PRESENTED

_____

TO

_____

BY

_____

ON

_____

THE
QUIET
BIBLE

NEW
INTERNATIONAL
VERSION

A LIFEGUIDE®
BIBLE

InterVarsity Press
Downers Grove, Illinois

Library of Congress Cataloging-in-Publication Data

18	17	16	15	14	13	12	11	10	9	8	7	6	5	4	3	2	1
11	10	09	08	07	06	05	04	03	02	01	00	99	98	97	96		

CONTENTS

Contributors —————— viii

Abbreviations —————— ix

Topical Bible Readings —— x

Bible Reading Plan ——— xi

Getting the Most Out of The
   NIV Quiet Time Bible ——— xv

Why Have a Quiet Time?
   John White ——— xvii

How to Have a Quiet Time
   Stephen D. Eyre ——— xviii

How to Study the Bible
   James F. Nyquist
   & Jack Kuhatschek ——— xx

Prayer and Journaling
   Bill Hybels ——— xxiii

Preface to the New
   International Version —— xxvi

Table of Weights and
   Measures ——— xxviii

The Old Testament ——— 1

The New Testament ——— 1149

Acknowledgments ——— 1595

Index of Quiet Time
   Subjects ——— 1597

Old Testament Books

Genesis ——————— 1

Exodus ——————— 66

Leviticus —————— 117

Numbers —————— 150

Deuteronomy ———— 195

Joshua ——————— 236

Judges ——————— 266

Ruth ———————— 297

1 Samuel —————— 302

2 Samuel —————— 341

1 Kings ——————— 372

2 Kings ——————— 407

1 Chronicles ————— 445

2 Chronicles ————— 481

Ezra ———————— 517

Nehemiah —————— 533

Esther ——————— 557

Job ————————— 571

Psalms ——————— 609

Proverbs —————— 745

Ecclesiastes ————— 782

Song of Songs ———— 800

Isaiah ——————— 809

Jeremiah —————— 887

Lamentations ————— 963

Ezekiel ——————— 972

Daniel ——————— 1032

Hosea ——————— 1056

Joel ———————— 1071

Amos ——————— 1077

Obadiah —————— 1089

Jonah ——————— 1092

Micah ——————— 1097

Nahum ——————— 1107

Habakkuk —————— 1112

Zephaniah —————— 1117

Haggai ——————— 1123

Zechariah —————— 1126

Malachi ——————— 1142

New Testament Books

Matthew —————— 1149

Mark ———————— 1194

Luke ———————— 1125

John ———————— 1275

Acts ———————— 1315

Romans —————— 1361

1 Corinthians ———— 1387

2 Corinthians ———— 1409

Galatians —————— 1426

Ephesians —————— 1439

Philippians ————— 1451

Colossians —————— 1460

1 Thessalonians ——— 1470

2 Thessalonians ——— 1477

1 Timothy —————— 1481

2 Timothy —————— 1490

Titus ———————— 1496

Philemon —————— 1499

Hebrews —————— 1502

James ——————— 1522

1 Peter ——————— 1532

2 Peter ——————— 1542

1 John ——————— 1548

2 John ——————— 1560

3 John ——————— 1562

Jude ———————— 1564

Revelation —————— 1567

THE NIV QUIET TIME BIBLE
STAFF & CONTRIBUTORS

GENERAL EDITOR
Cindy Bunch

EDITORIAL ADVISORS
Ken DeRuiter, James Hoover, Nancy Iglesias, Andrew T.
Le Peau and Don Stephenson

DESIGNER
Kathy Lay Burrows

WORD PROCESSING
Gloria Duncan-Bevilacqua

PROOFREADING
Michele Pelton-Fall, Al Hsu and Rebecca Cooper

PRODUCTION
Nancy Fox, Don Frye and Marjorie Sire

QUIET TIME WRITERS
Genesis: Charles and Anne Hummel
Exodus: James Reapsome
Leviticus: Dale and Sandy Larsen, Carolyn Nystrom
and Ruth Goring
Numbers: Rob Suggs and Gladys Hunt
Deuteronomy: Stephen Eyre
Joshua: Donald Baker
Judges: Donald Baker
Ruth: Gladys Hunt
1 Samuel: Jack Kuhatschek, Pete Scazzero,
Hazel Offner and Gladys Hunt
2 Samuel: Jack Kuhatschek, Brian Wallace, Cindy
Bunch and Scott Hotaling
1 Kings: Carolyn Nystrom, Pete Scazzero, Cindy Bunch
and Phyllis J. Le Peau
2 Kings: Carolyn Nystrom, Andrea and Howard
Louthan, Gladys Hunt and Phyllis J. Le Peau
1 Chronicles: Dale and Sandy Larsen and Jack
Kuhatschek
2 Chronicles: Dale and Sandy Larsen, Carolyn
Nystrom, Cindy Bunch and Scott Hotaling
Ezra: Tom Parker
Nehemiah: Don Fields
Esther: Patty Pell
Job: Paul Stevens
Psalms: Cindy Bunch, Isaac Canales, Stephen Eyre,
Phyllis J. Le Peau, Jack Kuhatschek, Mary Fisher, Linda
Gehrs, Dietrich Gruen, Dan Harrison, David Healey,

Carolyn Nystrom, Hazel Offner, Eugene Peterson,
Dale and Juanita Ryan, Bill Syrios and Brian Wallace
Proverbs: William Mouser
Ecclesiastes: Bill and Teresa Syrios
Song of Songs: Cindy Bunch
Isaiah: Howard Peskett
Jeremiah: Stephen Eyre, Dale and Sandy Larsen
Lamentations: Lin Johnson
Ezekiel: Paul Stevens
Daniel: Douglas Connelly
Hosea: Tom Parker
Joel: Doug and Doris Haugen
Amos: Doug and Doris Haugen
Obadiah: Dale and Sandy Larsen
Jonah: Doug and Doris Haugen
Micah: Tom Parker
Nahum: Rob Suggs
Habakkuk: Bob and Carolyn Hunter, Carolyn Nystrom
Zephaniah: Lin Johnson
Haggai: Lin Johnson
Zechariah: Jack Kuhatschek
Malachi: Carolyn Nystrom
Matthew: Stephen and Jacalyn Eyre
Mark: James Hoover
Luke: Ada Lum
John: Douglas Connelly
Acts: Phyllis J. Le Peau
Romans: Jack Kuhatschek
1 Corinthians: Paul Stevens and Dan Williams
2 Corinthians: Paul Stevens
Galatians: Jack Kuhatschek
Ephesians: Andrew T. and Phyllis J. Le Peau
Philippians: Donald Baker
Colossians: Martha Reapsome
1 & 2 Thessalonians: Donald Baker
1 & 2 Timothy: Pete Sommer
Titus: Pete Sommer
Philemon: Martha Reapsome
Hebrews: James Reapsome
James: Andrew T. and Phyllis J. Le Peau
1 & 2 Peter: Carolyn Nystrom
1, 2, 3 John: Ron Blankley
Jude: Carolyn Nystrom
Revelation: Paul Stevens and Scott Hotaling

ABBREVIATIONS

Books of the Bible

Genesis	Ge	Isaiah	Is	Romans	Ro
Exodus	Ex	Jeremiah	Jer	1 Corinthians	1Co
Leviticus	Lev	Lamentations	La	2 Corinthians	2Co
Numbers	Nu	Ezekiel	Eze	Galatians	Gal
Deuteronomy	Dt	Daniel	Da	Ephesians	Eph
Joshua	Jos	Hosea	Hos	Philippians	Php
Judges	Jdg	Joel	Joel	Colossians	Col
Ruth	Ru	Amos	Am	1 Thessalonians	1Th
1 Samuel	1Sa	Obadiah	Ob	2 Thessalonians	2Th
2 Samuel	2Sa	Jonah	Jnh	1 Timothy	1Ti
1 Kings	1Ki	Micah	Mic	2 Timothy	2Ti
2 Kings	2Ki	Nahum	Na	Titus	Tit
1 Chronicles	1Ch	Habakkuk	Hab	Philemon	Phm
2 Chronicles	2Ch	Zephaniah	Zep	Hebrews	Heb
Ezra	Ezr	Haggai	Hag	James	Jas
Nehemiah	Ne	Zechariah	Zec	1 Peter	1Pe
Esther	Est	Malachi	Mal	2 Peter	2Pe
Job	Job	Matthew	Mt	1 John	1Jn
Psalms	Ps	Mark	Mk	2 John	2Jn
Proverbs	Pr	Luke	Lk	3 John	3Jn
Ecclesiastes	Ecc	John	Jn	Jude	Jude
Song of Songs	SS	Acts	Ac	Revelation	Rev

TOPICAL BIBLE READINGS

Here are some quiet times you can turn to when you are looking for some answers to questions you are facing, encouragement from God through the difficult times or when you want to rejoice and praise God for the good things in your life. More topics are listed in the index on pages 1597-1601.

Angels Around Us
Psalm 91
Hebrews 1
Revelation 8—9

Assurance of Salvation
Psalms 25, 73
Luke 13:22—14:35
2 Corinthians 1:1-11

Battling Temptation
2 Samuel 11
Daniel 3
Mark 1:1-15
John 18:1-27

Comfort from God
Psalms 19, 86, 145
John 14
1 Peter 5

Decision-Making
Psalm 119:1-24
1 Corinthians 3
Revelation 14—15

Experiencing Burnout
1 Kings 19:1-18
Mark 6:6-56

Expressing Anger
Job 9—10
Psalms 4; 18:1-24; 94;
109
Jonah 4
Nahum 1
Mark 11:1-25

Facing Pressure
Daniel 1
Psalm 31
Mark 2:18—3:35
Galatians 6:11-18
Revelation 2

Feeling Lonely
Psalms 3, 22
Luke 6:12-49
John 12
2 Timothy 1

Finding Joy in God
Psalms 66, 126
Romans 5
Philippians 3:1-21

Grieving
Psalm 102
2 Corinthians
6:14—7:16

Handling Guilt
Leviticus 16
Psalm 130
1 Timothy 1

Loving Others
1 John 4:1-12
2 John 1-13

The Power of God
Nahum 3
Acts 9:32—10:48

Repentance
Psalm 32
Luke 3:1-20

Sources of Hope
Genesis 45:16—47:31
Psalms 33, 42—43, 146
Isaiah 11—12; 49;
65:17—66:24
Luke 1
Romans 4
1 Peter 1:1-12
Revelation 1:1-8

Spiritual Battles
Joshua 5:13—6:27
Psalm 110

John 7:1-52
Ephesians 6:10-24
1 John 5:1-12
Revelation 12, 13

Suffering
Job 20—21
Psalm 6
Lamentations 3, 4—5
John 18:28—19:16
Acts 8
2 Corinthians 12
Philippians 1:12-30
Hebrews 4:14—5:10
1 Peter 3:8-22; 4

Thanking God
Psalms 47, 50, 65
Philippians 4:10-23
Colossians 1:1-14

Times of Waiting
Psalms 27, 40, 44
Mark 13:1-37
Hebrews 9

BIBLE READING PLAN

The plan outlined below offers some variety in reading between Old and New Testament and types of literature with some effort to follow a historical sequence of events. Following it will help you better understand the whole of Scripture. Check off the boxes as you go to keep track of your reading. You can also use this plan and follow a different order; just look for the italic book titles and check off each passage. The quiet times cover all of the New Testament and selected passages from every Old Testament book. Bold type indicates that there is a quiet time with the passage. Every verse is represented in a readable unit, whether or not there is a quiet time. If you complete one quiet time each day, you will cover all of the quiet times in two years.

John
- ☑ **Jn 1**
- ☑ **Jn 2**
- ☑ **Jn 3**
- ☑ **Jn 4**
- ☑ **Jn 5**
- ☐ Jn 6
- ☐ Jn 7:1-52
- ☐ Jn 7:53—8:11
- ☐ Jn 8:12-59
- ☐ Jn 9
- ☐ Jn 10
- ☐ Jn 11
- ☐ Jn 12
- ☐ Jn 13:1-17
- ☐ Jn 13:18-38
- ☐ Jn 14
- ☑ **Jn 15:1-17**
- ☐ Jn 15:18—16:4
- ☐ Jn 16:5-33
- ☐ Jn 17:1-26
- ☐ Jn 18:1-27
- ☐ Jn 18:28—19:16
- ☐ Jn 19:17-42
- ☐ Jn 20
- ☐ Jn 21

Genesis
- ☑ **Ge 1:1—2:3**
- ☑ **Ge 2:4-25**
- ☑ **Ge 3**
- ☑ **Ge 4—5**
- ☑ **Ge 6—7**
- ☑ **Ge 8:1—9:17**
- ☑ **Ge 9:18—11:32**
- ☑ **Ge 12—13**
- ☑ **Ge 14—15**
- ☑ **Ge 16—17**
- ☑ **Ge 18—19**
- ☑ **Ge 20—21**
- ☑ **Ge 22—23**
- ☑ **Ge 24:1—25:11**
- ☑ **Ge 25:12—27:40**
- ☑ **Ge 27:41—30:24**

- ☑ **Ge 30:25—31:55**
- ☑ **Ge 32—33**
- ☑ **Ge 34—36**
- ☑ **Ge 37—38**
- ☑ **Ge 39—40**
- ☐ Ge 41—42
- ☐ Ge 43:1—45:15
- ☐ Ge 45:16—47:31
- ☐ Ge 48—49
- ☐ Ge 50

Psalms 1—13
- ☐ Ps 1
- ☐ Ps 2
- ☐ Ps 3
- ☐ Ps 4
- ☐ Ps 5
- ☐ Ps 6
- ☐ Ps 7
- ☐ Ps 8
- ☐ Ps 9
- ☐ Ps 10
- ☐ Ps 11—12
- ☐ Ps 13

1 Thessalonians
- ☐ 1Th 1
- ☐ 1Th 2:1-16
- ☐ 1Th 2:17—3:13
- ☐ 1Th 4:1-12
- ☐ 1Th 4:13—5:11
- ☐ 1Th 5:12-28

2 Thessalonians
- ☐ 2Th 1
- ☐ 2Th 2
- ☐ 2Th 3

Exodus
- ☐ Ex 1
- ☐ Ex 2
- ☐ Ex 3—4
- ☐ Ex 5:1—7:7
- ☐ Ex 7:8—10:29

- ☐ Ex 11:1—12:28
- ☐ Ex 12:29—13:16
- ☐ Ex 13:17—14:31
- ☐ Ex 15:1-21
- ☐ Ex 15:22—17:16
- ☐ Ex 18
- ☐ Ex 19
- ☐ Ex 20:1-21
- ☐ Ex 20:22—23:19
- ☐ Ex 23:20—24:18
- ☐ Ex 25—27
- ☐ Ex 28:1—29:37
- ☐ Ex 29:38—31:18
- ☐ Ex 32
- ☐ Ex 33
- ☐ Ex 34
- ☐ Ex 35—36
- ☐ Ex 37:1—39:31
- ☐ Ex 39:32—40:38

Ecclesiastes
- ☑ **Ecc 1:1-11**
- ☑ **Ecc 1:12—2:16**
- ☑ **Ecc 2:17-26**
- ☑ **Ecc 3:1—4:3**
- ☑ **Ecc 4:4—5:7**
- ☑ **Ecc 5:8—6:12**
- ☐ Ecc 7:1—8:1
- ☐ Ecc 8:2-17
- ☐ Ecc 9:1-12
- ☐ Ecc 9:13—10:20
- ☐ Ecc 11:1—12:8
- ☐ Ecc 12:9-14

Song of Songs
- ☐ SS 1—2
- ☐ SS 3
- ☐ SS 4
- ☐ SS 5—6
- ☐ SS 7—8

Luke
- ☐ Lk 1
- ☐ Lk 2

- ☐ Lk 3:1-20
- ☐ Lk 3:21—4:13
- ☐ Lk 4:14—5:16
- ☐ Lk 5:17—6:11
- ☐ Lk 6:12-49
- ☐ Lk 7
- ☐ Lk 8:1-21
- ☐ Lk 8:22-56
- ☐ Lk 9:1-50
- ☐ Lk 9:51—10:24
- ☐ Lk 10:25—11:13
- ☐ Lk 11:14—12:12
- ☐ Lk 12:13—13:21
- ☐ Lk 13:22—14:35
- ☐ Lk 15
- ☐ Lk 16
- ☐ Lk 17:1—18:14
- ☐ Lk 18:15—19:10
- ☐ Lk 19:11-48
- ☐ Lk 20:1—21:4
- ☐ Lk 21:5-38
- ☐ Lk 22:1-46
- ☐ Lk 22:47—23:56
- ☐ Lk 24

Leviticus
- ☐ Lev 1
- ☐ Lev 2—4
- ☐ Lev 5—7
- ☐ **Lev 8**
- ☐ Lev 9
- ☐ **Lev 10**
- ☐ Lev 11—12
- ☐ Lev 13
- ☐ Lev 14—15
- ☐ **Lev 16**
- ☐ Lev 17—18
- ☐ **Lev 19**
- ☐ Lev 20—22
- ☐ **Lev 23**
- ☐ Lev 24
- ☐ **Lev 25**
- ☐ **Lev 26**
- ☐ Lev 27

Acts
- ☐ Ac 1
- ☐ Ac 2
- ☐ Ac 3
- ☐ Ac 4:1-31
- ☐ Ac 4:32—5:16
- ☐ Ac 5:17—6:7
- ☐ Ac 6:8—7:60
- ☐ Ac 8
- ☐ Ac 9:1-31
- ☐ Ac 9:32—10:48
- ☐ Ac 11
- ☐ Ac 12
- ☐ Ac 13—14
- ☐ Ac 15
- ☐ Ac 16
- ☐ Ac 17
- ☐ Ac 18
- ☐ Ac 19:1—20:12
- ☐ Ac 20:13-38
- ☐ Ac 21:1—22:21
- ☐ Ac 22:22—23:35
- ☐ Ac 24:1—25:12
- ☐ Ac 25:13—26:32
- ☐ Ac 27—28

Psalms 14—29
- ☐ Ps 14
- ☐ Ps 15
- ☐ Ps 16
- ☐ Ps 17
- ☐ Ps 18:1-24
- ☐ Ps 18:25-50
- ☐ Ps 19
- ☐ Ps 20—21
- ☐ Ps 22
- ☐ Ps 23
- ☐ Ps 24
- ☐ Ps 25
- ☐ Ps 26
- ☐ Ps 27
- ☐ Ps 28
- ☐ Ps 29

Jonah
☐ Jnh 1
☐ Jnh 2
☐ Jnh 3
☐ Jnh 4

Galatians
☐ Gal 1:1-10
☐ Gal 1:11—2:10
☐ Gal 2:11-21
☐ Gal 3:1-14
☐ Gal 3:15-29
☐ Gal 4:1-20
☐ Gal 4:21—5:1
☐ Gal 5:2-15
☐ Gal 5:16-26
☐ Gal 6:1-10
☐ Gal 6:11-18

Isaiah
☐ Isa 1
☐ Isa 2
☐ Isa 3—4
☐ Isa 5
☐ Isa 6
☐ Isa 7
☐ Isa 8:1-10
☐ Isa 8:11—9:7
☐ Isa 9:8—10:34
☐ Isa 11—12
☐ Isa 13—14
☐ Isa 15—16
☐ Isa 17—18
☐ Isa 19—20
☐ Isa 21—22
☐ Isa 23
☐ Isa 24
☐ Isa 25
☐ Isa 26—27
☐ Isa 28—29
☐ Isa 30:1-18
☐ Isa 30:19—32:20
☐ Isa 33—35
☐ Isa 36—37
☐ Isa 38—39
☐ Isa 40
☐ Isa 41
☐ Isa 42
☐ Isa 43:1—44:5
☐ Isa 44:6-28
☐ Isa 45
☐ Isa 46—48
☐ Isa 49
☐ Isa 50:1—52:12
☐ Isa 52:13—53:12
☐ Isa 54—55
☐ Isa 56—57
☐ Isa 58
☐ Isa 59—60
☐ Isa 61

☐ Isa 62
☐ Isa 63:1-6
☐ Isa 63:7—64:12
☐ Isa 65:1-16
☐ Isa 65:17—66:24

Matthew
☐ Mt 1—2
☐ Mt 3
☐ Mt 4
☐ Mt 5:1—6:18
☐ Mt 6:19—7:29
☐ Mt 8:1—9:34
☐ Mt 9:35—11:30
☐ Mt 12
☐ Mt 13
☐ Mt 14
☐ Mt 15:1—16:20
☐ Mt 16:21—17:27
☐ Mt 18
☐ Mt 19—20
☐ Mt 21:1-27
☐ Mt 21:28—22:46
☐ Mt 23
☐ Mt 24
☐ Mt 25
☐ Mt 26
☐ Mt 27
☐ Mt 28

Psalms 30—41
☐ Ps 30
☐ Ps 31
☐ Ps 32
☐ Ps 33
☐ Ps 34
☐ Ps 35
☐ Ps 36
☐ Ps 37:1-17
☐ Ps 37:18-40
☐ Ps 38
☐ Ps 39
☐ Ps 40
☐ Ps 41

Romans
☐ Rm 1:1-17
☐ Rm 1:18-32
☐ Rm 2
☐ Rm 3:1-20
☐ Rm 3:21-31
☐ Rm 4
☐ Rm 5
☐ Rm 6:1—7:6
☐ Rm 7:7-25
☐ Rm 8:1-17
☐ Rm 8:18-39
☐ Rm 9:1-29
☐ Rm 9:30—10:21
☐ Rm 11

☐ Rm 12
☐ Rm 13
☐ Rm 14
☐ Rm 15:1-13
☐ Rm 15:14—16:27

Numbers
☐ Nu 1
☐ Nu 2—3
☐ Nu 4—6
☐ Nu 7
☐ Nu 8
☐ Nu 9
☐ Nu 10
☐ Nu 11
☐ Nu 12
☐ Nu 13:1—14:12
☐ Nu 14:13—15:41
☐ Nu 16
☐ Nu 17
☐ Nu 18—19
☐ Nu 20:1-13
☐ Nu 20:14-29
☐ Nu 21:1-9
☐ Nu 21:10—22:41
☐ Nu 23—25
☐ Nu 26:1—27:11
☐ Nu 27:12-23
☐ Nu 28—29
☐ Nu 30—31
☐ Nu 32
☐ Nu 33—34
☐ Nu 35—36

Amos
☐ Am 1—2
☐ Am 3
☐ Am 4
☐ Am 5—6
☐ Am 7—8
☐ Am 9

Hosea
☐ Hos 1:1—2:1
☐ Hos 2:2—3:5
☐ Hos 4
☐ Hos 5:1—6:11
☐ Hos 6:11—8:14
☐ Hos 9—10
☐ Hos 11:1-11
☐ Hos 11:12—13:16
☐ Hos 14

1 Corinthians
☐ 1 Co 1
☐ 1 Co 2
☐ 1 Co 3
☐ 1 Co 4
☐ 1 Co 5—6
☐ 1 Co 7

☐ 1 Co 8—9
☐ 1 Co 10:1—11:1
☐ 1 Co 11:2-34
☐ 1 Co 12
☐ 1 Co 13
☐ 1 Co 14
☐ 1 Co 15—16

Deuteronomy
☐ Dt 1
☐ Dt 2:1—3:20
☐ Dt 3:21-29
☐ Dt 4:1-14
☐ Dt 4:15-40
☐ Dt 4:41-49
☐ Dt 5
☐ Dt 6
☐ Dt 7
☐ Dt 8
☐ Dt 9—10
☐ Dt 11
☐ Dt 12:1-14
☐ Dt 12:15—13:18
☐ Dt 14
☐ Dt 15:1-11
☐ Dt 15:12—16:20
☐ Dt 16:21—18:22
☐ Dt 19—20
☐ Dt 21:1—23:14
☐ Dt 23:15-25
☐ Dt 24—25
☐ Dt 26—27
☐ Dt 28
☐ Dt 29
☐ Dt 30
☐ Dt 31:1-13
☐ Dt 31:14—34:12

2 Corinthians
☐ 2 Co 1:1-11
☐ 2 Co 1:12—2:11
☐ 2 Co 2:12—3:6
☐ 2 Co 3:7-18
☐ 2 Co 4:1—5:10
☐ 2 Co 5:11—6:13
☐ 2 Co 6:14—7:16
☐ 2 Co 8:1—9:15
☐ 2 Co 10
☐ 2 Co 11
☐ 2 Co 12
☐ 2 Co 13

Psalms 42—61
☐ Ps 42—43
☐ Ps 44
☐ Ps 45
☐ Ps 46
☐ Ps 47
☐ Ps 48—49
☐ Ps 50

☐ Ps 51
☐ Ps 52—54
☐ Ps 55
☐ Ps 56
☐ Ps 57
☐ Ps 58—59
☐ Ps 60—61

Micah
☐ Mic 1
☐ Mic 2
☐ Mic 3
☐ Mic 4
☐ Mic 5
☐ Mic 6
☐ Mic 7

Joshua
☐ Jos 1
☐ Jos 2
☐ Jos 3:1—5:12
☐ Jos 5:13—6:27
☐ Jos 7—8
☐ Jos 9
☐ Jos 10—12
☐ Jos 13
☐ Jos 14—18
☐ Jos 19
☐ Jos 20—21
☐ Jos 22
☐ Jos 23
☐ Jos 24

1 Timothy
☐ 1Ti 1
☐ 1Ti 2
☐ 1Ti 3
☐ 1Ti 4
☐ 1Ti 5:1—6:2
☐ 1Ti 6:3-20

Joel
☐ Joel 1
☐ Joel 2:1-27
☐ Joel 2:28—3:21

2 Timothy
☐ 2Ti 1
☐ 2Ti 2
☐ 2Ti 3
☐ 2Ti 4

Obadiah
☐ Ob 1-21

Titus
☐ Tit 1—3

Judges
☐ Jdg 1:1—2:5

- ☐ Jdg 2:6-23
- ☐ Jdg 3:1-11
- ☐ **Jdg 3:12-31**
- ☐ **Jdg 4**
- ☐ Jdg 5
- ☐ **Jdg 6:1-32**
- ☐ **Jdg 6:33—7:25**
- ☐ Jdg 8
- ☐ **Jdg 9**
- ☐ Jdg 10
- ☐ **Jdg 11—12**
- ☐ **Jdg 13**
- ☐ **Jdg 14—15**
- ☐ **Jdg 16**
- ☐ **Jdg 17—18**
- ☐ Jdg 19—20
- ☐ **Jdg 21**

Ruth
- ☐ **Ru 1—2**
- ☐ **Ru 3—4**

1 Samuel
- ☐ **1Sa 1:1—2:11**
- ☐ 1Sa 2:12-36
- ☐ **1Sa 3**
- ☐ **1Sa 4—5**
- ☐ 1Sa 6—7
- ☐ **1Sa 8**
- ☐ **1Sa 9:1—10:8**
- ☐ 1Sa 10:9—12:25
- ☐ **1Sa 13—14**
- ☐ **1Sa 15**
- ☐ **1Sa 16**
- ☐ **1Sa 17**
- ☐ **1Sa 18**
- ☐ 1Sa 19
- ☐ **1Sa 20**
- ☐ 1Sa 21—23
- ☐ **1Sa 24**
- ☐ **1Sa 25**
- ☐ **1Sa 26**
- ☐ 1Sa 27—29
- ☐ **1Sa 30**
- ☐ 1Sa 31

Ephesians
- ☐ **Eph 1:1-14**
- ☐ **Eph 1:15-23**
- ☐ **Eph 2:1-10**
- ☐ **Eph 2:11-22**
- ☐ **Eph 3**
- ☐ **Eph 4:1-16**
- ☐ **Eph 4:17-32**
- ☐ **Eph 5:1-20**
- ☐ **Eph 5:21-33**
- ☐ **Eph 6:1-9**
- ☐ **Eph 6:10-24**

2 Samuel
- ☐ 2Sa 1—2
- ☐ 2Sa 3—5
- ☐ **2Sa 6**
- ☐ **2Sa 7**
- ☐ 2Sa 8
- ☐ **2Sa 9**
- ☐ 2Sa 10
- ☐ **2Sa 11**
- ☐ **2Sa 12**
- ☐ **2Sa 13**
- ☐ 2Sa 14
- ☐ **2Sa 15**
- ☐ 2Sa 16:1—18:18
- ☐ **2Sa 18:19—19:10**
- ☐ 2Sa 19:11—20:26
- ☐ 2Sa 21—22
- ☐ 2Sa 23—24

Psalms 62—84
- ☐ **Ps 62**
- ☐ **Ps 63**
- ☐ **Ps 64**
- ☐ **Ps 65**
- ☐ **Ps 66**
- ☐ **Ps 67**
- ☐ Ps 68
- ☐ Ps 69—70
- ☐ Ps 71
- ☐ Ps 72
- ☐ **Ps 73**
- ☐ Ps 74
- ☐ Ps 75—76
- ☐ **Ps 77**
- ☐ Ps 78
- ☐ Ps 79
- ☐ Ps 80—81
- ☐ Ps 82—83
- ☐ **Ps 84**

1 Kings
- ☐ 1Ki 1
- ☐ 1Ki 2
- ☐ **1Ki 3**
- ☐ 1Ki 4
- ☐ 1Ki 5—6
- ☐ 1Ki 7
- ☐ 1Ki 8
- ☐ 1Ki 9—10
- ☐ **1Ki 11**
- ☐ **1Ki 12**
- ☐ 1Ki 13—14
- ☐ 1Ki 15—16
- ☐ **1Ki 17**
- ☐ **1Ki 18**
- ☐ **1Ki 19:1-18**
- ☐ 1Ki 19:19—20:43
- ☐ **1Ki 21**
- ☐ **1Ki 22:1-40**
- ☐ 1Ki 22:41-53

2 Kings
- ☐ 2Ki 1
- ☐ **2Ki 2**
- ☐ 2Ki 3:1—4:7
- ☐ **2Ki 4:8-37**
- ☐ 2Ki 4:38-44
- ☐ **2Ki 5**
- ☐ 2Ki 6:1-23
- ☐ **2Ki 6:24—7:20**
- ☐ 2Ki 8
- ☐ **2Ki 9—10**
- ☐ 2Ki 11—12
- ☐ **2Ki 13**
- ☐ 2Ki 14—15
- ☐ **2Ki 16**
- ☐ **2Ki 17**
- ☐ 2Ki 18:1-16
- ☐ **2Ki 18:17-37**
- ☐ **2Ki 19**
- ☐ **2Ki 20:1—21:18**
- ☐ 2Ki 21:19-26
- ☐ **2Ki 22:1—23:35**
- ☐ **2Ki 23:36—25:30**

Philippians
- ☐ **Php 1:1-11**
- ☐ **Php 1:12-30**
- ☐ **Php 2:1-18**
- ☐ **Php 2:19-30**
- ☐ **Php 3**
- ☐ **Php 4:1-9**
- ☐ **Php 4:10-23**

1 Chronicles
- ☐ 1Ch 1—4
- ☐ 1Ch 5—6
- ☐ 1Ch 7—8
- ☐ 1Ch 9—10
- ☐ **1Ch 11**
- ☐ 1Ch 12—14
- ☐ **1Ch 15:1—16:6**
- ☐ 1Ch 16:7-43
- ☐ **1Ch 17**
- ☐ 1Ch 18
- ☐ **1Ch 19**
- ☐ 1Ch 20
- ☐ **1Ch 21:1—22:1**
- ☐ 1Ch 22:2—23:32
- ☐ 1Ch 24—27
- ☐ **1Ch 28**
- ☐ **1Ch 29**

2 Chronicles
- ☐ **2Ch 1**
- ☐ 2Ch 2—3
- ☐ 2Ch 4—5
- ☐ **2Ch 6—7**
- ☐ 2Ch 8—9
- ☐ 2Ch 10—11
- ☐ 2Ch 12—13

- ☐ **2Ch 14—15**
- ☐ 2Ch 16—17
- ☐ **2Ch 18:1—19:3**
- ☐ 2Ch 19:4-11
- ☐ **2Ch 20:1-30**
- ☐ 2Ch 20:31—22:12
- ☐ **2Ch 23—24**
- ☐ 2Ch 25—26
- ☐ 2Ch 27—28
- ☐ **2Ch 29**
- ☐ 2Ch 30—31
- ☐ 2Ch 32—33
- ☐ **2Ch 34**
- ☐ 2Ch 35—36

Colossians
- ☐ **Col 1:1-14**
- ☐ **Col 1:15-23**
- ☐ **Col 1:24—2:5**
- ☐ **Col 2:6-23**
- ☐ **Col 3:1-11**
- ☐ **Col 3:12-17**
- ☐ **Col 3:18—4:1**
- ☐ **Col 4:2-18**

Philemon
- ☐ **Phm 1-25**

Esther
- ☐ **Est 1**
- ☐ **Est 2**
- ☐ **Est 3**
- ☐ **Est 4**
- ☐ **Est 5**
- ☐ **Est 6**
- ☐ **Est 7**
- ☐ **Est 8**
- ☐ **Est 9—10**

Ezra
- ☐ **Ezr 1—2**
- ☐ **Ezr 3**
- ☐ **Ezr 4**
- ☐ **Ezr 5—6**
- ☐ **Ezr 7**
- ☐ **Ezr 8**
- ☐ **Ezr 9**
- ☐ **Ezr 10**

1 Peter
- ☐ **1Pe 1:1-12**
- ☐ **1Pe 1:13-25**
- ☐ **1Pe 2:1-12**
- ☐ **1Pe 2:13—3:7**
- ☐ **1Pe 3:8-22**
- ☐ **1Pe 4**
- ☐ **1Pe 5**

Nehemiah
- ☐ **Ne 1**

- ☐ **Ne 2**
- ☐ **Ne 3**
- ☐ **Ne 4**
- ☐ **Ne 5**
- ☐ **Ne 6**
- ☐ **Ne 7**
- ☐ **Ne 8**
- ☐ **Ne 9**
- ☐ **Ne 10**
- ☐ **Ne 11**
- ☐ **Ne 12**
- ☐ **Ne 13**

2 Peter
- ☐ **2Pe 1:1-11**
- ☐ **2Pe 1:12-21**
- ☐ **2Pe 2**
- ☐ **2Pe 3**

Jude
- ☐ **Jude 1-25**

Psalms 85—106
- ☐ **Ps 85**
- ☐ **Ps 86**
- ☐ Ps 87
- ☐ **Ps 88**
- ☐ Ps 89
- ☐ **Ps 90**
- ☐ **Ps 91**
- ☐ Ps 92—93
- ☐ **Ps 94**
- ☐ **Ps 95**
- ☐ **Ps 96**
- ☐ Ps 97—98
- ☐ **Ps 99**
- ☐ **Ps 100**
- ☐ Ps 101
- ☐ Ps 102
- ☐ **Ps 103**
- ☐ Ps 104
- ☐ Ps 105
- ☐ **Ps 106**

Job
- ☐ **Job 1:1—2:10**
- ☐ **Job 2:11—4:17**
- ☐ Job 4:18—5:27
- ☐ **Job 6**
- ☐ Job 7—8
- ☐ **Job 9—10**
- ☐ Job 11—12
- ☐ **Job 13—14**
- ☐ **Job 15**
- ☐ **Job 16—17**
- ☐ Job 18—19
- ☐ **Job 20—21**
- ☐ Job 22
- ☐ **Job 23**
- ☐ Job 24—26

□ Job 27—28
□ Job 29—31
□ Job 32—33
□ Job 34
□ Job 35
□ Job 36—37
□ Job 38
□ Job 39
□ Job 40
□ Job 41
□ Job 42

James
□ Jas 1:1-18
□ Jas 1:19-27
□ Jas 2:1-13
□ Jas 2:14-26
□ Jas 3:1-12
□ Jas 3:13—4:10
□ Jas 4:11-17
□ Jas 5:1-11
□ Jas 5:12-20

Proverbs
□ Pr 1
□ Pr 2—3
□ Pr 4—5
□ Pr 6:1-19
□ Pr 6:20-35
□ Pr 7
□ Pr 8
□ Pr 9
□ Pr 10
□ Pr 11—12
□ Pr 13—14
□ Pr 15—16
□ Pr 17—18
□ Pr 19
□ Pr 20
□ Pr 21
□ Pr 22:1—24:22
□ Pr 24:23-34
□ Pr 25—26
□ Pr 27
□ Pr 28—29
□ Pr 30
□ Pr 31

Zephaniah
□ Zep 1
□ Zep 2
□ Zep 3

Nahum
□ Na 1
□ Na 2
□ Na 3

Ezekiel
□ Eze 1

□ Eze 2:1—3:15
□ Eze 3:16-27
□ Eze 4—5
□ Eze 6—7
□ Eze 8
□ Eze 9—10
□ Eze 11
□ Eze 12—13
□ Eze 14—15
□ Eze 16
□ Eze 17
□ Eze 18
□ Eze 19—20
□ Eze 21—22
□ Eze 23:1—24:14
□ Eze 24:15-27
□ Eze 25—26
□ Eze 27—28
□ Eze 29—30
□ Eze 31—32
□ Eze 33
□ Eze 34
□ Eze 35—36
□ Eze 37
□ Eze 38—39
□ Eze 40—41
□ Eze 42
□ Eze 43:1-12
□ Eze 43:13—44:31
□ Eze 45—46
□ Eze 47:1-12
□ Eze 47:13—48:35

1 John
□ 1Jn 1
□ 1Jn 2:1-11
□ 1Jn 2:12-17
□ 1Jn 2:18-27
□ 1Jn 2:28—3:10
□ 1Jn 3:11-24
□ 1Jn 4:1-12
□ 1Jn 4:13-21
□ 1Jn 5:1-12
□ 1Jn 5:13-21

Habakkuk
□ Hab 1:1—2:1
□ Hab 2:2-20
□ Hab 3

2 John
□ 2Jn 1-13

3 John
□ 3Jn 1-14

Jeremiah
□ Jer 1
□ Jer 2:1—3:5
□ Jer 3:6—4:4

□ Jer 4:5-31
□ Jer 5
□ Jer 6
□ Jer 7:1-20
□ Jer 7:21—8:22
□ Jer 9
□ Jer 10:1-16
□ Jer 10:17—11:23
□ Jer 12
□ Jer 13
□ Jer 14—15
□ Jer 16:1—17:4
□ Jer 17:5-18
□ Jer 17:19-27
□ Jer 18:1-17
□ Jer 18:18—19:15
□ Jer 20—21
□ Jer 22
□ Jer 23
□ Jer 24
□ Jer 25:1-14
□ Jer 25:15-38
□ Jer 26
□ Jer 27
□ Jer 28
□ Jer 29:1-23
□ Jer 29:24—30:24
□ Jer 31
□ Jer 32:1-25
□ Jer 32:26-44
□ Jer 33
□ Jer 34—35
□ Jer 36
□ Jer 37
□ Jer 38
□ Jer 39—40
□ Jer 41—43
□ Jer 44
□ Jer 45—47
□ Jer 48—49
□ Jer 50:1-20
□ Jer 50:21—51:64
□ Jer 52

Psalms 107—129
□ Ps 107
□ Ps 108
□ Ps 109
□ Ps 110
□ Ps 111—114
□ Ps 115
□ Ps 116
□ Ps 117
□ Ps 118
□ Ps 119:1-24
□ Ps 119:25-40
□ Ps 119:41—120:7
□ Ps 121
□ Ps 122
□ Ps 123—125

□ Ps 126
□ Ps 127
□ Ps 128—129

Lamentations
□ La 1—2
□ La 3
□ La 4—5

Haggai
□ Hag 1—2

Mark
□ Mk 1:1-15
□ Mk 1:16-39
□ Mk 1:40—2:17
□ Mk 2:18—3:35
□ Mk 4:1-34
□ Mk 4:35—6:6
□ Mk 6:6-56
□ Mk 7
□ Mk 8:1—9:1
□ Mk 9:2-32
□ Mk 9:33-50
□ Mk 10:1-31
□ Mk 10:32-52
□ Mk 11:1-25
□ Mk 11:27—12:27
□ Mk 12:28-44
□ Mk 13
□ Mk 14:1-42
□ Mk 14:43-72
□ Mk 15:1—16:8

Zechariah
□ Zec 1
□ Zec 2—3
□ Zec 4—5
□ Zec 6
□ Zec 7
□ Zec 8
□ Zec 9—10
□ Zec 11
□ Zec 12—13
□ Zec 14

Daniel
□ Da 1
□ Da 2:1-30
□ Da 2:31-49
□ Da 3
□ Da 4
□ Da 5
□ Da 6
□ Da 7
□ Da 8
□ Da 9
□ Da 10:1—11:35
□ Da 11:36—12:13

Malachi
□ Mal 1:1—2:16
□ Mal 2:17—3:18
□ Mal 4

Hebrews
□ Heb 1
□ Heb 2
□ Heb 3
□ Heb 4:1-13
□ Heb 4:14—5:10
□ Heb 5:11—6:20
□ Heb 7
□ Heb 8
□ Heb 9
□ Heb 10
□ Heb 11
□ Heb 12
□ Heb 13

Psalms 130—150
□ Ps 130
□ Ps 131—132
□ Ps 133
□ Ps 134—135
□ Ps 136
□ Ps 137
□ Ps 138
□ Ps 139
□ Ps 140—141
□ Ps 142
□ Ps 143
□ Ps 144
□ Ps 145
□ Ps 146
□ Ps 147
□ Ps 148
□ Ps 149
□ Ps 150

Revelation
□ Rev 1:1-8
□ Rev 1:9-20
□ Rev 2
□ Rev 3
□ Rev 4—5
□ Rev 6
□ Rev 7
□ Rev 8—9
□ Rev 10—11
□ Rev 12
□ Rev 13
□ Rev 14—15
□ Rev 16
□ Rev 17—18
□ Rev 19
□ Rev 20
□ Rev 21—22

Getting the Most Out of
The NIV Quiet Time Bible

Cindy Bunch & Andrew T. Le Peau

Quiet time can seem like an impossible dream to many of us. We face so many demands—work, family, friends, maintaining a home, schoolwork, church obligations each day—that we have little time left for peaceful reflection. Yet this can be one of the most renewing and vitalizing experiences of our Christian lives.

Whether you call it quiet time, devotions, or Bible study and prayer, what we are talking about is a portion of your day that is set aside to be in solitude. It is a time to connect with God and to hear what he has to say to you, to study Scripture, to apply the Word to your life, to offer praise and worship to God, and to pray. This may also be a time when you record what you are learning in a spiritual journal.

God is calling us to be with him. We cannot neglect this honor.

Why a Quiet Time Bible?

The NIV Quiet Time Bible puts us in direct touch with God's Word. It leads us to discover what the Bible says rather than simply telling us what it says. In the same way, this Bible does not tell you how to apply the Word to your life; rather it guides us with God's help to apply the Scripture ourselves. It uncovers the questions we have, the issues we face and the challenges that lie ahead. In this way, God's Word becomes as current as this morning's breakfast conversations.

How does *The NIV Quiet Time Bible* accomplish all this? Not by giving you study notes, extensive background notes or cross-references. Instead, it helps you discover for yourself the meaning of Scripture by asking thought-provoking questions. This question format is known as *inductive Bible study*.

We tend to remember very little of what others tell us. But we remember a large percentage of what we discover ourselves. As it has been said, "Tell me, and I will forget. Show me, and I may remember.

Involve me, and I will understand." This is why inductive study works so well. Even if other sources of spiritual nourishment are hard to find, if we learn how to feed ourselves from the Word of God, we will never go hungry.

The quiet times in this Bible are personal. The questions expose us to the promises, assurances, exhortations and challenges of God's Word. They are designed to allow the Scriptures to renew our minds so that we can be transformed by the Spirit of God. Our goal as Christians is not just to know *about* God, but to actually know him as one person knows another. He is our Friend, our Father, our Comforter, our Helper, our Guide and our Lord. Knowing him in this way, talking with him in this way calls for responses of joy, of worship, of repentance and sorrow, of hope and expectation. Loving God more. That's what this Bible is all about.

How to Use *The NIV Quiet Time Bible*

Because you will be making discoveries about yourself and about God, you may want to keep a special notebook to record what you are learning each day. You may want to note commitments that you make and keep a list of prayer concerns so that you can look back and discover how God has been working in your life.

At the beginning of each book of the Bible you will find a brief introduction which provides important information on who wrote the book, who it was written to and why it was written. The outline in each introduction provides an overview of all the quiet times in each book (but excludes text not covered in the quiet times). It will also include historical background and maps or charts in some cases. All of this is important to understanding each book.

Each quiet time has several components:

Warming Up to God. Sometimes a question that draws you into the theme for the day, sometimes a topic to reflect on or pray about, this portion is designed to help you prepare your heart and mind for what you will be learning from Scripture.

Daily Scripture Reading. Read and reread the assigned Bible passage to familiarize yourself with what the author is saying. When you begin a new section you may want to read the entire book along with the introduction to that book. This will give you a helpful overview of its contents. It might be good to have a Bible dictionary handy. You could use it to look up any unfamiliar words, names or places.

Discovering the Word. The studies ask three different kinds of questions. *Observation* questions help us to understand the content of the passage by asking about the basic facts: who, what, when, where and how. *Interpretation* questions delve into the meaning of the passage. *Application* questions help us discover its implications for growing in Christ. These three keys unlock the treasures of the biblical writings and help us live them out.

Applying the Word. This is your opportunity to make the study personal. How has God's Word spoken to you? What actions do you need to take as a result of what you have learned?

Responding in Prayer. The suggestion here is to help you begin to seek God's wisdom in the area you've studied. You will also want to pray about your daily concerns, for family and friends, and about national and world events.

The introductory articles that follow will help you to better understand each of the parts of the study and show you how to get the most out of them. If you've never had a quiet time before, you'll discover the reason to have one in John White's article. Steve Eyre offers help on how to approach the discipline of quiet time, while Jack Kuhatschek and James

Nyquist help with how Bible study works. Finally, Bill Hybels overviews the components of prayer and journaling.

The studies are designed to take fifteen or twenty minutes. You'll want to set aside additional time for prayer. Feel free to work at your own pace. Sometimes you may want to spend two days on one quiet time; other times you might want to do two in one day (one psalm and one New Testament study, for example). There are a total of 730 quiet times, which will allow you to read the Bible in two years. However, this schedule should not be something you feel bound to. Go at your own pace and as the Spirit leads you. Not all of the psalms are covered in the quiet times, but you may want to read them all as you go along.

A plan is provided at the front of the Bible interspersing the Old and New Testament books. You can follow that or can move around according to your needs and interests and keep track of what you have covered. Another option would be to read the New Testament and the Psalms in one year and the Old Testament in a second year. The topical index offers help in areas of personal need. It's a place to turn when you feel sad or lonely or are in need of forgiveness. Each quiet time is indexed at the end of the Bible so that you can locate particular topics. Generally, you'll find that you gain the best grasp of each Bible book if you work through the book from beginning to end, rather than skipping around.

If you are in a Bible study group, you may be interested in knowing that our LifeGuide® Bible Study Series includes companion guides on each New Testament book and many Old Testament books. You may want to double up on your learning by using those guides, which provide studies forty-five to sixty minutes long and include leader's notes, in a group context.

It is our hope that these quiet times will be an encouragement and a source of growth for your life with Christ. May the Holy Spirit be with you as you meet God each day.

Why Have a Quiet Time?

John White

Quiet times work. Prayer and Bible study change us—and the people around us. Our values alter once we start meeting regularly with God. Some things that once seemed important shrivel, while others swell in significance.

We see people differently. We pity people we once feared, and pray for people who once enraged us.

We will, to be sure, approach problems differently, feel different about our work, our studies, our job, our future. Our goals will have changed so that life slowly takes on new meaning. The changes are understandable since we are influenced by our Creator God who we spend time with daily.

But do I recommend that we have a daily quiet time solely for these reasons? As a matter of fact, no. There's much more to be gained.

To commune with God is to touch both infinity and eternity. We have opened a window to both a beyondness and an immediacy which time and space are powerless to provide and which we can experience in no other way. The most widely read person has only rubbed shoulders with a few obscurity-bound professors or dipped into a selection of "the world's great books"—a contradictory jumble of finite perspectives. Yet we are invited to private tutorials with the fountain of ultimate wisdom.

We are invited to collaborate in the creation of destiny, not to be a mere spectator but a coauthor. God does not want to determine all things in splendid solitude by the word of his power. He wants the painting of the future to be a family project in which we all play a part under his benign direction. Earth's policymakers are but actors in a drama written in heaven, and we are offered a pen to do some of the writing. Can we imagine anything better?

For Love's Sake

Yet not even for any of these reasons but for love's sake would I urge us to meet God daily!

As the deer pants for streams of water,
    so my soul pants for you, O God.

My soul thirsts for God, for the living God.
    When can I go and meet with God?
    (Ps 42:1-2)

Our quest must be that of a suitor too blinded by beauty to descend to calculating self-interest, too intoxicated with love to care about the cost or the consequences of his suit.

It must be the love of Mary, sitting at Jesus' feet, enchanted by his words and grace, but deaf and blind to the frustration of her resentful sister (Lk 10:38-42). An enchantment of that sort will not be broken, nor its pleasures denied. It is time we forgot about our spiritual performance and our spiritual needs and gave ourselves up to passion.

"Beautiful!" you sigh. "I wish I felt that way. But I don't love God like that. So what can I do? How can I love when my heart is cold, when all I experience is the nagging guilt of knowing my love is a sorry thing not worth offering?"

But wait. A moment ago when you read the words of the psalmist, wasn't there a faint stirring of envy in you, an echo of the longing the psalmist expressed? If there was—and it matters not how feeble or faint—then your love is not absent but suppressed. It lies dormant beneath the weight of unbelief and discouragement.

Our love for God lies within many of us like a coiled spring, inactive but straining for release. It is a potential volcano, a dangerous thing that we fear to set free lest we shall have to cope with raging fire. Unless we take the risk of loving, we will only be half alive. But we should not be afraid of the longing within; it is more than matched by the greater longing of a God who planted it there.

Come, then, for love's sake. Come boldly defying fears. Enter into a love-pact to meet Christ daily. Come trembling to confess inadequacies. He is gentle and will understand. He will not force us or hurry the pace beyond what we are able to tolerate.

Come to his footstool. Come trusting. And come for love of him.

How to Have a Quiet Time

Stephen D. Eyre

One of the questions I frequently ask in counseling and discipling is "How is your quiet time?" If the person is having one, usually there is a slight pause and then the answer "I am having it regularly." Or, "I have been studying the Scriptures diligently."

Both responses are good, but not what I am after. I want to know more than just frequency or diligence in Scripture. What I want to know is, What is happening in your personal encounter with God?

Only as I get a glimpse of what's happening in the heart in touch with God can I give helpful spiritual guidance. Is there a sense of worship, or a sense of deadness? Perhaps so many concerns come to mind that we can't focus on the Scriptures. Or our prayer may be jumbled and distracted. All these things mean something, indicating both our needs and what God may be doing in our hearts.

I also want to know what is happening in a quiet time because I have found that it is possible to be blind to the presence of God and not even know it. When this happens, quiet times become merely an empty formality. Scripture becomes a book of principles to be applied. Prayer is a shopping list of things God is supposed to do. Difficulties in life are problems God is supposed to solve.

When we are blind to God, what God is doing in us in the midst of difficulties is overlooked. That God might want us to listen rather than do all the talking in prayer never occurs to us. And that God might want to meet us in Scripture is lost in our search for principles.

The Presence of God

The Lord's presence is the birthright of every believer and the heart of every quiet time. Before Jesus was born he was named *Immanuel*—God with us. During his discipling of the apostles, Jesus promised them, and us, that he would not leave us as orphans but make his home with us (Jn 14:15-21). His last words in the Gospel of Matthew were his promise to be with us to the end of the age (Mt 28:20).

This is more than an abstract promise or an intellectual idea. Nor is it an exotic mystical experience. It is merely a matter of relationship. God intends for us to know that he is with us. Meeting with God is very similar to being with a friend when you know each other well. There is a sense of connection that is much deeper than what we say to each other or the things we do together.

Sometimes you can know the presence of the Lord as a warm, quiet affection that wells up as you sit quietly before him. At other times the sense of his presence may come as a deep sense of heaviness and grief over your sinfulness. Or perhaps you know the Lord is with you as you read the Scriptures—a sense of inner nourishment as you read about God's work in the lives of people in the Old and New Testaments.

God's presence gives strength for living. And, we should note, the presence of God with us is not merely for our benefit. Others too will sense a depth about our lives that stirs spiritual hunger within them.

Using Your Emotions

All relationships involve our emotions, and our relationship with God is no different. Just as ignoring our emotions will leave us feeling separate and distant from people, the same will be true of our relationship with God if we ignore its emotional dimension.

So if we are to grow in spiritual perception, then we need to understand that emotions play an important role. With my emotions I sense God's affection for me, embrace his Word and react to his commands.

I realize that to bring in emotions is to invite controversy. Talking about emotions among Christians can be, well, emotional. Some pride themselves on their emotional restraint. Others take pride in their ability to display emotion. For those who value emotional restraint, let me say that, while I am suggesting that we must open ourselves up to emotion, I am not necessarily advocating outward displays of emotion. For those who have found great benefit in the feeling side of faith, you should keep in mind that emotions are natural responses that vary from time to time and should not be forced or manipulated.

Both in Scripture and in history we see godly people whose emotions were central in their encounters with God. David, as many psalms testify, experienced tremendous heights and great depths. Elijah, Jeremiah, Jonah and Habakkuk, to mention a few, had their times of ups and lots of downs.

Our emotions are more than mere reactions. They mean something. The writer of Psalm 42 begins, "As the deer pants for streams of water, so my soul pants for you, O God." He continues, "Why are you downcast, O my soul? Why so disturbed within me?" (vv. 5, 11). Today we would just consider ourselves depressed. The psalmist, in contrast, knew that his soul was "downcast" for a reason; he was thirsty for a fresh encounter with God.

This is not to say that strong emotions are a guarantee that God's Spirit is at work. Satan can duplicate almost anything. The way to discern true spiritual affection is in our love for God. Are we growing in appreciation of God's might, majesty and beauty? And when we are emotionally down, are we pitying ourselves or are we reaching out to seek God's consolation?

Once we are open to our emotions before the Lord, fresh springs of spiritual life can open up. And there is no better place to embrace our emotions than in our quiet times.

Quiet Time Phases

Because knowing God is a dynamic personal relationship, just like any other relationship, it tends to shift and vary with time and circumstances. If we are unaware of this dynamic, we may expect the same thing to happen each time we sit down to enjoy time with God. But the reality is that our quiet times are full of variety. Sometimes they are rich and sweet, other times dry and boring. Sometimes they require great determination, and other times they seem fresh and spontaneous. Sometimes we may go for

long periods in which we do not consistently have quiet times, while at other times we are easily able to maintain the discipline of meeting God regularly.

We should not feel guilty about these ebbs and flows. If we think of quiet times as merely something we do, a method to be followed, then this variety will bother us. But if we know that our quiet times are always changing because our relationship with God is always growing and developing, then we can view these changes in our quiet times with deeper spiritual insight.

Personality and Spiritual Disciplines

Our temperaments have a great deal to do with our spiritual disciplines. I have observed that people who are methodical and detail oriented—accountants and engineers, for example—may have a hard time getting beyond staying in a routine, focusing on rigorously doing one's spiritual duty. On the other hand, those who tend to be spontaneous—say, artists, musicians and designers—may struggle to maintain a routine, but meet God on a more intimate level.

I am of the spontaneous temperament. I don't like to settle into one way of doing things for very long. I have a natural inclination to avoid set daily quiet times. I deal with this tendency in two ways. Sometimes I find it necessary to be very determined on a daily basis. At other times, I make it a goal to have four or five quiet times during the week and feel good about it if I have three or four.

Whatever our quiet time experience, there is no place for self-condemnation or pride. When we do well, it is surely a gift of God's grace to us. When we do poorly, being either irregular or legalistic, we shouldn't be surprised. God isn't. I don't condemn myself when I miss the mark. I am grateful for what times I have. I know the Lord is glad to be with me, and I determine to do better next time.

Each person has to move through the spiritual journey in his or her own way. Wherever we are in our spiritual lives, we should keep in mind that our goal in having a quiet time is to live with a heart-sense of devotion in the presence of God.

Inexpressible Joy

Quiet times are so much more than a duty. A quiet time is a divine encounter. God is with us. The purpose of a quiet time is to meet with him. If we are not listening for him, if we are not looking for him, we may miss the meeting.

On the other hand, if we are looking and listening through carefully developed spiritual disciplines, we will, in the words of Peter, be "filled with an inexpressible and glorious joy" (1Pe 1:8).

The Lord is present in his world, and all creation declares his glory. In our work, our family, our recreation, whatever we do, we can be filled with a sense of his presence.

However, unless we practice the discipline of a quiet time, we will be apt to miss his glory that swirls and sings around us. A fruitful quiet time will allow us to be before him in such a way that we sense his presence in everything we do.

How to Study the Bible

James F. Nyquist & Jack Kuhatschek

Sherlock Holmes was known for his brilliant powers of observation. One day a stranger came into Holmes's study. The detective looked over the gentleman carefully and then remarked to Watson: "Beyond the obvious facts that he has at some time done manual labour, that he takes snuff, that he is a Freemason, that he has been in China, and that he has done considerable amount of writing lately, I can deduce nothing else."[1]

Watson was so astounded by his abilities that he commented: "I could not help laughing at the ease with which he explained his process of deduction. 'When I hear you give your reasons,' I remarked, 'the thing always appears to me to be so ridiculously simple that I could easily do it myself, though at each successive instance of your reasoning I am baffled, until you explain your process. And yet I believe that my eyes are as good as yours.'

" 'Quite so,' he answered . . . throwing himself down into an armchair. 'You see, but you do not observe.' "[2]

Step One: Observation

The first step in personal Bible study is to make several *observations* about the passage or book you are studying. Like a good detective, we must train our eyes to see the obvious and the not so obvious. We can learn to do this by bombarding the book or passage with questions. Rudyard Kipling once wrote:

I have six faithful serving men
Who taught me all I know,
Their names are *What* and *Where* and *When*
And *How* and *Why* and *Who*.

Who—Who is the author of the book? To whom is he writing? Who are the major and minor characters?

Where—Where do the events occur? Are there any references to towns, cities, provinces? If you are reading a letter, where do the recipients live?

When—Are there any references to the time, day, month or year, or to when events took place in relation to other events?

What—What actions or events are taking place? What words or ideas are repeated or are central to the passage? What is the mood (joyous, somber)?

Why—Does the passage offer any reasons, explanations, statements of purpose?

How—How is the passage written? Is it a letter, speech, poem, parable? Does the author use any figures of speech (similes, metaphors)? How is it organized (around ideas, people, geography)?

The observation questions in the quiet times (which often begin with one of these six words) help us probe a book or passage and uncover many important facts. *Writing down* our observations in a notebook helps us make sure we are observing clearly and allows us to refer to these facts later in our study.

The importance of careful observation cannot be

overstressed since your observations will form the basis for your interpretations. In one of his most baffling cases, Sherlock Holmes commented to Watson: "I had . . . come to an entirely erroneous conclusion, which shows, my dear Watson, how dangerous it always is to reason from insufficient data."[3]

Sometimes observation may seem simplistic and dull. But it is extremely important. As Holmes suggests, faulty or inadequate data could lead us to wrong conclusions about what the passage means, which is the next step in the process.

Step Two: Interpretation

When we interpret we seek to understand those facts discovered through careful observation.

Were there any words you didn't understand? Define them.

Did the author use figurative language? This needs to be unraveled.

Were major ideas presented? Try to grasp their meaning and significance.

Did you encounter any difficulties? Seek to resolve them.

Meaning, significance, explanation—these are the goals of the interpreter. How do you reach these goals? And once you have reached them, how do you know you are not mistaken?

For example, have you ever been discussing a passage of Scripture with someone when suddenly he or she says, "That's just *your* interpretation," as if to say, "You have your interpretation and I have mine, and mine is just as good as yours!"

The person is half right. People often disagree on how the Bible should be interpreted. But just because there are many different interpretations of a passage doesn't mean they are all *good* interpretations. A good interpretation must pass one crucial test—it must conform to the *author's* intended meaning. You may have a seemingly wonderful interpretation of Scripture, but if it is different from what the author intended, it is incorrect.

How then can we discover the author's meaning? By following five steps:

1. Discover the historical context of the book. The events described in the Bible took place thousands of years ago. Therefore, we often lack important information regarding the background or context in which these events took place. For example, almost every New Testament letter was written to address a particular problem or set of problems: the Galatians were seeking to be justified by law; the Corinthians wanted answers to questions about marriage, spiritual gifts, meat offered to idols and so on; Timothy needed to know how to restore order to a church.

Sometimes the background or context of a psalm, prophetic book or New Testament letter can be found within the book or passage itself. For example, in 1 John we read, "I am writing these things to you about those who are trying to lead you astray" (1Jn 2:26). The introductions to each book in *The NIV Quiet Time Bible* also give you much of the basic information you'll need. If you want more, you can always consult a good reference work like the *New Bible Dictionary*.

2. Identify the type of literature you are studying. The biblical authors communicated in a variety of ways—through stories, letters, poems, proverbs, parables and symbols. The *way* they say things adds richness and beauty to *what* they say.

The literature of the Bible has been classified into various types. These include discourse (for example, the New Testament letters), prose narrative (the style used in the Gospels re-creating scenes and events from biblical history), poetry (the Psalms), proverbs (wise sayings such as those in the book of Proverbs), parables (Jesus used parables to explain a spiritual truth by means of a story or analogy), prophetic literature (for example, Isaiah) and apocalyptic literature (Revelation, which makes heavy use of symbolism, fits here).

3. Get an overview of the book. In Bible study it is helpful to get an overview of the book you are studying. And you may want to do this before starting on the quiet times in any given book. The parts of the book only take on their true significance in light of the whole. But remember that the way a book is put together will be closely related to its literary type. An epistle such as Romans is organized around ideas. Historical narratives are put together in a variety of ways. Genesis (after chapter 11) is organized around people: Abraham, Isaac, Jacob and Joseph. The Gospel of John focuses primarily on several "signs" which Jesus did. Psalm 119 is structured around the letters of the Hebrew alphabet!

Begin by reading quickly through the book. As you read, try to discover its overall theme. Next, look for major sections or divisions within the book. Look for connections or relationships between the sections, subsections and paragraphs. Look also for contracts, for cause and effect, for movement from general to specific and so on. Continually ask yourself how these paragraphs, subsections and sections contribute to the overall theme of the book.

4. *Study the book passage by passage.* Once you have an overview of the structure and contents of a book, begin studying it passage by passage, which are already clearly divided for you in this Bible. Many of the questions you will find in the quiet times will help you identify the main *subject* of the passage, what the author is *saying* about it, the *context* of the passage you are studying and its *atmosphere* or *mood.*

5. *Compare your interpretation with a good commentary.* Once you feel you have understood the main subject of the passage and what the author is saying about it, compare your interpretation with that of a good commentary, such as the *New Bible Commentary,* which can give you additional insights that you might have missed. It can also serve as a corrective if you have misunderstood something the author has said. But do your best to understand the passage on your own before consulting a commentary.

Step Three: Application

To properly apply the Scriptures, we must remember the nature of Scripture. We mentioned earlier that almost every book of the Bible was written to address specific problems, needs and questions of the people living *at that time.*

We face many of these same problems and questions today. It is still possible to take a fellow believer to court, and we still have questions about marriage. In fact there are hundreds of ways in which our problems and needs correspond to those faced by the people in the Bible. This is natural since we share a common humanity.

This leads us to the first principle of application:

Rule #1: Whenever our situation corresponds to that faced by the original readers, God's Word to us is exactly the same as it was to them.

But there are also situations from their day which do not have an exact counterpart today. This, too, is to be expected because of the differences between modern and biblical culture. In such cases we should follow the second principle of application:

Rule #2: Whenever our situation does not correspond to that faced by the original readers, we should look for the principle *underlying God's Word to them. We can then apply that principle to comparable situations today.*

For example, what was the principle underlying Paul's words about food sacrificed to idols? He was concerned that the Corinthians not do anything that would lead someone with a weak conscience to sin: "Therefore, if what I eat causes my brother to fall into sin, I will never eat meat again, so that I will not cause him to fall" (1Co 8:13). This principle might be applicable to many situations today, such as whether a Christian should drink alcoholic beverages around someone who is a former alcoholic—or drink at all.

Once we understand these principles of application, we can think of unlimited ways in which God's Word applies today.

Practice Makes Perfect (Well, Almost)

Learning to study the Bible is like learning any other skill—the more you do it, the easier it becomes. One of the side benefits of using *The NIV Quiet Time Bible* regularly is that you will be trained to better observe, interpret and apply Scripture. At first, it may seem mechanical, like learning how to type. And remember, you are not alone in Bible study. The Holy Spirit did not write Scripture in order to confuse us. He will help you to understand and apply the Bible as you pray, study diligently and make use of many of the study aids available today. Bon appetit!

[1]*The Illustrated Sherlock Holmes Treasury* (New York: Avenel Books, 1976), p. 17.
[2]Ibid., p. 2 (emphasis added).
[3]Ibid., p. 112.

Prayer and Journaling

Bill Hybels

According to a well-known business axiom, "if you want to know something, ask an expert." If you want to learn about sailboat racing, ask Dennis Connor. If you want to know about broadcast journalism, ask Diane Sawyer. If you want to find out how to turn around a large corporation, ask Lee Iacocca.

It makes sense, then, if you want to learn how to pray, to ask the number-one expert—Jesus Christ himself. Jesus' disciples recognized his expertise. Once they stumbled upon him while he was praying privately (see Lk 11:1). They were so moved by his earnestness and intensity that when he finally got up from his knees, one of them timidly asked, "Would you teach us to pray?" They knew that in comparison to their Master, they were mere neophytes—first-graders in the school of prayer.

Jesus did not object to their question. Instead, he took the opportunity to teach them how to pray. This is what he said:

When you pray, do not be like the hypocrites, for they love to pray standing in the synagogues and on the street corners to be seen by men. . . . When you pray, go into your room, close the door and pray to your Father, who is unseen. Then your Father, who sees what is done in secret, will reward you. And when you pray, do not keep on babbling like pagans, for they think they will be heard because of their many words. Do not be like them, for your Father knows what you need before you ask him.

This, then, is how you should pray:

"Our Father in heaven, hallowed be your name, your kingdom come, your will be done on earth as it is in heaven. Give us today our daily bread. Forgive us our debts, as we also have forgiven our debtors. And lead us not into temptation, but deliver us from the evil one." (Mt 6:5-13)

No other passage in Scripture tells so straightforwardly how to pray, and the advice Jesus offered his disciples two thousand years ago applies to all of us today: (1) pray secretly, (2) pray sincerely and (3) pray specifically.

Getting Away from Distractions

Some people pray in public places, at social gatherings and at mealtimes, just so they can be seen and heard and assumed to be religious. But prayer, Jesus says, is not a spectator sport. It is not something we are to engage in to give off signals of spirituality. Forget that idea, says Jesus. When you pray, go into your room and shut the door. Find a closet, an empty office, the workshop out in the garage, some secret place away from people and alone with God. That's where you can pray most effectively.

Why the emphasis on privacy? Why shut the door? First, there is an obvious, practical reason. A private place ensures a minimum of distractions, and most people find distractions deadly when it comes to making connection with God. Almost any kind of noise—voices, music, a ringing phone, kids, dogs, birds—can cause me to lose my concentration during a time of prayer. Even a ticking clock can catch me up in its rhythm until I'm tapping my foot and singing a country song to its beat. Jesus knows how our minds are put together, and he counsels, "Don't bother fighting distractions, because you'll lose. Avoid them. Find a quiet place where you can pray without interruption."

The practical reasons for privacy are important, but I think there is also a more subtle wisdom in Jesus' advice to pray in a secret place. Once you identify such a place and begin to use it regularly, a kind of aura surrounds it. Your prayer room becomes to you what the garden of Gethsemane became to Jesus—a holy place, the place where God meets with you.

I created such a prayer room near the credenza in a corner of my former office. In my prayer place I put an open Bible, a sign that says "God is able," a crown of thorns to remind me of the suffering

Savior and a shepherd's staff that I often hold up while making requests.

That office corner became a holy place for me. I arrived there around six o'clock in the morning when no one was around and the phone was unlikely to ring, and there I communed with the Lord. I poured out my heart to him, worshiped him, prayed for members of my congregation and received remarkable answers to my prayer.

My office has recently been relocated, and I now have a new prayer corner. But I miss the old one—not because there is anything holy about the corner itself, but because of what happened there. Every morning for several years I met with the Lord, and he met faithfully with me. Thinking of that corner is like thinking of home.

If you want to learn how to pray, find yourself a quiet place, free of distractions. It doesn't have to be a chapel. It can be the utility room, the kitchen pantry, the barn, your office or the front seat of your pickup truck, as long as the surroundings are familiar and quiet.

Meaning What We Say
Not only did Jesus tell his disciples to pray secretly; he also told them to pray sincerely. "Do not keep on babbling," he said. Be careful of clichés. Don't fall into the habit of using meaningless repetition.

How easy it is to use sanctified jargon while praying! Certain phrases sound so appropriate, so spiritual, so pious, that many believers learn to string them together and call that prayer. They may not even think of the implications of what they are saying.

For example, I sometimes hear a mature believer say very earnestly, "Dear Lord, please be with me as I go on this new job interview," or "Please be with me as I go on this trip." When you first hear it, this request sounds holy. Unfortunately, it doesn't make sense. I'm often tempted to ask the one doing the praying, "Why do you ask God to do what he is already doing?" We don't need to ask God to be with us if we are members of his family. Instead, we need to pray that we will be *aware* of his presence, that we will be confident because of it. Asking God to be with us when he is already there is one kind of "babbling."

Another kind of meaningless repetition is often heard at the dinner table. A believer sits down to a meal that is a nutritional nightmare. The grease is bubbling, the salt is glistening, the sugared drink stands ready to slosh the stuff down. "Dear Lord," the person prays, "bless this food to our bodies, and grant us strength and nourishment from it so that we may do your will." God's will might be for the believer to say, "Amen," push back from the table and give the meal to the dog—except that dogs matter to God too!

The apostle Paul tells us God's will in 1 Corinthians 6:20: "Honor God with your body." That means putting the right things into your body. Don't ask God to bless junk food and miraculously transform it so that it has nutritional value. Doing that is acting like the fifth-grader who, after taking the geography test, prayed, "Dear God, please make Detroit the capital of Michigan." That's not how God works.

Praying Specifically
God-honoring prayers are not simply shopping lists. They are more than cries for help, strength, mercy and miracles. Authentic prayer should include worship: "Our Father in heaven, hallowed be your name" (Mt 6:9). It should include submission: "Your will be done on earth as it is in heaven" (v. 10). Requests are certainly appropriate: "Give us today our daily bread" (v. 11); as are confessions: "Forgive us our debts, as we also have forgiven our debtors" (v. 12).

The Lord's Prayer is an excellent model, but it was never intended to be a magical incantation to get God's attention. Jesus didn't give this prayer as a paragraph to be recited; in fact, he had just warned against using repetitious phrases. Instead, he gave it as a pattern to suggest the variety of elements that should be included when we pray.

Putting Prayers on Paper
A good way to learn to pray specifically is to write out your prayers and then read them to God. Many people find they are better able to concentrate if they put pen to paper and arrange their assorted thoughts into an organized format. I've been doing this for several years, and I find that it helps me in several ways. It forces me to be specific; broad generalities don't look good on paper. It keeps my mind from wandering. And it helps me see when

God answers prayers.

At the end of each month, I read over my prayer journal and see where God has done miraculous things. Whenever my faith feels weak, I turn to my journal and see evidence that God is answering my prayers. If I can list a number of answers to specific prayers in January, I feel better prepared to trust God in February.

I write out my prayers every day; I have not been able to grow in my prayer life any other way. Experiment and see what works best for you. Try writing out your prayers once a week at first. If you find it helpful, do it more often. If it cramps your style and makes you uncomfortable, find another way that is more effective for you. But however you do it, pray Jesus' way: make your prayers private, sincere and specific.

Remember that God's prevailing power is released through prayer. He is interested in you and your needs. He is able to meet any need, and he has invited you to pray. His Son, Jesus, the expert on prayer, has given instructions so that you know just how to pray.

Here's an assignment to get your prayer routine started. Take a sheet of paper and draw three horizontal lines across it, dividing it into four sections. Label the sections A, C, T and S.

In the first section, write a paragraph of adoration. List God's characteristics that especially move you today. In the second, write a paragraph of confession. Specifically identify the sins that are on your conscience. (You can burn this paper when you're done with it!) In the third, list God's blessings for which you are thankful. And in the fourth, make your requests, whatever they may be.

Do this again tomorrow, and the next day. Experiment with the ACTS routine. Adapt the categories to fit your situation, but be sure to include each category each time you pray. Experience the blessings of balance.

And see what God does in your life.

PREFACE

The New International Version of the Holy Bible is a completely new translation made by over a hundred scholars working directly from the best available Greek texts. It had its beginning in 1965 when, after several years of exploratory study by committees from the Christian Reformed Church and the National Association of Evangelicals, a group of scholars met at Palos Heights, Illinois, and concurred in the need for a new translation of the Bible in contemporary English. This group, though not made up of official church representatives, was transdenominational. Its conclusion was endorsed by a large number of leaders from many denominations who met in Chicago in 1966.

Responsibility for the new version was delegated by the Palos Heights group to a self-governing body of fifteen, the Committee on Bible Translation, composed for the most part of biblical scholars from colleges, universities and seminaries. In 1967 the New York Bible Society (now the International Bible Society) generously undertook the financial sponsorship of the project—a sponsorship that made it possible to enlist the help of many distinguished scholars. The fact that participants from the United States, Great Britain, Canada, Australia and New Zealand worked together gave the project its international scope. That they were from many denominations—including Anglican, Assemblies of God, Baptist, Brethren, Christian Reformed, Church of Christ, Evangelical Free, Lutheran, Mennonite, Methodist, Nazarene, Presbyterian, Wesleyan and other churches helped to safeguard the translation from sectarian bias.

How it was made helps to give the New International Version its distinctiveness. The translation of each book was assigned to a team of scholars. Next, one of the Intermediate Editorial Committees revised the initial translation, with constant reference to the Hebrew, Aramaic or Greek. Their work then went to one of the General Editorial Committees, which checked it in detail and made another thorough revision. This revision in turn was carefully reviewed by the Committee on Bible Translation, which made further changes and then released the final version for publication. In this way the entire Bible underwent three revisions, during each of which the translation was examined for its faithfulness to the original languages and for its English style.

All this involved many thousands of hours of research and discussion regarding the meaning of the texts and the precise way of putting them into English. It may well be that no other translation has been made by a more thorough process of review and revision from committee to committee than this one.

From the beginning of the project, the Committee on Bible Translation held to certain goals for the New International Version: that it would be an accurate translation and one that would have clarity and literary quality and so prove suitable for public and private reading, teaching, preaching, memorizing and liturgical use. The Committee also sought to preserve some measure of continuity with the long tradition of translating the Scriptures into English.

In working toward these goals, the translators were united in their commitment to the authority and infallibility of the Bible as God's Word in written form. They believe that it contains the divine answer to the deepest needs of humanity, that it sheds unique light on our path in a dark world, and that it sets forth the way to our eternal well-being.

The first concern of the translators has been the accuracy of the translation and its fidelity to the thought of the biblical writers. They have striven for more than a word-for-word translation. Because thought patterns and syntax differ from language to language, faithful communication of the meaning of the writers of the Bible demands frequent modifications in sentence structure and constant regard for the contextual meanings of words.

The Committee on Bible Translation submitted the developing version to a number of stylistic consultants. Samples of the translation were tested for clarity and ease of reading by various kinds of people—young and old, highly educated and less well educated, ministers and laymen. Concern for clear and natural English motivated the translators and consultants. In view of the international use of English, the translators sought to avoid obvious Americanisms on the one hand and obvious Anglicisms on the other. A British edition reflects the comparatively few differences of significant idiom and of spelling.

As for the traditional pronouns "thou," "thee" and "thine" in reference to the Deity, the translators judged that to use these archaisms (along with the old verb forms such as "doest," "wouldest" and "hadst") would violate accuracy in translation. Greek does not use special pronouns for the persons of the Godhead. A present-day translation is not enhanced by forms that in the time of the King James Version were used in everyday speech, whether referring to God or man.

The Greek text used in translating the New Testament was an eclectic one. No other piece of ancient literature has such an abundance of manuscript witnesses as does the New Testament. Where existing manuscripts differ, the translators made their choice of readings according to accepted principles of New Testament textual criticism. Footnotes call attention to places where there was uncertainty about what the original text was. The best current printed texts of the Greek New Testament were used.

There is a sense in which the work of translation is never wholly finished. This applies to all great literature and uniquely so to the Bible. In 1973 the New Testament in the New International Version was published. Since then, suggestions for corrections and revisions have been received from various sources. The Committee on Bible Translation carefully considered the suggestions and adopted a number of them. These were incorporated in the first printing of the entire Bible in 1978. Additional revisions were made by the Committee on Bible Translation in 1983 and appear in printings after that date.

As in other ancient documents, the precise meaning of the biblical texts is sometimes uncertian. This is more often the case with the Hebrew and Aramaic texts than with the Greek text. Although archaeological and linguistic discoveries in this century aid in understanding difficult passages, some uncertainties remain. The more significant of these have been called to the reader's attention in the footnotes.

In regard to the divine name *YHWH,* commonly referred to as the *Tetragrammaton,* the translators adopted the device used in most English versions of rendering that name as "LORD" in capital letters to distinguish it from *Adonai,* another Hebrew word rendered "Lord," for which small letters are used. Wherever the two names stand together in the Old Testament as a compound name of God, they are rendered "Sovereign LORD."

Because for most readers today the phrases "the LORD of hosts" and "God of hosts" have little meaning, this version renders them "the LORD Almighty" and "God Almighty." These renderings convey the sense of the Hebrew, namely, "he who is sovereign over all the 'hosts' (powers) in heaven and on earth, especially over the 'hosts' (armies) of Israel." For readers unacquainted with Hebrew this does not make clear the distinction between *Sabaoth* ("hosts" or "Almighty") and *Shaddai* (which can also be translated "Almighty"), but the latter occurs infrequently and is always footnoted. When *Adonai* and *YHWH Sabaoth* occur together, they are rendered "the Lord, the LORD Almighty."

As for other proper nouns, the familiar spellings of the King James Version are generally retained. Names traditionally spelled with "ch," except where it is final, are usually spelled in this translation with "k" or "c," since the biblical languages do not have the sound that "ch" frequently indicates in English—for example, in *chant.* For well-known names such as Zechariah, however, the traditional spelling has been retained. Variation in the spelling of names in the original languages has usually not been indicated. Where a person or place has two or more different names in the Hebrew, Aramaic or Greek texts, the more familiar one has generally been used, with footnotes where needed.

To achieve clarity the translators sometimes supplied words not in the original texts but required by the context. If there was uncertainty about such material, it is enclosed in brackets. Also for the sake of clarity or style, nouns,

including some proper nouns, are sometimes substituted for pronouns, and vice versa. As an aid to the reader, italicized sectional headings are inserted in most of the books. They are not to be regarded as part of the NIV text, are not for oral reading, and are not intended to dictate the interpretation of the sections they head.

The footnotes in this version are of several kinds, most of which need no explanation. Those giving alternative translations begin with "Or" and generally introduce the alternative with the last word preceding it in the text, except when it is a single-word alternative; in poetry quoted in a footnote a slant mark indicates a line division. Footnotes introduced by "Or" do not have uniform significance. In some cases two possible translations were considered to have about equal validity. In other cases, though the translators were convinced that the translation in the text was correct, they judged that another interpretation was possible and of sufficient importance to be represented in a footnote.

In the New Testament, footnotes that refer to uncertainty regarding the original text are introduced by "Some manuscripts" or similar expressions. In the Old Testament, evidence for the reading chosen is given first and evidence for the alternative is added after a semicolon (for example: Septuagint; Hebrew *father*). In such notes the term "Hebrew" refers to the Masoretic Text.

It should be noted that minerals, flora and fauna, architectural details, articles of clothing and jewelry, musical instruments and other articles cannot always be identified with precision. Also measures of capacity in the biblical period are particularly uncertain.

Like all translations of the Bible, made as they are by imperfect man, this one undoubtedly falls short of its goals. Yet we are grateful to God for the extent to which he has enabled us to realize these goals and for the strength he has given us and our colleagues to complete our task. We offer this version of the Bible to him in whose name and for whose glory it has been made. We pray that it will lead many into a better understanding of the Holy Scriptures and a fuller knowledge of Jesus Christ the incarnate Word, of whom the Scriptures so faithfully testify.

The Committee on Bible Translation

June 1978
(Revised August 1983)

Names of the translators and editors
may be secured
from the International Bible Society,
translation sponsors of the
New International Version,
P.O. Box 62970,
Colorado Springs, Colorado
80962-2970 U.S.A.

TABLE OF WEIGHTS AND MEASURES

Biblical Unit		Approximate American Equivalent	Approximate Metric Equivalent

WEIGHTS

talent	(60 minas)	75 pounds	34 kilograms
mina	(50 shekels)	1¼ pounds	0.6 kilogram
shekel	(2 bekas)	³/₅ ounce	11.5 grams
pim	(²/₃ shekel)	¹/₃ ounce	7.6 grams
beka	(10 gerahs)	¹/₅ ounce	5.5 grams
gerah		¹/₅₀ ounce	0.6 gram

LENGTH

cubit		18 inches	0.5 meter
span		9 inches	23 centimeters
handbreadth		3 inches	8 centimeters

CAPACITY
Dry Measure

cor [homer]	(10 ephahs)	6 bushels	220 liters
lethek	(5 ephahs)	3 bushels	110 liters
ephah	(10 omers)	³/₅ bushel	22 liters
seah	(¹/₃ ephah)	7 quarts	7.3 liters
omer	(¹/₁₀ ephah)	2 quarts	2 liters
cab	(¹/₁₈ ephah)	1 quart	1 liter

Liquid Measure

bath	(1 ephah)	6 gallons	22 liters
hin	(¹/₆ bath)	4 quarts	4 liters
log	(¹/₇₂ bath)	¹/₃ quart	0.3 liter

The figures of the table are calculated on the basis of a shekel equaling 11.5 grams, a cubit equaling 18 inches and an ephah equaling 22 liters. The quart referred to is either a dry quart (slightly larger than a liter) or a liquid quart (slightly smaller than a liter), whichever is applicable. The ton referred to in the footnotes is the American ton of 2,000 pounds.

This table is based on the best available information, but it is not intended to be mathematically precise; like the measurement equivalents in the footnotes, it merely gives approximate amounts and distances. Weights and measures differed somewhat at various times and places in the ancient world. There is uncertainty particularly about the ephah and the bath; further discoveries may give more light on these units of capacity.

THE
OLD TESTAMENT

Genesis

We all look back and wonder about beginnings. Children are fascinated with stories of their birth and babyhood. Families trace their genealogies. Nations produce histories of their origin. The pressures of the present and hopes for the future take on new meaning when we know more about how it all began.

Genesis is a book of beginnings: the origin of the universe, birth of the human race and founding of the Hebrew nation. Yet this book is more than a record of origins. It provides the foundation for many of the great themes so prominent throughout the Old and New Testaments. Here we learn about God, humanity and nature in their mutual relationships. The Creator and Controller of the universe reveals himself as the Lord and Judge of history, which has both a purpose and a goal. Concepts of covenant and grace, election and redemption permeate God's saving activity to overcome the consequences of evil and sin. These great doctrines of creation, sin and salvation trace their beginnings to this remarkable book.

It should not surprise us that Genesis, more than any other part of the Bible, has been the scene of historical, literary, theological and scientific battles. Some of these issues have made their way out of church and seminary into our schools and courts. Since much discussion of these controversial questions is based on misinformation and secondhand opinion, we should find out for ourselves what the text says and, equally important, what it does *not* say. The purpose of these quiet times is to help you discover the meaning of Genesis for those who first heard its message and then for us today. You may be surprised to find how clear Genesis is when we let the author have his say and refrain from importing questions he never intended to answer.

Historical Context

Genesis is the first of five books called the Pentateuch. The New Testament attributes these writings to Moses. During the last century many critics have questioned the Mosaic authorship of the Pentateuch. Liberal scholarship attributes these writings to unknown authors or redactors long after Moses, probably late in the monarchy. Nevertheless, a strong case can be made for the traditional view that Moses wrote most of the Pentateuch, even though he may have used existing sources for Genesis and some of the material may have been edited after his death. At any rate, we will assume that the message of Genesis was given to Israel during their years in the wilderness, around 1250 B.C. Therefore, we need to know something of Israel's cultural and religious situation in order to understand what the author intends to teach.

For about four hundred years the Hebrews had languished in Egypt, far from the land promised to Abraham. Those centuries took a spiritual as well as a physical toll. The Hebrews had no Scriptures, only some oral patriarchal traditions. Except for a few midwives who remained faithful, the people had supplanted the fear of the Lord with cultic worship of the gods of other nations. Even after they were miraculously delivered from slavery and led toward Canaan, the people apparently had little knowledge of the God of their forefather Abraham.

When the Hebrews arrived at Mount Sinai, their worldview and lifestyle differed little from that of neighboring nations. Their culture was essentially pagan. Now God was calling them to keep his covenant, to become "a kingdom of priests and a holy nation" (Ex 19:6). Although the people assented enthusiastically, their yes was just the beginning of a long, painful process by which God would create a new culture to fulfill their vocation.

Moses faced a formidable task. The people needed a radically different theology to know God and his purpose in history, a new religious institution to guide their worship, another lifestyle for moral and ethical living, and a new cosmology to reorient their attitudes toward the natural world. These five books of Moses were designed to make the Hebrews a people of God through a new, divinely instituted culture. For this reason the Pentateuch provides strong antipagan teaching to help God's people make a clean break with the past and learn to look at all of life from his point of view.

The Role of Genesis

This first book opens with an account of the beginning of the universe that lays the foundation for Israel's new cosmology. The narrative strikes hard not only at the nature gods worshiped by Israel's pagan neighbors but also at an array of false philosophies which have led large sections of the human race astray in every century.

The creation of the world culminates in God's forming a man and woman. But they soon rebel against their Creator and plunge humanity into sin, with devastating consequences. From then on Genesis recounts the drama of God's mighty acts of judgment and mercy as his redemptive purpose unfolds.

Throughout these narratives a central and organizing motif is the "call of God." His creative word initially calls the whole creation into being. God then calls into existence a covenant community to be his special people. Genesis and the whole Old Testament look forward to his new creation and covenant in Jesus Christ, into whose fellowship we also are called.

Outline

Part 1: Creation and Primeval History

1/ Genesis 1:1—2:3 ———————————— Our Place in the World

2/ Genesis 2:4—25 ———————————— Life as God Intended It

3/ Genesis 3 ———————————— How Can We Deal with Temptation?

4/ Genesis 4—5 ———————————— Consequences of Sin

5/ Genesis 6—7 ——————————— How Should We Live?

6/ Genesis 8:1—9:17 ——————— God's Promises

7/ Genesis 9:18—11:32 ——————— Family Problems

Part 2: The Emergence of Israel

8/ Genesis 12—13 ——————————— Following God into the Unknown

9/ Genesis 14—15 ——————————— Tests of Faith

10/ Genesis 16—17 ——————————— When Faith Falters

11/ Genesis 18—19 ——————————— God's Judgment on Society

12/ Genesis 20—21 ——————————— The Consequences of Unbelief

13/ Genesis 22—23 ——————————— Ultimate Faith

14/ Genesis 24:1—25:11 ——————— God's Guidance and Care

15/ Genesis 25:12—27:40 ——————— A Family Feud

16/ Genesis 27:41—30:24 ——————— God's Mercy and Justice

17/ Genesis 30:25—31:55 ——————— Rivalry and Its Results

18/ Genesis 32—33 ——————————— Planning and Praying

19/ Genesis 34—36 ——————————— The Cost of Discipleship

Part 3: Migration to Egypt

20/ Genesis 37—38 ——————————— Pride and Prejudice

21/ Genesis 39—40 ——————————— Performance Under Pressure

22/ Genesis 41—42 ——————————— Faithful Service Rewarded

23/ Genesis 43:1—45:15 ——————— Family Reconciliation

24/ Genesis 45:16—47:31 ——————— God Preserves His People

25/ Genesis 48—49 ——————————— The Life of Faith

26/ Genesis 50 ————————————— Spiritual Maturity

1 / *Genesis 1:1—2:3*
Our Place in the World

Imagine being a live spectater of the creation—Wow!

HAVE YOU EVER been involved in a discussion about creation? Do you wonder why this first chapter of Genesis generates so much controversy and what it is really meant to teach? This study will help you understand the author's purpose in writing and what his message taught Israel about their God, his creation and their special place in the natural world. It will also help you to consider how this account is relevant today. Remember that Genesis 1, like other books in the Bible, describes natural events in popular and nontechnical language. It reports them as they appear to the average person without explaining exactly *how* they took place. The emphasis is on the *who* and *why*, the Creator and his purposes in creation.

 Warming Up to God Isn't it amazing? The Creator of the universe is also the God who wants to be with you today. Sit quietly and let him come to you now.

 Read Genesis 1:1—2:3.

1 In the beginning God created the heavens and the earth. ²Now the earth was*ᵃ* formless and empty, darkness was over the surface of the deep, and the Spirit of God was hovering over the waters.

³And God said, "Let there be light," and there was light. ⁴God saw that the light was good, and he separated the light from the darkness. ⁵God called the light "day," and the darkness he called "night." And there was evening, and there was morning—the first day.

⁶And God said, "Let there be an expanse between the waters to separate water from water." ⁷So God made the expanse and separated the water under the expanse from the water above it. And it was so. ⁸God called the expanse "sky." And there was evening, and there was morning—the second day.

⁹And God said, "Let the water under the sky be gathered to one place, and let dry ground appear." And it was so. ¹⁰God called the dry ground "land," and the gathered waters he called "seas." And God saw that it was good.

¹¹Then God said, "Let the land produce vegetation: seed-bearing plants and trees on the land that bear fruit with seed in it, according to their various kinds." And it was so. ¹²The land produced vegetation: plants bearing seed according to their kinds and trees bearing fruit with seed in it according to their kinds. And God saw that it was good. ¹³And there was evening, and there was morning—the third day.

¹⁴And God said, "Let there be lights in the expanse of the sky to separate the day from the night, and let them serve as signs to mark seasons and days and years, ¹⁵and let them be lights in the expanse of the sky to give light on the earth." And it was so. ¹⁶God made two great lights—the greater light to govern the day and the lesser light to govern the night. He also made the stars. ¹⁷God set them in the expanse of the sky to give light on the earth, ¹⁸to govern the day and the night, and to separate light from darkness. And God saw that it was good. ¹⁹And there was evening, and there was morning—the fourth day.

²⁰And God said, "Let the water teem with living creatures, and let birds fly above the earth across the expanse of the sky." ²¹So God created the great creatures of the sea and every living and moving thing with which the water teems, according to their kinds, and every winged bird according to its kind. And God saw that it was good. ²²God blessed them and said, "Be fruitful and increase in number and fill the water in the seas, and let the birds increase on the earth." ²³And there was evening, and there was morning—the fifth day.

²⁴And God said, "Let the land produce living creatures according to their kinds: livestock, creatures that move along the ground, and wild animals, each according to its kind." And it was so. ²⁵God made the wild animals according to their kinds, the livestock according to their kinds, and all the creatures that move along the ground according to their kinds. And God saw that it was good.

²⁶Then God said, "Let us make man in our

ᵃ2 Or possibly became

image, in our likeness, and let them rule over the fish of the sea and the birds of the air, over the livestock, over all the earth,[b] and over all the creatures that move along the ground."

27So God created man in his own image,
    in the image of God he created him;
    male and female he created them.

28God blessed them and said to them, "Be fruitful and increase in number; fill the earth and subdue it. Rule over the fish of the sea and the birds of the air and over every living creature that moves on the ground." 29Then God said, "I give you every seed-bearing plant on the face of the whole earth and every tree that has fruit with seed in it. They will be yours for food. 30And to all the beasts of the earth and all the birds of the

air and all the creatures that move on the ground—everything that has the breath of life in it—I give every green plant for food." And it was so.

31God saw all that he had made, and it was very good. And there was evening, and there was morning—the sixth day.

2 Thus the heavens and the earth were completed in all their vast array.

2By the seventh day God had finished the work he had been doing; so on the seventh day he rested[c] from all his work. 3And God blessed the seventh day and made it holy, because on it he rested from all the work of creating that he had done.

[b]26 Hebrew; Syriac all the wild animals   [c]2 Or ceased; also in verse 3

 Discovering the Word   1. In what ways do God's creative commands during the first three days add form to the formless earth (1:3–13)?   2. How do God's commands during the next three days add fullness to the empty earth (1:14–25)?   3. In what ways do you think God views his creation as being good (1:4, 10, 12, 18, 21, 25)?   4. In what ways are man and woman unique among God's creation (1:26–27)?   5. What special commands and provisions does God give to the man and woman in his creation (1:28–31)?   6. According to 1:26, the man and woman are made in the image and likeness of God. What similarities are there between God's own work in creation and the commands and responsibilities he gives to the man and woman?

 Applying the Word   1. The creation account reveals that God brings order, beauty and harmony out of an originally chaotic situation. In what areas do you need to trust God to produce these qualities in your life?   2. As you look around at God's creation, how does it give you a greater appreciation for the Creator?

Responding in Prayer   Thank God for the magnificence of his creation and for allowing you to play such an important role in it.

---

2 / *Genesis 2:4–25*
Life as God Intended It

God intended something WONDERFUL! We've messed it up c̄ sin, etc. He was gracious enough to also give us a free will — but we chose against Him.

> *For of all sad words of tongue or pen,*
> *The saddest are these: "It might have been!"*

THESE WORDS TAKE on special significance when we consider life as God originally intended it. Genesis 2 still provides the basis for understanding who we were meant to be in relation to God, nature and each other. This narrative is different from the first in both content and style. It quickly moves from the world at large to the narrow stage of "a garden in the east." The literary style also changes significantly with its more colorful and detailed descriptions. Yet it continues to be history, rather than parable or myth, as it supplements the brief account of the creation of man and woman in 1:26–30.

 Warming Up to God   Close your eyes and think of a lush tropical forest, gloriously scented and teeming with life. Drink in the beautiful world God made for his people. Allow thanksgiving to well up inside until you are a bubbling spring of praise for God.

Read Genesis 2:4–25.

⁴This is the account of the heavens and the earth when they were created.

When the Lᴏʀᴅ God made the earth and the heavens— ⁵and no shrub of the field had yet appeared on the earth*ᵈ* and no plant of the field had yet sprung up, for the Lᴏʀᴅ God had not sent rain on the earth*ᵈ* and there was no man to work the ground, ⁶but streams*ᵉ* came up from the earth and watered the whole surface of the ground— ⁷the Lᴏʀᴅ God formed the man*ᶠ* from the dust of the ground and breathed into his nostrils the breath of life, and the man became a living being.

⁸Now the Lᴏʀᴅ God had planted a garden in the east, in Eden; and there he put the man he had formed. ⁹And the Lᴏʀᴅ God made all kinds of trees grow out of the ground—trees that were pleasing to the eye and good for food. In the middle of the garden were the tree of life and the tree of the knowledge of good and evil.

¹⁰A river watering the garden flowed from Eden; from there it was separated into four headwaters. ¹¹The name of the first is the Pishon; it winds through the entire land of Havilah, where there is gold. ¹²(The gold of that land is good; aromatic resin*ᵍ* and onyx are also there.) ¹³The name of the second river is the Gihon; it winds through the entire land of Cush.*ʰ* ¹⁴The name of the third river is the Tigris; it runs along the east side of Asshur. And the fourth river is the Euphrates.

¹⁵The Lᴏʀᴅ God took the man and put him in the Garden of Eden to work it and take care of it. ¹⁶And the Lᴏʀᴅ God commanded the man, "You are free to eat from any tree in the garden; ¹⁷but

you must not eat from the tree of the knowledge of good and evil, for when you eat of it you will surely die."

¹⁸The Lᴏʀᴅ God said, "It is not good for the man to be alone. I will make a helper suitable for him."

¹⁹Now the Lᴏʀᴅ God had formed out of the ground all the beasts of the field and all the birds of the air. He brought them to the man to see what he would name them; and whatever the man called each living creature, that was its name. ²⁰So the man gave names to all the livestock, the birds of the air and all the beasts of the field.

But for Adam*ⁱ* no suitable helper was found. ²¹So the Lᴏʀᴅ God caused the man to fall into a deep sleep; and while he was sleeping, he took one of the man's ribs*ʲ* and closed up the place with flesh. ²²Then the Lᴏʀᴅ God made a woman from the rib*ᵏ* he had taken out of the man, and he brought her to the man.

²³The man said,

"This is now bone of my bones
    and flesh of my flesh;
she shall be called 'woman,'*ˡ*
    for she was taken out of man."

²⁴For this reason a man will leave his father and mother and be united to his wife, and they will become one flesh.

²⁵The man and his wife were both naked, and they felt no shame.

ᵈ5 Or land; also in verse 6   ᵉ6 Or mist   ᶠ7 The Hebrew for man (adam) sounds like and may be related to the Hebrew for ground (adamah); it is also the name Adam (see Gen. 2:20).   ᵍ12 Or good; pearls   ʰ13 Possibly southeast Mesopotamia   ⁱ20 Or the man   ʲ21 Or took part of the man's side   ᵏ22 Or part   ˡ23 The Hebrew for woman sounds like the Hebrew for man.

 Discovering the Word 1. The author describes the creation of man in verse 7. In what ways is his creation unique? 2. What are we told about the garden God has prepared for Adam (vv. 8–14)? 3. What responsibility, freedom and limitation does God give to the man (vv. 15–17)? 4. How does Adam's name for his new partner reflect his appreciation of her (v. 23)? 5. Explain in your own words what verse 24 teaches about marriage.

Applying the Word 1. Note the social dimension of being created in the image of God (v. 18). What implications does this have for your relationships with other people? 2. How has this passage helped you understand who you were created to be in relation to God, nature and other people?

Responding in Prayer Thank your heavenly Father for making you in his image and likeness.

3 / *Genesis 3*
How Can We Deal with Temptation?

IF GOD IS good and powerful, why does he allow so much evil and pain? Although the Bible doesn't answer this question directly, it shows how sin and its consequences entered the world. The last chapter left Adam and Eve in Eden at peace with God, themselves and the natural world over which they had been given stewardship. They had the freedom to fulfill this responsibility and eat any fruit in the garden, with one exception. The tree of the knowledge of good and evil would be the test of their obedience to the Creator. In this study we see how they met this test and what lessons we can learn from their experience.

Warming Up to God Remember that no sin is any different or worse than the first sin in the Garden of Eden. Tell Jesus about your sin—and let him forgive you.

Read Genesis 3.

---

3 Now the serpent was more crafty than any of the wild animals the LORD God had made. He said to the woman, "Did God really say, 'You must not eat from any tree in the garden'?"

²The woman said to the serpent, "We may eat fruit from the trees in the garden, ³but God did say, 'You must not eat fruit from the tree that is in the middle of the garden, and you must not touch it, or you will die.' "

⁴"You will not surely die," the serpent said to the woman. ⁵"For God knows that when you eat of it your eyes will be opened, and you will be like God, knowing good and evil."

⁶When the woman saw that the fruit of the tree was good for food and pleasing to the eye, and also desirable for gaining wisdom, she took some and ate it. She also gave some to her husband, who was with her, and he ate it. ⁷Then the eyes of both of them were opened, and they realized they were naked; so they sewed fig leaves together and made coverings for themselves.

⁸Then the man and his wife heard the sound of the LORD God as he was walking in the garden in the cool of the day, and they hid from the LORD God among the trees of the garden. ⁹But the LORD God called to the man, "Where are you?"

¹⁰He answered, "I heard you in the garden, and I was afraid because I was naked; so I hid."

¹¹And he said, "Who told you that you were naked? Have you eaten from the tree that I commanded you not to eat from?"

¹²The man said, "The woman you put here with me—she gave me some fruit from the tree, and I ate it."

¹³Then the LORD God said to the woman, "What is this you have done?"

The woman said, "The serpent deceived me, and I ate."

¹⁴So the LORD God said to the serpent, "Because you have done this,

"Cursed are you above all the livestock
   and all the wild animals!
You will crawl on your belly
   and you will eat dust
   all the days of your life.
¹⁵And I will put enmity
   between you and the woman,
   and between your offspring^m and hers;
he will crush^n your head,
   and you will strike his heel."

¹⁶To the woman he said,

"I will greatly increase your pains in
   childbearing;
   with pain you will give birth to children.
Your desire will be for your husband,
   and he will rule over you."

¹⁷To Adam he said, "Because you listened to your wife and ate from the tree about which I commanded you, 'You must not eat of it,'

"Cursed is the ground because of you;
   through painful toil you will eat of it
   all the days of your life.
¹⁸It will produce thorns and thistles for you,
   and you will eat the plants of the field.
¹⁹By the sweat of your brow
   you will eat your food
until you return to the ground,

^{m}15 Or *seed* ^{n}15 Or *strike*

since from it you were taken;
for dust you are
   and to dust you will return."

²⁰Adam° named his wife Eve,ᵖ because she would become the mother of all the living.

²¹The LORD God made garments of skin for Adam and his wife and clothed them. ²²And the LORD God said, "The man has now become like one of us, knowing good and evil. He must not be allowed to reach out his hand and take also from the tree of life and eat, and live forever." ²³So the LORD God banished him from the Garden of Eden to work the ground from which he had been taken. ²⁴After he drove the man out, he placed on the east side𝑞 of the Garden of Eden cherubim and a flaming sword flashing back and forth to guard the way to the tree of life.

°20 Or *The man*   ᵖ20 *Eve* probably means *living.*   𝑞24 Or *placed in front*

Discovering the Word   1. How does Eve's answer misrepresent God's command (vv. 2–3)?   2. The serpent now becomes more direct (vv. 4–5). What statements does he make about the purpose and results of the command?   3. How have the serpent's words distorted Eve's thinking (v. 6)?   4. How did Adam and Eve's sin immediately affect their attitude toward themselves, each other and God (vv. 7–13)?   5. What judgments does the Lord God pronounce on the serpent (vv. 14–15), the woman (v. 16) and the man (vv. 17–19)? (Describe them in your own words.)   6. What actions does God finally take to end this era in Eden (vv. 21–24)?

Applying the Word   1. Adam and Eve made several mistakes: they listened to a creature instead of the Creator, followed their own impressions against his instructions, doubted God's concern for their best interests and made self-fulfillment their goal. In what situations have any of these led you to disobey a command of God?   2. What one lesson have you learned from this study that can help you recognize and resist a temptation you are facing?

Responding in Prayer   Romans 5:12 and 15 tell us that in the same way that sin entered the world through one person, it is redeemed by one man, our Lord Jesus Christ. Thank him for his love that erased our first sin in the garden and gave his wonderful grace.

---

4 / *Genesis 4—5*
Consequences of Sin

A LUTHERAN BISHOP in East Germany who suffered persecution first by the Nazis and then the Communists declared: "When God is not God, man is not man!" He had seen how the rejection of divine authority inevitably led to inhuman actions. In the previous chapter Adam and Eve's disobedience to God fractured their relationship with him. Now we see sin spreading to family relationships as hateful attitudes lead to violent actions.

   Warming Up to God   Jesus your Savior wants to care for you today. Hide under his shadow and tell him your concerns. He is listening and offers you peace.

   Read Genesis 4—5.

Adam𝑟 lay with his wife Eve, and she became pregnant and gave birth to Cain.𝑠 She said, "With the help of the LORD I have brought forth𝑡 a man." ²Later she gave birth to his brother Abel.

Now Abel kept flocks, and Cain worked the soil. ³In the course of time Cain brought some of the fruits of the soil as an offering to the LORD. ⁴But Abel brought fat portions from some of the firstborn of his flock. The LORD looked with favor on Abel and his offering, ⁵but on Cain and his offering he did not look with favor. So Cain was very angry, and his face was downcast.

⁶Then the LORD said to Cain, "Why are you angry? Why is your face downcast? ⁷If you do what is right, will you not be accepted? But if you

𝑟1 Or *The man*   𝑠1 *Cain* sounds like the Hebrew for *brought forth* or *acquired.*   𝑡1 Or *have acquired* do not do what is right, sin is crouching at your door; it desires to have you, but you must master it."

8Now Cain said to his brother Abel, "Let's go out to the field."ᵘ And while they were in the field, Cain attacked his brother Abel and killed him.

9Then the LORD said to Cain, "Where is your brother Abel?"

"I don't know," he replied. "Am I my brother's keeper?"

10The LORD said, "What have you done? Listen! Your brother's blood cries out to me from the ground. 11Now you are under a curse and driven from the ground, which opened its mouth to receive your brother's blood from your hand. 12When you work the ground, it will no longer yield its crops for you. You will be a restless wanderer on the earth."

13Cain said to the LORD, "My punishment is more than I can bear. 14Today you are driving me from the land, and I will be hidden from your presence; I will be a restless wanderer on the earth, and whoever finds me will kill me."

15But the LORD said to him, "Not soᵛ; if anyone kills Cain, he will suffer vengeance seven times over." Then the LORD put a mark on Cain so that no one who found him would kill him. 16So Cain went out from the LORD's presence and lived in the land of Nod,ʷ east of Eden.

17Cain lay with his wife, and she became pregnant and gave birth to Enoch. Cain was then building a city, and he named it after his son Enoch. 18To Enoch was born Irad, and Irad was the father of Mehujael, and Mehujael was the father of Methushael, and Methushael was the father of Lamech.

19Lamech married two women, one named Adah and the other Zillah. 20Adah gave birth to Jabal; he was the father of those who live in tents and raise livestock. 21His brother's name was Jubal; he was the father of all who play the harp and flute. 22Zillah also had a son, Tubal-Cain, who forged all kinds of tools out ofˣ bronze and iron. Tubal-Cain's sister was Naamah.

23Lamech said to his wives,

"Adah and Zillah, listen to me;
    wives of Lamech, hear my words.
I have killedʸ a man for wounding me,
    a young man for injuring me.
24If Cain is avenged seven times,

then Lamech seventy-seven times."

25Adam lay with his wife again, and she gave birth to a son and named him Seth,ᶻ saying, "God has granted me another child in place of Abel, since Cain killed him." 26Seth also had a son, and he named him Enosh.

At that time men began to call onᵃ the name of the LORD.

5 This is the written account of Adam's line.

When God created man, he made him in the likeness of God. 2He created them male and female and blessed them. And when they were created, he called them "man.ᵇ"

3When Adam had lived 130 years, he had a son in his own likeness, in his own image; and he named him Seth. 4After Seth was born, Adam lived 800 years and had other sons and daughters. 5Altogether, Adam lived 930 years, and then he died.

6When Seth had lived 105 years, he became the fatherᶜ of Enosh. 7And after he became the father of Enosh, Seth lived 807 years and had other sons and daughters. 8Altogether, Seth lived 912 years, and then he died.

9When Enosh had lived 90 years, he became the father of Kenan. 10And after he became the father of Kenan, Enosh lived 815 years and had other sons and daughters. 11Altogether, Enosh lived 905 years, and then he died.

12When Kenan had lived 70 years, he became the father of Mahalalel. 13And after he became the father of Mahalalel, Kenan lived 840 years and had other sons and daughters. 14Altogether, Kenan lived 910 years, and then he died.

15When Mahalalel had lived 65 years, he became the father of Jared. 16And after he became the father of Jared, Mahalalel lived 830 years and had other sons and daughters. 17Altogether, Mahalalel lived 895 years, and then he died.

18When Jared had lived 162 years, he became the father of Enoch. 19And after he became the father of Enoch, Jared lived 800 years and had other sons and daughters. 20Altogether, Jared lived 962 years, and then he died.

21When Enoch had lived 65 years, he became

ᵘ8 Samaritan Pentateuch, Septuagint, Vulgate and Syriac; Masoretic Text does not have *"Let's go out to the field."*   ᵛ15 Septuagint, Vulgate and Syriac; Hebrew *Very well*   ʷ16 *Nod* means *wandering* (see verses 12 and 14).   ˣ22 Or *who instructed all who work in*   ʸ23 Or *I will kill*   ᶻ25 *Seth* probably means *granted.*   ᵃ26 Or *to proclaim*   ᵇ2 Hebrew *adam*   ᶜ6 *Father* may mean *ancestor;* also in verses 7-26.

the father of Methuselah. 22And after he became the father of Methuselah, Enoch walked with God 300 years and had other sons and daughters. 23Altogether, Enoch lived 365 years. 24Enoch walked with God; then he was no more, because God took him away.

25When Methuselah had lived 187 years, he became the father of Lamech. 26And after he became the father of Lamech, Methuselah lived 782 years and had other sons and daughters. 27Altogether, Methuselah lived 969 years, and then he died.

28When Lamech had lived 182 years, he had a son. 29He named him Noah*d* and said, "He will comfort us in the labor and painful toil of our hands caused by the ground the LORD has cursed." 30After Noah was born, Lamech lived 595 years and had other sons and daughters. 31Altogether, Lamech lived 777 years, and then he died.

32After Noah was 500 years old, he became the father of Shem, Ham and Japheth.

d29 Noah sounds like the Hebrew for comfort.

 Discovering the Word 1. Why do you think the Lord looked with favor on Abel and his offering but not on Cain and his offering (vv. 3–7)? 2. How does 4:7 illustrate the nature of sin and our response to it? 3. The Lord confronts Adam, Eve and Cain with their sin by using a question (3:11, 13; 4:9–10). What might be some of the reasons for this approach? 4. In what way is Cain's punishment (4:10–16) a logical consequence of his sin? 5. How do Lamech's attitude and action expressed in his taunting song go beyond that of Cain's (4:23–24)?

Applying the Word 1. The lifestyle of Cain's family is a picture of humanity—technical progress matched by moral decline. How do you see this trend reflected in our own civilization? 2. How have you experienced God's judgment as a logical result of a wrong action? 3. How has this chapter helped you to understand the nature and consequences of sin?

Responding in Prayer Ask God to heal relationships in your life damaged by the effects of the Fall.

5 / *Genesis 6—7*
How Should We Live?

DOES IT REALLY make much difference how we live? Good so often goes unrewarded while evil persists without punishment. No wonder that we find life so perplexing. Even though these chapters don't answer all our questions, they show that eventually God's justice becomes evident in human affairs. The last chapter recorded how sin became more flagrant in Cain's family. Now the author describes the spread of this moral cancer throughout the human race. He contrasts two radically different ways of living and their results.

 Warming Up to God Today is a day full of sin and struggle—and it is a day made and consecrated by the Lord. Tell him about the events of your day and let anxiety slip away.

 Read Genesis 6—7.

6When men began to increase in number on the earth and daughters were born to them, 2the sons of God saw that the daughters of men were beautiful, and they married any of them they chose. 3Then the LORD said, "My Spirit will not contend with*e* man forever, for he is mortal*f*; his days will be a hundred and twenty years."

4The Nephilim were on the earth in those days—and also afterward—when the sons of God went to the daughters of men and had children by them. They were the heroes of old, men of renown.

5The LORD saw how great man's wickedness on the earth had become, and that every inclination of the thoughts of his heart was only evil all the time. 6The LORD was grieved that he had made

e3 Or My spirit will not remain in   f3 Or corrupt

man on the earth, and his heart was filled with pain. [7]So the LORD said, "I will wipe mankind, whom I have created, from the face of the earth—men and animals, and creatures that move along the ground, and birds of the air—for I am grieved that I have made them." [8]But Noah found favor in the eyes of the LORD.

[9]This is the account of Noah.

Noah was a righteous man, blameless among the people of his time, and he walked with God. [10]Noah had three sons: Shem, Ham and Japheth.

[11]Now the earth was corrupt in God's sight and was full of violence. [12]God saw how corrupt the earth had become, for all the people on earth had corrupted their ways. [13]So God said to Noah, "I am going to put an end to all people, for the earth is filled with violence because of them. I am surely going to destroy both them and the earth. [14]So make yourself an ark of cypress[g] wood; make rooms in it and coat it with pitch inside and out. [15]This is how you are to build it: The ark is to be 450 feet long, 75 feet wide and 45 feet high.[h] [16]Make a roof for it and finish[i] the ark to within 18 inches[j] of the top. Put a door in the side of the ark and make lower, middle and upper decks. [17]I am going to bring floodwaters on the earth to destroy all life under the heavens, every creature that has the breath of life in it. Everything on earth will perish. [18]But I will establish my covenant with you, and you will enter the ark—you and your sons and your wife and your sons' wives with you. [19]You are to bring into the ark two of all living creatures, male and female, to keep them alive with you. [20]Two of every kind of bird, of every kind of animal and of every kind of creature that moves along the ground will come to you to be kept alive. [21]You are to take every kind of food that is to be eaten and store it away as food for you and for them."

[22]Noah did everything just as God commanded him.

7 The LORD then said to Noah, "Go into the ark, you and your whole family, because I have found you righteous in this generation. [2]Take with you seven[k] of every kind of clean animal, a male and its mate, and two of every kind of unclean animal, a male and its mate, [3]and also seven of every kind of bird, male and female, to keep their various kinds alive throughout the earth. [4]Seven days from now I will send rain on the earth for forty days and forty nights, and I will wipe from the face of the earth every living creature I have made."

[5]And Noah did all that the LORD commanded him.

[6]Noah was six hundred years old when the floodwaters came on the earth. [7]And Noah and his sons and his wife and his sons' wives entered the ark to escape the waters of the flood. [8]Pairs of clean and unclean animals, of birds and of all creatures that move along the ground, [9]male and female, came to Noah and entered the ark, as God had commanded Noah. [10]And after the seven days the floodwaters came on the earth.

[11]In the six hundredth year of Noah's life, on the seventeenth day of the second month—on that day all the springs of the great deep burst forth, and the floodgates of the heavens were opened. [12]And rain fell on the earth forty days and forty nights.

[13]On that very day Noah and his sons, Shem, Ham and Japheth, together with his wife and the wives of his three sons, entered the ark. [14]They had with them every wild animal according to its kind, all livestock according to their kinds, every creature that moves along the ground according to its kind and every bird according to its kind, everything with wings. [15]Pairs of all creatures that have the breath of life in them came to Noah and entered the ark. [16]The animals going in were male and female of every living thing, as God had commanded Noah. Then the LORD shut him in.

[17]For forty days the flood kept coming on the earth, and as the waters increased they lifted the ark high above the earth. [18]The waters rose and increased greatly on the earth, and the ark floated on the surface of the water. [19]They rose greatly on the earth, and all the high mountains under the entire heavens were covered. [20]The waters rose and covered the mountains to a depth of more than twenty feet.[l,m] [21]Every living thing that moved on the earth perished—birds, livestock, wild animals, all the creatures that swarm over the earth, and all mankind. [22]Everything on dry land that had the breath of life in its nostrils died. [23]Every living thing on the face of the earth was wiped out; men and animals and the creatures that move along the ground and the birds of the

g14 The meaning of the Hebrew for this word is uncertain.
h15 Hebrew 300 cubits long, 50 cubits wide and 30 cubits high (about 140 meters long, 23 meters wide and 13.5 meters high)   i16 Or Make an opening for light by finishing   j16 Hebrew a cubit (about 0.5 meter)   k2 Or seven pairs; also in verse 3   l20 Hebrew fifteen cubits (about 6.9 meters)   m20 Or rose more than twenty feet, and the mountains were covered

air were wiped from the earth. Only Noah was left, and those with him in the ark.

²⁴The waters flooded the earth for a hundred and fifty days.

Discovering the Word 1. When the Lord looks at the human condition in the time of Noah, what does he see (6:5–13)? 2. How has God's attitude toward creation changed since the beginning (1:31; 6:6–7, 11–13, 17)? 3. How is Noah different from his contemporaries (6:9; 7:1)? 4. What provisions does God make for Noah and for the various living creatures to preserve life after the flood (7:14–22)? 5. What details are given about the flood and its results (7:17–24)?

Applying the Word 1. In what situations have you felt embarrassed because of your obedience to God? 2. What do chapters 6 and 7 reveal about the severity and grace of God? 3. The New Testament compares the severe judgment in the days of Noah with the judgment that will be poured out at the return of Christ. How can you urge those around you to seek refuge in Christ?

Responding in Prayer Think of someone you want to come to salvation. Pray to God and ask him to "flood" that person with love and forgiveness.

---

6 / *Genesis 8:1—9:17*
God's Promises

HOW DO YOU feel when you see the long-awaited fulfillment of one of God's promises? Perhaps your response is similar to that of Noah and his family. In the previous study we saw them safe within the ark as the deluge destroyed all life on earth and eventually covered the mountains. Now we see how God fulfills his promises to them and how Noah's response can be an example to us today.

Warming Up to God As you come to Jesus today, let the truth of his love that was poured out for you sink into your soul. Reflect quietly for a few moments on the beauty of his love.

Read Genesis 8:1—9:17.

---

8 But God remembered Noah and all the wild animals and the livestock that were with him in the ark, and he sent a wind over the earth, and the waters receded. ²Now the springs of the deep and the floodgates of the heavens had been closed, and the rain had stopped falling from the sky. ³The water receded steadily from the earth. At the end of the hundred and fifty days the water had gone down, ⁴and on the seventeenth day of the seventh month the ark came to rest on the mountains of Ararat. ⁵The waters continued to recede until the tenth month, and on the first day of the tenth month the tops of the mountains became visible.

⁶After forty days Noah opened the window he had made in the ark ⁷and sent out a raven, and it kept flying back and forth until the water had dried up from the earth. ⁸Then he sent out a dove to see if the water had receded from the surface of the ground. ⁹But the dove could find no place to set its feet because there was water over all the surface of the earth; so it returned to Noah in the ark. He reached out his hand and took the dove and brought it back to himself in the ark. ¹⁰He waited seven more days and again sent out the dove from the ark. ¹¹When the dove returned to him in the evening, there in its beak was a freshly plucked olive leaf! Then Noah knew that the water had receded from the earth. ¹²He waited seven more days and sent the dove out again, but this time it did not return to him.

¹³By the first day of the first month of Noah's six hundred and first year, the water had dried up from the earth. Noah then removed the covering from the ark and saw that the surface of the ground was dry. ¹⁴By the twenty-seventh day of the second month the earth was completely dry.

¹⁵Then God said to Noah, ¹⁶"Come out of the ark, you and your wife and your sons and their wives. ¹⁷Bring out every kind of living creature

that is with you—the birds, the animals, and all the creatures that move along the ground—so they can multiply on the earth and be fruitful and increase in number upon it."

[18]So Noah came out, together with his sons and his wife and his sons' wives. [19]All the animals and all the creatures that move along the ground and all the birds—everything that moves on the earth—came out of the ark, one kind after another.

[20]Then Noah built an altar to the LORD and, taking some of all the clean animals and clean birds, he sacrificed burnt offerings on it. [21]The LORD smelled the pleasing aroma and said in his heart: "Never again will I curse the ground because of man, even though[n] every inclination of his heart is evil from childhood. And never again will I destroy all living creatures, as I have done.

[22]"As long as the earth endures,
    seedtime and harvest,
    cold and heat,
    summer and winter,
    day and night
    will never cease."

9 Then God blessed Noah and his sons, saying to them, "Be fruitful and increase in number and fill the earth. [2]The fear and dread of you will fall upon all the beasts of the earth and all the birds of the air, upon every creature that moves along the ground, and upon all the fish of the sea; they are given into your hands. [3]Everything that lives and moves will be food for you. Just as I gave you the green plants, I now give you everything.

[4]"But you must not eat meat that has its lifeblood still in it. [5]And for your lifeblood I will surely demand an accounting. I will demand an accounting from every animal. And from each man, too, I will demand an accounting for the life of his fellow man.

[6]"Whoever sheds the blood of man,
    by man shall his blood be shed;
for in the image of God
    has God made man.

[7]As for you, be fruitful and increase in number; multiply on the earth and increase upon it."

[8]Then God said to Noah and to his sons with him: [9]"I now establish my covenant with you and with your descendants after you [10]and with every living creature that was with you—the birds, the livestock and all the wild animals, all those that came out of the ark with you—every living creature on earth. [11]I establish my covenant with you: Never again will all life be cut off by the waters of a flood; never again will there be a flood to destroy the earth."

[12]And God said, "This is the sign of the covenant I am making between me and you and every living creature with you, a covenant for all generations to come: [13]I have set my rainbow in the clouds, and it will be the sign of the covenant between me and the earth. [14]Whenever I bring clouds over the earth and the rainbow appears in the clouds, [15]I will remember my covenant between me and you and all living creatures of every kind. Never again will the waters become a flood to destroy all life. [16]Whenever the rainbow appears in the clouds, I will see it and remember the everlasting covenant between God and all living creatures of every kind on the earth."

[17]So God said to Noah, "This is the sign of the covenant I have established between me and all life on the earth."

[n]21 Or man, for

Discovering the Word   1. What do we learn about God's concern for the passengers of the ark and his activity to end the flood (8:1–5)?   2. What initiative does Noah take during this period (8:6–12)?   3. Noah's first action after emptying the ark is to offer a sacrifice to God (8:20). What does this reveal about his priorities amid the pressure of urgent tasks calling for immediate attention?   4. What commission does God now give Noah and his family (9:1–7)?   5. In 9:17 God makes a covenant as unconditional as it is undeserved. What do we learn about the extent and purpose of this first covenant?

Applying the Word   1. How has God's grace been evident throughout this passage?   2. How has his grace been evident in your life lately?   3. What aspect of Noah's example—his obedience, faith, courage, endurance—is most meaningful to you in a situation you are facing?

 Responding in Prayer   Spend time in prayer, thanking God for his grace to you, who deserve his judgment.

7 / *Genesis 9:18—11:32*
Family Problems

A RECURRING PROBLEM in every generation is self-centered disrespect for authority, both human and divine. This attitude continued after the flood in Noah's own family, then on a larger scale in society. In the previous study we saw that Noah's new commission was similar to the one given to Adam. Now we see how sin again spreads from father to son to succeeding generations in both the private and public realms as self-indulgence generates waves of evil in ever-widening circles.

 Warming Up to God Does the evil in this world sometimes weigh heavily on you? Tell Jesus your frustrations and let him renew your hope in his sovereignty.

 Read Genesis 9:18—11:32.

¹⁸The sons of Noah who came out of the ark were Shem, Ham and Japheth. (Ham was the father of Canaan.) ¹⁹These were the three sons of Noah, and from them came the people who were scattered over the earth.

²⁰Noah, a man of the soil, proceeded*ᵒ* to plant a vineyard. ²¹When he drank some of its wine, he became drunk and lay uncovered inside his tent. ²²Ham, the father of Canaan, saw his father's nakedness and told his two brothers outside. ²³But Shem and Japheth took a garment and laid it across their shoulders; then they walked in backward and covered their father's nakedness. Their faces were turned the other way so that they would not see their father's nakedness.

²⁴When Noah awoke from his wine and found out what his youngest son had done to him, ²⁵he said,

"Cursed be Canaan!
    The lowest of slaves
    will he be to his brothers."

²⁶He also said,

"Blessed be the LORD, the God of Shem!
    May Canaan be the slave of Shem.*ᵖ*
²⁷May God extend the territory of Japheth*q*;
    may Japheth live in the tents of Shem,
    and may Canaan be his*ʳ* slave."

²⁸After the flood Noah lived 350 years. ²⁹Altogether, Noah lived 950 years, and then he died.

10 This is the account of Shem, Ham and Japheth, Noah's sons, who themselves had sons after the flood.
²The sons*ˢ* of Japheth:

Gomer, Magog, Madai, Javan, Tubal, Meshech and Tiras.
³The sons of Gomer:
    Ashkenaz, Riphath and Togarmah.
⁴The sons of Javan:
    Elishah, Tarshish, the Kittim and the Rodanim.*ᵗ* ⁵(From these the maritime peoples spread out into their territories by their clans within their nations, each with its own language.)
⁶The sons of Ham:
    Cush, Mizraim,*ᵘ* Put and Canaan.
⁷The sons of Cush:
    Seba, Havilah, Sabtah, Raamah and Sabteca.
The sons of Raamah:
    Sheba and Dedan.

⁸Cush was the father*ᵛ* of Nimrod, who grew to be a mighty warrior on the earth. ⁹He was a mighty hunter before the LORD; that is why it is said, "Like Nimrod, a mighty hunter before the LORD." ¹⁰The first centers of his kingdom were Babylon, Erech, Akkad and Calneh, in*ʷ* Shinar.*ˣ* ¹¹From that land he went to Assyria, where he built Nineveh, Rehoboth Ir,*ʸ* Calah ¹²and Resen, which is between Nineveh and Calah; that is the great city.

¹³Mizraim was the father of
    the Ludites, Anamites, Lehabites, Naphtuhites, ¹⁴Pathrusites, Casluhites (from

ᵒ20 Or *soil, was the first*   *ᵖ26* Or *be his slave*   *q27 Japheth* sounds like the Hebrew for *extend.*   *ʳ27* Or *their*   *ˢ2 Sons* may mean *descendants* or *successors* or *nations;* also in verses 3, 4, 6, 7, 20-23, 29 and 31.   *ᵗ4* Some manuscripts of the Masoretic Text and Samaritan Pentateuch (see also Septuagint and 1 Chron. 1:7); most manuscripts of the Masoretic Text *Dodanim*   *ᵘ6* That is, Egypt; also in verse 13   *ᵛ8 Father* may mean *ancestor* or *predecessor* or *founder;* also in verses 13, 15, 24 and 26.

whom the Philistines came) and Caphtorites.

¹⁵Canaan was the father of
Sidon his firstborn,ᶻ and of the Hittites,
¹⁶Jebusites, Amorites, Girgashites, ¹⁷Hi-
vites, Arkites, Sinites, ¹⁸Arvadites, Zemarites and Hamathites.

Later the Canaanite clans scattered ¹⁹and the
borders of Canaan reached from Sidon toward
Gerar as far as Gaza, and then toward Sodom,
Gomorrah, Admah and Zeboiim, as far as Lasha.

²⁰These are the sons of Ham by their clans and
languages, in their territories and nations.

²¹Sons were also born to Shem, whose older
brother wasᵃ Japheth; Shem was the ancestor of
all the sons of Eber.

²²The sons of Shem:
Elam, Asshur, Arphaxad, Lud and Aram.
²³The sons of Aram:
Uz, Hul, Gether and Meshech.ᵇ
²⁴Arphaxad was the father ofᶜ Shelah,
and Shelah the father of Eber.
²⁵Two sons were born to Eber:
One was named Peleg,ᵈ because in his
time the earth was divided; his brother
was named Joktan.
²⁶Joktan was the father of
Almodad, Sheleph, Hazarmaveth, Jerah,
²⁷Hadoram, Uzal, Diklah, ²⁸Obal, Abimael, Sheba, ²⁹Ophir, Havilah and Jobab.
All these were sons of Joktan.

³⁰The region where they lived stretched from Mesha toward Sephar, in the eastern hill country.

³¹These are the sons of Shem by their clans and
languages, in their territories and nations.

³²These are the clans of Noah's sons, according
to their lines of descent, within their nations.
From these the nations spread out over the earth
after the flood.

11

Now the whole world had one language and a common speech. ²As
men moved eastward,ᵉ they found
a plain in Shinarˣ and settled there.

³They said to each other, "Come, let's make
bricks and bake them thoroughly." They used
brick instead of stone, and tar for mortar. ⁴Then
they said, "Come, let us build ourselves a city,

with a tower that reaches to the heavens, so that
we may make a name for ourselves and not be
scattered over the face of the whole earth."

⁵But the LORD came down to see the city and
the tower that the men were building. ⁶The LORD
said, "If as one people speaking the same language they have begun to do this, then nothing
they plan to do will be impossible for them.
⁷Come, let us go down and confuse their language so they will not understand each other."

⁸So the LORD scattered them from there over all
the earth, and they stopped building the city.
⁹That is why it was called Babelᶠ—because there
the LORD confused the language of the whole
world. From there the LORD scattered them over
the face of the whole earth.

¹⁰This is the account of Shem.

Two years after the flood, when Shem was 100
years old, he became the fatherᵍ of Arphaxad.
¹¹And after he became the father of Arphaxad,
Shem lived 500 years and had other sons and
daughters.

¹²When Arphaxad had lived 35 years, he became the father of Shelah. ¹³And after he became
the father of Shelah, Arphaxad lived 403 years
and had other sons and daughters.ʰ

¹⁴When Shelah had lived 30 years, he became
the father of Eber. ¹⁵And after he became the father of Eber, Shelah lived 403 years and had other
sons and daughters.

¹⁶When Eber had lived 34 years, he became the
father of Peleg. ¹⁷And after he became the father
of Peleg, Eber lived 430 years and had other sons
and daughters.

¹⁸When Peleg had lived 30 years, he became
the father of Reu. ¹⁹And after he became the father of Reu, Peleg lived 209 years and had other
sons and daughters.

²⁰When Reu had lived 32 years, he became the
father of Serug. ²¹And after he became the father
of Serug, Reu lived 207 years and had other sons
and daughters.

ʷ10 Or Erech and Akkad—all of them in   ˣ10,2 That is, Babylonia
ʸ11 Or Nineveh with its city squares   ᶻ15 Or of the Sidonians, the
foremost   ᵃ21 Or Shem, the older brother of   ᵇ23 See Septuagint
and 1 Chron. 1:17; Hebrew Mash   ᶜ24 Hebrew; Septuagint father of
Cainan, and Cainan was the father of   ᵈ25 Peleg means division.
ᵉ2 Or from the east; or in the east   ᶠ9 That is, Babylon; Babel sounds
like the Hebrew for confused.   ᵍ10 Father may mean ancestor; also
in verses 11-25.   ʰ12,13 Hebrew; Septuagint (see also Luke 3:35, 36
and note at Gen. 10:24) 35 years, he became the father of Cainan. ¹³And
after he became the father of Cainan, Arphaxad lived 430 years and had
other sons and daughters, and then he died. When Cainan had lived 130
years, he became the father of Shelah. And after he became the father of
Shelah, Cainan lived 330 years and had other sons and daughters

²²When Serug had lived 30 years, he became the father of Nahor. ²³And after he became the father of Nahor, Serug lived 200 years and had other sons and daughters.

²⁴When Nahor had lived 29 years, he became the father of Terah. ²⁵And after he became the father of Terah, Nahor lived 119 years and had other sons and daughters.

²⁶After Terah had lived 70 years, he became the father of Abram, Nahor and Haran.

²⁷This is the account of Terah.

Terah became the father of Abram, Nahor and Haran. And Haran became the father of Lot. ²⁸While his father Terah was still alive, Haran died in Ur of the Chaldeans, in the land of his birth. ²⁹Abram and Nahor both married. The name of Abram's wife was Sarai, and the name of Nahor's wife was Milcah; she was the daughter of Haran, the father of both Milcah and Iscah. ³⁰Now Sarai was barren; she had no children.

³¹Terah took his son Abram, his grandson Lot son of Haran, and his daughter-in-law Sarai, the wife of his son Abram, and together they set out from Ur of the Chaldeans to go to Canaan. But when they came to Haran, they settled there.

³²Terah lived 205 years, and he died in Haran.

 Discovering the Word **1.** Describe what happens in the brief story of Noah and his three sons (9:20–23). **2.** What curse does Noah pronounce on Canaan (Ham's son) and his descendants (9:24–27)? **3.** What interesting facts does chapter 10 reveal about the spread of humanity after the flood? (Note especially 10:5, 8–15, 25.) **4.** What action do the people of Babel take, and what is their motive (11:1–9)? **5.** It is amusing that the Lord must come down (11:5) to see this tower that will reach to the heavens. What is his reaction (11:5–9)? **6.** Genesis 11:10–32 traces the line from Shem to Abram. Why do you think the author is beginning to shift from all the families of the earth to one family?

 Applying the Word **1.** In what specific ways do families today suffer from a disrespect for parents and animosity among the children? **2.** How have you recently hurt someone through failure to communicate, and what steps toward healing can you take?

 Responding in Prayer Ask the Father to show you one specific way you can be a minister of the gospel of Christ to your family or community.

Abram left for the unknown, obeying & trusting God one step at a time.

8 / *Genesis 12—13*
Following God into the Unknown

SUPPOSE GOD CALLED you to leave all that is familiar—your home, family, friends—and follow him into another part of the country or world with a radically different lifestyle. How would you feel as you said goodby and moved out into the unknown? In this study we see how Abram responds to such a call and how his faith matures.

Warming Up to God Free your hands of books or pencils and fold them across your lap. Close your eyes and think of the characteristics of God. Let God draw near to you in these quiet moments.

Read Genesis 12—13.

12 The Lord had said to Abram, "Leave your country, your people and your father's household and go to the land I will show you.

²"I will make you into a great nation
  and I will bless you;
I will make your name great,
  and you will be a blessing.

[3]I will bless those who bless you,
  and whoever curses you I will curse;
and all peoples on earth
  will be blessed through you."

No questions, complete obedience to God.

[4]So Abram left, as the LORD had told him; and Lot went with him. Abram was seventy-five years old when he set out from Haran. [5]He took his wife Sarai, his nephew Lot, all the possessions they had accumulated and the people they had acquired in Haran, and they set out for the land of Canaan, and they arrived there.

[6]Abram traveled through the land as far as the site of the great tree of Moreh at Shechem. At that time the Canaanites were in the land. [7]The LORD appeared to Abram and said, "To your offspring[i] I will give this land." So he built an altar there to the LORD, who had appeared to him.

[8]From there he went on toward the hills east of Bethel and pitched his tent, with Bethel on the west and Ai on the east. There he built an altar to the LORD and called on the name of the LORD. [9]Then Abram set out and continued toward the Negev.

[10]Now there was a famine in the land, and Abram went down to Egypt to live there for a while because the famine was severe. [11]As he was about to enter Egypt, he said to his wife Sarai, "I know what a beautiful woman you are. [12]When the Egyptians see you, they will say, 'This is his wife.' Then they will kill me but will let you live. [13]Say you are my sister, so that I will be treated well for your sake and my life will be spared because of you."

[14]When Abram came to Egypt, the Egyptians saw that she was a very beautiful woman. [15]And when Pharaoh's officials saw her, they praised her to Pharaoh, and she was taken into his palace. [16]He treated Abram well for her sake, and Abram acquired sheep and cattle, male and female donkeys, menservants and maidservants, and camels.

[17]But the LORD inflicted serious diseases on Pharaoh and his household because of Abram's wife Sarai. [18]So Pharaoh summoned Abram. "What have you done to me?" he said. "Why didn't you tell me she was your wife? [19]Why did you say, 'She is my sister,' so that I took her to be my wife? Now then, here is your wife. Take her and go!" [20]Then Pharaoh gave orders about Abram to his men, and they sent him on his way, with his wife and everything he had.

13

So Abram went up from Egypt to the Negev, with his wife and everything he had, and Lot went with him. [2]Abram had become very wealthy in livestock and in silver and gold.

[3]From the Negev he went from place to place until he came to Bethel, to the place between Bethel and Ai where his tent had been earlier [4]and where he had first built an altar. There Abram called on the name of the LORD.

[5]Now Lot, who was moving about with Abram, also had flocks and herds and tents. [6]But the land could not support them while they stayed together, for their possessions were so great that they were not able to stay together. [7]And quarreling arose between Abram's herdsmen and the herdsmen of Lot. The Canaanites and Perizzites were also living in the land at that time.

[8]So Abram said to Lot, "Let's not have any quarreling between you and me, or between your herdsmen and mine, for we are brothers. [9]Is not the whole land before you? Let's part company. If you go to the left, I'll go to the right; if you go to the right, I'll go to the left."

[10]Lot looked up and saw that the whole plain of the Jordan was well watered, like the garden of the LORD, like the land of Egypt, toward Zoar. (This was before the LORD destroyed Sodom and Gomorrah.) [11]So Lot chose for himself the whole plain of the Jordan and set out toward the east. The two men parted company: [12]Abram lived in the land of Canaan, while Lot lived among the cities of the plain and pitched his tents near Sodom. [13]Now the men of Sodom were wicked and were sinning greatly against the LORD.

[14]The LORD said to Abram after Lot had parted from him, "Lift up your eyes from where you are and look north and south, east and west. [15]All the land that you see I will give to you and your offspring[j] forever. [16]I will make your offspring like the dust of the earth, so that if anyone could count the dust, then your offspring could be counted. [17]Go, walk through the length and breadth of the land, for I am giving it to you."

[18]So Abram moved his tents and went to live near the great trees of Mamre at Hebron, where he built an altar to the LORD.

[i]7 Or seed   [j]15 Or seed; also in verse 16

Discovering the Word 1. What command and promise does the Lord give to Abram (12:1–3)? 2. What additional promise and encouragement does God give to Abram as he arrives in Canaan (12:6–9)? 3. How does Abram's scheming about himself and Sarai evidence a lack of faith (12:10–16)? 4. Describe the problem which arises between Abram and Lot (13:1–7). 5. Abram, as the older man, has the right to choose the best land. How does his action here demonstrate a greater confidence in God's promise to take care of him (13:8–13)? 6. What renewed and expanded promises does the Lord give to Abram (13:14–17)?

Applying the Word 1. Describe a time when you took matters into your own hands instead of trusting in God's faithfulness. 2. How can Abram's experiences in chapters 12 and 13 encourage you to entrust your needs more fully to God?

Responding in Prayer Thank God for his faithfulness in keeping promises—and ask him to increase your faith while you wait to see your requests come to fruition.

9 / *Genesis 14—15*
Tests of Faith

IF YOU WANT your faith to increase, don't be surprised or disheartened over difficulties which demand faith. The muscles of faith grow strong through training and testing that is sometimes painful. Abram continues to learn this lesson after parting from his nephew Lot. In this study we see Abram's trials and the resources God provides to help him meet the challenge and persevere.

 Warming Up to God What do you think really makes your faith grow? Write down any specific events in your life that God has used to increase your faith.

 Read Genesis 14—15.

14 At this time Amraphel king of Shinar,[k] Arioch king of Ellasar, Kedorlaomer king of Elam and Tidal king of Goiim ²went to war against Bera king of Sodom, Birsha king of Gomorrah, Shinab king of Admah, Shemeber king of Zeboiim, and the king of Bela (that is, Zoar). ³All these latter kings joined forces in the Valley of Siddim (the Salt Sea[l]). ⁴For twelve years they had been subject to Kedorlaomer, but in the thirteenth year they rebelled.

⁵In the fourteenth year, Kedorlaomer and the kings allied with him went out and defeated the Rephaites in Ashteroth Karnaim, the Zuzites in Ham, the Emites in Shaveh Kiriathaim ⁶and the Horites in the hill country of Seir, as far as El Paran near the desert. ⁷Then they turned back and went to En Mishpat (that is, Kadesh), and they conquered the whole territory of the Amalekites, as well as the Amorites who were living in Hazazon Tamar.

⁸Then the king of Sodom, the king of Gomorrah, the king of Admah, the king of Zeboiim and the king of Bela (that is, Zoar) marched out and drew up their battle lines in the Valley of Siddim ⁹against Kedorlaomer king of Elam, Tidal king of Goiim, Amraphel king of Shinar and Arioch king of Ellasar—four kings against five. ¹⁰Now the Valley of Siddim was full of tar pits, and when the kings of Sodom and Gomorrah fled, some of the men fell into them and the rest fled to the hills. ¹¹The four kings seized all the goods of Sodom and Gomorrah and all their food; then they went away. ¹²They also carried off Abram's nephew Lot and his possessions, since he was living in Sodom.

¹³One who had escaped came and reported this to Abram the Hebrew. Now Abram was living near the great trees of Mamre the Amorite, a brother[m] of Eshcol and Aner, all of whom were allied with Abram. ¹⁴When Abram heard that his relative had been taken captive, he called out the 318 trained men born in his household and went in pursuit as far as Dan. ¹⁵During the night

---

k1 That is, Babylonia; also in verse 9   *l3* That is, the Dead Sea
m13 Or *a relative; or an ally*

Abram divided his men to attack them and he routed them, pursuing them as far as Hobah, north of Damascus. ¹⁶He recovered all the goods and brought back his relative Lot and his possessions, together with the women and the other people.

¹⁷After Abram returned from defeating Kedorlaomer and the kings allied with him, the king of Sodom came out to meet him in the Valley of Shaveh (that is, the King's Valley).

¹⁸Then Melchizedek king of Salem*n* brought out bread and wine. He was priest of God Most High, ¹⁹and he blessed Abram, saying,

"Blessed be Abram by God Most High,
    Creator*o* of heaven and earth.
²⁰And blessed be*p* God Most High,
    who delivered your enemies into your
        hand."

Then Abram gave him a tenth of everything.

²¹The king of Sodom said to Abram, "Give me the people and keep the goods for yourself."

²²But Abram said to the king of Sodom, "I have raised my hand to the Lord, God Most High, Creator of heaven and earth, and have taken an oath ²³that I will accept nothing belonging to you, not even a thread or the thong of a sandal, so that you will never be able to say, 'I made Abram rich.' ²⁴I will accept nothing but what my men have eaten and the share that belongs to the men who went with me—to Aner, Eshcol and Mamre. Let them have their share."

15

After this, the word of the Lord came to Abram in a vision:

"Do not be afraid, Abram.
I am your shield,*q*
your very great reward.*r*"

²But Abram said, "O Sovereign Lord, what can you give me since I remain childless and the one who will inherit*s* my estate is Eliezer of Damascus?" ³And Abram said, "You have given me no children; so a servant in my household will be my heir."

⁴Then the word of the Lord came to him: "This man will not be your heir, but a son coming from your own body will be your heir." ⁵He took him outside and said, "Look up at the heavens and count the stars—if indeed you can count them." Then he said to him, "So shall your offspring be."

⁶Abram believed the Lord, and he credited it to him as righteousness.

⁷He also said to him, "I am the Lord, who brought you out of Ur of the Chaldeans to give you this land to take possession of it."

⁸But Abram said, "O Sovereign Lord, how can I know that I will gain possession of it?"

⁹So the Lord said to him, "Bring me a heifer, a goat and a ram, each three years old, along with a dove and a young pigeon."

¹⁰Abram brought all these to him, cut them in two and arranged the halves opposite each other; the birds, however, he did not cut in half. ¹¹Then birds of prey came down on the carcasses, but Abram drove them away.

¹²As the sun was setting, Abram fell into a deep sleep, and a thick and dreadful darkness came over him. ¹³Then the Lord said to him, "Know for certain that your descendants will be strangers in a country not their own, and they will be enslaved and mistreated four hundred years. ¹⁴But I will punish the nation they serve as slaves, and afterward they will come out with great possessions. ¹⁵You, however, will go to your fathers in peace and be buried at a good old age. ¹⁶In the fourth generation your descendants will come back here, for the sin of the Amorites has not yet reached its full measure."

¹⁷When the sun had set and darkness had fallen, a smoking firepot with a blazing torch appeared and passed between the pieces. ¹⁸On that day the Lord made a covenant with Abram and said, "To your descendants I give this land, from the river*t* of Egypt to the great river, the Euphrates— ¹⁹the land of the Kenites, Kenizzites, Kadmonites, ²⁰Hittites, Perizzites, Rephaites, ²¹Amorites, Canaanites, Girgashites and Jebusites."

---

n18 That is, Jerusalem   *o19* Or *Possessor*; also in verse 22
p20 Or *And praise be to*   *q1* Or *sovereign*   *r1* Or *shield; / your
reward will be very great*   *s2* The meaning of the Hebrew for this
phrase is uncertain.   *t18* Or *Wadi*

🔖 **Discovering the Word** 1. What political and military situation is described in 14:1–4, and how is it similar to today? 2. Since Abram lived in tents away from the cities, his people were not involved in this military campaign. When he learns of Lot's capture, what strategy does Abram devise (14:13–16)? 3. Who is Melchizedek, and what does he do (14:18–20)? 4. What is Abram's main problem in chapter 15, and how does he propose to solve it (15:2–3)? 5. How would God's message to Abram at this point renew his confidence (15:1, 4, 5)?

6. Genesis 15:6 is the first time we read that Abram *believes* the Lord. Explain in your own words what it means that his faith is credited to him as righteousness.

 Applying the Word **1.** What evidence do you find of Abram's growing confidence in God? **2.** If you have ever had to wait a long time for God to fulfill a promise, what did you learn in the process about yourself, the Lord and his way of working with you?

Responding in Prayer Thank Jesus for his death, which enables our belief to be credited as righteousness in God's eyes.

10 / *Genesis 16—17*
When Faith Falters

DO YOU EVER get tired of waiting for God to act? Do you sometimes wonder whether your faith is simply foolishness? At such times it is tempting to become an activist. "If *God* won't help me, I'll do it *myself!*" As this passage opens, we find that Sarai and Abram are frustrated by the passing of years without a son. Taking matters into their own hands, they devise their own strategy for "fulfilling" God's promise.

 Warming Up to God You are like a jar of clay filled with the Spirit of Christ. Pour out to him your weariness, sin or discouragement and let him pour into you his cool water of grace and peace.

 Read Genesis 16—17.

16 Now Sarai, Abram's wife, had borne him no children. But she had an Egyptian maidservant named Hagar; ²so she said to Abram, "The LORD has kept me from having children. Go, sleep with my maidservant; perhaps I can build a family through her."

Abram agreed to what Sarai said. ³So after Abram had been living in Canaan ten years, Sarai his wife took her Egyptian maidservant Hagar and gave her to her husband to be his wife. ⁴He slept with Hagar, and she conceived.

When she knew she was pregnant, she began to despise her mistress. ⁵Then Sarai said to Abram, "You are responsible for the wrong I am suffering. I put my servant in your arms, and now that she knows she is pregnant, she despises me. May the LORD judge between you and me."

⁶"Your servant is in your hands," Abram said. "Do with her whatever you think best." Then Sarai mistreated Hagar; so she fled from her.

⁷The angel of the LORD found Hagar near a spring in the desert; it was the spring that is beside the road to Shur. ⁸And he said, "Hagar, servant of Sarai, where have you come from, and where are you going?"

"I'm running away from my mistress Sarai," she answered.

⁹Then the angel of the LORD told her, "Go back to your mistress and submit to her." ¹⁰The angel added, "I will so increase your descendants that they will be too numerous to count."

¹¹The angel of the LORD also said to her:

Submission to authority, even when being wronged.

"You are now with child
    and you will have a son.
You shall name him Ishmael,ᵘ
    for the LORD has heard of your misery.
¹²He will be a wild donkey of a man;
    his hand will be against everyone
    and everyone's hand against him,
and he will live in hostility
    towardᵛ all his brothers."

¹³She gave this name to the LORD who spoke to her: "You are the God who sees me," for she said, "I have now seenʷ the One who sees me." ¹⁴That is why the well was called Beer Lahai Roiˣ; it is still there, between Kadesh and Bered.

¹⁵So Hagar bore Abram a son, and Abram gave the name Ishmael to the son she had borne. ¹⁶Abram was eighty-six years old when Hagar bore him Ishmael.

ᵘ11 *Ishmael* means *God hears.*   ᵛ12 Or *live to the east / of*
ʷ13 Or *seen the back of*   ˣ14 *Beer Lahai Roi* means *well of the Living One who sees me.*

17

When Abram was ninety-nine years old, the LORD appeared to him and said, "I am God Almighty[y]; walk before me and be blameless. ²I will confirm my covenant between me and you and will greatly increase your numbers."

³Abram fell facedown, and God said to him, ⁴"As for me, this is my covenant with you: You will be the father of many nations. ⁵No longer will you be called Abram[z]; your name will be Abraham,[a] for I have made you a father of many nations. ⁶I will make you very fruitful; I will make nations of you, and kings will come from you. ⁷I will establish my covenant as an everlasting covenant between me and you and your descendants after you for the generations to come, to be your God and the God of your descendants after you. ⁸The whole land of Canaan, where you are now an alien, I will give as an everlasting possession to you and your descendants after you; and I will be their God."

⁹Then God said to Abraham, "As for you, you must keep my covenant, you and your descendants after you for the generations to come. ¹⁰This is my covenant with you and your descendants after you, the covenant you are to keep: Every male among you shall be circumcised. ¹¹You are to undergo circumcision, and it will be the sign of the covenant between me and you. ¹²For the generations to come every male among you who is eight days old must be circumcised, including those born in your household or bought with money from a foreigner—those who are not your offspring. ¹³Whether born in your household or bought with your money, they must be circumcised. My covenant in your flesh is to be an everlasting covenant. ¹⁴Any uncircumcised male, who has not been circumcised in the flesh, will be cut off from his people; he has broken my covenant."

¹⁵God also said to Abraham, "As for Sarai your wife, you are no longer to call her Sarai; her name will be Sarah. ¹⁶I will bless her and will surely give you a son by her. I will bless her so that she will be the mother of nations; kings of peoples will come from her."

¹⁷Abraham fell facedown; he laughed and said to himself, "Will a son be born to a man a hundred years old? Will Sarah bear a child at the age of ninety?" ¹⁸And Abraham said to God, "If only Ishmael might live under your blessing!"

¹⁹Then God said, "Yes, but your wife Sarah will bear you a son, and you will call him Isaac.[b] I will establish my covenant with him as an everlasting covenant for his descendants after him. ²⁰And as for Ishmael, I have heard you: I will surely bless him; I will make him fruitful and will greatly increase his numbers. He will be the father of twelve rulers, and I will make him into a great nation. ²¹But my covenant I will establish with Isaac, whom Sarah will bear to you by this time next year." ²²When he had finished speaking with Abraham, God went up from him.

²³On that very day Abraham took his son Ishmael and all those born in his household or bought with his money, every male in his household, and circumcised them, as God told him. ²⁴Abraham was ninety-nine years old when he was circumcised, ²⁵and his son Ishmael was thirteen; ²⁶Abraham and his son Ishmael were both circumcised on that same day. ²⁷And every male in Abraham's household, including those born in his household or bought from a foreigner, was circumcised with him.

---

y1 Hebrew *El-Shaddai*   *z5* Abram means *exalted father.*
a5 Abraham means *father of many.*   *b19* Isaac means *he laughs.*

Discovering the Word **1.** Sarai and Abram's action seems strange to us, but it was an acceptable custom in ancient Near Eastern culture. Yet how might their action indicate a lack of faith? **2.** Hagar flees to the wilderness of Shur on the northeast frontier of Egypt, her native land. What promises and encouragement does the angel give to her (16:7–12)? **3.** What does Hagar learn about the Lord through this traumatic experience (16:13–14)? **4.** In 17:1–8 "God Almighty" appears to Abram and, ironically, changes his name from *Abram* ("exalted father") to *Abraham* ("father of many"). What covenant promises does the Lord reiterate in these verses? **5.** In 17:18 Abraham expressed his concern about Ishmael. How does God respond to Abraham's request (17:19–22)? **6.** How did Abraham fulfill his responsibility in the covenant (17:23–27)?

Applying the Word **1.** How can impatience with God's timetable and way of working lead us to unbelief and even disobedience? **2.** Have you ever gone through a difficult time in which you gained new insight into God's concern for you? Explain.

Responding in Prayer Ask God to teach you to be obedient in the face of ambiguous or difficult circumstances.

11/ *Genesis 18—19*
God's Judgment on Society

CONTEMPORARY CHRISTIANITY HAS been described as "privately engaging but socially irrelevant." Many of us concern ourselves only with family and church to the neglect of the broader arenas of work and community—the economic, social and political fabric of our society. So far we have seen Abraham wrapped up in his personal and family concerns. But in this passage he broadens his perspective. He becomes involved in the problems of a neighboring city whose lifestyle is the antithesis of everything he stands for. Abraham's reaction to the news of impending judgment can instruct us today concerning responsible Christian action in our own society.

 Warming Up to God What problems do you see in your community that weigh on your heart and mind?

 Read Genesis 18—19.

---

18 The LORD appeared to Abraham near the great trees of Mamre while he was sitting at the entrance to his tent in the heat of the day. ²Abraham looked up and saw three men standing nearby. When he saw them, he hurried from the entrance of his tent to meet them and bowed low to the ground.

³He said, "If I have found favor in your eyes, my lord,ᶜ do not pass your servant by. ⁴Let a little water be brought, and then you may all wash your feet and rest under this tree. ⁵Let me get you something to eat, so you can be refreshed and then go on your way—now that you have come to your servant."

"Very well," they answered, "do as you say."

⁶So Abraham hurried into the tent to Sarah. "Quick," he said, "get three seahsᵈ of fine flour and knead it and bake some bread."

⁷Then he ran to the herd and selected a choice, tender calf and gave it to a servant, who hurried to prepare it. ⁸He then brought some curds and milk and the calf that had been prepared, and set these before them. While they ate, he stood near them under a tree.

⁹"Where is your wife Sarah?" they asked him.

"There, in the tent," he said.

¹⁰Then the LORDᵉ said, "I will surely return to you about this time next year, and Sarah your wife will have a son."

Now Sarah was listening at the entrance to the tent, which was behind him. ¹¹Abraham and Sarah were already old and well advanced in years, and Sarah was past the age of childbearing. ¹²So Sarah laughed to herself as she thought, "After I am worn out and my

masterᶠ is old, will I now have this pleasure?"

¹³Then the LORD said to Abraham, "Why did Sarah laugh and say, 'Will I really have a child, now that I am old?' ¹⁴Is anything too hard for the LORD? I will return to you at the appointed time next year and Sarah will have a son."

¹⁵Sarah was afraid, so she lied and said, "I did not laugh."

But he said, "Yes, you did laugh."

¹⁶When the men got up to leave, they looked down toward Sodom, and Abraham walked along with them to see them on their way. ¹⁷Then the LORD said, "Shall I hide from Abraham what I am about to do? ¹⁸Abraham will surely become a great and powerful nation, and all nations on earth will be blessed through him. ¹⁹For I have chosen him, so that he will direct his children and his household after him to keep the way of the LORD by doing what is right and just, so that the LORD will bring about for Abraham what he has promised him."

²⁰Then the LORD said, "The outcry against Sodom and Gomorrah is so great and their sin so grievous ²¹that I will go down and see if what they have done is as bad as the outcry that has reached me. If not, I will know."

²²The men turned away and went toward Sodom, but Abraham remained standing before the LORD.ᵍ ²³Then Abraham approached him and said: "Will you sweep away the righteous with the wicked? ²⁴What if there are fifty righteous people

---

ᶜ3 Or *O Lord*   ᵈ6 That is, probably about 20 quarts (about 22 liters)   ᵉ10 Hebrew *Then he*   ᶠ12 Or *husband*   ᵍ22 Masoretic Text; an ancient Hebrew scribal tradition *but the* LORD *remained standing before Abraham* in the city? Will you really sweep it away and not spare[h] the place for the sake of the fifty righteous people in it? 25Far be it from you to do such a thing—to kill the righteous with the wicked, treating the righteous and the wicked alike. Far be it from you! Will not the Judge[i] of all the earth do right?"

26The LORD said, "If I find fifty righteous people in the city of Sodom, I will spare the whole place for their sake."

27Then Abraham spoke up again: "Now that I have been so bold as to speak to the Lord, though I am nothing but dust and ashes, 28what if the number of the righteous is five less than fifty? Will you destroy the whole city because of five people?"

"If I find forty-five there," he said, "I will not destroy it."

29Once again he spoke to him, "What if only forty are found there?"

He said, "For the sake of forty, I will not do it."

30Then he said, "May the Lord not be angry, but let me speak. What if only thirty can be found there?"

He answered, "I will not do it if I find thirty there."

31Abraham said, "Now that I have been so bold as to speak to the Lord, what if only twenty can be found there?"

He said, "For the sake of twenty, I will not destroy it."

32Then he said, "May the Lord not be angry, but let me speak just once more. What if only ten can be found there?"

He answered, "For the sake of ten, I will not destroy it."

33When the LORD had finished speaking with Abraham, he left, and Abraham returned home.

19

The two angels arrived at Sodom in the evening, and Lot was sitting in the gateway of the city. When he saw them, he got up to meet them and bowed down with his face to the ground. 2"My lords," he said, "please turn aside to your servant's house. You can wash your feet and spend the night and then go on your way early in the morning."

"No," they answered, "we will spend the night in the square."

3But he insisted so strongly that they did go with him and entered his house. He prepared a meal for them, baking bread without yeast, and they ate. 4Before they had gone to bed, all the men from every part of the city of Sodom—both young and old—surrounded the house. 5They called to Lot, "Where are the men who came to you tonight? Bring them out to us so that we can have sex with them."

6Lot went outside to meet them and shut the door behind him 7and said, "No, my friends. Don't do this wicked thing. 8Look, I have two daughters who have never slept with a man. Let me bring them out to you, and you can do what you like with them. But don't do anything to these men, for they have come under the protection of my roof."

9"Get out of our way," they replied. And they said, "This fellow came here as an alien, and now he wants to play the judge! We'll treat you worse than them." They kept bringing pressure on Lot and moved forward to break down the door.

10But the men inside reached out and pulled Lot back into the house and shut the door. 11Then they struck the men who were at the door of the house, young and old, with blindness so that they could not find the door.

12The two men said to Lot, "Do you have anyone else here—sons-in-law, sons or daughters, or anyone else in the city who belongs to you? Get them out of here, 13because we are going to destroy this place. The outcry to the LORD against its people is so great that he has sent us to destroy it."

14So Lot went out and spoke to his sons-in-law, who were pledged to marry[j] his daughters. He said, "Hurry and get out of this place, because the LORD is about to destroy the city!" But his sons-in-law thought he was joking.

15With the coming of dawn, the angels urged Lot, saying, "Hurry! Take your wife and your two daughters who are here, or you will be swept away when the city is punished."

16When he hesitated, the men grasped his hand and the hands of his wife and of his two daughters and led them safely out of the city, for the LORD was merciful to them. 17As soon as they had brought them out, one of them said, "Flee for

---

h24 Or forgive; also in verse 26   i25 Or Ruler   j14 Or were married to your lives! Don't look back, and don't stop any-where in the plain! Flee to the mountains or you will be swept away!"

¹⁸But Lot said to them, "No, my lords,ᵏ please! ¹⁹Yourˡ servant has found favor in yourˡ eyes, and youˡ have shown great kindness to me in sparing my life. But I can't flee to the mountains; this disaster will overtake me, and I'll die. ²⁰Look, here is a town near enough to run to, and it is small. Let me flee to it—it is very small, isn't it? Then my life will be spared."

²¹He said to him, "Very well, I will grant this request too; I will not overthrow the town you speak of. ²²But flee there quickly, because I can-not do anything until you reach it." (That is why the town was called Zoar.ᵐ)

²³By the time Lot reached Zoar, the sun had risen over the land. ²⁴Then the LORD rained down burning sulfur on Sodom and Gomor-rah—from the LORD out of the heavens. ²⁵Thus he overthrew those cities and the entire plain, including all those living in the cities—and also the vegetation in the land. ²⁶But Lot's wife looked back, and she became a pillar of salt.

²⁷Early the next morning Abraham got up and returned to the place where he had stood before the LORD. ²⁸He looked down toward Sodom and Gomorrah, toward all the land of the plain, and he saw dense smoke rising from the land, like smoke from a furnace.

²⁹So when God destroyed the cities of the plain, he remembered Abraham, and he brought Lot out of the catastrophe that overthrew the cit-ies where Lot had lived.

³⁰Lot and his two daughters left Zoar and set-tled in the mountains, for he was afraid to stay in Zoar. He and his two daughters lived in a cave. ³¹One day the older daughter said to the younger, "Our father is old, and there is no man around here to lie with us, as is the custom all over the earth. ³²Let's get our father to drink wine and then lie with him and preserve our family line through our father."

³³That night they got their father to drink wine, and the older daughter went in and lay with him. He was not aware of it when she lay down or when she got up.

³⁴The next day the older daughter said to the younger, "Last night I lay with my father. Let's get him to drink wine again tonight, and you go in and lie with him so we can preserve our family line through our father." ³⁵So they got their father to drink wine that night also, and the younger daughter went and lay with him. Again he was not aware of it when she lay down or when she got up.

³⁶So both of Lot's daughters became pregnant by their father. ³⁷The older daughter had a son, and she named him Moabⁿ; he is the father of the Moabites of today. ³⁸The younger daugh-ter also had a son, and she named him Ben-Ammiᵒ; he is the father of the Ammonites of today.

ᵏ18 Or *No, Lord*; or *No, my lord*   ˡ19 The Hebrew is singular.
ᵐ22 *Zoar* means *small.*   ⁿ37 *Moab* sounds like the Hebrew for *from father.*   ᵒ38 *Ben-Ammi* means *son of my people.*

Discovering the Word 1. In 18:1–8 what elements of hospitality does Abraham show even to visiting strangers? 2. Why does the Lord decide to tell Abraham about his decision to destroy Sodom and Gomorrah (18:16–19)? 3. In the long conversation that follows (18:20–33), what do you learn about Abraham's attitude toward the wicked cities and toward the Lord? 4. In chapter 19 we get a close look at the people in Sodom. How do their actions help us understand why they were under God's judgment? 5. How is the Lord's mercy evident in his treatment of Lot and his family (19:10–22)? 6. Describe how God's judgment works out in Sodom and in Lot's family (19:23–28).

Applying the Word 1. In what areas could we intercede with God for our city, state or country because of its sins? 2. What can we do to avert the judgment of God on ourselves and those around us?

Responding in Prayer Pray for the city or town you live in, that you might be spared God's judgment.

12 / *Genesis 20—21*
The Consequences of Unbelief

HAVE YOU EVER gotten into trouble because you didn't trust God to take care of you? Did you take matters into your own hands and in the process cut some moral or ethical corners? If so, you have company. Even Abraham gave in to his fears and failed to tell the truth in a potentially dangerous situation. The Bible has no plaster saints. It doesn't cover over the sins of its heroes. So we can learn from their *failures* as well as their successes. In the previous study we saw Abraham at his best as he showed concern for a sinful city. In this study we find him near his worst as he pursues a course of action with potentially disastrous consequences for everyone concerned.

 Warming Up to God What have you struggled with recently? Tell Christ about it and let him take it from you as you come near to him in Scripture.

 Read Genesis 20—21.

20 Now Abraham moved on from there into the region of the Negev and lived between Kadesh and Shur. For a while he stayed in Gerar, ²and there Abraham said of his wife Sarah, "She is my sister." Then Abimelech king of Gerar sent for Sarah and took her.

³But God came to Abimelech in a dream one night and said to him, "You are as good as dead because of the woman you have taken; she is a married woman."

⁴Now Abimelech had not gone near her, so he said, "Lord, will you destroy an innocent nation? ⁵Did he not say to me, 'She is my sister,' and didn't she also say, 'He is my brother'? I have done this with a clear conscience and clean hands."

⁶Then God said to him in the dream, "Yes, I know you did this with a clear conscience, and so I have kept you from sinning against me. That is why I did not let you touch her. ⁷Now return the man's wife, for he is a prophet, and he will pray for you and you will live. But if you do not return her, you may be sure that you and all yours will die."

⁸Early the next morning Abimelech summoned all his officials, and when he told them all that had happened, they were very much afraid. ⁹Then Abimelech called Abraham in and said, "What have you done to us? How have I wronged you that you have brought such great guilt upon me and my kingdom? You have done things to me that should not be done." ¹⁰And Abimelech asked Abraham, "What was your reason for doing this?"

¹¹Abraham replied, "I said to myself, 'There is surely no fear of God in this place, and they will kill me because of my wife.' ¹²Besides, she really is my sister, the daughter of my father though not of my mother; and she became my wife. ¹³And when God had me wander from my father's household, I said to her, 'This is how you can show your love to me: Everywhere we go, say of me, "He is my brother." ' "

¹⁴Then Abimelech brought sheep and cattle and male and female slaves and gave them to Abraham, and he returned Sarah his wife to him. ¹⁵And Abimelech said, "My land is before you; live wherever you like."

¹⁶To Sarah he said, "I am giving your brother a thousand shekels*ᵖ* of silver. This is to cover the offense against you before all who are with you; you are completely vindicated."

¹⁷Then Abraham prayed to God, and God healed Abimelech, his wife and his slave girls so they could have children again, ¹⁸for the LORD had closed up every womb in Abimelech's household because of Abraham's wife Sarah.

21 Now the LORD was gracious to Sarah as he had said, and the LORD did for Sarah what he had promised. ²Sarah became pregnant and bore a son to Abraham in his old age, at the very time God had promised him. ³Abraham gave the name Isaac*q* to the son Sarah bore him. ⁴When his son Isaac was eight days old, Abraham circumcised him, as God commanded him. ⁵Abraham was a hundred years old when his son Isaac was born to him.

⁶Sarah said, "God has brought me laughter, and everyone who hears about this will laugh with me." ⁷And she added, "Who would have said to

P16 That is, about 25 pounds (about 11.5 kilograms)   q3 Isaac means *he laughs.*

Abraham that Sarah would nurse children? Yet I have borne him a son in his old age."

8The child grew and was weaned, and on the day Isaac was weaned Abraham held a great feast. 9But Sarah saw that the son whom Hagar the Egyptian had borne to Abraham was mocking, 10and she said to Abraham, "Get rid of that slave woman and her son, for that slave woman's son will never share in the inheritance with my son Isaac."

11The matter distressed Abraham greatly because it concerned his son. 12But God said to him, "Do not be so distressed about the boy and your maidservant. Listen to whatever Sarah tells you, because it is through Isaac that your offspring*r* will be reckoned. 13I will make the son of the maidservant into a nation also, because he is your offspring."

14Early the next morning Abraham took some food and a skin of water and gave them to Hagar. He set them on her shoulders and then sent her off with the boy. She went on her way and wandered in the desert of Beersheba.

15When the water in the skin was gone, she put the boy under one of the bushes. 16Then she went off and sat down nearby, about a bowshot away, for she thought, "I cannot watch the boy die." And as she sat there nearby, she*s* began to sob.

17God heard the boy crying, and the angel of God called to Hagar from heaven and said to her, "What is the matter, Hagar? Do not be afraid; God has heard the boy crying as he lies there. 18Lift the boy up and take him by the hand, for I will make him into a great nation."

19Then God opened her eyes and she saw a well of water. So she went and filled the skin with water and gave the boy a drink.

20God was with the boy as he grew up. He lived in the desert and became an archer. 21While he was living in the Desert of Paran, his mother got a wife for him from Egypt.

22At that time Abimelech and Phicol the commander of his forces said to Abraham, "God is with you in everything you do. 23Now swear to me here before God that you will not deal falsely with me or my children or my descendants. Show to me and the country where you are living as an alien the same kindness I have shown to you."

24Abraham said, "I swear it."

25Then Abraham complained to Abimelech about a well of water that Abimelech's servants had seized. 26But Abimelech said, "I don't know who has done this. You did not tell me, and I heard about it only today."

27So Abraham brought sheep and cattle and gave them to Abimelech, and the two men made a treaty. 28Abraham set apart seven ewe lambs from the flock, 29and Abimelech asked Abraham, "What is the meaning of these seven ewe lambs you have set apart by themselves?"

30He replied, "Accept these seven lambs from my hand as a witness that I dug this well."

31So that place was called Beersheba,*t* because the two men swore an oath there.

32After the treaty had been made at Beersheba, Abimelech and Phicol the commander of his forces returned to the land of the Philistines. 33Abraham planted a tamarisk tree in Beersheba, and there he called upon the name of the LORD, the Eternal God. 34And Abraham stayed in the land of the Philistines for a long time.

*r*12 Or *seed*   *s*16 Hebrew; Septuagint *the child*   *t*31 *Beersheba* can mean *well of seven* or *well of the oath.*

Discovering the Word 1. Describe Abraham's situation and how God deals with it (20:1–7). 2. What do the questions Abimelech asks the next day reveal about his attitude toward Abraham (20:8–10)? 3. How does the patriarch try to explain his way out of this difficulty (20:11–13)? 4. The name *Isaac* means "he laughs." Describe Sarah's reaction and how she feels after waiting so long for this joyful event (21:1–7). 5. What problem does Abraham face in 21:8–14, and how is it resolved? 6. How does God help and encourage Hagar in her hour of crisis (21:15–21)?

Applying the Word 1. Think of a difficult situation in which fear or unbelief led you to a course of action that didn't honor God. What were the consequences and lessons you learned? 2. How can Sarah and Abraham's experience encourage us to be more patient and faithful in waiting for unanswered prayer?

 Responding in Prayer Thank your Father for the laughter he's brought into your heart.

13 / *Genesis 22—23*
Ultimate Faith

Abraham responds immediately to God — He sacrifice's his most beloved possession

SUPPOSE GOD ASKED you to give up someone or something at the very center of your life—a loved one, your home, profession or plans for the future. How would you respond? In this study we walk with Abraham through such a valley of testing. He comes to the climax of his career as he faces a soul-shattering event. Abraham's experience can teach us how God provides for those who honor him with such faith and obedience.

 Warming Up to God   Tell God about any pain you are suffering right now. Remember that James says trials develop perseverance. Ask God to purify your character while you endure.

 Read Genesis 22—23.

22 Some time later God tested Abraham. He said to him, "Abraham!" "Here I am," he replied.

²Then God said, "Take your son, your only son, Isaac, whom you love, and go to the region of Moriah. Sacrifice him there as a burnt offering on one of the mountains I will tell you about."

³Early the next morning Abraham got up and saddled his donkey. He took with him two of his servants and his son Isaac. When he had cut enough wood for the burnt offering, he set out for the place God had told him about. ⁴On the third day Abraham looked up and saw the place in the distance. ⁵He said to his servants, "Stay here with the donkey while I and the boy go over there. We will worship and then we will come back to you."

⁶Abraham took the wood for the burnt offering and placed it on his son Isaac, and he himself carried the fire and the knife. As the two of them went on together, ⁷Isaac spoke up and said to his father Abraham, "Father?"

"Yes, my son?" Abraham replied.

"The fire and wood are here," Isaac said, "but where is the lamb for the burnt offering?"

⁸Abraham answered, "God himself will provide the lamb for the burnt offering, my son." And the two of them went on together.

⁹When they reached the place God had told him about, Abraham built an altar there and arranged the wood on it. He bound his son Isaac and laid him on the altar, on top of the wood. ¹⁰Then he reached out his hand and took the knife to slay his son. ¹¹But the angel of the Lord called out to him from heaven, "Abraham! Abraham!"

"Here I am," he replied.

¹²"Do not lay a hand on the boy," he said. "Do not do anything to him. Now I know that you fear God, because you have not withheld from me your son, your only son."

¹³Abraham looked up and there in a thicket he saw a ram ᵘ caught by its horns. He went over and took the ram and sacrificed it as a burnt offering instead of his son. ¹⁴So Abraham called that place The Lord Will Provide. And to this day it is said, "On the mountain of the Lord it will be provided."

¹⁵The angel of the Lord called to Abraham from heaven a second time ¹⁶and said, "I swear by myself, declares the Lord, that because you have done this and have not withheld your son, your only son, ¹⁷I will surely bless you and make your descendants as numerous as the stars in the sky and as the sand on the seashore. Your descendants will take possession of the cities of their enemies, ¹⁸and through your offspring ᵛ all nations on earth will be blessed, because you have obeyed me."

¹⁹Then Abraham returned to his servants, and they set off together for Beersheba. And Abraham stayed in Beersheba.

²⁰Some time later Abraham was told, "Milcah is also a mother; she has borne sons to your brother Nahor: ²¹Uz the firstborn, Buz his brother, Kemuel (the father of Aram), ²²Kesed, Hazo, Pildash, Jidlaph and Bethuel." ²³Bethuel became the father of Rebekah. Milcah bore these eight sons to Abraham's brother Nahor. ²⁴His concubine, whose name was Reumah, also had sons: Tebah, Gaham, Tahash and Maacah.

ᵘ13 Many manuscripts of the Masoretic Text, Samaritan Pentateuch, Septuagint and Syriac; most manuscripts of the Masoretic Text *a ram behind him*   ᵛ18 Or *seed*

23

Sarah lived to be a hundred and twenty-seven years old. ²She died at Kiriath Arba (that is, Hebron) in the land of Canaan, and Abraham went to mourn for Sarah and to weep over her.

³Then Abraham rose from beside his dead wife and spoke to the Hittites.ʷ He said, ⁴"I am an alien and a stranger among you. Sell me some property for a burial site here so I can bury my dead."

⁵The Hittites replied to Abraham, ⁶"Sir, listen to us. You are a mighty prince among us. Bury your dead in the choicest of our tombs. None of us will refuse you his tomb for burying your dead."

⁷Then Abraham rose and bowed down before the people of the land, the Hittites. ⁸He said to them, "If you are willing to let me bury my dead, then listen to me and intercede with Ephron son of Zohar on my behalf ⁹so he will sell me the cave of Machpelah, which belongs to him and is at the end of his field. Ask him to sell it to me for the full price as a burial site among you."

¹⁰Ephron the Hittite was sitting among his people and he replied to Abraham in the hearing of all the Hittites who had come to the gate of his city. ¹¹"No, my lord," he said. "Listen to me; I giveˣ you the field, and I giveˣ you the cave that

is in it. I giveˣ it to you in the presence of my people. Bury your dead."

¹²Again Abraham bowed down before the people of the land ¹³and he said to Ephron in their hearing, "Listen to me, if you will. I will pay the price of the field. Accept it from me so I can bury my dead there."

¹⁴Ephron answered Abraham, ¹⁵"Listen to me, my lord; the land is worth four hundred shekelsʸ of silver, but what is that between me and you? Bury your dead."

¹⁶Abraham agreed to Ephron's terms and weighed out for him the price he had named in the hearing of the Hittites: four hundred shekels of silver, according to the weight current among the merchants.

¹⁷So Ephron's field in Machpelah near Mamre—both the field and the cave in it, and all the trees within the borders of the field—was deeded ¹⁸to Abraham as his property in the presence of all the Hittites who had come to the gate of the city. ¹⁹Afterward Abraham buried his wife Sarah in the cave in the field of Machpelah near Mamre (which is at Hebron) in the land of Canaan. ²⁰So the field and the cave in it were deeded to Abraham by the Hittites as a burial site.

ʷ3 Or *the sons of Heth;* also in verses 5, 7, 10, 16, 18 and 20
ˣ11 Or *sell* ʸ15 That is, about 10 pounds (about 4.5 kilograms)

 Discovering the Word 1. In God's command to Abraham what phrases emphasize the magnitude and painfulness of this sacrifice (22:1–2)? 2. What do the details of the narrative reveal about Abraham's response to this incredibly difficult situation (22:3–10)? 3. How does God's provision for Abraham in 22:13–14 fulfill the confidence he expressed earlier (22:5, 8)? 4. When Abraham decides to bury Sarah among the Hittites, how do they react to his first request (23:1–6)? 5. What steps does Abraham go through to observe the laws of the land (23:7–16)? 6. At the time of Sarah's death, she and Abraham had not seen the fulfillment of most of God's promises. How was her burial a silent testimony to their future fulfillment (23:17–19)?

Applying the Word 1. In 22:12 the Lord says, "Now I know that you fear God, because you have not withheld from me your son, your only son." Based on Abraham's example, what do you think it means to fear God? 2. Have you ever faced a situation in which obedience to God required you to give up someone or something you loved? Explain.

Responding in Prayer Praise God for this foreshadowing of his ultimate act of sacrifice—the willful surrender of his Son's life to give us forgiveness and salvation.

14 / *Genesis 24:1—25:11*
God's Guidance and Care

HOW DO YOU go about discovering God's will in a specific situation? When you think you understand his will, do you simply wait for it or do you work toward its fulfillment? Although the Bible gives no formulas or blueprints, it does illustrate certain principles we can apply. In this study Abraham continues to wind up his affairs by arranging for the sure succession of his line. Here we have the fascinating story of the way he went about securing the right wife for his son Isaac.

 Warming Up to God God wants to give you the desires of your heart. What are you yearning for today?

 Read Genesis 24:1—25:11.

24 Abraham was now old and well advanced in years, and the LORD had blessed him in every way. ²He said to the chief*z* servant in his household, the one in charge of all that he had, "Put your hand under my thigh. ³I want you to swear by the LORD, the God of heaven and the God of earth, that you will not get a wife for my son from the daughters of the Canaanites, among whom I am living, ⁴but will go to my country and my own relatives and get a wife for my son Isaac."

⁵The servant asked him, "What if the woman is unwilling to come back with me to this land? Shall I then take your son back to the country you came from?"

⁶"Make sure that you do not take my son back there," Abraham said. ⁷"The LORD, the God of heaven, who brought me out of my father's household and my native land and who spoke to me and promised me on oath, saying, 'To your offspring*a* I will give this land'—he will send his angel before you so that you can get a wife for my son from there. ⁸If the woman is unwilling to come back with you, then you will be released from this oath of mine. Only do not take my son back there." ⁹So the servant put his hand under the thigh of his master Abraham and swore an oath to him concerning this matter.

¹⁰Then the servant took ten of his master's camels and left, taking with him all kinds of good things from his master. He set out for Aram Naharaim*b* and made his way to the town of Nahor. ¹¹He had the camels kneel down near the well outside the town; it was toward evening, the time the women go out to draw water.

¹²Then he prayed, "O LORD, God of my master Abraham, give me success today, and show kindness to my master Abraham. ¹³See, I am standing beside this spring, and the daughters of the townspeople are coming out to draw water. ¹⁴May it be that when I say to a girl, 'Please let down your jar that I may have a drink,' and she says, 'Drink, and I'll water your camels too'—let her be the one you have chosen for your servant Isaac. By this I will know that you have shown kindness to my master."

¹⁵Before he had finished praying, Rebekah came out with her jar on her shoulder. She was the daughter of Bethuel son of Milcah, who was the wife of Abraham's brother Nahor. ¹⁶The girl was very beautiful, a virgin; no man had ever lain with her. She went down to the spring, filled her jar and came up again.

¹⁷The servant hurried to meet her and said, "Please give me a little water from your jar."

¹⁸"Drink, my lord," she said, and quickly lowered the jar to her hands and gave him a drink.

¹⁹After she had given him a drink, she said, "I'll draw water for your camels too, until they have finished drinking." ²⁰So she quickly emptied her jar into the trough, ran back to the well to draw more water, and drew enough for all his camels. ²¹Without saying a word, the man watched her closely to learn whether or not the LORD had made his journey successful.

²²When the camels had finished drinking, the man took out a gold nose ring weighing a beka*c* and two gold bracelets weighing ten shekels.*d* ²³Then he asked, "Whose daughter are you? Please tell me, is there room in your father's house for us to spend the night?"

²⁴She answered him, "I am the daughter of Be-

---

*z*2 Or *oldest*   *a*7 Or *seed*   *b*10 That is, Northwest Mesopotamia
*c*22 That is, about 1/5 ounce (about 5.5 grams)   *d*22 That is, about 4 ounces (about 110 grams)

thuel, the son that Milcah bore to Nahor." 25And she added, "We have plenty of straw and fodder, as well as room for you to spend the night."

26Then the man bowed down and worshiped the LORD, 27saying, "Praise be to the LORD, the God of my master Abraham, who has not abandoned his kindness and faithfulness to my master. As for me, the LORD has led me on the journey to the house of my master's relatives."

28The girl ran and told her mother's household about these things. 29Now Rebekah had a brother named Laban, and he hurried out to the man at the spring. 30As soon as he had seen the nose ring, and the bracelets on his sister's arms, and had heard Rebekah tell what the man said to her, he went out to the man and found him standing by the camels near the spring. 31"Come, you who are blessed by the LORD," he said. "Why are you standing out here? I have prepared the house and a place for the camels."

32So the man went to the house, and the camels were unloaded. Straw and fodder were brought for the camels, and water for him and his men to wash their feet. 33Then food was set before him, but he said, "I will not eat until I have told you what I have to say."

"Then tell us," ⌊Laban⌋ said.

34So he said, "I am Abraham's servant. 35The LORD has blessed my master abundantly, and he has become wealthy. He has given him sheep and cattle, silver and gold, menservants and maidservants, and camels and donkeys. 36My master's wife Sarah has borne him a son in her e old age, and he has given him everything he owns. 37And my master made me swear an oath, and said, 'You must not get a wife for my son from the daughters of the Canaanites, in whose land I live, 38but go to my father's family and to my own clan, and get a wife for my son.'

39"Then I asked my master, 'What if the woman will not come back with me?'

40"He replied, 'The LORD, before whom I have walked, will send his angel with you and make your journey a success, so that you can get a wife for my son from my own clan and from my father's family. 41Then, when you go to my clan, you will be released from my oath even if they refuse to give her to you—you will be released from my oath.'

42"When I came to the spring today, I said, 'O LORD, God of my master Abraham, if you will, please grant success to the journey on which I have come. 43See, I am standing beside this spring; if a maiden comes out to draw water and I say to her, "Please let me drink a little water from your jar," 44and if she says to me, "Drink, and I'll draw water for your camels too," let her be the one the LORD has chosen for my master's son.'

45"Before I finished praying in my heart, Rebekah came out, with her jar on her shoulder. She went down to the spring and drew water, and I said to her, 'Please give me a drink.'

46"She quickly lowered her jar from her shoulder and said, 'Drink, and I'll water your camels too.' So I drank, and she watered the camels also.

47"I asked her, 'Whose daughter are you?'

"She said, 'The daughter of Bethuel son of Nahor, whom Milcah bore to him.'

"Then I put the ring in her nose and the bracelets on her arms, 48and I bowed down and worshiped the LORD. I praised the LORD, the God of my master Abraham, who had led me on the right road to get the granddaughter of my master's brother for his son. 49Now if you will show kindness and faithfulness to my master, tell me; and if not, tell me, so I may know which way to turn."

50Laban and Bethuel answered, "This is from the LORD; we can say nothing to you one way or the other. 51Here is Rebekah; take her and go, and let her become the wife of your master's son, as the LORD has directed."

52When Abraham's servant heard what they said, he bowed down to the ground before the LORD. 53Then the servant brought out gold and silver jewelry and articles of clothing and gave them to Rebekah; he also gave costly gifts to her brother and to her mother. 54Then he and the men who were with him ate and drank and spent the night there.

When they got up the next morning, he said, "Send me on my way to my master."

55But her brother and her mother replied, "Let the girl remain with us ten days or so; then you f may go."

56But he said to them, "Do not detain me, now that the LORD has granted success to my journey. Send me on my way so I may go to my master."

57Then they said, "Let's call the girl and ask her about it." 58So they called Rebekah and asked her, "Will you go with this man?"

"I will go," she said.

Rebekah responds immediately to God's call

e36 Or his   f55 Or she

⁵⁹So they sent their sister Rebekah on her way, along with her nurse and Abraham's servant and his men. ⁶⁰And they blessed Rebekah and said to her,

"Our sister, may you increase
    to thousands upon thousands;
may your offspring possess
    the gates of their enemies."

⁶¹Then Rebekah and her maids got ready and mounted their camels and went back with the man. So the servant took Rebekah and left.

⁶²Now Isaac had come from Beer Lahai Roi, for he was living in the Negev. ⁶³He went out to the field one evening to meditate,ᵍ and as he looked up, he saw camels approaching. ⁶⁴Rebekah also looked up and saw Isaac. She got down from her camel ⁶⁵and asked the servant, "Who is that man in the field coming to meet us?"

"He is my master," the servant answered. So she took her veil and covered herself.

⁶⁶Then the servant told Isaac all he had done. ⁶⁷Isaac brought her into the tent of his mother Sarah, and he married Rebekah. So she became his wife, and he loved her; and Isaac was comforted after his mother's death.

25 Abraham tookʰ another wife, whose name was Keturah. ²She bore him Zimran, Jokshan, Medan, Midian, Ishbak and Shuah. ³Jokshan was the father of Sheba and Dedan; the descendants of Dedan were the Asshurites, the Letushites and the Leummites. ⁴The sons of Midian were Ephah, Epher, Hanoch, Abida and Eldaah. All these were descendants of Keturah.

⁵Abraham left everything he owned to Isaac. ⁶But while he was still living, he gave gifts to the sons of his concubines and sent them away from his son Isaac to the land of the east.

⁷Altogether, Abraham lived a hundred and seventy-five years. ⁸Then Abraham breathed his last and died at a good old age, an old man and full of years; and he was gathered to his people. ⁹His sons Isaac and Ishmael buried him in the cave of Machpelah near Mamre, in the field of Ephron son of Zohar the Hittite, ¹⁰the field Abraham had bought from the Hittites.ⁱ There Abraham was buried with his wife Sarah. ¹¹After Abraham's death, God blessed his son Isaac, who then lived near Beer Lahai Roi.

ᵍ63 The meaning of the Hebrew for this word is uncertain.   ʰ1 Or *had taken*   ⁱ10 Or *the sons of Heth*

 Discovering the Word 1. What main concerns are evident in Abraham's commands to his servant (24:1–9)? 2. As the servant arrives at Nahor he offers the first prayer for personal guidance recorded in the Bible. What does he specifically ask of God (24:12–14)? 3. How does the servant's account in 24:33–49 reveal his excitement and awe at the Lord's guidance? 4. How does Rebekah's family react to these sudden, unexpected events (24:50–53)? 5. In what way is Rebekah involved in the decision to go with the servant (24:54–60)? 6. What do we learn about Abraham's final years (25:1–11)?

Applying the Word 1. The servant had not asked for a vision or miraculous event but for guidance through clear signs in natural circumstances. When has God guided you in this way? 2. What is the most important lesson you have learned from studying the life of Abraham?

Responding in Prayer Thank the Lord for giving you the model of the not-so-perfect, but God-directed, life of Abraham.

---

15 / *Genesis 25:12—27:40*
A Family Feud

CONTROVERSY AND QUARRELING among brothers, euphemistically called sibling rivalry, is prevalent in most families and is a part of growing up. It can be contained, however, if it is dealt with consistently and fairly. But when the parents show partiality and take sides, this struggle often becomes malignant and fatal to family unity. This study opens with the joy of long-awaited birth. After twenty years, Isaac and Rebekah have not just one son but twins. As the boys grow up, parental partiality develops with tragic consequences for family relationships. Yet throughout these events God works out his sovereign purpose and remains merciful to this family in spite of their failures. Not only can we profit from their mistakes, but we can also be encouraged by God's love for us even when we fail.

 Warming Up to God What one new event or piece of news can you share with Jesus today? Tell him a story and ask him to teach you as you continue reading the stories of Abraham, Isaac and now Jacob.

 Read Genesis 25:12—27:40.

---

¹²This is the account of Abraham's son Ishmael, whom Sarah's maidservant, Hagar the Egyptian, bore to Abraham.

¹³These are the names of the sons of Ishmael, listed in the order of their birth: Nebaioth the firstborn of Ishmael, Kedar, Adbeel, Mibsam, ¹⁴Mishma, Dumah, Massa, ¹⁵Hadad, Tema, Jetur, Naphish and Kedemah. ¹⁶These were the sons of Ishmael, and these are the names of the twelve tribal rulers according to their settlements and camps. ¹⁷Altogether, Ishmael lived a hundred and thirty-seven years. He breathed his last and died, and he was gathered to his people. ¹⁸His descendants settled in the area from Havilah to Shur, near the border of Egypt, as you go toward Asshur. And they lived in hostility toward^j all their brothers.

¹⁹This is the account of Abraham's son Isaac.

Abraham became the father of Isaac, ²⁰and Isaac was forty years old when he married Rebekah daughter of Bethuel the Aramean from Paddan Aram^k and sister of Laban the Aramean. ²¹Isaac prayed to the Lord on behalf of his wife, because she was barren. The Lord answered his prayer, and his wife Rebekah became pregnant. ²²The babies jostled each other within her, and she said, "Why is this happening to me?" So she went to inquire of the Lord.

²³The Lord said to her,

"Two nations are in your womb,
  and two peoples from within you will be
    separated;
one people will be stronger than the other,
  and the older will serve the younger."

²⁴When the time came for her to give birth, there were twin boys in her womb. ²⁵The first to come out was red, and his whole body was like a hairy garment; so they named him Esau.^{l} ²⁶After this, his brother came out, with his hand grasping Esau's heel; so he was named Jacob.^{m} Isaac was sixty years old when Rebekah gave birth to them.

²⁷The boys grew up, and Esau became a skillful hunter, a man of the open country, while Jacob was a quiet man, staying among the tents. ²⁸Isaac, who had a taste for wild game, loved Esau, but Rebekah loved Jacob.

²⁹Once when Jacob was cooking some stew, Esau came in from the open country, famished. ³⁰He said to Jacob, "Quick, let me have some of that red stew! I'm famished!" (That is why he was also called Edom.^{n})

³¹Jacob replied, "First sell me your birthright."

³²"Look, I am about to die," Esau said. "What good is the birthright to me?"

³³But Jacob said, "Swear to me first." So he swore an oath to him, selling his birthright to Jacob.

³⁴Then Jacob gave Esau some bread and some lentil stew. He ate and drank, and then got up and left.

So Esau despised his birthright.

26 Now there was a famine in the land—besides the earlier famine of Abraham's time—and Isaac went to Abimelech king of the Philistines in Gerar. ²The Lord appeared to Isaac and said, "Do not go down to Egypt; live in the land where I tell you to live. ³Stay in this land for a while, and I will be with you and will bless you. For to you and your descendants I will give all these lands and will confirm the oath I swore to your father Abraham. ⁴I will make your descendants as numerous as the stars in the sky and will give them all these lands, and through your offspring^o all nations on earth will be blessed, ⁵because Abraham obeyed me and kept my requirements, my commands, my decrees and my laws." ⁶So Isaac stayed in Gerar.

⁷When the men of that place asked him about his wife, he said, "She is my sister," because he was afraid to say, "She is my wife." He thought, "The men of this place might kill me on account of Rebekah, because she is beautiful."

⁸When Isaac had been there a long time, Abim-

---

^{j}18 Or lived to the east of ^{k}20 That is, Northwest Mesopotamia
^{l}25 Esau may mean hairy; he was also called Edom, which means red.
^{m}26 Jacob means he grasps the heel (figuratively, he deceives).
^{n}30 Edom means red. ^{o}4 Or seed

elech king of the Philistines looked down from a window and saw Isaac caressing his wife Rebekah. ⁹So Abimelech summoned Isaac and said, "She is really your wife! Why did you say, 'She is my sister'?"

Isaac answered him, "Because I thought I might lose my life on account of her."

¹⁰Then Abimelech said, "What is this you have done to us? One of the men might well have slept with your wife, and you would have brought guilt upon us."

¹¹So Abimelech gave orders to all the people: "Anyone who molests this man or his wife shall surely be put to death."

¹²Isaac planted crops in that land and the same year reaped a hundredfold, because the LORD blessed him. ¹³The man became rich, and his wealth continued to grow until he became very wealthy. ¹⁴He had so many flocks and herds and servants that the Philistines envied him. ¹⁵So all the wells that his father's servants had dug in the time of his father Abraham, the Philistines stopped up, filling them with earth.

¹⁶Then Abimelech said to Isaac, "Move away from us; you have become too powerful for us."

¹⁷So Isaac moved away from there and encamped in the Valley of Gerar and settled there. ¹⁸Isaac reopened the wells that had been dug in the time of his father Abraham, which the Philistines had stopped up after Abraham died, and he gave them the same names his father had given them.

¹⁹Isaac's servants dug in the valley and discovered a well of fresh water there. ²⁰But the herdsmen of Gerar quarreled with Isaac's herdsmen and said, "The water is ours!" So he named the well Esek,ᵖ because they disputed with him. ²¹Then they dug another well, but they quarreled over that one also; so he named it Sitnah.�q ²²He moved on from there and dug another well, and no one quarreled over it. He named it Rehoboth,ʳ saying, "Now the LORD has given us room and we will flourish in the land."

²³From there he went up to Beersheba. ²⁴That night the LORD appeared to him and said, "I am the God of your father Abraham. Do not be afraid, for I am with you; I will bless you and will increase the number of your descendants for the sake of my servant Abraham."

²⁵Isaac built an altar there and called on the name of the LORD. There he pitched his tent, and there his servants dug a well.

²⁶Meanwhile, Abimelech had come to him from Gerar, with Ahuzzath his personal adviser and Phicol the commander of his forces. ²⁷Isaac asked them, "Why have you come to me, since you were hostile to me and sent me away?"

²⁸They answered, "We saw clearly that the LORD was with you; so we said, 'There ought to be a sworn agreement between us'—between us and you. Let us make a treaty with you ²⁹that you will do us no harm, just as we did not molest you but always treated you well and sent you away in peace. And now you are blessed by the LORD."

³⁰Isaac then made a feast for them, and they ate and drank. ³¹Early the next morning the men swore an oath to each other. Then Isaac sent them on their way, and they left him in peace.

³²That day Isaac's servants came and told him about the well they had dug. They said, "We've found water!" ³³He called it Shibah,ˢ and to this day the name of the town has been Beersheba.ᵗ

³⁴When Esau was forty years old, he married Judith daughter of Beeri the Hittite, and also Basemath daughter of Elon the Hittite. ³⁵They were a source of grief to Isaac and Rebekah.

27

When Isaac was old and his eyes were so weak that he could no longer see, he called for Esau his older son and said to him, "My son."

"Here I am," he answered.

²Isaac said, "I am now an old man and don't know the day of my death. ³Now then, get your weapons—your quiver and bow—and go out to the open country to hunt some wild game for me. ⁴Prepare me the kind of tasty food I like and bring it to me to eat, so that I may give you my blessing before I die."

⁵Now Rebekah was listening as Isaac spoke to his son Esau. When Esau left for the open country to hunt game and bring it back, ⁶Rebekah said to her son Jacob, "Look, I overheard your father say to your brother Esau, ⁷'Bring me some game and prepare me some tasty food to eat, so that I may give you my blessing in the presence of the LORD before I die.' ⁸Now, my son, listen carefully and do what I tell you: ⁹Go out to the flock and bring me two choice young goats, so I can prepare some tasty food for your father, just the way he likes it. ¹⁰Then take it to your father to eat, so that he may give you his blessing before he dies."

ᵖ20 *Esek* means *dispute.*   q21 *Sitnah* means *opposition.*
ʳ22 *Rehoboth* means *room.*   ˢ33 *Shibah* can mean *oath* or *seven.*
ᵗ33 *Beersheba* can mean *well of the oath* or *well of seven.*

¹¹Jacob said to Rebekah his mother, "But my brother Esau is a hairy man, and I'm a man with smooth skin. ¹²What if my father touches me? I would appear to be tricking him and would bring down a curse on myself rather than a blessing."

¹³His mother said to him, "My son, let the curse fall on me. Just do what I say; go and get them for me."

¹⁴So he went and got them and brought them to his mother, and she prepared some tasty food, just the way his father liked it. ¹⁵Then Rebekah took the best clothes of Esau her older son, which she had in the house, and put them on her younger son Jacob. ¹⁶She also covered his hands and the smooth part of his neck with the goatskins. ¹⁷Then she handed to her son Jacob the tasty food and the bread she had made.

¹⁸He went to his father and said, "My father."

"Yes, my son," he answered. "Who is it?"

¹⁹Jacob said to his father, "I am Esau your first-born. I have done as you told me. Please sit up and eat some of my game so that you may give me your blessing."

²⁰Isaac asked his son, "How did you find it so quickly, my son?"

"The LORD your God gave me success," he replied.

²¹Then Isaac said to Jacob, "Come near so I can touch you, my son, to know whether you really are my son Esau or not."

²²Jacob went close to his father Isaac, who touched him and said, "The voice is the voice of Jacob, but the hands are the hands of Esau." ²³He did not recognize him, for his hands were hairy like those of his brother Esau; so he blessed him. ²⁴"Are you really my son Esau?" he asked.

"I am," he replied.

²⁵Then he said, "My son, bring me some of your game to eat, so that I may give you my blessing."

Jacob brought it to him and he ate; and he brought some wine and he drank. ²⁶Then his father Isaac said to him, "Come here, my son, and kiss me."

²⁷So he went to him and kissed him. When Isaac caught the smell of his clothes, he blessed him and said,

"Ah, the smell of my son
    is like the smell of a field
    that the LORD has blessed.
²⁸May God give you of heaven's dew

and of earth's richness—
    an abundance of grain and new wine.
²⁹May nations serve you
    and peoples bow down to you.
Be lord over your brothers,
    and may the sons of your mother bow
        down to you.
May those who curse you be cursed
    and those who bless you be blessed."

³⁰After Isaac finished blessing him and Jacob had scarcely left his father's presence, his brother Esau came in from hunting. ³¹He too prepared some tasty food and brought it to his father. Then he said to him, "My father, sit up and eat some of my game, so that you may give me your blessing."

³²His father Isaac asked him, "Who are you?"

"I am your son," he answered, "your firstborn, Esau."

³³Isaac trembled violently and said, "Who was it, then, that hunted game and brought it to me? I ate it just before you came and I blessed him—and indeed he will be blessed!"

³⁴When Esau heard his father's words, he burst out with a loud and bitter cry and said to his father, "Bless me—me too, my father!"

³⁵But he said, "Your brother came deceitfully and took your blessing."

³⁶Esau said, "Isn't he rightly named Jacob[u]? He has deceived me these two times: He took my birthright, and now he's taken my blessing!" Then he asked, "Haven't you reserved any blessing for me?"

³⁷Isaac answered Esau, "I have made him lord over you and have made all his relatives his servants, and I have sustained him with grain and new wine. So what can I possibly do for you, my son?"

³⁸Esau said to his father, "Do you have only one blessing, my father? Bless me too, my father!" Then Esau wept aloud.

³⁹His father Isaac answered him,

"Your dwelling will be
    away from the earth's richness,
    away from the dew of heaven above.
⁴⁰You will live by the sword
    and you will serve your brother.
But when you grow restless,
    you will throw his yoke
    from off your neck."

ᵘ36 *Jacob* means *he grasps the heel* (figuratively, *he deceives*).

Discovering the Word 1. What difficulties and tests of faith do Isaac and Rebekah encounter in connection with the birth of their sons (25:19–22)? 2. What does the incident in 25:29–34 reveal about the character of the two brothers? 3. What specific promises does the Lord make to Isaac in reaffirming his covenant with Abraham (26:2–6, 23–25)? 4. In 25:28 we learned that "Isaac, who had a taste for wild game, loved Esau, but Rebekah loved Jacob." How does this parental favoritism work itself out in the struggle recounted in 27:1–17? 5. How does Jacob succeed in deceiving his father (27:18–29)?

Applying the Word 1. Verse 34 states that Esau despised his birthright (his double portion of the inheritance and future role as head of the family). In what areas are you tempted to give up something spiritually valuable for the sake of something of little or no value? 2. In what ways have you experienced the strength of your parents or been influenced by their weaknesses? 3. How can you show equal love and care to family members with radically different personalities?

Responding in Prayer Ask God to show you how to encourage better relationships in your own family or living situation.

16 / *Genesis 27:41—30:24*
God's Mercy and Justice

HOW DO YOU cope with the consequences of sin in your life? What effect does your disobedience to God have on his purposes for you? Jacob's experience can provide helpful answers to these questions. In the last study we saw how parental partiality increased the natural rivalry between Esau and Jacob. As Isaac and Rebekah took sides to work against each other, the family relationships became strained. In this study we see how they finally fractured, with unforeseen consequences.

Warming Up to God What words would you use to describe the mercy of God? Thank him for each way he has shown mercy to you.

Read Genesis 27:41—30:24.

⁴¹Esau held a grudge against Jacob because of the blessing his father had given him. He said to himself, "The days of mourning for my father are near; then I will kill my brother Jacob."

⁴²When Rebekah was told what her older son Esau had said, she sent for her younger son Jacob and said to him, "Your brother Esau is consoling himself with the thought of killing you. ⁴³Now then, my son, do what I say: Flee at once to my brother Laban in Haran. ⁴⁴Stay with him for a while until your brother's fury subsides. ⁴⁵When your brother is no longer angry with you and forgets what you did to him, I'll send word for you to come back from there. Why should I lose both of you in one day?"

⁴⁶Then Rebekah said to Isaac, "I'm disgusted with living because of these Hittite women. If Jacob takes a wife from among the women of this land, from Hittite women like these, my life will not be worth living."

28 So Isaac called for Jacob and blessedᵛ him and commanded him: "Do not marry a Canaanite woman. ²Go at once to Paddan Aram,ʷ to the house of your mother's father Bethuel. Take a wife for yourself there, from among the daughters of Laban, your mother's brother. ³May God Almightyˣ bless you and make you fruitful and increase your numbers until you become a community of peoples. ⁴May he give you and your descendants the blessing given to Abraham, so that you may take possession of the land where you now live as an alien, the land God gave to Abraham." ⁵Then Isaac sent Jacob on his way, and he went to Paddan Aram, to Laban son of Bethuel the Aramean, the brother of Rebekah, who was the mother of Jacob and Esau.

⁶Now Esau learned that Isaac had blessed Jacob and had sent him to Paddan Aram to take a wife

ᵛ1 Or *greeted*   ʷ2 That is, Northwest Mesopotamia; also in verses 5, 6 and 7   ˣ3 Hebrew *El-Shaddai* from there, and that when he blessed him he commanded him, "Do not marry a Canaanite woman," ⁷and that Jacob had obeyed his father and mother and had gone to Paddan Aram. ⁸Esau then realized how displeasing the Canaanite women were to his father Isaac; ⁹so he went to Ishmael and married Mahalath, the sister of Nebaioth and daughter of Ishmael son of Abraham, in addition to the wives he already had.

¹⁰Jacob left Beersheba and set out for Haran. ¹¹When he reached a certain place, he stopped for the night because the sun had set. Taking one of the stones there, he put it under his head and lay down to sleep. ¹²He had a dream in which he saw a stairway^y resting on the earth, with its top reaching to heaven, and the angels of God were ascending and descending on it. ¹³There above it^z stood the Lᴏʀᴅ, and he said: "I am the Lᴏʀᴅ, the God of your father Abraham and the God of Isaac. I will give you and your descendants the land on which you are lying. ¹⁴Your descendants will be like the dust of the earth, and you will spread out to the west and to the east, to the north and to the south. All peoples on earth will be blessed through you and your offspring. ¹⁵I am with you and will watch over you wherever you go, and I will bring you back to this land. I will not leave you until I have done what I have promised you."

¹⁶When Jacob awoke from his sleep, he thought, "Surely the Lᴏʀᴅ is in this place, and I was not aware of it." ¹⁷He was afraid and said, "How awesome is this place! This is none other than the house of God; this is the gate of heaven."

¹⁸Early the next morning Jacob took the stone he had placed under his head and set it up as a pillar and poured oil on top of it. ¹⁹He called that place Bethel,^{a} though the city used to be called Luz.

²⁰Then Jacob made a vow, saying, "If God will be with me and will watch over me on this journey I am taking and will give me food to eat and clothes to wear ²¹so that I return safely to my father's house, then the Lᴏʀᴅ^b will be my God ²²and^c this stone that I have set up as a pillar will be God's house, and of all that you give me I will give you a tenth."

29 Then Jacob continued on his journey and came to the land of the eastern peoples. ²There he saw a well in the field, with three flocks of sheep lying near it because the flocks were watered from that well. The stone over the mouth of the well was large. ³When all the flocks were gathered there, the shepherds would roll the stone away from the well's mouth and water the sheep. Then they would return the stone to its place over the mouth of the well.

⁴Jacob asked the shepherds, "My brothers, where are you from?"

"We're from Haran," they replied.

⁵He said to them, "Do you know Laban, Nahor's grandson?"

"Yes, we know him," they answered.

⁶Then Jacob asked them, "Is he well?"

"Yes, he is," they said, "and here comes his daughter Rachel with the sheep."

⁷"Look," he said, "the sun is still high; it is not time for the flocks to be gathered. Water the sheep and take them back to pasture."

⁸"We can't," they replied, "until all the flocks are gathered and the stone has been rolled away from the mouth of the well. Then we will water the sheep."

⁹While he was still talking with them, Rachel came with her father's sheep, for she was a shepherdess. ¹⁰When Jacob saw Rachel daughter of Laban, his mother's brother, and Laban's sheep, he went over and rolled the stone away from the mouth of the well and watered his uncle's sheep. ¹¹Then Jacob kissed Rachel and began to weep aloud. ¹²He had told Rachel that he was a relative of her father and a son of Rebekah. So she ran and told her father.

¹³As soon as Laban heard the news about Jacob, his sister's son, he hurried to meet him. He embraced him and kissed him and brought him to his home, and there Jacob told him all these things. ¹⁴Then Laban said to him, "You are my own flesh and blood."

After Jacob had stayed with him for a whole month, ¹⁵Laban said to him, "Just because you are a relative of mine, should you work for me for nothing? Tell me what your wages should be."

¹⁶Now Laban had two daughters; the name of the older was Leah, and the name of the younger was Rachel. ¹⁷Leah had weak^d eyes, but Rachel was lovely in form, and beautiful. ¹⁸Jacob was in love with Rachel and said, "I'll work for you seven years in return for your younger daughter Rachel."

---

^{y}12 Or *ladder* ^{z}13 Or *There beside him* ^{a}19 *Bethel* means *house of God.* ^{b}20,21 Or *Since God . . . father's house, the* Lᴏʀᴅ ^{c}21,22 Or *house, and the* Lᴏʀᴅ *will be my God,* 22*then* ^{d}17 Or *delicate*

¹⁹Laban said, "It's better that I give her to you than to some other man. Stay here with me." ²⁰So Jacob served seven years to get Rachel, but they seemed like only a few days to him because of his love for her.

²¹Then Jacob said to Laban, "Give me my wife. My time is completed, and I want to lie with her."

²²So Laban brought together all the people of the place and gave a feast. ²³But when evening came, he took his daughter Leah and gave her to Jacob, and Jacob lay with her. ²⁴And Laban gave his servant girl Zilpah to his daughter as her maidservant.

²⁵When morning came, there was Leah! So Jacob said to Laban, "What is this you have done to me? I served you for Rachel, didn't I? Why have you deceived me?"

²⁶Laban replied, "It is not our custom here to give the younger daughter in marriage before the older one. ²⁷Finish this daughter's bridal week; then we will give you the younger one also, in return for another seven years of work."

²⁸And Jacob did so. He finished the week with Leah, and then Laban gave him his daughter Rachel to be his wife. ²⁹Laban gave his servant girl Bilhah to his daughter Rachel as her maidservant. ³⁰Jacob lay with Rachel also, and he loved Rachel more than Leah. And he worked for Laban another seven years.

³¹When the Lord saw that Leah was not loved, he opened her womb, but Rachel was barren. ³²Leah became pregnant and gave birth to a son. She named him Reuben,ᵉ for she said, "It is because the Lord has seen my misery. Surely my husband will love me now."

³³She conceived again, and when she gave birth to a son she said, "Because the Lord heard that I am not loved, he gave me this one too." So she named him Simeon.ᶠ

³⁴Again she conceived, and when she gave birth to a son she said, "Now at last my husband will become attached to me, because I have borne him three sons." So he was named Levi.ᵍ

³⁵She conceived again, and when she gave birth to a son she said, "This time I will praise the Lord." So she named him Judah.ʰ Then she stopped having children.

30

When Rachel saw that she was not bearing Jacob any children, she became jealous of her sister. So she said to Jacob, "Give me children, or I'll die!"

²Jacob became angry with her and said, "Am I in the place of God, who has kept you from having children?"

³Then she said, "Here is Bilhah, my maidservant. Sleep with her so that she can bear children for me and that through her I too can build a family."

⁴So she gave him her servant Bilhah as a wife. Jacob slept with her, ⁵and she became pregnant and bore him a son. ⁶Then Rachel said, "God has vindicated me; he has listened to my plea and given me a son." Because of this she named him Dan.ⁱ

⁷Rachel's servant Bilhah conceived again and bore Jacob a second son. ⁸Then Rachel said, "I have had a great struggle with my sister, and I have won." So she named him Naphtali.ʲ

⁹When Leah saw that she had stopped having children, she took her maidservant Zilpah and gave her to Jacob as a wife. ¹⁰Leah's servant Zilpah bore Jacob a son. ¹¹Then Leah said, "What good fortune!"ᵏ So she named him Gad.ˡ

¹²Leah's servant Zilpah bore Jacob a second son. ¹³Then Leah said, "How happy I am! The women will call me happy." So she named him Asher.ᵐ

¹⁴During wheat harvest, Reuben went out into the fields and found some mandrake plants, which he brought to his mother Leah. Rachel said to Leah, "Please give me some of your son's mandrakes."

¹⁵But she said to her, "Wasn't it enough that you took away my husband? Will you take my son's mandrakes too?"

"Very well," Rachel said, "he can sleep with you tonight in return for your son's mandrakes."

¹⁶So when Jacob came in from the fields that evening, Leah went out to meet him. "You must sleep with me," she said. "I have hired you with my son's mandrakes." So he slept with her that night.

¹⁷God listened to Leah, and she became pregnant and bore Jacob a fifth son. ¹⁸Then Leah said, "God has rewarded me for giving my maidservant to my husband." So she named him Issachar.ⁿ

¹⁹Leah conceived again and bore Jacob a sixth son. ²⁰Then Leah said, "God has presented me

---

ᵉ32 Reuben sounds like the Hebrew for he has seen my misery; the name means see, a son.   ᶠ33 Simeon probably means one who hears.   ᵍ34 Levi sounds like and may be derived from the Hebrew for attached.   ʰ35 Judah sounds like and may be derived from the Hebrew for praise.   ⁱ6 Dan here means he has vindicated.   ʲ8 Naphtali means my struggle.   ᵏ11 Or "A troop is coming!"   ˡ11 Gad can mean good fortune or a troop.   ᵐ13 Asher means happy.   ⁿ18 Issachar sounds like the Hebrew for reward.

with a precious gift. This time my husband will treat me with honor, because I have borne him six sons." So she named him Zebulun.ᵒ

²¹Some time later she gave birth to a daughter and named her Dinah.

²²Then God remembered Rachel; he listened to her and opened her womb. ²³She became preg-

nant and gave birth to a son and said, "God has taken away my disgrace." ²⁴She named him Jo-seph,ᵖ and said, "May the LORD add to me an-other son."

ᵒ20 *Zebulun* probably means *honor*.   ᵖ24 *Joseph* means *may he add*.

Discovering the Word 1. When Rebekah hears of Esau's plan to kill Jacob, what strategy does she devise, and how does she persuade her son and husband to carry it out (27:41–46)? 2. Describe what happens to Jacob on his first night away from home (28:10–15). 3. From Jacob's response to the dream, what clue can we get about his relationship to God at this point (28:16–22)? 4. In what ways is Jacob's initial experience in Haran similar to and different from that of Abraham's chief servant many years earlier (29:1–18; see also 24:10–28)? 5. Jacob meets his match and means of discipline in Laban. In what way does the latter's trickery repay Jacob for the exploitation of his father's blindness (29:19–24), and how is this situation resolved (29:25–30)? 6. What impresses you about the relationships between Rachel and Leah (30:1–24)?

Applying the Word 1. A past sin or disobedience to God can leave us with a burden of guilt or failure. How can Jacob's experience renew our confidence in God's grace? 2. Spiritual maturity often comes through suffering. In what difficult situation do you now believe God is working to strengthen your faith and character?

Responding in Prayer Spend time thanking God for his care and discipline in your life.

---

17 / *Genesis 30:25—31:55*
Rivalry and Its Results

DO YOU CURRENTLY have a strained or fractured relationship with a family member, friend or colleague at work? Has the cancer of resentment or anger been eating away at you? In this passage we find Jacob and Laban in just such a situation. In the previous chapter, after marrying both Leah and Rachel, Jacob was obligated to serve their father for another seven years. Now he wants to return to his homeland with his family. But Laban persuades Jacob to stay on with a new contract. We will see how the rivalry between these two men escalates to the point of open conflict.

Warming Up to God Why are you coming to be with the Lord today? Tell him with honesty and frankness your thoughts and feelings. Extend them as gifts of obedience, and he will accept them as a fragrant offering.

Read Genesis 30:25—31:55.

---

²⁵After Rachel gave birth to Joseph, Jacob said to Laban, "Send me on my way so I can go back to my own homeland. ²⁶Give me my wives and children, for whom I have served you, and I will be on my way. You know how much work I've done for you."

²⁷But Laban said to him, "If I have found favor in your eyes, please stay. I have learned by divina-tion that�q the LORD has blessed me because of

you." ²⁸He added, "Name your wages, and I will pay them."

²⁹Jacob said to him, "You know how I have worked for you and how your livestock has fared under my care. ³⁰The little you had before I came has increased greatly, and the LORD has blessed you wherever I have been. But now, when may I do something for my own household?"

 q27 Or possibly *have become rich and*

³¹"What shall I give you?" he asked.

"Don't give me anything," Jacob replied. "But if you will do this one thing for me, I will go on tending your flocks and watching over them: ³²Let me go through all your flocks today and remove from them every speckled or spotted sheep, every dark-colored lamb and every spotted or speckled goat. They will be my wages. ³³And my honesty will testify for me in the future, whenever you check on the wages you have paid me. Any goat in my possession that is not speckled or spotted, or any lamb that is not dark-colored, will be considered stolen."

³⁴"Agreed," said Laban. "Let it be as you have said." ³⁵That same day he removed all the male goats that were streaked or spotted, and all the speckled or spotted female goats (all that had white on them) and all the dark-colored lambs, and he placed them in the care of his sons. ³⁶Then he put a three-day journey between himself and Jacob, while Jacob continued to tend the rest of Laban's flocks.

³⁷Jacob, however, took fresh-cut branches from poplar, almond and plane trees and made white stripes on them by peeling the bark and exposing the white inner wood of the branches. ³⁸Then he placed the peeled branches in all the watering troughs, so that they would be directly in front of the flocks when they came to drink. When the flocks were in heat and came to drink, ³⁹they mated in front of the branches. And they bore young that were streaked or speckled or spotted. ⁴⁰Jacob set apart the young of the flock by themselves, but made the rest face the streaked and dark-colored animals that belonged to Laban. Thus he made separate flocks for himself and did not put them with Laban's animals. ⁴¹Whenever the stronger females were in heat, Jacob would place the branches in the troughs in front of the animals so they would mate near the branches, ⁴²but if the animals were weak, he would not place them there. So the weak animals went to Laban and the strong ones to Jacob. ⁴³In this way the man grew exceedingly prosperous and came to own large flocks, and maidservants and menservants, and camels and donkeys.

31

Jacob heard that Laban's sons were saying, "Jacob has taken everything our father owned and has gained all this wealth from what belonged to our father." ²And Jacob noticed that Laban's attitude toward him was not what it had been.

³Then the LORD said to Jacob, "Go back to the land of your fathers and to your relatives, and I will be with you."

⁴So Jacob sent word to Rachel and Leah to come out to the fields where his flocks were. ⁵He said to them, "I see that your father's attitude toward me is not what it was before, but the God of my father has been with me. ⁶You know that I've worked for your father with all my strength, ⁷yet your father has cheated me by changing my wages ten times. However, God has not allowed him to harm me. ⁸If he said, 'The speckled ones will be your wages,' then all the flocks gave birth to speckled young; and if he said, 'The streaked ones will be your wages,' then all the flocks bore streaked young. ⁹So God has taken away your father's livestock and has given them to me.

¹⁰"In breeding season I once had a dream in which I looked up and saw that the male goats mating with the flock were streaked, speckled or spotted. ¹¹The angel of God said to me in the dream, 'Jacob.' I answered, 'Here I am.' ¹²And he said, 'Look up and see that all the male goats mating with the flock are streaked, speckled or spotted, for I have seen all that Laban has been doing to you. ¹³I am the God of Bethel, where you anointed a pillar and where you made a vow to me. Now leave this land at once and go back to your native land.' "

¹⁴Then Rachel and Leah replied, "Do we still have any share in the inheritance of our father's estate? ¹⁵Does he not regard us as foreigners? Not only has he sold us, but he has used up what was paid for us. ¹⁶Surely all the wealth that God took away from our father belongs to us and our children. So do whatever God has told you."

¹⁷Then Jacob put his children and his wives on camels, ¹⁸and he drove all his livestock ahead of him, along with all the goods he had accumulated in Paddan Aram,ʳ to go to his father Isaac in the land of Canaan.

¹⁹When Laban had gone to shear his sheep, Rachel stole her father's household gods. ²⁰Moreover, Jacob deceived Laban the Aramean by not telling him he was running away. ²¹So he fled with all he had, and crossing the River,ˢ he headed for the hill country of Gilead.

²²On the third day Laban was told that Jacob had fled. ²³Taking his relatives with him, he pursued Jacob for seven days and caught up with him

ʳ18 That is, Northwest Mesopotamia   ˢ21 That is, the Euphrates in the hill country of Gilead. ²⁴Then God came to Laban the Aramean in a dream at night and said to him, "Be careful not to say anything to Jacob, either good or bad."

²⁵Jacob had pitched his tent in the hill country of Gilead when Laban overtook him, and Laban and his relatives camped there too. ²⁶Then Laban said to Jacob, "What have you done? You've deceived me, and you've carried off my daughters like captives in war. ²⁷Why did you run off secretly and deceive me? Why didn't you tell me, so I could send you away with joy and singing to the music of tambourines and harps? ²⁸You didn't even let me kiss my grandchildren and my daughters good-by. You have done a foolish thing. ²⁹I have the power to harm you; but last night the God of your father said to me, 'Be careful not to say anything to Jacob, either good or bad.' ³⁰Now you have gone off because you longed to return to your father's house. But why did you steal my gods?"

³¹Jacob answered Laban, "I was afraid, because I thought you would take your daughters away from me by force. ³²But if you find anyone who has your gods, he shall not live. In the presence of our relatives, see for yourself whether there is anything of yours here with me; and if so, take it." Now Jacob did not know that Rachel had stolen the gods.

³³So Laban went into Jacob's tent and into Leah's tent and into the tent of the two maidservants, but he found nothing. After he came out of Leah's tent, he entered Rachel's tent. ³⁴Now Rachel had taken the household gods and put them inside her camel's saddle and was sitting on them. Laban searched through everything in the tent but found nothing.

³⁵Rachel said to her father, "Don't be angry, my lord, that I cannot stand up in your presence; I'm having my period." So he searched but could not find the household gods.

³⁶Jacob was angry and took Laban to task. "What is my crime?" he asked Laban. "What sin have I committed that you hunt me down? ³⁷Now that you have searched through all my goods, what have you found that belongs to your household? Put it here in front of your relatives and mine, and let them judge between the two of us.

³⁸"I have been with you for twenty years now. Your sheep and goats have not miscarried, nor have I eaten rams from your flocks. ³⁹I did not bring you animals torn by wild beasts; I bore the loss myself. And you demanded payment from me for whatever was stolen by day or night. ⁴⁰This was my situation: The heat consumed me in the daytime and the cold at night, and sleep fled from my eyes. ⁴¹It was like this for the twenty years I was in your household. I worked for you fourteen years for your two daughters and six years for your flocks, and you changed my wages ten times. ⁴²If the God of my father, the God of Abraham and the Fear of Isaac, had not been with me, you would surely have sent me away empty-handed. But God has seen my hardship and the toil of my hands, and last night he rebuked you."

⁴³Laban answered Jacob, "The women are my daughters, the children are my children, and the flocks are my flocks. All you see is mine. Yet what can I do today about these daughters of mine, or about the children they have borne? ⁴⁴Come now, let's make a covenant, you and I, and let it serve as a witness between us."

⁴⁵So Jacob took a stone and set it up as a pillar. ⁴⁶He said to his relatives, "Gather some stones." So they took stones and piled them in a heap, and they ate there by the heap. ⁴⁷Laban called it Jegar Sahadutha,ᵗ and Jacob called it Galeed.ᵘ

⁴⁸Laban said, "This heap is a witness between you and me today." That is why it was called Galeed. ⁴⁹It was also called Mizpah,ᵛ because he said, "May the LORD keep watch between you and me when we are away from each other. ⁵⁰If you mistreat my daughters or if you take any wives besides my daughters, even though no one is with us, remember that God is a witness between you and me."

⁵¹Laban also said to Jacob, "Here is this heap, and here is this pillar I have set up between you and me. ⁵²This heap is a witness, and this pillar is a witness, that I will not go past this heap to your side to harm you and that you will not go past this heap and pillar to my side to harm me. ⁵³May the God of Abraham and the God of Nahor, the God of their father, judge between us."

So Jacob took an oath in the name of the Fear of his father Isaac. ⁵⁴He offered a sacrifice there in the hill country and invited his relatives to a meal. After they had eaten, they spent the night there.

⁵⁵Early the next morning Laban kissed his grandchildren and his daughters and blessed them. Then he left and returned home.

ᵗ47 The Aramaic *Jegar Sahadutha* means *witness heap.*   ᵘ47 The Hebrew *Galeed* means *witness heap.*   ᵛ49 *Mizpah* means *watchtower.*

Discovering the Word 1. Why does Jacob want to leave, and why does Laban want him to stay (30:25–30)? 2. Describe Jacob's way of getting back at Laban to increase the strength of his own flocks (30:37–43). 3. What new factors in Jacob's situation now prompt his decision to leave Laban's employ and return home (31:1–13)? 4. How has God protected and provided for Jacob in the midst of his unjust treatment by Laban (31:1–21)? 5. How do Laban and Jacob reconcile their differences (31:43–55)?

 Applying the Word 1. Why is it often so difficult for us to see the other person's point of view in a controversy? 2. What have we learned in this passage that can help us in dealing with a strained or fractured relationship?

 Responding in Prayer Decide now what steps you can take in a personal conflict you face, and pray for courage to follow through.

18 / *Genesis 32—33*
Planning and Praying

THE CHRISTIAN LIFE is a mysterious mixture of God's work and ours, his gracious provision and our effort. Sometimes we are perplexed over who should make the next move. We see this pattern in the life of Jacob, whose planning and praying, laboring and believing are prominent in this narrative. The previous study ended with reconciliation and peaceful departure. Now Jacob resolutely heads toward another confrontation with his adversary of twenty years earlier—his brother Esau, whom he cheated. Jacob combines planning and prayer as he obeys God's command to return to his country and relatives. His struggle can teach us how to redress past wrongs and effect reconciliation with someone we have injured.

Warming Up to God As you sit before your Father, remember that he has also come to be with you. Rest with him and enjoy his presence while he teaches you about himself.

Read Genesis 32—33.

---

32 Jacob also went on his way, and the angels of God met him. ²When Jacob saw them, he said, "This is the camp of God!" So he named that place Mahanaim.ʷ

³Jacob sent messengers ahead of him to his brother Esau in the land of Seir, the country of Edom. ⁴He instructed them: "This is what you are to say to my master Esau: 'Your servant Jacob says, I have been staying with Laban and have remained there till now. ⁵I have cattle and donkeys, sheep and goats, menservants and maidservants. Now I am sending this message to my lord, that I may find favor in your eyes.' "

⁶When the messengers returned to Jacob, they said, "We went to your brother Esau, and now he is coming to meet you, and four hundred men are with him."

⁷In great fear and distress Jacob divided the people who were with him into two groups,ˣ and the flocks and herds and camels as well. ⁸He thought, "If Esau comes and attacks one group,ʸ the groupʸ that is left may escape."

⁹Then Jacob prayed, "O God of my father Abraham, God of my father Isaac, O Lᴏʀᴅ, who said to me, 'Go back to your country and your relatives, and I will make you prosper,' ¹⁰I am unworthy of all the kindness and faithfulness you have shown your servant. I had only my staff when I crossed this Jordan, but now I have become two groups. ¹¹Save me, I pray, from the hand of my brother Esau, for I am afraid he will come and attack me, and also the mothers with their children. ¹²But you have said, 'I will surely make you prosper and will make your descendants like the sand of the sea, which cannot be counted.' "

¹³He spent the night there, and from what he had with him he selected a gift for his brother Esau: ¹⁴two hundred female goats and twenty male goats, two hundred ewes and twenty rams, ¹⁵thirty female camels with their young, forty

ʷ2 *Mahanaim* means *two camps.*   ˣ7 Or *camps;* also in verse 10
ʸ8 Or *camp*

cows and ten bulls, and twenty female donkeys and ten male donkeys. ¹⁶He put them in the care of his servants, each herd by itself, and said to his servants, "Go ahead of me, and keep some space between the herds."

¹⁷He instructed the one in the lead: "When my brother Esau meets you and asks, 'To whom do you belong, and where are you going, and who owns all these animals in front of you?' ¹⁸then you are to say, 'They belong to your servant Jacob. They are a gift sent to my lord Esau, and he is coming behind us.'"

¹⁹He also instructed the second, the third and all the others who followed the herds: "You are to say the same thing to Esau when you meet him. ²⁰And be sure to say, 'Your servant Jacob is coming behind us.'" For he thought, "I will pacify him with these gifts I am sending on ahead; later, when I see him, perhaps he will receive me." ²¹So Jacob's gifts went on ahead of him, but he himself spent the night in the camp.

²²That night Jacob got up and took his two wives, his two maidservants and his eleven sons and crossed the ford of the Jabbok. ²³After he had sent them across the stream, he sent over all his possessions. ²⁴So Jacob was left alone, and a man wrestled with him till daybreak. ²⁵When the man saw that he could not overpower him, he touched the socket of Jacob's hip so that his hip was wrenched as he wrestled with the man. ²⁶Then the man said, "Let me go, for it is daybreak."

But Jacob replied, "I will not let you go unless you bless me."

²⁷The man asked him, "What is your name?"

"Jacob," he answered.

²⁸Then the man said, "Your name will no longer be Jacob, but Israel,ᶻ because you have struggled with God and with men and have overcome."

²⁹Jacob said, "Please tell me your name."

But he replied, "Why do you ask my name?" Then he blessed him there.

³⁰So Jacob called the place Peniel,ᵃ saying, "It is because I saw God face to face, and yet my life was spared."

³¹The sun rose above him as he passed Peniel,ᵇ and he was limping because of his hip. ³²Therefore to this day the Israelites do not eat the tendon attached to the socket of the hip, because the socket of Jacob's hip was touched near the tendon.

33 Jacob looked up and there was Esau, coming with his four hundred men; so he divided the children among Leah, Rachel and the two maidservants. ²He put the maidservants and their children in front, Leah and her children next, and Rachel and Joseph in the rear. ³He himself went on ahead and bowed down to the ground seven times as he approached his brother.

⁴But Esau ran to meet Jacob and embraced him; he threw his arms around his neck and kissed him. And they wept. ⁵Then Esau looked up and saw the women and children. "Who are these with you?" he asked.

Jacob answered, "They are the children God has graciously given your servant."

⁶Then the maidservants and their children approached and bowed down. ⁷Next, Leah and her children came and bowed down. Last of all came Joseph and Rachel, and they too bowed down.

⁸Esau asked, "What do you mean by all these droves I met?"

"To find favor in your eyes, my lord," he said.

⁹But Esau said, "I already have plenty, my brother. Keep what you have for yourself."

¹⁰"No, please!" said Jacob. "If I have found favor in your eyes, accept this gift from me. For to see your face is like seeing the face of God, now that you have received me favorably. ¹¹Please accept the present that was brought to you, for God has been gracious to me and I have all I need." And because Jacob insisted, Esau accepted it.

¹²Then Esau said, "Let us be on our way; I'll accompany you."

¹³But Jacob said to him, "My lord knows that the children are tender and that I must care for the ewes and cows that are nursing their young. If they are driven hard just one day, all the animals will die. ¹⁴So let my lord go on ahead of his servant, while I move along slowly at the pace of the droves before me and that of the children, until I come to my lord in Seir."

¹⁵Esau said, "Then let me leave some of my men with you."

"But why do that?" Jacob asked. "Just let me find favor in the eyes of my lord."

¹⁶So that day Esau started on his way back to Seir. ¹⁷Jacob, however, went to Succoth, where he built a place for himself and made shelters for his

---

ᶻ28 Israel means he struggles with God.   ᵃ30 Peniel means face of God.   ᵇ31 Hebrew Penuel, a variant of Peniel.

livestock. That is why the place is called Suc-coth.*

¹⁸After Jacob came from Paddan Aram,ᵈ he arrived safely at theᵉ city of Shechem in Canaan and camped within sight of the city. ¹⁹For a hundred pieces of silver,ᶠ he bought from the sons of Hamor, the father of Shechem, the plot of

ground where he pitched his tent. ²⁰There he set up an altar and called it El Elohe Israel.ᵍ

ᶜ17 *Succoth* means *shelters.*   ᵈ18 That is, Northwest Mesopotamia
ᵉ18 Or *arrived at Shalem, a*   ᶠ19 Hebrew *hundred kesitahs;* a kesitah was a unit of money of unknown weight and value.   ᵍ20 *El Elohe Israel* can mean *God, the God of Israel* or *mighty is the God of Israel.*

Discovering the Word 1. After Jacob receives the ominous report brought back by the servants (32:6), he alternately plans and prays. How does his prayer in 32:9–12 reflect his relationship with God at this point? 2. To what extent do you think Jacob's plans are consistent or inconsistent with his prayer (32:13–21)? 3. How does the struggle with the unknown man give insight into Jacob's personality (32:22–32)? 4. How does the change of Jacob's name from *he deceives* to *he struggles with God* indicate the development of his character? 5. In what ways does this meeting between Jacob and Esau (chapter 33) contrast with the last time they saw each other (chapter 27)?

Applying the Word 1. In what ways can Jacob's prayer be a model for our own praying? 2. In what areas do you struggle to trust and obey the Lord? 3. In what areas can Jacob's actions toward Esau be a model for us of repentance and reconciliation?

Responding in Prayer Praise the God of the world, your Father, for being a God who changes names. Ask him to "rename" you as one in the image of his Son.

19 / *Genesis 34—36*
The Cost of Discipleship

IN OUR CHRISTIAN life both compromise and commitment are costly. When we falter and compromise, the consequences take their toll on us personally and often on our family and friends. Nevertheless, God graciously calls us to repentance and renewed commitment. In the last chapter Jacob bought a plot of land in Shechem among the Canaanites instead of going on to Bethel as God commanded. Now his compromise with a pagan community results in a multiple tragedy. We see how God again rescues his servant from a dangerous situation and reaffirms his covenant promise.

Warming Up to God What expectations do you place on this time with the Lord? (Do you feel pressure to "accomplish" something?) Allow yourself to just *be* with Jesus today.

Read Genesis 34—36.

34 Now Dinah, the daughter Leah had borne to Jacob, went out to visit the women of the land. ²When Shechem son of Hamor the Hivite, the ruler of that area, saw her, he took her and violated her. ³His heart was drawn to Dinah daughter of Jacob, and he loved the girl and spoke tenderly to her. ⁴And Shechem said to his father Hamor, "Get me this girl as my wife."

⁵When Jacob heard that his daughter Dinah had been defiled, his sons were in the fields with

his livestock; so he kept quiet about it until they came home.

⁶Then Shechem's father Hamor went out to talk with Jacob. ⁷Now Jacob's sons had come in from the fields as soon as they heard what had happened. They were filled with grief and fury, because Shechem had done a disgraceful thing inʰ Israel by lying with Jacob's daughter—a thing that should not be done.

⁸But Hamor said to them, "My son Shechem has his heart set on your daughter. Please give her

ʰ7 Or *against*

to him as his wife. ⁹Intermarry with us; give us your daughters and take our daughters for yourselves. ¹⁰You can settle among us; the land is open to you. Live in it, trade[i] in it, and acquire property in it."

¹¹Then Shechem said to Dinah's father and brothers, "Let me find favor in your eyes, and I will give you whatever you ask. ¹²Make the price for the bride and the gift I am to bring as great as you like, and I'll pay whatever you ask me. Only give me the girl as my wife."

¹³Because their sister Dinah had been defiled, Jacob's sons replied deceitfully as they spoke to Shechem and his father Hamor. ¹⁴They said to them, "We can't do such a thing; we can't give our sister to a man who is not circumcised. That would be a disgrace to us. ¹⁵We will give our consent to you on one condition only: that you become like us by circumcising all your males. ¹⁶Then we will give you our daughters and take your daughters for ourselves. We'll settle among you and become one people with you. ¹⁷But if you will not agree to be circumcised, we'll take our sister[j] and go."

¹⁸Their proposal seemed good to Hamor and his son Shechem. ¹⁹The young man, who was the most honored of all his father's household, lost no time in doing what they said, because he was delighted with Jacob's daughter. ²⁰So Hamor and his son Shechem went to the gate of their city to speak to their fellow townsmen. ²¹"These men are friendly toward us," they said. "Let them live in our land and trade in it; the land has plenty of room for them. We can marry their daughters and they can marry ours. ²²But the men will consent to live with us as one people only on the condition that our males be circumcised, as they themselves are. ²³Won't their livestock, their property and all their other animals become ours? So let us give our consent to them, and they will settle among us."

²⁴All the men who went out of the city gate agreed with Hamor and his son Shechem, and every male in the city was circumcised.

²⁵Three days later, while all of them were still in pain, two of Jacob's sons, Simeon and Levi, Dinah's brothers, took their swords and attacked the unsuspecting city, killing every male. ²⁶They put Hamor and his son Shechem to the sword and took Dinah from Shechem's house and left. ²⁷The sons of Jacob came upon the dead bodies and looted the city where[k] their sister had been defiled. ²⁸They seized their flocks and herds and donkeys and everything else of theirs in the city and out in the fields. ²⁹They carried off all their wealth and all their women and children, taking as plunder everything in the houses.

³⁰Then Jacob said to Simeon and Levi, "You have brought trouble on me by making me a stench to the Canaanites and Perizzites, the people living in this land. We are few in number, and if they join forces against me and attack me, I and my household will be destroyed."

³¹But they replied, "Should he have treated our sister like a prostitute?"

35

Then God said to Jacob, "Go up to Bethel and settle there, and build an altar there to God, who appeared to you when you were fleeing from your brother Esau."

²So Jacob said to his household and to all who were with him, "Get rid of the foreign gods you have with you, and purify yourselves and change your clothes. ³Then come, let us go up to Bethel, where I will build an altar to God, who answered me in the day of my distress and who has been with me wherever I have gone." ⁴So they gave Jacob all the foreign gods they had and the rings in their ears, and Jacob buried them under the oak at Shechem. ⁵Then they set out, and the terror of God fell upon the towns all around them so that no one pursued them.

⁶Jacob and all the people with him came to Luz (that is, Bethel) in the land of Canaan. ⁷There he built an altar, and he called the place El Bethel,[l] because it was there that God revealed himself to him when he was fleeing from his brother.

⁸Now Deborah, Rebekah's nurse, died and was buried under the oak below Bethel. So it was named Allon Bacuth.[m]

⁹After Jacob returned from Paddan Aram,[n] God appeared to him again and blessed him. ¹⁰God said to him, "Your name is Jacob,[o] but you will no longer be called Jacob; your name will be Israel.[p]" So he named him Israel.

¹¹And God said to him, "I am God Almighty[q]; be fruitful and increase in number. A nation and a community of nations will come from you, and kings will come from your body. ¹²The land I

i10 Or move about freely; also in verse 21   j17 Hebrew daughter
k27 Or because   l7 El Bethel means God of Bethel.   m8 Allon
Bacuth means oak of weeping.   n9 That is, Northwest Mesopotamia;
also in verse 26   o10 Jacob means he grasps the heel (figuratively, he
deceives).   p10 Israel means he struggles with God.   q11 Hebrew
El-Shaddai

gave to Abraham and Isaac I also give to you, and I will give this land to your descendants after you." ¹³Then God went up from him at the place where he had talked with him.

¹⁴Jacob set up a stone pillar at the place where God had talked with him, and he poured out a drink offering on it; he also poured oil on it. ¹⁵Jacob called the place where God had talked with him Bethel.ʳ

¹⁶Then they moved on from Bethel. While they were still some distance from Ephrath, Rachel began to give birth and had great difficulty. ¹⁷And as she was having great difficulty in childbirth, the midwife said to her, "Don't be afraid, for you have another son." ¹⁸As she breathed her last—for she was dying—she named her son Ben-Oni.ˢ But his father named him Benjamin.ᵗ

¹⁹So Rachel died and was buried on the way to Ephrath (that is, Bethlehem). ²⁰Over her tomb Jacob set up a pillar, and to this day that pillar marks Rachel's tomb.

²¹Israel moved on again and pitched his tent beyond Migdal Eder. ²²While Israel was living in that region, Reuben went in and slept with his father's concubine Bilhah, and Israel heard of it.

Jacob had twelve sons:

²³The sons of Leah:
    Reuben the firstborn of Jacob,
    Simeon, Levi, Judah, Issachar and Zebulun.

²⁴The sons of Rachel:
    Joseph and Benjamin.

²⁵The sons of Rachel's maidservant Bilhah:
    Dan and Naphtali.

²⁶The sons of Leah's maidservant Zilpah:
    Gad and Asher.

These were the sons of Jacob, who were born to him in Paddan Aram.

²⁷Jacob came home to his father Isaac in Mamre, near Kiriath Arba (that is, Hebron), where Abraham and Isaac had stayed. ²⁸Isaac lived a hundred and eighty years. ²⁹Then he breathed his last and died and was gathered to his people, old and full of years. And his sons Esau and Jacob buried him.

36 This is the account of Esau (that is, Edom).

²Esau took his wives from the women of Canaan: Adah daughter of Elon the Hittite, and Oholibamah daughter of Anah and granddaughter of Zibeon the Hivite— ³also Basemath daughter of Ishmael and sister of Nebaioth.

⁴Adah bore Eliphaz to Esau, Basemath bore Reuel, ⁵and Oholibamah bore Jeush, Jalam and Korah. These were the sons of Esau, who were born to him in Canaan.

⁶Esau took his wives and sons and daughters and all the members of his household, as well as his livestock and all his other animals and all the goods he had acquired in Canaan, and moved to a land some distance from his brother Jacob. ⁷Their possessions were too great for them to remain together; the land where they were staying could not support them both because of their livestock. ⁸So Esau (that is, Edom) settled in the hill country of Seir.

⁹This is the account of Esau the father of the Edomites in the hill country of Seir.

¹⁰These are the names of Esau's sons:
    Eliphaz, the son of Esau's wife Adah, and
    Reuel, the son of Esau's wife Basemath.

¹¹The sons of Eliphaz:
    Teman, Omar, Zepho, Gatam and Kenaz.

¹²Esau's son Eliphaz also had a concubine named Timna, who bore him Amalek. These were grandsons of Esau's wife Adah.

¹³The sons of Reuel:
    Nahath, Zerah, Shammah and Mizzah. These were grandsons of Esau's wife Basemath.

¹⁴The sons of Esau's wife Oholibamah daughter of Anah and granddaughter of Zibeon, whom she bore to Esau:
    Jeush, Jalam and Korah.

¹⁵These were the chiefs among Esau's descendants:

The sons of Eliphaz the firstborn of Esau:
    Chiefs Teman, Omar, Zepho, Kenaz, ¹⁶Korah,ᵘ Gatam and Amalek. These were the chiefs descended from Eliphaz in Edom; they were grandsons of Adah.

¹⁷The sons of Esau's son Reuel:
    Chiefs Nahath, Zerah, Shammah and Mizzah. These were the chiefs descended

---

ʳ15 Bethel means house of God.   ˢ18 Ben-Oni means son of my trouble.   ᵗ18 Benjamin means son of my right hand.
ᵘ16 Masoretic Text; Samaritan Pentateuch (see also Gen. 36:11 and 1 Chron. 1:36) does not have Korah.

from Reuel in Edom; they were grand-sons of Esau's wife Basemath.

¹⁸The sons of Esau's wife Oholibamah:

Chiefs Jeush, Jalam and Korah. These were the chiefs descended from Esau's wife Oholibamah daughter of Anah.

¹⁹These were the sons of Esau (that is, Edom), and these were their chiefs.

²⁰These were the sons of Seir the Horite, who were living in the region:

Lotan, Shobal, Zibeon, Anah, ²¹Dishon, Ezer and Dishan. These sons of Seir in Edom were Horite chiefs.

²²The sons of Lotan:

Hori and Homam.ᵛ Timna was Lotan's sister.

²³The sons of Shobal:

Alvan, Manahath, Ebal, Shepho and Onam.

²⁴The sons of Zibeon:

Aiah and Anah. This is the Anah who discovered the hot springsʷ in the desert while he was grazing the donkeys of his father Zibeon.

²⁵The children of Anah:

Dishon and Oholibamah daughter of Anah.

²⁶The sons of Dishonˣ:

Hemdan, Eshban, Ithran and Keran.

²⁷The sons of Ezer:

Bilhan, Zaavan and Akan.

²⁸The sons of Dishan:

Uz and Aran.

²⁹These were the Horite chiefs:

Lotan, Shobal, Zibeon, Anah, ³⁰Dishon, Ezer and Dishan. These were the Horite chiefs, according to their divisions, in the land of Seir.

³¹These were the kings who reigned in Edom before any Israelite king reignedʸ:

³²Bela son of Beor became king of Edom. His city was named Dinhabah.

³³When Bela died, Jobab son of Zerah from Bozrah succeeded him as king.

³⁴When Jobab died, Husham from the land of the Temanites succeeded him as king.

³⁵When Husham died, Hadad son of Bedad, who defeated Midian in the country of Moab, succeeded him as king. His city was named Avith.

³⁶When Hadad died, Samlah from Masrekah succeeded him as king.

³⁷When Samlah died, Shaul from Rehoboth on the riverᶻ succeeded him as king.

³⁸When Shaul died, Baal-Hanan son of Acbor succeeded him as king.

³⁹When Baal-Hanan son of Acbor died, Hadadᵃ succeeded him as king. His city was named Pau, and his wife's name was Mehetabel daughter of Matred, the daughter of Me-Zahab.

⁴⁰These were the chiefs descended from Esau, by name, according to their clans and regions:

Timna, Alvah, Jetheth, ⁴¹Oholibamah, Elah, Pinon, ⁴²Kenaz, Teman, Mibzar, ⁴³Magdiel and Iram. These were the chiefs of Edom, according to their settlements in the land they occupied.

This was Esau the father of the Edomites.

ᵛ22 Hebrew *Hemam*, a variant of *Homam* (see 1 Chron. 1:39)
ʷ24 Vulgate; Syriac *discovered water;* the meaning of the Hebrew for this word is uncertain.   ˣ26 Hebrew *Dishan*, a variant of *Dishon*
ʸ31 Or *before an Israelite king reigned over them*   ᶻ37 Possibly the Euphrates   ᵃ39 Many manuscripts of the Masoretic Text, Samaritan Pentateuch and Syriac (see also 1 Chron. 1:50); most manuscripts of the Masoretic Text *Hadar*

 Discovering the Word 1. What is Shechem's attitude toward Dinah (34:1–4)? 2. In Genesis 35:1 God renews his call for Jacob to settle in Bethel. What is the cost of this commitment for Jacob and the members of his household (35:2–7)? 3. What specific promises does God reaffirm to Jacob and to his descendants (35:9–13)? 4. What new griefs come into Jacob's life (35:16–29)? 5. What do the comments in 35:29 and 36:6–8 show about the relationship between Jacob and Esau?

Applying the Word 1. In what way does this tragedy illustrate the dangers of spiritual compromise or disobedience? 2. Have you become aware of any "foreign god" in your life, something which is taking the place of God? Explain. 3. How can we, like Jacob, transform the pain of losing someone we love into confidence and courage for the future?

Responding in Prayer Praise God for the remarkable example of his faithfulness to his chosen children through the life of Jacob.

20 / *Genesis 37—38*
Pride and Prejudice

WE OFTEN SEE how children tend to duplicate the weaknesses as well as the strengths of their parents. This is evident in many families of the Old Testament. Jacob suffered from parental favoritism as a boy. Now we see how he perpetuates this practice in his relationship with Joseph—with disastrous results.

 Warming Up to God   How have you seen the harmful effects of "playing favorites" in your family?

 Read Genesis 37—38.

37 Jacob lived in the land where his father had stayed, the land of Canaan.

²This is the account of Jacob.

Joseph, a young man of seventeen, was tending the flocks with his brothers, the sons of Bilhah and the sons of Zilpah, his father's wives, and he brought their father a bad report about them.

³Now Israel loved Joseph more than any of his other sons, because he had been born to him in his old age; and he made a richly ornamented[b] robe for him. ⁴When his brothers saw that their father loved him more than any of them, they hated him and could not speak a kind word to him.

⁵Joseph had a dream, and when he told it to his brothers, they hated him all the more. ⁶He said to them, "Listen to this dream I had: ⁷We were binding sheaves of grain out in the field when suddenly my sheaf rose and stood upright, while your sheaves gathered around mine and bowed down to it."

⁸His brothers said to him, "Do you intend to reign over us? Will you actually rule us?" And they hated him all the more because of his dream and what he had said.

⁹Then he had another dream, and he told it to his brothers. "Listen," he said, "I had another dream, and this time the sun and moon and eleven stars were bowing down to me."

¹⁰When he told his father as well as his brothers, his father rebuked him and said, "What is this dream you had? Will your mother and I and your brothers actually come and bow down to the ground before you?" ¹¹His brothers were jealous of him, but his father kept the matter in mind.

¹²Now his brothers had gone to graze their father's flocks near Shechem, ¹³and Israel said to Joseph, "As you know, your brothers are grazing the flocks near Shechem. Come, I am going to send you to them."

"Very well," he replied.

¹⁴So he said to him, "Go and see if all is well with your brothers and with the flocks, and bring word back to me." Then he sent him off from the Valley of Hebron.

When Joseph arrived at Shechem, ¹⁵a man found him wandering around in the fields and asked him, "What are you looking for?"

¹⁶He replied, "I'm looking for my brothers. Can you tell me where they are grazing their flocks?"

¹⁷"They have moved on from here," the man answered. "I heard them say, 'Let's go to Dothan.'"

So Joseph went after his brothers and found them near Dothan. ¹⁸But they saw him in the distance, and before he reached them, they plotted to kill him.

¹⁹"Here comes that dreamer!" they said to each other. ²⁰"Come now, let's kill him and throw him into one of these cisterns and say that a ferocious animal devoured him. Then we'll see what comes of his dreams."

²¹When Reuben heard this, he tried to rescue him from their hands. "Let's not take his life," he said. ²²"Don't shed any blood. Throw him into this cistern here in the desert, but don't lay a hand on him." Reuben said this to rescue him from them and take him back to his father.

²³So when Joseph came to his brothers, they stripped him of his robe—the richly ornamented robe he was wearing— ²⁴and they took him and threw him into the cistern. Now the cistern was empty; there was no water in it.

²⁵As they sat down to eat their meal, they

_____

b3 The meaning of the Hebrew for richly ornamented is uncertain; also in verses 23 and 32.

looked up and saw a caravan of Ishmaelites coming from Gilead. Their camels were loaded with spices, balm and myrrh, and they were on their way to take them down to Egypt.

²⁶Judah said to his brothers, "What will we gain if we kill our brother and cover up his blood? ²⁷Come, let's sell him to the Ishmaelites and not lay our hands on him; after all, he is our brother, our own flesh and blood." His brothers agreed.

²⁸So when the Midianite merchants came by, his brothers pulled Joseph up out of the cistern and sold him for twenty shekels*ᶜ* of silver to the Ishmaelites, who took him to Egypt.

²⁹When Reuben returned to the cistern and saw that Joseph was not there, he tore his clothes. ³⁰He went back to his brothers and said, "The boy isn't there! Where can I turn now?"

³¹Then they got Joseph's robe, slaughtered a goat and dipped the robe in the blood. ³²They took the ornamented robe back to their father and said, "We found this. Examine it to see whether it is your son's robe."

³³He recognized it and said, "It is my son's robe! Some ferocious animal has devoured him. Joseph has surely been torn to pieces."

³⁴Then Jacob tore his clothes, put on sackcloth and mourned for his son many days. ³⁵All his sons and daughters came to comfort him, but he refused to be comforted. "No," he said, "in mourning will I go down to the grave*ᵈ* to my son." So his father wept for him.

³⁶Meanwhile, the Midianites*ᵉ* sold Joseph in Egypt to Potiphar, one of Pharaoh's officials, the captain of the guard.

38

At that time, Judah left his brothers and went down to stay with a man of Adullam named Hirah. ²There Judah met the daughter of a Canaanite man named Shua. He married her and lay with her; ³she became pregnant and gave birth to a son, who was named Er. ⁴She conceived again and gave birth to a son and named him Onan. ⁵She gave birth to still another son and named him Shelah. It was at Kezib that she gave birth to him.

⁶Judah got a wife for Er, his firstborn, and her name was Tamar. ⁷But Er, Judah's firstborn, was wicked in the LORD's sight; so the LORD put him to death.

⁸Then Judah said to Onan, "Lie with your brother's wife and fulfill your duty to her as a brother-in-law to produce offspring for your brother." ⁹But Onan knew that the offspring would not be his; so whenever he lay with his brother's wife, he spilled his semen on the ground to keep from producing offspring for his brother. ¹⁰What he did was wicked in the LORD's sight; so he put him to death also.

¹¹Judah then said to his daughter-in-law Tamar, "Live as a widow in your father's house until my son Shelah grows up." For he thought, "He may die too, just like his brothers." So Tamar went to live in her father's house.

¹²After a long time Judah's wife, the daughter of Shua, died. When Judah had recovered from his grief, he went up to Timnah, to the men who were shearing his sheep, and his friend Hirah the Adullamite went with him.

¹³When Tamar was told, "Your father-in-law is on his way to Timnah to shear his sheep," ¹⁴she took off her widow's clothes, covered herself with a veil to disguise herself, and then sat down at the entrance to Enaim, which is on the road to Timnah. For she saw that, though Shelah had now grown up, she had not been given to him as his wife.

¹⁵When Judah saw her, he thought she was a prostitute, for she had covered her face. ¹⁶Not realizing that she was his daughter-in-law, he went over to her by the roadside and said, "Come now, let me sleep with you."

"And what will you give me to sleep with you?" she asked.

¹⁷"I'll send you a young goat from my flock," he said.

"Will you give me something as a pledge until you send it?" she asked.

¹⁸He said, "What pledge should I give you?"

"Your seal and its cord, and the staff in your hand," she answered. So he gave them to her and slept with her, and she became pregnant by him. ¹⁹After she left, she took off her veil and put on her widow's clothes again.

²⁰Meanwhile Judah sent the young goat by his friend the Adullamite in order to get his pledge back from the woman, but he did not find her. ²¹He asked the men who lived there, "Where is the shrine prostitute who was beside the road at Enaim?"

"There hasn't been any shrine prostitute here," they said.

*ᶜ28 That is, about 8 ounces (about 0.2 kilogram)   ᵈ35 Hebrew Sheol
ᵉ36 Samaritan Pentateuch, Septuagint, Vulgate and Syriac (see also verse 28); Masoretic Text Medanites*

22So he went back to Judah and said, "I didn't find her. Besides, the men who lived there said, 'There hasn't been any shrine prostitute here.' "

23Then Judah said, "Let her keep what she has, or we will become a laughingstock. After all, I did send her this young goat, but you didn't find her."

24About three months later Judah was told, "Your daughter-in-law Tamar is guilty of prostitution, and as a result she is now pregnant."

Judah said, "Bring her out and have her burned to death!"

25As she was being brought out, she sent a message to her father-in-law. "I am pregnant by the man who owns these," she said. And she added, "See if you recognize whose seal and cord and staff these are."

26Judah recognized them and said, "She is more righteous than I, since I wouldn't give her to my son Shelah." And he did not sleep with her again.

27When the time came for her to give birth, there were twin boys in her womb. 28As she was giving birth, one of them put out his hand; so the midwife took a scarlet thread and tied it on his wrist and said, "This one came out first." 29But when he drew back his hand, his brother came out, and she said, "So this is how you have broken out!" And he was named Perez.ſ 30Then his brother, who had the scarlet thread on his wrist, came out and he was given the name Zerah.g

ſ29 *Perez* means *breaking out.*   g30 *Zerah* can mean *scarlet* or *brightness.*

 Discovering the Word 1. Describe the family relationships at the outset of the story (37:1–4). 2. We have already seen in the examples of Abimelech, Jacob and Laban that dreams are a medium through which God reveals his will. This time, however, the communication is not through words. How are the symbols in Joseph's two dreams interpreted by his family (37:5–11)? 3. What are the varied reactions of Joseph's brothers when they see him approaching (37:12–22)? 4. What motive do you see in the way the brothers report to their father the news of Joseph's disappearance (37:29–35)? 5. In spite of having three sons, how does Judah find his lineage to be in jeopardy (38:1–11)? 6. What strategy does Tamar work out to establish her status as matriarch of Judah's line (38:12–30)?

Applying the Word 1. Jacob's favoritism, Joseph's arrogance and the brothers' envy contribute to this tragedy of rivalry and hatred. To what extent are you involved in a family situation, either your own or that of a friend, with some of these elements? 2. Perez (38:29) is listed in the genealogies of David (Ru 4:18–22) and Joseph, the husband of Mary (Mt 1:3). How can this fact help us to appreciate God's grace?

Responding in Prayer Ask God to give you endurance when painful circumstances make his will seem unsure.

---

21 / *Genesis 39—40*
Performance Under Pressure

HOW DO YOU react when you are treated unjustly? How do you feel when you do everything you can to serve God well, only to have the bottom drop out of your life? Joseph faced these difficulties after he became a slave in Egypt. His example of perseverance under pressure and the way he coped with a shattering reversal can be instructive to us in similar situations.

 Warming Up to God Like Joseph, we sometimes face hardships we don't understand. Tell God about your worries, and ask him to remind you of his faithfulness to you, his child.

 Read Genesis 39—40.

Joseph took even the lowliest of tasks & did a good job

39

Now Joseph had been taken down to Egypt. Potiphar, an Egyptian who was one of Pharaoh's officials, the captain of the guard, bought him from the Ishmaelites who had taken him there.

²The LORD was with Joseph and he prospered, and he lived in the house of his Egyptian master. ³When his master saw that the LORD was with him and that the LORD gave him success in everything he did, ⁴Joseph found favor in his eyes and became his attendant. Potiphar put him in charge of his household, and he entrusted to his care everything he owned. ⁵From the time he put him in charge of his household and of all that he owned, the LORD blessed the household of the Egyptian because of Joseph. The blessing of the LORD was on everything Potiphar had, both in the house and in the field. ⁶So he left in Joseph's care everything he had; with Joseph in charge, he did not concern himself with anything except the food he ate.

Now Joseph was well-built and handsome, ⁷and after a while his master's wife took notice of Joseph and said, "Come to bed with me!"

⁸But he refused. "With me in charge," he told her, "my master does not concern himself with anything in the house; everything he owns he has entrusted to my care. ⁹No one is greater in this house than I am. My master has withheld nothing from me except you, because you are his wife. How then could I do such a wicked thing and sin against God?" ¹⁰And though she spoke to Joseph day after day, he refused to go to bed with her or even be with her.

¹¹One day he went into the house to attend to his duties, and none of the household servants was inside. ¹²She caught him by his cloak and said, "Come to bed with me!" But he left his cloak in her hand and ran out of the house.

¹³When she saw that he had left his cloak in her hand and had run out of the house, ¹⁴she called her household servants. "Look," she said to them, "this Hebrew has been brought to us to make sport of us! He came in here to sleep with me, but I screamed. ¹⁵When he heard me scream for help, he left his cloak beside me and ran out of the house."

¹⁶She kept his cloak beside her until his master came home. ¹⁷Then she told him this story: "That Hebrew slave you brought us came to me to make sport of me. ¹⁸But as soon as I screamed for help, he left his cloak beside me and ran out of the house."

¹⁹When his master heard the story his wife told him, saying, "This is how your slave treated me," he burned with anger. ²⁰Joseph's master took him and put him in prison, the place where the king's prisoners were confined.

But while Joseph was there in the prison, ²¹the LORD was with him; he showed him kindness and granted him favor in the eyes of the prison warden. ²²So the warden put Joseph in charge of all those held in the prison, and he was made responsible for all that was done there. ²³The warden paid no attention to anything under Joseph's care, because the LORD was with Joseph and gave him success in whatever he did.

40

Some time later, the cupbearer and the baker of the king of Egypt offended their master, the king of Egypt. ²Pharaoh was angry with his two officials, the chief cupbearer and the chief baker, ³and put them in custody in the house of the captain of the guard, in the same prison where Joseph was confined. ⁴The captain of the guard assigned them to Joseph, and he attended them.

After they had been in custody for some time, ⁵each of the two men—the cupbearer and the baker of the king of Egypt, who were being held in prison—had a dream the same night, and each dream had a meaning of its own.

⁶When Joseph came to them the next morning, he saw that they were dejected. ⁷So he asked Pharaoh's officials who were in custody with him in his master's house, "Why are your faces so sad today?"

⁸"We both had dreams," they answered, "but there is no one to interpret them."

Then Joseph said to them, "Do not interpretations belong to God? Tell me your dreams."

⁹So the chief cupbearer told Joseph his dream. He said to him, "In my dream I saw a vine in front of me, ¹⁰and on the vine were three branches. As soon as it budded, it blossomed, and its clusters ripened into grapes. ¹¹Pharaoh's cup was in my hand, and I took the grapes, squeezed them into Pharaoh's cup and put the cup in his hand."

¹²"This is what it means," Joseph said to him. "The three branches are three days. ¹³Within three days Pharaoh will lift up your head and restore you to your position, and you will put Pharaoh's cup in his hand, just as you used to do when you were his cupbearer. ¹⁴But when all goes

well with you, remember me and show me kindness; mention me to Pharaoh and get me out of
this prison. ¹⁵For I was forcibly carried off from
the land of the Hebrews, and even here I have
done nothing to deserve being put in a dungeon."

¹⁶When the chief baker saw that Joseph had
given a favorable interpretation, he said to Joseph, "I too had a dream: On my head were three
baskets of bread.ʰ ¹⁷In the top basket were all
kinds of baked goods for Pharaoh, but the birds
were eating them out of the basket on my head."

¹⁸"This is what it means," Joseph said. "The
three baskets are three days. ¹⁹Within three days
Pharaoh will lift off your head and hang you

on a tree.ⁱ And the birds will eat away your
flesh."

²⁰Now the third day was Pharaoh's birthday,
and he gave a feast for all his officials. He lifted up
the heads of the chief cupbearer and the chief
baker in the presence of his officials: ²¹He restored the chief cupbearer to his position, so that
he once again put the cup into Pharaoh's hand,
²²but he hangedʲ the chief baker, just as Joseph
had said to them in his interpretation.

²³The chief cupbearer, however, did not remember Joseph; he forgot him.

ʰ16 Or *three wicker baskets*   ⁱ19 Or *and impale you on a pole*
ʲ22 Or *impaled*

Discovering the Word 1. Trace the development of Joseph's ability and responsibility from the time
he enters Potiphar's house (39:1–6). 2. Describe the temptation and increasing pressure Joseph now
experiences (39:6–12). 3. Notice the symmetry between verses 1–6 and 20–23 in chapter 39. From the latter
description of Joseph's activities, what can we surmise about his attitude toward his new, more humiliating situation? 4. Describe the new situation in which Joseph finds himself (40:1–8). 5. In 40:9–19 what similarities and
differences do you find in the cupbearer's and baker's dreams and Joseph's interpretations? 6. What are the
consequences for the three men (40:20–23)?

Applying the Word 1. In what situation have you been treated unjustly for taking a moral stand or
refusing to do something wrong? 2. What impresses you about Joseph's performance under these incredible pressures, reverses and disappointments?

Responding in Prayer Ask your heavenly Father, your shield and protector, to give you moral courage
and stamina during these difficult days.

---

22 / *Genesis 41—42*
Faithful Service Rewarded

WE OFTEN TAKE a short-term view of the Christian life that concentrates on what God does *for* us *now*. Yet God
has longer-range purposes that focus on what he wants to accomplish *in* us for the *future*. This principle has been
at work in Joseph's life. Through adversity and disappointment God developed his character and gave him invalu-
able training. Now a sudden crisis and opportunity reveal what kind of person he has become—an example that
can encourage us in our life and service for God.

Warming Up to God What are some tangible ways that God has blessed you recently? Thank him for
each gift. Rejoice that every day is full of his blessings.

Read Genesis 41—42.

4 1 When two full years had passed,
Pharaoh had a dream: He was
standing by the Nile, ²when out of
the river there came up seven cows, sleek and fat,
and they grazed among the reeds. ³After them,
seven other cows, ugly and gaunt, came up out of

the Nile and stood beside those on the riverbank.
⁴And the cows that were ugly and gaunt ate up
the seven sleek, fat cows. Then Pharaoh woke up.

⁵He fell asleep again and had a second dream:
Seven heads of grain, healthy and good, were
growing on a single stalk. ⁶After them, seven

other heads of grain sprouted—thin and scorched by the east wind. ⁷The thin heads of grain swallowed up the seven healthy, full heads. Then Pharaoh woke up; it had been a dream.

⁸In the morning his mind was troubled, so he sent for all the magicians and wise men of Egypt. Pharaoh told them his dreams, but no one could interpret them for him.

⁹Then the chief cupbearer said to Pharaoh, "Today I am reminded of my shortcomings. ¹⁰Pharaoh was once angry with his servants, and he imprisoned me and the chief baker in the house of the captain of the guard. ¹¹Each of us had a dream the same night, and each dream had a meaning of its own. ¹²Now a young Hebrew was there with us, a servant of the captain of the guard. We told him our dreams, and he interpreted them for us, giving each man the interpretation of his dream. ¹³And things turned out exactly as he interpreted them to us: I was restored to my position, and the other man was hanged.ᵏ"

¹⁴So Pharaoh sent for Joseph, and he was quickly brought from the dungeon. When he had shaved and changed his clothes, he came before Pharaoh.

¹⁵Pharaoh said to Joseph, "I had a dream, and no one can interpret it. But I have heard it said of you that when you hear a dream you can interpret it."

¹⁶"I cannot do it," Joseph replied to Pharaoh, "but God will give Pharaoh the answer he desires."

¹⁷Then Pharaoh said to Joseph, "In my dream I was standing on the bank of the Nile, ¹⁸when out of the river there came up seven cows, fat and sleek, and they grazed among the reeds. ¹⁹After them, seven other cows came up—scrawny and very ugly and lean. I had never seen such ugly cows in all the land of Egypt. ²⁰The lean, ugly cows ate up the seven fat cows that came up first. ²¹But even after they ate them, no one could tell that they had done so; they looked just as ugly as before. Then I woke up.

²²"In my dreams I also saw seven heads of grain, full and good, growing on a single stalk. ²³After them, seven other heads sprouted—withered and thin and scorched by the east wind. ²⁴The thin heads of grain swallowed up the seven good heads. I told this to the magicians, but none could explain it to me."

²⁵Then Joseph said to Pharaoh, "The dreams of Pharaoh are one and the same. God has revealed to Pharaoh what he is about to do. ²⁶The seven good cows are seven years, and the seven good heads of grain are seven years; it is one and the same dream. ²⁷The seven lean, ugly cows that came up afterward are seven years, and so are the seven worthless heads of grain scorched by the east wind: They are seven years of famine.

²⁸"It is just as I said to Pharaoh: God has shown Pharaoh what he is about to do. ²⁹Seven years of great abundance are coming throughout the land of Egypt, ³⁰but seven years of famine will follow them. Then all the abundance in Egypt will be forgotten, and the famine will ravage the land. ³¹The abundance in the land will not be remembered, because the famine that follows it will be so severe. ³²The reason the dream was given to Pharaoh in two forms is that the matter has been firmly decided by God, and God will do it soon.

³³"And now let Pharaoh look for a discerning and wise man and put him in charge of the land of Egypt. ³⁴Let Pharaoh appoint commissioners over the land to take a fifth of the harvest of Egypt during the seven years of abundance. ³⁵They should collect all the food of these good years that are coming and store up the grain under the authority of Pharaoh, to be kept in the cities for food. ³⁶This food should be held in reserve for the country, to be used during the seven years of famine that will come upon Egypt, so that the country may not be ruined by the famine."

³⁷The plan seemed good to Pharaoh and to all his officials. ³⁸So Pharaoh asked them, "Can we find anyone like this man, one in whom is the spirit of Godˡ?"

³⁹Then Pharaoh said to Joseph, "Since God has made all this known to you, there is no one so discerning and wise as you. ⁴⁰You shall be in charge of my palace, and all my people are to submit to your orders. Only with respect to the throne will I be greater than you."

⁴¹So Pharaoh said to Joseph, "I hereby put you in charge of the whole land of Egypt." ⁴²Then Pharaoh took his signet ring from his finger and put it on Joseph's finger. He dressed him in robes of fine linen and put a gold chain around his neck. ⁴³He had him ride in a chariot as his second-in-command,ᵐ and men shouted before

ᵏ13 Or *impaled*   ˡ38 Or *of the gods*   ᵐ43 Or *in the chariot of his second-in-command*; or *in his second chariot* him, "Make way[n]!" Thus he put him in charge of the whole land of Egypt.

[44]Then Pharaoh said to Joseph, "I am Pharaoh, but without your word no one will lift hand or foot in all Egypt." [45]Pharaoh gave Joseph the name Zaphenath-Paneah and gave him Asenath daughter of Potiphera, priest of On,[o] to be his wife. And Joseph went throughout the land of Egypt.

[46]Joseph was thirty years old when he entered the service of Pharaoh king of Egypt. And Joseph went out from Pharaoh's presence and traveled throughout Egypt. [47]During the seven years of abundance the land produced plentifully. [48]Joseph collected all the food produced in those seven years of abundance in Egypt and stored it in the cities. In each city he put the food grown in the fields surrounding it. [49]Joseph stored up huge quantities of grain, like the sand of the sea; it was so much that he stopped keeping records because it was beyond measure.

[50]Before the years of famine came, two sons were born to Joseph by Asenath daughter of Potiphera, priest of On. [51]Joseph named his first-born Manasseh[p] and said, "It is because God has made me forget all my trouble and all my father's household." [52]The second son he named Ephraim[q] and said, "It is because God has made me fruitful in the land of my suffering."

[53]The seven years of abundance in Egypt came to an end, [54]and the seven years of famine began, just as Joseph had said. There was famine in all the other lands, but in the whole land of Egypt there was food. [55]When all Egypt began to feel the famine, the people cried to Pharaoh for food. Then Pharaoh told all the Egyptians, "Go to Joseph and do what he tells you."

[56]When the famine had spread over the whole country, Joseph opened the storehouses and sold grain to the Egyptians, for the famine was severe throughout Egypt. [57]And all the countries came to Egypt to buy grain from Joseph, because the famine was severe in all the world.

42 When Jacob learned that there was grain in Egypt, he said to his sons, "Why do you just keep looking at each other?" [2]He continued, "I have heard that there is grain in Egypt. Go down there and buy some for us, so that we may live and not die."

[3]Then ten of Joseph's brothers went down to buy grain from Egypt. [4]But Jacob did not send Benjamin, Joseph's brother, with the others, because he was afraid that harm might come to him. [5]So Israel's sons were among those who went to buy grain, for the famine was in the land of Canaan also.

[6]Now Joseph was the governor of the land, the one who sold grain to all its people. So when Joseph's brothers arrived, they bowed down to him with their faces to the ground. [7]As soon as Joseph saw his brothers, he recognized them, but he pretended to be a stranger and spoke harshly to them. "Where do you come from?" he asked.

"From the land of Canaan," they replied, "to buy food."

[8]Although Joseph recognized his brothers, they did not recognize him. [9]Then he remembered his dreams about them and said to them, "You are spies! You have come to see where our land is unprotected."

[10]"No, my lord," they answered. "Your servants have come to buy food. [11]We are all the sons of one man. Your servants are honest men, not spies."

[12]"No!" he said to them. "You have come to see where our land is unprotected."

[13]But they replied, "Your servants were twelve brothers, the sons of one man, who lives in the land of Canaan. The youngest is now with our father, and one is no more."

[14]Joseph said to them, "It is just as I told you: You are spies! [15]And this is how you will be tested: As surely as Pharaoh lives, you will not leave this place unless your youngest brother comes here. [16]Send one of your number to get your brother; the rest of you will be kept in prison, so that your words may be tested to see if you are telling the truth. If you are not, then as surely as Pharaoh lives, you are spies!" [17]And he put them all in custody for three days.

[18]On the third day, Joseph said to them, "Do this and you will live, for I fear God: [19]If you are honest men, let one of your brothers stay here in prison, while the rest of you go and take grain back for your starving households. [20]But you must bring your youngest brother to me, so that your words may be verified and that you may not die." This they proceeded to do.

[21]They said to one another, "Surely we are being punished because of our brother. We saw how distressed he was when he pleaded with us

[n]43 Or *Bow down*   [o]45 That is, Heliopolis; also in verse 50
[p]51 *Manasseh* sounds like and may be derived from the Hebrew for *forget.*   [q]52 *Ephraim* sounds like the Hebrew for *twice fruitful.*

for his life, but we would not listen; that's why this distress has come upon us."

²²Reuben replied, "Didn't I tell you not to sin against the boy? But you wouldn't listen! Now we must give an accounting for his blood." ²³They did not realize that Joseph could understand them, since he was using an interpreter.

²⁴He turned away from them and began to weep, but then turned back and spoke to them again. He had Simeon taken from them and bound before their eyes.

²⁵Joseph gave orders to fill their bags with grain, to put each man's silver back in his sack, and to give them provisions for their journey. After this was done for them, ²⁶they loaded their grain on their donkeys and left.

²⁷At the place where they stopped for the night one of them opened his sack to get feed for his donkey, and he saw his silver in the mouth of his sack. ²⁸"My silver has been returned," he said to his brothers. "Here it is in my sack."

Their hearts sank and they turned to each other trembling and said, "What is this that God has done to us?"

²⁹When they came to their father Jacob in the land of Canaan, they told him all that had happened to them. They said, ³⁰"The man who is lord over the land spoke harshly to us and treated us as though we were spying on the land. ³¹But we said to him, 'We are honest men; we are not spies.

³²We were twelve brothers, sons of one father. One is no more, and the youngest is now with our father in Canaan.'

³³"Then the man who is lord over the land said to us, 'This is how I will know whether you are honest men: Leave one of your brothers here with me, and take food for your starving households and go. ³⁴But bring your youngest brother to me so I will know that you are not spies but honest men. Then I will give your brother back to you, and you can trade^r in the land.' "

³⁵As they were emptying their sacks, there in each man's sack was his pouch of silver! When they and their father saw the money pouches, they were frightened. ³⁶Their father Jacob said to them, "You have deprived me of my children. Joseph is no more and Simeon is no more, and now you want to take Benjamin. Everything is against me!"

³⁷Then Reuben said to his father, "You may put both of my sons to death if I do not bring him back to you. Entrust him to my care, and I will bring him back."

³⁸But Jacob said, "My son will not go down there with you; his brother is dead and he is the only one left. If harm comes to him on the journey you are taking, you will bring my gray head down to the grave^s in sorrow."

^r34 Or *move about freely*   ^s38 Hebrew *Sheol*

Discovering the Word 1. How does Joseph's sudden opportunity come about (41:8–14)? 2. How do Joseph's interpretation and proposal demonstrate discernment and wisdom (41:15–36)? 3. Describe Joseph's new position and the responsibilities Pharaoh gives him (41:37–49). 4. Joseph's brothers sold him into slavery twenty years before this event. He is now about thirty-seven (see 37:2; 41:46). Trace the events which lead Joseph's brothers into his presence and fulfill his earlier dreams (42:1–9). 5. Do you think the brothers are genuinely repentant at this point (42:21–22)? Explain. 6. How does Reuben's response to his father's despair show his willingness to shoulder family responsibility (42:35–37)?

Applying the Word 1. How have you seen God use a difficult assignment to prepare you for a later responsibility? 2. How has adversity or pressure helped you become more mature in your responsibility for others?

Responding in Prayer Ask God to help you strive for excellence in all that you do to the glory of his name (1Co 10:31).

23 / *Genesis 43:1—45:15*
Family Reconciliation

WHAT MAKES RECONCILIATION possible? What elements are necessary on each side of a hurt or wrong to heal a damaged relationship? This study provides answers to these crucial questions. Joseph's brothers have now returned home from Egypt with a report of their traumatic experience. As the grain purchased on the first visit to Egypt runs out, Jacob and his sons face increasingly difficult decisions. Although our experience may be less traumatic, we can learn principles of reconciliation from this complex family situation.

Warming Up to God Why does it seem so hard to freely accept God's forgiveness? Today, let yourself rest with confidence in the truth that God's forgiveness covers over every one of your sins. Jesus forgives you now.

Read Genesis 43:1—45:15.

43 Now the famine was still severe in the land. ²So when they had eaten all the grain they had brought from Egypt, their father said to them, "Go back and buy us a little more food."

³But Judah said to him, "The man warned us solemnly, 'You will not see my face again unless your brother is with you.' ⁴If you will send our brother along with us, we will go down and buy food for you. ⁵But if you will not send him, we will not go down, because the man said to us, 'You will not see my face again unless your brother is with you.' "

⁶Israel asked, "Why did you bring this trouble on me by telling the man you had another brother?"

⁷They replied, "The man questioned us closely about ourselves and our family. 'Is your father still living?' he asked us. 'Do you have another brother?' We simply answered his questions. How were we to know he would say, 'Bring your brother down here'?"

⁸Then Judah said to Israel his father, "Send the boy along with me and we will go at once, so that we and you and our children may live and not die. ⁹I myself will guarantee his safety; you can hold me personally responsible for him. If I do not bring him back to you and set him here before you, I will bear the blame before you all my life. ¹⁰As it is, if we had not delayed, we could have gone and returned twice."

¹¹Then their father Israel said to them, "If it must be, then do this: Put some of the best products of the land in your bags and take them down to the man as a gift—a little balm and a little honey, some spices and myrrh, some pistachio nuts and almonds. ¹²Take double the amount of silver with you, for you must return the silver that was put back into the mouths of your sacks. Perhaps it was a mistake. ¹³Take your brother also and go back to the man at once. ¹⁴And may God Almighty¹ grant you mercy before the man so that he will let your other brother and Benjamin come back with you. As for me, if I am bereaved, I am bereaved."

¹⁵So the men took the gifts and double the amount of silver, and Benjamin also. They hurried down to Egypt and presented themselves to Joseph. ¹⁶When Joseph saw Benjamin with them, he said to the steward of his house, "Take these men to my house, slaughter an animal and prepare dinner; they are to eat with me at noon."

¹⁷The man did as Joseph told him and took the men to Joseph's house. ¹⁸Now the men were frightened when they were taken to his house. They thought, "We were brought here because of the silver that was put back into our sacks the first time. He wants to attack us and overpower us and seize us as slaves and take our donkeys."

¹⁹So they went up to Joseph's steward and spoke to him at the entrance to the house. ²⁰"Please, sir," they said, "we came down here the first time to buy food. ²¹But at the place where we stopped for the night we opened our sacks and each of us found his silver—the exact weight—in the mouth of his sack. So we have brought it back with us. ²²We have also brought additional silver with us to buy food. We don't know who put our silver in our sacks."

²³"It's all right," he said. "Don't be afraid. Your God, the God of your father, has given you trea-

¹14 Hebrew *El-Shaddai*

sure in your sacks; I received your silver." Then he brought Simeon out to them.

²⁴The steward took the men into Joseph's house, gave them water to wash their feet and provided fodder for their donkeys. ²⁵They prepared their gifts for Joseph's arrival at noon, because they had heard that they were to eat there.

²⁶When Joseph came home, they presented to him the gifts they had brought into the house, and they bowed down before him to the ground. ²⁷He asked them how they were, and then he said, "How is your aged father you told me about? Is he still living?"

²⁸They replied, "Your servant our father is still alive and well." And they bowed low to pay him honor.

²⁹As he looked about and saw his brother Benjamin, his own mother's son, he asked, "Is this your youngest brother, the one you told me about?" And he said, "God be gracious to you, my son." ³⁰Deeply moved at the sight of his brother, Joseph hurried out and looked for a place to weep. He went into his private room and wept there.

³¹After he had washed his face, he came out and, controlling himself, said, "Serve the food."

³²They served him by himself, the brothers by themselves, and the Egyptians who ate with him by themselves, because Egyptians could not eat with Hebrews, for that is detestable to Egyptians. ³³The men had been seated before him in the order of their ages, from the firstborn to the youngest; and they looked at each other in astonishment. ³⁴When portions were served to them from Joseph's table, Benjamin's portion was five times as much as anyone else's. So they feasted and drank freely with him.

44 Now Joseph gave these instructions to the steward of his house: "Fill the men's sacks with as much food as they can carry, and put each man's silver in the mouth of his sack. ²Then put my cup, the silver one, in the mouth of the youngest one's sack, along with the silver for his grain." And he did as Joseph said.

³As morning dawned, the men were sent on their way with their donkeys. ⁴They had not gone far from the city when Joseph said to his steward, "Go after those men at once, and when you catch up with them, say to them, 'Why have you repaid good with evil? ⁵Isn't this the cup my master

drinks from and also uses for divination? This is a wicked thing you have done.' "

⁶When he caught up with them, he repeated these words to them. ⁷But they said to him, "Why does my lord say such things? Far be it from your servants to do anything like that! ⁸We even brought back to you from the land of Canaan the silver we found inside the mouths of our sacks. So why would we steal silver or gold from your master's house? ⁹If any of your servants is found to have it, he will die; and the rest of us will become my lord's slaves."

¹⁰"Very well, then," he said, "let it be as you say. Whoever is found to have it will become my slave; the rest of you will be free from blame."

¹¹Each of them quickly lowered his sack to the ground and opened it. ¹²Then the steward proceeded to search, beginning with the oldest and ending with the youngest. And the cup was found in Benjamin's sack. ¹³At this, they tore their clothes. Then they all loaded their donkeys and returned to the city.

¹⁴Joseph was still in the house when Judah and his brothers came in, and they threw themselves to the ground before him. ¹⁵Joseph said to them, "What is this you have done? Don't you know that a man like me can find things out by divination?"

¹⁶"What can we say to my lord?" Judah replied. "What can we say? How can we prove our innocence? God has uncovered your servants' guilt. We are now my lord's slaves—we ourselves and the one who was found to have the cup."

¹⁷But Joseph said, "Far be it from me to do such a thing! Only the man who was found to have the cup will become my slave. The rest of you, go back to your father in peace."

¹⁸Then Judah went up to him and said: "Please, my lord, let your servant speak a word to my lord. Do not be angry with your servant, though you are equal to Pharaoh himself. ¹⁹My lord asked his servants, 'Do you have a father or a brother?' ²⁰And we answered, 'We have an aged father, and there is a young son born to him in his old age. His brother is dead, and he is the only one of his mother's sons left, and his father loves him.'

²¹"Then you said to your servants, 'Bring him down to me so I can see him for myself.' ²²And we said to my lord, 'The boy cannot leave his father; if he leaves him, his father will die.' ²³But you told your servants, 'Unless your youngest brother comes down with you, you will not see my face

again.' 24When we went back to your servant my father, we told him what my lord had said.

25"Then our father said, 'Go back and buy a little more food.' 26But we said, 'We cannot go down. Only if our youngest brother is with us will we go. We cannot see the man's face unless our youngest brother is with us.'

27"Your servant my father said to us, 'You know that my wife bore me two sons. 28One of them went away from me, and I said, "He has surely been torn to pieces." And I have not seen him since. 29If you take this one from me too and harm comes to him, you will bring my gray head down to the grave[u] in misery.'

30"So now, if the boy is not with us when I go back to your servant my father and if my father, whose life is closely bound up with the boy's life, 31sees that the boy isn't there, he will die. Your servants will bring the gray head of our father down to the grave in sorrow. 32Your servant guaranteed the boy's safety to my father. I said, 'If I do not bring him back to you, I will bear the blame before you, my father, all my life!'

33"Now then, please let your servant remain here as my lord's slave in place of the boy, and let the boy return with his brothers. 34How can I go back to my father if the boy is not with me? No! Do not let me see the misery that would come upon my father."

45

Then Joseph could no longer control himself before all his attendants, and he cried out, "Have everyone leave my presence!" So there was no one with Joseph when he made himself known to his brothers. 2And he wept so loudly that the Egyptians heard him, and Pharaoh's household heard about it.

3Joseph said to his brothers, "I am Joseph! Is my father still living?" But his brothers were not able to answer him, because they were terrified at his presence.

4Then Joseph said to his brothers, "Come close to me." When they had done so, he said, "I am your brother Joseph, the one you sold into Egypt! 5And now, do not be distressed and do not be angry with yourselves for selling me here, because it was to save lives that God sent me ahead of you. 6For two years now there has been famine in the land, and for the next five years there will not be plowing and reaping. 7But God sent me ahead of you to preserve for you a remnant on earth and to save your lives by a great deliverance.[v]

8"So then, it was not you who sent me here, but God. He made me father to Pharaoh, lord of his entire household and ruler of all Egypt. 9Now hurry back to my father and say to him, 'This is what your son Joseph says: God has made me lord of all Egypt. Come down to me; don't delay. 10You shall live in the region of Goshen and be near me—you, your children and grandchildren, your flocks and herds, and all you have. 11I will provide for you there, because five years of famine are still to come. Otherwise you and your household and all who belong to you will become destitute.'

12"You can see for yourselves, and so can my brother Benjamin, that it is really I who am speaking to you. 13Tell my father about all the honor accorded me in Egypt and about everything you have seen. And bring my father down here quickly."

14Then he threw his arms around his brother Benjamin and wept, and Benjamin embraced him, weeping. 15And he kissed all his brothers and wept over them. Afterward his brothers talked with him.

u29 Hebrew *Sheol*; also in verse 31   v7 Or *save you as a great band of survivors*

Discovering the Word 1. As Jacob instructs his sons and takes the risk of losing Benjamin, where does his confidence lie (43:11–14)? 2. What insights do verses 26–34 of chapter 43 give us into Joseph's character? 3. The stage is now set for the climax of this drama (chapter 44). What final strategy does Joseph devise in verses 1–17? 4. Judah's appeal is one of the great intercessions in the Bible. How does his attitude differ from that shown by him and his brothers twenty-three years earlier (44:18–34)? 5. How does Joseph explain to his brothers the reason for his being sold into Egypt and the purpose of his sufferings (45:1–11)?

Applying the Word 1. Think of a difficult situation you are currently facing. How can you entrust it to God Almighty, the one for whom nothing is impossible? 2. Restoring a relationship fractured by injustice and injury requires repentance, confession and acceptance of responsibility for the consequences. In what way have you, like Joseph's brothers, been involved in such a process? 3. How can this perspective toward your own suffering make it possible for you to forgive someone who has grievously wronged or hurt you?

Responding in Prayer Think of one step you need to take to encourage reconciliation with someone you know. Ask God to give you the love, patience and courage to follow through.

24 / *Genesis 45:16—47:31*
God Preserves His People

DO YOU EVER wonder how the bits and pieces of your life fit together? This study shows how the seemingly unrelated and perplexing events of the preceding chapters now serve God's purpose to preserve Jacob's family during the coming famine. This account can strengthen our faith and hope as we work through difficult situations we cannot understand.

 Warming Up to God After years of separation and trials, Jacob and Joseph are reunited. What relationships or areas of your life seem untouchable by God's grace? Pray for God to renew your hope—and to answer your "hopeless" requests.

 Read Genesis 45:16—47:31.

¹⁶When the news reached Pharaoh's palace that Joseph's brothers had come, Pharaoh and all his officials were pleased. ¹⁷Pharaoh said to Joseph, "Tell your brothers, 'Do this: Load your animals and return to the land of Canaan, ¹⁸and bring your father and your families back to me. I will give you the best of the land of Egypt and you can enjoy the fat of the land.'

¹⁹"You are also directed to tell them, 'Do this: Take some carts from Egypt for your children and your wives, and get your father and come. ²⁰Never mind about your belongings, because the best of all Egypt will be yours.' "

²¹So the sons of Israel did this. Joseph gave them carts, as Pharaoh had commanded, and he also gave them provisions for their journey. ²²To each of them he gave new clothing, but to Benjamin he gave three hundred shekels[w] of silver and five sets of clothes. ²³And this is what he sent to his father: ten donkeys loaded with the best things of Egypt, and ten female donkeys loaded with grain and bread and other provisions for his journey. ²⁴Then he sent his brothers away, and as they were leaving he said to them, "Don't quarrel on the way!"

²⁵So they went up out of Egypt and came to their father Jacob in the land of Canaan. ²⁶They told him, "Joseph is still alive! In fact, he is ruler of all Egypt." Jacob was stunned; he did not believe them. ²⁷But when they told him everything Joseph had said to them, and when he saw the carts Joseph had sent to carry him back, the spirit of their father Jacob revived. ²⁸And Israel said, "I'm convinced! My son Joseph is still alive. I will go and see him before I die."

46 So Israel set out with all that was his, and when he reached Beersheba, he offered sacrifices to the God of his father Isaac.

²And God spoke to Israel in a vision at night and said, "Jacob! Jacob!"

"Here I am," he replied.

³"I am God, the God of your father," he said. "Do not be afraid to go down to Egypt, for I will make you into a great nation there. ⁴I will go down to Egypt with you, and I will surely bring you back again. And Joseph's own hand will close your eyes."

⁵Then Jacob left Beersheba, and Israel's sons took their father Jacob and their children and their wives in the carts that Pharaoh had sent to transport him. ⁶They also took with them their livestock and the possessions they had acquired in Canaan, and Jacob and all his offspring went to Egypt. ⁷He took with him to Egypt his sons and grandsons and his daughters and granddaughters—all his offspring.

⁸These are the names of the sons of Israel (Jacob and his descendants) who went to Egypt:

Reuben the firstborn of Jacob.
⁹The sons of Reuben:

[w] 22 That is, about 7 1/2 pounds (about 3.5 kilograms)

Hanoch, Pallu, Hezron and Carmi.

[10]The sons of Simeon:

Jemuel, Jamin, Ohad, Jakin, Zohar and Shaul the son of a Canaanite woman.

[11]The sons of Levi:

Gershon, Kohath and Merari.

[12]The sons of Judah:

Er, Onan, Shelah, Perez and Zerah (but Er and Onan had died in the land of Canaan).

The sons of Perez:

Hezron and Hamul.

[13]The sons of Issachar:

Tola, Puah,[x] Jashub[y] and Shimron.

[14]The sons of Zebulun:

Sered, Elon and Jahleel.

[15]These were the sons Leah bore to Jacob in Paddan Aram,[z] besides his daughter Dinah. These sons and daughters of his were thirty-three in all.

[16]The sons of Gad:

Zephon,[a] Haggi, Shuni, Ezbon, Eri, Arodi and Areli.

[17]The sons of Asher:

Imnah, Ishvah, Ishvi and Beriah.

Their sister was Serah.

The sons of Beriah:

Heber and Malkiel.

[18]These were the children born to Jacob by Zilpah, whom Laban had given to his daughter Leah—sixteen in all.

[19]The sons of Jacob's wife Rachel:

Joseph and Benjamin. [20]In Egypt, Manasseh and Ephraim were born to Joseph by Asenath daughter of Potiphera, priest of On.[b]

[21]The sons of Benjamin:

Bela, Beker, Ashbel, Gera, Naaman, Ehi, Rosh, Muppim, Huppim and Ard.

[22]These were the sons of Rachel who were born to Jacob—fourteen in all.

[23]The son of Dan:

Hushim.

[24]The sons of Naphtali:

Jahziel, Guni, Jezer and Shillem.

[25]These were the sons born to Jacob by Bilhah, whom Laban had given to his daughter Rachel—seven in all.

[26]All those who went to Egypt with Jacob—those who were his direct descendants, not counting his sons' wives—numbered sixty-six persons. [27]With the two sons[c] who had been born to Joseph in Egypt, the members of Jacob's family, which went to Egypt, were seventy[d] in all.

[28]Now Jacob sent Judah ahead of him to Joseph to get directions to Goshen. When they arrived in the region of Goshen, [29]Joseph had his chariot made ready and went to Goshen to meet his father Israel. As soon as Joseph appeared before him, he threw his arms around his father[e] and wept for a long time.

[30]Israel said to Joseph, "Now I am ready to die, since I have seen for myself that you are still alive."

[31]Then Joseph said to his brothers and to his father's household, "I will go up and speak to Pharaoh and will say to him, 'My brothers and my father's household, who were living in the land of Canaan, have come to me. [32]The men are shepherds; they tend livestock, and they have brought along their flocks and herds and everything they own.' [33]When Pharaoh calls you in and asks, 'What is your occupation?' [34]you should answer, 'Your servants have tended livestock from our boyhood on, just as our fathers did.' Then you will be allowed to settle in the region of Goshen, for all shepherds are detestable to the Egyptians."

47

Joseph went and told Pharaoh, "My father and brothers, with their flocks and herds and everything they own, have come from the land of Canaan and are now in Goshen." [2]He chose five of his brothers and presented them before Pharaoh.

[3]Pharaoh asked the brothers, "What is your occupation?"

"Your servants are shepherds," they replied to Pharaoh, "just as our fathers were." [4]They also said to him, "We have come to live here awhile, because the famine is severe in Canaan and your servants' flocks have no pasture. So now, please let your servants settle in Goshen."

[5]Pharaoh said to Joseph, "Your father and your brothers have come to you, [6]and the land of Egypt is before you; settle your father and your brothers in the best part of the land. Let them live

x13 Samaritan Pentateuch and Syriac (see also 1 Chron. 7:1); Masoretic Text *Puvah*   y13 Samaritan Pentateuch and some Septuagint manuscripts (see also Num. 26:24 and 1 Chron. 7:1); Masoretic Text *Iob*   z15 That is, Northwest Mesopotamia   a16 Samaritan Pentateuch and Septuagint (see also Num. 26:15); Masoretic Text *Ziphion*   b20 That is, Heliopolis   c27 Hebrew; Septuagint *the nine children*   d27 Hebrew (see also Exodus 1:5 and footnote); Septuagint (see also Acts 7:14) *seventy-five*   e29 Hebrew *around him* in Goshen. And if you know of any among them with special ability, put them in charge of my own livestock."

[7]Then Joseph brought his father Jacob in and presented him before Pharaoh. After Jacob blessed[f] Pharaoh, [8]Pharaoh asked him, "How old are you?"

[9]And Jacob said to Pharaoh, "The years of my pilgrimage are a hundred and thirty. My years have been few and difficult, and they do not equal the years of the pilgrimage of my fathers." [10]Then Jacob blessed[g] Pharaoh and went out from his presence.

[11]So Joseph settled his father and his brothers in Egypt and gave them property in the best part of the land, the district of Rameses, as Pharaoh directed. [12]Joseph also provided his father and his brothers and all his father's household with food, according to the number of their children.

[13]There was no food, however, in the whole region because the famine was severe; both Egypt and Canaan wasted away because of the famine. [14]Joseph collected all the money that was to be found in Egypt and Canaan in payment for the grain they were buying, and he brought it to Pharaoh's palace. [15]When the money of the people of Egypt and Canaan was gone, all Egypt came to Joseph and said, "Give us food. Why should we die before your eyes? Our money is used up."

[16]"Then bring your livestock," said Joseph. "I will sell you food in exchange for your livestock, since your money is gone." [17]So they brought their livestock to Joseph, and he gave them food in exchange for their horses, their sheep and goats, their cattle and donkeys. And he brought them through that year with food in exchange for all their livestock.

[18]When that year was over, they came to him the following year and said, "We cannot hide from our lord the fact that since our money is gone and our livestock belongs to you, there is nothing left for our lord except our bodies and our land. [19]Why should we perish before your eyes—we and our land as well? Buy us and our land in exchange for food, and we with our land will be in bondage to Pharaoh. Give us seed so

that we may live and not die, and that the land may not become desolate."

[20]So Joseph bought all the land in Egypt for Pharaoh. The Egyptians, one and all, sold their fields, because the famine was too severe for them. The land became Pharaoh's, [21]and Joseph reduced the people to servitude,[h] from one end of Egypt to the other. [22]However, he did not buy the land of the priests, because they received a regular allotment from Pharaoh and had food enough from the allotment Pharaoh gave them. That is why they did not sell their land.

[23]Joseph said to the people, "Now that I have bought you and your land today for Pharaoh, here is seed for you so you can plant the ground. [24]But when the crop comes in, give a fifth of it to Pharaoh. The other four-fifths you may keep as seed for the fields and as food for yourselves and your households and your children."

[25]"You have saved our lives," they said. "May we find favor in the eyes of our lord; we will be in bondage to Pharaoh."

[26]So Joseph established it as a law concerning land in Egypt—still in force today—that a fifth of the produce belongs to Pharaoh. It was only the land of the priests that did not become Pharaoh's.

[27]Now the Israelites settled in Egypt in the region of Goshen. They acquired property there and were fruitful and increased greatly in number.

[28]Jacob lived in Egypt seventeen years, and the years of his life were a hundred and forty-seven. [29]When the time drew near for Israel to die, he called for his son Joseph and said to him, "If I have found favor in your eyes, put your hand under my thigh and promise that you will show me kindness and faithfulness. Do not bury me in Egypt, [30]but when I rest with my fathers, carry me out of Egypt and bury me where they are buried."

"I will do as you say," he said.

[31]"Swear to me," he said. Then Joseph swore to him, and Israel worshiped as he leaned on the top of his staff.[i]

[f]7 Or greeted   [g]10 Or said farewell to   [h]21 Samaritan Pentateuch and Septuagint (see also Vulgate); Masoretic Text and he moved the people into the cities   [i]31 Or Israel bowed down at the head of his bed

---

Discovering the Word 1. What is Pharaoh's reaction to the news that Joseph's brothers have arrived (45:16–24)? 2. Beersheba had been Isaac's center of worship. As God confirms this move to Egypt, what encouragement does he give Jacob for both the immediate and distant future (46:1–4)? 3. How do verses 5–27 of chapter 46 underscore God's faithfulness to the promises he made to Abraham, Isaac and Jacob? **4.** How does Joseph's skill as a planner and administrator continue to show itself as he arranges for his father's family to settle in Goshen (46:28–34)? **5.** What does 47:13–27 reveal about God's purpose in bringing Joseph to Egypt? **6.** How does Jacob's last request of Joseph show his faith in God's promise regarding his descendants and their own land (47:28–30)?

 Applying the Word 1. Has God ever allowed you to see how seemingly unrelated events fit into the tapestry of his will? Explain. 2. What important promise or prayer request are you patiently waiting for God to fulfill?

 Responding in Prayer Thank God for his loving control over the lives of Abraham, Isaac and Jacob. Praise him for ordering your steps according to his benevolent will.

25 / *Genesis 48—49*
The Life of Faith

OUR SELF-CENTERED TECHNOLOGICAL society seeks instant gratification and immediate results. The good life emblazoned on television is measured by what we have and use now. The elderly are usually considered obsolete rather than examples of how to live fully for the long run. But for those with eyes to see, Jacob can teach us valuable lessons about the satisfaction of persevering in the life of faith. This study views his final days as he evaluates the past and peers into the future.

 Warming Up to God Paint a picture of God in your mind. What is he like? Write down what you see. Let God come to you now and broaden your perspective.

 Read Genesis 48—49.

48 Some time later Joseph was told, "Your father is ill." So he took his two sons Manasseh and Ephraim along with him. ²When Jacob was told, "Your son Joseph has come to you," Israel rallied his strength and sat up on the bed.

³Jacob said to Joseph, "God Almighty^j appeared to me at Luz in the land of Canaan, and there he blessed me ⁴and said to me, 'I am going to make you fruitful and will increase your numbers. I will make you a community of peoples, and I will give this land as an everlasting possession to your descendants after you.'

⁵"Now then, your two sons born to you in Egypt before I came to you here will be reckoned as mine; Ephraim and Manasseh will be mine, just as Reuben and Simeon are mine. ⁶Any children born to you after them will be yours; in the territory they inherit they will be reckoned under the names of their brothers. ⁷As I was returning from Paddan,^k to my sorrow Rachel died in the land of Canaan while we were still on the way, a little distance from Ephrath. So I buried her there beside the road to Ephrath" (that is, Bethlehem).

⁸When Israel saw the sons of Joseph, he asked, "Who are these?"

⁹"They are the sons God has given me here," Joseph said to his father.

Then Israel said, "Bring them to me so I may bless them."

¹⁰Now Israel's eyes were failing because of old age, and he could hardly see. So Joseph brought his sons close to him, and his father kissed them and embraced them.

¹¹Israel said to Joseph, "I never expected to see your face again, and now God has allowed me to see your children too."

¹²Then Joseph removed them from Israel's knees and bowed down with his face to the ground. ¹³And Joseph took both of them, Ephraim on his right toward Israel's left hand and Manasseh on his left toward Israel's right hand, and brought them close to him. ¹⁴But Israel reached out his right hand and put it on Ephraim's head, though he was the younger, and crossing his arms, he put his left hand on Manas-

j3 Hebrew El-Shaddai   *k7 That is, Northwest Mesopotamia* seh's head, even though Manasseh was the first-born.

¹⁵Then he blessed Joseph and said,

"May the God before whom my fathers
    Abraham and Isaac walked,
the God who has been my shepherd
    all my life to this day,
¹⁶the Angel who has delivered me from all
    harm
    —may he bless these boys.
May they be called by my name
    and the names of my fathers Abraham and
      Isaac,
and may they increase greatly
    upon the earth."

¹⁷When Joseph saw his father placing his right hand on Ephraim's head he was displeased; so he took hold of his father's hand to move it from Ephraim's head to Manasseh's head. ¹⁸Joseph said to him, "No, my father, this one is the firstborn; put your right hand on his head."

¹⁹But his father refused and said, "I know, my son, I know. He too will become a people, and he too will become great. Nevertheless, his younger brother will be greater than he, and his descendants will become a group of nations." ²⁰He blessed them that day and said,

"In your^l name will Israel pronounce this
    blessing:
'May God make you like Ephraim and
    Manasseh.' "

So he put Ephraim ahead of Manasseh.

²¹Then Israel said to Joseph, "I am about to die, but God will be with you^m and take you^m back to the land of your^m fathers. ²²And to you, as one who is over your brothers, I give the ridge of landⁿ I took from the Amorites with my sword and my bow."

49

Then Jacob called for his sons and said: "Gather around so I can tell you what will happen to you in days to come.

²"Assemble and listen, sons of Jacob;
    listen to your father Israel.

³"Reuben, you are my firstborn,
    my might, the first sign of my strength,
    excelling in honor, excelling in power.
⁴Turbulent as the waters, you will no longer
    excel,

for you went up onto your father's bed,
    onto my couch and defiled it.

⁵"Simeon and Levi are brothers—
    their swords^o are weapons of violence.
⁶Let me not enter their council,
    let me not join their assembly,
for they have killed men in their anger
    and hamstrung oxen as they pleased.
⁷Cursed be their anger, so fierce,
    and their fury, so cruel!
I will scatter them in Jacob
    and disperse them in Israel.

⁸"Judah,^p your brothers will praise you;
    your hand will be on the neck of your
      enemies;
    your father's sons will bow down to you.
⁹You are a lion's cub, O Judah;
    you return from the prey, my son.
Like a lion he crouches and lies down,
    like a lioness—who dares to rouse him?
¹⁰The scepter will not depart from Judah,
    nor the ruler's staff from between his feet,
until he comes to whom it belongs^q
    and the obedience of the nations is his.
¹¹He will tether his donkey to a vine,
    his colt to the choicest branch;
he will wash his garments in wine,
    his robes in the blood of grapes.
¹²His eyes will be darker than wine,
    his teeth whiter than milk.^r

¹³"Zebulun will live by the seashore
    and become a haven for ships;
    his border will extend toward Sidon.

¹⁴"Issachar is a rawboned^s donkey
    lying down between two saddlebags.^t
¹⁵When he sees how good is his resting place
    and how pleasant is his land,
he will bend his shoulder to the burden
    and submit to forced labor.

¹⁶"Dan^u will provide justice for his people
    as one of the tribes of Israel.
¹⁷Dan will be a serpent by the roadside,
    a viper along the path,
that bites the horse's heels
    so that its rider tumbles backward.

^l20 The Hebrew is singular.   ^m21 The Hebrew is plural.   ⁿ22 Or *And to you I give one portion more than to your brothers—the portion*   ^o5 The meaning of the Hebrew for this word is uncertain.   ^p8 *Judah* sounds like and may be derived from the Hebrew for *praise.*   ^q10 Or *until Shiloh comes; or until he comes to whom tribute belongs*   ^r12 Or *will be dull from wine, / his teeth white from milk*   ^s14 Or *strong*   ^t14 Or *campfires*   ^u16 *Dan* here means *he provides justice.*

18"I look for your deliverance, O LORD.

19"Gad[v] will be attacked by a band of raiders,
    but he will attack them at their heels.

20"Asher's food will be rich;
    he will provide delicacies fit for a king.

21"Naphtali is a doe set free
    that bears beautiful fawns.[w]

22"Joseph is a fruitful vine,
    a fruitful vine near a spring,
    whose branches climb over a wall.[x]

23With bitterness archers attacked him;
    they shot at him with hostility.

24But his bow remained steady,
    his strong arms stayed[y] limber,
because of the hand of the Mighty One of
    Jacob,
    because of the Shepherd, the Rock of Israel,

25because of your father's God, who helps you,
    because of the Almighty,[z] who blesses you
with blessings of the heavens above,
    blessings of the deep that lies below,
    blessings of the breast and womb.

26Your father's blessings are greater
    than the blessings of the ancient mountains,
    than[a] the bounty of the age-old hills.
Let all these rest on the head of Joseph,

on the brow of the prince among[b] his
    brothers.

27"Benjamin is a ravenous wolf;
    in the morning he devours the prey,
    in the evening he divides the plunder."

28All these are the twelve tribes of Israel, and this is what their father said to them when he blessed them, giving each the blessing appropriate to him.

29Then he gave them these instructions: "I am about to be gathered to my people. Bury me with my fathers in the cave in the field of Ephron the Hittite, 30the cave in the field of Machpelah, near Mamre in Canaan, which Abraham bought as a burial place from Ephron the Hittite, along with the field. 31There Abraham and his wife Sarah were buried, there Isaac and his wife Rebekah were buried, and there I buried Leah. 32The field and the cave in it were bought from the Hittites.[c]"

33When Jacob had finished giving instructions to his sons, he drew his feet up into the bed, breathed his last and was gathered to his people.

[v]19 *Gad* can mean *attack* and *band of raiders*.   [w]21 Or *free; / he utters beautiful words*   [x]22 Or *Joseph is a wild colt, / a wild colt near a spring, / a wild donkey on a terraced hill*   [y]23,24 Or *archers will attack . . . will shoot . . . will remain . . . will stay*   [z]25 Hebrew *Shaddai*   [a]26 Or *of my progenitors, / as great as*   [b]26 Or *the one separated from*   [c]32 Or *the sons of Heth*

 Discovering the Word   1. In what ways is Jacob's faith evident as he blesses Ephraim and Manasseh (48:8–20)?   2. In 49:3–7 how are the blessings given to Reuben, Simeon and Levi related to their past actions (see Ge 34; 35:22)?   3. What future does Jacob see for Judah (49:8–12)?   4. After blessing six of his other sons (49:13–21), Jacob gives a rich and lengthy blessing to Joseph. How is Joseph's blessing related to his past actions (49:22–26)?   5. Recall events in Joseph's life which illustrate the names given to God in 49:24–25.   6. How do Jacob's last words demonstrate the faith and hope with which he finished the course of his life (48:21–22; 49:29–32)?

Applying the Word   1. Although our past failures and sins affect our future, how can God's forgiveness and grace help us triumph over these consequences?   2. In what specific areas are you having to trust God for the future?

Responding in Prayer   Ask God to help you remember that his plans are much greater than our own. Praise him for the miracles he's shown you in the life of Jacob.

26 / *Genesis 50*
Spiritual Maturity

LIKE A FINE painting or sculpture, God's work takes time, but its beauty is a tribute to the artist. The previous studies have shown how God used the years of hardship and suffering to produce in Joseph a spiritual maturity unsurpassed in the Old Testament. In this final chapter of Genesis we see how Joseph's life reflects the character of God. He provides a model for the way we should relate to God and others.

 Warming Up to God Reflect for a few moments on what God has taught you about himself through Genesis. Thank God for the ways you've grown, and ask him to teach you more.

 Read Genesis 50.

50 Joseph threw himself upon his father and wept over him and kissed him. ²Then Joseph directed the physicians in his service to embalm his father Israel. So the physicians embalmed him, ³taking a full forty days, for that was the time required for embalming. And the Egyptians mourned for him seventy days.

⁴When the days of mourning had passed, Joseph said to Pharaoh's court, "If I have found favor in your eyes, speak to Pharaoh for me. Tell him, ⁵'My father made me swear an oath and said, "I am about to die; bury me in the tomb I dug for myself in the land of Canaan." Now let me go up and bury my father; then I will return.' "

⁶Pharaoh said, "Go up and bury your father, as he made you swear to do."

⁷So Joseph went up to bury his father. All Pharaoh's officials accompanied him—the dignitaries of his court and all the dignitaries of Egypt— ⁸besides all the members of Joseph's household and his brothers and those belonging to his father's household. Only their children and their flocks and herds were left in Goshen. ⁹Chariots and horsemen*d* also went up with him. It was a very large company.

¹⁰When they reached the threshing floor of Atad, near the Jordan, they lamented loudly and bitterly; and there Joseph observed a seven-day period of mourning for his father. ¹¹When the Canaanites who lived there saw the mourning at the threshing floor of Atad, they said, "The Egyptians are holding a solemn ceremony of mourning." That is why that place near the Jordan is called Abel Mizraim.*e*

¹²So Jacob's sons did as he had commanded them: ¹³They carried him to the land of Canaan and buried him in the cave in the field of Machpe-

lah, near Mamre, which Abraham had bought as a burial place from Ephron the Hittite, along with the field. ¹⁴After burying his father, Joseph returned to Egypt, together with his brothers and all the others who had gone with him to bury his father.

¹⁵When Joseph's brothers saw that their father was dead, they said, "What if Joseph holds a grudge against us and pays us back for all the wrongs we did to him?" ¹⁶So they sent word to Joseph, saying, "Your father left these instructions before he died: ¹⁷'This is what you are to say to Joseph: I ask you to forgive your brothers the sins and the wrongs they committed in treating you so badly.' Now please forgive the sins of the servants of the God of your father." When their message came to him, Joseph wept.

¹⁸His brothers then came and threw themselves down before him. "We are your slaves," they said.

¹⁹But Joseph said to them, "Don't be afraid. Am I in the place of God? ²⁰You intended to harm me, but God intended it for good to accomplish what is now being done, the saving of many lives. ²¹So then, don't be afraid. I will provide for you and your children." And he reassured them and spoke kindly to them.

²²Joseph stayed in Egypt, along with all his father's family. He lived a hundred and ten years ²³and saw the third generation of Ephraim's children. Also the children of Makir son of Manasseh were placed at birth on Joseph's knees.*f*

²⁴Then Joseph said to his brothers, "I am about to die. But God will surely come to your aid and take you up out of this land to the land he promised on oath to Abraham, Isaac and Jacob." ²⁵And Joseph made the sons of Israel swear an oath and

d9 Or *charioteers*   *e11* Abel Mizraim means *mourning of the Egyptians*.   *f23* That is, were counted as his said, "God will surely come to your aid, and then you must carry my bones up from this place."

²⁶So Joseph died at the age of a hundred and ten. And after they embalmed him, he was placed in a coffin in Egypt.

 Discovering the Word 1. How is Joseph's love and respect for his father evident? 2. Describe the reaction of Joseph's brothers after their father's burial and the strategy they devise to save themselves (vv. 15–18). 3. What does Joseph's answer to his brothers reveal about his attitude toward being treated unjustly (vv. 19–20)? 4. How does Joseph show his brothers that he not only forgives but genuinely loves them (v. 21)? 5. One hundred and ten years was considered to be the ideal life span in ancient Egypt. How are Joseph's final years and words similar to his father's (vv. 22–26)?

Applying the Word 1. Think of someone who has injured you. What is your attitude toward that person? 2. As you look back over this chapter, describe some of the ways Joseph demonstrates the qualities of faith, love and hope. 3. In the Genesis narrative we have seen that Abraham, Isaac, Jacob and Joseph all died in faith, looking forward to promises they did not see fulfilled in their lifetime. How does their example provide a model for our hope as Christians?

Responding in Prayer Take time to thank God for his goodness, grace and faithfulness in each generation, including our own.

Exodus

When we're young we can hardly wait to get our independence. Responsibility rarely crosses our minds. Our parents, on the other hand, think about responsibility a great deal. They cautiously increase our independence bit by bit, anxiously waiting for signs of growing maturity. But that's just the beginning. For the rest of our lives we walk the tightrope between independence and responsibility.

Long ago this issue was dramatized for us in ancient Israel's struggle to gain its independence and to show responsible obedience to God. Moses was "the anxious parent" deputized by God to lead the nation to independence and to teach them responsible freedom.

The book of Exodus tells it all. Written by Moses himself, Exodus is the story of abject slavery and glorious liberation. God patiently teaches what human responsibility means, both in worship and in our relationships with others.

Just like children struggling through adolescence to responsible adulthood, Israel had its good and bad days. Their exodus to freedom did not give them the right to do as they pleased. They had to learn loyalty and obedience to God as a consequence of his giving them their independence. For them, learning to trust and obey God was rooted in God's gracious deliverance from bondage.

In effect, God owned them because he had redeemed them from bondage. The story of Israel's exodus thus becomes a prototype of every Christian's exodus from the enslaving power of sin. Jesus Christ the redeemer becomes Lord of those who would acknowledge his saving love and power.

All this and more is bound up in the book of Exodus. Serious students will find a gold mine of insight and practical values that relate to living today. This is history with a punch. Allow yourself the benefit of careful reflection. Take time to cross 3,500 years and think about both victories and defeats among God's people. Thrill to Moses' encounters with Pharaoh, with his own rebellious people and with God at Mount Sinai. Grasp the significance of the Ten Commandments and the worship of the true and living God. Meditate on new ideas about the meaning of worship, music, and the consecration of one's possessions and talents to the glory of God.

Exodus begins with Moses' account of cruel bondage in Egypt, moves through the bitter struggle with Pharaoh for deliverance, continues on to Mount Sinai and the giving of the Ten

Commandments, and climaxes with the building of a place of worship and the establishment of a priesthood. It covers a period of close to one hundred years.

Major themes include the name and glory of God, the covenants (agreements) between God and Israel, the Law and the tabernacle. The institution of the Passover points to salvation through the death of Christ. The tabernacle and the priesthood speak of the God-given principles of how we worship God and the privileges we have to praise and glorify him.

Because there is much historical data to be covered, some of it is not included in the questions. The quiet times are organized around the major events in the story, their significance for Israel and what we can learn from them about Christian living. You will need to develop the skill of scanning blocks of text, looking for highlights. Pertinent New Testament doctrines and applications for Christian living are also considered.

The questions are designed to help you discover the facts and reflect on their significance for your life. The apostle Paul wrote that these ancient accounts were given to teach and warn us (1Co 10:11). May God help you to grasp life-changing truth as you grow in your ability to trust and obey him.

Outline

1/ Exodus 1 —————————— *Evil Plans, Courageous Resistance*

2/ Exodus 2 —————————— *A Mother's Faith, a Son's Brashness*

3/ Exodus 3—4 ————————— *Stubborn Reluctance Overcome*

4/ Exodus 5:1—7:7 ———————— *Rebuff and Resolution*

5/ Exodus 7:8—10:29 ———————— *God's Power on the Line*

6/ Exodus 11:1—12:28 ——————— *Night of Death and Deliverance*

7/ Exodus 12:29—13:16 —————— *Freedom and Its Cost*

8/ Exodus 13:17—14:31 —————— *From Crisis to Triumph*

9/ Exodus 15:1—21 ———————— *Praise for the Past and Hope for the Future*

10/ Exodus 15:22—17:16 —————— *Adversities of the Desert*

11/ Exodus 18 ————————— *Wise Counsel*

12/ Exodus 19 ————————— *Preparing for God*

13/ Exodus 20:1—21 ———————— *Ten Keys to God's Character*

14/ Exodus 20:22—23:19 —————— *A Well-Ordered Society*

15/ Exodus 23:20—24:18 —————— *Ratifying the Covenant*

16/ Exodus 25—27 ———————— *God's Blueprint for Worship*

17/ Exodus 28:1—29:37 —————— *God's Holiness*

18/ Exodus 29:38—31:18 —————— *God's Revelation in People and Things*

19/ Exodus 32 ————————— *Idolatry's Fearful Toll*

20/ Exodus 33 ————————— *God's Presence and Glory*

21/ Exodus 34 ————————— *Renewing the Covenant*

22/ Exodus 35—36 ———————— *Building the Tabernacle*

23/ Exodus 37:1—39:31 —————— *God Speaks Powerfully in Wood, Gold, Silver, Linen and Wool*

24/ Exodus 39:32—40:38 —————— *Time for Praise and Reflection*

1 / *Exodus 1*
Evil Plans, Courageous Resistance

OPPRESSION IS A nasty word, but it grabs the headlines because it's the reason for much conflict today. Scenes out of this chapter fit totalitarian societies. Only the methods of oppression change. God's people were not spared in 1700 B.C., and they are not always spared now. But in this study you will find a bright spot of courageous resistance.

 Warming Up to God Today you begin the account of the nation of Israel, the descendants of the promises made to Abraham, Isaac and Jacob. How are you seeing God's promises fulfilled in your life?

 Read Exodus 1.

1 These are the names of the sons of Israel who went to Egypt with Jacob, each with his family: ²Reuben, Simeon, Levi and Judah; ³Issachar, Zebulun and Benjamin; ⁴Dan and Naphtali; Gad and Asher. ⁵The descendants of Jacob numbered seventy*a* in all; Joseph was already in Egypt.

⁶Now Joseph and all his brothers and all that generation died, ⁷but the Israelites were fruitful and multiplied greatly and became exceedingly numerous, so that the land was filled with them.

⁸Then a new king, who did not know about Joseph, came to power in Egypt. ⁹"Look," he said to his people, "the Israelites have become much too numerous for us. ¹⁰Come, we must deal shrewdly with them or they will become even more numerous and, if war breaks out, will join our enemies, fight against us and leave the country."

¹¹So they put slave masters over them to oppress them with forced labor, and they built Pithom and Rameses as store cities for Pharaoh. ¹²But the more they were oppressed, the more they multiplied and spread; so the Egyptians came to dread the Israelites ¹³and worked them ruthlessly. ¹⁴They made their lives bitter with hard labor in brick and mortar and with all kinds of work in the fields; in all their hard labor the Egyptians used them ruthlessly.

¹⁵The king of Egypt said to the Hebrew midwives, whose names were Shiphrah and Puah, ¹⁶"When you help the Hebrew women in childbirth and observe them on the delivery stool, if it is a boy, kill him; but if it is a girl, let her live." ¹⁷The midwives, however, feared God and did not do what the king of Egypt had told them to do; they let the boys live. ¹⁸Then the king of Egypt summoned the midwives and asked them, "Why have you done this? Why have you let the boys live?"

¹⁹The midwives answered Pharaoh, "Hebrew women are not like Egyptian women; they are vigorous and give birth before the midwives arrive."

²⁰So God was kind to the midwives and the people increased and became even more numerous. ²¹And because the midwives feared God, he gave them families of their own.

²²Then Pharaoh gave this order to all his people: "Every boy that is born*b* you must throw into the Nile, but let every girl live."

a5 Masoretic Text (see also Gen. 46:27); Dead Sea Scrolls and Septuagint (see also Acts 7:14 and note at Gen. 46:27) *seventy-five*
b22 Masoretic Text; Samaritan Pentateuch, Septuagint and Targums *born to the Hebrews*

 Discovering the Word **1.** How did "the sons of Israel" (Jacob's descendants) fare in Egypt (vv. 1–7)? **2.** What was their situation under a king who had forgotten Joseph's role (Ge 41) in saving the country (vv. 8–14)? **3.** Why did Pharaoh's strategy backfire (v. 12)? **4.** What new population control plans did Pharaoh devise (vv. 15–22)? **5.** Imagine the emotions of the king and the midwives when he summoned them (v. 18). What was the secret of the women's self-control and wisdom (vv. 17, 21)?

Applying the Word **1.** How does your fear of God motivate right moral conduct and give you the courage to withstand the temptation to do evil? **2.** In what circumstances have you felt oppressed by unreasonable demands? **3.** How did you find God's help?

Responding in Prayer Thank God for your personal freedom and ask him to give you endurance when you are faced with oppression.

2 / *Exodus 2*
A Mother's Faith, a Son's Brashness

WORKING DOWNTOWN ON an engineering maintenance project, the man knew that his friend's wife lay dying in a hospital only four blocks away. But he didn't go to see the woman. Lack of appropriate dress demolished his courage to do something bold in Christ's name. Few of us can brag about how bravely we have responded in crisis. Faith, for us, is a comfortable intellectual exercise, not something that demands bold action. That definition becomes even more attractive when we're not sure how to distinguish between faith and foolishness. This study contrasts a privileged kid's brashness with a woman's courageous faith in action.

 Warming Up to God What has been the most costly thing you have had to do for God?

 Read Exodus 2.

2 Now a man of the house of Levi married a Levite woman, ²and she became pregnant and gave birth to a son. When she saw that he was a fine child, she hid him for three months. ³But when she could hide him no longer, she got a papyrus basket for him and coated it with tar and pitch. Then she placed the child in it and put it among the reeds along the bank of the Nile. ⁴His sister stood at a distance to see what would happen to him.

⁵Then Pharaoh's daughter went down to the Nile to bathe, and her attendants were walking along the river bank. She saw the basket among the reeds and sent her slave girl to get it. ⁶She opened it and saw the baby. He was crying, and she felt sorry for him. "This is one of the Hebrew babies," she said.

⁷Then his sister asked Pharaoh's daughter, "Shall I go and get one of the Hebrew women to nurse the baby for you?"

⁸"Yes, go," she answered. And the girl went and got the baby's mother. ⁹Pharaoh's daughter said to her, "Take this baby and nurse him for me, and I will pay you." So the woman took the baby and nursed him. ¹⁰When the child grew older, she took him to Pharaoh's daughter and he became her son. She named him Moses,ᶜ saying, "I drew him out of the water."

¹¹One day, after Moses had grown up, he went out to where his own people were and watched them at their hard labor. He saw an Egyptian beating a Hebrew, one of his own people. ¹²Glancing this way and that and seeing no one, he killed the Egyptian and hid him in the sand. ¹³The next day he went out and saw two Hebrews fighting. He asked the one in the wrong, "Why are you hitting your fellow Hebrew?"

¹⁴The man said, "Who made you ruler and judge over us? Are you thinking of killing me as you killed the Egyptian?" Then Moses was afraid and thought, "What I did must have become known."

¹⁵When Pharaoh heard of this, he tried to kill Moses, but Moses fled from Pharaoh and went to live in Midian, where he sat down by a well. ¹⁶Now a priest of Midian had seven daughters, and they came to draw water and fill the troughs to water their father's flock. ¹⁷Some shepherds came along and drove them away, but Moses got up and came to their rescue and watered their flock.

¹⁸When the girls returned to Reuel their father, he asked them, "Why have you returned so early today?"

¹⁹They answered, "An Egyptian rescued us from the shepherds. He even drew water for us and watered the flock."

²⁰"And where is he?" he asked his daughters. "Why did you leave him? Invite him to have something to eat."

²¹Moses agreed to stay with the man, who gave his daughter Zipporah to Moses in marriage. ²²Zipporah gave birth to a son, and Moses named him Gershom,ᵈ saying, "I have become an alien in a foreign land."

²³During that long period, the king of Egypt died. The Israelites groaned in their slavery and

ᶜ10 *Moses* sounds like the Hebrew for *draw out.*   ᵈ22 *Gershom* sounds like the Hebrew for *an alien there.*

cried out, and their cry for help because of their slavery went up to God. ²⁴God heard their groaning and he remembered his covenant with Abraham, with Isaac and with Jacob. ²⁵So God looked on the Israelites and was concerned about them.

Discovering the Word 1. How did God plan for the infant Moses to survive Pharaoh's murderous edict (vv. 1–10)? 2. What did Moses' survival cost his mother? 3. Why did Moses flee to Midian (vv. 11–15)? (He was 40 years old at the time.) 4. Meanwhile, what was happening to the Israelites in Egypt (v. 23)? 5. How did their condition affect God and why (vv. 24–25)?

Applying the Word 1. How has God confronted you recently with a demand for courageous faith? 2. God hears the cries of his people today. What difference does that make when you are confronted by circumstances you are powerless to change?

Responding in Prayer Ask God to use you in his plans to creatively address the difficult situations in your life.

3 / *Exodus 3—4*
Stubborn Reluctance Overcome

THE MILESTONES OF history are marked by people who have met impossible demands. Battlefield monuments utter mute testimony to these events. Modern Turkey owes its existence to Kemal Ataturk, who rallied his troops with the impossible demand that they drive back the enemy from Gallipoli. Your most impossible demand may seem small in comparison—but not at the time the challenge presented itself. Perhaps it was writing an academic paper without adequate time or expertise. Or maybe it was the time when your church group decided to talk to people on the beach about Jesus Christ. This study shows how God put an impossible demand on Moses and propelled him into national leadership.

Warming Up to God Remember today that God has chosen you to do great works through him. Ask God to give you courage and to teach you from the example of Moses.

Read Exodus 3—4.

3 Now Moses was tending the flock of Jethro his father-in-law, the priest of Midian, and he led the flock to the far side of the desert and came to Horeb, the mountain of God. ²There the angel of the LORD appeared to him in flames of fire from within a bush. Moses saw that though the bush was on fire it did not burn up. ³So Moses thought, "I will go over and see this strange sight—why the bush does not burn up."

⁴When the LORD saw that he had gone over to look, God called to him from within the bush, "Moses! Moses!"

And Moses said, "Here I am."

⁵"Do not come any closer," God said. "Take off your sandals, for the place where you are standing is holy ground." ⁶Then he said, "I am the God of your father, the God of Abraham, the God of Isaac and the God of Jacob." At this, Moses hid his face, because he was afraid to look at God.

⁷The LORD said, "I have indeed seen the misery of my people in Egypt. I have heard them crying out because of their slave drivers, and I am concerned about their suffering. ⁸So I have come down to rescue them from the hand of the Egyptians and to bring them up out of that land into a good and spacious land, a land flowing with milk and honey—the home of the Canaanites, Hittites,

Amorites, Perizzites, Hivites and Jebusites. ⁹And now the cry of the Israelites has reached me, and I have seen the way the Egyptians are oppressing them. ¹⁰So now, go. I am sending you to Pharaoh to bring my people the Israelites out of Egypt."

¹¹But Moses said to God, "Who am I, that I should go to Pharaoh and bring the Israelites out of Egypt?"

¹²And God said, "I will be with you. And this will be the sign to you that it is I who have sent you: When you have brought the people out of Egypt, youᵉ will worship God on this mountain."

¹³Moses said to God, "Suppose I go to the Israelites and say to them, 'The God of your fathers has sent me to you,' and they ask me, 'What is his name?' Then what shall I tell them?"

¹⁴God said to Moses, "I AM WHO I AM.ᶠ This is what you are to say to the Israelites: 'I AM has sent me to you.' "

¹⁵God also said to Moses, "Say to the Israelites, 'The LORD,ᵍ the God of your fathers—the God of Abraham, the God of Isaac and the God of Jacob—has sent me to you.' This is my name forever, the name by which I am to be remembered from generation to generation.

¹⁶"Go, assemble the elders of Israel and say to them, 'The LORD, the God of your fathers—the God of Abraham, Isaac and Jacob—appeared to me and said: I have watched over you and have seen what has been done to you in Egypt. ¹⁷And I have promised to bring you up out of your misery in Egypt into the land of the Canaanites, Hittites, Amorites, Perizzites, Hivites and Jebusites—a land flowing with milk and honey.'

¹⁸"The elders of Israel will listen to you. Then you and the elders are to go to the king of Egypt and say to him, 'The LORD, the God of the Hebrews, has met with us. Let us take a three-day journey into the desert to offer sacrifices to the LORD our God.' ¹⁹But I know that the king of Egypt will not let you go unless a mighty hand compels him. ²⁰So I will stretch out my hand and strike the Egyptians with all the wonders that I will perform among them. After that, he will let you go.

²¹"And I will make the Egyptians favorably disposed toward this people, so that when you leave you will not go empty-handed. ²²Every woman is to ask her neighbor and any woman living in her house for articles of silver and gold and for cloth-ing, which you will put on your sons and daughters. And so you will plunder the Egyptians."

4 Moses answered, "What if they do not believe me or listen to me and say, 'The LORD did not appear to you'?"

²Then the LORD said to him, "What is that in your hand?"

"A staff," he replied.

³The LORD said, "Throw it on the ground."

Moses threw it on the ground and it became a snake, and he ran from it. ⁴Then the LORD said to him, "Reach out your hand and take it by the tail." So Moses reached out and took hold of the snake and it turned back into a staff in his hand. ⁵"This," said the LORD, "is so that they may believe that the LORD, the God of their fathers—the God of Abraham, the God of Isaac and the God of Jacob—has appeared to you."

⁶Then the LORD said, "Put your hand inside your cloak." So Moses put his hand into his cloak, and when he took it out, it was leprous,ʰ like snow.

⁷"Now put it back into your cloak," he said. So Moses put his hand back into his cloak, and when he took it out, it was restored, like the rest of his flesh.

⁸Then the LORD said, "If they do not believe you or pay attention to the first miraculous sign, they may believe the second. ⁹But if they do not believe these two signs or listen to you, take some water from the Nile and pour it on the dry ground. The water you take from the river will become blood on the ground."

¹⁰Moses said to the LORD, "O Lord, I have never been eloquent, neither in the past nor since you have spoken to your servant. I am slow of speech and tongue."

¹¹The LORD said to him, "Who gave man his mouth? Who makes him deaf or mute? Who gives him sight or makes him blind? Is it not I, the LORD? ¹²Now go; I will help you speak and will teach you what to say."

¹³But Moses said, "O Lord, please send someone else to do it."

¹⁴Then the LORD's anger burned against Moses and he said, "What about your brother, Aaron the Levite? I know he can speak well. He is already on his way to meet you, and his heart will be glad when he sees you. ¹⁵You shall speak to him and

---

ᵉ12 The Hebrew is plural.   ᶠ14 Or I WILL BE WHAT I WILL BE
ᵍ15 The Hebrew for LORD sounds like and may be derived from the Hebrew for I AM in verse 14.   ʰ6 The Hebrew word was used for various diseases affecting the skin—not necessarily leprosy.

put words in his mouth; I will help both of you speak and will teach you what to do. ¹⁶He will speak to the people for you, and it will be as if he were your mouth and as if you were God to him. ¹⁷But take this staff in your hand so you can perform miraculous signs with it."

¹⁸Then Moses went back to Jethro his father-in-law and said to him, "Let me go back to my own people in Egypt to see if any of them are still alive."

Jethro said, "Go, and I wish you well."

¹⁹Now the LORD had said to Moses in Midian, "Go back to Egypt, for all the men who wanted to kill you are dead." ²⁰So Moses took his wife and sons, put them on a donkey and started back to Egypt. And he took the staff of God in his hand.

²¹The LORD said to Moses, "When you return to Egypt, see that you perform before Pharaoh all the wonders I have given you the power to do. But I will harden his heart so that he will not let the people go. ²²Then say to Pharaoh, 'This is what the LORD says: Israel is my firstborn son, ²³and I told you, "Let my son go, so he may wor-

ship me." But you refused to let him go; so I will kill your firstborn son.'"

²⁴At a lodging place on the way, the LORD met ⌊Moses⌋ⁱ and was about to kill him. ²⁵But Zipporah took a flint knife, cut off her son's foreskin and touched ⌊Moses'⌋ feet with it.ʲ "Surely you are a bridegroom of blood to me," she said. ²⁶So the LORD let him alone. (At that time she said "bridegroom of blood," referring to circumcision.)

²⁷The LORD said to Aaron, "Go into the desert to meet Moses." So he met Moses at the mountain of God and kissed him. ²⁸Then Moses told Aaron everything the LORD had sent him to say, and also about all the miraculous signs he had commanded him to perform.

²⁹Moses and Aaron brought together all the elders of the Israelites, ³⁰and Aaron told them everything the LORD had said to Moses. He also performed the signs before the people, ³¹and they believed. And when they heard that the LORD was concerned about them and had seen their misery, they bowed down and worshiped.

ⁱ24 Or ⌊Moses' son⌋; Hebrew him   ʲ25 Or and drew near ⌊Moses'⌋ feet

---

 Discovering the Word 1. What motivates God to act on behalf of his people (3:7–10)? 2. How does Moses respond to God's assignment and why (3:11–13)? 3. What reassurance does God give Moses (3:12–22)? 4. What other doubts and fears does Moses have (4:1, 10)? 5. How does God deal with these inadequacies (4:2–9, 11–12)? 6. How do the events in 4:27–31 confirm the Lord's promises to Moses?

Applying the Word 1. When have you felt inadequate to do something God wanted you to do? 2. When you are sure God is speaking to you, and a specific "Yes, Lord" is expected of you, what things influence your answer?

Responding in Prayer Confess your fears and feelings of inadequacy to the Lord, and boldly ask him to call you to participate in his plans.

---

4 / *Exodus 5:1—7:7*
Rebuff and Resolution

THE CHRISTIAN STUDENT group discovered a sure-fire winner for its outreach meeting. Here was a famous businessman who was sure to attract a crowd. Confidently, the Christians plugged away at inviting their friends, and their work was rewarded with a packed room. An hour or so later they fled the room in defeat. They had tried to obey God, but their venture failed. In a word, their hero speaker bombed. Discouragement enveloped the group like a dense fog. No doubt Moses felt the same way, except the stakes were higher. In this study, he and Aaron are soundly rebuffed, though they doggedly pursue God's will with obedient courage.

 Warming Up to God What struggles have you faced today? Tell God about them, and let him show you through Scripture how he deals with evil.

Read Exodus 5:1—7:7.

5 Afterward Moses and Aaron went to Pharaoh and said, "This is what the LORD, the God of Israel, says: 'Let my people go, so that they may hold a festival to me in the desert.' "

²Pharaoh said, "Who is the LORD, that I should obey him and let Israel go? I do not know the LORD and I will not let Israel go."

³Then they said, "The God of the Hebrews has met with us. Now let us take a three-day journey into the desert to offer sacrifices to the LORD our God, or he may strike us with plagues or with the sword."

⁴But the king of Egypt said, "Moses and Aaron, why are you taking the people away from their labor? Get back to your work!" ⁵Then Pharaoh said, "Look, the people of the land are now numerous, and you are stopping them from working."

⁶That same day Pharaoh gave this order to the slave drivers and foremen in charge of the people: ⁷"You are no longer to supply the people with straw for making bricks; let them go and gather their own straw. ⁸But require them to make the same number of bricks as before; don't reduce the quota. They are lazy; that is why they are crying out, 'Let us go and sacrifice to our God.' ⁹Make the work harder for the men so that they keep working and pay no attention to lies."

¹⁰Then the slave drivers and the foremen went out and said to the people, "This is what Pharaoh says: 'I will not give you any more straw. ¹¹Go and get your own straw wherever you can find it, but your work will not be reduced at all.' " ¹²So the people scattered all over Egypt to gather stubble to use for straw. ¹³The slave drivers kept pressing them, saying, "Complete the work required of you for each day, just as when you had straw." ¹⁴The Israelite foremen appointed by Pharaoh's slave drivers were beaten and were asked, "Why didn't you meet your quota of bricks yesterday or today, as before?"

¹⁵Then the Israelite foremen went and appealed to Pharaoh: "Why have you treated your servants this way? ¹⁶Your servants are given no straw, yet we are told, 'Make bricks!' Your servants are being beaten, but the fault is with your own people."

¹⁷Pharaoh said, "Lazy, that's what you are— lazy! That is why you keep saying, 'Let us go and sacrifice to the LORD.' ¹⁸Now get to work. You will not be given any straw, yet you must produce your full quota of bricks."

¹⁹The Israelite foremen realized they were in trouble when they were told, "You are not to reduce the number of bricks required of you for each day." ²⁰When they left Pharaoh, they found Moses and Aaron waiting to meet them, ²¹and they said, "May the LORD look upon you and judge you! You have made us a stench to Pharaoh and his officials and have put a sword in their hand to kill us."

²²Moses returned to the LORD and said, "O Lord, why have you brought trouble upon this people? Is this why you sent me? ²³Ever since I went to Pharaoh to speak in your name, he has brought trouble upon this people, and you have not rescued your people at all."

6 Then the LORD said to Moses, "Now you will see what I will do to Pharaoh: Because of my mighty hand he will let them go; because of my mighty hand he will drive them out of his country."

²God also said to Moses, "I am the LORD. ³I appeared to Abraham, to Isaac and to Jacob as God Almighty,*ᵏ* but by my name the LORD*ˡ* I did not make myself known to them.*ᵐ* ⁴I also established my covenant with them to give them the land of Canaan, where they lived as aliens. ⁵Moreover, I have heard the groaning of the Israelites, whom the Egyptians are enslaving, and I have remembered my covenant.

⁶"Therefore, say to the Israelites: 'I am the LORD, and I will bring you out from under the yoke of the Egyptians. I will free you from being slaves to them, and I will redeem you with an outstretched arm and with mighty acts of judgment. ⁷I will take you as my own people, and I will be your God. Then you will know that I am the LORD your God, who brought you out from under the yoke of the Egyptians. ⁸And I will bring you to the land I swore with uplifted hand to give to Abraham, to Isaac and to Jacob. I will give it to you as a possession. I am the LORD.' "

⁹Moses reported this to the Israelites, but they

ᵏ3 Hebrew *El-Shaddai*   *ˡ3* See note at Exodus 3:15.   *ᵐ3* Or *Almighty, and by my name the* LORD *did I not let myself be known to them?*

did not listen to him because of their discouragement and cruel bondage.

¹⁰Then the LORD said to Moses, ¹¹"Go, tell Pharaoh king of Egypt to let the Israelites go out of his country."

¹²But Moses said to the LORD, "If the Israelites will not listen to me, why would Pharaoh listen to me, since I speak with faltering lips[n]?"

¹³Now the LORD spoke to Moses and Aaron about the Israelites and Pharaoh king of Egypt, and he commanded them to bring the Israelites out of Egypt.

¹⁴These were the heads of their families[o]:

The sons of Reuben the firstborn son of Israel were Hanoch and Pallu, Hezron and Carmi. These were the clans of Reuben.

¹⁵The sons of Simeon were Jemuel, Jamin, Ohad, Jakin, Zohar and Shaul the son of a Canaanite woman. These were the clans of Simeon.

¹⁶These were the names of the sons of Levi according to their records: Gershon, Kohath and Merari. Levi lived 137 years.

¹⁷The sons of Gershon, by clans, were Libni and Shimei.

¹⁸The sons of Kohath were Amram, Izhar, Hebron and Uzziel. Kohath lived 133 years.

¹⁹The sons of Merari were Mahli and Mushi.

These were the clans of Levi according to their records.

²⁰Amram married his father's sister Jochebed, who bore him Aaron and Moses. Amram lived 137 years.

²¹The sons of Izhar were Korah, Nepheg and Zicri.

²²The sons of Uzziel were Mishael, Elzaphan and Sithri.

²³Aaron married Elisheba, daughter of Amminadab and sister of Nahshon, and she bore him Nadab and Abihu, Eleazar and Ithamar.

²⁴The sons of Korah were Assir, Elkanah and Abiasaph. These were the Korahite clans.

²⁵Eleazar son of Aaron married one of the daughters of Putiel, and she bore him Phinehas.

These were the heads of the Levite families, clan by clan.

²⁶It was this same Aaron and Moses to whom the LORD said, "Bring the Israelites out of Egypt by their divisions." ²⁷They were the ones who spoke to Pharaoh king of Egypt about bringing the Israelites out of Egypt. It was the same Moses and Aaron.

²⁸Now when the LORD spoke to Moses in Egypt, ²⁹he said to him, "I am the LORD. Tell Pharaoh king of Egypt everything I tell you."

³⁰But Moses said to the LORD, "Since I speak with faltering lips, why would Pharaoh listen to me?"

7 Then the LORD said to Moses, "See, I have made you like God to Pharaoh, and your brother Aaron will be your prophet. ²You are to say everything I command you, and your brother Aaron is to tell Pharaoh to let the Israelites go out of his country. ³But I will harden Pharaoh's heart, and though I multiply my miraculous signs and wonders in Egypt, ⁴he will not listen to you. Then I will lay my hand on Egypt and with mighty acts of judgment I will bring out my divisions, my people the Israelites. ⁵And the Egyptians will know that I am the LORD when I stretch out my hand against Egypt and bring the Israelites out of it."

⁶Moses and Aaron did just as the LORD commanded them. ⁷Moses was eighty years old and Aaron eighty-three when they spoke to Pharaoh.

[n] 12 Hebrew *I am uncircumcised of lips*; also in verse 30   [o] 14 The Hebrew for *families* here and in verse 25 refers to units larger than clans.

Discovering the Word   1. What were the major outcomes of the first encounter between Moses and Aaron and Pharaoh (Ex 5)?   2. Describe Moses' feelings and the logic of his cry to God (5:22–23).   3. The statement "I am the LORD" is repeated four times in 6:1–8. What does God emphasize about himself in response to Moses' complaint (6:1–5)?   4. What does the Lord's message to Israel emphasize about his plans for them (6:6–8)?   5. Moses is concerned that Pharaoh won't listen to him (6:30). Yet how will Pharaoh's stubbornness help to fulfill God's plans for Egypt (7:3–5)?   6. In spite of defeat and discouragement (5:2; 6:9, 12, 30), Moses "did just as the LORD commanded" (7:6). What do you think brought him to this decisive obedience?

Applying the Word   1. Give an example from your life of when discouragement blurred the clarity of God's power and promises.   2. What definitive spiritual decision have you made during your life as a Christian?

 Responding in Prayer   Thank God for the people and circumstances he used to influence your walk with Christ.

5 / *Exodus 7:8—10:29*
God's Power on the Line

GOD'S AUTHORITY IS on the line any time a world leader like Pharaoh decides to take charge. It's also on the line when his children decide to play the game their own way. We have the benefit of looking at a historical book like Exodus to tell us the futility of resisting God. But somehow we find ourselves engaged in a recurring battle in our lives, not too dissimilar to Pharaoh's. Pharaoh opposed God, with devastating consequences. God will also challenge your right to do as you please. This lesson shows that it's futile to resist.

 Warming Up to God   When do you feel that the world is spinning out of control? What do you need from God in those times?

 Read Exodus 7:8—10:29.

⁸The Lord said to Moses and Aaron, ⁹"When Pharaoh says to you, 'Perform a miracle,' then say to Aaron, 'Take your staff and throw it down before Pharaoh,' and it will become a snake."

¹⁰So Moses and Aaron went to Pharaoh and did just as the Lord commanded. Aaron threw his staff down in front of Pharaoh and his officials, and it became a snake. ¹¹Pharaoh then summoned wise men and sorcerers, and the Egyptian magicians also did the same things by their secret arts: ¹²Each one threw down his staff and it became a snake. But Aaron's staff swallowed up their staffs. ¹³Yet Pharaoh's heart became hard and he would not listen to them, just as the Lord had said.

¹⁴Then the Lord said to Moses, "Pharaoh's heart is unyielding; he refuses to let the people go. ¹⁵Go to Pharaoh in the morning as he goes out to the water. Wait on the bank of the Nile to meet him, and take in your hand the staff that was changed into a snake. ¹⁶Then say to him, 'The Lord, the God of the Hebrews, has sent me to say to you: Let my people go, so that they may worship me in the desert. But until now you have not listened. ¹⁷This is what the Lord says: By this you will know that I am the Lord: With the staff that is in my hand I will strike the water of the Nile, and it will be changed into blood. ¹⁸The fish in the Nile will die, and the river will stink; the Egyptians will not be able to drink its water.' "

¹⁹The Lord said to Moses, "Tell Aaron, 'Take your staff and stretch out your hand over the waters of Egypt—over the streams and canals, over the ponds and all the reservoirs'—and they will turn to blood. Blood will be everywhere in Egypt, even in the wooden buckets and stone jars."

²⁰Moses and Aaron did just as the Lord had commanded. He raised his staff in the presence of Pharaoh and his officials and struck the water of the Nile, and all the water was changed into blood. ²¹The fish in the Nile died, and the river smelled so bad that the Egyptians could not drink its water. Blood was everywhere in Egypt.

²²But the Egyptian magicians did the same things by their secret arts, and Pharaoh's heart became hard; he would not listen to Moses and Aaron, just as the Lord had said. ²³Instead, he turned and went into his palace, and did not take even this to heart. ²⁴And all the Egyptians dug along the Nile to get drinking water, because they could not drink the water of the river.

²⁵Seven days passed after the Lord struck the Nile. ¹Then the Lord said to Moses, "Go to Pharaoh and say to him, 'This is what the Lord says: Let my people go, so that they may worship me. ²If you refuse to let them go, I will plague your whole country with frogs. ³The Nile will teem with frogs. They will come up into

your palace and your bedroom and onto your bed, into the houses of your officials and on your people, and into your ovens and kneading troughs. ⁴The frogs will go up on you and your people and all your officials.' "

⁵Then the LORD said to Moses, "Tell Aaron, 'Stretch out your hand with your staff over the streams and canals and ponds, and make frogs come up on the land of Egypt.' "

⁶So Aaron stretched out his hand over the waters of Egypt, and the frogs came up and covered the land. ⁷But the magicians did the same things by their secret arts; they also made frogs come up on the land of Egypt.

⁸Pharaoh summoned Moses and Aaron and said, "Pray to the LORD to take the frogs away from me and my people, and I will let your people go to offer sacrifices to the LORD."

⁹Moses said to Pharaoh, "I leave to you the honor of setting the time for me to pray for you and your officials and your people that you and your houses may be rid of the frogs, except for those that remain in the Nile."

¹⁰"Tomorrow," Pharaoh said.

Moses replied, "It will be as you say, so that you may know there is no one like the LORD our God. ¹¹The frogs will leave you and your houses, your officials and your people; they will remain only in the Nile."

¹²After Moses and Aaron left Pharaoh, Moses cried out to the LORD about the frogs he had brought on Pharaoh. ¹³And the LORD did what Moses asked. The frogs died in the houses, in the courtyards and in the fields. ¹⁴They were piled into heaps, and the land reeked of them. ¹⁵But when Pharaoh saw that there was relief, he hardened his heart and would not listen to Moses and Aaron, just as the LORD had said.

¹⁶Then the LORD said to Moses, "Tell Aaron, 'Stretch out your staff and strike the dust of the ground,' and throughout the land of Egypt the dust will become gnats." ¹⁷They did this, and when Aaron stretched out his hand with the staff and struck the dust of the ground, gnats came upon men and animals. All the dust throughout the land of Egypt became gnats. ¹⁸But when the magicians tried to produce gnats by their secret arts, they could not. And the gnats were on men and animals.

¹⁹The magicians said to Pharaoh, "This is the finger of God." But Pharaoh's heart was hard and he would not listen, just as the LORD had said.

²⁰Then the LORD said to Moses, "Get up early in the morning and confront Pharaoh as he goes to the water and say to him, 'This is what the LORD says: Let my people go, so that they may worship me. ²¹If you do not let my people go, I will send swarms of flies on you and your officials, on your people and into your houses. The houses of the Egyptians will be full of flies, and even the ground where they are.

²²" 'But on that day I will deal differently with the land of Goshen, where my people live; no swarms of flies will be there, so that you will know that I, the LORD, am in this land. ²³I will make a distinction*p* between my people and your people. This miraculous sign will occur tomorrow.' "

²⁴And the LORD did this. Dense swarms of flies poured into Pharaoh's palace and into the houses of his officials, and throughout Egypt the land was ruined by the flies.

²⁵Then Pharaoh summoned Moses and Aaron and said, "Go, sacrifice to your God here in the land."

²⁶But Moses said, "That would not be right. The sacrifices we offer the LORD our God would be detestable to the Egyptians. And if we offer sacrifices that are detestable in their eyes, will they not stone us? ²⁷We must take a three-day journey into the desert to offer sacrifices to the LORD our God, as he commands us."

²⁸Pharaoh said, "I will let you go to offer sacrifices to the LORD your God in the desert, but you must not go very far. Now pray for me."

²⁹Moses answered, "As soon as I leave you, I will pray to the LORD, and tomorrow the flies will leave Pharaoh and his officials and his people. Only be sure that Pharaoh does not act deceitfully again by not letting the people go to offer sacrifices to the LORD."

³⁰Then Moses left Pharaoh and prayed to the LORD, ³¹and the LORD did what Moses asked: The flies left Pharaoh and his officials and his people; not a fly remained. ³²But this time also Pharaoh hardened his heart and would not let the people go.

9 Then the LORD said to Moses, "Go to Pharaoh and say to him, 'This is what the LORD, the God of the Hebrews, says: "Let my people go, so that they may worship me." ²If you refuse to let them go and continue to hold

p23 Septuagint and Vulgate; Hebrew will put a deliverance

them back, ³the hand of the LORD will bring a terrible plague on your livestock in the field—on your horses and donkeys and camels and on your cattle and sheep and goats. ⁴But the LORD will make a distinction between the livestock of Israel and that of Egypt, so that no animal belonging to the Israelites will die.' "

⁵The LORD set a time and said, "Tomorrow the LORD will do this in the land." ⁶And the next day the LORD did it: All the livestock of the Egyptians died, but not one animal belonging to the Israelites died. ⁷Pharaoh sent men to investigate and found that not even one of the animals of the Israelites had died. Yet his heart was unyielding and he would not let the people go.

⁸Then the LORD said to Moses and Aaron, "Take handfuls of soot from a furnace and have Moses toss it into the air in the presence of Pharaoh. ⁹It will become fine dust over the whole land of Egypt, and festering boils will break out on men and animals throughout the land."

¹⁰So they took soot from a furnace and stood before Pharaoh. Moses tossed it into the air, and festering boils broke out on men and animals. ¹¹The magicians could not stand before Moses because of the boils that were on them and on all the Egyptians. ¹²But the LORD hardened Pharaoh's heart and he would not listen to Moses and Aaron, just as the LORD had said to Moses.

¹³Then the LORD said to Moses, "Get up early in the morning, confront Pharaoh and say to him, 'This is what the LORD, the God of the Hebrews, says: Let my people go, so that they may worship me, ¹⁴or this time I will send the full force of my plagues against you and against your officials and your people, so you may know that there is no one like me in all the earth. ¹⁵For by now I could have stretched out my hand and struck you and your people with a plague that would have wiped you off the earth. ¹⁶But I have raised you up*q* for this very purpose, that I might show you my power and that my name might be proclaimed in all the earth. ¹⁷You still set yourself against my people and will not let them go. ¹⁸Therefore, at this time tomorrow I will send the worst hailstorm that has ever fallen on Egypt, from the day it was founded till now. ¹⁹Give an order now to bring your livestock and everything you have in the field to a place of shelter, because the hail will fall on every man and animal that has not been brought in and is still out in the field, and they will die.' "

²⁰Those officials of Pharaoh who feared the word of the LORD hurried to bring their slaves and their livestock inside. ²¹But those who ignored the word of the LORD left their slaves and livestock in the field.

²²Then the LORD said to Moses, "Stretch out your hand toward the sky so that hail will fall all over Egypt—on men and animals and on everything growing in the fields of Egypt." ²³When Moses stretched out his staff toward the sky, the LORD sent thunder and hail, and lightning flashed down to the ground. So the LORD rained hail on the land of Egypt; ²⁴hail fell and lightning flashed back and forth. It was the worst storm in all the land of Egypt since it had become a nation. ²⁵Throughout Egypt hail struck everything in the fields—both men and animals; it beat down everything growing in the fields and stripped every tree. ²⁶The only place it did not hail was the land of Goshen, where the Israelites were.

²⁷Then Pharaoh summoned Moses and Aaron. "This time I have sinned," he said to them. "The LORD is in the right, and I and my people are in the wrong. ²⁸Pray to the LORD, for we have had enough thunder and hail. I will let you go; you don't have to stay any longer."

²⁹Moses replied, "When I have gone out of the city, I will spread out my hands in prayer to the LORD. The thunder will stop and there will be no more hail, so you may know that the earth is the LORD's. ³⁰But I know that you and your officials still do not fear the LORD God."

³¹(The flax and barley were destroyed, since the barley had headed and the flax was in bloom. ³²The wheat and spelt, however, were not destroyed, because they ripen later.)

³³Then Moses left Pharaoh and went out of the city. He spread out his hands toward the LORD; the thunder and hail stopped, and the rain no longer poured down on the land. ³⁴When Pharaoh saw that the rain and hail and thunder had stopped, he sinned again: He and his officials hardened their hearts. ³⁵So Pharaoh's heart was hard and he would not let the Israelites go, just as the LORD had said through Moses.

10

Then the LORD said to Moses, "Go to Pharaoh, for I have hardened his heart and the hearts of his officials so that I may perform these miraculous signs of mine among them ²that you may tell your chil-

q16 Or have spared you

dren and grandchildren how I dealt harshly with the Egyptians and how I performed my signs among them, and that you may know that I am the LORD."

³So Moses and Aaron went to Pharaoh and said to him, "This is what the LORD, the God of the Hebrews, says: 'How long will you refuse to humble yourself before me? Let my people go, so that they may worship me. ⁴If you refuse to let them go, I will bring locusts into your country tomorrow. ⁵They will cover the face of the ground so that it cannot be seen. They will devour what little you have left after the hail, including every tree that is growing in your fields. ⁶They will fill your houses and those of all your officials and all the Egyptians—something neither your fathers nor your forefathers have ever seen from the day they settled in this land till now.'" Then Moses turned and left Pharaoh.

⁷Pharaoh's officials said to him, "How long will this man be a snare to us? Let the people go, so that they may worship the LORD their God. Do you not yet realize that Egypt is ruined?"

⁸Then Moses and Aaron were brought back to Pharaoh. "Go, worship the LORD your God," he said. "But just who will be going?"

⁹Moses answered, "We will go with our young and old, with our sons and daughters, and with our flocks and herds, because we are to celebrate a festival to the LORD."

¹⁰Pharaoh said, "The LORD be with you—if I let you go, along with your women and children! Clearly you are bent on evil.ʳ ¹¹No! Have only the men go; and worship the LORD, since that's what you have been asking for." Then Moses and Aaron were driven out of Pharaoh's presence.

¹²And the LORD said to Moses, "Stretch out your hand over Egypt so that locusts will swarm over the land and devour everything growing in the fields, everything left by the hail."

¹³So Moses stretched out his staff over Egypt, and the LORD made an east wind blow across the land all that day and all that night. By morning the wind had brought the locusts; ¹⁴they invaded all Egypt and settled down in every area of the country in great numbers. Never before had there

been such a plague of locusts, nor will there ever be again. ¹⁵They covered all the ground until it was black. They devoured all that was left after the hail—everything growing in the fields and the fruit on the trees. Nothing green remained on tree or plant in all the land of Egypt.

¹⁶Pharaoh quickly summoned Moses and Aaron and said, "I have sinned against the LORD your God and against you. ¹⁷Now forgive my sin once more and pray to the LORD your God to take this deadly plague away from me."

¹⁸Moses then left Pharaoh and prayed to the LORD. ¹⁹And the LORD changed the wind to a very strong west wind, which caught up the locusts and carried them into the Red Sea.ˢ Not a locust was left anywhere in Egypt. ²⁰But the LORD hardened Pharaoh's heart, and he would not let the Israelites go.

²¹Then the LORD said to Moses, "Stretch out your hand toward the sky so that darkness will spread over Egypt—darkness that can be felt." ²²So Moses stretched out his hand toward the sky, and total darkness covered all Egypt for three days. ²³No one could see anyone else or leave his place for three days. Yet all the Israelites had light in the places where they lived.

²⁴Then Pharaoh summoned Moses and said, "Go, worship the LORD. Even your women and children may go with you; only leave your flocks and herds behind."

²⁵But Moses said, "You must allow us to have sacrifices and burnt offerings to present to the LORD our God. ²⁶Our livestock too must go with us; not a hoof is to be left behind. We have to use some of them in worshiping the LORD our God, and until we get there we will not know what we are to use to worship the LORD."

²⁷But the LORD hardened Pharaoh's heart, and he was not willing to let them go. ²⁸Pharaoh said to Moses, "Get out of my sight! Make sure you do not appear before me again! The day you see my face you will die."

²⁹"Just as you say," Moses replied, "I will never appear before you again."

ʳ10 Or *Be careful, trouble is in store for you!*   ˢ19 Hebrew *Yam Suph*; that is, Sea of Reeds

---

🔦 **Discovering the Word** 1. What was the sign of God's supremacy (7:8–13)? 2. How did Pharaoh react to these "mighty acts of judgment," as God called them (7:4; 8:8, 25–32)? 3. What was the basic issue between God and Pharaoh (7:5, 17; 8:10, 22)? 4. What new disclosure does God make to Pharaoh about his power (8:22–23)? 5. Some of the Egyptians responded positively to this outbreak of judgments (9:20). How do people interpret natural disasters today?   6. What pattern of behavior has by this time become well established in Pharaoh (8:15, 30–32; 9:34–35)?

 Applying the Word   1. In what matters is God in conflict with earthly powers today?   2. When you are humbled by God, how can you regain your self-confidence and your trust in God?

 Responding in Prayer Give thanks to your loving, gracious Father, who "has raised you up for this very purpose"—to demonstrate his power and proclaim his name in all the earth.

6 / *Exodus 11:1—12:28*
Night of Death and Deliverance

DEATH IS A powerful, painful lesson. It gets our attention as nothing else does. It's also unavoidable. It was God's final recourse in showing both his supremacy to Pharaoh and his power to liberate his people. When Pharaoh refused God's ultimatum, thousands perished; when Israel heeded his way of deliverance, thousands lived. The final act of judgment is thus a stark portrayal of how every person's fate hinges on either believing or disbelieving the one true and living God in heaven.

 Warming Up to God Sit quietly for a few moments and recall the events of your salvation. Thank the Lord for the way he "drew you out of Egypt."

 Read Exodus 11:1—12:28.

11 Now the LORD had said to Moses, "I will bring one more plague on Pharaoh and on Egypt. After that, he will let you go from here, and when he does, he will drive you out completely. ²Tell the people that men and women alike are to ask their neighbors for articles of silver and gold." ³(The LORD made the Egyptians favorably disposed toward the people, and Moses himself was highly regarded in Egypt by Pharaoh's officials and by the people.)

⁴So Moses said, "This is what the LORD says: 'About midnight I will go throughout Egypt. ⁵Every firstborn son in Egypt will die, from the firstborn son of Pharaoh, who sits on the throne, to the firstborn son of the slave girl, who is at her hand mill, and all the firstborn of the cattle as well. ⁶There will be loud wailing throughout Egypt—worse than there has ever been or ever will be again. ⁷But among the Israelites not a dog will bark at any man or animal.' Then you will know that the LORD makes a distinction between Egypt and Israel. ⁸All these officials of yours will come to me, bowing down before me and saying, 'Go, you and all the people who follow you!' After that I will leave." Then Moses, hot with anger, left Pharaoh.

⁹The LORD had said to Moses, "Pharaoh will refuse to listen to you—so that my wonders may be multiplied in Egypt." ¹⁰Moses and Aaron performed all these wonders before Pharaoh, but the LORD hardened Pharaoh's heart, and he would not let the Israelites go out of his country.

12 The LORD said to Moses and Aaron in Egypt, ²"This month is to be for you the first month, the first month of your year. ³Tell the whole community of Israel that on the tenth day of this month each man is to take a lamb[†] for his family, one for each household. ⁴If any household is too small for a whole lamb, they must share one with their nearest neighbor, having taken into account the number of people there are. You are to determine the amount of lamb needed in accordance with what each person will eat. ⁵The animals you choose must be year-old males without defect, and you may take them from the sheep or the goats. ⁶Take care of them until the fourteenth day of the month, when all the people of the community of Israel must slaughter them at twilight. ⁷Then they are to take some of the blood and put it on the sides and tops of the doorframes of the houses where they eat the lambs. ⁸That same night they

†3 The Hebrew word can mean *lamb* or *kid*; also in verse 4.

are to eat the meat roasted over the fire, along with bitter herbs, and bread made without yeast. ⁹Do not eat the meat raw or cooked in water, but roast it over the fire—head, legs and inner parts. ¹⁰Do not leave any of it till morning; if some is left till morning, you must burn it. ¹¹This is how you are to eat it: with your cloak tucked into your belt, your sandals on your feet and your staff in your hand. Eat it in haste; it is the LORD's Passover.

¹²"On that same night I will pass through Egypt and strike down every firstborn—both men and animals—and I will bring judgment on all the gods of Egypt. I am the LORD. ¹³The blood will be a sign for you on the houses where you are; and when I see the blood, I will pass over you. No destructive plague will touch you when I strike Egypt.

¹⁴"This is a day you are to commemorate; for the generations to come you shall celebrate it as a festival to the LORD—a lasting ordinance. ¹⁵For seven days you are to eat bread made without yeast. On the first day remove the yeast from your houses, for whoever eats anything with yeast in it from the first day through the seventh must be cut off from Israel. ¹⁶On the first day hold a sacred assembly, and another one on the seventh day. Do no work at all on these days, except to prepare food for everyone to eat—that is all you may do.

¹⁷"Celebrate the Feast of Unleavened Bread, because it was on this very day that I brought your divisions out of Egypt. Celebrate this day as a lasting ordinance for the generations to come.

¹⁸In the first month you are to eat bread made without yeast, from the evening of the fourteenth day until the evening of the twenty-first day. ¹⁹For seven days no yeast is to be found in your houses. And whoever eats anything with yeast in it must be cut off from the community of Israel, whether he is an alien or native-born. ²⁰Eat nothing made with yeast. Wherever you live, you must eat unleavened bread."

²¹Then Moses summoned all the elders of Israel and said to them, "Go at once and select the animals for your families and slaughter the Passover lamb. ²²Take a bunch of hyssop, dip it into the blood in the basin and put some of the blood on the top and on both sides of the doorframe. Not one of you shall go out the door of his house until morning. ²³When the LORD goes through the land to strike down the Egyptians, he will see the blood on the top and sides of the doorframe and will pass over that doorway, and he will not permit the destroyer to enter your houses and strike you down.

²⁴"Obey these instructions as a lasting ordinance for you and your descendants. ²⁵When you enter the land that the LORD will give you as he promised, observe this ceremony. ²⁶And when your children ask you, 'What does this ceremony mean to you?' ²⁷then tell them, 'It is the Passover sacrifice to the LORD, who passed over the houses of the Israelites in Egypt and spared our homes when he struck down the Egyptians.' " Then the people bowed down and worshiped. ²⁸The Israelites did just what the LORD commanded Moses and Aaron.

Discovering the Word 1. What is God's promise and instruction to Moses (11:1–2)? 2. How do you account for the Egyptians' change in attitude toward God's people and Moses (11:3)? 3. What is to be the nature, scope and result of God's final judgment on Egypt (11:4–7)? 4. What steps are the Israelites to take to be spared (12:1–13)? 5. Why were they to eat the meal "in haste" (12:11)? 6. Describe the memorial Feast of Unleavened Bread (12:14–20).

Applying the Word 1. Like Moses, how can we continue to trust God in the face of seemingly irresistible unbelief among friends, family or relatives? 2. The shield against the "destroyer" (12:23) in Egypt was the blood of a perfect lamb. Christ's blood secures the Christian's deliverance from eternal death (Jn 1:29; Heb 9:14; Rev 5:13). As you reflect on the powerful imagery of the Lord's Passover, and also on Christ's sacrifice, what response and deeds would be appropriate?

Responding in Prayer Thank Jesus for being your Passover lamb and for the remarkable foreshadowing of his coming to earth in the Israelites' exodus from Egypt.

7 / *Exodus 12:29—13:16*
Freedom and Its Cost

FREEDOM HAS A high price. For some political refugees today it means a perilous sea journey along the coast of Southeast Asia. For others, a dangerous trek over Central American mountains. In Europe it often costs job and even family. In this study we find what Israel's freedom cost—for both the losers and the winners. God secured the liberation of his people, but this in turn cost them the rights to their most precious possessions.

 Warming Up to God What does it mean to be "free in Christ"?

 Read Exodus 12:29—13:16.

²⁹At midnight the LORD struck down all the firstborn in Egypt, from the firstborn of Pharaoh, who sat on the throne, to the firstborn of the prisoner, who was in the dungeon, and the firstborn of all the livestock as well. ³⁰Pharaoh and all his officials and all the Egyptians got up during the night, and there was loud wailing in Egypt, for there was not a house without someone dead.

³¹During the night Pharaoh summoned Moses and Aaron and said, "Up! Leave my people, you and the Israelites! Go, worship the LORD as you have requested. ³²Take your flocks and herds, as you have said, and go. And also bless me."

³³The Egyptians urged the people to hurry and leave the country. "For otherwise," they said, "we will all die!" ³⁴So the people took their dough before the yeast was added, and carried it on their shoulders in kneading troughs wrapped in clothing. ³⁵The Israelites did as Moses instructed and asked the Egyptians for articles of silver and gold and for clothing. ³⁶The LORD had made the Egyptians favorably disposed toward the people, and they gave them what they asked for; so they plundered the Egyptians.

³⁷The Israelites journeyed from Rameses to Succoth. There were about six hundred thousand men on foot, besides women and children. ³⁸Many other people went up with them, as well as large droves of livestock, both flocks and herds. ³⁹With the dough they had brought from Egypt, they baked cakes of unleavened bread. The dough was without yeast because they had been driven out of Egypt and did not have time to prepare food for themselves.

⁴⁰Now the length of time the Israelite people lived in Egypt[u] was 430 years. ⁴¹At the end of the 430 years, to the very day, all the LORD's divisions left Egypt. ⁴²Because the LORD kept vigil that night

to bring them out of Egypt, on this night all the Israelites are to keep vigil to honor the LORD for the generations to come.

⁴³The LORD said to Moses and Aaron, "These are the regulations for the Passover:

"No foreigner is to eat of it. ⁴⁴Any slave you have bought may eat of it after you have circumcised him, ⁴⁵but a temporary resident and a hired worker may not eat of it.

⁴⁶"It must be eaten inside one house; take none of the meat outside the house. Do not break any of the bones. ⁴⁷The whole community of Israel must celebrate it.

⁴⁸"An alien living among you who wants to celebrate the LORD's Passover must have all the males in his household circumcised; then he may take part like one born in the land. No uncircumcised male may eat of it. ⁴⁹The same law applies to the native-born and to the alien living among you."

⁵⁰All the Israelites did just what the LORD had commanded Moses and Aaron. ⁵¹And on that very day the LORD brought the Israelites out of Egypt by their divisions.

13 The LORD said to Moses, ²"Consecrate to me every firstborn male. The first offspring of every womb among the Israelites belongs to me, whether man or animal."

³Then Moses said to the people, "Commemorate this day, the day you came out of Egypt, out of the land of slavery, because the LORD brought you out of it with a mighty hand. Eat nothing containing yeast. ⁴Today, in the month of Abib, you are leaving. ⁵When the LORD brings you into the land of the Canaanites, Hittites, Amorites, Hivites and Jebusites—the land he swore to your

---

u 40 Masoretic Text; Samaritan Pentateuch and Septuagint *Egypt and Canaan* forefathers to give you, a land flowing with milk and honey—you are to observe this ceremony in this month: ⁶For seven days eat bread made without yeast and on the seventh day hold a festival to the LORD. ⁷Eat unleavened bread during those seven days; nothing with yeast in it is to be seen among you, nor shall any yeast be seen anywhere within your borders. ⁸On that day tell your son, 'I do this because of what the LORD did for me when I came out of Egypt.' ⁹This observance will be for you like a sign on your hand and a reminder on your forehead that the law of the LORD is to be on your lips. For the LORD brought you out of Egypt with his mighty hand. ¹⁰You must keep this ordinance at the appointed time year after year.

¹¹After the LORD brings you into the land of the Canaanites and gives it to you, as he promised on oath to you and your forefathers, ¹²you are to give over to the LORD the first offspring of every womb. All the firstborn males of your livestock belong to the LORD. ¹³Redeem with a lamb every firstborn donkey, but if you do not redeem it, break its neck. Redeem every firstborn among your sons.

¹⁴"In days to come, when your son asks you, 'What does this mean?' say to him, 'With a mighty hand the LORD brought us out of Egypt, out of the land of slavery. ¹⁵When Pharaoh stubbornly refused to let us go, the LORD killed every firstborn in Egypt, both man and animal. This is why I sacrifice to the LORD the first male offspring of every womb and redeem each of my firstborn sons.' ¹⁶And it will be like a sign on your hand and a symbol on your forehead that the LORD brought us out of Egypt with his mighty hand."

Discovering the Word 1. What contrasts do you observe between Pharaoh's attitude and behavior now and his earlier encounters with Moses and Aaron (12:29–32)? 2. God fulfilled his warnings and promises (see 3:20–22; 4:23). What significance would this have for Israel's understanding of God's nature and character? 3. How would the Passover restrictions (12:43–49) encourage foreigners and others to worship God and, at the same time, preserve Israel from religious compromise and contamination? 4. God calls Israel to dedicate to him that which he has just delivered—the whole nation, not just the firstborn of man and beast. What plan does God have for perpetuating this ordinance (13:8–10, 14–15)? 5. What was the basis of God's authority to claim the firstborn as his own?

Applying the Word 1. How can we guard the essential elements of our faith in Jesus Christ and, at the same time, extend his offer of salvation to all people? 2. How do you maintain fresh impressions of your own deliverance from the guilt and enslavement of sin?

Responding in Prayer Ask the Lord to show you how to balance freedom in him with the responsibilities of service.

---

8 / *Exodus 13:17—14:31*
From Crisis to Triumph

IMPOSSIBLE JAMS CONVERGE on us at the most unlikely moments. One minute we're cruising down the freeway at 60 mph, and the next instant we slam on the brakes. For the next two hours we're stuck. Wouldn't it be wonderful if we could wave a magic wand and unclog the whole mess? Life is like that. God leads us in and out of jams to test our mettle. In this study, Israel's moment of glorious freedom was shattered by an advancing army. Seemingly, disaster loomed. But God had some things to prove to Egypt, Israel and Moses. Painful lessons indeed.

Warming Up to God Think of a miracle you've experienced. Respond from your heart to the God who loves to surprise you with his tremendous power and creativity.

Read Exodus 13:17—14:31.

¹⁷When Pharaoh let the people go, God did not lead them on the road through the Philistine country, though that was shorter. For God said, "If they face war, they might change their minds and return to Egypt." ¹⁸So God led the people around by the desert road toward the Red Sea.ᵛ The Israelites went up out of Egypt armed for battle.

¹⁹Moses took the bones of Joseph with him because Joseph had made the sons of Israel swear an oath. He had said, "God will surely come to your aid, and then you must carry my bones up with you from this place."ʷ

²⁰After leaving Succoth they camped at Etham on the edge of the desert. ²¹By day the LORD went ahead of them in a pillar of cloud to guide them on their way and by night in a pillar of fire to give them light, so that they could travel by day or night. ²²Neither the pillar of cloud by day nor the pillar of fire by night left its place in front of the people.

14 Then the LORD said to Moses, ²"Tell the Israelites to turn back and encamp near Pi Hahiroth, between Migdol and the sea. They are to encamp by the sea, directly opposite Baal Zephon. ³Pharaoh will think, 'The Israelites are wandering around the land in confusion, hemmed in by the desert.' ⁴And I will harden Pharaoh's heart, and he will pursue them. But I will gain glory for myself through Pharaoh and all his army, and the Egyptians will know that I am the LORD." So the Israelites did this.

⁵When the king of Egypt was told that the people had fled, Pharaoh and his officials changed their minds about them and said, "What have we done? We have let the Israelites go and have lost their services!" ⁶So he had his chariot made ready and took his army with him. ⁷He took six hundred of the best chariots, along with all the other chariots of Egypt, with officers over all of them. ⁸The LORD hardened the heart of Pharaoh king of Egypt, so that he pursued the Israelites, who were marching out boldly. ⁹The Egyptians—all Pharaoh's horses and chariots, horsemenˣ and troops—pursued the Israelites and overtook them as they camped by the sea near Pi Hahiroth, opposite Baal Zephon.

¹⁰As Pharaoh approached, the Israelites looked up, and there were the Egyptians, marching after them. They were terrified and cried out to the LORD. ¹¹They said to Moses, "Was it because there were no graves in Egypt that you brought us to the desert to die? What have you done to us by bringing us out of Egypt? ¹²Didn't we say to you in Egypt, 'Leave us alone; let us serve the Egyptians'? It would have been better for us to serve the Egyptians than to die in the desert!"

¹³Moses answered the people, "Do not be afraid. Stand firm and you will see the deliverance the LORD will bring you today. The Egyptians you see today you will never see again. ¹⁴The LORD will fight for you; you need only to be still."

¹⁵Then the LORD said to Moses, "Why are you crying out to me? Tell the Israelites to move on. ¹⁶Raise your staff and stretch out your hand over the sea to divide the water so that the Israelites can go through the sea on dry ground. ¹⁷I will harden the hearts of the Egyptians so that they will go in after them. And I will gain glory through Pharaoh and all his army, through his chariots and his horsemen. ¹⁸The Egyptians will know that I am the LORD when I gain glory through Pharaoh, his chariots and his horsemen."

¹⁹Then the angel of God, who had been traveling in front of Israel's army, withdrew and went behind them. The pillar of cloud also moved from in front and stood behind them, ²⁰coming between the armies of Egypt and Israel. Throughout the night the cloud brought darkness to the one side and light to the other side; so neither went near the other all night long.

²¹Then Moses stretched out his hand over the sea, and all that night the LORD drove the sea back with a strong east wind and turned it into dry land. The waters were divided, ²²and the Israelites went through the sea on dry ground, with a wall of water on their right and on their left.

²³The Egyptians pursued them, and all Pharaoh's horses and chariots and horsemen followed them into the sea. ²⁴During the last watch of the night the LORD looked down from the pillar of fire and cloud at the Egyptian army and threw it into confusion. ²⁵He made the wheels of their chariots come offʸ so that they had difficulty driving. And the Egyptians said, "Let's get away from the Israelites! The LORD is fighting for them against Egypt."

²⁶Then the LORD said to Moses, "Stretch out your hand over the sea so that the waters may flow back over the Egyptians and their chariots

ᵛ18 Hebrew *Yam Suph*; that is, Sea of Reeds   ʷ19 See Gen. 50:25.
ˣ9 Or *charioteers*; also in verses 17, 18, 23, 26 and 28   ʸ25 Or *He jammed the wheels of their chariots* (see Samaritan Pentateuch, Septuagint and Syriac)

and horsemen." ²⁷Moses stretched out his hand over the sea, and at daybreak the sea went back to its place. The Egyptians were fleeing toward*z* it, and the LORD swept them into the sea. ²⁸The water flowed back and covered the chariots and horsemen—the entire army of Pharaoh that had followed the Israelites into the sea. Not one of them survived.

²⁹But the Israelites went through the sea on dry ground, with a wall of water on their right and on their left. ³⁰That day the LORD saved Israel from the hands of the Egyptians, and Israel saw the Egyptians lying dead on the shore. ³¹And when the Israelites saw the great power the LORD displayed against the Egyptians, the people feared the LORD and put their trust in him and in Moses his servant.

z27 Or from

 Discovering the Word 1. Why did God not take Israel the shortest route to Palestine? 2. What plan does God reveal to Moses (14:1–4)? 3. How did the Israelites react to the onslaught of the Egyptians and why (14:10–12)? 4. Compare each part of Moses' commands (14:13–14) with the Israelites' conditions and attitudes (14:10–12). 5. What did God's plan for escape require of Moses and the people (14:15–18)? 6. What was the outcome of this hair-raising experience for the Egyptians, Moses and Israel (14:17–18, 30–31)?

Applying the Word 1. Faith operates both long-range (Joseph) and short-range (following the cloud pillar). What areas of your life require long-range or short-range trust in God? 2. Think about times when you have felt like Israel, trapped between the Egyptians and the Red Sea. What did you do and why?

Responding in Prayer Thank the Lord for the ways he has miraculously delivered you—either physically or spiritually—from "the Egyptians" in your life.

---

9 / *Exodus 15:1–21*
Praise for the Past and Hope for the Future

MUSIC PLAYS A vital role in Christian worship. Sometimes, however, music causes contention: the old favorites versus the new gospel tunes; organs versus guitars. Overlooked is the fact that God gave us music and singing to praise and glorify his name. Nowhere is this seen more clearly than in the thrilling song service that broke out on the eastern shore of the Red Sea. Moses the statesman, Moses the voice of God became Israel's song leader. Praise and honor to God marked the final triumph over Egypt. How much more do Christians need to sing to God for his victory in Christ.

 Warming Up to God For what do you have reason to praise the Father? List the many ways God has blessed you.

 Read Exodus 15:1–21.

---

15 Then Moses and the Israelites sang this song to the LORD:

"I will sing to the LORD,
  for he is highly exalted.
The horse and its rider
  he has hurled into the sea.
²The LORD is my strength and my song;
  he has become my salvation.
He is my God, and I will praise him,
  my father's God, and I will exalt him.

³The LORD is a warrior;
  the LORD is his name.
⁴Pharaoh's chariots and his army
  he has hurled into the sea.
The best of Pharaoh's officers
  are drowned in the Red Sea.*a*
⁵The deep waters have covered them;
  they sank to the depths like a stone.
⁶"Your right hand, O LORD,

a4 Hebrew Yam Suph; that is, Sea of Reeds; also in verse 22

was majestic in power.
Your right hand, O LORD,
  shattered the enemy.
7In the greatness of your majesty
  you threw down those who opposed you.
You unleashed your burning anger;
  it consumed them like stubble.
8By the blast of your nostrils
  the waters piled up.
The surging waters stood firm like a wall;
  the deep waters congealed in the heart of
    the sea.

9"The enemy boasted,
  'I will pursue, I will overtake them.
I will divide the spoils;
  I will gorge myself on them.
I will draw my sword
  and my hand will destroy them.'
10But you blew with your breath,
  and the sea covered them.
They sank like lead
  in the mighty waters.

11"Who among the gods is like you, O LORD?
  Who is like you—
    majestic in holiness,
    awesome in glory,
    working wonders?
12You stretched out your right hand
  and the earth swallowed them.

13"In your unfailing love you will lead
  the people you have redeemed.
In your strength you will guide them
  to your holy dwelling.

14The nations will hear and tremble;
  anguish will grip the people of Philistia.
15The chiefs of Edom will be terrified,
  the leaders of Moab will be seized with
    trembling,
the people^b of Canaan will melt away;
16 terror and dread will fall upon them.
By the power of your arm
  they will be as still as a stone—
until your people pass by, O LORD,
  until the people you bought^c pass by.
17You will bring them in and plant them
  on the mountain of your inheritance—
the place, O LORD, you made for your
    dwelling,
  the sanctuary, O Lord, your hands
    established.
18The LORD will reign
  for ever and ever."

19When Pharaoh's horses, chariots and horse-men^d went into the sea, the LORD brought the waters of the sea back over them, but the Israelites walked through the sea on dry ground. 20Then Miriam the prophetess, Aaron's sister, took a tambourine in her hand, and all the women followed her, with tambourines and dancing. 21Miriam sang to them:

"Sing to the LORD,
  for he is highly exalted.
The horse and its rider
  he has hurled into the sea."

^b15 Or rulers   ^c16 Or created   ^d19 Or charioteers

 Discovering the Word 1. What inspired this song of victory (v. 1)? 2. What conclusions about God do the people draw from the Red Sea victory (vv. 3–11)? 3. After rehearsing the past, the people look to the future. What enemies lie ahead (vv. 14–15)? 4. What will be the effect of the exodus on these nations (vv. 14–16)? 5. On what basis do the people exude confidence for their future (vv. 13–18)? 6. What role did Miriam and the other women play in the victory celebration and why (vv. 20–21)?

Applying the Word 1. Against what adversaries do you need to see a demonstration of God's power, majesty and holiness? 2. How does the knowledge of God's character and past faithfulness encourage you in anticipation of the future?

Responding in Prayer Pray aloud and tell God his characteristics and qualities.

10 / *Exodus 15:22—17:16*
Adversities of the Desert

ONE OF THE premier sports events in America is the Super Bowl, a football game played each January for the championship of the National Football League. Contending teams get two weeks to prepare. Players and coaches get the best of everything in order to win. Suppose the teams ran out of water and food. Suppose the players mutinied. If that happened, suppose you were the coach. Could you possibly concentrate on your game plans? Of course not. But that's what confronted Moses as he led team Israel. This study chronicles not only defection in the ranks but also attack from outside. Not a pretty picture, really, until we see how God intervened.

 Warming Up to God What needs or longings do you have? Present them to God—and let his peace dwell in your heart and the knowledge that God promises to meet your needs.

 Read Exodus 15:22—17:16.

---

²²Then Moses led Israel from the Red Sea and they went into the Desert of Shur. For three days they traveled in the desert without finding water. ²³When they came to Marah, they could not drink its water because it was bitter. (That is why the place is called Marah.ᵉ) ²⁴So the people grumbled against Moses, saying, "What are we to drink?"

²⁵Then Moses cried out to the Lord, and the Lord showed him a piece of wood. He threw it into the water, and the water became sweet.

There the Lord made a decree and a law for them, and there he tested them. ²⁶He said, "If you listen carefully to the voice of the Lord your God and do what is right in his eyes, if you pay attention to his commands and keep all his decrees, I will not bring on you any of the diseases I brought on the Egyptians, for I am the Lord, who heals you."

²⁷Then they came to Elim, where there were twelve springs and seventy palm trees, and they camped there near the water.

16 The whole Israelite community set out from Elim and came to the Desert of Sin, which is between Elim and Sinai, on the fifteenth day of the second month after they had come out of Egypt. ²In the desert the whole community grumbled against Moses and Aaron. ³The Israelites said to them, "If only we had died by the Lord's hand in Egypt! There we sat around pots of meat and ate all the food we wanted, but you have brought us out into this desert to starve this entire assembly to death."

⁴Then the Lord said to Moses, "I will rain down bread from heaven for you. The people are to go out each day and gather enough for that day. In this way I will test them and see whether they will follow my instructions. ⁵On the sixth day they are to prepare what they bring in, and that is to be twice as much as they gather on the other days."

⁶So Moses and Aaron said to all the Israelites, "In the evening you will know that it was the Lord who brought you out of Egypt, ⁷and in the morning you will see the glory of the Lord, because he has heard your grumbling against him. Who are we, that you should grumble against us?" ⁸Moses also said, "You will know that it was the Lord when he gives you meat to eat in the evening and all the bread you want in the morning, because he has heard your grumbling against him. Who are we? You are not grumbling against us, but against the Lord."

⁹Then Moses told Aaron, "Say to the entire Israelite community, 'Come before the Lord, for he has heard your grumbling.' "

¹⁰While Aaron was speaking to the whole Israelite community, they looked toward the desert, and there was the glory of the Lord appearing in the cloud.

¹¹The Lord said to Moses, ¹²"I have heard the grumbling of the Israelites. Tell them, 'At twilight you will eat meat, and in the morning you will be filled with bread. Then you will know that I am the Lord your God.' "

¹³That evening quail came and covered the camp, and in the morning there was a layer of dew around the camp. ¹⁴When the dew was gone, thin flakes like frost on the ground appeared on the desert floor. ¹⁵When the Israelites saw it, they

ᵉ23 *Marah* means *bitter.*

said to each other, "What is it?" For they did not know what it was.

Moses said to them, "It is the bread the LORD has given you to eat. ¹⁶This is what the LORD has commanded: 'Each one is to gather as much as he needs. Take an omer^f for each person you have in your tent.' "

¹⁷The Israelites did as they were told; some gathered much, some little. ¹⁸And when they measured it by the omer, he who gathered much did not have too much, and he who gathered little did not have too little. Each one gathered as much as he needed.

¹⁹Then Moses said to them, "No one is to keep any of it until morning."

²⁰However, some of them paid no attention to Moses; they kept part of it until morning, but it was full of maggots and began to smell. So Moses was angry with them.

²¹Each morning everyone gathered as much as he needed, and when the sun grew hot, it melted away. ²²On the sixth day, they gathered twice as much—two omers^g for each person—and the leaders of the community came and reported this to Moses. ²³He said to them, "This is what the LORD commanded: 'Tomorrow is to be a day of rest, a holy Sabbath to the LORD. So bake what you want to bake and boil what you want to boil. Save whatever is left and keep it until morning.' "

²⁴So they saved it until morning, as Moses commanded, and it did not stink or get maggots in it. ²⁵"Eat it today," Moses said, "because today is a Sabbath to the LORD. You will not find any of it on the ground today. ²⁶Six days you are to gather it, but on the seventh day, the Sabbath, there will not be any."

²⁷Nevertheless, some of the people went out on the seventh day to gather it, but they found none. ²⁸Then the LORD said to Moses, "How long will you^h refuse to keep my commands and my instructions? ²⁹Bear in mind that the LORD has given you the Sabbath; that is why on the sixth day he gives you bread for two days. Everyone is to stay where he is on the seventh day; no one is to go out." ³⁰So the people rested on the seventh day.

³¹The people of Israel called the bread manna.^i It was white like coriander seed and tasted like wafers made with honey. ³²Moses said, "This is what the LORD has commanded: 'Take an omer of manna and keep it for the generations to come, so they can see the bread I gave you to eat in the desert when I brought you out of Egypt.' "

³³So Moses said to Aaron, "Take a jar and put an omer of manna in it. Then place it before the LORD to be kept for the generations to come."

³⁴As the LORD commanded Moses, Aaron put the manna in front of the Testimony, that it might be kept. ³⁵The Israelites ate manna forty years, until they came to a land that was settled; they ate manna until they reached the border of Canaan.

³⁶(An omer is one tenth of an ephah.)

17 The whole Israelite community set out from the Desert of Sin, traveling from place to place as the LORD commanded. They camped at Rephidim, but there was no water for the people to drink. ²So they quarreled with Moses and said, "Give us water to drink."

Moses replied, "Why do you quarrel with me? Why do you put the LORD to the test?"

³But the people were thirsty for water there, and they grumbled against Moses. They said, "Why did you bring us up out of Egypt to make us and our children and livestock die of thirst?"

⁴Then Moses cried out to the LORD, "What am I to do with these people? They are almost ready to stone me."

⁵The LORD answered Moses, "Walk on ahead of the people. Take with you some of the elders of Israel and take in your hand the staff with which you struck the Nile, and go. ⁶I will stand there before you by the rock at Horeb. Strike the rock, and water will come out of it for the people to drink." So Moses did this in the sight of the elders of Israel. ⁷And he called the place Massah^j and Meribah^k because the Israelites quarreled and because they tested the LORD saying, "Is the LORD among us or not?"

⁸The Amalekites came and attacked the Israelites at Rephidim. ⁹Moses said to Joshua, "Choose some of our men and go out to fight the Amalekites. Tomorrow I will stand on top of the hill with the staff of God in my hands."

¹⁰So Joshua fought the Amalekites as Moses had ordered, and Moses, Aaron and Hur went to the top of the hill. ¹¹As long as Moses held up his hands, the Israelites were winning, but whenever he lowered his hands, the Amalekites were winning. ¹²When Moses' hands grew tired, they took a stone and put it under him and he sat on it. Aaron and Hur held his hands up—one on one

---

^f16 That is, probably about 2 quarts (about 2 liters); also in verses 18, 32, 33 and 36   ^g22 That is, probably about 4 quarts (about 4.5 liters)   ^h28 The Hebrew is plural.   ^i31 *Manna* means *What is it?* (see verse 15).   ^j7 *Massah* means *testing.*   ^k7 *Meribah* means *quarreling.*

side, one on the other—so that his hands remained steady till sunset. ¹³So Joshua overcame the Amalekite army with the sword.

¹⁴Then the LORD said to Moses, "Write this on a scroll as something to be remembered and make sure that Joshua hears it, because I will completely blot out the memory of Amalek from under heaven."

¹⁵Moses built an altar and called it The LORD is my Banner. ¹⁶He said, "For hands were lifted up to the throne of the LORD. The¹ LORD will be at war against the Amalekites from generation to generation."

¹16 Or "Because a hand was against the throne of the LORD, the

 Discovering the Word 1. Put yourself in the shoes of an Israelite three days into the desert with no water. How would you feel? 2. Faced with starvation, the Israelites attacked Moses and Aaron (16:1–3). In what sense were they groaning against God (16:7–8)? 3. Why and how did God respond to Israel's complaints (16:9–15)? 4. In what ways did Israel violate God's commands and why (16:16–30)? 5. Israel's next hurdle is an enemy attack (17:8–16). What was God's plan for victory over the Amalekites? 6. Reflect on how Moses summarized the day. What did he do, what did he emphasize, and why (17:15–16)?

 Applying the Word 1. When you have reached the end of the rope, what do you say to God and to those whom you think are to blame? Why? 2. Reflect on God's meeting your needs in emergencies. How might you be able to keep such events as a testimony to future generations?

 Responding in Prayer What happens after the miracle? Ask God to help you be obedient even after he "parts the Red Sea."

11 / *Exodus 18*
Wise Counsel

IN-LAWS ARE THE favorite butt of jokes. Rarely are they portrayed in a positive light. But God places us in extended families to give us added wisdom and to shave off our rough edges. Jethro, Moses' father-in-law, brought Moses' wife and sons back to him. He also brought praise and worship to God. But he didn't stop there. This study shows how he made Moses face up to a weak link in his command. Jethro could be accused of meddling, but he was God's deliverer for Moses and Israel, just as much as Joshua and his soldiers were (17:8–16). Jethro forces us to examine our motives in doing Christian service.

Warming Up to God What burdens have you felt today as a result of your responsibilities? Tell God about them and let your anxiety slip away.

Read Exodus 18.

18 Now Jethro, the priest of Midian and father-in-law of Moses, heard of everything God had done for Moses and for his people Israel, and how the LORD had brought Israel out of Egypt.

²After Moses had sent away his wife Zipporah, his father-in-law Jethro received her ³and her two sons. One son was named Gershom,ᵐ for Moses

said, "I have become an alien in a foreign land"; ⁴and the other was named Eliezer,ⁿ for he said, "My father's God was my helper; he saved me from the sword of Pharaoh."

⁵Jethro, Moses' father-in-law, together with Moses' sons and wife, came to him in the desert,

ᵐ3 *Gershom sounds like the Hebrew for an alien there.*   ⁿ4 *Eliezer means my God is helper.*

where he was camped near the mountain of God. [6]Jethro had sent word to him, "I, your father-in-law Jethro, am coming to you with your wife and her two sons."

[7]So Moses went out to meet his father-in-law and bowed down and kissed him. They greeted each other and then went into the tent. [8]Moses told his father-in-law about everything the LORD had done to Pharaoh and the Egyptians for Israel's sake and about all the hardships they had met along the way and how the LORD had saved them.

[9]Jethro was delighted to hear about all the good things the LORD had done for Israel in rescuing them from the hand of the Egyptians. [10]He said, "Praise be to the LORD, who rescued you from the hand of the Egyptians and of Pharaoh, and who rescued the people from the hand of the Egyptians. [11]Now I know that the LORD is greater than all other gods, for he did this to those who had treated Israel arrogantly." [12]Then Jethro, Moses' father-in-law, brought a burnt offering and other sacrifices to God, and Aaron came with all the elders of Israel to eat bread with Moses' father-in-law in the presence of God.

[13]The next day Moses took his seat to serve as judge for the people, and they stood around him from morning till evening. [14]When his father-in-law saw all that Moses was doing for the people, he said, "What is this you are doing for the people? Why do you alone sit as judge, while all these people stand around you from morning till evening?"

[15]Moses answered him, "Because the people come to me to seek God's will. [16]Whenever they have a dispute, it is brought to me, and I decide between the parties and inform them of God's decrees and laws."

[17]Moses' father-in-law replied, "What you are doing is not good. [18]You and these people who come to you will only wear yourselves out. The work is too heavy for you; you cannot handle it alone. [19]Listen now to me and I will give you some advice, and may God be with you. You must be the people's representative before God and bring their disputes to him. [20]Teach them the decrees and laws, and show them the way to live and the duties they are to perform. [21]But select capable men from all the people—men who fear God, trustworthy men who hate dishonest gain—and appoint them as officials over thousands, hundreds, fifties and tens. [22]Have them serve as judges for the people at all times, but have them bring every difficult case to you; the simple cases they can decide themselves. That will make your load lighter, because they will share it with you. [23]If you do this and God so commands, you will be able to stand the strain, and all these people will go home satisfied."

[24]Moses listened to his father-in-law and did everything he said. [25]He chose capable men from all Israel and made them leaders of the people, officials over thousands, hundreds, fifties and tens. [26]They served as judges for the people at all times. The difficult cases they brought to Moses, but the simple ones they decided themselves.

[27]Then Moses sent his father-in-law on his way, and Jethro returned to his own country.

Discovering the Word   1. What facts do we learn about Jethro and Moses' family (vv. 1–4)?   2. What do the names of Moses' sons recall for him and his family (vv. 3–4)?   3. Why was worship the appropriate response to Moses' report (vv. 9–12)?   4. What did Jethro observe about Moses' daily routine and the toll this was taking on Moses and the people (vv. 13–18)?   5. How did Moses respond to Jethro's counsel (vv. 19–26)?

Applying the Word   1. What impressions do you have of Moses' ego at this time in his life?   2. Why could it have been easy to overlook God's hand at work in this family reunion, compared to his provision of water, food and victories over the Egyptians and the Amalekites?   3. If you are in a leadership position, think about planning to share the load. What will this do for you, for others and especially for younger leaders coming along?

 Responding in Prayer   Thank God for the people in your life who have given you wise counsel.

12 / *Exodus 19*
Preparing for God

DO YOU TUNE in or tune out when the pastor stands to read the Scripture? You've heard it before? Probably. How then can Christians who have heard the Bible so often recapture the expectancy of hearing it for the first time? A very practical problem indeed. When God spoke to his people the first time, a thunderstorm erupted. We can't expect that every Sunday, so perhaps we have to look within. How eager are we to hear God speak? To listen and obey? In this study we find not only thunder and lightning but a prepared, excited—even fearful—people. The New Testament reminds us that God is still a consuming fire.

 Warming Up to God Spend some time quietly meditating on the nature of God. Prepare your heart to be met by the Lord today.

 Read Exodus 19.

19 In the third month after the Israelites left Egypt—on the very day— they came to the Desert of Sinai. ²After they set out from Rephidim, they entered the Desert of Sinai, and Israel camped there in the desert in front of the mountain.

³Then Moses went up to God, and the LORD called to him from the mountain and said, "This is what you are to say to the house of Jacob and what you are to tell the people of Israel: ⁴'You yourselves have seen what I did to Egypt, and how I carried you on eagles' wings and brought you to myself. ⁵Now if you obey me fully and keep my covenant, then out of all nations you will be my treasured possession. Although the whole earth is mine, ⁶you° will be for me a kingdom of priests and a holy nation.' These are the words you are to speak to the Israelites."

⁷So Moses went back and summoned the elders of the people and set before them all the words the LORD had commanded him to speak. ⁸The people all responded together, "We will do everything the LORD has said." So Moses brought their answer back to the LORD.

⁹The LORD said to Moses, "I am going to come to you in a dense cloud, so that the people will hear me speaking with you and will always put their trust in you." Then Moses told the LORD what the people had said.

¹⁰And the LORD said to Moses, "Go to the people and consecrate them today and tomorrow. Have them wash their clothes ¹¹and be ready by the third day, because on that day the LORD will come down on Mount Sinai in the sight of all the people. ¹²Put limits for the people around the mountain and tell them, 'Be careful that you do not go up the mountain or touch the foot of it. Whoever touches the mountain shall surely be put to death. ¹³He shall surely be stoned or shot with arrows; not a hand is to be laid on him. Whether man or animal, he shall not be permitted to live.' Only when the ram's horn sounds a long blast may they go up to the mountain."

¹⁴After Moses had gone down the mountain to the people, he consecrated them, and they washed their clothes. ¹⁵Then he said to the people, "Prepare yourselves for the third day. Abstain from sexual relations."

¹⁶On the morning of the third day there was thunder and lightning, with a thick cloud over the mountain, and a very loud trumpet blast. Everyone in the camp trembled. ¹⁷Then Moses led the people out of the camp to meet with God, and they stood at the foot of the mountain. ¹⁸Mount Sinai was covered with smoke, because the LORD descended on it in fire. The smoke billowed up from it like smoke from a furnace, the whole mountainᵖ trembled violently, ¹⁹and the sound of the trumpet grew louder and louder. Then Moses spoke and the voice of God answered him.�q

²⁰The LORD descended to the top of Mount Sinai and called Moses to the top of the mountain. So Moses went up ²¹and the LORD said to him, "Go down and warn the people so they do not force their way through to see the LORD and many of them perish. ²²Even the priests, who approach the LORD, must consecrate themselves, or the LORD will break out against them."

²³Moses said to the LORD, "The people cannot come up Mount Sinai, because you yourself

ᵒ5,6 Or *possession, for the whole earth is mine.* 6*You*   ᵖ18 Most Hebrew manuscripts; a few Hebrew manuscripts and Septuagint *all the people*   q19 Or *and God answered him with thunder* warned us, 'Put limits around the mountain and set it apart as holy.'"

²⁴The LORD replied, "Go down and bring Aaron up with you. But the priests and the people must not force their way through to come up to the LORD, or he will break out against them."

²⁵So Moses went down to the people and told them.

 Discovering the Word 1. What prospect did God hold out for his people after three months on the road (vv. 1–6)? 2. What preparations did the people have to make for God's appearance and why (vv. 10–15)? 3. What message was God conveying about himself and about his words (vv. 6, 23)? 4. How and why did the people react to the signs of God's presence on the mountain (vv. 16–19)? 5. Why would the Israelites be tempted to "force their way through to see the LORD" (v. 21)?

 Applying the Word 1. Moses "consecrated" the people so they could meet God (v. 14). What is required of you to meet him? Why? 2. Moses acts as mediator between God and his people. In what sense is Jesus our mediator now (1Ti 2:5–6)? 3. The events of these days cause the people to hear and obey. How can we hold God's Word in holy awe?

 Responding in Prayer Ask the Lord to help you prepare your heart for worship before you come to church.

---

13 / *Exodus 20:1–21*
Ten Keys to God's Character

THE MOST CONVINCING orders are those issued in simple words: Stop! Go! No misunderstanding them. In military training, soldiers learn split-second obedience to concise commands. Their survival depends on it! In Exodus 20, God speaks ten words—the most majestic moral commands ever spoken, the clearest rules for humanity's welfare. They are the foundation of personal and national life. They also reveal God's character. In this passage Israel learns that God is much more than the God of food, water, military victories and natural calamities.

Warming Up to God What part, if any, have the Ten Commandments had in forming your faith?

Read Exodus 20:1–21.

---

20 And God spoke all these words:

²"I am the LORD your God, who brought you out of Egypt, out of the land of slavery.

³"You shall have no other gods beforeʳ me.

⁴"You shall not make for yourself an idol in the form of anything in heaven above or on the earth beneath or in the waters below. ⁵You shall not bow down to them or worship them; for I, the LORD your God, am a jealous God, punishing the children for the sin of the fathers to the third and fourth generation of those who hate me, ⁶but showing love to a thousand ⌊generations⌋ of those who love me and keep my commandments.

⁷"You shall not misuse the name of the LORD your God, for the LORD will not hold anyone guiltless who misuses his name.

⁸"Remember the Sabbath day by keeping it holy. ⁹Six days you shall labor and do all your work, ¹⁰but the seventh day is a Sabbath to the LORD your God. On it you shall not do any work, neither you, nor your son or daughter, nor your manservant or maidservant, nor your animals, nor the alien within your gates. ¹¹For in six days the LORD made the heavens and the earth, the sea, and

ʳ3 Or besides

all that is in them, but he rested on the seventh day. Therefore the LORD blessed the Sabbath day and made it holy.

12"Honor your father and your mother, so that you may live long in the land the LORD your God is giving you.

13"You shall not murder.

14"You shall not commit adultery.

15"You shall not steal.

16"You shall not give false testimony against your neighbor.

17"You shall not covet your neighbor's house. You shall not covet your neighbor's wife, or his manservant or maidser-

vant, his ox or donkey, or anything that belongs to your neighbor."

18When the people saw the thunder and lightning and heard the trumpet and saw the mountain in smoke, they trembled with fear. They stayed at a distance 19and said to Moses, "Speak to us yourself and we will listen. But do not have God speak to us or we will die."

20Moses said to the people, "Do not be afraid. God has come to test you, so that the fear of God will be with you to keep you from sinning."

21The people remained at a distance, while Moses approached the thick darkness where God was.

 Discovering the Word   1. What right did God have to issue these commands (v. 2)?   2. What reasons does God give for prohibiting idolatry (v. 4)?   3. How would you interpret the promise given to those who honor their parents (v. 12)?   4. Murder and adultery (vv. 13–14) are not just external acts; they are matters of the heart (see Mt 5:21–30). What, then, does it mean to obey these commands?   5. In what way is coveting (v. 17) a wrong not only against our neighbor but against God?

 Applying the Word   1. What "other gods" or idols compete for your allegiance?   2. In today's world, how can we observe God's sabbath principle (vv. 8–11)?

Responding in Prayer   Reflect on all the commands and, as needed, follow the promise of 1 John 1:9, asking God to purify your heart and life anew.

---

14 / *Exodus 20:22—23:19*
A Well-Ordered Society

"DO NOT COOK a young goat in its mother's milk." That law seems to have about as much relevance as the 55 mph speed limit. But long before Congress got into the act, God gave laws to his nation that addressed serious social ills that still plague us today. Not goat's-milk stew or speed limits—but what about murder, robbery and rape? What about justice and bribery? Who cares for the helpless? In this study Moses conveys God's plan for a newly born nation, whose fundamental credo was "You are to be my holy people" (22:31). Holiness is never outdated.

 Warming Up to God   What is the purpose for rules in society? Think of ways God's law has protected you, and thank God for instituting it.

 Read Exodus 20:22—23:19.

22Then the LORD said to Moses, "Tell the Israelites this: 'You have seen for yourselves that I have spoken to you from heaven: 23Do not make any gods to be alongside me; do not make for yourselves gods of silver or gods of gold. 24" 'Make an altar of earth for me and sacrifice on it your burnt offerings and fellowship offerings,⁵ your sheep and goats and your cattle.

Wherever I cause my name to be honored, I will come to you and bless you. 25If you make an altar of stones for me, do not build it with dressed stones, for you will defile it if you use a tool on it. 26And do not go up to my altar on steps, lest your nakedness be exposed on it.'

⁵24 Traditionally *peace offerings*

21

"These are the laws you are to set before them:

2"If you buy a Hebrew servant, he is to serve you for six years. But in the seventh year, he shall go free, without paying anything. 3If he comes alone, he is to go free alone; but if he has a wife when he comes, she is to go with him. 4If his master gives him a wife and she bears him sons or daughters, the woman and her children shall belong to her master, and only the man shall go free.

5"But if the servant declares, 'I love my master and my wife and children and do not want to go free,' 6then his master must take him before the judges.[t] He shall take him to the door or the doorpost and pierce his ear with an awl. Then he will be his servant for life.

7"If a man sells his daughter as a servant, she is not to go free as menservants do. 8If she does not please the master who has selected her for himself,[u] he must let her be redeemed. He has no right to sell her to foreigners, because he has broken faith with her. 9If he selects her for his son, he must grant her the rights of a daughter. 10If he marries another woman, he must not deprive the first one of her food, clothing and marital rights. 11If he does not provide her with these three things, she is to go free, without any payment of money.

12"Anyone who strikes a man and kills him shall surely be put to death. 13However, if he does not do it intentionally, but God lets it happen, he is to flee to a place I will designate. 14But if a man schemes and kills another man deliberately, take him away from my altar and put him to death.

15"Anyone who attacks[v] his father or his mother must be put to death.

16"Anyone who kidnaps another and either sells him or still has him when he is caught must be put to death.

17"Anyone who curses his father or mother must be put to death.

18"If men quarrel and one hits the other with a stone or with his fist[w] and he does not die but is confined to bed, 19the one who struck the blow will not be held responsible if the other gets up and walks around outside with his staff; however, he must pay the injured man for the loss of his time and see that he is completely healed.

20"If a man beats his male or female slave with a rod and the slave dies as a direct result, he must be punished, 21but he is not to be punished if the slave gets up after a day or two, since the slave is his property.

22"If men who are fighting hit a pregnant woman and she gives birth prematurely[x] but there is no serious injury, the offender must be fined whatever the woman's husband demands and the court allows. 23But if there is serious injury, you are to take life for life, 24eye for eye, tooth for tooth, hand for hand, foot for foot, 25burn for burn, wound for wound, bruise for bruise.

26"If a man hits a manservant or maidservant in the eye and destroys it, he must let the servant go free to compensate for the eye. 27And if he knocks out the tooth of a manservant or maidservant, he must let the servant go free to compensate for the tooth.

28"If a bull gores a man or a woman to death, the bull must be stoned to death, and its meat must not be eaten. But the owner of the bull will not be held responsible. 29If, however, the bull has had the habit of goring and the owner has been warned but has not kept it penned up and it kills a man or woman, the bull must be stoned and the owner also must be put to death. 30However, if payment is demanded of him, he may redeem his life by paying whatever is demanded. 31This law also applies if the bull gores a son or daughter. 32If the bull gores a male or female slave, the owner must pay thirty shekels[y] of silver to the master of the slave, and the bull must be stoned.

33"If a man uncovers a pit or digs one and fails to cover it and an ox or a donkey falls into it, 34the owner of the pit must pay for the loss; he must pay its owner, and the dead animal will be his.

35"If a man's bull injures the bull of another and it dies, they are to sell the live one and divide both the money and the dead animal equally. 36However, if it was known that the bull had the habit of goring, yet the owner did not keep it penned up, the owner must pay, animal for animal, and the dead animal will be his.

22

"If a man steals an ox or a sheep and slaughters it or sells it, he must pay back five head of cattle for the ox and four sheep for the sheep.

---

t6 Or before God   u8 Or master so that he does not choose her
v15 Or kills   w18 Or with a tool   x22 Or she has a miscarriage
y32 That is, about 12 ounces (about 0.3 kilogram)

²"If a thief is caught breaking in and is struck so that he dies, the defender is not guilty of bloodshed; ³but if it happens_z after sunrise, he is guilty of bloodshed.

"A thief must certainly make restitution, but if he has nothing, he must be sold to pay for his theft.

⁴"If the stolen animal is found alive in his possession—whether ox or donkey or sheep—he must pay back double.

⁵"If a man grazes his livestock in a field or vineyard and lets them stray and they graze in another man's field, he must make restitution from the best of his own field or vineyard.

⁶"If a fire breaks out and spreads into thornbushes so that it burns shocks of grain or standing grain or the whole field, the one who started the fire must make restitution.

⁷"If a man gives his neighbor silver or goods for safekeeping and they are stolen from the neighbor's house, the thief, if he is caught, must pay back double. ⁸But if the thief is not found, the owner of the house must appear before the judges_a to determine whether he has laid his hands on the other man's property. ⁹In all cases of illegal possession of an ox, a donkey, a sheep, a garment, or any other lost property about which somebody says, 'This is mine,' both parties are to bring their cases before the judges. The one whom the judges declare_b guilty must pay back double to his neighbor.

¹⁰"If a man gives a donkey, an ox, a sheep or any other animal to his neighbor for safekeeping and it dies or is injured or is taken away while no one is looking, ¹¹the issue between them will be settled by the taking of an oath before the Lord that the neighbor did not lay hands on the other person's property. The owner is to accept this, and no restitution is required. ¹²But if the animal was stolen from the neighbor, he must make restitution to the owner. ¹³If it was torn to pieces by a wild animal, he shall bring in the remains as evidence and he will not be required to pay for the torn animal.

¹⁴"If a man borrows an animal from his neighbor and it is injured or dies while the owner is not present, he must make restitution. ¹⁵But if the owner is with the animal, the borrower will not have to pay. If the animal was hired, the money paid for the hire covers the loss.

¹⁶"If a man seduces a virgin who is not pledged to be married and sleeps with her, he must pay the bride-price, and she shall be his wife. ¹⁷If her father absolutely refuses to give her to him, he must still pay the bride-price for virgins.

¹⁸"Do not allow a sorceress to live.

¹⁹"Anyone who has sexual relations with an animal must be put to death.

²⁰"Whoever sacrifices to any god other than the Lord must be destroyed._c

²¹"Do not mistreat an alien or oppress him, for you were aliens in Egypt.

²²"Do not take advantage of a widow or an orphan. ²³If you do and they cry out to me, I will certainly hear their cry. ²⁴My anger will be aroused, and I will kill you with the sword; your wives will become widows and your children fatherless.

²⁵"If you lend money to one of my people among you who is needy, do not be like a moneylender; charge him no interest._d ²⁶If you take your neighbor's cloak as a pledge, return it to him by sunset, ²⁷because his cloak is the only covering he has for his body. What else will he sleep in? When he cries out to me, I will hear, for I am compassionate.

²⁸"Do not blaspheme God_e or curse the ruler of your people.

²⁹"Do not hold back offerings from your granaries or your vats._f

"You must give me the firstborn of your sons. ³⁰Do the same with your cattle and your sheep. Let them stay with their mothers for seven days, but give them to me on the eighth day.

³¹"You are to be my holy people. So do not eat the meat of an animal torn by wild beasts; throw it to the dogs.

23

"Do not spread false reports. Do not help a wicked man by being a malicious witness.

²"Do not follow the crowd in doing wrong. When you give testimony in a lawsuit, do not pervert justice by siding with the crowd, ³and do not show favoritism to a poor man in his lawsuit.

⁴"If you come across your enemy's ox or donkey wandering off, be sure to take it back to him. ⁵If you see the donkey of someone who hates you fallen down under its load, do not leave it there; be sure you help him with it.

⁶"Do not deny justice to your poor people in

_z_3 Or _if he strikes him_   _a_8 Or _before God;_ also in verse 9   _b_9 Or _whom God declares_   _c_20 The Hebrew term refers to the irrevocable giving over of things or persons to the Lord, often by totally destroying them.   _d_25 Or _excessive interest_   _e_28 Or _Do not revile the judges_   _f_29 The meaning of the Hebrew for this phrase is uncertain.

their lawsuits. ⁷Have nothing to do with a false charge and do not put an innocent or honest person to death, for I will not acquit the guilty.

⁸"Do not accept a bribe, for a bribe blinds those who see and twists the words of the righteous.

⁹"Do not oppress an alien; you yourselves know how it feels to be aliens, because you were aliens in Egypt.

¹⁰"For six years you are to sow your fields and harvest the crops, ¹¹but during the seventh year let the land lie unplowed and unused. Then the poor among your people may get food from it, and the wild animals may eat what they leave. Do the same with your vineyard and your olive grove.

¹²"Six days do your work, but on the seventh day do not work, so that your ox and your donkey may rest and the slave born in your household, and the alien as well, may be refreshed.

¹³"Be careful to do everything I have said to you. Do not invoke the names of other gods; do not let them be heard on your lips.

¹⁴"Three times a year you are to celebrate a festival to me.

¹⁵"Celebrate the Feast of Unleavened Bread; for seven days eat bread made without yeast, as I commanded you. Do this at the appointed time in the month of Abib, for in that month you came out of Egypt.

"No one is to appear before me empty-handed.

¹⁶"Celebrate the Feast of Harvest with the firstfruits of the crops you sow in your field.

"Celebrate the Feast of Ingathering at the end of the year, when you gather in your crops from the field.

¹⁷"Three times a year all the men are to appear before the Sovereign LORD.

¹⁸"Do not offer the blood of a sacrifice to me along with anything containing yeast.

"The fat of my festival offerings must not be kept until morning.

¹⁹"Bring the best of the firstfruits of your soil to the house of the LORD your God.

"Do not cook a young goat in its mother's milk.

Discovering the Word 1. These laws were intended to improve the conditions of slaves. Why do you think slavery of any kind was permitted (21:1–11)? 2. What crimes are subject to capital punishment and why (21:12–17)? 3. What legal principle underlies punishment of those guilty of causing personal injuries (21:23–25)? 4. Restitution had to be made in certain cases. How does being liable for restitution contribute to the protection of property (22:1–15)? 5. In these miscellaneous laws, what do you sense is God's prime concern (22:16–31)? Why? 6. How does God's concern for justice and mercy stand out here (23:1–9)?

Applying the Word 1. How would you explain your social responsibilities based on the principles here? 2. Compared to what Israel's religious festivals might cost the average Israelite (23:10–19), what does your worship of God cost you?

Responding in Prayer Ask the Lord to give you a proper perspective of the law in your life.

---

15 / *Exodus 23:20—24:18*
Ratifying the Covenant

PEACE TREATIES AND home mortgages are ratified by signatures of the parties involved. Marriages are ratified by vows spoken before witnesses. The point is the same: promises are made and solemnly sealed. God called forth such an agreement at the birth of Israel. A written document was agreed to. Public vows were made. The blood of sacrificial animals sealed the covenant—a landmark in Israel's history. A marriage, as it were, was begun between God and his people. As this study reveals, our commitments to God carry awesome responsibilities.

Warming Up to God List three promises in Scripture given to you by the Father. Let these promises encourage your heart and give you peace as you seek the face of God today.

Read Exodus 23:20—24:18.

20"See, I am sending an angel ahead of you to guard you along the way and to bring you to the place I have prepared. 21Pay attention to him and listen to what he says. Do not rebel against him; he will not forgive your rebellion, since my Name is in him. 22If you listen carefully to what he says and do all that I say, I will be an enemy to your enemies and will oppose those who oppose you. 23My angel will go ahead of you and bring you into the land of the Amorites, Hittites, Perizzites, Canaanites, Hivites and Jebusites, and I will wipe them out. 24Do not bow down before their gods or worship them or follow their practices. You must demolish them and break their sacred stones to pieces. 25Worship the LORD your God, and his blessing will be on your food and water. I will take away sickness from among you, 26and none will miscarry or be barren in your land. I will give you a full life span.

27"I will send my terror ahead of you and throw into confusion every nation you encounter. I will make all your enemies turn their backs and run. 28I will send the hornet ahead of you to drive the Hivites, Canaanites and Hittites out of your way. 29But I will not drive them out in a single year, because the land would become desolate and the wild animals too numerous for you. 30Little by little I will drive them out before you, until you have increased enough to take possession of the land.

31"I will establish your borders from the Red Sea[g] to the Sea of the Philistines,[h] and from the desert to the River.[i] I will hand over to you the people who live in the land and you will drive them out before you. 32Do not make a covenant with them or with their gods. 33Do not let them live in your land, or they will cause you to sin against me, because the worship of their gods will certainly be a snare to you."

24 Then he said to Moses, "Come up to the LORD, you and Aaron, Nadab and Abihu, and seventy of the elders of Israel. You are to worship at a distance, 2but Moses alone is to approach the LORD; the others must not come near. And the people may not come up with him."

3When Moses went and told the people all the LORD's words and laws, they responded with one voice, "Everything the LORD has said we will do." 4Moses then wrote down everything the LORD had said.

He got up early the next morning and built an altar at the foot of the mountain and set up twelve stone pillars representing the twelve tribes of Israel. 5Then he sent young Israelite men, and they offered burnt offerings and sacrificed young bulls as fellowship offerings[j] to the LORD. 6Moses took half of the blood and put it in bowls, and the other half he sprinkled on the altar. 7Then he took the Book of the Covenant and read it to the people. They responded, "We will do everything the LORD has said; we will obey."

8Moses then took the blood, sprinkled it on the people and said, "This is the blood of the covenant that the LORD has made with you in accordance with all these words."

9Moses and Aaron, Nadab and Abihu, and the seventy elders of Israel went up 10and saw the God of Israel. Under his feet was something like a pavement made of sapphire,[k] clear as the sky itself. 11But God did not raise his hand against these leaders of the Israelites; they saw God, and they ate and drank.

12The LORD said to Moses, "Come up to me on the mountain and stay here, and I will give you the tablets of stone, with the law and commands I have written for their instruction."

13Then Moses set out with Joshua his aide, and Moses went up on the mountain of God. 14He said to the elders, "Wait here for us until we come back to you. Aaron and Hur are with you, and anyone involved in a dispute can go to them."

15When Moses went up on the mountain, the cloud covered it, 16and the glory of the LORD settled on Mount Sinai. For six days the cloud covered the mountain, and on the seventh day the LORD called to Moses from within the cloud. 17To the Israelites the glory of the LORD looked like a consuming fire on top of the mountain. 18Then Moses entered the cloud as he went on up the mountain. And he stayed on the mountain forty days and forty nights.

g31 Hebrew *Yam Suph*; that is, Sea of Reeds   h31 That is, the Mediterranean   i31 That is, the Euphrates   j5 Traditionally *peace offerings*   k10 Or *lapis lazuli*

Discovering the Word 1. What perils and temptations lie ahead for the Israelites? 2. In light of these, what commands and promises does God give? 3. After Israel's response (24:3) and Moses' steps to ensure that a public record of the laws would be kept (24:4), why was sacrifice appropriate (24:5)? 4. How would you summarize the basic points of this agreement (covenant) between God and his people? 5. What is the purpose of this mountaintop meeting with God (24:9–18)?

 Applying the Word 1. What perils or temptations are you facing? 2. How does God help you to meet them? 3. God showed his glory to Israel (24:15–18). In what ways have you seen God display his glory in your life?

Responding in Prayer Praise God for his incredible covenant—the solid assurance that God will always be with his children and you, his child.

16 / *Exodus 25—27*
God's Blueprint for Worship

CHURCH BUILDINGS TODAY appear to be designed primarily for functional purposes. We don't build Gothic cathedrals anymore. We struggle to find God's presence in our sanctuaries. For some, architecture is unimportant. For others, it's a prime source of inspiration. Moses and the Israelites didn't have to debate the matter. God gave them his plan for their sanctuary. Beyond the plans, however, were important spiritual lessons. Fortunately for us, the New Testament gives us the fulfillment of these plans in Christ and his church.

 Warming Up to God Where in your life do you need God's guidance? Reflect on this question and ask God to show you the correct path.

 Read Exodus 25—27.

25 The LORD said to Moses, 2"Tell the Israelites to bring me an offering. You are to receive the offering for me from each man whose heart prompts him to give. 3These are the offerings you are to receive from them: gold, silver and bronze; 4blue, purple and scarlet yarn and fine linen; goat hair; 5ram skins dyed red and hides of sea cows[l]; acacia wood; 6olive oil for the light; spices for the anointing oil and for the fragrant incense; 7and onyx stones and other gems to be mounted on the ephod and breastpiece.

8"Then have them make a sanctuary for me, and I will dwell among them. 9Make this tabernacle and all its furnishings exactly like the pattern I will show you.

10"Have them make a chest of acacia wood— two and a half cubits long, a cubit and a half wide, and a cubit and a half high.[m] 11Overlay it with pure gold, both inside and out, and make a gold molding around it. 12Cast four gold rings for it and fasten them to its four feet, with two rings on one side and two rings on the other. 13Then make poles of acacia wood and overlay them with gold. 14Insert the poles into the rings on the sides of the chest to carry it. 15The poles are to remain in the rings of this ark; they are not to be removed. 16Then put in the ark the Testimony, which I will give you.

17"Make an atonement cover[n] of pure gold— two and a half cubits long and a cubit and a half wide.[o] 18And make two cherubim out of hammered gold at the ends of the cover. 19Make one cherub on one end and the second cherub on the other; make the cherubim of one piece with the cover, at the two ends. 20The cherubim are to have their wings spread upward, overshadowing the cover with them. The cherubim are to face each other, looking toward the cover. 21Place the cover on top of the ark and put in the ark the Testimony, which I will give you. 22There, above the cover between the two cherubim that are over the ark of the Testimony, I will meet with you

l5 That is, dugongs   *m10 That is, about 3 3/4 feet (about 1.1 meters) long and 2 1/4 feet (about 0.7 meter) wide and high*
n17 Traditionally a mercy seat   *o17 That is, about 3 3/4 feet (about 1.1 meters) long and 2 1/4 feet (about 0.7 meter) wide*

and give you all my commands for the Israelites.

²³"Make a table of acacia wood—two cubits long, a cubit wide and a cubit and a half high.ᵖ ²⁴Overlay it with pure gold and make a gold molding around it. ²⁵Also make around it a rim a handbreadth�q wide and put a gold molding on the rim. ²⁶Make four gold rings for the table and fasten them to the four corners, where the four legs are. ²⁷The rings are to be close to the rim to hold the poles used in carrying the table. ²⁸Make the poles of acacia wood, overlay them with gold and carry the table with them. ²⁹And make its plates and dishes of pure gold, as well as its pitchers and bowls for the pouring out of offerings. ³⁰Put the bread of the Presence on this table to be before me at all times.

³¹"Make a lampstand of pure gold and hammer it out, base and shaft; its flowerlike cups, buds and blossoms shall be of one piece with it. ³²Six branches are to extend from the sides of the lampstand—three on one side and three on the other. ³³Three cups shaped like almond flowers with buds and blossoms are to be on one branch, three on the next branch, and the same for all six branches extending from the lampstand. ³⁴And on the lampstand there are to be four cups shaped like almond flowers with buds and blossoms. ³⁵One bud shall be under the first pair of branches extending from the lampstand, a second bud under the second pair, and a third bud under the third pair—six branches in all. ³⁶The buds and branches shall all be of one piece with the lampstand, hammered out of pure gold.

³⁷"Then make its seven lamps and set them up on it so that they light the space in front of it. ³⁸Its wick trimmers and trays are to be of pure gold. ³⁹A talentʳ of pure gold is to be used for the lampstand and all these accessories. ⁴⁰See that you make them according to the pattern shown you on the mountain.

26 "Make the tabernacle with ten curtains of finely twisted linen and blue, purple and scarlet yarn, with cherubim worked into them by a skilled craftsman. ²All the curtains are to be the same size—twenty-eight cubits long and four cubits wide.ˢ ³Join five of the curtains together, and do the same with the other five. ⁴Make loops of blue material along the edge of the end curtain in one set, and do the same with the end curtain in the other set. ⁵Make fifty loops on one curtain and fifty loops on the end curtain of the other set,

with the loops opposite each other. ⁶Then make fifty gold clasps and use them to fasten the curtains together so that the tabernacle is a unit.

⁷"Make curtains of goat hair for the tent over the tabernacle—eleven altogether. ⁸All eleven curtains are to be the same size—thirty cubits long and four cubits wide.ᵗ ⁹Join five of the curtains together into one set and the other six into another set. Fold the sixth curtain double at the front of the tent. ¹⁰Make fifty loops along the edge of the end curtain in one set and also along the edge of the end curtain in the other set. ¹¹Then make fifty bronze clasps and put them in the loops to fasten the tent together as a unit. ¹²As for the additional length of the tent curtains, the half curtain that is left over is to hang down at the rear of the tabernacle. ¹³The tent curtains will be a cubitᵘ longer on both sides; what is left will hang over the sides of the tabernacle so as to cover it. ¹⁴Make for the tent a covering of ram skins dyed red, and over that a covering of hides of sea cows.ᵛ

¹⁵"Make upright frames of acacia wood for the tabernacle. ¹⁶Each frame is to be ten cubits long and a cubit and a half wide,ʷ ¹⁷with two projections set parallel to each other. Make all the frames of the tabernacle in this way. ¹⁸Make twenty frames for the south side of the tabernacle ¹⁹and make forty silver bases to go under them—two bases for each frame, one under each projection. ²⁰For the other side, the north side of the tabernacle, make twenty frames ²¹and forty silver bases—two under each frame. ²²Make six frames for the far end, that is, the west end of the tabernacle, ²³and make two frames for the corners at the far end. ²⁴At these two corners they must be double from the bottom all the way to the top, and fitted into a single ring; both shall be like that. ²⁵So there will be eight frames and sixteen silver bases—two under each frame.

²⁶"Also make crossbars of acacia wood: five for the frames on one side of the tabernacle, ²⁷five for those on the other side, and five for the frames on the west, at the far end of the tabernacle. ²⁸The center crossbar is to extend from end to end at the middle of the frames. ²⁹Overlay the frames

ᵖ23 That is, about 3 feet (about 0.9 meter) long and 1 1/2 feet (about 0.5 meter) wide and 2 1/4 feet (about 0.7 meter) high   q25 That is, about 3 inches (about 8 centimeters)   ʳ39 That is, about 75 pounds (about 34 kilograms)   ˢ2 That is, about 42 feet (about 12.5 meters) long and 6 feet (about 1.8 meters) wide   ᵗ8 That is, about 45 feet (about 13.5 meters) long and 6 feet (about 1.8 meters) wide
ᵘ13 That is, about 1 1/2 feet (about 0.5 meter)   ᵛ14 That is, dugongs   ʷ16 That is, about 15 feet (about 4.5 meters) long and 2 1/4 feet (about 0.7 meter) wide

with gold and make gold rings to hold the cross-bars. Also overlay the crossbars with gold.

30"Set up the tabernacle according to the plan shown you on the mountain.

31"Make a curtain of blue, purple and scarlet yarn and finely twisted linen, with cherubim worked into it by a skilled craftsman. 32Hang it with gold hooks on four posts of acacia wood overlaid with gold and standing on four silver bases. 33Hang the curtain from the clasps and place the ark of the Testimony behind the curtain. The curtain will separate the Holy Place from the Most Holy Place. 34Put the atonement cover on the ark of the Testimony in the Most Holy Place. 35Place the table outside the curtain on the north side of the tabernacle and put the lampstand opposite it on the south side.

36"For the entrance to the tent make a curtain of blue, purple and scarlet yarn and finely twisted linen—the work of an embroiderer. 37Make gold hooks for this curtain and five posts of acacia wood overlaid with gold. And cast five bronze bases for them.

27 "Build an altar of acacia wood, three cubits^x high; it is to be square, five cubits long and five cubits wide.^{y} 2Make a horn at each of the four corners, so that the horns and the altar are of one piece, and overlay the altar with bronze. 3Make all its utensils of bronze—its pots to remove the ashes, and its shovels, sprinkling bowls, meat forks and firepans. 4Make a grating for it, a bronze network, and make a bronze ring at each of the four corners of the network. 5Put it under the ledge of the altar so that it is halfway up the altar. 6Make poles of acacia wood for the altar and overlay them with bronze. 7The poles are to be inserted into the rings so they will be on two sides of the altar when it is carried. 8Make the altar hollow, out of boards. It is to be made just as you were shown on the mountain.

9"Make a courtyard for the tabernacle. The south side shall be a hundred cubits^z long and is to have curtains of finely twisted linen, 10with twenty posts and twenty bronze bases and with silver hooks and bands on the posts. 11The north side shall also be a hundred cubits long and is to have curtains, with twenty posts and twenty bronze bases and with silver hooks and bands on the posts.

12"The west end of the courtyard shall be fifty cubits^a wide and have curtains, with ten posts and ten bases. 13On the east end, toward the sunrise, the courtyard shall also be fifty cubits wide. 14Curtains fifteen cubits^b long are to be on one side of the entrance, with three posts and three bases, 15and curtains fifteen cubits long are to be on the other side, with three posts and three bases.

16"For the entrance to the courtyard, provide a curtain twenty cubits^c long, of blue, purple and scarlet yarn and finely twisted linen—the work of an embroiderer—with four posts and four bases. 17All the posts around the courtyard are to have silver bands and hooks, and bronze bases. 18The courtyard shall be a hundred cubits long and fifty cubits wide,^{d} with curtains of finely twisted linen five cubits^e high, and with bronze bases. 19All the other articles used in the service of the tabernacle, whatever their function, including all the tent pegs for it and those for the courtyard, are to be of bronze.

20"Command the Israelites to bring you clear oil of pressed olives for the light so that the lamps may be kept burning. 21In the Tent of Meeting, outside the curtain that is in front of the Testimony, Aaron and his sons are to keep the lamps burning before the LORD from evening till morning. This is to be a lasting ordinance among the Israelites for the generations to come.

^{x}1 That is, about 4 1/2 feet (about 1.3 meters) ^{y}1 That is, about 7 1/2 feet (about 2.3 meters) long and wide ^{z}9 That is, about 150 feet (about 46 meters); also in verse 11 ^{a}12 That is, about 75 feet (about 23 meters); also in verse 13 ^{b}14 That is, about 22 1/2 feet (about 6.9 meters); also in verse 15 ^{c}16 That is, about 30 feet (about 9 meters) ^{d}18 That is, about 150 feet (about 46 meters) long and 75 feet (about 23 meters) wide ^{e}18 That is, about 7 1/2 feet (about 2.3 meters)

Discovering the Word 1. Why would an Israelite feel prompted to give building materials for the tabernacle (25:2)? 2. What was the purpose of the sanctuary (25:8)? 3. Since God does not dwell in a building now (Eph 2:19–22), why should we have church sanctuaries? 4. The wooden chest called the ark held God's Law ("the Testimony"). God promised to meet his people there and teach them his commands (25:16, 22). As Christians, how is our access to God and his commands superior to what is described here? 5. The bread of the Presence (25:30) symbolized that the fruit of our labors comes from and belongs to God. Why would Israel need this daily reminder? 6. What does the value of the materials that went into the tabernacle suggest about the message God was trying to convey to his people (Ex 26)?

Applying the Word 1. Israel's tabernacle "was only a copy of the true one . . . heaven itself" (Heb 9:24). How does this fact enhance your appreciation of what Jesus has done and is doing for you (Heb 9:1–5, 23–28)? 2. How can we carry on the tradition of the bread of the Presence, reminding ourselves that all we have comes from God?

Responding in Prayer Ask God to fill his tabernacle, your heart, with his glory and mercy.

17 / *Exodus 28:1—29:37*
God's Holiness

DEPENDING ON YOUR religious background, you might venerate, despise or just tolerate priests. Regardless of our church affiliation and the various names we give our leaders, we recognize their role in corporate worship. Too often we see the man or woman in leadership and fail to focus on God himself. The focal point of worship is, after all, God, and not the priest or pastor. God's plan for Israel's priesthood pointed to his own holiness and to human sin. Priests and worshipers alike needed atonement for their sins. This study will help you examine your own motives in worship.

 Warming Up to God What do you need to tell God before you read his Word? Confess today's sin or today's frustrations—and let God listen to you as your loving Father.

 Read Exodus 28:1—29:37.

28 "Have Aaron your brother brought to you from among the Israelites, along with his sons Nadab and Abihu, Eleazar and Ithamar, so they may serve me as priests. ²Make sacred garments for your brother Aaron, to give him dignity and honor. ³Tell all the skilled men to whom I have given wisdom in such matters that they are to make garments for Aaron, for his consecration, so he may serve me as priest. ⁴These are the garments they are to make: a breastpiece, an ephod, a robe, a woven tunic, a turban and a sash. They are to make these sacred garments for your brother Aaron and his sons, so they may serve me as priests. ⁵Have them use gold, and blue, purple and scarlet yarn, and fine linen.

⁶"Make the ephod of gold, and of blue, purple and scarlet yarn, and of finely twisted linen—the work of a skilled craftsman. ⁷It is to have two shoulder pieces attached to two of its corners, so it can be fastened. ⁸Its skillfully woven waistband is to be like it—of one piece with the ephod and made with gold, and with blue, purple and scarlet yarn, and with finely twisted linen.

⁹"Take two onyx stones and engrave on them the names of the sons of Israel ¹⁰in the order of their birth—six names on one stone and the re-maining six on the other. ¹¹Engrave the names of the sons of Israel on the two stones the way a gem cutter engraves a seal. Then mount the stones in gold filigree settings ¹²and fasten them on the shoulder pieces of the ephod as memorial stones for the sons of Israel. Aaron is to bear the names on his shoulders as a memorial before the LORD. ¹³Make gold filigree settings ¹⁴and two braided chains of pure gold, like a rope, and attach the chains to the settings.

¹⁵"Fashion a breastpiece for making decisions—the work of a skilled craftsman. Make it like the ephod: of gold, and of blue, purple and scarlet yarn, and of finely twisted linen. ¹⁶It is to be square—a span*f* long and a span wide—and folded double. ¹⁷Then mount four rows of precious stones on it. In the first row there shall be a ruby, a topaz and a beryl; ¹⁸in the second row a turquoise, a sapphire*g* and an emerald; ¹⁹in the third row a jacinth, an agate and an amethyst; ²⁰in the fourth row a chrysolite, an onyx and a jasper.*h* Mount them in gold filigree settings. ²¹There are to be twelve stones, one for each of the names of the sons of Israel, each engraved like

*f*16 That is, about 9 inches (about 22 centimeters)   *g*18 Or *lapis lazuli*   *h*20 The precise identification of some of these precious stones is uncertain.

a seal with the name of one of the twelve tribes.

²²"For the breastpiece make braided chains of pure gold, like a rope. ²³Make two gold rings for it and fasten them to two corners of the breastpiece. ²⁴Fasten the two gold chains to the rings at the corners of the breastpiece, ²⁵and the other ends of the chains to the two settings, attaching them to the shoulder pieces of the ephod at the front. ²⁶Make two gold rings and attach them to the other two corners of the breastpiece on the inside edge next to the ephod. ²⁷Make two more gold rings and attach them to the bottom of the shoulder pieces on the front of the ephod, close to the seam just above the waistband of the ephod. ²⁸The rings of the breastpiece are to be tied to the rings of the ephod with blue cord, connecting it to the waistband, so that the breastpiece will not swing out from the ephod.

²⁹"Whenever Aaron enters the Holy Place, he will bear the names of the sons of Israel over his heart on the breastpiece of decision as a continuing memorial before the LORD. ³⁰Also put the Urim and the Thummim in the breastpiece, so they may be over Aaron's heart whenever he enters the presence of the LORD. Thus Aaron will always bear the means of making decisions for the Israelites over his heart before the LORD.

³¹"Make the robe of the ephod entirely of blue cloth, ³²with an opening for the head in its center. There shall be a woven edge like a collarⁱ around this opening, so that it will not tear. ³³Make pomegranates of blue, purple and scarlet yarn around the hem of the robe, with gold bells between them. ³⁴The gold bells and the pomegranates are to alternate around the hem of the robe. ³⁵Aaron must wear it when he ministers. The sound of the bells will be heard when he enters the Holy Place before the LORD and when he comes out, so that he will not die.

³⁶"Make a plate of pure gold and engrave on it as on a seal: HOLY TO THE LORD. ³⁷Fasten a blue cord to it to attach it to the turban; it is to be on the front of the turban. ³⁸It will be on Aaron's forehead, and he will bear the guilt involved in the sacred gifts the Israelites consecrate, whatever their gifts may be. It will be on Aaron's forehead continually so that they will be acceptable to the LORD.

³⁹"Weave the tunic of fine linen and make the turban of fine linen. The sash is to be the work of an embroiderer. ⁴⁰Make tunics, sashes and headbands for Aaron's sons, to give them dignity and honor. ⁴¹After you put these clothes on your brother Aaron and his sons, anoint and ordain them. Consecrate them so they may serve me as priests.

⁴²"Make linen undergarments as a covering for the body, reaching from the waist to the thigh. ⁴³Aaron and his sons must wear them whenever they enter the Tent of Meeting or approach the altar to minister in the Holy Place, so that they will not incur guilt and die.

"This is to be a lasting ordinance for Aaron and his descendants.

29

"This is what you are to do to consecrate them, so they may serve me as priests: Take a young bull and two rams without defect. ²And from fine wheat flour, without yeast, make bread, and cakes mixed with oil, and wafers spread with oil. ³Put them in a basket and present them in it—along with the bull and the two rams. ⁴Then bring Aaron and his sons to the entrance to the Tent of Meeting and wash them with water. ⁵Take the garments and dress Aaron with the tunic, the robe of the ephod, the ephod itself and the breastpiece. Fasten the ephod on him by its skillfully woven waistband. ⁶Put the turban on his head and attach the sacred diadem to the turban. ⁷Take the anointing oil and anoint him by pouring it on his head. ⁸Bring his sons and dress them in tunics ⁹and put headbands on them. Then tie sashes on Aaron and his sons.^j The priesthood is theirs by a lasting ordinance. In this way you shall ordain Aaron and his sons.

¹⁰"Bring the bull to the front of the Tent of Meeting, and Aaron and his sons shall lay their hands on its head. ¹¹Slaughter it in the LORD's presence at the entrance to the Tent of Meeting. ¹²Take some of the bull's blood and put it on the horns of the altar with your finger, and pour out the rest of it at the base of the altar. ¹³Then take all the fat around the inner parts, the covering of the liver, and both kidneys with the fat on them, and burn them on the altar. ¹⁴But burn the bull's flesh and its hide and its offal outside the camp. It is a sin offering.

¹⁵"Take one of the rams, and Aaron and his sons shall lay their hands on its head. ¹⁶Slaughter it and take the blood and sprinkle it against the altar on all sides. ¹⁷Cut the ram into pieces and wash the inner parts and the legs, putting them

ⁱ32 The meaning of the Hebrew for this word is uncertain.
^j9 Hebrew; Septuagint *on them*

with the head and the other pieces. ¹⁸Then burn the entire ram on the altar. It is a burnt offering to the LORD, a pleasing aroma, an offering made to the LORD by fire.

¹⁹"Take the other ram, and Aaron and his sons shall lay their hands on its head. ²⁰Slaughter it, take some of its blood and put it on the lobes of the right ears of Aaron and his sons, on the thumbs of their right hands, and on the big toes of their right feet. Then sprinkle blood against the altar on all sides. ²¹And take some of the blood on the altar and some of the anointing oil and sprinkle it on Aaron and his garments and on his sons and their garments. Then he and his sons and their garments will be consecrated.

²²"Take from this ram the fat, the fat tail, the fat around the inner parts, the covering of the liver, both kidneys with the fat on them, and the right thigh. (This is the ram for the ordination.) ²³From the basket of bread made without yeast, which is before the LORD, take a loaf, and a cake made with oil, and a wafer. ²⁴Put all these in the hands of Aaron and his sons and wave them before the LORD as a wave offering. ²⁵Then take them from their hands and burn them on the altar along with the burnt offering for a pleasing aroma to the LORD, an offering made to the LORD by fire. ²⁶After you take the breast of the ram for Aaron's ordination, wave it before the LORD as a wave offering, and it will be your share.

²⁷"Consecrate those parts of the ordination ram that belong to Aaron and his sons: the breast that was waved and the thigh that was presented. ²⁸This is always to be the regular share from the Israelites for Aaron and his sons. It is the contribution the Israelites are to make to the LORD from their fellowship offerings.ᵏ

²⁹"Aaron's sacred garments will belong to his descendants so that they can be anointed and ordained in them. ³⁰The son who succeeds him as priest and comes to the Tent of Meeting to minister in the Holy Place is to wear them seven days.

³¹"Take the ram for the ordination and cook the meat in a sacred place. ³²At the entrance to the Tent of Meeting, Aaron and his sons are to eat the meat of the ram and the bread that is in the basket. ³³They are to eat these offerings by which atonement was made for their ordination and consecration. But no one else may eat them, because they are sacred. ³⁴And if any of the meat of the ordination ram or any bread is left over till morning, burn it up. It must not be eaten, because it is sacred.

³⁵"Do for Aaron and his sons everything I have commanded you, taking seven days to ordain them. ³⁶Sacrifice a bull each day as a sin offering to make atonement. Purify the altar by making atonement for it, and anoint it to consecrate it. ³⁷For seven days make atonement for the altar and consecrate it. Then the altar will be most holy, and whatever touches it will be holy.

ᵏ28 Traditionally *peace offerings*

 Discovering the Word 1. How and why did God give special status to the sons of Aaron? 2. What would the precious stones mean to the Israelites in their relationship with God (28:9–12, 21, 29)? 3. What facts about God's nature are emphasized by these garments (28:35–36, 38, 43)? 4. What do they teach about our spiritual condition and its consequences? 5. What offerings were made for the priests (29:1–3)? 6. Why do you think God went to such elaborate measures for his priests' garments and for their ordination?

Applying the Word 1. How can we develop an appreciation of our own sin and God's holiness in our worship? 2. If you had been one of Aaron's sons, what would have been your major feelings and impressions about God and about your ministry? 3. Jesus is our great high priest. What benefits do we receive from him (Heb 2:14–18; 5:1–3, 7–10; 9:11–15; 10:19–25)?

Responding in Prayer Pour out your requests to God, knowing that Jesus, your High Priest, will plead to the Father on your behalf.

18 / *Exodus 29:38—31:18*
God's Revelation in People and Things

"BACK TO THE drawing board" is often said after a failed experiment or project. Sometimes Christians behave as though the worship of God is a do-it-yourself project. Some lack a sense of responding to God himself. Church leaders experiment and fiddle with changes in the order of worship. But God is a God of economy and order. No wasted, botched plans or experiments with him. Moses and the Israelites received a specific plan, precise in every detail and dimension. Each part of the plan said something about God. Careful study of the plan pays off in new insights about God and about worship.

 Warming Up to God As you sit before the Bible allow yourself to sit spiritually before the Lord. Rest silently for a few minutes and allow yourself to become relaxed and focused before you begin your study.

 Read Exodus 29:38—31:18.

---

³⁸"This is what you are to offer on the altar regularly each day: two lambs a year old. ³⁹Offer one in the morning and the other at twilight. ⁴⁰With the first lamb offer a tenth of an ephah[l] of fine flour mixed with a quarter of a hin[m] of oil from pressed olives, and a quarter of a hin of wine as a drink offering. ⁴¹Sacrifice the other lamb at twilight with the same grain offering and its drink offering as in the morning—a pleasing aroma, an offering made to the LORD by fire.

⁴²"For the generations to come this burnt offering is to be made regularly at the entrance to the Tent of Meeting before the LORD. There I will meet you and speak to you; ⁴³there also I will meet with the Israelites, and the place will be consecrated by my glory.

⁴⁴"So I will consecrate the Tent of Meeting and the altar and will consecrate Aaron and his sons to serve me as priests. ⁴⁵Then I will dwell among the Israelites and be their God. ⁴⁶They will know that I am the LORD their God, who brought them out of Egypt so that I might dwell among them. I am the LORD their God.

30 "Make an altar of acacia wood for burning incense. ²It is to be square, a cubit long and a cubit wide, and two cubits high[n]—its horns of one piece with it. ³Overlay the top and all the sides and the horns with pure gold, and make a gold molding around it. ⁴Make two gold rings for the altar below the molding—two on opposite sides—to hold the poles used to carry it. ⁵Make the poles of acacia wood and overlay them with gold. ⁶Put the altar in front of the curtain that is before the ark of the Testimony—before the atonement cover that is over the Testimony—where I will meet with you.

⁷"Aaron must burn fragrant incense on the altar every morning when he tends the lamps. ⁸He must burn incense again when he lights the lamps at twilight so incense will burn regularly before the LORD for the generations to come. ⁹Do not offer on this altar any other incense or any burnt offering or grain offering, and do not pour a drink offering on it. ¹⁰Once a year Aaron shall make atonement on its horns. This annual atonement must be made with the blood of the atoning sin offering for the generations to come. It is most holy to the LORD."

¹¹Then the LORD said to Moses, ¹²"When you take a census of the Israelites to count them, each one must pay the LORD a ransom for his life at the time he is counted. Then no plague will come on them when you number them. ¹³Each one who crosses over to those already counted is to give a half shekel,[o] according to the sanctuary shekel, which weighs twenty gerahs. This half shekel is an offering to the LORD. ¹⁴All who cross over, those twenty years old or more, are to give an offering to the LORD. ¹⁵The rich are not to give more than a half shekel and the poor are not to give less when you make the offering to the LORD to atone for your lives. ¹⁶Receive the atonement money from the Israelites and use it for the service of the Tent of Meeting. It will be a memorial for the Israelites before the LORD, making atonement for your lives."

¹⁷Then the LORD said to Moses, ¹⁸"Make a

---

[l]40 That is, probably about 2 quarts (about 2 liters)   [m]40 That is, probably about 1 quart (about 1 liter)   [n]2 That is, about 1 1/2 feet (about 0.5 meter) long and wide and about 3 feet (about 0.9 meter) high   [o]13 That is, about 1/5 ounce (about 6 grams); also in verse 15

bronze basin, with its bronze stand, for washing. Place it between the Tent of Meeting and the altar, and put water in it. ¹⁹Aaron and his sons are to wash their hands and feet with water from it. ²⁰Whenever they enter the Tent of Meeting, they shall wash with water so that they will not die. Also, when they approach the altar to minister by presenting an offering made to the Lord by fire, ²¹they shall wash their hands and feet so that they will not die. This is to be a lasting ordinance for Aaron and his descendants for the generations to come."

²²Then the Lord said to Moses, ²³"Take the following fine spices: 500 shekels*ᵖ* of liquid myrrh, half as much (that is, 250 shekels) of fragrant cinnamon, 250 shekels of fragrant cane, ²⁴500 shekels of cassia—all according to the sanctuary shekel—and a hin*�q* of olive oil. ²⁵Make these into a sacred anointing oil, a fragrant blend, the work of a perfumer. It will be the sacred anointing oil. ²⁶Then use it to anoint the Tent of Meeting, the ark of the Testimony, ²⁷the table and all its articles, the lampstand and its accessories, the altar of incense, ²⁸the altar of burnt offering and all its utensils, and the basin with its stand. ²⁹You shall consecrate them so they will be most holy, and whatever touches them will be holy.

³⁰"Anoint Aaron and his sons and consecrate them so they may serve me as priests. ³¹Say to the Israelites, 'This is to be my sacred anointing oil for the generations to come. ³²Do not pour it on men's bodies and do not make any oil with the same formula. It is sacred, and you are to consider it sacred. ³³Whoever makes perfume like it and whoever puts it on anyone other than a priest must be cut off from his people.'"

³⁴Then the Lord said to Moses, "Take fragrant spices—gum resin, onycha and galbanum—and pure frankincense, all in equal amounts, ³⁵and make a fragrant blend of incense, the work of a perfumer. It is to be salted and pure and sacred. ³⁶Grind some of it to powder and place it in front of the Testimony in the Tent of Meeting, where I will meet with you. It shall be most holy to you. ³⁷Do not make any incense with this formula for yourselves; consider it holy to the Lord. ³⁸Whoever makes any like it to enjoy its fragrance must be cut off from his people."

31

Then the Lord said to Moses, ²"See, I have chosen Bezalel son of Uri, the son of Hur, of the tribe of Judah, ³and I have filled him with the Spirit of God, with skill, ability and knowledge in all kinds of crafts— ⁴to make artistic designs for work in gold, silver and bronze, ⁵to cut and set stones, to work in wood, and to engage in all kinds of craftsmanship. ⁶Moreover, I have appointed Oholiab son of Ahisamach, of the tribe of Dan, to help him. Also I have given skill to all the craftsmen to make everything I have commanded you: ⁷the Tent of Meeting, the ark of the Testimony with the atonement cover on it, and all the other furnishings of the tent— ⁸the table and its articles, the pure gold lampstand and all its accessories, the altar of incense, ⁹the altar of burnt offering and all its utensils, the basin with its stand— ¹⁰and also the woven garments, both the sacred garments for Aaron the priest and the garments for his sons when they serve as priests, ¹¹and the anointing oil and fragrant incense for the Holy Place. They are to make them just as I commanded you."

¹²Then the Lord said to Moses, ¹³"Say to the Israelites, 'You must observe my Sabbaths. This will be a sign between me and you for the generations to come, so you may know that I am the Lord, who makes you holy.*ʳ*

¹⁴"'Observe the Sabbath, because it is holy to you. Anyone who desecrates it must be put to death; whoever does any work on that day must be cut off from his people. ¹⁵For six days, work is to be done, but the seventh day is a Sabbath of rest, holy to the Lord. Whoever does any work on the Sabbath day must be put to death. ¹⁶The Israelites are to observe the Sabbath, celebrating it for the generations to come as a lasting covenant. ¹⁷It will be a sign between me and the Israelites forever, for in six days the Lord made the heavens and the earth, and on the seventh day he abstained from work and rested.'"

¹⁸When the Lord finished speaking to Moses on Mount Sinai, he gave him the two tablets of the Testimony, the tablets of stone inscribed by the finger of God.

ᵖ23 That is, about 12 1/2 pounds (about 6 kilograms)   �q24 That is, probably about 4 quarts (about 4 liters)   ʳ13 Or *who sanctifies you; or who sets you apart as holy*

Discovering the Word 1. How does God summarize the purposes of worship (29:42–46)? 2. Incense speaks of the prayers of God's people (Rev 5:8). Why would Israel need such a reminder (30:1–10)? 3. What aspect of worship would be inspired by paying atonement money (30:11–16)? 4. Why do you think it was important that rich and poor gave the same small amount (30:15)? 5. The shepherds of Israel had neither artistic skills nor craftsmanship. What does God's plan to remedy this reveal about his concern for beauty (31:1–11)? 6. Exodus 31:12–18 is the third instruction and warning regarding the Sabbath (see 20:8–11; 23:10–13). What new emphasis is added here regarding the purpose of the Sabbath and the punishment of those who disregard it?

Applying the Word 1. The Bible speaks of the cleansing effect of Scripture (Ps 119:9; Jn 15:3). Why is it important to be washed daily by God's Word? 2. From these forty days' instructions (Ex 25—31) from God, what major impressions do you receive about him and about worshiping him?

Responding in Prayer Spend time worshiping the Lord. Choose your own way to express yourself and ascribe worth to God.

19 / *Exodus 32*
Idolatry's Fearful Toll

PROBABLY NOTHING SHOCKS us as much as defection. Selling out to the enemy is hard to understand. Loyalty rightly stands near the top of qualities we admire. When traitors are exposed, we smugly assume that we would never do such a thing. But who knows where we are the most vulnerable? On the heels of glorious triumph Israel plunged into idolatry with the flimsiest of excuses. God's nation flunked the loyalty test, with disastrous consequences.

 Warming Up to God Sit quietly as you recall recent events in your life. Confess your sins to Jesus and acknowledge that every one of them is forgiven and blotted from the memory of the Father.

 Read Exodus 32.

32 When the people saw that Moses was so long in coming down from the mountain, they gathered around Aaron and said, "Come, make us gods[s] who will go before us. As for this fellow Moses who brought us up out of Egypt, we don't know what has happened to him."

²Aaron answered them, "Take off the gold earrings that your wives, your sons and your daughters are wearing, and bring them to me." ³So all the people took off their earrings and brought them to Aaron. ⁴He took what they handed him and made it into an idol cast in the shape of a calf, fashioning it with a tool. Then they said, "These are your gods,[t] O Israel, who brought you up out of Egypt."

⁵When Aaron saw this, he built an altar in front of the calf and announced, "Tomorrow there will be a festival to the LORD." ⁶So the next day the people rose early and sacrificed burnt offerings and presented fellowship offerings.[u] Afterward they sat down to eat and drink and got up to indulge in revelry.

⁷Then the LORD said to Moses, "Go down, because your people, whom you brought up out of Egypt, have become corrupt. ⁸They have been quick to turn away from what I commanded them and have made themselves an idol cast in the shape of a calf. They have bowed down to it and sacrificed to it and have said, 'These are your gods, O Israel, who brought you up out of Egypt.'

⁹"I have seen these people," the LORD said to Moses, "and they are a stiff-necked people. ¹⁰Now leave me alone so that my anger may burn against them and that I may destroy them. Then I will make you into a great nation."

¹¹But Moses sought the favor of the LORD his God. "O LORD," he said, "why should your anger burn against your people, whom you brought out of Egypt with great power and a mighty hand? ¹²Why should the Egyptians say, 'It was with evil

---

[s]1 Or *a god*; also in verses 23 and 31   [t]4 Or *This is your god*; also in verse 8   [u]6 Traditionally *peace offerings*

intent that he brought them out, to kill them in the mountains and to wipe them off the face of the earth'? Turn from your fierce anger; relent and do not bring disaster on your people. ¹³Remember your servants Abraham, Isaac and Israel, to whom you swore by your own self: 'I will make your descendants as numerous as the stars in the sky and I will give your descendants all this land I promised them, and it will be their inheritance forever.' " ¹⁴Then the LORD relented and did not bring on his people the disaster he had threatened.

¹⁵Moses turned and went down the mountain with the two tablets of the Testimony in his hands. They were inscribed on both sides, front and back. ¹⁶The tablets were the work of God; the writing was the writing of God, engraved on the tablets.

¹⁷When Joshua heard the noise of the people shouting, he said to Moses, "There is the sound of war in the camp."

¹⁸Moses replied:

"It is not the sound of victory,
　it is not the sound of defeat;
　it is the sound of singing that I hear."

¹⁹When Moses approached the camp and saw the calf and the dancing, his anger burned and he threw the tablets out of his hands, breaking them to pieces at the foot of the mountain. ²⁰And he took the calf they had made and burned it in the fire; then he ground it to powder, scattered it on the water and made the Israelites drink it.

²¹He said to Aaron, "What did these people do to you, that you led them into such great sin?"

²²"Do not be angry, my lord," Aaron answered. "You know how prone these people are to evil. ²³They said to me, 'Make us gods who will go before us. As for this fellow Moses who brought

us up out of Egypt, we don't know what has happened to him.' ²⁴So I told them, 'Whoever has any gold jewelry, take it off.' Then they gave me the gold, and I threw it into the fire, and out came this calf!"

²⁵Moses saw that the people were running wild and that Aaron had let them get out of control and so become a laughingstock to their enemies. ²⁶So he stood at the entrance to the camp and said, "Whoever is for the LORD, come to me." And all the Levites rallied to him.

²⁷Then he said to them, "This is what the LORD, the God of Israel, says: 'Each man strap a sword to his side. Go back and forth through the camp from one end to the other, each killing his brother and friend and neighbor.' " ²⁸The Levites did as Moses commanded, and that day about three thousand of the people died. ²⁹Then Moses said, "You have been set apart to the LORD today, for you were against your own sons and brothers, and he has blessed you this day."

³⁰The next day Moses said to the people, "You have committed a great sin. But now I will go up to the LORD; perhaps I can make atonement for your sin."

³¹So Moses went back to the LORD and said, "Oh, what a great sin these people have committed! They have made themselves gods of gold. ³²But now, please forgive their sin—but if not, then blot me out of the book you have written."

³³The LORD replied to Moses, "Whoever has sinned against me I will blot out of my book. ³⁴Now go, lead the people to the place I spoke of, and my angel will go before you. However, when the time comes for me to punish, I will punish them for their sin."

³⁵And the LORD struck the people with a plague because of what they did with the calf Aaron had made.

 Discovering the Word 1. Who instigated the idolatry and why (v. 1)? 2. What impresses you about the dialogue between God and Moses (vv. 9–14)? 3. How did Moses react when he saw the Israelites' idolatrous worship (vv. 19–24)? 4. How was God's judgment against idolatry carried out (vv. 27–28, 35)? 5. What did it cost the Levites to take a public stand for God? 6. Moses offered his life to atone for Israel's sin (vv. 30–32). What did God promise instead (vv. 33–34)?

 Applying the Word 1. In what ways can we emulate Moses in our relation to God and in our care for sinning people? 2. What spiritual disciplines could help you maintain faithfulness to God?

Responding in Prayer Praise God for this example of grace—even in Exodus, long before Christ ever came to earth.

20 / *Exodus 33*
God's Presence and Glory

I REMEMBER TAKING my son to school the first time. I dragged him all the way. My presence was not enough to enable him to face this terrible prospect. The command to go was clear, but that wasn't enough for him. In the same way God commanded Israel to go to the good land he had promised to give them. God's leader asked for God's presence before he would move out. In this study we see more of God's loving patience with Moses and Israel and how this speaks to our own basic spiritual goals.

 Warming Up to God Sit quietly and imagine you are a glass of water, full of words, thoughts, ideas and sins that distract. Pour yourself out in front of the Lord and let the Spirit refill you with his good, refreshing water.

 Read Exodus 33.

---

33 Then the LORD said to Moses, "Leave this place, you and the people you brought up out of Egypt, and go up to the land I promised on oath to Abraham, Isaac and Jacob, saying, 'I will give it to your descendants.' ²I will send an angel before you and drive out the Canaanites, Amorites, Hittites, Perizzites, Hivites and Jebusites. ³Go up to the land flowing with milk and honey. But I will not go with you, because you are a stiff-necked people and I might destroy you on the way."

⁴When the people heard these distressing words, they began to mourn and no one put on any ornaments. ⁵For the LORD had said to Moses, "Tell the Israelites, 'You are a stiff-necked people. If I were to go with you even for a moment, I might destroy you. Now take off your ornaments and I will decide what to do with you.'" ⁶So the Israelites stripped off their ornaments at Mount Horeb.

⁷Now Moses used to take a tent and pitch it outside the camp some distance away, calling it the "tent of meeting." Anyone inquiring of the LORD would go to the tent of meeting outside the camp. ⁸And whenever Moses went out to the tent, all the people rose and stood at the entrances to their tents, watching Moses until he entered the tent. ⁹As Moses went into the tent, the pillar of cloud would come down and stay at the entrance, while the LORD spoke with Moses. ¹⁰Whenever the people saw the pillar of cloud standing at the entrance to the tent, they all stood and worshiped, each at the entrance to his tent. ¹¹The LORD would speak to Moses face to face, as a man speaks with his friend. Then Moses would return to the camp, but his young aide Joshua son of Nun did not leave the tent.

¹²Moses said to the LORD, "You have been telling me, 'Lead these people,' but you have not let me know whom you will send with me. You have said, 'I know you by name and you have found favor with me.' ¹³If you are pleased with me, teach me your ways so I may know you and continue to find favor with you. Remember that this nation is your people."

¹⁴The LORD replied, "My Presence will go with you, and I will give you rest."

¹⁵Then Moses said to him, "If your Presence does not go with us, do not send us up from here. ¹⁶How will anyone know that you are pleased with me and with your people unless you go with us? What else will distinguish me and your people from all the other people on the face of the earth?"

¹⁷And the LORD said to Moses, "I will do the very thing you have asked, because I am pleased with you and I know you by name."

¹⁸Then Moses said, "Now show me your glory."

¹⁹And the LORD said, "I will cause all my goodness to pass in front of you, and I will proclaim my name, the LORD, in your presence. I will have mercy on whom I will have mercy, and I will have compassion on whom I will have compassion. ²⁰But," he said, "you cannot see my face, for no one may see me and live."

²¹Then the LORD said, "There is a place near me where you may stand on a rock. ²²When my glory passes by, I will put you in a cleft in the rock and cover you with my hand until I have passed by. ²³Then I will remove my hand and you will see my back; but my face must not be seen."

Discovering the Word 1. What commands, promises and warnings did God give Israel? 2. What occurred at the tent of meeting and why? 3. What do these verses reveal about Moses' relationship with God and the effect it had on others? 4. Look at the development of Moses' requests (vv. 13, 15, 18). How do they increase in spiritual wisdom and depth and reveal Moses' deepest desire? 5. In God's answer to Moses (vv. 19–23), what do you learn about his nature and character?

Applying the Word 1. Moses could not see God's face. What is our privilege and responsibility in light of John 14:8–14 and Hebrews 1:1–4? 2. In what ways do you demonstrate a desire to know God and to see his glory?

Responding in Prayer Thank the Father for showing you his glory incarnate in his son, Jesus Christ.

21 / *Exodus 34*
Renewing the Covenant

THE CYNICAL STATEMENT of some historians is that treaties are made to be broken. Sadly, that's often been the case. Humanity's record of keeping treaties is abysmal, but nations keep on making treaties, hoping for a more secure future. Israel fell into idolatry and soon broke faith with God (Ex 19:8; 24:3). Likewise, we can recall solemn vows and promises shattered by expediency, fear and unfaithfulness. But God doesn't quit on us. That's not his nature. In this study, he calls Moses to the mountain a second time and reaffirms principles of holy living.

 Warming Up to God Think of an experience in which you were given a second chance. How did it make you feel? Why?

 Read Exodus 34.

34 The LORD said to Moses, "Chisel out two stone tablets like the first ones, and I will write on them the words that were on the first tablets, which you broke. ²Be ready in the morning, and then come up on Mount Sinai. Present yourself to me there on top of the mountain. ³No one is to come with you or be seen anywhere on the mountain; not even the flocks and herds may graze in front of the mountain."

⁴So Moses chiseled out two stone tablets like the first ones and went up Mount Sinai early in the morning, as the LORD had commanded him; and he carried the two stone tablets in his hands. ⁵Then the LORD came down in the cloud and stood there with him and proclaimed his name, the LORD. ⁶And he passed in front of Moses, proclaiming, "The LORD, the LORD, the compassionate and gracious God, slow to anger, abounding in love and faithfulness, ⁷maintaining love to thousands, and forgiving wickedness, rebellion and sin. Yet he does not leave the guilty unpunished; he punishes the children and their children for

the sin of the fathers to the third and fourth generation."

⁸Moses bowed to the ground at once and worshiped. ⁹"O Lord, if I have found favor in your eyes," he said, "then let the Lord go with us. Although this is a stiff-necked people, forgive our wickedness and our sin, and take us as your inheritance."

¹⁰Then the LORD said: "I am making a covenant with you. Before all your people I will do wonders never before done in any nation in all the world. The people you live among will see how awesome is the work that I, the LORD, will do for you. ¹¹Obey what I command you today. I will drive out before you the Amorites, Canaanites, Hittites, Perizzites, Hivites and Jebusites. ¹²Be careful not to make a treaty with those who live in the land where you are going, or they will be a snare among you. ¹³Break down their altars, smash their sacred stones and cut down their Asherah poles.ᵛ ¹⁴Do not worship any other god, for the LORD, whose name is Jealous, is a jealous God.

ᵛ 13 That is, symbols of the goddess Asherah

¹⁵"Be careful not to make a treaty with those who live in the land; for when they prostitute themselves to their gods and sacrifice to them, they will invite you and you will eat their sacrifices. ¹⁶And when you choose some of their daughters as wives for your sons and those daughters prostitute themselves to their gods, they will lead your sons to do the same.

¹⁷"Do not make cast idols.

¹⁸"Celebrate the Feast of Unleavened Bread. For seven days eat bread made without yeast, as I commanded you. Do this at the appointed time in the month of Abib, for in that month you came out of Egypt.

¹⁹"The first offspring of every womb belongs to me, including all the firstborn males of your livestock, whether from herd or flock. ²⁰Redeem the firstborn donkey with a lamb, but if you do not redeem it, break its neck. Redeem all your firstborn sons.

"No one is to appear before me empty-handed.

²¹"Six days you shall labor, but on the seventh day you shall rest; even during the plowing season and harvest you must rest.

²²"Celebrate the Feast of Weeks with the firstfruits of the wheat harvest, and the Feast of Ingathering at the turn of the year.ʷ ²³Three times a year all your men are to appear before the Sovereign Lᴏʀᴅ, the God of Israel. ²⁴I will drive out nations before you and enlarge your territory, and no one will covet your land when you go up three times each year to appear before the Lᴏʀᴅ your God.

²⁵"Do not offer the blood of a sacrifice to me along with anything containing yeast, and do not let any of the sacrifice from the Passover Feast remain until morning.

²⁶"Bring the best of the firstfruits of your soil to the house of the Lᴏʀᴅ your God.

"Do not cook a young goat in its mother's milk."

²⁷Then the Lᴏʀᴅ said to Moses, "Write down these words, for in accordance with these words I have made a covenant with you and with Israel." ²⁸Moses was there with the Lᴏʀᴅ forty days and forty nights without eating bread or drinking water. And he wrote on the tablets the words of the covenant—the Ten Commandments.

²⁹When Moses came down from Mount Sinai with the two tablets of the Testimony in his hands, he was not aware that his face was radiant because he had spoken with the Lᴏʀᴅ. ³⁰When Aaron and all the Israelites saw Moses, his face was radiant, and they were afraid to come near him. ³¹But Moses called to them; so Aaron and all the leaders of the community came back to him, and he spoke to them. ³²Afterward all the Israelites came near him, and he gave them all the commands the Lᴏʀᴅ had given him on Mount Sinai.

³³When Moses finished speaking to them, he put a veil over his face. ³⁴But whenever he entered the Lᴏʀᴅ's presence to speak with him, he removed the veil until he came out. And when he came out and told the Israelites what he had been commanded, ³⁵they saw that his face was radiant. Then Moses would put the veil back over his face until he went in to speak with the Lᴏʀᴅ.

ʷ 22 That is, in the fall

Discovering the Word 1. In order to meet God, what was required of Moses (vv. 1–3)? 2. How would you describe God, based on what he proclaimed to Moses (vv. 6–7)? 3. What request did Moses make and why (vv. 8–9)? 4. How would you summarize the covenant God made with Israel? 5. What effect did this meeting with God have on Moses, the leaders and the people (vv. 29–32)? 6. What practice was then established and why (vv. 33–35)?

Applying the Word 1. God calls us to live among those who do not honor his name. In what ways can they be a "snare" for us (v. 12)? 2. What principles of godly living in the New Testament would correspond to God's concern for Israel here (Gal 5:16–26; Eph 4:20–32)?

 Responding in Prayer Praise God for being a God of second chances.

22 / *Exodus 35—36*
Building the Tabernacle

HARDLY A DAY passes that we aren't asked to contribute to some worthy cause or implored to work on a needed project. The avalanche of appeals dulls our senses and makes it hard to sort out priorities. It's tempting to do nothing. In this study, God launches a tabernacle building project. He asks for money (donated goods) and services (labor). Israel was called a "stiff-necked people"—not the best prospects for a building fund drive—but their response to God is surprising.

Warming Up to God Spend a few minutes telling God about the events of your day—your joys and worries. Lay them at his feet and leave them behind as you look into the Word.

Read Exodus 35—36.

---

35 Moses assembled the whole Israelite community and said to them, "These are the things the LORD has commanded you to do: ²For six days, work is to be done, but the seventh day shall be your holy day, a Sabbath of rest to the LORD. Whoever does any work on it must be put to death. ³Do not light a fire in any of your dwellings on the Sabbath day."

⁴Moses said to the whole Israelite community, "This is what the LORD has commanded: ⁵From what you have, take an offering for the LORD. Everyone who is willing is to bring to the LORD an offering of gold, silver and bronze; ⁶blue, purple and scarlet yarn and fine linen; goat hair; ⁷ram skins dyed red and hides of sea cowsˣ; acacia wood; ⁸olive oil for the light; spices for the anointing oil and for the fragrant incense; ⁹and onyx stones and other gems to be mounted on the ephod and breastpiece.

¹⁰"All who are skilled among you are to come and make everything the LORD has commanded: ¹¹the tabernacle with its tent and its covering, clasps, frames, crossbars, posts and bases; ¹²the ark with its poles and the atonement cover and the curtain that shields it; ¹³the table with its poles and all its articles and the bread of the Presence; ¹⁴the lampstand that is for light with its accessories, lamps and oil for the light; ¹⁵the altar of incense with its poles, the anointing oil and the fragrant incense; the curtain for the doorway at the entrance to the tabernacle; ¹⁶the altar of burnt offering with its bronze grating, its poles and all its utensils; the bronze basin with its stand; ¹⁷the curtains of the courtyard with its posts and bases, and the curtain for the entrance to the courtyard; ¹⁸the tent pegs for the tabernacle and for the courtyard, and their ropes; ¹⁹the woven garments worn for ministering in the sanctuary—both the sacred garments for Aaron the priest and the garments for his sons when they serve as priests."

²⁰Then the whole Israelite community withdrew from Moses' presence, ²¹and everyone who was willing and whose heart moved him came and brought an offering to the LORD for the work on the Tent of Meeting, for all its service, and for the sacred garments. ²²All who were willing, men and women alike, came and brought gold jewelry of all kinds: brooches, earrings, rings and ornaments. They all presented their gold as a wave offering to the LORD. ²³Everyone who had blue, purple or scarlet yarn or fine linen, or goat hair, ram skins dyed red or hides of sea cows brought them. ²⁴Those presenting an offering of silver or bronze brought it as an offering to the LORD, and everyone who had acacia wood for any part of the work brought it. ²⁵Every skilled woman spun with her hands and brought what she had spun—blue, purple or scarlet yarn or fine linen. ²⁶And all the women who were willing and had the skill spun the goat hair. ²⁷The leaders brought onyx stones and other gems to be mounted on the ephod and breastpiece. ²⁸They also brought spices and olive oil for the light and for the anointing oil and for the fragrant incense. ²⁹All the Israelite men and women who were willing brought to the LORD freewill offerings for all the work the LORD through Moses had commanded them to do.

³⁰Then Moses said to the Israelites, "See, the LORD has chosen Bezalel son of Uri, the son of Hur, of the tribe of Judah, ³¹and he has filled him with the Spirit of God, with skill, ability and

ˣ7 That is, dugongs; also in verse 23

knowledge in all kinds of crafts— ³²to make artistic designs for work in gold, silver and bronze, ³³to cut and set stones, to work in wood and to engage in all kinds of artistic craftsmanship. ³⁴And he has given both him and Oholiab son of Ahisamach, of the tribe of Dan, the ability to teach others. ³⁵He has filled them with skill to do all kinds of work as craftsmen, designers, embroiderers in blue, purple and scarlet yarn and fine linen, and weavers—all of them master craftsmen and designers.

36

¹So Bezalel, Oholiab and every skilled person to whom the LORD has given skill and ability to know how to carry out all the work of constructing the sanctuary are to do the work just as the Lord has commanded."

²Then Moses summoned Bezalel and Oholiab and every skilled person to whom the LORD had given ability and who was willing to come and do the work. ³They received from Moses all the offerings the Israelites had brought to carry out the work of constructing the sanctuary. And the people continued to bring freewill offerings morning after morning. ⁴So all the skilled craftsmen who were doing all the work on the sanctuary left their work ⁵and said to Moses, "The people are bringing more than enough for doing the work the LORD commanded to be done."

⁶Then Moses gave an order and they sent this word throughout the camp: "No man or woman is to make anything else as an offering for the sanctuary." And so the people were restrained from bringing more, ⁷because what they already had was more than enough to do all the work.

⁸All the skilled men among the workmen made the tabernacle with ten curtains of finely twisted linen and blue, purple and scarlet yarn, with cherubim worked into them by a skilled craftsman. ⁹All the curtains were the same size—twenty-eight cubits long and four cubits wide.ʸ ¹⁰They joined five of the curtains together and did the same with the other five. ¹¹Then they made loops of blue material along the edge of the end curtain in one set, and the same was done with the end curtain in the other set. ¹²They also made fifty loops on one curtain and fifty loops on the end curtain of the other set, with the loops opposite each other. ¹³Then they made fifty gold clasps and used them to fasten the two sets of curtains together so that the tabernacle was a unit.

¹⁴They made curtains of goat hair for the tent over the tabernacle—eleven altogether. ¹⁵All eleven curtains were the same size—thirty cubits long and four cubits wide.ᶻ ¹⁶They joined five of the curtains into one set and the other six into another set. ¹⁷Then they made fifty loops along the edge of the end curtain in one set and also along the edge of the end curtain in the other set. ¹⁸They made fifty bronze clasps to fasten the tent together as a unit. ¹⁹Then they made for the tent a covering of ram skins dyed red, and over that a covering of hides of sea cows.ᵃ

²⁰They made upright frames of acacia wood for the tabernacle. ²¹Each frame was ten cubits long and a cubit and a half wide,ᵇ ²²with two projections set parallel to each other. They made all the frames of the tabernacle in this way. ²³They made twenty frames for the south side of the tabernacle ²⁴and made forty silver bases to go under them— two bases for each frame, one under each projection. ²⁵For the other side, the north side of the tabernacle, they made twenty frames ²⁶and forty silver bases—two under each frame. ²⁷They made six frames for the far end, that is, the west end of the tabernacle, ²⁸and two frames were made for the corners of the tabernacle at the far end. ²⁹At these two corners the frames were double from the bottom all the way to the top and fitted into a single ring; both were made alike. ³⁰So there were eight frames and sixteen silver bases—two under each frame.

³¹They also made crossbars of acacia wood: five for the frames on one side of the tabernacle, ³²five for those on the other side, and five for the frames on the west, at the far end of the tabernacle. ³³They made the center crossbar so that it extended from end to end at the middle of the frames. ³⁴They overlaid the frames with gold and made gold rings to hold the crossbars. They also overlaid the crossbars with gold.

³⁵They made the curtain of blue, purple and scarlet yarn and finely twisted linen, with cherubim worked into it by a skilled craftsman. ³⁶They made four posts of acacia wood for it and overlaid them with gold. They made gold hooks for them and cast their four silver bases. ³⁷For the entrance to the tent they made a curtain of blue, purple and scarlet yarn and finely twisted linen—the

ʸ9 That is, about 42 feet (about 12.5 meters) long and 6 feet (about 1.8 meters) wide   ᶻ15 That is, about 45 feet (about 13.5 meters) long and 6 feet (about 1.8 meters) wide   ᵃ19 That is, dugongs   ᵇ21 That is, about 15 feet (about 4.5 meters) long and 2 1/4 feet (about 0.7 meter) wide work of an embroiderer; ³⁸and they made five posts with hooks for them. They overlaid the tops of the posts and their bands with gold and made their five bases of bronze.

Discovering the Word 1. What was God's plan for the provision of materials (vv. 4–9)? 2. Of what value and importance would it be for the Israelites to give their own possessions and to build the tabernacle themselves (35:10)? 3. The Israelites responded to God's call for an offering (35:20–29). How do you account for this outpouring of goods and materials (see 36:3–7)? 4. In God's plan, how was it possible for everyone to give something (see 3:21–22; 12:35–36)? 5. How did the nomadic Israelites—shepherds in Egypt for more than four centuries—suddenly develop skills in design, building and craftsmanship (35:30–35)? 6. Who came to do the work (36:1–2)?

Applying the Word 1. What possessions and abilities do you have for God to use? 2. What keeps God's people today from giving willingly, sacrificially and generously?

Responding in Prayer Ask the Lord to teach you how to give graciously.

23 / *Exodus 37:1—39:31*
God Speaks Powerfully in Wood, Gold, Silver, Linen and Wool

HOW IMPORTANT IS the furniture in your church? What about the clothes people wear? What do they say to you and others? In God's plan for Israel's worship, he spoke powerfully through furniture and clothing. God has also given us spiritual dress—both inner qualities and outward deeds—to help people know and understand him. He also speaks to us in the beauty of the sanctuary. This study looks at outward things, so look for their hidden meaning and significance. The medium is the message in this case.

Warming Up to God Confess the ways you've forgotten your Savior today. Let his forgiveness fall on you like gentle rain—and regain your strength to press on.

Read Exodus 37:1—39:31.

37 Bezalel made the ark of acacia wood—two and a half cubits long, a cubit and a half wide, and a cubit and a half high.ᶜ ²He overlaid it with pure gold, both inside and out, and made a gold molding around it. ³He cast four gold rings for it and fastened them to its four feet, with two rings on one side and two rings on the other. ⁴Then he made poles of acacia wood and overlaid them with gold. ⁵And he inserted the poles into the rings on the sides of the ark to carry it.

⁶He made the atonement cover of pure gold—two and a half cubits long and a cubit and a half wide.ᵈ ⁷Then he made two cherubim out of hammered gold at the ends of the cover. ⁸He made one cherub on one end and the second cherub on the other; at the two ends he made them of one piece with the cover. ⁹The cherubim had their wings spread upward, overshadowing the cover with them. The cherubim faced each other, looking toward the cover.

¹⁰Theyᵉ made the table of acacia wood—two cubits long, a cubit wide, and a cubit and a half high.ᶠ ¹¹Then they overlaid it with pure gold and made a gold molding around it. ¹²They also made around it a rim a handbreadthᵍ wide and put a gold molding on the rim. ¹³They cast four gold rings for the table and fastened them to the four corners, where the four legs were. ¹⁴The rings were put close to the rim to hold the poles used

ᶜ1 That is, about 3 3/4 feet (about 1.1 meters) long and 2 1/4 feet (about 0.7 meter) wide and high　ᵈ6 That is, about 3 3/4 feet (about 1.1 meters) long and 2 1/4 feet (about 0.7 meter) wide　ᵉ10 Or He; also in verses 11-29　ᶠ10 That is, about 3 feet (about 0.9 meter) long, 1 1/2 feet (about 0.5 meter) wide, and 2 1/4 feet (about 0.7 meter) high　ᵍ12 That is, about 3 inches (about 8 centimeters) in carrying the table. ¹⁵The poles for carrying the table were made of acacia wood and were overlaid with gold. ¹⁶And they made from pure gold the articles for the table—its plates and dishes and bowls and its pitchers for the pouring out of drink offerings.

¹⁷They made the lampstand of pure gold and hammered it out, base and shaft; its flowerlike cups, buds and blossoms were of one piece with it. ¹⁸Six branches extended from the sides of the lampstand—three on one side and three on the other. ¹⁹Three cups shaped like almond flowers with buds and blossoms were on one branch, three on the next branch and the same for all six branches extending from the lampstand. ²⁰And on the lampstand were four cups shaped like almond flowers with buds and blossoms. ²¹One bud was under the first pair of branches extending from the lampstand, a second bud under the second pair, and a third bud under the third pair—six branches in all. ²²The buds and the branches were all of one piece with the lampstand, hammered out of pure gold.

²³They made its seven lamps, as well as its wick trimmers and trays, of pure gold. ²⁴They made the lampstand and all its accessories from one talent[h] of pure gold.

²⁵They made the altar of incense out of acacia wood. It was square, a cubit long and a cubit wide, and two cubits high[i]—its horns of one piece with it. ²⁶They overlaid the top and all the sides and the horns with pure gold, and made a gold molding around it. ²⁷They made two gold rings below the molding—two on opposite sides—to hold the poles used to carry it. ²⁸They made the poles of acacia wood and overlaid them with gold.

²⁹They also made the sacred anointing oil and the pure, fragrant incense—the work of a perfumer.

38 They[j] built the altar of burnt offering of acacia wood, three cubits[k] high; it was square, five cubits long and five cubits wide.[l] ²They made a horn at each of the four corners, so that the horns and the altar were of one piece, and they overlaid the altar with bronze. ³They made all its utensils of bronze—its pots, shovels, sprinkling bowls, meat forks and firepans. ⁴They made a grating for the altar, a bronze network, to be under its ledge, halfway up the altar. ⁵They cast bronze rings to hold the poles for the four corners of the bronze grating. ⁶They made the poles of acacia wood and overlaid them with bronze. ⁷They inserted the poles into the rings so they would be on the sides of the altar for carrying it. They made it hollow, out of boards.

⁸They made the bronze basin and its bronze stand from the mirrors of the women who served at the entrance to the Tent of Meeting.

⁹Next they made the courtyard. The south side was a hundred cubits[m] long and had curtains of finely twisted linen, ¹⁰with twenty posts and twenty bronze bases, and with silver hooks and bands on the posts. ¹¹The north side was also a hundred cubits long and had twenty posts and twenty bronze bases, with silver hooks and bands on the posts.

¹²The west end was fifty cubits[n] wide and had curtains, with ten posts and ten bases, with silver hooks and bands on the posts. ¹³The east end, toward the sunrise, was also fifty cubits wide. ¹⁴Curtains fifteen cubits[o] long were on one side of the entrance, with three posts and three bases, ¹⁵and curtains fifteen cubits long were on the other side of the entrance to the courtyard, with three posts and three bases. ¹⁶All the curtains around the courtyard were of finely twisted linen. ¹⁷The bases for the posts were bronze. The hooks and bands on the posts were silver, and their tops were overlaid with silver; so all the posts of the courtyard had silver bands.

¹⁸The curtain for the entrance to the courtyard was of blue, purple and scarlet yarn and finely twisted linen—the work of an embroiderer. It was twenty cubits[p] long and, like the curtains of the courtyard, five cubits[q] high, ¹⁹with four posts and four bronze bases. Their hooks and bands were silver, and their tops were overlaid with silver. ²⁰All the tent pegs of the tabernacle and of the surrounding courtyard were bronze. □

²¹These are the amounts of the materials used for the tabernacle, the tabernacle of the Testimony, which were recorded at Moses' command by the Levites under the direction of Ithamar son of Aaron, the priest. ²²(Bezalel son of Uri, the son of Hur, of the tribe of Judah, made everything the LORD commanded Moses; ²³with him was Oholiab

---

h24 That is, about 75 pounds (about 34 kilograms)   i25 That is, about 1 1/2 feet (about 0.5 meter) long and wide, and about 3 feet (about 0.9 meter) high   j1 Or He; also in verses 2-9   k1 That is, about 4 1/2 feet (about 1.3 meters)   l1 That is, about 7 1/2 feet (about 2.3 meters) long and wide   m9 That is, about 150 feet (about 46 meters)   n12 That is, about 75 feet (about 23 meters)   o14 That is, about 22 1/2 feet (about 6.9 meters)   p18 That is, about 30 feet (about 9 meters)   q18 That is, about 7 1/2 feet (about 2.3 meters) son of Ahisamach, of the tribe of Dan—a crafts-man and designer, and an embroiderer in blue, purple and scarlet yarn and fine linen.) ²⁴The to-tal amount of the gold from the wave offering used for all the work on the sanctuary was 29 talents and 730 shekels,ʳ according to the sanc-tuary shekel.

²⁵The silver obtained from those of the com-munity who were counted in the census was 100 talents and 1,775 shekels,ˢ according to the sanctuary shekel— ²⁶one beka per person, that is, half a shekel,ᵗ according to the sanctuary shekel, from everyone who had crossed over to those counted, twenty years old or more, a total of 603,550 men. ²⁷The 100 talentsᵘ of silver were used to cast the bases for the sanctuary and for the curtain—100 bases from the 100 talents, one talent for each base. ²⁸They used the 1,775 shek-elsᵛ to make the hooks for the posts, to overlay the tops of the posts, and to make their bands.

²⁹The bronze from the wave offering was 70 talents and 2,400 shekels.ʷ ³⁰They used it to make the bases for the entrance to the Tent of Meeting, the bronze altar with its bronze grating and all its utensils, ³¹the bases for the surround-ing courtyard and those for its entrance and all the tent pegs for the tabernacle and those for the surrounding courtyard.

39

From the blue, purple and scarlet yarn they made woven garments for ministering in the sanctuary. They also made sacred garments for Aaron, as the LORD commanded Moses.

²Theyˣ made the ephod of gold, and of blue, purple and scarlet yarn, and of finely twisted linen. ³They hammered out thin sheets of gold and cut strands to be worked into the blue, pur-ple and scarlet yarn and fine linen—the work of a skilled craftsman. ⁴They made shoulder pieces for the ephod, which were attached to two of its corners, so it could be fastened. ⁵Its skillfully wo-ven waistband was like it—of one piece with the ephod and made with gold, and with blue, purple and scarlet yarn, and with finely twisted linen, as the LORD commanded Moses.

⁶They mounted the onyx stones in gold filigree settings and engraved them like a seal with the names of the sons of Israel. ⁷Then they fastened them on the shoulder pieces of the ephod as me-morial stones for the sons of Israel, as the LORD commanded Moses.

⁸They fashioned the breastpiece—the work of a skilled craftsman. They made it like the ephod: of gold, and of blue, purple and scarlet yarn, and of finely twisted linen. ⁹It was square—a spanʸ long and a span wide—and folded double. ¹⁰Then they mounted four rows of precious stones on it. In the first row there was a ruby, a topaz and a beryl; ¹¹in the second row a turquoise, a sap-phireᶻ and an emerald; ¹²in the third row a ja-cinth, an agate and an amethyst; ¹³in the fourth row a chrysolite, an onyx and a jasper.ᵃ They were mounted in gold filigree settings. ¹⁴There were twelve stones, one for each of the names of the sons of Israel, each engraved like a seal with the name of one of the twelve tribes.

¹⁵For the breastpiece they made braided chains of pure gold, like a rope. ¹⁶They made two gold filigree settings and two gold rings, and fastened the rings to two of the corners of the breastpiece. ¹⁷They fastened the two gold chains to the rings at the corners of the breastpiece, ¹⁸and the other ends of the chains to the two settings, attaching them to the shoulder pieces of the ephod at the front. ¹⁹They made two gold rings and attached them to the other two corners of the breastpiece on the inside edge next to the ephod. ²⁰Then they made two more gold rings and attached them to the bottom of the shoulder pieces on the front of the ephod, close to the seam just above the waist-band of the ephod. ²¹They tied the rings of the breastpiece to the rings of the ephod with blue cord, connecting it to the waistband so that the breastpiece would not swing out from the ephod—as the LORD commanded Moses.

²²They made the robe of the ephod entirely of blue cloth—the work of a weaver— ²³with an opening in the center of the robe like the opening of a collar,ᵇ and a band around this opening, so that it would not tear. ²⁴They made pomegranates of blue, purple and scarlet yarn and finely twisted linen around the hem of the robe. ²⁵And they made bells of pure gold and attached them around the hem between the pomegranates. ²⁶The bells and pomegranates alternated around the

ʳ24 The weight of the gold was a little over one ton (about 1 metric ton).   ˢ25 The weight of the silver was a little over 3 3/4 tons (about 3.4 metric tons).   ᵗ26 That is, about 1/5 ounce (about 5.5 grams)
ᵘ27 That is, about 3 3/4 tons (about 3.4 metric tons)   ᵛ28 That is, about 45 pounds (about 20 kilograms)   ʷ29 The weight of the bronze was about 2 1/2 tons (about 2.4 metric tons).   ˣ2 Or He; also in verses 7, 8 and 22   ʸ9 That is, about 9 inches (about 22 centimeters)
ᶻ11 Or lapis lazuli   ᵃ13 The precise identification of some of these precious stones is uncertain.   ᵇ23 The meaning of the Hebrew for this word is uncertain.

hem of the robe to be worn for ministering, as the LORD commanded Moses.

²⁷For Aaron and his sons, they made tunics of fine linen—the work of a weaver— ²⁸and the turban of fine linen, the linen headbands and the undergarments of finely twisted linen. ²⁹The sash was of finely twisted linen and blue, purple and scarlet yarn—the work of an embroiderer—as the LORD commanded Moses.

³⁰They made the plate, the sacred diadem, out of pure gold and engraved on it, like an inscription on a seal: HOLY TO THE LORD. ³¹Then they fastened a blue cord to it to attach it to the turban, as the LORD commanded Moses.

 Discovering the Word 1. How would the ark, table, lampstand, altar of incense and altar of burnt offering assist the Israelites in their worship of God? 2. What aspect of God's nature and character does each article depict? 3. How does each article illustrate some aspect of our own relation to God? 4. What message was God trying to convey about himself and worship through the priests' ephod, breastpiece, robe and tunic (Ex 39)?

 Applying the Word 1. What advantages do we have in knowing and worshiping God that the Israelites did not have (Heb 9:1–15)? 2. The New Testament refers to Christians as priests (1Pe 2:5, 9). What is our function as priests? 3. What priestly garments are we called to wear (Col 3:12–14)?

 Responding in Prayer Praise God for revealing himself to us. Pray that he will use you in his service.

---

24 / *Exodus 39:32—40:38*
Time for Praise and Reflection

DEDICATIONS OF NEW churches are special. Such services evoke pride and appreciation. But with every privilege and blessing from God comes new responsibilities. Our church buildings, in a sense, call us to faithful worship, witness and obedience to God's will. Although God's glory may not be visible, it is present in our hearts. Join with Moses and the Israelites in this study and celebrate God's goodness to them and to us.

Warming Up to God What have you learned about God through these quiet times in Exodus? Reflect on the ways you've grown and thank God for molding you in the image of his Son.

Read Exodus 39:32—40:38.

---

³²So all the work on the tabernacle, the Tent of Meeting, was completed. The Israelites did everything just as the LORD commanded Moses. ³³Then they brought the tabernacle to Moses: the tent and all its furnishings, its clasps, frames, crossbars, posts and bases; ³⁴the covering of ram skins dyed red, the covering of hides of sea cowsᶜ and the shielding curtain; ³⁵the ark of the Testimony with its poles and the atonement cover; ³⁶the table with all its articles and the bread of the Presence; ³⁷the pure gold lampstand with its row of lamps and all its accessories, and the oil for the light; ³⁸the gold altar, the anointing oil, the fragrant incense, and the curtain for the entrance to the tent; ³⁹the bronze altar with its bronze grating, its poles and all its utensils; the basin with its stand; ⁴⁰the curtains of the courtyard with its posts and bases, and the curtain for the entrance

to the courtyard; the ropes and tent pegs for the courtyard; all the furnishings for the tabernacle, the Tent of Meeting; ⁴¹and the woven garments worn for ministering in the sanctuary, both the sacred garments for Aaron the priest and the garments for his sons when serving as priests.

⁴²The Israelites had done all the work just as the LORD had commanded Moses. ⁴³Moses inspected the work and saw that they had done it just as the LORD had commanded. So Moses blessed them.

40 Then the LORD said to Moses: ²"Set up the tabernacle, the Tent of Meeting, on the first day of the first month. ³Place the ark of the Testimony in it and shield the ark with the curtain. ⁴Bring in the table

ᶜ34 That is, dugongs

and set out what belongs on it. Then bring in the lampstand and set up its lamps. 5Place the gold altar of incense in front of the ark of the Testimony and put the curtain at the entrance to the tabernacle.

6"Place the altar of burnt offering in front of the entrance to the tabernacle, the Tent of Meeting; 7place the basin between the Tent of Meeting and the altar and put water in it. 8Set up the courtyard around it and put the curtain at the entrance to the courtyard.

9"Take the anointing oil and anoint the tabernacle and everything in it; consecrate it and all its furnishings, and it will be holy. 10Then anoint the altar of burnt offering and all its utensils; consecrate the altar, and it will be most holy. 11Anoint the basin and its stand and consecrate them.

12"Bring Aaron and his sons to the entrance to the Tent of Meeting and wash them with water. 13Then dress Aaron in the sacred garments, anoint him and consecrate him so he may serve me as priest. 14Bring his sons and dress them in tunics. 15Anoint them just as you anointed their father, so they may serve me as priests. Their anointing will be to a priesthood that will continue for all generations to come." 16Moses did everything just as the LORD commanded him.

17So the tabernacle was set up on the first day of the first month in the second year. 18When Moses set up the tabernacle, he put the bases in place, erected the frames, inserted the crossbars and set up the posts. 19Then he spread the tent over the tabernacle and put the covering over the tent, as the LORD commanded him.

20He took the Testimony and placed it in the ark, attached the poles to the ark and put the atonement cover over it. 21Then he brought the ark into the tabernacle and hung the shielding curtain and shielded the ark of the Testimony, as the LORD commanded him.

22Moses placed the table in the Tent of Meeting on the north side of the tabernacle outside the curtain 23and set out the bread on it before the LORD, as the LORD commanded him.

24He placed the lampstand in the Tent of Meeting opposite the table on the south side of the tabernacle 25and set up the lamps before the LORD, as the LORD commanded him.

26Moses placed the gold altar in the Tent of Meeting in front of the curtain 27and burned fragrant incense on it, as the LORD commanded him. 28Then he put up the curtain at the entrance to the tabernacle.

29He set the altar of burnt offering near the entrance to the tabernacle, the Tent of Meeting, and offered on it burnt offerings and grain offerings, as the LORD commanded him.

30He placed the basin between the Tent of Meeting and the altar and put water in it for washing, 31and Moses and Aaron and his sons used it to wash their hands and feet. 32They washed whenever they entered the Tent of Meeting or approached the altar, as the LORD commanded Moses.

33Then Moses set up the courtyard around the tabernacle and altar and put up the curtain at the entrance to the courtyard. And so Moses finished the work.

34Then the cloud covered the Tent of Meeting, and the glory of the LORD filled the tabernacle. 35Moses could not enter the Tent of Meeting because the cloud had settled upon it, and the glory of the LORD filled the tabernacle.

36In all the travels of the Israelites, whenever the cloud lifted from above the tabernacle, they would set out; 37but if the cloud did not lift, they did not set out—until the day it lifted. 38So the cloud of the LORD was over the tabernacle by day, and fire was in the cloud by night, in the sight of all the house of Israel during all their travels.

Discovering the Word 1. What feelings do you think the Israelites had in working "just as the Lord had commanded" and in showing their work to Moses? 2. Why was it necessary to anoint everything, burn incense and make offerings (40:9–10, 26–29)? 3. Buildings and furnishings today are not holy, as the tabernacle and its furnishings were. What are the components of God's dwelling place today (Eph 2:19–22)? 4. How did God reveal his presence (40:34–38)?

Applying the Word 1. As you invest your life for God, what satisfaction have you gained from following his plan? 2. In what circumstances have you especially felt God's presence? 3. How does God reveal his glory and presence in our midst today?

Responding in Prayer Thank God for the ways he has used the stories of Exodus to strengthen you and draw you closer to himself.

Leviticus

"**Y**ou're spending your quiet time reading *Leviticus*? Isn't it just a list of laws? And hasn't that all been replaced by grace?"

Those are some of the astonished responses you're likely to get when you tell people you're reading this book of the Bible. It's true, Leviticus has never made popular devotional reading. But for those who dare to venture into it daily, it brings us face to face with realities about God, the world and ourselves.

The book is concerned with living out the sacred trust of holiness. *Leviticus* means "pertaining to the Levites." To the descendants of Levi, Jacob's son, God gave special responsibilities for worship (Nu 1:47–53; 3:5–13). The Lord set them apart as his priests who were to make sure that the tabernacle—and the people—remained holy.

The first seven chapters are instructions for various offerings. Chapters 8—10 relate the ordination of Aaron and his sons as priests. Chapters 11—15 are about cleansing. In chapter 16 the all-important Day of Atonement (Yom Kippur) is instituted. The last eleven chapters deal with moral laws for everyday living, priestly behavior, festivals and the results to be expected from obeying or disobeying God.

Except for brief narrative portions, the book presents itself as spoken by God to Moses. No proof is offered. It simply says, "The Lord said to Moses," or sometimes, "The Lord said to Moses and Aaron." The time is shortly after the Israelites' exodus from Egypt, an event long dated c. 1220 B.C., though recent discoveries indicate it may have been earlier, c. 1440 B.C.

This is all historically interesting and deserves study—but is it appropriate for a Christian's quiet time? Why concern ourselves with Old Testament sacrifices and purification when Christ has fulfilled all the law? What do we gain today from a devotional reading of Leviticus?

First of all, Leviticus shows us God. It says that God is holy, a truth that made the prophet Isaiah cry out, "Woe is me!" Yet this holy God talks to Moses, a man sometimes of timidity and temper, and, through Moses, he talks to ordinary people, explaining how to live and how to know him.

Leviticus also shows us ourselves. It tells us we can know God. It says that we are not holy unless God makes us so. It portrays people trying to get around God's laws—something we all still try in various ways. And it promises that a broken relationship with God can be restored through his mercy.

Finally, Leviticus shows us the world, mostly indirectly, by telling us how God's people are different from the world. Some differences are external, but they are primarily internal because God has already made us different from the rest of humanity. Leviticus tells us that as we live in this world we are bound to be distinctive simply because we belong to God.

God commands his people: "Be holy, because I am holy" (Lev 11:44). He also assures us: "I am the LORD, who makes you holy" (Lev 20:8). May you grow in holiness as you meditate on this book of holiness.

Outline

1/ Leviticus 1 ——————————————— *A Holy Sacrifice*

2/ Leviticus 8 ——————————————— *A Chosen Priesthood*

3/ Leviticus 10 —————————————— *Where Flippancy Doesn't Fit*

4/ Leviticus 16 —————————————— *Facing Temptation*

5/ Leviticus 19 —————————————— *Laws with a Purpose*

6/ Leviticus 23 —————————————— *Feasts of Remembrance*

7/ Leviticus 25 —————————————— *A Garden to Tend*

8/ Leviticus 26 —————————————— *Reaping Results*

1 / *Leviticus 1*
A Holy Sacrifice

DROPPING A FEW coins in the Salvation Army kettle at Christmas or giving used items to Goodwill Industries has become routine for most of us. But what if you were asked to contribute your best suit or your best set of china? God asked the Israelites to give their best as a sacrifice to him. No doubt some did it with secret grumblings, while others did it with joy.

 Warming Up to God Reflect on a time when you made some difficult sacrifices and the Lord made the cost worth it. Allow your words of praise and gratitude to well up in response.

 Read Leviticus 1.

1 The Lord called to Moses and spoke to him from the Tent of Meeting. He said, ²"Speak to the Israelites and say to them: 'When any of you brings an offering to the Lord, bring as your offering an animal from either the herd or the flock.

³" 'If the offering is a burnt offering from the herd, he is to offer a male without defect. He must present it at the entrance to the Tent of Meeting so that it*a* will be acceptable to the Lord. ⁴He is to lay his hand on the head of the burnt offering, and it will be accepted on his behalf to make atonement for him. ⁵He is to slaughter the young bull before the Lord, and then Aaron's sons the priests shall bring the blood and sprinkle it against the altar on all sides at the entrance to the Tent of Meeting. ⁶He is to skin the burnt offering and cut it into pieces. ⁷The sons of Aaron the priest are to put fire on the altar and arrange wood on the fire. ⁸Then Aaron's sons the priests shall arrange the pieces, including the head and the fat, on the burning wood that is on the altar. ⁹He is to wash the inner parts and the legs with water, and the priest is to burn all of it on the altar. It is a burnt offering, an offering made by fire, an aroma pleasing to the Lord.

¹⁰" 'If the offering is a burnt offering from the flock, from either the sheep or the goats, he is to offer a male without defect. ¹¹He is to slaughter it at the north side of the altar before the Lord, and Aaron's sons the priests shall sprinkle its blood against the altar on all sides. ¹²He is to cut it into pieces, and the priest shall arrange them, including the head and the fat, on the burning wood that is on the altar. ¹³He is to wash the inner parts and the legs with water, and the priest is to bring all of it and burn it on the altar. It is a burnt offering, an offering made by fire, an aroma pleasing to the Lord.

¹⁴" 'If the offering to the Lord is a burnt offering of birds, he is to offer a dove or a young pigeon. ¹⁵The priest shall bring it to the altar, wring off the head and burn it on the altar; its blood shall be drained out on the side of the altar. ¹⁶He is to remove the crop with its contents*b* and throw it to the east side of the altar, where the ashes are. ¹⁷He shall tear it open by the wings, not severing it completely, and then the priest shall burn it on the wood that is on the fire on the altar. It is a burnt offering, an offering made by fire, an aroma pleasing to the Lord.

*a*3 Or he   *b*16 Or crop and the feathers; the meaning of the Hebrew for this word is uncertain.

Discovering the Word 1. When the Israelites brought offerings from their herds or flocks, what requirements did they need to meet (vv. 3–10)? 2. How were the givers to identify themselves with the offering (v. 4)? 3. What was the purpose of the offering (v. 4)? 4. What part did the priests play in the offering (vv. 5–17)? 5. How was an offering of birds different from one from the herd or flock (vv. 14–17)?

Applying the Word 1. In Romans 12:1 Paul urges us: "Offer your bodies as living sacrifices, holy and pleasing to God—this is your spiritual act of worship." How is this sacrifice different from the burnt offerings of Leviticus 1? How is it the same? 2. Verses 9, 13 and 17 describe how the offering creates "an aroma pleasing to the Lord." How is your life pleasing to God?

Responding in Prayer Give thanks for Christ's sacrifice and the salvation it has made available to you. Pray for guidance in how you can offer your body as a living sacrifice today.

Leviticus 2—7

2 " 'When someone brings a grain offering to the LORD, his offering is to be of fine flour. He is to pour oil on it, put incense on it ²and take it to Aaron's sons the priests. The priest shall take a handful of the fine flour and oil, together with all the incense, and burn this as a memorial portion on the altar, an offering made by fire, an aroma pleasing to the LORD. ³The rest of the grain offering belongs to Aaron and his sons; it is a most holy part of the offerings made to the LORD by fire.

⁴" 'If you bring a grain offering baked in an oven, it is to consist of fine flour: cakes made without yeast and mixed with oil, orᶜ wafers made without yeast and spread with oil. ⁵If your grain offering is prepared on a griddle, it is to be made of fine flour mixed with oil, and without yeast. ⁶Crumble it and pour oil on it; it is a grain offering. ⁷If your grain offering is cooked in a pan, it is to be made of fine flour and oil. ⁸Bring the grain offering made of these things to the LORD; present it to the priest, who shall take it to the altar. ⁹He shall take out the memorial portion from the grain offering and burn it on the altar as an offering made by fire, an aroma pleasing to the LORD. ¹⁰The rest of the grain offering belongs to Aaron and his sons; it is a most holy part of the offerings made to the LORD by fire.

¹¹" 'Every grain offering you bring to the LORD must be made without yeast, for you are not to burn any yeast or honey in an offering made to the LORD by fire. ¹²You may bring them to the LORD as an offering of the firstfruits, but they are not to be offered on the altar as a pleasing aroma. ¹³Season all your grain offerings with salt. Do not leave the salt of the covenant of your God out of your grain offerings; add salt to all your offerings.

¹⁴" 'If you bring a grain offering of firstfruits to the LORD, offer crushed heads of new grain roasted in the fire. ¹⁵Put oil and incense on it; it is a grain offering. ¹⁶The priest shall burn the memorial portion of the crushed grain and the oil, together with all the incense, as an offering made to the LORD by fire.

3 " 'If someone's offering is a fellowship offering,ᵈ and he offers an animal from the herd, whether male or female, he is to present before the LORD an animal without defect. ²He is to lay his hand on the head of his offering and slaughter it at the entrance to the Tent of Meeting. Then Aaron's sons the priests shall sprinkle the blood against the altar on all sides. ³From the fellowship offering he is to bring a sacrifice made to the LORD by fire: all the fat that covers the inner parts or is connected to them, ⁴both kidneys with the fat on them near the loins, and the covering of the liver, which he will remove with the kidneys. ⁵Then Aaron's sons are to burn it on the altar on top of the burnt offering that is on the burning wood, as an offering made by fire, an aroma pleasing to the LORD.

⁶" 'If he offers an animal from the flock as a fellowship offering to the LORD, he is to offer a male or female without defect. ⁷If he offers a lamb, he is to present it before the LORD. ⁸He is to lay his hand on the head of his offering and slaughter it in front of the Tent of Meeting. Then Aaron's sons shall sprinkle its blood against the altar on all sides. ⁹From the fellowship offering he is to bring a sacrifice made to the LORD by fire: its fat, the entire fat tail cut off close to the backbone, all the fat that covers the inner parts or is connected to them, ¹⁰both kidneys with the fat on them near the loins, and the covering of the liver, which he will remove with the kidneys. ¹¹The priest shall burn them on the altar as food, an offering made to the LORD by fire.

¹²" 'If his offering is a goat, he is to present it before the LORD. ¹³He is to lay his hand on its head and slaughter it in front of the Tent of Meeting. Then Aaron's sons shall sprinkle its blood against the altar on all sides. ¹⁴From what he offers he is to make this offering to the LORD by fire: all the fat that covers the inner parts or is connected to them, ¹⁵both kidneys with the fat on them near the loins, and the covering of the liver, which he will remove with the kidneys. ¹⁶The

ᶜ4 Or and   ᵈ1 Traditionally *peace offering;* also in verses 3, 6 and 9 priest shall burn them on the altar as food, an offering made by fire, a pleasing aroma. All the fat is the Lord's.

¹⁷" 'This is a lasting ordinance for the generations to come, wherever you live: You must not eat any fat or any blood.' "

4 The Lord said to Moses, ²"Say to the Israelites: 'When anyone sins unintentionally and does what is forbidden in any of the Lord's commands—

³" 'If the anointed priest sins, bringing guilt on the people, he must bring to the Lord a young bull without defect as a sin offering for the sin he has committed. ⁴He is to present the bull at the entrance to the Tent of Meeting before the Lord. He is to lay his hand on its head and slaughter it before the Lord. ⁵Then the anointed priest shall take some of the bull's blood and carry it into the Tent of Meeting. ⁶He is to dip his finger into the blood and sprinkle some of it seven times before the Lord, in front of the curtain of the sanctuary. ⁷The priest shall then put some of the blood on the horns of the altar of fragrant incense that is before the Lord in the Tent of Meeting. The rest of the bull's blood he shall pour out at the base of the altar of burnt offering at the entrance to the Tent of Meeting. ⁸He shall remove all the fat from the bull of the sin offering—the fat that covers the inner parts or is connected to them, ⁹both kidneys with the fat on them near the loins, and the covering of the liver, which he will remove with the kidneys— ¹⁰just as the fat is removed from the ox*ᵉ* sacrificed as a fellowship offering.*ᶠ* Then the priest shall burn them on the altar of burnt offering. ¹¹But the hide of the bull and all its flesh, as well as the head and legs, the inner parts and offal— ¹²that is, all the rest of the bull—he must take outside the camp to a place ceremonially clean, where the ashes are thrown, and burn it in a wood fire on the ash heap.

¹³" 'If the whole Israelite community sins unintentionally and does what is forbidden in any of the Lord's commands, even though the community is unaware of the matter, they are guilty. ¹⁴When they become aware of the sin they committed, the assembly must bring a young bull as a sin offering and present it before the Tent of Meeting. ¹⁵The elders of the community are to lay their hands on the bull's head before the Lord, and the bull shall be slaughtered before the Lord. ¹⁶Then the anointed priest is to take some of the

bull's blood into the Tent of Meeting. ¹⁷He shall dip his finger into the blood and sprinkle it before the Lord seven times in front of the curtain. ¹⁸He is to put some of the blood on the horns of the altar that is before the Lord in the Tent of Meeting. The rest of the blood he shall pour out at the base of the altar of burnt offering at the entrance to the Tent of Meeting. ¹⁹He shall remove all the fat from it and burn it on the altar, ²⁰and do with this bull just as he did with the bull for the sin offering. In this way the priest will make atonement for them, and they will be forgiven. ²¹Then he shall take the bull outside the camp and burn it as he burned the first bull. This is the sin offering for the community.

²²" 'When a leader sins unintentionally and does what is forbidden in any of the commands of the Lord his God, he is guilty. ²³When he is made aware of the sin he committed, he must bring as his offering a male goat without defect. ²⁴He is to lay his hand on the goat's head and slaughter it at the place where the burnt offering is slaughtered before the Lord. It is a sin offering. ²⁵Then the priest shall take some of the blood of the sin offering with his finger and put it on the horns of the altar of burnt offering and pour out the rest of the blood at the base of the altar. ²⁶He shall burn all the fat on the altar as he burned the fat of the fellowship offering. In this way the priest will make atonement for the man's sin, and he will be forgiven.

²⁷" 'If a member of the community sins unintentionally and does what is forbidden in any of the Lord's commands, he is guilty. ²⁸When he is made aware of the sin he committed, he must bring as his offering for the sin he committed a female goat without defect. ²⁹He is to lay his hand on the head of the sin offering and slaughter it at the place of the burnt offering. ³⁰Then the priest is to take some of the blood with his finger and put it on the horns of the altar of burnt offering and pour out the rest of the blood at the base of the altar. ³¹He shall remove all the fat, just as the fat is removed from the fellowship offering, and the priest shall burn it on the altar as an aroma pleasing to the Lord. In this way the priest will make atonement for him, and he will be forgiven.

³²" 'If he brings a lamb as his sin offering, he is to bring a female without defect. ³³He is to lay his

ᵉ10 The Hebrew word can include both male and female.
ᶠ10 Traditionally *peace offering*; also in verses 26, 31 and 35

hand on its head and slaughter it for a sin offering at the place where the burnt offering is slaughtered. ³⁴Then the priest shall take some of the blood of the sin offering with his finger and put it on the horns of the altar of burnt offering and pour out the rest of the blood at the base of the altar. ³⁵He shall remove all the fat, just as the fat is removed from the lamb of the fellowship offering, and the priest shall burn it on the altar on top of the offerings made to the Lord by fire. In this way the priest will make atonement for him for the sin he has committed, and he will be forgiven.

5 " 'If a person sins because he does not speak up when he hears a public charge to testify regarding something he has seen or learned about, he will be held responsible.

²" 'Or if a person touches anything ceremonially unclean—whether the carcasses of unclean wild animals or of unclean livestock or of unclean creatures that move along the ground—even though he is unaware of it, he has become unclean and is guilty.

³" 'Or if he touches human uncleanness—anything that would make him unclean—even though he is unaware of it, when he learns of it he will be guilty.

⁴" 'Or if a person thoughtlessly takes an oath to do anything, whether good or evil—in any matter one might carelessly swear about—even though he is unaware of it, in any case when he learns of it he will be guilty.

⁵" 'When anyone is guilty in any of these ways, he must confess in what way he has sinned ⁶and, as a penalty for the sin he has committed, he must bring to the Lord a female lamb or goat from the flock as a sin offering; and the priest shall make atonement for him for his sin.

⁷" 'If he cannot afford a lamb, he is to bring two doves or two young pigeons to the Lord as a penalty for his sin—one for a sin offering and the other for a burnt offering. ⁸He is to bring them to the priest, who shall first offer the one for the sin offering. He is to wring its head from its neck, not severing it completely, ⁹and is to sprinkle some of the blood of the sin offering against the side of the altar; the rest of the blood must be drained out at the base of the altar. It is a sin offering. ¹⁰The priest shall then offer the other as a burnt offering in the prescribed way and make atonement for him for the sin he has committed, and he will be forgiven.

¹¹" 'If, however, he cannot afford two doves or two young pigeons, he is to bring as an offering for his sin a tenth of an ephah^g of fine flour for a sin offering. He must not put oil or incense on it, because it is a sin offering. ¹²He is to bring it to the priest, who shall take a handful of it as a memorial portion and burn it on the altar on top of the offerings made to the Lord by fire. It is a sin offering. ¹³In this way the priest will make atonement for him for any of these sins he has committed, and he will be forgiven. The rest of the offering will belong to the priest, as in the case of the grain offering.' "

¹⁴The Lord said to Moses: ¹⁵"When a person commits a violation and sins unintentionally in regard to any of the Lord's holy things, he is to bring to the Lord as a penalty a ram from the flock, one without defect and of the proper value in silver, according to the sanctuary shekel.^h It is a guilt offering. ¹⁶He must make restitution for what he has failed to do in regard to the holy things, add a fifth of the value to that and give it all to the priest, who will make atonement for him with the ram as a guilt offering, and he will be forgiven.

¹⁷"If a person sins and does what is forbidden in any of the Lord's commands, even though he does not know it, he is guilty and will be held responsible. ¹⁸He is to bring to the priest as a guilt offering a ram from the flock, one without defect and of the proper value. In this way the priest will make atonement for him for the wrong he has committed unintentionally, and he will be forgiven. ¹⁹It is a guilt offering; he has been guilty ofⁱ wrongdoing against the Lord."

6 The Lord said to Moses: ²"If anyone sins and is unfaithful to the Lord by deceiving his neighbor about something entrusted to him or left in his care or stolen, or if he cheats him, ³or if he finds lost property and lies about it, or if he swears falsely, or if he commits any such sin that people may do— ⁴when he thus sins and becomes guilty, he must return what he has stolen or taken by extortion, or what was entrusted to him, or the lost property he found, ⁵or whatever it was he swore falsely about. He must make restitution in full, add a fifth of the value to it and give it all to the owner on the day he presents his guilt offering. ⁶And as a penalty he must bring to

^g11 That is, probably about 2 quarts (about 2 liters)   ^h15 That is, about 2/5 ounce (about 11.5 grams)   ⁱ19 Or has made full expiation for his

the priest, that is, to the LORD, his guilt offering, a ram from the flock, one without defect and of the proper value. ⁷In this way the priest will make atonement for him before the LORD, and he will be forgiven for any of these things he did that made him guilty.”

⁸The LORD said to Moses: ⁹“Give Aaron and his sons this command: ‘These are the regulations for the burnt offering: The burnt offering is to remain on the altar hearth throughout the night, till morning, and the fire must be kept burning on the altar. ¹⁰The priest shall then put on his linen clothes, with linen undergarments next to his body, and shall remove the ashes of the burnt offering that the fire has consumed on the altar and place them beside the altar. ¹¹Then he is to take off these clothes and put on others, and carry the ashes outside the camp to a place that is ceremonially clean. ¹²The fire on the altar must be kept burning; it must not go out. Every morning the priest is to add firewood and arrange the burnt offering on the fire and burn the fat of the fellowship offerings[j] on it. ¹³The fire must be kept burning on the altar continuously; it must not go out.

¹⁴“ ‘These are the regulations for the grain offering: Aaron's sons are to bring it before the LORD, in front of the altar. ¹⁵The priest is to take a handful of fine flour and oil, together with all the incense on the grain offering, and burn the memorial portion on the altar as an aroma pleasing to the LORD. ¹⁶Aaron and his sons shall eat the rest of it, but it is to be eaten without yeast in a holy place; they are to eat it in the courtyard of the Tent of Meeting. ¹⁷It must not be baked with yeast; I have given it as their share of the offerings made to me by fire. Like the sin offering and the guilt offering, it is most holy. ¹⁸Any male descendant of Aaron may eat it. It is his regular share of the offerings made to the LORD by fire for the generations to come. Whatever touches them will become holy.[k] ’ ”

¹⁹The LORD also said to Moses, ²⁰“This is the offering Aaron and his sons are to bring to the LORD on the day he[l] is anointed: a tenth of an ephah[m] of fine flour as a regular grain offering, half of it in the morning and half in the evening. ²¹Prepare it with oil on a griddle; bring it well-mixed and present the grain offering broken[n] in pieces as an aroma pleasing to the LORD. ²²The son who is to succeed him as anointed priest shall prepare it. It is the LORD's regular share and is to

be burned completely. ²³Every grain offering of a priest shall be burned completely; it must not be eaten.”

²⁴The LORD said to Moses, ²⁵“Say to Aaron and his sons: ‘These are the regulations for the sin offering: The sin offering is to be slaughtered before the LORD in the place the burnt offering is slaughtered; it is most holy. ²⁶The priest who offers it shall eat it; it is to be eaten in a holy place, in the courtyard of the Tent of Meeting. ²⁷Whatever touches any of the flesh will become holy, and if any of the blood is spattered on a garment, you must wash it in a holy place. ²⁸The clay pot the meat is cooked in must be broken; but if it is cooked in a bronze pot, the pot is to be scoured and rinsed with water. ²⁹Any male in a priest's family may eat it; it is most holy. ³⁰But any sin offering whose blood is brought into the Tent of Meeting to make atonement in the Holy Place must not be eaten; it must be burned.

7 “ ‘These are the regulations for the guilt offering, which is most holy: ²The guilt offering is to be slaughtered in the place where the burnt offering is slaughtered, and its blood is to be sprinkled against the altar on all sides. ³All its fat shall be offered: the fat tail and the fat that covers the inner parts, ⁴both kidneys with the fat on them near the loins, and the covering of the liver, which is to be removed with the kidneys. ⁵The priest shall burn them on the altar as an offering made to the LORD by fire. It is a guilt offering. ⁶Any male in a priest's family may eat it, but it must be eaten in a holy place; it is most holy.

⁷“ ‘The same law applies to both the sin offering and the guilt offering: They belong to the priest who makes atonement with them. ⁸The priest who offers a burnt offering for anyone may keep its hide for himself. ⁹Every grain offering baked in an oven or cooked in a pan or on a griddle belongs to the priest who offers it, ¹⁰and every grain offering, whether mixed with oil or dry, belongs equally to all the sons of Aaron.

¹¹“ ‘These are the regulations for the fellowship offering[o] a person may present to the LORD:

¹²“ ‘If he offers it as an expression of thankfulness, then along with this thank offering he is to offer cakes of bread made without yeast and

---

[j]12 Traditionally *peace offerings be holy*; similarly in verse 27   [k]18 Or *Whoever touches them must be holy*; similarly in verse 27   [l]20 Or *each*   [m]20 That is, probably about 2 quarts (about 2 liters)   [n]21 The meaning of the Hebrew for this word is uncertain.   [o]11 Traditionally *peace offering*; also in verses 13-37

mixed with oil, wafers made without yeast and spread with oil, and cakes of fine flour well-kneaded and mixed with oil. ¹³Along with his fellowship offering of thanksgiving he is to present an offering with cakes of bread made with yeast. ¹⁴He is to bring one of each kind as an offering, a contribution to the LORD; it belongs to the priest who sprinkles the blood of the fellowship offerings. ¹⁵The meat of his fellowship offering of thanksgiving must be eaten on the day it is offered; he must leave none of it till morning.

¹⁶ 'If, however, his offering is the result of a vow or is a freewill offering, the sacrifice shall be eaten on the day he offers it, but anything left over may be eaten on the next day. ¹⁷Any meat of the sacrifice left over till the third day must be burned up. ¹⁸If any meat of the fellowship offering is eaten on the third day, it will not be accepted. It will not be credited to the one who offered it, for it is impure; the person who eats any of it will be held responsible.

¹⁹ 'Meat that touches anything ceremonially unclean must not be eaten; it must be burned up. As for other meat, anyone ceremonially clean may eat it. ²⁰But if anyone who is unclean eats any meat of the fellowship offering belonging to the LORD, that person must be cut off from his people. ²¹If anyone touches something unclean—whether human uncleanness or an unclean animal or any unclean, detestable thing—and then eats any of the meat of the fellowship offering belonging to the LORD, that person must be cut off from his people.' "

²²The LORD said to Moses, ²³"Say to the Israelites: 'Do not eat any of the fat of cattle, sheep or goats. ²⁴The fat of an animal found dead or torn by wild animals may be used for any other purpose, but you must not eat it. ²⁵Anyone who eats the fat of an animal from which an offering by fire may beᵖ made to the LORD must be cut off from his people. ²⁶And wherever you live, you must not eat the blood of any bird or animal. ²⁷If anyone eats blood, that person must be cut off from his people.' "

²⁸The LORD said to Moses, ²⁹"Say to the Israelites: 'Anyone who brings a fellowship offering to the LORD is to bring part of it as his sacrifice to the LORD. ³⁰With his own hands he is to bring the offering made to the LORD by fire; he is to bring the fat, together with the breast, and wave the breast before the LORD as a wave offering. ³¹The priest shall burn the fat on the altar, but the breast belongs to Aaron and his sons. ³²You are to give the right thigh of your fellowship offerings to the priest as a contribution. ³³The son of Aaron who offers the blood and the fat of the fellowship offering shall have the right thigh as his share. ³⁴From the fellowship offerings of the Israelites, I have taken the breast that is waved and the thigh that is presented and have given them to Aaron the priest and his sons as their regular share from the Israelites.' "

³⁵This is the portion of the offerings made to the LORD by fire that were allotted to Aaron and his sons on the day they were presented to serve the LORD as priests. ³⁶On the day they were anointed, the LORD commanded that the Israelites give this to them as their regular share for the generations to come.

³⁷These, then, are the regulations for the burnt offering, the grain offering, the sin offering, the guilt offering, the ordination offering and the fellowship offering, ³⁸which the LORD gave Moses on Mount Sinai on the day he commanded the Israelites to bring their offerings to the LORD, in the Desert of Sinai.

ᵖ25 Or *fire is*

2 / *Leviticus 8*
A Chosen Priesthood

"YOU HAVE BEEN selected for this once-in-a-lifetime opportunity to own a piece of Paradise!" Maybe we'd feel more specially chosen if the sales letter weren't a computer-generated form letter. We would like to be singled out personally for a gift or an honor. The Lord is building all believers into a "holy priesthood" (1Pe 2:5). Our priesthood is foreshadowed in the original ordination ceremony of the priests of the Lord.

Warming Up to God Recall a time you felt called by the Lord for a particular task or role. Thank him for how he helped you fulfill it and for what the experience showed you about yourself and about God.

Read Leviticus 8.

8 The LORD said to Moses, ²"Bring Aaron and his sons, their garments, the anointing oil, the bull for the sin offering, the two rams and the basket containing bread made without yeast, ³and gather the entire assembly at the entrance to the Tent of Meeting." ⁴Moses did as the LORD commanded him, and the assembly gathered at the entrance to the Tent of Meeting.

⁵Moses said to the assembly, "This is what the LORD has commanded to be done." ⁶Then Moses brought Aaron and his sons forward and washed them with water. ⁷He put the tunic on Aaron, tied the sash around him, clothed him with the robe and put the ephod on him. He also tied the ephod to him by its skillfully woven waistband; so it was fastened on him. ⁸He placed the breastpiece on him and put the Urim and Thummim in the breastpiece. ⁹Then he placed the turban on Aaron's head and set the gold plate, the sacred diadem, on the front of it, as the LORD commanded Moses.

¹⁰Then Moses took the anointing oil and anointed the tabernacle and everything in it, and so consecrated them. ¹¹He sprinkled some of the oil on the altar seven times, anointing the altar and all its utensils and the basin with its stand, to consecrate them. ¹²He poured some of the anointing oil on Aaron's head and anointed him to consecrate him. ¹³Then he brought Aaron's sons forward, put tunics on them, tied sashes around them and put headbands on them, as the LORD commanded Moses.

¹⁴He then presented the bull for the sin offering, and Aaron and his sons laid their hands on its head. ¹⁵Moses slaughtered the bull and took some of the blood, and with his finger he put it on all the horns of the altar to purify the altar. He poured out the rest of the blood at the base of the altar. So he consecrated it to make atonement for it. ¹⁶Moses also took all the fat around the inner parts, the covering of the liver, and both kidneys and their fat, and burned it on the altar. ¹⁷But the bull with its hide and its flesh and its offal he burned up outside the camp, as the LORD commanded Moses.

¹⁸He then presented the ram for the burnt offering, and Aaron and his sons laid their hands on its head. ¹⁹Then Moses slaughtered the ram and sprinkled the blood against the altar on all sides. ²⁰He cut the ram into pieces and burned the head, the pieces and the fat. ²¹He washed the inner parts and the legs with water and burned the whole ram on the altar as a burnt offering, a pleasing aroma, an offering made to the LORD by fire, as the LORD commanded Moses.

²²He then presented the other ram, the ram for the ordination, and Aaron and his sons laid their hands on its head. ²³Moses slaughtered the ram and took some of its blood and put it on the lobe of Aaron's right ear, on the thumb of his right hand and on the big toe of his right foot. ²⁴Moses also brought Aaron's sons forward and put some of the blood on the lobes of their right ears, on the thumbs of their right hands and on the big toes of their right feet. Then he sprinkled blood against the altar on all sides. ²⁵He took the fat, the fat tail, all the fat around the inner parts, the covering of the liver, both kidneys and their fat and the right thigh. ²⁶Then from the basket of bread made without yeast, which was before the LORD, he took a cake of bread, and one made with oil, and a wafer; he put these on the fat portions and on the right thigh. ²⁷He put all these in the hands of Aaron and his sons and waved them before the LORD as a wave offering. ²⁸Then Moses took them from their hands and burned them on the altar on top of the burnt offering as an ordination offering, a pleasing aroma, an offering made to the LORD by fire. ²⁹He also took the breast—Moses' share of the ordination ram—and waved it before the LORD as a wave offering, as the LORD commanded Moses.

³⁰Then Moses took some of the anointing oil and some of the blood from the altar and sprinkled them on Aaron and his garments and on his sons and their garments. So he consecrated Aaron and his garments and his sons and their garments.

³¹Moses then said to Aaron and his sons, "Cook the meat at the entrance to the Tent of Meeting and eat it there with the bread from the basket of ordination offerings, as I commanded,

saying,^{q} 'Aaron and his sons are to eat it.' ³²Then burn up the rest of the meat and the bread. ³³Do not leave the entrance to the Tent of Meeting for seven days, until the days of your ordination are completed, for your ordination will last seven days. ³⁴What has been done today was commanded by the LORD to make atonement for you. ³⁵You must stay at the entrance to the Tent of Meeting day and night for seven days and do what the LORD requires, so you will not die; for that is what I have been commanded." ³⁶So Aaron and his sons did everything the LORD commanded through Moses.

^{q} 31 Or I was commanded:

Discovering the Word 1. How were Aaron and his sons singled out in front of the assembly of all the Israelites (vv. 1–13)? 2. Recalling the atonement sacrifice (Lev 1:4), what is the significance of Aaron and his sons' laying their hands on the heads of the offerings (vv. 14, 18, 22)? 3. How was the blood of the ordination lamb used to anoint Aaron and his sons (vv. 23–24)? 4. What message would this ceremony carry to the watching Israelites? 5. How would Aaron and his sons feel honored by this ceremony of ordination as God's priests? 6. How might they feel inadequate for the job?

Applying the Word 1. How do you feel honored for the role in which God has placed you? 2. In what ways do you feel inadequate?

Responding in Prayer Thank the Lord for the privileges and responsibilities of your priesthood. Bring your sins, fears and inadequacies to him for his cleansing and renewing.

Leviticus 9

9 On the eighth day Moses summoned Aaron and his sons and the elders of Israel. ²He said to Aaron, "Take a bull calf for your sin offering and a ram for your burnt offering, both without defect, and present them before the LORD. ³Then say to the Israelites: 'Take a male goat for a sin offering, a calf and a lamb—both a year old and without defect—for a burnt offering, ⁴and an ox^r and a ram for a fellowship offering^s to sacrifice before the LORD, together with a grain offering mixed with oil. For today the LORD will appear to you.' "

⁵They took the things Moses commanded to the front of the Tent of Meeting, and the entire assembly came near and stood before the LORD. ⁶Then Moses said, "This is what the LORD has commanded you to do, so that the glory of the LORD may appear to you."

⁷Moses said to Aaron, "Come to the altar and sacrifice your sin offering and your burnt offering and make atonement for yourself and the people; sacrifice the offering that is for the people and make atonement for them, as the LORD has commanded."

⁸So Aaron came to the altar and slaughtered the calf as a sin offering for himself. ⁹His sons brought the blood to him, and he dipped his finger into the blood and put it on the horns of the altar; the rest of the blood he poured out at the base of the altar. ¹⁰On the altar he burned the fat, the kidneys and the covering of the liver from the sin offering, as the LORD commanded Moses; ¹¹the flesh and the hide he burned up outside the camp.

¹²Then he slaughtered the burnt offering. His sons handed him the blood, and he sprinkled it against the altar on all sides. ¹³They handed him the burnt offering piece by piece, including the head, and he burned them on the altar. ¹⁴He washed the inner parts and the legs and burned them on top of the burnt offering on the altar.

¹⁵Aaron then brought the offering that was for the people. He took the goat for the people's sin offering and slaughtered it and offered it for a sin offering as he did with the first one.

¹⁶He brought the burnt offering and offered it in the prescribed way. ¹⁷He also brought the grain offering, took a handful of it and burned it on the altar in addition to the morning's burnt offering.

¹⁸He slaughtered the ox and the ram as the fellowship offering for the people. His sons

^{r} 4 The Hebrew word can include both male and female; also in verses 18 and 19. ^{s} 4 Traditionally peace offering; also in verses 18 and 22 handed him the blood, and he sprinkled it against the altar on all sides. ¹⁹But the fat portions of the ox and the ram—the fat tail, the layer of fat, the kidneys and the covering of the liver— ²⁰these they laid on the breasts, and then Aaron burned the fat on the altar. ²¹Aaron waved the breasts and the right thigh before the Lord as a wave offering, as Moses commanded.

²²Then Aaron lifted his hands toward the people and blessed them. And having sacrificed the sin offering, the burnt offering and the fellowship offering, he stepped down.

²³Moses and Aaron then went into the Tent of Meeting. When they came out, they blessed the people; and the glory of the Lord appeared to all the people. ²⁴Fire came out from the presence of the Lord and consumed the burnt offering and the fat portions on the altar. And when all the people saw it, they shouted for joy and fell face-down.

3 / *Leviticus 10*
Where Flippancy Doesn't Fit

"THE PRESIDENT IS on the phone!" "It's the Queen calling—she wants to talk to you!" Most of us would gulp and take the phone with a shaking hand. We're far less nervous about approaching the Lord. Certainly we do have confident access to God through Christ. Still it's all too easy to forget that God is holy and only through his mercy can we approach at all.

 Warming Up to God Think about your focus when you enter a worship service. Are you preoccupied with responsibilities and other plans, or are you aware of the wonder of worshiping a holy God?

 Read Leviticus 10.

10 Aaron's sons Nadab and Abihu took their censers, put fire in them and added incense; and they offered unauthorized fire before the Lord, contrary to his command. ²So fire came out from the presence of the Lord and consumed them, and they died before the Lord. ³Moses then said to Aaron, "This is what the Lord spoke of when he said:

" 'Among those who approach me
   I will show myself holy;
in the sight of all the people
   I will be honored.' "

Aaron remained silent.

⁴Moses summoned Mishael and Elzaphan, sons of Aaron's uncle Uzziel, and said to them, "Come here; carry your cousins outside the camp, away from the front of the sanctuary." ⁵So they came and carried them, still in their tunics, outside the camp, as Moses ordered.

⁶Then Moses said to Aaron and his sons Eleazar and Ithamar, "Do not let your hair become unkempt,ᶠ and do not tear your clothes, or you will die and the Lord will be angry with the whole community. But your relatives, all the house of Israel, may mourn for those the Lord has destroyed by fire. ⁷Do not leave the entrance to the Tent of Meeting or you will die, because the Lord's anointing oil is on you." So they did as Moses said.

⁸Then the Lord said to Aaron, ⁹"You and your sons are not to drink wine or other fermented drink whenever you go into the Tent of Meeting, or you will die. This is a lasting ordinance for the generations to come. ¹⁰You must distinguish between the holy and the common, between the unclean and the clean, ¹¹and you must teach the Israelites all the decrees the Lord has given them through Moses."

¹²Moses said to Aaron and his remaining sons, Eleazar and Ithamar, "Take the grain offering left over from the offerings made to the Lord by fire and eat it prepared without yeast beside the altar, for it is most holy. ¹³Eat it in a holy place, because it is your share and your sons' share of the offerings made to the Lord by fire; for so I have been commanded. ¹⁴But you and your sons and your

ᶠ6 Or *Do not uncover your heads*

daughters may eat the breast that was waved and the thigh that was presented. Eat them in a ceremonially clean place; they have been given to you and your children as your share of the Israelites' fellowship offerings.ᵘ ¹⁵The thigh that was presented and the breast that was waved must be brought with the fat portions of the offerings made by fire, to be waved before the LORD as a wave offering. This will be the regular share for you and your children, as the LORD has commanded."

¹⁶When Moses inquired about the goat of the sin offering and found that it had been burned up, he was angry with Eleazar and Ithamar, Aaron's remaining sons, and asked, ¹⁷"Why didn't you eat the sin offering in the sanctuary area? It is most holy; it was given to you to take away the guilt of the community by making atonement for them before the LORD. ¹⁸Since its blood was not taken into the Holy Place, you should have eaten the goat in the sanctuary area, as I commanded."

¹⁹Aaron replied to Moses, "Today they sacrificed their sin offering and their burnt offering before the LORD, but such things as this have happened to me. Would the LORD have been pleased if I had eaten the sin offering today?" ²⁰When Moses heard this, he was satisfied.

ᵘ14 Traditionally *peace offerings*

Discovering the Word 1. What led to Nadab and Abihu's tragedy (vv. 1–2)? 2. What reason did Moses offer for God's extreme reaction (vv. 2–3)? 3. How were Aaron and his two surviving sons to mourn differently from the rest of the people (vv. 6–7)? 4. How else was God's holiness to be esteemed by the priests (vv. 8–11)? 5. Notice the detailed instructions Moses gives regarding the remains of offerings (vv. 12–20). How do his admonitions reflect his concern for the holiness of God?

Applying the Word 1. During worship, what typically distracts you from the sense of God's holy presence? 2. In what ways have you approached God with presumption?

Responding in Prayer We don't have to attend a worship service to approach the Lord. Acknowledge God's holy presence with you now, and worship him in your heart.

Leviticus 11—15

11 The LORD said to Moses and Aaron, ²"Say to the Israelites: 'Of all the animals that live on land, these are the ones you may eat: ³You may eat any animal that has a split hoof completely divided and that chews the cud.

⁴" 'There are some that only chew the cud or only have a split hoof, but you must not eat them. The camel, though it chews the cud, does not have a split hoof; it is ceremonially unclean for you. ⁵The coney,ᵛ though it chews the cud, does not have a split hoof; it is unclean for you. ⁶The rabbit, though it chews the cud, does not have a split hoof; it is unclean for you. ⁷And the pig, though it has a split hoof completely divided, does not chew the cud; it is unclean for you. ⁸You must not eat their meat or touch their carcasses; they are unclean for you.

⁹" 'Of all the creatures living in the water of the seas and the streams, you may eat any that have fins and scales. ¹⁰But all creatures in the seas or streams that do not have fins and scales— whether among all the swarming things or among all the other living creatures in the water—you are to detest. ¹¹And since you are to detest them, you must not eat their meat and you must detest their carcasses. ¹²Anything living in the water that does not have fins and scales is to be detestable to you.

¹³" 'These are the birds you are to detest and not eat because they are detestable: the eagle, the vulture, the black vulture, ¹⁴the red kite, any kind of black kite, ¹⁵any kind of raven, ¹⁶the horned owl, the screech owl, the gull, any kind of hawk, ¹⁷the little owl, the cormorant, the great owl, ¹⁸the white owl, the desert owl, the osprey, ¹⁹the stork, any kind of heron, the hoopoe and the bat.ʷ

²⁰" 'All flying insects that walk on all fours are to be detestable to you. ²¹There are, however,

ᵛ5 That is, the hyrax or rock badger   ʷ19 The precise identification of some of the birds, insects and animals in this chapter is uncertain.

some winged creatures that walk on all fours that you may eat: those that have jointed legs for hopping on the ground. ²²Of these you may eat any kind of locust, katydid, cricket or grasshopper. ²³But all other winged creatures that have four legs you are to detest.

²⁴" 'You will make yourselves unclean by these; whoever touches their carcasses will be unclean till evening. ²⁵Whoever picks up one of their carcasses must wash his clothes, and he will be unclean till evening.

²⁶" 'Every animal that has a split hoof not completely divided or that does not chew the cud is unclean for you; whoever touches ⌊the carcass of⌋ any of them will be unclean. ²⁷Of all the animals that walk on all fours, those that walk on their paws are unclean for you; whoever touches their carcasses will be unclean till evening. ²⁸Anyone who picks up their carcasses must wash his clothes, and he will be unclean till evening. They are unclean for you.

²⁹" 'Of the animals that move about on the ground, these are unclean for you: the weasel, the rat, any kind of great lizard, ³⁰the gecko, the monitor lizard, the wall lizard, the skink and the chameleon. ³¹Of all those that move along the ground, these are unclean for you. Whoever touches them when they are dead will be unclean till evening. ³²When one of them dies and falls on something, that article, whatever its use, will be unclean, whether it is made of wood, cloth, hide or sackcloth. Put it in water; it will be unclean till evening, and then it will be clean. ³³If one of them falls into a clay pot, everything in it will be unclean, and you must break the pot. ³⁴Any food that could be eaten but has water on it from such a pot is unclean, and any liquid that could be drunk from it is unclean. ³⁵Anything that one of their carcasses falls on becomes unclean; an oven or cooking pot must be broken up. They are unclean, and you are to regard them as unclean. ³⁶A spring, however, or a cistern for collecting water remains clean, but anyone who touches one of these carcasses is unclean. ³⁷If a carcass falls on any seeds that are to be planted, they remain clean. ³⁸But if water has been put on the seed and a carcass falls on it, it is unclean for you.

³⁹" 'If an animal that you are allowed to eat dies, anyone who touches the carcass will be unclean till evening. ⁴⁰Anyone who eats some of the carcass must wash his clothes, and he will be unclean till evening. Anyone who picks up the carcass must wash his clothes, and he will be unclean till evening.

⁴¹" 'Every creature that moves about on the ground is detestable; it is not to be eaten. ⁴²You are not to eat any creature that moves about on the ground, whether it moves on its belly or walks on all fours or on many feet; it is detestable. ⁴³Do not defile yourselves by any of these creatures. Do not make yourselves unclean by means of them or be made unclean by them. ⁴⁴I am the Lord your God; consecrate yourselves and be holy, because I am holy. Do not make yourselves unclean by any creature that moves about on the ground. ⁴⁵I am the Lord who brought you up out of Egypt to be your God; therefore be holy, because I am holy.

⁴⁶" 'These are the regulations concerning animals, birds, every living thing that moves in the water and every creature that moves about on the ground. ⁴⁷You must distinguish between the unclean and the clean, between living creatures that may be eaten and those that may not be eaten.' "

12

The Lord said to Moses, ²"Say to the Israelites: 'A woman who becomes pregnant and gives birth to a son will be ceremonially unclean for seven days, just as she is unclean during her monthly period. ³On the eighth day the boy is to be circumcised. ⁴Then the woman must wait thirty-three days to be purified from her bleeding. She must not touch anything sacred or go to the sanctuary until the days of her purification are over. ⁵If she gives birth to a daughter, for two weeks the woman will be unclean, as during her period. Then she must wait sixty-six days to be purified from her bleeding.

⁶" 'When the days of her purification for a son or daughter are over, she is to bring to the priest at the entrance to the Tent of Meeting a year-old lamb for a burnt offering and a young pigeon or a dove for a sin offering. ⁷He shall offer them before the Lord to make atonement for her, and then she will be ceremonially clean from her flow of blood.

" 'These are the regulations for the woman who gives birth to a boy or a girl. ⁸If she cannot afford a lamb, she is to bring two doves or two young pigeons, one for a burnt offering and the other for a sin offering. In this way the priest will make atonement for her, and she will be clean.' "

13

The LORD said to Moses and Aaron, [2]"When anyone has a swelling or a rash or a bright spot on his skin that may become an infectious skin disease,[x] he must be brought to Aaron the priest or to one of his sons[y] who is a priest. [3]The priest is to examine the sore on his skin, and if the hair in the sore has turned white and the sore appears to be more than skin deep,[z] it is an infectious skin disease. When the priest examines him, he shall pronounce him ceremonially unclean. [4]If the spot on his skin is white but does not appear to be more than skin deep and the hair in it has not turned white, the priest is to put the infected person in isolation for seven days. [5]On the seventh day the priest is to examine him, and if he sees that the sore is unchanged and has not spread in the skin, he is to keep him in isolation another seven days. [6]On the seventh day the priest is to examine him again, and if the sore has faded and has not spread in the skin, the priest shall pronounce him clean; it is only a rash. The man must wash his clothes, and he will be clean. [7]But if the rash does spread in his skin after he has shown himself to the priest to be pronounced clean, he must appear before the priest again. [8]The priest is to examine him, and if the rash has spread in the skin, he shall pronounce him unclean; it is an infectious disease.

[9]"When anyone has an infectious skin disease, he must be brought to the priest. [10]The priest is to examine him, and if there is a white swelling in the skin that has turned the hair white and if there is raw flesh in the swelling, [11]it is a chronic skin disease and the priest shall pronounce him unclean. He is not to put him in isolation, because he is already unclean.

[12]"If the disease breaks out all over his skin and, so far as the priest can see, it covers all the skin of the infected person from head to foot, [13]the priest is to examine him, and if the disease has covered his whole body, he shall pronounce that person clean. Since it has all turned white, he is clean. [14]But whenever raw flesh appears on him, he will be unclean. [15]When the priest sees the raw flesh, he shall pronounce him unclean. The raw flesh is unclean; he has an infectious disease. [16]Should the raw flesh change and turn white, he must go to the priest. [17]The priest is to examine him, and if the sores have turned white, the priest shall pronounce the infected person clean; then he will be clean.

[18]"When someone has a boil on his skin and it heals, [19]and in the place where the boil was, a white swelling or reddish-white spot appears, he must present himself to the priest. [20]The priest is to examine it, and if it appears to be more than skin deep and the hair in it has turned white, the priest shall pronounce him unclean. It is an infectious skin disease that has broken out where the boil was. [21]But if, when the priest examines it, there is no white hair in it and it is not more than skin deep and has faded, then the priest is to put him in isolation for seven days. [22]If it is spreading in the skin, the priest shall pronounce him unclean; it is infectious. [23]But if the spot is unchanged and has not spread, it is only a scar from the boil, and the priest shall pronounce him clean.

[24]"When someone has a burn on his skin and a reddish-white or white spot appears in the raw flesh of the burn, [25]the priest is to examine the spot, and if the hair in it has turned white, and it appears to be more than skin deep, it is an infectious disease that has broken out in the burn. The priest shall pronounce him unclean; it is an infectious skin disease. [26]But if the priest examines it and there is no white hair in the spot and if it is not more than skin deep and has faded, then the priest is to put him in isolation for seven days. [27]On the seventh day the priest is to examine him, and if it is spreading in the skin, the priest shall pronounce him unclean; it is an infectious skin disease. [28]If, however, the spot is unchanged and has not spread in the skin but has faded, it is a swelling from the burn, and the priest shall pronounce him clean; it is only a scar from the burn.

[29]"If a man or woman has a sore on the head or on the chin, [30]the priest is to examine the sore, and if it appears to be more than skin deep and the hair in it is yellow and thin, the priest shall pronounce that person unclean; it is an itch, an infectious disease of the head or chin. [31]But if, when the priest examines this kind of sore, it does not seem to be more than skin deep and there is no black hair in it, then the priest is to put the infected person in isolation for seven days. [32]On the seventh day the priest is to examine the sore, and if the itch has not spread and there is no yellow hair in it and it does not appear to be more than skin deep, [33]he must be shaved

---

[x]2 Traditionally *leprosy*; the Hebrew word was used for various diseases affecting the skin—not necessarily leprosy; also elsewhere in this chapter. [y]2 Or *descendants* [z]3 Or *be lower than the rest of the skin*; also elsewhere in this chapter

except for the diseased area, and the priest is to keep him in isolation another seven days. ³⁴On the seventh day the priest is to examine the itch, and if it has not spread in the skin and appears to be no more than skin deep, the priest shall pronounce him clean. He must wash his clothes, and he will be clean. ³⁵But if the itch does spread in the skin after he is pronounced clean, ³⁶the priest is to examine him, and if the itch has spread in the skin, the priest does not need to look for yellow hair; the person is unclean. ³⁷If, however, in his judgment it is unchanged and black hair has grown in it, the itch is healed. He is clean, and the priest shall pronounce him clean.

³⁸"When a man or woman has white spots on the skin, ³⁹the priest is to examine them, and if the spots are dull white, it is a harmless rash that has broken out on the skin; that person is clean. ⁴⁰"When a man has lost his hair and is bald, he is clean. ⁴¹If he has lost his hair from the front of his scalp and has a bald forehead, he is clean. ⁴²But if he has a reddish-white sore on his bald head or forehead, it is an infectious disease breaking out on his head or forehead. ⁴³The priest is to examine him, and if the swollen sore on his head or forehead is reddish-white like an infectious skin disease, ⁴⁴the man is diseased and is unclean. The priest shall pronounce him unclean because of the sore on his head.

⁴⁵"The person with such an infectious disease must wear torn clothes, let his hair be unkempt,ᵃ cover the lower part of his face and cry out, 'Unclean! Unclean!' ⁴⁶As long as he has the infection he remains unclean. He must live alone; he must live outside the camp.

⁴⁷"If any clothing is contaminated with mildew—any woolen or linen clothing, ⁴⁸any woven or knitted material of linen or wool, any leather or anything made of leather— ⁴⁹and if the contamination in the clothing, or leather, or woven or knitted material, or any leather article, is greenish or reddish, it is a spreading mildew and must be shown to the priest. ⁵⁰The priest is to examine the mildew and isolate the affected article for seven days. ⁵¹On the seventh day he is to examine it, and if the mildew has spread in the clothing, or the woven or knitted material, or the leather, whatever its use, it is a destructive mildew; the article is unclean. ⁵²He must burn up the clothing, or the woven or knitted material of wool or linen, or any leather article that has the con-

tamination in it, because the mildew is destructive; the article must be burned up.

⁵³"But if, when the priest examines it, the mildew has not spread in the clothing, or the woven or knitted material, or the leather article, ⁵⁴he shall order that the contaminated article be washed. Then he is to isolate it for another seven days. ⁵⁵After the affected article has been washed, the priest is to examine it, and if the mildew has not changed its appearance, even though it has not spread, it is unclean. Burn it with fire, whether the mildew has affected one side or the other. ⁵⁶If, when the priest examines it, the mildew has faded after the article has been washed, he is to tear the contaminated part out of the clothing, or the leather, or the woven or knitted material. ⁵⁷But if it reappears in the clothing, or in the woven or knitted material, or in the leather article, it is spreading, and whatever has the mildew must be burned with fire. ⁵⁸The clothing, or the woven or knitted material, or any leather article that has been washed and is rid of the mildew, must be washed again, and it will be clean."

⁵⁹These are the regulations concerning contamination by mildew in woolen or linen clothing, woven or knitted material, or any leather article, for pronouncing them clean or unclean.

14 The Lᴏʀᴅ said to Moses, ²"These are the regulations for the diseased person at the time of his ceremonial cleansing, when he is brought to the priest: ³The priest is to go outside the camp and examine him. If the person has been healed of his infectious skin disease,ᵇ ⁴the priest shall order that two live clean birds and some cedar wood, scarlet yarn and hyssop be brought for the one to be cleansed. ⁵Then the priest shall order that one of the birds be killed over fresh water in a clay pot. ⁶He is then to take the live bird and dip it, together with the cedar wood, the scarlet yarn and the hyssop, into the blood of the bird that was killed over the fresh water. ⁷Seven times he shall sprinkle the one to be cleansed of the infectious disease and pronounce him clean. Then he is to release the live bird in the open fields.

⁸"The person to be cleansed must wash his clothes, shave off all his hair and bathe with water; then he will be ceremonially clean. After this he may come into the camp, but he must stay

ᵃ45 Or clothes, uncover his head   ᵇ3 Traditionally leprosy; the Hebrew word was used for various diseases affecting the skin—not necessarily leprosy; also elsewhere in this chapter.

outside his tent for seven days. ⁹On the seventh day he must shave off all his hair; he must shave his head, his beard, his eyebrows and the rest of his hair. He must wash his clothes and bathe himself with water, and he will be clean.

¹⁰"On the eighth day he must bring two male lambs and one ewe lamb a year old, each without defect, along with three-tenths of an ephah*c* of fine flour mixed with oil for a grain offering, and one log*d* of oil. ¹¹The priest who pronounces him clean shall present both the one to be cleansed and his offerings before the Lord at the entrance to the Tent of Meeting.

¹²"Then the priest is to take one of the male lambs and offer it as a guilt offering, along with the log of oil; he shall wave them before the Lord as a wave offering. ¹³He is to slaughter the lamb in the holy place where the sin offering and the burnt offering are slaughtered. Like the sin offering, the guilt offering belongs to the priest; it is most holy. ¹⁴The priest is to take some of the blood of the guilt offering and put it on the lobe of the right ear of the one to be cleansed, on the thumb of his right hand and on the big toe of his right foot. ¹⁵The priest shall then take some of the log of oil, pour it in the palm of his own left hand, ¹⁶dip his right forefinger into the oil in his palm, and with his finger sprinkle some of it before the Lord seven times. ¹⁷The priest is to put some of the oil remaining in his palm on the lobe of the right ear of the one to be cleansed, on the thumb of his right hand and on the big toe of his right foot, on top of the blood of the guilt offering. ¹⁸The rest of the oil in his palm the priest shall put on the head of the one to be cleansed and make atonement for him before the Lord.

¹⁹"Then the priest is to sacrifice the sin offering and make atonement for the one to be cleansed from his uncleanness. After that, the priest shall slaughter the burnt offering ²⁰and offer it on the altar, together with the grain offering, and make atonement for him, and he will be clean.

²¹"If, however, he is poor and cannot afford these, he must take one male lamb as a guilt offering to be waved to make atonement for him, together with a tenth of an ephah*e* of fine flour mixed with oil for a grain offering, a log of oil, ²²and two doves or two young pigeons, which he can afford, one for a sin offering and the other for a burnt offering.

²³"On the eighth day he must bring them for his cleansing to the priest at the entrance to the Tent of Meeting, before the Lord. ²⁴The priest is to take the lamb for the guilt offering, together with the log of oil, and wave them before the Lord as a wave offering. ²⁵He shall slaughter the lamb for the guilt offering and take some of its blood and put it on the lobe of the right ear of the one to be cleansed, on the thumb of his right hand and on the big toe of his right foot. ²⁶The priest is to pour some of the oil into the palm of his own left hand, ²⁷and with his right forefinger sprinkle some of the oil from his palm seven times before the Lord. ²⁸Some of the oil in his palm he is to put on the same places he put the blood of the guilt offering—on the lobe of the right ear of the one to be cleansed, on the thumb of his right hand and on the big toe of his right foot. ²⁹The rest of the oil in his palm the priest shall put on the head of the one to be cleansed, to make atonement for him before the Lord. ³⁰Then he shall sacrifice the doves or the young pigeons, which the person can afford, ³¹one*f* as a sin offering and the other as a burnt offering, together with the grain offering. In this way the priest will make atonement before the Lord on behalf of the one to be cleansed."

³²These are the regulations for anyone who has an infectious skin disease and who cannot afford the regular offerings for his cleansing.

³³The Lord said to Moses and Aaron, ³⁴"When you enter the land of Canaan, which I am giving you as your possession, and I put a spreading mildew in a house in that land, ³⁵the owner of the house must go and tell the priest, 'I have seen something that looks like mildew in my house.' ³⁶The priest is to order the house to be emptied before he goes in to examine the mildew, so that nothing in the house will be pronounced unclean. After this the priest is to go in and inspect the house. ³⁷He is to examine the mildew on the walls, and if it has greenish or reddish depressions that appear to be deeper than the surface of the wall, ³⁸the priest shall go out the doorway of the house and close it up for seven days. ³⁹On the seventh day the priest shall return to inspect the house. If the mildew has spread on the walls, ⁴⁰he is to order that the contaminated stones be torn out and thrown into an unclean place outside the town. ⁴¹He must have all the inside walls of the house scraped and the material that is scraped off

c10 That is, probably about 6 quarts (about 6.5 liters) d10 That is, probably about 2/3 pint (about 0.3 liter); also in verses 12, 15, 21 and 24 e21 That is, probably about 2 quarts (about 2 liters)
f31 Septuagint and Syriac; Hebrew 31such as the person can afford, one

dumped into an unclean place outside the town. ⁴²Then they are to take other stones to replace these and take new clay and plaster the house.

⁴³"If the mildew reappears in the house after the stones have been torn out and the house scraped and plastered, ⁴⁴the priest is to go and examine it and, if the mildew has spread in the house, it is a destructive mildew; the house is unclean. ⁴⁵It must be torn down—its stones, timbers and all the plaster—and taken out of the town to an unclean place.

⁴⁶"Anyone who goes into the house while it is closed up will be unclean till evening. ⁴⁷Anyone who sleeps or eats in the house must wash his clothes.

⁴⁸"But if the priest comes to examine it and the mildew has not spread after the house has been plastered, he shall pronounce the house clean, because the mildew is gone. ⁴⁹To purify the house he is to take two birds and some cedar wood, scarlet yarn and hyssop. ⁵⁰He shall kill one of the birds over fresh water in a clay pot. ⁵¹Then he is to take the cedar wood, the hyssop, the scarlet yarn and the live bird, dip them into the blood of the dead bird and the fresh water, and sprinkle the house seven times. ⁵²He shall purify the house with the bird's blood, the fresh water, the live bird, the cedar wood, the hyssop and the scarlet yarn. ⁵³Then he is to release the live bird in the open fields outside the town. In this way he will make atonement for the house, and it will be clean."

⁵⁴These are the regulations for any infectious skin disease, for an itch, ⁵⁵for mildew in clothing or in a house, ⁵⁶and for a swelling, a rash or a bright spot, ⁵⁷to determine when something is clean or unclean.

These are the regulations for infectious skin diseases and mildew.

15

The LORD said to Moses and Aaron, ²"Speak to the Israelites and say to them: 'When any man has a bodily discharge, the discharge is unclean. ³Whether it continues flowing from his body or is blocked, it will make him unclean. This is how his discharge will bring about uncleanness:

⁴" 'Any bed the man with a discharge lies on will be unclean, and anything he sits on will be unclean. ⁵Anyone who touches his bed must wash his clothes and bathe with water, and he will be unclean till evening. ⁶Whoever sits on anything that the man with a discharge sat on must wash his clothes and bathe with water, and he will be unclean till evening.

⁷" 'Whoever touches the man who has a discharge must wash his clothes and bathe with water, and he will be unclean till evening.

⁸" 'If the man with the discharge spits on someone who is clean, that person must wash his clothes and bathe with water, and he will be unclean till evening.

⁹" 'Everything the man sits on when riding will be unclean, ¹⁰and whoever touches any of the things that were under him will be unclean till evening; whoever picks up those things must wash his clothes and bathe with water, and he will be unclean till evening.

¹¹" 'Anyone the man with a discharge touches without rinsing his hands with water must wash his clothes and bathe with water, and he will be unclean till evening.

¹²" 'A clay pot that the man touches must be broken, and any wooden article is to be rinsed with water.

¹³" 'When a man is cleansed from his discharge, he is to count off seven days for his ceremonial cleansing; he must wash his clothes and bathe himself with fresh water, and he will be clean. ¹⁴On the eighth day he must take two doves or two young pigeons and come before the LORD to the entrance to the Tent of Meeting and give them to the priest. ¹⁵The priest is to sacrifice them, the one for a sin offering and the other for a burnt offering. In this way he will make atonement before the LORD for the man because of his discharge.

¹⁶" 'When a man has an emission of semen, he must bathe his whole body with water, and he will be unclean till evening. ¹⁷Any clothing or leather that has semen on it must be washed with water, and it will be unclean till evening. ¹⁸When a man lies with a woman and there is an emission of semen, both must bathe with water, and they will be unclean till evening.

¹⁹" 'When a woman has her regular flow of blood, the impurity of her monthly period will last seven days, and anyone who touches her will be unclean till evening.

²⁰" 'Anything she lies on during her period will be unclean, and anything she sits on will be unclean. ²¹Whoever touches her bed must wash his clothes and bathe with water, and he will be unclean till evening. ²²Whoever touches anything she sits on must wash his clothes and bathe with

water, and he will be unclean till evening. 23Whether it is the bed or anything she was sitting on, when anyone touches it, he will be unclean till evening.

24" 'If a man lies with her and her monthly flow touches him, he will be unclean for seven days; any bed he lies on will be unclean.

25" 'When a woman has a discharge of blood for many days at a time other than her monthly period or has a discharge that continues beyond her period, she will be unclean as long as she has the discharge, just as in the days of her period. 26Any bed she lies on while her discharge continues will be unclean, as is her bed during her monthly period, and anything she sits on will be unclean, as during her period. 27Whoever touches them will be unclean; he must wash his clothes and bathe with water, and he will be unclean till evening.

28" 'When she is cleansed from her discharge, she must count off seven days, and after that she will be ceremonially clean. 29On the eighth day she must take two doves or two young pigeons and bring them to the priest at the entrance to the Tent of Meeting. 30The priest is to sacrifice one for a sin offering and the other for a burnt offering. In this way he will make atonement for her before the LORD for the uncleanness of her discharge.

31" 'You must keep the Israelites separate from things that make them unclean, so they will not die in their uncleanness for defiling my dwelling place,g which is among them.' "

32These are the regulations for a man with a discharge, for anyone made unclean by an emission of semen, 33for a woman in her monthly period, for a man or a woman with a discharge, and for a man who lies with a woman who is ceremonially unclean.

g31 Or *my tabernacle*

---

4 / *Leviticus 16*
Facing Temptation

"I HAVEN'T SINNED for seventeen years," says one fervent Christian.
"I sin every day," says another, equally fervent.
These two Christians may define *sin* differently, but each knows the insistent battle of temptation. One knows the constant guardedness it takes to resist a small lie, a cutting remark, an inclination to laziness. The other knows the equally constant wash of God's grace as confession assures forgiveness and a continued walk with Christ. But no matter how we view sin, temptation is a battle for us all. And guilt often results from our battles with sin.

 Warming Up to God   Sit quietly before God. What have you felt guilty about recently? Talk to God about it.

 Read Leviticus 16.

---

16 The LORD spoke to Moses after the death of the two sons of Aaron who died when they approached the LORD. 2The LORD said to Moses: "Tell your brother Aaron not to come whenever he chooses into the Most Holy Place behind the curtain in front of the atonement cover on the ark, or else he will die, because I appear in the cloud over the atonement cover.

3"This is how Aaron is to enter the sanctuary area: with a young bull for a sin offering and a ram for a burnt offering. 4He is to put on the sacred linen tunic, with linen undergarments next to his body; he is to tie the linen sash around him and put on the linen turban. These are sacred garments; so he must bathe himself with water before he puts them on. 5From the Israelite community he is to take two male goats for a sin offering and a ram for a burnt offering.

6"Aaron is to offer the bull for his own sin offering to make atonement for himself and his household. 7Then he is to take the two goats and present them before the LORD at the entrance to the Tent of Meeting. 8He is to cast lots for the two goats—one lot for the Lord and the other for the scapegoat.[h] 9Aaron shall bring the goat whose lot falls to the Lord and sacrifice it for a sin offering. 10But the goat chosen by lot as the scapegoat shall be presented alive before the Lord to be used for making atonement by sending it into the desert as a scapegoat.

11"Aaron shall bring the bull for his own sin offering to make atonement for himself and his household, and he is to slaughter the bull for his own sin offering. 12He is to take a censer full of burning coals from the altar before the Lord and two handfuls of finely ground fragrant incense and take them behind the curtain. 13He is to put the incense on the fire before the Lord, and the smoke of the incense will conceal the atonement cover above the Testimony, so that he will not die. 14He is to take some of the bull's blood and with his finger sprinkle it on the front of the atonement cover; then he shall sprinkle some of it with his finger seven times before the atonement cover.

15"He shall then slaughter the goat for the sin offering for the people and take its blood behind the curtain and do with it as he did with the bull's blood: He shall sprinkle it on the atonement cover and in front of it. 16In this way he will make atonement for the Most Holy Place because of the uncleanness and rebellion of the Israelites, whatever their sins have been. He is to do the same for the Tent of Meeting, which is among them in the midst of their uncleanness. 17No one is to be in the Tent of Meeting from the time Aaron goes in to make atonement in the Most Holy Place until he comes out, having made atonement for himself, his household and the whole community of Israel.

18"Then he shall come out to the altar that is before the Lord and make atonement for it. He shall take some of the bull's blood and some of the goat's blood and put it on all the horns of the altar. 19He shall sprinkle some of the blood on it with his finger seven times to cleanse it and to consecrate it from the uncleanness of the Israelites.

20"When Aaron has finished making atonement for the Most Holy Place, the Tent of Meeting and the altar, he shall bring forward the live goat. 21He is to lay both hands on the head of the live goat and confess over it all the wickedness and rebellion of the Israelites—all their sins—and put them on the goat's head. He shall send the goat away into the desert in the care of a man appointed for the task. 22The goat will carry on itself all their sins to a solitary place; and the man shall release it in the desert.

23"Then Aaron is to go into the Tent of Meeting and take off the linen garments he put on before he entered the Most Holy Place, and he is to leave them there. 24He shall bathe himself with water in a holy place and put on his regular garments. Then he shall come out and sacrifice the burnt offering for himself and the burnt offering for the people, to make atonement for himself and for the people. 25He shall also burn the fat of the sin offering on the altar.

26"The man who releases the goat as a scapegoat must wash his clothes and bathe himself with water; afterward he may come into the camp. 27The bull and the goat for the sin offerings, whose blood was brought into the Most Holy Place to make atonement, must be taken outside the camp; their hides, flesh and offal are to be burned up. 28The man who burns them must wash his clothes and bathe himself with water; afterward he may come into the camp.

29"This is to be a lasting ordinance for you: On the tenth day of the seventh month you must deny yourselves[i] and not do any work—whether native-born or an alien living among you— 30because on this day atonement will be made for you, to cleanse you. Then, before the Lord, you will be clean from all your sins. 31It is a sabbath of rest, and you must deny yourselves; it is a lasting ordinance. 32The priest who is anointed and ordained to succeed his father as high priest is to make atonement. He is to put on the sacred linen garments 33and make atonement for the Most Holy Place, for the Tent of Meeting and the altar, and for the priests and all the people of the community.

34"This is to be a lasting ordinance for you: Atonement is to be made once a year for all the sins of the Israelites."

And it was done, as the Lord commanded Moses.

h8 That is, the goat of removal; Hebrew azazel; also in verses 10 and 26   i29 Or must fast; also in verse 31

Discovering the Word 1. As you visualize all that was to happen on the Day of Atonement, what pictures remind you that God is holy and that he expects holiness from his people? 2. What personal preparation was Aaron to make for his work of atonement (vv. 1–14)? 3. What did this preparation symbolize about Aaron and his role before God and the people? 4. How is each sacrificial goat a visual symbol of sin (vv. 7–10, 15–19, 20–24)? 5. What practical good could come from this method of atoning for sin?

Applying the Word 1. Imagine yourself as a Hebrew of this era. How do you think you would feel on the days just before and just after the Day of Atonement? 2. What do you do when you feel guilty about something?

Responding in Prayer If this study points to sin that needs to be confessed, do so now. If you have already done this, ask God to help you experience his forgiveness.

Leviticus 17—18

17 The Lord said to Moses, 2"Speak to Aaron and his sons and to all the Israelites and say to them: 'This is what the Lord has commanded: 3Any Israelite who sacrifices an ox,ʲ a lamb or a goat in the camp or outside of it 4instead of bringing it to the entrance to the Tent of Meeting to present it as an offering to the Lord in front of the tabernacle of the Lord—that man shall be considered guilty of bloodshed; he has shed blood and must be cut off from his people. 5This is so the Israelites will bring to the Lord the sacrifices they are now making in the open fields. They must bring them to the priest, that is, to the Lord, at the entrance to the Tent of Meeting and sacrifice them as fellowship offerings.ᵏ 6The priest is to sprinkle the blood against the altar of the Lord at the entrance to the Tent of Meeting and burn the fat as an aroma pleasing to the Lord. 7They must no longer offer any of their sacrifices to the goat idolsˡ to whom they prostitute themselves. This is to be a lasting ordinance for them and for the generations to come.'

8"Say to them: 'Any Israelite or any alien living among them who offers a burnt offering or sacrifice 9and does not bring it to the entrance to the Tent of Meeting to sacrifice it to the Lord—that man must be cut off from his people.

10" 'Any Israelite or any alien living among them who eats any blood—I will set my face against that person who eats blood and will cut him off from his people. 11For the life of a creature is in the blood, and I have given it to you to make atonement for yourselves on the altar; it is the blood that makes atonement for one's life. 12Therefore I say to the Israelites, "None of you may eat blood, nor may an alien living among you eat blood."

13" 'Any Israelite or any alien living among you who hunts any animal or bird that may be eaten must drain out the blood and cover it with earth, 14because the life of every creature is its blood. That is why I have said to the Israelites, "You must not eat the blood of any creature, because the life of every creature is its blood; anyone who eats it must be cut off."

15" 'Anyone, whether native-born or alien, who eats anything found dead or torn by wild animals must wash his clothes and bathe with water, and he will be ceremonially unclean till evening; then he will be clean. 16But if he does not wash his clothes and bathe himself, he will be held responsible.' "

18 The Lord said to Moses, 2"Speak to the Israelites and say to them: 'I am the Lord your God. 3You must not do as they do in Egypt, where you used to live, and you must not do as they do in the land of Canaan, where I am bringing you. Do not follow their practices. 4You must obey my laws and be careful to follow my decrees. I am the Lord your God. 5Keep my decrees and laws, for the man who obeys them will live by them. I am the Lord.

6" 'No one is to approach any close relative to have sexual relations. I am the Lord.

7" 'Do not dishonor your father by having sexual relations with your mother. She is your mother; do not have relations with her.

8" 'Do not have sexual relations with your father's wife; that would dishonor your father.

ʲ3 The Hebrew word can include both male and female.
ᵏ5 Traditionally *peace offerings*   ˡ7 Or *demons*

9" 'Do not have sexual relations with your sister, either your father's daughter or your mother's daughter, whether she was born in the same home or elsewhere.

10" 'Do not have sexual relations with your son's daughter or your daughter's daughter; that would dishonor you.

11" 'Do not have sexual relations with the daughter of your father's wife, born to your father; she is your sister.

12" 'Do not have sexual relations with your father's sister; she is your father's close relative.

13" 'Do not have sexual relations with your mother's sister, because she is your mother's close relative.

14" 'Do not dishonor your father's brother by approaching his wife to have sexual relations; she is your aunt.

15" 'Do not have sexual relations with your daughter-in-law. She is your son's wife; do not have relations with her.

16" 'Do not have sexual relations with your brother's wife; that would dishonor your brother.

17" 'Do not have sexual relations with both a woman and her daughter. Do not have sexual relations with either her son's daughter or her daughter's daughter; they are her close relatives. That is wickedness.

18" 'Do not take your wife's sister as a rival wife and have sexual relations with her while your wife is living.

19" 'Do not approach a woman to have sexual relations during the uncleanness of her monthly period.

20" 'Do not have sexual relations with your neighbor's wife and defile yourself with her.

21" 'Do not give any of your children to be sacrificed[m] to Molech, for you must not profane the name of your God. I am the Lord.

22" 'Do not lie with a man as one lies with a woman; that is detestable.

23" 'Do not have sexual relations with an animal and defile yourself with it. A woman must not present herself to an animal to have sexual relations with it; that is a perversion.

24" 'Do not defile yourselves in any of these ways, because this is how the nations that I am going to drive out before you became defiled. 25Even the land was defiled; so I punished it for its sin, and the land vomited out its inhabitants. 26But you must keep my decrees and my laws. The native-born and the aliens living among you must not do any of these detestable things, 27for all these things were done by the people who lived in the land before you, and the land became defiled. 28And if you defile the land, it will vomit you out as it vomited out the nations that were before you.

29" 'Everyone who does any of these detestable things—such persons must be cut off from their people. 30Keep my requirements and do not follow any of the detestable customs that were practiced before you came and do not defile yourselves with them. I am the Lord your God.' "

[m] 21 Or to be passed through ⌊the fire⌋

---

5 / *Leviticus 19*
Laws with a Purpose

"A POLICY? WHAT do we need a policy for?" That's how a group of junior highers reacted when we announced a policy for an upcoming overnight trip. They knew "policy" was a fancy name for "rules." But when it came to curbing the behavior of certain obnoxious group members, they saw a need for rules. Good rules have a purpose beyond rule-keeping. God's rules, faithfully followed, will yield a better life for people.

 Warming Up to God Think about the rules you've had to follow in life. When have you found following rules difficult? Some rules are better than others. Compare your experiences with unreasonable rules to what it's like to follow God's laws. Allow this to be a source of praise to God for caring enough to give us his good laws.

Read Leviticus 19.

19

The LORD said to Moses, [2]"Speak to the entire assembly of Israel and say to them: 'Be holy because I, the LORD your God, am holy.

[3]" 'Each of you must respect his mother and father, and you must observe my Sabbaths. I am the LORD your God.

[4]" 'Do not turn to idols or make gods of cast metal for yourselves. I am the LORD your God.

[5]" 'When you sacrifice a fellowship offering[n] to the LORD, sacrifice it in such a way that it will be accepted on your behalf. [6]It shall be eaten on the day you sacrifice it or on the next day; anything left over until the third day must be burned up. [7]If any of it is eaten on the third day, it is impure and will not be accepted. [8]Whoever eats it will be held responsible because he has desecrated what is holy to the LORD; that person must be cut off from his people.

[9]" 'When you reap the harvest of your land, do not reap to the very edges of your field or gather the gleanings of your harvest. [10]Do not go over your vineyard a second time or pick up the grapes that have fallen. Leave them for the poor and the alien. I am the LORD your God.

[11]" 'Do not steal.

" 'Do not lie.

" 'Do not deceive one another.

[12]" 'Do not swear falsely by my name and so profane the name of your God. I am the LORD.

[13]" 'Do not defraud your neighbor or rob him.

" 'Do not hold back the wages of a hired man overnight.

[14]" 'Do not curse the deaf or put a stumbling block in front of the blind, but fear your God. I am the LORD.

[15]" 'Do not pervert justice; do not show partiality to the poor or favoritism to the great, but judge your neighbor fairly.

[16]" 'Do not go about spreading slander among your people.

" 'Do not do anything that endangers your neighbor's life. I am the LORD.

[17]" 'Do not hate your brother in your heart. Rebuke your neighbor frankly so you will not share in his guilt.

[18]" 'Do not seek revenge or bear a grudge against one of your people, but love your neighbor as yourself. I am the LORD.

[19]" 'Keep my decrees.

" 'Do not mate different kinds of animals.

" 'Do not plant your field with two kinds of seed.

" 'Do not wear clothing woven of two kinds of material.

[20]" 'If a man sleeps with a woman who is a slave girl promised to another man but who has not been ransomed or given her freedom, there must be due punishment. Yet they are not to be put to death, because she had not been freed. [21]The man, however, must bring a ram to the entrance to the Tent of Meeting for a guilt offering to the LORD. [22]With the ram of the guilt offering the priest is to make atonement for him before the LORD for the sin he has committed, and his sin will be forgiven.

[23]" 'When you enter the land and plant any kind of fruit tree, regard its fruit as forbidden.[o] For three years you are to consider it forbidden[o]; it must not be eaten. [24]In the fourth year all its fruit will be holy, an offering of praise to the LORD. [25]But in the fifth year you may eat its fruit. In this way your harvest will be increased. I am the LORD your God.

[26]" 'Do not eat any meat with the blood still in it.

" 'Do not practice divination or sorcery.

[27]" 'Do not cut the hair at the sides of your head or clip off the edges of your beard.

[28]" 'Do not cut your bodies for the dead or put tattoo marks on yourselves. I am the LORD.

[29]" 'Do not degrade your daughter by making her a prostitute, or the land will turn to prostitution and be filled with wickedness.

[30]" 'Observe my Sabbaths and have reverence for my sanctuary. I am the LORD.

[31]" 'Do not turn to mediums or seek out spiritists, for you will be defiled by them. I am the LORD your God.

[32]" 'Rise in the presence of the aged, show respect for the elderly and revere your God. I am the LORD.

[33]" 'When an alien lives with you in your land, do not mistreat him. [34]The alien living with you must be treated as one of your native-born. Love him as yourself, for you were aliens in Egypt. I am the LORD your God.

[35]" 'Do not use dishonest standards when mea-

---

[n]5 Traditionally *peace offering*   [o]23 Hebrew *uncircumcised*

suring length, weight or quantity. 36Use honest scales and honest weights, an honest ephah*p* and an honest hin.*q* I am the LORD your God, who brought you out of Egypt.

37" 'Keep all my decrees and all my laws and follow them. I am the LORD.' "

p36 An ephah was a dry measure.   *q36* A hin was a liquid measure.

Discovering the Word   1. God said, "Be holy because I, the LORD your God, am holy" (v. 2). What do the various laws that follow reveal about the holiness of God?   2. Consider the laws in verses 3, 11, 16–17, 32 and 35–36. How would obedience to these laws create better relationships between people?   3. Consider the laws in verses 9–10, 14 and 33–34, and imagine a society observing these laws. How would life be better for disadvantaged people?   4. Jesus quoted "love your neighbor as yourself" (v. 18) as one of the two greatest commandments, second only to loving God. Why is it a good summary of all the laws in this chapter (as well as all God's other laws)?   5. What do these laws reveal about God's concern for his people?

Applying the Word   1. Which of the laws in this chapter particularly stir your heart with their "rightness" (that is, you're glad to find them in the Bible)?   2. Which of the laws would you find hardest to obey?

Responding in Prayer   Praise God for showing you his character through his principles. Ask for his continuing help in living as he wants.

Leviticus 20—22

20 The LORD said to Moses, 2"Say to the Israelites: 'Any Israelite or any alien living in Israel who gives*r* any of his children to Molech must be put to death. The people of the community are to stone him. 3I will set my face against that man and I will cut him off from his people; for by giving his children to Molech, he has defiled my sanctuary and profaned my holy name. 4If the people of the community close their eyes when that man gives one of his children to Molech and they fail to put him to death, 5I will set my face against that man and his family and will cut off from their people both him and all who follow him in prostituting themselves to Molech.

6" 'I will set my face against the person who turns to mediums and spiritists to prostitute himself by following them, and I will cut him off from his people.

7" 'Consecrate yourselves and be holy, because I am the LORD your God. 8Keep my decrees and follow them. I am the LORD, who makes you holy.*s*

9" 'If anyone curses his father or mother, he must be put to death. He has cursed his father or his mother, and his blood will be on his own head.

10" 'If a man commits adultery with another man's wife—with the wife of his neighbor—both the adulterer and the adulteress must be put to death.

11" 'If a man sleeps with his father's wife, he has dishonored his father. Both the man and the woman must be put to death; their blood will be on their own heads.

12" 'If a man sleeps with his daughter-in-law, both of them must be put to death. What they have done is a perversion; their blood will be on their own heads.

13" 'If a man lies with a man as one lies with a woman, both of them have done what is detestable. They must be put to death; their blood will be on their own heads.

14" 'If a man marries both a woman and her mother, it is wicked. Both he and they must be burned in the fire, so that no wickedness will be among you.

15" 'If a man has sexual relations with an animal, he must be put to death, and you must kill the animal.

16" 'If a woman approaches an animal to have sexual relations with it, kill both the woman and the animal. They must be put to death; their blood will be on their own heads.

17" 'If a man marries his sister, the daughter of either his father or his mother, and they have sexual relations, it is a disgrace. They must be cut off before the eyes of their people. He has dishonored his sister and will be held responsible.

r2 Or *sacrifices*; also in verses 3 and 4   *s8* Or *who sanctifies you*; or *who sets you apart as holy*

18" 'If a man lies with a woman during her monthly period and has sexual relations with her, he has exposed the source of her flow, and she has also uncovered it. Both of them must be cut off from their people.

19" 'Do not have sexual relations with the sister of either your mother or your father, for that would dishonor a close relative; both of you would be held responsible.

20" 'If a man sleeps with his aunt, he has dishonored his uncle. They will be held responsible; they will die childless.

21" 'If a man marries his brother's wife, it is an act of impurity; he has dishonored his brother. They will be childless.

22" 'Keep all my decrees and laws and follow them, so that the land where I am bringing you to live may not vomit you out. 23You must not live according to the customs of the nations I am going to drive out before you. Because they did all these things, I abhorred them. 24But I said to you, "You will possess their land; I will give it to you as an inheritance, a land flowing with milk and honey." I am the LORD your God, who has set you apart from the nations.

25" 'You must therefore make a distinction between clean and unclean animals and between unclean and clean birds. Do not defile yourselves by any animal or bird or anything that moves along the ground—those which I have set apart as unclean for you. 26You are to be holy to me[t] because I, the LORD, am holy, and I have set you apart from the nations to be my own.

27" 'A man or woman who is a medium or spiritist among you must be put to death. You are to stone them; their blood will be on their own heads.' "

21 The LORD said to Moses, "Speak to the priests, the sons of Aaron, and say to them: 'A priest must not make himself ceremonially unclean for any of his people who die, 2except for a close relative, such as his mother or father, his son or daughter, his brother, 3or an unmarried sister who is dependent on him since she has no husband—for her he may make himself unclean. 4He must not make himself unclean for people related to him by marriage,[u] and so defile himself.

5" 'Priests must not shave their heads or shave off the edges of their beards or cut their bodies. 6They must be holy to their God and must not

profane the name of their God. Because they present the offerings made to the LORD by fire, the food of their God, they are to be holy.

7" 'They must not marry women defiled by prostitution or divorced from their husbands, because priests are holy to their God. 8Regard them as holy, because they offer up the food of your God. Consider them holy, because I the LORD am holy—I who make you holy.[v]

9" 'If a priest's daughter defiles herself by becoming a prostitute, she disgraces her father; she must be burned in the fire.

10" 'The high priest, the one among his brothers who has had the anointing oil poured on his head and who has been ordained to wear the priestly garments, must not let his hair become unkempt[w] or tear his clothes. 11He must not enter a place where there is a dead body. He must not make himself unclean, even for his father or mother, 12nor leave the sanctuary of his God or desecrate it, because he has been dedicated by the anointing oil of his God. I am the LORD.

13" 'The woman he marries must be a virgin. 14He must not marry a widow, a divorced woman, or a woman defiled by prostitution, but only a virgin from his own people, 15so he will not defile his offspring among his people. I am the LORD, who makes him holy.[x] ' "

16The LORD said to Moses, 17"Say to Aaron: 'For the generations to come none of your descendants who has a defect may come near to offer the food of his God. 18No man who has any defect may come near: no man who is blind or lame, disfigured or deformed; 19no man with a crippled foot or hand, 20or who is hunchbacked or dwarfed, or who has any eye defect, or who has festering or running sores or damaged testicles. 21No descendant of Aaron the priest who has any defect is to come near to present the offerings made to the LORD by fire. He has a defect; he must not come near to offer the food of his God. 22He may eat the most holy food of his God, as well as the holy food; 23yet because of his defect, he must not go near the curtain or approach the altar, and so desecrate my sanctuary. I am the LORD, who makes them holy.[y] ' "

24So Moses told this to Aaron and his sons and to all the Israelites.

22

The LORD said to Moses, [2]"Tell Aaron and his sons to treat with respect the sacred offerings the Israelites consecrate to me, so they will not profane my holy name. I am the LORD.

[3]"Say to them: 'For the generations to come, if any of your descendants is ceremonially unclean and yet comes near the sacred offerings that the Israelites consecrate to the LORD, that person must be cut off from my presence. I am the LORD.

[4]" 'If a descendant of Aaron has an infectious skin disease[z] or a bodily discharge, he may not eat the sacred offerings until he is cleansed. He will also be unclean if he touches something defiled by a corpse or by anyone who has an emission of semen, [5]or if he touches any crawling thing that makes him unclean, or any person who makes him unclean, whatever the uncleanness may be. [6]The one who touches any such thing will be unclean till evening. He must not eat any of the sacred offerings unless he has bathed himself with water. [7]When the sun goes down, he will be clean, and after that he may eat the sacred offerings, for they are his food. [8]He must not eat anything found dead or torn by wild animals, and so become unclean through it. I am the LORD.

[9]" 'The priests are to keep my requirements so that they do not become guilty and die for treating them with contempt. I am the LORD, who makes them holy.[a]

[10]" 'No one outside a priest's family may eat the sacred offering, nor may the guest of a priest or his hired worker eat it. [11]But if a priest buys a slave with money, or if a slave is born in his household, that slave may eat his food. [12]If a priest's daughter marries anyone other than a priest, she may not eat any of the sacred contributions. [13]But if a priest's daughter becomes a widow or is divorced, yet has no children, and she returns to live in her father's house as in her youth, she may eat of her father's food. No unauthorized person, however, may eat any of it.

[14]" 'If anyone eats a sacred offering by mistake, he must make restitution to the priest for the offering and add a fifth of the value to it. [15]The priests must not desecrate the sacred offerings the Israelites present to the LORD [16]by allowing them to eat the sacred offerings and so bring upon them guilt requiring payment. I am the LORD, who makes them holy.' "

[17]The LORD said to Moses, [18]"Speak to Aaron and his sons and to all the Israelites and say to them: 'If any of you—either an Israelite or an alien living in Israel—presents a gift for a burnt offering to the LORD, either to fulfill a vow or as a freewill offering, [19]you must present a male without defect from the cattle, sheep or goats in order that it may be accepted on your behalf. [20]Do not bring anything with a defect, because it will not be accepted on your behalf. [21]When anyone brings from the herd or flock a fellowship offering[b] to the LORD to fulfill a special vow or as a freewill offering, it must be without defect or blemish to be acceptable. [22]Do not offer to the LORD the blind, the injured or the maimed, or anything with warts or festering or running sores. Do not place any of these on the altar as an offering made to the LORD by fire. [23]You may, however, present as a freewill offering an ox[c] or a sheep that is deformed or stunted, but it will not be accepted in fulfillment of a vow. [24]You must not offer to the LORD an animal whose testicles are bruised, crushed, torn or cut. You must not do this in your own land, [25]and you must not accept such animals from the hand of a foreigner and offer them as the food of your God. They will not be accepted on your behalf, because they are deformed and have defects.' "

[26]The LORD said to Moses, [27]"When a calf, a lamb or a goat is born, it is to remain with its mother for seven days. From the eighth day on, it will be acceptable as an offering made to the LORD by fire. [28]Do not slaughter a cow or a sheep and its young on the same day.

[29]"When you sacrifice a thank offering to the LORD, sacrifice it in such a way that it will be accepted on your behalf. [30]It must be eaten that same day; leave none of it till morning. I am the LORD.

[31]"Keep my commands and follow them. I am the LORD. [32]Do not profane my holy name. I must be acknowledged as holy by the Israelites. I am the LORD, who makes[d] you holy[e] [33]and who brought you out of Egypt to be your God. I am the LORD."

---

[z]4 Traditionally *leprosy*; the Hebrew word was used for various diseases affecting the skin—not necessarily leprosy.   [a]9 Or *who sanctifies them; or who sets them apart as holy*; also in verse 16   [b]21 Traditionally *peace offering*   [c]23 The Hebrew word can include both male and female.   [d]32 Or *made*   [e]32 Or *who sanctifies you; or who sets you apart as holy*

6 / *Leviticus 23*
Feasts of Remembrance

"I CAN'T COME to class tomorrow," Tanya told me. "It's my mother's birthday, and we're going to lay flowers on her grave." A birthday is not a time we normally think of visiting a grave, and we certainly wouldn't miss an entire day of school to do it. Tanya, however, was one of my students in the Ukraine, where both birthdays and visits to graves are momentous occasions—times of remembrance. From the flow of the Israelites' year God carved out regular celebrations of remembrance so they would never forget who they were and where they came from.

 Warming Up to God What observances help you most to celebrate your history with the Lord? (They may be ones common to all Christians, such as Christmas and Easter, or your own private remembrances, such as the date of your salvation or baptism.)

Read Leviticus 23.

---

23 The Lord said to Moses, 2"Speak to the Israelites and say to them: 'These are my appointed feasts, the appointed feasts of the Lord, which you are to proclaim as sacred assemblies.

3" 'There are six days when you may work, but the seventh day is a Sabbath of rest, a day of sacred assembly. You are not to do any work; wherever you live, it is a Sabbath to the Lord.

4" 'These are the Lord's appointed feasts, the sacred assemblies you are to proclaim at their appointed times: 5The Lord's Passover begins at twilight on the fourteenth day of the first month. 6On the fifteenth day of that month the Lord's Feast of Unleavened Bread begins; for seven days you must eat bread made without yeast. 7On the first day hold a sacred assembly and do no regular work. 8For seven days present an offering made to the Lord by fire. And on the seventh day hold a sacred assembly and do no regular work.' "

9The Lord said to Moses, 10"Speak to the Israelites and say to them: 'When you enter the land I am going to give you and you reap its harvest, bring to the priest a sheaf of the first grain you harvest. 11He is to wave the sheaf before the Lord so it will be accepted on your behalf; the priest is to wave it on the day after the Sabbath. 12On the day you wave the sheaf, you must sacrifice as a burnt offering to the Lord a lamb a year old without defect, 13together with its grain offering of two-tenths of an ephah*f* of fine flour mixed with oil—an offering made to the Lord by fire, a pleasing aroma—and its drink offering of a quarter of a hin*g* of wine. 14You must not eat any bread, or roasted or new grain, until the very day you bring this offering to your God. This is to be a lasting ordinance for the generations to come, wherever you live.

15" 'From the day after the Sabbath, the day you brought the sheaf of the wave offering, count off seven full weeks. 16Count off fifty days up to the day after the seventh Sabbath, and then present an offering of new grain to the Lord. 17From wherever you live, bring two loaves made of two-tenths of an ephah of fine flour, baked with yeast, as a wave offering of firstfruits to the Lord. 18Present with this bread seven male lambs, each a year old and without defect, one young bull and two rams. They will be a burnt offering to the Lord, together with their grain offerings and drink offerings—an offering made by fire, an aroma pleasing to the Lord. 19Then sacrifice one male goat for a sin offering and two lambs, each a year old, for a fellowship offering.*h* 20The priest is to wave the two lambs before the Lord as a wave offering, together with the bread of the firstfruits. They are a sacred offering to the Lord for the priest. 21On that same day you are to proclaim a sacred assembly and do no regular work. This is to be a lasting ordinance for the generations to come, wherever you live.

22" 'When you reap the harvest of your land, do not reap to the very edges of your field or gather the gleanings of your harvest. Leave them for the poor and the alien. I am the Lord your God.' "

23The Lord said to Moses, 24"Say to the Israelites: 'On the first day of the seventh month you are to have a day of rest, a sacred assembly commemorated with trumpet blasts. 25Do no regular

*f13 That is, probably about 4 quarts (about 4.5 liters); also in verse 17
g13 That is, probably about 1 quart (about 1 liter) h19 Traditionally peace offering*

work, but present an offering made to the Lord by fire.' "

26The Lord said to Moses, 27"The tenth day of this seventh month is the Day of Atonement. Hold a sacred assembly and deny yourselves,i and present an offering made to the Lord by fire. 28Do no work on that day, because it is the Day of Atonement, when atonement is made for you before the Lord your God. 29Anyone who does not deny himself on that day must be cut off from his people. 30I will destroy from among his people anyone who does any work on that day. 31You shall do no work at all. This is to be a lasting ordinance for the generations to come, wherever you live. 32It is a sabbath of rest for you, and you must deny yourselves. From the evening of the ninth day of the month until the following evening you are to observe your sabbath."

33The Lord said to Moses, 34"Say to the Israelites: 'On the fifteenth day of the seventh month the Lord's Feast of Tabernacles begins, and it lasts for seven days. 35The first day is a sacred assembly; do no regular work. 36For seven days present offerings made to the Lord by fire, and on the eighth day hold a sacred assembly and present an offering made to the Lord by fire. It is the closing assembly; do no regular work.

37(" 'These are the Lord's appointed feasts, which you are to proclaim as sacred assemblies for bringing offerings made to the Lord by fire— the burnt offerings and grain offerings, sacrifices and drink offerings required for each day. 38These offerings are in addition to those for the Lord's Sabbaths andj in addition to your gifts and whatever you have vowed and all the freewill offerings you give to the Lord.)

39" 'So beginning with the fifteenth day of the seventh month, after you have gathered the crops of the land, celebrate the festival to the Lord for seven days; the first day is a day of rest, and the eighth day also is a day of rest. 40On the first day you are to take choice fruit from the trees, and palm fronds, leafy branches and poplars, and rejoice before the Lord your God for seven days. 41Celebrate this as a festival to the Lord for seven days each year. This is to be a lasting ordinance for the generations to come; celebrate it in the seventh month. 42Live in booths for seven days: All native-born Israelites are to live in booths 43so your descendants will know that I had the Israelites live in booths when I brought them out of Egypt. I am the Lord your God.' "

44So Moses announced to the Israelites the appointed feasts of the Lord.

i27 Or and fast; also in verses 29 and 32   j38 Or These feasts are in addition to the Lord's Sabbaths, and these offerings are

---

Discovering the Word 1. What are the various feasts ordained by God? 2. There are variations in the feasts, but what features do they have in common? 3. Notice the place offerings have in the feasts (vv. 8, 12–13, 16–19, 27, 36–37). Why do you think they included offerings? 4. What value would the feasts have in the yearly cycle of life for Israel? 5. How would giving common dates of remembrance to all Israel help ensure their observance?

Applying the Word 1. What do we gain from regular—even enforced—remembrance of our past? 2. What is the value of celebrating what God has done "by the calendar" and not just whenever we feel like it? 3. How can you commemorate some particular act of God on your behalf? (Remember these feasts were joyful parties!)

Responding in Prayer Thank the Lord for his faithfulness to you and to all his people. Ask him to bring to your mind some of his acts for you that you have forgotten.

Leviticus 24

24 The Lord said to Moses, 2"Command the Israelites to bring you clear oil of pressed olives for the light so that the lamps may be kept burning continually. 3Outside the curtain of the Testimony in the Tent of Meeting, Aaron is to tend the lamps before the Lord from evening till morning, continually. This is to be a lasting ordinance for the generations to come. 4The lamps on the pure gold lampstand before the Lord must be tended continually.

5"Take fine flour and bake twelve loaves of

bread, using two-tenths of an ephah[k] for each loaf. [6]Set them in two rows, six in each row, on the table of pure gold before the LORD. [7]Along each row put some pure incense as a memorial portion to represent the bread and to be an offering made to the LORD by fire. [8]This bread is to be set out before the LORD regularly, Sabbath after Sabbath, on behalf of the Israelites, as a lasting covenant. [9]It belongs to Aaron and his sons, who are to eat it in a holy place, because it is a most holy part of their regular share of the offerings made to the LORD by fire."

[10]Now the son of an Israelite mother and an Egyptian father went out among the Israelites, and a fight broke out in the camp between him and an Israelite. [11]The son of the Israelite woman blasphemed the Name with a curse; so they brought him to Moses. (His mother's name was Shelomith, the daughter of Dibri the Danite.) [12]They put him in custody until the will of the LORD should be made clear to them.

[13]Then the LORD said to Moses: [14]"Take the blasphemer outside the camp. All those who heard him are to lay their hands on his head, and the entire assembly is to stone him. [15]Say to the Israelites: 'If anyone curses his God, he will be held responsible; [16]anyone who blasphemes the name of the LORD must be put to death. The entire assembly must stone him. Whether an alien or native-born, when he blasphemes the Name, he must be put to death.

[17]" 'If anyone takes the life of a human being, he must be put to death. [18]Anyone who takes the life of someone's animal must make restitution—life for life. [19]If anyone injures his neighbor, whatever he has done must be done to him: [20]fracture for fracture, eye for eye, tooth for tooth. As he has injured the other, so he is to be injured. [21]Whoever kills an animal must make restitution, but whoever kills a man must be put to death. [22]You are to have the same law for the alien and the native-born. I am the LORD your God.' "

[23]Then Moses spoke to the Israelites, and they took the blasphemer outside the camp and stoned him. The Israelites did as the LORD commanded Moses.

[k]5 That is, probably about 4 quarts (about 4.5 liters)

---

7 / *Leviticus 25*
A Garden to Tend

FOR MANY OF us, farming—even gardening—is an alien occupation practiced by loners who wear flannel shirts and overalls and are separated from neighbors by many miles. Most of us live severed from the earth, unaware of our profound daily dependence on its bounty. God gave Israel, an agricultural society, guidelines for establishing just practices. Even those of us who are urban need to understand the link between environmental stewardship and justice.

 Warming Up to God　Today's quiet time deals with how we are to care for God's creation. Recall a place in nature that has touched you. As you bring that place to mind, praise God for how he created it.

 Read Leviticus 25.

---

25 The LORD said to Moses on Mount Sinai, [2]"Speak to the Israelites and say to them: 'When you enter the land I am going to give you, the land itself must observe a sabbath to the LORD. [3]For six years sow your fields, and for six years prune your vineyards and gather their crops. [4]But in the seventh year the land is to have a sabbath of rest, a sabbath to the LORD. Do not sow your fields or prune your vineyards. [5]Do not reap what grows of itself or harvest the grapes of your untended vines. The land is to have a year of rest. [6]Whatever the land yields during the sabbath year will be food for you—for yourself, your manservant and maidservant, and the hired worker and temporary resident who live among you, [7]as well as for your livestock and the wild animals in your land. Whatever the land produces may be eaten.

8" 'Count off seven sabbaths of years—seven times seven years—so that the seven sabbaths of years amount to a period of forty-nine years. 9Then have the trumpet sounded everywhere on the tenth day of the seventh month; on the Day of Atonement sound the trumpet throughout your land. 10Consecrate the fiftieth year and proclaim liberty throughout the land to all its inhabitants. It shall be a jubilee for you; each one of you is to return to his family property and each to his own clan. 11The fiftieth year shall be a jubilee for you; do not sow and do not reap what grows of itself or harvest the untended vines. 12For it is a jubilee and is to be holy for you; eat only what is taken directly from the fields.

13" 'In this Year of Jubilee everyone is to return to his own property.

14" 'If you sell land to one of your countrymen or buy any from him, do not take advantage of each other. 15You are to buy from your countryman on the basis of the number of years since the Jubilee. And he is to sell to you on the basis of the number of years left for harvesting crops. 16When the years are many, you are to increase the price, and when the years are few, you are to decrease the price, because what he is really selling you is the number of crops. 17Do not take advantage of each other, but fear your God. I am the LORD your God.

18" 'Follow my decrees and be careful to obey my laws, and you will live safely in the land. 19Then the land will yield its fruit, and you will eat your fill and live there in safety. 20You may ask, "What will we eat in the seventh year if we do not plant or harvest our crops?" 21I will send you such a blessing in the sixth year that the land will yield enough for three years. 22While you plant during the eighth year, you will eat from the old crop and will continue to eat from it until the harvest of the ninth year comes in.

23" 'The land must not be sold permanently, because the land is mine and you are but aliens and my tenants. 24Throughout the country that you hold as a possession, you must provide for the redemption of the land.

25" 'If one of your countrymen becomes poor and sells some of his property, his nearest relative is to come and redeem what his countryman has sold. 26If, however, a man has no one to redeem it for him but he himself prospers and acquires sufficient means to redeem it, 27he is to determine the value for the years since he sold it and refund the balance to the man to whom he sold it; he can then go back to his own property. 28But if he does not acquire the means to repay him, what he sold will remain in the possession of the buyer until the Year of Jubilee. It will be returned in the Jubilee, and he can then go back to his property.

29" 'If a man sells a house in a walled city, he retains the right of redemption a full year after its sale. During that time he may redeem it. 30If it is not redeemed before a full year has passed, the house in the walled city shall belong permanently to the buyer and his descendants. It is not to be returned in the Jubilee. 31But houses in villages without walls around them are to be considered as open country. They can be redeemed, and they are to be returned in the Jubilee.

32" 'The Levites always have the right to redeem their houses in the Levitical towns, which they possess. 33So the property of the Levites is redeemable—that is, a house sold in any town they hold—and is to be returned in the Jubilee, because the houses in the towns of the Levites are their property among the Israelites. 34But the pastureland belonging to their towns must not be sold; it is their permanent possession.

35" 'If one of your countrymen becomes poor and is unable to support himself among you, help him as you would an alien or a temporary resident, so he can continue to live among you. 36Do not take interest of any kind[l] from him, but fear your God, so that your countryman may continue to live among you. 37You must not lend him money at interest or sell him food at a profit. 38I am the LORD your God, who brought you out of Egypt to give you the land of Canaan and to be your God.

39" 'If one of your countrymen becomes poor among you and sells himself to you, do not make him work as a slave. 40He is to be treated as a hired worker or a temporary resident among you; he is to work for you until the Year of Jubilee. 41Then he and his children are to be released, and he will go back to his own clan and to the property of his forefathers. 42Because the Israelites are my servants, whom I brought out of Egypt, they must not be sold as slaves. 43Do not rule over them ruthlessly, but fear your God.

44" 'Your male and female slaves are to come from the nations around you; from them you may

l36 Or take excessive interest; similarly in verse 37

buy slaves. ⁴⁵You may also buy some of the temporary residents living among you and members of their clans born in your country, and they will become your property. ⁴⁶You can will them to your children as inherited property and can make them slaves for life, but you must not rule over your fellow Israelites ruthlessly.

⁴⁷" 'If an alien or a temporary resident among you becomes rich and one of your countrymen becomes poor and sells himself to the alien living among you or to a member of the alien's clan, ⁴⁸he retains the right of redemption after he has sold himself. One of his relatives may redeem him: ⁴⁹An uncle or a cousin or any blood relative in his clan may redeem him. Or if he prospers, he may redeem himself. ⁵⁰He and his buyer are to count the time from the year he sold himself up to the Year of Jubilee. The price for his release is to be based on the rate paid to a hired man for that number of years. ⁵¹If many years remain, he must pay for his redemption a larger share of the price paid for him. ⁵²If only a few years remain until the Year of Jubilee, he is to compute that and pay for his redemption accordingly. ⁵³He is to be treated as a man hired from year to year; you must see to it that his owner does not rule over him ruthlessly.

⁵⁴" 'Even if he is not redeemed in any of these ways, he and his children are to be released in the Year of Jubilee, ⁵⁵for the Israelites belong to me as servants. They are my servants, whom I brought out of Egypt. I am the LORD your God.

Discovering the Word 1. What is the primary way the Israelites are to care for their land (vv. 3–5, 11)? 2. What would a sabbath year for the land be like for the people of Israel (vv. 4–7)? 3. What are the key provisions of the Year of Jubilee (vv. 13–22)? 4. How do the guidelines for observing the Year of Jubilee show the link that exists between care of the land and justice for people? 5. What images does the phrase "redemption of the land" bring to mind (v. 24)? 6. Verses 25–55 contain principles for living on the land with others. What do these principles tell you about God's desires for the land and the people?

Applying the Word 1. In what ways is taking good care of the land linked to justice for people in today's world? 2. How is the misuse of land related to the oppression of people?

Responding in Prayer Pray for those who suffer because we do not properly care for God's creation.

---

8 / *Leviticus 26*
Reaping Results

"SHE HAD IT coming." "I should have known." "It was his own fault." "Well, what did they expect?" In these and a hundred other ways we affirm that people reap what they sow. While that is often said negatively, it can be positive too: "It really paid off." "That's your reward." "You earned it!" Before Israel entered the Promised Land, the Lord told them what they could expect from both obedience and disobedience.

Warming Up to God In what ways has God rewarded your faith and obedience to him?

Read Leviticus 26.

---

26 " 'Do not make idols or set up an image or a sacred stone for yourselves, and do not place a carved stone in your land to bow down before it. I am the LORD your God.

²" 'Observe my Sabbaths and have reverence for my sanctuary. I am the LORD.

³" 'If you follow my decrees and are careful to obey my commands, ⁴I will send you rain in its season, and the ground will yield its crops and

the trees of the field their fruit. ⁵Your threshing will continue until grape harvest and the grape harvest will continue until planting, and you will eat all the food you want and live in safety in your land.

⁶" 'I will grant peace in the land, and you will lie down and no one will make you afraid. I will remove savage beasts from the land, and the sword will not pass through your country. ⁷You will pursue your enemies, and they will fall by the sword before you. ⁸Five of you will chase a hundred, and a hundred of you will chase ten thousand, and your enemies will fall by the sword before you.

⁹" 'I will look on you with favor and make you fruitful and increase your numbers, and I will keep my covenant with you. ¹⁰You will still be eating last year's harvest when you will have to move it out to make room for the new. ¹¹I will put my dwelling place[m] among you, and I will not abhor you. ¹²I will walk among you and be your God, and you will be my people. ¹³I am the LORD your God, who brought you out of Egypt so that you would no longer be slaves to the Egyptians; I broke the bars of your yoke and enabled you to walk with heads held high.

¹⁴" 'But if you will not listen to me and carry out all these commands, ¹⁵and if you reject my decrees and abhor my laws and fail to carry out all my commands and so violate my covenant, ¹⁶then I will do this to you: I will bring upon you sudden terror, wasting diseases and fever that will destroy your sight and drain away your life. You will plant seed in vain, because your enemies will eat it. ¹⁷I will set my face against you so that you will be defeated by your enemies; those who hate you will rule over you, and you will flee even when no one is pursuing you.

¹⁸" 'If after all this you will not listen to me, I will punish you for your sins seven times over. ¹⁹I will break down your stubborn pride and make the sky above you like iron and the ground beneath you like bronze. ²⁰Your strength will be spent in vain, because your soil will not yield its crops, nor will the trees of the land yield their fruit.

²¹" 'If you remain hostile toward me and refuse to listen to me, I will multiply your afflictions seven times over, as your sins deserve. ²²I will send wild animals against you, and they will rob you of your children, destroy your cattle and

make you so few in number that your roads will be deserted.

²³" 'If in spite of these things you do not accept my correction but continue to be hostile toward me, ²⁴I myself will be hostile toward you and will afflict you for your sins seven times over. ²⁵And I will bring the sword upon you to avenge the breaking of the covenant. When you withdraw into your cities, I will send a plague among you, and you will be given into enemy hands. ²⁶When I cut off your supply of bread, ten women will be able to bake your bread in one oven, and they will dole out the bread by weight. You will eat, but you will not be satisfied.

²⁷" 'If in spite of this you still do not listen to me but continue to be hostile toward me, ²⁸then in my anger I will be hostile toward you, and I myself will punish you for your sins seven times over. ²⁹You will eat the flesh of your sons and the flesh of your daughters. ³⁰I will destroy your high places, cut down your incense altars and pile your dead bodies on the lifeless forms of your idols, and I will abhor you. ³¹I will turn your cities into ruins and lay waste your sanctuaries, and I will take no delight in the pleasing aroma of your offerings. ³²I will lay waste the land, so that your enemies who live there will be appalled. ³³I will scatter you among the nations and will draw out my sword and pursue you. Your land will be laid waste, and your cities will lie in ruins. ³⁴Then the land will enjoy its sabbath years all the time that it lies desolate and you are in the country of your enemies; then the land will rest and enjoy its sabbaths. ³⁵All the time that it lies desolate, the land will have the rest it did not have during the sabbaths you lived in it.

³⁶" 'As for those of you who are left, I will make their hearts so fearful in the lands of their enemies that the sound of a windblown leaf will put them to flight. They will run as though fleeing from the sword, and they will fall, even though no one is pursuing them. ³⁷They will stumble over one another as though fleeing from the sword, even though no one is pursuing them. So you will not be able to stand before your enemies. ³⁸You will perish among the nations; the land of your enemies will devour you. ³⁹Those of you who are left will waste away in the lands of their enemies because of their sins; also be-

m 11 Or *my tabernacle*

cause of their fathers' sins they will waste away.

⁴⁰"'But if they will confess their sins and the sins of their fathers—their treachery against me and their hostility toward me, ⁴¹which made me hostile toward them so that I sent them into the land of their enemies—then when their uncircumcised hearts are humbled and they pay for their sin, ⁴²I will remember my covenant with Jacob and my covenant with Isaac and my covenant with Abraham, and I will remember the land. ⁴³For the land will be deserted by them and will enjoy its sabbaths while it lies desolate without them. They will pay for their sins because

they rejected my laws and abhorred my decrees. ⁴⁴Yet in spite of this, when they are in the land of their enemies, I will not reject them or abhor them so as to destroy them completely, breaking my covenant with them. I am the LORD their God. ⁴⁵But for their sake I will remember the covenant with their ancestors whom I brought out of Egypt in the sight of the nations to be their God. I am the LORD.' "

⁴⁶These are the decrees, the laws and the regulations that the LORD established on Mount Sinai between himself and the Israelites through Moses.

Discovering the Word   1. How would the Lord bless Israel for obeying him (vv. 3–13)?   2. How would he chastise them for disobeying (vv. 14–39)?   3. How do verses 18, 21, 23 and 27 show that God would keep giving Israel another chance to obey?   4. Even after the extreme chastisement of being banished from their land, what did God promise if they repented (vv. 40–45)?   5. How do the punishments, as well as the rewards, demonstrate God's generous grace?

Applying the Word   1. This Scripture should not lead us to interpret *every* event as God's reward or punishment. Nevertheless, we can all think of events through which God spoke to us about our behavior. How has the Lord affirmed or reprimanded you through something that happened?   2. When remarkable events occur, how open are you to what the Lord might be saying to you through them?

Responding in Prayer   Thank the Lord for communicating to you through happenings in your life. Renew your commitment to follow him in obedience.

Leviticus 27

27 The LORD said to Moses, ²"Speak to the Israelites and say to them: 'If anyone makes a special vow to dedicate persons to the LORD by giving equivalent values, ³set the value of a male between the ages of twenty and sixty at fifty shekels*ⁿ* of silver, according to the sanctuary shekel*ᵒ*; ⁴and if it is a female, set her value at thirty shekels.*ᵖ* ⁵If it is a person between the ages of five and twenty, set the value of a male at twenty shekels*�q* and of a female at ten shekels.*ʳ* ⁶If it is a person between one month and five years, set the value of a male at five shekels*ˢ* of silver and that of a female at three shekels*ᵗ* of silver. ⁷If it is a person sixty years old or more, set the value of a male at fifteen shekels*ᵘ* and of a female at ten shekels. ⁸If anyone making the vow is too poor to pay the specified amount, he is to present the person to the priest, who will set the value for him according to what the man making the vow can afford.

⁹"'If what he vowed is an animal that is accept-

able as an offering to the LORD, such an animal given to the LORD becomes holy. ¹⁰He must not exchange it or substitute a good one for a bad one, or a bad one for a good one; if he should substitute one animal for another, both it and the substitute become holy. ¹¹If what he vowed is a ceremonially unclean animal—one that is not acceptable as an offering to the LORD—the animal must be presented to the priest, ¹²who will judge its quality as good or bad. Whatever value the priest then sets, that is what it will be. ¹³If the owner wishes to redeem the animal, he must add a fifth to its value.

¹⁴"'If a man dedicates his house as something holy to the LORD, the priest will judge its quality as good or bad. Whatever value the priest then

---

ⁿ3 That is, about 1 1/4 pounds (about 0.6 kilogram); also in verse 16   *ᵒ3* That is, about 2/5 ounce (about 11.5 grams); also in verse 25   *ᵖ4* That is, about 12 ounces (about 0.3 kilogram)   *q5* That is, about 8 ounces (about 0.2 kilogram)   *ʳ5* That is, about 4 ounces (about 110 grams); also in verse 7   *ˢ6* That is, about 2 ounces (about 55 grams)   *ᵗ6* That is, about 1 1/4 ounces (about 35 grams)   *ᵘ7* That is, about 6 ounces (about 170 grams) sets, so it will remain. ¹⁵If the man who dedicates his house redeems it, he must add a fifth to its value, and the house will again become his.

¹⁶" 'If a man dedicates to the LORD part of his family land, its value is to be set according to the amount of seed required for it—fifty shekels of silver to a homer ᵛ of barley seed. ¹⁷If he dedicates his field during the Year of Jubilee, the value that has been set remains. ¹⁸But if he dedicates his field after the Jubilee, the priest will determine the value according to the number of years that remain until the next Year of Jubilee, and its set value will be reduced. ¹⁹If the man who dedicates the field wishes to redeem it, he must add a fifth to its value, and the field will again become his. ²⁰If, however, he does not redeem the field, or if he has sold it to someone else, it can never be redeemed. ²¹When the field is released in the Jubilee, it will become holy, like a field devoted to the LORD; it will become the property of the priests. ʷ

²²" 'If a man dedicates to the LORD a field he has bought, which is not part of his family land, ²³the priest will determine its value up to the Year of Jubilee, and the man must pay its value on that day as something holy to the LORD. ²⁴In the Year of Jubilee the field will revert to the person from whom he bought it, the one whose land it was. ²⁵Every value is to be set according to the sanctuary shekel, twenty gerahs to the shekel.

²⁶" 'No one, however, may dedicate the first-born of an animal, since the firstborn already belongs to the LORD; whether an ox ˣ or a sheep, it is the LORD's. ²⁷If it is one of the unclean animals, he may buy it back at its set value, adding a fifth of the value to it. If he does not redeem it, it is to be sold at its set value.

²⁸" 'But nothing that a man owns and devotes ʸ to the LORD—whether man or animal or family land—may be sold or redeemed; everything so devoted is most holy to the LORD.

²⁹" 'No person devoted to destruction ᶻ may be ransomed; he must be put to death.

³⁰" 'A tithe of everything from the land, whether grain from the soil or fruit from the trees, belongs to the LORD; it is holy to the LORD. ³¹If a man redeems any of his tithe, he must add a fifth of the value to it. ³²The entire tithe of the herd and flock—every tenth animal that passes under the shepherd's rod—will be holy to the LORD. ³³He must not pick out the good from the bad or make any substitution. If he does make a substitution, both the animal and its substitute become holy and cannot be redeemed.' "

³⁴These are the commands the LORD gave Moses on Mount Sinai for the Israelites.

ᵛ16 That is, probably about 6 bushels (about 220 liters)   ʷ21 Or *priest*   ˣ26 The Hebrew word can include both male and female.   ʸ28 The Hebrew term refers to the irrevocable giving over of things or persons to the LORD.   ᶻ29 The Hebrew term refers to the irrevocable giving over of things or persons to the LORD, often by totally destroying them.

Numbers

O ne month after the close of the book of Exodus, Moses commands a census of all the Jews. He finds that an Israelite army would number 603,550 fighting men. A generation later (Nu 26) he will commission a new count. These human inventories —the numbering of God's people—provide the title of the Pentateuch's fourth book.

But the ancients had another name for this account: they called it "In the Wilderness." That title is a fitting one for the story of a wandering people caught in transition between slavery and freedom. Having fled Pharaoh's tyranny in Egypt, God's people seek the permanent homeland of their dreams. But reality interferes with their dreams; they face the crises and trials of nomadic life.

Along with its colorful and gripping narrative, Numbers offers a metaphor for the wilderness experience every human must encounter. We experience life as a pilgrimage like that of Moses and his people, with past struggles behind us and dreams yet to fulfill. Along the way, there is heartbreak and disappointment. But the voice of God is consistent, calling on us to face every challenge with steadfast obedience. Like the Israelites, we discover that the hardest times produce the strongest lessons, and that at the other end of the wilderness journey we find ourselves wiser and more capable. To obey God is to move forward in life with direction and purpose.

But disobedience has consequences. When God's people rebel against his command to enter Canaan, the results are painful and far-reaching. We learn that our own failures have implications for generations yet unborn. There is nowhere in the Bible a more graphic picture of the social consequences of sin.

Numbers begins with the exodus generation. It ends thirty-nine years later with the story of their children fighting to solidify their place in Canaan. It begins shortly after the Israelites receive the Law from Mount Sinai. It ends as they struggle to live by that Law in a world of hostile neighbors. It begins with a leader, Moses, at the peak of his power. It ends as Moses, forbidden from entering the Promised Land, gives way to a new leader. These are thirty-nine pivotal years in the spiritual history of a nation.

As you study Numbers, watch for these themes: obedience, purity, leadership, guidance, discouragement, deliverance. What can you learn and apply from the lessons of Moses' people? As those themes play out in the book of Numbers, so will they be repeated in the wilderness experiences of our own lives.

Outline

1/ Numbers 1 ———————————————— *People Count!*

2/ Numbers 9 ———————————————— *Looking Back; Looking Ahead*

3/ Numbers 11 ———————————————— *No Thanks*

4/ Numbers 12 ———————————————— *A Critical Spirit*

5/ Numbers 13:1—14:12 ————————— *Taking Risks*

6/ Numbers 17 ———————————————— *Budding Leadership*

7/ Numbers 20:1–13 —————————— *God's Work; God's Way*

8/ Numbers 21:1–9 ———————————— *The Serpent That Saved*

9/ Numbers 27:12–23 ————————— *Passing the Torch*

10/ Numbers 32 ———————————————— *United We Stand*

1 / *Numbers 1*
People Count!

WE LIVE IN the age of the survey. Demographic studies measure every possible facet of modern life. We seem to have an obsession with categorizing people. In Numbers categories play an important part—two censuses are recorded. The Israelites have secured their freedom from Egyptian slavery, and Moses calls for a count of the twelve tribes.

 Warming Up to God   What groups do you feel particularly a part of and identify with?

 Read Numbers 1.

The Lord spoke to Moses in the Tent of Meeting in the Desert of Sinai on the first day of the second month of the second year after the Israelites came out of Egypt. He said: ²"Take a census of the whole Israelite community by their clans and families, listing every man by name, one by one. ³You and Aaron are to number by their divisions all the men in Israel twenty years old or more who are able to serve in the army. ⁴One man from each tribe, each the head of his family, is to help you. ⁵These are the names of the men who are to assist you:

  from Reuben, Elizur son of Shedeur;
  ⁶from Simeon, Shelumiel son of Zurishaddai;
  ⁷from Judah, Nahshon son of Amminadab;
  ⁸from Issachar, Nethanel son of Zuar;
  ⁹from Zebulun, Eliab son of Helon;
  ¹⁰from the sons of Joseph:
     from Ephraim, Elishama son of Ammihud;
     from Manasseh, Gamaliel son of Pedahzur;
  ¹¹from Benjamin, Abidan son of Gideoni;
  ¹²from Dan, Ahiezer son of Ammishaddai;
  ¹³from Asher, Pagiel son of Ocran;
  ¹⁴from Gad, Eliasaph son of Deuel;
  ¹⁵from Naphtali, Ahira son of Enan."

¹⁶These were the men appointed from the community, the leaders of their ancestral tribes. They were the heads of the clans of Israel.

¹⁷Moses and Aaron took these men whose names had been given, ¹⁸and they called the whole community together on the first day of the second month. The people indicated their ancestry by their clans and families, and the men twenty years old or more were listed by name, one by one, ¹⁹as the Lord commanded Moses. And so he counted them in the Desert of Sinai:

²⁰From the descendants of Reuben the firstborn son of Israel:

All the men twenty years old or more who were able to serve in the army were listed by name, one by one, according to the records of their clans and families. ²¹The number from the tribe of Reuben was 46,500.

²²From the descendants of Simeon:

All the men twenty years old or more who were able to serve in the army were counted and listed by name, one by one, according to the records of their clans and families. ²³The number from the tribe of Simeon was 59,300.

²⁴From the descendants of Gad:

All the men twenty years old or more who were able to serve in the army were listed by name, according to the records of their clans and families. ²⁵The number from the tribe of Gad was 45,650.

²⁶From the descendants of Judah:

All the men twenty years old or more who were able to serve in the army were listed by name, according to the records of their clans and families. ²⁷The number from the tribe of Judah was 74,600.

²⁸From the descendants of Issachar:

All the men twenty years old or more who were able to serve in the army were listed by name, according to the records of their clans and families. ²⁹The number from the tribe of Issachar was 54,400.

³⁰From the descendants of Zebulun:
All the men twenty years old or more who were able to serve in the army were listed by name, according to the records of their clans and families. ³¹The number from the tribe of Zebulun was 57,400.

³²From the sons of Joseph:
From the descendants of Ephraim:
All the men twenty years old or more who were able to serve in the army were listed by name, according to the records of their clans and families. ³³The number from the tribe of Ephraim was 40,500.

³⁴From the descendants of Manasseh:
All the men twenty years old or more who were able to serve in the army were listed by name, according to the records of their clans and families. ³⁵The number from the tribe of Manasseh was 32,200.

³⁶From the descendants of Benjamin:
All the men twenty years old or more who were able to serve in the army were listed by name, according to the records of their clans and families. ³⁷The number from the tribe of Benjamin was 35,400.

³⁸From the descendants of Dan:
All the men twenty years old or more who were able to serve in the army were listed by name, according to the records of their clans and families. ³⁹The number from the tribe of Dan was 62,700.

⁴⁰From the descendants of Asher:
All the men twenty years old or more who were able to serve in the army were listed by name, according to the records of their clans and families. ⁴¹The number from the tribe of Asher was 41,500.

⁴²From the descendants of Naphtali:
All the men twenty years old or more who were able to serve in the army were listed by name, according to the records of their clans and families. ⁴³The number from the tribe of Naphtali was 53,400.

⁴⁴These were the men counted by Moses and Aaron and the twelve leaders of Israel, each one representing his family. ⁴⁵All the Israelites twenty years old or more who were able to serve in Israel's army were counted according to their families. ⁴⁶The total number was 603,550.

⁴⁷The families of the tribe of Levi, however, were not counted along with the others. ⁴⁸The LORD had said to Moses: ⁴⁹"You must not count the tribe of Levi or include them in the census of the other Israelites. ⁵⁰Instead, appoint the Levites to be in charge of the tabernacle of the Testimony—over all its furnishings and everything belonging to it. They are to carry the tabernacle and all its furnishings; they are to take care of it and encamp around it. ⁵¹Whenever the tabernacle is to move, the Levites are to take it down, and whenever the tabernacle is to be set up, the Levites shall do it. Anyone else who goes near it shall be put to death. ⁵²The Israelites are to set up their tents by divisions, each man in his own camp under his own standard. ⁵³The Levites, however, are to set up their tents around the tabernacle of the Testimony so that wrath will not fall on the Israelite community. The Levites are to be responsible for the care of the tabernacle of the Testimony."

⁵⁴The Israelites did all this just as the LORD commanded Moses.

Discovering the Word 1. For what reasons does God ask Moses to take a census of all the people (vv. 2–3)? 2. Why do you think it was important for the Israelites to maintain their tribal identities? 3. God sets apart the Levites to take care of the tabernacle (vv. 47–53). Why is it important for those with spiritual responsibilities to be singled out? 4. What special challenges might there have been for nomadic people maintaining the tabernacle and God's laws?

Applying the Word 1. What personal characteristics about you might God count as most important? 2. How can you specifically build up your "tribe" (this could mean family, church or group) as a unit mobilized to serve God?

 Responding in Prayer In God's eyes people count. Praise him for caring about the details of our lives. Ask him to help you today to make your "tribe" a stronger one.

Numbers 2—8

2 The LORD said to Moses and Aaron: [2]"The Israelites are to camp around the Tent of Meeting some distance from it, each man under his standard with the banners of his family."

[3]On the east, toward the sunrise, the divisions of the camp of Judah are to encamp under their standard. The leader of the people of Judah is Nahshon son of Amminadab. [4]His division numbers 74,600.

[5]The tribe of Issachar will camp next to them. The leader of the people of Issachar is Nethanel son of Zuar. [6]His division numbers 54,400.

[7]The tribe of Zebulun will be next. The leader of the people of Zebulun is Eliab son of Helon. [8]His division numbers 57,400.

[9]All the men assigned to the camp of Judah, according to their divisions, number 186,400. They will set out first.

[10]On the south will be the divisions of the camp of Reuben under their standard. The leader of the people of Reuben is Elizur son of Shedeur. [11]His division numbers 46,500.

[12]The tribe of Simeon will camp next to them. The leader of the people of Simeon is Shelumiel son of Zurishaddai. [13]His division numbers 59,300.

[14]The tribe of Gad will be next. The leader of the people of Gad is Eliasaph son of Deuel.[a] [15]His division numbers 45,650.

[16]All the men assigned to the camp of Reuben, according to their divisions, number 151,450. They will set out second.

[17]Then the Tent of Meeting and the camp of the Levites will set out in the middle of the camps. They will set out in the same order as they encamp, each in his own place under his standard.

[18]On the west will be the divisions of the camp of Ephraim under their standard. The leader of the people of Ephraim is Elishama son of Ammihud. [19]His division numbers 40,500.

[20]The tribe of Manasseh will be next to them. The leader of the people of Manasseh is Gamaliel son of Pedahzur. [21]His division numbers 32,200.

[22]The tribe of Benjamin will be next. The leader of the people of Benjamin is Abidan son of Gideoni. [23]His division numbers 35,400.

[24]All the men assigned to the camp of Ephraim, according to their divisions, number 108,100. They will set out third.

[25]On the north will be the divisions of the camp of Dan, under their standard. The leader of the people of Dan is Ahiezer son of Ammishaddai. [26]His division numbers 62,700.

[27]The tribe of Asher will camp next to them. The leader of the people of Asher is Pagiel son of Ocran. [28]His division numbers 41,500.

[29]The tribe of Naphtali will be next. The leader of the people of Naphtali is Ahira son of Enan. [30]His division numbers 53,400.

[31]All the men assigned to the camp of Dan number 157,600. They will set out last, under their standards.

[32]These are the Israelites, counted according to their families. All those in the camps, by their divisions, number 603,550. [33]The Levites, however, were not counted along with the other Israelites, as the LORD commanded Moses.

[34]So the Israelites did everything the LORD commanded Moses; that is the way they encamped under their standards, and that is the way they set out, each with his clan and family.

3 This is the account of the family of Aaron and Moses at the time the LORD talked with Moses on Mount Sinai.

[2]The names of the sons of Aaron were Nadab the firstborn and Abihu, Eleazar and Ithamar. [3]Those were the names of Aaron's sons, the anointed priests, who were ordained to serve as priests. [4]Nadab and Abihu, however, fell dead before the LORD when they made an offering with unauthorized fire before him in the Desert of Sinai. They had no sons; so only Eleazar and Itha-

---

a14 Many manuscripts of the Masoretic Text, Samaritan Pentateuch and Vulgate (see also Num. 1:14); most manuscripts of the Masoretic Text *Reuel* mar served as priests during the lifetime of their father Aaron.

5The LORD said to Moses, 6"Bring the tribe of Levi and present them to Aaron the priest to assist him. 7They are to perform duties for him and for the whole community at the Tent of Meeting by doing the work of the tabernacle. 8They are to take care of all the furnishings of the Tent of Meeting, fulfilling the obligations of the Israelites by doing the work of the tabernacle. 9Give the Levites to Aaron and his sons; they are the Israelites who are to be given wholly to him.b 10Appoint Aaron and his sons to serve as priests; anyone else who approaches the sanctuary must be put to death."

11The LORD also said to Moses, 12"I have taken the Levites from among the Israelites in place of the first male offspring of every Israelite woman. The Levites are mine, 13for all the firstborn are mine. When I struck down all the firstborn in Egypt, I set apart for myself every firstborn in Israel, whether man or animal. They are to be mine. I am the LORD."

14The LORD said to Moses in the Desert of Sinai, 15"Count the Levites by their families and clans. Count every male a month old or more." 16So Moses counted them, as he was commanded by the word of the LORD.

17These were the names of the sons of Levi:
Gershon, Kohath and Merari.

18These were the names of the Gershonite clans:
Libni and Shimei.

19The Kohathite clans:
Amram, Izhar, Hebron and Uzziel.

20The Merarite clans:
Mahli and Mushi.

These were the Levite clans, according to their families.

21To Gershon belonged the clans of the Libnites and Shimeites; these were the Gershonite clans. 22The number of all the males a month old or more who were counted was 7,500. 23The Gershonite clans were to camp on the west, behind the tabernacle. 24The leader of the families of the Gershonites was Eliasaph son of Lael. 25At the Tent of Meeting the Gershonites were responsible for the care of the tabernacle and tent, its coverings, the curtain at the entrance to the Tent of Meeting, 26the curtains of the courtyard, the curtain at the entrance to the courtyard surrounding

the tabernacle and altar, and the ropes—and everything related to their use.

27To Kohath belonged the clans of the Amramites, Izharites, Hebronites and Uzzielites; these were the Kohathite clans. 28The number of all the males a month old or more was 8,600.c The Kohathites were responsible for the care of the sanctuary. 29The Kohathite clans were to camp on the south side of the tabernacle. 30The leader of the families of the Kohathite clans was Elizaphan son of Uzziel. 31They were responsible for the care of the ark, the table, the lampstand, the altars, the articles of the sanctuary used in ministering, the curtain, and everything related to their use. 32The chief leader of the Levites was Eleazar son of Aaron, the priest. He was appointed over those who were responsible for the care of the sanctuary.

33To Merari belonged the clans of the Mahlites and the Mushites; these were the Merarite clans. 34The number of all the males a month old or more who were counted was 6,200. 35The leader of the families of the Merarite clans was Zuriel son of Abihail; they were to camp on the north side of the tabernacle. 36The Merarites were appointed to take care of the frames of the tabernacle, its crossbars, posts, bases, all its equipment, and everything related to their use, 37as well as the posts of the surrounding courtyard with their bases, tent pegs and ropes.

38Moses and Aaron and his sons were to camp to the east of the tabernacle, toward the sunrise, in front of the Tent of Meeting. They were responsible for the care of the sanctuary on behalf of the Israelites. Anyone else who approached the sanctuary was to be put to death.

39The total number of Levites counted at the LORD's command by Moses and Aaron according to their clans, including every male a month old or more, was 22,000.

40The LORD said to Moses, "Count all the firstborn Israelite males who are a month old or more and make a list of their names. 41Take the Levites for me in place of all the firstborn of the Israelites, and the livestock of the Levites in place of all the firstborn of the livestock of the Israelites. I am the LORD."

b9 Most manuscripts of the Masoretic Text; some manuscripts of the Masoretic Text, Samaritan Pentateuch and Septuagint (see also Num. 8:16) to me   c28 Hebrew; some Septuagint manuscripts 8,300

⁴²So Moses counted all the firstborn of the Israelites, as the LORD commanded him. ⁴³The total number of firstborn males a month old or more, listed by name, was 22,273.

⁴⁴The LORD also said to Moses, ⁴⁵"Take the Levites in place of all the firstborn of Israel, and the livestock of the Levites in place of their livestock. The Levites are to be mine. I am the LORD. ⁴⁶To redeem the 273 firstborn Israelites who exceed the number of the Levites, ⁴⁷collect five shekels*d* for each one, according to the sanctuary shekel, which weighs twenty gerahs. ⁴⁸Give the money for the redemption of the additional Israelites to Aaron and his sons."

⁴⁹So Moses collected the redemption money from those who exceeded the number redeemed by the Levites. ⁵⁰From the firstborn of the Israelites he collected silver weighing 1,365 shekels,*e* according to the sanctuary shekel. ⁵¹Moses gave the redemption money to Aaron and his sons, as he was commanded by the word of the LORD.

4 The LORD said to Moses and Aaron: ²"Take a census of the Kohathite branch of the Levites by their clans and families. ³Count all the men from thirty to fifty years of age who come to serve in the work in the Tent of Meeting.

⁴"This is the work of the Kohathites in the Tent of Meeting: the care of the most holy things. ⁵When the camp is to move, Aaron and his sons are to go in and take down the shielding curtain and cover the ark of the Testimony with it. ⁶Then they are to cover this with hides of sea cows,*f* spread a cloth of solid blue over that and put the poles in place.

⁷"Over the table of the Presence they are to spread a blue cloth and put on it the plates, dishes and bowls, and the jars for drink offerings; the bread that is continually there is to remain on it. ⁸Over these they are to spread a scarlet cloth, cover that with hides of sea cows and put its poles in place.

⁹"They are to take a blue cloth and cover the lampstand that is for light, together with its lamps, its wick trimmers and trays, and all its jars for the oil used to supply it. ¹⁰Then they are to wrap it and all its accessories in a covering of hides of sea cows and put it on a carrying frame.

¹¹"Over the gold altar they are to spread a blue cloth and cover that with hides of sea cows and put its poles in place.

¹²"They are to take all the articles used for ministering in the sanctuary, wrap them in a blue cloth, cover that with hides of sea cows and put them on a carrying frame.

¹³"They are to remove the ashes from the bronze altar and spread a purple cloth over it. ¹⁴Then they are to place on it all the utensils used for ministering at the altar, including the firepans, meat forks, shovels and sprinkling bowls. Over it they are to spread a covering of hides of sea cows and put its poles in place.

¹⁵"After Aaron and his sons have finished covering the holy furnishings and all the holy articles, and when the camp is ready to move, the Kohathites are to come to do the carrying. But they must not touch the holy things or they will die. The Kohathites are to carry those things that are in the Tent of Meeting.

¹⁶"Eleazar son of Aaron, the priest, is to have charge of the oil for the light, the fragrant incense, the regular grain offering and the anointing oil. He is to be in charge of the entire tabernacle and everything in it, including its holy furnishings and articles."

¹⁷The LORD said to Moses and Aaron, ¹⁸"See that the Kohathite tribal clans are not cut off from the Levites. ¹⁹So that they may live and not die when they come near the most holy things, do this for them: Aaron and his sons are to go into the sanctuary and assign to each man his work and what he is to carry. ²⁰But the Kohathites must not go in to look at the holy things, even for a moment, or they will die."

²¹The LORD said to Moses, ²²"Take a census also of the Gershonites by their families and clans. ²³Count all the men from thirty to fifty years of age who come to serve in the work at the Tent of Meeting.

²⁴"This is the service of the Gershonite clans as they work and carry burdens: ²⁵They are to carry the curtains of the tabernacle, the Tent of Meeting, its covering and the outer covering of hides of sea cows, the curtains for the entrance to the Tent of Meeting, ²⁶the curtains of the courtyard surrounding the tabernacle and altar, the curtain for the entrance, the ropes and all the equipment used in its service. The Gershonites are to do all that needs to be done with these things. ²⁷All their service, whether carrying or doing other work, is to be done under the direction of Aaron

---

d47 That is, about 2 ounces (about 55 grams)   *e50* That is, about 35 pounds (about 15.5 kilograms)   *f6* That is, dugongs; also in verses 8, 10, 11, 12, 14 and 25 and his sons. You shall assign to them as their responsibility all they are to carry. ²⁸This is the service of the Gershonite clans at the Tent of Meeting. Their duties are to be under the direction of Ithamar son of Aaron, the priest.

²⁹"Count the Merarites by their clans and families. ³⁰Count all the men from thirty to fifty years of age who come to serve in the work at the Tent of Meeting. ³¹This is their duty as they perform service at the Tent of Meeting: to carry the frames of the tabernacle, its crossbars, posts and bases, ³²as well as the posts of the surrounding courtyard with their bases, tent pegs, ropes, all their equipment and everything related to their use. Assign to each man the specific things he is to carry. ³³This is the service of the Merarite clans as they work at the Tent of Meeting under the direction of Ithamar son of Aaron, the priest."

³⁴Moses, Aaron and the leaders of the community counted the Kohathites by their clans and families. ³⁵All the men from thirty to fifty years of age who came to serve in the work in the Tent of Meeting, ³⁶counted by clans, were 2,750. ³⁷This was the total of all those in the Kohathite clans who served in the Tent of Meeting. Moses and Aaron counted them according to the LORD's command through Moses.

³⁸The Gershonites were counted by their clans and families. ³⁹All the men from thirty to fifty years of age who came to serve in the work at the Tent of Meeting, ⁴⁰counted by their clans and families, were 2,630. ⁴¹This was the total of those in the Gershonite clans who served at the Tent of Meeting. Moses and Aaron counted them according to the LORD's command.

⁴²The Merarites were counted by their clans and families. ⁴³All the men from thirty to fifty years of age who came to serve in the work at the Tent of Meeting, ⁴⁴counted by their clans, were 3,200. ⁴⁵This was the total of those in the Merarite clans. Moses and Aaron counted them according to the LORD's command through Moses.

⁴⁶So Moses, Aaron and the leaders of Israel counted all the Levites by their clans and families. ⁴⁷All the men from thirty to fifty years of age who came to do the work of serving and carrying the Tent of Meeting ⁴⁸numbered 8,580. ⁴⁹At the LORD's command through Moses, each was assigned his work and told what to carry.

Thus they were counted, as the LORD commanded Moses.

5 The LORD said to Moses, ²"Command the Israelites to send away from the camp anyone who has an infectious skin disease^g or a discharge of any kind, or who is ceremonially unclean because of a dead body. ³Send away male and female alike; send them outside the camp so they will not defile their camp, where I dwell among them." ⁴The Israelites did this; they sent them outside the camp. They did just as the LORD had instructed Moses.

⁵The LORD said to Moses, ⁶"Say to the Israelites: 'When a man or woman wrongs another in any way^h and so is unfaithful to the LORD, that person is guilty ⁷and must confess the sin he has committed. He must make full restitution for his wrong, add one fifth to it and give it all to the person he has wronged. ⁸But if that person has no close relative to whom restitution can be made for the wrong, the restitution belongs to the LORD and must be given to the priest, along with the ram with which atonement is made for him. ⁹All the sacred contributions the Israelites bring to a priest will belong to him. ¹⁰Each man's sacred gifts are his own, but what he gives to the priest will belong to the priest.' "

¹¹Then the LORD said to Moses, ¹²"Speak to the Israelites and say to them: 'If a man's wife goes astray and is unfaithful to him ¹³by sleeping with another man, and this is hidden from her husband and her impurity is undetected (since there is no witness against her and she has not been caught in the act), ¹⁴and if feelings of jealousy come over her husband and he suspects his wife and she is impure—or if he is jealous and suspects her even though she is not impure— ¹⁵then he is to take his wife to the priest. He must also take an offering of a tenth of an ephah^i of barley flour on her behalf. He must not pour oil on it or put incense on it, because it is a grain offering for jealousy, a reminder offering to draw attention to guilt.

¹⁶" 'The priest shall bring her and have her stand before the LORD. ¹⁷Then he shall take some holy water in a clay jar and put some dust from the tabernacle floor into the water. ¹⁸After the priest has had the woman stand before the LORD, he shall loosen her hair and place in her hands the reminder offering, the grain offering for jealousy, while he himself holds the bitter water that

---

g2 Traditionally *leprosy*; the Hebrew word was used for various diseases affecting the skin—not necessarily leprosy.   *h6* Or *woman commits any wrong common to mankind*   *i15* That is, probably about 2 quarts (about 2 liters) brings a curse. ¹⁹Then the priest shall put the woman under oath and say to her, "If no other man has slept with you and you have not gone astray and become impure while married to your husband, may this bitter water that brings a curse not harm you. ²⁰But if you have gone astray while married to your husband and you have defiled yourself by sleeping with a man other than your husband"— ²¹here the priest is to put the woman under this curse of the oath—"may the LORD cause your people to curse and denounce you when he causes your thigh to waste away and your abdomen to swell.ʲ ²²May this water that brings a curse enter your body so that your abdomen swells and your thigh wastes away.ᵏ"

" 'Then the woman is to say, "Amen. So be it."

²³" 'The priest is to write these curses on a scroll and then wash them off into the bitter water. ²⁴He shall have the woman drink the bitter water that brings a curse, and this water will enter her and cause bitter suffering. ²⁵The priest is to take from her hands the grain offering for jealousy, wave it before the LORD and bring it to the altar. ²⁶The priest is then to take a handful of the grain offering as a memorial offering and burn it on the altar; after that, he is to have the woman drink the water. ²⁷If she has defiled herself and been unfaithful to her husband, then when she is made to drink the water that brings a curse, it will go into her and cause bitter suffering; her abdomen will swell and her thigh waste away,ˡ and she will become accursed among her people. ²⁸If, however, the woman has not defiled herself and is free from impurity, she will be cleared of guilt and will be able to have children.

²⁹" 'This, then, is the law of jealousy when a woman goes astray and defiles herself while married to her husband, ³⁰or when feelings of jealousy come over a man because he suspects his wife. The priest is to have her stand before the LORD and is to apply this entire law to her. ³¹The husband will be innocent of any wrongdoing, but the woman will bear the consequences of her sin.' "

6 The LORD said to Moses, ²"Speak to the Israelites and say to them: 'If a man or woman wants to make a special vow, a vow of separation to the LORD as a Nazirite, ³he must abstain from wine and other fermented drink and must not drink vinegar made from wine or from other fermented drink. He must not drink grape juice or eat grapes or raisins. ⁴As long as he is a Nazirite, he must not eat anything that comes from the grapevine, not even the seeds or skins.

⁵" 'During the entire period of his vow of separation no razor may be used on his head. He must be holy until the period of his separation to the LORD is over; he must let the hair of his head grow long. ⁶Throughout the period of his separation to the LORD he must not go near a dead body. ⁷Even if his own father or mother or brother or sister dies, he must not make himself ceremonially unclean on account of them, because the symbol of his separation to God is on his head. ⁸Throughout the period of his separation he is consecrated to the LORD.

⁹" 'If someone dies suddenly in his presence, thus defiling the hair he has dedicated, he must shave his head on the day of his cleansing—the seventh day. ¹⁰Then on the eighth day he must bring two doves or two young pigeons to the priest at the entrance to the Tent of Meeting. ¹¹The priest is to offer one as a sin offering and the other as a burnt offering to make atonement for him because he sinned by being in the presence of the dead body. That same day he is to consecrate his head. ¹²He must dedicate himself to the LORD for the period of his separation and must bring a year-old male lamb as a guilt offering. The previous days do not count, because he became defiled during his separation.

¹³" 'Now this is the law for the Nazirite when the period of his separation is over. He is to be brought to the entrance to the Tent of Meeting. ¹⁴There he is to present his offerings to the LORD: a year-old male lamb without defect for a burnt offering, a year-old ewe lamb without defect for a sin offering, a ram without defect for a fellowship offering,ᵐ ¹⁵together with their grain offerings and drink offerings, and a basket of bread made without yeast—cakes made of fine flour mixed with oil, and wafers spread with oil.

¹⁶" 'The priest is to present them before the LORD and make the sin offering and the burnt offering. ¹⁷He is to present the basket of unleavened bread and is to sacrifice the ram as a fellowship offering to the LORD, together with its grain offering and drink offering.

¹⁸" 'Then at the entrance to the Tent of Meeting, the Nazirite must shave off the hair that he

---

ʲ21 Or causes you to have a miscarrying womb and barrenness
ᵏ22 Or body and cause you to be barren and have a miscarrying womb
ˡ27 Or suffering; she will have barrenness and a miscarrying womb
ᵐ14 Traditionally peace offering; also in verses 17 and 18

dedicated. He is to take the hair and put it in the fire that is under the sacrifice of the fellowship offering.

19" 'After the Nazirite has shaved off the hair of his dedication, the priest is to place in his hands a boiled shoulder of the ram, and a cake and a wafer from the basket, both made without yeast. 20The priest shall then wave them before the LORD as a wave offering; they are holy and belong to the priest, together with the breast that was waved and the thigh that was presented. After that, the Nazirite may drink wine.

21" 'This is the law of the Nazirite who vows his offering to the LORD in accordance with his separation, in addition to whatever else he can afford. He must fulfill the vow he has made, according to the law of the Nazirite.' "

22The LORD said to Moses, 23"Tell Aaron and his sons, 'This is how you are to bless the Israelites. Say to them:

24" ' "The LORD bless you
        and keep you;
25the LORD make his face shine upon you
        and be gracious to you;
26the LORD turn his face toward you
        and give you peace." '

27"So they will put my name on the Israelites, and I will bless them."

7 When Moses finished setting up the tabernacle, he anointed it and consecrated it and all its furnishings. He also anointed and consecrated the altar and all its utensils. 2Then the leaders of Israel, the heads of families who were the tribal leaders in charge of those who were counted, made offerings. 3They brought as their gifts before the LORD six covered carts and twelve oxen—an ox from each leader and a cart from every two. These they presented before the tabernacle.

4The LORD said to Moses, 5"Accept these from them, that they may be used in the work at the Tent of Meeting. Give them to the Levites as each man's work requires."

6So Moses took the carts and oxen and gave them to the Levites. 7He gave two carts and four oxen to the Gershonites, as their work required, 8and he gave four carts and eight oxen to the Merarites, as their work required. They were all under the direction of Ithamar son of Aaron, the priest. 9But Moses did not give any to the Kohathites, because they were to carry on their shoulders

the holy things, for which they were responsible.

10When the altar was anointed, the leaders brought their offerings for its dedication and presented them before the altar. 11For the LORD had said to Moses, "Each day one leader is to bring his offering for the dedication of the altar."

12The one who brought his offering on the first day was Nahshon son of Amminadab of the tribe of Judah.

13His offering was one silver plate weighing a hundred and thirty shekels,[n] and one silver sprinkling bowl weighing seventy shekels,[o] both according to the sanctuary shekel, each filled with fine flour mixed with oil as a grain offering; 14one gold dish weighing ten shekels,[p] filled with incense; 15one young bull, one ram and one male lamb a year old, for a burnt offering; 16one male goat for a sin offering; 17and two oxen, five rams, five male goats and five male lambs a year old, to be sacrificed as a fellowship offering.[q] This was the offering of Nahshon son of Amminadab.

18On the second day Nethanel son of Zuar, the leader of Issachar, brought his offering.

19The offering he brought was one silver plate weighing a hundred and thirty shekels, and one silver sprinkling bowl weighing seventy shekels, both according to the sanctuary shekel, each filled with fine flour mixed with oil as a grain offering; 20one gold dish weighing ten shekels, filled with incense; 21one young bull, one ram and one male lamb a year old, for a burnt offering; 22one male goat for a sin offering; 23and two oxen, five rams, five male goats and five male lambs a year old, to be sacrificed as a fellowship offering. This was the offering of Nethanel son of Zuar.

24On the third day, Eliab son of Helon, the leader of the people of Zebulun, brought his offering.

25His offering was one silver plate weighing a hundred and thirty shekels, and one silver sprinkling bowl weighing seventy shekels, both according to the sanctuary shekel, each filled with fine flour mixed with oil as a grain offering; 26one gold dish weighing ten

---

n13 That is, about 3 1/4 pounds (about 1.5 kilograms); also elsewhere in this chapter   o13 That is, about 1 3/4 pounds (about 0.8 kilogram); also elsewhere in this chapter   p14 That is, about 4 ounces (about 110 grams); also elsewhere in this chapter   q17 Traditionally peace offering; also elsewhere in this chapter shekels, filled with incense; ²⁷one young bull, one ram and one male lamb a year old, for a burnt offering; ²⁸one male goat for a sin offering; ²⁹and two oxen, five rams, five male goats and five male lambs a year old, to be sacrificed as a fellowship offering. This was the offering of Eliab son of Helon.

³⁰On the fourth day Elizur son of Shedeur, the leader of the people of Reuben, brought his offering.

³¹His offering was one silver plate weighing a hundred and thirty shekels, and one silver sprinkling bowl weighing seventy shekels, both according to the sanctuary shekel, each filled with fine flour mixed with oil as a grain offering; ³²one gold dish weighing ten shekels, filled with incense; ³³one young bull, one ram and one male lamb a year old, for a burnt offering; ³⁴one male goat for a sin offering; ³⁵and two oxen, five rams, five male goats and five male lambs a year old, to be sacrificed as a fellowship offering. This was the offering of Elizur son of Shedeur.

³⁶On the fifth day Shelumiel son of Zurishaddai, the leader of the people of Simeon, brought his offering.

³⁷His offering was one silver plate weighing a hundred and thirty shekels, and one silver sprinkling bowl weighing seventy shekels, both according to the sanctuary shekel, each filled with fine flour mixed with oil as a grain offering; ³⁸one gold dish weighing ten shekels, filled with incense; ³⁹one young bull, one ram and one male lamb a year old, for a burnt offering; ⁴⁰one male goat for a sin offering; ⁴¹and two oxen, five rams, five male goats and five male lambs a year old, to be sacrificed as a fellowship offering. This was the offering of Shelumiel son of Zurishaddai.

⁴²On the sixth day Eliasaph son of Deuel, the leader of the people of Gad, brought his offering. ⁴³His offering was one silver plate weighing a hundred and thirty shekels, and one silver sprinkling bowl weighing seventy shekels, both according to the sanctuary shekel, each filled with fine flour mixed with oil as a grain offering; ⁴⁴one gold dish weighing ten shekels, filled with incense; ⁴⁵one young bull, one ram and one male lamb a year old, for a burnt offering; ⁴⁶one male goat for a sin

offering; ⁴⁷and two oxen, five rams, five male goats and five male lambs a year old, to be sacrificed as a fellowship offering. This was the offering of Eliasaph son of Deuel.

⁴⁸On the seventh day Elishama son of Ammihud, the leader of the people of Ephraim, brought his offering.

⁴⁹His offering was one silver plate weighing a hundred and thirty shekels, and one silver sprinkling bowl weighing seventy shekels, both according to the sanctuary shekel, each filled with fine flour mixed with oil as a grain offering; ⁵⁰one gold dish weighing ten shekels, filled with incense; ⁵¹one young bull, one ram and one male lamb a year old, for a burnt offering; ⁵²one male goat for a sin offering; ⁵³and two oxen, five rams, five male goats and five male lambs a year old, to be sacrificed as a fellowship offering. This was the offering of Elishama son of Ammihud.

⁵⁴On the eighth day Gamaliel son of Pedahzur, the leader of the people of Manasseh, brought his offering.

⁵⁵His offering was one silver plate weighing a hundred and thirty shekels, and one silver sprinkling bowl weighing seventy shekels, both according to the sanctuary shekel, each filled with fine flour mixed with oil as a grain offering; ⁵⁶one gold dish weighing ten shekels, filled with incense; ⁵⁷one young bull, one ram and one male lamb a year old, for a burnt offering; ⁵⁸one male goat for a sin offering; ⁵⁹and two oxen, five rams, five male goats and five male lambs a year old, to be sacrificed as a fellowship offering. This was the offering of Gamaliel son of Pedahzur.

⁶⁰On the ninth day Abidan son of Gideoni, the leader of the people of Benjamin, brought his offering.

⁶¹His offering was one silver plate weighing a hundred and thirty shekels, and one silver sprinkling bowl weighing seventy shekels, both according to the sanctuary shekel, each filled with fine flour mixed with oil as a grain offering; ⁶²one gold dish weighing ten shekels, filled with incense; ⁶³one young bull, one ram and one male lamb a year old, for a burnt offering; ⁶⁴one male goat for a sin offering; ⁶⁵and two oxen, five rams, five male goats and five male lambs a year old, to be

sacrificed as a fellowship offering. This was the offering of Abidan son of Gideoni.

66On the tenth day Ahiezer son of Ammishaddai, the leader of the people of Dan, brought his offering.

67His offering was one silver plate weighing a hundred and thirty shekels, and one silver sprinkling bowl weighing seventy shekels, both according to the sanctuary shekel, each filled with fine flour mixed with oil as a grain offering; 68one gold dish weighing ten shekels, filled with incense; 69one young bull, one ram and one male lamb a year old, for a burnt offering; 70one male goat for a sin offering; 71and two oxen, five rams, five male goats and five male lambs a year old, to be sacrificed as a fellowship offering. This was the offering of Ahiezer son of Ammishaddai.

72On the eleventh day Pagiel son of Ocran, the leader of the people of Asher, brought his offering.

73His offering was one silver plate weighing a hundred and thirty shekels, and one silver sprinkling bowl weighing seventy shekels, both according to the sanctuary shekel, each filled with fine flour mixed with oil as a grain offering; 74one gold dish weighing ten shekels, filled with incense; 75one young bull, one ram and one male lamb a year old, for a burnt offering; 76one male goat for a sin offering; 77and two oxen, five rams, five male goats and five male lambs a year old, to be sacrificed as a fellowship offering. This was the offering of Pagiel son of Ocran.

78On the twelfth day Ahira son of Enan, the leader of the people of Naphtali, brought his offering.

79His offering was one silver plate weighing a hundred and thirty shekels, and one silver sprinkling bowl weighing seventy shekels, both according to the sanctuary shekel, each filled with fine flour mixed with oil as a grain offering; 80one gold dish weighing ten shekels, filled with incense; 81one young bull, one ram and one male lamb a year old, for a burnt offering; 82one male goat for a sin offering; 83and two oxen, five rams, five male goats and five male lambs a year old, to be sacrificed as a fellowship offering. This was the offering of Ahira son of Enan.

84These were the offerings of the Israelite leaders for the dedication of the altar when it was anointed: twelve silver plates, twelve silver sprinkling bowls and twelve gold dishes. 85Each silver plate weighed a hundred and thirty shekels, and each sprinkling bowl seventy shekels. Altogether, the silver dishes weighed two thousand four hundred shekels,r according to the sanctuary shekel. 86The twelve gold dishes filled with incense weighed ten shekels each, according to the sanctuary shekel. Altogether, the gold dishes weighed a hundred and twenty shekels.s 87The total number of animals for the burnt offering came to twelve young bulls, twelve rams and twelve male lambs a year old, together with their grain offering. Twelve male goats were used for the sin offering. 88The total number of animals for the sacrifice of the fellowship offering came to twenty-four oxen, sixty rams, sixty male goats and sixty male lambs a year old. These were the offerings for the dedication of the altar after it was anointed.

89When Moses entered the Tent of Meeting to speak with the Lord, he heard the voice speaking to him from between the two cherubim above the atonement cover on the ark of the Testimony. And he spoke with him.

8 The Lord said to Moses, 2"Speak to Aaron and say to him, 'When you set up the seven lamps, they are to light the area in front of the lampstand.' "

3Aaron did so; he set up the lamps so that they faced forward on the lampstand, just as the Lord commanded Moses. 4This is how the lampstand was made: It was made of hammered gold—from its base to its blossoms. The lampstand was made exactly like the pattern the Lord had shown Moses.

5The Lord said to Moses: 6"Take the Levites from among the other Israelites and make them ceremonially clean. 7To purify them, do this: Sprinkle the water of cleansing on them; then have them shave their whole bodies and wash their clothes, and so purify themselves. 8Have them take a young bull with its grain offering of fine flour mixed with oil; then you are to take a second young bull for a sin offering. 9Bring the Levites to the front of the Tent of Meeting and assemble the whole Israelite community. 10You are to bring the Levites before the Lord, and the

r85 That is, about 60 pounds (about 28 kilograms)   s86 That is, about 3 pounds (about 1.4 kilograms)

Israelites are to lay their hands on them. [11]Aaron is to present the Levites before the Lord as a wave offering from the Israelites, so that they may be ready to do the work of the Lord.

[12]"After the Levites lay their hands on the heads of the bulls, use the one for a sin offering to the Lord and the other for a burnt offering, to make atonement for the Levites. [13]Have the Levites stand in front of Aaron and his sons and then present them as a wave offering to the Lord. [14]In this way you are to set the Levites apart from the other Israelites, and the Levites will be mine.

[15]"After you have purified the Levites and presented them as a wave offering, they are to come to do their work at the Tent of Meeting. [16]They are the Israelites who are to be given wholly to me. I have taken them as my own in place of the firstborn, the first male offspring from every Israelite woman. [17]Every firstborn male in Israel, whether man or animal, is mine. When I struck down all the firstborn in Egypt, I set them apart for myself. [18]And I have taken the Levites in place of all the firstborn sons in Israel. [19]Of all the Isra-

elites, I have given the Levites as gifts to Aaron and his sons to do the work at the Tent of Meeting on behalf of the Israelites and to make atonement for them so that no plague will strike the Israelites when they go near the sanctuary."

[20]Moses, Aaron and the whole Israelite community did with the Levites just as the Lord commanded Moses. [21]The Levites purified themselves and washed their clothes. Then Aaron presented them as a wave offering before the Lord and made atonement for them to purify them. [22]After that, the Levites came to do their work at the Tent of Meeting under the supervision of Aaron and his sons. They did with the Levites just as the Lord commanded Moses.

[23]The Lord said to Moses, [24]"This applies to the Levites: Men twenty-five years old or more shall come to take part in the work at the Tent of Meeting, [25]but at the age of fifty, they must retire from their regular service and work no longer. [26]They may assist their brothers in performing their duties at the Tent of Meeting, but they themselves must not do the work. This, then, is how you are to assign the responsibilities of the Levites."

2 / *Numbers 9*
Looking Back; Looking Ahead

WHAT TRADITIONS DO you look forward to each year? Caroling at Christmas? Decorating Easter eggs? A family cookout in July? The Bible deals frequently with the importance of tradition and commemoration of important events. In Numbers 9 we learn the power of remembering the past as we face the future.

 Warming Up to God Think of a tradition that is meaningful for you. How does it nurture you? Thank God for the joy you gain through traditions.

 Read Numbers 9.

9 The Lord spoke to Moses in the Desert of Sinai in the first month of the second year after they came out of Egypt. He said, [2]"Have the Israelites celebrate the Passover at the appointed time. [3]Celebrate it at the appointed time, at twilight on the fourteenth day of this month, in accordance with all its rules and regulations."

[4]So Moses told the Israelites to celebrate the Passover, [5]and they did so in the Desert of Sinai at twilight on the fourteenth day of the first month.

The Israelites did everything just as the Lord commanded Moses.

[6]But some of them could not celebrate the Passover on that day because they were ceremonially unclean on account of a dead body. So they came to Moses and Aaron that same day [7]and said to Moses, "We have become unclean because of a dead body, but why should we be kept from presenting the Lord's offering with the other Israelites at the appointed time?"

⁸Moses answered them, "Wait until I find out what the LORD commands concerning you."

⁹Then the LORD said to Moses, ¹⁰"Tell the Israelites: 'When any of you or your descendants are unclean because of a dead body or are away on a journey, they may still celebrate the LORD's Passover. ¹¹They are to celebrate it on the fourteenth day of the second month at twilight. They are to eat the lamb, together with unleavened bread and bitter herbs. ¹²They must not leave any of it till morning or break any of its bones. When they celebrate the Passover, they must follow all the regulations. ¹³But if a man who is ceremonially clean and not on a journey fails to celebrate the Passover, that person must be cut off from his people because he did not present the LORD's offering at the appointed time. That man will bear the consequences of his sin.

¹⁴" 'An alien living among you who wants to celebrate the LORD's Passover must do so in accordance with its rules and regulations. You must have the same regulations for the alien and the native-born.' "

¹⁵On the day the tabernacle, the Tent of the Testimony, was set up, the cloud covered it. From evening till morning the cloud above the taberna-cle looked like fire. ¹⁶That is how it continued to be; the cloud covered it, and at night it looked like fire. ¹⁷Whenever the cloud lifted from above the Tent, the Israelites set out; wherever the cloud settled, the Israelites encamped. ¹⁸At the LORD's command the Israelites set out, and at his command they encamped. As long as the cloud stayed over the tabernacle, they remained in camp. ¹⁹When the cloud remained over the tabernacle a long time, the Israelites obeyed the LORD's order and did not set out. ²⁰Sometimes the cloud was over the tabernacle only a few days; at the LORD's command they would encamp, and then at his command they would set out. ²¹Sometimes the cloud stayed only from evening till morning, and when it lifted in the morning, they set out. Whether by day or by night, whenever the cloud lifted, they set out. ²²Whether the cloud stayed over the tabernacle for two days or a month or a year, the Israelites would remain in camp and not set out; but when it lifted, they would set out. ²³At the LORD's command they encamped, and at the LORD's command they set out. They obeyed the LORD's order, in accordance with his command through Moses.

 Discovering the Word 1. God establishes celebration of the Passover at the beginning of chapter 9 (Exodus 12 provides the background). Why might he want the Israelites to commemorate this recent spiritual event? 2. Verses 6–13 involve purity during the Passover celebration. What is the relationship between purity and worship? 3. Soon after, God begins to lead the Israelites using a cloud (vv. 15–23). How will it help the Israelites to keep a sense of the past as they move into the future? 4. What do the "cloud patterns" (that is, the cloud's day-to-day status) reveal about the process of following God's guidance?

 Applying the Word 1. How can you commemorate the important events in your personal spiritual pilgrimage? 2. In what direction is God leading you in current life decisions?

Responding in Prayer Praise God for the strength he gives us through memories, and ask him to help you be patient in the guidance he provides from day to day.

Numbers 10

10 The LORD said to Moses: ²"Make two trumpets of hammered silver, and use them for calling the community together and for having the camps set out. ³When both are sounded, the whole community is to assemble before you at the entrance to the Tent of Meeting. ⁴If only one is sounded, the leaders—the heads of the clans of Israel—are to assemble before you. ⁵When a trumpet blast is sounded, the tribes camping on the east are to set out. ⁶At the sounding of a second blast, the camps on the south are to set out. The blast will be the signal for setting out. ⁷To gather the assembly, blow the trumpets, but not with the same signal.

⁸"The sons of Aaron, the priests, are to blow the trumpets. This is to be a lasting ordinance for you and the generations to come. ⁹When you go into battle in your own land against an enemy

who is oppressing you, sound a blast on the trumpets. Then you will be remembered by the Lord your God and rescued from your enemies. ¹⁰Also at your times of rejoicing—your appointed feasts and New Moon festivals—you are to sound the trumpets over your burnt offerings and fellowship offerings,ᶦ and they will be a memorial for you before your God. I am the Lord your God."

¹¹On the twentieth day of the second month of the second year, the cloud lifted from above the tabernacle of the Testimony. ¹²Then the Israelites set out from the Desert of Sinai and traveled from place to place until the cloud came to rest in the Desert of Paran. ¹³They set out, this first time, at the Lord's command through Moses.

¹⁴The divisions of the camp of Judah went first, under their standard. Nahshon son of Amminadab was in command. ¹⁵Nethanel son of Zuar was over the division of the tribe of Issachar, ¹⁶and Eliab son of Helon was over the division of the tribe of Zebulun. ¹⁷Then the tabernacle was taken down, and the Gershonites and Merarites, who carried it, set out.

¹⁸The divisions of the camp of Reuben went next, under their standard. Elizur son of Shedeur was in command. ¹⁹Shelumiel son of Zurishaddai was over the division of the tribe of Simeon, ²⁰and Eliasaph son of Deuel was over the division of the tribe of Gad. ²¹Then the Kohathites set out, carrying the holy things. The tabernacle was to be set up before they arrived.

²²The divisions of the camp of Ephraim went next, under their standard. Elishama son of Ammihud was in command. ²³Gamaliel son of Pedahzur was over the division of the tribe of Manasseh, ²⁴and Abidan son of Gideoni was over the division of the tribe of Benjamin.

²⁵Finally, as the rear guard for all the units, the divisions of the camp of Dan set out, under their standard. Ahiezer son of Ammishaddai was in command. ²⁶Pagiel son of Ocran was over the division of the tribe of Asher, ²⁷and Ahira son of Enan was over the division of the tribe of Naphtali. ²⁸This was the order of march for the Israelite divisions as they set out.

²⁹Now Moses said to Hobab son of Reuel the Midianite, Moses' father-in-law, "We are setting out for the place about which the Lord said, 'I will give it to you.' Come with us and we will treat you well, for the Lord has promised good things to Israel."

³⁰He answered, "No, I will not go; I am going back to my own land and my own people."

³¹But Moses said, "Please do not leave us. You know where we should camp in the desert, and you can be our eyes. ³²If you come with us, we will share with you whatever good things the Lord gives us."

³³So they set out from the mountain of the Lord and traveled for three days. The ark of the covenant of the Lord went before them during those three days to find them a place to rest. ³⁴The cloud of the Lord was over them by day when they set out from the camp.

³⁵Whenever the ark set out, Moses said,

"Rise up, O Lord!
　May your enemies be scattered;
　may your foes flee before you."

³⁶Whenever it came to rest, he said,

"Return, O Lord,
　to the countless thousands of Israel."

ᶦ10 Traditionally *peace offerings*

---

3 / *Numbers 11*
No Thanks

"WHAT HAVE YOU done for me lately?" It's just human nature. We quickly take for granted what we have, and wish we had more. In this chapter, God's people begin to grumble, forgetting the many blessings and miracles they've experienced on the journey.

Warming Up to God Some things we take completely for granted; it takes losing them to fully appreciate them. When have you had this experience? Thank God for three good things in your life you would normally ignore.

Read Numbers 11.

11 Now the people complained about their hardships in the hearing of the LORD, and when he heard them his anger was aroused. Then fire from the LORD burned among them and consumed some of the outskirts of the camp. ²When the people cried out to Moses, he prayed to the LORD and the fire died down. ³So that place was called Taberah,ᵘ because fire from the LORD had burned among them.

⁴The rabble with them began to crave other food, and again the Israelites started wailing and said, "If only we had meat to eat! ⁵We remember the fish we ate in Egypt at no cost—also the cucumbers, melons, leeks, onions and garlic. ⁶But now we have lost our appetite; we never see anything but this manna!"

⁷The manna was like coriander seed and looked like resin. ⁸The people went around gathering it, and then ground it in a handmill or crushed it in a mortar. They cooked it in a pot or made it into cakes. And it tasted like something made with olive oil. ⁹When the dew settled on the camp at night, the manna also came down.

¹⁰Moses heard the people of every family wailing, each at the entrance to his tent. The LORD became exceedingly angry, and Moses was troubled. ¹¹He asked the LORD, "Why have you brought this trouble on your servant? What have I done to displease you that you put the burden of all these people on me? ¹²Did I conceive all these people? Did I give them birth? Why do you tell me to carry them in my arms, as a nurse carries an infant, to the land you promised on oath to their forefathers? ¹³Where can I get meat for all these people? They keep wailing to me, 'Give us meat to eat!' ¹⁴I cannot carry all these people by myself; the burden is too heavy for me. ¹⁵If this is how you are going to treat me, put me to death right now—if I have found favor in your eyes—and do not let me face my own ruin."

¹⁶The LORD said to Moses: "Bring me seventy of Israel's elders who are known to you as leaders and officials among the people. Have them come to the Tent of Meeting, that they may stand there with you. ¹⁷I will come down and speak with you there, and I will take of the Spirit that is on you and put the Spirit on them. They will help you carry the burden of the people so that you will not have to carry it alone.

¹⁸"Tell the people: 'Consecrate yourselves in preparation for tomorrow, when you will eat meat. The LORD heard you when you wailed, "If only we had meat to eat! We were better off in Egypt!" Now the LORD will give you meat, and you will eat it. ¹⁹You will not eat it for just one day, or two days, or five, ten or twenty days, ²⁰but for a whole month—until it comes out of your nostrils and you loathe it—because you have rejected the LORD, who is among you, and have wailed before him, saying, "Why did we ever leave Egypt?" ' "

²¹But Moses said, "Here I am among six hundred thousand men on foot, and you say, 'I will give them meat to eat for a whole month!' ²²Would they have enough if flocks and herds were slaughtered for them? Would they have enough if all the fish in the sea were caught for them?"

²³The LORD answered Moses, "Is the LORD's arm too short? You will now see whether or not what I say will come true for you."

²⁴So Moses went out and told the people what the LORD had said. He brought together seventy of their elders and had them stand around the Tent. ²⁵Then the LORD came down in the cloud and spoke with him, and he took of the Spirit that was on him and put the Spirit on the seventy elders. When the Spirit rested on them, they prophesied, but they did not do so again.ᵛ

²⁶However, two men, whose names were Eldad and Medad, had remained in the camp. They were listed among the elders, but did not go out to the Tent. Yet the Spirit also rested on them, and they prophesied in the camp. ²⁷A young man ran and told Moses, "Eldad and Medad are prophesying in the camp."

²⁸Joshua son of Nun, who had been Moses' aide since youth, spoke up and said, "Moses, my lord, stop them!"

²⁹But Moses replied, "Are you jealous for my sake? I wish that all the LORD's people were prophets and that the LORD would put his Spirit on them!" ³⁰Then Moses and the elders of Israel returned to the camp.

³¹Now a wind went out from the LORD and drove quail in from the sea. It brought themʷ

ᵘ3 *Taberah* means *burning.*   ᵛ25 Or *prophesied and continued to do so*   ʷ31 Or *They flew*

down all around the camp to about three feet×
above the ground, as far as a day's walk in any
direction. ³²All that day and night and all the next
day the people went out and gathered quail. No
one gathered less than ten homers.ʸ Then they
spread them out all around the camp. ³³But while
the meat was still between their teeth and before
it could be consumed, the anger of the Lᴏʀᴅ
burned against the people, and he struck them

with a severe plague. ³⁴Therefore the place was
named Kibroth Hattaavah,ᶻ because there they
buried the people who had craved other food.

³⁵From Kibroth Hattaavah the people traveled
to Hazeroth and stayed there.

×31 Hebrew *two cubits* (about 1 meter)   ʸ32 That is, probably about
60 bushels (about 2.2 kiloliters)   ᶻ34 *Kibroth Hattaavah* means
graves of craving.

Discovering the Word   1. What do you learn about the Israelites from these verses?   2. Considering God's method for feeding the people, why do you think he is particularly angered by their response (vv. 4–10)?   3. Moses himself complains to God (vv. 11–15). Why do you think God takes his complaint seriously? 4. If Moses were a discontented person, how might he have reacted differently to the events in verses 24–28? 5. What lesson does God teach the people through granting their request (vv. 18–20, 31–35)?

Applying the Word   1. How should God's statement in verse 23 influence your tendency to complain? 2. With what area of your life do you most often feel dissatisfaction?   3. What can you do to keep God's blessings before you in such a way that you will be more grateful?

Responding in Prayer   Spend time in prayer exclusively thanking God for all he has provided—even those things that are hard to appreciate. Then, follow Moses' example in presenting your frustrations honestly as you seek his guidance.

---

4 / *Numbers 12*
A Critical Spirit

WHO HASN'T BEEN critical of someone else and said, either aloud or inwardly, "Who does he think he is?" Often we don't understand the details of someone's actions or have all the facts. Our anxiety comes out of our mouths, and we not only hurt ourselves but sometimes damage the loyalty and well-being of others. This passage warns us about the dangers of criticism. When the children of Israel left Egypt, they had little sense of national identity and were not used to following a leader. Imagine what could have happened to Moses' confidence and to the people when the members of Moses' own family began to criticize his leadership.

 Warming Up to God   What have you been thinking critical thoughts about lately?

 Read Numbers 12.

---

12 Miriam and Aaron began to talk against Moses because of his Cushite wife, for he had married a Cushite. ²"Has the Lᴏʀᴅ spoken only through Moses?" they asked. "Hasn't he also spoken through us?" And the Lᴏʀᴅ heard this.

³(Now Moses was a very humble man, more humble than anyone else on the face of the earth.)

⁴At once the Lᴏʀᴅ said to Moses, Aaron and Miriam, "Come out to the Tent of Meeting, all

three of you." So the three of them came out. ⁵Then the Lᴏʀᴅ came down in a pillar of cloud; he stood at the entrance to the Tent and summoned Aaron and Miriam. When both of them stepped forward, ⁶he said, "Listen to my words:

"When a prophet of the Lᴏʀᴅ is among you,
    I reveal myself to him in visions,
    I speak to him in dreams.
⁷But this is not true of my servant Moses;
    he is faithful in all my house.
⁸With him I speak face to face,

clearly and not in riddles;
he sees the form of the LORD.
Why then were you not afraid
to speak against my servant Moses?"

⁹The anger of the LORD burned against them, and he left them.

¹⁰When the cloud lifted from above the Tent, there stood Miriam—leprous,ᵃ like snow. Aaron turned toward her and saw that she had leprosy; ¹¹and he said to Moses, "Please, my lord, do not hold against us the sin we have so foolishly committed. ¹²Do not let her be like a stillborn infant coming from its mother's womb with its flesh half eaten away."

¹³So Moses cried out to the LORD, "O God, please heal her!"

¹⁴The LORD replied to Moses, "If her father had spit in her face, would she not have been in disgrace for seven days? Confine her outside the camp for seven days; after that she can be brought back." ¹⁵So Miriam was confined outside the camp for seven days, and the people did not move on till she was brought back.

¹⁶After that, the people left Hazeroth and encamped in the Desert of Paran.

ᵃ10 The Hebrew word was used for various diseases affecting the skin—not necessarily leprosy.

Discovering the Word   1. Of what two things are Miriam and Aaron critical?   2. How does their view differ from God's evaluation of Moses?   3. Miriam and Aaron's attack on their brother may have been provoked by his appointing seventy elders over Israel (11:16–17). How might the appointment of elders affect Miriam's status and feelings?   4. How does the Lord respond to the criticisms of Miriam and Aaron (vv. 4–10)?   5. What do we learn about Aaron and Moses from their response to this traumatic event (vv. 10–13)?   6. Why do you think God carried out a seven-day punishment for Miriam (vv. 14–15)? Why didn't he punish Aaron in the same way?

Applying the Word   1. How do you react when you feel your status or position is threatened?   2. Why is the criticism of spiritual leaders especially dangerous?

Responding in Prayer   Sometimes God does give us important insights into situations. Pray that God will give you the knowledge to use this insight with a godly spirit, not a critical spirit.

---

5 / *Numbers 13:1—14:12*
Taking Risks

THOSE WHO CHALLENGE society's standards risk disapproval or even ostracism. We are constantly warned about the folly of taking risks. From life insurance to safe long-term investments, we are encouraged to save and conserve our resources. While this might be prudent financial advice, it can have a dangerous effect in the lives of Christians. We tend to adapt all too easily to a safe and comfortable lifestyle. In our walk with Christ we often follow the path of least resistance, avoiding challenges which intimidate us. Today's passage reminds us that an essential element of faithfulness to Christ is the willingness to risk. On the threshold of the Promised Land the children of Israel are faced with a critical choice. They can opt for the path of least resistance or dare to trust their God.

Warming Up to God   What aspect of following Christ frightens or challenges you the most? God knows your fears and wants to comfort you.

Read Numbers 13:1—14:12.

13 The LORD said to Moses, ²"Send some men to explore the land of Canaan, which I am giving to the Israelites. From each ancestral tribe send one of its leaders."

³So at the LORD's command Moses sent them out from the Desert of Paran. All of them were leaders of the Israelites. ⁴These are their names:

from the tribe of Reuben, Shammua son of Zaccur;

⁵from the tribe of Simeon, Shaphat son of Hori;

⁶from the tribe of Judah, Caleb son of Jephunneh;

⁷from the tribe of Issachar, Igal son of Joseph;

⁸from the tribe of Ephraim, Hoshea son of Nun;

⁹from the tribe of Benjamin, Palti son of Raphu;

¹⁰from the tribe of Zebulun, Gaddiel son of Sodi;

¹¹from the tribe of Manasseh (a tribe of Joseph), Gaddi son of Susi;

¹²from the tribe of Dan, Ammiel son of Gemalli;

¹³from the tribe of Asher, Sethur son of Michael;

¹⁴from the tribe of Naphtali, Nahbi son of Vophsi;

¹⁵from the tribe of Gad, Geuel son of Maki.

¹⁶These are the names of the men Moses sent to explore the land. (Moses gave Hoshea son of Nun the name Joshua.)

¹⁷When Moses sent them to explore Canaan, he said, "Go up through the Negev and on into the hill country. ¹⁸See what the land is like and whether the people who live there are strong or weak, few or many. ¹⁹What kind of land do they live in? Is it good or bad? What kind of towns do they live in? Are they unwalled or fortified? ²⁰How is the soil? Is it fertile or poor? Are there trees on it or not? Do your best to bring back some of the fruit of the land." (It was the season for the first ripe grapes.)

²¹So they went up and explored the land from the Desert of Zin as far as Rehob, toward Lebo*b* Hamath. ²²They went up through the Negev and came to Hebron, where Ahiman, Sheshai and Talmai, the descendants of Anak, lived. (Hebron had been built seven years before Zoan in Egypt.) ²³When they reached the Valley of Eshcol,*c* they cut off a branch bearing a single cluster of grapes. Two of them carried it on a pole between them, along with some pomegranates and figs. ²⁴That place was called the Valley of Eshcol because of the cluster of grapes the Israelites cut off there. ²⁵At the end of forty days they returned from exploring the land.

²⁶They came back to Moses and Aaron and the whole Israelite community at Kadesh in the Desert of Paran. There they reported to them and to the whole assembly and showed them the fruit of the land. ²⁷They gave Moses this account: "We went into the land to which you sent us, and it does flow with milk and honey! Here is its fruit. ²⁸But the people who live there are powerful, and the cities are fortified and very large. We even saw descendants of Anak there. ²⁹The Amalekites live in the Negev; the Hittites, Jebusites and Amorites live in the hill country; and the Canaanites live near the sea and along the Jordan."

³⁰Then Caleb silenced the people before Moses and said, "We should go up and take possession of the land, for we can certainly do it."

³¹But the men who had gone up with him said, "We can't attack those people; they are stronger than we are." ³²And they spread among the Israelites a bad report about the land they had explored. They said, "The land we explored devours those living in it. All the people we saw there are of great size. ³³We saw the Nephilim there (the descendants of Anak come from the Nephilim). We seemed like grasshoppers in our own eyes, and we looked the same to them."

14 That night all the people of the community raised their voices and wept aloud. ²All the Israelites grumbled against Moses and Aaron, and the whole assembly said to them, "If only we had died in Egypt! Or in this desert! ³Why is the Lord bringing us to this land only to let us fall by the sword? Our wives and children will be taken as plunder. Wouldn't it be better for us to go back to Egypt?" ⁴And they said to each other, "We should choose a leader and go back to Egypt."

⁵Then Moses and Aaron fell facedown in front of the whole Israelite assembly gathered there. ⁶Joshua son of Nun and Caleb son of Jephunneh, who were among those who had explored the land, tore their clothes ⁷and said to the entire Israelite assembly, "The land we passed through and explored is exceedingly good. ⁸If the Lord is pleased with us, he will lead us into that land, a land flowing with milk and honey, and will give it to us. ⁹Only do not rebel against the Lord. And do not be afraid of the people of the land, because we will swallow them up. Their protection is gone, but the Lord is with us. Do not be afraid of them."

b21 Or *toward the entrance to*   *c23 Eshcol* means *cluster;* also in verse 24.

¹⁰But the whole assembly talked about stoning them. Then the glory of the Lᴏʀᴅ appeared at the Tent of Meeting to all the Israelites. ¹¹The Lᴏʀᴅ said to Moses, "How long will these people treat me with contempt? How long will they refuse to believe in me, in spite of all the miraculous signs I have performed among them? ¹²I will strike them down with a plague and destroy them, but I will make you into a nation greater and stronger than they."

Discovering the Word 1. What kind of information does Moses ask the Israelite leaders to gather (13:18–20)? 2. What negative and positive aspects of the land do the spies describe in their report to the Israelite community (13:27–29)? 3. How does Caleb's perception of the situation (13:30) contrast with that of the other spies (13:31–33)? 4. How do the Israelites respond to the conflicting assessments of the land the spies have explored (14:1–4)? 5. What do Caleb and Joshua remind the people about their identity (14:8–9)?

Applying the Word 1. In your Christian experience, have you ever reached a point when you wanted to "go back to Egypt"? Explain. 2. In verse 10 the people respond to Moses, Aaron, Joshua and Caleb by talking about stoning them. Clearly, their stance for God had put them in physical danger. What type of risks might Christians in your situation face by trusting God despite the opposition of a majority? 3. Where might God be calling you to step out in faith in a risky situation?

Responding in Prayer Ask God to make you a person who is ready to take risks for his sake.

Numbers 14:13—16:50

¹³Moses said to the Lᴏʀᴅ, "Then the Egyptians will hear about it! By your power you brought these people up from among them. ¹⁴And they will tell the inhabitants of this land about it. They have already heard that you, O Lᴏʀᴅ, are with these people and that you, O Lᴏʀᴅ, have been seen face to face, that your cloud stays over them, and that you go before them in a pillar of cloud by day and a pillar of fire by night. ¹⁵If you put these people to death all at one time, the nations who have heard this report about you will say, ¹⁶'The Lᴏʀᴅ was not able to bring these people into the land he promised them on oath; so he slaughtered them in the desert.'

¹⁷"Now may the Lord's strength be displayed, just as you have declared: ¹⁸'The Lᴏʀᴅ is slow to anger, abounding in love and forgiving sin and rebellion. Yet he does not leave the guilty unpunished; he punishes the children for the sin of the fathers to the third and fourth generation.' ¹⁹In accordance with your great love, forgive the sin of these people, just as you have pardoned them from the time they left Egypt until now."

²⁰The Lᴏʀᴅ replied, "I have forgiven them, as you asked. ²¹Nevertheless, as surely as I live and as surely as the glory of the Lᴏʀᴅ fills the whole earth, ²²not one of the men who saw my glory and the miraculous signs I performed in Egypt and in the desert but who disobeyed me and tested me ten times— ²³not one of them will ever see the land I promised on oath to their forefathers. No one who has treated me with contempt will ever see it. ²⁴But because my servant Caleb has a different spirit and follows me wholeheartedly, I will bring him into the land he went to, and his descendants will inherit it. ²⁵Since the Amalekites and Canaanites are living in the valleys, turn back tomorrow and set out toward the desert along the route to the Red Sea.ᵈ"

²⁶The Lᴏʀᴅ said to Moses and Aaron: ²⁷"How long will this wicked community grumble against me? I have heard the complaints of these grumbling Israelites. ²⁸So tell them, 'As surely as I live, declares the Lᴏʀᴅ, I will do to you the very things I heard you say: ²⁹In this desert your bodies will fall—every one of you twenty years old or more who was counted in the census and who has grumbled against me. ³⁰Not one of you will enter the land I swore with uplifted hand to make your home, except Caleb son of Jephunneh and Joshua son of Nun. ³¹As for your children that you said would be taken as plunder, I will bring them in to enjoy the land you have rejected. ³²But you—your bodies will fall in this desert. ³³Your children will be shepherds here for forty years, suffer-

ᵈ25 Hebrew *Yam Suph*; that is, Sea of Reeds

ing for your unfaithfulness, until the last of your bodies lies in the desert. ³⁴For forty years—one year for each of the forty days you explored the land—you will suffer for your sins and know what it is like to have me against you.' ³⁵I, the LORD, have spoken, and I will surely do these things to this whole wicked community, which has banded together against me. They will meet their end in this desert; here they will die."

³⁶So the men Moses had sent to explore the land, who returned and made the whole community grumble against him by spreading a bad report about it— ³⁷these men responsible for spreading the bad report about the land were struck down and died of a plague before the LORD. ³⁸Of the men who went to explore the land, only Joshua son of Nun and Caleb son of Jephunneh survived.

³⁹When Moses reported this to all the Israelites, they mourned bitterly. ⁴⁰Early the next morning they went up toward the high hill country. "We have sinned," they said. "We will go up to the place the LORD promised."

⁴¹But Moses said, "Why are you disobeying the LORD's command? This will not succeed! ⁴²Do not go up, because the LORD is not with you. You will be defeated by your enemies, ⁴³for the Amalekites and Canaanites will face you there. Because you have turned away from the LORD, he will not be with you and you will fall by the sword."

⁴⁴Nevertheless, in their presumption they went up toward the high hill country, though neither Moses nor the ark of the LORD's covenant moved from the camp. ⁴⁵Then the Amalekites and Canaanites who lived in that hill country came down and attacked them and beat them down all the way to Hormah.

15 The LORD said to Moses, ²"Speak to the Israelites and say to them: 'After you enter the land I am giving you as a home ³and you present to the LORD offerings made by fire, from the herd or the flock, as an aroma pleasing to the LORD—whether burnt offerings or sacrifices, for special vows or freewill offerings or festival offerings— ⁴then the one who brings his offering shall present to the LORD a grain offering of a tenth of an ephah^e of fine flour mixed with a quarter of a hin^f of oil. ⁵With each lamb for the burnt offering or the sacrifice, prepare a quarter of a hin of wine as a drink offering.

⁶" 'With a ram prepare a grain offering of two-tenths of an ephah^g of fine flour mixed with a third of a hin^h of oil, ⁷and a third of a hin of wine as a drink offering. Offer it as an aroma pleasing to the LORD.

⁸" 'When you prepare a young bull as a burnt offering or sacrifice, for a special vow or a fellowship offering^i to the LORD, ⁹bring with the bull a grain offering of three-tenths of an ephah^j of fine flour mixed with half a hin^k of oil. ¹⁰Also bring half a hin of wine as a drink offering. It will be an offering made by fire, an aroma pleasing to the LORD. ¹¹Each bull or ram, each lamb or young goat, is to be prepared in this manner. ¹²Do this for each one, for as many as you prepare.

¹³" 'Everyone who is native-born must do these things in this way when he brings an offering made by fire as an aroma pleasing to the LORD. ¹⁴For the generations to come, whenever an alien or anyone else living among you presents an offering made by fire as an aroma pleasing to the LORD, he must do exactly as you do. ¹⁵The community is to have the same rules for you and for the alien living among you; this is a lasting ordinance for the generations to come. You and the alien shall be the same before the LORD: ¹⁶The same laws and regulations will apply both to you and to the alien living among you.' "

¹⁷The LORD said to Moses, ¹⁸"Speak to the Israelites and say to them: 'When you enter the land to which I am taking you ¹⁹and you eat the food of the land, present a portion as an offering to the LORD. ²⁰Present a cake from the first of your ground meal and present it as an offering from the threshing floor. ²¹Throughout the generations to come you are to give this offering to the LORD from the first of your ground meal.

²²" 'Now if you unintentionally fail to keep any of these commands the LORD gave Moses— ²³any of the LORD's commands to you through him, from the day the LORD gave them and continuing through the generations to come— ²⁴and if this is done unintentionally without the community being aware of it, then the whole community is to offer a young bull for a burnt offering as an aroma pleasing to the LORD, along with its prescribed grain offering and drink offering, and a male goat for a sin offering. ²⁵The priest is to make atone-

---

^e4 That is, probably about 2 quarts (about 2 liters)   ^f4 That is, probably about 1 quart (about 1 liter); also in verse 5   ^g6 That is, probably about 4 quarts (about 4.5 liters)   ^h6 That is, probably about 1 1/4 quarts (about 1.2 liters); also in verse 7   ^i8 Traditionally *peace offering*   ^j9 That is, probably about 6 quarts (about 6.5 liters)   ^k9 That is, probably about 2 quarts (about 2 liters); also in verse 10 ment for the whole Israelite community, and they will be forgiven, for it was not intentional and they have brought to the LORD for their wrong an offering made by fire and a sin offering. ²⁶The whole Israelite community and the aliens living among them will be forgiven, because all the people were involved in the unintentional wrong.

²⁷" 'But if just one person sins unintentionally, he must bring a year-old female goat for a sin offering. ²⁸The priest is to make atonement before the LORD for the one who erred by sinning unintentionally, and when atonement has been made for him, he will be forgiven. ²⁹One and the same law applies to everyone who sins unintentionally, whether he is a native-born Israelite or an alien.

³⁰" 'But anyone who sins defiantly, whether native-born or alien, blasphemes the LORD, and that person must be cut off from his people. ³¹Because he has despised the LORD's word and broken his commands, that person must surely be cut off; his guilt remains on him.' "

³²While the Israelites were in the desert, a man was found gathering wood on the Sabbath day. ³³Those who found him gathering wood brought him to Moses and Aaron and the whole assembly, ³⁴and they kept him in custody, because it was not clear what should be done to him. ³⁵Then the LORD said to Moses, "The man must die. The whole assembly must stone him outside the camp." ³⁶So the assembly took him outside the camp and stoned him to death, as the LORD commanded Moses.

³⁷The LORD said to Moses, ³⁸"Speak to the Israelites and say to them: 'Throughout the generations to come you are to make tassels on the corners of your garments, with a blue cord on each tassel. ³⁹You will have these tassels to look at and so you will remember all the commands of the LORD, that you may obey them and not prostitute yourselves by going after the lusts of your own hearts and eyes. ⁴⁰Then you will remember to obey all my commands and will be consecrated to your God. ⁴¹I am the LORD your God, who brought you out of Egypt to be your God. I am the LORD your God.' "

16

Korah son of Izhar, the son of Kohath, the son of Levi, and certain Reubenites—Dathan and Abiram, sons of Eliab, and On son of Peleth—became insolent¹ ²and rose up against Moses. With them were 250 Israelite men, well-known community leaders who had been appointed members of the

council. ³They came as a group to oppose Moses and Aaron and said to them, "You have gone too far! The whole community is holy, every one of them, and the LORD is with them. Why then do you set yourselves above the LORD's assembly?"

⁴When Moses heard this, he fell facedown. ⁵Then he said to Korah and all his followers: "In the morning the LORD will show who belongs to him and who is holy, and he will have that person come near him. The man he chooses he will cause to come near him. ⁶You, Korah, and all your followers are to do this: Take censers ⁷and tomorrow put fire and incense in them before the LORD. The man the LORD chooses will be the one who is holy. You Levites have gone too far!"

⁸Moses also said to Korah, "Now listen, you Levites! ⁹Isn't it enough for you that the God of Israel has separated you from the rest of the Israelite community and brought you near himself to do the work at the LORD's tabernacle and to stand before the community and minister to them? ¹⁰He has brought you and all your fellow Levites near himself, but now you are trying to get the priesthood too. ¹¹It is against the LORD that you and all your followers have banded together. Who is Aaron that you should grumble against him?"

¹²Then Moses summoned Dathan and Abiram, the sons of Eliab. But they said, "We will not come! ¹³Isn't it enough that you have brought us up out of a land flowing with milk and honey to kill us in the desert? And now you also want to lord it over us? ¹⁴Moreover, you haven't brought us into a land flowing with milk and honey or given us an inheritance of fields and vineyards. Will you gouge out the eyes ofᵐ these men? No, we will not come!"

¹⁵Then Moses became very angry and said to the LORD, "Do not accept their offering. I have not taken so much as a donkey from them, nor have I wronged any of them."

¹⁶Moses said to Korah, "You and all your followers are to appear before the LORD tomorrow— you and they and Aaron. ¹⁷Each man is to take his censer and put incense in it—250 censers in all— and present it before the LORD. You and Aaron are to present your censers also." ¹⁸So each man took his censer, put fire and incense in it, and stood with Moses and Aaron at the entrance to the Tent of Meeting. ¹⁹When Korah had gathered all his followers in opposition to them at the entrance to

¹1 Or Peleth—took ⌐men⌐   ᵐ14 Or you make slaves of; or you deceive

the Tent of Meeting, the glory of the LORD appeared to the entire assembly. [20]The LORD said to Moses and Aaron, [21]"Separate yourselves from this assembly so I can put an end to them at once."

[22]But Moses and Aaron fell facedown and cried out, "O God, God of the spirits of all mankind, will you be angry with the entire assembly when only one man sins?"

[23]Then the LORD said to Moses, [24]"Say to the assembly, 'Move away from the tents of Korah, Dathan and Abiram.' "

[25]Moses got up and went to Dathan and Abiram, and the elders of Israel followed him. [26]He warned the assembly, "Move back from the tents of these wicked men! Do not touch anything belonging to them, or you will be swept away because of all their sins." [27]So they moved away from the tents of Korah, Dathan and Abiram. Dathan and Abiram had come out and were standing with their wives, children and little ones at the entrances to their tents.

[28]Then Moses said, "This is how you will know that the LORD has sent me to do all these things and that it was not my idea: [29]If these men die a natural death and experience only what usually happens to men, then the LORD has not sent me. [30]But if the LORD brings about something totally new, and the earth opens its mouth and swallows them, with everything that belongs to them, and they go down alive into the grave,[n] then you will know that these men have treated the LORD with contempt."

[31]As soon as he finished saying all this, the ground under them split apart [32]and the earth opened its mouth and swallowed them, with their households and all Korah's men and all their possessions. [33]They went down alive into the grave, with everything they owned; the earth closed over them, and they perished and were gone from the community. [34]At their cries, all the Israelites around them fled, shouting, "The earth is going to swallow us too!"

[35]And fire came out from the LORD and consumed the 250 men who were offering the incense.

[36]The LORD said to Moses, [37]"Tell Eleazar son of Aaron, the priest, to take the censers out of the smoldering remains and scatter the coals some distance away, for the censers are holy— [38]the censers of the men who sinned at the cost of their lives. Hammer the censers into sheets to overlay the altar, for they were presented before the LORD and have become holy. Let them be a sign to the Israelites."

[39]So Eleazar the priest collected the bronze censers brought by those who had been burned up, and he had them hammered out to overlay the altar, [40]as the LORD directed him through Moses. This was to remind the Israelites that no one except a descendant of Aaron should come to burn incense before the LORD, or he would become like Korah and his followers.

[41]The next day the whole Israelite community grumbled against Moses and Aaron. "You have killed the LORD's people," they said.

[42]But when the assembly gathered in opposition to Moses and Aaron and turned toward the Tent of Meeting, suddenly the cloud covered it and the glory of the LORD appeared. [43]Then Moses and Aaron went to the front of the Tent of Meeting, [44]and the LORD said to Moses, [45]"Get away from this assembly so I can put an end to them at once." And they fell facedown.

[46]Then Moses said to Aaron, "Take your censer and put incense in it, along with fire from the altar, and hurry to the assembly to make atonement for them. Wrath has come out from the LORD; the plague has started." [47]So Aaron did as Moses said, and ran into the midst of the assembly. The plague had already started among the people, but Aaron offered the incense and made atonement for them. [48]He stood between the living and the dead, and the plague stopped. [49]But 14,700 people died from the plague, in addition to those who had died because of Korah. [50]Then Aaron returned to Moses at the entrance to the Tent of Meeting, for the plague had stopped.

[n]30 Hebrew *Sheol*; also in verse 33

6 / *Numbers 17*
Budding Leadership

WANTED: STRONG LEADERS. No matter what group or organization is being discussed, that statement applies. Good leaders are hard to find, hard to train, and hard to keep. In Numbers 17 God affirms the leaders set before Israel in a time of crisis.

 Warming Up to God Think of the leaders who have made a difference in your life. They might be from church, family or school. Reflect on the leadership gifts that most impressed and influenced you, and thank God for bringing them into your life.

Read Numbers 17.

17 The LORD said to Moses, ²"Speak to the Israelites and get twelve staffs from them, one from the leader of each of their ancestral tribes. Write the name of each man on his staff. ³On the staff of Levi write Aaron's name, for there must be one staff for the head of each ancestral tribe. ⁴Place them in the Tent of Meeting in front of the Testimony, where I meet with you. ⁵The staff belonging to the man I choose will sprout, and I will rid myself of this constant grumbling against you by the Israelites."

⁶So Moses spoke to the Israelites, and their leaders gave him twelve staffs, one for the leader of each of their ancestral tribes, and Aaron's staff was among them. ⁷Moses placed the staffs before the LORD in the Tent of the Testimony.

⁸The next day Moses entered the Tent of the Testimony and saw that Aaron's staff, which represented the house of Levi, had not only sprouted but had budded, blossomed and produced almonds. ⁹Then Moses brought out all the staffs from the LORD's presence to all the Israelites. They looked at them, and each man took his own staff.

¹⁰The LORD said to Moses, "Put back Aaron's staff in front of the Testimony, to be kept as a sign to the rebellious. This will put an end to their grumbling against me, so that they will not die." ¹¹Moses did just as the LORD commanded him.

¹²The Israelites said to Moses, "We will die! We are lost, we are all lost! ¹³Anyone who even comes near the tabernacle of the LORD will die. Are we all going to die?"

Discovering the Word 1. Why does God set up this test (v. 5)? 2. Why do you think he uses this test instead of simply punishing the troublemakers? 3. How does the staff make an appropriate object for God's lesson (see, for example, Ps 23:4)? 4. Why do you think the staffs are placed in front of the ark and Ten Commandments? 5. How would the display of the staffs serve as a good deterrent to grumbling (v. 10)?

 Applying the Word 1. How can you provide stronger support to those in leadership in your church or fellowship? 2. How can you seek confirmation of God's approval for your own service?

 Responding in Prayer Ask God to make you aware of the place of leadership in daily life. Pray for the wisdom to be a stronger supporter and a wiser leader.

Numbers 18—19

18 The LORD said to Aaron, "You, your sons and your father's family are to bear the responsibility for offenses against the sanctuary, and you and your sons alone are to bear the responsibility for offenses against the priesthood. ²Bring your fellow Levites from your ancestral tribe to join you and assist you when you and your sons minister before the Tent of the Testimony. ³They are to be responsible to you and are to perform all the duties of the Tent, but they must not go near the furnishings of the sanctuary or the altar, or both they and you

will die. ⁴They are to join you and be responsible for the care of the Tent of Meeting—all the work at the Tent—and no one else may come near where you are.

⁵"You are to be responsible for the care of the sanctuary and the altar, so that wrath will not fall on the Israelites again. ⁶I myself have selected your fellow Levites from among the Israelites as a gift to you, dedicated to the Lord to do the work at the Tent of Meeting. ⁷But only you and your sons may serve as priests in connection with everything at the altar and inside the curtain. I am giving you the service of the priesthood as a gift. Anyone else who comes near the sanctuary must be put to death."

⁸Then the Lord said to Aaron, "I myself have put you in charge of the offerings presented to me; all the holy offerings the Israelites give me I give to you and your sons as your portion and regular share. ⁹You are to have the part of the most holy offerings that is kept from the fire. From all the gifts they bring me as most holy offerings, whether grain or sin or guilt offerings, that part belongs to you and your sons. ¹⁰Eat it as something most holy; every male shall eat it. You must regard it as holy.

¹¹"This also is yours: whatever is set aside from the gifts of all the wave offerings of the Israelites. I give this to you and your sons and daughters as your regular share. Everyone in your household who is ceremonially clean may eat it.

¹²"I give you all the finest olive oil and all the finest new wine and grain they give the Lord as the firstfruits of their harvest. ¹³All the land's firstfruits that they bring to the Lord will be yours. Everyone in your household who is ceremonially clean may eat it.

¹⁴"Everything in Israel that is devoted⁰ to the Lord is yours. ¹⁵The first offspring of every womb, both man and animal, that is offered to the Lord is yours. But you must redeem every firstborn son and every firstborn male of unclean animals. ¹⁶When they are a month old, you must redeem them at the redemption price set at five shekelsᵖ of silver, according to the sanctuary shekel, which weighs twenty gerahs.

¹⁷"But you must not redeem the firstborn of an ox, a sheep or a goat; they are holy. Sprinkle their blood on the altar and burn their fat as an offering made by fire, an aroma pleasing to the Lord. ¹⁸Their meat is to be yours, just as the breast of the wave offering and the right thigh are yours.

¹⁹Whatever is set aside from the holy offerings the Israelites present to the Lord I give to you and your sons and daughters as your regular share. It is an everlasting covenant of salt before the Lord for both you and your offspring."

²⁰The Lord said to Aaron, "You will have no inheritance in their land, nor will you have any share among them; I am your share and your inheritance among the Israelites.

²¹"I give to the Levites all the tithes in Israel as their inheritance in return for the work they do while serving at the Tent of Meeting. ²²From now on the Israelites must not go near the Tent of Meeting, or they will bear the consequences of their sin and will die. ²³It is the Levites who are to do the work at the Tent of Meeting and bear the responsibility for offenses against it. This is a lasting ordinance for the generations to come. They will receive no inheritance among the Israelites. ²⁴Instead, I give to the Levites as their inheritance the tithes that the Israelites present as an offering to the Lord. That is why I said concerning them: 'They will have no inheritance among the Israelites.' "

²⁵The Lord said to Moses, ²⁶"Speak to the Levites and say to them: 'When you receive from the Israelites the tithe I give you as your inheritance, you must present a tenth of that tithe as the Lord's offering. ²⁷Your offering will be reckoned to you as grain from the threshing floor or juice from the winepress. ²⁸In this way you also will present an offering to the Lord from all the tithes you receive from the Israelites. From these tithes you must give the Lord's portion to Aaron the priest. ²⁹You must present as the Lord's portion the best and holiest part of everything given to you.'

³⁰"Say to the Levites: 'When you present the best part, it will be reckoned to you as the product of the threshing floor or the winepress. ³¹You and your households may eat the rest of it anywhere, for it is your wages for your work at the Tent of Meeting. ³²By presenting the best part of it you will not be guilty in this matter; then you will not defile the holy offerings of the Israelites, and you will not die.' "

19 The Lord said to Moses and Aaron: ²"This is a requirement of the law that the Lord has commanded: Tell the Israelites to bring you a red heifer without

---

⁰14 The Hebrew term refers to the irrevocable giving over of things or persons to the Lord. ᵖ16 That is, about 2 ounces (about 55 grams)

defect or blemish and that has never been under a yoke. ³Give it to Eleazar the priest; it is to be taken outside the camp and slaughtered in his presence. ⁴Then Eleazar the priest is to take some of its blood on his finger and sprinkle it seven times toward the front of the Tent of Meeting. ⁵While he watches, the heifer is to be burned—its hide, flesh, blood and offal. ⁶The priest is to take some cedar wood, hyssop and scarlet wool and throw them onto the burning heifer. ⁷After that, the priest must wash his clothes and bathe himself with water. He may then come into the camp, but he will be ceremonially unclean till evening. ⁸The man who burns it must also wash his clothes and bathe with water, and he too will be unclean till evening.

⁹"A man who is clean shall gather up the ashes of the heifer and put them in a ceremonially clean place outside the camp. They shall be kept by the Israelite community for use in the water of cleansing; it is for purification from sin. ¹⁰The man who gathers up the ashes of the heifer must also wash his clothes, and he too will be unclean till evening. This will be a lasting ordinance both for the Israelites and for the aliens living among them.

¹¹"Whoever touches the dead body of anyone will be unclean for seven days. ¹²He must purify himself with the water on the third day and on the seventh day; then he will be clean. But if he does not purify himself on the third and seventh days, he will not be clean. ¹³Whoever touches the dead body of anyone and fails to purify himself defiles the LORD's tabernacle. That person must be cut off from Israel. Because the water of cleansing has not been sprinkled on him, he is unclean; his uncleanness remains on him.

¹⁴"This is the law that applies when a person dies in a tent: Anyone who enters the tent and anyone who is in it will be unclean for seven days, ¹⁵and every open container without a lid fastened on it will be unclean.

¹⁶"Anyone out in the open who touches someone who has been killed with a sword or someone who has died a natural death, or anyone who touches a human bone or a grave, will be unclean for seven days.

¹⁷"For the unclean person, put some ashes from the burned purification offering into a jar and pour fresh water over them. ¹⁸Then a man who is ceremonially clean is to take some hyssop, dip it in the water and sprinkle the tent and all the furnishings and the people who were there. He must also sprinkle anyone who has touched a human bone or a grave or someone who has been killed or someone who has died a natural death. ¹⁹The man who is clean is to sprinkle the unclean person on the third and seventh days, and on the seventh day he is to purify him. The person being cleansed must wash his clothes and bathe with water, and that evening he will be clean. ²⁰But if a person who is unclean does not purify himself, he must be cut off from the community, because he has defiled the sanctuary of the LORD. The water of cleansing has not been sprinkled on him, and he is unclean. ²¹This is a lasting ordinance for them.

"The man who sprinkles the water of cleansing must also wash his clothes, and anyone who touches the water of cleansing will be unclean till evening. ²²Anything that an unclean person touches becomes unclean, and anyone who touches it becomes unclean till evening."

7 / *Numbers 20:1–13*
God's Work; God's Way

THERE'S NO JOY in being left out—especially when you feel you've earned something. Imagine how Moses must have felt. For nearly forty years he had led the Israelites through the wilderness, often serving as the only influence for godly obedience. But in Numbers 20, the leader discovers he will never realize his goal. What sin could be great enough to bear such a price? This chapter reveals the answer.

 Warming Up to God What is your greatest personal dream? What would happen if you were told today you would never attain it? Could you still trust God?

📖 **Read Numbers 20:1–13.**

20

In the first month the whole Israelite community arrived at the Desert of Zin, and they stayed at Kadesh. There Miriam died and was buried.

²Now there was no water for the community, and the people gathered in opposition to Moses and Aaron. ³They quarreled with Moses and said, "If only we had died when our brothers fell dead before the LORD! ⁴Why did you bring the LORD's community into this desert, that we and our livestock should die here? ⁵Why did you bring us up out of Egypt to this terrible place? It has no grain or figs, grapevines or pomegranates. And there is no water to drink!"

⁶Moses and Aaron went from the assembly to the entrance to the Tent of Meeting and fell facedown, and the glory of the LORD appeared to them. ⁷The LORD said to Moses, ⁸"Take the staff, and you and your brother Aaron gather the assembly together. Speak to that rock before their eyes and it will pour out its water. You will bring water out of the rock for the community so they and their livestock can drink."

⁹So Moses took the staff from the LORD's presence, just as he commanded him. ¹⁰He and Aaron gathered the assembly together in front of the rock and Moses said to them, "Listen, you rebels, must we bring you water out of this rock?" ¹¹Then Moses raised his arm and struck the rock twice with his staff. Water gushed out, and the community and their livestock drank.

¹²But the LORD said to Moses and Aaron, "Because you did not trust in me enough to honor me as holy in the sight of the Israelites, you will not bring this community into the land I give them."

¹³These were the waters of Meribah,�q where the Israelites quarreled with the LORD and where he showed himself holy among them.

q13 *Meribah* means *quarreling.*

🔦 **Discovering the Word** 1. This story is set at the very place a similar rebellion had happened twenty years earlier (see Ex 17:1–7). How would this fact affect the thinking of Moses and of the people? 2. How do Moses' actions compare with or differ from those in Exodus 17? 3. What is it about Moses' actions that so angers God? 4. What effect do you think this lesson had on the observers?

💧 **Applying the Word** 1. What external pressures are likely to influence the way in which you carry out God's commands? 2. What good things might you currently be doing in ways and with attitudes other than God's? List a few.

🙏 **Responding in Prayer** Take some time to reflect on the current pressures and conflicts in your life. Acknowledge God as sovereign over them. Thank him for giving you wisdom to handle these, and ask him to especially guard your spirit in today's events.

Numbers 20:14–29

¹⁴Moses sent messengers from Kadesh to the king of Edom, saying:

"This is what your brother Israel says: You know about all the hardships that have come upon us. ¹⁵Our forefathers went down into Egypt, and we lived there many years. The Egyptians mistreated us and our fathers, ¹⁶but when we cried out to the LORD, he heard our cry and sent an angel and brought us out of Egypt.

"Now we are here at Kadesh, a town on the edge of your territory. ¹⁷Please let us pass through your country. We will not go through any field or vineyard, or drink water from any well. We will travel along the king's highway and not turn to the right or to the left until we have passed through your territory."

¹⁸But Edom answered:

"You may not pass through here; if you

try, we will march out and attack you with the sword."

19The Israelites replied:

"We will go along the main road, and if we or our livestock drink any of your water, we will pay for it. We only want to pass through on foot—nothing else."

20Again they answered:

"You may not pass through."

Then Edom came out against them with a large and powerful army. 21Since Edom refused to let them go through their territory, Israel turned away from them.

22The whole Israelite community set out from Kadesh and came to Mount Hor. 23At Mount Hor, near the border of Edom, the LORD said to Moses and Aaron, 24"Aaron will be gathered to his people. He will not enter the land I give the Israelites, because both of you rebelled against my command at the waters of Meribah. 25Get Aaron and his son Eleazar and take them up Mount Hor. 26Remove Aaron's garments and put them on his son Eleazar, for Aaron will be gathered to his people; he will die there."

27Moses did as the LORD commanded: They went up Mount Hor in the sight of the whole community. 28Moses removed Aaron's garments and put them on his son Eleazar. And Aaron died there on top of the mountain. Then Moses and Eleazar came down from the mountain, 29and when the whole community learned that Aaron had died, the entire house of Israel mourned for him thirty days.

8 / *Numbers 21:1–9*
The Serpent That Saved

CRISIS STRIKES. WE feel surrounded by uncontrollable forces and a hopeless situation. At times like this the weakest fall into sin; the strongest lift their eyes to God and find new power. In this remarkable story, we learn of God's provision in the wilderness for those who believe. And we see in the incident the foreshadowing of God's provision through Christ, more than a thousand years later.

Warming Up to God What is the most difficult crisis you've faced over the past couple of years? How did you seek God in that situation?

Read Numbers 21:1–9.

21 When the Canaanite king of Arad, who lived in the Negev, heard that Israel was coming along the road to Atharim, he attacked the Israelites and captured some of them. 2Then Israel made this vow to the LORD: "If you will deliver these people into our hands, we will totally destroyʳ their cities." 3The LORD listened to Israel's plea and gave the Canaanites over to them. They completely destroyed them and their towns; so the place was named Hormah.ˢ

4They traveled from Mount Hor along the route to the Red Sea,ᵗ to go around Edom. But the people grew impatient on the way; 5they spoke against God and against Moses, and said, "Why have you brought us up out of Egypt to die in the desert? There is no bread! There is no water! And we detest this miserable food!"

6Then the LORD sent venomous snakes among them; they bit the people and many Israelites died. 7The people came to Moses and said, "We sinned when we spoke against the LORD and against you. Pray that the LORD will take the snakes away from us." So Moses prayed for the people.

8The LORD said to Moses, "Make a snake and put it up on a pole; anyone who is bitten can look

ʳ2 The Hebrew term refers to the irrevocable giving over of things or persons to the LORD, often by totally destroying them; also in verse 3. ˢ3 *Hormah* means *destruction*.   ᵗ4 Hebrew *Yam Suph*; that is, Sea of Reeds at it and live." 9So Moses made a bronze snake and put it up on a pole. Then when anyone was bitten by a snake and looked at the bronze snake, he lived.

Discovering the Word 1. In the previous chapter, Aaron and Miriam have died; Moses has been punished. How would the state of mind of the Israelites contribute to this crisis? 2. How do the Israelites' complaints in verses 4–5 contrast with the events of verses 1–3? 3. Why do you think God chooses a snake as the central symbol of his salvation, considering how snakes have just been used (vv. 6–9)? 4. John 3:14–15 compares Jesus to the bronze snake. What similarities can you find?

Applying the Word 1. Crisis events seem to separate the strong from the weak. If an unforeseen catastrophe happened today, how would you look to God for strength? 2. How can you help others to seek God in trying times?

Responding in Prayer Praise God the deliverer as you seek him in prayer today. Review the times he has been there to provide comfort and deliverance. Particularly give thanks that he has lifted up his Son, like the snake, so that we can keep our vision focused.

Numbers 21:10—27:11

10The Israelites moved on and camped at Oboth. 11Then they set out from Oboth and camped in Iye Abarim, in the desert that faces Moab toward the sunrise. 12From there they moved on and camped in the Zered Valley. 13They set out from there and camped alongside the Arnon, which is in the desert extending into Amorite territory. The Arnon is the border of Moab, between Moab and the Amorites. 14That is why the Book of the Wars of the LORD says:

". . . Waheb in Suphah[u] and the ravines,
the Arnon 15and[v] the slopes of the ravines
that lead to the site of Ar
and lie along the border of Moab."

16From there they continued on to Beer, the well where the LORD said to Moses, "Gather the people together and I will give them water."

17Then Israel sang this song:

"Spring up, O well!
Sing about it,
18about the well that the princes dug,
that the nobles of the people sank—
the nobles with scepters and staffs."

Then they went from the desert to Mattanah, 19from Mattanah to Nahaliel, from Nahaliel to Bamoth, 20and from Bamoth to the valley in Moab where the top of Pisgah overlooks the wasteland.

21Israel sent messengers to say to Sihon king of the Amorites:

22"Let us pass through your country. We will not turn aside into any field or vineyard, or drink water from any well. We will travel along the king's highway until we have passed through your territory."

23But Sihon would not let Israel pass through his territory. He mustered his entire army and marched out into the desert against Israel. When he reached Jahaz, he fought with Israel. 24Israel, however, put him to the sword and took over his land from the Arnon to the Jabbok, but only as far as the Ammonites, because their border was fortified. 25Israel captured all the cities of the Amorites and occupied them, including Heshbon and all its surrounding settlements. 26Heshbon was the city of Sihon king of the Amorites, who had fought against the former king of Moab and had taken from him all his land as far as the Arnon.

27That is why the poets say:

"Come to Heshbon and let it be rebuilt;
let Sihon's city be restored.

28"Fire went out from Heshbon,
a blaze from the city of Sihon.
It consumed Ar of Moab,
the citizens of Arnon's heights.
29Woe to you, O Moab!
You are destroyed, O people of Chemosh!
He has given up his sons as fugitives

---

u14 The meaning of the Hebrew for this phrase is uncertain.
v14,15 Or "I have been given from Suphah and the ravines / of the Arnon 15to

and his daughters as captives
to Sihon king of the Amorites.

30"But we have overthrown them;
Heshbon is destroyed all the way to Dibon.
We have demolished them as far as Nophah,
which extends to Medeba."

31So Israel settled in the land of the Amorites.

32After Moses had sent spies to Jazer, the Israelites captured its surrounding settlements and drove out the Amorites who were there. 33Then they turned and went up along the road toward Bashan, and Og king of Bashan and his whole army marched out to meet them in battle at Edrei.

34The LORD said to Moses, "Do not be afraid of him, for I have handed him over to you, with his whole army and his land. Do to him what you did to Sihon king of the Amorites, who reigned in Heshbon."

35So they struck him down, together with his sons and his whole army, leaving them no survivors. And they took possession of his land.

22 Then the Israelites traveled to the plains of Moab and camped along the Jordan across from Jericho.w

2Now Balak son of Zippor saw all that Israel had done to the Amorites, 3and Moab was terrified because there were so many people. Indeed, Moab was filled with dread because of the Israelites.

4The Moabites said to the elders of Midian, "This horde is going to lick up everything around us, as an ox licks up the grass of the field."

So Balak son of Zippor, who was king of Moab at that time, 5sent messengers to summon Balaam son of Beor, who was at Pethor, near the River,x in his native land. Balak said:

"A people has come out of Egypt; they cover the face of the land and have settled next to me. 6Now come and put a curse on these people, because they are too powerful for me. Perhaps then I will be able to defeat them and drive them out of the country. For I know that those you bless are blessed, and those you curse are cursed."

7The elders of Moab and Midian left, taking with them the fee for divination. When they came to Balaam, they told him what Balak had said.

8"Spend the night here," Balaam said to them, "and I will bring you back the answer the LORD

gives me." So the Moabite princes stayed with him.

9God came to Balaam and asked, "Who are these men with you?"

10Balaam said to God, "Balak son of Zippor, king of Moab, sent me this message: 11'A people that has come out of Egypt covers the face of the land. Now come and put a curse on them for me. Perhaps then I will be able to fight them and drive them away.'"

12But God said to Balaam, "Do not go with them. You must not put a curse on those people, because they are blessed."

13The next morning Balaam got up and said to Balak's princes, "Go back to your own country, for the LORD has refused to let me go with you."

14So the Moabite princes returned to Balak and said, "Balaam refused to come with us."

15Then Balak sent other princes, more numerous and more distinguished than the first. 16They came to Balaam and said:

"This is what Balak son of Zippor says: Do not let anything keep you from coming to me, 17because I will reward you handsomely and do whatever you say. Come and put a curse on these people for me."

18But Balaam answered them, "Even if Balak gave me his palace filled with silver and gold, I could not do anything great or small to go beyond the command of the LORD my God. 19Now stay here tonight as the others did, and I will find out what else the LORD will tell me."

20That night God came to Balaam and said, "Since these men have come to summon you, go with them, but do only what I tell you."

21Balaam got up in the morning, saddled his donkey and went with the princes of Moab. 22But God was very angry when he went, and the angel of the LORD stood in the road to oppose him. Balaam was riding on his donkey, and his two servants were with him. 23When the donkey saw the angel of the LORD standing in the road with a drawn sword in his hand, she turned off the road into a field. Balaam beat her to get her back on the road.

24Then the angel of the LORD stood in a narrow path between two vineyards, with walls on both sides. 25When the donkey saw the angel of the

---

w1 Hebrew *Jordan of Jericho*; possibly an ancient name for the Jordan
River   x5 That is, the Euphrates

LORD, she pressed close to the wall, crushing Balaam's foot against it. So he beat her again.

²⁶Then the angel of the LORD moved on ahead and stood in a narrow place where there was no room to turn, either to the right or to the left. ²⁷When the donkey saw the angel of the LORD, she lay down under Balaam, and he was angry and beat her with his staff. ²⁸Then the LORD opened the donkey's mouth, and she said to Balaam, "What have I done to you to make you beat me these three times?"

²⁹Balaam answered the donkey, "You have made a fool of me! If I had a sword in my hand, I would kill you right now."

³⁰The donkey said to Balaam, "Am I not your own donkey, which you have always ridden, to this day? Have I been in the habit of doing this to you?"

"No," he said.

³¹Then the LORD opened Balaam's eyes, and he saw the angel of the LORD standing in the road with his sword drawn. So he bowed low and fell facedown.

³²The angel of the LORD asked him, "Why have you beaten your donkey these three times? I have come here to oppose you because your path is a reckless one before me.ʸ ³³The donkey saw me and turned away from me these three times. If she had not turned away, I would certainly have killed you by now, but I would have spared her."

³⁴Balaam said to the angel of the LORD, "I have sinned. I did not realize you were standing in the road to oppose me. Now if you are displeased, I will go back."

³⁵The angel of the LORD said to Balaam, "Go with the men, but speak only what I tell you." So Balaam went with the princes of Balak.

³⁶When Balak heard that Balaam was coming, he went out to meet him at the Moabite town on the Arnon border, at the edge of his territory. ³⁷Balak said to Balaam, "Did I not send you an urgent summons? Why didn't you come to me? Am I really not able to reward you?"

³⁸"Well, I have come to you now," Balaam replied. "But can I say just anything? I must speak only what God puts in my mouth."

³⁹Then Balaam went with Balak to Kiriath Huzoth. ⁴⁰Balak sacrificed cattle and sheep, and gave some to Balaam and the princes who were with him. ⁴¹The next morning Balak took Balaam up to Bamoth Baal, and from there he saw part of the people.

23

Balaam said, "Build me seven altars here, and prepare seven bulls and seven rams for me." ²Balak did as Balaam said, and the two of them offered a bull and a ram on each altar.

³Then Balaam said to Balak, "Stay here beside your offering while I go aside. Perhaps the LORD will come to meet with me. Whatever he reveals to me I will tell you." Then he went off to a barren height.

⁴God met with him, and Balaam said, "I have prepared seven altars, and on each altar I have offered a bull and a ram."

⁵The LORD put a message in Balaam's mouth and said, "Go back to Balak and give him this message."

⁶So he went back to him and found him standing beside his offering, with all the princes of Moab. ⁷Then Balaam uttered his oracle:

"Balak brought me from Aram,
　the king of Moab from the eastern
　　mountains.
'Come,' he said, 'curse Jacob for me;
　come, denounce Israel.'
⁸How can I curse
　those whom God has not cursed?
How can I denounce
　those whom the LORD has not denounced?
⁹From the rocky peaks I see them,
　from the heights I view them.
I see a people who live apart
　and do not consider themselves one of the
　　nations.
¹⁰Who can count the dust of Jacob
　or number the fourth part of Israel?
Let me die the death of the righteous,
　and may my end be like theirs!"

¹¹Balak said to Balaam, "What have you done to me? I brought you to curse my enemies, but you have done nothing but bless them!"

¹²He answered, "Must I not speak what the LORD puts in my mouth?"

¹³Then Balak said to him, "Come with me to another place where you can see them; you will see only a part but not all of them. And from there, curse them for me." ¹⁴So he took him to the field of Zophim on the top of Pisgah, and there he built seven altars and offered a bull and a ram on each altar.

ʸ32 The meaning of the Hebrew for this clause is uncertain.

15Balaam said to Balak, "Stay here beside your offering while I meet with him over there."

16The Lord met with Balaam and put a message in his mouth and said, "Go back to Balak and give him this message."

17So he went to him and found him standing beside his offering, with the princes of Moab. Balak asked him, "What did the Lord say?"

18Then he uttered his oracle:

"Arise, Balak, and listen;
    hear me, son of Zippor.
19God is not a man, that he should lie,
    nor a son of man, that he should change
        his mind.
Does he speak and then not act?
Does he promise and not fulfill?
20I have received a command to bless;
    he has blessed, and I cannot change it.

21"No misfortune is seen in Jacob,
    no misery observed in Israel.z
The Lord their God is with them;
    the shout of the King is among them.
22God brought them out of Egypt;
    they have the strength of a wild ox.
23There is no sorcery against Jacob,
    no divination against Israel.
It will now be said of Jacob
    and of Israel, 'See what God has done!'
24The people rise like a lioness;
    they rouse themselves like a lion
that does not rest till he devours his prey
    and drinks the blood of his victims."

25Then Balak said to Balaam, "Neither curse them at all nor bless them at all!"

26Balaam answered, "Did I not tell you I must do whatever the Lord says?"

27Then Balak said to Balaam, "Come, let me take you to another place. Perhaps it will please God to let you curse them for me from there." 28And Balak took Balaam to the top of Peor, overlooking the wasteland.

29Balaam said, "Build me seven altars here, and prepare seven bulls and seven rams for me." 30Balak did as Balaam had said, and offered a bull and a ram on each altar.

24 Now when Balaam saw that it pleased the Lord to bless Israel, he did not resort to sorcery as at other times, but turned his face toward the desert. 2When Balaam looked out and saw Israel en-camped tribe by tribe, the Spirit of God came upon him 3and he uttered his oracle:

"The oracle of Balaam son of Beor,
    the oracle of one whose eye sees clearly,
4the oracle of one who hears the words of
        God,
    who sees a vision from the Almighty,a
    who falls prostrate, and whose eyes are
        opened:

5"How beautiful are your tents, O Jacob,
    your dwelling places, O Israel!

6"Like valleys they spread out,
    like gardens beside a river,
 like aloes planted by the Lord,
    like cedars beside the waters.
7Water will flow from their buckets;
    their seed will have abundant water.

"Their king will be greater than Agag;
    their kingdom will be exalted.

8"God brought them out of Egypt;
    they have the strength of a wild ox.
They devour hostile nations
    and break their bones in pieces;
    with their arrows they pierce them.
9Like a lion they crouch and lie down,
    like a lioness—who dares to rouse them?

"May those who bless you be blessed
    and those who curse you be cursed!"

10Then Balak's anger burned against Balaam. He struck his hands together and said to him, "I summoned you to curse my enemies, but you have blessed them these three times. 11Now leave at once and go home! I said I would reward you handsomely, but the Lord has kept you from being rewarded."

12Balaam answered Balak, "Did I not tell the messengers you sent me, 13'Even if Balak gave me his palace filled with silver and gold, I could not do anything of my own accord, good or bad, to go beyond the command of the Lord—and I must say only what the Lord says'? 14Now I am going back to my people, but come, let me warn you of what this people will do to your people in days to come."

15Then he uttered his oracle:

"The oracle of Balaam son of Beor,

z21 Or He has not looked on Jacob's offenses / or on the wrongs found in Israel.   a4 Hebrew Shaddai; also in verse 16

the oracle of one whose eye sees clearly,
[16]the oracle of one who hears the words of
God,
who has knowledge from the Most High,
who sees a vision from the Almighty,
who falls prostrate, and whose eyes are
opened:

[17]"I see him, but not now;
I behold him, but not near.
A star will come out of Jacob;
a scepter will rise out of Israel.
He will crush the foreheads of Moab,
the skulls[b] of[c] all the sons of Sheth.[d]
[18]Edom will be conquered;
Seir, his enemy, will be conquered,
but Israel will grow strong.
[19]A ruler will come out of Jacob
and destroy the survivors of the city."

[20]Then Balaam saw Amalek and uttered his oracle:

"Amalek was first among the nations,
but he will come to ruin at last."

[21]Then he saw the Kenites and uttered his oracle:

"Your dwelling place is secure,
your nest is set in a rock;
[22]yet you Kenites will be destroyed
when Asshur takes you captive."

[23]Then he uttered his oracle:

"Ah, who can live when God does this?[e]
[24]   Ships will come from the shores of Kittim;
they will subdue Asshur and Eber,
but they too will come to ruin."

[25]Then Balaam got up and returned home and
Balak went his own way.

25 While Israel was staying in Shittim,
the men began to indulge in sexual
immorality with Moabite women,
[2]who invited them to the sacrifices to their gods.
The people ate and bowed down before these
gods. [3]So Israel joined in worshiping the Baal of
Peor. And the LORD's anger burned against them.
[4]The LORD said to Moses, "Take all the leaders
of these people, kill them and expose them in
broad daylight before the LORD, so that the LORD's
fierce anger may turn away from Israel."
[5]So Moses said to Israel's judges, "Each of you

must put to death those of your men who have
joined in worshiping the Baal of Peor."

[6]Then an Israelite man brought to his family a
Midianite woman right before the eyes of Moses
and the whole assembly of Israel while they were
weeping at the entrance to the Tent of Meeting.
[7]When Phinehas son of Eleazar, the son of Aaron,
the priest, saw this, he left the assembly, took a
spear in his hand [8]and followed the Israelite into
the tent. He drove the spear through both of
them—through the Israelite and into the
woman's body. Then the plague against the Israelites was stopped; [9]but those who died in the
plague numbered 24,000.

[10]The LORD said to Moses, [11]"Phinehas son of
Eleazar, the son of Aaron, the priest, has turned
my anger away from the Israelites; for he was as
zealous as I am for my honor among them, so that
in my zeal I did not put an end to them. [12]Therefore tell him I am making my covenant of peace
with him. [13]He and his descendants will have a
covenant of a lasting priesthood, because he was
zealous for the honor of his God and made atonement for the Israelites."

[14]The name of the Israelite who was killed with
the Midianite woman was Zimri son of Salu, the
leader of a Simeonite family. [15]And the name of
the Midianite woman who was put to death was
Cozbi daughter of Zur, a tribal chief of a Midianite family.

[16]The LORD said to Moses, [17]"Treat the Midianites as enemies and kill them, [18]because they
treated you as enemies when they deceived you
in the affair of Peor and their sister Cozbi, the
daughter of a Midianite leader, the woman who
was killed when the plague came as a result of
Peor."

26 After the plague the LORD said to
Moses and Eleazar son of Aaron,
the priest, [2]"Take a census of the
whole Israelite community by families—all those
twenty years old or more who are able to serve in
the army of Israel." [3]So on the plains of Moab by
the Jordan across from Jericho,[f] Moses and Eleazar the priest spoke with them and said, [4]"Take a
census of the men twenty years old or more, as
the LORD commanded Moses."

---

[b]17 Samaritan Pentateuch (see also Jer. 48:45); the meaning of the word
in the Masoretic Text is uncertain.   [c]17 Or possibly *Moab, / batter*
[d]17 Or *all the noisy boasters*   [e]23 Masoretic Text; with a different
word division of the Hebrew *A people will gather from the north.*
[f]3 Hebrew *Jordan of Jericho*; possibly an ancient name for the Jordan
River; also in verse 63

These were the Israelites who came out of Egypt:

⁵The descendants of Reuben, the firstborn son of Israel, were:

through Hanoch, the Hanochite clan;
through Pallu, the Palluite clan;
⁶through Hezron, the Hezronite clan;
through Carmi, the Carmite clan.

⁷These were the clans of Reuben; those numbered were 43,730.

⁸The son of Pallu was Eliab, ⁹and the sons of Eliab were Nemuel, Dathan and Abiram. The same Dathan and Abiram were the community officials who rebelled against Moses and Aaron and were among Korah's followers when they rebelled against the LORD. ¹⁰The earth opened its mouth and swallowed them along with Korah, whose followers died when the fire devoured the 250 men. And they served as a warning sign. ¹¹The line of Korah, however, did not die out.

¹²The descendants of Simeon by their clans were:

through Nemuel, the Nemuelite clan;
through Jamin, the Jaminite clan;
through Jakin, the Jakinite clan;
¹³through Zerah, the Zerahite clan;
through Shaul, the Shaulite clan.

¹⁴These were the clans of Simeon; there were 22,200 men.

¹⁵The descendants of Gad by their clans were:

through Zephon, the Zephonite clan;
through Haggi, the Haggite clan;
through Shuni, the Shunite clan;
¹⁶through Ozni, the Oznite clan;
through Eri, the Erite clan;
¹⁷through Arodi,ᵍ the Arodite clan;
through Areli, the Arelite clan.

¹⁸These were the clans of Gad; those numbered were 40,500.

¹⁹Er and Onan were sons of Judah, but they died in Canaan.

²⁰The descendants of Judah by their clans were:

through Shelah, the Shelanite clan;
through Perez, the Perezite clan;
through Zerah, the Zerahite clan.
²¹The descendants of Perez were:
through Hezron, the Hezronite clan;
through Hamul, the Hamulite clan.

²²These were the clans of Judah; those numbered were 76,500.

²³The descendants of Issachar by their clans were:

through Tola, the Tolaite clan;
through Puah, the Puiteʰ clan;
²⁴through Jashub, the Jashubite clan;
through Shimron, the Shimronite clan.

²⁵These were the clans of Issachar; those numbered were 64,300.

²⁶The descendants of Zebulun by their clans were:

through Sered, the Seredite clan;
through Elon, the Elonite clan;
through Jahleel, the Jahleelite clan.

²⁷These were the clans of Zebulun; those numbered were 60,500.

²⁸The descendants of Joseph by their clans through Manasseh and Ephraim were:

²⁹The descendants of Manasseh:

through Makir, the Makirite clan (Makir was the father of Gilead);
through Gilead, the Gileadite clan.
³⁰These were the descendants of Gilead:
through Iezer, the Iezerite clan;
through Helek, the Helekite clan;
³¹through Asriel, the Asrielite clan;
through Shechem, the Shechemite clan;
³²through Shemida, the Shemidaite clan;
through Hepher, the Hepherite clan.
³³(Zelophehad son of Hepher had no sons; he had only daughters, whose names were Mahlah, Noah, Hoglah, Milcah and Tirzah.)

³⁴These were the clans of Manasseh; those numbered were 52,700.

³⁵These were the descendants of Ephraim by their clans:

through Shuthelah, the Shuthelahite clan;
through Beker, the Bekerite clan;
through Tahan, the Tahanite clan.
³⁶These were the descendants of Shuthelah:
through Eran, the Eranite clan.

³⁷These were the clans of Ephraim; those numbered were 32,500.

These were the descendants of Joseph by their clans.

³⁸The descendants of Benjamin by their clans were:

ᵍ17 Samaritan Pentateuch and Syriac (see also Gen. 46:16); Masoretic Text *Arod*   ʰ23 Samaritan Pentateuch, Septuagint, Vulgate and Syriac (see also 1 Chron. 7:1); Masoretic Text *through Puvah, the Punite* through Bela, the Belaite clan;

through Ashbel, the Ashbelite clan;

through Ahiram, the Ahiramite clan;

³⁹through Shupham,ⁱ the Shuphamite clan;

through Hupham, the Huphamite clan.

⁴⁰The descendants of Bela through Ard and Naaman were:

through Ard,ʲ the Ardite clan;

through Naaman, the Naamite clan.

⁴¹These were the clans of Benjamin; those numbered were 45,600.

⁴²These were the descendants of Dan by their clans:

through Shuham, the Shuhamite clan.

These were the clans of Dan: ⁴³All of them were Shuhamite clans; and those numbered were 64,400.

⁴⁴The descendants of Asher by their clans were:

through Imnah, the Imnite clan;

through Ishvi, the Ishvite clan;

through Beriah, the Beriite clan;

⁴⁵and through the descendants of Beriah:

through Heber, the Heberite clan;

through Malkiel, the Malkielite clan.

⁴⁶(Asher had a daughter named Serah.)

⁴⁷These were the clans of Asher; those numbered were 53,400.

⁴⁸The descendants of Naphtali by their clans were:

through Jahzeel, the Jahzeelite clan;

through Guni, the Gunite clan;

⁴⁹through Jezer, the Jezerite clan;

through Shillem, the Shillemite clan.

⁵⁰These were the clans of Naphtali; those numbered were 45,400.

⁵¹The total number of the men of Israel was 601,730.

⁵²The LORD said to Moses, ⁵³"The land is to be allotted to them as an inheritance based on the number of names. ⁵⁴To a larger group give a larger inheritance, and to a smaller group a smaller one; each is to receive its inheritance according to the number of those listed. ⁵⁵Be sure that the land is distributed by lot. What each group inherits will be according to the names for its ancestral tribe. ⁵⁶Each inheritance is to be distributed by lot among the larger and smaller groups."

⁵⁷These were the Levites who were counted by their clans:

through Gershon, the Gershonite clan;

through Kohath, the Kohathite clan;

through Merari, the Merarite clan.

⁵⁸These also were Levite clans:

the Libnite clan,

the Hebronite clan,

the Mahlite clan,

the Mushite clan,

the Korahite clan.

(Kohath was the forefather of Amram; ⁵⁹the name of Amram's wife was Jochebed, a descendant of Levi, who was born to the Levitesᵏ in Egypt. To Amram she bore Aaron, Moses and their sister Miriam. ⁶⁰Aaron was the father of Nadab and Abihu, Eleazar and Ithamar. ⁶¹But Nadab and Abihu died when they made an offering before the LORD with unauthorized fire.)

⁶²All the male Levites a month old or more numbered 23,000. They were not counted along with the other Israelites because they received no inheritance among them.

⁶³These are the ones counted by Moses and Eleazar the priest when they counted the Israelites on the plains of Moab by the Jordan across from Jericho. ⁶⁴Not one of them was among those counted by Moses and Aaron the priest when they counted the Israelites in the Desert of Sinai. ⁶⁵For the LORD had told those Israelites they would surely die in the desert, and not one of them was left except Caleb son of Jephunneh and Joshua son of Nun.

27

The daughters of Zelophehad son of Hepher, the son of Gilead, the son of Makir, the son of Manasseh, belonged to the clans of Manasseh son of Joseph. The names of the daughters were Mahlah, Noah, Hoglah, Milcah and Tirzah. They approached ²the entrance to the Tent of Meeting and stood before Moses, Eleazar the priest, the leaders and the whole assembly, and said, ³"Our father died in the desert. He was not among Korah's followers, who banded together against the LORD, but he died for his own sin and left no sons. ⁴Why

---

ⁱ39 A few manuscripts of the Masoretic Text, Samaritan Pentateuch, Vulgate and Syriac (see also Septuagint); most manuscripts of the Masoretic Text *Shephupham* ʲ40 Samaritan Pentateuch and Vulgate (see also Septuagint); Masoretic Text does not have *through Ard*. ᵏ59 Or *Jochebed, a daughter of Levi, who was born to Levi* should our father's name disappear from his clan because he had no son? Give us property among our father's relatives."

⁵So Moses brought their case before the LORD ⁶and the LORD said to him, ⁷"What Zelophehad's daughters are saying is right. You must certainly give them property as an inheritance among their father's relatives and turn their father's inheritance over to them.

⁸"Say to the Israelites, 'If a man dies and leaves no son, turn his inheritance over to his daughter. ⁹If he has no daughter, give his inheritance to his brothers. ¹⁰If he has no brothers, give his inheritance to his father's brothers. ¹¹If his father had no brothers, give his inheritance to the nearest relative in his clan, that he may possess it. This is to be a legal requirement for the Israelites, as the LORD commanded Moses.' "

9 / *Numbers 27:12–23*
Passing the Torch

WHO CARRIES ON for the great leaders? The best of them become living legends and seem irreplaceable. Moses led the Israelites for forty years. A generation had grown up who had known no other leader. But the time came, even for Moses, to pass the torch. Numbers 27:12–23 details how God's people can make such a transition.

 Warming Up to God   Think of a time you have lost a beloved pastor, Sunday-school teacher or important spiritual influence. How did you accept the new leader?

 Read Numbers 27:12–23.

¹²Then the LORD said to Moses, "Go up this mountain in the Abarim range and see the land I have given the Israelites. ¹³After you have seen it, you too will be gathered to your people, as your brother Aaron was, ¹⁴for when the community rebelled at the waters in the Desert of Zin, both of you disobeyed my command to honor me as holy before their eyes." (These were the waters of Meribah Kadesh, in the Desert of Zin.)

¹⁵Moses said to the LORD, ¹⁶"May the LORD, the God of the spirits of all mankind, appoint a man over this community ¹⁷to go out and come in before them, one who will lead them out and bring them in, so the LORD's people will not be like sheep without a shepherd."

¹⁸So the LORD said to Moses, "Take Joshua son of Nun, a man in whom is the spirit,ⁱ and lay

your hand on him. ¹⁹Have him stand before Eleazar the priest and the entire assembly and commission him in their presence. ²⁰Give him some of your authority so the whole Israelite community will obey him. ²¹He is to stand before Eleazar the priest, who will obtain decisions for him by inquiring of the Urim before the LORD. At his command he and the entire community of the Israelites will go out, and at his command they will come in."

²²Moses did as the LORD commanded him. He took Joshua and had him stand before Eleazar the priest and the whole assembly. ²³Then he laid his hands on him and commissioned him, as the LORD instructed through Moses.

ⁱ18 Or *Spirit*

 Discovering the Word   1. Moses has been forbidden from entering the Promised Land. How do you account for God's command for Moses to look at the land from the mountains (vv. 12–14)?   2. What does Moses' statement (vv. 15–17) reveal about his state of mind?   3. From this passage (v. 18) and Numbers 14 (vv. 6–9, 30, 36–38) what do you know about Joshua's credentials for leadership?   4. What formalities are commanded for the installation of Joshua (vv. 19–21)?   5. Why is it important for Joshua to be commissioned in this way?

Applying the Word   1. What credentials should you seek in a spiritual leader?   2. How can you build and affirm trust in your church's or Christian group's leaders?

Responding in Prayer Thank God for the wise leaders he has provided in the past, as well as the ones he has placed before you now. Affirm to him that you will respect and support those leaders.

Numbers 28—31

28 The LORD said to Moses, [2]"Give this command to the Israelites and say to them: 'See that you present to me at the appointed time the food for my offerings made by fire, as an aroma pleasing to me.' [3]Say to them: 'This is the offering made by fire that you are to present to the LORD: two lambs a year old without defect, as a regular burnt offering each day. [4]Prepare one lamb in the morning and the other at twilight, [5]together with a grain offering of a tenth of an ephah[m] of fine flour mixed with a quarter of a hin[n] of oil from pressed olives. [6]This is the regular burnt offering instituted at Mount Sinai as a pleasing aroma, an offering made to the LORD by fire. [7]The accompanying drink offering is to be a quarter of a hin of fermented drink with each lamb. Pour out the drink offering to the LORD at the sanctuary. [8]Prepare the second lamb at twilight, along with the same kind of grain offering and drink offering that you prepare in the morning. This is an offering made by fire, an aroma pleasing to the LORD.

[9]" 'On the Sabbath day, make an offering of two lambs a year old without defect, together with its drink offering and a grain offering of two-tenths of an ephah[o] of fine flour mixed with oil. [10]This is the burnt offering for every Sabbath, in addition to the regular burnt offering and its drink offering.

[11]" 'On the first of every month, present to the LORD a burnt offering of two young bulls, one ram and seven male lambs a year old, all without defect. [12]With each bull there is to be a grain offering of three-tenths of an ephah[p] of fine flour mixed with oil; with the ram, a grain offering of two-tenths of an ephah of fine flour mixed with oil; [13]and with each lamb, a grain offering of a tenth of an ephah of fine flour mixed with oil. This is for a burnt offering, a pleasing aroma, an offering made to the LORD by fire. [14]With each bull there is to be a drink offering of half a hin[q] of wine; with the ram, a third of a hin[r]; and with each lamb, a quarter of a hin. This is the monthly burnt offering to be made at each new moon during the year. [15]Besides the regular burnt offering

with its drink offering, one male goat is to be presented to the LORD as a sin offering.

[16]" 'On the fourteenth day of the first month the LORD's Passover is to be held. [17]On the fifteenth day of this month there is to be a festival; for seven days eat bread made without yeast. [18]On the first day hold a sacred assembly and do no regular work. [19]Present to the LORD an offering made by fire, a burnt offering of two young bulls, one ram and seven male lambs a year old, all without defect. [20]With each bull prepare a grain offering of three-tenths of an ephah of fine flour mixed with oil; with the ram, two-tenths; [21]and with each of the seven lambs, one-tenth. [22]Include one male goat as a sin offering to make atonement for you. [23]Prepare these in addition to the regular morning burnt offering. [24]In this way prepare the food for the offering made by fire every day for seven days as an aroma pleasing to the LORD; it is to be prepared in addition to the regular burnt offering and its drink offering. [25]On the seventh day hold a sacred assembly and do no regular work.

[26]" 'On the day of firstfruits, when you present to the LORD an offering of new grain during the Feast of Weeks, hold a sacred assembly and do no regular work. [27]Present a burnt offering of two young bulls, one ram and seven male lambs a year old as an aroma pleasing to the LORD. [28]With each bull there is to be a grain offering of three-tenths of an ephah of fine flour mixed with oil; with the ram, two-tenths; [29]and with each of the seven lambs, one-tenth. [30]Include one male goat to make atonement for you. [31]Prepare these together with their drink offerings, in addition to the regular burnt offering and its grain offering. Be sure the animals are without defect.

29 " 'On the first day of the seventh month hold a sacred assembly and do no regular work. It is a day for

[m]5 That is, probably about 2 quarts (about 2 liters); also in verses 13, 21 and 29   [n]5 That is, probably about 1 quart (about 1 liter); also in verses 7 and 14   [o]9 That is, probably about 4 quarts (about 4.5 liters); also in verses 12, 20 and 28   [p]12 That is, probably about 6 quarts (about 6.5 liters); also in verses 20 and 28   [q]14 That is, probably about 2 quarts (about 2 liters)   [r]14 That is, probably about 1 1/4 quarts (about 1.2 liters)

you to sound the trumpets. ²As an aroma pleasing to the LORD, prepare a burnt offering of one young bull, one ram and seven male lambs a year old, all without defect. ³With the bull prepare a grain offering of three-tenths of an ephah[s] of fine flour mixed with oil; with the ram, two-tenths[t]; ⁴and with each of the seven lambs, one-tenth.[u] ⁵Include one male goat as a sin offering to make atonement for you. ⁶These are in addition to the monthly and daily burnt offerings with their grain offerings and drink offerings as specified. They are offerings made to the LORD by fire—a pleasing aroma.

⁷" 'On the tenth day of this seventh month hold a sacred assembly. You must deny yourselves[v] and do no work. ⁸Present as an aroma pleasing to the LORD a burnt offering of one young bull, one ram and seven male lambs a year old, all without defect. ⁹With the bull prepare a grain offering of three-tenths of an ephah of fine flour mixed with oil; with the ram, two-tenths; ¹⁰and with each of the seven lambs, one-tenth. ¹¹Include one male goat as a sin offering, in addition to the sin offering for atonement and the regular burnt offering with its grain offering, and their drink offerings.

¹²" 'On the fifteenth day of the seventh month, hold a sacred assembly and do no regular work. Celebrate a festival to the LORD for seven days. ¹³Present an offering made by fire as an aroma pleasing to the LORD, a burnt offering of thirteen young bulls, two rams and fourteen male lambs a year old, all without defect. ¹⁴With each of the thirteen bulls prepare a grain offering of three-tenths of an ephah of fine flour mixed with oil; with each of the two rams, two-tenths; ¹⁵and with each of the fourteen lambs, one-tenth. ¹⁶Include one male goat as a sin offering, in addition to the regular burnt offering with its grain offering and drink offering.

¹⁷" 'On the second day prepare twelve young bulls, two rams and fourteen male lambs a year old, all without defect. ¹⁸With the bulls, rams and lambs, prepare their grain offerings and drink offerings according to the number specified. ¹⁹Include one male goat as a sin offering, in addition to the regular burnt offering with its grain offering, and their drink offerings.

²⁰" 'On the third day prepare eleven bulls, two rams and fourteen male lambs a year old, all without defect. ²¹With the bulls, rams and lambs, prepare their grain offerings and drink offerings according to the number specified. ²²Include one male goat as a sin offering, in addition to the regular burnt offering with its grain offering and drink offering.

²³" 'On the fourth day prepare ten bulls, two rams and fourteen male lambs a year old, all without defect. ²⁴With the bulls, rams and lambs, prepare their grain offerings and drink offerings according to the number specified. ²⁵Include one male goat as a sin offering, in addition to the regular burnt offering with its grain offering and drink offering.

²⁶" 'On the fifth day prepare nine bulls, two rams and fourteen male lambs a year old, all without defect. ²⁷With the bulls, rams and lambs, prepare their grain offerings and drink offerings according to the number specified. ²⁸Include one male goat as a sin offering, in addition to the regular burnt offering with its grain offering and drink offering.

²⁹" 'On the sixth day prepare eight bulls, two rams and fourteen male lambs a year old, all without defect. ³⁰With the bulls, rams and lambs, prepare their grain offerings and drink offerings according to the number specified. ³¹Include one male goat as a sin offering, in addition to the regular burnt offering with its grain offering and drink offering.

³²" 'On the seventh day prepare seven bulls, two rams and fourteen male lambs a year old, all without defect. ³³With the bulls, rams and lambs, prepare their grain offerings and drink offerings according to the number specified. ³⁴Include one male goat as a sin offering, in addition to the regular burnt offering with its grain offering and drink offering.

³⁵" 'On the eighth day hold an assembly and do no regular work. ³⁶Present an offering made by fire as an aroma pleasing to the LORD, a burnt offering of one bull, one ram and seven male lambs a year old, all without defect. ³⁷With the bull, the ram and the lambs, prepare their grain offerings and drink offerings according to the number specified. ³⁸Include one male goat as a sin offering, in addition to the regular burnt offering with its grain offering and drink offering.

³⁹" 'In addition to what you vow and your freewill offerings, prepare these for the LORD at your appointed feasts: your burnt offerings, grain offerings, drink offerings and fellowship offerings.[w]' "

---

[s]3 That is, probably about 6 quarts (about 6.5 liters); also in verses 9 and 14   [t]3 That is, probably about 4 quarts (about 4.5 liters); also in verses 9 and 14   [u]4 That is, probably about 2 quarts (about 2 liters); also in verses 10 and 15   [v]7 Or *must fast*   [w]39 Traditionally *peace offerings*

⁴⁰Moses told the Israelites all that the Lᴏʀᴅ commanded him.

30

Moses said to the heads of the tribes of Israel: "This is what the Lᴏʀᴅ commands: ²When a man makes a vow to the Lᴏʀᴅ or takes an oath to obligate himself by a pledge, he must not break his word but must do everything he said.

³"When a young woman still living in her father's house makes a vow to the Lᴏʀᴅ or obligates herself by a pledge ⁴and her father hears about her vow or pledge but says nothing to her, then all her vows and every pledge by which she obligated herself will stand. ⁵But if her father forbids her when he hears about it, none of her vows or the pledges by which she obligated herself will stand; the Lᴏʀᴅ will release her because her father has forbidden her.

⁶"If she marries after she makes a vow or after her lips utter a rash promise by which she obligates herself ⁷and her husband hears about it but says nothing to her, then her vows or the pledges by which she obligated herself will stand. ⁸But if her husband forbids her when he hears about it, he nullifies the vow that obligates her or the rash promise by which she obligates herself, and the Lᴏʀᴅ will release her.

⁹"Any vow or obligation taken by a widow or divorced woman will be binding on her.

¹⁰"If a woman living with her husband makes a vow or obligates herself by a pledge under oath ¹¹and her husband hears about it but says nothing to her and does not forbid her, then all her vows or the pledges by which she obligated herself will stand. ¹²But if her husband nullifies them when he hears about them, then none of the vows or pledges that came from her lips will stand. Her husband has nullified them, and the Lᴏʀᴅ will release her. ¹³Her husband may confirm or nullify any vow she makes or any sworn pledge to deny herself. ¹⁴But if her husband says nothing to her about it from day to day, then he confirms all her vows or the pledges binding on her. He confirms them by saying nothing to her when he hears about them. ¹⁵If, however, he nullifies them some time after he hears about them, then he is responsible for her guilt."

¹⁶These are the regulations the Lᴏʀᴅ gave Moses concerning relationships between a man and his wife, and between a father and his young daughter still living in his house.

31

The Lᴏʀᴅ said to Moses, ²"Take vengeance on the Midianites for the Israelites. After that, you will be gathered to your people."

³So Moses said to the people, "Arm some of your men to go to war against the Midianites and to carry out the Lᴏʀᴅ's vengeance on them. ⁴Send into battle a thousand men from each of the tribes of Israel." ⁵So twelve thousand men armed for battle, a thousand from each tribe, were supplied from the clans of Israel. ⁶Moses sent them into battle, a thousand from each tribe, along with Phinehas son of Eleazar, the priest, who took with him articles from the sanctuary and the trumpets for signaling.

⁷They fought against Midian, as the Lᴏʀᴅ commanded Moses, and killed every man. ⁸Among their victims were Evi, Rekem, Zur, Hur and Reba—the five kings of Midian. They also killed Balaam son of Beor with the sword. ⁹The Israelites captured the Midianite women and children and took all the Midianite herds, flocks and goods as plunder. ¹⁰They burned all the towns where the Midianites had settled, as well as all their camps. ¹¹They took all the plunder and spoils, including the people and animals, ¹²and brought the captives, spoils and plunder to Moses and Eleazar the priest and the Israelite assembly at their camp on the plains of Moab, by the Jordan across from Jericho.ˣ

¹³Moses, Eleazar the priest and all the leaders of the community went to meet them outside the camp. ¹⁴Moses was angry with the officers of the army—the commanders of thousands and commanders of hundreds—who returned from the battle.

¹⁵"Have you allowed all the women to live?" he asked them. ¹⁶"They were the ones who followed Balaam's advice and were the means of turning the Israelites away from the Lᴏʀᴅ in what happened at Peor, so that a plague struck the Lᴏʀᴅ's people. ¹⁷Now kill all the boys. And kill every woman who has slept with a man, ¹⁸but save for yourselves every girl who has never slept with a man.

¹⁹"All of you who have killed anyone or touched anyone who was killed must stay outside the camp seven days. On the third and seventh days you must purify yourselves and your cap-

ˣ12 Hebrew *Jordan of Jericho*; possibly an ancient name for the Jordan River tives. ²⁰Purify every garment as well as everything made of leather, goat hair or wood."

²¹Then Eleazar the priest said to the soldiers who had gone into battle, "This is the requirement of the law that the LORD gave Moses: ²²Gold, silver, bronze, iron, tin, lead ²³and anything else that can withstand fire must be put through the fire, and then it will be clean. But it must also be purified with the water of cleansing. And whatever cannot withstand fire must be put through that water. ²⁴On the seventh day wash your clothes and you will be clean. Then you may come into the camp."

²⁵The LORD said to Moses, ²⁶"You and Eleazar the priest and the family heads of the community are to count all the people and animals that were captured. ²⁷Divide the spoils between the soldiers who took part in the battle and the rest of the community. ²⁸From the soldiers who fought in the battle, set apart as tribute for the LORD one out of every five hundred, whether persons, cattle, donkeys, sheep or goats. ²⁹Take this tribute from their half share and give it to Eleazar the priest as the LORD's part. ³⁰From the Israelites' half, select one out of every fifty, whether persons, cattle, donkeys, sheep, goats or other animals. Give them to the Levites, who are responsible for the care of the LORD's tabernacle." ³¹So Moses and Eleazar the priest did as the LORD commanded Moses.

³²The plunder remaining from the spoils that the soldiers took was 675,000 sheep, ³³72,000 cattle, ³⁴61,000 donkeys ³⁵and 32,000 women who had never slept with a man.

³⁶The half share of those who fought in battle was:

337,500 sheep, ³⁷of which the tribute for the LORD was 675;

³⁸36,000 cattle, of which the tribute for the LORD was 72;

³⁹30,500 donkeys, of which the tribute for the LORD was 61;

⁴⁰16,000 people, of which the tribute for the LORD was 32.

⁴¹Moses gave the tribute to Eleazar the priest as the LORD's part, as the LORD commanded Moses.

⁴²The half belonging to the Israelites, which Moses set apart from that of the fighting men— ⁴³the community's half—was 337,500 sheep, ⁴⁴36,000 cattle, ⁴⁵30,500 donkeys ⁴⁶and 16,000 people. ⁴⁷From the Israelites' half, Moses selected one out of every fifty persons and animals, as the LORD commanded him, and gave them to the Levites, who were responsible for the care of the LORD's tabernacle.

⁴⁸Then the officers who were over the units of the army—the commanders of thousands and commanders of hundreds—went to Moses ⁴⁹and said to him, "Your servants have counted the soldiers under our command, and not one is missing. ⁵⁰So we have brought as an offering to the LORD the gold articles each of us acquired—armlets, bracelets, signet rings, earrings and necklaces—to make atonement for ourselves before the LORD."

⁵¹Moses and Eleazar the priest accepted from them the gold—all the crafted articles. ⁵²All the gold from the commanders of thousands and commanders of hundreds that Moses and Eleazar presented as a gift to the LORD weighed 16,750 shekels.^y ⁵³Each soldier had taken plunder for himself. ⁵⁴Moses and Eleazar the priest accepted the gold from the commanders of thousands and commanders of hundreds and brought it into the Tent of Meeting as a memorial for the Israelites before the LORD.

^y52 That is, about 420 pounds (about 190 kilograms)

10 / *Numbers 32*
United We Stand

NEARLY FORTY YEARS together in the wilderness—and now the great moment has arrived. It's time for the Israelites to cross the Jordan, face the opposition, and claim their land. But two tribes announce their intention not to make the trip. Are they exercising their prerogative? Or are the destinies of the twelve tribes intertwined? To what extent must we consider the effect on others when making a decision?

Warming Up to God Finish this sentence: Others depend on me for . . . What would happen if you were to abandon a large responsibility at home, work or school? Who would suffer? Ask God to make you aware of your important leadership roles.

Read Numbers 32.

32 The Reubenites and Gadites, who had very large herds and flocks, saw that the lands of Jazer and Gilead were suitable for livestock. ²So they came to Moses and Eleazar the priest and to the leaders of the community, and said, ³"Ataroth, Dibon, Jazer, Nimrah, Heshbon, Elealeh, Sebam, Nebo and Beon— ⁴the land the LORD subdued before the people of Israel—are suitable for livestock, and your servants have livestock. ⁵If we have found favor in your eyes," they said, "let this land be given to your servants as our possession. Do not make us cross the Jordan."

⁶Moses said to the Gadites and Reubenites, "Shall your countrymen go to war while you sit here? ⁷Why do you discourage the Israelites from going over into the land the LORD has given them? ⁸This is what your fathers did when I sent them from Kadesh Barnea to look over the land. ⁹After they went up to the Valley of Eshcol and viewed the land, they discouraged the Israelites from entering the land the LORD had given them. ¹⁰The LORD's anger was aroused that day and he swore this oath: ¹¹'Because they have not followed me wholeheartedly, not one of the men twenty years old or more who came up out of Egypt will see the land I promised on oath to Abraham, Isaac and Jacob— ¹²not one except Caleb son of Jephunneh the Kenizzite and Joshua son of Nun, for they followed the LORD wholeheartedly.' ¹³The LORD's anger burned against Israel and he made them wander in the desert forty years, until the whole generation of those who had done evil in his sight was gone.

¹⁴"And here you are, a brood of sinners, standing in the place of your fathers and making the LORD even more angry with Israel. ¹⁵If you turn away from following him, he will again leave all this people in the desert, and you will be the cause of their destruction."

¹⁶Then they came up to him and said, "We would like to build pens here for our livestock and cities for our women and children. ¹⁷But we are ready to arm ourselves and go ahead of the Israelites until we have brought them to their place. Meanwhile our women and children will live in fortified cities, for protection from the inhabitants of the land. ¹⁸We will not return to our homes until every Israelite has received his inheritance. ¹⁹We will not receive any inheritance with them on the other side of the Jordan, because our inheritance has come to us on the east side of the Jordan."

²⁰Then Moses said to them, "If you will do this—if you will arm yourselves before the LORD for battle, ²¹and if all of you will go armed over the Jordan before the LORD until he has driven his enemies out before him— ²²then when the land is subdued before the LORD, you may return and be free from your obligation to the LORD and to Israel. And this land will be your possession before the LORD.

²³"But if you fail to do this, you will be sinning against the LORD; and you may be sure that your sin will find you out. ²⁴Build cities for your women and children, and pens for your flocks, but do what you have promised."

²⁵The Gadites and Reubenites said to Moses, "We your servants will do as our lord commands. ²⁶Our children and wives, our flocks and herds will remain here in the cities of Gilead. ²⁷But your servants, every man armed for battle, will cross over to fight before the LORD, just as our lord says."

²⁸Then Moses gave orders about them to Eleazar the priest and Joshua son of Nun and to the family heads of the Israelite tribes. ²⁹He said to them, "If the Gadites and Reubenites, every man armed for battle, cross over the Jordan with you before the LORD, then when the land is subdued before you, give them the land of Gilead as their possession. ³⁰But if they do not cross over with you armed, they must accept their possession with you in Canaan."

³¹The Gadites and Reubenites answered, "Your servants will do what the LORD has said. ³²We will cross over before the LORD into Canaan armed, but the property we inherit will be on this side of the Jordan."

³³Then Moses gave to the Gadites, the Reubenites and the half-tribe of Manasseh son of Joseph the kingdom of Sihon king of the Amorites and

the kingdom of Og king of Bashan—the whole land with its cities and the territory around them.

³⁴The Gadites built up Dibon, Ataroth, Aroer, ³⁵Atroth Shophan, Jazer, Jogbehah, ³⁶Beth Nimrah and Beth Haran as fortified cities, and built pens for their flocks. ³⁷And the Reubenites rebuilt Heshbon, Elealeh and Kiriathaim, ³⁸as well as Nebo and Baal Meon (these names were changed) and Sibmah. They gave names to the cities they rebuilt.

³⁹The descendants of Makir son of Manasseh went to Gilead, captured it and drove out the Amorites who were there. ⁴⁰So Moses gave Gilead to the Makirites, the descendants of Manasseh, and they settled there. ⁴¹Jair, a descendant of Manasseh, captured their settlements and called them Havvoth Jair.ᶻ ⁴²And Nobah captured Kenath and its surrounding settlements and called it Nobah after himself.

ᶻ41 Or *them the settlements of Jair*

Discovering the Word 1. How would you evaluate the two tribes' justification for not crossing the river into Canaan (vv. 1–5)? 2. What important principles does Moses remind them of (vv. 6–15)? 3. What practical considerations might have concerned Moses about the division in destinations? 4. How would you evaluate the compromise offered by the two tribes (vv. 16–19)? 5. Why was this arrangement satisfactory to Moses (vv. 20–24)?

Applying the Word 1. What real or potential divisions can you detect in your church or Christian group? 2. Like Moses, how can you guard unity among believers?

Responding in Prayer Reflect on the importance of keeping everyone together as we follow God's leadership. Ask God to show you ways you can promote unity in your fellowship and enhance a sense of common goals.

Numbers 33—36

33 Here are the stages in the journey of the Israelites when they came out of Egypt by divisions under the leadership of Moses and Aaron. ²At the Lord's command Moses recorded the stages in their journey. This is their journey by stages:

³The Israelites set out from Rameses on the fifteenth day of the first month, the day after the Passover. They marched out boldly in full view of all the Egyptians, ⁴who were burying all their firstborn, whom the Lord had struck down among them; for the Lord had brought judgment on their gods.

⁵The Israelites left Rameses and camped at Succoth.

⁶They left Succoth and camped at Etham, on the edge of the desert.

⁷They left Etham, turned back to Pi Hahiroth, to the east of Baal Zephon, and camped near Migdol.

⁸They left Pi Hahirothᵃ and passed through the sea into the desert, and when they had traveled for three days in the Desert of Etham, they camped at Marah.

⁹They left Marah and went to Elim, where there were twelve springs and seventy palm trees, and they camped there.

¹⁰They left Elim and camped by the Red Sea.ᵇ

¹¹They left the Red Sea and camped in the Desert of Sin.

¹²They left the Desert of Sin and camped at Dophkah.

¹³They left Dophkah and camped at Alush.

¹⁴They left Alush and camped at Rephidim, where there was no water for the people to drink.

¹⁵They left Rephidim and camped in the Desert of Sinai.

¹⁶They left the Desert of Sinai and camped at Kibroth Hattaavah.

¹⁷They left Kibroth Hattaavah and camped at Hazeroth.

ᵃ8 Many manuscripts of the Masoretic Text, Samaritan Pentateuch and Vulgate; most manuscripts of the Masoretic Text *left from before Hahiroth*
ᵇ10 Hebrew *Yam Suph*; that is, Sea of Reeds; also in verse 11

18They left Hazeroth and camped at Rithmah.

19They left Rithmah and camped at Rimmon Perez.

20They left Rimmon Perez and camped at Libnah.

21They left Libnah and camped at Rissah.

22They left Rissah and camped at Kehelathah.

23They left Kehelathah and camped at Mount Shepher.

24They left Mount Shepher and camped at Haradah.

25They left Haradah and camped at Makheloth.

26They left Makheloth and camped at Tahath.

27They left Tahath and camped at Terah.

28They left Terah and camped at Mithcah.

29They left Mithcah and camped at Hashmonah.

30They left Hashmonah and camped at Moseroth.

31They left Moseroth and camped at Bene Jaakan.

32They left Bene Jaakan and camped at Hor Haggidgad.

33They left Hor Haggidgad and camped at Jotbathah.

34They left Jotbathah and camped at Abronah.

35They left Abronah and camped at Ezion Geber.

36They left Ezion Geber and camped at Kadesh, in the Desert of Zin.

37They left Kadesh and camped at Mount Hor, on the border of Edom. 38At the Lord's command Aaron the priest went up Mount Hor, where he died on the first day of the fifth month of the fortieth year after the Israelites came out of Egypt. 39Aaron was a hundred and twenty-three years old when he died on Mount Hor.

40The Canaanite king of Arad, who lived in the Negev of Canaan, heard that the Israelites were coming.

41They left Mount Hor and camped at Zalmonah.

42They left Zalmonah and camped at Punon.

43They left Punon and camped at Oboth.

44They left Oboth and camped at Iye Abarim, on the border of Moab.

45They left Iyim^c and camped at Dibon Gad.

46They left Dibon Gad and camped at Almon Diblathaim.

47They left Almon Diblathaim and camped in the mountains of Abarim, near Nebo.

48They left the mountains of Abarim and camped on the plains of Moab by the Jordan across from Jericho.^d 49There on the plains of Moab they camped along the Jordan from Beth Jeshimoth to Abel Shittim.

50On the plains of Moab by the Jordan across from Jericho the Lord said to Moses, 51"Speak to the Israelites and say to them: 'When you cross the Jordan into Canaan, 52drive out all the inhabitants of the land before you. Destroy all their carved images and their cast idols, and demolish all their high places. 53Take possession of the land and settle in it, for I have given you the land to possess. 54Distribute the land by lot, according to your clans. To a larger group give a larger inheritance, and to a smaller group a smaller one. Whatever falls to them by lot will be theirs. Distribute it according to your ancestral tribes.

55" 'But if you do not drive out the inhabitants of the land, those you allow to remain will become barbs in your eyes and thorns in your sides. They will give you trouble in the land where you will live. 56And then I will do to you what I plan to do to them.' "

34 The Lord said to Moses, 2"Command the Israelites and say to them: 'When you enter Canaan, the land that will be allotted to you as an inheritance will have these boundaries:

3" 'Your southern side will include some of the Desert of Zin along the border of Edom. On the east, your southern boundary will start from the end of the Salt Sea,^e 4cross south of Scorpion^f Pass, continue on to Zin and go south of Kadesh Barnea. Then it will go to Hazar Addar and over to Azmon, 5where it will turn, join the Wadi of Egypt and end at the Sea.^g

6" 'Your western boundary will be the coast of the Great Sea. This will be your boundary on the west.

---

^c45 That is, Iye Abarim   ^d48 Hebrew *Jordan of Jericho*; possibly an ancient name for the Jordan River; also in verse 50   ^e3 That is, the Dead Sea; also in verse 12   ^f4 Hebrew *Akrabbim*   ^g5 That is, the Mediterranean; also in verses 6 and 7

7" 'For your northern boundary, run a line from the Great Sea to Mount Hor 8and from Mount Hor to Lebo[h] Hamath. Then the boundary will go to Zedad, 9continue to Ziphron and end at Hazar Enan. This will be your boundary on the north.

10" 'For your eastern boundary, run a line from Hazar Enan to Shepham. 11The boundary will go down from Shepham to Riblah on the east side of Ain and continue along the slopes east of the Sea of Kinnereth.[i] 12Then the boundary will go down along the Jordan and end at the Salt Sea.

" 'This will be your land, with its boundaries on every side.' "

13Moses commanded the Israelites: "Assign this land by lot as an inheritance. The LORD has ordered that it be given to the nine and a half tribes, 14because the families of the tribe of Reuben, the tribe of Gad and the half-tribe of Manasseh have received their inheritance. 15These two and a half tribes have received their inheritance on the east side of the Jordan of Jericho,[j] toward the sunrise."

16The LORD said to Moses, 17"These are the names of the men who are to assign the land for you as an inheritance: Eleazar the priest and Joshua son of Nun. 18And appoint one leader from each tribe to help assign the land. 19These are their names:

Caleb son of Jephunneh,
    from the tribe of Judah;
20Shemuel son of Ammihud,
    from the tribe of Simeon;
21Elidad son of Kislon,
    from the tribe of Benjamin;
22Bukki son of Jogli,
    the leader from the tribe of Dan;
23Hanniel son of Ephod,
    the leader from the tribe of Manasseh son of Joseph;
24Kemuel son of Shiphtan,
    the leader from the tribe of Ephraim son of Joseph;
25Elizaphan son of Parnach,
    the leader from the tribe of Zebulun;
26Paltiel son of Azzan,
    the leader from the tribe of Issachar;
27Ahihud son of Shelomi,
    the leader from the tribe of Asher;
28Pedahel son of Ammihud,
    the leader from the tribe of Naphtali."

29These are the men the LORD commanded to assign the inheritance to the Israelites in the land of Canaan.

35 On the plains of Moab by the Jordan across from Jericho,[k] the LORD said to Moses, 2"Command the Israelites to give the Levites towns to live in from the inheritance the Israelites will possess. And give them pasturelands around the towns. 3Then they will have towns to live in and pasturelands for their cattle, flocks and all their other livestock.

4"The pasturelands around the towns that you give the Levites will extend out fifteen hundred feet[l] from the town wall. 5Outside the town, measure three thousand feet[m] on the east side, three thousand on the south side, three thousand on the west and three thousand on the north, with the town in the center. They will have this area as pastureland for the towns.

6"Six of the towns you give the Levites will be cities of refuge, to which a person who has killed someone may flee. In addition, give them forty-two other towns. 7In all you must give the Levites forty-eight towns, together with their pasturelands. 8The towns you give the Levites from the land the Israelites possess are to be given in proportion to the inheritance of each tribe: Take many towns from a tribe that has many, but few from one that has few."

9Then the LORD said to Moses: 10"Speak to the Israelites and say to them: 'When you cross the Jordan into Canaan, 11select some towns to be your cities of refuge, to which a person who has killed someone accidentally may flee. 12They will be places of refuge from the avenger, so that a person accused of murder may not die before he stands trial before the assembly. 13These six towns you give will be your cities of refuge. 14Give three on this side of the Jordan and three in Canaan as cities of refuge. 15These six towns will be a place of refuge for Israelites, aliens and any other people living among them, so that anyone who has killed another accidentally can flee there.

16" 'If a man strikes someone with an iron object so that he dies, he is a murderer; the murderer shall be put to death. 17Or if anyone has a

h8 Or to the entrance to   i11 That is, Galilee   j15 Jordan of Jericho was possibly an ancient name for the Jordan River.
k1 Hebrew Jordan of Jericho; possibly an ancient name for the Jordan River   l4 Hebrew a thousand cubits (about 450 meters)
m5 Hebrew two thousand cubits (about 900 meters)

stone in his hand that could kill, and he strikes someone so that he dies, he is a murderer; the murderer shall be put to death. ¹⁸Or if anyone has a wooden object in his hand that could kill, and he hits someone so that he dies, he is a murderer; the murderer shall be put to death. ¹⁹The avenger of blood shall put the murderer to death; when he meets him, he shall put him to death. ²⁰If anyone with malice aforethought shoves another or throws something at him intentionally so that he dies ²¹or if in hostility he hits him with his fist so that he dies, that person shall be put to death; he is a murderer. The avenger of blood shall put the murderer to death when he meets him.

²²" 'But if without hostility someone suddenly shoves another or throws something at him unintentionally ²³or, without seeing him, drops a stone on him that could kill him, and he dies, then since he was not his enemy and he did not intend to harm him, ²⁴the assembly must judge between him and the avenger of blood according to these regulations. ²⁵The assembly must protect the one accused of murder from the avenger of blood and send him back to the city of refuge to which he fled. He must stay there until the death of the high priest, who was anointed with the holy oil.

²⁶" 'But if the accused ever goes outside the limits of the city of refuge to which he has fled ²⁷and the avenger of blood finds him outside the city, the avenger of blood may kill the accused without being guilty of murder. ²⁸The accused must stay in his city of refuge until the death of the high priest; only after the death of the high priest may he return to his own property.

²⁹" 'These are to be legal requirements for you throughout the generations to come, wherever you live.

³⁰" 'Anyone who kills a person is to be put to death as a murderer only on the testimony of witnesses. But no one is to be put to death on the testimony of only one witness.

³¹" 'Do not accept a ransom for the life of a murderer, who deserves to die. He must surely be put to death.

³²" 'Do not accept a ransom for anyone who has fled to a city of refuge and so allow him to go back and live on his own land before the death of the high priest.

³³" 'Do not pollute the land where you are. Bloodshed pollutes the land, and atonement cannot be made for the land on which blood has been shed, except by the blood of the one who shed it. ³⁴Do not defile the land where you live and where I dwell, for I, the LORD, dwell among the Israelites.' "

36

The family heads of the clan of Gilead son of Makir, the son of Manasseh, who were from the clans of the descendants of Joseph, came and spoke before Moses and the leaders, the heads of the Israelite families. ²They said, "When the LORD commanded my lord to give the land as an inheritance to the Israelites by lot, he ordered you to give the inheritance of our brother Zelophehad to his daughters. ³Now suppose they marry men from other Israelite tribes; then their inheritance will be taken from our ancestral inheritance and added to that of the tribe they marry into. And so part of the inheritance allotted to us will be taken away. ⁴When the Year of Jubilee for the Israelites comes, their inheritance will be added to that of the tribe into which they marry, and their property will be taken from the tribal inheritance of our forefathers."

⁵Then at the LORD's command Moses gave this order to the Israelites: "What the tribe of the descendants of Joseph is saying is right. ⁶This is what the LORD commands for Zelophehad's daughters: They may marry anyone they please as long as they marry within the tribal clan of their father. ⁷No inheritance in Israel is to pass from tribe to tribe, for every Israelite shall keep the tribal land inherited from his forefathers. ⁸Every daughter who inherits land in any Israelite tribe must marry someone in her father's tribal clan, so that every Israelite will possess the inheritance of his fathers. ⁹No inheritance may pass from tribe to tribe, for each Israelite tribe is to keep the land it inherits."

¹⁰So Zelophehad's daughters did as the LORD commanded Moses. ¹¹Zelophehad's daughters—Mahlah, Tirzah, Hoglah, Milcah and Noah—married their cousins on their father's side. ¹²They married within the clans of the descendants of Manasseh son of Joseph, and their inheritance remained in their father's clan and tribe.

¹³These are the commands and regulations the LORD gave through Moses to the Israelites on the plains of Moab by the Jordan across from Jericho.ⁿ

ⁿ13 Hebrew *Jordan of Jericho*; possibly an ancient name for the Jordan River

Deuteronomy

Outline

1. Deuteronomy 1-3 ....
2. Deuteronomy 4:1-43 ....
3. Deuteronomy 4:1-40 ....
4. Deuteronomy 5 ....
5. Deuteronomy 6 ....
6. Deuteronomy 7 ....
7. Deuteronomy 8 ....
8. Deuteronomy 12:1-14 ....
9. Deuteronomy 13:1-18 ....

D euteronomy offers great riches of wisdom to strengthen and sustain our faith. It is striking that all three of Jesus' quotes from Scripture as he resisted the temptations of Satan came from Deuteronomy (Lk 4:4, 8, 12). A book so significant in the life of our Lord must have much to say to us as well.

The word *Deuteronomy* means "the second giving of the law." It's an appropriate title, because that is what the book of Deuteronomy is. The Ten Commandments were given at Mount Sinai forty years earlier. Now, in Deuteronomy Moses repeats the Ten Commandments, reminding the nation of Israel about the circumstances under which they were given and explaining again what they mean.

The difference between the first and second giving of the law is striking. The first time Israel had just been delivered from slavery in Egypt. They hardly knew God at all, and Moses was their new leader. Now they have had forty years of experience following God under Moses' direction. The first time the law was given, they were merely a collection of slaves who had just fled from Pharaoh. They were terrified of the people whose land they were about to invade. Now they are a unified nation experienced in combat.

The book of Deuteronomy is divided into four sections. In the first three sections Moses reminds the nation of what they need to know before they march into the land. In 1:1—4:44 Moses rehearses their history. The second section, 4:44—28:68, contains the Ten Commandments and the covenant commitments that God and Israel have made to each other. In the third section Moses address the consequences of unfaithfulness to the law and issues a call to determined and heartfelt commitment to God. The final section, 29—34, records Moses' goodbys and his death.

Moses was laying down his burden of leadership and turning it over to Joshua. For forty years he had lead the nation. How hard it must have been for him to let go! With great care and passion Moses speaks from his heart. You can feel his aching desire to make sure that he had done everything possible to get his people ready for the blessings and challenges of life in the Promised Land.

As we read the words of Moses in Deuteronomy, there is much we can learn about being the people of God today. Throughout the book, Moses issues a call that rings down through the centuries, through the Old Testament to the New: "Love the LORD your God with all your heart and with all your soul and with all your strength" (6:5). That is something we need to hear again and again and again.

Outline

1/ Deuteronomy 3:21–29 —————————— Passing the Baton

2/ Deuteronomy 4:1–14 —————————— Remembering When and Why

3/ Deuteronomy 4:15–40 —————————— Only God Can Save

4/ Deuteronomy 5 —————————— Keeping God at a Distance

5/ Deuteronomy 6 —————————— Loving and Fearing the Law Giver

6/ Deuteronomy 7 —————————— Being a Holy People

7/ Deuteronomy 8 —————————— Remembering to Be Grateful

8/ Deuteronomy 12:1–14 —————————— One Place of Worship

9/ Deuteronomy 15:1–11 —————————— The Year of Freedom

10/ Deuteronomy 23:15–25 —————————— The Laws of Freedom

11/ Deuteronomy 30 —————————— A Scattered Future

12/ Deuteronomy 31:1–13 —————————— Saying Goodby

Deuteronomy 1:1—3:20

1 These are the words Moses spoke to all Israel in the desert east of the Jordan—that is, in the Arabah—opposite Suph, between Paran and Tophel, Laban, Hazeroth and Dizahab. ²(It takes eleven days to go from Horeb to Kadesh Barnea by the Mount Seir road.)

³In the fortieth year, on the first day of the eleventh month, Moses proclaimed to the Israelites all that the LORD had commanded him concerning them. ⁴This was after he had defeated Sihon king of the Amorites, who reigned in Heshbon, and at Edrei had defeated Og king of Bashan, who reigned in Ashtaroth.

⁵East of the Jordan in the territory of Moab, Moses began to expound this law, saying:

⁶The LORD our God said to us at Horeb, "You have stayed long enough at this mountain. ⁷Break camp and advance into the hill country of the Amorites; go to all the neighboring peoples in the Arabah, in the mountains, in the western foothills, in the Negev and along the coast, to the land of the Canaanites and to Lebanon, as far as the great river, the Euphrates. ⁸See, I have given you this land. Go in and take possession of the land that the LORD swore he would give to your fathers—to Abraham, Isaac and Jacob—and to their descendants after them."

⁹At that time I said to you, "You are too heavy a burden for me to carry alone. ¹⁰The LORD your God has increased your numbers so that today you are as many as the stars in the sky. ¹¹May the LORD, the God of your fathers, increase you a thousand times and bless you as he has promised! ¹²But how can I bear your problems and your burdens and your disputes all by myself? ¹³Choose some wise, understanding and respected men from each of your tribes, and I will set them over you."

¹⁴You answered me, "What you propose to do is good."

¹⁵So I took the leading men of your tribes, wise and respected men, and appointed them to have authority over you—as commanders of thousands, of hundreds, of fifties and of tens and as tribal officials. ¹⁶And I charged your judges at that time: Hear the disputes between your brothers and judge fairly, whether the case is between brother Israelites or between one of them and an alien. ¹⁷Do not show partiality in judging; hear both small and great alike. Do not be afraid of any man, for judgment belongs to God. Bring me any case too hard for you, and I will hear it. ¹⁸And at that time I told you everything you were to do.

¹⁹Then, as the LORD our God commanded us, we set out from Horeb and went toward the hill country of the Amorites through all that vast and dreadful desert that you have seen, and so we reached Kadesh Barnea. ²⁰Then I said to you, "You have reached the hill country of the Amorites, which the LORD our God is giving us. ²¹See, the LORD your God has given you the land. Go up and take possession of it as the LORD, the God of your fathers, told you. Do not be afraid; do not be discouraged."

²²Then all of you came to me and said, "Let us send men ahead to spy out the land for us and bring back a report about the route we are to take and the towns we will come to."

²³The idea seemed good to me; so I selected twelve of you, one man from each tribe. ²⁴They left and went up into the hill country, and came to the Valley of Eshcol and explored it. ²⁵Taking with them some of the fruit of the land, they brought it down to us and reported, "It is a good land that the LORD our God is giving us."

²⁶But you were unwilling to go up; you rebelled against the command of the LORD your God. ²⁷You grumbled in your tents and said, "The LORD hates us; so he brought us out of Egypt to deliver us into the hands of the Amorites to destroy us. ²⁸Where can we go? Our brothers have made us lose heart. They say, 'The people are stronger and taller than we are; the cities are large, with walls up to the sky. We even saw the Anakites there.' "

²⁹Then I said to you, "Do not be terrified; do not be afraid of them. ³⁰The LORD your God, who is going before you, will fight for you, as he did for you in Egypt, before your very eyes, ³¹and in the desert. There you saw how the LORD your God carried you, as a father carries his son, all the way you went until you reached this place."

³²In spite of this, you did not trust in the LORD your God, ³³who went ahead of you on your journey, in fire by night and in a cloud by day, to search out places for you to camp and to show you the way you should go.

³⁴When the LORD heard what you said, he was

angry and solemnly swore: ³⁵"Not a man of this evil generation shall see the good land I swore to give your forefathers, ³⁶except Caleb son of Jephunneh. He will see it, and I will give him and his descendants the land he set his feet on, because he followed the LORD wholeheartedly."

³⁷Because of you the LORD became angry with me also and said, "You shall not enter it, either. ³⁸But your assistant, Joshua son of Nun, will enter it. Encourage him, because he will lead Israel to inherit it. ³⁹And the little ones that you said would be taken captive, your children who do not yet know good from bad—they will enter the land. I will give it to them and they will take possession of it. ⁴⁰But as for you, turn around and set out toward the desert along the route to the Red Sea.ᵃ"

⁴¹Then you replied, "We have sinned against the LORD. We will go up and fight, as the LORD our God commanded us." So every one of you put on his weapons, thinking it easy to go up into the hill country.

⁴²But the LORD said to me, "Tell them, 'Do not go up and fight, because I will not be with you. You will be defeated by your enemies.'"

⁴³So I told you, but you would not listen. You rebelled against the LORD's command and in your arrogance you marched up into the hill country. ⁴⁴The Amorites who lived in those hills came out against you; they chased you like a swarm of bees and beat you down from Seir all the way to Hormah. ⁴⁵You came back and wept before the LORD, but he paid no attention to your weeping and turned a deaf ear to you. ⁴⁶And so you stayed in Kadesh many days—all the time you spent there.

2 Then we turned back and set out toward the desert along the route to the Red Sea,ᵃ as the LORD had directed me. For a long time we made our way around the hill country of Seir.

²Then the LORD said to me, ³"You have made your way around this hill country long enough; now turn north. ⁴Give the people these orders: 'You are about to pass through the territory of your brothers the descendants of Esau, who live in Seir. They will be afraid of you, but be very careful. ⁵Do not provoke them to war, for I will not give you any of their land, not even enough to put your foot on. I have given Esau the hill country of Seir as his own. ⁶You are to pay them in silver for the food you eat and the water you drink.'"

⁷The LORD your God has blessed you in all the work of your hands. He has watched over your journey through this vast desert. These forty years the LORD your God has been with you, and you have not lacked anything.

⁸So we went on past our brothers the descendants of Esau, who live in Seir. We turned from the Arabah road, which comes up from Elath and Ezion Geber, and traveled along the desert road of Moab.

⁹Then the LORD said to me, "Do not harass the Moabites or provoke them to war, for I will not give you any part of their land. I have given Ar to the descendants of Lot as a possession."

¹⁰(The Emites used to live there—a people strong and numerous, and as tall as the Anakites. ¹¹Like the Anakites, they too were considered Rephaites, but the Moabites called them Emites. ¹²Horites used to live in Seir, but the descendants of Esau drove them out. They destroyed the Horites from before them and settled in their place, just as Israel did in the land the LORD gave them as their possession.)

¹³And the LORD said, "Now get up and cross the Zered Valley." So we crossed the valley.

¹⁴Thirty-eight years passed from the time we left Kadesh Barnea until we crossed the Zered Valley. By then, that entire generation of fighting men had perished from the camp, as the LORD had sworn to them. ¹⁵The LORD's hand was against them until he had completely eliminated them from the camp.

¹⁶Now when the last of these fighting men among the people had died, ¹⁷the LORD said to me, ¹⁸"Today you are to pass by the region of Moab at Ar. ¹⁹When you come to the Ammonites, do not harass them or provoke them to war, for I will not give you possession of any land belonging to the Ammonites. I have given it as a possession to the descendants of Lot."

²⁰(That too was considered a land of the Rephaites, who used to live there; but the Ammonites called them Zamzummites. ²¹They were a people strong and numerous, and as tall as the Anakites. The LORD destroyed them from before the Ammonites, who drove them out and settled in their place. ²²The LORD had done the same for the descendants of Esau, who lived in Seir, when he destroyed the Horites from before them. They drove them out and have lived in their place to

ᵃ40,1 Hebrew *Yam Suph*; that is, Sea of Reeds

this day. 23And as for the Avvites who lived in villages as far as Gaza, the Caphtorites coming out from Caphtor*b* destroyed them and settled in their place.)

24"Set out now and cross the Arnon Gorge. See, I have given into your hand Sihon the Amorite, king of Heshbon, and his country. Begin to take possession of it and engage him in battle. 25This very day I will begin to put the terror and fear of you on all the nations under heaven. They will hear reports of you and will tremble and be in anguish because of you."

26From the desert of Kedemoth I sent messengers to Sihon king of Heshbon offering peace and saying, 27"Let us pass through your country. We will stay on the main road; we will not turn aside to the right or to the left. 28Sell us food to eat and water to drink for their price in silver. Only let us pass through on foot— 29as the descendants of Esau, who live in Seir, and the Moabites, who live in Ar, did for us—until we cross the Jordan into the land the LORD our God is giving us." 30But Sihon king of Heshbon refused to let us pass through. For the LORD your God had made his spirit stubborn and his heart obstinate in order to give him into your hands, as he has now done.

31The LORD said to me, "See, I have begun to deliver Sihon and his country over to you. Now begin to conquer and possess his land."

32When Sihon and all his army came out to meet us in battle at Jahaz, 33the LORD our God delivered him over to us and we struck him down, together with his sons and his whole army. 34At that time we took all his towns and completely destroyed*c* them—men, women and children. We left no survivors. 35But the livestock and the plunder from the towns we had captured we carried off for ourselves. 36From Aroer on the rim of the Arnon Gorge, and from the town in the gorge, even as far as Gilead, not one town was too strong for us. The LORD our God gave us all of them. 37But in accordance with the command of the LORD our God, you did not encroach on any of the land of the Ammonites, neither the land along the course of the Jabbok nor that around the towns in the hills.

3 Next we turned and went up along the road toward Bashan, and Og king of Bashan with his whole army marched out to meet us in battle at Edrei. 2The LORD said to me, "Do not be afraid of him, for I have handed him over to you with his whole army and his land. Do to him what you did to Sihon king of the Amorites, who reigned in Heshbon."

3So the LORD our God also gave into our hands Og king of Bashan and all his army. We struck them down, leaving no survivors. 4At that time we took all his cities. There was not one of the sixty cities that we did not take from them—the whole region of Argob, Og's kingdom in Bashan. 5All these cities were fortified with high walls and with gates and bars, and there were also a great many unwalled villages. 6We completely destroyed*c* them, as we had done with Sihon king of Heshbon, destroying*c* every city—men, women and children. 7But all the livestock and the plunder from their cities we carried off for ourselves.

8So at that time we took from these two kings of the Amorites the territory east of the Jordan, from the Arnon Gorge as far as Mount Hermon. 9(Hermon is called Sirion by the Sidonians; the Amorites call it Senir.) 10We took all the towns on the plateau, and all Gilead, and all Bashan as far as Salecah and Edrei, towns of Og's kingdom in Bashan. 11(Only Og king of Bashan was left of the remnant of the Rephaites. His bed*d* was made of iron and was more than thirteen feet long and six feet wide.*e* It is still in Rabbah of the Ammonites.)

12Of the land that we took over at that time, I gave the Reubenites and the Gadites the territory north of Aroer by the Arnon Gorge, including half the hill country of Gilead, together with its towns. 13The rest of Gilead and also all of Bashan, the kingdom of Og, I gave to the half tribe of Manasseh. (The whole region of Argob in Bashan used to be known as a land of the Rephaites. 14Jair, a descendant of Manasseh, took the whole region of Argob as far as the border of the Geshurites and the Maacathites; it was named after him, so that to this day Bashan is called Havvoth Jair.*f*) 15And I gave Gilead to Makir. 16But to the Reubenites and the Gadites I gave the territory extending from Gilead down to the Arnon Gorge (the middle of the gorge being the border) and out to the Jabbok River, which is the border of the Ammonites. 17Its western border was the Jordan in the Arabah, from Kinnereth to the Sea of

---

*b*23 That is, Crete   *c*34,6 The Hebrew term refers to the irrevocable giving over of things or persons to the LORD, often by totally destroying them.   *d*11 Or *sarcophagus*   *e*11 Hebrew *nine cubits long and four cubits wide* (about 4 meters long and 1.8 meters wide)   *f*14 Or *called the settlements of Jair* the Arabah (the Salt Sea⁸), below the slopes of Pisgah.

¹⁸I commanded you at that time: "The LORD your God has given you this land to take possession of it. But all your able-bodied men, armed for battle, must cross over ahead of your brother Israelites. ¹⁹However, your wives, your children and your livestock (I know you have much live-stock) may stay in the towns I have given you, ²⁰until the LORD gives rest to your brothers as he has to you, and they too have taken over the land that the LORD your God is giving them, across the Jordan. After that, each of you may go back to the possession I have given you."

g17 That is, the Dead Sea

1 / *Deuteronomy 3:21–29*
Passing the Baton

I KNEW THAT a new training position would be necessary in the next couple of years for our ministry, and I wanted to be the one who got it. However, it went to someone else. I was angry with those in authority who passed me over; I was angry with my friends who didn't support me; I was angry at God who had the power to make things come out differently. I had to work through the grief and pain back to the point of trusting that God knew what he was doing. And I had to come to terms with the fact that I cannot always have things my way. Moses also had to face a bitter disappointment. He didn't get to take the people of Israel into the Promised Land. That job, one that he had been waiting for all his life, was to go to Joshua. Moses was disappointed with God and angry at others.

 Warming Up to God This is a time of transition for Moses and the Israelites, moving from the wilderness to the Promised Land and changing from one leader to another. What major transitions in your personal, professional or spiritual life have you faced, and how did they affect you?

 Read Deuteronomy 3:21–29.

²¹At that time I commanded Joshua: "You have seen with your own eyes all that the LORD your God has done to these two kings. The LORD will do the same to all the kingdoms over there where you are going. ²²Do not be afraid of them; the LORD your God himself will fight for you."

²³At that time I pleaded with the LORD: ²⁴"O Sovereign LORD, you have begun to show to your servant your greatness and your strong hand. For what god is there in heaven or on earth who can do the deeds and mighty works you do? ²⁵Let me go over and see the good land beyond the Jordan—that fine hill country and Lebanon."

²⁶But because of you the LORD was angry with me and would not listen to me. "That is enough," the LORD said. "Do not speak to me anymore about this matter. ²⁷Go up to the top of Pisgah and look west and north and south and east. Look at the land with your own eyes, since you are not going to cross this Jordan. ²⁸But commission Joshua, and encourage and strengthen him, for he will lead this people across and will cause them to inherit the land that you will see." ²⁹So we stayed in the valley near Beth Peor.

Discovering the Word 1. What issues is Moses facing as he comes to the end of his life and ministry? 2. As Moses recounts his "forced retirement," how would you describe his interaction with God? 3. What is Moses doing to see that things carry on when he is gone (vv. 21–22, 28)? 4. What might Moses have felt as he stood on the top of Pisgah and looked over at the Promised Land (v. 27)?

Applying the Word 1. Moses had to turn over the leadership of Israel. Recall tasks that you have had to turn over to someone else. What was difficult about doing this? 2. Moses encouraged Joshua to take up leadership responsibilities for Israel. What responsibilities do you have, and how do you feel a need for encouragement? **3.** Moses bolstered Joshua's confidence by reminding him of battles that had been won through the help of God. As you reflect on your life, what "battles" has God helped you to win?

Responding in Prayer Pray that the leaders in your church will have the wisdom to know when to take charge and when to step back. Ask God to give you a sense of his empowering presence as you face the responsibilities he has called you to.

2 / *Deuteronomy 4:1–14*
Remembering When and Why

WEDDINGS ARE life-changing events for everyone from the bride and groom to their parents and their friends. That may be one of the reasons that so much planning goes into a wedding and the service is so elaborate. The bride in her white dress accompanied by her attendants, the groom and groomsmen in their tuxedos, the walk down the aisle. These rituals show outwardly that this is a turning point in life. In the years to come the wedding service will become a fond memory to be shared with children and mused on in passing moments between husband and wife.

The giving of the Ten Commandments was just such a life-changing event. Not just for two people, but for a couple of million people. In fact, in many ways it was like a marriage ceremony. Israel was making a commitment to God and God was making a commitment to Israel. And so God made sure that there was an elaborate display of his glory. God wanted to create an event that would be recalled with reverence and awe by generations to come.

 Warming Up to God Recall a time when God seemed very close and caring. What impressed you about him, and what difference did it make in your life? How can recalling that previous experience be a help and encouragement to you right now?

 Read Deuteronomy 4:1–14.

4 Hear now, O Israel, the decrees and laws I am about to teach you. Follow them so that you may live and may go in and take possession of the land that the LORD, the God of your fathers, is giving you. ²Do not add to what I command you and do not subtract from it, but keep the commands of the LORD your God that I give you.

³You saw with your own eyes what the LORD did at Baal Peor. The LORD your God destroyed from among you everyone who followed the Baal of Peor, ⁴but all of you who held fast to the LORD your God are still alive today.

⁵See, I have taught you decrees and laws as the LORD my God commanded me, so that you may follow them in the land you are entering to take possession of it. ⁶Observe them carefully, for this will show your wisdom and understanding to the nations, who will hear about all these decrees and say, "Surely this great nation is a wise and understanding people." ⁷What other nation is so great as to have their gods near them the way the LORD our God is near us whenever we pray to him? ⁸And what other nation is so great as to have such

righteous decrees and laws as this body of laws I am setting before you today?

⁹Only be careful, and watch yourselves closely so that you do not forget the things your eyes have seen or let them slip from your heart as long as you live. Teach them to your children and to their children after them. ¹⁰Remember the day you stood before the LORD your God at Horeb, when he said to me, "Assemble the people before me to hear my words so that they may learn to revere me as long as they live in the land and may teach them to their children." ¹¹You came near and stood at the foot of the mountain while it blazed with fire to the very heavens, with black clouds and deep darkness. ¹²Then the LORD spoke to you out of the fire. You heard the sound of words but saw no form; there was only a voice. ¹³He declared to you his covenant, the Ten Commandments, which he commanded you to follow and then wrote them on two stone tablets. ¹⁴And the LORD directed me at that time to teach you the decrees and laws you are to follow in the land that you are crossing the Jordan to possess.

Discovering the Word 1. What responsibilities do the Israelites have regarding the law (look throughout the passage)? 2. What benefits were to come to Israel through the Ten Commandments? 3. How was the law to make Israel an international witness (vv. 6–8)? 4. If you were standing at the mountain when the law was given, according to verses 11–13, what would you have seen and heard? 5. How would it have affected your attitude toward the law?

Applying the Word 1. In what ways might we add to or subtract from God's law (v. 2)? 2. What benefits have come to you through God's laws? 3. Moses warns Israel to be careful so they won't forget or let God's Word "slip" from their hearts. Note several things you can do to keep God's laws fresh in your heart and mind.

Responding in Prayer Ask God to give you an appreciation for his law. Pray that your faithful obedience to his law will make you a witness to others who don't yet know the privilege and freedom of obedience to him.

3 / *Deuteronomy 4:15–40*
Only God Can Save

SOMETIMES I FORGET what Christianity is all about. In the midst of Bible studies, worship services, committee meetings and service projects I end up just going through the motions. Somehow the Christian faith collapses into a set of obligations that I am required to fulfill and a set of activities that I am supposed to be doing. And then, as sunlight coming through the clouds, the central truth breaks through. I am reminded that God is a saving God, a liberating God, a God who wants freedom for his people. The passage that you are about to read is one you need to fix in your mind and read from time to time. It summarizes the central message of the Bible. God took his people from slavery in Egypt to freedom. There is no one like him. When that shift takes place in my mind, the pressure of obligation changes to gratitude and heartfelt service.

 Warming Up to God List your obligations regarding church, work and family. As you do, commit them to the Lord's keeping. Sit in quiet for a few moments and practice gratitude for the freedom that he brings to you.

 Read Deuteronomy 4:15–40.

¹⁵You saw no form of any kind the day the LORD spoke to you at Horeb out of the fire. Therefore watch yourselves very carefully, ¹⁶so that you do not become corrupt and make for yourselves an idol, an image of any shape, whether formed like a man or a woman, ¹⁷or like any animal on earth or any bird that flies in the air, ¹⁸or like any creature that moves along the ground or any fish in the waters below. ¹⁹And when you look up to the sky and see the sun, the moon and the stars—all the heavenly array—do not be enticed into bowing down to them and worshiping things the LORD your God has apportioned to all the nations under heaven. ²⁰But as for you, the LORD took you and brought you out of the iron-smelting furnace, out of Egypt, to be the people of his inheritance, as you now are.

²¹The LORD was angry with me because of you, and he solemnly swore that I would not cross the Jordan and enter the good land the LORD your God is giving you as your inheritance. ²²I will die in this land; I will not cross the Jordan; but you are about to cross over and take possession of that good land. ²³Be careful not to forget the covenant of the LORD your God that he made with you; do not make for yourselves an idol in the form of anything the LORD your God has forbidden. ²⁴For the LORD your God is a consuming fire, a jealous God.

²⁵After you have had children and grandchildren and have lived in the land a long time—if you then become corrupt and make any kind of idol, doing evil in the eyes of the LORD your God and provoking him to anger, ²⁶I call heaven and earth as witnesses against you this day that you will quickly perish from the land that you are crossing the Jordan to possess. You will not live there long but will certainly be destroyed. ²⁷The

LORD will scatter you among the peoples, and only a few of you will survive among the nations to which the LORD will drive you. 28There you will worship man-made gods of wood and stone, which cannot see or hear or eat or smell. 29But if from there you seek the LORD your God, you will find him if you look for him with all your heart and with all your soul. 30When you are in distress and all these things have happened to you, then in later days you will return to the LORD your God and obey him. 31For the LORD your God is a merciful God; he will not abandon or destroy you or forget the covenant with your forefathers, which he confirmed to them by oath.

32Ask now about the former days, long before your time, from the day God created man on the earth; ask from one end of the heavens to the other. Has anything so great as this ever happened, or has anything like it ever been heard of? 33Has any other people heard the voice of God[h] speaking out of fire, as you have, and lived? 34Has any god ever tried to take for himself one nation out of another nation, by testings, by miraculous signs and wonders, by war, by a mighty hand and

an outstretched arm, or by great and awesome deeds, like all the things the LORD your God did for you in Egypt before your very eyes?

35You were shown these things so that you might know that the LORD is God; besides him there is no other. 36From heaven he made you hear his voice to discipline you. On earth he showed you his great fire, and you heard his words from out of the fire. 37Because he loved your forefathers and chose their descendants after them, he brought you out of Egypt by his Presence and his great strength, 38to drive out before you nations greater and stronger than you and to bring you into their land to give it to you for your inheritance, as it is today.

39Acknowledge and take to heart this day that the LORD is God in heaven above and on the earth below. There is no other. 40Keep his decrees and commands, which I am giving you today, so that it may go well with you and your children after you and that you may live long in the land the LORD your God gives you for all time.

[h]33 Or of a god

 Discovering the Word 1. What different types of idolatry are the people warned against (vv. 15–31)? 2. What are the results of idolatry (vv. 21–31)? 3. Look at verses 32–38. What had God done to achieve Israel's salvation? 4. What response should Israel have to God's saving work (vv. 35, 39–40)? 5. What benefits will come to the people if they take this admonition to heart (vv. 37–40)?

Applying the Word 1. Israel's salvation was deliverance from slavery. A Christian's salvation is deliverance from sin. How is God's power at work in both? 2. For Israel, one of the gifts coming with their salvation was the Promised Land. What are some of the benefits that come to Christians through Christ's achievement of salvation on the cross? 3. What can you do to keep from taking your salvation for granted as Israel was in danger of doing?

Responding in Prayer Ask God to give you a heart of gratitude for his saving work in Jesus Christ. Pray that you would grow in your exclusive commitment to him and responsiveness to his leading and law.

Deuteronomy 4:41–49

41Then Moses set aside three cities east of the Jordan, 42to which anyone who had killed a person could flee if he had unintentionally killed his neighbor without malice aforethought. He could flee into one of these cities and save his life. 43The cities were these: Bezer in the desert plateau, for the Reubenites; Ramoth in Gilead, for the Gadites; and Golan in Bashan, for the Manassites.

44This is the law Moses set before the Israelites. 45These are the stipulations, decrees and laws Moses gave them when they came out of Egypt 46and were in the valley near Beth Peor east of the Jordan, in the land of Sihon king of the Amorites, who reigned in Heshbon and was defeated by Moses and the Israelites as they came out of Egypt. 47They took possession of his land and the land of

Og king of Bashan, the two Amorite kings east of the Jordan. ⁴⁸This land extended from Aroer on the rim of the Arnon Gorge to Mount Siyon[i] (that is, Hermon), ⁴⁹and included all the Arabah east of the Jordan, as far as the Sea of the Arabah,[j] below the slopes of Pisgah.

ⁱ48 Hebrew, Syriac (see also Deut. 3:9) *Sirion*   ^j49 That is, the Dead Sea

---

4 / *Deuteronomy 5*
Keeping God at a Distance

ONE OF THE most memorable passages for me in C. S. Lewis's Chronicles of Narnia comes in the first book, *The Lion, the Witch and the Wardrobe*. When Peter, Susan and Lucy first hear about Aslan, the lion Lord of Narnia, they experience a thrill of fear. One of the children asks if Aslan's "safe." The answer is "No, he's not safe, but he's good."

With those words Lewis captures the heart of the passage you are about to read. As God reveals his glory at Mount Sinai, his voice thunders the Ten Commandments, and the top of the mountain is ablaze with fire. The response of the people, appropriately, is fear. But God is interested in creating a special kind of fear, a fear that is afraid of evil and disobedience and is respectfully desirous of doing good. The writer of Proverbs summarizes it this way, "The fear of the LORD is the beginning of knowledge" (1:7).

 Warming Up to God Approaching God creates a variety of heart responses. Often we experience a sense of gratitude. And, frequently, we should have a sense of awe and respect. Pause now to consider the expanse of the galaxies and the brutality of Christ's cross. Write down any responses you have.

Read Deuteronomy 5.

---

5 Moses summoned all Israel and said:
Hear, O Israel, the decrees and laws I declare in your hearing today. Learn them and be sure to follow them. ²The LORD our God made a covenant with us at Horeb. ³It was not with our fathers that the LORD made this covenant, but with us, with all of us who are alive here today. ⁴The LORD spoke to you face to face out of the fire on the mountain. ⁵(At that time I stood between the LORD and you to declare to you the word of the LORD, because you were afraid of the fire and did not go up the mountain.) And he said:

> ⁶"I am the LORD your God, who brought you out of Egypt, out of the land of slavery.
>
> ⁷"You shall have no other gods before[k] me.
>
> ⁸"You shall not make for yourself an idol in the form of anything in heaven above or on the earth beneath or in the waters below. ⁹You shall not bow down to them or worship them; for I, the LORD your God, am a jealous God, punishing the children for the sin of the fathers to the third and fourth generation of

> those who hate me, ¹⁰but showing love to a thousand ⌊generations⌋ of those who love me and keep my commandments.
>
> ¹¹"You shall not misuse the name of the LORD your God, for the LORD will not hold anyone guiltless who misuses his name.
>
> ¹²"Observe the Sabbath day by keeping it holy, as the LORD your God has commanded you. ¹³Six days you shall labor and do all your work, ¹⁴but the seventh day is a Sabbath to the LORD your God. On it you shall not do any work, neither you, nor your son or daughter, nor your manservant or maidservant, nor your ox, your donkey or any of your animals, nor the alien within your gates, so that your manservant and maidservant may rest, as you do. ¹⁵Remember that you were slaves in Egypt and that the LORD your God brought you out of there with a mighty hand and an outstretched arm. Therefore the

^k7 Or *besides*

LORD your God has commanded you to observe the Sabbath day.

16"Honor your father and your mother, as the LORD your God has commanded you, so that you may live long and that it may go well with you in the land the LORD your God is giving you.

17"You shall not murder.

18"You shall not commit adultery.

19"You shall not steal.

20"You shall not give false testimony against your neighbor.

21"You shall not covet your neighbor's wife. You shall not set your desire on your neighbor's house or land, his manservant or maidservant, his ox or donkey, or anything that belongs to your neighbor."

22These are the commandments the LORD proclaimed in a loud voice to your whole assembly there on the mountain from out of the fire, the cloud and the deep darkness; and he added nothing more. Then he wrote them on two stone tablets and gave them to me. 23When you heard the voice out of the darkness, while the mountain was ablaze with fire, all the leading men of your tribes and your elders came to me. 24And you said, "The LORD our God has shown us his glory and his majesty, and we have heard his voice from the fire. Today we have seen that a man can live even if God speaks with him. 25But now, why should we die? This great fire will consume us, and we will die if we hear the voice of the LORD our God any longer. 26For what mortal man has ever heard the voice of the living God speaking out of fire, as we have, and survived? 27Go near and listen to all that the LORD our God says. Then tell us whatever the LORD our God tells you. We will listen and obey."

28The LORD heard you when you spoke to me and the LORD said to me, "I have heard what this people said to you. Everything they said was good. 29Oh, that their hearts would be inclined to fear me and keep all my commands always, so that it might go well with them and their children forever!

30"Go, tell them to return to their tents. 31But you stay here with me so that I may give you all the commands, decrees and laws you are to teach them to follow in the land I am giving them to possess."

32So be careful to do what the LORD your God has commanded you; do not turn aside to the right or to the left. 33Walk in all the way that the LORD your God has commanded you, so that you may live and prosper and prolong your days in the land that you will possess.

Discovering the Word 1. What positive and negative aspects of fear run through these verses? 2. Note the response of the people in verses 23–27. Why do you think the experience of receiving the law produced such fear? 3. In response to the law, what role is Moses given by the people (vv. 24–27)? 4. According to verses 28–29, how does God feel about the suggestion of the Israelite leaders regarding Moses' role? 5. What benefits are to come to the nation from living by the law?

Applying the Word 1. How can the fear of the Lord be a positive influence in your life and conduct? 2. In what way may the fear of the Lord be a problem for you that keeps you from spending time with him? 3. In Jesus Christ we no longer come to God through a mediator. How does this encourage a more personal relationship with him than the people had in the Old Testament?

Responding in Prayer Ask God to give you the courage to seek his presence, and then spend some time in quiet worship. Pray that the fear of the Lord would be a helpful presence in guiding your heartfelt obedience.

5 / *Deuteronomy 6*
Loving and Fearing the Law Giver

WHILE KNOWLEDGE BEGINS with the fear of the Lord (Pr 1:7), it is not the end. Fearing God goes hand-in-hand with heartfelt love. Yet this fact often slips from our minds and hearts. What we need to fix in our minds as firmly as we can is that God loves us, and he wants us to love him. The Scriptures are the tool that he has given us to keep our hearts alive. They are to be logs on the hearth of hearts feeding the flame of devotion. As we read the record of his loving acts as recorded in Scripture, we are to be reminded that he is the God who saves us from our chains and provides abundantly for our needs.

 Warming Up to God   God deserves our love. From the cross of Jesus Christ to the food that you have eaten today, make a record of things to be grateful for. Offer your praise to the Lord from that list. Ask him to breathe life into the embers of your heart. Sit with him and cultivate a quiet that is filled with heartfelt affection.

📖 **Read Deuteronomy 6.**

6 These are the commands, decrees and laws the Lord your God directed me to teach you to observe in the land that you are crossing the Jordan to possess, ²so that you, your children and their children after them may fear the Lord your God as long as you live by keeping all his decrees and commands that I give you, and so that you may enjoy long life. ³Hear, O Israel, and be careful to obey so that it may go well with you and that you may increase greatly in a land flowing with milk and honey, just as the Lord, the God of your fathers, promised you.

⁴Hear, O Israel: The Lord our God, the Lord is one.¹ ⁵Love the Lord your God with all your heart and with all your soul and with all your strength. ⁶These commandments that I give you today are to be upon your hearts. ⁷Impress them on your children. Talk about them when you sit at home and when you walk along the road, when you lie down and when you get up. ⁸Tie them as symbols on your hands and bind them on your foreheads. ⁹Write them on the doorframes of your houses and on your gates.

¹⁰When the Lord your God brings you into the land he swore to your fathers, to Abraham, Isaac and Jacob, to give you—a land with large, flourishing cities you did not build, ¹¹houses filled with all kinds of good things you did not provide, wells you did not dig, and vineyards and olive groves you did not plant—then when you eat and are satisfied, ¹²be careful that you do not forget the Lord, who brought you out of Egypt, out of the land of slavery.

¹³Fear the Lord your God, serve him only and take your oaths in his name. ¹⁴Do not follow other gods, the gods of the peoples around you; ¹⁵for the Lord your God, who is among you, is a jealous God and his anger will burn against you, and he will destroy you from the face of the land. ¹⁶Do not test the Lord your God as you did at Massah. ¹⁷Be sure to keep the commands of the Lord your God and the stipulations and decrees he has given you. ¹⁸Do what is right and good in the Lord's sight, so that it may go well with you and you may go in and take over the good land that the Lord promised on oath to your forefathers, ¹⁹thrusting out all your enemies before you, as the Lord said.

²⁰In the future, when your son asks you, "What is the meaning of the stipulations, decrees and laws the Lord our God has commanded you?" ²¹tell him: "We were slaves of Pharaoh in Egypt, but the Lord brought us out of Egypt with a mighty hand. ²²Before our eyes the Lord sent miraculous signs and wonders—great and terrible—upon Egypt and Pharaoh and his whole household. ²³But he brought us out from there to bring us in and give us the land that he promised on oath to our forefathers. ²⁴The Lord commanded us to obey all these decrees and to fear the Lord our God, so that we might always prosper and be kept alive, as is the case today. ²⁵And if we are careful to obey all this law before the Lord our God, as he has commanded us, that will be our righteousness."

¹4 Or *The Lord our God is one Lord*; or *The Lord is our God, the Lord is one*; or *The Lord is our God, the Lord alone*

Discovering the Word 1. How are both fear and love important motivations in these verses? 2. How is love of the Lord to affect the way children are to be raised in the new land (vv. 4–9)? 3. What is the difference between passing the law on out of obligation and passing it on out of love? 4. What dangers will the Israelites face, and how will the fear of the Lord be helpful (vv. 10–19)? 5. How will the law be an aid in keeping the memory of God's salvation fresh (vv. 20–25)?

Applying the Word 1. Love for God was to be passed on from generation to generation. What attitudes have you picked up toward God from your parents? (If you are a parent, consider as well what attitudes toward God you are passing on to your children.) 2. Consider your own motivations. In what areas do you live by God's law out of obligation and in what ways do you follow God's law because of your affection for him? 3. The Israelites were to be careful not to take God's gift of the new land for granted. What do you tend to take for granted about God's saving work in your life?

Responding in Prayer Ask God to help you grow in a love-filled faith. Pray that the members of your church would pass on a love for God from adults to children.

6 / *Deuteronomy 7*
Being a Holy People

STEPPING ACROSS THE border from the U.S. to Mexico or getting off a plane at Heathrow airport in London, you know that you are in a different country. Expressed in the difference in clothes and architecture are attitudes, values and beliefs which make each country unique. And behind all the differences is the way God or a god is worshiped. In the midst of the cultural and racial mix of the Middle East God wanted to make his people distinct. God set up firm limits as if to say to his children, "We don't do that in our family." In their customs, relationships, government and religion they were to be a distinct people of freedom, salvation and liberation for all the world to see.

 Warming Up to God How do your experiences of worship, both on Sunday morning at church and on your own, affect the way you live?

 Read Deuteronomy 7.

7 When the LORD your God brings you into the land you are entering to possess and drives out before you many nations—the Hittites, Girgashites, Amorites, Canaanites, Perizzites, Hivites and Jebusites, seven nations larger and stronger than you— ²and when the LORD your God has delivered them over to you and you have defeated them, then you must destroy them totally.*m* Make no treaty with them, and show them no mercy. ³Do not intermarry with them. Do not give your daughters to their sons or take their daughters for your sons, ⁴for they will turn your sons away from following me to serve other gods, and the LORD's anger will burn against you and will quickly destroy you. ⁵This is what you are to do to them: Break down their altars, smash their sacred stones, cut down their Asherah poles*n* and burn their idols in the fire. ⁶For you are a people holy to the LORD your God. The LORD your God has chosen you out of all the peoples on the face of the earth to be his people, his treasured possession.

⁷The LORD did not set his affection on you and choose you because you were more numerous than other peoples, for you were the fewest of all peoples. ⁸But it was because the LORD loved you and kept the oath he swore to your forefathers that he brought you out with a mighty hand and redeemed you from the land of slavery, from the power of Pharaoh king of Egypt. ⁹Know therefore that the LORD your God is God; he is the faithful God, keeping his covenant of love to a thousand generations of those who love him and keep his commands. ¹⁰But

those who hate him he will repay to their face
by destruction;

*m2 The Hebrew term refers to the irrevocable giving over of things or persons to the LORD, often by totally destroying them; also in verse 26.
n5 That is, symbols of the goddess Asherah; here and elsewhere in Deuteronomy*

he will not be slow to repay to their face
    those who hate him.

¹¹Therefore, take care to follow the commands, decrees and laws I give you today.

¹²If you pay attention to these laws and are careful to follow them, then the LORD your God will keep his covenant of love with you, as he swore to your forefathers. ¹³He will love you and bless you and increase your numbers. He will bless the fruit of your womb, the crops of your land—your grain, new wine and oil—the calves of your herds and the lambs of your flocks in the land that he swore to your forefathers to give you. ¹⁴You will be blessed more than any other people; none of your men or women will be childless, nor any of your livestock without young. ¹⁵The LORD will keep you free from every disease. He will not inflict on you the horrible diseases you knew in Egypt, but he will inflict them on all who hate you. ¹⁶You must destroy all the peoples the LORD your God gives over to you. Do not look on them with pity and do not serve their gods, for that will be a snare to you.

¹⁷You may say to yourselves, "These nations are stronger than we are. How can we drive them out?" ¹⁸But do not be afraid of them; remember well what the LORD your God did to Pharaoh and to all Egypt. ¹⁹You saw with your own eyes the great trials, the miraculous signs and wonders, the mighty hand and outstretched arm, with which the LORD your God brought you out. The LORD your God will do the same to all the peoples you now fear. ²⁰Moreover, the LORD your God will send the hornet among them until even the survivors who hide from you have perished. ²¹Do not be terrified by them, for the LORD your God, who is among you, is a great and awesome God. ²²The LORD your God will drive out those nations before you, little by little. You will not be allowed to eliminate them all at once, or the wild animals will multiply around you. ²³But the LORD your God will deliver them over to you, throwing them into great confusion until they are destroyed. ²⁴He will give their kings into your hand, and you will wipe out their names from under heaven. No one will be able to stand up against you; you will destroy them. ²⁵The images of their gods you are to burn in the fire. Do not covet the silver and gold on them, and do not take it for yourselves, or you will be ensnared by it, for it is detestable to the LORD your God. ²⁶Do not bring a detestable thing into your house or you, like it, will be set apart for destruction. Utterly abhor and detest it, for it is set apart for destruction.

Discovering the Word 1. What obligations come to Israel in its special relationship with God? 2. From these verses, how would you define the word *holy*? 3. Intermarriage was forbidden and destruction of foreign altars was required (vv. 1–7). Why would you think these instructions are so harsh and uncompromising? 4. Israel is told that they have a special relationship with God (v. 6). How does Moses seek to deal with the potential danger of national arrogance (vv. 7–11)? 5. What blessings come with keeping these laws (vv. 12–26)?

Applying the Word 1. How do you seek to be separate from ungodly forms of worship and behavior? 2. What are some sources of temptation that cause you to turn from the Lord? 3. As Christians, we are also God's chosen people. How is this a cause for both gratitude and humility?

Responding in Prayer Ask the Lord to teach you what it means to be *in* but not *of* the world. Ask God to make your church a place where people feel special and important in Christ.

---

7 / *Deuteronomy 8*
Remembering to Be Grateful

I HAVE A houseful of stuff now, but I can remember when I could put everything I owned in the trunk and back seat of my car. I had some good times in those student days, but I am having some good times now too. I suppose the real difference is that I've got more to be thankful for. I wonder if the depth of my gratitude has kept pace with the increase in God's blessings? I don't think so. Gratitude is a skill that requires disciplined cultivation throughout our lives. After all, God continues to give and give. Shouldn't we continue to say we appreciate it?

Warming Up to God Considering your current state of spiritual gratitude in comparison to the blessings you have been given, how would you rate yourself? After you have done that, make a list of as many things as you can to thank God for.

 Read Deuteronomy 8.

8 Be careful to follow every command I am giving you today, so that you may live and increase and may enter and possess the land that the LORD promised on oath to your forefathers. ²Remember how the LORD your God led you all the way in the desert these forty years, to humble you and to test you in order to know what was in your heart, whether or not you would keep his commands. ³He humbled you, causing you to hunger and then feeding you with manna, which neither you nor your fathers had known, to teach you that man does not live on bread alone but on every word that comes from the mouth of the LORD. ⁴Your clothes did not wear out and your feet did not swell during these forty years. ⁵Know then in your heart that as a man disciplines his son, so the LORD your God disciplines you.

⁶Observe the commands of the LORD your God, walking in his ways and revering him. ⁷For the LORD your God is bringing you into a good land— a land with streams and pools of water, with springs flowing in the valleys and hills; ⁸a land with wheat and barley, vines and fig trees, pomegranates, olive oil and honey; ⁹a land where bread will not be scarce and you will lack nothing; a land where the rocks are iron and you can dig copper out of the hills.

¹⁰When you have eaten and are satisfied, praise the LORD your God for the good land he has given you. ¹¹Be careful that you do not forget the LORD your God, failing to observe his commands, his laws and his decrees that I am giving you this day. ¹²Otherwise, when you eat and are satisfied, when you build fine houses and settle down, ¹³and when your herds and flocks grow large and your silver and gold increase and all you have is multiplied, ¹⁴then your heart will become proud and you will forget the LORD your God, who brought you out of Egypt, out of the land of slavery. ¹⁵He led you through the vast and dreadful desert, that thirsty and waterless land, with its venomous snakes and scorpions. He brought you water out of hard rock. ¹⁶He gave you manna to eat in the desert, something your fathers had never known, to humble and to test you so that in the end it might go well with you. ¹⁷You may say to yourself, "My power and the strength of my hands have produced this wealth for me." ¹⁸But remember the LORD your God, for it is he who gives you the ability to produce wealth, and so confirms his covenant, which he swore to your forefathers, as it is today.

¹⁹If you ever forget the LORD your God and follow other gods and worship and bow down to them, I testify against you today that you will surely be destroyed. ²⁰Like the nations the LORD destroyed before you, so you will be destroyed for not obeying the LORD your God.

Discovering the Word 1. Summarize what Israel needs to know to continually enjoy the fruits of the Promised Land. 2. Describe the character of God's discipline (vv. 1–5). 3. How might the discipline of God have prepared Israel for living in the Promised Land? 4. Why was the testing and waiting in the wilderness worth the wait (vv. 6–9)? 5. What were the dangers to be faced in the Promised Land (vv. 10–18)? 6. Describe the relationship between forgetfulness and disobedience (vv. 19–20).

Applying the Word 1. While God disciplined and tested Israel, he also provided for "daily bread" during their time of testing. How has God provided for you during times of testing? 2. After God's time of testing, he brought Israel into the blessing of the Promised Land. What parallels can you draw to your own experience of God's leading in your life?

 Responding in Prayer Ask God to give you a grateful heart that trusts and obeys in the times of blessing and testing.

Deuteronomy 9—11

9 Hear, O Israel. You are now about to cross the Jordan to go in and dispossess nations greater and stronger than you, with large cities that have walls up to the sky. ²The people are strong and tall—Anakites! You know about them and have heard it said: "Who can stand up against the Anakites?" ³But be assured today that the LORD your God is the one who goes across ahead of you like a devouring fire. He will destroy them; he will subdue them before you. And you will drive them out and annihilate them quickly, as the LORD has promised you.

⁴After the LORD your God has driven them out before you, do not say to yourself, "The LORD has brought me here to take possession of this land because of my righteousness." No, it is on account of the wickedness of these nations that the LORD is going to drive them out before you. ⁵It is not because of your righteousness or your integrity that you are going in to take possession of their land; but on account of the wickedness of these nations, the LORD your God will drive them out before you, to accomplish what he swore to your fathers, to Abraham, Isaac and Jacob. ⁶Understand, then, that it is not because of your righteousness that the LORD your God is giving you this good land to possess, for you are a stiff-necked people.

⁷Remember this and never forget how you provoked the LORD your God to anger in the desert. From the day you left Egypt until you arrived here, you have been rebellious against the LORD. ⁸At Horeb you aroused the LORD's wrath so that he was angry enough to destroy you. ⁹When I went up on the mountain to receive the tablets of stone, the tablets of the covenant that the LORD had made with you, I stayed on the mountain forty days and forty nights; I ate no bread and drank no water. ¹⁰The LORD gave me two stone tablets inscribed by the finger of God. On them were all the commandments the LORD proclaimed to you on the mountain out of the fire, on the day of the assembly.

¹¹At the end of the forty days and forty nights, the LORD gave me the two stone tablets, the tablets of the covenant. ¹²Then the LORD told me, "Go down from here at once, because your people whom you brought out of Egypt have become corrupt. They have turned away quickly from what I commanded them and have made a cast idol for themselves."

¹³And the LORD said to me, "I have seen this people, and they are a stiff-necked people indeed! ¹⁴Let me alone, so that I may destroy them and blot out their name from under heaven. And I will make you into a nation stronger and more numerous than they."

¹⁵So I turned and went down from the mountain while it was ablaze with fire. And the two tablets of the covenant were in my hands.ᵒ ¹⁶When I looked, I saw that you had sinned against the LORD your God; you had made for yourselves an idol cast in the shape of a calf. You had turned aside quickly from the way that the LORD had commanded you. ¹⁷So I took the two tablets and threw them out of my hands, breaking them to pieces before your eyes.

¹⁸Then once again I fell prostrate before the LORD for forty days and forty nights; I ate no bread and drank no water, because of all the sin you had committed, doing what was evil in the LORD's sight and so provoking him to anger. ¹⁹I feared the anger and wrath of the LORD, for he was angry enough with you to destroy you. But again the LORD listened to me. ²⁰And the LORD was angry enough with Aaron to destroy him, but at that time I prayed for Aaron too. ²¹Also I took that sinful thing of yours, the calf you had made, and burned it in the fire. Then I crushed it and ground it to powder as fine as dust and threw the dust into a stream that flowed down the mountain.

²²You also made the LORD angry at Taberah, at Massah and at Kibroth Hattaavah.

²³And when the LORD sent you out from Kadesh Barnea, he said, "Go up and take possession of the land I have given you." But you rebelled against the command of the LORD your God. You did not trust him or obey him. ²⁴You have been rebellious against the LORD ever since I have known you.

²⁵I lay prostrate before the LORD those forty days and forty nights because the LORD had said he would destroy you. ²⁶I prayed to the LORD and said, "O Sovereign LORD, do not destroy your peo-

ᵒ15 Or And I had the two tablets of the covenant with me, one in each hand ple, your own inheritance that you redeemed by your great power and brought out of Egypt with a mighty hand. 27Remember your servants Abraham, Isaac and Jacob. Overlook the stubbornness of this people, their wickedness and their sin. 28Otherwise, the country from which you brought us will say, 'Because the LORD was not able to take them into the land he had promised them, and because he hated them, he brought them out to put them to death in the desert.' 29But they are your people, your inheritance that you brought out by your great power and your outstretched arm."

10 At that time the LORD said to me, "Chisel out two stone tablets like the first ones and come up to me on the mountain. Also make a wooden chest.p 2I will write on the tablets the words that were on the first tablets, which you broke. Then you are to put them in the chest."

3So I made the ark out of acacia wood and chiseled out two stone tablets like the first ones, and I went up on the mountain with the two tablets in my hands. 4The LORD wrote on these tablets what he had written before, the Ten Commandments he had proclaimed to you on the mountain, out of the fire, on the day of the assembly. And the LORD gave them to me. 5Then I came back down the mountain and put the tablets in the ark I had made, as the LORD commanded me, and they are there now.

6(The Israelites traveled from the wells of the Jaakanites to Moserah. There Aaron died and was buried, and Eleazar his son succeeded him as priest. 7From there they traveled to Gudgodah and on to Jotbathah, a land with streams of water. 8At that time the LORD set apart the tribe of Levi to carry the ark of the covenant of the LORD, to stand before the LORD to minister and to pronounce blessings in his name, as they still do today. 9That is why the Levites have no share or inheritance among their brothers; the LORD is their inheritance, as the LORD your God told them.)

10Now I had stayed on the mountain forty days and nights, as I did the first time, and the LORD listened to me at this time also. It was not his will to destroy you. 11"Go," the LORD said to me, "and lead the people on their way, so that they may enter and possess the land that I swore to their fathers to give them."

12And now, O Israel, what does the LORD your God ask of you but to fear the LORD your God, to walk in all his ways, to love him, to serve the LORD your God with all your heart and with all your soul, 13and to observe the LORD's commands and decrees that I am giving you today for your own good?

14To the LORD your God belong the heavens, even the highest heavens, the earth and everything in it. 15Yet the LORD set his affection on your forefathers and loved them, and he chose you, their descendants, above all the nations, as it is today. 16Circumcise your hearts, therefore, and do not be stiff-necked any longer. 17For the LORD your God is God of gods and Lord of lords, the great God, mighty and awesome, who shows no partiality and accepts no bribes. 18He defends the cause of the fatherless and the widow, and loves the alien, giving him food and clothing. 19And you are to love those who are aliens, for you yourselves were aliens in Egypt. 20Fear the LORD your God and serve him. Hold fast to him and take your oaths in his name. 21He is your praise; he is your God, who performed for you those great and awesome wonders you saw with your own eyes. 22Your forefathers who went down into Egypt were seventy in all, and now the LORD your God has made you as numerous as the stars in the sky.

11 Love the LORD your God and keep his requirements, his decrees, his laws and his commands always. 2Remember today that your children were not the ones who saw and experienced the discipline of the LORD your God: his majesty, his mighty hand, his outstretched arm; 3the signs he performed and the things he did in the heart of Egypt, both to Pharaoh king of Egypt and to his whole country; 4what he did to the Egyptian army, to its horses and chariots, how he overwhelmed them with the waters of the Red Seaq as they were pursuing you, and how the LORD brought lasting ruin on them. 5It was not your children who saw what he did for you in the desert until you arrived at this place, 6and what he did to Dathan and Abiram, sons of Eliab the Reubenite, when the earth opened its mouth right in the middle of all Israel and swallowed them up with their households, their tents and every living thing that belonged to them. 7But it was your own eyes that saw all these great things the LORD has done.

8Observe therefore all the commands I am giv-

p1 That is, an ark   q4 Hebrew *Yam Suph*; that is, Sea of Reeds ing you today, so that you may have the strength to go in and take over the land that you are crossing the Jordan to possess, ⁹and so that you may live long in the land that the LORD swore to your forefathers to give to them and their descendants, a land flowing with milk and honey. ¹⁰The land you are entering to take over is not like the land of Egypt, from which you have come, where you planted your seed and irrigated it by foot as in a vegetable garden. ¹¹But the land you are crossing the Jordan to take possession of is a land of mountains and valleys that drinks rain from heaven. ¹²It is a land the LORD your God cares for; the eyes of the LORD your God are continually on it from the beginning of the year to its end.

¹³So if you faithfully obey the commands I am giving you today—to love the LORD your God and to serve him with all your heart and with all your soul— ¹⁴then I will send rain on your land in its season, both autumn and spring rains, so that you may gather in your grain, new wine and oil. ¹⁵I will provide grass in the fields for your cattle, and you will eat and be satisfied.

¹⁶Be careful, or you will be enticed to turn away and worship other gods and bow down to them. ¹⁷Then the LORD's anger will burn against you, and he will shut the heavens so that it will not rain and the ground will yield no produce, and you will soon perish from the good land the LORD is giving you. ¹⁸Fix these words of mine in your hearts and minds; tie them as symbols on your hands and bind them on your foreheads. ¹⁹Teach them to your children, talking about them when you sit at home and when you walk along the road, when you lie down and when you get up. ²⁰Write them on the doorframes of your houses and on your gates, ²¹so that your days and the days of your children may be many in the land

that the LORD swore to give your forefathers, as many as the days that the heavens are above the earth.

²²If you carefully observe all these commands I am giving you to follow—to love the LORD your God, to walk in all his ways and to hold fast to him— ²³then the LORD will drive out all these nations before you, and you will dispossess nations larger and stronger than you. ²⁴Every place where you set your foot will be yours: Your territory will extend from the desert to Lebanon, and from the Euphrates River to the western sea.ʳ ²⁵No man will be able to stand against you. The LORD your God, as he promised you, will put the terror and fear of you on the whole land, wherever you go.

²⁶See, I am setting before you today a blessing and a curse— ²⁷the blessing if you obey the commands of the LORD your God that I am giving you today; ²⁸the curse if you disobey the commands of the LORD your God and turn from the way that I command you today by following other gods, which you have not known. ²⁹When the LORD your God has brought you into the land you are entering to possess, you are to proclaim on Mount Gerizim the blessings, and on Mount Ebal the curses. ³⁰As you know, these mountains are across the Jordan, west of the road,ˢ toward the setting sun, near the great trees of Moreh, in the territory of those Canaanites living in the Arabah in the vicinity of Gilgal. ³¹You are about to cross the Jordan to enter and take possession of the land the LORD your God is giving you. When you have taken it over and are living there, ³²be sure that you obey all the decrees and laws I am setting before you today.

ʳ24 That is, the Mediterranean   ˢ30 Or *Jordan, westward*

8 / *Deuteronomy 12:1–14*
One Place of Worship

VISIT LONDON AND two of the "must sees" are Westminster Abbey and St. Paul's Cathedral. In Paris Notre Dame will be on your sightseeing list. And a cathedral will be on your tour of many other major cities in Europe. Wandering through these huge buildings with their myriad statues, soaring arches and rainbow-colored windows, you may pause to consider what motivated such massive efforts of religious construction. Why is it that some continue to serve living communities of faith and others are only museums? A place of worship embodies the values, beliefs and practices that unify a people and contributes to their formation as a community.

Warming Up to God How does your church building contribute to (or hinder) your experience of worship?

Read Deuteronomy 12:1–14.

12 These are the decrees and laws you must be careful to follow in the land that the LORD, the God of your fathers, has given you to possess—as long as you live in the land. ²Destroy completely all the places on the high mountains and on the hills and under every spreading tree where the nations you are dispossessing worship their gods. ³Break down their altars, smash their sacred stones and burn their Asherah poles in the fire; cut down the idols of their gods and wipe out their names from those places.

⁴You must not worship the LORD your God in their way. ⁵But you are to seek the place the LORD your God will choose from among all your tribes to put his Name there for his dwelling. To that place you must go; ⁶there bring your burnt offerings and sacrifices, your tithes and special gifts, what you have vowed to give and your free-will offerings, and the firstborn of your herds and flocks. ⁷There, in the presence of the LORD your God, you and your families shall eat and shall rejoice in everything you have put your

hand to, because the LORD your God has blessed you.

⁸You are not to do as we do here today, everyone as he sees fit, ⁹since you have not yet reached the resting place and the inheritance the LORD your God is giving you. ¹⁰But you will cross the Jordan and settle in the land the LORD your God is giving you as an inheritance, and he will give you rest from all your enemies around you so that you will live in safety. ¹¹Then to the place the LORD your God will choose as a dwelling for his Name—there you are to bring everything I command you: your burnt offerings and sacrifices, your tithes and special gifts, and all the choice possessions you have vowed to the LORD. ¹²And there rejoice before the LORD your God, you, your sons and daughters, your menservants and maidservants, and the Levites from your towns, who have no allotment or inheritance of their own. ¹³Be careful not to sacrifice your burnt offerings anywhere you please. ¹⁴Offer them only at the place the LORD will choose in one of your tribes, and there observe everything I command you.

Discovering the Word 1. How will the worship of God change after Israel enters the land? 2. What verbs are used in verses 2–3 to describe how Israel is to treat the worship centers of the Canaanite gods? What's the point? 3. From verses 7 and 12 describe the tone of a typical worship experience in the land. 4. How would the plan for worship described here be superior to the current practices—"everyone as he sees fit" (v. 8)? 5. What limitations would having a national worship center place on the frequency and style of the worship in Israel? 6. What benefits and protection might a central place of worship provide for Israel as they enter the land?

Applying the Word 1. Although a central place of worship was abolished with the coming of Christ, Christians still gather at church—the place which has become our worship center. What benefits do you get out of your church's worship? 2. Israel's worship was to be characterized by rejoicing in the presence of the Lord for his blessings of prosperity. How would you describe your church's worship? 3. Israel needed a centralized place of worship to counter the influence of Canaanite idolatry. What worship guidelines might you need to counter the patterns of ungodliness of our present time?

Responding in Prayer Ask God to make worship a time of gratitude and celebration in your life, and praise him for the places where Jesus Christ is worshiped that are scattered all around the world.

Deuteronomy 12:15—14:29

¹⁵Nevertheless, you may slaughter your animals in any of your towns and eat as much of the meat as you want, as if it were gazelle or deer, according to the blessing the LORD your God gives you. Both the ceremonially unclean and the clean may eat it. ¹⁶But you must not eat the blood; pour it out on the ground like water. ¹⁷You must not eat in your own towns the tithe of your grain and new wine and oil, or the firstborn of your herds and flocks, or whatever you have vowed to give, or your freewill offerings or special gifts. ¹⁸Instead, you are to eat them in the presence of the LORD your God at the place the LORD your God will choose—you, your sons and daughters, your menservants and maidservants, and the Levites from your towns—and you are to rejoice before the LORD your God in everything you put your hand to. ¹⁹Be careful not to neglect the Levites as long as you live in your land.

²⁰When the LORD your God has enlarged your territory as he promised you, and you crave meat and say, "I would like some meat," then you may eat as much of it as you want. ²¹If the place where the LORD your God chooses to put his Name is too far away from you, you may slaughter animals from the herds and flocks the LORD has given you, as I have commanded you, and in your own towns you may eat as much of them as you want. ²²Eat them as you would gazelle or deer. Both the ceremonially unclean and the clean may eat. ²³But be sure you do not eat the blood, because the blood is the life, and you must not eat the life with the meat. ²⁴You must not eat the blood; pour it out on the ground like water. ²⁵Do not eat it, so that it may go well with you and your children after you, because you will be doing what is right in the eyes of the LORD.

²⁶But take your consecrated things and whatever you have vowed to give, and go to the place the LORD will choose. ²⁷Present your burnt offerings on the altar of the LORD your God, both the meat and the blood. The blood of your sacrifices must be poured beside the altar of the LORD your God, but you may eat the meat. ²⁸Be careful to obey all these regulations I am giving you, so that it may always go well with you and your children after you, because you will be doing what is good and right in the eyes of the LORD your God.

²⁹The LORD your God will cut off before you the nations you are about to invade and dispossess. But when you have driven them out and settled in their land, ³⁰and after they have been destroyed before you, be careful not to be ensnared by inquiring about their gods, saying, "How do these nations serve their gods? We will do the same." ³¹You must not worship the LORD your God in their way, because in worshiping their gods, they do all kinds of detestable things the LORD hates. They even burn their sons and daughters in the fire as sacrifices to their gods.

³²See that you do all I command you; do not add to it or take away from it.

13 If a prophet, or one who foretells by dreams, appears among you and announces to you a miraculous sign or wonder, ²and if the sign or wonder of which he has spoken takes place, and he says, "Let us follow other gods" (gods you have not known) "and let us worship them," ³you must not listen to the words of that prophet or dreamer. The LORD your God is testing you to find out whether you love him with all your heart and with all your soul. ⁴It is the LORD your God you must follow, and him you must revere. Keep his commands and obey him; serve him and hold fast to him. ⁵That prophet or dreamer must be put to death, because he preached rebellion against the LORD your God, who brought you out of Egypt and redeemed you from the land of slavery; he has tried to turn you from the way the LORD your God commanded you to follow. You must purge the evil from among you.

⁶If your very own brother, or your son or daughter, or the wife you love, or your closest friend secretly entices you, saying, "Let us go and worship other gods" (gods that neither you nor your fathers have known, ⁷gods of the peoples around you, whether near or far, from one end of the land to the other), ⁸do not yield to him or listen to him. Show him no pity. Do not spare him or shield him. ⁹You must certainly put him to death. Your hand must be the first in putting him to death, and then the hands of all the people. ¹⁰Stone him to death, because he tried to turn you away from the LORD your God, who brought you out of Egypt, out of the land of slavery. ¹¹Then all Israel will hear and be afraid, and no one among you will do such an evil thing again.

¹²If you hear it said about one of the towns the LORD your God is giving you to live in ¹³that wicked men have arisen among you and have led the people of their town astray, saying, "Let us go and worship other gods" (gods you have not known), ¹⁴then you must inquire, probe and investigate it thoroughly. And if it is true and it has been proved that this detestable thing has been done among you, ¹⁵you must certainly put to the sword all who live in that town. Destroy it completely,ᵗ both its people and its livestock. ¹⁶Gather all the plunder of the town into the middle of the public square and completely burn the town and all its plunder as a whole burnt offering to the LORD your God. It is to remain a ruin forever, never to be rebuilt. ¹⁷None of those condemned thingsᵗ shall be found in your hands, so that the LORD will turn from his fierce anger; he will show you mercy, have compassion on you, and increase your numbers, as he promised on oath to your forefathers, ¹⁸because you obey the LORD your God, keeping all his commands that I am giving you today and doing what is right in his eyes.

14 You are the children of the LORD your God. Do not cut yourselves or shave the front of your heads for the dead, ²for you are a people holy to the LORD your God. Out of all the peoples on the face of the earth, the LORD has chosen you to be his treasured possession.

³Do not eat any detestable thing. ⁴These are the animals you may eat: the ox, the sheep, the goat, ⁵the deer, the gazelle, the roe deer, the wild goat, the ibex, the antelope and the mountain sheep.ᵘ ⁶You may eat any animal that has a split hoof divided in two and that chews the cud. ⁷However, of those that chew the cud or that have a split hoof completely divided you may not eat the camel, the rabbit or the coney.ᵛ Although they chew the cud, they do not have a split hoof; they are ceremonially unclean for you. ⁸The pig is also unclean; although it has a split hoof, it does not chew the cud. You are not to eat their meat or touch their carcasses.

⁹Of all the creatures living in the water, you may eat any that has fins and scales. ¹⁰But anything that does not have fins and scales you may not eat; for you it is unclean.

¹¹You may eat any clean bird. ¹²But these you may not eat: the eagle, the vulture, the black vulture, ¹³the red kite, the black kite, any kind of falcon, ¹⁴any kind of raven, ¹⁵the horned owl, the screech owl, the gull, any kind of hawk, ¹⁶the little owl, the great owl, the white owl, ¹⁷the desert owl, the osprey, the cormorant, ¹⁸the stork, any kind of heron, the hoopoe and the bat.

¹⁹All flying insects that swarm are unclean to you; do not eat them. ²⁰But any winged creature that is clean you may eat.

²¹Do not eat anything you find already dead. You may give it to an alien living in any of your towns, and he may eat it, or you may sell it to a foreigner. But you are a people holy to the LORD your God.

Do not cook a young goat in its mother's milk.

²²Be sure to set aside a tenth of all that your fields produce each year. ²³Eat the tithe of your grain, new wine and oil, and the firstborn of your herds and flocks in the presence of the LORD your God at the place he will choose as a dwelling for his Name, so that you may learn to revere the LORD your God always. ²⁴But if that place is too distant and you have been blessed by the LORD your God and cannot carry your tithe (because the place where the LORD will choose to put his Name is so far away), ²⁵then exchange your tithe for silver, and take the silver with you and go to the place the LORD your God will choose. ²⁶Use the silver to buy whatever you like: cattle, sheep, wine or other fermented drink, or anything you wish. Then you and your household shall eat there in the presence of the LORD your God and rejoice. ²⁷And do not neglect the Levites living in your towns, for they have no allotment or inheritance of their own.

²⁸At the end of every three years, bring all the tithes of that year's produce and store it in your towns, ²⁹so that the Levites (who have no allotment or inheritance of their own) and the aliens, the fatherless and the widows who live in your towns may come and eat and be satisfied, and so that the LORD your God may bless you in all the work of your hands.

ᵗ15,17 The Hebrew term refers to the irrevocable giving over of things or persons to the LORD, often by totally destroying them.   ᵘ5 The precise identification of some of the birds and animals in this chapter is uncertain.   ᵛ7 That is, the hyrax or rock badger

9 / *Deuteronomy 15:1–11*
The Year of Freedom

IT SEEMS LIKE every couple of nights I get a phone call from some credit card company. They offer me the opportunity to go further into debt through the use of their card at some great interest rate. My response is "No, thanks. I'm deep enough in debt as it is." No one has ever called up and offered to take the load of my debt and cancel it, no interest, no charge. It's inconceivable. Yet in ancient Israel something equivalent to that happened every seven years. Why? God's salvation is an offer of freedom—not just religious freedom, not just political freedom, but economic freedom as well.

 Warming Up to God Jesus teaches us to pray, "Give us this day our daily bread." What difference would it make in your attitude toward your work today if you didn't feel that earning your living was totally up to you?

 Read Deuteronomy 15:1–11.

15 At the end of every seven years you must cancel debts. ²This is how it is to be done: Every creditor shall cancel the loan he has made to his fellow Israelite. He shall not require payment from his fellow Israelite or brother, because the LORD's time for canceling debts has been proclaimed. ³You may require payment from a foreigner, but you must cancel any debt your brother owes you. ⁴However, there should be no poor among you, for in the land the LORD your God is giving you to possess as your inheritance, he will richly bless you, ⁵if only you fully obey the LORD your God and are careful to follow all these commands I am giving you today. ⁶For the LORD your God will bless you as he has promised, and you will lend to many nations but will borrow from none. You will rule over many nations but none will rule over you.

⁷If there is a poor man among your brothers in any of the towns of the land that the LORD your God is giving you, do not be hardhearted or tight-fisted toward your poor brother. ⁸Rather be open-handed and freely lend him whatever he needs. ⁹Be careful not to harbor this wicked thought: "The seventh year, the year for canceling debts, is near," so that you do not show ill will toward your needy brother and give him nothing. He may then appeal to the LORD against you, and you will be found guilty of sin. ¹⁰Give generously to him and do so without a grudging heart; then because of this the LORD your God will bless you in all your work and in everything you put your hand to. ¹¹There will always be poor people in the land. Therefore I command you to be open-handed toward your brothers and toward the poor and needy in your land.

Discovering the Word 1. What provisions are being made for the poor after they enter the land? 2. Note the colorful words in verses 7–10 which describe those who refuse to follow this law. What attitude does Moses want to see among the citizens of the land? 3. What provision is made for those who would seek to avoid the spirit of this law (vv. 8–9)? 4. Moses sets high standards, yet he is also realistic. How would you explain the apparent conflict between verses 4 and 11?

Applying the Word 1. What is there about the intent of this law that could be applied in your country? 2. What is there about the intent of this law that could be applied in the church? 3. How will the spirit of these economic principles make a difference in the way that you use your money?

Responding in Prayer Pray for those who have financial needs in your church. Ask God to touch the hearts of members of your church to be a help to them. Pray for those who have adequate financial resources, that they would be willing to be an aid and resource for those in need.

Deuteronomy 15:12—23:14

¹²If a fellow Hebrew, a man or a woman, sells himself to you and serves you six years, in the seventh year you must let him go free. ¹³And when you release him, do not send him away empty-handed. ¹⁴Supply him liberally from your flock, your threshing floor and your winepress. Give to him as the LORD your God has blessed you. ¹⁵Remember that you were slaves in Egypt and the LORD your God redeemed you. That is why I give you this command today.

¹⁶But if your servant says to you, "I do not want to leave you," because he loves you and your family and is well off with you, ¹⁷then take an awl and push it through his ear lobe into the door, and he will become your servant for life. Do the same for your maidservant.

¹⁸Do not consider it a hardship to set your servant free, because his service to you these six years has been worth twice as much as that of a hired hand. And the LORD your God will bless you in everything you do.

¹⁹Set apart for the LORD your God every firstborn male of your herds and flocks. Do not put the firstborn of your oxen to work, and do not shear the firstborn of your sheep. ²⁰Each year you and your family are to eat them in the presence of the LORD your God at the place he will choose. ²¹If an animal has a defect, is lame or blind, or has any serious flaw, you must not sacrifice it to the LORD your God. ²²You are to eat it in your own towns. Both the ceremonially unclean and the clean may eat it, as if it were gazelle or deer. ²³But you must not eat the blood; pour it out on the ground like water.

16 Observe the month of Abib and celebrate the Passover of the LORD your God, because in the month of Abib he brought you out of Egypt by night. ²Sacrifice as the Passover to the LORD your God an animal from your flock or herd at the place the LORD will choose as a dwelling for his Name. ³Do not eat it with bread made with yeast, but for seven days eat unleavened bread, the bread of affliction, because you left Egypt in haste—so that all the days of your life you may remember the time of your departure from Egypt. ⁴Let no yeast be found in your possession in all your land for seven days. Do not let any of the meat you sacrifice on the evening of the first day remain until morning.

⁵You must not sacrifice the Passover in any town the LORD your God gives you ⁶except in the place he will choose as a dwelling for his Name. There you must sacrifice the Passover in the evening, when the sun goes down, on the anniversary[w] of your departure from Egypt. ⁷Roast it and eat it at the place the LORD your God will choose. Then in the morning return to your tents. ⁸For six days eat unleavened bread and on the seventh day hold an assembly to the LORD your God and do no work.

⁹Count off seven weeks from the time you begin to put the sickle to the standing grain. ¹⁰Then celebrate the Feast of Weeks to the LORD your God by giving a freewill offering in proportion to the blessings the LORD your God has given you. ¹¹And rejoice before the LORD your God at the place he will choose as a dwelling for his Name— you, your sons and daughters, your menservants and maidservants, the Levites in your towns, and the aliens, the fatherless and the widows living among you. ¹²Remember that you were slaves in Egypt, and follow carefully these decrees.

¹³Celebrate the Feast of Tabernacles for seven days after you have gathered the produce of your threshing floor and your winepress. ¹⁴Be joyful at your Feast—you, your sons and daughters, your menservants and maidservants, and the Levites, the aliens, the fatherless and the widows who live in your towns. ¹⁵For seven days celebrate the Feast to the LORD your God at the place the LORD will choose. For the LORD your God will bless you in all your harvest and in all the work of your hands, and your joy will be complete.

¹⁶Three times a year all your men must appear before the LORD your God at the place he will choose: at the Feast of Unleavened Bread, the Feast of Weeks and the Feast of Tabernacles. No man should appear before the LORD empty-handed: ¹⁷Each of you must bring a gift in proportion to the way the LORD your God has blessed you.

¹⁸Appoint judges and officials for each of your tribes in every town the LORD your God is giving you, and they shall judge the people fairly. ¹⁹Do not pervert justice or show partiality. Do not ac-

w 6 Or *down, at the time of day*

cept a bribe, for a bribe blinds the eyes of the wise and twists the words of the righteous. ²⁰Follow justice and justice alone, so that you may live and possess the land the LORD your God is giving you.

²¹Do not set up any wooden Asherah pole˟ beside the altar you build to the LORD your God, ²²and do not erect a sacred stone, for these the LORD your God hates.

17 Do not sacrifice to the LORD your God an ox or a sheep that has any defect or flaw in it, for that would be detestable to him.

²If a man or woman living among you in one of the towns the LORD gives you is found doing evil in the eyes of the LORD your God in violation of his covenant, ³and contrary to my command has worshiped other gods, bowing down to them or to the sun or the moon or the stars of the sky, ⁴and this has been brought to your attention, then you must investigate it thoroughly. If it is true and it has been proved that this detestable thing has been done in Israel, ⁵take the man or woman who has done this evil deed to your city gate and stone that person to death. ⁶On the testimony of two or three witnesses a man shall be put to death, but no one shall be put to death on the testimony of only one witness. ⁷The hands of the witnesses must be the first in putting him to death, and then the hands of all the people. You must purge the evil from among you.

⁸If cases come before your courts that are too difficult for you to judge—whether bloodshed, lawsuits or assaults—take them to the place the LORD your God will choose. ⁹Go to the priests, who are Levites, and to the judge who is in office at that time. Inquire of them and they will give you the verdict. ¹⁰You must act according to the decisions they give you at the place the LORD will choose. Be careful to do everything they direct you to do. ¹¹Act according to the law they teach you and the decisions they give you. Do not turn aside from what they tell you, to the right or to the left. ¹²The man who shows contempt for the judge or for the priest who stands ministering there to the LORD your God must be put to death. You must purge the evil from Israel. ¹³All the people will hear and be afraid, and will not be contemptuous again.

¹⁴When you enter the land the LORD your God is giving you and have taken possession of it and settled in it, and you say, "Let us set a king over us like all the nations around us," ¹⁵be sure to appoint over you the king the LORD your God chooses. He must be from among your own brothers. Do not place a foreigner over you, one who is not a brother Israelite. ¹⁶The king, moreover, must not acquire great numbers of horses for himself or make the people return to Egypt to get more of them, for the LORD has told you, "You are not to go back that way again." ¹⁷He must not take many wives, or his heart will be led astray. He must not accumulate large amounts of silver and gold.

¹⁸When he takes the throne of his kingdom, he is to write for himself on a scroll a copy of this law, taken from that of the priests, who are Levites. ¹⁹It is to be with him, and he is to read it all the days of his life so that he may learn to revere the LORD his God and follow carefully all the words of this law and these decrees ²⁰and not consider himself better than his brothers and turn from the law to the right or to the left. Then he and his descendants will reign a long time over his kingdom in Israel.

18 The priests, who are Levites—indeed the whole tribe of Levi—are to have no allotment or inheritance with Israel. They shall live on the offerings made to the LORD by fire, for that is their inheritance. ²They shall have no inheritance among their brothers; the LORD is their inheritance, as he promised them.

³This is the share due the priests from the people who sacrifice a bull or a sheep: the shoulder, the jowls and the inner parts. ⁴You are to give them the firstfruits of your grain, new wine and oil, and the first wool from the shearing of your sheep, ⁵for the LORD your God has chosen them and their descendants out of all your tribes to stand and minister in the LORD's name always.

⁶If a Levite moves from one of your towns anywhere in Israel where he is living, and comes in all earnestness to the place the LORD will choose, ⁷he may minister in the name of the LORD his God like all his fellow Levites who serve there in the presence of the LORD. ⁸He is to share equally in their benefits, even though he has received money from the sale of family possessions.

⁹When you enter the land the LORD your God is giving you, do not learn to imitate the detestable ways of the nations there. ¹⁰Let no one be found among you who sacrifices his son or daughter

˟21 Or *Do not plant any tree dedicated to Asherah*

in^y the fire, who practices divination or sorcery, interprets omens, engages in witchcraft, ¹¹or casts spells, or who is a medium or spiritist or who consults the dead. ¹²Anyone who does these things is detestable to the LORD, and because of these detestable practices the LORD your God will drive out those nations before you. ¹³You must be blameless before the LORD your God.

¹⁴The nations you will dispossess listen to those who practice sorcery or divination. But as for you, the LORD your God has not permitted you to do so. ¹⁵The LORD your God will raise up for you a prophet like me from among your own brothers. You must listen to him. ¹⁶For this is what you asked of the LORD your God at Horeb on the day of the assembly when you said, "Let us not hear the voice of the LORD our God nor see this great fire anymore, or we will die."

¹⁷The LORD said to me: "What they say is good. ¹⁸I will raise up for them a prophet like you from among their brothers; I will put my words in his mouth, and he will tell them everything I command him. ¹⁹If anyone does not listen to my words that the prophet speaks in my name, I myself will call him to account. ²⁰But a prophet who presumes to speak in my name anything I have not commanded him to say, or a prophet who speaks in the name of other gods, must be put to death."

²¹You may say to yourselves, "How can we know when a message has not been spoken by the LORD?" ²²If what a prophet proclaims in the name of the LORD does not take place or come true, that is a message the LORD has not spoken. That prophet has spoken presumptuously. Do not be afraid of him.

19

When the LORD your God has destroyed the nations whose land he is giving you, and when you have driven them out and settled in their towns and houses, ²then set aside for yourselves three cities centrally located in the land the LORD your God is giving you to possess. ³Build roads to them and divide into three parts the land the LORD your God is giving you as an inheritance, so that anyone who kills a man may flee there.

⁴This is the rule concerning the man who kills another and flees there to save his life—one who kills his neighbor unintentionally, without malice aforethought. ⁵For instance, a man may go into the forest with his neighbor to cut wood, and as he swings his ax to fell a tree, the head may fly off and hit his neighbor and kill him. That man may flee to one of these cities and save his life. ⁶Otherwise, the avenger of blood might pursue him in a rage, overtake him if the distance is too great, and kill him even though he is not deserving of death, since he did it to his neighbor without malice aforethought. ⁷This is why I command you to set aside for yourselves three cities.

⁸If the LORD your God enlarges your territory, as he promised on oath to your forefathers, and gives you the whole land he promised them, ⁹because you carefully follow all these laws I command you today—to love the LORD your God and to walk always in his ways—then you are to set aside three more cities. ¹⁰Do this so that innocent blood will not be shed in your land, which the LORD your God is giving you as your inheritance, and so that you will not be guilty of bloodshed.

¹¹But if a man hates his neighbor and lies in wait for him, assaults and kills him, and then flees to one of these cities, ¹²the elders of his town shall send for him, bring him back from the city, and hand him over to the avenger of blood to die. ¹³Show him no pity. You must purge from Israel the guilt of shedding innocent blood, so that it may go well with you.

¹⁴Do not move your neighbor's boundary stone set up by your predecessors in the inheritance you receive in the land the LORD your God is giving you to possess.

¹⁵One witness is not enough to convict a man accused of any crime or offense he may have committed. A matter must be established by the testimony of two or three witnesses.

¹⁶If a malicious witness takes the stand to accuse a man of a crime, ¹⁷the two men involved in the dispute must stand in the presence of the LORD before the priests and the judges who are in office at the time. ¹⁸The judges must make a thorough investigation, and if the witness proves to be a liar, giving false testimony against his brother, ¹⁹then do to him as he intended to do to his brother. You must purge the evil from among you. ²⁰The rest of the people will hear of this and be afraid, and never again will such an evil thing be done among you. ²¹Show no pity: life for life, eye for eye, tooth for tooth, hand for hand, foot for foot.

^{y}10 Or *who makes his son or daughter pass through*

20

When you go to war against your enemies and see horses and chariots and an army greater than yours, do not be afraid of them, because the Lord your God, who brought you up out of Egypt, will be with you. ²When you are about to go into battle, the priest shall come forward and address the army. ³He shall say: "Hear, O Israel, today you are going into battle against your enemies. Do not be fainthearted or afraid; do not be terrified or give way to panic before them. ⁴For the Lord your God is the one who goes with you to fight for you against your enemies to give you victory."

⁵The officers shall say to the army: "Has anyone built a new house and not dedicated it? Let him go home, or he may die in battle and someone else may dedicate it. ⁶Has anyone planted a vineyard and not begun to enjoy it? Let him go home, or he may die in battle and someone else enjoy it. ⁷Has anyone become pledged to a woman and not married her? Let him go home, or he may die in battle and someone else marry her." ⁸Then the officers shall add, "Is any man afraid or fainthearted? Let him go home so that his brothers will not become disheartened too." ⁹When the officers have finished speaking to the army, they shall appoint commanders over it.

¹⁰When you march up to attack a city, make its people an offer of peace. ¹¹If they accept and open their gates, all the people in it shall be subject to forced labor and shall work for you. ¹²If they refuse to make peace and they engage you in battle, lay siege to that city. ¹³When the Lord your God delivers it into your hand, put to the sword all the men in it. ¹⁴As for the women, the children, the livestock and everything else in the city, you may take these as plunder for yourselves. And you may use the plunder the Lord your God gives you from your enemies. ¹⁵This is how you are to treat all the cities that are at a distance from you and do not belong to the nations nearby.

¹⁶However, in the cities of the nations the Lord your God is giving you as an inheritance, do not leave alive anything that breathes. ¹⁷Completely destroy² them—the Hittites, Amorites, Canaanites, Perizzites, Hivites and Jebusites—as the Lord your God has commanded you. ¹⁸Otherwise, they will teach you to follow all the detestable things they do in worshiping their gods, and you will sin against the Lord your God.

¹⁹When you lay siege to a city for a long time, fighting against it to capture it, do not destroy its trees by putting an ax to them, because you can eat their fruit. Do not cut them down. Are the trees of the field people, that you should besiege them?ᵃ ²⁰However, you may cut down trees that you know are not fruit trees and use them to build siege works until the city at war with you falls.

21

If a man is found slain, lying in a field in the land the Lord your God is giving you to possess, and it is not known who killed him, ²your elders and judges shall go out and measure the distance from the body to the neighboring towns. ³Then the elders of the town nearest the body shall take a heifer that has never been worked and has never worn a yoke ⁴and lead her down to a valley that has not been plowed or planted and where there is a flowing stream. There in the valley they are to break the heifer's neck. ⁵The priests, the sons of Levi, shall step forward, for the Lord your God has chosen them to minister and to pronounce blessings in the name of the Lord and to decide all cases of dispute and assault. ⁶Then all the elders of the town nearest the body shall wash their hands over the heifer whose neck was broken in the valley, ⁷and they shall declare: "Our hands did not shed this blood, nor did our eyes see it done. ⁸Accept this atonement for your people Israel, whom you have redeemed, O Lord, and do not hold your people guilty of the blood of an innocent man." And the bloodshed will be atoned for. ⁹So you will purge from yourselves the guilt of shedding innocent blood, since you have done what is right in the eyes of the Lord.

¹⁰When you go to war against your enemies and the Lord your God delivers them into your hands and you take captives, ¹¹if you notice among the captives a beautiful woman and are attracted to her, you may take her as your wife. ¹²Bring her into your home and have her shave her head, trim her nails ¹³and put aside the clothes she was wearing when captured. After she has lived in your house and mourned her father and mother for a full month, then you may go to her and be her husband and she shall be your wife. ¹⁴If you are not pleased with her, let her go wherever she wishes. You must not sell her or treat her as a slave, since you have dishonored her.

ᶻ17 The Hebrew term refers to the irrevocable giving over of things or persons to the Lord, often by totally destroying them.   ᵃ19 Or *down to use in the siege, for the fruit trees are for the benefit of man.*

[15]If a man has two wives, and he loves one but not the other, and both bear him sons but the firstborn is the son of the wife he does not love, [16]when he wills his property to his sons, he must not give the rights of the firstborn to the son of the wife he loves in preference to his actual firstborn, the son of the wife he does not love. [17]He must acknowledge the son of his unloved wife as the firstborn by giving him a double share of all he has. That son is the first sign of his father's strength. The right of the firstborn belongs to him.

[18]If a man has a stubborn and rebellious son who does not obey his father and mother and will not listen to them when they discipline him, [19]his father and mother shall take hold of him and bring him to the elders at the gate of his town. [20]They shall say to the elders, "This son of ours is stubborn and rebellious. He will not obey us. He is a profligate and a drunkard." [21]Then all the men of his town shall stone him to death. You must purge the evil from among you. All Israel will hear of it and be afraid.

[22]If a man guilty of a capital offense is put to death and his body is hung on a tree, [23]you must not leave his body on the tree overnight. Be sure to bury him that same day, because anyone who is hung on a tree is under God's curse. You must not desecrate the land the LORD your God is giving you as an inheritance.

22 If you see your brother's ox or sheep straying, do not ignore it but be sure to take it back to him. [2]If the brother does not live near you or if you do not know who he is, take it home with you and keep it until he comes looking for it. Then give it back to him. [3]Do the same if you find your brother's donkey or his cloak or anything he loses. Do not ignore it.

[4]If you see your brother's donkey or his ox fallen on the road, do not ignore it. Help him get it to its feet.

[5]A woman must not wear men's clothing, nor a man wear women's clothing, for the LORD your God detests anyone who does this.

[6]If you come across a bird's nest beside the road, either in a tree or on the ground, and the mother is sitting on the young or on the eggs, do not take the mother with the young. [7]You may take the young, but be sure to let the mother go, so that it may go well with you and you may have a long life.

[8]When you build a new house, make a parapet around your roof so that you may not bring the guilt of bloodshed on your house if someone falls from the roof.

[9]Do not plant two kinds of seed in your vineyard; if you do, not only the crops you plant but also the fruit of the vineyard will be defiled.[b]

[10]Do not plow with an ox and a donkey yoked together.

[11]Do not wear clothes of wool and linen woven together.

[12]Make tassels on the four corners of the cloak you wear.

[13]If a man takes a wife and, after lying with her, dislikes her [14]and slanders her and gives her a bad name, saying, "I married this woman, but when I approached her, I did not find proof of her virginity," [15]then the girl's father and mother shall bring proof that she was a virgin to the town elders at the gate. [16]The girl's father will say to the elders, "I gave my daughter in marriage to this man, but he dislikes her. [17]Now he has slandered her and said, 'I did not find your daughter to be a virgin.' But here is the proof of my daughter's virginity." Then her parents shall display the cloth before the elders of the town, [18]and the elders shall take the man and punish him. [19]They shall fine him a hundred shekels of silver[c] and give them to the girl's father, because this man has given an Israelite virgin a bad name. She shall continue to be his wife; he must not divorce her as long as he lives.

[20]If, however, the charge is true and no proof of the girl's virginity can be found, [21]she shall be brought to the door of her father's house and there the men of her town shall stone her to death. She has done a disgraceful thing in Israel by being promiscuous while still in her father's house. You must purge the evil from among you.

[22]If a man is found sleeping with another man's wife, both the man who slept with her and the woman must die. You must purge the evil from Israel.

[23]If a man happens to meet in a town a virgin pledged to be married and he sleeps with her, [24]you shall take both of them to the gate of that town and stone them to death—the girl because she was in a town and did not scream for help, and the man because he violated another man's wife. You must purge the evil from among you.

---

b9 Or *be forfeited to the sanctuary*   *c19* That is, about 2 1/2 pounds (about 1 kilogram)

²⁵But if out in the country a man happens to meet a girl pledged to be married and rapes her, only the man who has done this shall die. ²⁶Do nothing to the girl; she has committed no sin deserving death. This case is like that of someone who attacks and murders his neighbor, ²⁷for the man found the girl out in the country, and though the betrothed girl screamed, there was no one to rescue her.

²⁸If a man happens to meet a virgin who is not pledged to be married and rapes her and they are discovered, ²⁹he shall pay the girl's father fifty shekels of silver.ᵈ He must marry the girl, for he has violated her. He can never divorce her as long as he lives.

³⁰A man is not to marry his father's wife; he must not dishonor his father's bed.

23 No one who has been emasculated by crushing or cutting may enter the assembly of the LORD.

²No one born of a forbidden marriageᵉ nor any of his descendants may enter the assembly of the LORD, even down to the tenth generation.

³No Ammonite or Moabite or any of his descendants may enter the assembly of the LORD, even down to the tenth generation. ⁴For they did not come to meet you with bread and water on your way when you came out of Egypt, and they hired Balaam son of Beor from Pethor in Aram Naharaimᶠ to pronounce a curse on you. ⁵However, the LORD your God would not listen to Balaam but turned the curse into a blessing for you, because the LORD your God loves you. ⁶Do not seek a treaty of friendship with them as long as you live.

⁷Do not abhor an Edomite, for he is your brother. Do not abhor an Egyptian, because you lived as an alien in his country. ⁸The third generation of children born to them may enter the assembly of the LORD.

⁹When you are encamped against your enemies, keep away from everything impure. ¹⁰If one of your men is unclean because of a nocturnal emission, he is to go outside the camp and stay there. ¹¹But as evening approaches he is to wash himself, and at sunset he may return to the camp.

¹²Designate a place outside the camp where you can go to relieve yourself. ¹³As part of your equipment have something to dig with, and when you relieve yourself, dig a hole and cover up your excrement. ¹⁴For the LORD your God moves about in your camp to protect you and to deliver your enemies to you. Your camp must be holy, so that he will not see among you anything indecent and turn away from you.

ᵈ29 That is, about 1 1/4 pounds (about 0.6 kilogram) ᵉ2 Or one of illegitimate birth ᶠ4 That is, Northwest Mesopotamia

10 / *Deuteronomy 23:15–25*
The Laws of Freedom

ONE CHARACTERISTIC OF a good insurance policy is the details. Every contingency is covered—no possibilities are left open. The verses you read in this section of Scripture fit into the category of the insurance policy. They are a collection of miscellaneous laws that don't appear to be intrinsically related to each other, but they are worth considering, as are other difficult passages. What you will discover is that God's wise care for the freedom of his people extends to the smallest details of personal conduct and community concerns.

 Warming Up to God God reveals himself to us in the details of our daily experiences. Think back over your activities for the past several days. Consider how God might have been caring, guiding and instructing you through all that you've experienced.

 Read Deuteronomy 23:15–25.

---

¹⁵If a slave has taken refuge with you, do not hand him over to his master. ¹⁶Let him live among you wherever he likes and in whatever town he chooses. Do not oppress him.

¹⁷No Israelite man or woman is to become a shrine prostitute. ¹⁸You must not bring the earn-

ings of a female prostitute or of a male prosti-tute^g into the house of the LORD your God to pay any vow, because the LORD your God detests them both.

¹⁹Do not charge your brother interest, whether on money or food or anything else that may earn interest. ²⁰You may charge a foreigner interest, but not a brother Israelite, so that the LORD your God may bless you in everything you put your hand to in the land you are entering to possess.

²¹If you make a vow to the LORD your God, do not be slow to pay it, for the LORD your God will certainly demand it of you and you will be guilty

of sin. ²²But if you refrain from making a vow, you will not be guilty. ²³Whatever your lips utter you must be sure to do, because you made your vow freely to the LORD your God with your own mouth.

²⁴If you enter your neighbor's vineyard, you may eat all the grapes you want, but do not put any in your basket. ²⁵If you enter your neighbor's grainfield, you may pick kernels with your hands, but you must not put a sickle to his standing grain.

g18 Hebrew of a dog

 Discovering the Word 1. What different community problems are addressed in these verses? 2. In what different ways do these laws protect the Israelites and encourage them to live as a community of freed people? 3. What abuses of worship are addressed in verses 17–18 and 21–23? 4. What do these provisions tell you about how worship is to be approached? 5. What potential problems in a farming community do verses 24–25 address?

Applying the Word 1. God's law is meant to maintain the freedom he gave Israel when he rescued them from slavery in Egypt. How can this insight affect the way you read both the Old and New Testament? 2. The law about shrine prostitution addresses the issue of acceptable offerings. What do you think God expects from you when you make a pledge or an offering at your church? 3. Look at verses 19–20. The laws in Deuteronomy were given for an agricultural society. What principles regarding the use of money might we draw from these verses for a capitalist society that is built on the principle of lending and interest?

Responding in Prayer Thank God for the freedom his law brings. Pray that God will make you wise and honest in the use of the financial resources he has given to you.

Deuteronomy 24—29

24

If a man marries a woman who be-comes displeasing to him because he finds something indecent about her, and he writes her a certificate of divorce, gives it to her and sends her from his house, ²and if after she leaves his house she becomes the wife of another man, ³and her second husband dislikes her and writes her a certificate of divorce, gives it to her and sends her from his house, or if he dies, ⁴then her first husband, who divorced her, is not allowed to marry her again after she has been defiled. That would be detestable in the eyes of the LORD. Do not bring sin upon the land the LORD your God is giving you as an inheritance.

⁵If a man has recently married, he must not be sent to war or have any other duty laid on him. For one year he is to be free to stay at home and bring happiness to the wife he has married.

⁶Do not take a pair of millstones—not even the upper one—as security for a debt, because that would be taking a man's livelihood as security.

⁷If a man is caught kidnapping one of his brother Israelites and treats him as a slave or sells him, the kidnapper must die. You must purge the evil from among you.

⁸In cases of leprous^h diseases be very careful to do exactly as the priests, who are Levites, instruct you. You must follow carefully what I have commanded them. ⁹Remember what the LORD your God did to Miriam along the way after you came out of Egypt.

¹⁰When you make a loan of any kind to your neighbor, do not go into his house to get what he is offering as a pledge. ¹¹Stay outside and let the

h8 The Hebrew word was used for various diseases affecting the skin—not necessarily leprosy.

man to whom you are making the loan bring the pledge out to you. ¹²If the man is poor, do not go to sleep with his pledge in your possession. ¹³Return his cloak to him by sunset so that he may sleep in it. Then he will thank you, and it will be regarded as a righteous act in the sight of the Lᴏʀᴅ your God.

¹⁴Do not take advantage of a hired man who is poor and needy, whether he is a brother Israelite or an alien living in one of your towns. ¹⁵Pay him his wages each day before sunset, because he is poor and is counting on it. Otherwise he may cry to the Lᴏʀᴅ against you, and you will be guilty of sin.

¹⁶Fathers shall not be put to death for their children, nor children put to death for their fathers; each is to die for his own sin.

¹⁷Do not deprive the alien or the fatherless of justice, or take the cloak of the widow as a pledge. ¹⁸Remember that you were slaves in Egypt and the Lᴏʀᴅ your God redeemed you from there. That is why I command you to do this.

¹⁹When you are harvesting in your field and you overlook a sheaf, do not go back to get it. Leave it for the alien, the fatherless and the widow, so that the Lᴏʀᴅ your God may bless you in all the work of your hands. ²⁰When you beat the olives from your trees, do not go over the branches a second time. Leave what remains for the alien, the fatherless and the widow. ²¹When you harvest the grapes in your vineyard, do not go over the vines again. Leave what remains for the alien, the fatherless and the widow. ²²Remember that you were slaves in Egypt. That is why I command you to do this.

25 When men have a dispute, they are to take it to court and the judges will decide the case, acquitting the innocent and condemning the guilty. ²If the guilty man deserves to be beaten, the judge shall make him lie down and have him flogged in his presence with the number of lashes his crime deserves, ³but he must not give him more than forty lashes. If he is flogged more than that, your brother will be degraded in your eyes.

⁴Do not muzzle an ox while it is treading out the grain.

⁵If brothers are living together and one of them dies without a son, his widow must not marry outside the family. Her husband's brother shall take her and marry her and fulfill the duty of a brother-in-law to her. ⁶The first son she bears shall carry on the name of the dead brother so that his name will not be blotted out from Israel.

⁷However, if a man does not want to marry his brother's wife, she shall go to the elders at the town gate and say, "My husband's brother refuses to carry on his brother's name in Israel. He will not fulfill the duty of a brother-in-law to me." ⁸Then the elders of his town shall summon him and talk to him. If he persists in saying, "I do not want to marry her," ⁹his brother's widow shall go up to him in the presence of the elders, take off one of his sandals, spit in his face and say, "This is what is done to the man who will not build up his brother's family line." ¹⁰That man's line shall be known in Israel as The Family of the Unsandaled.

¹¹If two men are fighting and the wife of one of them comes to rescue her husband from his assailant, and she reaches out and seizes him by his private parts, ¹²you shall cut off her hand. Show her no pity.

¹³Do not have two differing weights in your bag—one heavy, one light. ¹⁴Do not have two differing measures in your house—one large, one small. ¹⁵You must have accurate and honest weights and measures, so that you may live long in the land the Lᴏʀᴅ your God is giving you. ¹⁶For the Lᴏʀᴅ your God detests anyone who does these things, anyone who deals dishonestly.

¹⁷Remember what the Amalekites did to you along the way when you came out of Egypt. ¹⁸When you were weary and worn out, they met you on your journey and cut off all who were lagging behind; they had no fear of God. ¹⁹When the Lᴏʀᴅ your God gives you rest from all the enemies around you in the land he is giving you to possess as an inheritance, you shall blot out the memory of Amalek from under heaven. Do not forget!

26 When you have entered the land the Lᴏʀᴅ your God is giving you as an inheritance and have taken possession of it and settled in it, ²take some of the firstfruits of all that you produce from the soil of the land the Lᴏʀᴅ your God is giving you and put them in a basket. Then go to the place the Lᴏʀᴅ your God will choose as a dwelling for his Name ³and say to the priest in office at the time, "I declare today to the Lᴏʀᴅ your God that I have come to the land the Lᴏʀᴅ swore to our forefathers to give us." ⁴The priest shall take the basket from your hands and set it down in front of the altar of the LORD your God. ⁵Then you shall declare before the LORD your God: "My father was a wandering Aramean, and he went down into Egypt with a few people and lived there and became a great nation, powerful and numerous. ⁶But the Egyptians mistreated us and made us suffer, putting us to hard labor. ⁷Then we cried out to the LORD, the God of our fathers, and the LORD heard our voice and saw our misery, toil and oppression. ⁸So the LORD brought us out of Egypt with a mighty hand and an outstretched arm, with great terror and with miraculous signs and wonders. ⁹He brought us to this place and gave us this land, a land flowing with milk and honey; ¹⁰and now I bring the firstfruits of the soil that you, O LORD, have given me." Place the basket before the LORD your God and bow down before him. ¹¹And you and the Levites and the aliens among you shall rejoice in all the good things the LORD your God has given to you and your household.

¹²When you have finished setting aside a tenth of all your produce in the third year, the year of the tithe, you shall give it to the Levite, the alien, the fatherless and the widow, so that they may eat in your towns and be satisfied. ¹³Then say to the LORD your God: "I have removed from my house the sacred portion and have given it to the Levite, the alien, the fatherless and the widow, according to all you commanded. I have not turned aside from your commands nor have I forgotten any of them. ¹⁴I have not eaten any of the sacred portion while I was in mourning, nor have I removed any of it while I was unclean, nor have I offered any of it to the dead. I have obeyed the LORD my God; I have done everything you commanded me. ¹⁵Look down from heaven, your holy dwelling place, and bless your people Israel and the land you have given us as you promised on oath to our forefathers, a land flowing with milk and honey."

¹⁶The LORD your God commands you this day to follow these decrees and laws; carefully observe them with all your heart and with all your soul. ¹⁷You have declared this day that the LORD is your God and that you will walk in his ways, that you will keep his decrees, commands and laws, and that you will obey him. ¹⁸And the LORD has declared this day that you are his people, his treasured possession as he promised, and that you are to keep all his commands. ¹⁹He has declared that he will set you in praise, fame and honor high above all the nations he has made and that you

will be a people holy to the LORD your God, as he promised.

27

Moses and the elders of Israel commanded the people: "Keep all these commands that I give you today. ²When you have crossed the Jordan into the land the LORD your God is giving you, set up some large stones and coat them with plaster. ³Write on them all the words of this law when you have crossed over to enter the land the LORD your God is giving you, a land flowing with milk and honey, just as the LORD, the God of your fathers, promised you. ⁴And when you have crossed the Jordan, set up these stones on Mount Ebal, as I command you today, and coat them with plaster. ⁵Build there an altar to the LORD your God, an altar of stones. Do not use any iron tool upon them. ⁶Build the altar of the LORD your God with fieldstones and offer burnt offerings on it to the LORD your God. ⁷Sacrifice fellowship offeringsᶦ there, eating them and rejoicing in the presence of the LORD your God. ⁸And you shall write very clearly all the words of this law on these stones you have set up."

⁹Then Moses and the priests, who are Levites, said to all Israel, "Be silent, O Israel, and listen! You have now become the people of the LORD your God. ¹⁰Obey the LORD your God and follow his commands and decrees that I give you today."

¹¹On the same day Moses commanded the people:

¹²When you have crossed the Jordan, these tribes shall stand on Mount Gerizim to bless the people: Simeon, Levi, Judah, Issachar, Joseph and Benjamin. ¹³And these tribes shall stand on Mount Ebal to pronounce curses: Reuben, Gad, Asher, Zebulun, Dan and Naphtali.

¹⁴The Levites shall recite to all the people of Israel in a loud voice:

¹⁵"Cursed is the man who carves an image or casts an idol—a thing detestable to the LORD, the work of the craftsman's hands—and sets it up in secret."

Then all the people shall say, "Amen!"

¹⁶"Cursed is the man who dishonors his father or his mother."

Then all the people shall say, "Amen!"

¹⁷"Cursed is the man who moves his neighbor's boundary stone."

Then all the people shall say, "Amen!"

ᶦ7 Traditionally *peace offerings*

¹⁸"Cursed is the man who leads the blind astray on the road."

Then all the people shall say, "Amen!"
¹⁹"Cursed is the man who withholds justice from the alien, the fatherless or the widow."

Then all the people shall say, "Amen!"
²⁰"Cursed is the man who sleeps with his father's wife, for he dishonors his father's bed."

Then all the people shall say, "Amen!"
²¹"Cursed is the man who has sexual relations with any animal."

Then all the people shall say, "Amen!"
²²"Cursed is the man who sleeps with his sister, the daughter of his father or the daughter of his mother."

Then all the people shall say, "Amen!"
²³"Cursed is the man who sleeps with his mother-in-law."

Then all the people shall say, "Amen!"
²⁴"Cursed is the man who kills his neighbor secretly."

Then all the people shall say, "Amen!"
²⁵"Cursed is the man who accepts a bribe to kill an innocent person."

Then all the people shall say, "Amen!"
²⁶"Cursed is the man who does not uphold the words of this law by carrying them out."

Then all the people shall say, "Amen!"

28 If you fully obey the Lord your God and carefully follow all his commands I give you today, the Lord your God will set you high above all the nations on earth. ²All these blessings will come upon you and accompany you if you obey the Lord your God:

³You will be blessed in the city and blessed in the country.

⁴The fruit of your womb will be blessed, and the crops of your land and the young of your livestock—the calves of your herds and the lambs of your flocks.

⁵Your basket and your kneading trough will be blessed.

⁶You will be blessed when you come in and blessed when you go out.

⁷The Lord will grant that the enemies who rise up against you will be defeated before you. They will come at you from one direction but flee from you in seven.

⁸The Lord will send a blessing on your barns and on everything you put your hand to. The Lord your God will bless you in the land he is giving you.

⁹The Lord will establish you as his holy people, as he promised you on oath, if you keep the commands of the Lord your God and walk in his ways. ¹⁰Then all the peoples on earth will see that you are called by the name of the Lord, and they will fear you. ¹¹The Lord will grant you abundant prosperity—in the fruit of your womb, the young of your livestock and the crops of your ground—in the land he swore to your forefathers to give you.

¹²The Lord will open the heavens, the storehouse of his bounty, to send rain on your land in season and to bless all the work of your hands. You will lend to many nations but will borrow from none. ¹³The Lord will make you the head, not the tail. If you pay attention to the commands of the Lord your God that I give you this day and carefully follow them, you will always be at the top, never at the bottom. ¹⁴Do not turn aside from any of the commands I give you today, to the right or to the left, following other gods and serving them.

¹⁵However, if you do not obey the Lord your God and do not carefully follow all his commands and decrees I am giving you today, all these curses will come upon you and overtake you:

¹⁶You will be cursed in the city and cursed in the country.

¹⁷Your basket and your kneading trough will be cursed.

¹⁸The fruit of your womb will be cursed, and the crops of your land, and the calves of your herds and the lambs of your flocks.

¹⁹You will be cursed when you come in and cursed when you go out.

²⁰The Lord will send on you curses, confusion and rebuke in everything you put your hand to, until you are destroyed and come to sudden ruin because of the evil you have done in forsaking him.^j ²¹The Lord will plague you with diseases until he has destroyed you from the land you are entering to possess. ²²The Lord will strike you with wasting disease, with fever and inflamma-

^j20 Hebrew *me*

tion, with scorching heat and drought, with blight and mildew, which will plague you until you perish. ²³The sky over your head will be bronze, the ground beneath you iron. ²⁴The Lord will turn the rain of your country into dust and powder; it will come down from the skies until you are destroyed.

²⁵The Lord will cause you to be defeated before your enemies. You will come at them from one direction but flee from them in seven, and you will become a thing of horror to all the kingdoms on earth. ²⁶Your carcasses will be food for all the birds of the air and the beasts of the earth, and there will be no one to frighten them away. ²⁷The Lord will afflict you with the boils of Egypt and with tumors, festering sores and the itch, from which you cannot be cured. ²⁸The Lord will afflict you with madness, blindness and confusion of mind. ²⁹At midday you will grope about like a blind man in the dark. You will be unsuccessful in everything you do; day after day you will be oppressed and robbed, with no one to rescue you.

³⁰You will be pledged to be married to a woman, but another will take her and ravish her. You will build a house, but you will not live in it. You will plant a vineyard, but you will not even begin to enjoy its fruit. ³¹Your ox will be slaughtered before your eyes, but you will eat none of it. Your donkey will be forcibly taken from you and will not be returned. Your sheep will be given to your enemies, and no one will rescue them. ³²Your sons and daughters will be given to another nation, and you will wear out your eyes watching for them day after day, powerless to lift a hand. ³³A people that you do not know will eat what your land and labor produce, and you will have nothing but cruel oppression all your days. ³⁴The sights you see will drive you mad. ³⁵The Lord will afflict your knees and legs with painful boils that cannot be cured, spreading from the soles of your feet to the top of your head.

³⁶The Lord will drive you and the king you set over you to a nation unknown to you or your fathers. There you will worship other gods, gods of wood and stone. ³⁷You will become a thing of horror and an object of scorn and ridicule to all the nations where the Lord will drive you.

³⁸You will sow much seed in the field but you will harvest little, because locusts will devour it. ³⁹You will plant vineyards and cultivate them but you will not drink the wine or gather the grapes, because worms will eat them. ⁴⁰You will have ol-

ive trees throughout your country but you will not use the oil, because the olives will drop off. ⁴¹You will have sons and daughters but you will not keep them, because they will go into captivity. ⁴²Swarms of locusts will take over all your trees and the crops of your land.

⁴³The alien who lives among you will rise above you higher and higher, but you will sink lower and lower. ⁴⁴He will lend to you, but you will not lend to him. He will be the head, but you will be the tail.

⁴⁵All these curses will come upon you. They will pursue you and overtake you until you are destroyed, because you did not obey the Lord your God and observe the commands and decrees he gave you. ⁴⁶They will be a sign and a wonder to you and your descendants forever. ⁴⁷Because you did not serve the Lord your God joyfully and gladly in the time of prosperity, ⁴⁸therefore in hunger and thirst, in nakedness and dire poverty, you will serve the enemies the Lord sends against you. He will put an iron yoke on your neck until he has destroyed you.

⁴⁹The Lord will bring a nation against you from far away, from the ends of the earth, like an eagle swooping down, a nation whose language you will not understand, ⁵⁰a fierce-looking nation without respect for the old or pity for the young. ⁵¹They will devour the young of your livestock and the crops of your land until you are destroyed. They will leave you no grain, new wine or oil, nor any calves of your herds or lambs of your flocks until you are ruined. ⁵²They will lay siege to all the cities throughout your land until the high fortified walls in which you trust fall down. They will besiege all the cities throughout the land the Lord your God is giving you.

⁵³Because of the suffering that your enemy will inflict on you during the siege, you will eat the fruit of the womb, the flesh of the sons and daughters the Lord your God has given you. ⁵⁴Even the most gentle and sensitive man among you will have no compassion on his own brother or the wife he loves or his surviving children, ⁵⁵and he will not give to one of them any of the flesh of his children that he is eating. It will be all he has left because of the suffering your enemy will inflict on you during the siege of all your cities. ⁵⁶The most gentle and sensitive woman among you—so sensitive and gentle that she would not venture to touch the ground with the sole of her foot—will begrudge the husband she

loves and her own son or daughter ⁵⁷the after-birth from her womb and the children she bears. For she intends to eat them secretly during the siege and in the distress that your enemy will inflict on you in your cities.

⁵⁸If you do not carefully follow all the words of this law, which are written in this book, and do not revere this glorious and awesome name—the LORD your God— ⁵⁹the LORD will send fearful plagues on you and your descendants, harsh and prolonged disasters, and severe and lingering illnesses. ⁶⁰He will bring upon you all the diseases of Egypt that you dreaded, and they will cling to you. ⁶¹The LORD will also bring on you every kind of sickness and disaster not recorded in this Book of the Law, until you are destroyed. ⁶²You who were as numerous as the stars in the sky will be left but few in number, because you did not obey the LORD your God. ⁶³Just as it pleased the LORD to make you prosper and increase in number, so it will please him to ruin and destroy you. You will be uprooted from the land you are entering to possess.

⁶⁴Then the LORD will scatter you among all nations, from one end of the earth to the other. There you will worship other gods—gods of wood and stone, which neither you nor your fathers have known. ⁶⁵Among those nations you will find no repose, no resting place for the sole of your foot. There the LORD will give you an anxious mind, eyes weary with longing, and a despairing heart. ⁶⁶You will live in constant suspense, filled with dread both night and day, never sure of your life. ⁶⁷In the morning you will say, "If only it were evening!" and in the evening, "If only it were morning!"—because of the terror that will fill your hearts and the sights that your eyes will see. ⁶⁸The LORD will send you back in ships to Egypt on a journey I said you should never make again. There you will offer yourselves for sale to your enemies as male and female slaves, but no one will buy you.

29 These are the terms of the covenant the LORD commanded Moses to make with the Israelites in Moab, in addition to the covenant he had made with them at Horeb.

²Moses summoned all the Israelites and said to them:

Your eyes have seen all that the LORD did in Egypt to Pharaoh, to all his officials and to all his land. ³With your own eyes you saw those great trials, those miraculous signs and great wonders. ⁴But to this day the LORD has not given you a mind that understands or eyes that see or ears that hear. ⁵During the forty years that I led you through the desert, your clothes did not wear out, nor did the sandals on your feet. ⁶You ate no bread and drank no wine or other fermented drink. I did this so that you might know that I am the LORD your God.

⁷When you reached this place, Sihon king of Heshbon and Og king of Bashan came out to fight against us, but we defeated them. ⁸We took their land and gave it as an inheritance to the Reubenites, the Gadites and the half-tribe of Manasseh.

⁹Carefully follow the terms of this covenant, so that you may prosper in everything you do. ¹⁰All of you are standing today in the presence of the LORD your God—your leaders and chief men, your elders and officials, and all the other men of Israel, ¹¹together with your children and your wives, and the aliens living in your camps who chop your wood and carry your water. ¹²You are standing here in order to enter into a covenant with the LORD your God, a covenant the LORD is making with you this day and sealing with an oath, ¹³to confirm you this day as his people, that he may be your God as he promised you and as he swore to your fathers, Abraham, Isaac and Jacob. ¹⁴I am making this covenant, with its oath, not only with you ¹⁵who are standing here with us today in the presence of the LORD our God but also with those who are not here today.

¹⁶You yourselves know how we lived in Egypt and how we passed through the countries on the way here. ¹⁷You saw among them their detestable images and idols of wood and stone, of silver and gold. ¹⁸Make sure there is no man or woman, clan or tribe among you today whose heart turns away from the LORD our God to go and worship the gods of those nations; make sure there is no root among you that produces such bitter poison.

¹⁹When such a person hears the words of this oath, he invokes a blessing on himself and therefore thinks, "I will be safe, even though I persist in going my own way." This will bring disaster on the watered land as well as the dry.ᵏ ²⁰The LORD will never be willing to forgive him; his wrath and zeal will burn against that man. All the curses written in this book will fall upon him, and the

ᵏ19 Or way, in order to add drunkenness to thirst."

Lord will blot out his name from under heaven. 21The Lord will single him out from all the tribes of Israel for disaster, according to all the curses of the covenant written in this Book of the Law.

22Your children who follow you in later generations and foreigners who come from distant lands will see the calamities that have fallen on the land and the diseases with which the Lord has afflicted it. 23The whole land will be a burning waste of salt and sulfur—nothing planted, nothing sprouting, no vegetation growing on it. It will be like the destruction of Sodom and Gomorrah, Admah and Zeboiim, which the Lord overthrew in fierce anger. 24All the nations will ask: "Why has the Lord done this to this land? Why this fierce, burning anger?"

25And the answer will be: "It is because this people abandoned the covenant of the Lord, the God of their fathers, the covenant he made with them when he brought them out of Egypt. 26They went off and worshiped other gods and bowed down to them, gods they did not know, gods he had not given them. 27Therefore the Lord's anger burned against this land, so that he brought on it all the curses written in this book. 28In furious anger and in great wrath the Lord uprooted them from their land and thrust them into another land, as it is now."

29The secret things belong to the Lord our God, but the things revealed belong to us and to our children forever, that we may follow all the words of this law.

11 / *Deuteronomy 30*
A Scattered Future

THE HISTORY OF Israel for the past three thousand years has been a turbulent one. They have experienced numerous invasions and massive deportation and persecution. I find it amazing that they were able to maintain their sense of national identity for nearly two thousand years without sovereign control of their homeland. The hand of God has been at work. Moses foretold the dispersion even before they set foot in the land. As he is giving his final words, he tells the people that they will not stay faithful to the covenant. And he wants Israel to know in no uncertain terms that they will be severely disciplined for future unfaithfulness. However, threat of judgment is not the last word. As Moses looks into the future, he gives Israel hope on the other side of judgment.

 Warming Up to God In the Ten Commandments God describes himself as a jealous God. What are some of the painful and positive consequences of worshiping a God who cares whether you love him or ignore him?

 Read Deuteronomy 30.

30 When all these blessings and curses I have set before you come upon you and you take them to heart wherever the Lord your God disperses you among the nations, 2and when you and your children return to the Lord your God and obey him with all your heart and with all your soul according to everything I command you today, 3then the Lord your God will restore your fortunes[1] and have compassion on you and gather you again from all the nations where he scattered you. 4Even if you have been banished to the most distant land under the heavens, from there the Lord your God will gather you and bring you back. 5He will bring you to the land that belonged to your fathers, and you will take possession of it. He will make you more prosperous and numerous than your fathers. 6The Lord your God will circumcise your hearts and the hearts of your descendants, so that you may love him with all your heart and with all your soul, and live. 7The Lord your God will put all these curses on your enemies who hate and persecute you. 8You will again obey the Lord and follow all his commands I am giving you today. 9Then the Lord your God will make you most prosperous in all the work of your hands and in the fruit of your womb, the young of your livestock and the crops of your land. The Lord will

[1] 3 Or *will bring you back from captivity*

again delight in you and make you prosperous, just as he delighted in your fathers, ¹⁰if you obey the LORD your God and keep his commands and decrees that are written in this Book of the Law and turn to the LORD your God with all your heart and with all your soul.

¹¹Now what I am commanding you today is not too difficult for you or beyond your reach. ¹²It is not up in heaven, so that you have to ask, "Who will ascend into heaven to get it and proclaim it to us so we may obey it?" ¹³Nor is it beyond the sea, so that you have to ask, "Who will cross the sea to get it and proclaim it to us so we may obey it?" ¹⁴No, the word is very near you; it is in your mouth and in your heart so you may obey it.

¹⁵See, I set before you today life and prosperity, death and destruction. ¹⁶For I command you today to love the LORD your God, to walk in his ways, and to keep his commands, decrees and laws; then you will live and increase, and the LORD your God will bless you in the land you are entering to possess.

¹⁷But if your heart turns away and you are not obedient, and if you are drawn away to bow down to other gods and worship them, ¹⁸I declare to you this day that you will certainly be destroyed. You will not live long in the land you are crossing the Jordan to enter and possess.

¹⁹This day I call heaven and earth as witnesses against you that I have set before you life and death, blessings and curses. Now choose life, so that you and your children may live ²⁰and that you may love the LORD your God, listen to his voice, and hold fast to him. For the LORD is your life, and he will give you many years in the land he swore to give to your fathers, Abraham, Isaac and Jacob.

 Discovering the Word 1. What is going to happen to Israel in the future? 2. How is the Lord's justice and mercy embodied in these verses? 3. How might an Israelite who had yet to enter the land respond to the warnings here? 4. Compare and contrast the choice between life and death (vv. 11–20). What is involved in each? 5. Read the passage again. What issues of the heart are woven throughout? 6. How are these verses a summary of the entire book?

Applying the Word 1. The curses and the blessings for obedience were aimed at cultivating a community of people with spiritually responsive hearts. How would you characterize the spiritual responsiveness of your own heart? 2. In what area of your life do you need the reassurance of verses 11–14, that you are able to follow God's commands?

Responding in Prayer Thank God for his love that won't let you live in disobedience. Pray that God will give you a heart that is open to learning from his loving discipline.

---

12 / *Deuteronomy 31:1–13*
Saying Goodby

"DO YOU HAVE your notebook? How about your lunch? What about your coat? Don't forget the permission slip I signed for you last night." These are the questions a parent asks as a child leaves for school. So it is with Moses as he prepares Israel for their entrance into the Promised Land without him. How hard it must have been to turn over the reins of leadership and step out of the way! And how must the people have felt? Moses was the only leader they had ever known. He knew God, he knew the law, and he always seemed to know what to do. No doubt about it, the parting, for all, was difficult. However, both Moses and the nation needed to understand that the nation had made a covenant with God, not with Moses. They needed to grasp that God was their Savior, not Moses. If Moses had continued, it wouldn't have been good for the nation, nor would it have been good for Moses himself.

 Warming Up to God We must look beyond our spiritual leaders to the God they serve. Think of someone who has been a spiritual influence in your life. Consider how they have been a means of pointing to the presence and character of God. Thank God for that person and for his grace in working through him or her.

 Read Deuteronomy 31:1–13.

31

Then Moses went out and spoke these words to all Israel: ²"I am now a hundred and twenty years old and I am no longer able to lead you. The Lord has said to me, 'You shall not cross the Jordan.' ³The Lord your God himself will cross over ahead of you. He will destroy these nations before you, and you will take possession of their land. Joshua also will cross over ahead of you, as the Lord said. ⁴And the Lord will do to them what he did to Sihon and Og, the kings of the Amorites, whom he destroyed along with their land. ⁵The Lord will deliver them to you, and you must do to them all that I have commanded you. ⁶Be strong and courageous. Do not be afraid or terrified because of them, for the Lord your God goes with you; he will never leave you nor forsake you."

⁷Then Moses summoned Joshua and said to him in the presence of all Israel, "Be strong and courageous, for you must go with this people into the land that the Lord swore to their forefathers to give them, and you must divide it among them as their inheritance. ⁸The Lord himself goes before you and will be with you; he will never leave you nor forsake you. Do not be afraid; do not be discouraged."

⁹So Moses wrote down this law and gave it to the priests, the sons of Levi, who carried the ark of the covenant of the Lord, and to all the elders of Israel. ¹⁰Then Moses commanded them: "At the end of every seven years, in the year for canceling debts, during the Feast of Tabernacles, ¹¹when all Israel comes to appear before the Lord your God at the place he will choose, you shall read this law before them in their hearing. ¹²Assemble the people—men, women and children, and the aliens living in your towns—so they can listen and learn to fear the Lord your God and follow carefully all the words of this law. ¹³Their children, who do not know this law, must hear it and learn to fear the Lord your God as long as you live in the land you are crossing the Jordan to possess."

🖊️ **Discovering the Word** 1. How would you characterize the tone of these goodby words from Moses? 2. What is the Lord's part and what is Israel's part in taking the land (vv. 3–6)? 3. How would you describe Joshua's commission from Moses (vv. 7–8)? 4. What provision is made for keeping the law a central part of the nation's life (vv. 9–13)? 5. Look through the whole chapter again. In what specific ways does Moses assure the people that the presence of God will be a help to them?

💧 **Applying the Word** 1. Moses reminds the people of what God has done as they prepare to enter the land. How does the knowledge of what God did for Israel help you to trust him for the challenges you face? 2. The presence of God was to provide a sense of confidence and courage in the time of leadership transition. How can the presence of God provide confidence and courage as you face your tasks and transitions? 3. The presence of God does not take away the need to "be strong and courageous." In what areas do you need to exercise strength and courage?

✋ **Responding in Prayer** Pray that the leaders of your church would find their strength and courage in the presence of God. Ask that God would give you a love for his law that will keep you stable and faithful throughout the duration of your Christian pilgrimage.

Deuteronomy 31:14—34:12

¹⁴The Lord said to Moses, "Now the day of your death is near. Call Joshua and present yourselves at the Tent of Meeting, where I will commission him." So Moses and Joshua came and presented themselves at the Tent of Meeting.

¹⁵Then the Lord appeared at the Tent in a pillar of cloud, and the cloud stood over the entrance to the Tent. ¹⁶And the Lord said to Moses: "You are going to rest with your fathers, and these people will soon prostitute themselves to the foreign gods of the land they are entering. They will forsake me and break the covenant I made with them. ¹⁷On that day I will become angry with them and forsake them; I will hide my face from them, and they will be destroyed. Many disasters and difficulties will come upon them, and on that day they will ask, 'Have not these disasters come upon us because our God is not with us?' ¹⁸And

I will certainly hide my face on that day because of all their wickedness in turning to other gods.

19"Now write down for yourselves this song and teach it to the Israelites and have them sing it, so that it may be a witness for me against them. 20When I have brought them into the land flowing with milk and honey, the land I promised on oath to their forefathers, and when they eat their fill and thrive, they will turn to other gods and worship them, rejecting me and breaking my covenant. 21And when many disasters and difficulties come upon them, this song will testify against them, because it will not be forgotten by their descendants. I know what they are disposed to do, even before I bring them into the land I promised them on oath." 22So Moses wrote down this song that day and taught it to the Israelites.

23The LORD gave this command to Joshua son of Nun: "Be strong and courageous, for you will bring the Israelites into the land I promised them on oath, and I myself will be with you."

24After Moses finished writing in a book the words of this law from beginning to end, 25he gave this command to the Levites who carried the ark of the covenant of the LORD: 26"Take this Book of the Law and place it beside the ark of the covenant of the LORD your God. There it will remain as a witness against you. 27For I know how rebellious and stiff-necked you are. If you have been rebellious against the LORD while I am still alive and with you, how much more will you rebel after I die! 28Assemble before me all the elders of your tribes and all your officials, so that I can speak these words in their hearing and call heaven and earth to testify against them. 29For I know that after my death you are sure to become utterly corrupt and to turn from the way I have commanded you. In days to come, disaster will fall upon you because you will do evil in the sight of the LORD and provoke him to anger by what your hands have made."

30And Moses recited the words of this song from beginning to end in the hearing of the whole assembly of Israel:

32

Listen, O heavens, and I will speak;
   hear, O earth, the words of my mouth.
2Let my teaching fall like rain
   and my words descend like dew,
like showers on new grass,

like abundant rain on tender plants.
3I will proclaim the name of the LORD.
   Oh, praise the greatness of our God!
4He is the Rock, his works are perfect,
   and all his ways are just.
A faithful God who does no wrong,
   upright and just is he.

5They have acted corruptly toward him;
   to their shame they are no longer his children,
   but a warped and crooked generation.m
6Is this the way you repay the LORD,
   O foolish and unwise people?
Is he not your Father, your Creator,n
   who made you and formed you?

7Remember the days of old;
   consider the generations long past.
Ask your father and he will tell you,
   your elders, and they will explain to you.
8When the Most High gave the nations their inheritance,
   when he divided all mankind,
he set up boundaries for the peoples
   according to the number of the sons of Israel.o
9For the LORD's portion is his people,
   Jacob his allotted inheritance.

10In a desert land he found him,
   in a barren and howling waste.
He shielded him and cared for him;
   he guarded him as the apple of his eye,
11like an eagle that stirs up its nest
   and hovers over its young,
that spreads its wings to catch them
   and carries them on its pinions.
12The LORD alone led him;
   no foreign god was with him.

13He made him ride on the heights of the land
   and fed him with the fruit of the fields.
He nourished him with honey from the rock,
   and with oil from the flinty crag,
14with curds and milk from herd and flock
   and with fattened lambs and goats,
with choice rams of Bashan
   and the finest kernels of wheat.
You drank the foaming blood of the grape.

---

m 5 Or Corrupt are they and not his children, / a generation warped and twisted to their shame   n 6 Or Father, who bought you
o 8 Masoretic Text; Dead Sea Scrolls (see also Septuagint) sons of God

¹⁵Jeshurunᵖ grew fat and kicked;
    filled with food, he became heavy and
        sleek.
He abandoned the God who made him
    and rejected the Rock his Savior.
¹⁶They made him jealous with their foreign
        gods
    and angered him with their detestable idols.
¹⁷They sacrificed to demons, which are not
        God—
    gods they had not known,
    gods that recently appeared,
    gods your fathers did not fear.
¹⁸You deserted the Rock, who fathered you;
    you forgot the God who gave you birth.

¹⁹The Lord saw this and rejected them
    because he was angered by his sons and
        daughters.
²⁰"I will hide my face from them," he said,
    "and see what their end will be;
for they are a perverse generation,
    children who are unfaithful.
²¹They made me jealous by what is no god
    and angered me with their worthless idols.
I will make them envious by those who are
        not a people;
    I will make them angry by a nation that has
        no understanding.
²²For a fire has been kindled by my wrath,
    one that burns to the realm of death�q
        below.
It will devour the earth and its harvests
    and set afire the foundations of the
        mountains.

²³"I will heap calamities upon them
    and spend my arrows against them.
²⁴I will send wasting famine against them,
    consuming pestilence and deadly plague;
I will send against them the fangs of wild
        beasts,
    the venom of vipers that glide in the dust.
²⁵In the street the sword will make them
        childless;
    in their homes terror will reign.
Young men and young women will perish,
    infants and gray-haired men.
²⁶I said I would scatter them
    and blot out their memory from mankind,
²⁷but I dreaded the taunt of the enemy,
    lest the adversary misunderstand
    and say, 'Our hand has triumphed;

the Lord has not done all this.' "

²⁸They are a nation without sense,
    there is no discernment in them.
²⁹If only they were wise and would understand
        this
    and discern what their end will be!
³⁰How could one man chase a thousand,
    or two put ten thousand to flight,
unless their Rock had sold them,
    unless the Lord had given them up?
³¹For their rock is not like our Rock,
    as even our enemies concede.
³²Their vine comes from the vine of Sodom
    and from the fields of Gomorrah.
Their grapes are filled with poison,
    and their clusters with bitterness.
³³Their wine is the venom of serpents,
    the deadly poison of cobras.

³⁴"Have I not kept this in reserve
    and sealed it in my vaults?
³⁵It is mine to avenge; I will repay.
    In due time their foot will slip;
their day of disaster is near
    and their doom rushes upon them."

³⁶The Lord will judge his people
    and have compassion on his servants
when he sees their strength is gone
    and no one is left, slave or free.
³⁷He will say: "Now where are their gods,
    the rock they took refuge in,
³⁸the gods who ate the fat of their sacrifices
    and drank the wine of their drink offerings?
Let them rise up to help you!
    Let them give you shelter!

³⁹"See now that I myself am He!
    There is no god besides me.
I put to death and I bring to life,
    I have wounded and I will heal,
    and no one can deliver out of my hand.
⁴⁰I lift my hand to heaven and declare:
    As surely as I live forever,
⁴¹when I sharpen my flashing sword
    and my hand grasps it in judgment,
I will take vengeance on my adversaries
    and repay those who hate me.
⁴²I will make my arrows drunk with blood,
    while my sword devours flesh:
the blood of the slain and the captives,

p15 Jeshurun means the upright one, that is, Israel.   q22 Hebrew to Sheol the heads of the enemy leaders."

⁴³Rejoice, O nations, with his people,ʳˑˢ
for he will avenge the blood of his servants;
he will take vengeance on his enemies
and make atonement for his land and
people.

⁴⁴Moses came with Joshuaᵗ son of Nun and spoke all the words of this song in the hearing of the people. ⁴⁵When Moses finished reciting all these words to all Israel, ⁴⁶he said to them, "Take to heart all the words I have solemnly declared to you this day, so that you may command your children to obey carefully all the words of this law. ⁴⁷They are not just idle words for you—they are your life. By them you will live long in the land you are crossing the Jordan to possess."

⁴⁸On that same day the LORD told Moses, ⁴⁹"Go up into the Abarim Range to Mount Nebo in Moab, across from Jericho, and view Canaan, the land I am giving the Israelites as their own possession. ⁵⁰There on the mountain that you have climbed you will die and be gathered to your people, just as your brother Aaron died on Mount Hor and was gathered to his people. ⁵¹This is because both of you broke faith with me in the presence of the Israelites at the waters of Meribah Kadesh in the Desert of Zin and because you did not uphold my holiness among the Israelites. ⁵²Therefore, you will see the land only from a distance; you will not enter the land I am giving to the people of Israel."

33

This is the blessing that Moses the man of God pronounced on the Israelites before his death. ²He said:

"The LORD came from Sinai
and dawned over them from Seir;
he shone forth from Mount Paran.
He came withᵘ myriads of holy ones
from the south, from his mountain
slopes.ᵛ
³Surely it is you who love the people;
all the holy ones are in your hand.
At your feet they all bow down,
and from you receive instruction,
⁴the law that Moses gave us,
the possession of the assembly of Jacob.
⁵He was king over Jeshurunʷ
when the leaders of the people assembled,
along with the tribes of Israel.

⁶"Let Reuben live and not die,

nor* his men be few."

⁷And this he said about Judah:

"Hear, O LORD, the cry of Judah;
bring him to his people.
With his own hands he defends his cause.
Oh, be his help against his foes!"

⁸About Levi he said:

"Your Thummim and Urim belong
to the man you favored.
You tested him at Massah;
you contended with him at the waters of
Meribah.
⁹He said of his father and mother,
'I have no regard for them.'
He did not recognize his brothers
or acknowledge his own children,
but he watched over your word
and guarded your covenant.
¹⁰He teaches your precepts to Jacob
and your law to Israel.
He offers incense before you
and whole burnt offerings on your altar.
¹¹Bless all his skills, O LORD,
and be pleased with the work of his hands.
Smite the loins of those who rise up against
him;
strike his foes till they rise no more."

¹²About Benjamin he said:

"Let the beloved of the LORD rest secure in
him,
for he shields him all day long,
and the one the LORD loves rests between
his shoulders."

¹³About Joseph he said:

"May the LORD bless his land
with the precious dew from heaven above
and with the deep waters that lie below;
¹⁴with the best the sun brings forth
and the finest the moon can yield;
¹⁵with the choicest gifts of the ancient
mountains
and the fruitfulness of the everlasting hills;
¹⁶with the best gifts of the earth and its fullness

ʳ43 Or *Make his people rejoice, O nations*   ˢ43 Masoretic Text; Dead Sea Scrolls (see also Septuagint) *people, / and let all the angels worship him /*   ᵗ44 Hebrew *Hoshea,* a variant of *Joshua*   ᵘ2 Or *from*   ᵛ2 The meaning of the Hebrew for this phrase is uncertain.   ʷ5 *Jeshurun* means *the upright one,* that is, Israel; also in verse 26.   ˣ6 Or *but let*

and the favor of him who dwelt in the
burning bush.
Let all these rest on the head of Joseph,
on the brow of the prince among[y] his
brothers.

[17]In majesty he is like a firstborn bull;
his horns are the horns of a wild ox.
With them he will gore the nations,
even those at the ends of the earth.
Such are the ten thousands of Ephraim;
such are the thousands of Manasseh."

[18]About Zebulun he said:

"Rejoice, Zebulun, in your going out,
and you, Issachar, in your tents.
[19]They will summon peoples to the mountain
and there offer sacrifices of righteousness;
they will feast on the abundance of the seas,
on the treasures hidden in the sand."

[20]About Gad he said:

"Blessed is he who enlarges Gad's domain!
Gad lives there like a lion,
tearing at arm or head.
[21]He chose the best land for himself;
the leader's portion was kept for him.
When the heads of the people assembled,
he carried out the LORD's righteous will,
and his judgments concerning Israel."

[22]About Dan he said:

"Dan is a lion's cub,
springing out of Bashan."

[23]About Naphtali he said:

"Naphtali is abounding with the favor of the
LORD
and is full of his blessing;
he will inherit southward to the lake."

[24]About Asher he said:

"Most blessed of sons is Asher;
let him be favored by his brothers,
and let him bathe his feet in oil.
[25]The bolts of your gates will be iron and
bronze,
and your strength will equal your days.

[26]"There is no one like the God of Jeshurun,
who rides on the heavens to help you
and on the clouds in his majesty.
[27]The eternal God is your refuge,
and underneath are the everlasting arms.

He will drive out your enemy before you,
saying, 'Destroy him!'
[28]So Israel will live in safety alone;
Jacob's spring is secure
in a land of grain and new wine,
where the heavens drop dew.
[29]Blessed are you, O Israel!
Who is like you,
a people saved by the LORD?
He is your shield and helper
and your glorious sword.
Your enemies will cower before you,
and you will trample down their high
places.[z]"

34

Then Moses climbed Mount Nebo
from the plains of Moab to the top
of Pisgah, across from Jericho.
There the LORD showed him the whole land—
from Gilead to Dan, [2]all of Naphtali, the territory
of Ephraim and Manasseh, all the land of Judah
as far as the western sea,[a] [3]the Negev and the
whole region from the Valley of Jericho, the City
of Palms, as far as Zoar. [4]Then the LORD said to
him, "This is the land I promised on oath to Abraham, Isaac and Jacob when I said, 'I will give it to
your descendants.' I have let you see it with your
eyes, but you will not cross over into it."

[5]And Moses the servant of the LORD died there
in Moab, as the LORD had said. [6]He buried him[b]
in Moab, in the valley opposite Beth Peor, but to
this day no one knows where his grave is. [7]Moses
was a hundred and twenty years old when he
died, yet his eyes were not weak nor his strength
gone. [8]The Israelites grieved for Moses in the
plains of Moab thirty days, until the time of weeping and mourning was over.

[9]Now Joshua son of Nun was filled with the
spirit[c] of wisdom because Moses had laid his
hands on him. So the Israelites listened to him
and did what the LORD had commanded Moses.

[10]Since then, no prophet has risen in Israel like
Moses, whom the LORD knew face to face, [11]who
did all those miraculous signs and wonders the
LORD sent him to do in Egypt—to Pharaoh and to
all his officials and to his whole land. [12]For no
one has ever shown the mighty power or performed the awesome deeds that Moses did in the
sight of all Israel.

[y]16 Or of the one separated from   [z]29 Or will tread upon their bodies
[a]2 That is, the Mediterranean   [b]6 Or He was buried   [c]9 Or Spirit

Joshua

Can we count on God to keep his promises?

Thousands of years ago God promised Abraham, "I will make you into a great nation" (Ge 12:2). "To your descendants I give this land, from the river of Egypt to the great river, the Euphrates" (Ge 15:18). These same promises were renewed with each generation of Abraham's descendants, but hundreds of years passed and his children still had no land to call their own. Even worse, they lived as slaves for four hundred years and wandered in the desert forty years after that. They hardly qualified as a great nation!

The book of Joshua is the story of God's making good on his promises. It tells how Israel entered and conquered the land God had promised them. In fact, God's faithfulness is so complete that at the end of the book we hear this proclamation: "You know with all your heart and soul that not one of all the good promises the LORD your God gave you has failed. Every promise has been fulfilled; not one has failed" (Jos 23:14).

Can we count on God to keep his promises? The answer from Joshua is a resounding yes! God is utterly dependable, and we can trust him completely. Joshua is a book for those whose prayers seem to go unanswered, for those who wonder if God is really alive and active, and for those who desire fresh assurance of God's dependability.

Joshua is also a fast-paced book. In it we share the excitement of the Israelites, who through God's power saw a river dry up and a city wall tumble. We watch them face overwhelming odds and emerge victorious.

The book of Joshua picks up the story of Israel's history after the death of Moses and carries it through the entry, conquest and division of the Promised Land. The events recorded began around 1406 B.C. and ended about twenty-four years later.

Although the author of the book is not identified, the traditional view is that it was written by Joshua himself, with a few additions made by Eleazar or Phinehas (for example, the reference to Joshua's death in 24:29–30). However, some scholars believe that the book may have been written by a younger contemporary of Joshua, and still others think it was not written until the beginning of the monarchy by someone who had access to various records of the actual events.

Outline

1/ Joshua 1 ———————————— *Get Ready to Go*

2/ Joshua 2 ———————————— *Rahab's Life-Changing Faith*

3/ Joshua 3:1—5:12 ———————— *Crossing the Jordan*

4/ Joshua 5:13—6:27 ———————— *Jericho Falls*

5/ Joshua 7—8 ————————— *Defeat, Confession and Victory*

6/ Joshua 9 ———————————— *Deceived*

7/ Joshua 10—12 ———————— *The Lord Fights for Israel*

8/ Joshua 14—18 ———————— *Joshua Divides the Land*

9/ Joshua 20—21 ———————— *The Lord Fulfills His Promises*

10/ Joshua 22 ———————————— *Will the Nation Survive?*

11/ Joshua 23 ———————————— *Joshua's Farewell*

12/ Joshua 24 ———————————— *Who Will Serve the Lord?*

1 / *Joshua 1*
Get Ready to Go

GOD SOMETIMES ASKS us to do things that seem far beyond our abilities. He might ask us to assume a position of leadership, or take on a demanding project, or begin a Bible study with our non-Christian friends. At such times it is easy to feel underqualified and overwhelmed. Imagine trying to fill the shoes of someone as legendary as Moses! This was the task Joshua faced. You will notice that the name Moses pops up many times in the book of Joshua. At times Joshua must have felt that the memory of Moses hung over him like a dark cloud. Now that it was his turn to lead, Joshua needed to know if the people would follow him as they had Moses. More importantly, he needed to know if God intended to help him as he had Moses.

 Warming Up to God   God has a unique task for you. It is possible that he is calling you to do some work for him even now. Ask God to make you open to doing his will.

 Read Joshua 1.

1 After the death of Moses the servant of the LORD, the LORD said to Joshua son of Nun, Moses' aide: ²"Moses my servant is dead. Now then, you and all these people, get ready to cross the Jordan River into the land I am about to give to them—to the Israelites. ³I will give you every place where you set your foot, as I promised Moses. ⁴Your territory will extend from the desert to Lebanon, and from the great river, the Euphrates—all the Hittite country—to the Great Sea*ᵃ* on the west. ⁵No one will be able to stand up against you all the days of your life. As I was with Moses, so I will be with you; I will never leave you nor forsake you.

⁶"Be strong and courageous, because you will lead these people to inherit the land I swore to their forefathers to give them. ⁷Be strong and very courageous. Be careful to obey all the law my servant Moses gave you; do not turn from it to the right or to the left, that you may be successful wherever you go. ⁸Do not let this Book of the Law depart from your mouth; meditate on it day and night, so that you may be careful to do everything written in it. Then you will be prosperous and successful. ⁹Have I not commanded you? Be strong and courageous. Do not be terrified; do not be discouraged, for the LORD your God will be with you wherever you go."

¹⁰So Joshua ordered the officers of the people: ¹¹"Go through the camp and tell the people, 'Get your supplies ready. Three days from now you will cross the Jordan here to go in and take possession of the land the LORD your God is giving you for your own.' "

¹²But to the Reubenites, the Gadites and the half-tribe of Manasseh, Joshua said, ¹³"Remember the command that Moses the servant of the LORD gave you: 'The LORD your God is giving you rest and has granted you this land.' ¹⁴Your wives, your children and your livestock may stay in the land that Moses gave you east of the Jordan, but all your fighting men, fully armed, must cross over ahead of your brothers. You are to help your brothers ¹⁵until the LORD gives them rest, as he has done for you, and until they too have taken possession of the land that the LORD your God is giving them. After that, you may go back and occupy your own land, which Moses the servant of the LORD gave you east of the Jordan toward the sunrise."

¹⁶Then they answered Joshua, "Whatever you have commanded us we will do, and wherever you send us we will go. ¹⁷Just as we fully obeyed Moses, so we will obey you. Only may the LORD your God be with you as he was with Moses. ¹⁸Whoever rebels against your word and does not obey your words, whatever you may command them, will be put to death. Only be strong and courageous!"

ᵃ4 That is, the Mediterranean

Discovering the Word 1. What promises does the Lord make to Joshua (vv. 1–9)? 2. How would these promises strengthen and encourage Joshua? 3. What commands does the Lord give to Joshua (vv. 6–9)? 4. What is the relationship between God's promises and his commands? 5. How is God's presence made evident in the response he receives from the tribes (vv. 16–18)?

Applying the Word 1. How do you react when faced with something you feel totally unqualified to do? 2. What challenging task do you face in the near future?

Responding in Prayer Thank God for his presence and strength as you seek to obey him in the challenges you face.

2 / *Joshua 2*
Rahab's Life-Changing Faith

HOW CAN WE recognize genuine faith? What does it look like? How does it act? In this study we meet a woman of faith, a member of the only family in Jericho God allowed Israel to spare. Because of Rahab's faith, not only was her life spared but God extended to her the promises he had made to Israel. She became an ancestor of both King David and Jesus. She is mentioned in James as an example of saving faith. She is also honored in Hebrews 11, "The Faith Hall of Fame." Not bad for someone known throughout history as "Rahab the prostitute"!

Warming Up to God Reflect on the past week. How has your faith made a difference in your life? Praise God for his care for you.

Read Joshua 2.

2 Then Joshua son of Nun secretly sent two spies from Shittim. "Go, look over the land," he said, "especially Jericho." So they went and entered the house of a prostitute[b] named Rahab and stayed there.

²The king of Jericho was told, "Look! Some of the Israelites have come here tonight to spy out the land." ³So the king of Jericho sent this message to Rahab: "Bring out the men who came to you and entered your house, because they have come to spy out the whole land."

⁴But the woman had taken the two men and hidden them. She said, "Yes, the men came to me, but I did not know where they had come from. ⁵At dusk, when it was time to close the city gate, the men left. I don't know which way they went. Go after them quickly. You may catch up with them." ⁶(But she had taken them up to the roof and hidden them under the stalks of flax she had laid out on the roof.) ⁷So the men set out in pursuit of the spies on the road that leads to the fords of the Jordan, and as soon as the pursuers had gone out, the gate was shut.

⁸Before the spies lay down for the night, she went up on the roof ⁹and said to them, "I know that the LORD has given this land to you and that a great fear of you has fallen on us, so that all who live in this country are melting in fear because of you. ¹⁰We have heard how the LORD dried up the water of the Red Sea[c] for you when you came out of Egypt, and what you did to Sihon and Og, the two kings of the Amorites east of the Jordan, whom you completely destroyed.[d] ¹¹When we heard of it, our hearts melted and everyone's courage failed because of you, for the LORD your God is God in heaven above and on the earth below. ¹²Now then, please swear to me by the LORD that you will show kindness to my family, because I have shown kindness to you. Give me a sure sign ¹³that you will spare the lives of my father and mother, my brothers and sisters, and all who belong to them, and that you will save us from death."

¹⁴"Our lives for your lives!" the men assured her. "If you don't tell what we are doing, we will treat you kindly and faithfully when the LORD gives us the land."

¹⁵So she let them down by a rope through the

---

b 1 Or possibly *an innkeeper*   *c 10* Hebrew *Yam Suph*; that is, Sea of Reeds   *d 10* The Hebrew term refers to the irrevocable giving over of things or persons to the LORD, often by totally destroying them.

window, for the house she lived in was part of the city wall. ¹⁶Now she had said to them, "Go to the hills so the pursuers will not find you. Hide yourselves there three days until they return, and then go on your way."

¹⁷The men said to her, "This oath you made us swear will not be binding on us ¹⁸unless, when we enter the land, you have tied this scarlet cord in the window through which you let us down, and unless you have brought your father and mother, your brothers and all your family into your house. ¹⁹If anyone goes outside your house into the street, his blood will be on his own head; we will not be responsible. As for anyone who is in the house with you, his blood will be on our head if a hand is laid on him. ²⁰But if you tell

what we are doing, we will be released from the oath you made us swear."

²¹"Agreed," she replied. "Let it be as you say." So she sent them away and they departed. And she tied the scarlet cord in the window.

²²When they left, they went into the hills and stayed there three days, until the pursuers had searched all along the road and returned without finding them. ²³Then the two men started back. They went down out of the hills, forded the river and came to Joshua son of Nun and told him everything that had happened to them. ²⁴They said to Joshua, "The LORD has surely given the whole land into our hands; all the people are melting in fear because of us."

Discovering the Word 1. What risks does Rahab take in protecting the spies (vv. 1–7)? 2. What does Rahab know and believe about the God of Israel (vv. 8–11)? 3. What deal does Rahab make in exchange for helping the spies (vv. 12–16)? 4. What conditions must she and her family fulfill in order to be saved (vv. 17–21)? 5. A missionary named Jim Elliot once made the statement "He is no fool who gives what he cannot keep to gain what he cannot lose." How might this statement apply to Rahab? 6. Why must a genuine faith express itself in actions?

Applying the Word 1. What actions have you taken recently as a direct result of your faith in Christ? 2. How can our faith have a positive effect on both Christians and non-Christians?

Responding in Prayer Ask God to make you ready to take the risks your faith requires.

---

3 / *Joshua 3:1—5:12*
Crossing the Jordan

GOD'S BLESSINGS ARE given for a purpose. He wants us to grow in our love for him as we experience kindness upon kindness. These chapters contain several reminders of all God did in leading Israel from Egypt to the Promised Land. They teach us the importance of remembering and celebrating what God has done for us.

 Warming Up to God How have God's blessings recently encouraged growth in your life?

 Read Joshua 3:1—5:12.

---

3 Early in the morning Joshua and all the Israelites set out from Shittim and went to the Jordan, where they camped before crossing over. ²After three days the officers went throughout the camp, ³giving orders to the people: "When you see the ark of the covenant of the LORD your God, and the priests, who are Levites,

carrying it, you are to move out from your positions and follow it. ⁴Then you will know which way to go, since you have never been this way before. But keep a distance of about a thousand yardsᵉ between you and the ark; do not go near it."

ᵉ4 Hebrew *about two thousand cubits* (about 900 meters)

⁵Joshua told the people, "Consecrate yourselves, for tomorrow the LORD will do amazing things among you."

⁶Joshua said to the priests, "Take up the ark of the covenant and pass on ahead of the people." So they took it up and went ahead of them.

⁷And the LORD said to Joshua, "Today I will begin to exalt you in the eyes of all Israel, so they may know that I am with you as I was with Moses. ⁸Tell the priests who carry the ark of the covenant: 'When you reach the edge of the Jordan's waters, go and stand in the river.'"

⁹Joshua said to the Israelites, "Come here and listen to the words of the LORD your God. ¹⁰This is how you will know that the living God is among you and that he will certainly drive out before you the Canaanites, Hittites, Hivites, Perizzites, Girgashites, Amorites and Jebusites. ¹¹See, the ark of the covenant of the Lord of all the earth will go into the Jordan ahead of you. ¹²Now then, choose twelve men from the tribes of Israel, one from each tribe. ¹³And as soon as the priests who carry the ark of the LORD—the Lord of all the earth—set foot in the Jordan, its waters flowing downstream will be cut off and stand up in a heap."

¹⁴So when the people broke camp to cross the Jordan, the priests carrying the ark of the covenant went ahead of them. ¹⁵Now the Jordan is at flood stage all during harvest. Yet as soon as the priests who carried the ark reached the Jordan and their feet touched the water's edge, ¹⁶the water from upstream stopped flowing. It piled up in a heap a great distance away, at a town called Adam in the vicinity of Zarethan, while the water flowing down to the Sea of the Arabah (the Salt Sea ʃ) was completely cut off. So the people crossed over opposite Jericho. ¹⁷The priests who carried the ark of the covenant of the LORD stood firm on dry ground in the middle of the Jordan, while all Israel passed by until the whole nation had completed the crossing on dry ground.

4 When the whole nation had finished crossing the Jordan, the LORD said to Joshua, ²"Choose twelve men from among the people, one from each tribe, ³and tell them to take up twelve stones from the middle of the Jordan from right where the priests stood and to carry them over with you and put them down at the place where you stay tonight."

⁴So Joshua called together the twelve men he had appointed from the Israelites, one from each tribe, ⁵and said to them, "Go over before the ark of the LORD your God into the middle of the Jordan. Each of you is to take up a stone on his shoulder, according to the number of the tribes of the Israelites, ⁶to serve as a sign among you. In the future, when your children ask you, 'What do these stones mean?' ⁷tell them that the flow of the Jordan was cut off before the ark of the covenant of the LORD. When it crossed the Jordan, the waters of the Jordan were cut off. These stones are to be a memorial to the people of Israel forever."

⁸So the Israelites did as Joshua commanded them. They took twelve stones from the middle of the Jordan, according to the number of the tribes of the Israelites, as the LORD had told Joshua; and they carried them over with them to their camp, where they put them down. ⁹Joshua set up the twelve stones that had beenᵍ in the middle of the Jordan at the spot where the priests who carried the ark of the covenant had stood. And they are there to this day.

¹⁰Now the priests who carried the ark remained standing in the middle of the Jordan until everything the LORD had commanded Joshua was done by the people, just as Moses had directed Joshua. The people hurried over, ¹¹and as soon as all of them had crossed, the ark of the LORD and the priests came to the other side while the people watched. ¹²The men of Reuben, Gad and the half-tribe of Manasseh crossed over, armed, in front of the Israelites, as Moses had directed them. ¹³About forty thousand armed for battle crossed over before the LORD to the plains of Jericho for war.

¹⁴That day the LORD exalted Joshua in the sight of all Israel; and they revered him all the days of his life, just as they had revered Moses.

¹⁵Then the LORD said to Joshua, ¹⁶"Command the priests carrying the ark of the Testimony to come up out of the Jordan."

¹⁷So Joshua commanded the priests, "Come up out of the Jordan."

¹⁸And the priests came up out of the river carrying the ark of the covenant of the LORD. No sooner had they set their feet on the dry ground than the waters of the Jordan returned to their place and ran at flood stage as before.

¹⁹On the tenth day of the first month the people went up from the Jordan and camped at Gilgal on the eastern border of Jericho. ²⁰And Joshua set

ʃ16 That is, the Dead Sea   g9 Or Joshua also set up twelve stones up at Gilgal the twelve stones they had taken out of the Jordan. ²¹He said to the Israelites, "In the future when your descendants ask their fathers, 'What do these stones mean?' ²²tell them, 'Israel crossed the Jordan on dry ground.' ²³For the LORD your God dried up the Jordan before you until you had crossed over. The LORD your God did to the Jordan just what he had done to the Red Sea*ʰ* when he dried it up before us until we had crossed over. ²⁴He did this so that all the peoples of the earth might know that the hand of the LORD is powerful and so that you might always fear the LORD your God."

5 Now when all the Amorite kings west of the Jordan and all the Canaanite kings along the coast heard how the LORD had dried up the Jordan before the Israelites until we had crossed over, their hearts melted and they no longer had the courage to face the Israelites.

²At that time the LORD said to Joshua, "Make flint knives and circumcise the Israelites again." ³So Joshua made flint knives and circumcised the Israelites at Gibeath Haaraloth.*ⁱ*

⁴Now this is why he did so: All those who came out of Egypt—all the men of military age—died in the desert on the way after leaving Egypt. ⁵All the people that came out had been circumcised, but all the people born in the desert during the journey from Egypt had not. ⁶The Israelites had

moved about in the desert forty years until all the men who were of military age when they left Egypt had died, since they had not obeyed the LORD. For the LORD had sworn to them that they would not see the land that he had solemnly promised their fathers to give us, a land flowing with milk and honey. ⁷So he raised up their sons in their place, and these were the ones Joshua circumcised. They were still uncircumcised because they had not been circumcised on the way. ⁸And after the whole nation had been circumcised, they remained where they were in camp until they were healed.

⁹Then the LORD said to Joshua, "Today I have rolled away the reproach of Egypt from you." So the place has been called Gilgal*ʲ* to this day.

¹⁰On the evening of the fourteenth day of the month, while camped at Gilgal on the plains of Jericho, the Israelites celebrated the Passover. ¹¹The day after the Passover, that very day, they ate some of the produce of the land: unleavened bread and roasted grain. ¹²The manna stopped the day after*ᵏ* they ate this food from the land; there was no longer any manna for the Israelites, but that year they ate of the produce of Canaan.

ʰ23 Hebrew Yam Suph; *that is, Sea of Reeds ⁱ3 Gibeath Haaraloth means* hill of foreskins. *ʲ9 Gilgal sounds like the Hebrew for roll. ᵏ12 Or the day*

Discovering the Word 1. Picture life with the Israelites during their three days of encampment along the Jordan. What thoughts and conversations do you imagine they had? 2. Describe the sequence of events the Israelites would have seen as they crossed the Jordan (3:3–4, 8–17). 3. Why was this miraculous crossing especially important for Joshua's leadership (3:7 and 4:14)? 4. What other goals did this miracle accomplish (3:10; 4:24; see 5:1)? 5. How would the twelve stones from the Jordan River serve as a memorial for future generations (4:1–7, 19–24)? 6. Circumcision was the sign of the covenant between God and Israel. Why was it important for the Israelites to be circumcised at this time?

Applying the Word 1. What memorials do you have to remind yourself and future generations of what God has done? 2. What have these chapters taught you about remembering and celebrating the things God has done?

Responding in Prayer Praise God for the things you have seen him do—in your life and your church.

4 / *Joshua 5:13—6:27*
Jericho Falls

WE FIGHT MANY battles in life—financial, physical, emotional and spiritual. How can we be victorious in these struggles, especially when the odds against us seem overwhelming?

Conquering the Promised Land was an enormous task. Forty years earlier the Israelites had lamented, "The land we explored devours those living in it. All the people we saw there are of great size. . . . We seemed like grasshoppers in our own eyes, and we looked the same to them" (Nu 13:32–33). Yet in spite of these obstacles, Joshua and the people of Israel now set out to conquer the first Canaanite stronghold—Jericho. As they do so, the Lord teaches them and us how to be victorious.

 Warming Up to God When have you felt that God was fighting your battles for you? How did you feel?

 Read Joshua 5:13—6:27.

---

¹³Now when Joshua was near Jericho, he looked up and saw a man standing in front of him with a drawn sword in his hand. Joshua went up to him and asked, "Are you for us or for our enemies?"

¹⁴"Neither," he replied, "but as commander of the army of the Lord I have now come." Then Joshua fell facedown to the ground in reverence, and asked him, "What message does my Lord*l* have for his servant?"

¹⁵The commander of the Lord's army replied, "Take off your sandals, for the place where you are standing is holy." And Joshua did so.

6 Now Jericho was tightly shut up because of the Israelites. No one went out and no one came in.

²Then the Lord said to Joshua, "See, I have delivered Jericho into your hands, along with its king and its fighting men. ³March around the city once with all the armed men. Do this for six days. ⁴Have seven priests carry trumpets of rams' horns in front of the ark. On the seventh day, march around the city seven times, with the priests blowing the trumpets. ⁵When you hear them sound a long blast on the trumpets, have all the people give a loud shout; then the wall of the city will collapse and the people will go up, every man straight in."

⁶So Joshua son of Nun called the priests and said to them, "Take up the ark of the covenant of the Lord and have seven priests carry trumpets in front of it." ⁷And he ordered the people, "Advance! March around the city, with the armed guard going ahead of the ark of the Lord."

⁸When Joshua had spoken to the people, the seven priests carrying the seven trumpets before the Lord went forward, blowing their trumpets, and the ark of the Lord's covenant followed them. ⁹The armed guard marched ahead of the priests who blew the trumpets, and the rear guard followed the ark. All this time the trumpets were sounding. ¹⁰But Joshua had commanded the people, "Do not give a war cry, do not raise your voices, do not say a word until the day I tell you to shout. Then shout!" ¹¹So he had the ark of the Lord carried around the city, circling it once. Then the people returned to camp and spent the night there.

¹²Joshua got up early the next morning and the priests took up the ark of the Lord. ¹³The seven priests carrying the seven trumpets went forward, marching before the ark of the Lord and blowing the trumpets. The armed men went ahead of them and the rear guard followed the ark of the Lord, while the trumpets kept sounding. ¹⁴So on the second day they marched around the city once and returned to the camp. They did this for six days.

¹⁵On the seventh day, they got up at daybreak and marched around the city seven times in the same manner, except that on that day they circled the city seven times. ¹⁶The seventh time around, when the priests sounded the trumpet blast, Joshua commanded the people, "Shout! For the Lord has given you the city! ¹⁷The city and all that is in it are to be devoted*m* to the Lord. Only Rahab the prostitute*n* and all who are with her in

*l*14 Or *lord*　　*m*17 The Hebrew term refers to the irrevocable giving over of things or persons to the Lord, often by totally destroying them; also in verses 18 and 21.　　*n*17 Or possibly *innkeeper*; also in verses 22 and 25 her house shall be spared, because she hid the spies we sent. ¹⁸But keep away from the devoted things, so that you will not bring about your own destruction by taking any of them. Otherwise you will make the camp of Israel liable to destruction and bring trouble on it. ¹⁹All the silver and gold and the articles of bronze and iron are sacred to the LORD and must go into his treasury."

²⁰When the trumpets sounded, the people shouted, and at the sound of the trumpet, when the people gave a loud shout, the wall collapsed; so every man charged straight in, and they took the city. ²¹They devoted the city to the LORD and destroyed with the sword every living thing in it—men and women, young and old, cattle, sheep and donkeys.

²²Joshua said to the two men who had spied out the land, "Go into the prostitute's house and bring her out and all who belong to her, in accordance with your oath to her." ²³So the young men who had done the spying went in and brought out Rahab, her father and mother and brothers

and all who belonged to her. They brought out her entire family and put them in a place outside the camp of Israel.

²⁴Then they burned the whole city and everything in it, but they put the silver and gold and the articles of bronze and iron into the treasury of the LORD's house. ²⁵But Joshua spared Rahab the prostitute, with her family and all who belonged to her, because she hid the men Joshua had sent as spies to Jericho—and she lives among the Israelites to this day.

²⁶At that time Joshua pronounced this solemn oath: "Cursed before the LORD is the man who undertakes to rebuild this city, Jericho:

"At the cost of his firstborn son
    will he lay its foundations;
at the cost of his youngest
    will he set up its gates."

²⁷So the LORD was with Joshua, and his fame spread throughout the land.

 Discovering the Word 1. How do you think the visit by the commander of the army of the Lord affected Joshua (5:13–15)? 2. In what ways do the Lord's instructions for the conquest of Jericho seem strange (6:1–5)? 3. How do you think the Israelites felt during this seven-day spectacle (6:6–16)? 4. What lessons was God teaching the Israelites during their seven days of marching? 5. What did it mean for this city and its contents to be devoted to the Lord (6:17–25)? 6. Why didn't God allow the Israelites to keep any of the spoils of war (6:19, 24)?

 Applying the Word 1. How is our spiritual warfare today similar to and different from Israel's conquest of Jericho (see 2Co 10:3–5)? 2. What spiritual battles are you currently fighting?

Responding in Prayer Pray for victory for yourself and others you know who are fighting spiritual battles.

---

5 / *Joshua 7—8*
Defeat, Confession and Victory

SUCCESS CAN LEAD to complacency. We feel confident, in control, optimistic—then suddenly the bottom drops out of our lives. Israel had tasted success. They had entered the Promised Land, they had won an important battle, and God was obviously with them. Conquering the city of Ai would be a piece of cake! But their confidence collapsed when they attacked the city and were routed. What had gone wrong? Had God failed them? Why hadn't God kept his promise?

 Warming Up to God Think of a time when you failed at something. How did you feel, and why?

 Read Joshua 7—8.

7 But the Israelites acted unfaithfully in regard to the devoted things[o]; Achan son of Carmi, the son of Zimri,[p] the son of Zerah, of the tribe of Judah, took some of them. So the LORD's anger burned against Israel.

²Now Joshua sent men from Jericho to Ai, which is near Beth Aven to the east of Bethel, and told them, "Go up and spy out the region." So the men went up and spied out Ai.

³When they returned to Joshua, they said, "Not all the people will have to go up against Ai. Send two or three thousand men to take it and do not weary all the people, for only a few men are there." ⁴So about three thousand men went up; but they were routed by the men of Ai, ⁵who killed about thirty-six of them. They chased the Israelites from the city gate as far as the stone quarries[q] and struck them down on the slopes. At this the hearts of the people melted and became like water.

⁶Then Joshua tore his clothes and fell facedown to the ground before the ark of the LORD, remaining there till evening. The elders of Israel did the same, and sprinkled dust on their heads. ⁷And Joshua said, "Ah, Sovereign LORD, why did you ever bring this people across the Jordan to deliver us into the hands of the Amorites to destroy us? If only we had been content to stay on the other side of the Jordan! ⁸O Lord, what can I say, now that Israel has been routed by its enemies? ⁹The Canaanites and the other people of the country will hear about this and they will surround us and wipe out our name from the earth. What then will you do for your own great name?"

¹⁰The LORD said to Joshua, "Stand up! What are you doing down on your face? ¹¹Israel has sinned; they have violated my covenant, which I commanded them to keep. They have taken some of the devoted things; they have stolen, they have lied, they have put them with their own possessions. ¹²That is why the Israelites cannot stand against their enemies; they turn their backs and run because they have been made liable to destruction. I will not be with you anymore unless you destroy whatever among you is devoted to destruction.

¹³"Go, consecrate the people. Tell them, 'Consecrate yourselves in preparation for tomorrow; for this is what the LORD, the God of Israel, says: That which is devoted is among you, O Israel. You cannot stand against your enemies until you remove it.

¹⁴" 'In the morning, present yourselves tribe by tribe. The tribe that the LORD takes shall come forward clan by clan; the clan that the LORD takes shall come forward family by family; and the family that the LORD takes shall come forward man by man. ¹⁵He who is caught with the devoted things shall be destroyed by fire, along with all that belongs to him. He has violated the covenant of the LORD and has done a disgraceful thing in Israel!' "

¹⁶Early the next morning Joshua had Israel come forward by tribes, and Judah was taken. ¹⁷The clans of Judah came forward, and he took the Zerahites. He had the clan of the Zerahites come forward by families, and Zimri was taken. ¹⁸Joshua had his family come forward man by man, and Achan son of Carmi, the son of Zimri, the son of Zerah, of the tribe of Judah, was taken.

¹⁹Then Joshua said to Achan, "My son, give glory to the LORD,[r] the God of Israel, and give him the praise.[s] Tell me what you have done; do not hide it from me."

²⁰Achan replied, "It is true! I have sinned against the LORD, the God of Israel. This is what I have done: ²¹When I saw in the plunder a beautiful robe from Babylonia,[t] two hundred shekels[u] of silver and a wedge of gold weighing fifty shekels,[v] I coveted them and took them. They are hidden in the ground inside my tent, with the silver underneath."

²²So Joshua sent messengers, and they ran to the tent, and there it was, hidden in his tent, with the silver underneath. ²³They took the things from the tent, brought them to Joshua and all the Israelites and spread them out before the LORD.

²⁴Then Joshua, together with all Israel, took Achan son of Zerah, the silver, the robe, the gold wedge, his sons and daughters, his cattle, donkeys and sheep, his tent and all that he had, to the Valley of Achor. ²⁵Joshua said, "Why have you brought this trouble on us? The LORD will bring trouble on you today."

Then all Israel stoned him, and after they had stoned the rest, they burned them. ²⁶Over Achan they heaped up a large pile of rocks, which remains to this day. Then the LORD turned from his

---

o 1 The Hebrew term refers to the irrevocable giving over of things or persons to the LORD, often by totally destroying them; also in verses 11, 12, 13 and 15.   *p 1* See Septuagint and 1 Chron. 2:6; Hebrew *Zabdi*; also in verses 17 and 18.   *q 5* Or *as far as Shebarim*   *r 19* A solemn charge to tell the truth   *s 19* Or *and confess to him* *t 21* Hebrew *Shinar*   *u 21* That is, about 5 pounds (about 2.3 kilograms)   *v 21* That is, about 1 1/4 pounds (about 0.6 kilogram) fierce anger. Therefore that place has been called the Valley of Achor[w] ever since.

8 Then the LORD said to Joshua, "Do not be afraid; do not be discouraged. Take the whole army with you, and go up and attack Ai. For I have delivered into your hands the king of Ai, his people, his city and his land. ²You shall do to Ai and its king as you did to Jericho and its king, except that you may carry off their plunder and livestock for yourselves. Set an ambush behind the city."

³So Joshua and the whole army moved out to attack Ai. He chose thirty thousand of his best fighting men and sent them out at night ⁴with these orders: "Listen carefully. You are to set an ambush behind the city. Don't go very far from it. All of you be on the alert. ⁵I and all those with me will advance on the city, and when the men come out against us, as they did before, we will flee from them. ⁶They will pursue us until we have lured them away from the city, for they will say, 'They are running away from us as they did before.' So when we flee from them, ⁷you are to rise up from ambush and take the city. The LORD your God will give it into your hand. ⁸When you have taken the city, set it on fire. Do what the LORD has commanded. See to it; you have my orders."

⁹Then Joshua sent them off, and they went to the place of ambush and lay in wait between Bethel and Ai, to the west of Ai—but Joshua spent that night with the people.

¹⁰Early the next morning Joshua mustered his men, and he and the leaders of Israel marched before them to Ai. ¹¹The entire force that was with him marched up and approached the city and arrived in front of it. They set up camp north of Ai, with the valley between them and the city. ¹²Joshua had taken about five thousand men and set them in ambush between Bethel and Ai, to the west of the city. ¹³They had the soldiers take up their positions—all those in the camp to the north of the city and the ambush to the west of it. That night Joshua went into the valley.

¹⁴When the king of Ai saw this, he and all the men of the city hurried out early in the morning to meet Israel in battle at a certain place overlooking the Arabah. But he did not know that an ambush had been set against him behind the city. ¹⁵Joshua and all Israel let themselves be driven back before them, and they fled toward the desert. ¹⁶All the men of Ai were called to pursue them, and they pursued Joshua and were lured away from the city. ¹⁷Not a man remained in Ai or Bethel who did not go after Israel. They left the city open and went in pursuit of Israel.

¹⁸Then the LORD said to Joshua, "Hold out toward Ai the javelin that is in your hand, for into your hand I will deliver the city." So Joshua held out his javelin toward Ai. ¹⁹As soon as he did this, the men in the ambush rose quickly from their position and rushed forward. They entered the city and captured it and quickly set it on fire.

²⁰The men of Ai looked back and saw the smoke of the city rising against the sky, but they had no chance to escape in any direction, for the Israelites who had been fleeing toward the desert had turned back against their pursuers. ²¹For when Joshua and all Israel saw that the ambush had taken the city and that smoke was going up from the city, they turned around and attacked the men of Ai. ²²The men of the ambush also came out of the city against them, so that they were caught in the middle, with Israelites on both sides. Israel cut them down, leaving them neither survivors nor fugitives. ²³But they took the king of Ai alive and brought him to Joshua.

²⁴When Israel had finished killing all the men of Ai in the fields and in the desert where they had chased them, and when every one of them had been put to the sword, all the Israelites returned to Ai and killed those who were in it. ²⁵Twelve thousand men and women fell that day—all the people of Ai. ²⁶For Joshua did not draw back the hand that held out his javelin until he had destroyed[x] all who lived in Ai. ²⁷But Israel did carry off for themselves the livestock and plunder of this city, as the LORD had instructed Joshua.

²⁸So Joshua burned Ai and made it a permanent heap of ruins, a desolate place to this day. ²⁹He hung the king of Ai on a tree and left him there until evening. At sunset, Joshua ordered them to take his body from the tree and throw it down at the entrance of the city gate. And they raised a large pile of rocks over it, which remains to this day.

³⁰Then Joshua built on Mount Ebal an altar to the LORD, the God of Israel, ³¹as Moses the servant of the LORD had commanded the Israelites. He built it according to what is written in the Book of the Law of Moses—an altar of uncut stones, on

---

w26 *Achor* means *trouble.*   *x26* The Hebrew term refers to the irrevocable giving over of things or persons to the LORD, often by totally destroying them.

which no iron tool had been used. On it they offered to the LORD burnt offerings and sacrificed fellowship offerings.ʸ ³²There, in the presence of the Israelites, Joshua copied on stones the law of Moses, which he had written. ³³All Israel, aliens and citizens alike, with their elders, officials and judges, were standing on both sides of the ark of the covenant of the LORD, facing those who carried it—the priests, who were Levites. Half of the people stood in front of Mount Gerizim and half of them in front of Mount Ebal, as Moses the servant of the LORD had formerly commanded when he gave instructions to bless the people of Israel.

³⁴Afterward, Joshua read all the words of the law—the blessings and the curses—just as it is written in the Book of the Law. ³⁵There was not a word of all that Moses had commanded that Joshua did not read to the whole assembly of Israel, including the women and children, and the aliens who lived among them.

y31 Traditionally peace offerings

 Discovering the Word   1. What are Joshua's concerns after this defeat (7:6–9)?   2. How do God's concerns differ from Joshua's (7:10–15)?   3. Joshua urged Achan to "give glory to the LORD" by admitting his crime (7:19). How does confession glorify God?   4. How did the second attack on Ai differ from the first (8:1–29)?   5. If you had been an Israelite, what thoughts would have come to mind each time you saw the rock piles mentioned in 7:26 and 8:29?   6. What impact would the reading of the law have had on the Israelites (8:32–35)?

 Applying the Word   1. Joshua stated that Achan was being stoned because he had brought disaster on the Israelites (7:25). Thirty-six Israelite warriors had already died because of Achan's sin. How might our sins affect others?   2. What reminders can help keep us from sinning?

 Responding in Prayer   Bring any sin in your life before God. Confess it to him with a penitent heart.

---

6 / *Joshua 9*
Deceived

SATAN'S PRIMARY STRATEGY is deceit. He seduces us into believing that a lie is truth, that evil is good and that a "suicidal plunge is really a leap into life" (Derek Kidner, *Genesis* [Downers Grove, Ill.: InterVarsity Press, 1967], p. 68).

Warming Up to God   How do you decide whether to make a decision on your own or to pray about it first?

Read Joshua 9.

---

9 Now when all the kings west of the Jordan heard about these things—those in the hill country, in the western foothills, and along the entire coast of the Great Seaᶻ as far as Lebanon (the kings of the Hittites, Amorites, Canaanites, Perizzites, Hivites and Jebusites)— ²they came together to make war against Joshua and Israel.

³However, when the people of Gibeon heard what Joshua had done to Jericho and Ai, ⁴they resorted to a ruse: They went as a delegation whose donkeys were loadedᵃ with worn-out sacks and old wineskins, cracked and mended. ⁵The men put worn and patched sandals on their feet and wore old clothes. All the bread of their food supply was dry and moldy. ⁶Then they went to Joshua in the camp at Gilgal and said to him and the men of Israel, "We have come from a distant country; make a treaty with us."

z1 That is, the Mediterranean   a4 Most Hebrew manuscripts; some Hebrew manuscripts, Vulgate and Syriac (see also Septuagint) They prepared provisions and loaded their donkeys

⁷The men of Israel said to the Hivites, "But perhaps you live near us. How then can we make a treaty with you?"

⁸"We are your servants," they said to Joshua.

But Joshua asked, "Who are you and where do you come from?"

⁹They answered: "Your servants have come from a very distant country because of the fame of the LORD your God. For we have heard reports of him: all that he did in Egypt, ¹⁰and all that he did to the two kings of the Amorites east of the Jordan—Sihon king of Heshbon, and Og king of Bashan, who reigned in Ashtaroth. ¹¹And our elders and all those living in our country said to us, 'Take provisions for your journey; go and meet them and say to them, "We are your servants; make a treaty with us." ' ¹²This bread of ours was warm when we packed it at home on the day we left to come to you. But now see how dry and moldy it is. ¹³And these wineskins that we filled were new, but see how cracked they are. And our clothes and sandals are worn out by the very long journey."

¹⁴The men of Israel sampled their provisions but did not inquire of the LORD. ¹⁵Then Joshua made a treaty of peace with them to let them live, and the leaders of the assembly ratified it by oath.

¹⁶Three days after they made the treaty with the Gibeonites, the Israelites heard that they were neighbors, living near them. ¹⁷So the Israelites set out and on the third day came to their cities: Gibeon, Kephirah, Beeroth and Kiriath Jearim. ¹⁸But the Israelites did not attack them, because the leaders of the assembly had sworn an oath to them by the LORD, the God of Israel.

The whole assembly grumbled against the leaders, ¹⁹but all the leaders answered, "We have given them our oath by the LORD, the God of Israel, and we cannot touch them now. ²⁰This is what we will do to them: We will let them live, so that wrath will not fall on us for breaking the oath we swore to them." ²¹They continued, "Let them live, but let them be woodcutters and water carriers for the entire community." So the leaders' promise to them was kept.

²²Then Joshua summoned the Gibeonites and said, "Why did you deceive us by saying, 'We live a long way from you,' while actually you live near us? ²³You are now under a curse: You will never cease to serve as woodcutters and water carriers for the house of my God."

²⁴They answered Joshua, "Your servants were clearly told how the LORD your God had commanded his servant Moses to give you the whole land and to wipe out all its inhabitants from before you. So we feared for our lives because of you, and that is why we did this. ²⁵We are now in your hands. Do to us whatever seems good and right to you."

²⁶So Joshua saved them from the Israelites, and they did not kill them. ²⁷That day he made the Gibeonites woodcutters and water carriers for the community and for the altar of the LORD at the place the LORD would choose. And that is what they are to this day.

Discovering the Word 1. When they hear about Israel's victories, how does the Gibeonites' reaction differ from that of the kings west of the Jordan (vv. 1–6)? 2. What made the Gibeonites' deception so convincing to the Israelites (vv. 7–13)? 3. The Israelites were fooled because they "did not inquire of the LORD" (v. 14). Why should they have known that this was not a decision to be made on their own? 4. Why did the Israelites take their oath so seriously, even though it was based on a lie (vv. 16–19)? 5. The Gibeonites are similar to Rahab in that, for both, their faith led them to lie (vv. 22–27). Why aren't the Gibeonites commended for their faith as Rahab was?

Applying the Word 1. What tricks does Satan use to keep us from seeking God's guidance? 2. In what areas are we tempted to make peace with a sinful world?

Responding in Prayer Pray for those who are even now under Satan's deceitful influence.

7 / *Joshua 10—12*
The Lord Fights for Israel

GOD DEMONSTRATES HIS faithfulness to every Christian. He strengthens us when we are weak, comforts us when we are suffering, heals us when we are sick. He provides for all of our physical, emotional and spiritual needs. After all this, why do we often find it difficult to trust him? Joshua and Israel had miraculously crossed the Jordan and conquered the cities of Jericho and Ai. Yet in spite of these victories, they still needed to be reassured that God was with them.

 Warming Up to God Why is it often hard to trust God for the future even though he has been faithful in the past?

 Read Joshua 10—12.

10 Now Adoni-Zedek king of Jerusalem heard that Joshua had taken Ai and totally destroyed[b] it, doing to Ai and its king as he had done to Jericho and its king, and that the people of Gibeon had made a treaty of peace with Israel and were living near them. [2]He and his people were very much alarmed at this, because Gibeon was an important city, like one of the royal cities; it was larger than Ai, and all its men were good fighters. [3]So Adoni-Zedek king of Jerusalem appealed to Hoham king of Hebron, Piram king of Jarmuth, Japhia king of Lachish and Debir king of Eglon. [4]"Come up and help me attack Gibeon," he said, "because it has made peace with Joshua and the Israelites."

[5]Then the five kings of the Amorites—the kings of Jerusalem, Hebron, Jarmuth, Lachish and Eglon—joined forces. They moved up with all their troops and took up positions against Gibeon and attacked it.

[6]The Gibeonites then sent word to Joshua in the camp at Gilgal: "Do not abandon your servants. Come up to us quickly and save us! Help us, because all the Amorite kings from the hill country have joined forces against us."

[7]So Joshua marched up from Gilgal with his entire army, including all the best fighting men. [8]The LORD said to Joshua, "Do not be afraid of them; I have given them into your hand. Not one of them will be able to withstand you."

[9]After an all-night march from Gilgal, Joshua took them by surprise. [10]The LORD threw them into confusion before Israel, who defeated them in a great victory at Gibeon. Israel pursued them along the road going up to Beth Horon and cut them down all the way to Azekah and Makkedah. [11]As they fled before Israel on the road down

from Beth Horon to Azekah, the LORD hurled large hailstones down on them from the sky, and more of them died from the hailstones than were killed by the swords of the Israelites.

[12]On the day the LORD gave the Amorites over to Israel, Joshua said to the LORD in the presence of Israel:

"O sun, stand still over Gibeon,
   O moon, over the Valley of Aijalon."
[13]So the sun stood still,
   and the moon stopped,
      till the nation avenged itself on[c] its
         enemies,

as it is written in the Book of Jashar.

The sun stopped in the middle of the sky and delayed going down about a full day. [14]There has never been a day like it before or since, a day when the LORD listened to a man. Surely the LORD was fighting for Israel!

[15]Then Joshua returned with all Israel to the camp at Gilgal.

[16]Now the five kings had fled and hidden in the cave at Makkedah. [17]When Joshua was told that the five kings had been found hiding in the cave at Makkedah, [18]he said, "Roll large rocks up to the mouth of the cave, and post some men there to guard it. [19]But don't stop! Pursue your enemies, attack them from the rear and don't let them reach their cities, for the LORD your God has given them into your hand."

[20]So Joshua and the Israelites destroyed them completely—almost to a man—but the few who were left reached their fortified cities. [21]The whole army then returned safely to Joshua in the

---

b 1 The Hebrew term refers to the irrevocable giving over of things or persons to the LORD, often by totally destroying them; also in verses 28, 35, 37, 39 and 40.   c 13 Or nation triumphed over camp at Makkedah, and no one uttered a word against the Israelites.

²²Joshua said, "Open the mouth of the cave and bring those five kings out to me." ²³So they brought the five kings out of the cave—the kings of Jerusalem, Hebron, Jarmuth, Lachish and Eglon. ²⁴When they had brought these kings to Joshua, he summoned all the men of Israel and said to the army commanders who had come with him, "Come here and put your feet on the necks of these kings." So they came forward and placed their feet on their necks.

²⁵Joshua said to them, "Do not be afraid; do not be discouraged. Be strong and courageous. This is what the LORD will do to all the enemies you are going to fight." ²⁶Then Joshua struck and killed the kings and hung them on five trees, and they were left hanging on the trees until evening.

²⁷At sunset Joshua gave the order and they took them down from the trees and threw them into the cave where they had been hiding. At the mouth of the cave they placed large rocks, which are there to this day.

²⁸That day Joshua took Makkedah. He put the city and its king to the sword and totally destroyed everyone in it. He left no survivors. And he did to the king of Makkedah as he had done to the king of Jericho.

²⁹Then Joshua and all Israel with him moved on from Makkedah to Libnah and attacked it. ³⁰The LORD also gave that city and its king into Israel's hand. The city and everyone in it Joshua put to the sword. He left no survivors there. And he did to its king as he had done to the king of Jericho.

³¹Then Joshua and all Israel with him moved on from Libnah to Lachish; he took up positions against it and attacked it. ³²The LORD handed Lachish over to Israel, and Joshua took it on the second day. The city and everyone in it he put to the sword, just as he had done to Libnah. ³³Meanwhile, Horam king of Gezer had come up to help Lachish, but Joshua defeated him and his army—until no survivors were left.

³⁴Then Joshua and all Israel with him moved on from Lachish to Eglon; they took up positions against it and attacked it. ³⁵They captured it that same day and put it to the sword and totally destroyed everyone in it, just as they had done to Lachish.

³⁶Then Joshua and all Israel with him went up from Eglon to Hebron and attacked it. ³⁷They took the city and put it to the sword, together with its king, its villages and everyone in it. They left no survivors. Just as at Eglon, they totally destroyed it and everyone in it.

³⁸Then Joshua and all Israel with him turned around and attacked Debir. ³⁹They took the city, its king and its villages, and put them to the sword. Everyone in it they totally destroyed. They left no survivors. They did to Debir and its king as they had done to Libnah and its king and to Hebron.

⁴⁰So Joshua subdued the whole region, including the hill country, the Negev, the western foothills and the mountain slopes, together with all their kings. He left no survivors. He totally destroyed all who breathed, just as the LORD, the God of Israel, had commanded. ⁴¹Joshua subdued them from Kadesh Barnea to Gaza and from the whole region of Goshen to Gibeon. ⁴²All these kings and their lands Joshua conquered in one campaign, because the LORD, the God of Israel, fought for Israel.

⁴³Then Joshua returned with all Israel to the camp at Gilgal.

11

When Jabin king of Hazor heard of this, he sent word to Jobab king of Madon, to the kings of Shimron and Acshaph, ²and to the northern kings who were in the mountains, in the Arabah south of Kinnereth, in the western foothills and in Naphoth Dor^d on the west; ³to the Canaanites in the east and west; to the Amorites, Hittites, Perizzites and Jebusites in the hill country; and to the Hivites below Hermon in the region of Mizpah. ⁴They came out with all their troops and a large number of horses and chariots—a huge army, as numerous as the sand on the seashore. ⁵All these kings joined forces and made camp together at the Waters of Merom, to fight against Israel.

⁶The LORD said to Joshua, "Do not be afraid of them, because by this time tomorrow I will hand all of them over to Israel, slain. You are to hamstring their horses and burn their chariots."

⁷So Joshua and his whole army came against them suddenly at the Waters of Merom and attacked them, ⁸and the LORD gave them into the

^d2 Or *in the heights of Dor*

hand of Israel. They defeated them and pursued them all the way to Greater Sidon, to Misrephoth Maim, and to the Valley of Mizpah on the east, until no survivors were left. ⁹Joshua did to them as the LORD had directed: He hamstrung their horses and burned their chariots.

¹⁰At that time Joshua turned back and captured Hazor and put its king to the sword. (Hazor had been the head of all these kingdoms.) ¹¹Everyone in it they put to the sword. They totally destroyed[e] them, not sparing anything that breathed, and he burned up Hazor itself.

¹²Joshua took all these royal cities and their kings and put them to the sword. He totally destroyed them, as Moses the servant of the LORD had commanded. ¹³Yet Israel did not burn any of the cities built on their mounds—except Hazor, which Joshua burned. ¹⁴The Israelites carried off for themselves all the plunder and livestock of these cities, but all the people they put to the sword until they completely destroyed them, not sparing anyone that breathed. ¹⁵As the LORD commanded his servant Moses, so Moses commanded Joshua, and Joshua did it; he left nothing undone of all that the LORD commanded Moses.

¹⁶So Joshua took this entire land: the hill country, all the Negev, the whole region of Goshen, the western foothills, the Arabah and the mountains of Israel with their foothills, ¹⁷from Mount Halak, which rises toward Seir, to Baal Gad in the Valley of Lebanon below Mount Hermon. He captured all their kings and struck them down, putting them to death. ¹⁸Joshua waged war against all these kings for a long time. ¹⁹Except for the Hivites living in Gibeon, not one city made a treaty of peace with the Israelites, who took them all in battle. ²⁰For it was the LORD himself who hardened their hearts to wage war against Israel, so that he might destroy them totally, exterminating them without mercy, as the LORD had commanded Moses.

²¹At that time Joshua went and destroyed the Anakites from the hill country: from Hebron, Debir and Anab, from all the hill country of Judah, and from all the hill country of Israel. Joshua totally destroyed them and their towns. ²²No Anakites were left in Israelite territory; only in Gaza, Gath and Ashdod did any survive. ²³So Joshua took the entire land, just as the LORD had directed Moses, and he gave it as an inheritance to Israel according to their tribal divisions.

Then the land had rest from war.

12

These are the kings of the land whom the Israelites had defeated and whose territory they took over east of the Jordan, from the Arnon Gorge to Mount Hermon, including all the eastern side of the Arabah:

²Sihon king of the Amorites,
who reigned in Heshbon. He ruled from Aroer on the rim of the Arnon Gorge—from the middle of the gorge—to the Jabbok River, which is the border of the Ammonites. This included half of Gilead. ³He also ruled over the eastern Arabah from the Sea of Kinnereth[f] to the Sea of the Arabah (the Salt Sea[g]), to Beth Jeshimoth, and then southward below the slopes of Pisgah.

⁴And the territory of Og king of Bashan,
one of the last of the Rephaites, who reigned in Ashtaroth and Edrei. ⁵He ruled over Mount Hermon, Salecah, all of Bashan to the border of the people of Geshur and Maacah, and half of Gilead to the border of Sihon king of Heshbon.

⁶Moses, the servant of the LORD, and the Israelites conquered them. And Moses the servant of the LORD gave their land to the Reubenites, the Gadites and the half-tribe of Manasseh to be their possession.

⁷These are the kings of the land that Joshua and the Israelites conquered on the west side of the Jordan, from Baal Gad in the Valley of Lebanon to Mount Halak, which rises toward Seir (their lands Joshua gave as an inheritance to the tribes of Israel according to their tribal divisions— ⁸the hill country, the western foothills, the Arabah, the mountain slopes, the desert and the Negev—the lands of the Hittites, Amorites, Canaanites, Perizzites, Hivites and Jebusites):

⁹the king of Jericho	one
the king of Ai (near Bethel)	one
¹⁰the king of Jerusalem	one
the king of Hebron	one
¹¹the king of Jarmuth	one
the king of Lachish	one
¹²the king of Eglon	one
the king of Gezer	one
¹³the king of Debir	one

---

e11 The Hebrew term refers to the irrevocable giving over of things or persons to the LORD, often by totally destroying them; also in verses 12, 20 and 21.   f3 That is, Galilee   g3 That is, the Dead Sea

the king of Geder	one	20the king of Shimron Meron	one
14the king of Hormah	one	the king of Acshaph	one
the king of Arad	one	21the king of Taanach	one
15the king of Libnah	one	the king of Megiddo	one
the king of Adullam	one	22the king of Kedesh	one
16the king of Makkedah	one	the king of Jokneam in Carmel	one
the king of Bethel	one	23the king of Dor (in Naphoth Dorʰ)	one
17the king of Tappuah	one	the king of Goyim in Gilgal	one
the king of Hepher	one	24the king of Tirzah	one
18the king of Aphek	one	thirty-one kings in all.	
the king of Lasharon	one		
19the king of Madon	one	ʰ23 Or *in the heights of Dor*	
the king of Hazor	one		

Discovering the Word 1. The Lord tells Joshua, "Do not be afraid of them; I have given them into your hand" (10:8). After miraculously crossing the Jordan and conquering Jericho and Ai, why would Joshua need this reassurance? 2. Verse 14 concludes, "Surely the Lᴏʀᴅ was fighting for Israel!" How is this obvious from 10:9–15? 3. After the Lord reassures him, how does Joshua reassure his army about future battles (10:16–27)? 4. How does the Lord demonstrate his faithfulness to Israel during the southern campaign (10:29–43)? 5. During the northern campaign, how does Joshua demonstrate his obedience to the Lord (11:6–23)? 6. In chapters 11—12 we do not read of any miraculous intervention by God as we did in previous chapters. How did the Israelites know that God was still the one giving them the victory?

Applying the Word 1. In spite of past victories, in what areas do you need to be reassured of God's presence and power? Explain. 2. What can we do to encourage others about God's faithfulness? 3. Why is our obedience an important factor if we wish to see God's power?

Responding in Prayer Pray that God would make his presence real to you.

Joshua 13

13 When Joshua was old and well advanced in years, the Lᴏʀᴅ said to him, "You are very old, and there are still very large areas of land to be taken over.

2"This is the land that remains: all the regions of the Philistines and Geshurites: 3from the Shihor River on the east of Egypt to the territory of Ekron on the north, all of it counted as Canaanite (the territory of the five Philistine rulers in Gaza, Ashdod, Ashkelon, Gath and Ekron—that of the Avites); 4from the south, all the land of the Canaanites, from Arah of the Sidonians as far as Aphek, the region of the Amorites, 5the area of the Gebalitesⁱ; and all Lebanon to the east, from Baal Gad below Mount Hermon to Leboʲ Hamath.

6"As for all the inhabitants of the mountain re-

gions from Lebanon to Misrephoth Maim, that is, all the Sidonians, I myself will drive them out before the Israelites. Be sure to allocate this land to Israel for an inheritance, as I have instructed you, 7and divide it as an inheritance among the nine tribes and half of the tribe of Manasseh."

8The other half of Manasseh,ᵏ the Reubenites and the Gadites had received the inheritance that Moses had given them east of the Jordan, as he, the servant of the Lᴏʀᴅ, had assigned it to them.

9It extended from Aroer on the rim of the Arnon Gorge, and from the town in the middle of the gorge, and included the whole plateau of Medeba as far as Dibon, 10and all the towns of Sihon king of the Amorites, who ruled in Heshbon, out to the border of the

ⁱ5 That is, the area of Byblos ʲ5 Or *to the entrance to*
ᵏ8 Hebrew *With it* (that is, with the other half of Manasseh)

Ammonites. ¹¹It also included Gilead, the territory of the people of Geshur and Maacah, all of Mount Hermon and all Bashan as far as Salecah— ¹²that is, the whole kingdom of Og in Bashan, who had reigned in Ashtaroth and Edrei and had survived as one of the last of the Rephaites. Moses had defeated them and taken over their land. ¹³But the Israelites did not drive out the people of Geshur and Maacah, so they continue to live among the Israelites to this day.

¹⁴But to the tribe of Levi he gave no inheritance, since the offerings made by fire to the LORD, the God of Israel, are their inheritance, as he promised them.

¹⁵This is what Moses had given to the tribe of Reuben, clan by clan:

¹⁶The territory from Aroer on the rim of the Arnon Gorge, and from the town in the middle of the gorge, and the whole plateau past Medeba ¹⁷to Heshbon and all its towns on the plateau, including Dibon, Bamoth Baal, Beth Baal Meon, ¹⁸Jahaz, Kedemoth, Mephaath, ¹⁹Kiriathaim, Sibmah, Zereth Shahar on the hill in the valley, ²⁰Beth Peor, the slopes of Pisgah, and Beth Jeshimoth ²¹—all the towns on the plateau and the entire realm of Sihon king of the Amorites, who ruled at Heshbon. Moses had defeated him and the Midianite chiefs, Evi, Rekem, Zur, Hur and Reba—princes allied with Sihon—who lived in that country. ²²In addition to those slain in battle, the Israelites had put to the sword Balaam son of Beor, who practiced divination. ²³The boundary of the Reubenites was the bank of the Jordan. These towns and their villages were the inheritance of the Reubenites, clan by clan.

²⁴This is what Moses had given to the tribe of Gad, clan by clan:

²⁵The territory of Jazer, all the towns of Gilead and half the Ammonite country as far as Aroer, near Rabbah; ²⁶and from Heshbon to Ramath Mizpah and Betonim, and from Mahanaim to the territory of Debir; ²⁷and in the valley, Beth Haram, Beth Nimrah, Succoth and Zaphon with the rest of the realm of Sihon king of Heshbon (the east side of the Jordan, the territory up to the end of the Sea of Kinnereth[l]). ²⁸These towns and their villages were the inheritance of the Gadites, clan by clan.

²⁹This is what Moses had given to the half-tribe of Manasseh, that is, to half the family of the descendants of Manasseh, clan by clan:

³⁰The territory extending from Mahanaim and including all of Bashan, the entire realm of Og king of Bashan—all the settlements of Jair in Bashan, sixty towns, ³¹half of Gilead, and Ashtaroth and Edrei (the royal cities of Og in Bashan). This was for the descendants of Makir son of Manasseh—for half of the sons of Makir, clan by clan.

³²This is the inheritance Moses had given when he was in the plains of Moab across the Jordan east of Jericho. ³³But to the tribe of Levi, Moses had given no inheritance; the LORD, the God of Israel, is their inheritance, as he promised them.

¹27 That is, Galilee

8 / *Joshua 14—18*
Joshua Divides the Land

CHRISTIANS OFTEN FEEL more like captives than conquerors. What hinders our spiritual progress? Why do we sometimes experience so little when we are promised so much? God had proven himself to Israel throughout their many battles. He had promised to be with them in the conquest of Canaan and had kept his promise. Yet in spite of many victories, much of the land remained to be conquered. These chapters look at why Israel had failed to possess all that God had promised.

Warming Up to God In what one area of your life would you most like to see spiritual progress?

Read Joshua 14—18.

14 Now these are the areas the Israelites received as an inheritance in the land of Canaan, which Eleazar the priest, Joshua son of Nun and the heads of the tribal clans of Israel allotted to them. ²Their inheritances were assigned by lot to the nine-and-a-half tribes, as the Lord had commanded through Moses. ³Moses had granted the two-and-a-half tribes their inheritance east of the Jordan but had not granted the Levites an inheritance among the rest, ⁴for the sons of Joseph had become two tribes—Manasseh and Ephraim. The Levites received no share of the land but only towns to live in, with pasturelands for their flocks and herds. ⁵So the Israelites divided the land, just as the Lord had commanded Moses.

⁶Now the men of Judah approached Joshua at Gilgal, and Caleb son of Jephunneh the Kenizzite said to him, "You know what the Lord said to Moses the man of God at Kadesh Barnea about you and me. ⁷I was forty years old when Moses the servant of the Lord sent me from Kadesh Barnea to explore the land. And I brought him back a report according to my convictions, ⁸but my brothers who went up with me made the hearts of the people melt with fear. I, however, followed the Lord my God wholeheartedly. ⁹So on that day Moses swore to me, 'The land on which your feet have walked will be your inheritance and that of your children forever, because you have followed the Lord my God wholeheartedly.'ᵐ

¹⁰"Now then, just as the Lord promised, he has kept me alive for forty-five years since the time he said this to Moses, while Israel moved about in the desert. So here I am today, eighty-five years old! ¹¹I am still as strong today as the day Moses sent me out; I'm just as vigorous to go out to battle now as I was then. ¹²Now give me this hill country that the Lord promised me that day. You yourself heard then that the Anakites were there and their cities were large and fortified, but, the Lord helping me, I will drive them out just as he said."

¹³Then Joshua blessed Caleb son of Jephunneh and gave him Hebron as his inheritance. ¹⁴So Hebron has belonged to Caleb son of Jephunneh the Kenizzite ever since, because he followed the Lord, the God of Israel, wholeheartedly. ¹⁵(Hebron used to be called Kiriath Arba after Arba, who was the greatest man among the Anakites.)

Then the land had rest from war.

15 The allotment for the tribe of Judah, clan by clan, extended down to the territory of Edom, to the Desert of Zin in the extreme south.

²Their southern boundary started from the bay at the southern end of the Salt Sea,ⁿ ³crossed south of Scorpionᵒ Pass, continued on to Zin and went over to the south of Kadesh Barnea. Then it ran past Hezron up to Addar and curved around to Karka. ⁴It then passed along to Azmon and joined the Wadi of Egypt, ending at the sea. This is theirᵖ southern boundary.

⁵The eastern boundary is the Salt Sea as far as the mouth of the Jordan.

The northern boundary started from the bay of the sea at the mouth of the Jordan, ⁶went up to Beth Hoglah and continued north of Beth Arabah to the Stone of Bohan son of Reuben. ⁷The boundary then went up to Debir from the Valley of Achor and turned north to Gilgal, which faces the Pass of Adummim south of the gorge. It continued along to the waters of En Shemesh and came out at En Rogel. ⁸Then it ran up the Valley of Ben Hinnom along the southern slope of the Jebusite city (that is, Jerusalem). From there it climbed to the top of the hill west of the Hinnom Valley at the northern end of the Valley of Rephaim. ⁹From the hilltop the boundary headed toward the spring of the waters of Nephtoah, came out at the towns of Mount Ephron and went down toward Baalah (that is, Kiriath Jearim). ¹⁰Then it curved westward from Baalah to Mount Seir, ran along the northern slope of Mount Jearim (that is, Kesalon), continued down to Beth Shemesh and crossed to Timnah. ¹¹It went to the northern slope of Ekron, turned toward Shikkeron, passed along to Mount

ᵐ9 Deut. 1:36   ⁿ2 That is, the Dead Sea; also in verse 5
ᵒ3 Hebrew *Akrabbim*   ᵖ4 Hebrew *your*

Baalah and reached Jabneel. The boundary ended at the sea.

¹²The western boundary is the coastline of the Great Sea. ⁹

These are the boundaries around the people of Judah by their clans.

¹³In accordance with the LORD's command to him, Joshua gave to Caleb son of Jephunneh a portion in Judah—Kiriath Arba, that is, Hebron. (Arba was the forefather of Anak.) ¹⁴From Hebron Caleb drove out the three Anakites—Sheshai, Ahiman and Talmai—descendants of Anak. ¹⁵From there he marched against the people living in Debir (formerly called Kiriath Sepher). ¹⁶And Caleb said, "I will give my daughter Acsah in marriage to the man who attacks and captures Kiriath Sepher." ¹⁷Othniel son of Kenaz, Caleb's brother, took it; so Caleb gave his daughter Acsah to him in marriage.

¹⁸One day when she came to Othniel, she urged him ʳ to ask her father for a field. When she got off her donkey, Caleb asked her, "What can I do for you?"

¹⁹She replied, "Do me a special favor. Since you have given me land in the Negev, give me also springs of water." So Caleb gave her the upper and lower springs.

²⁰This is the inheritance of the tribe of Judah, clan by clan:

²¹The southernmost towns of the tribe of Judah in the Negev toward the boundary of Edom were:

Kabzeel, Eder, Jagur, ²²Kinah, Dimonah, Adadah, ²³Kedesh, Hazor, Ithnan, ²⁴Ziph, Telem, Bealoth, ²⁵Hazor Hadattah, Kerioth Hezron (that is, Hazor), ²⁶Amam, Shema, Moladah, ²⁷Hazar Gaddah, Heshmon, Beth Pelet, ²⁸Hazar Shual, Beersheba, Biziothiah, ²⁹Baalah, Iim, Ezem, ³⁰Eltolad, Kesil, Hormah, ³¹Ziklag, Madmannah, Sansannah, ³²Lebaoth, Shilhim, Ain and Rimmon—a total of twenty-nine towns and their villages.

³³In the western foothills:

Eshtaol, Zorah, Ashnah, ³⁴Zanoah, En Gannim, Tappuah, Enam, ³⁵Jarmuth, Adullam, Socoh, Azekah, ³⁶Shaaraim, Adithaim and Gederah (or Gederothaim)ˢ—fourteen towns and their villages.

³⁷Zenan, Hadashah, Migdal Gad, ³⁸Dilean, Mizpah, Joktheel, ³⁹Lachish, Bozkath, Eglon, ⁴⁰Cabbon, Lahmas, Kitlish, ⁴¹Gederoth, Beth Dagon, Naamah and Makkedah—sixteen towns and their villages.

⁴²Libnah, Ether, Ashan, ⁴³Iphtah, Ashnah, Nezib, ⁴⁴Keilah, Aczib and Mareshah—nine towns and their villages.

⁴⁵Ekron, with its surrounding settlements and villages; ⁴⁶west of Ekron, all that were in the vicinity of Ashdod, together with their villages; ⁴⁷Ashdod, its surrounding settlements and villages; and Gaza, its settlements and villages, as far as the Wadi of Egypt and the coastline of the Great Sea.

⁴⁸In the hill country:

Shamir, Jattir, Socoh, ⁴⁹Dannah, Kiriath Sannah (that is, Debir), ⁵⁰Anab, Eshtemoh, Anim, ⁵¹Goshen, Holon and Giloh—eleven towns and their villages.

⁵²Arab, Dumah, Eshan, ⁵³Janim, Beth Tappuah, Aphekah, ⁵⁴Humtah, Kiriath Arba (that is, Hebron) and Zior—nine towns and their villages.

⁵⁵Maon, Carmel, Ziph, Juttah, ⁵⁶Jezreel, Jokdeam, Zanoah, ⁵⁷Kain, Gibeah and Timnah—ten towns and their villages.

⁵⁸Halhul, Beth Zur, Gedor, ⁵⁹Maarath, Beth Anoth and Eltekon—six towns and their villages.

⁶⁰Kiriath Baal (that is, Kiriath Jearim) and Rabbah—two towns and their villages.

⁶¹In the desert:

Beth Arabah, Middin, Secacah, ⁶²Nibshan, the City of Salt and En Gedi—six towns and their villages.

⁶³Judah could not dislodge the Jebusites, who were living in Jerusalem; to this day the Jebusites live there with the people of Judah.

16 The allotment for Joseph began at the Jordan of Jericho, ᵗ east of the waters of Jericho, and went up from there through the desert into the hill country of Bethel. ²It went on from Bethel (that is, Luz), ᵘ crossed over to the territory of the Arkites in Ataroth, ³descended westward to the territory of the Japhletites as far as the region of Lower Beth Horon and on to Gezer, ending at the sea.

⁹12 That is, the Mediterranean; also in verse 47   ʳ18 Hebrew and some Septuagint manuscripts; other Septuagint manuscripts (see also note at Judges 1:14) *Othniel, he urged her*   ˢ36 Or *Gederah and Gederothaim*   ᵗ1 *Jordan of Jericho* was possibly an ancient name for the Jordan River.   ᵘ2 Septuagint; Hebrew *Bethel to Luz*

4So Manasseh and Ephraim, the descendants of Joseph, received their inheritance.

5This was the territory of Ephraim, clan by clan:

The boundary of their inheritance went from Ataroth Addar in the east to Upper Beth Horon 6and continued to the sea. From Micmethath on the north it curved eastward to Taanath Shiloh, passing by it to Janoah on the east. 7Then it went down from Janoah to Ataroth and Naarah, touched Jericho and came out at the Jordan. 8From Tappuah the border went west to the Kanah Ravine and ended at the sea. This was the inheritance of the tribe of the Ephraimites, clan by clan. 9It also included all the towns and their villages that were set aside for the Ephraimites within the inheritance of the Manassites.

10They did not dislodge the Canaanites living in Gezer; to this day the Canaanites live among the people of Ephraim but are required to do forced labor.

17 This was the allotment for the tribe of Manasseh as Joseph's firstborn, that is, for Makir, Manasseh's firstborn. Makir was the ancestor of the Gileadites, who had received Gilead and Bashan because the Makirites were great soldiers. 2So this allotment was for the rest of the people of Manasseh—the clans of Abiezer, Helek, Asriel, Shechem, Hepher and Shemida. These are the other male descendants of Manasseh son of Joseph by their clans.

3Now Zelophehad son of Hepher, the son of Gilead, the son of Makir, the son of Manasseh, had no sons but only daughters, whose names were Mahlah, Noah, Hoglah, Milcah and Tirzah. 4They went to Eleazar the priest, Joshua son of Nun, and the leaders and said, "The Lord commanded Moses to give us an inheritance among our brothers." So Joshua gave them an inheritance along with the brothers of their father, according to the Lord's command. 5Manasseh's share consisted of ten tracts of land besides Gilead and Bashan east of the Jordan, 6because the daughters of the tribe of Manasseh received an inheritance among the sons. The land of Gilead belonged to the rest of the descendants of Manasseh.

7The territory of Manasseh extended from Asher to Micmethath east of Shechem. The boundary ran southward from there to include the people living at En Tappuah. 8(Manasseh had the land of Tappuah, but Tappuah itself, on the boundary of Manasseh, belonged to the Ephraimites.) 9Then the boundary continued south to the Kanah Ravine. There were towns belonging to Ephraim lying among the towns of Manasseh, but the boundary of Manasseh was the northern side of the ravine and ended at the sea. 10On the south the land belonged to Ephraim, on the north to Manasseh. The territory of Manasseh reached the sea and bordered Asher on the north and Issachar on the east.

11Within Issachar and Asher, Manasseh also had Beth Shan, Ibleam and the people of Dor, Endor, Taanach and Megiddo, together with their surrounding settlements (the third in the list is Naphoth v).

12Yet the Manassites were not able to occupy these towns, for the Canaanites were determined to live in that region. 13However, when the Israelites grew stronger, they subjected the Canaanites to forced labor but did not drive them out completely.

14The people of Joseph said to Joshua, "Why have you given us only one allotment and one portion for an inheritance? We are a numerous people and the Lord has blessed us abundantly."

15"If you are so numerous," Joshua answered, "and if the hill country of Ephraim is too small for you, go up into the forest and clear land for yourselves there in the land of the Perizzites and Rephaites."

16The people of Joseph replied, "The hill country is not enough for us, and all the Canaanites who live in the plain have iron chariots, both those in Beth Shan and its settlements and those in the Valley of Jezreel."

17But Joshua said to the house of Joseph—to Ephraim and Manasseh—"You are numerous and very powerful. You will have not only one allotment 18but the forested hill country as well. Clear it, and its farthest limits will be yours; though the Canaanites have iron chariots and though they are strong, you can drive them out."

18 The whole assembly of the Israelites gathered at Shiloh and set up the Tent of Meeting there. The country was brought under their control, 2but

v 11 That is, Naphoth Dor

there were still seven Israelite tribes who had not yet received their inheritance.

³So Joshua said to the Israelites: "How long will you wait before you begin to take possession of the land that the Lord, the God of your fathers, has given you? ⁴Appoint three men from each tribe. I will send them out to make a survey of the land and to write a description of it, according to the inheritance of each. Then they will return to me. ⁵You are to divide the land into seven parts. Judah is to remain in its territory on the south and the house of Joseph in its territory on the north. ⁶After you have written descriptions of the seven parts of the land, bring them here to me and I will cast lots for you in the presence of the Lord our God. ⁷The Levites, however, do not get a portion among you, because the priestly service of the Lord is their inheritance. And Gad, Reuben and the half-tribe of Manasseh have already received their inheritance on the east side of the Jordan. Moses the servant of the Lord gave it to them."

⁸As the men started on their way to map out the land, Joshua instructed them, "Go and make a survey of the land and write a description of it. Then return to me, and I will cast lots for you here at Shiloh in the presence of the Lord." ⁹So the men left and went through the land. They wrote its description on a scroll, town by town, in seven parts, and returned to Joshua in the camp at Shiloh. ¹⁰Joshua then cast lots for them in Shiloh in the presence of the Lord, and there he distributed the land to the Israelites according to their tribal divisions.

¹¹The lot came up for the tribe of Benjamin, clan by clan. Their allotted territory lay between the tribes of Judah and Joseph:

¹²On the north side their boundary began at the Jordan, passed the northern slope of Jericho and headed west into the hill country, coming out at the desert of Beth Aven. ¹³From there it crossed to the south slope of Luz (that is, Bethel) and went down to Ata-

roth Addar on the hill south of Lower Beth Horon.

¹⁴From the hill facing Beth Horon on the south the boundary turned south along the western side and came out at Kiriath Baal (that is, Kiriath Jearim), a town of the people of Judah. This was the western side.

¹⁵The southern side began at the outskirts of Kiriath Jearim on the west, and the boundary came out at the spring of the waters of Nephtoah. ¹⁶The boundary went down to the foot of the hill facing the Valley of Ben Hinnom, north of the Valley of Rephaim. It continued down the Hinnom Valley along the southern slope of the Jebusite city and so to En Rogel. ¹⁷It then curved north, went to En Shemesh, continued to Geliloth, which faces the Pass of Adummim, and ran down to the Stone of Bohan son of Reuben. ¹⁸It continued to the northern slope of Beth Arabah[w] and on down into the Arabah. ¹⁹It then went to the northern slope of Beth Hoglah and came out at the northern bay of the Salt Sea,[x] at the mouth of the Jordan in the south. This was the southern boundary.

²⁰The Jordan formed the boundary on the eastern side.

These were the boundaries that marked out the inheritance of the clans of Benjamin on all sides.

²¹The tribe of Benjamin, clan by clan, had the following cities:

Jericho, Beth Hoglah, Emek Keziz, ²²Beth Arabah, Zemaraim, Bethel, ²³Avvim, Parah, Ophrah, ²⁴Kephar Ammoni, Ophni and Geba—twelve towns and their villages.

²⁵Gibeon, Ramah, Beeroth, ²⁶Mizpah, Kephirah, Mozah, ²⁷Rekem, Irpeel, Taralah, ²⁸Zelah, Haeleph, the Jebusite city (that is, Jerusalem), Gibeah and Kiriath—fourteen towns and their villages.

This was the inheritance of Benjamin for its clans.

w 18 Septuagint; Hebrew *slope facing the Arabah*   x 19 That is, the Dead Sea

---

Discovering the Word 1. How is Caleb's faith just as strong at eighty-five as it had been at forty? 2. Note 15:63, 16:10 and 17:12–13. God had promised to drive these Canaanites out of the land. Why then do you think Israel had difficulty dislodging them (see also Ex 23:29–30 and Dt 7:22–24)? 3. How does the attitude of the people of Joseph contrast with that of Caleb? 4. How does Joshua deal with their complaint (17:17–18)? 5. Seven tribes had not yet received their inheritance. What was their problem (18:1–10)? 6. As you look back over these chapters, what reasons can you give for why Israel had difficulty taking full possession of the land?

Applying the Word 1. Which reasons help to explain why God's promises to us are sometimes only partially fulfilled? (For example, his promise to purify our lives of sin.) Explain. 2. We sometimes act like the people of Joseph, complaining about how little God has given us when we have not fully used what we have. How do you think Joshua would respond to our complaints and excuses?

Responding in Prayer Ask God to mold your faith to be like Caleb's.

Joshua 19

19 The second lot came out for the tribe of Simeon, clan by clan. Their inheritance lay within the territory of Judah. ²It included:

Beersheba (or Sheba),ʸ Moladah, ³Hazar Shual, Balah, Ezem, ⁴Eltolad, Bethul, Hormah, ⁵Ziklag, Beth Marcaboth, Hazar Susah, ⁶Beth Lebaoth and Sharuhen—thirteen towns and their villages;

⁷Ain, Rimmon, Ether and Ashan—four towns and their villages— ⁸and all the villages around these towns as far as Baalath Beer (Ramah in the Negev).

This was the inheritance of the tribe of the Simeonites, clan by clan. ⁹The inheritance of the Simeonites was taken from the share of Judah, because Judah's portion was more than they needed. So the Simeonites received their inheritance within the territory of Judah.

¹⁰The third lot came up for Zebulun, clan by clan:

The boundary of their inheritance went as far as Sarid. ¹¹Going west it ran to Maralah, touched Dabbesheth, and extended to the ravine near Jokneam. ¹²It turned east from Sarid toward the sunrise to the territory of Kisloth Tabor and went on to Daberath and up to Japhia. ¹³Then it continued eastward to Gath Hepher and Eth Kazin; it came out at Rimmon and turned toward Neah. ¹⁴There the boundary went around on the north to Hannathon and ended at the Valley of Iphtah El. ¹⁵Included were Kattath, Nahalal, Shimron, Idalah and Bethlehem. There were twelve towns and their villages.

¹⁶These towns and their villages were the inheritance of Zebulun, clan by clan.

¹⁷The fourth lot came out for Issachar, clan by clan. ¹⁸Their territory included:

Jezreel, Kesulloth, Shunem, ¹⁹Hapharaim, Shion, Anaharath, ²⁰Rabbith, Kishion, Ebez,

²¹Remeth, En Gannim, En Haddah and Beth Pazzez. ²²The boundary touched Tabor, Shahazumah and Beth Shemesh, and ended at the Jordan. There were sixteen towns and their villages.

²³These towns and their villages were the inheritance of the tribe of Issachar, clan by clan.

²⁴The fifth lot came out for the tribe of Asher, clan by clan. ²⁵Their territory included:

Helkath, Hali, Beten, Acshaph, ²⁶Allammelech, Amad and Mishal. On the west the boundary touched Carmel and Shihor Libnath. ²⁷It then turned east toward Beth Dagon, touched Zebulun and the Valley of Iphtah El, and went north to Beth Emek and Neiel, passing Cabul on the left. ²⁸It went to Abdon,ᶻ Rehob, Hammon and Kanah, as far as Greater Sidon. ²⁹The boundary then turned back toward Ramah and went to the fortified city of Tyre, turned toward Hosah and came out at the sea in the region of Aczib, ³⁰Ummah, Aphek and Rehob. There were twenty-two towns and their villages.

³¹These towns and their villages were the inheritance of the tribe of Asher, clan by clan.

³²The sixth lot came out for Naphtali, clan by clan:

³³Their boundary went from Heleph and the large tree in Zaanannim, passing Adami Nekeb and Jabneel to Lakkum and ending at the Jordan. ³⁴The boundary ran west through Aznoth Tabor and came out at Hukkok. It touched Zebulun on the south, Asher on the west and the Jordanᵃ on the east. ³⁵The fortified cities were Ziddim, Zer, Hammath, Rakkath, Kinnereth, ³⁶Adamah, Ramah, Hazor, ³⁷Kedesh, Edrei, En Hazor,

ʸ2 Or *Beersheba, Sheba*; 1 Chron. 4:28 does not have *Sheba*.
ᶻ28 Some Hebrew manuscripts (see also Joshua 21:30); most Hebrew manuscripts *Ebron*   ᵃ34 Septuagint; Hebrew *west, and Judah, the Jordan,*

³⁸Iron, Migdal El, Horem, Beth Anath and Beth Shemesh. There were nineteen towns and their villages.

³⁹These towns and their villages were the inheritance of the tribe of Naphtali, clan by clan.

⁴⁰The seventh lot came out for the tribe of Dan, clan by clan. ⁴¹The territory of their inheritance included:

Zorah, Eshtaol, Ir Shemesh, ⁴²Shaalabbin, Aijalon, Ithlah, ⁴³Elon, Timnah, Ekron, ⁴⁴Eltekeh, Gibbethon, Baalath, ⁴⁵Jehud, Bene Berak, Gath Rimmon, ⁴⁶Me Jarkon and Rakkon, with the area facing Joppa.

⁴⁷(But the Danites had difficulty taking possession of their territory, so they went up and attacked Leshem, took it, put it to the sword and occupied it. They settled in Leshem and named it Dan after their forefather.)

⁴⁸These towns and their villages were the inheritance of the tribe of Dan, clan by clan.

⁴⁹When they had finished dividing the land into its allotted portions, the Israelites gave Joshua son of Nun an inheritance among them, ⁵⁰as the LORD had commanded. They gave him the town he asked for—Timnath Serah*ᵇ* in the hill country of Ephraim. And he built up the town and settled there.

⁵¹These are the territories that Eleazar the priest, Joshua son of Nun and the heads of the tribal clans of Israel assigned by lot at Shiloh in the presence of the LORD at the entrance to the Tent of Meeting. And so they finished dividing the land.

ᵇ50 Also known as *Timnath Heres* (see Judges 2:9)

9 / *Joshua 20—21*
The Lord Fulfills His Promises

HOW DOES FAITH differ from wishful thinking? Why should we expect God to answer our prayers, to provide us with food and clothing, or to be involved in jobs or family? How do we know our faith isn't simply foolishness? Scripture tells us that true faith must be grounded in God's promises. If God has promised to do something, then we can trust him wholeheartedly. If he has not promised to do something, then all the faith in the world won't make it happen. In Joshua 20—21 we see the final outcome of God's promises to Israel.

 Warming Up to God Think of a time recently when you trusted God for something. Which of his promises applied to that situation?

 Read Joshua 20—21.

20 Then the LORD said to Joshua: ²"Tell the Israelites to designate the cities of refuge, as I instructed you through Moses, ³so that anyone who kills a person accidentally and unintentionally may flee there and find protection from the avenger of blood.

⁴"When he flees to one of these cities, he is to stand in the entrance of the city gate and state his case before the elders of that city. Then they are to admit him into their city and give him a place to live with them. ⁵If the avenger of blood pursues him, they must not surrender the one accused, because he killed his neighbor unintentionally and without malice aforethought. ⁶He is

to stay in that city until he has stood trial before the assembly and until the death of the high priest who is serving at that time. Then he may go back to his own home in the town from which he fled."

⁷So they set apart Kedesh in Galilee in the hill country of Naphtali, Shechem in the hill country of Ephraim, and Kiriath Arba (that is, Hebron) in the hill country of Judah. ⁸On the east side of the Jordan of Jerichoᶜ they designated Bezer in the desert on the plateau in the tribe of Reuben, Ramoth in Gilead in the tribe of Gad, and Golan in Bashan in the tribe of Manasseh. ⁹Any of the Israelites or any alien living among them who killed

ᶜ8 *Jordan of Jericho* was possibly an ancient name for the Jordan River.

someone accidentally could flee to these designated cities and not be killed by the avenger of blood prior to standing trial before the assembly.

21

Now the family heads of the Levites approached Eleazar the priest, Joshua son of Nun, and the heads of the other tribal families of Israel ²at Shiloh in Canaan and said to them, "The LORD commanded through Moses that you give us towns to live in, with pasturelands for our livestock." ³So, as the LORD had commanded, the Israelites gave the Levites the following towns and pasturelands out of their own inheritance:

⁴The first lot came out for the Kohathites, clan by clan. The Levites who were descendants of Aaron the priest were allotted thirteen towns from the tribes of Judah, Simeon and Benjamin. ⁵The rest of Kohath's descendants were allotted ten towns from the clans of the tribes of Ephraim, Dan and half of Manasseh.

⁶The descendants of Gershon were allotted thirteen towns from the clans of the tribes of Issachar, Asher, Naphtali and the half-tribe of Manasseh in Bashan.

⁷The descendants of Merari, clan by clan, received twelve towns from the tribes of Reuben, Gad and Zebulun.

⁸So the Israelites allotted to the Levites these towns and their pasturelands, as the LORD had commanded through Moses.

⁹From the tribes of Judah and Simeon they allotted the following towns by name ¹⁰(these towns were assigned to the descendants of Aaron who were from the Kohathite clans of the Levites, because the first lot fell to them):

¹¹They gave them Kiriath Arba (that is, Hebron), with its surrounding pastureland, in the hill country of Judah. (Arba was the forefather of Anak.) ¹²But the fields and villages around the city they had given to Caleb son of Jephunneh as his possession.

¹³So to the descendants of Aaron the priest they gave Hebron (a city of refuge for one accused of murder), Libnah, ¹⁴Jattir, Eshtemoa, ¹⁵Holon, Debir, ¹⁶Ain, Juttah and Beth Shemesh, together with their pasturelands—nine towns from these two tribes.

¹⁷And from the tribe of Benjamin they gave them Gibeon, Geba, ¹⁸Anathoth and Almon, together with their pasturelands—four towns.

¹⁹All the towns for the priests, the descendants of Aaron, were thirteen, together with their pasturelands.

²⁰The rest of the Kohathite clans of the Levites were allotted towns from the tribe of Ephraim:

²¹In the hill country of Ephraim they were given Shechem (a city of refuge for one accused of murder) and Gezer, ²²Kibzaim and Beth Horon, together with their pasturelands—four towns.

²³Also from the tribe of Dan they received Eltekeh, Gibbethon, ²⁴Aijalon and Gath Rimmon, together with their pasturelands—four towns.

²⁵From half the tribe of Manasseh they received Taanach and Gath Rimmon, together with their pasturelands—two towns.

²⁶All these ten towns and their pasturelands were given to the rest of the Kohathite clans.

²⁷The Levite clans of the Gershonites were given:
from the half-tribe of Manasseh,
Golan in Bashan (a city of refuge for one accused of murder) and Be Eshtarah, together with their pasturelands—two towns;
²⁸from the tribe of Issachar,
Kishion, Daberath, ²⁹Jarmuth and En Gannim, together with their pasturelands—four towns;
³⁰from the tribe of Asher,
Mishal, Abdon, ³¹Helkath and Rehob, together with their pasturelands—four towns;
³²from the tribe of Naphtali,
Kedesh in Galilee (a city of refuge for one accused of murder), Hammoth Dor and Kartan, together with their pasturelands—three towns.
³³All the towns of the Gershonite clans were thirteen, together with their pasturelands.

³⁴The Merarite clans (the rest of the Levites) were given:
from the tribe of Zebulun,
Jokneam, Kartah, ³⁵Dimnah and Nahalal, together with their pasturelands—four towns;
³⁶from the tribe of Reuben,
Bezer, Jahaz, ³⁷Kedemoth and Mephaath, together with their pasturelands—four towns;
³⁸from the tribe of Gad,
Ramoth in Gilead (a city of refuge for one accused of murder), Mahanaim, ³⁹Heshbon

and Jazer, together with their pasturelands—
four towns in all.
⁴⁰All the towns allotted to the Merarite clans, who
were the rest of the Levites, were twelve.

⁴¹The towns of the Levites in the territory held
by the Israelites were forty-eight in all, together
with their pasturelands. ⁴²Each of these towns
had pasturelands surrounding it; this was true for
all these towns.

⁴³So the LORD gave Israel all the land he had
sworn to give their forefathers, and they took possession of it and settled there. ⁴⁴The LORD gave
them rest on every side, just as he had sworn to
their forefathers. Not one of their enemies with-
stood them; the LORD handed all their enemies
over to them. ⁴⁵Not one of all the LORD's good
promises to the house of Israel failed; every one
was fulfilled.

Discovering the Word 1. What was the purpose of the cities of refuge (20:1–6)? 2. What does the command to establish these cities teach us about the Lord? 3. How did the Levites differ from the other tribes (see 13:14, 33; 14:3–4; 18:7)? 4. What do you think God's purpose was in scattering the Levites throughout the land? 5. How does 21:43–45 provide the climax to the book of Joshua?

Applying the Word 1. What are some of the promises God has made to us as Christians? 2. In what ways have you seen God fulfill these promises in your life?

Responding in Prayer Praise God for his faithfulness in keeping his promises to us.

10 / *Joshua 22*
Will the Nation Survive?

THE TRIBES WHICH had been given land on the east side of the Jordan had fulfilled their commitment to the rest of Israel. They had entered the Promised Land with the others and had helped them to fight. Now it was time for them to return to their own homes. But since the Israelites would be living on both sides of the river, the Jordan Rift Valley became a natural barrier which hindered the unity of the twelve tribes. Could Israel still remain unified? Their response to a national crisis illustrates principles for maintaining Christian unity.

Warming Up to God God is glorified by your praise and worship. Spend some time offering your thanks for who he is.

Read Joshua 22.

22 Then Joshua summoned the Reubenites, the Gadites and the half-
tribe of Manasseh ²and said to
them, "You have done all that Moses the servant
of the LORD commanded, and you have obeyed me
in everything I commanded. ³For a long time
now—to this very day—you have not deserted
your brothers but have carried out the mission
the LORD your God gave you. ⁴Now that the LORD
your God has given your brothers rest as he
promised, return to your homes in the land that
Moses the servant of the LORD gave you on the
other side of the Jordan. ⁵But be very careful
to keep the commandment and the law that

Moses the servant of the LORD gave you: to love
the LORD your God, to walk in all his ways, to
obey his commands, to hold fast to him and
to serve him with all your heart and all your
soul."

⁶Then Joshua blessed them and sent them
away, and they went to their homes. ⁷(To the
half-tribe of Manasseh Moses had given land in
Bashan, and to the other half of the tribe Joshua
gave land on the west side of the Jordan with
their brothers.) When Joshua sent them home, he
blessed them, ⁸saying, "Return to your homes
with your great wealth—with large herds of livestock, with silver, gold, bronze and iron, and a

great quantity of clothing—and divide with your brothers the plunder from your enemies."

⁹So the Reubenites, the Gadites and the half-tribe of Manasseh left the Israelites at Shiloh in Canaan to return to Gilead, their own land, which they had acquired in accordance with the command of the LORD through Moses.

¹⁰When they came to Geliloth near the Jordan in the land of Canaan, the Reubenites, the Gadites and the half-tribe of Manasseh built an imposing altar there by the Jordan. ¹¹And when the Israelites heard that they had built the altar on the border of Canaan at Geliloth near the Jordan on the Israelite side, ¹²the whole assembly of Israel gathered at Shiloh to go to war against them.

¹³So the Israelites sent Phinehas son of Eleazar, the priest, to the land of Gilead—to Reuben, Gad and the half-tribe of Manasseh. ¹⁴With him they sent ten of the chief men, one for each of the tribes of Israel, each the head of a family division among the Israelite clans.

¹⁵When they went to Gilead—to Reuben, Gad and the half-tribe of Manasseh—they said to them: ¹⁶"The whole assembly of the LORD says: 'How could you break faith with the God of Israel like this? How could you turn away from the LORD and build yourselves an altar in rebellion against him now? ¹⁷Was not the sin of Peor enough for us? Up to this very day we have not cleansed ourselves from that sin, even though a plague fell on the community of the LORD! ¹⁸And are you now turning away from the LORD?

" 'If you rebel against the LORD today, tomorrow he will be angry with the whole community of Israel. ¹⁹If the land you possess is defiled, come over to the LORD's land, where the LORD's tabernacle stands, and share the land with us. But do not rebel against the LORD or against us by building an altar for yourselves, other than the altar of the LORD our God. ²⁰When Achan son of Zerah acted unfaithfully regarding the devoted things,ᵈ did not wrath come upon the whole community of Israel? He was not the only one who died for his sin.' "

²¹Then Reuben, Gad and the half-tribe of Manasseh replied to the heads of the clans of Israel: ²²"The Mighty One, God, the LORD! The Mighty One, God, the LORD! He knows! And let Israel know! If this has been in rebellion or disobedience to the LORD, do not spare us this day. ²³If we have built our own altar to turn away from the LORD and to offer burnt offerings and grain offer-

ings, or to sacrifice fellowship offeringsᵉ on it, may the LORD himself call us to account.

²⁴"No! We did it for fear that some day your descendants might say to ours, 'What do you have to do with the LORD, the God of Israel? ²⁵The LORD has made the Jordan a boundary between us and you—you Reubenites and Gadites! You have no share in the LORD.' So your descendants might cause ours to stop fearing the LORD.

²⁶"That is why we said, 'Let us get ready and build an altar—but not for burnt offerings or sacrifices.' ²⁷On the contrary, it is to be a witness between us and you and the generations that follow, that we will worship the LORD at his sanctuary with our burnt offerings, sacrifices and fellowship offerings. Then in the future your descendants will not be able to say to ours, 'You have no share in the LORD.'

²⁸"And we said, 'If they ever say this to us, or to our descendants, we will answer: Look at the replica of the LORD's altar, which our fathers built, not for burnt offerings and sacrifices, but as a witness between us and you.'

²⁹"Far be it from us to rebel against the LORD and turn away from him today by building an altar for burnt offerings, grain offerings and sacrifices, other than the altar of the LORD our God that stands before his tabernacle."

³⁰When Phinehas the priest and the leaders of the community—the heads of the clans of the Israelites—heard what Reuben, Gad and Manasseh had to say, they were pleased. ³¹And Phinehas son of Eleazar, the priest, said to Reuben, Gad and Manasseh, "Today we know that the LORD is with us, because you have not acted unfaithfully toward the LORD in this matter. Now you have rescued the Israelites from the LORD's hand."

³²Then Phinehas son of Eleazar, the priest, and the leaders returned to Canaan from their meeting with the Reubenites and Gadites in Gilead and reported to the Israelites. ³³They were glad to hear the report and praised God. And they talked no more about going to war against them to devastate the country where the Reubenites and the Gadites lived.

³⁴And the Reubenites and the Gadites gave the altar this name: A Witness Between Us that the LORD is God.

ᵈ20 The Hebrew term refers to the irrevocable giving over of things or persons to the LORD, often by totally destroying them.
ᵉ23 Traditionally peace offerings; also in verse 27

Discovering the Word   1. Why does Joshua commend the tribes of Reuben, Gad and Manasseh (vv. 1–4)?   2. What blessings had these tribes received from God because of their faithful service (vv. 6–9)?   3. Why were the western tribes prepared to do battle over the issue of the altar (vv. 10–20; see also Deut 12:1–14)?   4. What reasons did the eastern tribes have for building the altar (vv. 21–29)?   5. How did both sides in this dispute show that they were honoring God (vv. 30–34)?

Applying the Word   1. What can we learn from this story about confronting those whose actions seem offensive?   2. What should our attitude be toward those who have misunderstood our actions?   3. What principles do you find in this chapter for restoring and maintaining unity in your church or fellowship group?

Responding in Prayer   Pray that God would bring unity to his church around the world.

11 / *Joshua 23*
Joshua's Farewell

GREAT LEADERS INSPIRE us to obey God. We depend on their encouragement and their example. But what happens when such leaders are no longer around? About twenty years elapsed between the end of the war and Joshua's death. During that time, Joshua's influence kept Israel loyal to God. Now Joshua knows that he is about to die, and he is concerned that Israel's loyalty to God might not continue in his absence. Therefore, he calls the Israelites together to hear a farewell message of challenge and warning.

 Warming Up to God   If you were giving a farewell address, what words of thanks would you offer to God?

 Read Joshua 23.

23 After a long time had passed and the LORD had given Israel rest from all their enemies around them, Joshua, by then old and well advanced in years, ²summoned all Israel—their elders, leaders, judges and officials—and said to them: "I am old and well advanced in years. ³You yourselves have seen everything the LORD your God has done to all these nations for your sake; it was the LORD your God who fought for you. ⁴Remember how I have allotted as an inheritance for your tribes all the land of the nations that remain—the nations I conquered—between the Jordan and the Great Sea*ʄ* in the west. ⁵The LORD your God himself will drive them out of your way. He will push them out before you, and you will take possession of their land, as the LORD your God promised you.

⁶"Be very strong; be careful to obey all that is written in the Book of the Law of Moses, without turning aside to the right or to the left. ⁷Do not associate with these nations that remain among you; do not invoke the names of their gods or swear by them. You must not serve them or bow down to them. ⁸But you are to hold fast to the LORD your God, as you have until now.

⁹"The LORD has driven out before you great and powerful nations; to this day no one has been able to withstand you. ¹⁰One of you routs a thousand, because the LORD your God fights for you, just as he promised. ¹¹So be very careful to love the LORD your God.

¹²"But if you turn away and ally yourselves with the survivors of these nations that remain among you and if you intermarry with them and associate with them, ¹³then you may be sure that the LORD your God will no longer drive out these nations before you. Instead, they will become snares and traps for you, whips on your backs and thorns in your eyes, until you perish from this good land, which the LORD your God has given you.

¹⁴"Now I am about to go the way of all the earth. You know with all your heart and soul that not one of all the good promises the LORD your God gave you has failed. Every promise has been fulfilled; not one has failed. ¹⁵But just as every good promise of the LORD your God has come true, so the LORD will bring on you all the evil he has threatened, until he has destroyed you from

ʄ4 That is, the Mediterranean

this good land he has given you. ¹⁶If you violate the covenant of the LORD your God, which he commanded you, and go and serve other gods and bow down to them, the LORD's anger will burn against you, and you will quickly perish from the good land he has given you."

Discovering the Word 1. How does Joshua exalt God in his farewell address? 2. What promises and commands does Joshua give to Israel (vv. 5–11)? 3. What does it mean for us to "hold fast to the LORD" and "to love the LORD" (vv. 8, 11)? 4. Why weren't the Israelites allowed to associate with the nations around them (vv. 7–8, 12–13)? 5. Joshua warns that the Lord is faithful not only to his promises but also to his threats (vv. 14–16). What threats had the Lord made to Israel (vv. 15–16)?

Applying the Word 1. Today, what aspects of non-Christian culture can become snares, traps, whips on our backs and thorns in our eyes? 2. We obviously cannot and should not avoid non-Christians today. How then can we resist the temptation to live like them? 3. How does Joshua's farewell address motivate you to be faithful to the Lord?

Responding in Prayer Ask God to make you faithful. Pray that your pastor and the leaders of your church would be faithful as well.

12 / *Joshua 24*
Who Will Serve the Lord?

THROUGHOUT THE BOOK of Joshua the Lord has demonstrated his faithfulness and his power. Every promise he made was fulfilled; every battle he fought was won. Now at the conclusion of the book he asks Israel and us to reaffirm the most important decision of our lives: "Choose for yourselves this day whom you will serve" (v. 15).

Warming Up to God God has given us the ability to make choices. What are some of the inherent benefits and dangers of this freedom for you?

Read Joshua 24.

24 Then Joshua assembled all the tribes of Israel at Shechem. He summoned the elders, leaders, judges and officials of Israel, and they presented themselves before God.

²Joshua said to all the people, "This is what the LORD, the God of Israel, says: 'Long ago your forefathers, including Terah the father of Abraham and Nahor, lived beyond the River*ᵍ* and worshiped other gods. ³But I took your father Abraham from the land beyond the River and led him throughout Canaan and gave him many descendants. I gave him Isaac, ⁴and to Isaac I gave Jacob and Esau. I assigned the hill country of Seir to Esau, but Jacob and his sons went down to Egypt.

⁵" 'Then I sent Moses and Aaron, and I afflicted the Egyptians by what I did there, and I brought you out. ⁶When I brought your fathers out of Egypt, you came to the sea, and the Egyptians pursued them with chariots and horsemen*ʰ* as far as the Red Sea.*ⁱ* ⁷But they cried to the LORD

for help, and he put darkness between you and the Egyptians; he brought the sea over them and covered them. You saw with your own eyes what I did to the Egyptians. Then you lived in the desert for a long time.

⁸" 'I brought you to the land of the Amorites who lived east of the Jordan. They fought against you, but I gave them into your hands. I destroyed them from before you, and you took possession of their land. ⁹When Balak son of Zippor, the king of Moab, prepared to fight against Israel, he sent for Balaam son of Beor to put a curse on you. ¹⁰But I would not listen to Balaam, so he blessed you again and again, and I delivered you out of his hand.

¹¹" 'Then you crossed the Jordan and came to Jericho. The citizens of Jericho fought against you, as did also the Amorites, Perizzites, Canaanites, Hittites, Girgashites, Hivites and Jebusites,

ᵍ2 That is, the Euphrates; also in verses 3, 14 and 15   ʰ6 Or charioteers   ⁱ6 Hebrew Yam Suph; that is, Sea of Reeds but I gave them into your hands. ¹²I sent the hornet ahead of you, which drove them out before you—also the two Amorite kings. You did not do it with your own sword and bow. ¹³So I gave you a land on which you did not toil and cities you did not build; and you live in them and eat from vineyards and olive groves that you did not plant.'

¹⁴"Now fear the LORD and serve him with all faithfulness. Throw away the gods your forefathers worshiped beyond the River and in Egypt, and serve the LORD. ¹⁵But if serving the LORD seems undesirable to you, then choose for yourselves this day whom you will serve, whether the gods your forefathers served beyond the River, or the gods of the Amorites, in whose land you are living. But as for me and my household, we will serve the LORD."

¹⁶Then the people answered, "Far be it from us to forsake the LORD to serve other gods! ¹⁷It was the LORD our God himself who brought us and our fathers up out of Egypt, from that land of slavery, and performed those great signs before our eyes. He protected us on our entire journey and among all the nations through which we traveled. ¹⁸And the LORD drove out before us all the nations, including the Amorites, who lived in the land. We too will serve the LORD, because he is our God."

¹⁹Joshua said to the people, "You are not able to serve the LORD. He is a holy God; he is a jealous God. He will not forgive your rebellion and your sins. ²⁰If you forsake the LORD and serve foreign gods, he will turn and bring disaster on you and make an end of you, after he has been good to you."

²¹But the people said to Joshua, "No! We will serve the LORD."

²²Then Joshua said, "You are witnesses against yourselves that you have chosen to serve the LORD."

"Yes, we are witnesses," they replied.

²³"Now then," said Joshua, "throw away the foreign gods that are among you and yield your hearts to the LORD, the God of Israel."

²⁴And the people said to Joshua, "We will serve the LORD our God and obey him."

²⁵On that day Joshua made a covenant for the people, and there at Shechem he drew up for them decrees and laws. ²⁶And Joshua recorded these things in the Book of the Law of God. Then he took a large stone and set it up there under the oak near the holy place of the LORD.

²⁷"See!" he said to all the people. "This stone will be a witness against us. It has heard all the words the LORD has said to us. It will be a witness against you if you are untrue to your God."

²⁸Then Joshua sent the people away, each to his own inheritance.

²⁹After these things, Joshua son of Nun, the servant of the LORD, died at the age of a hundred and ten. ³⁰And they buried him in the land of his inheritance, at Timnath Serah[j] in the hill country of Ephraim, north of Mount Gaash.

³¹Israel served the LORD throughout the lifetime of Joshua and of the elders who outlived him and who had experienced everything the LORD had done for Israel.

³²And Joseph's bones, which the Israelites had brought up from Egypt, were buried at Shechem in the tract of land that Jacob bought for a hundred pieces of silver[k] from the sons of Hamor, the father of Shechem. This became the inheritance of Joseph's descendants.

³³And Eleazar son of Aaron died and was buried at Gibeah, which had been allotted to his son Phinehas in the hill country of Ephraim.

---

j30 Also known as Timnath Heres (see Judges 2:9)   k32 Hebrew hundred kesitahs; a kesitah was a unit of money of unknown weight and value.

Discovering the Word 1. Why do you think the Lord recounts Israel's history from beginning to end (vv. 1–13)? 2. Joshua and the Israelites repeat the word *serve* thirteen times in verses 14–27. Why is this a good word to describe our duty to God? 3. Why might serving the Lord seem undesirable to the Israelites (v. 15)? 4. Why doesn't Joshua accept the Israelites' first pledge to serve the Lord (v. 19)? 5. What is the purpose of the witnesses mentioned in verses 22 and 27?

Applying the Word 1. Israel must choose whom they will serve (v. 15). What choices to you have about whom to serve? 2. In what ways is serving the Lord difficult for you? 3. What makes serving him worthwhile?

Responding in Prayer Pray that God will give you courage to rise to the challenge of Joshua—to obey God more fully.

Judges

Despicable people doing deplorable things. That pretty much sums up the book of Judges. Why would the Bible even contain such trashy tales about dysfunctional characters? As I read the book, I find it difficult to find any sympathy for those—even the heroes—involved in these violent and abusive accounts.

Who can love people who maltreat others? Who would care about people who complicate and sabotage their own lives and then refuse the hope that is offered? Who would have patience with people who refuse to learn from their mistakes but instead pass them on as a legacy to the next generation? The answer is that only God could care about creatures such as these. So the book of Judges is not really about the judges who held court in Israel. It is about the God of mercy and patience who loves even the most dysfunctional and resistant among us.

The book of Judges covers the history of Israel between the death of Joshua and the appearance of Samuel (approximately 1220–1050 B.C.). For Israel this was a time without a formal government. The people were supposed to look to God for leadership, but when they failed to do so, they were doomed to a continuing cycle of disobedience, suffering, cries for help and deliverance.

How can you benefit from the book of Judges? You will learn of the great depth of God's love and mercy as you see it continually offered to people who do not deserve or appreciate it. You will be able to learn from the mistakes of others. Perhaps you will be able to break cycles of dysfunction which persist in your own life or home. Most of all, the study of Judges should help you to hand the throne of your life over to God, the true king. The writer of the book of Judges often uses the phrase "in those days Israel had no king." Without God reigning in our hearts, our lives are destined to become as disastrous as the characters of this book.

To gain these benefits, it is important to study the book of Judges correctly. If you look to the characters of these stories as role models, you will be sorely disappointed. Even the judges whom God uses to save Israel are depraved and fallen creatures. The point of these stories is not the character qualities of the judges, but the fact that God works through people such as these. The only true hero of this book is God.

It is also important that you refrain from becoming smug about your own enlightenment. As you read Judges, you will encounter characters who treat women as possessions and who settle problems with angry outbursts of violence (and these are supposedly the good guys!). These are stories of people in a much more primitive time who were struggling to understand God, themselves and forgiveness. Although they acted out in a much more dramatic and childish way, their passions and their rebellion against God were the same as yours and mine. So as you read, look for the sins you have in common with the characters and ask yourself what would happen if you were to give full reign to every passion.

In your quiet times, may you come to understand the condition of humankind and the mercy of God with new clarity and depth.

Outline

1/ Judges 2:6–23 ———————————— The Cycle of Misery

2/ Judges 3:12–31 ——————————— A Left-Handed Leader

3/ Judges 4 ————————————————— Trust and Betrayal

4/ Judges 6:1–32 ——————————— Real Repentance

5/ Judges 6:33—7:25 ————————— Building Faith

6/ Judges 9 ————————————————— Integrity Lost

7/ Judges 11—12 ——————————— God's Dysfunctional Family

8/ Judges 13 ——————————————— God Forges a New Tool

9/ Judges 14—15 ———————————— The Need for Conflict

10/ Judges 16 ——————————————— Victorious Defeat

11/ Judges 17—18 —————————— A Moral Collapse

12/ Judges 21 ——————————————— The Aftermath of Moral Decay

Judges 1:1—2:5

1 After the death of Joshua, the Israelites asked the LORD, "Who will be the first to go up and fight for us against the Canaanites?"

2The LORD answered, "Judah is to go; I have given the land into their hands."

3Then the men of Judah said to the Simeonites their brothers, "Come up with us into the territory allotted to us, to fight against the Canaanites. We in turn will go with you into yours." So the Simeonites went with them.

4When Judah attacked, the LORD gave the Canaanites and Perizzites into their hands and they struck down ten thousand men at Bezek. 5It was there that they found Adoni-Bezek and fought against him, putting to rout the Canaanites and Perizzites. 6Adoni-Bezek fled, but they chased him and caught him, and cut off his thumbs and big toes.

7Then Adoni-Bezek said, "Seventy kings with their thumbs and big toes cut off have picked up scraps under my table. Now God has paid me back for what I did to them." They brought him to Jerusalem, and he died there.

8The men of Judah attacked Jerusalem also and took it. They put the city to the sword and set it on fire.

9After that, the men of Judah went down to fight against the Canaanites living in the hill country, the Negev and the western foothills. 10They advanced against the Canaanites living in Hebron (formerly called Kiriath Arba) and defeated Sheshai, Ahiman and Talmai.

11From there they advanced against the people living in Debir (formerly called Kiriath Sepher). 12And Caleb said, "I will give my daughter Acsah in marriage to the man who attacks and captures Kiriath Sepher." 13Othniel son of Kenaz, Caleb's younger brother, took it; so Caleb gave his daughter Acsah to him in marriage.

14One day when she came to Othniel, she urged him[a] to ask her father for a field. When she got off her donkey, Caleb asked her, "What can I do for you?"

15She replied, "Do me a special favor. Since you have given me land in the Negev, give me also springs of water." Then Caleb gave her the upper and lower springs.

16The descendants of Moses' father-in-law, the Kenite, went up from the City of Palms[b] with the men of Judah to live among the people of the Desert of Judah in the Negev near Arad.

17Then the men of Judah went with the Simeonites their brothers and attacked the Canaanites living in Zephath, and they totally destroyed[c] the city. Therefore it was called Hormah.[d] 18The men of Judah also took[e] Gaza, Ashkelon and Ekron—each city with its territory.

19The LORD was with the men of Judah. They took possession of the hill country, but they were unable to drive the people from the plains, because they had iron chariots. 20As Moses had promised, Hebron was given to Caleb, who drove from it the three sons of Anak. 21The Benjamites, however, failed to dislodge the Jebusites, who were living in Jerusalem; to this day the Jebusites live there with the Benjamites.

22Now the house of Joseph attacked Bethel, and the LORD was with them. 23When they sent men to spy out Bethel (formerly called Luz), 24the spies saw a man coming out of the city and they said to him, "Show us how to get into the city and we will see that you are treated well." 25So he showed them, and they put the city to the sword but spared the man and his whole family. 26He then went to the land of the Hittites, where he built a city and called it Luz, which is its name to this day.

27But Manasseh did not drive out the people of Beth Shan or Taanach or Dor or Ibleam or Megiddo and their surrounding settlements, for the Canaanites were determined to live in that land. 28When Israel became strong, they pressed the Canaanites into forced labor but never drove them out completely. 29Nor did Ephraim drive out the Canaanites living in Gezer, but the Canaanites continued to live there among them. 30Neither did Zebulun drive out the Canaanites living in Kitron or Nahalol, who remained among them; but they did subject them to forced labor. 31Nor did Asher drive out those living in Acco or

---

*a*14 Hebrew; Septuagint and Vulgate *Othniel, he urged her*   *b*16 That is, Jericho   *c*17 The Hebrew term refers to the irrevocable giving over of things or persons to the LORD, often by totally destroying them. *d*17 *Hormah means destruction.*   *e*18 Hebrew; Septuagint *Judah did not take*

Sidon or Ahlab or Aczib or Helbah or Aphek or Rehob, ³²and because of this the people of Asher lived among the Canaanite inhabitants of the land. ³³Neither did Naphtali drive out those living in Beth Shemesh or Beth Anath; but the Naphtalites too lived among the Canaanite inhabitants of the land, and those living in Beth Shemesh and Beth Anath became forced laborers for them. ³⁴The Amorites confined the Danites to the hill country, not allowing them to come down into the plain. ³⁵And the Amorites were determined also to hold out in Mount Heres, Aijalon and Shaalbim, but when the power of the house of Joseph increased, they too were pressed into forced labor. ³⁶The boundary of the Amorites was from Scorpion*f* Pass to Sela and beyond.

2

The angel of the LORD went up from Gilgal to Bokim and said, "I brought you up out of Egypt and led you into the land that I swore to give to your forefathers. I said, 'I will never break my covenant with you, ²and you shall not make a covenant with the people of this land, but you shall break down their altars.' Yet you have disobeyed me. Why have you done this? ³Now therefore I tell you that I will not drive them out before you; they will be ⌊thorns⌋ in your sides and their gods will be a snare to you."

⁴When the angel of the LORD had spoken these things to all the Israelites, the people wept aloud, ⁵and they called that place Bokim.*g* There they offered sacrifices to the LORD.

f 36 Hebrew Akrabbim   g 5 Bokim means weepers.

1 / *Judges 2:6–23*
The Cycle of Misery

UNDER THE INSPIRED leadership of Joshua, the Israelite people marched into the land which God had promised to give them. Through many brilliant military campaigns, the pagan populace was destroyed and the Israelites were left clearly in charge. Joshua had been able to retire with pride, leaving a bright and promising future for the young nation. However, it wasn't long before the golden future turned to hopeless despair. The people had foolishly destroyed the gift they had been given and now they needed to be rescued. It was the first round of a cycle that was to be repeated again and again.

 Warming Up to God It is said that "no one touches a hot stove twice." What "hot stoves" have plagued your life?

 Read Judges 2:6–23.

⁶After Joshua had dismissed the Israelites, they went to take possession of the land, each to his own inheritance. ⁷The people served the LORD throughout the lifetime of Joshua and of the elders who outlived him and who had seen all the great things the LORD had done for Israel.

⁸Joshua son of Nun, the servant of the LORD, died at the age of a hundred and ten. ⁹And they buried him in the land of his inheritance, at Timnath Heres*h* in the hill country of Ephraim, north of Mount Gaash.

¹⁰After that whole generation had been gathered to their fathers, another generation grew up, who knew neither the LORD nor what he had done for Israel. ¹¹Then the Israelites did evil in the eyes of the LORD and served the Baals. ¹²They forsook the LORD, the God of their fathers, who had brought them out of Egypt. They followed and worshiped various gods of the peoples around them. They provoked the LORD to anger ¹³because they forsook him and served Baal and the Ashtoreths. ¹⁴In his anger against Israel the LORD handed them over to raiders who plundered them. He sold them to their enemies all around, whom they were no longer able to resist. ¹⁵Whenever Israel went out to fight, the hand of the LORD was against them to defeat them, just as he had sworn to them. They were in great distress.

¹⁶Then the LORD raised up judges,*i* who saved them out of the hands of these raiders. ¹⁷Yet they

h 9 Also known as Timnath Serah (see Joshua 19:50 and 24:30)
i 16 Or leaders; similarly in verses 17-19

would not listen to their judges but prostituted themselves to other gods and worshiped them. Unlike their fathers, they quickly turned from the way in which their fathers had walked, the way of obedience to the Lord's commands. 18Whenever the Lord raised up a judge for them, he was with the judge and saved them out of the hands of their enemies as long as the judge lived; for the Lord had compassion on them as they groaned under those who oppressed and afflicted them. 19But when the judge died, the people returned to ways even more corrupt than those of their fathers, following other gods and serving and wor-

shiping them. They refused to give up their evil practices and stubborn ways.

20Therefore the Lord was very angry with Israel and said, "Because this nation has violated the covenant that I laid down for their forefathers and has not listened to me, 21I will no longer drive out before them any of the nations Joshua left when he died. 22I will use them to test Israel and see whether they will keep the way of the Lord and walk in it as their forefathers did." 23The Lord had allowed those nations to remain; he did not drive them out at once by giving them into the hands of Joshua.

 Discovering the Word 1. What cycle of behavior do these verses describe? 2. How did the second generation differ from the first (vv. 10–15)? 3. What does God's work through the judges reveal about his character (vv. 16–19)? 4. Why do you think the Israelites refused to listen to the judges? 5. In what ways did God use and control the enemies of Israel (vv. 20–23)?

Applying the Word 1. When are you likely to refuse to listen to godly advice? 2. The cycle of misery which trapped these Israelites is still at work today. How has the cycle of disobedience—distress—rescue—disobedience affected you?

Responding in Prayer Consider how you might be currently disobeying God. Let your memories of his past faithfulness to you call you back to obedience.

Judges 3:1–11

3These are the nations the Lord left to test all those Israelites who had not experienced any of the wars in Canaan 2(he did this only to teach warfare to the descendants of the Israelites who had not had previous battle experience): 3the five rulers of the Philistines, all the Canaanites, the Sidonians, and the Hivites living in the Lebanon mountains from Mount Baal Hermon to Lebo Hamath. 4They were left to test the Israelites to see whether they would obey the Lord's commands, which he had given their forefathers through Moses.

5The Israelites lived among the Canaanites, Hittites, Amorites, Perizzites, Hivites and Jebusites. 6They took their daughters in marriage and gave their own daughters to their sons, and served their gods.

7The Israelites did evil in the eyes of the Lord; they forgot the Lord their God and served the Baals and the Asherahs. 8The anger of the Lord burned against Israel so that he sold them into the hands of Cushan-Rishathaim king of Aram Naharaim,k to whom the Israelites were subject for eight years. 9But when they cried out to the Lord, he raised up for them a deliverer, Othniel son of Kenaz, Caleb's younger brother, who saved them. 10The Spirit of the Lord came upon him, so that he became Israel's judgel and went to war. The Lord gave Cushan-Rishathaim king of Aram into the hands of Othniel, who overpowered him. 11So the land had peace for forty years, until Othniel son of Kenaz died.

j3 Or *to the entrance to*   k8 That is, Northwest Mesopotamia
l10 Or *leader*

2 / *Judges 3:12–31*
A Left-Handed Leader

IN ONE OF those cheaply produced local television commercials, a large, smirking man smoking a huge cigar is identified as the greedy landlord. He is grabbing money from a line of discouraged-looking tenants and stuffing it into his already full pockets. But when the announcer shows how you can buy a new home and make payments lower than rent, the tenants triumphantly toss Mr. Landlord into his swimming pool. Like those discouraged tenants, the Israelites found themselves paying tribute to a greedy king. Their unwise choices to ignore God had caused the loss of their independence, so they were desperate for someone like the television announcer who would help them throw the greedy king off their back.

 Warming Up to God What would happen in your life if you gradually stopped worshiping God? Ask God to use this passage to strengthen your character through your worship.

 Read Judges 3:12–31.

¹²Once again the Israelites did evil in the eyes of the LORD, and because they did this evil the LORD gave Eglon king of Moab power over Israel. ¹³Getting the Ammonites and Amalekites to join him, Eglon came and attacked Israel, and they took possession of the City of Palms.^m ¹⁴The Israelites were subject to Eglon king of Moab for eighteen years.

¹⁵Again the Israelites cried out to the LORD, and he gave them a deliverer—Ehud, a left-handed man, the son of Gera the Benjamite. The Israelites sent him with tribute to Eglon king of Moab. ¹⁶Now Ehud had made a double-edged sword about a foot and a half^n long, which he strapped to his right thigh under his clothing. ¹⁷He presented the tribute to Eglon king of Moab, who was a very fat man. ¹⁸After Ehud had presented the tribute, he sent on their way the men who had carried it. ¹⁹At the idols^o near Gilgal he himself turned back and said, "I have a secret message for you, O king."

The king said, "Quiet!" And all his attendants left him.

²⁰Ehud then approached him while he was sitting alone in the upper room of his summer palace^p and said, "I have a message from God for you." As the king rose from his seat, ²¹Ehud reached with his left hand, drew the sword from his right thigh and plunged it into the king's belly. ²²Even the handle sank in after the blade, which came out his back. Ehud did not pull the sword out, and the fat closed in over it. ²³Then

Ehud went out to the porch^q; he shut the doors of the upper room behind him and locked them. ²⁴After he had gone, the servants came and found the doors of the upper room locked. They said, "He must be relieving himself in the inner room of the house." ²⁵They waited to the point of embarrassment, but when he did not open the doors of the room, they took a key and unlocked them. There they saw their lord fallen to the floor, dead.

²⁶While they waited, Ehud got away. He passed by the idols and escaped to Seirah. ²⁷When he arrived there, he blew a trumpet in the hill country of Ephraim, and the Israelites went down with him from the hills, with him leading them.

²⁸"Follow me," he ordered, "for the LORD has given Moab, your enemy, into your hands." So they followed him down and, taking possession of the fords of the Jordan that led to Moab, they allowed no one to cross over. ²⁹At that time they struck down about ten thousand Moabites, all vigorous and strong; not a man escaped. ³⁰That day Moab was made subject to Israel, and the land had peace for eighty years.

³¹After Ehud came Shamgar son of Anath, who struck down six hundred Philistines with an oxgoad. He too saved Israel.

---

^m 13 That is, Jericho   ^n 16 Hebrew *a cubit* (about 0.5 meter)
^o 19 Or *the stone quarries*; also in verse 26   ^p 20 The meaning of the Hebrew for this phrase is uncertain.   ^q 23 The meaning of the Hebrew for this word is uncertain.

Discovering the Word 1. How do the attitudes and emotions of the Israelite people change in this story (vv. 12–15, 27–30)? 2. The conquering Moabites attempted to keep Israel weak by forcing them to pay a heavy tax called *tribute*. In verses 15–19 Ehud delivers the tribute to King Eglon. How does this picture highlight the painful consequences of poor choices? 3. Why do you think the Bible gives such a gory description of how Israel was saved? 4. Which of Ehud's qualities did God use in fulfilling his plan? 5. Ehud's left-handedness was considered to be a handicap. What does this tell you about God's surprises?

Applying the Word 1. The Israelites paid a high price for ignoring God. What has been the price of your bad choices? 2. Which of your weaknesses would you be surprised to find God developing into assets? 3. What has this story taught you about the way back to God?

Responding in Prayer What bad choices have you recently made? Make confession a part of your prayer as you ask God to build your character.

3 / *Judges 4*
Trust and Betrayal

"ET TU, BRUTE?" These words from the Shakespearean play *Julius Caesar* sum up the shock and pain of betrayal. The dagger twisted in the back by a trusted friend is a double agony. But it isn't only our friends who betray us. After a recent earthquake, Californians talked about their fears that they couldn't trust the ground to remain firm. A friend who lost hours of computer input during a power failure said he felt betrayed by technology. If friends, nature, knowledge and things all have the potential to turn against us, then where can we turn in a time of crisis?

 Warming Up to God What people and things have you assumed would be there to rescue you if you needed them?

 Read Judges 4.

4 After Ehud died, the Israelites once again did evil in the eyes of the LORD. ²So the LORD sold them into the hands of Jabin, a king of Canaan, who reigned in Hazor. The commander of his army was Sisera, who lived in Harosheth Haggoyim. ³Because he had nine hundred iron chariots and had cruelly oppressed the Israelites for twenty years, they cried to the LORD for help.

⁴Deborah, a prophetess, the wife of Lappidoth, was leading' Israel at that time. ⁵She held court under the Palm of Deborah between Ramah and Bethel in the hill country of Ephraim, and the Israelites came to her to have their disputes decided. ⁶She sent for Barak son of Abinoam from Kedesh in Naphtali and said to him, "The LORD, the God of Israel, commands you: 'Go, take with you ten thousand men of Naphtali and Zebulun and lead the way to Mount Tabor. ⁷I will lure Sisera, the commander of Jabin's army, with his chariots and his troops to the Kishon River and give him into your hands.' "

⁸Barak said to her, "If you go with me, I will go; but if you don't go with me, I won't go."

⁹"Very well," Deborah said, "I will go with you. But because of the way you are going about this,⁵ the honor will not be yours, for the LORD will hand Sisera over to a woman." So Deborah went with Barak to Kedesh, ¹⁰where he summoned Zebulun and Naphtali. Ten thousand men followed him, and Deborah also went with him.

¹¹Now Heber the Kenite had left the other Kenites, the descendants of Hobab, Moses' brother-in-law,ᵗ and pitched his tent by the great tree in Zaanannim near Kedesh.

¹²When they told Sisera that Barak son of Abinoam had gone up to Mount Tabor, ¹³Sisera gathered together his nine hundred iron chariots and all the men with him, from Harosheth Haggoyim to the Kishon River.

¹⁴Then Deborah said to Barak, "Go! This is the day the LORD has given Sisera into your hands. Has not the LORD gone ahead of you?" So Barak

ʳ4 Traditionally *judging*   ˢ9 Or *But on the expedition you are undertaking*   ᵗ11 Or *father-in-law* went down Mount Tabor, followed by ten thousand men. ¹⁵At Barak's advance, the LORD routed Sisera and all his chariots and army by the sword, and Sisera abandoned his chariot and fled on foot. ¹⁶But Barak pursued the chariots and army as far as Harosheth Haggoyim. All the troops of Sisera fell by the sword; not a man was left.

¹⁷Sisera, however, fled on foot to the tent of Jael, the wife of Heber the Kenite, because there were friendly relations between Jabin king of Hazor and the clan of Heber the Kenite.

¹⁸Jael went out to meet Sisera and said to him, "Come, my lord, come right in. Don't be afraid." So he entered her tent, and she put a covering over him.

¹⁹"I'm thirsty," he said. "Please give me some water." She opened a skin of milk, gave him a drink, and covered him up.

²⁰"Stand in the doorway of the tent," he told her. "If someone comes by and asks you, 'Is anyone here?' say 'No.' "

²¹But Jael, Heber's wife, picked up a tent peg and a hammer and went quietly to him while he lay fast asleep, exhausted. She drove the peg through his temple into the ground, and he died.

²²Barak came by in pursuit of Sisera, and Jael went out to meet him. "Come," she said, "I will show you the man you're looking for." So he went in with her, and there lay Sisera with the tent peg through his temple—dead.

²³On that day God subdued Jabin, the Canaanite king, before the Israelites. ²⁴And the hand of the Israelites grew stronger and stronger against Jabin, the Canaanite king, until they destroyed him.

 Discovering the Word 1. What gifts and skills did Deborah possess (vv. 4–14)? 2. What difference did Deborah's presence make during a godless period of Israel's history? 3. Why was it wrong for Barak to ask Deborah to go with him (v. 8)? 4. What assumptions did Sisera make regarding his safety (vv. 15–21)? 5. How did each of the things Sisera trusted to protect him fail?

Applying the Word 1. Consider where each of the leading characters of this story—Deborah, Barak, Jael and Sisera—put his or her trust. Which of them are you most like? Why? 2. What has this study helped you to discover about your trust in God?

Responding in Prayer Ask God to show you where your trust is. Ask him to be the stable foundation of your trust.

Judges 5

5 On that day Deborah and Barak son of Abinoam sang this song:

²"When the princes in Israel take the
        lead,
  when the people willingly offer
        themselves—
  praise the LORD!

³"Hear this, you kings! Listen, you rulers!
  I will sing toᵘ the LORD, I will sing;
  I will make music toᵛ the LORD, the God of
        Israel.

⁴"O LORD, when you went out from Seir,
  when you marched from the land of Edom,

  the earth shook, the heavens poured,
        the clouds poured down water.
⁵The mountains quaked before the LORD, the
        One of Sinai,
  before the LORD, the God of Israel.

⁶"In the days of Shamgar son of Anath,
  in the days of Jael, the roads were
        abandoned;
  travelers took to winding paths.
⁷Village lifeʷ in Israel ceased,
  ceased until I,ˣ Deborah, arose,
  arose a mother in Israel.
⁸When they chose new gods,

ᵘ3 Or of   ᵛ3 Or / with song I will praise   ʷ7 Or Warriors
ˣ7 Or you

war came to the city gates,
and not a shield or spear was seen
among forty thousand in Israel.
⁹My heart is with Israel's princes,
with the willing volunteers among the
people.
Praise the LORD!

¹⁰"You who ride on white donkeys,
sitting on your saddle blankets,
and you who walk along the road,
consider ¹¹the voice of the singers⁽ʸ⁾ at the
watering places.
They recite the righteous acts of the LORD,
the righteous acts of his warriors⁽ᶻ⁾ in
Israel.

"Then the people of the LORD
went down to the city gates.
¹²'Wake up, wake up, Deborah!
Wake up, wake up, break out in song!
Arise, O Barak!
Take captive your captives, O son of
Abinoam.'

¹³"Then the men who were left
came down to the nobles;
the people of the LORD
came to me with the mighty.
¹⁴Some came from Ephraim, whose roots were
in Amalek;
Benjamin was with the people who
followed you.
From Makir captains came down,
from Zebulun those who bear a
commander's staff.
¹⁵The princes of Issachar were with Deborah;
yes, Issachar was with Barak,
rushing after him into the valley.
In the districts of Reuben
there was much searching of heart.
¹⁶Why did you stay among the campfires⁽ᵃ⁾
to hear the whistling for the flocks?
In the districts of Reuben
there was much searching of heart.
¹⁷Gilead stayed beyond the Jordan.
And Dan, why did he linger by the ships?
Asher remained on the coast
and stayed in his coves.
¹⁸The people of Zebulun risked their very lives;
so did Naphtali on the heights of the field.

¹⁹"Kings came, they fought;
the kings of Canaan fought
at Taanach by the waters of Megiddo,
but they carried off no silver, no plunder.
²⁰From the heavens the stars fought,
from their courses they fought against
Sisera.
²¹The river Kishon swept them away,
the age-old river, the river Kishon.
March on, my soul; be strong!
²²Then thundered the horses' hoofs—
galloping, galloping go his mighty steeds.
²³'Curse Meroz,' said the angel of the LORD.
'Curse its people bitterly,
because they did not come to help the LORD,
to help the LORD against the mighty.'

²⁴"Most blessed of women be Jael,
the wife of Heber the Kenite,
most blessed of tent-dwelling women.
²⁵He asked for water, and she gave him milk;
in a bowl fit for nobles she brought him
curdled milk.
²⁶Her hand reached for the tent peg,
her right hand for the workman's hammer.
She struck Sisera, she crushed his head,
she shattered and pierced his temple.
²⁷At her feet he sank,
he fell; there he lay.
At her feet he sank, he fell;
where he sank, there he fell—dead.

²⁸"Through the window peered Sisera's mother;
behind the lattice she cried out,
'Why is his chariot so long in coming?
Why is the clatter of his chariots delayed?'
²⁹The wisest of her ladies answer her;
indeed, she keeps saying to herself,
³⁰'Are they not finding and dividing the spoils:
a girl or two for each man,
colorful garments as plunder for Sisera,
colorful garments embroidered,
highly embroidered garments for my
neck—
all this as plunder?'

³¹"So may all your enemies perish, O LORD!
But may they who love you be like the sun
when it rises in its strength."

Then the land had peace forty years.

ʸ11 Or *archers*; the meaning of the Hebrew for this word is uncertain.
ᶻ11 Or *villagers*   ᵃ16 Or *saddlebags*

4 / *Judges 6:1–32*
Real Repentance

OH, NO! GOD'S people are at it again. By this time in your study, you are probably getting used to the disappointing litany "Again the Israelites did evil in the eyes of the LORD." You know what's coming: punishment, repentance and rescue. But what happens when the people become so hard-hearted that even punishment fails to cause them to see the error of their ways? What happens when their cry to God carries only regret and no repentance? In Judges 6 you will see God take the initiative to win his people back to himself.

 Warming Up to God   In what ways was God at work in your life even before you met him?

 Read Judges 6:1–32.

6 Again the Israelites did evil in the eyes of the LORD, and for seven years he gave them into the hands of the Midianites. ²Because the power of Midian was so oppressive, the Israelites prepared shelters for themselves in mountain clefts, caves and strongholds. ³Whenever the Israelites planted their crops, the Midianites, Amalekites and other eastern peoples invaded the country. ⁴They camped on the land and ruined the crops all the way to Gaza and did not spare a living thing for Israel, neither sheep nor cattle nor donkeys. ⁵They came up with their livestock and their tents like swarms of locusts. It was impossible to count the men and their camels; they invaded the land to ravage it. ⁶Midian so impoverished the Israelites that they cried out to the LORD for help.

⁷When the Israelites cried to the LORD because of Midian, ⁸he sent them a prophet, who said, "This is what the LORD, the God of Israel, says: I brought you up out of Egypt, out of the land of slavery. ⁹I snatched you from the power of Egypt and from the hand of all your oppressors. I drove them from before you and gave you their land. ¹⁰I said to you, 'I am the LORD your God; do not worship the gods of the Amorites, in whose land you live.' But you have not listened to me."

¹¹The angel of the LORD came and sat down under the oak in Ophrah that belonged to Joash the Abiezrite, where his son Gideon was threshing wheat in a winepress to keep it from the Midianites. ¹²When the angel of the LORD appeared to Gideon, he said, "The LORD is with you, mighty warrior."

¹³"But sir," Gideon replied, "if the LORD is with us, why has all this happened to us? Where are all his wonders that our fathers told us about when they said, 'Did not the LORD bring us up out of Egypt?' But now the LORD has abandoned us and put us into the hand of Midian."

¹⁴The LORD turned to him and said, "Go in the strength you have and save Israel out of Midian's hand. Am I not sending you?"

¹⁵"But Lord,ᵇ" Gideon asked, "how can I save Israel? My clan is the weakest in Manasseh, and I am the least in my family."

¹⁶The LORD answered, "I will be with you, and you will strike down all the Midianites together."

¹⁷Gideon replied, "If now I have found favor in your eyes, give me a sign that it is really you talking to me. ¹⁸Please do not go away until I come back and bring my offering and set it before you."

And the LORD said, "I will wait until you return."

¹⁹Gideon went in, prepared a young goat, and from an ephahᶜ of flour he made bread without yeast. Putting the meat in a basket and its broth in a pot, he brought them out and offered them to him under the oak.

²⁰The angel of God said to him, "Take the meat and the unleavened bread, place them on this rock, and pour out the broth." And Gideon did so. ²¹With the tip of the staff that was in his hand, the angel of the LORD touched the meat and the unleavened bread. Fire flared from the rock, consuming the meat and the bread. And the angel of the LORD disappeared. ²²When Gideon realized that it was the angel of the LORD, he exclaimed, "Ah, Sovereign LORD! I have seen the angel of the LORD face to face!"

²³But the LORD said to him, "Peace! Do not be afraid. You are not going to die."

ᵇ15 Or *sir*   ᶜ19 That is, probably about 3/5 bushel (about 22 liters)

24So Gideon built an altar to the LORD there and called it The LORD is Peace. To this day it stands in Ophrah of the Abiezrites.

25That same night the LORD said to him, "Take the second bull from your father's herd, the one seven years old.*d* Tear down your father's altar to Baal and cut down the Asherah pole*e* beside it. 26Then build a proper kind of*f* altar to the LORD your God on the top of this height. Using the wood of the Asherah pole that you cut down, offer the second*g* bull as a burnt offering."

27So Gideon took ten of his servants and did as the LORD told him. But because he was afraid of his family and the men of the town, he did it at night rather than in the daytime.

28In the morning when the men of the town got up, there was Baal's altar, demolished, with the Asherah pole beside it cut down and the second bull sacrificed on the newly built altar!

29They asked each other, "Who did this?"

When they carefully investigated, they were told, "Gideon son of Joash did it."

30The men of the town demanded of Joash, "Bring out your son. He must die, because he has broken down Baal's altar and cut down the Asherah pole beside it."

31But Joash replied to the hostile crowd around him, "Are you going to plead Baal's cause? Are you trying to save him? Whoever fights for him shall be put to death by morning! If Baal really is a god, he can defend himself when someone breaks down his altar." 32So that day they called Gideon "Jerub-Baal,*h*" saying, "Let Baal contend with him," because he broke down Baal's altar.

*d*25 Or *Take a full-grown, mature bull from your father's herd* *e*25 That is, a symbol of the goddess Asherah; here and elsewhere in Judges   *f*26 Or *build with layers of stone an*   *g*26 Or *full-grown*; also in verse 28   *h*32 *Jerub-Baal* means *let Baal contend.*

 Discovering the Word 1. Imagine life during the years of Midianite occupation (vv. 1–6). What about this situation would have been most distressing to you? 2. When the Israelites finally cried out to God, he first sent a prophet (vv. 7–10). What evidence is there that the Israelites' repentance was not real? 3. Compare the words of God to the words of Gideon in verses 7–15. How did Gideon's view of the problem and its solution differ from God's? 4. How did the miracle of verse 21 change Gideon? 5. God's first command to Gideon was to tear down his father's altar to Baal (vv. 25–27). How did Gideon's obedience differ from God's intention? 6. How could true obedience have made an even greater impact on Gideon's family and community (vv. 28–30)?

 Applying the Word 1. When has your repentance and obedience been less than complete? 2. What have been the results of false repentance in your life?

Responding in Prayer Take some time to thank God for his initiative in your life. Ask him to guide you to true repentance.

---

5 / Judges 6:33—7:25
Building Faith

"FAITH IS [OUR] response to God's initiative," says John White in *The Fight* (Downers Grove, Ill.: InterVarsity Press, 1976, p. 97). Given this definition, faith is shown not in how devotedly we believe, but in how powerfully we take action. It can be illustrated by Gideon, who entered public life as a timid and uncertain man, constantly second-guessing himself. Yet Gideon took action when God asked him to do so. Our passage for this study chronicles the metamorphosis of Gideon from reluctant leader to confident man of faith.

 Warming Up to God How has John White's definition of faith been true in your life?

 Read Judges 6:33—7:25.

33Now all the Midianites, Amalekites and other eastern peoples joined forces and crossed over the Jordan and camped in the Valley of Jezreel. 34Then the Spirit of the LORD came upon Gideon, and he blew a trumpet, summoning the Abiezrites to follow him. 35He sent messengers throughout Manasseh, calling them to arms, and also into Asher, Zebulun and Naphtali, so that they too went up to meet them.

36Gideon said to God, "If you will save Israel by my hand as you have promised— 37look, I will place a wool fleece on the threshing floor. If there is dew only on the fleece and all the ground is dry, then I will know that you will save Israel by my hand, as you said." 38And that is what happened. Gideon rose early the next day; he squeezed the fleece and wrung out the dew—a bowlful of water.

39Then Gideon said to God, "Do not be angry with me. Let me make just one more request. Allow me one more test with the fleece. This time make the fleece dry and the ground covered with dew." 40That night God did so. Only the fleece was dry; all the ground was covered with dew.

7 Early in the morning, Jerub-Baal (that is, Gideon) and all his men camped at the spring of Harod. The camp of Midian was north of them in the valley near the hill of Moreh. 2The LORD said to Gideon, "You have too many men for me to deliver Midian into their hands. In order that Israel may not boast against me that her own strength has saved her, 3announce now to the people, 'Anyone who trembles with fear may turn back and leave Mount Gilead.'" So twenty-two thousand men left, while ten thousand remained.

4But the LORD said to Gideon, "There are still too many men. Take them down to the water, and I will sift them for you there. If I say, 'This one shall go with you,' he shall go; but if I say, 'This one shall not go with you,' he shall not go."

5So Gideon took the men down to the water. There the LORD told him, "Separate those who lap the water with their tongues like a dog from those who kneel down to drink." 6Three hundred men lapped with their hands to their mouths. All the rest got down on their knees to drink. 7The LORD said to Gideon, "With the three hundred men that lapped I will save you and give the Midianites into your hands. Let all the other men go, each to his own place." 8So Gideon sent the rest of the Israelites to their tents but kept the three hundred, who took over the provisions and trumpets of the others.

Now the camp of Midian lay below him in the valley. 9During that night the LORD said to Gideon, "Get up, go down against the camp, because I am going to give it into your hands. 10If you are afraid to attack, go down to the camp with your servant Purah 11and listen to what they are saying. Afterward, you will be encouraged to attack the camp." So he and Purah his servant went down to the outposts of the camp. 12The Midianites, the Amalekites and all the other eastern peoples had settled in the valley, thick as locusts. Their camels could no more be counted than the sand on the seashore.

13Gideon arrived just as a man was telling a friend his dream. "I had a dream," he was saying. "A round loaf of barley bread came tumbling into the Midianite camp. It struck the tent with such force that the tent overturned and collapsed."

14His friend responded, "This can be nothing other than the sword of Gideon son of Joash, the Israelite. God has given the Midianites and the whole camp into his hands."

15When Gideon heard the dream and its interpretation, he worshiped God. He returned to the camp of Israel and called out, "Get up! The LORD has given the Midianite camp into your hands." 16Dividing the three hundred men into three companies, he placed trumpets and empty jars in the hands of all of them, with torches inside.

17"Watch me," he told them. "Follow my lead. When I get to the edge of the camp, do exactly as I do. 18When I and all who are with me blow our trumpets, then from all around the camp blow yours and shout, 'For the LORD and for Gideon.'"

19Gideon and the hundred men with him reached the edge of the camp at the beginning of the middle watch, just after they had changed the guard. They blew their trumpets and broke the jars that were in their hands. 20The three companies blew the trumpets and smashed the jars. Grasping the torches in their left hands and holding in their right hands the trumpets they were to blow, they shouted, "A sword for the LORD and for Gideon!" 21While each man held his position around the camp, all the Midianites ran, crying out as they fled.

22When the three hundred trumpets sounded, the LORD caused the men throughout the camp to turn on each other with their swords. The army fled to Beth Shittah toward Zererah as far as the border of Abel Meholah near Tabbath. ²³Israelites from Naphtali, Asher and all Manasseh were called out, and they pursued the Midianites. ²⁴Gideon sent messengers throughout the hill country of Ephraim, saying, "Come down against the Midianites and seize the waters of the Jordan ahead of them as far as Beth Barah."

So all the men of Ephraim were called out and they took the waters of the Jordan as far as Beth Barah. ²⁵They also captured two of the Midianite leaders, Oreb and Zeeb. They killed Oreb at the rock of Oreb, and Zeeb at the winepress of Zeeb. They pursued the Midianites and brought the heads of Oreb and Zeeb to Gideon, who was by the Jordan.

Discovering the Word 1. Gideon called the people to battle (6:34–35) before he laid out the fleece (6:36–40). What do you think would have happened if he had asked for the proof first? 2. Many people have sought spiritual guidance by asking for a specific sign. Because they base this on what Gideon did, this practice is sometimes referred to as "fleecing." What does Gideon's experience teach you about this practice? 3. How would Gideon have felt when over two-thirds of his men went home (7:3)? 4. How were Gideon and the Israelite army like a barley loaf (7:13–15)? 5. How was Gideon changed by these events (7:15–25)?

Applying the Word 1. How do you seek God's guidance? 2. How has God given you encouragement when you wavered in your faith?

Responding in Prayer Pray that God will give you faith to carry out the tasks that he has for you.

Judges 8

8 Now the Ephraimites asked Gideon, "Why have you treated us like this? Why didn't you call us when you went to fight Midian?" And they criticized him sharply.

²But he answered them, "What have I accomplished compared to you? Aren't the gleanings of Ephraim's grapes better than the full grape harvest of Abiezer? ³God gave Oreb and Zeeb, the Midianite leaders, into your hands. What was I able to do compared to you?" At this, their resentment against him subsided.

⁴Gideon and his three hundred men, exhausted yet keeping up the pursuit, came to the Jordan and crossed it. ⁵He said to the men of Succoth, "Give my troops some bread; they are worn out, and I am still pursuing Zebah and Zalmunna, the kings of Midian."

⁶But the officials of Succoth said, "Do you already have the hands of Zebah and Zalmunna in your possession? Why should we give bread to your troops?"

⁷Then Gideon replied, "Just for that, when the LORD has given Zebah and Zalmunna into my hand, I will tear your flesh with desert thorns and briers."

⁸From there he went up to Peniel[i] and made the same request of them, but they answered as

the men of Succoth had. ⁹So he said to the men of Peniel, "When I return in triumph, I will tear down this tower."

¹⁰Now Zebah and Zalmunna were in Karkor with a force of about fifteen thousand men, all that were left of the armies of the eastern peoples; a hundred and twenty thousand swordsmen had fallen. ¹¹Gideon went up by the route of the nomads east of Nobah and Jogbehah and fell upon the unsuspecting army. ¹²Zebah and Zalmunna, the two kings of Midian, fled, but he pursued them and captured them, routing their entire army.

¹³Gideon son of Joash then returned from the battle by the Pass of Heres. ¹⁴He caught a young man of Succoth and questioned him, and the young man wrote down for him the names of the seventy-seven officials of Succoth, the elders of the town. ¹⁵Then Gideon came and said to the men of Succoth, "Here are Zebah and Zalmunna, about whom you taunted me by saying, 'Do you already have the hands of Zebah and Zalmunna in your possession? Why should we give bread to your exhausted men?' " ¹⁶He took the elders of the town and taught the men of Succoth a lesson by punishing them with desert thorns and briers.

ⁱ8 Hebrew *Penuel*, a variant of *Peniel*; also in verses 9 and 17

¹⁷He also pulled down the tower of Peniel and killed the men of the town.

¹⁸Then he asked Zebah and Zalmunna, "What kind of men did you kill at Tabor?"

"Men like you," they answered, "each one with the bearing of a prince."

¹⁹Gideon replied, "Those were my brothers, the sons of my own mother. As surely as the LORD lives, if you had spared their lives, I would not kill you." ²⁰Turning to Jether, his oldest son, he said, "Kill them!" But Jether did not draw his sword, because he was only a boy and was afraid.

²¹Zebah and Zalmunna said, "Come, do it yourself. 'As is the man, so is his strength.'" So Gideon stepped forward and killed them, and took the ornaments off their camels' necks.

²²The Israelites said to Gideon, "Rule over us—you, your son and your grandson—because you have saved us out of the hand of Midian."

²³But Gideon told them, "I will not rule over you, nor will my son rule over you. The LORD will rule over you." ²⁴And he said, "I do have one request, that each of you give me an earring from your share of the plunder." (It was the custom of the Ishmaelites to wear gold earrings.)

²⁵They answered, "We'll be glad to give them." So they spread out a garment, and each man threw a ring from his plunder onto it. ²⁶The weight of the gold rings he asked for came to seventeen hundred shekels,ʲ not counting the ornaments, the pendants and the purple garments worn by the kings of Midian or the chains that were on their camels' necks. ²⁷Gideon made the gold into an ephod, which he placed in Ophrah, his town. All Israel prostituted themselves by worshiping it there, and it became a snare to Gideon and his family.

²⁸Thus Midian was subdued before the Israelites and did not raise its head again. During Gideon's lifetime, the land enjoyed peace forty years.

²⁹Jerub-Baal son of Joash went back home to live. ³⁰He had seventy sons of his own, for he had many wives. ³¹His concubine, who lived in Shechem, also bore him a son, whom he named Abimelech. ³²Gideon son of Joash died at a good old age and was buried in the tomb of his father Joash in Ophrah of the Abiezrites.

³³No sooner had Gideon died than the Israelites again prostituted themselves to the Baals. They set up Baal-Berith as their god and ³⁴did not remember the LORD their God, who had rescued them from the hands of all their enemies on every side. ³⁵They also failed to show kindness to the family of Jerub-Baal (that is, Gideon) for all the good things he had done for them.

ʲ26 That is, about 43 pounds (about 19.5 kilograms)

6 / *Judges 9*
Integrity Lost

A MOTTO ON the wall of a German school read:
> When wealth is lost, nothing is lost;
> When health is lost, something is lost;
> When character is lost, all is lost!

The people of Shechem serve as an illustration of this motto. By failing to stand up for what was right, they soon found their lives ruled by evil. Once character was gone, they lost freedom. All of the choices presented to them were merely different paths through a vile maze which led inexorably to a final death trap.

 Warming Up to God When have you felt pressured to make a decision you were uncomfortable with?

 Read Judges 9.

9 Abimelech son of Jerub-Baal went to his mother's brothers in Shechem and said to them and to all his mother's clan, ²"Ask all the citizens of Shechem, 'Which is better for you: to have all seventy of Jerub-Baal's sons rule over you, or just one man?' Remember, I am your flesh and blood."

³When the brothers repeated all this to the citizens of Shechem, they were inclined to follow Abimelech, for they said, "He is our brother." ⁴They gave him seventy shekels*ᵏ* of silver from the temple of Baal-Berith, and Abimelech used it to hire reckless adventurers, who became his followers. ⁵He went to his father's home in Ophrah and on one stone murdered his seventy brothers, the sons of Jerub-Baal. But Jotham, the youngest son of Jerub-Baal, escaped by hiding. ⁶Then all the citizens of Shechem and Beth Millo gathered beside the great tree at the pillar in Shechem to crown Abimelech king.

⁷When Jotham was told about this, he climbed up on the top of Mount Gerizim and shouted to them, "Listen to me, citizens of Shechem, so that God may listen to you. ⁸One day the trees went out to anoint a king for themselves. They said to the olive tree, 'Be our king.'

⁹"But the olive tree answered, 'Should I give up my oil, by which both gods and men are honored, to hold sway over the trees?'

¹⁰"Next, the trees said to the fig tree, 'Come and be our king.'

¹¹"But the fig tree replied, 'Should I give up my fruit, so good and sweet, to hold sway over the trees?'

¹²"Then the trees said to the vine, 'Come and be our king.'

¹³"But the vine answered, 'Should I give up my wine, which cheers both gods and men, to hold sway over the trees?'

¹⁴"Finally all the trees said to the thornbush, 'Come and be our king.'

¹⁵"The thornbush said to the trees, 'If you really want to anoint me king over you, come and take refuge in my shade; but if not, then let fire come out of the thornbush and consume the cedars of Lebanon!'

¹⁶"Now if you have acted honorably and in good faith when you made Abimelech king, and if you have been fair to Jerub-Baal and his family, and if you have treated him as he deserves— ¹⁷and to think that my father fought for you, risked his life to rescue you from the hand of Midian ¹⁸(but today you have revolted against my father's family, murdered his seventy sons on a single stone, and made Abimelech, the son of his slave girl, king over the citizens of Shechem because he is your brother)— ¹⁹if then you have acted honorably and in good faith toward Jerub-Baal and his family today, may Abimelech be your joy, and may you be his, too! ²⁰But if you have not, let fire come out from Abimelech and consume you, citizens of Shechem and Beth Millo, and let fire come out from you, citizens of Shechem and Beth Millo, and consume Abimelech!"

²¹Then Jotham fled, escaping to Beer, and he lived there because he was afraid of his brother Abimelech.

²²After Abimelech had governed Israel three years, ²³God sent an evil spirit between Abimelech and the citizens of Shechem, who acted treacherously against Abimelech. ²⁴God did this in order that the crime against Jerub-Baal's seventy sons, the shedding of their blood, might be avenged on their brother Abimelech and on the citizens of Shechem, who had helped him murder his brothers. ²⁵In opposition to him these citizens of Shechem set men on the hilltops to ambush and rob everyone who passed by, and this was reported to Abimelech.

²⁶Now Gaal son of Ebed moved with his brothers into Shechem, and its citizens put their confidence in him. ²⁷After they had gone out into the fields and gathered the grapes and trodden them, they held a festival in the temple of their god. While they were eating and drinking, they cursed Abimelech. ²⁸Then Gaal son of Ebed said, "Who is Abimelech, and who is Shechem, that we should be subject to him? Isn't he Jerub-Baal's son, and isn't Zebul his deputy? Serve the men of Hamor, Shechem's father! Why should we serve Abimelech? ²⁹If only this people were under my command! Then I would get rid of him. I would say to Abimelech, 'Call out your whole army!' "*ˡ*

³⁰When Zebul the governor of the city heard what Gaal son of Ebed said, he was very angry. ³¹Under cover he sent messengers to Abimelech, saying, "Gaal son of Ebed and his brothers have come to Shechem and are stirring up the city against you. ³²Now then, during the night you and your men should come and lie in wait in the fields. ³³In the morning at sunrise, advance against the city. When Gaal and his men come

ᵏ4 That is, about 1 3/4 pounds (about 0.8 kilogram)   *ˡ29* Septuagint; Hebrew *him.*" Then he said to Abimelech, "Call out your whole army!"

out against you, do whatever your hand finds to do."

³⁴So Abimelech and all his troops set out by night and took up concealed positions near Shechem in four companies. ³⁵Now Gaal son of Ebed had gone out and was standing at the entrance to the city gate just as Abimelech and his soldiers came out from their hiding place.

³⁶When Gaal saw them, he said to Zebul, "Look, people are coming down from the tops of the mountains!"

Zebul replied, "You mistake the shadows of the mountains for men."

³⁷But Gaal spoke up again: "Look, people are coming down from the center of the land, and a company is coming from the direction of the soothsayers' tree."

³⁸Then Zebul said to him, "Where is your big talk now, you who said, 'Who is Abimelech that we should be subject to him?' Aren't these the men you ridiculed? Go out and fight them!"

³⁹So Gaal led out ᵐ the citizens of Shechem and fought Abimelech. ⁴⁰Abimelech chased him, and many fell wounded in the flight—all the way to the entrance to the gate. ⁴¹Abimelech stayed in Arumah, and Zebul drove Gaal and his brothers out of Shechem.

⁴²The next day the people of Shechem went out to the fields, and this was reported to Abimelech. ⁴³So he took his men, divided them into three companies and set an ambush in the fields. When he saw the people coming out of the city, he rose to attack them. ⁴⁴Abimelech and the companies with him rushed forward to a position at the entrance to the city gate. Then two companies rushed upon those in the fields and struck them down. ⁴⁵All that day Abimelech pressed his attack against the city until he had captured it and killed its people. Then he destroyed the city and scattered salt over it.

⁴⁶On hearing this, the citizens in the tower of Shechem went into the stronghold of the temple of El-Berith. ⁴⁷When Abimelech heard that they had assembled there, ⁴⁸he and all his men went up Mount Zalmon. He took an ax and cut off some branches, which he lifted to his shoulders. He ordered the men with him, "Quick! Do what you have seen me do!" ⁴⁹So all the men cut branches and followed Abimelech. They piled them against the stronghold and set it on fire over the people inside. So all the people in the tower of Shechem, about a thousand men and women, also died.

⁵⁰Next Abimelech went to Thebez and besieged it and captured it. ⁵¹Inside the city, however, was a strong tower, to which all the men and women—all the people of the city—fled. They locked themselves in and climbed up on the tower roof. ⁵²Abimelech went to the tower and stormed it. But as he approached the entrance to the tower to set it on fire, ⁵³a woman dropped an upper millstone on his head and cracked his skull.

⁵⁴Hurriedly he called to his armor-bearer, "Draw your sword and kill me, so that they can't say, 'A woman killed him.' " So his servant ran him through, and he died. ⁵⁵When the Israelites saw that Abimelech was dead, they went home.

⁵⁶Thus God repaid the wickedness that Abimelech had done to his father by murdering his seventy brothers. ⁵⁷God also made the men of Shechem pay for all their wickedness. The curse of Jotham son of Jerub-Baal came on them.

ᵐ39 Or *Gaal went out in the sight of*

Discovering the Word 1. If you were assigned the task of writing an obituary for Abimelech, what would you say about him? 2. When the people offered to make Gideon their king, he turned them down (8:22–23). His children apparently didn't feel the same way. What dilemmas did this present for the people of Shechem (vv. 1–6)? 3. What truths was Jotham attempting to illustrate by his fable (vv. 7–15)? 4. Jotham had shouted, "If then you have acted honorably and in good faith toward Jerub-Baal and his family today, may Abimelech be your joy, and may you be his, too!" (v. 19). What prevented this blessing of joy from occurring? 5. How was Jotham's prophecy in verse 20 fulfilled?

Applying the Word 1. The story ends by stating, "Thus God repaid the wickedness" (v. 56). What does this passage teach you about God's justice and integrity? 2. What do you as a citizen learn from this passage about the importance of choosing leaders who have integrity?

 Responding in Prayer Pray that your spiritual leaders and elected officials would be people of character and integrity.

Judges 10

10 After the time of Abimelech a man of Issachar, Tola son of Puah, the son of Dodo, rose to save Israel. He lived in Shamir, in the hill country of Ephraim. ²He led[n] Israel twenty-three years; then he died, and was buried in Shamir.

³He was followed by Jair of Gilead, who led Israel twenty-two years. ⁴He had thirty sons, who rode thirty donkeys. They controlled thirty towns in Gilead, which to this day are called Havvoth Jair.[o] ⁵When Jair died, he was buried in Kamon.

⁶Again the Israelites did evil in the eyes of the LORD. They served the Baals and the Ashtoreths, and the gods of Aram, the gods of Sidon, the gods of Moab, the gods of the Ammonites and the gods of the Philistines. And because the Israelites forsook the LORD and no longer served him, ⁷he became angry with them. He sold them into the hands of the Philistines and the Ammonites, ⁸who that year shattered and crushed them. For eighteen years they oppressed all the Israelites on the east side of the Jordan in Gilead, the land of the Amorites. ⁹The Ammonites also crossed the Jordan to fight against Judah, Benjamin and the house of Ephraim; and Israel was in great distress. ¹⁰Then the Israelites cried out to the LORD, "We have sinned against you, forsaking our God and serving the Baals."

¹¹The LORD replied, "When the Egyptians, the Amorites, the Ammonites, the Philistines, ¹²the Sidonians, the Amalekites and the Maonites[p] oppressed you and you cried to me for help, did I not save you from their hands? ¹³But you have forsaken me and served other gods, so I will no longer save you. ¹⁴Go and cry out to the gods you have chosen. Let them save you when you are in trouble!"

¹⁵But the Israelites said to the LORD, "We have sinned. Do with us whatever you think best, but please rescue us now." ¹⁶Then they got rid of the foreign gods among them and served the LORD. And he could bear Israel's misery no longer.

¹⁷When the Ammonites were called to arms and camped in Gilead, the Israelites assembled and camped at Mizpah. ¹⁸The leaders of the people of Gilead said to each other, "Whoever will launch the attack against the Ammonites will be the head of all those living in Gilead."

---

[n]2 Traditionally *judged*; also in verse 3   [o]4 Or *called the settlements of Jair*   [p]12 Hebrew; some Septuagint manuscripts *Midianites*

---

7 / Judges 11—12
God's Dysfunctional Family

IF OUR FAMILIES were perfect, none of us would ever feel worthless or unloved, our relationships with each other would bring joy and satisfaction, and we would experience intimacy with God. Unfortunately, we are all products of a fallen world. Pains from our past continue to bring a destructive element into our present relationships. The intimacy and acceptance we crave slip away from us. Does God love us even when our own dysfunctions cause us to run from him? In the story of Jephthah, God uses this man with a broken and hurting past to illustrate what he will do to heal a broken, pain-driven world.

Warming Up to God What effect do past pains have on your current relationships? Prepare your heart for God's healing through the story in this passage.

Read Judges 11—12.

11 Jephthah the Gileadite was a mighty warrior. His father was Gilead; his mother was a prostitute. ²Gilead's wife also bore him sons, and when they were grown up, they drove Jephthah away. "You are not going to get any inheritance in our family," they said, "because you are the son of another woman." ³So Jephthah fled from his brothers and settled in the land of Tob, where a group of adventurers gathered around him and followed him.

⁴Some time later, when the Ammonites made war on Israel, ⁵the elders of Gilead went to get Jephthah from the land of Tob. ⁶"Come," they said, "be our commander, so we can fight the Ammonites."

⁷Jephthah said to them, "Didn't you hate me and drive me from my father's house? Why do you come to me now, when you're in trouble?"

⁸The elders of Gilead said to him, "Nevertheless, we are turning to you now; come with us to fight the Ammonites, and you will be our head over all who live in Gilead."

⁹Jephthah answered, "Suppose you take me back to fight the Ammonites and the LORD gives them to me—will I really be your head?"

¹⁰The elders of Gilead replied, "The LORD is our witness; we will certainly do as you say." ¹¹So Jephthah went with the elders of Gilead, and the people made him head and commander over them. And he repeated all his words before the LORD in Mizpah.

¹²Then Jephthah sent messengers to the Ammonite king with the question: "What do you have against us that you have attacked our country?"

¹³The king of the Ammonites answered Jephthah's messengers, "When Israel came up out of Egypt, they took away my land from the Arnon to the Jabbok, all the way to the Jordan. Now give it back peaceably."

¹⁴Jephthah sent back messengers to the Ammonite king, ¹⁵saying:

"This is what Jephthah says: Israel did not take the land of Moab or the land of the Ammonites. ¹⁶But when they came up out of Egypt, Israel went through the desert to the Red Sea𐞥 and on to Kadesh. ¹⁷Then Israel sent messengers to the king of Edom, saying, 'Give us permission to go through your country,' but the king of Edom would not

listen. They sent also to the king of Moab, and he refused. So Israel stayed at Kadesh.

¹⁸"Next they traveled through the desert, skirted the lands of Edom and Moab, passed along the eastern side of the country of Moab, and camped on the other side of the Arnon. They did not enter the territory of Moab, for the Arnon was its border.

¹⁹"Then Israel sent messengers to Sihon king of the Amorites, who ruled in Heshbon, and said to him, 'Let us pass through your country to our own place.' ²⁰Sihon, however, did not trust Israelʳ to pass through his territory. He mustered all his men and encamped at Jahaz and fought with Israel.

²¹"Then the LORD, the God of Israel, gave Sihon and all his men into Israel's hands, and they defeated them. Israel took over all the land of the Amorites who lived in that country, ²²capturing all of it from the Arnon to the Jabbok and from the desert to the Jordan.

²³"Now since the LORD, the God of Israel, has driven the Amorites out before his people Israel, what right have you to take it over? ²⁴Will you not take what your god Chemosh gives you? Likewise, whatever the LORD our God has given us, we will possess. ²⁵Are you better than Balak son of Zippor, king of Moab? Did he ever quarrel with Israel or fight with them? ²⁶For three hundred years Israel occupied Heshbon, Aroer, the surrounding settlements and all the towns along the Arnon. Why didn't you retake them during that time? ²⁷I have not wronged you, but you are doing me wrong by waging war against me. Let the LORD, the Judge,ˢ decide the dispute this day between the Israelites and the Ammonites."

²⁸The king of Ammon, however, paid no attention to the message Jephthah sent him.

²⁹Then the Spirit of the LORD came upon Jephthah. He crossed Gilead and Manasseh, passed through Mizpah of Gilead, and from there he advanced against the Ammonites. ³⁰And Jephthah made a vow to the LORD: "If you give the Ammonites into my hands, ³¹whatever comes out of the door of my house to meet me when I return in triumph from the Ammonites will be the LORD's, and I will sacrifice it as a burnt offering."

𐞥16 Hebrew *Yam Suph*; that is, Sea of Reeds   ʳ20 Or *however, would not make an agreement for Israel*   ˢ27 Or *Ruler*

³²Then Jephthah went over to fight the Ammonites, and the LORD gave them into his hands. ³³He devastated twenty towns from Aroer to the vicinity of Minnith, as far as Abel Keramim. Thus Israel subdued Ammon.

³⁴When Jephthah returned to his home in Mizpah, who should come out to meet him but his daughter, dancing to the sound of tambourines! She was an only child. Except for her he had neither son nor daughter. ³⁵When he saw her, he tore his clothes and cried, "Oh! My daughter! You have made me miserable and wretched, because I have made a vow to the LORD that I cannot break."

³⁶"My father," she replied, "you have given your word to the LORD. Do to me just as you promised, now that the LORD has avenged you of your enemies, the Ammonites. ³⁷But grant me this one request," she said. "Give me two months to roam the hills and weep with my friends, because I will never marry."

³⁸"You may go," he said. And he let her go for two months. She and the girls went into the hills and wept because she would never marry. ³⁹After the two months, she returned to her father and he did to her as he had vowed. And she was a virgin. From this comes the Israelite custom ⁴⁰that each year the young women of Israel go out for four days to commemorate the daughter of Jephthah the Gileadite.

12 The men of Ephraim called out their forces, crossed over to Zaphon and said to Jephthah, "Why did you go to fight the Ammonites without calling us to go with you? We're going to burn down your house over your head."

²Jephthah answered, "I and my people were engaged in a great struggle with the Ammonites, and although I called, you didn't save me out of their hands. ³When I saw that you wouldn't help, I took my life in my hands and crossed over to fight the Ammonites, and the LORD gave me the victory over them. Now why have you come up today to fight me?"

⁴Jephthah then called together the men of Gilead and fought against Ephraim. The Gileadites struck them down because the Ephraimites had said, "You Gileadites are renegades from Ephraim and Manasseh." ⁵The Gileadites captured the fords of the Jordan leading to Ephraim, and whenever a survivor of Ephraim said, "Let me cross over," the men of Gilead asked him, "Are you an Ephraimite?" If he replied, "No," ⁶they said, "All right, say 'Shibboleth.'" If he said, "Sibboleth," because he could not pronounce the word correctly, they seized him and killed him at the fords of the Jordan. Forty-two thousand Ephraimites were killed at that time.

⁷Jephthah led¹ Israel six years. Then Jephthah the Gileadite died, and was buried in a town in Gilead.

⁸After him, Ibzan of Bethlehem led Israel. ⁹He had thirty sons and thirty daughters. He gave his daughters away in marriage to those outside his clan, and for his sons he brought in thirty young women as wives from outside his clan. Ibzan led Israel seven years. ¹⁰Then Ibzan died, and was buried in Bethlehem.

¹¹After him, Elon the Zebulunite led Israel ten years. ¹²Then Elon died, and was buried in Aijalon in the land of Zebulun.

¹³After him, Abdon son of Hillel, from Pirathon, led Israel. ¹⁴He had forty sons and thirty grandsons, who rode on seventy donkeys. He led Israel eight years. ¹⁵Then Abdon son of Hillel died, and was buried at Pirathon in Ephraim, in the hill country of the Amalekites.

¹⁷ Traditionally *judged*; also in verses 8-14

Discovering the Word 1. Imagine that you are a psychologist and that Jephthah and the people of Israel have come to your office for family counseling. What problems do you see in this family? 2. What expectations did Jephthah and the people of Gilead bring to their reconciliation (11:4–11)? 3. Why did Jephthah make and keep his tragic vow to God (11:30–35)? 4. After winning a great victory and sacrificing a beloved daughter, Jephthah still did not find the approval he craved (12:1). How does Jephthah deal with this latest rejection? 5. Even though God provided a great victory, the characters in this story were unable to celebrate or appreciate it. How did their dysfunctions prevent them from celebrating God's mighty act?

Applying the Word 1. How have you dealt with rejection in your life? 2. When have your own relational dysfunctions caused you to miss celebrating a gift from God? 3. How could changes in the way you relate to other people make a positive difference in the way you relate to God?

 Responding in Prayer Pray that God will build you into a person of gentleness and discernment so that you can show acceptance to others.

8 / *Judges 13*
God Forges a New Tool

FINDING A GOOD pair of scissors in my house can often be difficult. One day in frustration, I bought a new pair, put them in my private drawer and forbid the rest of the family to touch them. Since that day, I (almost always) have been able to locate scissors when I need them. God's sending of Samson was similar to my purchase of scissors. Samson was to be set apart for God's use alone. When it was time to once again save the Israelites, God's implement of salvation would be readily at hand.

 Warming Up to God   Imagine yourself as God's tool. How would you describe yourself? For example, would you say that you are in the toolbox waiting to be used? misplaced and can't be found? in God's hands? Or being used for someone else's project?

 Read Judges 13.

---

13 Again the Israelites did evil in the eyes of the LORD, so the LORD delivered them into the hands of the Philistines for forty years.

²A certain man of Zorah, named Manoah, from the clan of the Danites, had a wife who was sterile and remained childless. ³The angel of the LORD appeared to her and said, "You are sterile and childless, but you are going to conceive and have a son. ⁴Now see to it that you drink no wine or other fermented drink and that you do not eat anything unclean, ⁵because you will conceive and give birth to a son. No razor may be used on his head, because the boy is to be a Nazirite, set apart to God from birth, and he will begin the deliverance of Israel from the hands of the Philistines."

⁶Then the woman went to her husband and told him, "A man of God came to me. He looked like an angel of God, very awesome. I didn't ask him where he came from, and he didn't tell me his name. ⁷But he said to me, 'You will conceive and give birth to a son. Now then, drink no wine or other fermented drink and do not eat anything unclean, because the boy will be a Nazirite of God from birth until the day of his death.' "

⁸Then Manoah prayed to the LORD: "O Lord, I beg you, let the man of God you sent to us come again to teach us how to bring up the boy who is to be born."

⁹God heard Manoah, and the angel of God came again to the woman while she was out in the field; but her husband Manoah was not with her. ¹⁰The woman hurried to tell her husband,

"He's here! The man who appeared to me the other day!"

¹¹Manoah got up and followed his wife. When he came to the man, he said, "Are you the one who talked to my wife?"

"I am," he said.

¹²So Manoah asked him, "When your words are fulfilled, what is to be the rule for the boy's life and work?"

¹³The angel of the LORD answered, "Your wife must do all that I have told her. ¹⁴She must not eat anything that comes from the grapevine, nor drink any wine or other fermented drink nor eat anything unclean. She must do everything I have commanded her."

¹⁵Manoah said to the angel of the LORD, "We would like you to stay until we prepare a young goat for you."

¹⁶The angel of the LORD replied, "Even though you detain me, I will not eat any of your food. But if you prepare a burnt offering, offer it to the LORD." (Manoah did not realize that it was the angel of the LORD.)

¹⁷Then Manoah inquired of the angel of the LORD, "What is your name, so that we may honor you when your word comes true?"

¹⁸He replied, "Why do you ask my name? It is beyond understanding.ᵘ" ¹⁹Then Manoah took a

ᵘ 18 Or is *wonderful*

young goat, together with the grain offering, and sacrificed it on a rock to the LORD. And the LORD did an amazing thing while Manoah and his wife watched: 20As the flame blazed up from the altar toward heaven, the angel of the LORD ascended in the flame. Seeing this, Manoah and his wife fell with their faces to the ground. 21When the angel of the LORD did not show himself again to Manoah and his wife, Manoah realized that it was the angel of the LORD.

22"We are doomed to die!" he said to his wife. "We have seen God!"

23But his wife answered, "If the LORD had meant to kill us, he would not have accepted a burnt offering and grain offering from our hands, nor shown us all these things or now told us this."

24The woman gave birth to a boy and named him Samson. He grew and the LORD blessed him, 25and the Spirit of the LORD began to stir him while he was in Mahaneh Dan, between Zorah and Eshtaol.

Discovering the Word　1. What did God require of Manoah, his wife and Samson (vv. 4–5)?　2. How would keeping the Nazirite vow have prepared Samson for God's service?　3. What does God's second visit to Samson's parents add to the first (vv. 9–21)?　4. What does God reveal about himself to Samson's parents, and what does he hold back (vv. 16–21)?　5. Why were Samson's parents afraid when they realized they had seen God (vv. 22–23)?

Applying the Word　1. What does this passage teach you about how God prepares us for service?　2. How has God prepared you for his service?

Responding in Prayer　Ask God to make you a useful tool in his service.

---

9 / *Judges 14—15*
The Need for Conflict

"THERE IS IN truth no such thing as harmonious co-existence between church and world, for where there is no conflict it is because the world has taken over," writes Michael Wilcock (*The Message of Judges* [Downers Grove, Ill.: InterVarsity Press, 1992], p. 142). In each of the previous occupations described in Judges, there is conflict. We are at least told that the people cry out to God for deliverance. Not so with the Philistine conquest. The people have lived under the Philistines' thumb for forty years without complaining. In surprising ways God uses Samson to create conflict where none existed. The message to today's church is clear—conflict is a necessary part of our message.

Warming Up to God　What conflict do you see between the church and the world today? In what ways do you feel caught up in that conflict?

Read Judges 14—15.

---

14 Samson went down to Timnah and saw there a young Philistine woman. 2When he returned, he said to his father and mother, "I have seen a Philistine woman in Timnah; now get her for me as my wife."

3His father and mother replied, "Isn't there an acceptable woman among your relatives or among all our people? Must you go to the uncircumcised Philistines to get a wife?"

But Samson said to his father, "Get her for me. She's the right one for me." 4(His parents did not know that this was from the LORD, who was seeking an occasion to confront the Philistines; for at that time they were ruling over Israel.) 5Samson went down to Timnah together with his father and mother. As they approached the vineyards of Timnah, suddenly a young lion came roaring toward him. ⁶The Spirit of the Lord came upon him in power so that he tore the lion apart with his bare hands as he might have torn a young goat. But he told neither his father nor his mother what he had done. ⁷Then he went down and talked with the woman, and he liked her.

⁸Some time later, when he went back to marry her, he turned aside to look at the lion's carcass. In it was a swarm of bees and some honey, ⁹which he scooped out with his hands and ate as he went along. When he rejoined his parents, he gave them some, and they too ate it. But he did not tell them that he had taken the honey from the lion's carcass.

¹⁰Now his father went down to see the woman. And Samson made a feast there, as was customary for bridegrooms. ¹¹When he appeared, he was given thirty companions.

¹²"Let me tell you a riddle," Samson said to them. "If you can give me the answer within the seven days of the feast, I will give you thirty linen garments and thirty sets of clothes. ¹³If you can't tell me the answer, you must give me thirty linen garments and thirty sets of clothes."

"Tell us your riddle," they said. "Let's hear it." ¹⁴He replied,

"Out of the eater, something to eat;
    out of the strong, something sweet."

For three days they could not give the answer.

¹⁵On the fourthᵛ day, they said to Samson's wife, "Coax your husband into explaining the riddle for us, or we will burn you and your father's household to death. Did you invite us here to rob us?"

¹⁶Then Samson's wife threw herself on him, sobbing, "You hate me! You don't really love me. You've given my people a riddle, but you haven't told me the answer."

"I haven't even explained it to my father or mother," he replied, "so why should I explain it to you?" ¹⁷She cried the whole seven days of the feast. So on the seventh day he finally told her, because she continued to press him. She in turn explained the riddle to her people.

¹⁸Before sunset on the seventh day the men of the town said to him,

"What is sweeter than honey?
    What is stronger than a lion?"

Samson said to them,

"If you had not plowed with my heifer,
    you would not have solved my riddle."

¹⁹Then the Spirit of the Lord came upon him in power. He went down to Ashkelon, struck down thirty of their men, stripped them of their belongings and gave their clothes to those who had explained the riddle. Burning with anger, he went up to his father's house. ²⁰And Samson's wife was given to the friend who had attended him at his wedding.

15 Later on, at the time of wheat harvest, Samson took a young goat and went to visit his wife. He said, "I'm going to my wife's room." But her father would not let him go in.

²"I was so sure you thoroughly hated her," he said, "that I gave her to your friend. Isn't her younger sister more attractive? Take her instead."

³Samson said to them, "This time I have a right to get even with the Philistines; I will really harm them." ⁴So he went out and caught three hundred foxes and tied them tail to tail in pairs. He then fastened a torch to every pair of tails, ⁵lit the torches and let the foxes loose in the standing grain of the Philistines. He burned up the shocks and standing grain, together with the vineyards and olive groves.

⁶When the Philistines asked, "Who did this?" they were told, "Samson, the Timnite's son-in-law, because his wife was given to his friend."

So the Philistines went up and burned her and her father to death. ⁷Samson said to them, "Since you've acted like this, I won't stop until I get my revenge on you." ⁸He attacked them viciously and slaughtered many of them. Then he went down and stayed in a cave in the rock of Etam.

⁹The Philistines went up and camped in Judah, spreading out near Lehi. ¹⁰The men of Judah asked, "Why have you come to fight us?"

"We have come to take Samson prisoner," they answered, "to do to him as he did to us."

¹¹Then three thousand men from Judah went down to the cave in the rock of Etam and said to Samson, "Don't you realize that the Philistines are rulers over us? What have you done to us?"

He answered, "I merely did to them what they did to me."

¹²They said to him, "We've come to tie you up and hand you over to the Philistines."

ᵛ15 Some Septuagint manuscripts and Syriac; Hebrew *seventh*

Samson said, "Swear to me that you won't kill me yourselves."

¹³"Agreed," they answered. "We will only tie you up and hand you over to them. We will not kill you." So they bound him with two new ropes and led him up from the rock. ¹⁴As he approached Lehi, the Philistines came toward him shouting. The Spirit of the LORD came upon him in power. The ropes on his arms became like charred flax, and the bindings dropped from his hands. ¹⁵Finding a fresh jawbone of a donkey, he grabbed it and struck down a thousand men.

¹⁶Then Samson said,

"With a donkey's jawbone
    I have made donkeys of them.ʷ
With a donkey's jawbone

I have killed a thousand men."

¹⁷When he finished speaking, he threw away the jawbone; and the place was called Ramath Lehi.ˣ

¹⁸Because he was very thirsty, he cried out to the LORD, "You have given your servant this great victory. Must I now die of thirst and fall into the hands of the uncircumcised?" ¹⁹Then God opened up the hollow place in Lehi, and water came out of it. When Samson drank, his strength returned and he revived. So the spring was called En Hakkore,ʸ and it is still there in Lehi.

²⁰Samson ledᶻ Israel for twenty years in the days of the Philistines.

ʷ16 Or *made a heap or two*; the Hebrew for *donkey* sounds like the Hebrew for *heap.*   ˣ17 *Ramath Lehi* means *jawbone hill.*   ʸ19 *En Hakkore* means *caller's spring.*   ᶻ20 Traditionally *judged*

 Discovering the Word 1. What did Samson's parents seem to expect their son would be like (14:1–4)? 2. What did Samson's marriage and subsequent acts of vengeance accomplish (14:19—15:8)? 3. What do Samson's actions reveal about his character? 4. What attitude did the men of Judah have toward the Philistines (15:9–13)? 5. Samson was the only judge without an army. All of his exploits were performed single-handedly. What does this tell you about the moral and spiritual condition of Israel?

Applying the Word 1. What similarities do you see between Israel's situation and the moral and spiritual conditions of today? 2. What action might God be calling you to take that would be in conflict with the ways of the world?

Responding in Prayer Pray that the Christian church will be united in facing conflict with a world that rejects God.

10 / *Judges 16*
Victorious Defeat

IMAGINE A PASSION play starring a notorious sinner in the role of Jesus. Instead of traveling the countryside preaching and healing, this hero visits brothels and brawls in bar fights. You would probably walk out of such a sacrilegious production, yet this is what God presents to us in the story of Samson. Samson represents both the best and the worst in each of us; called by the grace of God, bound to him by promise, repeatedly empowered, greatly gifted, yet faithless, self-indulgent, and only too ready to fraternize with the enemy.

 Warming Up to God When has a "sinner" surprised you by demonstrating God's grace?

 Read Judges 16.

16 One day Samson went to Gaza, where he saw a prostitute. He went in to spend the night with her. ²The people of Gaza were told, "Samson is here!" So they surrounded the place and lay in wait for him all night at the city gate. They made no move during the night, saying, "At dawn we'll kill him."

³But Samson lay there only until the middle of the night. Then he got up and took hold of the doors of the city gate, together with the two

posts, and tore them loose, bar and all. He lifted them to his shoulders and carried them to the top of the hill that faces Hebron.

4Some time later, he fell in love with a woman in the Valley of Sorek whose name was Delilah. 5The rulers of the Philistines went to her and said, "See if you can lure him into showing you the secret of his great strength and how we can overpower him so we may tie him up and subdue him. Each one of us will give you eleven hundred shekels*a* of silver."

6So Delilah said to Samson, "Tell me the secret of your great strength and how you can be tied up and subdued."

7Samson answered her, "If anyone ties me with seven fresh thongs*b* that have not been dried, I'll become as weak as any other man."

8Then the rulers of the Philistines brought her seven fresh thongs that had not been dried, and she tied him with them. 9With men hidden in the room, she called to him, "Samson, the Philistines are upon you!" But he snapped the thongs as easily as a piece of string snaps when it comes close to a flame. So the secret of his strength was not discovered.

10Then Delilah said to Samson, "You have made a fool of me; you lied to me. Come now, tell me how you can be tied."

11He said, "If anyone ties me securely with new ropes that have never been used, I'll become as weak as any other man."

12So Delilah took new ropes and tied him with them. Then, with men hidden in the room, she called to him, "Samson, the Philistines are upon you!" But he snapped the ropes off his arms as if they were threads.

13Delilah then said to Samson, "Until now, you have been making a fool of me and lying to me. Tell me how you can be tied."

He replied, "If you weave the seven braids of my head into the fabric ⌐on the loom⌐ and tighten it with the pin, I'll become as weak as any other man." So while he was sleeping, Delilah took the seven braids of his head, wove them into the fabric 14and*c* tightened it with the pin.

Again she called to him, "Samson, the Philistines are upon you!" He awoke from his sleep and pulled up the pin and the loom, with the fabric.

15Then she said to him, "How can you say, 'I love you,' when you won't confide in me? This is the third time you have made a fool of me and haven't told me the secret of your great strength."

16With such nagging she prodded him day after day until he was tired to death.

17So he told her everything. "No razor has ever been used on my head," he said, "because I have been a Nazirite set apart to God since birth. If my head were shaved, my strength would leave me, and I would become as weak as any other man."

18When Delilah saw that he had told her everything, she sent word to the rulers of the Philistines, "Come back once more; he has told me everything." So the rulers of the Philistines returned with the silver in their hands. 19Having put him to sleep on her lap, she called a man to shave off the seven braids of his hair, and so began to subdue him.*d* And his strength left him.

20Then she called, "Samson, the Philistines are upon you!"

He awoke from his sleep and thought, "I'll go out as before and shake myself free." But he did not know that the LORD had left him.

21Then the Philistines seized him, gouged out his eyes and took him down to Gaza. Binding him with bronze shackles, they set him to grinding in the prison. 22But the hair on his head began to grow again after it had been shaved.

23Now the rulers of the Philistines assembled to offer a great sacrifice to Dagon their god and to celebrate, saying, "Our god has delivered Samson, our enemy, into our hands."

24When the people saw him, they praised their god, saying,

"Our god has delivered our enemy
   into our hands,
the one who laid waste our land
   and multiplied our slain."

25While they were in high spirits, they shouted, "Bring out Samson to entertain us." So they called Samson out of the prison, and he performed for them.

When they stood him among the pillars, 26Samson said to the servant who held his hand, "Put me where I can feel the pillars that support the temple, so that I may lean against them." 27Now the temple was crowded with men and women; all the rulers of the Philistines were there, and on the roof were about three thousand men and women watching Samson perform.

---

*a*5 That is, about 28 pounds (about 13 kilograms)   *b*7 Or *bowstrings*; also in verses 8 and 9   *c*13,14 Some Septuagint manuscripts; Hebrew *"I can, if you weave the seven braids of my head into the fabric ⌐on the loom.⌐" 14So she*   *d*19 Hebrew; some Septuagint manuscripts *and he began to weaken*

28Then Samson prayed to the LORD, "O Sovereign LORD, remember me. O God, please strengthen me just once more, and let me with one blow get revenge on the Philistines for my two eyes." 29Then Samson reached toward the two central pillars on which the temple stood. Bracing himself against them, his right hand on the one and his left hand on the other, 30Samson said, "Let me die with the Philistines!" Then he pushed with all his might, and down came the temple on the rul-

ers and all the people in it. Thus he killed many more when he died than while he lived.

31Then his brothers and his father's whole family went down to get him. They brought him back and buried him between Zorah and Eshtaol in the tomb of Manoah his father. He had led*e* Israel twenty years.

e31 Traditionally *judged*

Discovering the Word 1. What clues suggest Samson's spiritual condition at the beginning of this chapter (vv. 1–4)? 2. Why do you think Samson revealed the secret of his strength to Delilah (vv. 15–17)? 3. Imagine the scene in verse 20 when Samson discovers that the Lord has left him. What thoughts, emotions and regrets would have gone through his mind? 4. How did Samson change after his capture (vv. 25–30)? 5. What has Samson taught you?

Applying the Word 1. In what ways do you, like Samson, take God's gifts for granted? 2. How would your life be different if the Lord suddenly "left" you?

Responding in Prayer In his arrest and death Samson can remind us of Jesus' great gift to us. Tell Jesus how grateful you are for his sacrifice.

11 / *Judges 17—18*
A Moral Collapse

IN HIS JANUARY 27, 1838, address before the Young Men's Lyceum, Springfield, Illinois, Abraham Lincoln said:
At what point shall we expect the approach of danger? By what means shall we fortify against it? Shall we expect some trans-Atlantic military giant, to step the ocean, and crush us at a blow?
Never!
At what point then is the approach of danger to be expected?
I answer, if it ever reaches us, it must spring up amongst us. It cannot come from abroad. If destruction be our lot, we ourselves must be its author and finisher. As a nation of free men, we must live through all times, or die by suicide.
The last five chapters of Judges show us a picture of a society destroying itself by a moral and spiritual collapse.

Warming Up to God What dangers are your nation, church and family facing? God grieves when we turn from him. Take some time to reflect on how God must feel as he looks on the world he created.

Read Judges 17—18.

17 Now a man named Micah from the hill country of Ephraim 2said to his mother, "The eleven hundred shekels*f* of silver that were taken from you and about which I heard you utter a curse—I have that silver with me; I took it."

Then his mother said, "The LORD bless you, my son!"

3When he returned the eleven hundred shekels

of silver to his mother, she said, "I solemnly consecrate my silver to the LORD for my son to make a carved image and a cast idol. I will give it back to you."

4So he returned the silver to his mother, and she took two hundred shekels*g* of silver and gave them to a silversmith, who made them into the

f2 That is, about 28 pounds (about 13 kilograms) *g4* That is, about 5 pounds (about 2.3 kilograms) image and the idol. And they were put in Micah's house.

⁵Now this man Micah had a shrine, and he made an ephod and some idols and installed one of his sons as his priest. ⁶In those days Israel had no king; everyone did as he saw fit.

⁷A young Levite from Bethlehem in Judah, who had been living within the clan of Judah, ⁸left that town in search of some other place to stay. On his wayʰ he came to Micah's house in the hill country of Ephraim.

⁹Micah asked him, "Where are you from?"

"I'm a Levite from Bethlehem in Judah," he said, "and I'm looking for a place to stay."

¹⁰Then Micah said to him, "Live with me and be my father and priest, and I'll give you ten shekelsⁱ of silver a year, your clothes and your food." ¹¹So the Levite agreed to live with him, and the young man was to him like one of his sons. ¹²Then Micah installed the Levite, and the young man became his priest and lived in his house. ¹³And Micah said, "Now I know that the LORD will be good to me, since this Levite has become my priest."

18 In those days Israel had no king. And in those days the tribe of the Danites was seeking a place of their own where they might settle, because they had not yet come into an inheritance among the tribes of Israel. ²So the Danites sent five warriors from Zorah and Eshtaol to spy out the land and explore it. These men represented all their clans. They told them, "Go, explore the land."

The men entered the hill country of Ephraim and came to the house of Micah, where they spent the night. ³When they were near Micah's house, they recognized the voice of the young Levite; so they turned in there and asked him, "Who brought you here? What are you doing in this place? Why are you here?"

⁴He told them what Micah had done for him, and said, "He has hired me and I am his priest."

⁵Then they said to him, "Please inquire of God to learn whether our journey will be successful."

⁶The priest answered them, "Go in peace. Your journey has the LORD's approval."

⁷So the five men left and came to Laish, where they saw that the people were living in safety, like the Sidonians, unsuspecting and secure. And since their land lacked nothing, they were prosperous.ʲ Also, they lived a long way from the Sidonians and had no relationship with anyone else.ᵏ

⁸When they returned to Zorah and Eshtaol, their brothers asked them, "How did you find things?"

⁹They answered, "Come on, let's attack them! We have seen that the land is very good. Aren't you going to do something? Don't hesitate to go there and take it over. ¹⁰When you get there, you will find an unsuspecting people and a spacious land that God has put into your hands, a land that lacks nothing whatever."

¹¹Then six hundred men from the clan of the Danites, armed for battle, set out from Zorah and Eshtaol. ¹²On their way they set up camp near Kiriath Jearim in Judah. This is why the place west of Kiriath Jearim is called Mahaneh Danˡ to this day. ¹³From there they went on to the hill country of Ephraim and came to Micah's house.

¹⁴Then the five men who had spied out the land of Laish said to their brothers, "Do you know that one of these houses has an ephod, other household gods, a carved image and a cast idol? Now you know what to do." ¹⁵So they turned in there and went to the house of the young Levite at Micah's place and greeted him. ¹⁶The six hundred Danites, armed for battle, stood at the entrance to the gate. ¹⁷The five men who had spied out the land went inside and took the carved image, the ephod, the other household gods and the cast idol while the priest and the six hundred armed men stood at the entrance to the gate.

¹⁸When these men went into Micah's house and took the carved image, the ephod, the other household gods and the cast idol, the priest said to them, "What are you doing?"

¹⁹They answered him, "Be quiet! Don't say a word. Come with us, and be our father and priest. Isn't it better that you serve a tribe and clan in Israel as priest rather than just one man's household?" ²⁰Then the priest was glad. He took the ephod, the other household gods and the carved image and went along with the people. ²¹Putting their little children, their livestock and their possessions in front of them, they turned away and left.

²²When they had gone some distance from Micah's house, the men who lived near Micah were

ʰ8 Or *To carry on his profession*   ⁱ10 That is, about 4 ounces (about 110 grams)   ʲ7 The meaning of the Hebrew for this clause is uncertain.   ᵏ7 Hebrew; some Septuagint manuscripts *with the Arameans*   ˡ12 *Mahaneh Dan* means *Dan's camp.*

called together and overtook the Danites. ²³As they shouted after them, the Danites turned and said to Micah, "What's the matter with you that you called out your men to fight?"

²⁴He replied, "You took the gods I made, and my priest, and went away. What else do I have? How can you ask, 'What's the matter with you?' "

²⁵The Danites answered, "Don't argue with us, or some hot-tempered men will attack you, and you and your family will lose your lives." ²⁶So the Danites went their way, and Micah, seeing that they were too strong for him, turned around and went back home.

²⁷Then they took what Micah had made, and his priest, and went on to Laish, against a peaceful and unsuspecting people. They attacked them with the sword and burned down their city.

²⁸There was no one to rescue them because they lived a long way from Sidon and had no relationship with anyone else. The city was in a valley near Beth Rehob.

The Danites rebuilt the city and settled there. ²⁹They named it Dan after their forefather Dan, who was born to Israel—though the city used to be called Laish. ³⁰There the Danites set up for themselves the idols, and Jonathan son of Gershom, the son of Moses,ᵐ and his sons were priests for the tribe of Dan until the time of the captivity of the land. ³¹They continued to use the idols Micah had made, all the time the house of God was in Shiloh.

ᵐ30 An ancient Hebrew scribal tradition, some Septuagint manuscripts and Vulgate; Masoretic Text *Manasseh*

Discovering the Word 1. What happens to the stolen silver throughout this tale? 2. Describe Micah's mother (17:1–4). What was her relationship to God and to her son? 3. What actions does Micah take in this narrative (17:1–3, 10–13; 18:22–26)? 4. How did the Levite pervert religion (17:10–13; 18:4–6, 18–20)? 5. What do you learn about the tribe of Dan?

Applying the Word 1. What individuals or groups in your community most resemble Micah's mother, Micah, the Levite and the Danites? 2. By which of their sins are you most tempted? 3. What role could you have in calling people back to God?

Responding in Prayer Pray for the people in your city or town and for yourself.

Judges 19—20

19 In those days Israel had no king. Now a Levite who lived in a remote area in the hill country of Ephraim took a concubine from Bethlehem in Judah. ²But she was unfaithful to him. She left him and went back to her father's house in Bethlehem, Judah. After she had been there four months, ³her husband went to her to persuade her to return. He had with him his servant and two donkeys. She took him into her father's house, and when her father saw him, he gladly welcomed him. ⁴His father-in-law, the girl's father, prevailed upon him to stay; so he remained with him three days, eating and drinking, and sleeping there.

⁵On the fourth day they got up early and he prepared to leave, but the girl's father said to his son-in-law, "Refresh yourself with something to eat; then you can go." ⁶So the two of them sat down to eat and drink together. Afterward the girl's father said, "Please stay tonight and enjoy yourself." ⁷And when the man got up to go, his father-in-law persuaded him, so he stayed there that night. ⁸On the morning of the fifth day, when he rose to go, the girl's father said, "Refresh yourself. Wait till afternoon!" So the two of them ate together.

⁹Then when the man, with his concubine and his servant, got up to leave, his father-in-law, the girl's father, said, "Now look, it's almost evening. Spend the night here; the day is nearly over. Stay and enjoy yourself. Early tomorrow morning you can get up and be on your way home." ¹⁰But, unwilling to stay another night, the man left and went toward Jebus (that is, Jerusalem), with his two saddled donkeys and his concubine.

¹¹When they were near Jebus and the day was almost gone, the servant said to his master,

"Come, let's stop at this city of the Jebusites and spend the night."

¹²His master replied, "No. We won't go into an alien city, whose people are not Israelites. We will go on to Gibeah." ¹³He added, "Come, let's try to reach Gibeah or Ramah and spend the night in one of those places." ¹⁴So they went on, and the sun set as they neared Gibeah in Benjamin. ¹⁵There they stopped to spend the night. They went and sat in the city square, but no one took them into his home for the night.

¹⁶That evening an old man from the hill country of Ephraim, who was living in Gibeah (the men of the place were Benjamites), came in from his work in the fields. ¹⁷When he looked and saw the traveler in the city square, the old man asked, "Where are you going? Where did you come from?"

¹⁸He answered, "We are on our way from Bethlehem in Judah to a remote area in the hill country of Ephraim where I live. I have been to Bethlehem in Judah and now I am going to the house of the LORD. No one has taken me into his house. ¹⁹We have both straw and fodder for our donkeys and bread and wine for ourselves your servants— me, your maidservant, and the young man with us. We don't need anything."

²⁰"You are welcome at my house," the old man said. "Let me supply whatever you need. Only don't spend the night in the square." ²¹So he took him into his house and fed his donkeys. After they had washed their feet, they had something to eat and drink.

²²While they were enjoying themselves, some of the wicked men of the city surrounded the house. Pounding on the door, they shouted to the old man who owned the house, "Bring out the man who came to your house so we can have sex with him."

²³The owner of the house went outside and said to them, "No, my friends, don't be so vile. Since this man is my guest, don't do this disgraceful thing. ²⁴Look, here is my virgin daughter, and his concubine. I will bring them out to you now, and you can use them and do to them whatever you wish. But to this man, don't do such a disgraceful thing."

²⁵But the men would not listen to him. So the man took his concubine and sent her outside to them, and they raped her and abused her throughout the night, and at dawn they let her go. ²⁶At daybreak the woman went back to the house where her master was staying, fell down at the door and lay there until daylight.

²⁷When her master got up in the morning and opened the door of the house and stepped out to continue on his way, there lay his concubine, fallen in the doorway of the house, with her hands on the threshold. ²⁸He said to her, "Get up; let's go." But there was no answer. Then the man put her on his donkey and set out for home.

²⁹When he reached home, he took a knife and cut up his concubine, limb by limb, into twelve parts and sent them into all the areas of Israel. ³⁰Everyone who saw it said, "Such a thing has never been seen or done, not since the day the Israelites came up out of Egypt. Think about it! Consider it! Tell us what to do!"

20

Then all the Israelites from Dan to Beersheba and from the land of Gilead came out as one man and assembled before the LORD in Mizpah. ²The leaders of all the people of the tribes of Israel took their places in the assembly of the people of God, four hundred thousand soldiers armed with swords. ³(The Benjamites heard that the Israelites had gone up to Mizpah.) Then the Israelites said, "Tell us how this awful thing happened."

⁴So the Levite, the husband of the murdered woman, said, "I and my concubine came to Gibeah in Benjamin to spend the night. ⁵During the night the men of Gibeah came after me and surrounded the house, intending to kill me. They raped my concubine, and she died. ⁶I took my concubine, cut her into pieces and sent one piece to each region of Israel's inheritance, because they committed this lewd and disgraceful act in Israel. ⁷Now, all you Israelites, speak up and give your verdict."

⁸All the people rose as one man, saying, "None of us will go home. No, not one of us will return to his house. ⁹But now this is what we'll do to Gibeah: We'll go up against it as the lot directs. ¹⁰We'll take ten men out of every hundred from all the tribes of Israel, and a hundred from a thousand, and a thousand from ten thousand, to get provisions for the army. Then, when the army arrives at Gibeah[n] in Benjamin, it can give them what they deserve for all this vileness done in Israel." ¹¹So all the men of Israel got together and united as one man against the city.

¹²The tribes of Israel sent men throughout the

---

[n]10 One Hebrew manuscript; most Hebrew manuscripts *Geba,* a variant of *Gibeah*

tribe of Benjamin, saying, "What about this awful crime that was committed among you? ¹³Now surrender those wicked men of Gibeah so that we may put them to death and purge the evil from Israel."

But the Benjamites would not listen to their fellow Israelites. ¹⁴From their towns they came together at Gibeah to fight against the Israelites. ¹⁵At once the Benjamites mobilized twenty-six thousand swordsmen from their towns, in addition to seven hundred chosen men from those living in Gibeah. ¹⁶Among all these soldiers there were seven hundred chosen men who were left-handed, each of whom could sling a stone at a hair and not miss.

¹⁷Israel, apart from Benjamin, mustered four hundred thousand swordsmen, all of them fighting men.

¹⁸The Israelites went up to Bethel⁰ and inquired of God. They said, "Who of us shall go first to fight against the Benjamites?"

The LORD replied, "Judah shall go first."

¹⁹The next morning the Israelites got up and pitched camp near Gibeah. ²⁰The men of Israel went out to fight the Benjamites and took up battle positions against them at Gibeah. ²¹The Benjamites came out of Gibeah and cut down twenty-two thousand Israelites on the battlefield that day. ²²But the men of Israel encouraged one another and again took up their positions where they had stationed themselves the first day. ²³The Israelites went up and wept before the LORD until evening, and they inquired of the LORD. They said, "Shall we go up again to battle against the Benjamites, our brothers?"

The LORD answered, "Go up against them."

²⁴Then the Israelites drew near to Benjamin the second day. ²⁵This time, when the Benjamites came out from Gibeah to oppose them, they cut down another eighteen thousand Israelites, all of them armed with swords.

²⁶Then the Israelites, all the people, went up to Bethel, and there they sat weeping before the LORD. They fasted that day until evening and presented burnt offerings and fellowship offeringsᵖ to the LORD. ²⁷And the Israelites inquired of the LORD. (In those days the ark of the covenant of God was there, ²⁸with Phinehas son of Eleazar, the son of Aaron, ministering before it.) They asked, "Shall we go up again to battle with Benjamin our brother, or not?"

The LORD responded, "Go, for tomorrow I will give them into your hands."

²⁹Then Israel set an ambush around Gibeah. ³⁰They went up against the Benjamites on the third day and took up positions against Gibeah as they had done before. ³¹The Benjamites came out to meet them and were drawn away from the city. They began to inflict casualties on the Israelites as before, so that about thirty men fell in the open field and on the roads—the one leading to Bethel and the other to Gibeah.

³²While the Benjamites were saying, "We are defeating them as before," the Israelites were saying, "Let's retreat and draw them away from the city to the roads."

³³All the men of Israel moved from their places and took up positions at Baal Tamar, and the Israelite ambush charged out of its place on the west�q of Gibeah.ʳ ³⁴Then ten thousand of Israel's finest men made a frontal attack on Gibeah. The fighting was so heavy that the Benjamites did not realize how near disaster was. ³⁵The LORD defeated Benjamin before Israel, and on that day the Israelites struck down 25,100 Benjamites, all armed with swords. ³⁶Then the Benjamites saw that they were beaten.

Now the men of Israel had given way before Benjamin, because they relied on the ambush they had set near Gibeah. ³⁷The men who had been in ambush made a sudden dash into Gibeah, spread out and put the whole city to the sword. ³⁸The men of Israel had arranged with the ambush that they should send up a great cloud of smoke from the city, ³⁹and then the men of Israel would turn in the battle.

The Benjamites had begun to inflict casualties on the men of Israel (about thirty), and they said, "We are defeating them as in the first battle." ⁴⁰But when the column of smoke began to rise from the city, the Benjamites turned and saw the smoke of the whole city going up into the sky. ⁴¹Then the men of Israel turned on them, and the men of Benjamin were terrified, because they realized that disaster had come upon them. ⁴²So they fled before the Israelites in the direction of the desert, but they could not escape the battle. And the men of Israel who came out of the towns cut them down there. ⁴³They surrounded the

---

⁰18 Or *to the house of God*; also in verse 26   ᵖ26 Traditionally *peace offerings*   q33 Some Septuagint manuscripts and Vulgate; the meaning of the Hebrew for this word is uncertain.   ʳ33 Hebrew *Geba,* a variant of *Gibeah*

Benjamites, chased them and easily⁵ overran them in the vicinity of Gibeah on the east. ⁴⁴Eighteen thousand Benjamites fell, all of them valiant fighters. ⁴⁵As they turned and fled toward the desert to the rock of Rimmon, the Israelites cut down five thousand men along the roads. They kept pressing after the Benjamites as far as Gidom and struck down two thousand more.

⁴⁶On that day twenty-five thousand Benjamite swordsmen fell, all of them valiant fighters. ⁴⁷But six hundred men turned and fled into the desert to the rock of Rimmon, where they stayed four months. ⁴⁸The men of Israel went back to Benjamin and put all the towns to the sword, including the animals and everything else they found. All the towns they came across they set on fire.

⁵43 The meaning of the Hebrew for this word is uncertain.

12 / *Judges 21*
The Aftermath of Moral Decay

THE MORAL DECAY of Israel continued to grow worse. In Judges 19 we are told the story of a man and his concubine who, while traveling, had stopped for the night in the town of Gibeah. Instead of offering hospitality, the residents of Gibeah tried to rape the man. To save himself, he gave the townsfolk his concubine instead. The poor woman was gang-raped and left dead on the doorstep. In an attempt to gain sympathy and to justify himself, the enraged lover cut the body of his concubine into twelve pieces and sent one to each tribe of Israel with a message demanding that justice be done. This incident resulted in a bloody and devastating civil war against not only the town of Gibeah but also the entire tribe of Benjamin (Jdg 20). In the aftermath of the civil war, the Israelites began to regret what they had done. All of the women from the tribe of Benjamin had been killed and only six hundred men remained alive.

Warming Up to God   When have you made a promise foolishly? What should be done about foolish promises?

Read Judges 21.

21 The men of Israel had taken an oath at Mizpah: "Not one of us will give his daughter in marriage to a Benjamite."

²The people went to Bethel,ᵗ where they sat before God until evening, raising their voices and weeping bitterly. ³"O LORD, the God of Israel," they cried, "why has this happened to Israel? Why should one tribe be missing from Israel today?"

⁴Early the next day the people built an altar and presented burnt offerings and fellowship offerings.ᵘ

⁵Then the Israelites asked, "Who from all the tribes of Israel has failed to assemble before the LORD?" For they had taken a solemn oath that anyone who failed to assemble before the LORD at Mizpah should certainly be put to death.

⁶Now the Israelites grieved for their brothers, the Benjamites. "Today one tribe is cut off from Israel," they said. ⁷"How can we provide wives for those who are left, since we have taken an oath by the LORD not to give them any of our daughters in marriage?" ⁸Then they asked, "Which one of the tribes of Israel failed to assemble before the LORD at Mizpah?" They discovered that no one from Jabesh Gilead had come to the camp for the assembly. ⁹For when they counted the people, they found that none of the people of Jabesh Gilead were there.

¹⁰So the assembly sent twelve thousand fighting men with instructions to go to Jabesh Gilead and put to the sword those living there, including the women and children. ¹¹"This is what you are to do," they said. "Kill every male and every woman who is not a virgin." ¹²They found among the people living in Jabesh Gilead four hundred young women who had never slept with a man, and they took them to the camp at Shiloh in Canaan.

¹³Then the whole assembly sent an offer of

ᵗ2 Or *to the house of God*   ᵘ4 Traditionally *peace offerings* peace to the Benjamites at the rock of Rimmon. ¹⁴So the Benjamites returned at that time and were given the women of Jabesh Gilead who had been spared. But there were not enough for all of them.

¹⁵The people grieved for Benjamin, because the Lord had made a gap in the tribes of Israel. ¹⁶And the elders of the assembly said, "With the women of Benjamin destroyed, how shall we provide wives for the men who are left? ¹⁷The Benjamite survivors must have heirs," they said, "so that a tribe of Israel will not be wiped out. ¹⁸We can't give them our daughters as wives, since we Israelites have taken this oath: 'Cursed be anyone who gives a wife to a Benjamite.' ¹⁹But look, there is the annual festival of the Lord in Shiloh, to the north of Bethel, and east of the road that goes from Bethel to Shechem, and to the south of Lebonah."

²⁰So they instructed the Benjamites, saying,

"Go and hide in the vineyards ²¹and watch. When the girls of Shiloh come out to join in the dancing, then rush from the vineyards and each of you seize a wife from the girls of Shiloh and go to the land of Benjamin. ²²When their fathers or brothers complain to us, we will say to them, 'Do us a kindness by helping them, because we did not get wives for them during the war, and you are innocent, since you did not give your daughters to them.' "

²³So that is what the Benjamites did. While the girls were dancing, each man caught one and carried her off to be his wife. Then they returned to their inheritance and rebuilt the towns and settled in them.

²⁴At that time the Israelites left that place and went home to their tribes and clans, each to his own inheritance.

²⁵In those days Israel had no king; everyone did as he saw fit.

Discovering the Word 1. The Israelites ask God, "Why has this happened to Israel? Why should one tribe be missing from Israel today?" (v. 3). How would you answer their question? 2. What is right and what is wrong about the Israelites' actions in this chapter? 3. What do you learn from this story about the importance of and the process for reconciliation? 4. What did the Israelites understand about the making and keeping of vows, and where had they gone wrong in their vow making (vv. 7, 12–23)? 5. The book of Judges ends with a phrase that is repeated often, especially in the last five chapters: "In those days Israel had no king; everyone did as he saw fit." Why is the author so concerned that we know this?

Applying the Word 1. With whom might God be calling you to reconcile? 2. How can you do this? 3. What foolish promise do you need to reconsider today?

Responding in Prayer Ask God to give you wisdom in your relationships as you reconcile brokenness and make and keep promises.

Ruth

L oyalty is a rare virtue. "I'll go with you unless someone better comes along" is a popular way to act with friends and sometimes even spouses. Who are the friends who have stuck by you during the hard times? Hopefully, a few people come to mind. These are most likely people of unusual character and courage.

Ruth was written during the period of the judges (c. 1380–1050 B.C.), which were dark and turbulent days for Israel. It provides a glimpse into the lives of ordinary people who show a care and loyalty for each other that reflect God's character.

Ruth was a Moabite. Her people descended from Lot's oldest daughter, who, though rescued from the destruction of Sodom and Gomorrah, chose to live apart from God's people (Ge 19:37). Ruth's choices are in sharp contrast to this.

After Ruth marries into an Israelite family, she becomes very devoted to them, especially to her mother-in-law, Naomi. Because Ruth chooses to identify with the people of God, she is given a place in the genealogy of Jesus Christ (Mt 1:1, 5) as the great-grandmother of David. From Ruth we learn that simple obedience, faith and loyalty can have far-reaching results.

Outline

1/ Ruth 1—2 ——————————————— The Cost of Loyalty
2/ Ruth 3—4 ——————————————— Sadness Swallowed Up by Joy

1 / *Ruth 1—2*
The Cost of Loyalty

A UNIVERSITY STUDENT wrote to J. R. R. Tolkien after reading *Lord of the Rings,* "You have made loyalty and courage more meaningful to me." Loyalty doesn't get much "press" today. It's present in the lives of many, but isn't heralded like it used to be when people signed their letters "Your loyal friend." In Ruth we find a model of loyalty that would bring much to our friendships today.

 Warming Up to God What makes it hard to be loyal to another person?

 Read Ruth 1—2.

---

1 In the days when the judges ruled,[a] there was a famine in the land, and a man from Bethlehem in Judah, together with his wife and two sons, went to live for a while in the country of Moab. ²The man's name was Elimelech, his wife's name Naomi, and the names of his two sons were Mahlon and Kilion. They were Ephrathites from Bethlehem, Judah. And they went to Moab and lived there.

³Now Elimelech, Naomi's husband, died, and she was left with her two sons. ⁴They married Moabite women, one named Orpah and the other Ruth. After they had lived there about ten years, ⁵both Mahlon and Kilion also died, and Naomi was left without her two sons and her husband.

⁶When she heard in Moab that the LORD had come to the aid of his people by providing food for them, Naomi and her daughters-in-law prepared to return home from there. ⁷With her two daughters-in-law she left the place where she had been living and set out on the road that would take them back to the land of Judah.

⁸Then Naomi said to her two daughters-in-law, "Go back, each of you, to your mother's home. May the LORD show kindness to you, as you have shown to your dead and to me. ⁹May the LORD grant that each of you will find rest in the home of another husband."

Then she kissed them and they wept aloud ¹⁰and said to her, "We will go back with you to your people."

¹¹But Naomi said, "Return home, my daughters. Why would you come with me? Am I going to have any more sons, who could become your husbands? ¹²Return home, my daughters; I am too old to have another husband. Even if I thought there was still hope for me—even if I had a husband tonight and then gave birth to sons— ¹³would you wait until they grew up? Would you remain unmarried for them? No, my daughters. It is more bitter for me than for you, because the LORD's hand has gone out against me!"

¹⁴At this they wept again. Then Orpah kissed her mother-in-law good-by, but Ruth clung to her.

¹⁵"Look," said Naomi, "your sister-in-law is going back to her people and her gods. Go back with her."

¹⁶But Ruth replied, "Don't urge me to leave you or to turn back from you. Where you go I will go, and where you stay I will stay. Your people will be my people and your God my God. ¹⁷Where you die I will die, and there I will be buried. May the LORD deal with me, be it ever so severely, if anything but death separates you and me." ¹⁸When Naomi realized that Ruth was determined to go with her, she stopped urging her.

¹⁹So the two women went on until they came to Bethlehem. When they arrived in Bethlehem, the whole town was stirred because of them, and the women exclaimed, "Can this be Naomi?"

²⁰"Don't call me Naomi,[b]" she told them. "Call me Mara,[c] because the Almighty[d] has made my life very bitter. ²¹I went away full, but the LORD has brought me back empty. Why call me Naomi? The LORD has afflicted[e] me; the Almighty has brought misfortune upon me."

²²So Naomi returned from Moab accompanied by Ruth the Moabitess, her daughter-in-law, arriving in Bethlehem as the barley harvest was beginning.

---

[a]1 Traditionally *judged*   [b]20 *Naomi* means *pleasant*; also in verse 21.
[c]20 *Mara* means *bitter*.   [d]20 Hebrew *Shaddai*; also in verse 21
[e]21 Or *has testified against*

2 Now Naomi had a relative on her husband's side, from the clan of Elimelech, a man of standing, whose name was Boaz. ²And Ruth the Moabitess said to Naomi, "Let me go to the fields and pick up the leftover grain behind anyone in whose eyes I find favor."

Naomi said to her, "Go ahead, my daughter." ³So she went out and began to glean in the fields behind the harvesters. As it turned out, she found herself working in a field belonging to Boaz, who was from the clan of Elimelech.

⁴Just then Boaz arrived from Bethlehem and greeted the harvesters, "The LORD be with you!"

"The LORD bless you!" they called back.

⁵Boaz asked the foreman of his harvesters, "Whose young woman is that?"

⁶The foreman replied, "She is the Moabitess who came back from Moab with Naomi. ⁷She said, 'Please let me glean and gather among the sheaves behind the harvesters.' She went into the field and has worked steadily from morning till now, except for a short rest in the shelter."

⁸So Boaz said to Ruth, "My daughter, listen to me. Don't go and glean in another field and don't go away from here. Stay here with my servant girls. ⁹Watch the field where the men are harvesting, and follow along after the girls. I have told the men not to touch you. And whenever you are thirsty, go and get a drink from the water jars the men have filled."

¹⁰At this, she bowed down with her face to the ground. She exclaimed, "Why have I found such favor in your eyes that you notice me—a foreigner?"

¹¹Boaz replied, "I've been told all about what you have done for your mother-in-law since the death of your husband—how you left your father and mother and your homeland and came to live with a people you did not know before. ¹²May the LORD repay you for what you have done. May you be richly rewarded by the LORD, the God of Israel, under whose wings you have come to take refuge."

¹³"May I continue to find favor in your eyes, my lord," she said. "You have given me comfort and have spoken kindly to your servant—though I do not have the standing of one of your servant girls."

¹⁴At mealtime Boaz said to her, "Come over here. Have some bread and dip it in the wine vinegar."

When she sat down with the harvesters, he offered her some roasted grain. She ate all she wanted and had some left over. ¹⁵As she got up to glean, Boaz gave orders to his men, "Even if she gathers among the sheaves, don't embarrass her. ¹⁶Rather, pull out some stalks for her from the bundles and leave them for her to pick up, and don't rebuke her."

¹⁷So Ruth gleaned in the field until evening. Then she threshed the barley she had gathered, and it amounted to about an ephah.ʃ ¹⁸She carried it back to town, and her mother-in-law saw how much she had gathered. Ruth also brought out and gave her what she had left over after she had eaten enough.

¹⁹Her mother-in-law asked her, "Where did you glean today? Where did you work? Blessed be the man who took notice of you!"

Then Ruth told her mother-in-law about the one at whose place she had been working. "The name of the man I worked with today is Boaz," she said.

²⁰"The LORD bless him!" Naomi said to her daughter-in-law. "He has not stopped showing his kindness to the living and the dead." She added, "That man is our close relative; he is one of our kinsman-redeemers."

²¹Then Ruth the Moabitess said, "He even said to me, 'Stay with my workers until they finish harvesting all my grain.' "

²²Naomi said to Ruth her daughter-in-law, "It will be good for you, my daughter, to go with his girls, because in someone else's field you might be harmed."

²³So Ruth stayed close to the servant girls of Boaz to glean until the barley and wheat harvests were finished. And she lived with her mother-in-law.

ʃ17 That is, probably about 3/5 bushel (about 22 liters)

Discovering the Word 1. How does Ruth's relationship with Naomi differ from Orpah's (1:10, 14, 16–18)? 2. What are the practical implications of the choice Ruth makes in contrast to the choice Orpah makes? 3. Naomi and Ruth arrive in Bethlehem at the time of the barley harvest (1:22). What does Ruth's willingness to be a gleaner tell us about her (2:2)? 4. How does the regard that Boaz has for Ruth and her position in Israel (2:11–12) differ from Ruth's concept of herself (2:10, 13)? 5. Put yourself in Ruth's place. How would it feel to be a foreigner, needing to work hard to support your mother-in-law?

Applying the Word   1. What motivates your own loyalty?   2. What loyalties are important to you as a Christian, regardless of cost?

Responding in Prayer   Ask God to build you into a person of loyalty.

2 / *Ruth 3—4*
Sadness Swallowed Up by Joy

LIFE IS LIKE a grindstone, someone once said, and whether it grinds you down or polishes you depends on the stuff you are made of. It also depends on your view of God. Some people seem to get more hard knocks in life than others, and if you say, "That's not fair," you are probably right. Life isn't always fair. But the question is, even in the hardest circumstances is God in control? If he is, that means he can change the bitterness of our hard experiences.

Warming Up to God   Naomi is a case study in hardship. Despite Naomi's trials, Ruth's insistence on returning with her is strong indication of God's care. Gradually it dawns on Naomi that God has provided for her and Ruth in ways she had never expected. In these two chapters we see Naomi's bitterness turned to joy.

Read Ruth 3—4.

3 One day Naomi her mother-in-law said to her, "My daughter, should I not try to find a home^g for you, where you will be well provided for? ²Is not Boaz, with whose servant girls you have been, a kinsman of ours? Tonight he will be winnowing barley on the threshing floor. ³Wash and perfume yourself, and put on your best clothes. Then go down to the threshing floor, but don't let him know you are there until he has finished eating and drinking. ⁴When he lies down, note the place where he is lying. Then go and uncover his feet and lie down. He will tell you what to do."

⁵"I will do whatever you say," Ruth answered. ⁶So she went down to the threshing floor and did everything her mother-in-law told her to do.

⁷When Boaz had finished eating and drinking and was in good spirits, he went over to lie down at the far end of the grain pile. Ruth approached quietly, uncovered his feet and lay down. ⁸In the middle of the night something startled the man, and he turned and discovered a woman lying at his feet.

⁹"Who are you?" he asked.

"I am your servant Ruth," she said. "Spread the corner of your garment over me, since you are a kinsman-redeemer."

¹⁰"The LORD bless you, my daughter," he replied. "This kindness is greater than that which you showed earlier: You have not run after the younger men, whether rich or poor. ¹¹And now, my daughter, don't be afraid. I will do for you all you ask. All my fellow townsmen know that you are a woman of noble character. ¹²Although it is true that I am near of kin, there is a kinsman-redeemer nearer than I. ¹³Stay here for the night, and in the morning if he wants to redeem, good; let him redeem. But if he is not willing, as surely as the LORD lives I will do it. Lie here until morning."

¹⁴So she lay at his feet until morning, but got up before anyone could be recognized; and he said, "Don't let it be known that a woman came to the threshing floor."

¹⁵He also said, "Bring me the shawl you are wearing and hold it out." When she did so, he poured into it six measures of barley and put it on her. Then he^h went back to town.

¹⁶When Ruth came to her mother-in-law, Naomi asked, "How did it go, my daughter?"

Then she told her everything Boaz had done for her ¹⁷and added, "He gave me these six measures of barley, saying, 'Don't go back to your mother-in-law empty-handed.' "

¹⁸Then Naomi said, "Wait, my daughter, until you find out what happens. For the man will not rest until the matter is settled today."

g1 Hebrew find rest (see Ruth 1:9)   h15 Most Hebrew manuscripts; many Hebrew manuscripts, Vulgate and Syriac she

4 Meanwhile Boaz went up to the town gate and sat there. When the kinsman-redeemer he had mentioned came along, Boaz said, "Come over here, my friend, and sit down." So he went over and sat down.

²Boaz took ten of the elders of the town and said, "Sit here," and they did so. ³Then he said to the kinsman-redeemer, "Naomi, who has come back from Moab, is selling the piece of land that belonged to our brother Elimelech. ⁴I thought I should bring the matter to your attention and suggest that you buy it in the presence of these seated here and in the presence of the elders of my people. If you will redeem it, do so. But if you[i] will not, tell me, so I will know. For no one has the right to do it except you, and I am next in line."

"I will redeem it," he said.

⁵Then Boaz said, "On the day you buy the land from Naomi and from Ruth the Moabitess, you acquire[j] the dead man's widow, in order to maintain the name of the dead with his property."

⁶At this, the kinsman-redeemer said, "Then I cannot redeem it because I might endanger my own estate. You redeem it yourself. I cannot do it."

⁷(Now in earlier times in Israel, for the redemption and transfer of property to become final, one party took off his sandal and gave it to the other. This was the method of legalizing transactions in Israel.)

⁸So the kinsman-redeemer said to Boaz, "Buy it yourself." And he removed his sandal.

⁹Then Boaz announced to the elders and all the people, "Today you are witnesses that I have bought from Naomi all the property of Elimelech, Kilion and Mahlon. ¹⁰I have also acquired Ruth the Moabitess, Mahlon's widow, as my wife, in order to maintain the name of the dead with his property, so that his name will not disappear from among his family or from the town records. Today you are witnesses!"

¹¹Then the elders and all those at the gate said, "We are witnesses. May the LORD make the woman who is coming into your home like Rachel and Leah, who together built up the house of Israel. May you have standing in Ephrathah and be famous in Bethlehem. ¹²Through the offspring the LORD gives you by this young woman, may your family be like that of Perez, whom Tamar bore to Judah."

¹³So Boaz took Ruth and she became his wife. Then he went to her, and the LORD enabled her to conceive, and she gave birth to a son. ¹⁴The women said to Naomi: "Praise be to the LORD, who this day has not left you without a kinsman-redeemer. May he become famous throughout Israel! ¹⁵He will renew your life and sustain you in your old age. For your daughter-in-law, who loves you and who is better to you than seven sons, has given him birth."

¹⁶Then Naomi took the child, laid him in her lap and cared for him. ¹⁷The women living there said, "Naomi has a son." And they named him Obed. He was the father of Jesse, the father of David.

¹⁸This, then, is the family line of Perez:

Perez was the father of Hezron,
¹⁹Hezron the father of Ram,
Ram the father of Amminadab,
²⁰Amminadab the father of Nahshon,
Nahshon the father of Salmon,[k]
²¹Salmon the father of Boaz,
Boaz the father of Obed,
²²Obed the father of Jesse,
and Jesse the father of David.

i4 Many Hebrew manuscripts, Septuagint, Vulgate and Syriac; most Hebrew manuscripts he   j5 Hebrew; Vulgate and Syriac Naomi, you acquire Ruth the Moabitess,   k20 A few Hebrew manuscripts, some Septuagint manuscripts and Vulgate (see also verse 21 and Septuagint of 1 Chron. 2:11); most Hebrew manuscripts Salma

---

Discovering the Word 1. How does Naomi plan for Ruth's future (3:1–4)? 2. "To spread the corners of your garment over me" (3:9) was a request for marriage. Why might this be a risky plan? 3. How would you evaluate Boaz's character from his actions in these two chapters? 4. What does the birth of Obed mean to Naomi (4:13–17)? 5. What is the turning point in Naomi's life from the bitterness she expressed as she returned to Bethlehem (1:20) to the joy she feels at the end of the story (4:16)?

Applying the Word 1. Naomi's grandson becomes an ancestor of King David and is mentioned in the genealogy of Jesus in Matthew 1:5. What do you learn about God from the amazing ways in which he blesses Naomi after all her tragedies? 2. In what ways has God shown his faithfulness to you and changed your sorrow to joy?

Responding in Prayer Praise God for the Redeemer he has given us in Jesus Christ. Thank him for the joy that he brings into your life.

1 Samuel

When I was a child, my hero was Superman. Like him, I wanted to be faster than a speeding bullet, able to leap tall buildings in a single bound and bend steel in my bare hands. Using a bath towel for my cape, I flew around the house, performing imaginary feats of strength and courage.

As I grew up, however, I discovered that Superman was not the best kind of hero. I found it impossible to be like him, no matter how hard I tried. Bullets simply wouldn't bounce off me and neither would harsh words, fears, disappointments, illnesses or a hundred other weaknesses that are common to frail, fallen humanity.

Bullets didn't bounce off David either. As I read about his life, I am astonished at how open and vulnerable he was. He records his weaknesses and struggles for all the world to read: "I am worn out from groaning; all night long I flood my bed with weeping and drench my couch with tears. My eyes grow weak with sorrow; they fail because of all my foes." "I know my transgressions, and my sin is always before me. Against you, you only, have I sinned and done what is evil in your sight" (Ps 6:6–7; 51:3–4).

Yet in spite of all his weaknesses, fears, doubts and sins, David was also a man of faith. His life illustrates a tenacious trust in God and an intense desire to know him: "The Lord is my light and my salvation—whom shall I fear? The Lord is the stronghold of my life—of whom shall I be afraid?" "One thing I ask of the Lord, this is what I seek: that I may dwell in the house of the Lord . . . and to seek him in his temple" (Ps 27:1, 4). Because of these qualities, God was able to use David mightily, molding and shaping him into a man after his own heart.

I believe we need this kind of three-dimensional role model today—someone who allows us to be fully human, yet who inspires us to look beyond our weaknesses and frailties to the Living God. You will meet David in these quiet times in 1 Samuel.

David's life extended from around 1040 to 970 B.C. Second Samuel 5 records that "David was thirty years old when he became king, and he reigned forty years. In Hebron he reigned over Judah seven years and six months, and in Jerusalem he reigned over all Israel and Judah thirty-three years" (vv. 4–5). The biblical writers view David as the greatest of Israel's kings and the one through whom the ultimate king, the Messiah, eventually came (see Mt 1:1; Lk 3:31).

It is my prayer that as you study 1 Samuel, you too will develop a passionate heart for God.

Outline

1/ 1 Samuel 1:1—2:11 ————————— *From Misery to Praise*

2/ 1 Samuel 3 ——————————————— *Hearing God's Voice*

3/ 1 Samuel 8 ——————————————— *Status Symbols*

4/ 1 Samuel 9:1—10:8 ——————————— *Citizenship*

5/ 1 Samuel 15 ——————————————— *Doing Almost All of God's Will*

6/ 1 Samuel 16 ——————————————— *The Lord Looks at the Heart*

7/ 1 Samuel 17 ——————————————— *The Battle Is the Lord's*

8/ 1 Samuel 18 ——————————————— *Bitterness*

9/ 1 Samuel 20 ——————————————— *True Friendship*

10/ 1 Samuel 24 ——————————————— *A Matter of Conscience*

11/ 1 Samuel 25 ——————————————— *Secure in the Lord*

12/ 1 Samuel 26 ——————————————— *Self-Control*

13/ 1 Samuel 30 ——————————————— *Finding Strength in the Lord*

1 / *1 Samuel 1:1—2:11*
From Misery to Praise

WAITING IS ONE of the hardest things we do. So much of life involves waiting, and in an age of instant products, waiting irritates us. But waiting is hardest when we see the clock running on, the years going by and still our hopes and dreams are unfulfilled. Hannah knew about waiting. In a society that measured a woman's worth by her children, Hannah was barren. Year after year she waited in misery for the answer to her prayers. She had two choices: to be bitter or to continue seeking God's help. This quiet time looks at Hannah's journey from misery to praise.

 Warming Up to God   What cherished hope do you increasingly fear may never be realized in your life? Talk openly with God about your physical, emotional and spiritual response to this experience of waiting.

 Read 1 Samuel 1:1—2:11.

1 There was a certain man from Ramathaim, a Zuphite[a] from the hill country of Ephraim, whose name was Elkanah son of Jeroham, the son of Elihu, the son of Tohu, the son of Zuph, an Ephraimite. [2]He had two wives; one was called Hannah and the other Peninnah. Peninnah had children, but Hannah had none.

[3]Year after year this man went up from his town to worship and sacrifice to the LORD Almighty at Shiloh, where Hophni and Phinehas, the two sons of Eli, were priests of the LORD. [4]Whenever the day came for Elkanah to sacrifice, he would give portions of the meat to his wife Peninnah and to all her sons and daughters. [5]But to Hannah he gave a double portion because he loved her, and the LORD had closed her womb. [6]And because the LORD had closed her womb, her rival kept provoking her in order to irritate her. [7]This went on year after year. Whenever Hannah went up to the house of the LORD, her rival provoked her till she wept and would not eat. [8]Elkanah her husband would say to her, "Hannah, why are you weeping? Why don't you eat? Why are you downhearted? Don't I mean more to you than ten sons?"

[9]Once when they had finished eating and drinking in Shiloh, Hannah stood up. Now Eli the priest was sitting on a chair by the doorpost of the LORD's temple.[b] [10]In bitterness of soul Hannah wept much and prayed to the LORD. [11]And she made a vow, saying, "O LORD Almighty, if you will only look upon your servant's misery and remember me, and not forget your servant but give her a son, then I will give him to the LORD for all the days of his life, and no razor will ever be used on his head."

[12]As she kept on praying to the LORD, Eli observed her mouth. [13]Hannah was praying in her heart, and her lips were moving but her voice was not heard. Eli thought she was drunk [14]and said to her, "How long will you keep on getting drunk? Get rid of your wine."

[15]"Not so, my lord," Hannah replied, "I am a woman who is deeply troubled. I have not been drinking wine or beer; I was pouring out my soul to the LORD. [16]Do not take your servant for a wicked woman; I have been praying here out of my great anguish and grief."

[17]Eli answered, "Go in peace, and may the God of Israel grant you what you have asked of him."

[18]She said, "May your servant find favor in your eyes." Then she went her way and ate something, and her face was no longer downcast.

[19]Early the next morning they arose and worshiped before the LORD and then went back to their home at Ramah. Elkanah lay with Hannah his wife, and the LORD remembered her. [20]So in the course of time Hannah conceived and gave birth to a son. She named him Samuel,[c] saying, "Because I asked the LORD for him."

[21]When the man Elkanah went up with all his family to offer the annual sacrifice to the LORD and to fulfill his vow, [22]Hannah did not go. She said to her husband, "After the boy is weaned, I will take him and present him before the LORD, and he will live there always."

[23]"Do what seems best to you," Elkanah her husband told her. "Stay here until you have

---

a1 Or from Ramathaim Zuphim   *b9 That is, tabernacle*
c20 Samuel sounds like the Hebrew for heard of God.

weaned him; only may the LORD make good his[d] word." So the woman stayed at home and nursed her son until she had weaned him.

²⁴After he was weaned, she took the boy with her, young as he was, along with a three-year-old bull,[e] an ephah[f] of flour and a skin of wine, and brought him to the house of the LORD at Shiloh. ²⁵When they had slaughtered the bull, they brought the boy to Eli, ²⁶and she said to him, "As surely as you live, my lord, I am the woman who stood here beside you praying to the LORD. ²⁷I prayed for this child, and the LORD has granted me what I asked of him. ²⁸So now I give him to the LORD. For his whole life he will be given over to the LORD." And he worshiped the LORD there.

2 Then Hannah prayed and said:

"My heart rejoices in the LORD;
    in the LORD my horn[g] is lifted high.
My mouth boasts over my enemies,
    for I delight in your deliverance.

²"There is no one holy[h] like the LORD;
    there is no one besides you;
    there is no Rock like our God.

³"Do not keep talking so proudly
    or let your mouth speak such arrogance,
for the LORD is a God who knows,
    and by him deeds are weighed.

⁴"The bows of the warriors are broken,
    but those who stumbled are armed with
        strength.
⁵Those who were full hire themselves out for
        food,

but those who were hungry hunger no
        more.
She who was barren has borne seven children,
    but she who has had many sons pines
        away.
⁶"The LORD brings death and makes alive;
    he brings down to the grave[i] and raises
        up.
⁷The LORD sends poverty and wealth;
    he humbles and he exalts.
⁸He raises the poor from the dust
    and lifts the needy from the ash heap;
he seats them with princes
    and has them inherit a throne of honor.

"For the foundations of the earth are the
        LORD's;
    upon them he has set the world.
⁹He will guard the feet of his saints,
    but the wicked will be silenced in darkness.

"It is not by strength that one prevails;
¹⁰   those who oppose the LORD will be
        shattered.
He will thunder against them from heaven;
    the LORD will judge the ends of the earth.

"He will give strength to his king
    and exalt the horn of his anointed."

¹¹Then Elkanah went home to Ramah, but the boy ministered before the LORD under Eli the priest.

---

[d]23 Masoretic Text; Dead Sea Scrolls, Septuagint and Syriac *your*   [e]24 Dead Sea Scrolls, Septuagint and Syriac; Masoretic Text *with three bulls*   [f]24 That is, probably about 3/5 bushel (about 22 liters)   [g]1 *Horn* here symbolizes strength; also in verse 10.   [h]2 Or *no Holy One*   [i]6 Hebrew *Sheol*

 Discovering the Word 1. Why is Hannah's pain so intense (1:2–7)? **2.** Hannah turns to God in desperation. What does her prayer reveal about her (1:9–11)? **3.** Look at chapter 2. What shift do you see in Hannah's focus between chapters 1 and 2? **4.** What does Hannah believe about God? (Find several strong beliefs.) **5.** If you were describing Hannah to a friend, what would you say about her? about her gifts? about her spiritual life?

 Applying the Word 1. When you are bitter about your disappointments, to whom (or what) do you turn? **2.** What specific things can you learn from Hannah about the solution to the pain of unfulfilled hopes?

Responding in Prayer Try speaking or writing out your own song of praise, telling God what you believe about him.

1 Samuel 2:12–36

¹²Eli's sons were wicked men; they had no regard for the Lord. ¹³Now it was the practice of the priests with the people that whenever anyone offered a sacrifice and while the meat was being boiled, the servant of the priest would come with a three-pronged fork in his hand. ¹⁴He would plunge it into the pan or kettle or caldron or pot, and the priest would take for himself whatever the fork brought up. This is how they treated all the Israelites who came to Shiloh. ¹⁵But even before the fat was burned, the servant of the priest would come and say to the man who was sacrificing, "Give the priest some meat to roast; he won't accept boiled meat from you, but only raw."

¹⁶If the man said to him, "Let the fat be burned up first, and then take whatever you want," the servant would then answer, "No, hand it over now; if you don't, I'll take it by force."

¹⁷This sin of the young men was very great in the Lord's sight, for they[j] were treating the Lord's offering with contempt.

¹⁸But Samuel was ministering before the Lord—a boy wearing a linen ephod. ¹⁹Each year his mother made him a little robe and took it to him when she went up with her husband to offer the annual sacrifice. ²⁰Eli would bless Elkanah and his wife, saying, "May the Lord give you children by this woman to take the place of the one she prayed for and gave to the Lord." Then they would go home. ²¹And the Lord was gracious to Hannah; she conceived and gave birth to three sons and two daughters. Meanwhile, the boy Samuel grew up in the presence of the Lord.

²²Now Eli, who was very old, heard about everything his sons were doing to all Israel and how they slept with the women who served at the entrance to the Tent of Meeting. ²³So he said to them, "Why do you do such things? I hear from all the people about these wicked deeds of yours. ²⁴No, my sons; it is not a good report that I hear spreading among the Lord's people. ²⁵If a man sins against another man, God[k] may mediate for him; but if a man sins against the Lord, who will intercede for him?" His sons, however, did not

listen to their father's rebuke, for it was the Lord's will to put them to death.

²⁶And the boy Samuel continued to grow in stature and in favor with the Lord and with men.

²⁷Now a man of God came to Eli and said to him, "This is what the Lord says: 'Did I not clearly reveal myself to your father's house when they were in Egypt under Pharaoh? ²⁸I chose your father out of all the tribes of Israel to be my priest, to go up to my altar, to burn incense, and to wear an ephod in my presence. I also gave your father's house all the offerings made with fire by the Israelites. ²⁹Why do you[l] scorn my sacrifice and offering that I prescribed for my dwelling? Why do you honor your sons more than me by fattening yourselves on the choice parts of every offering made by my people Israel?'

³⁰"Therefore the Lord, the God of Israel, declares: 'I promised that your house and your father's house would minister before me forever.' But now the Lord declares: 'Far be it from me! Those who honor me I will honor, but those who despise me will be disdained. ³¹The time is coming when I will cut short your strength and the strength of your father's house, so that there will not be an old man in your family line ³²and you will see distress in my dwelling. Although good will be done to Israel, in your family line there will never be an old man. ³³Every one of you that I do not cut off from my altar will be spared only to blind your eyes with tears and to grieve your heart, and all your descendants will die in the prime of life.

³⁴" 'And what happens to your two sons, Hophni and Phinehas, will be a sign to you—they will both die on the same day. ³⁵I will raise up for myself a faithful priest, who will do according to what is in my heart and mind. I will firmly establish his house, and he will minister before my anointed one always. ³⁶Then everyone left in your family line will come and bow down before him for a piece of silver and a crust of bread and plead, "Appoint me to some priestly office so I can have food to eat." ' "

[j]17 Or men   [k]25 Or the judges   [l]29 The Hebrew is plural.

2 / 1 Samuel 3
Hearing God's Voice

AMID THE HUSTLE and bustle of daily life, we often find it hard to hear God's voice. Many "voices" shout for our attention—deadlines to meet, bills to pay, meetings to attend, phone calls to make, children to care for. We try to read our Bible but struggle to be still and receive a word from God.

In the days of Samuel few people were listening to God's voice. Politically and spiritually Israel was in terrible shape as they "had no king" and "everyone did as he saw fit" (Jdg 21:25). In this study we observe Samuel as a young man, hearing the word of the Lord for the first time and beginning his prophetic ministry.

 Warming Up to God   How have you heard God speak to you?

 Read 1 Samuel 3.

3 The boy Samuel ministered before the LORD under Eli. In those days the word of the LORD was rare; there were not many visions.

²One night Eli, whose eyes were becoming so weak that he could barely see, was lying down in his usual place. ³The lamp of God had not yet gone out, and Samuel was lying down in the temple*m* of the LORD, where the ark of God was. ⁴Then the LORD called Samuel.

Samuel answered, "Here I am." ⁵And he ran to Eli and said, "Here I am; you called me."

But Eli said, "I did not call; go back and lie down." So he went and lay down.

⁶Again the LORD called, "Samuel!" And Samuel got up and went to Eli and said, "Here I am; you called me."

"My son," Eli said, "I did not call; go back and lie down."

⁷Now Samuel did not yet know the LORD: The word of the LORD had not yet been revealed to him.

⁸The LORD called Samuel a third time, and Samuel got up and went to Eli and said, "Here I am; you called me."

Then Eli realized that the LORD was calling the boy. ⁹So Eli told Samuel, "Go and lie down, and if he calls you, say, 'Speak, LORD, for your servant is listening.'" So Samuel went and lay down in his place.

¹⁰The LORD came and stood there, calling as at the other times, "Samuel! Samuel!"

Then Samuel said, "Speak, for your servant is listening."

¹¹And the LORD said to Samuel: "See, I am about to do something in Israel that will make the ears of everyone who hears of it tingle. ¹²At that time I will carry out against Eli everything I spoke against his family—from beginning to end. ¹³For I told him that I would judge his family forever because of the sin he knew about; his sons made themselves contemptible,*n* and he failed to restrain them. ¹⁴Therefore, I swore to the house of Eli, 'The guilt of Eli's house will never be atoned for by sacrifice or offering.'"

¹⁵Samuel lay down until morning and then opened the doors of the house of the LORD. He was afraid to tell Eli the vision, ¹⁶but Eli called him and said, "Samuel, my son."

Samuel answered, "Here I am."

¹⁷"What was it he said to you?" Eli asked. "Do not hide it from me. May God deal with you, be it ever so severely, if you hide from me anything he told you." ¹⁸So Samuel told him everything, hiding nothing from him. Then Eli said, "He is the LORD; let him do what is good in his eyes."

¹⁹The LORD was with Samuel as he grew up, and he let none of his words fall to the ground. ²⁰And all Israel from Dan to Beersheba recognized that Samuel was attested as a prophet of the LORD. ²¹The LORD continued to appear at Shiloh, and there he revealed himself to Samuel through his word.

m 3 That is, tabernacle   *n 13* Masoretic Text; an ancient Hebrew scribal tradition and Septuagint *sons blasphemed God*

Discovering the Word 1. Why do you think Samuel has difficulty discerning God's voice from Eli's (vv. 4–8)? 2. What do you think Samuel thought and felt as he listened to Eli and then returned to his bed (vv. 9–10)? 3. Why is the attitude "Speak, for your servant is listening" (v. 10) so important in order to hear from God? 4. Why would God's message in verses 11–14 have been particularly hard for Samuel to hear? 5. How does Samuel's obedience affect his relationship to God and his future ministry (vv. 19–21)?

Applying the Word 1. How does Samuel's openness to hear from God compare with yours? 2. When are you most tempted to hide God's word from others? Explain. 3. What is the greatest obstacle that prevents you from hearing God's voice?

Responding in Prayer Ask God to make you more open and attentive to his voice.

1 Samuel 4—7

4 And Samuel's word came to all Israel.

Now the Israelites went out to fight against the Philistines. The Israelites camped at Ebenezer, and the Philistines at Aphek. ²The Philistines deployed their forces to meet Israel, and as the battle spread, Israel was defeated by the Philistines, who killed about four thousand of them on the battlefield. ³When the soldiers returned to camp, the elders of Israel asked, "Why did the LORD bring defeat upon us today before the Philistines? Let us bring the ark of the LORD's covenant from Shiloh, so that itᵒ may go with us and save us from the hand of our enemies."

⁴So the people sent men to Shiloh, and they brought back the ark of the covenant of the LORD Almighty, who is enthroned between the cherubim. And Eli's two sons, Hophni and Phinehas, were there with the ark of the covenant of God.

⁵When the ark of the LORD's covenant came into the camp, all Israel raised such a great shout that the ground shook. ⁶Hearing the uproar, the Philistines asked, "What's all this shouting in the Hebrew camp?"

When they learned that the ark of the LORD had come into the camp, ⁷the Philistines were afraid. "A god has come into the camp," they said. "We're in trouble! Nothing like this has happened before. ⁸Woe to us! Who will deliver us from the hand of these mighty gods? They are the gods who struck the Egyptians with all kinds of plagues in the desert. ⁹Be strong, Philistines! Be men, or you will be subject to the Hebrews, as they have been to you. Be men, and fight!"

¹⁰So the Philistines fought, and the Israelites were defeated and every man fled to his tent. The slaughter was very great; Israel lost thirty thousand foot soldiers. ¹¹The ark of God was captured, and Eli's two sons, Hophni and Phinehas, died.

¹²That same day a Benjamite ran from the battle line and went to Shiloh, his clothes torn and dust on his head. ¹³When he arrived, there was Eli sitting on his chair by the side of the road, watching, because his heart feared for the ark of God. When the man entered the town and told what had happened, the whole town sent up a cry.

¹⁴Eli heard the outcry and asked, "What is the meaning of this uproar?"

The man hurried over to Eli, ¹⁵who was ninety-eight years old and whose eyes were set so that he could not see. ¹⁶He told Eli, "I have just come from the battle line; I fled from it this very day."

Eli asked, "What happened, my son?"

¹⁷The man who brought the news replied, "Israel fled before the Philistines, and the army has suffered heavy losses. Also your two sons, Hophni and Phinehas, are dead, and the ark of God has been captured."

¹⁸When he mentioned the ark of God, Eli fell backward off his chair by the side of the gate. His neck was broken and he died, for he was an old man and heavy. He had ledᵖ Israel forty years.

¹⁹His daughter-in-law, the wife of Phinehas, was pregnant and near the time of delivery. When she heard the news that the ark of God had been captured and that her father-in-law and her husband were dead, she went into labor and gave birth, but was overcome by her labor pains. ²⁰As she was dying, the women attending her said,

ᵒ3 Or *he*　　ᵖ18 Traditionally *judged*

"Don't despair; you have given birth to a son." But she did not respond or pay any attention.

²¹She named the boy Ichabod,�q saying, "The glory has departed from Israel"—because of the capture of the ark of God and the deaths of her father-in-law and her husband. ²²She said, "The glory has departed from Israel, for the ark of God has been captured."

5 After the Philistines had captured the ark of God, they took it from Ebenezer to Ashdod. ²Then they carried the ark into Dagon's temple and set it beside Dagon. ³When the people of Ashdod rose early the next day, there was Dagon, fallen on his face on the ground before the ark of the LORD! They took Dagon and put him back in his place. ⁴But the following morning when they rose, there was Dagon, fallen on his face on the ground before the ark of the LORD! His head and hands had been broken off and were lying on the threshold; only his body remained. ⁵That is why to this day neither the priests of Dagon nor any others who enter Dagon's temple at Ashdod step on the threshold.

⁶The LORD's hand was heavy upon the people of Ashdod and its vicinity; he brought devastation upon them and afflicted them with tumors.ʳ ⁷When the men of Ashdod saw what was happening, they said, "The ark of the god of Israel must not stay here with us, because his hand is heavy upon us and upon Dagon our god." ⁸So they called together all the rulers of the Philistines and asked them, "What shall we do with the ark of the god of Israel?"

They answered, "Have the ark of the god of Israel moved to Gath." So they moved the ark of the God of Israel.

⁹But after they had moved it, the LORD's hand was against that city, throwing it into a great panic. He afflicted the people of the city, both young and old, with an outbreak of tumors.ˢ ¹⁰So they sent the ark of God to Ekron.

As the ark of God was entering Ekron, the people of Ekron cried out, "They have brought the ark of the god of Israel around to us to kill us and our people." ¹¹So they called together all the rulers of the Philistines and said, "Send the ark of the god of Israel away; let it go back to its own place, or itᵗ will kill us and our people." For death had filled the city with panic; God's hand was very heavy upon it. ¹²Those who did not die were afflicted with tumors, and the outcry of the city went up to heaven.

6 When the ark of the LORD had been in Philistine territory seven months, ²the Philistines called for the priests and the diviners and said, "What shall we do with the ark of the LORD? Tell us how we should send it back to its place."

³They answered, "If you return the ark of the god of Israel, do not send it away empty, but by all means send a guilt offering to him. Then you will be healed, and you will know why his hand has not been lifted from you."

⁴The Philistines asked, "What guilt offering should we send to him?"

They replied, "Five gold tumors and five gold rats, according to the number of the Philistine rulers, because the same plague has struck both you and your rulers. ⁵Make models of the tumors and of the rats that are destroying the country, and pay honor to Israel's god. Perhaps he will lift his hand from you and your gods and your land. ⁶Why do you harden your hearts as the Egyptians and Pharaoh did? When heᵘ treated them harshly, did they not send the Israelites out so they could go on their way?

⁷"Now then, get a new cart ready, with two cows that have calved and have never been yoked. Hitch the cows to the cart, but take their calves away and pen them up. ⁸Take the ark of the LORD and put it on the cart, and in a chest beside it put the gold objects you are sending back to him as a guilt offering. Send it on its way, ⁹but keep watching it. If it goes up to its own territory, toward Beth Shemesh, then the LORD has brought this great disaster on us. But if it does not, then we will know that it was not his hand that struck us and that it happened to us by chance."

¹⁰So they did this. They took two such cows and hitched them to the cart and penned up their calves. ¹¹They placed the ark of the LORD on the cart and along with it the chest containing the gold rats and the models of the tumors. ¹²Then the cows went straight up toward Beth Shemesh, keeping on the road and lowing all the way; they did not turn to the right or to the left. The rulers of the Philistines followed them as far as the border of Beth Shemesh.

¹³Now the people of Beth Shemesh were harvesting their wheat in the valley, and when they

---

q21 Ichabod means no glory.   r6 Hebrew; Septuagint and Vulgate tumors. And rats appeared in their land, and death and destruction were throughout the city   s9 Or with tumors in the groin (see Septuagint)   t11 Or he   u6 That is, God looked up and saw the ark, they rejoiced at the sight. ¹⁴The cart came to the field of Joshua of Beth Shemesh, and there it stopped beside a large rock. The people chopped up the wood of the cart and sacrificed the cows as a burnt offering to the LORD. ¹⁵The Levites took down the ark of the LORD, together with the chest containing the gold objects, and placed them on the large rock. On that day the people of Beth Shemesh offered burnt offerings and made sacrifices to the LORD. ¹⁶The five rulers of the Philistines saw all this and then returned that same day to Ekron.

¹⁷These are the gold tumors the Philistines sent as a guilt offering to the LORD—one each for Ashdod, Gaza, Ashkelon, Gath and Ekron. ¹⁸And the number of the gold rats was according to the number of Philistine towns belonging to the five rulers—the fortified towns with their country villages. The large rock, on which ᵛ they set the ark of the LORD, is a witness to this day in the field of Joshua of Beth Shemesh.

¹⁹But God struck down some of the men of Beth Shemesh, putting seventy ʷ of them to death because they had looked into the ark of the LORD. The people mourned because of the heavy blow the LORD had dealt them, ²⁰and the men of Beth Shemesh asked, "Who can stand in the presence of the LORD, this holy God? To whom will the ark go up from here?"

²¹Then they sent messengers to the people of Kiriath Jearim, saying, "The Philistines have returned the ark of the LORD. Come down and take it up to your place." ¹So the men of Kiriath Jearim came and took up the ark of the LORD. They took it to Abinadab's house on the hill and consecrated Eleazar his son to guard the ark of the LORD.

²It was a long time, twenty years in all, that the ark remained at Kiriath Jearim, and all the people of Israel mourned and sought after the LORD. ³And Samuel said to the whole house of Israel, "If you are returning to the LORD with all your hearts, then rid yourselves of the foreign gods and the Ashtoreths and commit yourselves to the LORD and serve him only, and he will deliver you out of the hand of the Philistines." ⁴So the Israelites put away their Baals and Ashtoreths, and served the LORD only.

⁵Then Samuel said, "Assemble all Israel at Mizpah and I will intercede with the LORD for you." ⁶When they had assembled at Mizpah, they drew water and poured it out before the LORD. On that day they fasted and there they confessed, "We have sinned against the LORD." And Samuel was leader ˣ of Israel at Mizpah.

⁷When the Philistines heard that Israel had assembled at Mizpah, the rulers of the Philistines came up to attack them. And when the Israelites heard of it, they were afraid because of the Philistines. ⁸They said to Samuel, "Do not stop crying out to the LORD our God for us, that he may rescue us from the hand of the Philistines." ⁹Then Samuel took a suckling lamb and offered it up as a whole burnt offering to the LORD. He cried out to the LORD on Israel's behalf, and the LORD answered him.

¹⁰While Samuel was sacrificing the burnt offering, the Philistines drew near to engage Israel in battle. But that day the LORD thundered with loud thunder against the Philistines and threw them into such a panic that they were routed before the Israelites. ¹¹The men of Israel rushed out of Mizpah and pursued the Philistines, slaughtering them along the way to a point below Beth Car.

¹²Then Samuel took a stone and set it up between Mizpah and Shen. He named it Ebenezer,ʸ saying, "Thus far has the LORD helped us." ¹³So the Philistines were subdued and did not invade Israelite territory again.

Throughout Samuel's lifetime, the hand of the LORD was against the Philistines. ¹⁴The towns from Ekron to Gath that the Philistines had captured from Israel were restored to her, and Israel delivered the neighboring territory from the power of the Philistines. And there was peace between Israel and the Amorites.

¹⁵Samuel continued as judge over Israel all the days of his life. ¹⁶From year to year he went on a circuit from Bethel to Gilgal to Mizpah, judging Israel in all those places. ¹⁷But he always went back to Ramah, where his home was, and there he also judged Israel. And he built an altar there to the LORD.

ᵛ 18 A few Hebrew manuscripts (see also Septuagint); most Hebrew manuscripts *villages as far as Greater Abel, where*   ʷ 19 A few Hebrew manuscripts; most Hebrew manuscripts and Septuagint *50,070*   ˣ 6 Traditionally *judge*   ʸ 12 *Ebenezer* means *stone of help.*

3 / *1 Samuel 8*
Status Symbols

DO YOU REMEMBER the alligators? For a while the Izod symbol was the trendiest inch-long animal to have positioned on the left side of your knit shirt. In rebellion I wore a shirt with a small frog on it. Trends come and go, but they inevitably carry us along. In this passage the Israelites decide that a king would be a great status symbol so they could be like the countries around them.

 Warming Up to God Reflect on your own patterns of living—home, clothing, car, possessions, even your yard. In what ways has your imagination been captured by current trends?

 Read 1 Samuel 8.

---

8 When Samuel grew old, he appointed his sons as judges for Israel. ²The name of his firstborn was Joel and the name of his second was Abijah, and they served at Beersheba. ³But his sons did not walk in his ways. They turned aside after dishonest gain and accepted bribes and perverted justice.

⁴So all the elders of Israel gathered together and came to Samuel at Ramah. ⁵They said to him, "You are old, and your sons do not walk in your ways; now appoint a king to lead*z* us, such as all the other nations have."

⁶But when they said, "Give us a king to lead us," this displeased Samuel; so he prayed to the LORD. ⁷And the LORD told him: "Listen to all that the people are saying to you; it is not you they have rejected, but they have rejected me as their king. ⁸As they have done from the day I brought them up out of Egypt until this day, forsaking me and serving other gods, so they are doing to you. ⁹Now listen to them; but warn them solemnly and let them know what the king who will reign over them will do."

¹⁰Samuel told all the words of the LORD to the people who were asking him for a king. ¹¹He said, "This is what the king who will reign over you will do: He will take your sons and make them serve with his chariots and horses, and they will run in front of his chariots. ¹²Some he will assign to be commanders of thousands and commanders of fifties, and others to plow his ground and reap his harvest, and still others to make weapons of war and equipment for his chariots. ¹³He will take your daughters to be perfumers and cooks and bakers. ¹⁴He will take the best of your fields and vineyards and olive groves and give them to his attendants. ¹⁵He will take a tenth of your grain and of your vintage and give it to his officials and attendants. ¹⁶Your menservants and maidservants and the best of your cattle*a* and donkeys he will take for his own use. ¹⁷He will take a tenth of your flocks, and you yourselves will become his slaves. ¹⁸When that day comes, you will cry out for relief from the king you have chosen, and the LORD will not answer you in that day."

¹⁹But the people refused to listen to Samuel. "No!" they said. "We want a king over us. ²⁰Then we will be like all the other nations, with a king to lead us and to go out before us and fight our battles."

²¹When Samuel heard all that the people said, he repeated it before the LORD. ²²The LORD answered, "Listen to them and give them a king."

Then Samuel said to the men of Israel, "Everyone go back to his town."

z5 Traditionally *judge*; also in verses 6 and 20   *a16* Septuagint; Hebrew *young men*

 Discovering the Word 1. What do we learn about Samuel's sons in verses 1–3? 2. What reasons do the elders give for wanting a king (vv. 4–5)? 3. It seems that the elders have good reasons for being dissatisfied with Samuel's sons, but what other motivations are behind their request (vv. 7–8, 19–20)? 4. Notice all the terrible results that will come from having a king (vv. 11–18). Why do you think the people continue asking despite these warnings? 5. Why do you think the Lord repeatedly tells Samuel to "listen to the people" (vv. 7, 9, 22)?

Applying the Word 1. When are you most likely to be influenced by trends? 2. What trends are you following despite the warnings you may have had?

Responding in Prayer Tell the Lord how you have replaced him as king (v. 7) with status symbols. Ask him to help you reform your ways.

4 / 1 Samuel 9:1—10:8
Citizenship

LEIF SERVES ON his local public school board. The board must make a decision about a public health clinic located in the high school. The health clinic provides immunizations and physical examinations, and gives emergency care for injuries. It provides counsel to students with drug and alcohol problems. It supplies nutrition advice for pregnant women, birth control information, adoption agency referrals and phone numbers for abortion clinics. Recently the board has received a rash of complaints about the health clinic. One side says that the public school ought to be in the business of education, not providing fancy health services. The other complaints are from those who want birth control and abortion information ceased. And they want the clinic closed if that's what it takes.

Leif believes that abortion is wrong. And he believes that sex outside of marriage is wrong. He also knows that a certain percentage of these high-school students will have problem pregnancies—whether or not the clinic is open. And without the clinic, many kids at that high school will get no medical care at all. What position should Leif take on the upcoming school board decision?

 Warming Up to God In what area of your life do you see potential conflict between civil policy and moral principle?

 Read 1 Samuel 9:1—10:8.

9 There was a Benjamite, a man of standing, whose name was Kish son of Abiel, the son of Zeror, the son of Becorath, the son of Aphiah of Benjamin. ²He had a son named Saul, an impressive young man without equal among the Israelites—a head taller than any of the others.

³Now the donkeys belonging to Saul's father Kish were lost, and Kish said to his son Saul, "Take one of the servants with you and go and look for the donkeys." ⁴So he passed through the hill country of Ephraim and through the area around Shalisha, but they did not find them. They went on into the district of Shaalim, but the donkeys were not there. Then he passed through the territory of Benjamin, but they did not find them.

⁵When they reached the district of Zuph, Saul said to the servant who was with him, "Come, let's go back, or my father will stop thinking about the donkeys and start worrying about us."

⁶But the servant replied, "Look, in this town there is a man of God; he is highly respected, and everything he says comes true. Let's go there now. Perhaps he will tell us what way to take."

⁷Saul said to his servant, "If we go, what can we give the man? The food in our sacks is gone. We

have no gift to take to the man of God. What do we have?"

⁸The servant answered him again. "Look," he said, "I have a quarter of a shekel*ᵇ* of silver. I will give it to the man of God so that he will tell us what way to take." ⁹(Formerly in Israel, if a man went to inquire of God, he would say, "Come, let us go to the seer," because the prophet of today used to be called a seer.)

¹⁰"Good," Saul said to his servant. "Come, let's go." So they set out for the town where the man of God was.

¹¹As they were going up the hill to the town, they met some girls coming out to draw water, and they asked them, "Is the seer here?"

¹²"He is," they answered. "He's ahead of you. Hurry now; he has just come to our town today, for the people have a sacrifice at the high place. ¹³As soon as you enter the town, you will find him before he goes up to the high place to eat. The people will not begin eating until he comes, because he must bless the sacrifice; afterward, those who are invited will eat. Go up now; you should find him about this time."

¹⁴They went up to the town, and as they were

ᵇ8 That is, about 1/10 ounce (about 3 grams)

entering it, there was Samuel, coming toward them on his way up to the high place.

¹⁵Now the day before Saul came, the Lord had revealed this to Samuel: ¹⁶"About this time tomorrow I will send you a man from the land of Benjamin. Anoint him leader over my people Israel; he will deliver my people from the hand of the Philistines. I have looked upon my people, for their cry has reached me."

¹⁷When Samuel caught sight of Saul, the Lord said to him, "This is the man I spoke to you about; he will govern my people."

¹⁸Saul approached Samuel in the gateway and asked, "Would you please tell me where the seer's house is?"

¹⁹"I am the seer," Samuel replied. "Go up ahead of me to the high place, for today you are to eat with me, and in the morning I will let you go and will tell you all that is in your heart. ²⁰As for the donkeys you lost three days ago, do not worry about them; they have been found. And to whom is all the desire of Israel turned, if not to you and all your father's family?"

²¹Saul answered, "But am I not a Benjamite, from the smallest tribe of Israel, and is not my clan the least of all the clans of the tribe of Benjamin? Why do you say such a thing to me?"

²²Then Samuel brought Saul and his servant into the hall and seated them at the head of those who were invited—about thirty in number. ²³Samuel said to the cook, "Bring the piece of meat I gave you, the one I told you to lay aside."

²⁴So the cook took up the leg with what was on it and set it in front of Saul. Samuel said, "Here is what has been kept for you. Eat, because it was set aside for you for this occasion, from the time I said, 'I have invited guests.'" And Saul dined with Samuel that day.

²⁵After they came down from the high place to the town, Samuel talked with Saul on the roof of his house. ²⁶They rose about daybreak and Samuel called to Saul on the roof, "Get ready, and I will send you on your way." When Saul got ready, he and Samuel went outside together. ²⁷As they were going down to the edge of the town, Samuel said to Saul, "Tell the servant to go on ahead of us"—and the servant did so—"but you stay here awhile, so that I may give you a message from God."

10

Then Samuel took a flask of oil and poured it on Saul's head and kissed him, saying, "Has not the Lord anointed you leader over his inheritance?ᶜ ²When you leave me today, you will meet two men near Rachel's tomb, at Zelzah on the border of Benjamin. They will say to you, 'The donkeys you set out to look for have been found. And now your father has stopped thinking about them and is worried about you. He is asking, "What shall I do about my son?" '

³"Then you will go on from there until you reach the great tree of Tabor. Three men going up to God at Bethel will meet you there. One will be carrying three young goats, another three loaves of bread, and another a skin of wine. ⁴They will greet you and offer you two loaves of bread, which you will accept from them.

⁵"After that you will go to Gibeah of God, where there is a Philistine outpost. As you approach the town, you will meet a procession of prophets coming down from the high place with lyres, tambourines, flutes and harps being played before them, and they will be prophesying. ⁶The Spirit of the Lord will come upon you in power, and you will prophesy with them; and you will be changed into a different person. ⁷Once these signs are fulfilled, do whatever your hand finds to do, for God is with you.

⁸"Go down ahead of me to Gilgal. I will surely come down to you to sacrifice burnt offerings and fellowship offerings,ᵈ but you must wait seven days until I come to you and tell you what you are to do."

ᶜ1 Hebrew; Septuagint and Vulgate over his people Israel? You will reign over the Lord's people and save them from the power of their enemies round about. And this will be a sign to you that the Lord has anointed you leader over his inheritance: ᵈ8 Traditionally peace offerings

---

Discovering the Word 1. What events lead to a meeting between Saul and Samuel? 2. What reasons did Saul have to trust Samuel? 3. Given the information here, what do you see as Samuel's civil responsibilities? 4. What do you see as Samuel's spiritual responsibilities? 5. What do you think would be hard about Samuel's dual position?

Applying the Word 1. Review the dilemma Leif faced with his school board. If you were Leif, what decision would you urge on your fellow board members? 2. How would the recommendation you have chosen meet your responsibilities to all of the people in your school district? 3. How would it meet your responsibilities as a heavenly citizen?

Responding in Prayer Take time now to pray for one of your own civil leaders.

1 Samuel 10:9—14:52

⁹As Saul turned to leave Samuel, God changed Saul's heart, and all these signs were fulfilled that day. ¹⁰When they arrived at Gibeah, a procession of prophets met him; the Spirit of God came upon him in power, and he joined in their prophesying. ¹¹When all those who had formerly known him saw him prophesying with the prophets, they asked each other, "What is this that has happened to the son of Kish? Is Saul also among the prophets?"

¹²A man who lived there answered, "And who is their father?" So it became a saying: "Is Saul also among the prophets?" ¹³After Saul stopped prophesying, he went to the high place.

¹⁴Now Saul's uncle asked him and his servant, "Where have you been?"

"Looking for the donkeys," he said. "But when we saw they were not to be found, we went to Samuel."

¹⁵Saul's uncle said, "Tell me what Samuel said to you."

¹⁶Saul replied, "He assured us that the donkeys had been found." But he did not tell his uncle what Samuel had said about the kingship.

¹⁷Samuel summoned the people of Israel to the Lord at Mizpah ¹⁸and said to them, "This is what the Lord, the God of Israel, says: 'I brought Israel up out of Egypt, and I delivered you from the power of Egypt and all the kingdoms that oppressed you.' ¹⁹But you have now rejected your God, who saves you out of all your calamities and distresses. And you have said, 'No, set a king over us.' So now present yourselves before the Lord by your tribes and clans."

²⁰When Samuel brought all the tribes of Israel near, the tribe of Benjamin was chosen. ²¹Then he brought forward the tribe of Benjamin, clan by clan, and Matri's clan was chosen. Finally Saul son of Kish was chosen. But when they looked for him, he was not to be found. ²²So they inquired further of the Lord, "Has the man come here yet?"

And the Lord said, "Yes, he has hidden himself among the baggage."

²³They ran and brought him out, and as he stood among the people he was a head taller than any of the others. ²⁴Samuel said to all the people, "Do you see the man the Lord has chosen? There is no one like him among all the people."

Then the people shouted, "Long live the king!"

²⁵Samuel explained to the people the regulations of the kingship. He wrote them down on a scroll and deposited it before the Lord. Then Samuel dismissed the people, each to his own home.

²⁶Saul also went to his home in Gibeah, accompanied by valiant men whose hearts God had touched. ²⁷But some troublemakers said, "How can this fellow save us?" They despised him and brought him no gifts. But Saul kept silent.

11 Nahash the Ammonite went up and besieged Jabesh Gilead. And all the men of Jabesh said to him, "Make a treaty with us, and we will be subject to you."

²But Nahash the Ammonite replied, "I will make a treaty with you only on the condition that I gouge out the right eye of every one of you and so bring disgrace on all Israel."

³The elders of Jabesh said to him, "Give us seven days so we can send messengers throughout Israel; if no one comes to rescue us, we will surrender to you."

⁴When the messengers came to Gibeah of Saul and reported these terms to the people, they all wept aloud. ⁵Just then Saul was returning from the fields, behind his oxen, and he asked, "What is wrong with the people? Why are they weeping?" Then they repeated to him what the men of Jabesh had said.

⁶When Saul heard their words, the Spirit of God came upon him in power, and he burned with anger. ⁷He took a pair of oxen, cut them into pieces, and sent the pieces by messengers throughout Israel, proclaiming, "This is what will

be done to the oxen of anyone who does not follow Saul and Samuel." Then the terror of the LORD fell on the people, and they turned out as one man. ⁸When Saul mustered them at Bezek, the men of Israel numbered three hundred thousand and the men of Judah thirty thousand.

⁹They told the messengers who had come, "Say to the men of Jabesh Gilead, 'By the time the sun is hot tomorrow, you will be delivered.'" When the messengers went and reported this to the men of Jabesh, they were elated. ¹⁰They said to the Ammonites, "Tomorrow we will surrender to you, and you can do to us whatever seems good to you."

¹¹The next day Saul separated his men into three divisions; during the last watch of the night they broke into the camp of the Ammonites and slaughtered them until the heat of the day. Those who survived were scattered, so that no two of them were left together.

¹²The people then said to Samuel, "Who was it that asked, 'Shall Saul reign over us?' Bring these men to us and we will put them to death."

¹³But Saul said, "No one shall be put to death today, for this day the LORD has rescued Israel."

¹⁴Then Samuel said to the people, "Come, let us go to Gilgal and there reaffirm the kingship." ¹⁵So all the people went to Gilgal and confirmed Saul as king in the presence of the LORD. There they sacrificed fellowship offerings^e before the LORD, and Saul and all the Israelites held a great celebration.

12 Samuel said to all Israel, "I have listened to everything you said to me and have set a king over you. ²Now you have a king as your leader. As for me, I am old and gray, and my sons are here with you. I have been your leader from my youth until this day. ³Here I stand. Testify against me in the presence of the LORD and his anointed. Whose ox have I taken? Whose donkey have I taken? Whom have I cheated? Whom have I oppressed? From whose hand have I accepted a bribe to make me shut my eyes? If I have done any of these, I will make it right."

⁴"You have not cheated or oppressed us," they replied. "You have not taken anything from anyone's hand."

⁵Samuel said to them, "The LORD is witness against you, and also his anointed is witness this day, that you have not found anything in my hand."

"He is witness," they said.

⁶Then Samuel said to the people, "It is the LORD who appointed Moses and Aaron and brought your forefathers up out of Egypt. ⁷Now then, stand here, because I am going to confront you with evidence before the LORD as to all the righteous acts performed by the LORD for you and your fathers.

⁸"After Jacob entered Egypt, they cried to the LORD for help, and the LORD sent Moses and Aaron, who brought your forefathers out of Egypt and settled them in this place.

⁹"But they forgot the LORD their God; so he sold them into the hand of Sisera, the commander of the army of Hazor, and into the hands of the Philistines and the king of Moab, who fought against them. ¹⁰They cried out to the LORD and said, 'We have sinned; we have forsaken the LORD and served the Baals and the Ashtoreths. But now deliver us from the hands of our enemies, and we will serve you.' ¹¹Then the LORD sent Jerub-Baal,^f Barak,^g Jephthah and Samuel,^h and he delivered you from the hands of your enemies on every side, so that you lived securely.

¹²"But when you saw that Nahash king of the Ammonites was moving against you, you said to me, 'No, we want a king to rule over us'—even though the LORD your God was your king. ¹³Now here is the king you have chosen, the one you asked for; see, the LORD has set a king over you. ¹⁴If you fear the LORD and serve and obey him and do not rebel against his commands, and if both you and the king who reigns over you follow the LORD your God—good! ¹⁵But if you do not obey the LORD, and if you rebel against his commands, his hand will be against you, as it was against your fathers.

¹⁶"Now then, stand still and see this great thing the LORD is about to do before your eyes! ¹⁷Is it not wheat harvest now? I will call upon the LORD to send thunder and rain. And you will realize what an evil thing you did in the eyes of the LORD when you asked for a king."

¹⁸Then Samuel called upon the LORD, and that same day the LORD sent thunder and rain. So all the people stood in awe of the LORD and of Samuel.

¹⁹The people all said to Samuel, "Pray to the LORD your God for your servants so that we will

---

^e15 Traditionally *peace offerings*   ^f11 Also called *Gideon*
^g11 Some Septuagint manuscripts and Syriac; Hebrew *Bedan*
^h11 Hebrew; some Septuagint manuscripts and Syriac *Samson*

not die, for we have added to all our other sins the evil of asking for a king."

20"Do not be afraid," Samuel replied. "You have done all this evil; yet do not turn away from the LORD, but serve the LORD with all your heart. 21Do not turn away after useless idols. They can do you no good, nor can they rescue you, because they are useless. 22For the sake of his great name the LORD will not reject his people, because the LORD was pleased to make you his own. 23As for me, far be it from me that I should sin against the LORD by failing to pray for you. And I will teach you the way that is good and right. 24But be sure to fear the LORD and serve him faithfully with all your heart; consider what great things he has done for you. 25Yet if you persist in doing evil, both you and your king will be swept away."

13

Saul was ⌊thirty⌋[i] years old when he became king, and he reigned over Israel ⌊forty-⌋[j] two years.

2Saul[k] chose three thousand men from Israel; two thousand were with him at Micmash and in the hill country of Bethel, and a thousand were with Jonathan at Gibeah in Benjamin. The rest of the men he sent back to their homes.

3Jonathan attacked the Philistine outpost at Geba, and the Philistines heard about it. Then Saul had the trumpet blown throughout the land and said, "Let the Hebrews hear!" 4So all Israel heard the news: "Saul has attacked the Philistine outpost, and now Israel has become a stench to the Philistines." And the people were summoned to join Saul at Gilgal.

5The Philistines assembled to fight Israel, with three thousand[l] chariots, six thousand charioteers, and soldiers as numerous as the sand on the seashore. They went up and camped at Micmash, east of Beth Aven. 6When the men of Israel saw that their situation was critical and that their army was hard pressed, they hid in caves and thickets, among the rocks, and in pits and cisterns. 7Some Hebrews even crossed the Jordan to the land of Gad and Gilead.

Saul remained at Gilgal, and all the troops with him were quaking with fear. 8He waited seven days, the time set by Samuel; but Samuel did not come to Gilgal, and Saul's men began to scatter. 9So he said, "Bring me the burnt offering and the fellowship offerings.[m]" And Saul offered up the burnt offering. 10Just as he finished making the

offering, Samuel arrived, and Saul went out to greet him.

11"What have you done?" asked Samuel.

Saul replied, "When I saw that the men were scattering, and that you did not come at the set time, and that the Philistines were assembling at Micmash, 12I thought, 'Now the Philistines will come down against me at Gilgal, and I have not sought the LORD's favor.' So I felt compelled to offer the burnt offering."

13"You acted foolishly," Samuel said. "You have not kept the command the LORD your God gave you; if you had, he would have established your kingdom over Israel for all time. 14But now your kingdom will not endure; the LORD has sought out a man after his own heart and appointed him leader of his people, because you have not kept the LORD's command."

15Then Samuel left Gilgal[n] and went up to Gibeah in Benjamin, and Saul counted the men who were with him. They numbered about six hundred.

16Saul and his son Jonathan and the men with them were staying in Gibeah[o] in Benjamin, while the Philistines camped at Micmash. 17Raiding parties went out from the Philistine camp in three detachments. One turned toward Ophrah in the vicinity of Shual, 18another toward Beth Horon, and the third toward the borderland overlooking the Valley of Zeboim facing the desert.

19Not a blacksmith could be found in the whole land of Israel, because the Philistines had said, "Otherwise the Hebrews will make swords or spears!" 20So all Israel went down to the Philistines to have their plowshares, mattocks, axes and sickles[p] sharpened. 21The price was two thirds of a shekel[q] for sharpening plowshares and mattocks, and a third of a shekel[r] for sharpening forks and axes and for repointing goads.

22So on the day of the battle not a soldier with Saul and Jonathan had a sword or spear in his hand; only Saul and his son Jonathan had them.

23Now a detachment of Philistines had gone

---

[i]1 A few late manuscripts of the Septuagint; Hebrew does not have thirty.   [j]1 See the round number in Acts 13:21; Hebrew does not have forty-.   [k]1,2 Or *and when he had reigned over Israel two years,* 2he   [l]5 Some Septuagint manuscripts and Syriac; Hebrew *thirty thousand*   [m]9 Traditionally *peace offerings*   [n]15 Hebrew; Septuagint *Gilgal and went his way; the rest of the people went after Saul to meet the army, and they went out of Gilgal*   [o]16 Two Hebrew manuscripts; most Hebrew manuscripts *Geba,* a variant of *Gibeah*   [p]20 Septuagint; Hebrew *plowshares*   [q]21 Hebrew *pim;* that is, about 1/4 ounce (about 8 grams)   [r]21 That is, about 1/8 ounce (about 4 grams)

14

out to the pass at Micmash. ¹One day Jonathan son of Saul said to the young man bearing his armor, "Come, let's go over to the Philistine outpost on the other side." But he did not tell his father.

²Saul was staying on the outskirts of Gibeah under a pomegranate tree in Migron. With him were about six hundred men, ³among whom was Ahijah, who was wearing an ephod. He was a son of Ichabod's brother Ahitub son of Phinehas, the son of Eli, the LORD's priest in Shiloh. No one was aware that Jonathan had left.

⁴On each side of the pass that Jonathan intended to cross to reach the Philistine outpost was a cliff; one was called Bozez, and the other Seneh. ⁵One cliff stood to the north toward Micmash, the other to the south toward Geba.

⁶Jonathan said to his young armor-bearer, "Come, let's go over to the outpost of those uncircumcised fellows. Perhaps the LORD will act in our behalf. Nothing can hinder the LORD from saving, whether by many or by few."

⁷"Do all that you have in mind," his armor-bearer said. "Go ahead; I am with you heart and soul."

⁸Jonathan said, "Come, then; we will cross over toward the men and let them see us. ⁹If they say to us, 'Wait there until we come to you,' we will stay where we are and not go up to them. ¹⁰But if they say, 'Come up to us,' we will climb up, because that will be our sign that the LORD has given them into our hands."

¹¹So both of them showed themselves to the Philistine outpost. "Look!" said the Philistines. "The Hebrews are crawling out of the holes they were hiding in." ¹²The men of the outpost shouted to Jonathan and his armor-bearer, "Come up to us and we'll teach you a lesson."

So Jonathan said to his armor-bearer, "Climb up after me; the LORD has given them into the hand of Israel."

¹³Jonathan climbed up, using his hands and feet, with his armor-bearer right behind him. The Philistines fell before Jonathan, and his armor-bearer followed and killed behind him. ¹⁴In that first attack Jonathan and his armor-bearer killed some twenty men in an area of about half an acre.ˢ

¹⁵Then panic struck the whole army—those in the camp and field, and those in the outposts and raiding parties—and the ground shook. It was a panic sent by God.ᵗ

¹⁶Saul's lookouts at Gibeah in Benjamin saw the army melting away in all directions. ¹⁷Then Saul said to the men who were with him, "Muster the forces and see who has left us." When they did, it was Jonathan and his armor-bearer who were not there.

¹⁸Saul said to Ahijah, "Bring the ark of God." (At that time it was with the Israelites.)ᵘ ¹⁹While Saul was talking to the priest, the tumult in the Philistine camp increased more and more. So Saul said to the priest, "Withdraw your hand."

²⁰Then Saul and all his men assembled and went to the battle. They found the Philistines in total confusion, striking each other with their swords. ²¹Those Hebrews who had previously been with the Philistines and had gone up with them to their camp went over to the Israelites who were with Saul and Jonathan. ²²When all the Israelites who had hidden in the hill country of Ephraim heard that the Philistines were on the run, they joined the battle in hot pursuit. ²³So the LORD rescued Israel that day, and the battle moved on beyond Beth Aven.

²⁴Now the men of Israel were in distress that day, because Saul had bound the people under an oath, saying, "Cursed be any man who eats food before evening comes, before I have avenged myself on my enemies!" So none of the troops tasted food.

²⁵The entire armyᵛ entered the woods, and there was honey on the ground. ²⁶When they went into the woods, they saw the honey oozing out, yet no one put his hand to his mouth, because they feared the oath. ²⁷But Jonathan had not heard that his father had bound the people with the oath, so he reached out the end of the staff that was in his hand and dipped it into the honeycomb. He raised his hand to his mouth, and his eyes brightened.ʷ ²⁸Then one of the soldiers told him, "Your father bound the army under a strict oath, saying, 'Cursed be any man who eats food today!' That is why the men are faint."

²⁹Jonathan said, "My father has made trouble for the country. See how my eyes brightenedˣ when I tasted a little of this honey. ³⁰How much better it would have been if the men had eaten today some of the plunder they took from their

---

ˢ14 Hebrew *half a yoke*; a "yoke" was the land plowed by a yoke of oxen in one day.   ᵗ15 Or *a terrible panic*   ᵘ18 Hebrew; Septuagint *"Bring the ephod." (At that time he wore the ephod before the Israelites.)*   ᵛ25 Or *Now all the people of the land*   ʷ27 Or *his strength was renewed*   ˣ29 Or *my strength was renewed* enemies. Would not the slaughter of the Philistines have been even greater?"

[31]That day, after the Israelites had struck down the Philistines from Micmash to Aijalon, they were exhausted. [32]They pounced on the plunder and, taking sheep, cattle and calves, they butchered them on the ground and ate them, together with the blood. [33]Then someone said to Saul, "Look, the men are sinning against the LORD by eating meat that has blood in it."

"You have broken faith," he said. "Roll a large stone over here at once." [34]Then he said, "Go out among the men and tell them, 'Each of you bring me your cattle and sheep, and slaughter them here and eat them. Do not sin against the LORD by eating meat with blood still in it.' "

So everyone brought his ox that night and slaughtered it there. [35]Then Saul built an altar to the LORD; it was the first time he had done this.

[36]Saul said, "Let us go down after the Philistines by night and plunder them till dawn, and let us not leave one of them alive."

"Do whatever seems best to you," they replied.

But the priest said, "Let us inquire of God here."

[37]So Saul asked God, "Shall I go down after the Philistines? Will you give them into Israel's hand?" But God did not answer him that day.

[38]Saul therefore said, "Come here, all you who are leaders of the army, and let us find out what sin has been committed today. [39]As surely as the LORD who rescues Israel lives, even if it lies with my son Jonathan, he must die." But not one of the men said a word.

[40]Saul then said to all the Israelites, "You stand over there; I and Jonathan my son will stand over here."

"Do what seems best to you," the men replied.

[41]Then Saul prayed to the LORD, the God of Israel, "Give me the right answer."[y] And Jonathan and Saul were taken by lot, and the men

were cleared. [42]Saul said, "Cast the lot between me and Jonathan my son." And Jonathan was taken.

[43]Then Saul said to Jonathan, "Tell me what you have done."

So Jonathan told him, "I merely tasted a little honey with the end of my staff. And now must I die?"

[44]Saul said, "May God deal with me, be it ever so severely, if you do not die, Jonathan."

[45]But the men said to Saul, "Should Jonathan die—he who has brought about this great deliverance in Israel? Never! As surely as the LORD lives, not a hair of his head will fall to the ground, for he did this today with God's help." So the men rescued Jonathan, and he was not put to death.

[46]Then Saul stopped pursuing the Philistines, and they withdrew to their own land.

[47]After Saul had assumed rule over Israel, he fought against their enemies on every side: Moab, the Ammonites, Edom, the kings[z] of Zobah, and the Philistines. Wherever he turned, he inflicted punishment on them.[a] [48]He fought valiantly and defeated the Amalekites, delivering Israel from the hands of those who had plundered them.

[49]Saul's sons were Jonathan, Ishvi and Malki-Shua. The name of his older daughter was Merab, and that of the younger was Michal. [50]His wife's name was Ahinoam daughter of Ahimaaz. The name of the commander of Saul's army was Abner son of Ner, and Ner was Saul's uncle. [51]Saul's father Kish and Abner's father Ner were sons of Abiel.

[52]All the days of Saul there was bitter war with the Philistines, and whenever Saul saw a mighty or brave man, he took him into his service.

[y]41 Hebrew; Septuagint "Why have you not answered your servant today? If the fault is in me or my son Jonathan, respond with Urim, but if the men of Israel are at fault, respond with Thummim."
[z]47 Masoretic Text; Dead Sea Scrolls and Septuagint king
[a]47 Hebrew; Septuagint he was victorious

5 / 1 Samuel 15
Doing Almost All of God's Will

PERHAPS ONE OF the cleverest schemes of the Enemy is to convince us that doing most of God's will is enough, and that by doing it we will receive God's blessings. King Saul fell into such a temptation. Instructed by God to fight and to destroy the Amalekites, he succumbed to the wishes of his fighting men and did only part of God's command.

 Warming Up to God When does pressure from the people around you have a greater influence on your life than God does?

 Read 1 Samuel 15.

15 Samuel said to Saul, "I am the one the LORD sent to anoint you king over his people Israel; so listen now to the message from the LORD. ²This is what the LORD Almighty says: 'I will punish the Amalekites for what they did to Israel when they waylaid them as they came up from Egypt. ³Now go, attack the Amalekites and totally destroy*ᵇ* everything that belongs to them. Do not spare them; put to death men and women, children and infants, cattle and sheep, camels and donkeys.' "

⁴So Saul summoned the men and mustered them at Telaim—two hundred thousand foot soldiers and ten thousand men from Judah. ⁵Saul went to the city of Amalek and set an ambush in the ravine. ⁶Then he said to the Kenites, "Go away, leave the Amalekites so that I do not destroy you along with them; for you showed kindness to all the Israelites when they came up out of Egypt." So the Kenites moved away from the Amalekites.

⁷Then Saul attacked the Amalekites all the way from Havilah to Shur, to the east of Egypt. ⁸He took Agag king of the Amalekites alive, and all his people he totally destroyed with the sword. ⁹But Saul and the army spared Agag and the best of the sheep and cattle, the fat calves*ᶜ* and lambs—everything that was good. These they were unwilling to destroy completely, but everything that was despised and weak they totally destroyed.

¹⁰Then the word of the LORD came to Samuel: ¹¹"I am grieved that I have made Saul king, because he has turned away from me and has not carried out my instructions." Samuel was troubled, and he cried out to the LORD all that night.

¹²Early in the morning Samuel got up and went to meet Saul, but he was told, "Saul has gone to Carmel. There he has set up a monument in his

own honor and has turned and gone on down to Gilgal."

¹³When Samuel reached him, Saul said, "The LORD bless you! I have carried out the LORD's instructions."

¹⁴But Samuel said, "What then is this bleating of sheep in my ears? What is this lowing of cattle that I hear?"

¹⁵Saul answered, "The soldiers brought them from the Amalekites; they spared the best of the sheep and cattle to sacrifice to the LORD your God, but we totally destroyed the rest."

¹⁶"Stop!" Samuel said to Saul. "Let me tell you what the LORD said to me last night."

"Tell me," Saul replied.

¹⁷Samuel said, "Although you were once small in your own eyes, did you not become the head of the tribes of Israel? The LORD anointed you king over Israel. ¹⁸And he sent you on a mission, saying, 'Go and completely destroy those wicked people, the Amalekites; make war on them until you have wiped them out.' ¹⁹Why did you not obey the LORD? Why did you pounce on the plunder and do evil in the eyes of the LORD?"

²⁰"But I did obey the LORD," Saul said. "I went on the mission the LORD assigned me. I completely destroyed the Amalekites and brought back Agag their king. ²¹The soldiers took sheep and cattle from the plunder, the best of what was devoted to God, in order to sacrifice them to the LORD your God at Gilgal."

²²But Samuel replied:

"Does the LORD delight in burnt offerings and
       sacrifices

ᵇ3 The Hebrew term refers to the irrevocable giving over of things or persons to the LORD, often by totally destroying them; also in verses 8, 9, 15, 18, 20 and 21.   *ᶜ9* Or *the grown bulls*; the meaning of the Hebrew for this phrase is uncertain.

as much as in obeying the voice of the
     LORD?
To obey is better than sacrifice,
    and to heed is better than the fat of rams.
²³For rebellion is like the sin of divination,
    and arrogance like the evil of idolatry.
Because you have rejected the word of the
     LORD,
    he has rejected you as king."

²⁴Then Saul said to Samuel, "I have sinned. I violated the LORD's command and your instructions. I was afraid of the people and so I gave in to them. ²⁵Now I beg you, forgive my sin and come back with me, so that I may worship the LORD."

²⁶But Samuel said to him, "I will not go back with you. You have rejected the word of the LORD, and the LORD has rejected you as king over Israel!"

²⁷As Samuel turned to leave, Saul caught hold of the hem of his robe, and it tore. ²⁸Samuel said to him, "The LORD has torn the kingdom of Israel from you today and has given it to one of your neighbors—to one better than you. ²⁹He who is the Glory of Israel does not lie or change his mind; for he is not a man, that he should change his mind."

³⁰Saul replied, "I have sinned. But please honor me before the elders of my people and before Israel; come back with me, so that I may worship the LORD your God." ³¹So Samuel went back with Saul, and Saul worshiped the LORD.

³²Then Samuel said, "Bring me Agag king of the Amalekites."

Agag came to him confidently,[d] thinking, "Surely the bitterness of death is past."

³³But Samuel said,

"As your sword has made women childless,
    so will your mother be childless among
      women."

And Samuel put Agag to death before the LORD at Gilgal.

³⁴Then Samuel left for Ramah, but Saul went up to his home in Gibeah of Saul. ³⁵Until the day Samuel died, he did not go to see Saul again, though Samuel mourned for him. And the LORD was grieved that he had made Saul king over Israel.

d32 Or him trembling, yet

Discovering the Word   **1.** What message from the Lord does Samuel deliver to Saul, and why (vv. 1–3)? **2.** How does Saul begin to obey God but later change his mind (vv. 4–9)? **3.** What factors contributed to Saul's unwillingness to carry out God's explicit command (vv. 12, 24, 30)? **4.** Why do you think God equates disobedience with idolatry (vv. 22–23)? **5.** Although Saul finally confesses his sin in verse 24, what do his actions suggest about the sincerity of his repentance (vv. 24–30)?

Applying the Word   **1.** How does the description of Saul's disobedience (vv. 22–23) differ from the way we view our sin when we do not do all of God's will? **2.** What "burnt offerings" and "sacrifices" do we sometimes offer to compensate for our lack of obedience? **3.** Think of one area where you have been content to do almost all of God's will. What steps should you take to complete your obedience to God?

 Responding in Prayer   Ask God for courage to give him your obedience.

---

6 / 1 Samuel 16
The Lord Looks at the Heart

IN THE BOOK *Selling of the President*, author Joe McGinniss emphasized that in politics, image is everything. A candidate must exude confidence, charm and good looks. Never mind the real issues of the campaign. A broad smile, a warm handshake and the ability to look good on camera are much more important for selling the political product to the ultimate consumer—the registered voter. Israel's first king, Saul, was this sort of candidate—tall, handsome and impressive. Unfortunately, he was also foolish and disobedient. As Israel's second king is chosen, the Lord rejects worldly standards of leadership and selects David, a man after his own heart.

Warming Up to God How does a person's appearance affect your initial opinion of him or her?

Read 1 Samuel 16.

16 The LORD said to Samuel, "How long will you mourn for Saul, since I have rejected him as king over Israel? Fill your horn with oil and be on your way; I am sending you to Jesse of Bethlehem. I have chosen one of his sons to be king."

²But Samuel said, "How can I go? Saul will hear about it and kill me."

The LORD said, "Take a heifer with you and say, 'I have come to sacrifice to the LORD.' ³Invite Jesse to the sacrifice, and I will show you what to do. You are to anoint for me the one I indicate."

⁴Samuel did what the LORD said. When he arrived at Bethlehem, the elders of the town trembled when they met him. They asked, "Do you come in peace?"

⁵Samuel replied, "Yes, in peace; I have come to sacrifice to the LORD. Consecrate yourselves and come to the sacrifice with me." Then he consecrated Jesse and his sons and invited them to the sacrifice.

⁶When they arrived, Samuel saw Eliab and thought, "Surely the LORD's anointed stands here before the LORD."

⁷But the LORD said to Samuel, "Do not consider his appearance or his height, for I have rejected him. The LORD does not look at the things man looks at. Man looks at the outward appearance, but the LORD looks at the heart."

⁸Then Jesse called Abinadab and had him pass in front of Samuel. But Samuel said, "The LORD has not chosen this one either." ⁹Jesse then had Shammah pass by, but Samuel said, "Nor has the LORD chosen this one." ¹⁰Jesse had seven of his sons pass before Samuel, but Samuel said to him, "The LORD has not chosen these." ¹¹So he asked Jesse, "Are these all the sons you have?"

"There is still the youngest," Jesse answered, "but he is tending the sheep."

Samuel said, "Send for him; we will not sit down*ᶜ* until he arrives."

¹²So he sent and had him brought in. He was ruddy, with a fine appearance and handsome features.

Then the LORD said, "Rise and anoint him; he is the one."

¹³So Samuel took the horn of oil and anointed him in the presence of his brothers, and from that day on the Spirit of the LORD came upon David in power. Samuel then went to Ramah.

¹⁴Now the Spirit of the LORD had departed from Saul, and an evilᶠ spirit from the LORD tormented him.

¹⁵Saul's attendants said to him, "See, an evil spirit from God is tormenting you. ¹⁶Let our lord command his servants here to search for someone who can play the harp. He will play when the evil spirit from God comes upon you, and you will feel better."

¹⁷So Saul said to his attendants, "Find someone who plays well and bring him to me."

¹⁸One of the servants answered, "I have seen a son of Jesse of Bethlehem who knows how to play the harp. He is a brave man and a warrior. He speaks well and is a fine-looking man. And the LORD is with him."

¹⁹Then Saul sent messengers to Jesse and said, "Send me your son David, who is with the sheep." ²⁰So Jesse took a donkey loaded with bread, a skin of wine and a young goat and sent them with his son David to Saul.

²¹David came to Saul and entered his service. Saul liked him very much, and David became one of his armor-bearers. ²²Then Saul sent word to Jesse, saying, "Allow David to remain in my service, for I am pleased with him."

²³Whenever the spirit from God came upon Saul, David would take his harp and play. Then relief would come to Saul; he would feel better, and the evil spirit would leave him.

ᶜ11 Some Septuagint manuscripts; Hebrew not gather around ᶠ14 Or injurious; also in verses 15, 16 and 23

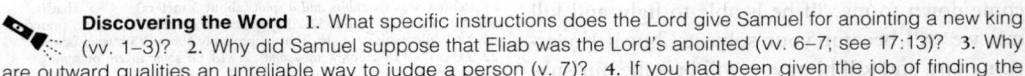

Discovering the Word 1. What specific instructions does the Lord give Samuel for anointing a new king (vv. 1–3)? 2. Why did Samuel suppose that Eliab was the Lord's anointed (vv. 6–7; see 17:13)? 3. Why are outward qualities an unreliable way to judge a person (v. 7)? 4. If you had been given the job of finding the next king of Israel, why would David have been an unlikely choice?   5. In what sense was he also a good choice (vv. 14–23)?

 Applying the Word   1. The Lord tells Samuel, "Man looks at the outward appearance" (v. 7). What sorts of "outward" things do we tend to look at in people?   2. How does our culture reinforce our emphasis on appearance?   3. When the Lord looks at our hearts, what specific qualities do you think he values most? Explain.

Responding in Prayer   Take time to pray, asking the Lord to develop these qualities within you.

7 / *1 Samuel 17*
The Battle Is the Lord's

ONE OF THE myths of our culture is "If you set your mind to it, you can do anything." The heroes of that myth are self-made men and women, those who climb from obscurity to fame through sheer willpower and determination. The message is clear: victory goes to the strong, and the spoils of victory to those who are powerful. The Bible presents a very different message: " 'Not by might nor by power, but by my Spirit,' says the LORD Almighty" (Zec 4:6). In this chapter David confronts not only Goliath but also our myths of human adequacy.

 Warming Up to God   When you are faced with a challenge that seems beyond your abilities, how do you tend to respond?

 Read 1 Samuel 17.

17 Now the Philistines gathered their forces for war and assembled at Socoh in Judah. They pitched camp at at Ephes Dammim, between Socoh and Azekah. ²Saul and the Israelites assembled and camped in the Valley of Elah and drew up their battle line to meet the Philistines. ³The Philistines occupied one hill and the Israelites another, with the valley between them.

⁴A champion named Goliath, who was from Gath, came out of the Philistine camp. He was over nine feet*ᵍ* tall. ⁵He had a bronze helmet on his head and wore a coat of scale armor of bronze weighing five thousand shekels*ʰ*; ⁶on his legs he wore bronze greaves, and a bronze javelin was slung on his back. ⁷His spear shaft was like a weaver's rod, and its iron point weighed six hundred shekels.*ⁱ* His shield bearer went ahead of him.

⁸Goliath stood and shouted to the ranks of Israel, "Why do you come out and line up for battle? Am I not a Philistine, and are you not the servants of Saul? Choose a man and have him come down to me. ⁹If he is able to fight and kill me, we will become your subjects; but if I overcome him and kill him, you will become our sub-

jects and serve us." ¹⁰Then the Philistine said, "This day I defy the ranks of Israel! Give me a man and let us fight each other." ¹¹On hearing the Philistine's words, Saul and all the Israelites were dismayed and terrified.

¹²Now David was the son of an Ephrathite named Jesse, who was from Bethlehem in Judah. Jesse had eight sons, and in Saul's time he was old and well advanced in years. ¹³Jesse's three oldest sons had followed Saul to the war: The firstborn was Eliab; the second, Abinadab; and the third, Shammah. ¹⁴David was the youngest. The three oldest followed Saul, ¹⁵but David went back and forth from Saul to tend his father's sheep at Bethlehem.

¹⁶For forty days the Philistine came forward every morning and evening and took his stand.

¹⁷Now Jesse said to his son David, "Take this ephah*ʲ* of roasted grain and these ten loaves of bread for your brothers and hurry to their camp. ¹⁸Take along these ten cheeses to the commander of their unit.*ᵏ* See how your brothers are and bring back some assurance*ˡ* from them. ¹⁹They

ᵍ4 Hebrew *was six cubits and a span* (about 3 meters)   *ʰ5* That is, about 125 pounds (about 57 kilograms)   *ⁱ7* That is, about 15 pounds (about 7 kilograms)   *ʲ17* That is, probably about 3/5 bushel (about 22 liters)   *ᵏ18* Hebrew *thousand*   *ˡ18* Or *some token; or some pledge of spoils* are with Saul and all the men of Israel in the Valley of Elah, fighting against the Philistines."

²⁰Early in the morning David left the flock with a shepherd, loaded up and set out, as Jesse had directed. He reached the camp as the army was going out to its battle positions, shouting the war cry. ²¹Israel and the Philistines were drawing up their lines facing each other. ²²David left his things with the keeper of supplies, ran to the battle lines and greeted his brothers. ²³As he was talking with them, Goliath, the Philistine champion from Gath, stepped out from his lines and shouted his usual defiance, and David heard it. ²⁴When the Israelites saw the man, they all ran from him in great fear.

²⁵Now the Israelites had been saying, "Do you see how this man keeps coming out? He comes out to defy Israel. The king will give great wealth to the man who kills him. He will also give him his daughter in marriage and will exempt his father's family from taxes in Israel."

²⁶David asked the men standing near him, "What will be done for the man who kills this Philistine and removes this disgrace from Israel? Who is this uncircumcised Philistine that he should defy the armies of the living God?"

²⁷They repeated to him what they had been saying and told him, "This is what will be done for the man who kills him."

²⁸When Eliab, David's oldest brother, heard him speaking with the men, he burned with anger at him and asked, "Why have you come down here? And with whom did you leave those few sheep in the desert? I know how conceited you are and how wicked your heart is; you came down only to watch the battle."

²⁹"Now what have I done?" said David. "Can't I even speak?" ³⁰He then turned away to someone else and brought up the same matter, and the men answered him as before. ³¹What David said was overheard and reported to Saul, and Saul sent for him.

³²David said to Saul, "Let no one lose heart on account of this Philistine; your servant will go and fight him."

³³Saul replied, "You are not able to go out against this Philistine and fight him; you are only a boy, and he has been a fighting man from his youth."

³⁴But David said to Saul, "Your servant has been keeping his father's sheep. When a lion or a bear came and carried off a sheep from the flock,

³⁵I went after it, struck it and rescued the sheep from its mouth. When it turned on me, I seized it by its hair, struck it and killed it. ³⁶Your servant has killed both the lion and the bear; this uncircumcised Philistine will be like one of them, because he has defied the armies of the living God. ³⁷The LORD who delivered me from the paw of the lion and the paw of the bear will deliver me from the hand of this Philistine."

Saul said to David, "Go, and the LORD be with you."

³⁸Then Saul dressed David in his own tunic. He put a coat of armor on him and a bronze helmet on his head. ³⁹David fastened on his sword over the tunic and tried walking around, because he was not used to them.

"I cannot go in these," he said to Saul, "because I am not used to them." So he took them off. ⁴⁰Then he took his staff in his hand, chose five smooth stones from the stream, put them in the pouch of his shepherd's bag and, with his sling in his hand, approached the Philistine.

⁴¹Meanwhile, the Philistine, with his shield bearer in front of him, kept coming closer to David. ⁴²He looked David over and saw that he was only a boy, ruddy and handsome, and he despised him. ⁴³He said to David, "Am I a dog, that you come at me with sticks?" And the Philistine cursed David by his gods. ⁴⁴"Come here," he said, "and I'll give your flesh to the birds of the air and the beasts of the field!"

⁴⁵David said to the Philistine, "You come against me with sword and spear and javelin, but I come against you in the name of the LORD Almighty, the God of the armies of Israel, whom you have defied. ⁴⁶This day the LORD will hand you over to me, and I'll strike you down and cut off your head. Today I will give the carcasses of the Philistine army to the birds of the air and the beasts of the earth, and the whole world will know that there is a God in Israel. ⁴⁷All those gathered here will know that it is not by sword or spear that the LORD saves; for the battle is the LORD's, and he will give all of you into our hands."

⁴⁸As the Philistine moved closer to attack him, David ran quickly toward the battle line to meet him. ⁴⁹Reaching into his bag and taking out a stone, he slung it and struck the Philistine on the forehead. The stone sank into his forehead, and he fell facedown on the ground.

⁵⁰So David triumphed over the Philistine with a

sling and a stone; without a sword in his hand he struck down the Philistine and killed him.

⁵¹David ran and stood over him. He took hold of the Philistine's sword and drew it from the scabbard. After he killed him, he cut off his head with the sword.

When the Philistines saw that their hero was dead, they turned and ran. ⁵²Then the men of Israel and Judah surged forward with a shout and pursued the Philistines to the entrance of Gath ͫ and to the gates of Ekron. Their dead were strewn along the Shaaraim road to Gath and Ekron. ⁵³When the Israelites returned from chasing the Philistines, they plundered their camp. ⁵⁴David took the Philistine's head and brought it to Jerusalem, and he put the Philistine's weapons in his own tent.

⁵⁵As Saul watched David going out to meet the Philistine, he said to Abner, commander of the army, "Abner, whose son is that young man?"

Abner replied, "As surely as you live, O king, I don't know."

⁵⁶The king said, "Find out whose son this young man is."

⁵⁷As soon as David returned from killing the Philistine, Abner took him and brought him before Saul, with David still holding the Philistine's head.

⁵⁸"Whose son are you, young man?" Saul asked him.

David said, "I am the son of your servant Jesse of Bethlehem."

ͫ 52 Some Septuagint manuscripts; Hebrew *a valley*

Discovering the Word 1. Humanly speaking, why were the Israelites justly terrified of Goliath (vv. 1–11)? 2. As David reaches the army camp, what does he learn about their situation (vv. 12–27)? 3. Why do you think David's brother is so harsh with him (vv. 28–30)? 4. From a human standpoint, why was David an unlikely choice as the champion of Israel (vv. 15, 33, 38–40)? 5. What impresses you about the conversation and battle between David and Goliath (vv. 41–49)?

Applying the Word 1. Normally, we select people who are humanly qualified to do a job. Likewise, we normally take on responsibilities for which we feel qualified. Does faith remove the need for human qualifications? Why or why not? 2. When is it proper to trust God to overcome our deficiencies? 3. What "Goliaths" are you currently facing—either at work or home or in your personal life?

Responding in Prayer Praise God for the past spiritual victories he's given you. Let those victories be a source of encouragement.

---

8 / *1 Samuel 18*
Bitterness

ONE OF THE darkest times in my life was when I allowed bitterness to root and grow in my heart. I was hurt. I refused to forgive or to risk being hurt again. My whole person was becoming engulfed by this monstrous plant that was growing inside of me. Others were defiled by it. If I had continued to disobey God in this way, I would have been destroyed.

Saul, ancient Israel's first king, knew those feelings. They were directed toward David, a young man from the hill country. David had changed the course of a forty-day stand-off with the Philistine army by singlehandedly killing their giant leader. Suddenly, all the people were praising this boy from the sheep pastures. Rumor had it that David would someday be king.

Warming Up to God How do you usually respond when you are afraid that someone or something important to you will be taken away?

Read 1 Samuel 18.

18

After David had finished talking with Saul, Jonathan became one in spirit with David, and he loved him as himself. [2]From that day Saul kept David with him and did not let him return to his father's house. [3]And Jonathan made a covenant with David because he loved him as himself. [4]Jonathan took off the robe he was wearing and gave it to David, along with his tunic, and even his sword, his bow and his belt.

[5]Whatever Saul sent him to do, David did it so successfully[n] that Saul gave him a high rank in the army. This pleased all the people, and Saul's officers as well.

[6]When the men were returning home after David had killed the Philistine, the women came out from all the towns of Israel to meet King Saul with singing and dancing, with joyful songs and with tambourines and lutes. [7]As they danced, they sang:

"Saul has slain his thousands,
    and David his tens of thousands."

[8]Saul was very angry; this refrain galled him. "They have credited David with tens of thousands," he thought, "but me with only thousands. What more can he get but the kingdom?" [9]And from that time on Saul kept a jealous eye on David.

[10]The next day an evil[o] spirit from God came forcefully upon Saul. He was prophesying in his house, while David was playing the harp, as he usually did. Saul had a spear in his hand [11]and he hurled it, saying to himself, "I'll pin David to the wall." But David eluded him twice.

[12]Saul was afraid of David, because the LORD was with David but had left Saul. [13]So he sent David away from him and gave him command over a thousand men, and David led the troops in their campaigns. [14]In everything he did he had great success,[p] because the LORD was with him. [15]When Saul saw how successful[q] he was, he was afraid of him. [16]But all Israel and Judah loved David, because he led them in their campaigns.

[17]Saul said to David, "Here is my older daughter Merab. I will give her to you in marriage; only serve me bravely and fight the battles of the LORD." For Saul said to himself, "I will not raise a hand against him. Let the Philistines do that!"

[18]But David said to Saul, "Who am I, and what is my family or my father's clan in Israel, that I should become the king's son-in-law?" [19]So[r] when the time came for Merab, Saul's daughter, to be given to David, she was given in marriage to Adriel of Meholah.

[20]Now Saul's daughter Michal was in love with David, and when they told Saul about it, he was pleased. [21]"I will give her to him," he thought, "so that she may be a snare to him and so that the hand of the Philistines may be against him." So Saul said to David, "Now you have a second opportunity to become my son-in-law."

[22]Then Saul ordered his attendants: "Speak to David privately and say, 'Look, the king is pleased with you, and his attendants all like you; now become his son-in-law.'"

[23]They repeated these words to David. But David said, "Do you think it is a small matter to become the king's son-in-law? I'm only a poor man and little known."

[24]When Saul's servants told him what David had said, [25]Saul replied, "Say to David, 'The king wants no other price for the bride than a hundred Philistine foreskins, to take revenge on his enemies.'" Saul's plan was to have David fall by the hands of the Philistines.

[26]When the attendants told David these things, he was pleased to become the king's son-in-law. So before the allotted time elapsed, [27]David and his men went out and killed two hundred Philistines. He brought their foreskins and presented the full number to the king so that he might become the king's son-in-law. Then Saul gave him his daughter Michal in marriage.

[28]When Saul realized that the LORD was with David and that his daughter Michal loved David, [29]Saul became still more afraid of him, and he remained his enemy the rest of his days.

[30]The Philistine commanders continued to go out to battle, and as often as they did, David met with more success[s] than the rest of Saul's officers, and his name became well known.

---

n5 Or wisely   o10 Or injurious   p14 Or he was very wise
q15 Or wise   r19 Or However,   s30 Or David acted more wisely

---

Discovering the Word   1. What causes can you find for Saul's hostile feelings?   2. Often, if not always, fear is behind anger. What specifically was Saul afraid of (vv. 8, 12, 15, 28)?   3. How was Saul affected by the bitterness that he allowed to grow within himself?   4. What do you think is the difference between anger and bitterness? **5.** What evidence is there that the problem became not only an emotional battle but a spiritual battle (vv. 10, 12, 28)? **6.** What warnings do we get from this passage about the destructive nature of bitterness?

 Applying the Word **1.** Think about a time when you were bitter. What were you afraid of? **2.** How was your relationship with others affected? **3.** How was your relationship with God affected?

 Responding in Prayer Ask God to help you recognize the fears and/or anger in you that could lead to bitterness. Ask him to make you sensitive to those fears in others.

1 Samuel 19

19 Saul told his son Jonathan and all the attendants to kill David. But Jonathan was very fond of David ²and warned him, "My father Saul is looking for a chance to kill you. Be on your guard tomorrow morning; go into hiding and stay there. ³I will go out and stand with my father in the field where you are. I'll speak to him about you and will tell you what I find out."

⁴Jonathan spoke well of David to Saul his father and said to him, "Let not the king do wrong to his servant David; he has not wronged you, and what he has done has benefited you greatly. ⁵He took his life in his hands when he killed the Philistine. The LORD won a great victory for all Israel, and you saw it and were glad. Why then would you do wrong to an innocent man like David by killing him for no reason?"

⁶Saul listened to Jonathan and took this oath: "As surely as the LORD lives, David will not be put to death."

⁷So Jonathan called David and told him the whole conversation. He brought him to Saul, and David was with Saul as before.

⁸Once more war broke out, and David went out and fought the Philistines. He struck them with such force that they fled before him.

⁹But an evil¹ spirit from the LORD came upon Saul as he was sitting in his house with his spear in his hand. While David was playing the harp, ¹⁰Saul tried to pin him to the wall with his spear, but David eluded him as Saul drove the spear into the wall. That night David made good his escape.

¹¹Saul sent men to David's house to watch it and to kill him in the morning. But Michal, David's wife, warned him, "If you don't run for your life tonight, tomorrow you'll be killed." ¹²So Michal let David down through a window, and he fled and escaped. ¹³Then Michal took an idol¹¹

and laid it on the bed, covering it with a garment and putting some goats' hair at the head.

¹⁴When Saul sent the men to capture David, Michal said, "He is ill."

¹⁵Then Saul sent the men back to see David and told them, "Bring him up to me in his bed so that I may kill him." ¹⁶But when the men entered, there was the idol in the bed, and at the head was some goats' hair.

¹⁷Saul said to Michal, "Why did you deceive me like this and send my enemy away so that he escaped?"

Michal told him, "He said to me, 'Let me get away. Why should I kill you?' "

¹⁸When David had fled and made his escape, he went to Samuel at Ramah and told him all that Saul had done to him. Then he and Samuel went to Naioth and stayed there. ¹⁹Word came to Saul: "David is in Naioth at Ramah"; ²⁰so he sent men to capture him. But when they saw a group of prophets prophesying, with Samuel standing there as their leader, the Spirit of God came upon Saul's men and they also prophesied. ²¹Saul was told about it, and he sent more men, and they prophesied too. Saul sent men a third time, and they also prophesied. ²²Finally, he himself left for Ramah and went to the great cistern at Secu. And he asked, "Where are Samuel and David?"

"Over in Naioth at Ramah," they said.

²³So Saul went to Naioth at Ramah. But the Spirit of God came even upon him, and he walked along prophesying until he came to Naioth. ²⁴He stripped off his robes and also prophesied in Samuel's presence. He lay that way all that day and night. This is why people say, "Is Saul also among the prophets?"

¹9 Or *injurious*   ¹¹13 Hebrew *teraphim*; also in verse 16

9 / *1 Samuel 20*
True Friendship

WHEN I WAS growing up, I had a friend named David Miller. David and I met in grammar school. In the third grade we were in Cub Scouts together. In the fourth grade we both had the same girlfriend. In sixth and seventh grade we went to camp together. Our relationship continued through high school, then we lost touch with each other, and later I moved to another city.

After many years, I went home for a visit and decided to stop by and see David. He was living in the same house—now with his wife and children. After the initial shock and joy at seeing each other, he invited me in. As I stepped inside, I felt as though I was stepping back in time. All the childhood memories associated with his house flooded back into my mind. What good friends we'd been!

In this study we will explore the strong relationship between David and Jonathan. It helps us see and appreciate the qualities of true friendship.

Warming Up to God What qualities do you appreciate most in a friend, and why?

Read 1 Samuel 20.

20 Then David fled from Naioth at Ramah and went to Jonathan and asked, "What have I done? What is my crime? How have I wronged your father, that he is trying to take my life?"

²"Never!" Jonathan replied. "You are not going to die! Look, my father doesn't do anything, great or small, without confiding in me. Why would he hide this from me? It's not so!"

³But David took an oath and said, "Your father knows very well that I have found favor in your eyes, and he has said to himself, 'Jonathan must not know this or he will be grieved.' Yet as surely as the LORD lives and as you live, there is only a step between me and death."

⁴Jonathan said to David, "Whatever you want me to do, I'll do for you."

⁵So David said, "Look, tomorrow is the New Moon festival, and I am supposed to dine with the king; but let me go and hide in the field until the evening of the day after tomorrow. ⁶If your father misses me at all, tell him, 'David earnestly asked my permission to hurry to Bethlehem, his hometown, because an annual sacrifice is being made there for his whole clan.' ⁷If he says, 'Very well,' then your servant is safe. But if he loses his temper, you can be sure that he is determined to harm me. ⁸As for you, show kindness to your servant, for you have brought him into a covenant with you before the LORD. If I am guilty, then kill me yourself! Why hand me over to your father?"

⁹"Never!" Jonathan said. "If I had the least in-

kling that my father was determined to harm you, wouldn't I tell you?"

¹⁰David asked, "Who will tell me if your father answers you harshly?"

¹¹"Come," Jonathan said, "let's go out into the field." So they went there together.

¹²Then Jonathan said to David: "By the LORD, the God of Israel, I will surely sound out my father by this time the day after tomorrow! If he is favorably disposed toward you, will I not send you word and let you know? ¹³But if my father is inclined to harm you, may the LORD deal with me, be it ever so severely, if I do not let you know and send you away safely. May the LORD be with you as he has been with my father. ¹⁴But show me unfailing kindness like that of the LORD as long as I live, so that I may not be killed, ¹⁵and do not ever cut off your kindness from my family—not even when the LORD has cut off every one of David's enemies from the face of the earth."

¹⁶So Jonathan made a covenant with the house of David, saying, "May the LORD call David's enemies to account." ¹⁷And Jonathan had David reaffirm his oath out of love for him, because he loved him as he loved himself.

¹⁸Then Jonathan said to David: "Tomorrow is the New Moon festival. You will be missed, because your seat will be empty. ¹⁹The day after tomorrow, toward evening, go to the place where you hid when this trouble began, and wait by the stone Ezel. ²⁰I will shoot three arrows to the side of it, as though I were shooting at a target. ²¹Then I will send a boy and say, 'Go, find the arrows.' If

I say to him, 'Look, the arrows are on this side of you; bring them here,' then come, because, as surely as the LORD lives, you are safe; there is no danger. ²²But if I say to the boy, 'Look, the arrows are beyond you,' then you must go, because the LORD has sent you away. ²³And about the matter you and I discussed—remember, the LORD is witness between you and me forever."

²⁴So David hid in the field, and when the New Moon festival came, the king sat down to eat. ²⁵He sat in his customary place by the wall, opposite Jonathan,ᵛ and Abner sat next to Saul, but David's place was empty. ²⁶Saul said nothing that day, for he thought, "Something must have happened to David to make him ceremonially unclean—surely he is unclean." ²⁷But the next day, the second day of the month, David's place was empty again. Then Saul said to his son Jonathan, "Why hasn't the son of Jesse come to the meal, either yesterday or today?"

²⁸Jonathan answered, "David earnestly asked me for permission to go to Bethlehem. ²⁹He said, 'Let me go, because our family is observing a sacrifice in the town and my brother has ordered me to be there. If I have found favor in your eyes, let me get away to see my brothers.' That is why he has not come to the king's table."

³⁰Saul's anger flared up at Jonathan and he said to him, "You son of a perverse and rebellious woman! Don't I know that you have sided with the son of Jesse to your own shame and to the shame of the mother who bore you? ³¹As long as the son of Jesse lives on this earth, neither you nor your kingdom will be established. Now send and bring him to me, for he must die!"

³²"Why should he be put to death? What has he done?" Jonathan asked his father. ³³But Saul hurled his spear at him to kill him. Then Jonathan knew that his father intended to kill David.

³⁴Jonathan got up from the table in fierce anger; on that second day of the month he did not eat, because he was grieved at his father's shameful treatment of David.

³⁵In the morning Jonathan went out to the field for his meeting with David. He had a small boy with him, ³⁶and he said to the boy, "Run and find the arrows I shoot." As the boy ran, he shot an arrow beyond him. ³⁷When the boy came to the place where Jonathan's arrow had fallen, Jonathan called out after him, "Isn't the arrow beyond you?" ³⁸Then he shouted, "Hurry! Go quickly! Don't stop!" The boy picked up the arrow and returned to his master. ³⁹(The boy knew nothing of all this; only Jonathan and David knew.) ⁴⁰Then Jonathan gave his weapons to the boy and said, "Go, carry them back to town."

⁴¹After the boy had gone, David got up from the south side ⌊of the stone⌋ and bowed down before Jonathan three times, with his face to the ground. Then they kissed each other and wept together—but David wept the most.

⁴²Jonathan said to David, "Go in peace, for we have sworn friendship with each other in the name of the LORD, saying, 'The LORD is witness between you and me, and between your descendants and my descendants forever.'" Then David left, and Jonathan went back to the town.

ᵛ25 Septuagint; Hebrew wall. Jonathan arose

 Discovering the Word 1. In 1 Samuel 18:1–4 David and Jonathan make a covenant with one another. This is put to the test when Saul tries to kill David (chapter 19). What impresses you about Jonathan's and David's love for each other? 2. How does their love express itself in their commitment to each other? 3. How does Jonathan's experience with Saul demonstrate some of the cost of friendship (vv. 30–42)? 4. What do we learn about the level of intimacy between Jonathan and David (vv. 41–42)?

Applying the Word 1. What factors enhance or inhibit intimacy in a relationship? 2. Think of your closest friend. If you could pick one area in which you'd like your friendship to be more like Jonathan's and David's, what would it be? 3. What specific steps can you take to achieve that goal?

Responding in Prayer Praise God for the friends he has given you. Ask him to help you show his love to them.

1 Samuel 21—23

21 David went to Nob, to Ahimelech the priest. Ahimelech trembled when he met him, and asked, "Why are you alone? Why is no one with you?"

²David answered Ahimelech the priest, "The king charged me with a certain matter and said to me, 'No one is to know anything about your mission and your instructions.' As for my men, I have told them to meet me at a certain place. ³Now then, what do you have on hand? Give me five loaves of bread, or whatever you can find."

⁴But the priest answered David, "I don't have any ordinary bread on hand; however, there is some consecrated bread here—provided the men have kept themselves from women."

⁵David replied, "Indeed women have been kept from us, as usual whenever*ʷ* I set out. The men's things*ˣ* are holy even on missions that are not holy. How much more so today!" ⁶So the priest gave him the consecrated bread, since there was no bread there except the bread of the Presence that had been removed from before the Lord and replaced by hot bread on the day it was taken away.

⁷Now one of Saul's servants was there that day, detained before the Lord; he was Doeg the Edomite, Saul's head shepherd.

⁸David asked Ahimelech, "Don't you have a spear or a sword here? I haven't brought my sword or any other weapon, because the king's business was urgent."

⁹The priest replied, "The sword of Goliath the Philistine, whom you killed in the Valley of Elah, is here; it is wrapped in a cloth behind the ephod. If you want it, take it; there is no sword here but that one."

David said, "There is none like it; give it to me."

¹⁰That day David fled from Saul and went to Achish king of Gath. ¹¹But the servants of Achish said to him, "Isn't this David, the king of the land? Isn't he the one they sing about in their dances:

" 'Saul has slain his thousands,
  and David his tens of thousands'?"

¹²David took these words to heart and was very much afraid of Achish king of Gath. ¹³So he pretended to be insane in their presence; and while he was in their hands he acted like a madman, making marks on the doors of the gate and letting saliva run down his beard.

¹⁴Achish said to his servants, "Look at the man! He is insane! Why bring him to me? ¹⁵Am I so short of madmen that you have to bring this fellow here to carry on like this in front of me? Must this man come into my house?"

22 David left Gath and escaped to the cave of Adullam. When his brothers and his father's household heard about it, they went down to him there. ²All those who were in distress or in debt or discontented gathered around him, and he became their leader. About four hundred men were with him.

³From there David went to Mizpah in Moab and said to the king of Moab, "Would you let my father and mother come and stay with you until I learn what God will do for me?" ⁴So he left them with the king of Moab, and they stayed with him as long as David was in the stronghold.

⁵But the prophet Gad said to David, "Do not stay in the stronghold. Go into the land of Judah." So David left and went to the forest of Hereth.

⁶Now Saul heard that David and his men had been discovered. And Saul, spear in hand, was seated under the tamarisk tree on the hill at Gibeah, with all his officials standing around him. ⁷Saul said to them, "Listen, men of Benjamin! Will the son of Jesse give all of you fields and vineyards? Will he make all of you commanders of thousands and commanders of hundreds? ⁸Is that why you have all conspired against me? No one tells me when my son makes a covenant with the son of Jesse. None of you is concerned about me or tells me that my son has incited my servant to lie in wait for me, as he does today."

⁹But Doeg the Edomite, who was standing with Saul's officials, said, "I saw the son of Jesse come to Ahimelech son of Ahitub at Nob. ¹⁰Ahimelech inquired of the Lord for him; he also gave him provisions and the sword of Goliath the Philistine."

¹¹Then the king sent for the priest Ahimelech son of Ahitub and his father's whole family, who were the priests at Nob, and they all came to the king. ¹²Saul said, "Listen now, son of Ahitub."

ʷ5 Or *from us in the past few days since*   ˣ5 Or *bodies*

"Yes, my lord," he answered.

¹³Saul said to him, "Why have you conspired against me, you and the son of Jesse, giving him bread and a sword and inquiring of God for him, so that he has rebelled against me and lies in wait for me, as he does today?"

¹⁴Ahimelech answered the king, "Who of all your servants is as loyal as David, the king's son-in-law, captain of your bodyguard and highly respected in your household? ¹⁵Was that day the first time I inquired of God for him? Of course not! Let not the king accuse your servant or any of his father's family, for your servant knows nothing at all about this whole affair."

¹⁶But the king said, "You will surely die, Ahimelech, you and your father's whole family."

¹⁷Then the king ordered the guards at his side: "Turn and kill the priests of the LORD, because they too have sided with David. They knew he was fleeing, yet they did not tell me."

But the king's officials were not willing to raise a hand to strike the priests of the LORD.

¹⁸The king then ordered Doeg, "You turn and strike down the priests." So Doeg the Edomite turned and struck them down. That day he killed eighty-five men who wore the linen ephod. ¹⁹He also put to the sword Nob, the town of the priests, with its men and women, its children and infants, and its cattle, donkeys and sheep.

²⁰But Abiathar, a son of Ahimelech son of Ahitub, escaped and fled to join David. ²¹He told David that Saul had killed the priests of the LORD. ²²Then David said to Abiathar: "That day, when Doeg the Edomite was there, I knew he would be sure to tell Saul. I am responsible for the death of your father's whole family. ²³Stay with me; don't be afraid; the man who is seeking your life is seeking mine also. You will be safe with me."

23 When David was told, "Look, the Philistines are fighting against Keilah and are looting the threshing floors," ²he inquired of the LORD, saying, "Shall I go and attack these Philistines?"

The LORD answered him, "Go, attack the Philistines and save Keilah."

³But David's men said to him, "Here in Judah we are afraid. How much more, then, if we go to Keilah against the Philistine forces!"

⁴Once again David inquired of the LORD, and the LORD answered him, "Go down to Keilah, for I am going to give the Philistines into your hand."

⁵So David and his men went to Keilah, fought the Philistines and carried off their livestock. He inflicted heavy losses on the Philistines and saved the people of Keilah. ⁶(Now Abiathar son of Ahimelech had brought the ephod down with him when he fled to David at Keilah.)

⁷Saul was told that David had gone to Keilah, and he said, "God has handed him over to me, for David has imprisoned himself by entering a town with gates and bars." ⁸And Saul called up all his forces for battle, to go down to Keilah to besiege David and his men.

⁹When David learned that Saul was plotting against him, he said to Abiathar the priest, "Bring the ephod." ¹⁰David said, "O LORD, God of Israel, your servant has heard definitely that Saul plans to come to Keilah and destroy the town on account of me. ¹¹Will the citizens of Keilah surrender me to him? Will Saul come down, as your servant has heard? O LORD, God of Israel, tell your servant."

And the LORD said, "He will."

¹²Again David asked, "Will the citizens of Keilah surrender me and my men to Saul?"

And the LORD said, "They will."

¹³So David and his men, about six hundred in number, left Keilah and kept moving from place to place. When Saul was told that David had escaped from Keilah, he did not go there.

¹⁴David stayed in the desert strongholds and in the hills of the Desert of Ziph. Day after day Saul searched for him, but God did not give David into his hands.

¹⁵While David was at Horesh in the Desert of Ziph, he learned that Saul had come out to take his life. ¹⁶And Saul's son Jonathan went to David at Horesh and helped him find strength in God. ¹⁷"Don't be afraid," he said. "My father Saul will not lay a hand on you. You will be king over Israel, and I will be second to you. Even my father Saul knows this." ¹⁸The two of them made a covenant before the LORD. Then Jonathan went home, but David remained at Horesh.

¹⁹The Ziphites went up to Saul at Gibeah and said, "Is not David hiding among us in the strongholds at Horesh, on the hill of Hakilah, south of Jeshimon? ²⁰Now, O king, come down whenever it pleases you to do so, and we will be responsible for handing him over to the king."

²¹Saul replied, "The LORD bless you for your concern for me. ²²Go and make further preparation. Find out where David usually goes and who has seen him there. They tell me he is very crafty.

23Find out about all the hiding places he uses and come back to me with definite information.y Then I will go with you; if he is in the area, I will track him down among all the clans of Judah."

24So they set out and went to Ziph ahead of Saul. Now David and his men were in the Desert of Maon, in the Arabah south of Jeshimon. 25Saul and his men began the search, and when David was told about it, he went down to the rock and stayed in the Desert of Maon. When Saul heard this, he went into the Desert of Maon in pursuit of David.

26Saul was going along one side of the moun-

tain, and David and his men were on the other side, hurrying to get away from Saul. As Saul and his forces were closing in on David and his men to capture them, 27a messenger came to Saul, saying, "Come quickly! The Philistines are raiding the land." 28Then Saul broke off his pursuit of David and went to meet the Philistines. That is why they call this place Sela Hammahlekoth.z 29And David went up from there and lived in the strongholds of En Gedi.

y23 Or me at Nacon   z28 Sela Hammahlekoth means rock of parting.

10/ *1 Samuel 24*
A Matter of Conscience

HOW DO WE determine God's will? Do we look to circumstances? the counsel of friends? the words of Scripture? In 1 Samuel 24 everything seems to indicate that David should kill Saul and take his place on the throne of Israel. Yet David rejects conventional wisdom and uses a different method for deciding what is right. His attitude should cause us to reexamine our own notions about guidance.

Warming Up to God As you begin this quiet time, consider in what area of your life you need God's guidance. Ask God to use this study to direct you.

Read 1 Samuel 24.

24 After Saul returned from pursuing the Philistines, he was told, "David is in the Desert of En Gedi." 2So Saul took three thousand chosen men from all Israel and set out to look for David and his men near the Crags of the Wild Goats.

3He came to the sheep pens along the way; a cave was there, and Saul went in to relieve himself. David and his men were far back in the cave. 4The men said, "This is the day the LORD spoke of when he saida to you, 'I will give your enemy into your hands for you to deal with as you wish.'" Then David crept up unnoticed and cut off a corner of Saul's robe.

5Afterward, David was conscience-stricken for having cut off a corner of his robe. 6He said to his men, "The LORD forbid that I should do such a thing to my master, the LORD's anointed, or lift my hand against him; for he is the anointed of the LORD." 7With these words David rebuked his men and did not allow them to

attack Saul. And Saul left the cave and went his way.

8Then David went out of the cave and called out to Saul, "My lord the king!" When Saul looked behind him, David bowed down and prostrated himself with his face to the ground. 9He said to Saul, "Why do you listen when men say, 'David is bent on harming you'? 10This day you have seen with your own eyes how the LORD delivered you into my hands in the cave. Some urged me to kill you, but I spared you; I said, 'I will not lift my hand against my master, because he is the LORD's anointed.' 11See, my father, look at this piece of your robe in my hand! I cut off the corner of your robe but did not kill you. Now understand and recognize that I am not guilty of wrongdoing or rebellion. I have not wronged you, but you are hunting me down to take my life. 12May the LORD judge between you and me. And

a4 Or "Today the LORD is saying

may the LORD avenge the wrongs you have done to me, but my hand will not touch you. ¹³As the old saying goes, 'From evildoers come evil deeds,' so my hand will not touch you.

¹⁴"Against whom has the king of Israel come out? Whom are you pursuing? A dead dog? A flea? ¹⁵May the LORD be our judge and decide between us. May he consider my cause and uphold it; may he vindicate me by delivering me from your hand."

¹⁶When David finished saying this, Saul asked, "Is that your voice, David my son?" And he wept aloud. ¹⁷"You are more righteous than I," he said. "You have treated me well, but I have treated you

badly. ¹⁸You have just now told me of the good you did to me; the LORD delivered me into your hands, but you did not kill me. ¹⁹When a man finds his enemy, does he let him get away unharmed? May the LORD reward you well for the way you treated me today. ²⁰I know that you will surely be king and that the kingdom of Israel will be established in your hands. ²¹Now swear to me by the LORD that you will not cut off my descendants or wipe out my name from my father's family."

²²So David gave his oath to Saul. Then Saul returned home, but David and his men went up to the stronghold.

Discovering the Word   1. What factors might have convinced David that it was God's will for him to kill Saul (vv. 1–7)?   2. Why do you think David places such importance on respecting the Lord's anointed (vv. 6, 10)?   3. What arguments does David use to convince Saul of his innocence (vv. 8–15)?   4. How does Saul respond to David's words (vv. 16–22)?   5. What do David's actions force Saul to conclude about David?

Applying the Word   1. We often rely on circumstances and the counsel of friends when making important decisions. To what extent are these reliable guides?   2. Is it ever right to go against conscience in a small area for the sake of a supposedly greater good? Explain.   3. How can we know when to take matters into our own hands and when to leave them in God's hands?

Responding in Prayer   Ask God to give you wisdom in the area you are struggling with. Ask him to show you how to take action—or wait on him.

11 / *1 Samuel 25*
Secure in the Lord

IN THE TV series *The Honeymooners* Ralph Cramden used to threaten to knock his wife clear to the moon. "One of these days, Alice, *bang . . . zoom!*" We all give similar threats at one time or another: "I'll get you for this!" "You'll be sorry you ever treated me like that!" "You'll wish you had never been born!" When people mistreat us, we instinctively want revenge. We want to get even, to show them how it feels. In 1 Samuel 25 David is insulted by a man named Nabal. David's response gives us both a positive and negative example of how we should respond to those who mistreat us.

Warming Up to God   How have you felt mistreated by others this week?

Read 1 Samuel 25.

25 Now Samuel died, and all Israel assembled and mourned for him; and they buried him at his home in Ramah.

Then David moved down into the Desert of Maon.ᵇ ²A certain man in Maon, who had property there at Carmel, was very wealthy. He had a

thousand goats and three thousand sheep, which he was shearing in Carmel. ³His name was Nabal and his wife's name was Abigail. She was an intelligent and beautiful woman, but her husband, a Calebite, was surly and mean in his dealings.

⁴While David was in the desert, he heard that

ᵇ1 Some Septuagint manuscripts; Hebrew *Paran*

Nabal was shearing sheep. ⁵So he sent ten young men and said to them, "Go up to Nabal at Carmel and greet him in my name. ⁶Say to him: 'Long life to you! Good health to you and your household! And good health to all that is yours!

⁷" 'Now I hear that it is sheep-shearing time. When your shepherds were with us, we did not mistreat them, and the whole time they were at Carmel nothing of theirs was missing. ⁸Ask your own servants and they will tell you. Therefore be favorable toward my young men, since we come at a festive time. Please give your servants and your son David whatever you can find for them.' "

⁹When David's men arrived, they gave Nabal this message in David's name. Then they waited.

¹⁰Nabal answered David's servants, "Who is this David? Who is this son of Jesse? Many servants are breaking away from their masters these days. ¹¹Why should I take my bread and water, and the meat I have slaughtered for my shearers, and give it to men coming from who knows where?"

¹²David's men turned around and went back. When they arrived, they reported every word. ¹³David said to his men, "Put on your swords!" So they put on their swords, and David put on his. About four hundred men went up with David, while two hundred stayed with the supplies.

¹⁴One of the servants told Nabal's wife Abigail: "David sent messengers from the desert to give our master his greetings, but he hurled insults at them. ¹⁵Yet these men were very good to us. They did not mistreat us, and the whole time we were out in the fields near them nothing was missing. ¹⁶Night and day they were a wall around us all the time we were herding our sheep near them. ¹⁷Now think it over and see what you can do, because disaster is hanging over our master and his whole household. He is such a wicked man that no one can talk to him."

¹⁸Abigail lost no time. She took two hundred loaves of bread, two skins of wine, five dressed sheep, five seahsᶜ of roasted grain, a hundred cakes of raisins and two hundred cakes of pressed figs, and loaded them on donkeys. ¹⁹Then she told her servants, "Go on ahead; I'll follow you." But she did not tell her husband Nabal.

²⁰As she came riding her donkey into a mountain ravine, there were David and his men descending toward her, and she met them. ²¹David had just said, "It's been useless—all my watching over this fellow's property in the desert so that nothing of his was missing. He has paid me back evil for good. ²²May God deal with David,ᵈ be it ever so severely, if by morning I leave alive one male of all who belong to him!"

²³When Abigail saw David, she quickly got off her donkey and bowed down before David with her face to the ground. ²⁴She fell at his feet and said: "My lord, let the blame be on me alone. Please let your servant speak to you; hear what your servant has to say. ²⁵May my lord pay no attention to that wicked man Nabal. He is just like his name—his name is Fool, and folly goes with him. But as for me, your servant, I did not see the men my master sent.

²⁶"Now since the LORD has kept you, my master, from bloodshed and from avenging yourself with your own hands, as surely as the LORD lives and as you live, may your enemies and all who intend to harm my master be like Nabal. ²⁷And let this gift, which your servant has brought to my master, be given to the men who follow you. ²⁸Please forgive your servant's offense, for the LORD will certainly make a lasting dynasty for my master, because he fights the LORD's battles. Let no wrongdoing be found in you as long as you live. ²⁹Even though someone is pursuing you to take your life, the life of my master will be bound securely in the bundle of the living by the LORD your God. But the lives of your enemies he will hurl away as from the pocket of a sling. ³⁰When the LORD has done for my master every good thing he promised concerning him and has appointed him leader over Israel, ³¹my master will not have on his conscience the staggering burden of needless bloodshed or of having avenged himself. And when the LORD has brought my master success, remember your servant."

³²David said to Abigail, "Praise be to the LORD, the God of Israel, who has sent you today to meet me. ³³May you be blessed for your good judgment and for keeping me from bloodshed this day and from avenging myself with my own hands. ³⁴Otherwise, as surely as the LORD, the God of Israel, lives, who has kept me from harming you, if you had not come quickly to meet me, not one male belonging to Nabal would have been left alive by daybreak."

³⁵Then David accepted from her hand what she had brought him and said, "Go home in peace.

ᶜ18 That is, probably about a bushel (about 37 liters)   ᵈ22 Some Septuagint manuscripts; Hebrew with David's enemies

I have heard your words and granted your request."

³⁶When Abigail went to Nabal, he was in the house holding a banquet like that of a king. He was in high spirits and very drunk. So she told him nothing until daybreak. ³⁷Then in the morning, when Nabal was sober, his wife told him all these things, and his heart failed him and he became like a stone. ³⁸About ten days later, the LORD struck Nabal and he died.

³⁹When David heard that Nabal was dead, he said, "Praise be to the LORD, who has upheld my cause against Nabal for treating me with contempt. He has kept his servant from doing wrong and has brought Nabal's wrongdoing down on his own head."

Then David sent word to Abigail, asking her to become his wife. ⁴⁰His servants went to Carmel and said to Abigail, "David has sent us to you to take you to become his wife."

⁴¹She bowed down with her face to the ground and said, "Here is your maidservant, ready to serve you and wash the feet of my master's servants." ⁴²Abigail quickly got on a donkey and, attended by her five maids, went with David's messengers and became his wife. ⁴³David had also married Ahinoam of Jezreel, and they both were his wives. ⁴⁴But Saul had given his daughter Michal, David's wife, to Paltielᵉ son of Laish, who was from Gallim.

ᵉ44 Hebrew *Palti*, a variant of *Paltiel*

Discovering the Word 1. What does the author tell us about the two new characters in this drama (vv. 2–3)? 2. Why is David so offended by Nabal's response to his request (vv. 4–13, 21–22)? 3. Even if David's offense is justified, how would you evaluate his plan to get even with Nabal (vv. 13, 34)? 4. What impresses you about Abigail's response when she finds out what has happened (vv. 14–32)? 5. The events in this chapter are deliberately sandwiched between two accounts of David sparing Saul's life. How is David's relationship with Nabal similar to his relationship with Saul?

Applying the Word 1. What methods do we sometimes use to "get even" with those who mistreat us? 2. Think of someone who has recently mistreated you. How can this study affect your attitude and actions toward that person?

Responding in Prayer Pray for your enemies.

---

12 / 1 Samuel 26
Self-Control

YOU'RE ON A diet. As you pick up a magazine, you turn innocently to the food section. "After all," you say to yourself, "pictures aren't fattening." As you pore over every page, each dessert looks better than the last one. You decide to read in the kitchen because "the light is better." After a few minutes, you begin thinking about the ice cream in the freezer. A model of restraint, you decide to get only one spoonful—well, two at the most. Pretty soon you've eaten the whole quart! Sound familiar? We all struggle with self-control. And temptations often blind our better judgment. In 1 Samuel 26 David faces the powerful temptation of choosing between self-gratification and self-control. His response can encourage us in our struggles.

Warming Up to God In what area of your life would you like to have greater self-control?

Read 1 Samuel 26.

26

The Ziphites went to Saul at Gibeah and said, "Is not David hiding on the hill of Hakilah, which faces Jeshimon?"

2So Saul went down to the Desert of Ziph, with his three thousand chosen men of Israel, to search there for David. 3Saul made his camp beside the road on the hill of Hakilah facing Jeshimon, but David stayed in the desert. When he saw that Saul had followed him there, 4he sent out scouts and learned that Saul had definitely arrived.ʃ

5Then David set out and went to the place where Saul had camped. He saw where Saul and Abner son of Ner, the commander of the army, had lain down. Saul was lying inside the camp, with the army encamped around him.

6David then asked Ahimelech the Hittite and Abishai son of Zeruiah, Joab's brother, "Who will go down into the camp with me to Saul?"

"I'll go with you," said Abishai.

7So David and Abishai went to the army by night, and there was Saul, lying asleep inside the camp with his spear stuck in the ground near his head. Abner and the soldiers were lying around him.

8Abishai said to David, "Today God has delivered your enemy into your hands. Now let me pin him to the ground with one thrust of my spear; I won't strike him twice."

9But David said to Abishai, "Don't destroy him! Who can lay a hand on the LORD's anointed and be guiltless? 10As surely as the LORD lives," he said, "the LORD himself will strike him; either his time will come and he will die, or he will go into battle and perish. 11But the LORD forbid that I should lay a hand on the LORD's anointed. Now get the spear and water jug that are near his head, and let's go."

12So David took the spear and water jug near Saul's head, and they left. No one saw or knew about it, nor did anyone wake up. They were all sleeping, because the LORD had put them into a deep sleep.

13Then David crossed over to the other side and stood on top of the hill some distance away; there was a wide space between them. 14He called out to the army and to Abner son of Ner, "Aren't you going to answer me, Abner?"

Abner replied, "Who are you who calls to the king?"

15David said, "You're a man, aren't you? And who is like you in Israel? Why didn't you guard your lord the king? Someone came to destroy your lord the king. 16What you have done is not good. As surely as the LORD lives, you and your men deserve to die, because you did not guard your master, the LORD's anointed. Look around you. Where are the king's spear and water jug that were near his head?"

17Saul recognized David's voice and said, "Is that your voice, David my son?"

David replied, "Yes it is, my lord the king." 18And he added, "Why is my lord pursuing his servant? What have I done, and what wrong am I guilty of? 19Now let my lord the king listen to his servant's words. If the LORD has incited you against me, then may he accept an offering. If, however, men have done it, may they be cursed before the LORD! They have now driven me from my share in the LORD's inheritance and have said, 'Go, serve other gods.' 20Now do not let my blood fall to the ground far from the presence of the LORD. The king of Israel has come out to look for a flea—as one hunts a partridge in the mountains."

21Then Saul said, "I have sinned. Come back, David my son. Because you considered my life precious today, I will not try to harm you again. Surely I have acted like a fool and have erred greatly."

22"Here is the king's spear," David answered. "Let one of your young men come over and get it. 23The LORD rewards every man for his righteousness and faithfulness. The LORD delivered you into my hands today, but I would not lay a hand on the LORD's anointed. 24As surely as I valued your life today, so may the LORD value my life and deliver me from all trouble."

25Then Saul said to David, "May you be blessed, my son David; you will do great things and surely triumph."

So David went on his way, and Saul returned home.

ʃ4 Or *had come to Nacon*

Discovering the Word 1. Describe the tension and dangers involved in David's plan (vv. 5–7). 2. Abishai tells David to seize this golden opportunity to kill Saul (v. 8). Why would this be a tempting suggestion? 3. Why does David resist the temptation to take matters into his own hands (vv. 9–11)? 4. From a safe distance David calls out to Abner (vv. 13–16). How would his words to Abner make Saul more receptive to him? 5. What does the passage teach about how God regards human life (vv. 21–24)?

Applying the Word 1. When we are tempted to sin, how can our attitude toward God's will affect the outcome? 2. If we know God is present to help us in our struggle, how can it be easier to exercise self-control? 3. In what ways can our commitment to doing God's will affect Christians and non-Christians as they observe us?

Responding in Prayer Think again about that area where you desire greater self-control. Ask God's Spirit to cultivate this fruit within you.

1 Samuel 27—29

27 But David thought to himself, "One of these days I will be destroyed by the hand of Saul. The best thing I can do is to escape to the land of the Philistines. Then Saul will give up searching for me anywhere in Israel, and I will slip out of his hand."

²So David and the six hundred men with him left and went over to Achish son of Maoch king of Gath. ³David and his men settled in Gath with Achish. Each man had his family with him, and David had his two wives: Ahinoam of Jezreel and Abigail of Carmel, the widow of Nabal. ⁴When Saul was told that David had fled to Gath, he no longer searched for him.

⁵Then David said to Achish, "If I have found favor in your eyes, let a place be assigned to me in one of the country towns, that I may live there. Why should your servant live in the royal city with you?"

⁶So on that day Achish gave him Ziklag, and it has belonged to the kings of Judah ever since. ⁷David lived in Philistine territory a year and four months.

⁸Now David and his men went up and raided the Geshurites, the Girzites and the Amalekites. (From ancient times these peoples had lived in the land extending to Shur and Egypt.) ⁹Whenever David attacked an area, he did not leave a man or woman alive, but took sheep and cattle, donkeys and camels, and clothes. Then he returned to Achish.

¹⁰When Achish asked, "Where did you go raiding today?" David would say, "Against the Negev of Judah" or "Against the Negev of Jerahmeel" or "Against the Negev of the Kenites." ¹¹He did not leave a man or woman alive to be brought to Gath, for he thought, "They might inform on us and say, 'This is what David did.' " And such was his practice as long as he lived in Philistine territory. ¹²Achish trusted David and said to himself, "He has become so odious to his people, the Israelites, that he will be my servant forever."

28 In those days the Philistines gathered their forces to fight against Israel. Achish said to David, "You must understand that you and your men will accompany me in the army."

²David said, "Then you will see for yourself what your servant can do."

Achish replied, "Very well, I will make you my bodyguard for life."

³Now Samuel was dead, and all Israel had mourned for him and buried him in his own town of Ramah. Saul had expelled the mediums and spiritists from the land.

⁴The Philistines assembled and came and set up camp at Shunem, while Saul gathered all the Israelites and set up camp at Gilboa. ⁵When Saul saw the Philistine army, he was afraid; terror filled his heart. ⁶He inquired of the LORD, but the LORD did not answer him by dreams or Urim or prophets. ⁷Saul then said to his attendants, "Find me a woman who is a medium, so I may go and inquire of her."

"There is one in Endor," they said.

⁸So Saul disguised himself, putting on other clothes, and at night he and two men went to the woman. "Consult a spirit for me," he said, "and bring up for me the one I name."

⁹But the woman said to him, "Surely you know what Saul has done. He has cut off the mediums

and spiritists from the land. Why have you set a trap for my life to bring about my death?"

¹⁰Saul swore to her by the LORD, "As surely as the LORD lives, you will not be punished for this."

¹¹Then the woman asked, "Whom shall I bring up for you?"

"Bring up Samuel," he said.

¹²When the woman saw Samuel, she cried out at the top of her voice and said to Saul, "Why have you deceived me? You are Saul!"

¹³The king said to her, "Don't be afraid. What do you see?"

The woman said, "I see a spirit⁸ coming up out of the ground."

¹⁴"What does he look like?" he asked.

"An old man wearing a robe is coming up," she said.

Then Saul knew it was Samuel, and he bowed down and prostrated himself with his face to the ground.

¹⁵Samuel said to Saul, "Why have you disturbed me by bringing me up?"

"I am in great distress," Saul said. "The Philistines are fighting against me, and God has turned away from me. He no longer answers me, either by prophets or by dreams. So I have called on you to tell me what to do."

¹⁶Samuel said, "Why do you consult me, now that the LORD has turned away from you and become your enemy? ¹⁷The LORD has done what he predicted through me. The LORD has torn the kingdom out of your hands and given it to one of your neighbors—to David. ¹⁸Because you did not obey the LORD or carry out his fierce wrath against the Amalekites, the LORD has done this to you today. ¹⁹The LORD will hand over both Israel and you to the Philistines, and tomorrow you and your sons will be with me. The LORD will also hand over the army of Israel to the Philistines."

²⁰Immediately Saul fell full length on the ground, filled with fear because of Samuel's words. His strength was gone, for he had eaten nothing all that day and night.

²¹When the woman came to Saul and saw that he was greatly shaken, she said, "Look, your maidservant has obeyed you. I took my life in my hands and did what you told me to do. ²²Now please listen to your servant and let me give you some food so you may eat and have the strength to go on your way."

²³He refused and said, "I will not eat."

But his men joined the woman in urging him, and he listened to them. He got up from the ground and sat on the couch.

²⁴The woman had a fattened calf at the house, which she butchered at once. She took some flour, kneaded it and baked bread without yeast. ²⁵Then she set it before Saul and his men, and they ate. That same night they got up and left.

29 The Philistines gathered all their forces at Aphek, and Israel camped by the spring in Jezreel. ²As the Philistine rulers marched with their units of hundreds and thousands, David and his men were marching at the rear with Achish. ³The commanders of the Philistines asked, "What about these Hebrews?"

Achish replied, "Is this not David, who was an officer of Saul king of Israel? He has already been with me for over a year, and from the day he left Saul until now, I have found no fault in him."

⁴But the Philistine commanders were angry with him and said, "Send the man back, that he may return to the place you assigned him. He must not go with us into battle, or he will turn against us during the fighting. How better could he regain his master's favor than by taking the heads of our own men? ⁵Isn't this the David they sang about in their dances:

" 'Saul has slain his thousands,
    and David his tens of thousands'?"

⁶So Achish called David and said to him, "As surely as the LORD lives, you have been reliable, and I would be pleased to have you serve with me in the army. From the day you came to me until now, I have found no fault in you, but the rulers don't approve of you. ⁷Turn back and go in peace; do nothing to displease the Philistine rulers."

⁸"But what have I done?" asked David. "What have you found against your servant from the day I came to you until now? Why can't I go and fight against the enemies of my lord the king?"

⁹Achish answered, "I know that you have been as pleasing in my eyes as an angel of God; nevertheless, the Philistine commanders have said, 'He must not go up with us into battle.' ¹⁰Now get up

⁸13 Or see spirits; or see gods

early, along with your master's servants who have come with you, and leave in the morning as soon as it is light."

11So David and his men got up early in the morning to go back to the land of the Philistines, and the Philistines went up to Jezreel.

13 / *1 Samuel 30*
Finding Strength in the Lord

IN A CHAPTER entitled "The False Hope of Modern Christianity," Larry Crabb writes, "Modern Christianity, in dramatic reversal of its biblical form, promises to relieve the pain of living in a fallen world. The message, whether it's from fundamentalists requiring us to live by a favored set of rules or from charismatics urging a deeper surrender of the Spirit's power, is too often the same: The promise of bliss is for NOW! Complete satisfaction can be ours this side of Heaven" (*Inside Out* [Colorado Springs: NavPress, 1988], p. 15). The life of David exposes the inadequacy of that view. In this chapter David and his men experience a devastating crisis. Yet in the midst of the crisis, they also find strength and help in the Lord.

 Warming Up to God The Christian life is often portrayed as a before-and-after story, with everything "after" being sweetness and light. How do you respond to that kind of portrayal?

 Read 1 Samuel 30.

30 David and his men reached Ziklag on the third day. Now the Amalekites had raided the Negev and Ziklag. They had attacked Ziklag and burned it, 2and had taken captive the women and all who were in it, both young and old. They killed none of them, but carried them off as they went on their way.

3When David and his men came to Ziklag, they found it destroyed by fire and their wives and sons and daughters taken captive. 4So David and his men wept aloud until they had no strength left to weep. 5David's two wives had been captured—Ahinoam of Jezreel and Abigail, the widow of Nabal of Carmel. 6David was greatly distressed because the men were talking of stoning him; each one was bitter in spirit because of his sons and daughters. But David found strength in the LORD his God.

7Then David said to Abiathar the priest, the son of Ahimelech, "Bring me the ephod." Abiathar brought it to him, 8and David inquired of the LORD, "Shall I pursue this raiding party? Will I overtake them?"

"Pursue them," he answered. "You will certainly overtake them and succeed in the rescue."

9David and the six hundred men with him came to the Besor Ravine, where some stayed behind, 10for two hundred men were too exhausted to cross the ravine. But David and four hundred men continued the pursuit.

11They found an Egyptian in a field and brought him to David. They gave him water to drink and food to eat— 12part of a cake of pressed figs and two cakes of raisins. He ate and was revived, for he had not eaten any food or drunk any water for three days and three nights.

13David asked him, "To whom do you belong, and where do you come from?"

He said, "I am an Egyptian, the slave of an Amalekite. My master abandoned me when I became ill three days ago. 14We raided the Negev of the Kerethites and the territory belonging to Judah and the Negev of Caleb. And we burned Ziklag."

15David asked him, "Can you lead me down to this raiding party?"

He answered, "Swear to me before God that you will not kill me or hand me over to my master, and I will take you down to them." 16He led David down, and there they were, scattered over the countryside, eating, drinking and reveling because of the great amount of plunder they had taken from the land of the Philistines and from Judah. 17David fought them from dusk until the evening of the next day, and none of them got away, except four hundred young

men who rode off on camels and fled. ¹⁸David
recovered everything the Amalekites had taken,
including his two wives. ¹⁹Nothing was missing:
young or old, boy or girl, plunder or anything
else they had taken. David brought everything
back. ²⁰He took all the flocks and herds, and his
men drove them ahead of the other livestock, saying, "This is David's plunder."

²¹Then David came to the two hundred men
who had been too exhausted to follow him and
who were left behind at the Besor Ravine. They
came out to meet David and the people with him.
As David and his men approached, he greeted
them. ²²But all the evil men and troublemakers
among David's followers said, "Because they did
not go out with us, we will not share with them
the plunder we recovered. However, each man
may take his wife and children and go."

²³David replied, "No, my brothers, you must
not do that with what the LORD has given us. He
has protected us and handed over to us the forces
that came against us. ²⁴Who will listen to what
you say? The share of the man who stayed with
the supplies is to be the same as that of him who
went down to the battle. All will share alike."
²⁵David made this a statute and ordinance for Israel from that day to this.

²⁶When David arrived in Ziklag, he sent some
of the plunder to the elders of Judah, who were
his friends, saying, "Here is a present for you
from the plunder of the LORD's enemies."

²⁷He sent it to those who were in Bethel, Ramoth Negev and Jattir; ²⁸to those in Aroer, Siph-
moth, Eshtemoa ²⁹and Racal; to those in the
towns of the Jerahmeelites and the Kenites; ³⁰to
those in Hormah, Bor Ashan, Athach ³¹and Hebron; and to those in all the other places where
David and his men had roamed.

Discovering the Word 1. When David and his men return to their home in Ziklag, what do they find
(vv. 1–3)? 2. What are we told about the depths of their distress (vv. 4–6)? 3. After David has found
strength in the Lord, how does he also find help from the Lord (vv. 7–20)? 4. What was wrong with the logic of
those who said, "Because they did not go out with us, we will not share with them the plunder we recovered"
(v. 22)? 5. David declares that the Lord "has protected us and handed over to us the forces that came against us"
(v. 23). If the Lord was able to do all that, why do you think he allowed the problem to arise in the first place?

Applying the Word 1. How can David's experience help us to have a realistic view of the difficulties we
might face as Christians? 2. Reflect on a difficulty or distress you are currently facing. How can David's
experience give you hope?

 Responding in Prayer Ask God to sustain you with hope through your crisis.

---

1 Samuel 31

31 Now the Philistines fought against
Israel; the Israelites fled before
them, and many fell slain on Mount
Gilboa. ²The Philistines pressed hard after Saul
and his sons, and they killed his sons Jonathan,
Abinadab and Malki-Shua. ³The fighting grew
fierce around Saul, and when the archers overtook him, they wounded him critically.

⁴Saul said to his armor-bearer, "Draw your
sword and run me through, or these uncircumcised fellows will come and run me through and
abuse me."

But his armor-bearer was terrified and would
not do it; so Saul took his own sword and fell on
it. ⁵When the armor-bearer saw that Saul was
dead, he too fell on his sword and died with him.
⁶So Saul and his three sons and his armor-bearer
and all his men died together that same day.

⁷When the Israelites along the valley and those
across the Jordan saw that the Israelite army had
fled and that Saul and his sons had died, they
abandoned their towns and fled. And the Philistines came and occupied them.

⁸The next day, when the Philistines came to
strip the dead, they found Saul and his three sons
fallen on Mount Gilboa. ⁹They cut off his head
and stripped off his armor, and they sent messengers throughout the land of the Philistines to proclaim the news in the temple of their idols and
among their people. ¹⁰They put his armor in the

temple of the Ashtoreths and fastened his body to the wall of Beth Shan.

[11]When the people of Jabesh Gilead heard of what the Philistines had done to Saul, [12]all their valiant men journeyed through the night to Beth Shan. They took down the bodies of Saul and his sons from the wall of Beth Shan and went to Jabesh, where they burned them. [13]Then they took their bones and buried them under a tamarisk tree at Jabesh, and they fasted seven days.

2 Samuel

Highs and lows. David's life, like our lives, was full of extremes. For David, however, God played a part through it all.

Second Samuel highlights some of David's high moments, winning battles and bringing prosperity to Israel. Chapter 7 contains God's promise that his dynasty would live forever.

In chapters 10—20 we move to the darker moments of David's life as we see him succumb to temptation and murder. The results of his sin follow him through life and are seen in the lives of his children.

At the end of the book we discover that David has not lost his hope in the Lord. Chapters 22 and 23 record his songs of praise to God. May you, like David, find that the Lord is your rock, your fortress and your deliverer (22:2) through the ups and downs of life.

Outline

1/ 2 Samuel 6 —————————— God's Wrath & Blessing

2/ 2 Samuel 7 —————————— God's Promise to David

3/ 2 Samuel 9 —————————— Integrity

4/ 2 Samuel 11 ————————— Facing Temptation

5/ 2 Samuel 12 ————————— God's Severe Mercy

6/ 2 Samuel 13 ————————— Sexual Violence

7/ 2 Samuel 15 ————————— Difficult Days

8/ 2 Samuel 18:19—19:10 ———— Receiving Counsel

2 Samuel 1—5

After the death of Saul, David returned from defeating the Amalekites and stayed in Ziklag two days. ²On the third day a man arrived from Saul's camp, with his clothes torn and with dust on his head. When he came to David, he fell to the ground to pay him honor.

³"Where have you come from?" David asked him.

He answered, "I have escaped from the Israelite camp."

⁴"What happened?" David asked. "Tell me."

He said, "The men fled from the battle. Many of them fell and died. And Saul and his son Jonathan are dead."

⁵Then David said to the young man who brought him the report, "How do you know that Saul and his son Jonathan are dead?"

⁶"I happened to be on Mount Gilboa," the young man said, "and there was Saul, leaning on his spear, with the chariots and riders almost upon him. ⁷When he turned around and saw me, he called out to me, and I said, 'What can I do?'

⁸"He asked me, 'Who are you?'

" 'An Amalekite,' I answered.

⁹"Then he said to me, 'Stand over me and kill me! I am in the throes of death, but I'm still alive.'

¹⁰"So I stood over him and killed him, because I knew that after he had fallen he could not survive. And I took the crown that was on his head and the band on his arm and have brought them here to my lord."

¹¹Then David and all the men with him took hold of their clothes and tore them. ¹²They mourned and wept and fasted till evening for Saul and his son Jonathan, and for the army of the Lord and the house of Israel, because they had fallen by the sword.

¹³David said to the young man who brought him the report, "Where are you from?"

"I am the son of an alien, an Amalekite," he answered.

¹⁴David asked him, "Why were you not afraid to lift your hand to destroy the Lord's anointed?"

¹⁵Then David called one of his men and said, "Go, strike him down!" So he struck him down, and he died. ¹⁶For David had said to him, "Your blood be on your own head. Your own mouth testified against you when you said, 'I killed the Lord's anointed.' "

¹⁷David took up this lament concerning Saul and his son Jonathan, ¹⁸and ordered that the men of Judah be taught this lament of the bow (it is written in the Book of Jashar):

¹⁹"Your glory, O Israel, lies slain on your
    heights.
  How the mighty have fallen!

²⁰"Tell it not in Gath,
    proclaim it not in the streets of Ashkelon,
  lest the daughters of the Philistines be glad,
    lest the daughters of the uncircumcised
      rejoice.

²¹"O mountains of Gilboa,
    may you have neither dew nor rain,
    nor fields that yield offerings ⌞of grain⌟.
  For there the shield of the mighty was defiled,
    the shield of Saul—no longer rubbed with
      oil.
²²From the blood of the slain,
    from the flesh of the mighty,
  the bow of Jonathan did not turn back,
    the sword of Saul did not return
      unsatisfied.

²³"Saul and Jonathan—
    in life they were loved and gracious,
    and in death they were not parted.
  They were swifter than eagles,
    they were stronger than lions.

²⁴"O daughters of Israel,
    weep for Saul,
  who clothed you in scarlet and finery,
    who adorned your garments with
      ornaments of gold.

²⁵"How the mighty have fallen in battle!
    Jonathan lies slain on your heights.
²⁶I grieve for you, Jonathan my brother;
    you were very dear to me.
  Your love for me was wonderful,
    more wonderful than that of women.

²⁷"How the mighty have fallen!
    The weapons of war have perished!"

In the course of time, David inquired of the Lord. "Shall I go up to one of the towns of Judah?" he asked.

The Lord said, "Go up."

David asked, "Where shall I go?"

"To Hebron," the LORD answered.

²So David went up there with his two wives, Ahinoam of Jezreel and Abigail, the widow of Nabal of Carmel. ³David also took the men who were with him, each with his family, and they settled in Hebron and its towns. ⁴Then the men of Judah came to Hebron and there they anointed David king over the house of Judah.

When David was told that it was the men of Jabesh Gilead who had buried Saul, ⁵he sent messengers to the men of Jabesh Gilead to say to them, "The LORD bless you for showing this kindness to Saul your master by burying him. ⁶May the LORD now show you kindness and faithfulness, and I too will show you the same favor because you have done this. ⁷Now then, be strong and brave, for Saul your master is dead, and the house of Judah has anointed me king over them."

⁸Meanwhile, Abner son of Ner, the commander of Saul's army, had taken Ish-Bosheth son of Saul and brought him over to Mahanaim. ⁹He made him king over Gilead, Ashuri*a* and Jezreel, and also over Ephraim, Benjamin and all Israel.

¹⁰Ish-Bosheth son of Saul was forty years old when he became king over Israel, and he reigned two years. The house of Judah, however, followed David. ¹¹The length of time David was king in Hebron over the house of Judah was seven years and six months.

¹²Abner son of Ner, together with the men of Ish-Bosheth son of Saul, left Mahanaim and went to Gibeon. ¹³Joab son of Zeruiah and David's men went out and met them at the pool of Gibeon. One group sat down on one side of the pool and one group on the other side.

¹⁴Then Abner said to Joab, "Let's have some of the young men get up and fight hand to hand in front of us."

"All right, let them do it," Joab said.

¹⁵So they stood up and were counted off—twelve men for Benjamin and Ish-Bosheth son of Saul, and twelve for David. ¹⁶Then each man grabbed his opponent by the head and thrust his dagger into his opponent's side, and they fell down together. So that place in Gibeon was called Helkath Hazzurim.*b*

¹⁷The battle that day was very fierce, and Abner and the men of Israel were defeated by David's men.

¹⁸The three sons of Zeruiah were there: Joab, Abishai and Asahel. Now Asahel was as fleet-footed as a wild gazelle. ¹⁹He chased Abner, turning neither to the right nor to the left as he pursued him. ²⁰Abner looked behind him and asked, "Is that you, Asahel?"

"It is," he answered.

²¹Then Abner said to him, "Turn aside to the right or to the left; take on one of the young men and strip him of his weapons." But Asahel would not stop chasing him.

²²Again Abner warned Asahel, "Stop chasing me! Why should I strike you down? How could I look your brother Joab in the face?"

²³But Asahel refused to give up the pursuit; so Abner thrust the butt of his spear into Asahel's stomach, and the spear came out through his back. He fell there and died on the spot. And every man stopped when he came to the place where Asahel had fallen and died.

²⁴But Joab and Abishai pursued Abner, and as the sun was setting, they came to the hill of Ammah, near Giah on the way to the wasteland of Gibeon. ²⁵Then the men of Benjamin rallied behind Abner. They formed themselves into a group and took their stand on top of a hill.

²⁶Abner called out to Joab, "Must the sword devour forever? Don't you realize that this will end in bitterness? How long before you order your men to stop pursuing their brothers?"

²⁷Joab answered, "As surely as God lives, if you had not spoken, the men would have continued the pursuit of their brothers until morning.*c*"

²⁸So Joab blew the trumpet, and all the men came to a halt; they no longer pursued Israel, nor did they fight anymore.

²⁹All that night Abner and his men marched through the Arabah. They crossed the Jordan, continued through the whole Bithron*d* and came to Mahanaim.

³⁰Then Joab returned from pursuing Abner and assembled all his men. Besides Asahel, nineteen of David's men were found missing. ³¹But David's men had killed three hundred and sixty Benjamites who were with Abner. ³²They took Asahel and buried him in his father's tomb at Bethlehem. Then Joab and his men marched all night and arrived at Hebron by daybreak.

---

*a*9 Or *Asher*   *b*16 *Helkath Hazzurim* means *field of daggers* or *field of hostilities.*   *c*27 Or *spoken this morning, the men would not have taken up the pursuit of their brothers;* or *spoken, the men would have given up the pursuit of their brothers by morning*   *d*29 Or *morning;* or *ravine;* the meaning of the Hebrew for this word is uncertain.

3 The war between the house of Saul and the house of David lasted a long time. David grew stronger and stronger, while the house of Saul grew weaker and weaker.

²Sons were born to David in Hebron:

His firstborn was Amnon the son of Ahinoam of Jezreel;

³his second, Kileab the son of Abigail the widow of Nabal of Carmel;

the third, Absalom the son of Maacah daughter of Talmai king of Geshur;

⁴the fourth, Adonijah the son of Haggith;

the fifth, Shephatiah the son of Abital;

⁵and the sixth, Ithream the son of David's wife Eglah.

These were born to David in Hebron.

⁶During the war between the house of Saul and the house of David, Abner had been strengthening his own position in the house of Saul. ⁷Now Saul had had a concubine named Rizpah daughter of Aiah. And Ish-Bosheth said to Abner, "Why did you sleep with my father's concubine?"

⁸Abner was very angry because of what Ish-Bosheth said and he answered, "Am I a dog's head—on Judah's side? This very day I am loyal to the house of your father Saul and to his family and friends. I haven't handed you over to David. Yet now you accuse me of an offense involving this woman! ⁹May God deal with Abner, be it ever so severely, if I do not do for David what the LORD promised him on oath ¹⁰and transfer the kingdom from the house of Saul and establish David's throne over Israel and Judah from Dan to Beersheba." ¹¹Ish-Bosheth did not dare to say another word to Abner, because he was afraid of him.

¹²Then Abner sent messengers on his behalf to say to David, "Whose land is it? Make an agreement with me, and I will help you bring all Israel over to you."

¹³"Good," said David. "I will make an agreement with you. But I demand one thing of you: Do not come into my presence unless you bring Michal daughter of Saul when you come to see me." ¹⁴Then David sent messengers to Ish-Bosheth son of Saul, demanding, "Give me my wife Michal, whom I betrothed to myself for the price of a hundred Philistine foreskins."

¹⁵So Ish-Bosheth gave orders and had her taken away from her husband Paltiel son of Laish. ¹⁶Her husband, however, went with her, weeping behind her all the way to Bahurim. Then Abner said to him, "Go back home!" So he went back.

¹⁷Abner conferred with the elders of Israel and said, "For some time you have wanted to make David your king. ¹⁸Now do it! For the LORD promised David, 'By my servant David I will rescue my people Israel from the hand of the Philistines and from the hand of all their enemies.' "

¹⁹Abner also spoke to the Benjamites in person. Then he went to Hebron to tell David everything that Israel and the whole house of Benjamin wanted to do. ²⁰When Abner, who had twenty men with him, came to David at Hebron, David prepared a feast for him and his men. ²¹Then Abner said to David, "Let me go at once and assemble all Israel for my lord the king, so that they may make a compact with you, and that you may rule over all that your heart desires." So David sent Abner away, and he went in peace.

²²Just then David's men and Joab returned from a raid and brought with them a great deal of plunder. But Abner was no longer with David in Hebron, because David had sent him away, and he had gone in peace. ²³When Joab and all the soldiers with him arrived, he was told that Abner son of Ner had come to the king and that the king had sent him away and that he had gone in peace.

²⁴So Joab went to the king and said, "What have you done? Look, Abner came to you. Why did you let him go? Now he is gone! ²⁵You know Abner son of Ner; he came to deceive you and observe your movements and find out everything you are doing."

²⁶Joab then left David and sent messengers after Abner, and they brought him back from the well of Sirah. But David did not know it. ²⁷Now when Abner returned to Hebron, Joab took him aside into the gateway, as though to speak with him privately. And there, to avenge the blood of his brother Asahel, Joab stabbed him in the stomach, and he died.

²⁸Later, when David heard about this, he said, "I and my kingdom are forever innocent before the LORD concerning the blood of Abner son of Ner. ²⁹May his blood fall upon the head of Joab and upon all his father's house! May Joab's house never be without someone who has a running sore or leprosyᵉ or who leans on a crutch or who falls by the sword or who lacks food."

³⁰(Joab and his brother Abishai murdered Ab-

ᵉ29 The Hebrew word was used for various diseases affecting the skin—not necessarily leprosy.

ner because he had killed their brother Asahel in the battle at Gibeon.)

31Then David said to Joab and all the people with him, "Tear your clothes and put on sackcloth and walk in mourning in front of Abner." King David himself walked behind the bier. 32They buried Abner in Hebron, and the king wept aloud at Abner's tomb. All the people wept also.

33The king sang this lament for Abner:

"Should Abner have died as the lawless die?
34   Your hands were not bound,
       your feet were not fettered.
You fell as one falls before wicked men."

And all the people wept over him again.

35Then they all came and urged David to eat something while it was still day; but David took an oath, saying, "May God deal with me, be it ever so severely, if I taste bread or anything else before the sun sets!"

36All the people took note and were pleased; indeed, everything the king did pleased them. 37So on that day all the people and all Israel knew that the king had no part in the murder of Abner son of Ner.

38Then the king said to his men, "Do you not realize that a prince and a great man has fallen in Israel this day? 39And today, though I am the anointed king, I am weak, and these sons of Zeruiah are too strong for me. May the LORD repay the evildoer according to his evil deeds!"

4 When Ish-Bosheth son of Saul heard that Abner had died in Hebron, he lost courage, and all Israel became alarmed. 2Now Saul's son had two men who were leaders of raiding bands. One was named Baanah and the other Recab; they were sons of Rimmon the Beerothite from the tribe of Benjamin—Beeroth is considered part of Benjamin, 3because the people of Beeroth fled to Gittaim and have lived there as aliens to this day.

4(Jonathan son of Saul had a son who was lame in both feet. He was five years old when the news about Saul and Jonathan came from Jezreel. His nurse picked him up and fled, but as she hurried to leave, he fell and became crippled. His name was Mephibosheth.)

5Now Recab and Baanah, the sons of Rimmon the Beerothite, set out for the house of Ish-Bosheth, and they arrived there in the heat of the day while he was taking his noonday rest. 6They

went into the inner part of the house as if to get some wheat, and they stabbed him in the stomach. Then Recab and his brother Baanah slipped away.

7They had gone into the house while he was lying on the bed in his bedroom. After they stabbed and killed him, they cut off his head. Taking it with them, they traveled all night by way of the Arabah. 8They brought the head of Ish-Bosheth to David at Hebron and said to the king, "Here is the head of Ish-Bosheth son of Saul, your enemy, who tried to take your life. This day the LORD has avenged my lord the king against Saul and his offspring."

9David answered Recab and his brother Baanah, the sons of Rimmon the Beerothite, "As surely as the LORD lives, who has delivered me out of all trouble, 10when a man told me, 'Saul is dead,' and thought he was bringing good news, I seized him and put him to death in Ziklag. That was the reward I gave him for his news! 11How much more—when wicked men have killed an innocent man in his own house and on his own bed—should I not now demand his blood from your hand and rid the earth of you!"

12So David gave an order to his men, and they killed them. They cut off their hands and feet and hung the bodies by the pool in Hebron. But they took the head of Ish-Bosheth and buried it in Abner's tomb at Hebron.

5 All the tribes of Israel came to David at Hebron and said, "We are your own flesh and blood. 2In the past, while Saul was king over us, you were the one who led Israel on their military campaigns. And the LORD said to you, 'You will shepherd my people Israel, and you will become their ruler.' "

3When all the elders of Israel had come to King David at Hebron, the king made a compact with them at Hebron before the LORD, and they anointed David king over Israel.

4David was thirty years old when he became king, and he reigned forty years. 5In Hebron he reigned over Judah seven years and six months, and in Jerusalem he reigned over all Israel and Judah thirty-three years.

6The king and his men marched to Jerusalem to attack the Jebusites, who lived there. The Jebusites said to David, "You will not get in here; even the blind and the lame can ward you off." They thought, "David cannot get in here." 7Nevertheless, David captured the fortress of Zion, the City of David.

⁸On that day, David said, "Anyone who conquers the Jebusites will have to use the water shaftᶠ to reach those 'lame and blind' who are David's enemies.ᵍ" That is why they say, "The 'blind and lame' will not enter the palace."

⁹David then took up residence in the fortress and called it the City of David. He built up the area around it, from the supporting terracesʰ inward. ¹⁰And he became more and more powerful, because the LORD God Almighty was with him.

¹¹Now Hiram king of Tyre sent messengers to David, along with cedar logs and carpenters and stonemasons, and they built a palace for David. ¹²And David knew that the LORD had established him as king over Israel and had exalted his kingdom for the sake of his people Israel.

¹³After he left Hebron, David took more concubines and wives in Jerusalem, and more sons and daughters were born to him. ¹⁴These are the names of the children born to him there: Shammua, Shobab, Nathan, Solomon, ¹⁵Ibhar, Elishua, Nepheg, Japhia, ¹⁶Elishama, Eliada and Eliphelet.

¹⁷When the Philistines heard that David had been anointed king over Israel, they went up in full force to search for him, but David heard about it and went down to the stronghold. ¹⁸Now the Philistines had come and spread out in the Valley of Rephaim; ¹⁹so David inquired of the LORD, "Shall I go and attack the Philistines? Will you hand them over to me?"

The LORD answered him, "Go, for I will surely hand the Philistines over to you."

²⁰So David went to Baal Perazim, and there he defeated them. He said, "As waters break out, the LORD has broken out against my enemies before me." So that place was called Baal Perazim.ⁱ ²¹The Philistines abandoned their idols there, and David and his men carried them off.

²²Once more the Philistines came up and spread out in the Valley of Rephaim; ²³so David inquired of the LORD, and he answered, "Do not go straight up, but circle around behind them and attack them in front of the balsam trees. ²⁴As soon as you hear the sound of marching in the tops of the balsam trees, move quickly, because that will mean the LORD has gone out in front of you to strike the Philistine army." ²⁵So David did as the LORD commanded him, and he struck down the Philistines all the way from Gibeonʲ to Gezer.

ᶠ8 Or use scaling hooks   ᵍ8 Or are hated by David   ʰ9 Or the Millo   ⁱ20 Baal Perazim means the lord who breaks out.   ʲ25 Septuagint (see also 1 Chron. 14:16); Hebrew Geba

1 / 2 Samuel 6
God's Wrath & Blessing

IN THE CHRONICLES of Narnia we are introduced to Aslan, the son of the great Emperor-Beyond-the-Sea, in this way:
    "Don't you know who is the King of Beasts? Aslan is a lion—the Lion, the great Lion."
    "Ooh!" said Susan, "I'd thought he was a man. Is he—quite safe? I shall feel rather nervous about meeting a lion."
    "That you will, dearie, and no mistake," said Mrs. Beaver. "If there's anyone who can appear before Aslan without their knees knocking, they're either braver than most or else just silly."
    "Then he isn't safe?" said Lucy.
    "Safe!" said Mr. Beaver. "Don't you hear what Mrs. Beaver tells you? Who said anything about safe? 'Course he isn't safe. But he's good."
In this chapter David learns in a terrible way that the Lord, the God of Israel, isn't safe. But he also gains a greater appreciation of God's goodness.

 Warming Up to God When you think of God's holiness, what ideas or images come to mind?

 Read 2 Samuel 6.

6 David again brought together out of Israel chosen men, thirty thousand in all. [2]He and all his men set out from Baalah of Judah[k] to bring up from there the ark of God, which is called by the Name,[l] the name of the LORD Almighty, who is enthroned between the cherubim that are on the ark. [3]They set the ark of God on a new cart and brought it from the house of Abinadab, which was on the hill. Uzzah and Ahio, sons of Abinadab, were guiding the new cart [4]with the ark of God on it,[m] and Ahio was walking in front of it. [5]David and the whole house of Israel were celebrating with all their might before the LORD, with songs[n] and with harps, lyres, tambourines, sistrums and cymbals.

[6]When they came to the threshing floor of Nacon, Uzzah reached out and took hold of the ark of God, because the oxen stumbled. [7]The LORD's anger burned against Uzzah because of his irreverent act; therefore God struck him down and he died there beside the ark of God.

[8]Then David was angry because the LORD's wrath had broken out against Uzzah, and to this day that place is called Perez Uzzah.[o]

[9]David was afraid of the LORD that day and said, "How can the ark of the LORD ever come to me?" [10]He was not willing to take the ark of the LORD to be with him in the City of David. Instead, he took it aside to the house of Obed-Edom the Gittite. [11]The ark of the LORD remained in the house of Obed-Edom the Gittite for three months, and the LORD blessed him and his entire household.

[12]Now King David was told, "The LORD has blessed the household of Obed-Edom and everything he has, because of the ark of God." So David went down and brought up the ark of God from the house of Obed-Edom to the City of David with rejoicing. [13]When those who were carrying the ark of the LORD had taken six steps, he sacrificed a bull and a fattened calf. [14]David, wearing a linen ephod, danced before the LORD with all his might, [15]while he and the entire house of Israel brought up the ark of the LORD with shouts and the sound of trumpets.

[16]As the ark of the LORD was entering the City of David, Michal daughter of Saul watched from a window. And when she saw King David leaping and dancing before the LORD, she despised him in her heart.

[17]They brought the ark of the LORD and set it in its place inside the tent that David had pitched for it, and David sacrificed burnt offerings and fellowship offerings[p] before the LORD. [18]After he had finished sacrificing the burnt offerings and fellowship offerings, he blessed the people in the name of the LORD Almighty. [19]Then he gave a loaf of bread, a cake of dates and a cake of raisins to each person in the whole crowd of Israelites, both men and women. And all the people went to their homes.

[20]When David returned home to bless his household, Michal daughter of Saul came out to meet him and said, "How the king of Israel has distinguished himself today, disrobing in the sight of the slave girls of his servants as any vulgar fellow would!"

[21]David said to Michal, "It was before the LORD, who chose me rather than your father or anyone from his house when he appointed me ruler over the LORD's people Israel—I will celebrate before the LORD. [22]I will become even more undignified than this, and I will be humiliated in my own eyes. But by these slave girls you spoke of, I will be held in honor."

[23]And Michal daughter of Saul had no children to the day of her death.

[k]2 That is, Kiriath Jearim; Hebrew *Baale Judah*, a variant of *Baalah of Judah*   [l]2 Hebrew; Septuagint and Vulgate do not have *the Name.*   [m]3,4 Dead Sea Scrolls and some Septuagint manuscripts; Masoretic Text *cart* [4]*and they brought it with the ark of God from the house of Abinadab, which was on the hill*   [n]5 See Dead Sea Scrolls, Septuagint and 1 Chronicles 13:8; Masoretic Text *celebrating before the LORD with all kinds of instruments made of pine.*   [o]8 *Perez Uzzah* means *outbreak against Uzzah.*   [p]17 Traditionally *peace offerings*; also in verse 18

Discovering the Word 1. What words would you use to describe the mood of those bringing the ark to Jerusalem (vv. 1–5)? 2. Uzzah's act of taking hold of the ark seems well intentioned (v. 6). Why then did the Lord's anger burn against him (v. 17; see also 1Ch 15:11–15)? 3. After Uzzah died, David become both angry and afraid of the Lord (vv. 8–9). How would you evaluate his emotional response? 4. Although the Lord had struck down Uzzah, he blessed the house of Obed-Edom (vv. 10–11). What was the Lord saying about himself through these events? 5. What new precautions does David take as he moves the ark to Jerusalem (vv. 12–15)? 6. In what other ways was this event marked by celebration?

Applying the Word 1. Do your times of worship tend to be somber or joyous? Explain. 2. In what ways might we make our times of worship more of a joyous celebration? 3. How does this chapter help you to understand God's holiness?

Responding in Prayer Ask God to teach you about his holiness, that you might respond in reverence to the one who is good—but not safe.

2 / 2 *Samuel 7*
God's Promise to David

AT SOME POINT in our lives, most of us want to do great things for God. We may imagine ourselves as world-famous evangelists, proclaiming the good news to thousands. Or we may aspire to be great Bible expositors, holding people spellbound with our oratory. Or perhaps we will be the next Mother Teresa, bringing care to the sick and needy. David wanted to build a magnificent temple for the Lord. However, in this passage he is surprised to discover that God's plans for David are far greater than David's plans for God.

 Warming Up to God Have you ever wanted to do great things for God? Explain.

 Read 2 Samuel 7.

7 After the king was settled in his palace and the LORD had given him rest from all his enemies around him, ²he said to Nathan the prophet, "Here I am, living in a palace of cedar, while the ark of God remains in a tent."

³Nathan replied to the king, "Whatever you have in mind, go ahead and do it, for the LORD is with you."

⁴That night the word of the LORD came to Nathan, saying:

⁵"Go and tell my servant David, 'This is what the LORD says: Are you the one to build me a house to dwell in? ⁶I have not dwelt in a house from the day I brought the Israelites up out of Egypt to this day. I have been moving from place to place with a tent as my dwelling. ⁷Wherever I have moved with all the Israelites, did I ever say to any of their rulers whom I commanded to shepherd my people Israel, "Why have you not built me a house of cedar?" '

⁸"Now then, tell my servant David, 'This is what the LORD Almighty says: I took you from the pasture and from following the flock to be ruler over my people Israel. ⁹I have been with you wherever you have gone, and I have cut off all your enemies from before you. Now I will make your name great, like the names of the greatest men of the earth. ¹⁰And I will provide a place for my people Israel and will plant them so that they can have a home of their own and no longer be disturbed. Wicked people will not oppress them anymore, as they did at the beginning ¹¹and have done ever since the time I appointed leaders*q* over my people Israel. I will also give you rest from all your enemies.

" 'The LORD declares to you that the LORD himself will establish a house for you: ¹²When your days are over and you rest with your fathers, I will raise up your offspring to succeed you, who will come from your own body, and I will establish his kingdom. ¹³He is the one who will build a house for my Name, and I will establish the throne of his kingdom forever. ¹⁴I will be his father, and he will be my son. When he does wrong, I will punish him with the rod of men, with floggings inflicted by men. ¹⁵But my love will never be taken away from him, as I took it away from Saul, whom I removed from before you. ¹⁶Your house and your kingdom will endure forever before me*r*; your throne will be established forever.' "

¹⁷Nathan reported to David all the words of this entire revelation.

¹⁸Then King David went in and sat before the LORD, and he said:

q11 Traditionally judges *r16 Some Hebrew manuscripts and Septuagint; most Hebrew manuscripts you*

"Who am I, O Sovereign LORD, and what is my family, that you have brought me this far? ¹⁹And as if this were not enough in your sight, O Sovereign LORD, you have also spoken about the future of the house of your servant. Is this your usual way of dealing with man, O Sovereign LORD?

²⁰"What more can David say to you? For you know your servant, O Sovereign LORD. ²¹For the sake of your word and according to your will, you have done this great thing and made it known to your servant.

²²"How great you are, O Sovereign LORD! There is no one like you, and there is no God but you, as we have heard with our own ears. ²³And who is like your people Israel—the one nation on earth that God went out to redeem as a people for himself, and to make a name for himself, and to perform great and awesome wonders by driving out nations and their gods from before your people, whom you redeemed from Egypt?ˢ ²⁴You have established your people Israel as your very own forever, and you, O LORD, have become their God.

²⁵"And now, LORD God, keep forever the promise you have made concerning your servant and his house. Do as you promised, ²⁶so that your name will be great forever. Then men will say, 'The LORD Almighty is God over Israel!' And the house of your servant David will be established before you.

²⁷"O LORD Almighty, God of Israel, you have revealed this to your servant, saying, 'I will build a house for you.' So your servant has found courage to offer you this prayer. ²⁸O Sovereign LORD, you are God! Your words are trustworthy, and you have promised these good things to your servant. ²⁹Now be pleased to bless the house of your servant, that it may continue forever in your sight; for you, O Sovereign LORD, have spoken, and with your blessing the house of your servant will be blessed forever."

ˢ23 See Septuagint and 1 Chron. 17:21; Hebrew *wonders for your land and before your people, whom you redeemed from Egypt, from the nations and their gods.*

Discovering the Word 1. What prompts David to want to build a house for the Lord (vv. 1–3)? 2. Throughout history, sincere people have built monuments for the Lord that he never asked for (vv. 4–7). How can we avoid involvement in these misguided projects? 3. Verses 8–16 have been called the Davidic covenant. What specific promises does God make to David? 4. How do the promises in verses 8–16 find their ultimate fulfillment in Jesus Christ (see, for example, Lk 1:30–33)? 5. After hearing God's promises to him, David prays (v. 18). Why is he astonished not only with the promises but with God himself (vv. 18–24)? 6. After praising God for his greatness, what requests does David make (vv. 25–29)?

Applying the Word 1. What insights does this passage give us into the relationship between God's sovereignty and our responsibility? 2. When have you been astonished to discover that both God and his plans are far greater than you imagined? 3. In what ways has the Lord demonstrated his greatness or goodness to you recently?

Responding in Prayer Take time to thank him for all that he has done for you.

2 Samuel 8

8 In the course of time, David defeated the Philistines and subdued them, and he took Metheg Ammah from the control of the Philistines.

²David also defeated the Moabites. He made them lie down on the ground and measured them off with a length of cord. Every two lengths of them were put to death, and the third length was allowed to live. So the Moabites became subject to David and brought tribute.

³Moreover, David fought Hadadezer son of Rehob, king of Zobah, when he went to restore his control along the Euphrates River. ⁴David captured a thousand of his chariots, seven thousand charioteersᵗ and twenty thousand foot soldiers.

ᵗ4 Septuagint (see also Dead Sea Scrolls and 1 Chron. 18:4); Masoretic Text *captured seventeen hundred of his charioteers*

He hamstrung all but a hundred of the chariot horses.

⁵When the Arameans of Damascus came to help Hadadezer king of Zobah, David struck down twenty-two thousand of them. ⁶He put garrisons in the Aramean kingdom of Damascus, and the Arameans became subject to him and brought tribute. The LORD gave David victory wherever he went.

⁷David took the gold shields that belonged to the officers of Hadadezer and brought them to Jerusalem. ⁸From Tebah ᵘ and Berothai, towns that belonged to Hadadezer, King David took a great quantity of bronze.

⁹When Tou ᵛ king of Hamath heard that David had defeated the entire army of Hadadezer, ¹⁰he sent his son Joram ʷ to King David to greet him and congratulate him on his victory in battle over Hadadezer, who had been at war with Tou. Joram brought with him articles of silver and gold and bronze.

¹¹King David dedicated these articles to the LORD, as he had done with the silver and gold

from all the nations he had subdued: ¹²Edom ˣ and Moab, the Ammonites and the Philistines, and Amalek. He also dedicated the plunder taken from Hadadezer son of Rehob, king of Zobah.

¹³And David became famous after he returned from striking down eighteen thousand Edomites ʸ in the Valley of Salt.

¹⁴He put garrisons throughout Edom, and all the Edomites became subject to David. The LORD gave David victory wherever he went.

¹⁵David reigned over all Israel, doing what was just and right for all his people. ¹⁶Joab son of Zeruiah was over the army; Jehoshaphat son of Ahilud was recorder; ¹⁷Zadok son of Ahitub and Ahimelech son of Abiathar were priests; Seraiah was secretary; ¹⁸Benaiah son of Jehoiada was over the Kerethites and Pelethites; and David's sons were royal advisers. ᶻ

ᵘ8 See some Septuagint manuscripts (see also 1 Chron. 18:8); Hebrew *Betah.*   ᵛ9 Hebrew *Toi,* a variant of *Tou;* also in verse 10   ʷ10 A variant of *Hadoram*   ˣ12 Some Hebrew manuscripts, Septuagint and Syriac (see also 1 Chron. 18:11); most Hebrew manuscripts *Aram*   ʸ13 A few Hebrew manuscripts, Septuagint and Syriac (see also 1 Chron. 18:12); most Hebrew manuscripts *Aram* (that is, Arameans)   ᶻ18 Or *were priests*

---

3 / 2 *Samuel 9*
Integrity

I WAS IN a minor accident not long ago. It caused so little damage that the owner of the other car suggested we settle privately, without the help of our insurance companies and the police. This was an attractive offer, since the accident was my fault and I'd probably get a ticket. But I wanted to do the right thing . . . and besides, someone had already called the police. That week I felt good about having done the right thing. However, the next week when I paid my ticket and my insurance premium went up, I felt frustrated. I caught myself wishing I had taken the man's suggestion. I learned through this incident that, though I value being a man of integrity, I'm not so wild about the costs that sometimes go along with it.

 Warming Up to God   What is real integrity? Give an example of someone who has demonstrated strong integrity.

 Read 2 Samuel 9.

---

9 David asked, "Is there anyone still left of the house of Saul to whom I can show kindness for Jonathan's sake?"

²Now there was a servant of Saul's household named Ziba. They called him to appear before David, and the king said to him, "Are you Ziba?"

"Your servant," he replied.

³The king asked, "Is there no one still left of

the house of Saul to whom I can show God's kindness?"

Ziba answered the king, "There is still a son of Jonathan; he is crippled in both feet."

⁴"Where is he?" the king asked.

Ziba answered, "He is at the house of Makir son of Ammiel in Lo Debar."

⁵So King David had him brought from Lo Debar, from the house of Makir son of Ammiel.

6When Mephibosheth son of Jonathan, the son of Saul, came to David, he bowed down to pay him honor.

David said, "Mephibosheth!"

"Your servant," he replied.

7"Don't be afraid," David said to him, "for I will surely show you kindness for the sake of your father Jonathan. I will restore to you all the land that belonged to your grandfather Saul, and you will always eat at my table."

8Mephibosheth bowed down and said, "What is your servant, that you should notice a dead dog like me?"

9Then the king summoned Ziba, Saul's servant, and said to him, "I have given your master's grandson everything that belonged to Saul and his family. 10You and your sons and your servants are to farm the land for him and bring in the crops, so that your master's grandson may be provided for. And Mephibosheth, grandson of your master, will always eat at my table." (Now Ziba had fifteen sons and twenty servants.)

11Then Ziba said to the king, "Your servant will do whatever my lord the king commands his servant to do." So Mephibosheth ate at David's*a* table like one of the king's sons.

12Mephibosheth had a young son named Mica, and all the members of Ziba's household were servants of Mephibosheth. 13And Mephibosheth lived in Jerusalem, because he always ate at the king's table, and he was crippled in both feet.

*a*11 Septuagint; Hebrew *my*

 Discovering the Word 1. What is Mephibosheth's relationship to Jonathan and to Saul? 2. In 1 Samuel 20:12–17 David made a covenant with Jonathan. In what way is David's care for Mephibosheth a fulfillment of his promise to Jonathan? 3. What kindness does David show Mephibosheth, and what does it cost him (vv. 7–15)? 4. What does this tell us about David's character? 5. What does this say about David's attitude toward his promises?

Applying the Word 1. In what situations are you most tempted to compromise your integrity? Why? 2. What are some of the real and potential costs you may incur to maintain your integrity? 3. How can you emulate David's integrity in day-to-day situations?

Responding in Prayer Pray for God's strength as you work toward being a person of integrity.

---

2 Samuel 10

10 In the course of time, the king of the Ammonites died, and his son Hanun succeeded him as king. 2David thought, "I will show kindness to Hanun son of Nahash, just as his father showed kindness to me." So David sent a delegation to express his sympathy to Hanun concerning his father.

When David's men came to the land of the Ammonites, 3the Ammonite nobles said to Hanun their lord, "Do you think David is honoring your father by sending men to you to express sympathy? Hasn't David sent them to you to explore the city and spy it out and overthrow it?" 4So Hanun seized David's men, shaved off half of each man's beard, cut off their garments in the middle at the buttocks, and sent them away.

5When David was told about this, he sent messengers to meet the men, for they were greatly humiliated. The king said, "Stay at Jericho till your beards have grown, and then come back."

6When the Ammonites realized that they had become a stench in David's nostrils, they hired twenty thousand Aramean foot soldiers from Beth Rehob and Zobah, as well as the king of Maacah with a thousand men, and also twelve thousand men from Tob.

7On hearing this, David sent Joab out with the entire army of fighting men. 8The Ammonites came out and drew up in battle formation at the entrance to their city gate, while the Arameans of Zobah and Rehob and the men of Tob and Maacah were by themselves in the open country.

9Joab saw that there were battle lines in front of him and behind him; so he selected some of the best troops in Israel and deployed them against the Arameans. ¹⁰He put the rest of the men under the command of Abishai his brother and deployed them against the Ammonites. ¹¹Joab said, "If the Arameans are too strong for me, then you are to come to my rescue; but if the Ammonites are too strong for you, then I will come to rescue you. ¹²Be strong and let us fight bravely for our people and the cities of our God. The Lord will do what is good in his sight."

¹³Then Joab and the troops with him advanced to fight the Arameans, and they fled before him. ¹⁴When the Ammonites saw that the Arameans were fleeing, they fled before Abishai and went inside the city. So Joab returned from fighting the Ammonites and came to Jerusalem.

¹⁵After the Arameans saw that they had been routed by Israel, they regrouped. ¹⁶Hadadezer had Arameans brought from beyond the Riverᵇ; they went to Helam, with Shobach the commander of Hadadezer's army leading them.

¹⁷When David was told of this, he gathered all Israel, crossed the Jordan and went to Helam. The Arameans formed their battle lines to meet David and fought against him. ¹⁸But they fled before Israel, and David killed seven hundred of their charioteers and forty thousand of their foot soldiers.ᶜ He also struck down Shobach the commander of their army, and he died there. ¹⁹When all the kings who were vassals of Hadadezer saw that they had been defeated by Israel, they made peace with the Israelites and became subject to them.

So the Arameans were afraid to help the Ammonites anymore.

ᵇ16 That is, the Euphrates   ᶜ18 Some Septuagint manuscripts (see also 1 Chron. 19:18); Hebrew *horsemen*

---

4 / 2 Samuel 11
Facing Temptation

IN *LAKE WOBEGON Days* Garrison Keillor describes a priest named Father Emil, who presides over Our Lady of Perpetual Responsibility Catholic Church. Every year Father Emil faithfully delivers a sermon on the evils of birth control. He entitles it "If You Didn't Want to Go to Minneapolis, Why Did You Get on the Train?" His point, of course, is that if we want to avoid certain consequences, we must avoid certain actions. The story of David and Bathsheba reveals how a series of smaller sins can build to tragic and devastating results. We also discover what forces can lead "a man after God's own heart" to commit adultery and murder.

 Warming Up to God When have you failed to be honest with God about sin in your life? If you have not yet done so, confess that sin to God.

 Read 2 Samuel 11.

---

11 In the spring, at the time when kings go off to war, David sent Joab out with the king's men and the whole Israelite army. They destroyed the Ammonites and besieged Rabbah. But David remained in Jerusalem.

²One evening David got up from his bed and walked around on the roof of the palace. From the roof he saw a woman bathing. The woman was very beautiful, ³and David sent someone to find out about her. The man said, "Isn't this Bathsheba, the daughter of Eliam and the wife of Uriah the Hittite?" ⁴Then David sent messengers to get her. She came to him, and he slept with her. (She had purified herself from her uncleanness.) Thenᵈ she went back home. ⁵The woman conceived and sent word to David, saying, "I am pregnant."

⁶So David sent this word to Joab: "Send me Uriah the Hittite." And Joab sent him to David. ⁷When Uriah came to him, David asked him how Joab was, how the soldiers were and how the war was going. ⁸Then David said to Uriah, "Go down to your house and wash your feet." So Uriah left the palace, and a gift from the king was sent after him. ⁹But Uriah slept at the entrance to the palace with all his master's servants and did not go down to his house.

ᵈ4 Or *with her. When she purified herself from her uncleanness,*

¹⁰When David was told, "Uriah did not go home," he asked him, "Haven't you just come from a distance? Why didn't you go home?"

¹¹Uriah said to David, "The ark and Israel and Judah are staying in tents, and my master Joab and my lord's men are camped in the open fields. How could I go to my house to eat and drink and lie with my wife? As surely as you live, I will not do such a thing!"

¹²Then David said to him, "Stay here one more day, and tomorrow I will send you back." So Uriah remained in Jerusalem that day and the next. ¹³At David's invitation, he ate and drank with him, and David made him drunk. But in the evening Uriah went out to sleep on his mat among his master's servants; he did not go home.

¹⁴In the morning David wrote a letter to Joab and sent it with Uriah. ¹⁵In it he wrote, "Put Uriah in the front line where the fighting is fiercest. Then withdraw from him so he will be struck down and die."

¹⁶So while Joab had the city under siege, he put Uriah at a place where he knew the strongest defenders were. ¹⁷When the men of the city came out and fought against Joab, some of the men in David's army fell; moreover, Uriah the Hittite died.

¹⁸Joab sent David a full account of the battle. ¹⁹He instructed the messenger: "When you have finished giving the king this account of the battle,

²⁰the king's anger may flare up, and he may ask you, 'Why did you get so close to the city to fight? Didn't you know they would shoot arrows from the wall? ²¹Who killed Abimelech son of Jerub-Beshethᵉ? Didn't a woman throw an upper millstone on him from the wall, so that he died in Thebez? Why did you get so close to the wall?' If he asks you this, then say to him, 'Also, your servant Uriah the Hittite is dead.'"

²²The messenger set out, and when he arrived he told David everything Joab had sent him to say. ²³The messenger said to David, "The men overpowered us and came out against us in the open, but we drove them back to the entrance to the city gate. ²⁴Then the archers shot arrows at your servants from the wall, and some of the king's men died. Moreover, your servant Uriah the Hittite is dead."

²⁵David told the messenger, "Say this to Joab: 'Don't let this upset you; the sword devours one as well as another. Press the attack against the city and destroy it.' Say this to encourage Joab."

²⁶When Uriah's wife heard that her husband was dead, she mourned for him. ²⁷After the time of mourning was over, David had her brought to his house, and she became his wife and bore him a son. But the thing David had done displeased the Lord.

ᵉ21 Also known as *Jerub-Baal* (that is, Gideon)

 Discovering the Word 1. Sin often begins with a series of temptations, each one leading to the next. What steps led to David's sin with Bathsheba (vv. 1–5)? 2. At each stage of his temptation, what might David have done to keep from taking the next step? (Be specific.) 3. What plan does David devise to cover up his sin (vv. 6–13)? How does Uriah thwart David's plan—at least initially? 4. When deceit fails to work, how does David's plan become vicious (vv. 14–15)? 5. What other people does David draw into the wake of his sin? 6. From this chapter, how would you explain what led "a man after God's own heart" to commit adultery and murder?

 Applying the Word 1. At what point does a temptation become sin? 2. Why are we tempted to cover up our sins rather than confess them? 3. In what specific ways is David's experience a warning to you?

Responding in Prayer Pray that you would be faithful in the "little things" so that you would not be led into temptation.

5 / 2 Samuel 12
God's Severe Mercy

IT OFTEN SEEMS easier to cover up our sin than to confess it and accept the consequences. In the previous chapter, David sought desperately to hide what he had done. After his plan was frustrated again and again, he cold-bloodedly killed the one who threatened to expose his sin. The chapter concluded with the ominous words "But the thing David had done displeased the LORD." Then, when David assumes his "problem" is safely behind him, Nathan appears with a message from God. This chapter gives us a powerful example of God's severe mercy.

 Warming Up to God How do you tend to respond when someone confronts you about something you know you've done wrong?

 Read 2 Samuel 12.

12 The LORD sent Nathan to David. When he came to him, he said, "There were two men in a certain town, one rich and the other poor. ²The rich man had a very large number of sheep and cattle, ³but the poor man had nothing except one little ewe lamb he had bought. He raised it, and it grew up with him and his children. It shared his food, drank from his cup and even slept in his arms. It was like a daughter to him.

⁴"Now a traveler came to the rich man, but the rich man refrained from taking one of his own sheep or cattle to prepare a meal for the traveler who had come to him. Instead, he took the ewe lamb that belonged to the poor man and prepared it for the one who had come to him."

⁵David burned with anger against the man and said to Nathan, "As surely as the LORD lives, the man who did this deserves to die! ⁶He must pay for that lamb four times over, because he did such a thing and had no pity."

⁷Then Nathan said to David, "You are the man! This is what the LORD, the God of Israel, says: 'I anointed you king over Israel, and I delivered you from the hand of Saul. ⁸I gave you your master's house to you, and your master's wives into your arms. I gave you the house of Israel and Judah. And if all this had been too little, I would have given you even more. ⁹Why did you despise the word of the LORD by doing what is evil in his eyes? You struck down Uriah the Hittite with the sword and took his wife to be your own. You killed him with the sword of the Ammonites. ¹⁰Now, therefore, the sword will never depart from your house, because you despised me and took the wife of Uriah the Hittite to be your own.'

¹¹"This is what the LORD says: 'Out of your own household I am going to bring calamity upon you. Before your very eyes I will take your wives and give them to one who is close to you, and he will lie with your wives in broad daylight. ¹²You did it in secret, but I will do this thing in broad daylight before all Israel.' "

¹³Then David said to Nathan, "I have sinned against the LORD."

Nathan replied, "The LORD has taken away your sin. You are not going to die. ¹⁴But because by doing this you have made the enemies of the LORD show utter contempt,ᶠ the son born to you will die."

¹⁵After Nathan had gone home, the LORD struck the child that Uriah's wife had borne to David, and he became ill. ¹⁶David pleaded with God for the child. He fasted and went into his house and spent the nights lying on the ground. ¹⁷The elders of his household stood beside him to get him up from the ground, but he refused, and he would not eat any food with them.

¹⁸On the seventh day the child died. David's servants were afraid to tell him that the child was dead, for they thought, "While the child was still living, we spoke to David but he would not listen to us. How can we tell him the child is dead? He may do something desperate."

¹⁹David noticed that his servants were whispering among themselves and he realized the child was dead. "Is the child dead?" he asked.

"Yes," they replied, "he is dead."

²⁰Then David got up from the ground. After he had washed, put on lotions and changed his clothes, he went into the house of the LORD and

---

ᶠ14 Masoretic Text; an ancient Hebrew scribal tradition *this you have shown utter contempt for the LORD* worshiped. Then he went to his own house, and at his request they served him food, and he ate.

²¹His servants asked him, "Why are you acting this way? While the child was alive, you fasted and wept, but now that the child is dead, you get up and eat!"

²²He answered, "While the child was still alive, I fasted and wept. I thought, 'Who knows? The LORD may be gracious to me and let the child live.' ²³But now that he is dead, why should I fast? Can I bring him back again? I will go to him, but he will not return to me."

²⁴Then David comforted his wife Bathsheba, and he went to her and lay with her. She gave birth to a son, and they named him Solomon. The LORD loved him; ²⁵and because the LORD loved him, he sent word through Nathan the prophet to name him Jedidiah.ᵍ

²⁶Meanwhile Joab fought against Rabbah of the Ammonites and captured the royal citadel. ²⁷Joab then sent messengers to David, saying, "I have fought against Rabbah and taken its water supply. ²⁸Now muster the rest of the troops and besiege the city and capture it. Otherwise I will take the city, and it will be named after me."

²⁹So David mustered the entire army and went to Rabbah, and attacked and captured it. ³⁰He took the crown from the head of their kingʰ—its weight was a talentⁱ of gold, and it was set with precious stones—and it was placed on David's head. He took a great quantity of plunder from the city ³¹and brought out the people who were there, consigning them to labor with saws and with iron picks and axes, and he made them work at brickmaking.ʲ He did this to all the Ammonite towns. Then David and his entire army returned to Jerusalem.

ᵍ25 *Jedidiah* means *loved by the* LORD.   ʰ30 Or *of Milcom* (that is, Molech)   ⁱ30 That is, about 75 pounds (about 34 kilograms)   ʲ31 The meaning of the Hebrew for this clause is uncertain.

Discovering the Word 1. Why do you think Nathan tells David a story rather than confronting him directly about his sin (vv. 1–6)? 2. Why is the Lord amazed that David despised both him and his word (vv. 7–10)? 3. How is God's justice and mercy revealed in his decision about David's sin (vv. 10–14)? 4. We normally assume that God disciplines us for our benefit (see Heb 12:5–13). Is God's treatment of David an example of beneficial discipline, or is God merely demanding a penalty for David's sin? Explain. 5. How does David respond to the news that his child is ill (vv. 15–17)? 6. After the child dies, how is God's grace again evident in David's life (vv. 23–25)?

Applying the Word 1. Why is it so difficult for us to be objective about our own sin? 2. The author of Hebrews writes: "No discipline seems pleasant at the time, but painful. Later on, however, it produces a harvest of righteousness and peace for those who have been trained by it" (12:11). In what ways has God's painful discipline had that effect in your life?

Responding in Prayer What is God trying to teach you at this point in your life? Ask him to make you open to his voice.

---

6 / *2 Samuel 13*
Sexual Violence

IN PREPARATION FOR writing *Stolen Childhood*, Alice Huskey did a survey of female students at a Christian college. Nineteen percent of the students reported sexual abuse before the age of eighteen. Five percent reported incest. Of those abused, eighty-nine percent knew the abuser. Less than half of the victims had told another person. Often those who did tell were ignored or even punished ([Downers Grove, Ill.: InterVarsity Press, 1989], p. 35). As these statistics show, sexual violence, among both Christians and non-Christians, is all too common. In this study we will see some of the far-reaching implications of this tragic fact.

Warming Up to God How has sexual violence affected you or someone you know? Ask God to prepare you to study this difficult topic.

Read 2 Samuel 13.

13

In the course of time, Amnon son of David fell in love with Tamar, the beautiful sister of Absalom son of David.

²Amnon became frustrated to the point of illness on account of his sister Tamar, for she was a virgin, and it seemed impossible for him to do anything to her.

³Now Amnon had a friend named Jonadab son of Shimeah, David's brother. Jonadab was a very shrewd man. ⁴He asked Amnon, "Why do you, the king's son, look so haggard morning after morning? Won't you tell me?"

Amnon said to him, "I'm in love with Tamar, my brother Absalom's sister."

⁵"Go to bed and pretend to be ill," Jonadab said. "When your father comes to see you, say to him, 'I would like my sister Tamar to come and give me something to eat. Let her prepare the food in my sight so I may watch her and then eat it from her hand.' "

⁶So Amnon lay down and pretended to be ill. When the king came to see him, Amnon said to him, "I would like my sister Tamar to come and make some special bread in my sight, so I may eat from her hand."

⁷David sent word to Tamar at the palace: "Go to the house of your brother Amnon and prepare some food for him." ⁸So Tamar went to the house of her brother Amnon, who was lying down. She took some dough, kneaded it, made the bread in his sight and baked it. ⁹Then she took the pan and served him the bread, but he refused to eat.

"Send everyone out of here," Amnon said. So everyone left him. ¹⁰Then Amnon said to Tamar, "Bring the food here into my bedroom so I may eat from your hand." And Tamar took the bread she had prepared and brought it to her brother Amnon in his bedroom. ¹¹But when she took it to him to eat, he grabbed her and said, "Come to bed with me, my sister."

¹²"Don't, my brother!" she said to him. "Don't force me. Such a thing should not be done in Israel! Don't do this wicked thing. ¹³What about me? Where could I get rid of my disgrace? And what about you? You would be like one of the wicked fools in Israel. Please speak to the king; he will not keep me from being married to you."

¹⁴But he refused to listen to her, and since he was stronger than she, he raped her.

¹⁵Then Amnon hated her with intense hatred. In fact, he hated her more than he had loved her. Amnon said to her, "Get up and get out!"

¹⁶"No!" she said to him. "Sending me away would be a greater wrong than what you have already done to me."

But he refused to listen to her. ¹⁷He called his personal servant and said, "Get this woman out of here and bolt the door after her." ¹⁸So his servant put her out and bolted the door after her. She was wearing a richly ornamented[k] robe, for this was the kind of garment the virgin daughters of the king wore. ¹⁹Tamar put ashes on her head and tore the ornamented[l] robe she was wearing. She put her hand on her head and went away, weeping aloud as she went.

²⁰Her brother Absalom said to her, "Has that Amnon, your brother, been with you? Be quiet now, my sister; he is your brother. Don't take this thing to heart." And Tamar lived in her brother Absalom's house, a desolate woman.

²¹When King David heard all this, he was furious. ²²Absalom never said a word to Amnon, either good or bad; he hated Amnon because he had disgraced his sister Tamar.

²³Two years later, when Absalom's sheepshearers were at Baal Hazor near the border of Ephraim, he invited all the king's sons to come there. ²⁴Absalom went to the king and said, "Your servant has had shearers come. Will the king and his officials please join me?"

²⁵"No, my son," the king replied. "All of us should not go; we would only be a burden to you." Although Absalom urged him, he still refused to go, but gave him his blessing.

²⁶Then Absalom said, "If not, please let my brother Amnon come with us."

The king asked him, "Why should he go with you?" ²⁷But Absalom urged him, so he sent with him Amnon and the rest of the king's sons.

²⁸Absalom ordered his men, "Listen! When Amnon is in high spirits from drinking wine and I say to you, 'Strike Amnon down,' then kill him. Don't be afraid. Have not I given you this order? Be strong and brave." ²⁹So Absalom's men did to

---

k 18 The meaning of the Hebrew for this phrase is uncertain.   l 19 The meaning of the Hebrew for this word is uncertain.

Amnon what Absalom had ordered. Then all the king's sons got up, mounted their mules and fled.

³⁰While they were on their way, the report came to David: "Absalom has struck down all the king's sons; not one of them is left." ³¹The king stood up, tore his clothes and lay down on the ground; and all his servants stood by with their clothes torn.

³²But Jonadab son of Shimeah, David's brother, said, "My lord should not think that they killed all the princes; only Amnon is dead. This has been Absalom's expressed intention ever since the day Amnon raped his sister Tamar. ³³My lord the king should not be concerned about the report that all the king's sons are dead. Only Amnon is dead."

³⁴Meanwhile, Absalom had fled.

Now the man standing watch looked up and saw many people on the road west of him, com-ing down the side of the hill. The watchman went and told the king, "I see men in the direction of Horonaim, on the side of the hill."[m]

³⁵Jonadab said to the king, "See, the king's sons are here; it has happened just as your servant said."

³⁶As he finished speaking, the king's sons came in, wailing loudly. The king, too, and all his servants wept very bitterly.

³⁷Absalom fled and went to Talmai son of Ammihud, the king of Geshur. But King David mourned for his son every day.

³⁸After Absalom fled and went to Geshur, he stayed there three years. ³⁹And the spirit of the king[n] longed to go to Absalom, for he was consoled concerning Amnon's death.

---

[m] 34 Septuagint; Hebrew does not have this sentence.   [n] 39 Dead Sea Scrolls and some Septuagint manuscripts; Masoretic Text *But ⌊the spirit of⌋ David the king*

Discovering the Word 1. Summarize Amnon's situation as it is described in verses 1–2. 2. Why do you think Amnon chooses to confide in Jonadab (vv. 3–4)? 3. How does Tamar respond to Amnon's advances (vv. 11–13)? 4. Why do you think Amnon's reaction after the encounter was hatred (vv. 15–17)? 5. What is the effect of Amnon's actions on family relations (vv. 21–22, 32)?

Applying the Word 1. What are some of the effects of sexual violence on our culture? 2. What can we do with our friends or in our churches to address the issue of sexual violence? Consider both victims and perpetrators.

Responding in Prayer Absalom tells Tamar not to take it to heart, yet she is described as a "desolate woman." Pray for those who have felt the pain of sexual violence. What results of sexual violence have you seen in victims in our culture (yourself, someone you know, someone you've heard or read about)?

---

2 Samuel 14

14 Joab son of Zeruiah knew that the king's heart longed for Absalom. ²So Joab sent someone to Tekoa and had a wise woman brought from there. He said to her, "Pretend you are in mourning. Dress in mourning clothes, and don't use any cosmetic lotions. Act like a woman who has spent many days grieving for the dead. ³Then go to the king and speak these words to him." And Joab put the words in her mouth.

⁴When the woman from Tekoa went[o] to the king, she fell with her face to the ground to pay him honor, and she said, "Help me, O king!"

⁵The king asked her, "What is troubling you?"

She said, "I am indeed a widow; my husband is dead. ⁶I your servant had two sons. They got into a fight with each other in the field, and no one was there to separate them. One struck the other and killed him. ⁷Now the whole clan has risen up against your servant; they say, 'Hand over the one who struck his brother down, so that we may put him to death for the life of his brother whom he killed; then we will get rid of the heir as well.' They would put out the only burning coal I have left, leaving my husband neither name nor descendant on the face of the earth."

⁸The king said to the woman, "Go home, and I will issue an order in your behalf."

⁹But the woman from Tekoa said to him, "My lord the king, let the blame rest on me and on my

---

[o] 4 Many Hebrew manuscripts, Septuagint, Vulgate and Syriac; most Hebrew manuscripts *spoke*

father's family, and let the king and his throne be without guilt."

¹⁰The king replied, "If anyone says anything to you, bring him to me, and he will not bother you again."

¹¹She said, "Then let the king invoke the Lord his God to prevent the avenger of blood from adding to the destruction, so that my son will not be destroyed."

"As surely as the Lord lives," he said, "not one hair of your son's head will fall to the ground."

¹²Then the woman said, "Let your servant speak a word to my lord the king."

"Speak," he replied.

¹³The woman said, "Why then have you devised a thing like this against the people of God? When the king says this, does he not convict himself, for the king has not brought back his banished son? ¹⁴Like water spilled on the ground, which cannot be recovered, so we must die. But God does not take away life; instead, he devises ways so that a banished person may not remain estranged from him.

¹⁵"And now I have come to say this to my lord the king because the people have made me afraid. Your servant thought, 'I will speak to the king; perhaps he will do what his servant asks. ¹⁶Perhaps the king will agree to deliver his servant from the hand of the man who is trying to cut off both me and my son from the inheritance God gave us.'

¹⁷"And now your servant says, 'May the word of my lord the king bring me rest, for my lord the king is like an angel of God in discerning good and evil. May the Lord your God be with you.'"

¹⁸Then the king said to the woman, "Do not keep from me the answer to what I am going to ask you."

"Let my lord the king speak," the woman said.

¹⁹The king asked, "Isn't the hand of Joab with you in all this?"

The woman answered, "As surely as you live, my lord the king, no one can turn to the right or to the left from anything my lord the king says. Yes, it was your servant Joab who instructed me to do this and who put all these words into the mouth of your servant. ²⁰Your servant Joab did this to change the present situation. My lord has

wisdom like that of an angel of God—he knows everything that happens in the land."

²¹The king said to Joab, "Very well, I will do it. Go, bring back the young man Absalom."

²²Joab fell with his face to the ground to pay him honor, and he blessed the king. Joab said, "Today your servant knows that he has found favor in your eyes, my lord the king, because the king has granted his servant's request."

²³Then Joab went to Geshur and brought Absalom back to Jerusalem. ²⁴But the king said, "He must go to his own house; he must not see my face." So Absalom went to his own house and did not see the face of the king.

²⁵In all Israel there was not a man so highly praised for his handsome appearance as Absalom. From the top of his head to the sole of his foot there was no blemish in him. ²⁶Whenever he cut the hair of his head—he used to cut his hair from time to time when it became too heavy for him—he would weigh it, and its weight was two hundred shekelsᵖ by the royal standard.

²⁷Three sons and a daughter were born to Absalom. The daughter's name was Tamar, and she became a beautiful woman.

²⁸Absalom lived two years in Jerusalem without seeing the king's face. ²⁹Then Absalom sent for Joab in order to send him to the king, but Joab refused to come to him. So he sent a second time, but he refused to come. ³⁰Then he said to his servants, "Look, Joab's field is next to mine, and he has barley there. Go and set it on fire." So Absalom's servants set the field on fire.

³¹Then Joab did go to Absalom's house and he said to him, "Why have your servants set my field on fire?"

³²Absalom said to Joab, "Look, I sent word to you and said, 'Come here so I can send you to the king to ask, "Why have I come from Geshur? It would be better for me if I were still there!"' Now then, I want to see the king's face, and if I am guilty of anything, let him put me to death."

³³So Joab went to the king and told him this. Then the king summoned Absalom, and he came in and bowed down with his face to the ground before the king. And the king kissed Absalom.

ᵖ26 That is, about 5 pounds (about 2.3 kilograms)

7 / 2 Samuel 15
Difficult Days

STRESS HAS BECOME a part of our Western culture. We are all familiar with it, and it affects us all in our own way. Some can't eat, some get grumpy, some sleep. Me, well, I stay awake at night. My mind and heart cannot stop thinking about the issue at hand. My body is zonked, but my head keeps going a mile a minute.

One night a few years ago, while wrestling with a sudden case of insomnia brought on by balancing the family checkbook, I was struck by how void my worry was of thoughts of God. I had considered every option a thousand times in my head, but I hadn't prayed. I had not stopped to consider God's character or the promises of his Word. That night I learned that my lack of sleep is directly linked to my lack of faith. I still occasionally find myself unable to sleep, but I now have an option that brings my heart rest. I remember God, and I give it to him.

 Warming Up to God What are you feeling worried about right now? How has God been part of your process of working through your stress?

 Read 2 Samuel 15.

15 In the course of time, Absalom provided himself with a chariot and horses and with fifty men to run ahead of him. ²He would get up early and stand by the side of the road leading to the city gate. Whenever anyone came with a complaint to be placed before the king for a decision, Absalom would call out to him, "What town are you from?" He would answer, "Your servant is from one of the tribes of Israel." ³Then Absalom would say to him, "Look, your claims are valid and proper, but there is no representative of the king to hear you." ⁴And Absalom would add, "If only I were appointed judge in the land! Then everyone who has a complaint or case could come to me and I would see that he gets justice."

⁵Also, whenever anyone approached him to bow down before him, Absalom would reach out his hand, take hold of him and kiss him. ⁶Absalom behaved in this way toward all the Israelites who came to the king asking for justice, and so he stole the hearts of the men of Israel.

⁷At the end of four*�q* years, Absalom said to the king, "Let me go to Hebron and fulfill a vow I made to the LORD. ⁸While your servant was living at Geshur in Aram, I made this vow: 'If the LORD takes me back to Jerusalem, I will worship the LORD in Hebron.*ʳ* '"

⁹The king said to him, "Go in peace." So he went to Hebron.

¹⁰Then Absalom sent secret messengers throughout the tribes of Israel to say, "As soon as you hear the sound of the trumpets, then say, 'Absalom is king in Hebron.' " ¹¹Two hundred men from Jerusalem had accompanied Absalom.

They had been invited as guests and went quite innocently, knowing nothing about the matter. ¹²While Absalom was offering sacrifices, he also sent for Ahithophel the Gilonite, David's counselor, to come from Giloh, his hometown. And so the conspiracy gained strength, and Absalom's following kept on increasing.

¹³A messenger came and told David, "The hearts of the men of Israel are with Absalom."

¹⁴Then David said to all his officials who were with him in Jerusalem, "Come! We must flee, or none of us will escape from Absalom. We must leave immediately, or he will move quickly to overtake us and bring ruin upon us and put the city to the sword."

¹⁵The king's officials answered him, "Your servants are ready to do whatever our lord the king chooses."

¹⁶The king set out, with his entire household following him; but he left ten concubines to take care of the palace. ¹⁷So the king set out, with all the people following him, and they halted at a place some distance away. ¹⁸All his men marched past him, along with all the Kerethites and Pelethites; and all the six hundred Gittites who had accompanied him from Gath marched before the king.

¹⁹The king said to Ittai the Gittite, "Why should you come along with us? Go back and stay with King Absalom. You are a foreigner, an exile from your homeland. ²⁰You came only yesterday. And today shall I make you wander about with us, when I do not know where I am going? Go

q7 Some Septuagint manuscripts, Syriac and Josephus; Hebrew forty
r8 Some Septuagint manuscripts; Hebrew does not have in Hebron.

back, and take your countrymen. May kindness and faithfulness be with you."

²¹But Ittai replied to the king, "As surely as the Lord lives, and as my lord the king lives, wherever my lord the king may be, whether it means life or death, there will your servant be."

²²David said to Ittai, "Go ahead, march on." So Ittai the Gittite marched on with all his men and the families that were with him.

²³The whole countryside wept aloud as all the people passed by. The king also crossed the Kidron Valley, and all the people moved on toward the desert.

²⁴Zadok was there, too, and all the Levites who were with him were carrying the ark of the covenant of God. They set down the ark of God, and Abiathar offered sacrifices⁵ until all the people had finished leaving the city.

²⁵Then the king said to Zadok, "Take the ark of God back into the city. If I find favor in the Lord's eyes, he will bring me back and let me see it and his dwelling place again. ²⁶But if he says, 'I am not pleased with you,' then I am ready; let him do to me whatever seems good to him."

²⁷The king also said to Zadok the priest, "Aren't you a seer? Go back to the city in peace, with your son Ahimaaz and Jonathan son of Abiathar. You and Abiathar take your two sons with you. ²⁸I will wait at the fords in the desert until word comes from you to inform me." ²⁹So Zadok

and Abiathar took the ark of God back to Jerusalem and stayed there.

³⁰But David continued up the Mount of Olives, weeping as he went; his head was covered and he was barefoot. All the people with him covered their heads too and were weeping as they went up. ³¹Now David had been told, "Ahithophel is among the conspirators with Absalom." So David prayed, "O Lord, turn Ahithophel's counsel into foolishness."

³²When David arrived at the summit, where people used to worship God, Hushai the Arkite was there to meet him, his robe torn and dust on his head. ³³David said to him, "If you go with me, you will be a burden to me. ³⁴But if you return to the city and say to Absalom, 'I will be your servant, O king; I was your father's servant in the past, but now I will be your servant,' then you can help me by frustrating Ahithophel's advice. ³⁵Won't the priests Zadok and Abiathar be there with you? Tell them anything you hear in the king's palace. ³⁶Their two sons, Ahimaaz son of Zadok and Jonathan son of Abiathar, are there with them. Send them to me with anything you hear."

³⁷So David's friend Hushai arrived at Jerusalem as Absalom was entering the city.

ˢ24 Or *Abiathar went up*

 Discovering the Word   1. What is Absalom's strategy against David (vv. 1–12)?   2. Identify Absalom's unethical behavior. What does it tell us about him?   3. What does David do in defense against Absalom's attack?   4. Why does David tell Ittai to go back at first (vv. 19–20)?   5. What does the devotion of the people tell you about David (vv. 16, 21, 23, 30)?   6. In what ways does David demonstrate and act on his faith and trust in God?

Applying the Word   1. In 2 Samuel we learn that David took some steps in his own defense; yet he also looked to God for a sign of favor.   2. What truth or truths about God might help you respond to stressful situations with rest and peace?

Responding in Prayer   Spend some time praying through the issues that are troubling you.

2 Samuel 16:1—18:18

16 When David had gone a short distance beyond the summit, there was Ziba, the steward of Mephibosheth, waiting to meet him. He had a string of donkeys saddled and loaded with two hundred loaves of bread, a hundred cakes of raisins, a hundred cakes of figs and a skin of wine.

²The king asked Ziba, "Why have you brought these?"

Ziba answered, "The donkeys are for the king's household to ride on, the bread and fruit are for the men to eat, and the wine is to refresh those who become exhausted in the desert."

³The king then asked, "Where is your master's grandson?"

Ziba said to him, "He is staying in Jerusalem, because he thinks, 'Today the house of Israel will give me back my grandfather's kingdom.' "

⁴Then the king said to Ziba, "All that belonged to Mephibosheth is now yours."

"I humbly bow," Ziba said. "May I find favor in your eyes, my lord the king."

⁵As King David approached Bahurim, a man from the same clan as Saul's family came out from there. His name was Shimei son of Gera, and he cursed as he came out. ⁶He pelted David and all the king's officials with stones, though all the troops and the special guard were on David's right and left. ⁷As he cursed, Shimei said, "Get out, get out, you man of blood, you scoundrel! ⁸The LORD has repaid you for all the blood you shed in the household of Saul, in whose place you have reigned. The LORD has handed the kingdom over to your son Absalom. You have come to ruin because you are a man of blood!"

⁹Then Abishai son of Zeruiah said to the king, "Why should this dead dog curse my lord the king? Let me go over and cut off his head."

¹⁰But the king said, "What do you and I have in common, you sons of Zeruiah? If he is cursing because the LORD said to him, 'Curse David,' who can ask, 'Why do you do this?' "

¹¹David then said to Abishai and all his officials, "My son, who is of my own flesh, is trying to take my life. How much more, then, this Benjamite! Leave him alone; let him curse, for the LORD has told him to. ¹²It may be that the LORD will see my distress and repay me with good for the cursing I am receiving today."

¹³So David and his men continued along the road while Shimei was going along the hillside opposite him, cursing as he went and throwing stones at him and showering him with dirt. ¹⁴The king and all the people with him arrived at their destination exhausted. And there he refreshed himself.

¹⁵Meanwhile, Absalom and all the men of Israel came to Jerusalem, and Ahithophel was with him. ¹⁶Then Hushai the Arkite, David's friend, went to Absalom and said to him, "Long live the king! Long live the king!"

¹⁷Absalom asked Hushai, "Is this the love you show your friend? Why didn't you go with your friend?"

¹⁸Hushai said to Absalom, "No, the one chosen by the LORD, by these people, and by all the men of Israel—his I will be, and I will remain with him. ¹⁹Furthermore, whom should I serve? Should I not serve the son? Just as I served your father, so I will serve you."

²⁰Absalom said to Ahithophel, "Give us your advice. What should we do?"

²¹Ahithophel answered, "Lie with your father's concubines whom he left to take care of the palace. Then all Israel will hear that you have made yourself a stench in your father's nostrils, and the hands of everyone with you will be strengthened." ²²So they pitched a tent for Absalom on the roof, and he lay with his father's concubines in the sight of all Israel.

²³Now in those days the advice Ahithophel gave was like that of one who inquires of God. That was how both David and Absalom regarded all of Ahithophel's advice.

17 Ahithophel said to Absalom, "I would* choose twelve thousand men and set out tonight in pursuit of David. ²I would* attack him while he is weary and weak. I would* strike him with terror, and then all the people with him will flee. I would* strike down only the king ³and bring all the people back to you. The death of the man you seek will mean the return of all; all the people will be unharmed." ⁴This plan seemed good to Absalom and to all the elders of Israel.

⁵But Absalom said, "Summon also Hushai the Arkite, so we can hear what he has to say."

*1 Or *Let me*   *2 Or will*

⁶When Hushai came to him, Absalom said, "Ahithophel has given this advice. Should we do what he says? If not, give us your opinion."

⁷Hushai replied to Absalom, "The advice Ahithophel has given is not good this time. ⁸You know your father and his men; they are fighters, and as fierce as a wild bear robbed of her cubs. Besides, your father is an experienced fighter; he will not spend the night with the troops. ⁹Even now, he is hidden in a cave or some other place. If he should attack your troops first,ᵛ whoever hears about it will say, 'There has been a slaughter among the troops who follow Absalom.' ¹⁰Then even the bravest soldier, whose heart is like the heart of a lion, will melt with fear, for all Israel knows that your father is a fighter and that those with him are brave.

¹¹"So I advise you: Let all Israel, from Dan to Beersheba—as numerous as the sand on the seashore—be gathered to you, with you yourself leading them into battle. ¹²Then we will attack him wherever he may be found, and we will fall on him as dew settles on the ground. Neither he nor any of his men will be left alive. ¹³If he withdraws into a city, then all Israel will bring ropes to that city, and we will drag it down to the valley until not even a piece of it can be found."

¹⁴Absalom and all the men of Israel said, "The advice of Hushai the Arkite is better than that of Ahithophel." For the Lᴏʀᴅ had determined to frustrate the good advice of Ahithophel in order to bring disaster on Absalom.

¹⁵Hushai told Zadok and Abiathar, the priests, "Ahithophel has advised Absalom and the elders of Israel to do such and such, but I have advised them to do so and so. ¹⁶Now send a message immediately and tell David, 'Do not spend the night at the fords in the desert; cross over without fail, or the king and all the people with him will be swallowed up.' "

¹⁷Jonathan and Ahimaaz were staying at En Rogel. A servant girl was to go and inform them, and they were to go and tell King David, for they could not risk being seen entering the city. ¹⁸But a young man saw them and told Absalom. So the two of them left quickly and went to the house of a man in Bahurim. He had a well in his courtyard, and they climbed down into it. ¹⁹His wife took a covering and spread it out over the opening of the well and scattered grain over it. No one knew anything about it.

²⁰When Absalom's men came to the woman at the house, they asked, "Where are Ahimaaz and Jonathan?"

The woman answered them, "They crossed over the brook."ʷ The men searched but found no one, so they returned to Jerusalem.

²¹After the men had gone, the two climbed out of the well and went to inform King David. They said to him, "Set out and cross the river at once; Ahithophel has advised such and such against you." ²²So David and all the people with him set out and crossed the Jordan. By daybreak, no one was left who had not crossed the Jordan.

²³When Ahithophel saw that his advice had not been followed, he saddled his donkey and set out for his house in his hometown. He put his house in order and then hanged himself. So he died and was buried in his father's tomb.

²⁴David went to Mahanaim, and Absalom crossed the Jordan with all the men of Israel. ²⁵Absalom had appointed Amasa over the army in place of Joab. Amasa was the son of a man named Jether,ˣ an Israeliteʸ who had married Abigail,ᶻ the daughter of Nahash and sister of Zeruiah the mother of Joab. ²⁶The Israelites and Absalom camped in the land of Gilead.

²⁷When David came to Mahanaim, Shobi son of Nahash from Rabbah of the Ammonites, and Makir son of Ammiel from Lo Debar, and Barzillai the Gileadite from Rogelim ²⁸brought bedding and bowls and articles of pottery. They also brought wheat and barley, flour and roasted grain, beans and lentils,ᵃ ²⁹honey and curds, sheep, and cheese from cows' milk for David and his people to eat. For they said, "The people have become hungry and tired and thirsty in the desert."

18
David mustered the men who were with him and appointed over them commanders of thousands and commanders of hundreds. ²David sent the troops out—a third under the command of Joab, a third under Joab's brother Abishai son of Zeruiah, and a third under Ittai the Gittite. The king told the troops, "I myself will surely march out with you."

³But the men said, "You must not go out; if we are forced to flee, they won't care about us. Even if half of us die, they won't care; but you are

ᵛ9 Or *When some of the men fall at the first attack* ʷ20 Or "They *passed by the sheep pen toward the water.*" ˣ25 Hebrew *Ithra,* a variant of *Jether* ʸ25 Hebrew and some Septuagint manuscripts; other Septuagint manuscripts (see also 1 Chron. 2:17) *Ishmaelite* or *Jezreelite* ᶻ25 Hebrew *Abigal,* a variant of *Abigail* ᵃ28 Most Septuagint manuscripts and Syriac; Hebrew *lentils, and roasted grain* worth ten thousand of us.*b* It would be better now for you to give us support from the city."

⁴The king answered, "I will do whatever seems best to you."

So the king stood beside the gate while all the men marched out in units of hundreds and of thousands. ⁵The king commanded Joab, Abishai and Ittai, "Be gentle with the young man Absalom for my sake." And all the troops heard the king giving orders concerning Absalom to each of the commanders.

⁶The army marched into the field to fight Israel, and the battle took place in the forest of Ephraim. ⁷There the army of Israel was defeated by David's men, and the casualties that day were great—twenty thousand men. ⁸The battle spread out over the whole countryside, and the forest claimed more lives that day than the sword.

⁹Now Absalom happened to meet David's men. He was riding his mule, and as the mule went under the thick branches of a large oak, Absalom's head got caught in the tree. He was left hanging in midair, while the mule he was riding kept on going.

¹⁰When one of the men saw this, he told Joab, "I just saw Absalom hanging in an oak tree."

¹¹Joab said to the man who had told him this, "What! You saw him? Why didn't you strike him to the ground right there? Then I would have had to give you ten shekels*c* of silver and a warrior's belt."

¹²But the man replied, "Even if a thousand shekels*d* were weighed out into my hands, I would not lift my hand against the king's son. In our hearing the king commanded you and Abishai and Ittai, 'Protect the young man Absalom for my sake.*e*' ¹³And if I had put my life in jeopardy*f*—and nothing is hidden from the king—you would have kept your distance from me."

¹⁴Joab said, "I'm not going to wait like this for you." So he took three javelins in his hand and plunged them into Absalom's heart while Absalom was still alive in the oak tree. ¹⁵And ten of Joab's armor-bearers surrounded Absalom, struck him and killed him.

¹⁶Then Joab sounded the trumpet, and the troops stopped pursuing Israel, for Joab halted them. ¹⁷They took Absalom, threw him into a big pit in the forest and piled up a large heap of rocks over him. Meanwhile, all the Israelites fled to their homes.

¹⁸During his lifetime Absalom had taken a pillar and erected it in the King's Valley as a monument to himself, for he thought, "I have no son to carry on the memory of my name." He named the pillar after himself, and it is called Absalom's Monument to this day.

---

*b*3 Two Hebrew manuscripts, some Septuagint manuscripts and Vulgate; most Hebrew manuscripts *care; for now there are ten thousand like us*   *c*11 That is, about 4 ounces (about 115 grams)   *d*12 That is, about 25 pounds (about 11 kilograms)   *e*12 A few Hebrew manuscripts, Septuagint, Vulgate and Syriac; most Hebrew manuscripts may be translated *Absalom, whoever you may be.*   *f*13 Or *Otherwise, if I had acted treacherously toward him*

8 / *2 Samuel 18:19—19:10*
Receiving Counsel

I HATE LOOKING silly—looking as if I don't know what I am doing. Sometimes this fear keeps me from the simplest of tasks (asking directions, for instance). This aversion was so strong in my youth that it kept me from trying the things I enjoy so much today, like basketball and golf. I was so paralyzed by fear that I even refused instruction.

Maturity and a growing security in God's love for me have freed me from so many fears—but some still linger. Like I said, I'm occasionally stereotypically male in my reluctance to ask for directions. But experience has taught me that I'll be much better off if I seek other people's advice. I may not always look like the competent man I think people expect me to be, but I'm learning, growing and becoming more like God in humility.

 Warming Up to God When has asking for advice or instruction been of significant benefit to you?

 Read 2 Samuel 18:19—19:10.

¹⁹Now Ahimaaz son of Zadok said, "Let me run and take the news to the king that the LORD has delivered him from the hand of his enemies."

²⁰"You are not the one to take the news today," Joab told him. "You may take the news another time, but you must not do so today, because the king's son is dead."

²¹Then Joab said to a Cushite, "Go, tell the king what you have seen." The Cushite bowed down before Joab and ran off.

²²Ahimaaz son of Zadok again said to Joab, "Come what may, please let me run behind the Cushite."

But Joab replied, "My son, why do you want to go? You don't have any news that will bring you a reward."

²³He said, "Come what may, I want to run."

So Joab said, "Run!" Then Ahimaaz ran by way of the plainᵍ and outran the Cushite.

²⁴While David was sitting between the inner and outer gates, the watchman went up to the roof of the gateway by the wall. As he looked out, he saw a man running alone. ²⁵The watchman called out to the king and reported it.

The king said, "If he is alone, he must have good news." And the man came closer and closer.

²⁶Then the watchman saw another man running, and he called down to the gatekeeper, "Look, another man running alone!"

The king said, "He must be bringing good news, too."

²⁷The watchman said, "It seems to me that the first one runs like Ahimaaz son of Zadok."

"He's a good man," the king said. "He comes with good news."

²⁸Then Ahimaaz called out to the king, "All is well!" He bowed down before the king with his face to the ground and said, "Praise be to the LORD your God! He has delivered up the men who lifted their hands against my lord the king."

²⁹The king asked, "Is the young man Absalom safe?"

Ahimaaz answered, "I saw great confusion just as Joab was about to send the king's servant and me, your servant, but I don't know what it was."

³⁰The king said, "Stand aside and wait here." So he stepped aside and stood there.

³¹Then the Cushite arrived and said, "My lord the king, hear the good news! The LORD has delivered you today from all who rose up against you."

³²The king asked the Cushite, "Is the young man Absalom safe?"

The Cushite replied, "May the enemies of my lord the king and all who rise up to harm you be like that young man."

³³The king was shaken. He went up to the room over the gateway and wept. As he went, he said: "O my son Absalom! My son, my son Absalom! If only I had died instead of you—O Absalom, my son, my son!"

19

Joab was told, "The king is weeping and mourning for Absalom." ²And for the whole army the victory that day was turned into mourning, because on that day the troops heard it said, "The king is grieving for his son." ³The men stole into the city that day as men steal in who are ashamed when they flee from battle. ⁴The king covered his face and cried aloud, "O my son Absalom! O Absalom, my son, my son!"

⁵Then Joab went into the house to the king and said, "Today you have humiliated all your men, who have just saved your life and the lives of your sons and daughters and the lives of your wives and concubines. ⁶You love those who hate you and hate those who love you. You have made it clear today that the commanders and their men mean nothing to you. I see that you would be pleased if Absalom were alive today and all of us were dead. ⁷Now go out and encourage your men. I swear by the LORD that if you don't go out, not a man will be left with you by nightfall. This will be worse for you than all the calamities that have come upon you from your youth till now."

⁸So the king got up and took his seat in the gateway. When the men were told, "The king is sitting in the gateway," they all came before him.

Meanwhile, the Israelites had fled to their homes. ⁹Throughout the tribes of Israel, the people were all arguing with each other, saying, "The king delivered us from the hand of our enemies; he is the one who rescued us from the hand of the Philistines. But now he has fled the country because of Absalom; ¹⁰and Absalom, whom we anointed to rule over us, has died in battle. So why do you say nothing about bringing the king back?"

ᵍ23 That is, the plain of the Jordan

Discovering the Word 1. What seems to be David's mood in 18:24–32? 2. Absalom was killed in 18:14 while trying to forcibly take the kingdom from David. Describe the extent of David's grief. 3. Why is David's mourning his son's death upsetting to his army (19:5–6)? 4. In your own words, what was Joab's advice to David (19:7)? 5. What did it cost David to follow the advice given to him (19:9–10)?

Applying the Word 1. What kind of advice are you eager to receive? Explain. 2. Are you good at hearing criticism? Why or why not? 3. From David's example, what are some principles we should apply when we try to evaluate advice given to us?

Responding in Prayer Ask God to build in you the character traits of humility and wisdom.

2 Samuel 19:11—24:25

[11]King David sent this message to Zadok and Abiathar, the priests: "Ask the elders of Judah, 'Why should you be the last to bring the king back to his palace, since what is being said throughout Israel has reached the king at his quarters? [12]You are my brothers, my own flesh and blood. So why should you be the last to bring back the king?' [13]And say to Amasa, 'Are you not my own flesh and blood? May God deal with me, be it ever so severely, if from now on you are not the commander of my army in place of Joab.' "

[14]He won over the hearts of all the men of Judah as though they were one man. They sent word to the king, "Return, you and all your men." [15]Then the king returned and went as far as the Jordan.

Now the men of Judah had come to Gilgal to go out and meet the king and bring him across the Jordan. [16]Shimei son of Gera, the Benjamite from Bahurim, hurried down with the men of Judah to meet King David. [17]With him were a thousand Benjamites, along with Ziba, the steward of Saul's household, and his fifteen sons and twenty servants. They rushed to the Jordan, where the king was. [18]They crossed at the ford to take the king's household over and to do whatever he wished.

When Shimei son of Gera crossed the Jordan, he fell prostrate before the king [19]and said to him, "May my lord not hold me guilty. Do not remember how your servant did wrong on the day my lord the king left Jerusalem. May the king put it out of his mind. [20]For I your servant know that I have sinned, but today I have come here as the first of the whole house of Joseph to come down and meet my lord the king."

[21]Then Abishai son of Zeruiah said, "Shouldn't Shimei be put to death for this? He cursed the Lord's anointed."

[22]David replied, "What do you and I have in common, you sons of Zeruiah? This day you have become my adversaries! Should anyone be put to death in Israel today? Do I not know that today I am king over Israel?" [23]So the king said to Shimei, "You shall not die." And the king promised him on oath.

[24]Mephibosheth, Saul's grandson, also went down to meet the king. He had not taken care of his feet or trimmed his mustache or washed his clothes from the day the king left until the day he returned safely. [25]When he came from Jerusalem to meet the king, the king asked him, "Why didn't you go with me, Mephibosheth?"

[26]He said, "My lord the king, since I your servant am lame, I said, 'I will have my donkey saddled and will ride on it, so I can go with the king.' But Ziba my servant betrayed me. [27]And he has slandered your servant to my lord the king. My lord the king is like an angel of God; so do whatever pleases you. [28]All my grandfather's descendants deserved nothing but death from my lord the king, but you gave your servant a place among those who eat at your table. So what right do I have to make any more appeals to the king?"

[29]The king said to him, "Why say more? I order you and Ziba to divide the fields."

[30]Mephibosheth said to the king, "Let him take everything, now that my lord the king has arrived home safely."

[31]Barzillai the Gileadite also came down from Rogelim to cross the Jordan with the king and to send him on his way from there. [32]Now Barzillai was a very old man, eighty years of age. He had provided for the king during his stay in Mahanaim, for he was a very wealthy man. [33]The king said to Barzillai, "Cross over with me and stay

with me in Jerusalem, and I will provide for you."

³⁴But Barzillai answered the king, "How many more years will I live, that I should go up to Jerusalem with the king? ³⁵I am now eighty years old. Can I tell the difference between what is good and what is not? Can your servant taste what he eats and drinks? Can I still hear the voices of men and women singers? Why should your servant be an added burden to my lord the king? ³⁶Your servant will cross over the Jordan with the king for a short distance, but why should the king reward me in this way? ³⁷Let your servant return, that I may die in my own town near the tomb of my father and mother. But here is your servant Kimham. Let him cross over with my lord the king. Do for him whatever pleases you."

³⁸The king said, "Kimham shall cross over with me, and I will do for him whatever pleases you. And anything you desire from me I will do for you."

³⁹So all the people crossed the Jordan, and then the king crossed over. The king kissed Barzillai and gave him his blessing, and Barzillai returned to his home.

⁴⁰When the king crossed over to Gilgal, Kimham crossed with him. All the troops of Judah and half the troops of Israel had taken the king over.

⁴¹Soon all the men of Israel were coming to the king and saying to him, "Why did our brothers, the men of Judah, steal the king away and bring him and his household across the Jordan, together with all his men?"

⁴²All the men of Judah answered the men of Israel, "We did this because the king is closely related to us. Why are you angry about it? Have we eaten any of the king's provisions? Have we taken anything for ourselves?"

⁴³Then the men of Israel answered the men of Judah, "We have ten shares in the king; and besides, we have a greater claim on David than you have. So why do you treat us with contempt? Were we not the first to speak of bringing back our king?"

But the men of Judah responded even more harshly than the men of Israel.

20

Now a troublemaker named Sheba son of Bicri, a Benjamite, happened to be there. He sounded the trumpet and shouted,

"We have no share in David,
no part in Jesse's son!
Every man to his tent, O Israel!"

²So all the men of Israel deserted David to follow Sheba son of Bicri. But the men of Judah stayed by their king all the way from the Jordan to Jerusalem.

³When David returned to his palace in Jerusalem, he took the ten concubines he had left to take care of the palace and put them in a house under guard. He provided for them, but did not lie with them. They were kept in confinement till the day of their death, living as widows.

⁴Then the king said to Amasa, "Summon the men of Judah to come to me within three days, and be here yourself." ⁵But when Amasa went to summon Judah, he took longer than the time the king had set for him.

⁶David said to Abishai, "Now Sheba son of Bicri will do us more harm than Absalom did. Take your master's men and pursue him, or he will find fortified cities and escape from us." ⁷So Joab's men and the Kerethites and Pelethites and all the mighty warriors went out under the command of Abishai. They marched out from Jerusalem to pursue Sheba son of Bicri.

⁸While they were at the great rock in Gibeon, Amasa came to meet them. Joab was wearing his military tunic, and strapped over it at his waist was a belt with a dagger in its sheath. As he stepped forward, it dropped out of its sheath.

⁹Joab said to Amasa, "How are you, my brother?" Then Joab took Amasa by the beard with his right hand to kiss him. ¹⁰Amasa was not on his guard against the dagger in Joab's hand, and Joab plunged it into his belly, and his intestines spilled out on the ground. Without being stabbed again, Amasa died. Then Joab and his brother Abishai pursued Sheba son of Bicri.

¹¹One of Joab's men stood beside Amasa and said, "Whoever favors Joab, and whoever is for David, let him follow Joab!" ¹²Amasa lay wallowing in his blood in the middle of the road, and the man saw that all the troops came to a halt there. When he realized that everyone who came up to Amasa stopped, he dragged him from the road into a field and threw a garment over him. ¹³After Amasa had been removed from the road, all the men went on with Joab to pursue Sheba son of Bicri.

¹⁴Sheba passed through all the tribes of Israel to Abel Beth Maacahʰ and through the entire region of the Berites, who gathered together and followed him. ¹⁵All the troops with Joab came

ʰ 14 Or Abel, even Beth Maacah; also in verse 15

and besieged Sheba in Abel Beth Maacah. They built a siege ramp up to the city, and it stood against the outer fortifications. While they were battering the wall to bring it down, ¹⁶a wise woman called from the city, "Listen! Listen! Tell Joab to come here so I can speak to him." ¹⁷He went toward her, and she asked, "Are you Joab?"

"I am," he answered.

She said, "Listen to what your servant has to say."

"I'm listening," he said.

¹⁸She continued, "Long ago they used to say, 'Get your answer at Abel,' and that settled it. ¹⁹We are the peaceful and faithful in Israel. You are trying to destroy a city that is a mother in Israel. Why do you want to swallow up the LORD's inheritance?"

²⁰"Far be it from me!" Joab replied, "Far be it from me to swallow up or destroy! ²¹That is not the case. A man named Sheba son of Bicri, from the hill country of Ephraim, has lifted up his hand against the king, against David. Hand over this one man, and I'll withdraw from the city."

The woman said to Joab, "His head will be thrown to you from the wall."

²²Then the woman went to all the people with her wise advice, and they cut off the head of Sheba son of Bicri and threw it to Joab. So he sounded the trumpet, and his men dispersed from the city, each returning to his home. And Joab went back to the king in Jerusalem.

²³Joab was over Israel's entire army; Benaiah son of Jehoiada was over the Kerethites and Pelethites; ²⁴Adoniram[i] was in charge of forced labor; Jehoshaphat son of Ahilud was recorder; ²⁵Sheva was secretary; Zadok and Abiathar were priests; ²⁶and Ira the Jairite was David's priest.

21

During the reign of David, there was a famine for three successive years; so David sought the face of the LORD. The LORD said, "It is on account of Saul and his blood-stained house; it is because he put the Gibeonites to death."

²The king summoned the Gibeonites and spoke to them. (Now the Gibeonites were not a part of Israel but were survivors of the Amorites; the Israelites had sworn to ⌊spare⌋ them, but Saul in his zeal for Israel and Judah had tried to annihilate them.) ³David asked the Gibeonites, "What shall I do for you? How shall I make amends so that you will bless the LORD's inheritance?"

⁴The Gibeonites answered him, "We have no right to demand silver or gold from Saul or his family, nor do we have the right to put anyone in Israel to death."

"What do you want me to do for you?" David asked.

⁵They answered the king, "As for the man who destroyed us and plotted against us so that we have been decimated and have no place anywhere in Israel, ⁶let seven of his male descendants be given to us to be killed and exposed before the LORD at Gibeah of Saul—the LORD's chosen one."

So the king said, "I will give them to you."

⁷The king spared Mephibosheth son of Jonathan, the son of Saul, because of the oath before the LORD between David and Jonathan son of Saul. ⁸But the king took Armoni and Mephibosheth, the two sons of Aiah's daughter Rizpah, whom she had borne to Saul, together with the five sons of Saul's daughter Merab,[j] whom she had borne to Adriel son of Barzillai the Meholathite. ⁹He handed them over to the Gibeonites, who killed and exposed them on a hill before the LORD. All seven of them fell together; they were put to death during the first days of the harvest, just as the barley harvest was beginning.

¹⁰Rizpah daughter of Aiah took sackcloth and spread it out for herself on a rock. From the beginning of the harvest till the rain poured down from the heavens on the bodies, she did not let the birds of the air touch them by day or the wild animals by night. ¹¹When David was told what Aiah's daughter Rizpah, Saul's concubine, had done, ¹²he went and took the bones of Saul and his son Jonathan from the citizens of Jabesh Gilead. (They had taken them secretly from the public square at Beth Shan, where the Philistines had hung them after they struck Saul down on Gilboa.) ¹³David brought the bones of Saul and his son Jonathan from there, and the bones of those who had been killed and exposed were gathered up.

¹⁴They buried the bones of Saul and his son Jonathan in the tomb of Saul's father Kish, at Zela in Benjamin, and did everything the king commanded. After that, God answered prayer in behalf of the land.

¹⁵Once again there was a battle between the Philistines and Israel. David went down with his men to fight against the Philistines, and he be-

i24 Some Septuagint manuscripts (see also 1 Kings 4:6 and 5:14); Hebrew *Adoram*   j8 Two Hebrew manuscripts, some Septuagint manuscripts and Syriac (see also 1 Samuel 18:19); most Hebrew and Septuagint manuscripts *Michal* came exhausted. [16]And Ishbi-Benob, one of the descendants of Rapha, whose bronze spearhead weighed three hundred shekels[k] and who was armed with a new ⌊sword⌋, said he would kill David. [17]But Abishai son of Zeruiah came to David's rescue; he struck the Philistine down and killed him. Then David's men swore to him, saying, "Never again will you go out with us to battle, so that the lamp of Israel will not be extinguished."

[18]In the course of time, there was another battle with the Philistines, at Gob. At that time Sibbecai the Hushathite killed Saph, one of the descendants of Rapha.

[19]In another battle with the Philistines at Gob, Elhanan son of Jaare-Oregim[l] the Bethlehemite killed Goliath[m] the Gittite, who had a spear with a shaft like a weaver's rod.

[20]In still another battle, which took place at Gath, there was a huge man with six fingers on each hand and six toes on each foot—twenty-four in all. He also was descended from Rapha. [21]When he taunted Israel, Jonathan son of Shimeah, David's brother, killed him.

[22]These four were descendants of Rapha in Gath, and they fell at the hands of David and his men.

22

David sang to the LORD the words of this song when the LORD delivered him from the hand of all his enemies and from the hand of Saul. [2]He said:

"The LORD is my rock, my fortress and my
    deliverer;
[3] my God is my rock, in whom I take refuge,
    my shield and the horn[n] of my salvation.
He is my stronghold, my refuge and my
    savior—
    from violent men you save me.
[4]I call to the LORD, who is worthy of praise,
    and I am saved from my enemies.

[5]"The waves of death swirled about me;
    the torrents of destruction overwhelmed
    me.
[6]The cords of the grave[o] coiled around me;
    the snares of death confronted me.
[7]In my distress I called to the LORD;
    I called out to my God.
From his temple he heard my voice;
    my cry came to his ears.

[8]"The earth trembled and quaked,
    the foundations of the heavens[p] shook;

they trembled because he was angry.
[9]Smoke rose from his nostrils;
    consuming fire came from his mouth,
    burning coals blazed out of it.
[10]He parted the heavens and came down;
    dark clouds were under his feet.
[11]He mounted the cherubim and flew;
    he soared[q] on the wings of the wind.
[12]He made darkness his canopy around him—
    the dark[r] rain clouds of the sky.
[13]Out of the brightness of his presence
    bolts of lightning blazed forth.
[14]The LORD thundered from heaven;
    the voice of the Most High resounded.
[15]He shot arrows and scattered ⌊the enemies⌋,
    bolts of lightning and routed them.
[16]The valleys of the sea were exposed
    and the foundations of the earth laid bare
at the rebuke of the LORD,
    at the blast of breath from his nostrils.

[17]"He reached down from on high and took
        hold of me;
    he drew me out of deep waters.
[18]He rescued me from my powerful enemy,
    from my foes, who were too strong for me.
[19]They confronted me in the day of my disaster,
    but the LORD was my support.
[20]He brought me out into a spacious place;
    he rescued me because he delighted in me.

[21]"The LORD has dealt with me according to my
        righteousness;
    according to the cleanness of my hands he
        has rewarded me.
[22]For I have kept the ways of the LORD;
    I have not done evil by turning from my
        God.
[23]All his laws are before me;
    I have not turned away from his decrees.
[24]I have been blameless before him
    and have kept myself from sin.
[25]The LORD has rewarded me according to my
        righteousness,
    according to my cleanness[s] in his sight.

[k]16 That is, about 7 1/2 pounds (about 3.5 kilograms)   [l]19 Or son of Jair the weaver   [m]19 Hebrew and Septuagint; 1 Chron. 20:5 son of Jair killed Lahmi the brother of Goliath   [n]3 Horn here symbolizes strength.   [o]6 Hebrew Sheol   [p]8 Hebrew; Vulgate and Syriac (see also Psalm 18:7) mountains   [q]11 Many Hebrew manuscripts (see also Psalm 18:10); most Hebrew manuscripts appeared   [r]12 Septuagint and Vulgate (see also Psalm 18:11); Hebrew massed   [s]25 Hebrew; Septuagint and Vulgate (see also Psalm 18:24) to the cleanness of my hands

²⁶"To the faithful you show yourself faithful,
  to the blameless you show yourself
    blameless,
²⁷to the pure you show yourself pure,
  but to the crooked you show yourself
    shrewd.
²⁸You save the humble,
  but your eyes are on the haughty to bring
    them low.
²⁹You are my lamp, O Lord;
  the Lord turns my darkness into light.
³⁰With your help I can advance against a
    troopᵗ;
  with my God I can scale a wall.

³¹"As for God, his way is perfect;
  the word of the Lord is flawless.
He is a shield
  for all who take refuge in him.
³²For who is God besides the Lord?
  And who is the Rock except our God?
³³It is God who arms me with strengthᵘ
  and makes my way perfect.
³⁴He makes my feet like the feet of a deer;
  he enables me to stand on the heights.
³⁵He trains my hands for battle;
  my arms can bend a bow of bronze.
³⁶You give me your shield of victory;
  you stoop down to make me great.
³⁷You broaden the path beneath me,
  so that my ankles do not turn.

³⁸"I pursued my enemies and crushed them;
  I did not turn back till they were destroyed.
³⁹I crushed them completely, and they could
    not rise;
  they fell beneath my feet.
⁴⁰You armed me with strength for battle;
  you made my adversaries bow at my feet.
⁴¹You made my enemies turn their backs in
    flight,
  and I destroyed my foes.
⁴²They cried for help, but there was no one to
    save them—
  to the Lord, but he did not answer.
⁴³I beat them as fine as the dust of the earth;
  I pounded and trampled them like mud in
    the streets.
⁴⁴"You have delivered me from the attacks of
    my people;
  you have preserved me as the head of
    nations.
People I did not know are subject to me,

⁴⁵ and foreigners come cringing to me;
  as soon as they hear me, they obey me.
⁴⁶They all lose heart;
  they come tremblingᵛ from their
    strongholds.

⁴⁷"The Lord lives! Praise be to my Rock!
  Exalted be God, the Rock, my Savior!
⁴⁸He is the God who avenges me,
  who puts the nations under me,
⁴⁹ who sets me free from my enemies.
You exalted me above my foes;
  from violent men you rescued me.
⁵⁰Therefore I will praise you, O Lord, among
    the nations;
  I will sing praises to your name.
⁵¹He gives his king great victories;
  he shows unfailing kindness to his
    anointed,
  to David and his descendants forever."

23

These are the last words of David:

"The oracle of David son of Jesse,
  the oracle of the man exalted by
    the Most High,
the man anointed by the God of Jacob,
Israel's singer of songsʷ:

²"The Spirit of the Lord spoke through me;
  his word was on my tongue.
³The God of Israel spoke,
  the Rock of Israel said to me:
'When one rules over men in righteousness,
  when he rules in the fear of God,
⁴he is like the light of morning at sunrise
  on a cloudless morning,
like the brightness after rain
  that brings the grass from the earth.'

⁵"Is not my house right with God?
  Has he not made with me an everlasting
    covenant,
  arranged and secured in every part?
Will he not bring to fruition my salvation
  and grant me my every desire?
⁶But evil men are all to be cast aside like
    thorns,
  which are not gathered with the hand.
⁷Whoever touches thorns
  uses a tool of iron or the shaft of a spear;
  they are burned up where they lie."

ᵗ30 Or *can run through a barricade*   ᵘ33 Dead Sea Scrolls,
some Septuagint manuscripts, Vulgate and Syriac (see also Psalm 18:32);
Masoretic Text *who is my strong refuge*   ᵛ46 Some Septuagint
manuscripts and Vulgate (see also Psalm 18:45); Masoretic Text *they
arm themselves.*   ʷ1 Or *Israel's beloved singer*

8These are the names of David's mighty men:

Josheb-Basshebeth,[x] a Tahkemonite,[y] was chief of the Three; he raised his spear against eight hundred men, whom he killed[z] in one encounter.

9Next to him was Eleazar son of Dodai the Ahohite. As one of the three mighty men, he was with David when they taunted the Philistines gathered ⌊at Pas Dammim⌋[a] for battle. Then the men of Israel retreated, 10but he stood his ground and struck down the Philistines till his hand grew tired and froze to the sword. The LORD brought about a great victory that day. The troops returned to Eleazar, but only to strip the dead.

11Next to him was Shammah son of Agee the Hararite. When the Philistines banded together at a place where there was a field full of lentils, Israel's troops fled from them. 12But Shammah took his stand in the middle of the field. He defended it and struck the Philistines down, and the LORD brought about a great victory.

13During harvest time, three of the thirty chief men came down to David at the cave of Adullam, while a band of Philistines was encamped in the Valley of Rephaim. 14At that time David was in the stronghold, and the Philistine garrison was at Bethlehem. 15David longed for water and said, "Oh, that someone would get me a drink of water from the well near the gate of Bethlehem!" 16So the three mighty men broke through the Philistine lines, drew water from the well near the gate of Bethlehem and carried it back to David. But he refused to drink it; instead, he poured it out before the LORD. 17"Far be it from me, O LORD, to do this!" he said. "Is it not the blood of men who went at the risk of their lives?" And David would not drink it.

Such were the exploits of the three mighty men.

18Abishai the brother of Joab son of Zeruiah was chief of the Three.[b] He raised his spear against three hundred men, whom he killed, and so he became as famous as the Three. 19Was he not held in greater honor than the Three? He became their commander, even though he was not included among them.

20Benaiah son of Jehoiada was a valiant fighter from Kabzeel, who performed great exploits. He struck down two of Moab's best men. He also went down into a pit on a snowy day and killed a lion. 21And he struck down a huge Egyptian. Although the Egyptian had a spear in his hand, Be-

naiah went against him with a club. He snatched the spear from the Egyptian's hand and killed him with his own spear. 22Such were the exploits of Benaiah son of Jehoiada; he too was as famous as the three mighty men. 23He was held in greater honor than any of the Thirty, but he was not included among the Three. And David put him in charge of his bodyguard.

24Among the Thirty were:

Asahel the brother of Joab,

Elhanan son of Dodo from Bethlehem,

25Shammah the Harodite,

Elika the Harodite,

26Helez the Paltite,

Ira son of Ikkesh from Tekoa,

27Abiezer from Anathoth,

Mebunnai[c] the Hushathite,

28Zalmon the Ahohite,

Maharai the Netophathite,

29Heled[d] son of Baanah the Netophathite,

Ithai son of Ribai from Gibeah in Benjamin,

30Benaiah the Pirathonite,

Hiddai[e] from the ravines of Gaash,

31Abi-Albon the Arbathite,

Azmaveth the Barhumite,

32Eliahba the Shaalbonite,

the sons of Jashen,

Jonathan 33son of[f] Shammah the Hararite,

Ahiam son of Sharar[g] the Hararite,

34Eliphelet son of Ahasbai the Maacathite,

Eliam son of Ahithophel the Gilonite,

35Hezro the Carmelite,

Paarai the Arbite,

36Igal son of Nathan from Zobah,

the son of Hagri,[h]

37Zelek the Ammonite,

Naharai the Beerothite, the armor-bearer of Joab son of Zeruiah,

38Ira the Ithrite,

Gareb the Ithrite

x8 Hebrew; some Septuagint manuscripts suggest Ish-Bosheth, that is, Esh-Baal (see also 1 Chron. 11:11 Jashobeam).   y8 Probably a variant of Hacmonite (see 1 Chron. 11:11)   z8 Some Septuagint manuscripts (see also 1 Chron. 11:11); Hebrew and other Septuagint manuscripts Three; it was Adino the Eznite who killed eight hundred men   a9 See 1 Chron. 11:13; Hebrew gathered there.   b18 Most Hebrew manuscripts (see also 1 Chron. 11:20); two Hebrew manuscripts and Syriac Thirty   c27 Hebrew; some Septuagint manuscripts (see also 1 Chron. 11:29) Sibbecai   d29 Some Hebrew manuscripts and Vulgate (see also 1 Chron. 11:30); most Hebrew manuscripts Heleb   e30 Hebrew; some Septuagint manuscripts (see also 1 Chron. 11:32) Hurai   f33 Some Septuagint manuscripts (see also 1 Chron. 11:34); Hebrew does not have son of.   g33 Hebrew; some Septuagint manuscripts (see also 1 Chron. 11:35) Sacar   h36 Some Septuagint manuscripts (see also 1 Chron. 11:38); Hebrew Haggadi

³⁹and Uriah the Hittite.
There were thirty-seven in all.

24

Again the anger of the Lord burned against Israel, and he incited David against them, saying, "Go and take a census of Israel and Judah."

²So the king said to Joab and the army commanders[i] with him, "Go throughout the tribes of Israel from Dan to Beersheba and enroll the fighting men, so that I may know how many there are."

³But Joab replied to the king, "May the Lord your God multiply the troops a hundred times over, and may the eyes of my lord the king see it. But why does my lord the king want to do such a thing?"

⁴The king's word, however, overruled Joab and the army commanders; so they left the presence of the king to enroll the fighting men of Israel.

⁵After crossing the Jordan, they camped near Aroer, south of the town in the gorge, and then went through Gad and on to Jazer. ⁶They went to Gilead and the region of Tahtim Hodshi, and on to Dan Jaan and around toward Sidon. ⁷Then they went toward the fortress of Tyre and all the towns of the Hivites and Canaanites. Finally, they went on to Beersheba in the Negev of Judah.

⁸After they had gone through the entire land, they came back to Jerusalem at the end of nine months and twenty days.

⁹Joab reported the number of the fighting men to the king: In Israel there were eight hundred thousand able-bodied men who could handle a sword, and in Judah five hundred thousand.

¹⁰David was conscience-stricken after he had counted the fighting men, and he said to the Lord, "I have sinned greatly in what I have done. Now, O Lord, I beg you, take away the guilt of your servant. I have done a very foolish thing."

¹¹Before David got up the next morning, the word of the Lord had come to Gad the prophet, David's seer: ¹²"Go and tell David, 'This is what the Lord says: I am giving you three options. Choose one of them for me to carry out against you.' "

¹³So Gad went to David and said to him, "Shall there come upon you three[j] years of famine in your land? Or three months of fleeing from your enemies while they pursue you? Or three days of plague in your land? Now then, think it over and decide how I should answer the one who sent me."

¹⁴David said to Gad, "I am in deep distress. Let us fall into the hands of the Lord, for his mercy is great; but do not let me fall into the hands of men."

¹⁵So the Lord sent a plague on Israel from that morning until the end of the time designated, and seventy thousand of the people from Dan to Beersheba died. ¹⁶When the angel stretched out his hand to destroy Jerusalem, the Lord was grieved because of the calamity and said to the angel who was afflicting the people, "Enough! Withdraw your hand." The angel of the Lord was then at the threshing floor of Araunah the Jebusite.

¹⁷When David saw the angel who was striking down the people, he said to the Lord, "I am the one who has sinned and done wrong. These are but sheep. What have they done? Let your hand fall upon me and my family."

¹⁸On that day Gad went to David and said to him, "Go up and build an altar to the Lord on the threshing floor of Araunah the Jebusite." ¹⁹So David went up, as the Lord had commanded through Gad. ²⁰When Araunah looked and saw the king and his men coming toward him, he went out and bowed down before the king with his face to the ground.

²¹Araunah said, "Why has my lord the king come to his servant?"

"To buy your threshing floor," David answered, "so I can build an altar to the Lord, that the plague on the people may be stopped."

²²Araunah said to David, "Let my lord the king take whatever pleases him and offer it up. Here are oxen for the burnt offering, and here are threshing sledges and ox yokes for the wood. ²³O king, Araunah gives all this to the king." Araunah also said to him, "May the Lord your God accept you."

²⁴But the king replied to Araunah, "No, I insist on paying you for it. I will not sacrifice to the Lord my God burnt offerings that cost me nothing."

So David bought the threshing floor and the oxen and paid fifty shekels[k] of silver for them. ²⁵David built an altar to the Lord there and sacrificed burnt offerings and fellowship offerings.[l] Then the Lord answered prayer in behalf of the land, and the plague on Israel was stopped.

---

*i*2 Septuagint (see also verse 4 and 1 Chron. 21:2); Hebrew *Joab the army commander*   *j*13 Septuagint (see also 1 Chron. 21:12); Hebrew *seven*   *k*24 That is, about 1 1/4 pounds (about 0.6 kilogram)
*l*25 Traditionally *peace offerings*

1 Kings

W hat good will it do us twenty-first century Christians to study the kings who ruled a nation of Hebrews three thousand years ago? For people who get excited about battles and dates and ancient political maneuverings, the answer is obvious. All history, even Hebrew history, is great.

But what about the rest of us? God must have had some reason for designing his Holy Book so that one-third of the Old Testament recounts historical events. He wasn't just entertaining history buffs. A look at the issues surrounding these kings will give us some clues.

We see Solomon, who prayed as if he knew exactly what God desired to give, then fell into paganism under the influence of his seven hundred(!) wives. And we ask, "Do I ever place the people I love ahead of God?"

We see Jeroboam and Rehoboam, who split their nation in civil war and then split their places of worship. (Who among us has endured civil war within our church that could end in separate places of worship?)

We see Ahab, who ignored God even though prophets shouted into his spiritually deaf ears. And we look with dread upon our own potential deafness.

They ruled for four centuries, these Hebrew kings. There were forty-two of them. Some ruled only days, others for a lifetime. Some were so minor that they rate only a line of text. Others fill whole books. Some were evil; some were good. The biblical text evaluates each one at the end of his life. A reminder that we ourselves will undergo the same evaluation.

Outline

1/ 1 Kings 3 —————————— Praying with God's Values

2/ 1 Kings 11 —————————— Faithless in Love

3/ 1 Kings 12 —————————— Internal Conflict

4/ 1 Kings 17 —————————— Serving Each Other

5/ 1 Kings 18 —————————— Knowing God's Power

6/ 1 Kings 19:1–18 —————————— Caring for the Whole Person

7/ 1 Kings 21 —————————— Manipulation

8/ 1 Kings 22:1–40 —————————— Deaf to God

Israel and Judah

0 10 20 30 miles

1 Kings 1—2

1 When King David was old and well advanced in years, he could not keep warm even when they put covers over him. ²So his servants said to him, "Let us look for a young virgin to attend the king and take care of him. She can lie beside him so that our lord the king may keep warm."

³Then they searched throughout Israel for a beautiful girl and found Abishag, a Shunammite, and brought her to the king. ⁴The girl was very beautiful; she took care of the king and waited on him, but the king had no intimate relations with her.

⁵Now Adonijah, whose mother was Haggith, put himself forward and said, "I will be king." So he got chariots and horses*a* ready, with fifty men to run ahead of him. ⁶(His father had never interfered with him by asking, "Why do you behave as you do?" He was also very handsome and was born next after Absalom.)

⁷Adonijah conferred with Joab son of Zeruiah and with Abiathar the priest, and they gave him their support. ⁸But Zadok the priest, Benaiah son of Jehoiada, Nathan the prophet, Shimei and Rei*b* and David's special guard did not join Adonijah.

⁹Adonijah then sacrificed sheep, cattle and fattened calves at the Stone of Zoheleth near En Rogel. He invited all his brothers, the king's sons, and all the men of Judah who were royal officials, ¹⁰but he did not invite Nathan the prophet or Benaiah or the special guard or his brother Solomon.

¹¹Then Nathan asked Bathsheba, Solomon's mother, "Have you not heard that Adonijah, the son of Haggith, has become king without our lord David's knowing it? ¹²Now then, let me advise you how you can save your own life and the life of your son Solomon. ¹³Go in to King David and say to him, 'My lord the king, did you not swear to me your servant: "Surely Solomon your son shall be king after me, and he will sit on my throne"? Why then has Adonijah become king?' ¹⁴While you are still there talking to the king, I will come in and confirm what you have said."

¹⁵So Bathsheba went to see the aged king in his room, where Abishag the Shunammite was attending him. ¹⁶Bathsheba bowed low and knelt before the king.

"What is it you want?" the king asked.

¹⁷She said to him, "My lord, you yourself swore to me your servant by the Lord your God: 'Solomon your son shall be king after me, and he will sit on my throne.' ¹⁸But now Adonijah has become king, and you, my lord the king, do not know about it. ¹⁹He has sacrificed great numbers of cattle, fattened calves, and sheep, and has invited all the king's sons, Abiathar the priest and Joab the commander of the army, but he has not invited Solomon your servant. ²⁰My lord the king, the eyes of all Israel are on you, to learn from you who will sit on the throne of my lord the king after him. ²¹Otherwise, as soon as my lord the king is laid to rest with his fathers, I and my son Solomon will be treated as criminals."

²²While she was still speaking with the king, Nathan the prophet arrived. ²³And they told the king, "Nathan the prophet is here." So he went before the king and bowed with his face to the ground.

²⁴Nathan said, "Have you, my lord the king, declared that Adonijah shall be king after you, and that he will sit on your throne? ²⁵Today he has gone down and sacrificed great numbers of cattle, fattened calves, and sheep. He has invited all the king's sons, the commanders of the army and Abiathar the priest. Right now they are eating and drinking with him and saying, 'Long live King Adonijah!' ²⁶But me your servant, and Zadok the priest, and Benaiah son of Jehoiada, and your servant Solomon he did not invite. ²⁷Is this something my lord the king has done without letting his servants know who should sit on the throne of my lord the king after him?"

²⁸Then King David said, "Call in Bathsheba." So she came into the king's presence and stood before him.

²⁹The king then took an oath: "As surely as the Lord lives, who has delivered me out of every trouble, ³⁰I will surely carry out today what I swore to you by the Lord, the God of Israel: Solomon your son shall be king after me, and he will sit on my throne in my place."

³¹Then Bathsheba bowed low with her face to the ground and, kneeling before the king, said, "May my lord King David live forever!"

³²King David said, "Call in Zadok the priest,

a5 Or charioteers   *b8 Or and his friends*

Nathan the prophet and Benaiah son of Jehoiada." When they came before the king, ³³he said to them: "Take your lord's servants with you and set Solomon my son on my own mule and take him down to Gihon. ³⁴There have Zadok the priest and Nathan the prophet anoint him king over Israel. Blow the trumpet and shout, 'Long live King Solomon!' ³⁵Then you are to go up with him, and he is to come and sit on my throne and reign in my place. I have appointed him ruler over Israel and Judah."

³⁶Benaiah son of Jehoiada answered the king, "Amen! May the LORD, the God of my lord the king, so declare it. ³⁷As the LORD was with my lord the king, so may he be with Solomon to make his throne even greater than the throne of my lord King David!"

³⁸So Zadok the priest, Nathan the prophet, Benaiah son of Jehoiada, the Kerethites and the Pelethites went down and put Solomon on King David's mule and escorted him to Gihon. ³⁹Zadok the priest took the horn of oil from the sacred tent and anointed Solomon. Then they sounded the trumpet and all the people shouted, "Long live King Solomon!" ⁴⁰And all the people went up after him, playing flutes and rejoicing greatly, so that the ground shook with the sound.

⁴¹Adonijah and all the guests who were with him heard it as they were finishing their feast. On hearing the sound of the trumpet, Joab asked, "What's the meaning of all the noise in the city?"

⁴²Even as he was speaking, Jonathan son of Abiathar the priest arrived. Adonijah said, "Come in. A worthy man like you must be bringing good news."

⁴³"Not at all!" Jonathan answered. "Our lord King David has made Solomon king. ⁴⁴The king has sent with him Zadok the priest, Nathan the prophet, Benaiah son of Jehoiada, the Kerethites and the Pelethites, and they have put him on the king's mule, ⁴⁵and Zadok the priest and Nathan the prophet have anointed him king at Gihon. From there they have gone up cheering, and the city resounds with it. That's the noise you hear. ⁴⁶Moreover, Solomon has taken his seat on the royal throne. ⁴⁷Also, the royal officials have come to congratulate our lord King David, saying, 'May your God make Solomon's name more famous than yours and his throne greater than yours!' And the king bowed in worship on his bed ⁴⁸and said, 'Praise be to the LORD, the God of Israel, who

has allowed my eyes to see a successor on my throne today.' "

⁴⁹At this, all Adonijah's guests rose in alarm and dispersed. ⁵⁰But Adonijah, in fear of Solomon, went and took hold of the horns of the altar. ⁵¹Then Solomon was told, "Adonijah is afraid of King Solomon and is clinging to the horns of the altar. He says, 'Let King Solomon swear to me today that he will not put his servant to death with the sword.' "

⁵²Solomon replied, "If he shows himself to be a worthy man, not a hair of his head will fall to the ground; but if evil is found in him, he will die." ⁵³Then King Solomon sent men, and they brought him down from the altar. And Adonijah came and bowed down to King Solomon, and Solomon said, "Go to your home."

2 When the time drew near for David to die, he gave a charge to Solomon his son. ²"I am about to go the way of all the earth," he said. "So be strong, show yourself a man, ³and observe what the LORD your God requires: Walk in his ways, and keep his decrees and commands, his laws and requirements, as written in the Law of Moses, so that you may prosper in all you do and wherever you go, ⁴and that the LORD may keep his promise to me: 'If your descendants watch how they live, and if they walk faithfully before me with all their heart and soul, you will never fail to have a man on the throne of Israel.'

⁵"Now you yourself know what Joab son of Zeruiah did to me—what he did to the two commanders of Israel's armies, Abner son of Ner and Amasa son of Jether. He killed them, shedding their blood in peacetime as if in battle, and with that blood stained the belt around his waist and the sandals on his feet. ⁶Deal with him according to your wisdom, but do not let his gray head go down to the grave[c] in peace.

⁷"But show kindness to the sons of Barzillai of Gilead and let them be among those who eat at your table. They stood by me when I fled from your brother Absalom.

⁸"And remember, you have with you Shimei son of Gera, the Benjamite from Bahurim, who called down bitter curses on me the day I went to Mahanaim. When he came down to meet me at the Jordan, I swore to him by the LORD: 'I will not put you to death by the sword.' ⁹But now, do not

c6 Hebrew Sheol; also in verse 9

consider him innocent. You are a man of wisdom; you will know what to do to him. Bring his gray head down to the grave in blood."

[10]Then David rested with his fathers and was buried in the City of David. [11]He had reigned forty years over Israel—seven years in Hebron and thirty-three in Jerusalem. [12]So Solomon sat on the throne of his father David, and his rule was firmly established.

[13]Now Adonijah, the son of Haggith, went to Bathsheba, Solomon's mother. Bathsheba asked him, "Do you come peacefully?"

He answered, "Yes, peacefully." [14]Then he added, "I have something to say to you."

"You may say it," she replied.

[15]"As you know," he said, "the kingdom was mine. All Israel looked to me as their king. But things changed, and the kingdom has gone to my brother; for it has come to him from the LORD. [16]Now I have one request to make of you. Do not refuse me."

"You may make it," she said.

[17]So he continued, "Please ask King Solomon—he will not refuse you—to give me Abishag the Shunammite as my wife."

[18]"Very well," Bathsheba replied, "I will speak to the king for you."

[19]When Bathsheba went to King Solomon to speak to him for Adonijah, the king stood up to meet her, bowed down to her and sat down on his throne. He had a throne brought for the king's mother, and she sat down at his right hand.

[20]"I have one small request to make of you," she said. "Do not refuse me."

The king replied, "Make it, my mother; I will not refuse you."

[21]So she said, "Let Abishag the Shunammite be given in marriage to your brother Adonijah."

[22]King Solomon answered his mother, "Why do you request Abishag the Shunammite for Adonijah? You might as well request the kingdom for him—after all, he is my older brother—yes, for him and for Abiathar the priest and Joab son of Zeruiah!"

[23]Then King Solomon swore by the LORD: "May God deal with me, be it ever so severely, if Adonijah does not pay with his life for this request! [24]And now, as surely as the LORD lives—he who has established me securely on the throne of my father David and has founded a dynasty for me as he promised—Adonijah shall be put to death today!" [25]So King Solomon gave orders to Benaiah

son of Jehoiada, and he struck down Adonijah and he died.

[26]To Abiathar the priest the king said, "Go back to your fields in Anathoth. You deserve to die, but I will not put you to death now, because you carried the ark of the Sovereign LORD before my father David and shared all my father's hardships." [27]So Solomon removed Abiathar from the priesthood of the LORD, fulfilling the word the LORD had spoken at Shiloh about the house of Eli.

[28]When the news reached Joab, who had conspired with Adonijah though not with Absalom, he fled to the tent of the LORD and took hold of the horns of the altar. [29]King Solomon was told that Joab had fled to the tent of the LORD and was beside the altar. Then Solomon ordered Benaiah son of Jehoiada, "Go, strike him down!"

[30]So Benaiah entered the tent of the LORD and said to Joab, "The king says, 'Come out!' "

But he answered, "No, I will die here."

Benaiah reported to the king, "This is how Joab answered me."

[31]Then the king commanded Benaiah, "Do as he says. Strike him down and bury him, and so clear me and my father's house of the guilt of the innocent blood that Joab shed. [32]The LORD will repay him for the blood he shed, because without the knowledge of my father David he attacked two men and killed them with the sword. Both of them—Abner son of Ner, commander of Israel's army, and Amasa son of Jether, commander of Judah's army—were better men and more upright than he. [33]May the guilt of their blood rest on the head of Joab and his descendants forever. But on David and his descendants, his house and his throne, may there be the LORD's peace forever."

[34]So Benaiah son of Jehoiada went up and struck down Joab and killed him, and he was buried on his own land[d] in the desert. [35]The king put Benaiah son of Jehoiada over the army in Joab's position and replaced Abiathar with Zadok the priest.

[36]Then the king sent for Shimei and said to him, "Build yourself a house in Jerusalem and live there, but do not go anywhere else. [37]The day you leave and cross the Kidron Valley, you can be sure you will die; your blood will be on your own head."

[38]Shimei answered the king, "What you say is good. Your servant will do as my lord the king

[d]34 Or *buried in his tomb*

has said." And Shimei stayed in Jerusalem for a long time.

39But three years later, two of Shimei's slaves ran off to Achish son of Maacah, king of Gath, and Shimei was told, "Your slaves are in Gath." 40At this, he saddled his donkey and went to Achish at Gath in search of his slaves. So Shimei went away and brought the slaves back from Gath.

41When Solomon was told that Shimei had gone from Jerusalem to Gath and had returned, 42the king summoned Shimei and said to him, "Did I not make you swear by the LORD and warn you, 'On the day you leave to go anywhere else, you can be sure you will die'? At that time you said to me, 'What you say is good. I will obey.' 43Why then did you not keep your oath to the LORD and obey the command I gave you?"

44The king also said to Shimei, "You know in your heart all the wrong you did to my father David. Now the LORD will repay you for your wrongdoing. 45But King Solomon will be blessed, and David's throne will remain secure before the LORD forever."

46Then the king gave the order to Benaiah son of Jehoiada, and he went out and struck Shimei down and killed him.

The kingdom was now firmly established in Solomon's hands.

1 / 1 Kings 3
Praying with God's Values

"HELLO, MARY? I need a listening ear. Do you have time?" Haltingly, I poured out my disappointment and sorrow about a problem that had been plaguing me for days. Mary made sympathetic noises, offered a few corrective comments and promised to pray. The situation was unchanged; yet, as the day progressed, I felt the cloud of sadness lift. I knew Mary was praying. And God, in his generosity, was granting the requests of her prayer.

Why had I chosen Mary? Because she was approachable? Partly. But more because I knew her spiritual walk. It was carefully metered by God's laws. And because she was comfortable with prayer, her prayers were specific and to the point. Like her spiritual walk, her prayers seemed closely matched to God's values.

 Warming Up to God   In what area of your life would you like to have someone's prayers?

 Read 1 Kings 3.

3 Solomon made an alliance with Pharaoh king of Egypt and married his daughter. He brought her to the City of David until he finished building his palace and the temple of the LORD, and the wall around Jerusalem. 2The people, however, were still sacrificing at the high places, because a temple had not yet been built for the Name of the LORD. 3Solomon showed his love for the LORD by walking according to the statutes of his father David, except that he offered sacrifices and burned incense on the high places.

4The king went to Gibeon to offer sacrifices, for that was the most important high place, and Solomon offered a thousand burnt offerings on that altar. 5At Gibeon the LORD appeared to Solomon during the night in a dream, and God said, "Ask for whatever you want me to give you."

6Solomon answered, "You have shown great kindness to your servant, my father David, because he was faithful to you and righteous and upright in heart. You have continued this great kindness to him and have given him a son to sit on his throne this very day.

7"Now, O LORD my God, you have made your servant king in place of my father David. But I am only a little child and do not know how to carry out my duties. 8Your servant is here among the people you have chosen, a great people, too numerous to count or number. 9So give your servant a discerning heart to govern your people and to distinguish between right and wrong. For who is able to govern this great people of yours?"

10The Lord was pleased that Solomon had asked for this. 11So God said to him, "Since you have asked for this and not for long life or wealth for yourself, nor have asked for the death of your enemies but for discernment in administering justice, ¹²I will do what you have asked. I will give you a wise and discerning heart, so that there will never have been anyone like you, nor will there ever be. ¹³Moreover, I will give you what you have not asked for—both riches and honor—so that in your lifetime you will have no equal among kings. ¹⁴And if you walk in my ways and obey my statutes and commands as David your father did, I will give you a long life." ¹⁵Then Solomon awoke—and he realized it had been a dream.

He returned to Jerusalem, stood before the ark of the Lord's covenant and sacrificed burnt offerings and fellowship offerings.ᵉ Then he gave a feast for all his court.

¹⁶Now two prostitutes came to the king and stood before him. ¹⁷One of them said, "My lord, this woman and I live in the same house. I had a baby while she was there with me. ¹⁸The third day after my child was born, this woman also had a baby. We were alone; there was no one in the house but the two of us.

¹⁹"During the night this woman's son died because she lay on him. ²⁰So she got up in the middle of the night and took my son from my side while I your servant was asleep. She put him by her breast and put her dead son by my breast. ²¹The next morning, I got up to nurse my son—

and he was dead! But when I looked at him closely in the morning light, I saw that it wasn't the son I had borne."

²²The other woman said, "No! The living one is my son; the dead one is yours."

But the first one insisted, "No! The dead one is yours; the living one is mine." And so they argued before the king.

²³The king said, "This one says, 'My son is alive and your son is dead,' while that one says, 'No! Your son is dead and mine is alive.' "

²⁴Then the king said, "Bring me a sword." So they brought a sword for the king. ²⁵He then gave an order: "Cut the living child in two and give half to one and half to the other."

²⁶The woman whose son was alive was filled with compassion for her son and said to the king, "Please, my lord, give her the living baby! Don't kill him!"

But the other said, "Neither I nor you shall have him. Cut him in two!"

²⁷Then the king gave his ruling: "Give the living baby to the first woman. Do not kill him; she is his mother."

²⁸When all Israel heard the verdict the king had given, they held the king in awe, because they saw that he had wisdom from God to administer justice.

ᵉ15 Traditionally *peace offerings*

Discovering the Word 1. What do Solomon's actions in the early years of his reign (vv. 1–4) say about his character? 2. Solomon answered God's question with a prayer (vv. 5–9). What does Solomon's prayer suggest about his attitude toward himself, his job and his God? 3. What did God promise Solomon (vv. 10–14)? 4. How would you describe a discerning heart? 5. In verses 16–28 we see Solomon's wisdom put to the test. Do you agree that Solomon's method of judgment was wise? Why or why not?

Applying the Word 1. Think of one of your current responsibilities that seems a bit too big for you. What would you *like* to ask of God in that area? 2. How can you begin to bring your prayers more into line with God's values?

Responding in Prayer Think of one person who particularly needs a discerning heart right now. Pray one or two sentences asking God's help for that person.

1 Kings 4—10

4 So King Solomon ruled over all Israel. ²And these were his chief officials:

Azariah son of Zadok—the priest;
³Elihoreph and Ahijah, sons of Shisha—secretaries;
Jehoshaphat son of Ahilud—recorder;
⁴Benaiah son of Jehoiada—commander in chief;
Zadok and Abiathar—priests;
⁵Azariah son of Nathan—in charge of the district officers;
Zabud son of Nathan—a priest and personal adviser to the king;
⁶Ahishar—in charge of the palace;
Adoniram son of Abda—in charge of forced labor.

⁷Solomon also had twelve district governors over all Israel, who supplied provisions for the king and the royal household. Each one had to provide supplies for one month in the year. ⁸These are their names:

Ben-Hur—in the hill country of Ephraim;
⁹Ben-Deker—in Makaz, Shaalbim, Beth Shemesh and Elon Bethhanan;
¹⁰Ben-Hesed—in Arubboth (Socoh and all the land of Hepher were his);
¹¹Ben-Abinadab—in Naphoth Dor ʲ (he was married to Taphath daughter of Solomon);
¹²Baana son of Ahilud—in Taanach and Megiddo, and in all of Beth Shan next to Zarethan below Jezreel, from Beth Shan to Abel Meholah across to Jokmeam;
¹³Ben-Geber—in Ramoth Gilead (the settlements of Jair son of Manasseh in Gilead were his, as well as the district of Argob in Bashan and its sixty large walled cities with bronze gate bars);
¹⁴Ahinadab son of Iddo—in Mahanaim;
¹⁵Ahimaaz—in Naphtali (he had married Basemath daughter of Solomon);
¹⁶Baana son of Hushai—in Asher and in Aloth;
¹⁷Jehoshaphat son of Paruah—in Issachar;
¹⁸Shimei son of Ela—in Benjamin;
¹⁹Geber son of Uri—in Gilead (the country of Sihon king of the Amorites and the country of Og king of Bashan). He was the only governor over the district.

²⁰The people of Judah and Israel were as numerous as the sand on the seashore; they ate, they drank and they were happy. ²¹And Solomon ruled over all the kingdoms from the River ᵍ to the land of the Philistines, as far as the border of Egypt. These countries brought tribute and were Solomon's subjects all his life.

²²Solomon's daily provisions were thirty cors ʰ of fine flour and sixty cors ⁱ of meal, ²³ten head of stall-fed cattle, twenty of pasture-fed cattle and a hundred sheep and goats, as well as deer, gazelles, roebucks and choice fowl. ²⁴For he ruled over all the kingdoms west of the River, from Tiphsah to Gaza, and had peace on all sides. ²⁵During Solomon's lifetime Judah and Israel, from Dan to Beersheba, lived in safety, each man under his own vine and fig tree.

²⁶Solomon had four ʲ thousand stalls for chariot horses, and twelve thousand horses. ᵏ ²⁷The district officers, each in his month, supplied provisions for King Solomon and all who came to the king's table. They saw to it that nothing was lacking. ²⁸They also brought to the proper place their quotas of barley and straw for the chariot horses and the other horses.

²⁹God gave Solomon wisdom and very great insight, and a breadth of understanding as measureless as the sand on the seashore. ³⁰Solomon's wisdom was greater than the wisdom of all the men of the East, and greater than all the wisdom of Egypt. ³¹He was wiser than any other man, including Ethan the Ezrahite—wiser than Heman, Calcol and Darda, the sons of Mahol. And his fame spread to all the surrounding nations. ³²He spoke three thousand proverbs and his songs numbered a thousand and five. ³³He described plant life, from the cedar of Lebanon to the hyssop that grows out of walls. He also taught about animals and birds, reptiles and fish. ³⁴Men of all nations came to listen to Solomon's wisdom, sent by all the kings of the world, who had heard of his wisdom.

ʲ11 Or *in the heights of Dor*   ᵍ21 That is, the Euphrates; also in verse 24   ʰ22 That is, probably about 185 bushels (about 6.6 kiloliters)
ⁱ22 That is, probably about 375 bushels (about 13.2 kiloliters)
ʲ26 Some Septuagint manuscripts (see also 2 Chron. 9:25); Hebrew *forty*
ᵏ26 Or *charioteers*

5

When Hiram king of Tyre heard that Solomon had been anointed king to succeed his father David, he sent his envoys to Solomon, because he had always been on friendly terms with David. ²Solomon sent back this message to Hiram:

³"You know that because of the wars waged against my father David from all sides, he could not build a temple for the Name of the Lord his God until the Lord put his enemies under his feet. ⁴But now the Lord my God has given me rest on every side, and there is no adversary or disaster. ⁵I intend, therefore, to build a temple for the Name of the Lord my God, as the Lord told my father David, when he said, 'Your son whom I will put on the throne in your place will build the temple for my Name.'

⁶"So give orders that cedars of Lebanon be cut for me. My men will work with yours, and I will pay you for your men whatever wages you set. You know that we have no one so skilled in felling timber as the Sidonians."

⁷When Hiram heard Solomon's message, he was greatly pleased and said, "Praise be to the Lord today, for he has given David a wise son to rule over this great nation."

⁸So Hiram sent word to Solomon:

"I have received the message you sent me and will do all you want in providing the cedar and pine logs. ⁹My men will haul them down from Lebanon to the sea, and I will float them in rafts by sea to the place you specify. There I will separate them and you can take them away. And you are to grant my wish by providing food for my royal household."

¹⁰In this way Hiram kept Solomon supplied with all the cedar and pine logs he wanted, ¹¹and Solomon gave Hiram twenty thousand cors^l of wheat as food for his household, in addition to twenty thousand baths^{m,n} of pressed olive oil. Solomon continued to do this for Hiram year after year. ¹²The Lord gave Solomon wisdom, just as he had promised him. There were peaceful relations between Hiram and Solomon, and the two of them made a treaty.

¹³King Solomon conscripted laborers from all Israel—thirty thousand men. ¹⁴He sent them off to Lebanon in shifts of ten thousand a month, so that they spent one month in Lebanon and two months at home. Adoniram was in charge of the forced labor. ¹⁵Solomon had seventy thousand carriers and eighty thousand stonecutters in the hills, ¹⁶as well as thirty-three hundred^o foremen who supervised the project and directed the workmen. ¹⁷At the king's command they removed from the quarry large blocks of quality stone to provide a foundation of dressed stone for the temple. ¹⁸The craftsmen of Solomon and Hiram and the men of Gebal^p cut and prepared the timber and stone for the building of the temple.

6

In the four hundred and eightieth^q year after the Israelites had come out of Egypt, in the fourth year of Solomon's reign over Israel, in the month of Ziv, the second month, he began to build the temple of the Lord.

²The temple that King Solomon built for the Lord was sixty cubits long, twenty wide and thirty high.^{r} ³The portico at the front of the main hall of the temple extended the width of the temple, that is twenty cubits,^{s} and projected ten cubits^t from the front of the temple. ⁴He made narrow clerestory windows in the temple. ⁵Against the walls of the main hall and inner sanctuary he built a structure around the building, in which there were side rooms. ⁶The lowest floor was five cubits^u wide, the middle floor six cubits^v and the third floor seven.^{w} He made offset ledges around the outside of the temple so that nothing would be inserted into the temple walls.

⁷In building the temple, only blocks dressed at the quarry were used, and no hammer, chisel or any other iron tool was heard at the temple site while it was being built.

⁸The entrance to the lowest^x floor was on the south side of the temple; a stairway led up to the middle level and from there to the third. ⁹So he built the temple and completed it, roofing it with beams and cedar planks. ¹⁰And he built the side rooms all along the temple. The height of each was five cubits, and they were attached to the temple by beams of cedar.

^{l}11 That is, probably about 125,000 bushels (about 4,400 kiloliters)
^{m}11 Septuagint (see also 2 Chron. 2:10); Hebrew *twenty cors*
^{n}11 That is, about 115,000 gallons (about 440 kiloliters)
^{o}16 Hebrew; some Septuagint manuscripts (see also 2 Chron. 2:2, 18) *thirty-six hundred* ^{p}18 That is, Byblos ^{q}1 Hebrew; Septuagint *four hundred and fortieth* ^{r}2 That is, about 90 feet (about 27 meters) long and 30 feet (about 9 meters) wide and 45 feet (about 13.5 meters) high ^{s}3 That is, about 30 feet (about 9 meters) ^{t}3 That is, about 15 feet (about 4.5 meters) ^{u}6 That is, about 7 1/2 feet (about 2.3 meters); also in verses 10 and 24 ^{v}6 That is, about 9 feet (about 2.7 meters) ^{w}6 That is, about 10 1/2 feet (about 3.1 meters)
^{x}8 Septuagint; Hebrew *middle*

¹¹The word of the Lord came to Solomon: ¹²"As for this temple you are building, if you follow my decrees, carry out my regulations and keep all my commands and obey them, I will fulfill through you the promise I gave to David your father. ¹³And I will live among the Israelites and will not abandon my people Israel."

¹⁴So Solomon built the temple and completed it. ¹⁵He lined its interior walls with cedar boards, paneling them from the floor of the temple to the ceiling, and covered the floor of the temple with planks of pine. ¹⁶He partitioned off twenty cubitsʸ at the rear of the temple with cedar boards from floor to ceiling to form within the temple an inner sanctuary, the Most Holy Place. ¹⁷The main hall in front of this room was forty cubitsᶻ long. ¹⁸The inside of the temple was cedar, carved with gourds and open flowers. Everything was cedar; no stone was to be seen.

¹⁹He prepared the inner sanctuary within the temple to set the ark of the covenant of the Lord there. ²⁰The inner sanctuary was twenty cubits long, twenty wide and twenty high.ᵃ He overlaid the inside with pure gold, and he also overlaid the altar of cedar. ²¹Solomon covered the inside of the temple with pure gold, and he extended gold chains across the front of the inner sanctuary, which was overlaid with gold. ²²So he overlaid the whole interior with gold. He also overlaid with gold the altar that belonged to the inner sanctuary.

²³In the inner sanctuary he made a pair of cherubim of olive wood, each ten cubitsᵇ high. ²⁴One wing of the first cherub was five cubits long, and the other wing five cubits—ten cubits from wing tip to wing tip. ²⁵The second cherub also measured ten cubits, for the two cherubim were identical in size and shape. ²⁶The height of each cherub was ten cubits. ²⁷He placed the cherubim inside the innermost room of the temple, with their wings spread out. The wing of one cherub touched one wall, while the wing of the other touched the other wall, and their wings touched each other in the middle of the room. ²⁸He overlaid the cherubim with gold.

²⁹On the walls all around the temple, in both the inner and outer rooms, he carved cherubim, palm trees and open flowers. ³⁰He also covered the floors of both the inner and outer rooms of the temple with gold.

³¹For the entrance of the inner sanctuary he made doors of olive wood with five-sided jambs.

³²And on the two olive wood doors he carved cherubim, palm trees and open flowers, and overlaid the cherubim and palm trees with beaten gold. ³³In the same way he made four-sided jambs of olive wood for the entrance to the main hall. ³⁴He also made two pine doors, each having two leaves that turned in sockets. ³⁵He carved cherubim, palm trees and open flowers on them and overlaid them with gold hammered evenly over the carvings.

³⁶And he built the inner courtyard of three courses of dressed stone and one course of trimmed cedar beams.

³⁷The foundation of the temple of the Lord was laid in the fourth year, in the month of Ziv. ³⁸In the eleventh year in the month of Bul, the eighth month, the temple was finished in all its details according to its specifications. He had spent seven years building it.

7 It took Solomon thirteen years, however, to complete the construction of his palace. ²He built the Palace of the Forest of Lebanon a hundred cubits long, fifty wide and thirty high,ᶜ with four rows of cedar columns supporting trimmed cedar beams. ³It was roofed with cedar above the beams that rested on the columns—forty-five beams, fifteen to a row. ⁴Its windows were placed high in sets of three, facing each other. ⁵All the doorways had rectangular frames; they were in the front part in sets of three, facing each other.ᵈ

⁶He made a colonnade fifty cubits long and thirty wide.ᵉ In front of it was a portico, and in front of that were pillars and an overhanging roof.

⁷He built the throne hall, the Hall of Justice, where he was to judge, and he covered it with cedar from floor to ceiling.ᶠ ⁸And the palace in which he was to live, set farther back, was similar in design. Solomon also made a palace like this hall for Pharaoh's daughter, whom he had married.

⁹All these structures, from the outside to the great courtyard and from foundation to eaves, were made of blocks of high-grade stone cut to size and trimmed with a saw on their inner and outer faces. ¹⁰The foundations were laid with

---

ʸ16 That is, about 30 feet (about 9 meters)   ᶻ17 That is, about 60 feet (about 18 meters)   ᵃ20 That is, about 30 feet (about 9 meters) long, wide and high   ᵇ23 That is, about 15 feet (about 4.5 meters) ᶜ2 That is, about 150 feet (about 46 meters) long, 75 feet (about 23 meters) wide and 45 feet (about 13.5 meters) high   ᵈ5 The meaning of the Hebrew for this verse is uncertain.   ᵉ6 That is, about 75 feet (about 23 meters) long and 45 feet (about 13.5 meters) wide ᶠ7 Vulgate and Syriac; Hebrew *floor* large stones of good quality, some measuring ten cubits^g and some eight.^h ¹¹Above were high-grade stones, cut to size, and cedar beams. ¹²The great courtyard was surrounded by a wall of three courses of dressed stone and one course of trimmed cedar beams, as was the inner courtyard of the temple of the LORD with its portico.

¹³King Solomon sent to Tyre and brought Hu-ram,ⁱ ¹⁴whose mother was a widow from the tribe of Naphtali and whose father was a man of Tyre and a craftsman in bronze. Huram was highly skilled and experienced in all kinds of bronze work. He came to King Solomon and did all the work assigned to him.

¹⁵He cast two bronze pillars, each eighteen cu-bits high and twelve cubits around,^j by line. ¹⁶He also made two capitals of cast bronze to set on the tops of the pillars; each capital was five cubits^k high. ¹⁷A network of interwoven chains festooned the capitals on top of the pillars, seven for each capital. ¹⁸He made pomegranates in two rows^l encircling each network to decorate the capitals on top of the pillars.^m He did the same for each capital. ¹⁹The capitals on top of the pil-lars in the portico were in the shape of lilies, four cubitsⁿ high. ²⁰On the capitals of both pillars, above the bowl-shaped part next to the network, were the two hundred pomegranates in rows all around. ²¹He erected the pillars at the portico of the temple. The pillar to the south he named Ja-kin^o and the one to the north Boaz.^p ²²The capi-tals on top were in the shape of lilies. And so the work on the pillars was completed.

²³He made the Sea of cast metal, circular in shape, measuring ten cubits^g from rim to rim and five cubits high. It took a line of thirty cu-bits^q to measure around it. ²⁴Below the rim, gourds encircled it—ten to a cubit. The gourds were cast in two rows in one piece with the Sea. ²⁵The Sea stood on twelve bulls, three facing north, three facing west, three facing south and three facing east. The Sea rested on top of them, and their hindquarters were toward the center. ²⁶It was a handbreadth^r in thickness, and its rim was like the rim of a cup, like a lily blossom. It held two thousand baths.^s

²⁷He also made ten movable stands of bronze; each was four cubits long, four wide and three high.^t ²⁸This is how the stands were made: They had side panels attached to uprights. ²⁹On the panels between the uprights were lions, bulls and cherubim—and on the uprights as well. Above

and below the lions and bulls were wreaths of hammered work. ³⁰Each stand had four bronze wheels with bronze axles, and each had a basin resting on four supports, cast with wreaths on each side. ³¹On the inside of the stand there was an opening that had a circular frame one cubit^u deep. This opening was round, and with its base-work it measured a cubit and a half.^v Around its opening there was engraving. The panels of the stands were square, not round. ³²The four wheels were under the panels, and the axles of the wheels were attached to the stand. The diameter of each wheel was a cubit and a half. ³³The wheels were made like chariot wheels; the axles, rims, spokes and hubs were all of cast metal.

³⁴Each stand had four handles, one on each corner, projecting from the stand. ³⁵At the top of the stand there was a circular band half a cubit^w deep. The supports and panels were attached to the top of the stand. ³⁶He engraved cherubim, lions and palm trees on the surfaces of the sup-ports and on the panels, in every available space, with wreaths all around. ³⁷This is the way he made the ten stands. They were all cast in the same molds and were identical in size and shape.

³⁸He then made ten bronze basins, each hold-ing forty baths^x and measuring four cubits across, one basin to go on each of the ten stands. ³⁹He placed five of the stands on the south side of the temple and five on the north. He placed the Sea on the south side, at the southeast corner of the temple. ⁴⁰He also made the basins and shovels and sprinkling bowls.

So Huram finished all the work he had under-taken for King Solomon in the temple of the LORD:

⁴¹the two pillars;
  the two bowl-shaped capitals on top of the
    pillars;
  the two sets of network decorating the two
    bowl-shaped capitals on top of the pillars;

---

^g10,23 That is, about 15 feet (about 4.5 meters)   ^h10 That is, about 12 feet (about 3.6 meters)   ⁱ13 Hebrew *Hiram*, a variant of *Huram*; also in verses 40 and 45   ^j15 That is, about 27 feet (about 8.1 meters) high and 18 feet (about 5.4 meters) around   ^k16 That is, about 7 1/2 feet (about 2.3 meters); also in verse 23   ^l18 Two Hebrew manuscripts and Septuagint; most Hebrew manuscripts *made the pillars, and there were two rows*   ^m18 Many Hebrew manuscripts and Syriac; most Hebrew manuscripts *pomegranates*   ⁿ19 That is, about 6 feet (about 1.8 meters); also in verse 38   ^o21 *Jakin* probably means *he establishes.*   ^p21 *Boaz* probably means *in him is strength.*   ^q23 That is, about 45 feet (about 13.5 meters)   ^r26 That is, about 3 inches (about 8 centimeters)   ^s26 That is, probably about 11,500 gallons (about 44 kiloliters); the Septuagint does not have this sentence.   ^t27 That is, about 6 feet (about 1.8 meters) long and wide and about 4 1/2 feet (about 1.3 meters) high   ^u31 That is, about 1 1/2 feet (about 0.5 meter)   ^v31 That is, about 2 1/4 feet (about 0.7 meter); also in verse 32   ^w35 That is, about 3/4 foot (about 0.2 meter)   ^x38 That is, about 230 gallons (about 880 liters)

⁴²the four hundred pomegranates for the two sets of network (two rows of pomegranates for each network, decorating the bowl-shaped capitals on top of the pillars);
⁴³the ten stands with their ten basins;
⁴⁴the Sea and the twelve bulls under it;
⁴⁵the pots, shovels and sprinkling bowls.

All these objects that Huram made for King Solomon for the temple of the LORD were of burnished bronze. ⁴⁶The king had them cast in clay molds in the plain of the Jordan between Succoth and Zarethan. ⁴⁷Solomon left all these things unweighed, because there were so many; the weight of the bronze was not determined.

⁴⁸Solomon also made all the furnishings that were in the LORD's temple:

the golden altar;
the golden table on which was the bread of the Presence;
⁴⁹the lampstands of pure gold (five on the right and five on the left, in front of the inner sanctuary);
the gold floral work and lamps and tongs;
⁵⁰the pure gold basins, wick trimmers, sprinkling bowls, dishes and censers;
and the gold sockets for the doors of the innermost room, the Most Holy Place, and also for the doors of the main hall of the temple.

⁵¹When all the work King Solomon had done for the temple of the LORD was finished, he brought in the things his father David had dedicated—the silver and gold and the furnishings—and he placed them in the treasuries of the LORD's temple.

8 Then King Solomon summoned into his presence at Jerusalem the elders of Israel, all the heads of the tribes and the chiefs of the Israelite families, to bring up the ark of the LORD's covenant from Zion, the City of David. ²All the men of Israel came together to King Solomon at the time of the festival in the month of Ethanim, the seventh month.

³When all the elders of Israel had arrived, the priests took up the ark, ⁴and they brought up the ark of the LORD and the Tent of Meeting and all the sacred furnishings in it. The priests and Levites carried them up, ⁵and King Solomon and the entire assembly of Israel that had gathered about

him were before the ark, sacrificing so many sheep and cattle that they could not be recorded or counted.

⁶The priests then brought the ark of the LORD's covenant to its place in the inner sanctuary of the temple, the Most Holy Place, and put it beneath the wings of the cherubim. ⁷The cherubim spread their wings over the place of the ark and overshadowed the ark and its carrying poles. ⁸These poles were so long that their ends could be seen from the Holy Place in front of the inner sanctuary, but not from outside the Holy Place; and they are still there today. ⁹There was nothing in the ark except the two stone tablets that Moses had placed in it at Horeb, where the LORD made a covenant with the Israelites after they came out of Egypt.

¹⁰When the priests withdrew from the Holy Place, the cloud filled the temple of the LORD. ¹¹And the priests could not perform their service because of the cloud, for the glory of the LORD filled his temple.

¹²Then Solomon said, "The LORD has said that he would dwell in a dark cloud; ¹³I have indeed built a magnificent temple for you, a place for you to dwell forever."

¹⁴While the whole assembly of Israel was standing there, the king turned around and blessed them. ¹⁵Then he said:

"Praise be to the LORD, the God of Israel, who with his own hand has fulfilled what he promised with his own mouth to my father David. For he said, ¹⁶'Since the day I brought my people Israel out of Egypt, I have not chosen a city in any tribe of Israel to have a temple built for my Name to be there, but I have chosen David to rule my people Israel.'

¹⁷"My father David had it in his heart to build a temple for the Name of the LORD, the God of Israel. ¹⁸But the LORD said to my father David, 'Because it was in your heart to build a temple for my Name, you did well to have this in your heart. ¹⁹Nevertheless, you are not the one to build the temple, but your son, who is your own flesh and blood—he is the one who will build the temple for my Name.'

²⁰"The LORD has kept the promise he made: I have succeeded David my father and now I sit on the throne of Israel, just as the LORD promised, and I have built the temple

for the Name of the LORD, the God of Israel. ²¹I have provided a place there for the ark, in which is the covenant of the LORD that he made with our fathers when he brought them out of Egypt."

²²Then Solomon stood before the altar of the LORD in front of the whole assembly of Israel, spread out his hands toward heaven ²³and said:

"O LORD, God of Israel, there is no God like you in heaven above or on earth below—you who keep your covenant of love with your servants who continue wholeheartedly in your way. ²⁴You have kept your promise to your servant David my father; with your mouth you have promised and with your hand you have fulfilled it—as it is today.

²⁵"Now LORD, God of Israel, keep for your servant David my father the promises you made to him when you said, 'You shall never fail to have a man to sit before me on the throne of Israel, if only your sons are careful in all they do to walk before me as you have done.' ²⁶And now, O God of Israel, let your word that you promised your servant David my father come true.

²⁷"But will God really dwell on earth? The heavens, even the highest heaven, cannot contain you. How much less this temple I have built! ²⁸Yet give attention to your servant's prayer and his plea for mercy, O LORD my God. Hear the cry and the prayer that your servant is praying in your presence this day. ²⁹May your eyes be open toward this temple night and day, this place of which you said, 'My Name shall be there,' so that you will hear the prayer your servant prays toward this place. ³⁰Hear the supplication of your servant and of your people Israel when they pray toward this place. Hear from heaven, your dwelling place, and when you hear, forgive.

³¹"When a man wrongs his neighbor and is required to take an oath and he comes and swears the oath before your altar in this temple, ³²then hear from heaven and act. Judge between your servants, condemning the guilty and bringing down on his own head what he has done. Declare the innocent not guilty, and so establish his innocence.

³³"When your people Israel have been de-

feated by an enemy because they have sinned against you, and when they turn back to you and confess your name, praying and making supplication to you in this temple, ³⁴then hear from heaven and forgive the sin of your people Israel and bring them back to the land you gave to their fathers.

³⁵"When the heavens are shut up and there is no rain because your people have sinned against you, and when they pray toward this place and confess your name and turn from their sin because you have afflicted them, ³⁶then hear from heaven and forgive the sin of your servants, your people Israel. Teach them the right way to live, and send rain on the land you gave your people for an inheritance.

³⁷"When famine or plague comes to the land, or blight or mildew, locusts or grasshoppers, or when an enemy besieges them in any of their cities, whatever disaster or disease may come, ³⁸and when a prayer or plea is made by any of your people Israel—each one aware of the afflictions of his own heart, and spreading out his hands toward this temple— ³⁹then hear from heaven, your dwelling place. Forgive and act; deal with each man according to all he does, since you know his heart (for you alone know the hearts of all men), ⁴⁰so that they will fear you all the time they live in the land you gave our fathers.

⁴¹"As for the foreigner who does not belong to your people Israel but has come from a distant land because of your name— ⁴²for men will hear of your great name and your mighty hand and your outstretched arm— when he comes and prays toward this temple, ⁴³then hear from heaven, your dwelling place, and do whatever the foreigner asks of you, so that all the peoples of the earth may know your name and fear you, as do your own people Israel, and may know that this house I have built bears your Name.

⁴⁴"When your people go to war against their enemies, wherever you send them, and when they pray to the LORD toward the city you have chosen and the temple I have built for your Name, ⁴⁵then hear from heaven their prayer and their plea, and uphold their cause.

⁴⁶"When they sin against you—for there is

no one who does not sin—and you become angry with them and give them over to the enemy, who takes them captive to his own land, far away or near; ⁴⁷and if they have a change of heart in the land where they are held captive, and repent and plead with you in the land of their conquerors and say, 'We have sinned, we have done wrong, we have acted wickedly'; ⁴⁸and if they turn back to you with all their heart and soul in the land of their enemies who took them captive, and pray to you toward the land you gave their fathers, toward the city you have chosen and the temple I have built for your Name; ⁴⁹then from heaven, your dwelling place, hear their prayer and their plea, and uphold their cause. ⁵⁰And forgive your people, who have sinned against you; forgive all the offenses they have committed against you, and cause their conquerors to show them mercy; ⁵¹for they are your people and your inheritance, whom you brought out of Egypt, out of that iron-smelting furnace.

⁵²"May your eyes be open to your servant's plea and to the plea of your people Israel, and may you listen to them whenever they cry out to you. ⁵³For you singled them out from all the nations of the world to be your own inheritance, just as you declared through your servant Moses when you, O Sovereign Lord, brought our fathers out of Egypt."

⁵⁴When Solomon had finished all these prayers and supplications to the Lord, he rose from before the altar of the Lord, where he had been kneeling with his hands spread out toward heaven. ⁵⁵He stood and blessed the whole assembly of Israel in a loud voice, saying:

⁵⁶"Praise be to the Lord, who has given rest to his people Israel just as he promised. Not one word has failed of all the good promises he gave through his servant Moses. ⁵⁷May the Lord our God be with us as he was with our fathers; may he never leave us nor forsake us. ⁵⁸May he turn our hearts to him, to walk in all his ways and to keep the commands, decrees and regulations he gave our fathers. ⁵⁹And may these words of mine, which I have prayed before the Lord, be near to the Lord our God day and night, that he may uphold the cause of his servant and the

cause of his people Israel according to each day's need, ⁶⁰so that all the peoples of the earth may know that the Lord is God and that there is no other. ⁶¹But your hearts must be fully committed to the Lord our God, to live by his decrees and obey his commands, as at this time."

⁶²Then the king and all Israel with him offered sacrifices before the Lord. ⁶³Solomon offered a sacrifice of fellowship offeringsʸ to the Lord: twenty-two thousand cattle and a hundred and twenty thousand sheep and goats. So the king and all the Israelites dedicated the temple of the Lord.

⁶⁴On that same day the king consecrated the middle part of the courtyard in front of the temple of the Lord, and there he offered burnt offerings, grain offerings and the fat of the fellowship offerings, because the bronze altar before the Lord was too small to hold the burnt offerings, the grain offerings and the fat of the fellowship offerings.

⁶⁵So Solomon observed the festival at that time, and all Israel with him—a vast assembly, people from Leboᶻ Hamath to the Wadi of Egypt. They celebrated it before the Lord our God for seven days and seven days more, fourteen days in all. ⁶⁶On the following day he sent the people away. They blessed the king and then went home, joyful and glad in heart for all the good things the Lord had done for his servant David and his people Israel.

9 When Solomon had finished building the temple of the Lord and the royal palace, and had achieved all he had desired to do, ²the Lord appeared to him a second time, as he had appeared to him at Gibeon. ³The Lord said to him:

"I have heard the prayer and plea you have made before me; I have consecrated this temple, which you have built, by putting my Name there forever. My eyes and my heart will always be there.

⁴"As for you, if you walk before me in integrity of heart and uprightness, as David your father did, and do all I command and observe my decrees and laws, ⁵I will establish your royal throne over Israel forever, as I promised David your father when I said,

ʸ63 Traditionally *peace offerings*; also in verse 64   ᶻ65 Or *from the entrance to*

'You shall never fail to have a man on the throne of Israel.'

6"But if you[a] or your sons turn away from me and do not observe the commands and decrees I have given you[a] and go off to serve other gods and worship them, 7then I will cut off Israel from the land I have given them and will reject this temple I have consecrated for my Name. Israel will then become a byword and an object of ridicule among all peoples. 8And though this temple is now imposing, all who pass by will be appalled and will scoff and say, 'Why has the LORD done such a thing to this land and to this temple?' 9People will answer, 'Because they have forsaken the LORD their God, who brought their fathers out of Egypt, and have embraced other gods, worshiping and serving them—that is why the LORD brought all this disaster on them.' "

10At the end of twenty years, during which Solomon built these two buildings—the temple of the LORD and the royal palace— 11King Solomon gave twenty towns in Galilee to Hiram king of Tyre, because Hiram had supplied him with all the cedar and pine and gold he wanted. 12But when Hiram went from Tyre to see the towns that Solomon had given him, he was not pleased with them. 13"What kind of towns are these you have given me, my brother?" he asked. And he called them the Land of Cabul,[b] a name they have to this day. 14Now Hiram had sent to the king 120 talents[c] of gold.

15Here is the account of the forced labor King Solomon conscripted to build the LORD's temple, his own palace, the supporting terraces,[d] the wall of Jerusalem, and Hazor, Megiddo and Gezer. 16(Pharaoh king of Egypt had attacked and captured Gezer. He had set it on fire. He killed its Canaanite inhabitants and then gave it as a wedding gift to his daughter, Solomon's wife. 17And Solomon rebuilt Gezer.) He built up Lower Beth Horon, 18Baalath, and Tadmor[e] in the desert, within his land, 19as well as all his store cities and the towns for his chariots and for his horses[f]— whatever he desired to build in Jerusalem, in Lebanon and throughout all the territory he ruled.

20All the people left from the Amorites, Hittites, Perizzites, Hivites and Jebusites (these peoples were not Israelites), 21that is, their descendants remaining in the land, whom the Israelites

could not exterminate[g]—these Solomon conscripted for his slave labor force, as it is to this day. 22But Solomon did not make slaves of any of the Israelites; they were his fighting men, his government officials, his officers, his captains, and the commanders of his chariots and charioteers. 23They were also the chief officials in charge of Solomon's projects—550 officials supervising the men who did the work.

24After Pharaoh's daughter had come up from the City of David to the palace Solomon had built for her, he constructed the supporting terraces.

25Three times a year Solomon sacrificed burnt offerings and fellowship offerings[h] on the altar he had built for the LORD, burning incense before the LORD along with them, and so fulfilled the temple obligations.

26King Solomon also built ships at Ezion Geber, which is near Elath in Edom, on the shore of the Red Sea.[i] 27And Hiram sent his men—sailors who knew the sea—to serve in the fleet with Solomon's men. 28They sailed to Ophir and brought back 420 talents[j] of gold, which they delivered to King Solomon.

10

When the queen of Sheba heard about the fame of Solomon and his relation to the name of the LORD, she came to test him with hard questions. 2Arriving at Jerusalem with a very great caravan—with camels carrying spices, large quantities of gold, and precious stones—she came to Solomon and talked with him about all that she had on her mind. 3Solomon answered all her questions; nothing was too hard for the king to explain to her. 4When the queen of Sheba saw all the wisdom of Solomon and the palace he had built, 5the food on his table, the seating of his officials, the attending servants in their robes, his cupbearers, and the burnt offerings he made at[k] the temple of the LORD, she was overwhelmed.

6She said to the king, "The report I heard in my own country about your achievements and your wisdom is true. 7But I did not believe these things until I came and saw with my own eyes. Indeed, not even half was told me; in wisdom and wealth you have far exceeded the report I heard. 8How

---

[a]6 The Hebrew is plural.　[b]13 Cabul sounds like the Hebrew for good-for-nothing.　[c]14 That is, about 4 1/2 tons (about 4 metric tons)　[d]15 Or the Millo; also in verse 24　[e]18 The Hebrew may also be read Tamar.　[f]19 Or charioteers　[g]21 The Hebrew term refers to the irrevocable giving over of things or persons to the LORD, often by totally destroying them.　[h]25 Traditionally peace offerings　[i]26 Hebrew Yam Suph; that is, Sea of Reeds　[j]28 That is, about 16 tons (about 14.5 metric tons)　[k]5 Or the ascent by which he went up to

happy your men must be! How happy your officials, who continually stand before you and hear your wisdom! ⁹Praise be to the Lord your God, who has delighted in you and placed you on the throne of Israel. Because of the Lord's eternal love for Israel, he has made you king, to maintain justice and righteousness."

¹⁰And she gave the king 120 talents[l] of gold, large quantities of spices, and precious stones. Never again were so many spices brought in as those the queen of Sheba gave to King Solomon.

¹¹(Hiram's ships brought gold from Ophir; and from there they brought great cargoes of almugwood[m] and precious stones. ¹²The king used the almugwood to make supports for the temple of the Lord and for the royal palace, and to make harps and lyres for the musicians. So much almugwood has never been imported or seen since that day.)

¹³King Solomon gave the queen of Sheba all she desired and asked for, besides what he had given her out of his royal bounty. Then she left and returned with her retinue to her own country.

¹⁴The weight of the gold that Solomon received yearly was 666 talents,[n] ¹⁵not including the revenues from merchants and traders and from all the Arabian kings and the governors of the land.

¹⁶King Solomon made two hundred large shields of hammered gold; six hundred bekas[o] of gold went into each shield. ¹⁷He also made three hundred small shields of hammered gold, with three minas[p] of gold in each shield. The king put them in the Palace of the Forest of Lebanon.

¹⁸Then the king made a great throne inlaid with ivory and overlaid with fine gold. ¹⁹The throne had six steps, and its back had a rounded top. On both sides of the seat were armrests, with

a lion standing beside each of them. ²⁰Twelve lions stood on the six steps, one at either end of each step. Nothing like it had ever been made for any other kingdom. ²¹All King Solomon's goblets were gold, and all the household articles in the Palace of the Forest of Lebanon were pure gold. Nothing was made of silver, because silver was considered of little value in Solomon's days. ²²The king had a fleet of trading ships[q] at sea along with the ships of Hiram. Once every three years it returned, carrying gold, silver and ivory, and apes and baboons.

²³King Solomon was greater in riches and wisdom than all the other kings of the earth. ²⁴The whole world sought audience with Solomon to hear the wisdom God had put in his heart. ²⁵Year after year, everyone who came brought a gift—articles of silver and gold, robes, weapons and spices, and horses and mules.

²⁶Solomon accumulated chariots and horses; he had fourteen hundred chariots and twelve thousand horses,[r] which he kept in the chariot cities and also with him in Jerusalem. ²⁷The king made silver as common in Jerusalem as stones, and cedar as plentiful as sycamore-fig trees in the foothills. ²⁸Solomon's horses were imported from Egypt[s] and from Kue[t]—the royal merchants purchased them from Kue. ²⁹They imported a chariot from Egypt for six hundred shekels[u] of silver, and a horse for a hundred and fifty.[p] They also exported them to all the kings of the Hittites and of the Arameans.

---

[l]10 That is, about 4 1/2 tons (about 4 metric tons)   [m]11 Probably a variant of *algumwood*; also in verse 12   [n]14 That is, about 25 tons (about 23 metric tons)   [o]16 That is, about 7 1/2 pounds (about 3.5 kilograms)   [p]17,29 That is, about 3 3/4 pounds (about 1.7 kilograms)   [q]22 Hebrew *of ships of Tarshish*   [r]26 Or *charioteers*   [s]28 Or possibly *Muzur*, a region in Cilicia; also in verse 29   [t]28 Probably Cilicia   [u]29 That is, about 15 pounds (about 7 kilograms)

---

2 / 1 Kings 11
Faithless in Love

"I WANT TO do God's will—if only I knew what it was," the young woman said to her pastor. "God has brought Bill and me together, and he has created a great love between us. Bill wants to marry me, but I'm not sure."

'But has Bill given himself to Jesus Christ?" her pastor probed.

"No, not yet," she hesitated. "But I think he will—perhaps after we're married . . ." Her voice trailed off under her pastor's firm gaze.

"God has already shown you his will, I think," her pastor replied. "You know Paul's writings to the Christians at Corinth: 'Do not be yoked together with unbelievers.' "

God's laws may seem harsh, but they are less harsh than the results of living by our own guidelines. God seems to know what works. Solomon had occasion to discover this truth.

 Warming Up to God What effect does it have on you when spiritual values are kept separate from your everyday life?

 Read 1 Kings 11.

11 King Solomon, however, loved many foreign women besides Pharaoh's daughter—Moabites, Ammonites, Edomites, Sidonians and Hittites. ²They were from nations about which the LORD had told the Israelites, "You must not intermarry with them, because they will surely turn your hearts after their gods." Nevertheless, Solomon held fast to them in love. ³He had seven hundred wives of royal birth and three hundred concubines, and his wives led him astray. ⁴As Solomon grew old, his wives turned his heart after other gods, and his heart was not fully devoted to the LORD his God, as the heart of David his father had been. ⁵He followed Ashtoreth the goddess of the Sidonians, and Molech ᵛ the detestable god of the Ammonites. ⁶So Solomon did evil in the eyes of the LORD; he did not follow the LORD completely, as David his father had done.

⁷On a hill east of Jerusalem, Solomon built a high place for Chemosh the detestable god of Moab, and for Molech the detestable god of the Ammonites. ⁸He did the same for all his foreign wives, who burned incense and offered sacrifices to their gods.

⁹The LORD became angry with Solomon because his heart had turned away from the LORD, the God of Israel, who had appeared to him twice. ¹⁰Although he had forbidden Solomon to follow other gods, Solomon did not keep the LORD's command. ¹¹So the LORD said to Solomon, "Since this is your attitude and you have not kept my covenant and my decrees, which I commanded you, I will most certainly tear the kingdom away from you and give it to one of your subordinates. ¹²Nevertheless, for the sake of David your father, I will not do it during your lifetime. I will tear it out of the hand of your son. ¹³Yet I will not tear the whole kingdom from him, but will give him one tribe for the sake of David my servant and for the sake of Jerusalem, which I have chosen."

¹⁴Then the LORD raised up against Solomon an adversary, Hadad the Edomite, from the royal line of Edom. ¹⁵Earlier when David was fighting with Edom, Joab the commander of the army, who had gone up to bury the dead, had struck down all the men in Edom. ¹⁶Joab and all the Israelites stayed there for six months, until they had destroyed all the men in Edom. ¹⁷But Hadad, still only a boy, fled to Egypt with some Edomite officials who had served his father. ¹⁸They set out from Midian and went to Paran. Then taking men from Paran with them, they went to Egypt, to Pharaoh king of Egypt, who gave Hadad a house and land and provided him with food.

¹⁹Pharaoh was so pleased with Hadad that he gave him a sister of his own wife, Queen Tahpenes, in marriage. ²⁰The sister of Tahpenes bore him a son named Genubath, whom Tahpenes brought up in the royal palace. There Genubath lived with Pharaoh's own children.

²¹While he was in Egypt, Hadad heard that David rested with his fathers and that Joab the commander of the army was also dead. Then Hadad said to Pharaoh, "Let me go, that I may return to my own country."

²²"What have you lacked here that you want to go back to your own country?" Pharaoh asked.

"Nothing," Hadad replied, "but do let me go!"

²³And God raised up against Solomon another adversary, Rezon son of Eliada, who had fled from his master, Hadadezer king of Zobah. ²⁴He gathered men around him and became the leader of a band of rebels when David destroyed the forces ʷ ⌞of Zobah⌟; the rebels went to Damascus, where they settled and took control. ²⁵Rezon was Israel's adversary as long as Solomon lived, adding to the trouble caused by Hadad. So Rezon ruled in Aram and was hostile toward Israel.

²⁶Also, Jeroboam son of Nebat rebelled against the king. He was one of Solomon's officials, an Ephraimite from Zeredah, and his mother was a widow named Zeruah.

²⁷Here is the account of how he rebelled against the king: Solomon had built the supporting terraces ˣ and had filled in the gap in the wall of the city of David his father. ²⁸Now Jeroboam

ᵛ5 Hebrew *Milcom;* also in verse 33   ʷ24 Hebrew *destroyed them*
ˣ27 Or *the Millo*

was a man of standing, and when Solomon saw how well the young man did his work, he put him in charge of the whole labor force of the house of Joseph.

²⁹About that time Jeroboam was going out of Jerusalem, and Ahijah the prophet of Shiloh met him on the way, wearing a new cloak. The two of them were alone out in the country, ³⁰and Ahijah took hold of the new cloak he was wearing and tore it into twelve pieces. ³¹Then he said to Jeroboam, "Take ten pieces for yourself, for this is what the LORD, the God of Israel, says: 'See, I am going to tear the kingdom out of Solomon's hand and give you ten tribes. ³²But for the sake of my servant David and the city of Jerusalem, which I have chosen out of all the tribes of Israel, he will have one tribe. ³³I will do this because they haveʸ forsaken me and worshiped Ashtoreth the goddess of the Sidonians, Chemosh the god of the Moabites, and Molech the god of the Ammonites, and have not walked in my ways, nor done what is right in my eyes, nor kept my statutes and laws as David, Solomon's father, did.

³⁴" 'But I will not take the whole kingdom out of Solomon's hand; I have made him ruler all the days of his life for the sake of David my servant, whom I chose and who observed my commands and statutes. ³⁵I will take the kingdom from his son's hands and give you ten tribes. ³⁶I will give one tribe to his son so that David my servant may always have a lamp before me in Jerusalem, the city where I chose to put my Name. ³⁷However, as for you, I will take you, and you will rule over all that your heart desires; you will be king over Israel. ³⁸If you do whatever I command you and walk in my ways and do what is right in my eyes by keeping my statutes and commands, as David my servant did, I will be with you. I will build you a dynasty as enduring as the one I built for David and will give Israel to you. ³⁹I will humble David's descendants because of this, but not forever.' "

⁴⁰Solomon tried to kill Jeroboam, but Jeroboam fled to Egypt, to Shishak the king, and stayed there until Solomon's death.

⁴¹As for the other events of Solomon's reign—all he did and the wisdom he displayed—are they not written in the book of the annals of Solomon? ⁴²Solomon reigned in Jerusalem over all Israel forty years. ⁴³Then he rested with his fathers and was buried in the city of David his father. And Rehoboam his son succeeded him as king.

ʸ33 Hebrew; Septuagint, Vulgate and Syriac *because he has*

Discovering the Word 1. In what ways did Solomon break the first commandment, "You shall have no other gods before me" (vv. 1–13)? 2. In verse 13 God says that the consequence of Solomon's sin will be that his kingdom will be taken away. What mercy does God promise? Why? 3. What indications do you see that Hadad had the potential to become a serious threat to Solomon (vv. 14–22)? 4. What about Rezon (vv. 23–25)? 5. If Jeroboam chose to benefit from the experience of Israel's previous two kings (David and Solomon), how would it affect his reign?

Applying the Word 1. Solomon allowed his acquisition of wives to ease out his faith in God. When has your own love for a person created tensions with your faith? 2. How can we balance our love for the important people in our lives with our love for God? 3. Solomon's marriages to pagans testified to his lack of wholehearted commitment to God. In what area of your life do you struggle to keep your actions in line with your beliefs?

 Responding in Prayer Verse 6 characterizes Solomon's life: "So Solomon did evil in the eyes of the LORD." Pray that your life will be characterized by faithfulness.

3 / *1 Kings 12*
Internal Conflict

CIVIL WAR. AMERICAN minds turn to Yankee blue battling Confederate gray; brothers, cousins and neighbors pitted against each other; a wantonly destructive march to the sea, forever an embarrassment to both sides; a president on his knees, in tears. Three thousand years ago, Israel, too, suffered civil war with many of the same griefs. As in the U.S. Civil War, family members had to decide which side they were on. Geography wasn't always the most important factor, for this war was not only a war of politics. It was also, at least at the outset, a war of faith.

 Warming Up to God How do you respond to conflict within your church or fellowship group? How does that kind of conflict affect your faith?

 Read 1 Kings 12.

12 Rehoboam went to Shechem, for all the Israelites had gone there to make him king. ²When Jeroboam son of Nebat heard this (he was still in Egypt, where he had fled from King Solomon), he returned from² Egypt. ³So they sent for Jeroboam, and he and the whole assembly of Israel went to Rehoboam and said to him: ⁴"Your father put a heavy yoke on us, but now lighten the harsh labor and the heavy yoke he put on us, and we will serve you."

⁵Rehoboam answered, "Go away for three days and then come back to me." So the people went away.

⁶Then King Rehoboam consulted the elders who had served his father Solomon during his lifetime. "How would you advise me to answer these people?" he asked.

⁷They replied, "If today you will be a servant to these people and serve them and give them a favorable answer, they will always be your servants."

⁸But Rehoboam rejected the advice the elders gave him and consulted the young men who had grown up with him and were serving him. ⁹He asked them, "What is your advice? How should we answer these people who say to me, 'Lighten the yoke your father put on us'?"

¹⁰The young men who had grown up with him replied, "Tell these people who have said to you, 'Your father put a heavy yoke on us, but make our yoke lighter'—tell them, 'My little finger is thicker than my father's waist. ¹¹My father laid on you a heavy yoke; I will make it even heavier. My father scourged you with whips; I will scourge you with scorpions.' "

¹²Three days later Jeroboam and all the people returned to Rehoboam, as the king had said, "Come back to me in three days." ¹³The king answered the people harshly. Rejecting the advice given him by the elders, ¹⁴he followed the advice of the young men and said, "My father made your yoke heavy; I will make it even heavier. My father scourged you with whips; I will scourge you with scorpions." ¹⁵So the king did not listen to the people, for this turn of events was from the LORD, to fulfill the word the LORD had spoken to Jeroboam son of Nebat through Ahijah the Shilonite.

¹⁶When all Israel saw that the king refused to listen to them, they answered the king:

"What share do we have in David,
    what part in Jesse's son?
To your tents, O Israel!
    Look after your own house, O David!"

So the Israelites went home. ¹⁷But as for the Israelites who were living in the towns of Judah, Rehoboam still ruled over them.

¹⁸King Rehoboam sent out Adoniram,ᵃ who was in charge of forced labor, but all Israel stoned him to death. King Rehoboam, however, managed to get into his chariot and escape to Jerusalem. ¹⁹So Israel has been in rebellion against the house of David to this day.

²⁰When all the Israelites heard that Jeroboam had returned, they sent and called him to the assembly and made him king over all Israel. Only the tribe of Judah remained loyal to the house of David.

²¹When Rehoboam arrived in Jerusalem, he mustered the whole house of Judah and the tribe of Benjamin—a hundred and eighty thousand

---

z2 Or *he remained in*   *a18* Some Septuagint manuscripts and Syriac (see also 1 Kings 4:6 and 5:14); Hebrew *Adoram* fighting men—to make war against the house of Israel and to regain the kingdom for Rehoboam son of Solomon.

²²But this word of God came to Shemaiah the man of God: ²³"Say to Rehoboam son of Solomon king of Judah, to the whole house of Judah and Benjamin, and to the rest of the people, ²⁴'This is what the Lord says: Do not go up to fight against your brothers, the Israelites. Go home, every one of you, for this is my doing.' " So they obeyed the word of the Lord and went home again, as the Lord had ordered.

²⁵Then Jeroboam fortified Shechem in the hill country of Ephraim and lived there. From there he went out and built up Peniel.ᵇ

²⁶Jeroboam thought to himself, "The kingdom will now likely revert to the house of David. ²⁷If these people go up to offer sacrifices at the temple of the Lord in Jerusalem, they will again give their allegiance to their lord, Rehoboam king of Judah. They will kill me and return to King Rehoboam."

²⁸After seeking advice, the king made two golden calves. He said to the people, "It is too much for you to go up to Jerusalem. Here are your gods, O Israel, who brought you up out of Egypt." ²⁹One he set up in Bethel, and the other in Dan. ³⁰And this thing became a sin; the people went even as far as Dan to worship the one there.

³¹Jeroboam built shrines on high places and appointed priests from all sorts of people, even though they were not Levites. ³²He instituted a festival on the fifteenth day of the eighth month, like the festival held in Judah, and offered sacrifices on the altar. This he did in Bethel, sacrificing to the calves he had made. And at Bethel he also installed priests at the high places he had made. ³³On the fifteenth day of the eighth month, a month of his own choosing, he offered sacrifices on the altar he had built at Bethel. So he instituted the festival for the Israelites and went up to the altar to make offerings.

ᵇ25 Hebrew *Penuel*, a variant of *Peniel*

Discovering the Word 1. What steps in verses 1–19 led to the division recorded in verse 20? 2. At what points did reconciliation seem possible? 3. What indications do you find that God had not abandoned his people during this time of conflict? 4. What spiritual results for the people of Israel would you expect to grow out of Jeroboam's new places of worship (vv. 26–30)? 5. What did Jeroboam do that was contrary to God's law (vv. 31–33)?

Applying the Word 1. If you were a godly person living under Jeroboam's rule, what choices would you have to make? 2. In what ways do your actions show a take-it-for-granted attitude toward your current opportunities to worship? 3. What conflict are you currently facing, and how do you need God's help to resolve it?

Responding in Prayer Praise God for the freedom you have to worship. Pray for those who don't have religious freedom.

---

1 Kings 13—16

13

By the word of the Lord a man of God came from Judah to Bethel, as Jeroboam was standing by the altar to make an offering. ²He cried out against the altar by the word of the Lord: "O altar, altar! This is what the Lord says: 'A son named Josiah will be born to the house of David. On you he will sacrifice the priests of the high places who now make offerings here, and human bones will be burned on you.' " ³That same day the man of God gave a sign: "This is the sign the Lord has declared: The altar will be split apart and the ashes on it will be poured out."

⁴When King Jeroboam heard what the man of God cried out against the altar at Bethel, he stretched out his hand from the altar and said, "Seize him!" But the hand he stretched out toward the man shriveled up, so that he could not pull it back. ⁵Also, the altar was split apart and its ashes poured out according to the sign given by the man of God by the word of the Lord.

⁶Then the king said to the man of God, "Intercede with the Lord your God and pray for me that my hand may be restored." So the man of God interceded with the Lord, and the king's hand was restored and became as it was before.

⁷The king said to the man of God, "Come home with me and have something to eat, and I will give you a gift."

⁸But the man of God answered the king, "Even if you were to give me half your possessions, I would not go with you, nor would I eat bread or drink water here. ⁹For I was commanded by the word of the LORD: 'You must not eat bread or drink water or return by the way you came.'" ¹⁰So he took another road and did not return by the way he had come to Bethel.

¹¹Now there was a certain old prophet living in Bethel, whose sons came and told him all that the man of God had done there that day. They also told their father what he had said to the king. ¹²Their father asked them, "Which way did he go?" And his sons showed him which road the man of God from Judah had taken. ¹³So he said to his sons, "Saddle the donkey for me." And when they had saddled the donkey for him, he mounted it ¹⁴and rode after the man of God. He found him sitting under an oak tree and asked, "Are you the man of God who came from Judah?"

"I am," he replied.

¹⁵So the prophet said to him, "Come home with me and eat."

¹⁶The man of God said, "I cannot turn back and go with you, nor can I eat bread or drink water with you in this place. ¹⁷I have been told by the word of the LORD: 'You must not eat bread or drink water there or return by the way you came.'"

¹⁸The old prophet answered, "I too am a prophet, as you are. And an angel said to me by the word of the LORD: 'Bring him back with you to your house so that he may eat bread and drink water.'" (But he was lying to him.) ¹⁹So the man of God returned with him and ate and drank in his house.

²⁰While they were sitting at the table, the word of the LORD came to the old prophet who had brought him back. ²¹He cried out to the man of God who had come from Judah, "This is what the LORD says: 'You have defied the word of the LORD and have not kept the command the LORD your God gave you. ²²You came back and ate bread and drank water in the place where he told you not to eat or drink. Therefore your body will not be buried in the tomb of your fathers.'"

²³When the man of God had finished eating and drinking, the prophet who had brought him back saddled his donkey for him. ²⁴As he went on

his way, a lion met him on the road and killed him, and his body was thrown down on the road, with both the donkey and the lion standing beside it. ²⁵Some people who passed by saw the body thrown down there, with the lion standing beside the body, and they went and reported it in the city where the old prophet lived.

²⁶When the prophet who had brought him back from his journey heard of it, he said, "It is the man of God who defied the word of the LORD. The LORD has given him over to the lion, which has mauled him and killed him, as the word of the LORD had warned him."

²⁷The prophet said to his sons, "Saddle the donkey for me," and they did so. ²⁸Then he went out and found the body thrown down on the road, with the donkey and the lion standing beside it. The lion had neither eaten the body nor mauled the donkey. ²⁹So the prophet picked up the body of the man of God, laid it on the donkey, and brought it back to his own city to mourn for him and bury him. ³⁰Then he laid the body in his own tomb, and they mourned over him and said, "Oh, my brother!"

³¹After burying him, he said to his sons, "When I die, bury me in the grave where the man of God is buried; lay my bones beside his bones. ³²For the message he declared by the word of the LORD against the altar in Bethel and against all the shrines on the high places in the towns of Samaria will certainly come true."

³³Even after this, Jeroboam did not change his evil ways, but once more appointed priests for the high places from all sorts of people. Anyone who wanted to become a priest he consecrated for the high places. ³⁴This was the sin of the house of Jeroboam that led to its downfall and to its destruction from the face of the earth.

14 At that time Abijah son of Jeroboam became ill, ²and Jeroboam said to his wife, "Go, disguise yourself, so you won't be recognized as the wife of Jeroboam. Then go to Shiloh. Ahijah the prophet is there—the one who told me I would be king over this people. ³Take ten loaves of bread with you, some cakes and a jar of honey, and go to him. He will tell you what will happen to the boy." ⁴So Jeroboam's wife did what he said and went to Ahijah's house in Shiloh.

Now Ahijah could not see; his sight was gone because of his age. ⁵But the LORD had told Ahijah, "Jeroboam's wife is coming to ask you about her son, for he is ill, and you are to give her such and such an answer. When she arrives, she will pretend to be someone else."

⁶So when Ahijah heard the sound of her footsteps at the door, he said, "Come in, wife of Jeroboam. Why this pretense? I have been sent to you with bad news. ⁷Go, tell Jeroboam that this is what the LORD, the God of Israel, says: 'I raised you up from among the people and made you a leader over my people Israel. ⁸I tore the kingdom away from the house of David and gave it to you, but you have not been like my servant David, who kept my commands and followed me with all his heart, doing only what was right in my eyes. ⁹You have done more evil than all who lived before you. You have made for yourself other gods, idols made of metal; you have provoked me to anger and thrust me behind your back.

¹⁰" 'Because of this, I am going to bring disaster on the house of Jeroboam. I will cut off from Jeroboam every last male in Israel—slave or free. I will burn up the house of Jeroboam as one burns dung, until it is all gone. ¹¹Dogs will eat those belonging to Jeroboam who die in the city, and the birds of the air will feed on those who die in the country. The LORD has spoken!'

¹²"As for you, go back home. When you set foot in your city, the boy will die. ¹³All Israel will mourn for him and bury him. He is the only one belonging to Jeroboam who will be buried, because he is the only one in the house of Jeroboam in whom the LORD, the God of Israel, has found anything good.

¹⁴"The LORD will raise up for himself a king over Israel who will cut off the family of Jeroboam. This is the day! What? Yes, even now.ᶜ ¹⁵And the LORD will strike Israel, so that it will be like a reed swaying in the water. He will uproot Israel from this good land that he gave to their forefathers and scatter them beyond the River,ᵈ because they provoked the LORD to anger by making Asherah poles.ᵉ ¹⁶And he will give Israel up because of the sins Jeroboam has committed and has caused Israel to commit."

¹⁷Then Jeroboam's wife got up and left and went to Tirzah. As soon as she stepped over the threshold of the house, the boy died. ¹⁸They buried him, and all Israel mourned for him, as the LORD had said through his servant the prophet Ahijah.

¹⁹The other events of Jeroboam's reign, his wars and how he ruled, are written in the book of the annals of the kings of Israel. ²⁰He reigned for twenty-two years and then rested with his fathers. And Nadab his son succeeded him as king.

²¹Rehoboam son of Solomon was king in Judah. He was forty-one years old when he became king, and he reigned seventeen years in Jerusalem, the city the LORD had chosen out of all the tribes of Israel in which to put his Name. His mother's name was Naamah; she was an Ammonite.

²²Judah did evil in the eyes of the LORD. By the sins they committed they stirred up his jealous anger more than their fathers had done. ²³They also set up for themselves high places, sacred stones and Asherah poles on every high hill and under every spreading tree. ²⁴There were even male shrine prostitutes in the land; the people engaged in all the detestable practices of the nations the LORD had driven out before the Israelites.

²⁵In the fifth year of King Rehoboam, Shishak king of Egypt attacked Jerusalem. ²⁶He carried off the treasures of the temple of the LORD and the treasures of the royal palace. He took everything, including all the gold shields Solomon had made. ²⁷So King Rehoboam made bronze shields to replace them and assigned these to the commanders of the guard on duty at the entrance to the royal palace. ²⁸Whenever the king went to the LORD's temple, the guards bore the shields, and afterward they returned them to the guardroom.

²⁹As for the other events of Rehoboam's reign, and all he did, are they not written in the book of the annals of the kings of Judah? ³⁰There was continual warfare between Rehoboam and Jeroboam. ³¹And Rehoboam rested with his fathers and was buried with them in the City of David. His mother's name was Naamah; she was an Ammonite. And Abijahᶠ his son succeeded him as king.

15

In the eighteenth year of the reign of Jeroboam son of Nebat, Abijahᵍ became king of Judah, ²and he reigned in Jerusalem three years. His mother's name was Maacah daughter of Abishalom.ʰ

³He committed all the sins his father had done before him; his heart was not fully devoted to the LORD his God, as the heart of David his forefather

ᶜ14 The meaning of the Hebrew for this sentence is uncertain. ᵈ15 That is, the Euphrates ᵉ15 That is, symbols of the goddess Asherah; here and elsewhere in 1 Kings ᶠ31 Some Hebrew manuscripts and Septuagint (see also 2 Chron. 12:16); most Hebrew manuscripts *Abijam* ᵍ1 Some Hebrew manuscripts and Septuagint (see also 2 Chron. 12:16); most Hebrew manuscripts *Abijam*; also in verses 7 and 8 ʰ2 A variant of *Absalom*; also in verse 10 had been. [4]Nevertheless, for David's sake the LORD his God gave him a lamp in Jerusalem by raising up a son to succeed him and by making Jerusalem strong. [5]For David had done what was right in the eyes of the LORD and had not failed to keep any of the LORD's commands all the days of his life—except in the case of Uriah the Hittite.

[6]There was war between Rehoboam[i] and Jeroboam throughout ˌAbijah'sˌ lifetime. [7]As for the other events of Abijah's reign, and all he did, are they not written in the book of the annals of the kings of Judah? There was war between Abijah and Jeroboam. [8]And Abijah rested with his fathers and was buried in the City of David. And Asa his son succeeded him as king.

[9]In the twentieth year of Jeroboam king of Israel, Asa became king of Judah, [10]and he reigned in Jerusalem forty-one years. His grandmother's name was Maacah daughter of Abishalom.

[11]Asa did what was right in the eyes of the LORD, as his father David had done. [12]He expelled the male shrine prostitutes from the land and got rid of all the idols his fathers had made. [13]He even deposed his grandmother Maacah from her position as queen mother, because she had made a repulsive Asherah pole. Asa cut the pole down and burned it in the Kidron Valley. [14]Although he did not remove the high places, Asa's heart was fully committed to the LORD all his life. [15]He brought into the temple of the LORD the silver and gold and the articles that he and his father had dedicated.

[16]There was war between Asa and Baasha king of Israel throughout their reigns. [17]Baasha king of Israel went up against Judah and fortified Ramah to prevent anyone from leaving or entering the territory of Asa king of Judah.

[18]Asa then took all the silver and gold that was left in the treasuries of the LORD's temple and of his own palace. He entrusted it to his officials and sent them to Ben-Hadad son of Tabrimmon, the son of Hezion, the king of Aram, who was ruling in Damascus. [19]"Let there be a treaty between me and you," he said, "as there was between my father and your father. See, I am sending you a gift of silver and gold. Now break your treaty with Baasha king of Israel so he will withdraw from me."

[20]Ben-Hadad agreed with King Asa and sent the commanders of his forces against the towns of Israel. He conquered Ijon, Dan, Abel Beth Maacah and all Kinnereth in addition to Naphtali. [21]When Baasha heard this, he stopped building Ramah and withdrew to Tirzah. [22]Then King Asa issued an order to all Judah—no one was exempt—and they carried away from Ramah the stones and timber Baasha had been using there. With them King Asa built up Geba in Benjamin, and also Mizpah.

[23]As for all the other events of Asa's reign, all his achievements, all he did and the cities he built, are they not written in the book of the annals of the kings of Judah? In his old age, however, his feet became diseased. [24]Then Asa rested with his fathers and was buried with them in the city of his father David. And Jehoshaphat his son succeeded him as king.

[25]Nadab son of Jeroboam became king of Israel in the second year of Asa king of Judah, and he reigned over Israel two years. [26]He did evil in the eyes of the LORD, walking in the ways of his father and in his sin, which he had caused Israel to commit.

[27]Baasha son of Ahijah of the house of Issachar plotted against him, and he struck him down at Gibbethon, a Philistine town, while Nadab and all Israel were besieging it. [28]Baasha killed Nadab in the third year of Asa king of Judah and succeeded him as king.

[29]As soon as he began to reign, he killed Jeroboam's whole family. He did not leave Jeroboam anyone that breathed, but destroyed them all, according to the word of the LORD given through his servant Ahijah the Shilonite— [30]because of the sins Jeroboam had committed and had caused Israel to commit, and because he provoked the LORD, the God of Israel, to anger.

[31]As for the other events of Nadab's reign, and all he did, are they not written in the book of the annals of the kings of Israel? [32]There was war between Asa and Baasha king of Israel throughout their reigns.

[33]In the third year of Asa king of Judah, Baasha son of Ahijah became king of all Israel in Tirzah, and he reigned twenty-four years. [34]He did evil in the eyes of the LORD, walking in the ways of Jeroboam and in his sin, which he had caused Israel to commit.

16 Then the word of the LORD came to Jehu son of Hanani against Baasha: [2]"I lifted you up from the dust and made you leader of my people Israel, but you walked in the ways of Jeroboam and caused my people Israel to sin and to provoke me to anger by

[i]6 Most Hebrew manuscripts; some Hebrew manuscripts and Syriac *Abijam* (that is, Abijah)

their sins. ³So I am about to consume Baasha and his house, and I will make your house like that of Jeroboam son of Nebat. ⁴Dogs will eat those belonging to Baasha who die in the city, and the birds of the air will feed on those who die in the country."

⁵As for the other events of Baasha's reign, what he did and his achievements, are they not written in the book of the annals of the kings of Israel? ⁶Baasha rested with his fathers and was buried in Tirzah. And Elah his son succeeded him as king.

⁷Moreover, the word of the LORD came through the prophet Jehu son of Hanani to Baasha and his house, because of all the evil he had done in the eyes of the LORD, provoking him to anger by the things he did, and becoming like the house of Jeroboam—and also because he destroyed it.

⁸In the twenty-sixth year of Asa king of Judah, Elah son of Baasha became king of Israel, and he reigned in Tirzah two years.

⁹Zimri, one of his officials, who had command of half his chariots, plotted against him. Elah was in Tirzah at the time, getting drunk in the home of Arza, the man in charge of the palace at Tirzah. ¹⁰Zimri came in, struck him down and killed him in the twenty-seventh year of Asa king of Judah. Then he succeeded him as king.

¹¹As soon as he began to reign and was seated on the throne, he killed off Baasha's whole family. He did not spare a single male, whether relative or friend. ¹²So Zimri destroyed the whole family of Baasha, in accordance with the word of the LORD spoken against Baasha through the prophet Jehu— ¹³because of all the sins Baasha and his son Elah had committed and had caused Israel to commit, so that they provoked the LORD, the God of Israel, to anger by their worthless idols.

¹⁴As for the other events of Elah's reign, and all he did, are they not written in the book of the annals of the kings of Israel?

¹⁵In the twenty-seventh year of Asa king of Judah, Zimri reigned in Tirzah seven days. The army was encamped near Gibbethon, a Philistine town. ¹⁶When the Israelites in the camp heard that Zimri had plotted against the king and murdered him, they proclaimed Omri, the commander of the army, king over Israel that very day there in the camp. ¹⁷Then Omri and all the Israelites with him withdrew from Gibbethon and laid siege to Tirzah. ¹⁸When Zimri saw that the city was taken, he went into the citadel of the royal palace and set the palace on fire around him. So he died, ¹⁹because of the sins he had committed,

doing evil in the eyes of the LORD and walking in the ways of Jeroboam and in the sin he had committed and had caused Israel to commit.

²⁰As for the other events of Zimri's reign, and the rebellion he carried out, are they not written in the book of the annals of the kings of Israel?

²¹Then the people of Israel were split into two factions; half supported Tibni son of Ginath for king, and the other half supported Omri. ²²But Omri's followers proved stronger than those of Tibni son of Ginath. So Tibni died and Omri became king.

²³In the thirty-first year of Asa king of Judah, Omri became king of Israel, and he reigned twelve years, six of them in Tirzah. ²⁴He bought the hill of Samaria from Shemer for two talents^j of silver and built a city on the hill, calling it Samaria, after Shemer, the name of the former owner of the hill.

²⁵But Omri did evil in the eyes of the LORD and sinned more than all those before him. ²⁶He walked in all the ways of Jeroboam son of Nebat and in his sin, which he had caused Israel to commit, so that they provoked the LORD, the God of Israel, to anger by their worthless idols.

²⁷As for the other events of Omri's reign, what he did and the things he achieved, are they not written in the book of the annals of the kings of Israel? ²⁸Omri rested with his fathers and was buried in Samaria. And Ahab his son succeeded him as king.

²⁹In the thirty-eighth year of Asa king of Judah, Ahab son of Omri became king of Israel, and he reigned in Samaria over Israel twenty-two years. ³⁰Ahab son of Omri did more evil in the eyes of the LORD than any of those before him. ³¹He not only considered it trivial to commit the sins of Jeroboam son of Nebat, but he also married Jezebel daughter of Ethbaal king of the Sidonians, and began to serve Baal and worship him. ³²He set up an altar for Baal in the temple of Baal that he built in Samaria. ³³Ahab also made an Asherah pole and did more to provoke the LORD, the God of Israel, to anger than did all the kings of Israel before him.

³⁴In Ahab's time, Hiel of Bethel rebuilt Jericho. He laid its foundations at the cost of his firstborn son Abiram, and he set up its gates at the cost of his youngest son Segub, in accordance with the word of the LORD spoken by Joshua son of Nun.

---

^{j}24 That is, about 150 pounds (about 70 kilograms)

4 / 1 Kings 17
Serving Each Other

IT SEEMED TO Elijah that he was the only person in Israel who served God. Ahab had just become the king, and he was already more evil than his father, Omri, had been. And now God was asking Elijah to give a dire prophecy about no rain in the land. All Elijah wanted to do was get away from everything and not do anything important. Most of all, he wanted someone to take care of *him* for once.

Warming Up to God When have you felt that you didn't want to be responsible to anyone else, that you just wanted to be taken care of?

Read 1 Kings 17.

17 Now Elijah the Tishbite, from Tishbe*ᵏ* in Gilead, said to Ahab, "As the LORD, the God of Israel, lives, whom I serve, there will be neither dew nor rain in the next few years except at my word."

²Then the word of the LORD came to Elijah: ³"Leave here, turn eastward and hide in the Kerith Ravine, east of the Jordan. ⁴You will drink from the brook, and I have ordered the ravens to feed you there."

⁵So he did what the LORD had told him. He went to the Kerith Ravine, east of the Jordan, and stayed there. ⁶The ravens brought him bread and meat in the morning and bread and meat in the evening, and he drank from the brook.

⁷Some time later the brook dried up because there had been no rain in the land. ⁸Then the word of the LORD came to him: ⁹"Go at once to Zarephath of Sidon and stay there. I have commanded a widow in that place to supply you with food." ¹⁰So he went to Zarephath. When he came to the town gate, a widow was there gathering sticks. He called to her and asked, "Would you bring me a little water in a jar so I may have a drink?" ¹¹As she was going to get it, he called, "And bring me, please, a piece of bread."

¹²"As surely as the LORD your God lives," she replied, "I don't have any bread—only a handful of flour in a jar and a little oil in a jug. I am gathering a few sticks to take home and make a meal for myself and my son, that we may eat it—and die."

¹³Elijah said to her, "Don't be afraid. Go home and do as you have said. But first make a small cake of bread for me from what you have and bring it to me, and then make something for yourself and your son. ¹⁴For this is what the LORD, the God of Israel, says: 'The jar of flour will not be used up and the jug of oil will not run dry until the day the LORD gives rain on the land.' "

¹⁵She went away and did as Elijah had told her. So there was food every day for Elijah and for the woman and her family. ¹⁶For the jar of flour was not used up and the jug of oil did not run dry, in keeping with the word of the LORD spoken by Elijah.

¹⁷Some time later the son of the woman who owned the house became ill. He grew worse and worse, and finally stopped breathing. ¹⁸She said to Elijah, "What do you have against me, man of God? Did you come to remind me of my sin and kill my son?"

¹⁹"Give me your son," Elijah replied. He took him from her arms, carried him to the upper room where he was staying, and laid him on his bed. ²⁰Then he cried out to the LORD, "O LORD my God, have you brought tragedy also upon this widow I am staying with, by causing her son to die?" ²¹Then he stretched himself out on the boy three times and cried to the LORD, "O LORD my God, let this boy's life return to him!"

²²The LORD heard Elijah's cry, and the boy's life returned to him, and he lived. ²³Elijah picked up the child and carried him down from the room into the house. He gave him to his mother and said, "Look, your son is alive!"

²⁴Then the woman said to Elijah, "Now I know that you are a man of God and that the word of the LORD from your mouth is the truth."

ᵏ1 Or Tishbite, of the settlers

Discovering the Word 1. Why does God send Elijah first into the Kerith ravine and then to the widow at Zarephath (v. 1)? 2. What service does the widow render to Elijah (vv. 7–15)? 3. What service does Elijah render to the widow (vv. 13–14, 22)? 4. How is the widow's response to her son's coming back to life (v. 24) different from her statement in verse 18? 5. What two (or more) things are accomplished by the relationship between the widow and Elijah?

Applying the Word 1. At what time in your life did you help someone in a difficult situation and find that that person had helped you also? 2. Sometimes God can't use us in the way he used the widow and Elijah in each other's lives because we aren't open to the possibility of mutual service. How do you need to change in order to be open to such a relationship?

Responding in Prayer Pray for awareness of the blessings you can give and receive through Christian service.

5 / 1 Kings 18
Knowing God's Power

IMAGINE YOURSELF LIVING in a country where everyone is following other gods. There are no churches, no Bible studies, no fellowship, no Christian literature. As far as you know, you are the only Christian in the land. How would you respond? The prophet Elijah faced such odds. Israel had abandoned the Lord for another god, Baal. They had rejected Elijah in favor of the four hundred and fifty prophets of Baal. Yet in spite of these odds, Elijah challenged Baal and his prophets to a contest with God.

 Warming Up to God How would you feel if every Christian you know abandoned the faith, and you had to stand alone in your commitment to Jesus? Consider this prayerfully and honestly before God.

 Read 1 Kings 18.

18 After a long time, in the third year, the word of the Lord came to Elijah: "Go and present yourself to Ahab, and I will send rain on the land." ²So Elijah went to present himself to Ahab.

Now the famine was severe in Samaria, ³and Ahab had summoned Obadiah, who was in charge of his palace. (Obadiah was a devout believer in the Lord. ⁴While Jezebel was killing off the Lord's prophets, Obadiah had taken a hundred prophets and hidden them in two caves, fifty in each, and had supplied them with food and water.) ⁵Ahab had said to Obadiah, "Go through the land to all the springs and valleys. Maybe we can find some grass to keep the horses and mules alive so we will not have to kill any of our animals." ⁶So they divided the land they were to cover, Ahab going in one direction and Obadiah in another.

⁷As Obadiah was walking along, Elijah met him. Obadiah recognized him, bowed down to the ground, and said, "Is it really you, my lord Elijah?"

⁸"Yes," he replied. "Go tell your master, 'Elijah is here.' "

⁹"What have I done wrong," asked Obadiah, "that you are handing your servant over to Ahab to be put to death? ¹⁰As surely as the Lord your God lives, there is not a nation or kingdom where my master has not sent someone to look for you. And whenever a nation or kingdom claimed you were not there, he made them swear they could not find you. ¹¹But now you tell me to go to my master and say, 'Elijah is here.' ¹²I don't know where the Spirit of the Lord may carry you when I leave you. If I go and tell Ahab and he doesn't find you, he will kill me. Yet I your servant have worshiped the Lord since my youth. ¹³Haven't you heard, my lord, what I did while Jezebel was

killing the prophets of the LORD? I hid a hundred of the LORD's prophets in two caves, fifty in each, and supplied them with food and water. ¹⁴And now you tell me to go to my master and say, 'Elijah is here.' He will kill me!"

¹⁵Elijah said, "As the LORD Almighty lives, whom I serve, I will surely present myself to Ahab today."

¹⁶So Obadiah went to meet Ahab and told him, and Ahab went to meet Elijah. ¹⁷When he saw Elijah, he said to him, "Is that you, you troubler of Israel?"

¹⁸"I have not made trouble for Israel," Elijah replied. "But you and your father's family have. You have abandoned the LORD's commands and have followed the Baals. ¹⁹Now summon the people from all over Israel to meet me on Mount Carmel. And bring the four hundred and fifty prophets of Baal and the four hundred prophets of Asherah, who eat at Jezebel's table."

²⁰So Ahab sent word throughout all Israel and assembled the prophets on Mount Carmel. ²¹Elijah went before the people and said, "How long will you waver between two opinions? If the LORD is God, follow him; but if Baal is God, follow him."

But the people said nothing.

²²Then Elijah said to them, "I am the only one of the LORD's prophets left, but Baal has four hundred and fifty prophets. ²³Get two bulls for us. Let them choose one for themselves, and let them cut it into pieces and put it on the wood but not set fire to it. I will prepare the other bull and put it on the wood but not set fire to it. ²⁴Then you call on the name of your god, and I will call on the name of the LORD. The god who answers by fire— he is God."

Then all the people said, "What you say is good."

²⁵Elijah said to the prophets of Baal, "Choose one of the bulls and prepare it first, since there are so many of you. Call on the name of your god, but do not light the fire." ²⁶So they took the bull given them and prepared it.

Then they called on the name of Baal from morning till noon. "O Baal, answer us!" they shouted. But there was no response; no one answered. And they danced around the altar they had made.

²⁷At noon Elijah began to taunt them. "Shout louder!" he said. "Surely he is a god! Perhaps he

is deep in thought, or busy, or traveling. Maybe he is sleeping and must be awakened." ²⁸So they shouted louder and slashed themselves with swords and spears, as was their custom, until their blood flowed. ²⁹Midday passed, and they continued their frantic prophesying until the time for the evening sacrifice. But there was no response, no one answered, no one paid attention.

³⁰Then Elijah said to all the people, "Come here to me." They came to him, and he repaired the altar of the LORD, which was in ruins. ³¹Elijah took twelve stones, one for each of the tribes descended from Jacob, to whom the word of the LORD had come, saying, "Your name shall be Israel." ³²With the stones he built an altar in the name of the LORD, and he dug a trench around it large enough to hold two seahs¹ of seed. ³³He arranged the wood, cut the bull into pieces and laid it on the wood. Then he said to them, "Fill four large jars with water and pour it on the offering and on the wood."

³⁴"Do it again," he said, and they did it again.

"Do it a third time," he ordered, and they did it the third time. ³⁵The water ran down around the altar and even filled the trench.

³⁶At the time of sacrifice, the prophet Elijah stepped forward and prayed: "O LORD, God of Abraham, Isaac and Israel, let it be known today that you are God in Israel and that I am your servant and have done all these things at your command. ³⁷Answer me, O LORD, answer me, so these people will know that you, O LORD, are God, and that you are turning their hearts back again."

³⁸Then the fire of the LORD fell and burned up the sacrifice, the wood, the stones and the soil, and also licked up the water in the trench.

³⁹When all the people saw this, they fell prostrate and cried, "The LORD—he is God! The LORD—he is God!"

⁴⁰Then Elijah commanded them, "Seize the prophets of Baal. Don't let anyone get away!" They seized them, and Elijah had them brought down to the Kishon Valley and slaughtered there.

⁴¹And Elijah said to Ahab, "Go, eat and drink, for there is the sound of a heavy rain." ⁴²So Ahab went off to eat and drink, but Elijah climbed to

¹32 That is, probably about 13 quarts (about 15 liters)

the top of Carmel, bent down to the ground and put his face between his knees.

43"Go and look toward the sea," he told his servant. And he went up and looked.

"There is nothing there," he said.

Seven times Elijah said, "Go back."

44The seventh time the servant reported, "A cloud as small as a man's hand is rising from the sea."

So Elijah said, "Go and tell Ahab, 'Hitch up your chariot and go down before the rain stops you.'"

45Meanwhile, the sky grew black with clouds, the wind rose, a heavy rain came on and Ahab rode off to Jezreel. 46The power of the LORD came upon Elijah and, tucking his cloak into his belt, he ran ahead of Ahab all the way to Jezreel.

 Discovering the Word 1. Describe the difficult position Obadiah finds himself in (vv. 9–15). 2. Why do you think Ahab agrees to Elijah's demand for a contest? 3. Elijah challenges the people of Israel at Mount Carmel (vv. 20–21). What does their failure to answer indicate? 4. What is pathetic about the frenzied activities of Baal's prophets and the taunts of Elijah (vv. 26–29)? 5. What do Elijah's actions indicate about his knowledge of God's reality and power (vv. 30–37)? 6. Summarize the dramatic outcome of the contest between Elijah and the prophets of Baal (vv. 38–40).

Applying the Word 1. In what ways are you or the people around you wavering between two gods? (For example, wavering between materialism, personal desires or ambitions and the Lord Jesus Christ.) 2. What are the "Mount Carmel" situations in which you face overwhelming odds today? (For example, at work, at school, in your family or neighborhood.) 3. How can you, like Elijah, rely on God's power in that situation? (Take into account what your part and God's part might be.)

Responding in Prayer Spend time in prayer, committing your situation to God's powerful care.

6 / *1 Kings 19:1–18*
Caring for the Whole Person

ELIJAH EXPERIENCED A thrilling victory over the prophets of Baal in chapter 18. Impressed, the people worshiped the Lord. Then they helped Elijah kill all the prophets of Baal. Life was going well until suddenly Queen Jezebel stepped into Elijah's scene.

Often we are quick to blame discontent on spiritual need. But Elijah had experienced great spiritual victory. In this passage his emotional and physical needs became evident. We are whole people—body, soul (emotions, mind and will) and spirit. And God ministered to Elijah's whole being.

 Warming Up to God Why is it sometimes difficult to hear the Lord's voice when you are feeling especially busy and successful "doing the Lord's work"?

 Read 1 Kings 19:1–18.

19 Now Ahab told Jezebel everything Elijah had done and how he had killed all the prophets with the sword. 2So Jezebel sent a messenger to Elijah to say, "May the gods deal with me, be it ever so severely, if by this time tomorrow I do not make your life like that of one of them."

3Elijah was afraid m and ran for his life. When he came to Beersheba in Judah, he left his servant there, 4while he himself went a day's journey into the desert. He came to a broom tree, sat down under it and prayed that he might die. "I have had enough, LORD," he said. "Take my life; I am no better than my ancestors." 5Then he lay down under the tree and fell asleep.

m 3 Or *Elijah saw*

All at once an angel touched him and said, "Get up and eat." [6]He looked around, and there by his head was a cake of bread baked over hot coals, and a jar of water. He ate and drank and then lay down again.

[7]The angel of the Lord came back a second time and touched him and said, "Get up and eat, for the journey is too much for you." [8]So he got up and ate and drank. Strengthened by that food, he traveled forty days and forty nights until he reached Horeb, the mountain of God. [9]There he went into a cave and spent the night.

And the word of the Lord came to him: "What are you doing here, Elijah?"

[10]He replied, "I have been very zealous for the Lord God Almighty. The Israelites have rejected your covenant, broken down your altars, and put your prophets to death with the sword. I am the only one left, and now they are trying to kill me too."

[11]The Lord said, "Go out and stand on the mountain in the presence of the Lord, for the Lord is about to pass by."

Then a great and powerful wind tore the mountains apart and shattered the rocks before the Lord, but the Lord was not in the wind. After the wind there was an earthquake, but the Lord was not in the earthquake. [12]After the earthquake came a fire, but the Lord was not in the fire. And after the fire came a gentle whisper. [13]When Elijah heard it, he pulled his cloak over his face and went out and stood at the mouth of the cave.

Then a voice said to him, "What are you doing here, Elijah?"

[14]He replied, "I have been very zealous for the Lord God Almighty. The Israelites have rejected your covenant, broken down your altars, and put your prophets to death with the sword. I am the only one left, and now they are trying to kill me too."

[15]The Lord said to him, "Go back the way you came, and go to the Desert of Damascus. When you get there, anoint Hazael king over Aram. [16]Also, anoint Jehu son of Nimshi king over Israel, and anoint Elisha son of Shaphat from Abel Meholah to succeed you as prophet. [17]Jehu will put to death any who escape the sword of Hazael, and Elisha will put to death any who escape the sword of Jehu. [18]Yet I reserve seven thousand in Israel—all whose knees have not bowed down to Baal and all whose mouths have not kissed him."

 Discovering the Word 1. As you look through the passage, what do you see of Elijah's emotional needs (vv. 3–4, 10, 14), physical needs (vv. 5–8) and spiritual needs (vv. 8, 10–11, 13–14)? 2. What do you think happened to the faith Elijah had so dramatically demonstrated in the previous chapters? 3. In what different ways did the angel minister to Elijah's needs (vv. 5–9)? 4. What do you think is the significance of the Lord *not* being in the wind, the earthquake or the fire—but in a gentle whisper (vv. 11–12)? 5. What emotional as well as spiritual needs of Elijah were met by his encounter with God?

 Applying the Word 1. What factors in your life cause you to miss the "gentle whisper" of God? 2. What helps you to hear it?

Responding in Prayer Thank God for making you a whole person. Ask him to meet the emotional, physical and spiritual needs you have right now.

---

1 Kings 19:19—20:43

[19]So Elijah went from there and found Elisha son of Shaphat. He was plowing with twelve yoke of oxen, and he himself was driving the twelfth pair. Elijah went up to him and threw his cloak around him. [20]Elisha then left his oxen and ran after Elijah. "Let me kiss my father and mother good-by," he said, "and then I will come with you."

"Go back," Elijah replied. "What have I done to you?"

[21]So Elisha left him and went back. He took his yoke of oxen and slaughtered them. He burned the plowing equipment to cook the meat and gave it to the people, and they ate. Then he set out to follow Elijah and became his attendant.

20

Now Ben-Hadad king of Aram mustered his entire army. Accompanied by thirty-two kings with their horses and chariots, he went up and besieged Samaria and attacked it. 2He sent messengers into the city to Ahab king of Israel, saying, "This is what Ben-Hadad says: 3'Your silver and gold are mine, and the best of your wives and children are mine.' "

4The king of Israel answered, "Just as you say, my lord the king. I and all I have are yours."

5The messengers came again and said, "This is what Ben-Hadad says: 'I sent to demand your silver and gold, your wives and your children. 6But about this time tomorrow I am going to send my officials to search your palace and the houses of your officials. They will seize everything you value and carry it away.' "

7The king of Israel summoned all the elders of the land and said to them, "See how this man is looking for trouble! When he sent for my wives and my children, my silver and my gold, I did not refuse him."

8The elders and the people all answered, "Don't listen to him or agree to his demands."

9So he replied to Ben-Hadad's messengers, "Tell my lord the king, 'Your servant will do all you demanded the first time, but this demand I cannot meet.' " They left and took the answer back to Ben-Hadad.

10Then Ben-Hadad sent another message to Ahab: "May the gods deal with me, be it ever so severely, if enough dust remains in Samaria to give each of my men a handful."

11The king of Israel answered, "Tell him: 'One who puts on his armor should not boast like one who takes it off.' "

12Ben-Hadad heard this message while he and the kings were drinking in their tents,[n] and he ordered his men: "Prepare to attack." So they prepared to attack the city.

13Meanwhile a prophet came to Ahab king of Israel and announced, "This is what the Lord says: 'Do you see this vast army? I will give it into your hand today, and then you will know that I am the Lord.' "

14"But who will do this?" asked Ahab.

The prophet replied, "This is what the Lord says: 'The young officers of the provincial commanders will do it.' "

"And who will start the battle?" he asked.

The prophet answered, "You will."

15So Ahab summoned the young officers of the provincial commanders, 232 men. Then he assembled the rest of the Israelites, 7,000 in all. 16They set out at noon while Ben-Hadad and the 32 kings allied with him were in their tents getting drunk. 17The young officers of the provincial commanders went out first.

Now Ben-Hadad had dispatched scouts, who reported, "Men are advancing from Samaria."

18He said, "If they have come out for peace, take them alive; if they have come out for war, take them alive."

19The young officers of the provincial commanders marched out of the city with the army behind them 20and each one struck down his opponent. At that, the Arameans fled, with the Israelites in pursuit. But Ben-Hadad king of Aram escaped on horseback with some of his horsemen. 21The king of Israel advanced and overpowered the horses and chariots and inflicted heavy losses on the Arameans.

22Afterward, the prophet came to the king of Israel and said, "Strengthen your position and see what must be done, because next spring the king of Aram will attack you again."

23Meanwhile, the officials of the king of Aram advised him, "Their gods are gods of the hills. That is why they were too strong for us. But if we fight them on the plains, surely we will be stronger than they. 24Do this: Remove all the kings from their commands and replace them with other officers. 25You must also raise an army like the one you lost—horse for horse and chariot for chariot—so we can fight Israel on the plains. Then surely we will be stronger than they." He agreed with them and acted accordingly.

26The next spring Ben-Hadad mustered the Arameans and went up to Aphek to fight against Israel. 27When the Israelites were also mustered and given provisions, they marched out to meet them. The Israelites camped opposite them like two small flocks of goats, while the Arameans covered the countryside.

28The man of God came up and told the king of Israel, "This is what the Lord says: 'Because the Arameans think the Lord is a god of the hills and not a god of the valleys, I will deliver this vast army into your hands, and you will know that I am the Lord.' "

29For seven days they camped opposite each

n12 Or in Succoth; also in verse 16

other, and on the seventh day the battle was joined. The Israelites inflicted a hundred thousand casualties on the Aramean foot soldiers in one day. ³⁰The rest of them escaped to the city of Aphek, where the wall collapsed on twenty-seven thousand of them. And Ben-Hadad fled to the city and hid in an inner room.

³¹His officials said to him, "Look, we have heard that the kings of the house of Israel are merciful. Let us go to the king of Israel with sackcloth around our waists and ropes around our heads. Perhaps he will spare your life."

³²Wearing sackcloth around their waists and ropes around their heads, they went to the king of Israel and said, "Your servant Ben-Hadad says: 'Please let me live.'"

The king answered, "Is he still alive? He is my brother."

³³The men took this as a good sign and were quick to pick up his word. "Yes, your brother Ben-Hadad!" they said.

"Go and get him," the king said. When Ben-Hadad came out, Ahab had him come up into his chariot.

³⁴"I will return the cities my father took from your father," Ben-Hadad offered. "You may set up your own market areas in Damascus, as my father did in Samaria."

⌐Ahab said,⌐ "On the basis of a treaty I will set you free." So he made a treaty with him, and let him go.

³⁵By the word of the LORD one of the sons of the prophets said to his companion, "Strike me with your weapon," but the man refused.

³⁶So the prophet said, "Because you have not obeyed the LORD, as soon as you leave me a lion will kill you." And after the man went away, a lion found him and killed him.

³⁷The prophet found another man and said, "Strike me, please." So the man struck him and wounded him. ³⁸Then the prophet went and stood by the road waiting for the king. He disguised himself with his headband down over his eyes. ³⁹As the king passed by, the prophet called out to him, "Your servant went into the thick of the battle, and someone came to me with a captive and said, 'Guard this man. If he is missing, it will be your life for his life, or you must pay a talentᵒ of silver.' ⁴⁰While your servant was busy here and there, the man disappeared."

"That is your sentence," the king of Israel said. "You have pronounced it yourself."

⁴¹Then the prophet quickly removed the headband from his eyes, and the king of Israel recognized him as one of the prophets. ⁴²He said to the king, "This is what the LORD says: 'You have set free a man I had determined should die.ᵖ Therefore it is your life for his life, your people for his people.'" ⁴³Sullen and angry, the king of Israel went to his palace in Samaria.

ᵒ39 That is, about 75 pounds (about 34 kilograms)   ᵖ42 The Hebrew term refers to the irrevocable giving over of things or persons to the LORD, often by totally destroying them.

---

7 / 1 Kings 21
Manipulation

A RECENT BOOK released by a Christian publisher entitled *Not Just Any Man: A Guide to Finding Mr. Right* explains that the way to find a husband is to practice careful manipulation. For example, the author suggests that a woman should compliment men often. At the office she could say, "I really think you are the best salesman in the company." At church she might "comment on how much more perceptive he is than others or how much more he's thought through his beliefs than other men." The author concludes by saying, "Of course you should base your comparison on some supporting evidence, but don't be too literal." This kind of advice is not new. But since Old Testament days the results of manipulation have been both sin and compromise.

 Warming Up to God Think of a recent time when you manipulated events to your advantage. What factors prompted you to do this? Discuss your sin openly with God.

 Read 1 Kings 21.

21 Some time later there was an incident involving a vineyard belonging to Naboth the Jezreelite. The vineyard was in Jezreel, close to the palace of Ahab king of Samaria. ²Ahab said to Naboth, "Let me have your vineyard to use for a vegetable garden, since it is close to my palace. In exchange I will give you a better vineyard or, if you prefer, I will pay you whatever it is worth."

³But Naboth replied, "The LORD forbid that I should give you the inheritance of my fathers."

⁴So Ahab went home, sullen and angry because Naboth the Jezreelite had said, "I will not give you the inheritance of my fathers." He lay on his bed sulking and refused to eat.

⁵His wife Jezebel came in and asked him, "Why are you so sullen? Why won't you eat?"

⁶He answered her, "Because I said to Naboth the Jezreelite, 'Sell me your vineyard; or if you prefer, I will give you another vineyard in its place.' But he said, 'I will not give you my vineyard.'"

⁷Jezebel his wife said, "Is this how you act as king over Israel? Get up and eat! Cheer up. I'll get you the vineyard of Naboth the Jezreelite."

⁸So she wrote letters in Ahab's name, placed his seal on them, and sent them to the elders and nobles who lived in Naboth's city with him. ⁹In those letters she wrote:

"Proclaim a day of fasting and seat Naboth in a prominent place among the people. ¹⁰But seat two scoundrels opposite him and have them testify that he has cursed both God and the king. Then take him out and stone him to death."

¹¹So the elders and nobles who lived in Naboth's city did as Jezebel directed in the letters she had written to them. ¹²They proclaimed a fast and seated Naboth in a prominent place among the people. ¹³Then two scoundrels came and sat opposite him and brought charges against Naboth before the people, saying, "Naboth has cursed both God and the king." So they took him outside the city and stoned him to death. ¹⁴Then they sent word to Jezebel: "Naboth has been stoned and is dead."

¹⁵As soon as Jezebel heard that Naboth had been stoned to death, she said to Ahab, "Get up and take possession of the vineyard of Naboth the Jezreelite that he refused to sell you. He is no longer alive, but dead." ¹⁶When Ahab heard that Naboth was dead, he got up and went down to take possession of Naboth's vineyard.

¹⁷Then the word of the LORD came to Elijah the Tishbite: ¹⁸"Go down to meet Ahab king of Israel, who rules in Samaria. He is now in Naboth's vineyard, where he has gone to take possession of it. ¹⁹Say to him, 'This is what the LORD says: Have you not murdered a man and seized his property?' Then say to him, 'This is what the LORD says: In the place where dogs licked up Naboth's blood, dogs will lick up your blood—yes, yours!'"

²⁰Ahab said to Elijah, "So you have found me, my enemy!"

"I have found you," he answered, "because you have sold yourself to do evil in the eyes of the LORD. ²¹I am going to bring disaster on you. I will consume your descendants and cut off from Ahab every last male in Israel—slave or free. ²²I will make your house like that of Jeroboam son of Nebat and that of Baasha son of Ahijah, because you have provoked me to anger and have caused Israel to sin.'

²³"And also concerning Jezebel the LORD says: 'Dogs will devour Jezebel by the wall of*q* Jezreel.'

²⁴"Dogs will eat those belonging to Ahab who die in the city, and the birds of the air will feed on those who die in the country."

²⁵(There was never a man like Ahab, who sold himself to do evil in the eyes of the LORD, urged on by Jezebel his wife. ²⁶He behaved in the vilest manner by going after idols, like the Amorites the LORD drove out before Israel.)

²⁷When Ahab heard these words, he tore his clothes, put on sackcloth and fasted. He lay in sackcloth and went around meekly.

²⁸Then the word of the LORD came to Elijah the Tishbite: ²⁹"Have you noticed how Ahab has humbled himself before me? Because he has humbled himself, I will not bring this disaster in his day, but I will bring it on his house in the days of his son."

----

*q*23 Most Hebrew manuscripts; a few Hebrew manuscripts, Vulgate and Syriac (see also 2 Kings 9:26) *the plot of ground at*

Discovering the Word 1. Naboth refuses Ahab's request because he believes the land has been given to his family by the Lord, and he wants to keep it as his family's inheritance in the Promised Land. Describe Ahab's response from verse 4. 2. How does Jezebel react to her husband's behavior (vv. 5–7)? 3. In what ways do you think Ahab's behavior was manipulative? 4. How does Jezebel attempt to resolve the problem (vv. 8–16)? 5. After Ahab's direct approach fails, Jezebel is able to manipulate the situation to Ahab's advantage. Sometimes manipulation seems to work. However, what is the end result (vv. 17–28)?

Applying the Word 1. What kinds of actions define manipulation? 2. How does our culture encourage the use of manipulative tactics to achieve our goals and desires? 3. Think of a situation or relationship in which you are tempted to manipulate. What would be a more Christlike approach?

Responding in Prayer Recognizing the manipulative patterns in your life is a major step in overcoming them. Ask God to give you insight into the patterns in your life and courage to overcome them.

8 / *1 Kings 22:1–40*
Deaf to God

WE EACH HAVE our own methods of tuning out God. For example, singing an entire hymn without a single word registering in the mind; meticulously compiling a things-to-do list during the sermon; accidentally leaving a Bible at church and not missing it for days; feeling no compunction about a pattern of daily prayer long since abandoned and hardly remembered. There are many paths by which we can become deaf to God. Ahab's life (and death) warns us against such a route.

 Warming Up to God What do you do that sometimes makes you "deaf" to God?

 Read 1 Kings 22:1–40.

22 For three years there was no war between Aram and Israel. ²But in the third year Jehoshaphat king of Judah went down to see the king of Israel. ³The king of Israel had said to his officials, "Don't you know that Ramoth Gilead belongs to us and yet we are doing nothing to retake it from the king of Aram?"

⁴So he asked Jehoshaphat, "Will you go with me to fight against Ramoth Gilead?"

Jehoshaphat replied to the king of Israel, "I am as you are, my people as your people, my horses as your horses." ⁵But Jehoshaphat also said to the king of Israel, "First seek the counsel of the LORD."

⁶So the king of Israel brought together the prophets—about four hundred men—and asked them, "Shall I go to war against Ramoth Gilead, or shall I refrain?"

"Go," they answered, "for the Lord will give it into the king's hand."

⁷But Jehoshaphat asked, "Is there not a prophet of the LORD here whom we can inquire of?"

⁸The king of Israel answered Jehoshaphat, "There is still one man through whom we can inquire of the LORD, but I hate him because he never prophesies anything good about me, but always bad. He is Micaiah son of Imlah."

"The king should not say that," Jehoshaphat replied.

⁹So the king of Israel called one of his officials and said, "Bring Micaiah son of Imlah at once."

¹⁰Dressed in their royal robes, the king of Israel and Jehoshaphat king of Judah were sitting on their thrones at the threshing floor by the entrance of the gate of Samaria, with all the prophets prophesying before them. ¹¹Now Zedekiah son of Kenaanah had made iron horns and he declared, "This is what the LORD says: 'With these you will gore the Arameans until they are destroyed.' "

¹²All the other prophets were prophesying the same thing. "Attack Ramoth Gilead and be victo-

rious," they said, "for the LORD will give it into the king's hand."

¹³The messenger who had gone to summon Micaiah said to him, "Look, as one man the other prophets are predicting success for the king. Let your word agree with theirs, and speak favorably."

¹⁴But Micaiah said, "As surely as the LORD lives, I can tell him only what the LORD tells me."

¹⁵When he arrived, the king asked him, "Micaiah, shall we go to war against Ramoth Gilead, or shall I refrain?"

"Attack and be victorious," he answered, "for the LORD will give it into the king's hand."

¹⁶The king said to him, "How many times must I make you swear to tell me nothing but the truth in the name of the LORD?"

¹⁷Then Micaiah answered, "I saw all Israel scattered on the hills like sheep without a shepherd, and the LORD said, 'These people have no master. Let each one go home in peace.' "

¹⁸The king of Israel said to Jehoshaphat, "Didn't I tell you that he never prophesies anything good about me, but only bad?"

¹⁹Micaiah continued, "Therefore hear the word of the LORD: I saw the LORD sitting on his throne with all the host of heaven standing around him on his right and on his left. ²⁰And the LORD said, 'Who will entice Ahab into attacking Ramoth Gilead and going to his death there?'

"One suggested this, and another that. ²¹Finally, a spirit came forward, stood before the LORD and said, 'I will entice him.'

²²" 'By what means?' the LORD asked.

" 'I will go out and be a lying spirit in the mouths of all his prophets,' he said.

" 'You will succeed in enticing him,' said the LORD. 'Go and do it.'

²³"So now the LORD has put a lying spirit in the mouths of all these prophets of yours. The LORD has decreed disaster for you."

²⁴Then Zedekiah son of Kenaanah went up and slapped Micaiah in the face. "Which way did the spirit from* the LORD go when he went from me to speak to you?" he asked.

²⁵Micaiah replied, "You will find out on the day you go to hide in an inner room."

²⁶The king of Israel then ordered, "Take Micaiah and send him back to Amon the ruler of the city and to Joash the king's son ²⁷and say, 'This is what the king says: Put this fellow in prison and give him nothing but bread and water until I return safely.' "

²⁸Micaiah declared, "If you ever return safely, the LORD has not spoken through me." Then he added, "Mark my words, all you people!"

²⁹So the king of Israel and Jehoshaphat king of Judah went up to Ramoth Gilead. ³⁰The king of Israel said to Jehoshaphat, "I will enter the battle in disguise, but you wear your royal robes." So the king of Israel disguised himself and went into battle.

³¹Now the king of Aram had ordered his thirty-two chariot commanders, "Do not fight with anyone, small or great, except the king of Israel." ³²When the chariot commanders saw Jehoshaphat, they thought, "Surely this is the king of Israel." So they turned to attack him, but when Jehoshaphat cried out, ³³the chariot commanders saw that he was not the king of Israel and stopped pursuing him.

³⁴But someone drew his bow at random and hit the king of Israel between the sections of his armor. The king told his chariot driver, "Wheel around and get me out of the fighting. I've been wounded." ³⁵All day long the battle raged, and the king was propped up in his chariot facing the Arameans. The blood from his wound ran onto the floor of the chariot, and that evening he died. ³⁶As the sun was setting, a cry spread through the army: "Every man to his town; everyone to his land!"

³⁷So the king died and was brought to Samaria, and they buried him there. ³⁸They washed the chariot at a pool in Samaria (where the prostitutes bathed),ˢ and the dogs licked up his blood, as the word of the LORD had declared.

³⁹As for the other events of Ahab's reign, including all he did, the palace he built and inlaid with ivory, and the cities he fortified, are they not written in the book of the annals of the kings of Israel? ⁴⁰Ahab rested with his fathers. And Ahaziah his son succeeded him as king.

ʳ24 Or *Spirit of*   ˢ38 Or *Samaria and cleaned the weapons*

Discovering the Word 1. What was Ahab's proposal (vv. 1–4)? 2. How did the two kings view the project differently (vv. 4–8)? 3. What was hard about Micaiah's job (vv. 9–16)? 4. Look again at Micaiah's statements in verses 17–23. Why do you think that Ahab was easy prey for the lying prophets? 5. What did it cost Micaiah to speak God's truth? 6. During the course of his life, Ahab had many opportunities for hearing truths from God. In view of this, what do you see as the difference between hearing and receiving God's Word?

Applying the Word 1. Why do you sometimes hesitate to talk about what you know to be God's truth? 2. What precautions could you take to keep from acquiring Ahab's kind of deafness?

Responding in Prayer Ask God to give you ears to hear his truth (Mt 13:16).

1 Kings 22:41–53

⁴¹Jehoshaphat son of Asa became king of Judah in the fourth year of Ahab king of Israel. ⁴²Jehoshaphat was thirty-five years old when he became king, and he reigned in Jerusalem twenty-five years. His mother's name was Azubah daughter of Shilhi. ⁴³In everything he walked in the ways of his father Asa and did not stray from them; he did what was right in the eyes of the LORD. The high places, however, were not removed, and the people continued to offer sacrifices and burn incense there. ⁴⁴Jehoshaphat was also at peace with the king of Israel.

⁴⁵As for the other events of Jehoshaphat's reign, the things he achieved and his military exploits, are they not written in the book of the annals of the kings of Judah? ⁴⁶He rid the land of the rest of the male shrine prostitutes who remained there even after the reign of his father Asa. ⁴⁷There was then no king in Edom; a deputy ruled.

⁴⁸Now Jehoshaphat built a fleet of trading ships[f] to go to Ophir for gold, but they never set sail—they were wrecked at Ezion Geber. ⁴⁹At that time Ahaziah son of Ahab said to Jehoshaphat, "Let my men sail with your men," but Jehoshaphat refused.

⁵⁰Then Jehoshaphat rested with his fathers and was buried with them in the city of David his father. And Jehoram his son succeeded him.

⁵¹Ahaziah son of Ahab became king of Israel in Samaria in the seventeenth year of Jehoshaphat king of Judah, and he reigned over Israel two years. ⁵²He did evil in the eyes of the LORD, because he walked in the ways of his father and mother and in the ways of Jeroboam son of Nebat, who caused Israel to sin. ⁵³He served and worshiped Baal and provoked the LORD, the God of Israel, to anger, just as his father had done.

᠌⁴⁸ Hebrew *of ships of Tarshish*

2 Kings

The Old Testament kings faltered and failed in many ways. As we examine their lives, we can learn much about following God. We see Ahaz, who, when faced with trouble, stopped believing in God. And we wonder about our own ability to keep faith in the face of circumstantial despair.

We see Hoshea, who angered God so much by his determination to serve other gods that God destroyed his nation. And we pray for our own national leaders, and thereby for ourselves.

We see Hezekiah, who when faced with terminal illness, cried out to God. And God extended his life, which Hezekiah may have later regretted. And we wonder whether we will die with grace, or fear, or both.

We see Manasseh, the most wicked king of all. Yet God let him reign for forty-five years, the longest reign of any Hebrew king. We wonder how our faith, rattled by an afternoon of inconvenience, would endure in an era when the king killed God-worshipers every day.

We see Josiah, who became king at the age of eight, yet turned his nation to worship God. And we wonder about our influence for God on our own children—and the results of their influence on others.

We see Zedekiah, the last Hebrew king, presiding over a nation already dead. And we look for hope from a God who is not stopped by death.

When the narrative of the kings ends with the fall of Judah in 587 B.C., their names are not forgotten. In the opening pages of the New Testament, they live again. It seems that when God chose a family for his son, the infant Jesus, he chose from a line of kings. And so we read Joseph's genealogy, and we find, among all those hard-to-pronounce names, a familiar line: the kings of Israel.

Let us read from them and learn. None was perfect, and neither are we. But God was sovereign—even over the kings. And he is sovereign over us as well.

Outline

1/ 2 Kings 2 —————————— *Transition*

2/ 2 Kings 4:8–37 —————————— *Taking the Initiative*

3/ 2 Kings 5 ———————————— *Physical Healing*

4/ 2 Kings 6:24—7:20 ——————— *Faith in Hard Times*

5/ 2 Kings 9—10 ————————— *God's Avenger*

6/ 2 Kings 13 ———————————— *Facing Losses*

7/ 2 Kings 16 ———————————— *Faithless in Trouble*

8/ 2 Kings 17 ———————————— *Idolatry's Reward*

9/ 2 Kings 18:17–37 ——————— *Identity*

10/ 2 Kings 19 ————————— *Asking for Help*

11/ 2 Kings 20:1—21:18 ————— *One Giant Step Backward*

12/ 2 Kings 22:1—23:35 ————— *Following God's Law*

13/ 2 Kings 23:36—25:30 ———— *End of the Line*

Empires from 960—587 B.C.

2 Kings 1

1 After Ahab's death, Moab rebelled against Israel. ²Now Ahaziah had fallen through the lattice of his upper room in Samaria and injured himself. So he sent messengers, saying to them, "Go and consult Baal-Zebub, the god of Ekron, to see if I will recover from this injury."

³But the angel of the LORD said to Elijah the Tishbite, "Go up and meet the messengers of the king of Samaria and ask them, 'Is it because there is no God in Israel that you are going off to consult Baal-Zebub, the god of Ekron?' ⁴Therefore this is what the LORD says: 'You will not leave the bed you are lying on. You will certainly die!' " So Elijah went.

⁵When the messengers returned to the king, he asked them, "Why have you come back?"

⁶"A man came to meet us," they replied. "And he said to us, 'Go back to the king who sent you and tell him, "This is what the LORD says: Is it because there is no God in Israel that you are sending men to consult Baal-Zebub, the god of Ekron? Therefore you will not leave the bed you are lying on. You will certainly die!" ' "

⁷The king asked them, "What kind of man was it who came to meet you and told you this?"

⁸They replied, "He was a man with a garment of hair and with a leather belt around his waist."

The king said, "That was Elijah the Tishbite."

⁹Then he sent to Elijah a captain with his company of fifty men. The captain went up to Elijah, who was sitting on the top of a hill, and said to him, "Man of God, the king says, 'Come down!' "

¹⁰Elijah answered the captain, "If I am a man of God, may fire come down from heaven and consume you and your fifty men!" Then fire fell from heaven and consumed the captain and his men.

¹¹At this the king sent to Elijah another captain with his fifty men. The captain said to him, "Man of God, this is what the king says, 'Come down at once!' "

¹²"If I am a man of God," Elijah replied, "may fire come down from heaven and consume you and your fifty men!" Then the fire of God fell from heaven and consumed him and his fifty men.

¹³So the king sent a third captain with his fifty men. This third captain went up and fell on his knees before Elijah. "Man of God," he begged, "please have respect for my life and the lives of these fifty men, your servants! ¹⁴See, fire has fallen from heaven and consumed the first two captains and all their men. But now have respect for my life!"

¹⁵The angel of the LORD said to Elijah, "Go down with him; do not be afraid of him." So Elijah got up and went down with him to the king.

¹⁶He told the king, "This is what the LORD says: Is it because there is no God in Israel for you to consult that you have sent messengers to consult Baal-Zebub, the god of Ekron? Because you have done this, you will never leave the bed you are lying on. You will certainly die!" ¹⁷So he died, according to the word of the LORD that Elijah had spoken.

Because Ahaziah had no son, Joram*a* succeeded him as king in the second year of Jehoram son of Jehoshaphat king of Judah. ¹⁸As for all the other events of Ahaziah's reign, and what he did, are they not written in the book of the annals of the kings of Israel?

*a*17 Hebrew *Jehoram*, a variant of *Joram*

1 / 2 Kings 2
Transition

WHEN OUR OLDEST daughter, Sheri, left for college, it was a big transition for our family. She played all four stringed instruments—and several instruments of other varieties. Her part-time job during high school was to teach younger music students. At the same time our next-oldest daughter, Lori, a cellist and a flutist, was being asked to consider picking up some of Sheri's students. It was a scary thought, walking in the footsteps of a respected older sister. Sure, Lori had studied hard and practiced a lot. But she was younger and inexperienced. The mantle was on the ground. Would she pick it up? Elisha had to make the same decision.

2 When the Lord was about to take Elijah up to heaven in a whirlwind, Elijah and Elisha were on their way from Gilgal. ²Elijah said to Elisha, "Stay here; the Lord has sent me to Bethel."

But Elisha said, "As surely as the Lord lives and as you live, I will not leave you." So they went down to Bethel.

³The company of the prophets at Bethel came out to Elisha and asked, "Do you know that the Lord is going to take your master from you today?"

"Yes, I know," Elisha replied, "but do not speak of it."

⁴Then Elijah said to him, "Stay here, Elisha; the Lord has sent me to Jericho."

And he replied, "As surely as the Lord lives and as you live, I will not leave you." So they went to Jericho.

⁵The company of the prophets at Jericho went up to Elisha and asked him, "Do you know that the Lord is going to take your master from you today?"

"Yes, I know," he replied, "but do not speak of it."

⁶Then Elijah said to him, "Stay here; the Lord has sent me to the Jordan."

And he replied, "As surely as the Lord lives and as you live, I will not leave you." So the two of them walked on.

⁷Fifty men of the company of the prophets went and stood at a distance, facing the place where Elijah and Elisha had stopped at the Jordan. ⁸Elijah took his cloak, rolled it up and struck the water with it. The water divided to the right and to the left, and the two of them crossed over on dry ground.

⁹When they had crossed, Elijah said to Elisha, "Tell me, what can I do for you before I am taken from you?"

"Let me inherit a double portion of your spirit," Elisha replied.

¹⁰"You have asked a difficult thing," Elijah said, "yet if you see me when I am taken from you, it will be yours—otherwise not."

¹¹As they were walking along and talking together, suddenly a chariot of fire and horses of fire appeared and separated the two of them, and Elijah went up to heaven in a whirlwind. ¹²Elisha saw this and cried out, "My father! My father! The chariots and horsemen of Israel!" And Elisha saw him no more. Then he took hold of his own clothes and tore them apart.

¹³He picked up the cloak that had fallen from Elijah and went back and stood on the bank of the Jordan. ¹⁴Then he took the cloak that had fallen from him and struck the water with it. "Where now is the Lord, the God of Elijah?" he asked. When he struck the water, it divided to the right and to the left, and he crossed over.

¹⁵The company of the prophets from Jericho, who were watching, said, "The spirit of Elijah is resting on Elisha." And they went to meet him and bowed to the ground before him. ¹⁶"Look," they said, "we your servants have fifty able men. Let them go and look for your master. Perhaps the Spirit of the Lord has picked him up and set him down on some mountain or in some valley."

"No," Elisha replied, "do not send them."

¹⁷But they persisted until he was too ashamed to refuse. So he said, "Send them." And they sent fifty men, who searched for three days but did not find him. ¹⁸When they returned to Elisha, who was staying in Jericho, he said to them, "Didn't I tell you not to go?"

¹⁹The men of the city said to Elisha, "Look, our lord, this town is well situated, as you can see, but the water is bad and the land is unproductive."

²⁰"Bring me a new bowl," he said, "and put salt in it." So they brought it to him.

²¹Then he went out to the spring and threw the salt into it, saying, "This is what the Lord says: 'I have healed this water. Never again will it cause death or make the land unproductive.'" ²²And the water has remained wholesome to this day, according to the word Elisha had spoken.

²³From there Elisha went up to Bethel. As he was walking along the road, some youths came out of the town and jeered at him. "Go on up, you baldhead!" they said. "Go on up, you baldhead!" ²⁴He turned around, looked at them and called down a curse on them in the name of the Lord.

Then two bears came out of the woods and mauled forty-two of the youths. ²⁵And he went on to Mount Carmel and from there returned to Samaria.

 Discovering the Word 1. Why do you think Elijah kept telling Elisha to "stay here" (vv. 2, 4, 6)? 2. Why do you think Elisha insisted on following Elijah? 3. How did Elijah show that the gift Elisha requested was not within his authority to give (vv. 9–12)? 4. Three miracles occur (vv. 14, 19–22, 23–25). What effect would each have on Elisha's ministry? 5. In what ways did God provide support for Elisha in the job he had given him to do? (Use the whole chapter.)

Applying the Word 1. Think of at least one job that you are reasonably sure God has assigned to you. What help has God given you so far in doing that job? 2. What obstacles and discouragements are you likely to face in this job? 3. How might your past experiences of God's support help you through future obstacles?

Responding in Prayer Ask God to encourage you through the time of transition that you face.

---

2 Kings 3:1—4:7

3 Joram*ᵇ* son of Ahab became king of Israel in Samaria in the eighteenth year of Jehoshaphat king of Judah, and he reigned twelve years. ²He did evil in the eyes of the LORD, but not as his father and mother had done. He got rid of the sacred stone of Baal that his father had made. ³Nevertheless he clung to the sins of Jeroboam son of Nebat, which he had caused Israel to commit; he did not turn away from them.

⁴Now Mesha king of Moab raised sheep, and he had to supply the king of Israel with a hundred thousand lambs and with the wool of a hundred thousand rams. ⁵But after Ahab died, the king of Moab rebelled against the king of Israel. ⁶So at that time King Joram set out from Samaria and mobilized all Israel. ⁷He also sent this message to Jehoshaphat king of Judah: "The king of Moab has rebelled against me. Will you go with me to fight against Moab?"

"I will go with you," he replied. "I am as you are, my people as your people, my horses as your horses."

⁸"By what route shall we attack?" he asked.

"Through the Desert of Edom," he answered.

⁹So the king of Israel set out with the king of Judah and the king of Edom. After a roundabout march of seven days, the army had no more water for themselves or for the animals with them.

¹⁰"What!" exclaimed the king of Israel. "Has the LORD called us three kings together only to hand us over to Moab?"

¹¹But Jehoshaphat asked, "Is there no prophet of the LORD here, that we may inquire of the LORD through him?"

An officer of the king of Israel answered, "Elisha son of Shaphat is here. He used to pour water on the hands of Elijah.*ᶜ*"

¹²Jehoshaphat said, "The word of the LORD is with him." So the king of Israel and Jehoshaphat and the king of Edom went down to him.

¹³Elisha said to the king of Israel, "What do we have to do with each other? Go to the prophets of your father and the prophets of your mother."

"No," the king of Israel answered, "because it was the LORD who called us three kings together to hand us over to Moab."

¹⁴Elisha said, "As surely as the LORD Almighty lives, whom I serve, if I did not have respect for the presence of Jehoshaphat king of Judah, I would not look at you or even notice you. ¹⁵But now bring me a harpist."

While the harpist was playing, the hand of the LORD came upon Elisha ¹⁶and he said, "This is what the LORD says: Make this valley full of ditches. ¹⁷For this is what the LORD says: You will see neither wind nor rain, yet this valley will be filled with water, and you, your cattle and your other animals will drink. ¹⁸This is an easy thing in the eyes of the LORD; he will also hand Moab over to you. ¹⁹You will overthrow every fortified city

ᵇ1 Hebrew Jehoram, a variant of Joram; also in verse 6   ᶜ11 That is, he was Elijah's personal servant.

and every major town. You will cut down every good tree, stop up all the springs, and ruin every good field with stones."

20The next morning, about the time for offering the sacrifice, there it was—water flowing from the direction of Edom! And the land was filled with water.

21Now all the Moabites had heard that the kings had come to fight against them; so every man, young and old, who could bear arms was called up and stationed on the border. 22When they got up early in the morning, the sun was shining on the water. To the Moabites across the way, the water looked red—like blood. 23"That's blood!" they said. "Those kings must have fought and slaughtered each other. Now to the plunder, Moab!"

24But when the Moabites came to the camp of Israel, the Israelites rose up and fought them until they fled. And the Israelites invaded the land and slaughtered the Moabites. 25They destroyed the towns, and each man threw a stone on every good field until it was covered. They stopped up all the springs and cut down every good tree. Only Kir Hareseth was left with its stones in place, but men armed with slings surrounded it and attacked it as well.

26When the king of Moab saw that the battle had gone against him, he took with him seven hundred swordsmen to break through to the king of Edom, but they failed. 27Then he took his firstborn son, who was to succeed him as king, and offered him as a sacrifice on the city wall. The fury against Israel was great; they withdrew and returned to their own land.

4 The wife of a man from the company of the prophets cried out to Elisha, "Your servant my husband is dead, and you know that he revered the LORD. But now his creditor is coming to take my two boys as his slaves."

2Elisha replied to her, "How can I help you? Tell me, what do you have in your house?"

"Your servant has nothing there at all," she said, "except a little oil."

3Elisha said, "Go around and ask all your neighbors for empty jars. Don't ask for just a few. 4Then go inside and shut the door behind you and your sons. Pour oil into all the jars, and as each is filled, put it to one side."

5She left him and afterward shut the door behind her and her sons. They brought the jars to her and she kept pouring. 6When all the jars were full, she said to her son, "Bring me another one."

But he replied, "There is not a jar left." Then the oil stopped flowing.

7She went and told the man of God, and he said, "Go, sell the oil and pay your debts. You and your sons can live on what is left."

2 / 2 Kings 4:8–37
Taking the Initiative

"I THOUGHT HE must be a Christian when he took me to his home for dinner and overnight," said a visiting Chinese scholar, recounting how a stranger at the airport had offered him hospitality when he was stranded. Hospitality is a trait repeatedly commended in the Bible. God is hospitable, and he wants his children to be also. In this story a woman welcomes "the man of God" into her home and is rewarded for doing so—or so it seems until the day her son dies. The initiative she shows in offering hospitality leads her to a deeper faith in expecting God to act on her behalf. Her faith and boldness, as well as her generosity, are a model for us.

 Warming Up to God   When is it hard for you to show hospitality?

 Read 2 Kings 4:8–37.

8One day Elisha went to Shunem. And a well-to-do woman was there, who urged him to stay for a meal. So whenever he came by, he stopped there to eat. 9She said to her husband, "I know that this man who often comes our way is a holy man of God. 10Let's make a small room on the roof and put in it a bed and a table, a chair and a lamp for him. Then he can stay there whenever he comes to us."

11One day when Elisha came, he went up to his

room and lay down there. ¹²He said to his servant Gehazi, "Call the Shunammite." So he called her, and she stood before him. ¹³Elisha said to him, "Tell her, 'You have gone to all this trouble for us. Now what can be done for you? Can we speak on your behalf to the king or the commander of the army?' "

She replied, "I have a home among my own people."

¹⁴"What can be done for her?" Elisha asked.

Gehazi said, "Well, she has no son and her husband is old."

¹⁵Then Elisha said, "Call her." So he called her, and she stood in the doorway. ¹⁶"About this time next year," Elisha said, "you will hold a son in your arms."

"No, my lord," she objected. "Don't mislead your servant, O man of God!"

¹⁷But the woman became pregnant, and the next year about that same time she gave birth to a son, just as Elisha had told her.

¹⁸The child grew, and one day he went out to his father, who was with the reapers. ¹⁹"My head! My head!" he said to his father.

His father told a servant, "Carry him to his mother." ²⁰After the servant had lifted him up and carried him to his mother, the boy sat on her lap until noon, and then he died. ²¹She went up and laid him on the bed of the man of God, then shut the door and went out.

²²She called her husband and said, "Please send me one of the servants and a donkey so I can go to the man of God quickly and return."

²³"Why go to him today?" he asked. "It's not the New Moon or the Sabbath."

"It's all right," she said.

²⁴She saddled the donkey and said to her servant, "Lead on; don't slow down for me unless I tell you." ²⁵So she set out and came to the man of God at Mount Carmel.

When he saw her in the distance, the man of God said to his servant Gehazi, "Look! There's the Shunammite! ²⁶Run to meet her and ask her, 'Are you all right? Is your husband all right? Is your child all right?' "

"Everything is all right," she said.

²⁷When she reached the man of God at the mountain, she took hold of his feet. Gehazi came over to push her away, but the man of God said, "Leave her alone! She is in bitter distress, but the Lord has hidden it from me and has not told me why."

²⁸"Did I ask you for a son, my lord?" she said. "Didn't I tell you, 'Don't raise my hopes'?"

²⁹Elisha said to Gehazi, "Tuck your cloak into your belt, take my staff in your hand and run. If you meet anyone, do not greet him, and if anyone greets you, do not answer. Lay my staff on the boy's face."

³⁰But the child's mother said, "As surely as the Lord lives and as you live, I will not leave you." So he got up and followed her.

³¹Gehazi went on ahead and laid the staff on the boy's face, but there was no sound or response. So Gehazi went back to meet Elisha and told him, "The boy has not awakened."

³²When Elisha reached the house, there was the boy lying dead on his couch. ³³He went in, shut the door on the two of them and prayed to the Lord. ³⁴Then he got on the bed and lay upon the boy, mouth to mouth, eyes to eyes, hands to hands. As he stretched himself out upon him, the boy's body grew warm. ³⁵Elisha turned away and walked back and forth in the room and then got on the bed and stretched out upon him once more. The boy sneezed seven times and opened his eyes.

³⁶Elisha summoned Gehazi and said, "Call the Shunammite." And he did. When she came, he said, "Take your son." ³⁷She came in, fell at his feet and bowed to the ground. Then she took her son and went out.

Discovering the Word 1. What do you know about the life circumstances of the Shunammite woman from this story? 2. Why did the woman use her resources to help Elisha? 3. What do you think Elisha's concern for her needs (vv. 12–14) meant to the Shunammite woman? 4. After being given a son and raising him to boyhood, the woman now faces a terrible loss (vv. 18–20). How does she respond to the death of her son (vv. 21–30)? 5. What is the woman's strong resolve in the face of her son's death?

Applying the Word 1. Compare your own use of resources to that of the woman in this story. How can you show hospitality even with limited resources? 2. When have you spoken "accusing words" like these to God or to others? 3. Why is it important to lay a foundation of faith and trust in God before times of crisis come to us?

Responding in Prayer What wonderful works has God done on your behalf? Offer him your praise.

2 Kings 4:38–44

38Elisha returned to Gilgal and there was a famine in that region. While the company of the prophets was meeting with him, he said to his servant, "Put on the large pot and cook some stew for these men."

39One of them went out into the fields to gather herbs and found a wild vine. He gathered some of its gourds and filled the fold of his cloak. When he returned, he cut them up into the pot of stew, though no one knew what they were. 40The stew was poured out for the men, but as they began to eat it, they cried out, "O man of God, there is death in the pot!" And they could not eat it.

41Elisha said, "Get some flour." He put it into the pot and said, "Serve it to the people to eat." And there was nothing harmful in the pot.

42A man came from Baal Shalishah, bringing the man of God twenty loaves of barley bread baked from the first ripe grain, along with some heads of new grain. "Give it to the people to eat," Elisha said.

43"How can I set this before a hundred men?" his servant asked.

But Elisha answered, "Give it to the people to eat. For this is what the LORD says: 'They will eat and have some left over.' " 44Then he set it before them, and they ate and had some left over, according to the word of the LORD.

---

3 / 2 Kings 5
Physical Healing

I KNEW DIANA was growing when she was able to say, "I have come to realize that there are others all around me who are in pain. I am not the only one who is suffering. Until now I could not see the pain of others because I was so focused on mine." Often, the first step in being used by God in meeting others' needs is being able to identify those needs. Three thousand years ago, Naaman, the pagan commander of a large army, was sick. In that setting, a take-charge man learned about need—from a servant girl. And he met a God who cared.

 Warming Up to God When you are in physical need, what kinds of responses or activities from people communicate to you that someone cares?

 Read 2 Kings 5.

5Now Naaman was commander of the army of the king of Aram. He was a great man in the sight of his master and highly regarded, because through him the LORD had given victory to Aram. He was a valiant soldier, but he had leprosy.d

2Now bands from Aram had gone out and had taken captive a young girl from Israel, and she served Naaman's wife. 3She said to her mistress, "If only my master would see the prophet who is in Samaria! He would cure him of his leprosy."

4Naaman went to his master and told him what the girl from Israel had said. 5"By all means, go," the king of Aram replied. "I will send a letter to the king of Israel." So Naaman left, taking with him ten talentse of silver, six thousand shekelsf of gold and ten sets of clothing. 6The letter that he took to the king of Israel read: "With this letter I am sending my servant Naaman to you so that you may cure him of his leprosy."

7As soon as the king of Israel read the letter, he tore his robes and said, "Am I God? Can I kill and bring back to life? Why does this fellow send someone to me to be cured of his leprosy? See how he is trying to pick a quarrel with me!"

8When Elisha the man of God heard that the king of Israel had torn his robes, he sent him this message: "Why have you torn your robes? Have the man come to me and he will know that there is a prophet in Israel." 9So Naaman went with his horses and chariots and stopped at the door of

d1 The Hebrew word was used for various diseases affecting the skin—not necessarily leprosy; also in verses 3, 6, 7, 11 and 27. e5 That is, about 750 pounds (about 340 kilograms)   f5 That is, about 150 pounds (about 70 kilograms)

Elisha's house. ¹⁰Elisha sent a messenger to say to him, "Go, wash yourself seven times in the Jordan, and your flesh will be restored and you will be cleansed."

¹¹But Naaman went away angry and said, "I thought that he would surely come out to me and stand and call on the name of the Lord his God, wave his hand over the spot and cure me of my leprosy. ¹²Are not Abana and Pharpar, the rivers of Damascus, better than any of the waters of Israel? Couldn't I wash in them and be cleansed?" So he turned and went off in a rage.

¹³Naaman's servants went to him and said, "My father, if the prophet had told you to do some great thing, would you not have done it? How much more, then, when he tells you, 'Wash and be cleansed'!" ¹⁴So he went down and dipped himself in the Jordan seven times, as the man of God had told him, and his flesh was restored and became clean like that of a young boy.

¹⁵Then Naaman and all his attendants went back to the man of God. He stood before him and said, "Now I know that there is no God in all the world except in Israel. Please accept now a gift from your servant."

¹⁶The prophet answered, "As surely as the Lord lives, whom I serve, I will not accept a thing." And even though Naaman urged him, he refused.

¹⁷"If you will not," said Naaman, "please let me, your servant, be given as much earth as a pair of mules can carry, for your servant will never again make burnt offerings and sacrifices to any other god but the Lord. ¹⁸But may the Lord forgive your servant for this one thing: When my master enters the temple of Rimmon to bow down and he is leaning on my arm and I bow there also—when I bow down in the temple of Rimmon, may the Lord forgive your servant for this."

¹⁹"Go in peace," Elisha said.

After Naaman had traveled some distance, ²⁰Gehazi, the servant of Elisha the man of God, said to himself, "My master was too easy on Naaman, this Aramean, by not accepting from him what he brought. As surely as the Lord lives, I will run after him and get something from him."

²¹So Gehazi hurried after Naaman. When Naaman saw him running toward him, he got down from the chariot to meet him. "Is everything all right?" he asked.

²²"Everything is all right," Gehazi answered. "My master sent me to say, 'Two young men from the company of the prophets have just come to me from the hill country of Ephraim. Please give them a talent⁸ of silver and two sets of clothing.' "

²³"By all means, take two talents," said Naaman. He urged Gehazi to accept them, and then tied up the two talents of silver in two bags, with two sets of clothing. He gave them to two of his servants, and they carried them ahead of Gehazi. ²⁴When Gehazi came to the hill, he took the things from the servants and put them away in the house. He sent the men away and they left. ²⁵Then he went in and stood before his master Elisha.

"Where have you been, Gehazi?" Elisha asked.

"Your servant didn't go anywhere," Gehazi answered.

²⁶But Elisha said to him, "Was not my spirit with you when the man got down from his chariot to meet you? Is this the time to take money, or to accept clothes, olive groves, vineyards, flocks, herds, or menservants and maidservants? ²⁷Naaman's leprosy will cling to you and to your descendants forever." Then Gehazi went from Elisha's presence and he was leprous, as white as snow.

⁸22 That is, about 75 pounds (about 34 kilograms)

 Discovering the Word   1. What are ways that people reached out to Naaman throughout this passage? 2. Describe Naaman and the servant girl (vv. 1–3). 3. Why was Naaman angry at Elisha (vv. 10–13)? 4. What was Naaman's response when he was cured (v. 15)? 5. Why did Gehazi follow Naaman (vv. 20–22)?

Applying the Word   1. When have you been upset because of the way God chose to work when you or someone else was in need? 2. We have considered the benefits to Naaman of the help people gave him. What benefits do you think came to those who helped? 3. What benefits do you receive from seeing others helped?

Responding in Prayer   Pray that God will make you sensitive to the needs of others and will help you to gently lead them in the right steps toward healing.

2 Kings 6:1–23

6 The company of the prophets said to Elisha, "Look, the place where we meet with you is too small for us. ²Let us go to the Jordan, where each of us can get a pole; and let us build a place there for us to live."

And he said, "Go."

³Then one of them said, "Won't you please come with your servants?"

"I will," Elisha replied. ⁴And he went with them.

They went to the Jordan and began to cut down trees. ⁵As one of them was cutting down a tree, the iron axhead fell into the water. "Oh, my lord," he cried out, "it was borrowed!"

⁶The man of God asked, "Where did it fall?" When he showed him the place, Elisha cut a stick and threw it there, and made the iron float. ⁷"Lift it out," he said. Then the man reached out his hand and took it.

⁸Now the king of Aram was at war with Israel. After conferring with his officers, he said, "I will set up my camp in such and such a place."

⁹The man of God sent word to the king of Israel: "Beware of passing that place, because the Arameans are going down there." ¹⁰So the king of Israel checked on the place indicated by the man of God. Time and again Elisha warned the king, so that he was on his guard in such places.

¹¹This enraged the king of Aram. He summoned his officers and demanded of them, "Will you not tell me which of us is on the side of the king of Israel?"

¹²"None of us, my lord the king," said one of his officers, "but Elisha, the prophet who is in Israel, tells the king of Israel the very words you speak in your bedroom."

¹³"Go, find out where he is," the king ordered, "so I can send men and capture him." The report came back: "He is in Dothan." ¹⁴Then he sent horses and chariots and a strong force there. They went by night and surrounded the city.

¹⁵When the servant of the man of God got up and went out early the next morning, an army with horses and chariots had surrounded the city. "Oh, my lord, what shall we do?" the servant asked.

¹⁶"Don't be afraid," the prophet answered. "Those who are with us are more than those who are with them."

¹⁷And Elisha prayed, "O LORD, open his eyes so he may see." Then the LORD opened the servant's eyes, and he looked and saw the hills full of horses and chariots of fire all around Elisha.

¹⁸As the enemy came down toward him, Elisha prayed to the LORD, "Strike these people with blindness." So he struck them with blindness, as Elisha had asked.

¹⁹Elisha told them, "This is not the road and this is not the city. Follow me, and I will lead you to the man you are looking for." And he led them to Samaria.

²⁰After they entered the city, Elisha said, "LORD, open the eyes of these men so they can see." Then the LORD opened their eyes and they looked, and there they were, inside Samaria.

²¹When the king of Israel saw them, he asked Elisha, "Shall I kill them, my father? Shall I kill them?"

²²"Do not kill them," he answered. "Would you kill men you have captured with your own sword or bow? Set food and water before them so that they may eat and drink and then go back to their master." ²³So he prepared a great feast for them, and after they had finished eating and drinking, he sent them away, and they returned to their master. So the bands from Aram stopped raiding Israel's territory.

4 / 2 Kings 6:24—7:20
Faith in Hard Times

I HAVE A friend who has been plagued by seeming disasters: One daughter joined a cult; another daughter couldn't seem to stay married—to anyone; a son died of cancer; her husband requires frequent psychiatric care.

What has she done wrong? Nothing really. She has done a better-than-average job of parenting and she possesses a more-than-normal dose of stability. Through all the trauma, she has maintained an uncomplicated trust in God. And occasionally we see a glimmer of purpose around her string of disasters. This larger view shows all of us close to her that her trust is justified.

 Warming Up to God What is the biggest disaster you have had to face since you began to trust God? What did that period in your life teach you about God?

 Read 2 Kings 6:24—7:20.

²⁴Some time later, Ben-Hadad king of Aram mobilized his entire army and marched up and laid siege to Samaria. ²⁵There was a great famine in the city; the siege lasted so long that a donkey's head sold for eighty shekels[h] of silver, and a quarter of a cab[i] of seed pods[j] for five shekels.[k]

²⁶As the king of Israel was passing by on the wall, a woman cried to him, "Help me, my lord the king!"

²⁷The king replied, "If the LORD does not help you, where can I get help for you? From the threshing floor? From the winepress?" ²⁸Then he asked her, "What's the matter?"

She answered, "This woman said to me, 'Give up your son so we may eat him today, and tomorrow we'll eat my son.' ²⁹So we cooked my son and ate him. The next day I said to her, 'Give up your son so we may eat him,' but she had hidden him."

³⁰When the king heard the woman's words, he tore his robes. As he went along the wall, the people looked, and there, underneath, he had sackcloth on his body. ³¹He said, "May God deal with me, be it ever so severely, if the head of Elisha son of Shaphat remains on his shoulders today!"

³²Now Elisha was sitting in his house, and the elders were sitting with him. The king sent a messenger ahead, but before he arrived, Elisha said to the elders, "Don't you see how this murderer is sending someone to cut off my head? Look, when the messenger comes, shut the door and hold it shut against him. Is not the sound of his master's footsteps behind him?"

³³While he was still talking to them, the messenger came down to him. And ⌊the king⌋ said, "This disaster is from the LORD. Why should I wait for the LORD any longer?"

7 Elisha said, "Hear the word of the LORD. This is what the LORD says: About this time tomorrow, a seah[l] of flour will sell

for a shekel[m] and two seahs[n] of barley for a shekel at the gate of Samaria."

²The officer on whose arm the king was leaning said to the man of God, "Look, even if the LORD should open the floodgates of the heavens, could this happen?"

"You will see it with your own eyes," answered Elisha, "but you will not eat any of it!"

³Now there were four men with leprosy[o] at the entrance of the city gate. They said to each other, "Why stay here until we die? ⁴If we say, 'We'll go into the city'—the famine is there, and we will die. And if we stay here, we will die. So let's go over to the camp of the Arameans and surrender. If they spare us, we live; if they kill us, then we die."

⁵At dusk they got up and went to the camp of the Arameans. When they reached the edge of the camp, not a man was there, ⁶for the Lord had caused the Arameans to hear the sound of chariots and horses and a great army, so that they said to one another, "Look, the king of Israel has hired the Hittite and Egyptian kings to attack us!" ⁷So they got up and fled in the dusk and abandoned their tents and their horses and donkeys. They left the camp as it was and ran for their lives.

⁸The men who had leprosy reached the edge of the camp and entered one of the tents. They ate and drank, and carried away silver, gold and clothes, and went off and hid them. They returned and entered another tent and took some things from it and hid them also.

⁹Then they said to each other, "We're not doing right. This is a day of good news and we are keeping it to ourselves. If we wait until daylight,

---

ʰ25 That is, about 2 pounds (about 1 kilogram)   ⁱ25 That is, probably about 1/2 pint (about 0.3 liter)   ʲ25 Or *of dove's dung*   ᵏ25 That is, about 2 ounces (about 55 grams)   ˡ1 That is, probably about 7 quarts (about 7.3 liters); also in verses 16 and 18   ᵐ1 That is, about 2/5 ounce (about 11 grams); also in verses 16 and 18   ⁿ1 That is, probably about 13 quarts (about 15 liters); also in verses 16 and 18   ᵒ3 The Hebrew word is used for various diseases affecting the skin—not necessarily leprosy; also in verse 8.

punishment will overtake us. Let's go at once and report this to the royal palace."

¹⁰So they went and called out to the city gate-keepers and told them, "We went into the Aramean camp and not a man was there—not a sound of anyone—only tethered horses and donkeys, and the tents left just as they were." ¹¹The gatekeepers shouted the news, and it was reported within the palace.

¹²The king got up in the night and said to his officers, "I will tell you what the Arameans have done to us. They know we are starving; so they have left the camp to hide in the countryside, thinking, 'They will surely come out, and then we will take them alive and get into the city.' "

¹³One of his officers answered, "Have some men take five of the horses that are left in the city. Their plight will be like that of all the Israelites left here—yes, they will only be like all these Israelites who are doomed. So let us send them to find out what happened."

¹⁴So they selected two chariots with their horses, and the king sent them after the Aramean army. He commanded the drivers, "Go and find out what has happened." ¹⁵They followed them as far as the Jordan, and they found the whole road strewn with the clothing and equipment the Arameans had thrown away in their headlong flight. So the messengers returned and reported to the king. ¹⁶Then the people went out and plundered the camp of the Arameans. So a seah of flour sold for a shekel, and two seahs of barley sold for a shekel, as the LORD had said.

¹⁷Now the king had put the officer on whose arm he leaned in charge of the gate, and the people trampled him in the gateway, and he died, just as the man of God had foretold when the king came down to his house. ¹⁸It happened as the man of God had said to the king: "About this time tomorrow, a seah of flour will sell for a shekel and two seahs of barley for a shekel at the gate of Samaria."

¹⁹The officer had said to the man of God, "Look, even if the LORD should open the floodgates of the heavens, could this happen?" The man of God had replied, "You will see it with your own eyes, but you will not eat any of it!" ²⁰And that is exactly what happened to him, for the people trampled him in the gateway, and he died.

Discovering the Word 1. What indications do you see that the situation in Samaria was desperate (6:24—7:2)? 2. Notice each reference to God in 6:24—7:2. What does each speaker seem to believe about God's relationship to the siege? 3. Why did the four lepers go to the Aramean camp (7:3–4)? 4. If you had been one of those lepers, what would you have done when you discovered the Aramean camp deserted (vv. 8–9)? 5. Why do you think the king's officer died (vv. 17–20)?

Applying the Word 1. Why is it hard to trust God during hard times? 2. What can you do during times of relative calm that would prepare you to trust God when times are hard?

Responding in Prayer Pray about the hard times you face in your life and pray for those around the world who face famine and war.

---

2 Kings 8

8 Now Elisha had said to the woman whose son he had restored to life, "Go away with your family and stay for a while wherever you can, because the LORD has decreed a famine in the land that will last seven years." ²The woman proceeded to do as the man of God said. She and her family went away and stayed in the land of the Philistines seven years.

³At the end of the seven years she came back from the land of the Philistines and went to the king to beg for her house and land. ⁴The king was talking to Gehazi, the servant of the man of God,

and had said, "Tell me about all the great things Elisha has done." ⁵Just as Gehazi was telling the king how Elisha had restored the dead to life, the woman whose son Elisha had brought back to life came to beg the king for her house and land.

Gehazi said, "This is the woman, my lord the king, and this is her son whom Elisha restored to life." ⁶The king asked the woman about it, and she told him.

Then he assigned an official to her case and said to him, "Give back everything that belonged to her, including all the income from her land from the day she left the country until now."

⁷Elisha went to Damascus, and Ben-Hadad king of Aram was ill. When the king was told, "The man of God has come all the way up here," ⁸he said to Hazael, "Take a gift with you and go to meet the man of God. Consult the LORD through him; ask him, 'Will I recover from this illness?' "

⁹Hazael went to meet Elisha, taking with him as a gift forty camel-loads of all the finest wares of Damascus. He went in and stood before him, and said, "Your son Ben-Hadad king of Aram has sent me to ask, 'Will I recover from this illness?' "

¹⁰Elisha answered, "Go and say to him, 'You will certainly recover'; butᵖ the LORD has revealed to me that he will in fact die." ¹¹He stared at him with a fixed gaze until Hazael felt ashamed. Then the man of God began to weep.

¹²"Why is my lord weeping?" asked Hazael.

"Because I know the harm you will do to the Israelites," he answered. "You will set fire to their fortified places, kill their young men with the sword, dash their little children to the ground, and rip open their pregnant women."

¹³Hazael said, "How could your servant, a mere dog, accomplish such a feat?"

"The LORD has shown me that you will become king of Aram," answered Elisha.

¹⁴Then Hazael left Elisha and returned to his master. When Ben-Hadad asked, "What did Elisha say to you?" Hazael replied, "He told me that you would certainly recover." ¹⁵But the next day he took a thick cloth, soaked it in water and spread it over the king's face, so that he died. Then Hazael succeeded him as king.

¹⁶In the fifth year of Joram son of Ahab king of Israel, when Jehoshaphat was king of Judah, Jehoram son of Jehoshaphat began his reign as king of Judah. ¹⁷He was thirty-two years old when he became king, and he reigned in Jerusalem eight years. ¹⁸He walked in the ways of the kings of Israel, as the house of Ahab had done, for he married a daughter of Ahab. He did evil in the eyes of the LORD. ¹⁹Nevertheless, for the sake of his servant David, the LORD was not willing to destroy Judah. He had promised to maintain a lamp for David and his descendants forever.

²⁰In the time of Jehoram, Edom rebelled against Judah and set up its own king. ²¹So Jehoram�q went to Zair with all his chariots. The Edomites surrounded him and his chariot commanders, but he rose up and broke through by night; his army, however, fled back home. ²²To this day Edom has been in rebellion against Judah. Libnah revolted at the same time.

²³As for the other events of Jehoram's reign, and all he did, are they not written in the book of the annals of the kings of Judah? ²⁴Jehoram rested with his fathers and was buried with them in the City of David. And Ahaziah his son succeeded him as king.

²⁵In the twelfth year of Joram son of Ahab king of Israel, Ahaziah son of Jehoram king of Judah began to reign. ²⁶Ahaziah was twenty-two years old when he became king, and he reigned in Jerusalem one year. His mother's name was Athaliah, a granddaughter of Omri king of Israel. ²⁷He walked in the ways of the house of Ahab and did evil in the eyes of the LORD, as the house of Ahab had done, for he was related by marriage to Ahab's family.

²⁸Ahaziah went with Joram son of Ahab to war against Hazael king of Aram at Ramoth Gilead. The Arameans wounded Joram; ²⁹so King Joram returned to Jezreel to recover from the wounds the Arameans had inflicted on him at Ramothʳ in his battle with Hazael king of Aram.

Then Ahaziah son of Jehoram king of Judah went down to Jezreel to see Joram son of Ahab, because he had been wounded.

ᵖ10 The Hebrew may also be read *Go and say, 'You will certainly not recover,' for.*   q21 Hebrew *Joram*, a variant of *Jehoram*; also in verses 23 and 24   ʳ29 Hebrew *Ramah*, a variant of *Ramoth*

5 / 2 Kings 9—10
God's Avenger

GOD'S EXECUTIONER

Fly, killer Jehu
Riding your chariot
A madman across the plains

"He drives like Jehu?"
Swallows my messengers
And spits them out his tail

Tremble Ahab in your grave
You spilt your seed on the ground
One-hundred-fold
And Jehu rides to lick it up

 Warming Up to God In what way or on whom would you like to exercise vengeance?

 Read 2 Kings 9—10.

9 The prophet Elisha summoned a man from the company of the prophets and said to him, "Tuck your cloak into your belt, take this flask of oil with you and go to Ramoth Gilead. ²When you get there, look for Jehu son of Jehoshaphat, the son of Nimshi. Go to him, get him away from his companions and take him into an inner room. ³Then take the flask and pour the oil on his head and declare, 'This is what the LORD says: I anoint you king over Israel.' Then open the door and run; don't delay!"

⁴So the young man, the prophet, went to Ramoth Gilead. ⁵When he arrived, he found the army officers sitting together. "I have a message for you, commander," he said.

"For which of us?" asked Jehu.

"For you, commander," he replied.

⁶Jehu got up and went into the house. Then the prophet poured the oil on Jehu's head and declared, "This is what the LORD, the God of Israel, says: 'I anoint you king over the LORD's people Israel. ⁷You are to destroy the house of Ahab your master, and I will avenge the blood of my servants the prophets and the blood of all the LORD's servants shed by Jezebel. ⁸The whole house of Ahab will perish. I will cut off from Ahab every last male in Israel—slave or free. ⁹I will make the house of Ahab like the house of Jeroboam son of Nebat and like the house of Baasha son of Ahijah. ¹⁰As for Jezebel, dogs will devour her on the plot

of ground at Jezreel, and no one will bury her.' " Then he opened the door and ran.

¹¹When Jehu went out to his fellow officers, one of them asked him, "Is everything all right? Why did this madman come to you?"

"You know the man and the sort of things he says," Jehu replied.

¹²"That's not true!" they said. "Tell us."

Jehu said, "Here is what he told me: 'This is what the LORD says: I anoint you king over Israel.' "

¹³They hurried and took their cloaks and spread them under him on the bare steps. Then they blew the trumpet and shouted, "Jehu is king!"

¹⁴So Jehu son of Jehoshaphat, the son of Nimshi, conspired against Joram. (Now Joram and all Israel had been defending Ramoth Gilead against Hazael king of Aram, ¹⁵but King Joramˢ had returned to Jezreel to recover from the wounds the Arameans had inflicted on him in the battle with Hazael king of Aram.) Jehu said, "If this is the way you feel, don't let anyone slip out of the city to go and tell the news in Jezreel." ¹⁶Then he got into his chariot and rode to Jezreel, because Joram was resting there and Ahaziah king of Judah had gone down to see him.

¹⁷When the lookout standing on the tower in

ˢ15 Hebrew *Jehoram,* a variant of *Joram*; also in verses 17 and 21-24

Jezreel saw Jehu's troops approaching, he called out, "I see some troops coming."

"Get a horseman," Joram ordered. "Send him to meet them and ask, 'Do you come in peace?' "

18The horseman rode off to meet Jehu and said, "This is what the king says: 'Do you come in peace?' "

"What do you have to do with peace?" Jehu replied. "Fall in behind me."

The lookout reported, "The messenger has reached them, but he isn't coming back."

19So the king sent out a second horseman. When he came to them he said, "This is what the king says: 'Do you come in peace?' "

Jehu replied, "What do you have to do with peace? Fall in behind me."

20The lookout reported, "He has reached them, but he isn't coming back either. The driving is like that of Jehu son of Nimshi—he drives like a madman."

21"Hitch up my chariot," Joram ordered. And when it was hitched up, Joram king of Israel and Ahaziah king of Judah rode out, each in his own chariot, to meet Jehu. They met him at the plot of ground that had belonged to Naboth the Jezreelite. 22When Joram saw Jehu he asked, "Have you come in peace, Jehu?"

"How can there be peace," Jehu replied, "as long as all the idolatry and witchcraft of your mother Jezebel abound?"

23Joram turned about and fled, calling out to Ahaziah, "Treachery, Ahaziah!"

24Then Jehu drew his bow and shot Joram between the shoulders. The arrow pierced his heart and he slumped down in his chariot. 25Jehu said to Bidkar, his chariot officer, "Pick him up and throw him on the field that belonged to Naboth the Jezreelite. Remember how you and I were riding together in chariots behind Ahab his father when the LORD made this prophecy about him: 26'Yesterday I saw the blood of Naboth and the blood of his sons, declares the LORD, and I will surely make you pay for it on this plot of ground, declares the LORD.'t Now then, pick him up and throw him on that plot, in accordance with the word of the LORD."

27When Ahaziah king of Judah saw what had happened, he fled up the road to Beth Haggan.u Jehu chased him, shouting, "Kill him too!" They wounded him in his chariot on the way up to Gur near Ibleam, but he escaped to Megiddo and died there. 28His servants took him by chariot to Jeru-

salem and buried him with his fathers in his tomb in the City of David. 29(In the eleventh year of Joram son of Ahab, Ahaziah had become king of Judah.)

30Then Jehu went to Jezreel. When Jezebel heard about it, she painted her eyes, arranged her hair and looked out of a window. 31As Jehu entered the gate, she asked, "Have you come in peace, Zimri, you murderer of your master?"v

32He looked up at the window and called out, "Who is on my side? Who?" Two or three eunuchs looked down at him. 33"Throw her down!" Jehu said. So they threw her down, and some of her blood spattered the wall and the horses as they trampled her underfoot.

34Jehu went in and ate and drank. "Take care of that cursed woman," he said, "and bury her, for she was a king's daughter." 35But when they went out to bury her, they found nothing except her skull, her feet and her hands. 36They went back and told Jehu, who said, "This is the word of the LORD that he spoke through his servant Elijah the Tishbite: On the plot of ground at Jezreel dogs will devour Jezebel's flesh.w 37Jezebel's body will be like refuse on the ground in the plot at Jezreel, so that no one will be able to say, 'This is Jezebel.' "

10 Now there were in Samaria seventy sons of the house of Ahab. So Jehu wrote letters and sent them to Samaria: to the officials of Jezreel,x to the elders and to the guardians of Ahab's children. He said, 2"As soon as this letter reaches you, since your master's sons are with you and you have chariots and horses, a fortified city and weapons, 3choose the best and most worthy of your master's sons and set him on his father's throne. Then fight for your master's house."

4But they were terrified and said, "If two kings could not resist him, how can we?"

5So the palace administrator, the city governor, the elders and the guardians sent this message to Jehu: "We are your servants and we will do anything you say. We will not appoint anyone as king; you do whatever you think best."

6Then Jehu wrote them a second letter, saying, "If you are on my side and will obey me, take the heads of your master's sons and come to me in Jezreel by this time tomorrow."

t26 See 1 Kings 21:19.   u27 Or fled by way of the garden house
v31 Or "Did Zimri have peace, who murdered his master?"   w36 See
1 Kings 21:23.   x1 Hebrew; some Septuagint manuscripts and Vulgate
of the city

Now the royal princes, seventy of them, were with the leading men of the city, who were rearing them. [7]When the letter arrived, these men took the princes and slaughtered all seventy of them. They put their heads in baskets and sent them to Jehu in Jezreel. [8]When the messenger arrived, he told Jehu, "They have brought the heads of the princes."

Then Jehu ordered, "Put them in two piles at the entrance of the city gate until morning."

[9]The next morning Jehu went out. He stood before all the people and said, "You are innocent. It was I who conspired against my master and killed him, but who killed all these? [10]Know then, that not a word the Lord has spoken against the house of Ahab will fail. The Lord has done what he promised through his servant Elijah." [11]So Jehu killed everyone in Jezreel who remained of the house of Ahab, as well as all his chief men, his close friends and his priests, leaving him no survivor.

[12]Jehu then set out and went toward Samaria. At Beth Eked of the Shepherds, [13]he met some relatives of Ahaziah king of Judah and asked, "Who are you?"

They said, "We are relatives of Ahaziah, and we have come down to greet the families of the king and of the queen mother."

[14]"Take them alive!" he ordered. So they took them alive and slaughtered them by the well of Beth Eked—forty-two men. He left no survivor.

[15]After he left there, he came upon Jehonadab son of Recab, who was on his way to meet him. Jehu greeted him and said, "Are you in accord with me, as I am with you?"

"I am," Jehonadab answered.

"If so," said Jehu, "give me your hand." So he did, and Jehu helped him up into the chariot. [16]Jehu said, "Come with me and see my zeal for the Lord." Then he had him ride along in his chariot.

[17]When Jehu came to Samaria, he killed all who were left there of Ahab's family; he destroyed them, according to the word of the Lord spoken to Elijah.

[18]Then Jehu brought all the people together and said to them, "Ahab served Baal a little; Jehu will serve him much. [19]Now summon all the prophets of Baal, all his ministers and all his priests. See that no one is missing, because I am going to hold a great sacrifice for Baal. Anyone who fails to come will no longer live." But Jehu

was acting deceptively in order to destroy the ministers of Baal.

[20]Jehu said, "Call an assembly in honor of Baal." So they proclaimed it. [21]Then he sent word throughout Israel, and all the ministers of Baal came; not one stayed away. They crowded into the temple of Baal until it was full from one end to the other. [22]And Jehu said to the keeper of the wardrobe, "Bring robes for all the ministers of Baal." So he brought out robes for them.

[23]Then Jehu and Jehonadab son of Recab went into the temple of Baal. Jehu said to the ministers of Baal, "Look around and see that no servants of the Lord are here with you—only ministers of Baal." [24]So they went in to make sacrifices and burnt offerings. Now Jehu had posted eighty men outside with this warning: "If one of you lets any of the men I am placing in your hands escape, it will be your life for his life."

[25]As soon as Jehu had finished making the burnt offering, he ordered the guards and officers: "Go in and kill them; let no one escape." So they cut them down with the sword. The guards and officers threw the bodies out and then entered the inner shrine of the temple of Baal. [26]They brought the sacred stone out of the temple of Baal and burned it. [27]They demolished the sacred stone of Baal and tore down the temple of Baal, and people have used it for a latrine to this day.

[28]So Jehu destroyed Baal worship in Israel. [29]However, he did not turn away from the sins of Jeroboam son of Nebat, which he had caused Israel to commit—the worship of the golden calves at Bethel and Dan.

[30]The Lord said to Jehu, "Because you have done well in accomplishing what is right in my eyes and have done to the house of Ahab all I had in mind to do, your descendants will sit on the throne of Israel to the fourth generation." [31]Yet Jehu was not careful to keep the law of the Lord, the God of Israel, with all his heart. He did not turn away from the sins of Jeroboam, which he had caused Israel to commit.

[32]In those days the Lord began to reduce the size of Israel. Hazael overpowered the Israelites throughout their territory [33]east of the Jordan in all the land of Gilead (the region of Gad, Reuben and Manasseh), from Aroer by the Arnon Gorge through Gilead to Bashan.

[34]As for the other events of Jehu's reign, all he did, and all his achievements, are they not written in the book of the annals of the kings of Israel?

³⁵Jehu rested with his fathers and was buried in Samaria. And Jehoahaz his son succeeded him as king. ³⁶The time that Jehu reigned over Israel in Samaria was twenty-eight years.

 Discovering the Word 1. What disturbs you most about this account? 2. What did God tell Jehu to do (9:3–10)? 3. Note all the people Jehu killed. How was each a part of his strategy for securing his own position as king? 4. What evidence do you see that when Jehu killed the leaders of Baal-worship it was not simply because of his desire to worship the true God (10:28–31)? 5. Would you classify Jehu as a good or an evil king? Why? 6. Why do you think God allowed this slaughter by Jehu?

 Applying the Word 1. If God is good and God is sovereign, how do you explain wholesale violence in our world? 2. What do you think should be the attitude of Christians toward violence?

Responding in Prayer Pray that God's justice will be exercised in the parts of the world where people suffer.

---

2 Kings 11—12

11 When Athaliah the mother of Ahaziah saw that her son was dead, she proceeded to destroy the whole royal family. ²But Jehosheba, the daughter of King Jehoramʸ and sister of Ahaziah, took Joash son of Ahaziah and stole him away from among the royal princes, who were about to be murdered. She put him and his nurse in a bedroom to hide him from Athaliah; so he was not killed. ³He remained hidden with his nurse at the temple of the LORD for six years while Athaliah ruled the land.

⁴In the seventh year Jehoiada sent for the commanders of units of a hundred, the Carites and the guards and had them brought to him at the temple of the LORD. He made a covenant with them and put them under oath at the temple of the LORD. Then he showed them the king's son. ⁵He commanded them, saying, "This is what you are to do: You who are in the three companies that are going on duty on the Sabbath—a third of you guarding the royal palace, ⁶a third at the Sur Gate, and a third at the gate behind the guard, who take turns guarding the temple— ⁷and you who are in the other two companies that normally go off Sabbath duty are all to guard the temple for the king. ⁸Station yourselves around the king, each man with his weapon in his hand. Anyone who approaches your ranksᶻ must be put to death. Stay close to the king wherever he goes."

⁹The commanders of units of a hundred did just as Jehoiada the priest ordered. Each one took his men—those who were going on duty on the Sabbath and those who were going off duty—and came to Jehoiada the priest. ¹⁰Then he gave the commanders the spears and shields that had belonged to King David and that were in the temple of the LORD. ¹¹The guards, each with his weapon in his hand, stationed themselves around the king—near the altar and the temple, from the south side to the north side of the temple.

¹²Jehoiada brought out the king's son and put the crown on him; he presented him with a copy of the covenant and proclaimed him king. They anointed him, and the people clapped their hands and shouted, "Long live the king!"

¹³When Athaliah heard the noise made by the guards and the people, she went to the people at the temple of the LORD. ¹⁴She looked and there was the king, standing by the pillar, as the custom was. The officers and the trumpeters were beside the king, and all the people of the land were rejoicing and blowing trumpets. Then Athaliah tore her robes and called out, "Treason! Treason!"

¹⁵Jehoiada the priest ordered the commanders of units of a hundred, who were in charge of the troops: "Bring her out between the ranksᵃ and put to the sword anyone who follows her." For the priest had said, "She must not be put to death in the temple of the LORD." ¹⁶So they seized her as she reached the place where the horses enter the palace grounds, and there she was put to death.

¹⁷Jehoiada then made a covenant between the LORD and the king and people that they would be the LORD's people. He also made a covenant be-

ʸ2 Hebrew *Joram*, a variant of *Jehoram*   ᶻ8 Or *approaches the precincts*   ᵃ15 Or *out from the precincts* tween the king and the people. ¹⁸All the people of the land went to the temple of Baal and tore it down. They smashed the altars and idols to pieces and killed Mattan the priest of Baal in front of the altars.

Then Jehoiada the priest posted guards at the temple of the LORD. ¹⁹He took with him the commanders of hundreds, the Carites, the guards and all the people of the land, and together they brought the king down from the temple of the LORD and went into the palace, entering by way of the gate of the guards. The king then took his place on the royal throne, ²⁰and all the people of the land rejoiced. And the city was quiet, because Athaliah had been slain with the sword at the palace.

²¹Joash[b] was seven years old when he began to reign.

12

In the seventh year of Jehu, Joash[c] became king, and he reigned in Jerusalem forty years. His mother's name was Zibiah; she was from Beersheba. ²Joash did what was right in the eyes of the LORD all the years Jehoiada the priest instructed him. ³The high places, however, were not removed; the people continued to offer sacrifices and burn incense there.

⁴Joash said to the priests, "Collect all the money that is brought as sacred offerings to the temple of the LORD—the money collected in the census, the money received from personal vows and the money brought voluntarily to the temple. ⁵Let every priest receive the money from one of the treasurers, and let it be used to repair whatever damage is found in the temple."

⁶But by the twenty-third year of King Joash the priests still had not repaired the temple. ⁷Therefore King Joash summoned Jehoiada the priest and the other priests and asked them, "Why aren't you repairing the damage done to the temple? Take no more money from your treasurers, but hand it over for repairing the temple." ⁸The priests agreed that they would not collect any more money from the people and that they would not repair the temple themselves.

⁹Jehoiada the priest took a chest and bored a hole in its lid. He placed it beside the altar, on the right side as one enters the temple of the LORD. The priests who guarded the entrance put into the chest all the money that was brought to the temple of the LORD. ¹⁰Whenever they saw that there was a large amount of money in the chest, the royal secretary and the high priest came, counted the money that had been brought into the temple of the LORD and put it into bags. ¹¹When the amount had been determined, they gave the money to the men appointed to supervise the work on the temple. With it they paid those who worked on the temple of the LORD— the carpenters and builders, ¹²the masons and stonecutters. They purchased timber and dressed stone for the repair of the temple of the LORD, and met all the other expenses of restoring the temple.

¹³The money brought into the temple was not spent for making silver basins, wick trimmers, sprinkling bowls, trumpets or any other articles of gold or silver for the temple of the LORD; ¹⁴it was paid to the workmen, who used it to repair the temple. ¹⁵They did not require an accounting from those to whom they gave the money to pay the workers, because they acted with complete honesty. ¹⁶The money from the guilt offerings and sin offerings was not brought into the temple of the LORD; it belonged to the priests.

¹⁷About this time Hazael king of Aram went up and attacked Gath and captured it. Then he turned to attack Jerusalem. ¹⁸But Joash king of Judah took all the sacred objects dedicated by his fathers—Jehoshaphat, Jehoram and Ahaziah, the kings of Judah—and the gifts he himself had dedicated and all the gold found in the treasuries of the temple of the LORD and of the royal palace, and he sent them to Hazael king of Aram, who then withdrew from Jerusalem.

¹⁹As for the other events of the reign of Joash, and all he did, are they not written in the book of the annals of the kings of Judah? ²⁰His officials conspired against him and assassinated him at Beth Millo, on the road down to Silla. ²¹The officials who murdered him were Jozabad son of Shimeath and Jehozabad son of Shomer. He died and was buried with his fathers in the City of David. And Amaziah his son succeeded him as king.

---

[b]21 Hebrew Jehoash, a variant of Joash   [c]1 Hebrew Jehoash, a variant of Joash; also in verses 2, 4, 6, 7 and 18

6 / *2 Kings 13*
Facing Losses

MY FRIEND JAN sat at her kitchen table and cried. Her husband had lost his job. Their living room now stood warehouse-vacant; the furniture had been repossessed. The large country home in which they lived was next in line; the bank would no longer carry the loan. And now (surprise) a new baby was on the way. Jan would also have to give up her job. Losses like these make us take a hard look at ourselves. Have we displeased God? Have we made foolish errors in planning? Or are we simply caught in the fallout of a world that is overrun by sin? Sometimes we can find no answers, but if we bring the questions to God, we will come away with something of value to sustain us through that time.

 Warming Up to God How has a personal loss of your own or of a friend or relative caused you to feel abandoned by God?

 Read 2 Kings 13.

---

13 In the twenty-third year of Joash son of Ahaziah king of Judah, Jehoahaz son of Jehu became king of Israel in Samaria, and he reigned seventeen years. ²He did evil in the eyes of the LORD by following the sins of Jeroboam son of Nebat, which he had caused Israel to commit, and he did not turn away from them. ³So the LORD's anger burned against Israel, and for a long time he kept them under the power of Hazael king of Aram and Ben-Hadad his son.

⁴Then Jehoahaz sought the LORD's favor, and the LORD listened to him, for he saw how severely the king of Aram was oppressing Israel. ⁵The LORD provided a deliverer for Israel, and they escaped from the power of Aram. So the Israelites lived in their own homes as they had before. ⁶But they did not turn away from the sins of the house of Jeroboam, which he had caused Israel to commit; they continued in them. Also, the Asherah pole*d* remained standing in Samaria.

⁷Nothing had been left of the army of Jehoahaz except fifty horsemen, ten chariots and ten thousand foot soldiers, for the king of Aram had destroyed the rest and made them like the dust at threshing time.

⁸As for the other events of the reign of Jehoahaz, all he did and his achievements, are they not written in the book of the annals of the kings of Israel? ⁹Jehoahaz rested with his fathers and was buried in Samaria. And Jehoash*e* his son succeeded him as king.

¹⁰In the thirty-seventh year of Joash king of Judah, Jehoash son of Jehoahaz became king of Israel in Samaria, and he reigned sixteen years.

¹¹He did evil in the eyes of the LORD and did not turn away from any of the sins of Jeroboam son of Nebat, which he had caused Israel to commit; he continued in them.

¹²As for the other events of the reign of Jehoash, all he did and his achievements, including his war against Amaziah king of Judah, are they not written in the book of the annals of the kings of Israel? ¹³Jehoash rested with his fathers, and Jeroboam succeeded him on the throne. Jehoash was buried in Samaria with the kings of Israel.

¹⁴Now Elisha was suffering from the illness from which he died. Jehoash king of Israel went down to see him and wept over him. "My father! My father!" he cried. "The chariots and horsemen of Israel!"

¹⁵Elisha said, "Get a bow and some arrows," and he did so. ¹⁶"Take the bow in your hands," he said to the king of Israel. When he had taken it, Elisha put his hands on the king's hands.

¹⁷"Open the east window," he said, and he opened it. "Shoot!" Elisha said, and he shot. "The LORD's arrow of victory, the arrow of victory over Aram!" Elisha declared. "You will completely destroy the Arameans at Aphek."

¹⁸Then he said, "Take the arrows," and the king took them. Elisha told him, "Strike the ground." He struck it three times and stopped. ¹⁹The man of God was angry with him and said, "You should have struck the ground five or six times; then you would have defeated Aram and completely destroyed it. But now you will defeat it only three times."

---

d6 That is, a symbol of the goddess Asherah; here and elsewhere in 2 Kings   *e9* Hebrew *Joash*, a variant of *Jehoash*; also in verses 12-14 and 25

²⁰Elisha died and was buried.

Now Moabite raiders used to enter the country every spring. ²¹Once while some Israelites were burying a man, suddenly they saw a band of raiders; so they threw the man's body into Elisha's tomb. When the body touched Elisha's bones, the man came to life and stood up on his feet.

²²Hazael king of Aram oppressed Israel throughout the reign of Jehoahaz. ²³But the LORD was gracious to them and had compassion and showed concern for them because of his covenant with Abraham, Isaac and Jacob. To this day he has been unwilling to destroy them or banish them from his presence.

²⁴Hazael king of Aram died, and Ben-Hadad his son succeeded him as king. ²⁵Then Jehoash son of Jehoahaz recaptured from Ben-Hadad son of Hazael the towns he had taken in battle from his father Jehoahaz. Three times Jehoash defeated him, and so he recovered the Israelite towns.

 Discovering the Word 1. Describe the conditions in Israel during the reign of Jehoahaz and Jehoash (vv. 13–10). 2. What do you think King Jehoash meant when he said to Elisha, "My father! My father! . . . The chariots and horsemen of Israel" (v. 14)? 3. Why do you think Elisha had Jehoash act out his message from God (vv. 15–19)? 4. What effect was Elisha's final miracle likely to have on the Israelites who saw it (vv. 20–21)? 5. Why did God bring relief from Hazael's attacks (vv. 22–25)?

 Applying the Word 1. When have you seen evidence of God's mercy in a time of personal loss? 2. How has personal loss increased your trust in God?

Responding in Prayer Pray that God will teach you about himself through the losses you experience.

---

2 Kings 14—15

14 In the second year of Jehoash*ʲ* son of Jehoahaz king of Israel, Amaziah son of Joash king of Judah began to reign. ²He was twenty-five years old when he became king, and he reigned in Jerusalem twenty-nine years. His mother's name was Jehoaddin; she was from Jerusalem. ³He did what was right in the eyes of the LORD, but not as his father David had done. In everything he followed the example of his father Joash. ⁴The high places, however, were not removed; the people continued to offer sacrifices and burn incense there.

⁵After the kingdom was firmly in his grasp, he executed the officials who had murdered his father the king. ⁶Yet he did not put the sons of the assassins to death, in accordance with what is written in the Book of the Law of Moses where the LORD commanded: "Fathers shall not be put to death for their children, nor children put to death for their fathers; each is to die for his own sins."*ᵍ*

⁷He was the one who defeated ten thousand Edomites in the Valley of Salt and captured Sela in battle, calling it Joktheel, the name it has to this day.

⁸Then Amaziah sent messengers to Jehoash son of Jehoahaz, the son of Jehu, king of Israel, with the challenge: "Come, meet me face to face."

⁹But Jehoash king of Israel replied to Amaziah king of Judah: "A thistle in Lebanon sent a message to a cedar in Lebanon, 'Give your daughter to my son in marriage.' Then a wild beast in Lebanon came along and trampled the thistle underfoot. ¹⁰You have indeed defeated Edom and now you are arrogant. Glory in your victory, but stay at home! Why ask for trouble and cause your own downfall and that of Judah also?"

¹¹Amaziah, however, would not listen, so Jehoash king of Israel attacked. He and Amaziah king of Judah faced each other at Beth Shemesh in Judah. ¹²Judah was routed by Israel, and every man fled to his home. ¹³Jehoash king of Israel captured Amaziah king of Judah, the son of Joash, the son of Ahaziah, at Beth Shemesh. Then Jehoash went to Jerusalem and broke down the wall of Jerusalem from the Ephraim Gate to the Corner Gate—a section about six hundred feet long.*ʰ* ¹⁴He took all the gold and silver and all the articles found in the temple of the LORD and in the treasuries of the

ʲ1 Hebrew *Joash,* a variant of *Jehoash;* also in verses 13, 23 and 27
ᵍ6 Deut. 24:16   *ʰ13* Hebrew *four hundred cubits* (about 180 meters)

royal palace. He also took hostages and returned to Samaria.

15As for the other events of the reign of Jehoash, what he did and his achievements, including his war against Amaziah king of Judah, are they not written in the book of the annals of the kings of Israel? 16Jehoash rested with his fathers and was buried in Samaria with the kings of Israel. And Jeroboam his son succeeded him as king.

17Amaziah son of Joash king of Judah lived for fifteen years after the death of Jehoash son of Jehoahaz king of Israel. 18As for the other events of Amaziah's reign, are they not written in the book of the annals of the kings of Judah?

19They conspired against him in Jerusalem, and he fled to Lachish, but they sent men after him to Lachish and killed him there. 20He was brought back by horse and was buried in Jerusalem with his fathers, in the City of David.

21Then all the people of Judah took Azariah,i who was sixteen years old, and made him king in place of his father Amaziah. 22He was the one who rebuilt Elath and restored it to Judah after Amaziah rested with his fathers.

23In the fifteenth year of Amaziah son of Joash king of Judah, Jeroboam son of Jehoash king of Israel became king in Samaria, and he reigned forty-one years. 24He did evil in the eyes of the LORD and did not turn away from any of the sins of Jeroboam son of Nebat, which he had caused Israel to commit. 25He was the one who restored the boundaries of Israel from Leboj Hamath to the Sea of the Arabah,k in accordance with the word of the LORD, the God of Israel, spoken through his servant Jonah son of Amittai, the prophet from Gath Hepher.

26The LORD had seen how bitterly everyone in Israel, whether slave or free, was suffering; there was no one to help them. 27And since the LORD had not said he would blot out the name of Israel from under heaven, he saved them by the hand of Jeroboam son of Jehoash.

28As for the other events of Jeroboam's reign, all he did, and his military achievements, including how he recovered for Israel both Damascus and Hamath, which had belonged to Yaudi,l are they not written in the book of the annals of the kings of Israel? 29Jeroboam rested with his fathers, the kings of Israel. And Zechariah his son succeeded him as king.

15 In the twenty-seventh year of Jeroboam king of Israel, Azariah son of Amaziah king of Judah began to reign. 2He was sixteen years old when he became king, and he reigned in Jerusalem fifty-two years. His mother's name was Jecoliah; she was from Jerusalem. 3He did what was right in the eyes of the LORD, just as his father Amaziah had done. 4The high places, however, were not removed; the people continued to offer sacrifices and burn incense there.

5The LORD afflicted the king with leprosym until the day he died, and he lived in a separate house.n Jotham the king's son had charge of the palace and governed the people of the land.

6As for the other events of Azariah's reign, and all he did, are they not written in the book of the annals of the kings of Judah? 7Azariah rested with his fathers and was buried near them in the City of David. And Jotham his son succeeded him as king.

8In the thirty-eighth year of Azariah king of Judah, Zechariah son of Jeroboam became king of Israel in Samaria, and he reigned six months. 9He did evil in the eyes of the LORD, as his fathers had done. He did not turn away from the sins of Jeroboam son of Nebat, which he had caused Israel to commit.

10Shallum son of Jabesh conspired against Zechariah. He attacked him in front of the people,o assassinated him and succeeded him as king. 11The other events of Zechariah's reign are written in the book of the annals of the kings of Israel. 12So the word of the LORD spoken to Jehu was fulfilled: "Your descendants will sit on the throne of Israel to the fourth generation."p

13Shallum son of Jabesh became king in the thirty-ninth year of Uzziah king of Judah, and he reigned in Samaria one month. 14Then Menahem son of Gadi went from Tirzah up to Samaria. He attacked Shallum son of Jabesh in Samaria, assassinated him and succeeded him as king.

15The other events of Shallum's reign, and the conspiracy he led, are written in the book of the annals of the kings of Israel.

16At that time Menahem, starting out from Tirzah, attacked Tiphsah and everyone in the city and its vicinity, because they refused to open

---

i21 Also called Uzziah   j25 Or from the entrance to   k25 That is, the Dead Sea   l28 Or Judah   m5 The Hebrew word was used for various diseases affecting the skin—not necessarily leprosy.   n5 Or in a house where he was relieved of responsibility   o10 Hebrew; some Septuagint manuscripts in Ibleam   p12 2 Kings 10:30

their gates. He sacked Tiphsah and ripped open all the pregnant women.

17In the thirty-ninth year of Azariah king of Judah, Menahem son of Gadi became king of Israel, and he reigned in Samaria ten years. 18He did evil in the eyes of the Lord. During his entire reign he did not turn away from the sins of Jeroboam son of Nebat, which he had caused Israel to commit.

19Then Pul*q* king of Assyria invaded the land, and Menahem gave him a thousand talents*r* of silver to gain his support and strengthen his own hold on the kingdom. 20Menahem exacted this money from Israel. Every wealthy man had to contribute fifty shekels*s* of silver to be given to the king of Assyria. So the king of Assyria withdrew and stayed in the land no longer.

21As for the other events of Menahem's reign, and all he did, are they not written in the book of the annals of the kings of Israel? 22Menahem rested with his fathers. And Pekahiah his son succeeded him as king.

23In the fiftieth year of Azariah king of Judah, Pekahiah son of Menahem became king of Israel in Samaria, and he reigned two years. 24Pekahiah did evil in the eyes of the Lord. He did not turn away from the sins of Jeroboam son of Nebat, which he had caused Israel to commit. 25One of his chief officers, Pekah son of Remaliah, conspired against him. Taking fifty men of Gilead with him, he assassinated Pekahiah, along with Argob and Arieh, in the citadel of the royal palace at Samaria. So Pekah killed Pekahiah and succeeded him as king.

26The other events of Pekahiah's reign, and all he did, are written in the book of the annals of the kings of Israel.

27In the fifty-second year of Azariah king of

Judah, Pekah son of Remaliah became king of Israel in Samaria, and he reigned twenty years. 28He did evil in the eyes of the Lord. He did not turn away from the sins of Jeroboam son of Nebat, which he had caused Israel to commit.

29In the time of Pekah king of Israel, Tiglath-Pileser king of Assyria came and took Ijon, Abel Beth Maacah, Janoah, Kedesh and Hazor. He took Gilead and Galilee, including all the land of Naphtali, and deported the people to Assyria. 30Then Hoshea son of Elah conspired against Pekah son of Remaliah. He attacked and assassinated him, and then succeeded him as king in the twentieth year of Jotham son of Uzziah.

31As for the other events of Pekah's reign, and all he did, are they not written in the book of the annals of the kings of Israel?

32In the second year of Pekah son of Remaliah king of Israel, Jotham son of Uzziah king of Judah began to reign. 33He was twenty-five years old when he became king, and he reigned in Jerusalem sixteen years. His mother's name was Jerusha daughter of Zadok. 34He did what was right in the eyes of the Lord, just as his father Uzziah had done. 35The high places, however, were not removed; the people continued to offer sacrifices and burn incense there. Jotham rebuilt the Upper Gate of the temple of the Lord.

36As for the other events of Jotham's reign, and what he did, are they not written in the book of the annals of the kings of Judah? 37(In those days the Lord began to send Rezin king of Aram and Pekah son of Remaliah against Judah.) 38Jotham rested with his fathers and was buried with them in the City of David, the city of his father. And Ahaz his son succeeded him as king.

q19 Also called *Tiglath-Pileser*   *r19* That is, about 37 tons (about 34 metric tons)   *s20* That is, about 1 1/4 pounds (about 0.6 kilogram)

---

7 / *2 Kings 16*
Faithless in Trouble

WE HAD TWO girls, but we had planned two more children—boys, we hoped. Already, I had lost one baby in the first trimester. Pregnant again, I prayed my way through those first three months. Shortly into the second trimester I lost the baby. And I was mad! I had done all the right things. I had been especially careful about diet, medicines, activities. I had prayed constantly. But the baby had died inside me anyway. I prayed one angry prayer to God and then stopped praying altogether. For a while. But God is merciful. He gave us two boys (adopted). Later I had to ask, "Why was I so mad? Is God only God for the good times?" My response to trouble was not so different from that of King Ahaz. When the going got tough, Ahaz switched sides.

 Warming Up to God Think of difficult times you have experienced, for example, a fight within your church, the death of someone you have prayed for, unemployment, family or friends going through a divorce. What are some negative ways you have responded to such situations? What are some positive ways you have responded?

Read 2 Kings 16.

16

In the seventeenth year of Pekah son of Remaliah, Ahaz son of Jotham king of Judah began to reign. ²Ahaz was twenty years old when he became king, and he reigned in Jerusalem sixteen years. Unlike David his father, he did not do what was right in the eyes of the LORD his God. ³He walked in the ways of the kings of Israel and even sacrificed his son in[t] the fire, following the detestable ways of the nations the LORD had driven out before the Israelites. ⁴He offered sacrifices and burned incense at the high places, on the hilltops and under every spreading tree.

⁵Then Rezin king of Aram and Pekah son of Remaliah king of Israel marched up to fight against Jerusalem and besieged Ahaz, but they could not overpower him. ⁶At that time, Rezin king of Aram recovered Elath for Aram by driving out the men of Judah. Edomites then moved into Elath and have lived there to this day.

⁷Ahaz sent messengers to say to Tiglath-Pileser king of Assyria, "I am your servant and vassal. Come up and save me out of the hand of the king of Aram and of the king of Israel, who are attacking me." ⁸And Ahaz took the silver and gold found in the temple of the LORD and in the treasuries of the royal palace and sent it as a gift to the king of Assyria. ⁹The king of Assyria complied by attacking Damascus and capturing it. He deported its inhabitants to Kir and put Rezin to death.

¹⁰Then King Ahaz went to Damascus to meet Tiglath-Pileser king of Assyria. He saw an altar in Damascus and sent to Uriah the priest a sketch of the altar, with detailed plans for its construction. ¹¹So Uriah the priest built an altar in accordance with all the plans that King Ahaz had sent from Damascus and finished it before King Ahaz re-

turned. ¹²When the king came back from Damascus and saw the altar, he approached it and presented offerings[u] on it. ¹³He offered up his burnt offering and grain offering, poured out his drink offering, and sprinkled the blood of his fellowship offerings[v] on the altar. ¹⁴The bronze altar that stood before the LORD he brought from the front of the temple—from between the new altar and the temple of the LORD—and put it on the north side of the new altar.

¹⁵King Ahaz then gave these orders to Uriah the priest: "On the large new altar, offer the morning burnt offering and the evening grain offering, the king's burnt offering and his grain offering, and the burnt offering of all the people of the land, and their grain offering and their drink offering. Sprinkle on the altar all the blood of the burnt offerings and sacrifices. But I will use the bronze altar for seeking guidance." ¹⁶And Uriah the priest did just as King Ahaz had ordered.

¹⁷King Ahaz took away the side panels and removed the basins from the movable stands. He removed the Sea from the bronze bulls that supported it and set it on a stone base. ¹⁸He took away the Sabbath canopy[w] that had been built at the temple and removed the royal entryway outside the temple of the LORD, in deference to the king of Assyria.

¹⁹As for the other events of the reign of Ahaz, and what he did, are they not written in the book of the annals of the kings of Judah? ²⁰Ahaz rested with his fathers and was buried with them in the City of David. And Hezekiah his son succeeded him as king.

t3 Or even made his son pass through   u12 Or and went up
v13 Traditionally peace offerings   w18 Or the dais of his throne (see Septuagint)

Discovering the Word 1. In what different ways did Ahaz express his idolatry? 2. What military crisis did Ahaz face (vv. 5–6)? (Use the map in the introduction to picture this.) 3. Why do you think Ahaz appealed to Assyria (vv. 7–9)? 4. What specific changes did Ahaz make in the temple (vv. 8, 10–18)? 5. God gave Moses specific instructions for arrangements in his tabernacle. In view of this, what was Ahaz saying by his actions in the temple?

 Applying the Word 1. In what ways does your response to trouble seem to be a search for other gods and other altars? 2. To what extent does your response to trouble reflect a determined faith in God? 3. Much of our worship can become, like Ahaz's, an attempt to get what we want out of God. When this occurs, we need to ask ourselves, "Who is my god: God or me?" How can you make your worship less self-centered and more God centered?

 Responding in Prayer Focus your prayers on God, reflecting on his character and good works.

---

8 / 2 Kings 17
Idolatry's Reward

WE HAD JUST bought a new house on an acre of land. I could plant fruit trees and a vegetable garden. Our children could run and yell without disturbing neighbors. All six of us could sit down at the kitchen table. Best of all, there were windows everywhere. When my brother visited, he asked matter-of-factly, "Is this house your goal in life?" He meant, "Do you plan to stay here, or are you planning to 'move up'?"

I knew what he meant, but I chose to answer what he actually asked. "No, of course not," I said stoutly. "I don't think any house could be my goal in life." I could answer with confidence because I'm just not a house person, as my grubby kitchen floor and cluttered linen closet will testify. But had Dan chosen another topic (such as work, friends, family, church), I might have had to squirm a little. Idolatry is insidious to us all.

Warming Up to God Take a private inventory of your own temptations by jotting down answers to the following questions:
I couldn't live without _____. When my mind is idle, it automatically turns to _____. If I could have anything in the world, I would choose _____. The most important thing (or person) to me is _____. I know God wants me to _____, but I can't.

Read 2 Kings 17.

17 In the twelfth year of Ahaz king of Judah, Hoshea son of Elah became king of Israel in Samaria, and he reigned nine years. ²He did evil in the eyes of the LORD, but not like the kings of Israel who preceded him.

³Shalmaneser king of Assyria came up to attack Hoshea, who had been Shalmaneser's vassal and had paid him tribute. ⁴But the king of Assyria discovered that Hoshea was a traitor, for he had sent envoys to So^x king of Egypt, and he no longer paid tribute to the king of Assyria, as he had done year by year. Therefore Shalmaneser seized him and put him in prison. ⁵The king of Assyria invaded the entire land, marched against Samaria and laid siege to it for three years. ⁶In the ninth year of Hoshea, the king of Assyria captured Samaria and deported the Israelites to As-syria. He settled them in Halah, in Gozan on the Habor River and in the towns of the Medes.

⁷All this took place because the Israelites had sinned against the LORD their God, who had brought them up out of Egypt from under the power of Pharaoh king of Egypt. They worshiped other gods ⁸and followed the practices of the nations the LORD had driven out before them, as well as the practices that the kings of Israel had introduced. ⁹The Israelites secretly did things against the LORD their God that were not right. From watchtower to fortified city they built themselves high places in all their towns. ¹⁰They set up sacred stones and Asherah poles on every high hill and under every spreading tree. ¹¹At every high place they burned incense, as the nations whom the LORD had driven out before them had done.

$^x4$ Or *to Sais, to the; So* is possibly an abbreviation for *Osorkon*.

They did wicked things that provoked the LORD to anger. ¹²They worshiped idols, though the LORD had said, "You shall not do this."ʸ ¹³The LORD warned Israel and Judah through all his prophets and seers: "Turn from your evil ways. Observe my commands and decrees, in accordance with the entire Law that I commanded your fathers to obey and that I delivered to you through my servants the prophets."

¹⁴But they would not listen and were as stiff-necked as their fathers, who did not trust in the LORD their God. ¹⁵They rejected his decrees and the covenant he had made with their fathers and the warnings he had given them. They followed worthless idols and themselves became worthless. They imitated the nations around them although the LORD had ordered them, "Do not do as they do," and they did the things the LORD had forbidden them to do.

¹⁶They forsook all the commands of the LORD their God and made for themselves two idols cast in the shape of calves, and an Asherah pole. They bowed down to all the starry hosts, and they worshiped Baal. ¹⁷They sacrificed their sons and daughters inᶻ the fire. They practiced divination and sorcery and sold themselves to do evil in the eyes of the LORD, provoking him to anger.

¹⁸So the LORD was very angry with Israel and removed them from his presence. Only the tribe of Judah was left, ¹⁹and even Judah did not keep the commands of the LORD their God. They followed the practices Israel had introduced. ²⁰Therefore the LORD rejected all the people of Israel; he afflicted them and gave them into the hands of plunderers, until he thrust them from his presence.

²¹When he tore Israel away from the house of David, they made Jeroboam son of Nebat their king. Jeroboam enticed Israel away from following the LORD and caused them to commit a great sin. ²²The Israelites persisted in all the sins of Jeroboam and did not turn away from them ²³until the LORD removed them from his presence, as he had warned through all his servants the prophets. So the people of Israel were taken from their homeland into exile in Assyria, and they are still there.

²⁴The king of Assyria brought people from Babylon, Cuthah, Avva, Hamath and Sepharvaim and settled them in the towns of Samaria to replace the Israelites. They took over Samaria and lived in its towns. ²⁵When they first lived there, they did not worship the LORD; so he sent lions among them and they killed some of the people. ²⁶It was reported to the king of Assyria: "The people you deported and resettled in the towns of Samaria do not know what the god of that country requires. He has sent lions among them, which are killing them off, because the people do not know what he requires."

²⁷Then the king of Assyria gave this order: "Have one of the priests you took captive from Samaria go back to live there and teach the people what the god of the land requires." ²⁸So one of the priests who had been exiled from Samaria came to live in Bethel and taught them how to worship the LORD.

²⁹Nevertheless, each national group made its own gods in the several towns where they settled, and set them up in the shrines the people of Samaria had made at the high places. ³⁰The men from Babylon made Succoth Benoth, the men from Cuthah made Nergal, and the men from Hamath made Ashima; ³¹the Avvites made Nibhaz and Tartak, and the Sepharvites burned their children in the fire as sacrifices to Adrammelech and Anammelech, the gods of Sepharvaim. ³²They worshiped the LORD, but they also appointed all sorts of their own people to officiate for them as priests in the shrines at the high places. ³³They worshiped the LORD, but they also served their own gods in accordance with the customs of the nations from which they had been brought.

³⁴To this day they persist in their former practices. They neither worship the LORD nor adhere to the decrees and ordinances, the laws and commands that the LORD gave the descendants of Jacob, whom he named Israel. ³⁵When the LORD made a covenant with the Israelites, he commanded them: "Do not worship any other gods or bow down to them, serve them or sacrifice to them. ³⁶But the LORD, who brought you up out of Egypt with mighty power and outstretched arm, is the one you must worship. To him you shall bow down and to him offer sacrifices. ³⁷You must always be careful to keep the decrees and ordinances, the laws and commands he wrote for you. Do not worship other gods. ³⁸Do not forget the covenant I have made with you, and do not worship other gods. ³⁹Rather, worship the LORD your God; it is he who will deliver you from the hand of all your enemies."

ʸ12 Exodus 20:4, 5   ᶻ17 Or *They made their sons and daughters pass through*

⁴⁰They would not listen, however, but persisted in their former practices. ⁴¹Even while these people were worshiping the LORD, they were serving their idols. To this day their children and grandchildren continue to do as their fathers did.

Discovering the Word 1. Notice the people and places in verses 1–6. How do these verses outline the final steps to Israel's death as a nation? 2. Review the list of sins (there are about twenty) in verses 7–22. What common characteristics do you find? 3. The writer of 2 Kings says repeatedly of Israel, "The LORD removed them from his presence." Consider the events of this chapter. What did it mean to Israel in practical terms to be removed from the presence of God (vv. 18, 20 and 23)? 4. Do you think that it is possible for people or nations today to be removed from the presence of God? Explain. 5. Why did the new Samaritans find it hard to serve one God alone (vv. 24–33)?

Applying the Word 1. Looking back to your inventory of temptations, in what areas of your life do you need to be alert to the temptation of idolatry? 2. What steps can you take to keep normal healthy interests in the world around you from turning into idolatry?

Responding in Prayer Confess your areas of weakness to the Lord. Ask him to protect you from idolatry.

---

2 Kings 18:1–16

18 In the third year of Hoshea son of Elah king of Israel, Hezekiah son of Ahaz king of Judah began to reign. ²He was twenty-five years old when he became king, and he reigned in Jerusalem twenty-nine years. His mother's name was Abijah*ᵃ* daughter of Zechariah. ³He did what was right in the eyes of the LORD, just as his father David had done. ⁴He removed the high places, smashed the sacred stones and cut down the Asherah poles. He broke into pieces the bronze snake Moses had made, for up to that time the Israelites had been burning incense to it. (It was called*ᵇ* Nehushtan.*ᶜ*)

⁵Hezekiah trusted in the LORD, the God of Israel. There was no one like him among all the kings of Judah, either before him or after him. ⁶He held fast to the LORD and did not cease to follow him; he kept the commands the LORD had given Moses. ⁷And the LORD was with him; he was successful in whatever he undertook. He rebelled against the king of Assyria and did not serve him. ⁸From watchtower to fortified city, he defeated the Philistines, as far as Gaza and its territory.

⁹In King Hezekiah's fourth year, which was the seventh year of Hoshea son of Elah king of Israel, Shalmaneser king of Assyria marched against Samaria and laid siege to it. ¹⁰At the end of three years the Assyrians took it. So Samaria was captured in Hezekiah's sixth year, which was the ninth year of Hoshea king of Israel. ¹¹The king of Assyria deported Israel to Assyria and settled them in Halah, in Gozan on the Habor River and in towns of the Medes. ¹²This happened because they had not obeyed the LORD their God, but had violated his covenant—all that Moses the servant of the LORD commanded. They neither listened to the commands nor carried them out.

¹³In the fourteenth year of King Hezekiah's reign, Sennacherib king of Assyria attacked all the fortified cities of Judah and captured them. ¹⁴So Hezekiah king of Judah sent this message to the king of Assyria at Lachish: "I have done wrong. Withdraw from me, and I will pay whatever you demand of me." The king of Assyria exacted from Hezekiah king of Judah three hundred talents*ᵈ* of silver and thirty talents*ᵉ* of gold. ¹⁵So Hezekiah gave him all the silver that was found in the temple of the LORD and in the treasuries of the royal palace.

¹⁶At this time Hezekiah king of Judah stripped off the gold with which he had covered the doors and doorposts of the temple of the LORD, and gave it to the king of Assyria.

ᵃ2 Hebrew *Abi,* a variant of *Abijah*   *ᵇ4* Or *He called it*
ᶜ4 Nehushtan sounds like the Hebrew for *bronze* and *snake* and *unclean thing.*   *ᵈ14* That is, about 11 tons (about 10 metric tons)
ᵉ14 That is, about 1 ton (about 1 metric ton)

9 / *2 Kings 18:17–37*
Identity

OUR SOCIETY IS locked in a longstanding identity crisis. From the troubled teen years beset with self-image problems to the midlife crisis and beyond, many of those around us do not know who they are. After the Sunday message many Christians walk out into the world only to sink back into the quagmire of their own identity crisis. We shouldn't be surprised that so many of us wrestle with this problem. God's Word makes it clear that his people live in a halfway house between heaven and hell, adherents to God's truth within a world of lies. The following passage from 2 Kings gives one such example. Besieging Jerusalem with a powerful army, the Assyrian king, Sennacherib, issues not only a threat to King Hezekiah and the kingdom of Judah but also a direct challenge to the entire identity of God's people.

 Warming Up to God   Every day we are challenged by our society. Sometimes our culture intimidates us and attempts to erode confidence in our identity as God's people. In what ways do you struggle with this?

 Read 2 Kings 18:17–37.

---

[17]The king of Assyria sent his supreme commander, his chief officer and his field commander with a large army, from Lachish to King Hezekiah at Jerusalem. They came up to Jerusalem and stopped at the aqueduct of the Upper Pool, on the road to the Washerman's Field. [18]They called for the king; and Eliakim son of Hilkiah the palace administrator, Shebna the secretary, and Joah son of Asaph the recorder went out to them.

[19]The field commander said to them, "Tell Hezekiah:

" 'This is what the great king, the king of Assyria, says: On what are you basing this confidence of yours? [20]You say you have strategy and military strength—but you speak only empty words. On whom are you depending, that you rebel against me? [21]Look now, you are depending on Egypt, that splintered reed of a staff, which pierces a man's hand and wounds him if he leans on it! Such is Pharaoh king of Egypt to all who depend on him. [22]And if you say to me, "We are depending on the LORD our God"—isn't he the one whose high places and altars Hezekiah removed, saying to Judah and Jerusalem, "You must worship before this altar in Jerusalem"?

[23]" 'Come now, make a bargain with my master, the king of Assyria: I will give you two thousand horses—if you can put riders on them! [24]How can you repulse one officer of the least of my master's officials, even though you are depending on Egypt for chariots and horsemen*f*? [25]Furthermore, have I

come to attack and destroy this place without word from the LORD? The LORD himself told me to march against this country and destroy it.' "

[26]Then Eliakim son of Hilkiah, and Shebna and Joah said to the field commander, "Please speak to your servants in Aramaic, since we understand it. Don't speak to us in Hebrew in the hearing of the people on the wall."

[27]But the commander replied, "Was it only to your master and you that my master sent me to say these things, and not to the men sitting on the wall—who, like you, will have to eat their own filth and drink their own urine?"

[28]Then the commander stood and called out in Hebrew: "Hear the word of the great king, the king of Assyria! [29]This is what the king says: Do not let Hezekiah deceive you. He cannot deliver you from my hand. [30]Do not let Hezekiah persuade you to trust in the LORD when he says, 'The LORD will surely deliver us; this city will not be given into the hand of the king of Assyria.'

[31]"Do not listen to Hezekiah. This is what the king of Assyria says: Make peace with me and come out to me. Then every one of you will eat from his own vine and fig tree and drink water from his own cistern, [32]until I come and take you to a land like your own, a land of grain and new wine, a land of bread and vineyards, a land of olive trees and honey. Choose life and not death!

"Do not listen to Hezekiah, for he is misleading you when he says, 'The LORD will deliver us.'

f24 Or charioteers

³³Has the god of any nation ever delivered his land from the hand of the king of Assyria? ³⁴Where are the gods of Hamath and Arpad? Where are the gods of Sepharvaim, Hena and Ivvah? Have they rescued Samaria from my hand? ³⁵Who of all the gods of these countries has been able to save his land from me? How then can the LORD deliver Jerusalem from my hand?"

³⁶But the people remained silent and said nothing in reply, because the king had commanded, "Do not answer him."

³⁷Then Eliakim son of Hilkiah the palace administrator, Shebna the secretary and Joah son of Asaph the recorder went to Hezekiah, with their clothes torn, and told him what the field commander had said.

 Discovering the Word 1. Speaking through the field commander, Sennacherib, the king of Assyria, addresses Hezekiah and his assistants. What kinds of questions does Sennacherib raise in verses 19–20? 2. How does Sennacherib try to shake Judah's confidence in verses 21–24? 3. Compare Hezekiah's exhortation (v. 30) with the offer of the king of Assyria (vv. 31–33). What are the relative benefits of these two appeals? 4. In what sense does the king of Assyria attempt to undermine their identity as God's chosen people (vv. 33–35)?

 Applying the Word 1. What tactics does our culture use to cause us to question our identity as God's people? 2. In what aspect of your identity do you feel particularly vulnerable to attack? 3. What would it mean for you to "trust in the LORD" (v. 30) in responding to this threat?

 Responding in Prayer Ask God to teach you what trust means for you today.

---

10 / *2 Kings 19*
Asking for Help

"I AM AN island." This unbiblical thought is steeped in Western culture. However, if we are to stand against the world, we must stand together. And we can start by asking God for help as Hezekiah does.

Warming Up to God How do you tend to feel and respond when your faith or confidence in God is tested?

Read 2 Kings 19.

---

19 When King Hezekiah heard this, he tore his clothes and put on sackcloth and went into the temple of the LORD. ²He sent Eliakim the palace administrator, Shebna the secretary and the leading priests, all wearing sackcloth, to the prophet Isaiah son of Amoz. ³They told him, "This is what Hezekiah says: This day is a day of distress and rebuke and disgrace, as when children come to the point of birth and there is no strength to deliver them. ⁴It may be that the LORD your God will hear all the words of the field commander, whom his master, the king of Assyria, has sent to ridicule the living God, and that he will rebuke him for the words the LORD your God has heard. Therefore pray for the remnant that still survives."

⁵When King Hezekiah's officials came to Isaiah, ⁶Isaiah said to them, "Tell your master, 'This is what the LORD says: Do not be afraid of what you have heard—those words with which the underlings of the king of Assyria have blasphemed me. ⁷Listen! I am going to put such a spirit in him that when he hears a certain report, he will return to his own country, and there I will have him cut down with the sword.' "

⁸When the field commander heard that the king of Assyria had left Lachish, he withdrew and found the king fighting against Libnah.

⁹Now Sennacherib received a report that Tirhakah, the Cushite^g king ⌊of Egypt⌋, was marching out to fight against him. So he again sent messen-

8,9 That is, from the upper Nile region

gers to Hezekiah with this word: ^{10}"Say to Hezekiah king of Judah: Do not let the god you depend on deceive you when he says, 'Jerusalem will not be handed over to the king of Assyria.' ^{11}Surely you have heard what the kings of Assyria have done to all the countries, destroying them completely. And will you be delivered? ^{12}Did the gods of the nations that were destroyed by my forefathers deliver them: the gods of Gozan, Haran, Rezeph and the people of Eden who were in Tel Assar? ^{13}Where is the king of Hamath, the king of Arpad, the king of the city of Sepharvaim, or of Hena or Ivvah?"

^{14}Hezekiah received the letter from the messengers and read it. Then he went up to the temple of the LORD and spread it out before the LORD. ^{15}And Hezekiah prayed to the LORD: "O LORD, God of Israel, enthroned between the cherubim, you alone are God over all the kingdoms of the earth. You have made heaven and earth. ^{16}Give ear, O LORD, and hear; open your eyes, O LORD, and see; listen to the words Sennacherib has sent to insult the living God.

^{17}"It is true, O LORD, that the Assyrian kings have laid waste these nations and their lands. ^{18}They have thrown their gods into the fire and destroyed them, for they were not gods but only wood and stone, fashioned by men's hands. ^{19}Now, O LORD our God, deliver us from his hand, so that all kingdoms on earth may know that you alone, O LORD, are God."

^{20}Then Isaiah son of Amoz sent a message to Hezekiah: "This is what the LORD, the God of Israel, says: I have heard your prayer concerning Sennacherib king of Assyria. ^{21}This is the word that the LORD has spoken against him:

" 'The Virgin Daughter of Zion
    despises you and mocks you.
The Daughter of Jerusalem
    tosses her head as you flee.
^{22}Who is it you have insulted and blasphemed?
    Against whom have you raised your voice
and lifted your eyes in pride?
    Against the Holy One of Israel!
^{23}By your messengers
    you have heaped insults on the Lord.
And you have said,
    "With my many chariots
I have ascended the heights of the mountains,
    the utmost heights of Lebanon.
I have cut down its tallest cedars,

the choicest of its pines.
I have reached its remotest parts,
    the finest of its forests.
^{24}I have dug wells in foreign lands
    and drunk the water there.
With the soles of my feet
    I have dried up all the streams of Egypt."

^{25}" 'Have you not heard?
    Long ago I ordained it.
In days of old I planned it;
    now I have brought it to pass,
that you have turned fortified cities
    into piles of stone.
^{26}Their people, drained of power,
    are dismayed and put to shame.
They are like plants in the field,
    like tender green shoots,
like grass sprouting on the roof,
    scorched before it grows up.

^{27}" 'But I know where you stay
    and when you come and go
    and how you rage against me.
^{28}Because you rage against me
    and your insolence has reached my ears,
I will put my hook in your nose
    and my bit in your mouth,
and I will make you return
    by the way you came.'

^{29}"This will be the sign for you, O Hezekiah:

"This year you will eat what grows by itself,
    and the second year what springs from that.
But in the third year sow and reap,
    plant vineyards and eat their fruit.
^{30}Once more a remnant of the house of Judah
    will take root below and bear fruit above.
^{31}For out of Jerusalem will come a remnant,
    and out of Mount Zion a band of survivors.

The zeal of the LORD Almighty will accomplish this.

^{32}"Therefore this is what the LORD says concerning the king of Assyria:

"He will not enter this city
    or shoot an arrow here.
He will not come before it with shield
    or build a siege ramp against it.
^{33}By the way that he came he will return;
    he will not enter this city,
                    declares the LORD.

³⁴I will defend this city and save it,
    for my sake and for the sake of David my
      servant."

³⁵That night the angel of the Lord went out and put to death a hundred and eighty-five thousand men in the Assyrian camp. When the people got up the next morning—there were all the dead bodies! ³⁶So Sennacherib king of Assyria broke camp and withdrew. He returned to Nineveh and stayed there.

³⁷One day, while he was worshiping in the temple of his god Nisroch, his sons Adrammelech and Sharezer cut him down with the sword, and they escaped to the land of Ararat. And Esarhaddon his son succeeded him as king.

Discovering the Word **1.** Describe Hezekiah's attitude and actions in response to the ominous words of the king (vv. 1–4). **2.** Compare Sennacherib's view of God and the Assyrian army (vv. 9–13) with the picture presented in Isaiah's prophecy (vv. 6–7). How do they differ? **3.** Confronted with his own crisis, Hezekiah brings his dilemma before the Lord. Reread verses 3–4 and Hezekiah's prayer in verses 15–19. How has Hezekiah's perception changed? **4.** Review Sennacherib's boasts in verses 10–13. How does Hezekiah now evaluate Sennacherib's claims (vv. 17–18)? **5.** What assurances does Isaiah offer in his prophecy (vv. 20–34)?

Applying the Word **1.** What can we learn from Hezekiah's example about confronting the lies the world feeds us? **2.** How would a reaffirmation of God's character be of help when we face overt or subtle attacks on our identity as Christians?

Responding in Prayer Ask God for the help you need in the difficult situations you are facing.

---

11 / *2 Kings 20:1—21:18*
One Giant Step Backward

MY FRIENDS BOB and Dottie and their children are missionaries to a primitive tribe of Indians in South America. After some initial awkwardness, they were well received. They donned the long white tunics of the tribal people, carried their woven handbags and wore tiny beaded necklaces. They ate native food. The Indians helped Bob and Dottie learn the language. God seemed ready to use them to help bring these people into his kingdom. Then drug traffic swept the area. Speculators bought the land or simply massacred Indians reluctant to sell. Twentieth-century viruses decimated the tribe. Only two-thirds of the Indians remained alive. And some who were left looked at my friends with hostile eyes. Can we still trust God when all the trends point counter to what we know of his purposes? One of the advantages of studying the Old Testament is seeing, in a few pages, God moving through hundreds of years of history. It may help us trust God's unseen purposes for our own small page.

Warming Up to God When in your life has it been hard to understand God's purposes?

Read 2 Kings 20:1—21:18.

---

20 In those days Hezekiah became ill and was at the point of death. The prophet Isaiah son of Amoz went to him and said, "This is what the Lord says: Put your house in order, because you are going to die; you will not recover."

²Hezekiah turned his face to the wall and prayed to the Lord, ³"Remember, O Lord, how I

have walked before you faithfully and with wholehearted devotion and have done what is good in your eyes." And Hezekiah wept bitterly.

⁴Before Isaiah had left the middle court, the word of the Lord came to him: ⁵"Go back and tell Hezekiah, the leader of my people, 'This is what the Lord, the God of your father David, says: I

have heard your prayer and seen your tears; I will heal you. On the third day from now you will go up to the temple of the LORD. ⁶I will add fifteen years to your life. And I will deliver you and this city from the hand of the king of Assyria. I will defend this city for my sake and for the sake of my servant David.' "

⁷Then Isaiah said, "Prepare a poultice of figs." They did so and applied it to the boil, and he recovered.

⁸Hezekiah had asked Isaiah, "What will be the sign that the LORD will heal me and that I will go up to the temple of the LORD on the third day from now?"

⁹Isaiah answered, "This is the LORD's sign to you that the LORD will do what he has promised: Shall the shadow go forward ten steps, or shall it go back ten steps?"

¹⁰"It is a simple matter for the shadow to go forward ten steps," said Hezekiah. "Rather, have it go back ten steps."

¹¹Then the prophet Isaiah called upon the LORD, and the LORD made the shadow go back the ten steps it had gone down on the stairway of Ahaz.

¹²At that time Merodach-Baladan son of Baladan king of Babylon sent Hezekiah letters and a gift, because he had heard of Hezekiah's illness. ¹³Hezekiah received the messengers and showed them all that was in his storehouses—the silver, the gold, the spices and the fine oil—his armory and everything found among his treasures. There was nothing in his palace or in all his kingdom that Hezekiah did not show them.

¹⁴Then Isaiah the prophet went to King Hezekiah and asked, "What did those men say, and where did they come from?"

"From a distant land," Hezekiah replied. "They came from Babylon."

¹⁵The prophet asked, "What did they see in your palace?"

"They saw everything in my palace," Hezekiah said. "There is nothing among my treasures that I did not show them."

¹⁶Then Isaiah said to Hezekiah, "Hear the word of the LORD: ¹⁷The time will surely come when everything in your palace, and all that your fathers have stored up until this day, will be carried off to Babylon. Nothing will be left, says the LORD. ¹⁸And some of your descendants, your own flesh and blood, that will be born to you, will be taken away, and they will become eunuchs in the palace of the king of Babylon."

¹⁹"The word of the LORD you have spoken is good," Hezekiah replied. For he thought, "Will there not be peace and security in my lifetime?"

²⁰As for the other events of Hezekiah's reign, all his achievements and how he made the pool and the tunnel by which he brought water into the city, are they not written in the book of the annals of the kings of Judah? ²¹Hezekiah rested with his fathers. And Manasseh his son succeeded him as king.

21

Manasseh was twelve years old when he became king, and he reigned in Jerusalem fifty-five years. His mother's name was Hephzibah. ²He did evil in the eyes of the LORD, following the detestable practices of the nations the LORD had driven out before the Israelites. ³He rebuilt the high places his father Hezekiah had destroyed; he also erected altars to Baal and made an Asherah pole, as Ahab king of Israel had done. He bowed down to all the starry hosts and worshiped them. ⁴He built altars in the temple of the LORD, of which the LORD had said, "In Jerusalem I will put my Name." ⁵In both courts of the temple of the LORD, he built altars to all the starry hosts. ⁶He sacrificed his own son in^h the fire, practiced sorcery and divination, and consulted mediums and spiritists. He did much evil in the eyes of the LORD, provoking him to anger.

⁷He took the carved Asherah pole he had made and put it in the temple, of which the LORD had said to David and to his son Solomon, "In this temple and in Jerusalem, which I have chosen out of all the tribes of Israel, I will put my Name forever. ⁸I will not again make the feet of the Israelites wander from the land I gave their forefathers, if only they will be careful to do everything I commanded them and will keep the whole Law that my servant Moses gave them." ⁹But the people did not listen. Manasseh led them astray, so that they did more evil than the nations the LORD had destroyed before the Israelites.

¹⁰The LORD said through his servants the prophets: ¹¹"Manasseh king of Judah has committed these detestable sins. He has done more evil

^h6 Or *He made his own son pass through*

than the Amorites who preceded him and has led Judah into sin with his idols. ¹²Therefore this is what the LORD, the God of Israel, says: I am going to bring such disaster on Jerusalem and Judah that the ears of everyone who hears of it will tingle. ¹³I will stretch out over Jerusalem the measuring line used against Samaria and the plumb line used against the house of Ahab. I will wipe out Jerusalem as one wipes a dish, wiping it and turning it upside down. ¹⁴I will forsake the remnant of my inheritance and hand them over to their enemies. They will be looted and plundered by all their foes, ¹⁵because they have done evil in my eyes and have provoked me to anger from the day their forefathers came out of Egypt until this day."

¹⁶Moreover, Manasseh also shed so much innocent blood that he filled Jerusalem from end to end—besides the sin that he had caused Judah to commit, so that they did evil in the eyes of the LORD.

¹⁷As for the other events of Manasseh's reign, and all he did, including the sin he committed, are they not written in the book of the annals of the kings of Judah? ¹⁸Manasseh rested with his fathers and was buried in his palace garden, the garden of Uzza. And Amon his son succeeded him as king.

Discovering the Word 1. What do the details in the communication between God and Hezekiah reveal about their relationship (20:1–11)? 2. Why do you think Hezekiah treated the messengers from Babylon the way he did (20:15)? 3. What explanation can you offer for Hezekiah's response to Isaiah's prophecy (20:16–19)? 4. When you try to imagine life in Judah under Manasseh's reign, what pictures come to your mind? 5. Find as many references to the people of Judah as you can in 21:7–15. How do these help explain why Manasseh was able to make such a total reversal of his father's reforms? 6. Look back at Hezekiah's situation in 20:1–11. If Hezekiah could have known the future, including the birth of his son, do you think he would have wanted God to add fifteen years to his life? Why or why not?

Applying the Word 1. What do you know about God that helps you to stand against popular trends that go against what you know is right? 2. How can you serve God in your response to these trends?

Responding in Prayer Ask God to teach you how to trust in him even during times when the world only seems to be getting worse.

---

2 Kings 21:19–26

¹⁹Amon was twenty-two years old when he became king, and he reigned in Jerusalem two years. His mother's name was Meshullemeth daughter of Haruz; she was from Jotbah. ²⁰He did evil in the eyes of the LORD, as his father Manasseh had done. ²¹He walked in all the ways of his father; he worshiped the idols his father had worshiped, and bowed down to them. ²²He forsook the LORD, the God of his fathers, and did not walk in the way of the LORD.

²³Amon's officials conspired against him and assassinated the king in his palace. ²⁴Then the people of the land killed all who had plotted against King Amon, and they made Josiah his son king in his place.

²⁵As for the other events of Amon's reign, and what he did, are they not written in the book of the annals of the kings of Judah? ²⁶He was buried in his grave in the garden of Uzza. And Josiah his son succeeded him as king.

12 / *2 Kings 22:1—23:35*
Following God's Law

SENIORS IN HIGH school typically get a little huffy about restrictive school rules such as hall passes and washroom permits. Sometimes even teachers are not immune to similar feelings. When my daughter's music teacher, accustomed to working with diligent honors students, was confronted with the request for one more hall pass for an in-building errand, he wrote, "Sheri has my permission to be in the hall so that she can check the drug supply in her locker. Antonia is her bodyguard." (They weren't stopped.) There's something inside us that grates against laws—of any kind—unless, of course, we've had to live a long time without them. Judah had such an experience.

 Warming Up to God Much of today's culture ignores God's laws. What pressures do you feel to follow the culture rather than the law of God?

 Read 2 Kings 22:1—23:35.

22 Josiah was eight years old when he became king, and he reigned in Jerusalem thirty-one years. His mother's name was Jedidah daughter of Adaiah; she was from Bozkath. ²He did what was right in the eyes of the LORD and walked in all the ways of his father David, not turning aside to the right or to the left.

³In the eighteenth year of his reign, King Josiah sent the secretary, Shaphan son of Azaliah, the son of Meshullam, to the temple of the LORD. He said: ⁴"Go up to Hilkiah the high priest and have him get ready the money that has been brought into the temple of the LORD, which the doorkeepers have collected from the people. ⁵Have them entrust it to the men appointed to supervise the work on the temple. And have these men pay the workers who repair the temple of the LORD— ⁶the carpenters, the builders and the masons. Also have them purchase timber and dressed stone to repair the temple. ⁷But they need not account for the money entrusted to them, because they are acting faithfully."

⁸Hilkiah the high priest said to Shaphan the secretary, "I have found the Book of the Law in the temple of the LORD." He gave it to Shaphan, who read it. ⁹Then Shaphan the secretary went to the king and reported to him: "Your officials have paid out the money that was in the temple of the LORD and have entrusted it to the workers and supervisors at the temple." ¹⁰Then Shaphan the secretary informed the king, "Hilkiah the priest has given me a book." And Shaphan read from it in the presence of the king.

¹¹When the king heard the words of the Book of the Law, he tore his robes. ¹²He gave these orders to Hilkiah the priest, Ahikam son of Shaphan, Acbor son of Micaiah, Shaphan the secretary and Asaiah the king's attendant: ¹³"Go and inquire of the LORD for me and for the people and for all Judah about what is written in this book that has been found. Great is the LORD's anger that burns against us because our fathers have not obeyed the words of this book; they have not acted in accordance with all that is written there concerning us."

¹⁴Hilkiah the priest, Ahikam, Acbor, Shaphan and Asaiah went to speak to the prophetess Huldah, who was the wife of Shallum son of Tikvah, the son of Harhas, keeper of the wardrobe. She lived in Jerusalem, in the Second District.

¹⁵She said to them, "This is what the LORD, the God of Israel, says: Tell the man who sent you to me, ¹⁶'This is what the LORD says: I am going to bring disaster on this place and its people, according to everything written in the book the king of Judah has read. ¹⁷Because they have forsaken me and burned incense to other gods and provoked me to anger by all the idols their hands have made,ⁱ my anger will burn against this place and will not be quenched.' ¹⁸Tell the king of Judah, who sent you to inquire of the LORD, 'This is what the LORD, the God of Israel, says concerning the words you heard: ¹⁹Because your heart was responsive and you humbled yourself before the LORD when you heard what I have spoken against this place and its people, that they would become accursed and laid waste, and because you tore your robes and wept in my presence, I have heard you, declares the LORD. ²⁰Therefore I will gather you to your fathers, and you will be buried

ⁱ17 Or *by everything they have done*

in peace. Your eyes will not see all the disaster I am going to bring on this place.' "

So they took her answer back to the king.

23

Then the king called together all the elders of Judah and Jerusalem. [2]He went up to the temple of the LORD with the men of Judah, the people of Jerusalem, the priests and the prophets—all the people from the least to the greatest. He read in their hearing all the words of the Book of the Covenant, which had been found in the temple of the LORD. [3]The king stood by the pillar and renewed the covenant in the presence of the LORD—to follow the LORD and keep his commands, regulations and decrees with all his heart and all his soul, thus confirming the words of the covenant written in this book. Then all the people pledged themselves to the covenant.

[4]The king ordered Hilkiah the high priest, the priests next in rank and the doorkeepers to remove from the temple of the LORD all the articles made for Baal and Asherah and all the starry hosts. He burned them outside Jerusalem in the fields of the Kidron Valley and took the ashes to Bethel. [5]He did away with the pagan priests appointed by the kings of Judah to burn incense on the high places of the towns of Judah and on those around Jerusalem—those who burned incense to Baal, to the sun and moon, to the constellations and to all the starry hosts. [6]He took the Asherah pole from the temple of the LORD to the Kidron Valley outside Jerusalem and burned it there. He ground it to powder and scattered the dust over the graves of the common people. [7]He also tore down the quarters of the male shrine prostitutes, which were in the temple of the LORD and where women did weaving for Asherah.

[8]Josiah brought all the priests from the towns of Judah and desecrated the high places, from Geba to Beersheba, where the priests had burned incense. He broke down the shrines[j] at the gates—at the entrance to the Gate of Joshua, the city governor, which is on the left of the city gate. [9]Although the priests of the high places did not serve at the altar of the LORD in Jerusalem, they ate unleavened bread with their fellow priests.

[10]He desecrated Topheth, which was in the Valley of Ben Hinnom, so no one could use it to sacrifice his son or daughter in[k] the fire to Molech. [11]He removed from the entrance to the temple of the LORD the horses that the kings of Judah had dedicated to the sun. They were in the court

near the room of an official named Nathan-Melech. Josiah then burned the chariots dedicated to the sun.

[12]He pulled down the altars the kings of Judah had erected on the roof near the upper room of Ahaz, and the altars Manasseh had built in the two courts of the temple of the LORD. He removed them from there, smashed them to pieces and threw the rubble into the Kidron Valley. [13]The king also desecrated the high places that were east of Jerusalem on the south of the Hill of Corruption—the ones Solomon king of Israel had built for Ashtoreth the vile goddess of the Sidonians, for Chemosh the vile god of Moab, and for Molech[l] the detestable god of the people of Ammon. [14]Josiah smashed the sacred stones and cut down the Asherah poles and covered the sites with human bones.

[15]Even the altar at Bethel, the high place made by Jeroboam son of Nebat, who had caused Israel to sin—even that altar and high place he demolished. He burned the high place and ground it to powder, and burned the Asherah pole also. [16]Then Josiah looked around, and when he saw the tombs that were there on the hillside, he had the bones removed from them and burned on the altar to defile it, in accordance with the word of the LORD proclaimed by the man of God who foretold these things.

[17]The king asked, "What is that tombstone I see?"

The men of the city said, "It marks the tomb of the man of God who came from Judah and pronounced against the altar of Bethel the very things you have done to it."

[18]"Leave it alone," he said. "Don't let anyone disturb his bones." So they spared his bones and those of the prophet who had come from Samaria.

[19]Just as he had done at Bethel, Josiah removed and defiled all the shrines at the high places that the kings of Israel had built in the towns of Samaria that had provoked the LORD to anger. [20]Josiah slaughtered all the priests of those high places on the altars and burned human bones on them. Then he went back to Jerusalem.

[21]The king gave this order to all the people: "Celebrate the Passover to the LORD your God, as it is written in this Book of the Covenant." [22]Not since the days of the judges who led Israel, nor throughout the days of the kings of Israel and the

_____

j8 Or high places   k10 Or to make his son or daughter pass through
l13 Hebrew Milcom

kings of Judah, had any such Passover been observed. ²³But in the eighteenth year of King Josiah, this Passover was celebrated to the LORD in Jerusalem.

²⁴Furthermore, Josiah got rid of the mediums and spiritists, the household gods, the idols and all the other detestable things seen in Judah and Jerusalem. This he did to fulfill the requirements of the law written in the book that Hilkiah the priest had discovered in the temple of the LORD. ²⁵Neither before nor after Josiah was there a king like him who turned to the LORD as he did—with all his heart and with all his soul and with all his strength, in accordance with all the Law of Moses.

²⁶Nevertheless, the LORD did not turn away from the heat of his fierce anger, which burned against Judah because of all that Manasseh had done to provoke him to anger. ²⁷So the LORD said, "I will remove Judah also from my presence as I removed Israel, and I will reject Jerusalem, the city I chose, and this temple, about which I said, 'There shall my Name be.'ᵐ"

²⁸As for the other events of Josiah's reign, and all he did, are they not written in the book of the annals of the kings of Judah?

²⁹While Josiah was king, Pharaoh Neco king of Egypt went up to the Euphrates River to help the king of Assyria. King Josiah marched out to meet him in battle, but Neco faced him and killed him at Megiddo. ³⁰Josiah's servants brought his body in a chariot from Megiddo to Jerusalem and buried him in his own tomb. And the people of the land took Jehoahaz son of Josiah and anointed him and made him king in place of his father.

³¹Jehoahaz was twenty-three years old when he became king, and he reigned in Jerusalem three months. His mother's name was Hamutal daughter of Jeremiah; she was from Libnah. ³²He did evil in the eyes of the LORD, just as his fathers had done. ³³Pharaoh Neco put him in chains at Riblah in the land of Hamathⁿ so that he might not reign in Jerusalem, and he imposed on Judah a levy of a hundred talentsᵒ of silver and a talentᵖ of gold. ³⁴Pharaoh Neco made Eliakim son of Josiah king in place of his father Josiah and changed Eliakim's name to Jehoiakim. But he took Jehoahaz and carried him off to Egypt, and there he died. ³⁵Jehoiakim paid Pharaoh Neco the silver and gold he demanded. In order to do so, he taxed the land and exacted the silver and gold from the people of the land according to their assessments.

ᵐ27 1 Kings 8:29   ⁿ33 Hebrew; Septuagint (see also 2 Chron. 36:3) *Neco at Riblah in Hamath removed him*   ᵒ33 That is, about 3 3/4 tons (about 3.4 metric tons)   ᵖ33 That is, about 75 pounds (about 34 kilograms)

 Discovering the Word 1. What steps led to finding the Book of the Law (22:1–8)? 2. What can you know about Huldah from verses 14–20? 3. What effect would you expect the scene in 23:1–3 to have on the people? 4. From 23:2–24 list some sixteen religious reforms that Josiah instituted. As you read through these reforms, what do you learn about the spiritual practices of the people before Josiah became king? 5. How does the description of Josiah in 23:25 contrast with the description of Jehoahaz in 23:31–34?

Applying the Word 1. What relationship do you see between our response to God's law and our concept of God? 2. Study more carefully the words in 2 Kings 23:25 describing Josiah's commitment to God and to God's law. What aspect of that description would you like to make more a part of your own commitment? 3. God's law is tied to his character. As you think of your own natural resistance to law, what steps could you take to bring your response to God's law into line with what you believe to be true of God?

Responding in Prayer Make 2 Kings 23:25 your prayer that you would turn to the Lord with all your heart, soul and strength.

13 / *2 Kings 23:36—25:30*
End of the Line

EZEKIEL 8

Dig you prophet, Dig in the wall
Probe the hole that opens to the night
Weep Ezekiel, Weep for your call

Crumble small the whitewash with your awl
Daubed by holy priests who smothered light
Dig you prophet, Dig in the wall

Dig you deeper, Dig back to the fall
Hasten shepherd, see your flock's in flight
Weep Ezekiel, Weep for your call

Hide your eyes and shrink from the small
Door that dries your bones as if you might
Not dig. You watchman, Dig in the wall

Seventy elders, sentries of God's law
Worship beasts and creatures slimed with blight
Weep Ezekiel, Weep for your call

Watch the Spirit flee among the tall
Cherubim, who bear Him out of sight
Hear the curse of God upon your wall
Weep you watchman, Weep for your call

—*Carolyn Nystrom, 1980*

 Warming Up to God How do you feel when a Christian leader falls deep into sin?

 Read 2 Kings 23:36—25:30.

³⁶Jehoiakim was twenty-five years old when he became king, and he reigned in Jerusalem eleven years. His mother's name was Zebidah daughter of Pedaiah; she was from Rumah. ³⁷And he did evil in the eyes of the LORD, just as his fathers had done.

24 During Jehoiakim's reign, Nebuchadnezzar king of Babylon invaded the land, and Jehoiakim became his vassal for three years. But then he changed his mind and rebelled against Nebuchadnezzar. ²The LORD sent Babylonian,�q Aramean, Moabite and Ammonite raiders against him. He sent them to destroy Judah, in accordance with the word of the LORD proclaimed by his servants the prophets. ³Surely these things happened to Judah according to the LORD's command, in order to remove them from his presence because of the sins of Manasseh and all he had done, ⁴including the shedding of innocent blood. For he had filled

Jerusalem with innocent blood, and the LORD was not willing to forgive.

⁵As for the other events of Jehoiakim's reign, and all he did, are they not written in the book of the annals of the kings of Judah? ⁶Jehoiakim rested with his fathers. And Jehoiachin his son succeeded him as king.

⁷The king of Egypt did not march out from his own country again, because the king of Babylon had taken all his territory, from the Wadi of Egypt to the Euphrates River.

⁸Jehoiachin was eighteen years old when he became king, and he reigned in Jerusalem three months. His mother's name was Nehushta daughter of Elnathan; she was from Jerusalem. ⁹He did evil in the eyes of the LORD, just as his father had done.

¹⁰At that time the officers of Nebuchadnezzar king of Babylon advanced on Jerusalem and laid

q2 Or Chaldean

siege to it, [11]and Nebuchadnezzar himself came up to the city while his officers were besieging it. [12]Jehoiachin king of Judah, his mother, his attendants, his nobles and his officials all surrendered to him.

In the eighth year of the reign of the king of Babylon, he took Jehoiachin prisoner. [13]As the LORD had declared, Nebuchadnezzar removed all the treasures from the temple of the LORD and from the royal palace, and took away all the gold articles that Solomon king of Israel had made for the temple of the LORD. [14]He carried into exile all Jerusalem: all the officers and fighting men, and all the craftsmen and artisans—a total of ten thousand. Only the poorest people of the land were left.

[15]Nebuchadnezzar took Jehoiachin captive to Babylon. He also took from Jerusalem to Babylon the king's mother, his wives, his officials and the leading men of the land. [16]The king of Babylon also deported to Babylon the entire force of seven thousand fighting men, strong and fit for war, and a thousand craftsmen and artisans. [17]He made Mattaniah, Jehoiachin's uncle, king in his place and changed his name to Zedekiah.

[18]Zedekiah was twenty-one years old when he became king, and he reigned in Jerusalem eleven years. His mother's name was Hamutal daughter of Jeremiah; she was from Libnah. [19]He did evil in the eyes of the LORD, just as Jehoiakim had done. [20]It was because of the LORD's anger that all this happened to Jerusalem and Judah, and in the end he thrust them from his presence.

Now Zedekiah rebelled against the king of Babylon.

25

So in the ninth year of Zedekiah's reign, on the tenth day of the tenth month, Nebuchadnezzar king of Babylon marched against Jerusalem with his whole army. He encamped outside the city and built siege works all around it. [2]The city was kept under siege until the eleventh year of King Zedekiah. [3]By the ninth day of the ⌊fourth⌋[r] month the famine in the city had become so severe that there was no food for the people to eat. [4]Then the city wall was broken through, and the whole army fled at night through the gate between the two walls near the king's garden, though the Babylonians[s] were surrounding the city. They fled toward the Arabah,[t] [5]but the Babylonian[u] army pursued the king and overtook him in the plains of Jericho. All his soldiers were separated from

him and scattered, [6]and he was captured. He was taken to the king of Babylon at Riblah, where sentence was pronounced on him. [7]They killed the sons of Zedekiah before his eyes. Then they put out his eyes, bound him with bronze shackles and took him to Babylon.

[8]On the seventh day of the fifth month, in the nineteenth year of Nebuchadnezzar king of Babylon, Nebuzaradan commander of the imperial guard, an official of the king of Babylon, came to Jerusalem. [9]He set fire to the temple of the LORD, the royal palace and all the houses of Jerusalem. Every important building he burned down. [10]The whole Babylonian army, under the commander of the imperial guard, broke down the walls around Jerusalem. [11]Nebuzaradan the commander of the guard carried into exile the people who remained in the city, along with the rest of the populace and those who had gone over to the king of Babylon. [12]But the commander left behind some of the poorest people of the land to work the vineyards and fields.

[13]The Babylonians broke up the bronze pillars, the movable stands and the bronze Sea that were at the temple of the LORD and they carried the bronze to Babylon. [14]They also took away the pots, shovels, wick trimmers, dishes and all the bronze articles used in the temple service. [15]The commander of the imperial guard took away the censers and sprinkling bowls—all that were made of pure gold or silver.

[16]The bronze from the two pillars, the Sea and the movable stands, which Solomon had made for the temple of the LORD, was more than could be weighed. [17]Each pillar was twenty-seven feet[v] high. The bronze capital on top of one pillar was four and a half feet[w] high and was decorated with a network and pomegranates of bronze all around. The other pillar, with its network, was similar.

[18]The commander of the guard took as prisoners Seraiah the chief priest, Zephaniah the priest next in rank and the three doorkeepers. [19]Of those still in the city, he took the officer in charge of the fighting men and five royal advisers. He also took the secretary who was chief officer in charge of conscripting the people of the land and sixty of his men who were found in the city. [20]Nebuzaradan the commander took them all and

[r]3 See Jer. 52:6.   [s]4 Or *Chaldeans*; also in verses 13, 25 and 26
[t]4 Or *the Jordan Valley*   [u]5 Or *Chaldean*; also in verses 10 and 24
[v]17 Hebrew *eighteen cubits* (about 8.1 meters)   [w]17 Hebrew *three cubits* (about 1.3 meters)

brought them to the king of Babylon at Riblah. ²¹There at Riblah, in the land of Hamath, the king had them executed.

So Judah went into captivity, away from her land.

²²Nebuchadnezzar king of Babylon appointed Gedaliah son of Ahikam, the son of Shaphan, to be over the people he had left behind in Judah. ²³When all the army officers and their men heard that the king of Babylon had appointed Gedaliah as governor, they came to Gedaliah at Mizpah— Ishmael son of Nethaniah, Johanan son of Kareah, Seraiah son of Tanhumeth the Netophathite, Jaazaniah the son of the Maacathite, and their men. ²⁴Gedaliah took an oath to reassure them and their men. "Do not be afraid of the Babylonian officials," he said. "Settle down in the land and serve the king of Babylon, and it will go well with you."

²⁵In the seventh month, however, Ishmael son of Nethaniah, the son of Elishama, who was of royal blood, came with ten men and assassinated Gedaliah and also the men of Judah and the Babylonians who were with him at Mizpah. ²⁶At this, all the people from the least to the greatest, together with the army officers, fled to Egypt for fear of the Babylonians.

²⁷In the thirty-seventh year of the exile of Jehoiachin king of Judah, in the year Evil-Merodach˟ became king of Babylon, he released Jehoiachin from prison on the twenty-seventh day of the twelfth month. ²⁸He spoke kindly to him and gave him a seat of honor higher than those of the other kings who were with him in Babylon. ²⁹So Jehoiachin put aside his prison clothes and for the rest of his life ate regularly at the king's table. ³⁰Day by day the king gave Jehoiachin a regular allowance as long as he lived.

˟27 Also called *Amel-Marduk*

Discovering the Word 1. Using the material you've read, trace the final steps of the nation of Judah. 2. What events in those final years make the strongest impression on your mind? Why? 3. Consider the history of Israel and Judah. What turning points do you see that led to this kind of end? 4. During the time that Zedekiah and his people were about to be deported to Babylon, the prophet Jeremiah wrote a letter to the Hebrew people already captive in Babylon. Read God's words to them in Jeremiah 29:10–14. If you had been a Hebrew captive in Babylon, what effect would these words have on the way you conducted your life during captivity?

Applying the Word 1. How might this study of Jewish history affect the way you pray for your own nation and its leaders? 2. What personal hope do the words from Jeremiah offer to you?

Responding in Prayer Take time to pray for specific national needs and leaders.

1 Chronicles

A flood devastates a community. Houses that were not swept away are filled knee-deep with mud. As the waters recede at last, the residents return and look at the damage. At first they're numb, then grief-stricken over their losses. Finally, they take courage and tackle the job of rebuilding, and soon a renewed community emerges from the wreckage.

That's the sort of situation that faced the Jews on their return to Jerusalem after their exile to Babylon. Their city and temple had been ransacked by Nebuchadnezzar in 587 B.C. (2Ki 25:8–12). After Persia took over Babylon, King Cyrus gave the Jews permission to return and rebuild. Nehemiah made an inspection tour and found massive destruction (Ne 2:11–17). It was enough to dishearten even the most loyal Jew.

Enter Ezra, the priest, traditionally considered the author of the Chronicles. (They were originally written as one book but later divided, probably because the single scroll was unwieldy for reading aloud in the synagogue.) Ezra was a man with a purpose. He made the journey back to Jerusalem to help rebuild the temple and restore the worship of God (Ezr 7:6–10). With everything in ruins, surrounded by unfriendly non-Jews who had been imported by Nebuchadnezzar, the people needed encouragement to begin—and finish—the work. They also needed admonitions to stay faithful to the Lord. The books of 1 and 2 Chronicles were apparently written to provide that encouragement and admonition.

At first glance the Chronicles don't look very encouraging! First Chronicles begins with one of those dreaded "name" lists: genealogies beginning all the way back with Adam. While it's not very interesting for us to read nine chapters of someone else's family tree, it must have been fascinating for the returning Jews to reestablish contact with their broken history.

After the genealogies, 1 Chronicles briefly sums up the life of Israel's first king, Saul, then begins a lengthy account of the life of King David. Skipping over David's sins and failures—we have to go to 2 Samuel to find those—it relates in adventure-story style the conquest of Jerusalem, triumphs of David and his warriors, the bringing of the ark of the covenant to Jerusalem, and David's dying in honor and high regard. Throughout the book the Lord's hand is seen, blessing obedience and faithfulness with success.

Our circumstances are different, but we still need encouragement to continue the work God has given us. What needs to be renewed in your life? During your quiet times in 1 Chronicles, you will discover those places where you need to seek renewal—and the courage you need to begin the process. You can praise God along with David: "In your hands are strength and power to exalt and give strength to all" (1Ch 29:12).

Outline

1/ 1 Chronicles 11 ———————————— *Famous for Bravery*

2/ 1 Chronicles 15:1—16:6 ———————— *Joyful Celebration*

3/ 1 Chronicles 17 ———————————— *Honored by God's Promises*

4/ 1 Chronicles 19 ———————————— *Misunderstood Sympathy*

5/ 1 Chronicles 21:1—22:1 ———————— *Misplaced Trust*

6/ 1 Chronicles 28 ———————————— *A Legacy of Humble Service*

7/ 1 Chronicles 29 ———————————— *Generous Giving*

1 Chronicles 1—10

1 Adam, Seth, Enosh, ²Kenan, Mahalalel, Jared, ³Enoch, Methuselah, Lamech, Noah.

⁴The sons of Noah:ª
Shem, Ham and Japheth.

⁵The sonsᵇ of Japheth:
Gomer, Magog, Madai, Javan, Tubal, Meshech and Tiras.
⁶The sons of Gomer:
Ashkenaz, Riphathᶜ and Togarmah.
⁷The sons of Javan:
Elishah, Tarshish, the Kittim and the Rodanim.

⁸The sons of Ham:
Cush, Mizraim,ᵈ Put and Canaan.
⁹The sons of Cush:
Seba, Havilah, Sabta, Raamah and Sabteca.
The sons of Raamah:
Sheba and Dedan.
¹⁰Cush was the fatherᵉ of
Nimrod, who grew to be a mighty warrior on earth.

¹¹Mizraim was the father of
the Ludites, Anamites, Lehabites, Naphtuhites, ¹²Pathrusites, Casluhites (from whom the Philistines came) and Caphtorites.

¹³Canaan was the father of
Sidon his firstborn,ᶠ and of the Hittites, ¹⁴Jebusites, Amorites, Girgashites, ¹⁵Hivites, Arkites, Sinites, ¹⁶Arvadites, Zemarites and Hamathites.

¹⁷The sons of Shem:
Elam, Asshur, Arphaxad, Lud and Aram.
The sons of Aram�g:
Uz, Hul, Gether and Meshech.
¹⁸Arphaxad was the father of Shelah,
and Shelah the father of Eber.
¹⁹Two sons were born to Eber:
One was named Peleg,ʰ because in his time the earth was divided; his brother was named Joktan.
²⁰Joktan was the father of
Almodad, Sheleph, Hazarmaveth, Jerah, ²¹Hadoram, Uzal, Diklah, ²²Obal,ⁱ

Abimael, Sheba, ²³Ophir, Havilah and Jobab. All these were sons of Joktan.

²⁴Shem, Arphaxad,ʲ Shelah,
²⁵Eber, Peleg, Reu,
²⁶Serug, Nahor, Terah
²⁷and Abram (that is, Abraham).

²⁸The sons of Abraham:
Isaac and Ishmael.

²⁹These were their descendants:
Nebaioth the firstborn of Ishmael, Kedar, Adbeel, Mibsam, ³⁰Mishma, Dumah, Massa, Hadad, Tema, ³¹Jetur, Naphish and Kedemah. These were the sons of Ishmael.

³²The sons born to Keturah, Abraham's concubine:
Zimran, Jokshan, Medan, Midian, Ishbak and Shuah.
The sons of Jokshan:
Sheba and Dedan.
³³The sons of Midian:
Ephah, Epher, Hanoch, Abida and Eldaah.
All these were descendants of Keturah.

³⁴Abraham was the father of Isaac.
The sons of Isaac:
Esau and Israel.
³⁵The sons of Esau:
Eliphaz, Reuel, Jeush, Jalam and Korah.
³⁶The sons of Eliphaz:
Teman, Omar, Zepho,ᵏ Gatam and Kenaz;
by Timna: Amalek.ˡ
³⁷The sons of Reuel:
Nahath, Zerah, Shammah and Mizzah.

³⁸The sons of Seir:

ª4 Septuagint; Hebrew does not have *The sons of Noah:*   ᵇ5 *Sons* may mean *descendants* or *successors* or *nations;* also in verses 6-10, 17 and 20.   ᶜ6 Many Hebrew manuscripts and Vulgate (see also Septuagint and Gen. 10:3); most Hebrew manuscripts *Diphath* ᵈ8 That is, Egypt; also in verse 11   ᵉ10 *Father* may mean *ancestor* or *predecessor* or *founder;* also in verses 11, 13, 18 and 20.   ᶠ13 Or *of the Sidonians, the foremost*   ᵍ17 One Hebrew manuscript and some Septuagint manuscripts (see also Gen. 10:23); most Hebrew manuscripts do not have this line.   ʰ19 *Peleg* means *division.*   ⁱ22 Some Hebrew manuscripts and Syriac (see also Gen. 10:28); most Hebrew manuscripts *Ebal*   ʲ24 Hebrew; some Septuagint manuscripts *Arphaxad, Cainan* (see also note at Gen. 11:10)   ᵏ36 Many Hebrew manuscripts, some Septuagint manuscripts and Syriac (see also Gen. 36:11); most Hebrew manuscripts *Zephi*   ˡ36 Some Septuagint manuscripts (see also Gen. 36:12); Hebrew *Gatam, Kenaz, Timna and Amalek*

Lotan, Shobal, Zibeon, Anah, Dishon, Ezer and Dishan.

[39]The sons of Lotan:

Hori and Homam. Timna was Lotan's sister.

[40]The sons of Shobal:

Alvan,[m] Manahath, Ebal, Shepho and Onam.

The sons of Zibeon:

Aiah and Anah.

[41]The son of Anah:

Dishon.

The sons of Dishon:

Hemdan,[n] Eshban, Ithran and Keran.

[42]The sons of Ezer:

Bilhan, Zaavan and Akan.[o]

The sons of Dishan[p]:

Uz and Aran.

[43]These were the kings who reigned in Edom before any Israelite king reigned[q]:

Bela son of Beor, whose city was named Dinhabah.

[44]When Bela died, Jobab son of Zerah from Bozrah succeeded him as king.

[45]When Jobab died, Husham from the land of the Temanites succeeded him as king.

[46]When Husham died, Hadad son of Bedad, who defeated Midian in the country of Moab, succeeded him as king. His city was named Avith.

[47]When Hadad died, Samlah from Masrekah succeeded him as king.

[48]When Samlah died, Shaul from Rehoboth on the river[r] succeeded him as king.

[49]When Shaul died, Baal-Hanan son of Acbor succeeded him as king.

[50]When Baal-Hanan died, Hadad succeeded him as king. His city was named Pau,[s] and his wife's name was Mehetabel daughter of Matred, the daughter of Me-Zahab. [51]Hadad also died.

The chiefs of Edom were:

Timna, Alvah, Jetheth, [52]Oholibamah, Elah, Pinon, [53]Kenaz, Teman, Mibzar, [54]Magdiel and Iram. These were the chiefs of Edom.

2 These were the sons of Israel:

Reuben, Simeon, Levi, Judah, Issachar, Zebulun, [2]Dan, Joseph, Benjamin, Naphtali, Gad and Asher.

[3]The sons of Judah:

Er, Onan and Shelah. These three were born to him by a Canaanite woman, the daughter of Shua. Er, Judah's firstborn, was wicked in the LORD's sight; so the LORD put him to death. [4]Tamar, Judah's daughter-in-law, bore him Perez and Zerah. Judah had five sons in all.

[5]The sons of Perez:

Hezron and Hamul.

[6]The sons of Zerah:

Zimri, Ethan, Heman, Calcol and Darda[t]—five in all.

[7]The son of Carmi:

Achar,[u] who brought trouble on Israel by violating the ban on taking devoted things.[v]

[8]The son of Ethan:

Azariah.

[9]The sons born to Hezron were:

Jerahmeel, Ram and Caleb.[w]

[10]Ram was the father of

Amminadab, and Amminadab the father of Nahshon, the leader of the people of Judah. [11]Nahshon was the father of Salmon,[x] Salmon the father of Boaz, [12]Boaz the father of Obed and Obed the father of Jesse.

[13]Jesse was the father of

Eliab his firstborn; the second son was Abinadab, the third Shimea, [14]the fourth Nethanel, the fifth Raddai, [15]the sixth Ozem and the seventh David. [16]Their sisters were Zeruiah and Abigail. Zeruiah's three sons were Abishai, Joab and Asahel. [17]Abigail was the mother of Amasa, whose father was Jether the Ishmaelite.

[18]Caleb son of Hezron had children by his wife Azubah (and by Jerioth). These were her sons: Jesher, Shobab and Ardon. [19]When Azubah died, Caleb married Eph-

[m]40 Many Hebrew manuscripts and some Septuagint manuscripts (see also Gen. 36:23); most Hebrew manuscripts *Alian*   [n]41 Many Hebrew manuscripts and some Septuagint manuscripts (see also Gen. 36:26); most Hebrew manuscripts *Hamran*   [o]42 Many Hebrew and Septuagint manuscripts (see also Gen. 36:27); most Hebrew manuscripts *Zaavan, Jaakan*   [p]42 Hebrew *Dishon*, a variant of *Dishan*   [q]43 Or *before an Israelite king reigned over them*   [r]48 Possibly the Euphrates   [s]50 Many Hebrew manuscripts, some Septuagint manuscripts, Vulgate and Syriac (see also Gen. 36:39); most Hebrew manuscripts *Pai*   [t]6 Many Hebrew manuscripts, some Septuagint manuscripts and Syriac (see also 1 Kings 4:31); most Hebrew manuscripts *Dara*   [u]7 *Achar* means *trouble*; *Achar* is called *Achan* in Joshua.   [v]7 The Hebrew term refers to the irrevocable giving over of things or persons to the LORD, often by totally destroying them.   [w]9 Hebrew *Kelubai*, a variant of *Caleb*   [x]11 Septuagint (see also Ruth 4:21); Hebrew *Salma*

rath, who bore him Hur. ²⁰Hur was the father of Uri, and Uri the father of Bezalel.

²¹Later, Hezron lay with the daughter of Makir the father of Gilead (he had married her when he was sixty years old), and she bore him Segub. ²²Segub was the father of Jair, who controlled twenty-three towns in Gilead. ²³(But Geshur and Aram captured Havvoth Jair,ʸ as well as Kenath with its surrounding settlements—sixty towns.) All these were descendants of Makir the father of Gilead.

²⁴After Hezron died in Caleb Ephrathah, Abijah the wife of Hezron bore him Ashhur the fatherᶻ of Tekoa.

²⁵The sons of Jerahmeel the firstborn of Hezron:
Ram his firstborn, Bunah, Oren, Ozem andᵃ Ahijah. ²⁶Jerahmeel had another wife, whose name was Atarah; she was the mother of Onam.

²⁷The sons of Ram the firstborn of Jerahmeel:
Maaz, Jamin and Eker.

²⁸The sons of Onam:
Shammai and Jada.
The sons of Shammai:
Nadab and Abishur.

²⁹Abishur's wife was named Abihail, who bore him Ahban and Molid.

³⁰The sons of Nadab:
Seled and Appaim. Seled died without children.

³¹The son of Appaim:
Ishi, who was the father of Sheshan.
Sheshan was the father of Ahlai.

³²The sons of Jada, Shammai's brother:
Jether and Jonathan. Jether died without children.

³³The sons of Jonathan:
Peleth and Zaza.
These were the descendants of Jerahmeel.

³⁴Sheshan had no sons—only daughters.
He had an Egyptian servant named Jarha. ³⁵Sheshan gave his daughter in marriage to his servant Jarha, and she bore him Attai.

³⁶Attai was the father of Nathan,
Nathan the father of Zabad,
³⁷Zabad the father of Ephlal,
Ephlal the father of Obed,

³⁸Obed the father of Jehu,
Jehu the father of Azariah,
³⁹Azariah the father of Helez,
Helez the father of Eleasah,
⁴⁰Eleasah the father of Sismai,
Sismai the father of Shallum,
⁴¹Shallum the father of Jekamiah,
and Jekamiah the father of Elishama.

⁴²The sons of Caleb the brother of Jerahmeel:
Mesha his firstborn, who was the father of Ziph, and his son Mareshah,ᵇ who was the father of Hebron.

⁴³The sons of Hebron:
Korah, Tappuah, Rekem and Shema. ⁴⁴Shema was the father of Raham, and Raham the father of Jorkeam. Rekem was the father of Shammai. ⁴⁵The son of Shammai was Maon, and Maon was the father of Beth Zur.

⁴⁶Caleb's concubine Ephah was the mother of Haran, Moza and Gazez. Haran was the father of Gazez.

⁴⁷The sons of Jahdai:
Regem, Jotham, Geshan, Pelet, Ephah and Shaaph.

⁴⁸Caleb's concubine Maacah was the mother of Sheber and Tirhanah. ⁴⁹She also gave birth to Shaaph the father of Madmannah and to Sheva the father of Macbenah and Gibea. Caleb's daughter was Acsah. ⁵⁰These were the descendants of Caleb.

The sons of Hur the firstborn of Ephrathah:
Shobal the father of Kiriath Jearim, ⁵¹Salma the father of Bethlehem, and Hareph the father of Beth Gader.

⁵²The descendants of Shobal the father of Kiriath Jearim were:
Haroeh, half the Manahathites, ⁵³and the clans of Kiriath Jearim: the Ithrites, Puthites, Shumathites and Mishraites. From these descended the Zorathites and Eshtaolites.

⁵⁴The descendants of Salma:
Bethlehem, the Netophathites, Atroth Beth Joab, half the Manahathites, the Zorites, ⁵⁵and the clans of scribesᶜ who lived at Jabez: the Tirathites, Shimeathites and Sucathites. These are the Kenites

---

ʸ23 Or *captured the settlements of Jair*   ᶻ24 *Father* may mean *civic leader* or *military leader*; also in verses 42, 45, 49-52 and possibly elsewhere.   ᵃ25 Or *Oren and Ozem, by*   ᵇ42 The meaning of the Hebrew for this phrase is uncertain.   ᶜ55 Or *of the Sopherites* who came from Hammath, the father of the house of Recab.[d]

3 These were the sons of David born to him in Hebron:

The firstborn was Amnon the son of Ahinoam of Jezreel;

the second, Daniel the son of Abigail of Carmel;

²the third, Absalom the son of Maacah daughter of Talmai king of Geshur;

the fourth, Adonijah the son of Haggith;

³the fifth, Shephatiah the son of Abital;

and the sixth, Ithream, by his wife Eglah.

⁴These six were born to David in Hebron, where he reigned seven years and six months.

David reigned in Jerusalem thirty-three years, ⁵and these were the children born to him there:

Shammua,[e] Shobab, Nathan and Solomon. These four were by Bathsheba[f] daughter of Ammiel. ⁶There were also Ibhar, Elishua,[g] Eliphelet, ⁷Nogah, Nepheg, Japhia, ⁸Elishama, Eliada and Eliphelet—nine in all. ⁹All these were the sons of David, besides his sons by his concubines. And Tamar was their sister.

¹⁰Solomon's son was Rehoboam,

Abijah his son,

Asa his son,

Jehoshaphat his son,

¹¹Jehoram[h] his son,

Ahaziah his son,

Joash his son,

¹²Amaziah his son,

Azariah his son,

Jotham his son,

¹³Ahaz his son,

Hezekiah his son,

Manasseh his son,

¹⁴Amon his son,

Josiah his son.

¹⁵The sons of Josiah:

Johanan the firstborn,

Jehoiakim the second son,

Zedekiah the third,

Shallum the fourth.

¹⁶The successors of Jehoiakim:

Jehoiachin[i] his son,

and Zedekiah.

¹⁷The descendants of Jehoiachin the captive:

Shealtiel his son, ¹⁸Malkiram, Pedaiah, Shenazzar, Jekamiah, Hoshama and Nedabiah.

¹⁹The sons of Pedaiah:

Zerubbabel and Shimei.

The sons of Zerubbabel:

Meshullam and Hananiah.

Shelomith was their sister.

²⁰There were also five others:

Hashubah, Ohel, Berekiah, Hasadiah and Jushab-Hesed.

²¹The descendants of Hananiah:

Pelatiah and Jeshaiah, and the sons of Rephaiah, of Arnan, of Obadiah and of Shecaniah.

²²The descendants of Shecaniah:

Shemaiah and his sons:

Hattush, Igal, Bariah, Neariah and Shaphat—six in all.

²³The sons of Neariah:

Elioenai, Hizkiah and Azrikam—three in all.

²⁴The sons of Elioenai:

Hodaviah, Eliashib, Pelaiah, Akkub, Johanan, Delaiah and Anani—seven in all.

4 The descendants of Judah:

Perez, Hezron, Carmi, Hur and Shobal.

²Reaiah son of Shobal was the father of Jahath, and Jahath the father of Ahumai and Lahad. These were the clans of the Zorathites.

³These were the sons[j] of Etam:

Jezreel, Ishma and Idbash. Their sister was named Hazzelelponi. ⁴Penuel was the father of Gedor, and Ezer the father of Hushah.

These were the descendants of Hur, the firstborn of Ephrathah and father[k] of Bethlehem.

⁵Ashhur the father of Tekoa had two wives, Helah and Naarah.

⁶Naarah bore him Ahuzzam, Hepher, Temeni and Haahashtari. These were the descendants of Naarah.

⁷The sons of Helah:

d55 Or father of Beth Recab   e5 Hebrew Shimea, a variant of Shammua   f5 One Hebrew manuscript and Vulgate (see also Septuagint and 2 Samuel 11:3); most Hebrew manuscripts Bathshua   g6 Two Hebrew manuscripts (see also 2 Samuel 5:15 and 1 Chron. 14:5); most Hebrew manuscripts Elishama   h11 Hebrew Joram, a variant of Jehoram   i16 Hebrew Jeconiah, a variant of Jehoiachin; also in verse 17   j3 Some Septuagint manuscripts (see also Vulgate); Hebrew father   k4 Father may mean civic leader or military leader; also in verses 12, 14, 17, 18 and possibly elsewhere.

Zereth, Zohar, Ethnan, ⁸and Koz, who was the father of Anub and Hazzobebah and of the clans of Aharhel son of Harum.

⁹Jabez was more honorable than his brothers. His mother had named him Jabez,^l saying, "I gave birth to him in pain." ¹⁰Jabez cried out to the God of Israel, "Oh, that you would bless me and enlarge my territory! Let your hand be with me, and keep me from harm so that I will be free from pain." And God granted his request.

¹¹Kelub, Shuhah's brother, was the father of Mehir, who was the father of Eshton. ¹²Eshton was the father of Beth Rapha, Paseah and Tehinnah the father of Ir Nahash.^m These were the men of Recah.

¹³The sons of Kenaz:
Othniel and Seraiah.
The sons of Othniel:
Hathath and Meonothai.ⁿ ¹⁴Meonothai was the father of Ophrah.
Seraiah was the father of Joab,
the father of Ge Harashim.^o It was called this because its people were craftsmen.
¹⁵The sons of Caleb son of Jephunneh:
Iru, Elah and Naam.
The son of Elah:
Kenaz.
¹⁶The sons of Jehallelel:
Ziph, Ziphah, Tiria and Asarel.
¹⁷The sons of Ezrah:
Jether, Mered, Epher and Jalon. One of Mered's wives gave birth to Miriam, Shammai and Ishbah the father of Eshtemoa. ¹⁸(His Judean wife gave birth to Jered the father of Gedor, Heber the father of Soco, and Jekuthiel the father of Zanoah.) These were the children of Pharaoh's daughter Bithiah, whom Mered had married.
¹⁹The sons of Hodiah's wife, the sister of Naham:
the father of Keilah the Garmite, and Eshtemoa the Maacathite.
²⁰The sons of Shimon:
Amnon, Rinnah, Ben-Hanan and Tilon.
The descendants of Ishi:
Zoheth and Ben-Zoheth.
²¹The sons of Shelah son of Judah:
Er the father of Lecah, Laadah the father of Mareshah and the clans of the linen

workers at Beth Ashbea, ²²Jokim, the men of Cozeba, and Joash and Saraph, who ruled in Moab and Jashubi Lehem. (These records are from ancient times.) ²³They were the potters who lived at Netaim and Gederah; they stayed there and worked for the king.

²⁴The descendants of Simeon:
Nemuel, Jamin, Jarib, Zerah and Shaul;
²⁵Shallum was Shaul's son, Mibsam his son and Mishma his son.
²⁶The descendants of Mishma:
Hammuel his son, Zaccur his son and Shimei his son.
²⁷Shimei had sixteen sons and six daughters, but his brothers did not have many children; so their entire clan did not become as numerous as the people of Judah. ²⁸They lived in Beersheba, Moladah, Hazar Shual, ²⁹Bilhah, Ezem, Tolad, ³⁰Bethuel, Hormah, Ziklag, ³¹Beth Marcaboth, Hazar Susim, Beth Biri and Shaaraim. These were their towns until the reign of David. ³²Their surrounding villages were Etam, Ain, Rimmon, Token and Ashan—five towns— ³³and all the villages around these towns as far as Baalath.^p These were their settlements. And they kept a genealogical record.

³⁴Meshobab, Jamlech, Joshah son of Amaziah, ³⁵Joel, Jehu son of Joshibiah, the son of Seraiah, the son of Asiel, ³⁶also Elioenai, Jaakobah, Jeshohaiah, Asaiah, Adiel, Jesimiel, Benaiah, ³⁷and Ziza son of Shiphi, the son of Allon, the son of Jedaiah, the son of Shimri, the son of Shemaiah.

³⁸The men listed above by name were leaders of their clans. Their families increased greatly, ³⁹and they went to the outskirts of Gedor to the east of the valley in search of pasture for their flocks. ⁴⁰They found rich, good pasture, and the land was spacious, peaceful and quiet. Some Hamites had lived there formerly.

⁴¹The men whose names were listed came in the days of Hezekiah king of Judah. They attacked the Hamites in their dwellings and also the Meunites who were there and completely destroyed^q them, as is evident to this day. Then

^l9 Jabez sounds like the Hebrew for pain.   ^m12 Or of the city of Nahash   ⁿ13 Some Septuagint manuscripts and Vulgate; Hebrew does not have and Meonothai.   ^o14 Ge Harashim means valley of craftsmen.   ^p33 Some Septuagint manuscripts (see also Joshua 19:8); Hebrew Baal   ^q41 The Hebrew term refers to the irrevocable giving over of things or persons to the LORD, often by totally destroying them.

they settled in their place, because there was pasture for their flocks. ⁴²And five hundred of these Simeonites, led by Pelatiah, Neariah, Rephaiah and Uzziel, the sons of Ishi, invaded the hill country of Seir. ⁴³They killed the remaining Amalekites who had escaped, and they have lived there to this day.

5 The sons of Reuben the firstborn of Israel (he was the firstborn, but when he defiled his father's marriage bed, his rights as firstborn were given to the sons of Joseph son of Israel; so he could not be listed in the genealogical record in accordance with his birthright, ²and though Judah was the strongest of his brothers and a ruler came from him, the rights of the firstborn belonged to Joseph)— ³the sons of Reuben the firstborn of Israel:

Hanoch, Pallu, Hezron and Carmi.
⁴The descendants of Joel:
Shemaiah his son, Gog his son,
Shimei his son, ⁵Micah his son,
Reaiah his son, Baal his son,
⁶and Beerah his son, whom Tiglath-Pileser[r] king of Assyria took into exile. Beerah was a leader of the Reubenites.

⁷Their relatives by clans, listed according to their genealogical records:

Jeiel the chief, Zechariah, ⁸and Bela son of Azaz, the son of Shema, the son of Joel. They settled in the area from Aroer to Nebo and Baal Meon. ⁹To the east they occupied the land up to the edge of the desert that extends to the Euphrates River, because their livestock had increased in Gilead.

¹⁰During Saul's reign they waged war against the Hagrites, who were defeated at their hands; they occupied the dwellings of the Hagrites throughout the entire region east of Gilead.

¹¹The Gadites lived next to them in Bashan, as far as Salecah:

¹²Joel was the chief, Shapham the second, then Janai and Shaphat, in Bashan.

¹³Their relatives, by families, were:
Michael, Meshullam, Sheba, Jorai, Jacan, Zia and Eber—seven in all.

¹⁴These were the sons of Abihail son of Huri, the son of Jaroah, the son of Gilead, the son of Michael, the son of Jeshishai, the son of Jahdo, the son of Buz.

¹⁵Ahi son of Abdiel, the son of Guni, was head of their family.

¹⁶The Gadites lived in Gilead, in Bashan and its outlying villages, and on all the pasturelands of Sharon as far as they extended.

¹⁷All these were entered in the genealogical records during the reigns of Jotham king of Judah and Jeroboam king of Israel.

¹⁸The Reubenites, the Gadites and the half-tribe of Manasseh had 44,760 men ready for military service—able-bodied men who could handle shield and sword, who could use a bow, and who were trained for battle. ¹⁹They waged war against the Hagrites, Jetur, Naphish and Nodab. ²⁰They were helped in fighting them, and God handed the Hagrites and all their allies over to them, because they cried out to him during the battle. He answered their prayers, because they trusted in him. ²¹They seized the livestock of the Hagrites—fifty thousand camels, two hundred fifty thousand sheep and two thousand donkeys. They also took one hundred thousand people captive, ²²and many others fell slain, because the battle was God's. And they occupied the land until the exile.

²³The people of the half-tribe of Manasseh were numerous; they settled in the land from Bashan to Baal Hermon, that is, to Senir (Mount Hermon).

²⁴These were the heads of their families: Epher, Ishi, Eliel, Azriel, Jeremiah, Hodaviah and Jahdiel. They were brave warriors, famous men, and heads of their families. ²⁵But they were unfaithful to the God of their fathers and prostituted themselves to the gods of the peoples of the land, whom God had destroyed before them. ²⁶So the God of Israel stirred up the spirit of Pul king of Assyria (that is, Tiglath-Pileser king of Assyria), who took the Reubenites, the Gadites and the half-tribe of Manasseh into exile. He took them to Halah, Habor, Hara and the river of Gozan, where they are to this day.

6 The sons of Levi:
Gershon, Kohath and Merari.
²The sons of Kohath:
Amram, Izhar, Hebron and Uzziel.
³The children of Amram:
Aaron, Moses and Miriam.
The sons of Aaron:
Nadab, Abihu, Eleazar and Ithamar.

ʳ6 Hebrew *Tilgath-Pilneser*, a variant of *Tiglath-Pileser*; also in verse 26

⁴Eleazar was the father of Phinehas,
Phinehas the father of Abishua,
⁵Abishua the father of Bukki,
Bukki the father of Uzzi,
⁶Uzzi the father of Zerahiah,
Zerahiah the father of Meraioth,
⁷Meraioth the father of Amariah,
Amariah the father of Ahitub,
⁸Ahitub the father of Zadok,
Zadok the father of Ahimaaz,
⁹Ahimaaz the father of Azariah,
Azariah the father of Johanan,
¹⁰Johanan the father of Azariah (it was he
who served as priest in the temple Solomon built in Jerusalem),
¹¹Azariah the father of Amariah,
Amariah the father of Ahitub,
¹²Ahitub the father of Zadok,
Zadok the father of Shallum,
¹³Shallum the father of Hilkiah,
Hilkiah the father of Azariah,
¹⁴Azariah the father of Seraiah,
and Seraiah the father of Jehozadak.
¹⁵Jehozadak was deported when the LORD sent
Judah and Jerusalem into exile by the hand
of Nebuchadnezzar.

¹⁶The sons of Levi:
Gershon,ˢ Kohath and Merari.
¹⁷These are the names of the sons of Gershon:
Libni and Shimei.
¹⁸The sons of Kohath:
Amram, Izhar, Hebron and Uzziel.
¹⁹The sons of Merari:
Mahli and Mushi.

These are the clans of the Levites listed ac-
cording to their fathers:
²⁰Of Gershon:
Libni his son, Jehath his son,
Zimmah his son, ²¹Joah his son,
Iddo his son, Zerah his son
and Jeatherai his son.
²²The descendants of Kohath:
Amminadab his son, Korah his son,
Assir his son, ²³Elkanah his son,
Ebiasaph his son, Assir his son,
²⁴Tahath his son, Uriel his son,
Uzziah his son and Shaul his son.
²⁵The descendants of Elkanah:
Amasai, Ahimoth,
²⁶Elkanah his son,ᵗ Zophai his son,
Nahath his son, ²⁷Eliab his son,

Jeroham his son, Elkanah his son
and Samuel his son.ᵘ
²⁸The sons of Samuel:
Joelᵛ the firstborn
and Abijah the second son.
²⁹The descendants of Merari:
Mahli, Libni his son,
Shimei his son, Uzzah his son,
³⁰Shimea his son, Haggiah his son
and Asaiah his son.

³¹These are the men David put in charge of the
music in the house of the LORD after the ark came
to rest there. ³²They ministered with music before
the tabernacle, the Tent of Meeting, until Solomon built the temple of the LORD in Jerusalem.
They performed their duties according to the regulations laid down for them.
³³Here are the men who served, together with
their sons:

From the Kohathites:
Heman, the musician,
the son of Joel, the son of Samuel,
³⁴the son of Elkanah, the son of Jeroham,
the son of Eliel, the son of Toah,
³⁵the son of Zuph, the son of Elkanah,
the son of Mahath, the son of Amasai,
³⁶the son of Elkanah, the son of Joel,
the son of Azariah, the son of Zephaniah,
³⁷the son of Tahath, the son of Assir,
the son of Ebiasaph, the son of Korah,
³⁸the son of Izhar, the son of Kohath,
the son of Levi, the son of Israel;
³⁹and Heman's associate Asaph, who served at
his right hand:
Asaph son of Berekiah, the son of Shimea,
⁴⁰the son of Michael, the son of Baaseiah,ʷ
the son of Malkijah, ⁴¹the son of Ethni,
the son of Zerah, the son of Adaiah,
⁴²the son of Ethan, the son of Zimmah,
the son of Shimei, ⁴³the son of Jahath,
the son of Gershon, the son of Levi;
⁴⁴and from their associates, the Merarites, at
his left hand:
Ethan son of Kishi, the son of Abdi,

ˢ16 Hebrew Gershom, a variant of Gershon; also in verses 17, 20, 43,
62 and 71   ᵗ26 Some Hebrew manuscripts, Septuagint and Syriac;
most Hebrew manuscripts Ahimoth 26and Elkanah. The sons of Elkanah:
ᵘ27 Some Septuagint manuscripts (see also 1 Samuel 1:19,20 and
1 Chron. 6:33,34); Hebrew does not have and Samuel his son.
ᵛ28 Some Septuagint manuscripts and Syriac (see also 1 Samuel 8:2 and
1 Chron. 6:33); Hebrew does not have Joel.   ʷ40 Most Hebrew
manuscripts; some Hebrew manuscripts, one Septuagint manuscript and
Syriac Maaseiah

the son of Malluch, ⁴⁵the son of Hashabiah,
the son of Amaziah, the son of Hilkiah,
⁴⁶the son of Amzi, the son of Bani,
the son of Shemer, ⁴⁷the son of Mahli,
the son of Mushi, the son of Merari,
the son of Levi.

⁴⁸Their fellow Levites were assigned to all the other duties of the tabernacle, the house of God. ⁴⁹But Aaron and his descendants were the ones who presented offerings on the altar of burnt offering and on the altar of incense in connection with all that was done in the Most Holy Place, making atonement for Israel, in accordance with all that Moses the servant of God had commanded.

⁵⁰These were the descendants of Aaron:
Eleazar his son, Phinehas his son,
Abishua his son, ⁵¹Bukki his son,
Uzzi his son, Zerahiah his son,
⁵²Meraioth his son, Amariah his son,
Ahitub his son, ⁵³Zadok his son
and Ahimaaz his son.

⁵⁴These were the locations of their settlements allotted as their territory (they were assigned to the descendants of Aaron who were from the Kohathite clan, because the first lot was for them):
⁵⁵They were given Hebron in Judah with its surrounding pasturelands. ⁵⁶But the fields and villages around the city were given to Caleb son of Jephunneh.
⁵⁷So the descendants of Aaron were given Hebron (a city of refuge), and Libnah,^x Jattir, Eshtemoa, ⁵⁸Hilen, Debir, ⁵⁹Ashan, Juttah^y and Beth Shemesh, together with their pasturelands. ⁶⁰And from the tribe of Benjamin they were given Gibeon,^z Geba, Alemeth and Anathoth, together with their pasturelands.
These towns, which were distributed among the Kohathite clans, were thirteen in all.

⁶¹The rest of Kohath's descendants were allotted ten towns from the clans of half the tribe of Manasseh.

⁶²The descendants of Gershon, clan by clan, were allotted thirteen towns from the tribes of Issachar, Asher and Naphtali, and from the part of the tribe of Manasseh that is in Bashan.

⁶³The descendants of Merari, clan by clan, were allotted twelve towns from the tribes of Reuben, Gad and Zebulun.

⁶⁴So the Israelites gave the Levites these towns and their pasturelands. ⁶⁵From the tribes of Judah, Simeon and Benjamin they allotted the previously named towns.

⁶⁶Some of the Kohathite clans were given as their territory towns from the tribe of Ephraim.
⁶⁷In the hill country of Ephraim they were given Shechem (a city of refuge), and Gezer,^a ⁶⁸Jokmeam, Beth Horon, ⁶⁹Aijalon and Gath Rimmon, together with their pasturelands.
⁷⁰And from half the tribe of Manasseh the Israelites gave Aner and Bileam, together with their pasturelands, to the rest of the Kohathite clans.

⁷¹The Gershonites received the following:
From the clan of the half-tribe of Manasseh they received Golan in Bashan and also Ashtaroth, together with their pasturelands;
⁷²from the tribe of Issachar
they received Kedesh, Daberath, ⁷³Ramoth and Anem, together with their pasturelands;
⁷⁴from the tribe of Asher
they received Mashal, Abdon, ⁷⁵Hukok and Rehob, together with their pasturelands;
⁷⁶and from the tribe of Naphtali
they received Kedesh in Galilee, Hammon and Kiriathaim, together with their pasturelands.

⁷⁷The Merarites (the rest of the Levites) received the following:
From the tribe of Zebulun
they received Jokneam, Kartah,^b Rimmono and Tabor, together with their pasturelands;
⁷⁸from the tribe of Reuben across the Jordan east of Jericho
they received Bezer in the desert, Jahzah, ⁷⁹Kedemoth and Mephaath, together with their pasturelands;
⁸⁰and from the tribe of Gad

^x57 See Joshua 21:13; Hebrew *given the cities of refuge: Hebron, Libnah*.
^y59 Syriac (see also Septuagint and Joshua 21:16); Hebrew does not have *Juttah*.   ^z60 See Joshua 21:17; Hebrew does not have *Gibeon*.
^a67 See Joshua 21:21; Hebrew *given the cities of refuge: Shechem, Gezer*.
^b77 See Septuagint and Joshua 21:34; Hebrew does not have *Jokneam, Kartah*.

they received Ramoth in Gilead, Mahanaim, ⁸¹Heshbon and Jazer, together with
their pasturelands.

7 The sons of Issachar:
Tola, Puah, Jashub and Shimron—four
in all.
²The sons of Tola:
Uzzi, Rephaiah, Jeriel, Jahmai, Ibsam and
Samuel—heads of their families. During
the reign of David, the descendants of
Tola listed as fighting men in their genealogy numbered 22,600.
³The son of Uzzi:
Izrahiah.

The sons of Izrahiah:
Michael, Obadiah, Joel and Isshiah. All
five of them were chiefs. ⁴According to
their family genealogy, they had 36,000
men ready for battle, for they had many
wives and children.
⁵The relatives who were fighting men belonging to all the clans of Issachar, as
listed in their genealogy, were 87,000 in
all.

⁶Three sons of Benjamin:
Bela, Beker and Jediael.
⁷The sons of Bela:
Ezbon, Uzzi, Uzziel, Jerimoth and Iri,
heads of families—five in all. Their genealogical record listed 22,034 fighting
men.
⁸The sons of Beker:
Zemirah, Joash, Eliezer, Elioenai, Omri,
Jeremoth, Abijah, Anathoth and Alemeth.
All these were the sons of Beker. ⁹Their
genealogical record listed the heads of
families and 20,200 fighting men.
¹⁰The son of Jediael:
Bilhan.

The sons of Bilhan:
Jeush, Benjamin, Ehud, Kenaanah, Ze-
than, Tarshish and Ahishahar. ¹¹All these
sons of Jediael were heads of families.
There were 17,200 fighting men ready to
go out to war.
¹²The Shuppites and Huppites were the
descendants of Ir, and the Hushites the
descendants of Aher.

¹³The sons of Naphtali:

Jahziel, Guni, Jezer and Shillem*ᶜ*—the
descendants of Bilhah.

¹⁴The descendants of Manasseh:
Asriel was his descendant through his Aramean concubine. She gave birth to Makir
the father of Gilead. ¹⁵Makir took a wife
from among the Huppites and Shuppites.
His sister's name was Maacah.

Another descendant was named Zelophehad, who had only daughters.

¹⁶Makir's wife Maacah gave birth to a son
and named him Peresh. His brother was
named Sheresh, and his sons were Ulam
and Rakem.
¹⁷The son of Ulam:
Bedan.

These were the sons of Gilead son of Makir,
the son of Manasseh. ¹⁸His sister Ham-
moleketh gave birth to Ishhod, Abiezer
and Mahlah.
¹⁹The sons of Shemida were:
Ahian, Shechem, Likhi and Aniam.

²⁰The descendants of Ephraim:
Shuthelah, Bered his son,
Tahath his son, Eleadah his son,
Tahath his son, ²¹Zabad his son
and Shuthelah his son.

Ezer and Elead were killed by the native-
born men of Gath, when they went down to
seize their livestock. ²²Their father Ephraim
mourned for them many days, and his relatives came to comfort him. ²³Then he lay
with his wife again, and she became pregnant and gave birth to a son. He named him
Beriah,*ᵈ* because there had been misfortune in his family. ²⁴His daughter was Sheerah, who built Lower and Upper Beth Horon as well as Uzzen Sheerah.

²⁵Rephah was his son, Resheph his son,*ᵉ*
Telah his son, Tahan his son,
²⁶Ladan his son, Ammihud his son,
Elishama his son, ²⁷Nun his son
and Joshua his son.

²⁸Their lands and settlements included Bethel
and its surrounding villages, Naaran to the east,
Gezer and its villages to the west, and Shechem
and its villages all the way to Ayyah and its villages. ²⁹Along the borders of Manasseh were Beth

ᶜ13 Some Hebrew and Septuagint manuscripts (see also Gen. 46:24 and
Num. 26:49); most Hebrew manuscripts *Shallum*   *ᵈ23 Beriah* sounds
like the Hebrew for *misfortune.*   *ᵉ25* Some Septuagint manuscripts;
Hebrew does not have *his son.*

Shan, Taanach, Megiddo and Dor, together with their villages. The descendants of Joseph son of Israel lived in these towns.

³⁰The sons of Asher:

Imnah, Ishvah, Ishvi and Beriah. Their sister was Serah.

³¹The sons of Beriah:

Heber and Malkiel, who was the father of Birzaith.

³²Heber was the father of Japhlet, Shomer and Hotham and of their sister Shua.

³³The sons of Japhlet:

Pasach, Bimhal and Ashvath. These were Japhlet's sons.

³⁴The sons of Shomer:

Ahi, Rohgah,ʲ Hubbah and Aram.

³⁵The sons of his brother Helem:

Zophah, Imna, Shelesh and Amal.

³⁶The sons of Zophah:

Suah, Harnepher, Shual, Beri, Imrah, ³⁷Bezer, Hod, Shamma, Shilshah, Ithranᵍ and Beera.

³⁸The sons of Jether:

Jephunneh, Pispah and Ara.

³⁹The sons of Ulla:

Arah, Hanniel and Rizia.

⁴⁰All these were descendants of Asher—heads of families, choice men, brave warriors and outstanding leaders. The number of men ready for battle, as listed in their genealogy, was 26,000.

8 Benjamin was the father of Bela his firstborn,

Ashbel the second son, Aharah the third,

²Nohah the fourth and Rapha the fifth.

³The sons of Bela were:

Addar, Gera, Abihud,ʰ ⁴Abishua, Naaman, Ahoah, ⁵Gera, Shephuphan and Huram.

⁶These were the descendants of Ehud, who were heads of families of those living in Geba and were deported to Manahath:

⁷Naaman, Ahijah, and Gera, who deported them and who was the father of Uzza and Ahihud.

⁸Sons were born to Shaharaim in Moab after he had divorced his wives Hushim and Baara. ⁹By his wife Hodesh he had Jobab, Zibia, Mesha, Malcam, ¹⁰Jeuz, Sakia and Mirmah. These were his sons, heads of families. ¹¹By Hushim he had Abitub and Elpaal.

¹²The sons of Elpaal:

Eber, Misham, Shemed (who built Ono and Lod with its surrounding villages), ¹³and Beriah and Shema, who were heads of families of those living in Aijalon and who drove out the inhabitants of Gath.

¹⁴Ahio, Shashak, Jeremoth, ¹⁵Zebadiah, Arad, Eder, ¹⁶Michael, Ishpah and Joha were the sons of Beriah.

¹⁷Zebadiah, Meshullam, Hizki, Heber, ¹⁸Ishmerai, Izliah and Jobab were the sons of Elpaal.

¹⁹Jakim, Zicri, Zabdi, ²⁰Elienai, Zillethai, Eliel, ²¹Adaiah, Beraiah and Shimrath were the sons of Shimei.

²²Ishpan, Eber, Eliel, ²³Abdon, Zicri, Hanan, ²⁴Hananiah, Elam, Anthothijah, ²⁵Iphdeiah and Penuel were the sons of Shashak.

²⁶Shamsherai, Shehariah, Athaliah, ²⁷Jaareshiah, Elijah and Zicri were the sons of Jeroham.

²⁸All these were heads of families, chiefs as listed in their genealogy, and they lived in Jerusalem.

²⁹Jeielⁱ the fatherʲ of Gibeon lived in Gibeon.

His wife's name was Maacah, ³⁰and his firstborn son was Abdon, followed by Zur, Kish, Baal, Ner,ᵏ Nadab, ³¹Gedor, Ahio, Zeker ³²and Mikloth, who was the father of Shimeah. They too lived near their relatives in Jerusalem.

³³Ner was the father of Kish, Kish the father of Saul, and Saul the father of Jonathan, Malki-Shua, Abinadab and Esh-Baal.ˡ

³⁴The son of Jonathan:

Merib-Baal,ᵐ who was the father of Micah.

³⁵The sons of Micah:

Pithon, Melech, Tarea and Ahaz.

³⁶Ahaz was the father of Jehoaddah, Jehoaddah was the father of Alemeth, Azmaveth and Zimri, and Zimri was the father of Moza. ³⁷Moza was the father of Binea;

ʲ34 Or *of his brother Shomer: Rohgah*   ᵍ37 Possibly a variant of *Jether*   ʰ3 Or *Gera the father of Ehud*   ⁱ29 Some Septuagint manuscripts (see also 1 Chron. 9:35); Hebrew does not have *Jeiel*.   ʲ29 *Father* may mean *civic leader* or *military leader*.   ᵏ30 Some Septuagint manuscripts (see also 1 Chron. 9:36); Hebrew does not have *Ner*.   ˡ33 Also known as *Ish-Bosheth*   ᵐ34 Also known as *Mephibosheth*

Raphah was his son, Eleasah his son and Azel his son.

[38]Azel had six sons, and these were their names:

Azrikam, Bokeru, Ishmael, Sheariah, Obadiah and Hanan. All these were the sons of Azel.

[39]The sons of his brother Eshek:

Ulam his firstborn, Jeush the second son and Eliphelet the third. [40]The sons of Ulam were brave warriors who could handle the bow. They had many sons and grandsons—150 in all.

All these were the descendants of Benjamin.

9 All Israel was listed in the genealogies recorded in the book of the kings of Israel.

The people of Judah were taken captive to Babylon because of their unfaithfulness. [2]Now the first to resettle on their own property in their own towns were some Israelites, priests, Levites and temple servants.

[3]Those from Judah, from Benjamin, and from Ephraim and Manasseh who lived in Jerusalem were:

[4]Uthai son of Ammihud, the son of Omri, the son of Imri, the son of Bani, a descendant of Perez son of Judah.

[5]Of the Shilonites:

Asaiah the firstborn and his sons.

[6]Of the Zerahites:

Jeuel.

The people from Judah numbered 690.

[7]Of the Benjamites:

Sallu son of Meshullam, the son of Hodaviah, the son of Hassenuah;

[8]Ibneiah son of Jeroham; Elah son of Uzzi, the son of Micri; and Meshullam son of Shephatiah, the son of Reuel, the son of Ibnijah.

[9]The people from Benjamin, as listed in their genealogy, numbered 956. All these men were heads of their families.

[10]Of the priests:

Jedaiah; Jehoiarib; Jakin;

[11]Azariah son of Hilkiah, the son of Meshullam, the son of Zadok, the son of Meraioth, the son of Ahitub, the official in charge of the house of God;

[12]Adaiah son of Jeroham, the son of Pashhur, the son of Malkijah; and Maasai son of Adiel, the son of Jahzerah, the son of

Meshullam, the son of Meshillemith, the son of Immer.

[13]The priests, who were heads of families, numbered 1,760. They were able men, responsible for ministering in the house of God.

[14]Of the Levites:

Shemaiah son of Hasshub, the son of Azrikam, the son of Hashabiah, a Merarite; [15]Bakbakkar, Heresh, Galal and Mattaniah son of Mica, the son of Zicri, the son of Asaph; [16]Obadiah son of Shemaiah, the son of Galal, the son of Jeduthun; and Berekiah son of Asa, the son of Elkanah, who lived in the villages of the Netophathites.

[17]The gatekeepers:

Shallum, Akkub, Talmon, Ahiman and their brothers, Shallum their chief [18]being stationed at the King's Gate on the east, up to the present time. These were the gatekeepers belonging to the camp of the Levites. [19]Shallum son of Kore, the son of Ebiasaph, the son of Korah, and his fellow gatekeepers from his family (the Korahites) were responsible for guarding the thresholds of the Tent[n] just as their fathers had been responsible for guarding the entrance to the dwelling of the LORD. [20]In earlier times Phinehas son of Eleazar was in charge of the gatekeepers, and the LORD was with him. [21]Zechariah son of Meshelemiah was the gatekeeper at the entrance to the Tent of Meeting.

[22]Altogether, those chosen to be gatekeepers at the thresholds numbered 212. They were registered by genealogy in their villages. The gatekeepers had been assigned to their positions of trust by David and Samuel the seer. [23]They and their descendants were in charge of guarding the gates of the house of the LORD—the house called the Tent. [24]The gatekeepers were on the four sides: east, west, north and south. [25]Their brothers in their villages had to come from time to time and share their duties for seven-day periods. [26]But the four principal gatekeepers, who were Levites, were entrusted with the responsibility for the rooms and treasuries in the house of God. [27]They would spend the night stationed around the house of God, because they had to guard it; and

[n]19 That is, the temple; also in verses 21 and 23

they had charge of the key for opening it each morning.

28Some of them were in charge of the articles used in the temple service; they counted them when they were brought in and when they were taken out. 29Others were assigned to take care of the furnishings and all the other articles of the sanctuary, as well as the flour and wine, and the oil, incense and spices. 30But some of the priests took care of mixing the spices. 31A Levite named Mattithiah, the firstborn son of Shallum the Korahite, was entrusted with the responsibility for baking the offering bread. 32Some of their Kohathite brothers were in charge of preparing for every Sabbath the bread set out on the table.

33Those who were musicians, heads of Levite families, stayed in the rooms of the temple and were exempt from other duties because they were responsible for the work day and night.

34All these were heads of Levite families, chiefs as listed in their genealogy, and they lived in Jerusalem.

35Jeiel the father*o* of Gibeon lived in Gibeon. His wife's name was Maacah, 36and his firstborn son was Abdon, followed by Zur, Kish, Baal, Ner, Nadab, 37Gedor, Ahio, Zechariah and Mikloth. 38Mikloth was the father of Shimeam. They too lived near their relatives in Jerusalem.

39Ner was the father of Kish, Kish the father of Saul, and Saul the father of Jonathan, Malki-Shua, Abinadab and Esh-Baal.*p*

40The son of Jonathan:

Merib-Baal,*q* who was the father of Micah.

41The sons of Micah:

Pithon, Melech, Tahrea and Ahaz.*r*

42Ahaz was the father of Jadah, Jadah*s* was the father of Alemeth, Azmaveth and Zimri, and Zimri was the father of Moza. 43Moza was the father of Binea; Rephaiah was his son, Eleasah his son and Azel his son.

44Azel had six sons, and these were their names:

Azrikam, Bokeru, Ishmael, Sheariah,

Obadiah and Hanan. These were the sons of Azel.

10 Now the Philistines fought against Israel; the Israelites fled before them, and many fell slain on Mount Gilboa. 2The Philistines pressed hard after Saul and his sons, and they killed his sons Jonathan, Abinadab and Malki-Shua. 3The fighting grew fierce around Saul, and when the archers overtook him, they wounded him.

4Saul said to his armor-bearer, "Draw your sword and run me through, or these uncircumcised fellows will come and abuse me."

But his armor-bearer was terrified and would not do it; so Saul took his own sword and fell on it. 5When the armor-bearer saw that Saul was dead, he too fell on his sword and died. 6So Saul and his three sons died, and all his house died together.

7When all the Israelites in the valley saw that the army had fled and that Saul and his sons had died, they abandoned their towns and fled. And the Philistines came and occupied them.

8The next day, when the Philistines came to strip the dead, they found Saul and his sons fallen on Mount Gilboa. 9They stripped him and took his head and his armor, and sent messengers throughout the land of the Philistines to proclaim the news among their idols and their people. 10They put his armor in the temple of their gods and hung up his head in the temple of Dagon.

11When all the inhabitants of Jabesh Gilead heard of everything the Philistines had done to Saul, 12all their valiant men went and took the bodies of Saul and his sons and brought them to Jabesh. Then they buried their bones under the great tree in Jabesh, and they fasted seven days.

13Saul died because he was unfaithful to the LORD; he did not keep the word of the LORD and even consulted a medium for guidance, 14and did not inquire of the LORD. So the LORD put him to death and turned the kingdom over to David son of Jesse.

---

*o*35 *Father* may mean *civic leader* or *military leader.*   *p*39 Also known as *Ish-Bosheth*   *q*40 Also known as *Mephibosheth*   *r*41 Vulgate and Syriac (see also Septuagint and 1 Chron. 8:35); Hebrew does not have *and Ahaz.*   *s*42 Some Hebrew manuscripts and Septuagint (see also 1 Chron. 8:36); most Hebrew manuscripts *Jarah, Jarah*

1 / *1 Chronicles 11*
Famous for Bravery

"YOU MAY NOT be the best person, but you may be the only person." I pondered my friend's comment for a long time as I thought about doing something that would take nerve—nerve I didn't feel I had. I finally concluded that she meant, "Somebody else might do a better job, but nobody else is willing—except you." Sometimes that's how bravery is born. A dangerous job lies ahead of us, and we choose to go ahead and do it.

 Warming Up to God When has the Lord given you courage to take a risk for him?

 Read 1 Chronicles 11.

11 All Israel came together to David at Hebron and said, "We are your own flesh and blood. ²In the past, even while Saul was king, you were the one who led Israel on their military campaigns. And the LORD your God said to you, 'You will shepherd my people Israel, and you will become their ruler.'"

³When all the elders of Israel had come to King David at Hebron, he made a compact with them at Hebron before the LORD, and they anointed David king over Israel, as the LORD had promised through Samuel.

⁴David and all the Israelites marched to Jerusalem (that is, Jebus). The Jebusites who lived there ⁵said to David, "You will not get in here." Nevertheless, David captured the fortress of Zion, the City of David.

⁶David had said, "Whoever leads the attack on the Jebusites will become commander-in-chief." Joab son of Zeruiah went up first, and so he received the command.

⁷David then took up residence in the fortress, and so it was called the City of David. ⁸He built up the city around it, from the supporting terraces*ᵗ* to the surrounding wall, while Joab restored the rest of the city. ⁹And David became more and more powerful, because the LORD Almighty was with him.

¹⁰These were the chiefs of David's mighty men—they, together with all Israel, gave his kingship strong support to extend it over the whole land, as the LORD had promised— ¹¹this is the list of David's mighty men:

Jashobeam,*ᵘ* a Hacmonite, was chief of the officers*ᵛ*; he raised his spear against three hundred men, whom he killed in one encounter.

¹²Next to him was Eleazar son of Dodai the Ahohite, one of the three mighty men. ¹³He was with David at Pas Dammim when the Philistines gathered there for battle. At a place where there was a field full of barley, the troops fled from the Philistines. ¹⁴But they took their stand in the middle of the field. They defended it and struck the Philistines down, and the LORD brought about a great victory.

¹⁵Three of the thirty chiefs came down to David to the rock at the cave of Adullam, while a band of Philistines was encamped in the Valley of Rephaim. ¹⁶At that time David was in the stronghold, and the Philistine garrison was at Bethlehem. ¹⁷David longed for water and said, "Oh, that someone would get me a drink of water from the well near the gate of Bethlehem!" ¹⁸So the Three broke through the Philistine lines, drew water from the well near the gate of Bethlehem and carried it back to David. But he refused to drink it; instead, he poured it out before the LORD. ¹⁹"God forbid that I should do this!" he said. "Should I drink the blood of these men who went at the risk of their lives?" Because they risked their lives to bring it back, David would not drink it.

Such were the exploits of the three mighty men.

²⁰Abishai the brother of Joab was chief of the Three. He raised his spear against three hundred men, whom he killed, and so he became as famous as the Three. ²¹He was doubly honored above the Three and became their commander, even though he was not included among them.

²²Benaiah son of Jehoiada was a valiant fighter from Kabzeel, who performed great exploits. He struck down two of Moab's best men. He also went down into a pit on a snowy day and killed a lion. ²³And he struck down an Egyptian who was

ᵗ8 Or the Millo ᵘ11 Possibly a variant of Jashob-Baal ᵛ11 Or Thirty; some Septuagint manuscripts Three (see also 2 Samuel 23:8) seven and a half feet[w] tall. Although the Egyptian had a spear like a weaver's rod in his hand, Benaiah went against him with a club. He snatched the spear from the Egyptian's hand and killed him with his own spear. **24**Such were the exploits of Benaiah son of Jehoiada; he too was as famous as the three mighty men. **25**He was held in greater honor than any of the Thirty, but he was not included among the Three. And David put him in charge of his bodyguard.

26The mighty men were:

Asahel the brother of Joab,
Elhanan son of Dodo from Bethlehem,
27Shammoth the Harorite,
Helez the Pelonite,
28Ira son of Ikkesh from Tekoa,
Abiezer from Anathoth,
29Sibbecai the Hushathite,
Ilai the Ahohite,
30Maharai the Netophathite,
Heled son of Baanah the Netophathite,
31Ithai son of Ribai from Gibeah in Benjamin,
Benaiah the Pirathonite,
32Hurai from the ravines of Gaash,
Abiel the Arbathite,
33Azmaveth the Baharumite,
Eliahba the Shaalbonite,
34the sons of Hashem the Gizonite,
Jonathan son of Shagee the Hararite,
35Ahiam son of Sacar the Hararite,
Eliphal son of Ur,
36Hepher the Mekerathite,
Ahijah the Pelonite,
37Hezro the Carmelite,
Naarai son of Ezbai,
38Joel the brother of Nathan,
Mibhar son of Hagri,
39Zelek the Ammonite,
Naharai the Berothite, the armor-bearer of Joab son of Zeruiah,
40Ira the Ithrite,
Gareb the Ithrite,
41Uriah the Hittite,
Zabad son of Ahlai,
42Adina son of Shiza the Reubenite, who was chief of the Reubenites, and the thirty with him,
43Hanan son of Maacah,
Joshaphat the Mithnite,
44Uzzia the Ashterathite,
Shama and Jeiel the sons of Hotham the Aroerite,
45Jediael son of Shimri,
his brother Joha the Tizite,
46Eliel the Mahavite,
Jeribai and Joshaviah the sons of Elnaam,
Ithmah the Moabite,
47Eliel, Obed and Jaasiel the Mezobaite.

[w]23 Hebrew *five cubits* (about 2.3 meters)

 Discovering the Word 1. How had David inspired others to bravery (vv. 1–2)? 2. In what ways did the capture of Zion require courageous action (vv. 4–9)? 3. How did David's "mighty men" exhibit courage (vv. 11–25)? 4. Why did David refuse the water he had longed for (vv. 17–19)? 5. How would you say this passage defines heroism?

Applying the Word 1. How do you think these "mighty men" handled their natural fears? 2. How does faith in God help us act more courageously? 3. What challenge are you now facing which requires bravery?

Responding in Prayer Bring your fears to the Lord. Trust him to be with you as you do whatever is necessary. Take the step to act in spite of your fears.

1 Chronicles 12—14

12 These were the men who came to David at Ziklag, while he was banished from the presence of Saul son of Kish (they were among the warriors who helped him in battle; ²they were armed with bows and were able to shoot arrows or to sling stones right-handed or left-handed; they were kinsmen of Saul from the tribe of Benjamin):

³Ahiezer their chief and Joash the sons of Shemaah the Gibeathite; Jeziel and Pelet the sons of Azmaveth; Beracah, Jehu the Anathothite, ⁴and Ishmaiah the Gibeonite, a mighty man among the Thirty, who was a leader of the Thirty; Jeremiah, Jahaziel, Johanan, Jozabad the Gederathite, ⁵Eluzai, Jerimoth, Bealiah, Shemariah and Shephatiah the Haruphite; ⁶Elkanah, Isshiah, Azarel, Joezer and Jashobeam the Korahites; ⁷and Joelah and Zebadiah the sons of Jeroham from Gedor.

⁸Some Gadites defected to David at his stronghold in the desert. They were brave warriors, ready for battle and able to handle the shield and spear. Their faces were the faces of lions, and they were as swift as gazelles in the mountains.

⁹Ezer was the chief,
  Obadiah the second in command, Eliab the third,
¹⁰Mishmannah the fourth, Jeremiah the fifth,
¹¹Attai the sixth, Eliel the seventh,
¹²Johanan the eighth, Elzabad the ninth,
¹³Jeremiah the tenth and Macbannai the eleventh.

¹⁴These Gadites were army commanders; the least was a match for a hundred, and the greatest for a thousand. ¹⁵It was they who crossed the Jordan in the first month when it was overflowing all its banks, and they put to flight everyone living in the valleys, to the east and to the west.

¹⁶Other Benjamites and some men from Judah also came to David in his stronghold. ¹⁷David went out to meet them and said to them, "If you have come to me in peace, to help me, I am ready to have you unite with me. But if you have come to betray me to my enemies when my hands are free from violence, may the God of our fathers see it and judge you."

¹⁸Then the Spirit came upon Amasai, chief of the Thirty, and he said:

"We are yours, O David!
  We are with you, O son of Jesse!
Success, success to you,
  and success to those who help you,
    for your God will help you."

So David received them and made them leaders of his raiding bands.

¹⁹Some of the men of Manasseh defected to David when he went with the Philistines to fight against Saul. (He and his men did not help the Philistines because, after consultation, their rulers sent him away. They said, "It will cost us our heads if he deserts to his master Saul.") ²⁰When David went to Ziklag, these were the men of Manasseh who defected to him: Adnah, Jozabad, Jediael, Michael, Jozabad, Elihu and Zillethai, leaders of units of a thousand in Manasseh. ²¹They helped David against raiding bands, for all of them were brave warriors, and they were commanders in his army. ²²Day after day men came to help David, until he had a great army, like the army of God.ˣ

²³These are the numbers of the men armed for battle who came to David at Hebron to turn Saul's kingdom over to him, as the Lᴏʀᴅ had said:
²⁴men of Judah, carrying shield and spear—
  6,800 armed for battle;
²⁵men of Simeon, warriors ready for battle—
  7,100;
²⁶men of Levi—4,600, ²⁷including Jehoiada,
  leader of the family of Aaron, with 3,700
  men, ²⁸and Zadok, a brave young warrior,
  with 22 officers from his family;
²⁹men of Benjamin, Saul's kinsmen—3,000,
  most of whom had remained loyal to
  Saul's house until then;
³⁰men of Ephraim, brave warriors, famous in
  their own clans—20,800;
³¹men of half the tribe of Manasseh, designated by name to come and make David
  king—18,000;
³²men of Issachar, who understood the times
  and knew what Israel should do—200

ˣ22 Or *a great and mighty army*

chiefs, with all their relatives under their command;

33men of Zebulun, experienced soldiers prepared for battle with every type of weapon, to help David with undivided loyalty—50,000;

34men of Naphtali—1,000 officers, together with 37,000 men carrying shields and spears;

35men of Dan, ready for battle—28,600;

36men of Asher, experienced soldiers prepared for battle—40,000;

37and from east of the Jordan, men of Reuben, Gad and the half-tribe of Manasseh, armed with every type of weapon—120,000.

38All these were fighting men who volunteered to serve in the ranks. They came to Hebron fully determined to make David king over all Israel. All the rest of the Israelites were also of one mind to make David king. 39The men spent three days there with David, eating and drinking, for their families had supplied provisions for them. 40Also, their neighbors from as far away as Issachar, Zebulun and Naphtali came bringing food on donkeys, camels, mules and oxen. There were plentiful supplies of flour, fig cakes, raisin cakes, wine, oil, cattle and sheep, for there was joy in Israel.

13 David conferred with each of his officers, the commanders of thousands and commanders of hundreds. 2He then said to the whole assembly of Israel, "If it seems good to you and if it is the will of the LORD our God, let us send word far and wide to the rest of our brothers throughout the territories of Israel, and also to the priests and Levites who are with them in their towns and pasturelands, to come and join us. 3Let us bring the ark of our God back to us, for we did not inquire of*y* it*z* during the reign of Saul." 4The whole assembly agreed to do this, because it seemed right to all the people.

5So David assembled all the Israelites, from the Shihor River in Egypt to Lebo*a* Hamath, to bring the ark of God from Kiriath Jearim. 6David and all the Israelites with him went to Baalah of Judah (Kiriath Jearim) to bring up from there the ark of God the LORD, who is enthroned between the cherubim—the ark that is called by the Name.

7They moved the ark of God from Abinadab's house on a new cart, with Uzzah and Ahio guiding it. 8David and all the Israelites were celebrat-

ing with all their might before God, with songs and with harps, lyres, tambourines, cymbals and trumpets.

9When they came to the threshing floor of Kidon, Uzzah reached out his hand to steady the ark, because the oxen stumbled. 10The LORD's anger burned against Uzzah, and he struck him down because he had put his hand on the ark. So he died there before God.

11Then David was angry because the LORD's wrath had broken out against Uzzah, and to this day that place is called Perez Uzzah.*b*

12David was afraid of God that day and asked, "How can I ever bring the ark of God to me?" 13He did not take the ark to be with him in the City of David. Instead, he took it aside to the house of Obed-Edom the Gittite. 14The ark of God remained with the family of Obed-Edom in his house for three months, and the LORD blessed his household and everything he had.

14 Now Hiram king of Tyre sent messengers to David, along with cedar logs, stonemasons and carpenters to build a palace for him. 2And David knew that the LORD had established him as king over Israel and that his kingdom had been highly exalted for the sake of his people Israel.

3In Jerusalem David took more wives and became the father of more sons and daughters. 4These are the names of the children born to him there: Shammua, Shobab, Nathan, Solomon, 5Ibhar, Elishua, Elpelet, 6Nogah, Nepheg, Japhia, 7Elishama, Beeliada*c* and Eliphelet.

8When the Philistines heard that David had been anointed king over all Israel, they went up in full force to search for him, but David heard about it and went out to meet them. 9Now the Philistines had come and raided the Valley of Rephaim; 10so David inquired of God: "Shall I go and attack the Philistines? Will you hand them over to me?"

The LORD answered him, "Go, I will hand them over to you."

11So David and his men went up to Baal Perazim, and there he defeated them. He said, "As waters break out, God has broken out against my enemies by my hand." So that place was called Baal Perazim.*d* 12The Philistines had abandoned

*y*3 Or *we neglected*   *z*3 Or *him*   *a*5 Or *to the entrance to*
*b*11 *Perez Uzzah* means *outbreak against Uzzah.*   *c*7 A variant of *Eliada*   *d*11 *Baal Perazim* means *the lord who breaks out.*

their gods there, and David gave orders to burn them in the fire.

¹³Once more the Philistines raided the valley; ¹⁴so David inquired of God again, and God answered him, "Do not go straight up, but circle around them and attack them in front of the balsam trees. ¹⁵As soon as you hear the sound of marching in the tops of the balsam trees, move out to battle, because that will mean God has gone out in front of you to strike the Philistine army." ¹⁶So David did as God commanded him, and they struck down the Philistine army, all the way from Gibeon to Gezer.

¹⁷So David's fame spread throughout every land, and the LORD made all the nations fear him.

2 / 1 Chronicles 15:1—16:6
Joyful Celebration

THE BACKYARD WEDDING two doors away was getting noisy. It was late; everybody was singing. Fortunately, the couple seemed to have all musical friends and family, because the sound was glorious. It must have been a similar event when David and the priests and singers brought the ark of the covenant to its new place in Jerusalem in a noisy, joyful procession.

 Warming Up to God   What makes you feel like celebrating the Lord?

 Read 1 Chronicles 15:1—16:6.

15 After David had constructed buildings for himself in the City of David, he prepared a place for the ark of God and pitched a tent for it. ²Then David said, "No one but the Levites may carry the ark of God, because the LORD chose them to carry the ark of the LORD and to minister before him forever."

³David assembled all Israel in Jerusalem to bring up the ark of the LORD to the place he had prepared for it. ⁴He called together the descendants of Aaron and the Levites:

⁵From the descendants of Kohath,
Uriel the leader and 120 relatives;
⁶from the descendants of Merari,
Asaiah the leader and 220 relatives;
⁷from the descendants of Gershon,ᵉ
Joel the leader and 130 relatives;
⁸from the descendants of Elizaphan,
Shemaiah the leader and 200 relatives;
⁹from the descendants of Hebron,
Eliel the leader and 80 relatives;
¹⁰from the descendants of Uzziel,
Amminadab the leader and 112 relatives.

¹¹Then David summoned Zadok and Abiathar the priests, and Uriel, Asaiah, Joel, Shemaiah, Eliel and Amminadab the Levites. ¹²He said to them, "You are the heads of the Levitical families; you and your fellow Levites are to consecrate yourselves and bring up the ark of the LORD, the God of Israel, to the place I have prepared for it. ¹³It was because you, the Levites, did not bring it up the first time that the LORD our God broke out in anger against us. We did not inquire of him about how to do it in the prescribed way." ¹⁴So the priests and Levites consecrated themselves in order to bring up the ark of the LORD, the God of Israel. ¹⁵And the Levites carried the ark of God with the poles on their shoulders, as Moses had commanded in accordance with the word of the LORD.

¹⁶David told the leaders of the Levites to appoint their brothers as singers to sing joyful songs, accompanied by musical instruments: lyres, harps and cymbals.

¹⁷So the Levites appointed Heman son of Joel; from his brothers, Asaph son of Berekiah; and from their brothers the Merarites, Ethan son of Kushaiah; ¹⁸and with them their brothers next in rank: Zechariah,ᶠ Jaaziel, Shemiramoth, Jehiel,

---

ᵉ7 Hebrew *Gershom*, a variant of *Gershon*   ᶠ18 Three Hebrew manuscripts and most Septuagint manuscripts (see also verse 20 and 1 Chron. 16:5); most Hebrew manuscripts *Zechariah son and* or *Zechariah, Ben and*

Unni, Eliab, Benaiah, Maaseiah, Mattithiah, Eliphelehu, Mikneiah, Obed-Edom and Jeiel,^g the gatekeepers.

¹⁹The musicians Heman, Asaph and Ethan were to sound the bronze cymbals; ²⁰Zechariah, Aziel, Shemiramoth, Jehiel, Unni, Eliab, Maaseiah and Benaiah were to play the lyres according to *alamoth,*^h ²¹and Mattithiah, Eliphelehu, Mikneiah, Obed-Edom, Jeiel and Azaziah were to play the harps, directing according to *sheminith.*^h ²²Kenaniah the head Levite was in charge of the singing; that was his responsibility because he was skillful at it.

²³Berekiah and Elkanah were to be doorkeepers for the ark. ²⁴Shebaniah, Joshaphat, Nethanel, Amasai, Zechariah, Benaiah and Eliezer the priests were to blow trumpets before the ark of God. Obed-Edom and Jehiah were also to be doorkeepers for the ark.

²⁵So David and the elders of Israel and the commanders of units of a thousand went to bring up the ark of the covenant of the Lord from the house of Obed-Edom, with rejoicing. ²⁶Because God had helped the Levites who were carrying the ark of the covenant of the Lord, seven bulls and seven rams were sacrificed. ²⁷Now David was clothed in a robe of fine linen, as were all the Levites who were carrying the ark, and as were the singers, and Kenaniah, who was in charge of the singing of the choirs. David also wore a linen ephod. ²⁸So all Israel brought up the ark of the

covenant of the Lord with shouts, with the sounding of rams' horns and trumpets, and of cymbals, and the playing of lyres and harps.

²⁹As the ark of the covenant of the Lord was entering the City of David, Michal daughter of Saul watched from a window. And when she saw King David dancing and celebrating, she despised him in her heart.

16 They brought the ark of God and set it inside the tent that David had pitched for it, and they presented burnt offerings and fellowship offeringsⁱ before God. ²After David had finished sacrificing the burnt offerings and fellowship offerings, he blessed the people in the name of the Lord. ³Then he gave a loaf of bread, a cake of dates and a cake of raisins to each Israelite man and woman.

⁴He appointed some of the Levites to minister before the ark of the Lord, to make petition, to give thanks, and to praise the Lord, the God of Israel: ⁵Asaph was the chief, Zechariah second, then Jeiel, Shemiramoth, Jehiel, Mattithiah, Eliab, Benaiah, Obed-Edom and Jeiel. They were to play the lyres and harps, Asaph was to sound the cymbals, ⁶and Benaiah and Jahaziel the priests were to blow the trumpets regularly before the ark of the covenant of God.

^g18 Hebrew; Septuagint (see also verse 21) *Jeiel and Azaziah*   ^h20,21 Probably a musical term   ⁱ1 Traditionally *peace offerings;* also in verse 2

Discovering the Word 1. Before this, the ark of the covenant was in temporary lodging. It had never been in Jerusalem. How did King David make preparations for bringing it into his new capital (15:1–15)? 2. What was the importance of singing as the ark was moved (15:16–22)? 3. How did David conduct himself during the procession (15:25–29)? 4. If you had been an observer there, what would you have thought of the king? 5. Why do you think Michal, one of David's wives, reacted negatively (15:29)? 6. In what ways did they celebrate when they got the ark inside the tent (16:1–6)?

Applying the Word 1. How do you feel about unrestrained celebration by Christians in worship? 2. How open are you to worship styles different from the one you prefer? 3. What helps you to express your joy in the Lord?

Responding in Prayer Praise the Lord in some joyful way today through motion, spoken words, music, writing, artwork or whatever is natural to you.

1 Chronicles 16:7–43

⁷That day David first committed to Asaph and his associates this psalm of thanks to the LORD:

⁸Give thanks to the LORD, call on his name;
  make known among the nations what he
    has done.
⁹Sing to him, sing praise to him;
  tell of all his wonderful acts.
¹⁰Glory in his holy name;
  let the hearts of those who seek the LORD
    rejoice.
¹¹Look to the LORD and his strength;
  seek his face always.
¹²Remember the wonders he has done,
  his miracles, and the judgments he
    pronounced,
¹³O descendants of Israel his servant,
  O sons of Jacob, his chosen ones.

¹⁴He is the LORD our God;
  his judgments are in all the earth.
¹⁵He remembersʲ his covenant forever,
  the word he commanded, for a thousand
    generations,
¹⁶the covenant he made with Abraham,
  the oath he swore to Isaac.
¹⁷He confirmed it to Jacob as a decree,
  to Israel as an everlasting covenant:
¹⁸"To you I will give the land of Canaan
  as the portion you will inherit."

¹⁹When they were but few in number,
  few indeed, and strangers in it,
²⁰theyᵏ wandered from nation to nation,
  from one kingdom to another.
²¹He allowed no man to oppress them;
  for their sake he rebuked kings:
²²"Do not touch my anointed ones;
  do my prophets no harm."

²³Sing to the LORD, all the earth;
  proclaim his salvation day after day.
²⁴Declare his glory among the nations,
  his marvelous deeds among all peoples.
²⁵For great is the LORD and most worthy of
    praise;
  he is to be feared above all gods.
²⁶For all the gods of the nations are idols,
  but the LORD made the heavens.
²⁷Splendor and majesty are before him;
  strength and joy in his dwelling place.

²⁸Ascribe to the LORD, O families of nations,
  ascribe to the LORD glory and strength,
²⁹ ascribe to the LORD the glory due his name.
  Bring an offering and come before him;
    worship the LORD in the splendor of hisˡ
      holiness.
³⁰Tremble before him, all the earth!
  The world is firmly established; it cannot
    be moved.
³¹Let the heavens rejoice, let the earth be glad;
  let them say among the nations, "The LORD
    reigns!"
³²Let the sea resound, and all that is in it;
  let the fields be jubilant, and everything in
    them!
³³Then the trees of the forest will sing,
  they will sing for joy before the LORD,
  for he comes to judge the earth.

³⁴Give thanks to the LORD, for he is good;
  his love endures forever.
³⁵Cry out, "Save us, O God our Savior;
  gather us and deliver us from the nations,
  that we may give thanks to your holy name,
  that we may glory in your praise."
³⁶Praise be to the LORD, the God of Israel,
  from everlasting to everlasting.

Then all the people said "Amen" and "Praise the
LORD."

³⁷David left Asaph and his associates before the ark of the covenant of the LORD to minister there regularly, according to each day's requirements. ³⁸He also left Obed-Edom and his sixty-eight associates to minister with them. Obed-Edom son of Jeduthun, and also Hosah, were gatekeepers.

³⁹David left Zadok the priest and his fellow priests before the tabernacle of the LORD at the high place in Gibeon ⁴⁰to present burnt offerings to the LORD on the altar of burnt offering regularly, morning and evening, in accordance with everything written in the Law of the LORD, which he had given Israel. ⁴¹With them were Heman and Jeduthun and the rest of those chosen and designated by name to give thanks to the LORD,

ʲ15 Some Septuagint manuscripts (see also Psalm 105:8); Hebrew
Remember   ᵏ18-20 One Hebrew manuscript, Septuagint and Vulgate
(see also Psalm 105:12); most Hebrew manuscripts inherit, / ¹⁹though
you are but few in number, / few indeed, and strangers in it." / ²⁰They
ˡ29 Or LORD with the splendor of

"for his love endures forever." ⁴²Heman and Jeduthun were responsible for the sounding of the trumpets and cymbals and for the playing of the other instruments for sacred song.

The sons of Jeduthun were stationed at the gate.

⁴³Then all the people left, each for his own home, and David returned home to bless his family.

3 / 1 Chronicles 17
Honored by God's Promises

A MAGAZINE AD campaign has for its theme "a promise." The picture always shows people who are committed to each other, and the words give lavish promises of security. I find the ads unclear, but apparently this insurance company will help the people in the ad keep their promises. Sometimes we extract promises from people against their will. In today's Scripture God gave David an unexpected promise.

 Warming Up to God Think about a time the Lord kept a promise to you. How did it deepen your relationship with him?

 Read 1 Chronicles 17.

17 After David was settled in his palace, he said to Nathan the prophet, "Here I am, living in a palace of cedar, while the ark of the covenant of the LORD is under a tent."

²Nathan replied to David, "Whatever you have in mind, do it, for God is with you."

³That night the word of God came to Nathan, saying:

⁴"Go and tell my servant David, 'This is what the LORD says: You are not the one to build me a house to dwell in. ⁵I have not dwelt in a house from the day I brought Israel up out of Egypt to this day. I have moved from one tent site to another, from one dwelling place to another. ⁶Wherever I have moved with all the Israelites, did I ever say to any of their leaders^m whom I commanded to shepherd my people, "Why have you not built me a house of cedar?" '

⁷"Now then, tell my servant David, 'This is what the LORD Almighty says: I took you from the pasture and from following the flock, to be ruler over my people Israel. ⁸I have been with you wherever you have gone, and I have cut off all your enemies from before you. Now I will make your name like the names of the greatest men of the earth. ⁹And I will provide a place for my people Israel and will plant them so that they can

have a home of their own and no longer be disturbed. Wicked people will not oppress them anymore, as they did at the beginning ¹⁰and have done ever since the time I appointed leaders over my people Israel. I will also subdue all your enemies.

" 'I declare to you that the LORD will build a house for you: ¹¹When your days are over and you go to be with your fathers, I will raise up your offspring to succeed you, one of your own sons, and I will establish his kingdom. ¹²He is the one who will build a house for me, and I will establish his throne forever. ¹³I will be his father, and he will be my son. I will never take my love away from him, as I took it away from your predecessor. ¹⁴I will set him over my house and my kingdom forever; his throne will be established forever.' "

¹⁵Nathan reported to David all the words of this entire revelation.

¹⁶Then King David went in and sat before the LORD, and he said:

"Who am I, O LORD God, and what is my family, that you have brought me this far? ¹⁷And as if this were not enough in your

^m 6 Traditionally *judges*; also in verse 10

sight, O God, you have spoken about the future of the house of your servant. You have looked on me as though I were the most exalted of men, O LORD God.

18"What more can David say to you for honoring your servant? For you know your servant, 19O LORD. For the sake of your servant and according to your will, you have done this great thing and made known all these great promises.

20"There is no one like you, O LORD, and there is no God but you, as we have heard with our own ears. 21And who is like your people Israel—the one nation on earth whose God went out to redeem a people for himself, and to make a name for yourself, and to perform great and awesome wonders by driving out nations from before your people, whom you redeemed from Egypt? 22You made your people Israel your very own forever, and you, O LORD, have become their God.

23"And now, LORD, let the promise you have made concerning your servant and his house be established forever. Do as you promised, 24so that it will be established and that your name will be great forever. Then men will say, 'The LORD Almighty, the God over Israel, is Israel's God!' And the house of your servant David will be established before you.

25"You, my God, have revealed to your servant that you will build a house for him. So your servant has found courage to pray to you. 26O LORD, you are God! You have promised these good things to your servant. 27Now you have been pleased to bless the house of your servant, that it may continue forever in your sight; for you, O LORD, have blessed it, and it will be blessed forever."

Discovering the Word 1. The ark of the covenant had been brought to Jerusalem and set up in the tabernacle (tent). What did David plan to do next (v. 1)? 2. How did God use Nathan to intervene in David's plans (vv. 2–6)? 3. What did the Lord promise David (vv. 7–14)? 4. David could have gotten huffy about the Lord not letting *him* build a temple. Instead, how did he respond to the revelation of this unexpected promise (vv. 16–19)? 5. How did David express his confidence in God's promise (vv. 20–27)?

Applying the Word 1. How do you feel about the promises God makes to us? 2. In times of anxiety, what promises of God do you hold on to?

Responding in Prayer Thank the Lord for his promises. Think of specific ones and how they apply to you, and praise him for his faithfulness.

---

1 Chronicles 18

18 In the course of time, David defeated the Philistines and subdued them, and he took Gath and its surrounding villages from the control of the Philistines.

2David also defeated the Moabites, and they became subject to him and brought tribute.

3Moreover, David fought Hadadezer king of Zobah, as far as Hamath, when he went to establish his control along the Euphrates River. 4David captured a thousand of his chariots, seven thousand charioteers and twenty thousand foot soldiers. He hamstrung all but a hundred of the chariot horses.

5When the Arameans of Damascus came to help Hadadezer king of Zobah, David struck down twenty-two thousand of them. 6He put garrisons in the Aramean kingdom of Damascus, and the Arameans became subject to him and brought tribute. The LORD gave David victory everywhere he went.

7David took the gold shields carried by the officers of Hadadezer and brought them to Jerusalem. 8From Tebah[n] and Cun, towns that belonged to Hadadezer, David took a great quantity of bronze, which Solomon used to make the bronze Sea, the pillars and various bronze articles.

9When Tou king of Hamath heard that David had defeated the entire army of Hadadezer king of

---

n8 Hebrew *Tibhath,* a variant of *Tebah*

Zobah, ¹⁰he sent his son Hadoram to King David to greet him and congratulate him on his victory in battle over Hadadezer, who had been at war with Tou. Hadoram brought all kinds of articles of gold and silver and bronze.

¹¹King David dedicated these articles to the LORD, as he had done with the silver and gold he had taken from all these nations: Edom and Moab, the Ammonites and the Philistines, and Amalek.

¹²Abishai son of Zeruiah struck down eighteen thousand Edomites in the Valley of Salt. ¹³He put garrisons in Edom, and all the Edomites became subject to David. The LORD gave David victory everywhere he went.

¹⁴David reigned over all Israel, doing what was just and right for all his people. ¹⁵Joab son of Zeruiah was over the army; Jehoshaphat son of Ahilud was recorder; ¹⁶Zadok son of Ahitub and Ahimelech*ᵒ* son of Abiathar were priests; Shavsha was secretary; ¹⁷Benaiah son of Jehoiada was over the Kerethites and Pelethites; and David's sons were chief officials at the king's side.

ᵒ16 Some Hebrew manuscripts, Vulgate and Syriac (see also 2 Samuel 8:17); most Hebrew manuscripts Abimelech

4 / 1 Chronicles 19
Misunderstood Sympathy

WE KNOW ONE home where it's not safe to inquire about family members; you might mention the name of whoever's in the doghouse right now. In many families and workplaces—even churches—there's one person who keeps things stirred up with rumors. When we start guessing and second-guessing people's motives, there's no end in sight. In this case a misunderstanding inflated into war.

Warming Up to God When have your motives been misunderstood? How did God help you deal with it?

Read 1 Chronicles 19.

19 In the course of time, Nahash king of the Ammonites died, and his son succeeded him as king. ²David thought, "I will show kindness to Hanun son of Nahash, because his father showed kindness to me." So David sent a delegation to express his sympathy to Hanun concerning his father.

When David's men came to Hanun in the land of the Ammonites to express sympathy to him, ³the Ammonite nobles said to Hanun, "Do you think David is honoring your father by sending men to you to express sympathy? Haven't his men come to you to explore and spy out the country and overthrow it?" ⁴So Hanun seized David's men, shaved them, cut off their garments in the middle at the buttocks, and sent them away.

⁵When someone came and told David about the men, he sent messengers to meet them, for they were greatly humiliated. The king said, "Stay at Jericho till your beards have grown, and then come back."

⁶When the Ammonites realized that they had become a stench in David's nostrils, Hanun and the Ammonites sent a thousand talents*ᵖ* of silver to hire chariots and charioteers from Aram Naharaim,*ᵠ* Aram Maacah and Zobah. ⁷They hired thirty-two thousand chariots and charioteers, as well as the king of Maacah with his troops, who came and camped near Medeba, while the Ammonites were mustered from their towns and moved out for battle.

⁸On hearing this, David sent Joab out with the entire army of fighting men. ⁹The Ammonites came out and drew up in battle formation at the entrance to their city, while the kings who had come were by themselves in the open country.

¹⁰Joab saw that there were battle lines in front of him and behind him; so he selected some of the best troops in Israel and deployed them against the Arameans. ¹¹He put the rest of the

ᵖ6 That is, about 37 tons (about 34 metric tons)   ᵠ6 That is, Northwest Mesopotamia men under the command of Abishai his brother, and they were deployed against the Ammonites. ¹²Joab said, "If the Arameans are too strong for me, then you are to rescue me; but if the Ammonites are too strong for you, then I will rescue you. ¹³Be strong and let us fight bravely for our people and the cities of our God. The LORD will do what is good in his sight."

¹⁴Then Joab and the troops with him advanced to fight the Arameans, and they fled before him. ¹⁵When the Ammonites saw that the Arameans were fleeing, they too fled before his brother Abishai and went inside the city. So Joab went back to Jerusalem.

¹⁶After the Arameans saw that they had been routed by Israel, they sent messengers and had Arameans brought from beyond the River,ʳ with

Shophach the commander of Hadadezer's army leading them.

¹⁷When David was told of this, he gathered all Israel and crossed the Jordan; he advanced against them and formed his battle lines opposite them. David formed his lines to meet the Arameans in battle, and they fought against him. ¹⁸But they fled before Israel, and David killed seven thousand of their charioteers and forty thousand of their foot soldiers. He also killed Shophach the commander of their army.

¹⁹When the vassals of Hadadezer saw that they had been defeated by Israel, they made peace with David and became subject to him.

So the Arameans were not willing to help the Ammonites anymore.

ʳ16 That is, the Euphrates

Discovering the Word   1. What was David's intention in sending the delegation to the Ammonites (vv. 1–2)? 2. How did suspicion poison their mission (vv. 3–4)? 3. How did the Ammonites escalate their aggression against Israel (vv. 6–7)? 4. What was the outcome of the conflict (vv. 14–19)? 5. How could the conflict have been avoided?

Applying the Word   1. Why are we so prone to take offense at what might be innocent gestures? 2. When have you seen something innocent escalate into a fight? 3. What can you do to prevent such tragic misunderstandings?

Responding in Prayer   Pray for patience and wisdom to avoid leaping to conclusions about other people's motives.

---

1 Chronicles 20

20 In the spring, at the time when kings go off to war, Joab led out the armed forces. He laid waste the land of the Ammonites and went to Rabbah and besieged it, but David remained in Jerusalem. Joab attacked Rabbah and left it in ruins. ²David took the crown from the head of their kingˢ—its weight was found to be a talentᵗ of gold, and it was set with precious stones—and it was placed on David's head. He took a great quantity of plunder from the city ³and brought out the people who were there, consigning them to labor with saws and with iron picks and axes. David did this to all the Ammonite towns. Then David and his entire army returned to Jerusalem.

⁴In the course of time, war broke out with the Philistines, at Gezer. At that time Sibbecai the

Hushathite killed Sippai, one of the descendants of the Rephaites, and the Philistines were subjugated.

⁵In another battle with the Philistines, Elhanan son of Jair killed Lahmi the brother of Goliath the Gittite, who had a spear with a shaft like a weaver's rod.

⁶In still another battle, which took place at Gath, there was a huge man with six fingers on each hand and six toes on each foot—twenty-four in all. He also was descended from Rapha. ⁷When he taunted Israel, Jonathan son of Shimea, David's brother, killed him.

⁸These were descendants of Rapha in Gath, and they fell at the hands of David and his men.

ˢ2 Or of Milcom, that is, Molech   ᵗ2 That is, about 75 pounds (about 34 kilograms)

5 / *1 Chronicles 21:1—22:1*
Misplaced Trust

WHAT MAKES YOU feel secure? Is it a steady job? a large savings account? good health? family and friends? Each of these can be a gift from the Lord and a reason for giving thanks. However, when we begin to trust in the gift rather than the Giver, we are headed for trouble. In this chapter David discovers the terrible consequences of misplaced trust.

 Warming Up to God What sorts of things contribute to your feelings of security?

 Read 1 Chronicles 21:1—22:1.

21 Satan rose up against Israel and incited David to take a census of Israel. ²So David said to Joab and the commanders of the troops, "Go and count the Israelites from Beersheba to Dan. Then report back to me so that I may know how many there are."

³But Joab replied, "May the Lord multiply his troops a hundred times over. My lord the king, are they not all my lord's subjects? Why does my lord want to do this? Why should he bring guilt on Israel?"

⁴The king's word, however, overruled Joab; so Joab left and went throughout Israel and then came back to Jerusalem. ⁵Joab reported the number of the fighting men to David: In all Israel there were one million one hundred thousand men who could handle a sword, including four hundred and seventy thousand in Judah.

⁶But Joab did not include Levi and Benjamin in the numbering, because the king's command was repulsive to him. ⁷This command was also evil in the sight of God; so he punished Israel.

⁸Then David said to God, "I have sinned greatly by doing this. Now, I beg you, take away the guilt of your servant. I have done a very foolish thing."

⁹The Lord said to Gad, David's seer, ¹⁰"Go and tell David, 'This is what the Lord says: I am giving you three options. Choose one of them for me to carry out against you.'"

¹¹So Gad went to David and said to him, "This is what the Lord says: 'Take your choice: ¹²three years of famine, three months of being swept away[u] before your enemies, with their swords overtaking you, or three days of the sword of the Lord—days of plague in the land, with the angel of the Lord ravaging every part of Israel.' Now

then, decide how I should answer the one who sent me."

¹³David said to Gad, "I am in deep distress. Let me fall into the hands of the Lord, for his mercy is very great; but do not let me fall into the hands of men."

¹⁴So the Lord sent a plague on Israel, and seventy thousand men of Israel fell dead. ¹⁵And God sent an angel to destroy Jerusalem. But as the angel was doing so, the Lord saw it and was grieved because of the calamity and said to the angel who was destroying the people, "Enough! Withdraw your hand." The angel of the Lord was then standing at the threshing floor of Araunah[v] the Jebusite.

¹⁶David looked up and saw the angel of the Lord standing between heaven and earth, with a drawn sword in his hand extended over Jerusalem. Then David and the elders, clothed in sackcloth, fell facedown.

¹⁷David said to God, "Was it not I who ordered the fighting men to be counted? I am the one who has sinned and done wrong. These are but sheep. What have they done? O Lord my God, let your hand fall upon me and my family, but do not let this plague remain on your people."

¹⁸Then the angel of the Lord ordered Gad to tell David to go up and build an altar to the Lord on the threshing floor of Araunah the Jebusite. ¹⁹So David went up in obedience to the word that Gad had spoken in the name of the Lord.

²⁰While Araunah was threshing wheat, he turned and saw the angel; his four sons who were with him hid themselves. ²¹Then David approached, and when Araunah looked and saw

[u]*12 Hebrew; Septuagint and Vulgate (see also 2 Samuel 24:13) of fleeing*
[v]*15 Hebrew Ornan, a variant of Araunah; also in verses 18-28*

him, he left the threshing floor and bowed down before David with his face to the ground.

²²David said to him, "Let me have the site of your threshing floor so I can build an altar to the LORD, that the plague on the people may be stopped. Sell it to me at the full price."

²³Araunah said to David, "Take it! Let my lord the king do whatever pleases him. Look, I will give the oxen for the burnt offerings, the threshing sledges for the wood, and the wheat for the grain offering. I will give all this."

²⁴But King David replied to Araunah, "No, I insist on paying the full price. I will not take for the LORD what is yours, or sacrifice a burnt offering that costs me nothing."

²⁵So David paid Araunah six hundred shekels^w of gold for the site. ²⁶David built an altar to the LORD there and sacrificed burnt offerings and fel-

lowship offerings.^{x} He called on the LORD, and the LORD answered him with fire from heaven on the altar of burnt offering.

²⁷Then the LORD spoke to the angel, and he put his sword back into its sheath. ²⁸At that time, when David saw that the LORD had answered him on the threshing floor of Araunah the Jebusite, he offered sacrifices there. ²⁹The tabernacle of the LORD, which Moses had made in the desert, and the altar of burnt offering were at that time on the high place at Gibeon. ³⁰But David could not go before it to inquire of God, because he was afraid of the sword of the angel of the LORD.

22 Then David said, "The house of the LORD God is to be here, and also the altar of burnt offering for Israel."

^{w}25 That is, about 15 pounds (about 15 kilograms) ^{x}26 Traditionally *peace offerings*

Discovering the Word 1. In what ways does the author make it clear that David's action was evil (21:1, 3, 6, 8)? 2. Unfortunately, the author does not tell us *why* David's action was sinful. Why might the Lord have viewed David's action as sinful? 3. In what sense was the plague on Israel (21:14) an appropriate punishment for David's sin? 4. What contributes to the mood of fear and urgency in 21:16–27? 5. Why was this an appropriate site for building the house of the Lord (22:1)?

Applying the Word 1. Why are we often tempted to trust in human strength and resources rather than in the Lord? 2. Animal sacrifices are no longer necessary to atone for our sins (Heb 10:11–12). What then should we do when we discover we are guilty of misplaced trust?

Responding in Prayer If you are aware of any such areas of your life, take time now to confess them to the Lord. Thank him for the forgiveness and security we have in Christ.

---

1 Chronicles 22:2—27:34

²So David gave orders to assemble the aliens living in Israel, and from among them he appointed stonecutters to prepare dressed stone for building the house of God. ³He provided a large amount of iron to make nails for the doors of the gateways and for the fittings, and more bronze than could be weighed. ⁴He also provided more cedar logs than could be counted, for the Sidonians and Tyrians had brought large numbers of them to David.

⁵David said, "My son Solomon is young and inexperienced, and the house to be built for the LORD should be of great magnificence and fame and splendor in the sight of all the nations. Therefore I will make preparations for it." So David made extensive preparations before his death.

⁶Then he called for his son Solomon and

charged him to build a house for the LORD, the God of Israel. ⁷David said to Solomon: "My son, I had it in my heart to build a house for the Name of the LORD my God. ⁸But this word of the LORD came to me: 'You have shed much blood and have fought many wars. You are not to build a house for my Name, because you have shed much blood on the earth in my sight. ⁹But you will have a son who will be a man of peace and rest, and I will give him rest from all his enemies on every side. His name will be Solomon,^{y} and I will grant Israel peace and quiet during his reign. ¹⁰He is the one who will build a house for my Name. He will be my son, and I will be his father. And I will

^{y}9 *Solomon* sounds like and may be derived from the Hebrew for *peace*.

establish the throne of his kingdom over Israel forever.'

¹¹"Now, my son, the LORD be with you, and may you have success and build the house of the LORD your God, as he said you would. ¹²May the LORD give you discretion and understanding when he puts you in command over Israel, so that you may keep the law of the LORD your God. ¹³Then you will have success if you are careful to observe the decrees and laws that the LORD gave Moses for Israel. Be strong and courageous. Do not be afraid or discouraged.

¹⁴"I have taken great pains to provide for the temple of the LORD a hundred thousand talents[z] of gold, a million talents[a] of silver, quantities of bronze and iron too great to be weighed, and wood and stone. And you may add to them. ¹⁵You have many workmen: stonecutters, masons and carpenters, as well as men skilled in every kind of work ¹⁶in gold and silver, bronze and iron— craftsmen beyond number. Now begin the work, and the LORD be with you."

¹⁷Then David ordered all the leaders of Israel to help his son Solomon. ¹⁸He said to them, "Is not the LORD your God with you? And has he not granted you rest on every side? For he has handed the inhabitants of the land over to me, and the land is subject to the LORD and to his people. ¹⁹Now devote your heart and soul to seeking the LORD your God. Begin to build the sanctuary of the LORD God, so that you may bring the ark of the covenant of the LORD and the sacred articles belonging to God into the temple that will be built for the Name of the LORD."

23

When David was old and full of years, he made his son Solomon king over Israel.

²He also gathered together all the leaders of Israel, as well as the priests and Levites. ³The Levites thirty years old or more were counted, and the total number of men was thirty-eight thousand. ⁴David said, "Of these, twenty-four thousand are to supervise the work of the temple of the LORD and six thousand are to be officials and judges. ⁵Four thousand are to be gatekeepers and four thousand are to praise the LORD with the musical instruments I have provided for that purpose."

⁶David divided the Levites into groups corresponding to the sons of Levi: Gershon, Kohath and Merari.

⁷Belonging to the Gershonites:
Ladan and Shimei.

⁸The sons of Ladan:
Jehiel the first, Zetham and Joel—three in all.

⁹The sons of Shimei:
Shelomoth, Haziel and Haran—three in all.
These were the heads of the families of Ladan.

¹⁰And the sons of Shimei:
Jahath, Ziza,[b] Jeush and Beriah.
These were the sons of Shimei—four in all.

¹¹Jahath was the first and Ziza the second, but Jeush and Beriah did not have many sons; so they were counted as one family with one assignment.

¹²The sons of Kohath:
Amram, Izhar, Hebron and Uzziel—four in all.

¹³The sons of Amram:
Aaron and Moses.
Aaron was set apart, he and his descendants forever, to consecrate the most holy things, to offer sacrifices before the LORD, to minister before him and to pronounce blessings in his name forever. ¹⁴The sons of Moses the man of God were counted as part of the tribe of Levi.

¹⁵The sons of Moses:
Gershom and Eliezer.

¹⁶The descendants of Gershom:
Shubael was the first.

¹⁷The descendants of Eliezer:
Rehabiah was the first.
Eliezer had no other sons, but the sons of Rehabiah were very numerous.

¹⁸The sons of Izhar:
Shelomith was the first.

¹⁹The sons of Hebron:
Jeriah the first, Amariah the second, Jahaziel the third and Jekameam the fourth.

²⁰The sons of Uzziel:
Micah the first and Isshiah the second.

²¹The sons of Merari:
Mahli and Mushi.
The sons of Mahli:

---

z14 That is, about 3,750 tons (about 3,450 metric tons)   a14 That is, about 37,500 tons (about 34,500 metric tons)   b10 One Hebrew manuscript, Septuagint and Vulgate (see also verse 11); most Hebrew manuscripts Zina

Eleazar and Kish.

²²Eleazar died without having sons: he had only daughters. Their cousins, the sons of Kish, married them.

²³The sons of Mushi:

Mahli, Eder and Jerimoth—three in all.

²⁴These were the descendants of Levi by their families—the heads of families as they were registered under their names and counted individually, that is, the workers twenty years old or more who served in the temple of the LORD. ²⁵For David had said, "Since the LORD, the God of Israel, has granted rest to his people and has come to dwell in Jerusalem forever, ²⁶the Levites no longer need to carry the tabernacle or any of the articles used in its service." ²⁷According to the last instructions of David, the Levites were counted from those twenty years old or more.

²⁸The duty of the Levites was to help Aaron's descendants in the service of the temple of the LORD: to be in charge of the courtyards, the side rooms, the purification of all sacred things and the performance of other duties at the house of God. ²⁹They were in charge of the bread set out on the table, the flour for the grain offerings, the unleavened wafers, the baking and the mixing, and all measurements of quantity and size. ³⁰They were also to stand every morning to thank and praise the LORD. They were to do the same in the evening ³¹and whenever burnt offerings were presented to the LORD on Sabbaths and at New Moon festivals and at appointed feasts. They were to serve before the LORD regularly in the proper number and in the way prescribed for them.

³²And so the Levites carried out their responsibilities for the Tent of Meeting, for the Holy Place and, under their brothers the descendants of Aaron, for the service of the temple of the LORD.

24

These were the divisions of the sons of Aaron:

The sons of Aaron were Nadab, Abihu, Eleazar and Ithamar. ²But Nadab and Abihu died before their father did, and they had no sons; so Eleazar and Ithamar served as the priests. ³With the help of Zadok a descendant of Eleazar and Ahimelech a descendant of Ithamar, David separated them into divisions for their appointed order of ministering. ⁴A larger number of leaders were found among Eleazar's descendants than among Ithamar's, and they were divided accordingly: sixteen heads of families from Eleazar's

descendants and eight heads of families from Ithamar's descendants. ⁵They divided them impartially by drawing lots, for there were officials of the sanctuary and officials of God among the descendants of both Eleazar and Ithamar.

⁶The scribe Shemaiah son of Nethanel, a Levite, recorded their names in the presence of the king and of the officials: Zadok the priest, Ahimelech son of Abiathar and the heads of families of the priests and of the Levites—one family being taken from Eleazar and then one from Ithamar.

⁷The first lot fell to Jehoiarib,
  the second to Jedaiah,
⁸the third to Harim,
  the fourth to Seorim,
⁹the fifth to Malkijah,
  the sixth to Mijamin,
¹⁰the seventh to Hakkoz,
  the eighth to Abijah,
¹¹the ninth to Jeshua,
  the tenth to Shecaniah,
¹²the eleventh to Eliashib,
  the twelfth to Jakim,
¹³the thirteenth to Huppah,
  the fourteenth to Jeshebeab,
¹⁴the fifteenth to Bilgah,
  the sixteenth to Immer,
¹⁵the seventeenth to Hezir,
  the eighteenth to Happizzez,
¹⁶the nineteenth to Pethahiah,
  the twentieth to Jehezkel,
¹⁷the twenty-first to Jakin,
  the twenty-second to Gamul,
¹⁸the twenty-third to Delaiah
  and the twenty-fourth to Maaziah.

¹⁹This was their appointed order of ministering when they entered the temple of the LORD, according to the regulations prescribed for them by their forefather Aaron, as the LORD, the God of Israel, had commanded him.

²⁰As for the rest of the descendants of Levi:
  from the sons of Amram: Shubael;
    from the sons of Shubael: Jehdeiah.
  ²¹As for Rehabiah, from his sons:
    Isshiah was the first.
²²From the Izharites: Shelomoth;
  from the sons of Shelomoth: Jahath.
²³The sons of Hebron: Jeriah the first,ᶜ Ama-

ᶜ23 Two Hebrew manuscripts and some Septuagint manuscripts (see also 1 Chron. 23:19); most Hebrew manuscripts *The sons of Jeriah:*

riah the second, Jahaziel the third and Jekameam the fourth. ²⁴The son of Uzziel: Micah;
        from the sons of Micah: Shamir.
    ²⁵The brother of Micah: Isshiah;
        from the sons of Isshiah: Zechariah.
²⁶The sons of Merari: Mahli and Mushi.
    The son of Jaaziah: Beno.
²⁷The sons of Merari:
        from Jaaziah: Beno, Shoham, Zaccur and
        Ibri.
²⁸From Mahli: Eleazar, who had no sons.
²⁹From Kish: the son of Kish:
    Jerahmeel.
³⁰And the sons of Mushi: Mahli, Eder and Jer-
    imoth.

These were the Levites, according to their families. ³¹They also cast lots, just as their brothers the descendants of Aaron did, in the presence of King David and of Zadok, Ahimelech, and the heads of families of the priests and of the Levites. The families of the oldest brother were treated the same as those of the youngest.

25

David, together with the commanders of the army, set apart some of the sons of Asaph, Heman and Jeduthun for the ministry of prophesying, accompanied by harps, lyres and cymbals. Here is the list of the men who performed this service:

²From the sons of Asaph:
    Zaccur, Joseph, Nethaniah and Asarelah. The sons of Asaph were under the supervision of Asaph, who prophesied under the king's supervision.
³As for Jeduthun, from his sons:
    Gedaliah, Zeri, Jeshaiah, Shimei,^d Hashabiah and Mattithiah, six in all, under the supervision of their father Jeduthun, who prophesied, using the harp in thanking and praising the LORD.
⁴As for Heman, from his sons:
    Bukkiah, Mattaniah, Uzziel, Shubael and Jerimoth; Hananiah, Hanani, Eliathah, Giddalti and Romamti-Ezer; Joshbekashah, Mallothi, Hothir and Mahazioth. ⁵All these were sons of Heman the king's seer. They were given him through the promises of God to exalt him.^e God gave Heman fourteen sons and three daughters.

⁶All these men were under the supervision of

their fathers for the music of the temple of the LORD, with cymbals, lyres and harps, for the ministry at the house of God. Asaph, Jeduthun and Heman were under the supervision of the king. ⁷Along with their relatives—all of them trained and skilled in music for the LORD—they numbered 288. ⁸Young and old alike, teacher as well as student, cast lots for their duties.

⁹The first lot, which was for Asaph, fell to
    Joseph,
        his sons and relatives,^f   12^g
    the second to Gedaliah,
        he and his relatives and sons,   12
¹⁰the third to Zaccur,
        his sons and relatives,   12
¹¹the fourth to Izri,^h
        his sons and relatives,   12
¹²the fifth to Nethaniah,
        his sons and relatives,   12
¹³the sixth to Bukkiah,
        his sons and relatives,   12
¹⁴the seventh to Jesarelah,ⁱ
        his sons and relatives,   12
¹⁵the eighth to Jeshaiah,
        his sons and relatives,   12
¹⁶the ninth to Mattaniah,
        his sons and relatives,   12
¹⁷the tenth to Shimei,
        his sons and relatives,   12
¹⁸the eleventh to Azarel,^j
        his sons and relatives,   12
¹⁹the twelfth to Hashabiah,
        his sons and relatives,   12
²⁰the thirteenth to Shubael,
        his sons and relatives,   12
²¹the fourteenth to Mattithiah,
        his sons and relatives,   12
²²the fifteenth to Jerimoth,
        his sons and relatives,   12
²³the sixteenth to Hananiah,
        his sons and relatives,   12
²⁴the seventeenth to Joshbekashah,
        his sons and relatives,   12
²⁵the eighteenth to Hanani,
        his sons and relatives,   12
²⁶the nineteenth to Mallothi,
        his sons and relatives,   12

^d3 One Hebrew manuscript and some Septuagint manuscripts (see also verse 17); most Hebrew manuscripts do not have *Shimei.*   ^e5 Hebrew *exalt the horn*   ^f9 See Septuagint; Hebrew does not have *his sons and relatives.*   ^g9 See the total in verse 7; Hebrew does not have *twelve.*   ^h11 A variant of *Zeri*   ⁱ14 A variant of *Asarelah*   ^j18 A variant of *Uzziel*

27the twentieth to Eliathah,
   his sons and relatives,   12
28the twenty-first to Hothir,
   his sons and relatives,   12
29the twenty-second to Giddalti,
   his sons and relatives,   12
30the twenty-third to Mahazioth,
   his sons and relatives,   12
31the twenty-fourth to Romamti-Ezer,
   his sons and relatives,   12

26 The divisions of the gatekeepers:
From the Korahites: Meshele-
miah son of Kore, one of the
sons of Asaph.
2Meshelemiah had sons:
   Zechariah the firstborn,
   Jediael the second,
   Zebadiah the third,
   Jathniel the fourth,
   3Elam the fifth,
   Jehohanan the sixth
   and Eliehoenai the seventh.
4Obed-Edom also had sons:
   Shemaiah the firstborn,
   Jehozabad the second,
   Joah the third,
   Sacar the fourth,
   Nethanel the fifth,
   5Ammiel the sixth,
   Issachar the seventh
   and Peullethai the eighth.
   (For God had blessed Obed-Edom.)

6His son Shemaiah also had sons, who were
leaders in their father's family because
they were very capable men. 7The sons of
Shemaiah: Othni, Rephael, Obed and Elzabad; his relatives Elihu and Semakiah
were also able men. 8All these were
descendants of Obed-Edom; they and
their sons and their relatives were capable
men with the strength to do the work—
descendants of Obed-Edom, 62 in all.
9Meshelemiah had sons and relatives, who
were able men—18 in all.

10Hosah the Merarite had sons: Shimri the
first (although he was not the firstborn,
his father had appointed him the first),
11Hilkiah the second, Tabaliah the third
and Zechariah the fourth. The sons and
relatives of Hosah were 13 in all.

12These divisions of the gatekeepers, through
their chief men, had duties for ministering in the
temple of the LORD, just as their relatives had.
13Lots were cast for each gate, according to their
families, young and old alike.
14The lot for the East Gate fell to Shelemiah.[k]
Then lots were cast for his son Zechariah, a wise
counselor, and the lot for the North Gate fell to
him. 15The lot for the South Gate fell to Obed-
Edom, and the lot for the storehouse fell to his
sons. 16The lots for the West Gate and the Shalle-
keth Gate on the upper road fell to Shuppim and
Hosah.

Guard was alongside of guard: 17There were six
Levites a day on the east, four a day on the north,
four a day on the south and two at a time at the
storehouse. 18As for the court to the west, there
were four at the road and two at the court itself.

19These were the divisions of the gatekeepers
who were descendants of Korah and Merari.

20Their fellow Levites were[l] in charge of the
treasuries of the house of God and the treasuries
for the dedicated things.

21The descendants of Ladan, who were Gershonites through Ladan and who were heads of
families belonging to Ladan the Gershonite, were
Jehieli, 22the sons of Jehieli, Zetham and his
brother Joel. They were in charge of the treasuries
of the temple of the LORD.

23From the Amramites, the Izharites, the Hebronites and the Uzzielites:

24Shubael, a descendant of Gershom son of
Moses, was the officer in charge of the
treasuries. 25His relatives through Eliezer:
Rehabiah his son, Jeshaiah his son, Joram
his son, Zicri his son and Shelomith his
son. 26Shelomith and his relatives were in
charge of all the treasuries for the things
dedicated by King David, by the heads of
families who were the commanders of
thousands and commanders of hundreds,
and by the other army commanders.
27Some of the plunder taken in battle they
dedicated for the repair of the temple of
the LORD. 28And everything dedicated by
Samuel the seer and by Saul son of Kish,
Abner son of Ner and Joab son of Zeruiah, and all the other dedicated things

k 14 A variant of Meshelemiah   l 20 Septuagint; Hebrew As for the
Levites, Ahijah was

were in the care of Shelomith and his relatives. ²⁹From the Izharites: Kenaniah and his sons were assigned duties away from the temple, as officials and judges over Israel. ³⁰From the Hebronites: Hashabiah and his relatives—seventeen hundred able men—were responsible in Israel west of the Jordan for all the work of the LORD and for the king's service. ³¹As for the Hebronites, Jeriah was their chief according to the genealogical records of their families. In the fortieth year of David's reign a search was made in the records, and capable men among the Hebronites were found at Jazer in Gilead. ³²Jeriah had twenty-seven hundred relatives, who were able men and heads of families, and King David put them in charge of the Reubenites, the Gadites and the half-tribe of Manasseh for every matter pertaining to God and for the affairs of the king.

27

This is the list of the Israelites—heads of families, commanders of thousands and commanders of hundreds, and their officers, who served the king in all that concerned the army divisions that were on duty month by month throughout the year. Each division consisted of 24,000 men.

²In charge of the first division, for the first month, was Jashobeam son of Zabdiel. There were 24,000 men in his division. ³He was a descendant of Perez and chief of all the army officers for the first month. ⁴In charge of the division for the second month was Dodai the Ahohite; Mikloth was the leader of his division. There were 24,000 men in his division. ⁵The third army commander, for the third month, was Benaiah son of Jehoiada the priest. He was chief and there were 24,000 men in his division. ⁶This was the Benaiah who was a mighty man among the Thirty and was over the Thirty. His son Ammizabad was in charge of his division. ⁷The fourth, for the fourth month, was Asahel the brother of Joab; his son Zebadiah was his successor. There were 24,000 men in his division. ⁸The fifth, for the fifth month, was the commander Shamhuth the Izrahite. There were 24,000 men in his division. ⁹The sixth, for the sixth month, was Ira the son of Ikkesh the Tekoite. There were 24,000 men in his division. ¹⁰The seventh, for the seventh month, was Helez the Pelonite, an Ephraimite. There were 24,000 men in his division. ¹¹The eighth, for the eighth month, was Sibbecai the Hushathite, a Zerahite. There were 24,000 men in his division. ¹²The ninth, for the ninth month, was Abiezer the Anathothite, a Benjamite. There were 24,000 men in his division. ¹³The tenth, for the tenth month, was Maharai the Netophathite, a Zerahite. There were 24,000 men in his division. ¹⁴The eleventh, for the eleventh month, was Benaiah the Pirathonite, an Ephraimite. There were 24,000 men in his division. ¹⁵The twelfth, for the twelfth month, was Heldai the Netophathite, from the family of Othniel. There were 24,000 men in his division.

¹⁶The officers over the tribes of Israel:

over the Reubenites: Eliezer son of Zicri;
over the Simeonites: Shephatiah son of Maacah;
¹⁷over Levi: Hashabiah son of Kemuel;
over Aaron: Zadok;
¹⁸over Judah: Elihu, a brother of David;
over Issachar: Omri son of Michael;
¹⁹over Zebulun: Ishmaiah son of Obadiah;
over Naphtali: Jerimoth son of Azriel;
²⁰over the Ephraimites: Hoshea son of Azaziah;
over half the tribe of Manasseh: Joel son of Pedaiah;
²¹over the half-tribe of Manasseh in Gilead: Iddo son of Zechariah;
over Benjamin: Jaasiel son of Abner;
²²over Dan: Azarel son of Jeroham.
These were the officers over the tribes of Israel.

²³David did not take the number of the men twenty years old or less, because the LORD had promised to make Israel as numerous as the stars in the sky. ²⁴Joab son of Zeruiah began to count the men but did not finish. Wrath came on Israel on account of this numbering, and the number

was not entered in the book[m] of the annals of King David.

²⁵Azmaveth son of Adiel was in charge of the royal storehouses.

Jonathan son of Uzziah was in charge of the storehouses in the outlying districts, in the towns, the villages and the watchtowers.

²⁶Ezri son of Kelub was in charge of the field workers who farmed the land.

²⁷Shimei the Ramathite was in charge of the vineyards.

Zabdi the Shiphmite was in charge of the produce of the vineyards for the wine vats.

²⁸Baal-Hanan the Gederite was in charge of the olive and sycamore-fig trees in the western foothills.

Joash was in charge of the supplies of olive oil.

²⁹Shitrai the Sharonite was in charge of the herds grazing in Sharon.

Shaphat son of Adlai was in charge of the herds in the valleys.

³⁰Obil the Ishmaelite was in charge of the camels.

Jehdeiah the Meronothite was in charge of the donkeys.

³¹Jaziz the Hagrite was in charge of the flocks.

All these were the officials in charge of King David's property.

³²Jonathan, David's uncle, was a counselor, a man of insight and a scribe. Jehiel son of Hacmoni took care of the king's sons.

³³Ahithophel was the king's counselor.

Hushai the Arkite was the king's friend. ³⁴Ahithophel was succeeded by Jehoiada son of Benaiah and by Abiathar.

Joab was the commander of the royal army.

[m]24 Septuagint; Hebrew *number*

6 / 1 Chronicles 28
A Legacy of Humble Service

OUR CHURCH IS full of plaques memorializing those who gave the stained glass windows, the organ, the furnishings in the small chapel, the ceiling lights. The names go largely unnoticed, but what would the building be like without those things? People several generations back started the Sunday school, began the choir, collected the first missions offering. Today we carry on the work they started. As David passes his dreams for the temple on to Solomon—despite his disappointment at not being able to build it himself—he too leaves a legacy for those to come.

Warming Up to God How much of your work for the Lord was actually started by a previous generation? Consider the people who came before you to lay the foundation, and thank God for them.

Read 1 Chronicles 28.

28 David summoned all the officials of Israel to assemble at Jerusalem: the officers over the tribes, the commanders of the divisions in the service of the king, the commanders of thousands and commanders of hundreds, and the officials in charge of all the property and livestock belonging to the king and his sons, together with the palace officials, the mighty men and all the brave warriors.

²King David rose to his feet and said: "Listen to me, my brothers and my people. I had it in my heart to build a house as a place of rest for the ark of the covenant of the LORD, for the footstool of our God, and I made plans to build it. ³But God said to me, 'You are not to build a house for my Name, because you are a warrior and have shed blood.'

⁴"Yet the LORD, the God of Israel, chose me from my whole family to be king over Israel forever. He chose Judah as leader, and from the house of Judah he chose my family, and from my father's sons he was pleased to make me king over all Israel. ⁵Of all my sons—and the LORD has given me many—he has chosen my son Solomon to sit on the throne of the kingdom of the LORD over Israel. ⁶He said to me: 'Solomon your son is

the one who will build my house and my courts, for I have chosen him to be my son, and I will be his father. [7]I will establish his kingdom forever if he is unswerving in carrying out my commands and laws, as is being done at this time.'

[8]"So now I charge you in the sight of all Israel and of the assembly of the LORD, and in the hearing of our God: Be careful to follow all the commands of the LORD your God, that you may possess this good land and pass it on as an inheritance to your descendants forever.

[9]"And you, my son Solomon, acknowledge the God of your father, and serve him with wholehearted devotion and with a willing mind, for the LORD searches every heart and understands every motive behind the thoughts. If you seek him, he will be found by you; but if you forsake him, he will reject you forever. [10]Consider now, for the LORD has chosen you to build a temple as a sanctuary. Be strong and do the work."

[11]Then David gave his son Solomon the plans for the portico of the temple, its buildings, its storerooms, its upper parts, its inner rooms and the place of atonement. [12]He gave him the plans of all that the Spirit had put in his mind for the courts of the temple of the LORD and all the surrounding rooms, for the treasuries of the temple of God and for the treasuries for the dedicated things. [13]He gave him instructions for the divisions of the priests and Levites, and for all the work of serving in the temple of the LORD, as well as for all the articles to be used in its service. [14]He

designated the weight of gold for all the gold articles to be used in various kinds of service, and the weight of silver for all the silver articles to be used in various kinds of service: [15]the weight of gold for the gold lampstands and their lamps, with the weight for each lampstand and its lamps; and the weight of silver for each silver lampstand and its lamps, according to the use of each lampstand; [16]the weight of gold for each table for consecrated bread; the weight of silver for the silver tables; [17]the weight of pure gold for the forks, sprinkling bowls and pitchers; the weight of gold for each gold dish; the weight of silver for each silver dish; [18]and the weight of the refined gold for the altar of incense. He also gave him the plan for the chariot, that is, the cherubim of gold that spread their wings and shelter the ark of the covenant of the LORD.

[19]"All this," David said, "I have in writing from the hand of the LORD upon me, and he gave me understanding in all the details of the plan."

[20]David also said to Solomon his son, "Be strong and courageous, and do the work. Do not be afraid or discouraged, for the LORD God, my God, is with you. He will not fail you or forsake you until all the work for the service of the temple of the LORD is finished. [21]The divisions of the priests and Levites are ready for all the work on the temple of God, and every willing man skilled in any craft will help you in all the work. The officials and all the people will obey your every command."

Discovering the Word 1. David was admitting to the officials that the Lord had denied him the privilege of building the temple in favor of his son Solomon. What do his actions throughout this passage tell you about how he's handling this news? 2. How did David encourage Solomon to act (vv. 9–10)? 3. How did David provide for Solomon to carry out the building of the temple (vv. 11–19)? 4. How did David conclude his address (vv. 20–21)? 5. What do you learn about David's character from his reaction to this disappointment?

Applying the Word 1. When are you likely to pout about God's plans for you? (For example, when God gives someone else a job you'd like to have.) 2. How can your attitude be helped by getting the "long view" of God's plans in the world? 3. In what ways would you like to handle disappointment more like David does?

Responding in Prayer If you are aware of being overpossessive about some aspect of your life or ministry, confess your attitude to the Lord. Ask him to teach you humility and give you energy to serve him in the places he's called you to.

7 / *1 Chronicles 29*
Generous Giving

GIVING HAS BECOME a sore spot for many Christians. Every day we are bombarded with appeals for money—from television and radio evangelists, from missionaries, from parachurch organizations, from relief agencies, and from our own churches. Sometimes we feel like shouting, "Enough is enough!" David had a very different attitude toward giving. In this chapter he illustrates what it means to give joyously and generously to the Lord.

 Warming Up to God   Reflect on a time when you have recently enjoyed giving something to someone else. Thank God for the joy of giving.

 Read 1 Chronicles 29.

29 Then King David said to the whole assembly: "My son Solomon, the one whom God has chosen, is young and inexperienced. The task is great, because this palatial structure is not for man but for the LORD God. ²With all my resources I have provided for the temple of my God—gold for the gold work, silver for the silver, bronze for the bronze, iron for the iron and wood for the wood, as well as onyx for the settings, turquoise,ⁿ stones of various colors, and all kinds of fine stone and marble—all of these in large quantities. ³Besides, in my devotion to the temple of my God I now give my personal treasures of gold and silver for the temple of my God, over and above everything I have provided for this holy temple: ⁴three thousand talentsᵒ of gold (gold of Ophir) and seven thousand talentsᵖ of refined silver, for the overlaying of the walls of the buildings, ⁵for the gold work and the silver work, and for all the work to be done by the craftsmen. Now, who is willing to consecrate himself today to the LORD?"

⁶Then the leaders of families, the officers of the tribes of Israel, the commanders of thousands and commanders of hundreds, and the officials in charge of the king's work gave willingly. ⁷They gave toward the work on the temple of God five thousand talentsᑫ and ten thousand daricsʳ of gold, ten thousand talentsˢ of silver, eighteen thousand talentsᵗ of bronze and a hundred thousand talentsᵘ of iron. ⁸Any who had precious stones gave them to the treasury of the temple of the LORD in the custody of Jehiel the Gershonite. ⁹The people rejoiced at the willing response of their leaders, for they had given freely and wholeheartedly to the LORD. David the king also rejoiced greatly.

¹⁰David praised the LORD in the presence of the whole assembly, saying,

"Praise be to you, O LORD,
    God of our father Israel,
    from everlasting to everlasting.
¹¹Yours, O LORD, is the greatness and the power
    and the glory and the majesty and the
        splendor,
    for everything in heaven and earth is yours.
Yours, O LORD, is the kingdom;
    you are exalted as head over all.
¹²Wealth and honor come from you;
    you are the ruler of all things.
In your hands are strength and power
    to exalt and give strength to all.
¹³Now, our God, we give you thanks,
    and praise your glorious name.

¹⁴"But who am I, and who are my people, that we should be able to give as generously as this? Everything comes from you, and we have given you only what comes from your hand. ¹⁵We are aliens and strangers in your sight, as were all our forefathers. Our days on earth are like a shadow, without hope. ¹⁶O LORD our God, as for all this abundance that we have provided for building you a temple for your Holy Name, it comes from your hand, and all of it belongs to you. ¹⁷I know, my God, that you test the heart and are pleased with integrity. All these things have I given willingly and with honest intent. And now I have seen with joy how willingly your people who are here have given to you. ¹⁸O LORD, God of our fa-

---

ⁿ2 The meaning of the Hebrew for this word is uncertain.   ᵒ4 That is, about 110 tons (about 100 metric tons)   ᵖ4 That is, about 260 tons (about 240 metric tons)   ᑫ7 That is, about 190 tons (about 170 metric tons)   ʳ7 That is, about 185 pounds (about 84 kilograms)   ˢ7 That is, about 375 tons (about 345 metric tons)   ᵗ7 That is, about 675 tons (about 610 metric tons)   ᵘ7 That is, about 3,750 tons (about 3,450 metric tons) thers Abraham, Isaac and Israel, keep this desire in the hearts of your people forever, and keep their hearts loyal to you. ¹⁹And give my son Solomon the wholehearted devotion to keep your commands, requirements and decrees and to do everything to build the palatial structure for which I have provided."

²⁰Then David said to the whole assembly, "Praise the Lᴏʀᴅ your God." So they all praised the Lᴏʀᴅ, the God of their fathers; they bowed low and fell prostrate before the Lᴏʀᴅ and the king.

²¹The next day they made sacrifices to the Lᴏʀᴅ and presented burnt offerings to him: a thousand bulls, a thousand rams and a thousand male lambs, together with their drink offerings, and other sacrifices in abundance for all Israel. ²²They ate and drank with great joy in the presence of the Lᴏʀᴅ that day.

Then they acknowledged Solomon son of David as king a second time, anointing him before the Lᴏʀᴅ to be ruler and Zadok to be priest. ²³So Solomon sat on the throne of the Lᴏʀᴅ as king in place of his father David. He prospered and all Israel obeyed him. ²⁴All the officers and mighty men, as well as all of King David's sons, pledged their submission to King Solomon.

²⁵The Lᴏʀᴅ highly exalted Solomon in the sight of all Israel and bestowed on him royal splendor such as no king over Israel ever had before.

²⁶David son of Jesse was king over all Israel. ²⁷He ruled over Israel forty years—seven in Hebron and thirty-three in Jerusalem. ²⁸He died at a good old age, having enjoyed long life, wealth and honor. His son Solomon succeeded him as king.

²⁹As for the events of King David's reign, from beginning to end, they are written in the records of Samuel the seer, the records of Nathan the prophet and the records of Gad the seer, ³⁰together with the details of his reign and power, and the circumstances that surrounded him and Israel and the kingdoms of all the other lands.

Discovering the Word 1. How does David provide an excellent example of what it means to give generously to God (vv. 1–5)? 2. What effect does David's example have on the leaders of Israel and the people (vv. 6–9)? 3. What does David's prayer in verses 10–13 reveal about his view of God? 4. David might have felt boastful about his giving. What do verses 14–19 reveal about his reasons for humility? 5. David might also have felt remorse about parting with so much of his wealth. Instead, what spiritual and emotional impact did it have on him and the people (vv. 20–25)?

Applying the Word 1. How is our view of God related to our willingness or unwillingness to give generously? 2. In what ways have you been motivated to give more generously or to dedicate yourself more fully by observing the personal example of Christian leaders? 3. In what ways have you been challenged by David's example?

 Responding in Prayer Ask God to show you how you should be giving of your resources (time, money, talent and so on).

2 Chronicles

What do you want out of life? Money? Prestige? Significant relationships? God told Solomon to ask for whatever he wanted. Second Chronicles begins with Solomon's answer. You may find it surprising!

Solomon was given the huge responsibility of building the temple that his father, David, had put much of his life into planning. Several chapters of lavish detail are devoted to the construction and dedication of the temple in Jerusalem. The temple continues to be prominent throughout the book.

Revolt soon splits Solomon's kingdom in two (Israel and Judah) when Jeroboam rebels against Solomon's son Rehoboam. Though the sins of ungodly kings are briefly mentioned and condemned, most of the book is devoted to spiritual reform and renewal under the Judean kings Asa, Jehoshaphat, Joash, Hezekiah and Josiah. Perhaps the most dramatic moment comes when among the debris of the unused temple, Hilkiah the priest finds the lost Torah—the law of Moses (34:14–32). The fall of Jerusalem to Nebuchadnezzar is explained as the result of sin, but the book ends positively, with Cyrus king of Persia authorizing the rebuilding of the temple.

Throughout 2 Chronicles the Lord's hand is seen blessing obedience with success. This book will be an encouragement to you as you try to stay faithful to the Lord. It was said of King Uzziah, "As long as he sought the LORD, God gave him success" (26:5).

What places in your life would you like to rebuild? In 2 Chronicles you'll find courage to begin the process and see it through to completion.

Outline

1/ 2 Chronicles 1 —————————— *Give Me Wisdom*

2/ 2 Chronicles 6—7 —————————— *Bearing God's Name*

3/ 2 Chronicles 14—15 —————————— *Seeking God*

4/ 2 Chronicles 18:1—19:3 —————————— *Unpopular Prophecy*

5/ 2 Chronicles 20:1—30 —————————— *Battle Weary*

6/ 2 Chronicles 23—24 —————————— *Protégé to a Priest*

7/ 2 Chronicles 34 —————————— *Loving God*

1 / 2 Chronicles 1
Give Me Wisdom

POWERFUL TECHNOLOGICAL CONNECTIONS are bringing us almost unlimited access to information. Yet we have been unable to achieve our highest ideals of human rights and strong families. Knowledge is power, but power does not necessarily bring morality. Solomon asked for godly wisdom, the kind of knowledge that would make him a fit leader for God's people.

 Warming Up to God Reflect on a time that you did not know what to do and God gave you insight and direction.

 Read 2 Chronicles 1.

1 Solomon son of David established himself firmly over his kingdom, for the LORD his God was with him and made him exceedingly great.

²Then Solomon spoke to all Israel—to the commanders of thousands and commanders of hundreds, to the judges and to all the leaders in Israel, the heads of families— ³and Solomon and the whole assembly went to the high place at Gibeon, for God's Tent of Meeting was there, which Moses the LORD's servant had made in the desert. ⁴Now David had brought up the ark of God from Kiriath Jearim to the place he had prepared for it, because he had pitched a tent for it in Jerusalem. ⁵But the bronze altar that Bezalel son of Uri, the son of Hur, had made was in Gibeon in front of the tabernacle of the LORD; so Solomon and the assembly inquired of him there. ⁶Solomon went up to the bronze altar before the LORD in the Tent of Meeting and offered a thousand burnt offerings on it.

⁷That night God appeared to Solomon and said to him, "Ask for whatever you want me to give you."

⁸Solomon answered God, "You have shown great kindness to David my father and have made me king in his place. ⁹Now, LORD God, let your promise to my father David be confirmed, for you have made me king over a people who are as numerous as the dust of the earth. ¹⁰Give me wisdom and knowledge, that I may lead this people, for who is able to govern this great people of yours?"

¹¹God said to Solomon, "Since this is your heart's desire and you have not asked for wealth, riches or honor, nor for the death of your enemies, and since you have not asked for a long life but for wisdom and knowledge to govern my people over whom I have made you king, ¹²therefore wisdom and knowledge will be given you. And I will also give you wealth, riches and honor, such as no king who was before you ever had and none after you will have."

¹³Then Solomon went to Jerusalem from the high place at Gibeon, from before the Tent of Meeting. And he reigned over Israel.

¹⁴Solomon accumulated chariots and horses; he had fourteen hundred chariots and twelve thousand horses,ᵃ which he kept in the chariot cities and also with him in Jerusalem. ¹⁵The king made silver and gold as common in Jerusalem as stones, and cedar as plentiful as sycamore-fig trees in the foothills. ¹⁶Solomon's horses were imported from Egyptᵇ and from Kueᶜ—the royal merchants purchased them from Kue. ¹⁷They imported a chariot from Egypt for six hundred shekelsᵈ of silver, and a horse for a hundred and fifty.ᵉ They also exported them to all the kings of the Hittites and of the Arameans.

ᵃ14 Or *charioteers*   ᵇ16 Or possibly *Muzur, a region in Cilicia; also in verse 17*   ᶜ16 Probably Cilicia   ᵈ17 That is, about 15 pounds (about 7 kilograms)   ᵉ17 That is, about 3 3/4 pounds (about 1.7 kilograms)

Discovering the Word 1. What does verse 1 tell you about the relationship between God and Solomon? 2. What significant choices does Solomon make as he goes to worship God in verses 2–6? (Consider the people involved, the place and the symbolism of the elements he includes.) 3. What does the way in which God approaches Solomon suggest about their relationship (v. 7)? 4. What did Solomon ask of God, and why (vv. 8–10)? 5. How did God fulfill even what Solomon had not asked for (vv. 11–17)?

Applying the Word 1. In what area of your life do you need wisdom and knowledge? 2. In order to make your request of God, what must you believe about him?

Responding in Prayer Bring to the Lord all situations where you feel bewildered or stymied. Admit that you don't know what to do, and trust him for an answer.

2 Chronicles 2—5

2 Solomon gave orders to build a temple for the Name of the LORD and a royal palace for himself. ²He conscripted seventy thousand men as carriers and eighty thousand as stonecutters in the hills and thirty-six hundred as foremen over them.

³Solomon sent this message to Hiram*ƒ* king of Tyre:

"Send me cedar logs as you did for my father David when you sent him cedar to build a palace to live in. ⁴Now I am about to build a temple for the Name of the LORD my God and to dedicate it to him for burning fragrant incense before him, for setting out the consecrated bread regularly, and for making burnt offerings every morning and evening and on Sabbaths and New Moons and at the appointed feasts of the LORD our God. This is a lasting ordinance for Israel.

⁵"The temple I am going to build will be great, because our God is greater than all other gods. ⁶But who is able to build a temple for him, since the heavens, even the highest heavens, cannot contain him? Who then am I to build a temple for him, except as a place to burn sacrifices before him?

⁷"Send me, therefore, a man skilled to work in gold and silver, bronze and iron, and in purple, crimson and blue yarn, and experienced in the art of engraving, to work in Judah and Jerusalem with my skilled craftsmen, whom my father David provided.

⁸"Send me also cedar, pine and algum*ᵍ* logs from Lebanon, for I know that your men are skilled in cutting timber there. My men will work with yours ⁹to provide me with plenty of lumber, because the temple I build must be large and magnificent. ¹⁰I will give your servants, the woodsmen who cut the timber, twenty thousand cors*ʰ* of ground wheat, twenty thousand cors of barley,

twenty thousand baths*ⁱ* of wine and twenty thousand baths of olive oil."

¹¹Hiram king of Tyre replied by letter to Solomon:

"Because the LORD loves his people, he has made you their king."

¹²And Hiram added:

"Praise be to the LORD, the God of Israel, who made heaven and earth! He has given King David a wise son, endowed with intelligence and discernment, who will build a temple for the LORD and a palace for himself.

¹³"I am sending you Huram-Abi, a man of great skill, ¹⁴whose mother was from Dan and whose father was from Tyre. He is trained to work in gold and silver, bronze and iron, stone and wood, and with purple and blue and crimson yarn and fine linen. He is experienced in all kinds of engraving and can execute any design given to him. He will work with your craftsmen and with those of my lord, David your father.

¹⁵"Now let my lord send his servants the wheat and barley and the olive oil and wine he promised, ¹⁶and we will cut all the logs from Lebanon that you need and will float them in rafts by sea down to Joppa. You can then take them up to Jerusalem."

¹⁷Solomon took a census of all the aliens who were in Israel, after the census his father David had taken; and they were found to be 153,600. ¹⁸He assigned 70,000 of them to be carriers and 80,000 to be stonecutters in the hills, with 3,600 foremen over them to keep the people working.

ƒ3 Hebrew *Huram,* a variant of *Hiram;* also in verses 11 and 12 *ᵍ8* Probably a variant of *almug;* possibly juniper   *ʰ10* That is, probably about 125,000 bushels (about 4,400 kiloliters)   *ⁱ10* That is, probably about 115,000 gallons (about 440 kiloliters)

3 Then Solomon began to build the temple of the LORD in Jerusalem on Mount Moriah, where the LORD had appeared to his father David. It was on the threshing floor of Araunah[j] the Jebusite, the place provided by David. ²He began building on the second day of the second month in the fourth year of his reign.

³The foundation Solomon laid for building the temple of God was sixty cubits long and twenty cubits wide[k] (using the cubit of the old standard). ⁴The portico at the front of the temple was twenty cubits[l] long across the width of the building and twenty cubits[m] high.

He overlaid the inside with pure gold. ⁵He paneled the main hall with pine and covered it with fine gold and decorated it with palm tree and chain designs. ⁶He adorned the temple with precious stones. And the gold he used was gold of Parvaim. ⁷He overlaid the ceiling beams, doorframes, walls and doors of the temple with gold, and he carved cherubim on the walls.

⁸He built the Most Holy Place, its length corresponding to the width of the temple—twenty cubits long and twenty cubits wide. He overlaid the inside with six hundred talents[n] of fine gold. ⁹The gold nails weighed fifty shekels.[o] He also overlaid the upper parts with gold.

¹⁰In the Most Holy Place he made a pair of sculptured cherubim and overlaid them with gold. ¹¹The total wingspan of the cherubim was twenty cubits. One wing of the first cherub was five cubits[p] long and touched the temple wall, while its other wing, also five cubits long, touched the wing of the other cherub. ¹²Similarly one wing of the second cherub was five cubits long and touched the other temple wall, and its other wing, also five cubits long, touched the wing of the first cherub. ¹³The wings of these cherubim extended twenty cubits. They stood on their feet, facing the main hall.[q]

¹⁴He made the curtain of blue, purple and crimson yarn and fine linen, with cherubim worked into it.

¹⁵In the front of the temple he made two pillars, which ⌞together⌟ were thirty-five cubits[r] long, each with a capital on top measuring five cubits. ¹⁶He made interwoven chains[s] and put them on top of the pillars. He also made a hundred pomegranates and attached them to the chains. ¹⁷He erected the pillars in the front of the temple, one to the south and one to the north.

The one to the south he named Jakin[t] and the one to the north Boaz.[u]

4 He made a bronze altar twenty cubits long, twenty cubits wide and ten cubits high.[v] ²He made the Sea of cast metal, circular in shape, measuring ten cubits from rim to rim and five cubits[w] high. It took a line of thirty cubits[x] to measure around it. ³Below the rim, figures of bulls encircled it—ten to a cubit.[y] The bulls were cast in two rows in one piece with the Sea.

⁴The Sea stood on twelve bulls, three facing north, three facing west, three facing south and three facing east. The Sea rested on top of them, and their hindquarters were toward the center. ⁵It was a handbreadth[z] in thickness, and its rim was like the rim of a cup, like a lily blossom. It held three thousand baths.[a]

⁶He then made ten basins for washing and placed five on the south side and five on the north. In them the things to be used for the burnt offerings were rinsed, but the Sea was to be used by the priests for washing.

⁷He made ten gold lampstands according to the specifications for them and placed them in the temple, five on the south side and five on the north.

⁸He made ten tables and placed them in the temple, five on the south side and five on the north. He also made a hundred gold sprinkling bowls.

⁹He made the courtyard of the priests, and the large court and the doors for the court, and overlaid the doors with bronze. ¹⁰He placed the Sea on the south side, at the southeast corner.

¹¹He also made the pots and shovels and sprinkling bowls.

So Huram finished the work he had undertaken for King Solomon in the temple of God:

¹²the two pillars;

[j]1 Hebrew *Ornan*, a variant of *Araunah*   [k]3 That is, about 90 feet (about 27 meters) long and 30 feet (about 9 meters) wide   [l]4 That is, about 30 feet (about 9 meters); also in verses 8, 11 and 13   [m]4 Some Septuagint and Syriac manuscripts; Hebrew *and a hundred and twenty*   [n]8 That is, about 23 tons (about 21 metric tons)   [o]9 That is, about 1 1/4 pounds (about 0.6 kilogram)   [p]11 That is, about 7 1/2 feet (about 2.3 meters); also in verse 15   [q]13 Or *facing inward*   [r]15 That is, about 52 feet (about 16 meters)   [s]16 Or possibly *made chains in the inner sanctuary*; the meaning of the Hebrew for this phrase is uncertain.   [t]17 *Jakin* probably means *he establishes*.   [u]17 *Boaz* probably means *in him is strength*.   [v]1 That is, about 30 feet (about 9 meters) long and wide, and about 15 feet (about 4.5 meters) high   [w]2 That is, about 7 1/2 feet (about 2.3 meters)   [x]2 That is, about 45 feet (about 13.5 meters)   [y]3 That is, about 1 1/2 feet (about 0.5 meter)   [z]5 That is, about 3 inches (about 8 centimeters)   [a]5 That is, about 17,500 gallons (about 66 kiloliters)

the two bowl-shaped capitals on top of the
pillars;
the two sets of network decorating the two
bowl-shaped capitals on top of the pillars;
¹³the four hundred pomegranates for the two
sets of network (two rows of pomegranates for each network, decorating the
bowl-shaped capitals on top of the pillars);
¹⁴the stands with their basins;
¹⁵the Sea and the twelve bulls under it;
¹⁶the pots, shovels, meat forks and all related
articles.

All the objects that Huram-Abi made for King
Solomon for the temple of the LORD were of polished bronze. ¹⁷The king had them cast in clay
molds in the plain of the Jordan between Succoth
and Zarethan.ᵇ ¹⁸All these things that Solomon
made amounted to so much that the weight of the
bronze was not determined.

¹⁹Solomon also made all the furnishings that
were in God's temple:

the golden altar;
the tables on which was the bread of the
Presence;
²⁰the lampstands of pure gold with their
lamps, to burn in front of the inner sanctuary as prescribed;
²¹the gold floral work and lamps and tongs
(they were solid gold);
²²the pure gold wick trimmers, sprinkling
bowls, dishes and censers; and the gold
doors of the temple: the inner doors to
the Most Holy Place and the doors of the
main hall.

5 When all the work Solomon had done for
the temple of the LORD was finished, he
brought in the things his father David had
dedicated—the silver and gold and all the furnishings—and he placed them in the treasuries of
God's temple.

²Then Solomon summoned to Jerusalem the elders of Israel, all the heads of the tribes and the
chiefs of the Israelite families, to bring up the ark
of the LORD's covenant from Zion, the City of Da-

vid. ³And all the men of Israel came together to
the king at the time of the festival in the seventh
month.

⁴When all the elders of Israel had arrived, the
Levites took up the ark, ⁵and they brought up the
ark and the Tent of Meeting and all the sacred
furnishings in it. The priests, who were Levites,
carried them up; ⁶and King Solomon and the entire assembly of Israel that had gathered about
him were before the ark, sacrificing so many
sheep and cattle that they could not be recorded
or counted.

⁷The priests then brought the ark of the LORD's
covenant to its place in the inner sanctuary of the
temple, the Most Holy Place, and put it beneath
the wings of the cherubim. ⁸The cherubim spread
their wings over the place of the ark and covered
the ark and its carrying poles. ⁹These poles were
so long that their ends, extending from the ark,
could be seen from in front of the inner sanctuary, but not from outside the Holy Place; and they
are still there today. ¹⁰There was nothing in the
ark except the two tablets that Moses had placed
in it at Horeb, where the LORD made a covenant
with the Israelites after they came out of Egypt.

¹¹The priests then withdrew from the Holy
Place. All the priests who were there had consecrated themselves, regardless of their divisions.
¹²All the Levites who were musicians—Asaph,
Heman, Jeduthun and their sons and relatives—
stood on the east side of the altar, dressed in fine
linen and playing cymbals, harps and lyres. They
were accompanied by 120 priests sounding trumpets. ¹³The trumpeters and singers joined in unison, as with one voice, to give praise and thanks
to the LORD. Accompanied by trumpets, cymbals
and other instruments, they raised their voices in
praise to the LORD and sang:

"He is good;
his love endures forever."

Then the temple of the LORD was filled with a
cloud, ¹⁴and the priests could not perform their
service because of the cloud, for the glory of the
LORD filled the temple of God.

ᵇ17 Hebrew *Zeredatha,* a variant of *Zarethan*

2 / 2 Chronicles 6—7
Bearing God's Name

"I NOW PRONOUNCE you husband and wife. What God has joined, let no man put asunder." With these traditional words, a wedding ends. Two people who entered the church separately leave united. They even carry the same last name. And after that point anything that one or the other does will reflect on that name. Reasonable or not, the reputation of each person will rise and fall with the partner's behavior. It's enough to give a newly engaged couple some very solemn thoughts. But God himself takes the same risk—and not with just one person, but with a whole group. God calls them "my people, who are called by my Name" (7:14). What a great privilege to be linked to the name of God. And what a heavy responsibility.

 Warming Up to God   In what ways have you been a bearer of God's name this week?

 Read 2 Chronicles 6—7.

6 Then Solomon said, "The LORD has said that he would dwell in a dark cloud; ²I have built a magnificent temple for you, a place for you to dwell forever."

³While the whole assembly of Israel was standing there, the king turned around and blessed them. ⁴Then he said:

"Praise be to the LORD, the God of Israel, who with his hands has fulfilled what he promised with his mouth to my father David. For he said, ⁵'Since the day I brought my people out of Egypt, I have not chosen a city in any tribe of Israel to have a temple built for my Name to be there, nor have I chosen anyone to be the leader over my people Israel. ⁶But now I have chosen Jerusalem for my Name to be there, and I have chosen David to rule my people Israel.'

⁷"My father David had it in his heart to build a temple for the Name of the LORD, the God of Israel. ⁸But the LORD said to my father David, 'Because it was in your heart to build a temple for my Name, you did well to have this in your heart. ⁹Nevertheless, you are not the one to build the temple, but your son, who is your own flesh and blood—he is the one who will build the temple for my Name.'

¹⁰"The LORD has kept the promise he made. I have succeeded David my father and now I sit on the throne of Israel, just as the LORD promised, and I have built the temple for the Name of the LORD, the God of Israel. ¹¹There I have placed the ark, in which is the covenant of the LORD that he made with the people of Israel."

¹²Then Solomon stood before the altar of the LORD in front of the whole assembly of Israel and spread out his hands. ¹³Now he had made a bronze platform, five cubits*c* long, five cubits wide and three cubits*d* high, and had placed it in the center of the outer court. He stood on the platform and then knelt down before the whole assembly of Israel and spread out his hands toward heaven. ¹⁴He said:

"O LORD, God of Israel, there is no God like you in heaven or on earth—you who keep your covenant of love with your servants who continue wholeheartedly in your way. ¹⁵You have kept your promise to your servant David my father; with your mouth you have promised and with your hand you have fulfilled it—as it is today.

¹⁶"Now LORD, God of Israel, keep for your servant David my father the promises you made to him when you said, 'You shall never fail to have a man to sit before me on the throne of Israel, if only your sons are careful in all they do to walk before me according to my law, as you have done.' ¹⁷And now, O LORD, God of Israel, let your word that you promised your servant David come true.

¹⁸"But will God really dwell on earth with men? The heavens, even the highest heavens, cannot contain you. How much less this temple I have built! ¹⁹Yet give attention to your servant's prayer and his plea for mercy, O LORD my God. Hear the cry and the prayer that your servant is praying in your pres-

c13 That is, about 7 1/2 feet (about 2.3 meters)   d13 That is, about 4 1/2 feet (about 1.3 meters) ence. ²⁰May your eyes be open toward this temple day and night, this place of which you said you would put your Name there. May you hear the prayer your servant prays toward this place. ²¹Hear the supplications of your servant and of your people Israel when they pray toward this place. Hear from heaven, your dwelling place; and when you hear, forgive.

²²"When a man wrongs his neighbor and is required to take an oath and he comes and swears the oath before your altar in this temple, ²³then hear from heaven and act. Judge between your servants, repaying the guilty by bringing down on his own head what he has done. Declare the innocent not guilty and so establish his innocence.

²⁴"When your people Israel have been defeated by an enemy because they have sinned against you and when they turn back and confess your name, praying and making supplication before you in this temple, ²⁵then hear from heaven and forgive the sin of your people Israel and bring them back to the land you gave to them and their fathers.

²⁶"When the heavens are shut up and there is no rain because your people have sinned against you, and when they pray toward this place and confess your name and turn from their sin because you have afflicted them, ²⁷then hear from heaven and forgive the sin of your servants, your people Israel. Teach them the right way to live, and send rain on the land you gave your people for an inheritance.

²⁸"When famine or plague comes to the land, or blight or mildew, locusts or grasshoppers, or when enemies besiege them in any of their cities, whatever disaster or disease may come, ²⁹and when a prayer or plea is made by any of your people Israel—each one aware of his afflictions and pains, and spreading out his hands toward this temple— ³⁰then hear from heaven, your dwelling place. Forgive, and deal with each man according to all he does, since you know his heart (for you alone know the hearts of men), ³¹so that they will fear you and walk in your ways all the time they live in the land you gave our fathers.

³²"As for the foreigner who does not belong to your people Israel but has come from a distant land because of your great name and your mighty hand and your outstretched arm—when he comes and prays toward this temple, ³³then hear from heaven, your dwelling place, and do whatever the foreigner asks of you, so that all the peoples of the earth may know your name and fear you, as do your own people Israel, and may know that this house I have built bears your Name.

³⁴"When your people go to war against their enemies, wherever you send them, and when they pray to you toward this city you have chosen and the temple I have built for your Name, ³⁵then hear from heaven their prayer and their plea, and uphold their cause.

³⁶"When they sin against you—for there is no one who does not sin—and you become angry with them and give them over to the enemy, who takes them captive to a land far away or near; ³⁷and if they have a change of heart in the land where they are held captive, and repent and plead with you in the land of their captivity and say, 'We have sinned, we have done wrong and acted wickedly'; ³⁸and if they turn back to you with all their heart and soul in the land of their captivity where they were taken, and pray toward the land you gave their fathers, toward the city you have chosen and toward the temple I have built for your Name; ³⁹then from heaven, your dwelling place, hear their prayer and their pleas, and uphold their cause. And forgive your people, who have sinned against you.

⁴⁰"Now, my God, may your eyes be open and your ears attentive to the prayers offered in this place.

⁴¹"Now arise, O LORD God, and come to
　　your resting place,
　you and the ark of your might.
May your priests, O LORD God, be
　　clothed with salvation,
　may your saints rejoice in your
　　goodness.
⁴²O LORD God, do not reject your anointed
　　one.
　Remember the great love promised to
　　David your servant."

7 When Solomon finished praying, fire came down from heaven and consumed the burnt offering and the sacrifices, and the glory of the LORD filled the temple. ²The priests could not enter the temple of the LORD because the glory of the LORD filled it. ³When all the Israelites saw the fire coming down and the glory of the LORD above the temple, they knelt on the pavement with their faces to the ground, and they worshiped and gave thanks to the LORD, saying,

"He is good;
his love endures forever."

⁴Then the king and all the people offered sacrifices before the LORD. ⁵And King Solomon offered a sacrifice of twenty-two thousand head of cattle and a hundred and twenty thousand sheep and goats. So the king and all the people dedicated the temple of God. ⁶The priests took their positions, as did the Levites with the LORD's musical instruments, which King David had made for praising the LORD and which were used when he gave thanks, saying, "His love endures forever." Opposite the Levites, the priests blew their trumpets, and all the Israelites were standing.

⁷Solomon consecrated the middle part of the courtyard in front of the temple of the LORD, and there he offered burnt offerings and the fat of the fellowship offerings,ᵉ because the bronze altar he had made could not hold the burnt offerings, the grain offerings and the fat portions.

⁸So Solomon observed the festival at that time for seven days, and all Israel with him—a vast assembly, people from Leboᶠ Hamath to the Wadi of Egypt. ⁹On the eighth day they held an assembly, for they had celebrated the dedication of the altar for seven days and the festival for seven days more. ¹⁰On the twenty-third day of the seventh month he sent the people to their homes, joyful and glad in heart for the good things the LORD had done for David and Solomon and for his people Israel.

¹¹When Solomon had finished the temple of the LORD and the royal palace, and had succeeded in carrying out all he had in mind to do in the temple of the LORD and in his own palace, ¹²the LORD appeared to him at night and said:

"I have heard your prayer and have chosen this place for myself as a temple for sacrifices.

¹³"When I shut up the heavens so that there is no rain, or command locusts to devour the land or send a plague among my people, ¹⁴if my people, who are called by my name, will humble themselves and pray and seek my face and turn from their wicked ways, then will I hear from heaven and will forgive their sin and will heal their land. ¹⁵Now my eyes will be open and my ears attentive to the prayers offered in this place. ¹⁶I have chosen and consecrated this temple so that my Name may be there forever. My eyes and my heart will always be there.

¹⁷"As for you, if you walk before me as David your father did, and do all I command, and observe my decrees and laws, ¹⁸I will establish your royal throne, as I covenanted with David your father when I said, 'You shall never fail to have a man to rule over Israel.'

¹⁹"But if youᵍ turn away and forsake the decrees and commands I have given youᵍ and go off to serve other gods and worship them, ²⁰then I will uproot Israel from my land, which I have given them, and will reject this temple I have consecrated for my Name. I will make it a byword and an object of ridicule among all peoples. ²¹And though this temple is now so imposing, all who pass by will be appalled and say, 'Why has the LORD done such a thing to this land and to this temple?' ²²People will answer, 'Because they have forsaken the LORD, the God of their fathers, who brought them out of Egypt, and have embraced other gods, worshiping and serving them—that is why he brought all this disaster on them.' "

ᵉ7 Traditionally *peace offerings*   ᶠ8 Or *from the entrance to*
ᵍ19 The Hebrew is plural.

✎ Discovering the Word   1. What qualities of God are revealed in Solomon's account of Jewish history (6:1–11)?   2. What did Solomon express by the position of his body during his prayer (6:13)?   3. How does Solomon answer his own question in 6:18: "But will God really dwell on earth with men?" What does he not expect (6:19–21)?   4. In 6:22–42 what all is Solomon asking God to do?   5. In what ways did the people express their worship of God (7:1–10)? **6.** What steps could the people take to restore their relationship with God (7:12–22)?

 Applying the Word 1. If chapter 6 accurately describes God's nature, why might you need and want his forgiveness? **2.** Prayerfully read again 7:14. Think of a group of people whose relationship with God needs restoring (your family, your church, your community, your nation). How could you, as a part of that group, begin to contribute to a restored relationship with God?

Responding in Prayer Pray for the group you thought of above and for your role in the restoration process.

2 Chronicles 8—13

8 At the end of twenty years, during which Solomon built the temple of the LORD and his own palace, ²Solomon rebuilt the villages that Hiram^h had given him, and settled Israelites in them. ³Solomon then went to Hamath Zobah and captured it. ⁴He also built up Tadmor in the desert and all the store cities he had built in Hamath. ⁵He rebuilt Upper Beth Horon and Lower Beth Horon as fortified cities, with walls and with gates and bars, ⁶as well as Baalath and all his store cities, and all the cities for his chariots and for his horses^i—whatever he desired to build in Jerusalem, in Lebanon and throughout all the territory he ruled.

⁷All the people left from the Hittites, Amorites, Perizzites, Hivites and Jebusites (these peoples were not Israelites), ⁸that is, their descendants remaining in the land, whom the Israelites had not destroyed—these Solomon conscripted for his slave labor force, as it is to this day. ⁹But Solomon did not make slaves of the Israelites for his work; they were his fighting men, commanders of his captains, and commanders of his chariots and charioteers. ¹⁰They were also King Solomon's chief officials—two hundred and fifty officials supervising the men.

¹¹Solomon brought Pharaoh's daughter up from the City of David to the palace he had built for her, for he said, "My wife must not live in the palace of David king of Israel, because the places the ark of the LORD has entered are holy."

¹²On the altar of the LORD that he had built in front of the portico, Solomon sacrificed burnt offerings to the LORD, ¹³according to the daily requirement for offerings commanded by Moses for Sabbaths, New Moons and the three annual feasts—the Feast of Unleavened Bread, the Feast of Weeks and the Feast of Tabernacles. ¹⁴In keeping with the ordinance of his father David, he appointed the divisions of the priests for their duties, and the Levites to lead the praise and to assist the priests according to each day's requirement. He also appointed the gatekeepers by divisions for the various gates, because this was what David the man of God had ordered. ¹⁵They did not deviate from the king's commands to the priests or to the Levites in any matter, including that of the treasuries.

¹⁶All Solomon's work was carried out, from the day the foundation of the temple of the LORD was laid until its completion. So the temple of the LORD was finished.

¹⁷Then Solomon went to Ezion Geber and Elath on the coast of Edom. ¹⁸And Hiram sent him ships commanded by his own officers, men who knew the sea. These, with Solomon's men, sailed to Ophir and brought back four hundred and fifty talents^j of gold, which they delivered to King Solomon.

9 When the queen of Sheba heard of Solomon's fame, she came to Jerusalem to test him with hard questions. Arriving with a very great caravan—with camels carrying spices, large quantities of gold, and precious stones—she came to Solomon and talked with him about all she had on her mind. ²Solomon answered all her questions; nothing was too hard for him to explain to her. ³When the queen of Sheba saw the wisdom of Solomon, as well as the palace he had built, ⁴the food on his table, the seating of his officials, the attending servants in their robes, the cupbearers in their robes and the burnt offerings he made at^k the temple of the LORD, she was overwhelmed.

⁵She said to the king, "The report I heard in my

---

^h2 Hebrew *Huram*, a variant of *Hiram*; also in verse 18   ^i6 Or *charioteers*   ^j18 That is, about 17 tons (about 16 metric tons)
^k4 Or *the ascent by which he went up to*

own country about your achievements and your wisdom is true. 6But I did not believe what they said until I came and saw with my own eyes. Indeed, not even half the greatness of your wisdom was told me; you have far exceeded the report I heard. 7How happy your men must be! How happy your officials, who continually stand before you and hear your wisdom! 8Praise be to the LORD your God, who has delighted in you and placed you on his throne as king to rule for the LORD your God. Because of the love of your God for Israel and his desire to uphold them forever, he has made you king over them, to maintain justice and righteousness."

9Then she gave the king 120 talents[i] of gold, large quantities of spices, and precious stones. There had never been such spices as those the queen of Sheba gave to King Solomon.

10(The men of Hiram and the men of Solomon brought gold from Ophir; they also brought algumwood[m] and precious stones. 11The king used the algumwood to make steps for the temple of the LORD and for the royal palace, and to make harps and lyres for the musicians. Nothing like them had ever been seen in Judah.)

12King Solomon gave the queen of Sheba all she desired and asked for; he gave her more than she had brought to him. Then she left and returned with her retinue to her own country.

13The weight of the gold that Solomon received yearly was 666 talents,[n] 14not including the revenues brought in by merchants and traders. Also all the kings of Arabia and the governors of the land brought gold and silver to Solomon.

15King Solomon made two hundred large shields of hammered gold; six hundred bekas[o] of hammered gold went into each shield. 16He also made three hundred small shields of hammered gold, with three hundred bekas[p] of gold in each shield. The king put them in the Palace of the Forest of Lebanon.

17Then the king made a great throne inlaid with ivory and overlaid with pure gold. 18The throne had six steps, and a footstool of gold was attached to it. On both sides of the seat were armrests, with a lion standing beside each of them. 19Twelve lions stood on the six steps, one at either end of each step. Nothing like it had ever been made for any other kingdom. 20All King Solomon's goblets were gold, and all the household articles in the Palace of the Forest of Lebanon were pure gold. Nothing was made of silver, because silver was considered of little value in Solomon's day. 21The king had a fleet of trading ships[q] manned by Hiram's[r] men. Once every three years it returned, carrying gold, silver and ivory, and apes and baboons.

22King Solomon was greater in riches and wisdom than all the other kings of the earth. 23All the kings of the earth sought audience with Solomon to hear the wisdom God had put in his heart. 24Year after year, everyone who came brought a gift—articles of silver and gold, and robes, weapons and spices, and horses and mules.

25Solomon had four thousand stalls for horses and chariots, and twelve thousand horses,[s] which he kept in the chariot cities and also with him in Jerusalem. 26He ruled over all the kings from the River[t] to the land of the Philistines, as far as the border of Egypt. 27The king made silver as common in Jerusalem as stones, and cedar as plentiful as sycamore-fig trees in the foothills. 28Solomon's horses were imported from Egypt[u] and from all other countries.

29As for the other events of Solomon's reign, from beginning to end, are they not written in the records of Nathan the prophet, in the prophecy of Ahijah the Shilonite and in the visions of Iddo the seer concerning Jeroboam son of Nebat? 30Solomon reigned in Jerusalem over all Israel forty years. 31Then he rested with his fathers and was buried in the city of David his father. And Rehoboam his son succeeded him as king.

10 Rehoboam went to Shechem, for all the Israelites had gone there to make him king. 2When Jeroboam son of Nebat heard this (he was in Egypt, where he had fled from King Solomon), he returned from Egypt. 3So they sent for Jeroboam, and he and all Israel went to Rehoboam and said to him: 4"Your father put a heavy yoke on us, but now lighten the harsh labor and the heavy yoke he put on us, and we will serve you."

5Rehoboam answered, "Come back to me in three days." So the people went away.

6Then King Rehoboam consulted the elders who had served his father Solomon during his lifetime. "How would you advise me to answer these people?" he asked.

---

l9 That is, about 4 1/2 tons (about 4 metric tons)   m10 Probably a variant of *almugwood*   n13 That is, about 25 tons (about 23 metric tons)   o15 That is, about 7 1/2 pounds (about 3.5 kilograms)   p16 That is, about 3 3/4 pounds (about 1.7 kilograms)   q21 Hebrew *of ships that could go to Tarshish*   r21 Hebrew *Huram*, a variant of *Hiram*   s25 Or *charioteers*   t26 That is, the Euphrates   u28 Or possibly *Muzur*, a region in Cilicia

⁷They replied, "If you will be kind to these people and please them and give them a favorable answer, they will always be your servants."

⁸But Rehoboam rejected the advice the elders gave him and consulted the young men who had grown up with him and were serving him. ⁹He asked them, "What is your advice? How should we answer these people who say to me, 'Lighten the yoke your father put on us'?"

¹⁰The young men who had grown up with him replied, "Tell the people who have said to you, 'Your father put a heavy yoke on us, but make our yoke lighter'—tell them, 'My little finger is thicker than my father's waist. ¹¹My father laid on you a heavy yoke; I will make it even heavier. My father scourged you with whips; I will scourge you with scorpions.' "

¹²Three days later Jeroboam and all the people returned to Rehoboam, as the king had said, "Come back to me in three days." ¹³The king answered them harshly. Rejecting the advice of the elders, ¹⁴he followed the advice of the young men and said, "My father made your yoke heavy; I will make it even heavier. My father scourged you with whips; I will scourge you with scorpions." ¹⁵So the king did not listen to the people, for this turn of events was from God, to fulfill the word the LORD had spoken to Jeroboam son of Nebat through Ahijah the Shilonite.

¹⁶When all Israel saw that the king refused to listen to them, they answered the king:

"What share do we have in David,
    what part in Jesse's son?
To your tents, O Israel!
Look after your own house, O David!"

So all the Israelites went home. ¹⁷But as for the Israelites who were living in the towns of Judah, Rehoboam still ruled over them.

¹⁸King Rehoboam sent out Adoniram,ᵛ who was in charge of forced labor, but the Israelites stoned him to death. King Rehoboam, however, managed to get into his chariot and escape to Jerusalem. ¹⁹So Israel has been in rebellion against the house of David to this day.

11 When Rehoboam arrived in Jerusalem, he mustered the house of Judah and Benjamin—a hundred and eighty thousand fighting men—to make war against Israel and to regain the kingdom for Rehoboam.

²But this word of the LORD came to Shemaiah

the man of God: ³"Say to Rehoboam son of Solomon king of Judah and to all the Israelites in Judah and Benjamin, ⁴'This is what the LORD says: Do not go up to fight against your brothers. Go home, every one of you, for this is my doing.' " So they obeyed the words of the LORD and turned back from marching against Jeroboam.

⁵Rehoboam lived in Jerusalem and built up towns for defense in Judah: ⁶Bethlehem, Etam, Tekoa, ⁷Beth Zur, Soco, Adullam, ⁸Gath, Mareshah, Ziph, ⁹Adoraim, Lachish, Azekah, ¹⁰Zorah, Aijalon and Hebron. These were fortified cities in Judah and Benjamin. ¹¹He strengthened their defenses and put commanders in them, with supplies of food, olive oil and wine. ¹²He put shields and spears in all the cities, and made them very strong. So Judah and Benjamin were his.

¹³The priests and Levites from all their districts throughout Israel sided with him. ¹⁴The Levites even abandoned their pasturelands and property, and came to Judah and Jerusalem because Jeroboam and his sons had rejected them as priests of the LORD. ¹⁵And he appointed his own priests for the high places and for the goat and calf idols he had made. ¹⁶Those from every tribe of Israel who set their hearts on seeking the LORD, the God of Israel, followed the Levites to Jerusalem to offer sacrifices to the LORD, the God of their fathers. ¹⁷They strengthened the kingdom of Judah and supported Rehoboam son of Solomon three years, walking in the ways of David and Solomon during this time.

¹⁸Rehoboam married Mahalath, who was the daughter of David's son Jerimoth and of Abihail, the daughter of Jesse's son Eliab. ¹⁹She bore him sons: Jeush, Shemariah and Zaham. ²⁰Then he married Maacah daughter of Absalom, who bore him Abijah, Attai, Ziza and Shelomith. ²¹Rehoboam loved Maacah daughter of Absalom more than any of his other wives and concubines. In all, he had eighteen wives and sixty concubines, twenty-eight sons and sixty daughters.

²²Rehoboam appointed Abijah son of Maacah to be the chief prince among his brothers, in order to make him king. ²³He acted wisely, dispersing some of his sons throughout the districts of Judah and Benjamin, and to all the fortified cities. He gave them abundant provisions and took many wives for them.

ᵛ18 Hebrew *Hadoram*, a variant of *Adoniram*

12

After Rehoboam's position as king was established and he had become strong, he and all Israel[w] with him abandoned the law of the LORD. ²Because they had been unfaithful to the LORD, Shishak king of Egypt attacked Jerusalem in the fifth year of King Rehoboam. ³With twelve hundred chariots and sixty thousand horsemen and the innumerable troops of Libyans, Sukkites and Cushites[x] that came with him from Egypt, ⁴he captured the fortified cities of Judah and came as far as Jerusalem.

⁵Then the prophet Shemaiah came to Rehoboam and to the leaders of Judah who had assembled in Jerusalem for fear of Shishak, and he said to them, "This is what the LORD says, 'You have abandoned me; therefore, I now abandon you to Shishak.' "

⁶The leaders of Israel and the king humbled themselves and said, "The LORD is just."

⁷When the LORD saw that they humbled themselves, this word of the LORD came to Shemaiah: "Since they have humbled themselves, I will not destroy them but will soon give them deliverance. My wrath will not be poured out on Jerusalem through Shishak. ⁸They will, however, become subject to him, so that they may learn the difference between serving me and serving the kings of other lands."

⁹When Shishak king of Egypt attacked Jerusalem, he carried off the treasures of the temple of the LORD and the treasures of the royal palace. He took everything, including the gold shields Solomon had made. ¹⁰So King Rehoboam made bronze shields to replace them and assigned these to the commanders of the guard on duty at the entrance to the royal palace. ¹¹Whenever the king went to the LORD's temple, the guards went with him, bearing the shields, and afterward they returned them to the guardroom.

¹²Because Rehoboam humbled himself, the LORD's anger turned from him, and he was not totally destroyed. Indeed, there was some good in Judah.

¹³King Rehoboam established himself firmly in Jerusalem and continued as king. He was forty-one years old when he became king, and he reigned seventeen years in Jerusalem, the city the LORD had chosen out of all the tribes of Israel in which to put his Name. His mother's name was Naamah; she was an Ammonite. ¹⁴He did evil because he had not set his heart on seeking the LORD.

¹⁵As for the events of Rehoboam's reign, from beginning to end, are they not written in the records of Shemaiah the prophet and of Iddo the seer that deal with genealogies? There was continual warfare between Rehoboam and Jeroboam. ¹⁶Rehoboam rested with his fathers and was buried in the City of David. And Abijah his son succeeded him as king.

13

In the eighteenth year of the reign of Jeroboam, Abijah became king of Judah, ²and he reigned in Jerusalem three years. His mother's name was Maacah,[y] a daughter[z] of Uriel of Gibeah.

There was war between Abijah and Jeroboam. ³Abijah went into battle with a force of four hundred thousand able fighting men, and Jeroboam drew up a battle line against him with eight hundred thousand able troops.

⁴Abijah stood on Mount Zemaraim, in the hill country of Ephraim, and said, "Jeroboam and all Israel, listen to me! ⁵Don't you know that the LORD, the God of Israel, has given the kingship of Israel to David and his descendants forever by a covenant of salt? ⁶Yet Jeroboam son of Nebat, an official of Solomon son of David, rebelled against his master. ⁷Some worthless scoundrels gathered around him and opposed Rehoboam son of Solomon when he was young and indecisive and not strong enough to resist them.

⁸"And now you plan to resist the kingdom of the LORD, which is in the hands of David's descendants. You are indeed a vast army and have with you the golden calves that Jeroboam made to be your gods. ⁹But didn't you drive out the priests of the LORD, the sons of Aaron, and the Levites, and make priests of your own as the peoples of other lands do? Whoever comes to consecrate himself with a young bull and seven rams may become a priest of what are not gods.

¹⁰"As for us, the LORD is our God, and we have not forsaken him. The priests who serve the LORD are sons of Aaron, and the Levites assist them. ¹¹Every morning and evening they present burnt offerings and fragrant incense to the LORD. They set out the bread on the ceremonially clean table and light the lamps on the gold lampstand every evening. We are observing the requirements of the LORD our God. But you have forsaken him. ¹²God is with us; he is our leader. His priests with

---

w1 That is, Judah, as frequently in 2 Chronicles   x3 That is, people from the upper Nile region   y2 Most Septuagint manuscripts and Syriac (see also 2 Chron. 11:20 and 1 Kings 15:2); Hebrew *Micaiah*   z2 Or *granddaughter* their trumpets will sound the battle cry against you. Men of Israel, do not fight against the LORD, the God of your fathers, for you will not succeed."

¹³Now Jeroboam had sent troops around to the rear, so that while he was in front of Judah the ambush was behind them. ¹⁴Judah turned and saw that they were being attacked at both front and rear. Then they cried out to the LORD. The priests blew their trumpets ¹⁵and the men of Judah raised the battle cry. At the sound of their battle cry, God routed Jeroboam and all Israel before Abijah and Judah. ¹⁶The Israelites fled before Judah, and God delivered them into their hands. ¹⁷Abijah and his men inflicted heavy losses on them, so that there were five hun-

dred thousand casualties among Israel's able men. ¹⁸The men of Israel were subdued on that occasion, and the men of Judah were victorious because they relied on the LORD, the God of their fathers.

¹⁹Abijah pursued Jeroboam and took from him the towns of Bethel, Jeshanah and Ephron, with their surrounding villages. ²⁰Jeroboam did not regain power during the time of Abijah. And the LORD struck him down and he died.

²¹But Abijah grew in strength. He married fourteen wives and had twenty-two sons and sixteen daughters.

²²The other events of Abijah's reign, what he did and what he said, are written in the annotations of the prophet Iddo.

---

3 / 2 Chronicles 14—15
Seeking God

MY FRIEND SUSAN, emotionally raw from a recent divorce, attended a Fourth of July picnic with some friends, only to discover that the one thing more lonely than being alone is being alone in a crowd. She came home feeling not only husbandless, but also that her life was without God. For twenty years she had willed God out of existence. Now, more alone than ever, she stretched out on her empty bed and spoke the hesitant beginnings of prayer: "God, if you are there . . ." So began a torturous journey toward faith—a seeking after God. And God heard her prayer; bit by bit, God Almighty revealed himself to Susan.

 Warming Up to God   How does God draw you to himself?

 Read 2 Chronicles 14—15.

---

14 And Abijah rested with his fathers and was buried in the City of David. Asa his son succeeded him as king, and in his days the country was at peace for ten years.

²Asa did what was good and right in the eyes of the LORD his God. ³He removed the foreign altars and the high places, smashed the sacred stones and cut down the Asherah poles.ᵃ ⁴He commanded Judah to seek the LORD, the God of their fathers, and to obey his laws and commands. ⁵He removed the high places and incense altars in every town in Judah, and the kingdom was at peace under him. ⁶He built up the fortified cities of Judah, since the land was at peace. No one was at war with him during those years, for the LORD gave him rest.

⁷"Let us build up these towns," he said to Judah, "and put walls around them, with towers, gates and bars. The land is still ours, because we have sought the LORD our God; we sought him and he has given us rest on every side." So they built and prospered.

⁸Asa had an army of three hundred thousand men from Judah, equipped with large shields and with spears, and two hundred and eighty thousand from Benjamin, armed with small shields and with bows. All these were brave fighting men.

⁹Zerah the Cushite marched out against them with a vast armyᵇ and three hundred chariots,

---

ᵃ3 That is, symbols of the goddess Asherah; here and elsewhere in 2 Chronicles   ᵇ9 Hebrew *with an army of a thousand thousands* or *with an army of thousands upon thousands* and came as far as Mareshah. ¹⁰Asa went out to meet him, and they took up battle positions in the Valley of Zephathah near Mareshah.

¹¹Then Asa called to the Lord his God and said, "Lord, there is no one like you to help the powerless against the mighty. Help us, O Lord our God, for we rely on you, and in your name we have come against this vast army. O Lord, you are our God; do not let man prevail against you."

¹²The Lord struck down the Cushites before Asa and Judah. The Cushites fled, ¹³and Asa and his army pursued them as far as Gerar. Such a great number of Cushites fell that they could not recover; they were crushed before the Lord and his forces. The men of Judah carried off a large amount of plunder. ¹⁴They destroyed all the villages around Gerar, for the terror of the Lord had fallen upon them. They plundered all these villages, since there was much booty there. ¹⁵They also attacked the camps of the herdsmen and carried off droves of sheep and goats and camels. Then they returned to Jerusalem.

15 The Spirit of God came upon Azariah son of Oded. ²He went out to meet Asa and said to him, "Listen to me, Asa and all Judah and Benjamin. The Lord is with you when you are with him. If you seek him, he will be found by you, but if you forsake him, he will forsake you. ³For a long time Israel was without the true God, without a priest to teach and without the law. ⁴But in their distress they turned to the Lord, the God of Israel, and sought him, and he was found by them. ⁵In those days it was not safe to travel about, for all the inhabitants of the lands were in great turmoil. ⁶One nation was being crushed by another and one city by another, because God was troubling them with every kind of distress. ⁷But as for you, be strong and do not give up, for your work will be rewarded."

⁸When Asa heard these words and the proph-

ecy of Azariah son of[c] Oded the prophet, he took courage. He removed the detestable idols from the whole land of Judah and Benjamin and from the towns he had captured in the hills of Ephraim. He repaired the altar of the Lord that was in front of the portico of the Lord's temple.

⁹Then he assembled all Judah and Benjamin and the people from Ephraim, Manasseh and Simeon who had settled among them, for large numbers had come over to him from Israel when they saw that the Lord his God was with him.

¹⁰They assembled at Jerusalem in the third month of the fifteenth year of Asa's reign. ¹¹At that time they sacrificed to the Lord seven hundred head of cattle and seven thousand sheep and goats from the plunder they had brought back. ¹²They entered into a covenant to seek the Lord, the God of their fathers, with all their heart and soul. ¹³All who would not seek the Lord, the God of Israel, were to be put to death, whether small or great, man or woman. ¹⁴They took an oath to the Lord with loud acclamation, with shouting and with trumpets and horns. ¹⁵All Judah rejoiced about the oath because they had sworn it wholeheartedly. They sought God eagerly, and he was found by them. So the Lord gave them rest on every side.

¹⁶King Asa also deposed his grandmother Maacah from her position as queen mother, because she had made a repulsive Asherah pole. Asa cut the pole down, broke it up and burned it in the Kidron Valley. ¹⁷Although he did not remove the high places from Israel, Asa's heart was fully committed ⌊to the Lord⌋ all his life. ¹⁸He brought into the temple of God the silver and gold and the articles that he and his father had dedicated.

¹⁹There was no more war until the thirty-fifth year of Asa's reign.

ᶜ8 Vulgate and Syriac (see also Septuagint and verse 1); Hebrew does not have *Azariah son of*.

 Discovering the Word 1. List the action words in 14:1–7. 2. What do these words tell you about Asa? 3. What does Asa's prayer (14:11) reveal about his relationship with God? 4. Looking at 15:1–7, what past conditions in Israel might cause Asa to listen carefully to God's message? 5. What information can you gather from this prophecy about what God expects from his followers? 6. What words and phrases in 15:8–19 show the wholeheartedness with which Asa and his people turned to God?

 Applying the Word 1. These chapters show that if you seek the Lord, you will find him. What does this suggest about the nature of spiritual development?

Responding in Prayer Ask God to reveal himself to you and increase your faith so that you can believe more strongly in him.

2 Chronicles 16—17

16 In the thirty-sixth year of Asa's reign Baasha king of Israel went up against Judah and fortified Ramah to prevent anyone from leaving or entering the territory of Asa king of Judah.

2 Asa then took the silver and gold out of the treasuries of the LORD's temple and of his own palace and sent it to Ben-Hadad king of Aram, who was ruling in Damascus. 3 "Let there be a treaty between me and you," he said, "as there was between my father and your father. See, I am sending you silver and gold. Now break your treaty with Baasha king of Israel so he will withdraw from me."

4 Ben-Hadad agreed with King Asa and sent the commanders of his forces against the towns of Israel. They conquered Ijon, Dan, Abel Maim[d] and all the store cities of Naphtali. 5 When Baasha heard this, he stopped building Ramah and abandoned his work. 6 Then King Asa brought all the men of Judah, and they carried away from Ramah the stones and timber Baasha had been using. With them he built up Geba and Mizpah.

7 At that time Hanani the seer came to Asa king of Judah and said to him: "Because you relied on the king of Aram and not on the LORD your God, the army of the king of Aram has escaped from your hand. 8 Were not the Cushites[e] and Libyans a mighty army with great numbers of chariots and horsemen[f]? Yet when you relied on the LORD, he delivered them into your hand. 9 For the eyes of the LORD range throughout the earth to strengthen those whose hearts are fully committed to him. You have done a foolish thing, and from now on you will be at war."

10 Asa was angry with the seer because of this; he was so enraged that he put him in prison. At the same time Asa brutally oppressed some of the people.

11 The events of Asa's reign, from beginning to end, are written in the book of the kings of Judah and Israel. 12 In the thirty-ninth year of his reign Asa was afflicted with a disease in his feet. Though his disease was severe, even in his illness he did not seek help from the LORD, but only from the physicians. 13 Then in the forty-first year of his reign Asa died and rested with his fathers. 14 They buried him in the tomb that he had cut out for himself in the City of David. They laid

him on a bier covered with spices and various blended perfumes, and they made a huge fire in his honor.

17 Jehoshaphat his son succeeded him as king and strengthened himself against Israel. 2 He stationed troops in all the fortified cities of Judah and put garrisons in Judah and in the towns of Ephraim that his father Asa had captured.

3 The LORD was with Jehoshaphat because in his early years he walked in the ways his father David had followed. He did not consult the Baals 4 but sought the God of his father and followed his commands rather than the practices of Israel. 5 The LORD established the kingdom under his control; and all Judah brought gifts to Jehoshaphat, so that he had great wealth and honor. 6 His heart was devoted to the ways of the LORD; furthermore, he removed the high places and the Asherah poles from Judah.

7 In the third year of his reign he sent his officials Ben-Hail, Obadiah, Zechariah, Nethanel and Micaiah to teach in the towns of Judah. 8 With them were certain Levites—Shemaiah, Nethaniah, Zebadiah, Asahel, Shemiramoth, Jehonathan, Adonijah, Tobijah and Tob-Adonijah—and the priests Elishama and Jehoram. 9 They taught throughout Judah, taking with them the Book of the Law of the LORD; they went around to all the towns of Judah and taught the people.

10 The fear of the LORD fell on all the kingdoms of the lands surrounding Judah, so that they did not make war with Jehoshaphat. 11 Some Philistines brought Jehoshaphat gifts and silver as tribute, and the Arabs brought him flocks: seven thousand seven hundred rams and seven thousand seven hundred goats.

12 Jehoshaphat became more and more powerful; he built forts and store cities in Judah 13 and had large supplies in the towns of Judah. He also kept experienced fighting men in Jerusalem. 14 Their enrollment by families was as follows:

From Judah, commanders of units of 1,000:
Adnah the commander, with 300,000 fighting men;

d4 Also known as *Abel Beth Maacah*　　e8 That is, people from the upper Nile region　　f8 Or *charioteers*

¹⁵next, Jehohanan the commander, with 280,000;

¹⁶next, Amasiah son of Zicri, who volunteered himself for the service of the LORD, with 200,000.

¹⁷From Benjamin:

Eliada, a valiant soldier, with 200,000 men armed with bows and shields;

¹⁸next, Jehozabad, with 180,000 men armed for battle.

¹⁹These were the men who served the king, besides those he stationed in the fortified cities throughout Judah.

4 / 2 Chronicles 18:1—19:3
Unpopular Prophecy

"THAT WILL NEVER work." "Give up." "It's no use trying." Some people specialize in telling other people why their plans are hopeless. While nobody likes a wet blanket, there are times when God looks at our plans and says, "Don't do it." At those times we have to be open to change.

 Warming Up to God How have you seen God at work in shaping your plans?

 Read 2 Chronicles 18:1—19:3.

18 Now Jehoshaphat had great wealth and honor, and he allied himself with Ahab by marriage. ²Some years later he went down to visit Ahab in Samaria. Ahab slaughtered many sheep and cattle for him and the people with him and urged him to attack Ramoth Gilead. ³Ahab king of Israel asked Jehoshaphat king of Judah, "Will you go with me against Ramoth Gilead?"

Jehoshaphat replied, "I am as you are, and my people as your people; we will join you in the war." ⁴But Jehoshaphat also said to the king of Israel, "First seek the counsel of the LORD."

⁵So the king of Israel brought together the prophets—four hundred men—and asked them, "Shall we go to war against Ramoth Gilead, or shall I refrain?"

"Go," they answered, "for God will give it into the king's hand."

⁶But Jehoshaphat asked, "Is there not a prophet of the LORD here whom we can inquire of?"

⁷The king of Israel answered Jehoshaphat, "There is still one man through whom we can inquire of the LORD, but I hate him because he never prophesies anything good about me, but always bad. He is Micaiah son of Imlah."

"The king should not say that," Jehoshaphat replied.

⁸So the king of Israel called one of his officials and said, "Bring Micaiah son of Imlah at once."

⁹Dressed in their royal robes, the king of Israel and Jehoshaphat king of Judah were sitting on their thrones at the threshing floor by the entrance to the gate of Samaria, with all the prophets prophesying before them. ¹⁰Now Zedekiah son of Kenaanah had made iron horns, and he declared, "This is what the LORD says: 'With these you will gore the Arameans until they are destroyed.' "

¹¹All the other prophets were prophesying the same thing. "Attack Ramoth Gilead and be victorious," they said, "for the LORD will give it into the king's hand."

¹²The messenger who had gone to summon Micaiah said to him, "Look, as one man the other prophets are predicting success for the king. Let your word agree with theirs, and speak favorably."

¹³But Micaiah said, "As surely as the LORD lives, I can tell him only what my God says."

¹⁴When he arrived, the king asked him, "Micaiah, shall we go to war against Ramoth Gilead, or shall I refrain?"

"Attack and be victorious," he answered, "for they will be given into your hand."

¹⁵The king said to him, "How many times must I make you swear to tell me nothing but the truth in the name of the LORD?"

¹⁶Then Micaiah answered, "I saw all Israel scattered on the hills like sheep without a shepherd, and the LORD said, 'These people have no master. Let each one go home in peace.'"

¹⁷The king of Israel said to Jehoshaphat, "Didn't I tell you that he never prophesies anything good about me, but only bad?"

¹⁸Micaiah continued, "Therefore hear the word of the LORD: I saw the LORD sitting on his throne with all the host of heaven standing on his right and on his left. ¹⁹And the LORD said, 'Who will entice Ahab king of Israel into attacking Ramoth Gilead and going to his death there?'

"One suggested this, and another that. ²⁰Finally, a spirit came forward, stood before the LORD and said, 'I will entice him.'

"'By what means?' the LORD asked.

²¹"'I will go and be a lying spirit in the mouths of all his prophets,' he said.

"'You will succeed in enticing him,' said the LORD. 'Go and do it.'

²²"So now the LORD has put a lying spirit in the mouths of these prophets of yours. The LORD has decreed disaster for you."

²³Then Zedekiah son of Kenaanah went up and slapped Micaiah in the face. "Which way did the spirit from*ᵍ the LORD go when he went from me to speak to you?" he asked.

²⁴Micaiah replied, "You will find out on the day you go to hide in an inner room."

²⁵The king of Israel then ordered, "Take Micaiah and send him back to Amon the ruler of the city and to Joash the king's son, ²⁶and say, 'This is what the king says: Put this fellow in prison and give him nothing but bread and water until I return safely.'"

²⁷Micaiah declared, "If you ever return safely, the LORD has not spoken through me." Then he added, "Mark my words, all you people!"

²⁸So the king of Israel and Jehoshaphat king of Judah went up to Ramoth Gilead. ²⁹The king of Israel said to Jehoshaphat, "I will enter the battle in disguise, but you wear your royal robes." So the king of Israel disguised himself and went into battle.

³⁰Now the king of Aram had ordered his chariot commanders, "Do not fight with anyone, small or great, except the king of Israel." ³¹When the chariot commanders saw Jehoshaphat, they thought, "This is the king of Israel." So they turned to attack him, but Jehoshaphat cried out, and the LORD helped him. God drew them away from him, ³²for when the chariot commanders saw that he was not the king of Israel, they stopped pursuing him.

³³But someone drew his bow at random and hit the king of Israel between the sections of his armor. The king told the chariot driver, "Wheel around and get me out of the fighting. I've been wounded." ³⁴All day long the battle raged, and the king of Israel propped himself up in his chariot facing the Arameans until evening. Then at sunset he died.

19 When Jehoshaphat king of Judah returned safely to his palace in Jerusalem, ²Jehu the seer, the son of Hanani, went out to meet him and said to the king, "Should you help the wicked and loveʰ those who hate the LORD? Because of this, the wrath of the LORD is upon you. ³There is, however, some good in you, for you have rid the land of the Asherah poles and have set your heart on seeking God."

ᵍ23 Or Spirit of   ʰ2 Or and make alliances with

Discovering the Word 1. Ahab asked Jehoshaphat to join him in battle against Ramoth Gilead. How was God's will revealed concerning this plan? 2. Why was Ahab reluctant to inquire of Micaiah (18:7)? 3. It appears that Micaiah was speaking ironically in 18:14 or testing the king in some way. How does Micaiah's prophecy about the result of the battle change when the king insists Micaiah speak in the Lord's name (18:16–19)? 4. How did Ahab try to protect himself (18:28–29)? 5. How was Micaiah's prophecy fulfilled (18:33–34)?

Applying the Word 1. When do you resist hearing any discouraging words about your plans? 2. What set plans do you have that need to be opened up for God's examination?

Responding in Prayer Put your favorite plans and goals before the Lord. Ask him to sort out your motives and even change your plans if it's his will.

2 Chronicles 19:4–11

⁴Jehoshaphat lived in Jerusalem, and he went out again among the people from Beersheba to the hill country of Ephraim and turned them back to the LORD, the God of their fathers. ⁵He appointed judges in the land, in each of the fortified cities of Judah. ⁶He told them, "Consider carefully what you do, because you are not judging for man but for the LORD, who is with you whenever you give a verdict. ⁷Now let the fear of the LORD be upon you. Judge carefully, for with the LORD our God there is no injustice or partiality or bribery."

⁸In Jerusalem also, Jehoshaphat appointed some of the Levites, priests and heads of Israelite families to administer the law of the LORD and to settle disputes. And they lived in Jerusalem. ⁹He

gave them these orders: "You must serve faithfully and wholeheartedly in the fear of the LORD. ¹⁰In every case that comes before you from your fellow countrymen who live in the cities—whether bloodshed or other concerns of the law, commands, decrees or ordinances—you are to warn them not to sin against the LORD; otherwise his wrath will come on you and your brothers. Do this, and you will not sin.

¹¹"Amariah the chief priest will be over you in any matter concerning the LORD, and Zebadiah son of Ishmael, the leader of the tribe of Judah, will be over you in any matter concerning the king, and the Levites will serve as officials before you. Act with courage, and may the LORD be with those who do well."

5 / 2 Chronicles 20:1–30
Battle Weary

BATTLES IN JEHOSHAPHAT'S life took the form of armies marching across the Palestinian wilderness, bloody conflicts in the valleys, hunting and hiding in the mountains. My battles are of a different kind. They are often battles of time: four children, countless ensemble rehearsals for the girls, sports practices for the boys, two weekly Bible studies, a prayer group, a seventy-family Sunday school to superintend, a weepy neighbor to console, music practice to oversee ("No, a dotted half gets three beats"), homework to enforce, a neglected manuscript scattered over the dining-room table. I am battle weary.

I once experienced God's momentary deliverance from this battle. It took the form of a Midwestern snowstorm. Each jingle of the phone announced a cancellation. Our family had a day to lounge around a popping fire with the chords of Handel's *Messiah* in the background. I did not have to fight the battle that day.

Warming Up to God What weariness do you bring to God today?

Read 2 Chronicles 20:1–30.

20 After this, the Moabites and Ammonites with some of the Meunites[i] came to make war on Jehoshaphat.

²Some men came and told Jehoshaphat, "A vast army is coming against you from Edom,[j] from the other side of the Sea.[k] It is already in Haza-

zon Tamar" (that is, En Gedi). ³Alarmed, Jehoshaphat resolved to inquire of the LORD, and he proclaimed a fast for all Judah. ⁴The people of Judah came together to seek help from the LORD; indeed,

[i]1 Some Septuagint manuscripts; Hebrew *Ammonites*   [j]2 One Hebrew manuscript; most Hebrew manuscripts, Septuagint and Vulgate *Aram*
[k]2 That is, the Dead Sea

they came from every town in Judah to seek him.

⁵Then Jehoshaphat stood up in the assembly of Judah and Jerusalem at the temple of the Lord in the front of the new courtyard ⁶and said:

"O Lord, God of our fathers, are you not the God who is in heaven? You rule over all the kingdoms of the nations. Power and might are in your hand, and no one can withstand you. ⁷O our God, did you not drive out the inhabitants of this land before your people Israel and give it forever to the descendants of Abraham your friend? ⁸They have lived in it and have built in it a sanctuary for your Name, saying, ⁹'If calamity comes upon us, whether the sword of judgment, or plague or famine, we will stand in your presence before this temple that bears your Name and will cry out to you in our distress, and you will hear us and save us.'

¹⁰"But now here are men from Ammon, Moab and Mount Seir, whose territory you would not allow Israel to invade when they came from Egypt; so they turned away from them and did not destroy them. ¹¹See how they are repaying us by coming to drive us out of the possession you gave us as an inheritance. ¹²O our God, will you not judge them? For we have no power to face this vast army that is attacking us. We do not know what to do, but our eyes are upon you."

¹³All the men of Judah, with their wives and children and little ones, stood there before the Lord.

¹⁴Then the Spirit of the Lord came upon Jahaziel son of Zechariah, the son of Benaiah, the son of Jeiel, the son of Mattaniah, a Levite and descendant of Asaph, as he stood in the assembly.

¹⁵He said: "Listen, King Jehoshaphat and all who live in Judah and Jerusalem! This is what the Lord says to you: 'Do not be afraid or discouraged because of this vast army. For the battle is not yours, but God's. ¹⁶Tomorrow march down against them. They will be climbing up by the Pass of Ziz, and you will find them at the end of the gorge in the Desert of Jeruel. ¹⁷You will not have to fight this battle. Take up your positions; stand firm and see the deliverance the Lord will give you, O Judah and Jerusalem. Do not be afraid; do not be discouraged. Go out to face them tomorrow, and the Lord will be with you.' "

¹⁸Jehoshaphat bowed with his face to the ground, and all the people of Judah and Jerusalem fell down in worship before the Lord. ¹⁹Then some Levites from the Kohathites and Korahites stood up and praised the Lord, the God of Israel, with very loud voice.

²⁰Early in the morning they left for the Desert of Tekoa. As they set out, Jehoshaphat stood and said, "Listen to me, Judah and people of Jerusalem! Have faith in the Lord your God and you will be upheld; have faith in his prophets and you will be successful." ²¹After consulting the people, Jehoshaphat appointed men to sing to the Lord and to praise him for the splendor of his[l] holiness as they went out at the head of the army, saying:

"Give thanks to the Lord,
    for his love endures forever."

²²As they began to sing and praise, the Lord set ambushes against the men of Ammon and Moab and Mount Seir who were invading Judah, and they were defeated. ²³The men of Ammon and Moab rose up against the men from Mount Seir to destroy and annihilate them. After they finished slaughtering the men from Seir, they helped to destroy one another.

²⁴When the men of Judah came to the place that overlooks the desert and looked toward the vast army, they saw only dead bodies lying on the ground; no one had escaped. ²⁵So Jehoshaphat and his men went to carry off their plunder, and they found among them a great amount of equipment and clothing[m] and also articles of value— more than they could take away. There was so much plunder that it took three days to collect it. ²⁶On the fourth day they assembled in the Valley of Beracah, where they praised the Lord. This is why it is called the Valley of Beracah[n] to this day.

²⁷Then, led by Jehoshaphat, all the men of Judah and Jerusalem returned joyfully to Jerusalem, for the Lord had given them cause to rejoice over their enemies. ²⁸They entered Jerusalem and went to the temple of the Lord with harps and lutes and trumpets.

²⁹The fear of God came upon all the kingdoms

---

[l]21 Or *him with the splendor of*   [m]25 Some Hebrew manuscripts and Vulgate; most Hebrew manuscripts *corpses*   [n]26 *Beracah* means *praise.*

of the countries when they heard how the LORD had fought against the enemies of Israel. ³⁰And the kingdom of Jehoshaphat was at peace, for his God had given him rest on every side.

Discovering the Word 1. How did Jehoshaphat and his people respond to the news of the army's approach (vv. 1–4)? 2. What elements of praise do you find in Jehoshaphat's prayer (vv. 6–12)? 3. Imagine yourself standing in the crowd of people described in verse 13. How would you have felt about Jahaziel's words in verses 15–17? Why? 4. What methods did God use to fulfill his prophecy of the previous day (vv. 22–24)? 5. In what different ways did the people of Judah worship God (vv. 18–30)?

Applying the Word 1. Look again at the words in 2 Chronicles 20:15–17: "For the battle is not yours. . . . You will not have to fight this battle." When do you most need to hear this kind of message from God? 2. What can you learn from Jehoshaphat about the way to pray during such situations? 3. God will not fight all of our battles for us. (He didn't fight all of Jehoshaphat's. Besides, we might even be in the wrong battle!) But what can you learn from Jehoshaphat's walk with God that will help you cope when you feel battle weary?

Responding in Prayer Pray for a spirit of peace and contentment even in what worries you most just now.

---

2 Chronicles 20:31—22:12

³¹So Jehoshaphat reigned over Judah. He was thirty-five years old when he became king of Judah, and he reigned in Jerusalem twenty-five years. His mother's name was Azubah daughter of Shilhi. ³²He walked in the ways of his father Asa and did not stray from them; he did what was right in the eyes of the LORD. ³³The high places, however, were not removed, and the people still had not set their hearts on the God of their fathers.

³⁴The other events of Jehoshaphat's reign, from beginning to end, are written in the annals of Jehu son of Hanani, which are recorded in the book of the kings of Israel.

³⁵Later, Jehoshaphat king of Judah made an alliance with Ahaziah king of Israel, who was guilty of wickedness. ³⁶He agreed with him to construct a fleet of trading ships.ᵒ After these were built at Ezion Geber, ³⁷Eliezer son of Dodavahu of Mareshah prophesied against Jehoshaphat, saying, "Because you have made an alliance with Ahaziah, the LORD will destroy what you have made." The ships were wrecked and were not able to set sail to trade.ᵖ

21 Then Jehoshaphat rested with his fathers and was buried with them in the City of David. And Jehoram his son succeeded him as king. ²Jehoram's brothers, the sons of Jehoshaphat, were Azariah, Jehiel, Zechariah, Azariahu, Michael and Shephatiah. All these were sons of Jehoshaphat king of Israel.�q

³Their father had given them many gifts of silver and gold and articles of value, as well as fortified cities in Judah, but he had given the kingdom to Jehoram because he was his firstborn son.

⁴When Jehoram established himself firmly over his father's kingdom, he put all his brothers to the sword along with some of the princes of Israel. ⁵Jehoram was thirty-two years old when he became king, and he reigned in Jerusalem eight years. ⁶He walked in the ways of the kings of Israel, as the house of Ahab had done, for he married a daughter of Ahab. He did evil in the eyes of the LORD. ⁷Nevertheless, because of the covenant the LORD had made with David, the LORD was not willing to destroy the house of David. He had promised to maintain a lamp for him and his descendants forever.

⁸In the time of Jehoram, Edom rebelled against Judah and set up its own king. ⁹So Jehoram went there with his officers and all his chariots. The Edomites surrounded him and his chariot commanders, but he rose up and broke through by night. ¹⁰To this day Edom has been in rebellion against Judah.

Libnah revolted at the same time, because Jehoram had forsaken the LORD, the God of his fathers. ¹¹He had also built high places on the hills of Judah and had caused the people of Jerusalem to prostitute themselves and had led Judah astray.

ᵒ36 Hebrew *of ships that could go to Tarshish*   ᵖ37 Hebrew *sail for Tarshish*   q2 That is, Judah, as frequently in 2 Chronicles

[12]Jehoram received a letter from Elijah the prophet, which said:

"This is what the Lord, the God of your father David, says: 'You have not walked in the ways of your father Jehoshaphat or of Asa king of Judah. [13]But you have walked in the ways of the kings of Israel, and you have led Judah and the people of Jerusalem to prostitute themselves, just as the house of Ahab did. You have also murdered your own brothers, members of your father's house, men who were better than you. [14]So now the Lord is about to strike your people, your sons, your wives and everything that is yours, with a heavy blow. [15]You yourself will be very ill with a lingering disease of the bowels, until the disease causes your bowels to come out.' "

[16]The Lord aroused against Jehoram the hostility of the Philistines and of the Arabs who lived near the Cushites. [17]They attacked Judah, invaded it and carried off all the goods found in the king's palace, together with his sons and wives. Not a son was left to him except Ahaziah,[r] the youngest.

[18]After all this, the Lord afflicted Jehoram with an incurable disease of the bowels. [19]In the course of time, at the end of the second year, his bowels came out because of the disease, and he died in great pain. His people made no fire in his honor, as they had for his fathers.

[20]Jehoram was thirty-two years old when he became king, and he reigned in Jerusalem eight years. He passed away, to no one's regret, and was buried in the City of David, but not in the tombs of the kings.

22 The people of Jerusalem made Ahaziah, Jehoram's youngest son, king in his place, since the raiders, who came with the Arabs into the camp, had killed all the older sons. So Ahaziah son of Jehoram king of Judah began to reign.

[2]Ahaziah was twenty-two[s] years old when he became king, and he reigned in Jerusalem one year. His mother's name was Athaliah, a granddaughter of Omri.

[3]He too walked in the ways of the house of Ahab, for his mother encouraged him in doing wrong. [4]He did evil in the eyes of the Lord, as the house of Ahab had done, for after his father's death they became his advisers, to his undoing. [5]He also followed their counsel when he went with Joram[t] son of Ahab king of Israel to war against Hazael king of Aram at Ramoth Gilead. The Arameans wounded Joram; [6]so he returned to Jezreel to recover from the wounds they had inflicted on him at Ramoth[u] in his battle with Hazael king of Aram.

Then Ahaziah[v] son of Jehoram king of Judah went down to Jezreel to see Joram son of Ahab because he had been wounded.

[7]Through Ahaziah's visit to Joram, God brought about Ahaziah's downfall. When Ahaziah arrived, he went out with Joram to meet Jehu son of Nimshi, whom the Lord had anointed to destroy the house of Ahab. [8]While Jehu was executing judgment on the house of Ahab, he found the princes of Judah and the sons of Ahaziah's relatives, who had been attending Ahaziah, and he killed them. [9]He then went in search of Ahaziah, and his men captured him while he was hiding in Samaria. He was brought to Jehu and put to death. They buried him, for they said, "He was a son of Jehoshaphat, who sought the Lord with all his heart." So there was no one in the house of Ahaziah powerful enough to retain the kingdom.

[10]When Athaliah the mother of Ahaziah saw that her son was dead, she proceeded to destroy the whole royal family of the house of Judah. [11]But Jehosheba,[w] the daughter of King Jehoram, took Joash son of Ahaziah and stole him away from among the royal princes who were about to be murdered and put him and his nurse in a bedroom. Because Jehosheba,[w] the daughter of King Jehoram and wife of the priest Jehoiada, was Ahaziah's sister, she hid the child from Athaliah so she could not kill him. [12]He remained hidden with them at the temple of God for six years while Athaliah ruled the land.

[r]17 Hebrew Jehoahaz, a variant of Ahaziah   [s]2 Some Septuagint manuscripts and Syriac (see also 2 Kings 8:26); Hebrew forty-two   [t]5 Hebrew Jehoram, a variant of Joram; also in verses 6 and 7   [u]6 Hebrew Ramah, a variant of Ramoth   [v]6 Some Hebrew manuscripts, Septuagint, Vulgate and Syriac (see also 2 Kings 8:29); most Hebrew manuscripts Azariah   [w]11 Hebrew Jehoshabeath, a variant of Jehosheba

6 / 2 Chronicles 23—24
Protégé to a Priest

A CAR LOADED with household goods stands waiting in the driveway. I hug my spiritual mentor, my best friend, goodby. I close the car door behind her and watch her drive away while a gnawing emptiness digs at my gut. My mind goes back over our intense times of searching the Scriptures together, comfortable walks in the woods, shouting rides on a snow sled, tearful problem solving, brief honest prayers for one another. And I know I can never relive those times. They are gone, with her, to the West Coast.

It hasn't happened—yet. But the scene has crossed my mind often enough for me to ask myself some hard questions: Where is my faith anchored? In her or in God? If she goes, where will I turn for spiritual nurture? Am I a grown woman, able to find constructive ways to meet my own needs? Or am I still wandering, umbilical cord in hand, looking for a place to plug it in?

Warming Up to God What person is most responsible for your own spiritual development? How has that person nurtured you?

Read 2 Chronicles 23—24.

23 In the seventh year Jehoiada showed his strength. He made a covenant with the commanders of units of a hundred: Azariah son of Jeroham, Ishmael son of Jehohanan, Azariah son of Obed, Maaseiah son of Adaiah, and Elishaphat son of Zicri. ²They went throughout Judah and gathered the Levites and the heads of Israelite families from all the towns. When they came to Jerusalem, ³the whole assembly made a covenant with the king at the temple of God.

Jehoiada said to them, "The king's son shall reign, as the LORD promised concerning the descendants of David. ⁴Now this is what you are to do: A third of you priests and Levites who are going on duty on the Sabbath are to keep watch at the doors, ⁵a third of you at the royal palace and a third at the Foundation Gate, and all the other men are to be in the courtyards of the temple of the LORD. ⁶No one is to enter the temple of the LORD except the priests and Levites on duty; they may enter because they are consecrated, but all the other men are to guard what the LORD has assigned to them.ˣ ⁷The Levites are to station themselves around the king, each man with his weapons in his hand. Anyone who enters the temple must be put to death. Stay close to the king wherever he goes."

⁸The Levites and all the men of Judah did just as Jehoiada the priest ordered. Each one took his men—those who were going on duty on the Sabbath and those who were going off duty—for Jehoiada the priest had not released any of the divisions. ⁹Then he gave the commanders of units of a hundred the spears and the large and small shields that had belonged to King David and that were in the temple of God. ¹⁰He stationed all the men, each with his weapon in his hand, around the king—near the altar and the temple, from the south side to the north side of the temple.

¹¹Jehoiada and his sons brought out the king's son and put the crown on him; they presented him with a copy of the covenant and proclaimed him king. They anointed him and shouted, "Long live the king!"

¹²When Athaliah heard the noise of the people running and cheering the king, she went to them at the temple of the LORD. ¹³She looked, and there was the king, standing by his pillar at the entrance. The officers and the trumpeters were beside the king, and all the people of the land were rejoicing and blowing trumpets, and singers with musical instruments were leading the praises. Then Athaliah tore her robes and shouted, "Treason! Treason!"

¹⁴Jehoiada the priest sent out the commanders of units of a hundred, who were in charge of the troops, and said to them: "Bring her out between the ranksʸ and put to the sword anyone who follows her." For the priest had said, "Do not put her to death at the temple of the LORD." ¹⁵So they seized her as she reached the entrance of the Horse Gate on the palace grounds, and there they put her to death.

¹⁶Jehoiada then made a covenant that he and

ˣ6 Or to observe the LORD's command ⌐not to enter⌐   ʸ14 Or out from the precincts the people and the king^z would be the LORD's people. ¹⁷All the people went to the temple of Baal and tore it down. They smashed the altars and idols and killed Mattan the priest of Baal in front of the altars.

¹⁸Then Jehoiada placed the oversight of the temple of the LORD in the hands of the priests, who were Levites, to whom David had made assignments in the temple, to present the burnt offerings of the LORD as written in the Law of Moses, with rejoicing and singing, as David had ordered. ¹⁹He also stationed doorkeepers at the gates of the LORD's temple so that no one who was in any way unclean might enter.

²⁰He took with him the commanders of hundreds, the nobles, the rulers of the people and all the people of the land and brought the king down from the temple of the LORD. They went into the palace through the Upper Gate and seated the king on the royal throne, ²¹and all the people of the land rejoiced. And the city was quiet, because Athaliah had been slain with the sword.

24 Joash was seven years old when he became king, and he reigned in Jerusalem forty years. His mother's name was Zibiah; she was from Beersheba. ²Joash did what was right in the eyes of the LORD all the years of Jehoiada the priest. ³Jehoiada chose two wives for him, and he had sons and daughters.

⁴Some time later Joash decided to restore the temple of the LORD. ⁵He called together the priests and Levites and said to them, "Go to the towns of Judah and collect the money due annually from all Israel, to repair the temple of your God. Do it now." But the Levites did not act at once.

⁶Therefore the king summoned Jehoiada the chief priest and said to him, "Why haven't you required the Levites to bring in from Judah and Jerusalem the tax imposed by Moses the servant of the LORD and by the assembly of Israel for the Tent of the Testimony?"

⁷Now the sons of that wicked woman Athaliah had broken into the temple of God and had used even its sacred objects for the Baals.

⁸At the king's command, a chest was made and placed outside, at the gate of the temple of the LORD. ⁹A proclamation was then issued in Judah and Jerusalem that they should bring to the LORD the tax that Moses the servant of God had required of Israel in the desert. ¹⁰All the officials and all the people brought their contributions gladly, dropping them into the chest until it was full. ¹¹Whenever the chest was brought in by the Levites to the king's officials and they saw that there was a large amount of money, the royal secretary and the officer of the chief priest would come and empty the chest and carry it back to its place. They did this regularly and collected a great amount of money. ¹²The king and Jehoiada gave it to the men who carried out the work required for the temple of the LORD. They hired masons and carpenters to restore the LORD's temple, and also workers in iron and bronze to repair the temple.

¹³The men in charge of the work were diligent, and the repairs progressed under them. They rebuilt the temple of God according to its original design and reinforced it. ¹⁴When they had finished, they brought the rest of the money to the king and Jehoiada, and with it were made articles for the LORD's temple: articles for the service and for the burnt offerings, and also dishes and other objects of gold and silver. As long as Jehoiada lived, burnt offerings were presented continually in the temple of the LORD.

¹⁵Now Jehoiada was old and full of years, and he died at the age of a hundred and thirty. ¹⁶He was buried with the kings in the City of David, because of the good he had done in Israel for God and his temple.

¹⁷After the death of Jehoiada, the officials of Judah came and paid homage to the king, and he listened to them. ¹⁸They abandoned the temple of the LORD, the God of their fathers, and worshiped Asherah poles and idols. Because of their guilt, God's anger came upon Judah and Jerusalem. ¹⁹Although the LORD sent prophets to the people to bring them back to him, and though they testified against them, they would not listen.

²⁰Then the Spirit of God came upon Zechariah son of Jehoiada the priest. He stood before the people and said, "This is what God says: 'Why do you disobey the LORD's commands? You will not prosper. Because you have forsaken the LORD, he has forsaken you.'"

²¹But they plotted against him, and by order of the king they stoned him to death in the courtyard of the LORD's temple. ²²King Joash did not remember the kindness Zechariah's father Jehoiada had shown him but killed his son, who said as he lay dying, "May the LORD see this and call you to account."

^z16 Or covenant between ⌊the LORD⌋ and the people and the king that they (see 2 Kings 11:17)

²³At the turn of the year,ᵃ the army of Aram marched against Joash; it invaded Judah and Jerusalem and killed all the leaders of the people. They sent all the plunder to their king in Damascus. ²⁴Although the Aramean army had come with only a few men, the LORD delivered into their hands a much larger army. Because Judah had forsaken the LORD, the God of their fathers, judgment was executed on Joash. ²⁵When the Arameans withdrew, they left Joash severely wounded. His officials conspired against him for murdering the son of Jehoiada the priest, and they killed him in his bed. So he died and was buried in the City of David, but not in the tombs of the kings.

²⁶Those who conspired against him were Zabad,ᵇ son of Shimeath an Ammonite woman, and Jehozabad, son of Shimrithᶜ a Moabite woman. ²⁷The account of his sons, the many prophecies about him, and the record of the restoration of the temple of God are written in the annotations on the book of the kings. And Amaziah his son succeeded him as king.

ᵃ23 Probably in the spring   ᵇ26 A variant of *Jozabad*   ᶜ26 A variant of *Shomer*

 Discovering the Word 1. What groundwork did Jehoiada lay to ensure that the child Joash would safely become king (23:3–7)? 2. What steps did Jehoiada take to establish spiritual change in Judah (23:12—24:3)? 3. How would you describe the relationship between Jehoiada and Joash? 4. What indications do you see that Joash tried to make restoring the temple an honest process (24:4–14)? 5. What changes came to Judah after Jehoiada's death (24:17–27)? 6. Why would you not expect Joash to take this kind of turn?

Applying the Word 1. What could you be doing that would help you to continue to mature spiritually if your spiritual leader were removed from your life? 2. Think of one person for whom you are a spiritual guardian. How could you help that person continue growing spiritually even if you were no longer available to help?

Responding in Prayer Thank God for both those who have gone before you to lead the way of faith and those who follow after who you are privileged to lead.

---

2 Chronicles 25—33

25 Amaziah was twenty-five years old when he became king, and he reigned in Jerusalem twenty-nine years. His mother's name was Jehoaddinᵈ; she was from Jerusalem. ²He did what was right in the eyes of the LORD, but not wholeheartedly. ³After the kingdom was firmly in his control, he executed the officials who had murdered his father the king. ⁴Yet he did not put their sons to death, but acted in accordance with what is written in the Law, in the Book of Moses, where the LORD commanded: "Fathers shall not be put to death for their children, nor children put to death for their fathers; each is to die for his own sins."ᵉ

⁵Amaziah called the people of Judah together and assigned them according to their families to commanders of thousands and commanders of hundreds for all Judah and Benjamin. He then mustered those twenty years old or more and found that there were three hundred thousand men ready for military service, able to handle the spear and shield. ⁶He also hired a hundred thousand fighting men from Israel for a hundred talentsᶠ of silver.

⁷But a man of God came to him and said, "O king, these troops from Israel must not march with you, for the LORD is not with Israel—not with any of the people of Ephraim. ⁸Even if you go and fight courageously in battle, God will overthrow you before the enemy, for God has the power to help or to overthrow."

⁹Amaziah asked the man of God, "But what about the hundred talents I paid for these Israelite troops?"

The man of God replied, "The LORD can give you much more than that."

¹⁰So Amaziah dismissed the troops who had come to him from Ephraim and sent them home. They were furious with Judah and left for home in a great rage.

¹¹Amaziah then marshaled his strength and led his army to the Valley of Salt, where he killed ten thousand men of Seir. ¹²The army of Judah also

---

ᵈ1 Hebrew *Jehoaddan*, a variant of *Jehoaddin*   ᵉ4 Deut. 24:16
ᶠ6 That is, about 3 3/4 tons (about 3.4 metric tons); also in verse 9

captured ten thousand men alive, took them to the top of a cliff and threw them down so that all were dashed to pieces.

13Meanwhile the troops that Amaziah had sent back and had not allowed to take part in the war raided Judean towns from Samaria to Beth Horon. They killed three thousand people and carried off great quantities of plunder.

14When Amaziah returned from slaughtering the Edomites, he brought back the gods of the people of Seir. He set them up as his own gods, bowed down to them and burned sacrifices to them. 15The anger of the LORD burned against Amaziah, and he sent a prophet to him, who said, "Why do you consult this people's gods, which could not save their own people from your hand?"

16While he was still speaking, the king said to him, "Have we appointed you an adviser to the king? Stop! Why be struck down?"

So the prophet stopped but said, "I know that God has determined to destroy you, because you have done this and have not listened to my counsel."

17After Amaziah king of Judah consulted his advisers, he sent this challenge to Jehoash^g son of Jehoahaz, the son of Jehu, king of Israel: "Come, meet me face to face."

18But Jehoash king of Israel replied to Amaziah king of Judah: "A thistle in Lebanon sent a message to a cedar in Lebanon, 'Give your daughter to my son in marriage.' Then a wild beast in Lebanon came along and trampled the thistle underfoot. 19You say to yourself that you have defeated Edom, and now you are arrogant and proud. But stay at home! Why ask for trouble and cause your own downfall and that of Judah also?"

20Amaziah, however, would not listen, for God so worked that he might hand them over to ⌐Jehoash⌐, because they sought the gods of Edom. 21So Jehoash king of Israel attacked. He and Amaziah king of Judah faced each other at Beth Shemesh in Judah. 22Judah was routed by Israel, and every man fled to his home. 23Jehoash king of Israel captured Amaziah king of Judah, the son of Joash, the son of Ahaziah,^{h} at Beth Shemesh. Then Jehoash brought him to Jerusalem and broke down the wall of Jerusalem from the Ephraim Gate to the Corner Gate—a section about six hundred feet^i long. 24He took all the gold and silver and all the articles found in the temple of God that had been in the care of Obed-

Edom, together with the palace treasures and the hostages, and returned to Samaria.

25Amaziah son of Joash king of Judah lived for fifteen years after the death of Jehoash son of Jehoahaz king of Israel. 26As for the other events of Amaziah's reign, from beginning to end, are they not written in the book of the kings of Judah and Israel? 27From the time that Amaziah turned away from following the LORD, they conspired against him in Jerusalem and he fled to Lachish, but they sent men after him to Lachish and killed him there. 28He was brought back by horse and was buried with his fathers in the City of Judah.

26 Then all the people of Judah took Uzziah,^{j} who was sixteen years old, and made him king in place of his father Amaziah. 2He was the one who rebuilt Elath and restored it to Judah after Amaziah rested with his fathers.

3Uzziah was sixteen years old when he became king, and he reigned in Jerusalem fifty-two years. His mother's name was Jecoliah; she was from Jerusalem. 4He did what was right in the eyes of the LORD, just as his father Amaziah had done. 5He sought God during the days of Zechariah, who instructed him in the fear^k of God. As long as he sought the LORD, God gave him success.

6He went to war against the Philistines and broke down the walls of Gath, Jabneh and Ashdod. He then rebuilt towns near Ashdod and elsewhere among the Philistines. 7God helped him against the Philistines and against the Arabs who lived in Gur Baal and against the Meunites. 8The Ammonites brought tribute to Uzziah, and his fame spread as far as the border of Egypt, because he had become very powerful.

9Uzziah built towers in Jerusalem at the Corner Gate, at the Valley Gate and at the angle of the wall, and he fortified them. 10He also built towers in the desert and dug many cisterns, because he had much livestock in the foothills and in the plain. He had people working his fields and vineyards in the hills and in the fertile lands, for he loved the soil.

11Uzziah had a well-trained army, ready to go out by divisions according to their numbers as mustered by Jeiel the secretary and Maaseiah the officer under the direction of Hananiah, one of

^{g}17 Hebrew *Joash*, a variant of *Jehoash*; also in verses 18, 21, 23 and 25 ^{h}23 Hebrew *Jehoahaz*, a variant of *Ahaziah* ^{i}23 Hebrew *four hundred cubits* (about 180 meters) ^{j}1 Also called *Azariah* ^{k}5 Many Hebrew manuscripts, Septuagint and Syriac; other Hebrew manuscripts *vision* the royal officials. [12]The total number of family leaders over the fighting men was 2,600. [13]Under their command was an army of 307,500 men trained for war, a powerful force to support the king against his enemies. [14]Uzziah provided shields, spears, helmets, coats of armor, bows and slingstones for the entire army. [15]In Jerusalem he made machines designed by skillful men for use on the towers and on the corner defenses to shoot arrows and hurl large stones. His fame spread far and wide, for he was greatly helped until he became powerful.

[16]But after Uzziah became powerful, his pride led to his downfall. He was unfaithful to the LORD his God, and entered the temple of the LORD to burn incense on the altar of incense. [17]Azariah the priest with eighty other courageous priests of the LORD followed him in. [18]They confronted him and said, "It is not right for you, Uzziah, to burn incense to the LORD. That is for the priests, the descendants of Aaron, who have been consecrated to burn incense. Leave the sanctuary, for you have been unfaithful; and you will not be honored by the LORD God."

[19]Uzziah, who had a censer in his hand ready to burn incense, became angry. While he was raging at the priests in their presence before the incense altar in the LORD's temple, leprosy[l] broke out on his forehead. [20]When Azariah the chief priest and all the other priests looked at him, they saw that he had leprosy on his forehead, so they hurried him out. Indeed, he himself was eager to leave, because the LORD had afflicted him.

[21]King Uzziah had leprosy until the day he died. He lived in a separate house[m]—leprous, and excluded from the temple of the LORD. Jotham his son had charge of the palace and governed the people of the land.

[22]The other events of Uzziah's reign, from beginning to end, are recorded by the prophet Isaiah son of Amoz. [23]Uzziah rested with his fathers and was buried near them in a field for burial that belonged to the kings, for people said, "He had leprosy." And Jotham his son succeeded him as king.

27 Jotham was twenty-five years old when he became king, and he reigned in Jerusalem sixteen years. His mother's name was Jerusha daughter of Zadok. [2]He did what was right in the eyes of the LORD, just as his father Uzziah had done, but unlike him he did not enter the temple of the LORD.

The people, however, continued their corrupt practices. [3]Jotham rebuilt the Upper Gate of the temple of the LORD and did extensive work on the wall at the hill of Ophel. [4]He built towns in the Judean hills and forts and towers in the wooded areas.

[5]Jotham made war on the king of the Ammonites and conquered them. That year the Ammonites paid him a hundred talents[n] of silver, ten thousand cors[o] of wheat and ten thousand cors of barley. The Ammonites brought him the same amount also in the second and third years.

[6]Jotham grew powerful because he walked steadfastly before the LORD his God.

[7]The other events in Jotham's reign, including all his wars and the other things he did, are written in the book of the kings of Israel and Judah. [8]He was twenty-five years old when he became king, and he reigned in Jerusalem sixteen years. [9]Jotham rested with his fathers and was buried in the City of David. And Ahaz his son succeeded him as king.

28 Ahaz was twenty years old when he became king, and he reigned in Jerusalem sixteen years. Unlike David his father, he did not do what was right in the eyes of the LORD. [2]He walked in the ways of the kings of Israel and also made cast idols for worshiping the Baals. [3]He burned sacrifices in the Valley of Ben Hinnom and sacrificed his sons in the fire, following the detestable ways of the nations the LORD had driven out before the Israelites. [4]He offered sacrifices and burned incense at the high places, on the hilltops and under every spreading tree.

[5]Therefore the LORD his God handed him over to the king of Aram. The Arameans defeated him and took many of his people as prisoners and brought them to Damascus.

He was also given into the hands of the king of Israel, who inflicted heavy casualties on him. [6]In one day Pekah son of Remaliah killed a hundred and twenty thousand soldiers in Judah—because Judah had forsaken the LORD, the God of their fathers. [7]Zicri, an Ephraimite warrior, killed Maaseiah the king's son, Azrikam the officer in charge of the palace, and Elkanah, second to the king. [8]The Israelites took captive from their kinsmen

---

[l]19 The Hebrew word was used for various diseases affecting the skin—not necessarily leprosy; also in verses 20, 21 and 23. [m]21 Or *in a house where he was relieved of responsibilities* [n]5 That is, about 3 3/4 tons (about 3.4 metric tons) [o]5 That is, probably about 62,000 bushels (about 2,200 kiloliters)

two hundred thousand wives, sons and daughters. They also took a great deal of plunder, which they carried back to Samaria.

9But a prophet of the LORD named Oded was there, and he went out to meet the army when it returned to Samaria. He said to them, "Because the LORD, the God of your fathers, was angry with Judah, he gave them into your hand. But you have slaughtered them in a rage that reaches to heaven. 10And now you intend to make the men and women of Judah and Jerusalem your slaves. But aren't you also guilty of sins against the LORD your God? 11Now listen to me! Send back your fellow countrymen you have taken as prisoners, for the LORD's fierce anger rests on you."

12Then some of the leaders in Ephraim—Azariah son of Jehohanan, Berekiah son of Meshillemoth, Jehizkiah son of Shallum, and Amasa son of Hadlai—confronted those who were arriving from the war. 13"You must not bring those prisoners here," they said, "or we will be guilty before the LORD. Do you intend to add to our sin and guilt? For our guilt is already great, and his fierce anger rests on Israel."

14So the soldiers gave up the prisoners and plunder in the presence of the officials and all the assembly. 15The men designated by name took the prisoners, and from the plunder they clothed all who were naked. They provided them with clothes and sandals, food and drink, and healing balm. All those who were weak they put on donkeys. So they took them back to their fellow countrymen at Jericho, the City of Palms, and returned to Samaria.

16At that time King Ahaz sent to the kingᵖ of Assyria for help. 17The Edomites had again come and attacked Judah and carried away prisoners, 18while the Philistines had raided towns in the foothills and in the Negev of Judah. They captured and occupied Beth Shemesh, Aijalon and Gederoth, as well as Soco, Timnah and Gimzo, with their surrounding villages. 19The LORD had humbled Judah because of Ahaz king of Israel,�q for he had promoted wickedness in Judah and had been most unfaithful to the LORD. 20Tiglath-Pileserʳ king of Assyria came to him, but he gave him trouble instead of help. 21Ahaz took some of the things from the temple of the LORD and from the royal palace and from the princes and presented them to the king of Assyria, but that did not help him.

22In his time of trouble King Ahaz became even more unfaithful to the LORD. 23He offered sacrifices to the gods of Damascus, who had defeated him; for he thought, "Since the gods of the kings of Aram have helped them, I will sacrifice to them so they will help me." But they were his downfall and the downfall of all Israel.

24Ahaz gathered together the furnishings from the temple of God and took them away.ˢ He shut the doors of the LORD's temple and set up altars at every street corner in Jerusalem. 25In every town in Judah he built high places to burn sacrifices to other gods and provoked the LORD, the God of his fathers, to anger.

26The other events of his reign and all his ways, from beginning to end, are written in the book of the kings of Judah and Israel. 27Ahaz rested with his fathers and was buried in the city of Jerusalem, but he was not placed in the tombs of the kings of Israel. And Hezekiah his son succeeded him as king.

29 Hezekiah was twenty-five years old when he became king, and he reigned in Jerusalem twenty-nine years. His mother's name was Abijah daughter of Zechariah. 2He did what was right in the eyes of the LORD, just as his father David had done.

3In the first month of the first year of his reign, he opened the doors of the temple of the LORD and repaired them. 4He brought in the priests and the Levites, assembled them in the square on the east side 5and said: "Listen to me, Levites! Consecrate yourselves now and consecrate the temple of the LORD, the God of your fathers. Remove all defilement from the sanctuary. 6Our fathers were unfaithful; they did evil in the eyes of the LORD our God and forsook him. They turned their faces away from the LORD's dwelling place and turned their backs on him. 7They also shut the doors of the portico and put out the lamps. They did not burn incense or present any burnt offerings at the sanctuary to the God of Israel. 8Therefore, the anger of the LORD has fallen on Judah and Jerusalem; he has made them an object of dread and horror and scorn, as you can see with your own eyes. 9This is why our fathers have fallen by the sword and why our sons and daughters and our wives are in captivity. 10Now I intend to make a covenant with the LORD, the God of Israel, so that his fierce anger will turn away from us. 11My

ᵖ16 One Hebrew manuscript, Septuagint and Vulgate (see also 2 Kings 16:7); most Hebrew manuscripts kings   �q19 That is, Judah, as frequently in 2 Chronicles   ʳ20 Hebrew Tilgath-Pilneser, a variant of Tiglath-Pileser   ˢ24 Or and cut them up sons, do not be negligent now, for the LORD has chosen you to stand before him and serve him, to minister before him and to burn incense."

12Then these Levites set to work:

from the Kohathites,
Mahath son of Amasai and Joel son of Azariah;
from the Merarites,
Kish son of Abdi and Azariah son of Jehallelel;
from the Gershonites,
Joah son of Zimmah and Eden son of Joah;
13from the descendants of Elizaphan,
Shimri and Jeiel;
from the descendants of Asaph,
Zechariah and Mattaniah;
14from the descendants of Heman,
Jehiel and Shimei;
from the descendants of Jeduthun,
Shemaiah and Uzziel.

15When they had assembled their brothers and consecrated themselves, they went in to purify the temple of the LORD, as the king had ordered, following the word of the LORD. 16The priests went into the sanctuary of the LORD to purify it. They brought out to the courtyard of the LORD's temple everything unclean that they found in the temple of the LORD. The Levites took it and carried it out to the Kidron Valley. 17They began the consecration on the first day of the first month, and by the eighth day of the month they reached the portico of the LORD. For eight more days they consecrated the temple of the LORD itself, finishing on the sixteenth day of the first month.

18Then they went in to King Hezekiah and reported: "We have purified the entire temple of the LORD, the altar of burnt offering with all its utensils, and the table for setting out the consecrated bread, with all its articles. 19We have prepared and consecrated all the articles that King Ahaz removed in his unfaithfulness while he was king. They are now in front of the LORD's altar."

20Early the next morning King Hezekiah gathered the city officials together and went up to the temple of the LORD. 21They brought seven bulls, seven rams, seven male lambs and seven male goats as a sin offering for the kingdom, for the sanctuary and for Judah. The king commanded the priests, the descendants of Aaron, to offer these on the altar of the LORD. 22So they slaughtered the bulls, and the priests took the blood and sprinkled it on the altar; next they slaughtered the rams and sprinkled their blood on the altar; then they slaughtered the lambs and sprinkled their blood on the altar. 23The goats for the sin offering were brought before the king and the assembly, and they laid their hands on them. 24The priests then slaughtered the goats and presented their blood on the altar for a sin offering to atone for all Israel, because the king had ordered the burnt offering and the sin offering for all Israel.

25He stationed the Levites in the temple of the LORD with cymbals, harps and lyres in the way prescribed by David and Gad the king's seer and Nathan the prophet; this was commanded by the LORD through his prophets. 26So the Levites stood ready with David's instruments, and the priests with their trumpets.

27Hezekiah gave the order to sacrifice the burnt offering on the altar. As the offering began, singing to the LORD began also, accompanied by trumpets and the instruments of David king of Israel. 28The whole assembly bowed in worship, while the singers sang and the trumpeters played. All this continued until the sacrifice of the burnt offering was completed.

29When the offerings were finished, the king and everyone present with him knelt down and worshiped. 30King Hezekiah and his officials ordered the Levites to praise the LORD with the words of David and of Asaph the seer. So they sang praises with gladness and bowed their heads and worshiped.

31Then Hezekiah said, "You have now dedicated yourselves to the LORD. Come and bring sacrifices and thank offerings to the temple of the LORD." So the assembly brought sacrifices and thank offerings, and all whose hearts were willing brought burnt offerings.

32The number of burnt offerings the assembly brought was seventy bulls, a hundred rams and two hundred male lambs—all of them for burnt offerings to the LORD. 33The animals consecrated as sacrifices amounted to six hundred bulls and three thousand sheep and goats. 34The priests, however, were too few to skin all the burnt offerings; so their kinsmen the Levites helped them until the task was finished and until other priests had been consecrated, for the Levites had been more conscientious in consecrating themselves than the priests had been. 35There were burnt offerings in abundance, together with the fat of the fellowship offerings[t] and the drink offerings that accompanied the burnt offerings.

So the service of the temple of the LORD was reestablished. [36]Hezekiah and all the people rejoiced at what God had brought about for his people, because it was done so quickly.

30

Hezekiah sent word to all Israel and Judah and also wrote letters to Ephraim and Manasseh, inviting them to come to the temple of the LORD in Jerusalem and celebrate the Passover to the LORD, the God of Israel. [2]The king and his officials and the whole assembly in Jerusalem decided to celebrate the Passover in the second month. [3]They had not been able to celebrate it at the regular time because not enough priests had consecrated themselves and the people had not assembled in Jerusalem. [4]The plan seemed right both to the king and to the whole assembly. [5]They decided to send a proclamation throughout Israel, from Beersheba to Dan, calling the people to come to Jerusalem and celebrate the Passover to the LORD, the God of Israel. It had not been celebrated in large numbers according to what was written.

[6]At the king's command, couriers went throughout Israel and Judah with letters from the king and from his officials, which read:

"People of Israel, return to the LORD, the God of Abraham, Isaac and Israel, that he may return to you who are left, who have escaped from the hand of the kings of Assyria. [7]Do not be like your fathers and brothers, who were unfaithful to the LORD, the God of their fathers, so that he made them an object of horror, as you see. [8]Do not be stiff-necked, as your fathers were; submit to the LORD. Come to the sanctuary, which he has consecrated forever. Serve the LORD your God, so that his fierce anger will turn away from you. [9]If you return to the LORD, then your brothers and your children will be shown compassion by their captors and will come back to this land, for the LORD your God is gracious and compassionate. He will not turn his face from you if you return to him."

[10]The couriers went from town to town in Ephraim and Manasseh, as far as Zebulun, but the people scorned and ridiculed them. [11]Nevertheless, some men of Asher, Manasseh and Zebulun humbled themselves and went to Jerusalem.

[12]Also in Judah the hand of God was on the people to give them unity of mind to carry out what the king and his officials had ordered, following the word of the LORD.

[13]A very large crowd of people assembled in Jerusalem to celebrate the Feast of Unleavened Bread in the second month. [14]They removed the altars in Jerusalem and cleared away the incense altars and threw them into the Kidron Valley.

[15]They slaughtered the Passover lamb on the fourteenth day of the second month. The priests and the Levites were ashamed and consecrated themselves and brought burnt offerings to the temple of the LORD. [16]Then they took up their regular positions as prescribed in the Law of Moses the man of God. The priests sprinkled the blood handed to them by the Levites. [17]Since many in the crowd had not consecrated themselves, the Levites had to kill the Passover lambs for all those who were not ceremonially clean and could not consecrate ⌞their lambs⌟ to the LORD. [18]Although most of the many people who came from Ephraim, Manasseh, Issachar and Zebulun had not purified themselves, yet they ate the Passover, contrary to what was written. But Hezekiah prayed for them, saying, "May the LORD, who is good, pardon everyone [19]who sets his heart on seeking God—the LORD, the God of his fathers— even if he is not clean according to the rules of the sanctuary." [20]And the LORD heard Hezekiah and healed the people.

[21]The Israelites who were present in Jerusalem celebrated the Feast of Unleavened Bread for seven days with great rejoicing, while the Levites and priests sang to the LORD every day, accompanied by the LORD's instruments of praise.[u]

[22]Hezekiah spoke encouragingly to all the Levites, who showed good understanding of the service of the LORD. For the seven days they ate their assigned portion and offered fellowship offerings[t] and praised the LORD, the God of their fathers.

[23]The whole assembly then agreed to celebrate the festival seven more days; so for another seven days they celebrated joyfully. [24]Hezekiah king of Judah provided a thousand bulls and seven thousand sheep and goats for the assembly, and the officials provided them with a thousand bulls and ten thousand sheep and goats. A great number of priests consecrated themselves. [25]The entire as-

---

[t] 35,22 Traditionally *peace offerings*   [u] 21 Or *priests praised the LORD every day with resounding instruments belonging to the LORD*

sembly of Judah rejoiced, along with the priests and Levites and all who had assembled from Israel, including the aliens who had come from Israel and those who lived in Judah. ²⁶There was great joy in Jerusalem, for since the days of Solomon son of David king of Israel there had been nothing like this in Jerusalem. ²⁷The priests and the Levites stood to bless the people, and God heard them, for their prayer reached heaven, his holy dwelling place.

31 When all this had ended, the Israelites who were there went out to the towns of Judah, smashed the sacred stones and cut down the Asherah poles. They destroyed the high places and the altars throughout Judah and Benjamin and in Ephraim and Manasseh. After they had destroyed all of them, the Israelites returned to their own towns and to their own property.

²Hezekiah assigned the priests and Levites to divisions—each of them according to their duties as priests or Levites—to offer burnt offerings and fellowship offerings,ᵛ to minister, to give thanks and to sing praises at the gates of the LORD's dwelling. ³The king contributed from his own possessions for the morning and evening burnt offerings and for the burnt offerings on the Sabbaths, New Moons and appointed feasts as written in the Law of the LORD. ⁴He ordered the people living in Jerusalem to give the portion due the priests and Levites so they could devote themselves to the Law of the LORD. ⁵As soon as the order went out, the Israelites generously gave the firstfruits of their grain, new wine, oil and honey and all that the fields produced. They brought a great amount, a tithe of everything. ⁶The men of Israel and Judah who lived in the towns of Judah also brought a tithe of their herds and flocks and a tithe of the holy things dedicated to the LORD their God, and they piled them in heaps. ⁷They began doing this in the third month and finished in the seventh month. ⁸When Hezekiah and his officials came and saw the heaps, they praised the LORD and blessed his people Israel.

⁹Hezekiah asked the priests and Levites about the heaps; ¹⁰and Azariah the chief priest, from the family of Zadok, answered, "Since the people began to bring their contributions to the temple of the LORD, we have had enough to eat and plenty to spare, because the LORD has blessed his people, and this great amount is left over."

¹¹Hezekiah gave orders to prepare storerooms in the temple of the LORD, and this was done. ¹²Then they faithfully brought in the contributions, tithes and dedicated gifts. Conaniah, a Levite, was in charge of these things, and his brother Shimei was next in rank. ¹³Jehiel, Azaziah, Nahath, Asahel, Jerimoth, Jozabad, Eliel, Ismakiah, Mahath and Benaiah were supervisors under Conaniah and Shimei his brother, by appointment of King Hezekiah and Azariah the official in charge of the temple of God.

¹⁴Kore son of Imnah the Levite, keeper of the East Gate, was in charge of the freewill offerings given to God, distributing the contributions made to the LORD and also the consecrated gifts. ¹⁵Eden, Miniamin, Jeshua, Shemaiah, Amariah and Shecaniah assisted him faithfully in the towns of the priests, distributing to their fellow priests according to their divisions, old and young alike.

¹⁶In addition, they distributed to the males three years old or more whose names were in the genealogical records—all who would enter the temple of the LORD to perform the daily duties of their various tasks, according to their responsibilities and their divisions. ¹⁷And they distributed to the priests enrolled by their families in the genealogical records and likewise to the Levites twenty years old or more, according to their responsibilities and their divisions. ¹⁸They included all the little ones, the wives, and the sons and daughters of the whole community listed in these genealogical records. For they were faithful in consecrating themselves.

¹⁹As for the priests, the descendants of Aaron, who lived on the farm lands around their towns or in any other towns, men were designated by name to distribute portions to every male among them and to all who were recorded in the genealogies of the Levites.

²⁰This is what Hezekiah did throughout Judah, doing what was good and right and faithful before the LORD his God. ²¹In everything that he undertook in the service of God's temple and in obedience to the law and the commands, he sought his God and worked wholeheartedly. And so he prospered.

32 After all that Hezekiah had so faithfully done, Sennacherib king of Assyria came and invaded Judah. He laid siege to the fortified cities, thinking to con-

ᵛ2 Traditionally *peace offerings*

quer them for himself. ²When Hezekiah saw that Sennacherib had come and that he intended to make war on Jerusalem, ³he consulted with his officials and military staff about blocking off the water from the springs outside the city, and they helped him. ⁴A large force of men assembled, and they blocked all the springs and the stream that flowed through the land. "Why should the kingsʷ of Assyria come and find plenty of water?" they said. ⁵Then he worked hard repairing all the broken sections of the wall and building towers on it. He built another wall outside that one and reinforced the supporting terracesˣ of the City of David. He also made large numbers of weapons and shields.

⁶He appointed military officers over the people and assembled them before him in the square at the city gate and encouraged them with these words: ⁷"Be strong and courageous. Do not be afraid or discouraged because of the king of Assyria and the vast army with him, for there is a greater power with us than with him. ⁸With him is only the arm of flesh, but with us is the Lord our God to help us and to fight our battles." And the people gained confidence from what Hezekiah the king of Judah said.

⁹Later, when Sennacherib king of Assyria and all his forces were laying siege to Lachish, he sent his officers to Jerusalem with this message for Hezekiah king of Judah and for all the people of Judah who were there:

¹⁰"This is what Sennacherib king of Assyria says: On what are you basing your confidence, that you remain in Jerusalem under siege? ¹¹When Hezekiah says, 'The Lord our God will save us from the hand of the king of Assyria,' he is misleading you, to let you die of hunger and thirst. ¹²Did not Hezekiah himself remove this god's high places and altars, saying to Judah and Jerusalem, 'You must worship before one altar and burn sacrifices on it'?

¹³"Do you not know what I and my fathers have done to all the peoples of the other lands? Were the gods of those nations ever able to deliver their land from my hand? ¹⁴Who of all the gods of these nations that my fathers destroyed has been able to save his people from me? How then can your god deliver you from my hand? ¹⁵Now do not let Hezekiah deceive you and mislead you like

this. Do not believe him, for no god of any nation or kingdom has been able to deliver his people from my hand or the hand of my fathers. How much less will your god deliver you from my hand!"

¹⁶Sennacherib's officers spoke further against the Lord God and against his servant Hezekiah. ¹⁷The king also wrote letters insulting the Lord, the God of Israel, and saying this against him: "Just as the gods of the peoples of the other lands did not rescue their people from my hand, so the god of Hezekiah will not rescue his people from my hand." ¹⁸Then they called out in Hebrew to the people of Jerusalem who were on the wall, to terrify them and make them afraid in order to capture the city. ¹⁹They spoke about the God of Jerusalem as they did about the gods of the other peoples of the world—the work of men's hands.

²⁰King Hezekiah and the prophet Isaiah son of Amoz cried out in prayer to heaven about this. ²¹And the Lord sent an angel, who annihilated all the fighting men and the leaders and officers in the camp of the Assyrian king. So he withdrew to his own land in disgrace. And when he went into the temple of his god, some of his sons cut him down with the sword.

²²So the Lord saved Hezekiah and the people of Jerusalem from the hand of Sennacherib king of Assyria and from the hand of all others. He took care of themʸ on every side. ²³Many brought offerings to Jerusalem for the Lord and valuable gifts for Hezekiah king of Judah. From then on he was highly regarded by all the nations.

²⁴In those days Hezekiah became ill and was at the point of death. He prayed to the Lord, who answered him and gave him a miraculous sign. ²⁵But Hezekiah's heart was proud and he did not respond to the kindness shown him; therefore the Lord's wrath was on him and on Judah and Jerusalem. ²⁶Then Hezekiah repented of the pride of his heart, as did the people of Jerusalem; therefore the Lord's wrath did not come upon them during the days of Hezekiah.

²⁷Hezekiah had very great riches and honor, and he made treasuries for his silver and gold and for his precious stones, spices, shields and all kinds of valuables. ²⁸He also made buildings to

---

ʷ4 Hebrew; Septuagint and Syriac *king*   ˣ5 Or *the Millo*
ʸ22 Hebrew; Septuagint and Vulgate *He gave them rest*

store the harvest of grain, new wine and oil; and he made stalls for various kinds of cattle, and pens for the flocks. 29He built villages and acquired great numbers of flocks and herds, for God had given him very great riches.

30It was Hezekiah who blocked the upper outlet of the Gihon spring and channeled the water down to the west side of the City of David. He succeeded in everything he undertook. 31But when envoys were sent by the rulers of Babylon to ask him about the miraculous sign that had occurred in the land, God left him to test him and to know everything that was in his heart.

32The other events of Hezekiah's reign and his acts of devotion are written in the vision of the prophet Isaiah son of Amoz in the book of the kings of Judah and Israel. 33Hezekiah rested with his fathers and was buried on the hill where the tombs of David's descendants are. All Judah and the people of Jerusalem honored him when he died. And Manasseh his son succeeded him as king.

33 Manasseh was twelve years old when he became king, and he reigned in Jerusalem fifty-five years. 2He did evil in the eyes of the LORD, following the detestable practices of the nations the LORD had driven out before the Israelites. 3He rebuilt the high places his father Hezekiah had demolished; he also erected altars to the Baals and made Asherah poles. He bowed down to all the starry hosts and worshiped them. 4He built altars in the temple of the LORD, of which the LORD had said, "My Name will remain in Jerusalem forever." 5In both courts of the temple of the LORD, he built altars to all the starry hosts. 6He sacrificed his sons inᶻ the fire in the Valley of Ben Hinnom, practiced sorcery, divination and witchcraft, and consulted mediums and spiritists. He did much evil in the eyes of the LORD, provoking him to anger.

7He took the carved image he had made and put it in God's temple, of which God had said to David and to his son Solomon, "In this temple and in Jerusalem, which I have chosen out of all the tribes of Israel, I will put my Name forever. 8I will not again make the feet of the Israelites leave the land I assigned to your forefathers, if only they will be careful to do everything I commanded them concerning all the laws, decrees and ordinances given through Moses."

9But Manasseh led Judah and the people of Jerusalem astray, so that they did more evil than the nations the LORD had destroyed before the Israelites.

10The LORD spoke to Manasseh and his people, but they paid no attention. 11So the LORD brought against them the army commanders of the king of Assyria, who took Manasseh prisoner, put a hook in his nose, bound him with bronze shackles and took him to Babylon. 12In his distress he sought the favor of the LORD his God and humbled himself greatly before the God of his fathers. 13And when he prayed to him, the LORD was moved by his entreaty and listened to his plea; so he brought him back to Jerusalem and to his kingdom. Then Manasseh knew that the LORD is God.

14Afterward he rebuilt the outer wall of the City of David, west of the Gihon spring in the valley, as far as the entrance of the Fish Gate and encircling the hill of Ophel; he also made it much higher. He stationed military commanders in all the fortified cities in Judah.

15He got rid of the foreign gods and removed the image from the temple of the LORD, as well as all the altars he had built on the temple hill and in Jerusalem; and he threw them out of the city. 16Then he restored the altar of the LORD and sacrificed fellowship offeringsᵃ and thank offerings on it, and told Judah to serve the LORD, the God of Israel. 17The people, however, continued to sacrifice at the high places, but only to the LORD their God.

18The other events of Manasseh's reign, including his prayer to his God and the words the seers spoke to him in the name of the LORD, the God of Israel, are written in the annals of the kings of Israel.ᵇ 19His prayer and how God was moved by his entreaty, as well as all his sins and unfaithfulness, and the sites where he built high places and set up Asherah poles and idols before he humbled himself—all are written in the records of the seers.ᶜ 20Manasseh rested with his fathers and was buried in his palace. And Amon his son succeeded him as king.

21Amon was twenty-two years old when he became king, and he reigned in Jerusalem two years. 22He did evil in the eyes of the LORD, as his

---

ᶻ6 Or *He made his sons pass through*   ᵃ16 Traditionally *peace offerings*   ᵇ18 That is, Judah, as frequently in 2 Chronicles
ᶜ19 One Hebrew manuscript and Septuagint; most Hebrew manuscripts of *Hozai*

father Manasseh had done. Amon worshiped and offered sacrifices to all the idols Manasseh had made. 23But unlike his father Manasseh, he did not humble himself before the LORD; Amon increased his guilt.

24Amon's officials conspired against him and assassinated him in his palace. 25Then the people of the land killed all who had plotted against King Amon, and they made Josiah his son king in his place.

7 / 2 Chronicles 34
Loving God

ONE OF THE most frustrating aspects of being a Christian is our need for "proof" that God cares about our daily lives. Often, when we are left to ourselves, we have real doubts that God even notices our efforts to do what is right. King Josiah found himself in this situation when his servants found the book of the Law and read it to him.

 Warming Up to God Think about a time when you really wanted to know that God cared about what you were doing. How did God communicate his love for you?

 Read 2 Chronicles 34.

34 Josiah was eight years old when he became king, and he reigned in Jerusalem thirty-one years. 2He did what was right in the eyes of the LORD and walked in the ways of his father David, not turning aside to the right or to the left.

3In the eighth year of his reign, while he was still young, he began to seek the God of his father David. In his twelfth year he began to purge Judah and Jerusalem of high places, Asherah poles, carved idols and cast images. 4Under his direction the altars of the Baals were torn down; he cut to pieces the incense altars that were above them, and smashed the Asherah poles, the idols and the images. These he broke to pieces and scattered over the graves of those who had sacrificed to them. 5He burned the bones of the priests on their altars, and so he purged Judah and Jerusalem. 6In the towns of Manasseh, Ephraim and Simeon, as far as Naphtali, and in the ruins around them, 7he tore down the altars and the Asherah poles and crushed the idols to powder and cut to pieces all the incense altars throughout Israel. Then he went back to Jerusalem.

8In the eighteenth year of Josiah's reign, to purify the land and the temple, he sent Shaphan son of Azaliah and Maaseiah the ruler of the city, with Joah son of Joahaz, the recorder, to repair the temple of the LORD his God.

9They went to Hilkiah the high priest and gave him the money that had been brought into the temple of God, which the Levites who were the doorkeepers had collected from the people of Manasseh, Ephraim and the entire remnant of Israel and from all the people of Judah and Benjamin and the inhabitants of Jerusalem. 10Then they entrusted it to the men appointed to supervise the work on the LORD's temple. These men paid the workers who repaired and restored the temple. 11They also gave money to the carpenters and builders to purchase dressed stone, and timber for joists and beams for the buildings that the kings of Judah had allowed to fall into ruin.

12The men did the work faithfully. Over them to direct them were Jahath and Obadiah, Levites descended from Merari, and Zechariah and Meshullam, descended from Kohath. The Levites— all who were skilled in playing musical instruments— 13had charge of the laborers and supervised all the workers from job to job. Some of the Levites were secretaries, scribes and doorkeepers.

14While they were bringing out the money that had been taken into the temple of the LORD, Hilkiah the priest found the Book of the Law of the LORD that had been given through Moses. ¹⁵Hilkiah said to Shaphan the secretary, "I have found the Book of the Law in the temple of the LORD." He gave it to Shaphan.

¹⁶Then Shaphan took the book to the king and reported to him: "Your officials are doing everything that has been committed to them. ¹⁷They have paid out the money that was in the temple of the LORD and have entrusted it to the supervisors and workers." ¹⁸Then Shaphan the secretary informed the king, "Hilkiah the priest has given me a book." And Shaphan read from it in the presence of the king.

¹⁹When the king heard the words of the Law, he tore his robes. ²⁰He gave these orders to Hilkiah, Ahikam son of Shaphan, Abdon son of Micah,[d] Shaphan the secretary and Asaiah the king's attendant: ²¹"Go and inquire of the LORD for me and for the remnant in Israel and Judah about what is written in this book that has been found. Great is the LORD's anger that is poured out on us because our fathers have not kept the word of the LORD; they have not acted in accordance with all that is written in this book."

²²Hilkiah and those the king had sent with him[e] went to speak to the prophetess Huldah, who was the wife of Shallum son of Tokhath,[f] the son of Hasrah,[g] keeper of the wardrobe. She lived in Jerusalem, in the Second District.

²³She said to them, "This is what the LORD, the God of Israel, says: Tell the man who sent you to me, ²⁴'This is what the LORD says: I am going to bring disaster on this place and its people—all the curses written in the book that has been read in the presence of the king of Judah. ²⁵Because they have forsaken me and burned incense to other gods and provoked me to anger by all that their hands have made,[h] my anger will be poured out on this place and will not be quenched.' ²⁶Tell the king of Judah, who sent you to inquire of the LORD, 'This is what the LORD, the God of Israel, says concerning the words you heard: ²⁷Because your heart was responsive and you humbled yourself before God when you heard what he spoke against this place and its people, and because you humbled yourself before me and tore your robes and wept in my presence, I have heard you, declares the LORD. ²⁸Now I will gather you to your fathers, and you will be buried in peace. Your eyes will not see all the disaster I am going to bring on this place and on those who live here.' "

So they took her answer back to the king.

²⁹Then the king called together all the elders of Judah and Jerusalem. ³⁰He went up to the temple of the LORD with the men of Judah, the people of Jerusalem, the priests and the Levites—all the people from the least to the greatest. He read in their hearing all the words of the Book of the Covenant, which had been found in the temple of the LORD. ³¹The king stood by his pillar and renewed the covenant in the presence of the LORD—to follow the LORD and keep his commands, regulations and decrees with all his heart and all his soul, and to obey the words of the covenant written in this book.

³²Then he had everyone in Jerusalem and Benjamin pledge themselves to it; the people of Jerusalem did this in accordance with the covenant of God, the God of their fathers.

³³Josiah removed all the detestable idols from all the territory belonging to the Israelites, and he had all who were present in Israel serve the LORD their God. As long as he lived, they did not fail to follow the LORD, the God of their fathers.

d20 Also called Acbor son of Micaiah   e22 One Hebrew manuscript, Vulgate and Syriac; most Hebrew manuscripts do not have had sent with him.   f22 Also called Tikvah   g22 Also called Harhas   h25 Or by everything they have done

---

Discovering the Word 1. What do verses 1–7 reveal about Josiah's relationship with God? 2. Describe the nature of the work in verses 8–13. 3. The book of the Law that was read to Josiah was most likely Deuteronomy 12—26 and 28. The guidelines for worship in this passage are specifically what Josiah's predecessors disobeyed. What image of God do you think Josiah had? (Note his reaction in verse 19.) 4. Why did Josiah send messengers for Huldah (vv. 20–21)? 5. What feelings do you think Josiah had in response to Huldah's message (vv. 23–28)? 6. What image of God did Huldah communicate to Josiah?

Applying the Word 1. Think of someone who has helped you to see God more clearly. How has this person affected you? 2. How has this experience helped you to obey God?

Responding in Prayer Thank God for the different people in your daily life whom God uses to communicate his love to you.

2 Chronicles 35—36

35 Josiah celebrated the Passover to the LORD in Jerusalem, and the Passover lamb was slaughtered on the fourteenth day of the first month. ²He appointed the priests to their duties and encouraged them in the service of the LORD's temple. ³He said to the Levites, who instructed all Israel and who had been consecrated to the LORD: "Put the sacred ark in the temple that Solomon son of David king of Israel built. It is not to be carried about on your shoulders. Now serve the LORD your God and his people Israel. ⁴Prepare yourselves by families in your divisions, according to the directions written by David king of Israel and by his son Solomon.

⁵"Stand in the holy place with a group of Levites for each subdivision of the families of your fellow countrymen, the lay people. ⁶Slaughter the Passover lambs, consecrate yourselves and prepare ˎthe lambsˎ for your fellow countrymen, doing what the LORD commanded through Moses."

⁷Josiah provided for all the lay people who were there a total of thirty thousand sheep and goats for the Passover offerings, and also three thousand cattle—all from the king's own possessions.

⁸His officials also contributed voluntarily to the people and the priests and Levites. Hilkiah, Zechariah and Jehiel, the administrators of God's temple, gave the priests twenty-six hundred Passover offerings and three hundred cattle. ⁹Also Conaniah along with Shemaiah and Nethanel, his brothers, and Hashabiah, Jeiel and Jozabad, the leaders of the Levites, provided five thousand Passover offerings and five hundred head of cattle for the Levites.

¹⁰The service was arranged and the priests stood in their places with the Levites in their divisions as the king had ordered. ¹¹The Passover lambs were slaughtered, and the priests sprinkled the blood handed to them, while the Levites skinned the animals. ¹²They set aside the burnt offerings to give them to the subdivisions of the families of the people to offer to the LORD, as is written in the Book of Moses. They did the same with the cattle. ¹³They roasted the Passover animals over the fire as prescribed, and boiled the holy offerings in pots, caldrons and pans and served them quickly to all the people. ¹⁴After this,

they made preparations for themselves and for the priests, because the priests, the descendants of Aaron, were sacrificing the burnt offerings and the fat portions until nightfall. So the Levites made preparations for themselves and for the Aaronic priests.

¹⁵The musicians, the descendants of Asaph, were in the places prescribed by David, Asaph, Heman and Jeduthun the king's seer. The gatekeepers at each gate did not need to leave their posts, because their fellow Levites made the preparations for them.

¹⁶So at that time the entire service of the LORD was carried out for the celebration of the Passover and the offering of burnt offerings on the altar of the LORD, as King Josiah had ordered. ¹⁷The Israelites who were present celebrated the Passover at that time and observed the Feast of Unleavened Bread for seven days. ¹⁸The Passover had not been observed like this in Israel since the days of the prophet Samuel; and none of the kings of Israel had ever celebrated such a Passover as did Josiah, with the priests, the Levites and all Judah and Israel who were there with the people of Jerusalem. ¹⁹This Passover was celebrated in the eighteenth year of Josiah's reign.

²⁰After all this, when Josiah had set the temple in order, Neco king of Egypt went up to fight at Carchemish on the Euphrates, and Josiah marched out to meet him in battle. ²¹But Neco sent messengers to him, saying, "What quarrel is there between you and me, O king of Judah? It is not you I am attacking at this time, but the house with which I am at war. God has told me to hurry; so stop opposing God, who is with me, or he will destroy you."

²²Josiah, however, would not turn away from him, but disguised himself to engage him in battle. He would not listen to what Neco had said at God's command but went to fight him on the plain of Megiddo.

²³Archers shot King Josiah, and he told his officers, "Take me away; I am badly wounded." ²⁴So they took him out of his chariot, put him in the other chariot he had and brought him to Jerusalem, where he died. He was buried in the tombs of his fathers, and all Judah and Jerusalem mourned for him.

²⁵Jeremiah composed laments for Josiah, and to

this day all the men and women singers commemorate Josiah in the laments. These became a tradition in Israel and are written in the Laments.

26The other events of Josiah's reign and his acts of devotion, according to what is written in the Law of the LORD— 27all the events, from beginning to end, are written in the book of the kings of Israel and Judah.

36 1And the people of the land took Jehoahaz son of Josiah and made him king in Jerusalem in place of his father.

2Jehoahaz*i* was twenty-three years old when he became king, and he reigned in Jerusalem three months. 3The king of Egypt dethroned him in Jerusalem and imposed on Judah a levy of a hundred talents*j* of silver and a talent*k* of gold. 4The king of Egypt made Eliakim, a brother of Jehoahaz, king over Judah and Jerusalem and changed Eliakim's name to Jehoiakim. But Neco took Eliakim's brother Jehoahaz and carried him off to Egypt.

5Jehoiakim was twenty-five years old when he became king, and he reigned in Jerusalem eleven years. He did evil in the eyes of the LORD his God. 6Nebuchadnezzar king of Babylon attacked him and bound him with bronze shackles to take him to Babylon. 7Nebuchadnezzar also took to Babylon articles from the temple of the LORD and put them in his temple*l* there.

8The other events of Jehoiakim's reign, the detestable things he did and all that was found against him, are written in the book of the kings of Israel and Judah. And Jehoiachin his son succeeded him as king.

9Jehoiachin was eighteen*m* years old when he became king, and he reigned in Jerusalem three months and ten days. He did evil in the eyes of the LORD. 10In the spring, King Nebuchadnezzar sent for him and brought him to Babylon, together with articles of value from the temple of the LORD, and he made Jehoiachin's uncle,*n* Zedekiah, king over Judah and Jerusalem.

11Zedekiah was twenty-one years old when he became king, and he reigned in Jerusalem eleven years. 12He did evil in the eyes of the LORD his God and did not humble himself before Jeremiah the prophet, who spoke the word of the LORD. 13He also rebelled against King Nebuchadnezzar, who had made him take an oath in God's name.

He became stiff-necked and hardened his heart and would not turn to the LORD, the God of Israel. 14Furthermore, all the leaders of the priests and the people became more and more unfaithful, following all the detestable practices of the nations and defiling the temple of the LORD, which he had consecrated in Jerusalem.

15The LORD, the God of their fathers, sent word to them through his messengers again and again, because he had pity on his people and on his dwelling place. 16But they mocked God's messengers, despised his words and scoffed at his prophets until the wrath of the LORD was aroused against his people and there was no remedy. 17He brought up against them the king of the Babylonians,*o* who killed their young men with the sword in the sanctuary, and spared neither young man nor young woman, old man or aged. God handed all of them over to Nebuchadnezzar. 18He carried to Babylon all the articles from the temple of God, both large and small, and the treasures of the LORD's temple and the treasures of the king and his officials. 19They set fire to God's temple and broke down the wall of Jerusalem; they burned all the palaces and destroyed everything of value there.

20He carried into exile to Babylon the remnant, who escaped from the sword, and they became servants to him and his sons until the kingdom of Persia came to power. 21The land enjoyed its sabbath rests; all the time of its desolation it rested, until the seventy years were completed in fulfillment of the word of the LORD spoken by Jeremiah.

22In the first year of Cyrus king of Persia, in order to fulfill the word of the LORD spoken by Jeremiah, the LORD moved the heart of Cyrus king of Persia to make a proclamation throughout his realm and to put it in writing:

23"This is what Cyrus king of Persia says:

" 'The LORD, the God of heaven, has given me all the kingdoms of the earth and he has appointed me to build a temple for him at Jerusalem in Judah. Anyone of his people among you—may the LORD his God be with him, and let him go up.' "

---

*i*2 Hebrew *Joahaz*, a variant of *Jehoahaz*; also in verse 4   *j*3 That is, about 3 3/4 tons (about 3.4 metric tons)   *k*3 That is, about 75 pounds (about 34 kilograms)   *l*7 Or *palace*   *m*9 One Hebrew manuscript, some Septuagint manuscripts and Syriac (see also 2 Kings 24:8); most Hebrew manuscripts *eight*   *n*10 Hebrew *brother,* that is, relative (see 2 Kings 24:17)   *o*17 Or *Chaldeans*

Ezra

*I*f you were in prison, what words would you like most to hear from your captors? Would they be "You can go home now"? King Cyrus of Persia said this to the Israelites when he freed them from captivity. And he also sent them back to their homeland with all of the treasures of the former temple of Jerusalem and with money and supplies to build a new altar and temple.

This would have been momentous to the people of Israel. More than two hundred years before (722 B.C.) the Assyrians destroyed the northern kingdom, Israel. In 587 B.C. the Babylonians conquered what remained of the southern kingdom, Judah. They destroyed the temple and took the leaders of the people into exile. Psalm 137:4 gives us a glimpse into the crisis that this was for the people of Israel: "How can we sing the songs of the Lord while in a foreign land?" The sense of loss and grief was profound.

Then came Cyrus the Persian in 538 B.C., who conquered Babylon and set in motion policies of religious tolerance and encouragement that would largely characterize the attitude of the Persian kings to follow, Darius and Artaxerxes. This policy enabled and encouraged the people of Israel to return to their homeland. No doubt it was advantageous for the kings to have a loyal buffer between them and the other major superpower of the day, Egypt, but whatever the motives of the Persian kings, the author makes it clear that God is the one who controls history.

Ezra is the first part of a divided book. Nehemiah is the second half. The Hebrew Bible treated the two books as one. They became separated due to Christian influence. If you read the two books together, the story will make better sense. There are three different return trips that take place (Ezr 1—6, 7—10; Ne 1—7), and the book concludes by a gathering of the congregation of Israel for repentance and rejoicing.

The book of Ezra focuses on several themes: the continuity of the leaders before and after the exile, the place of the community in bringing about God's work, the rebuilding of the altar and the temple, and the importance of holiness within the community. It is clear from this book that the freedom that the Israelites have received is from God. We can take encouragement for our lives from this picture of a God who is faithful to his promises.

Outline

1/ Ezra 1—2 ———————— Return from Exile

2/ Ezra 3 ———————— The Priorities of God's People

3/ Ezra 4 ———————— Words That Hurt

4/ Ezra 5—6 ———————— God's Surprises

5/ Ezra 7 ———————— Powerful Friends

6/ Ezra 8 ———————— Practical Spirituality

7/ Ezra 9 ———————— Turning Away from God

8/ Ezra 10 ———————— Compromise

If you were in prison, what in the world would you like most to hear from your captors? Would it, maybe be: You can go home now? King Cyrus of Persia said this to the Israelites when he freed them from captivity. And he also sent them back to their homeland, with all of the treasures of the former temple of Jerusalem and with money and supplies to build a new altar and temple.

This would have been momentous to the people of Israel. More than two hundred years before (722 B.C.), the Assyrians destroyed the northern kingdom, Israel. In 587 B.C. the Babylonians conquered what remained of the southern kingdom, Judah. They destroyed the temple and took the leaders of the people into exile. Psalm 137:4 gives us a glimpse into the crisis that this was for the people of Israel. How can we sing the songs of the Lord while in a foreign land? The sense of loss and grief was profound.

Then came Cyrus the Persian (in 539 B.C.), who conquered Babylon and set in motion policies of religious tolerance and encouragement that would largely characterize the attitude of the Persian throne to follow. Darius and Artaxerxes. This policy enabled and encouraged the people of Israel to return to their homeland. No doubt it was advantageous for the Persians to have a loyal buffer between them and the other major superpower of the day, Egypt, but whatever the motives of the Persian kings, the author makes it clear that God is the one who controls history.

Ezra is the first part of a unified book. Nehemiah is the second half of the Hebrew Bible, treated the two books as one. They became separate due to Christian tradition. If you read the two books together, the story will make better sense. There are three different parts that take place (Ezra 1—6; Neh 1—7) and the book concludes on a gathering of the congregation of Israel for repentance and rejoicing.

The book of Ezra focuses on several themes: the community of the leaders before and after the exile, the place of the community in bringing about God's work, the rebuilding of the altar and the temple, and the importance of holiness within the community. It is clear from this book that the need of that the Israelites have received is from God. We can take encouragement in our lives from this picture of a God who is faithful to fulfill his promises.

1 / *Ezra 1—2*
Return from Exile

EXILE. THEIR HOMELAND was destroyed. They were forcibly removed to a strange land. There they were foreigners, losers, third-class inhabitants. Feelings ran deep—anger, shame, alienation and isolation. What hope could possibly exist in people who had not seen their homeland for over fifty years? This is where the book of Ezra starts.

 Warming Up to God Have you ever had an experience of being physically or emotionally far from home? How would you describe that experience of exile?

 Read Ezra 1—2.

1 In the first year of Cyrus king of Persia, in order to fulfill the word of the LORD spoken by Jeremiah, the LORD moved the heart of Cyrus king of Persia to make a proclamation throughout his realm and to put it in writing:

²"This is what Cyrus king of Persia says:

" 'The LORD, the God of heaven, has given me all the kingdoms of the earth and he has appointed me to build a temple for him at Jerusalem in Judah. ³Anyone of his people among you—may his God be with him, and let him go up to Jerusalem in Judah and build the temple of the LORD, the God of Israel, the God who is in Jerusalem. ⁴And the people of any place where survivors may now be living are to provide him with silver and gold, with goods and livestock, and with freewill offerings for the temple of God in Jerusalem.' "

⁵Then the family heads of Judah and Benjamin, and the priests and Levites—everyone whose heart God had moved—prepared to go up and build the house of the LORD in Jerusalem. ⁶All their neighbors assisted them with articles of silver and gold, with goods and livestock, and with valuable gifts, in addition to all the freewill offerings. ⁷Moreover, King Cyrus brought out the articles belonging to the temple of the LORD, which Nebuchadnezzar had carried away from Jerusalem and had placed in the temple of his god.ᵃ ⁸Cyrus king of Persia had them brought by Mithredath the treasurer, who counted them out to Sheshbazzar the prince of Judah.

⁹This was the inventory:

gold dishes	30
silver dishes	1,000
silver pansᵇ	29
¹⁰gold bowls	30
matching silver bowls	410
other articles	1,000

¹¹In all, there were 5,400 articles of gold and of silver. Sheshbazzar brought all these along when the exiles came up from Babylon to Jerusalem.

2 Now these are the people of the province who came up from the captivity of the exiles, whom Nebuchadnezzar king of Babylon had taken captive to Babylon (they returned to Jerusalem and Judah, each to his own town, ²in company with Zerubbabel, Jeshua, Nehemiah, Seraiah, Reelaiah, Mordecai, Bilshan, Mispar, Bigvai, Rehum and Baanah):

The list of the men of the people of Israel:

³the descendants of Parosh	2,172
⁴of Shephatiah	372
⁵of Arah	775
⁶of Pahath-Moab (through the line of Jeshua and Joab)	2,812
⁷of Elam	1,254
⁸of Zattu	945
⁹of Zaccai	760
¹⁰of Bani	642
¹¹of Bebai	623
¹²of Azgad	1,222
¹³of Adonikam	666
¹⁴of Bigvai	2,056
¹⁵of Adin	454
¹⁶of Ater (through Hezekiah)	98
¹⁷of Bezai	323
¹⁸of Jorah	112
¹⁹of Hashum	223
²⁰of Gibbar	95
²¹the men of Bethlehem	123
²²of Netophah	56

ᵃ7 Or *gods* ᵇ9 The meaning of the Hebrew for this word is uncertain.

23of Anathoth	128
24of Azmaveth	42
25of Kiriath Jearim,ᶜ Kephirah and Beeroth	743
26of Ramah and Geba	621
27of Micmash	122
28of Bethel and Ai	223
29of Nebo	52
30of Magbish	156
31of the other Elam	1,254
32of Harim	320
33of Lod, Hadid and Ono	725
34of Jericho	345
35of Senaah	3,630

36The priests:

the descendants of Jedaiah (through the family of Jeshua)	973
37of Immer	1,052
38of Pashhur	1,247
39of Harim	1,017

40The Levites:

the descendants of Jeshua and Kadmiel (through the line of Hodaviah)	74

41The singers:

the descendants of Asaph	128

42The gatekeepers of the temple:

the descendants of Shallum, Ater, Talmon, Akkub, Hatita and Shobai	139

43The temple servants:

the descendants of
Ziha, Hasupha, Tabbaoth,
44Keros, Siaha, Padon,
45Lebanah, Hagabah, Akkub,
46Hagab, Shalmai, Hanan,
47Giddel, Gahar, Reaiah,
48Rezin, Nekoda, Gazzam,
49Uzza, Paseah, Besai,
50Asnah, Meunim, Nephussim,
51Bakbuk, Hakupha, Harhur,
52Bazluth, Mehida, Harsha,
53Barkos, Sisera, Temah,
54Neziah and Hatipha

55The descendants of the servants of Solomon:

the descendants of
Sotai, Hassophereth, Peruda,
56Jaala, Darkon, Giddel,
57Shephatiah, Hattil,
Pokereth-Hazzebaim and Ami

58The temple servants and the descendants of the servants of Solomon	392

59The following came up from the towns of Tel Melah, Tel Harsha, Kerub, Addon and Immer, but they could not show that their families were descended from Israel:

60The descendants of Delaiah, Tobiah and Nekoda	652

61And from among the priests:

The descendants of
Hobaiah, Hakkoz and Barzillai (a man who had married a daughter of Barzillai the Gileadite and was called by that name).

62These searched for their family records, but they could not find them and so were excluded from the priesthood as unclean. 63The governor ordered them not to eat any of the most sacred food until there was a priest ministering with the Urim and Thummim.

64The whole company numbered 42,360, 65besides their 7,337 menservants and maidservants; and they also had 200 men and women singers. 66They had 736 horses, 245 mules, 67435 camels and 6,720 donkeys.

68When they arrived at the house of the LORD in Jerusalem, some of the heads of the families gave freewill offerings toward the rebuilding of the house of God on its site. 69According to their ability they gave to the treasury for this work 61,000 drachmasᵈ of gold, 5,000 minasᵉ of silver and 100 priestly garments.

70The priests, the Levites, the singers, the gatekeepers and the temple servants settled in their own towns, along with some of the other people, and the rest of the Israelites settled in their towns.

ᶜ25 See Septuagint (see also Neh. 7:29); Hebrew *Kiriath Arim.*
ᵈ69 That is, about 1,100 pounds (about 500 kilograms)   ᵉ69 That is, about 3 tons (about 2.9 metric tons)

Discovering the Word 1. What would it have been like to have heard the proclamation of King Cyrus (1:1–4)? 2. What were the Israelites provided with beyond their freedom (1:3–11)? 3. What might have been the thoughts and feelings of those who were chosen to return to Israel (2:1–66)? 4. Why were the returnees so generous in the offering (2:68–69) to rebuild the temple? 5. How would the prophecy of Jeremiah (2Ch 36:21) affect them as they resettled Israel (2:70)?

Applying the Word 1. How might God be calling you to return to a place or a group? 2. How can the profound gratitude of the Israelites in 2:68–69 impact your response to God?

Responding in Prayer Offer the Lord your thanks for bringing you back from the exile of sin.

---

2 / *Ezra 3*
The Priorities of God's People

IF YOU HAD to move away from your country next month, what would be on your "To Do" list? Cleaning and packing, of course. But who would you want to spend time with? People from work, the neighborhood or social clubs? You might find that it's the people you worship with each Sunday who are most important. Once you arrive in the new place, what would be your highest priorities? In this chapter we learn a lot about the Israelites' priorities.

Warming Up to God List your priorities as you think about establishing yourself in a new place. What stands out to you in the goals you would set for yourself?

Read Ezra 3.

---

3 When the seventh month came and the Israelites had settled in their towns, the people assembled as one man in Jerusalem. ²Then Jeshua son of Jozadak and his fellow priests and Zerubbabel son of Shealtiel and his associates began to build the altar of the God of Israel to sacrifice burnt offerings on it, in accordance with what is written in the Law of Moses the man of God. ³Despite their fear of the peoples around them, they built the altar on its foundation and sacrificed burnt offerings on it to the LORD, both the morning and evening sacrifices. ⁴Then in accordance with what is written, they celebrated the Feast of Tabernacles with the required number of burnt offerings prescribed for each day. ⁵After that, they presented the regular burnt offerings, the New Moon sacrifices and the sacrifices for all the appointed sacred feasts of the LORD, as well as those brought as freewill offerings to the LORD. ⁶On the first day of the seventh month they began to offer burnt offerings to the LORD, though the foundation of the LORD's temple had not yet been laid.

⁷Then they gave money to the masons and carpenters, and gave food and drink and oil to the people of Sidon and Tyre, so that they would bring cedar logs by sea from Lebanon to Joppa, as authorized by Cyrus king of Persia.

⁸In the second month of the second year after their arrival at the house of God in Jerusalem, Zerubbabel son of Shealtiel, Jeshua son of Jozadak and the rest of their brothers (the priests and the Levites and all who had returned from the captivity to Jerusalem) began the work, appointing Levites twenty years of age and older to supervise the building of the house of the LORD. ⁹Jeshua and his sons and brothers and Kadmiel and his sons (descendants of Hodaviah*f*) and the sons of Henadad and their sons and brothers—all Levites—joined together in supervising those working on the house of God.

¹⁰When the builders laid the foundation of the temple of the LORD, the priests in their vestments and with trumpets, and the Levites (the sons of Asaph) with cymbals, took their places to praise the LORD, as prescribed by David king of Israel. ¹¹With praise and thanksgiving they sang to the LORD:

f 9 Hebrew *Yehudah*, probably a variant of *Hodaviah*

"He is good;
    his love to Israel endures forever."

And all the people gave a great shout of praise to the LORD, because the foundation of the house of the LORD was laid. ¹²But many of the older priests and Levites and family heads, who had seen the former temple, wept aloud when they saw the foundation of this temple being laid, while many others shouted for joy. ¹³No one could distinguish the sound of the shouts of joy from the sound of weeping, because the people made so much noise. And the sound was heard far away.

 Discovering the Word 1. Besides the obvious task of settling back in their homeland, what was the first priority for the returned exiles (vv. 1–2)? 2. How did the Israelites deal with their reasonable and real fears (v. 3)? 3. The seventh month was one of the most sacred and worshipful, yet the entire temple lay demolished. How did they "make do" (v. 6)? 4. What does the next project the Israelites turn their attention to tell you about their priorities (vv. 7–9)? 5. In what various ways did the people express themselves in worship (vv. 10–13)?

 Applying the Word 1. How can the God-given priority of worshiping with God's people (Heb 10:25) grow in your life? 2. How could you follow the example of the Israelites in facing your fears?

Responding in Prayer Ask God to help you make your worship of him first and foremost in your life.

---

3 / *Ezra 4*
Words That Hurt

HAS SOMEONE EVER written or said something about you that was designed to hurt you? How much of it was true? false? To show the continued opposition Israel faced, the author jumps ahead in time to tell of a time when their neighbors wrote to the king in order to damage Israel.

 Warming Up to God Talk to God about how the words of others have hurt you.

 Read Ezra 4.

When the enemies of Judah and Benjamin heard that the exiles were building a temple for the LORD, the God of Israel, ²they came to Zerubbabel and to the heads of the families and said, "Let us help you build because, like you, we seek your God and have been sacrificing to him since the time of Esarhaddon king of Assyria, who brought us here."

³But Zerubbabel, Jeshua and the rest of the heads of the families of Israel answered, "You have no part with us in building a temple to our God. We alone will build it for the LORD, the God of Israel, as King Cyrus, the king of Persia, commanded us."

⁴Then the peoples around them set out to discourage the people of Judah and make them afraid to go on building.ᵍ ⁵They hired counselors to work against them and frustrate their plans during the entire reign of Cyrus king of Persia and down to the reign of Darius king of Persia.

⁶At the beginning of the reign of Xerxes,ʰ they lodged an accusation against the people of Judah and Jerusalem.

⁷And in the days of Artaxerxes king of Persia, Bishlam, Mithredath, Tabeel and the rest of his associates wrote a letter to Artaxerxes. The letter was written in Aramaic script and in the Aramaic language.ⁱʲ

---

g4 Or and troubled them as they built   ʰ6 Hebrew Ahasuerus, a variant of Xerxes' Persian name   ⁱ7 Or written in Aramaic and translated   ʲ7 The text of Ezra 4:8—6:18 is in Aramaic.

⁸Rehum the commanding officer and Shimshai the secretary wrote a letter against Jerusalem to Artaxerxes the king as follows:

⁹Rehum the commanding officer and Shimshai the secretary, together with the rest of their associates—the judges and officials over the men from Tripolis, Persia,ᵏ Erech and Babylon, the Elamites of Susa, ¹⁰and the other people whom the great and honorable Ashurbanipalˡ deported and settled in the city of Samaria and elsewhere in Trans-Euphrates.

¹¹(This is a copy of the letter they sent him.)

To King Artaxerxes,

From your servants, the men of Trans-Euphrates:

¹²The king should know that the Jews who came up to us from you have gone to Jerusalem and are rebuilding that rebellious and wicked city. They are restoring the walls and repairing the foundations.

¹³Furthermore, the king should know that if this city is built and its walls are restored, no more taxes, tribute or duty will be paid, and the royal revenues will suffer. ¹⁴Now since we are under obligation to the palace and it is not proper for us to see the king dishonored, we are sending this message to inform the king, ¹⁵so that a search may be made in the archives of your predecessors. In these records you will find that this city is a rebellious city, troublesome to kings and provinces, a place of rebellion from ancient times. That is why this city was destroyed. ¹⁶We inform the king that if this city is built and its walls are restored, you will be left with nothing in Trans-Euphrates.

¹⁷The king sent this reply:

To Rehum the commanding officer, Shimshai the secretary and the rest of their associates living in Samaria and elsewhere in Trans-Euphrates:

Greetings.

¹⁸The letter you sent us has been read and translated in my presence. ¹⁹I issued an order and a search was made, and it was found that this city has a long history of revolt against kings and has been a place of rebellion and sedition. ²⁰Jerusalem has had powerful kings ruling over the whole of Trans-Euphrates, and taxes, tribute and duty were paid to them. ²¹Now issue an order to these men to stop work, so that this city will not be rebuilt until I so order. ²²Be careful not to neglect this matter. Why let this threat grow, to the detriment of the royal interests?

²³As soon as the copy of the letter of King Artaxerxes was read to Rehum and Shimshai the secretary and their associates, they went immediately to the Jews in Jerusalem and compelled them by force to stop.

²⁴Thus the work on the house of God in Jerusalem came to a standstill until the second year of the reign of Darius king of Persia.

ᵏ9 Or *officials, magistrates and governors over the men from*
ˡ10 Aramaic *Osnappar*, a variant of *Ashurbanipal*

 Discovering the Word 1. If you could use one word to sum up the events in this passage, what word would it be? 2. Describe the response of the "neighbors" (vv. 1–5). 3. What reasons are given to King Artaxerxes to persuade him to stop the building in Jerusalem (vv. 12–16)? 4. Which of these reasons are true and which are not? 5. What reasons does King Artaxerxes give for having the work stopped (vv. 17–22)? 6. What do you think it was like for the Israelites to stop this long-awaited work for a year (v. 24)?

 Applying the Word 1. What is it like for someone to tell the truth about you in order to hurt you? 2. How does it feel if someone lies about you? 3. What would be a godly response?

Responding in Prayer Praise God for the fact that his work continues even when it looks to us like it has been stopped dead by slander and other sins. Pray for those you know who have been hurt by lies.

4 / *Ezra 5—6*
God's Surprises

WHO WOULD YOU say is the most powerful person on earth today? Imagine you receive a letter from that person stating that they wanted to help your Christian community fulfill its mission and that all they wanted from you was a list of your needs so that they could be sure that they sent enough supplies and money. This was the joyful experience of the Israelites.

 Warming Up to God Reflect on how powerful God is. What signs of his power have you recently witnessed?

 Read Ezra 5—6.

5 Now Haggai the prophet and Zechariah the prophet, a descendant of Iddo, prophesied to the Jews in Judah and Jerusalem in the name of the God of Israel, who was over them. ²Then Zerubbabel son of Shealtiel and Jeshua son of Jozadak set to work to rebuild the house of God in Jerusalem. And the prophets of God were with them, helping them.

³At that time Tattenai, governor of Trans-Euphrates, and Shethar-Bozenai and their associates went to them and asked, "Who authorized you to rebuild this temple and restore this structure?" ⁴They also asked, "What are the names of the men constructing this building?"*ᵐ* ⁵But the eye of their God was watching over the elders of the Jews, and they were not stopped until a report could go to Darius and his written reply be received.

⁶This is a copy of the letter that Tattenai, governor of Trans-Euphrates, and Shethar-Bozenai and their associates, the officials of Trans-Euphrates, sent to King Darius. ⁷The report they sent him read as follows:

To King Darius:

Cordial greetings.

⁸The king should know that we went to the district of Judah, to the temple of the great God. The people are building it with large stones and placing the timbers in the walls. The work is being carried on with diligence and is making rapid progress under their direction.

⁹We questioned the elders and asked them, "Who authorized you to rebuild this temple and restore this structure?" ¹⁰We also asked them their names, so that we could write down the names of their leaders for your information.

¹¹This is the answer they gave us:

"We are the servants of the God of heaven and earth, and we are rebuilding the temple that was built many years ago, one that a great king of Israel built and finished. ¹²But because our fathers angered the God of heaven, he handed them over to Nebuchadnezzar the Chaldean, king of Babylon, who destroyed this temple and deported the people to Babylon.

¹³"However, in the first year of Cyrus king of Babylon, King Cyrus issued a decree to rebuild this house of God. ¹⁴He even removed from the temple*ⁿ* of Babylon the gold and silver articles of the house of God, which Nebuchadnezzar had taken from the temple in Jerusalem and brought to the temple*ⁿ* in Babylon.

"Then King Cyrus gave them to a man named Sheshbazzar, whom he had appointed governor, ¹⁵and he told him, 'Take these articles and go and deposit them in the temple in Jerusalem. And rebuild the house of God on its site.' ¹⁶So this Sheshbazzar came and laid the foundations of the house of God in Jerusalem. From that day to the present it has been under construction but is not yet finished."

¹⁷Now if it pleases the king, let a search be made in the royal archives of Babylon to see if King Cyrus did in fact issue a decree to rebuild this house of God in Jerusalem. Then

ᵐ4 See Septuagint; Aramaic ⁴We told them the names of the men constructing this building. *ⁿ14 Or palace* let the king send us his decision in this matter.

6 King Darius then issued an order, and they searched in the archives stored in the treasury at Babylon. ²A scroll was found in the citadel of Ecbatana in the province of Media, and this was written on it:

Memorandum:

³In the first year of King Cyrus, the king issued a decree concerning the temple of God in Jerusalem:

Let the temple be rebuilt as a place to present sacrifices, and let its foundations be laid. It is to be ninety feet*ᵒ* high and ninety feet wide, ⁴with three courses of large stones and one of timbers. The costs are to be paid by the royal treasury. ⁵Also, the gold and silver articles of the house of God, which Nebuchadnezzar took from the temple in Jerusalem and brought to Babylon, are to be returned to their places in the temple in Jerusalem; they are to be deposited in the house of God.

⁶Now then, Tattenai, governor of Trans-Euphrates, and Shethar-Bozenai and you, their fellow officials of that province, stay away from there. ⁷Do not interfere with the work on this temple of God. Let the governor of the Jews and the Jewish elders rebuild this house of God on its site.

⁸Moreover, I hereby decree what you are to do for these elders of the Jews in the construction of this house of God:

The expenses of these men are to be fully paid out of the royal treasury, from the revenues of Trans-Euphrates, so that the work will not stop. ⁹Whatever is needed—young bulls, rams, male lambs for burnt offerings to the God of heaven, and wheat, salt, wine and oil, as requested by the priests in Jerusalem—must be given them daily without fail, ¹⁰so that they may offer sacrifices pleasing to the God of heaven and pray for the well-being of the king and his sons.

¹¹Furthermore, I decree that if anyone changes this edict, a beam is to be pulled from his house and he is to be lifted up and impaled on it. And for this crime his house is to be made a pile of rubble. ¹²May God, who has caused his Name to dwell there, overthrow any king or people who lifts a hand to change this decree or to destroy this temple in Jerusalem.

I Darius have decreed it. Let it be carried out with diligence.

¹³Then, because of the decree King Darius had sent, Tattenai, governor of Trans-Euphrates, and Shethar-Bozenai and their associates carried it out with diligence. ¹⁴So the elders of the Jews continued to build and prosper under the preaching of Haggai the prophet and Zechariah, a descendant of Iddo. They finished building the temple according to the command of the God of Israel and the decrees of Cyrus, Darius and Artaxerxes, kings of Persia. ¹⁵The temple was completed on the third day of the month Adar, in the sixth year of the reign of King Darius.

¹⁶Then the people of Israel—the priests, the Levites and the rest of the exiles—celebrated the dedication of the house of God with joy. ¹⁷For the dedication of this house of God they offered a hundred bulls, two hundred rams, four hundred male lambs and, as a sin offering for all Israel, twelve male goats, one for each of the tribes of Israel. ¹⁸And they installed the priests in their divisions and the Levites in their groups for the service of God at Jerusalem, according to what is written in the Book of Moses.

¹⁹On the fourteenth day of the first month, the exiles celebrated the Passover. ²⁰The priests and Levites had purified themselves and were all ceremonially clean. The Levites slaughtered the Passover lamb for all the exiles, for their brothers the priests and for themselves. ²¹So the Israelites who had returned from the exile ate it, together with all who had separated themselves from the unclean practices of their Gentile neighbors in order to seek the LORD, the God of Israel. ²²For seven days they celebrated with joy the Feast of Unleavened Bread, because the LORD had filled them with joy by changing the attitude of the king of Assyria, so that he assisted them in the work on the house of God, the God of Israel.

ᵒ3 Aramaic *sixty cubits* (about 27 meters)

Discovering the Word 1. How do these chapters compare and contrast with chapter 4? 2. How would you feel after an encounter like the one in 5:3–4? 3. What good news did the Israelites hear in the letter of King Cyrus (6:1–12)? 4. How do you suppose the people of Israel felt when the temple was finally complete (6:13–15)? 5. What did they do when the temple was completed (6:16–22)?

Applying the Word 1. How can chapter 5 help you to press on in doing God's work in the face of opposition? 2. What does it mean to you that God is able to use the most powerful people on earth (like Cyrus) to further his purpose? 3. How can worship be a stronger part of your response to God's faithfulness?

Responding in Prayer Praise the God who holds the hearts and minds of the most powerful rulers in his hands.

5 / *Ezra 7*
Powerful Friends

LIFE IN A FOREIGN country can be difficult. There are new foods, unexpected customs, new ways of speaking or even a new language, different ways of dressing and much more. Something that helps a great deal in such a situation is a friend from the new culture who can help you make the adjustment and introduce you around. In this chapter Ezra finds a friend—and a benefactor—in the king. As a result, many good things come to his people as well.

Warming Up to God What connections, friends, privileges or abilities do you have which you can use to benefit the church?

Read Ezra 7.

7 After these things, during the reign of Artaxerxes king of Persia, Ezra son of Seraiah, the son of Azariah, the son of Hilkiah, ²the son of Shallum, the son of Zadok, the son of Ahitub, ³the son of Amariah, the son of Azariah, the son of Meraioth, ⁴the son of Zerahiah, the son of Uzzi, the son of Bukki, ⁵the son of Abishua, the son of Phinehas, the son of Eleazar, the son of Aaron the chief priest— ⁶this Ezra came up from Babylon. He was a teacher well versed in the Law of Moses, which the LORD, the God of Israel, had given. The king had granted him everything he asked, for the hand of the LORD his God was on him. ⁷Some of the Israelites, including priests, Levites, singers, gatekeepers and temple servants, also came up to Jerusalem in the seventh year of King Artaxerxes.

⁸Ezra arrived in Jerusalem in the fifth month of the seventh year of the king. ⁹He had begun his journey from Babylon on the first day of the first month, and he arrived in Jerusalem on the first day of the fifth month, for the gracious hand of his God was on him. ¹⁰For Ezra had devoted himself to the study and observance of the Law of the

LORD, and to teaching its decrees and laws in Israel.

¹¹This is a copy of the letter King Artaxerxes had given to Ezra the priest and teacher, a man learned in matters concerning the commands and decrees of the LORD for Israel:

¹²ᵖArtaxerxes, king of kings,

To Ezra the priest, a teacher of the Law of the God of heaven:

Greetings.

¹³Now I decree that any of the Israelites in my kingdom, including priests and Levites, who wish to go to Jerusalem with you, may go. ¹⁴You are sent by the king and his seven advisers to inquire about Judah and Jerusalem with regard to the Law of your God, which is in your hand. ¹⁵Moreover, you are to take with you the silver and gold that the king and his advisers have freely given to the God of Israel, whose dwelling is in Jerusalem, ¹⁶together with all the silver and gold

P12 The text of Ezra 7:12-26 is in Aramaic.

you may obtain from the province of Babylon, as well as the freewill offerings of the people and priests for the temple of their God in Jerusalem. ¹⁷With this money be sure to buy bulls, rams and male lambs, together with their grain offerings and drink offerings, and sacrifice them on the altar of the temple of your God in Jerusalem.

¹⁸You and your brother Jews may then do whatever seems best with the rest of the silver and gold, in accordance with the will of your God. ¹⁹Deliver to the God of Jerusalem all the articles entrusted to you for worship in the temple of your God. ²⁰And anything else needed for the temple of your God that you may have occasion to supply, you may provide from the royal treasury.

²¹Now I, King Artaxerxes, order all the treasurers of Trans-Euphrates to provide with diligence whatever Ezra the priest, a teacher of the Law of the God of heaven, may ask of you— ²²up to a hundred talents*q* of silver, a hundred cors*r* of wheat, a hundred baths*s* of wine, a hundred baths*s* of olive oil, and salt without limit. ²³Whatever the God of heaven has prescribed, let it be done with diligence for the temple of the God of heaven. Why should there be wrath against the realm of the king and of his sons? ²⁴You are also to know that you have no authority to impose taxes, tribute or duty on any of the priests, Levites, singers, gatekeepers, temple servants or other workers at this house of God.

²⁵And you, Ezra, in accordance with the wisdom of your God, which you possess, appoint magistrates and judges to administer justice to all the people of Trans-Euphrates—all who know the laws of your God. And you are to teach any who do not know them. ²⁶Whoever does not obey the law of your God and the law of the king must surely be punished by death, banishment, confiscation of property, or imprisonment.

²⁷Praise be to the LORD, the God of our fathers, who has put it into the king's heart to bring honor to the house of the LORD in Jerusalem in this way ²⁸and who has extended his good favor to me before the king and his advisers and all the king's powerful officials. Because the hand of the LORD my God was on me, I took courage and gathered leading men from Israel to go up with me.

q22 That is, about 3 3/4 tons (about 3.4 metric tons)   r22 That is, probably about 600 bushels (about 22 kiloliters)   s22 That is, probably about 600 gallons (about 2.2 kiloliters)

Discovering the Word 1. What qualities of Ezra would have helped him to find favor in the eyes of the king (vv. 5–6, 9–10)? 2. Describe the king's generosity to Ezra and his people (vv. 13–22). 3. What commission is Ezra given by King Artaxerxes (vv. 25–26)? 4. This is most likely the same Artaxerxes who wrote the letter stopping all building in chapter 4. What does the letter suggest about why the king changed his mind about the temple (vv. 23, 27–28)? 5. Since Israel lay between the kingdom of Persia and Egypt (the other superpower of the day), it was undoubtedly useful for the king to have friendly allies as a buffer. How can God use this king with mixed motives?

Applying the Word 1. If God is able to change a king's heart as he did with Artaxerxes, how might that change your faith in God and your prayer life? 2. Ezra's lifelong preparation and faithfulness to God put him in a pivotal place to be used of God. How can you faithfully prepare yourself for such a day?

 Responding in Prayer Pray for those in leadership in your country and around the world. Affirm your trust in God alone.

---

6 / *Ezra 8*
Practical Spirituality

IT'S DARK, AND you are in a part of town that is known to be dangerous. Unfortunately, you and those with you have to travel on foot to your destination. You naturally turn to prayer. This was the situation Ezra found himself in. And the pressure was on because he had bragged that God would protect those "who look to him." Now he had to put his life where his mouth was.

 Warming Up to God We typically turn to God in crisis and forget to rely on him in daily life. In what part of your life should you particularly be looking to God for guidance? Spend some time in quiet with the Lord.

 Read Ezra 8.

8 These are the family heads and those registered with them who came up with me from Babylon during the reign of King Artaxerxes:

²of the descendants of Phinehas, Gershom;
of the descendants of Ithamar, Daniel;
of the descendants of David, Hattush ³of the descendants of Shecaniah;

of the descendants of Parosh, Zechariah, and with him were registered 150 men;

⁴of the descendants of Pahath-Moab, Eliehoenai son of Zerahiah, and with him 200 men;

⁵of the descendants of Zattu,ᵗ Shecaniah son of Jahaziel, and with him 300 men;

⁶of the descendants of Adin, Ebed son of Jonathan, and with him 50 men;

⁷of the descendants of Elam, Jeshaiah son of Athaliah, and with him 70 men;

⁸of the descendants of Shephatiah, Zebadiah son of Michael, and with him 80 men;

⁹of the descendants of Joab, Obadiah son of Jehiel, and with him 218 men;

¹⁰of the descendants of Bani,ᵘ Shelomith son of Josiphiah, and with him 160 men;

¹¹of the descendants of Bebai, Zechariah son of Bebai, and with him 28 men;

¹²of the descendants of Azgad, Johanan son of Hakkatan, and with him 110 men;

¹³of the descendants of Adonikam, the last ones, whose names were Eliphelet, Jeuel and Shemaiah, and with them 60 men;

¹⁴of the descendants of Bigvai, Uthai and Zaccur, and with them 70 men.

¹⁵I assembled them at the canal that flows toward Ahava, and we camped there three days. When I checked among the people and the priests, I found no Levites there. ¹⁶So I summoned Eliezer, Ariel, Shemaiah, Elnathan, Jarib, Elnathan, Nathan, Zechariah and Meshullam, who were leaders, and Joiarib and Elnathan, who were men of learning, ¹⁷and I sent them to Iddo, the leader in Casiphia. I told them what to say to Iddo and his kinsmen, the temple servants in Casiphia, so that they might bring attendants to us for the house of our God. ¹⁸Because the gracious hand of our God was on us, they brought us Sherebiah, a capable man, from the descendants of Mahli son of Levi, the son of Israel, and Sherebiah's sons and brothers, 18 men; ¹⁹and Hasahabiah, together with Jeshaiah from the descendants of Merari, and his brothers and nephews, 20 men. ²⁰They also brought 220 of the temple servants— a body that David and the officials had established to assist the Levites. All were registered by name.

²¹There, by the Ahava Canal, I proclaimed a fast, so that we might humble ourselves before our God and ask him for a safe journey for us and our children, with all our possessions. ²²I was ashamed to ask the king for soldiers and horsemen to protect us from enemies on the road, because we had told the king, "The gracious hand of our God is on everyone who looks to him, but his great anger is against all who forsake him." ²³So we fasted and petitioned our God about this, and he answered our prayer.

²⁴Then I set apart twelve of the leading priests, together with Sherebiah, Hashabiah and ten of their brothers, ²⁵and I weighed out to them the offering of silver and gold and the articles that the king, his advisers, his officials and all Israel present there had donated for the house of our God. ²⁶I weighed out to them 650 talentsᵛ of silver, silver articles weighing 100 talents,ʷ 100 talentsʷ of gold, ²⁷20 bowls

---

ᵗ5 Some Septuagint manuscripts (also 1 Esdras 8:32); Hebrew does not have *Zattu*.   ᵘ10 Some Septuagint manuscripts (also 1 Esdras 8:36); Hebrew does not have *Bani*.   ᵛ26 That is, about 25 tons (about 22 metric tons)   ʷ26 That is, about 3 3/4 tons (about 3.4 metric tons) of gold valued at 1,000 darics,ˣ and two fine articles of polished bronze, as precious as gold.

²⁸I said to them, "You as well as these articles are consecrated to the LORD. The silver and gold are a freewill offering to the LORD, the God of your fathers. ²⁹Guard them carefully until you weigh them out in the chambers of the house of the LORD in Jerusalem before the leading priests and the Levites and the family heads of Israel." ³⁰Then the priests and Levites received the silver and gold and sacred articles that had been weighed out to be taken to the house of our God in Jerusalem.

³¹On the twelfth day of the first month we set out from the Ahava Canal to go to Jerusalem. The hand of our God was on us, and he protected us from enemies and bandits along the way. ³²So we arrived in Jerusalem, where we rested three days.

³³On the fourth day, in the house of our God, we weighed out the silver and gold and the sacred articles into the hands of Meremoth son of Uriah, the priest. Eleazar son of Phinehas was with him, and so were the Levites Jozabad son of Jeshua and Noadiah son of Binnui. ³⁴Everything was accounted for by number and weight, and the entire weight was recorded at that time.

³⁵Then the exiles who had returned from captivity sacrificed burnt offerings to the God of Israel: twelve bulls for all Israel, ninety-six rams, seventy-seven male lambs and, as a sin offering, twelve male goats. All this was a burnt offering to the LORD. ³⁶They also delivered the king's orders to the royal satraps and to the governors of Trans-Euphrates, who then gave assistance to the people and to the house of God.

ˣ27 That is, about 19 pounds (about 8.5 kilograms)

 Discovering the Word 1. Notice those mentioned in verses 1–14. What would it have been like for Ezra as the leader to gather all these people together (v. 15)? 2. Ezra sees that among those who are returning there are no Levites to assist in the day-to-day routine of the temple, so what does he do (vv. 15–20)? 3. What steps does Ezra take to prepare for the journey (vv. 21–30)? 4. What would be the benefit of weighing out (and weighing in) the articles given into his trust (vv. 24–26, 33–34)? 5. How did Ezra and the people respond to God after safely returning to Israel (vv. 35–36)? 6. Sometimes "being spiritual" is seen as better than "being practical." In what ways do you see both in Ezra?

Applying the Word 1. How can practical accountability safeguards (like weighing the gifts in vv. 24–34) protect the reputation of Christ's church and its leaders? 2. In what ways are you torn between being spiritual and being practical?

Responding in Prayer Ask God to help you see that being practical can be spiritual and that being spiritual can be practical. Pray that you will grow in both areas.

---

7 / *Ezra 9*
Turning Away from God

SEVEN HUNDRED WIVES! Though jokes come to mind quickly when we think of Solomon's household, the Bible does not give this fact to shock or amuse, but to warn. Besides the obvious show of pride and abuse of power, Solomon violated God's law by having foreign women among his wives. These were not foreign women who followed God like Rahab and Ruth; these were women who worshiped other gods—and led Solomon to do so as well. In today's passage Ezra receives news that his people have fallen into the same trap.

 Warming Up to God How has a relationship with a non-Christian (friendship, coworker, dating, marriage) led you away from your commitment to God in some way?

 Read Ezra 9.

9 After these things had been done, the leaders came to me and said, "The people of Israel, including the priests and the Levites, have not kept themselves separate from the neighboring peoples with their detestable practices, like those of the Canaanites, Hittites, Perizzites, Jebusites, Ammonites, Moabites, Egyptians and Amorites. ²They have taken some of their daughters as wives for themselves and their sons, and have mingled the holy race with the peoples around them. And the leaders and officials have led the way in this unfaithfulness."

³When I heard this, I tore my tunic and cloak, pulled hair from my head and beard and sat down appalled. ⁴Then everyone who trembled at the words of the God of Israel gathered around me because of this unfaithfulness of the exiles. And I sat there appalled until the evening sacrifice.

⁵Then, at the evening sacrifice, I rose from my self-abasement, with my tunic and cloak torn, and fell on my knees with my hands spread out to the Lord my God ⁶and prayed:

"O my God, I am too ashamed and disgraced to lift up my face to you, my God, because our sins are higher than our heads and our guilt has reached to the heavens. ⁷From the days of our forefathers until now, our guilt has been great. Because of our sins, we and our kings and our priests have been subjected to the sword and captivity, to pillage and humiliation at the hand of foreign kings, as it is today.

⁸"But now, for a brief moment, the Lord our God has been gracious in leaving us a remnant and giving us a firm place in his sanctuary, and so our God gives light to our eyes and a little relief in our bondage. ⁹Though we are slaves, our God has not deserted us in our bondage. He has shown us kindness in the sight of the kings of Persia: He has granted us new life to rebuild the house of our God and repair its ruins, and he has given us a wall of protection in Judah and Jerusalem.

¹⁰"But now, O our God, what can we say after this? For we have disregarded the commands ¹¹you gave through your servants the prophets when you said: 'The land you are entering to possess is a land polluted by the corruption of its peoples. By their detestable practices they have filled it with their impurity from one end to the other. ¹²Therefore, do not give your daughters in marriage to their sons or take their daughters for your sons. Do not seek a treaty of friendship with them at any time, that you may be strong and eat the good things of the land and leave it to your children as an everlasting inheritance.'

¹³"What has happened to us is a result of our evil deeds and our great guilt, and yet, our God, you have punished us less than our sins have deserved and have given us a remnant like this. ¹⁴Shall we again break your commands and intermarry with the peoples who commit such detestable practices? Would you not be angry enough with us to destroy us, leaving us no remnant or survivor? ¹⁵O Lord, God of Israel, you are righteous! We are left this day as a remnant. Here we are before you in our guilt, though because of it not one of us can stand in your presence."

 Discovering the Word 1. Some Jewish men were breaking their marriages to marry women who worshiped pagan gods (vv. 1–2, see also Mal 2:11–14). Describe Ezra's reaction to this news (vv. 3–5). 2. How would you outline the prayer of Ezra (vv. 6–15)? 3. What seems to be the problem with taking a foreign spouse (vv. 10–12)? 4. How would Ezra answer the question "Why hasn't God punished us yet?" (vv. 13–15)? 5. What in this passages shows that Ezra takes the holiness of God seriously?

Applying the Word 1. What compromises in the Christian community need to be mourned and confessed? 2. How can Ezra's prayer inform the way you confess your sins and the sins of your community? 3. How can you separate yourself from "detestable" practices of our culture and still reach out to those who desperately need the hope you have in Jesus?

Responding in Prayer Thank the Lord for not always treating us as we deserve to be treated. Pray that you will not take his mercy for granted, but instead take it wherever you go.

8 / *Ezra 10*
Compromise

HAVE YOU EVER compromised yourself and your beliefs? When did you realize this? The exiles who had returned a generation before Ezra had begun to merge with the neighboring cultures by marrying those who followed "detestable practices" (9:2). This lack of faithfulness broke Ezra's heart and caused him to pray the prayer found in chapter 9. When the people saw his passionate praying on their behalf, they realized their need for change.

 Warming Up to God Ask God's Spirit to help you to see areas where you are giving in to your culture and compromising your faith.

 Read Ezra 10.

---

10 While Ezra was praying and confessing, weeping and throwing himself down before the house of God, a large crowd of Israelites—men, women and children—gathered around him. They too wept bitterly. ²Then Shecaniah son of Jehiel, one of the descendants of Elam, said to Ezra, "We have been unfaithful to our God by marrying foreign women from the peoples around us. But in spite of this, there is still hope for Israel. ³Now let us make a covenant before our God to send away all these women and their children, in accordance with the counsel of my lord and of those who fear the commands of our God. Let it be done according to the Law. ⁴Rise up; this matter is in your hands. We will support you, so take courage and do it."

⁵So Ezra rose up and put the leading priests and Levites and all Israel under oath to do what had been suggested. And they took the oath. ⁶Then Ezra withdrew from before the house of God and went to the room of Jehohanan son of Eliashib. While he was there, he ate no food and drank no water, because he continued to mourn over the unfaithfulness of the exiles.

⁷A proclamation was then issued throughout Judah and Jerusalem for all the exiles to assemble in Jerusalem. ⁸Anyone who failed to appear within three days would forfeit all his property, in accordance with the decision of the officials and elders, and would himself be expelled from the assembly of the exiles.

⁹Within the three days, all the men of Judah and Benjamin had gathered in Jerusalem. And on the twentieth day of the ninth month, all the people were sitting in the square before the house of God, greatly distressed by the occasion and because of the rain. ¹⁰Then Ezra the priest stood up and said to them, "You have been unfaithful; you have married foreign women, adding to Israel's guilt. ¹¹Now make confession to the LORD, the God of your fathers, and do his will. Separate yourselves from the peoples around you and from your foreign wives."

¹²The whole assembly responded with a loud voice: "You are right! We must do as you say. ¹³But there are many people here and it is the rainy season; so we cannot stand outside. Besides, this matter cannot be taken care of in a day or two, because we have sinned greatly in this thing. ¹⁴Let our officials act for the whole assembly. Then let everyone in our towns who has married a foreign woman come at a set time, along with the elders and judges of each town, until the fierce anger of our God in this matter is turned away from us." ¹⁵Only Jonathan son of Asahel and Jahzeiah son of Tikvah, supported by Meshullam and Shabbethai the Levite, opposed this.

¹⁶So the exiles did as was proposed. Ezra the priest selected men who were family heads, one from each family division, and all of them designated by name. On the first day of the tenth month they sat down to investigate the cases, ¹⁷and by the first day of the first month they finished dealing with all the men who had married foreign women.

¹⁸Among the descendants of the priests, the following had married foreign women:

From the descendants of Jeshua son of Jozadak, and his brothers: Maaseiah, Eliezer, Jarib and Gedaliah. ¹⁹(They all gave their hands in pledge to put away their wives, and for their guilt they each presented a ram from the flock as a guilt offering.)

20From the descendants of Immer:

Hanani and Zebadiah.

21From the descendants of Harim:

Maaseiah, Elijah, Shemaiah, Jehiel and Uzziah.

22From the descendants of Pashhur:

Elioenai, Maaseiah, Ishmael, Nethanel, Jozabad and Elasah.

23Among the Levites:

Jozabad, Shimei, Kelaiah (that is, Kelita), Pethahiah, Judah and Eliezer.

24From the singers:

Eliashib.

From the gatekeepers:

Shallum, Telem and Uri.

25And among the other Israelites:

From the descendants of Parosh:

Ramiah, Izziah, Malkijah, Mijamin, Eleazar, Malkijah and Benaiah.

26From the descendants of Elam:

Mattaniah, Zechariah, Jehiel, Abdi, Jeremoth and Elijah.

27From the descendants of Zattu:

Elioenai, Eliashib, Mattaniah, Jeremoth, Zabad and Aziza.

28From the descendants of Bebai:

Jehohanan, Hananiah, Zabbai and Athlai.

29From the descendants of Bani:

Meshullam, Malluch, Adaiah, Jashub, Sheal and Jeremoth.

30From the descendants of Pahath-Moab:

Adna, Kelal, Benaiah, Maaseiah, Mattaniah, Bezalel, Binnui and Manasseh.

31From the descendants of Harim:

Eliezer, Ishijah, Malkijah, Shemaiah, Shimeon, 32Benjamin, Malluch and Shemariah.

33From the descendants of Hashum:

Mattenai, Mattattah, Zabad, Eliphelet, Jeremai, Manasseh and Shimei.

34From the descendants of Bani:

Maadai, Amram, Uel, 35Benaiah, Bedeiah, Keluhi, 36Vaniah, Meremoth, Eliashib, 37Mattaniah, Mattenai and Jaasu.

38From the descendants of Binnui:ʸ

Shimei, 39Shelemiah, Nathan, Adaiah, 40Macnadebai, Shashai, Sharai, 41Azarel, Shelemiah, Shemariah, 42Shallum, Amariah and Joseph.

43From the descendants of Nebo:

Jeiel, Mattithiah, Zabad, Zebina, Jaddai, Joel and Benaiah.

44All these had married foreign women, and some of them had children by these wives.ᶻ

ʸ37,38 See Septuagint (also 1 Esdras 9:34); Hebrew *Jaasu* 38*and Bani and Binnui,*   ᶻ44 Or *and they sent them away with their children*

 Discovering the Word 1. How does Ezra demonstrate his concerns about the decisions his people have made (vv. 1, 6)? 2. What indications are there that the repentance of the people is sincere (vv. 1–5, 7–9)? 3. How do the people respond to the call for repentance (vv. 12–15)? 4. How does Ezra empower the people of God (vv. 12–17)? 5. What do you learn about those who intermarried from the list in verses 18–44?

Applying the Word 1. How can marriage or a deep friendship strengthen one's relationship with God, and how can it weaken it? 2. Ezra is obviously not a controlling individual. He is open to suggestions and willing to delegate authority. What can you and your community learn from his style of leadership?

Responding in Prayer Thank God for the example of Ezra's passionate faith that does not consume people but attracts them to the Lord. Pray that you will grow in such faith.

Nehemiah

Nehemiah was in leadership during an extraordinary time in Israel's history. He faced opposition from all sides—both from his own people and from outside forces. A little background will help set the stage for understanding the pressures Nehemiah faced.

From antiquity, Ezra and Nehemiah have been considered almost as one book. The two books cover a period of about one hundred years. In 587 B.C. Judah was removed from the land of Israel and deported to Babylon with only a few left in the land. In 538 B.C. Cyrus sent some of the people back to rebuild the temple. Nehemiah's second return would be around 430 B.C. Zerubbabel, Ezra and Nehemiah are all wrapped up in this history. Zerubbabel built the temple, Ezra brought the law back into Israel's life and Nehemiah rebuilt the wall that made Jerusalem secure.

The amazing thing is that Israel had more autonomy and distinctiveness than at any time of their existence as a sovereign state. The Persian empire allowed the people to practice their religious convictions with seriousness, and this probably accounts for why Israel had such a pristine religious life at this time.

While Zerubbabel and Ezra worked more in the religious realm, Nehemiah was really sent to Judah to be governor of the land, and that gave him considerably more ability to make some lasting changes in the life of the people. The people needed Nehemiah's strong leadership to handle the opposition to their work.

There were three primary opposers: Sanballat, Geshem and Tobiah. Sanballat was probably governor of Samaria and was not interested in Judah's becoming an independent nation again. Geshem is thought to have been a leader of a powerful block of Arab communities. Tobiah was probably governor of Ammon and a member of an influential Jewish family.

Derek Kidner describes the importance of this period of Israel's history:

The two centuries of the Persian empire were among the most formative periods of Jewish history. Out of the ruins of the little kingdom of Judah there had emerged the small community whose concern to be the people of God by pedigree and practice shaped it into the nation which meets us in the New Testament. Already the future prominence of the Temple and its priests of the law and its scribes, as well as the enmity between Jew and Samaritans, could be seen developing. Throughout this time the Persian regime was given a substantial part to play, both in sending and subsidizing the three expeditions of Zerubbabel, Ezra and Nehemiah, and in backing their authority with its own. It was not the first empire, nor the last, to be allotted some such role. (Derek Kidner, *Ezra & Nehemiah* [Downers Grove, Ill.: InterVarsity Press, 1979], p. 17.)

The Israelites living in the land were fairly passive at this point in history. They had to adapt to the culture around them because they were such a small remnant. Their intermarrying and political ties made this considerably worse.

Nehemiah's gifts in administration and perseverance enabled him to mold this people back into the "people of God" so they could obey God's commands and have a distinction from the people around them. This is where Nehemiah shines through. It was not enough to build just the wall—he had to build a people that would once again stand on their own as God led them. Putting some "backbone" back into the people was a large part of what Nehemiah had to accomplish—even if it required him to be harsh with them at times.

God has called each of us to important tasks, both as leaders and as followers. Reading Nehemiah will help us to have the courage we need to follow through even in the face of difficulty and persecution. God be with you as you study.

Outline

1/ Nehemiah 1 ——————————— *Depending on God*

2/ Nehemiah 2 ——————————— *The Planning Process*

3/ Nehemiah 3 ——————————— *Many Hands Make Lighter Work*

4/ Nehemiah 4 ——————————— *Opposition from the Outside*

5/ Nehemiah 5 ——————————— *Opposition from Within*

6/ Nehemiah 6 ——————————— *Facing Intimidation*

7/ Nehemiah 7 ——————————— *Family History*

8/ Nehemiah 8 ——————————— *Celebration and Revival*

9/ Nehemiah 9 ——————————— *Getting Back to Your Roots*

10/ Nehemiah 10 ——————————— *A Covenant with God*

11/ Nehemiah 11 ——————————— *Choosing Where to Live and Work*

12/ Nehemiah 12 ——————————— *Important Work*

13/ Nehemiah 13 ——————————— *Spiritual Decay*

1 / *Nehemiah 1*
Depending on God

AT ONE TIME or another, most of us have said, "I am too busy to pray!" If the work of God or the work that we want to do for God depended on our energy and insight, then it might be true. But of course, at least theoretically, we believe that God's work can only be done through his power (Ps 127:1, "Unless the LORD builds the house, its builders labor in vain"). Yet we don't think our biggest job is to pray. If we did, it might make a big difference in what we try to accomplish for the Lord! As we go before the Lord in prayer, we gain his perspective, and we gain confidence. In this study Nehemiah models dependency on the Lord for his strength.

 Warming Up to God Before you look into the Scriptures, sit quietly for a few moments and breathe deeply, allowing yourself to become relaxed and peaceful. Ask the Holy Spirit to give you discernment as you begin studying Nehemiah.

Read Nehemiah 1.

1 The words of Nehemiah son of Hacaliah:

In the month of Kislev in the twentieth year, while I was in the citadel of Susa, ²Hanani, one of my brothers, came from Judah with some other men, and I questioned them about the Jewish remnant that survived the exile, and also about Jerusalem.

³They said to me, "Those who survived the exile and are back in the province are in great trouble and disgrace. The wall of Jerusalem is broken down, and its gates have been burned with fire."

⁴When I heard these things, I sat down and wept. For some days I mourned and fasted and prayed before the God of heaven. ⁵Then I said:

"O LORD, God of heaven, the great and awesome God, who keeps his covenant of love with those who love him and obey his commands, ⁶let your ear be attentive and your eyes open to hear the prayer your servant is praying before you day and night for your servants, the people of Israel. I confess the sins we Israelites, including myself and my father's house, have committed against you. ⁷We have acted very wickedly toward you. We have not obeyed the commands, decrees and laws you gave your servant Moses.

⁸"Remember the instruction you gave your servant Moses, saying, 'If you are unfaithful, I will scatter you among the nations, ⁹but if you return to me and obey my commands, then even if your exiled people are at the farthest horizon, I will gather them from there and bring them to the place I have chosen as a dwelling for my Name.'

¹⁰"They are your servants and your people, whom you redeemed by your great strength and your mighty hand. ¹¹O Lord, let your ear be attentive to the prayer of this your servant and to the prayer of your servants who delight in revering your name. Give your servant success today by granting him favor in the presence of this man."

I was cupbearer to the king.

Discovering the Word 1. In verses 1–3 what event is being discussed? 2. What four things does Nehemiah do when he hears Hanani's report (v. 4)? 3. List the specific concerns that Nehemiah mentions in his prayer (vv. 5–11). 4. What evidence do you find here that Nehemiah believed God heard his prayer and would answer it? 5. What do you learn about Nehemiah's character from his reaction and his prayer?

Applying the Word 1. Nehemiah got more confident as he prayed and fasted. How does this compare with what you have experienced in prayer? 2. As you think about your ministry, are there any reports you are hearing that you need to petition God for? 3. What will you do to take a risk and become part of the answer for that prayer?

 Responding in Prayer Thank the Lord for using people just like you to carry out his plans. Ask him to give you courage as you participate in his work.

2 / *Nehemiah 2*
The Planning Process

ONCE DWIGHT L. Moody was sailing on an ocean vessel and a fire broke out. One of his traveling companions said, "Don't you think we should go and pray, Brother Moody?" Moody replied, "You can go and pray, brother, but I am going to man the water buckets. There is a time to pray and a time to put the fire out!" We tend to build a dichotomy between praying and doing. Usually what trips us up in the Christian life is not finding the balance between dependency on God and action on our part. Surely both must be important in God's eyes! In this chapter Nehemiah shows evidence of careful planning on both fronts.

 Warming Up to God What fears do you have that keep you from taking risks with your faith? Tell your Father about them—and let him show you how to overcome them with his strength.

 Read Nehemiah 2.

2 In the month of Nisan in the twentieth year of King Artaxerxes, when wine was brought for him, I took the wine and gave it to the king. I had not been sad in his presence before; ²so the king asked me, "Why does your face look so sad when you are not ill? This can be nothing but sadness of heart."

I was very much afraid, ³but I said to the king, "May the king live forever! Why should my face not look sad when the city where my fathers are buried lies in ruins, and its gates have been destroyed by fire?"

⁴The king said to me, "What is it you want?"

Then I prayed to the God of heaven, ⁵and I answered the king, "If it pleases the king and if your servant has found favor in his sight, let him send me to the city in Judah where my fathers are buried so that I can rebuild it."

⁶Then the king, with the queen sitting beside him, asked me, "How long will your journey take, and when will you get back?" It pleased the king to send me; so I set a time.

⁷I also said to him, "If it pleases the king, may I have letters to the governors of Trans-Euphrates, so that they will provide me safe-conduct until I arrive in Judah? ⁸And may I have a letter to Asaph, keeper of the king's forest, so he will give me timber to make beams for the gates of the citadel by the temple and for the city wall and for the residence I will occupy?" And because the gracious hand of my God was upon me, the king granted my requests. ⁹So I went to the governors of Trans-Euphrates and gave them the king's letters. The king had also sent army officers and cavalry with me.

¹⁰When Sanballat the Horonite and Tobiah the Ammonite official heard about this, they were very much disturbed that someone had come to promote the welfare of the Israelites.

¹¹I went to Jerusalem, and after staying there three days ¹²I set out during the night with a few men. I had not told anyone what my God had put in my heart to do for Jerusalem. There were no mounts with me except the one I was riding on.

¹³By night I went out through the Valley Gate toward the Jackal[a] Well and the Dung Gate, examining the walls of Jerusalem, which had been broken down, and its gates, which had been destroyed by fire. ¹⁴Then I moved on toward the Fountain Gate and the King's Pool, but there was not enough room for my mount to get through; ¹⁵so I went up the valley by night, examining the wall. Finally, I turned back and reentered through the Valley Gate. ¹⁶The officials did not know where I had gone or what I was doing, because as yet I had said nothing to the Jews or the priests or nobles or officials or any others who would be doing the work.

¹⁷Then I said to them, "You see the trouble we are in: Jerusalem lies in ruins, and its gates have been burned with fire. Come, let us rebuild the wall of Jerusalem, and we will no longer be in disgrace." ¹⁸I also told them about the gracious hand of my God upon me and what the king had said to me.

They replied, "Let us start rebuilding." So they began this good work.

¹⁹But when Sanballat the Horonite, Tobiah the Ammonite official and Geshem the Arab heard about it, they mocked and ridiculed us. "What is

---

ᵃ13 Or *Serpent* or *Fig*

this you are doing?" they asked. "Are you rebelling against the king?"

²⁰I answered them by saying, "The God of heaven will give us success. We his servants will start rebuilding, but as for you, you have no share in Jerusalem or any claim or historic right to it."

 Discovering the Word 1. How did Nehemiah give evidence of having a well-thought-through plan in verses 1–9? 2. What is the difference between the praying Nehemiah does in this chapter and what he did in chapter 1? 3. What evidences of thoroughness do you find in verses 11–16? 4. Why do you think Nehemiah appears so confident in verses 17–20? 5. From this chapter, what makes it reasonable for Nehemiah to be so hard-line with Sanballat, Tobiah and Geshem (vv. 18–20)?

Applying the Word 1. When you do a "great work for God," do you expect opposition? Explain. 2. Do you feel it is okay to say the "gracious hand of my God [is] upon me" (v. 18) regarding the work that you are doing? Explain why or why not.

Responding in Prayer Consider one risk or act of faith you need to take this week and ask the Lord to guide you through this test of your obedience.

---

3 / *Nehemiah 3*
Many Hands Make Lighter Work

A GIFTED LEADER can motivate others, but a job usually gets done because of prayer and unity among believers. This is so primarily because vision is spiritual and not material. When there is a lot of mundane work, like repairing a badly damaged wall, there must be unity for the job to be done. People need to feel they are part of the decision and the process. To miss this step of getting people "on board" dooms most projects to failure. This chapter shows how much the Israelites desired to work.

 Warming Up to God Where are you today, figuratively, with the Lord? Take stock of yourself in relationship with him, confessing your sins and acknowledging his grace for you. He is listening and desires to talk with you today.

 Read Nehemiah 3.

---

3 Eliashib the high priest and his fellow priests went to work and rebuilt the Sheep Gate. They dedicated it and set its doors in place, building as far as the Tower of the Hundred, which they dedicated, and as far as the Tower of Hananel. ²The men of Jericho built the adjoining section, and Zaccur son of Imri built next to them.

³The Fish Gate was rebuilt by the sons of Hassenaah. They laid its beams and put its doors and bolts and bars in place. ⁴Meremoth son of Uriah, the son of Hakkoz, repaired the next section. Next to him Meshullam son of Berekiah, the son of Meshezabel, made repairs, and next to him Zadok son of Baana also made repairs. ⁵The next section was repaired by the men of Tekoa, but their nobles would not put their

shoulders to the work under their supervisors.ᵇ

⁶The Jeshanahᶜ Gate was repaired by Joiada son of Paseah and Meshullam son of Besodeiah. They laid its beams and put its doors and bolts and bars in place. ⁷Next to them, repairs were made by men from Gibeon and Mizpah—Melatiah of Gibeon and Jadon of Meronoth—places under the authority of the governor of Trans-Euphrates. ⁸Uzziel son of Harhaiah, one of the goldsmiths, repaired the next section; and Hananiah, one of the perfume-makers, made repairs next to that. They restoredᵈ Jerusalem as far as the Broad Wall. ⁹Rephaiah son of Hur, ruler of a half-district of Jerusalem, repaired the next section. ¹⁰Adjoining this, Jedaiah son of Harumaph made

ᵇ5 Or *their Lord* or *the governor*   ᶜ6 Or *Old*   ᵈ8 Or *They left out part of* repairs opposite his house, and Hattush son of Hashabneiah made repairs next to him. ¹¹Malkijah son of Harim and Hasshub son of Pahath-Moab repaired another section and the Tower of the Ovens. ¹²Shallum son of Hallohesh, ruler of a half-district of Jerusalem, repaired the next section with the help of his daughters.

¹³The Valley Gate was repaired by Hanun and the residents of Zanoah. They rebuilt it and put its doors and bolts and bars in place. They also repaired five hundred yards* of the wall as far as the Dung Gate.

¹⁴The Dung Gate was repaired by Malkijah son of Recab, ruler of the district of Beth Hakkerem. He rebuilt it and put its doors and bolts and bars in place.

¹⁵The Fountain Gate was repaired by Shallun son of Col-Hozeh, ruler of the district of Mizpah. He rebuilt it, roofing it over and putting its doors and bolts and bars in place. He also repaired the wall of the Pool of Siloam,* by the King's Garden, as far as the steps going down from the City of David. ¹⁶Beyond him, Nehemiah son of Azbuk, ruler of a half-district of Beth Zur, made repairs up to a point opposite the tombs* of David, as far as the artificial pool and the House of the Heroes.

¹⁷Next to him, the repairs were made by the Levites under Rehum son of Bani. Beside him, Hashabiah, ruler of half the district of Keilah, carried out repairs for his district. ¹⁸Next to him, the repairs were made by their countrymen under Binnui* son of Henadad, ruler of the other half-district of Keilah. ¹⁹Next to him, Ezer son of Jeshua, ruler of Mizpah, repaired another section, from a point facing the ascent to the armory as far as the angle. ²⁰Next to him, Baruch son of Zabbai zealously repaired another section, from the angle to the entrance of the house of Eliashib the high

priest. ²¹Next to him, Meremoth son of Uriah, the son of Hakkoz, repaired another section, from the entrance of Eliashib's house to the end of it.

²²The repairs next to him were made by the priests from the surrounding region. ²³Beyond them, Benjamin and Hasshub made repairs in front of their house; and next to them, Azariah son of Maaseiah, the son of Ananiah, made repairs beside his house. ²⁴Next to him, Binnui son of Henadad repaired another section, from Azariah's house to the angle and the corner, ²⁵and Palal son of Uzai worked opposite the angle and the tower projecting from the upper palace near the court of the guard. Next to him, Pedaiah son of Parosh ²⁶and the temple servants living on the hill of Ophel made repairs up to a point opposite the Water Gate toward the east and the projecting tower. ²⁷Next to them, the men of Tekoa repaired another section, from the great projecting tower to the wall of Ophel.

²⁸Above the Horse Gate, the priests made repairs, each in front of his own house. ²⁹Next to them, Zadok son of Immer made repairs opposite his house. Next to him, Shemaiah son of Shecaniah, the guard at the East Gate, made repairs. ³⁰Next to him, Hananiah son of Shelemiah, and Hanun, the sixth son of Zalaph, repaired another section. Next to them, Meshullam son of Berekiah made repairs opposite his living quarters. ³¹Next to him, Malkijah, one of the goldsmiths, made repairs as far as the house of the temple servants and the merchants, opposite the Inspection Gate, and as far as the room above the corner; ³²and between the room above the corner and the Sheep Gate the goldsmiths and merchants made repairs.

*13 Hebrew *a thousand cubits* (about 450 meters)   *15 Hebrew *Shelah*, a variant of *Shiloah*, that is, Siloam   *16 Hebrew; Septuagint, some Vulgate manuscripts and Syriac *tomb*   *18 Two Hebrew manuscripts and Syriac (see also Septuagint and verse 24); most Hebrew manuscripts *Bavvai*

Discovering the Word   1. This chapter describes the hard work of building the wall around Jerusalem and repairing the gates. List the groups or individuals in this chapter who give themselves to the work. 2. What are some of the occupations of the repairers?   3. What was the place of women in this work (v. 12)? 4. From the chapter, what seems to be the motivation for people to work on their part of the wall?   5. Was Nehemiah privileged to have everyone committed to the work (v. 5)? Explain.

Applying the Word   1. How do you feel when facing what seems to be an impossible task—especially when there doesn't seem to be commitment from those you are working with?   2. How has cooperation played a significant part in your church or fellowship group's success in ministry?   3. Do you feel you are as motivated to work in your church or fellowship as this group of people is? Explain your response.

Responding in Prayer Ask the Lord to give you a helper or partner in your ministry—and ask him to teach you both how to work together.

4 / *Nehemiah 4*
Opposition from the Outside

"STICKS AND STONES may break my bones, but names will never hurt me!" We usually hear children say this. But when we want to oppose something because it is getting in our way, we adults have a slightly more sophisticated way of doing the same thing.

The enemies of Israel started out at the "sticks and stones" level, but they were soon into slander, intimidation and threatening with weapons. Our enemy the devil is always going to oppose the work of God. We need to expect and be able to fight opposition, if we will do God's work.

Warming Up to God How have your plans for good and faithful service to the Lord been frustrated lately? Express your feelings to the Lord and give them over to him completely, trusting he will continue to do his will on earth.

Read Nehemiah 4.

4 When Sanballat heard that we were rebuilding the wall, he became angry and was greatly incensed. He ridiculed the Jews, ²and in the presence of his associates and the army of Samaria, he said, "What are those feeble Jews doing? Will they restore their wall? Will they offer sacrifices? Will they finish in a day? Can they bring the stones back to life from those heaps of rubble—burned as they are?"

³Tobiah the Ammonite, who was at his side, said, "What they are building—if even a fox climbed up on it, he would break down their wall of stones!"

⁴Hear us, O our God, for we are despised. Turn their insults back on their own heads. Give them over as plunder in a land of captivity. ⁵Do not cover up their guilt or blot out their sins from your sight, for they have thrown insults in the face of[i] the builders.

⁶So we rebuilt the wall till all of it reached half its height, for the people worked with all their heart.

⁷But when Sanballat, Tobiah, the Arabs, the Ammonites and the men of Ashdod heard that the repairs to Jerusalem's walls had gone ahead and that the gaps were being closed, they were very angry. ⁸They all plotted together to come and fight against Jerusalem and stir up trouble against

it. ⁹But we prayed to our God and posted a guard day and night to meet this threat.

¹⁰Meanwhile, the people in Judah said, "The strength of the laborers is giving out, and there is so much rubble that we cannot rebuild the wall."

¹¹Also our enemies said, "Before they know it or see us, we will be right there among them and will kill them and put an end to the work."

¹²Then the Jews who lived near them came and told us ten times over, "Wherever you turn, they will attack us."

¹³Therefore I stationed some of the people behind the lowest points of the wall at the exposed places, posting them by families, with their swords, spears and bows. ¹⁴After I looked things over, I stood up and said to the nobles, the officials and the rest of the people, "Don't be afraid of them. Remember the Lord, who is great and awesome, and fight for your brothers, your sons and your daughters, your wives and your homes."

¹⁵When our enemies heard that we were aware of their plot and that God had frustrated it, we all returned to the wall, each to his own work.

¹⁶From that day on, half of my men did the work, while the other half were equipped with spears, shields, bows and armor. The officers posted themselves behind all the people of Judah ¹⁷who were building the wall. Those who carried materials did their work with one hand and held

ⁱ5 Or *have provoked you to anger before*

a weapon in the other, ¹⁸and each of the builders wore his sword at his side as he worked. But the man who sounded the trumpet stayed with me.

¹⁹Then I said to the nobles, the officials and the rest of the people, "The work is extensive and spread out, and we are widely separated from each other along the wall. ²⁰Wherever you hear the sound of the trumpet, join us there. Our God will fight for us!"

²¹So we continued the work with half the men holding spears, from the first light of dawn till the stars came out. ²²At that time I also said to the people, "Have every man and his helper stay inside Jerusalem at night, so they can serve us as guards by night and workmen by day." ²³Neither I nor my brothers nor my men nor the guards with me took off our clothes; each had his weapon, even when he went for water.ʲ

ʲ23 The meaning of the Hebrew for this clause is uncertain.

 Discovering the Word 1. Describe the progression of seriousness in how Sanballat and Tobiah threaten the Jews and the building of the wall in verses 1–3. 2. List the ways Nehemiah responds to these forms of opposition (vv. 4–6). 3. Why do you think Nehemiah is so uncharitable in his prayer in verses 4–5? 4. Note that Sanballat has inside help in his intimidation of the Jews and Nehemiah. What is it (vv. 10 and 12)? 5. In verses 13–20, how does Nehemiah handle these threats? 6. What was Nehemiah trusting in to get the work done (vv. 9, 14 and 20)?

 Applying the Word 1. In what situation have you seen a creative solution keep the work moving forward? 2. Does opposition make you want to quit a job, or does it challenge you to work harder to complete it? Explain.

Responding in Prayer Pray verses 4 and 5 to the Lord, boldly asking for sinful oppression to be lifted from Christians today.

5 / *Nehemiah 5*
Opposition from Within

MOST ORGANIZATIONS AND nations fall apart because of opposition and deterioration from within rather than from without. An idea is conceived, gains adherence and grows to fruition. Then after it has served its purpose for a period of time, the work it took to get to that point is taken for granted and often personal aggrandizement corrupts the intended purpose. At the beginning there is sacrifice by the people, but someone usually figures out how to make money from the idea, and it is not long before that which helped people hurts people. That is what happens in this chapter of Nehemiah.

 Warming Up to God The Lord is excited to hear from you today and wants to listen to all you have to say. Tell him about your day and your feelings for a few minutes before you begin reading the Word.

 Read Nehemiah 5.

5 Now the men and their wives raised a great outcry against their Jewish brothers. ²Some were saying, "We and our sons and daughters are numerous; in order for us to eat and stay alive, we must get grain."

³Others were saying, "We are mortgaging our fields, our vineyards and our homes to get grain during the famine."

⁴Still others were saying, "We have had to borrow money to pay the king's tax on our fields and vineyards. ⁵Although we are of the same flesh and blood as our countrymen and though our sons are as good as theirs, yet we have to subject our sons and daughters to slavery. Some of our daughters have already been enslaved, but we are powerless, because our fields and our vineyards belong to others."

⁶When I heard their outcry and these charges, I was very angry. ⁷I pondered them in my mind and then accused the nobles and officials. I told

them, "You are exacting usury from your own countrymen!" So I called together a large meeting to deal with them ⁸and said: "As far as possible, we have bought back our Jewish brothers who were sold to the Gentiles. Now you are selling your brothers, only for them to be sold back to us!" They kept quiet, because they could find nothing to say.

⁹So I continued, "What you are doing is not right. Shouldn't you walk in the fear of our God to avoid the reproach of our Gentile enemies? ¹⁰I and my brothers and my men are also lending the people money and grain. But let the exacting of usury stop! ¹¹Give back to them immediately their fields, vineyards, olive groves and houses, and also the usury you are charging them—the hundredth part of the money, grain, new wine and oil."

¹²"We will give it back," they said. "And we will not demand anything more from them. We will do as you say."

Then I summoned the priests and made the nobles and officials take an oath to do what they had promised. ¹³I also shook out the folds of my robe and said, "In this way may God shake out of his house and possessions every man who does not keep this promise. So may such a man be shaken out and emptied!"

At this the whole assembly said, "Amen," and praised the LORD. And the people did as they had promised.

¹⁴Moreover, from the twentieth year of King Artaxerxes, when I was appointed to be their governor in the land of Judah, until his thirty-second year—twelve years—neither I nor my brothers ate the food allotted to the governor. ¹⁵But the earlier governors—those preceding me—placed a heavy burden on the people and took forty shekels[k] of silver from them in addition to food and wine. Their assistants also lorded it over the people. But out of reverence for God I did not act like that. ¹⁶Instead, I devoted myself to the work on this wall. All my men were assembled there for the work; we[l] did not acquire any land.

¹⁷Furthermore, a hundred and fifty Jews and officials ate at my table, as well as those who came to us from the surrounding nations. ¹⁸Each day one ox, six choice sheep and some poultry were prepared for me, and every ten days an abundant supply of wine of all kinds. In spite of all this, I never demanded the food allotted to the governor, because the demands were heavy on these people.

¹⁹Remember me with favor, O my God, for all I have done for these people.

k15 That is, about 1 pound (about 0.5 kilogram)   l16 Most Hebrew manuscripts; some Hebrew manuscripts, Septuagint, Vulgate and Syriac I

 Discovering the Word 1. List the three forms of internal opposition in verses 1–5 that are developing against the vision of building the wall. 2. Who seem to be the people responsible for this inequity? Why do you think they would do this? 3. Make two lists. In the first cite the practices of the nobles, officials, former governors and their servants (vv. 7–12). In the second list cite the practices of Nehemiah (vv. 14–18). 4. How would you define the kind of leadership that Nehemiah exercises in dealing with this internal opposition to the wall? 5. In what ways does the chapter show Nehemiah doing all he can to not be part of this internal opposition?

Applying the Word 1. In what ways are leaders (spiritual or secular) today likely to assume privileges as these nobles and officials did? 2. How do you determine what is culturally acceptable and what God's kingdom values are? 3. What kind of internal opposition could likely come up within your church or Christian group to divert you from your real objectives?

Responding in Prayer Ask the Lord to "remember you" as you strive to serve him and carry out his will.

6 / *Nehemiah 6*
Facing Intimidation

USING POWER TO create pressure is a very effective way to get at people, especially if they are not sure of themselves or what they should be doing. However, if the objects of intimidation are quite confident in what they are doing, they may not be at all bothered by this approach.

Nehemiah had wrestled with God so thoroughly about what he was doing in building the wall that he was not sidetracked by attempts to call him away from the work. When someone reacts like Nehemiah, then the intimidator must become more and more threatening. It eventually boils down to who can intimidate the most or who is the most confident in what God's will is for the occasion. Notice in this chapter that Nehemiah doesn't give in to the intimidation.

Warming Up to God Think of a time when you had to be aggressive to fight for something you thought was right. How did you feel and act? Write down your ideas and compare them to the actions of Nehemiah.

Read Nehemiah 6.

6 When word came to Sanballat, Tobiah, Geshem the Arab and the rest of our enemies that I had rebuilt the wall and not a gap was left in it—though up to that time I had not set the doors in the gates— ²Sanballat and Geshem sent me this message: "Come, let us meet together in one of the villages^m on the plain of Ono."

But they were scheming to harm me; ³so I sent messengers to them with this reply: "I am carrying on a great project and cannot go down. Why should the work stop while I leave it and go down to you?" ⁴Four times they sent me the same message, and each time I gave them the same answer.

⁵Then, the fifth time, Sanballat sent his aide to me with the same message, and in his hand was an unsealed letter ⁶in which was written:

"It is reported among the nations—and Geshem^n says it is true—that you and the Jews are plotting to revolt, and therefore you are building the wall. Moreover, according to these reports you are about to become their king ⁷and have even appointed prophets to make this proclamation about you in Jerusalem: 'There is a king in Judah!' Now this report will get back to the king; so come, let us confer together."

⁸I sent him this reply: "Nothing like what you are saying is happening; you are just making it up out of your head."

⁹They were all trying to frighten us, thinking, "Their hands will get too weak for the work, and it will not be completed."

⌊But I prayed,⌋ "Now strengthen my hands."

¹⁰One day I went to the house of Shemaiah son of Delaiah, the son of Mehetabel, who was shut in at his home. He said, "Let us meet in the house of God, inside the temple, and let us close the temple doors, because men are coming to kill you— by night they are coming to kill you."

¹¹But I said, "Should a man like me run away? Or should one like me go into the temple to save his life? I will not go!" ¹²I realized that God had not sent him, but that he had prophesied against me because Tobiah and Sanballat had hired him. ¹³He had been hired to intimidate me so that I would commit a sin by doing this, and then they would give me a bad name to discredit me.

¹⁴Remember Tobiah and Sanballat, O my God, because of what they have done; remember also the prophetess Noadiah and the rest of the prophets who have been trying to intimidate me.

¹⁵So the wall was completed on the twenty-fifth of Elul, in fifty-two days. ¹⁶When all our enemies heard about this, all the surrounding nations were afraid and lost their self-confidence, because they realized that this work had been done with the help of our God.

¹⁷Also, in those days the nobles of Judah were sending many letters to Tobiah, and replies from Tobiah kept coming to them. ¹⁸For many in Judah were under oath to him, since he was son-in-law to Shecaniah son of Arah, and his son Jehohanan had married the daughter of Meshullam son of Berekiah. ¹⁹Moreover, they kept reporting to me his good deeds and then telling him what I said. And Tobiah sent letters to intimidate me.

^m2 Or *in Kephirim*   ^n6 Hebrew *Gashmu*, a variant of *Geshem*

Discovering the Word 1. List all the efforts at intimidation in this chapter. 2. What kind of divided loyalties do you find in the people building the wall? 3. From this chapter, what guiding principles does Nehemiah give about how to cooperate with other religious groups? 4. How do the circumstances in verses 17–19 make it difficult for Nehemiah to keep his objectives clear?

 Applying the Word 1. How is the work God has called you to do a "great work" and worthy of your full attention? 2. How could your vision be made great and clear enough so that you will not be easily sidetracked (vv. 3, 8 and 11)? 3. What do you expect by way of opposition in the job you are doing for the Lord?

Responding in Prayer Ask God to give you singlemindedness and determination as you work to proclaim his truth to those around you.

7 / *Nehemiah 7*
Family History

I REMEMBER MY grandparents talking about our family genealogy, and I thought, "How boring," so I didn't listen. Now I have 4,600 names on my computer about my genealogy, and I wish that I had listened to those conversations, because now I have lost much of the information with no way to retrieve it. I have even started recording many of the oldest relatives on tape so that I get not only the information but also their voices on tape for future generations. In this chapter of Nehemiah, we find that if people could not trace their lineage back to a preexilic Jewish relative, they were not considered bona fide descendants and could not be counted. I wonder if some of them didn't wish they had listened more to their relatives when they were talking about great-grandpa and great-grandma.

 Warming Up to God Recall a fond family memory that you have from a holiday or your childhood. Thank the Lord for giving you your past as a remembrance and guide for the future.

 Read Nehemiah 7.

7 After the wall had been rebuilt and I had set the doors in place, the gatekeepers and the singers and the Levites were appointed. ²I put in charge of Jerusalem my brother Hanani, along with⁰ Hananiah the commander of the citadel, because he was a man of integrity and feared God more than most men do. ³I said to them, "The gates of Jerusalem are not to be opened until the sun is hot. While the gatekeepers are still on duty, have them shut the doors and bar them. Also appoint residents of Jerusalem as guards, some at their posts and some near their own houses."

⁴Now the city was large and spacious, but there were few people in it, and the houses had not yet been rebuilt. ⁵So my God put it into my heart to assemble the nobles, the officials and the common people for registration by families. I found the genealogical record of those who had been the first to return. This is what I found written there:

⁶These are the people of the province who came up from the captivity of the exiles whom Nebuchadnezzar king of Babylon had taken captive (they returned to Jerusalem and Judah, each to his own town, ⁷in company with Zerubbabel, Jeshua, Nehemiah, Azariah, Raamiah, Nahamani, Mordecai, Bilshan, Mispereth, Bigvai, Nehum and Baanah):

The list of the men of Israel:

⁸the descendants of Parosh	2,172
⁹of Shephatiah	372
¹⁰of Arah	652
¹¹of Pahath-Moab (through the line of Jeshua and Joab)	2,818
¹²of Elam	1,254
¹³of Zattu	845
¹⁴of Zaccai	760
¹⁵of Binnui	648
¹⁶of Bebai	628

⁰2 Or *Hanani, that is,*

17of Azgad	2,322
18of Adonikam	667
19of Bigvai	2,067
20of Adin	655
21of Ater (through Hezekiah)	98
22of Hashum	328
23of Bezai	324
24of Hariph	112
25of Gibeon	95

26the men of Bethlehem and Netophah	188
27of Anathoth	128
28of Beth Azmaveth	42
29of Kiriath Jearim, Kephirah and Beeroth	743
30of Ramah and Geba	621
31of Micmash	122
32of Bethel and Ai	123
33of the other Nebo	52
34of the other Elam	1,254
35of Harim	320
36of Jericho	345
37of Lod, Hadid and Ono	721
38of Senaah	3,930

39The priests:

the descendants of Jedaiah (through the family of Jeshua)	973
40of Immer	1,052
41of Pashhur	1,247
42of Harim	1,017

43The Levites:

the descendants of Jeshua (through Kadmiel through the line of Hodaviah)	74

44The singers:

the descendants of Asaph	148

45The gatekeepers:

the descendants of Shallum, Ater, Talmon, Akkub, Hatita and Shobai	138

46The temple servants:

the descendants of
Ziha, Hasupha, Tabbaoth,
47Keros, Sia, Padon,
48Lebana, Hagaba, Shalmai,
49Hanan, Giddel, Gahar,
50Reaiah, Rezin, Nekoda,
51Gazzam, Uzza, Paseah,
52Besai, Meunim, Nephussim,
53Bakbuk, Hakupha, Harhur,
54Bazluth, Mehida, Harsha,
55Barkos, Sisera, Temah,
56Neziah and Hatipha

57The descendants of the servants of Solomon:

the descendants of
Sotai, Sophereth, Perida,
58Jaala, Darkon, Giddel,
59Shephatiah, Hattil,
Pokereth-Hazzebaim and Amon

60The temple servants and the descendants of the servants of Solomon	392

61The following came up from the towns of Tel Melah, Tel Harsha, Kerub, Addon and Immer, but they could not show that their families were descended from Israel:

62the descendants of Delaiah, Tobiah and Nekoda	642

63And from among the priests:

the descendants of
Hobaiah, Hakkoz and Barzillai (a man who had married a daughter of Barzillai the Gileadite and was called by that name).

64These searched for their family records, but they could not find them and so were excluded from the priesthood as unclean. 65The governor, therefore, ordered them not to eat any of the most sacred food until there should be a priest ministering with the Urim and Thummim.

66The whole company numbered 42,360, 67besides their 7,337 menservants and maidservants; and they also had 245 men and women singers. 68There were 736 horses, 245 mules,*p* 69435 camels and 6,720 donkeys.

70Some of the heads of the families contributed to the work. The governor gave to the treasury 1,000 drachmas*q* of gold, 50 bowls and 530 garments for priests. 71Some of the heads of the families gave to the trea-

p68 Some Hebrew manuscripts (see also Ezra 2:66); most Hebrew manuscripts do not have this verse.   *q70* That is, about 19 pounds (about 8.5 kilograms) sury for the work 20,000 drachmas^r of gold and 2,200 minas^s of silver. ⁷²The total given by the rest of the people was 20,000 drachmas of gold, 2,000 minas^t of silver and 67 garments for priests.

⁷³The priests, the Levites, the gatekeepers,

the singers and the temple servants, along with certain of the people and the rest of the Israelites, settled in their own towns.

^r71 That is, about 375 pounds (about 170 kilograms); also in verse 72
^s71 That is, about 1 1/3 tons (about 1.2 metric tons)   ^t72 That is, about 1 1/4 tons (about 1.1 metric tons)

Discovering the Word 1. In verses 1–3, who is to guard the city, and what do you learn about where they are assigned to guard? 2. We previously met Hanani in 1:2. From the qualifications given in verse 2, why could Nehemiah trust him? 3. Nehemiah decides that the families who have returned should be registered. How would the registration deal with Israel's sin of mixing themselves with the people of the nations around Jerusalem (vv. 64–65)? 4. Look more closely at these lists. Why are there so many priests and so few Levites? 5. Why couldn't some of the people make connections with relatives? 6. What is significant about Nehemiah giving the priests 530 garments and the rest of the people only giving 67 garments?

Applying the Word 1. In what ways are you concerned about your family history and protecting it? 2. How does the thought that you will be in someone's Christian family tree affect you?

Responding in Prayer Think of one person you would like to invite into the family of God and ask the Lord to assist you as you witness to this person.

8 / *Nehemiah 8*
Celebration and Revival

A LOOK AT church history seems to indicate that mature Christians have a pretty wide variety of religious emotions. That is, they know how to laugh, and they know how to weep. Sometimes we avoid crying and laughing because it implies that we are not stable. When we deny the variety of religious emotions that we find in the Bible, we are robbing ourselves. In this chapter of Nehemiah we see real repentance, contrition and weeping as well as great celebration and joy in doing what God wants. Without the exhilaration of celebration our tears of repentance would lead us into morbid introspection—something that would do us no good, because only God can handle our sins and shortcomings. But without true repentance and contrition we really do not find joy of the kind this chapter demonstrates.

Warming Up to God What has God's forgiveness meant for you? Recall a specific instance when God's tangible grace intersected your life. Dwell upon it for a few moments and let the remembrance of God's overflowing goodness refresh your soul.

Read Nehemiah 8.

When the seventh month came and the Israelites had settled in their towns, ¹all the people assembled as one man in the square before the Water Gate. They told Ezra the scribe to bring out the Book of the Law of Moses, which the LORD had commanded for Israel.

²So on the first day of the seventh month Ezra the priest brought the Law before the assembly, which was made up of men and women and all who were able to understand. ³He read it aloud from daybreak till noon as he faced the square before the Water Gate in the presence of the men, women and others who could understand. And all the people listened attentively to the Book of the Law.

⁴Ezra the scribe stood on a high wooden platform built for the occasion. Beside him on his right stood Mattithiah, Shema, Anaiah, Uriah, Hilkiah and Maaseiah; and on his left were Pedaiah, Mishael, Malkijah, Hashum, Hashbaddanah, Zechariah and Meshullam.

⁵Ezra opened the book. All the people could see him because he was standing above them; and as he opened it, the people all stood up. ⁶Ezra praised the LORD, the great God; and all the people lifted their hands and responded, "Amen! Amen!" Then they bowed down and worshiped the LORD with their faces to the ground.

⁷The Levites—Jeshua, Bani, Sherebiah, Jamin, Akkub, Shabbethai, Hodiah, Maaseiah, Kelita, Azariah, Jozabad, Hanan and Pelaiah—instructed the people in the Law while the people were standing there. ⁸They read from the Book of the Law of God, making it clearᵘ and giving the meaning so that the people could understand what was being read.

⁹Then Nehemiah the governor, Ezra the priest and scribe, and the Levites who were instructing the people said to them all, "This day is sacred to the LORD your God. Do not mourn or weep." For all the people had been weeping as they listened to the words of the Law.

¹⁰Nehemiah said, "Go and enjoy choice food and sweet drinks, and send some to those who have nothing prepared. This day is sacred to our Lord. Do not grieve, for the joy of the LORD is your strength."

¹¹The Levites calmed all the people, saying, "Be still, for this is a sacred day. Do not grieve."

¹²Then all the people went away to eat and drink, to send portions of food and to celebrate with great joy, because they now understood the words that had been made known to them.

¹³On the second day of the month, the heads of all the families, along with the priests and the Levites, gathered around Ezra the scribe to give attention to the words of the Law. ¹⁴They found written in the Law, which the LORD had commanded through Moses, that the Israelites were to live in booths during the feast of the seventh month ¹⁵and that they should proclaim this word and spread it throughout their towns and in Jerusalem: "Go out into the hill country and bring back branches from olive and wild olive trees, and from myrtles, palms and shade trees, to make booths"—as it is written.ᵛ

¹⁶So the people went out and brought back branches and built themselves booths on their own roofs, in their courtyards, in the courts of the house of God and in the square by the Water Gate and the one by the Gate of Ephraim. ¹⁷The whole company that had returned from exile built booths and lived in them. From the days of Joshua son of Nun until that day, the Israelites had not celebrated it like this. And their joy was very great.

¹⁸Day after day, from the first day to the last, Ezra read from the Book of the Law of God. They celebrated the feast for seven days, and on the eighth day, in accordance with the regulation, there was an assembly.

ᵘ8 Or God, translating it   ᵛ15 See Lev. 23:37-40.

Discovering the Word 1. The seventh month was one of great importance to the Jews. It was to include several feasts as well as the great Day of Atonement. What prompted the people to meet together? 2. What were the qualifications of those who attended (vv. 2–3)? 3. What statements show the reverence and seriousness of the people as they receive the Word of God (vv. 3–12)? 4. Who assembles the second day (v. 13)? Why do you think this is? 5. Verse 17 says that all the people had great joy. What was the reason for this?

Applying the Word 1. How much is celebration a part of your regular Christian life? 2. How do Christians you know show the great joy they have from obeying God's Word? 3. Many Christians do not have much joy because they don't take obedience to God's Word seriously or make it a priority in their lives. How will you guard against that in your life?

Responding in Prayer Spend some time in prayer and celebrate all the many ways the Lord has provided for you and forgiven your sins.

9 / *Nehemiah 9*
Getting Back to Your Roots

FOR MANY OF us it is difficult to think about corporately confessing our sins in the sight and hearing of many people. Yet revival and renewal are always preceded by contrition and remorse for our sins. Israel is at the end of itself, and the Lord is the only one who can deliver them, so they are returning to him. We too must be humbled, broken and serious to be recipients of God's renewal.

Warming Up to God   How do we get beyond the sin that keeps us from true fellowship with Christ and find true healing? Ask God to show you as you read Nehemiah 9.

Read Nehemiah 9.

9 On the twenty-fourth day of the same month, the Israelites gathered together, fasting and wearing sackcloth and having dust on their heads. ²Those of Israelite descent had separated themselves from all foreigners. They stood in their places and confessed their sins and the wickedness of their fathers. ³They stood where they were and read from the Book of the Law of the Lᴏʀᴅ their God for a quarter of the day, and spent another quarter in confession and in worshiping the Lᴏʀᴅ their God. ⁴Standing on the stairs were the Levites—Jeshua, Bani, Kadmiel, Shebaniah, Bunni, Sherebiah, Bani and Kenani—who called with loud voices to the Lᴏʀᴅ their God. ⁵And the Levites—Jeshua, Kadmiel, Bani, Hashabneiah, Sherebiah, Hodiah, Shebaniah and Pethahiah—said: "Stand up and praise the Lᴏʀᴅ your God, who is from everlasting to everlasting.ʷ"

"Blessed be your glorious name, and may it be exalted above all blessing and praise. ⁶You alone are the Lᴏʀᴅ. You made the heavens, even the highest heavens, and all their starry host, the earth and all that is on it, the seas and all that is in them. You give life to everything, and the multitudes of heaven worship you.

⁷"You are the Lᴏʀᴅ God, who chose Abram and brought him out of Ur of the Chaldeans and named him Abraham. ⁸You found his heart faithful to you, and you made a covenant with him to give to his descendants the land of the Canaanites, Hittites, Amorites, Perizzites, Jebusites and Girgashites. You have kept your promise because you are righteous.

⁹"You saw the suffering of our forefathers in Egypt; you heard their cry at the Red Sea.ˣ ¹⁰You sent miraculous signs and wonders against Pharaoh, against all his officials and all the people of his land, for you knew how arrogantly the Egyptians treated them. You made a name for yourself, which remains to this day. ¹¹You divided the sea before them, so that they passed through it on dry ground, but you hurled their pursuers into the depths, like a stone into mighty waters. ¹²By day you led them with a pillar of cloud, and by night with a pillar of fire to give them light on the way they were to take.

¹³"You came down on Mount Sinai; you spoke to them from heaven. You gave them regulations and laws that are just and right, and decrees and commands that are good. ¹⁴You made known to them your holy Sabbath and gave them commands, decrees and laws through your servant Moses. ¹⁵In their hunger you gave them bread from heaven and in their thirst you brought them water from the rock; you told them to go in and take possession of the land you had sworn with uplifted hand to give them.

¹⁶"But they, our forefathers, became arrogant and stiff-necked, and did not obey your commands. ¹⁷They refused to listen and failed to remember the miracles you performed among them. They became stiff-necked and in their rebellion appointed a leader in order to return to their slavery. But you are a forgiving God, gracious and compassionate, slow to anger and abounding in love. Therefore you did not desert them, ¹⁸even when they cast for themselves an image of a calf and said, 'This is your god, who

ʷ5 Or *God for ever and ever*   ˣ9 Hebrew *Yam Suph*; that is, Sea of Reeds brought you up out of Egypt,' or when they committed awful blasphemies.

¹⁹"Because of your great compassion you did not abandon them in the desert. By day the pillar of cloud did not cease to guide them on their path, nor the pillar of fire by night to shine on the way they were to take. ²⁰You gave your good Spirit to instruct them. You did not withhold your manna from their mouths, and you gave them water for their thirst. ²¹For forty years you sustained them in the desert; they lacked nothing, their clothes did not wear out nor did their feet become swollen.

²²"You gave them kingdoms and nations, allotting to them even the remotest frontiers. They took over the country of Sihon*ʸ* king of Heshbon and the country of Og king of Bashan. ²³You made their sons as numerous as the stars in the sky, and you brought them into the land that you told their fathers to enter and possess. ²⁴Their sons went in and took possession of the land. You subdued before them the Canaanites, who lived in the land; you handed the Canaanites over to them, along with their kings and the peoples of the land, to deal with them as they pleased. ²⁵They captured fortified cities and fertile land; they took possession of houses filled with all kinds of good things, wells already dug, vineyards, olive groves and fruit trees in abundance. They ate to the full and were well-nourished; they reveled in your great goodness.

²⁶"But they were disobedient and rebelled against you; they put your law behind their backs. They killed your prophets, who had admonished them in order to turn them back to you; they committed awful blasphemies. ²⁷So you handed them over to their enemies, who oppressed them. But when they were oppressed they cried out to you. From heaven you heard them, and in your great compassion you gave them deliverers, who rescued them from the hand of their enemies.

²⁸"But as soon as they were at rest, they again did what was evil in your sight. Then you abandoned them to the hand of their enemies so that they ruled over them. And

when they cried out to you again, you heard from heaven, and in your compassion you delivered them time after time.

²⁹"You warned them to return to your law, but they became arrogant and disobeyed your commands. They sinned against your ordinances, by which a man will live if he obeys them. Stubbornly they turned their backs on you, became stiff-necked and refused to listen. ³⁰For many years you were patient with them. By your Spirit you admonished them through your prophets. Yet they paid no attention, so you handed them over to the neighboring peoples. ³¹But in your great mercy you did not put an end to them or abandon them, for you are a gracious and merciful God.

³²"Now therefore, O our God, the great, mighty and awesome God, who keeps his covenant of love, do not let all this hardship seem trifling in your eyes—the hardship that has come upon us, upon our kings and leaders, upon our priests and prophets, upon our fathers and all your people, from the days of the kings of Assyria until today. ³³In all that has happened to us, you have been just; you have acted faithfully, while we did wrong. ³⁴Our kings, our leaders, our priests and our fathers did not follow your law; they did not pay attention to your commands or the warnings you gave them. ³⁵Even while they were in their kingdom, enjoying your great goodness to them in the spacious and fertile land you gave them, they did not serve you or turn from their evil ways.

³⁶"But see, we are slaves today, slaves in the land you gave our forefathers so they could eat its fruit and the other good things it produces. ³⁷Because of our sins, its abundant harvest goes to the kings you have placed over us. They rule over our bodies and our cattle as they please. We are in great distress.

³⁸"In view of all this, we are making a binding agreement, putting it in writing, and our leaders, our Levites and our priests are affixing their seals to it."

ʸ22 One Hebrew manuscript and Septuagint; most Hebrew manuscripts *Sihon, that is, the country of the*

Discovering the Word 1. Note that the time frame is about three weeks after the first reading of the Law. Why do you think they were wearing sackcloth and putting dust on their heads? 2. A quarter of a day is probably two to three hours. Does it seem feasible to you that they could confess sins for that long? Explain. 3. Why do you think they spent so much time confessing the sins of their ancestors? 4. What are the evidences from this passage that Ezra did not lose hope, even though the sins of Israel were many?

Applying the Word 1. How freely in your Christian life can you move between repentance for your sins and experiencing the celebration of God's forgiveness? 2. It may be surprising that the Israelites could go back so far and remember so many sins. Do you have any sense of history regarding your family sins or shortcomings? Explain your answer. 3. Now picture a time of corporate confession for your church or fellowship group. What kinds of sins should you be repenting of as a group?

Responding in Prayer Think of one act of reconciliation you need to make with members of your family, friends and the Lord himself. Pray and ask for forgiveness and commit to following through on your commitment this week.

10 / *Nehemiah 10*
A Covenant with God

MUCH OF THE world thinks that Christianity is a rip-off. Because Christians see God as the Creator and therefore the owner of everything there is, we give a tithe, and even more, to the Lord as an appropriate response. Part of the confusion is that the non-Christian sees the church or Christian leaders as getting that money. While serious Christians see all they have as belonging to God, non-Christians basically see all they have as a result of their hard work! Christians must be very honest and responsible with the money they control. Otherwise they open the body of Christ to ridicule and suspicion by the non-Christian world. There is no way the body of Christ can function well unless all God's people support those who have forgone a secular job to do the full-time work of the Lord and the body. This chapter of Nehemiah is about making such a covenant of support.

Warming Up to God What promises have you made or do you need to make with the Lord? Discuss them with him and ask for renewed energy for renewed faithfulness.

Read Nehemiah 10.

10 Those who sealed it were:

Nehemiah the governor, the son of Hacaliah.

Zedekiah, ²Seraiah, Azariah, Jeremiah, ³Pashhur, Amariah, Malkijah, ⁴Hattush, Shebaniah, Malluch, ⁵Harim, Meremoth, Obadiah, ⁶Daniel, Ginnethon, Baruch, ⁷Meshullam, Abijah, Mijamin, ⁸Maaziah, Bilgai and Shemaiah.

These were the priests.

⁹The Levites:

Jeshua son of Azaniah, Binnui of the sons of Henadad, Kadmiel, ¹⁰and their associates: Shebaniah, Hodiah, Kelita, Pelaiah, Hanan,

¹¹Mica, Rehob, Hashabiah, ¹²Zaccur, Sherebiah, Shebaniah, ¹³Hodiah, Bani and Beninu.

¹⁴The leaders of the people:

Parosh, Pahath-Moab, Elam, Zattu, Bani, ¹⁵Bunni, Azgad, Bebai, ¹⁶Adonijah, Bigvai, Adin, ¹⁷Ater, Hezekiah, Azzur, ¹⁸Hodiah, Hashum, Bezai, ¹⁹Hariph, Anathoth, Nebai, ²⁰Magpiash, Meshullam, Hezir, ²¹Meshezabel, Zadok, Jaddua, ²²Pelatiah, Hanan, Anaiah, ²³Hoshea, Hananiah, Hasshub, ²⁴Hallohesh, Pilha, Shobek, ²⁵Rehum, Hashabnah, Maaseiah, ²⁶Ahiah, Hanan, Anan,

²⁷Malluch, Harim and Baanah.

²⁸"The rest of the people—priests, Levites, gatekeepers, singers, temple servants and all who separated themselves from the neighboring peoples for the sake of the Law of God, together with their wives and all their sons and daughters who are able to understand— ²⁹all these now join their brothers the nobles, and bind themselves with a curse and an oath to follow the Law of God given through Moses the servant of God and to obey carefully all the commands, regulations and decrees of the LORD our Lord.

³⁰"We promise not to give our daughters in marriage to the peoples around us or take their daughters for our sons.

³¹"When the neighboring peoples bring merchandise or grain to sell on the Sabbath, we will not buy from them on the Sabbath or on any holy day. Every seventh year we will forgo working the land and will cancel all debts.

³²"We assume the responsibility for carrying out the commands to give a third of a shekelᶻ each year for the service of the house of our God: ³³for the bread set out on the table; for the regular grain offerings and burnt offerings; for the offerings on the Sabbaths, New Moon festivals and appointed feasts; for the holy offerings; for sin offerings to make atonement for Israel; and for all the duties of the house of our God.

³⁴"We—the priests, the Levites and the people—have cast lots to determine when each of our families is to bring to the house of our God at set times each year a contribution of wood to burn on the altar of the LORD our God, as it is written in the Law.

³⁵"We also assume responsibility for bringing to the house of the LORD each year the firstfruits of our crops and of every fruit tree.

³⁶"As it is also written in the Law, we will bring the firstborn of our sons and of our cattle, of our herds and of our flocks to the house of our God, to the priests ministering there.

³⁷"Moreover, we will bring to the storerooms of the house of our God, to the priests, the first of our ground meal, of our ∟grain⌐ offerings, of the fruit of all our trees and of our new wine and oil. And we will bring a tithe of our crops to the Levites, for it is the Levites who collect the tithes in all the towns where we work. ³⁸A priest descended from Aaron is to accompany the Levites when they receive the tithes, and the Levites are to bring a tenth of the tithes up to the house of our God, to the storerooms of the treasury. ³⁹The people of Israel, including the Levites, are to bring their contributions of grain, new wine and oil to the storerooms where the articles for the sanctuary are kept and where the ministering priests, the gatekeepers and the singers stay.

"We will not neglect the house of our God."

ᶻ32 That is, about 1/8 ounce (about 4 grams)

Discovering the Word 1. The result of hearing the Law read (chapter 8) and the result of obeying the Law (chapter 9) now produce a written agreement in chapter 10 to obey God and his commandments. Who were the groups of people mentioned in this chapter? 2. What evidence is there that everyone was included in the covenant agreement (vv. 28–29)? 3. Make a list of the things that the people covenant to do before the Lord (vv. 30–39). 4. Why would it be very important in their situation not to intermarry? 5. Do you think verse 29 is still binding on us today as it was on the people in Nehemiah's day? Explain why you give the answer that you do. 6. Who collected the tithe, and to whom did these people tithe?

Applying the Word 1. What effect would the actions the people commit to have on their life and worship? 2. Do you feel you take material things and the tithing of them as seriously as they did in this passage? Why or why not?

Responding in Prayer Reflect upon your commitments to the Lord with family, at work or school, or in your times of fellowship with him alone. Rededicate yourself in specific ways to these commitments—and promise the Lord to have renewed effort and obedience.

11 / *Nehemiah 11*
Choosing Where to Live and Work

WHEN MY FRIEND Ken is deciding where to live and work, he bases the decision on where he feels God wants him to develop a ministry and be of help in the building up of the body of Christ. Certainly people with the world's values do not choose a place to live and work on that basis. But as a Christian, the more I think about it, the more it makes sense. Not just my money belongs to the Lord, but my profession and my gifts belong to him so they can be used in the body of Christ. God would surely know better than I where I should live and work so that I would fit his plans for the building of his kingdom! Only God can balance all the variables in a way that works best for his purposes.

 Warming Up to God What rests heavy on your heart today? Draw near to Jesus, who is waiting to put his arms around you as you tell him of your concerns. Let him listen to all your anxieties and allow them to become his worries for you.

 Read Nehemiah 11.

---

11 Now the leaders of the people settled in Jerusalem, and the rest of the people cast lots to bring one out of every ten to live in Jerusalem, the holy city, while the remaining nine were to stay in their own towns. ²The people commended all the men who volunteered to live in Jerusalem.

³These are the provincial leaders who settled in Jerusalem (now some Israelites, priests, Levites, temple servants and descendants of Solomon's servants lived in the towns of Judah, each on his own property in the various towns, ⁴while other people from both Judah and Benjamin lived in Jerusalem):

From the descendants of Judah:

Athaiah son of Uzziah, the son of Zechariah, the son of Amariah, the son of Shephatiah, the son of Mahalalel, a descendant of Perez; ⁵and Maaseiah son of Baruch, the son of Col-Hozeh, the son of Hazaiah, the son of Adaiah, the son of Joiarib, the son of Zechariah, a descendant of Shelah. ⁶The descendants of Perez who lived in Jerusalem totaled 468 able men.

⁷From the descendants of Benjamin:

Sallu son of Meshullam, the son of Joed, the son of Pedaiah, the son of Kolaiah, the son of Maaseiah, the son of Ithiel, the son of Jeshaiah, ⁸and his followers, Gabbai and Sallai—928 men. ⁹Joel son of Zicri was their chief officer, and Judah son of Hassenuah was over the Second District of the city.

¹⁰From the priests:

Jedaiah; the son of Joiarib; Jakin; ¹¹Seraiah son of Hilkiah, the son of Meshullam, the son of Zadok, the son of Meraioth, the son of Ahitub, supervisor in the house of God, ¹²and their associates, who carried on work for the temple—822 men; Adaiah son of Jeroham, the son of Pelaliah, the son of Amzi, the son of Zechariah, the son of Pashhur, the son of Malkijah, ¹³and his associates, who were heads of families—242 men; Amashsai son of Azarel, the son of Ahzai, the son of Meshillemoth, the son of Immer, ¹⁴and his*a* associates, who were able men—128. Their chief officer was Zabdiel son of Haggedolim.

¹⁵From the Levites:

Shemaiah son of Hasshub, the son of Azrikam, the son of Hashabiah, the son of Bunni; ¹⁶Shabbethai and Jozabad, two of the heads of the Levites, who had charge of the outside work of the house of God; ¹⁷Mattaniah son of Mica, the son of Zabdi, the son of Asaph, the director who led in thanksgiving and prayer; Bakbukiah, second among his associates; and Abda son of Shammua, the son of Galal, the son of Jeduthun. ¹⁸The Levites in the holy city totaled 284.

¹⁹The gatekeepers:

Akkub, Talmon and their associates, who kept watch at the gates—172 men.

²⁰The rest of the Israelites, with the priests and Levites, were in all the towns of Judah, each on his ancestral property.

a 14 Most Septuagint manuscripts; Hebrew their

²¹The temple servants lived on the hill of Ophel, and Ziha and Gishpa were in charge of them.

²²The chief officer of the Levites in Jerusalem was Uzzi son of Bani, the son of Hashabiah, the son of Mattaniah, the son of Mica. Uzzi was one of Asaph's descendants, who were the singers responsible for the service of the house of God. ²³The singers were under the king's orders, which regulated their daily activity.

²⁴Pethahiah son of Meshezabel, one of the descendants of Zerah son of Judah, was the king's agent in all affairs relating to the people.

²⁵As for the villages with their fields, some of the people of Judah lived in Kiriath Arba and its surrounding settlements, in Dibon and its settle- ments, in Jekabzeel and its villages, ²⁶in Jeshua, in Moladah, in Beth Pelet, ²⁷in Hazar Shual, in Beer- sheba and its settlements, ²⁸in Ziklag, in Meconah and its settlements, ²⁹in En Rimmon, in Zorah, in Jarmuth, ³⁰Zanoah, Adullam and their villages, in Lachish and its fields, and in Azekah and its set- tlements. So they were living all the way from Beersheba to the Valley of Hinnom.

³¹The descendants of the Benjamites from Geba lived in Micmash, Aija, Bethel and its settlements, ³²in Anathoth, Nob and Ananiah, ³³in Hazor, Ra- mah and Gittaim, ³⁴in Hadid, Zeboim and Nebal- lat, ³⁵in Lod and Ono, and in the Valley of the Craftsmen.

³⁶Some of the divisions of the Levites of Judah settled in Benjamin.

 Discovering the Word   1. How did the Jews in chapter 11 decide who would live in Jerusalem?   2. Why do you think the people did not want to live in Jerusalem (v. 2)?   3. What reasons can you think of for these five groups of people to live in Jerusalem (v. 3)?   4. How (from chapter 10) would all of these people be taken care of materially?   5. How was Nehemiah making the city ready for the people?

Applying the Word   1. What factors do you consider in determining where you should live? (Consider occupation, salary, school, church, ministry, family and so on.)   2. Since our barter system is money, in what ways does our lifestyle free us up to be more involved in kingdom building?   3. As you read this passage, what personal decisions (past or future) about where you live and how that impacts your service to God come to mind?

Responding in Prayer   Ask the Lord to help you live in obedience—your hardest daily decision no matter where God leads you.

---

12 / *Nehemiah 12*
Important Work

"IF A JOB is worth doing, it is worth doing well!" I would like to have a dollar for every time I heard that growing up. I don't think that I understood the saying nearly as well as I do after years of working on it. Integrity and respect come to those who do a good job. We recognize excellence when we see it, and we are offended by a job half-done. We would be of much better use to God, others and ourselves if we didn't volunteer for everything that came along, but rather did a better job on the things we can realistically complete. If I do my part faithfully, God will do the rest in building his kingdom.

 Warming Up to God   How is your kingdom workload? Are you feeling overwhelmed by commitments to your church or fellowship? Or are you ready for a new challenge? Reflect on your commitments of service to God before you begin.

Read Nehemiah 12.

12

These were the priests and Levites who returned with Zerubbabel son of Shealtiel and with Jeshua:
Seraiah, Jeremiah, Ezra, [2]Amariah, Malluch, Hattush, [3]Shecaniah, Rehum, Meremoth, [4]Iddo, Ginnethon,[b] Abijah, [5]Mijamin,[c] Moadiah, Bilgah, [6]Shemaiah, Joiarib, Jedaiah, [7]Sallu, Amok, Hilkiah and Jedaiah.
These were the leaders of the priests and their associates in the days of Jeshua.

[8]The Levites were Jeshua, Binnui, Kadmiel, Sherebiah, Judah, and also Mattaniah, who, together with his associates, was in charge of the songs of thanksgiving. [9]Bakbukiah and Unni, their associates, stood opposite them in the services.

[10]Jeshua was the father of Joiakim, Joiakim the father of Eliashib, Eliashib the father of Joiada, [11]Joiada the father of Jonathan, and Jonathan the father of Jaddua.

[12]In the days of Joiakim, these were the heads of the priestly families:
of Seraiah's family, Meraiah;
of Jeremiah's, Hananiah;
[13]of Ezra's, Meshullam;
of Amariah's, Jehohanan;
[14]of Malluch's, Jonathan;
of Shecaniah's,[d] Joseph;
[15]of Harim's, Adna;
of Meremoth's,[e] Helkai;
[16]of Iddo's, Zechariah;
of Ginnethon's, Meshullam;
[17]of Abijah's, Zicri;
of Miniamin's and of Moadiah's, Piltai;
[18]of Bilgah's, Shammua;
of Shemaiah's, Jehonathan;
[19]of Joiarib's, Mattenai;
of Jedaiah's, Uzzi;
[20]of Sallu's, Kallai;
of Amok's, Eber;
[21]of Hilkiah's, Hashabiah;
of Jedaiah's, Nethanel.

[22]The family heads of the Levites in the days of Eliashib, Joiada, Johanan and Jaddua, as well as those of the priests, were recorded in the reign of Darius the Persian. [23]The family heads among the descendants of Levi up to the time of Johanan son of Eliashib were recorded in the book of the annals. [24]And the leaders of the Levites were Hashabiah, Sherebiah, Jeshua son of Kadmiel, and their associates, who stood opposite them to give praise and thanksgiving, one section responding to the other, as prescribed by David the man of God.

[25]Mattaniah, Bakbukiah, Obadiah, Meshullam, Talmon and Akkub were gatekeepers who guarded the storerooms at the gates. [26]They served in the days of Joiakim son of Jeshua, the son of Jozadak, and in the days of Nehemiah the governor and of Ezra the priest and scribe.

[27]At the dedication of the wall of Jerusalem, the Levites were sought out from where they lived and were brought to Jerusalem to celebrate joyfully the dedication with songs of thanksgiving and with the music of cymbals, harps and lyres. [28]The singers also were brought together from the region around Jerusalem—from the villages of the Netophathites, [29]from Beth Gilgal, and from the area of Geba and Azmaveth, for the singers had built villages for themselves around Jerusalem. [30]When the priests and Levites had purified themselves ceremonially, they purified the people, the gates and the wall.

[31]I had the leaders of Judah go up on top[f] of the wall. I also assigned two large choirs to give thanks. One was to proceed on top[g] of the wall to the right, toward the Dung Gate. [32]Hoshaiah and half the leaders of Judah followed them, [33]along with Azariah, Ezra, Meshullam, [34]Judah, Benjamin, Shemaiah, Jeremiah, [35]as well as some priests with trumpets, and also Zechariah son of Jonathan, the son of Shemaiah, the son of Mattaniah, the son of Micaiah, the son of Zaccur, the son of Asaph, [36]and his associates—Shemaiah, Azarel, Milalai, Gilalai, Maai, Nethanel, Judah and Hanani—with musical instruments ∟prescribed by⌟ David the man of God. Ezra the scribe led the procession. [37]At the Fountain Gate they continued directly up the steps of the City of David on the ascent to the wall and passed above the house of David to the Water Gate on the east.

[38]The second choir proceeded in the opposite direction. I followed them on top[h] of the wall, together with half the people—past the Tower of the Ovens to the Broad Wall, [39]over the Gate of Ephraim, the Jeshanah[i] Gate, the Fish Gate, the Tower of Hananel and the Tower of the Hundred,

---

[b]4 Many Hebrew manuscripts and Vulgate (see also Neh. 12:16); most Hebrew manuscripts *Ginnethoi*   [c]5 A variant of *Miniamin*
[d]14 Very many Hebrew manuscripts, some Septuagint manuscripts and Syriac (see also Neh. 12:3); most Hebrew manuscripts *Shebaniah's*
[e]15 Some Septuagint manuscripts (see also Neh. 12:3); Hebrew *Meraioth's*   [f]31 Or *go alongside*   [g]31 Or *proceed alongside*
[h]38 Or *them alongside*   [i]39 Or *Old*

as far as the Sheep Gate. At the Gate of the Guard they stopped.

⁴⁰The two choirs that gave thanks then took their places in the house of God; so did I, together with half the officials, ⁴¹as well as the priests—Eliakim, Maaseiah, Miniamin, Micaiah, Elioenai, Zechariah and Hananiah with their trumpets—⁴²and also Maaseiah, Shemaiah, Eleazar, Uzzi, Jehohanan, Malkijah, Elam and Ezer. The choirs sang under the direction of Jezrahiah. ⁴³And on that day they offered great sacrifices, rejoicing because God had given them great joy. The women and children also rejoiced. The sound of rejoicing in Jerusalem could be heard far away.

⁴⁴At that time men were appointed to be in charge of the storerooms for the contributions, firstfruits and tithes. From the fields around the towns they were to bring into the storerooms the portions required by the Law for the priests and the Levites, for Judah was pleased with the ministering priests and Levites. ⁴⁵They performed the service of their God and the service of purification, as did also the singers and gatekeepers, according to the commands of David and his son Solomon. ⁴⁶For long ago, in the days of David and Asaph, there had been directors for the singers and for the songs of praise and thanksgiving to God. ⁴⁷So in the days of Zerubbabel and of Nehemiah, all Israel contributed the daily portions for the singers and gatekeepers. They also set aside the portion for the other Levites, and the Levites set aside the portion for the descendants of Aaron.

Discovering the Word   1. Why do you think the author mentions so many people in this chapter?   2. How would you feel if you were Meshullam in verse 25 and were recognized for guarding the storerooms?   3. Consider verses 8 and 24. Do you think most people would have wanted these jobs? Why or why not?   4. From the book of Nehemiah so far, what is the reason for their great rejoicing (v. 43)?   5. How important do you think the collection of these goods was to the effective running of Jerusalem and providing the worship and celebration that Jerusalem represented (vv. 44–47)?

Applying the Word   1. Since in our culture we see the up-front gifts as more significant than the supporting or helping gifts, would you see being in the choir as an important ministry? Why or why not?   2. What are some of the supporting roles you think of in the church?   3. How could you give (financially and with your encouragement) to sustain the supporting people (that is, pastors, missionaries, youth workers, denominational headquarters) in your church or fellowship?

Responding in Prayer   Thank the Lord for giving you a job in his kingdom, and recommit yourself to be faithful in your tasks.

13 / *Nehemiah 13*
Spiritual Decay

"I KNOW THEY are sinning against the Lord, but I love them too much to reprimand them." Sometimes we emphasize loving people and not endangering our relationships with them over challenging them to get right with the Lord. When we think like this, we have accepted the world's values and not kingdom values! If relationship with God is the most important thing in the world, then to help people get back into right relationship with God is the best thing we can do for them. When we don't do this, what we are really saying is that we are more concerned about what that person thinks than what God thinks. We must be freed from this kind of bondage, or we are not of much use to God, others or ourselves. When we are biblically directed, we will be respected and others will hear God's Word through us.

Warming Up to God   Do you need forgiveness from the Lord today? Stop now and tell him about your pride or selfishness today—and let the solid truth of 1 John 1:9 that you are forgiven and cleansed cause you to rejoice and be refreshed.

Read Nehemiah 13.

13

On that day the Book of Moses was read aloud in the hearing of the people and there it was found written that no Ammonite or Moabite should ever be admitted into the assembly of God, ²because they had not met the Israelites with food and water but had hired Balaam to call a curse down on them. (Our God, however, turned the curse into a blessing.) ³When the people heard this law, they excluded from Israel all who were of foreign descent.

⁴Before this, Eliashib the priest had been put in charge of the storerooms of the house of our God. He was closely associated with Tobiah, ⁵and he had provided him with a large room formerly used to store the grain offerings and incense and temple articles, and also the tithes of grain, new wine and oil prescribed for the Levites, singers and gatekeepers, as well as the contributions for the priests.

⁶But while all this was going on, I was not in Jerusalem, for in the thirty-second year of Artaxerxes king of Babylon I had returned to the king. Some time later I asked his permission ⁷and came back to Jerusalem. Here I learned about the evil thing Eliashib had done in providing Tobiah a room in the courts of the house of God. ⁸I was greatly displeased and threw all Tobiah's household goods out of the room. ⁹I gave orders to purify the rooms, and then I put back into them the equipment of the house of God, with the grain offerings and the incense.

¹⁰I also learned that the portions assigned to the Levites had not been given to them, and that all the Levites and singers responsible for the service had gone back to their own fields. ¹¹So I rebuked the officials and asked them, "Why is the house of God neglected?" Then I called them together and stationed them at their posts.

¹²All Judah brought the tithes of grain, new wine and oil into the storerooms. ¹³I put Shelemiah the priest, Zadok the scribe, and a Levite named Pedaiah in charge of the storerooms and made Hanan son of Zaccur, the son of Mattaniah, their assistant, because these men were considered trustworthy. They were made responsible for distributing the supplies to their brothers.

¹⁴Remember me for this, O my God, and do not blot out what I have so faithfully done for the house of my God and its services.

¹⁵In those days I saw men in Judah treading winepresses on the Sabbath and bringing in grain and loading it on donkeys, together with wine, grapes, figs and all other kinds of loads. And they were bringing all this into Jerusalem on the Sabbath. Therefore I warned them against selling food on that day. ¹⁶Men from Tyre who lived in Jerusalem were bringing in fish and all kinds of merchandise and selling them in Jerusalem on the Sabbath to the people of Judah. ¹⁷I rebuked the nobles of Judah and said to them, "What is this wicked thing you are doing—desecrating the Sabbath day? ¹⁸Didn't your forefathers do the same things, so that our God brought all this calamity upon us and upon this city? Now you are stirring up more wrath against Israel by desecrating the Sabbath."

¹⁹When evening shadows fell on the gates of Jerusalem before the Sabbath, I ordered the doors to be shut and not opened until the Sabbath was over. I stationed some of my own men at the gates so that no load could be brought in on the Sabbath day. ²⁰Once or twice the merchants and sellers of all kinds of goods spent the night outside Jerusalem. ²¹But I warned them and said, "Why do you spend the night by the wall? If you do this again, I will lay hands on you." From that time on they no longer came on the Sabbath. ²²Then I commanded the Levites to purify themselves and go and guard the gates in order to keep the Sabbath day holy.

Remember me for this also, O my God, and show mercy to me according to your great love.

²³Moreover, in those days I saw men of Judah who had married women from Ashdod, Ammon and Moab. ²⁴Half of their children spoke the language of Ashdod or the language of one of the other peoples, and did not know how to speak the language of Judah. ²⁵I rebuked them and called curses down on them. I beat some of the men and pulled out their hair. I made them take an oath in God's name and said: "You are not to give your daughters in marriage to their sons, nor are you to take their daughters in marriage for your sons or for yourselves. ²⁶Was it not because of marriages like these that Solomon king of Israel sinned? Among the many nations there was no king like him. He was loved by his

God, and God made him king over all Israel, but even he was led into sin by foreign women. ²⁷Must we hear now that you too are doing all this terrible wickedness and are being unfaithful to our God by marrying foreign women?"

²⁸One of the sons of Joiada son of Eliashib the high priest was son-in-law to Sanballat the Horonite. And I drove him away from me.

²⁹Remember them, O my God, because they defiled the priestly office and the covenant of the priesthood and of the Levites.

³⁰So I purified the priests and the Levites of everything foreign, and assigned them duties, each to his own task. ³¹I also made provision for contributions of wood at designated times, and for the firstfruits.

Remember me with favor, O my God.

 Discovering the Word 1. Note from 2:1 and 13:6 that Nehemiah spent twelve years in Jerusalem before going back to Artaxerxes. We don't know how long it was before Nehemiah came back to Jerusalem to check up on things, but it was probably several years. List the things in this chapter that indicate the Israelites have backslidden before the Lord. 2. Considering the people made such a strong covenant in chapter 10, how do you think they could have gone this far astray in chapter 13? 3. What does the passage reveal about how Nehemiah felt when he came back and saw how bad things were spiritually? 4. Compare 10:30 with 13:23–28. Do you see anything in the text that shows you why Israel has backslidden? 5. Nehemiah's response in verse 25 is very dramatic and physical. What principles does this suggest to you for how we should deal with sin today?

Applying the Word 1. Why is it so much harder to confront leaders who are sinning, as in this chapter? 2. In what ways do you need to be more direct with others about their sin? 3. How would you like others to help you in dealing with your own sin?

Responding in Prayer Ask the Lord to make you more like Nehemiah, who pursued righteousness and called others to holy living. Pray as he did: "Remember me with favor, O my God."

Esther

"Just Do It" has been a successful and popular slogan the past few years for the athletic company Nike. It refers to getting in shape and participating in athletics no matter what the physical or mental strain. But the slogan brings something else to my mind after spending time in the book of Esther: it reminds me to *just do it*—just do the right thing no matter what the consequences.

In the book of Esther we see the lives of several characters played out. There are those people who are selfish and prideful, seeking only personal recognition, and there are those who risk everything for others and choose integrity in the face of great opposition. Esther is a book about developing godly character. In the midst of a culture which emphasizes doing what is right, this book speaks to us in profound ways.

As we read through the events of Esther, we are given a description of what godly character is and what it is not. But there is another very strong theme that weaves in and around the theme of character. It is the idea that God is working in the circumstances and events of people's lives to bring about his plans. God is the director, the conductor, the weaver. As God works in our lives, we must choose what is right so that we can be a part of God's plan.

The events of this powerful book take place in Persia during the reign of King Xerxes from 486 to 465 B.C. It has been over one hundred years since the beginning of the exile, and some Jews have returned to Jerusalem. The story is set in the city of Susa, which is where the king has his winter palace. It involves the whole of the Jewish people, but revolves around the lives of King Xerxes; Esther; her cousin, Mordecai; and Haman, the king's highest noble.

Esther's story presents the last major threat to the Jewish people in the Old Testament period. The threat and the Jews' deliverance is recorded in this book. The Jewish festival of Purim, which is still celebrated today, is established in Esther, which accounts for the book's great popularity among the Jewish people. It is a wonderful story of God's providence and the character of his people told with humor, irony, repetition and contrast.

Esther will stir us to examine our character, the deep aspects of our hearts. It will encourage us in taking a stand for what is right and give us courage that God is still in control. It is a book that we need to study so that we can glorify God with our whole beings and begin to be witnesses in our world because of our integrity. If we allow the themes of Esther to penetrate our lives, we will begin to stop and question our actions and thoughts and align them with God's desire.

May your study in Esther produce in you a longing for consistent godly character.

Outline

1/ Esther 1 ——————————— *A Little Respect*

2/ Esther 2 ——————————— *Trusting God's Work*

3/ Esther 3 ——————————— *Evaluating Advice*

4/ Esther 4 ——————————— *Doing the Right Thing*

5/ Esther 5 ——————————— *The Heart of the Matter*

6/ Esther 6 ——————————— *Recognizing Unrighteousness*

7/ Esther 7 ——————————— *Character No Matter What*

8/ Esther 8 ——————————— *Praising God's Faithfulness*

9/ Esther 9—10 ——————————— *Remembering and Celebrating*

SLEEPLESS NIGHTS

READ:
Psalm 16

**My heart also instructs me in the night seasons.
—Psalm 16:7**

THE BIBLE IN ONE YEAR:
■ 1 Samuel 8–10

The psalmist David had his dark, lonely nights when everything seemed out of control. Doubts and fears assailed him, and there was no escape from his problems. He tossed and turned just as we do, but then he turned to his Shepherd (Psalm 23:1) and reminded himself of the Lord's presence. That brought peace to his anxious, troubled soul. David said, "Because He is at my right hand I shall not be moved" (16:8).

We too have occasions of wakefulness when anxious thoughts jostle one another for attention, when we curse the darkness, and when we long for sleep. But we mustn't fret, for darkness can be our friend. God is present in it, visiting us, counseling us, instructing us in the night. Perhaps on our beds, as nowhere else, we may hear God's voice. We can listen to His thoughts and meditate on His Word.

We can talk to the Lord about every concern, casting our care on Him (1 Peter 5:7). We can talk about our failures, our conflicts, our challenges, our anxieties, our frustrations over His lengthy delays—all the things that stress us out and render us sleepless—and listen to what He has to say. That's what can set us apart from ordinary insomniacs. That's the secret of quiet rest. —DHR

*I couldn't sleep last night, but did not toss
And count my wakefulness a dreadful loss;
Ah, no! I was quite glad to lose my sleep—
I had such wondrous company to keep!* —Seller

**WHEN YOU CAN'T SLEEP, DON'T COUNT SHEEP.
TALK TO THE SHEPHERD.**

March 17
Saturday

OUR GREATEST NEED

READ:
Psalm 42:1-4

Man shall not live by bread alone, but by every word that proceeds from the mouth of God.
—Matthew 4:4

THE BIBLE IN ONE YEAR:
■ 1 Samuel 11–13

We are creatures with all kinds of needs. Without air, water, or food, for instance, we can't go on living. In addition to these absolutely basic necessities, we have a host of others that must be met if we are to be healthy and happy. But these needs are not just physical, emotional, and social; they are also spiritual.

Anyone who thinks human beings are mere organisms is overlooking our most essential need. Douglas Coupland talks about this in his book *Life After God:* "Now here is my secret: I tell it to you with an openness of heart that I doubt I shall ever achieve again . . . . My secret is that I need God—that I am sick and can no longer make it alone. I need God to help me give, because I no longer seem to be capable of giving; to help me be kind, as I no longer seem capable of kindness; to help me love, as I seem beyond being able to love."

Do you recognize your need for God? The author of Psalm 42 certainly did (vv.1-2). That need can be met by entering into a personal relationship with Jesus Christ. As you confess your sin and believe that He'll forgive you, He will. Then, by His Holy Spirit, He will come to live in you and enable you to be kind, generous, and loving.

Christ meets our greatest need. —VCG

Eternal life is knowing God
Through Jesus Christ His only Son;
Such knowledge is life's greatest need—
Without it life has not begun. —D. De Haan

IF YOU'RE LOOKING FOR GOD, LOOK TO JESUS.

1 / *Esther 1*
A Little Respect

ONE OF MY favorite and most influential teachers was a high-school English teacher. His class was extremely difficult and challenging, but I loved it and worked diligently in order to do well. The reason I respected this teacher so much is that he listened to me and valued me. We would all like to be respected by others, and so we try many ways of gaining that respect. Some try to gain it through controlling others or by demanding it. However, one of the ways respect is gained is by appreciating others and showing them respect.

 Warming Up to God Think of one person whom you respect. What are some characteristics of this person? How did he or she gain your respect?

 Read Esther 1.

1 This is what happened during the time of Xerxes,ᵃ the Xerxes who ruled over 127 provinces stretching from India to Cushᵇ: ²At that time King Xerxes reigned from his royal throne in the citadel of Susa, ³and in the third year of his reign he gave a banquet for all his nobles and officials. The military leaders of Persia and Media, the princes, and the nobles of the provinces were present.

⁴For a full 180 days he displayed the vast wealth of his kingdom and the splendor and glory of his majesty. ⁵When these days were over, the king gave a banquet, lasting seven days, in the enclosed garden of the king's palace, for all the people from the least to the greatest, who were in the citadel of Susa. ⁶The garden had hangings of white and blue linen, fastened with cords of white linen and purple material to silver rings on marble pillars. There were couches of gold and silver on a mosaic pavement of porphyry, marble, mother-of-pearl and other costly stones. ⁷Wine was served in goblets of gold, each one different from the other, and the royal wine was abundant, in keeping with the king's liberality. ⁸By the king's command each guest was allowed to drink in his own way, for the king instructed all the wine stewards to serve each man what he wished.

⁹Queen Vashti also gave a banquet for the women in the royal palace of King Xerxes.

¹⁰On the seventh day, when King Xerxes was in high spirits from wine, he commanded the seven eunuchs who served him—Mehuman, Biztha, Harbona, Bigtha, Abagtha, Zethar and Carcas—¹¹to bring before him Queen Vashti, wearing her royal crown, in order to display her beauty to the people and nobles, for she was lovely to look at. ¹²But when the attendants delivered the king's command, Queen Vashti refused to come. Then the king became furious and burned with anger.

¹³Since it was customary for the king to consult experts in matters of law and justice, he spoke with the wise men who understood the times ¹⁴and were closest to the king—Carshena, Shethar, Admatha, Tarshish, Meres, Marsena and Memucan, the seven nobles of Persia and Media who had special access to the king and were highest in the kingdom.

¹⁵"According to law, what must be done to Queen Vashti?" he asked. "She has not obeyed the command of King Xerxes that the eunuchs have taken to her."

¹⁶Then Memucan replied in the presence of the king and the nobles, "Queen Vashti has done wrong, not only against the king but also against all the nobles and the peoples of all the provinces of King Xerxes. ¹⁷For the queen's conduct will become known to all the women, and so they will despise their husbands and say, 'King Xerxes commanded Queen Vashti to be brought before him, but she would not come.' ¹⁸This very day the Persian and Median women of the nobility who have heard about the queen's conduct will respond to all the king's nobles in the same way. There will be no end of disrespect and discord.

¹⁹"Therefore, if it pleases the king, let him issue a royal decree and let it be written in the laws of Persia and Media, which cannot be repealed, that Vashti is never again to enter the presence of King Xerxes. Also let the king give her royal position to someone else who is better than she. ²⁰Then

ᵃ1 Hebrew *Ahasuerus*, a variant of Xerxes' Persian name; here and throughout Esther   ᵇ1 That is, the upper Nile region when the king's edict is proclaimed throughout all his vast realm, all the women will respect their husbands, from the least to the greatest."

21The king and his nobles were pleased with this advice, so the king did as Memucan pro-posed. 22He sent dispatches to all parts of the kingdom, to each province in its own script and to each people in its own language, proclaiming in each people's tongue that every man should be ruler over his own household.

 Discovering the Word 1. Describe the celebration given by King Xerxes (vv. 2–8). 2. Why might the king have given such an extravagant party? 3. Why does King Xerxes ask Queen Vashti to come to him (vv. 10–11)? 4. Why did the wise men perceive Queen Vashti's refusal to be so dangerous to the kingdom (vv. 16–20)? 5. The wise men mention respect several times in this chapter. In their view how was respect gained and maintained?

 Applying the Word 1. In what ways have you been shown appreciation and regard by those around you? 2. Describe one thing that you can do this week to show someone respect.

Responding in Prayer Ask God to teach you how to give respect and to make you a person worthy of respect.

---

2 / *Esther 2*
Trusting God's Work

THE MOST IMPORTANT person in a play is not on the stage. The director is the one who has instructed the cast for months before on where to stand and sit and when and how to say a line. The director is behind the scenes giving final instructions, touching up makeup and encouraging the players—orchestrating every detail.

In the book of Esther God is not mentioned, but he is the key figure in the story. He works through the circum-stances to place everything in order so that his plans will be accomplished. God is the director of our lives as well. As we look back at different times in our lives, we can see his handprints all over. Our response to him is to look for his hand moving and to trust his direction.

 Warming Up to God Recall a time in your past when you saw God work through circumstances in your life to bring something about. Allow your praise for God's good work to well up in response.

 Read Esther 2.

Later when the anger of King Xerxes had subsided, he remembered Vashti and what she had done and what he had de-creed about her. 2Then the king's personal atten-dants proposed, "Let a search be made for beauti-ful young virgins for the king. 3Let the king appoint commissioners in every province of his realm to bring all these beautiful girls into the harem at the citadel of Susa. Let them be placed under the care of Hegai, the king's eunuch, who is in charge of the women; and let beauty treat-ments be given to them. 4Then let the girl who pleases the king be queen instead of Vashti." This advice appealed to the king, and he followed it.

5Now there was in the citadel of Susa a Jew of the tribe of Benjamin, named Mordecai son of Jair, the son of Shimei, the son of Kish, 6who had been carried into exile from Jerusalem by Nebu-chadnezzar king of Babylon, among those taken captive with Jehoiachin*c* king of Judah. 7Morde-cai had a cousin named Hadassah, whom he had brought up because she had neither father nor mother. This girl, who was also known as Esther, was lovely in form and features, and Mordecai had taken her as his own daughter when her fa-ther and mother died.

8When the king's order and edict had been pro-claimed, many girls were brought to the citadel of Susa and put under the care of Hegai. Esther also was taken to the king's palace and entrusted to Hegai, who had charge of the harem. 9The girl

c6 Hebrew Jeconiah, *a variant of* Jehoiachin

pleased him and won his favor. Immediately he provided her with her beauty treatments and special food. He assigned to her seven maids selected from the king's palace and moved her and her maids into the best place in the harem.

¹⁰Esther had not revealed her nationality and family background, because Mordecai had forbidden her to do so. ¹¹Every day he walked back and forth near the courtyard of the harem to find out how Esther was and what was happening to her.

¹²Before a girl's turn came to go in to King Xerxes, she had to complete twelve months of beauty treatments prescribed for the women, six months with oil of myrrh and six with perfumes and cosmetics. ¹³And this is how she would go to the king: Anything she wanted was given her to take with her from the harem to the king's palace. ¹⁴In the evening she would go there and in the morning return to another part of the harem to the care of Shaashgaz, the king's eunuch who was in charge of the concubines. She would not return to the king unless he was pleased with her and summoned her by name.

¹⁵When the turn came for Esther (the girl Mordecai had adopted, the daughter of his uncle Abihail) to go to the king, she asked for nothing other than what Hegai, the king's eunuch who was in charge of the harem, suggested. And Esther won the favor of everyone who saw her. ¹⁶She was taken to King Xerxes in the royal residence in the tenth month, the month of Tebeth, in the seventh year of his reign.

¹⁷Now the king was attracted to Esther more than to any of the other women, and she won his favor and approval more than any of the other virgins. So he set a royal crown on her head and made her queen instead of Vashti. ¹⁸And the king gave a great banquet, Esther's banquet, for all his nobles and officials. He proclaimed a holiday throughout the provinces and distributed gifts with royal liberality.

¹⁹When the virgins were assembled a second time, Mordecai was sitting at the king's gate. ²⁰But Esther had kept secret her family background and nationality just as Mordecai had told her to do, for she continued to follow Mordecai's instructions as she had done when he was bringing her up.

²¹During the time Mordecai was sitting at the king's gate, Bigthana[d] and Teresh, two of the king's officers who guarded the doorway, became angry and conspired to assassinate King Xerxes. ²²But Mordecai found out about the plot and told Queen Esther, who in turn reported it to the king, giving credit to Mordecai. ²³And when the report was investigated and found to be true, the two officials were hanged on a gallows.[e] All this was recorded in the book of the annals in the presence of the king.

d21 Hebrew Bigthan, a variant of Bigthana   e23 Or were hung (or impaled) on poles; similarly elsewhere in Esther

---

Discovering the Word 1. Summarize the plan to find a new queen that King Xerxes put into action (vv. 1–4). 2. How does Esther enter the story and become the queen (vv. 5–17)? 3. It is mentioned three times that Esther won approval in someone's eyes (vv. 9, 15, 17). What does this tell us about Esther? 4. How does Mordecai enter into the plot of the story (vv. 19–23)? 5. Even though God has not been directly mentioned in the book, where do you see his hand moving in the story so far?

Applying the Word 1. Where do you see God's hand moving in circumstances in your life right now? 2. How do you think he wants you to respond?

Responding in Prayer Ask God to give you confidence in his work in your life.

---

3 / *Esther 3*
Evaluating Advice

NO ONE HAS "any right to counsel others who is not ready to hear and follow the counsel of the Lord." This quote from A. W. Tozer reminds me of the responsibility we have in giving advice to others. It is a serious thing to give counsel, and it is also a serious step to take the counsel of our friends. So often we can give quick advice to one another without truly understanding the situation or without pure motives. Part of godly character is knowing how to evaluate the advice we receive and in turn to offer sound and wise counsel.

 Warming Up to God When in your life have you received good advice and when have you received poor advice?

 Read Esther 3.

---

3 After these events, King Xerxes honored Haman son of Hammedatha, the Agagite, elevating him and giving him a seat of honor higher than that of all the other nobles. ²All the royal officials at the king's gate knelt down and paid honor to Haman, for the king had commanded this concerning him. But Mordecai would not kneel down or pay him honor.

³Then the royal officials at the king's gate asked Mordecai, "Why do you disobey the king's command?" ⁴Day after day they spoke to him but he refused to comply. Therefore they told Haman about it to see whether Mordecai's behavior would be tolerated, for he had told them he was a Jew.

⁵When Haman saw that Mordecai would not kneel down or pay him honor, he was enraged. ⁶Yet having learned who Mordecai's people were, he scorned the idea of killing only Mordecai. Instead Haman looked for a way to destroy all Mordecai's people, the Jews, throughout the whole kingdom of Xerxes.

⁷In the twelfth year of King Xerxes, in the first month, the month of Nisan, they cast the *pur* (that is, the lot) in the presence of Haman to select a day and month. And the lot fell on*ʲ* the twelfth month, the month of Adar.

⁸Then Haman said to King Xerxes, "There is a certain people dispersed and scattered among the peoples in all the provinces of your kingdom whose customs are different from those of all other people and who do not obey the king's laws; it is not in the king's best interest to tolerate

them. ⁹If it pleases the king, let a decree be issued to destroy them, and I will put ten thousand talents*ᵍ* of silver into the royal treasury for the men who carry out this business."

¹⁰So the king took his signet ring from his finger and gave it to Haman son of Hammedatha, the Agagite, the enemy of the Jews. ¹¹"Keep the money," the king said to Haman, "and do with the people as you please."

¹²Then on the thirteenth day of the first month the royal secretaries were summoned. They wrote out in the script of each province and in the language of each people all Haman's orders to the king's satraps, the governors of the various provinces and the nobles of the various peoples. These were written in the name of King Xerxes himself and sealed with his own ring. ¹³Dispatches were sent by couriers to all the king's provinces with the order to destroy, kill and annihilate all the Jews—young and old, women and little children—on a single day, the thirteenth day of the twelfth month, the month of Adar, and to plunder their goods. ¹⁴A copy of the text of the edict was to be issued as law in every province and made known to the people of every nationality so they would be ready for that day.

¹⁵Spurred on by the king's command, the couriers went out, and the edict was issued in the citadel of Susa. The king and Haman sat down to drink, but the city of Susa was bewildered.

ʲ7 Septuagint; Hebrew does not have And the lot fell on. ᵍ9 That is, about 375 tons (about 345 metric tons)

 Discovering the Word 1. List all the words and phrases in this chapter which bring to mind tragedy or conflict. 2. What is the conflict between Haman and Mordecai which causes Haman's intense reaction to Mordecai (vv. 2–6)? 3. How does Haman persuade the king to adopt his plan to destroy the Jews (vv. 8–9)? 4. In verses 12–14 the words *each*, *every* and *all* are repeated frequently. What might the author have been trying to communicate in this detailed description of the edict? 5. This chapter gives us even more detail about who King Xerxes was. What do we learn about him?

Applying the Word 1. How might you guard against giving unwise advice? 2. What are some ways you can evaluate the advice you receive from others?

Responding in Prayer Pray that you will be given wise counselors who will give you godly advice.

4 / *Esther 4*
Doing the Right Thing

LASZLO TOKES WAS a pastor in Timisoara, Romania, during the reign of the communist regime under Ceausescu. He had dedicated his life to bringing about revival in the church in Romania despite opposition and danger. He risked his life to preach the gospel and stand up against the communist government. Because of his courage and integrity he helped the people to win their freedom. We may never face circumstances like those of Laszlo Tokes, but doing what is right means little things: giving back extra change when a cashier makes a mistake or letting the cable company know about the free service that's been coming in. Whether the stakes are large or small, it takes the same character qualities of courage and moral strength to choose what is right.

 Warming Up to God Recall an instance in your life where obeying God's call meant taking a risk or facing a difficulty. How did you feel? What did you pray?

 Read Esther 4.

When Mordecai learned of all that had been done, he tore his clothes, put on sackcloth and ashes, and went out into the city, wailing loudly and bitterly. ²But he went only as far as the king's gate, because no one clothed in sackcloth was allowed to enter it. ³In every province to which the edict and order of the king came, there was great mourning among the Jews, with fasting, weeping and wailing. Many lay in sackcloth and ashes.

⁴When Esther's maids and eunuchs came and told her about Mordecai, she was in great distress. She sent clothes for him to put on instead of his sackcloth, but he would not accept them. ⁵Then Esther summoned Hathach, one of the king's eunuchs assigned to attend her, and ordered him to find out what was troubling Mordecai and why.

⁶So Hathach went out to Mordecai in the open square of the city in front of the king's gate. ⁷Mordecai told him everything that had happened to him, including the exact amount of money Haman had promised to pay into the royal treasury for the destruction of the Jews. ⁸He also gave him a copy of the text of the edict for their annihilation, which had been published in Susa, to show to Esther and explain it to her, and he told him to

urge her to go into the king's presence to beg for mercy and plead with him for her people.

⁹Hathach went back and reported to Esther what Mordecai had said. ¹⁰Then she instructed him to say to Mordecai, ¹¹"All the king's officials and the people of the royal provinces know that for any man or woman who approaches the king in the inner court without being summoned the king has but one law: that he be put to death. The only exception to this is for the king to extend the gold scepter to him and spare his life. But thirty days have passed since I was called to go to the king."

¹²When Esther's words were reported to Mordecai, ¹³he sent back this answer: "Do not think that because you are in the king's house you alone of all the Jews will escape. ¹⁴For if you remain silent at this time, relief and deliverance for the Jews will arise from another place, but you and your father's family will perish. And who knows but that you have come to royal position for such a time as this?"

¹⁵Then Esther sent this reply to Mordecai: ¹⁶"Go, gather together all the Jews who are in Susa, and fast for me. Do not eat or drink for three days, night or day. I and my maids will fast as you do. When this is done, I will go to the

king, even though it is against the law. And if I perish, I perish."

¹⁷So Mordecai went away and carried out all of Esther's instructions.

 Discovering the Word 1. Describe the response of Mordecai and the Jews to Haman's plot (vv. 1–3). 2. Why do you think Mordecai was so confident in his plan to stop the annihilation of the Jews (vv. 6–8)? 3. What is Esther's first reaction to Mordecai's request that she go to the king (vv. 9–11)? 4. How do Mordecai's arguments in verses 12–14 persuade Esther to go to the king? 5. In this chapter how do we see God's sovereignty and people's responses working together? 6. What character qualities does Esther show in her response to Mordecai's second message?

Applying the Word 1. Think of a present context in which God has placed you to do his will. What risks do you face in doing the right thing in this context? 2. What character qualities must you exhibit in order to do the right thing?

Responding in Prayer Pray that doing the right thing will be more than a slogan for you—that it will be a way of life.

---

5 / *Esther 5*
The Heart of the Matter

MY SCHOOLTEACHER HUSBAND came home one day from work with an unpleasant note from a parent. The note expressed anger and concern over his performance as a teacher. In the face of a situation that could have led my husband to bitterness I watched him respond with courage, compassion and humility as he made an appointment to meet with the parent the next day. Because of his response, the misunderstanding was clarified and the relationship was reconciled.

Our character comes through especially in times where we are facing a difficult task or situations or people that anger us. Our response to these kinds of occurrences in our life tells a great deal about our character. Do we face them with courage and humility or with anger, bitterness and pride? In their contrasting responses Esther and Haman show the condition of their hearts.

 Warming Up to God What example comes to mind when you think of a person acting with courage or humility?

 Read Esther 5.

---

5 On the third day Esther put on her royal robes and stood in the inner court of the palace, in front of the king's hall. The king was sitting on his royal throne in the hall, facing the entrance. ²When he saw Queen Esther standing in the court, he was pleased with her and held out to her the gold scepter that was in his hand. So Esther approached and touched the tip of the scepter.

³Then the king asked, "What is it, Queen Esther? What is your request? Even up to half the kingdom, it will be given you."

⁴"If it pleases the king," replied Esther, "let the king, together with Haman, come today to a banquet I have prepared for him."

⁵"Bring Haman at once," the king said, "so that we may do what Esther asks."

So the king and Haman went to the banquet Esther had prepared. ⁶As they were drinking wine, the king again asked Esther, "Now what is your petition? It will be given you. And what is your request? Even up to half the kingdom, it will be granted."

⁷Esther replied, "My petition and my request is this: ⁸If the king regards me with favor and if it pleases the king to grant my petition and fulfill my request, let the king and Haman come tomorrow to the banquet I will prepare for them. Then I will answer the king's question."

⁹Haman went out that day happy and in high spirits. But when he saw Mordecai at the king's gate and observed that he neither rose nor showed fear in his presence, he was filled with rage against Mordecai. ¹⁰Nevertheless, Haman restrained himself and went home.

Calling together his friends and Zeresh, his wife, ¹¹Haman boasted to them about his vast wealth, his many sons, and all the ways the king had honored him and how he had elevated him above the other nobles and officials. ¹²"And that's not all," Haman added. "I'm the only person Queen Esther invited to accompany the king to the banquet she gave. And she has invited me along with the king tomorrow. ¹³But all this gives me no satisfaction as long as I see that Jew Mordecai sitting at the king's gate."

¹⁴His wife Zeresh and all his friends said to him, "Have a gallows built, seventy-five feet[h] high, and ask the king in the morning to have Mordecai hanged on it. Then go with the king to the dinner and be happy." This suggestion delighted Haman, and he had the gallows built.

ʰ14 Hebrew *fifty cubits* (about 23 meters)

Discovering the Word   1. What risks does Esther take in verses 1–8?   2. The second time the king asks Esther to make her request known, she answers him. What do her words reveal about her character (vv. 7–8)?   3. What characteristics do we see in Haman (vv. 9–14)?   4. Haman boasts about having everything: sons, wealth, position and recognition. Why do you think Haman is still so consumed with Mordecai?   5. How does the passage contrast Esther's character and Haman's character?

Applying the Word   1. Where in your own life do you see the qualities of Esther, and where do you see the qualities of Haman?   2. In what current situation can you try to respond with the courage and humility of Esther?   3. Esther 4:15–16 tells us how Esther was supported by the Jewish people. How could the support of other believers be helpful to you in the midst of a trial you are going through now?

Responding in Prayer   Pray that God will be molding you into a person of character who responds out of humility rather than pride.

6 / *Esther 6*
Recognizing Unrighteousness

WHEN I TAKE an honest look at myself, I see many ugly spots that mar my character. One of the ugliest traits is my desire to make myself look better than others. This ungodly character trait seeps into my relationships and damages intimacy. For each of us there are things about our character which are displeasing to God; perhaps it is pride or arrogance, selfish ambition or manipulation. Because we let those things grow in our lives rather than allowing God to remove them, we experience various consequences of our unrighteousness.

Warming Up to God   What is one aspect of your character you would like to be more Christlike? Take time to talk openly with God about how you want to change.

Read Esther 6.

6 That night the king could not sleep; so he ordered the book of the chronicles, the record of his reign, to be brought in and read to him. ²It was found recorded there that Mordecai had exposed Bigthana and Teresh, two of the king's officers who guarded the doorway, who had conspired to assassinate King Xerxes.

³"What honor and recognition has Mordecai received for this?" the king asked.

"Nothing has been done for him," his attendants answered.

⁴The king said, "Who is in the court?" Now Haman had just entered the outer court of the palace to speak to the king about hanging Mordecai on the gallows he had erected for him.

⁵His attendants answered, "Haman is standing in the court."

"Bring him in," the king ordered.

⁶When Haman entered, the king asked him, "What should be done for the man the king delights to honor?"

Now Haman thought to himself, "Who is there that the king would rather honor than me?" ⁷So he answered the king, "For the man the king delights to honor, ⁸have them bring a royal robe the king has worn and a horse the king has ridden, one with a royal crest placed on its head. ⁹Then let the robe and horse be entrusted to one of the king's most noble princes. Let them robe the man the king delights to honor, and lead him on the horse through the city streets, proclaiming before him, 'This is what is done for the man the king delights to honor!' "

¹⁰"Go at once," the king commanded Haman. "Get the robe and the horse and do just as you have suggested for Mordecai the Jew, who sits at the king's gate. Do not neglect anything you have recommended."

¹¹So Haman got the robe and the horse. He robed Mordecai, and led him on horseback through the city streets, proclaiming before him, "This is what is done for the man the king delights to honor!"

¹²Afterward Mordecai returned to the king's gate. But Haman rushed home, with his head covered in grief, ¹³and told Zeresh his wife and all his friends everything that had happened to him.

His advisers and his wife Zeresh said to him, "Since Mordecai, before whom your downfall has started, is of Jewish origin, you cannot stand against him—you will surely come to ruin!" ¹⁴While they were still talking with him, the king's eunuchs arrived and hurried Haman away to the banquet Esther had prepared.

Discovering the Word 1. How does the king respond to discovering Mordecai's role in thwarting the assassination plot (vv. 2–6)? 2. Where do you see irony in King Xerxes' and Haman's actions on this particular night (vv. 1–6 and 5:14)? 3. What else can we discern about Haman's character through his response to the king's question in verses 7–9? 4. Haman sought comfort from his wife and friends after his ride through the city with Mordecai, but he receives a very different response. How do his wife and advisors interpret the situation and react to Haman (vv. 12–14)? Why? 5. How has the ungodliness in Haman's character led to his humiliation?

Applying the Word 1. Think back to the characteristic in your life which is not always Christlike. What might be (or have been) some negative consequences of this trait? 2. What is one thing that you can do this week, with God's help, to reform your character?

Responding in Prayer Offer your praise to Jesus Christ for what you have learned about yourself through this study. Ask him for the help you need to become more like him.

---

7 / *Esther 7*
Character No Matter What

This is what the wicked are like—
always carefree, they increase in wealth.
Surely in vain have I kept my heart pure;
in vain have I washed my hands in innocence. (Ps 73:12–13)

THE PSALMIST IS wrestling with the fact that he does not see justice being carried out; instead, the wicked prosper and the righteous are plagued. In a similar way Esther and Mordecai have chosen to do what is right all along, yet they face destruction. Haman, who is prideful, angry and bitter, has been successful in plotting against the Jews. Finally, in chapter 7 Esther and Mordecai see justice taking place. However, in our lives we do not always see justice when we choose to do what is right. The people of God must have consistent character whether or not justice prevails in this life.

Warming Up to God When does the injustice of the world most weigh on your mind and heart?

Read Esther 7.

7 So the king and Haman went to dine with Queen Esther, ²and as they were drinking wine on that second day, the king again asked, "Queen Esther, what is your petition? It will be given you. What is your request? Even up to half the kingdom, it will be granted."

³Then Queen Esther answered, "If I have found favor with you, O king, and if it pleases your majesty, grant me my life—this is my petition. And spare my people—this is my request. ⁴For I and my people have been sold for destruction and slaughter and annihilation. If we had merely been sold as male and female slaves, I would have kept quiet, because no such distress would justify disturbing the king.ⁱ"

⁵King Xerxes asked Queen Esther, "Who is he? Where is the man who has dared to do such a thing?"

⁶Esther said, "The adversary and enemy is this vile Haman."

Then Haman was terrified before the king and queen. ⁷The king got up in a rage, left his wine and went out into the palace garden. But Haman, realizing that the king had already decided his fate, stayed behind to beg Queen Esther for his life.

⁸Just as the king returned from the palace garden to the banquet hall, Haman was falling on the couch where Esther was reclining.

The king exclaimed, "Will he even molest the queen while she is with me in the house?"

As soon as the word left the king's mouth, they covered Haman's face. ⁹Then Harbona, one of the eunuchs attending the king, said, "A gallows seventy-five feetʲ high stands by Haman's house. He had it made for Mordecai, who spoke up to help the king."

The king said, "Hang him on it!" ¹⁰So they hanged Haman on the gallows he had prepared for Mordecai. Then the king's fury subsided.

ⁱ4 Or *quiet, but the compensation our adversary offers cannot be compared with the loss the king would suffer*   ʲ9 Hebrew *fifty cubits* (about 23 meters)

 Discovering the Word 1. Name all of the truths that were previously hidden but are now revealed in this chapter. 2. This chapter revolves around Queen Esther, King Xerxes and Haman. What might each of them be feeling at the beginning of the banquet? 3. What thoughts and emotions might the king and Haman have experienced when Esther presented her request (vv. 6–7)? 4. How do you see justice carried out in the lives of Esther, Mordecai and Haman?

Applying the Word 1. As Christians, when should we expect to see justice served and when should we be satisfied with doing what is right? Give examples from your experience. 2. How can you seek justice in a situation where you currently see injustice? 3. How will you respond if justice is not served?

Responding in Prayer Justice begins with prayer. Ask God to show you how he would like to use you in the pursuit of justice.

---

8 / *Esther 8*
Praising God's Faithfulness

AS THE SUNSHINE filtered through the sanctuary windows, the pastor stood and asked for the congregation to tell how God had been faithful. One by one the people rose to their feet and spoke. There were testimonies about marriages restored, physical healings, new passion for service, children coming to Christ and spiritual growth. I listened with a joyful heart; certainly God was faithful!

The book of Esther shows that God brings justice in his time and in his way. But one thing remains certain: God is faithful. From overwhelming opposition to the smallest concern, God provides for us. In this chapter God provides not only for Esther and Mordecai, but for all of his people, and they respond with rejoicing and celebrating. Our response to God should be no different.

Warming Up to God Recall in detail a time when God has proven himself faithful to you in a difficult situation. Thank God for all the ways he helped you.

Read Esther 8.

8 That same day King Xerxes gave Queen Esther the estate of Haman, the enemy of the Jews. And Mordecai came into the presence of the king, for Esther had told how he was related to her. ²The king took off his signet ring, which he had reclaimed from Haman, and presented it to Mordecai. And Esther appointed him over Haman's estate.

³Esther again pleaded with the king, falling at his feet and weeping. She begged him to put an end to the evil plan of Haman the Agagite, which he had devised against the Jews. ⁴Then the king extended the gold scepter to Esther and she arose and stood before him.

⁵"If it pleases the king," she said, "and if he regards me with favor and thinks it the right thing to do, and if he is pleased with me, let an order be written overruling the dispatches that Haman son of Hammedatha, the Agagite, devised and wrote to destroy the Jews in all the king's provinces. ⁶For how can I bear to see disaster fall on my people? How can I bear to see the destruction of my family?"

⁷King Xerxes replied to Queen Esther and to Mordecai the Jew, "Because Haman attacked the Jews, I have given his estate to Esther, and they have hanged him on the gallows. ⁸Now write another decree in the king's name in behalf of the Jews as seems best to you, and seal it with the king's signet ring—for no document written in the king's name and sealed with his ring can be revoked."

⁹At once the royal secretaries were summoned—on the twenty-third day of the third month, the month of Sivan. They wrote out all Mordecai's orders to the Jews, and to the satraps, governors and nobles of the 127 provinces stretching from India to Cush.ᵏ These orders were written in the script of each province and the language of each people and also to the Jews in their own script and language. ¹⁰Mordecai wrote in the name of King Xerxes, sealed the dispatches with the king's signet ring, and sent them by mounted couriers, who rode fast horses especially bred for the king.

¹¹The king's edict granted the Jews in every city the right to assemble and protect themselves; to destroy, kill and annihilate any armed force of any nationality or province that might attack them and their women and children; and to plunder the property of their enemies. ¹²The day appointed for the Jews to do this in all the provinces of King Xerxes was the thirteenth day of the twelfth month, the month of Adar. ¹³A copy of the text of the edict was to be issued as law in every province and made known to the people of every nationality so that the Jews would be ready on that day to avenge themselves on their enemies.

¹⁴The couriers, riding the royal horses, raced out, spurred on by the king's command. And the edict was also issued in the citadel of Susa.

¹⁵Mordecai left the king's presence wearing royal garments of blue and white, a large crown of gold and a purple robe of fine linen. And the city of Susa held a joyous celebration. ¹⁶For the Jews it was a time of happiness and joy, gladness and honor. ¹⁷In every province and in every city, wherever the edict of the king went, there was joy and gladness among the Jews, with feasting and celebrating. And many people of other nationalities became Jews because fear of the Jews had seized them.

ᵏ9 That is, the upper Nile region

Discovering the Word 1. List all the ways in this chapter that Esther and Mordecai are rewarded by God through the actions of the king. 2. In verses 3–6 we see a little of Esther's heart. How does she feel toward her people? 3. How does King Xerxes respond to Esther's plea (vv. 7–10)? 4. God provides for the Jews through the edict Mordecai issued in the king's name. How did the edict (vv. 11–13) provide what Esther was asking for in verses 5–6 without breaking the first edict (3:12–14)? 5. Describe the response of the Jews to God's provision and protection (vv. 15–17).

Applying the Word 1. Esther felt deep concern and compassion for her people. For what person or group of people would you like to have that same kind of concern? 2. How might you develop your compassion for them? 3. How can we be faithful when we are waiting for God to act in our lives?

Responding in Prayer Think over the past week and share how God has been faithful to you. Express to God your joy and gladness about his provision for you.

9 / *Esther 9—10*
Remembering and Celebrating

IT WAS A beautiful spring day and I was walking along a dirt road that wound through the mountains outside Bear Trap Ranch in Colorado. I was pouring out my heart to God and wrestling with where he wanted to take me in my life. As I strolled among the pine trees, God opened my eyes to the abundant life that lay before me if I would commit my future to his service. It was that moment that changed the course of my life, and I am eternally grateful to the Lord. Every time I visit Bear Trap Ranch I walk along that very road and remember that moment and God's faithfulness to me. Celebrating God's goodness helps me keep my perspective and empowers me to go on in my commitment to his service.

 Warming Up to God What is something you or your family commemorated, and how was it celebrated?

 Read Esther 9—10.

9 On the thirteenth day of the twelfth month, the month of Adar, the edict commanded by the king was to be carried out. On this day the enemies of the Jews had hoped to overpower them, but now the tables were turned and the Jews got the upper hand over those who hated them. ²The Jews assembled in their cities in all the provinces of King Xerxes to attack those seeking their destruction. No one could stand against them, because the people of all the other nationalities were afraid of them. ³And all the nobles of the provinces, the satraps, the governors and the king's administrators helped the Jews, because fear of Mordecai had seized them. ⁴Mordecai was prominent in the palace; his reputation spread throughout the provinces, and he became more and more powerful.

⁵The Jews struck down all their enemies with the sword, killing and destroying them, and they did what they pleased to those who hated them. ⁶In the citadel of Susa, the Jews killed and destroyed five hundred men. ⁷They also killed Parshandatha, Dalphon, Aspatha, ⁸Poratha, Adalia, Aridatha, ⁹Parmashta, Arisai, Aridai and Vaizatha, ¹⁰the ten sons of Haman son of Hammedatha, the enemy of the Jews. But they did not lay their hands on the plunder.

¹¹The number of those slain in the citadel of Susa was reported to the king that same day. ¹²The king said to Queen Esther, "The Jews have killed and destroyed five hundred men and the ten sons of Haman in the citadel of Susa. What have they done in the rest of the king's provinces? Now what is your petition? It will be given you. What is your request? It will also be granted."

¹³"If it pleases the king," Esther answered, "give the Jews in Susa permission to carry out this day's edict tomorrow also, and let Haman's ten sons be hanged on gallows."

¹⁴So the king commanded that this be done. An edict was issued in Susa, and they hanged the ten sons of Haman. ¹⁵The Jews in Susa came together on the fourteenth day of the month of Adar, and they put to death in Susa three hundred men, but they did not lay their hands on the plunder.

¹⁶Meanwhile, the remainder of the Jews who were in the king's provinces also assembled to protect themselves and get relief from their enemies. They killed seventy-five thousand of them but did not lay their hands on the plunder. ¹⁷This happened on the thirteenth day of the month of Adar, and on the fourteenth they rested and made it a day of feasting and joy.

¹⁸The Jews in Susa, however, had assembled on the thirteenth and fourteenth, and then on the fifteenth they rested and made it a day of feasting and joy.

¹⁹That is why rural Jews—those living in villages—observe the fourteenth of the month of

Adar as a day of joy and feasting, a day for giving presents to each other.

²⁰Mordecai recorded these events, and he sent letters to all the Jews throughout the provinces of King Xerxes, near and far, ²¹to have them celebrate annually the fourteenth and fifteenth days of the month of Adar ²²as the time when the Jews got relief from their enemies, and as the month when their sorrow was turned into joy and their mourning into a day of celebration. He wrote them to observe the days as days of feasting and joy and giving presents of food to one another and gifts to the poor.

²³So the Jews agreed to continue the celebration they had begun, doing what Mordecai had written to them. ²⁴For Haman son of Hammedatha, the Agagite, the enemy of all the Jews, had plotted against the Jews to destroy them and had cast the *pur* (that is, the lot) for their ruin and destruction. ²⁵But when the plot came to the king's attention,¹ he issued written orders that the evil scheme Haman had devised against the Jews should come back onto his own head, and that he and his sons should be hanged on the gallows. ²⁶(Therefore these days were called Purim, from the word *pur*.) Because of everything written in this letter and because of what they had seen and what had happened to them, ²⁷the Jews took it upon themselves to establish the custom that they and their descendants and all who join them should without fail observe these two days every year, in the way prescribed and at the time appointed. ²⁸These days should be remembered

and observed in every generation by every family, and in every province and in every city. And these days of Purim should never cease to be celebrated by the Jews, nor should the memory of them die out among their descendants.

²⁹So Queen Esther, daughter of Abihail, along with Mordecai the Jew, wrote with full authority to confirm this second letter concerning Purim. ³⁰And Mordecai sent letters to all the Jews in the 127 provinces of the kingdom of Xerxes—words of goodwill and assurance— ³¹to establish these days of Purim at their designated times, as Mordecai the Jew and Queen Esther had decreed for them, and as they had established for themselves and their descendants in regard to their times of fasting and lamentation. ³²Esther's decree confirmed these regulations about Purim, and it was written down in the records.

10

King Xerxes imposed tribute throughout the empire, to its distant shores. ²And all his acts of power and might, together with a full account of the greatness of Mordecai to which the king had raised him, are they not written in the book of the annals of the kings of Media and Persia? ³Mordecai the Jew was second in rank to King Xerxes, preeminent among the Jews, and held in high esteem by his many fellow Jews, because he worked for the good of his people and spoke up for the welfare of all the Jews.

¹25 Or *when Esther came before the king*

 Discovering the Word 1. Summarize the events of the thirteenth, fourteenth and fifteenth days of Adar. 2. Describe the people that the Jews actually destroyed on these days in the month of Adar (9:5–17). 3. The author mentions three separate times that the Jews did not lay their hands on their enemies' plunder. Why might the Jews have left the plunder despite the king's permission to take it (9:10, 15–16)? 4. Mordecai and Esther proclaimed and established the celebration of Purim as a holiday for all the Jews. What was the purpose of the celebration (9:20–27)? 5. God has saved his people and blessed Esther and Mordecai for their obedience to him. Summarize what happens to Esther and Mordecai at the end of the story (9:29—10:3).

Applying the Word 1. Throughout Scripture God instructs his people to commemorate the times when he acted to provide and save his people. Why is remembering God's acts of faithfulness important for us as Christians? 2. What is one thing that God has done for you that you would truly like to remember? 3. What are some ways you could celebrate it?

Responding in Prayer Begin your tradition of celebrating right now by offering your praise and thanksgiving to God.

Job

One thing we can count on in this life is *trouble!* Becoming a Christian, contrary to what some say, does not so much deliver us from problems as delivers us *in* them. We still get sick, lose jobs, worry about our children and struggle with loneliness. On a deeper level a personal encounter with God brings at the same time exquisite joy and a new set of questions. Sometimes, like Job, we are led through a dark valley without seeing the path out, why we are suffering, whether God has a redeeming purpose in it all and how we are to respond. Are we to just patiently take it all?

Mention the name *Job* and one immediately thinks of patience, partly because of one misunderstood New Testament reference to this Old Testament saint (Jas 5:11). Job did suffer, but not patiently. He rebelled.

Job's saintly friends tried to "explain" his problems by appealing to the logic of good orthodox theology. In the end, Job's almost irreverent appeal to God for an explanation led to his justification and approval by God. While Job's orthodox friends were rejected (Job 42:7), he persevered; that is the real point of the New Testament reference. Perhaps among other things, this surprising reversal can be explained by the fact that Job spoke *to* God about his suffering while Job's friends spoke *about* God to Job. But this is not the only mystery encompassed by this fascinating Old Testament book.

Job raises as many questions as it answers. Indeed, when God finally speaks to Job in the whirlwind (chapters 38—41), God himself asks questions! Traditionally theology has wrestled with how a good and all-powerful God could at the same time allow or even *cause* (as Job claims) suffering and evil in the world. But the usual abstract arguments, spoken smoothly by Job's three friends—Eliphaz, Bildad and Zophar—are not only rejected by God and his beloved Job, they are not even the point of the book.

This is not a book of rational, systematic theology. This is the story of one human being—one very human and very righteous being—who loses his possessions, his family and his health. But it is a story that takes place within the household of faith. And it is faith that rebels and a God who loves the rebel that is the surprise of the story.

Job—and we—have problems with innocent suffering precisely because we have faith in God, whose goodness is known in the land of the living. There is no answer either in jettisoning belief in the goodness of God or in rejecting the hope that *in this life* there should be both satisfaction and justice. In the end, *and only in the end,* Job finds peace with God through his sufferings and not in spite of them. Ultimately, Job's passion points to the death, resurrection and vindication of Jesus as God's final answer to the problem of the innocent suffering.

The gospel-bearing quality of Job is all the more remarkable because the book may be very ancient. There is no mention of temple, monarchy or prophets. We do not know who wrote the book, when or where the author lived, though there is no adequate reason to deny the unity of the book. For date, authorship and textual questions read Francis I. Anderson, *Job,* Tyndale Old Testament Commentaries (Downers Grove, Ill.: InterVarsity Press, 1976), pages 15–76.

The book contains an astonishing mixture of riddles, hymns, curses, proverbs and nature poems. The introduction (1:1—2:13) and conclusion (42:7–17) are in prose, while the speeches of Job, the three friends, the young man Elihu and God himself (3:1—42:6) are in poetry. No wonder the Jewish rabbis were unsure where to place Job in Scripture. Though they eventually chose the Writings section, this book fits just as well alongside the great exodus, David and Ruth.

Like all biblical stories, this one catches us in its plot and invites us in its mysterious and ironic way to find God not in talking *about* God, but in talking *to* him at the point of our deepest questions about the meaning of life and of God himself, not in leisure-time spirituality, but in the middle of life where it is hardest. According to the *New Bible Commentary,* "The book takes its place in the testimony of the ages that there is a blank in the human heart which Jesus alone can fill."

Outline

1/ Job 1:1—2:10 ———————————————— *Dueling with the Devil*

2/ Job 2:11—4:17 ———————————————— *God in the Dark*

3/ Job 6 ———————————————— *God-Talk*

4/ Job 9—10 ———————————————— *If God Were Only Human!*

5/ Job 13—14 ———————————————— *The Faith That Rebels*

6/ Job 16—17 ———————————————— *Our Heavenly Guarantor*

7/ Job 20—21 ———————————————— *The Problem of Pain*

8/ Job 23 ———————————————— *The Silence of God*

9/ Job 35 ———————————————— *Songs in the Night*

10/ Job 38 ———————————————— *God in the Storm*

11/ Job 40 ———————————————— *The Joy of Repentance*

12/ Job 42 ———————————————— *Is Faith Always Worthwhile?*

1 / *Job 1:1—2:10*
Dueling with the Devil

IS IT POSSIBLE to love God for God's sake, and not merely for the benefits of being faithful, even when there *are* benefits? And what if these benefits are all removed and one is left with no benefit but God alone? This is the question Satan poses to God regarding his faithful servant, Job.

 Warming Up to God How would you respond to someone who charges that religion is only for those who can't make it on their own?

 Read Job 1:1—2:10.

---

1 In the land of Uz there lived a man whose name was Job. This man was blameless and upright; he feared God and shunned evil. ²He had seven sons and three daughters, ³and he owned seven thousand sheep, three thousand camels, five hundred yoke of oxen and five hundred donkeys, and had a large number of servants. He was the greatest man among all the people of the East.

⁴His sons used to take turns holding feasts in their homes, and they would invite their three sisters to eat and drink with them. ⁵When a period of feasting had run its course, Job would send and have them purified. Early in the morning he would sacrifice a burnt offering for each of them, thinking, "Perhaps my children have sinned and cursed God in their hearts." This was Job's regular custom.

⁶One day the angels*ª* came to present themselves before the LORD, and Satan*ᵇ* also came with them. ⁷The LORD said to Satan, "Where have you come from?"

Satan answered the LORD, "From roaming through the earth and going back and forth in it."

⁸Then the LORD said to Satan, "Have you considered my servant Job? There is no one on earth like him; he is blameless and upright, a man who fears God and shuns evil."

⁹"Does Job fear God for nothing?" Satan replied. ¹⁰"Have you not put a hedge around him and his household and everything he has? You have blessed the work of his hands, so that his flocks and herds are spread throughout the land. ¹¹But stretch out your hand and strike everything he has, and he will surely curse you to your face."

¹²The LORD said to Satan, "Very well, then, everything he has is in your hands, but on the man himself do not lay a finger."

Then Satan went out from the presence of the LORD.

¹³One day when Job's sons and daughters were feasting and drinking wine at the oldest brother's house, ¹⁴a messenger came to Job and said, "The oxen were plowing and the donkeys were grazing nearby, ¹⁵and the Sabeans attacked and carried them off. They put the servants to the sword, and I am the only one who has escaped to tell you!"

¹⁶While he was still speaking, another messenger came and said, "The fire of God fell from the sky and burned up the sheep and the servants, and I am the only one who has escaped to tell you!"

¹⁷While he was still speaking, another messenger came and said, "The Chaldeans formed three raiding parties and swept down on your camels and carried them off. They put the servants to the sword, and I am the only one who has escaped to tell you!"

¹⁸While he was still speaking, yet another messenger came and said, "Your sons and daughters were feasting and drinking wine at the oldest brother's house, ¹⁹when suddenly a mighty wind swept in from the desert and struck the four corners of the house. It collapsed on them and they are dead, and I am the only one who has escaped to tell you!"

²⁰At this, Job got up and tore his robe and shaved his head. Then he fell to the ground in worship ²¹and said:

"Naked I came from my mother's womb,
    and naked I will depart.*ᶜ*
The LORD gave and the LORD has taken away;
    may the name of the LORD be praised."

ª6 Hebrew the sons of God   ᵇ6 Satan means accuser.   ᶜ21 Or will return there

²²In all this, Job did not sin by charging God with wrongdoing.

2 On another day the angels*d* came to present themselves before the LORD, and Satan also came with them to present himself before him. ²And the LORD said to Satan, "Where have you come from?"

Satan answered the LORD, "From roaming through the earth and going back and forth in it."

³Then the LORD said to Satan, "Have you considered my servant Job? There is no one on earth like him; he is blameless and upright, a man who fears God and shuns evil. And he still maintains his integrity, though you incited me against him to ruin him without any reason."

⁴"Skin for skin!" Satan replied. "A man will give all he has for his own life. ⁵But stretch out your hand and strike his flesh and bones, and he will surely curse you to your face."

⁶The LORD said to Satan, "Very well, then, he is in your hands; but you must spare his life."

⁷So Satan went out from the presence of the LORD and afflicted Job with painful sores from the soles of his feet to the top of his head. ⁸Then Job took a piece of broken pottery and scraped himself with it as he sat among the ashes.

⁹His wife said to him, "Are you still holding on to your integrity? Curse God and die!"

¹⁰He replied, "You are talking like a foolish*e* woman. Shall we accept good from God, and not trouble?"

In all this, Job did not sin in what he said.

d1 Hebrew *the sons of God*   *e10* The Hebrew word rendered *foolish* denotes moral deficiency.

 Discovering the Word 1. What indications are there that Job's righteousness was not directly related to his being blessed with material prosperity (1:1–8)? 2. In this very ancient document Satan appears as an angelic adversary with free access to God's presence, unlike the devil in the New Testament. What does Satan accuse Job of (1:9–11)? 3. For what good reasons could God agree to a contest that would affect Job and his family so painfully? 4. How does Job react to the first test (1:20–22)? 5. Why do you think God agreed to the second test (2:1–6)? 6. Why would the suggestion Job's wife made be especially dangerous to Job's faith (2:9–10)?

Applying the Word 1. Suffering is a mystery, and the opening scenes of this book deepen the mystery by showing how inadequate are our "reasons" for misfortune. What have you already learned about accepting trouble from God (2:10)? 2. What difference will this make to your own attitude toward hard times?

Responding in Prayer This passage may have raised some difficult questions and feelings for you. Talk openly with God about your response to what you have read.

---

2 / *Job 2:11—4:17*
God in the Dark

FOR EVERY TEN people that can withstand the temptations of adversity, only one can stand prosperity—or so it is said. It was different with our Old Testament hero. Job has handled his prosperity as a ministry, and later defends his stewardship of abundance (29:7–25; 31:24–25). But now he is plunged into excruciating loss, a living death. This new test will examine whether his belief in the goodness of God can be subverted by hopelessly negative circumstances. Job will ask the questions that we asked when life is hardest.

 Warming Up to God When have you been tempted to doubt God's goodness? What questions did you ask? What thoughts, if any, did you have of God?

 Read Job 2:11—4:17.

---

¹¹When Job's three friends, Eliphaz the Temanite, Bildad the Shuhite and Zophar the Naamathite, heard about all the troubles that had come upon him, they set out from their homes and met together by agreement to go and sympathize with him and comfort him. ¹²When they saw him from

a distance, they could hardly recognize him; they began to weep aloud, and they tore their robes and sprinkled dust on their heads. ¹³Then they sat on the ground with him for seven days and seven nights. No one said a word to him, because they saw how great his suffering was.

3 After this, Job opened his mouth and cursed the day of his birth. ²He said:

³"May the day of my birth perish,
and the night it was said, 'A boy is born!'
⁴That day—may it turn to darkness;
may God above not care about it;
may no light shine upon it.
⁵May darkness and deep shadowᶠ claim it
once more;
may a cloud settle over it;
may blackness overwhelm its light.
⁶That night—may thick darkness seize it;
may it not be included among the days of
the year
nor be entered in any of the months.
⁷May that night be barren;
may no shout of joy be heard in it.
⁸May those who curse daysᵍ curse that day,
those who are ready to rouse Leviathan.
⁹May its morning stars become dark;
may it wait for daylight in vain
and not see the first rays of dawn,
¹⁰for it did not shut the doors of the womb on
me
to hide trouble from my eyes.

¹¹"Why did I not perish at birth,
and die as I came from the womb?
¹²Why were there knees to receive me
and breasts that I might be nursed?
¹³For now I would be lying down in peace;
I would be asleep and at rest
¹⁴with kings and counselors of the earth,
who built for themselves places now lying
in ruins,
¹⁵with rulers who had gold,
who filled their houses with silver.
¹⁶Or why was I not hidden in the ground like a
stillborn child,
like an infant who never saw the light of
day?
¹⁷There the wicked cease from turmoil,
and there the weary are at rest.
¹⁸Captives also enjoy their ease;
they no longer hear the slave driver's shout.
¹⁹The small and the great are there,

and the slave is freed from his master.

²⁰"Why is light given to those in misery,
and life to the bitter of soul,
²¹to those who long for death that does not
come,
who search for it more than for hidden
treasure,
²²who are filled with gladness
and rejoice when they reach the grave?
²³Why is life given to a man
whose way is hidden,
whom God has hedged in?
²⁴For sighing comes to me instead of food;
my groans pour out like water.
²⁵What I feared has come upon me;
what I dreaded has happened to me.
²⁶I have no peace, no quietness;
I have no rest, but only turmoil."

4 Then Eliphaz the Temanite replied:

²"If someone ventures a word with
you, will you be impatient?
But who can keep from speaking?
³Think how you have instructed many,
how you have strengthened feeble hands.
⁴Your words have supported those who
stumbled;
you have strengthened faltering knees.
⁵But now trouble comes to you, and you are
discouraged;
it strikes you, and you are dismayed.
⁶Should not your piety be your confidence
and your blameless ways your hope?

⁷"Consider now: Who, being innocent, has
ever perished?
Where were the upright ever destroyed?
⁸As I have observed, those who plow evil
and those who sow trouble reap it.
⁹At the breath of God they are destroyed;
at the blast of his anger they perish.
¹⁰The lions may roar and growl,
yet the teeth of the great lions are broken.
¹¹The lion perishes for lack of prey,
and the cubs of the lioness are scattered.

¹²"A word was secretly brought to me,
my ears caught a whisper of it.
¹³Amid disquieting dreams in the night,
when deep sleep falls on men,

ᶠ5 Or and the shadow of death   ᵍ8 Or the sea

¹⁴fear and trembling seized me
and made all my bones shake.
¹⁵A spirit glided past my face,
and the hair on my body stood on end.
¹⁶It stopped,

but I could not tell what it was.
A form stood before my eyes,
and I heard a hushed voice:
¹⁷'Can a mortal be more righteous than God?
Can a man be more pure than his Maker?

Discovering the Word 1. At this point in the story Job's three friends travel a considerable distance to console Job. What actions of the friends indicate they understood how deeply Job was suffering (2:11–13)? 2. From chapters 3 through 31 the story moves from prose to poetry as Job's three friends discuss the meaning of his adversity and where—if anywhere—God was present in the darkness. In what ways does Job's response to his suffering go beyond asking the usual why (3:1–10)? 3. What does Job think God's role is in all this (3:11, 16)? 4. What new questions does Job ask in 3:20–26? 5. Each of Job's three friends makes a speech, with Job responding—a cycle that gets repeated three times in the book. Eliphaz responds cautiously at first and then attacks. Why does Eliphaz think Job is suffering (4:7–11)?

Applying the Word 1. Eliphaz thinks he has God's word (4:12–17). Job only has dark questions. What have you learned so far about finding God in the midst of pain and loss? 2. How do you feel about living with unanswered questions?

Responding in Prayer Initially, Job's friends were good comforters (2:11–13) simply by being there. Pray for someone you know who needs comfort. Ask God to show you what you can offer that person.

Job 4:18—5:27

¹⁸If God places no trust in his servants,
if he charges his angels with error,
¹⁹how much more those who live in houses of
clay,
whose foundations are in the dust,
who are crushed more readily than a moth!
²⁰Between dawn and dusk they are broken to
pieces;
unnoticed, they perish forever.
²¹Are not the cords of their tent pulled up,
so that they die without wisdom?'ʰ

5 "Call if you will, but who will answer
you?
To which of the holy ones will you
turn?
²Resentment kills a fool,
and envy slays the simple.
³I myself have seen a fool taking root,
but suddenly his house was cursed.
⁴His children are far from safety,
crushed in court without a defender.
⁵The hungry consume his harvest,
taking it even from among thorns,
and the thirsty pant after his wealth.
⁶For hardship does not spring from the soil,
nor does trouble sprout from the ground.
⁷Yet man is born to trouble

as surely as sparks fly upward.

⁸"But if it were I, I would appeal to God;
I would lay my cause before him.
⁹He performs wonders that cannot be
fathomed,
miracles that cannot be counted.
¹⁰He bestows rain on the earth;
he sends water upon the countryside.
¹¹The lowly he sets on high,
and those who mourn are lifted to safety.
¹²He thwarts the plans of the crafty,
so that their hands achieve no success.
¹³He catches the wise in their craftiness,
and the schemes of the wily are swept
away.
¹⁴Darkness comes upon them in the daytime;
at noon they grope as in the night.
¹⁵He saves the needy from the sword in their
mouth;
he saves them from the clutches of the
powerful.
¹⁶So the poor have hope,
and injustice shuts its mouth.

¹⁷"Blessed is the man whom God corrects;

ʰ21 Some interpreters end the quotation after verse 17.

so do not despise the discipline of the
  Almighty.[i]
¹⁸For he wounds, but he also binds up;
  he injures, but his hands also heal.
¹⁹From six calamities he will rescue you;
  in seven no harm will befall you.
²⁰In famine he will ransom you from death,
  and in battle from the stroke of the sword.
²¹You will be protected from the lash of the
  tongue,
  and need not fear when destruction comes.
²²You will laugh at destruction and famine,
  and need not fear the beasts of the earth.
²³For you will have a covenant with the stones
  of the field,

and the wild animals will be at peace with
  you.
²⁴You will know that your tent is secure;
  you will take stock of your property and
  find nothing missing.
²⁵You will know that your children will be
  many,
  and your descendants like the grass of the
  earth.
²⁶You will come to the grave in full vigor,
  like sheaves gathered in season.
²⁷"We have examined this, and it is true.
  So hear it and apply it to yourself."

ⁱ17 Hebrew *Shaddai*; here and throughout Job

3 / Job 6
God-Talk

"WITH FRIENDS LIKE these, who needs enemies!" might well be Job's heart-cry, and sometimes our own. Even our worst experiences of friendship do not quench our desire for soul friends, people who will walk with us through life's hardest moments and who will point us to God without preaching at us or judging our spirituality. Most of us are lonely, as was our Old Testament hero. "Job's comforters," the cynical title given to Eliphaz, Bildad and Zophar— and later the young man Elihu—didn't help his situation.

 Warming Up to God Reflect on the friend who has been most encouraging in your spiritual journey. Use single words to characterize your relationship with that person.

 Read Job 6.

6 Then Job replied:

²"If only my anguish could be weighed
  and all my misery be placed on the scales!
³It would surely outweigh the sand of the
  seas—
  no wonder my words have been impetuous.
⁴The arrows of the Almighty are in me,
  my spirit drinks in their poison;
  God's terrors are marshaled against me.
⁵Does a wild donkey bray when it has grass,
  or an ox bellow when it has fodder?
⁶Is tasteless food eaten without salt,
  or is there flavor in the white of an egg[j]?
⁷I refuse to touch it;
  such food makes me ill.

⁸"Oh, that I might have my request,
  that God would grant what I hope for,

⁹that God would be willing to crush me,
  to let loose his hand and cut me off!
¹⁰Then I would still have this consolation—
  my joy in unrelenting pain—
  that I had not denied the words of the Holy
  One.

¹¹"What strength do I have, that I should still
  hope?
  What prospects, that I should be patient?
¹²Do I have the strength of stone?
  Is my flesh bronze?
¹³Do I have any power to help myself,
  now that success has been driven from me?

¹⁴"A despairing man should have the devotion
  of his friends,

ʲ6 The meaning of the Hebrew for this phrase is uncertain.

even though he forsakes the fear of the
Almighty.
¹⁵But my brothers are as undependable as
intermittent streams,
as the streams that overflow
¹⁶when darkened by thawing ice
and swollen with melting snow,
¹⁷but that cease to flow in the dry season,
and in the heat vanish from their channels.
¹⁸Caravans turn aside from their routes;
they go up into the wasteland and perish.
¹⁹The caravans of Tema look for water,
the traveling merchants of Sheba look in
hope.
²⁰They are distressed, because they had been
confident;
they arrive there, only to be disappointed.
²¹Now you too have proved to be of no help;
you see something dreadful and are afraid.
²²Have I ever said, 'Give something on my
behalf,
pay a ransom for me from your wealth,

²³deliver me from the hand of the enemy,
ransom me from the clutches of the
ruthless'?

²⁴"Teach me, and I will be quiet;
show me where I have been wrong.
²⁵How painful are honest words!
But what do your arguments prove?
²⁶Do you mean to correct what I say,
and treat the words of a despairing man as
wind?
²⁷You would even cast lots for the fatherless
and barter away your friend.

²⁸"But now be so kind as to look at me.
Would I lie to your face?
²⁹Relent, do not be unjust;
reconsider, for my integrity is at stake.ᵏ
³⁰Is there any wickedness on my lips?
Can my mouth not discern malice?

ᵏ29 Or my righteousness still stands

Discovering the Word 1. Instead of responding to Eliphaz's accusation that his suffering was a result of his sin or his children's sin, Job explores his problem on a deeper level. For what new reason does he want God to end it all (v. 10)? 2. What word pictures does Job use to describe his friends (vv. 15–21)? 3. What reason does Job see underlying his friends' failure to minister to him (v. 21)? 4. What does Job need from his friends in this time of suffering? 5. How could his friends have confidence in Job's integrity (v. 29) even though they have no explanation for his problem except God's discipline?

Applying the Word 1. Look at verse 14. Is it always right to maintain a friendship even if your friend "loses" faith or goes through a period of rebellion? 2. Later Job will comment, "Men at ease have contempt for misfortune" (12:5). What would enable you to be of help to others in the pit of despair even though you are doing fine yourself?

Responding in Prayer Reflect on the friends God has given you, and thank him for their gifts. Ask him to teach you to be a faithful friend.

Job 7—8

7 "Does not man have hard service on
earth?
Are not his days like those of a hired
man?
²Like a slave longing for the evening shadows,
or a hired man waiting eagerly for his
wages,
³so I have been allotted months of futility,
and nights of misery have been assigned to
me.

⁴When I lie down I think, 'How long before I
get up?'
The night drags on, and I toss till dawn.
⁵My body is clothed with worms and scabs,
my skin is broken and festering.

⁶"My days are swifter than a weaver's shuttle,
and they come to an end without hope.
⁷Remember, O God, that my life is but a
breath;

my eyes will never see happiness again.
8The eye that now sees me will see me no
        longer;
    you will look for me, but I will be no
        more.
9As a cloud vanishes and is gone,
    so he who goes down to the grave*l* does
        not return.
10He will never come to his house again;
    his place will know him no more.

11"Therefore I will not keep silent;
    I will speak out in the anguish of my
        spirit,
    I will complain in the bitterness of my
        soul.
12Am I the sea, or the monster of the deep,
    that you put me under guard?
13When I think my bed will comfort me
    and my couch will ease my complaint,
14even then you frighten me with dreams
    and terrify me with visions,
15so that I prefer strangling and death,
    rather than this body of mine.
16I despise my life; I would not live forever.
    Let me alone; my days have no meaning.

17"What is man that you make so much of
        him,
    that you give him so much attention,
18that you examine him every morning
    and test him every moment?
19Will you never look away from me,
    or let me alone even for an instant?
20If I have sinned, what have I done to you,
    O watcher of men?
    Why have you made me your target?
    Have I become a burden to you?*m*
21Why do you not pardon my offenses
    and forgive my sins?
    For I will soon lie down in the dust;
        you will search for me, but I will be no
            more."

8

Then Bildad the Shuhite replied:

2"How long will you say such things?
    Your words are a blustering wind.
3Does God pervert justice?
    Does the Almighty pervert what is right?

4When your children sinned against him,
    he gave them over to the penalty of their
        sin.
5But if you will look to God
    and plead with the Almighty,
6if you are pure and upright,
    even now he will rouse himself on your
        behalf
    and restore you to your rightful place.
7Your beginnings will seem humble,
    so prosperous will your future be.

8"Ask the former generations
    and find out what their fathers learned,
9for we were born only yesterday and know
        nothing,
    and our days on earth are but a shadow.
10Will they not instruct you and tell you?
    Will they not bring forth words from their
        understanding?
11Can papyrus grow tall where there is no
        marsh?
    Can reeds thrive without water?
12While still growing and uncut,
    they wither more quickly than grass.
13Such is the destiny of all who forget God;
    so perishes the hope of the godless.
14What he trusts in is fragile*n*;
    what he relies on is a spider's web.
15He leans on his web, but it gives way;
    he clings to it, but it does not hold.
16He is like a well-watered plant in the
        sunshine,
    spreading its shoots over the garden;
17it entwines its roots around a pile of rocks
    and looks for a place among the stones.
18But when it is torn from its spot,
    that place disowns it and says, 'I never saw
        you.'
19Surely its life withers away,
    and*o* from the soil other plants grow.

20"Surely God does not reject a blameless man
    or strengthen the hands of evildoers.
21He will yet fill your mouth with laughter
    and your lips with shouts of joy.
22Your enemies will be clothed in shame,
    and the tents of the wicked will be no
        more."

---

*l*9 Hebrew *Sheol*   *m*20 A few manuscripts of the Masoretic Text, an
ancient Hebrew scribal tradition and Septuagint; most manuscripts of the
Masoretic Text *I have become a burden to myself.*   *n*14 The meaning
of the Hebrew for this word is uncertain.   *o*19 Or *Surely all the joy it
has / is that*

4 / *Job 9—10*
If God Were Only Human!

WHEN THE BOTTOM falls out of life, we cry, "Where is God when I am hurting? Does he really understand? Can he *do* anything? Does God dwell in heaven unmoved by our cries?" Sometimes the Bible presents the most important truths not in a frontal attack or a prophetic pronouncement, but in a pregnant hint. This passage is a case in point. It takes us one step farther to the edge of the greatest of all discoveries, the gospel itself—that God should become a human being, making himself totally accessible to his own creature.

 Warming Up to God Try to remember your first pictures or impressions of God. Was God distant, close, awesomely different, totally unlike anyone human, or very similar to your earthly father or mother? Explain.

 Read Job 9—10.

9 Then Job replied:

2"Indeed, I know that this is true.
  But how can a mortal be righteous before
    God?
3Though one wished to dispute with him,
  he could not answer him one time out of a
    thousand.
4His wisdom is profound, his power is vast.
  Who has resisted him and come out
    unscathed?
5He moves mountains without their knowing it
  and overturns them in his anger.
6He shakes the earth from its place
  and makes its pillars tremble.
7He speaks to the sun and it does not shine;
  he seals off the light of the stars.
8He alone stretches out the heavens
  and treads on the waves of the sea.
9He is the Maker of the Bear and Orion,
  the Pleiades and the constellations of the
    south.
10He performs wonders that cannot be
    fathomed,
  miracles that cannot be counted.
11When he passes me, I cannot see him;
  when he goes by, I cannot perceive him.
12If he snatches away, who can stop him?
  Who can say to him, 'What are you doing?'
13God does not restrain his anger;
  even the cohorts of Rahab cowered at his
    feet.
14"How then can I dispute with him?
  How can I find words to argue with him?
15Though I were innocent, I could not answer
    him;
  I could only plead with my Judge for
    mercy.

16Even if I summoned him and he responded,
  I do not believe he would give me a
    hearing.
17He would crush me with a storm
  and multiply my wounds for no reason.
18He would not let me regain my breath
  but would overwhelm me with misery.
19If it is a matter of strength, he is mighty!
  And if it is a matter of justice, who will
    summon him[P]?
20Even if I were innocent, my mouth would
    condemn me;
  if I were blameless, it would pronounce me
    guilty.

21"Although I am blameless,
  I have no concern for myself;
  I despise my own life.
22It is all the same; that is why I say,
  'He destroys both the blameless and the
    wicked.'
23When a scourge brings sudden death,
  he mocks the despair of the innocent.
24When a land falls into the hands of the
    wicked,
  he blindfolds its judges.
  If it is not he, then who is it?

25"My days are swifter than a runner;
  they fly away without a glimpse of joy.
26They skim past like boats of papyrus,
  like eagles swooping down on their prey.
27If I say, 'I will forget my complaint,
  I will change my expression, and smile,'
28I still dread all my sufferings,
  for I know you will not hold me innocent.
29Since I am already found guilty,
  why should I struggle in vain?

P19 See Septuagint; Hebrew me.

30Even if I washed myself with soap[q]
and my hands with washing soda,
31you would plunge me into a slime pit
so that even my clothes would detest me.

32"He is not a man like me that I might answer
him,
that we might confront each other in court.
33If only there were someone to arbitrate
between us,
to lay his hand upon us both,
34someone to remove God's rod from me,
so that his terror would frighten me no
more.
35Then I would speak up without fear of him,
but as it now stands with me, I cannot.

10

"I loathe my very life;
therefore I will give free rein to
my complaint
and speak out in the bitterness of my soul.
2I will say to God: Do not condemn me,
but tell me what charges you have against
me.
3Does it please you to oppress me,
to spurn the work of your hands,
while you smile on the schemes of the
wicked?
4Do you have eyes of flesh?
Do you see as a mortal sees?
5Are your days like those of a mortal
or your years like those of a man,
6that you must search out my faults
and probe after my sin—
7though you know that I am not guilty
and that no one can rescue me from your
hand?

8"Your hands shaped me and made me.
Will you now turn and destroy me?
9Remember that you molded me like clay.
Will you now turn me to dust again?
10Did you not pour me out like milk

and curdle me like cheese,
11clothe me with skin and flesh
and knit me together with bones and
sinews?
12You gave me life and showed me kindness,
and in your providence watched over my
spirit.

13"But this is what you concealed in your heart,
and I know that this was in your mind:
14If I sinned, you would be watching me
and would not let my offense go
unpunished.
15If I am guilty—woe to me!
Even if I am innocent, I cannot lift my
head,
for I am full of shame
and drowned in[r] my affliction.
16If I hold my head high, you stalk me like a
lion
and again display your awesome power
against me.
17You bring new witnesses against me
and increase your anger toward me;
your forces come against me wave upon
wave.

18"Why then did you bring me out of the womb?
I wish I had died before any eye saw me.
19If only I had never come into being,
or had been carried straight from the womb
to the grave!
20Are not my few days almost over?
Turn away from me so I can have a
moment's joy
21before I go to the place of no return,
to the land of gloom and deep shadow,[s]
22to the land of deepest night,
of deep shadow and disorder,
where even the light is like darkness."

[q]30 Or *snow*   [r]15 Or *and aware of*   [s]21 Or *and the shadow of
death*; also in verse 22

 Discovering the Word 1. Notice that Job's friends talk *about* God, but Job talks *to* God. How does
Job characterize God (9:1–13)? 2. Why does Job feel it is becoming pointless to complain to God
(9:14–20)? 3. Why is it equally pointless to put on a happy face (9:27–31)? 4. What does Job feel is wrong about
his God (9:32–35 and 10:1–7)? 5. In none of his petitions does Job ask for his sickness to be cured. Describe
what it is he wants from God.

 Applying the Word 1. In what ways has Jesus Christ made Job's deepest dream a reality? 2. When
tragedy strikes what difference does it make to know that God has come in the flesh (Jn 1:14)?

Responding in Prayer Follow Job's model and talk *to* God about the concerns on your heart—even if you
are concerned about God's own character.

Job 11—12

11 Then Zophar the Naamathite replied:

2"Are all these words to go unanswered?
  Is this talker to be vindicated?
3Will your idle talk reduce men to silence?
  Will no one rebuke you when you mock?
4You say to God, 'My beliefs are flawless
  and I am pure in your sight.'
5Oh, how I wish that God would speak,
  that he would open his lips against you
6and disclose to you the secrets of wisdom,
  for true wisdom has two sides.
  Know this: God has even forgotten some of
    your sin.

7"Can you fathom the mysteries of God?
  Can you probe the limits of the Almighty?
8They are higher than the heavens—what can
    you do?
  They are deeper than the depths of the
    grave*—what can you know?
9Their measure is longer than the earth
  and wider than the sea.

10"If he comes along and confines you in prison
  and convenes a court, who can oppose
    him?
11Surely he recognizes deceitful men;
  and when he sees evil, does he not take
    note?
12But a witless man can no more become wise
  than a wild donkey's colt can be born a
    man.*

13"Yet if you devote your heart to him
  and stretch out your hands to him,
14if you put away the sin that is in your hand
  and allow no evil to dwell in your tent,
15then you will lift up your face without shame;
  you will stand firm and without fear.
16You will surely forget your trouble,
  recalling it only as waters gone by.
17Life will be brighter than noonday,
  and darkness will become like morning.
18You will be secure, because there is hope;
  you will look about you and take your rest
    in safety.
19You will lie down, with no one to make you
    afraid,

and many will court your favor.
20But the eyes of the wicked will fail,
  and escape will elude them;
  their hope will become a dying gasp."

12 Then Job replied:

2"Doubtless you are the people,
  and wisdom will die with you!
3But I have a mind as well as you;
  I am not inferior to you.
  Who does not know all these things?

4"I have become a laughingstock to my friends,
  though I called upon God and he
    answered—
  a mere laughingstock, though righteous and
    blameless!
5Men at ease have contempt for misfortune
  as the fate of those whose feet are slipping.
6The tents of marauders are undisturbed,
  and those who provoke God are secure—
  those who carry their god in their hands.*

7"But ask the animals, and they will teach you,
  or the birds of the air, and they will tell
    you;
8or speak to the earth, and it will teach you,
  or let the fish of the sea inform you.
9Which of all these does not know
  that the hand of the LORD has done this?
10In his hand is the life of every creature
  and the breath of all mankind.
11Does not the ear test words
  as the tongue tastes food?
12Is not wisdom found among the aged?
  Does not long life bring understanding?

13"To God belong wisdom and power;
  counsel and understanding are his.
14What he tears down cannot be rebuilt;
  the man he imprisons cannot be released.
15If he holds back the waters, there is drought;
  if he lets them loose, they devastate the
    land.
16To him belong strength and victory;
  both deceived and deceiver are his.
17He leads counselors away stripped
  and makes fools of judges.

*8 Hebrew *than Sheol*   *12 Or *wild donkey can be born tame*
*6 Or *secure / in what God's hand brings them*

¹⁸He takes off the shackles put on by kings
    and ties a loincloth^w around their waist.
¹⁹He leads priests away stripped
    and overthrows men long established.
²⁰He silences the lips of trusted advisers
    and takes away the discernment of elders.
²¹He pours contempt on nobles
    and disarms the mighty.
²²He reveals the deep things of darkness
    and brings deep shadows into the light.

²³He makes nations great, and destroys them;
    he enlarges nations, and disperses them.
²⁴He deprives the leaders of the earth of their
        reason;
    he sends them wandering through a
        trackless waste.
²⁵They grope in darkness with no light;
    he makes them stagger like drunkards.

^w 18 Or *shackles of kings / and ties a belt*

5 / *Job 13—14*
The Faith That Rebels

LOSS OF WORK, loss of loved ones, loss of opportunities, excruciating disease and withering judgments from close friends—these are experiences of the faithful. But how should we respond? Simply accept them, fight them or try to ignore them? No. Those who get blessed by God are not those who ask nothing of God but those who will do almost anything to know God. The kingdom is not for the mildly interested but the desperate (Ge 32:26). Jesus said it is for the hungry, the thirsty, the poor (Mt 5:3–6) and the bold (Lk 11:8).

Job is a case in point. He experienced the loss of everything, even the comfort of his best friends. Yet he refuses to accept his friends' explanations, or to accept the absence of God as God's final answer. There is more reverence in Job's "irreverence" than in the friends' deference. This study will show us that faith sometimes requires us to rebel—in the right direction!

 Warming Up to God In what life experiences have you been tempted to "lie down and take it" or give up compliantly?

 Read Job 13—14.

13
"My eyes have seen all this,
    my ears have heard and
    understood it.
²What you know, I also know;
    I am not inferior to you.
³But I desire to speak to the Almighty
    and to argue my case with God.
⁴You, however, smear me with lies;
    you are worthless physicians, all of you!
⁵If only you would be altogether silent!
    For you, that would be wisdom.
⁶Hear now my argument;
    listen to the plea of my lips.
⁷Will you speak wickedly on God's behalf?
    Will you speak deceitfully for him?
⁸Will you show him partiality?
    Will you argue the case for God?
⁹Would it turn out well if he examined you?
    Could you deceive him as you might
        deceive men?

¹⁰He would surely rebuke you
    if you secretly showed partiality.
¹¹Would not his splendor terrify you?
    Would not the dread of him fall on you?
¹²Your maxims are proverbs of ashes;
    your defenses are defenses of clay.

¹³"Keep silent and let me speak;
    then let come to me what may.
¹⁴Why do I put myself in jeopardy
    and take my life in my hands?
¹⁵Though he slay me, yet will I hope in him;
    I will surely^x defend my ways to his face.
¹⁶Indeed, this will turn out for my deliverance,
    for no godless man would dare come before
        him!
¹⁷Listen carefully to my words;
    let your ears take in what I say.
¹⁸Now that I have prepared my case,

^x 15 Or *He will surely slay me; I have no hope — / yet I will*

I know I will be vindicated.
¹⁹Can anyone bring charges against me?
　　If so, I will be silent and die.

²⁰"Only grant me these two things, O God,
　　and then I will not hide from you:
²¹Withdraw your hand far from me,
　　and stop frightening me with your terrors.
²²Then summon me and I will answer,
　　or let me speak, and you reply.
²³How many wrongs and sins have I
　　　committed?
　　Show me my offense and my sin.
²⁴Why do you hide your face
　　and consider me your enemy?
²⁵Will you torment a windblown leaf?
　　Will you chase after dry chaff?
²⁶For you write down bitter things against me
　　and make me inherit the sins of my youth.
²⁷You fasten my feet in shackles;
　　you keep close watch on all my paths
　　by putting marks on the soles of my feet.

²⁸"So man wastes away like something rotten,
　　like a garment eaten by moths.

14

"Man born of woman
is of few days and full of trouble.
²He springs up like a flower and
　withers away;
like a fleeting shadow, he does not endure.
³Do you fix your eye on such a one?
　Will you bring himʸ before you for
　　judgment?
⁴Who can bring what is pure from the impure?
　No one!
⁵Man's days are determined;
　you have decreed the number of his
　　months
and have set limits he cannot exceed.
⁶So look away from him and let him alone,
　till he has put in his time like a hired man.

⁷"At least there is hope for a tree:
　If it is cut down, it will sprout again,
　and its new shoots will not fail.

⁸Its roots may grow old in the ground
　and its stump die in the soil,
⁹yet at the scent of water it will bud
　and put forth shoots like a plant.
¹⁰But man dies and is laid low;
　he breathes his last and is no more.
¹¹As water disappears from the sea
　or a riverbed becomes parched and dry,
¹²so man lies down and does not rise;
　till the heavens are no more, men will not
　　awake
　or be roused from their sleep.

¹³"If only you would hide me in the graveᶻ
　and conceal me till your anger has passed!
　If only you would set me a time
　and then remember me!
¹⁴If a man dies, will he live again?
　All the days of my hard service
　I will wait for my renewalᵃ to come.
¹⁵You will call and I will answer you;
　you will long for the creature your hands
　　have made.
¹⁶Surely then you will count my steps
　but not keep track of my sin.
¹⁷My offenses will be sealed up in a bag;
　you will cover over my sin.

¹⁸"But as a mountain erodes and crumbles
　and as a rock is moved from its place,
¹⁹as water wears away stones
　and torrents wash away the soil,
　so you destroy man's hope.
²⁰You overpower him once for all, and he is
　　gone;
　you change his countenance and send him
　　away.
²¹If his sons are honored, he does not know it;
　if they are brought low, he does not see it.
²²He feels but the pain of his own body
　and mourns only for himself."

ʸ3 Septuagint, Vulgate and Syriac; Hebrew *me* 　ᶻ13 Hebrew *Sheol*
ᵃ14 Or *release*

Discovering the Word　1. The third of Job's friends, Zophar, has delivered his message (chapter 11). Why are the friends worthless physicians (13:4)?　2. Job speaks directly to God in 13:20–28. What does Job request of God (13:20–22)?　3. What makes Job feel hopeless (14:7–12), even though he claims to have hope in God (13:15)?　4. In what ways did Job rebel in the right direction?

Applying the Word　1. If you could speak directly with God, what unanswered questions would you ask?　2. What unfair experiences would you want God to explain?　3. What impact has this quiet time had on your own response to the hardest experiences of life?

Job 15

15

Then Eliphaz the Temanite replied:

2"Would a wise man answer with empty notions
or fill his belly with the hot east wind?
3Would he argue with useless words,
with speeches that have no value?
4But you even undermine piety
and hinder devotion to God.
5Your sin prompts your mouth;
you adopt the tongue of the crafty.
6Your own mouth condemns you, not mine;
your own lips testify against you.

7"Are you the first man ever born?
Were you brought forth before the hills?
8Do you listen in on God's council?
Do you limit wisdom to yourself?
9What do you know that we do not know?
What insights do you have that we do not have?
10The gray-haired and the aged are on our side,
men even older than your father.
11Are God's consolations not enough for you,
words spoken gently to you?
12Why has your heart carried you away,
and why do your eyes flash,
13so that you vent your rage against God
and pour out such words from your mouth?

14"What is man, that he could be pure,
or one born of woman, that he could be righteous?
15If God places no trust in his holy ones,
if even the heavens are not pure in his eyes,
16how much less man, who is vile and corrupt,
who drinks up evil like water!

17"Listen to me and I will explain to you;
let me tell you what I have seen,
18what wise men have declared,
hiding nothing received from their fathers
19(to whom alone the land was given
when no alien passed among them):

20All his days the wicked man suffers torment,
the ruthless through all the years stored up for him.
21Terrifying sounds fill his ears;
when all seems well, marauders attack him.
22He despairs of escaping the darkness;
he is marked for the sword.
23He wanders about—food for vultures[b];
he knows the day of darkness is at hand.
24Distress and anguish fill him with terror;
they overwhelm him, like a king poised to attack,
25because he shakes his fist at God
and vaunts himself against the Almighty,
26defiantly charging against him
with a thick, strong shield.

27"Though his face is covered with fat
and his waist bulges with flesh,
28he will inhabit ruined towns
and houses where no one lives,
houses crumbling to rubble.
29He will no longer be rich and his wealth will not endure,
nor will his possessions spread over the land.
30He will not escape the darkness;
a flame will wither his shoots,
and the breath of God's mouth will carry him away.
31Let him not deceive himself by trusting what is worthless,
for he will get nothing in return.
32Before his time he will be paid in full,
and his branches will not flourish.
33He will be like a vine stripped of its unripe grapes,
like an olive tree shedding its blossoms.
34For the company of the godless will be barren,
and fire will consume the tents of those who love bribes.
35They conceive trouble and give birth to evil;
their womb fashions deceit."

b23 Or about, looking for food

6 / *Job 16—17*
Our Heavenly Guarantor

WE LONG TO be sure—sure that we are accepted by God, sure that our sins are *really* forgiven, not to crop up again to haunt us like a long-suppressed secret, sure that we will be with God when we die and sure that God is *for* us. Mike Mason suggests that one of our deepest questions is whether God likes us. "Of course God loves us, he loves everybody, indiscriminately, even the people he is going to send to hell. . . . The real question is not whether God loves us, but whether he approves of us, whether we are pleasing to him" (as quoted in *Job* by Francis Andersen). In the end our question—like Job's—is "Is there a Friend in the universe?"

 Warming Up to God Of what do you feel most sure in your life at this point? Explain.

 Read Job 16—17.

16

Then Job replied:

²"I have heard many things like these;
    miserable comforters are you all!
³Will your long-winded speeches never end?
    What ails you that you keep on arguing?
⁴I also could speak like you,
    if you were in my place;
 I could make fine speeches against you
    and shake my head at you.
⁵But my mouth would encourage you;
    comfort from my lips would bring you
      relief.

⁶"Yet if I speak, my pain is not relieved;
    and if I refrain, it does not go away.
⁷Surely, O God, you have worn me out;
    you have devastated my entire household.
⁸You have bound me—and it has become a
      witness;
    my gauntness rises up and testifies against
      me.
⁹God assails me and tears me in his anger
    and gnashes his teeth at me;
    my opponent fastens on me his piercing
      eyes.
¹⁰Men open their mouths to jeer at me;
    they strike my cheek in scorn
    and unite together against me.
¹¹God has turned me over to evil men
    and thrown me into the clutches of the
      wicked.
¹²All was well with me, but he shattered me;
    he seized me by the neck and crushed me.
 He has made me his target;
¹³   his archers surround me.

Without pity, he pierces my kidneys
    and spills my gall on the ground.
¹⁴Again and again he bursts upon me;
    he rushes at me like a warrior.

¹⁵"I have sewed sackcloth over my skin
    and buried my brow in the dust.
¹⁶My face is red with weeping,
    deep shadows ring my eyes;
¹⁷yet my hands have been free of violence
    and my prayer is pure.

¹⁸"O earth, do not cover my blood;
    may my cry never be laid to rest!
¹⁹Even now my witness is in heaven;
    my advocate is on high.
²⁰My intercessor is my friend[c]
    as my eyes pour out tears to God;
²¹on behalf of a man he pleads with God
    as a man pleads for his friend.

²²"Only a few years will pass
    before I go on the journey of no return.

17

¹My spirit is broken,
    my days are cut short,
    the grave awaits me.
²Surely mockers surround me;
    my eyes must dwell on their hostility.

³"Give me, O God, the pledge you demand.
    Who else will put up security for me?
⁴You have closed their minds to
      understanding;
    therefore you will not let them triumph.
⁵If a man denounces his friends for reward,
    the eyes of his children will fail.

[c]20 Or *My friends treat me with scorn*

6"God has made me a byword to everyone,
  a man in whose face people spit.
7My eyes have grown dim with grief;
  my whole frame is but a shadow.
8Upright men are appalled at this;
  the innocent are aroused against the
    ungodly.
9Nevertheless, the righteous will hold to their
    ways,
  and those with clean hands will grow
    stronger.

10"But come on, all of you, try again!
  I will not find a wise man among you.
11My days have passed, my plans are shattered,

and so are the desires of my heart.
12These men turn night into day;
  in the face of darkness they say, 'Light is
    near.'
13If the only home I hope for is the grave,d
  if I spread out my bed in darkness,
14if I say to corruption, 'You are my father,'
  and to the worm, 'My mother' or 'My
    sister,'
15where then is my hope?
  Who can see any hope for me?
16Will it go down to the gates of deathd?
  Will we descend together into the dust?"

d13,16 Hebrew *Sheol*

 Discovering the Word 1. In chapter 15 Eliphaz started the second round of speeches, trying once again to cut Job down to size. What words does Job use to emphasize that not only his friends but also God has become his enemy (16:7–14)? 2. In what sense could Job say his "prayer is pure" (16:17)? 3. What certainty is impressed on Job's soul as he prays through his tears (16:18–21)? 4. Job looks to God for a pledge of security (17:3). How is it possible that Job could appeal for help from God when it is God who is apparently attacking him? 5. Look at Job 19:23–27. Bildad has had his second turn (chapter 18) at accusing Job. In what ways does this great breakthrough answer the deepest quest of his prayers?

Applying the Word 1. While discovering hope, Job must still exercise faith. Why is it important that the guarantees of our future should still require personal faith? 2. There are several images of God's provision in this study: witness, advocate, intercessor, guarantor, redeemer-kinsman. Which one especially gives you hope? 3. What difference will this make to the uncertainties you face?

Responding in Prayer Bring your insecurities to your heavenly Guarantor.

Job 18—19

18

Then Bildad the Shuhite replied:

2"When will you end these
    speeches?
Be sensible, and then we can talk.
3Why are we regarded as cattle
  and considered stupid in your sight?
4You who tear yourself to pieces in your anger,
  is the earth to be abandoned for your sake?
  Or must the rocks be moved from their
    place?

5"The lamp of the wicked is snuffed out;
  the flame of his fire stops burning.
6The light in his tent becomes dark;
  the lamp beside him goes out.
7The vigor of his step is weakened;
  his own schemes throw him down.

8His feet thrust him into a net
  and he wanders into its mesh.
9A trap seizes him by the heel;
  a snare holds him fast.
10A noose is hidden for him on the ground;
  a trap lies in his path.
11Terrors startle him on every side
  and dog his every step.
12Calamity is hungry for him;
  disaster is ready for him when he falls.
13It eats away parts of his skin;
  death's firstborn devours his limbs.
14He is torn from the security of his tent
  and marched off to the king of terrors.
15Fire residese in his tent;

e15 Or *Nothing he had remains*

burning sulfur is scattered over his
dwelling.
¹⁶His roots dry up below
and his branches wither above.
¹⁷The memory of him perishes from the earth;
he has no name in the land.
¹⁸He is driven from light into darkness
and is banished from the world.
¹⁹He has no offspring or descendants among his
people,
no survivor where once he lived.
²⁰Men of the west are appalled at his fate;
men of the east are seized with horror.
²¹Surely such is the dwelling of an evil man;
such is the place of one who knows not
God."

19

Then Job replied:

²"How long will you torment me
and crush me with words?
³Ten times now you have reproached me;
shamelessly you attack me.
⁴If it is true that I have gone astray,
my error remains my concern alone.
⁵If indeed you would exalt yourselves above
me
and use my humiliation against me,
⁶then know that God has wronged me
and drawn his net around me.

⁷"Though I cry, 'I've been wronged!' I get no
response;
though I call for help, there is no justice.
⁸He has blocked my way so I cannot pass;
he has shrouded my paths in darkness.
⁹He has stripped me of my honor
and removed the crown from my head.
¹⁰He tears me down on every side till I am
gone;
he uproots my hope like a tree.
¹¹His anger burns against me;
he counts me among his enemies.
¹²His troops advance in force;
they build a siege ramp against me
and encamp around my tent.

¹³"He has alienated my brothers from me;
my acquaintances are completely estranged
from me.

¹⁴My kinsmen have gone away;
my friends have forgotten me.
¹⁵My guests and my maidservants count me a
stranger;
they look upon me as an alien.
¹⁶I summon my servant, but he does not
answer,
though I beg him with my own mouth.
¹⁷My breath is offensive to my wife;
I am loathsome to my own brothers.
¹⁸Even the little boys scorn me;
when I appear, they ridicule me.
¹⁹All my intimate friends detest me;
those I love have turned against me.
²⁰I am nothing but skin and bones;
I have escaped with only the skin of my
teeth.ᶠ

²¹"Have pity on me, my friends, have pity,
for the hand of God has struck me.
²²Why do you pursue me as God does?
Will you never get enough of my flesh?

²³"Oh, that my words were recorded,
that they were written on a scroll,
²⁴that they were inscribed with an iron tool
onᵍ lead,
or engraved in rock forever!
²⁵I know that my Redeemerʰ lives,
and that in the end he will stand upon the
earth.ⁱ
²⁶And after my skin has been destroyed,
yetʲ inᵏ my flesh I will see God;
²⁷I myself will see him
with my own eyes—I, and not another.
How my heart yearns within me!

²⁸"If you say, 'How we will hound him,
since the root of the trouble lies in him,ˡ'
²⁹you should fear the sword yourselves;
for wrath will bring punishment by the
sword,
and then you will know that there is
judgment.ᵐ"

ᶠ20 Or *only my gums*   ᵍ24 Or *and*   ʰ25 Or *defender*   ⁱ25 Or
upon my grave   ʲ26 Or *And after I awake, / though this body has
been destroyed, / then*   ᵏ26 Or / *apart from*   ˡ28 Many Hebrew
manuscripts, Septuagint and Vulgate; most Hebrew manuscripts *me*
ᵐ29 Or / *that you may come to know the Almighty*

7 / *Job 20—21*
The Problem of Pain

WARS, DISEASE, CONGENITAL deformities, earthquakes and the seismic disturbances in our daily lives—all of these leave us with questions about the goodness of God and his active control of the world. Job himself suffered economic, familial, physical and social disaster, so much so that he despaired of life and longed for death. How could a good God cause all this (as Job firmly believed), or even allow this (as most moderns would say)? The classic way of putting the matter is this: If God is all-powerful, he is not good; if he is good, he is not all-powerful.

Job will not get his answer in these chapters. Indeed, he does not get a satisfying theological answer even in the end when God finally speaks—he will get something even better! But his dialogue with his friend Zophar will push his thinking and praying a step closer to the belief that God's love is not confined to rewards and punishments.

 Warming Up to God What have you witnessed or experienced in life that has made it difficult for you to believe there is a good God running the world?

 Read Job 20—21.

20 Then Zophar the Naamathite replied:

2"My troubled thoughts prompt me to answer
because I am greatly disturbed.
3I hear a rebuke that dishonors me,
and my understanding inspires me to reply.

4"Surely you know how it has been from of
old,
ever since man[n] was placed on the earth,
5that the mirth of the wicked is brief,
the joy of the godless lasts but a moment.
6Though his pride reaches to the heavens
and his head touches the clouds,
7he will perish forever, like his own dung;
those who have seen him will say, 'Where
is he?'
8Like a dream he flies away, no more to be
found,
banished like a vision of the night.
9The eye that saw him will not see him again;
his place will look on him no more.
10His children must make amends to the poor;
his own hands must give back his wealth.
11The youthful vigor that fills his bones
will lie with him in the dust.

12"Though evil is sweet in his mouth
and he hides it under his tongue,
13though he cannot bear to let it go
and keeps it in his mouth,
14yet his food will turn sour in his stomach;
it will become the venom of serpents within
him.

15He will spit out the riches he swallowed;
God will make his stomach vomit them up.
16He will suck the poison of serpents;
the fangs of an adder will kill him.
17He will not enjoy the streams,
the rivers flowing with honey and cream.
18What he toiled for he must give back
uneaten;
he will not enjoy the profit from his
trading.
19For he has oppressed the poor and left them
destitute;
he has seized houses he did not build.

20"Surely he will have no respite from his
craving;
he cannot save himself by his treasure.
21Nothing is left for him to devour;
his prosperity will not endure.
22In the midst of his plenty, distress will
overtake him;
the full force of misery will come upon
him.
23When he has filled his belly,
God will vent his burning anger against
him
and rain down his blows upon him.
24Though he flees from an iron weapon,
a bronze-tipped arrow pierces him.
25He pulls it out of his back,
the gleaming point out of his liver.
Terrors will come over him;
26   total darkness lies in wait for his treasures.

n4 Or Adam

A fire unfanned will consume him
and devour what is left in his tent.
²⁷The heavens will expose his guilt;
the earth will rise up against him.
²⁸A flood will carry off his house,
rushing waters° on the day of God's wrath.
²⁹Such is the fate God allots the wicked,
the heritage appointed for them by God."

21

Then Job replied:

²"Listen carefully to my words;
let this be the consolation you give me.
³Bear with me while I speak,
and after I have spoken, mock on.

⁴"Is my complaint directed to man?
Why should I not be impatient?
⁵Look at me and be astonished;
clap your hand over your mouth.
⁶When I think about this, I am terrified;
trembling seizes my body.
⁷Why do the wicked live on,
growing old and increasing in power?
⁸They see their children established around
them,
their offspring before their eyes.
⁹Their homes are safe and free from fear;
the rod of God is not upon them.
¹⁰Their bulls never fail to breed;
their cows calve and do not miscarry.
¹¹They send forth their children as a flock;
their little ones dance about.
¹²They sing to the music of tambourine and
harp;
they make merry to the sound of the flute.
¹³They spend their years in prosperity
and go down to the graveᵖ in peace.�q
¹⁴Yet they say to God, 'Leave us alone!
We have no desire to know your ways.
¹⁵Who is the Almighty, that we should serve
him?
What would we gain by praying to him?'
¹⁶But their prosperity is not in their own hands,
so I stand aloof from the counsel of the
wicked.

¹⁷"Yet how often is the lamp of the wicked
snuffed out?
How often does calamity come upon them,
the fate God allots in his anger?
¹⁸How often are they like straw before the
wind,

like chaff swept away by a gale?
¹⁹⌐It is said,⌐ 'God stores up a man's
punishment for his sons.'
Let him repay the man himself, so that he
will know it!
²⁰Let his own eyes see his destruction;
let him drink of the wrath of the
Almighty.ʳ
²¹For what does he care about the family he
leaves behind
when his allotted months come to an end?

²²"Can anyone teach knowledge to God,
since he judges even the highest?
²³One man dies in full vigor,
completely secure and at ease,
²⁴his bodyˢ well nourished,
his bones rich with marrow.
²⁵Another man dies in bitterness of soul,
never having enjoyed anything good.
²⁶Side by side they lie in the dust,
and worms cover them both.

²⁷"I know full well what you are thinking,
the schemes by which you would wrong
me.
²⁸You say, 'Where now is the great man's
house,
the tents where wicked men lived?'
²⁹Have you never questioned those who travel?
Have you paid no regard to their
accounts—
³⁰that the evil man is spared from the day of
calamity,
that he is delivered fromᵗ the day of
wrath?
³¹Who denounces his conduct to his face?
Who repays him for what he has done?
³²He is carried to the grave,
and watch is kept over his tomb.
³³The soil in the valley is sweet to him;
all men follow after him,
and a countless throng goesᵘ before him.

³⁴"So how can you console me with your
nonsense?
Nothing is left of your answers but
falsehood!"

°28 Or *The possessions in his house will be carried off, / washed away*
ᵖ13 Hebrew *Sheol*   q13 Or *in an instant*   ʳ17-20 Verses 17 and
18 may be taken as exclamations and 19 and 20 as declarations.
ˢ24 The meaning of the Hebrew for this word is uncertain.   ᵗ30 Or
man is reserved for the day of calamity, / that he is brought forth to
ᵘ33 Or / *as a countless throng went*

Discovering the Word 1. What words and phrases are used to describe the wicked in chapter 20? 2. What is Zophar's view of God's righteousness? 3. How does Job's reality check in chapter 21 contrast with Zophar's view (20:29)? 4. Job 21:14–15 expresses the spiritual question the wicked might ask: "What would we gain by praying to him?" On the basis of the discussion thus far, how do you think Zophar would answer that question? 5. How would Job reply?

Applying the Word 1. It has been said that Job and the others were trying to fit together the pieces of a puzzle without having all the pieces. How can the discoveries Job is making (consider the last study too) help you deal with the problem of pain? 2. What have you learned in this study about helping people find answers to questions about the goodness of God?

Responding in Prayer Ask God to help you grow in your understanding of who he is and how he works in the world.

Job 22

22
Then Eliphaz the Temanite replied:

²"Can a man be of benefit to God?
Can even a wise man benefit him?
³What pleasure would it give the Almighty if you were righteous?
What would he gain if your ways were blameless?

⁴"Is it for your piety that he rebukes you and brings charges against you?
⁵Is not your wickedness great?
Are not your sins endless?
⁶You demanded security from your brothers for no reason;
you stripped men of their clothing, leaving them naked.
⁷You gave no water to the weary and you withheld food from the hungry,
⁸though you were a powerful man, owning land—
an honored man, living on it.
⁹And you sent widows away empty-handed and broke the strength of the fatherless.
¹⁰That is why snares are all around you, why sudden peril terrifies you,
¹¹why it is so dark you cannot see, and why a flood of water covers you.

¹²"Is not God in the heights of heaven?
And see how lofty are the highest stars!
¹³Yet you say, 'What does God know?
Does he judge through such darkness?
¹⁴Thick clouds veil him, so he does not see us

as he goes about in the vaulted heavens.'
¹⁵Will you keep to the old path that evil men have trod?
¹⁶They were carried off before their time, their foundations washed away by a flood.
¹⁷They said to God, 'Leave us alone!
What can the Almighty do to us?'
¹⁸Yet it was he who filled their houses with good things,
so I stand aloof from the counsel of the wicked.

¹⁹"The righteous see their ruin and rejoice; the innocent mock them, saying,
²⁰'Surely our foes are destroyed, and fire devours their wealth.'

²¹"Submit to God and be at peace with him; in this way prosperity will come to you.
²²Accept instruction from his mouth and lay up his words in your heart.
²³If you return to the Almighty, you will be restored:
If you remove wickedness far from your tent
²⁴and assign your nuggets to the dust, your gold of Ophir to the rocks in the ravines,
²⁵then the Almighty will be your gold, the choicest silver for you.
²⁶Surely then you will find delight in the Almighty
and will lift up your face to God.
²⁷You will pray to him, and he will hear you, and you will fulfill your vows.

28What you decide on will be done,
and light will shine on your ways.
29When men are brought low and you say, 'Lift
them up!'

then he will save the downcast.
30He will deliver even one who is not innocent,
who will be delivered through the cleanness
of your hands."

8 / *Job 23*
The Silence of God

WE HAVE ALL experienced someone's mindless chatter or withering judgment at a moment when we needed to be deeply understood. But when we listen—really listen—we "speak" with our ears. We communicate our respect, prize the person and encourage the movement of God in someone's life. Could it be that it's the same with God? Does he communicate his love to us sometimes by listening as we pour out our hearts, rather than finishing our sentences for us and telling us how to feel, what to do, where to go? For twenty-two chapters God has not spoken directly to Job. But God has listened in silence.

 Warming Up to God   Recall a time when a friend or family member really listened to you. How did you feel? How did that person's listening help you?

 Read Job 23.

23 Then Job replied:

2"Even today my complaint is
bitter;
his hand[v] is heavy in spite of[w] my
groaning.
3If only I knew where to find him;
if only I could go to his dwelling!
4I would state my case before him
and fill my mouth with arguments.
5I would find out what he would answer me,
and consider what he would say.
6Would he oppose me with great power?
No, he would not press charges against me.
7There an upright man could present his case
before him,
and I would be delivered forever from my
judge.

8"But if I go to the east, he is not there;
if I go to the west, I do not find him.
9When he is at work in the north, I do not see
him;
when he turns to the south, I catch no
glimpse of him.

10But he knows the way that I take;
when he has tested me, I will come forth as
gold.
11My feet have closely followed his steps;
I have kept to his way without turning
aside.
12I have not departed from the commands of
his lips;
I have treasured the words of his mouth
more than my daily bread.

13"But he stands alone, and who can oppose
him?
He does whatever he pleases.
14He carries out his decree against me,
and many such plans he still has in store.
15That is why I am terrified before him;
when I think of all this, I fear him.
16God has made my heart faint;
the Almighty has terrified me.
17Yet I am not silenced by the darkness,
by the thick darkness that covers my face.

v2 Septuagint and Syriac; Hebrew / *the hand on me*   w2 Or *heavy on me in*

Discovering the Word   1. What does Job now want more than anything (see also 29:4–5)? Why?   2. Why do you think Job finds God so elusive (vv. 8–9)?   3. Job longs for an opportunity to renew friendship with God and present his case, and he is not simply waiting passively. What has he been doing (vv. 10–12)?

4. What appears to be Job's main remaining problem in establishing his righteousness with God (vv. 13–17)?
5. How does Job's experience show the difference between a God who comforts through silence and an absent god who is not really there at all?

 Applying the Word 1. Why do you think people sometimes find God unresponsive when they say they are seeking him wholeheartedly? 2. The Bible suggests that the people who received mystical experiences of God (Moses, Isaiah, John, and even Job—42:5) were not seeking an overwhelming encounter with God; these experiences were given by God at God's initiative. What does Job's case teach us about waiting? 3. How does Job's attitude help you to wait for God?

Responding in Prayer After you pray about the needs in your life, listen for God's response. Allow even silence to bring you comfort as you trust in his listening ear.

Job 24—34

24

"Why does the Almighty not set times for judgment?
Why must those who know him look in vain for such days?
²Men move boundary stones;
they pasture flocks they have stolen.
³They drive away the orphan's donkey
and take the widow's ox in pledge.
⁴They thrust the needy from the path
and force all the poor of the land into hiding.
⁵Like wild donkeys in the desert,
the poor go about their labor of foraging food;
the wasteland provides food for their children.
⁶They gather fodder in the fields
and glean in the vineyards of the wicked.
⁷Lacking clothes, they spend the night naked;
they have nothing to cover themselves in the cold.
⁸They are drenched by mountain rains
and hug the rocks for lack of shelter.
⁹The fatherless child is snatched from the breast;
the infant of the poor is seized for a debt.
¹⁰Lacking clothes, they go about naked;
they carry the sheaves, but still go hungry.
¹¹They crush olives among the terraces ˣ;
they tread the winepresses, yet suffer thirst.
¹²The groans of the dying rise from the city,
and the souls of the wounded cry out for help.
But God charges no one with wrongdoing.

¹³"There are those who rebel against the light,
who do not know its ways
or stay in its paths.
¹⁴When daylight is gone, the murderer rises up
and kills the poor and needy;
in the night he steals forth like a thief.
¹⁵The eye of the adulterer watches for dusk;
he thinks, 'No eye will see me,'
and he keeps his face concealed.
¹⁶In the dark, men break into houses,
but by day they shut themselves in;
they want nothing to do with the light.
¹⁷For all of them, deep darkness is their morning ʸ;
they make friends with the terrors of darkness. ᶻ

¹⁸"Yet they are foam on the surface of the water;
their portion of the land is cursed,
so that no one goes to the vineyards.
¹⁹As heat and drought snatch away the melted snow,
so the grave ᵃ snatches away those who have sinned.
²⁰The womb forgets them,
the worm feasts on them;
evil men are no longer remembered
but are broken like a tree.
²¹They prey on the barren and childless woman,
and to the widow show no kindness.
²²But God drags away the mighty by his power;
though they become established, they have no assurance of life.

ˣ11 Or *olives between the millstones*; the meaning of the Hebrew for this word is uncertain.   ʸ17 Or *them, their morning is like the shadow of death*   ᶻ17 Or *of the shadow of death*   ᵃ19 Hebrew *Sheol*

²³He may let them rest in a feeling of security,
  but his eyes are on their ways.
²⁴For a little while they are exalted, and then
    they are gone;
  they are brought low and gathered up like
    all others;
  they are cut off like heads of grain.

²⁵"If this is not so, who can prove me false
  and reduce my words to nothing?"

25

Then Bildad the Shuhite replied:

²"Dominion and awe belong to
    God;
  he establishes order in the heights of
    heaven.
³Can his forces be numbered?
  Upon whom does his light not rise?
⁴How then can a man be righteous before
    God?
  How can one born of woman be pure?
⁵If even the moon is not bright
  and the stars are not pure in his eyes,
⁶how much less man, who is but a maggot—
  a son of man, who is only a worm!"

26

Then Job replied:

²"How you have helped the
    powerless!
  How you have saved the arm that is feeble!
³What advice you have offered to one without
    wisdom!
  And what great insight you have displayed!
⁴Who has helped you utter these words?
  And whose spirit spoke from your mouth?

⁵"The dead are in deep anguish,
  those beneath the waters and all that live in
    them.
⁶Death*a* is naked before God;
  Destruction*b* lies uncovered.
⁷He spreads out the northern ⌊skies⌋ over
    empty space;
  he suspends the earth over nothing.
⁸He wraps up the waters in his clouds,
  yet the clouds do not burst under their
    weight.
⁹He covers the face of the full moon,
  spreading his clouds over it.
¹⁰He marks out the horizon on the face of the
    waters

for a boundary between light and darkness.
¹¹The pillars of the heavens quake,
  aghast at his rebuke.
¹²By his power he churned up the sea;
  by his wisdom he cut Rahab to pieces.
¹³By his breath the skies became fair;
  his hand pierced the gliding serpent.
¹⁴And these are but the outer fringe of his
    works;
  how faint the whisper we hear of him!
  Who then can understand the thunder of
    his power?"

27

And Job continued his discourse:

²"As surely as God lives, who has
    denied me justice,
  the Almighty, who has made me taste
    bitterness of soul,
³as long as I have life within me,
  the breath of God in my nostrils,
⁴my lips will not speak wickedness,
  and my tongue will utter no deceit.
⁵I will never admit you are in the right;
  till I die, I will not deny my integrity.
⁶I will maintain my righteousness and never let
    go of it;
  my conscience will not reproach me as long
    as I live.

⁷"May my enemies be like the wicked,
  my adversaries like the unjust!
⁸For what hope has the godless when he is cut
    off,
  when God takes away his life?
⁹Does God listen to his cry
  when distress comes upon him?
¹⁰Will he find delight in the Almighty?
  Will he call upon God at all times?

¹¹"I will teach you about the power of God;
  the ways of the Almighty I will not conceal.
¹²You have all seen this yourselves.
  Why then this meaningless talk?

¹³"Here is the fate God allots to the wicked,
  the heritage a ruthless man receives from
    the Almighty:
¹⁴However many his children, their fate is the
    sword;
  his offspring will never have enough to eat.
¹⁵The plague will bury those who survive him,

*a*6 Hebrew *Sheol*   *b*6 Hebrew *Abaddon*

and their widows will not weep for them.
[16]Though he heaps up silver like dust
   and clothes like piles of clay,
[17]what he lays up the righteous will wear,
   and the innocent will divide his silver.
[18]The house he builds is like a moth's cocoon,
   like a hut made by a watchman.
[19]He lies down wealthy, but will do so no
      more;
   when he opens his eyes, all is gone.
[20]Terrors overtake him like a flood;
   a tempest snatches him away in the night.
[21]The east wind carries him off, and he is gone;
   it sweeps him out of his place.
[22]It hurls itself against him without mercy
   as he flees headlong from its power.
[23]It claps its hands in derision
   and hisses him out of his place.

28

"There is a mine for silver
   and a place where gold is refined.
   [2]Iron is taken from the earth,
and copper is smelted from ore.
[3]Man puts an end to the darkness;
   he searches the farthest recesses
   for ore in the blackest darkness.
[4]Far from where people dwell he cuts a shaft,
   in places forgotten by the foot of man;
   far from men he dangles and sways.
[5]The earth, from which food comes,
   is transformed below as by fire;
[6]sapphires[c] come from its rocks,
   and its dust contains nuggets of gold.
[7]No bird of prey knows that hidden path,
   no falcon's eye has seen it.
[8]Proud beasts do not set foot on it,
   and no lion prowls there.
[9]Man's hand assaults the flinty rock
   and lays bare the roots of the mountains.
[10]He tunnels through the rock;
   his eyes see all its treasures.
[11]He searches[d] the sources of the rivers
   and brings hidden things to light.

[12]"But where can wisdom be found?
   Where does understanding dwell?
[13]Man does not comprehend its worth;
   it cannot be found in the land of the living.
[14]The deep says, 'It is not in me';
   the sea says, 'It is not with me.'
[15]It cannot be bought with the finest gold,
   nor can its price be weighed in silver.

[16]It cannot be bought with the gold of Ophir,
   with precious onyx or sapphires.
[17]Neither gold nor crystal can compare with it,
   nor can it be had for jewels of gold.
[18]Coral and jasper are not worthy of mention;
   the price of wisdom is beyond rubies.
[19]The topaz of Cush cannot compare with it;
   it cannot be bought with pure gold.

[20]"Where then does wisdom come from?
   Where does understanding dwell?
[21]It is hidden from the eyes of every living
      thing,
   concealed even from the birds of the air.
[22]Destruction[e] and Death say,
   'Only a rumor of it has reached our ears.'
[23]God understands the way to it
   and he alone knows where it dwells,
[24]for he views the ends of the earth
   and sees everything under the heavens.
[25]When he established the force of the wind
   and measured out the waters,
[26]when he made a decree for the rain
   and a path for the thunderstorm,
[27]then he looked at wisdom and appraised it;
   he confirmed it and tested it.
[28]And he said to man,
   'The fear of the Lord—that is wisdom,
   and to shun evil is understanding.' "

29

Job continued his discourse:
   [2]"How I long for the months
      gone by,
   for the days when God watched over me,
[3]when his lamp shone upon my head
   and by his light I walked through darkness!
[4]Oh, for the days when I was in my prime,
   when God's intimate friendship blessed my
      house,
[5]when the Almighty was still with me
   and my children were around me,
[6]when my path was drenched with cream
   and the rock poured out for me streams of
      olive oil.

[7]"When I went to the gate of the city
   and took my seat in the public square,
[8]the young men saw me and stepped aside
   and the old men rose to their feet;
[9]the chief men refrained from speaking
   and covered their mouths with their hands;

[c]6 Or *lapis lazuli*; also in verse 16   [d]11 Septuagint, Aquila and
Vulgate; Hebrew *He dams up*   [e]22 Hebrew *Abaddon*

¹⁰the voices of the nobles were hushed,
and their tongues stuck to the roof of their
mouths.
¹¹Whoever heard me spoke well of me,
and those who saw me commended me,
¹²because I rescued the poor who cried for
help,
and the fatherless who had none to assist
him.
¹³The man who was dying blessed me;
I made the widow's heart sing.
¹⁴I put on righteousness as my clothing;
justice was my robe and my turban.
¹⁵I was eyes to the blind
and feet to the lame.
¹⁶I was a father to the needy;
I took up the case of the stranger.
¹⁷I broke the fangs of the wicked
and snatched the victims from their teeth.

¹⁸"I thought, 'I will die in my own house,
my days as numerous as the grains of sand.
¹⁹My roots will reach to the water,
and the dew will lie all night on my
branches.
²⁰My glory will remain fresh in me,
the bow ever new in my hand.'

²¹"Men listened to me expectantly,
waiting in silence for my counsel.
²²After I had spoken, they spoke no more;
my words fell gently on their ears.
²³They waited for me as for showers
and drank in my words as the spring rain.
²⁴When I smiled at them, they scarcely believed
it;
the light of my face was precious to them.^f
²⁵I chose the way for them and sat as their chief;
I dwelt as a king among his troops;
I was like one who comforts mourners.

30

"But now they mock me,
men younger than I,
whose fathers I would have
disdained
to put with my sheep dogs.
²Of what use was the strength of their hands
to me,
since their vigor had gone from them?
³Haggard from want and hunger,
they roamed^g the parched land
in desolate wastelands at night.

⁴In the brush they gathered salt herbs,
and their food^h was the root of the broom
tree.
⁵They were banished from their fellow men,
shouted at as if they were thieves.
⁶They were forced to live in the dry stream
beds,
among the rocks and in holes in the
ground.
⁷They brayed among the bushes
and huddled in the undergrowth.
⁸A base and nameless brood,
they were driven out of the land.

⁹"And now their sons mock me in song;
I have become a byword among them.
¹⁰They detest me and keep their distance;
they do not hesitate to spit in my face.
¹¹Now that God has unstrung my bow and
afflicted me,
they throw off restraint in my presence.
¹²On my right the tribeⁱ attacks;
they lay snares for my feet,
they build their siege ramps against me.
¹³They break up my road;
they succeed in destroying me—
without anyone's helping them.^j
¹⁴They advance as through a gaping breach;
amid the ruins they come rolling in.
¹⁵Terrors overwhelm me;
my dignity is driven away as by the wind,
my safety vanishes like a cloud.

¹⁶"And now my life ebbs away;
days of suffering grip me.
¹⁷Night pierces my bones;
my gnawing pains never rest.
¹⁸In his great power ⌊God⌋ becomes like
clothing to me^k;
he binds me like the neck of my garment.
¹⁹He throws me into the mud,
and I am reduced to dust and ashes.

²⁰"I cry out to you, O God, but you do not
answer;
I stand up, but you merely look at me.
²¹You turn on me ruthlessly;
with the might of your hand you attack me.

---

^f24 The meaning of the Hebrew for this clause is uncertain.
^g3 Or gnawed   ^h4 Or fuel   ⁱ12 The meaning of the Hebrew for
this word is uncertain.   ^j13 Or me. / 'No one can help him,'
⌊they say⌋   ^k18 Hebrew; Septuagint ⌊God⌋ grasps my clothing

²²You snatch me up and drive me before the
　　wind;
　　you toss me about in the storm.
²³I know you will bring me down to death,
　　to the place appointed for all the living.

²⁴"Surely no one lays a hand on a broken man
　　when he cries for help in his distress.
²⁵Have I not wept for those in trouble?
　　Has not my soul grieved for the poor?
²⁶Yet when I hoped for good, evil came;
　　when I looked for light, then came
　　　darkness.
²⁷The churning inside me never stops;
　　days of suffering confront me.
²⁸I go about blackened, but not by the sun;
　　I stand up in the assembly and cry for help.
²⁹I have become a brother of jackals,
　　a companion of owls.
³⁰My skin grows black and peels;
　　my body burns with fever.
³¹My harp is tuned to mourning,
　　and my flute to the sound of wailing.

31

"I made a covenant with my eyes
not to look lustfully at a girl.
　²For what is man's lot from God
above,
　his heritage from the Almighty on high?
³Is it not ruin for the wicked,
　　disaster for those who do wrong?
⁴Does he not see my ways
　　and count my every step?

⁵"If I have walked in falsehood
　　or my foot has hurried after deceit—
⁶let God weigh me in honest scales
　　and he will know that I am blameless—
⁷if my steps have turned from the path,
　　if my heart has been led by my eyes,
　　or if my hands have been defiled,
⁸then may others eat what I have sown,
　　and may my crops be uprooted.

⁹"If my heart has been enticed by a woman,
　　or if I have lurked at my neighbor's door,
¹⁰then may my wife grind another man's grain,
　　and may other men sleep with her.
¹¹For that would have been shameful,
　　a sin to be judged.
¹²It is a fire that burns to Destructionˡ;
　　it would have uprooted my harvest.

¹³"If I have denied justice to my menservants
　　and maidservants
　　when they had a grievance against me,

¹⁴what will I do when God confronts me?
　　What will I answer when called to account?
¹⁵Did not he who made me in the womb make
　　them?
　　Did not the same one form us both within
　　　our mothers?

¹⁶"If I have denied the desires of the poor
　　or let the eyes of the widow grow weary,
¹⁷if I have kept my bread to myself,
　　not sharing it with the fatherless—
¹⁸but from my youth I reared him as would a
　　father,
　　and from my birth I guided the widow—
¹⁹if I have seen anyone perishing for lack of
　　clothing,
　　or a needy man without a garment,
²⁰and his heart did not bless me
　　for warming him with the fleece from my
　　　sheep,
²¹if I have raised my hand against the
　　fatherless,
　　knowing that I had influence in court,
²²then let my arm fall from the shoulder,
　　let it be broken off at the joint.
²³For I dreaded destruction from God,
　　and for fear of his splendor I could not do
　　　such things.

²⁴"If I have put my trust in gold
　　or said to pure gold, 'You are my security,'
²⁵if I have rejoiced over my great wealth,
　　the fortune my hands had gained,
²⁶if I have regarded the sun in its radiance
　　or the moon moving in splendor,
²⁷so that my heart was secretly enticed
　　and my hand offered them a kiss of
　　　homage,
²⁸then these also would be sins to be judged,
　　for I would have been unfaithful to God on
　　　high.

²⁹"If I have rejoiced at my enemy's misfortune
　　or gloated over the trouble that came to
　　　him—
³⁰I have not allowed my mouth to sin
　　by invoking a curse against his life—
³¹if the men of my household have never said,
　　'Who has not had his fill of Job's meat?'—
³²but no stranger had to spend the night in the
　　street,

ˡ12 Hebrew *Abaddon*

for my door was always open to the
　　traveler—
³³if I have concealed my sin as men do,ᵐ
　　by hiding my guilt in my heart
³⁴because I so feared the crowd
　　and so dreaded the contempt of the clans
　　that I kept silent and would not go outside

³⁵("Oh, that I had someone to hear me!
　　I sign now my defense—let the Almighty
　　　answer me;
　　let my accuser put his indictment in
　　　writing.
³⁶Surely I would wear it on my shoulder,
　　I would put it on like a crown.
³⁷I would give him an account of my every
　　　step;
　　like a prince I would approach him.)—

³⁸"if my land cries out against me
　　and all its furrows are wet with tears,
³⁹if I have devoured its yield without payment
　　or broken the spirit of its tenants,
⁴⁰then let briers come up instead of wheat
　　and weeds instead of barley."

The words of Job are ended.

32

So these three men stopped answering Job, because he was righteous in his own eyes. ²But Elihu son of Barakel the Buzite, of the family of Ram, became very angry with Job for justifying himself rather than God. ³He was also angry with the three friends, because they had found no way to refute Job, and yet had condemned him.ⁿ ⁴Now Elihu had waited before speaking to Job because they were older than he. ⁵But when he saw that the three men had nothing more to say, his anger was aroused.

⁶So Elihu son of Barakel the Buzite said:

"I am young in years,
　　and you are old;
that is why I was fearful,
　　not daring to tell you what I know.
⁷I thought, 'Age should speak;
　　advanced years should teach wisdom.'
⁸But it is the spiritᵒ in a man,
　　the breath of the Almighty, that gives him
　　　understanding.
⁹It is not only the oldᵖ who are wise,
　　not only the aged who understand what is
　　　right.

¹⁰"Therefore I say: Listen to me;
　　I too will tell you what I know.
¹¹I waited while you spoke,
　　I listened to your reasoning;
　　while you were searching for words,
¹²　I gave you my full attention.
　　But not one of you has proved Job wrong;
　　none of you has answered his arguments.
¹³Do not say, 'We have found wisdom;
　　let God refute him, not man.'
¹⁴But Job has not marshaled his words against
　　　me,
　　and I will not answer him with your
　　　arguments.

¹⁵"They are dismayed and have no more to say;
　　words have failed them.
¹⁶Must I wait, now that they are silent,
　　now that they stand there with no reply?
¹⁷I too will have my say;
　　I too will tell what I know.
¹⁸For I am full of words,
　　and the spirit within me compels me;
¹⁹inside I am like bottled-up wine,
　　like new wineskins ready to burst.
²⁰I must speak and find relief;
　　I must open my lips and reply.
²¹I will show partiality to no one,
　　nor will I flatter any man;
²²for if I were skilled in flattery,
　　my Maker would soon take me away.

33

"But now, Job, listen to my words;
　　pay attention to everything I say.
²I am about to open my mouth;
　　my words are on the tip of my tongue.
³My words come from an upright heart;
　　my lips sincerely speak what I know.
⁴The Spirit of God has made me;
　　the breath of the Almighty gives me life.
⁵Answer me then, if you can;
　　prepare yourself and confront me.
⁶I am just like you before God;
　　I too have been taken from clay.
⁷No fear of me should alarm you,
　　nor should my hand be heavy upon you.

⁸"But you have said in my hearing—
　　I heard the very words—

ᵐ33 Or as Adam did　ⁿ3 Masoretic Text; an ancient Hebrew scribal tradition Job, and so had condemned God　ᵒ8 Or Spirit; also in verse 18　ᵖ9 Or many; or great

⁹'I am pure and without sin;
    I am clean and free from guilt.
¹⁰Yet God has found fault with me;
    he considers me his enemy.
¹¹He fastens my feet in shackles;
    he keeps close watch on all my paths.'

¹²"But I tell you, in this you are not right,
    for God is greater than man.
¹³Why do you complain to him
    that he answers none of man's words*q*?
¹⁴For God does speak—now one way, now
        another—
    though man may not perceive it.
¹⁵In a dream, in a vision of the night,
    when deep sleep falls on men
    as they slumber in their beds,
¹⁶he may speak in their ears
    and terrify them with warnings,
¹⁷to turn man from wrongdoing
    and keep him from pride,
¹⁸to preserve his soul from the pit,*r*
    his life from perishing by the sword.*s*
¹⁹Or a man may be chastened on a bed of pain
    with constant distress in his bones,
²⁰so that his very being finds food repulsive
    and his soul loathes the choicest meal.
²¹His flesh wastes away to nothing,
    and his bones, once hidden, now stick out.
²²His soul draws near to the pit,*t*
    and his life to the messengers of death.*u*

²³"Yet if there is an angel on his side
    as a mediator, one out of a thousand,
    to tell a man what is right for him,
²⁴to be gracious to him and say,
    'Spare him from going down to the pit*v*;
    I have found a ransom for him'—
²⁵then his flesh is renewed like a child's;
    it is restored as in the days of his youth.
²⁶He prays to God and finds favor with him,
    he sees God's face and shouts for joy;
    he is restored by God to his righteous state.
²⁷Then he comes to men and says,
    'I sinned, and perverted what was right,
    but I did not get what I deserved.
²⁸He redeemed my soul from going down to the
        pit,*w*
    and I will live to enjoy the light.'

²⁹"God does all these things to a man—
    twice, even three times—
³⁰to turn back his soul from the pit,*x*

that the light of life may shine on him.

³¹"Pay attention, Job, and listen to me;
    be silent, and I will speak.
³²If you have anything to say, answer me;
    speak up, for I want you to be cleared.
³³But if not, then listen to me;
    be silent, and I will teach you wisdom."

34

Then Elihu said:

²"Hear my words, you wise men;
    listen to me, you men of learning.
³For the ear tests words
    as the tongue tastes food.
⁴Let us discern for ourselves what is right;
    let us learn together what is good.

⁵"Job says, 'I am innocent,
    but God denies me justice.
⁶Although I am right,
    I am considered a liar;
although I am guiltless,
    his arrow inflicts an incurable wound.'
⁷What man is like Job,
    who drinks scorn like water?
⁸He keeps company with evildoers;
    he associates with wicked men.
⁹For he says, 'It profits a man nothing
    when he tries to please God.'

¹⁰"So listen to me, you men of understanding.
    Far be it from God to do evil,
    from the Almighty to do wrong.
¹¹He repays a man for what he has done;
    he brings upon him what his conduct
        deserves.
¹²It is unthinkable that God would do wrong,
    that the Almighty would pervert justice.
¹³Who appointed him over the earth?
    Who put him in charge of the whole
        world?
¹⁴If it were his intention
    and he withdrew his spirit*y* and breath,
¹⁵all mankind would perish together
    and man would return to the dust.

¹⁶"If you have understanding, hear this;
    listen to what I say.
¹⁷Can he who hates justice govern?
    Will you condemn the just and mighty One?

---

q13 Or *that he does not answer for any of his actions*   *r18* Or
preserve him from the grave   *s18* Or *from crossing the River*
t22 Or *He draws near to the grave*   *u22* Or *to the dead*   *v24* Or
grave   *w28* Or *redeemed me from going down to the grave*   *x30* Or
turn him back from the grave   *y14* Or *Spirit*

¹⁸Is he not the One who says to kings, 'You are
worthless,'
and to nobles, 'You are wicked,'
¹⁹who shows no partiality to princes
and does not favor the rich over the poor,
for they are all the work of his hands?
²⁰They die in an instant, in the middle of the
night;
the people are shaken and they pass away;
the mighty are removed without human
hand.

²¹"His eyes are on the ways of men;
he sees their every step.
²²There is no dark place, no deep shadow,
where evildoers can hide.
²³God has no need to examine men further,
that they should come before him for
judgment.
²⁴Without inquiry he shatters the mighty
and sets up others in their place.
²⁵Because he takes note of their deeds,
he overthrows them in the night and they
are crushed.
²⁶He punishes them for their wickedness
where everyone can see them,
²⁷because they turned from following him
and had no regard for any of his ways.

²⁸They caused the cry of the poor to come
before him,
so that he heard the cry of the needy.
²⁹But if he remains silent, who can condemn
him?
If he hides his face, who can see him?
Yet he is over man and nation alike,
³⁰   to keep a godless man from ruling,
from laying snares for the people.

³¹"Suppose a man says to God,
'I am guilty but will offend no more.
³²Teach me what I cannot see;
if I have done wrong, I will not do so
again.'
³³Should God then reward you on your terms,
when you refuse to repent?
You must decide, not I;
so tell me what you know.

³⁴"Men of understanding declare,
wise men who hear me say to me,
³⁵'Job speaks without knowledge;
his words lack insight.'
³⁶Oh, that Job might be tested to the utmost
for answering like a wicked man!
³⁷To his sin he adds rebellion;
scornfully he claps his hands among us
and multiplies his words against God."

9 / *Job 35*
Songs in the Night

KIERKEGAARD ONCE SAID that whatever it may be that one comes to as a matter of course because of aging, it is not wisdom. So we see that Job's three friends, all senior, have tried to explain Job's suffering and to defend God. Now a young man, Elihu, comes into the picture. Elihu waited in the sidelines because, as he says, "Age should speak" (32:7). He is exasperated with Eliphaz, Bildad and Zophar because they have failed to deal adequately with Job. But he is also angry with Job "for justifying himself rather than God" (32:2). So he jumps into the discussion offering his only slightly revised version of the stock answers, with one important variation.

Warming Up to God Recall a situation in your life when someone "jumped to a conclusion." How did you feel?

Read Job 35.

35
Then Elihu said:
²"Do you think this is just?
You say, 'I will be cleared by God.^z'

³Yet you ask him, 'What profit is it to me,^a
and what do I gain by not sinning?'

^z2 Or *My righteousness is more than God's*   ^a3 Or *you*

4"I would like to reply to you
   and to your friends with you.
5Look up at the heavens and see;
   gaze at the clouds so high above you.
6If you sin, how does that affect him?
   If your sins are many, what does that do to
      him?
7If you are righteous, what do you give to him,
   or what does he receive from your hand?
8Your wickedness affects only a man like
      yourself,
   and your righteousness only the sons of
      men.

9"Men cry out under a load of oppression;
   they plead for relief from the arm of the
      powerful.
10But no one says, 'Where is God my Maker,
   who gives songs in the night,
11who teaches more to us than to[b] the beasts
   of the earth

and makes us wiser than[c] the birds of the
      air?'
12He does not answer when men cry out
   because of the arrogance of the wicked.
13Indeed, God does not listen to their empty
      plea;
   the Almighty pays no attention to it.
14How much less, then, will he listen
   when you say that you do not see him,
   that your case is before him
   and you must wait for him,
15and further, that his anger never punishes
   and he does not take the least notice of
      wickedness.[d]
16So Job opens his mouth with empty talk;
   without knowledge he multiplies words."

[b]11 Or *teaches us by*   [c]11 Or *us wise by*   [d]15 Symmachus,
Theodotion and Vulgate; the meaning of the Hebrew for this word is
uncertain.

Discovering the Word   1. In verse 3 Elihu claims that Job wants to know "What profit is it to me, and what do I gain by not sinning?" yet Job has never said this. Why is this question important to the discussion? 2. How does Elihu answer the question he poses (vv. 4–8)?   3. From verses 1–8 what is Elihu's view of God?   4. In verses 9–16 Elihu deals with a second question—one that *was* asked by Job: Why doesn't God answer prayer? What is Elihu's answer to this question?   5. Why does Elihu's "ministry" not offer any substantial help to Job?

Applying the Word   1. Not all of Elihu's advice is misguided. He does propose that God, if he were sought, would give cheer and comfort in the night when things seem more hopeless than ever (35:10). When, if ever, have you received from God a "song in the night"?   2. Chapter 36 is the last passage in which Job's friends attempt to explain his situation and comfort him. What have you learned about ministering to people in distress?

Responding in Prayer   Praise God for bringing us hope even in the midst of pain.

Job 36—37

36

Elihu continued:

2"Bear with me a little longer and
   I will show you
that there is more to be said in God's
      behalf.
3I get my knowledge from afar;
   I will ascribe justice to my Maker.
4Be assured that my words are not false;
   one perfect in knowledge is with you.

5"God is mighty, but does not despise men;

he is mighty, and firm in his purpose.
6He does not keep the wicked alive
   but gives the afflicted their rights.
7He does not take his eyes off the righteous;
   he enthrones them with kings
   and exalts them forever.
8But if men are bound in chains,
   held fast by cords of affliction,
9he tells them what they have done—
   that they have sinned arrogantly.
10He makes them listen to correction
   and commands them to repent of their evil.

¹¹If they obey and serve him,
    they will spend the rest of their days in
        prosperity
    and their years in contentment.
¹²But if they do not listen,
    they will perish by the sword*e*
    and die without knowledge.

¹³"The godless in heart harbor resentment;
    even when he fetters them, they do not cry
        for help.
¹⁴They die in their youth,
    among male prostitutes of the shrines.
¹⁵But those who suffer he delivers in their
        suffering;
    he speaks to them in their affliction.

¹⁶"He is wooing you from the jaws of distress
    to a spacious place free from restriction,
    to the comfort of your table laden with
        choice food.
¹⁷But now you are laden with the judgment due
        the wicked;
    judgment and justice have taken hold of
        you.
¹⁸Be careful that no one entices you by riches;
    do not let a large bribe turn you aside.
¹⁹Would your wealth
    or even all your mighty efforts
    sustain you so you would not be in
        distress?
²⁰Do not long for the night,
    to drag people away from their homes.*f*
²¹Beware of turning to evil,
    which you seem to prefer to affliction.

²²"God is exalted in his power.
    Who is a teacher like him?
²³Who has prescribed his ways for him,
    or said to him, 'You have done wrong'?
²⁴Remember to extol his work,
    which men have praised in song.
²⁵All mankind has seen it;
    men gaze on it from afar.
²⁶How great is God—beyond our
        understanding!
    The number of his years is past finding out.

²⁷"He draws up the drops of water,
    which distill as rain to the streams*g*;
²⁸the clouds pour down their moisture
    and abundant showers fall on mankind.
²⁹Who can understand how he spreads out the
        clouds,

    how he thunders from his pavilion?
³⁰See how he scatters his lightning about him,
    bathing the depths of the sea.
³¹This is the way he governs*h* the nations
    and provides food in abundance.
³²He fills his hands with lightning
    and commands it to strike its mark.
³³His thunder announces the coming storm;
    even the cattle make known its approach.*i*

37

    "At this my heart pounds
        and leaps from its place.
²Listen! Listen to the roar of his
        voice,
    to the rumbling that comes from his
        mouth.
³He unleashes his lightning beneath the whole
        heaven
    and sends it to the ends of the earth.
⁴After that comes the sound of his roar;
    he thunders with his majestic voice.
    When his voice resounds,
    he holds nothing back.
⁵God's voice thunders in marvelous ways;
    he does great things beyond our
        understanding.
⁶He says to the snow, 'Fall on the earth,'
    and to the rain shower, 'Be a mighty
        downpour.'
⁷So that all men he has made may know his
        work,
    he stops every man from his labor.*j*
⁸The animals take cover;
    they remain in their dens.
⁹The tempest comes out from its chamber,
    the cold from the driving winds.
¹⁰The breath of God produces ice,
    and the broad waters become frozen.
¹¹He loads the clouds with moisture;
    he scatters his lightning through them.
¹²At his direction they swirl around
    over the face of the whole earth
    to do whatever he commands them.
¹³He brings the clouds to punish men,
    or to water his earth*k* and show his love.

¹⁴"Listen to this, Job;
    stop and consider God's wonders.
¹⁵Do you know how God controls the clouds

e 12 Or will cross the River   *j 20 The meaning of the Hebrew for verses 18-20 is uncertain.*   *g 27 Or distill from the mist as rain*   *h 31 Or nourishes*   *i 33 Or announces his coming— / the One zealous against evil*   *j 7 Or / he fills all men with fear by his power*   *k 13 Or to favor them* and makes his lightning flash?

¹⁶Do you know how the clouds hang poised,
those wonders of him who is perfect in
knowledge?

¹⁷You who swelter in your clothes
when the land lies hushed under the south
wind,

¹⁸can you join him in spreading out the skies,
hard as a mirror of cast bronze?

¹⁹"Tell us what we should say to him;
we cannot draw up our case because of our
darkness.

²⁰Should he be told that I want to speak?
Would any man ask to be swallowed up?

²¹Now no one can look at the sun,
bright as it is in the skies
after the wind has swept them clean.

²²Out of the north he comes in golden
splendor;
God comes in awesome majesty.

²³The Almighty is beyond our reach and exalted
in power;
in his justice and great righteousness, he
does not oppress.

²⁴Therefore, men revere him,
for does he not have regard for all the wise
in heart?¹"

¹24 Or *for he does not have regard for any who think they are wise.*

10 / *Job 38*
God in the Storm

SURPRISE IS ONE thing you can count on when dealing with the living God. We have had thirty-seven chapters of gut-wrenching dialogue between Job and his friends, heart-rending prayers by Job to his elusive God, and life-and-death questions hurled by Job at God to make sense of the suffering of the innocent. Job, we think, deserves a comprehensive answer from the supreme Being of the universe. He gets a surprise. For four chapters God speaks in the whirlwind. This is no "still small voice" speaking. God is thundering. But what he thunders is *more questions*.

 Warming Up to God What experiences of God have led you to worship?

 Read Job 38.

38

Then the LORD answered Job out of
the storm. He said:

²"Who is this that darkens my
counsel
with words without knowledge?

³Brace yourself like a man;
I will question you,
and you shall answer me.

⁴"Where were you when I laid the earth's
foundation?
Tell me, if you understand.

⁵Who marked off its dimensions? Surely you
know!
Who stretched a measuring line across it?

⁶On what were its footings set,
or who laid its cornerstone—

⁷while the morning stars sang together
and all the angels^m shouted for joy?

⁸"Who shut up the sea behind doors
when it burst forth from the womb,

⁹when I made the clouds its garment
and wrapped it in thick darkness,

¹⁰when I fixed limits for it
and set its doors and bars in place,

¹¹when I said, 'This far you may come and no
farther;
here is where your proud waves halt'?

¹²"Have you ever given orders to the morning,
or shown the dawn its place,

¹³that it might take the earth by the edges
and shake the wicked out of it?

¹⁴The earth takes shape like clay under a seal;
its features stand out like those of a
garment.

¹⁵The wicked are denied their light,
and their uparaised arm is broken.

^m7 Hebrew *the sons of God*

¹⁶"Have you journeyed to the springs of the sea
or walked in the recesses of the deep?
¹⁷Have the gates of death been shown to you?
Have you seen the gates of the shadow of
deathⁿ?
¹⁸Have you comprehended the vast expanses of
the earth?
Tell me, if you know all this.

¹⁹"What is the way to the abode of light?
And where does darkness reside?
²⁰Can you take them to their places?
Do you know the paths to their dwellings?
²¹Surely you know, for you were already born!
You have lived so many years!

²²"Have you entered the storehouses of the
snow
or seen the storehouses of the hail,
²³which I reserve for times of trouble,
for days of war and battle?
²⁴What is the way to the place where the
lightning is dispersed,
or the place where the east winds are
scattered over the earth?
²⁵Who cuts a channel for the torrents of rain,
and a path for the thunderstorm,
²⁶to water a land where no man lives,
a desert with no one in it,
²⁷to satisfy a desolate wasteland
and make it sprout with grass?
²⁸Does the rain have a father?
Who fathers the drops of dew?
²⁹From whose womb comes the ice?
Who gives birth to the frost from the
heavens

³⁰when the waters become hard as stone,
when the surface of the deep is frozen?

³¹"Can you bind the beautiful^o Pleiades?
Can you loose the cords of Orion?
³²Can you bring forth the constellations in their
seasons^p
or lead out the Bear^q with its cubs?
³³Do you know the laws of the heavens?
Can you set up ⌊God's⌋ dominion over
the earth?

³⁴"Can you raise your voice to the clouds
and cover yourself with a flood of water?
³⁵Do you send the lightning bolts on their
way?
Do they report to you, 'Here we are'?
³⁶Who endowed the heart^s with wisdom
or gave understanding to the mind^s?
³⁷Who has the wisdom to count the clouds?
Who can tip over the water jars of the
heavens
³⁸when the dust becomes hard
and the clods of earth stick together?

³⁹"Do you hunt the prey for the lioness
and satisfy the hunger of the lions
⁴⁰when they crouch in their dens
or lie in wait in a thicket?
⁴¹Who provides food for the raven
when its young cry out to God
and wander about for lack of food?

ⁿ17 Or *gates of deep shadows*   ^o31 Or *the twinkling; or the chains of the*   ^p32 Or *the morning star in its season*   ^q32 Or *out Leo*   ^r33 Or *his; or their*   ^s36 The meaning of the Hebrew for this word is uncertain.

Discovering the Word 1. What common theme do all of God's questions have? 2. Why does God emphasize that Job was not around when he created the world (vv. 4–7)? 3. God lists more things that Job *cannot* do in verses 8–41. What kinds of things are under God's control? 4. What purpose can God have in telling Job that God does things which no human being will ever appreciate or even see? 5. What effect will all these questions have on Job's view of himself and of God?

Applying the Word 1. Do you think that in every complaint against God there is an implicit revolt against our being creatures? Explain. 2. Why do you think it is sometimes more important in our spiritual journey to get more questions than answers? 3. How have questions helped you to grow spiritually?

Responding in Prayer Thank God for allowing you to freely come to him with your questions.

Job 39

39 "Do you know when the
mountain goats give birth?
Do you watch when the doe bears
her fawn?
2Do you count the months till they bear?
Do you know the time they give birth?
3They crouch down and bring forth their young;
their labor pains are ended.
4Their young thrive and grow strong in the wilds;
they leave and do not return.

5"Who let the wild donkey go free?
Who untied his ropes?
6I gave him the wasteland as his home,
the salt flats as his habitat.
7He laughs at the commotion in the town;
he does not hear a driver's shout.
8He ranges the hills for his pasture
and searches for any green thing.

9"Will the wild ox consent to serve you?
Will he stay by your manger at night?
10Can you hold him to the furrow with a
harness?
Will he till the valleys behind you?
11Will you rely on him for his great strength?
Will you leave your heavy work to him?
12Can you trust him to bring in your grain
and gather it to your threshing floor?

13"The wings of the ostrich flap joyfully,
but they cannot compare with the pinions
and feathers of the stork.
14She lays her eggs on the ground
and lets them warm in the sand,
15unmindful that a foot may crush them,

that some wild animal may trample them.
16She treats her young harshly, as if they were
not hers;
she cares not that her labor was in vain,
17for God did not endow her with wisdom
or give her a share of good sense.
18Yet when she spreads her feathers to run,
she laughs at horse and rider.

19"Do you give the horse his strength
or clothe his neck with a flowing mane?
20Do you make him leap like a locust,
striking terror with his proud snorting?
21He paws fiercely, rejoicing in his strength,
and charges into the fray.
22He laughs at fear, afraid of nothing;
he does not shy away from the sword.
23The quiver rattles against his side,
along with the flashing spear and lance.
24In frenzied excitement he eats up the ground;
he cannot stand still when the trumpet
sounds.
25At the blast of the trumpet he snorts, 'Aha!'
He catches the scent of battle from afar,
the shout of commanders and the battle cry.

26"Does the hawk take flight by your wisdom
and spread his wings toward the south?
27Does the eagle soar at your command
and build his nest on high?
28He dwells on a cliff and stays there at night;
a rocky crag is his stronghold.
29From there he seeks out his food;
his eyes detect it from afar.
30His young ones feast on blood,
and where the slain are, there is he."

11 / Job 40
The Joy of Repentance

HARDLY ANYONE WOULD speak of repentance as desirable. But it is! Repentance is not joyless self-hatred but blessed God-discovery. Repentance is the experience of coming home. In this climactic chapter Job finally repents. *But of what?* That surely is one of the burning questions evoked by the book, the answer to which will provide a profound clue for our own spiritual journeys. Job is an exemplary saint (1:8) and has thus far rightly resisted caving in to his friends' insistence that he repent of a long list of moral failures. But Job is not exempt from the need to repent.

Warming Up to God How do you feel when someone tells you, "You *must* repent"?

Read Job 40.

40

The LORD said to Job:

2"Will the one who contends
with the Almighty correct him?
Let him who accuses God answer him!"

3Then Job answered the LORD:

4"I am unworthy—how can I reply to you?
I put my hand over my mouth.
5I spoke once, but I have no answer—
twice, but I will say no more."

6Then the LORD spoke to Job out of the storm:

7"Brace yourself like a man;
I will question you,
and you shall answer me.

8"Would you discredit my justice?
Would you condemn me to justify
yourself?
9Do you have an arm like God's,
and can your voice thunder like his?
10Then adorn yourself with glory and splendor,
and clothe yourself in honor and majesty.
11Unleash the fury of your wrath,
look at every proud man and bring him
low,
12look at every proud man and humble him,
crush the wicked where they stand.
13Bury them all in the dust together;

shroud their faces in the grave.
14Then I myself will admit to you
that your own right hand can save you.

15"Look at the behemoth,[t]
which I made along with you
and which feeds on grass like an ox.
16What strength he has in his loins,
what power in the muscles of his belly!
17His tail[u] sways like a cedar;
the sinews of his thighs are close-knit.
18His bones are tubes of bronze,
his limbs like rods of iron.
19He ranks first among the works of God,
yet his Maker can approach him with his
sword.
20The hills bring him their produce,
and all the wild animals play nearby.
21Under the lotus plants he lies,
hidden among the reeds in the marsh.
22The lotuses conceal him in their shadow;
the poplars by the stream surround him.
23When the river rages, he is not alarmed;
he is secure, though the Jordan should
surge against his mouth.
24Can anyone capture him by the eyes,[v]
or trap him and pierce his nose?

t15 Possibly the hippopotamus or the elephant   u17 Possibly trunk
v24 Or by a water hole

Discovering the Word 1. What three words does God use to describe what Job has been doing up until now (v. 2)? 2. Describe Job's first response to God's self-revelation (vv. 3–5). 3. What indication is there in verses 6–14 that Job has not fully repented even though he is in a more subdued frame of mind? 4. How has Job discredited God in his attempt to justify himself (v. 8)? 5. Through what means does God expand Job's grasp of his personal dilemma (vv. 15–24)?

Applying the Word 1. What have you learned from this passage about true repentance? 2. In what area of your life do you need to come to full repentance?

Responding in Prayer St. Teresa said, "As I see it, we shall never succeed in knowing ourselves unless we seek to know God." Reflect on this thought as you come before God in repentance.

Job 41

41 "Can you pull in the leviathan[w]
with a fishhook
or tie down his tongue with a
rope?
²Can you put a cord through his nose
or pierce his jaw with a hook?
³Will he keep begging you for mercy?
Will he speak to you with gentle words?
⁴Will he make an agreement with you
for you to take him as your slave for life?
⁵Can you make a pet of him like a bird
or put him on a leash for your girls?
⁶Will traders barter for him?
Will they divide him up among the
merchants?
⁷Can you fill his hide with harpoons
or his head with fishing spears?
⁸If you lay a hand on him,
you will remember the struggle and never
do it again!
⁹Any hope of subduing him is false;
the mere sight of him is overpowering.
¹⁰No one is fierce enough to rouse him.
Who then is able to stand against me?
¹¹Who has a claim against me that I must pay?
Everything under heaven belongs to me.

¹²"I will not fail to speak of his limbs,
his strength and his graceful form.
¹³Who can strip off his outer coat?
Who would approach him with a bridle?
¹⁴Who dares open the doors of his mouth,
ringed about with his fearsome teeth?
¹⁵His back has[x] rows of shields
tightly sealed together;
¹⁶each is so close to the next
that no air can pass between.
¹⁷They are joined fast to one another;
they cling together and cannot be parted.

¹⁸His snorting throws out flashes of light;
his eyes are like the rays of dawn.
¹⁹Firebrands stream from his mouth;
sparks of fire shoot out.
²⁰Smoke pours from his nostrils
as from a boiling pot over a fire of reeds.
²¹His breath sets coals ablaze,
and flames dart from his mouth.
²²Strength resides in his neck;
dismay goes before him.
²³The folds of his flesh are tightly joined;
they are firm and immovable.
²⁴His chest is hard as rock,
hard as a lower millstone.
²⁵When he rises up, the mighty are terrified;
they retreat before his thrashing.
²⁶The sword that reaches him has no effect,
nor does the spear or the dart or the
javelin.
²⁷Iron he treats like straw
and bronze like rotten wood.
²⁸Arrows do not make him flee;
slingstones are like chaff to him.
²⁹A club seems to him but a piece of straw;
he laughs at the rattling of the lance.
³⁰His undersides are jagged potsherds,
leaving a trail in the mud like a threshing
sledge.
³¹He makes the depths churn like a boiling
caldron
and stirs up the sea like a pot of ointment.
³²Behind him he leaves a glistening wake;
one would think the deep had white hair.
³³Nothing on earth is his equal—
a creature without fear.
³⁴He looks down on all that are haughty;
he is king over all that are proud."

[w]1 Possibly the crocodile   [x]15 Or His pride is his

12 / Job 42
Is Faith Always Worthwhile?

SO WHAT DO we get out of faith? Money? Power? Success? Every believer comes to these questions at some time or other. It is, after all, Satan's question in the first chapter. And so the fateful test is designed—the test to see whether Job's faith is without any ulterior motive or, as Satan believes, merely a commercial contract rather than a covenant of belonging. After Job prays for his friends, he has his fortune restored and is given a new family. The story ends with Job living happily ever after and dying "old and full of years." But was Satan right? Is unselfish faith possible? or even desirable?

Warming Up to God How do you react when you hear someone talking about the benefits of following Jesus (such as health and wealth) when you have never received some of these blessings?

Read Job 42.

42

Then Job replied to the Lord:

²"I know that you can do all things;
no plan of yours can be thwarted.
³⌜You asked,⌟ 'Who is this that obscures my counsel without knowledge?'
Surely I spoke of things I did not understand,
things too wonderful for me to know.
⁴⌜"You said,⌟ 'Listen now, and I will speak;
I will question you,
and you shall answer me.'
⁵My ears had heard of you
but now my eyes have seen you.
⁶Therefore I despise myself
and repent in dust and ashes."

⁷After the Lord had said these things to Job, he said to Eliphaz the Temanite, "I am angry with you and your two friends, because you have not spoken of me what is right, as my servant Job has. ⁸So now take seven bulls and seven rams and go to my servant Job and sacrifice a burnt offering for yourselves. My servant Job will pray for you, and I will accept his prayer and not deal with you according to your folly. You have not spoken of me what is right, as my servant Job has." ⁹So Eli-

phaz the Temanite, Bildad the Shuhite and Zophar the Naamathite did what the Lord told them; and the Lord accepted Job's prayer.

¹⁰After Job had prayed for his friends, the Lord made him prosperous again and gave him twice as much as he had before. ¹¹All his brothers and sisters and everyone who had known him before came and ate with him in his house. They comforted and consoled him over all the trouble the Lord had brought upon him, and each one gave him a piece of silverʸ and a gold ring.

¹²The Lord blessed the latter part of Job's life more than the first. He had fourteen thousand sheep, six thousand camels, a thousand yoke of oxen and a thousand donkeys. ¹³And he also had seven sons and three daughters. ¹⁴The first daughter he named Jemimah, the second Keziah and the third Keren-Happuch. ¹⁵Nowhere in all the land were there found women as beautiful as Job's daughters, and their father granted them an inheritance along with their brothers.

¹⁶After this, Job lived a hundred and forty years; he saw his children and their children to the fourth generation. ¹⁷And so he died, old and full of years.

ʸ11 Hebrew *him a kesitah*; a kesitah was a unit of money of unknown weight and value.

Discovering the Word 1. After God's speech in 40:15—41:34, Job is moved to full repentance. What words does Job use to describe his direct experience of God (vv. 1–6)? 2. What does Job now know about God and about himself? 3. What do verses 7–17 say about God's evaluation of each of the characters in the drama? 4. Job's friends would probably have agreed with all that God said to Job in chapters 38—41. Why is God angry with them? 5. In what sense has Job spoken of what is right about God (v. 7)? 6. How do you think Job would now answer the question "Why are you suffering?"

Applying the Word 1. In what sense may suffering Christians look forward to the blessing of God? 2. What have you learned through this study about loving God for God's sake?

Responding in Prayer Praise God for what you have learned about him and the way he works in the world through the book of Job.

Psalms

People look into mirrors to see how they look; they look into the Psalms to find out who they are. With a mirror we detect a new wrinkle here, an old wart there. We use a mirror when shaving or applying makeup to improve, if we can, the face we present to the world. With the Psalms we bring into awareness an ancient sorrow, we release a latent joy. We use the Psalms to present ourselves before God as honestly and thoroughly as we are able. A mirror shows us the shape of our nose and the curve of our chin, things we otherwise know only through the reports of others. The Psalms show us the shape of our souls and the curve of our sin, realities deep within us, hidden and obscured, for which we need focus and names.

The Psalms are poetry and the Psalms are prayer. These two features, the poetry and the prayer, need to be kept in mind always. If either is forgotten the Psalms will not only be misunderstood but misused.

Poetry is language used with intensity. It is not, as so many suppose, decorative speech. Poets tell us what our eyes, blurred with too much gawking, and our ears, dulled with too much chatter, miss around and within us. Poets use words to drag us into the depths of reality itself, not by reporting on how life is but by pushing/pulling us into the middle of it. Poetry gets at the heart of existence. Far from being cosmetic language, it is intestinal. It is root language. Poetry doesn't so much tell us something we never knew as bring into recognition what was latent or forgotten or overlooked. The Psalms are almost entirely this kind of language. Knowing this, we will not be looking primarily for ideas about God in the Psalms or for direction in moral conduct. We will expect, rather, to find exposed and sharpened what it means to be human beings before God.

Prayer is language used in relation to God. It gives utterance to what we sense or want or respond to before God. God speaks to us; our answers are our prayers. The answers are not always articulate. Silence, sighs, groaning—these also constitute responses. But God is always involved, whether in darkness or light, whether in faith or despair. This is hard to get used to. Our habit is to talk *about* God, not to him. We love discussing God. But the Psalms resist such discussions. They are provided not to teach us about God but to train us in responding to him. We don't learn the Psalms until we are praying them.

Those two features, the poetry and the prayer, account for both the excitement and the difficulty in studying the Psalms. The *poetry* requires that we deal with our actual humanity—these words dive beneath the surfaces of prose and pretense straight into the depths. We are more comfortable with prose, the laid-back language of our ordinary discourse. The *prayer* requires that we deal with God—this God who is determined on nothing less than the total renovation of our lives. We would rather have a religious bull session.

One editorial feature of the Psalms helps to keep these distinctive qualities of the Psalms before us. The Psalms are arranged into five books. At the end of Psalms 41, 72, 89, 106 and 150 formula sentences indicate a conclusion. Because of these miniconclusions the Psalms are usually printed (in English translations) as Book I (Psalms 1—41), Book II (42—72), Book III (73—89), Book IV (90—106) and Book V (107—150).

This five-book arrangement matches the five-book beginning of the Bible, deeply embedded in our minds as the five books of Moses. The five books of Moses are matched by the five books of David like two five-fingered hands clasping one another in greeting. In the five books of Moses God addresses us by his word, calling us into being and shaping our salvation. In the five books of David we personally respond to this word that addresses us. Prayer is answering speech. Every word that God speaks to us must be answered by us. God's Word has not done its complete work until it evokes an answer from us. All our answers are prayers. The Psalms train us in this answering speech, this language that responds to all God's creating and saving words targeted to our lives.

It is important to notice this well, for it shifts our interpretive stance. Our usual approach to God's Word is to ask, What is God saying to me? That is almost always the correct question when reading Scripture. But in the Psalms the question is, How do I answer the God who speaks to me? In the Psalms we do not primarily learn what God *says* to us, but how to honestly, devoutly and faithfully *answer* his words to us. In the course of acquiring language we learn how to answer our parents, our teachers, our employers and our friends, but we do not get very much practice in answering God. The Psalms train us in answering God. And so we bring a somewhat different mindset to the Psalms than we do to the rest of Scripture—we are learning to *pray*, not study, although the two activities will always be interconnected.

We know almost nothing of the circumstances in which the 150 psalms were written. David is the most named author, but most are anonymous. But that hardly matters, for the settings of the Psalms are not geographical or cultural but *interior*. Calvin called them "an anatomy of all the parts of the soul." Everything that anyone can feel or experience in relation to God is in these prayers. You will find them the best place in Scripture to explore all the parts of your life and then to say who you are and what is in you—guilt, anger, salvation, praise—to the God who loves, judges and saves you in Jesus Christ.

Outline

1/ Psalm 1 —————————————— *Praying Our Inattention*

2/ Psalm 2 —————————————— *Praying Our Intimidation*

3/ Psalm 3 —————————————— *Praying Our Trouble*

4/ Psalm 4 —————————————— *Dealing with Anger*

5/ Psalm 5 —————————————— *Relying on God*

6/ Psalm 6 —————————————— *Praying Our Tears*

7/ Psalm 8 ——————————— *Praying Our Creation*

8/ Psalm 10 ——————————— *A Prayer of Helplessness*

9/ Psalm 13 ——————————— *A Prayer of Self-Doubt*

10/ Psalm 15 ——————————— *A Person of Honesty*

11/ Psalm 16 ——————————— *Finding Balance in Life*

12/ Psalm 18:1–24 ——————————— *A Prayer for Justice*

13/ Psalm 18:25–50 ——————————— *A Prayer for Equipping*

14/ Psalm 19 ——————————— *Comfort from Scripture*

15/ Psalm 22 ——————————— *A Prayer of Anguish*

16/ Psalm 23 ——————————— *Praying Our Fear*

17/ Psalm 24 ——————————— *A Prayer of Ascension*

18/ Psalm 25 ——————————— *Integrity in Times of Doubt*

19/ Psalm 27 ——————————— *Waiting for the Lord*

20/ Psalm 29 ——————————— *The Voice of the Lord*

21/ Psalm 30 ——————————— *Waiting for Security*

22/ Psalm 31 ——————————— *Rescued from Idolaters*

23/ Psalm 32 ——————————— *Confession and Forgiveness*

24/ Psalm 33 ——————————— *Hoping in the Word*

25/ Psalm 34 ——————————— *Deliverance from Trouble*

26/ Psalm 35 ——————————— *Protection from My Enemies*

27/ Psalm 36 ——————————— *The Fountain of the Lord's Love*

28/ Psalm 37:1–17 ——————————— *The Peace of the Lord*

29/ Psalm 37:18–40 ——————————— *Our Inheritance*

30/ Psalm 38 ——————————— *Rebuke and Judgment*

31/ Psalm 39 ——————————— *Facing Life's End*

32/ Psalm 40 ——————————— *Learning to Wait on the Lord*

33/ Psalms 42—43 ——————————— *Hoping in the Lord*

34/ Psalm 44 ——————————— *A Prayer When God Is Silent*

35/ Psalm 45 ——————————— *A Wedding Song*

36/ Psalm 46 ——————————— *Still Point in a Turning World*

37/ Psalm 47 ——————————— *Being Devoted to God*

38/ Psalm 50 ——————————— *Offering Thanks*

39/ Psalm 51 ——————————— *Praying Our Sin*

40/ Psalm 55 ——————————— *Expressing Feelings to God*

41/ Psalm 57 ——————————— *A Prayer of Distress*

42/ Psalm 62 ——————————— *A Prayer of Trust*

43/ Psalm 63 ——————————— *A Prayer of Longing for God*

44/ Psalm 65 ——————————— *A Prayer of Gratitude*

45/ Psalm 66 ——————————— *A Prayer of Joy*

46/ Psalm 67 ——————————— *God's Love for All Creatures*

47/ Psalm 73 —————————— *Praying Our Doubt*

48/ Psalm 77 —————————— *Praying Our Discontent*

49/ Psalm 84 —————————— *A Prayer of Yearning*

50/ Psalm 86 —————————— *A Prayer of Dependence*

51/ Psalm 88 —————————— *A Prayer of Despair*

52/ Psalm 90 —————————— *Praying Our Death*

53/ Psalm 91 —————————— *Angels Among Us*

54/ Psalm 94 —————————— *A Prayer of Anger*

55/ Psalm 95 —————————— *A Psalm of Rest*

56/ Psalm 96 —————————— *Worldwide Worship*

57/ Psalm 99 —————————— *Hail to the King of Kings*

58/ Psalm 100 —————————— *Seeing Myself as Human*

59/ Psalm 102 —————————— *A Prayer of Grief*

60/ Psalm 103 —————————— *Praying Our Salvation*

61/ Psalm 104 —————————— *Protecting God's Creation*

62/ Psalm 107 —————————— *The Goodness of God*

63/ Psalm 109 —————————— *Feeling Anger*

64/ Psalm 110 —————————— *A Psalm of Submission*

65/ Psalm 115 —————————— *A Psalm of Praise*

66/ Psalm 116 —————————— *Talking to God*

67/ Psalm 118 —————————— *Enduring Love*

68/ Psalm 119:1–24 —————————— *Searching for God's Wisdom*

69/ Psalm 119:25–40 —————————— *Seeking God*

70/ Psalm 121 —————————— *A Prayer of Assurance*

71/ Psalm 122 —————————— *A Prayer for Peace*

72/ Psalm 126 —————————— *A Song of Joy*

73/ Psalm 127 —————————— *Worthwhile Work*

74/ Psalm 130 —————————— *A Prayer of Hope*

75/ Psalm 133 —————————— *Blessed Unity*

76/ Psalm 137 —————————— *Praying Our Hate*

77/ Psalm 139 —————————— *Wonderfully Made*

78/ Psalm 142 —————————— *A Prayer of Desperation*

79/ Psalm 143 —————————— *Asking for Guidance*

80/ Psalm 145 —————————— *Relying on God*

81/ Psalm 146 —————————— *The Source of Hope*

82/ Psalm 148 —————————— *A Symphony of Praise*

83/ Psalm 150 —————————— *Praying Our Praise*

1 / *Psalm 1*
Praying Our Inattention

PSALM 1 IS the biblical preparation for a life of prayer. Step by step it detaches us from activities and words that distract us from God so that we can be attentive before him. Most of us can't step immediately from the noisy, high-stimulus world into the quiet concentration of prayer. We need a way of transition. Psalm 1 provides a kind of entryway into the place of prayer.

 Warming Up to God Do you feel a gap (or chasm!) between "real life" (work, school, family) and your prayer life? Explain. Ask God to help you begin to make prayer a part of your life.

 Read Psalm 1.

BOOK I
Psalms 1–41

Psalm 1

¹Blessed is the man
who does not walk in the counsel of the
wicked
or stand in the way of sinners
or sit in the seat of mockers.
²But his delight is in the law of the LORD,
and on his law he meditates day and night.
³He is like a tree planted by streams of water,
which yields its fruit in season

and whose leaf does not wither.
Whatever he does prospers.

⁴Not so the wicked!
They are like chaff
that the wind blows away.
⁵Therefore the wicked will not stand in the
judgment,
nor sinners in the assembly of the
righteous.

⁶For the LORD watches over the way of the
righteous,
but the way of the wicked will perish.

Discovering the Word 1. What contrasts do you notice in the psalm? 2. What significance do you see in the progression from *walk* to *stand* to *sit* (v. 1)? 3. "The law of the LORD" is contrasted with the words *counsel, way* and *seat*. What does this contrast bring out? 4. *Tree* is the central metaphor of the psalm (v. 3). Put your imagination to use. How are law-delighting people like trees? 5. In what ways are the wicked like chaff (vv. 4–6)?

Applying the Word 1. How do these two radically different portraits (the tree-righteous and the chaff-wicked) motivate you to delight in God's Word? 2. How does meditation—listening to God speak to us through Scripture—prepare us for prayer? 3. A *life* of prayer requires preparation, a procedure for moving from inattention to attention. The same procedure will not suit everyone. How can you develop a procedure that fits your circumstances and development?

Responding in Prayer As you turn to prayer, spend careful time in preparation.

2 / *Psalm 2*
Praying Our Intimidation

WE WAKE UP each day in a world noisy with boasting, violent with guns, arrogant with money. How can we avoid being intimidated? What use can prayer have in the face of governments and armies and millionaires? None, if God is not at work; all, if God is. God is as much at work in the public sphere as he is in the personal, and our prayers are as needful there as in our personal lives.

 Warming Up to God How do you feel when you consider the needs of our world and try to pray for them? Know that God is in control. Spend time reflecting on that fact before you begin.

 Read Psalm 2.

Psalm 2

[1]Why do the nations conspire[a]
and the peoples plot in vain?
[2]The kings of the earth take their stand
and the rulers gather together
against the LORD
and against his Anointed One.[b]
[3]"Let us break their chains," they say,
"and throw off their fetters."

[4]The One enthroned in heaven laughs;
the Lord scoffs at them.
[5]Then he rebukes them in his anger
and terrifies them in his wrath, saying,
[6]"I have installed my King[c]
on Zion, my holy hill."

[7]I will proclaim the decree of the LORD:

He said to me, "You are my Son[d];

today I have become your Father.[e]
[8]Ask of me,
and I will make the nations your
inheritance,
the ends of the earth your possession.
[9]You will rule them with an iron scepter[f];
you will dash them to pieces like pottery."

[10]Therefore, you kings, be wise;
be warned, you rulers of the earth.
[11]Serve the LORD with fear
and rejoice with trembling.
[12]Kiss the Son, lest he be angry
and you be destroyed in your way,
for his wrath can flare up in a moment.
Blessed are all who take refuge in him.

[a]1 Hebrew; Septuagint *rage*   [b]2 Or *anointed one*   [c]6 Or *king*
[d]7 Or *son; also in verse 12*   [e]7 Or *have begotten you*   [f]9 Or *will break them with a rod of iron*

 Discovering the Word 1. Compare the opening nouns and verbs in Psalm 1:1–3 with those in Psalm 2:1–3. What differences in orientation do they suggest between these two psalms? 2. How does the Lord view the vaunted power of nations (vv. 4–6)? 3. "Anointed One" in verse 2 is a translation of the Hebrew word *Messiah*. What in this psalm reminds you of Jesus? 4. The psalm begins and ends with references to kings and rulers (vv. 2–3, 10–12). How do they relate to the King enthroned by the Lord (v. 6)?

 Applying the Word 1. It is always easier to pray for personal needs than political situations. But Psalm 2 is entirely political. Therefore, as citizens of Christ's kingdom, what responsibility do we have as citizens of an earthly nation? 2. How does Christ's relationship with kings and rulers impact your prayers for the world?

Responding in Prayer Think of three rulers (presidents, kings, prime ministers or dictators). Pray for them.

---

3 / *Psalm 3*
Praying Our Trouble

PRAYER BEGINS IN a realization that we cannot help ourselves, so we must reach out to God. "Help!" is the basic prayer. We are in trouble, deep trouble. If God cannot get us out, we are lost; if God can get us out, we are saved. If we don't know that we need help, prayer will always be peripheral to our lives, a matter of mood and good manners. But the moment we know we are in trouble, prayer is a life-or-death matter.

Warming Up to God What is the worst trouble you were in this last week? Where did you go for help? Did you get help? God is your help. Talk to him about what you need today.

Read Psalm 3.

Psalm 3

A psalm of David. When he fled from his
son Absalom.

¹O Lord, how many are my foes!
    How many rise up against me!
²Many are saying of me,
    "God will not deliver him."   *Selah*ᵍ

³But you are a shield around me, O Lord;
    you bestow glory on me and lift*ʰ* up my
        head.
⁴To the Lord I cry aloud,
    and he answers me from his holy
        hill.   *Selah*

⁵I lie down and sleep;
    I wake again, because the Lord sustains me.
⁶I will not fear the tens of thousands
    drawn up against me on every side.

⁷Arise, O Lord!
    Deliver me, O my God!
Strike all my enemies on the jaw;
    break the teeth of the wicked.

⁸From the Lord comes deliverance.
    May your blessing be on your
        people.   *Selah*

*g2 A word of uncertain meaning, occurring frequently in the Psalms;
possibly a musical term   h3 Or Lord, / my Glorious One, who lifts*

Discovering the Word   1. *Deliver/deliverance* is a key word in this psalm. What do we learn about the nature of deliverance through its various uses here?   **2.** David's prayer naturally divides into five sections: verses 1–2, 3–4, 5–6, 7 and 8. What progression do you see from each section to the next?   **3.** What actions is God described as taking in this psalm?   **4.** Are you used to thinking of God in these ways? Explain.   **5.** What actions is David described as taking in the psalm?

Applying the Word   1. David describes his foes in verses 1–2. Do you ever feel overwhelmed by threatening people or circumstances? Give an example.   **2.** What kind of trouble are you in right now?   **3.** What in this psalm do you think will help you to pray your trouble?

Responding in Prayer   Take an image or phrase from Psalm 3 and use it to pray your trouble.

---

4 / *Psalm 4*
Dealing with Anger

ANGER IS AN emotion common to all people. Anger in itself is not sin. It is simply an emotion, a God-given part of life as a human being. It's a natural reaction to threats or injuries; yet anger is all too often expressed in ways that spread the harm around. The Old Testament is full of references to God's righteous anger or indignation against sin, and this emotional aspect of God's character also appears in the New Testament through Christ. How can we learn to "be angry, but sin not"?

 Warming Up to God   How do you generally respond when you are angry? (For example, do you talk about it or do you keep it to yourself?)

 Read Psalm 4.

Psalm 4

For the director of music. With stringed instruments. A psalm of David.

¹Answer me when I call to you,
    O my righteous God.
Give me relief from my distress;
    be merciful to me and hear my prayer.

²How long, O men, will you turn my glory
        into shame[i]?
How long will you love delusions and seek
        false gods[j]?   *Selah*

³Know that the LORD has set apart the godly
        for himself;
    the LORD will hear when I call to him.

⁴In your anger do not sin;

when you are on your beds,
    search your hearts and be silent.   *Selah*
⁵Offer right sacrifices
    and trust in the LORD.

⁶Many are asking, "Who can show us any
        good?"
Let the light of your face shine upon us,
    O LORD.
⁷You have filled my heart with greater joy
    than when their grain and new wine
        abound.
⁸I will lie down and sleep in peace,
    for you alone, O LORD,
    make me dwell in safety.

i2 Or you dishonor my Glorious One   j2 Or seek lies

Discovering the Word   1. What is David angry about (v. 2)?   2. How does David deal with his anger (vv. 1, 3)?   3. In verse 4 David suggests that we can be angry and not sin. How do you think that could be possible?   4. What do you think David means by the phrase "search your hearts and be silent" (v. 4)?

Applying the Word   1. How can reflecting on angry feelings be a healthy way of dealing with anger?   2. How can knowing the joy of the Lord (vv. 6–7) help you deal with anger?

Responding in Prayer   Talk to God about any anger you are dealing with right now. Ask him to help you express it directly and not hold it in.

5 / *Psalm 5*
Relying on God

FEELING BETRAYED, PERSECUTED or fearful are common human experiences. Christians are not immune from such emotions. Indeed, because of the opposition of the fallen world to Christ, we will inevitably face them. How do we pray in these circumstances? Instead of allowing our fear or anger to dominate our thinking, we need to focus on God. Psalm 5 is one example of a prayer written in the face of opposition.

Warming Up to God   What happens to your relationship with God (especially your prayer life) when you find yourself facing opposition or persecution?

Read Psalm 5.

Psalm 5

For the director of music. For flutes.
    A psalm of David.

¹Give ear to my words, O LORD,
    consider my sighing.
²Listen to my cry for help,
    my King and my God,

for to you I pray.
³In the morning, O LORD, you hear my voice;
    in the morning I lay my requests before
        you
    and wait in expectation.

⁴You are not a God who takes pleasure in evil;
    with you the wicked cannot dwell.

⁵The arrogant cannot stand in your
     presence;
  you hate all who do wrong.
⁶You destroy those who tell lies;
  bloodthirsty and deceitful men
     the LORD abhors.

⁷But I, by your great mercy,
  will come into your house;
 in reverence will I bow down
  toward your holy temple.
⁸Lead me, O LORD, in your righteousness
  because of my enemies—
  make straight your way before me.

⁹Not a word from their mouth can
     be trusted;
  their heart is filled with destruction.

Their throat is an open grave;
  with their tongue they speak deceit.
¹⁰Declare them guilty, O God!
  Let their intrigues be their downfall.
Banish them for their many sins,
  for they have rebelled against you.

¹¹But let all who take refuge in you
     be glad;
  let them ever sing for joy.
Spread your protection over them,
  that those who love your name may rejoice
     in you.
¹²For surely, O LORD, you bless the
     righteous;
  you surround them with your favor as with
     a shield.

Discovering the Word 1. List the characteristics of the wicked and the righteous from David's descriptions in the passage. 2. When we are opposed or persecuted by others, it is easy to want to take revenge or become aggressive toward them. What is David's strategy for dealing with opposition? 3. David appears confident of God hearing his prayer and shielding him. What grounds are there in the passage for such confidence? 4. What does the passage show us about David's relationship with God? 5. David is clearly accustomed to beginning his day with prayer (v. 3). What are the benefits of this model?

Applying the Word 1. The psalm gives us a clear picture of how God opposes the wicked and deals with them. How does this help in coping with opposition or persecution on a day-to-day basis? 2. Both Christians and non-Christians often blame God for the pain, suffering or persecution that they encounter. How does Psalm 5 help us to understand the pain, suffering and persecution from God's perspective? 3. What aspects of David's prayer in this passage are a helpful model for you?

Responding in Prayer Think of any situations that represent a threat or pressure for you. Spend some time praying about those situations, trying to focus particularly on God's power and supremacy over the situation (while being realistic about the difficulties!).

---

6 / *Psalm 6*
Praying Our Tears

TEARS ARE A biological gift of God. They are a physical means for expressing emotional and spiritual experience. But it is hard to know what to do with them. If we indulge our tears, we cultivate self-pity. If we suppress our tears, we lose touch with our feelings. But if we *pray* our tears, we enter into sadnesses that integrate our sorrows with our Lord's sorrows and discover both the source of and the relief from our sadness.

 Warming Up to God How do you feel about crying (is it always negative, positive or mixed)?

 Read Psalm 6.

Psalm 6

For the director of music. With stringed
instruments. According to *sheminith.*[k]
A psalm of David.

[1] O Lord, do not rebuke me in your anger
or discipline me in your wrath.
[2] Be merciful to me, Lord, for I am faint;
O Lord, heal me, for my bones are in
agony.
[3] My soul is in anguish.
How long, O Lord, how long?

[4] Turn, O Lord, and deliver me;
save me because of your unfailing love.
[5] No one remembers you when he is dead.
Who praises you from the grave[l]?

[6] I am worn out from groaning;
all night long I flood my bed with weeping
and drench my couch with tears.
[7] My eyes grow weak with sorrow;
they fail because of all my foes.

[8] Away from me, all you who do evil,
for the Lord has heard my weeping.
[9] The Lord has heard my cry for mercy;
the Lord accepts my prayer.
[10] All my enemies will be ashamed and
dismayed;
they will turn back in sudden disgrace.

[k] Title: Probably a musical term   [l] 5 Hebrew *Sheol*

Discovering the Word 1. Compare the first verse with the last. Are the tears because of the Lord or the enemies? Explain. 2. What is the cumulative effect of the three verbs *turn, deliver* and *save* in verse 4? 3. The emotional center of this prayer is verses 6–7. How many different ways is weeping expressed? 4. Why the tears? (Go through the psalm and note every possible source.) 5. In verses 8–9 there are three phrases in parallel: *weeping*, *cry for mercy* and *prayer*. Are these aspects of one thing or three different things? Explain.

Applying the Word 1. "How long?" (v. 3) is a frequent question in prayer. Considering the frequency with which it is uttered in Scripture, God must welcome it. What in your life, past or present, evokes this question? 2. Tears are often considered a sign that something is wrong with us—depression, unhappiness, frustration—and are therefore to be either avoided or cured. But what if they are a sign of something right with us? What rightness could they be evidence of?

Responding in Prayer Who do you know who is in grief? Pray for them now, using phrases from Psalm 6 to express their sorrow.

Psalm 7

Psalm 7

A *shiggaion*[m] of David, which he sang to
the Lord concerning Cush, a Benjamite.

[1] O Lord my God, I take refuge in you;
save and deliver me from all who pursue
me,
[2] or they will tear me like a lion
and rip me to pieces with no one to rescue
me.

[3] O Lord my God, if I have done this
and there is guilt on my hands—
[4] if I have done evil to him who is at peace
with me
or without cause have robbed my foe—
[5] then let my enemy pursue and overtake me;
let him trample my life to the ground
and make me sleep in the dust.   *Selah*

[6] Arise, O Lord, in your anger;
rise up against the rage of my enemies.
Awake, my God; decree justice.
[7] Let the assembled peoples gather around you.
Rule over them from on high;
[8]   let the Lord judge the peoples.
Judge me, O Lord, according to my
righteousness,
according to my integrity, O Most High.
[9] O righteous God,
who searches minds and hearts,
bring to an end the violence of the wicked
and make the righteous secure.

[10] My shield[n] is God Most High,

[m] Title: Probably a literary or musical term   [n] 10 Or *sovereign*

who saves the upright in heart.
[11]God is a righteous judge,
    a God who expresses his wrath every day.
[12]If he does not relent,
    he[o] will sharpen his sword;
    he will bend and string his bow.
[13]He has prepared his deadly weapons;
    he makes ready his flaming arrows.

[14]He who is pregnant with evil
    and conceives trouble gives birth to
        disillusionment.

[15]He who digs a hole and scoops it out
    falls into the pit he has made.
[16]The trouble he causes recoils on himself;
    his violence comes down on his own head.

[17]I will give thanks to the LORD because of his
        righteousness
    and will sing praise to the name of the LORD
        Most High.

---

[o]12 Or *If a man does not repent, / God*

7 / *Psalm 8*
Praying Our Creation

DISORIENTATION IS A terrible experience. If we cannot locate our place, we are in confusion and anxiety. We are also in danger, for we are apt to act inappropriately. If we are among enemies and don't know it, we may lose our life. If we are among friends and don't know it, we may miss good relationships. If we are alongside a cliff and don't know it, we may lose our footing. In Psalm 8, we find out where we are and some important aspects of who we are.

 Warming Up to God When traveling, have you ever awakened and not known where you were? The bed is unfamiliar; the room is strange; you look out the window and don't recognize anything. What does it feel like to be disoriented?

Read Psalm 8.

Psalm 8

For the director of music. According to
gittith.[p] A psalm of David.

[1]O LORD, our Lord,
    how majestic is your name in all the earth!

You have set your glory
    above the heavens.
[2]From the lips of children and infants
    you have ordained praise[q]
because of your enemies,
    to silence the foe and the avenger.

[3]When I consider your heavens,
    the work of your fingers,
the moon and the stars,
    which you have set in place,

[4]what is man that you are mindful of him,
    the son of man that you care for him?
[5]You made him a little lower than the
        heavenly beings[r]
    and crowned him with glory and honor.

[6]You made him ruler over the works of your
        hands;
    you put everything under his feet:
[7]all flocks and herds,
    and the beasts of the field,
[8]the birds of the air,
    and the fish of the sea,
    all that swim the paths of the seas.

[9]O LORD, our Lord,
    how majestic is your name in all the earth!

---

[p]Title: Probably a musical term   [q]2 Or *strength*   [r]5 Or *than God*

Discovering the Word 1. Browse through the psalm and note every word that refers to what God has created. How do these things reveal God's glory? 2. Why do you think the psalmist contrasts what children and infants say with what foes and avengers say (v. 2)? 3. What evidence do we have that God is mindful of us, that he cares for us? 4. "Ruler" and "under his feet" (v. 6) can be twisted into excuses to exploit and pillage. What is there in this psalm to prevent such twisting?

Applying the Word 1. How does Psalm 8 compare with the way you view yourself? 2. What adjustments do you need to make to view yourself as God views you? 3. Some people think of themselves as "a little higher than the heavenly beings"; others think, "a little lower than the beasts of the field." In what area has Psalm 8 corrected your self-image?

Responding in Prayer Praise God and use this psalm as the basis for your praise.

Psalm 9

Psalm 9[s]

For the director of music. To ˻the tune of˼ "The Death of the Son." A psalm of David.

¹I will praise you, O LORD, with all my heart;
 I will tell of all your wonders.
²I will be glad and rejoice in you;
 I will sing praise to your name, O Most
 High.

³My enemies turn back;
 they stumble and perish before you.
⁴For you have upheld my right and my cause;
 you have sat on your throne, judging
 righteously.
⁵You have rebuked the nations and destroyed
 the wicked;
 you have blotted out their name for ever
 and ever.
⁶Endless ruin has overtaken the enemy,
 you have uprooted their cities;
 even the memory of them has perished.

⁷The LORD reigns forever;
 he has established his throne for judgment.
⁸He will judge the world in righteousness;
 he will govern the peoples with justice.
⁹The LORD is a refuge for the oppressed,
 a stronghold in times of trouble.
¹⁰Those who know your name will trust in you,
 for you, LORD, have never forsaken those
 who seek you.

¹¹Sing praises to the LORD, enthroned in Zion;
 proclaim among the nations what he has
 done.
¹²For he who avenges blood remembers;
 he does not ignore the cry of the afflicted.

¹³O LORD, see how my enemies persecute me!
 Have mercy and lift me up from the gates
 of death,
¹⁴that I may declare your praises
 in the gates of the Daughter of Zion
 and there rejoice in your salvation.
¹⁵The nations have fallen into the pit they have
 dug;
 their feet are caught in the net they have
 hidden.
¹⁶The LORD is known by his justice;
 the wicked are ensnared by the work of
 their hands.   *Higgaion.*[t] *Selah*
¹⁷The wicked return to the grave,[u]
 all the nations that forget God.
¹⁸But the needy will not always be forgotten,
 nor the hope of the afflicted ever perish.

¹⁹Arise, O LORD, let not man triumph;
 let the nations be judged in your presence.
²⁰Strike them with terror, O LORD;
 let the nations know they are but men.

        Selah

[s] Psalms 9 and 10 may have been originally a single acrostic poem, the stanzas of which begin with the successive letters of the Hebrew alphabet. In the Septuagint they constitute one psalm.   [t] 16 Or *Meditation*; possibly a musical notation   [u] 17 Hebrew *Sheol*

8 / *Psalm 10*
A Prayer of Helplessness

HELPLESSNESS. IT IS an experience shared by everyone. There is no way out. There are no alternatives. It is an experience full of fear, rage and despair. Because our culture places such a high value on individualism and self-reliance, the experience of helplessness is full of shame for us. We expect that others will blame us for letting it happen. And we end up blaming ourselves. In times of helplessness, however, shame and blame are not helpful. What might be helpful is to know that God understands helplessness and that he hears our prayers.

 Warming Up to God Recall a time when you felt helpless. Picture God in that situation with you as your protector and defender. How does that make you feel?

 Read Psalm 10.

Psalm 10ᵛ

¹Why, O Lord, do you stand far off?
　Why do you hide yourself in times of
　　trouble?

²In his arrogance the wicked man hunts down
　　the weak,
　who are caught in the schemes he
　　devises.
³He boasts of the cravings of his heart;
　he blesses the greedy and reviles
　　the Lord.
⁴In his pride the wicked does not seek him;
　in all his thoughts there is no room for
　　God.
⁵His ways are always prosperous;
　he is haughty and your laws are far from
　　him;
　he sneers at all his enemies.
⁶He says to himself, "Nothing will shake me;
　I'll always be happy and never have
　　trouble."
⁷His mouth is full of curses and lies and
　　threats;
　trouble and evil are under his tongue.
⁸He lies in wait near the villages;
　from ambush he murders the innocent,
　watching in secret for his victims.
⁹He lies in wait like a lion in cover;
　he lies in wait to catch the helpless;

he catches the helpless and drags them off
　in his net.
¹⁰His victims are crushed, they collapse;
　they fall under his strength.
¹¹He says to himself, "God has forgotten;
　he covers his face and never sees."

¹²Arise, Lord! Lift up your hand, O God.
　Do not forget the helpless.
¹³Why does the wicked man revile God?
　Why does he say to himself,
　"He won't call me to account"?
¹⁴But you, O God, do see trouble
　and grief;
　you consider it to take it in hand.
The victim commits himself to you;
　you are the helper of the fatherless.
¹⁵Break the arm of the wicked and evil man;
　call him to account for his wickedness
　that would not be found out.

¹⁶The Lord is King for ever and ever;
　the nations will perish from his land.
¹⁷You hear, O Lord, the desire of the afflicted;
　you encourage them, and you listen to their
　　cry,
¹⁸defending the fatherless and the oppressed,
　in order that man, who is of the earth, may
　　terrify no more.

ᵛPsalms 9 and 10 may have been originally a single acrostic poem, the
stanzas of which begin with the successive letters of the Hebrew
alphabet. In the Septuagint they constitute one psalm.

 Discovering the Word 1. The prayer begins with the question "Why, God, do you hide yourself?" Why is this such an urgent question when you are feeling helpless? 2. How does the author describe the person who is attacking him (vv. 3–11)? 3. What is the attitude of the wicked person toward God (vv. 3–4, 11)? 4. How does the writer describe the victim (vv. 2, 10, 14)? 5. How does the writer describe God and his actions on behalf of people who have been abused (vv. 12, 14–18)?

Applying the Word 1. Notice the author's various perspectives of God. The prayer begins with an absent God: "Where are you, God?" In the middle the author risks asking God to respond on his behalf: "Arise, Lord!" The prayer ends with praise to the God who hears and defends the oppressed. Which of these perspectives of God have you experienced? 2. When you feel helpless, how would it help you if you experienced God as acting on your behalf?

Responding in Prayer How would you like God to respond to your feelings of helplessness?

Psalms 11—12

Psalm 11

For the director of music. Of David.

[1]In the LORD I take refuge.
How then can you say to me:
"Flee like a bird to your mountain.
[2]For look, the wicked bend their bows;
they set their arrows against the
strings
to shoot from the shadows
at the upright in heart.
[3]When the foundations are being destroyed,
what can the righteous do[w]?"

[4]The LORD is in his holy temple;
the LORD is on his heavenly throne.
He observes the sons of men;
his eyes examine them.
[5]The LORD examines the righteous,
but the wicked[x] and those who love
violence
his soul hates.
[6]On the wicked he will rain
fiery coals and burning sulfur;
a scorching wind will be their lot.

[7]For the LORD is righteous,
he loves justice;
upright men will see his face.

Psalm 12

For the director of music. According to sheminith.[y] A psalm of David.

[1]Help, LORD, for the godly are no more;
the faithful have vanished from among
men.
[2]Everyone lies to his neighbor;
their flattering lips speak with deception.

[3]May the LORD cut off all flattering lips
and every boastful tongue
[4]that says, "We will triumph with our
tongues;
we own our lips[z]—who is our master?"

[5]"Because of the oppression of the weak
and the groaning of the needy,
I will now arise," says the LORD.
"I will protect them from those who malign
them."
[6]And the words of the LORD are flawless,
like silver refined in a furnace of clay,
purified seven times.

[7]O LORD, you will keep us safe
and protect us from such people forever.
[8]The wicked freely strut about
when what is vile is honored among men.

---

[w]3 Or *what is the Righteous One doing*
Righteous One, examines the wicked, /
[z]4 Or / *our lips are our plowshares*

[x]5 Or *The LORD, the*
[y]Title: Probably a musical term

9 / *Psalm 13*
A Prayer of Self-Doubt

PEOPLE ASK ABOUT God: "Why did God let this happen?" "Was he unable to respond to my prayers?" "Was it my fault?" "Was my faith too weak?" These painful questions and the doubts which they represent are difficult to discuss with other people. They can also be very difficult to share with God.

Fortunately, the Bible itself gives voice to these painful questions. God is not shocked by our struggles with doubt. May knowing that God is able to respond to doubt in helpful ways give you the courage to pray when your heart is full of unanswerable questions.

 Warming Up to God At what times in your life have you struggled with doubt? Talk openly with God about it; he wants to know your true feelings.

 Read Psalm 13.

Psalm 13

For the director of music. A psalm
of David.

¹How long, O Lᴏʀᴅ? Will you forget me
forever?
How long will you hide your face from me?
²How long must I wrestle with my thoughts
and every day have sorrow in my heart?
How long will my enemy triumph over me?

³Look on me and answer, O Lᴏʀᴅ my God.
Give light to my eyes, or I will sleep in
death;
⁴my enemy will say, "I have overcome him,"
and my foes will rejoice when I fall.

⁵But I trust in your unfailing love;
my heart rejoices in your salvation.
⁶I will sing to the Lᴏʀᴅ,
for he has been good to me.

 Discovering the Word 1. The author begins with two questions that express his doubts about God. What are his concerns? 2. In verse 2 what reasons does he give for his sorrow? 3. Why is it helpful to express our doubts to God? 4. The author not only has questions about God, he also has questions about himself. He asks, "How long must I wrestle with my thoughts and every day have sorrow in my heart?" What is it about the experience of doubt that causes people to question themselves? 5. The writer ends the prayer of doubt with a statement of trust (vv. 5–6). How is it possible to doubt and trust at the same time?

Applying the Word 1. When is it difficult for you to follow the writer's example in expressing your doubts about God? 2. How might it give you courage in your spiritual struggle to know that the Bible gives voice to doubts?

Responding in Prayer What doubts would you like to express to God?

Psalm 14

Psalm 14

For the director of music. Of David.

¹The fool*a* says in his heart,
"There is no God."
They are corrupt, their deeds are vile;
there is no one who does good.

²The Lᴏʀᴅ looks down from heaven
on the sons of men
to see if there are any who understand,
any who seek God.

---

a1 The Hebrew words rendered *fool* in Psalms denote one who is morally deficient.

³All have turned aside,
  they have together become corrupt;
there is no one who does good,
  not even one.

⁴Will evildoers never learn—
  those who devour my people as men eat
    bread
  and who do not call on the LORD?
⁵There they are, overwhelmed with dread,

for God is present in the company of the
  righteous.
⁶You evildoers frustrate the plans of the poor,
  but the LORD is their refuge.

⁷Oh, that salvation for Israel would come out
  of Zion!
When the LORD restores the fortunes of his
  people,
let Jacob rejoice and Israel be glad!

10 / *Psalm 15*
A Person of Honesty

A LIE CONTAMINATES everyone close to it. Worst of all, it rots the character of the person who tells the lie.

Warming Up to God   Reflect on the past week. How have you failed to be honest? Take your failings to Christ. What does he have to say to you?

Read Psalm 15.

Psalm 15

A psalm of David.

¹LORD, who may dwell in your sanctuary?
  Who may live on your holy hill?

²He whose walk is blameless
  and who does what is righteous,
who speaks the truth from his heart
³ and has no slander on his tongue,
who does his neighbor no wrong

and casts no slur on his fellowman,
⁴who despises a vile man
  but honors those who fear the LORD,
who keeps his oath
  even when it hurts,
⁵who lends his money without usury
  and does not accept a bribe against the
    innocent.

He who does these things
  will never be shaken.

Discovering the Word   1. What must a person do to be worthy to approach the Lord ("dwell in your sanctuary") (vv. 2–5)?   2. What, according to this psalm, keeps a person from being shaken?   3. What would it be like to live "on the holy hill" of the Lord?   4. When is it hard to keep a promise (v. 4)?

Applying the Word   1. How might this psalm help you to make specific choices for honesty in your dealings with other people?   2. What forms of self-discipline would you recommend to someone who wanted to become more truthful?   3. What help in being honest do you need?

Responding in Prayer   Ask God to help you to have a walk that is blameless.

11 / *Psalm 16*
Finding Balance in Life

JOE IS A Christian businessman. He has significant responsibility at work and puts in long hours. He enjoys his work and is productive. He is also active in his church, teaching Sunday school and serving as a deacon. His wife also works outside the home, so Joe often takes a turn cooking and cleaning. Additionally, he enjoys spending time with his family—playing a game of softball or going out to dinner together.

Joe is the Christian many of us strive to be. He is able to juggle many responsibilities and demands. He seems to be able to maintain a godly balance of values. But does he really exist? This study is about how we can discover God's values for our lives.

 Warming Up to God In what areas of your life do you struggle for balance?

 Read Psalm 16.

Psalm 16

A *miktam*[b] of David.

[1]Keep me safe, O God,
  for in you I take refuge.

[2]I said to the Lord, "You are my Lord;
  apart from you I have no good thing."

[3]As for the saints who are in the land,
  they are the glorious ones in whom is all
    my delight.[c]

[4]The sorrows of those will increase
  who run after other gods.
I will not pour out their libations of blood
  or take up their names on my lips.

[5]Lord, you have assigned me my portion and
    my cup;
  you have made my lot secure.
[6]The boundary lines have fallen for me in
    pleasant places;

surely I have a delightful inheritance.

[7]I will praise the Lord, who counsels me;
  even at night my heart instructs me.
[8]I have set the Lord always before me.
  Because he is at my right hand,
  I will not be shaken.

[9]Therefore my heart is glad and my tongue
    rejoices;
  my body also will rest secure,
[10]because you will not abandon me to the
    grave,[d]
  nor will you let your Holy One[e] see decay.
[11]You have made[f] known to me the path of
    life;
  you will fill me with joy in your presence,
  with eternal pleasures at your right hand.

[b]Title: Probably a literary or musical term [c]3 Or As for the pagan priests who are in the land / and the nobles in whom all delight, I said: [d]10 Hebrew Sheol [e]10 Or your faithful one [f]11 Or You will make

 Discovering the Word 1. According to this passage, what has the Lord done for David? 2. What body imagery does David use to describe his relationship with God (vv. 5, 7–11)? 3. Describe the spirit of David's comments about the land in verses 5–6. 4. What is the significance of the Lord's being at David's right hand (vv. 8–11)? 5. Look back through the entire passage. What is important to people who follow God? 6. How do those values contrast with worldly values?

 Applying the Word 1. In what specific ways do you need to bring your values in line with God's values? 2. What would help you to do that?

Responding in Prayer Make thanking God for the "inheritance" he has given you a focus for prayer. Try to be aware of the different roles (counselor, protector, sustainer, refuge) God plays in your daily life.

Psalm 17

Psalm 17

A prayer of David.

¹Hear, O LORD, my righteous plea;
  listen to my cry.
Give ear to my prayer—
  it does not rise from deceitful lips.
²May my vindication come from you;
  may your eyes see what is right.

³Though you probe my heart and examine me
    at night,
  though you test me, you will find
    nothing;
  I have resolved that my mouth will
    not sin.
⁴As for the deeds of men—
  by the word of your lips
  I have kept myself
  from the ways of the violent.
⁵My steps have held to your paths;
  my feet have not slipped.

⁶I call on you, O God, for you will
    answer me;
  give ear to me and hear my prayer.
⁷Show the wonder of your great love,
  you who save by your right hand
  those who take refuge in you from their
    foes.

⁸Keep me as the apple of your eye;
  hide me in the shadow of your wings
⁹from the wicked who assail me,
  from my mortal enemies who surround me.

¹⁰They close up their callous hearts,
  and their mouths speak with arrogance.
¹¹They have tracked me down, they now
    surround me,
  with eyes alert, to throw me to the
    ground.
¹²They are like a lion hungry for prey,
  like a great lion crouching in cover.

¹³Rise up, O LORD, confront them, bring them
    down;
  rescue me from the wicked by your sword.
¹⁴O LORD, by your hand save me from such
    men,
  from men of this world whose reward is in
    this life.

You still the hunger of those you cherish;
  their sons have plenty,
  and they store up wealth for their
    children.
¹⁵And I—in righteousness I will see
    your face;
  when I awake, I will be satisfied with
    seeing your likeness.

12 / *Psalm 18:1–24*
A Prayer for Justice

IT MAY COME as a surprise that God is angry at those who take advantage of others. God shares our anger at injustice. In the text for this study, the author suggests that God's response to the wicked is anger so intense that the earth itself trembles.

 Warming Up to God When have you felt angry at injustice toward you or toward others?

 Read Psalm 18:1–24.

Psalm 18

For the director of music. Of David the
servant of the Lord. He sang to the Lord
the words of this song when the Lord
delivered him from the hand of all his
enemies and from the hand of Saul. He
said:

¹I love you, O Lord, my strength.

²The Lord is my rock, my fortress and my
   deliverer;
 my God is my rock, in whom I take refuge.
 He is my shield and the horn*g* of my
   salvation, my stronghold.
³I call to the Lord, who is worthy of praise,
 and I am saved from my enemies.

⁴The cords of death entangled me;
 the torrents of destruction overwhelmed
   me.
⁵The cords of the grave*h* coiled around me;
 the snares of death confronted me.
⁶In my distress I called to the Lord;
 I cried to my God for help.
 From his temple he heard my voice;
 my cry came before him, into his ears.

⁷The earth trembled and quaked,
 and the foundations of the mountains
   shook;
 they trembled because he was angry.
⁸Smoke rose from his nostrils;
 consuming fire came from his mouth,
 burning coals blazed out of it.
⁹He parted the heavens and came down;
 dark clouds were under his feet.
¹⁰He mounted the cherubim and flew;
 he soared on the wings of the wind.
¹¹He made darkness his covering, his canopy
   around him—
 the dark rain clouds of the sky.

¹²Out of the brightness of his presence clouds
   advanced,
 with hailstones and bolts of lightning.
¹³The Lord thundered from heaven;
 the voice of the Most High resounded.*i*
¹⁴He shot his arrows and scattered ⌊the
   enemies⌋,
 great bolts of lightning and routed them.
¹⁵The valleys of the sea were exposed
 and the foundations of the earth laid bare
 at your rebuke, O Lord,
 at the blast of breath from your nostrils.

¹⁶He reached down from on high and took hold
   of me;
 he drew me out of deep waters.
¹⁷He rescued me from my powerful enemy,
 from my foes, who were too strong for me.
¹⁸They confronted me in the day of my disaster,
 but the Lord was my support.
¹⁹He brought me out into a spacious place;
 he rescued me because he delighted in me.

²⁰The Lord has dealt with me according to my
   righteousness;
 according to the cleanness of my hands he
   has rewarded me.
²¹For I have kept the ways of the Lord;
 I have not done evil by turning from my
   God.
²²All his laws are before me;
 I have not turned away from his decrees.
²³I have been blameless before him
 and have kept myself from sin.
²⁴The Lord has rewarded me according to my
   righteousness,
 according to the cleanness of my hands in
   his sight.

g2 Horn here symbolizes strength.   *h5* Hebrew *Sheol*   *i13* Some
Hebrew manuscripts and Septuagint (see also 2 Samuel 22:14); most
Hebrew manuscripts *resounded, / amid hailstones and bolts of lightning*

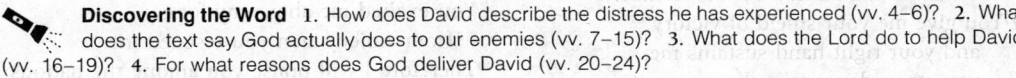

Discovering the Word **1.** How does David describe the distress he has experienced (vv. 4–6)? **2.** What
does the text say God actually does to our enemies (vv. 7–15)? **3.** What does the Lord do to help David
(vv. 16–19)? **4.** For what reasons does God deliver David (vv. 20–24)?

Applying the Word **1.** How do the author's feelings compare with your own? **2.** What thoughts and
feelings do you have as you read this powerful description of God's response to a cry for help?

Responding in Prayer What would you like to say to the God who shares your anger about injustice and
who delights in you?

13 / *Psalm 18:25–50*
A Prayer for Equipping

WRESTLERS, BOXERS AND fencers know that for every move there is an equal and opposite move meant to block it, counterpunch, or parry the thrust. So also God provides just the right protection and timely provision for his people. Here God enables David to alternately evade and thwart his enemies, particularly Saul, eventually overcoming and crushing them.

 Warming Up to God God is our fight coach too. The Lord does not guide where he does not also provide. Think about what battles God may be leading you into and what you need to emerge victorious. Thank God that he will make every provision to help you overcome enemies and obstacles along the way.

Read Psalm 18:25–50.

²⁵To the faithful you show yourself faithful,
   to the blameless you show yourself
      blameless,
²⁶to the pure you show yourself pure,
   but to the crooked you show yourself
      shrewd.
²⁷You save the humble
   but bring low those whose eyes are
      haughty.
²⁸You, O LORD, keep my lamp burning;
   my God turns my darkness into light.
²⁹With your help I can advance against a
      troopʲ;
   with my God I can scale a wall.

³⁰As for God, his way is perfect;
   the word of the LORD is flawless.
He is a shield
   for all who take refuge in him.
³¹For who is God besides the LORD?
   And who is the Rock except our God?
³²It is God who arms me with strength
   and makes my way perfect.
³³He makes my feet like the feet of a deer;
   he enables me to stand on the heights.
³⁴He trains my hands for battle;
   my arms can bend a bow of bronze.
³⁵You give me your shield of victory,
   and your right hand sustains me;
   you stoop down to make me great.
³⁶You broaden the path beneath me,
   so that my ankles do not turn.

³⁷I pursued my enemies and overtook them;
   I did not turn back till they were destroyed.
³⁸I crushed them so that they could not rise;
   they fell beneath my feet.

³⁹You armed me with strength for battle;
   you made my adversaries bow at my feet.
⁴⁰You made my enemies turn their backs in
      flight,
   and I destroyed my foes.
⁴¹They cried for help, but there was no one to
      save them—
   to the LORD, but he did not answer.
⁴²I beat them as fine as dust borne on the wind;
   I poured them out like mud in the streets.

⁴³You have delivered me from the attacks of the
      people;
   you have made me the head of nations;
   people I did not know are subject to me.
⁴⁴As soon as they hear me, they obey me;
   foreigners cringe before me.
⁴⁵They all lose heart;
   they come trembling from their
      strongholds.

⁴⁶The LORD lives! Praise be to my Rock!
   Exalted be God my Savior!
⁴⁷He is the God who avenges me,
   who subdues nations under me,
⁴⁸   who saves me from my enemies.
You exalted me above my foes;
   from violent men you rescued me.
⁴⁹Therefore I will praise you among the nations,
      O LORD;
   I will sing praises to your name.
⁵⁰He gives his king great victories;
   he shows unfailing kindness to his
      anointed,
   to David and his descendants forever.

ʲ29 Or can run through a barricade

Discovering the Word 1. Previously, the psalmist noted that the earth trembled and quaked as an expression of God's anger (v. 7). Now it's the enemies of God's people who tremble or quake in their boots (v. 45). What has God done on David's behalf to bring this about? 2. What was David's part in securing this victory in cooperation with God (vv. 25–29)? 3. In what ways did God the Warrior specifically equip or provide for the warrior David (vv. 30–36)? 4. What reversal of fortune do David and the surrounding nations experience as a result of the Lord coming to his rescue (vv. 37–45)? 5. How does the conclusion of this psalm (vv. 46–50) compare with its beginning (vv. 1–6)? 6. What does that tell you about God the warrior?

Applying the Word 1. At what points (feelings, circumstances, outcomes) can you identify with David? 2. Think about the fights God may be preparing you for. What equipping do you need? (Where can God strengthen a particular weakness of yours? What can you praise him for already?)

Responding in Prayer Trust God to fight evil and avenge any wrongs done to you. If you have experienced God's justice in the face of evil, praise him. Recount the ways he has led you and equipped you every step of the way.

14 / *Psalm 19*
Comfort from Scripture

TOM WAS FRIGHTENED before going to surgery. I shared thoughts with him from Psalm 23 about our Shepherd who gives us all we need and goes with us through dark valleys. Tom didn't have to be afraid, because Jesus was with him. He seemed to be at peace. Sharing Scripture may not always be the right thing to help someone, but often it is. Psalm 19 describes what Scripture is like and how it can offer comfort.

Warming Up to God Reflect on some of your favorite words from Scripture. You may want to turn to the passage and reread it. Drink in the comfort those familiar words bring.

Read Psalm 19.

Psalm 19

For the director of music. A psalm
of David.

¹The heavens declare the glory of God;
   the skies proclaim the work of his hands.
²Day after day they pour forth speech;
   night after night they display knowledge.
³There is no speech or language
   where their voice is not heard.ᵏ
⁴Their voiceˡ goes out into all the earth,
   their words to the ends of the world.

In the heavens he has pitched a tent for the
      sun,
⁵ which is like a bridegroom coming forth
      from his pavilion,
   like a champion rejoicing to run his course.
⁶It rises at one end of the heavens
   and makes its circuit to the other;
   nothing is hidden from its heat.

⁷The law of the LORD is perfect,
   reviving the soul.
The statutes of the LORD are trustworthy,
   making wise the simple.
⁸The precepts of the LORD are right,
   giving joy to the heart.
The commands of the LORD are radiant,
   giving light to the eyes.
⁹The fear of the LORD is pure,
   enduring forever.
The ordinances of the LORD are sure
   and altogether righteous.
¹⁰They are more precious than gold,
   than much pure gold;
they are sweeter than honey,
   than honey from the comb.
¹¹By them is your servant warned;
   in keeping them there is great reward.

¹²Who can discern his errors?

ᵏ3 Or *They have no speech, there are no words; / no sound is heard from them*   ˡ4 Septuagint, Jerome and Syriac; Hebrew *line*

Forgive my hidden faults.
¹³Keep your servant also from willful sins;
  may they not rule over me.
Then will I be blameless,
  innocent of great transgression.

¹⁴May the words of my mouth and the
  meditation of my heart
be pleasing in your sight,
  O LORD, my Rock and my Redeemer.

Discovering the Word 1. What does creation reveal about God (vv. 1–6)? **2.** The terms *law*, *statutes*, *precepts*, *commands* and *ordinances* in this passage are synonyms for Scripture. In verses 7–11, how are the Scriptures described? **3.** What do they do? **4.** What is the overall effect of the psalmist's encounter with God through nature and the Scriptures (vv. 12–14)?

Applying the Word 1. From which of the effects of Scripture listed in verses 7–11 have you benefited? **2.** How has this psalm been helpful to you by offering insight or comfort? **3.** Sharing Scripture can be done in three ways. The first and most obvious way is sharing a passage or verse directly. The second is sharing how we have been affected or changed by Scripture. The third is simply living out the principles of Scripture. How might you appropriately and effectively share Scripture with someone in need this week?

Responding in Prayer Ask God to make Scripture alive and active in you this week. Pray that he will help you share his Word, either directly or through actions, with someone in need.

Psalms 20—21

Psalm 20

For the director of music. A psalm
of David.

¹May the LORD answer you when you are in
  distress;
  may the name of the God of Jacob protect
    you.
²May he send you help from the sanctuary
  and grant you support from Zion.
³May he remember all your sacrifices
  and accept your burnt offerings.   *Selah*
⁴May he give you the desire of your heart
  and make all your plans succeed.
⁵We will shout for joy when you are victorious
  and will lift up our banners in the name of
    our God.
May the LORD grant all your requests.

⁶Now I know that the LORD saves his anointed;
  he answers him from his holy heaven
  with the saving power of his right hand.
⁷Some trust in chariots and some in horses,
  but we trust in the name of the LORD our
    God.
⁸They are brought to their knees and fall,
  but we rise up and stand firm.

⁹O LORD, save the king!
  Answer^m us when we call!

Psalm 21

For the director of music. A psalm
of David.

¹O LORD, the king rejoices in your strength.
  How great is his joy in the victories you
    give!
²You have granted him the desire of his heart
  and have not withheld the request of his
    lips.   *Selah*
³You welcomed him with rich blessings
  and placed a crown of pure gold on his
    head.
⁴He asked you for life, and you gave it to
    him—
  length of days, for ever and ever.
⁵Through the victories you gave, his glory is
    great;
  you have bestowed on him splendor and
    majesty.
⁶Surely you have granted him eternal blessings
  and made him glad with the joy of your
    presence.
⁷For the king trusts in the LORD;
  through the unfailing love of the Most High
  he will not be shaken.

⁸Your hand will lay hold on all your enemies;

^m9 Or *save! / O King, answer*

your right hand will seize your foes.
⁹At the time of your appearing
  you will make them like a fiery furnace.
In his wrath the Lord will swallow them up,
  and his fire will consume them.
¹⁰You will destroy their descendants from the
    earth,
  their posterity from mankind.

¹¹Though they plot evil against you
  and devise wicked schemes, they cannot
    succeed;
¹²for you will make them turn their backs
  when you aim at them with drawn bow.

¹³Be exalted, O Lord, in your strength;
  we will sing and praise your might.

15 / *Psalm 22*
A Prayer of Anguish

THIS PRAYER OF anguish parallels the experience of our Lord, who took Psalm 22 to heart and spoke it from the cross. No other psalm is quoted as often in the New Testament. Persecuted saints and lonely Christians ever since have used this prayer to draw near to their God at times when they feel most abandoned.

   Warming Up to God We jokingly refer to places we despise, or would never want to go near or visit again, as "Godforsaken." But being forsaken or abandoned by others is no laughing matter. Do you have a "Godforsaken place" in your past experience? What was that like?

Read Psalm 22.

Psalm 22

For the director of music. To ⌊the tune of⌋
  "The Doe of the Morning." A psalm
  of David.

¹My God, my God, why have you forsaken
    me?
  Why are you so far from saving me,
    so far from the words of my groaning?
²O my God, I cry out by day, but you do not
    answer,
  by night, and am not silent.

³Yet you are enthroned as the Holy One;
  you are the praise of Israel.ⁿ
⁴In you our fathers put their trust;
  they trusted and you delivered them.
⁵They cried to you and were saved;
  in you they trusted and were not
    disappointed.

⁶But I am a worm and not a man,
  scorned by men and despised by the
    people.
⁷All who see me mock me;
  they hurl insults, shaking their heads:
⁸"He trusts in the Lord;

let the Lord rescue him.
Let him deliver him,
  since he delights in him."

⁹Yet you brought me out of the womb;
  you made me trust in you
  even at my mother's breast.
¹⁰From birth I was cast upon you;
  from my mother's womb you have been my
    God.
¹¹Do not be far from me,
  for trouble is near
  and there is no one to help.

¹²Many bulls surround me;
  strong bulls of Bashan encircle me.
¹³Roaring lions tearing their prey
  open their mouths wide against me.
¹⁴I am poured out like water,
  and all my bones are out of joint.
  My heart has turned to wax;
    it has melted away within me.
¹⁵My strength is dried up like a potsherd,
  and my tongue sticks to the roof of my
    mouth;

ⁿ3 Or *Yet you are holy, / enthroned on the praises of Israel*

you lay me[o] in the dust of death.
16Dogs have surrounded me;
a band of evil men has encircled me,
they have pierced[p] my hands and my feet.
17I can count all my bones;
people stare and gloat over me.
18They divide my garments among them
and cast lots for my clothing.

19But you, O LORD, be not far off;
O my Strength, come quickly to help me.
20Deliver my life from the sword,
my precious life from the power of the
dogs.
21Rescue me from the mouth of the lions;
save[q] me from the horns of the wild oxen.

22I will declare your name to my brothers;
in the congregation I will praise you.
23You who fear the LORD, praise him!
All you descendants of Jacob, honor him!
Revere him, all you descendants of Israel!
24For he has not despised or disdained
the suffering of the afflicted one;
he has not hidden his face from him
but has listened to his cry for help.

25From you comes the theme of my praise in
the great assembly;
before those who fear you[r] will I fulfill my
vows.
26The poor will eat and be satisfied;
they who seek the LORD will praise him—
may your hearts live forever!
27All the ends of the earth
will remember and turn to the LORD,
and all the families of the nations
will bow down before him,
28for dominion belongs to the LORD
and he rules over the nations.
29All the rich of the earth will feast and
worship;
all who go down to the dust will kneel
before him—
those who cannot keep themselves alive.
30Posterity will serve him;
future generations will be told about the
Lord.
31They will proclaim his righteousness
to a people yet unborn—
for he has done it.

o 15 Or / *I am laid* *p 16* Some Hebrew manuscripts, Septuagint and Syriac; most Hebrew manuscripts / *like the lion,* *q 21* Or / *you have heard* *r 25* Hebrew *him*

Discovering the Word 1. David did not shrink back from asking tough "why" questions. Neither did Jesus in quoting verse 1 (Mt 27:46; Mk 15:34). What were David and Jesus experiencing at the time they prayed this prayer (vv. 1–2, 6–8)? 2. Being abandoned by friends and surrounded by enemies can feel all the more stark in contrast to one's history of being close to God and his people. What kind of relationship have this psalmist and his people enjoyed with their God (vv. 3–5, 9–10)? 3. What are his attackers like (vv. 12–18)? 4. What does he pray for (vv. 11, 19–21)? 5. In anticipation of God's sure deliverance, what does the psalmist vow (vv. 22, 25)? 6. Who joins him in this chorus of praise and why (vv. 23, 26–31)?

Applying the Word 1. This psalm conjures up images of sword fights, bull fights, dog fights and a lion's den. What scenes of violence contemporary to your experience does this psalm conjure up for you? 2. The Gospel writers applied this psalm to Jesus (see Mt 27:35, 39, 43 and 46). In what ways does Psalm 22 fit the circumstances of Jesus' crucifixion? 3. At what points can you identify with the psalmist or with Jesus?

Responding in Prayer Pour out your anguish before God, as he will listen to your cry for help. Trust God to deliver you from physical circumstances and emotional moods that cause you to feel forsaken. Remember what God has done for you in the past, and join others in praising God for what he will do in the future.

16 / *Psalm 23*
Praying Our Fear

THE WORLD IS a fearsome place. If we manage with the help of parents, teachers and friends to survive the dangers of infancy and childhood, we find ourselves launched in an adult world that is ringed with terror—accident, assault, disease, violence, conflicts. Prayer brings fear into focus and faces it. But prayer does more than bravely face fear; it affirms God's presence in it.

 Warming Up to God Spend some time trying to bring your fears into focus. Know that God is with you in the midst of your fear.

 Read Psalm 23.

Psalm 23

A psalm of David.

¹The LORD is my shepherd, I shall not be in
   want.
² He makes me lie down in green pastures,
he leads me beside quiet waters,
³ he restores my soul.
He guides me in paths of righteousness
   for his name's sake.
⁴Even though I walk
   through the valley of the shadow of
   death,ˢ
I will fear no evil,

for you are with me;
your rod and your staff,
   they comfort me.
⁵You prepare a table before me
   in the presence of my enemies.
You anoint my head with oil;
   my cup overflows.
⁶Surely goodness and love will follow me
   all the days of my life,
and I will dwell in the house of the LORD
   forever.

ˢ4 Or *through the darkest valley*

Discovering the Word 1. There are two large metaphors in the psalm: the shepherd (vv. 1–4) and the host (vv. 5–6). Compare and contrast these two images. 2. Look carefully at the shepherd. How exactly does he care for his sheep (vv. 1–4)? 3. "I will fear no evil" (v. 4) is a bold statement. What does it mean for you to say that? 4. Look carefully at the host. How exactly does he provide for his guest (vv. 5–6)?

Applying the Word 1. Enemies are prominent in the psalm prayers and appear here. Who are your enemies? 2. What is the most comforting thing that you have experienced in the life of faith? 3. Psalm 23 is a weapon against fear. What fear in your life will you go to war against with this prayer as your cannon?

Responding in Prayer Name your fears and ask Christ the Shepherd and Christ the Host to relieve them.

---

17 / *Psalm 24*
A Prayer of Ascension

DAVID MAY HAVE composed this psalm on the occasion of bringing the Ark of the Covenant back to Jerusalem or in commemoration of that historic event. This prayer by worshipers ascending to Mount Zion has long been used by the church to celebrate Christ's ascension to the heavenly Jerusalem, paving the way for others to follow and stand in God's holy presence. Psalm 24 affirms that Jerusalem is the royal site for inaugurating the kingdom of God.

Warming Up to God What is the longest journey or pilgrimage you have made? What was arriving like for you?

Read Psalm 24.

Psalm 24

Of David. A psalm.

¹The earth is the LORD's, and everything in it,
  the world, and all who live in it;
²for he founded it upon the seas
  and established it upon the waters.

³Who may ascend the hill of the LORD?
  Who may stand in his holy place?
⁴He who has clean hands and a pure heart,
  who does not lift up his soul to an idol
  or swear by what is false.ᵗ
⁵He will receive blessing from the LORD
  and vindication from God his Savior.
⁶Such is the generation of those who seek him,

who seek your face, O God of Jacob.ᵘ
                                    Selah

⁷Lift up your heads, O you gates;
  be lifted up, you ancient doors,
  that the King of glory may come in.
⁸Who is this King of glory?
  The LORD strong and mighty,
  the LORD mighty in battle.
⁹Lift up your heads, O you gates;
  lift them up, you ancient doors,
  that the King of glory may come in.
¹⁰Who is he, this King of glory?
  The LORD Almighty—
  he is the King of glory.   *Selah*

ᵗ4 Or *swear falsely* ᵘ6 Two Hebrew manuscripts and Syriac (see also Septuagint); most Hebrew manuscripts *face, Jacob*

Discovering the Word 1. Verses 1–2 echo themes from creation in reference to the founding of a city and the temple. What feelings and images does that backdrop evoke for this worshiper? 2. What kind of person may enter the Lord's sanctuary (vv. 3–6)? 3. Do these restrictions render the temple accessible to the public, only to priests, or to the one and only King? 4. Who is this "King of glory," and how is he described? 5. What glorious things has he done as Lord of creation (vv. 1–2) and God of Jacob (v. 6)?

Applying the Word 1. This psalm raises the doors of our hearts and the standards of readiness for corporate worship. What steps in preparation for worship does this psalm conjure up for you? 2. Paul quotes verse 1, which had become a Jewish blessing at mealtimes, to underscore the believer's freedom to eat meat without a troubled conscience (1Co 10:25–26). What new freedoms does knowing the sovereignty of God, affirmed in Psalm 24, give you?

Responding in Prayer As you seek God's face, prepare to meet his standards of acceptance—pure motives, integrity, trusting totally in God to vindicate you. This may prompt you to confession. Then lift up the gates and doors of your life, with thanksgiving and praise, to let more of the King into your worship.

---

18 / *Psalm 25*
Integrity in Times of Doubt

IN PHILIP YANCEY'S thoughtful book *Disappointment with God*, the writer speaks of Richard—a new and enthusiastic convert to the Christian faith. Richard studied the Bible with diligence and prayed every day. He transferred from a university to a Christian college, graduated, and went on to a Christian graduate school.

Then Richard's parents separated. Richard dropped out of school for a while to try to mend his family. He prayed constantly that God would bring his parents back together. His parents remained apart. Next Richard lost an important job. Then his fiancée jilted him. And his health began to deteriorate.

One night, Richard stayed up all night to pray. For four hours he pleaded with God to reveal himself. Nothing. Finally, Richard got up from his knees, gathered up his Bible and his theology textbooks, and went out to a backyard brick barbecue. There, in the last hours of darkness, Richard burned his books—and his faith.

Why? As Yancey said, "The theology he had learned in school and had written about in his book no longer *worked for him.*" He was disappointed with God. Is faith in God good only as long as it "works"?

 Warming Up to God When you are in a difficult situation, what kind of prayer are you likely to pray to God?

 Read Psalm 25.

Psalm 25[v]

Of David.

[1]To you, O L ORD , I lift up my soul;
[2]   in you I trust, O my God.
Do not let me be put to shame,
   nor let my enemies triumph over me.
[3]No one whose hope is in you
   will ever be put to shame,
but they will be put to shame
   who are treacherous without excuse.

[4]Show me your ways, O L ORD ,
   teach me your paths;
[5]guide me in your truth and teach me,
   for you are God my Savior,
   and my hope is in you all day long.
[6]Remember, O L ORD , your great mercy and
      love,
   for they are from of old.
[7]Remember not the sins of my youth
   and my rebellious ways;
   according to your love remember me,
   for you are good, O L ORD .

[8]Good and upright is the L ORD ;
   therefore he instructs sinners in
      his ways.
[9]He guides the humble in what is right
   and teaches them his way.
[10]All the ways of the L ORD are loving and
   faithful

for those who keep the demands of his
      covenant.
[11]For the sake of your name, O L ORD ,
   forgive my iniquity, though it is great.
[12]Who, then, is the man that fears the L ORD ?
   He will instruct him in the way chosen for
      him.
[13]He will spend his days in prosperity,
   and his descendants will inherit the land.
[14]The L ORD confides in those who fear him;
   he makes his covenant known to them.
[15]My eyes are ever on the L ORD ,
   for only he will release my feet from the
      snare.

[16]Turn to me and be gracious to me,
   for I am lonely and afflicted.
[17]The troubles of my heart have multiplied;
   free me from my anguish.
[18]Look upon my affliction and my distress
   and take away all my sins.
[19]See how my enemies have increased
   and how fiercely they hate me!
[20]Guard my life and rescue me;
   let me not be put to shame,
   for I take refuge in you.
[21]May integrity and uprightness protect me,
   because my hope is in you.

[22]Redeem Israel, O God,
   from all their troubles!

[v]This psalm is an acrostic poem, the verses of which begin with the successive letters of the Hebrew alphabet.

 Discovering the Word 1. Psalm 25 divides into four stanzas. Give a topic-title to each (vv. 1–3, 4–7, 8–15, 16–22). 2. What does it mean to "lift up" your soul to God? 3. Study stanza 2. What all does David ask God to do? 4. Study stanza 3. David began his prayer by saying that he trusted God. In what ways does stanza 3 show that God has integrity—and therefore ought to be trusted? 5. Study stanza 4. What words and phrases here help you to understand David's current situation? 6. Compare David's position, described in stanza 4, with what he hopes from God in verses 12–13. In view of the differences, what does David's prayer say about his own integrity?

Applying the Word 1. Three times David uses the term *remember*. What would you want God to remember (and not remember) about you? 2. What do you count on God to do and to be?

Responding in Prayer Before you pray, meditate on God's character as David did. Ask God to make you a person of integrity.

Psalm 26

Psalm 26

Of David.

¹Vindicate me, O Lord,
  for I have led a blameless life;
 I have trusted in the Lord
  without wavering.
²Test me, O Lord, and try me,
  examine my heart and my mind;
³for your love is ever before me,
  and I walk continually in your truth.
⁴I do not sit with deceitful men,
  nor do I consort with hypocrites;
⁵I abhor the assembly of evildoers
  and refuse to sit with the wicked.

⁶I wash my hands in innocence,
  and go about your altar, O Lord,
⁷proclaiming aloud your praise
  and telling of all your wonderful deeds.
⁸I love the house where you live, O Lord,
  the place where your glory dwells.

⁹Do not take away my soul along with sinners,
  my life with bloodthirsty men,
¹⁰in whose hands are wicked schemes,
  whose right hands are full of bribes.
¹¹But I lead a blameless life;
  redeem me and be merciful to me.

¹²My feet stand on level ground;
  in the great assembly I will praise the Lord.

19 / *Psalm 27*
Waiting for the Lord

ONE OF SAMUEL Beckett's most famous plays is entitled *Waiting for Godot*. Throughout the play the characters wait and wait for Godot to appear, but he never does. The play is Beckett's way of saying that hope is futile—especially hope in God.

In contrast to Beckett's despair, the Bible offers hope to the sufferer. When we feel overwhelmed and ready to give up, Psalm 27 encourages us to "wait for the Lord." When we see no possibility of relief, David assures us, "I am still confident of this: I will see the goodness of the Lord in the land of the living."

 Warming Up to God In what kinds of situations do you find it hardest to wait?

 Read Psalm 27.

Psalm 27

Of David.

¹The Lord is my light and my salvation—
  whom shall I fear?
 The Lord is the stronghold of my life—
  of whom shall I be afraid?
²When evil men advance against me
  to devour my flesh,ʷ

when my enemies and my foes attack me,
  they will stumble and fall.
³Though an army besiege me,
  my heart will not fear;
 though war break out against me,
  even then will I be confident.

⁴One thing I ask of the Lord,
  this is what I seek:

ʷ2 Or *to slander me*

that I may dwell in the house of the Lord
  all the days of my life,
to gaze upon the beauty of the Lord
  and to seek him in his temple.
⁵For in the day of trouble
  he will keep me safe in his dwelling;
he will hide me in the shelter of his
    tabernacle
  and set me high upon a rock.
⁶Then my head will be exalted
  above the enemies who surround me;
at his tabernacle will I sacrifice with shouts of
    joy;
  I will sing and make music to the Lord.

⁷Hear my voice when I call, O Lord;
  be merciful to me and answer me.
⁸My heart says of you, "Seek hisˣ face!"
  Your face, Lord, I will seek.
⁹Do not hide your face from me,
  do not turn your servant away in anger;

you have been my helper.
  Do not reject me or forsake me,
  O God my Savior.
¹⁰Though my father and mother forsake me,
  the Lord will receive me.
¹¹Teach me your way, O Lord;
  lead me in a straight path
  because of my oppressors.
¹²Do not turn me over to the desire of my foes,
  for false witnesses rise up against me,
  breathing out violence.

¹³I am still confident of this:
  I will see the goodness of the Lord
  in the land of the living.
¹⁴Wait for the Lord;
  be strong and take heart
  and wait for the Lord.

ˣ8 Or *To you, O my heart, he has said, "Seek my*

Discovering the Word **1.** Why is David able to be fearless in the face of evil men, armies, and even war (vv. 1–3)? **2.** What images of safety does David apply to the Lord in verses 1–2 and 5–6? **3.** David seeks not only the Lord's protection but also the Lord himself (v. 4). How is David's intense desire for God revealed in this psalm (vv. 4, 8, 11)? **4.** David's confident statements about the Lord (vv. 1–6) lead up to his prayer in verses 7–12. What is the substance of his prayer? **5.** What real dangers does he seem to be facing? **6.** Why must your hope not only be confident but also patient (v. 14)?

Applying the Word **1.** How does it give you hope to know that the Lord is your stronghold (or "mighty fortress") during battle and your shelter from life's storms? **2.** The psalm ends as it begins—with David's confidence in the Lord's help (vv. 13–14). How can David's view of God help you to "be strong and take heart" in the midst of suffering?

 Responding in Prayer Ask God to strengthen your confidence in his promises and to make you patient as you wait for his answers.

Psalm 28

Psalm 28

Of David.

¹To you I call, O Lord my Rock;
  do not turn a deaf ear to me.
For if you remain silent,
  I will be like those who have gone down to
    the pit.
²Hear my cry for mercy
  as I call to you for help,
as I lift up my hands
  toward your Most Holy Place.

³Do not drag me away with the wicked,
  with those who do evil,
who speak cordially with their neighbors
  but harbor malice in their hearts.
⁴Repay them for their deeds
  and for their evil work;
repay them for what their hands have done
  and bring back upon them what they
    deserve.
⁵Since they show no regard for the works of
    the Lord
  and what his hands have done,
he will tear them down

and never build them up again.

⁶Praise be to the LORD,
for he has heard my cry for mercy.
⁷The LORD is my strength and my shield;
my heart trusts in him, and I am helped.
My heart leaps for joy

and I will give thanks to him in song.

⁸The LORD is the strength of his people,
a fortress of salvation for his anointed one.
⁹Save your people and bless your inheritance;
be their shepherd and carry them forever.

20 / *Psalm 29*
The Voice of the Lord

WHAT ARE THE ways that God chooses to speak to us? He uses the counsel of friends or the subtlety of our own conscience, and often he uses his own Word. But sometimes he speaks so that he can be heard loud and clear, and so that no one can be mistaken about what he is saying. This passage explores the ways we hear the voice of the Lord.

Warming Up to God Recall a time in your life when you felt that God was speaking to you specifically. Thank him for coming to you, and ask him now to speak to your listening heart.

Read Psalm 29.

Psalm 29

A psalm of David.

¹Ascribe to the LORD, O mighty ones,
ascribe to the LORD glory and strength.
²Ascribe to the LORD the glory due his name;
worship the LORD in the splendor of his*y*
holiness.

³The voice of the LORD is over the waters;
the God of glory thunders,
the LORD thunders over the mighty waters.
⁴The voice of the LORD is powerful;
the voice of the LORD is majestic.
⁵The voice of the LORD breaks the cedars;
the LORD breaks in pieces the cedars of
Lebanon.

⁶He makes Lebanon skip like a calf,
Sirion*z* like a young wild ox.
⁷The voice of the LORD strikes
with flashes of lightning.
⁸The voice of the LORD shakes the desert;
the LORD shakes the Desert of Kadesh.
⁹The voice of the LORD twists the oaks*a*
and strips the forests bare.
And in his temple all cry, "Glory!"

¹⁰The LORD sits*b* enthroned over the flood;
the LORD is enthroned as King forever.
¹¹The LORD gives strength to his people;
the LORD blesses his people with peace.

y2 Or LORD with the splendor of   *z6 That is, Mount Hermon*
a9 Or LORD makes the deer give birth   *b10 Or sat*

Discovering the Word 1. The psalmist addresses a specific audience in verse 1—"mighty ones." Why do you think he speaks to them? 2. David urges his audience to "ascribe to the Lord glory and strength" (v. 1). How does his psalm accomplish this? 3. What does "the voice of the Lord" do (vv. 3–9)? 4. What characteristics of God do these verses bring to mind? 5. What does verse 9 tell us about the proper response to hearing the voice of God? 6. Most of Psalm 29 describes the actions of God as a mighty and powerful rainstorm, inspiring not only awe, but even fear. However, the psalm ends (v. 11) describing the actions of God in quite a different fashion. How does this complete the picture of God that David has painted?

Applying the Word 1. How does observing the power of God in both nature and in his own actions help us understand the nature and role of worship in our lives? 2. Sometimes God uses a storm to draw our attention to him and cause us to fall before him in awe, but he also "blesses his people with peace." How can this passage help you to better understand the ways of God and his workings in your life?

Responding in Prayer Take some time to "ascribe to the Lord" some of the marvelous deeds he has done for you.

21 / *Psalm 30*
Waiting for Security

MAJOR CORPORATIONS ARE laying off large numbers in the latest rage of downsizing. Those who have gotten a pink slip do their best to cover it, but you can see the pain in their eyes.

One of our basic human needs is security. In the end, if our security, in any area, is dependent on our own resources and abilities, then we must live in constant vigilance. How much better if the Creator of the universe were in charge of protecting us! In this psalm David relates the experience of looking to God for his security. He found it both a humbling and thrilling experience.

Warming Up to God Imagine that you have turned off the radio that is blaring away inside you. Sit for a while in the quiet. You may find that there are protests inside. What are your thoughts and impressions?

Read Psalm 30.

Psalm 30

A psalm. A song. For the dedication of the temple.*c* Of David.

¹I will exalt you, O LORD,
    for you lifted me out of the depths
    and did not let my enemies gloat over me.
²O LORD my God, I called to you for help
    and you healed me.
³O LORD, you brought me up from the grave*d*;
    you spared me from going down into the
      pit.

⁴Sing to the LORD, you saints of his;
    praise his holy name.
⁵For his anger lasts only a moment,
    but his favor lasts a lifetime;
weeping may remain for a night,
    but rejoicing comes in the morning.

⁶When I felt secure, I said,
    "I will never be shaken."
⁷O LORD, when you favored me,

you made my mountain*e* stand firm;
    but when you hid your face,
    I was dismayed.

⁸To you, O LORD, I called;
    to the Lord I cried for mercy:
⁹"What gain is there in my destruction,*f*
    in my going down into the pit?
Will the dust praise you?
    Will it proclaim your faithfulness?
¹⁰Hear, O LORD, and be merciful to me;
    O LORD, be my help."

¹¹You turned my wailing into dancing;
    you removed my sackcloth and clothed me
      with joy,
¹²that my heart may sing to you and not be
      silent.
    O LORD my God, I will give you thanks
      forever.

*c*Title: Or *palace*   *d*3 Hebrew *Sheol*   *e*7 Or *hill country*   *f*9 Or *there if I am silenced*

Discovering the Word 1. No one knows for sure what the problem was, but from the words "depths," "healed," "enemies," "grave" and "pit" what possible dangers may David have been facing? 2. Read the whole psalm again. List the range of emotions that is described. 3. What insight into life does David gain by acknowledging that painful as well as pleasurable experiences come from God (v. 5)? **4.** How do verses 6–7 describe David's sense of dependence on God? **5.** What reasons does David present to God in favor of his deliverance (vv. 9–10)? **6.** Look over the entire psalm. How would you describe David's relationship with God?

 Applying the Word **1.** Difficult circumstances can cause us to reflect on the character of God. How have the circumstances of your life affected your relationship with God? **2.** David expresses some of the ups and downs of his life. Consider the last six months to year of your life and chart your ups and downs. **3.** Picture the Lord with you through the ups and downs of your life. How does it help you to know God is with you?

Responding in Prayer Give thanks to God for the ways he has been a help to you in the hard places of your life.

22 / *Psalm 31*
Rescued from Idolaters

WE LIVE IN a turbulent time. While the turbulence created by clashing belief systems seems new, the clash has been going on in different forms for thousands of years. In this psalm David affirms his choice to trust in the Lord rather than the popular idols of his age. In the current culture war we need to do the same.

 Warming Up to God Make a list of everything you have to do and give it over to God. If God blesses you with a sense of peace, just sit for a while and enjoy his presence before you move on to study.

 Read Psalm 31.

Psalm 31

For the director of music. A psalm of David.

¹In you, O LORD, I have taken refuge;
  let me never be put to shame;
  deliver me in your righteousness.
²Turn your ear to me,
  come quickly to my rescue;
 be my rock of refuge,
  a strong fortress to save me.
³Since you are my rock and my fortress,
  for the sake of your name lead and guide
   me.
⁴Free me from the trap that is set for me,
  for you are my refuge.
⁵Into your hands I commit my spirit;
  redeem me, O LORD, the God of truth.

⁶I hate those who cling to worthless idols;
  I trust in the LORD.
⁷I will be glad and rejoice in your love,
  for you saw my affliction
  and knew the anguish of my soul.
⁸You have not handed me over to the enemy
  but have set my feet in a spacious place.

⁹Be merciful to me, O LORD, for I am in
   distress;
  my eyes grow weak with sorrow,
  my soul and my body with grief.
¹⁰My life is consumed by anguish
  and my years by groaning;
  my strength fails because of my affliction,ᵍ
  and my bones grow weak.
¹¹Because of all my enemies,
  I am the utter contempt of my neighbors;
 I am a dread to my friends—
  those who see me on the street flee from
    me.
¹²I am forgotten by them as though I were
    dead;
  I have become like broken pottery.
¹³For I hear the slander of many;
  there is terror on every side;
 they conspire against me
  and plot to take my life.

¹⁴But I trust in you, O LORD;
  I say, "You are my God."
¹⁵My times are in your hands;
  deliver me from my enemies
  and from those who pursue me.

ᵍ10 Or guilt

¹⁶Let your face shine on your servant;
    save me in your unfailing love.
¹⁷Let me not be put to shame, O LORD,
    for I have cried out to you;
  but let the wicked be put to shame
    and lie silent in the grave.ʰ
¹⁸Let their lying lips be silenced,
    for with pride and contempt
    they speak arrogantly against the
        righteous.

¹⁹How great is your goodness,
    which you have stored up for those who
        fear you,
  which you bestow in the sight of men
    on those who take refuge in you.
²⁰In the shelter of your presence you
        hide them
    from the intrigues of men;

in your dwelling you keep them safe
    from accusing tongues.

²¹Praise be to the LORD,
    for he showed his wonderful love
        to me
    when I was in a besieged city.
²²In my alarm I said,
    "I am cut off from your sight!"
  Yet you heard my cry for mercy
    when I called to you for help.

²³Love the LORD, all his saints!
    The LORD preserves the faithful,
    but the proud he pays back in full.
²⁴Be strong and take heart,
    all you who hope in the LORD.

ʰ17 Hebrew Sheol

Discovering the Word 1. This is a psalm of urgency. What does David want from God (vv. 1–4)? 2. David feels threatened. What words does he use in these verses to describe his plight? 3. What words and ideas in verses 9–13 convey David's sense of isolation? 4. According to verses 14–18, what are several of the things David wants from God? 5. David's response to God's help is praise. What specific things does David praise God for?

Applying the Word 1. Consider a time in your life when you felt that others (perhaps non-Christians) held you in contempt and avoided you. How did it affect you? 2. What was your relationship with God like at that time? 3. What encouragement from God do you need to continue in a harsh world?

Responding in Prayer Tell God that you trust him with the "times" of your life. Ask him to make himself known in new ways to you and your family.

---

23 / *Psalm 32*
Confession and Forgiveness

JUST AS CHOLESTEROL is the silent killer of the physical heart, guilt is the silent killer of our souls. Cholesterol accumulates slowly over the years, residue left by a poor diet, inadequate exercise and perhaps genetic malfunction. So it is with guilt. Little by little, with each act of envy, lust, anger, resentment or other sin, guilt accumulates around our spiritual hearts. The good news is that God won't let us succumb to guilt without many warnings. The exposure of guilt is not for the purpose of condemnation (as it is with Satan) but for cleansing our hearts and restoring the flow of his love.

Warming Up to God What is causing you to feel frustrated or envious or resentful today? Give your feelings over to God one by one.

Read Psalm 32.

Psalm 32

Of David. A *maskil*.[i]

¹Blessed is he
  whose transgressions are forgiven,
  whose sins are covered.
²Blessed is the man
  whose sin the Lord does not count against
      him
  and in whose spirit is no deceit.

³When I kept silent,
  my bones wasted away
  through my groaning all day long.
⁴For day and night
  your hand was heavy upon me;
my strength was sapped
  as in the heat of summer.   *Selah*
⁵Then I acknowledged my sin to you
  and did not cover up my iniquity.
I said, "I will confess
  my transgressions to the Lord"—
and you forgave
  the guilt of my sin.   *Selah*

⁶Therefore let everyone who is godly pray to
      you
  while you may be found;
surely when the mighty waters rise,
  they will not reach him.
⁷You are my hiding place;
  you will protect me from trouble
  and surround me with songs of deliverance.
                                                   Selah

⁸I will instruct you and teach you in the way
      you should go;
  I will counsel you and watch over you.
⁹Do not be like the horse or the mule,
  which have no understanding
but must be controlled by bit and bridle
  or they will not come to you.
¹⁰Many are the woes of the wicked,
  but the Lord's unfailing love
  surrounds the man who trusts in him.

¹¹Rejoice in the Lord and be glad, you
      righteous;
  sing, all you who are upright in heart!

[i] Title: Probably a literary or musical term

 Discovering the Word **1.** Verses 1 and 2 begin with the word *blessed*. How would you define *blessed* from the way David uses it in these verses? **2.** David had a responsive conscience. How did his unexpressed sin affect him (vv. 3–4)? **3.** It feels good to be forgiven. How does David respond in verses 6–11? **4.** It is interesting that David experienced a sense of protection after receiving forgiveness (v. 7). How might unconfessed sin have made him feel vulnerable and exposed? **5.** In verses 8–9 David records the Lord's promise of guidance. From these verses, what is the condition of receiving God's guidance?

Applying the Word **1.** Consider whether there are things in the past for which you are guilty but have never sought forgiveness. Name those things. **2.** Are there things in the past for which you feel guilty but for which there was really no wrong done? Explain.

Responding in Prayer Ask God's forgiveness for what you have done wrong, and experience his grace.

---

24 / *Psalm 33*
Hoping in the Word

AFTER MY CONVERSION I was shocked at what happened when I picked up the Bible. I found myself enticed, confronted, spoken to and challenged. I couldn't get enough of it. Now almost thirty years later, I still can't get enough. The words that God has spoken are never outdated. In this psalm David meditates on the powerful Word of God by which he creates and sustains his world. Because of the nature of God's Word, we need to open our ears to hear as we read to understand.

 Warming Up to God In order to spend time with God today—stop! Don't try to run your own life, and don't tell God what to do. Present your life to God. Ask God to bring in his order.

Read Psalm 33.

Psalm 33

¹Sing joyfully to the LORD, you righteous;
  it is fitting for the upright to praise him.
²Praise the LORD with the harp;
  make music to him on the ten-stringed
    lyre.
³Sing to him a new song;
  play skillfully, and shout for joy.

⁴For the word of the LORD is right and true;
  he is faithful in all he does.
⁵The LORD loves righteousness and justice;
  the earth is full of his unfailing love.

⁶By the word of the LORD were the heavens
    made,
  their starry host by the breath of his
    mouth.
⁷He gathers the waters of the sea into jarsʲ;
  he puts the deep into storehouses.
⁸Let all the earth fear the LORD;
  let all the people of the world revere him.
⁹For he spoke, and it came to be;
  he commanded, and it stood firm.
¹⁰The LORD foils the plans of the nations;
  he thwarts the purposes of the peoples.
¹¹But the plans of the LORD stand firm forever,

the purposes of his heart through all
    generations.

¹²Blessed is the nation whose God is the LORD,
  the people he chose for his inheritance.
¹³From heaven the LORD looks down
  and sees all mankind;
¹⁴from his dwelling place he watches
  all who live on earth—
¹⁵he who forms the hearts of all,
  who considers everything they do.

¹⁶No king is saved by the size of his army;
  no warrior escapes by his great strength.
¹⁷A horse is a vain hope for deliverance;
  despite all its great strength it cannot save.
¹⁸But the eyes of the LORD are on those who
    fear him,
  on those whose hope is in his unfailing
    love,
¹⁹to deliver them from death
  and keep them alive in famine.

²⁰We wait in hope for the LORD;
  he is our help and our shield.
²¹In him our hearts rejoice,
  for we trust in his holy name.
²²May your unfailing love rest upon us, O LORD,
  even as we put our hope in you.

j 7 Or sea as into a heap

 Discovering the Word **1.** What is the emotional tone of this psalm? **2.** The word of the Lord is one of the themes of this psalm. What can you learn about God's word from verses 1–11? **3.** This psalm gives a big picture of God. Other nations thought of their god as a national deity with a limited realm of authority. Over what things does Israel's God have power (vv. 6–11)? **4.** According to verses 12–22, what is God's relationship to the world he created? **5.** What is his special relationship with "those who fear him" (vv. 18–22)?

Applying the Word **1.** Imagine that God watched you conduct your day from beginning to end. What would he see about your actions? **2.** How do they express your priorities, values and commitments? **3.** What hopes for success do you have that are misdirected? (Consider whether you are trusting in your skills, your background, your education, your intelligence, your money, your influence, your friends . . . or a thousand other things.)

Responding in Prayer After you have identified your false hopes, turn them over to God. Ask him to take them from you.

25 / *Psalm 34*
Deliverance from Trouble

DAVID WRITES THIS psalm for the spiritually immature, who need to be instructed in the ways of God. One thing David thinks we need to know is how to live in a way that brings the blessing of God. How do we face the hard times? When we hurt, we want to know: Have we done something wrong? Has God deserted us? What do we need to do to receive God's help? These are good questions. If we pay attention to David, we will get some answers.

 Warming Up to God It assaults our pride to acknowledge that there are things we don't know or problems we can't overcome. But when we stop trying to do it ourselves, we are in a position to receive the help God sends. List questions that you have for God. Don't tell him what to do, just ask. Then sit quietly for a while and listen.

Read Psalm 34.

Psalm 34 ᵏ

Of David. When he pretended to be insane
  before Abimelech, who drove him away,
  and he left.

¹I will extol the LORD at all times;
  his praise will always be on my lips.
²My soul will boast in the LORD;
  let the afflicted hear and rejoice.
³Glorify the LORD with me;
  let us exalt his name together.

⁴I sought the LORD, and he answered me;
  he delivered me from all my fears.
⁵Those who look to him are radiant;
  their faces are never covered with shame.
⁶This poor man called, and the LORD heard
      him;
  he saved him out of all his troubles.
⁷The angel of the LORD encamps around those
      who fear him,
  and he delivers them.
⁸Taste and see that the LORD is good;
  blessed is the man who takes refuge in him.
⁹Fear the LORD, you his saints,
  for those who fear him lack nothing.
¹⁰The lions may grow weak and hungry,
  but those who seek the LORD lack no good
      thing.

¹¹Come, my children, listen to me;
  I will teach you the fear of the LORD.

¹²Whoever of you loves life
  and desires to see many good days,
¹³keep your tongue from evil
  and your lips from speaking lies.
¹⁴Turn from evil and do good;
  seek peace and pursue it.

¹⁵The eyes of the LORD are on the righteous
  and his ears are attentive to their cry;
¹⁶the face of the LORD is against those who do
      evil,
  to cut off the memory of them from the
      earth.

¹⁷The righteous cry out, and the LORD hears
      them;
  he delivers them from all their troubles.
¹⁸The LORD is close to the brokenhearted
  and saves those who are crushed in spirit.

¹⁹A righteous man may have many troubles,
  but the LORD delivers him from them all;
²⁰he protects all his bones,
  not one of them will be broken.

²¹Evil will slay the wicked;
  the foes of the righteous will be
      condemned.
²²The LORD redeems his servants;
  no one will be condemned who takes
      refuge in him.

ᵏThis psalm is an acrostic poem, the verses of which begin with the successive letters of the Hebrew alphabet.

Discovering the Word **1.** What words does David use in verses 1–10 to express his feelings toward God? **2.** What benefits are mentioned in verses 1–10 that come to those who seek God's help? **3.** What do you think David means by inviting his readers to "taste and see that the Lord is good"? **4.** From verses 11–22, describe a righteous person. 5. According to what David writes, righteousness doesn't guarantee a trouble-free life. What assurances of comfort do the righteous have during times of pain?

 Applying the Word 1. How can the goodness of God be a means of strength in the problems that you face? 2. *Fear of the Lord* is an Old Testament term for "respect and submission to God." We should be afraid of offending God with conscious acts of disobedience. What temptations are you facing now? 3. How can learning the fear of the Lord keep you acting and thinking righteously?

Responding in Prayer Ask God to increase your ability to "taste and see" that he is with you and that he is good.

26 / *Psalm 35*
Protection from My Enemies

YOU MIGHT BE tempted to look at this psalm as barbaric and primitive. It contains angry thoughts of revenge. When David feels hurt, the anger pours forth in an eloquent torrent. There is no sense of "I'm not supposed to feel this way." Christian maturity is not about reducing the highs and lows of emotions to a level plane, but of feeling deeply in a godly way. The issue is not how or what we feel, but what we do with our emotions. David shows the way.

 Warming Up to God Those who know God hunger for him. Before you begin your study, allow a desire for God to rise within you.

 Read Psalm 35.

Psalm 35
Of David.

¹Contend, O LORD, with those who contend
with me;
fight against those who fight against me.
²Take up shield and buckler;
arise and come to my aid.
³Brandish spear and javelin¹
against those who pursue me.
Say to my soul,
"I am your salvation."

⁴May those who seek my life
be disgraced and put to shame;
may those who plot my ruin
be turned back in dismay.
⁵May they be like chaff before the wind,
with the angel of the LORD driving them
away;
⁶may their path be dark and slippery,
with the angel of the LORD pursuing them.
⁷Since they hid their net for me without cause
and without cause dug a pit for me,
⁸may ruin overtake them by surprise—

may the net they hid entangle them,
may they fall into the pit, to their ruin.
⁹Then my soul will rejoice in the LORD
and delight in his salvation.
¹⁰My whole being will exclaim,
"Who is like you, O LORD?
You rescue the poor from those too strong for
them,
the poor and needy from those who rob
them."

¹¹Ruthless witnesses come forward;
they question me on things I know nothing
about.
¹²They repay me evil for good
and leave my soul forlorn.
¹³Yet when they were ill, I put on sackcloth
and humbled myself with fasting.
When my prayers returned to me
unanswered,
¹⁴ I went about mourning
as though for my friend or brother.
I bowed my head in grief
as though weeping for my mother.
¹⁵But when I stumbled, they gathered in glee;

13 Or *and block the way*

attackers gathered against me when I was
    unaware.
They slandered me without ceasing.
¹⁶Like the ungodly they maliciously mocked[m];
    they gnashed their teeth at me.
¹⁷O Lord, how long will you look on?
    Rescue my life from their ravages,
    my precious life from these lions.
¹⁸I will give you thanks in the great
        assembly;
    among throngs of people I will
        praise you.

¹⁹Let not those gloat over me
    who are my enemies without cause;
    let not those who hate me without reason
    maliciously wink the eye.
²⁰They do not speak peaceably,
    but devise false accusations
    against those who live quietly in
        the land.
²¹They gape at me and say, "Aha! Aha!
    With our own eyes we have seen it."

²²O Lord, you have seen this; be not silent.
    Do not be far from me, O Lord.

²³Awake, and rise to my defense!
    Contend for me, my God and Lord.
²⁴Vindicate me in your righteousness, O Lord
        my God;
    do not let them gloat over me.
²⁵Do not let them think, "Aha, just what we
        wanted!"
    or say, "We have swallowed him up."

²⁶May all who gloat over my distress
    be put to shame and confusion;
    may all who exalt themselves over me
    be clothed with shame and disgrace.
²⁷May those who delight in my vindication
    shout for joy and gladness;
    may they always say, "The Lord be
        exalted,
    who delights in the well-being of his
        servant."
²⁸My tongue will speak of your righteousness
    and of your praises all day long.

[m] 16 Septuagint; Hebrew may mean *ungodly circle of mockers*.

Discovering the Word 1. In your own words describe the different kinds of misfortune David would like to see inflicted on those who have hurt him (vv. 4–6, 8, 26). **2.** What reasons does David give for being so hurt and angry (vv. 4, 7, 11–16, 19–21)? **3.** What do verses 11–16 reveal about David's enemies? **4.** What does the cry "How long will you look on?" (v. 17) imply about David's sense of God's help? **5.** David continues with the description of his adversaries' behavior. What have his enemies done in verses 19–28 to hurt him?

Applying the Word 1. We may not feel gracious toward those who hurt us, but we choose to act that way, not from feelings but from obedience to Jesus Christ. Who do you feel hostility and anger toward? **2.** When we come through a trying experience with a sense of victory, it is natural to think about what a good job we have done and how cleverly we have faced our problems. David, however, avoids the temptation of personal boasting and gives praise to God. How does waiting on the Lord for help keep us from taking credit that belongs to God?

 Responding in Prayer Ask God to bless those who have hurt you.

---

27 / *Psalm 36*
The Fountain of the Lord's Love

I FIND LOVE difficult to talk about. For one thing, my need for love is embarrassing. When I acknowledge that I need love, it means that I am not complete in myself. To receive love, I must look to someone else. To make matters worse, I find that my need for love is inexhaustible. Yesterday's love is not enough for today.

Our need for love means we need people—friends, spouses, family members. However, our need for love is such that even if all those people loved us perfectly, we still wouldn't have enough love to meet our need. David celebrates the good news that God's supply of love is more than sufficient. God's love reaches to the heavens and has more substance than the biggest mountains.

 Warming Up to God Consider how open you are to receiving love from God, your family, friends and fellow Christians. Ask God to soften your heart as you prepare to spend time in his Word. Give over to God any hardening factors that you can discern.

Read Psalm 36.

Psalm 36

For the director of music. Of David the
servant of the Lord.

¹An oracle is within my heart
concerning the sinfulness of the
wicked:[n]
There is no fear of God
before his eyes.
²For in his own eyes he flatters himself
too much to detect or hate his sin.
³The words of his mouth are wicked and
deceitful;
he has ceased to be wise and to do
good.
⁴Even on his bed he plots evil;
he commits himself to a sinful course
and does not reject what is wrong.

⁵Your love, O Lord, reaches to the heavens,
your faithfulness to the skies.
⁶Your righteousness is like the mighty
mountains,

your justice like the great deep.
O Lord, you preserve both man and beast.
⁷ How priceless is your unfailing love!
Both high and low among men
find[o] refuge in the shadow of your
wings.
⁸They feast on the abundance of your
house;
you give them drink from your river of
delights.
⁹For with you is the fountain of life;
in your light we see light.

¹⁰Continue your love to those who know you,
your righteousness to the upright in heart.
¹¹May the foot of the proud not come against
me,
nor the hand of the wicked drive me away.
¹²See how the evildoers lie fallen—
thrown down, not able to rise!

[n]1 Or heart: / Sin proceeds from the wicked.   [o]7 Or love, O God! /
Men find; or love! / Both heavenly beings and men / find

 Discovering the Word 1. Describe the character of a wicked person from verses 1–4. 2. Describe the dynamics of a wicked person's relationship to God. 3. What decisions does a wicked person make that lead to a sinful life (vv. 2–4)? 4. David observes that there is no fear of the Lord before the eyes of the wicked. From verses 5–9, what is it that they are blind to? 5. Initially David seems to jump without transition from musing on the wicked to writing on the love of God. However, in verses 10–12 he ties the two themes together. What do these verses tell you about David's experiences?

Applying the Word 1. We all have sinful thoughts from time to time. The wicked, however, do not reject such thoughts. Instead they choose to entertain them and then make a commitment to act upon them. What are some thoughts you have chosen to reject recently because you knew they were wrong? 2. Consider your own ability to accept the Lord's love and his benefits. What hesitations do you have that the Lord loves you? 3. What would have to happen for you to be more open to his love?

Responding in Prayer After you have done that, give thanks to God that he has been so active in helping you choose what is right. If you find that you have let some ungodly ideas settle in your heart, reject them now and ask God to cleanse and redirect your thinking patterns.

28 / *Psalm 37:1–17*
The Peace of the Lord

COMING TO A narrow spot in the road during a Sunday afternoon ride, I got off and walked my bike. I'd gone only a short distance when a car swerved toward me. I dove for the ditch. As the car drove off, I was filled with indignation and rage. What the driver did was foolish, but I was surprised at the intensity of my fuming response. I wanted to yell and shake my fist. Something was out of place in my spirit. In my quiet time a couple of days later, I discovered a list of unresolved hurts and growing grudges. I set aside my Bible reading for the day and had a time of heart cleaning with the Lord.

David says that for us to enjoy peace in the land we have to "refrain from anger and turn from wrath." If you pay attention to what he says, then you will find a new way of coping with anger.

 Warming Up to God The first step in receiving God's peace is to stop shouting so loud. (If we aren't actually shouting out loud, we are usually doing so in our hearts.) Once we stop, he can sort things out. Put down the burdens and fights you face. Give them to God and allow him to speak peace to your heart.

Read Psalm 37:1–17.

Psalm 37ᵖ

Of David.

¹Do not fret because of evil men
    or be envious of those who do wrong;
²for like the grass they will soon wither,
    like green plants they will soon die away.

³Trust in the Lᴏʀᴅ and do good;
    dwell in the land and enjoy safe pasture.
⁴Delight yourself in the Lᴏʀᴅ
    and he will give you the desires of your
        heart.

⁵Commit your way to the Lᴏʀᴅ;
    trust in him and he will do this:
⁶He will make your righteousness shine like
        the dawn,
    the justice of your cause like the noonday
        sun.

⁷Be still before the Lᴏʀᴅ and wait patiently for
        him;
    do not fret when men succeed in their
        ways,
    when they carry out their wicked schemes.

⁸Refrain from anger and turn from wrath;
    do not fret—it leads only to evil.

⁹For evil men will be cut off,
    but those who hope in the Lᴏʀᴅ will inherit
        the land.

¹⁰A little while, and the wicked will be no
        more;
    though you look for them, they will not be
        found.
¹¹But the meek will inherit the land
    and enjoy great peace.

¹²The wicked plot against the righteous
    and gnash their teeth at them;
¹³but the Lord laughs at the wicked,
    for he knows their day is coming.

¹⁴The wicked draw the sword
    and bend the bow
    to bring down the poor and needy,
    to slay those whose ways are upright.
¹⁵But their swords will pierce their own hearts,
    and their bows will be broken.

¹⁶Better the little that the righteous have
    than the wealth of many wicked;
¹⁷for the power of the wicked will be broken,
    but the Lᴏʀᴅ upholds the righteous.

ᵖThis psalm is an acrostic poem, the stanzas of which begin with the successive letters of the Hebrew alphabet.

Discovering the Word 1. David gives an unusually extensive list of exhortations to his readers in verses 1–7. List them in your own words. 2. What benefits does God give to those who live this way? 3. We are not to worry when those who are evil succeed (v. 6). Why not? 4. What are the contrasts between the righteous and the wicked in verses 8–17? 5. Against the backdrop of the wicked, how is God's promise of peace and land an encouragement?

Applying the Word 1. David encourages you to "delight yourself in the Lord." What do you find delightful about knowing God? 2. What hesitations do you have that would keep you from delighting in God?

 Responding in Prayer Pray for those who are angry at you. Ask God to bless them.

---

29 / *Psalm 37:18–40*
Our Inheritance

AS A NEW Christian, I was sure that life would be easier than it had been. I had been in deep trouble emotionally, spiritually and academically. My salvation brought visible, revolutionary changes to all those areas. Everyone knew that *something* had happened. Now looking back several decades, the changes were real. But I'm not so quick to say that becoming a Christian makes life easier. However, it is worth it. This psalm is written from David's perspective of knowing God for over eighty years. David affirms that God keeps his promises and brings rewards to those who trust him.

 Warming Up to God Consider the staggering fact that the Creator of time and eternity loves you. Write down ten things you can think of about the love of God.

 Read Psalm 37:18–40.

---

¹⁸The days of the blameless are known to the
    Lᴏʀᴅ,
  and their inheritance will endure forever.
¹⁹In times of disaster they will not wither;
  in days of famine they will enjoy plenty.

²⁰But the wicked will perish:
  The Lᴏʀᴅ's enemies will be like the beauty
    of the fields,
  they will vanish—vanish like smoke.

²¹The wicked borrow and do not repay,
  but the righteous give generously;
²²those the Lᴏʀᴅ blesses will inherit the land,
  but those he curses will be cut off.

²³If the Lᴏʀᴅ delights in a man's way,
  he makes his steps firm;
²⁴though he stumble, he will not fall,
  for the Lᴏʀᴅ upholds him with his hand.

²⁵I was young and now I am old,
  yet I have never seen the righteous forsaken
  or their children begging bread.
²⁶They are always generous and lend freely;
  their children will be blessed.

²⁷Turn from evil and do good;
  then you will dwell in the land forever.
²⁸For the Lᴏʀᴅ loves the just
  and will not forsake his faithful ones.

They will be protected forever,
  but the offspring of the wicked will be cut
    off;
²⁹the righteous will inherit the land
  and dwell in it forever.

³⁰The mouth of the righteous man utters
    wisdom,
  and his tongue speaks what is just.
³¹The law of his God is in his heart;
  his feet do not slip.

³²The wicked lie in wait for the righteous,
  seeking their very lives;
³³but the Lᴏʀᴅ will not leave them in their
    power
  or let them be condemned when brought to
    trial.

³⁴Wait for the Lᴏʀᴅ
  and keep his way.
He will exalt you to inherit the land;
  when the wicked are cut off, you will see
    it.

³⁵I have seen a wicked and ruthless man
  flourishing like a green tree in its native
    soil,
³⁶but he soon passed away and was no more;
  though I looked for him, he could not be
    found.

37Consider the blameless, observe the upright;
  there is a future*q* for the man of peace.
38But all sinners will be destroyed;
  the future*r* of the wicked will be cut off.

39The salvation of the righteous comes from the
  LORD;

he is their stronghold in time of trouble.
40The LORD helps them and delivers them;
  he delivers them from the wicked and saves
    them,
  because they take refuge in him.

q37 Or there will be posterity   r38 Or posterity

 Discovering the Word   1. What are the contrasts between the blameless and the wicked in verses 18–24?   2. What can we know about the future of the wicked (vv. 20, 22, 28, 33–35)?   3. What are the benefits that come to the righteous in the end (vv. 18, 25, 28–29, 33, 37, 39–40)?   4. From verses 25–36, describe the character and actions of the righteous.   5. Describe the relationship between the wicked and the righteous in verses 32–40.

Applying the Word   1. David emphasizes the theme of inheritance in these verses. How can the anticipation of a future inheritance affect the way you live today in your relationships and the way you use your money and your possessions?   2. Let's get more specific. If you knew that all you could want would be coming to you in five years, how would it affect your actions and decisions today?

Responding in Prayer   Pray for those you know who are facing hard times. Ask God to bring his comfort, protection and provision.

30 / *Psalm 38*
Rebuke and Judgment

IF I AM willing to acknowledge that God blesses me, I must be willing to acknowledge that he disciplines me as well. As the author of Hebrews writes, "the Lord disciplines those he loves." God refuses to let me go my own way. This is good news indeed! At the same time, when I talk about the blessing or the judgment of God, I must be careful. I don't understand all that the Lord does. What appears to be a blessing may not be, while what appears to be judgment may not be either. Let's see if we can gain a little light on this difficult issue from David.

 Warming Up to God   God is constantly rescuing us from tight spots. Some of those tight spots we are aware of; most we are not. Make a list of thank-yous to God for as many instances of his help as you can think of.

 Read Psalm 38.

Psalm 38

A psalm of David. A petition.

1O LORD, do not rebuke me in your anger
  or discipline me in your wrath.
2For your arrows have pierced me,
  and your hand has come down upon me.
3Because of your wrath there is no health in
    my body;
  my bones have no soundness because of my
    sin.
4My guilt has overwhelmed me
  like a burden too heavy to bear.

5My wounds fester and are loathsome
  because of my sinful folly.
6I am bowed down and brought very low;
  all day long I go about mourning.
7My back is filled with searing pain;
  there is no health in my body.
8I am feeble and utterly crushed;
  I groan in anguish of heart.

9All my longings lie open before you, O Lord;
  my sighing is not hidden from you.
10My heart pounds, my strength fails me;
  even the light has gone from my eyes.

¹¹My friends and companions avoid me because
    of my wounds;
  my neighbors stay far away.
¹²Those who seek my life set their traps,
    those who would harm me talk of
    my ruin;
  all day long they plot deception.

¹³I am like a deaf man, who cannot
    hear,
  like a mute, who cannot open his
    mouth;
¹⁴I have become like a man who does
    not hear,
  whose mouth can offer no reply.
¹⁵I wait for you, O LORD;
  you will answer, O Lord my God.
¹⁶For I said, "Do not let them gloat

or exalt themselves over me when my foot
    slips."
¹⁷For I am about to fall,
  and my pain is ever with me.
¹⁸I confess my iniquity;
  I am troubled by my sin.
¹⁹Many are those who are my vigorous
    enemies;
  those who hate me without reason are
    numerous.
²⁰Those who repay my good with evil
  slander me when I pursue what is good.

²¹O LORD, do not forsake me;
  be not far from me, O my God.
²²Come quickly to help me,
  O Lord my Savior.

 Discovering the Word 1. David writes during a time of great pain. What images does he use to describe his situation (vv. 2–14)? 2. What reasons can you discover for his all-encompassing pain in these verses? 3. What physical, social and spiritual afflictions is David experiencing in these verses? 4. Describe David's attitude toward God in the midst of his afflictions. 5. What specific things does David want God to do to help him with his pain (vv. 15–16, 21–22)?

Applying the Word 1. What dangers and what benefits come from thinking of our physical, emotional and spiritual states as being the result of the discipline of God? 2. Although David is experiencing rejection and persecution, he acknowledges that he has sinned and shares in the responsibility for his affliction. When have you experienced pain that was at least partly your fault? How did you handle it? 3. What can you learn from David's example?

Responding in Prayer Pray for those whom you have offended this past year. Ask God's blessing on them.

---

31 / *Psalm 39*
Facing Life's End

JANE WALMSLEY, TELEVISION correspondent and commentator on American life, says that an essential element of the American psyche is the fervent belief and hope that somehow it is possible to elude death. That hope of eluding death flies in the face of reality. No one has. Life this side of the Fall is 100 percent fatal. There are some, and David would be among them, who would say that only those who have faced their death can really live life properly. In this psalm he asks God to help him take a long-term view of life, and as you shall read, that includes the impending prospect of death.

 Warming Up to God While we can never quite get our minds around this, the good news is that an eternal God can offer eternal life. Express praise and thanksgiving to our immortal God.

 Read Psalm 39.

Psalm 39

For the director of music. For Jeduthun.
A psalm of David.

¹I said, "I will watch my ways
and keep my tongue from sin;
I will put a muzzle on my mouth
as long as the wicked are in my presence."
²But when I was silent and still,
not even saying anything good,
my anguish increased.
³My heart grew hot within me,
and as I meditated, the fire burned;
then I spoke with my tongue:

⁴"Show me, O LORD, my life's end
and the number of my days;
let me know how fleeting is my life.
⁵You have made my days a mere handbreadth;
the span of my years is as nothing before
you.
Each man's life is but a breath. *Selah*
⁶Man is a mere phantom as he goes to and fro:

He bustles about, but only in vain;
he heaps up wealth, not knowing who will
get it.

⁷"But now, Lord, what do I look for?
My hope is in you.
⁸Save me from all my transgressions;
do not make me the scorn of fools.
⁹I was silent; I would not open my mouth,
for you are the one who has done this.
¹⁰Remove your scourge from me;
I am overcome by the blow of your hand.
¹¹You rebuke and discipline men for their sin;
you consume their wealth like a moth—
each man is but a breath. *Selah*

¹²"Hear my prayer, O LORD,
listen to my cry for help;
be not deaf to my weeping.
For I dwell with you as an alien,
a stranger, as all my fathers were.
¹³Look away from me, that I may rejoice again
before I depart and am no more."

Discovering the Word 1. Remembering that the psalms combine life experience, knowledge of God and emotions, how would you describe David's mood and situation in this psalm? 2. David chooses to be silent in the presence of some hostile people. What effect does David's silence have on him in verses 1–6? 3. When David breaks his silence, he does so by offering a prayer to face his mortality. What does David know (vv. 5–6), and what does he want to know (v. 4)? 4. This is a psalm of judgment. In your own words describe God's approach toward sin in verses 7–13. 5. What does David desire from God for himself (vv. 8, 10)? 6. How does David seem to have come to terms with his death at the end of this passage?

Applying the Word 1. How does considering your own mortality affect the way you think of the present and the future, your possessions, and your relationships? 2. How does the knowledge of eternal life through Jesus Christ affect your reflections?

Responding in Prayer Following David's example, ask God to help you see as much about your own mortality as you can handle. Sit quietly and wait for the Lord's insight. Write down what benefits you can perceive from facing your own death.

---

32 / *Psalm 40*
Learning to Wait on the Lord

JUDY HAD A portable phone beside her. Her son's wife was expecting, and Judy was about to become a grand-mother for the first time. During the entire Bible study, Judy contributed to our discussion. However, if that phone had rung with news of her daughter-in-law's labor, Judy would have been out of there in a minute. Just as Judy was prepared to receive a call and ready to respond when it came, so we should be waiting on the Lord.

Warming Up to God Jesus calls his disciples to deny themselves, take up their cross and follow him. Commit yourself, body and soul, to him. As reservations or objections rise to the surface, ask Jesus to take them from you.

Read Psalm 40.

Psalm 40

For the director of music. Of David.
A psalm.

¹I waited patiently for the LORD;
  he turned to me and heard my cry.
²He lifted me out of the slimy pit,
  out of the mud and mire;
he set my feet on a rock
  and gave me a firm place to stand.
³He put a new song in my mouth,
  a hymn of praise to our God.
Many will see and fear
  and put their trust in the LORD.

⁴Blessed is the man
  who makes the LORD his trust,
who does not look to the proud,
  to those who turn aside to false gods.ˢ
⁵Many, O LORD my God,
  are the wonders you have done.
The things you planned for us
  no one can recount to you;
were I to speak and tell of them,
  they would be too many to declare.

⁶Sacrifice and offering you did not desire,
  but my ears you have piercedᵗ,ᵘ;
burnt offerings and sin offerings
  you did not require.
⁷Then I said, "Here I am, I have come—
  it is written about me in the scroll.ᵛ
⁸I desire to do your will, O my God;
  your law is within my heart."

⁹I proclaim righteousness in the great
    assembly;
  I do not seal my lips,

as you know, O LORD.
¹⁰I do not hide your righteousness in my heart;
  I speak of your faithfulness and salvation.
I do not conceal your love and your truth
  from the great assembly.

¹¹Do not withhold your mercy from me,
    O LORD;
  may your love and your truth always
    protect me.
¹²For troubles without number surround me;
  my sins have overtaken me, and I cannot
    see.
They are more than the hairs of my head,
  and my heart fails within me.

¹³Be pleased, O LORD, to save me;
  O LORD, come quickly to help me.
¹⁴May all who seek to take my life
  be put to shame and confusion;
may all who desire my ruin
  be turned back in disgrace.
¹⁵May those who say to me, "Aha! Aha!"
  be appalled at their own shame.
¹⁶But may all who seek you
  rejoice and be glad in you;
may those who love your salvation always
    say,
  "The LORD be exalted!"

¹⁷Yet I am poor and needy;
  may the Lord think of me.
You are my help and my deliverer;
  O my God, do not delay.

ˢ4 Or *to falsehood*   ᵗ6 Hebrew; Septuagint *but a body you have
prepared for me* (see also Symmachus and Theodotion)   ᵘ6 Or
opened   ᵛ7 Or *come / with the scroll written for me*

Discovering the Word 1. In response to God's help, David proclaims righteousness, doesn't seal his lips, doesn't hide God's righteousness and does not conceal God's love. From your reading of verses 1–10, what is he eager to make known? 2. Compare verses 1–10 with verses 11–17. How does the psalm's tone change in the second half? 3. Considering David's attitude in these verses, put into your own words David's description of life's dilemma. 4. What effect does it have on him? 5. David begins this psalm by saying he waited patiently. He concludes by asking that God would not delay. What do the elements of patience and the need for a speedy answer contribute to your understanding of what it means to wait on God?

Applying the Word 1. Waiting in a slimy pit—what a graphic picture of needing God's help! Imagine that you are in a slimy pit from which you need deliverance. What things in your life have placed you in that pit, and what makes it "slimy"? 2. As you call out for God to deliver you, what is it like to wait on God? 3. Imagine that you knew Jesus Christ was coming back in one week. How would you spend your week waiting?

Responding in Prayer Pray for your loved ones that don't yet have a relationship with Jesus Christ. Ask the Spirit to give them hungry hearts for his love.

Psalm 41

Psalm 41

For the director of music. A psalm of David.

¹Blessed is he who has regard for the
    weak;
    the LORD delivers him in times of
    trouble.
²The LORD will protect him and preserve
    his life;
    he will bless him in the land
    and not surrender him to the desire of his
    foes.
³The LORD will sustain him on his sickbed
    and restore him from his bed of illness.
⁴I said, "O LORD, have mercy on me;
    heal me, for I have sinned against you."
⁵My enemies say of me in malice,
    "When will he die and his name perish?"
⁶Whenever one comes to see me,
    he speaks falsely, while his heart gathers
    slander;

then he goes out and spreads it abroad.
⁷All my enemies whisper together
    against me;
    they imagine the worst for me, saying,
⁸"A vile disease has beset him;
    he will never get up from the place where
    he lies."
⁹Even my close friend, whom I trusted,
    he who shared my bread,
    has lifted up his heel against me.

¹⁰But you, O LORD, have mercy on me;
    raise me up, that I may repay them.
¹¹I know that you are pleased with me,
    for my enemy does not triumph
    over me.
¹²In my integrity you uphold me
    and set me in your presence forever.

¹³Praise be to the LORD, the God of Israel,
    from everlasting to everlasting.
        Amen and Amen.

33 / *Psalms 42—43*
Hoping in the Lord

THE AUTHOR OF Psalm 42 was a musician who used to lead the procession of worshipers to the temple in Jerusalem. But now the holy temple of God lay in ruins; the fields and vineyards were burned, and this former spiritual leader sat six hundred miles away—an exile in Babylon.

The psalmist grieved over his circumstances. Like the other holy people of his era, he had linked drawing near to God with going up to God's temple. How could he worship God now? And, as his taunters reminded him, where was God anyway?

 Warming Up to God When is it hard for you to worship God? Talk honestly with God about your struggles.

 Read Psalms 42—43.

BOOK II
Psalms 42–72

Psalm 42[w]

For the director of music. A *maskil*[x] of the
Sons of Korah.

[1]As the deer pants for streams of water,
    so my soul pants for you, O God.
[2]My soul thirsts for God, for the living God.
    When can I go and meet with God?
[3]My tears have been my food
    day and night,
while men say to me all day long,
    "Where is your God?"
[4]These things I remember
    as I pour out my soul:
how I used to go with the multitude,
    leading the procession to the house of God,
with shouts of joy and thanksgiving
    among the festive throng.

[5]Why are you downcast, O my soul?
    Why so disturbed within me?
Put your hope in God,
    for I will yet praise him,
    my Savior and [6]my God.

My[y] soul is downcast within me;
    therefore I will remember you
from the land of the Jordan,
    the heights of Hermon—from Mount Mizar.
[7]Deep calls to deep
    in the roar of your waterfalls;
all your waves and breakers
    have swept over me.

[8]By day the LORD directs his love,
    at night his song is with me—
    a prayer to the God of my life.

[9]I say to God my Rock,

"Why have you forgotten me?
    Why must I go about mourning,
    oppressed by the enemy?"
[10]My bones suffer mortal agony
    as my foes taunt me,
saying to me all day long,
    "Where is your God?"

[11]Why are you downcast, O my soul?
    Why so disturbed within me?
Put your hope in God,
    for I will yet praise him,
    my Savior and my God.

Psalm 43[w]

[1]Vindicate me, O God,
    and plead my cause against an ungodly
        nation;
    rescue me from deceitful and wicked men.
[2]You are God my stronghold.
    Why have you rejected me?
Why must I go about mourning,
    oppressed by the enemy?
[3]Send forth your light and your truth,
    let them guide me;
let them bring me to your holy mountain,
    to the place where you dwell.
[4]Then will I go to the altar of God,
    to God, my joy and my delight.
I will praise you with the harp,
    O God, my God.

[5]Why are you downcast, O my soul?
    Why so disturbed within me?
Put your hope in God,
    for I will yet praise him,
    my Savior and my God.

[w]In many Hebrew manuscripts Psalms 42 and 43 constitute one psalm.
[x]Title: Probably a literary or musical term   [y]5,6 A few Hebrew
manuscripts, Septuagint and Syriac; most Hebrew manuscripts *praise him
for his saving help.* / [6]O my God, my

✎ Discovering the Word   1. 42:5 and 11 and 43:5 form a refrain for this psalm. What do you find in this refrain that makes it important enough to repeat?   2. The psalmist speaks honestly and openly to God. What words does he use to tell how he is feeling?   3. Why might the psalmist's honest words with God about his past and his present help to strengthen his faith?   4. Not all of what the psalmist says is about himself and his past. He also focuses on God. What aspects of God's character does he acknowledge (42:5, 8–9; 43:2, 3)?   5. How might a firm belief in a God of this character bring hope—even to an ancient Hebrew in exile?

⚷ Applying the Word   1. What kinds of things are likely to throw you into depression?   2. What do you talk about with God and with others when you are depressed?   3. Based on these psalms, when depression comes, what measures can you take to begin to cope with it?

Responding in Prayer Ask God to help you understand your own feelings of depression. Ask him to help you to focus on him and to more readily turn to him, both with your own depression and with that of a troubled friend.

34 / *Psalm 44*
A Prayer When God Is Silent

"IS NOT GOD silent about Stalingrad? What do we hear above and under its ruins? Do we not hear the roar of artillery, the tumult of the world and the cries of the dying? But where is the voice of God? When we think of God, is it not suddenly so quiet, so terribly quiet, in the witch's kitchen of this hell, that one can hear a pin drop even though grenades are bursting around us? There is neither voice nor answer" (*The Silence of God*, Helmut Thielicke [Grand Rapids, Mich.: Eerdmans, 1962]). The silence of God is perhaps one of life's most frightening experiences. What do we do, how do we proceed when God is silent? Do we withdraw in fear? Do we give up all hope? This is certainly our temptation. This psalm shows us another way. It opens the way for us to pursue God even when he is silent.

 Warming Up to God Think of a time when a friend did not respond to a letter or a phone message for a long time. What was your reaction to his or her silence?

 Read Psalm 44.

Psalm 44

For the director of music. Of the Sons of Korah. A *maskil.* ᶻ

¹We have heard with our ears, O God;
  our fathers have told us
what you did in their days,
  in days long ago.
²With your hand you drove out the nations
  and planted our fathers;
you crushed the peoples
  and made our fathers flourish.
³It was not by their sword that they won the
    land,
  nor did their arm bring them victory;
it was your right hand, your arm,
  and the light of your face, for you loved
    them.

⁴You are my King and my God,
  who decrees ᵃ victories for Jacob.
⁵Through you we push back our enemies;
  through your name we trample our foes.
⁶I do not trust in my bow,
  my sword does not bring me victory;
⁷but you give us victory over our enemies,
  you put our adversaries to shame.
⁸In God we make our boast all day long,

and we will praise your name forever. *Selah*

⁹But now you have rejected and humbled us;
  you no longer go out with our armies.
¹⁰You made us retreat before the enemy,
  and our adversaries have plundered us.
¹¹You gave us up to be devoured like sheep
  and have scattered us among the nations.
¹²You sold your people for a pittance,
  gaining nothing from their sale.

¹³You have made us a reproach to our
    neighbors,
  the scorn and derision of those around us.
¹⁴You have made us a byword among the
    nations;
  the peoples shake their heads at us.
¹⁵My disgrace is before me all day long,
  and my face is covered with shame
¹⁶at the taunts of those who reproach and revile
    me,
  because of the enemy, who is bent on
    revenge.

¹⁷All this happened to us,
  though we had not forgotten you
  or been false to your covenant.

ᶻTitle: Probably a literary or musical term   ᵃ4 Septuagint, Aquila and
Syriac; Hebrew *King, O God; I command*

18Our hearts had not turned back;
    our feet had not strayed from your path.
19But you crushed us and made us a haunt for
        jackals
    and covered us over with deep darkness.

20If we had forgotten the name of our God
    or spread out our hands to a foreign god,
21would not God have discovered it,
    since he knows the secrets of the heart?
22Yet for your sake we face death all day long;

we are considered as sheep to be
        slaughtered.

23Awake, O Lord! Why do you sleep?
    Rouse yourself! Do not reject us forever.
24Why do you hide your face
    and forget our misery and oppression?

25We are brought down to the dust;
    our bodies cling to the ground.
26Rise up and help us;
    redeem us because of your unfailing love.

 Discovering the Word 1. How does the writer contrast God in the past (vv. 1–8) with God in the present (vv. 9–16)? 2. The psalmist argues with God that the situation he and his people find themselves in is not fair. How does he express this (vv. 17–22)? 3. What is the significance of this plea for fairness and justice? 4. The psalmist summarizes his accusations of God in verses 23 and 24. What does he accuse God of? 5. In the final phrase of the psalm (v. 26), the writer appeals to God's unfailing love. This is a dramatic contrast to the accusations he has just made. How can these views of God be reconciled?

 Applying the Word 1. Think of a time when it seemed God was silent. How did your experience at that time compare with the experiences described in this psalm? 2. Think of a time when you experienced God's unfailing love. How would you describe that experience? 3. What encouragement does this psalm offer you for times when God seems silent?

 Responding in Prayer Ask God to help you to understand his ways and grant you peace when you are waiting for his voice.

35 / *Psalm 45*
A Wedding Song

THE EXCITEMENT OF a wedding day! Brides in beautiful gowns, an abundance of sweet-smelling flowers, nervous grooms and fathers waiting in the wings for the bride to make her entrance—and all are overflowing with a sense of expectancy that fills the air. The reason behind all of the extravagance, beyond the legal joining of two individuals together, is to celebrate a wonderful event and to capture it as something to remember for all time. This psalm is a celebration, both for the joy of the day and for the joy that is still to come.

Warming Up to God Reflect for a moment on the character of your God. He is the powerful judge and the Creator who flung the stars into space. But he is also the one who knows and loves you and became your Savior. Let this knowledge fill you with peace as you look to the words of God.

Read Psalm 45.

Psalm 45

For the director of music. To ˪the tune of˩
"Lilies." Of the Sons of Korah. A *maskil.*ᵇ
    A wedding song.

1My heart is stirred by a noble theme
    as I recite my verses for the king;
    my tongue is the pen of a skillful writer.

2You are the most excellent of men
    and your lips have been anointed with
        grace,
    since God has blessed you forever.
3Gird your sword upon your side, O mighty
        one;
    clothe yourself with splendor and majesty.

ᵇTitle: Probably a literary or musical term

⁴In your majesty ride forth victoriously
  in behalf of truth, humility and
    righteousness;
  let your right hand display awesome deeds.
⁵Let your sharp arrows pierce the hearts of the
    king's enemies;
  let the nations fall beneath your feet.
⁶Your throne, O God, will last for ever and
    ever;
  a scepter of justice will be the scepter of
    your kingdom.
⁷You love righteousness and hate wickedness;
  therefore God, your God, has set you above
    your companions
  by anointing you with the oil of joy.
⁸All your robes are fragrant with myrrh and
    aloes and cassia;
  from palaces adorned with ivory
  the music of the strings makes you glad.
⁹Daughters of kings are among your honored
    women;
  at your right hand is the royal bride in gold
    of Ophir.
¹⁰Listen, O daughter, consider and give ear:

Forget your people and your father's house.
¹¹The king is enthralled by your beauty;
  honor him, for he is your lord.
¹²The Daughter of Tyre will come with a gift,ᶜ
  men of wealth will seek your favor.

¹³All glorious is the princess within ᵇher
    chamberᶜ;
  her gown is interwoven with gold.
¹⁴In embroidered garments she is led to the
    king;
  her virgin companions follow her
  and are brought to you.
¹⁵They are led in with joy and gladness;
  they enter the palace of the king.

¹⁶Your sons will take the place of your fathers;
  you will make them princes throughout the
    land.
¹⁷I will perpetuate your memory through all
    generations;
  therefore the nations will praise you for
    ever and ever.

ᶜ12 Or A Tyrian robe is among the gifts

 Discovering the Word 1. Psalm 45 is a wedding song celebrating the marriage of a king of David's dynasty to a foreign princess. Twice in the psalm the poet refers to himself. What does he say are his purposes for writing (vv. 1, 17)? 2. What are the characteristics of this king? 3. How could these verses (particularly 6–7) refer to more than David's reign? 4. Verses 6 and 7 are quoted in Hebrews 1 and are used to describe the reign of Jesus Christ. How could the description of the king in this passage be applied to Christ? 5. What are the characteristics of the bride, and what is the attitude surrounding her coming (vv. 10–16)?

Applying the Word 1. We are Christ's bride. What promises do you see for yourself in this passage? 2. What kind of a response does seeing the majesty of Christ cause in your own life?

Responding in Prayer Thank God that your heart has been "stirred by a noble theme"—the promises of the King coming for his bride. Praise him for his majesty and the overwhelming awe that you feel because he has chosen *you* to be his bride.

---

36 / *Psalm 46*
Still Point in a Turning World

MARTIN LUTHER'S FAMOUS hymn "A Mighty Fortress Is Our God" is based on Psalm 46. This psalm celebrates Jerusalem as the city of God, the sure foundation for the kingdom of God. Today we can find spiritual strength and security in this psalm, especially when everything else is so topsy-turvy.

 Warming Up to God Consider the times of loss, tragedy or high anxiety when you thought your world was falling apart. How were you able to find the strength to face the dawn of another day?

Read Psalm 46.

Psalm 46

For the director of music. Of the Sons of
Korah. According to *alamoth.* ᵈ A song.

¹God is our refuge and strength,
 an ever-present help in trouble.
²Therefore we will not fear, though the earth
  give way
 and the mountains fall into the heart of the
  sea,
³though its waters roar and foam
 and the mountains quake with their
  surging.   *Selah*

⁴There is a river whose streams make glad the
  city of God,
 the holy place where the Most High dwells.
⁵God is within her, she will not fall;
 God will help her at break of day.

⁶Nations are in uproar, kingdoms fall;
 he lifts his voice, the earth melts.

⁷The Lord Almighty is with us;
 the God of Jacob is our fortress.   *Selah*

⁸Come and see the works of the Lord,
 the desolations he has brought on the
  earth.
⁹He makes wars cease to the ends of the earth;
 he breaks the bow and shatters the spear,
 he burns the shields*ᵉ* with fire.
¹⁰"Be still, and know that I am God;
 I will be exalted among the nations,
 I will be exalted in the earth."

¹¹The Lord Almighty is with us;
 the God of Jacob is our fortress.   *Selah*

^dTitle: Probably a musical term   *e*9 Or *chariots*

Discovering the Word 1. This psalm readily falls into three stanzas (vv. 1–3, 4–6 and 8–10) plus two refrains, or chorus lines (vv. 7, 11). What themes emerge in each section? 2. What images of a world falling apart do you see in these verses? 3. What truth about God is conveyed here in contrast to the world? 4. What effect does God's triumph over the nations have on the people who draw their strength from him (vv. 8–10)? 5. Where does one find stillness and security in the midst of violent forces unleashed all around (vv. 10–11)?

Applying the Word 1. What in your life is threatening or pounding away at your sense of security in God? 2. How can you remain still (v. 10) and know God's fortresslike strength (vv. 7, 11) in the midst of a world falling apart?

Responding in Prayer As God has triumphed, and will triumph, over all that wars against the city of Jerusalem and the soul of the believer, how can you exalt him among the nations? Spend some time being still and centering on him.

37 / *Psalm 47*
Being Devoted to God

THE SIGN OF a spiritually healthy heart is gratitude and affection. You will discover that after you have spent time with God, there rises from within your heart a deep sense of gratitude. Galatians 4:6 says, "Because you are sons, God sent the Spirit of his Son into our hearts, the Spirit who calls out, '*Abba*, Father.' " We can actually sense the Spirit within us as he cries, "Abba, Father."

Warming Up to God Make a list of things you are thankful for. While you may not be able to express gratitude right now, it will come in time if you continue to walk in this inner spiritual pilgrimage. If you do feel gratitude, sit for a while in heartfelt thanks to God.

Read Psalm 47.

Psalm 47

For the director of music. Of the Sons of
Korah. A psalm.

¹Clap your hands, all you nations;
shout to God with cries of joy.
²How awesome is the Lord Most High,
the great King over all the earth!
³He subdued nations under us,
peoples under our feet.
⁴He chose our inheritance for us,
the pride of Jacob, whom he loved.   *Selah*

⁵God has ascended amid shouts of joy,
the Lord amid the sounding of trumpets.
⁶Sing praises to God, sing praises;
sing praises to our King, sing praises.
⁷For God is the King of all the earth;
sing to him a psalm*ᶠ* of praise.
⁸God reigns over the nations;
God is seated on his holy throne.
⁹The nobles of the nations assemble
as the people of the God of Abraham,
for the kings*ᵍ* of the earth belong to God;
he is greatly exalted.

ᶠ7 Or a maskil (probably a literary or musical term)   *ᵍ9 Or shields*

 Discovering the Word 1. What is the psalmist thankful for (vv. 2–4)? 2. How is God described in each verse? 3. What is revealed about God's relationship with the people? 4. What actions of joy and gratitude do you see in these verses (vv. 1, 5–7)?

Applying the Word 1. How would you feel using the same outward expressions of joy as the psalmist? 2. The psalmist sings, claps, sacrifices and invites others to share in his joy in God. What ways can you outwardly show your joy in the Lord? 3. The Holy Spirit within us is continually offering praise. If you can, allow yourself to join the Spirit in praise. Try to write a psalm to the Lord, including in it reasons you enjoy knowing God. If you haven't come to the place of heartfelt worship, don't try to generate what you don't feel. You might want to sing a song or hymn that you can sing with meaning. Or perhaps play some recorded music that reflects your mood.

Responding in Prayer Ask God to give you the courage to walk in honesty until he brings you into the place of inner praise.

Psalms 48—49

Psalm 48

A song. A psalm of the Sons of Korah.

¹Great is the Lord, and most worthy of praise,
in the city of our God, his holy mountain.
²It is beautiful in its loftiness,
the joy of the whole earth.
Like the utmost heights of Zaphon*ʰ* is Mount
Zion,
the*ⁱ* city of the Great King.
³God is in her citadels;
he has shown himself to be her fortress.

⁴When the kings joined forces,
when they advanced together,
⁵they saw ⌊her⌋ and were astounded;
they fled in terror.
⁶Trembling seized them there,
pain like that of a woman in labor.
⁷You destroyed them like ships of Tarshish
shattered by an east wind.

⁸As we have heard,
so have we seen
in the city of the Lord Almighty,
in the city of our God:
God makes her secure forever.   *Selah*

⁹Within your temple, O God,
we meditate on your unfailing love.
¹⁰Like your name, O God,
your praise reaches to the ends of the earth;
your right hand is filled with righteousness.
¹¹Mount Zion rejoices,
the villages of Judah are glad
because of your judgments.

¹²Walk about Zion, go around her,

ʰ2 Zaphon can refer to a sacred mountain or the direction north.
ⁱ2 Or earth, / Mount Zion, on the northern side / of the

count her towers,
¹³consider well her ramparts,
    view her citadels,
that you may tell of them to the next
    generation.
¹⁴For this God is our God for ever and ever;
    he will be our guide even to the end.

Psalm 49

For the director of music. Of the Sons of
Korah. A psalm.

¹Hear this, all you peoples;
    listen, all who live in this world,
²both low and high,
    rich and poor alike:
³My mouth will speak words of wisdom;
    the utterance from my heart will give
    understanding.
⁴I will turn my ear to a proverb;
    with the harp I will expound my riddle:

⁵Why should I fear when evil days come,
    when wicked deceivers surround me—
⁶those who trust in their wealth
    and boast of their great riches?
⁷No man can redeem the life of another
    or give to God a ransom for him—
⁸the ransom for a life is costly,
    no payment is ever enough—
⁹that he should live on forever
    and not see decay.

¹⁰For all can see that wise men die;
    the foolish and the senseless alike perish
    and leave their wealth to others.

¹¹Their tombs will remain their houses[j]
    forever,
    their dwellings for endless generations,
    though they had[k] named lands after
    themselves.

¹²But man, despite his riches, does not endure;
    he is[l] like the beasts that perish.

¹³This is the fate of those who trust in
    themselves,
    and of their followers, who approve their
    sayings.   *Selah*
¹⁴Like sheep they are destined for the grave,[m]
    and death will feed on them.
The upright will rule over them in the
    morning;
    their forms will decay in the grave,[m]
    far from their princely mansions.
¹⁵But God will redeem my life[n] from the grave;
    he will surely take me to himself.   *Selah*

¹⁶Do not be overawed when a man grows rich,
    when the splendor of his house increases;
¹⁷for he will take nothing with him when he
    dies,
    his splendor will not descend with him.
¹⁸Though while he lived he counted himself
    blessed—
    and men praise you when you prosper—
¹⁹he will join the generation of his fathers,
    who will never see the light ⌊of life⌋.

²⁰A man who has riches without understanding
    is like the beasts that perish.

j 11 Septuagint and Syriac; Hebrew In their thoughts their houses will remain *k 11 Or I for they have* *l 12 Hebrew; Septuagint and Syriac read verse 12 the same as verse 20.* *m 14 Hebrew Sheol; also in verse 15* *n 15 Or soul*

38 / *Psalm 50*
Offering Thanks

"HOW ARE YOU?" we ask, and the response generally comes back, "Fine." Often we follow that with the question "Been busy?" and the answer is invariably yes. We live in a culture of busyness, and sometimes that overlaps into our Christian lives. We can become so busy working for God, doing good deeds, that we don't have time to offer him our praise and thanksgiving. This psalm helps us get our focus back to the fact that we are created to worship God.

Warming Up to God When have you gotten caught up in the things you *do* for God to the extent that you neglected worshiping him?

Read Psalm 50.

Psalm 50

A psalm of Asaph.

¹The Mighty One, God, the LORD,
   speaks and summons the earth
   from the rising of the sun to the place
      where it sets.
²From Zion, perfect in beauty,
   God shines forth.
³Our God comes and will not be silent;
   a fire devours before him,
   and around him a tempest rages.
⁴He summons the heavens above,
   and the earth, that he may judge his
      people:
⁵"Gather to me my consecrated ones,
   who made a covenant with me by
      sacrifice."
⁶And the heavens proclaim his righteousness,
   for God himself is judge.   *Selah*

⁷"Hear, O my people, and I will speak,
   O Israel, and I will testify against you:
   I am God, your God.
⁸I do not rebuke you for your sacrifices
   or your burnt offerings, which are ever
      before me.
⁹I have no need of a bull from your stall
   or of goats from your pens,
¹⁰for every animal of the forest is mine,
   and the cattle on a thousand hills.
¹¹I know every bird in the mountains,
   and the creatures of the field are mine.
¹²If I were hungry I would not tell you,

for the world is mine, and all that is in it.
¹³Do I eat the flesh of bulls
   or drink the blood of goats?
¹⁴Sacrifice thank offerings to God,
   fulfill your vows to the Most High,
¹⁵and call upon me in the day of trouble;
   I will deliver you, and you will honor me."

¹⁶But to the wicked, God says:

"What right have you to recite my laws
   or take my covenant on your lips?
¹⁷You hate my instruction
   and cast my words behind you.
¹⁸When you see a thief, you join with him;
   you throw in your lot with adulterers.
¹⁹You use your mouth for evil
   and harness your tongue to deceit.
²⁰You speak continually against your brother
   and slander your own mother's son.
²¹These things you have done and I kept silent;
   you thought I was altogether⁰ like you.
   But I will rebuke you
   and accuse you to your face.

²²"Consider this, you who forget God,
   or I will tear you to pieces, with none to
      rescue:
²³He who sacrifices thank offerings honors me,
   and he prepares the way
   so that I may show himᵖ the salvation of
      God."

⁰21 Or *thought the 'I* AM' *was*   ᵖ23 Or *and to him who considers his
way / I will show*

 Discovering the Word 1. How is God described in verses 1–6? 2. God does not say that sacrifices are wrong (v. 8), but what does he want the people to understand about their offerings to him (vv. 9–15)? 3. How does the tone of verses 16–22 change? 4. What evil deeds have the wicked done (vv. 16–22)? 5. How would "thank offerings" help them to understand salvation (vv. 14–15, 23)?

Applying the Word 1. What would a "thank offering" to God look like for you? 2. God promised that we can call upon him "in the day of trouble" and he will deliver us (v. 15). In what way would you like to call upon God today?

Responding in Prayer Make your prayers an offering of praise and thanksgiving for God's work in your life.

39 / *Psalm 51*
Praying Our Sin

ALONGSIDE THE BASIC fact that God made us good (Ps 8) is the equally basic fact that we have gone wrong. We pray our sins to get to the truth about ourselves and to find out how God treats sinners. Our experience of sin does not consist in doing some bad things but in being bad. It is a fundamental condition of our existence, not a temporary lapse into error. Praying our sin isn't resolving not to sin anymore; it is discovering what God has resolved to do with us as sinners.

Warming Up to God As Christians, we know we are sinful. Why then is it so painful to be confronted with a specific sin? What sin have you been avoiding talking to God about? Take it to God and experience his forgiveness.

Read Psalm 51.

Psalm 51

For the director of music. A psalm of David. When the prophet Nathan came to him after David had committed adultery with Bathsheba.

¹Have mercy on me, O God,
  according to your unfailing love;
according to your great compassion
  blot out my transgressions.
²Wash away all my iniquity
  and cleanse me from my sin.

³For I know my transgressions,
  and my sin is always before me.
⁴Against you, you only, have I sinned
  and done what is evil in your sight,
so that you are proved right when you speak
  and justified when you judge.
⁵Surely I was sinful at birth,
  sinful from the time my mother conceived
    me.
⁶Surely you desire truth in the inner parts*q*;
  you teach*r* me wisdom in the inmost
    place.

⁷Cleanse me with hyssop, and I will be clean;
  wash me, and I will be whiter than snow.
⁸Let me hear joy and gladness;
  let the bones you have crushed rejoice.
⁹Hide your face from my sins

and blot out all my iniquity.

¹⁰Create in me a pure heart, O God,
  and renew a steadfast spirit within me.
¹¹Do not cast me from your presence
  or take your Holy Spirit from me.
¹²Restore to me the joy of your salvation
  and grant me a willing spirit, to sustain me.

¹³Then I will teach transgressors your ways,
  and sinners will turn back to you.
¹⁴Save me from bloodguilt, O God,
  the God who saves me,
  and my tongue will sing of your
    righteousness.
¹⁵O Lord, open my lips,
  and my mouth will declare your praise.
¹⁶You do not delight in sacrifice, or I would
    bring it;
  you do not take pleasure in burnt offerings.
¹⁷The sacrifices of God are*s* a broken spirit;
  a broken and contrite heart,
  O God, you will not despise.

¹⁸In your good pleasure make Zion prosper;
  build up the walls of Jerusalem.
¹⁹Then there will be righteous sacrifices,
  whole burnt offerings to delight you;
  then bulls will be offered on your altar.

*q6 The meaning of the Hebrew for this phrase is uncertain.   r6 Or
you desired . . . ; / you taught   s17 Or My sacrifice, O God, is*

Discovering the Word 1. List the different synonyms for sin in David's prayer. 2. What is God asked to do about sin? (Count and name the verbs.) 3. Verse 10 is the center sentence. How does it center the prayer? 4. Forgiveness is an internal action with external consequences. What are some of them (vv. 13–17)? 5. What do you understand a "broken and contrite heart" to be (v. 17)? 6. According to verses 18–19, what is the relationship between personal forgiveness and social righteousness?

Applying the Word 1. When have you had a "broken and contrite heart"? 2. Psalm 51 makes us aware of how sinful we are, and it makes us less actively sinful. How do you see it working that way in you?

Responding in Prayer Be quiet before God. In silence confess your sins to him. Accept his forgiveness and grace.

Psalms 52—54

Psalm 52

For the director of music. A *maskil*[t]
of David. When Doeg the Edomite had
gone to Saul and told him: "David has gone
to the house of Ahimelech."

[1]Why do you boast of evil, you mighty man?
  Why do you boast all day long,
  you who are a disgrace in the eyes of God?
[2]Your tongue plots destruction;
  it is like a sharpened razor,
  you who practice deceit.
[3]You love evil rather than good,
  falsehood rather than speaking the truth.
                                        Selah

[4]You love every harmful word,
  O you deceitful tongue!

[5]Surely God will bring you down to everlasting
  ruin:
  He will snatch you up and tear you from
    your tent;
  he will uproot you from the land of the
    living.   *Selah*
[6]The righteous will see and fear;
  they will laugh at him, saying,
[7]"Here now is the man
  who did not make God his stronghold
  but trusted in his great wealth
  and grew strong by destroying others!"

[8]But I am like an olive tree
  flourishing in the house of God;
  I trust in God's unfailing love
  for ever and ever.
[9]I will praise you forever for what you have
    done;
  in your name I will hope, for your name is
    good.
  I will praise you in the presence of your
    saints.

Psalm 53

For the director of music. According to
  mahalath.[u] A *maskil*[t] of David.

[1]The fool says in his heart,
  "There is no God."
They are corrupt, and their ways
  are vile;
  there is no one who does good.

[2]God looks down from heaven
  on the sons of men
to see if there are any who understand,
  any who seek God.
[3]Everyone has turned away,
  they have together become corrupt;
  there is no one who does good,
  not even one.

[4]Will the evildoers never learn—
  those who devour my people as men eat
    bread
  and who do not call on God?
[5]There they were, overwhelmed with
    dread,
  where there was nothing to dread.
God scattered the bones of those who
    attacked you;
  you put them to shame, for God despised
    them.

[6]Oh, that salvation for Israel would come out
    of Zion!
  When God restores the fortunes of his
    people,
  let Jacob rejoice and Israel be glad!

[t]Title: Probably a literary or musical term   [u]Title: Probably a musical
term

Psalm 54

For the director of music. With stringed instruments. A *maskil*ᵛ of David. When the Ziphites had gone to Saul and said, "Is not David hiding among us?"

¹Save me, O God, by your name;
   vindicate me by your might.
²Hear my prayer, O God;
   listen to the words of my mouth.

³Strangers are attacking me;
   ruthless men seek my life—
   men without regard for God.   *Selah*

⁴Surely God is my help;
   the Lord is the one who sustains me.

⁵Let evil recoil on those who slander me;
   in your faithfulness destroy them.

⁶I will sacrifice a freewill offering to you;
   I will praise your name, O LORD,
   for it is good.
⁷For he has delivered me from all my troubles,
   and my eyes have looked in triumph on my
      foes.

ᵛ Title: Probably a literary or musical term

40 / *Psalm 55*
Expressing Feelings to God

"I WISH I could talk to God about this. But I just can't. I can't get the words out. I feel so guilty because I can't trust him with the things that are most important to me."

Learning to express our feelings to God is not easy. The passionate, emotionally unrestrained prayers of the Bible may not be the kind we grew up with. We may find, in fact, that the prayers of the Bible make us anxious. We wonder how God would respond if we told him what we really felt.

Learning to express our feelings to God is a vital part of growing in intimacy with him. When we can tell him of our sorrow and anger and confusion and joy, we will experience his faithful love in new ways. In his Word we find many models of godly people who openly expressed their deepest feelings to God.

 Warming Up to God When you are sad or angry and you are talking to God, how do you expect him to respond? Talk to God about your concerns and fears.

 Read Psalm 55.

Psalm 55

For the director of music. With stringed instruments. A *maskil*ʷ of David.

¹Listen to my prayer, O God,
   do not ignore my plea;
²   hear me and answer me.
My thoughts trouble me and I am distraught
³   at the voice of the enemy,
   at the stares of the wicked;
for they bring down suffering upon me
   and revile me in their anger.

⁴My heart is in anguish within me;
   the terrors of death assail me.
⁵Fear and trembling have beset me;
   horror has overwhelmed me.
⁶I said, "Oh, that I had the wings of a dove!

I would fly away and be at rest—
⁷I would flee far away
   and stay in the desert;   *Selah*
⁸I would hurry to my place of shelter,
   far from the tempest and storm."

⁹Confuse the wicked, O Lord, confound their
      speech,
   for I see violence and strife in the city.
¹⁰Day and night they prowl about on its walls;
   malice and abuse are within it.
¹¹Destructive forces are at work in the city;
   threats and lies never leave its streets.

¹²If an enemy were insulting me,
   I could endure it;
   if a foe were raising himself against me,

ʷ Title: Probably a literary or musical term

I could hide from him.
13But it is you, a man like myself,
  my companion, my close friend,
14with whom I once enjoyed sweet fellowship
  as we walked with the throng at the house
    of God.

15Let death take my enemies by surprise;
  let them go down alive to the grave,ˣ
  for evil finds lodging among them.

16But I call to God,
  and the LORD saves me.
17Evening, morning and noon
  I cry out in distress,
  and he hears my voice.
18He ransoms me unharmed
  from the battle waged against me,
  even though many oppose me.
19God, who is enthroned forever,
  will hear them and afflict them—   *Selah*

men who never change their ways
  and have no fear of God.

20My companion attacks his friends;
  he violates his covenant.
21His speech is smooth as butter,
  yet war is in his heart;
his words are more soothing than oil,
  yet they are drawn swords.

22Cast your cares on the LORD
  and he will sustain you;
  he will never let the righteous fall.
23But you, O God, will bring down the wicked
  into the pit of corruption;
  bloodthirsty and deceitful men
  will not live out half their days.

But as for me, I trust in you.

ˣ15 Hebrew *Sheol*

 Discovering the Word 1. What feelings are described in each section of Psalm 55? 2. Describe the image of God that you find in this passage. 3. What seems to be causing the psalmist to suffer (vv. 12–15, 20–21)? 4. What does the psalmist expect God to do for him (vv. 16–19, 22–23)?

Applying the Word 1. We often have a negative response to our "negative" feelings. What thoughts do you typically have in response to your feelings of anger, depression or fear? 2. How does it affect you to know that God is near to you when you are in pain?

Responding in Prayer How would you like God to help you to grow in your ability to express your feelings to him?

Psalm 56

Psalm 56

For the director of music. To ⌐the tune of⌐
"A Dove on Distant Oaks." Of David. A
*miktam.*ʸ When the Philistines had seized
      him in Gath.

1Be merciful to me, O God, for men hotly
      pursue me;
  all day long they press their attack.
2My slanderers pursue me all day long;
  many are attacking me in their pride.

3When I am afraid,
  I will trust in you.
4In God, whose word I praise,
  in God I trust; I will not be afraid.
  What can mortal man do to me?

5All day long they twist my words;
  they are always plotting to harm me.
6They conspire, they lurk,
  they watch my steps,
  eager to take my life.

7On no account let them escape;
  in your anger, O God, bring down the
    nations.
8Record my lament;
  list my tears on your scrollᶻ—
  are they not in your record?

9Then my enemies will turn back
  when I call for help.
  By this I will know that God is for me.

ʸTitle: Probably a literary or musical term   ᶻ8 Or / *put my tears in your wineskin*

¹⁰In God, whose word I praise,
  in the Lord, whose word I praise—
¹¹in God I trust; I will not be afraid.
  What can man do to me?

¹²I am under vows to you, O God;
  I will present my thank offerings to you.

¹³For you have delivered me^a from death
  and my feet from stumbling,
that I may walk before God
  in the light of life.^b

^a13 Or *my soul*   ^b13 Or *the land of the living*

41 / *Psalm 57*
A Prayer of Distress

OUR NEED FOR God's presence and care in our lives is a daily reality. However, when life is good we may be unaware of our need. As C. S. Lewis wrote in *A Grief Observed*, sometimes "life is so good," we may be "tempted to forget our need of him." But there are times in our lives when we are acutely aware of our need of God. In times of distress, when we are threatened with loss or harm or even with death, we remember our need for God and we turn to him with great urgency. Some people feel that they cannot bring their troubles to God. I have often heard people say, "I can't turn to God when I am in distress if I haven't been doing this all along." And I have heard other people say, "I can't bother God with this. There are many people hurting more than I am." But God invites us to turn to him when we are in distress. Repeatedly in the Scriptures God says to us, "Call on me in the day of trouble and I will answer you." This is exactly what this psalm helps us to do.

 Warming Up to God   What mental pictures does the word *distress* create for you?

 Read Psalm 57.

Psalm 57

For the director of music. ⌊To the tune of⌋
"Do Not Destroy." Of David. A *miktam*.^c
When he had fled from Saul into the cave.

¹Have mercy on me, O God, have mercy on
    me,
  for in you my soul takes refuge.
I will take refuge in the shadow of your wings
  until the disaster has passed.

²I cry out to God Most High,
  to God, who fulfills ⌊his purpose⌋ for me.
³He sends from heaven and saves me,
  rebuking those who hotly pursue me; *Selah*
God sends his love and his faithfulness.

⁴I am in the midst of lions;
  I lie among ravenous beasts—
men whose teeth are spears and arrows,
  whose tongues are sharp swords.

⁵Be exalted, O God, above the heavens;
  let your glory be over all the earth.

⁶They spread a net for my feet—
  I was bowed down in distress.
They dug a pit in my path—
  but they have fallen into it themselves.
                Selah

⁷My heart is steadfast, O God,
  my heart is steadfast;
  I will sing and make music.
⁸Awake, my soul!
  Awake, harp and lyre!
  I will awaken the dawn.

⁹I will praise you, O Lord, among the nations;
  I will sing of you among the peoples.
¹⁰For great is your love, reaching to the
    heavens;
  your faithfulness reaches to the skies.

¹¹Be exalted, O God, above the heavens;
  let your glory be over all the earth.

^cTitle: Probably a literary or musical term

Discovering the Word 1. The title and the introduction to this psalm suggest that this psalm was written by David when he fled into a cave, hiding from King Saul, who wanted to kill him. What image does David use in verse 1 to describe his experience of God as a safe shelter? 2. What metaphors does David use in verse 4 to describe the danger he found himself in? 3. In his time of distress David cried out to God (v. 2). What does it mean to "cry out" to God? 4. How did God intervene for David in his time of distress (vv. 3, 6)? 5. David responds to God's care in verse 7 by saying that his heart is steadfast. What is the significance of this response?

 Applying the Word 1. Think of a time when you were in distress. What was your experience of God like during that time? 2. How might this psalm encourage you in times of distress?

Responding in Prayer David responds to God's care with praise in verses 9–11. Offer your praises to God for his work in your life.

Psalms 58—61

Psalm 58

For the director of music. ⌊To the tune of⌋ "Do Not Destroy." Of David. A *miktam.*[d]

¹Do you rulers indeed speak justly?
  Do you judge uprightly among men?
²No, in your heart you devise injustice,
  and your hands mete out violence on the
    earth.
³Even from birth the wicked go astray;
  from the womb they are wayward and
    speak lies.
⁴Their venom is like the venom of a snake,
  like that of a cobra that has stopped its
    ears,
⁵that will not heed the tune of the charmer,
  however skillful the enchanter may be.
⁶Break the teeth in their mouths, O God;
  tear out, O LORD, the fangs of the lions!
⁷Let them vanish like water that flows away;
  when they draw the bow, let their arrows
    be blunted.
⁸Like a slug melting away as it moves along,
  like a stillborn child, may they not see the
    sun.
⁹Before your pots can feel ⌊the heat of⌋ the
    thorns—
  whether they be green or dry—the wicked
    will be swept away.[e]
¹⁰The righteous will be glad when they are
    avenged,
  when they bathe their feet in the blood of
    the wicked.
¹¹Then men will say,
  "Surely the righteous still are rewarded;

surely there is a God who judges the
    earth."

Psalm 59

For the director of music. ⌊To the tune of⌋ "Do Not Destroy." Of David. A *miktam.*[d]
When Saul had sent men to watch David's
    house in order to kill him.

¹Deliver me from my enemies, O God;
  protect me from those who rise up against
    me.
²Deliver me from evildoers
  and save me from bloodthirsty men.

³See how they lie in wait for me!
  Fierce men conspire against me
  for no offense or sin of mine, O LORD.
⁴I have done no wrong, yet they are ready to
    attack me.
  Arise to help me; look on my plight!
⁵O LORD God Almighty, the God of Israel,
  rouse yourself to punish all the nations;
  show no mercy to wicked traitors.   *Selah*

⁶They return at evening,
  snarling like dogs,
  and prowl about the city.
⁷See what they spew from their mouths—
  they spew out swords from their lips,
  and they say, "Who can hear us?"
⁸But you, O LORD, laugh at them;
  you scoff at all those nations.

⁹O my Strength, I watch for you;

---
[d] Title: Probably a literary or musical term   [e] 9 The meaning of the
Hebrew for this verse is uncertain.

you, O God, are my fortress, ¹⁰my loving
God.

God will go before me
and will let me gloat over those who
slander me.
¹¹But do not kill them, O Lord our shield,ᶠ
or my people will forget.
In your might make them wander about,
and bring them down.
¹²For the sins of their mouths,
for the words of their lips,
let them be caught in their pride.
For the curses and lies they utter,
¹³   consume them in wrath,
consume them till they are no more.
Then it will be known to the ends of the
earth
that God rules over Jacob.   *Selah*

¹⁴They return at evening,
snarling like dogs,
and prowl about the city.
¹⁵They wander about for food
and howl if not satisfied.
¹⁶But I will sing of your strength,
in the morning I will sing of your love;
for you are my fortress,
my refuge in times of trouble.

¹⁷O my Strength, I sing praise to you;
you, O God, are my fortress, my loving
God.

Psalm 60

For the director of music. To ⌜the tune of⌝
"The Lily of the Covenant." A *miktam*ᵍ of
David. For teaching. When he fought Aram
Naharaimʰ and Aram Zobah,ⁱ and when
Joab returned and struck down twelve
thousand Edomites in the Valley of Salt.

¹You have rejected us, O God, and burst forth
upon us;
you have been angry—now restore us!
²You have shaken the land and torn it open;
mend its fractures, for it is quaking.
³You have shown your people desperate times;
you have given us wine that makes us
stagger.

⁴But for those who fear you, you have raised a
banner
to be unfurled against the bow.   *Selah*

⁵Save us and help us with your right hand,
that those you love may be delivered.
⁶God has spoken from his sanctuary:
"In triumph I will parcel out Shechem
and measure off the Valley of Succoth.
⁷Gilead is mine, and Manasseh is mine;
Ephraim is my helmet,
Judah my scepter.
⁸Moab is my washbasin,
upon Edom I toss my sandal;
over Philistia I shout in triumph."

⁹Who will bring me to the fortified city?
Who will lead me to Edom?
¹⁰Is it not you, O God, you who have rejected
us
and no longer go out with our armies?
¹¹Give us aid against the enemy,
for the help of man is worthless.
¹²With God we will gain the victory,
and he will trample down our enemies.

Psalm 61

For the director of music. With stringed
instruments. Of David.

¹Hear my cry, O God;
listen to my prayer.

²From the ends of the earth I call to you,
I call as my heart grows faint;
lead me to the rock that is higher than I.
³For you have been my refuge,
a strong tower against the foe.

⁴I long to dwell in your tent forever
and take refuge in the shelter of your
wings.   *Selah*
⁵For you have heard my vows, O God;
you have given me the heritage of those
who fear your name.

⁶Increase the days of the king's life,
his years for many generations.
⁷May he be enthroned in God's presence
forever;
appoint your love and faithfulness to
protect him.

⁸Then will I ever sing praise to your name
and fulfill my vows day after day.

ᶠ11 Or *sovereign*   ᵍTitle: Probably a literary or musical term
ʰTitle: That is, Arameans of Northwest Mesopotamia   ⁱTitle: That is,
Arameans of central Syria

42 / *Psalm 62*
A Prayer of Trust

HUMANS COME INTO the world as vulnerable creatures, completely dependent on their parents for their survival. For people to develop a healthy capacity to trust, they need to experience an emotional attachment with a nurturing parent. If children are not greeted with nurturing, empathic responses to their physical, emotional and social needs, or if the relationship with the parent is disrupted, the attachment will be threatened and the capacity to trust will be damaged. Later in life it will be difficult for them to trust God. Trust is based on a person's character, ability and truthfulness. It is an act of committing oneself to another's good intentions and care. This psalm invites us to risk trusting. It calls us to commit ourselves to God's care.

 Warming Up to God What makes a person trustworthy?

 Read Psalm 62.

Psalm 62

For the director of music. For Jeduthun.
A psalm of David.

¹My soul finds rest in God alone;
  my salvation comes from him.
²He alone is my rock and my salvation;
  he is my fortress, I will never be shaken.

³How long will you assault a man?
  Would all of you throw him down—
  this leaning wall, this tottering fence?
⁴They fully intend to topple him
  from his lofty place;
  they take delight in lies.
With their mouths they bless,
  but in their hearts they curse.   *Selah*

⁵Find rest, O my soul, in God alone;
  my hope comes from him.
⁶He alone is my rock and my salvation;
  he is my fortress, I will not be shaken.

⁷My salvation and my honor depend on God*;
  he is my mighty rock, my refuge.
⁸Trust in him at all times, O people;
  pour out your hearts to him,
  for God is our refuge.   *Selah*

⁹Lowborn men are but a breath,
  the highborn are but a lie;
  if weighed on a balance, they are nothing;
  together they are only a breath.
¹⁰Do not trust in extortion
  or take pride in stolen goods;
  though your riches increase,
  do not set your heart on them.

¹¹One thing God has spoken,
  two things have I heard:
  that you, O God, are strong,
¹² and that you, O Lord, are loving.
  Surely you will reward each person
  according to what he has done.

/7 Or / God Most High is my salvation and my honor

 Discovering the Word 1. How does the writer contrast God and humanity? 2. The psalmist talks about resting in God. What pictures come to your mind with these words? 3. In verse 8, the psalmist draws a parallel between trusting in God and pouring out one's heart to God. How are these related? 4. Verse 10 warns against trusting in material wealth. Why is this such a strong temptation? 5. The last two verses depict God as strong and as loving. What images of a strong and loving God are presented in the psalm?

Applying the Word 1. Where else might you be tempted to place your trust, other than in God? 2. How does seeing God as strong help you to trust him? 3. How does seeing God as loving help you to trust him?

Responding in Prayer Express your hesitations and your desires to trust God.

43 / *Psalm 63*
A Prayer of Longing for God

SOMETIMES WE FEEL separated from God. During these times we may feel much like small children feel when they are separated from their parents—frightened, angry. And we may experience an intense longing for our Parent to return. Many things can create this sense of separation from God. It might come as a result of a loss or crisis in our life which leaves us feeling forgotten or uncared for by God. It might come during a time of personal sin or failure when we struggle with fear that God might condemn or reject us. It might come, as it did for this psalmist, as a result of being removed from our community of faith. Whatever the reason, a sense of separation from God can generate life's deepest pain, that of an intense longing for God. This psalm helps us express our longing for God in times when we feel separated from him.

 Warming Up to God Think of a time when you felt especially close to God. What was the experience like for you?

 Read Psalm 63.

Psalm 63

A psalm of David. When he was in the
Desert of Judah.

¹O God, you are my God,
earnestly I seek you;
my soul thirsts for you,
my body longs for you,
in a dry and weary land
where there is no water.

²I have seen you in the sanctuary
and beheld your power and your glory.
³Because your love is better than life,
my lips will glorify you.
⁴I will praise you as long as I live,
and in your name I will lift up my hands.
⁵My soul will be satisfied as with the richest of
foods;

with singing lips my mouth will praise you.

⁶On my bed I remember you;
I think of you through the watches of the
night.
⁷Because you are my help,
I sing in the shadow of your wings.
⁸My soul clings to you;
your right hand upholds me.

⁹They who seek my life will be destroyed;
they will go down to the depths of the
earth.
¹⁰They will be given over to the sword
and become food for jackals.

¹¹But the king will rejoice in God;
all who swear by God's name will praise
him,
while the mouths of liars will be silenced.

Discovering the Word 1. The psalmist describes his experience of longing for God in verse 1 with the strong physical metaphor of being thirsty in a desert with no sign of water. What does this image convey? 2. In verses 2 and 3 the psalmist describes how in the past he experienced God's presence. What did he experience of God? 3. Because of his longing for connection with God, the psalmist says he will seek God, he will remember God and he will cling to God. The first action he takes is to earnestly seek God. What does it mean to seek God? 4. The second action he takes is "remembering." Where, when, what and how does the psalmist say he "remembers" God? 5. The third action he describes is "clinging." In verse 8 he describes how he clings to God and how God holds him. What is your response to the image of clinging to God?

Applying the Word 1. Verse 1 describes a soul which is thirsty, with no chance of finding water. In stark contrast, verse 5 describes a soul which is satisfied with the richest of foods. These pictures contrast the experience of being separated from God and the experience of being close to God. What words or images would you use to describe times when you have felt separated from God? 2. What words or images would you use to describe times when you felt close to God? 3. As you think about the actions of seeking, remembering and clinging to God, which of these most closely describes what would be most helpful to you at this time? Explain.

Responding in Prayer Talk to God about your longing for him and your sense of deep satisfaction and joy in his presence.

Psalm 64

Psalm 64

For the director of music. A psalm
of David.

¹Hear me, O God, as I voice my
    complaint;
  protect my life from the threat of the
    enemy.
²Hide me from the conspiracy of the
    wicked,
  from that noisy crowd of evildoers.
³They sharpen their tongues like swords
  and aim their words like deadly arrows.
⁴They shoot from ambush at the innocent
    man;
  they shoot at him suddenly, without
    fear.
⁵They encourage each other in evil plans,
  they talk about hiding their snares;
  they say, "Who will see them[k]?"

⁶They plot injustice and say,
  "We have devised a perfect plan!"
  Surely the mind and heart of man are
    cunning.

⁷But God will shoot them with arrows;
  suddenly they will be struck down.
⁸He will turn their own tongues against
    them
  and bring them to ruin;
  all who see them will shake their heads
    in scorn.

⁹All mankind will fear;
  they will proclaim the works of God
  and ponder what he has done.
¹⁰Let the righteous rejoice in the LORD
  and take refuge in him;
  let all the upright in heart praise
    him!

[k] 5 Or us

44 / *Psalm 65*
A Prayer of Gratitude

BECAUSE I HAVE difficulty receiving gifts or compliments from others, I have had to remind myself to look people in the eyes when they offer me a gift or a compliment and say thank you. When we are unable to receive the good things that others offer us, we cheat ourselves, and we cheat them. When we are able to say thank you for gifts given, we are able to take the gift in, enjoy it and engage in a personal, intimate way with the giver of the gift. In the same way, when we express gratitude to God, we enter into a cycle of joyful relating with him. We take in his love, feel a deeper connection with him and experience joy. This psalm invites us to express gratitude to God for his good gifts.

 Warming Up to God What is it like for you to receive a gift or a compliment? What is it like for you to be on the receiving end of someone else's gratitude?

 Read Psalm 65.

Psalm 65

For the director of music. A psalm
of David. A song.

[1]Praise awaits[l] you, O God, in Zion;
    to you our vows will be fulfilled.
[2]O you who hear prayer,
    to you all men will come.
[3]When we were overwhelmed by sins,
    you forgave[m] our transgressions.
[4]Blessed are those you choose
    and bring near to live in your courts!
We are filled with the good things of your
        house,
    of your holy temple.

[5]You answer us with awesome deeds of
        righteousness,
    O God our Savior,
the hope of all the ends of the earth
    and of the farthest seas,
[6]who formed the mountains by your power,
    having armed yourself with strength,
[7]who stilled the roaring of the seas,
    the roaring of their waves,

and the turmoil of the nations.
[8]Those living far away fear your wonders;
    where morning dawns and evening fades
    you call forth songs of joy.

[9]You care for the land and water it;
    you enrich it abundantly.
The streams of God are filled with water
    to provide the people with grain,
    for so you have ordained it.[n]
[10]You drench its furrows
    and level its ridges;
you soften it with showers
    and bless its crops.
[11]You crown the year with your bounty,
    and your carts overflow with abundance.
[12]The grasslands of the desert overflow;
    the hills are clothed with gladness.
[13]The meadows are covered with flocks
    and the valleys are mantled with grain;
    they shout for joy and sing.

[l]1 Or *befits*; the meaning of the Hebrew for this word is uncertain.
[m]3 Or *made atonement for*   [n]9 Or *for that is how you prepare the land*

Discovering the Word   1. God's great power is acknowledged in this psalm. How is God's power a gift to us?   2. In verse 5 God is called "our Savior, the hope of all the ends of the earth and of the farthest seas." In what ways is God the hope of all the earth and seas?   3. The psalmist mentions several of God's awesome deeds in verses 6 and 7. What other awesome deeds might you add to the list?   4. Verse 8 offers a picture of the fears and joys common to all people of the earth. How do God's wonders cause us to experience fear?   5. How do God's wonders call forth songs of joy?

Applying the Word   1. Verses 9–13 describe the specific ways in which God tenderly loves and cares for the earth. What thoughts and feelings does this description evoke for you?   2. What implications does God's care for the earth have for the ways in which we treat the earth?   3. What personal value does expressing gratitude to God have for you?

Responding in Prayer   What are you grateful for today? Express your thanks to God.

---

45 / *Psalm 66*
A Prayer of Joy

LIFE WAS NOT intended by God to be a joyless ordeal. As much as it might surprise some of us, it is actually God's desire for us to experience joy. Joy is an act of relating to God with vulnerable, unselfconscious gratitude for the good gifts he gives. Joy comes when we experience and acknowledge God's love and care for us, when we allow ourselves to express our gratitude for his love with great energy. This psalm invites us to experience joy.

Warming Up to God Think of a time when you experienced joy. What evoked this feeling in you?

Read Psalm 66.

Psalm 66

For the director of music. A song. A psalm.

¹Shout with joy to God, all the earth!
² Sing the glory of his name;
  make his praise glorious!
³Say to God, "How awesome are your deeds!
  So great is your power
  that your enemies cringe before you.
⁴All the earth bows down to you;
  they sing praise to you,
  they sing praise to your name."   *Selah*

⁵Come and see what God has done,
  how awesome his works in man's behalf!
⁶He turned the sea into dry land,
  they passed through the waters on foot—
  come, let us rejoice in him.
⁷He rules forever by his power,
  his eyes watch the nations—
  let not the rebellious rise up against him.
                                          Selah

⁸Praise our God, O peoples,
  let the sound of his praise be heard;
⁹he has preserved our lives
  and kept our feet from slipping.
¹⁰For you, O God, tested us;

you refined us like silver.
¹¹You brought us into prison
  and laid burdens on our backs.
¹²You let men ride over our heads;
  we went through fire and water,
  but you brought us to a place of
  abundance.

¹³I will come to your temple with burnt
  offerings
  and fulfill my vows to you—
¹⁴vows my lips promised and my mouth spoke
  when I was in trouble.
¹⁵I will sacrifice fat animals to you
  and an offering of rams;
  I will offer bulls and goats.   *Selah*

¹⁶Come and listen, all you who fear God;
  let me tell you what he has done for me.
¹⁷I cried out to him with my mouth;
  his praise was on my tongue.
¹⁸If I had cherished sin in my heart,
  the Lord would not have listened;
¹⁹but God has surely listened
  and heard my voice in prayer.
²⁰Praise be to God,
  who has not rejected my prayer
  or withheld his love from me!

Discovering the Word 1. The writer calls us to action (vv. 1, 2, 3, 5, 8 and 16). What all does he call us to do? 2. How are each of these behaviors related to the experience or the expression of joy? 3. What does the section in the middle of this psalm (vv. 8–12) tell us about the cause for this particular expression of joy? 4. How might this kind of experience lead to joy? 5. Verses 16–20 are a more personal account of what the Lord has done. What does the writer say the Lord has done for him? 6. How might this kind of experience lead to joy?

Applying the Word 1. What other ways of expressing joy to God would you add to the psalmist's list? 2. Why is it important to allow ourselves to experience and express joy? 3. How might this psalm help you to experience and express joy?

Responding in Prayer What joy would you like to express to God?

46 / *Psalm 67*
God's Love for All Creatures

Jesus loves the little children—
All the children of the world.
Red, brown, yellow, black, and white—
They are precious in his sight.
Jesus loves the little children of the world.
JESUS LOVES EVERY culture he created. Its members are his little children, and he longs for them to fully experience the healing of his compassion. That's what redemption is all about. Because some of our sincere attempts to bring others into this love have been clumsy and insulting to other cultures, we are bombarded with accusations of destroying other cultures with Christianity. Some of those accusations are true and worth listening to. Yet these mistakes are not the true picture of our ministry. The gospel is good news to all societies, and God has always called and is still calling his people to bear his redemptive love to every place and people group on the earth.

 Warming Up to God   How have you recently seen God's power being revealed in your nation?

 Read Psalm 67.

Psalm 67

For the director of music. With stringed
    instruments. A psalm. A song.

¹May God be gracious to us and bless us
    and make his face shine upon us,   *Selah*
²that your ways may be known on earth,
    your salvation among all nations.

³May the peoples praise you, O God;
    may all the peoples praise you.

⁴May the nations be glad and sing
        for joy,
    for you rule the peoples justly
    and guide the nations of the earth.   *Selah*
⁵May the peoples praise you, O God;
    may all the peoples praise you.

⁶Then the land will yield its harvest,
    and God, our God, will bless us.
⁷God will bless us,
    and all the ends of the earth will
        fear him.

 Discovering the Word   1. What words do you notice being repeated throughout this passage?   2. Identify the blessings the Lord wants to bring to the nations.   3. What does this reveal about how God regards the nations?

 Applying the Word   1. What would these blessings look like if they came to your own culture?   2. How would these blessings affect some other nation in the world (say, Bosnia or South Africa)?

Responding in Prayer   Thank God for his compassion for the nations.

Psalms 68—72

Psalm 68

For the director of music. Of David.
A psalm. A song.

[1]May God arise, may his enemies be scattered;
    may his foes flee before him.
[2]As smoke is blown away by the wind,
    may you blow them away;
  as wax melts before the fire,
    may the wicked perish before God.
[3]But may the righteous be glad
    and rejoice before God;
    may they be happy and joyful.

[4]Sing to God, sing praise to his name,
    extol him who rides on the clouds[o]—
  his name is the LORD—
    and rejoice before him.
[5]A father to the fatherless, a defender of
      widows,
    is God in his holy dwelling.
[6]God sets the lonely in families,[p]
    he leads forth the prisoners with singing;
    but the rebellious live in a sun-scorched
      land.

[7]When you went out before your people, O
      God,
    when you marched through the wasteland,
                                    Selah
[8]the earth shook,
    the heavens poured down rain,
  before God, the One of Sinai,
    before God, the God of Israel.
[9]You gave abundant showers, O God;
    you refreshed your weary inheritance.
[10]Your people settled in it,
    and from your bounty, O God, you
      provided for the poor.

[11]The Lord announced the word,
    and great was the company of those who
      proclaimed it:
[12]"Kings and armies flee in haste;
    in the camps men divide the plunder.
[13]Even while you sleep among the campfires,[q]
    the wings of ⌐my⌐ dove are sheathed with
      silver,
    its feathers with shining gold."

[14]When the Almighty[r] scattered the kings in
      the land,
    it was like snow fallen on Zalmon.

[15]The mountains of Bashan are majestic
      mountains;
    rugged are the mountains of Bashan.
[16]Why gaze in envy, O rugged mountains,
    at the mountain where God chooses to
      reign,
    where the LORD himself will dwell forever?
[17]The chariots of God are tens of thousands
    and thousands of thousands;
    the Lord ⌐has come⌐ from Sinai into his
      sanctuary.
[18]When you ascended on high,
    you led captives in your train;
    you received gifts from men,
  even from[s] the rebellious—
    that you,[t] O LORD God, might dwell there.

[19]Praise be to the Lord, to God our Savior,
    who daily bears our burdens.   Selah
[20]Our God is a God who saves;
    from the Sovereign LORD comes escape from
      death.

[21]Surely God will crush the heads of his
      enemies,
    the hairy crowns of those who go on in
      their sins.
[22]The Lord says, "I will bring them from
      Bashan;
    I will bring them from the depths of the
      sea,
[23]that you may plunge your feet in the blood of
      your foes,
    while the tongues of your dogs have their
      share."

[24]Your procession has come into view, O God,
    the procession of my God and King into
      the sanctuary.
[25]In front are the singers, after them the
      musicians;
    with them are the maidens playing
      tambourines.
[26]Praise God in the great congregation;

---

[o]4 Or / prepare the way for him who rides through the deserts   [p]6 Or
the desolate in a homeland   [q]13 Or saddlebags   [r]14 Hebrew
Shaddai   [s]18 Or gifts for men, / even   [t]18 Or they

praise the LORD in the assembly of Israel.
²⁷There is the little tribe of Benjamin, leading
  them,
  there the great throng of Judah's princes,
  and there the princes of Zebulun and of
    Naphtali.

²⁸Summon your power, O God[u];
  show us your strength, O God, as you have
    done before.
²⁹Because of your temple at Jerusalem
  kings will bring you gifts.
³⁰Rebuke the beast among the reeds,
  the herd of bulls among the calves of the
    nations.
  Humbled, may it bring bars of silver.
  Scatter the nations who delight in war.
³¹Envoys will come from Egypt;
  Cush[v] will submit herself to God.

³²Sing to God, O kingdoms of the earth,
  sing praise to the Lord,   *Selah*
³³to him who rides the ancient skies above,
  who thunders with mighty voice.
³⁴Proclaim the power of God,
  whose majesty is over Israel,
  whose power is in the skies.
³⁵You are awesome, O God, in your sanctuary;
  the God of Israel gives power and strength
    to his people.

  Praise be to God!

Psalm 69

For the director of music. To ₍the tune of₎
  "Lilies." Of David.

¹Save me, O God,
  for the waters have come up to my neck.
²I sink in the miry depths,
  where there is no foothold.
  I have come into the deep waters;
  the floods engulf me.
³I am worn out calling for help;
  my throat is parched.
  My eyes fail,
  looking for my God.
⁴Those who hate me without reason
  outnumber the hairs of my head;
  many are my enemies without cause,
  those who seek to destroy me.
  I am forced to restore
  what I did not steal.

⁵You know my folly, O God;
  my guilt is not hidden from you.

⁶May those who hope in you
  not be disgraced because of me,
  O Lord, the LORD Almighty;
  may those who seek you
  not be put to shame because of me,
  O God of Israel.
⁷For I endure scorn for your sake,
  and shame covers my face.
⁸I am a stranger to my brothers,
  an alien to my own mother's sons;
⁹for zeal for your house consumes me,
  and the insults of those who insult you fall
    on me.
¹⁰When I weep and fast,
  I must endure scorn;
¹¹when I put on sackcloth,
  people make sport of me.
¹²Those who sit at the gate mock me,
  and I am the song of the drunkards.

¹³But I pray to you, O LORD,
  in the time of your favor;
  in your great love, O God,
  answer me with your sure salvation.
¹⁴Rescue me from the mire,
  do not let me sink;
  deliver me from those who hate me,
  from the deep waters.
¹⁵Do not let the floodwaters engulf me
  or the depths swallow me up
  or the pit close its mouth over me.
¹⁶Answer me, O LORD, out of the goodness of
    your love;
  in your great mercy turn to me.
¹⁷Do not hide your face from your servant;
  answer me quickly, for I am in trouble.
¹⁸Come near and rescue me;
  redeem me because of my foes.

¹⁹You know how I am scorned, disgraced and
    shamed;
  all my enemies are before you.
²⁰Scorn has broken my heart
  and has left me helpless;
  I looked for sympathy, but there was none,
  for comforters, but I found none.
²¹They put gall in my food
  and gave me vinegar for my thirst.

---

[u]*28 Many Hebrew manuscripts, Septuagint and Syriac; most Hebrew
manuscripts Your God has summoned power for you*   [v]*31 That is, the
upper Nile region*

²²May the table set before them become a snare;
  may it become retribution andʷ a trap.
²³May their eyes be darkened so they cannot
    see,
  and their backs be bent forever.
²⁴Pour out your wrath on them;
  let your fierce anger overtake them.
²⁵May their place be deserted;
  let there be no one to dwell in their tents.
²⁶For they persecute those you wound
  and talk about the pain of those you hurt.
²⁷Charge them with crime upon crime;
  do not let them share in your salvation.
²⁸May they be blotted out of the book of life
  and not be listed with the righteous.

²⁹I am in pain and distress;
  may your salvation, O God, protect me.

³⁰I will praise God's name in song
  and glorify him with thanksgiving.
³¹This will please the LORD more than an ox,
  more than a bull with its horns and hoofs.
³²The poor will see and be glad—
  you who seek God, may your hearts live!
³³The LORD hears the needy
  and does not despise his captive people.

³⁴Let heaven and earth praise him,
  the seas and all that move in them,
³⁵for God will save Zion
  and rebuild the cities of Judah.
  Then people will settle there and possess it;
³⁶ the children of his servants will inherit it,
  and those who love his name will dwell
    there.

Psalm 70

For the director of music. Of David.
A petition.

¹Hasten, O God, to save me;
  O LORD, come quickly to help me.
²May those who seek my life
  be put to shame and confusion;
  may all who desire my ruin
  be turned back in disgrace.
³May those who say to me, "Aha! Aha!"
  turn back because of their shame.
⁴But may all who seek you
  rejoice and be glad in you;
  may those who love your salvation always
    say,

"Let God be exalted!"

⁵Yet I am poor and needy;
  come quickly to me, O God.
You are my help and my deliverer;
  O LORD, do not delay.

Psalm 71

¹In you, O LORD, I have taken refuge;
  let me never be put to shame.
²Rescue me and deliver me in your
    righteousness;
  turn your ear to me and save me.
³Be my rock of refuge,
  to which I can always go;
  give the command to save me,
  for you are my rock and my fortress.
⁴Deliver me, O my God, from the hand of the
    wicked,
  from the grasp of evil and cruel men.

⁵For you have been my hope, O Sovereign
    LORD,
  my confidence since my youth.
⁶From birth I have relied on you;
  you brought me forth from my mother's
    womb.
  I will ever praise you.
⁷I have become like a portent to many,
  but you are my strong refuge.
⁸My mouth is filled with your praise,
  declaring your splendor all day long.

⁹Do not cast me away when I am old;
  do not forsake me when my strength is
    gone.
¹⁰For my enemies speak against me;
  those who wait to kill me conspire
    together.
¹¹They say, "God has forsaken him;
  pursue him and seize him,
  for no one will rescue him."
¹²Be not far from me, O God;
  come quickly, O my God, to help me.
¹³May my accusers perish in shame;
  may those who want to harm me
  be covered with scorn and disgrace.

¹⁴But as for me, I will always have hope;
  I will praise you more and more.
¹⁵My mouth will tell of your righteousness,
  of your salvation all day long,

ʷ22 Or snare / and their fellowship become

though I know not its measure.
¹⁶I will come and proclaim your mighty acts,
  O Sovereign LORD;
  I will proclaim your righteousness, yours
    alone.
¹⁷Since my youth, O God, you have taught me,
  and to this day I declare your marvelous
    deeds.
¹⁸Even when I am old and gray,
  do not forsake me, O God,
  till I declare your power to the next
    generation,
  your might to all who are to come.

¹⁹Your righteousness reaches to the skies, O
    God,
  you who have done great things.
  Who, O God, is like you?
²⁰Though you have made me see troubles,
    many and bitter,
  you will restore my life again;
  from the depths of the earth
  you will again bring me up.
²¹You will increase my honor
  and comfort me once again.

²²I will praise you with the harp
  for your faithfulness, O my God;
  I will sing praise to you with the lyre,
  O Holy One of Israel.
²³My lips will shout for joy
  when I sing praise to you—
  I, whom you have redeemed.
²⁴My tongue will tell of your righteous acts
    all day long,
  for those who wanted to harm me
  have been put to shame and confusion.

Psalm 72

Of Solomon.

¹Endow the king with your justice, O God,
  the royal son with your righteousness.
²He will^x judge your people in righteousness,
  your afflicted ones with justice.
³The mountains will bring prosperity to the
    people,
  the hills the fruit of righteousness.
⁴He will defend the afflicted among the people
  and save the children of the needy;
  he will crush the oppressor.

⁵He will endure^y as long as the sun,

as long as the moon, through all
    generations.
⁶He will be like rain falling on a mown field,
  like showers watering the earth.
⁷In his days the righteous will flourish;
  prosperity will abound till the moon is no
    more.

⁸He will rule from sea to sea
  and from the River^z to the ends of the
    earth.^{a}
⁹The desert tribes will bow before him
  and his enemies will lick the dust.
¹⁰The kings of Tarshish and of distant shores
  will bring tribute to him;
  the kings of Sheba and Seba
  will present him gifts.
¹¹All kings will bow down to him
  and all nations will serve him.

¹²For he will deliver the needy who cry out,
  the afflicted who have no one to help.
¹³He will take pity on the weak and the needy
  and save the needy from death.
¹⁴He will rescue them from oppression and
    violence,
  for precious is their blood in his sight.

¹⁵Long may he live!
  May gold from Sheba be given him.
  May people ever pray for him
  and bless him all day long.
¹⁶Let grain abound throughout the land;
  on the tops of the hills may it sway.
  Let its fruit flourish like Lebanon;
  let it thrive like the grass of the field.
¹⁷May his name endure forever;
  may it continue as long as the sun.

All nations will be blessed through him,
  and they will call him blessed.

¹⁸Praise be to the LORD God, the God of Israel,
  who alone does marvelous deeds.
¹⁹Praise be to his glorious name forever;
  may the whole earth be filled with his
    glory.
                    Amen and Amen.

²⁰This concludes the prayers of David son of
  Jesse.

---

^{x}2 Or *May he*; similarly in verses 3-11 and 17 ^{y}5 Septuagint;
Hebrew *You will be feared* ^{z}8 That is, the Euphrates ^{a}8 Or *the
end of the land*

47 / *Psalm 73*
Praying Our Doubt

DOUBT IS NOT a sin. It is an essential element in belief. Doubt is honesty. We see contradictions between what we believe and what we experience. What is going on here? Did God give us a bum steer? Why aren't things turning out the way we were taught to expect? No mature faith avoids or denies doubt. Doubt forces faith to bedrock.

 Warming Up to God   What doubts have you had or do you have about the Christian life? Express them to God without fear.

 Read Psalm 73.

BOOK III
Psalms 73–89

Psalm 73

A psalm of Asaph.

¹Surely God is good to Israel,
   to those who are pure in heart.

²But as for me, my feet had almost slipped;
   I had nearly lost my foothold.
³For I envied the arrogant
   when I saw the prosperity of the wicked.

⁴They have no struggles;
   their bodies are healthy and strong.*ᵇ*
⁵They are free from the burdens common to
     man;
   they are not plagued by human ills.
⁶Therefore pride is their necklace;
   they clothe themselves with violence.
⁷From their callous hearts comes iniquity*ᶜ*;
   the evil conceits of their minds know no
     limits.
⁸They scoff, and speak with malice;
   in their arrogance they threaten oppression.
⁹Their mouths lay claim to heaven,
   and their tongues take possession of the
     earth.
¹⁰Therefore their people turn to them
   and drink up waters in abundance.*ᵈ*
¹¹They say, "How can God know?
   Does the Most High have knowledge?"

¹²This is what the wicked are like—
   always carefree, they increase in wealth.

¹³Surely in vain have I kept my heart pure;

*ᵇ4 With a different word division of the Hebrew; Masoretic Text
struggles at their death; / their bodies are healthy   ᶜ7 Syriac (see also
Septuagint); Hebrew Their eyes bulge with fat   ᵈ10 The meaning of
the Hebrew for this verse is uncertain.*

   in vain have I washed my hands in
     innocence.
¹⁴All day long I have been plagued;
   I have been punished every morning.

¹⁵If I had said, "I will speak thus,"
   I would have betrayed your children.
¹⁶When I tried to understand all this,
   it was oppressive to me
¹⁷till I entered the sanctuary of God;
   then I understood their final destiny.

¹⁸Surely you place them on slippery ground;
   you cast them down to ruin.
¹⁹How suddenly are they destroyed,
   completely swept away by terrors!
²⁰As a dream when one awakes,
   so when you arise, O Lord,
   you will despise them as fantasies.

²¹When my heart was grieved
   and my spirit embittered,
²²I was senseless and ignorant;
   I was a brute beast before you.

²³Yet I am always with you;
   you hold me by my right hand.
²⁴You guide me with your counsel,
   and afterward you will take me into glory.
²⁵Whom have I in heaven but you?
   And earth has nothing I desire besides you.
²⁶My flesh and my heart may fail,
   but God is the strength of my heart
   and my portion forever.

²⁷Those who are far from you will perish;
   you destroy all who are unfaithful to you.
²⁸But as for me, it is good to be near God.
   I have made the Sovereign Lᴏʀᴅ my refuge;
   I will tell of all your deeds.

Discovering the Word 1. How would you paraphrase the doubt expressed in verses 2–12? 2. Who do you know who is, as they say, "getting away with murder"? 3. The key word and the pivotal center of the psalm is the word *till* in verse 17. What takes place here in the sanctuary? 4. The *yet* in verse 23 links two contrasting statements. What are they? 5. The prosperity of the wicked occupied the first part of the psalm (vv. 1–16). The presence of the Lord occupies the second (vv. 17–28). What is more vivid to you, the wicked or the Lord? Explain.

Applying the Word 1. Self-pity is like a deadly virus. How would you express, in terms of your own life, what the psalmist says in verses 13–14? 2. The appearance of the wicked whom we envy is in utter and complete contrast to their reality (vv. 18–20). How do you discern between what you *see* (and are tempted to envy) and what *is* (and so is affirmed in obedience)? 3. Worship is the pivotal act in this prayer. The Christian consensus is that it is the pivotal act every week. How can worship become a more pivotal part of your experience?

Responding in Prayer In your time of prayer spend five minutes in silence, savoring God's presence, letting him restore your perspective. Then speak your praises.

Psalms 74—76

Psalm 74

A *maskil*[e] of Asaph.

¹Why have you rejected us forever, O God?
  Why does your anger smolder against the
    sheep of your pasture?
²Remember the people you purchased of old,
  the tribe of your inheritance, whom you
    redeemed—
  Mount Zion, where you dwell.
³Turn your steps toward these everlasting
    ruins,
  all this destruction the enemy has brought
    on the sanctuary.

⁴Your foes roared in the place where you met
    with us;
  they set up their standards as signs.
⁵They behaved like men wielding axes
  to cut through a thicket of trees.
⁶They smashed all the carved paneling
  with their axes and hatchets.
⁷They burned your sanctuary to the ground;
  they defiled the dwelling place of your
    Name.
⁸They said in their hearts, "We will crush
    them completely!"
  They burned every place where God was
    worshiped in the land.
⁹We are given no miraculous signs;
  no prophets are left,
  and none of us knows how long this will
    be.

¹⁰How long will the enemy mock you, O God?
  Will the foe revile your name forever?
¹¹Why do you hold back your hand, your right
    hand?
  Take it from the folds of your garment and
    destroy them!

¹²But you, O God, are my king from of old;
  you bring salvation upon the earth.
¹³It was you who split open the sea by your
    power;
  you broke the heads of the monster in the
    waters.
¹⁴It was you who crushed the heads of
    Leviathan
  and gave him as food to the creatures of
    the desert.
¹⁵It was you who opened up springs and
    streams;
  you dried up the ever flowing rivers.
¹⁶The day is yours, and yours also the night;
  you established the sun and moon.
¹⁷It was you who set all the boundaries of the
    earth;
  you made both summer and winter.

¹⁸Remember how the enemy has mocked you,
    O LORD,
  how foolish people have reviled your name.
¹⁹Do not hand over the life of your dove to
    wild beasts;
  do not forget the lives of your afflicted
    people forever.

[e]Title: Probably a literary or musical term

²⁰Have regard for your covenant,
  because haunts of violence fill the dark
    places of the land.
²¹Do not let the oppressed retreat in disgrace;
  may the poor and needy praise your name.

²²Rise up, O God, and defend your cause;
  remember how fools mock you all day
    long.
²³Do not ignore the clamor of your adversaries,
  the uproar of your enemies, which rises
    continually.

Psalm 75

For the director of music. ⌊To the tune of⌋
  "Do Not Destroy." A psalm of Asaph.
    A song.

¹We give thanks to you, O God,
  we give thanks, for your Name is near;
    men tell of your wonderful deeds.

²You say, "I choose the appointed time;
  it is I who judge uprightly.
³When the earth and all its people quake,
  it is I who hold its pillars firm.   *Selah*
⁴To the arrogant I say, 'Boast no more,'
  and to the wicked, 'Do not lift up your
    horns.
⁵Do not lift your horns against heaven;
  do not speak with outstretched neck.' "

⁶No one from the east or the west
  or from the desert can exalt a man.
⁷But it is God who judges:
  He brings one down, he exalts another.
⁸In the hand of the LORD is a cup
  full of foaming wine mixed with spices;
he pours it out, and all the wicked of the
    earth
  drink it down to its very dregs.

⁹As for me, I will declare this forever;
  I will sing praise to the God of Jacob.
¹⁰I will cut off the horns of all the wicked,

but the horns of the righteous will be lifted
  up.

Psalm 76

For the director of music. With stringed
  instruments. A psalm of Asaph. A song.

¹In Judah God is known;
  his name is great in Israel.
²His tent is in Salem,
  his dwelling place in Zion.
³There he broke the flashing arrows,
  the shields and the swords, the weapons of
    war.   *Selah*

⁴You are resplendent with light,
  more majestic than mountains rich with
    game.
⁵Valiant men lie plundered,
  they sleep their last sleep;
not one of the warriors
  can lift his hands.
⁶At your rebuke, O God of Jacob,
  both horse and chariot lie still.
⁷You alone are to be feared.
  Who can stand before you when you are
    angry?
⁸From heaven you pronounced judgment,
  and the land feared and was quiet—
⁹when you, O God, rose up to judge,
  to save all the afflicted of the land.   *Selah*
¹⁰Surely your wrath against men brings you
    praise,
  and the survivors of your wrath are
    restrained.ᶠ

¹¹Make vows to the LORD your God and fulfill
    them;
  let all the neighboring lands
    bring gifts to the One to be feared.
¹²He breaks the spirit of rulers;
  he is feared by the kings of the earth.

ᶠ10 Or *Surely the wrath of men brings you praise, / and with the
remainder of wrath you arm yourself*

48 / *Psalm 77*
Praying Our Discontent

"THE ROOM IS too cold. Why were we seated way back in the corner? You'd think a restaurant like this would have more selection on the menu. When is our food going to get here? I don't even think this waitress deserves a tip . . ."

Perhaps you've had a meal with a person who complains like this. Some people are never satisfied with what they are given. Such people are tiring to be with. In contrast, the person who is aware of God's never-ending good gifts (and a person who seems to have comparatively less) is a joy to be around. Where do you fall on this spectrum?

 Warming Up to God Name three things you're grateful for. Reflect on your response. (How long did it take you to think of things you're grateful for? Did they come to mind quickly or slowly? How conscious are you of God's good gifts?) What did you learn about yourself?

Read Psalm 77.

Psalm 77

For the director of music. For Jeduthun.
Of Asaph. A psalm.

¹I cried out to God for help;
   I cried out to God to hear me.
²When I was in distress, I sought the Lord;
   at night I stretched out untiring hands
   and my soul refused to be comforted.

³I remembered you, O God, and I groaned;
   I mused, and my spirit grew faint.   *Selah*
⁴You kept my eyes from closing;
   I was too troubled to speak.
⁵I thought about the former days,
   the years of long ago;
⁶I remembered my songs in the night.
   My heart mused and my spirit inquired:

⁷"Will the Lord reject forever?
   Will he never show his favor again?
⁸Has his unfailing love vanished forever?
   Has his promise failed for all time?
⁹Has God forgotten to be merciful?
   Has he in anger withheld his compassion?"
                                           Selah

¹⁰Then I thought, "To this I will appeal:
   the years of the right hand of the Most
      High."

¹¹I will remember the deeds of the LORD;
   yes, I will remember your miracles of long
      ago.
¹²I will meditate on all your works
   and consider all your mighty deeds.

¹³Your ways, O God, are holy.
   What god is so great as our God?
¹⁴You are the God who performs miracles;
   you display your power among the peoples.
¹⁵With your mighty arm you redeemed your
      people,
   the descendants of Jacob and Joseph.   *Selah*

¹⁶The waters saw you, O God,
   the waters saw you and writhed;
   the very depths were convulsed.
¹⁷The clouds poured down water,
   the skies resounded with thunder;
   your arrows flashed back and forth.
¹⁸Your thunder was heard in the whirlwind,
   your lightning lit up the world;
   the earth trembled and quaked.
¹⁹Your path led through the sea,
   your way through the mighty waters,
   though your footprints were not seen.

²⁰You led your people like a flock
   by the hand of Moses and Aaron.

Discovering the Word   1. What words and phrases does the psalmist use to describe his emotion? **2.** Why does he "groan" at the memory of God (vv. 3–9)? **3.** How does the tone of the passage change in verses 10–15? **4.** What is the source of the change? **5.** How do verses 16–20 emphasize God's power?

Applying the Word   1. The psalmist's discontent makes him "too troubled to speak." When have you experienced this? **2.** Sometimes our culture leads us to believe that material things and achievements, such as a promotion at work, social status, the right relationship, a new car or the perfect house, will bring contentment. What false sources of contentment do you put faith in?   **3.** What in this passage could help you reform your thinking?

 Responding in Prayer The psalmist finds his source of contentment in who God is. Make God's character—rather than your needs—a focus of prayer.

Psalms 78—83

Psalm 78

A *maskil*ᵍ of Asaph.

¹O my people, hear my teaching;
   listen to the words of my mouth.
²I will open my mouth in parables,
   I will utter hidden things, things from of
      old—
³what we have heard and known,
   what our fathers have told us.
⁴We will not hide them from their children;
   we will tell the next generation
 the praiseworthy deeds of the LORD,
   his power, and the wonders he has done.
⁵He decreed statutes for Jacob
   and established the law in Israel,
 which he commanded our forefathers
   to teach their children,
⁶so the next generation would know them,
   even the children yet to be born,
   and they in turn would tell their children.
⁷Then they would put their trust in God
   and would not forget his deeds
   but would keep his commands.
⁸They would not be like their forefathers—
   a stubborn and rebellious generation,
 whose hearts were not loyal to God,
   whose spirits were not faithful to him.

⁹The men of Ephraim, though armed with
      bows,
   turned back on the day of battle;
¹⁰they did not keep God's covenant
   and refused to live by his law.
¹¹They forgot what he had done,
   the wonders he had shown them.
¹²He did miracles in the sight of their fathers
   in the land of Egypt, in the region of Zoan.
¹³He divided the sea and led them through;
   he made the water stand firm like a wall.
¹⁴He guided them with the cloud by day
   and with light from the fire all night.

¹⁵He split the rocks in the desert
   and gave them water as abundant as the
      seas;
¹⁶he brought streams out of a rocky crag
   and made water flow down like rivers.

¹⁷But they continued to sin against him,
   rebelling in the desert against the Most
      High.
¹⁸They willfully put God to the test
   by demanding the food they craved.
¹⁹They spoke against God, saying,
   "Can God spread a table in the desert?
²⁰When he struck the rock, water gushed out,
   and streams flowed abundantly.
 But can he also give us food?
   Can he supply meat for his people?"
²¹When the LORD heard them, he was very
      angry;
   his fire broke out against Jacob,
   and his wrath rose against Israel,
²²for they did not believe in God
   or trust in his deliverance.
²³Yet he gave a command to the skies above
   and opened the doors of the heavens;
²⁴he rained down manna for the people to eat,
   he gave them the grain of heaven.
²⁵Men ate the bread of angels;
   he sent them all the food they could eat.
²⁶He let loose the east wind from the heavens
   and led forth the south wind by his power.
²⁷He rained meat down on them like dust,
   flying birds like sand on the seashore.
²⁸He made them come down inside their camp,
   all around their tents.
²⁹They ate till they had more than enough,
   for he had given them what they craved.
³⁰But before they turned from the food they
      craved,
   even while it was still in their mouths,
³¹God's anger rose against them;
   he put to death the sturdiest among them,

ᵍTitle: Probably a literary or musical term

cutting down the young men of Israel.

³²In spite of all this, they kept on sinning;
  in spite of his wonders, they did not
    believe.
³³So he ended their days in futility
  and their years in terror.
³⁴Whenever God slew them, they would seek
    him;
  they eagerly turned to him again.
³⁵They remembered that God was their Rock,
  that God Most High was their Redeemer.
³⁶But then they would flatter him with their
    mouths,
  lying to him with their tongues;
³⁷their hearts were not loyal to him,
  they were not faithful to his covenant.
³⁸Yet he was merciful;
  he forgave their iniquities
    and did not destroy them.
  Time after time he restrained his anger
    and did not stir up his full wrath.
³⁹He remembered that they were but flesh,
  a passing breeze that does not return.

⁴⁰How often they rebelled against him in the
    desert
  and grieved him in the wasteland!
⁴¹Again and again they put God to the test;
  they vexed the Holy One of Israel.
⁴²They did not remember his power—
  the day he redeemed them from the
    oppressor,
⁴³the day he displayed his miraculous signs in
    Egypt,
  his wonders in the region of Zoan.
⁴⁴He turned their rivers to blood;
  they could not drink from their streams.
⁴⁵He sent swarms of flies that devoured them,
  and frogs that devastated them.
⁴⁶He gave their crops to the grasshopper,
  their produce to the locust.
⁴⁷He destroyed their vines with hail
  and their sycamore-figs with sleet.
⁴⁸He gave over their cattle to the hail,
  their livestock to bolts of lightning.
⁴⁹He unleashed against them his hot anger,
  his wrath, indignation and hostility—
    a band of destroying angels.
⁵⁰He prepared a path for his anger;
  he did not spare them from death
    but gave them over to the plague.
⁵¹He struck down all the firstborn of Egypt,

the firstfruits of manhood in the tents of
    Ham.
⁵²But he brought his people out like a flock;
  he led them like sheep through the desert.
⁵³He guided them safely, so they were unafraid;
  but the sea engulfed their enemies.
⁵⁴Thus he brought them to the border of his
    holy land,
  to the hill country his right hand had
    taken.
⁵⁵He drove out nations before them
  and allotted their lands to them as an
    inheritance;
  he settled the tribes of Israel in their
    homes.

⁵⁶But they put God to the test
  and rebelled against the Most High;
    they did not keep his statutes.
⁵⁷Like their fathers they were disloyal and
    faithless,
  as unreliable as a faulty bow.
⁵⁸They angered him with their high places;
  they aroused his jealousy with their idols.
⁵⁹When God heard them, he was very angry;
  he rejected Israel completely.
⁶⁰He abandoned the tabernacle of Shiloh,
  the tent he had set up among men.
⁶¹He sent ₎the ark of₎ his might into captivity,
  his splendor into the hands of the enemy.
⁶²He gave his people over to the sword;
  he was very angry with his inheritance.
⁶³Fire consumed their young men,
  and their maidens had no wedding songs;
⁶⁴their priests were put to the sword,
  and their widows could not weep.

⁶⁵Then the Lord awoke as from sleep,
  as a man wakes from the stupor of wine.
⁶⁶He beat back his enemies;
  he put them to everlasting shame.
⁶⁷Then he rejected the tents of Joseph,
  he did not choose the tribe of Ephraim;
⁶⁸but he chose the tribe of Judah,
  Mount Zion, which he loved.
⁶⁹He built his sanctuary like the heights,
  like the earth that he established forever.
⁷⁰He chose David his servant
  and took him from the sheep pens;
⁷¹from tending the sheep he brought him
  to be the shepherd of his people Jacob,
    of Israel his inheritance.

72And David shepherded them with integrity of
  heart;
  with skillful hands he led them.

Psalm 79

A psalm of Asaph.

1O God, the nations have invaded your
  inheritance;
  they have defiled your holy temple,
  they have reduced Jerusalem to rubble.
2They have given the dead bodies of your
  servants
  as food to the birds of the air,
  the flesh of your saints to the beasts of the
  earth.
3They have poured out blood like water
  all around Jerusalem,
  and there is no one to bury the dead.
4We are objects of reproach to our neighbors,
  of scorn and derision to those around us.

5How long, O LORD? Will you be angry
  forever?
  How long will your jealousy burn like fire?
6Pour out your wrath on the nations
  that do not acknowledge you,
 on the kingdoms
  that do not call on your name;
7for they have devoured Jacob
  and destroyed his homeland.
8Do not hold against us the sins of the fathers;
  may your mercy come quickly to meet us,
  for we are in desperate need.

9Help us, O God our Savior,
  for the glory of your name;
 deliver us and forgive our sins
  for your name's sake.
10Why should the nations say,
  "Where is their God?"
 Before our eyes, make known among the
  nations
  that you avenge the outpoured blood of
  your servants.
11May the groans of the prisoners come before
  you;
  by the strength of your arm
  preserve those condemned to die.

12Pay back into the laps of our neighbors seven
  times

 the reproach they have hurled at you,
  O Lord.
13Then we your people, the sheep of your
  pasture,
  will praise you forever;
 from generation to generation
  we will recount your praise.

Psalm 80

For the director of music. To ˻the tune of˼
"The Lilies of the Covenant." Of Asaph.
A psalm.

1Hear us, O Shepherd of Israel,
  you who lead Joseph like a flock;
 you who sit enthroned between the cherubim,
  shine forth
2 before Ephraim, Benjamin and Manasseh.
 Awaken your might;
  come and save us.

3Restore us, O God;
  make your face shine upon us,
  that we may be saved.

4O LORD God Almighty,
  how long will your anger smolder
  against the prayers of your people?
5You have fed them with the bread of tears;
  you have made them drink tears by the
  bowlful.
6You have made us a source of contention to
  our neighbors,
  and our enemies mock us.

7Restore us, O God Almighty;
  make your face shine upon us,
  that we may be saved.

8You brought a vine out of Egypt;
  you drove out the nations and planted it.
9You cleared the ground for it,
  and it took root and filled the land.
10The mountains were covered with its shade,
  the mighty cedars with its branches.
11It sent out its boughs to the Sea,[h]
  its shoots as far as the River.[i]

12Why have you broken down its walls
  so that all who pass by pick its grapes?
13Boars from the forest ravage it
  and the creatures of the field feed on it.
14Return to us, O God Almighty!

---

h11 Probably the Mediterranean   i11 That is, the Euphrates

Look down from heaven and see!
Watch over this vine,
15 the root your right hand has planted,
    the son[j] you have raised up for yourself.

16Your vine is cut down, it is burned with fire;
    at your rebuke your people perish.
17Let your hand rest on the man at your right
        hand,
    the son of man you have raised up for
        yourself.
18Then we will not turn away from you;
    revive us, and we will call on your name.

19Restore us, O LORD God Almighty;
    make your face shine upon us,
    that we may be saved.

Psalm 81

For the director of music. According to
gittith.[k] Of Asaph.

1Sing for joy to God our strength;
    shout aloud to the God of Jacob!
2Begin the music, strike the tambourine,
    play the melodious harp and lyre.

3Sound the ram's horn at the New Moon,
    and when the moon is full, on the day of
        our Feast;
4this is a decree for Israel,
    an ordinance of the God of Jacob.
5He established it as a statute for Joseph
    when he went out against Egypt,
    where we heard a language we did not
        understand.[l]

6He says, "I removed the burden from their
        shoulders;
    their hands were set free from the basket.
7In your distress you called and I rescued you,
    I answered you out of a thundercloud;
    I tested you at the waters of Meribah. *Selah*

8"Hear, O my people, and I will warn you—
    if you would but listen to me, O Israel!
9You shall have no foreign god among you;
    you shall not bow down to an alien god.
10I am the LORD your God,
    who brought you up out of Egypt.
    Open wide your mouth and I will fill it.

11"But my people would not listen to me;
    Israel would not submit to me.

12So I gave them over to their stubborn hearts
    to follow their own devices.

13"If my people would but listen to me,
    if Israel would follow my ways,
14how quickly would I subdue their enemies
    and turn my hand against their foes!
15Those who hate the LORD would cringe before
        him,
    and their punishment would last forever.
16But you would be fed with the finest of
        wheat;
    with honey from the rock I would satisfy
        you."

Psalm 82

A psalm of Asaph.

1God presides in the great assembly;
    he gives judgment among the "gods":

2"How long will you[m] defend the unjust
    and show partiality to the wicked?   *Selah*
3Defend the cause of the weak and fatherless;
    maintain the rights of the poor and
        oppressed.
4Rescue the weak and needy;
    deliver them from the hand of the wicked.

5"They know nothing, they understand
        nothing.
    They walk about in darkness;
    all the foundations of the earth are shaken.

6"I said, 'You are "gods";
    you are all sons of the Most High.'
7But you will die like mere men;
    you will fall like every other ruler."

8Rise up, O God, judge the earth,
    for all the nations are your inheritance.

Psalm 83

A song. A psalm of Asaph.

1O God, do not keep silent;
    be not quiet, O God, be not still.
2See how your enemies are astir,
    how your foes rear their heads.
3With cunning they conspire against your
        people;

---

j15 Or branch   *kTitle: Probably a musical term*   *l5 Or / and we
heard a voice we had not known*   *m2 The Hebrew is plural.*

they plot against those you cherish.
⁴"Come," they say, "let us destroy them as a nation,
that the name of Israel be remembered no more."

⁵With one mind they plot together;
they form an alliance against you—
⁶the tents of Edom and the Ishmaelites,
of Moab and the Hagrites,
⁷Gebal,ⁿ Ammon and Amalek,
Philistia, with the people of Tyre.
⁸Even Assyria has joined them
to lend strength to the descendants of Lot.
Selah

⁹Do to them as you did to Midian,
as you did to Sisera and Jabin at the river Kishon,
¹⁰who perished at Endor
and became like refuse on the ground.
¹¹Make their nobles like Oreb and Zeeb,

all their princes like Zebah and Zalmunna,
¹²who said, "Let us take possession
of the pasturelands of God."

¹³Make them like tumbleweed, O my God,
like chaff before the wind.
¹⁴As fire consumes the forest
or a flame sets the mountains ablaze,
¹⁵so pursue them with your tempest
and terrify them with your storm.
¹⁶Cover their faces with shame
so that men will seek your name, O Lᴏʀᴅ.

¹⁷May they ever be ashamed and dismayed;
may they perish in disgrace.
¹⁸Let them know that you, whose name is the Lᴏʀᴅ—
that you alone are the Most High over all the earth.

ⁿ7 That is, Byblos

49 / *Psalm 84*
A Prayer of Yearning

CONTINUOUS ACCESS AND warm intimacy with God is sometimes difficult to maintain. Times of spiritual dryness, "busyness" and adversity may capture our attention more and rob us of regular meeting times with God. Psalm 84 reflects a time of spiritual dryness common to many believers experientially and to Israel historically. This psalmist laments his forced and prolonged separation from God (likely during the Babylonian exile), which has robbed him of the appointed duties, freedom of access and the warm intimacy he once enjoyed.

Warming Up to God   Think back to where you were living when you were twelve years old. What was the center of warmth in your home then?

Read Psalm 84.

Psalm 84

For the director of music. According to *gittith.*ᵒ Of the Sons of Korah. A psalm.

¹How lovely is your dwelling place,
O Lᴏʀᴅ Almighty!
²My soul yearns, even faints,
for the courts of the Lᴏʀᴅ;
my heart and my flesh cry out
for the living God.

³Even the sparrow has found a home,
and the swallow a nest for herself,

where she may have her young—
a place near your altar,
O Lᴏʀᴅ Almighty, my King and my God.
⁴Blessed are those who dwell in your house;
they are ever praising you.   *Selah*

⁵Blessed are those whose strength is in you,
who have set their hearts on pilgrimage.
⁶As they pass through the Valley of Baca,
they make it a place of springs;
the autumn rains also cover it with pools.ᵖ

ᵒTitle: Probably a musical term   ᵖ6 Or *blessings*

⁷They go from strength to strength,
  till each appears before God in Zion.

⁸Hear my prayer, O Lord God Almighty;
  listen to me, O God of Jacob.   *Selah*

⁹Look upon our shield,�q O God;
  look with favor on your anointed one.

¹⁰Better is one day in your courts
  than a thousand elsewhere;
I would rather be a doorkeeper in the house
  of my God

than dwell in the tents of the wicked.
¹¹For the Lord God is a sun and shield;
  the Lord bestows favor and honor;
no good thing does he withhold
  from those whose walk is blameless.

¹²O Lord Almighty,
  blessed is the man who trusts in you.

q9 Or *sovereign*

Discovering the Word 1. What is the psalmist yearning for (vv. 2–3, 10)? 2. What names and metaphors for God can you find in this psalm? 3. The "Valley of Baca" (v. 6) was an arid stretch of desert that brought tears of adversity to pilgrims who had to traverse it en route to Jerusalem. What does that valley symbolize—historically and spiritually? 4. What are the benefits or blessings of trusting God as this psalmist does (vv. 4–5, 11–12)?

Applying the Word 1. If you could have one wish come true regarding your Christian life, what one thing would you yearn for? 2. How do you usually address God in prayer? Why? 3. Try to visualize where and when God has been closest to you. Put yourself in that picture as a "doorkeeper." How do you feel at those intimate times?

Responding in Prayer Spend time with the Lord of the universe in prayer, fellowship and worship.

Psalm 85

Psalm 85

For the director of music. Of the Sons of
Korah. A psalm.

¹You showed favor to your land, O Lord;
  you restored the fortunes of Jacob.
²You forgave the iniquity of your people
  and covered all their sins.   *Selah*
³You set aside all your wrath
  and turned from your fierce anger.

⁴Restore us again, O God our Savior,
  and put away your displeasure toward us.
⁵Will you be angry with us forever?
  Will you prolong your anger through all
    generations?
⁶Will you not revive us again,
  that your people may rejoice in you?
⁷Show us your unfailing love, O Lord,

and grant us your salvation.

⁸I will listen to what God the Lord will say;
  he promises peace to his people, his
    saints—
  but let them not return to folly.
⁹Surely his salvation is near those who fear
    him,
  that his glory may dwell in our land.

¹⁰Love and faithfulness meet together;
  righteousness and peace kiss each other.
¹¹Faithfulness springs forth from the earth,
  and righteousness looks down from heaven.
¹²The Lord will indeed give what is good,
  and our land will yield its harvest.
¹³Righteousness goes before him
  and prepares the way for his steps.

50 / *Psalm 86*
A Prayer of Dependence

OUR RELATIONSHIP WITH God is that of children to a parent, sheep to a shepherd, creators to the Creator. We are dependent on him for life, for breath, for sustenance, for help in trouble, for love, for forgiveness, for mercy. We may like to think of ourselves as independent and self-sufficient. But we are not. We need God. It is vital that we acknowledge our need for him because it is the beginning place of our relationship with him. This psalm helps us give voice to our dependence on God.

 Warming Up to God Think of a time when you needed to rely on someone for emotional or physical support. What feelings did you have about depending on them for help?

 Read Psalm 86.

Psalm 86

A prayer of David.

¹Hear, O Lᴏʀᴅ, and answer me,
for I am poor and needy.
²Guard my life, for I am devoted to you.
You are my God; save your servant
who trusts in you.
³Have mercy on me, O Lord,
for I call to you all day long.
⁴Bring joy to your servant,
for to you, O Lord,
I lift up my soul.

⁵You are forgiving and good, O Lord,
abounding in love to all who call
to you.
⁶Hear my prayer, O Lᴏʀᴅ;
listen to my cry for mercy.
⁷In the day of my trouble I will call
to you,
for you will answer me.

⁸Among the gods there is none like you,
O Lord;
no deeds can compare with yours.
⁹All the nations you have made
will come and worship before you, O Lord;
they will bring glory to your name.
¹⁰For you are great and do marvelous deeds;
you alone are God.

¹¹Teach me your way, O Lᴏʀᴅ,
and I will walk in your truth;
give me an undivided heart,
that I may fear your name.
¹²I will praise you, O Lord my God, with all
my heart;
I will glorify your name forever.
¹³For great is your love toward me;
you have delivered me from the depths of
the grave.ʳ

¹⁴The arrogant are attacking me,
O God;
a band of ruthless men seeks
my life—
men without regard for you.
¹⁵But you, O Lord, are a compassionate and
gracious God,
slow to anger, abounding in love and
faithfulness.
¹⁶Turn to me and have mercy on me;
grant your strength to your servant
and save the son of your maidservant.ˢ
¹⁷Give me a sign of your goodness,
that my enemies may see it and be put to
shame,
for you, O Lᴏʀᴅ, have helped me and
comforted me.

ʳ13 Hebrew *Sheol*   ˢ16 Or *save your faithful son*

Discovering the Word 1. What is the overall sense you get about the nature of the psalmist's relationship with God? 2. List the many requests the psalmist makes of God. 3. The psalmist sees God as loving, powerful and actively involved in caring for him. What are some of the specific statements he makes about God? 4. What impact would this view of God have on a person's ability to depend on God? 5. How does the psalmist show his dependence on God throughout this psalm?

Applying the Word 1. What reactions do you have to this kind of dependency on God? **2.** How might the psalmist's dependency on God encourage you to depend more fully on God? **3.** In what areas of your life do you need to acknowledge your dependence on God?

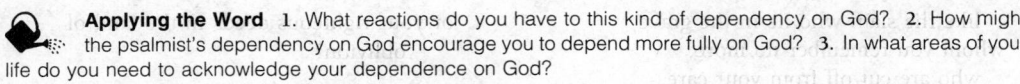 **Responding in Prayer** Freely express your sense of need for God and your struggles to depend on him.

Psalm 87

Psalm 87

Of the Sons of Korah. A psalm. A song.

¹He has set his foundation on the holy
    mountain;
² the Lord loves the gates of Zion
    more than all the dwellings of Jacob.
³Glorious things are said of you,
    O city of God: *Selah*
⁴"I will record Rahab^t and Babylon
    among those who acknowledge me—
Philistia too, and Tyre, along with
    Cush^u—

and will say, 'This^v one was born in
    Zion.'"
⁵Indeed, of Zion it will be said,
    "This one and that one were born in her,
    and the Most High himself will establish
    her."
⁶The Lord will write in the register of the
    peoples:
    "This one was born in Zion."   *Selah*
⁷As they make music they will sing,
    "All my fountains are in you."

t4 A poetic name for Egypt   u4 That is, the upper Nile region
v4 Or *"O Rahab and Babylon, / Philistia, Tyre and Cush, / I will record
concerning those who acknowledge me: / 'This*

51 / *Psalm 88*
A Prayer of Despair

"I GIVE UP," Nancy said as she buried her face in her hands. Nancy was not a passive person. She worked hard as a single mother to provide for her children. She had developed a good support system for herself. She was actively, compassionately engaged in life. But a series of losses had left her deeply shaken. Everything she had worked so hard for seemed to be gone. Nancy felt defeated. And without hope. Despair is giving up. Or, as the psalmist expresses it, despair is a time when "darkness" becomes our "closest friend."

 Warming Up to God What pictures come to mind when you think of a person who is experiencing despair?

 Read Psalm 88.

Psalm 88

A song. A psalm of the Sons of Korah. For
    the director of music. According to
mahalath leannoth.^w A *maskil*^x of Heman
    the Ezrahite.

¹O Lord, the God who saves me,
    day and night I cry out before you.
²May my prayer come before you;

turn your ear to my cry.

³For my soul is full of trouble
    and my life draws near the grave.^y
⁴I am counted among those who go down to
    the pit;
    I am like a man without strength.
⁵I am set apart with the dead,

w Title: Possibly a tune, "The Suffering of Affliction"   x Title: Probably a
literary or musical term   y3 Hebrew *Sheol*

like the slain who lie in the grave,
  whom you remember no more,
  who are cut off from your care.

⁶You have put me in the lowest pit,
  in the darkest depths.
⁷Your wrath lies heavily upon me;
  you have overwhelmed me with all your
    waves.   *Selah*
⁸You have taken from me my closest friends
  and have made me repulsive to them.
  I am confined and cannot escape;
⁹ my eyes are dim with grief.

I call to you, O LORD, every day;
  I spread out my hands to you.
¹⁰Do you show your wonders to the dead?
  Do those who are dead rise up and praise
    you?   *Selah*
¹¹Is your love declared in the grave,
  your faithfulness in Destructionᶻ?
¹²Are your wonders known in the place of
  darkness,

or your righteous deeds in the land of
  oblivion?

¹³But I cry to you for help, O LORD;
  in the morning my prayer comes before
    you.
¹⁴Why, O LORD, do you reject me
  and hide your face from me?

¹⁵From my youth I have been afflicted and
  close to death;
  I have suffered your terrors and am in
    despair.
¹⁶Your wrath has swept over me;
  your terrors have destroyed me.
¹⁷All day long they surround me like a flood;
  they have completely engulfed me.
¹⁸You have taken my companions and loved
  ones from me;
  the darkness is my closest friend.

ᶻ11 Hebrew *Abaddon*

Discovering the Word 1. What evidence is there of despair in this psalm? 2. What emotional impact did you experience as you read this psalm? 3. Contrast the first and last verses of this psalm. Most psalms which express strong doubts end with hope or praise. This psalm ends with doubt and despair. What is it like to be left with unresolved questions? 4. The writer blames God for his desperate situation. What does he say in blaming God (vv. 6–9, 15–18)? 5. In spite of his sense that God has rejected him and hurt him, the psalmist continues to talk with God. What does this say about his relationship with God?

Applying the Word 1. What reactions do you have to the psalmist blaming God? 2. Think of a time when it was difficult for you to talk to God. What was that experience like for you?

Responding in Prayer What would you like to say to God about the areas in life that feel "dark" or hopeless to you?

Psalm 89

Psalm 89

A *maskil*ᵃ of Ethan the Ezrahite.

¹I will sing of the LORD's great love
  forever;
  with my mouth I will make your
    faithfulness known through all
    generations.
²I will declare that your love stands firm
  forever,
  that you established your faithfulness in
    heaven itself.

³You said, "I have made a covenant with my
  chosen one,
  I have sworn to David my servant,
⁴'I will establish your line forever
  and make your throne firm through all
    generations.' "   *Selah*
⁵The heavens praise your wonders, O LORD,
  your faithfulness too, in the assembly of the
    holy ones.
⁶For who in the skies above can compare with
  the LORD?

ᵃTitle: Probably a literary or musical term

Who is like the LORD among the heavenly
   beings?
⁷In the council of the holy ones God is greatly
   feared;
   he is more awesome than all who surround
      him.
⁸O LORD God Almighty, who is like you?
   You are mighty, O LORD, and your
      faithfulness surrounds you.

⁹You rule over the surging sea;
   when its waves mount up, you still them.
¹⁰You crushed Rahab like one of the slain;
   with your strong arm you scattered your
      enemies.
¹¹The heavens are yours, and yours also the
   earth;
   you founded the world and all that is in it.
¹²You created the north and the south;
   Tabor and Hermon sing for joy at your
      name.
¹³Your arm is endued with power;
   your hand is strong, your right hand
      exalted.

¹⁴Righteousness and justice are the foundation
   of your throne;
   love and faithfulness go before you.
¹⁵Blessed are those who have learned to acclaim
   you,
   who walk in the light of your presence,
      O LORD.
¹⁶They rejoice in your name all day long;
   they exult in your righteousness.
¹⁷For you are their glory and strength,
   and by your favor you exalt our horn.^b
¹⁸Indeed, our shield^c belongs to the LORD,
   our king to the Holy One of Israel.

¹⁹Once you spoke in a vision,
   to your faithful people you said:
"I have bestowed strength on a warrior;
   I have exalted a young man from among
      the people.
²⁰I have found David my servant;
   with my sacred oil I have anointed him.
²¹My hand will sustain him;
   surely my arm will strengthen him.
²²No enemy will subject him to tribute;
   no wicked man will oppress him.
²³I will crush his foes before him
   and strike down his adversaries.
²⁴My faithful love will be with him,

and through my name his horn^d will be
   exalted.
²⁵I will set his hand over the sea,
   his right hand over the rivers.
²⁶He will call out to me, 'You are my Father,
   my God, the Rock my Savior.'
²⁷I will also appoint him my firstborn,
   the most exalted of the kings of the earth.
²⁸I will maintain my love to him forever,
   and my covenant with him will never fail.
²⁹I will establish his line forever,
   his throne as long as the heavens endure.

³⁰"If his sons forsake my law
   and do not follow my statutes,
³¹if they violate my decrees
   and fail to keep my commands,
³²I will punish their sin with the rod,
   their iniquity with flogging;
³³but I will not take my love from him,
   nor will I ever betray my faithfulness.
³⁴I will not violate my covenant
   or alter what my lips have uttered.
³⁵Once for all, I have sworn by my holiness—
   and I will not lie to David—
³⁶that his line will continue forever
   and his throne endure before me like the
      sun;
³⁷it will be established forever like the moon,
   the faithful witness in the sky."   *Selah*

³⁸But you have rejected, you have spurned,
   you have been very angry with your
      anointed one.
³⁹You have renounced the covenant with your
   servant
   and have defiled his crown in the dust.
⁴⁰You have broken through all his walls
   and reduced his strongholds to ruins.
⁴¹All who pass by have plundered him;
   he has become the scorn of his neighbors.
⁴²You have exalted the right hand of his foes;
   you have made all his enemies rejoice.
⁴³You have turned back the edge of his sword
   and have not supported him in battle.
⁴⁴You have put an end to his splendor
   and cast his throne to the ground.
⁴⁵You have cut short the days of his youth;
   you have covered him with a mantle of
      shame.   *Selah*

^b17 *Horn* here symbolizes strong one.   ^c18 Or *sovereign*
^d24 *Horn* here symbolizes strength.

⁴⁶How long, O Lᴏʀᴅ? Will you hide yourself
 forever?
 How long will your wrath burn like fire?
⁴⁷Remember how fleeting is my life.
 For what futility you have created all
 men!
⁴⁸What man can live and not see death,
 or save himself from the power of the
 graveᵉ? *Selah*
⁴⁹O Lord, where is your former great love,
 which in your faithfulness you swore to
 David?

⁵⁰Remember, Lord, how your servant hasᶠ
 been mocked,
 how I bear in my heart the taunts of all the
 nations,
⁵¹the taunts with which your enemies have
 mocked, O Lᴏʀᴅ,
 with which they have mocked every step of
 your anointed one.

⁵²Praise be to the Lᴏʀᴅ forever!
 Amen and Amen.

ᵉ48 Hebrew *Sheol* ᶠ50 Or *your servants have*

52 / *Psalm 90*
Praying Our Death

DEATH IS NOT a popular subject. We live in a society characterized by the denial of death. This is unusual. Most people who have lived on this earth have given a great deal of attention to death. Preparing for a good death has been, in every century except our own, an accepted goal in life. Psalm 90 has been part of that preparation for millions of Christians.

 Warming Up to God When you think about your own death, what do you think about? What do you feel?

 Read Psalm 90.

BOOK IV
Psalms 90–106

Psalm 90

A prayer of Moses the man of God.

¹Lord, you have been our dwelling place
 throughout all generations.
²Before the mountains were born
 or you brought forth the earth and the
 world,
 from everlasting to everlasting you are God.

³You turn men back to dust,
 saying, "Return to dust, O sons of men."
⁴For a thousand years in your sight
 are like a day that has just gone by,
 or like a watch in the night.
⁵You sweep men away in the sleep of death;
 they are like the new grass of the
 morning—
⁶though in the morning it springs up new,

by evening it is dry and withered.

⁷We are consumed by your anger
 and terrified by your indignation.
⁸You have set our iniquities before you,
 our secret sins in the light of your
 presence.
⁹All our days pass away under your wrath;
 we finish our years with a moan.
¹⁰The length of our days is seventy years—
 or eighty, if we have the strength;
 yet their spanᵍ is but trouble and sorrow,
 for they quickly pass, and we fly away.

¹¹Who knows the power of your anger?
 For your wrath is as great as the fear that is
 due you.
¹²Teach us to number our days aright,
 that we may gain a heart of wisdom.
¹³Relent, O Lᴏʀᴅ! How long will it be?
 Have compassion on your servants.

ᵍ10 Or *yet the best of them*

14Satisfy us in the morning with your unfailing
  love,
   that we may sing for joy and be glad all
     our days.
15Make us glad for as many days as you have
  afflicted us,
   for as many years as we have seen trouble.
16May your deeds be shown to your servants,

your splendor to their children.
17May the favor[h] of the Lord our God rest
  upon us;
   establish the work of our hands for us—
   yes, establish the work of our hands.

h17 Or *beauty*

 Discovering the Word 1. Read Psalm 90. Death sets a limit to our lives and stimulates reflection on the context of life, which is not death, but God. In verses 1–2 how does the psalmist set death within his view of God? 2. How does the psalmist describe God's anger and its effects on our lives (vv. 7–11)? 3. How do you integrate this view of God with John's well-known statement "God is love"? 4. Luther commented on verse 12: "Lord, teach us all to be such arithmeticians!" What does it mean to number our days aright? 5. Study the verbs in verses 14–17. What emerges as most important for you—what you do for the rest of your life or what God will do in your life? Explain.

Applying the Word 1. How long do you expect to live? 2. How do you plan to live the years left to you? 3. Plato believed that philosophy was nothing more than a study of death. In the Middle Ages pastoral care concentrated on preparing you for a good death. How does your meditation on death affect the way you live your life?

Responding in Prayer Express your awareness that you will die. In your prayers be conscious of Christ's death.

53 / *Psalm 91*
Angels Among Us

ANGEL STORIES ARE gaining wider acceptance today. People see angels taking various forms and functions—as messengers of glad tidings, spirits of people who have died, invisible guardians of our safety, angels in disguise as do-gooders or cherubs of romantic love. Many of the popular depictions of angels have nothing to do with the biblical perspective. The angels invoked in this psalm are heralds and harbingers of God's power. The psalm glows with testimony to the security of godly worshipers.

 Warming Up to God In your mind's eye, what do angels look like? What do they spend their time doing?

 Read Psalm 91.

Psalm 91

1He who dwells in the shelter of the Most
  High
   will rest in the shadow of the Almighty.[i]
2I will say[j] of the LORD, "He is my refuge and
  my fortress,
   my God, in whom I trust."

3Surely he will save you from the fowler's
  snare
   and from the deadly pestilence.

4He will cover you with his feathers,
   and under his wings you will find refuge;
   his faithfulness will be your shield and
     rampart.
5You will not fear the terror of night,
   nor the arrow that flies by day,
6nor the pestilence that stalks in the darkness,
   nor the plague that destroys at midday.
7A thousand may fall at your side,
   ten thousand at your right hand,

i1 Hebrew *Shaddai*   j2 Or *He says*

but it will not come near you.
⁸You will only observe with your eyes
and see the punishment of the wicked.

⁹If you make the Most High your dwelling—
even the Lord, who is my refuge—
¹⁰then no harm will befall you,
no disaster will come near your tent.
¹¹For he will command his angels concerning
you
to guard you in all your ways;
¹²they will lift you up in their hands,
so that you will not strike your foot against
a stone.

¹³You will tread upon the lion and the cobra;
you will trample the great lion and the
serpent.

¹⁴"Because he loves me," says the Lord, "I will
rescue him;
I will protect him, for he acknowledges my
name.
¹⁵He will call upon me, and I will answer him;
I will be with him in trouble,
I will deliver him and honor him.
¹⁶With long life will I satisfy him
and show him my salvation."

Discovering the Word 1. The psalm divides into two stanzas: vv. 1–8 and vv. 9–16. What theme is common to the opening couplet of each stanza (vv. 1–2, 9–10)? 2. What threatens the security of the believer, even those who take refuge in God (vv. 3–6, 13)? 3. Is the godly believer protected *from* calamity and sorrow, or is he promised God's presence *amidst* terrible circumstances? Explain your answer from the passage. 4. What is the basis for the psalmist's assurance that he will be safe and secure (vv. 9–12, 14–15)? 5. In this psalm, what does "my [God's] salvation" (v. 16) look like?

Applying the Word 1. What are you particularly anxious about these days, for which God is waiting on you to call his name and acknowledge your need? 2. How can you make God your dwelling place, your refuge, your shield in times of trouble?

Responding in Prayer God is waiting to hear from his people who love him and acknowledge their need of him. Tell him whatever is on your mind, whatever fears you have and whatever terrible circumstances you are facing. Trust him to answer.

Psalms 92—93

Psalm 92

A psalm. A song. For the Sabbath day.

¹It is good to praise the Lord
and make music to your name, O Most
High,
²to proclaim your love in the morning
and your faithfulness at night,
³to the music of the ten-stringed lyre
and the melody of the harp.

⁴For you make me glad by your deeds, O Lord;
I sing for joy at the works of your hands.
⁵How great are your works, O Lord,
how profound your thoughts!
⁶The senseless man does not know,
fools do not understand,
⁷that though the wicked spring up like grass
and all evildoers flourish,
they will be forever destroyed.

⁸But you, O Lord, are exalted forever.

⁹For surely your enemies, O Lord,
surely your enemies will perish;
all evildoers will be scattered.
¹⁰You have exalted my horn*ᵏ* like that of a
wild ox;
fine oils have been poured upon me.
¹¹My eyes have seen the defeat of my
adversaries;
my ears have heard the rout of my wicked
foes.

¹²The righteous will flourish like a palm tree,
they will grow like a cedar of Lebanon;
¹³planted in the house of the Lord,
they will flourish in the courts of our God.
¹⁴They will still bear fruit in old age,
they will stay fresh and green,

ᵏ10 Horn here symbolizes strength.

¹⁵proclaiming, "The LORD is upright;
    he is my Rock, and there is no wickedness
        in him."

Psalm 93

¹The LORD reigns, he is robed in majesty;
    the LORD is robed in majesty
    and is armed with strength.
The world is firmly established;
    it cannot be moved.
²Your throne was established long ago;
    you are from all eternity.

³The seas have lifted up, O LORD,
    the seas have lifted up their voice;
    the seas have lifted up their pounding
        waves.
⁴Mightier than the thunder of the great waters,
    mightier than the breakers of the sea—
    the LORD on high is mighty.

⁵Your statutes stand firm;
    holiness adorns your house
    for endless days, O LORD.

54 / *Psalm 94*
A Prayer of Anger

MIKE AND JOHN had something in common—they had both been ripped off by their business partners and they were both angry. Very angry. As they shared their experiences with each other, they discovered an important difference, however. Mike was baffled by what to do with his strong feelings. His anger frightened him and did not seem very spiritual, so most of the time he kept quiet about his sense of outrage at the unfairness of it all. John, on the other hand, had grown up in a church that prayed the psalms together. Together they had spoken the words of anger and outrage to God. As a result, John was able to talk to God about his anger. He knew he had been grievously wronged and that he was deeply angry. And he knew he could take his anger to God. This psalm is one of the psalms that can help us speak freely to God about our anger.

 Warming Up to God Is it difficult or relatively easy for you to tell God about your anger? Explain.

 Read Psalm 94.

Psalm 94

¹O LORD, the God who avenges,
    O God who avenges, shine forth.
²Rise up, O Judge of the earth;
    pay back to the proud what they deserve.
³How long will the wicked, O LORD,
    how long will the wicked be jubilant?

⁴They pour out arrogant words;
    all the evildoers are full of boasting.
⁵They crush your people, O LORD;
    they oppress your inheritance.
⁶They slay the widow and the alien;
    they murder the fatherless.
⁷They say, "The LORD does not see;
    the God of Jacob pays no heed."

⁸Take heed, you senseless ones among the
        people;

    you fools, when will you become wise?
⁹Does he who implanted the ear not hear?
    Does he who formed the eye not see?
¹⁰Does he who disciplines nations not punish?
    Does he who teaches man lack knowledge?
¹¹The LORD knows the thoughts of man;
    he knows that they are futile.

¹²Blessed is the man you discipline, O LORD,
    the man you teach from your law;
¹³you grant him relief from days of trouble,
    till a pit is dug for the wicked.
¹⁴For the LORD will not reject his people;
    he will never forsake his inheritance.
¹⁵Judgment will again be founded on
        righteousness,
    and all the upright in heart will follow it.

¹⁶Who will rise up for me against the wicked?

Who will take a stand for me against
   evildoers?
17Unless the LORD had given me help,
   I would soon have dwelt in the silence of
      death.
18When I said, "My foot is slipping,"
   your love, O LORD, supported me.
19When anxiety was great within me,
   your consolation brought joy to my soul.

20Can a corrupt throne be allied with you—

one that brings on misery by its decrees?
21They band together against the righteous
   and condemn the innocent to death.
22But the LORD has become my fortress,
   and my God the rock in whom I take
      refuge.
23He will repay them for their sins
   and destroy them for their wickedness;
   the LORD our God will destroy them.

 Discovering the Word 1. The psalmist addresses God as the Judge and as the one who avenges (vv. 1–2). What is the meaning of this for the psalmist? 2. In pleading his case before God, what does the psalmist say the wicked have done (vv. 4–7)? 3. In verses 8, 9 and 10 the psalmist asks several rhetorical questions of God. What statement is he making in these questions? 4. What hope does the psalmist express in verses 12–15? 5. Verse 16 captures the question the psalmist is wrestling with. What words would you use to express this question? 6. In verses 17 through 19 the psalmist expresses himself in vulnerable terms. How does he describe the experience of danger and fear that generated his anger?

Applying the Word 1. The psalmist concludes with statements that God will take care of justice, that God will judge. Why is this important to remember when we are feeling powerless and outraged in the face of injustice? 2. This psalm models several constructive ways we can behave when we are angry. It models honesty with ourselves and with God, stating our case to God, acknowledging our vulnerability, trusting God's care and letting God take care of justice. How might this example help you in times of anger? 3. Which of these behavioral examples might be especially important for you to follow when you are angry? Explain.

Responding in Prayer Talk to God about any feelings of anger—fresh or lingering—that you have.

---

55 / *Psalm 95*
A Psalm of Rest

SO OFTEN GOD gives us the consequences of our choices; other times he withholds or spares us the punishment our rebellion or hardheartedness deserves. That is an act of his mercy, for which this psalmist and all believers can give thanks. This psalm acknowledges God as Lord of the earth and Shepherd King of his people. The writer reflects on times of rebellion when the Israelites put God to the test and ended up missing out on God's rest.

 Warming Up to God Picture the place where you go to enjoy peace and serenity, rest from your labors, and listen to God. If you don't have a place like that, make one up. Where is that place? (Does it have mountain peaks, sandy beaches, desert calm, green pastures?)

Read Psalm 95.

Psalm 95

1Come, let us sing for joy to the LORD;
   let us shout aloud to the Rock of our
      salvation.
2Let us come before him with thanksgiving
   and extol him with music and song.

3For the LORD is the great God,
   the great King above all gods.
4In his hand are the depths of the earth,
   and the mountain peaks belong to him.
5The sea is his, for he made it,
   and his hands formed the dry land.

⁶Come, let us bow down in worship,
   let us kneel before the LORD our Maker;
⁷for he is our God
   and we are the people of his pasture,
   the flock under his care.

Today, if you hear his voice,
⁸ do not harden your hearts as you did at
     Meribah,ˡ
   as you did that day at Massahᵐ in the
     desert,

⁹where your fathers tested and tried me,
   though they had seen what I did.
¹⁰For forty years I was angry with that
     generation;
   I said, "They are a people whose hearts go
     astray,
   and they have not known my ways."
¹¹So I declared on oath in my anger,
   "They shall never enter my rest."

ˡ8 *Meribah* means *quarreling.*   ᵐ8 *Massah* means *testing.*

Discovering the Word 1. Where does this psalmist envision God ruling as Lord and King (vv. 3–5)? 2. Meribah and Massah are places where the Israelites rebelled in the desert and tested the Lord about whether he was with them or not (vv. 8–9). What happened as a result of that testing (vv. 10–11)? 3. What is the "rest" from which the rebellious Israelites were banned with an oath of God, but which a later generation would enjoy (v. 11)? 4. Imagine life without God's promised rest. What must that have been like? 5. What warning does the psalmist derive from that experience as he contemplates "Meribah" and "Massah" recurring for the present generation of God's people?

Applying the Word 1. Imagine life for you without God's promised rest. If your life and well-being were constantly threatened with adversaries in the land where you live and work, what would you be praying for? 2. During those times in your past when your heart strayed from God's ways (v. 10), how did God bring you back to himself? 3. As you listen to God's voice "today" (v. 7), what is he saying to you?

Responding in Prayer Whatever the past or present circumstances of your relationship with him may be, this psalm invites you to come into God's presence today. Try kneeling in his presence, acknowledging him as Lord of your life, even during those times you have strayed. Soften your heart and give him the praise and thanksgiving he deserves.

56 / *Psalm 96*
Worldwide Worship

OUR GOD IS a missionary God. He wants all nations, every living thing, to bow down in worship of him. And God wants us to take that message—in word and deed, in song and praise—to the ends of the earth. The psalmist bids us to be most inclusive in our worship of the one true God.

 Warming Up to God Think about the greatness of God. What hymns come to mind that prompt you with the melody, the lyrics and reasons to praise him for the great things he has done?

 Read Psalm 96.

Psalm 96

¹Sing to the LORD a new song;
   sing to the LORD, all the earth.
²Sing to the LORD, praise his name;
   proclaim his salvation day after
     day.
³Declare his glory among the nations,
   his marvelous deeds among all peoples.

⁴For great is the LORD and most worthy of
     praise;
   he is to be feared above all gods.
⁵For all the gods of the nations are idols,
   but the LORD made the heavens.
⁶Splendor and majesty are before him;
   strength and glory are in his sanctuary.

⁷Ascribe to the LORD, O families of nations,

ascribe to the LORD glory and strength.

[8] Ascribe to the LORD the glory due his name;
bring an offering and come into his courts.
[9] Worship the LORD in the splendor of his[n]
holiness;
tremble before him, all the earth.

[10] Say among the nations, "The LORD reigns."
The world is firmly established, it cannot
be moved;
he will judge the peoples with equity.
[11] Let the heavens rejoice, let the earth be glad;

let the sea resound, and all that is in it;
[12] let the fields be jubilant, and everything in
them.
Then all the trees of the forest will sing for
joy;
[13] they will sing before the LORD, for he
comes,
he comes to judge the earth.
He will judge the world in righteousness
and the peoples in his truth.

[n]9 Or LORD with the splendor of

Discovering the Word 1. This psalm is divided up into four parts that are identifiable by repeated words or refrains: verses 1–3, 4–6, 7–9 and 10–13. What repetition do you see in each of these sections? 2. What "marvelous deeds" (v. 3) come to mind that would prompt a believer to sing God's praises? 3. Why is the Lord "most worthy of" (entitled to) praise (vv. 4–6, 10, 13)? 4. Like an orchestra conductor that bids different sections to join in the ensemble, the psalmist bids different sections to join in the chorus of praise to God. How extensive or inclusive is this call to "ascribe glory to" (worship) God (vv. 7–13)?

Applying the Word 1. In light of this universal call to worship, think of those around you and on the other side of the globe. What does the psalmist prompt you to do about those who don't know God? 2. This psalm invites us to sing a "new song" declaring his glory to others (in witness) and ascribing glory directly to God (in worship). How would someone who is not musically inclined be creative in this kind of witness and worship? 3. Let the joy of knowing God bubble up within you and burst forth in a "new song" of worship. Be spontaneous and let this psalm be the wellspring for singing out or jotting down words of praise. (Later see if you, or someone you know, could set those words to music.)

Responding in Prayer Pray for someone who does not yet know God. Pray about inviting that person to join you in worship.

Psalms 97—98

Psalm 97

[1] The LORD reigns, let the earth be glad;
let the distant shores rejoice.

[2] Clouds and thick darkness surround him;
righteousness and justice are the foundation
of his throne.
[3] Fire goes before him
and consumes his foes on every side.
[4] His lightning lights up the world;
the earth sees and trembles.
[5] The mountains melt like wax before the LORD,
before the Lord of all the earth.
[6] The heavens proclaim his righteousness,
and all the peoples see his glory.

[7] All who worship images are put to shame,

those who boast in idols—
worship him, all you gods!

[8] Zion hears and rejoices
and the villages of Judah are glad
because of your judgments, O LORD.
[9] For you, O LORD, are the Most High over all
the earth;
you are exalted far above all gods.

[10] Let those who love the LORD hate evil,
for he guards the lives of his faithful ones
and delivers them from the hand of the
wicked.
[11] Light is shed upon the righteous
and joy on the upright in heart.
[12] Rejoice in the LORD, you who are righteous,
and praise his holy name.

Psalm 98

A psalm.

¹Sing to the LORD a new song,
  for he has done marvelous things;
his right hand and his holy arm
  have worked salvation for him.
²The LORD has made his salvation known
  and revealed his righteousness to the
    nations.
³He has remembered his love
  and his faithfulness to the house of Israel;
all the ends of the earth have seen
  the salvation of our God.

⁴Shout for joy to the LORD, all the earth,

burst into jubilant song with music;
⁵make music to the LORD with the harp,
  with the harp and the sound of singing,
⁶with trumpets and the blast of the ram's
    horn—
  shout for joy before the LORD, the King.

⁷Let the sea resound, and everything in it,
  the world, and all who live in it.
⁸Let the rivers clap their hands,
  let the mountains sing together for joy;
⁹let them sing before the LORD,
  for he comes to judge the earth.
He will judge the world in righteousness
  and the peoples with equity.

---

57 / *Psalm 99*
Hail to the King of Kings

THE ATTRIBUTES AND actions of our holy God inspire praise, awe and obedience in those who call on his name. This psalm calls to mind the special relationship that he had with Moses, Aaron and Samuel—a relationship that is representative and possible for all of God's people.

 Warming Up to God Think about the holiness of God. What hymns come to mind that prompt you to praise God for his holiness, the justice and rightness of his ways? How do those hymns make you feel about approaching God?

Read Psalm 99.

Psalm 99

¹The LORD reigns,
  let the nations tremble;
he sits enthroned between the cherubim,
  let the earth shake.
²Great is the LORD in Zion;
  he is exalted over all the nations.
³Let them praise your great and awesome
    name—
  he is holy.

⁴The King is mighty, he loves justice—
  you have established equity;
in Jacob you have done
  what is just and right.
⁵Exalt the LORD our God
  and worship at his footstool;
  he is holy.

⁶Moses and Aaron were among his priests,
  Samuel was among those who called on his
    name;
they called on the LORD
  and he answered them.
⁷He spoke to them from the pillar of cloud;
  they kept his statutes and the decrees he
    gave them.

⁸O LORD our God,
  you answered them;
you were to Israel⁰ a forgiving God,
  though you punished their misdeeds.ᴾ
⁹Exalt the LORD our God
  and worship at his holy mountain,
  for the LORD our God is holy.

⁰8 Hebrew *them*   ᴾ8 Or *| an avenger of the wrongs done to them*

Discovering the Word 1. This psalm speaks of the Lord in different ways a total of seven times. (Seven is a symbol of completeness.) What aspects or characteristics of this complete Lord does the psalmist affirm? 2. Study the verbs. How do or should others respond in relation to the exalted Lord? 3. Consider the causes and effects, also the actions and explanations, in this psalm. Why should God's people worship this Lord (vv. 4–8)? 4. Out of reverence for God's unapproachable holiness, the people went through intermediaries to God. Priests such as Moses, Aaron and Samuel were the go-betweens (v. 6). How did God speak with them (vv. 6–8)?

Applying the Word 1. God is terribly awesome and holy, forgiving and punishing. What does that say about the casual God-is-my-buddy approach or the presumptuous God-is-my-bellhop approach we often take in worship and prayer? 2. What does God expect you to do in response to his holy character and righteous decrees? 3. This psalm invites us to tremble, praise, exalt and worship this Lord. How do you do that each day?

Responding in Prayer Let the awe of knowing this holy God sink in. Pray for a desire to be and do and love the things that characterize this holy God.

---

58 / *Psalm 100*
Seeing Myself as Human

"IT MAKES ME nervous when people say, 'I'm only human,'" said Bob. "I'm afraid that if I give myself excuses like that I will let myself off the hook instead of doing my best. I don't know why, but I need to keep pushing myself beyond my limits or I become terribly anxious."

We may not consciously think that we are superhuman, but we often try to act that way in order to avoid our vulnerability and our neediness. We may not consciously think we are subhuman either, but we may feel that way about ourselves when we cannot escape our finitude and dependency. To be human, for us, is to be a long list of things we would rather avoid. We do not like the vulnerability, the limits, the dependency or the needs. And so, all too often, we defend ourselves against our fears by trying to be God. But, we are not God. The more we are able to embrace this most fundamental of realities—that we are creatures and God is our Creator—the freer our lives can become. The text for this study will help us to see ourselves as belonging to God.

 Warming Up to God God invites you to see yourself as a child of God. What obstacles might keep you from seeing yourself in this way?

 Read Psalm 100.

Psalm 100

A psalm. For giving thanks.

¹Shout for joy to the LORD, all the earth.
² Worship the LORD with gladness;
   come before him with joyful songs.
³Know that the LORD is God.
   It is he who made us, and we are his*q*;
   we are his people, the sheep of his pasture.

⁴Enter his gates with thanksgiving
   and his courts with praise;
   give thanks to him and praise his name.
⁵For the LORD is good and his love endures
      forever;
   his faithfulness continues through all
      generations.

q 3 Or and not we ourselves

 Discovering the Word 1. According to this psalm, who is God and what is he like? 2. This psalm also tells us about ourselves. According to this psalm, who are we? 3. The text instructs us to "know that LORD is God." What does it mean to "know that the LORD is God"? 4. What freedom might knowing this provide? 5. What things are we invited to do in response to God?

Applying the Word   1. In what area of your life do you need to quit trying to be superhuman?   2. How might it help you personally to "know that the LORD is God," that you are a creature, and "the sheep of his pasture"?

 Responding in Prayer   We are invited by this psalm to worship the Lord with gladness. Offer a brief song or poem or prayer of worship or praise to God.

Psalm 101

Psalm 101

Of David. A psalm.

¹I will sing of your love and justice;
   to you, O LORD, I will sing praise.
²I will be careful to lead a blameless life—
   when will you come to me?

I will walk in my house
   with blameless heart.
³I will set before my eyes
   no vile thing.

The deeds of faithless men I hate;
   they will not cling to me.
⁴Men of perverse heart shall be far
      from me;
   I will have nothing to do with evil.

⁵Whoever slanders his neighbor in
      secret,

him will I put to silence;
   whoever has haughty eyes and a proud
      heart,
   him will I not endure.

⁶My eyes will be on the faithful in the
      land,
   that they may dwell with me;
he whose walk is blameless
   will minister to me.

⁷No one who practices deceit
   will dwell in my house;
no one who speaks falsely
   will stand in my presence.

⁸Every morning I will put to silence
   all the wicked in the land;
I will cut off every evildoer
   from the city of the LORD.

59 / *Psalm 102*
A Prayer of Grief

AND GRIEF STILL feels like fear. Perhaps, more strictly, like suspense. Or like waiting; just hanging around waiting for something to happen. It gives life a permanently provisional feeling. . . . The act of living is different all through. Her absence is like the sky, spread over everything. (C. S. Lewis, *A Grief Observed*, [New York: Bantam, 1976], pp. 39, 13)

Grief is an experience of deep sorrow over a significant loss. Whether the loss we have suffered is the loss of a loved one, a job, our health or our home, the physical, emotional and spiritual suffering is intense. This psalm speaks our anguish to God in times of grief.

 Warming Up to God   How would you describe the experience of grief?

 Read Psalm 102.

Psalm 102

A prayer of an afflicted man. When he is faint and pours out his lament before the LORD.

¹Hear my prayer, O LORD;
  let my cry for help come to you.
²Do not hide your face from me
  when I am in distress.
 Turn your ear to me;
  when I call, answer me quickly.

³For my days vanish like smoke;
  my bones burn like glowing embers.
⁴My heart is blighted and withered like grass;
  I forget to eat my food.
⁵Because of my loud groaning
  I am reduced to skin and bones.
⁶I am like a desert owl,
  like an owl among the ruins.
⁷I lie awake; I have become
  like a bird alone on a roof.
⁸All day long my enemies taunt me;
  those who rail against me use my name as
    a curse.
⁹For I eat ashes as my food
  and mingle my drink with tears
¹⁰because of your great wrath,
  for you have taken me up and thrown me
    aside.
¹¹My days are like the evening shadow;
  I wither away like grass.

¹²But you, O LORD, sit enthroned forever;
  your renown endures through all
    generations.
¹³You will arise and have compassion on Zion,
  for it is time to show favor to her;
  the appointed time has come.
¹⁴For her stones are dear to your servants;
  her very dust moves them to pity.
¹⁵The nations will fear the name of the LORD,

all the kings of the earth will revere your
    glory.
¹⁶For the LORD will rebuild Zion
  and appear in his glory.
¹⁷He will respond to the prayer of the
    destitute;
  he will not despise their plea.

¹⁸Let this be written for a future generation,
  that a people not yet created may praise the
    LORD:
¹⁹"The LORD looked down from his sanctuary on
    high,
  from heaven he viewed the earth,
²⁰to hear the groans of the prisoners
  and release those condemned to death."
²¹So the name of the LORD will be declared in
    Zion
  and his praise in Jerusalem
²²when the peoples and the kingdoms
  assemble to worship the LORD.

²³In the course of my life[r] he broke my
    strength;
  he cut short my days.
²⁴So I said:
 "Do not take me away, O my God, in the
    midst of my days;
  your years go on through all generations.
²⁵In the beginning you laid the foundations of
    the earth,
  and the heavens are the work of your
    hands.
²⁶They will perish, but you remain;
  they will all wear out like a garment.
 Like clothing you will change them
  and they will be discarded.
²⁷But you remain the same,
  and your years will never end.
²⁸The children of your servants will live in your
    presence;
  their descendants will be established before
    you."

[r]23 Or By his power

Discovering the Word 1. In verses 1–2 the psalmist pleads for God to hear him. Why is this need so urgent in times of grief and distress? 2. How does the psalmist describe his current physical and emotional state (vv. 2–11)? 3. The psalmist seems to be blaming God and pleading with God (vv. 1–2, 24) at the same time. What does he blame God for (vv. 8, 10, 23)? 4. The writer seems to have mixed feelings about God. What positive perspectives does he express about God (vv. 12–22, 25–28)? 5. Mixed feelings about God are common in times of suffering and grief. What is it about times of grief that might create these mixed feelings?

Applying the Word 1. How do the psalmist's descriptions compare with your experiences of grief? 2. What experience have you had with mixed feelings toward God in times of grief? 3. What grief are you aware of (over a loss you have suffered—recent or long past) that you need to express to God?

Responding in Prayer Express your feelings of grief to God, and pray for others you know who are grieving.

60 / *Psalm 103*
Praying Our Salvation

WHAT GOD HAS done for us far exceeds anything we have done for or against him. The summary word for this excessive, undeserved, unexpected act by God is *salvation*. Prayer explores the country of salvation, tramping the contours, smelling the flowers, touching the outcroppings. There is more to do than recognize the sheer fact of salvation and witness to it; there are unnumbered details of grace, of mercy, of blessing to be appreciated and savored. Prayer is the means by which we do this.

Warming Up to God Reflect on the meaning of your salvation. Allow praise for God to arise from your joy.

Read Psalm 103.

Psalm 103

Of David.

¹Praise the LORD, O my soul;
    all my inmost being, praise his holy
        name.
²Praise the LORD, O my soul,
    and forget not all his benefits—
³who forgives all your sins
    and heals all your diseases,
⁴who redeems your life from the pit
    and crowns you with love and
        compassion,
⁵who satisfies your desires with good things
    so that your youth is renewed like the
        eagle's.

⁶The LORD works righteousness
    and justice for all the oppressed.

⁷He made known his ways to Moses,
    his deeds to the people of Israel:
⁸The LORD is compassionate and gracious,
    slow to anger, abounding in love.
⁹He will not always accuse,
    nor will he harbor his anger forever;
¹⁰he does not treat us as our sins deserve

or repay us according to our iniquities.
¹¹For as high as the heavens are above the
        earth,
    so great is his love for those who fear him;
¹²as far as the east is from the west,
    so far has he removed our transgressions
        from us.
¹³As a father has compassion on his children,
    so the LORD has compassion on those who
        fear him;
¹⁴for he knows how we are formed,
    he remembers that we are dust.
¹⁵As for man, his days are like grass,
    he flourishes like a flower of the field;
¹⁶the wind blows over it and it is gone,
    and its place remembers it no more.
¹⁷But from everlasting to everlasting
    the LORD's love is with those who fear
        him,
    and his righteousness with their children's
        children—
¹⁸with those who keep his covenant
    and remember to obey his precepts.

¹⁹The LORD has established his throne in
        heaven,
    and his kingdom rules over all.

²⁰Praise the LORD, you his angels,
  you mighty ones who do his bidding,
  who obey his word.
²¹Praise the LORD, all his heavenly hosts,
  you his servants who do his will.

²²Praise the LORD, all his works
  everywhere in his dominion.

  Praise the LORD, O my soul.

 Discovering the Word 1. Note the first and last sentences. How does this bracketing affect your understanding of the psalm's contents? 2. Salvation is more richly complex than we sometimes think. What five actions of God add up to salvation (vv. 3–5)? 3. How did God make his ways known to Moses and Israel (v. 7)? 4. What astounding statements about God does the psalmist make in verses 8–14? 5. Carefully observe the contrast between us (vv. 15–16) and God (vv. 17–19). Does this make you feel better or worse about yourself? Explain.

 Applying the Word 1. How have you benefited from your salvation? 2. How do verses 8–14 show you ways in which you would like to expand your thinking about God?

Responding in Prayer Add your personal praise to the praise in this psalm.

---

61 / *Psalm 104*
Protecting God's Creation

ONE NIGHT LAST summer, I stretched flat on my back in the grass of Trail Ridge Camp Sherith in central Wisconsin. "The stars are great at camp," my kids had all said. I was there to find out.

They emerged slowly at first, a few in the central heavens, but none near the still-lighted horizon. Could I count them? Almost. Then more and more came out. The first ones glared trumpetlike against the inky black, while others danced a gentle harmony. Even the horizon forgot the glow of sun and took on hundreds of thousands of lesser lights. Constellations, those artificial lines connecting stars like so many games of dot-to-dot, followed the patterns of my schoolgirl memory. A shooting star streaked across the sky, as if to connect the dots for me in some new constellation. Should I wish upon it?

I prayed instead. But what could I say to a God who had made all this and had somehow created in me the ability to enjoy it? For a long time I lay silent. Perhaps silence was the most sensible part of my prayer.

 Warming Up to God When have you felt that God's creation helped you to know him?

 Read Psalm 104.

Psalm 104

¹Praise the LORD, O my soul.

O LORD my God, you are very great;
  you are clothed with splendor and majesty.
²He wraps himself in light as with a garment;
  he stretches out the heavens like a tent
³ and lays the beams of his upper chambers
    on their waters.
He makes the clouds his chariot
  and rides on the wings of the wind.
⁴He makes winds his messengers,ˢ

flames of fire his servants.

⁵He set the earth on its foundations;
  it can never be moved.
⁶You covered it with the deep as with a
    garment;
  the waters stood above the mountains.
⁷But at your rebuke the waters fled,
  at the sound of your thunder they took to
    flight;

ˢ4 Or *angels*

8they flowed over the mountains,
  they went down into the valleys,
  to the place you assigned for them.
9You set a boundary they cannot cross;
  never again will they cover the earth.

10He makes springs pour water into the ravines;
  it flows between the mountains.
11They give water to all the beasts of the field;
  the wild donkeys quench their thirst.
12The birds of the air nest by the waters;
  they sing among the branches.
13He waters the mountains from his upper
    chambers;
  the earth is satisfied by the fruit of his
    work.
14He makes grass grow for the cattle,
  and plants for man to cultivate—
  bringing forth food from the earth:
15wine that gladdens the heart of man,
  oil to make his face shine,
  and bread that sustains his heart.
16The trees of the LORD are well watered,
  the cedars of Lebanon that he planted.
17There the birds make their nests;
  the stork has its home in the pine trees.
18The high mountains belong to the wild goats;
  the crags are a refuge for the coneys.ᵗ

19The moon marks off the seasons,
  and the sun knows when to go down.
20You bring darkness, it becomes night,
  and all the beasts of the forest prowl.
21The lions roar for their prey
  and seek their food from God.
22The sun rises, and they steal away;
  they return and lie down in their dens.
23Then man goes out to his work,
  to his labor until evening.

24How many are your works, O LORD!
  In wisdom you made them all;

the earth is full of your creatures.
25There is the sea, vast and spacious,
  teeming with creatures beyond number—
  living things both large and small.
26There the ships go to and fro,
  and the leviathan, which you formed to
    frolic there.

27These all look to you
  to give them their food at the proper time.
28When you give it to them,
  they gather it up;
  when you open your hand,
  they are satisfied with good things.
29When you hide your face,
  they are terrified;
  when you take away their breath,
  they die and return to the dust.
30When you send your Spirit,
  they are created,
  and you renew the face of the earth.

31May the glory of the LORD endure forever;
  may the LORD rejoice in his works—
32he who looks at the earth, and it trembles,
  who touches the mountains, and they
    smoke.

33I will sing to the LORD all my life;
  I will sing praise to my God as long as I
    live.
34May my meditation be pleasing to him,
  as I rejoice in the LORD.
35But may sinners vanish from the earth
  and the wicked be no more.

  Praise the LORD, O my soul.

  Praise the LORD.ᵘ

ᵗ18 That is, the hyrax or rock badger ᵘ35 Hebrew *Hallelu Yah*; in
the Septuagint this line stands at the beginning of Psalm 105.

 Discovering the Word 1. Study verses 1–4. How does the sky serve God? 2. Study verses 5–9. What
elements of earth's creation show God at work? 3. Study verses 10–18. What relationships does this
description of God's creation reveal? 4. Study verses 19–26. How do these verses express an orderliness to what
God has made? 5. Study verses 27–30. How do these verses show that God not only created but also personally
takes care of what he has made? 6. Study verses 31–35. What responses to God are triggered by the psalmist's
meditation on creation?

 Applying the Word 1. When have you enjoyed some aspect of the natural rhythms described here?
2. As you meditate on what God has made, how would you like to respond to God?

Responding in Prayer Praise God for the glory of his creation.

Psalms 105—106

Psalm 105

¹Give thanks to the LORD, call on his name;
  make known among the nations what he
    has done.
²Sing to him, sing praise to him;
  tell of all his wonderful acts.
³Glory in his holy name;
  let the hearts of those who seek the LORD
    rejoice.
⁴Look to the LORD and his strength;
  seek his face always.

⁵Remember the wonders he has done,
  his miracles, and the judgments he
    pronounced,
⁶O descendants of Abraham his servant,
  O sons of Jacob, his chosen ones.
⁷He is the LORD our God;
  his judgments are in all the earth.

⁸He remembers his covenant forever,
  the word he commanded, for a thousand
    generations,
⁹the covenant he made with Abraham,
  the oath he swore to Isaac.
¹⁰He confirmed it to Jacob as a decree,
  to Israel as an everlasting covenant:
¹¹"To you I will give the land of Canaan
  as the portion you will inherit."

¹²When they were but few in number,
  few indeed, and strangers in it,
¹³they wandered from nation to nation,
  from one kingdom to another.
¹⁴He allowed no one to oppress them;
  for their sake he rebuked kings:
¹⁵"Do not touch my anointed ones;
  do my prophets no harm."

¹⁶He called down famine on the land
  and destroyed all their supplies of food;
¹⁷and he sent a man before them—
  Joseph, sold as a slave.
¹⁸They bruised his feet with shackles,
  his neck was put in irons,
¹⁹till what he foretold came to pass,
  till the word of the LORD proved him true.
²⁰The king sent and released him,
  the ruler of peoples set him free.
²¹He made him master of his household,

ruler over all he possessed,
²²to instruct his princes as he pleased
  and teach his elders wisdom.

²³Then Israel entered Egypt;
  Jacob lived as an alien in the land of Ham.
²⁴The LORD made his people very fruitful;
  he made them too numerous for their foes,
²⁵whose hearts he turned to hate his people,
  to conspire against his servants.
²⁶He sent Moses his servant,
  and Aaron, whom he had chosen.
²⁷They performed his miraculous signs among
    them,
  his wonders in the land of Ham.
²⁸He sent darkness and made the land dark—
  for had they not rebelled against his words?
²⁹He turned their waters into blood,
  causing their fish to die.
³⁰Their land teemed with frogs,
  which went up into the bedrooms of their
    rulers.
³¹He spoke, and there came swarms of flies,
  and gnats throughout their country.
³²He turned their rain into hail,
  with lightning throughout their land;
³³he struck down their vines and fig trees
  and shattered the trees of their country.
³⁴He spoke, and the locusts came,
  grasshoppers without number;
³⁵they ate up every green thing in their land,
  ate up the produce of their soil.
³⁶Then he struck down all the firstborn in their
    land,
  the firstfruits of all their manhood.

³⁷He brought out Israel, laden with silver and
    gold,
  and from among their tribes no one
    faltered.
³⁸Egypt was glad when they left,
  because dread of Israel had fallen on them.
³⁹He spread out a cloud as a covering,
  and a fire to give light at night.
⁴⁰They asked, and he brought them quail
  and satisfied them with the bread of
    heaven.
⁴¹He opened the rock, and water gushed out;
  like a river it flowed in the desert.

⁴²For he remembered his holy promise
   given to his servant Abraham.
⁴³He brought out his people with rejoicing,
   his chosen ones with shouts of joy;
⁴⁴he gave them the lands of the nations,
   and they fell heir to what others had toiled
      for—
⁴⁵that they might keep his precepts
   and observe his laws.

Praise the Lord.ᵛ

Psalm 106

¹Praise the Lord.ʷ

Give thanks to the Lord, for he is good;
   his love endures forever.
²Who can proclaim the mighty acts of the Lord
   or fully declare his praise?
³Blessed are they who maintain justice,
   who constantly do what is right.
⁴Remember me, O Lord, when you show favor
      to your people,
   come to my aid when you save them,
⁵that I may enjoy the prosperity of your
      chosen ones,
   that I may share in the joy of your nation
   and join your inheritance in giving praise.

⁶We have sinned, even as our fathers did;
   we have done wrong and acted wickedly.
⁷When our fathers were in Egypt,
   they gave no thought to your miracles;
   they did not remember your many kindnesses,
   and they rebelled by the sea, the Red Sea.ˣ
⁸Yet he saved them for his name's sake,
   to make his mighty power known.
⁹He rebuked the Red Sea, and it dried up;
   he led them through the depths as through
      a desert.
¹⁰He saved them from the hand of the foe;
   from the hand of the enemy he redeemed
      them.
¹¹The waters covered their adversaries;
   not one of them survived.
¹²Then they believed his promises
   and sang his praise.

¹³But they soon forgot what he had done
   and did not wait for his counsel.
¹⁴In the desert they gave in to their craving;
   in the wasteland they put God to the test.
¹⁵So he gave them what they asked for,

but sent a wasting disease upon them.
¹⁶In the camp they grew envious of Moses
   and of Aaron, who was consecrated to the
      Lord.
¹⁷The earth opened up and swallowed Dathan;
   it buried the company of Abiram.
¹⁸Fire blazed among their followers;
   a flame consumed the wicked.
¹⁹At Horeb they made a calf
   and worshiped an idol cast from metal.
²⁰They exchanged their Glory
   for an image of a bull, which eats grass.
²¹They forgot the God who saved them,
   who had done great things in Egypt,
²²miracles in the land of Ham
   and awesome deeds by the Red Sea.
²³So he said he would destroy them—
   had not Moses, his chosen one,
   stood in the breach before him
   to keep his wrath from destroying them.

²⁴Then they despised the pleasant land;
   they did not believe his promise.
²⁵They grumbled in their tents
   and did not obey the Lord.
²⁶So he swore to them with uplifted hand
   that he would make them fall in the desert,
²⁷make their descendants fall among the nations
   and scatter them throughout the lands.

²⁸They yoked themselves to the Baal of Peor
   and ate sacrifices offered to lifeless gods;
²⁹they provoked the Lord to anger by their
      wicked deeds,
   and a plague broke out among them.
³⁰But Phinehas stood up and intervened,
   and the plague was checked.
³¹This was credited to him as righteousness
   for endless generations to come.

³²By the waters of Meribah they angered the
      Lord,
   and trouble came to Moses because of
      them;
³³for they rebelled against the Spirit of God,
   and rash words came from Moses' lips.ʸ

³⁴They did not destroy the peoples
   as the Lord had commanded them,
³⁵but they mingled with the nations

ᵛ45 Hebrew *Hallelu Yah*   ʷ1 Hebrew *Hallelu Yah*; also in verse 48
ˣ7 Hebrew *Yam Suph*; that is, Sea of Reeds; also in verses 9 and 22
ʸ33 Or *against his spirit, / and rash words came from his lips*

and adopted their customs.
³⁶They worshiped their idols,
    which became a snare to them.
³⁷They sacrificed their sons
    and their daughters to demons.
³⁸They shed innocent blood,
    the blood of their sons and daughters,
  whom they sacrificed to the idols of Canaan,
    and the land was desecrated by their blood.
³⁹They defiled themselves by what they did;
    by their deeds they prostituted themselves.

⁴⁰Therefore the LORD was angry with his people
    and abhorred his inheritance.
⁴¹He handed them over to the nations,
    and their foes ruled over them.
⁴²Their enemies oppressed them
    and subjected them to their power.
⁴³Many times he delivered them,

but they were bent on rebellion
    and they wasted away in their sin.

⁴⁴But he took note of their distress
    when he heard their cry;
⁴⁵for their sake he remembered his covenant
    and out of his great love he relented.
⁴⁶He caused them to be pitied
    by all who held them captive.

⁴⁷Save us, O LORD our God,
    and gather us from the nations,
  that we may give thanks to your holy name
    and glory in your praise.

⁴⁸Praise be to the LORD, the God of Israel,
    from everlasting to everlasting.
  Let all the people say, "Amen!"

  Praise the LORD.

62 / *Psalm 107*
The Goodness of God

PSALM 107 IS the classic exposition of God's goodness. J. I. Packer writes: "The whole psalm is a majestic panorama of the operations of divine goodness, transforming human lives" (*Knowing God* [Downers Grove, Ill.: InterVarsity Press, 1973], p. 148). God's actions reveal goodness in its highest and purest form. His goodness provides the standard for developing this fruit in our own lives.

 Warming Up to God   Try to imagine what it would be like if God were to withdraw all his goodness from you. How would your life be changed? Respond to God with praise for his presence with you.

 Read Psalm 107.

BOOK V
Psalms 107–150

Psalm 107

¹Give thanks to the LORD, for he is good;
    his love endures forever.
²Let the redeemed of the LORD say this—
    those he redeemed from the hand of the
      foe,
³those he gathered from the lands,
    from east and west, from north and
      south.ᶻ

⁴Some wandered in desert wastelands,
    finding no way to a city where they could
      settle.

⁵They were hungry and thirsty,
    and their lives ebbed away.
⁶Then they cried out to the LORD in their
      trouble,
    and he delivered them from their distress.
⁷He led them by a straight way
    to a city where they could settle.
⁸Let them give thanks to the LORD for his
      unfailing love
    and his wonderful deeds for men,
⁹for he satisfies the thirsty
    and fills the hungry with good things.

¹⁰Some sat in darkness and the deepest gloom,
    prisoners suffering in iron chains,

ᶻ3 Hebrew *north and the sea*

11for they had rebelled against the words of
God
and despised the counsel of the Most High.
12So he subjected them to bitter labor;
they stumbled, and there was no one to
help.
13Then they cried to the LORD in their trouble,
and he saved them from their distress.
14He brought them out of darkness and the
deepest gloom
and broke away their chains.
15Let them give thanks to the LORD for his
unfailing love
and his wonderful deeds for men,
16for he breaks down gates of bronze
and cuts through bars of iron.

17Some became fools through their rebellious
ways
and suffered affliction because of their
iniquities.
18They loathed all food
and drew near the gates of death.
19Then they cried to the LORD in their trouble,
and he saved them from their distress.
20He sent forth his word and healed them;
he rescued them from the grave.
21Let them give thanks to the LORD for his
unfailing love
and his wonderful deeds for men.
22Let them sacrifice thank offerings
and tell of his works with songs of joy.

23Others went out on the sea in ships;
they were merchants on the mighty
waters.
24They saw the works of the LORD,
his wonderful deeds in the deep.
25For he spoke and stirred up a tempest
that lifted high the waves.
26They mounted up to the heavens and went
down to the depths;
in their peril their courage melted away.
27They reeled and staggered like drunken men;
they were at their wits' end.

28Then they cried out to the LORD in their
trouble,
and he brought them out of their distress.
29He stilled the storm to a whisper;
the waves of the sea were hushed.
30They were glad when it grew calm,
and he guided them to their desired haven.
31Let them give thanks to the LORD for his
unfailing love
and his wonderful deeds for men.
32Let them exalt him in the assembly of the
people
and praise him in the council of the elders.

33He turned rivers into a desert,
flowing springs into thirsty ground,
34and fruitful land into a salt waste,
because of the wickedness of those who
lived there.
35He turned the desert into pools of water
and the parched ground into flowing
springs;
36there he brought the hungry to live,
and they founded a city where they could
settle.
37They sowed fields and planted vineyards
that yielded a fruitful harvest;
38he blessed them, and their numbers greatly
increased,
and he did not let their herds diminish.

39Then their numbers decreased, and they were
humbled
by oppression, calamity and sorrow;
40he who pours contempt on nobles
made them wander in a trackless waste.
41But he lifted the needy out of their affliction
and increased their families like flocks.
42The upright see and rejoice,
but all the wicked shut their mouths.

43Whoever is wise, let him heed these
things
and consider the great love of the LORD.

Discovering the Word 1. How do verses 1–3 introduce the major themes of the psalm? 2. The psalmist
gives four illustrations of God's goodness in verses 4–9, 10–16, 17–22 and 23–32. What do each of these
illustrations have in common? 3. What needs do the people have in each of these sections? 4. According to the
psalmist, what are some ways we should give thanks to God for his goodness and love (vv. 22, 32)? 5. What do
verses 33–42 reveal about the ups and downs of life?

Applying the Word 1. Are you likely to call out to God in the midst of your trouble as those in this passage did? Why or why not? 2. In what ways can we imitate the goodness of God displayed in this psalm?

Responding in Prayer Thank God for his goodness and unfailing love. Ask him to help you develop the fruit of goodness in your life.

Psalm 108

Psalm 108

A song. A psalm of David.

¹My heart is steadfast, O God;
　I will sing and make music with all my
　　soul.
²Awake, harp and lyre!
　I will awaken the dawn.
³I will praise you, O LORD, among the nations;
　I will sing of you among the peoples.
⁴For great is your love, higher than the
　　heavens;
　your faithfulness reaches to the skies.
⁵Be exalted, O God, above the heavens,
　and let your glory be over all the earth.

⁶Save us and help us with your right hand,
　that those you love may be delivered.
⁷God has spoken from his sanctuary:

"In triumph I will parcel out Shechem
　and measure off the Valley of Succoth.
⁸Gilead is mine, Manasseh is mine;
　Ephraim is my helmet,
　Judah my scepter.
⁹Moab is my washbasin,
　upon Edom I toss my sandal;
　over Philistia I shout in triumph."

¹⁰Who will bring me to the fortified city?
　Who will lead me to Edom?
¹¹Is it not you, O God, you who have rejected
　　us
　and no longer go out with our armies?
¹²Give us aid against the enemy,
　for the help of man is worthless.
¹³With God we will gain the victory,
　and he will trample down our enemies.

63 / *Psalm 109*
Feeling Anger

FOR MOST OF us, anger is not a comfortable emotion. For some of us, it is a terrifying emotion. We know the damage that anger can do. We know the pain it can cause. We fear our own capacity for evil when we are angry. We recognize our desire for revenge. We know that we have been hurt, and we know that anger feeds our longing to hurt back. However, avoiding anger will not make it go away, but can instead allow it to grow into bitterness. Feeling anger and expressing it honestly to God and to others makes it possible for us to continue growing toward forgiveness. There are, of course, both helpful and unhelpful things we can do with our anger. Denying, avoiding, minimizing and blaming others for it are just a few of the many unhelpful ways of responding to anger.

Warming Up to God What do you usually do when you are angry with someone who is important to you?

Read Psalm 109.

Psalm 109

For the director of music. Of David.
A psalm.

¹O God, whom I praise,
do not remain silent,
²for wicked and deceitful men
have opened their mouths against me;
they have spoken against me with lying
tongues.
³With words of hatred they surround me;
they attack me without cause.
⁴In return for my friendship they accuse me,
but I am a man of prayer.
⁵They repay me evil for good,
and hatred for my friendship.

⁶Appoint*ᵃ* an evil man*ᵇ* to oppose him;
let an accuser*ᶜ* stand at his right hand.
⁷When he is tried, let him be found guilty,
and may his prayers condemn him.
⁸May his days be few;
may another take his place of leadership.
⁹May his children be fatherless
and his wife a widow.
¹⁰May his children be wandering beggars;
may they be driven*ᵈ* from their ruined
homes.
¹¹May a creditor seize all he has;
may strangers plunder the fruits of his
labor.
¹²May no one extend kindness to him
or take pity on his fatherless children.
¹³May his descendants be cut off,
their names blotted out from the next
generation.
¹⁴May the iniquity of his fathers be remembered
before the LORD;
may the sin of his mother never be blotted
out.
¹⁵May their sins always remain before the LORD,
that he may cut off the memory of them
from the earth.

¹⁶For he never thought of doing a kindness,
but hounded to death the poor

and the needy and the brokenhearted.
¹⁷He loved to pronounce a curse—
may it*ᵉ* come on him;
he found no pleasure in blessing—
may it be*ᶠ* far from him.
¹⁸He wore cursing as his garment;
it entered into his body like water,
into his bones like oil.
¹⁹May it be like a cloak wrapped about him,
like a belt tied forever around him.
²⁰May this be the LORD's payment to my
accusers,
to those who speak evil of me.

²¹But you, O Sovereign LORD,
deal well with me for your name's sake;
out of the goodness of your love, deliver
me.
²²For I am poor and needy,
and my heart is wounded within me.
²³I fade away like an evening shadow;
I am shaken off like a locust.
²⁴My knees give way from fasting;
my body is thin and gaunt.
²⁵I am an object of scorn to my accusers;
when they see me, they shake their heads.

²⁶Help me, O LORD my God;
save me in accordance with your love.
²⁷Let them know that it is your hand,
that you, O LORD, have done it.
²⁸They may curse, but you will bless;
when they attack they will be put to shame,
but your servant will rejoice.
²⁹My accusers will be clothed with disgrace
and wrapped in shame as in a cloak.

³⁰With my mouth I will greatly extol the LORD;
in the great throng I will praise him.
³¹For he stands at the right hand of the needy
one,
to save his life from those who condemn
him.

ᵃ6 Or ⌊They say:⌋ "Appoint (with quotation marks at the end of verse
19)   ᵇ6 Or the Evil One   ᶜ6 Or let Satan   ᵈ10 Septuagint;
Hebrew sought   ᵉ17 Or curse, / and it has   ᶠ17 Or blessing, / and
it is

Discovering the Word 1. To what painful experiences is the author reacting (vv. 2–5)? 2. The speaker
is particularly outraged at the injustice of his accusers. "They repay me evil for good, and hatred for my
friendship" (v. 5). How does this add to his sense of rage? 3. What does the author ask God to do to his enemies
(vv. 6–20, 28–29)? 4. What does the author want God to do for him (vv. 20–26)?

Applying the Word 1. God is described in verse 31 as being on the side of the "needy" and "condemned." How could seeing God in this way be a practical help to you when you are angry? 2. How would expressing your anger to God be helpful to you? 3. How can other people be helpful to you in your struggle with anger?

Responding in Prayer What anger do you want to express to God today?

---

64 / *Psalm 110*
A Psalm of Submission

THINK ABOUT THE enemies you have. Bring to mind people you know who are opposed to Christianity. Picture them (and yourself) one day coming to Christ who will settle all disputes and rule with an iron hand. Psalm 110 acknowledges God as the eternal King-Priest who will, in fact, settle all disputes and judge all nations. This coronation hymn, although used for other kings of Israel, was viewed by Jews and Christians alike as clearly Messianic and forward-looking. Writers of the New Testament quote verses 1 and 4 on numerous occasions, making this psalm one of the most prophetic.

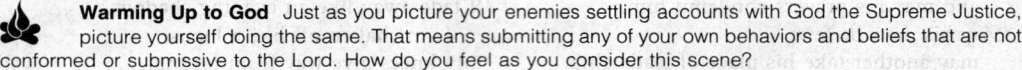 **Warming Up to God** Just as you picture your enemies settling accounts with God the Supreme Justice, picture yourself doing the same. That means submitting any of your own behaviors and beliefs that are not conformed or submissive to the Lord. How do you feel as you consider this scene?

 Read Psalm 110.

Psalm 110

Of David. A psalm.

¹The LORD says to my Lord:
 "Sit at my right hand
until I make your enemies
 a footstool for your feet."

²The LORD will extend your mighty scepter
 from Zion;
 you will rule in the midst of your enemies.
³Your troops will be willing
 on your day of battle.
Arrayed in holy majesty,
 from the womb of the dawn

you will receive the dew of your youth.ᵍ

⁴The LORD has sworn
 and will not change his mind:
 "You are a priest forever,
 in the order of Melchizedek."

⁵The Lord is at your right hand;
 he will crush kings on the day of his wrath.
⁶He will judge the nations, heaping up the
 dead
 and crushing the rulers of the whole earth.
⁷He will drink from a brook beside the wayʰ;
 therefore he will lift up his head.

g3 Or / your young men will come to you like the dew   h7 Or / The One who grants succession will set him in authority

---

Discovering the Word 1. Who is the psalmist referring to as "my Lord" (v. 1; see Mt 22:41–45)? 2. How will that Lord rule, and over whom (vv. 1–3, 5, 6)? 3. What is significant about the Lord swearing with a covenant oath (v. 4; Heb 6:16–18; 7:20–22)? 4. Melchizedek was the original king-priest of the God Most High in Jerusalem, who received a tithe from Abraham. His priesthood was a prototype of Christ's eternal priesthood (v. 4). What is significant about a priesthood for God's people that is permanent and irrevocable? 5. What is significant about this Lord sitting at the right hand of God (vv. 1, 5)?

Applying the Word 1. The troops are freewill offerings (v. 3) in the service of their Lord. What is your sacrificial offering to the Lord? 2. The Lord rules over all the powers that be, even enemies of his kingdom, with an iron hand and the undiminished vigor of youth (vv. 2–3). How is that good news to you and the battles you face?

Responding in Prayer Whatever battles you are engaged in right now, rest assured that the Lord will ultimately triumph and that the Lord's army will attack those problems with you. What battles or problem areas can you turn over to him now for his intercession and judgment?

Psalms 111—114

Psalm 111[i]

[1]Praise the LORD.[j]

I will extol the LORD with all my heart
  in the council of the upright and in the
    assembly.

[2]Great are the works of the LORD;
  they are pondered by all who delight in
    them.
[3]Glorious and majestic are his deeds,
  and his righteousness endures forever.
[4]He has caused his wonders to be remembered;
  the LORD is gracious and compassionate.
[5]He provides food for those who fear him;
  he remembers his covenant forever.
[6]He has shown his people the power of his
    works,
  giving them the lands of other nations.
[7]The works of his hands are faithful and just;
  all his precepts are trustworthy.
[8]They are steadfast for ever and ever,
  done in faithfulness and uprightness.
[9]He provided redemption for his people;
  he ordained his covenant forever—
  holy and awesome is his name.

[10]The fear of the LORD is the beginning of
    wisdom;
  all who follow his precepts have good
    understanding.
  To him belongs eternal praise.

Psalm 112[i]

[1]Praise the LORD.[j]

Blessed is the man who fears the LORD,
  who finds great delight in his commands.

[2]His children will be mighty in the land;
  the generation of the upright will be
    blessed.
[3]Wealth and riches are in his house,
  and his righteousness endures forever.
[4]Even in darkness light dawns for the upright,

for the gracious and compassionate and
  righteous man.[k]
[5]Good will come to him who is generous and
    lends freely,
  who conducts his affairs with justice.
[6]Surely he will never be shaken;
  a righteous man will be remembered
    forever.
[7]He will have no fear of bad news;
  his heart is steadfast, trusting in the LORD.
[8]His heart is secure, he will have no fear;
  in the end he will look in triumph on his
    foes.
[9]He has scattered abroad his gifts to the poor,
  his righteousness endures forever;
  his horn[l] will be lifted high in honor.

[10]The wicked man will see and be vexed,
  he will gnash his teeth and waste away;
  the longings of the wicked will come to
    nothing.

Psalm 113

[1]Praise the LORD.[m]

Praise, O servants of the LORD,
  praise the name of the LORD.
[2]Let the name of the LORD be praised,
  both now and forevermore.
[3]From the rising of the sun to the place where
    it sets,
  the name of the LORD is to be praised.

[4]The LORD is exalted over all the nations,
  his glory above the heavens.
[5]Who is like the LORD our God,
  the One who sits enthroned on high,
[6]who stoops down to look
  on the heavens and the earth?

[7]He raises the poor from the dust
  and lifts the needy from the ash heap;

[i]This psalm is an acrostic poem, the lines of which begin with the successive letters of the Hebrew alphabet.   [j]1 Hebrew *Hallelu Yah*
[k]4 Or *for* the LORD *is gracious and compassionate and righteous*
[l]9 *Horn* here symbolizes dignity.   [m]1 Hebrew *Hallelu Yah*; also in verse 9

[8]he seats them with princes,
with the princes of their people.
[9]He settles the barren woman in her home
as a happy mother of children.

Praise the LORD.

Psalm 114

[1]When Israel came out of Egypt,
the house of Jacob from a people of foreign
tongue,
[2]Judah became God's sanctuary,
Israel his dominion.

[3]The sea looked and fled,
the Jordan turned back;
[4]the mountains skipped like rams,
the hills like lambs.

[5]Why was it, O sea, that you fled,
O Jordan, that you turned back,
[6]you mountains, that you skipped like rams,
you hills, like lambs?

[7]Tremble, O earth, at the presence of the Lord,
at the presence of the God of Jacob,
[8]who turned the rock into a pool,
the hard rock into springs of water.

65 / *Psalm 115*
A Psalm of Praise

THIS PSALM PRAISES God as the one true Lord and ridicules the many cheap imitations and pretenders to the throne that prevail in the surrounding culture. The liturgical exchange between people and priests in this psalm makes it a very appropriate lead-in for public worship. In this liturgy, the cares and snares of the world are left behind and the people are called to trust God, who will abundantly bless them and receive the praise of his people.

 Warming Up to God When has God seemed distant or unresponsive to you (in the past or present)? Open yourself up to the possibilities of God blessing you and your family afresh.

 Read Psalm 115.

Psalm 115

[1]Not to us, O LORD, not to us
but to your name be the glory,
because of your love and faithfulness.

[2]Why do the nations say,
"Where is their God?"
[3]Our God is in heaven;
he does whatever pleases him.
[4]But their idols are silver and gold,
made by the hands of men.
[5]They have mouths, but cannot speak,
eyes, but they cannot see;
[6]they have ears, but cannot hear,
noses, but they cannot smell;
[7]they have hands, but cannot feel,
feet, but they cannot walk;
nor can they utter a sound with their
throats.
[8]Those who make them will be like them,

and so will all who trust in them.
[9]O house of Israel, trust in the LORD—
he is their help and shield.
[10]O house of Aaron, trust in the LORD—
he is their help and shield.
[11]You who fear him, trust in the LORD—
he is their help and shield.

[12]The LORD remembers us and will bless us:
He will bless the house of Israel,
he will bless the house of Aaron,
[13]he will bless those who fear the LORD—
small and great alike.

[14]May the LORD make you increase,
both you and your children.
[15]May you be blessed by the LORD,
the Maker of heaven and earth.
[16]The highest heavens belong to the LORD,
but the earth he has given to man.
[17]It is not the dead who praise the LORD,

those who go down to silence;   Praise the Lord.ⁿ
¹⁸it is we who extol the Lord,
    both now and forevermore.   ⁿ18 Hebrew *Hallelu Yah*

 Discovering the Word 1. Note that this psalm divides into five parts: three stanzas spoken by the respondents—a taunt song (vv. 1–8), confession of trust (vv. 12–13) and the closing doxology (vv. 16–18)—interspersed with an invocation (vv. 9–11) and benediction (vv. 14–15) spoken by the priests. What does this response-and-revelation rhythm call forth from the worship participants and leaders? 2. How do the idols that others worship compare to the God that Israel worships (vv. 1–8)? 3. Why should anyone, but especially Israel, trust in the Lord (vv. 9–11)? 4. Who will the Lord bless, why and how (vv. 12–15)? 5. What is the reason for living granted to those who have survived the exile and a whole lot more (vv. 16–18)?

Applying the Word 1. The Lord is not the only person or object that people trust to get them through the day. What else do people trust in these days for their salvation or their guidance? 2. For what have you recently trusted God alone to provide? 3. How did God prove to be your help and shield?

Responding in Prayer Consider how vastly superior God is to all idols. Ask God to help you forsake the idols of your culture.

---

66 / *Psalm 116*
Talking to God

HONESTY IS A NECESSARY ingredient to all intimate relationships. If we are to grow in our intimacy with God, we will need to learn to be honest with him. This will require us to challenge our distorted images of God and to grow in our understanding of him. God invites us to talk to him. He has promised to pay attention. He does not require us to do any physical, mental or spiritual gymnastics to get his attention. He does not insist that we have our lives "together" before we can talk to him. We can talk to him even when we are in trouble. We will always find him interested and compassionate.

 Warming Up to God Imagine yourself as one of the little children whom Jesus invited to come to him. Imagine yourself standing next to Jesus. Take a few minutes to close your eyes and experience his arm around your shoulder as you stand next to him. Tell him what you are thinking and feeling. What thoughts and feelings did you have during this meditation?

Read Psalm 116.

Psalm 116

¹I love the Lord, for he heard my voice;
    he heard my cry for mercy.
²Because he turned his ear to me,
    I will call on him as long as I live.

³The cords of death entangled me,
    the anguish of the graveᵒ came upon me;
    I was overcome by trouble and sorrow.
⁴Then I called on the name of the Lord:
    "O Lord, save me!"

⁵The Lord is gracious and righteous;
    our God is full of compassion.
⁶The Lord protects the simplehearted;
    when I was in great need, he saved me.

⁷Be at rest once more, O my soul,
    for the Lord has been good to you.

⁸For you, O Lord, have delivered my soul from death,

ᵒ3 Hebrew *Sheol*

my eyes from tears,
my feet from stumbling,
⁹that I may walk before the LORD
in the land of the living.
¹⁰I believed; therefore^p I said,
"I am greatly afflicted."
¹¹And in my dismay I said,
"All men are liars."

¹²How can I repay the LORD
for all his goodness to me?
¹³I will lift up the cup of salvation
and call on the name of the LORD.
¹⁴I will fulfill my vows to the LORD
in the presence of all his people.

¹⁵Precious in the sight of the LORD
is the death of his saints.

¹⁶O LORD, truly I am your servant;
I am your servant, the son of your
maidservant^q;
you have freed me from my chains.

¹⁷I will sacrifice a thank offering to you
and call on the name of the LORD.
¹⁸I will fulfill my vows to the LORD
in the presence of all his people,
¹⁹in the courts of the house of the LORD—
in your midst, O Jerusalem.

Praise the LORD.^r

p10 Or *believed even when*   q16 Or *servant, your faithful
son*   r19 Hebrew *Hallelu Yah*

 Discovering the Word 1. What images of God are presented here? 2. What did the author of the psalm experience when he called on God? 3. How does the psalmist respond to God (vv. 12–19)? 4. God invites us to talk to him about our troubles. He does not ask us to ignore them or minimize them or take care of them ourselves. How does this compare or contrast with your expectations of God?

Applying the Word 1. Think of a time when you had difficulty calling on God. What made it difficult for you? 2. Recall a time when you did call on God and he "answered you and showed you great and mighty things." What was this experience like for you?

Responding in Prayer What do you need to talk with God about today?

Psalm 117

Psalm 117

¹Praise the LORD, all you nations;
extol him, all you peoples.
²For great is his love toward us,

and the faithfulness of the LORD endures
forever.

Praise the LORD.^s

s2 Hebrew *Hallelu Yah*

67 / *Psalm 118*
Enduring Love

REMEMBER WHEN YOUR parents used to force you to write thank-you notes for the Christmas and birthday gifts you received from your out-of-town relatives? Although it may have been painful at the time, this discipline of thanksgiving helped you develop a grateful heart.

In like manner, the psalmist expresses thanks to God for delivering Israel from her many enemies. The historic occasion for Psalm 118 may have been Israel's defeat of a confederacy of nations or her deliverance from the Babylonian exile. In either event, the Israelites had much to thank God for, especially his love which endures forever. We who know the love of God in Christ have even more reason to give thanks through this psalm.

 Warming Up to God Think of all the things and relationships in your life that have passed on or proven temporary. Contrast that with the most enduring love relationship you know, or with the times that come to mind when you hum that ditty "Happy Days Are Here Again." How does that relationship or those days compare with the enduring love of God?

Read Psalm 118.

Psalm 118

¹Give thanks to the Lord, for he is good;
　his love endures forever.

²Let Israel say:
　"His love endures forever."
³Let the house of Aaron say:
　"His love endures forever."
⁴Let those who fear the Lord say:
　"His love endures forever."

⁵In my anguish I cried to the Lord,
　and he answered by setting me free.
⁶The Lord is with me; I will not be afraid.
　What can man do to me?
⁷The Lord is with me; he is my helper.
　I will look in triumph on my enemies.

⁸It is better to take refuge in the Lord
　than to trust in man.
⁹It is better to take refuge in the Lord
　than to trust in princes.

¹⁰All the nations surrounded me,
　but in the name of the Lord I cut them off.
¹¹They surrounded me on every side,
　but in the name of the Lord I cut them off.
¹²They swarmed around me like bees,
　but they died out as quickly as burning
　　thorns;
　in the name of the Lord I cut them off.

¹³I was pushed back and about to fall,
　but the Lord helped me.
¹⁴The Lord is my strength and my song;
　he has become my salvation.

¹⁵Shouts of joy and victory
　resound in the tents of the righteous:
　"The Lord's right hand has done mighty
　　things!

¹⁶The Lord's right hand is lifted high;
　the Lord's right hand has done mighty
　　things!"

¹⁷I will not die but live,
　and will proclaim what the Lord has done.
¹⁸The Lord has chastened me severely,
　but he has not given me over to death.

¹⁹Open for me the gates of righteousness;
　I will enter and give thanks to the Lord.
²⁰This is the gate of the Lord
　through which the righteous may enter.
²¹I will give you thanks, for you answered me;
　you have become my salvation.

²²The stone the builders rejected
　has become the capstone;
²³the Lord has done this,
　and it is marvelous in our eyes.
²⁴This is the day the Lord has made;
　let us rejoice and be glad in it.

²⁵O Lord, save us;
　O Lord, grant us success.
²⁶Blessed is he who comes in the name of the
　　Lord.
　From the house of the Lord we bless you.ᵗ
²⁷The Lord is God,
　and he has made his light shine upon us.
　With boughs in hand, join in the festal
　　procession
　upᵘ to the horns of the altar.

²⁸You are my God, and I will give you thanks;
　you are my God, and I will exalt you.
²⁹Give thanks to the Lord, for he is good;
　his love endures forever.

ᵗ26 The Hebrew is plural.　　ᵘ27 Or *Bind the festal sacrifice with ropes / and take it*

Discovering the Word **1.** Note that this psalm divides into five parts: a liturgical call to praise at the beginning (vv. 1–4) and end (v. 29)—which sandwiches the leader's song of thanksgiving (vv. 5–21), the people's response (vv. 22–27) and the leader's final prompting (v. 28). What indicators do you see that suggest a change of voice or speaker in each section? **2.** What is the significance of the many double and triple repetitions found throughout this psalm? **3.** What has the Lord done for the king and/or representatively for the people (vv. 5–21)? **4.** As an Israelite prompted to give thanks on the occasion of this psalm, what redemptive occasions in the life of your people come to mind? **5.** What is the significance of the stone-turned-capstone (v. 22), which is being celebrated on this festive day (v. 23)?

Applying the Word **1.** The early church applied verse 22 to Jesus. How is Jesus like this stone-turned-capstone? **2.** For what events in your life are you particularly grateful to God? **3.** How did God prove to be your helper, your strength or your salvation?

Responding in Prayer Praise God for the day(s) he has given you to rejoice (v. 24).

68 / *Psalm 119:1–24*
Searching for God's Wisdom

FEW SITUATIONS BRING life to a grinding halt like losing a contact lens. Have you ever seen it happen to a major-league baseball pitcher? Frustration turns to comedy as fellow players trickle out from the dugout and hunch over the mound on hands and knees. Fans get restless. Commentators start reminiscing about recent games. The TV audience goes on commercial break.

If we are going to have the vision to see life from God's perspective, we will regularly have to stop everything, hunker down and find out just what that perspective is. Like finding a contact lens, finding God's wisdom is simply worth whatever inconveniences may come in its pursuit.

 Warming Up to God In what area of your life do you need God's wisdom?

 Read Psalm 119:1–24.

Psalm 119[v]

א Aleph

¹Blessed are they whose ways are blameless,
 who walk according to the law of the LORD.
²Blessed are they who keep his statutes
 and seek him with all their heart.
³They do nothing wrong;
 they walk in his ways.
⁴You have laid down precepts
 that are to be fully obeyed.
⁵Oh, that my ways were steadfast
 in obeying your decrees!
⁶Then I would not be put to shame
 when I consider all your commands.
⁷I will praise you with an upright heart
 as I learn your righteous laws.
⁸I will obey your decrees;
 do not utterly forsake me.

ב Beth

⁹How can a young man keep his way pure?
 By living according to your word.
¹⁰I seek you with all my heart;
 do not let me stray from your commands.
¹¹I have hidden your word in my heart
 that I might not sin against you.
¹²Praise be to you, O LORD;
 teach me your decrees.
¹³With my lips I recount
 all the laws that come from your mouth.
¹⁴I rejoice in following your statutes
 as one rejoices in great riches.
¹⁵I meditate on your precepts
 and consider your ways.
¹⁶I delight in your decrees;

[v]This psalm is an acrostic poem; the verses of each stanza begin with the same letter of the Hebrew alphabet.

I will not neglect your word.

ג Gimel

¹⁷Do good to your servant, and I will live;
    I will obey your word.
¹⁸Open my eyes that I may see
    wonderful things in your law.
¹⁹I am a stranger on earth;
    do not hide your commands from me.

²⁰My soul is consumed with longing
    for your laws at all times.
²¹You rebuke the arrogant, who are cursed
    and who stray from your commands.
²²Remove from me scorn and contempt,
    for I keep your statutes.
²³Though rulers sit together and slander me,
    your servant will meditate on your decrees.
²⁴Your statutes are my delight;
    they are my counselors.

Discovering the Word 1. What different words does the psalmist use to describe God's Word? 2. What benefits of knowing and following God's Word does the psalmist mention in verses 1–8? 3. How does God's Word help us to deal with sin (vv. 9–16)? 4. How does God's Word enlighten us about God's ways (vv. 17–24)? 5. What are the consequences of *not* knowing or following God's Word (vv. 5–6, 9–11, 21–22)?

Applying the Word 1. What is a way you have experienced frustration in studying Scripture? 2. What in the psalmist's example can bring encouragement to us to meditate on and delight in God's Word?

Responding in Prayer Ask God to guide you as you turn to his Word for wisdom.

69 / *Psalm 119:25–40*
Seeking God

PRAYER AND MEDITATION are not easy disciplines. Many of us have used prayer as a magical device for controlling God or for acquiring God's favor. Similarly, many use meditation as a magical tool for control. But there is nothing magical about the spiritual disciplines of prayer and meditation. Both are ways to focus our attention on God. We can talk (pray) openly, honestly, vulnerably to God, and we can listen (meditate) with humility. It is this dynamic of speaking/listening, prayer/meditation that makes it possible for us to increase our contact with God. We can experience loving and being loved by our Creator.

Warming Up to God What difficulties do you experience with prayer and meditation?

Read Psalm 119:25–40.

ד Daleth

²⁵I am laid low in the dust;
    preserve my life according to your word.
²⁶I recounted my ways and you answered me;
    teach me your decrees.
²⁷Let me understand the teaching of your
        precepts;
    then I will meditate on your wonders.
²⁸My soul is weary with sorrow;
    strengthen me according to your word.
²⁹Keep me from deceitful ways;
    be gracious to me through your law.

³⁰I have chosen the way of truth;
    I have set my heart on your laws.
³¹I hold fast to your statutes, O LORD;
    do not let me be put to shame.
³²I run in the path of your commands,
    for you have set my heart free.

ה He

³³Teach me, O LORD, to follow your decrees;
    then I will keep them to the end.
³⁴Give me understanding, and I will keep your
        law

and obey it with all my heart.
³⁵Direct me in the path of your commands,
    for there I find delight.
³⁶Turn my heart toward your statutes
    and not toward selfish gain.
³⁷Turn my eyes away from worthless things;
    preserve my life according to your word.ʷ
³⁸Fulfill your promise to your servant,

so that you may be feared.
³⁹Take away the disgrace I dread,
    for your laws are good.
⁴⁰How I long for your precepts!
    Preserve my life in your righteousness.

ʷ37 Two manuscripts of the Masoretic Text and Dead Sea Scrolls; most manuscripts of the Masoretic Text *life in your way*

 Discovering the Word 1. Restate in your own words the requests the psalmist makes of God. 2. What major needs and desires is the psalmist expressing in these requests? 3. How do these needs/desires compare with your own at this time? 4. How does the psalmist describe what he has done and what he desires to do in his pursuit of God? 5. What benefits does the psalmist suggest might come from prayer and meditation (vv. 32–40)?

Applying the Word 1. The psalmist describes himself as "laid low in the dust" and as "weary with sorrow." Describe a time when you experienced these feelings. 2. In your experience, how can prayer and meditation improve our contact with God?

Responding in Prayer Ask God to help you practice the disciplines of prayer and meditation.

Psalm 119:41—120:7

ו Waw

⁴¹May your unfailing love come to me, O LORD,
    your salvation according to your promise;
⁴²then I will answer the one who taunts me,
    for I trust in your word.
⁴³Do not snatch the word of truth from my
        mouth,
    for I have put my hope in your laws.
⁴⁴I will always obey your law,
    for ever and ever.
⁴⁵I will walk about in freedom,
    for I have sought out your precepts.
⁴⁶I will speak of your statutes before kings
    and will not be put to shame,
⁴⁷for I delight in your commands
    because I love them.
⁴⁸I lift up my hands toˣ your commands,
        which I love,
    and I meditate on your decrees.

ז Zayin

⁴⁹Remember your word to your servant,
    for you have given me hope.

⁵⁰My comfort in my suffering is this:
    Your promise preserves my life.
⁵¹The arrogant mock me without restraint,
    but I do not turn from your law.
⁵²I remember your ancient laws, O LORD,
    and I find comfort in them.
⁵³Indignation grips me because of the wicked,
    who have forsaken your law.
⁵⁴Your decrees are the theme of my song
    wherever I lodge.
⁵⁵In the night I remember your name, O LORD,
    and I will keep your law.
⁵⁶This has been my practice:
    I obey your precepts.

ח Heth

⁵⁷You are my portion, O LORD;
    I have promised to obey your words.
⁵⁸I have sought your face with all my heart;
    be gracious to me according to your
        promise.
⁵⁹I have considered my ways

ˣ48 Or *for*

and have turned my steps to your statutes.
⁶⁰I will hasten and not delay
    to obey your commands.
⁶¹Though the wicked bind me with ropes,
    I will not forget your law.
⁶²At midnight I rise to give you thanks
    for your righteous laws.
⁶³I am a friend to all who fear you,
    to all who follow your precepts.
⁶⁴The earth is filled with your love, O LORD;
    teach me your decrees.

ט Teth

⁶⁵Do good to your servant
    according to your word, O LORD.
⁶⁶Teach me knowledge and good judgment,
    for I believe in your commands.
⁶⁷Before I was afflicted I went astray,
    but now I obey your word.
⁶⁸You are good, and what you do is good;
    teach me your decrees.
⁶⁹Though the arrogant have smeared me with
        lies,
    I keep your precepts with all my heart.
⁷⁰Their hearts are callous and unfeeling,
    but I delight in your law.
⁷¹It was good for me to be afflicted
    so that I might learn your decrees.
⁷²The law from your mouth is more precious to
        me
    than thousands of pieces of silver and gold.

י Yodh

⁷³Your hands made me and formed me;
    give me understanding to learn your
        commands.
⁷⁴May those who fear you rejoice when they see
        me,
    for I have put my hope in your word.
⁷⁵I know, O LORD, that your laws are righteous,
    and in faithfulness you have afflicted me.
⁷⁶May your unfailing love be my comfort,
    according to your promise to your servant.
⁷⁷Let your compassion come to me that I may
        live,
    for your law is my delight.
⁷⁸May the arrogant be put to shame for
        wronging me without cause;
    but I will meditate on your precepts.
⁷⁹May those who fear you turn to me,
    those who understand your statutes.
⁸⁰May my heart be blameless toward your
        decrees,
    that I may not be put to shame.

כ Kaph

⁸¹My soul faints with longing for your
        salvation,
    but I have put my hope in your word.
⁸²My eyes fail, looking for your promise;
    I say, "When will you comfort me?"
⁸³Though I am like a wineskin in the smoke,
    I do not forget your decrees.
⁸⁴How long must your servant wait?
    When will you punish my persecutors?
⁸⁵The arrogant dig pitfalls for me,
    contrary to your law.
⁸⁶All your commands are trustworthy;
    help me, for men persecute me without
        cause.
⁸⁷They almost wiped me from the earth,
    but I have not forsaken your precepts.
⁸⁸Preserve my life according to your love,
    and I will obey the statutes of your mouth.

ל Lamedh

⁸⁹Your word, O LORD, is eternal;
    it stands firm in the heavens.
⁹⁰Your faithfulness continues through all
        generations;
    you established the earth, and it endures.
⁹¹Your laws endure to this day,
    for all things serve you.
⁹²If your law had not been my delight,
    I would have perished in my affliction.
⁹³I will never forget your precepts,
    for by them you have preserved my life.
⁹⁴Save me, for I am yours;
    I have sought out your precepts.
⁹⁵The wicked are waiting to destroy me,
    but I will ponder your statutes.
⁹⁶To all perfection I see a limit;
    but your commands are boundless.

מ Mem

⁹⁷Oh, how I love your law!
    I meditate on it all day long.
⁹⁸Your commands make me wiser than my
        enemies,
    for they are ever with me.
⁹⁹I have more insight than all my teachers,

for I meditate on your statutes.
¹⁰⁰I have more understanding than the elders,
for I obey your precepts.
¹⁰¹I have kept my feet from every evil path
so that I might obey your word.
¹⁰²I have not departed from your laws,
for you yourself have taught me.
¹⁰³How sweet are your words to my taste,
sweeter than honey to my mouth!
¹⁰⁴I gain understanding from your precepts;
therefore I hate every wrong path.

ב Nun

¹⁰⁵Your word is a lamp to my feet
and a light for my path.
¹⁰⁶I have taken an oath and confirmed it,
that I will follow your righteous laws.
¹⁰⁷I have suffered much;
preserve my life, O Lord, according to your
word.
¹⁰⁸Accept, O Lord, the willing praise of my
mouth,
and teach me your laws.
¹⁰⁹Though I constantly take my life in my
hands,
I will not forget your law.
¹¹⁰The wicked have set a snare for me,
but I have not strayed from your precepts.
¹¹¹Your statutes are my heritage forever;
they are the joy of my heart.
¹¹²My heart is set on keeping your decrees
to the very end.

ס Samekh

¹¹³I hate double-minded men,
but I love your law.
¹¹⁴You are my refuge and my shield;
I have put my hope in your word.
¹¹⁵Away from me, you evildoers,
that I may keep the commands of my God!
¹¹⁶Sustain me according to your promise, and I
will live;
do not let my hopes be dashed.
¹¹⁷Uphold me, and I will be delivered;
I will always have regard for your decrees.
¹¹⁸You reject all who stray from your decrees,
for their deceitfulness is in vain.
¹¹⁹All the wicked of the earth you discard like
dross;
therefore I love your statutes.
¹²⁰My flesh trembles in fear of you;
I stand in awe of your laws.

ע Ayin

¹²¹I have done what is righteous and just;
do not leave me to my oppressors.
¹²²Ensure your servant's well-being;
let not the arrogant oppress me.
¹²³My eyes fail, looking for your salvation,
looking for your righteous promise.
¹²⁴Deal with your servant according to your
love
and teach me your decrees.
¹²⁵I am your servant; give me discernment
that I may understand your statutes.
¹²⁶It is time for you to act, O Lord;
your law is being broken.
¹²⁷Because I love your commands
more than gold, more than pure gold,
¹²⁸and because I consider all your precepts
right,
I hate every wrong path.

פ Pe

¹²⁹Your statutes are wonderful;
therefore I obey them.
¹³⁰The unfolding of your words gives light;
it gives understanding to the simple.
¹³¹I open my mouth and pant,
longing for your commands.
¹³²Turn to me and have mercy on me,
as you always do to those who love your
name.
¹³³Direct my footsteps according to your word;
let no sin rule over me.
¹³⁴Redeem me from the oppression of men,
that I may obey your precepts.
¹³⁵Make your face shine upon your servant
and teach me your decrees.
¹³⁶Streams of tears flow from my eyes,
for your law is not obeyed.

צ Tsadhe

¹³⁷Righteous are you, O Lord,
and your laws are right.
¹³⁸The statutes you have laid down are
righteous;
they are fully trustworthy.
¹³⁹My zeal wears me out,
for my enemies ignore your words.
¹⁴⁰Your promises have been thoroughly tested,
and your servant loves them.
¹⁴¹Though I am lowly and despised,
I do not forget your precepts.

142Your righteousness is everlasting
   and your law is true.
143Trouble and distress have come upon me,
   but your commands are my delight.
144Your statutes are forever right;
   give me understanding that I may live.

ק   Qoph

145I call with all my heart; answer me, O LORD,
   and I will obey your decrees.
146I call out to you; save me
   and I will keep your statutes.
147I rise before dawn and cry for help;
   I have put my hope in your word.
148My eyes stay open through the watches of
      the night,
   that I may meditate on your promises.
149Hear my voice in accordance with your love;
   preserve my life, O LORD, according to your
      laws.
150Those who devise wicked schemes are near,
   but they are far from your law.
151Yet you are near, O LORD,
   and all your commands are true.
152Long ago I learned from your statutes
   that you established them to last forever.

ר   Resh

153Look upon my suffering and deliver me,
   for I have not forgotten your law.
154Defend my cause and redeem me;
   preserve my life according to your promise.
155Salvation is far from the wicked,
   for they do not seek out your decrees.
156Your compassion is great, O LORD;
   preserve my life according to your laws.
157Many are the foes who persecute me,
   but I have not turned from your statutes.
158I look on the faithless with loathing,
   for they do not obey your word.
159See how I love your precepts;
   preserve my life, O LORD, according to your
      love.
160All your words are true;
   all your righteous laws are eternal.

ש   Sin and Shin

161Rulers persecute me without cause,
   but my heart trembles at your word.
162I rejoice in your promise
   like one who finds great spoil.
163I hate and abhor falsehood

but I love your law.
164Seven times a day I praise you
   for your righteous laws.
165Great peace have they who love your law,
   and nothing can make them stumble.
166I wait for your salvation, O LORD,
   and I follow your commands.
167I obey your statutes,
   for I love them greatly.
168I obey your precepts and your statutes,
   for all my ways are known to you.

ת   Taw

169May my cry come before you, O LORD;
   give me understanding according to your
      word.
170May my supplication come before you;
   deliver me according to your promise.
171May my lips overflow with praise,
   for you teach me your decrees.
172May my tongue sing of your word,
   for all your commands are righteous.
173May your hand be ready to help me,
   for I have chosen your precepts.
174I long for your salvation, O LORD,
   and your law is my delight.
175Let me live that I may praise you,
   and may your laws sustain me.
176I have strayed like a lost sheep.
   Seek your servant,
   for I have not forgotten your commands.

Psalm 120

A song of ascents.

1I call on the LORD in my distress,
   and he answers me.
2Save me, O LORD, from lying lips
   and from deceitful tongues.

3What will he do to you,
   and what more besides, O deceitful tongue?
4He will punish you with a warrior's sharp
      arrows,
   with burning coals of the broom tree.

5Woe to me that I dwell in Meshech,
   that I live among the tents of Kedar!
6Too long have I lived
   among those who hate peace.
7I am a man of peace;
   but when I speak, they are for war.

70 / *Psalm 121*
A Prayer of Assurance

THE JEWS WERE on an uphill journey to Jerusalem and the temple at Mount Zion. This psalm is among the many "songs of ascent" sung (or inwardly affirmed) by individuals in the caravan along the way. Any pilgrim facing an uphill climb of faith, and all of us on life's pilgrimage from this earthly existence to the heavenly glory, will find assurance in repeating the confession of this psalm.

 Warming Up to God   Imagine a battle of faith that you may be facing. Think of all helpful resources you may have turned to, or could be turning to, for help. Then face the Lord who watched you go to and fro. How do you imagine God making a difference in that situation?

Read Psalm 121.

Psalm 121

A song of ascents.

¹I lift up my eyes to the hills—
    where does my help come from?
²My help comes from the LORD,
    the Maker of heaven and earth.

³He will not let your foot slip—
    he who watches over you will not slumber;
⁴indeed, he who watches over Israel

will neither slumber nor sleep.

⁵The LORD watches over you—
    the LORD is your shade at your right hand;
⁶the sun will not harm you by day,
    nor the moon by night.

⁷The LORD will keep you from all harm—
    he will watch over your life;
⁸the LORD will watch over your coming and
        going
    both now and forevermore.

Discovering the Word   1. Judging from the words and phrases most often repeated in this psalm, what is its major theme?   2. How does the second verse in each of the four verse pairs (vv. 2, 4, 6, 8) expand on the minitheme of the introductory line in each pair (vv. 1, 3, 5, 7)?   3. What kind of help does the Lord provide his people along the journey (in contrast to those idols who may slumber or slouch on the job)?   4. In light of the assurances offered in this psalm, how do you account for the fact that some people do slip and fall into harm's way?

Applying the Word   1. Imagine you are an Israelite making this pilgrimage to Mount Zion and dialoguing your way through this psalm of confession and assurance. What parts do you find most reassuring for yourself?   2. What parts do you find most reassuring for a fellow pilgrim who you know is struggling along the way?   3. Consider one time, day or night, when you slipped badly and fell into harm's way. How was God watching over you in that situation?

Responding in Prayer   Consider using Psalm 121 as an appropriate prayer for all your comings and goings. Offer it at mealtimes, office breaks and bedtimes. Let it influence the prayers and counsel you offer family, friends and work associates, especially anyone facing an uphill battle.

---

71 / *Psalm 122*
A Prayer for Peace

PRAYER FOR THE "peace of Jerusalem" (vv. 6–9) distinguished this Zion hymn. (For other Zion songs, see Ps 46, 48, 76, 84, 126, 129, 137.) This prayer is not just for fellow worshipers, but for the policies and programs that bring "peace and prosperity" to the city. This call to pray for the decision-makers in government confers a benediction on their work, the result of which would be shalom for the "City of Peace."

Warming Up to God When you think about doing good and seeking the welfare of others, who comes to mind? Mentally open up today's newspaper along with the Bible to see the people and the needs that God cares most about in your city.

 Read Psalm 122.

Psalm 122

A song of ascents. Of David.

[1]I rejoiced with those who said to me,
  "Let us go to the house of the
    LORD."
[2]Our feet are standing
  in your gates, O Jerusalem.

[3]Jerusalem is built like a city
  that is closely compacted together.
[4]That is where the tribes go up,
  the tribes of the LORD,
to praise the name of the LORD

according to the statute given to
    Israel.
[5]There the thrones for judgment stand,
  the thrones of the house of David.

[6]Pray for the peace of Jerusalem:
  "May those who love you be secure.
[7]May there be peace within your walls
  and security within your citadels."
[8]For the sake of my brothers and friends,
  I will say, "Peace be within you."
[9]For the sake of the house of the LORD our
    God,
  I will seek your prosperity.

Discovering the Word 1. What was it like for these worshipers to go to the house of the Lord in Jerusalem (Mount Zion)? 2. Describe the city of Jerusalem (vv. 3–5). 3. What things does the psalmist pray will be given to the city (vv. 6–9)? 4. What would this psalmist say to someone who wanted to first meet his own needs or those of his family before seeking the peace and prosperity of the city?

Applying the Word 1. Worship at Mount Zion was both a regular obligation (although a joyous event) and a bonding experience for temple-bound worshipers. What is "going to church" like for you? 2. Psalm 122 also evokes memories of how Jesus revered and wept over Jerusalem (Lk 9:51; 13:31–35; 19:41–44). By comparison, what tears have you shed over your beloved city? 3. "Peace within *your* walls" and "security within *your* citadels" (author's italics, v. 7) will also benefit believers, but the city itself is the end in view here, not believers. How do you go about working for the good of the city where you live and worship?

Responding in Prayer Scan the city news section of your newspaper for events and people that need God's "shalom" (peace and prosperity). Bring to God in prayer everyone you know in city hall and the key urban areas that need shalom.

Psalms 123—125

Psalm 123

A song of ascents.

[1]I lift up my eyes to you,
  to you whose throne is in heaven.
[2]As the eyes of slaves look to the hand of their
    master,
  as the eyes of a maid look to the hand of
    her mistress,

so our eyes look to the LORD our God,
  till he shows us his mercy.

[3]Have mercy on us, O LORD, have mercy
    on us,
  for we have endured much contempt.
[4]We have endured much ridicule from the
    proud,
  much contempt from the arrogant.

Psalm 124

A song of ascents. Of David.

[1]If the LORD had not been on our side—
  let Israel say—
[2]if the LORD had not been on our side
  when men attacked us,
[3]when their anger flared against us,
  they would have swallowed us alive;
[4]the flood would have engulfed us,
  the torrent would have swept over us,
[5]the raging waters
  would have swept us away.

[6]Praise be to the LORD,
  who has not let us be torn by their
    teeth.
[7]We have escaped like a bird
  out of the fowler's snare;
the snare has been broken,
  and we have escaped.
[8]Our help is in the name of the LORD,
  the Maker of heaven and earth.

Psalm 125

A song of ascents.

[1]Those who trust in the LORD are like Mount
    Zion,
  which cannot be shaken but endures
    forever.
[2]As the mountains surround Jerusalem,
  so the LORD surrounds his people
  both now and forevermore.

[3]The scepter of the wicked will not remain
    over the land allotted to the righteous,
  for then the righteous might use
    their hands to do evil.

[4]Do good, O LORD, to those who are good,
  to those who are upright in heart.
[5]But those who turn to crooked ways
  the LORD will banish with the evildoers.

Peace be upon Israel.

---

72 / Psalm 126
A Song of Joy

ONE IMAGE OF happiness that sticks out in my mind is the suppertime dance that Snoopy does in the "Peanuts" comic strip. His head is flung back, his ears are flopping about, and his feet pound furiously. Have you ever felt like dancing for joy? In this passage the Israelites do.

 Warming Up to God What do you do when you are filled with joy?

 Read Psalm 126.

Psalm 126

A song of ascents.

[1]When the LORD brought back the captives to[a]
    Zion,
  we were like men who dreamed.[b]
[2]Our mouths were filled with laughter,
  our tongues with songs of joy.
Then it was said among the nations,
  "The LORD has done great things for them."
[3]The LORD has done great things for us,

and we are filled with joy.

[4]Restore our fortunes,[c] O LORD,
  like streams in the Negev.
[5]Those who sow in tears
  will reap with songs of joy.
[6]He who goes out weeping,
  carrying seed to sow,
will return with songs of joy,
  carrying sheaves with him.

*a*1 Or LORD *restored the fortunes of*   *b*1 Or *men restored to health*
*c*4 Or *Bring back our captives*

Discovering the Word 1. This is a song of celebration by the exiles who returned to Zion. What emotions do you see expressed throughout this psalm? 2. What imagery is used in verses 1–2 to describe the joy the writers feel? 3. How do verses 4–6 reflect a balance between cause and effect? 4. How are sadness and joy intertwined (vv. 5–6)?

 Applying the Word 1. The Israelites give God the credit for the "great things" that have happened. How do you do with giving God the credit? 2. When do you feel inhibited about freely expressing your joy?

Responding in Prayer What do you need to praise God for? Share your joy with him.

73 / *Psalm 127*
Worthwhile Work

WILL WE ALLOW technology and our society's definition of personhood to drive a wedge into our community? It can and does happen almost naturally—without our help.

As we respond to Jesus, there will be purpose in our lives and meaning within our relationships. It is the context of relationships with God and other persons that should give meaning to our work. Unfortunately, our culture elevates the possession of things and applauds compulsive work habits. We need to intervene where God's image in people is being destroyed by our society and structures. These passages encourage us to take the lead in bringing God's kingdom back into our relationships.

 Warming Up to God What challenges to faith are you currently facing in your workplace?

 Read Psalm 127.

Psalm 127

A song of ascents. Of Solomon.

[1]Unless the LORD builds the house,
  its builders labor in vain.
Unless the LORD watches over the city,
  the watchmen stand guard in vain.
[2]In vain you rise early
  and stay up late,
toiling for food to eat—
  for he grants sleep to[d] those he loves.

[3]Sons are a heritage from the LORD,
  children a reward from him.
[4]Like arrows in the hands of a warrior
  are sons born in one's youth.
[5]Blessed is the man
  whose quiver is full of them.
They will not be put to shame
  when they contend with their enemies in
    the gate.

d2 Or eat— / for while they sleep he provides for

 Discovering the Word 1. What basis is offered in this passage for the worth of our work (v. 1)? 2. Why is it foolish to work long hours (v. 2)? 3. Children (v. 3) are a gift from God and are a sign of his favor on those who do worthwhile work. In what ways has God rewarded you for good work?

 Applying the Word 1. How does your attitude toward work shape how you view your personal relationships? 2. In what way do you need the rest that the Lord grants "to those he loves"?

Responding in Prayer Ask God to build in you the attitude toward work that he wants you to have.

Psalms 128—129

Psalm 128

A song of ascents.

¹Blessed are all who fear the LORD,
  who walk in his ways.
²You will eat the fruit of your
    labor;
  blessings and prosperity will be
    yours.
³Your wife will be like a fruitful
    vine
  within your house;
 your sons will be like olive shoots
  around your table.
⁴Thus is the man blessed
  who fears the LORD.

⁵May the LORD bless you from Zion
  all the days of your life;
 may you see the prosperity of
    Jerusalem,
⁶   and may you live to see your
    children's children.

Peace be upon Israel.

Psalm 129

A song of ascents.

¹They have greatly oppressed me from my
    youth—
  let Israel say—
²they have greatly oppressed me from my
    youth,
  but they have not gained the victory over
    me.
³Plowmen have plowed my back
  and made their furrows long.
⁴But the LORD is righteous;
  he has cut me free from the cords of the
    wicked.

⁵May all who hate Zion
  be turned back in shame.
⁶May they be like grass on the roof,
  which withers before it can grow;
⁷with it the reaper cannot fill his hands,
  nor the one who gathers fill his arms.
⁸May those who pass by not say,
  "The blessing of the LORD be upon you;
  we bless you in the name of the LORD."

74 / Psalm 130
A Prayer of Hope

HOPE IS NECESSARY. It gives us the strength to keep going through the tough times. It gives life joy and meaning in the good times. However, when hope has been repeatedly disappointed, it slips away. This psalm offers a picture of this struggle. The writer is without much hope. Yet he puts himself in a place of allowing for the possibility of hope. As we pray with him, we too can begin to wait with growing expectation. We too can nurture our hope.

 Warming Up to God How would you describe the experience of hope? How would you describe the experience of hopelessness?

 Read Psalm 130.

Psalm 130

A song of ascents.

¹Out of the depths I cry to you, O LORD;
² O Lord, hear my voice.
 Let your ears be attentive
  to my cry for mercy.

³If you, O LORD, kept a record of sins,
  O Lord, who could stand?
⁴But with you there is forgiveness;
  therefore you are feared.

⁵I wait for the LORD, my soul waits,
  and in his word I put my hope.
⁶My soul waits for the Lord

more than watchmen wait for the morning,
more than watchmen wait for the morning.

⁷O Israel, put your hope in the Lᴏʀᴅ,

for with the Lᴏʀᴅ is unfailing love
and with him is full redemption.
⁸He himself will redeem Israel
from all their sins.

Discovering the Word 1. The psalm begins with a cry to the Lord from "out of the depths" (v. 1). What pictures come to mind as you read this phrase? 2. The psalmist's distress seems to be related to a struggle with guilt. How can guilt lead to hopelessness? 3. Verses 3 and 4 tell us that God forgives. How does the promise of forgiveness contribute to hope? 4. Verse 5 says, "I wait, . . . my soul waits." What is the relationship between waiting and hope? 5. The psalmist then uses the metaphor of watchmen (v. 6) to describe the experience of hope. What does he convey with this image? 6. What reasons does the psalmist give for hoping in the Lord (vv. 7–8)?

Applying the Word 1. What area of life is it difficult for you to be hopeful about? 2. What reasons do you have for hoping in the Lord?

Responding in Prayer Thank God for being the source of hope. Pray for courage when you face hopelessness.

Psalms 131—132

Psalm 131

A song of ascents. Of David.

¹My heart is not proud, O Lᴏʀᴅ,
 my eyes are not haughty;
 I do not concern myself with great matters
 or things too wonderful for me.
²But I have stilled and quieted my soul;
 like a weaned child with its mother,
 like a weaned child is my soul within me.

³O Israel, put your hope in the Lᴏʀᴅ
 both now and forevermore.

Psalm 132

A song of ascents.

¹O Lᴏʀᴅ, remember David
 and all the hardships he endured.

²He swore an oath to the Lᴏʀᴅ
 and made a vow to the Mighty One of
  Jacob:
³"I will not enter my house
 or go to my bed—
⁴I will allow no sleep to my eyes,
 no slumber to my eyelids,
⁵till I find a place for the Lᴏʀᴅ,
 a dwelling for the Mighty One of Jacob."

⁶We heard it in Ephrathah,

we came upon it in the fields of Jaarᵉ꞉ᶠ
⁷"Let us go to his dwelling place;
 let us worship at his footstool—
⁸arise, O Lᴏʀᴅ, and come to your resting place,
 you and the ark of your might.
⁹May your priests be clothed with
  righteousness;
 may your saints sing for joy."

¹⁰For the sake of David your servant,
 do not reject your anointed one.

¹¹The Lᴏʀᴅ swore an oath to David,
 a sure oath that he will not revoke:
"One of your own descendants
 I will place on your throne—
¹²if your sons keep my covenant
 and the statutes I teach them,
then their sons will sit
 on your throne for ever and ever."

¹³For the Lᴏʀᴅ has chosen Zion,
 he has desired it for his dwelling:
¹⁴"This is my resting place for ever and ever;
 here I will sit enthroned, for I have desired
  it—
¹⁵I will bless her with abundant provisions;
 her poor will I satisfy with food.
¹⁶I will clothe her priests with salvation,
 and her saints will ever sing for joy.

ᵉ6 That is, Kiriath Jearim   ᶠ6 Or *heard of it in Ephrathah, / we found*
it in the fields of Jaar. (And no quotes around verses 7-9)

17"Here I will make a horn^g grow for David
  and set up a lamp for my anointed
  one.
18I will clothe his enemies with shame,

but the crown on his head will be
  resplendent."

^g17 *Horn* here symbolizes strong one, that is, king.

75 / *Psalm 133*
Blessed Unity

THINK ABOUT THE many brother-to-brother and sister-to-sister loyalties and rivalries that are celebrated in our society—fraternities and sororities, sports teams, family corporations, class reunions, the Mafia (that is, "the Brotherhood"). In your mind's eye, or from your own experience, how do you picture those relationships? Do you envision any fraternal unity so blessed that it fairly oozes and drips with sweetness? David does. He waxes eloquent on this theme. Many contemporary songs which extol the blessedness of "mystic sweet communion" are based, in part, on this psalm.

 Warming Up to God How does the "mystic sweet communion" enjoyed by God's people compare to the kinds of unity that you have witnessed or experienced firsthand with others? As you get into this brief Bible study, surround yourself with images of warm Christian fellowship.

 Read Psalm 133.

Psalm 133

A song of ascents. Of David.

¹How good and pleasant it is
  when brothers live together in unity!
²It is like precious oil poured on the head,

running down on the beard,
running down on Aaron's beard,
  down upon the collar of his robes.
³It is as if the dew of Hermon
  were falling on Mount Zion.
For there the LORD bestows his blessing,
  even life forevermore.

Discovering the Word 1. What is so good or pleasant or blessed about brothers living together in unity (v. 1)? 2. To what is this blessedness compared (vv. 2–3)? 3. If the oil of anointing that saturated Aaron's beard and priestly robes was so precious and sanctifying (v. 2; Ex 29:7; Lev 21:10), what does that say about harmony running its course through the fellowship of God's people? 4. Mount Hermon rises 9,000 feet at three snow-covered peaks, its many glaciers stretching across 20 miles in northern Israel, watering the Jordan River valleys and cities below. However, during the summer, its snow and glaciers produce a heavy dew that envelops Mount Hermon, leaving much of the surroundings arid. For the "dew of Hermon" to fall on Mount Zion (v. 3) would be most unusual. What does that say about the blessing of brotherly unity?

Applying the Word 1. What does this psalm say to those who know only the brotherhood and sisterhood as it is portrayed in the media (consider fraternity hazing, sports teams that brawl, family corporations divided by sibling rivalry)? 2. Where are you experiencing strong brother-to-brother or sister-to-sister bonds and blessings that sanctify and sustain God's people, as does "oil" and "dew"? 3. In what way could you experience more of the priestly "oil" and Mount Hermon's "dew"?

Responding in Prayer Think about the spiritual refreshment and moral accountability that strong fellowship provides you. Thank God for the brothers and sisters he has given you to sanctify and sustain you. Consider ways that you can live in harmony with your family of faith, and pray toward that end.

Psalms 134—136

Psalm 134

A song of ascents.

¹Praise the Lord, all you servants of the Lord
  who minister by night in the house of the
    Lord.
²Lift up your hands in the sanctuary
  and praise the Lord.

³May the Lord, the Maker of heaven and earth,
  bless you from Zion.

Psalm 135

¹Praise the Lord.*ʰ*

 Praise the name of the Lord;
  praise him, you servants of the Lord,
²you who minister in the house of the Lord,
  in the courts of the house of our God.

³Praise the Lord, for the Lord is good;
  sing praise to his name, for that is pleasant.
⁴For the Lord has chosen Jacob to be his own,
  Israel to be his treasured possession.

⁵I know that the Lord is great,
  that our Lord is greater than all gods.
⁶The Lord does whatever pleases him,
  in the heavens and on the earth,
  in the seas and all their depths.
⁷He makes clouds rise from the ends of the
    earth;
  he sends lightning with the rain
  and brings out the wind from his
    storehouses.

⁸He struck down the firstborn of Egypt,
  the firstborn of men and animals.
⁹He sent his signs and wonders into your
    midst, O Egypt,
  against Pharaoh and all his servants.
¹⁰He struck down many nations
  and killed mighty kings—
¹¹Sihon king of the Amorites,
  Og king of Bashan
  and all the kings of Canaan—
¹²and he gave their land as an inheritance,
  an inheritance to his people Israel.

¹³Your name, O Lord, endures forever,
  your renown, O Lord, through all
    generations.
¹⁴For the Lord will vindicate his people

and have compassion on his servants.

¹⁵The idols of the nations are silver and gold,
  made by the hands of men.
¹⁶They have mouths, but cannot speak,
  eyes, but they cannot see;
¹⁷they have ears, but cannot hear,
  nor is there breath in their mouths.
¹⁸Those who make them will be like them,
  and so will all who trust in them.

¹⁹O house of Israel, praise the Lord;
  O house of Aaron, praise the Lord;
²⁰O house of Levi, praise the Lord;
  you who fear him, praise the Lord.
²¹Praise be to the Lord from Zion,
  to him who dwells in Jerusalem.

 Praise the Lord.

Psalm 136

¹Give thanks to the Lord, for he is good.
        His love endures forever.
²Give thanks to the God of gods.
        His love endures forever.
³Give thanks to the Lord of lords:
        His love endures forever.

⁴to him who alone does great wonders,
        His love endures forever.
⁵who by his understanding made the heavens,
        His love endures forever.
⁶who spread out the earth upon the waters,
        His love endures forever.
⁷who made the great lights—
        His love endures forever.
⁸the sun to govern the day,
        His love endures forever.
⁹the moon and stars to govern the night;
        His love endures forever.

¹⁰to him who struck down the firstborn of
    Egypt,
        His love endures forever.
¹¹and brought Israel out from among them
        His love endures forever.
¹²with a mighty hand and outstretched arm;
        His love endures forever.
¹³to him who divided the Red Seaⁱ asunder
        His love endures forever.

ʰ1 Hebrew *Hallelu Yah*; also in verses 3 and 21   ⁱ13 Hebrew *Yam Suph*; that is, Sea of Reeds; also in verse 15

¹⁴and brought Israel through the midst of it,
His love endures forever.
¹⁵but swept Pharaoh and his army into the Red Sea;
His love endures forever.
¹⁶to him who led his people through the desert,
His love endures forever.
¹⁷who struck down great kings,
His love endures forever.
¹⁸and killed mighty kings—
His love endures forever.
¹⁹Sihon king of the Amorites
His love endures forever.
²⁰and Og king of Bashan—
His love endures forever.

²¹and gave their land as an inheritance,
His love endures forever.
²²an inheritance to his servant Israel;
His love endures forever.

²³to the One who remembered us in our low estate
His love endures forever.
²⁴and freed us from our enemies,
His love endures forever.
²⁵and who gives food to every creature.
His love endures forever.

²⁶Give thanks to the God of heaven.
His love endures forever.

76 / *Psalm 137*
Praying Our Hate

WE PUT ON our "Sunday best" in our prayers. But when we pray the prayers of God's people, the Psalms, we find that will not do. We must pray who we actually are, not who we think we should be. Here is a prayer that brings out not the best but the worst in us; vile, venomous, vicious hate.

 Warming Up to God Everyone has hated at one time or another. It is one of the basic human experiences. Be honest before God. Whom have you hated? Why?

 Read Psalm 137.

Psalm 137

¹By the rivers of Babylon we sat and wept
when we remembered Zion.
²There on the poplars
we hung our harps,
³for there our captors asked us for songs,
our tormentors demanded songs of joy;
they said, "Sing us one of the songs of Zion!"

⁴How can we sing the songs of the LORD
while in a foreign land?
⁵If I forget you, O Jerusalem,
may my right hand forget ⌊its skill⌋.
⁶May my tongue cling to the roof of my mouth

if I do not remember you,
if I do not consider Jerusalem
my highest joy.

⁷Remember, O LORD, what the Edomites did
on the day Jerusalem fell.
"Tear it down," they cried,
"tear it down to its foundations!"

⁸O Daughter of Babylon, doomed to destruction,
happy is he who repays you
for what you have done to us—
⁹he who seizes your infants
and dashes them against the rocks.

Discovering the Word 1. This psalm combines the loveliest lyric we can sing with the ugliest emotion we can feel. What makes verses 1–6 lovely? 2. What makes verses 7–9 ugly? 3. Homesickness is understandable. Sometimes it is evidence of loyalty. Sometimes it is simply irresponsibility. Remembering your own experiences of this, how would you evaluate verses 4–6? 4. The two dominant emotions in this prayer are self-pity

(vv. 1–6) and avenging hate (vv. 7–9), neither of them particularly commendable. Praying our sins doesn't, as such, launder them. What does it do?

 Applying the Word   1. Jesus said, "Love your enemies and pray for those who persecute you" (Mt 5:44). How can we possibly love and pray for such people? **2.** Most of us suppress our negative emotions (unless, neurotically, we advertise them). The way of prayer is not to cover them up so we will appear respectable, but to expose them so we can be healed. What negative emotion would you like healed?

Responding in Prayer   Take any hate or dislike that you have uncovered and give it voice as you pray.

Psalm 138

Psalm 138

Of David.

¹I will praise you, O Lord, with all my heart;
   before the "gods" I will sing your praise.
²I will bow down toward your holy temple
   and will praise your name
   for your love and your faithfulness,
for you have exalted above all things
   your name and your word.
³When I called, you answered me;
   you made me bold and stouthearted.

⁴May all the kings of the earth praise you,
   O Lord,

when they hear the words of your mouth.
⁵May they sing of the ways of the Lord,
   for the glory of the Lord is great.

⁶Though the Lord is on high, he looks upon
      the lowly,
   but the proud he knows from afar.
⁷Though I walk in the midst of trouble,
   you preserve my life;
you stretch out your hand against the anger
      of my foes,
   with your right hand you save me.
⁸The Lord will fulfill ⌐his purpose⌐ for me;
   your love, O Lord, endures forever—
   do not abandon the works of your hands.

77 / *Psalm 139*
Wonderfully Made

A CRAFTSMAN IN medieval times would work for months on a special piece that displayed his finest artistic skill. Finally, when the work was finished, he would present it to the craftsmen's guild in hopes of achieving the rank of master. The work was called his masterpiece. In Psalm 139 we see God the master craftsman, lovingly at work on his masterpiece. The psalm can have a profound impact on the way we view ourselves.

 Warming Up to God   Do you think of yourself as God's artwork, his masterpiece? Why or why not? Ask God to help you see yourself through his eyes as you begin this study.

 Read Psalm 139.

Psalm 139

For the director of music. Of David.
A psalm.

¹O Lord, you have searched me
   and you know me.

²You know when I sit and when I rise;
   you perceive my thoughts from afar.
³You discern my going out and my lying
      down;
   you are familiar with all my ways.
⁴Before a word is on my tongue
   you know it completely, O Lord.

⁵You hem me in—behind and before;
   you have laid your hand upon me.
⁶Such knowledge is too wonderful for me,
   too lofty for me to attain.

⁷Where can I go from your Spirit?
   Where can I flee from your presence?
⁸If I go up to the heavens, you are there;
   if I make my bed in the depths,ʲ you are
      there.
⁹If I rise on the wings of the dawn,
   if I settle on the far side of the sea,
¹⁰even there your hand will guide me,
   your right hand will hold me fast.

¹¹If I say, "Surely the darkness will hide me
   and the light become night around me,"
¹²even the darkness will not be dark to you;
   the night will shine like the day,
   for darkness is as light to you.

¹³For you created my inmost being;
   you knit me together in my mother's
      womb.
¹⁴I praise you because I am fearfully and
      wonderfully made;
   your works are wonderful,
   I know that full well.
¹⁵My frame was not hidden from you
   when I was made in the secret place.

When I was woven together in the depths of
      the earth,
¹⁶   your eyes saw my unformed body.
All the days ordained for me
   were written in your book
   before one of them came to be.

¹⁷How precious toᵏ me are your thoughts,
      O God!
   How vast is the sum of them!
¹⁸Were I to count them,
   they would outnumber the grains of sand.
When I awake,
   I am still with you.

¹⁹If only you would slay the wicked, O God!
   Away from me, you bloodthirsty men!
²⁰They speak of you with evil intent;
   your adversaries misuse your name.
²¹Do I not hate those who hate you, O Lᴏʀᴅ,
   and abhor those who rise up against you?
²²I have nothing but hatred for them;
   I count them my enemies.

²³Search me, O God, and know my heart;
   test me and know my anxious thoughts.
²⁴See if there is any offensive way in me,
   and lead me in the way everlasting.

ʲ8 Hebrew *Sheol*   ᵏ17 Or *concerning*

Discovering the Word 1. According to the psalmist, what specific things does the Lord know about us (vv. 1–6)? **2.** The psalmist declares that God's knowledge of him is wonderful (v. 6). Yet why do you think he also feels an urge to flee from God's presence (vv. 7–12)? **3.** What words are used to describe God's activity and artistry in making us (vv. 13–16)?

Applying the Word 1. How do you hide your true self from God? **2.** When do you hide your true self from others? **3.** How does this psalm help you to feel more loved and valued by God?

Responding in Prayer Take time to thank God for the fact that you are "fearfully and wonderfully made." Put verses 23–24 in your own words and express them to God in prayer.

Psalms 140—141

Psalm 140

For the director of music. A psalm
of David.

¹Rescue me, O Lᴏʀᴅ, from evil men;
   protect me from men of violence,
²who devise evil plans in their hearts
   and stir up war every day.

³They make their tongues as sharp as a
      serpent's;
   the poison of vipers is on their lips.   *Selah*

⁴Keep me, O Lᴏʀᴅ, from the hands of the
      wicked;
   protect me from men of violence
   who plan to trip my feet.
⁵Proud men have hidden a snare for me;

they have spread out the cords of their net
and have set traps for me along my path.
                                        Selah

⁶O Lᴏʀᴅ, I say to you, "You are my God."
    Hear, O Lᴏʀᴅ, my cry for mercy.
⁷O Sovereign Lᴏʀᴅ, my strong deliverer,
    who shields my head in the day of battle—
⁸do not grant the wicked their desires, O Lᴏʀᴅ;
    do not let their plans succeed,
    or they will become proud.   *Selah*

⁹Let the heads of those who surround me
    be covered with the trouble their lips have
        caused.
¹⁰Let burning coals fall upon them;
    may they be thrown into the fire,
    into miry pits, never to rise.
¹¹Let slanderers not be established in the land;
    may disaster hunt down men of violence.

¹²I know that the Lᴏʀᴅ secures justice for the
        poor
    and upholds the cause of the needy.
¹³Surely the righteous will praise your name
    and the upright will live before you.

Psalm 141

A psalm of David.

¹O Lᴏʀᴅ, I call to you; come quickly to me.
    Hear my voice when I call to you.
²May my prayer be set before you like incense;
    may the lifting up of my hands be like the
        evening sacrifice.

³Set a guard over my mouth, O Lᴏʀᴅ;
    keep watch over the door of my lips.
⁴Let not my heart be drawn to what is evil,
    to take part in wicked deeds
with men who are evildoers;
    let me not eat of their delicacies.

⁵Let a righteous man¹ strike me—it is a
        kindness;
    let him rebuke me—it is oil on my head.
    My head will not refuse it.

Yet my prayer is ever against the deeds of
        evildoers;
⁶   their rulers will be thrown down from the
        cliffs,
    and the wicked will learn that my words
        were well spoken.
⁷⌊They will say,⌋ "As one plows and breaks up
        the earth,
    so our bones have been scattered at the
        mouth of the grave.ᵐ"

⁸But my eyes are fixed on you, O Sovereign
        Lᴏʀᴅ;
    in you I take refuge—do not give me over
        to death.
⁹Keep me from the snares they have laid for
        me,
    from the traps set by evildoers.
¹⁰Let the wicked fall into their own nets,
    while I pass by in safety.

_____
¹ 5 Or *Let the Righteous One*   ᵐ 7 Hebrew *Sheol*

78 / *Psalm 142*
A Prayer of Desperation

"IT'S CANCER." THE words shattered the tension in the room. I had been waiting with my friend to find out the results of her biopsy. My friend was calm. She was probably too stunned to feel. I, however, felt desperate. I wanted to scream "No!" I felt frightened, powerless, outraged. Desperation is an experience of extreme need and helplessness. We feel desperate when life's circumstances overpower us. We feel desperate when our well-being is threatened and we feel unable to affect the outcome. This psalm gives voice to our experiences of desperation.

 Warming Up to God Think of a time when you felt desperate. What phrases or images would you use to describe the situation you faced?

 Read Psalm 142.

Psalm 142

A *maskil*[n] of David. When he was in the cave. A prayer.

[1]I cry aloud to the LORD;
  I lift up my voice to the LORD
    for mercy.
[2]I pour out my complaint before him;
  before him I tell my trouble.

[3]When my spirit grows faint within
    me,
  it is you who know my way.
 In the path where I walk
  men have hidden a snare for me.
[4]Look to my right and see;
  no one is concerned for me.
 I have no refuge;
  no one cares for my life.

[5]I cry to you, O LORD;
  I say, "You are my refuge,
  my portion in the land of the
    living."
[6]Listen to my cry,
  for I am in desperate need;
 rescue me from those who pursue me,
  for they are too strong for me.
[7]Set me free from my prison,
  that I may praise your name.

Then the righteous will gather
    about me
  because of your goodness to me.

[n]Title: Probably a literary or musical term

Discovering the Word 1. This psalm was written by David when he was in a cave, perhaps when he was hiding from Saul. How would you describe David's emotional state? 2. What phrases and images does David use to describe the situation he faces (vv. 3, 6 and 7)? 3. What contrast do you see between David's experiences with people and his experience with God? 4. How would you compare his view of his personal power with his view of God's power?

Applying the Word 1. What is the significance of the contrast between our power and God's power when we feel desperate? 2. Are you able to pray with this kind of directness and urgency in times of personal need? Why or why not?

Responding in Prayer Write a psalm of your own, allowing yourself to cry out to God on your own behalf or on behalf of someone else who faces a desperate situation.

---

79 / *Psalm 143*
Asking for Guidance

"THE WAY I was taught to pray," explained Sue, "was to list for God the things I wanted done. I would give God a long list of 'requests' that were really thinly disguised expectations or demands. It amazes me now, but I really felt I knew what everyone needed and that my job was to bring these needs to God's attention. I would decide what needed to be done and God would do it. Sound backwards? I think so. I was surprised to discover a humbler way to pray. I learned to say, 'show me your will today and give me the power to carry it out.' I stopped telling God what to do and started to ask for guidance and help. Now I pray with an awareness that I am talking to my Creator, who knows me better than I know me, who loves me more than I love me, and who is personally involved in my life."

Warming Up to God What fears might keep you from seeking to know and to do God's will?

Read Psalm 143.

Psalm 143

A psalm of David.

¹O LORD, hear my prayer,
    listen to my cry for mercy;
  in your faithfulness and righteousness
    come to my relief.
²Do not bring your servant into judgment,
    for no one living is righteous before you.

³The enemy pursues me,
    he crushes me to the ground;
  he makes me dwell in darkness
    like those long dead.
⁴So my spirit grows faint within me;
    my heart within me is dismayed.

⁵I remember the days of long ago;
    I meditate on all your works
  and consider what your hands have done.
⁶I spread out my hands to you;
    my soul thirsts for you like a parched land.
                                                    Selah

⁷Answer me quickly, O LORD;

my spirit fails.
  Do not hide your face from me
    or I will be like those who go down to the
      pit.
⁸Let the morning bring me word of your
      unfailing love,
    for I have put my trust in you.
  Show me the way I should go,
    for to you I lift up my soul.
⁹Rescue me from my enemies, O LORD,
    for I hide myself in you.
¹⁰Teach me to do your will,
    for you are my God;
  may your good Spirit
    lead me on level ground.

¹¹For your name's sake, O LORD, preserve my
      life;
    in your righteousness, bring me out of
      trouble.
¹²In your unfailing love, silence my enemies;
    destroy all my foes,
    for I am your servant.

 Discovering the Word 1. What specifically does the psalmist say he longs for in this text (vv. 1, 7)? 2. What does the psalmist fear might happen (vv. 2, 7)? 3. Why does the psalmist need God's help (vv. 3–6)? 4. The psalmist asks for knowledge of God's will and the power to carry it out. What specifically does he ask for (vv. 8–12)? 5. The psalmist reminds God: "I have put my trust in you. . . . To you I lift up my soul. . . . I hide myself in you" (vv. 8–9). What do you think the psalmist is trying to communicate to God?

 Applying the Word 1. In what area of life do you feel a need for knowledge of God's will? 2. What knowledge of God's will have you received, but are hesitant and needing power to carry out?

Responding in Prayer What guidance would you like to ask God for today?

Psalm 144

Psalm 144

Of David.

¹Praise be to the LORD my Rock,
    who trains my hands for war,
    my fingers for battle.
²He is my loving God and my fortress,
    my stronghold and my deliverer,
  my shield, in whom I take refuge,
    who subdues peoples*ᵒ* under me.

³O LORD, what is man that you care for him,
    the son of man that you think of him?

⁴Man is like a breath;
    his days are like a fleeting shadow.

⁵Part your heavens, O LORD, and come down;
    touch the mountains, so that they smoke.
⁶Send forth lightning and scatter ⌊the enemies⌋;
    shoot your arrows and rout them.
⁷Reach down your hand from on high;
    deliver me and rescue me
  from the mighty waters,
    from the hands of foreigners

ᵒ2 Many manuscripts of the Masoretic Text, Dead Sea Scrolls, Aquila, Jerome and Syriac; most manuscripts of the Masoretic Text subdues my people

8whose mouths are full of lies,
　　whose right hands are deceitful.

9I will sing a new song to you, O God;
　　on the ten-stringed lyre I will make music
　　　to you,
10to the One who gives victory to kings,
　　who delivers his servant David from the
　　　deadly sword.

11Deliver me and rescue me
　　from the hands of foreigners
whose mouths are full of lies,
　　whose right hands are deceitful.

12Then our sons in their youth
　　will be like well-nurtured plants,

and our daughters will be like pillars
　　carved to adorn a palace.
13Our barns will be filled
　　with every kind of provision.
Our sheep will increase by thousands,
　　by tens of thousands in our fields;
14　our oxen will draw heavy loads.*p*
There will be no breaching of walls,
　　no going into captivity,
　　no cry of distress in our streets.

15Blessed are the people of whom this is true;
　　blessed are the people whose God is the
　　　Lord.

p14 Or our chieftains will be firmly established

80 / *Psalm 145*
Relying on God

PEOPLE WHO HAVE experienced repeated disappointments with parents or other significant people can develop an image of an unreliable God. He is seen as a God who cannot be counted on. He makes promises he may not keep. He may be loving one day and unaccountably angry the next. People who have experienced unreliable parents may ask: "How do I know God will keep his promises? How do I know he listens to me? How do I know he will answer me or help me?" The image of an unreliable God stands in stark contrast to biblical images of God. The God of the Bible is the Faithful One, the Rock, the Fortress. He is the same yesterday, today and forever.

 Warming Up to God　Think of a person whom you see as reliable. Describe the person and your response to his or her reliability.

 Read Psalm 145.

Psalm 145*q*

A psalm of praise. Of David.

1I will exalt you, my God the King;
　　I will praise your name for ever and ever.
2Every day I will praise you
　　and extol your name for ever and ever.

3Great is the Lord and most worthy of praise;
　　his greatness no one can fathom.
4One generation will commend your works to
　　another;
　　they will tell of your mighty acts.
5They will speak of the glorious splendor of
　　your majesty,
　　and I will meditate on your wonderful
　　works.*r*

6They will tell of the power of your awesome
　　works,
　　and I will proclaim your great deeds.
7They will celebrate your abundant goodness
　　and joyfully sing of your righteousness.

8The Lord is gracious and compassionate,
　　slow to anger and rich in love.
9The Lord is good to all;
　　he has compassion on all he has made.
10All you have made will praise you, O Lord;
　　your saints will extol you.
11They will tell of the glory of your kingdom
　　and speak of your might,
12so that all men may know of your mighty acts

*q*This psalm is an acrostic poem, the verses of which (including verse 13b) begin with the successive letters of the Hebrew alphabet. *r5* Dead Sea Scrolls and Syriac (see also Septuagint); Masoretic Text *On the glorious splendor of your majesty / and on your wonderful works I will meditate*

and the glorious splendor of your kingdom.
¹³Your kingdom is an everlasting kingdom,
and your dominion endures through all
generations.

The Lord is faithful to all his promises
and loving toward all he has made.ˢ
¹⁴The Lord upholds all those who fall
and lifts up all who are bowed down.
¹⁵The eyes of all look to you,
and you give them their food at the proper
time.
¹⁶You open your hand
and satisfy the desires of every living thing.

¹⁷The Lord is righteous in all his ways

and loving toward all he has made.
¹⁸The Lord is near to all who call on him,
to all who call on him in truth.
¹⁹He fulfills the desires of those who fear him;
he hears their cry and saves them.
²⁰The Lord watches over all who love him,
but all the wicked he will destroy.
²¹My mouth will speak in praise of the Lord.
Let every creature praise his holy name
for ever and ever.

ˢ13 One manuscript of the Masoretic Text, Dead Sea Scrolls and Syriac
(see also Septuagint); most manuscripts of the Masoretic Text do not
have the last two lines of verse 13.

 Discovering the Word 1. What descriptive words and phrases are used about God in this prayer? 2. What phrases suggest that God is reliable? 3. How does God help those who are in need (vv. 14–20)? 4. What image of God comes through to you most clearly?

 Applying the Word 1. How does the picture of God here compare or contrast with your image of God's reliability? 2. Why is it important for you to know that God is reliable?

 Responding in Prayer Offer God your thanks for his faithfulness.

81 / *Psalm 146*
The Source of Hope

"MY OWN MOM and Dad failed me," Linda said in her support group meeting. "Then my marriage fell apart. And then my health fell apart. Life has always been hard. I don't see why I should expect it to ever get any better. If anything, it will probably get worse. How is it possible for me to have hope?"

The Bible teaches that there is more to the story of our lives than our experiences of loss and disappointment. The planet may be fallen, but it is not forsaken by God. God is actively present in our lives, bringing gifts of life and joy into the midst of our darkness. We can dare to hope because of who God is.

 Warming Up to God In what area of life is it hard for you to find hope?

 Read Psalm 146.

Psalm 146

¹Praise the Lord.ᶦ

Praise the Lord, O my soul.
² I will praise the Lord all my life;
I will sing praise to my God as long as I
live.

³Do not put your trust in princes,
in mortal men, who cannot save.

⁴When their spirit departs, they return to the
ground;
on that very day their plans come to
nothing.

⁵Blessed is he whose help is the God of Jacob,
whose hope is in the Lord his God,
⁶the Maker of heaven and earth,

ᶦ1 Hebrew *Hallelu Yah*; also in verse 10

the sea, and everything in them—
the LORD, who remains faithful forever.
⁷He upholds the cause of the oppressed
and gives food to the hungry.
The LORD sets prisoners free,
⁸ the LORD gives sight to the blind,
the LORD lifts up those who are bowed down,
the LORD loves the righteous.

⁹The LORD watches over the alien
and sustains the fatherless and the widow,
but he frustrates the ways of the wicked.

¹⁰The LORD reigns forever,
your God, O Zion, for all generations.

Praise the LORD.

Discovering the Word 1. How does this psalm contrast the experience of hoping in God with the experience of hoping in people? 2. The psalmist mentions eight kinds of circumstances that might seem hopeless. List these situations/conditions and the reasons why they might seem hopeless. 3. Describe how God responds to people in each of these situations. 4. What do these responses from God to people in hopeless situations suggest to you about God's character?

Applying the Word 1. Which of the eight images of hopelessness do you most strongly relate to at this time? Explain. 2. Take a few minutes and allow yourself to picture God responding to you in the way this text describes God's response. What thoughts and feelings do you have in response to this image of God's care for you?

Responding in Prayer What would you like to say to God who is the source of your hope?

Psalm 147

Psalm 147

¹Praise the LORD. ᵘ

How good it is to sing praises to our God,
how pleasant and fitting to praise him!

²The LORD builds up Jerusalem;
he gathers the exiles of Israel.
³He heals the brokenhearted
and binds up their wounds.

⁴He determines the number of the stars
and calls them each by name.
⁵Great is our Lord and mighty in power;
his understanding has no limit.
⁶The LORD sustains the humble
but casts the wicked to the ground.

⁷Sing to the LORD with thanksgiving;
make music to our God on the harp.
⁸He covers the sky with clouds;
he supplies the earth with rain
and makes grass grow on the hills.
⁹He provides food for the cattle
and for the young ravens when they call.

¹⁰His pleasure is not in the strength of the
horse,

nor his delight in the legs of a man;
¹¹the LORD delights in those who fear him,
who put their hope in his unfailing love.

¹²Extol the LORD, O Jerusalem;
praise your God, O Zion,
¹³for he strengthens the bars of your gates
and blesses your people within you.
¹⁴He grants peace to your borders
and satisfies you with the finest of wheat.

¹⁵He sends his command to the earth;
his word runs swiftly.
¹⁶He spreads the snow like wool
and scatters the frost like ashes.
¹⁷He hurls down his hail like pebbles.
Who can withstand his icy blast?
¹⁸He sends his word and melts them;
he stirs up his breezes, and the waters flow.

¹⁹He has revealed his word to Jacob,
his laws and decrees to Israel.
²⁰He has done this for no other nation;
they do not know his laws.

Praise the LORD.

ᵘ1 Hebrew *Hallelu Yah*; also in verse 20

82 / *Psalm 148*
A Symphony of Praise

THIS CALL TO praise, if heeded by all of creation, would make for quite a symphony of praise. Perhaps it would sound more like a cacophony than a symphony. Judging from the noises that all of God's creatures make individually, it boggles the mind (never mind the eardrums!) to imagine the concert called for in Psalm 148. Its location at the end of the book suggests that Psalm 148 is meant to wrap everything up on a high praise note.

 Warming Up to God   Think about an exciting time of corporate praise that you have been a part of. How does seeing others engaged in worship inspire your worship?

 Read Psalm 148.

Psalm 148

¹Praise the LORD. ᵛ

Praise the LORD from the heavens,
    praise him in the heights above.
²Praise him, all his angels,
    praise him, all his heavenly hosts.
³Praise him, sun and moon,
    praise him, all you shining stars.
⁴Praise him, you highest heavens
    and you waters above the skies.
⁵Let them praise the name of the LORD,
    for he commanded and they were created.
⁶He set them in place for ever and ever;
    he gave a decree that will never pass away.

⁷Praise the LORD from the earth,
    you great sea creatures and all ocean
        depths,
⁸lightning and hail, snow and clouds,
    stormy winds that do his bidding,

⁹you mountains and all hills,
    fruit trees and all cedars,
¹⁰wild animals and all cattle,
    small creatures and flying birds,
¹¹kings of the earth and all nations,
    you princes and all rulers on earth,
¹²young men and maidens,
    old men and children.

¹³Let them praise the name of the LORD,
    for his name alone is exalted;
    his splendor is above the earth and the
        heavens.
¹⁴He has raised up for his people a horn, ʷ
    the praise of all his saints,
    of Israel, the people close to his heart.

Praise the LORD.

ᵛ1 Hebrew *Hallelu Yah*; also in verse 14   ʷ14 *Horn* here symbolizes strong one, that is, king.

 Discovering the Word   1. This psalm divides into two six-verse stanzas (vv. 1–6 and 7–12), with a recap that underscores the motivation to praise (vv. 13–14). What two major chorus groups are appealed to here?   2. Within those two major choral divisions, who joins in praising God?   3. Do you see this as mere figurative (symbolic or exaggerated) language used by the psalmist to call all things in heaven and on earth, or is there some way that all the various elements actually praise God?   4. Why praise God at all (vv. 5–6, 13–14)?

Applying the Word   1. What is the closest you have come, this side of heaven, to experiencing a worldwide worship service such as this psalm announces?   2. Do you look forward to heaven when this psalm finds its fulfillment, or does praising God all day long sound boring to you?   3. How does this psalm provide a new or fresh picture of praise for you?

Responding in Prayer   Imagine what it would be like to have every man, woman and child—young and old alike—participating in your church's choir. Pray (and practice) toward that end.

Psalm 149

Psalm 149

¹Praise the LORD.ˣ

Sing to the LORD a new song,
    his praise in the assembly of the saints.
²Let Israel rejoice in their Maker;
    let the people of Zion be glad in their King.
³Let them praise his name with dancing
    and make music to him with tambourine
        and harp.
⁴For the LORD takes delight in his people;
    he crowns the humble with salvation.
⁵Let the saints rejoice in this honor

and sing for joy on their beds.

⁶May the praise of God be in their mouths
    and a double-edged sword in their hands,
⁷to inflict vengeance on the nations
    and punishment on the peoples,
⁸to bind their kings with fetters,
    their nobles with shackles of iron,
⁹to carry out the sentence written against
        them.
    This is the glory of all his saints.

Praise the LORD.

ˣ1 Hebrew *Hallelu Yah*; also in verse 9

83 / *Psalm 150*
Praying Our Praise

ALL PRAYER FINALLY, in one way or another, becomes praise. Psalm 150 is deliberately placed as the concluding prayer of the church's book of prayers. No matter how much we suffer, no matter our doubts—everything finds its way into praise, the final consummating prayer.

Warming Up to God What circumstances or feelings in the last year have, however momentarily, made a praising person out of you? Reflect on that again in joy, celebrating with Christ.

Read Psalm 150.

Psalm 150

¹Praise the LORD.ʸ

Praise God in his sanctuary;
    praise him in his mighty heavens.
²Praise him for his acts of power;
    praise him for his surpassing greatness.
³Praise him with the sounding of the trumpet,
    praise him with the harp and lyre,

⁴praise him with tambourine and dancing,
    praise him with the strings and flute,
⁵praise him with the clash of cymbals,
    praise him with resounding cymbals.

⁶Let everything that has breath praise the LORD.

Praise the LORD.

ʸ1 Hebrew *Hallelu Yah*; also in verse 6

Discovering the Word **1.** How many times is the word *praise* used in the psalm? **2.** Verse 1 tells us *where* the Lord is to be praised. What is the meaning of "in his sanctuary" and "in his mighty heavens"? **3.** Verse 2 tells us *why* he is to be praised. What reasons does the psalmist give? **4.** Verses 3–5 tell us *how* to praise the Lord. As you read these verses, what kind of scene do you imagine?

Applying the Word **1.** Building on verse 2, what reasons can you give for praising God? **2.** There are no shortcuts to praise. We can see this in many psalms that express pain. What difficult circumstances in your life have found their way into praise? **3.** Augustine claimed that a "Christian should be a hallelujah from head to foot." What needs to be done to get to that point?

Responding in Prayer Gather the reflections and insights that have come from your study and turn them into a time of concluding and celebrative praise.

Proverbs

Every year thousands of books published have titles with the same first two words—*How to . . .* By reading these books you can learn how to paint like the old masters, how to get a job, how to get federal grants, a divorce, free publicity, a mortgage or even a nightclub gig. You can read about how to buy a car, a house, a small business or a personal computer. You can become a balloon artist, an astrologer, an athlete, a golfer, a fashion designer, a good dancer, a pilot, a master manipulator, a mechanic or a vampire. Experts out there will make *you* expert at petting a cat, picking lottery numbers, losing five pounds fast, building fences or bearing children.

All these books are offering us *wisdom*—skill in one area or another. Books like these proliferate because we all need wisdom to live successfully. Wisdom brings success and prosperity in our work, in dealings with family and friends, and in our relationship with God. One book of the Bible—the Proverbs of Solomon—specializes in wisdom. It gives us direction and guidance that is practical, concrete, reasonable, wholesome, understandable, shrewd and fruitful. By reading it we gain skill in *all* areas of life.

Where Did the Book of Proverbs Come From?

The book of Proverbs begins with the notice "The Proverbs of Solomon, Son of David, King of Israel." This does not mean, however, that Solomon authored every word of the book. In 1 Kings 4:32 we learn that Solomon "spoke three thousand proverbs." Undoubtedly he composed a substantial number of these proverbs himself. First Kings 4:34 mentions that kings of surrounding nations sent delegations to hear Solomon's wisdom. On the other hand, an exchange of wisdom must have developed between Solomon and those who came to learn from him.

The book of Proverbs reflects this interchange. Approximately three hundred proverbs are labeled "Proverbs of Solomon" in Proverbs 10:1—22:16. Perhaps this section formed the nucleus of the collection. Some years later, King Hezekiah's scribes added about 130 additional Solomonic proverbs, found in Proverbs 25:1—29:27. "Sayings of the Wise" appear in Proverbs 22:17—24:22, followed by "Further Sayings of the Wise" in Proverbs 24:23–34. Then come "Sayings of Agur" in Proverbs 30, "Sayings of King Lemuel" in Proverbs 31:1–9, and the acrostic poem on the virtuous wife in Proverbs 31:10–31. Clearly, the book of Proverbs as it comes to us contains a broad collection of proverbs, from a diversity of wise men and at least one woman who is identified as King Lemuel's mother.

Comparing the book of Proverbs with other ancient Near Eastern wisdom literature sheds light on how the collection arose in the first place. In order to instruct their sons, court officials in many lands would pull together the wisdom they had acquired in a lifetime of diplomatic service. From Egypt we have at least ten such collections, including *The Instruction of Ka-gem-ni* and *The Instruction of Prince Hor-dedef*, dating from the Old Kingdom (2686–2160 B.C.), and the *The Instruction of Onchsheshonqy* in the fourth or fifth century B.C. An Akkadian translation of a Sumerian original entitled *The Instructions of Shurruppak* dates from approximately 1300 B.C. Ahiquar, who served as vizier to the Assyrian kings Sennacherib and Esarhaddon in the seventh century B.C., left the *Words of Ahiquar*. The Proverbs of Solomon, Son of David, King of Israel takes its place alongside these and other collections. Prophetic authorities added Solomon's proverbs to the canon of Scripture. A manual of instruction for the king's son became available to all of God's children.

What Will Solomon's Proverbs Do for Me?
    Solomon tells us the purpose of the collection in Proverbs 1:2–6:
        For attaining wisdom and discipline;
            for understanding words of insight;
        for acquiring a disciplined and prudent life,
            doing what is right and just and fair;
        for giving prudence to the simple,
            knowledge and discretion to the young—
        let the wise listen and add to their learning,
            and let the discerning get guidance—
        for understanding proverbs and parables,
            the sayings and riddles of the wise.

Outline

1/ Proverbs 6:1–19 ——————————— Bad Words

2/ Proverbs 7 ————————————— The Simple

3/ Proverbs 9 ————————————— Two Dinner Invitations

4/ Proverbs 10 ———————————— Good Words

5/ Proverbs 13—14 ———————————— Finding Wisdom

6/ Proverbs 15—16 ———————————— Prayer

7/ Proverbs 17—18 ———————————— Avoiding the Fool

8/ Proverbs 19 ———————————— Giving

9/ Proverbs 21 ———————————— Planning the Future

10/ Proverbs 24:23–34 ——————————— The Sluggard

11/ Proverbs 27 ———————————— Friends

12/ Proverbs 30 ———————————— Wealth & Poverty

Proverbs 1—5

1 The proverbs of Solomon son of David, king of Israel:

2for attaining wisdom and discipline;
  for understanding words of insight;
3for acquiring a disciplined and prudent life,
  doing what is right and just and fair;
4for giving prudence to the simple,
  knowledge and discretion to the young—
5let the wise listen and add to their learning,
  and let the discerning get guidance—
6for understanding proverbs and parables,
  the sayings and riddles of the wise.

7The fear of the LORD is the beginning of
    knowledge,
  but fools*a* despise wisdom and discipline.

8Listen, my son, to your father's instruction
  and do not forsake your mother's teaching.
9They will be a garland to grace your head
  and a chain to adorn your neck.

10My son, if sinners entice you,
  do not give in to them.
11If they say, "Come along with us;
  let's lie in wait for someone's blood,
  let's waylay some harmless soul;
12let's swallow them alive, like the grave,*b*
  and whole, like those who go down to the
    pit;
13we will get all sorts of valuable things
  and fill our houses with plunder;
14throw in your lot with us,
  and we will share a common purse"—
15my son, do not go along with them,
  do not set foot on their paths;
16for their feet rush into sin,
  they are swift to shed blood.
17How useless to spread a net
  in full view of all the birds!
18These men lie in wait for their own blood;
  they waylay only themselves!
19Such is the end of all who go after ill-gotten
    gain;
  it takes away the lives of those who get it.

20Wisdom calls aloud in the street,
  she raises her voice in the public squares;
21at the head of the noisy streets*c* she cries
    out,

in the gateways of the city she makes her
    speech:

22"How long will you simple ones*d* love your
    simple ways?
  How long will mockers delight in mockery
  and fools hate knowledge?
23If you had responded to my rebuke,
  I would have poured out my heart to you
  and made my thoughts known to you.
24But since you rejected me when I called
  and no one gave heed when I stretched out
    my hand,
25since you ignored all my advice
  and would not accept my rebuke,
26I in turn will laugh at your disaster;
  I will mock when calamity overtakes you—
27when calamity overtakes you like a storm,
  when disaster sweeps over you like a
    whirlwind,
  when distress and trouble overwhelm you.

28"Then they will call to me but I will not
    answer;
  they will look for me but will not find me.
29Since they hated knowledge
  and did not choose to fear the LORD,
30since they would not accept my advice
  and spurned my rebuke,
31they will eat the fruit of their ways
  and be filled with the fruit of their
    schemes.
32For the waywardness of the simple will kill
    them,
  and the complacency of fools will destroy
    them;
33but whoever listens to me will live in safety
  and be at ease, without fear of harm."

2 My son, if you accept my words
  and store up my commands within you,
2turning your ear to wisdom
  and applying your heart to understanding,
3and if you call out for insight
  and cry aloud for understanding,
4and if you look for it as for silver
  and search for it as for hidden treasure,

a7 The Hebrew words rendered *fool* in Proverbs, and often elsewhere
in the Old Testament, denote one who is morally deficient.
b12 Hebrew *Sheol*   *c21* Hebrew; Septuagint / *on the tops of the walls*
d22 The Hebrew word rendered *simple* in Proverbs generally denotes
one without moral direction and inclined to evil.

⁵then you will understand the fear of the LORD
and find the knowledge of God.
⁶For the LORD gives wisdom,
and from his mouth come knowledge and
understanding.
⁷He holds victory in store for the upright,
he is a shield to those whose walk is
blameless,
⁸for he guards the course of the just
and protects the way of his faithful ones.

⁹Then you will understand what is right and
just
and fair—every good path.
¹⁰For wisdom will enter your heart,
and knowledge will be pleasant to your
soul.
¹¹Discretion will protect you,
and understanding will guard you.

¹²Wisdom will save you from the ways of
wicked men,
from men whose words are perverse,
¹³who leave the straight paths
to walk in dark ways,
¹⁴who delight in doing wrong
and rejoice in the perverseness of evil,
¹⁵whose paths are crooked
and who are devious in their ways.

¹⁶It will save you also from the adulteress,
from the wayward wife with her seductive
words,
¹⁷who has left the partner of her youth
and ignored the covenant she made before
God.*e*
¹⁸For her house leads down to death
and her paths to the spirits of the dead.
¹⁹None who go to her return
or attain the paths of life.

²⁰Thus you will walk in the ways of good men
and keep to the paths of the righteous.
²¹For the upright will live in the land,
and the blameless will remain in it;
²²but the wicked will be cut off from the land,
and the unfaithful will be torn from it.

3 My son, do not forget my teaching,
but keep my commands in your heart,
²for they will prolong your life many
years
and bring you prosperity.

³Let love and faithfulness never leave you;

bind them around your neck,
write them on the tablet of your heart.
⁴Then you will win favor and a good name
in the sight of God and man.

⁵Trust in the LORD with all your heart
and lean not on your own understanding;
⁶in all your ways acknowledge him,
and he will make your paths straight.*f*

⁷Do not be wise in your own eyes;
fear the LORD and shun evil.
⁸This will bring health to your body
and nourishment to your bones.

⁹Honor the LORD with your wealth,
with the firstfruits of all your crops;
¹⁰then your barns will be filled to overflowing,
and your vats will brim over with new
wine.

¹¹My son, do not despise the LORD's discipline
and do not resent his rebuke,
¹²because the LORD disciplines those he loves,
as a father*g* the son he delights in.

¹³Blessed is the man who finds wisdom,
the man who gains understanding,
¹⁴for she is more profitable than silver
and yields better returns than gold.
¹⁵She is more precious than rubies;
nothing you desire can compare with her.
¹⁶Long life is in her right hand;
in her left hand are riches and honor.
¹⁷Her ways are pleasant ways,
and all her paths are peace.
¹⁸She is a tree of life to those who embrace her;
those who lay hold of her will be blessed.

¹⁹By wisdom the LORD laid the earth's
foundations,
by understanding he set the heavens in
place;
²⁰by his knowledge the deeps were divided,
and the clouds let drop the dew.

²¹My son, preserve sound judgment and
discernment,
do not let them out of your sight;
²²they will be life for you,
an ornament to grace your neck.
²³Then you will go on your way in safety,
and your foot will not stumble;

e17 Or covenant of her God   *f6 Or will direct your paths*
g12 Hebrew; Septuagint / and he punishes

²⁴when you lie down, you will not be afraid;
  when you lie down, your sleep will be
    sweet.
²⁵Have no fear of sudden disaster
  or of the ruin that overtakes the wicked,
²⁶for the LORD will be your confidence
  and will keep your foot from being snared.

²⁷Do not withhold good from those who
    deserve it,
  when it is in your power to act.
²⁸Do not say to your neighbor,
  "Come back later; I'll give it tomorrow"—
  when you now have it with you.

²⁹Do not plot harm against your neighbor,
  who lives trustfully near you.
³⁰Do not accuse a man for no reason—
  when he has done you no harm.

³¹Do not envy a violent man
  or choose any of his ways,
³²for the LORD detests a perverse man
  but takes the upright into his confidence.

³³The LORD's curse is on the house of the
    wicked,
  but he blesses the home of the righteous.
³⁴He mocks proud mockers
  but gives grace to the humble.
³⁵The wise inherit honor,
  but fools he holds up to shame.

4 Listen, my sons, to a father's
    instruction;
  pay attention and gain understanding.
²I give you sound learning,
  so do not forsake my teaching.
³When I was a boy in my father's house,
  still tender, and an only child of my
    mother,
⁴he taught me and said,
  "Lay hold of my words with all your heart;
  keep my commands and you will live.
⁵Get wisdom, get understanding;
  do not forget my words or swerve from
    them.
⁶Do not forsake wisdom, and she will protect
    you;
  love her, and she will watch over you.
⁷Wisdom is supreme; therefore get wisdom.
  Though it cost all you have,ʰ get
    understanding.

⁸Esteem her, and she will exalt you;
  embrace her, and she will honor you.
⁹She will set a garland of grace on your head
  and present you with a crown of
    splendor."

¹⁰Listen, my son, accept what I say,
  and the years of your life will be many.
¹¹I guide you in the way of wisdom
  and lead you along straight paths.
¹²When you walk, your steps will not be
    hampered;
  when you run, you will not stumble.
¹³Hold on to instruction, do not let it go;
  guard it well, for it is your life.
¹⁴Do not set foot on the path of the wicked
  or walk in the way of evil men.
¹⁵Avoid it, do not travel on it;
  turn from it and go on your way.
¹⁶For they cannot sleep till they do evil;
  they are robbed of slumber till they make
    someone fall.
¹⁷They eat the bread of wickedness
  and drink the wine of violence.

¹⁸The path of the righteous is like the first
    gleam of dawn,
  shining ever brighter till the full light of
    day.
¹⁹But the way of the wicked is like deep
    darkness;
  they do not know what makes them
    stumble.

²⁰My son, pay attention to what I say;
  listen closely to my words.
²¹Do not let them out of your sight,
  keep them within your heart;
²²for they are life to those who find them
  and health to a man's whole body.
²³Above all else, guard your heart,
  for it is the wellspring of life.
²⁴Put away perversity from your mouth;
  keep corrupt talk far from your lips.
²⁵Let your eyes look straight ahead,
  fix your gaze directly before you.
²⁶Make levelⁱ paths for your feet
  and take only ways that are firm.
²⁷Do not swerve to the right or the left;
  keep your foot from evil.

ʰ7 Or *Whatever else you get*   ⁱ26 Or *Consider the*

5 My son, pay attention to my wisdom,
listen well to my words of insight,
  ²that you may maintain discretion
and your lips may preserve knowledge.
³For the lips of an adulteress drip honey,
and her speech is smoother than oil;
⁴but in the end she is bitter as gall,
sharp as a double-edged sword.
⁵Her feet go down to death;
her steps lead straight to the grave.ʲ
⁶She gives no thought to the way of life;
her paths are crooked, but she knows it
not.

⁷Now then, my sons, listen to me;
do not turn aside from what I say.
⁸Keep to a path far from her,
do not go near the door of her house,
⁹lest you give your best strength to others
and your years to one who is cruel,
¹⁰lest strangers feast on your wealth
and your toil enrich another man's house.
¹¹At the end of your life you will groan,
when your flesh and body are spent.
¹²You will say, "How I hated discipline!
How my heart spurned correction!
¹³I would not obey my teachers
or listen to my instructors.

¹⁴I have come to the brink of utter ruin
in the midst of the whole assembly."

¹⁵Drink water from your own cistern,
running water from your own well.
¹⁶Should your springs overflow in the streets,
your streams of water in the public
squares?
¹⁷Let them be yours alone,
never to be shared with strangers.
¹⁸May your fountain be blessed,
and may you rejoice in the wife of your
youth.
¹⁹A loving doe, a graceful deer—
may her breasts satisfy you always,
may you ever be captivated by her love.
²⁰Why be captivated, my son, by an adulteress?
Why embrace the bosom of another man's
wife?

²¹For a man's ways are in full view of the LORD,
and he examines all his paths.
²²The evil deeds of a wicked man ensnare him;
the cords of his sin hold him fast.
²³He will die for lack of discipline,
led astray by his own great folly.

j5 Hebrew *Sheol*

1 / *Proverbs 6:1–19*
Bad Words

A CHILDHOOD TAUNT says, "Sticks and stones may break my bones, but words will never hurt me." The sentiment may be brave, but we know from painful memory that words can be exceedingly painful. Solomon's proverbs speak straightforwardly of the harm that words can work—harm when they are spoken to us, by us or about us. And for all their power to work evil, bad words can be surprisingly (and disconcertingly) pleasant to hear or to speak! The world is awash with bad words. The wise man or woman knows how to recognize them, not only so they can purge bad words from their own speech, but also to escape the menace of bad words from others.

 Warming Up to God   How have your words betrayed you this week—through malicious talk, gossip, sarcasm, rudeness or in other ways? Ask God to make you open to discovering how he wants you to talk.

 Read Proverbs 6:1–19.

6 My son, if you have put up security for
your neighbor,
if you have struck hands in pledge for
another,
  ²if you have been trapped by what you said,

ensnared by the words of your mouth,
  ³then do this, my son, to free yourself,
since you have fallen into your neighbor's
hands:
Go and humble yourself;

press your plea with your neighbor!
⁴Allow no sleep to your eyes,
  no slumber to your eyelids.
⁵Free yourself, like a gazelle from the hand of
    the hunter,
  like a bird from the snare of the fowler.

⁶Go to the ant, you sluggard;
  consider its ways and be wise!
⁷It has no commander,
  no overseer or ruler,
⁸yet it stores its provisions in summer
  and gathers its food at harvest.

⁹How long will you lie there, you sluggard?
  When will you get up from your sleep?
¹⁰A little sleep, a little slumber,
  a little folding of the hands to rest—
¹¹and poverty will come on you like a bandit
  and scarcity like an armed man. *ᵏ*

¹²A scoundrel and villain,
  who goes about with a corrupt mouth,

¹³ who winks with his eye,
  signals with his feet
  and motions with his fingers,
¹⁴ who plots evil with deceit in his heart—
  he always stirs up dissension.
¹⁵Therefore disaster will overtake him in an
    instant;
  he will suddenly be destroyed—without
    remedy.

¹⁶There are six things the LORD hates,
  seven that are detestable to him:
¹⁷   haughty eyes,
    a lying tongue,
    hands that shed innocent blood,
¹⁸   a heart that devises wicked schemes,
    feet that are quick to rush into evil,
¹⁹   a false witness who pours out lies
    and a man who stirs up dissension
      among brothers.

ᵏ11 Or like a vagrant / and scarcity like a beggar

 Discovering the Word 1. What words and phrases are used to describe the effects of bad words (vv. 2, 12, 14–15, 17–19)? 2. Evil communication can occur without a word being spoken (vv. 12–14). 3. Why do you think a mischief-maker communicates in that way? 4. Why is *receiving* that kind of communication dangerous to you? 5. How are bad words a part of the seven things that are "detestable" to the Lord?

Applying the Word 1. Like smog, bad words are difficult to escape when they're "in the air." What can you do to reduce your exposure to such words in the coming weeks? 2. How can you resist adding to the pollution?

Responding in Prayer Bad words stir up dissention. Pray that your words will build unity.

Proverbs 6:20–35

²⁰My son, keep your father's commands
  and do not forsake your mother's teaching.
²¹Bind them upon your heart forever;
  fasten them around your neck.
²²When you walk, they will guide you;
  when you sleep, they will watch over you;
  when you awake, they will speak to you.
²³For these commands are a lamp,
  this teaching is a light,
  and the corrections of discipline
  are the way to life,
²⁴keeping you from the immoral woman,
  from the smooth tongue of the wayward
    wife.

²⁵Do not lust in your heart after her beauty
  or let her captivate you with her eyes,
²⁶for the prostitute reduces you to a loaf of
    bread,
  and the adulteress preys upon your very
    life.
²⁷Can a man scoop fire into his lap
  without his clothes being burned?
²⁸Can a man walk on hot coals
  without his feet being scorched?
²⁹So is he who sleeps with another man's wife;
  no one who touches her will go
    unpunished.

³⁰Men do not despise a thief if he steals

to satisfy his hunger when he is starving.
³¹Yet if he is caught, he must pay sevenfold,
    though it costs him all the wealth of his
    house.
³²But a man who commits adultery lacks
    judgment;
    whoever does so destroys himself.

³³Blows and disgrace are his lot,
    and his shame will never be wiped away;
³⁴for jealousy arouses a husband's fury,
    and he will show no mercy when he takes
    revenge.
³⁵He will not accept any compensation;
    he will refuse the bribe, however great it is.

2 / *Proverbs 7*
The Simple

AS P. T. BARNUM was fond of saying, "A sucker is born every minute." The book of Proverbs agrees! Proverbs teaches through images and metaphors like that of the simple young man. The tale of his seduction serves as a concrete example of the way in which folly can capture a simple-minded person. From Solomon's point of view, every one of us is born "simple"—that is, gullible, credulous, naive. But while Barnum saw human gullibility as an opportunity for profit, the proverbs see the condition as a character weakness to be corrected. All around us people appeal to our gullibility in one area or another. If we're to escape with our money, health and integrity intact, we need to develop what the proverbs call *prudence*. The first practical step to wisdom is to identify the simpleton in ourselves. The proverbs in this study are a mirror which lets us see where and how we are naive. And more than that, they will set us on the road to wisdom.

Warming Up to God All of us would agree that young children are naive or simple in all areas of life. But all of us *remain* naive or simple in some areas. In what way might this be true of you?

Read Proverbs 7.

7 My son, keep my words
    and store up my commands within you.
    ²Keep my commands and you will live;
    guard my teachings as the apple of your
    eye.
³Bind them on your fingers;
    write them on the tablet of your heart.
⁴Say to wisdom, "You are my sister,"
    and call understanding your kinsman;
⁵they will keep you from the adulteress,
    from the wayward wife with her seductive
    words.

⁶At the window of my house
    I looked out through the lattice.
⁷I saw among the simple,
    I noticed among the young men,
    a youth who lacked judgment.
⁸He was going down the street near her
    corner,
    walking along in the direction of her house
⁹at twilight, as the day was fading,
    as the dark of night set in.

¹⁰Then out came a woman to meet him,
    dressed like a prostitute and with crafty
    intent.
¹¹(She is loud and defiant,
    her feet never stay at home;
¹²now in the street, now in the squares,
    at every corner she lurks.)
¹³She took hold of him and kissed him
    and with a brazen face she said:

¹⁴"I have fellowship offerings¹ at home;
    today I fulfilled my vows.
¹⁵So I came out to meet you;
    I looked for you and have found you!
¹⁶I have covered my bed
    with colored linens from Egypt.
¹⁷I have perfumed my bed
    with myrrh, aloes and cinnamon.
¹⁸Come, let's drink deep of love till morning;
    let's enjoy ourselves with love!
¹⁹My husband is not at home;
    he has gone on a long journey.

¹14 Traditionally *peace offerings*

²⁰He took his purse filled with money
    and will not be home till full moon."

²¹With persuasive words she led him astray;
    she seduced him with her smooth talk.
²²All at once he followed her
    like an ox going to the slaughter,
    like a deer[m] stepping into a noose[n]
²³   till an arrow pierces his liver,
    like a bird darting into a snare,
        little knowing it will cost him his life.

²⁴Now then, my sons, listen to me;
    pay attention to what I say.
²⁵Do not let your heart turn to her ways
    or stray into her paths.
²⁶Many are the victims she has brought down;
    her slain are a mighty throng.
²⁷Her house is a highway to the grave,[o]
    leading down to the chambers of death.

m 22 Syriac (see also Septuagint); Hebrew fool   n 22 The meaning of the Hebrew for this line is uncertain.   o 27 Hebrew Sheol

---

 Discovering the Word   1. Proverbs 7:6–23 gives us the first full-blown portrait of the simpleton. What does the seductress say that is probably true?   2. What does she say (or imply) that is actually false?   3. Men and women "without judgment" can be persuaded to do foolish things other than adultery. From your own recollections, describe a case of persuasion which follows the same pattern as Proverbs 7.   4. How are the comparisons to animals drawn in verses 22–23 appropriate?   5. Does the warning in verses 24–27 seem overly dramatic to you? Why or why not?

Applying the Word   1. All of us have spheres of living where we, like the simpleton in Proverbs 7, have little choice but to believe what we are told. What are some of these areas in your life?   2. It's one thing to know we're naive in this or that respect, and quite another to develop the character strength called *prudence*. What can you begin doing now that will make you more prudent in the future?

Responding in Prayer   Jesus said, "Be as shrewd as snakes and as innocent as doves" (Mt 10:16). Pray for wisdom like that.

Proverbs 8

8 Does not wisdom call out?
    Does not understanding raise her voice?
  ²On the heights along the way,
    where the paths meet, she takes her stand;
³beside the gates leading into the city,
    at the entrances, she cries aloud:
⁴"To you, O men, I call out;
    I raise my voice to all mankind.
⁵You who are simple, gain prudence;
    you who are foolish, gain understanding.
⁶Listen, for I have worthy things to say;
    I open my lips to speak what is right.
⁷My mouth speaks what is true,
    for my lips detest wickedness.
⁸All the words of my mouth are just;
    none of them is crooked or perverse.
⁹To the discerning all of them are right;
    they are faultless to those who have
        knowledge.
¹⁰Choose my instruction instead of silver,
    knowledge rather than choice gold,
¹¹for wisdom is more precious than rubies,

and nothing you desire can compare with
    her.

¹²"I, wisdom, dwell together with prudence;
    I possess knowledge and discretion.
¹³To fear the Lᴏʀᴅ is to hate evil;
    I hate pride and arrogance,
        evil behavior and perverse speech.
¹⁴Counsel and sound judgment are mine;
    I have understanding and power.
¹⁵By me kings reign
    and rulers make laws that are just;
¹⁶by me princes govern,
    and all nobles who rule on earth.[p]
¹⁷I love those who love me,
    and those who seek me find me.
¹⁸With me are riches and honor,
    enduring wealth and prosperity.
¹⁹My fruit is better than fine gold;
    what I yield surpasses choice silver.
²⁰I walk in the way of righteousness,

p 16 Many Hebrew manuscripts and Septuagint; most Hebrew manuscripts and nobles—all righteous rulers

along the paths of justice,
²¹bestowing wealth on those who love me
and making their treasuries full.

²²"The Lᴏʀᴅ brought me forth as the first of his
works,�q,ʳ
before his deeds of old;
²³I was appointedˢ from eternity,
from the beginning, before the world began.
²⁴When there were no oceans, I was given
birth,
when there were no springs abounding with
water;
²⁵before the mountains were settled in place,
before the hills, I was given birth,
²⁶before he made the earth or its fields
or any of the dust of the world.
²⁷I was there when he set the heavens in place,
when he marked out the horizon on the
face of the deep,
²⁸when he established the clouds above
and fixed securely the fountains of the
deep,
²⁹when he gave the sea its boundary

so the waters would not overstep his
command,
and when he marked out the foundations of
the earth.
³⁰ Then I was the craftsman at his side.
I was filled with delight day after day,
rejoicing always in his presence,
³¹rejoicing in his whole world
and delighting in mankind.

³²"Now then, my sons, listen to me;
blessed are those who keep my ways.
³³Listen to my instruction and be wise;
do not ignore it.
³⁴Blessed is the man who listens to me,
watching daily at my doors,
waiting at my doorway.
³⁵For whoever finds me finds life
and receives favor from the Lᴏʀᴅ.
³⁶But whoever fails to find me harms himself;
all who hate me love death."

*q22 Or way; or dominion   ʳ22 Or The Lᴏʀᴅ possessed me at the
beginning of his work; or The Lᴏʀᴅ brought me forth at the beginning of
his work   ˢ23 Or fashioned*

3 / *Proverbs 9*
Two Dinner Invitations

AN INVITATION TO dinner is always welcome, until you get invitations to two *different* dinners, each held at the same time as the other. Then you have to decide which one to accept and which one to decline. Proverbs 9 presents this very dilemma—invitations to two dinners held simultaneously. How do you decide which invitation to accept? No doubt you'll make your decision based on many factors—the reputation of the host and hostess, the prospects for a good time, your own tastes in people and food. All these factors appear in the two invitations that conclude Solomon's introduction to the book of Proverbs. Other factors appear as well—such as how long you'll live and how prosperous you'll be. You see, these are no ordinary dinners, and the invitations come from no ordinary hostesses. Which one you attend will largely determine your health, your wealth and your happiness for the rest of your life.

 Warming Up to God   Where or how are you currently finding happiness in life?

 Read Proverbs 9.

 Wisdom has built her house;
she has hewn out its seven pillars.
²She has prepared her meat and mixed
her wine;
she has also set her table.
³She has sent out her maids, and she calls

from the highest point of the city.
⁴"Let all who are simple come in here!"
she says to those who lack judgment.
⁵"Come, eat my food
and drink the wine I have mixed.
⁶Leave your simple ways and you will live;

walk in the way of understanding.

7"Whoever corrects a mocker invites insult;
    whoever rebukes a wicked man incurs
        abuse.
8Do not rebuke a mocker or he will hate you;
    rebuke a wise man and he will love you.
9Instruct a wise man and he will be wiser still;
    teach a righteous man and he will add to
        his learning.

10"The fear of the LORD is the beginning of
        wisdom,
    and knowledge of the Holy One is
        understanding.
11For through me your days will be many,
    and years will be added to your life.
12If you are wise, your wisdom will reward you;
    if you are a mocker, you alone will suffer."

13The woman Folly is loud;
    she is undisciplined and without
        knowledge.
14She sits at the door of her house,
    on a seat at the highest point of the city,
15calling out to those who pass by,
    who go straight on their way.
16"Let all who are simple come in here!"
    she says to those who lack judgment.
17"Stolen water is sweet;
    food eaten in secret is delicious!"
18But little do they know that the dead are
        there,
    that her guests are in the depths of the
        grave.ᶦ

ᶦ18 Hebrew Sheol

 Discovering the Word 1. Do Lady Wisdom and Woman Folly invite the same people or different people to their feasts? Explain. 2. Which hostess has the greater resources to deploy in her guests' behalf? Explain. 3. What do verses 7–12 tell us about how Lady Wisdom imparts benefits to her guests? 4. After reading verse 10, do you think that knowledge and understanding must be explicitly Judeo-Christian in order to be genuine? Why or why not? 5. No matter which "invitation" you accept, your decision will result in both pleasure and pain. How do the pleasure and pain from dining at Lady Wisdom's house differ from the pleasure and pain one finds at Woman Folly's abode?

Applying the Word 1. Proverbs 9 is, of course, an extended metaphor—an allegory. Wisdom is *like* a wealthy woman inviting guests to a feast. What people do you know who embody the person of Lady Wisdom in their relationship to you? 2. In whom, or where, or in what circumstances have you encountered Woman Folly?

Responding in Prayer Pray that you would be made worthy of dinner with Lady Wisdom.

---

4 / *Proverbs 10*
Good Words

JESUS POWERFULLY UNDERSCORED the immense power of words to shape our destiny. Speaking of the final judgment, he said, "By your words you will be acquitted, and by your words you will be condemned" (Mt 12:37). He was reflecting a similar idea found in Proverbs 18:21: "The tongue has the power of life and death, and those who love it will eat its fruit."

Proverbs 6 displayed the awesome power for evil which words have. But they also have an awesome power for good. For all that, words are not magic; their power lies not so much in themselves as in the characters of those who speak them and those who hear them. You'll uncover some of the ways you can wisely fashion words for wholesome ends.

 Warming Up to God Would you describe yourself as a person of few or many words? Explain.

 Read Proverbs 10.

10

The proverbs of Solomon:

A wise son brings joy to his
father,
but a foolish son grief to his mother.

²Ill-gotten treasures are of no value,
but righteousness delivers from death.

³The Lord does not let the righteous go hungry
but he thwarts the craving of the wicked.

⁴Lazy hands make a man poor,
but diligent hands bring wealth.

⁵He who gathers crops in summer is a wise
son,
but he who sleeps during harvest is a
disgraceful son.

⁶Blessings crown the head of the righteous,
but violence overwhelms the mouth of the
wicked.ᵘ

⁷The memory of the righteous will be a
blessing,
but the name of the wicked will rot.

⁸The wise in heart accept commands,
but a chattering fool comes to ruin.

⁹The man of integrity walks securely,
but he who takes crooked paths will be
found out.

¹⁰He who winks maliciously causes grief,
and a chattering fool comes to ruin.

¹¹The mouth of the righteous is a fountain of
life,
but violence overwhelms the mouth of the
wicked.

¹²Hatred stirs up dissension,
but love covers over all wrongs.

¹³Wisdom is found on the lips of the
discerning,
but a rod is for the back of him who lacks
judgment.

¹⁴Wise men store up knowledge,
but the mouth of a fool invites ruin.

¹⁵The wealth of the rich is their fortified city,
but poverty is the ruin of the poor.

¹⁶The wages of the righteous bring them life,

but the income of the wicked brings them
punishment.

¹⁷He who heeds discipline shows the way to
life,
but whoever ignores correction leads others
astray.

¹⁸He who conceals his hatred has lying lips,
and whoever spreads slander is a fool.

¹⁹When words are many, sin is not absent,
but he who holds his tongue is wise.

²⁰The tongue of the righteous is choice silver,
but the heart of the wicked is of little
value.

²¹The lips of the righteous nourish many,
but fools die for lack of judgment.

²²The blessing of the Lord brings wealth,
and he adds no trouble to it.

²³A fool finds pleasure in evil conduct,
but a man of understanding delights in
wisdom.

²⁴What the wicked dreads will overtake him;
what the righteous desire will be granted.

²⁵When the storm has swept by, the wicked are
gone,
but the righteous stand firm forever.

²⁶As vinegar to the teeth and smoke to the eyes,
so is a sluggard to those who send him.

²⁷The fear of the Lord adds length to life,
but the years of the wicked are cut short.

²⁸The prospect of the righteous is joy,
but the hopes of the wicked come to
nothing.

²⁹The way of the Lord is a refuge for the
righteous,
but it is the ruin of those who do evil.

³⁰The righteous will never be uprooted,
but the wicked will not remain in the land.

³¹The mouth of the righteous brings forth
wisdom,
but a perverse tongue will be cut out.

ᵘ6 Or *but the mouth of the wicked conceals violence; also in verse 11*

32The lips of the righteous know what is
fitting,

but the mouth of the wicked only what is
perverse.

 Discovering the Word 1. How are wise words and foolish words contrasted (vv. 8, 10, 13–14, 18–21, 31–32)? 2. The phrase "chattering fool" is used in verses 8 and 10. What images does it bring to mind? 3. Verse 19 insists that the mere quantity of words produces sin. 4. When have words been like "choice silver" (v. 20) and nourished you (v. 21)? 5. Sometimes we are able to say just the right thing in a situation. When have your lips known what was fitting (v. 32)?

Applying the Word 1. Now that you have surveyed what the proverbs say about good and bad speech, which do you think is easier—to rid yourself of unwholesome speech habits or to build wholesome speech habits? Explain. 2. What strategy might you employ to reduce or eliminate your wordiness? (Hint: don't ignore the help that a friend or spouse can provide in these settings.) 3. Who do you need to encourage with good words?

Responding in Prayer Thank God for those who have nourished you with good words. Pray that you will be like them.

Proverbs 11—12

11

The Lord abhors dishonest scales,
but accurate weights are his
delight.

2When pride comes, then comes disgrace,
but with humility comes wisdom.

3The integrity of the upright guides them,
but the unfaithful are destroyed by their
duplicity.

4Wealth is worthless in the day of wrath,
but righteousness delivers from death.

5The righteousness of the blameless makes a
straight way for them,
but the wicked are brought down by their
own wickedness.

6The righteousness of the upright delivers
them,
but the unfaithful are trapped by evil
desires.

7When a wicked man dies, his hope perishes;
all he expected from his power comes to
nothing.

8The righteous man is rescued from trouble,
and it comes on the wicked instead.

9With his mouth the godless destroys his
neighbor,
but through knowledge the righteous
escape.

10When the righteous prosper, the city rejoices;
when the wicked perish, there are shouts of
joy.

11Through the blessing of the upright a city is
exalted,
but by the mouth of the wicked it is
destroyed.

12A man who lacks judgment derides his
neighbor,
but a man of understanding holds his
tongue.

13A gossip betrays a confidence,
but a trustworthy man keeps a secret.

14For lack of guidance a nation falls,
but many advisers make victory sure.

15He who puts up security for another will
surely suffer,
but whoever refuses to strike hands in
pledge is safe.

16A kindhearted woman gains respect,
but ruthless men gain only wealth.

17A kind man benefits himself,
but a cruel man brings trouble on himself.

18The wicked man earns deceptive wages,
but he who sows righteousness reaps a sure
reward.

19The truly righteous man attains life,

but he who pursues evil goes to his death.

²⁰The Lord detests men of perverse heart
but he delights in those whose ways are
blameless.

²¹Be sure of this: The wicked will not go
unpunished,
but those who are righteous will go free.

²²Like a gold ring in a pig's snout
is a beautiful woman who shows no
discretion.

²³The desire of the righteous ends only in good,
but the hope of the wicked only in wrath.

²⁴One man gives freely, yet gains even more;
another withholds unduly, but comes to
poverty.

²⁵A generous man will prosper;
he who refreshes others will himself be
refreshed.

²⁶People curse the man who hoards grain,
but blessing crowns him who is willing to
sell.

²⁷He who seeks good finds goodwill,
but evil comes to him who searches for it.

²⁸Whoever trusts in his riches will fall,
but the righteous will thrive like a green
leaf.

²⁹He who brings trouble on his family will
inherit only wind,
and the fool will be servant to the wise.

³⁰The fruit of the righteous is a tree of life,
and he who wins souls is wise.

³¹If the righteous receive their due on earth,
how much more the ungodly and the
sinner!

12 Whoever loves discipline loves
knowledge,
but he who hates correction is
stupid.

²A good man obtains favor from the Lord,
but the Lord condemns a crafty man.

³A man cannot be established through
wickedness,
but the righteous cannot be uprooted.

⁴A wife of noble character is her husband's
crown,
but a disgraceful wife is like decay in his
bones.

⁵The plans of the righteous are just,
but the advice of the wicked is deceitful.

⁶The words of the wicked lie in wait for blood,
but the speech of the upright rescues them.

⁷Wicked men are overthrown and are no more,
but the house of the righteous stands firm.

⁸A man is praised according to his wisdom,
but men with warped minds are despised.

⁹Better to be a nobody and yet have a servant
than pretend to be somebody and have no
food.

¹⁰A righteous man cares for the needs of his
animal,
but the kindest acts of the wicked are cruel.

¹¹He who works his land will have abundant
food,
but he who chases fantasies lacks judgment.

¹²The wicked desire the plunder of evil men,
but the root of the righteous flourishes.

¹³An evil man is trapped by his sinful talk,
but a righteous man escapes trouble.

¹⁴From the fruit of his lips a man is filled with
good things
as surely as the work of his hands rewards
him.

¹⁵The way of a fool seems right to him,
but a wise man listens to advice.

¹⁶A fool shows his annoyance at once,
but a prudent man overlooks an insult.

¹⁷A truthful witness gives honest testimony,
but a false witness tells lies.

¹⁸Reckless words pierce like a sword,
but the tongue of the wise brings healing.

¹⁹Truthful lips endure forever,
but a lying tongue lasts only a moment.

²⁰There is deceit in the hearts of those who plot
evil,
but joy for those who promote peace.

²¹No harm befalls the righteous,

but the wicked have their fill of trouble.

²²The Lord detests lying lips,
　　but he delights in men who are truthful.

²³A prudent man keeps his knowledge to
　　　himself,
　　but the heart of fools blurts out folly.

²⁴Diligent hands will rule,
　　but laziness ends in slave labor.

²⁵An anxious heart weighs a man down,
　　but a kind word cheers him up.

²⁶A righteous man is cautious in friendship,ᵛ
　　but the way of the wicked leads them
　　　astray.

²⁷The lazy man does not roastʷ his game,
　　but the diligent man prizes his
　　　possessions.

²⁸In the way of righteousness there is life;
　　along that path is immortality.

ᵛ26 Or *man is a guide to his neighbor*　　ʷ27 The meaning of the
Hebrew for this word is uncertain.

5 / *Proverbs 13—14*
Finding Wisdom

A FACTORY MANAGER'S assembly line was down, so he summoned a consultant to suggest remedies. After inspecting a huge piece of machinery, the consultant produced a small hammer, reached between some gears, and gave a small tap. The assembly line worked again, and the factory manager got a bill for $10,000. Aghast, the manager demanded another bill itemizing the charges. When it came, the second bill read: Tapping with hammer: $5.00/Knowing where to tap: $9,995.00.

Wisdom is "knowing where to tap." When we need some tapping done, we'll do it ourselves if we're wise enough; otherwise we'll need someone who knows where to tap. The book of Proverbs points us in both directions—by showing us "where to tap" in many areas of life, and by helping us seek out those who understand what we cannot yet perceive. The proverbs not only show us wisdom, they show us how to seek wisdom.

 Warming Up to God　Who do you think of when you ponder "wisdom"? Thank God for that person and
what he or she has taught you as you begin.

 Read Proverbs 13—14.

13 A wise son heeds his father's
instruction,
　　but a mocker does not listen to
rebuke.

²From the fruit of his lips a man enjoys good
　　things,
　　but the unfaithful have a craving for
　　　violence.

³He who guards his lips guards his life,
　　but he who speaks rashly will come to ruin.

⁴The sluggard craves and gets nothing,
　　but the desires of the diligent are fully
　　　satisfied.

⁵The righteous hate what is false,
　　but the wicked bring shame and disgrace.

⁶Righteousness guards the man of integrity,
　　but wickedness overthrows the sinner.

⁷One man pretends to be rich, yet has nothing;
　　another pretends to be poor, yet has great
　　　wealth.

⁸A man's riches may ransom his life,
　　but a poor man hears no threat.

⁹The light of the righteous shines brightly,
　　but the lamp of the wicked is snuffed out.

¹⁰Pride only breeds quarrels,
　　but wisdom is found in those who take
　　　advice.

¹¹Dishonest money dwindles away,
　　but he who gathers money little by little
　　　makes it grow.

¹²Hope deferred makes the heart sick,
　　but a longing fulfilled is a tree of life.

¹³He who scorns instruction will pay for it,
　　but he who respects a command is
　　　rewarded.

¹⁴The teaching of the wise is a fountain of life,
　　turning a man from the snares of death.

¹⁵Good understanding wins favor,
　　but the way of the unfaithful is hard.ˣ

¹⁶Every prudent man acts out of knowledge,
　　but a fool exposes his folly.

¹⁷A wicked messenger falls into trouble,
　　but a trustworthy envoy brings healing.

¹⁸He who ignores discipline comes to poverty
　　and shame,
　　but whoever heeds correction is honored.

¹⁹A longing fulfilled is sweet to the soul,
　　but fools detest turning from evil.

²⁰He who walks with the wise grows wise,
　　but a companion of fools suffers harm.

²¹Misfortune pursues the sinner,
　　but prosperity is the reward of the
　　　righteous.

²²A good man leaves an inheritance for his
　　children's children,
　　but a sinner's wealth is stored up for the
　　　righteous.

²³A poor man's field may produce abundant
　　food,
　　but injustice sweeps it away.

²⁴He who spares the rod hates his son,
　　but he who loves him is careful to
　　　discipline him.

²⁵The righteous eat to their hearts' content,
　　but the stomach of the wicked goes hungry.

14 The wise woman builds her
house,
　　but with her own hands the
foolish one tears hers down.

²He whose walk is upright fears the LORD,
　　but he whose ways are devious despises
　　　him.

³A fool's talk brings a rod to his back,
　　but the lips of the wise protect them.

⁴Where there are no oxen, the manger is
　　empty,
　　but from the strength of an ox comes an
　　　abundant harvest.

⁵A truthful witness does not deceive,
　　but a false witness pours out lies.

⁶The mocker seeks wisdom and finds none,
　　but knowledge comes easily to the
　　　discerning.

⁷Stay away from a foolish man,
　　for you will not find knowledge on his lips.

⁸The wisdom of the prudent is to give thought
　　to their ways,
　　but the folly of fools is deception.

⁹Fools mock at making amends for sin,
　　but goodwill is found among the upright.

¹⁰Each heart knows its own bitterness,
　　and no one else can share its joy.

¹¹The house of the wicked will be destroyed,
　　but the tent of the upright will flourish.

¹²There is a way that seems right to a man,
　　but in the end it leads to death.

¹³Even in laughter the heart may ache,
　　and joy may end in grief.

¹⁴The faithless will be fully repaid for their
　　ways,
　　and the good man rewarded for his.

¹⁵A simple man believes anything,
　　but a prudent man gives thought to his
　　　steps.

¹⁶A wise man fears the LORD and shuns evil,
　　but a fool is hotheaded and reckless.

¹⁷A quick-tempered man does foolish things,
　　and a crafty man is hated.

¹⁸The simple inherit folly,
　　but the prudent are crowned with
　　　knowledge.

¹⁹Evil men will bow down in the presence of
　　the good,
　　and the wicked at the gates of the
　　　righteous.

ˣ15 Or *unfaithful does not endure*

²⁰The poor are shunned even by their
    neighbors,
  but the rich have many friends.

²¹He who despises his neighbor sins,
  but blessed is he who is kind to the needy.

²²Do not those who plot evil go astray?
  But those who plan what is good find^y
    love and faithfulness.

²³All hard work brings a profit,
  but mere talk leads only to poverty.

²⁴The wealth of the wise is their crown,
  but the folly of fools yields folly.

²⁵A truthful witness saves lives,
  but a false witness is deceitful.

²⁶He who fears the LORD has a secure fortress,
  and for his children it will be a refuge.

²⁷The fear of the LORD is a fountain of life,
  turning a man from the snares of death.

²⁸A large population is a king's glory,
  but without subjects a prince is ruined.

²⁹A patient man has great understanding,
  but a quick-tempered man displays folly.

³⁰A heart at peace gives life to the body,
  but envy rots the bones.

³¹He who oppresses the poor shows contempt
    for their Maker,
  but whoever is kind to the needy honors
    God.

³²When calamity comes, the wicked are brought
    down,
  but even in death the righteous have a
    refuge.

³³Wisdom reposes in the heart of the discerning
  and even among fools she lets herself be
    known.^{z}

³⁴Righteousness exalts a nation,
  but sin is a disgrace to any people.

³⁵A king delights in a wise servant,
  but a shameful servant incurs his wrath.

^{y}22 Or *show* ^{z}33 Hebrew; Septuagint and Syriac / *but in the heart of
fools she is not known*

Discovering the Word **1.** We often say that someone is "street smart," meaning that the person has become shrewd through enrollment in the "School of Hard Knocks." Can we get wisdom without the "hard knocks"? Defend your answer from the proverbs themselves. **2.** In Solomon's day, the wisdom of Proverbs was probably taught in two places—the home and wisdom schools. Today the "wisdom school" takes many forms, from apprenticeships in trade unions to enrollment in universities. Using the proverbs above as a guide, what would you look for when trying to select such a school? **3.** What do you learn from these proverbs about advice? **4.** Why do you think there is often such a huge gulf between what seems right to us and what is truly wise (14:12)? **5.** Wanting wisdom isn't enough. To get it we must be able to receive it. From each of the proverbs in this study, suggest a character weakness which hinders a person from becoming wise—one character weakness per proverb.

Applying the Word **1.** In Proverbs to seek wisdom is to seek skill. What specific types of skill would you like to acquire in your work or in your relationships? **2.** What can you do in the week ahead to begin acquiring wisdom?

  Responding in Prayer Proverbs 14:33 says, "Wisdom reposes in the heart of the discerning." Pray for a discerning heart.

---

6 / *Proverbs 15—16*
Prayer

IF YOU SURVEYED books on prayer in a Christian bookstore, you'd find varied and often conflicting advice. Some authorities insist that successful prayer is scheduled; others favor impromptu prayer. One writer says fasting should accompany prayer, but another tells us to pray in any circumstance. Still another says that prayer is best done when alone, though someone else urges us to join with others. Some claim that prayer requires careful preparation and thought, while a conflicting authority says prayer should flow spontaneously from our hearts. Wisdom is needed as much for prayer as for any other area of human living. These proverbs furnish us wisdom for bringing our requests to God as we seek to live wisely.

Warming Up to God What has your pattern of prayer been over recent days, weeks, months, years? Where are you struggling? How are you growing? Spend some time reflecting on your prayer life.

Read Proverbs 15—16.

15

A gentle answer turns away wrath,
but a harsh word stirs up anger.

²The tongue of the wise
commends knowledge,
but the mouth of the fool gushes folly.

³The eyes of the Lord are everywhere,
keeping watch on the wicked and the good.

⁴The tongue that brings healing is a tree of
life,
but a deceitful tongue crushes the spirit.

⁵A fool spurns his father's discipline,
but whoever heeds correction shows
prudence.

⁶The house of the righteous contains great
treasure,
but the income of the wicked brings them
trouble.

⁷The lips of the wise spread knowledge;
not so the hearts of fools.

⁸The Lord detests the sacrifice of the wicked,
but the prayer of the upright pleases him.

⁹The Lord detests the way of the wicked
but he loves those who pursue
righteousness.

¹⁰Stern discipline awaits him who leaves the
path;
he who hates correction will die.

¹¹Death and Destruction*a* lie open before the
Lord—
how much more the hearts of men!

¹²A mocker resents correction;
he will not consult the wise.

¹³A happy heart makes the face cheerful,
but heartache crushes the spirit.

¹⁴The discerning heart seeks knowledge,
but the mouth of a fool feeds on folly.

¹⁵All the days of the oppressed are wretched,

but the cheerful heart has a continual feast.

¹⁶Better a little with the fear of the Lord
than great wealth with turmoil.

¹⁷Better a meal of vegetables where there is love
than a fattened calf with hatred.

¹⁸A hot-tempered man stirs up dissension,
but a patient man calms a quarrel.

¹⁹The way of the sluggard is blocked with
thorns,
but the path of the upright is a highway.

²⁰A wise son brings joy to his father,
but a foolish man despises his mother.

²¹Folly delights a man who lacks judgment,
but a man of understanding keeps a straight
course.

²²Plans fail for lack of counsel,
but with many advisers they succeed.

²³A man finds joy in giving an apt reply—
and how good is a timely word!

²⁴The path of life leads upward for the wise
to keep him from going down to the
grave.*b*

²⁵The Lord tears down the proud man's house
but he keeps the widow's boundaries intact.

²⁶The Lord detests the thoughts of the wicked,
but those of the pure are pleasing to him.

²⁷A greedy man brings trouble to his family,
but he who hates bribes will live.

²⁸The heart of the righteous weighs its answers,
but the mouth of the wicked gushes evil.

²⁹The Lord is far from the wicked
but he hears the prayer of the righteous.

³⁰A cheerful look brings joy to the heart,
and good news gives health to the bones.

³¹He who listens to a life-giving rebuke

a11 Hebrew *Sheol and Abaddon*   *b24* Hebrew *Sheol*

will be at home among the wise.

³²He who ignores discipline despises himself,
but whoever heeds correction gains
understanding.

³³The fear of the LORD teaches a man wisdom,^c
and humility comes before honor.

16

To man belong the plans of the
heart,
but from the LORD comes the reply
of the tongue.

²All a man's ways seem innocent to him,
but motives are weighed by the LORD.

³Commit to the LORD whatever you do,
and your plans will succeed.

⁴The LORD works out everything for his own
ends—
even the wicked for a day of disaster.

⁵The LORD detests all the proud of heart.
Be sure of this: They will not go
unpunished.

⁶Through love and faithfulness sin is atoned
for;
through the fear of the LORD a man avoids
evil.

⁷When a man's ways are pleasing to the LORD,
he makes even his enemies live at peace
with him.

⁸Better a little with righteousness
than much gain with injustice.

⁹In his heart a man plans his course,
but the LORD determines his steps.

¹⁰The lips of a king speak as an oracle,
and his mouth should not betray justice.

¹¹Honest scales and balances are from the LORD;
all the weights in the bag are of his
making.

¹²Kings detest wrongdoing,
for a throne is established through
righteousness.

¹³Kings take pleasure in honest lips;
they value a man who speaks the truth.

¹⁴A king's wrath is a messenger of death,
but a wise man will appease it.

¹⁵When a king's face brightens, it means life;
his favor is like a rain cloud in spring.

¹⁶How much better to get wisdom than gold,
to choose understanding rather than silver!

¹⁷The highway of the upright avoids evil;
he who guards his way guards his life.

¹⁸Pride goes before destruction,
a haughty spirit before a fall.

¹⁹Better to be lowly in spirit and among the
oppressed
than to share plunder with the proud.

²⁰Whoever gives heed to instruction prospers,
and blessed is he who trusts in the LORD.

²¹The wise in heart are called discerning,
and pleasant words promote instruction.^d

²²Understanding is a fountain of life to those
who have it,
but folly brings punishment to fools.

²³A wise man's heart guides his mouth,
and his lips promote instruction.^e

²⁴Pleasant words are a honeycomb,
sweet to the soul and healing to the bones.

²⁵There is a way that seems right to a man,
but in the end it leads to death.

²⁶The laborer's appetite works for him;
his hunger drives him on.

²⁷A scoundrel plots evil,
and his speech is like a scorching fire.

²⁸A perverse man stirs up dissension,
and a gossip separates close friends.

²⁹A violent man entices his neighbor
and leads him down a path that is not
good.

³⁰He who winks with his eye is plotting
perversity;
he who purses his lips is bent on evil.

³¹Gray hair is a crown of splendor;
it is attained by a righteous life.

³²Better a patient man than a warrior,

^c33 Or Wisdom teaches the fear of the LORD   ^d21 Or words make a
man persuasive   ^e23 Or mouth / and makes his lips persuasive

a man who controls his temper than one
who takes a city.

³³The lot is cast into the lap,
but its every decision is from the LORD.

 Discovering the Word 1. In contrast to many books on prayer, Proverbs 15:8 and 15:29 ignore the context and style of praying to focus on another factor. What is it? 2. Why is this factor sufficient by itself to account for whether God hears our prayers or not? 3. Proverbs 28:13 and other passages tell us that sin is present in everyone. How, then, can we ever be called "upright" or "righteous" in the sense of 15:8 or 15:29? 4. What does it mean to *commit* something to the Lord (16:3)? 5. What part do you think prayer plays in committing whatever you do to the Lord? 6. Proverbs 16:3 seems to promise unqualified success to those who commit their plans to the Lord. If this is not a "blank check" (and it's probably not), what is presupposed about our plans here?

Applying the Word 1. Think a moment about your own prayers. How might you begin praying more wisely? 2. In what ways does your character need to change so that your prayers will be those of the righteous?

Responding in Prayer Ask God to teach you how to pray.

---

7 / *Proverbs 17—18*
Avoiding the Fool

PROVERBS 27:22 MAKES one very clear point about fools—they're incorrigible: "Though you grind a fool in a mortar, grinding him like grain with a pestle, you will not remove his folly from him." But if fools can't be reformed, why do we find such an abundance of proverbs about them? The answer is simple—to help us recognize fools, their foolish behavior, and to warn us about the consequences of both. Our greatest danger from fools is meeting them unexpectedly, not recognizing them until it's too late. Recognizing and avoiding fools is our only defense from being undone by their folly. Defensive driving techniques protect us from foolish drivers. The proverbs in this study equip us for "defensive living."

 Warming Up to God One of the signs of a fool we'll explore in this passage is foolish talk. What foolish talk (gossip, lies and so on) do you need to confess to God as you begin?

 Read Proverbs 17—18.

---

17 Better a dry crust with peace and
quiet
than a house full of feasting,ʃ
with strife.

²A wise servant will rule over a disgraceful
son,
and will share the inheritance as one of the
brothers.

³The crucible for silver and the furnace for
gold,
but the LORD tests the heart.

⁴A wicked man listens to evil lips;
a liar pays attention to a malicious tongue.

⁵He who mocks the poor shows contempt for
their Maker;

whoever gloats over disaster will not go
unpunished.

⁶Children's children are a crown to the aged,
and parents are the pride of their children.

⁷Arrogantᵍ lips are unsuited to a fool—
how much worse lying lips to a ruler!

⁸A bribe is a charm to the one who gives it;
wherever he turns, he succeeds.

⁹He who covers over an offense promotes love,
but whoever repeats the matter separates
close friends.

¹⁰A rebuke impresses a man of discernment
more than a hundred lashes a fool.

ʃ1 Hebrew *sacrifices*   87 Or *Eloquent*

11An evil man is bent only on rebellion;
  a merciless official will be sent against him.

12Better to meet a bear robbed of her cubs
  than a fool in his folly.

13If a man pays back evil for good,
  evil will never leave his house.

14Starting a quarrel is like breaching a dam;
  so drop the matter before a dispute breaks
    out.

15Acquitting the guilty and condemning the
    innocent—
  the LORD detests them both.

16Of what use is money in the hand of a fool,
  since he has no desire to get wisdom?

17A friend loves at all times,
  and a brother is born for adversity.

18A man lacking in judgment strikes hands in
    pledge
  and puts up security for his neighbor.

19He who loves a quarrel loves sin;
  he who builds a high gate invites
    destruction.

20A man of perverse heart does not prosper;
  he whose tongue is deceitful falls into
    trouble.

21To have a fool for a son brings grief;
  there is no joy for the father of a fool.

22A cheerful heart is good medicine,
  but a crushed spirit dries up the bones.

23A wicked man accepts a bribe in secret
  to pervert the course of justice.

24A discerning man keeps wisdom in view,
  but a fool's eyes wander to the ends of the
    earth.

25A foolish son brings grief to his father
  and bitterness to the one who bore him.

26It is not good to punish an innocent man,
  or to flog officials for their integrity.

27A man of knowledge uses words with
    restraint,
  and a man of understanding is
    even-tempered.

28Even a fool is thought wise if he keeps silent,
  and discerning if he holds his tongue.

18 An unfriendly man pursues selfish
     ends;
  he defies all sound judgment.

2A fool finds no pleasure in understanding
  but delights in airing his own opinions.

3When wickedness comes, so does contempt,
  and with shame comes disgrace.

4The words of a man's mouth are deep waters,
  but the fountain of wisdom is a bubbling
    brook.

5It is not good to be partial to the wicked
  or to deprive the innocent of justice.

6A fool's lips bring him strife,
  and his mouth invites a beating.

7A fool's mouth is his undoing,
  and his lips are a snare to his soul.

8The words of a gossip are like choice morsels;
  they go down to a man's inmost parts.

9One who is slack in his work
  is brother to one who destroys.

10The name of the LORD is a strong tower;
  the righteous run to it and are safe.

11The wealth of the rich is their fortified city;
  they imagine it an unscalable wall.

12Before his downfall a man's heart is proud,
  but humility comes before honor.

13He who answers before listening—
  that is his folly and his shame.

14A man's spirit sustains him in sickness,
  but a crushed spirit who can bear?

15The heart of the discerning acquires
    knowledge;
  the ears of the wise seek it out.

16A gift opens the way for the giver
  and ushers him into the presence of the
    great.

17The first to present his case seems right,
  till another comes forward and questions
    him.

18Casting the lot settles disputes
    and keeps strong opponents apart.

19An offended brother is more unyielding than
    a fortified city,
and disputes are like the barred gates of a
    citadel.

20From the fruit of his mouth a man's stomach
    is filled;
with the harvest from his lips he is
    satisfied.

21The tongue has the power of life and death,
    and those who love it will eat its fruit.

22He who finds a wife finds what is good
    and receives favor from the LORD.

23A poor man pleads for mercy,
    but a rich man answers harshly.

24A man of many companions may come to
    ruin,
but there is a friend who sticks closer than
    a brother.

 Discovering the Word 1. Which verses in Proverbs 17—18 speak about fools? 2. Proverbs 17:12 poses a riddle—why are you better off meeting a rampaging mother bear rather than meeting a fool in his folly? 3. Describe an episode from your experience or from the experience of someone you know which illustrates the point of Proverbs 17:12. 4. Proverbs 18:2 tells us that opinionated people are apt to be fools—they're always ready with a viewpoint and ever eager to broadcast it. How would you expect a prudent or wise person to behave differently from the fool? 5. When have you seen a fool's mouth become his or her undoing (18:17)? 6. How does 18:2 account for the truth of 18:7?

 Applying the Word 1. Jesus warned, "Do not judge, or you too will be judged" (Mt 7:1). When we use the proverbs about the fool to evaluate people and conclude they are indeed foolish, do we ignore Jesus' warning? Why or why not? 2. What areas of your own character that might need work do these proverbs point to?

 Responding in Prayer Who do you know that has been taken in by a fool? Pray for that person.

8 / *Proverbs 19*
Giving

WITH THE POOR come knotty questions for all who view them with compassion: How can I meet so much need from my limited resources? How do I choose whom to help and whom to pass by? How do I balance the needs of the poor with the requests for help from my children, my aged parents or my extended family? The proverbs in this study help us in two ways. First, they guide us through the moral conflicts we encounter when confronted with the material neediness of others. Second, they give an antidote to the folly which exalts acquisitiveness as a social and economic virtue. Our prosperity, it turns out, may be a result of our *giving* rather than our getting.

Warming Up to God Recall a time when you have been in need and received a gift that encouraged you. Thank God for that provision.

Read Proverbs 19.

19 Better a poor man whose walk is
    blameless
    than a fool whose lips are
    perverse.

2It is not good to have zeal without
    knowledge,
    nor to be hasty and miss the way.

3A man's own folly ruins his life,
    yet his heart rages against the LORD.

4Wealth brings many friends,
    but a poor man's friend deserts him.

5A false witness will not go unpunished,
    and he who pours out lies will not go free.

⁶Many curry favor with a ruler,
and everyone is the friend of a man who
gives gifts.

⁷A poor man is shunned by all his relatives—
how much more do his friends avoid him!
Though he pursues them with pleading,
they are nowhere to be found.ʰ

⁸He who gets wisdom loves his own soul;
he who cherishes understanding prospers.

⁹A false witness will not go unpunished,
and he who pours out lies will perish.

¹⁰It is not fitting for a fool to live in luxury—
how much worse for a slave to rule over
princes!

¹¹A man's wisdom gives him patience;
it is to his glory to overlook an offense.

¹²A king's rage is like the roar of a lion,
but his favor is like dew on the grass.

¹³A foolish son is his father's ruin,
and a quarrelsome wife is like a constant
dripping.

¹⁴Houses and wealth are inherited from parents,
but a prudent wife is from the LORD.

¹⁵Laziness brings on deep sleep,
and the shiftless man goes hungry.

¹⁶He who obeys instructions guards his life,
but he who is contemptuous of his ways
will die.

¹⁷He who is kind to the poor lends to the LORD,
and he will reward him for what he has
done.

¹⁸Discipline your son, for in that there is hope;
do not be a willing party to his death.

¹⁹A hot-tempered man must pay the penalty;
if you rescue him, you will have to do it
again.

²⁰Listen to advice and accept instruction,
and in the end you will be wise.

²¹Many are the plans in a man's heart,
but it is the LORD's purpose that prevails.

²²What a man desires is unfailing loveⁱ;
better to be poor than a liar.

²³The fear of the LORD leads to life:
Then one rests content, untouched by
trouble.

²⁴The sluggard buries his hand in the dish;
he will not even bring it back to his
mouth!

²⁵Flog a mocker, and the simple will learn
prudence;
rebuke a discerning man, and he will gain
knowledge.

²⁶He who robs his father and drives out his
mother
is a son who brings shame and disgrace.

²⁷Stop listening to instruction, my son,
and you will stray from the words of
knowledge.

²⁸A corrupt witness mocks at justice,
and the mouth of the wicked gulps down
evil.

²⁹Penalties are prepared for mockers,
and beatings for the backs of fools.

h 7 The meaning of the Hebrew for this sentence is uncertain.   i 22 Or
A man's greed is his shame

Discovering the Word 1. When is it better to be poor (vv. 1, 22)? 2. What do you learn about the difficulties of poverty from Proverbs 19 (vv. 3, 7)? 3. What experience have you had with the problem mentioned in verse 6? 4. How can we avoid that problem? 5. Verse 17 implies a motive for giving that is almost never mentioned or, if mentioned, viewed as sub-Christian. What is it? 6. Why do you think people are uncomfortable with that kind of motive?

Applying the Word 1. When is giving to the poor difficult for you? 2. Beginning this week, how can your giving to the poor reflect the wisdom of these proverbs?

Responding in Prayer Pray for "unfailing love" (v. 22) that will allow you to give as God would want you to.

Proverbs 20

20 Wine is a mocker and beer a brawler;
whoever is led astray by them is not wise.

²A king's wrath is like the roar of a lion;
he who angers him forfeits his life.

³It is to a man's honor to avoid strife,
but every fool is quick to quarrel.

⁴A sluggard does not plow in season;
so at harvest time he looks but finds nothing.

⁵The purposes of a man's heart are deep waters,
but a man of understanding draws them out.

⁶Many a man claims to have unfailing love,
but a faithful man who can find?

⁷The righteous man leads a blameless life;
blessed are his children after him.

⁸When a king sits on his throne to judge,
he winnows out all evil with his eyes.

⁹Who can say, "I have kept my heart pure;
I am clean and without sin"?

¹⁰Differing weights and differing measures—
the Lord detests them both.

¹¹Even a child is known by his actions,
by whether his conduct is pure and right.

¹²Ears that hear and eyes that see—
the Lord has made them both.

¹³Do not love sleep or you will grow poor;
stay awake and you will have food to spare.

¹⁴"It's no good, it's no good!" says the buyer;
then off he goes and boasts about his purchase.

¹⁵Gold there is, and rubies in abundance,
but lips that speak knowledge are a rare jewel.

¹⁶Take the garment of one who puts up security for a stranger;
hold it in pledge if he does it for a wayward woman.

¹⁷Food gained by fraud tastes sweet to a man,
but he ends up with a mouth full of gravel.

¹⁸Make plans by seeking advice;
if you wage war, obtain guidance.

¹⁹A gossip betrays a confidence;
so avoid a man who talks too much.

²⁰If a man curses his father or mother,
his lamp will be snuffed out in pitch darkness.

²¹An inheritance quickly gained at the beginning
will not be blessed at the end.

²²Do not say, "I'll pay you back for this wrong!"
Wait for the Lord, and he will deliver you.

²³The Lord detests differing weights,
and dishonest scales do not please him.

²⁴A man's steps are directed by the Lord.
How then can anyone understand his own way?

²⁵It is a trap for a man to dedicate something rashly
and only later to consider his vows.

²⁶A wise king winnows out the wicked;
he drives the threshing wheel over them.

²⁷The lamp of the Lord searches the spirit of a man[j];
it searches out his inmost being.

²⁸Love and faithfulness keep a king safe;
through love his throne is made secure.

²⁹The glory of young men is their strength,
gray hair the splendor of the old.

³⁰Blows and wounds cleanse away evil,
and beatings purge the inmost being.

j27 Or The spirit of man is the Lord's lamp

9 / *Proverbs 21*
Planning the Future

NO DOUBT YOU'VE glanced once or twice at an astrologer's predictions in the newspaper. Even if you felt guilty or silly for doing it, you'd hardly fault yourself for wanting every possible advantage in planning your future. Planning for the future, after all, is a major industry. Hundreds of billions of dollars ride on the forecasts of economists, investment counselors, analysts of every sort, and even astrologers! Legions of advisors will sell you opinions on what will happen in the near term and long term; whether or not you take their advice, someone else will. And that person's actions may in turn affect your prosperity, health and happiness. For all their focus on the here and now, the proverbs keep a canny eye on the future. Many proverbs, in fact, offer wisdom on how to make plans, why to make them, and what we can expect of the best plans we make. With these proverbs you'll begin training for planning your future.

 Warming Up to God   How often do you think about and plan for the future?

 Read Proverbs 21.

21
The king's heart is in the hand of
the LORD;
   he directs it like a watercourse
wherever he pleases.

²All a man's ways seem right to him,
   but the LORD weighs the heart.

³To do what is right and just
   is more acceptable to the LORD than
      sacrifice.

⁴Haughty eyes and a proud heart,
   the lamp of the wicked, are sin!

⁵The plans of the diligent lead to profit
   as surely as haste leads to poverty.

⁶A fortune made by a lying tongue
   is a fleeting vapor and a deadly snare.ᵏ

⁷The violence of the wicked will drag them
      away,
   for they refuse to do what is right.

⁸The way of the guilty is devious,
   but the conduct of the innocent is upright.

⁹Better to live on a corner of the roof
   than share a house with a quarrelsome
      wife.

¹⁰The wicked man craves evil;
   his neighbor gets no mercy from him.

¹¹When a mocker is punished, the simple gain
      wisdom;
   when a wise man is instructed, he gets
      knowledge.

¹²The Righteous Oneˡ takes note of the house
      of the wicked
   and brings the wicked to ruin.

¹³If a man shuts his ears to the cry of the poor,
   he too will cry out and not be answered.

¹⁴A gift given in secret soothes anger,
   and a bribe concealed in the cloak pacifies
      great wrath.

¹⁵When justice is done, it brings joy to the
      righteous
   but terror to evildoers.

¹⁶A man who strays from the path of
      understanding
   comes to rest in the company of the dead.

¹⁷He who loves pleasure will become poor;
   whoever loves wine and oil will never be
      rich.

¹⁸The wicked become a ransom for the
      righteous,
   and the unfaithful for the upright.

¹⁹Better to live in a desert
   than with a quarrelsome and ill-tempered
      wife.

²⁰In the house of the wise are stores of choice
      food and oil,
   but a foolish man devours all he has.

²¹He who pursues righteousness and love

ᵏ6 Some Hebrew manuscripts, Septuagint and Vulgate; most Hebrew
manuscripts *vapor for those who seek death*   ˡ12 Or *The righteous
man*

finds life, prosperity[m] and honor.

²²A wise man attacks the city of the mighty
　and pulls down the stronghold in which
　　they trust.

²³He who guards his mouth and his tongue
　keeps himself from calamity.

²⁴The proud and arrogant man—"Mocker" is
　his name;
　he behaves with overweening pride.

²⁵The sluggard's craving will be the death of
　him,
　because his hands refuse to work.

²⁶All day long he craves for more,
　but the righteous give without sparing.

²⁷The sacrifice of the wicked is detestable—

how much more so when brought with evil
　intent!

²⁸A false witness will perish,
　and whoever listens to him will be
　　destroyed forever.[n]

²⁹A wicked man puts up a bold front,
　but an upright man gives thought to his
　　ways.

³⁰There is no wisdom, no insight, no plan
　that can succeed against the LORD.

³¹The horse is made ready for the day of battle,
　but victory rests with the LORD.

[m]21 Or *righteousness*　　[n]28 Or *1 but the words of an obedient man will live on*

Discovering the Word 1. The proverbs insist that character affects the success or failure of the plans a person makes. What character qualities mentioned in Proverbs 21 hinder our efforts to plan for the future (vv. 1–8, 16–17, 20–21, 23–26, 29–31)? 2. We usually evaluate a plan according to its merits, not on the basis of the character of the planner. Why does a planner's character make a difference? 3. Verse 2 points to a trap that we often fall into. Describe it. 4. Verse 5 says that a good plan by itself is not enough to yield success. Suppose you plan a picnic for a large number of people. Suppose further that you are diligent. How would your actions differ from those of a person who was not diligent? 5. Why do you think verse 21 points to just two qualities—righteousness and love—as the source of life, prosperity and honor? 6. An atheist could profitably apply much of the wisdom we've seen in these studies. Yet how do verses 30–31 also point to a divine dimension in the plans we make (and, indeed, in all wisdom)?

Applying the Word 1. When has one of your plans failed for one of the reasons mentioned in these proverbs? 2. What truths from this passage can help you with your current planning?

Responding in Prayer "Victory rests with the LORD" (v. 31). Allow that hope and promise to shape your prayers.

Proverbs 22:1—24:22

22 A good name is more desirable
　than great riches;
　to be esteemed is better than
　silver or gold.

²Rich and poor have this in common:
　The LORD is the Maker of them all.

³A prudent man sees danger and takes refuge,
　but the simple keep going and suffer for it.

⁴Humility and the fear of the LORD
　bring wealth and honor and life.

⁵In the paths of the wicked lie thorns and
　snares,

but he who guards his soul stays far from
　them.

⁶Train[o] a child in the way he should go,
　and when he is old he will not turn from
　　it.

⁷The rich rule over the poor,
　and the borrower is servant to the lender.

⁸He who sows wickedness reaps trouble,
　and the rod of his fury will be destroyed.

⁹A generous man will himself be blessed,
　for he shares his food with the poor.

[o]6 Or *Start*

¹⁰Drive out the mocker, and out goes strife;
  quarrels and insults are ended.

¹¹He who loves a pure heart and whose speech
      is gracious
  will have the king for his friend.

¹²The eyes of the LORD keep watch over
      knowledge,
  but he frustrates the words of the
      unfaithful.

¹³The sluggard says, "There is a lion outside!"
  or, "I will be murdered in the streets!"

¹⁴The mouth of an adulteress is a deep pit;
  he who is under the LORD's wrath will fall
      into it.

¹⁵Folly is bound up in the heart of a child,
  but the rod of discipline will drive it far
      from him.

¹⁶He who oppresses the poor to increase his
      wealth
  and he who gives gifts to the rich—both
      come to poverty.

¹⁷Pay attention and listen to the sayings of the
      wise;
  apply your heart to what I teach,
¹⁸for it is pleasing when you keep them in your
      heart
  and have all of them ready on your lips.
¹⁹So that your trust may be in the LORD,
  I teach you today, even you.
²⁰Have I not written thirtyᵖ sayings for you,
  sayings of counsel and knowledge,
²¹teaching you true and reliable words,
  so that you can give sound answers
      to him who sent you?

²²Do not exploit the poor because they are poor
  and do not crush the needy in court,
²³for the LORD will take up their case
  and will plunder those who plunder them.

²⁴Do not make friends with a hot-tempered
      man,
  do not associate with one easily angered,
²⁵or you may learn his ways
  and get yourself ensnared.

²⁶Do not be a man who strikes hands in pledge
  or puts up security for debts;
²⁷if you lack the means to pay,

your very bed will be snatched from under
  you.

²⁸Do not move an ancient boundary stone
  set up by your forefathers.

²⁹Do you see a man skilled in his work?
  He will serve before kings;
  he will not serve before obscure men.

23 When you sit to dine with a ruler,
    note well what�q is before you,
    ²and put a knife to your throat
  if you are given to gluttony.
³Do not crave his delicacies,
  for that food is deceptive.

⁴Do not wear yourself out to get rich;
  have the wisdom to show restraint.
⁵Cast but a glance at riches, and they are gone,
  for they will surely sprout wings
  and fly off to the sky like an eagle.

⁶Do not eat the food of a stingy man,
  do not crave his delicacies;
⁷for he is the kind of man
  who is always thinking about the cost.ʳ
  "Eat and drink," he says to you,
  but his heart is not with you.
⁸You will vomit up the little you have eaten
  and will have wasted your compliments.

⁹Do not speak to a fool,
  for he will scorn the wisdom of your
      words.

¹⁰Do not move an ancient boundary stone
  or encroach on the fields of the fatherless,
¹¹for their Defender is strong;
  he will take up their case against you.

¹²Apply your heart to instruction
  and your ears to words of knowledge.

¹³Do not withhold discipline from a child;
  if you punish him with the rod, he will not
      die.
¹⁴Punish him with the rod
  and save his soul from death.ˢ

¹⁵My son, if your heart is wise,
  then my heart will be glad;
¹⁶my inmost being will rejoice
  when your lips speak what is right.

ᵖ20 Or *not formerly written; or not written excellent*   �q1 Or *who*
ʳ7 Or *for as he thinks within himself, / so he is; or for as he puts on a
feast, / so he is*   ˢ14 Hebrew *Sheol*

¹⁷Do not let your heart envy sinners,
    but always be zealous for the fear of the
        LORD.
¹⁸There is surely a future hope for you,
    and your hope will not be cut off.

¹⁹Listen, my son, and be wise,
    and keep your heart on the right path.
²⁰Do not join those who drink too much wine
    or gorge themselves on meat,
²¹for drunkards and gluttons become poor,
    and drowsiness clothes them in rags.

²²Listen to your father, who gave you life,
    and do not despise your mother when she
        is old.
²³Buy the truth and do not sell it;
    get wisdom, discipline and understanding.
²⁴The father of a righteous man has great joy;
    he who has a wise son delights in him.
²⁵May your father and mother be glad;
    may she who gave you birth rejoice!

²⁶My son, give me your heart
    and let your eyes keep to my ways,
²⁷for a prostitute is a deep pit
    and a wayward wife is a narrow well.
²⁸Like a bandit she lies in wait,
    and multiplies the unfaithful among men.

²⁹Who has woe? Who has sorrow?
    Who has strife? Who has complaints?
    Who has needless bruises? Who has
        bloodshot eyes?
³⁰Those who linger over wine,
    who go to sample bowls of mixed wine.
³¹Do not gaze at wine when it is red,
    when it sparkles in the cup,
    when it goes down smoothly!
³²In the end it bites like a snake
    and poisons like a viper.
³³Your eyes will see strange sights
    and your mind imagine confusing things.
³⁴You will be like one sleeping on the high
        seas,
    lying on top of the rigging.
³⁵"They hit me," you will say, "but I'm not
        hurt!
    They beat me, but I don't feel it!
    When will I wake up
        so I can find another drink?"

24

Do not envy wicked men,
    do not desire their company;
    ²for their hearts plot violence,
and their lips talk about making trouble.

³By wisdom a house is built,
    and through understanding it is established;
⁴through knowledge its rooms are filled
    with rare and beautiful treasures.

⁵A wise man has great power,
    and a man of knowledge increases strength;
⁶for waging war you need guidance,
    and for victory many advisers.

⁷Wisdom is too high for a fool;
    in the assembly at the gate he has nothing
        to say.

⁸He who plots evil
    will be known as a schemer.
⁹The schemes of folly are sin,
    and men detest a mocker.

¹⁰If you falter in times of trouble,
    how small is your strength!
¹¹Rescue those being led away to death;
    hold back those staggering toward
        slaughter.
¹²If you say, "But we knew nothing about this,"
    does not he who weighs the heart perceive
        it?
    Does not he who guards your life know it?
    Will he not repay each person according to
        what he has done?

¹³Eat honey, my son, for it is good;
    honey from the comb is sweet to your taste.
¹⁴Know also that wisdom is sweet to your soul;
    if you find it, there is a future hope for
        you,
    and your hope will not be cut off.

¹⁵Do not lie in wait like an outlaw against a
        righteous man's house,
    do not raid his dwelling place;
¹⁶for though a righteous man falls seven times,
        he rises again,
    but the wicked are brought down by
        calamity.

¹⁷Do not gloat when your enemy falls;
    when he stumbles, do not let your heart
        rejoice,
¹⁸or the LORD will see and disapprove

and turn his wrath away from him.

¹⁹Do not fret because of evil men
  or be envious of the wicked,
²⁰for the evil man has no future hope,
  and the lamp of the wicked will be snuffed
    out.

²¹Fear the LORD and the king, my son,
  and do not join with the rebellious,
²²for those two will send sudden destruction
    upon them,
  and who knows what calamities they can
    bring?

---

10 / *Proverbs 24:23–34*
The Sluggard

YOU'VE FELT THE urge before; you've attended the soft voice that says: "The messy garage will still be there tomorrow; the chaotic closet won't run away. You've done enough for today. Leave that weedy flower bed till the weekend. Wait a few more days for the rest of the bills to arrive, and then you can pay them all at once! If you wash the car now, it'll rain, and then where will you be?" These seductions routinely beset a character the proverbs call *the sluggard.* We're apt to laugh in sympathy with the sluggard's feeble struggles to develop personal industry. After all, don't we know too well the sensual pleasures of a catnap? The proverbs laugh too, but it's more a snicker of scorn. The proverbs in this quiet time afford a bracing look at the sluggard.

 Warming Up to God   What tasks are you most tempted to put off until tomorrow?

 Read Proverbs 24:23–34.

---

²³These also are sayings of the wise:

To show partiality in judging is not good:
²⁴Whoever says to the guilty, "You are
    innocent"—
  peoples will curse him and nations
    denounce him.
²⁵But it will go well with those who convict the
    guilty,
  and rich blessing will come upon them.

²⁶An honest answer
  is like a kiss on the lips.

²⁷Finish your outdoor work
  and get your fields ready;
  after that, build your house.

²⁸Do not testify against your neighbor without
    cause,

or use your lips to deceive.
²⁹Do not say, "I'll do to him as he has done to
    me;
  I'll pay that man back for what he did."

³⁰I went past the field of the sluggard,
  past the vineyard of the man who lacks
    judgment;
³¹thorns had come up everywhere,
  the ground was covered with weeds,
  and the stone wall was in ruins.
³²I applied my heart to what I observed
  and learned a lesson from what I saw:
³³A little sleep, a little slumber,
  a little folding of the hands to rest—
³⁴and poverty will come on you like a bandit
  and scarcity like an armed man.ᶠ

ᶠ34 Or *like a vagrant / and scarcity like a beggar*

Discovering the Word   **1.** Although most of us are no longer farmers, how could verse 27 be good advice for us?   **2.** What characteristics of the sluggard do you notice (vv. 30–34)?   **3.** In 6:6–8 we see how the ant, in contrast, stores up provisions. How could you apply the remedy suggested by the ant to the one area of sluggardliness you mentioned previously?   **4.** How is the poverty that overcomes the sluggard like a bandit or an armed man (v. 34)? (What characteristics, for example, do such poverty and a bandit have in common?)

5. The proverbs hold out little hope for reforming a committed fool. On the other hand, why might there be some hope for reforming a sluggard?

 Applying the Word 1. Sometimes we need to rest! What is the difference between resting and being a sluggard? 2. Describe one area of your life where two or three characteristics of a sluggard are evident (for example, housework, desk, various chores, yardwork, grooming, wardrobe and so on). Be honest!

Responding in Prayer Ask God to make you a good steward of the time and resources he's given you.

Proverbs 25—26

25 These are more proverbs of Solomon, copied by the men of Hezekiah king of Judah:

²It is the glory of God to conceal a matter;
  to search out a matter is the glory of kings.

³As the heavens are high and the earth is deep,
  so the hearts of kings are unsearchable.

⁴Remove the dross from the silver,
  and out comes material forᵘ the
    silversmith;
⁵remove the wicked from the king's presence,
  and his throne will be established through
    righteousness.

⁶Do not exalt yourself in the king's presence,
  and do not claim a place among great men;
⁷it is better for him to say to you, "Come up
    here,"
  than for him to humiliate you before a
    nobleman.

What you have seen with your eyes
⁸ do not bringᵛ hastily to court,
  for what will you do in the end
  if your neighbor puts you to shame?

⁹If you argue your case with a neighbor,
  do not betray another man's confidence,
¹⁰or he who hears it may shame you
  and you will never lose your bad
    reputation.

¹¹A word aptly spoken
  is like apples of gold in settings of silver.

¹²Like an earring of gold or an ornament of fine
    gold
  is a wise man's rebuke to a listening ear.

¹³Like the coolness of snow at harvest time

is a trustworthy messenger to those who
    send him;
  he refreshes the spirit of his masters.

¹⁴Like clouds and wind without rain
  is a man who boasts of gifts he does not
    give.

¹⁵Through patience a ruler can be persuaded,
  and a gentle tongue can break a bone.

¹⁶If you find honey, eat just enough—
  too much of it, and you will vomit.

¹⁷Seldom set foot in your neighbor's house—
  too much of you, and he will hate you.

¹⁸Like a club or a sword or a sharp arrow
  is the man who gives false testimony
    against his neighbor.

¹⁹Like a bad tooth or a lame foot
  is reliance on the unfaithful in times of
    trouble.

²⁰Like one who takes away a garment on a cold
    day,
  or like vinegar poured on soda,
  is one who sings songs to a heavy heart.

²¹If your enemy is hungry, give him food to eat;
  if he is thirsty, give him water to drink.
²²In doing this, you will heap burning coals on
    his head,
  and the LORD will reward you.

²³As a north wind brings rain,
  so a sly tongue brings angry looks.

²⁴Better to live on a corner of the roof
  than share a house with a quarrelsome
    wife.

²⁵Like cold water to a weary soul

ᵘ4 Or comes a vessel from   ᵛ7,8 Or nobleman / on whom you had set
your eyes. / ⁸Do not go

is good news from a distant land.

²⁶Like a muddied spring or a polluted well
  is a righteous man who gives way to the
    wicked.

²⁷It is not good to eat too much honey,
  nor is it honorable to seek one's own
    honor.

²⁸Like a city whose walls are broken down
  is a man who lacks self-control.

26

Like snow in summer or rain in
  harvest,
honor is not fitting for a fool.

²Like a fluttering sparrow or a darting swallow,
  an undeserved curse does not come to rest.

³A whip for the horse, a halter for the donkey,
  and a rod for the backs of fools!

⁴Do not answer a fool according to his folly,
  or you will be like him yourself.

⁵Answer a fool according to his folly,
  or he will be wise in his own eyes.

⁶Like cutting off one's feet or drinking violence
  is the sending of a message by the hand of
    a fool.

⁷Like a lame man's legs that hang limp
  is a proverb in the mouth of a fool.

⁸Like tying a stone in a sling
  is the giving of honor to a fool.

⁹Like a thornbush in a drunkard's hand
  is a proverb in the mouth of a fool.

¹⁰Like an archer who wounds at random
  is he who hires a fool or any passer-by.

¹¹As a dog returns to its vomit,
  so a fool repeats his folly.

¹²Do you see a man wise in his own eyes?
  There is more hope for a fool than for him.

¹³The sluggard says, "There is a lion in the
    road,

a fierce lion roaming the streets!"

¹⁴As a door turns on its hinges,
  so a sluggard turns on his bed.

¹⁵The sluggard buries his hand in the dish;
  he is too lazy to bring it back to his mouth.

¹⁶The sluggard is wiser in his own eyes
  than seven men who answer discreetly.

¹⁷Like one who seizes a dog by the ears
  is a passer-by who meddles in a quarrel not
    his own.

¹⁸Like a madman shooting
    firebrands or deadly arrows
¹⁹is a man who deceives his neighbor
  and says, "I was only joking!"

²⁰Without wood a fire goes out;
  without gossip a quarrel dies down.

²¹As charcoal to embers and as wood to fire,
  so is a quarrelsome man for kindling strife.

²²The words of a gossip are like choice morsels;
  they go down to a man's inmost parts.

²³Like a coating of glazeʷ over earthenware
  are fervent lips with an evil heart.

²⁴A malicious man disguises himself with his
    lips,
  but in his heart he harbors deceit.
²⁵Though his speech is charming, do not
    believe him,
  for seven abominations fill his heart.
²⁶His malice may be concealed by deception,
  but his wickedness will be exposed in the
    assembly.

²⁷If a man digs a pit, he will fall into it;
  if a man rolls a stone, it will roll back on
    him.

²⁸A lying tongue hates those it hurts,
  and a flattering mouth works ruin.

ʷ23 With a different word division of the Hebrew; Masoretic Text *of
silver dross*

11 / *Proverbs 27*
Friends

AS E. C. McKENZIE said, "Some people make enemies instead of friends, because it is less trouble." It takes even less effort to alienate the friends we already have. On the other hand, finding and keeping a friend requires all the skill we can muster. But the reward for that effort is correspondingly great. The proverbs in this study give advice on friendship—its maintenance, how it is strengthened or weakened, and the special value of a friend. This wisdom is particularly valuable when applied to husband and wife, parent and child. But the wonder of friendship is its capacity to transcend age and gender, and to forge bonds stronger than blood.

 Warming Up to God   How have you recently been encouraged to spiritual growth by a friend?

 Read Proverbs 27.

27 Do not boast about tomorrow,
for you do not know what a day
may bring forth.

²Let another praise you, and not your own
mouth;
someone else, and not your own lips.

³Stone is heavy and sand a burden,
but provocation by a fool is heavier than
both.

⁴Anger is cruel and fury overwhelming,
but who can stand before jealousy?

⁵Better is open rebuke
than hidden love.

⁶Wounds from a friend can be trusted,
but an enemy multiplies kisses.

⁷He who is full loathes honey,
but to the hungry even what is bitter tastes
sweet.

⁸Like a bird that strays from its nest
is a man who strays from his home.

⁹Perfume and incense bring joy to the heart,
and the pleasantness of one's friend springs
from his earnest counsel.

¹⁰Do not forsake your friend and the friend of
your father,
and do not go to your brother's house
when disaster strikes you—
better a neighbor nearby than a brother far
away.

¹¹Be wise, my son, and bring joy to my heart;

then I can answer anyone who treats me
with contempt.

¹²The prudent see danger and take refuge,
but the simple keep going and suffer for it.

¹³Take the garment of one who puts up security
for a stranger;
hold it in pledge if he does it for a
wayward woman.

¹⁴If a man loudly blesses his neighbor early in
the morning,
it will be taken as a curse.

¹⁵A quarrelsome wife is like
a constant dripping on a rainy day;
¹⁶restraining her is like restraining the wind
or grasping oil with the hand.

¹⁷As iron sharpens iron,
so one man sharpens another.

¹⁸He who tends a fig tree will eat its fruit,
and he who looks after his master will be
honored.

¹⁹As water reflects a face,
so a man's heart reflects the man.

²⁰Death and Destruction[x] are never satisfied,
and neither are the eyes of man.

²¹The crucible for silver and the furnace for
gold,
but man is tested by the praise he receives.

²²Though you grind a fool in a mortar,
grinding him like grain with a pestle,

[x]20 Hebrew *Sheol and Abaddon*

you will not remove his folly from him.

²³Be sure you know the condition of your
    flocks,
    give careful attention to your herds;
²⁴for riches do not endure forever,
    and a crown is not secure for all
        generations.

²⁵When the hay is removed and new growth
        appears
    and the grass from the hills is gathered in,
²⁶the lambs will provide you with clothing,
    and the goats with the price of a field.
²⁷You will have plenty of goats' milk
    to feed you and your family
    and to nourish your servant girls.

Discovering the Word 1. *Friend* in English is flexible enough in its meaning to cover everything from a casual acquaintance to an intimate soul-mate. What type of friend is being described in these verses? 2. Our enemies do not actually kiss us, any more than our friends actually wreak damage on our bodies. *Kisses* and *wounds* are figures of speech. How would you paraphrase verse 6 without using the words *kisses, wounds* or any other figurative language? 3. Describe a "kiss" you've received from an enemy and a "wound" you've received from a friend. 4. How are the kind words of friends a special pleasure (vv. 2, 17)? 5. Ancient people knew, as we do, that only a harder material effectively sharpens a softer material. What happens when two objects of the same material sharpen one another (v. 17)?

Applying the Word 1. What friendship do you currently have in which you are sharpening one another? How are you doing that? 2. How many friends (in the sense that the proverbs use the term) do you think you want? Explain.

 Responding in Prayer Thank God for the friends you have who speak honestly with you—whether encouraging or rebuking—and build your relationship with Christ.

Proverbs 28—29

28 The wicked man flees though no
    one pursues,
    but the righteous are as bold as a
        lion.

²When a country is rebellious, it has many
        rulers,
    but a man of understanding and knowledge
        maintains order.

³A ruler^y who oppresses the poor
    is like a driving rain that leaves no crops.

⁴Those who forsake the law praise the wicked,
    but those who keep the law resist them.

⁵Evil men do not understand justice,
    but those who seek the Lᴏʀᴅ understand it
        fully.

⁶Better a poor man whose walk is blameless
    than a rich man whose ways are perverse.

⁷He who keeps the law is a discerning son,
    but a companion of gluttons disgraces his
        father.

⁸He who increases his wealth by exorbitant
        interest
    amasses it for another, who will be kind to
        the poor.

⁹If anyone turns a deaf ear to the law,
    even his prayers are detestable.

¹⁰He who leads the upright along an evil path
    will fall into his own trap,
    but the blameless will receive a good
        inheritance.

¹¹A rich man may be wise in his own eyes,
    but a poor man who has discernment sees
        through him.

¹²When the righteous triumph, there is great
        elation;
    but when the wicked rise to power, men go
        into hiding.

¹³He who conceals his sins does not prosper,
    but whoever confesses and renounces them
        finds mercy.

y3 Or *A poor man*

¹⁴Blessed is the man who always fears the LORD,
    but he who hardens his heart falls into
        trouble.

¹⁵Like a roaring lion or a charging bear
    is a wicked man ruling over a helpless
        people.

¹⁶A tyrannical ruler lacks judgment,
    but he who hates ill-gotten gain will enjoy
        a long life.

¹⁷A man tormented by the guilt of murder
    will be a fugitive till death;
    let no one support him.

¹⁸He whose walk is blameless is kept safe,
    but he whose ways are perverse will
        suddenly fall.

¹⁹He who works his land will have abundant
        food,
    but the one who chases fantasies will have
        his fill of poverty.

²⁰A faithful man will be richly blessed,
    but one eager to get rich will not go
        unpunished.

²¹To show partiality is not good—
    yet a man will do wrong for a piece of
        bread.

²²A stingy man is eager to get rich
    and is unaware that poverty awaits him.

²³He who rebukes a man will in the end gain
        more favor
    than he who has a flattering tongue.

²⁴He who robs his father or mother
    and says, "It's not wrong"—
    he is partner to him who destroys.

²⁵A greedy man stirs up dissension,
    but he who trusts in the LORD will prosper.

²⁶He who trusts in himself is a fool,
    but he who walks in wisdom is kept safe.

²⁷He who gives to the poor will lack nothing,
    but he who closes his eyes to them receives
        many curses.

²⁸When the wicked rise to power, people go
        into hiding;
    but when the wicked perish, the righteous
        thrive.

29 A man who remains stiff-necked
    after many rebukes
      will suddenly be destroyed—
    without remedy.

²When the righteous thrive, the people rejoice;
    when the wicked rule, the people groan.

³A man who loves wisdom brings joy to his
        father,
    but a companion of prostitutes squanders
        his wealth.

⁴By justice a king gives a country stability,
    but one who is greedy for bribes tears it
        down.

⁵Whoever flatters his neighbor
    is spreading a net for his feet.

⁶An evil man is snared by his own sin,
    but a righteous one can sing and be glad.

⁷The righteous care about justice for the poor,
    but the wicked have no such concern.

⁸Mockers stir up a city,
    but wise men turn away anger.

⁹If a wise man goes to court with a fool,
    the fool rages and scoffs, and there is no
        peace.

¹⁰Bloodthirsty men hate a man of integrity
    and seek to kill the upright.

¹¹A fool gives full vent to his anger,
    but a wise man keeps himself under
        control.

¹²If a ruler listens to lies,
    all his officials become wicked.

¹³The poor man and the oppressor have this in
        common:
    The LORD gives sight to the eyes of both.

¹⁴If a king judges the poor with fairness,
    his throne will always be secure.

¹⁵The rod of correction imparts wisdom,
    but a child left to himself disgraces his
        mother.

¹⁶When the wicked thrive, so does sin,
    but the righteous will see their downfall.

¹⁷Discipline your son, and he will give you
        peace;
    he will bring delight to your soul.

¹⁸Where there is no revelation, the people cast
off restraint;
but blessed is he who keeps the law.

¹⁹A servant cannot be corrected by mere words;
though he understands, he will not
respond.

²⁰Do you see a man who speaks in haste?
There is more hope for a fool than for him.

²¹If a man pampers his servant from youth,
he will bring grief ᶻ in the end.

²²An angry man stirs up dissension,
and a hot-tempered one commits many
sins.

²³A man's pride brings him low,
but a man of lowly spirit gains honor.

²⁴The accomplice of a thief is his own enemy;
he is put under oath and dare not testify.

²⁵Fear of man will prove to be a snare,
but whoever trusts in the LORD is kept safe.

²⁶Many seek an audience with a ruler,
but it is from the LORD that man gets
justice.

²⁷The righteous detest the dishonest;
the wicked detest the upright.

ᶻ21 The meaning of the Hebrew for this word is uncertain.

12 / *Proverbs 30*
Wealth & Poverty

WHEN OTHERS ARE obviously rich or poor, we infer many things about their talents, education, personality, tastes and personal influence. But, from the perspective of the proverbs, wealth and poverty are poor standards to use in judging others. Furthermore, Proverbs tells us it is foolish to suppose that wealth is an unmixed blessing and that poverty is always a curse. In a world that views wealth and poverty from faulty and imperfect perspectives, we need the precise, pithy standards in the proverbs to guide our steps away from snares that lie on every side.

  Warming Up to God Whether we think we're rich or poor often depends on our point of view. In what circumstances would you "feel" wealthy or poor? (Remember, we're thinking of *material* wealth and poverty.)

  Read Proverbs 30.

30 The sayings of Agur son of Jakeh—
an oracle ᵃ:

This man declared to Ithiel,
to Ithiel and to Ucal: ᵇ

²"I am the most ignorant of men;
I do not have a man's understanding.
³I have not learned wisdom,
nor have I knowledge of the Holy One.
⁴Who has gone up to heaven and come down?
Who has gathered up the wind in the
hollow of his hands?
Who has wrapped up the waters in his cloak?
Who has established all the ends of the
earth?
What is his name, and the name of his son?
Tell me if you know!

⁵"Every word of God is flawless;
he is a shield to those who take refuge in
him.
⁶Do not add to his words,
or he will rebuke you and prove you a liar.

⁷"Two things I ask of you, O LORD;
do not refuse me before I die:
⁸Keep falsehood and lies far from me;
give me neither poverty nor riches,
but give me only my daily bread.
⁹Otherwise, I may have too much and disown
you
and say, 'Who is the LORD?'
Or I may become poor and steal,

ᵃ1 Or *Jakeh of Massa*   ᵇ1 Masoretic Text; with a different word
division of the Hebrew *declared, "I am weary, O God; / I am weary, O
God, and faint.*

and so dishonor the name of my God.

¹⁰"Do not slander a servant to his master,
　or he will curse you, and you will pay for
　　it.

¹¹"There are those who curse their fathers
　and do not bless their mothers;
¹²those who are pure in their own eyes
　and yet are not cleansed of their filth;
¹³those whose eyes are ever so haughty,
　whose glances are so disdainful;
¹⁴those whose teeth are swords
　and whose jaws are set with knives
to devour the poor from the earth,
　the needy from among mankind.

¹⁵"The leech has two daughters.
　'Give! Give!' they cry.

"There are three things that are never
　　satisfied,
　four that never say, 'Enough!':
¹⁶the grave,ᶜ the barren womb,
　land, which is never satisfied with water,
　and fire, which never says, 'Enough!'

¹⁷"The eye that mocks a father,
　that scorns obedience to a mother,
will be pecked out by the ravens of the valley,
　will be eaten by the vultures.

¹⁸"There are three things that are too amazing
　　for me,
　four that I do not understand:
¹⁹the way of an eagle in the sky,
　the way of a snake on a rock,
　the way of a ship on the high seas,
　and the way of a man with a maiden.

²⁰"This is the way of an adulteress:

She eats and wipes her mouth
　and says, 'I've done nothing wrong.'

²¹"Under three things the earth trembles,
　under four it cannot bear up:
²²a servant who becomes king,
　a fool who is full of food,
²³an unloved woman who is married,
　and a maidservant who displaces her
　　mistress.

²⁴"Four things on earth are small,
　yet they are extremely wise:
²⁵Ants are creatures of little strength,
　yet they store up their food in the summer;
²⁶coneysᵈ are creatures of little power,
　yet they make their home in the crags;
²⁷locusts have no king,
　yet they advance together in ranks;
²⁸a lizard can be caught with the hand,
　yet it is found in kings' palaces.

²⁹"There are three things that are stately in
　　their stride,
　four that move with stately bearing:
³⁰a lion, mighty among beasts,
　who retreats before nothing;
³¹a strutting rooster, a he-goat,
　and a king with his army around him.ᵉ

³²"If you have played the fool and exalted
　　yourself,
　or if you have planned evil,
　clap your hand over your mouth!
³³For as churning the milk produces butter,
　and as twisting the nose produces blood,
　so stirring up anger produces strife."

ᶜ16 Hebrew *Sheol*　　ᵈ26 That is, the hyrax or rock badger　　ᵉ31 Or
king secure against revolt

Discovering the Word 1. According to verses 8–9, what do you see to be some of the disadvantages
of wealth? 2. What are the disadvantages of poverty? 3. It is simple to know if we're extravagantly rich
or pitifully poor. But between these extremes the boundaries between poverty and wealth are hard to see. How
does the prayer in verses 8–9 help us know when we are becoming perilously rich or poor? 4. How is extreme
wealth or poverty like those things that are never satisfied (vv. 15–16)? 5. How do verses 24–28 further illustrate
the need for balance in life?

Applying the Word 1. Cite an example from your experience (or the experience of someone you know
about) where an increase in wealth proved *disadvantageous*. 2. Can you think of a situation where your
poverty (actual or perceived) proved to be an advantage to you? Explain. 3. To what extent have you embraced
the attitude "Give me only my daily bread"? Explain.

Responding in Prayer Pray for those you know who might be in danger because of having too much or
not enough. Pray for yourself as well.

Proverbs 31

31 The sayings of King Lemuel—an
oracle[f] his mother taught him:

²"O my son, O son of my womb,
O son of my vows,[g]
³do not spend your strength on women,
your vigor on those who ruin kings.

⁴"It is not for kings, O Lemuel—
not for kings to drink wine,
not for rulers to crave beer,
⁵lest they drink and forget what the law
decrees,
and deprive all the oppressed of their
rights.
⁶Give beer to those who are perishing,
wine to those who are in anguish;
⁷let them drink and forget their poverty
and remember their misery no more.

⁸"Speak up for those who cannot speak for
themselves,
for the rights of all who are destitute.
⁹Speak up and judge fairly;
defend the rights of the poor and needy."

¹⁰[h]A wife of noble character who can find?
She is worth far more than rubies.
¹¹Her husband has full confidence in her
and lacks nothing of value.
¹²She brings him good, not harm,
all the days of her life.
¹³She selects wool and flax
and works with eager hands.
¹⁴She is like the merchant ships,
bringing her food from afar.
¹⁵She gets up while it is still dark;
she provides food for her family
and portions for her servant girls.
¹⁶She considers a field and buys it;

out of her earnings she plants a vineyard.
¹⁷She sets about her work vigorously;
her arms are strong for her tasks.
¹⁸She sees that her trading is profitable,
and her lamp does not go out at night.
¹⁹In her hand she holds the distaff
and grasps the spindle with her fingers.
²⁰She opens her arms to the poor
and extends her hands to the needy.
²¹When it snows, she has no fear for her
household;
for all of them are clothed in scarlet.
²²She makes coverings for her bed;
she is clothed in fine linen and purple.
²³Her husband is respected at the city gate,
where he takes his seat among the elders of
the land.
²⁴She makes linen garments and sells them,
and supplies the merchants with sashes.
²⁵She is clothed with strength and dignity;
she can laugh at the days to come.
²⁶She speaks with wisdom,
and faithful instruction is on her tongue.
²⁷She watches over the affairs of her household
and does not eat the bread of idleness.
²⁸Her children arise and call her blessed;
her husband also, and he praises her:
²⁹"Many women do noble things,
but you surpass them all."
³⁰Charm is deceptive, and beauty is fleeting;
but a woman who fears the LORD is to be
praised.
³¹Give her the reward she has earned,
and let her works bring her praise at the
city gate.

---

f1 Or *of Lemuel king of Massa, which*   *g2* Or / *the answer to my
prayers*   *h10* Verses 10-31 are an acrostic, each verse beginning with
a successive letter of the Hebrew alphabet.

Ecclesiastes

L ike an apple tree in the middle of an orange grove stands the book of Ecclesiastes among the other books of the Bible. At first glance, it just does not seem to fit. What place does a book which flaunts the daring assertion "Meaningless! Meaningless! Everything is meaningless" have in Scripture that intends to reveal the saving work of God?

Along with the book of Job, Ecclesiastes reminds us that God is bigger, and our life in this world more unpredictable, than we might think. The book invites us to take a realistic tour of life. The sightseeing stops will likely leave those who enjoy nice tidy answers a bit perplexed, if not downright frustrated.

Our guide for this adventure is introduced by the Hebrew title *qoheleth*. The title, which translated into Greek is *ekklēsiastēs*, comes from a Hebrew word for assembling. It suggests a type of office-bearer. Thus we have such translations as "the Preacher" (KJV, RSV, NASB), "the Speaker" (NEB), "the Philosopher" (TEV) and the one used in the NIV, "the Teacher."

The Teacher identifies himself as "son of David, king in Jerusalem" (1:1). Such an identification naturally links him with the wisest of all Israel's sages, King Solomon. Many commentators, however, believe that the Teacher was not actually Solomon but someone who wrote in the tradition and from the perspective of Solomon. (For a full discussion of Ecclesiastes' authorship, as well as other related issues, including background and date, see Michael Eaton, *Ecclesiastes*, Tyndale Old Testament Commentaries [Downers Grove, Ill.: InterVarsity Press, 1983], or Derek Kidner, *The Wisdom of Proverbs, Job and Ecclesiastes: An Introduction to Wisdom Literature* [Downers Grove, Ill.: InterVarsity Press, 1985]. Two other helpful commentaries on Ecclesiastes are Charles Swindoll, *Living on the Ragged Edge Bible Study Guide* [Fullerton, Calif.: Insight for Living, 1986], and Derek Kidner, *The Message of Ecclesiastes* [Downers Grove, Ill.: InterVarsity Press, 1976].)

The depth of insight found in the book would certainly argue for an author endowed with the kind of wisdom God granted to Solomon (see 1Ki 3:5–12). If the Teacher was not actually King Solomon, he surely qualified as a star disciple of this master sage.

As a wise man, the Teacher represented a group whose influence grew to virtual equality with Israel's prophets and priests. Israel's wise men observed the interworkings of nature and experience. From this storehouse of wisdom they made general pronouncements concerning life's most perplexing issues and counseled people who faced difficult decisions.

The three most notable works of Israel's wise men include Ecclesiastes, Job and Proverbs. Their mark on Old Testament literature may also be seen in the Song of Songs, Lamentations and a number of the psalms (such as 1, 37, 49, 73, 127, 133). This body of writing, called wisdom literature, has a strong influence on portions of the New Testament. Jesus frequently quotes proverbs and uses wise sayings. Paul often talks about the wisdom of God (see 1 Co 1:18—2:16 as an example). And the book of James provides counsel in a style similar to Old Testament wisdom literature.

The Teacher's message seems particularly aimed at the secularists—those who seek to find life's meaning outside of a practical faith in God. With despairing perception, the author explores a grim reality he calls "life under the sun"—life outside of God's control and goodness. He addresses some of life's most sensitive questions: Where can we find satisfaction? Who is really in control? What does it take to be content? How do we live wisely?

Much of the time God is left out of the discussion. But when he is introduced, everything changes. "Life under the sun" becomes "life from the hand of God." Chasing after meaning is transformed into the pursuit of God. This exploration of life's meaninglessness outside of knowing God thus becomes an invitation to know him. In its own unique way, Ecclesiastes is ultimately an introduction to the One who "came that we might have life abundantly"—Jesus Christ himself. It highlights the dilemma voiced by Peter but faced by all of us: "Lord, to whom shall we go? You have the words of eternal life" (Jn 6:68).

Understandably, then, Ecclesiastes warrants special study by anyone in a formative period of life. Colleges would do well to set up a course for their freshmen and sophomores with Ecclesiastes as required reading. They could call it "Basic Living 101."

These quiet times will help you plunge into the pessimism of Ecclesiastes in order to see the hope of a God-centered lifestyle. May the Lord use your study of Ecclesiastes as an encouragement to follow him closely in this unique and perplexing adventure we call *life*.

Outline

Part 1: Making Sense Out of Life

1/ Ecclesiastes 1:1–11 —————————— *Is It All Meaningless?*

2/ Ecclesiastes 1:12—2:16 ——————— *Where Can We Find Fulfillment?*

3/ Ecclesiastes 2:17–26 ——————— *What Is the Value of Work?*

4/ Ecclesiastes 3:1—4:3 ——————— *Who Is Really in Control?*

5/ Ecclesiastes 4:4—5:7 ——————— *What Attitudes Should We Embrace?*

6/ Ecclesiastes 5:8—6:12 ——————— *What Does It Take to Be Content?*

Part 2: Living Life Sensibly

7/ Ecclesiastes 7:1—8:1 ——————— *Where Can We Find Wisdom?*

8/ Ecclesiastes 8:2–17 ——————— *How Shall We Live Under Authority?*

9/ Ecclesiastes 9:1–12 ——————— *What Meaning Does Death Bring to Life?*

10/ Ecclesiastes 9:13—10:20 ——————— *How Do We Live Sensibly?*

11/ Ecclesiastes 11:1—12:8 ——————— *How Shall We Then Live?*

12/ Ecclesiastes 12:9–14 ——————— *What Makes Life Meaningful?*

1 / *Ecclesiastes 1:1–11*
Is It All Meaningless?

THE WATER IN the glass measures exactly at the halfway point. Now comes the classic test to determine whether you are a pessimist or an optimist: Do you consider the glass of water to be half-empty or half-full? If you answered half-empty, you will find Ecclesiastes' author, the Teacher, a fast friend. If you answered half-full, you may find it harder to relate to him. But either way, realize he is delivering pessimism with a purpose. In his introduction he answers a question before he even raises it. The question is, "Can meaning in life come outside of a God-centered universe?" The answer? Well, hang on for some of Scripture's most brutal language.

 Warming Up to God Draw or imagine a line with *pure pessimist* on the left and *outrageous optimist* on the right. Where would you place yourself on the continuum? Regardless of your response, what gives you hope today?

 Read Ecclesiastes 1:1–11.

1 The words of the Teacher,[a] son of David,
king in Jerusalem:

²"Meaningless! Meaningless!"
says the Teacher.
"Utterly meaningless!
Everything is meaningless."

³What does man gain from all his labor
at which he toils under the sun?
⁴Generations come and generations go,
but the earth remains forever.
⁵The sun rises and the sun sets,
and hurries back to where it rises.
⁶The wind blows to the south
and turns to the north;
round and round it goes,
ever returning on its course.
⁷All streams flow into the sea,
yet the sea is never full.

To the place the streams come from,
there they return again.
⁸All things are wearisome,
more than one can say.
The eye never has enough of seeing,
nor the ear its fill of hearing.
⁹What has been will be again,
what has been done will be done again;
there is nothing new under the sun.
¹⁰Is there anything of which one can say,
"Look! This is something new"?
It was here already, long ago;
it was here before our time.
¹¹There is no remembrance of men of old,
and even those who are yet to come
will not be remembered
by those who follow.

a1 Or *leader of the assembly*; also in verses 2 and 12

 Discovering the Word 1. How do you react to the theme (or thesis) of the book which the Teacher states in verses 2–3? 2. How do examples of nature support his thesis that "everything is meaningless" (vv. 5–7)? 3. From verses 9–10 describe the Teacher's view of history. 4. What might he say to a person who believes that educating people will eventually solve humanity's problems? 5. How does human mortality (vv. 4 and 11) bring the Teacher's argument to a climax?

Applying the Word 1. According to verse 8, seeking new experiences will not bring lasting satisfaction. Give a personal example to illustrate this. 2. As a Christian, on what basis would you seek to refute the Teacher's thesis? 3. What is one area in your life that has recently seemed futile or meaningless?

Responding in Prayer Reflect on ways you sense that your life lacks meaning or purpose. Ask God to help you draw on his resources to resist meaningless living and pursue his purposes.

2 / *Ecclesiastes 1:12—2:16*
Where Can We Find Fulfillment?

IMAGINE A TOTAL plunge into hedonism—following every possible avenue of self-seeking pleasure and satisfaction. Now let your imagination grow further, having the political and financial means to indulge yourself to the fullest possible extent. Imagination turns to reality in this section of Ecclesiastes—surely one of the most colorful passages in the Bible. Here is one person's attempt at something many only dream about.

 Warming Up to God If by some sudden shift in perspective wordly pleasure suddenly became your overriding goal, what would you likely do? With what results? Talk to God about your deeper desires to forsake short-term self-indulgence for the long-term gain of knowing him.

 Read Ecclesiastes 1:12—2:16.

---

¹²I, the Teacher, was king over Israel in Jerusalem. ¹³I devoted myself to study and to explore by wisdom all that is done under heaven. What a heavy burden God has laid on men! ¹⁴I have seen all the things that are done under the sun; all of them are meaningless, a chasing after the wind.

¹⁵What is twisted cannot be straightened;
  what is lacking cannot be counted.

¹⁶I thought to myself, "Look, I have grown and increased in wisdom more than anyone who has ruled over Jerusalem before me; I have experienced much of wisdom and knowledge." ¹⁷Then I applied myself to the understanding of wisdom, and also of madness and folly, but I learned that this, too, is a chasing after the wind.

¹⁸For with much wisdom comes much sorrow;
  the more knowledge, the more grief.

2 I thought in my heart, "Come now, I will test you with pleasure to find out what is good." But that also proved to be meaningless. ²"Laughter," I said, "is foolish. And what does pleasure accomplish?" ³I tried cheering myself with wine, and embracing folly—my mind still guiding me with wisdom. I wanted to see what was worthwhile for men to do under heaven during the few days of their lives.

⁴I undertook great projects: I built houses for myself and planted vineyards. ⁵I made gardens and parks and planted all kinds of fruit trees in them. ⁶I made reservoirs to water groves of flourishing trees. ⁷I bought male and female slaves and had other slaves who were born in my house. I also owned more herds and flocks than anyone in Jerusalem before me. ⁸I amassed silver and gold for myself, and the treasure of kings and provinces. I acquired men and women singers, and a harem*ᵇ* as well—the delights of the heart of man. ⁹I became greater by far than anyone in Jerusalem before me. In all this my wisdom stayed with me.

¹⁰I denied myself nothing my eyes desired;
  I refused my heart no pleasure.
My heart took delight in all my work,
  and this was the reward for all my labor.
¹¹Yet when I surveyed all that my hands had done
  and what I had toiled to achieve,
everything was meaningless, a chasing after the wind;
  nothing was gained under the sun.

¹²Then I turned my thoughts to consider wisdom,
  and also madness and folly.
What more can the king's successor do
  than what has already been done?
¹³I saw that wisdom is better than folly,
  just as light is better than darkness.
¹⁴The wise man has eyes in his head,
  while the fool walks in the darkness;
but I came to realize
  that the same fate overtakes them both.

¹⁵Then I thought in my heart,

"The fate of the fool will overtake me also.
  What then do I gain by being wise?"
I said in my heart,
  "This too is meaningless."

ᵇ8 The meaning of the Hebrew for this phrase is uncertain.

¹⁶For the wise man, like the fool, will not be   in days to come both will be forgotten.
    long remembered;   Like the fool, the wise man too must die!

Discovering the Word **1.** How does the Teacher describe himself and his quest? **2.** Why does the author call his search for wisdom "a heavy burden" (1:13)? **3.** Describe the various avenues the Teacher tested in his quest for fulfillment (2:1–16). **4.** In 2:12–16 he outlines two approaches to discovering meaning in life. What are the advantages and limitations of these two approaches? **5.** What prompts his change of perspective (2:14–16)? **6.** In the first six chapters the Teacher repeats his thesis that "everything is meaningless" 21 times. How does he show that life is meaningless in 1:12—2:16?

Applying the Word **1.** How have you been convinced of the meaninglessness of living outside of Christ's lordship? **2.** What would help you turn your desire for meaning in life into a wholehearted pursuit of God?

Responding in Prayer Matthew 7:8 promises that all who seek shall find. Knock on Jesus' door right now and ask him to give you a hunger to find meaning in life through knowing him better each day.

3 / *Ecclesiastes 2:17–26*
What Is the Value of Work?

GARY HATES HIS job. The tasks are repetitive, his boss is a grouch, the other employees bicker. The job, however, pays better than anything else he could find, and his son has a medical condition that would make him uninsurable if he changes companies. Gary feels trapped. Nothing can be quite as frustrating as work. And while most of us can't fully identify with Gary, many of us can readily understand something about his predicament. In this section of Ecclesiastes, the Teacher will look back at his own life's work. If anyone had a great job, he did. Even so, he asks, "Does it really amount to anything significant?"

Warming Up to God Do you feel more like God's dutiful employee or his valued friend? Explore your perspective and tell him your heart. Remember that he is your most patient listener and he's eager to hear how you're doing.

Read Ecclesiastes 2:17–26.

¹⁷So I hated life, because the work that is done under the sun was grievous to me. All of it is meaningless, a chasing after the wind. ¹⁸I hated all the things I had toiled for under the sun, because I must leave them to the one who comes after me. ¹⁹And who knows whether he will be a wise man or a fool? Yet he will have control over all the work into which I have poured my effort and skill under the sun. This too is meaningless. ²⁰So my heart began to despair over all my toilsome labor under the sun. ²¹For a man may do his work with wisdom, knowledge and skill, and then he must leave all he owns to someone who has not worked for it. This too is meaningless and

a great misfortune. ²²What does a man get for all the toil and anxious striving with which he labors under the sun? ²³All his days his work is pain and grief; even at night his mind does not rest. This too is meaningless.

²⁴A man can do nothing better than to eat and drink and find satisfaction in his work. This too, I see, is from the hand of God, ²⁵for without him, who can eat or find enjoyment? ²⁶To the man who pleases him, God gives wisdom, knowledge and happiness, but to the sinner he gives the task of gathering and storing up wealth to hand it over to the one who pleases God. This too is meaningless, a chasing after the wind.

Discovering the Word **1.** How would you describe the Teacher's emotional state as a result of his quest for meaning so far? **2.** The phrase "under the sun" appears often throughout Ecclesiastes—five times in this passage (vv. 17, 18, 19, 20, 22). Describe the "under the sun" mentality. **3.** What does the Teacher say about work (vv. 21–23)? **4.** What shift do you see in the way the Teacher views work (vv. 24–26)? **5.** Describe the contrast between seeking pleasure (vv. 10–11) and finding enjoyment (vv. 24–26).

 Applying the Word **1.** When have you experienced the kind of satisfying enjoyment described here? **2.** If you were to view your work as a gift from God to be enjoyed, how could that change your attitude about it?

Responding in Prayer Commit your work to the Lord and ask him to give you a heart that desires to glorify him in that context.

4 / *Ecclesiastes 3:1—4:3*
Who Is Really in Control?

"WHY DO THE innocent suffer?" is a question that has plagued the conscience of humankind. And we wonder, "Why do the unrighteous prosper?" Both of these questions can lead to despair, suggesting that life is indeed meaningless. But this famous chapter of Ecclesiastes poses a solution for life's apparent dilemma. The solution hinges on how one answers a third question—"Who is in control?" If humanity is in charge, then life is a game of chance whose rules are controlled by the most powerful among us. But if a just and loving God is in charge, then life becomes a set of ordained appointments which open the windows of eternity to us.

 Warming Up to God What was a situation in which you felt as though your life was out of control? Write down a few words to describe your feelings at that time. Now speak to the Lord about them—and leave your fears and frustrations in his hands.

 Read Ecclesiastes 3:1—4:3.

There is a time for everything,
    and a season for every activity under
        heaven:

2   a time to be born and a time to die,
    a time to plant and a time to uproot,
3   a time to kill and a time to heal,
    a time to tear down and a time to build,
4   a time to weep and a time to laugh,
    a time to mourn and a time to dance,
5   a time to scatter stones and a time to
        gather them,
    a time to embrace and a time to refrain,
6   a time to search and a time to give up,
    a time to keep and a time to throw away,
7   a time to tear and a time to mend,
    a time to be silent and a time to speak,
8   a time to love and a time to hate,
    a time for war and a time for peace.

⁹What does the worker gain from his toil? ¹⁰I have seen the burden God has laid on men. ¹¹He has made everything beautiful in its time. He has also set eternity in the hearts of men; yet they cannot fathom what God has done from begin-

ning to end. ¹²I know that there is nothing better for men than to be happy and do good while they live. ¹³That everyone may eat and drink, and find satisfaction in all his toil—this is the gift of God. ¹⁴I know that everything God does will endure forever; nothing can be added to it and nothing taken from it. God does it so that men will revere him.

¹⁵Whatever is has already been,
    and what will be has been before;
    and God will call the past to account.*

¹⁶And I saw something else under the sun:

In the place of judgment—wickedness was
        there,
    in the place of justice—wickedness was
        there.

¹⁷I thought in my heart,

"God will bring to judgment
    both the righteous and the wicked,

*15 Or *God calls back the past*

for there will be a time for every activity,
a time for every deed."

¹⁸I also thought, "As for men, God tests them so that they may see that they are like the animals. ¹⁹Man's fate is like that of the animals; the same fate awaits them both: As one dies, so dies the other. All have the same breath*d*; man has no advantage over the animal. Everything is meaningless. ²⁰All go to the same place; all come from dust, and to dust all return. ²¹Who knows if the spirit of man rises upward and if the spirit of the animal*e* goes down into the earth?"

²²So I saw that there is nothing better for a man than to enjoy his work, because that is his lot. For who can bring him to see what will happen after him?

4 Again I looked and saw all the oppression
that was taking place under the sun:

I saw the tears of the oppressed—
and they have no comforter;
power was on the side of their oppressors—
and they have no comforter.
²And I declared that the dead,
who had already died,
are happier than the living,
who are still alive.
³But better than both
is he who has not yet been,
who has not seen the evil
that is done under the sun.

d19 Or spirit   e21 Or Who knows the spirit of man, which rises upward, or the spirit of the animal, which

---

 Discovering the Word 1. Describe the Teacher's view of time in 3:1–8. 2. What negative and positive things does the Teacher say about time in 3:9–15? 3. What observations does the Teacher make in 3:16 and 4:1–3 about human wickedness? 4. In the future God will bring judgment (3:17). For the present, however, God brings us a test (3:18–22). What is the test and its desired results? 5. What kind of perspective results from seeing wickedness from a temporal viewpoint (4:1–3)? 6. What kind of perspective results from looking at wickedness from an eternal viewpoint (3:17)?

 Applying the Word 1. How would you live your life differently if you believed God had no control? 2. How do you struggle with the tension of *knowing* God is in control and yet *seeing* wickedness in control?

Responding in Prayer Praise God for setting eternity in our hearts, and thank him for being unchangingly faithful in the midst of life in a paradoxical world.

---

5 / *Ecclesiastes 4:4—5:7*
What Attitudes Should We Embrace?

"THE CHURCH IS full of hypocrites!" Christians often hear this from those outside the church. We like to respond by saying, "Yes, but if you think they're bad now, you should have seen them before God got hold of them!" One way or another, when it comes to how faith should change a person's life, expectations are high. And rightly so. We become like those we live around, and if that includes the Lord, then we will see our lives begin to reflect his. In this passage the Teacher explores some everyday values and attitudes that a relationship with God should influence.

 Warming Up to God Consider your usual approach to life. If you could remove one negative attitude that you struggle with, which one would it be? What difference would it make in your life if you turned this negative into a positive?

Read Ecclesiastes 4:4—5:7.

---

⁴And I saw that all labor and all achievement spring from man's envy of his neighbor. This too is meaningless, a chasing after the wind.

⁵The fool folds his hands
and ruins himself.
⁶Better one handful with tranquillity

than two handfuls with toil
and chasing after the wind.

⁷Again I saw something meaningless under the
sun:

⁸There was a man all alone;
    he had neither son nor brother.
There was no end to his toil,
    yet his eyes were not content with his
        wealth.
"For whom am I toiling," he asked,
    "and why am I depriving myself of
        enjoyment?"
This too is meaningless—
    a miserable business!

⁹Two are better than one,
    because they have a good return for their
        work:
¹⁰If one falls down,
    his friend can help him up.
But pity the man who falls
    and has no one to help him up!
¹¹Also, if two lie down together, they will keep
        warm.
    But how can one keep warm alone?
¹²Though one may be overpowered,
    two can defend themselves.
A cord of three strands is not quickly broken.

¹³Better a poor but wise youth than an old but
foolish king who no longer knows how to take
warning. ¹⁴The youth may have come from prison

to the kingship, or he may have been born in
poverty within his kingdom. ¹⁵I saw that all who
lived and walked under the sun followed the
youth, the king's successor. ¹⁶There was no end
to all the people who were before them. But those
who came later were not pleased with the successor. This too is meaningless, a chasing after the
wind.

5 Guard your steps when you go to the
house of God. Go near to listen rather
than to offer the sacrifice of fools, who do
not know that they do wrong.

²Do not be quick with your mouth,
    do not be hasty in your heart
        to utter anything before God.
God is in heaven
    and you are on earth,
        so let your words be few.
³As a dream comes when there are many cares,
    so the speech of a fool when there are
        many words.

⁴When you make a vow to God, do not delay in
fulfilling it. He has no pleasure in fools; fulfill
your vow. ⁵It is better not to vow than to make a
vow and not fulfill it. ⁶Do not let your mouth lead
you into sin. And do not protest to the ⌐temple⌐
messenger, "My vow was a mistake." Why should
God be angry at what you say and destroy the
work of your hands? ⁷Much dreaming and many
words are meaningless. Therefore stand in awe of
God.

📖 **Discovering the Word** 1. What are negative consequences of the two extreme attitudes described in
4:4–5? 2. What irony concerning the workaholic's efforts is spoken about in 4:7–8? 3. What are the
benefits of partnership (4:9–12)? 4. Ecclesiastes 4:13–16 outlines a "rags to riches" story. What, however, is the
ironic twist to its ending? 5. Contrast the two approaches to God described in 5:1–7.

💧 **Applying the Word** 1. On a scale of 1 to 10 (1 being lazy and 10 being a workaholic), how would you
rate yourself? Explain. 2. In terms of your need for other people, are you primarily a dependent or an
independent person? Explain. 3. How does the Teacher's wisdom challenge you toward growth in interdependence with others?

🤲 **Responding in Prayer** This passage ends with the words "Therefore stand in awe of God." Pray quietly
to the Lord for a few moments, allowing yourself to stand in awe of him. Humbly be silent before him who
made you and is making you into his child.

under the sun = away from or not for God

6 / *Ecclesiastes 5:8—6:12*
What Does It Take to Be Content?

IF THE ADVERTISERS are right, we have a lot to feel discontent about. We don't have enough possessions, and we don't have them soon enough or up to date enough. Fulfillment is equated with wearing the right kind of clothes, driving the right kind of car, drinking the right kind of beverage. This lifestyle of discontent held similar sway for many of the Teacher's contemporaries. In this section he challenges his reader to stop seeking satisfaction from accumulating things. Instead he offers an alternative, one that leads to a lifestyle of contentment.

 Warming Up to God In what areas of life do you find yourself least content? Consider Psalm 118:24: "This is the day the LORD has made; let us rejoice and be glad in it." For what do you have reason to rejoice today? Praise your God, the Lover of your soul, today before you look into his Word.

 Read Ecclesiastes 5:8—6:12.

---

⁸If you see the poor oppressed in a district, and justice and rights denied, do not be surprised at such things; for one official is eyed by a higher one, and over them both are others higher still. ⁹The increase from the land is taken by all; the king himself profits from the fields.

¹⁰Whoever loves money never has money
    enough;
    whoever loves wealth is never satisfied with
        his income.
This too is meaningless.

¹¹As goods increase,
    so do those who consume them.
And what benefit are they to the owner
    except to feast his eyes on them?

¹²The sleep of a laborer is sweet,
    whether he eats little or much,
but the abundance of a rich man
    permits him no sleep.

¹³I have seen a grievous evil under the sun:

wealth hoarded to the harm of its owner,
¹⁴ or wealth lost through some misfortune,
    so that when he has a son
        there is nothing left for him.
¹⁵Naked a man comes from his mother's womb,
    and as he comes, so he departs.
He takes nothing from his labor
    that he can carry in his hand.

¹⁶This too is a grievous evil:

As a man comes, so he departs,
    and what does he gain,
        since he toils for the wind?
¹⁷All his days he eats in darkness,

with great frustration, affliction and anger.

¹⁸Then I realized that it is good and proper for a man to eat and drink, and to find satisfaction in his toilsome labor under the sun during the few days of life God has given him—for this is his lot. ¹⁹Moreover, when God gives any man wealth and possessions, and enables him to enjoy them, to accept his lot and be happy in his work—this is a gift of God. ²⁰He seldom reflects on the days of his life, because God keeps him occupied with gladness of heart.

6 I have seen another evil under the sun, and it weighs heavily on men: ²God gives a man wealth, possessions and honor, so that he lacks nothing his heart desires, but God does not enable him to enjoy them, and a stranger enjoys them instead. This is meaningless, a grievous evil.

³A man may have a hundred children and live many years; yet no matter how long he lives, if he cannot enjoy his prosperity and does not receive proper burial, I say that a stillborn child is better off than he. ⁴It comes without meaning, it departs in darkness, and in darkness its name is shrouded. ⁵Though it never saw the sun or knew anything, it has more rest than does that man— ⁶even if he lives a thousand years twice over but fails to enjoy his prosperity. Do not all go to the same place?

⁷All man's efforts are for his mouth,
    yet his appetite is never satisfied.
⁸What advantage has a wise man
    over a fool?
What does a poor man gain

by knowing how to conduct himself before
others?
⁹Better what the eye sees
than the roving of the appetite.
This too is meaningless,
a chasing after the wind.

¹⁰Whatever exists has already been named,
and what man is has been known;
no man can contend

with one who is stronger than he.
¹¹The more the words,
the less the meaning,
and how does that profit anyone?

¹²For who knows what is good for a man in
life, during the few and meaningless days he
passes through like a shadow? Who can tell
him what will happen under the sun after he is
gone?

 Discovering the Word 1. How does the Teacher describe the nature of wealth? 2. What negative effects does the desire for wealth have in public life (5:8–9) and in personal life (5:10–17)? 3. Note the contrast between 5:18–20 and 6:1–2. What role does God have in the satisfaction which wealth, possessions and honor can bring? 4. Many children and a long life were considered the greatest of blessings in the Old Testament (6:3–6). What does our society define as "the good life"? 5. In 6:7–12 the Teacher uses questions to challenge his readers. How would the questions challenge an unbeliever (see especially v. 12)?

 Applying the Word 1. On a scale of 1 to 10 (1 being very little, 10 being very much), how would you rate your attachment to the things you own? 2. Give an example of how viewing possessions as a gift from God would help to change your attachment to them. 3. How could you exercise trust in God for an area in which you lack contentment?

 Responding in Prayer Confess any discontent to God and ask him to help you value his goodness and sufficiency.

---

7 / *Ecclesiastes 7:1—8:1*
Where Can We Find Wisdom?

WHO AMONG US does not look back in regret over a past decision? Sometimes we had inadequate information to make the right judgment. But often we simply lacked the necessary wisdom to make the right choice at the right time. In this section the Teacher will address where such wisdom comes from and how we can capitalize on it for future decisions.

Warming Up to God In what way do you feel that you lack wisdom? Ask God to give you insight into his wisdom as you grow through the study of his Word.

Read Ecclesiastes 7:1—8:1.

---

7 A good name is better than fine
perfume,
and the day of death better than the day
of birth.
²It is better to go to a house of mourning
than to go to a house of feasting,
for death is the destiny of every man;
the living should take this to heart.
³Sorrow is better than laughter,
because a sad face is good for the heart.

⁴The heart of the wise is in the house of
mourning,
but the heart of fools is in the house of
pleasure.
⁵It is better to heed a wise man's rebuke
than to listen to the song of fools.
⁶Like the crackling of thorns under the
pot,
so is the laughter of fools.
This too is meaningless.

⁷Extortion turns a wise man into a fool,
  and a bribe corrupts the heart.

⁸The end of a matter is better than its
    beginning,
  and patience is better than pride.
⁹Do not be quickly provoked in your spirit,
  for anger resides in the lap of fools.

¹⁰Do not say, "Why were the old days better
    than these?"
  For it is not wise to ask such questions.

¹¹Wisdom, like an inheritance, is a good thing
  and benefits those who see the sun.
¹²Wisdom is a shelter
  as money is a shelter,
but the advantage of knowledge is this:
  that wisdom preserves the life of its
    possessor.

¹³Consider what God has done:

Who can straighten
  what he has made crooked?
¹⁴When times are good, be happy;
  but when times are bad, consider:
God has made the one
  as well as the other.
Therefore, a man cannot discover
  anything about his future.

¹⁵In this meaningless life of mine I have seen
both of these:

a righteous man perishing in his
    righteousness,
  and a wicked man living long in his
    wickedness.
¹⁶Do not be overrighteous,
  neither be overwise—
  why destroy yourself?
¹⁷Do not be overwicked,
  and do not be a fool—
  why die before your time?
¹⁸It is good to grasp the one
  and not let go of the other.
  The man who fears God will avoid all
    ⌞extremes⌟.ᶠ

¹⁹Wisdom makes one wise man more powerful
  than ten rulers in a city.

²⁰There is not a righteous man on earth
  who does what is right and never sins.

²¹Do not pay attention to every word people
    say,
  or you may hear your servant cursing
    you—
²²for you know in your heart
  that many times you yourself have cursed
    others.

²³All this I tested by wisdom and I said,

"I am determined to be wise"—
  but this was beyond me.
²⁴Whatever wisdom may be,
  it is far off and most profound—
  who can discover it?
²⁵So I turned my mind to understand,
  to investigate and to search out wisdom
    and the scheme of things
and to understand the stupidity of wickedness
  and the madness of folly.

²⁶I find more bitter than death
  the woman who is a snare,
whose heart is a trap
  and whose hands are chains.
The man who pleases God will escape her,
  but the sinner she will ensnare.

²⁷"Look," says the Teacher,ᵍ "this is what I
have discovered:

"Adding one thing to another to discover the
    scheme of things—
²⁸ while I was still searching
  but not finding—
I found one ⌞upright⌟ man among a thousand,
  but not one ⌞upright⌟ woman among them
    all.
²⁹This only have I found:
  God made mankind upright,
  but men have gone in search of many
    schemes."

8 Who is like the wise man?
  Who knows the explanation of things?
  Wisdom brightens a man's face
  and changes its hard appearance.

ᶠ18 *Or* will follow them both   ᵍ27 *Or* leader of the assembly

Discovering the Word 1. What are some ways the Teacher describes wisdom? 2. Are you surprised by any of the comparisons of 7:1–6? Explain. 3. What dangers does the Teacher warn against in verses 7–10? 4. Why does he give the warning of verses 16–18 in the terms he uses? 5. Describe how fearing God puts life into perspective (v. 18). 6. What perspective does wisdom provide according to verses 19–22?

Applying the Word 1. How can suffering and sorrow offer instruction for living? 2. From this section of Ecclesiastes, Chuck Swindoll defines wisdom as "the God-given ability to see life with rare objectivity and to handle life with rare stability" (*Living on the Ragged Edge Bible Study Guide*). In what areas of your Christian life do you presently need such objectivity and stability?

Responding in Prayer Tell the Lord about one area of your life in which you need wisdom and guidance. Ask him to direct your choices and then relax in the truth that God desires to give his children good gifts.

8 / *Ecclesiastes 8:2–17*
How Shall We Live Under Authority?

DOES YOUR FOOT automatically come off the accelerator pedal when you buzz by a police car on the side of the road? Do your eyes then anxiously glance up to the rearview mirror? Sure we respect authority. But do we really appreciate how living under authority can greatly enrich our lives? In this study, the Teacher outlines some positive benefits of relating to both human and divine authority.

Warming Up to God Tell the Lord about events in your life or in world affairs that have angered you. How have you responded to that anger? Allow God to share your feelings, and remember that he too seeks an end to pain and despair.

Read Ecclesiastes 8:2–17.

²Obey the king's command, I say, because you took an oath before God. ³Do not be in a hurry to leave the king's presence. Do not stand up for a bad cause, for he will do whatever he pleases. ⁴Since a king's word is supreme, who can say to him, "What are you doing?"

⁵Whoever obeys his command will come to no
    harm,
    and the wise heart will know the proper
        time and procedure.
⁶For there is a proper time and procedure for
        every matter,
    though a man's misery weighs heavily upon
        him.

⁷Since no man knows the future,
    who can tell him what is to come?
⁸No man has power over the wind to contain
        it[h];
    so no one has power over the day of his
        death.
    As no one is discharged in time of war,

so wickedness will not release those who
        practice it.

⁹All this I saw, as I applied my mind to everything done under the sun. There is a time when a man lords it over others to his own[i] hurt. ¹⁰Then too, I saw the wicked buried—those who used to come and go from the holy place and receive praise[j] in the city where they did this. This too is meaningless.

¹¹When the sentence for a crime is not quickly carried out, the hearts of the people are filled with schemes to do wrong. ¹²Although a wicked man commits a hundred crimes and still lives a long time, I know that it will go better with God-fearing men, who are reverent before God. ¹³Yet because the wicked do not fear God, it will not go well with them, and their days will not lengthen like a shadow.

¹⁴There is something else meaningless that oc-

h8 Or over his spirit to retain it   i9 Or to their   j10 Some Hebrew manuscripts and Septuagint (Aquila); most Hebrew manuscripts and are forgotten curs on earth: righteous men who get what the wicked deserve, and wicked men who get what the righteous deserve. This too, I say, is meaningless. ¹⁵So I commend the enjoyment of life, because nothing is better for a man under the sun than to eat and drink and be glad. Then joy will accompany him in his work all the days of the life God has given him under the sun.

¹⁶When I applied my mind to know wisdom and to observe man's labor on earth—his eyes not seeing sleep day or night— ¹⁷then I saw all that God has done. No one can comprehend what goes on under the sun. Despite all his efforts to search it out, man cannot discover its meaning. Even if a wise man claims he knows, he cannot really comprehend it.

Discovering the Word 1. Why does the Teacher encourage obedience to authority? 2. What is significant about the fact that human authority is limited (v. 8)? 3. What unjust uses of authority are described (vv. 9–11, 14)? 4. How would you characterize the Teacher's answer to these injustices in verses 12–13? 5. How does God's authority, alluded to in verses 15–17, contrast with human limitations in verses 7–8? 6. In the face of life's injustices and uncertainties, the Teacher argues for enjoying life (v. 15). Why?

Applying the Word 1. According to verses 16–17, human wisdom is very limited. How should knowing this fact encourage you to fear and trust God? 2. What is an unsettled situation in life that you need to entrust to God?

Responding in Prayer Ask your Father to increase your faith and hope as you seek to follow him despite difficult circumstances that you do not fully understand.

9 / *Ecclesiastes 9:1–12*
What Meaning Does Death Bring to Life?

ON THE EDGE of the University of Oregon campus lies a sizable historical cemetery. For years university officials have eyed with envy this valuable slice of real estate that divides their campus. At one point some even entertained suggestions to build a superstructure of above-ground buildings over the plots! For many students the cemetery represents an unfortunate obstacle as they crisscross the campus from one class to the next. I doubt if the Teacher would share this objection. What better reminder for young people seeking to fashion lifelong values? Contemplation of death gives us the wisdom to live.

Warming Up to God When you think of your own death, what are some of your fears, anxieties—and hopes? Present these to God in prayer.

Read Ecclesiastes 9:1–12.

9 So I reflected on all this and concluded that the righteous and the wise and what they do are in God's hands, but no man knows whether love or hate awaits him. ²All share a common destiny—the righteous and the wicked, the good and the bad,ᵏ the clean and the unclean, those who offer sacrifices and those who do not.

As it is with the good man,
    so with the sinner;
as it is with those who take oaths,
    so with those who are afraid to take them.

³This is the evil in everything that happens under the sun: The same destiny overtakes all. The hearts of men, moreover, are full of evil and there is madness in their hearts while they live, and afterward they join the dead. ⁴Anyone who is among the living has hopeˡ—even a live dog is better off than a dead lion!

⁵For the living know that they will die,
    but the dead know nothing;
    they have no further reward,

ᵏ2 Septuagint (Aquila), Vulgate and Syriac; Hebrew does not have *and the bad.*   ˡ4 Or *What then is to be chosen? With all who live, there is hope*

and even the memory of them is forgotten.
⁶Their love, their hate

and their jealousy have long since vanished;
never again will they have a part
in anything that happens under the sun.

⁷Go, eat your food with gladness, and drink your wine with a joyful heart, for it is now that God favors what you do. ⁸Always be clothed in white, and always anoint your head with oil. ⁹Enjoy life with your wife, whom you love, all the days of this meaningless life that God has given you under the sun— all your meaningless days. For this is your lot in life and in your toilsome labor under the sun. ¹⁰Whatever your hand finds to do, do it with all your might, for in the grave,ᵐ where you are going, there is neither working nor planning nor knowledge nor wisdom.

¹¹I have seen something else under the sun:

The race is not to the swift
or the battle to the strong,
nor does food come to the wise
or wealth to the brilliant
or favor to the learned;
but time and chance happen to them all.

¹²Moreover, no man knows when his hour will come:

As fish are caught in a cruel net,
or birds are taken in a snare,
so men are trapped by evil times
that fall unexpectedly upon them.

ᵐ10 Hebrew *Sheol*

Discovering the Word 1. In what ways are the righteous and wicked described in verses 1–3? 2. What reaction might the Teacher hope to gain with his emphasis that a "common destiny" awaits all (vv. 1–3)? 3. What kind of hope does the Teacher offer in verses 4–6? 4. In what ways do verses 7–10 encourage us to enjoy life? 5. What uncertainty do the factors of time and chance bring to life (vv. 11–12)?

Applying the Word 1. What difference would it make in your life if you knew you were going to die within six months? 2. In what ways does taking death seriously help alter your values in the use of your money, time and energy? 3. How do Christ's death and resurrection give you hope in this life and in the one to come?

Responding in Prayer Reflect on the dilemna voiced by Peter but faced by all of us: "Lord, to whom shall we go? You have the words of eternal life" (Jn 6:68). Commit yourself to follow Jesus closely and thank him for the fulfillment such a life brings.

---

10 / *Ecclesiastes 9:13—10:20*
How Do We Live Sensibly?

COMMON SENSE. HAVE you felt that somehow you missed out on this body of wisdom that is supposedly so universal? Of course, we all lack commonsense judgment at times. But in this section, the Teacher addresses something deeper and darker, a lack of commonsense lifestyle. Such a lifestyle, called *foolishness,* results when human weakness and wickedness assert control. In this study, he will identify foolish behavior and tell us how to avoid it.

Warming Up to God When you need help making an important decision, who is your closest confidante? What qualities make that person a good listener and trusted advisor? Consider those characteristics as you read about some "contrasting" personality traits.

Read Ecclesiastes 9:13—10:20.

---

¹³I also saw under the sun this example of wisdom that greatly impressed me: ¹⁴There was once a small city with only a few people in it. And a

powerful king came against it, surrounded it and built huge siegeworks against it. ¹⁵Now there lived in that city a man poor but wise, and he saved the city by his wisdom. But nobody remembered that poor man. [16]So I said, "Wisdom is better than strength." But the poor man's wisdom is despised, and his words are no longer heeded.

[17]The quiet words of the wise are more to be heeded
  than the shouts of a ruler of fools.
[18]Wisdom is better than weapons of war,
  but one sinner destroys much good.

10 As dead flies give perfume a bad smell,
  so a little folly outweighs wisdom and honor.
[2]The heart of the wise inclines to the right,
  but the heart of the fool to the left.
[3]Even as he walks along the road,
  the fool lacks sense
  and shows everyone how stupid he is.
[4]If a ruler's anger rises against you,
  do not leave your post;
  calmness can lay great errors to rest.

[5]There is an evil I have seen under the sun,
  the sort of error that arises from a ruler:
[6]Fools are put in many high positions,
  while the rich occupy the low ones.
[7]I have seen slaves on horseback,
  while princes go on foot like slaves.

[8]Whoever digs a pit may fall into it;
  whoever breaks through a wall may be
    bitten by a snake.
[9]Whoever quarries stones may be injured by
    them;
  whoever splits logs may be endangered by
    them.
[10]If the ax is dull
  and its edge unsharpened,

more strength is needed
  but skill will bring success.

[11]If a snake bites before it is charmed,
  there is no profit for the charmer.

[12]Words from a wise man's mouth are gracious,
  but a fool is consumed by his own lips.
[13]At the beginning his words are folly;
  at the end they are wicked madness—
[14] and the fool multiplies words.

No one knows what is coming—
  who can tell him what will happen after
    him?
[15]A fool's work wearies him;
  he does not know the way to town.

[16]Woe to you, O land whose king was a
    servant[n]
  and whose princes feast in the morning.
[17]Blessed are you, O land whose king is of
    noble birth
  and whose princes eat at a proper time—
  for strength and not for drunkenness.

[18]If a man is lazy, the rafters sag;
  if his hands are idle, the house leaks.

[19]A feast is made for laughter,
  and wine makes life merry,
  but money is the answer for everything.

[20]Do not revile the king even in your thoughts,
  or curse the rich in your bedroom,
  because a bird of the air may carry your
    words,
  and a bird on the wing may report what
    you say.

[n]16 Or *king is a child*

Discovering the Word 1. Describe the ironies of wisdom and foolish behavior illustrated in 9:13–16. 2. How have you seen wisdom destroyed in the manner described in 9:18—10:1? 3. What is the significance of folly's description in 10:2–3? 4. List the common situations described in 10:8–11 that call for the exercise of good judgment. 5. What are the consequences of wise and foolish lifestyles according to 10:16–20?

Applying the Word 1. In reference to 9:17–18, do you find yourself giving more respect to those who have wisdom or to those who have status? Why? 2. What is an area of life in which you struggle to exercise good judgment? Explain. 3. James 1:5 says, "If any of you lacks wisdom, he should ask God, who gives generously." What current decision requires a wise attitude or action on your part?

Responding in Prayer Ask the Lord to teach you prayerful wisdom and to protect you from any inclination toward foolish actions. Ask for his wisdom in current decisions you must make. Ask him to nurture qualities of wisdom in your character.

11 / *Ecclesiastes 11:1—12:8*
How Shall We Then Live?

ALL WEEK I prepared myself to rappel off Inspiration II, a sheer cliff of 100 feet near Bear Trap Ranch in Colorado. Physical preparation included "learning the ropes" on smaller cliffs such as Inspiration I. Mental preparation involved watching and talking to veteran rappellers. The day that I was to go came, but I was busy with a camping trip. The next day no one was going. The day after that something else came up. From then until the end of the week I was going to make the rappelling trip . . . tomorrow. It never happened. To this day, twenty years later, I wonder: "Why didn't I go? Was I unsure of my skills, was I too timid to take up the challenge or . . . ?"

There is a risk to not taking risks. An opportunity to test our resolve or pursue a challenge may be lost forever. Failing to take spiritual risks in the life of faith has even greater consequences. In this section the Teacher will encourage us to "cast our bread upon the waters."

 Warming Up to God Create a brief list of your resources, skills, funds, time, energy and possessions. Bring this list to God in a prayer of thanks. What decisions do you have about using these assets that may lead you out of your comfort zone? Meditate on God's character as it relates to these decisions.

Read Ecclesiastes 11:1—12:8.

---

11 Cast your bread upon the waters,
for after many days you will find
it again.
²Give portions to seven, yes to eight,
for you do not know what disaster may
come upon the land.

³If clouds are full of water,
they pour rain upon the earth.
Whether a tree falls to the south or to the
north,
in the place where it falls, there will it lie.
⁴Whoever watches the wind will not plant;
whoever looks at the clouds will not reap.

⁵As you do not know the path of the wind,
or how the body is formed⁰ in a mother's
womb,
so you cannot understand the work of God,
the Maker of all things.

⁶Sow your seed in the morning,
and at evening let not your hands be idle,
for you do not know which will succeed,
whether this or that,
or whether both will do equally well.

⁷Light is sweet,
and it pleases the eyes to see the sun.
⁸However many years a man may live,
let him enjoy them all.
But let him remember the days of darkness,
for they will be many.
Everything to come is meaningless.

⁹Be happy, young man, while you are young,
and let your heart give you joy in the days
of your youth.
Follow the ways of your heart
and whatever your eyes see,
but know that for all these things
God will bring you to judgment.
¹⁰So then, banish anxiety from your heart
and cast off the troubles of your body,
for youth and vigor are meaningless.

12 Remember your Creator
in the days of your youth,
before the days of trouble come
and the years approach when you will say,
"I find no pleasure in them"—
²before the sun and the light
and the moon and the stars grow dark,
and the clouds return after the rain;
³when the keepers of the house tremble,
and the strong men stoop,
when the grinders cease because they are few,
and those looking through the windows
grow dim;
⁴when the doors to the street are closed
and the sound of grinding fades;
when men rise up at the sound of birds,
but all their songs grow faint;
⁵when men are afraid of heights
and of dangers in the streets;
when the almond tree blossoms
and the grasshopper drags himself along

⁰5 Or *know how life (or the spirit) / enters the body being formed*

and desire no longer is stirred.
Then man goes to his eternal home
and mourners go about the streets.

⁶Remember him—before the silver cord is
severed,
or the golden bowl is broken;
before the pitcher is shattered at the spring,
or the wheel broken at the well,

⁷and the dust returns to the ground it came
from,
and the spirit returns to God who gave it.

⁸"Meaningless! Meaningless!" says the
Teacher.ᵖ
"Everything is meaningless!"

P8 *Or the leader of the assembly; also in verses 9 and 10*

 Discovering the Word 1. What is the Teacher encouraging in 11:1–6? 2. Given what the Teacher has said in chapters 1—10, why would he encourage us to be risk-takers? 3. Describe the perspective on life found in 11:7–10. 4. What kind of relationship with God does the word *remember* imply (12:1, 6)? 5. What are the metaphors used to describe death (12:6–7)?

Applying the Word 1. What's something you've done which involved a great deal of risk? 2. How does the perspective of verses 7–10 encourage you to pursue joy? 3. Why should the eventuality of death be a strong encouragement to a risk-taking commitment to God?

Responding in Prayer Spend several minutes thanking the Lord for the life that you have found in him. Ask him to help you pursue the kind of faith-stretching life that taps into his vast resources.

---

12 / *Ecclesiastes 12:9–14*
What Makes Life Meaningful?

IF YOU WERE given the assignment to describe life with one word, what word would you choose? Few of us are comfortable with the Teacher's choice of *meaningless.* Consider this, however: in darkness, a few small lights will stand out clearly and become the focus of attention. These lights from Ecclesiastes—the purposes, values and priorities that should guide our lives—are now seen so much more clearly. In the final lines of the book, an observer comments on the life and writings of "the Teacher" who wrote this intriguing book. Let's take one last look at how to pursue meaning in life, Ecclesiates style.

 Warming Up to God If a person who knows you well tried to summarize what you have "taught" up to this point in your life, what do you think that person would say? Remember today that it is Jesus Christ who gives you hope and a purpose for your life. Meditate on the ways he has changed your life since you met him for the first time.

Read Ecclesiastes 12:9–14.

---

⁹Not only was the Teacher wise, but also he imparted knowledge to the people. He pondered and searched out and set in order many proverbs. ¹⁰The Teacher searched to find just the right words, and what he wrote was upright and true.

¹¹The words of the wise are like goads, their collected sayings like firmly embedded nails— given by one Shepherd. ¹²Be warned, my son, of anything in addition to them.

Of making many books there is no end, and much study wearies the body.

¹³Now all has been heard;
here is the conclusion of the matter:
Fear God and keep his commandments,
for this is the whole ⌞duty⌟ of man.
¹⁴For God will bring every deed into judgment,
including every hidden thing,
whether it is good or evil.

Discovering the Word 1. How is the Teacher's purpose described in verses 9–10? 2. Why is it significant that the Teacher's words are based on the authority of the "one Shepherd"? 3. Why do you think the commentator ends this book with the particular directives of verses 13–14? 4. Sum up the message of Ecclesiastes in a brief phrase or statement. 5. How would you characterize the Teacher's pursuit to find meaning in life? (See 1:12—6:12.)

Applying the Word 1. What does it mean for you to "fear God and keep his commandments"? 2. In light of your study of Ecclesiastes, on what basis is life meaningless to you and on what basis is it not? 3. Verse 11 says, "The words of the wise are like goads, their collected sayings like firmly embedded nails." What did you find in Ecclesiastes that goaded or irritated you toward wisdom?

Responding in Prayer Spend some time thanking the Shepherd for challenging you with the message of Ecclesiastes.

Song of Songs

"**S**exuality is a gift from God." "Our bodies are beautiful and should be enjoyed." You have probably heard statements like this, but are they true—for you?

Many people, even Christians, have heard negative messages, sometimes implicit—from their parents, friends or society—which inhibit them from understanding and appreciating their own sexuality. Perhaps you have been told: "Original sin started with Adam and Eve having sex." "Women should be very modest about what they wear so they won't cause men to lust." "God made sex just so we can procreate." If so, the Song of Songs will give you a new perspective.

Interpreters of the Song of Songs have struggled with whether it is an allegory about God's love for us, or if it should be read as a love song between two people. Understanding it either way can teach us about love. However, the Song of Songs is best seen as both:

How is one to understand the Song in terms of human and divine love? . . . The Bible suggests that these loves are united and not to be separated. . . . The union between man and woman became a primary symbol for the expression of the relationship of the Lord to His People. The covenant between God and His People is consistently portrayed as a marriage. (Roland Murphy O'Carm as quoted in Andrew Greeley, *Love Song*)

The Song of Songs is written as a play. The voice of the lover is most likely that of King Solomon, and the beloved is the feminine voice. Their friends serve as a chorus, adding dramatic effect, but perhaps also to show the importance of community relationship even in the midst of celebrating the marriage relationship. The first two chapters are the courtship between Solomon and his beloved, and chapter three describes their wedding procession. What follows is their declaration of love and their vows of commitment to the marriage.

It is our hope that these quiet times will bring you closer to God, our divine lover, and help you to understand the place of sexuality within marriage.

Outline

1/ Song of Songs 1—2 ——————— *Created for Love*

2/ Song of Songs 3 ——————— *Love Is Patient*

3/ Song of Songs 4 ——————— *God's Good Gift*

4/ Song of Songs 5—6 ——————— *Affirming One Another*

5/ Song of Songs 7—8 ——————— *Love for a Lifetime*

1 / *Song of Songs 1—2*
Created for Love

DO YOU REMEMBER the first time you read the Song of Songs? Perhaps you were in junior high, flipping through your Bible during a boring sermon. You were probably surprised by the explicit language and sensual images. The Song of Songs is a celebration of married love that includes open dialogue about physical love. It's an important part of the picture of married love as God created it to be.

 Warming Up to God Have you ever talked to God about how you feel about your sexual nature? Let him know of any apprehensions or positive feelings you have as you begin this book.

 Read Song of Songs 1—2.

1 Solomon's Song of Songs.

²Let him kiss me with the kisses of his
mouth—
for your love is more delightful than wine.
³Pleasing is the fragrance of your perfumes;
your name is like perfume poured out.
No wonder the maidens love you!
⁴Take me away with you—let us hurry!
Let the king bring me into his chambers.

We rejoice and delight in you*ᵃ*;
we will praise your love more than wine.
How right they are to adore you!

⁵Dark am I, yet lovely,
O daughters of Jerusalem,
dark like the tents of Kedar,
like the tent curtains of Solomon.*ᵇ*
⁶Do not stare at me because I am dark,
because I am darkened by the sun.
My mother's sons were angry with me
and made me take care of the vineyards;
my own vineyard I have neglected.
⁷Tell me, you whom I love, where you graze
your flock
and where you rest your sheep at midday.
Why should I be like a veiled woman
beside the flocks of your friends?
⁸If you do not know, most beautiful of women,
follow the tracks of the sheep
and graze your young goats
by the tents of the shepherds.
⁹I liken you, my darling, to a mare
harnessed to one of the chariots of
Pharaoh.
¹⁰Your cheeks are beautiful with earrings,
your neck with strings of jewels.
¹¹We will make you earrings of gold,
studded with silver.

¹²While the king was at his table,
my perfume spread its fragrance.
¹³My lover is to me a sachet of myrrh
resting between my breasts.
¹⁴My lover is to me a cluster of henna blossoms
from the vineyards of En Gedi.
¹⁵How beautiful you are, my darling!
Oh, how beautiful!
Your eyes are doves.
¹⁶How handsome you are, my lover!
Oh, how charming!
And our bed is verdant.
¹⁷The beams of our house are cedars;
our rafters are firs.

2 I am a rose*ᶜ* of Sharon,
a lily of the valleys.
²Like a lily among thorns
is my darling among the maidens.
³Like an apple tree among the trees of the
forest
is my lover among the young men.
I delight to sit in his shade,
and his fruit is sweet to my taste.
⁴He has taken me to the banquet hall,
and his banner over me is love.
⁵Strengthen me with raisins,
refresh me with apples,
for I am faint with love.
⁶His left arm is under my head,
and his right arm embraces me.
⁷Daughters of Jerusalem, I charge you
by the gazelles and by the does of the field:
Do not arouse or awaken love
until it so desires.

⁸Listen! My lover!
Look! Here he comes,

ᵃ4 The Hebrew is masculine singular.   *ᵇ5* Or *Salma*   *ᶜ1* Possibly a
member of the crocus family

leaping across the mountains,
  bounding over the hills.
⁹My lover is like a gazelle or a young stag.
  Look! There he stands behind our wall,
gazing through the windows,
  peering through the lattice.
¹⁰My lover spoke and said to me,
  "Arise, my darling,
  my beautiful one, and come with me.
¹¹See! The winter is past;
  the rains are over and gone.
¹²Flowers appear on the earth;
  the season of singing has come,
the cooing of doves
  is heard in our land.
¹³The fig tree forms its early fruit;
  the blossoming vines spread their fragrance.
Arise, come, my darling;
  my beautiful one, come with me."
¹⁴My dove in the clefts of the rock,

in the hiding places on the mountainside,
show me your face,
  let me hear your voice;
for your voice is sweet,
  and your face is lovely.
¹⁵Catch for us the foxes,
  the little foxes
that ruin the vineyards,
  our vineyards that are in bloom.
¹⁶My lover is mine and I am his;
  he browses among the lilies.
¹⁷Until the day breaks
  and the shadows flee,
turn, my lover,
  and be like a gazelle
or like a young stag
  on the rugged hills. ᵈ

ᵈ17 Or *the hills of Bether*

Discovering the Word 1. What sense do you get from this passage about how the "Beloved" and the "Lover" regard one another? 2. What images do they use to describe one another (1:3, 7, 9, 10, 12–14, 15; 2:2, 3, 8–9)? 3. What do these word pictures reflect about the nature of their relationship? 4. What fears and insecurities does the beloved reveal (1:3–4, 5–7)? 5. In 1:8 how do the friends pick up on the beloved's imagery and reassure her? 6. How does the lover reassure her (1:9–11)?

Applying the Word 1. Why is it important to have supportive friends involved in a marriage relationship? 2. How does knowing that the Song of Songs is included in Scripture affect your view of married relationships?

Responding in Prayer Reflect on your own sexuality and how you respond to this picture of passionate physical love. Talk to God about how you are feeling.

---

2 / *Song of Songs 3*
Love Is Patient

ONE OF THE many flaws in the *Playboy* approach to sex is that it makes people into things. *Playboy* magazine and all its derivatives are nothing more than a form of idolatry. No other aspect of the person, other than his or her body, is of any interest. This is a tragic distortion of God's good creation. True love requires time—and hard work. It may even include times of searching and insecurity.

Warming Up to God Perhaps you have recently used someone you love to satisfy your desires without considering the other person. Quietly consider this before God. Confess your sin to him. Wait for his forgiveness.

Read Song of Songs 3.

3 All night long on my bed
    I looked for the one my heart loves;
    I looked for him but did not find him.
²I will get up now and go about the city,
    through its streets and squares;
I will search for the one my heart loves.
So I looked for him but did not find him.
³The watchmen found me
    as they made their rounds in the city.
    "Have you seen the one my heart loves?"
⁴Scarcely had I passed them
    when I found the one my heart loves.
I held him and would not let him go
    till I had brought him to my mother's
        house,
to the room of the one who conceived me.
⁵Daughters of Jerusalem, I charge you
    by the gazelles and by the does of the field:
Do not arouse or awaken love
    until it so desires.

⁶Who is this coming up from the desert
    like a column of smoke,
perfumed with myrrh and incense

made from all the spices of the merchant?
⁷Look! It is Solomon's carriage,
    escorted by sixty warriors,
    the noblest of Israel,
⁸all of them wearing the sword,
    all experienced in battle,
each with his sword at his side,
    prepared for the terrors of the night.
⁹King Solomon made for himself the carriage;
    he made it of wood from Lebanon.
¹⁰Its posts he made of silver,
    its base of gold.
Its seat was upholstered with purple,
    its interior lovingly inlaid
    byᵉ the daughters of Jerusalem.
¹¹Come out, you daughters of Zion,
    and look at King Solomon wearing the
        crown,
    the crown with which his mother crowned
        him
on the day of his wedding,
    the day his heart rejoiced.

ᵉ10 Or its inlaid interior a gift of love / from

 Discovering the Word 1. What shift in tone do you notice in chapter 3? 2. Verses 1–3 describe some of the insecurities that love can bring. What is it about love that can make us feel this way? 3. Describe the reunion in verse 4. 4. "Do not arouse or awaken love until it so desires" (v. 5) is repeated from 2:7. What wisdom do you see in this saying? 5. Verses 6–11 are from the perspective of the friends. How do they describe the wedding procession?

Applying the Word 1. When are you likely to feel insecure about those you love? 2. The wedding procession in this passage is a time of publicly declaring love before others. What experience in your life confirmed the love someone (that is, the romantic love of a spouse or the love of a friend or family member) has for you?

Responding in Prayer Ask God to help you better show your love to those you care about.

---

3 / *Song of Songs 4*
God's Good Gift

Human passion . . . gives us a hint of God's passion for us. We are most like God's love for us when we are aroused in the presence of our beloved. And we best experience a hint of God's love for us when our beloved pursues us. (Andrew Greeley, *Love Song* [New York: Warner Books, 1989], p. 28.)

THIS EXCERPT FROM one of Andrew Greeley's novels is an appropriate description of what romantic love between a man and a woman is all about. God has given us this gift so that we can better understand what his love is like. And that is what the Song of Songs is all about.

Warming Up to God How do you feel about the quote above? Talk to God about how you experience his love.

Read Song of Songs 4.

4 How beautiful you are, my darling!
Oh, how beautiful!
Your eyes behind your veil are doves.
Your hair is like a flock of goats
descending from Mount Gilead.
²Your teeth are like a flock of sheep just
shorn,
coming up from the washing.
Each has its twin;
not one of them is alone.
³Your lips are like a scarlet ribbon;
your mouth is lovely.
Your temples behind your veil
are like the halves of a pomegranate.
⁴Your neck is like the tower of David,
built with elegance*ᶠ*;
on it hang a thousand shields,
all of them shields of warriors.
⁵Your two breasts are like two fawns,
like twin fawns of a gazelle
that browse among the lilies.
⁶Until the day breaks
and the shadows flee,
I will go to the mountain of myrrh
and to the hill of incense.
⁷All beautiful you are, my darling;
there is no flaw in you.

⁸Come with me from Lebanon, my bride,
come with me from Lebanon.
Descend from the crest of Amana,
from the top of Senir, the summit of
Hermon,
from the lions' dens
and the mountain haunts of the
leopards.
⁹You have stolen my heart, my sister, my
bride;

you have stolen my heart
with one glance of your eyes,
with one jewel of your necklace.
¹⁰How delightful is your love, my sister, my
bride!
How much more pleasing is your love than
wine,
and the fragrance of your perfume than any
spice!
¹¹Your lips drop sweetness as the honeycomb,
my bride;
milk and honey are under your tongue.
The fragrance of your garments is like that
of Lebanon.
¹²You are a garden locked up, my sister, my
bride;
you are a spring enclosed, a sealed
fountain.
¹³Your plants are an orchard of pomegranates
with choice fruits,
with henna and nard,
¹⁴ nard and saffron,
calamus and cinnamon,
with every kind of incense tree,
with myrrh and aloes
and all the finest spices.
¹⁵You are*ᵍ* a garden fountain,
a well of flowing water
streaming down from Lebanon.
¹⁶Awake, north wind,
and come, south wind!
Blow on my garden,
that its fragrance may spread abroad.
Let my lover come into his garden
and taste its choice fruits.

ᶠ4 The meaning of the Hebrew for this word is uncertain.   ᵍ15 Or I am (spoken by the Beloved)

Discovering the Word 1. What kinds of emotions do you notice throughout this passage? 2. What do the lover's explicit words describing his beloved's physical beauty (vv. 1–7) reveal about their relationship? 3. What words and phrases help you understand how Solomon feels about his beloved (vv. 9–15)? 4. How does the beloved respond to the praise and adoration that is lavished upon her? 5. What does their dialogue reveal about their attitude about themselves as sexual beings?

Applying the Word 1. How does this picture compare to and contrast with the depiction of married love in current media? 2. In what ways does this passage change and/or inform your attitude toward married love?

Responding in Prayer God pursues you like the lover pursues the beloved in this passage. Praise God for his love that never lets us go.

4 / *Song of Songs 5—6*
Affirming One Another

"THAT WAS A great meal." "You look fabulous." "Thanks for remembering." We all need to be noticed and appreciated. Sometimes we forget to affirm those we are closest to—yet they are the ones who most value our opinions. In the Song of Songs we have a picture of loving, mutual affirmation.

Warming Up to God In what area of your life would you most like to be praised?

Read Song of Songs 5—6.

5 I have come into my garden, my sister,
    my bride;
  I have gathered my myrrh with my
    spice.
I have eaten my honeycomb and my honey;
  I have drunk my wine and my milk.
Eat, O friends, and drink;
  drink your fill, O lovers.
²I slept but my heart was awake.
  Listen! My lover is knocking:
"Open to me, my sister, my darling,
  my dove, my flawless one.
My head is drenched with dew,
  my hair with the dampness of the night."
³I have taken off my robe—
  must I put it on again?
I have washed my feet—
  must I soil them again?
⁴My lover thrust his hand through the
    latch-opening;
  my heart began to pound for him.
⁵I arose to open for my lover,
  and my hands dripped with myrrh,
my fingers with flowing myrrh,
  on the handles of the lock.
⁶I opened for my lover,
  but my lover had left; he was gone.
  My heart sank at his departure.ʰ
I looked for him but did not find him.
  I called him but he did not answer.
⁷The watchmen found me
  as they made their rounds in the city.
They beat me, they bruised me;

they took away my cloak,
  those watchmen of the walls!
⁸O daughters of Jerusalem, I charge you—
  if you find my lover,
what will you tell him?
  Tell him I am faint with love.
⁹How is your beloved better than others,
  most beautiful of women?
How is your beloved better than others,
  that you charge us so?
¹⁰My lover is radiant and ruddy,
  outstanding among ten thousand.
¹¹His head is purest gold;
  his hair is wavy
  and black as a raven.
¹²His eyes are like doves
  by the water streams,
washed in milk,
  mounted like jewels.
¹³His cheeks are like beds of spice
  yielding perfume.
His lips are like lilies
  dripping with myrrh.
¹⁴His arms are rods of gold
  set with chrysolite.
His body is like polished ivory
  decorated with sapphires.ⁱ
¹⁵His legs are pillars of marble
  set on bases of pure gold.
His appearance is like Lebanon,
  choice as its cedars.
¹⁶His mouth is sweetness itself;

ʰ6 Or *heart had gone out to him when he spoke*   ⁱ14 Or *lapis lazuli*

he is altogether lovely.
This is my lover, this my friend,
O daughters of Jerusalem.

6 Where has your lover gone,
most beautiful of women?
Which way did your lover turn,
that we may look for him with you?

²My lover has gone down to his garden,
to the beds of spices,
to browse in the gardens
and to gather lilies.

³I am my lover's and my lover is mine;
he browses among the lilies.

⁴You are beautiful, my darling, as Tirzah,
lovely as Jerusalem,
majestic as troops with banners.

⁵Turn your eyes from me;
they overwhelm me.
Your hair is like a flock of goats
descending from Gilead.

⁶Your teeth are like a flock of sheep
coming up from the washing.
Each has its twin,
not one of them is alone.

⁷Your temples behind your veil
are like the halves of a pomegranate.

⁸Sixty queens there may be,
and eighty concubines,
and virgins beyond number;

⁹but my dove, my perfect one, is unique,
the only daughter of her mother,
the favorite of the one who bore her.
The maidens saw her and called her blessed;
the queens and concubines praised her.

¹⁰Who is this that appears like the dawn,
fair as the moon, bright as the sun,
majestic as the stars in procession?

¹¹I went down to the grove of nut trees
to look at the new growth in the valley,
to see if the vines had budded
or the pomegranates were in bloom.

¹²Before I realized it,
my desire set me among the royal chariots
of my people.ʲ

¹³Come back, come back, O Shulammite;
come back, come back, that we may gaze
on you!
Why would you gaze on the Shulammite
as on the dance of Mahanaim?

ʲ12 Or *among the chariots of Amminadab; or among the chariots of the people of the prince*

 Discovering the Word 1. The image of a garden runs through this passage and the whole book (5:1; 6:2–3) How is it appropriate to the picture of marital love? 2. Prompted by the friends in 5:9, the beloved describes her lover. 5:10–16 is the only place where she describes his appearance. We don't know whether he was present at that time. If he did hear her words—or if he heard about her praise—how would this have been meaningful to him? 3. Why is it important to make praise specific and concrete as in 5:10–16? 4. In 6:3 the beloved says, "I am my lover's and my lover is mine," while in 2:16 she says, "My lover is mine and I am his." What does this statement and the variation in wording tell you about the relationship?

Applying the Word 1. This is a picture of a couple who is actively adoring, courting and pursuing each other. What is the value of this in a marriage? 2. What have you seen happen when this aspect of the relationship is neglected? 3. Think of someone close to you, perhaps your spouse or a parent, that you need to affirm. How can you do this?

Responding in Prayer Ask God to make you a channel of love and affirmation to those you meet.

---

5 / *Song of Songs 7—8*
Love for a Lifetime

"LET'S PRETEND WE'RE married—oh, all night." This is love according to Prince. Popular songs tell us what love is. Jewelry advertisers tell us what love is. Movies show us what love is. Yet the definitions that popular culture gives us leave us empty—unfulfilled. The *NIV Student Bible* refers to the Song of Songs as "a poem about love the way it's meant to be." In this sense it shows us love as God envisions it, not as we usually see it.

 Warming Up to God When are you likely to be led astray by the media's depictions of love?

 Read Song of Songs 7—8.

7 How beautiful your sandaled feet,
     O prince's daughter!
     Your graceful legs are like jewels,
  the work of a craftsman's hands.
²Your navel is a rounded goblet
  that never lacks blended wine.
Your waist is a mound of wheat
  encircled by lilies.
³Your breasts are like two fawns,
  twins of a gazelle.
⁴Your neck is like an ivory tower.
Your eyes are the pools of Heshbon
  by the gate of Bath Rabbim.
Your nose is like the tower of Lebanon
  looking toward Damascus.
⁵Your head crowns you like Mount Carmel.
  Your hair is like royal tapestry;
  the king is held captive by its tresses.
⁶How beautiful you are and how pleasing,
  O love, with your delights!
⁷Your stature is like that of the palm,
  and your breasts like clusters of fruit.
⁸I said, "I will climb the palm tree;
  I will take hold of its fruit."
May your breasts be like the clusters of the
     vine,
  the fragrance of your breath like apples,
⁹ and your mouth like the best wine.
May the wine go straight to my lover,
  flowing gently over lips and teeth.ᵏ
¹⁰I belong to my lover,
  and his desire is for me.
¹¹Come, my lover, let us go to the
     countryside,
  let us spend the night in the villages.ˡ
¹²Let us go early to the vineyards
  to see if the vines have budded,
  if their blossoms have opened,
  and if the pomegranates are in bloom—
  there I will give you my love.
¹³The mandrakes send out their fragrance,
  and at our door is every delicacy,
both new and old,
  that I have stored up for you, my lover.

8 If only you were to me like a brother,
     who was nursed at my mother's breasts!
     Then, if I found you outside,
  I would kiss you,
  and no one would despise me.
²I would lead you
  and bring you to my mother's house—
  she who has taught me.
I would give you spiced wine to drink,
  the nectar of my pomegranates.
³His left arm is under my head
  and his right arm embraces me.
⁴Daughters of Jerusalem, I charge you:
  Do not arouse or awaken love
  until it so desires.
⁵Who is this coming up from the desert
  leaning on her lover?
Under the apple tree I roused you;
  there your mother conceived you,
  there she who was in labor gave you birth.
⁶Place me like a seal over your heart,
  like a seal on your arm;
for love is as strong as death,
  its jealousyᵐ unyielding as the grave.ⁿ
It burns like blazing fire,
  like a mighty flame.ᵒ
⁷Many waters cannot quench love;
  rivers cannot wash it away.
If one were to give
  all the wealth of his house for love,
  itᵖ would be utterly scorned.
⁸We have a young sister,
  and her breasts are not yet grown.
What shall we do for our sister
  for the day she is spoken for?
⁹If she is a wall,
  we will build towers of silver on her.
If she is a door,
  we will enclose her with panels of cedar.
¹⁰I am a wall,
  and my breasts are like towers.
Thus I have become in his eyes

ᵏ9 Septuagint, Aquila, Vulgate and Syriac; Hebrew *lips of sleepers*
ˡ11 Or *henna bushes*   ᵐ6 Or *ardor*   ⁿ6 Hebrew *Sheol*   ᵒ6 Or *l
like the very flame of the* Lᴏʀᴅ   ᵖ7 Or *he*

like one bringing contentment.
¹¹Solomon had a vineyard in Baal Hamon;
    he let out his vineyard to tenants.
Each was to bring for its fruit
    a thousand shekels^q of silver.
¹²But my own vineyard is mine to give;
    the thousand shekels are for you,
        O Solomon,
    and two hundred^r are for those who tend
        its fruit.

¹³You who dwell in the gardens
    with friends in attendance,
    let me hear your voice!
¹⁴Come away, my lover,
    and be like a gazelle
    or like a young stag
        on the spice-laden mountains.

^{q}11 That is, about 25 pounds (about 11.5 kilograms); also in verse 12
^{r}12 That is, about 5 pounds (about 2.3 kilograms)

Discovering the Word **1.** The lover offers his beloved praise in exquisite detail in 7:1–9. What does this reveal about their love? **2.** In 7:10 we see another variation of the refrain of 2:16 and 6:3. What truth about love and desire do you find here? **3.** How does sexual love within a marriage involve discoveries "both new and old" (7:13) that a one-night stand does not? **4.** The language of 8:6–7 is rich and beautiful. What qualities of love are named? **5.** How are these qualities unique to the long-term commitment of marriage? **6.** In what ways does marriage require a willingness to give one's self to your partner (8:12)?

Applying the Word **1.** When is it difficult for you to surrender yourself to those who love you? **2.** When is it difficult for you to surrender to God's love for you?

Responding in Prayer Ask God to make you responsive to his unending love for you.

Isaiah

We had planned, a pastor friend and I, a series of studies in Isaiah for his church. His enthusiasm for the studies was infectious. But when the time came, he did not attend. Why not? Some people would put it simply: "Cancer killed him." Yet from another perspective, we can say, "The Lord took him home into his presence." Thus, it was with a heart filled with sorrow and gratitude that I set off for the week in question. Filled with ideas and enthusiasm, I was convicted that "trusting God in troubled times" was the right theme for this bereaved church. I was loaded with emotion and the hope that our study times would be real encounters with God himself. And what times we had together! Times of worship, laughter and sober reflection. So it is to the memory of Eugene Kwa, to his wife, Ann Nai, and to the members of the church which he pastored that this is dedicated.

Trusting God in Troubled Times

Isaiah is a difficult and, therefore, often-neglected book. Why should we study Isaiah? First, because it is part of holy Scripture and is great literature. We should study Isaiah because it is very frequently quoted or alluded to in the New Testament. We should study these selected passages because trusting God is still essential and troubled times are our lot too.

These studies contain some fascinating passages, including (1) hard-hitting criticisms of empty religion; (2) panoramic and extraordinarily impressive views of God's coming day of judgment and the everlasting joys which follow it; (3) some of the most famous Messianic prophecies; (4) dramatic narratives of times of national crisis; (5) honest exposures of a rotten society and a heartfelt cry for revival; (6) the famous story of Isaiah's call and mysterious commission and meditations on what it means for us to be trustful, faithful servants of God; (7) robust assertions that God is the world's only Savior with worldwide purposes we are to carry out; (8) and many passages full of pastoral comfort for our "spiritual armory."

Isaiah lived through turbulent times. He was called to his work at the time when a famous Assyrian king was building his empire into the largest and cruelest that western Asia had ever seen. He saw the neighboring kingdom of Israel crack, collapse and vanish. For forty years Isaiah walked quietly in the corridors of power challenging a knock-kneed king to trust God even when he could see the campfires of the apparently invincible Assyrian army right outside his own city's locked gates and hear the threats of the general coming over the walls.

We know nothing of his wife, but Isaiah had two sons with names which were signposts to coming events. Isaiah was a social critic, remorselessly applying the yardstick of God's law to what he saw. He was a prophet—not an astrologer with cunningly ambiguous forecasts but a man who saw both the present and the future in an eternal light. He was a pastor looking with compassion on his fellow citizens and feeding them by teaching them. He was a poet, seeing events more fully, more deeply, more sharply.

It is our privilege to read his words, to be still, to observe, to receive, to meditate on what he said, and then to join in life-building, invigorating discussion in order that we too might trust God more, and thus with joy draw water from the wells of salvation.

Kosuke Koyama has pointedly contrasted Christianity as a noisy religion with the quiet religion of Buddhism. The barrage of words increases daily, amplified and multiplied by ever more sophisticated technology. We need some countermeasures. Isaiah's one hundred pages represent forty years of ministry. What then is his unusual impact? Most of the time *he lived what he talked*. By studying Isaiah, your life can also find a still center.

"This is what the Sovereign LORD, the Holy One of Israel, says: 'In repentance and rest is your salvation, in quietness and trust is your strength' " (Isa 30:15).

Outline

1/ Isaiah 1 ——————— A Hollow Religion

2/ Isaiah 2 ——————— The Revelation of God's Glory

3/ Isaiah 5 ——————— Judah's Wild Grapes

4/ Isaiah 6 ——————— In the Presence of God

5/ Isaiah 7 ——————— Stand Firm or Lose All

6/ Isaiah 8:11—9:7 ——————— To Us a Child Is Born

7/ Isaiah 11—12 ——————— The Earth Will Be Full of Knowledge

8/ Isaiah 24 ——————— Global Pollution

9/ Isaiah 25 ——————— Free at Last!

10/ Isaiah 30:1—18 ——————— Who Do You Rely On?

11/ Isaiah 36—37 ——————— An Extraordinary Deliverance

12/ Isaiah 38—39 ——————— Sovereign God and Forgetful King

13/ Isaiah 40 ——————— Unwearied Faith in an Unwearying God

14/ Isaiah 42 ——————— God's Servant: Image and Reality

15/ Isaiah 43:1—44:5 ——————— Rivers in the Desert

16/ Isaiah 45 ——————— Turning to God

17/ Isaiah 49 ——————— Foundations for Service

18/ Isaiah 52:13—53:12 ——————— The Heart of the Old Testament

19/ Isaiah 54—55 ——————— Shout for Joy

20/ Isaiah 58 ——————— Unfailing Spring

21/ Isaiah 61 ——————— A Garment of Praise for a Spirit of Despair

22/ Isaiah 62 ——————— The Refugees Return

23/ Isaiah 63:7—64:12 ——————— A Cry for Forgiveness and for Revival

24/ Isaiah 65:17—66:24 ——————— The Terror and the Glory

Map 1

Map 2

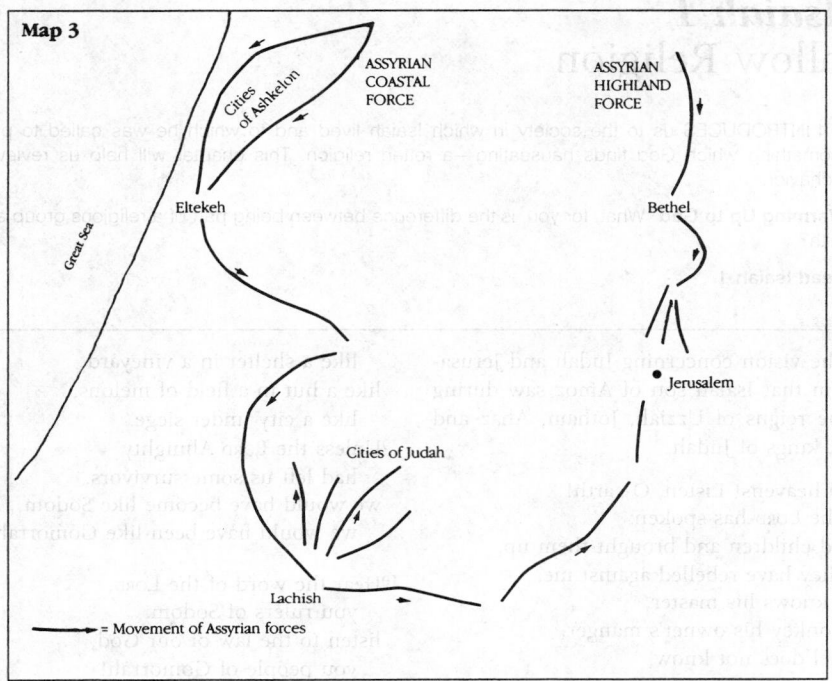

The Historical Background of Isaiah

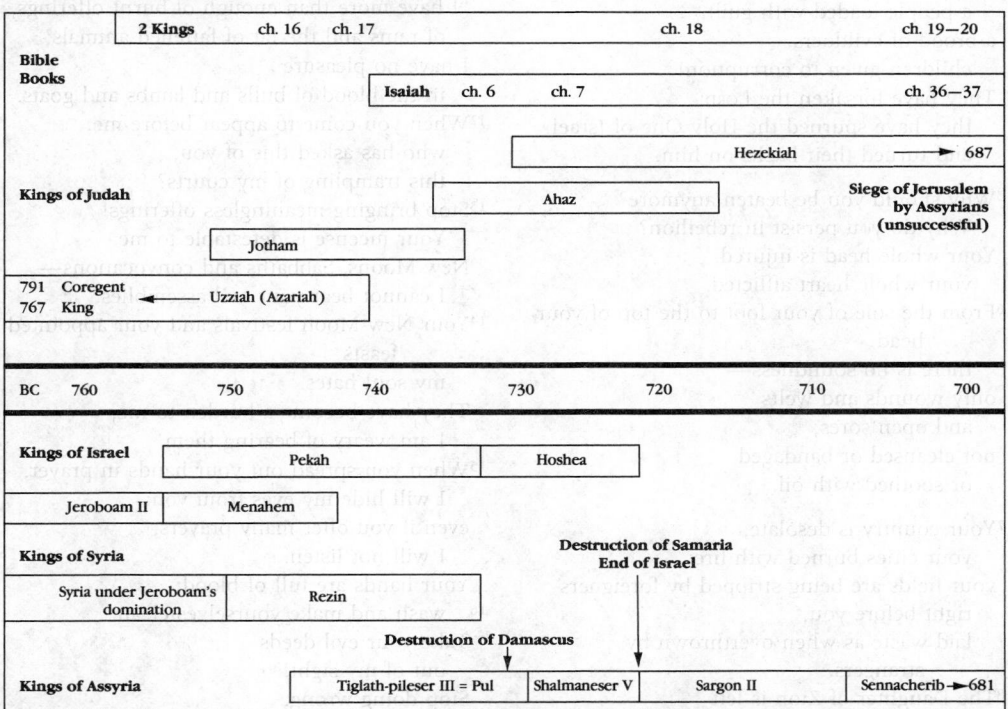

1 / *Isaiah 1*
A Hollow Religion

CHAPTER 1 INTRODUCES us to the society in which Isaiah lived and to which he was called to preach. We discover something which God finds nauseating—a rotten religion. This chapter will help us review our own religious behavior.

 Warming Up to God What, for you, is the difference between being part of a religious group and having faith?

 Read Isaiah 1.

1 The vision concerning Judah and Jerusalem that Isaiah son of Amoz saw during the reigns of Uzziah, Jotham, Ahaz and Hezekiah, kings of Judah.

²Hear, O heavens! Listen, O earth!
    For the LORD has spoken:
"I reared children and brought them up,
    but they have rebelled against me.
³The ox knows his master,
    the donkey his owner's manger,
but Israel does not know,
    my people do not understand."

⁴Ah, sinful nation,
    a people loaded with guilt,
a brood of evildoers,
    children given to corruption!
They have forsaken the LORD;
    they have spurned the Holy One of Israel
    and turned their backs on him.

⁵Why should you be beaten anymore?
    Why do you persist in rebellion?
Your whole head is injured,
    your whole heart afflicted.
⁶From the sole of your foot to the top of your
        head
    there is no soundness—
only wounds and welts
    and open sores,
not cleansed or bandaged
    or soothed with oil.

⁷Your country is desolate,
    your cities burned with fire;
your fields are being stripped by foreigners
    right before you,
    laid waste as when overthrown by
        strangers.
⁸The Daughter of Zion is left

like a shelter in a vineyard,
like a hut in a field of melons,
    like a city under siege.
⁹Unless the LORD Almighty
    had left us some survivors,
we would have become like Sodom,
    we would have been like Gomorrah.

¹⁰Hear the word of the LORD,
    you rulers of Sodom;
listen to the law of our God,
    you people of Gomorrah!
¹¹"The multitude of your sacrifices—
    what are they to me?" says the LORD.
"I have more than enough of burnt offerings,
    of rams and the fat of fattened animals;
I have no pleasure
    in the blood of bulls and lambs and goats.
¹²When you come to appear before me,
    who has asked this of you,
    this trampling of my courts?
¹³Stop bringing meaningless offerings!
    Your incense is detestable to me.
New Moons, Sabbaths and convocations—
    I cannot bear your evil assemblies.
¹⁴Your New Moon festivals and your appointed
        feasts
    my soul hates.
They have become a burden to me;
    I am weary of bearing them.
¹⁵When you spread out your hands in prayer,
    I will hide my eyes from you;
even if you offer many prayers,
    I will not listen.
Your hands are full of blood;
¹⁶   wash and make yourselves clean.
Take your evil deeds
    out of my sight!
Stop doing wrong,

17 learn to do right!
Seek justice,
encourage the oppressed.^a
Defend the cause of the fatherless,
plead the case of the widow.

18"Come now, let us reason together,"
says the LORD.
"Though your sins are like scarlet,
they shall be as white as snow;
though they are red as crimson,
they shall be like wool.
19If you are willing and obedient,
you will eat the best from the land;
20but if you resist and rebel,
you will be devoured by the sword."
For the mouth of the LORD has spoken.

21See how the faithful city
has become a harlot!
She once was full of justice;
righteousness used to dwell in her—
but now murderers!
22Your silver has become dross,
your choice wine is diluted with water.
23Your rulers are rebels,
companions of thieves;
they all love bribes
and chase after gifts.
They do not defend the cause of the
fatherless;

the widow's case does not come before
them.
24Therefore the Lord, the LORD Almighty,
the Mighty One of Israel, declares:
"Ah, I will get relief from my foes
and avenge myself on my enemies.
25I will turn my hand against you;
I will thoroughly purge away your dross
and remove all your impurities.
26I will restore your judges as in days of old,
your counselors as at the beginning.
Afterward you will be called
the City of Righteousness,
the Faithful City."

27Zion will be redeemed with justice,
her penitent ones with righteousness.
28But rebels and sinners will both be broken,
and those who forsake the LORD will perish.

29"You will be ashamed because of the sacred
oaks
in which you have delighted;
you will be disgraced because of the gardens
that you have chosen.
30You will be like an oak with fading leaves,
like a garden without water.
31The mighty man will become tinder
and his work a spark;
both will burn together,
with no one to quench the fire."

^a17 Or / rebuke the oppressor

Discovering the Word 1. In verses 2–3 the Lord summons heaven and earth to be witnesses of his accusations against his people. What is the force of the two metaphors the Lord uses to describe his people's unreasonable and rebellious conduct? 2. Both the nation (v. 4) and the country (v. 7) are in a shocking condition. What vivid pictures of sinfulness do verses 4–9 provide? 3. These people who verses 2–9 speak of were religious! How does God react in verses 10–15 to all of their religious commotion? 4. Describe the kind of life that God is asking them to lead instead (vv. 16–17). 5. Look at verses 21–26. You will notice that these verses are framed by reference to "the faithful city" (Jerusalem or Zion). Life in the capital reflects life in the nation. What picture do these verses give of life in Jerusalem? 6. Now return to verses 18–20. Some scholars think verse 18 is cynical, but traditionally it has been understood as a gracious invitation by humanity's Judge. What does this invitation offer?

Applying the Word 1. In what ways have heaven and earth witnessed the same sinfulness and the same results in your life and your society? 2. From your own experience, explain why it is much harder to fulfill the moral requirements of verses 16–17 than just to go through the ritual activities mentioned in verses 10–15. 3. Evaluate your own religious practices in the midst of your own society with all its needs. What reorientation does your life require if your religion is not to be just a burden—to you *and* to God?

 Responding in Prayer Confess your sins to God, knowing that he will make you pure.

2 / *Isaiah 2*
The Revelation of God's Glory

STANDING OUTSIDE THE Old City of Jerusalem is one of the most poignant memorials in Israel to the Six Day War of 1967. It is a futuristic sculpture made of wrecked military equipment with these words from Isaiah on it: "They will beat their swords into plowshares and their spears into pruning hooks. Nation will not take up sword against nation, nor will they train for war anymore" (Isa 2:4). These words still seem infinitely far from fulfillment. Globally, defense spending exceeds the income of the poorest half of the world's population. Yet this chapter of Isaiah tells us of a coming day of reckoning when there will be some incredible surprises. But the sorting and reassessment process begins now in people's response to God (and to Christ). Then, in that day, the process will be completed.

 Warming Up to God What would you do if you knew the world would end next week?

 Read Isaiah 2.

2 This is what Isaiah son of Amoz saw concerning Judah and Jerusalem:

²In the last days

the mountain of the LORD's temple will be
established
as chief among the mountains;
it will be raised above the hills,
and all nations will stream to it.

³Many peoples will come and say,

"Come, let us go up to the mountain of the
LORD,
to the house of the God of Jacob.
He will teach us his ways,
so that we may walk in his paths."
The law will go out from Zion,
the word of the LORD from Jerusalem.
⁴He will judge between the nations
and will settle disputes for many peoples.
They will beat their swords into plowshares
and their spears into pruning hooks.
Nation will not take up sword against nation,
nor will they train for war anymore.

⁵Come, O house of Jacob,
let us walk in the light of the LORD.

⁶You have abandoned your people,
the house of Jacob.
They are full of superstitions from the East;
they practice divination like the Philistines
and clasp hands with pagans.
⁷Their land is full of silver and gold;
there is no end to their treasures.
Their land is full of horses;

there is no end to their chariots.
⁸Their land is full of idols;
they bow down to the work of their hands,
to what their fingers have made.
⁹So man will be brought low
and mankind humbled—
do not forgive them.ᵇ

¹⁰Go into the rocks,
hide in the ground
from dread of the LORD
and the splendor of his majesty!
¹¹The eyes of the arrogant man will be humbled
and the pride of men brought low;
the LORD alone will be exalted in that day.

¹²The LORD Almighty has a day in store
for all the proud and lofty,
for all that is exalted
(and they will be humbled),
¹³for all the cedars of Lebanon, tall and lofty,
and all the oaks of Bashan,
¹⁴for all the towering mountains
and all the high hills,
¹⁵for every lofty tower
and every fortified wall,
¹⁶for every trading shipᶜ
and every stately vessel.
¹⁷The arrogance of man will be brought low
and the pride of men humbled;
the LORD alone will be exalted in that day,
18   and the idols will totally disappear.

¹⁹Men will flee to caves in the rocks
and to holes in the ground
from dread of the LORD

ᵇ9 Or *not raise them up*   ᶜ16 Hebrew *every ship of Tarshish*

and the splendor of his majesty,
  when he rises to shake the earth.
²⁰In that day men will throw away
  to the rodents and bats
their idols of silver and idols of
    gold,
  which they made to worship.
²¹They will flee to caverns in the rocks

and to the overhanging crags
from dread of the LORD
  and the splendor of his majesty,
  when he rises to shake the earth.

²²Stop trusting in man,
  who has but a breath in his nostrils.
Of what account is he?

Discovering the Word 1. To what period or periods do the words *day* and *days* refer (vv. 2, 11–12, 17, 20)? 2. According to verses 3–4, for what purpose and in what spirit do the nations stream toward Jerusalem? 3. Verses 6–9 provide a rather sad contrast to the vision of verses 2–4. What is the land full of according to these verses? 4. Verses 10–21 mention a number of great things, some natural and some synthetic, which will be brought low in the day when the splendor of God's majesty is revealed. What things are specifically mentioned? 5. What do you think is God's purpose in this process?

Applying the Word 1. In what practical ways can you express your own commitment to global peace? 2. What incentives and encouragements do chapters 1 and 2 of Isaiah give you to trust God in troubled times?

Responding in Prayer Ask God to teach you what it means to stop trusting in humanity (v. 22) and to only rely on him.

Isaiah 3—4

3 See now, the Lord,
  the LORD Almighty,
  is about to take from Jerusalem and
    Judah
both supply and support:
all supplies of food and all supplies of water,
² the hero and warrior,
the judge and prophet,
  the soothsayer and elder,
³the captain of fifty and man of rank,
  the counselor, skilled craftsman and clever
    enchanter.

⁴I will make boys their officials;
  mere children will govern them.
⁵People will oppress each other—
  man against man, neighbor against
    neighbor.
The young will rise up against the old,
  the base against the honorable.

⁶A man will seize one of his brothers
  at his father's home, and say,
"You have a cloak, you be our leader;
  take charge of this heap of ruins!"
⁷But in that day he will cry out,
  "I have no remedy.

I have no food or clothing in my house;
  do not make me the leader of the people."

⁸Jerusalem staggers,
  Judah is falling;
their words and deeds are against the LORD,
  defying his glorious presence.
⁹The look on their faces testifies against them;
  they parade their sin like Sodom;
  they do not hide it.
Woe to them!
  They have brought disaster upon
    themselves.

¹⁰Tell the righteous it will be well with them,
  for they will enjoy the fruit of their deeds.
¹¹Woe to the wicked! Disaster is upon them!
  They will be paid back for what their hands
    have done.

¹²Youths oppress my people,
  women rule over them.
O my people, your guides lead you astray;
  they turn you from the path.

¹³The LORD takes his place in court;
  he rises to judge the people.
¹⁴The LORD enters into judgment

against the elders and leaders of his people:
"It is you who have ruined my vineyard;
the plunder from the poor is in your
houses.
¹⁵What do you mean by crushing my people
and grinding the faces of the poor?"
declares the Lord, the LORD Almighty.

¹⁶The LORD says,
"The women of Zion are haughty,
walking along with outstretched necks,
flirting with their eyes,
tripping along with mincing steps,
with ornaments jingling on their ankles.
¹⁷Therefore the Lord will bring sores on the
heads of the women of Zion;
the LORD will make their scalps bald."

¹⁸In that day the Lord will snatch away their
finery: the bangles and headbands and crescent
necklaces, ¹⁹the earrings and bracelets and veils,
²⁰the headdresses and ankle chains and sashes,
the perfume bottles and charms, ²¹the signet rings
and nose rings, ²²the fine robes and the capes and
cloaks, the purses ²³and mirrors, and the linen
garments and tiaras and shawls.

²⁴Instead of fragrance there will be a stench;
instead of a sash, a rope;
instead of well-dressed hair, baldness;
instead of fine clothing, sackcloth;

instead of beauty, branding.
²⁵Your men will fall by the sword,
your warriors in battle.
²⁶The gates of Zion will lament and mourn;
destitute, she will sit on the ground.

4 In that day seven women
will take hold of one man
and say, "We will eat our own food
and provide our own clothes;
only let us be called by your name.
Take away our disgrace!"

²In that day the Branch of the LORD will be
beautiful and glorious, and the fruit of the land
will be the pride and glory of the survivors in
Israel. ³Those who are left in Zion, who remain
in Jerusalem, will be called holy, all who are recorded among the living in Jerusalem. ⁴The Lord
will wash away the filth of the women of Zion; he
will cleanse the bloodstains from Jerusalem by a
spirit^d of judgment and a spirit^d of fire. ⁵Then
the LORD will create over all of Mount Zion and
over those who assemble there a cloud of smoke
by day and a glow of flaming fire by night; over
all the glory will be a canopy. ⁶It will be a shelter
and shade from the heat of the day, and a refuge
and hiding place from the storm and rain.

d4 Or the Spirit

3 / *Isaiah 5*
Judah's Wild Grapes

"BE SURE YOUR sins will find you out." Do you think of this as just a quaint saying, used warningly by mothers to
their children? For Isaiah this fact is a grave reality which applies to nations as well as to individuals. The setting
of this chapter of Isaiah was probably during the grape harvest, a time famous for conversation and conviviality.
Isaiah uses a short parable to rouse his friends' consciences, and then with mounting vehemence attacks certain
sins directly.

Warming Up to God Have you ever been in a situation in which you needed to confront a friend with
inconsistencies in his or her lifestyle? What happened?

Read Isaiah 5.

5 I will sing for the one I love
a song about his vineyard:
My loved one had a vineyard
on a fertile hillside.

²He dug it up and cleared it of stones
and planted it with the choicest vines.
He built a watchtower in it
and cut out a winepress as well.

Then he looked for a crop of good grapes,
but it yielded only bad fruit.

³"Now you dwellers in Jerusalem and men of
Judah,
judge between me and my vineyard.
⁴What more could have been done for my
vineyard
than I have done for it?
When I looked for good grapes,
why did it yield only bad?
⁵Now I will tell you
what I am going to do to my vineyard:
I will take away its hedge,
and it will be destroyed;
I will break down its wall,
and it will be trampled.
⁶I will make it a wasteland,
neither pruned nor cultivated,
and briers and thorns will grow there.
I will command the clouds
not to rain on it."

⁷The vineyard of the LORD Almighty
is the house of Israel,
and the men of Judah
are the garden of his delight.
And he looked for justice, but saw bloodshed;
for righteousness, but heard cries of
distress.

⁸Woe to you who add house to house
and join field to field
till no space is left
and you live alone in the land.

⁹The LORD Almighty has declared in my hearing:

"Surely the great houses will become desolate,
the fine mansions left without occupants.
¹⁰A ten-acreᵉ vineyard will produce only a
bathᶠ of wine,
a homerᵍ of seed only an ephahʰ of
grain."

¹¹Woe to those who rise early in the morning
to run after their drinks,
who stay up late at night
till they are inflamed with wine.
¹²They have harps and lyres at their banquets,
tambourines and flutes and wine,
but they have no regard for the deeds of the
LORD,
no respect for the work of his hands.

¹³Therefore my people will go into exile
for lack of understanding;
their men of rank will die of hunger
and their masses will be parched with
thirst.
¹⁴Therefore the graveⁱ enlarges its appetite
and opens its mouth without limit;
into it will descend their nobles and masses
with all their brawlers and revelers.
¹⁵So man will be brought low
and mankind humbled,
the eyes of the arrogant humbled.
¹⁶But the LORD Almighty will be exalted by his
justice,
and the holy God will show himself holy
by his righteousness.
¹⁷Then sheep will graze as in their own pasture;
lambs will feedʲ among the ruins of the
rich.

¹⁸Woe to those who draw sin along with cords
of deceit,
and wickedness as with cart ropes,
¹⁹to those who say, "Let God hurry,
let him hasten his work
so we may see it.
Let it approach,
let the plan of the Holy One of Israel come,
so we may know it."

²⁰Woe to those who call evil good
and good evil,
who put darkness for light
and light for darkness,
who put bitter for sweet
and sweet for bitter.

²¹Woe to those who are wise in their own eyes
and clever in their own sight.

²²Woe to those who are heroes at drinking
wine
and champions at mixing drinks,
²³who acquit the guilty for a bribe,
but deny justice to the innocent.
²⁴Therefore, as tongues of fire lick up straw
and as dry grass sinks down in the flames,
so their roots will decay
and their flowers blow away like dust;

ᵉ10 Hebrew ten-yoke, that is, the land plowed by 10 yoke of oxen in
one day   ᶠ10 That is, probably about 6 gallons (about 22 liters)
ᵍ10 That is, probably about 6 bushels (about 220 liters)   ʰ10 That is,
probably about 3/5 bushel (about 22 liters)   ⁱ14 Hebrew Sheol
ʲ17 Septuagint; Hebrew / strangers will eat

for they have rejected the law of the LORD
Almighty
and spurned the word of the Holy One of
Israel.
²⁵Therefore the LORD's anger burns against his
people;
his hand is raised and he strikes them
down.
The mountains shake,
and the dead bodies are like refuse in the
streets.

Yet for all this, his anger is not turned away,
his hand is still upraised.

²⁶He lifts up a banner for the distant nations,
he whistles for those at the ends of the
earth.
Here they come,
swiftly and speedily!

²⁷Not one of them grows tired or stumbles,
not one slumbers or sleeps;
not a belt is loosened at the waist,
not a sandal thong is broken.
²⁸Their arrows are sharp,
all their bows are strung;
their horses' hoofs seem like flint,
their chariot wheels like a whirlwind.
²⁹Their roar is like that of the lion,
they roar like young lions;
they growl as they seize their prey
and carry it off with no one to
rescue.
³⁰In that day they will roar over it
like the roaring of the sea.
And if one looks at the land,
he will see darkness and distress;
even the light will be darkened by the
clouds.

 Discovering the Word 1. Choosing carefully the occasion and form (a love song), Isaiah introduces the subject of a dear friend's vineyard. Describe the care that was lavished on the vineyard and the owner's dismay when the final product was only evil-smelling, bitter, wild grapes (vv. 1–7). 2. Dropping the disguise of the parable, Isaiah rams home the lesson to his people directly in verse 7. Contrast what God has looked for among his people with what he has found. 3. Verses 8–23 fall into six sections introduced by the word *woe*. What are the sins described in each of these sections? 4. What do these woes reveal about the society at this time? 5. What punishment does the Lord announce in verses 9–10, 13–17 and 24–25?

Applying the Word 1. Give examples of ways in which God has lavished his care upon you, only to be rewarded by a bitter harvest. 2. Consider again the image of the vineyard in verses 1–3. How is God's work in you similar to that of the vineyard owner?

Responding in Prayer God calls you to respond to him. Pray for one specific sweet fruit to grow in your life.

4 / *Isaiah 6*
In the Presence of God

NO ONE ALIVE today would go into a nuclear reactor without protective clothing. In a similar way, during Old Testament times merely being in the presence of God was regarded as being fatal. In this chapter Isaiah comes before the presence of God. He is so overcome by the experience that he cries out, "Woe to me!" God is gracious to Isaiah, however, and gives him a special mission. Through this famous story we will learn something about God's call to us also.

 Warming Up to God When have you been confronted with the reality of God's surpassingly great holiness? How did you respond?

 Read Isaiah 6.

6 In the year that King Uzziah died, I saw the Lord seated on a throne, high and exalted, and the train of his robe filled the temple. ²Above him were seraphs, each with six wings: With two wings they covered their faces, with two they covered their feet, and with two they were flying. ³And they were calling to one another:

"Holy, holy, holy is the Lord Almighty;
the whole earth is full of his glory."

⁴At the sound of their voices the doorposts and thresholds shook and the temple was filled with smoke.

⁵"Woe to me!" I cried. "I am ruined! For I am a man of unclean lips, and I live among a people of unclean lips, and my eyes have seen the King, the Lord Almighty."

⁶Then one of the seraphs flew to me with a live coal in his hand, which he had taken with tongs from the altar. ⁷With it he touched my mouth and said, "See, this has touched your lips; your guilt is taken away and your sin atoned for."

⁸Then I heard the voice of the Lord saying, "Whom shall I send? And who will go for us?"

And I said, "Here am I. Send me!"

⁹He said, "Go and tell this people:

" 'Be ever hearing, but never understanding;
be ever seeing, but never perceiving.'
¹⁰Make the heart of this people calloused;
make their ears dull
and close their eyes.ᵏ
Otherwise they might see with their eyes,
hear with their ears,
understand with their hearts,
and turn and be healed."

¹¹Then I said, "For how long, O Lord?"
And he answered:

"Until the cities lie ruined
and without inhabitant,
until the houses are left deserted
and the fields ruined and ravaged,
¹²until the Lord has sent everyone far away
and the land is utterly forsaken.
¹³And though a tenth remains in the land,
it will again be laid waste.
But as the terebinth and oak
leave stumps when they are cut down,
so the holy seed will be the stump in the
land."

ᵏ9,10 Hebrew; Septuagint *'You will be ever hearing, but never understanding; / you will be ever seeing, but never perceiving.' / ¹⁰This people's heart has become calloused; / they hardly hear with their ears, / and they have closed their eyes*

 Discovering the Word **1.** Uzziah's long and prosperous reign came to an end under a cloud (see 2Ch 26:16–21). What do you think was Isaiah's purpose in verse 1 in describing God as occupying the throne? **2.** Describe in your own words, as vividly as possible, what Isaiah saw (vv. 2–4). **3.** What is the significance of Isaiah's cry in verse 5, especially his reference to his own and his people's lips? **4.** What wonderful answer did Isaiah get to his cry of pain (vv. 6–7)? **5.** In verses 8–10 Isaiah receives his call and commission. If we follow the punctuation very carefully, it appears that verse 9 is what Isaiah is to tell the people and verse 10 is God's summary of what will happen. Describe what Isaiah's ministry will be like. **6.** Isaiah's surprisingly cool response to this commission is to inquire how long he should continue (v. 11). What is God's answer to this question (vv. 11–13)?

 Applying the Word **1.** What does this chapter tell you about what it means to be called by God and the kind of response God requires? **2.** What is God calling you to?

Responding in Prayer Picture yourself in this scene in the presence of God. Respond to his holiness with worship and praise.

5 / *Isaiah 7*
Stand Firm or Lose All

IN THIS STUDY we see King Ahaz of Judah miss a crucial opportunity to trust God in troubled times. He was too frightened to trust God and too vain or proud to ask for the offered sign. Ahaz's leadership can be summarized in this way: "Faith played no part in his religion or his politics" (*The New Bible Commentary: Revised*). Isaiah's cool and calm trustfulness emerges in the most vivid contrast to Ahaz's maneuverings. Assyria was the incomparably brutal superpower of the day, threatening to engulf Syria, Israel and Judah at any time. The chill which it cast over the whole scene is comparable to modern armies like the Nazis, the Mau Mau, the Khmer Rouge and, most recently, Saddam Hussein's Republican Guard. Yet Isaiah was confident that even mighty Assyria was under his God's control.

 Warming Up to God Recall a time you experienced God's grace when you were in a very tight spot or in the midst of a personal crisis. Offer your praise to God for his faithfulness.

 Read Isaiah 7.

7 When Ahaz son of Jotham, the son of Uzziah, was king of Judah, King Rezin of Aram and Pekah son of Remaliah king of Israel marched up to fight against Jerusalem, but they could not overpower it.

²Now the house of David was told, "Aram has allied itself with[l] Ephraim"; so the hearts of Ahaz and his people were shaken, as the trees of the forest are shaken by the wind.

³Then the LORD said to Isaiah, "Go out, you and your son Shear-Jashub,[m] to meet Ahaz at the end of the aqueduct of the Upper Pool, on the road to the Washerman's Field. ⁴Say to him, 'Be careful, keep calm and don't be afraid. Do not lose heart because of these two smoldering stubs of firewood—because of the fierce anger of Rezin and Aram and of the son of Remaliah. ⁵Aram, Ephraim and Remaliah's son have plotted your ruin, saying, ⁶"Let us invade Judah; let us tear it apart and divide it among ourselves, and make the son of Tabeel king over it." ⁷Yet this is what the Sovereign LORD says:

" 'It will not take place,
    it will not happen,
⁸for the head of Aram is Damascus,
    and the head of Damascus is only Rezin.
Within sixty-five years
    Ephraim will be too shattered to be a
        people.
⁹The head of Ephraim is Samaria,
    and the head of Samaria is only Remaliah's
        son.
If you do not stand firm in your faith,
    you will not stand at all.' "

¹⁰Again the LORD spoke to Ahaz, ¹¹"Ask the LORD your God for a sign, whether in the deepest depths or in the highest heights."

¹²But Ahaz said, "I will not ask; I will not put the LORD to the test."

¹³Then Isaiah said, "Hear now, you house of David! Is it not enough to try the patience of men? Will you try the patience of my God also? ¹⁴Therefore the Lord himself will give you[n] a sign: The virgin will be with child and will give birth to a son, and[o] will call him Immanuel.[p] ¹⁵He will eat curds and honey when he knows enough to reject the wrong and choose the right. ¹⁶But before the boy knows enough to reject the wrong and choose the right, the land of the two kings you dread will be laid waste. ¹⁷The LORD will bring on you and on your people and on the house of your father a time unlike any since Ephraim broke away from Judah—he will bring the king of Assyria."

¹⁸In that day the LORD will whistle for flies from the distant streams of Egypt and for bees from the land of Assyria. ¹⁹They will all come and settle in the steep ravines and in the crevices in the rocks, on all the thornbushes and at all the water holes. ²⁰In that day the Lord will use a razor hired from beyond the River[q]—the king of Assyria—to shave your head and the hair of your legs, and to take off your beards also. ²¹In that day, a man will keep alive a young cow and two goats. ²²And because of the abundance of the milk they give, he will have curds to eat. All who remain in the land

---

[l]2 Or *has set up camp in*   [m]3 *Shear-Jashub* means *a remnant will return.*   [n]14 The Hebrew is plural.   [o]14 Masoretic Text; Dead Sea Scrolls *and he* or *and they*   [p]14 *Immanuel* means *God with us.*   [q]20 That is, the Euphrates

will eat curds and honey. ²³In that day, in every place where there were a thousand vines worth a thousand silver shekels,ʳ there will be only briers and thorns. ²⁴Men will go there with bow and arrow, for the land will be covered with briers and thorns. ²⁵As for all the hills once cultivated

by the hoe, you will no longer go there for fear of the briers and thorns; they will become places where cattle are turned loose and where sheep run.

ʳ23 That is, about 25 pounds (about 11.5 kilograms)

 Discovering the Word 1. Study map 1 (see introduction) to get a picture of the setting. How does God describe Ahaz's enemies in verses 3–6? 2. How does the Lord's statement "It will not happen" (vv. 7–9) challenge and encourage Ahaz to trust him? 3. Why do you think God was impatient with Ahaz (vv. 10–13)? 4. What is the significance of the sign of the virgin's child (vv. 14–17)? 5. Ahaz thought he was outwitting two small enemies by allying himself with his biggest one. What disastrous miscalculation did this involve according to verses 17 and 20? 6. Ahaz hoped to preserve his crown and kingdom, but his land would become a shambles. How do verses 18–25 expound the fateful consequences of his choice?

Applying the Word 1. When have you found verse 9—"If you do not stand firm in your faith, you will not stand at all"—to be true for you? 2. How can you better prepare to meet some real or imagined crisis by applying to yourself this very moment the exhortation that Isaiah gave to Ahaz, especially verses 4 and 9?

Responding in Prayer Pray that you will not lose heart.

Isaiah 8:1–10

8 The Lᴏʀᴅ said to me, "Take a large scroll and write on it with an ordinary pen: Maher-Shalal-Hash-Baz.ˢ ²And I will call in Uriah the priest and Zechariah son of Jeberekiah as reliable witnesses for me."

³Then I went to the prophetess, and she conceived and gave birth to a son. And the Lᴏʀᴅ said to me, "Name him Maher-Shalal-Hash-Baz. ⁴Before the boy knows how to say 'My father' or 'My mother,' the wealth of Damascus and the plunder of Samaria will be carried off by the king of Assyria."

⁵The Lᴏʀᴅ spoke to me again:

⁶"Because this people has rejected
   the gently flowing waters of Shiloah
and rejoices over Rezin
   and the son of Remaliah,
⁷therefore the Lord is about to bring against
   them
   the mighty floodwaters of the Riverᵗ—

the king of Assyria with all his pomp.
It will overflow all its channels,
   run over all its banks
⁸and sweep on into Judah, swirling over it,
   passing through it and reaching up to the
      neck.
Its outspread wings will cover the breadth of
   your land,
O Immanuelᵘ!"

⁹Raise the war cry,ᵛ you nations, and be
      shattered!
   Listen, all you distant lands.
Prepare for battle, and be shattered!
   Prepare for battle, and be shattered!
¹⁰Devise your strategy, but it will be thwarted;
   propose your plan, but it will not stand,
for God is with us.ʷ

ˢ1 *Maher-Shalal-Hash-Baz* means *quick to the plunder, swift to the spoil*; also in verse 3.   ᵗ7 That is, the Euphrates   ᵘ8 *Immanuel* means *God with us.*   ᵛ9 Or *Do your worst*   ʷ10 Hebrew *Immanuel*

6 / *Isaiah 8:11—9:7*
To Us a Child Is Born

JUDAH HAD TURNED away from the light into the dark: to mediums and spiritists, to ghosts that gibber and squeak (8:19–20). King Ahaz has turned away from the sign God offered him, but a greater King is coming to put things right. This King is a child rather than a mighty conqueror! Yet he has shoulders adequate to the task. He shares God's character as a Wonderful Counselor. He is described as Mighty God. Paradoxically, although a son, he is described as the Everlasting Father! He is the Prince of Peace, and his kingdom shares his character. He is a descendant of David and will rule his kingdom with justice and righteousness forever. All of these characteristics distinguish his kingdom from the chronic instability of Israel and the desperate wobbling of Judah.

 Warming Up to God Think of a time when you have been overwhelmed with the reality of the darkness and evil which is present in our world. How did you find comfort?

 Read Isaiah 8:11—9:7.

¹¹The Lord spoke to me with his strong hand upon me, warning me not to follow the way of this people. He said:

¹²"Do not call conspiracy
   everything that these people call
      conspiracy*;
do not fear what they fear,
   and do not dread it.
¹³The Lord Almighty is the one you are to
      regard as holy,
   he is the one you are to fear,
   he is the one you are to dread,
¹⁴and he will be a sanctuary;
   but for both houses of Israel he will be
a stone that causes men to stumble
   and a rock that makes them fall.
And for the people of Jerusalem he will be
   a trap and a snare.
¹⁵Many of them will stumble;
   they will fall and be broken,
   they will be snared and captured."

¹⁶Bind up the testimony
   and seal up the law among my disciples.
¹⁷I will wait for the Lord,
   who is hiding his face from the house of
      Jacob.
I will put my trust in him.

¹⁸Here am I, and the children the Lord has given me. We are signs and symbols in Israel from the Lord Almighty, who dwells on Mount Zion.
¹⁹When men tell you to consult mediums and spiritists, who whisper and mutter, should not a people inquire of their God? Why consult the dead on behalf of the living? ²⁰To the law and to the testimony! If they do not speak according to this word, they have no light of dawn. ²¹Distressed and hungry, they will roam through the land; when they are famished, they will become enraged and, looking upward, will curse their king and their God. ²²Then they will look toward the earth and see only distress and darkness and fearful gloom, and they will be thrust into utter darkness.

9 Nevertheless, there will be no more gloom for those who were in distress. In the past he humbled the land of Zebulun and the land of Naphtali, but in the future he will honor Galilee of the Gentiles, by the way of the sea, along the Jordan—

²The people walking in darkness
   have seen a great light;
on those living in the land of the shadow of
      death*y*
   a light has dawned.
³You have enlarged the nation
   and increased their joy;
they rejoice before you
   as people rejoice at the harvest,
as men rejoice
   when dividing the plunder.
⁴For as in the day of Midian's defeat,
   you have shattered
the yoke that burdens them,
   the bar across their shoulders,
   the rod of their oppressor.
⁵Every warrior's boot used in battle

x 12 Or Do not call for a treaty / every time these people call for a treaty
y 2 Or land of darkness

and every garment rolled in blood
will be destined for burning,
   will be fuel for the fire.
⁶For to us a child is born,
   to us a son is given,
   and the government will be on his
      shoulders.
 And he will be called
   Wonderful Counselor,ᶻ Mighty God,
   Everlasting Father, Prince of Peace.
⁷Of the increase of his government and peace

there will be no end.
He will reign on David's throne
   and over his kingdom,
establishing and upholding it
   with justice and righteousness
   from that time on and forever.
The zeal of the Lᴏʀᴅ Almighty
   will accomplish this.

ᶻ6 Or *Wonderful, Counselor*

Discovering the Word 1. Compare and contrast the ways of knowing God which are described in 8:11–22. 2. Where are the Israelites looking for wisdom according to 8:19–20? 3. The people are very distressed (8:21–22). Why do they curse their king and their God? 4. With the help of map 2 (in the introduction) find the regions of Zebulun, Naphtali and Galilee and the road called "the Way of the Sea." This road marked the western limits of Palestine, and the Jordan marked the eastern limits. What change from their present condition does Isaiah predict in 9:1–2? 5. The light dawns in 9:2–5. What specific changes does Isaiah predict? 6. In what ways is the coming of the kingdom of justice and righteousness mentioned in 9:7 good news for the poor, the needy and the oppressed?

Applying the Word 1. How has the Lord brought light into your dark corner of the world? 2. Which of these titles—"Wonderful Counselor, Mighty God, Everlasting Father, Prince of Peace"—particularly describes God as you have known him during a time of difficulty?

Responding in Prayer Praise God for his character and the way he has revealed himself to you.

Isaiah 9:8—10:34

⁸The Lord has sent a message against Jacob;
   it will fall on Israel.
⁹All the people will know it—
   Ephraim and the inhabitants of Samaria—
who say with pride
   and arrogance of heart,
¹⁰"The bricks have fallen down,
   but we will rebuild with dressed stone;
the fig trees have been felled,
   but we will replace them with cedars."
¹¹But the Lᴏʀᴅ has strengthened Rezin's foes
   against them
and has spurred their enemies on.
¹²Arameans from the east and Philistines from
   the west
have devoured Israel with open mouth.

Yet for all this, his anger is not turned away,
   his hand is still upraised.

¹³But the people have not returned to him who
   struck them,

nor have they sought the Lᴏʀᴅ Almighty.
¹⁴So the Lᴏʀᴅ will cut off from Israel both head
   and tail,
   both palm branch and reed in a single day;
¹⁵the elders and prominent men are the head,
   the prophets who teach lies are the tail.
¹⁶Those who guide this people mislead them,
   and those who are guided are led astray.
¹⁷Therefore the Lord will take no pleasure in
   the young men,
   nor will he pity the fatherless and widows,
for everyone is ungodly and wicked,
   every mouth speaks vileness.

Yet for all this, his anger is not turned away,
   his hand is still upraised.

¹⁸Surely wickedness burns like a fire;
   it consumes briers and thorns,
it sets the forest thickets ablaze,
   so that it rolls upward in a column of
      smoke.

¹⁹By the wrath of the LORD Almighty
    the land will be scorched
and the people will be fuel for the fire;
    no one will spare his brother.
²⁰On the right they will devour,
    but still be hungry;
on the left they will eat,
    but not be satisfied.
Each will feed on the flesh of his own
        offspring[a]:
²¹   Manasseh will feed on Ephraim, and
        Ephraim on Manasseh;
    together they will turn against Judah.

Yet for all this, his anger is not turned away,
    his hand is still upraised.

10 Woe to those who make unjust
        laws,
    to those who issue oppressive
        decrees,
²to deprive the poor of their rights
    and withhold justice from the oppressed of
        my people,
making widows their prey
    and robbing the fatherless.
³What will you do on the day of reckoning,
    when disaster comes from afar?
To whom will you run for help?
    Where will you leave your riches?
⁴Nothing will remain but to cringe among the
        captives
    or fall among the slain.

Yet for all this, his anger is not turned away,
    his hand is still upraised.

⁵"Woe to the Assyrian, the rod of my anger,
    in whose hand is the club of my wrath!
⁶I send him against a godless nation,
    I dispatch him against a people who anger
        me,
to seize loot and snatch plunder,
    and to trample them down like mud in the
        streets.
⁷But this is not what he intends,
    this is not what he has in mind;
his purpose is to destroy,
    to put an end to many nations.
⁸'Are not my commanders all kings?' he says.
⁹   'Has not Calno fared like Carchemish?
Is not Hamath like Arpad,
    and Samaria like Damascus?

¹⁰As my hand seized the kingdoms of the idols,
    kingdoms whose images excelled those of
        Jerusalem and Samaria—
¹¹shall I not deal with Jerusalem and her images
    as I dealt with Samaria and her idols?' "

¹²When the Lord has finished all his work
against Mount Zion and Jerusalem, he will say, "I
will punish the king of Assyria for the willful
pride of his heart and the haughty look in his
eyes. ¹³For he says:

" 'By the strength of my hand I have done
        this,
    and by my wisdom, because I have
        understanding.
I removed the boundaries of nations,
    I plundered their treasures;
    like a mighty one I subdued[b] their kings.
¹⁴As one reaches into a nest,
    so my hand reached for the wealth of the
        nations;
as men gather abandoned eggs,
    so I gathered all the countries;
not one flapped a wing,
    or opened its mouth to chirp.' "

¹⁵Does the ax raise itself above him who swings
        it,
    or the saw boast against him who uses it?
As if a rod were to wield him who lifts it up,
    or a club brandish him who is not wood!
¹⁶Therefore, the Lord, the LORD Almighty,
    will send a wasting disease upon his sturdy
        warriors;
under his pomp a fire will be kindled
    like a blazing flame.
¹⁷The Light of Israel will become a fire,
    their Holy One a flame;
in a single day it will burn and consume
    his thorns and his briers.
¹⁸The splendor of his forests and fertile fields
    it will completely destroy,
    as when a sick man wastes away.
¹⁹And the remaining trees of his forests will be
        so few
    that a child could write them down.

²⁰In that day the remnant of Israel,
    the survivors of the house of Jacob,
will no longer rely on him
    who struck them down

---

a20 Or *arm*   *b13* Or / *I subdued the mighty,*

but will truly rely on the LORD,
  the Holy One of Israel.
²¹A remnant will return,ᶜ a remnant of Jacob
  will return to the Mighty God.
²²Though your people, O Israel, be like the
    sand by the sea,
  only a remnant will return.
Destruction has been decreed,
  overwhelming and righteous.
²³The Lord, the LORD Almighty, will carry out
  the destruction decreed upon the whole
    land.

²⁴Therefore, this is what the Lord, the LORD Almighty, says:

"O my people who live in Zion,
  do not be afraid of the Assyrians,
who beat you with a rod
  and lift up a club against you, as Egypt did.
²⁵Very soon my anger against you will end
  and my wrath will be directed to their
    destruction."

²⁶The LORD Almighty will lash them with a
    whip,
  as when he struck down Midian at the rock
    of Oreb;
and he will raise his staff over the waters,
  as he did in Egypt.
²⁷In that day their burden will be lifted from
  your shoulders,

their yoke from your neck;
  the yoke will be broken
  because you have grown so fat.ᵈ

²⁸They enter Aiath;
  they pass through Migron;
  they store supplies at Micmash.
²⁹They go over the pass, and say,
  "We will camp overnight at Geba."
Ramah trembles;
  Gibeah of Saul flees.
³⁰Cry out, O Daughter of Gallim!
  Listen, O Laishah!
  Poor Anathoth!
³¹Madmenah is in flight;
  the people of Gebim take cover.
³²This day they will halt at Nob;
  they will shake their fist
at the mount of the Daughter of Zion,
  at the hill of Jerusalem.

³³See, the Lord, the LORD Almighty,
  will lop off the boughs with great power.
The lofty trees will be felled,
  the tall ones will be brought low.
³⁴He will cut down the forest thickets with an
    ax;
  Lebanon will fall before the Mighty One.

*ᶜ21 Hebrew shear-jashub; also in verse 22   ᵈ27 Hebrew; Septuagint
broken / from your shoulders*

7 / *Isaiah 11—12*
The Earth Will Be Full of Knowledge

IT IS ALWAYS helpful when going through a time of trouble if you find some reason to hold on to hope for the future. In the first ten chapters of Isaiah there is a remarkable alternation of the imagery of light and darkness. In this alternation we see the true ministry of a prophet—not good news without the bad news of humanity's sinfulness; but not the bad news without the good news of God's redeeming grace. The hope expressed here is not a blind and shallow optimism. It is not a "you have never had it so good" philosophy borne along on the crest of economic prosperity. Reading the whole of Isaiah 7—12 shows how difficult and depressing the days of Ahaz were in many respects. Yet this chapter holds out in both general and specific terms a thrilling hope for the future.

Warming Up to God What does the word *hope* mean to you?

Read Isaiah 11—12.

11

A shoot will come up from the
stump of Jesse;
from his roots a Branch will bear
fruit.
²The Spirit of the LORD will rest on him—
the Spirit of wisdom and of understanding,
the Spirit of counsel and of power,
the Spirit of knowledge and of the fear of
the LORD—
³and he will delight in the fear of the LORD.

He will not judge by what he sees with his
eyes,
or decide by what he hears with his ears;
⁴but with righteousness he will judge the
needy,
with justice he will give decisions for the
poor of the earth.
He will strike the earth with the rod of his
mouth;
with the breath of his lips he will slay the
wicked.
⁵Righteousness will be his belt
and faithfulness the sash around his waist.

⁶The wolf will live with the lamb,
the leopard will lie down with the goat,
the calf and the lion and the yearling[e]
together;
and a little child will lead them.
⁷The cow will feed with the bear,
their young will lie down together,
and the lion will eat straw like the ox.
⁸The infant will play near the hole of the
cobra,
and the young child put his hand into the
viper's nest.
⁹They will neither harm nor destroy
on all my holy mountain,
for the earth will be full of the knowledge of
the LORD
as the waters cover the sea.

¹⁰In that day the Root of Jesse will stand as a
banner for the peoples; the nations will rally to
him, and his place of rest will be glorious. ¹¹In
that day the Lord will reach out his hand a second
time to reclaim the remnant that is left of his
people from Assyria, from Lower Egypt, from Upper Egypt,[f] from Cush,[g] from Elam, from Babylonia,[h] from Hamath and from the islands of
the sea.

¹²He will raise a banner for the nations

and gather the exiles of Israel;
he will assemble the scattered people of Judah
from the four quarters of the earth.
¹³Ephraim's jealousy will vanish,
and Judah's enemies[i] will be cut off;
Ephraim will not be jealous of Judah,
nor Judah hostile toward Ephraim.
¹⁴They will swoop down on the slopes of
Philistia to the west;
together they will plunder the people to the
east.
They will lay hands on Edom and Moab,
and the Ammonites will be subject to them.
¹⁵The LORD will dry up
the gulf of the Egyptian sea;
with a scorching wind he will sweep his hand
over the Euphrates River.[j]
He will break it up into seven streams
so that men can cross over in sandals.
¹⁶There will be a highway for the remnant of
his people
that is left from Assyria,
as there was for Israel
when they came up from Egypt.

12

In that day you will say:

"I will praise you, O LORD.
Although you were angry with me,
your anger has turned away
and you have comforted me.
²Surely God is my salvation;
I will trust and not be afraid.
The LORD, the LORD, is my strength and my
song;
he has become my salvation."
³With joy you will draw water
from the wells of salvation.

⁴In that day you will say:

"Give thanks to the LORD, call on his name;
make known among the nations what he
has done,
and proclaim that his name is exalted.
⁵Sing to the LORD, for he has done glorious
things;
let this be known to all the world.
⁶Shout aloud and sing for joy, people of Zion,
for great is the Holy One of Israel among
you."

e6 Hebrew; Septuagint *lion will feed*   f11 Hebrew *from Pathros*
g11 That is, the upper Nile region   h11 Hebrew *Shinar*   i13 Or
hostility   j15 Hebrew *the River*

Discovering the Word 1. Summarize the character of the person described as the "Branch" in 11:2–5. 2. What do verses 6–9 teach about the character of the kingdom of the One who is called the "Branch"? 3. Show how the great homecoming spoken of in 11:10–16 spells out in detail what the prophecy of 11:9 predicts. 4. How are the Branch of 11:1 and the Root of 11:10 related? 5. What are the main themes of the songs of thanksgiving in chapter 12?

Applying the Word 1. Which of the qualities of the Holy Spirit listed in 11:2 do you most want the Spirit to work in your life at this time? Why? 2. How does your church or fellowship best reflect his kingdom as it is described here? 3. In situations in your life how does trusting God mean reaffirming the truths of 12:2?

Responding in Prayer Ask the Lord to show you what it means to live in hope for the future.

Isaiah 13—23

13 An oracle concerning Babylon that Isaiah son of Amoz saw:

²Raise a banner on a bare hilltop,
  shout to them;
beckon to them
  to enter the gates of the nobles.
³I have commanded my holy ones;
  I have summoned my warriors to carry out
    my wrath—
  those who rejoice in my triumph.

⁴Listen, a noise on the mountains,
  like that of a great multitude!
Listen, an uproar among the kingdoms,
  like nations massing together!
The Lord Almighty is mustering
  an army for war.
⁵They come from faraway lands,
  from the ends of the heavens—
the Lord and the weapons of his wrath—
  to destroy the whole country.

⁶Wail, for the day of the Lord is near;
  it will come like destruction from the
    Almighty.ᵏ
⁷Because of this, all hands will go limp,
  every man's heart will melt.
⁸Terror will seize them,
  pain and anguish will grip them;
  they will writhe like a woman in labor.
They will look aghast at each other,
  their faces aflame.

⁹See, the day of the Lord is coming
  —a cruel day, with wrath and fierce
    anger—
to make the land desolate

and destroy the sinners within it.
¹⁰The stars of heaven and their constellations
  will not show their light.
The rising sun will be darkened
  and the moon will not give its light.
¹¹I will punish the world for its evil,
  the wicked for their sins.
I will put an end to the arrogance of the
    haughty
  and will humble the pride of the ruthless.
¹²I will make man scarcer than pure gold,
  more rare than the gold of Ophir.
¹³Therefore I will make the heavens tremble;
  and the earth will shake from its place
at the wrath of the Lord Almighty,
  in the day of his burning anger.

¹⁴Like a hunted gazelle,
  like sheep without a shepherd,
each will return to his own people,
  each will flee to his native land.
¹⁵Whoever is captured will be thrust through;
  all who are caught will fall by the sword.
¹⁶Their infants will be dashed to pieces before
    their eyes;
  their houses will be looted and their wives
    ravished.

¹⁷See, I will stir up against them the Medes,
  who do not care for silver
  and have no delight in gold.
¹⁸Their bows will strike down the young men;
  they will have no mercy on infants
  nor will they look with compassion on
    children.
¹⁹Babylon, the jewel of kingdoms,

ᵏ6 Hebrew *Shaddai*

the glory of the Babylonians'[l] pride,
will be overthrown by God
like Sodom and Gomorrah.
[20]She will never be inhabited
or lived in through all generations;
no Arab will pitch his tent there,
no shepherd will rest his flocks there.
[21]But desert creatures will lie there,
jackals will fill her houses;
there the owls will dwell,
and there the wild goats will leap about.
[22]Hyenas will howl in her strongholds,
jackals in her luxurious palaces.
Her time is at hand,
and her days will not be prolonged.

14 The LORD will have compassion on Jacob;
once again he will choose Israel
and will settle them in their own land.
Aliens will join them
and unite with the house of Jacob.
[2]Nations will take them
and bring them to their own place.
And the house of Israel will possess the nations
as menservants and maidservants in the LORD's land.
They will make captives of their captors
and rule over their oppressors.

[3]On the day the LORD gives you relief from suffering and turmoil and cruel bondage, [4]you will take up this taunt against the king of Babylon:

How the oppressor has come to an end!
How his fury[m] has ended!
[5]The LORD has broken the rod of the wicked,
the scepter of the rulers,
[6]which in anger struck down peoples
with unceasing blows,
and in fury subdued nations
with relentless aggression.
[7]All the lands are at rest and at peace;
they break into singing.
[8]Even the pine trees and the cedars of Lebanon
exult over you and say,
"Now that you have been laid low,
no woodsman comes to cut us down."

[9]The grave[n] below is all astir
to meet you at your coming;

it rouses the spirits of the departed to greet you—
all those who were leaders in the world;
it makes them rise from their thrones—
all those who were kings over the nations.
[10]They will all respond,
they will say to you,
"You also have become weak, as we are;
you have become like us."
[11]All your pomp has been brought down to the grave,
along with the noise of your harps;
maggots are spread out beneath you
and worms cover you.

[12]How you have fallen from heaven,
O morning star, son of the dawn!
You have been cast down to the earth,
you who once laid low the nations!
[13]You said in your heart,
"I will ascend to heaven;
I will raise my throne
above the stars of God;
I will sit enthroned on the mount of assembly,
on the utmost heights of the sacred mountain.[o]
[14]I will ascend above the tops of the clouds;
I will make myself like the Most High."
[15]But you are brought down to the grave,
to the depths of the pit.

[16]Those who see you stare at you,
they ponder your fate:
"Is this the man who shook the earth
and made kingdoms tremble,
[17]the man who made the world a desert,
who overthrew its cities
and would not let his captives go home?"

[18]All the kings of the nations lie in state,
each in his own tomb.
[19]But you are cast out of your tomb
like a rejected branch;
you are covered with the slain,
with those pierced by the sword,
those who descend to the stones of the pit.
Like a corpse trampled underfoot,
[20] you will not join them in burial,
for you have destroyed your land
and killed your people.

[l]19 Or *Chaldeans'* [m]4 Dead Sea Scrolls, Septuagint and Syriac; the meaning of the word in the Masoretic Text is uncertain. [n]9 Hebrew *Sheol*; also in verses 11 and 15 [o]13 Or *the north*; Hebrew *Zaphon*

The offspring of the wicked
    will never be mentioned again.
[21]Prepare a place to slaughter his sons
    for the sins of their forefathers;
they are not to rise to inherit the land
    and cover the earth with their cities.

[22]"I will rise up against them,"
    declares the LORD Almighty.
"I will cut off from Babylon her name and
      survivors,
    her offspring and descendants,"
                   declares the LORD.
[23]"I will turn her into a place for owls
    and into swampland;
I will sweep her with the broom of
      destruction,"
    declares the LORD Almighty.

[24]The LORD Almighty has sworn,

"Surely, as I have planned, so it will be,
    and as I have purposed, so it will stand.
[25]I will crush the Assyrian in my land;
    on my mountains I will trample him down.
His yoke will be taken from my people,
    and his burden removed from their
      shoulders."

[26]This is the plan determined for the whole
      world;
    this is the hand stretched out over all
      nations.
[27]For the LORD Almighty has purposed, and who
      can thwart him?
    His hand is stretched out, and who can
      turn it back?

[28]This oracle came in the year King Ahaz died:

[29]Do not rejoice, all you Philistines,
    that the rod that struck you is broken;
from the root of that snake will spring up a
      viper,
    its fruit will be a darting, venomous
      serpent.
[30]The poorest of the poor will find pasture,
    and the needy will lie down in safety.
But your root I will destroy by famine;
    it will slay your survivors.

[31]Wail, O gate! Howl, O city!
    Melt away, all you Philistines!
A cloud of smoke comes from the north,
    and there is not a straggler in its ranks.

[32]What answer shall be given
    to the envoys of that nation?
"The LORD has established Zion,
    and in her his afflicted people will find
      refuge."

15

An oracle concerning Moab:

Ar in Moab is ruined,
  destroyed in a night!
Kir in Moab is ruined,
    destroyed in a night!
[2]Dibon goes up to its temple,
    to its high places to weep;
    Moab wails over Nebo and Medeba.
Every head is shaved
    and every beard cut off.
[3]In the streets they wear sackcloth;
    on the roofs and in the public squares
they all wail,
    prostrate with weeping.
[4]Heshbon and Elealeh cry out,
    their voices are heard all the way to Jahaz.
Therefore the armed men of Moab cry out,
    and their hearts are faint.

[5]My heart cries out over Moab;
    her fugitives flee as far as Zoar,
    as far as Eglath Shelishiyah.
They go up the way to Luhith,
    weeping as they go;
on the road to Horonaim
    they lament their destruction.
[6]The waters of Nimrim are dried up
    and the grass is withered;
the vegetation is gone
    and nothing green is left.
[7]So the wealth they have acquired and stored
      up
    they carry away over the Ravine of the
      Poplars.
[8]Their outcry echoes along the border of
      Moab;
    their wailing reaches as far as Eglaim,
    their lamentation as far as Beer Elim.
[9]Dimon's[p] waters are full of blood,
    but I will bring still more upon Dimon[p]—
a lion upon the fugitives of Moab
    and upon those who remain in the land.

p9 Masoretic Text; Dead Sea Scrolls, some Septuagint manuscripts and Vulgate Dibon

16

Send lambs as tribute
to the ruler of the land,
from Sela, across the desert,
to the mount of the Daughter of Zion.
²Like fluttering birds
pushed from the nest,
so are the women of Moab
at the fords of the Arnon.

³"Give us counsel,
render a decision.
Make your shadow like night—
at high noon.
Hide the fugitives,
do not betray the refugees.
⁴Let the Moabite fugitives stay with you;
be their shelter from the destroyer."

The oppressor will come to an end,
and destruction will cease;
the aggressor will vanish from the land.
⁵In love a throne will be established;
in faithfulness a man will sit on it—
one from the house �q of David—
one who in judging seeks justice
and speeds the cause of righteousness.

⁶We have heard of Moab's pride—
her overweening pride and conceit,
her pride and her insolence—
but her boasts are empty.
⁷Therefore the Moabites wail,
they wail together for Moab.
Lament and grieve
for the men ʳ of Kir Hareseth.
⁸The fields of Heshbon wither,
the vines of Sibmah also.
The rulers of the nations
have trampled down the choicest vines,
which once reached Jazer
and spread toward the desert.
Their shoots spread out
and went as far as the sea.
⁹So I weep, as Jazer weeps,
for the vines of Sibmah.
O Heshbon, O Elealeh,
I drench you with tears!
The shouts of joy over your ripened fruit
and over your harvests have been stilled.
¹⁰Joy and gladness are taken away from the
orchards;
no one sings or shouts in the vineyards;
no one treads out wine at the presses,

for I have put an end to the shouting.
¹¹My heart laments for Moab like a harp,
my inmost being for Kir Hareseth.
¹²When Moab appears at her high place,
she only wears herself out;
when she goes to her shrine to pray,
it is to no avail.

¹³This is the word the Lᴏʀᴅ has already spoken concerning Moab. ¹⁴But now the Lᴏʀᴅ says: "Within three years, as a servant bound by contract would count them, Moab's splendor and all her many people will be despised, and her survivors will be very few and feeble."

17

An oracle concerning Damascus:

"See, Damascus will no longer be
a city
but will become a heap of ruins.
²The cities of Aroer will be deserted
and left to flocks, which will lie down,
with no one to make them afraid.
³The fortified city will disappear from
Ephraim,
and royal power from Damascus;
the remnant of Aram will be
like the glory of the Israelites,"
declares the Lᴏʀᴅ Almighty.

⁴"In that day the glory of Jacob will fade;
the fat of his body will waste away.
⁵It will be as when a reaper gathers the
standing grain
and harvests the grain with his arm—
as when a man gleans heads of grain
in the Valley of Rephaim.
⁶Yet some gleanings will remain,
as when an olive tree is beaten,
leaving two or three olives on the topmost
branches,
four or five on the fruitful boughs,"
declares the Lᴏʀᴅ, the God of Israel.

⁷In that day men will look to their Maker
and turn their eyes to the Holy One of
Israel.
⁸They will not look to the altars,
the work of their hands,
and they will have no regard for the Asherah
poles ˢ

�q5 Hebrew *tent*   ʳ7 Or *"raisin cakes,"* a wordplay   ˢ8 That is, symbols of the goddess Asherah

and the incense altars their fingers have
made.

⁹In that day their strong cities, which they left
because of the Israelites, will be like places abandoned to thickets and undergrowth. And all will
be desolation.

¹⁰You have forgotten God your Savior;
    you have not remembered the Rock, your
        fortress.
Therefore, though you set out the finest
        plants
    and plant imported vines,
¹¹though on the day you set them out, you
        make them grow,
    and on the morning when you plant them,
        you bring them to bud,
yet the harvest will be as nothing
    in the day of disease and incurable pain.

¹²Oh, the raging of many nations—
    they rage like the raging sea!
Oh, the uproar of the peoples—
    they roar like the roaring of great waters!
¹³Although the peoples roar like the roar of
        surging waters,
    when he rebukes them they flee far away,
driven before the wind like chaff on the hills,
    like tumbleweed before a gale.
¹⁴In the evening, sudden terror!
    Before the morning, they are gone!
This is the portion of those who loot us,
    the lot of those who plunder us.

18 Woe to the land of whirring
        wings[t]
        along the rivers of Cush,[u]
²which sends envoys by sea
    in papyrus boats over the water.

Go, swift messengers,
    to a people tall and smooth-skinned,
    to a people feared far and wide,
an aggressive nation of strange speech,
    whose land is divided by rivers.

³All you people of the world,
    you who live on the earth,
when a banner is raised on the mountains,
    you will see it,
and when a trumpet sounds,
    you will hear it.
⁴This is what the LORD says to me:

"I will remain quiet and will look on from
    my dwelling place,
like shimmering heat in the sunshine,
    like a cloud of dew in the heat of harvest."
⁵For, before the harvest, when the blossom is
        gone
    and the flower becomes a ripening grape,
he will cut off the shoots with pruning
        knives,
    and cut down and take away the spreading
        branches.
⁶They will all be left to the mountain birds of
        prey
    and to the wild animals;
the birds will feed on them all summer,
    the wild animals all winter.

⁷At that time gifts will be brought to the LORD
Almighty

from a people tall and smooth-skinned,
    from a people feared far and wide,
an aggressive nation of strange speech,
    whose land is divided by rivers—

the gifts will be brought to Mount Zion, the place
of the Name of the LORD Almighty.

19 An oracle concerning Egypt:

    See, the LORD rides on a swift
        cloud
    and is coming to Egypt.
The idols of Egypt tremble before him,
    and the hearts of the Egyptians melt within
        them.

²"I will stir up Egyptian against Egyptian—
    brother will fight against brother,
    neighbor against neighbor,
    city against city,
    kingdom against kingdom.
³The Egyptians will lose heart,
    and I will bring their plans to nothing;
they will consult the idols and the spirits of
        the dead,
    the mediums and the spiritists.
⁴I will hand the Egyptians over
    to the power of a cruel master,
    and a fierce king will rule over them,"
declares the Lord, the LORD Almighty.

⁵The waters of the river will dry up,

---

t 1 Or of locusts   u 1 That is, the upper Nile region

and the riverbed will be parched and dry.
⁶The canals will stink;
  the streams of Egypt will dwindle and dry
    up.
The reeds and rushes will wither,
⁷   also the plants along the Nile,
    at the mouth of the river.
Every sown field along the Nile
  will become parched, will blow away and
    be no more.
⁸The fishermen will groan and lament,
  all who cast hooks into the Nile;
those who throw nets on the water
  will pine away.
⁹Those who work with combed flax will
    despair,
  the weavers of fine linen will lose hope.
¹⁰The workers in cloth will be dejected,
  and all the wage earners will be sick at
    heart.

¹¹The officials of Zoan are nothing but
    fools;
  the wise counselors of Pharaoh give
    senseless advice.
How can you say to Pharaoh,
  "I am one of the wise men,
    a disciple of the ancient kings"?

¹²Where are your wise men now?
  Let them show you and make known
what the LORD Almighty
  has planned against Egypt.
¹³The officials of Zoan have become fools,
  the leaders of Memphisᵛ are deceived;
the cornerstones of her peoples
  have led Egypt astray.
¹⁴The LORD has poured into them
  a spirit of dizziness;
they make Egypt stagger in all that she does,
  as a drunkard staggers around in his vomit.
¹⁵There is nothing Egypt can do—
  head or tail, palm branch or reed.

¹⁶In that day the Egyptians will be like women.
They will shudder with fear at the uplifted hand
that the LORD Almighty raises against them. ¹⁷And
the land of Judah will bring terror to the Egyptians; everyone to whom Judah is mentioned will
be terrified, because of what the LORD Almighty is
planning against them.

¹⁸In that day five cities in Egypt will speak the
language of Canaan and swear allegiance to the
LORD Almighty. One of them will be called the
City of Destruction.ʷ

¹⁹In that day there will be an altar to the LORD
in the heart of Egypt, and a monument to the
LORD at its border. ²⁰It will be a sign and witness
to the LORD Almighty in the land of Egypt. When
they cry out to the LORD because of their oppressors, he will send them a savior and defender, and
he will rescue them. ²¹So the LORD will make himself known to the Egyptians, and in that day they
will acknowledge the LORD. They will worship
with sacrifices and grain offerings; they will make
vows to the LORD and keep them. ²²The LORD
will strike Egypt with a plague; he will strike
them and heal them. They will turn to the LORD,
and he will respond to their pleas and heal
them.

²³In that day there will be a highway from
Egypt to Assyria. The Assyrians will go to Egypt
and the Egyptians to Assyria. The Egyptians and
Assyrians will worship together. ²⁴In that day Israel will be the third, along with Egypt and Assyria, a blessing on the earth. ²⁵The LORD Almighty will bless them, saying, "Blessed be Egypt
my people, Assyria my handiwork, and Israel my
inheritance."

20

In the year that the supreme commander, sent by Sargon king of Assyria, came to Ashdod and attacked
and captured it— ²at that time the LORD spoke
through Isaiah son of Amoz. He said to him,
"Take off the sackcloth from your body and the
sandals from your feet." And he did so, going
around stripped and barefoot.

³Then the LORD said, "Just as my servant Isaiah
has gone stripped and barefoot for three years, as
a sign and portent against Egypt and Cush,ˣ ⁴so
the king of Assyria will lead away stripped and
barefoot the Egyptian captives and Cushite exiles,
young and old, with buttocks bared—to Egypt's
shame. ⁵Those who trusted in Cush and boasted
in Egypt will be afraid and put to shame. ⁶In that
day the people who live on this coast will say, 'See
what has happened to those we relied on, those
we fled to for help and deliverance from the king
of Assyria! How then can we escape?' "

ᵛ13 Hebrew *Noph*   ʷ18 Most manuscripts of the Masoretic Text;
some manuscripts of the Masoretic Text, Dead Sea Scrolls and Vulgate
City of the Sun (that is, Heliopolis)   ˣ3 That is, the upper Nile
region; also in verse 5

21

An oracle concerning the Desert by
the Sea:

Like whirlwinds sweeping through
the southland,
an invader comes from the desert,
from a land of terror.

²A dire vision has been shown to me:
The traitor betrays, the looter takes loot.
Elam, attack! Media, lay siege!
I will bring to an end all the groaning she
caused.

³At this my body is racked with pain,
pangs seize me, like those of a woman in
labor;
I am staggered by what I hear,
I am bewildered by what I see.
⁴My heart falters,
fear makes me tremble;
the twilight I longed for
has become a horror to me.

⁵They set the tables,
they spread the rugs,
they eat, they drink!
Get up, you officers,
oil the shields!

⁶This is what the Lord says to me:

"Go, post a lookout
and have him report what he sees.
⁷When he sees chariots
with teams of horses,
riders on donkeys
or riders on camels,
let him be alert,
fully alert."

⁸And the lookout^y shouted,

"Day after day, my lord, I stand on the
watchtower;
every night I stay at my post.
⁹Look, here comes a man in a chariot
with a team of horses.
And he gives back the answer:
'Babylon has fallen, has fallen!
All the images of its gods
lie shattered on the ground!'"

¹⁰O my people, crushed on the threshing floor,
I tell you what I have heard
from the Lord Almighty,

from the God of Israel.

¹¹An oracle concerning Dumah^z:

Someone calls to me from Seir,
"Watchman, what is left of the night?
Watchman, what is left of the night?"
¹²The watchman replies,
"Morning is coming, but also the night.
If you would ask, then ask;
and come back yet again."

¹³An oracle concerning Arabia:

You caravans of Dedanites,
who camp in the thickets of Arabia,
¹⁴   bring water for the thirsty;
you who live in Tema,
bring food for the fugitives.
¹⁵They flee from the sword,
from the drawn sword,
from the bent bow
and from the heat of battle.

¹⁶This is what the Lord says to me: "Within one
year, as a servant bound by contract would count
it, all the pomp of Kedar will come to an end.
¹⁷The survivors of the bowmen, the warriors of
Kedar, will be few." The Lord, the God of Israel,
has spoken.

22

An oracle concerning the Valley of
Vision:

What troubles you now,
that you have all gone up on the roofs,
²O town full of commotion,
O city of tumult and revelry?
Your slain were not killed by the sword,
nor did they die in battle.
³All your leaders have fled together;
they have been captured without using the
bow.
All you who were caught were taken prisoner
together,
having fled while the enemy was still far
away.
⁴Therefore I said, "Turn away from me;
let me weep bitterly.
Do not try to console me
over the destruction of my people."

⁵The Lord, the Lord Almighty, has a day
of tumult and trampling and terror

---

*y 8 Dead Sea Scrolls and Syriac; Masoretic Text A lion   *z 11 Dumah*
means silence or stillness, a wordplay on Edom.*

in the Valley of Vision,
a day of battering down walls
    and of crying out to the mountains.
[6]Elam takes up the quiver,
    with her charioteers and horses;
    Kir uncovers the shield.
[7]Your choicest valleys are full of chariots,
    and horsemen are posted at the city gates;
[8]   the defenses of Judah are stripped away.

And you looked in that day
    to the weapons in the Palace of the Forest;
[9]you saw that the City of David
    had many breaches in its defenses;
you stored up water
    in the Lower Pool.
[10]You counted the buildings in Jerusalem
    and tore down houses to strengthen the
        wall.
[11]You built a reservoir between the two walls
    for the water of the Old Pool,
but you did not look to the One who made it,
    or have regard for the One who planned it
        long ago.

[12]The Lord, the LORD Almighty,
    called you on that day
to weep and to wail,
    to tear out your hair and put on sackcloth.
[13]But see, there is joy and revelry,
    slaughtering of cattle and killing of sheep,
    eating of meat and drinking of wine!
"Let us eat and drink," you say,
    "for tomorrow we die!"

[14]The LORD Almighty has revealed this in my
hearing: "Till your dying day this sin will not be
atoned for," says the Lord, the LORD Almighty.

[15]This is what the Lord, the LORD Almighty,
says:

"Go, say to this steward,
    to Shebna, who is in charge of the palace:
[16]What are you doing here and who gave you
        permission
    to cut out a grave for yourself here,
hewing your grave on the height
    and chiseling your resting place in the
        rock?

[17]"Beware, the LORD is about to take firm hold
        of you
    and hurl you away, O you mighty man.
[18]He will roll you up tightly like a ball

and throw you into a large country.
There you will die
    and there your splendid chariots will
        remain—
    you disgrace to your master's house!
[19]I will depose you from your office,
    and you will be ousted from your position.

[20]"In that day I will summon my servant, Eliakim son of Hilkiah. [21]I will clothe him with your
robe and fasten your sash around him and hand
your authority over to him. He will be a father to
those who live in Jerusalem and to the house of
Judah. [22]I will place on his shoulder the key to
the house of David; what he opens no one can
shut, and what he shuts no one can open. [23]I will
drive him like a peg into a firm place; he will be
a seat[a] of honor for the house of his father. [24]All
the glory of his family will hang on him: its offspring and offshoots—all its lesser vessels, from
the bowls to all the jars.

[25]"In that day," declares the LORD Almighty,
"the peg driven into the firm place will give way;
it will be sheared off and will fall, and the load
hanging on it will be cut down." The LORD has
spoken.

23

An oracle concerning Tyre:

Wail, O ships of Tarshish!
For Tyre is destroyed
    and left without house or harbor.
From the land of Cyprus[b]
    word has come to them.

[2]Be silent, you people of the island
    and you merchants of Sidon,
    whom the seafarers have enriched.
[3]On the great waters
    came the grain of the Shihor;
the harvest of the Nile[c] was the revenue of
        Tyre,
    and she became the marketplace of the
        nations.

[4]Be ashamed, O Sidon, and you, O fortress of
        the sea,
    for the sea has spoken:
"I have neither been in labor nor given birth;
    I have neither reared sons nor brought up
        daughters."

[a]23 Or throne   [b]1 Hebrew Kittim   [c]2,3 Masoretic Text; one Dead
Sea Scroll Sidon, / who cross over the sea; / your envoys [3]are on the great
waters. / The grain of the Shihor, / the harvest of the Nile,

[5]When word comes to Egypt,
   they will be in anguish at the report from
      Tyre.
[6]Cross over to Tarshish;
   wail, you people of the island.
[7]Is this your city of revelry,
   the old, old city,
whose feet have taken her
   to settle in far-off lands?
[8]Who planned this against Tyre,
   the bestower of crowns,
whose merchants are princes,
   whose traders are renowned in the earth?
[9]The LORD Almighty planned it,
   to bring low the pride of all glory
and to humble all who are renowned on
      the earth.
[10]Till[d] your land as along the Nile,
   O Daughter of Tarshish,
for you no longer have a harbor.
[11]The LORD has stretched out his hand over the
      sea
   and made its kingdoms tremble.
He has given an order concerning Phoenicia[e]
   that her fortresses be destroyed.
[12]He said, "No more of your reveling,
   O Virgin Daughter of Sidon, now crushed!

"Up, cross over to Cyprus[f];
   even there you will find no rest."

[13]Look at the land of the Babylonians,[g]
   this people that is now of no account!
The Assyrians have made it
   a place for desert creatures;
they raised up their siege towers,
   they stripped its fortresses bare
   and turned it into a ruin.

[14]Wail, you ships of Tarshish;
   your fortress is destroyed!

[15]At that time Tyre will be forgotten for seventy years, the span of a king's life. But at the end of these seventy years, it will happen to Tyre as in the song of the prostitute:

[16]"Take up a harp, walk through the city,
   O prostitute forgotten;
play the harp well, sing many a song,
   so that you will be remembered."

[17]At the end of seventy years, the LORD will deal with Tyre. She will return to her hire as a prostitute and will ply her trade with all the kingdoms on the face of the earth. [18]Yet her profit and her earnings will be set apart for the LORD; they will not be stored up or hoarded. Her profits will go to those who live before the LORD, for abundant food and fine clothes.

[d]10 Dead Sea Scrolls and some Septuagint manuscripts; Masoretic Text *Go through*   [e]11 Hebrew *Canaan*   [f]12 Hebrew *Kittim*   [g]13 Or *Chaldeans*

8 / *Isaiah 24*
Global Pollution

IS ECOLOGY JUST a field for freaks and romantics? Or is there something particularly appropriate for the believer in being concerned for the symphony of being between humanity and the environment? In a remarkable book inspired by this chapter of Isaiah, Clifford Hill, a British sociologist and theologian, examines the problems of pollution, war and materialism. Toward the end of *The Day Comes* he writes: "The time of the coming conflict is drawing near—very near! It will be in the lifetime of many now living. There is absolutely not the slightest doubt that these things will take place unless there is a radical and total change in our world-view."

   Warming Up to God If you can, spend your time with the Lord today outside—or look out a window. What do you see in God's creation that calls you to praise? Offer your thanks to him.

   Read Isaiah 24.

24
See, the LORD is going to lay waste
the earth
and devastate it;
he will ruin its face
and scatter its inhabitants—
²it will be the same
for priest as for people,
for master as for servant,
for mistress as for maid,
for seller as for buyer,
for borrower as for lender,
for debtor as for creditor.
³The earth will be completely laid waste
and totally plundered.
The LORD has spoken this word.

⁴The earth dries up and withers,
the world languishes and withers,
the exalted of the earth languish.
⁵The earth is defiled by its people;
they have disobeyed the laws,
violated the statutes
and broken the everlasting covenant.
⁶Therefore a curse consumes the earth;
its people must bear their guilt.
Therefore earth's inhabitants are burned up,
and very few are left.
⁷The new wine dries up and the vine withers;
all the merrymakers groan.
⁸The gaiety of the tambourines is stilled,
the noise of the revelers has stopped,
the joyful harp is silent.
⁹No longer do they drink wine with a song;
the beer is bitter to its drinkers.
¹⁰The ruined city lies desolate;
the entrance to every house is barred.
¹¹In the streets they cry out for wine;
all joy turns to gloom,
all gaiety is banished from the earth.
¹²The city is left in ruins,
its gate is battered to pieces.
¹³So will it be on the earth
and among the nations,
as when an olive tree is beaten,

or as when gleanings are left after the grape
harvest.

¹⁴They raise their voices, they shout for joy;
from the west they acclaim the LORD's
majesty.
¹⁵Therefore in the east give glory to the LORD;
exalt the name of the LORD, the God of
Israel,
in the islands of the sea.
¹⁶From the ends of the earth we hear singing:
"Glory to the Righteous One."

But I said, "I waste away, I waste away!
Woe to me!
The treacherous betray!
With treachery the treacherous betray!"
¹⁷Terror and pit and snare await you,
O people of the earth.
¹⁸Whoever flees at the sound of terror
will fall into a pit;
whoever climbs out of the pit
will be caught in a snare.

The floodgates of the heavens are opened,
the foundations of the earth shake.
¹⁹The earth is broken up,
the earth is split asunder,
the earth is thoroughly shaken.
²⁰The earth reels like a drunkard,
it sways like a hut in the wind;
so heavy upon it is the guilt of its rebellion
that it falls—never to rise again.

²¹In that day the LORD will punish
the powers in the heavens above
and the kings on the earth below.
²²They will be herded together
like prisoners bound in a dungeon;
they will be shut up in prison
and be punished ʰ after many days.
²³The moon will be abashed, the sun ashamed;
for the LORD Almighty will reign
on Mount Zion and in Jerusalem,
and before its elders, gloriously.

ʰ22 Or *released*

Discovering the Word 1. What key words describe the Lord's devastation of the earth (vv. 1, 3–4)? 2. What is the mood of verses 4–13? 3. According to verses 4–13, why will the devastation of the earth take place? 4. How do you account for the fragment of singing which bursts out in verses 14–16, only to be abruptly silenced by Isaiah's cry of pain in the latter part of verse 16? 5. What additional aspects of God's judgment are revealed in verses 2–3?

Applying the Word 1. These verses presuppose a close connection between the earth itself, the land and its inhabitants. In what ways can you see the godlessness of humanity taking its toll on the physical world today? 2. As a Christian, what do you believe is your responsibility to the earth?

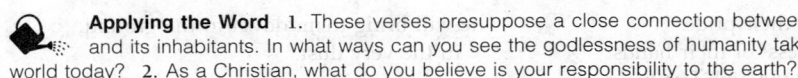 **Responding in Prayer** Ask God to teach you about your responsibility in caring for his creation.

9 / *Isaiah 25*
Free at Last!

> Free at last, free at last!
> Great God Almighty,
> Free at last!

THIS SONG, WITH eloquent simplicity, expresses the pervasive hope of oppressed, exploited and downtrodden people. Similarly, in this chapter a song of praise arises phoenixlike from the shattered world we saw at the end of chapter 24. Here we read of Israel's joy at the downfall of God's enemies, the end of death itself and God's final victory. Derek Kidner entitles this chapter "the great liberation," subtitling the sections: the end of tyranny (vv. 1–5), the end of darkness and death (vv. 6–8) and the end of pride (vv. 9–12). As we read of God's triumph, may it help to strengthen our faith in times of trouble.

 Warming Up to God Describe an experience you have had in driving rain, a snowstorm or some other natural disaster in which you knew that God was present with you.

 Read Isaiah 25.

25 O LORD, you are my God;
    I will exalt you and praise your
        name,
for in perfect faithfulness
    you have done marvelous things,
    things planned long ago.
2You have made the city a heap of rubble,
    the fortified town a ruin,
the foreigners' stronghold a city no more;
    it will never be rebuilt.
3Therefore strong peoples will honor you;
    cities of ruthless nations will revere you.
4You have been a refuge for the poor,
    a refuge for the needy in his distress,
a shelter from the storm
    and a shade from the heat.
For the breath of the ruthless
    is like a storm driving against a wall
5   and like the heat of the desert.
You silence the uproar of foreigners;
    as heat is reduced by the shadow of a
        cloud,
    so the song of the ruthless is stilled.

6On this mountain the LORD Almighty will
    prepare

a feast of rich food for all peoples,
    a banquet of aged wine—
    the best of meats and the finest of wines.
7On this mountain he will destroy
    the shroud that enfolds all peoples,
    the sheet that covers all nations;
8   he will swallow up death forever.
The Sovereign LORD will wipe away the tears
    from all faces;
he will remove the disgrace of his people
    from all the earth.
                    The LORD has spoken.

9In that day they will say,

"Surely this is our God;
    we trusted in him, and he saved us.
This is the LORD, we trusted in him;
    let us rejoice and be glad in his salvation."

10The hand of the LORD will rest on this
        mountain;
    but Moab will be trampled under him
    as straw is trampled down in the manure.
11They will spread out their hands in it,
    as a swimmer spreads out his hands to
        swim.

God will bring down their pride
   despite the cleverness[i] of their hands.
¹²He will bring down your high fortified walls
   and lay them low;

he will bring them down to the ground,
   to the very dust.

i11 The meaning of the Hebrew for this word is uncertain.

 Discovering the Word 1. How is God's character described in verse 1? 2. What repeated adjective reveals the main target of God's judgment in verses 2–5? 3. With what vivid metaphors does Isaiah describe God's relationship to the poor and needy (vv. 4–5)? 4. Look at the scene of God's banquet in verses 6–8. How does this wonderful imagery transform your understanding of death for the believer? 5. According to verses 10–12, what is the particular sin which characterized Moab (see also Isa 16:6)?

 Applying the Word 1. When are you most able to identify with the delighted response of verse 9? 2. To what present trial should you make a similar response?

Responding in Prayer Pray or write your own song of praise to God for the "marvelous things" he has planned (v. 1) for your life.

Isaiah 26—29

26

In that day this song will be sung in the land of Judah:

We have a strong city;
God makes salvation
   its walls and ramparts.
²Open the gates
   that the righteous nation may enter,
   the nation that keeps faith.
³You will keep in perfect peace
   him whose mind is steadfast,
   because he trusts in you.
⁴Trust in the LORD forever,
   for the LORD, the LORD, is the Rock eternal.
⁵He humbles those who dwell on high,
   he lays the lofty city low;
 he levels it to the ground
   and casts it down to the dust.
⁶Feet trample it down—
   the feet of the oppressed,
   the footsteps of the poor.

⁷The path of the righteous is level;
   O upright One, you make the way of the
      righteous smooth.
⁸Yes, LORD, walking in the way of your laws,[j]
   we wait for you;
 your name and renown
   are the desire of our hearts.
⁹My soul yearns for you in the night;
   in the morning my spirit longs for you.
When your judgments come upon the earth,
   the people of the world learn righteousness.

¹⁰Though grace is shown to the wicked,
   they do not learn righteousness;
even in a land of uprightness they go on
      doing evil
   and regard not the majesty of the LORD.
¹¹O LORD, your hand is lifted high,
   but they do not see it.
Let them see your zeal for your people and be
      put to shame;
   let the fire reserved for your enemies
      consume them.

¹²LORD, you establish peace for us;
   all that we have accomplished you have
      done for us.
¹³O LORD, our God, other lords besides you
      have ruled over us,
   but your name alone do we honor.
¹⁴They are now dead, they live no more;
   those departed spirits do not rise.
You punished them and brought them to
      ruin;
   you wiped out all memory of them.
¹⁵You have enlarged the nation, O LORD;
   you have enlarged the nation.
You have gained glory for yourself;
   you have extended all the borders of the
      land.

¹⁶LORD, they came to you in their distress;
   when you disciplined them,

j8 Or judgments

they could barely whisper a prayer.*k*

[17] As a woman with child and about to give
    birth
  writhes and cries out in her pain,
  so were we in your presence, O LORD.
[18] We were with child, we writhed in pain,
    but we gave birth to wind.
  We have not brought salvation to the earth;
    we have not given birth to people of the
    world.

[19] But your dead will live;
    their bodies will rise.
  You who dwell in the dust,
    wake up and shout for joy.
  Your dew is like the dew of the morning;
    the earth will give birth to her dead.

[20] Go, my people, enter your rooms
    and shut the doors behind you;
  hide yourselves for a little while
    until his wrath has passed by.
[21] See, the LORD is coming out of his dwelling
    to punish the people of the earth for their
    sins.
  The earth will disclose the blood shed upon
    her;
  she will conceal her slain no longer.

27 In that day,

    the LORD will punish with his
    sword,
  his fierce, great and powerful sword,
  Leviathan the gliding serpent,
  Leviathan the coiling serpent;
  he will slay the monster of the sea.

[2] In that day—

  "Sing about a fruitful vineyard:
[3]   I, the LORD, watch over it;
  I water it continually.
  I guard it day and night
    so that no one may harm it.
[4]   I am not angry.
  If only there were briers and thorns
    confronting me!
  I would march against them in battle;
    I would set them all on fire.
[5] Or else let them come to me for refuge;
    let them make peace with me,
  yes, let them make peace with me."

[6] In days to come Jacob will take root,

  Israel will bud and blossom
    and fill all the world with fruit.

[7] Has ⌐the LORD⌐ struck her
    as he struck down those who struck her?
  Has she been killed
    as those were killed who killed her?
[8] By warfare*l* and exile you contend with
    her—
  with his fierce blast he drives her out,
    as on a day the east wind blows.
[9] By this, then, will Jacob's guilt be atoned for,
    and this will be the full fruitage of the
    removal of his sin:
  When he makes all the altar stones
    to be like chalk stones crushed to pieces,
  no Asherah poles*m* or incense altars
    will be left standing.
[10] The fortified city stands desolate,
    an abandoned settlement, forsaken like the
    desert;
  there the calves graze,
    there they lie down;
  they strip its branches bare.
[11] When its twigs are dry, they are broken off
    and women come and make fires with
    them.
  For this is a people without understanding;
    so their Maker has no compassion on them,
    and their Creator shows them no favor.

[12] In that day the LORD will thresh from the
flowing Euphrates*n* to the Wadi of Egypt, and
you, O Israelites, will be gathered up one by one.
[13] And in that day a great trumpet will sound.
Those who were perishing in Assyria and those
who were exiled in Egypt will come and worship
the LORD on the holy mountain in Jerusalem.

28 Woe to that wreath, the pride of
    Ephraim's drunkards,
    to the fading flower, his glorious
    beauty,
  set on the head of a fertile valley—
    to that city, the pride of those laid low by
    wine!
[2] See, the Lord has one who is powerful and
    strong.
  Like a hailstorm and a destructive wind,
  like a driving rain and a flooding downpour,
  he will throw it forcefully to the ground.

---

k16 The meaning of the Hebrew for this clause is uncertain.   *l8* See
Septuagint; the meaning of the Hebrew for this word is uncertain.
m9 That is, symbols of the goddess Asherah   *n12* Hebrew *River*

3That wreath, the pride of Ephraim's
      drunkards,
  will be trampled underfoot.
4That fading flower, his glorious beauty,
  set on the head of a fertile valley,
  will be like a fig ripe before harvest—
    as soon as someone sees it and takes it in
      his hand,
  he swallows it.

5In that day the LORD Almighty
  will be a glorious crown,
  a beautiful wreath
  for the remnant of his people.
6He will be a spirit of justice
  to him who sits in judgment,
  a source of strength
  to those who turn back the battle at the
      gate.

7And these also stagger from wine
  and reel from beer:
  Priests and prophets stagger from beer
  and are befuddled with wine;
  they reel from beer,
  they stagger when seeing visions,
  they stumble when rendering decisions.
8All the tables are covered with vomit
  and there is not a spot without filth.

9"Who is it he is trying to teach?
  To whom is he explaining his message?
  To children weaned from their milk,
  to those just taken from the breast?
10For it is:
  Do and do, do and do,
  rule on rule, rule on rule°;
  a little here, a little there."

11Very well then, with foreign lips and strange
      tongues
  God will speak to this people,
12to whom he said,
  "This is the resting place, let the weary
      rest";
  and, "This is the place of repose"—
  but they would not listen.
13So then, the word of the LORD to them will
      become:
  Do and do, do and do,
  rule on rule, rule on rule;
  a little here, a little there—
  so that they will go and fall backward,
  be injured and snared and captured.

14Therefore hear the word of the LORD, you
      scoffers
  who rule this people in Jerusalem.
15You boast, "We have entered into a covenant
      with death,
  with the graveᵖ we have made an
      agreement.
  When an overwhelming scourge sweeps by,
  it cannot touch us,
  for we have made a lie our refuge
  and falsehood�q our hiding place."

16So this is what the Sovereign LORD says:

  "See, I lay a stone in Zion,
  a tested stone,
  a precious cornerstone for a sure foundation;
  the one who trusts will never be dismayed.
17I will make justice the measuring line
  and righteousness the plumb line;
  hail will sweep away your refuge, the lie,
  and water will overflow your hiding place.
18Your covenant with death will be annulled;
  your agreement with the grave will not
      stand.
  When the overwhelming scourge sweeps by,
  you will be beaten down by it.
19As often as it comes it will carry you away;
  morning after morning, by day and by
      night,
  it will sweep through."

The understanding of this message
  will bring sheer terror.
20The bed is too short to stretch out on,
  the blanket too narrow to wrap around
      you.
21The LORD will rise up as he did at Mount
      Perazim,
  he will rouse himself as in the Valley of
      Gibeon—
  to do his work, his strange work,
  and perform his task, his alien task.
22Now stop your mocking,
  or your chains will become heavier;
  the Lord, the LORD Almighty, has told me
  of the destruction decreed against the
      whole land.

23Listen and hear my voice;
  pay attention and hear what I say.

ᵒ10 Hebrew / sav lasav sav lasav / kav lakav kav lakav (possibly
meaningless sounds; perhaps a mimicking of the prophet's words); also
in verse 13   ᵖ15 Hebrew Sheol; also in verse 18   q15 Or false
gods

²⁴When a farmer plows for planting, does he
    plow continually?
  Does he keep on breaking up and
    harrowing the soil?
²⁵When he has leveled the surface,
    does he not sow caraway and scatter
      cummin?
  Does he not plant wheat in its place,ʳ
    barley in its plot,ʳ
    and spelt in its field?
²⁶His God instructs him
    and teaches him the right way.

²⁷Caraway is not threshed with a sledge,
    nor is a cartwheel rolled over cummin;
  caraway is beaten out with a rod,
    and cummin with a stick.
²⁸Grain must be ground to make bread;
    so one does not go on threshing it forever.
  Though he drives the wheels of his threshing
    cart over it,
    his horses do not grind it.
²⁹All this also comes from the Lord Almighty,
    wonderful in counsel and magnificent in
      wisdom.

29

Woe to you, Ariel, Ariel,
    the city where David settled!
  Add year to year
    and let your cycle of festivals go on.
²Yet I will besiege Ariel;
    she will mourn and lament,
    she will be to me like an altar hearth.ˢ
³I will encamp against you all around;
    I will encircle you with towers
    and set up my siege works against you.
⁴Brought low, you will speak from the ground;
    your speech will mumble out of the dust.
  Your voice will come ghostlike from the
      earth;
    out of the dust your speech will whisper.

⁵But your many enemies will become like fine
      dust,
    the ruthless hordes like blown chaff.
  Suddenly, in an instant,
⁶   the Lord Almighty will come
  with thunder and earthquake and great noise,
    with windstorm and tempest and flames of
      a devouring fire.
⁷Then the hordes of all the nations that fight
    against Ariel,

that attack her and her fortress and besiege
    her,
  will be as it is with a dream,
    with a vision in the night—
⁸as when a hungry man dreams that he is
      eating,
    but he awakens, and his hunger remains;
  as when a thirsty man dreams that he is
      drinking,
    but he awakens faint, with his thirst
      unquenched.
  So will it be with the hordes of all the nations
    that fight against Mount Zion.

⁹Be stunned and amazed,
    blind yourselves and be sightless;
  be drunk, but not from wine,
    stagger, but not from beer.
¹⁰The Lord has brought over you a deep sleep:
    He has sealed your eyes (the prophets);
    he has covered your heads (the seers).

¹¹For you this whole vision is nothing but
words sealed in a scroll. And if you give the scroll
to someone who can read, and say to him, "Read
this, please," he will answer, "I can't; it is sealed."
¹²Or if you give the scroll to someone who cannot
read, and say, "Read this, please," he will answer,
"I don't know how to read."

¹³The Lord says:

"These people come near to me with their
      mouth
    and honor me with their lips,
    but their hearts are far from me.
  Their worship of me
    is made up only of rules taught by men.ᵗ
¹⁴Therefore once more I will astound these
      people
    with wonder upon wonder;
  the wisdom of the wise will perish,
    the intelligence of the intelligent will
      vanish."
¹⁵Woe to those who go to great depths
    to hide their plans from the Lord,
  who do their work in darkness and think,
    "Who sees us? Who will know?"
¹⁶You turn things upside down,
    as if the potter were thought to be like the
      clay!

ʳ25 The meaning of the Hebrew for this word is uncertain.   ˢ2 The
Hebrew for *altar hearth* sounds like the Hebrew for *Ariel.*
ᵗ13 Hebrew; Septuagint *They worship me in vain; / their teachings are
but rules taught by men*

Shall what is formed say to him who formed
it,
"He did not make me"?
Can the pot say of the potter,
"He knows nothing"?

[17]In a very short time, will not Lebanon be
turned into a fertile field
and the fertile field seem like a forest?
[18]In that day the deaf will hear the words of the
scroll,
and out of gloom and darkness
the eyes of the blind will see.
[19]Once more the humble will rejoice in the
LORD;
the needy will rejoice in the Holy One of
Israel.
[20]The ruthless will vanish,
the mockers will disappear,
and all who have an eye for evil will be cut
down—

[21]those who with a word make a man out to be
guilty,
who ensnare the defender in court
and with false testimony deprive the
innocent of justice.

[22]Therefore this is what the LORD, who redeemed Abraham, says to the house of Jacob:

"No longer will Jacob be ashamed;
no longer will their faces grow pale.
[23]When they see among them their children,
the work of my hands,
they will keep my name holy;
they will acknowledge the holiness of the
Holy One of Jacob,
and will stand in awe of the God of Israel.
[24]Those who are wayward in spirit will gain
understanding;
those who complain will accept
instruction."

10 / *Isaiah 30:1–18*
Who Do You Rely On?

THE TITLE OF this study is taken from Isaiah 36:4, in which Hezekiah's court officials hear the Assyrian field commander scornfully mock Jewish military capability. And indeed there were apparently many in Judah who were not
at all sure that the Lord would be able to protect Jerusalem. Meanwhile, Isaiah still hammers away at the same
message he has been preaching all along: "Trust in the Lord at all times." Military alliances can do little to preserve
a society that is already corroded and rotten within.

 Warming Up to God Describe a time when it has been difficult for you to trust in God.

 Read Isaiah 30:1–18.

30 "Woe to the obstinate children,"
declares the LORD,
"to those who carry out plans that
are not mine,
forming an alliance, but not by my Spirit,
heaping sin upon sin;
[2]who go down to Egypt
without consulting me;
who look for help to Pharaoh's protection,
to Egypt's shade for refuge.
[3]But Pharaoh's protection will be to your
shame,
Egypt's shade will bring you disgrace.

[4]Though they have officials in Zoan
and their envoys have arrived in Hanes,
[5]everyone will be put to shame
because of a people useless to them,
who bring neither help nor advantage,
but only shame and disgrace."

[6]An oracle concerning the animals of the
Negev:

Through a land of hardship and distress,
of lions and lionesses,
of adders and darting snakes,

the envoys carry their riches on donkeys'
    backs,
  their treasures on the humps of camels,
to that unprofitable nation,
⁷ to Egypt, whose help is utterly useless.
Therefore I call her
  Rahab the Do-Nothing.

⁸Go now, write it on a tablet for them,
  inscribe it on a scroll,
that for the days to come
  it may be an everlasting witness.
⁹These are rebellious people, deceitful children,
  children unwilling to listen to the LORD's
    instruction.
¹⁰They say to the seers,
  "See no more visions!"
and to the prophets,
  "Give us no more visions of what is right!
Tell us pleasant things,
  prophesy illusions.
¹¹Leave this way,
  get off this path,
and stop confronting us
  with the Holy One of Israel!"

¹²Therefore, this is what the Holy One of Israel
says:

  "Because you have rejected this message,
    relied on oppression
  and depended on deceit,

¹³this sin will become for you
  like a high wall, cracked and bulging,
  that collapses suddenly, in an instant.
¹⁴It will break in pieces like pottery,
  shattered so mercilessly
that among its pieces not a fragment will be
    found
  for taking coals from a hearth
  or scooping water out of a cistern."

¹⁵This is what the Sovereign LORD, the Holy
One of Israel, says:

  "In repentance and rest is your salvation,
    in quietness and trust is your strength,
  but you would have none of it.
¹⁶You said, 'No, we will flee on horses.'
  Therefore you will flee!
You said, 'We will ride off on swift horses.'
  Therefore your pursuers will be swift!
¹⁷A thousand will flee
  at the threat of one;
at the threat of five
  you will all flee away,
till you are left
  like a flagstaff on a mountaintop,
  like a banner on a hill."

¹⁸Yet the LORD longs to be gracious to you;
  he rises to show you compassion.
For the LORD is a God of justice.
  Blessed are all who wait for him!

 Discovering the Word 1. Why does God object to Judah's taking shelter under the shadow of Egypt (vv. 1–5)? 2. How do verses 6–7 emphasize the utter futility of seeking Egypt's help? 3. From verses 8–11 describe the Israelites' behavior. 4. From verses 10–22 how do you think Isaiah was regarded by the people? 5. How is the metaphor Isaiah uses to depict God's judgment particularly appropriate to their sin (vv. 12–14)? 6. How do verses 16–17 depict the price of unbelief?

Applying the Word 1. What is the difference between faith and wishful thinking? 2. What sort of "Egypts" are we tempted to turn to today? 3. Consider some particular trouble you are facing at this time. What steps do you need to take in order to trust that God will be gracious to those who wait for him—as verse 18 promises?

Responding in Prayer Recall a time when you have experienced the kind of contentment verse 15 promises. Thank God for that gift, and pray that he will renew contentment in you.

Isaiah 30:19—35:10

¹⁹O people of Zion, who live in Jerusalem, you will weep no more. How gracious he will be when you cry for help! As soon as he hears, he will answer you. ²⁰Although the Lord gives you the bread of adversity and the water of affliction, your teachers will be hidden no more; with your own eyes you will see them. ²¹Whether you turn to the right or to the left, your ears will hear a voice behind you, saying, "This is the way; walk in it." ²²Then you will defile your idols overlaid with silver and your images covered with gold; you will throw them away like a menstrual cloth and say to them, "Away with you!"

²³He will also send you rain for the seed you sow in the ground, and the food that comes from the land will be rich and plentiful. In that day your cattle will graze in broad meadows. ²⁴The oxen and donkeys that work the soil will eat fodder and mash, spread out with fork and shovel. ²⁵In the day of great slaughter, when the towers fall, streams of water will flow on every high mountain and every lofty hill. ²⁶The moon will shine like the sun, and the sunlight will be seven times brighter, like the light of seven full days, when the Lord binds up the bruises of his people and heals the wounds he inflicted.

²⁷See, the Name of the Lord comes from afar,
 with burning anger and dense clouds of
  smoke;
his lips are full of wrath,
 and his tongue is a consuming fire.
²⁸His breath is like a rushing torrent,
 rising up to the neck.
He shakes the nations in the sieve of
  destruction;
 he places in the jaws of the peoples
  a bit that leads them astray.
²⁹And you will sing
 as on the night you celebrate a holy
  festival;
your hearts will rejoice
 as when people go up with flutes
to the mountain of the Lord,
 to the Rock of Israel.
³⁰The Lord will cause men to hear his majestic
  voice
and will make them see his arm coming
 down

with raging anger and consuming fire,
 with cloudburst, thunderstorm and hail.
³¹The voice of the Lord will shatter Assyria;
 with his scepter he will strike them down.
³²Every stroke the Lord lays on them
 with his punishing rod
will be to the music of tambourines and
  harps,
 as he fights them in battle with the blows
  of his arm.
³³Topheth has long been prepared;
 it has been made ready for the king.
Its fire pit has been made deep and wide,
 with an abundance of fire and wood;
the breath of the Lord,
 like a stream of burning sulfur,
  sets it ablaze.

31

Woe to those who go down to
 Egypt for help,
 who rely on horses,
who trust in the multitude of their chariots
 and in the great strength of their horsemen,
but do not look to the Holy One of Israel,
 or seek help from the Lord.
²Yet he too is wise and can bring disaster;
 he does not take back his words.
He will rise up against the house of the
  wicked,
 against those who help evildoers.
³But the Egyptians are men and not God;
 their horses are flesh and not spirit.
When the Lord stretches out his hand,
 he who helps will stumble,
 he who is helped will fall;
 both will perish together.

⁴This is what the Lord says to me:

"As a lion growls,
 a great lion over his prey—
and though a whole band of shepherds
 is called together against him,
he is not frightened by their shouts
 or disturbed by their clamor—
so the Lord Almighty will come down
 to do battle on Mount Zion and on its
  heights.
⁵Like birds hovering overhead,
 the Lord Almighty will shield Jerusalem;

he will shield it and deliver it,
    he will 'pass over' it and will rescue it."

⁶Return to him you have so greatly revolted against, O Israelites. ⁷For in that day every one of you will reject the idols of silver and gold your sinful hands have made.

⁸"Assyria will fall by a sword that is not of
    man;
    a sword, not of mortals, will devour them.
They will flee before the sword
    and their young men will be put to forced
        labor.
⁹Their stronghold will fall because of terror;
    at sight of the battle standard their
        commanders will panic,"
declares the LORD,
    whose fire is in Zion,
    whose furnace is in Jerusalem.

32 See, a king will reign in
    righteousness
    and rulers will rule with justice.
²Each man will be like a shelter from the wind
    and a refuge from the storm,
like streams of water in the desert
    and the shadow of a great rock in a thirsty
        land.

³Then the eyes of those who see will no longer
        be closed,
    and the ears of those who hear will listen.
⁴The mind of the rash will know and
        understand,
    and the stammering tongue will be fluent
        and clear.
⁵No longer will the fool be called noble
    nor the scoundrel be highly respected.
⁶For the fool speaks folly,
    his mind is busy with evil:
He practices ungodliness
    and spreads error concerning the LORD;
the hungry he leaves empty
    and from the thirsty he withholds water.
⁷The scoundrel's methods are wicked,
    he makes up evil schemes
to destroy the poor with lies,
    even when the plea of the needy is just.
⁸But the noble man makes noble plans,
    and by noble deeds he stands.

⁹You women who are so complacent,
    rise up and listen to me;

you daughters who feel secure,
    hear what I have to say!
¹⁰In little more than a year
    you who feel secure will tremble;
the grape harvest will fail,
    and the harvest of fruit will not come.
¹¹Tremble, you complacent women;
    shudder, you daughters who feel secure!
Strip off your clothes,
    put sackcloth around your waists.
¹²Beat your breasts for the pleasant fields,
    for the fruitful vines
¹³and for the land of my people,
    a land overgrown with thorns and briers—
yes, mourn for all houses of merriment
    and for this city of revelry.
¹⁴The fortress will be abandoned,
    the noisy city deserted;
citadel and watchtower will become a
        wasteland forever,
    the delight of donkeys, a pasture for flocks,
¹⁵till the Spirit is poured upon us from on high,
    and the desert becomes a fertile field,
    and the fertile field seems like a forest.
¹⁶Justice will dwell in the desert
    and righteousness live in the fertile field.
¹⁷The fruit of righteousness will be peace;
    the effect of righteousness will be quietness
        and confidence forever.
¹⁸My people will live in peaceful dwelling
        places,
    in secure homes,
    in undisturbed places of rest.
¹⁹Though hail flattens the forest
    and the city is leveled completely,
²⁰how blessed you will be,
    sowing your seed by every stream,
    and letting your cattle and donkeys range
        free.

33 Woe to you, O destroyer,
    you who have not been destroyed!
    Woe to you, O traitor,
    you who have not been betrayed!
When you stop destroying,
    you will be destroyed;
when you stop betraying,
    you will be betrayed.

²O LORD, be gracious to us;
    we long for you.
Be our strength every morning,
    our salvation in time of distress.

³At the thunder of your voice, the peoples flee;
  when you rise up, the nations scatter.
⁴Your plunder, O nations, is harvested as by
    young locusts;
  like a swarm of locusts men pounce on it.

⁵The LORD is exalted, for he dwells on high;
  he will fill Zion with justice and
    righteousness.
⁶He will be the sure foundation for your times,
  a rich store of salvation and wisdom and
    knowledge;
  the fear of the LORD is the key to this
    treasure.ᵘ

⁷Look, their brave men cry aloud in the
    streets;
  the envoys of peace weep bitterly.
⁸The highways are deserted,
  no travelers are on the roads.
The treaty is broken,
  its witnessesᵛ are despised,
  no one is respected.
⁹The land mournsʷ and wastes away,
  Lebanon is ashamed and withers;
Sharon is like the Arabah,
  and Bashan and Carmel drop their leaves.

¹⁰"Now will I arise," says the LORD.
  "Now will I be exalted;
  now will I be lifted up.
¹¹You conceive chaff,
  you give birth to straw;
  your breath is a fire that consumes you.
¹²The peoples will be burned as if to lime;
  like cut thornbushes they will be set
    ablaze."

¹³You who are far away, hear what I have done;
  you who are near, acknowledge my power!
¹⁴The sinners in Zion are terrified;
  trembling grips the godless:
"Who of us can dwell with the consuming
    fire?
Who of us can dwell with everlasting
    burning?"
¹⁵He who walks righteously
  and speaks what is right,
who rejects gain from extortion
  and keeps his hand from accepting bribes,
who stops his ears against plots of murder
  and shuts his eyes against contemplating
    evil—
¹⁶this is the man who will dwell on the heights,

whose refuge will be the mountain fortress.
His bread will be supplied,
  and water will not fail him.

¹⁷Your eyes will see the king in his beauty
  and view a land that stretches afar.
¹⁸In your thoughts you will ponder the former
    terror:
  "Where is that chief officer?
  Where is the one who took the revenue?
  Where is the officer in charge of the
    towers?"
¹⁹You will see those arrogant people no more,
  those people of an obscure speech,
  with their strange, incomprehensible
    tongue.

²⁰Look upon Zion, the city of our festivals;
  your eyes will see Jerusalem,
  a peaceful abode, a tent that will not be
    moved;
  its stakes will never be pulled up,
  nor any of its ropes broken.
²¹There the LORD will be our Mighty One.
  It will be like a place of broad rivers and
    streams.
No galley with oars will ride them,
  no mighty ship will sail them.
²²For the LORD is our judge,
  the LORD is our lawgiver,
the LORD is our king;
  it is he who will save us.

²³Your rigging hangs loose:
  The mast is not held secure,
  the sail is not spread.
Then an abundance of spoils will be divided
  and even the lame will carry off plunder.
²⁴No one living in Zion will say, "I am ill";
  and the sins of those who dwell there will
    be forgiven.

34

Come near, you nations, and
    listen;
  pay attention, you peoples!
Let the earth hear, and all that is in it,
  the world, and all that comes out of it!
²The LORD is angry with all nations;
  his wrath is upon all their armies.
He will totally destroyˣ them,
  he will give them over to slaughter.

ᵘ6 Or *is a treasure from him* ᵛ8 Dead Sea Scrolls; Masoretic Text /
the cities ʷ9 Or *dries up* ˣ2 The Hebrew term refers to the
irrevocable giving over of things or persons to the LORD, often by totally
destroying them; also in verse 5.

³Their slain will be thrown out,
    their dead bodies will send up a stench;
    the mountains will be soaked with their
        blood.
⁴All the stars of the heavens will be dissolved
    and the sky rolled up like a scroll;
all the starry host will fall
    like withered leaves from the vine,
    like shriveled figs from the fig tree.

⁵My sword has drunk its fill in the heavens;
    see, it descends in judgment on Edom,
    the people I have totally destroyed.
⁶The sword of the LORD is bathed in blood,
    it is covered with fat—
the blood of lambs and goats,
    fat from the kidneys of rams.
For the LORD has a sacrifice in Bozrah
    and a great slaughter in Edom.
⁷And the wild oxen will fall with them,
    the bull calves and the great bulls.
Their land will be drenched with blood,
    and the dust will be soaked with fat.

⁸For the LORD has a day of vengeance,
    a year of retribution, to uphold Zion's
        cause.
⁹Edom's streams will be turned into pitch,
    her dust into burning sulfur;
    her land will become blazing pitch!
¹⁰It will not be quenched night and day;
    its smoke will rise forever.
From generation to generation it will lie
        desolate;
    no one will ever pass through it again.
¹¹The desert owlʸ and screech owlʸ will
        possess it;
    the great owlʸ and the raven will nest
        there.
God will stretch out over Edom
    the measuring line of chaos
    and the plumb line of desolation.
¹²Her nobles will have nothing there to be
        called a kingdom,
    all her princes will vanish away.
¹³Thorns will overrun her citadels,
    nettles and brambles her strongholds.
She will become a haunt for jackals,
    a home for owls.
¹⁴Desert creatures will meet with hyenas,
    and wild goats will bleat to each other;
    there the night creatures will also repose
    and find for themselves places of rest.

¹⁵The owl will nest there and lay eggs,
    she will hatch them, and care for her young
        under the shadow of her wings;
there also the falcons will gather,
    each with its mate.

¹⁶Look in the scroll of the LORD and read:

None of these will be missing,
    not one will lack her mate.
For it is his mouth that has given the order,
    and his Spirit will gather them together.
¹⁷He allots their portions;
    his hand distributes them by measure.
They will possess it forever
    and dwell there from generation to
        generation.

35 The desert and the parched land
    will be glad;
    the wilderness will rejoice and
        blossom.
Like the crocus, ²it will burst into bloom;
    it will rejoice greatly and shout for joy.
The glory of Lebanon will be given to it,
    the splendor of Carmel and Sharon;
they will see the glory of the LORD,
    the splendor of our God.

³Strengthen the feeble hands,
    steady the knees that give way;
⁴say to those with fearful hearts,
    "Be strong, do not fear;
your God will come,
    he will come with vengeance;
with divine retribution
    he will come to save you."

⁵Then will the eyes of the blind be opened
    and the ears of the deaf unstopped.
⁶Then will the lame leap like a deer,
    and the mute tongue shout for joy.
Water will gush forth in the wilderness
    and streams in the desert.
⁷The burning sand will become a pool,
    the thirsty ground bubbling springs.
In the haunts where jackals once lay,
    grass and reeds and papyrus will grow.

⁸And a highway will be there;
    it will be called the Way of Holiness.
The unclean will not journey on it;
    it will be for those who walk in that Way;

ʸ11 The precise identification of these birds is uncertain.

wicked fools will not go about on it.ᶻ
⁹No lion will be there,
    nor will any ferocious beast get up on it;
    they will not be found there.
But only the redeemed will walk there,
10 and the ransomed of the LORD will return.

They will enter Zion with singing;
    everlasting joy will crown their heads.
Gladness and joy will overtake them,
    and sorrow and sighing will flee away.

ᶻ8 Or / *the simple will not stray from it*

---

11 / *Isaiah 36—37*
An Extraordinary Deliverance

HAVE YOU EVER been intimidated by someone's ability to present an argument? Have you ever been frustrated by someone's ability to twist your words and distort the truth? How do you respond in such situations? Isaiah and King Hezekiah were confronted with just such a situation. They remained confident in God, however, and were able to respond with force and conviction to the blasphemous words they heard.

 Warming Up to God Describe a time you have heard someone distort God's words.

 Read Isaiah 36—37.

36 In the fourteenth year of King Hezekiah's reign, Sennacherib king of Assyria attacked all the fortified cities of Judah and captured them. ²Then the king of Assyria sent his field commander with a large army from Lachish to King Hezekiah at Jerusalem. When the commander stopped at the aqueduct of the Upper Pool, on the road to the Washerman's Field, ³Eliakim son of Hilkiah the palace administrator, Shebna the secretary, and Joah son of Asaph the recorder went out to him.

⁴The field commander said to them, "Tell Hezekiah,

" 'This is what the great king, the king of Assyria, says: On what are you basing this confidence of yours? ⁵You say you have strategy and military strength—but you speak only empty words. On whom are you depending, that you rebel against me? ⁶Look now, you are depending on Egypt, that splintered reed of a staff, which pierces a man's hand and wounds him if he leans on it! Such is Pharaoh king of Egypt to all who depend on him. ⁷And if you say to me, "We are depending on the LORD our God"—isn't he the one whose high places and altars Hezekiah removed, saying to Judah and Jerusalem, "You must worship before this altar"?

⁸" 'Come now, make a bargain with my master, the king of Assyria: I will give you two thousand horses—if you can put riders on them! ⁹How then can you repulse one officer of the least of my master's officials, even though you are depending on Egypt for chariots and horsemen? ¹⁰Furthermore, have I come to attack and destroy this land without the LORD? The LORD himself told me to march against this country and destroy it.' "

¹¹Then Eliakim, Shebna and Joah said to the field commander, "Please speak to your servants in Aramaic, since we understand it. Don't speak to us in Hebrew in the hearing of the people on the wall."

¹²But the commander replied, "Was it only to your master and you that my master sent me to say these things, and not to the men sitting on the wall—who, like you, will have to eat their own filth and drink their own urine?"

¹³Then the commander stood and called out in Hebrew, "Hear the words of the great king, the king of Assyria! ¹⁴This is what the king says: Do not let Hezekiah deceive you. He cannot deliver you! ¹⁵Do not let Hezekiah persuade you to trust in the LORD when he says, 'The LORD will surely deliver us; this city will not be given into the hand of the king of Assyria.'

16"Do not listen to Hezekiah. This is what the king of Assyria says: Make peace with me and come out to me. Then every one of you will eat from his own vine and fig tree and drink water from his own cistern, 17until I come and take you to a land like your own—a land of grain and new wine, a land of bread and vineyards.

18"Do not let Hezekiah mislead you when he says, 'The LORD will deliver us.' Has the god of any nation ever delivered his land from the hand of the king of Assyria? 19Where are the gods of Hamath and Arpad? Where are the gods of Sepharvaim? Have they rescued Samaria from my hand? 20Who of all the gods of these countries has been able to save his land from me? How then can the LORD deliver Jerusalem from my hand?"

21But the people remained silent and said nothing in reply, because the king had commanded, "Do not answer him."

22Then Eliakim son of Hilkiah the palace administrator, Shebna the secretary, and Joah son of Asaph the recorder went to Hezekiah, with their clothes torn, and told him what the field commander had said.

37 When King Hezekiah heard this, he tore his clothes and put on sackcloth and went into the temple of the LORD. 2He sent Eliakim the palace administrator, Shebna the secretary, and the leading priests, all wearing sackcloth, to the prophet Isaiah son of Amoz. 3They told him, "This is what Hezekiah says: This day is a day of distress and rebuke and disgrace, as when children come to the point of birth and there is no strength to deliver them. 4It may be that the LORD your God will hear the words of the field commander, whom his master, the king of Assyria, has sent to ridicule the living God, and that he will rebuke him for the words the LORD your God has heard. Therefore pray for the remnant that still survives."

5When King Hezekiah's officials came to Isaiah, 6Isaiah said to them, "Tell your master, 'This is what the LORD says: Do not be afraid of what you have heard—those words with which the underlings of the king of Assyria have blasphemed me. 7Listen! I am going to put a spirit in him so that when he hears a certain report, he will return to his own country, and there I will have him cut down with the sword.' "

8When the field commander heard that the king of Assyria had left Lachish, he withdrew and found the king fighting against Libnah.

9Now Sennacherib received a report that Tirhakah, the Cushite[a] king ⌊of Egypt⌋, was marching out to fight against him. When he heard it, he sent messengers to Hezekiah with this word: 10"Say to Hezekiah king of Judah: Do not let the god you depend on deceive you when he says, 'Jerusalem will not be handed over to the king of Assyria.' 11Surely you have heard what the kings of Assyria have done to all the countries, destroying them completely. And will you be delivered? 12Did the gods of the nations that were destroyed by my forefathers deliver them—the gods of Gozan, Haran, Rezeph and the people of Eden who were in Tel Assar? 13Where is the king of Hamath, the king of Arpad, the king of the city of Sepharvaim, or of Hena or Ivvah?"

14Hezekiah received the letter from the messengers and read it. Then he went up to the temple of the LORD and spread it out before the LORD. 15And Hezekiah prayed to the LORD: 16"O LORD Almighty, God of Israel, enthroned between the cherubim, you alone are God over all the kingdoms of the earth. You have made heaven and earth. 17Give ear, O LORD, and hear; open your eyes, O LORD, and see; listen to all the words Sennacherib has sent to insult the living God.

18"It is true, O LORD, that the Assyrian kings have laid waste all these peoples and their lands. 19They have thrown their gods into the fire and destroyed them, for they were not gods but only wood and stone, fashioned by human hands. 20Now, O LORD our God, deliver us from his hand, so that all kingdoms on earth may know that you alone, O LORD, are God.[b]"

21Then Isaiah son of Amoz sent a message to Hezekiah: "This is what the LORD, the God of Israel, says: Because you have prayed to me concerning Sennacherib king of Assyria, 22this is the word the LORD has spoken against him:

"The Virgin Daughter of Zion
   despises and mocks you.
The Daughter of Jerusalem
   tosses her head as you flee.
23Who is it you have insulted and blasphemed?
   Against whom have you raised your voice
and lifted your eyes in pride?
   Against the Holy One of Israel!
24By your messengers
   you have heaped insults on the Lord.

a9 That is, from the upper Nile region   b20 Dead Sea Scrolls (see also 2 Kings 19:19); Masoretic Text *alone are the* LORD

And you have said,
'With my many chariots
I have ascended the heights of the mountains,
the utmost heights of Lebanon.
I have cut down its tallest cedars,
the choicest of its pines.
I have reached its remotest heights,
the finest of its forests.
25I have dug wells in foreign lands[c]
and drunk the water there.
With the soles of my feet
I have dried up all the streams of Egypt.'

26"Have you not heard?
Long ago I ordained it.
In days of old I planned it;
now I have brought it to pass,
that you have turned fortified cities
into piles of stone.
27Their people, drained of power,
are dismayed and put to shame.
They are like plants in the field,
like tender green shoots,
like grass sprouting on the roof,
scorched[d] before it grows up.
28"But I know where you stay
and when you come and go
and how you rage against me.
29Because you rage against me
and because your insolence has reached my
ears,
I will put my hook in your nose
and my bit in your mouth,
and I will make you return
by the way you came.

30"This will be the sign for you, O Hezekiah:

"This year you will eat what grows by itself,

and the second year what springs from that.
But in the third year sow and reap,
plant vineyards and eat their fruit.
31Once more a remnant of the house of Judah
will take root below and bear fruit above.
32For out of Jerusalem will come a remnant,
and out of Mount Zion a band of survivors.
The zeal of the LORD Almighty
will accomplish this.

33"Therefore this is what the LORD says concerning the king of Assyria:

"He will not enter this city
or shoot an arrow here.
He will not come before it with shield
or build a siege ramp against it.
34By the way that he came he will return;
he will not enter this city,"

declares the LORD.
35"I will defend this city and save it,
for my sake and for the sake of David my
servant!"

36Then the angel of the LORD went out and put to death a hundred and eighty-five thousand men in the Assyrian camp. When the people got up the next morning—there were all the dead bodies! 37So Sennacherib king of Assyria broke camp and withdrew. He returned to Nineveh and stayed there.

38One day, while he was worshiping in the temple of his god Nisroch, his sons Adrammelech and Sharezer cut him down with the sword, and they escaped to the land of Ararat. And Esarhaddon his son succeeded him as king.

c25 Dead Sea Scrolls (see also 2 Kings 19:24); Masoretic Text does not have in foreign lands. d27 Some manuscripts of the Masoretic Text, Dead Sea Scrolls and some Septuagint manuscripts (see also 2 Kings 19:26); most manuscripts of the Masoretic Text roof / and terraced fields

---

🔦 **Discovering the Word** 1. Use map 3 and the historical chart (in the introduction) to get a picture of the situation described in 36:1–3. (You may remember that the place where the Assyrian commander stood in verse 2 is the same spot where Isaiah had confronted Ahaz years earlier [see 7:3].) How do you think the Israelites and King Hezekiah were feeling at this point? 2. How does the field commander distort the truth in verse 7 and in verse 10? 3. What temptations does the king hold out in 36:16–20? 4. What attitudes are demonstrated in Hezekiah's message to Isaiah and Isaiah's reply (37:1–7)? 5. Sennacherib's response (37:9–13) is a cruder replay of the threats of his field commander in chapter 36. What is the substance of Isaiah's reply to Sennacherib's taunt? 6. Contrast the word of hope to Hezekiah (37:30–32) and the shockingly brief statement about the end of Sennacherib's campaign and the end of his life (37:36–38).

💧 **Applying the Word** 1. In what respects can you see parallels between the threats of the Assyrian general and the temptations you face? 2. In what respects can you take Hezekiah's and Isaiah's responses to Sennacherib as models for your own response to intimidation?

Responding in Prayer As you face a world that is hostile toward Christianity, pray that you will be made bold in faith.

12 / *Isaiah 38—39*
Sovereign God and Forgetful King

IT WAS A miracle. Hezekiah's life was extended by fifteen years! We might expect that he would live those fifteen years in unforgettable gratitude and trustfulness, but the Bible, with its usual dogged realism, records that it was not so. In the chapter which follows we will see how Hezekiah ignored the warnings he had been given and invited a treacherous enemy into his home.

Warming Up to God Which do you believe is more dangerous to faith—adversity or prosperity? Why?

Read Isaiah 38—39.

38 In those days Hezekiah became ill and was at the point of death. The prophet Isaiah son of Amoz went to him and said, "This is what the LORD says: Put your house in order, because you are going to die; you will not recover."

²Hezekiah turned his face to the wall and prayed to the LORD, ³"Remember, O LORD, how I have walked before you faithfully and with wholehearted devotion and have done what is good in your eyes." And Hezekiah wept bitterly.

⁴Then the word of the LORD came to Isaiah: ⁵"Go and tell Hezekiah, 'This is what the LORD, the God of your father David, says: I have heard your prayer and seen your tears; I will add fifteen years to your life. ⁶And I will deliver you and this city from the hand of the king of Assyria. I will defend this city.

⁷" 'This is the LORD's sign to you that the LORD will do what he has promised: ⁸I will make the shadow cast by the sun go back the ten steps it has gone down on the stairway of Ahaz.' " So the sunlight went back the ten steps it had gone down.

⁹A writing of Hezekiah king of Judah after his illness and recovery:

¹⁰I said, "In the prime of my life
    must I go through the gates of death*c*
    and be robbed of the rest of my years?"
¹¹I said, "I will not again see the LORD,
    the LORD, in the land of the living;

no longer will I look on mankind,
    or be with those who now dwell in this
        world.*f*
¹²Like a shepherd's tent my house
    has been pulled down and taken from me.
Like a weaver I have rolled up my life,
    and he has cut me off from the loom;
    day and night you made an end of me.
¹³I waited patiently till dawn,
    but like a lion he broke all my bones;
    day and night you made an end of me.
¹⁴I cried like a swift or thrush,
    I moaned like a mourning dove.
My eyes grew weak as I looked to the
        heavens.
    I am troubled; O Lord, come to my aid!"

¹⁵But what can I say?
    He has spoken to me, and he himself has
        done this.
I will walk humbly all my years
    because of this anguish of my soul.
¹⁶Lord, by such things men live;
    and my spirit finds life in them too.
You restored me to health
    and let me live.
¹⁷Surely it was for my benefit
    that I suffered such anguish.
In your love you kept me
    from the pit of destruction;
    you have put all my sins

*c*10 Hebrew *Sheol* *f*11 A few Hebrew manuscripts; most Hebrew manuscripts *in the place of cessation*

behind your back.
18For the grave[g] cannot praise you,
    death cannot sing your praise;
those who go down to the pit
    cannot hope for your faithfulness.
19The living, the living—they praise you,
    as I am doing today;
fathers tell their children
    about your faithfulness.

20The LORD will save me,
    and we will sing with stringed instruments
all the days of our lives
    in the temple of the LORD.

21Isaiah had said, "Prepare a poultice of figs and apply it to the boil, and he will recover." 22Hezekiah had asked, "What will be the sign that I will go up to the temple of the LORD?"

39

At that time Merodach-Baladan son of Baladan king of Babylon sent Hezekiah letters and a gift, because he had heard of his illness and recovery. 2Hezekiah received the envoys gladly and showed them what was in his storehouses—the silver, the gold, the spices, the fine oil, his entire armory and everything found among his treasures. There was nothing in his palace or in all his kingdom that Hezekiah did not show them.

3Then Isaiah the prophet went to King Hezekiah and asked, "What did those men say, and where did they come from?"

"From a distant land," Hezekiah replied. "They came to me from Babylon."

4The prophet asked, "What did they see in your palace?"

"They saw everything in my palace," Hezekiah said. "There is nothing among my treasures that I did not show them."

5Then Isaiah said to Hezekiah, "Hear the word of the LORD Almighty: 6The time will surely come when everything in your palace, and all that your fathers have stored up until this day, will be carried off to Babylon. Nothing will be left, says the LORD. 7And some of your descendants, your own flesh and blood who will be born to you, will be taken away, and they will become eunuchs in the palace of the king of Babylon."

8"The word of the LORD you have spoken is good," Hezekiah replied. For he thought, "There will be peace and security in my lifetime."

818 Hebrew *Sheol*

Discovering the Word 1. What do you learn about prayer from the events in 38:1–8? How do you reconcile the Lord's word in verse 1 that Hezekiah would not recover and his promise in verse 5 that Hezekiah would live fifteen more years? 2. With what vivid metaphors does Hezekiah describe his deathly sickness (38:10–14)? 3. What reassurance does Hezekiah find in God's love in 38:15–20? 4. What punishment did Isaiah announce for Hezekiah's disloyalty (39:5–7)? 5. How do you interpret Hezekiah's response—his words and his thoughts (39:8)?

Applying the Word 1. What abiding truths do you find in chapter 38 to hold on to firmly in times of sickness and misfortune? 2. In what ways does this passage expand or change your understanding of who God is and how he answers our prayers?

Responding in Prayer Tell the Lord your heart's desires with confidence that he answers prayer.

---

13 / *Isaiah 40*
Unwearied Faith in an Unwearying God

IN ISAIAH 40 and the chapters following, the ending of the Babylonian exile is presupposed, and it is the prophet's purpose to reconstruct his people's faith and hope with prophecies of liberation from captivity and a new calling to be God's servant and a light to the nations. Through all the vicissitudes of history, God the Holy One, God the Gracious One, unwearyingly speaks to his people, revealing himself as a God of grace, an incomparably great

God, and a God who is in charge of the movements of history, even when a tyrant arises to terrify the world. The nations in terror turn to their idols. But Israel is to trust God in such world-shaking times. And so are we.

 Warming Up to God What "idols" (for instance, money, power or sex) do you use as a source of comfort for your fears? Confess your sin to God and ask him to free you to hear his Word for you today.

 Read Isaiah 40.

---

40 Comfort, comfort my people,
  says your God.
   ²Speak tenderly to Jerusalem,
and proclaim to her
that her hard service has been completed,
  that her sin has been paid for,
that she has received from the LORD's hand
  double for all her sins.

³A voice of one calling:
"In the desert prepare
  the way for the LORD*ʰ*;
make straight in the wilderness
  a highway for our God.*ⁱ*
⁴Every valley shall be raised up,
  every mountain and hill made low;
the rough ground shall become level,
  the rugged places a plain.
⁵And the glory of the LORD will be revealed,
  and all mankind together will see it.
                    For the mouth of the LORD
                          has spoken."

⁶A voice says, "Cry out."
  And I said, "What shall I cry?"

"All men are like grass,
  and all their glory is like the flowers of the
    field.
⁷The grass withers and the flowers fall,
  because the breath of the LORD blows on
    them.
  Surely the people are grass.
⁸The grass withers and the flowers fall,
  but the word of our God stands forever."

⁹You who bring good tidings to Zion,
  go up on a high mountain.
You who bring good tidings to Jerusalem,*ʲ*
  lift up your voice with a shout,
lift it up, do not be afraid;
  say to the towns of Judah,
  "Here is your God!"
¹⁰See, the Sovereign LORD comes with power,
  and his arm rules for him.
  See, his reward is with him,

and his recompense accompanies him.
¹¹He tends his flock like a shepherd:
  He gathers the lambs in his arms
and carries them close to his heart;
  he gently leads those that have young.

¹²Who has measured the waters in the hollow
    of his hand,
  or with the breadth of his hand marked off
    the heavens?
Who has held the dust of the earth in a
    basket,
  or weighed the mountains on the scales
    and the hills in a balance?
¹³Who has understood the mind*ᵏ* of the LORD,
  or instructed him as his counselor?
¹⁴Whom did the LORD consult to enlighten him,
  and who taught him the right way?
Who was it that taught him knowledge
  or showed him the path of understanding?

¹⁵Surely the nations are like a drop in a bucket;
  they are regarded as dust on the scales;
  he weighs the islands as though they were
    fine dust.
¹⁶Lebanon is not sufficient for altar fires,
  nor its animals enough for burnt offerings.
¹⁷Before him all the nations are as nothing;
  they are regarded by him as worthless
    and less than nothing.

¹⁸To whom, then, will you compare God?
  What image will you compare him to?
¹⁹As for an idol, a craftsman casts it,
  and a goldsmith overlays it with gold
    and fashions silver chains for it.
²⁰A man too poor to present such an offering
  selects wood that will not rot.
  He looks for a skilled craftsman
    to set up an idol that will not topple.

²¹Do you not know?
  Have you not heard?

ʰ3 Or A voice of one calling in the desert: / "Prepare the way for the LORD   ⁱ3 Hebrew; Septuagint make straight the paths of our God   ʲ9 Or O Zion, bringer of good tidings, / go up on a high mountain. / O Jerusalem, bringer of good tidings   ᵏ13 Or Spirit; or spirit

Has it not been told you from the beginning?
  Have you not understood since the earth
    was founded?
²²He sits enthroned above the circle of the
    earth,
  and its people are like grasshoppers.
He stretches out the heavens like a canopy,
  and spreads them out like a tent to live in.
²³He brings princes to naught
  and reduces the rulers of this world to
    nothing.
²⁴No sooner are they planted,
  no sooner are they sown,
  no sooner do they take root in the ground,
than he blows on them and they wither,
  and a whirlwind sweeps them away like
    chaff.

²⁵"To whom will you compare me?
  Or who is my equal?" says the Holy One.
²⁶Lift your eyes and look to the heavens:
  Who created all these?
He who brings out the starry host one by one,
  and calls them each by name.

Because of his great power and mighty
    strength,
  not one of them is missing.

²⁷Why do you say, O Jacob,
  and complain, O Israel,
"My way is hidden from the Lord;
  my cause is disregarded by my God"?
²⁸Do you not know?
  Have you not heard?
The Lord is the everlasting God,
  the Creator of the ends of the earth.
He will not grow tired or weary,
  and his understanding no one can fathom.
²⁹He gives strength to the weary
  and increases the power of the weak.
³⁰Even youths grow tired and weary,
  and young men stumble and fall;
³¹but those who hope in the Lord
  will renew their strength.
They will soar on wings like eagles;
  they will run and not grow weary,
  they will walk and not be faint.

Discovering the Word 1. A tender, wooing voice speaks to God's people in verses 1 and 2. What are the implications of the three affirmations all introduced by the word *that*? 2. A second voice is raised in verses 6–8. What vivid contrast is made in these verses? 3. The third voice, in verse 9, says, "Here is your God!" What sort of a God is he according to verses 10 and 11? 4. In what different ways is the incomparable greatness of God affirmed by the avalanche of questions and statements in verses 12–17 and 21–26? 5. How does the prophet answer Israel's complaint in verse 27?

Applying the Word 1. Deserts, valleys and mountains are hindrances to transport and communication (vv. 3–5). If all humanity is to see the glory of the Lord, these obstacles must be removed. What obstacles do you and your group or church face in both your local witness and global missions efforts? 2. How can these obstacles be removed? 3. How do these verses bring you the encouragement you need?

Responding in Prayer Make verses 28–31 your prayer to the Lord today.

Isaiah 41

41 "Be silent before me, you islands!
  Let the nations renew their
    strength!
Let them come forward and speak;
  let us meet together at the place of
    judgment.

²"Who has stirred up one from the east,
  calling him in righteousness to his
    service¹?

He hands nations over to him
  and subdues kings before him.
He turns them to dust with his sword,
  to windblown chaff with his bow.
³He pursues them and moves on unscathed,
  by a path his feet have not traveled before.
⁴Who has done this and carried it through,

¹2 Or / *whom victory meets at every step*

calling forth the generations from the
    beginning?
I, the LORD—with the first of them
    and with the last—I am he."

⁵The islands have seen it and fear;
    the ends of the earth tremble.
They approach and come forward;
6   each helps the other
    and says to his brother, "Be strong!"
⁷The craftsman encourages the goldsmith,
    and he who smooths with the hammer
    spurs on him who strikes the anvil.
He says of the welding, "It is good."
    He nails down the idol so it will not topple.

⁸"But you, O Israel, my servant,
    Jacob, whom I have chosen,
    you descendants of Abraham my friend,
⁹I took you from the ends of the earth,
    from its farthest corners I called you.
I said, 'You are my servant';
    I have chosen you and have not rejected
    you.
¹⁰So do not fear, for I am with you;
    do not be dismayed, for I am your God.
I will strengthen you and help you;
    I will uphold you with my righteous right
    hand.

¹¹"All who rage against you
    will surely be ashamed and disgraced;
those who oppose you
    will be as nothing and perish.
¹²Though you search for your enemies,
    you will not find them.
Those who wage war against you
    will be as nothing at all.
¹³For I am the LORD, your God,
    who takes hold of your right hand
and says to you, Do not fear;
    I will help you.
¹⁴Do not be afraid, O worm Jacob,
    O little Israel,
for I myself will help you," declares the LORD,
    your Redeemer, the Holy One of Israel.
¹⁵"See, I will make you into a threshing sledge,
    new and sharp, with many teeth.
You will thresh the mountains and crush
    them,
    and reduce the hills to chaff.
¹⁶You will winnow them, the wind will pick
    them up,

and a gale will blow them away.
But you will rejoice in the LORD
    and glory in the Holy One of Israel.

¹⁷"The poor and needy search for water,
    but there is none;
    their tongues are parched with thirst.
But I the LORD will answer them;
    I, the God of Israel, will not forsake
    them.
¹⁸I will make rivers flow on barren heights,
    and springs within the valleys.
I will turn the desert into pools of water,
    and the parched ground into springs.
¹⁹I will put in the desert
    the cedar and the acacia, the myrtle and the
    olive.
I will set pines in the wasteland,
    the fir and the cypress together,
²⁰so that people may see and know,
    may consider and understand,
that the hand of the LORD has done this,
    that the Holy One of Israel has created it.

²¹"Present your case," says the LORD.
    "Set forth your arguments," says Jacob's
    King.
²²"Bring in ⌐ your idols⌐ to tell us
    what is going to happen.
Tell us what the former things were,
    so that we may consider them
    and know their final outcome.
Or declare to us the things to come,
23   tell us what the future holds,
    so we may know that you are gods.
Do something, whether good or bad,
    so that we will be dismayed and filled with
    fear.
²⁴But you are less than nothing
    and your works are utterly worthless;
    he who chooses you is detestable.

²⁵"I have stirred up one from the north, and he
    comes—
    one from the rising sun who calls on my
    name.
He treads on rulers as if they were mortar,
    as if he were a potter treading the clay.
²⁶Who told of this from the beginning, so we
    could know,
    or beforehand, so we could say, 'He was
    right'?
No one told of this,

no one foretold it,
  no one heard any words from you.
²⁷I was the first to tell Zion, 'Look, here they
      are!'
  I gave to Jerusalem a messenger of good
      tidings.

²⁸I look but there is no one—
  no one among them to give counsel,
  no one to give answer when I ask them.
²⁹See, they are all false!
  Their deeds amount to nothing;
  their images are but wind and confusion.

---

14 / *Isaiah 42*
God's Servant: Image and Reality

ONE OF JESUS' most memorable sayings is found in Mark 10:45: "The Son of Man did not come to be served, but to serve, and to give his life as a ransom for many." One of Jesus' most memorable actions took place in the upper room where he was having his last meal with his disciples. He washed the disciples' feet. Afterward he said, "You call me 'Teacher' and 'Lord,' and rightly so, for that is what I am.... I have set you an example that you should do as I have done for you" (Jn 13:13, 15). The roots of these memorable words and deeds of our Lord are in this chapter of Isaiah, in which God reveals, in gradually increasing detail, the character of the Deliverer whom he is going to provide for Israel, a mighty Deliverer who will yet be a lowly servant.

 Warming Up to God How do you feel when you picture Christ as a servant?

 Read Isaiah 42.

42 "Here is my servant, whom I
      uphold,
  my chosen one in whom I delight;
I will put my Spirit on him
  and he will bring justice to the nations.
²He will not shout or cry out,
  or raise his voice in the streets.
³A bruised reed he will not break,
  and a smoldering wick he will not snuff
      out.
In faithfulness he will bring forth justice;
⁴ he will not falter or be discouraged
till he establishes justice on earth.
  In his law the islands will put their hope."

⁵This is what God the LORD says—
he who created the heavens and stretched
      them out,
  who spread out the earth and all that
      comes out of it,
who gives breath to its people,
  and life to those who walk on it:
⁶"I, the LORD, have called you in righteousness;
  I will take hold of your hand.
I will keep you and will make you
  to be a covenant for the people

and a light for the Gentiles,
⁷to open eyes that are blind,
  to free captives from prison
  and to release from the dungeon those who
      sit in darkness.

⁸"I am the LORD; that is my name!
  I will not give my glory to another
  or my praise to idols.
⁹See, the former things have taken place,
  and new things I declare;
before they spring into being
  I announce them to you."

¹⁰Sing to the LORD a new song,
  his praise from the ends of the earth,
you who go down to the sea, and all that is
      in it,
  you islands, and all who live in them.
¹¹Let the desert and its towns raise their voices;
  let the settlements where Kedar lives
      rejoice.
Let the people of Sela sing for joy;
  let them shout from the mountaintops.
¹²Let them give glory to the LORD
  and proclaim his praise in the islands.
¹³The LORD will march out like a mighty man,

like a warrior he will stir up his zeal;
   with a shout he will raise the battle cry
   and will triumph over his enemies.

¹⁴"For a long time I have kept silent,
   I have been quiet and held myself back.
But now, like a woman in childbirth,
   I cry out, I gasp and pant.
¹⁵I will lay waste the mountains and hills
   and dry up all their vegetation;
I will turn rivers into islands
   and dry up the pools.
¹⁶I will lead the blind by ways they have not
     known,
   along unfamiliar paths I will guide them;
I will turn the darkness into light before them
   and make the rough places smooth.
These are the things I will do;
   I will not forsake them.
¹⁷But those who trust in idols,
   who say to images, 'You are our gods,'
   will be turned back in utter shame.

¹⁸"Hear, you deaf;
   look, you blind, and see!
¹⁹Who is blind but my servant,
   and deaf like the messenger I send?
Who is blind like the one committed to me,
   blind like the servant of the Lᴏʀᴅ?

²⁰You have seen many things, but have paid no
     attention;
   your ears are open, but you hear nothing."
²¹It pleased the Lᴏʀᴅ
   for the sake of his righteousness
   to make his law great and glorious.
²²But this is a people plundered and looted,
   all of them trapped in pits
   or hidden away in prisons.
They have become plunder,
   with no one to rescue them;
they have been made loot,
   with no one to say, "Send them back."

²³Which of you will listen to this
   or pay close attention in time to come?
²⁴Who handed Jacob over to become loot,
   and Israel to the plunderers?
Was it not the Lᴏʀᴅ,
   against whom we have sinned?
For they would not follow his ways;
   they did not obey his law.
²⁵So he poured out on them his burning anger,
   the violence of war.
It enveloped them in flames, yet they did not
     understand;
   it consumed them, but they did not take it
     to heart.

Discovering the Word 1. How would you summarize the servant's functions or duties according to verses 1–9? 2. What is the scope of the servant's ministry (vv. 4, 6)? 3. In what ways does the description of the servant and his ministry foreshadow our Lord's person and work? 4. What vivid metaphors do verses 10–17 use to describe the Lord at work? 5. How do verses 18–25 describe the state of the people of Israel?

Applying the Word 1. In what respect or respects does this passage challenge *you*—your character, your service? 2. Promises are needed because people are so often liars. But every word of God is a promise—what he says, he *will* do. Look in this chapter at the verbs which God is the subject of. Which one or ones can you take as a personal promise of God to you now?

 Responding in Prayer Praise God for what he has done for you in Jesus Christ.

---

15 / *Isaiah 43:1—44:5*
Rivers in the Desert

HOW DO YOU feel when you hear the words "I love you"? We should not be ashamed to express these feelings. But many of us have never, or seldom, heard these words. And sometimes, like a radio signal cluttered with static, the true meaning of the words is distorted by their overuse in countless songs, books and movies. In this passage we will hear these words afresh so that we can be made abundantly sure of God's love for us personally.

Warming Up to God On what do you base your sense of self-worth?

Read Isaiah 43:1—44:5.

43

But now, this is what the Lord
says—
he who created you, O Jacob,
he who formed you, O Israel:
"Fear not, for I have redeemed you;
I have summoned you by name; you are
mine.
2When you pass through the waters,
I will be with you;
and when you pass through the rivers,
they will not sweep over you.
When you walk through the fire,
you will not be burned;
the flames will not set you ablaze.
3For I am the Lord, your God,
the Holy One of Israel, your Savior;
I give Egypt for your ransom,
Cush*m* and Seba in your stead.
4Since you are precious and honored in my
sight,
and because I love you,
I will give men in exchange for you,
and people in exchange for your life.
5Do not be afraid, for I am with you;
I will bring your children from the east
and gather you from the west.
6I will say to the north, 'Give them up!'
and to the south, 'Do not hold them back.'
Bring my sons from afar
and my daughters from the ends of the
earth—
7everyone who is called by my name,
whom I created for my glory,
whom I formed and made."

8Lead out those who have eyes but are blind,
who have ears but are deaf.
9All the nations gather together
and the peoples assemble.
Which of them foretold this
and proclaimed to us the former things?
Let them bring in their witnesses to prove
they were right,
so that others may hear and say, "It is
true."
10"You are my witnesses," declares the Lord,
"and my servant whom I have chosen,

so that you may know and believe me
and understand that I am he.
Before me no god was formed,
nor will there be one after me.
11I, even I, am the Lord,
and apart from me there is no savior.
12I have revealed and saved and proclaimed—
I, and not some foreign god among you.
You are my witnesses," declares the Lord,
"that I am God.
13   Yes, and from ancient days I am he.
No one can deliver out of my hand.
When I act, who can reverse it?"

14This is what the Lord says—
your Redeemer, the Holy One of Israel:
"For your sake I will send to Babylon
and bring down as fugitives all the
Babylonians,*n*
in the ships in which they took pride.
15I am the Lord, your Holy One,
Israel's Creator, your King."

16This is what the Lord says—
he who made a way through the sea,
a path through the mighty waters,
17who drew out the chariots and horses,
the army and reinforcements together,
and they lay there, never to rise again,
extinguished, snuffed out like a wick:
18"Forget the former things;
do not dwell on the past.
19See, I am doing a new thing!
Now it springs up; do you not perceive it?
I am making a way in the desert
and streams in the wasteland.
20The wild animals honor me,
the jackals and the owls,
because I provide water in the desert
and streams in the wasteland,
to give drink to my people, my chosen,
21   the people I formed for myself
that they may proclaim my praise.

22"Yet you have not called upon me, O Jacob,
you have not wearied yourselves for me,
O Israel.

*m*3 That is, the upper Nile region   *n*14 Or *Chaldeans*

²³You have not brought me sheep for burnt
  offerings,
  nor honored me with your sacrifices.
I have not burdened you with grain offerings
  nor wearied you with demands for incense.
²⁴You have not bought any fragrant calamus for
  me,
  or lavished on me the fat of your sacrifices.
But you have burdened me with your sins
  and wearied me with your offenses.

²⁵"I, even I, am he who blots out
  your transgressions, for my own sake,
  and remembers your sins no more.
²⁶Review the past for me,
  let us argue the matter together;
  state the case for your innocence.
²⁷Your first father sinned;
  your spokesmen rebelled against me.
²⁸So I will disgrace the dignitaries of your
  temple,
  and I will consign Jacob to destruction⁰
  and Israel to scorn.

44 "But now listen, O Jacob, my
  servant,
  Israel, whom I have chosen.
²This is what the LORD says—
  he who made you, who formed you in the
  womb,
  and who will help you:
Do not be afraid, O Jacob, my servant,
  Jeshurun, whom I have chosen.
³For I will pour water on the thirsty land,
  and streams on the dry ground;
I will pour out my Spirit on your offspring,
  and my blessing on your descendants.
⁴They will spring up like grass in a meadow,
  like poplar trees by flowing streams.
⁵One will say, 'I belong to the LORD';
  another will call himself by the name of
  Jacob;
still another will write on his hand, 'The
  LORD's,'
  and will take the name Israel.

⁰28 The Hebrew term refers to the irrevocable giving over of things or
persons to the LORD, often by totally destroying them.

Discovering the Word 1. Pick out the verbs in 43:1–7 of which God is the subject and God's people (Israel and her descendants) are the object. 2. Israel is called to an international assembly of idol-worshipers and their idols in 43:8–13. To what does the Lord call Israel to witness? 3. What would the significance of 43:16–17 have been for the Israelites (see Ex 14:21–22)? 4. In 43:22–24 we see Israel's slavish religiosity, which does not please God. What promise does God repeat to his people (43:25)? 5. Just as the "but now" of 43:1 shines brightly against the dark background of 42:18–25, the "but now" of 44:1 shines brightly against the dark background of 43:22–28. God's patience has not expired. What does he promise his people in 44:1–5?

Applying the Word 1. How do you feel about being the object of the loving statements in 43:1–7? 2. We read in 43:19, "See, I am doing a new thing." God is a transforming, re-creative God. He is the One who makes all things new (Rev 21:5). He is the One who brings into existence things that did not exist (Rom 4:17). What new thing do you need to look, with expectant faith, for God to do for you?

Responding in Prayer Allow the words of 43:2 to be a personal encouragement to you from the Lord as you go to him in prayer.

Isaiah 44:6–28

⁶"This is what the LORD says—
  Israel's King and Redeemer, the LORD
  Almighty:
I am the first and I am the last;
  apart from me there is no God.
⁷Who then is like me? Let him proclaim it.
  Let him declare and lay out before me
what has happened since I established my
  ancient people,

and what is yet to come—
  yes, let him foretell what will come.
⁸Do not tremble, do not be afraid.
  Did I not proclaim this and foretell it long
  ago?
You are my witnesses. Is there any God
  besides me?
  No, there is no other Rock; I know not
  one."

⁹All who make idols are nothing,
  and the things they treasure are worthless.
Those who would speak up for them are
    blind;
  they are ignorant, to their own shame.
¹⁰Who shapes a god and casts an idol,
  which can profit him nothing?
¹¹He and his kind will be put to shame;
  craftsmen are nothing but men.
Let them all come together and take their
    stand;
  they will be brought down to terror and
    infamy.

¹²The blacksmith takes a tool
  and works with it in the coals;
he shapes an idol with hammers,
  he forges it with the might of his arm.
He gets hungry and loses his strength;
  he drinks no water and grows faint.
¹³The carpenter measures with a line
  and makes an outline with a marker;
he roughs it out with chisels
  and marks it with compasses.
He shapes it in the form of man,
  of man in all his glory,
  that it may dwell in a shrine.
¹⁴He cut down cedars,
  or perhaps took a cypress or oak.
He let it grow among the trees of the forest,
  or planted a pine, and the rain made it
    grow.
¹⁵It is man's fuel for burning;
  some of it he takes and warms himself,
  he kindles a fire and bakes bread.
But he also fashions a god and worships it;
  he makes an idol and bows down to it.
¹⁶Half of the wood he burns in the fire;
  over it he prepares his meal,
  he roasts his meat and eats his fill.
He also warms himself and says,
  "Ah! I am warm; I see the fire."
¹⁷From the rest he makes a god, his idol;
  he bows down to it and worships.
He prays to it and says,
  "Save me; you are my god."
¹⁸They know nothing, they understand nothing;
  their eyes are plastered over so they cannot
    see,
  and their minds closed so they cannot
    understand.
¹⁹No one stops to think,

no one has the knowledge or understanding
    to say,
"Half of it I used for fuel;
  I even baked bread over its coals,
  I roasted meat and I ate.
Shall I make a detestable thing from what is
    left?
  Shall I bow down to a block of wood?"
²⁰He feeds on ashes, a deluded heart misleads
    him;
  he cannot save himself, or say,
  "Is not this thing in my right hand a
    lie?"

²¹"Remember these things, O Jacob,
  for you are my servant, O Israel.
I have made you, you are my servant;
  O Israel, I will not forget you.
²²I have swept away your offenses like a
    cloud,
  your sins like the morning mist.
Return to me,
  for I have redeemed you."

²³Sing for joy, O heavens, for the LORD has done
    this;
  shout aloud, O earth beneath.
Burst into song, you mountains,
  you forests and all your trees,
for the LORD has redeemed Jacob,
  he displays his glory in Israel.
²⁴"This is what the LORD says—
  your Redeemer, who formed you in the
    womb:

I am the LORD,
  who has made all things,
  who alone stretched out the heavens,
  who spread out the earth by myself,

²⁵who foils the signs of false prophets
  and makes fools of diviners,
who overthrows the learning of the wise
  and turns it into nonsense,
²⁶who carries out the words of his servants
  and fulfills the predictions of his
    messengers,

who says of Jerusalem, 'It shall be inhabited,'
  of the towns of Judah, 'They shall be built,'
  and of their ruins, 'I will restore them,'
²⁷who says to the watery deep, 'Be dry,
  and I will dry up your streams,'
²⁸who says of Cyrus, 'He is my shepherd

and will accomplish all that I please;
he will say of Jerusalem, "Let it be rebuilt,"

and of the temple, "Let its foundations be laid." '

16 / *Isaiah 45*
Turning to God

THERE IS A well-known story of the conversion, on January 6, 1850, of the great Baptist preacher C. H. Spurgeon. One Sunday, while he was still a teenager, he attended a service at a Primitive Methodist Chapel. Because a snowstorm had prevented the appointed preacher from arriving, one of the stewards, a shoemaker, had to teach. Having nothing much to say, he stuck to the words of his text—Isaiah 45:22: "Turn to me and be saved, all you ends of the earth; for I am God, and there is no other." Finally, recognizing Spurgeon as a stranger, he said, "Young man, you look very miserable—look to Jesus. Look. Look. Look!"

"I looked," said Spurgeon, "until I could almost have looked my eyes away; and in heaven I will look still, in joy unutterable."

 Warming Up to God Spend some time looking at the Lord in worship and in awe. Focus yourself on him before you begin.

 Read Isaiah 45.

45 "This is what the LORD says to his anointed,
to Cyrus, whose right hand I take hold of
to subdue nations before him
and to strip kings of their armor,
to open doors before him
so that gates will not be shut:
²I will go before you
and will level the mountains*ᵖ*;
I will break down gates of bronze
and cut through bars of iron.
³I will give you the treasures of darkness,
riches stored in secret places,
so that you may know that I am the LORD,
the God of Israel, who summons you by name.
⁴For the sake of Jacob my servant,
of Israel my chosen,
I summon you by name
and bestow on you a title of honor,
though you do not acknowledge me.
⁵I am the LORD, and there is no other;
apart from me there is no God.
I will strengthen you,
though you have not acknowledged me,
⁶so that from the rising of the sun
to the place of its setting
men may know there is none besides me.

I am the LORD, and there is no other.
⁷I form the light and create darkness,
I bring prosperity and create disaster;
I, the LORD, do all these things.

⁸"You heavens above, rain down righteousness;
let the clouds shower it down.
Let the earth open wide,
let salvation spring up,
let righteousness grow with it;
I, the LORD, have created it.

⁹"Woe to him who quarrels with his Maker,
to him who is but a potsherd among the potsherds on the ground.
Does the clay say to the potter,
'What are you making?'
Does your work say,
'He has no hands'?
¹⁰Woe to him who says to his father,
'What have you begotten?'
or to his mother,
'What have you brought to birth?'

¹¹"This is what the LORD says—
the Holy One of Israel, and its Maker:
Concerning things to come,
do you question me about my children,

ᵖ2 Dead Sea Scrolls and Septuagint; the meaning of the word in the Masoretic Text is uncertain.

or give me orders about the work of my
   hands?
¹²It is I who made the earth
   and created mankind upon it.
My own hands stretched out the heavens;
   I marshaled their starry hosts.
¹³I will raise up Cyrus*q* in my righteousness:
   I will make all his ways straight.
He will rebuild my city
   and set my exiles free,
but not for a price or reward,
   says the LORD Almighty."

¹⁴This is what the LORD says:

"The products of Egypt and the merchandise
   of Cush,*r*
   and those tall Sabeans—
they will come over to you
   and will be yours;
they will trudge behind you,
   coming over to you in chains.
They will bow down before you
   and plead with you, saying,
'Surely God is with you, and there is no
     other;
   there is no other god.' "

¹⁵Truly you are a God who hides himself,
   O God and Savior of Israel.
¹⁶All the makers of idols will be put to shame
     and disgraced;
   they will go off into disgrace together.
¹⁷But Israel will be saved by the LORD
   with an everlasting salvation;
you will never be put to shame or disgraced,
   to ages everlasting.

¹⁸For this is what the LORD says—
he who created the heavens,
   he is God;
he who fashioned and made the earth,
   he founded it;

he did not create it to be empty,
   but formed it to be inhabited—
he says:
"I am the LORD,
   and there is no other.
¹⁹I have not spoken in secret,
   from somewhere in a land of darkness;
I have not said to Jacob's descendants,
   'Seek me in vain.'
I, the LORD, speak the truth;
   I declare what is right.

²⁰"Gather together and come;
   assemble, you fugitives from the nations.
Ignorant are those who carry about idols of
     wood,
who pray to gods that cannot save.
²¹Declare what is to be, present it—
   let them take counsel together.
Who foretold this long ago,
   who declared it from the distant past?
Was it not I, the LORD?
   And there is no God apart from me,
a righteous God and a Savior;
   there is none but me.

²²"Turn to me and be saved,
   all you ends of the earth;
   for I am God, and there is no other.
²³By myself I have sworn,
   my mouth has uttered in all integrity
   a word that will not be revoked:
Before me every knee will bow;
   by me every tongue will swear.
²⁴They will say of me, 'In the LORD alone
   are righteousness and strength.' "
All who have raged against him
   will come to him and be put to shame.
²⁵But in the LORD all the descendants of Israel
   will be found righteous and will exult.

q13 Hebrew *him*   *r14* That is, the upper Nile region

Discovering the Word **1.** In 44:28 God says of Cyrus (king of Babylon) that he is his shepherd who will cause Jerusalem and the temple to be rebuilt. What will God do for Cyrus according to 45:1–8? **2.** In verses 9–13 why does Israel complain and what is God's reply? **3.** What do verses 14–19 say about God's relationship with Israel? **4.** In verses 20–25 the horizons widen to the "ends of the earth." What are these foreigners summoned to do? **5.** What is the implication of the phrase "by myself I have sworn" in verse 23?

Applying the Word **1.** What practical conclusions follow from the statements of this chapter that behind the activities of a world conqueror (v. 1), behind darkness as well as light (v. 7), behind disaster as well as prosperity (v. 7) stands the sovereign Lord God? **2.** When have you complained to God? How did God reply? **3.** Might it be said of you that you find righteousness and strength in the Lord (v. 24)? Why or why not?

Responding in Prayer Pray for the salvation of family and friends who do not know the Lord.

Isaiah 46—48

46 Bel bows down, Nebo stoops low;
their idols are borne by beasts of
burden.⁵
The images that are carried about are
burdensome,
a burden for the weary.
²They stoop and bow down together;
unable to rescue the burden,
they themselves go off into captivity.

³"Listen to me, O house of Jacob,
all you who remain of the house of Israel,
you whom I have upheld since you were
conceived,
and have carried since your birth.
⁴Even to your old age and gray hairs
I am he, I am he who will sustain you.
I have made you and I will carry you;
I will sustain you and I will rescue you.

⁵"To whom will you compare me or count me
equal?
To whom will you liken me that we may be
compared?
⁶Some pour out gold from their bags
and weigh out silver on the scales;
they hire a goldsmith to make it into a god,
and they bow down and worship it.
⁷They lift it to their shoulders and carry it;
they set it up in its place, and there it
stands.
From that spot it cannot move.
Though one cries out to it, it does not
answer;
it cannot save him from his troubles.

⁸"Remember this, fix it in mind,
take it to heart, you rebels.
⁹Remember the former things, those of long
ago;
I am God, and there is no other;
I am God, and there is none like me.
¹⁰I make known the end from the beginning,
from ancient times, what is still to come.
I say: My purpose will stand,
and I will do all that I please.

¹¹From the east I summon a bird of prey;
from a far-off land, a man to fulfill my
purpose.
What I have said, that will I bring about;
what I have planned, that will I do.
¹²Listen to me, you stubborn-hearted,
you who are far from righteousness.
¹³I am bringing my righteousness near,
it is not far away;
and my salvation will not be delayed.
I will grant salvation to Zion,
my splendor to Israel.

47 "Go down, sit in the dust,
Virgin Daughter of Babylon;
sit on the ground without a
throne,
Daughter of the Babylonians.ᵗ
No more will you be called
tender or delicate.
²Take millstones and grind flour;
take off your veil.
Lift up your skirts, bare your legs,
and wade through the streams.
³Your nakedness will be exposed
and your shame uncovered.
I will take vengeance;
I will spare no one."

⁴Our Redeemer—the Lᴏʀᴅ Almighty is his
name—
is the Holy One of Israel.

⁵"Sit in silence, go into darkness,
Daughter of the Babylonians;
no more will you be called
queen of kingdoms.
⁶I was angry with my people
and desecrated my inheritance;
I gave them into your hand,
and you showed them no mercy.
Even on the aged
you laid a very heavy yoke.
⁷You said, 'I will continue forever—
the eternal queen!'

⁵1 Or *are but beasts and cattle*   ᵗ1 Or *Chaldeans*; also in verse 5

But you did not consider these things
  or reflect on what might happen.

⁸"Now then, listen, you wanton creature,
  lounging in your security
and saying to yourself,
  'I am, and there is none besides me.
I will never be a widow
  or suffer the loss of children.'
⁹Both of these will overtake you
  in a moment, on a single day:
  loss of children and widowhood.
They will come upon you in full measure,
  in spite of your many sorceries
  and all your potent spells.
¹⁰You have trusted in your wickedness
  and have said, 'No one sees me.'
Your wisdom and knowledge mislead you
  when you say to yourself,
  'I am, and there is none besides me.'
¹¹Disaster will come upon you,
  and you will not know how to conjure it
    away.
A calamity will fall upon you
  that you cannot ward off with a ransom;
a catastrophe you cannot foresee
  will suddenly come upon you.

¹²"Keep on, then, with your magic spells
  and with your many sorceries,
  which you have labored at since childhood.
Perhaps you will succeed,
  perhaps you will cause terror.
¹³All the counsel you have received has only
    worn you out!
Let your astrologers come forward,
  those stargazers who make predictions month
    by month,
  let them save you from what is coming
    upon you.
¹⁴Surely they are like stubble;
  the fire will burn them up.
They cannot even save themselves
  from the power of the flame.
Here are no coals to warm anyone;
  here is no fire to sit by.
¹⁵That is all they can do for you—
  these you have labored with
  and trafficked with since childhood.
Each of them goes on in his error;
  there is not one that can save you.

48

"Listen to this, O house of Jacob,
  you who are called by the name
    of Israel
and come from the line of Judah,
you who take oaths in the name of the Lord
  and invoke the God of Israel—
  but not in truth or righteousness—
²you who call yourselves citizens of the holy
    city
  and rely on the God of Israel—
  the Lord Almighty is his name:
³I foretold the former things long ago,
  my mouth announced them and I made
    them known;
  then suddenly I acted, and they came to
    pass.
⁴For I knew how stubborn you were;
  the sinews of your neck were iron,
  your forehead was bronze.
⁵Therefore I told you these things long ago;
  before they happened I announced them to
    you
so that you could not say,
  'My idols did them;
  my wooden image and metal god ordained
    them.'
⁶You have heard these things; look at them all.
  Will you not admit them?

"From now on I will tell you of new things,
  of hidden things unknown to you.
⁷They are created now, and not long ago;
  you have not heard of them before today.
So you cannot say,
  'Yes, I knew of them.'
⁸You have neither heard nor understood;
  from of old your ear has not been open.
Well do I know how treacherous you are;
  you were called a rebel from birth.
⁹For my own name's sake I delay my wrath;
  for the sake of my praise I hold it back
    from you,
  so as not to cut you off.
¹⁰See, I have refined you, though not as silver;
  I have tested you in the furnace of
    affliction.
¹¹For my own sake, for my own sake, I do this.
  How can I let myself be defamed?
  I will not yield my glory to another.

¹²"Listen to me, O Jacob,
  Israel, whom I have called:
  I am he;

I am the first and I am the last.
¹³My own hand laid the foundations of the
        earth,
    and my right hand spread out the heavens;
when I summon them,
    they all stand up together.

¹⁴"Come together, all of you, and listen:
    Which of ⌊the idols⌋ has foretold these
        things?
The Lord's chosen ally
    will carry out his purpose against Babylon;
    his arm will be against the Babylonians.ᵘ
¹⁵I, even I, have spoken;
    yes, I have called him.
I will bring him,
    and he will succeed in his mission.

    ¹⁶"Come near me and listen to this:

"From the first announcement I have not
        spoken in secret;
    at the time it happens, I am there."

And now the Sovereign Lord has sent me,
    with his Spirit.

¹⁷This is what the Lord says—
    your Redeemer, the Holy One of Israel:
"I am the Lord your God,
    who teaches you what is best for you,

who directs you in the way you should go.
¹⁸If only you had paid attention to my
        commands,
    your peace would have been like a river,
    your righteousness like the waves of the
        sea.
¹⁹Your descendants would have been like the
        sand,
    your children like its numberless grains;
    their name would never be cut off
    nor destroyed from before me."

²⁰Leave Babylon,
    flee from the Babylonians!
Announce this with shouts of joy
    and proclaim it.
Send it out to the ends of the earth;
    say, "The Lord has redeemed his servant
        Jacob."
²¹They did not thirst when he led them through
        the deserts;
    he made water flow for them from the
        rock;
    he split the rock
    and water gushed out.

²²"There is no peace," says the Lord, "for the
        wicked."

ᵘ14 Or Chaldeans; also in verse 20

17 / *Isaiah 49*
Foundations for Service

ISAIAH 42:1–25 WAS the first passage in which the Lord began to reveal to Isaiah the character of the Mighty Deliverer he was going to send, who would yet be a lowly servant. Isaiah 49 is the second so-called servant song which reveals more about the servant and what he will be like. The words apply preeminently to our Lord, but all his servants can take them too as a pattern for their ministry.

 Warming Up to God When depression, discouragement or despair comes your way, how do you deal with it?

 Read Isaiah 49.

49 Listen to me, you islands;
    hear this, you distant nations:
    Before I was born the Lord called
me;
    from my birth he has made mention of my
        name.

²He made my mouth like a sharpened sword,
    in the shadow of his hand he hid me;
he made me into a polished arrow
    and concealed me in his quiver.
³He said to me, "You are my servant,
    Israel, in whom I will display my splendor."

⁴But I said, "I have labored to no purpose;
    I have spent my strength in vain and for
        nothing.
Yet what is due me is in the Lord's hand,
    and my reward is with my God."

⁵And now the Lord says—
    he who formed me in the womb to be his
        servant
to bring Jacob back to him
    and gather Israel to himself,
for I am honored in the eyes of the Lord
    and my God has been my strength—
⁶he says:
"It is too small a thing for you to be my
        servant
    to restore the tribes of Jacob
    and bring back those of Israel I have kept.
I will also make you a light for the Gentiles,
    that you may bring my salvation to the
        ends of the earth."

⁷This is what the Lord says—
    the Redeemer and Holy One of Israel—
to him who was despised and abhorred by the
        nation,
    to the servant of rulers:
"Kings will see you and rise up,
    princes will see and bow down,
because of the Lord, who is faithful,
    the Holy One of Israel, who has chosen
        you."

⁸This is what the Lord says:

"In the time of my favor I will answer you,
    and in the day of salvation I will help you;
I will keep you and will make you
    to be a covenant for the people,
to restore the land
    and to reassign its desolate inheritances,
⁹to say to the captives, 'Come out,'
    and to those in darkness, 'Be free!'

"They will feed beside the roads
    and find pasture on every barren hill.
¹⁰They will neither hunger nor thirst,
    nor will the desert heat or the sun beat
        upon them.
He who has compassion on them will guide
        them
    and lead them beside springs of water.
¹¹I will turn all my mountains into roads,
    and my highways will be raised up.

¹²See, they will come from afar—
    some from the north, some from the west,
    some from the region of Aswan.ᵛ"

¹³Shout for joy, O heavens;
    rejoice, O earth;
    burst into song, O mountains!
For the Lord comforts his people
    and will have compassion on his afflicted
        ones.

¹⁴But Zion said, "The Lord has forsaken me,
    the Lord has forgotten me."

¹⁵"Can a mother forget the baby at her breast
    and have no compassion on the child she
        has borne?
Though she may forget,
    I will not forget you!
¹⁶See, I have engraved you on the palms of my
        hands;
    your walls are ever before me.
¹⁷Your sons hasten back,
    and those who laid you waste depart from
        you.
¹⁸Lift up your eyes and look around;
    all your sons gather and come to you.
As surely as I live," declares the Lord,
    "you will wear them all as ornaments;
    you will put them on, like a bride.

¹⁹"Though you were ruined and made desolate
    and your land laid waste,
now you will be too small for your people,
    and those who devoured you will be far
        away.
²⁰The children born during your bereavement
    will yet say in your hearing,
'This place is too small for us;
    give us more space to live in.'
²¹Then you will say in your heart,
    'Who bore me these?
I was bereaved and barren;
    I was exiled and rejected.
Who brought these up?
I was left all alone,
    but these—where have they come from?' "

²²This is what the Sovereign Lord says:

"See, I will beckon to the Gentiles,
    I will lift up my banner to the peoples;
they will bring your sons in their arms

ᵛ12 Dead Sea Scrolls; Masoretic Text *Sinim*

and carry your daughters on their
shoulders.
²³Kings will be your foster fathers,
and their queens your nursing mothers.
They will bow down before you with their
faces to the ground;
they will lick the dust at your feet.
Then you will know that I am the Lord;
those who hope in me will not be
disappointed."

²⁴Can plunder be taken from warriors,
or captives rescued from the fierce*ʷ*?

²⁵But this is what the Lord says:

"Yes, captives will be taken from warriors,
and plunder retrieved from the fierce;
I will contend with those who contend with
you,
and your children I will save.
²⁶I will make your oppressors eat their own
flesh;
they will be drunk on their own blood, as
with wine.
Then all mankind will know
that I, the Lord, am your Savior,
your Redeemer, the Mighty One of Jacob."

ʷ24 Dead Sea Scrolls, Vulgate and Syriac (see also Septuagint and verse
25); Masoretic Text *righteous*

Discovering the Word 1. Review the servant's reactions in verses 1–7 to the Lord's call. How does he look to the past and to the future for his encouragement? 2. The Lord is going to save his people, and the servant is going to be the mediator of his covenant with the people. How do verses 8–12 describe different aspects of God's salvation? 3. In what ways do verses 8–12 give a foretaste of the ministry of Jesus Christ? 4. Israel (Zion) responds with a complaint—not a song—in verse 14. By what arguments does the Lord refute the complaint in verses 15–18? 5. What promises are given to the Israelites in verses 22–26?

Applying the Word 1. When have you felt disappointed or hopeless in your relationship with God? 2. Review the forces marshaled in this passage for the battle against discouragement and despair. How does this knowledge help you with the daily battles you face?

Responding in Prayer Ask God to teach you how to put your hope in him.

Isaiah 50:1—52:12

50 This is what the Lord says:

"Where is your mother's
certificate of divorce
with which I sent her away?
Or to which of my creditors
did I sell you?
Because of your sins you were sold;
because of your transgressions your mother
was sent away.
²When I came, why was there no one?
When I called, why was there no one to
answer?
Was my arm too short to ransom you?
Do I lack the strength to rescue you?
By a mere rebuke I dry up the sea,
I turn rivers into a desert;
their fish rot for lack of water
and die of thirst.
³I clothe the sky with darkness

and make sackcloth its covering."

⁴The Sovereign Lord has given me an
instructed tongue,
to know the word that sustains the weary.
He wakens me morning by morning,
wakens my ear to listen like one being
taught.
⁵The Sovereign Lord has opened my ears,
and I have not been rebellious;
I have not drawn back.
⁶I offered my back to those who beat me,
my cheeks to those who pulled out my
beard;
I did not hide my face
from mocking and spitting.
⁷Because the Sovereign Lord helps me,
I will not be disgraced.
Therefore have I set my face like flint,
and I know I will not be put to shame.

⁸He who vindicates me is near.
  Who then will bring charges against me?
  Let us face each other!
  Who is my accuser?
  Let him confront me!
⁹It is the Sovereign LORD who helps me.
  Who is he that will condemn me?
  They will all wear out like a garment;
    the moths will eat them up.

¹⁰Who among you fears the LORD
    and obeys the word of his servant?
  Let him who walks in the dark,
    who has no light,
  trust in the name of the LORD
    and rely on his God.
¹¹But now, all you who light fires
    and provide yourselves with flaming
      torches,
  go, walk in the light of your fires
    and of the torches you have set ablaze.
  This is what you shall receive from my hand:
    You will lie down in torment.

51

"Listen to me, you who pursue
      righteousness
    and who seek the LORD:
  Look to the rock from which you were cut
    and to the quarry from which you were
      hewn;
²look to Abraham, your father,
    and to Sarah, who gave you birth.
  When I called him he was but one,
    and I blessed him and made him many.
³The LORD will surely comfort Zion
    and will look with compassion on all her
      ruins;
  he will make her deserts like Eden,
    her wastelands like the garden of the LORD.
  Joy and gladness will be found in her,
    thanksgiving and the sound of singing.

⁴"Listen to me, my people;
    hear me, my nation:
  The law will go out from me;
    my justice will become a light to the
      nations.
⁵My righteousness draws near speedily,
    my salvation is on the way,
    and my arm will bring justice to the
      nations.
  The islands will look to me
    and wait in hope for my arm.

⁶Lift up your eyes to the heavens,
    look at the earth beneath;
  the heavens will vanish like smoke,
    the earth will wear out like a garment
    and its inhabitants die like flies.
  But my salvation will last forever,
    my righteousness will never fail.

⁷"Hear me, you who know what is right,
    you people who have my law in your
      hearts:
  Do not fear the reproach of men
    or be terrified by their insults.
⁸For the moth will eat them up like a garment;
    the worm will devour them like wool.
  But my righteousness will last forever,
    my salvation through all generations."

⁹Awake, awake! Clothe yourself with strength,
    O arm of the LORD;
  awake, as in days gone by,
    as in generations of old.
  Was it not you who cut Rahab to pieces,
    who pierced that monster through?
¹⁰Was it not you who dried up the sea,
    the waters of the great deep,
  who made a road in the depths of the sea
    so that the redeemed might cross over?
¹¹The ransomed of the LORD will return.
    They will enter Zion with singing;
    everlasting joy will crown their heads.
  Gladness and joy will overtake them,
    and sorrow and sighing will flee away.

¹²"I, even I, am he who comforts you.
    Who are you that you fear mortal men,
    the sons of men, who are but grass,
¹³that you forget the LORD your Maker,
    who stretched out the heavens
    and laid the foundations of the earth,
  that you live in constant terror every day
    because of the wrath of the oppressor,
    who is bent on destruction?
  For where is the wrath of the oppressor?
¹⁴ The cowering prisoners will soon be set
      free;
  they will not die in their dungeon,
    nor will they lack bread.
¹⁵For I am the LORD your God,
    who churns up the sea so that its waves
      roar—
    the LORD Almighty is his name.
¹⁶I have put my words in your mouth

and covered you with the shadow of my
    hand—
I who set the heavens in place,
    who laid the foundations of the earth,
    and who say to Zion, 'You are my people.' "

17Awake, awake!
    Rise up, O Jerusalem,
you who have drunk from the hand of the
    LORD
    the cup of his wrath,
you who have drained to its dregs
    the goblet that makes men stagger.
18Of all the sons she bore
    there was none to guide her;
of all the sons she reared
    there was none to take her by the hand.
19These double calamities have come upon
    you—
    who can comfort you?—
ruin and destruction, famine and sword—
    who canˣ console you?
20Your sons have fainted;
    they lie at the head of every street,
    like antelope caught in a net.
They are filled with the wrath of the LORD
    and the rebuke of your God.

21Therefore hear this, you afflicted one,
    made drunk, but not with wine.
22This is what your Sovereign LORD says,
    your God, who defends his people:
"See, I have taken out of your hand
    the cup that made you stagger;
from that cup, the goblet of my wrath,
    you will never drink again.
23I will put it into the hands of your
    tormentors,
who said to you,
    'Fall prostrate that we may walk over you.'
And you made your back like the ground,
    like a street to be walked over."

52 Awake, awake, O Zion,
    clothe yourself with strength.
    Put on your garments of splendor,
O Jerusalem, the holy city.
The uncircumcised and defiled
    will not enter you again.
2Shake off your dust;
    rise up, sit enthroned, O Jerusalem.
Free yourself from the chains on your neck,
    O captive Daughter of Zion.

3For this is what the LORD says:

"You were sold for nothing,
    and without money you will be redeemed."

4For this is what the Sovereign LORD says:

"At first my people went down to Egypt to
    live;
    lately, Assyria has oppressed them.

5"And now what do I have here?" declares the
LORD.

"For my people have been taken away for
    nothing,
    and those who rule them mock,ʸ"
                 declares the LORD.

"And all day long
    my name is constantly blasphemed.
6Therefore my people will know my name;
    therefore in that day they will know
that it is I who foretold it.
    Yes, it is I."

7How beautiful on the mountains
    are the feet of those who bring good news,
who proclaim peace,
    who bring good tidings,
    who proclaim salvation,
who say to Zion,
    "Your God reigns!"
8Listen! Your watchmen lift up their voices;
    together they shout for joy.
When the LORD returns to Zion,
    they will see it with their own eyes.
9Burst into songs of joy together,
    you ruins of Jerusalem,
for the LORD has comforted his people,
    he has redeemed Jerusalem.
10The LORD will lay bare his holy arm
    in the sight of all the nations,
and all the ends of the earth will see
    the salvation of our God.

11Depart, depart, go out from there!
    Touch no unclean thing!
Come out from it and be pure,
    you who carry the vessels of the LORD.
12But you will not leave in haste
    or go in flight;
for the LORD will go before you,
    the God of Israel will be your rear guard.

ˣ19 Dead Sea Scrolls, Septuagint, Vulgate and Syriac; Masoretic Text /
how can I   ʸ5 Dead Sea Scrolls and Vulgate; Masoretic Text wail

18 / *Isaiah 52:13—53:12*
The Heart of the Old Testament

THERE IS A rising note of expectancy in chapters 51—52 as the time for the Jews' release from captivity draws nearer. Isaiah 51:9–11 records a prayer for God to act and pictures the exiles coming home to Zion "crowned with never-fading gladness." Then, in 52:1 Jerusalem is told to awake and arise from the dust. Why? A runner is approaching over the mountains with good news: God is about to deliver his people. It is time to leave Babylon. In this passage we are introduced again to the servant of the Lord, whose solitary agony is the price of his people's homecoming.

 Warming Up to God Think of a time when someone has suffered for you. Describe what you think the experience of suffering was like for that person.

 Read Isaiah 52:13—53:12.

---

¹³See, my servant will act wisely*z*;
  he will be raised and lifted up and highly
     exalted.
¹⁴Just as there were many who were appalled at
     him*a*—
  his appearance was so disfigured beyond
     that of any man
  and his form marred beyond human
     likeness—
¹⁵so will he sprinkle many nations,*b*
  and kings will shut their mouths because of
     him.
For what they were not told, they will see,
  and what they have not heard, they will
     understand.

53
Who has believed our message
and to whom has the arm of the
Lord been revealed?
²He grew up before him like a tender shoot,
  and like a root out of dry ground.
He had no beauty or majesty to attract us to
     him,
  nothing in his appearance that we should
     desire him.
³He was despised and rejected by men,
  a man of sorrows, and familiar with
     suffering.
Like one from whom men hide their faces
  he was despised, and we esteemed him not.

⁴Surely he took up our infirmities
  and carried our sorrows,
yet we considered him stricken by God,
  smitten by him, and afflicted.
⁵But he was pierced for our transgressions,
  he was crushed for our iniquities;

the punishment that brought us peace was
     upon him,
  and by his wounds we are healed.
⁶We all, like sheep, have gone astray,
  each of us has turned to his own way;
and the Lord has laid on him
  the iniquity of us all.

⁷He was oppressed and afflicted,
  yet he did not open his mouth;
he was led like a lamb to the slaughter,
  and as a sheep before her shearers is silent,
  so he did not open his mouth.
⁸By oppression*c* and judgment he was taken
     away.
  And who can speak of his descendants?
For he was cut off from the land of the living;
  for the transgression of my people he was
     stricken.*d*
⁹He was assigned a grave with the wicked,
  and with the rich in his death,
though he had done no violence,
  nor was any deceit in his mouth.

¹⁰Yet it was the Lord's will to crush him and
     cause him to suffer,
  and though the Lord makes*e* his life a
     guilt offering,
he will see his offspring and prolong his days,
  and the will of the Lord will prosper in his
     hand.
¹¹After the suffering of his soul,

---

*z13 Or will prosper   a14 Hebrew you   b15 Hebrew; Septuagint so
will many nations marvel at him   c8 Or From arrest   d8 or away.
/ Yet who of his generation considered / that he was cut off from the land
of the living / for the transgression of my people, / to whom the blow was
due?   e10 Hebrew though you make*

he will see the light ⌊of life⌋ᶠ and be
    satisfiedᵍ;
by his knowledgeʰ my righteous servant will
    justify many,
and he will bear their iniquities.
¹²Therefore I will give him a portion among the
    great,ⁱ
and he will divide the spoils with the
    strong,ʲ

because he poured out his life unto death,
    and was numbered with the transgressors.
For he bore the sin of many,
    and made intercession for the transgressors.

*ᶠ11 Dead Sea Scrolls (see also Septuagint); Masoretic Text does not have
the light ⌊of life⌋   ᵍ11 Or (with Masoretic Text) 11He will see the
result of the suffering of his soul / and be satisfied   ʰ11 Or by
knowledge of him   ⁱ12 Or many   ʲ12 Or numerous*

 Discovering the Word 1. What reaction do many people have to the servant? Why (52:14–15)? 2. In 52:10 we are told that the Lord is going to "lay bare his holy arm"; that is, act to save his people. But when he does so, what sort of person is revealed (53:1–3)? 3. How does 53:4–6 explain the servant's sufferings? 4. How did the servant conduct himself in the midst of his suffering (53:7–9)? 5. What will be the sequel to, the result of the servant's suffering (53:10–12)? 6. Compare 1 Peter 2:21–25 to Isaiah 53. What are the parallels?

 Applying the Word 1. Why do you think 53:5 is called the "burning heart" of the Old Testament and, indeed, of the whole Bible? 2. How do you respond to this graphic description of how Christ suffered for you?

Responding in Prayer Offer God your thanks and praise for Christ's suffering on your behalf.

---

19 / *Isaiah 54—55*
Shout for Joy

A VISITOR TO a harp shop observed that when the strings of the largest harp were plucked, all the other harps in the shop rang in unison with them. In this study the expectancy which has been heightening through previous chapters explodes into song and exhortation.

 Warming Up to God Recall a time when you have been overcome with the joy of knowing God in the midst of sorrow. Allow this memory to draw you close to him in an attitude of worship.

 Read Isaiah 54—55.

54

"Sing, O barren woman,
    you who never bore a child;
    burst into song, shout for joy,
you who were never in labor;
because more are the children of the desolate
    woman
than of her who has a husband,"
                   says the Lord.
²"Enlarge the place of your tent,
    stretch your tent curtains wide,
    do not hold back;
lengthen your cords,
    strengthen your stakes.
³For you will spread out to the right and to
    the left;

your descendants will dispossess nations
    and settle in their desolate cities.

⁴"Do not be afraid; you will not suffer
    shame.
Do not fear disgrace; you will not be
    humiliated.
You will forget the shame of your youth
    and remember no more the reproach of
        your widowhood.
⁵For your Maker is your husband—
    the Lord Almighty is his name—
the Holy One of Israel is your
        Redeemer;
he is called the God of all the earth.

6The LORD will call you back
  as if you were a wife deserted and
    distressed in spirit—
a wife who married young,
  only to be rejected," says your God.
7"For a brief moment I abandoned you,
  but with deep compassion I will bring you
    back.
8In a surge of anger
  I hid my face from you for a moment,
but with everlasting kindness
  I will have compassion on you,"
says the LORD your Redeemer.

9"To me this is like the days of Noah,
  when I swore that the waters of Noah
    would never again cover the earth.
So now I have sworn not to be angry with
    you,
  never to rebuke you again.
10Though the mountains be shaken
  and the hills be removed,
yet my unfailing love for you will not be
    shaken
  nor my covenant of peace be removed,"
says the LORD, who has compassion on you.

11"O afflicted city, lashed by storms and not
    comforted,
  I will build you with stones of turquoise,k
  your foundations with sapphires.l
12I will make your battlements of rubies,
  your gates of sparkling jewels,
  and all your walls of precious stones.
13All your sons will be taught by the LORD,
  and great will be your children's peace.
14In righteousness you will be established:
Tyranny will be far from you;
  you will have nothing to fear.
Terror will be far removed;
  it will not come near you.
15If anyone does attack you, it will not be my
    doing;
  whoever attacks you will surrender to you.

16"See, it is I who created the blacksmith
  who fans the coals into flame
  and forges a weapon fit for its work.
And it is I who have created the destroyer to
    work havoc;
17 no weapon forged against you will prevail,
  and you will refute every tongue that
    accuses you.

This is the heritage of the servants of the
    LORD,
  and this is their vindication from me,"
    declares the LORD.

55 "Come, all you who are thirsty,
  come to the waters;
  and you who have no money,
come, buy and eat!
Come, buy wine and milk
  without money and without cost.
2Why spend money on what is not bread,
  and your labor on what does not satisfy?
Listen, listen to me, and eat what is good,
  and your soul will delight in the richest of
    fare.
3Give ear and come to me;
  hear me, that your soul may live.
I will make an everlasting covenant with you,
  my faithful love promised to David.
4See, I have made him a witness to the
    peoples,
  a leader and commander of the peoples.
5Surely you will summon nations you know
    not,
  and nations that do not know you will
    hasten to you,
because of the LORD your God,
  the Holy One of Israel,
  for he has endowed you with splendor."

6Seek the LORD while he may be found;
  call on him while he is near.
7Let the wicked forsake his way
  and the evil man his thoughts.
Let him turn to the LORD, and he will have
    mercy on him,
  and to our God, for he will freely pardon.

8"For my thoughts are not your thoughts,
  neither are your ways my ways,"
    declares the LORD.
9"As the heavens are higher than the earth,
  so are my ways higher than your ways
  and my thoughts than your thoughts.
10As the rain and the snow
  come down from heaven,
  and do not return to it
  without watering the earth
  and making it bud and flourish,

k 11 The meaning of the Hebrew for this word is uncertain.   l 11 Or
lapis lazuli

so that it yields seed for the sower and
   bread for the eater,
¹¹so is my word that goes out from my mouth:
   It will not return to me empty,
but will accomplish what I desire
   and achieve the purpose for which I sent it.
¹²You will go out in joy
   and be led forth in peace;
the mountains and hills

will burst into song before you,
   and all the trees of the field
   will clap their hands.
¹³Instead of the thornbush will grow the pine
   tree,
   and instead of briers the myrtle will grow.
This will be for the Lord's renown,
   for an everlasting sign,
   which will not be destroyed."

Discovering the Word 1. Isaiah 54:1–10 is an extended, complex metaphor applied to the relationship between Jerusalem and the Lord. What is the metaphor? 2. In Isaiah 54:11–17 the metaphor changes to that of a rebuilt city. What will characterize this city? 3. Is the fulfillment of these marvelous promises to Jerusalem in the past, present or future? 4. An amazing offer is extended in 55:1–5. Who is invited and what are they invited to? 5. A note of urgency is introduced in 55:6–7. How do these verses outline the nature of true repentance? 6. What transformations do God's thoughts and words achieve according to 55:8–13?

Applying the Word 1. God's love for you is more unshakable than the mountains (54:10, the ancient world's most immovable objects). What are the implications of this statement for your life now? 2. Here again is the place where the eternal Word of God intersects with our lives today. In what way do you need to seek the Lord (55:6) for abundant life and for free pardon?

Responding in Prayer Make your prayer a time of refreshment and praise.

Isaiah 56—57

56

This is what the Lord says:

"Maintain justice
   and do what is right,
for my salvation is close at hand
   and my righteousness will soon be revealed.
²Blessed is the man who does this,
   the man who holds it fast,
who keeps the Sabbath without desecrating it,
   and keeps his hand from doing any evil."

³Let no foreigner who has bound himself to
   the Lord say,
   "The Lord will surely exclude me from his
    people."
And let not any eunuch complain,
   "I am only a dry tree."

⁴For this is what the Lord says:

"To the eunuchs who keep my Sabbaths,
   who choose what pleases me
   and hold fast to my covenant—
⁵to them I will give within my temple and its
   walls
   a memorial and a name

better than sons and daughters;
I will give them an everlasting name
   that will not be cut off.
⁶And foreigners who bind themselves to the
   Lord
   to serve him,
to love the name of the Lord,
   and to worship him,
all who keep the Sabbath without desecrating
   it
   and who hold fast to my covenant—
⁷these I will bring to my holy mountain
   and give them joy in my house of prayer.
Their burnt offerings and sacrifices
   will be accepted on my altar;
for my house will be called
   a house of prayer for all nations."
⁸The Sovereign Lord declares—
   he who gathers the exiles of Israel:
"I will gather still others to them
   besides those already gathered."

⁹Come, all you beasts of the field,
   come and devour, all you beasts of the
   forest!

¹⁰Israel's watchmen are blind,
    they all lack knowledge;
they are all mute dogs,
    they cannot bark;
they lie around and dream,
    they love to sleep.
¹¹They are dogs with mighty appetites;
    they never have enough.
They are shepherds who lack understanding;
    they all turn to their own way,
    each seeks his own gain.
¹²"Come," each one cries, "let me get wine!
    Let us drink our fill of beer!
And tomorrow will be like today,
    or even far better."

57

The righteous perish,
    and no one ponders it in his
    heart;
devout men are taken away,
    and no one understands
that the righteous are taken away
    to be spared from evil.
²Those who walk uprightly
    enter into peace;
    they find rest as they lie in death.

³"But you—come here, you sons of a
    sorceress,
    you offspring of adulterers and prostitutes!
⁴Whom are you mocking?
    At whom do you sneer
    and stick out your tongue?
Are you not a brood of rebels,
    the offspring of liars?
⁵You burn with lust among the oaks
    and under every spreading tree;
you sacrifice your children in the ravines
    and under the overhanging crags.
⁶ᴸThe idolsᴶ among the smooth stones of the
    ravines are your portion;
    they, they are your lot.
Yes, to them you have poured out drink
    offerings
    and offered grain offerings.
In the light of these things, should I relent?
⁷You have made your bed on a high and lofty
    hill;
    there you went up to offer your sacrifices.
⁸Behind your doors and your doorposts
    you have put your pagan symbols.
Forsaking me, you uncovered your bed,

you climbed into it and opened it wide;
you made a pact with those whose beds you
    love,
    and you looked on their nakedness.
⁹You went to Molechᵐ with olive oil
    and increased your perfumes.
You sent your ambassadorsⁿ far away;
    you descended to the graveᵒ itself!
¹⁰You were wearied by all your ways,
    but you would not say, 'It is hopeless.'
You found renewal of your strength,
    and so you did not faint.

¹¹"Whom have you so dreaded and feared
    that you have been false to me,
and have neither remembered me
    nor pondered this in your hearts?
Is it not because I have long been silent
    that you do not fear me?
¹²I will expose your righteousness and your
    works,
    and they will not benefit you.
¹³When you cry out for help,
    let your collection ᴸof idolsᴶ save you!
The wind will carry all of them off,
    a mere breath will blow them away.
But the man who makes me his refuge
    will inherit the land
    and possess my holy mountain."

¹⁴And it will be said:

"Build up, build up, prepare the road!
    Remove the obstacles out of the way of my
    people."
¹⁵For this is what the high and lofty One
    says—
    he who lives forever, whose name is
    holy:
"I live in a high and holy place,
    but also with him who is contrite and lowly
    in spirit,
to revive the spirit of the lowly
    and to revive the heart of the contrite.
¹⁶I will not accuse forever,
    nor will I always be angry,
for then the spirit of man would grow faint
    before me—
    the breath of man that I have created.
¹⁷I was enraged by his sinful greed;
    I punished him, and hid my face in anger,
    yet he kept on in his willful ways.

ᵐ9 Or *to the king*   ⁿ9 Or *idols*   ᵒ9 Hebrew *Sheol*

¹⁸I have seen his ways, but I will heal him;
    I will guide him and restore comfort to
        him,
¹⁹ creating praise on the lips of the mourners
        in Israel.
    Peace, peace, to those far and near,"

says the LORD. "And I will heal them."
²⁰But the wicked are like the tossing sea,
    which cannot rest,
    whose waves cast up mire and mud.
²¹"There is no peace," says my God, "for the
        wicked."

20 / *Isaiah 58*
Unfailing Spring

HAVE YOU EVER struggled with how to balance social action and a life of worship? Have you ever felt that God wasn't recognizing the work that you were doing for him? Have you ever wondered just what God requires of you? In chapters 56—66 we return to the homeland of Israel. And we quickly see that God's people are falling far short of God's idea of true worship. These chapters reveal how true worship will strengthen us and make us like a spring that never runs dry.

 Warming Up to God   What frustrations do you currently have regarding the way you serve God? Make this a time of honest dialogue with the Lord.

 Read Isaiah 58.

58 "Shout it aloud, do not hold back.
    Raise your voice like a trumpet.
    Declare to my people their
        rebellion
    and to the house of Jacob their sins.
²For day after day they seek me out;
    they seem eager to know my ways,
    as if they were a nation that does what is
        right
    and has not forsaken the commands of its
        God.
They ask me for just decisions
    and seem eager for God to come near them.
³'Why have we fasted,' they say,
    'and you have not seen it?
Why have we humbled ourselves,
    and you have not noticed?'

"Yet on the day of your fasting, you do as you
        please
    and exploit all your workers.
⁴Your fasting ends in quarreling and strife,
    and in striking each other with wicked fists.
You cannot fast as you do today
    and expect your voice to be heard on high.
⁵Is this the kind of fast I have chosen,
    only a day for a man to humble himself?
Is it only for bowing one's head like a reed

and for lying on sackcloth and ashes?
Is that what you call a fast,
    a day acceptable to the LORD?

⁶"Is not this the kind of fasting I have chosen:
    to loose the chains of injustice
    and untie the cords of the yoke,
    to set the oppressed free
    and break every yoke?
⁷Is it not to share your food with the hungry
    and to provide the poor wanderer with
        shelter—
when you see the naked, to clothe him,
    and not to turn away from your own flesh
        and blood?
⁸Then your light will break forth like the
        dawn,
    and your healing will quickly appear;
then your righteousness*ᴾ* will go before you,
    and the glory of the LORD will be your rear
        guard.
⁹Then you will call, and the LORD will answer;
    you will cry for help, and he will say: Here
        am I.

"If you do away with the yoke of oppression,
    with the pointing finger and malicious talk,

ᴾ8 Or your righteous One

¹⁰and if you spend yourselves in behalf of the
        hungry
    and satisfy the needs of the oppressed,
    then your light will rise in the darkness,
        and your night will become like the
        noonday.
¹¹The LORD will guide you always;
    he will satisfy your needs in a sun-scorched
        land
    and will strengthen your frame.
    You will be like a well-watered garden,
        like a spring whose waters never fail.
¹²Your people will rebuild the ancient ruins
    and will raise up the age-old foundations;
    you will be called Repairer of Broken Walls,
        Restorer of Streets with Dwellings.

¹³"If you keep your feet from breaking the
        Sabbath
    and from doing as you please on my holy
        day,
    if you call the Sabbath a delight
        and the LORD's holy day honorable,
    and if you honor it by not going your own
        way
    and not doing as you please or speaking
        idle words,
¹⁴then you will find your joy in the LORD,
    and I will cause you to ride on the heights
        of the land
    and to feast on the inheritance of your
        father Jacob."
                The mouth of the LORD has spoken.

Discovering the Word 1. In verses 1–3 the people *seem* very religious (after the destruction of Jerusalem, fast days were increased). They are puzzled by God's disinterest. What evaluation do these verses give of the people's religiosity? 2. God has some counter-questions for them in verses 3–5. Why does he refuse to take note of their fasting and to hear their prayers? 3. What positive requirements are laid out in verses 6–10 as those which the Lord desires and delights in? 4. What promises of the Lord's blessings are given in verses 6–12? 5. Philanthropy is not enough. Verses 13–14 introduce the subject of the Sabbath. How is our behavior on this holy day to be characterized?

Applying the Word 1. Meditate on the metaphors of verses 10–12. Which one (or ones) describes most vividly what you would like to see in your life? 2. How is the principle of keeping the Sabbath applicable today? 3. What steps do you need to take in your religious life and in your social behavior in order that your life may be a "well-watered garden" and a "spring whose waters never fail"?

 Responding in Prayer Pray that you will understand and experience true worship.

Isaiah 59—60

59
Surely the arm of the LORD is not
        too short to save,
        nor his ear too dull to hear.
²But your iniquities have separated
    you from your God;
    your sins have hidden his face from you,
        so that he will not hear.
³For your hands are stained with blood,
    your fingers with guilt.
    Your lips have spoken lies,
        and your tongue mutters wicked things.
⁴No one calls for justice;
    no one pleads his case with integrity.
    They rely on empty arguments and speak lies;
        they conceive trouble and give birth to evil.
⁵They hatch the eggs of vipers

    and spin a spider's web.
    Whoever eats their eggs will die,
        and when one is broken, an adder is
        hatched.
⁶Their cobwebs are useless for clothing;
    they cannot cover themselves with what
        they make.
    Their deeds are evil deeds,
        and acts of violence are in their hands.
⁷Their feet rush into sin;
    they are swift to shed innocent blood.
    Their thoughts are evil thoughts;
        ruin and destruction mark their ways.
⁸The way of peace they do not know;
    there is no justice in their paths.
    They have turned them into crooked roads;

no one who walks in them will know
    peace.

⁹So justice is far from us,
    and righteousness does not reach us.
We look for light, but all is darkness;
    for brightness, but we walk in deep
        shadows.
¹⁰Like the blind we grope along the wall,
    feeling our way like men without eyes.
At midday we stumble as if it were twilight;
    among the strong, we are like the dead.
¹¹We all growl like bears;
    we moan mournfully like doves.
We look for justice, but find none;
    for deliverance, but it is far away.

¹²For our offenses are many in your sight,
    and our sins testify against us.
Our offenses are ever with us,
    and we acknowledge our iniquities:
¹³rebellion and treachery against the LORD,
    turning our backs on our God,
fomenting oppression and revolt,
    uttering lies our hearts have conceived.
¹⁴So justice is driven back,
    and righteousness stands at a distance;
truth has stumbled in the streets,
    honesty cannot enter.
¹⁵Truth is nowhere to be found,
    and whoever shuns evil becomes a prey.

The LORD looked and was displeased
    that there was no justice.
¹⁶He saw that there was no one,
    he was appalled that there was no one to
        intervene;
so his own arm worked salvation for him,
    and his own righteousness sustained him.
¹⁷He put on righteousness as his breastplate,
    and the helmet of salvation on his head;
he put on the garments of vengeance
    and wrapped himself in zeal as in a cloak.
¹⁸According to what they have done,
    so will he repay
wrath to his enemies
    and retribution to his foes;
he will repay the islands their due.
¹⁹From the west, men will fear the name of the
    LORD,
and from the rising of the sun, they will
    revere his glory.
For he will come like a pent-up flood

that the breath of the LORD drives along.�q

²⁰"The Redeemer will come to Zion,
    to those in Jacob who repent of their sins,"
        declares the LORD.

²¹"As for me, this is my covenant with them,"
says the LORD. "My Spirit, who is on you, and my
words that I have put in your mouth will not
depart from your mouth, or from the mouths of
your children, or from the mouths of their
descendants from this time on and forever," says
the LORD.

60

"Arise, shine, for your light has
    come,
    and the glory of the LORD rises
        upon you.
²See, darkness covers the earth
    and thick darkness is over the peoples,
but the LORD rises upon you
    and his glory appears over you.
³Nations will come to your light,
    and kings to the brightness of your dawn.

⁴"Lift up your eyes and look about you:
    All assemble and come to you;
your sons come from afar,
    and your daughters are carried on the arm.
⁵Then you will look and be radiant,
    your heart will throb and swell with joy;
the wealth on the seas will be brought to you,
    to you the riches of the nations will come.
⁶Herds of camels will cover your land,
    young camels of Midian and Ephah.
And all from Sheba will come,
    bearing gold and incense
    and proclaiming the praise of the LORD.
⁷All Kedar's flocks will be gathered to you,
    the rams of Nebaioth will serve you;
they will be accepted as offerings on my altar,
    and I will adorn my glorious temple.

⁸"Who are these that fly along like clouds,
    like doves to their nests?
⁹Surely the islands look to me;
    in the lead are the ships of Tarshish,ʳ
bringing your sons from afar,
    with their silver and gold,
to the honor of the LORD your God,
    the Holy One of Israel,
    for he has endowed you with splendor.

q19 Or When the enemy comes in like a flood, / the Spirit of the LORD
will put him to flight   r9 Or the trading ships

10"Foreigners will rebuild your walls,
   and their kings will serve you.
Though in anger I struck you,
   in favor I will show you compassion.
11Your gates will always stand open,
   they will never be shut, day or night,
so that men may bring you the wealth of the
      nations—
   their kings led in triumphal procession.
12For the nation or kingdom that will not serve
      you will perish;
   it will be utterly ruined.

13"The glory of Lebanon will come to you,
   the pine, the fir and the cypress together,
to adorn the place of my sanctuary;
   and I will glorify the place of my feet.
14The sons of your oppressors will come
      bowing before you;
   all who despise you will bow down at your
      feet
and will call you the City of the LORD,
   Zion of the Holy One of Israel.

15"Although you have been forsaken and hated,
   with no one traveling through,
I will make you the everlasting pride
   and the joy of all generations.
16You will drink the milk of nations
   and be nursed at royal breasts.
Then you will know that I, the LORD, am your
      Savior,

your Redeemer, the Mighty One of Jacob.
17Instead of bronze I will bring you gold,
   and silver in place of iron.
Instead of wood I will bring you bronze,
   and iron in place of stones.
I will make peace your governor
   and righteousness your ruler.
18No longer will violence be heard in your land,
   nor ruin or destruction within your
      borders,
but you will call your walls Salvation
   and your gates Praise.
19The sun will no more be your light by day,
   nor will the brightness of the moon shine
      on you,
for the LORD will be your everlasting light,
   and your God will be your glory.
20Your sun will never set again,
   and your moon will wane no more;
the LORD will be your everlasting light,
   and your days of sorrow will end.
21Then will all your people be righteous
   and they will possess the land forever.
They are the shoot I have planted,
   the work of my hands,
   for the display of my splendor.
22The least of you will become a thousand,
   the smallest a mighty nation.
I am the LORD;
   in its time I will do this swiftly."

21 / *Isaiah 61*
A Garment of Praise for a Spirit of Despair

WHEN JERUSALEM WAS destroyed, some people contemptuously nicknamed her "Zion for whom no one cares" (Jer 30:17). She was utterly despised and alone. But God is the only one who can delete the indelible and heal the incurable. In this chapter we see his healing and restorative work through his servant. The healing depicted here is as long as time and as wide as the created world, and we can have a part in it as well.

Warming Up to God Think of a time you felt like an outcast. Who or what brought you comfort?

Read Isaiah 61.

61

The Spirit of the Sovereign LORD is on me,
because the LORD has anointed me
to preach good news to the poor.
He has sent me to bind up the brokenhearted,
to proclaim freedom for the captives
and release from darkness for the
prisoners,[5]
[2]to proclaim the year of the LORD's favor
and the day of vengeance of our God,
to comfort all who mourn,
[3] and provide for those who grieve in Zion—
to bestow on them a crown of beauty
instead of ashes,
the oil of gladness
instead of mourning,
and a garment of praise
instead of a spirit of despair.
They will be called oaks of righteousness,
a planting of the LORD
for the display of his splendor.

[4]They will rebuild the ancient ruins
and restore the places long devastated;
they will renew the ruined cities
that have been devastated for generations.
[5]Aliens will shepherd your flocks;
foreigners will work your fields and
vineyards.
[6]And you will be called priests of the LORD,
you will be named ministers of our God.
You will feed on the wealth of nations,
and in their riches you will boast.

[7]Instead of their shame
my people will receive a double portion,
and instead of disgrace
they will rejoice in their inheritance;
and so they will inherit a double portion in
their land,
and everlasting joy will be theirs.

[8]"For I, the LORD, love justice;
I hate robbery and iniquity.
In my faithfulness I will reward them
and make an everlasting covenant with
them.
[9]Their descendants will be known among the
nations
and their offspring among the peoples.
All who see them will acknowledge
that they are a people the LORD has
blessed."

[10]I delight greatly in the LORD;
my soul rejoices in my God.
For he has clothed me with garments of
salvation
and arrayed me in a robe of righteousness,
as a bridegroom adorns his head like a priest,
and as a bride adorns herself with her
jewels.
[11]For as the soil makes the sprout come up
and a garden causes seeds to grow,
so the Sovereign LORD will make righteousness
and praise
spring up before all nations.

[5]1 Hebrew; Septuagint *the blind*

Discovering the Word 1. Summarize the transforming ministry of the Lord's anointed servant in verses 1–3. 2. What is the significance of each metaphor in verse 3? 3. How do verses 4–9 depict Zion's transformed situation? 4. How are the two metaphors for righteousness found in the delighted outburst of song in verses 10–11 appropriate?

Applying the Word 1. How do verses 1–3 encourage you in areas of personal need? 2. There is a strong emphasis in this chapter on "righteousness" (vv. 3, 10–11) and "justice" (v. 8). How can you take a stand for justice this week for the glory of God's name?

Responding in Prayer Pray for the poor, the broken-hearted and prisoners.

22 / *Isaiah 62*
The Refugees Return

HAVE YOU EVER wondered what it is like to be a refugee? Have you ever wondered how it feels to pick up the few belongings you can carry and with a sick heart to leave your family home, your family farm, your family graves, your town, your country—perhaps never to return? But what if the chance comes to return home, for a new start under a new regime? The exultation and bridal joyousness of this chapter must be understood from the perspective of the returning refugees. The Israelites might have thought that Jerusalem had been irreversibly abandoned by the Lord—but it is not so.

 Warming Up to God Picture yourself as a refugee returning home to the Lord. What do you experience?

 Read Isaiah 62.

---

62 For Zion's sake I will not keep
        silent,
     for Jerusalem's sake I will not
        remain quiet,
   till her righteousness shines out like the
        dawn,
     her salvation like a blazing torch.
²The nations will see your righteousness,
     and all kings your glory;
   you will be called by a new name
     that the mouth of the LORD will bestow.
³You will be a crown of splendor in the LORD's
        hand,
     a royal diadem in the hand of your God.
⁴No longer will they call you Deserted,
     or name your land Desolate.
   But you will be called Hephzibah,ᵗ
     and your land Beulahᵘ;
   for the LORD will take delight in you,
     and your land will be married.
⁵As a young man marries a maiden,
     so will your sonsᵛ marry you;
   as a bridegroom rejoices over his bride,
     so will your God rejoice over you.

⁶I have posted watchmen on your walls,
        O Jerusalem;
     they will never be silent day or night.
   You who call on the LORD,
     give yourselves no rest,
⁷and give him no rest till he establishes
        Jerusalem

and makes her the praise of the earth.

⁸The LORD has sworn by his right hand
     and by his mighty arm:
   "Never again will I give your grain
     as food for your enemies,
   and never again will foreigners drink the new
        wine
     for which you have toiled;
⁹but those who harvest it will eat it
     and praise the LORD,
   and those who gather the grapes will drink it
     in the courts of my sanctuary."

¹⁰Pass through, pass through the gates!
     Prepare the way for the people.
   Build up, build up the highway!
     Remove the stones.
   Raise a banner for the nations.

¹¹The LORD has made proclamation
     to the ends of the earth:
   "Say to the Daughter of Zion,
     'See, your Savior comes!
   See, his reward is with him,
     and his recompense accompanies him.' "
¹²They will be called the Holy People,
     the Redeemed of the LORD;
   and you will be called Sought After,
     the City No Longer Deserted.

ᵗ4 *Hephzibah* means *my delight is in her.*   ᵘ4 *Beulah* means *married.*
ᵛ5 Or *Builder*

Discovering the Word 1. Isaiah has not kept silent about Judah's wickedness and her judgment. What motives does verse 1 reveal about his refusal to keep silent? 2. How do verses 2–5 describe the new relationship between God and Zion? 3. What will the role of Jerusalem's watchmen be (vv. 6–7)? 4. What is promised in verses 8–9? 5. Describe the scene which verse 10 sets up.

 Applying the Word 1. What role do celebratory processions and marches of witness have in the church today? 2. Pause and dwell on Zion's new names. *Hephzibah* means "my delight is in her," and *Beulah* means "married." How do you respond to these expressions of God's feelings toward you?

Responding in Prayer Respond in joyful prayer and worship to the God who calls you "Sought After, the City No Longer Deserted" (v. 12).

Isaiah 63:1–6

63
Who is this coming from Edom,
  from Bozrah, with his garments
  stained crimson?
Who is this, robed in splendor,
  striding forward in the greatness of his
  strength?

"It is I, speaking in righteousness,
  mighty to save."

²Why are your garments red,
  like those of one treading the winepress?

³"I have trodden the winepress alone;
  from the nations no one was with me.

I trampled them in my anger
  and trod them down in my wrath;
their blood spattered my garments,
  and I stained all my clothing.
⁴For the day of vengeance was in my heart,
  and the year of my redemption has come.
⁵I looked, but there was no one to help,
  I was appalled that no one gave support;
so my own arm worked salvation for me,
  and my own wrath sustained me.
⁶I trampled the nations in my anger;
  in my wrath I made them drunk
  and poured their blood on the ground."

---

23 / Isaiah 63:7—64:12
A Cry for Forgiveness and for Revival

HAVE YOU EVER been discouraged when you look at the people of God as they are today? Do you compare your church members to what they have been at various times in the past? Do you feel inadequate to the golden vision of what the church will be when Christ presents to God "a radiant church, without stain or wrinkle or any other blemish, but holy and blameless" (Eph 5:27)? It is a shattering experience for Isaiah too—to turn from the vision of radiant Zion in chapters 60—62 to Zion as she is.

 Warming Up to God When have you experienced spiritual revival in your life? Allow the joy of that time to well up within you.

 Read Isaiah 63:7—64:12.

---

⁷I will tell of the kindnesses of the LORD,
  the deeds for which he is to be praised,
  according to all the LORD has done for us—
yes, the many good things he has done
  for the house of Israel,

according to his compassion and many
  kindnesses.
⁸He said, "Surely they are my people,
  sons who will not be false to me";
and so he became their Savior.

⁹In all their distress he too was distressed,
  and the angel of his presence saved them.
In his love and mercy he redeemed them;
  he lifted them up and carried them
  all the days of old.
¹⁰Yet they rebelled
  and grieved his Holy Spirit.
So he turned and became their enemy
  and he himself fought against them.

¹¹Then his people recalled^w the days of old,
  the days of Moses and his people—
where is he who brought them through the
    sea,
  with the shepherd of his flock?
Where is he who set
  his Holy Spirit among them,
¹²who sent his glorious arm of power
  to be at Moses' right hand,
who divided the waters before them,
  to gain for himself everlasting renown,
¹³who led them through the depths?
Like a horse in open country,
  they did not stumble;
¹⁴like cattle that go down to the plain,
  they were given rest by the Spirit of the
    LORD.
This is how you guided your people
  to make for yourself a glorious name.

¹⁵Look down from heaven and see
  from your lofty throne, holy and glorious.
Where are your zeal and your might?
  Your tenderness and compassion are
    withheld from us.
¹⁶But you are our Father,
  though Abraham does not know us
  or Israel acknowledge us;
you, O LORD, are our Father,
  our Redeemer from of old is your name.
¹⁷Why, O LORD, do you make us wander from
    your ways
  and harden our hearts so we do not revere
    you?
Return for the sake of your servants,
  the tribes that are your inheritance.
¹⁸For a little while your people possessed your
    holy place,
  but now our enemies have trampled down
    your sanctuary.
¹⁹We are yours from of old;
  but you have not ruled over them,
  they have not been called by your name.^x

64

Oh, that you would rend the
heavens and come down,
  that the mountains would tremble
before you!
²As when fire sets twigs ablaze
  and causes water to boil,
come down to make your name known to
    your enemies
  and cause the nations to quake before you!
³For when you did awesome things that we
    did not expect,
  you came down, and the mountains
    trembled before you.
⁴Since ancient times no one has heard,
  no ear has perceived,
no eye has seen any God besides you,
  who acts on behalf of those who wait for
    him.
⁵You come to the help of those who gladly do
    right,
  who remember your ways.
But when we continued to sin against them,
  you were angry.
  How then can we be saved?
⁶All of us have become like one who is
    unclean,
  and all our righteous acts are like filthy
    rags;
we all shrivel up like a leaf,
  and like the wind our sins sweep us away.
⁷No one calls on your name
  or strives to lay hold of you;
for you have hidden your face from us
  and made us waste away because of our
    sins.

⁸Yet, O LORD, you are our Father.
  We are the clay, you are the potter;
  we are all the work of your hand.
⁹Do not be angry beyond measure, O LORD;
  do not remember our sins forever.
Oh, look upon us, we pray,
  for we are all your people.
¹⁰Your sacred cities have become a desert;
  even Zion is a desert, Jerusalem a
    desolation.
¹¹Our holy and glorious temple, where our
    fathers praised you,
  has been burned with fire,
  and all that we treasured lies in ruins.

^w11 Or But may he recall ^x19 Or We are like those you have never
ruled, / like those never called by your name

¹²After all this, O LORD, will you hold yourself
    back?

Will you keep silent and punish us beyond
    measure?

Discovering the Word 1. What do we learn from the way that Isaiah begins his long and passionate prayer in 63:7? 2. Isaiah 63:9 recalls how God brought his people out of slavery in Egypt. How do verses 8–9 describe the warmth of God's relationship with his people? 3. What do the chastened people remember about God's wonderful deeds (63:11–14)? 4. What striking phrase, repeated three times in 63:16—64:12, gives the prayer its special intensity (63:16; 64:8)? 5. How does Isaiah see God's hand in this sorry state of affairs, and how does Israel look to God to get them out of it (63:15, 17; 64:1, 4–5, 8)?

Applying the Word 1. God's interventions are always surprising. How do you see God's intervening in the world today through revival or in other ways? 2. How can following the model of this passage enrich and deepen your own prayer life?

Responding in Prayer Pray that God will bring revival to you and to your nation.

Isaiah 65:1–16

65 "I revealed myself to those who
    did not ask for me;
    I was found by those who did not
    seek me.
To a nation that did not call on my name,
    I said, 'Here am I, here am I.'
²All day long I have held out my hands
    to an obstinate people,
who walk in ways not good,
    pursuing their own imaginations—
³a people who continually provoke me
    to my very face,
offering sacrifices in gardens
    and burning incense on altars of brick;
⁴who sit among the graves
    and spend their nights keeping secret vigil;
who eat the flesh of pigs,
    and whose pots hold broth of unclean
      meat;
⁵who say, 'Keep away; don't come near me,
    for I am too sacred for you!'
Such people are smoke in my nostrils,
    a fire that keeps burning all day.

⁶"See, it stands written before me:
    I will not keep silent but will pay back in
      full;
    I will pay it back into their laps—
⁷both your sins and the sins of your fathers,"
    says the LORD.
"Because they burned sacrifices on the
    mountains

and defied me on the hills,
I will measure into their laps
    the full payment for their former deeds."

⁸This is what the LORD says:

"As when juice is still found in a cluster of
    grapes
    and men say, 'Don't destroy it,
    there is yet some good in it,'
so will I do in behalf of my servants;
    I will not destroy them all.
⁹I will bring forth descendants from Jacob,
    and from Judah those who will possess my
      mountains;
my chosen people will inherit them,
    and there will my servants live.
¹⁰Sharon will become a pasture for flocks,
    and the Valley of Achor a resting place for
      herds,
    for my people who seek me.

¹¹"But as for you who forsake the LORD
    and forget my holy mountain,
who spread a table for Fortune
    and fill bowls of mixed wine for Destiny,
¹²I will destine you for the sword,
    and you will all bend down for the
      slaughter;
for I called but you did not answer,
    I spoke but you did not listen.
You did evil in my sight
    and chose what displeases me."

¹³Therefore this is what the Sovereign Lord says:

"My servants will eat,
　but you will go hungry;
my servants will drink,
　but you will go thirsty;
my servants will rejoice,
　but you will be put to shame.
¹⁴My servants will sing
　out of the joy of their hearts,
but you will cry out
　from anguish of heart

and wail in brokenness of spirit.
¹⁵You will leave your name
　to my chosen ones as a curse;
the Sovereign Lord will put you to death,
　but to his servants he will give another
　　name.
¹⁶Whoever invokes a blessing in the land
　will do so by the God of truth;
he who takes an oath in the land
　will swear by the God of truth.
For the past troubles will be forgotten
　and hidden from my eyes.

24 / *Isaiah 65:17—66:24*
The Terror and the Glory

HOPE HAS A life-preserving character. Time and again, as prison-camp memoirs show, people who have something to live for survive, and those who lose hope die under the same conditions. All through Isaiah, the basic theme has been that God's faithful love should be the basis of his people's faithful trust. Now, as he brings his book to a climax, he describes the day when faith and hope will come to fruition. There will be a new heaven and a new earth in which love reigns. Yet this is not a fairy-tale ending. As in chapter 6, Isaiah cannot avert his eyes from the fact that some people *reject* the good news. One day their refusal will be irreversibly confirmed.

 Warming Up to God What people or events have recently given you hope regarding your future?

 Read Isaiah 65:17—66:24.

¹⁷"Behold, I will create
　new heavens and a new earth.
The former things will not be remembered,
　nor will they come to mind.
¹⁸But be glad and rejoice forever
　in what I will create,
for I will create Jerusalem to be a delight
　and its people a joy.
¹⁹I will rejoice over Jerusalem
　and take delight in my people;
the sound of weeping and of crying
　will be heard in it no more.

²⁰"Never again will there be in it
　an infant who lives but a few days,
　or an old man who does not live out his
　　years;
he who dies at a hundred
　will be thought a mere youth;
he who fails to reach ʸ a hundred

will be considered accursed.
²¹They will build houses and dwell in them;
　they will plant vineyards and eat their fruit.
²²No longer will they build houses and others
　live in them,
　or plant and others eat.
For as the days of a tree,
　so will be the days of my people;
my chosen ones will long enjoy
　the works of their hands.
²³They will not toil in vain
　or bear children doomed to misfortune;
for they will be a people blessed by the Lord,
　they and their descendants with them.
²⁴Before they call I will answer;
　while they are still speaking I will hear.
²⁵The wolf and the lamb will feed together,
　and the lion will eat straw like the ox,
　but dust will be the serpent's food.

ʸ20 Or / the sinner who reaches

They will neither harm nor destroy
  on all my holy mountain,"
                says the LORD.

66 This is what the LORD says:
    "Heaven is my throne,
and the earth is my footstool.
Where is the house you will build for me?
  Where will my resting place be?
²Has not my hand made all these things,
  and so they came into being?"
            declares the LORD.

"This is the one I esteem:
  he who is humble and contrite in spirit,
  and trembles at my word.
³But whoever sacrifices a bull
  is like one who kills a man,
and whoever offers a lamb,
  like one who breaks a dog's neck;
whoever makes a grain offering
  is like one who presents pig's blood,
and whoever burns memorial incense,
  like one who worships an idol.
They have chosen their own ways,
  and their souls delight in their
    abominations;
⁴so I also will choose harsh treatment for them
  and will bring upon them what they dread.
For when I called, no one answered,
  when I spoke, no one listened.
They did evil in my sight
  and chose what displeases me."

⁵Hear the word of the LORD,
  you who tremble at his word:
"Your brothers who hate you,
  and exclude you because of my name, have
    said,
'Let the LORD be glorified,
  that we may see your joy!'
  Yet they will be put to shame.
⁶Hear that uproar from the city,
  hear that noise from the temple!
It is the sound of the LORD
  repaying his enemies all they deserve.

⁷"Before she goes into labor,
  she gives birth;
before the pains come upon her,
  she delivers a son.
⁸Who has ever heard of such a thing?
  Who has ever seen such things?

Can a country be born in a day
  or a nation be brought forth in a moment?
Yet no sooner is Zion in labor
  than she gives birth to her children.
⁹Do I bring to the moment of birth
  and not give delivery?" says the LORD.
"Do I close up the womb
  when I bring to delivery?" says your God.
¹⁰"Rejoice with Jerusalem and be glad for her,
  all you who love her;
rejoice greatly with her,
  all you who mourn over her.
¹¹For you will nurse and be satisfied
  at her comforting breasts;
you will drink deeply
  and delight in her overflowing abundance."

¹²For this is what the LORD says:

"I will extend peace to her like a river,
  and the wealth of nations like a flooding
    stream;
you will nurse and be carried on her arm
  and dandled on her knees.
¹³As a mother comforts her child,
  so will I comfort you;
and you will be comforted over Jerusalem."

¹⁴When you see this, your heart will rejoice
  and you will flourish like grass;
the hand of the LORD will be made known to
    his servants,
  but his fury will be shown to his foes.
¹⁵See, the LORD is coming with fire,
  and his chariots are like a whirlwind;
he will bring down his anger with fury,
  and his rebuke with flames of fire.
¹⁶For with fire and with his sword
  the LORD will execute judgment upon all
    men,
  and many will be those slain by the LORD.

¹⁷"Those who consecrate and purify themselves to go into the gardens, following the one in the midst of[z] those who eat the flesh of pigs and rats and other abominable things—they will meet their end together," declares the LORD.

¹⁸"And I, because of their actions and their imaginations, am about to come[a] and gather all nations and tongues, and they will come and see my glory.

---

z 17 Or *gardens behind one of your temples, and*   a 18 The meaning of
the Hebrew for this clause is uncertain.

¹⁹"I will set a sign among them, and I will send some of those who survive to the nations—to Tarshish, to the Libyans[b] and Lydians (famous as archers), to Tubal and Greece, and to the distant islands that have not heard of my fame or seen my glory. They will proclaim my glory among the nations. ²⁰And they will bring all your brothers, from all the nations, to my holy mountain in Jerusalem as an offering to the LORD—on horses, in chariots and wagons, and on mules and camels," says the LORD. "They will bring them, as the Israelites bring their grain offerings, to the temple of the LORD in ceremonially clean vessels.

²¹And I will select some of them also to be priests and Levites," says the LORD.

²²"As the new heavens and the new earth that I make will endure before me," declares the LORD, "so will your name and descendants endure. ²³From one New Moon to another and from one Sabbath to another, all mankind will come and bow down before me," says the LORD. ²⁴"And they will go out and look upon the dead bodies of those who rebelled against me; their worm will not die, nor will their fire be quenched, and they will be loathsome to all mankind."

b19 Some Septuagint manuscripts *Put* (Libyans); Hebrew *Pul*

 Discovering the Word 1. What simple joys and pleasures characterize the new heaven and new earth (65:17–19, 24)? 2. What is God's complaint in 66:1–2? 3. Which worshipers please God and which displease him (66:2–4)? 4. According to 66:7–11, the apparently barren, abandoned and childless Zion is to have children. In what ways is childbirth an appropriate metaphor here? 5. What will it be like when God finally shows his glory (66:12–24)?

 Applying the Word 1. How can you best preserve the two poles of awe and intimacy that characterize true worship? 2. In what area of your life do you need to look to the Lord for hope?

Responding in Prayer Praise God for the growing trust in him that you have which enables you to have hope in a hopeless world.

Jeremiah

A s a teenager, I was delighted when my pastor started a series of sermons on prophecy. I hadn't been a Christian very long, and I had the impression that the Bible was a mysterious book that spoke about the future. I suppose at that time you could say that I put the Bible, Edgar Cayce and the works of Nostradamus in the same category.

My pastor brought some cold water to my youthful fancy. I learned that the future the prophets spoke about wasn't primarily some distant utopia that had to be deciphered by hocus–pocus and hidden wisdom. Instead, the prophets of the Old Testament were only partly concerned with the future. Their primary focus was on calling God's people back to faithful obedience and worship. When the prophets spoke of the future, they did so to let Israel know that they could expect defeat at the hands of their enemies if they didn't repent.

This was not at all what I expected. As my pastor developed the series, the prophets seemed to me to be strange characters wandering around thundering the message of an angry God to people who refused to obey him. After that series, I wasn't so eager to talk about prophecy anymore. I wasn't sure I liked the prophets or their message.

Eventually I got back to the prophets in my personal study. I was convinced that if the prophets were in the Scriptures, then I needed to study them. What I discovered at that time was that, yes, many of the prophets did strange things and proclaimed lots of wrath. What was off in my understanding, however, was the impression I got of God.

The thundering message of judgment came not because God is a short-tempered despot shouting angry curses at people who break his rules, but because he is so intensely caring for those he gave himself to. In and through the message of the prophets as they proclaimed the coming judgment is a message of love. I like the way the prophet Jeremiah says it: "I have loved you with an everlasting love; I have drawn you with loving-kindness" (Jer 31:3).

In this book you will find the prophet Jeremiah behaving strangely—proclaiming wrath and impending destruction. Jeremiah lived and wrote in a dark time. For over 250 years God had been sending prophets to warn his people to change their ways. And for over 250 years the prophets were ignored, persecuted or killed. As Jeremiah began his ministry somewhere around 620 B.C., God had already sent the northern half of the kingdom into exile a hundred years previously. For the southern kingdom, Jeremiah was their last messenger, their very last chance to turn things around. God and Jeremiah knew that it wouldn't work, but they rebuked and proclaimed anyway.

Studying the ministry of the prophet Jeremiah, you will get a glimpse of what it is like to have a personal relationship with God. God called Jeremiah to a painful ministry. But with that great burden, he gave Jeremiah a great gift, the gift of himself. When you study Jeremiah you get a glimpse of what it can be like for God and a human to be together. You will see a message of love that grows from a relationship of love—a hard love, a demanding love, but love nevertheless. What you will also discover, if you pay attention, is how you can grow in your own personal relationship to God. You will be stronger and more deeply open to the love of God than you were before.

The Shape of the Study

The book of Jeremiah is challenging. It is the second longest of all the prophetic works, with 52 chapters. There are three major sections:

Jeremiah 1—20 ——————————— The Impending Judgment
Jeremiah 21—45 ——————————— Living in the Midst of God's Judgment
Jeremiah 46—52 ——————————— Oracles of International Judgment

One of the ways that Jeremiah sought to get his message across was through the use of symbols. At one time he stands at the door of the temple and uses it as a backdrop. At another time he uses a linen belt, another time a potter's house, then a clay jar, later a basket of figs and then a yoke. We will look at these symbols and the messages that accompany them.

As we ponder the symbols of Jeremiah, we will touch on the major themes of his ministry:

☐ The defamation of the temple and the practice of false religion
☐ The breaking of the covenant bond with God
☐ The right of God to judge Judah for their sin
☐ Judah's spiritual adultery with false gods
☐ The failure of Judah's spiritual leaders
☐ God's promised blessing for the captives
☐ God's judgment of all the nations
☐ Jeremiah's experience of opposition from the false prophets
☐ God's promise to restore people to the land after the period of judgment

Through all the symbols and themes and the proclamations of judgment there is a commitment of love. Through Jeremiah, God says:

I will make an everlasting covenant with them: I will never stop doing good to them, and I will inspire them to fear me, so that they will never turn away from me. I will rejoice in doing them good and will assuredly plant them in this land with all my heart and soul. This is what the LORD says: As I have brought all this great calamity on this people, so I will give them all the prosperity I have promised them. (Jer 32:40-42)

When you stop to think about it, the prophets do speak of the future. God promised Israel a future on the other side of judgment and sin. It will be a time of peace, love and prosperity. A time of joy beyond which we can hardly imagine. The good news is that he invites those who have joined his people through faith in his son, Jesus Christ, to that future as well.

Outline

1/ Jeremiah 1 ——————————— Prophet to the Nations

2/ Jeremiah 3:6—4:4 ——————— The Call to Return

3/ Jeremiah 5 ——————————— Searching for Faithfulness

4/ Jeremiah 7:1–20 ———————— Empty Religion

5/ Jeremiah 10:1–16 ———————— God or Idols?

6/ Jeremiah 12 ————————— An Honest Complaint

7/ Jeremiah 13 ————————— Spoiled Bond

8/ Jeremiah 17:5–18 ———————— Blessings in Troubled Times

9/ Jeremiah 18:1–17 ———————— God's Shaping Hand

10/ Jeremiah 22 ————————— To Know the Lord

11/ Jeremiah 23 ————————— A Divine Coup

12/ Jeremiah 24 ————————— Living with God's Judgment

13/ Jeremiah 25:15–38 ——————— International Judgment

14/ Jeremiah 27 ————————— How to Prosper Anyway

15/ Jeremiah 28 ————————— Destroying False Hope

16/ Jeremiah 29:1–23 ———————— Living as Exiles

17/ Jeremiah 31 ————————— Restoration

18/ Jeremiah 32:1–25 ———————— The Promise of Renewed Land

19/ Jeremiah 33 ————————— The Sure and Certain Promise

20/ Jeremiah 36 ————————— The Burning Scroll

21/ Jeremiah 38 ————————— Sunk in the Mud

22/ Jeremiah 44 ————————— Self-Destruction

23/ Jeremiah 50:1–20 ———————— Babylon Shouldn't Gloat

24/ Jeremiah 52 ————————— Jerusalem Plundered

1 / *Jeremiah 1*
Prophet to the Nations

MAYBE IT'S BECAUSE I was in college in the sixties, but I've always wanted to do something significant with my life, to change the world. For this reason, coming into a relationship with God through Jesus Christ after my freshman year was exciting. What could be more meaningful than giving my life to God?

I've been following him for a couple of decades now. I have found it meaningful and fulfilling. But doing something significant wasn't quite what I thought it would be. Somehow I thought that making a difference would feel good and elicit loads of affirmation and appreciation from others. Well, sometimes it does and sometimes it doesn't! Jeremiah was called by God to a life of great meaning and significance. He also found lots of trouble. Why then did he do it? Read on and see.

 Warming Up to God Describe a time when you were given the opportunity to do something important. How did you feel?

 Read Jeremiah 1.

1 The words of Jeremiah son of Hilkiah, one of the priests at Anathoth in the territory of Benjamin. ²The word of the LORD came to him in the thirteenth year of the reign of Josiah son of Amon king of Judah, ³and through the reign of Jehoiakim son of Josiah king of Judah, down to the fifth month of the eleventh year of Zedekiah son of Josiah king of Judah, when the people of Jerusalem went into exile.

⁴The word of the LORD came to me, saying,

⁵"Before I formed you in the womb I knew*ᵃ* you,
before you were born I set you apart;
I appointed you as a prophet to the nations."

⁶"Ah, Sovereign LORD," I said, "I do not know how to speak; I am only a child."

⁷But the LORD said to me, "Do not say, 'I am only a child.' You must go to everyone I send you to and say whatever I command you. ⁸Do not be afraid of them, for I am with you and will rescue you," declares the LORD.

⁹Then the LORD reached out his hand and touched my mouth and said to me, "Now, I have put my words in your mouth. ¹⁰See, today I appoint you over nations and kingdoms to uproot and tear down, to destroy and overthrow, to build and to plant."

¹¹The word of the LORD came to me: "What do you see, Jeremiah?"

"I see the branch of an almond tree," I replied.

¹²The LORD said to me, "You have seen correctly, for I am watching*ᵇ* to see that my word is fulfilled."

¹³The word of the LORD came to me again: "What do you see?"

"I see a boiling pot, tilting away from the north," I answered.

¹⁴The LORD said to me, "From the north disaster will be poured out on all who live in the land. ¹⁵I am about to summon all the peoples of the northern kingdoms," declares the LORD.

"Their kings will come and set up their thrones
in the entrance of the gates of Jerusalem;
they will come against all her surrounding walls
and against all the towns of Judah.
¹⁶I will pronounce my judgments on my people
because of their wickedness in forsaking me,
in burning incense to other gods
and in worshiping what their hands have made.

¹⁷"Get yourself ready! Stand up and say to them whatever I command you. Do not be terrified by them, or I will terrify you before them. ¹⁸Today I have made you a fortified city, an iron pillar and a bronze wall to stand against the whole land—against the kings of Judah, its officials, its priests and the people of the land. ¹⁹They will fight against you but will not overcome you, for I am with you and will rescue you," declares the LORD.

ᵃ5 Or *chose*   *ᵇ12* The Hebrew for *watching* sounds like the Hebrew for *almond tree.*

Discovering the Word 1. The first three verses set the historical context. Jeremiah's ministry lasted about forty years, through one good king and then two wicked ones. From verses 1–3 alone, what do you think his ministry might have been like? 2. Describe Jeremiah's call in your own words (vv. 4–10). 3. How does the word of the Lord shape Jeremiah's identity (vv. 4–10)? 4. Jeremiah gets practice learning to see and hear God. What two pictures is he given, and how would each help the young prophet grow in his calling (vv. 11–16)? 5. Jeremiah's message will not be well received. What help does God offer him (vv. 17–19)?

Applying the Word 1. God's Word shapes the identity of all who hear it. How has it shaped you? 2. God addressed Jeremiah's fears of being too immature and inadequate. Are there ways that God has addressed your fears? 3. How might God's promise of protection and expectation of obedience be helpful for the challenges you face?

Responding in Prayer We are all called to witness of Christ's work. Pray that God will shape you into a servant who testifies of his work in you.

Jeremiah 2:1—3:5

2 The word of the LORD came to me: ²"Go and proclaim in the hearing of Jerusalem:

" 'I remember the devotion of your
      youth,
   how as a bride you loved me
and followed me through the desert,
   through a land not sown.
³Israel was holy to the LORD,
   the firstfruits of his harvest;
all who devoured her were held guilty,
   and disaster overtook them,' "
                              declares the LORD.

⁴Hear the word of the LORD, O house of Jacob,
   all you clans of the house of Israel.

⁵This is what the LORD says:

"What fault did your fathers find in me,
   that they strayed so far from me?
They followed worthless idols
   and became worthless themselves.
⁶They did not ask, 'Where is the LORD,
   who brought us up out of Egypt
and led us through the barren wilderness,
   through a land of deserts and rifts,
a land of drought and darkness,ᶜ
   a land where no one travels and no one
      lives?'
⁷I brought you into a fertile land
   to eat its fruit and rich produce.
But you came and defiled my land
   and made my inheritance detestable.
⁸The priests did not ask,
   'Where is the LORD?'

Those who deal with the law did not know
      me;
   the leaders rebelled against me.
The prophets prophesied by Baal,
   following worthless idols.

⁹"Therefore I bring charges against you again,"
                              declares the LORD.
"And I will bring charges against your
      children's children.
¹⁰Cross over to the coasts of Kittimᵈ and look,
   send to Kedarᵉ and observe closely;
   see if there has ever been anything like this:
¹¹Has a nation ever changed its gods?
   (Yet they are not gods at all.)
But my people have exchanged theirᶠ Glory
   for worthless idols.
¹²Be appalled at this, O heavens,
   and shudder with great horror,"
                              declares the LORD.
¹³"My people have committed two sins:
   They have forsaken me,
      the spring of living water,
   and have dug their own cisterns,
      broken cisterns that cannot hold water.
¹⁴Is Israel a servant, a slave by birth?
   Why then has he become plunder?
¹⁵Lions have roared;
   they have growled at him.
They have laid waste his land;
   his towns are burned and deserted.
¹⁶Also, the men of Memphisᵍ and Tahpanhes

ᶜ6 Or *and the shadow of death*   ᵈ10 That is, Cyprus and western coastlands   ᵉ10 The home of Bedouin tribes in the Syro-Arabian desert   ᶠ11 Masoretic Text; an ancient Hebrew scribal tradition *my* ᵍ16 Hebrew *Noph* have shaved the crown of your head.[h]

¹⁷Have you not brought this on yourselves
  by forsaking the LORD your God
  when he led you in the way?
¹⁸Now why go to Egypt
  to drink water from the Shihor[i]?
And why go to Assyria
  to drink water from the River[j]?
¹⁹Your wickedness will punish you;
  your backsliding will rebuke you.
Consider then and realize
  how evil and bitter it is for you
when you forsake the LORD your God
  and have no awe of me,"
          declares the Lord, the LORD Almighty.

²⁰"Long ago you broke off your yoke
  and tore off your bonds;
  you said, 'I will not serve you!'
Indeed, on every high hill
  and under every spreading tree
  you lay down as a prostitute.
²¹I had planted you like a choice vine
  of sound and reliable stock.
How then did you turn against me
  into a corrupt, wild vine?
²²Although you wash yourself with soda
  and use an abundance of soap,
  the stain of your guilt is still before me,"
          declares the Sovereign LORD.
²³"How can you say, 'I am not defiled;
  I have not run after the Baals'?
See how you behaved in the valley;
  consider what you have done.
You are a swift she-camel
  running here and there,
²⁴a wild donkey accustomed to the desert,
  sniffing the wind in her craving—
  in her heat who can restrain her?
Any males that pursue her need not tire
      themselves;
  at mating time they will find her.
²⁵Do not run until your feet are bare
  and your throat is dry.
But you said, 'It's no use!
  I love foreign gods,
  and I must go after them.'

²⁶"As a thief is disgraced when he is caught,
  so the house of Israel is disgraced—
they, their kings and their officials,
  their priests and their prophets.
²⁷They say to wood, 'You are my father,'

and to stone, 'You gave me birth.'
They have turned their backs to me
  and not their faces;
yet when they are in trouble, they say,
  'Come and save us!'
²⁸Where then are the gods you made for
      yourselves?
Let them come if they can save you
  when you are in trouble!
For you have as many gods
  as you have towns, O Judah.

²⁹"Why do you bring charges against me?
  You have all rebelled against me,"
          declares the LORD.
³⁰"In vain I punished your people;
  they did not respond to correction.
Your sword has devoured your prophets
  like a ravening lion.

³¹"You of this generation, consider the word of
the LORD:

"Have I been a desert to Israel
  or a land of great darkness?
Why do my people say, 'We are free to roam;
  we will come to you no more'?
³²Does a maiden forget her jewelry,
  a bride her wedding ornaments?
Yet my people have forgotten me,
  days without number.
³³How skilled you are at pursuing love!
  Even the worst of women can learn from
      your ways.
³⁴On your clothes men find
  the lifeblood of the innocent poor,
  though you did not catch them breaking in.
Yet in spite of all this
³⁵ you say, 'I am innocent;
  he is not angry with me.'
But I will pass judgment on you
  because you say, 'I have not sinned.'
³⁶Why do you go about so much,
  changing your ways?
You will be disappointed by Egypt
  as you were by Assyria.
³⁷You will also leave that place
  with your hands on your head,
for the LORD has rejected those you trust;
  you will not be helped by them.

^h16 Or *have cracked your skull*   ⁱ18 That is, a branch of the Nile
^j18 That is, the Euphrates

3 "If a man divorces his wife
　and she leaves him and marries another
　　man,
should he return to her again?
　Would not the land be completely defiled?
But you have lived as a prostitute with many
　　lovers—
　would you now return to me?"
　　　　　　　　　　　declares the LORD.
²"Look up to the barren heights and see.
　Is there any place where you have not been
　　ravished?
By the roadside you sat waiting for lovers,
　sat like a nomad[k] in the desert.

You have defiled the land
　with your prostitution and wickedness.
³Therefore the showers have been withheld,
　and no spring rains have fallen.
Yet you have the brazen look of a prostitute;
　you refuse to blush with shame.
⁴Have you not just called to me:
　'My Father, my friend from my youth,
⁵will you always be angry?
　Will your wrath continue forever?'
This is how you talk,
　but you do all the evil you can."

k 2 Or an Arab

---

2 / *Jeremiah 3:6—4:4*
The Call to Return

"COME BACK! COME back!" Whether called out to a small child, a rebellious teenager, a wandering spouse or even a straying pet, the words ring with desperation. Spoken by God to sinful humans, the words are heartbreaking. God the Creator allows his people the freedom of wandering from him. Still, he persists in calling them back to himself.

 Warming Up to God   In what areas might the Lord be calling you back to a closer walk with him?

 Read Jeremiah 3:6—4:4.

---

⁶During the reign of King Josiah, the LORD said to me, "Have you seen what faithless Israel has done? She has gone up on every high hill and under every spreading tree and has committed adultery there. ⁷I thought that after she had done all this she would return to me but she did not, and her unfaithful sister Judah saw it. ⁸I gave faithless Israel her certificate of divorce and sent her away because of all her adulteries. Yet I saw that her unfaithful sister Judah had no fear; she also went out and committed adultery. ⁹Because Israel's immorality mattered so little to her, she defiled the land and committed adultery with stone and wood. ¹⁰In spite of all this, her unfaithful sister Judah did not return to me with all her heart, but only in pretense," declares the LORD.

¹¹The LORD said to me, "Faithless Israel is more righteous than unfaithful Judah. ¹²Go, proclaim this message toward the north:

" 'Return, faithless Israel,' declares the LORD,

'I will frown on you no longer,
for I am merciful,' declares the LORD,
'I will not be angry forever.
¹³Only acknowledge your guilt—
　you have rebelled against the LORD your
　　God,
you have scattered your favors to foreign gods
　under every spreading tree,
　and have not obeyed me,' "
　　　　　　　　　　　declares the LORD.

¹⁴"Return, faithless people," declares the LORD, "for I am your husband. I will choose you—one from a town and two from a clan—and bring you to Zion. ¹⁵Then I will give you shepherds after my own heart, who will lead you with knowledge and understanding. ¹⁶In those days, when your numbers have increased greatly in the land," declares the LORD, "men will no longer say, 'The ark of the covenant of the LORD.' It will never enter their minds or be remembered; it will not be missed,

nor will another one be made. ¹⁷At that time they will call Jerusalem The Throne of the LORD, and all nations will gather in Jerusalem to honor the name of the LORD. No longer will they follow the stubbornness of their evil hearts. ¹⁸In those days the house of Judah will join the house of Israel, and together they will come from a northern land to the land I gave your forefathers as an inheritance.

¹⁹"I myself said,

" 'How gladly would I treat you like sons
   and give you a desirable land,
   the most beautiful inheritance of any
      nation.'
I thought you would call me 'Father'
   and not turn away from following me.
²⁰But like a woman unfaithful to her husband,
   so you have been unfaithful to me, O house
      of Israel,"

declares the LORD.

²¹A cry is heard on the barren heights,
   the weeping and pleading of the people of
      Israel,
because they have perverted their ways
   and have forgotten the LORD their God.

²²"Return, faithless people;
   I will cure you of backsliding."

"Yes, we will come to you,
   for you are the LORD our God.
²³Surely the ⌊idolatrous⌋ commotion on the hills
   and mountains is a deception;
surely in the LORD our God

is the salvation of Israel.
²⁴From our youth shameful gods have
      consumed
   the fruits of our fathers' labor—
their flocks and herds,
   their sons and daughters.
²⁵Let us lie down in our shame,
   and let our disgrace cover us.
We have sinned against the LORD our God,
   both we and our fathers;
from our youth till this day
   we have not obeyed the LORD our God."

4 "If you will return, O Israel,
   return to me,"

declares the LORD.

"If you put your detestable idols out of my
      sight
   and no longer go astray,
²and if in a truthful, just and righteous way
   you swear, 'As surely as the LORD lives,'
then the nations will be blessed by him
   and in him they will glory."

³This is what the LORD says to the men of Judah and to Jerusalem:

"Break up your unplowed ground
   and do not sow among thorns.
⁴Circumcise yourselves to the LORD,
   circumcise your hearts,
   you men of Judah and people of Jerusalem,
or my wrath will break out and burn like fire
   because of the evil you have done—
   burn with no one to quench it.

Discovering the Word 1. How had Israel been unfaithful to God (3:6–13)? 2. What does God promise if only Israel will return to him (3:14–18)? 3. What hopes did the Lord have for Israel (3:19–20)? 4. How do the people express their repentance (3:21–25)? 5. What warnings does God give Israel if they refuse to return to him (4:1–4)?

Applying the Word 1. Where have you given in to the temptation to be unfaithful to the Lord? (Think especially of "small" ways easily overlooked or excused.) 2. How do the Lord's promised blessings for repentance speak to you right now?

 Responding in Prayer Confess to the Lord any wanderings and rebellion against him. Thank him for his grace which keeps calling you back.

Jeremiah 4:5–31

⁵"Announce in Judah and proclaim in
    Jerusalem and say:
  'Sound the trumpet throughout the land!'
Cry aloud and say:
  'Gather together!
Let us flee to the fortified cities!'
⁶Raise the signal to go to Zion!
  Flee for safety without delay!
For I am bringing disaster from the north,
  even terrible destruction."

⁷A lion has come out of his lair;
  a destroyer of nations has set out.
He has left his place
  to lay waste your land.
Your towns will lie in ruins
  without inhabitant.
⁸So put on sackcloth,
  lament and wail,
for the fierce anger of the LORD
  has not turned away from us.

⁹"In that day," declares the LORD,
  "the king and the officials will lose heart,
the priests will be horrified,
  and the prophets will be appalled."

¹⁰Then I said, "Ah, Sovereign LORD, how completely you have deceived this people and Jerusalem by saying, 'You will have peace,' when the
sword is at our throats."

¹¹At that time this people and Jerusalem will be
told, "A scorching wind from the barren heights
in the desert blows toward my people, but not to
winnow or cleanse; ¹²a wind too strong for that
comes from me.ˡ Now I pronounce my judgments against them."

¹³Look! He advances like the clouds,
  his chariots come like a whirlwind,
his horses are swifter than eagles.
  Woe to us! We are ruined!
¹⁴O Jerusalem, wash the evil from your heart
  and be saved.
How long will you harbor wicked thoughts?
¹⁵A voice is announcing from Dan,
  proclaiming disaster from the hills of
    Ephraim.
¹⁶Tell this to the nations,
  proclaim it to Jerusalem:

'A besieging army is coming from a distant
  land,
raising a war cry against the cities of Judah.
¹⁷They surround her like men guarding a field,
  because she has rebelled against me,' "
                declares the LORD.
¹⁸"Your own conduct and actions
  have brought this upon you.
This is your punishment.
  How bitter it is!
  How it pierces to the heart!"

¹⁹Oh, my anguish, my anguish!
  I writhe in pain.
Oh, the agony of my heart!
  My heart pounds within me,
  I cannot keep silent.
For I have heard the sound of the trumpet;
  I have heard the battle cry.
²⁰Disaster follows disaster;
  the whole land lies in ruins.
In an instant my tents are destroyed,
  my shelter in a moment.
²¹How long must I see the battle standard
  and hear the sound of the trumpet?

²²"My people are fools;
  they do not know me.
They are senseless children;
  they have no understanding.
They are skilled in doing evil;
  they know not how to do good."

²³I looked at the earth,
  and it was formless and empty;
and at the heavens,
  and their light was gone.
²⁴I looked at the mountains,
  and they were quaking;
all the hills were swaying.
²⁵I looked, and there were no people;
  every bird in the sky had flown away.
²⁶I looked, and the fruitful land was a desert;
  all its towns lay in ruins
before the LORD, before his fierce anger.

²⁷This is what the LORD says:

"The whole land will be ruined,
  though I will not destroy it completely.

ˡ12 Or comes at my command

²⁸Therefore the earth will mourn
    and the heavens above grow dark,
because I have spoken and will not relent,
    I have decided and will not turn back."

²⁹At the sound of horsemen and archers
    every town takes to flight.
Some go into the thickets;
    some climb up among the rocks.
All the towns are deserted;
    no one lives in them.

³⁰What are you doing, O devastated one?
    Why dress yourself in scarlet

and put on jewels of gold?
Why shade your eyes with paint?
    You adorn yourself in vain.
Your lovers despise you;
    they seek your life.

³¹I hear a cry as of a woman in labor,
    a groan as of one bearing her first child—
the cry of the Daughter of Zion gasping for
        breath,
    stretching out her hands and saying,
"Alas! I am fainting;
    my life is given over to murderers."

3 / *Jeremiah 5*
Searching for Faithfulness

A NEWSPAPER AD reads "Christian carpenter. Reliable. Integrity counts." Is honesty so unusual that it merits advertisement as a unique feature of a person's work? This carpenter apparently thinks so. He is publicly committing himself to integrity and is willing to stake his work on his word. This is the sort of person God is looking for.

Warming Up to God To what extent would you say honesty characterizes your relationship with God?

Read Jeremiah 5.

5 "Go up and down the streets of
        Jerusalem,
    look around and consider,
    search through her squares.
If you can find but one person
    who deals honestly and seeks the truth,
    I will forgive this city.
²Although they say, 'As surely as the LORD
        lives,'
    still they are swearing falsely."

³O LORD, do not your eyes look for truth?
    You struck them, but they felt no pain;
    you crushed them, but they refused
        correction.
They made their faces harder than stone
    and refused to repent.
⁴I thought, "These are only the poor;
    they are foolish,
for they do not know the way of the LORD,
    the requirements of their God.
⁵So I will go to the leaders
    and speak to them;

surely they know the way of the LORD,
    the requirements of their God."
But with one accord they too had broken off
        the yoke
    and torn off the bonds.
⁶Therefore a lion from the forest will attack
        them,
    a wolf from the desert will ravage them,
a leopard will lie in wait near their towns
    to tear to pieces any who venture out,
for their rebellion is great
    and their backslidings many.

⁷"Why should I forgive you?
    Your children have forsaken me
    and sworn by gods that are not gods.
I supplied all their needs,
    yet they committed adultery
    and thronged to the houses of prostitutes.
⁸They are well-fed, lusty stallions,
    each neighing for another man's wife.
⁹Should I not punish them for this?"
    declares the LORD.

"Should I not avenge myself
   on such a nation as this?

¹⁰"Go through her vineyards and ravage them,
   but do not destroy them completely.
Strip off her branches,
   for these people do not belong to the LORD.
¹¹The house of Israel and the house of Judah
   have been utterly unfaithful to me,"
               declares the LORD.
¹²They have lied about the LORD;
   they said, "He will do nothing!
No harm will come to us;
   we will never see sword or famine.
¹³The prophets are but wind
   and the word is not in them;
   so let what they say be done to them."

¹⁴Therefore this is what the LORD God Almighty
says:

"Because the people have spoken these words,
   I will make my words in your mouth a fire
   and these people the wood it consumes.
¹⁵O house of Israel," declares the LORD,
   "I am bringing a distant nation against
      you—
  an ancient and enduring nation,
   a people whose language you do not know,
   whose speech you do not understand.
¹⁶Their quivers are like an open grave;
   all of them are mighty warriors.
¹⁷They will devour your harvests and food,
   devour your sons and daughters;
they will devour your flocks and herds,
   devour your vines and fig trees.
With the sword they will destroy
   the fortified cities in which you trust.

¹⁸"Yet even in those days," declares the LORD, "I
will not destroy you completely. ¹⁹And when the
people ask, 'Why has the LORD our God done all
this to us?' you will tell them, 'As you have forsaken me and served foreign gods in your own
land, so now you will serve foreigners in a land
not your own.'

²⁰"Announce this to the house of Jacob
   and proclaim it in Judah:
²¹Hear this, you foolish and senseless people,
   who have eyes but do not see,
   who have ears but do not hear:
²²Should you not fear me?" declares the LORD.
   "Should you not tremble in my presence?
I made the sand a boundary for the sea,
   an everlasting barrier it cannot cross.
The waves may roll, but they cannot prevail;
   they may roar, but they cannot cross it.
²³But these people have stubborn and rebellious
     hearts;
   they have turned aside and gone away.
²⁴They do not say to themselves,
  'Let us fear the LORD our God,
who gives autumn and spring rains in season,
   who assures us of the regular weeks of
     harvest.'
²⁵Your wrongdoings have kept these away;
   your sins have deprived you of good.

²⁶"Among my people are wicked men
   who lie in wait like men who snare birds
   and like those who set traps to catch men.
²⁷Like cages full of birds,
   their houses are full of deceit;
they have become rich and powerful
²⁸ and have grown fat and sleek.
   Their evil deeds have no limit;
   they do not plead the case of the fatherless
     to win it,
   they do not defend the rights of the poor.
²⁹Should I not punish them for this?"
   declares the LORD.
   "Should I not avenge myself
   on such a nation as this?

³⁰"A horrible and shocking thing
   has happened in the land:
³¹The prophets prophesy lies,
   the priests rule by their own authority,
and my people love it this way.
   But what will you do in the end?

 Discovering the Word 1. What was God searching for in the streets of Jerusalem (vv. 1–5)? 2. What did he find at different levels of society (vv. 2–5)? 3. How is mercy written into the judgments of God (vv. 6–19)? 4. How had the people lied about God and his prophets (vv. 12–13, 31)? 5. What truths about God were they ignoring or denying (vv. 21–25)?

Applying the Word 1. How will our relationship with the Lord change if we remember that he is the God of truth and hates lying? 2. In what areas can you be more honest with God, yourself and other people?

Responding in Prayer Come to the Lord in honesty about an area of life where you tend to be less than candid. Come boldly because you know God welcomes honesty and he is merciful.

Jeremiah 6

6 "Flee for safety, people of Benjamin!
Flee from Jerusalem!
Sound the trumpet in Tekoa!
Raise the signal over Beth Hakkerem!
For disaster looms out of the north,
even terrible destruction.
²I will destroy the Daughter of Zion,
so beautiful and delicate.
³Shepherds with their flocks will come against
her;
they will pitch their tents around her,
each tending his own portion."

⁴"Prepare for battle against her!
Arise, let us attack at noon!
But, alas, the daylight is fading,
and the shadows of evening grow long.
⁵So arise, let us attack at night
and destroy her fortresses!"

⁶This is what the Lord Almighty says:

"Cut down the trees
and build siege ramps against Jerusalem.
This city must be punished;
it is filled with oppression.
⁷As a well pours out its water,
so she pours out her wickedness.
Violence and destruction resound in her;
her sickness and wounds are ever before
me.
⁸Take warning, O Jerusalem,
or I will turn away from you
and make your land desolate
so no one can live in it."

⁹This is what the Lord Almighty says:

"Let them glean the remnant of Israel
as thoroughly as a vine;
pass your hand over the branches again,
like one gathering grapes."

¹⁰To whom can I speak and give warning?
Who will listen to me?
Their ears are closed*ᵐ*
so they cannot hear.
The word of the Lord is offensive to them;

they find no pleasure in it.
¹¹But I am full of the wrath of the Lord,
and I cannot hold it in.

"Pour it out on the children in the street
and on the young men gathered together;
both husband and wife will be caught in it,
and the old, those weighed down with
years.
¹²Their houses will be turned over to others,
together with their fields and their wives,
when I stretch out my hand
against those who live in the land,"
declares the Lord.
¹³"From the least to the greatest,
all are greedy for gain;
prophets and priests alike,
all practice deceit.
¹⁴They dress the wound of my people
as though it were not serious.
'Peace, peace,' they say,
when there is no peace.
¹⁵Are they ashamed of their loathsome conduct?
No, they have no shame at all;
they do not even know how to blush.
So they will fall among the fallen;
they will be brought down when I punish
them,"
says the Lord.

¹⁶This is what the Lord says:

"Stand at the crossroads and look;
ask for the ancient paths,
ask where the good way is, and walk in it,
and you will find rest for your souls.
But you said, 'We will not walk in it.'
¹⁷I appointed watchmen over you and said,
'Listen to the sound of the trumpet!'
But you said, 'We will not listen.'
¹⁸Therefore hear, O nations;
observe, O witnesses,
what will happen to them.
¹⁹Hear, O earth:
I am bringing disaster on this people,

ᵐ10 Hebrew uncircumcised

the fruit of their schemes,
because they have not listened to my words
   and have rejected my law.
²⁰What do I care about incense from Sheba
   or sweet calamus from a distant land?
Your burnt offerings are not acceptable;
   your sacrifices do not please me."

²¹Therefore this is what the Lᴏʀᴅ says:

"I will put obstacles before this people.
Fathers and sons alike will stumble over
      them;
   neighbors and friends will perish."

²²This is what the Lᴏʀᴅ says:

"Look, an army is coming
   from the land of the north;
a great nation is being stirred up
   from the ends of the earth.
²³They are armed with bow and spear;
   they are cruel and show no mercy.
They sound like the roaring sea
   as they ride on their horses;
they come like men in battle formation
   to attack you, O Daughter of Zion."

²⁴We have heard reports about them,
   and our hands hang limp.

Anguish has gripped us,
   pain like that of a woman in labor.
²⁵Do not go out to the fields
   or walk on the roads,
for the enemy has a sword,
   and there is terror on every side.
²⁶O my people, put on sackcloth
   and roll in ashes;
mourn with bitter wailing
   as for an only son,
for suddenly the destroyer
   will come upon us.

²⁷"I have made you a tester of metals
   and my people the ore,
that you may observe
   and test their ways.
²⁸They are all hardened rebels,
   going about to slander.
They are bronze and iron;
   they all act corruptly.
²⁹The bellows blow fiercely
   to burn away the lead with fire,
but the refining goes on in vain;
   the wicked are not purged out.
³⁰They are called rejected silver,
   because the Lᴏʀᴅ has rejected them."

---

4 / *Jeremiah 7:1–20*
Empty Religion

I AM AN ordained minster. I love the church. But there are days when I have my doubts about "organized" religion. I'm not exactly proud of the Crusades, the treatment of the Jews in the Middle Ages or the more recent fundraising scandals of the television evangelists. There are times when it seems that politics, power and social concerns are the primary moving and shaping forces of our churches. I am reminded on occasion that all that is done in the name of the Lord is not necessarily from the Lord. In front of the newly renovated temple Jeremiah called the people of Judah to examine their motives for their religious pursuits. What a shock it must have been for those who heard. Today, Jeremiah calls us to ponder: "Why do I serve God? Why am I going to church?"

 Warming Up to God What would you do if someone stood at the door of your newly renovated church and told you and everyone who entered that you were hypocrites under the judgment of God?

 Read Jeremiah 7:1–20.

7 This is the word that came to Jeremiah from the Lᴏʀᴅ: ²"Stand at the gate of the Lᴏʀᴅ's house and there proclaim this message:

" 'Hear the word of the Lᴏʀᴅ, all you people of Judah who come through these gates to worship the Lᴏʀᴅ. ³This is what the Lᴏʀᴅ Almighty, the God of Israel, says: Reform your ways and your actions, and I will let you live in this place. ⁴Do not trust in deceptive words and say, "This is the temple of the LORD, the temple of the LORD, the temple of the LORD!" ⁵If you really change your ways and your actions and deal with each other justly, ⁶if you do not oppress the alien, the fatherless or the widow and do not shed innocent blood in this place, and if you do not follow other gods to your own harm, ⁷then I will let you live in this place, in the land I gave your forefathers for ever and ever. ⁸But look, you are trusting in deceptive words that are worthless.

⁹" 'Will you steal and murder, commit adultery and perjury,ⁿ burn incense to Baal and follow other gods you have not known, ¹⁰and then come and stand before me in this house, which bears my Name, and say, "We are safe"—safe to do all these detestable things? ¹¹Has this house, which bears my Name, become a den of robbers to you? But I have been watching! declares the LORD.

¹²" 'Go now to the place in Shiloh where I first made a dwelling for my Name, and see what I did to it because of the wickedness of my people Israel. ¹³While you were doing all these things, declares the LORD, I spoke to you again and again, but you did not listen; I called you, but you did

not answer. ¹⁴Therefore, what I did to Shiloh I will now do to the house that bears my Name, the temple you trust in, the place I gave to you and your fathers. ¹⁵I will thrust you from my presence, just as I did all your brothers, the people of Ephraim.'

¹⁶"So do not pray for this people nor offer any plea or petition for them; do not plead with me, for I will not listen to you. ¹⁷Do you not see what they are doing in the towns of Judah and in the streets of Jerusalem? ¹⁸The children gather wood, the fathers light the fire, and the women knead the dough and make cakes of bread for the Queen of Heaven. They pour out drink offerings to other gods to provoke me to anger. ¹⁹But am I the one they are provoking? declares the LORD. Are they not rather harming themselves, to their own shame?

²⁰" 'Therefore this is what the Sovereign LORD says: My anger and my wrath will be poured out on this place, on man and beast, on the trees of the field and on the fruit of the ground, and it will burn and not be quenched.

ⁿ9 Or *and swear by false gods*

 Discovering the Word 1. Jeremiah stands at the door of the temple and confronts those who enter. What is his message in verses 1–11? 2. In verse 4 Jeremiah repeats the phrase "The temple of the LORD" three times. What do you think he is getting at? 3. Under the reign of Josiah, Judah's last good king, the temple had been renovated and the law, which had been lost, was rediscovered. How was the law being handled by the people (vv. 4–9)? 4. How does the experience of Shiloh illustrate Jeremiah's message (vv. 12–20)? 5. God was angry with their idolatry and promised to judge it (vv. 16–20). Why do you think he was so upset with their false worship?

Applying the Word 1. In verse 11 God declares that he is watching. If God were to tell you that he was especially watching your church, what do you think he would see and say? 2. God, not the temple, should have been the object of their faith. How is it possible that the focus of our faith can drift from a person, God, to an object, like the temple? 3. What can we do to see that our own personal worship is pleasing to God?

Responding in Prayer Offer your praise to the God who is worthy of our worship.

Jeremiah 7:21—9:26

²¹" 'This is what the LORD Almighty, the God of Israel, says: Go ahead, add your burnt offerings to your other sacrifices and eat the meat yourselves! ²²For when I brought your forefathers out of Egypt and spoke to them, I did not just give them commands about burnt offerings and sacrifices, ²³but I gave them this command: Obey me, and

I will be your God and you will be my people. Walk in all the ways I command you, that it may go well with you. ²⁴But they did not listen or pay attention; instead, they followed the stubborn inclinations of their evil hearts. They went backward and not forward. ²⁵From the time your forefathers left Egypt until now, day after day, again and again I sent you my servants the prophets. ²⁶But they did not listen to me or pay attention. They were stiff-necked and did more evil than their forefathers.'

²⁷"When you tell them all this, they will not listen to you; when you call to them, they will not answer. ²⁸Therefore say to them, 'This is the nation that has not obeyed the Lord its God or responded to correction. Truth has perished; it has vanished from their lips. ²⁹Cut off your hair and throw it away; take up a lament on the barren heights, for the Lord has rejected and abandoned this generation that is under his wrath.

³⁰" 'The people of Judah have done evil in my eyes, declares the Lord. They have set up their detestable idols in the house that bears my Name and have defiled it. ³¹They have built the high places of Topheth in the Valley of Ben Hinnom to burn their sons and daughters in the fire—something I did not command, nor did it enter my mind. ³²So beware, the days are coming, declares the Lord, when people will no longer call it Topheth or the Valley of Ben Hinnom, but the Valley of Slaughter, for they will bury the dead in Topheth until there is no more room. ³³Then the carcasses of this people will become food for the birds of the air and the beasts of the earth, and there will be no one to frighten them away. ³⁴I will bring an end to the sounds of joy and gladness and to the voices of bride and bridegroom in the towns of Judah and the streets of Jerusalem, for the land will become desolate.

8 " 'At that time, declares the Lord, the bones of the kings and officials of Judah, the bones of the priests and prophets, and the bones of the people of Jerusalem will be removed from their graves. ²They will be exposed to the sun and the moon and all the stars of the heavens, which they have loved and served and which they have followed and consulted and worshiped. They will not be gathered up or buried, but will be like refuse lying on the ground. ³Wherever I banish them, all the survivors of this evil nation will prefer death to life, declares the Lord Almighty.'

⁴"Say to them, 'This is what the Lord says:

" 'When men fall down, do they not get up?
    When a man turns away, does he not
        return?
⁵Why then have these people turned away?
    Why does Jerusalem always turn away?

They cling to deceit;
    they refuse to return.
⁶I have listened attentively,
    but they do not say what is right.
No one repents of his wickedness,
    saying, "What have I done?"
Each pursues his own course
    like a horse charging into battle.
⁷Even the stork in the sky
    knows her appointed seasons,
and the dove, the swift and the thrush
    observe the time of their migration.
But my people do not know
    the requirements of the Lord.

⁸" 'How can you say, "We are wise,
    for we have the law of the Lord,"
when actually the lying pen of the scribes
    has handled it falsely?
⁹The wise will be put to shame;
    they will be dismayed and trapped.
Since they have rejected the word of the Lord,
    what kind of wisdom do they have?
¹⁰Therefore I will give their wives to other men
    and their fields to new owners.
From the least to the greatest,
    all are greedy for gain;
prophets and priests alike,
    all practice deceit.
¹¹They dress the wound of my people
    as though it were not serious.
"Peace, peace," they say,
    when there is no peace.
¹²Are they ashamed of their loathsome conduct?
    No, they have no shame at all;
    they do not even know how to blush.
So they will fall among the fallen;
    they will be brought down when they are
        punished,
                            says the Lord.

¹³" 'I will take away their harvest,
                        declares the Lord.
    There will be no grapes on the vine.
There will be no figs on the tree,
    and their leaves will wither.
What I have given them
    will be taken from them.^o' "

¹⁴"Why are we sitting here?
    Gather together!
Let us flee to the fortified cities

---

^o13 The meaning of the Hebrew for this sentence is uncertain.

and perish there!
For the LORD our God has doomed us to
    perish
and given us poisoned water to drink,
because we have sinned against him.
¹⁵We hoped for peace
but no good has come,
for a time of healing
but there was only terror.
¹⁶The snorting of the enemy's horses
is heard from Dan;
at the neighing of their stallions
the whole land trembles.
They have come to devour
the land and everything in it,
the city and all who live there."

¹⁷"See, I will send venomous snakes among
    you,
vipers that cannot be charmed,
and they will bite you,"
                                    declares the LORD.

¹⁸O my Comforterᵖ in sorrow,
my heart is faint within me.
¹⁹Listen to the cry of my people
from a land far away:
"Is the LORD not in Zion?
Is her King no longer there?"

"Why have they provoked me to anger with
    their images,
with their worthless foreign idols?"

²⁰"The harvest is past,
the summer has ended,
and we are not saved."

²¹Since my people are crushed, I am crushed;
I mourn, and horror grips me.
²²Is there no balm in Gilead?
Is there no physician there?
Why then is there no healing
for the wound of my people?

9 ¹Oh, that my head were a spring of
    water
and my eyes a fountain of tears!
I would weep day and night
for the slain of my people.
²Oh, that I had in the desert
a lodging place for travelers,
so that I might leave my people
and go away from them;
for they are all adulterers,

a crowd of unfaithful people.

³"They make ready their tongue
like a bow, to shoot lies;
it is not by truth
that they triumph�q in the land.
They go from one sin to another;
they do not acknowledge me,"
                                    declares the LORD.

⁴"Beware of your friends;
do not trust your brothers.
For every brother is a deceiver,ʳ
and every friend a slanderer.
⁵Friend deceives friend,
and no one speaks the truth.
They have taught their tongues to lie;
they weary themselves with sinning.
⁶Youˢ live in the midst of deception;
in their deceit they refuse to acknowledge
    me,"
                                    declares the LORD.

⁷Therefore this is what the LORD Almighty says:
"See, I will refine and test them,
for what else can I do
because of the sin of my people?
⁸Their tongue is a deadly arrow;
it speaks with deceit.
With his mouth each speaks cordially to his
    neighbor,
but in his heart he sets a trap for him.
⁹Should I not punish them for this?"
    declares the LORD.
"Should I not avenge myself
on such a nation as this?"

¹⁰I will weep and wail for the mountains
and take up a lament concerning the desert
    pastures.
They are desolate and untraveled,
and the lowing of cattle is not heard.
The birds of the air have fled
and the animals are gone.

¹¹"I will make Jerusalem a heap of ruins,
a haunt of jackals;
and I will lay waste the towns of Judah
so no one can live there."

¹²What man is wise enough to understand this?
Who has been instructed by the LORD and can

ᵖ18 The meaning of the Hebrew for this word is uncertain.   q3 Or
lies; / they are not valiant for truth   ʳ4 Or a deceiving Jacob
ˢ6 That is, Jeremiah (the Hebrew is singular)

explain it? Why has the land been ruined and laid waste like a desert that no one can cross?

¹³The LORD said, "It is because they have forsaken my law, which I set before them; they have not obeyed me or followed my law. ¹⁴Instead, they have followed the stubbornness of their hearts; they have followed the Baals, as their fathers taught them." ¹⁵Therefore, this is what the LORD Almighty, the God of Israel, says: "See, I will make this people eat bitter food and drink poisoned water. ¹⁶I will scatter them among nations that neither they nor their fathers have known, and I will pursue them with the sword until I have destroyed them."

¹⁷This is what the LORD Almighty says:

"Consider now! Call for the wailing women
        to come;
    send for the most skillful of them.
¹⁸Let them come quickly
    and wail over us
till our eyes overflow with tears
    and water streams from our eyelids.
¹⁹The sound of wailing is heard from Zion:
    'How ruined we are!
    How great is our shame!
We must leave our land
    because our houses are in ruins.' "

²⁰Now, O women, hear the word of the LORD;
    open your ears to the words of his mouth.
Teach your daughters how to wail;
    teach one another a lament.

²¹Death has climbed in through our windows
    and has entered our fortresses;
it has cut off the children from the streets
    and the young men from the public
        squares.

²²Say, "This is what the LORD declares:

" 'The dead bodies of men will lie
    like refuse on the open field,
like cut grain behind the reaper,
    with no one to gather them.' "

²³This is what the LORD says:

"Let not the wise man boast of his wisdom
    or the strong man boast of his strength
    or the rich man boast of his riches,
²⁴but let him who boasts boast about this:
    that he understands and knows me,
that I am the LORD, who exercises kindness,
    justice and righteousness on earth,
    for in these I delight,"

                        declares the LORD.

²⁵"The days are coming," declares the LORD, "when I will punish all who are circumcised only in the flesh— ²⁶Egypt, Judah, Edom, Ammon, Moab and all who live in the desert in distant places.ᶠ For all these nations are really uncircumcised, and even the whole house of Israel is uncircumcised in heart."

ᶠ26 Or *desert and who clip the hair by their foreheads*

---

5 / *Jeremiah 10:1–16*
God or Idols?

A GARDEN CATALOG offers inflatable owls and fake falcons to scare away small birds from your fruit trees. For best effect, the catalog says, keep moving them around. Even the dumbest bird knows that a real owl or hawk doesn't sit frozen in the same spot day after day. Like those garden fakes, the idols of the nations surrounding Israel were lifeless and powerless.

 Warming Up to God   What has been an idol to you, and how did you come to reject it and choose the Lord?

 Read Jeremiah 10:1–16.

10

Hear what the LORD says to you, O house of Israel. ²This is what the LORD says:

"Do not learn the ways of the nations
  or be terrified by signs in the sky,
  though the nations are terrified by them.
³For the customs of the peoples are worthless;
  they cut a tree out of the forest,
  and a craftsman shapes it with his chisel.
⁴They adorn it with silver and gold;
  they fasten it with hammer and nails
  so it will not totter.
⁵Like a scarecrow in a melon patch,
  their idols cannot speak;
they must be carried
  because they cannot walk.
Do not fear them;
  they can do no harm
  nor can they do any good."

⁶No one is like you, O LORD;
  you are great,
  and your name is mighty in power.
⁷Who should not revere you,
  O King of the nations?
  This is your due.
Among all the wise men of the nations
  and in all their kingdoms,
  there is no one like you.
⁸They are all senseless and foolish;
  they are taught by worthless wooden idols.
⁹Hammered silver is brought from Tarshish
  and gold from Uphaz.
What the craftsman and goldsmith have made
  is then dressed in blue and purple—
all made by skilled workers.
¹⁰But the LORD is the true God;
  he is the living God, the eternal King.
When he is angry, the earth trembles;
  the nations cannot endure his wrath.

¹¹"Tell them this: 'These gods, who did not make the heavens and the earth, will perish from the earth and from under the heavens.' "ᵘ

¹²But God made the earth by his power;
  he founded the world by his wisdom
  and stretched out the heavens by his
    understanding.
¹³When he thunders, the waters in the heavens
    roar;
  he makes clouds rise from the ends of the
    earth.
He sends lightning with the rain
  and brings out the wind from his
    storehouses.

¹⁴Everyone is senseless and without knowledge;
  every goldsmith is shamed by his idols.
His images are a fraud;
  they have no breath in them.
¹⁵They are worthless, the objects of mockery;
  when their judgment comes, they will
    perish.
¹⁶He who is the Portion of Jacob is not like
    these,
  for he is the Maker of all things,
including Israel, the tribe of his inheritance—
  the LORD Almighty is his name.

ᵘ11 The text of this verse is in Aramaic.

Discovering the Word 1. Throughout this passage how is God contrasted with idols? 2. How do idols betray their powerlessness (v. 5)? 3. Why should people revere the Lord (vv. 6–7, 10, 12–13)? 4. What will be the fate of false gods (vv. 11, 15)? 5. How is the Lord's power shown in his creation (vv. 12–13, 16)?

Applying the Word 1. How can the humorous images in this passage, especially verses 4–5, give you a fresh perspective on the idols that tempt you? 2. In what ways is the Lord superior to your most appealing idols?

Responding in Prayer Praise the Lord for being the only true God. Commit yourself again to worshiping him alone.

Jeremiah 10:17—11:23

¹⁷Gather up your belongings to leave the land,
　　you who live under siege.
¹⁸For this is what the LORD says:
　　"At this time I will hurl out
　　　those who live in this land;
　I will bring distress on them
　　so that they may be captured."

¹⁹Woe to me because of my injury!
　　My wound is incurable!
　Yet I said to myself,
　　"This is my sickness, and I must endure it."
²⁰My tent is destroyed;
　　all its ropes are snapped.
　My sons are gone from me and are no more;
　　no one is left now to pitch my tent
　　or to set up my shelter.
²¹The shepherds are senseless
　　and do not inquire of the LORD;
　so they do not prosper
　　and all their flock is scattered.
²²Listen! The report is coming—
　　a great commotion from the land of the
　　　north!
　It will make the towns of Judah desolate,
　　a haunt of jackals.

²³I know, O LORD, that a man's life is not his
　　　own;
　　it is not for man to direct his steps.
²⁴Correct me, LORD, but only with justice—
　　not in your anger,
　　lest you reduce me to nothing.
²⁵Pour out your wrath on the nations
　　that do not acknowledge you,
　　on the peoples who do not call on your
　　　name.
　For they have devoured Jacob;
　　they have devoured him completely
　　and destroyed his homeland.

11 This is the word that came to Jeremiah from the LORD: ²"Listen to the terms of this covenant and tell them to the people of Judah and to those who live in Jerusalem. ³Tell them that this is what the LORD, the God of Israel, says: 'Cursed is the man who does not obey the terms of this covenant— ⁴the terms I commanded your forefathers when I brought them out of Egypt, out of the iron-smelt-ing furnace.' I said, 'Obey me and do everything I command you, and you will be my people, and I will be your God. ⁵Then I will fulfill the oath I swore to your forefathers, to give them a land flowing with milk and honey'—the land you possess today."

I answered, "Amen, LORD."

⁶The LORD said to me, "Proclaim all these words in the towns of Judah and in the streets of Jerusalem: 'Listen to the terms of this covenant and follow them. ⁷From the time I brought your forefathers up from Egypt until today, I warned them again and again, saying, "Obey me." ⁸But they did not listen or pay attention; instead, they followed the stubbornness of their evil hearts. So I brought on them all the curses of the covenant I had commanded them to follow but that they did not keep.' "

⁹Then the LORD said to me, "There is a conspiracy among the people of Judah and those who live in Jerusalem. ¹⁰They have returned to the sins of their forefathers, who refused to listen to my words. They have followed other gods to serve them. Both the house of Israel and the house of Judah have broken the covenant I made with their forefathers. ¹¹Therefore this is what the LORD says: 'I will bring on them a disaster they cannot escape. Although they cry out to me, I will not listen to them. ¹²The towns of Judah and the people of Jerusalem will go and cry out to the gods to whom they burn incense, but they will not help them at all when disaster strikes. ¹³You have as many gods as you have towns, O Judah; and the altars you have set up to burn incense to that shameful god Baal are as many as the streets of Jerusalem.'

¹⁴"Do not pray for this people nor offer any plea or petition for them, because I will not listen when they call to me in the time of their distress.

¹⁵"What is my beloved doing in my temple
　　as she works out her evil schemes with
　　　many?
　Can consecrated meat avert ⌐your
　　punishment⌐?
　When you engage in your wickedness,
　　then you rejoice.ᵛ"

ᵛ15 Or Could consecrated meat avert your punishment? / Then you would rejoice

¹⁶The L<small>ORD</small> called you a thriving olive tree
  with fruit beautiful in form.
But with the roar of a mighty storm
  he will set it on fire,
  and its branches will be broken.

¹⁷The L<small>ORD</small> Almighty, who planted you, has de-
creed disaster for you, because the house of Israel
and the house of Judah have done evil and provoked me to anger by burning incense to Baal.

¹⁸Because the L<small>ORD</small> revealed their plot to me, I
knew it, for at that time he showed me what they
were doing. ¹⁹I had been like a gentle lamb led to
the slaughter; I did not realize that they had plotted against me, saying,

"Let us destroy the tree and its fruit;
  let us cut him off from the land of the
    living,

that his name be remembered no
    more."

²⁰But, O L<small>ORD</small> Almighty, you who judge
    righteously
  and test the heart and mind,
let me see your vengeance upon them,
  for to you I have committed my cause.

²¹"Therefore this is what the L<small>ORD</small> says about
the men of Anathoth who are seeking your life
and saying, 'Do not prophesy in the name of the
L<small>ORD</small> or you will die by our hands'— ²²therefore
this is what the L<small>ORD</small> Almighty says: 'I will punish
them. Their young men will die by the sword,
their sons and daughters by famine. ²³Not even a
remnant will be left to them, because I will bring
disaster on the men of Anathoth in the year of
their punishment.' "

6 / *Jeremiah 12*
An Honest Complaint

GRIPE! GRIPE! NOBODY likes a griper. One of the most surprising things about the Bible is that it faithfully records
so many complaints against the Lord by his own people. God could have edited those protests out of the Scriptures, but he listened to them patiently and still lets us read them centuries later.

 Warming Up to God When are you most eager to complain to God, and when are you afraid to complain?

 Read Jeremiah 12.

¹² You are always righteous, O L<small>ORD</small>,
  when I bring a case before you.
  Yet I would speak with you about
    your justice:
Why does the way of the wicked prosper?
  Why do all the faithless live at ease?
²You have planted them, and they have taken
    root;
  they grow and bear fruit.
You are always on their lips
  but far from their hearts.
³Yet you know me, O L<small>ORD</small>;
  you see me and test my thoughts about
    you.
Drag them off like sheep to be butchered!
  Set them apart for the day of slaughter!
⁴How long will the land lie parched^w

and the grass in every field be withered?
Because those who live in it are wicked,
  the animals and birds have perished.
Moreover, the people are saying,
  "He will not see what happens to us."

⁵"If you have raced with men on foot
  and they have worn you out,
  how can you compete with horses?
If you stumble in safe country,^x
  how will you manage in the thickets by^y
    the Jordan?
⁶Your brothers, your own family—
  even they have betrayed you;
  they have raised a loud cry against you.
Do not trust them,

^w4 Or *land mourn*   ^x5 Or *If you put your trust in a land of safety*
^y5 Or *the flooding of*

though they speak well of you.

7"I will forsake my house,
  abandon my inheritance;
I will give the one I love
  into the hands of her enemies.
8My inheritance has become to me
  like a lion in the forest.
She roars at me;
  therefore I hate her.
9Has not my inheritance become to me
  like a speckled bird of prey
  that other birds of prey surround and
    attack?
Go and gather all the wild beasts;
  bring them to devour.
10Many shepherds will ruin my vineyard
  and trample down my field;
they will turn my pleasant field
  into a desolate wasteland.
11It will be made a wasteland,
  parched and desolate before me;
the whole land will be laid waste
  because there is no one who cares.
12Over all the barren heights in the desert

destroyers will swarm,
for the sword of the LORD will devour
  from one end of the land to the other;
  no one will be safe.
13They will sow wheat but reap thorns;
  they will wear themselves out but gain
    nothing.
So bear the shame of your harvest
  because of the LORD's fierce anger."

14This is what the LORD says: "As for all my wicked neighbors who seize the inheritance I gave my people Israel, I will uproot them from their lands and I will uproot the house of Judah from among them. 15But after I uproot them, I will again have compassion and will bring each of them back to his own inheritance and his own country. 16And if they learn well the ways of my people and swear by my name, saying, 'As surely as the LORD lives'—even as they once taught my people to swear by Baal—then they will be established among my people. 17But if any nation does not listen, I will completely uproot and destroy it," declares the LORD.

Discovering the Word   1. What irked Jeremiah (vv. 1–4)?   2. How did God challenge Jeremiah (vv. 5–6)?   3. What explanation did the Lord give for letting his people be trampled on (vv. 7–13)? 4. What would be the final fate of those who devoured Israel (vv. 14–17)?   5. How would God offer mercy to Israel's enemies (vv. 15–16)?

Applying the Word   1. Think of a time you shared Jeremiah's complaint. Perhaps that time is right now. How does this passage shed light on what might be going on behind the scenes?   2. What insights has the Lord given you in response to your complaints?   3. What have you learned that can help you turn your complaints into praise?

Responding in Prayer   Do not be afraid to honestly tell God how you feel about something unfair, and as you pray, stay open to what he wants to show you through unfair circumstances.

---

7 / *Jeremiah 13*
Spoiled Bond

FIRM COMMITMENTS ARE an important part of our lives. The bank you borrow money from wants to know your credit record and your assets to see if you can keep your commitment to repay your loan. And be careful about your business partners. Can they keep a commitment? You sign a binding contract with someone who has a history of breaking them at your peril. Think long and hard about the commitment marriage involves. Marry someone who has a series of former partners, and the chances are good that you will end up with a broken heart.

God especially doesn't like those who make commitments of convenience. He has high standards for us and for himself. When he makes a commitment, he stakes his life on it. Jesus Christ is the evidence. He expects the same sort of fidelity in return. Just as there are painful consequences when a business contract is broken or when a marriage partner cheats, so there are painful consequences when we default on our commitments to God.

 Warming Up to God 1. What were the consequences of someone failing to keep their commitment to you? How did you feel?

 Read Jeremiah 13.

13 This is what the LORD said to me: "Go and buy a linen belt and put it around your waist, but do not let it touch water." ²So I bought a belt, as the LORD directed, and put it around my waist.

³Then the word of the LORD came to me a second time: ⁴"Take the belt you bought and are wearing around your waist, and go now to Perath*z* and hide it there in a crevice in the rocks." ⁵So I went and hid it at Perath, as the LORD told me.

⁶Many days later the LORD said to me, "Go now to Perath and get the belt I told you to hide there." ⁷So I went to Perath and dug up the belt and took it from the place where I had hidden it, but now it was ruined and completely useless.

⁸Then the word of the LORD came to me: ⁹"This is what the LORD says: 'In the same way I will ruin the pride of Judah and the great pride of Jerusalem. ¹⁰These wicked people, who refuse to listen to my words, who follow the stubbornness of their hearts and go after other gods to serve and worship them, will be like this belt—completely useless! ¹¹For as a belt is bound around a man's waist, so I bound the whole house of Israel and the whole house of Judah to me,' declares the LORD, 'to be my people for my renown and praise and honor. But they have not listened.'

¹²"Say to them: 'This is what the LORD, the God of Israel, says: Every wineskin should be filled with wine.' And if they say to you, 'Don't we know that every wineskin should be filled with wine?' ¹³then tell them, 'This is what the LORD says: I am going to fill with drunkenness all who live in this land, including the kings who sit on David's throne, the priests, the prophets and all those living in Jerusalem. ¹⁴I will smash them one against the other, fathers and sons alike, declares the LORD. I will allow no pity or mercy or compassion to keep me from destroying them.' "

¹⁵Hear and pay attention,
    do not be arrogant,
    for the LORD has spoken.
¹⁶Give glory to the LORD your God

before he brings the darkness,
before your feet stumble
    on the darkening hills.
You hope for light,
    but he will turn it to thick darkness
    and change it to deep gloom.
¹⁷But if you do not listen,
    I will weep in secret
    because of your pride;
my eyes will weep bitterly,
    overflowing with tears,
    because the LORD's flock will be taken
        captive.

¹⁸Say to the king and to the queen mother,
    "Come down from your thrones,
for your glorious crowns
    will fall from your heads."
¹⁹The cities in the Negev will be shut up,
    and there will be no one to open them.
All Judah will be carried into exile,
    carried completely away.

²⁰Lift up your eyes and see
    those who are coming from the north.
Where is the flock that was entrusted to you,
    the sheep of which you boasted?
²¹What will you say when ⌊the LORD⌋ sets over
        you
    those you cultivated as your special allies?
Will not pain grip you
    like that of a woman in labor?
²²And if you ask yourself,
    "Why has this happened to me?"—
it is because of your many sins
    that your skirts have been torn off
    and your body mistreated.
²³Can the Ethiopian*a* change his skin
    or the leopard its spots?
Neither can you do good
    who are accustomed to doing evil.

²⁴"I will scatter you like chaff
    driven by the desert wind.

z4 Or possibly *the Euphrates*; also in verses 5-7   *a23* Hebrew
Cushite (probably a person from the upper Nile region)

²⁵This is your lot,
  the portion I have decreed for you,"
                    declares the LORD,
  "because you have forgotten me
  and trusted in false gods.
²⁶I will pull up your skirts over your face
  that your shame may be seen—

²⁷your adulteries and lustful
    neighings,
  your shameless prostitution!
I have seen your detestable acts
  on the hills and in the fields.
Woe to you, O Jerusalem!
  How long will you be unclean?"

 Discovering the Word 1. Describe the task that God gave to Jeremiah in verses 1–11. 2. What is the point of this object lesson (vv. 9–11)? 3. A linen belt was more than functional; it was an ornament of dignity and pride. How might Israel and Judah have been a source of pride to God? 4. Jeremiah's message in verses 12–17 is directed at the leaders. In what ways is pride and arrogance a problem in these verses? 5. What could be the remedy for the coming judgment (vv. 15–17, 20, 23, 25)?

Applying the Word 1. One purpose of a belt was to tie things together. What things might come apart in your life if you were no longer bound to the Lord? 2. God wants to take pride in a relationship with his people. How can this insight enrich your relationship with him? 3. How can God's Word strengthen our bonds and commitments?

Responding in Prayer Giving glory to God puts the focus back on him and puts us in our proper place. Give glory to God for yourself, your family, your work and your whole course of life.

Jeremiah 14:1—17:4

14 This is the word of the LORD to Jeremiah concerning the drought:

²"Judah mourns,
  her cities languish;
they wail for the land,
  and a cry goes up from Jerusalem.
³The nobles send their servants for water;
  they go to the cisterns
  but find no water.
They return with their jars unfilled;
  dismayed and despairing,
  they cover their heads.
⁴The ground is cracked
  because there is no rain in the land;
  the farmers are dismayed
  and cover their heads.
⁵Even the doe in the field
  deserts her newborn fawn
  because there is no grass.
⁶Wild donkeys stand on the barren heights
  and pant like jackals;
  their eyesight fails
  for lack of pasture."

⁷Although our sins testify against us,
  O LORD, do something for the sake of your
    name.

For our backsliding is great;
  we have sinned against you.
⁸O Hope of Israel,
  its Savior in times of distress,
why are you like a stranger in the land,
  like a traveler who stays only a night?
⁹Why are you like a man taken by surprise,
  like a warrior powerless to save?
You are among us, O LORD,
  and we bear your name;
  do not forsake us!

¹⁰This is what the LORD says about this people:

"They greatly love to wander;
  they do not restrain their feet.
So the LORD does not accept them;
  he will now remember their wickedness
  and punish them for their sins."

¹¹Then the LORD said to me, "Do not pray for the well-being of this people. ¹²Although they fast, I will not listen to their cry; though they offer burnt offerings and grain offerings, I will not accept them. Instead, I will destroy them with the sword, famine and plague."

¹³But I said, "Ah, Sovereign LORD, the prophets keep telling them, 'You will not see the sword or

suffer famine. Indeed, I will give you lasting peace in this place.' "

¹⁴Then the LORD said to me, "The prophets are prophesying lies in my name. I have not sent them or appointed them or spoken to them. They are prophesying to you false visions, divinations, idolatries*b* and the delusions of their own minds. ¹⁵Therefore, this is what the LORD says about the prophets who are prophesying in my name: I did not send them, yet they are saying, 'No sword or famine will touch this land.' Those same prophets will perish by sword and famine. ¹⁶And the people they are prophesying to will be thrown out into the streets of Jerusalem because of the famine and sword. There will be no one to bury them or their wives, their sons or their daughters. I will pour out on them the calamity they deserve.

¹⁷"Speak this word to them:

" 'Let my eyes overflow with tears
    night and day without ceasing;
for my virgin daughter—my people—
    has suffered a grievous wound,
    a crushing blow.
¹⁸If I go into the country,
    I see those slain by the sword;
if I go into the city,
    I see the ravages of famine.
Both prophet and priest
    have gone to a land they know not.' "

¹⁹Have you rejected Judah completely?
    Do you despise Zion?
Why have you afflicted us
    so that we cannot be healed?
We hoped for peace
    but no good has come,
for a time of healing
    but there is only terror.
²⁰O LORD, we acknowledge our wickedness
    and the guilt of our fathers;
    we have indeed sinned against you.
²¹For the sake of your name do not despise us;
    do not dishonor your glorious throne.
Remember your covenant with us
    and do not break it.
²²Do any of the worthless idols of the nations
        bring rain?
    Do the skies themselves send down
        showers?
No, it is you, O LORD our God.
    Therefore our hope is in you,

for you are the one who does all this.

15 Then the LORD said to me: "Even if Moses and Samuel were to stand before me, my heart would not go out to this people. Send them away from my presence! Let them go! ²And if they ask you, 'Where shall we go?' tell them, 'This is what the LORD says:

" 'Those destined for death, to death;
    those for the sword, to the sword;
    those for starvation, to starvation;
    those for captivity, to captivity.'

³"I will send four kinds of destroyers against them," declares the LORD, "the sword to kill and the dogs to drag away and the birds of the air and the beasts of the earth to devour and destroy. ⁴I will make them abhorrent to all the kingdoms of the earth because of what Manasseh son of Hezekiah king of Judah did in Jerusalem.

⁵"Who will have pity on you, O Jerusalem?
    Who will mourn for you?
    Who will stop to ask how you are?
⁶You have rejected me," declares the LORD.
    "You keep on backsliding.
So I will lay hands on you and destroy you;
    I can no longer show compassion.
⁷I will winnow them with a winnowing fork
    at the city gates of the land.
I will bring bereavement and destruction on
        my people,
    for they have not changed their ways.
⁸I will make their widows more numerous
    than the sand of the sea.
At midday I will bring a destroyer
    against the mothers of their young men;
suddenly I will bring down on them
    anguish and terror.
⁹The mother of seven will grow faint
    and breathe her last.
Her sun will set while it is still day;
    she will be disgraced and humiliated.
I will put the survivors to the sword
    before their enemies,"
                                    declares the LORD.

¹⁰Alas, my mother, that you gave me birth,
    a man with whom the whole land strives
        and contends!
I have neither lent nor borrowed,

─────────────────
*b*14 Or *visions, worthless divinations*

yet everyone curses me.

¹¹The LORD said,

"Surely I will deliver you for a good purpose;
  surely I will make your enemies plead with
    you
  in times of disaster and times of distress.

¹²"Can a man break iron—
  iron from the north—or bronze?
¹³Your wealth and your treasures
  I will give as plunder, without charge,
because of all your sins
  throughout your country.
¹⁴I will enslave you to your enemies
  in\(^c\) a land you do not know,
for my anger will kindle a fire
  that will burn against you."

¹⁵You understand, O LORD;
  remember me and care for me.
  Avenge me on my persecutors.
You are long-suffering—do not take me away;
  think of how I suffer reproach for your
    sake.
¹⁶When your words came, I ate them;
  they were my joy and my heart's delight,
for I bear your name,
  O LORD God Almighty.
¹⁷I never sat in the company of revelers,
  never made merry with them;
I sat alone because your hand was on me
  and you had filled me with indignation.
¹⁸Why is my pain unending
  and my wound grievous and incurable?
Will you be to me like a deceptive brook,
  like a spring that fails?

¹⁹Therefore this is what the LORD says:

"If you repent, I will restore you
  that you may serve me;
if you utter worthy, not worthless, words,
  you will be my spokesman.
Let this people turn to you,
  but you must not turn to them.
²⁰I will make you a wall to this people,
  a fortified wall of bronze;
they will fight against you
  but will not overcome you,
for I am with you
  to rescue and save you,"

declares the LORD.
²¹"I will save you from the hands of the wicked

and redeem you from the grasp of the
  cruel."

16 Then the word of the LORD came to
me: ²"You must not marry and have
sons or daughters in this place." ³For this is what the LORD says about the sons and daughters born in this land and about the women who are their mothers and the men who are their fathers: ⁴"They will die of deadly diseases. They will not be mourned or buried but will be like refuse lying on the ground. They will perish by sword and famine, and their dead bodies will become food for the birds of the air and the beasts of the earth."

⁵For this is what the LORD says: "Do not enter a house where there is a funeral meal; do not go to mourn or show sympathy, because I have withdrawn my blessing, my love and my pity from this people," declares the LORD. ⁶"Both high and low will die in this land. They will not be buried or mourned, and no one will cut himself or shave his head for them. ⁷No one will offer food to comfort those who mourn for the dead—not even for a father or a mother—nor will anyone give them a drink to console them.

⁸"And do not enter a house where there is feasting and sit down to eat and drink. ⁹For this is what the LORD Almighty, the God of Israel, says: Before your eyes and in your days I will bring an end to the sounds of joy and gladness and to the voices of bride and bridegroom in this place.

¹⁰"When you tell these people all this and they ask you, 'Why has the LORD decreed such a great disaster against us? What wrong have we done? What sin have we committed against the LORD our God?' ¹¹then say to them, 'It is because your fathers forsook me,' declares the LORD, 'and followed other gods and served and worshiped them. They forsook me and did not keep my law. ¹²But you have behaved more wickedly than your fathers. See how each of you is following the stubbornness of his evil heart instead of obeying me. ¹³So I will throw you out of this land into a land neither you nor your fathers have known, and there you will serve other gods day and night, for I will show you no favor.'

¹⁴"However, the days are coming," declares the LORD, "when men will no longer say, 'As surely as the LORD lives, who brought the Israelites up out

---

\(^c\)14 Some Hebrew manuscripts, Septuagint and Syriac (see also Jer. 17:4); most Hebrew manuscripts *I will cause your enemies to bring you / into* of Egypt,' ¹⁵but they will say, 'As surely as the LORD lives, who brought the Israelites up out of the land of the north and out of all the countries where he had banished them.' For I will restore them to the land I gave their forefathers.

¹⁶"But now I will send for many fishermen," declares the LORD, "and they will catch them. After that I will send for many hunters, and they will hunt them down on every mountain and hill and from the crevices of the rocks. ¹⁷My eyes are on all their ways; they are not hidden from me, nor is their sin concealed from my eyes. ¹⁸I will repay them double for their wickedness and their sin, because they have defiled my land with the lifeless forms of their vile images and have filled my inheritance with their detestable idols."

¹⁹O LORD, my strength and my fortress,
    my refuge in time of distress,
to you the nations will come
    from the ends of the earth and say,
"Our fathers possessed nothing but false gods,
    worthless idols that did them no good.
²⁰Do men make their own gods?
    Yes, but they are not gods!"

²¹"Therefore I will teach them—
    this time I will teach them

my power and might.
Then they will know
    that my name is the LORD.

17 "Judah's sin is engraved with an iron tool,
        inscribed with a flint point,
on the tablets of their hearts
    and on the horns of their altars.
²Even their children remember
    their altars and Asherah poles[d]
beside the spreading trees
    and on the high hills.
³My mountain in the land
    and your[e] wealth and all your treasures
I will give away as plunder,
    together with your high places,
    because of sin throughout your country.
⁴Through your own fault you will lose
    the inheritance I gave you.
I will enslave you to your enemies
    in a land you do not know,
for you have kindled my anger,
    and it will burn forever."

---

[d]2 That is, symbols of the goddess Asherah   [e]2,3 Or hills / ³and the mountains of the land. / Your

---

8 / *Jeremiah 17:5–18*
Blessings in Troubled Times

AFTER BEING BATTERED all day by a hot south wind, the squash vines and tomato plants in our garden drooped in the fading light. They practically cried out for water from the sprinkler. But the trees in the yard were green and flourishing, though they required far more water than the squash and tomatoes. The deep roots of the trees found a hidden source of water far below the surface where the garden plants struggled. Like those trees, people who trust in the Lord are not at the mercy of surface circumstances because we have deep roots to our eternal Source.

 Warming Up to God   When have you experienced God's strength in a difficult time?

 Read Jeremiah 17:5–18.

---

⁵This is what the LORD says:

"Cursed is the one who trusts in man,
    who depends on flesh for his strength
    and whose heart turns away from the LORD.
⁶He will be like a bush in the wastelands;
    he will not see prosperity when it comes.

He will dwell in the parched places of the desert,
    in a salt land where no one lives.

⁷"But blessed is the man who trusts in the LORD,
    whose confidence is in him.

8He will be like a tree planted by the water
  that sends out its roots by the stream.
It does not fear when heat comes;
  its leaves are always green.
It has no worries in a year of drought
  and never fails to bear fruit."

9The heart is deceitful above all things
  and beyond cure.
Who can understand it?

10"I the LORD search the heart
  and examine the mind,
to reward a man according to his conduct,
  according to what his deeds deserve."

11Like a partridge that hatches eggs it did not
    lay
  is the man who gains riches by unjust
    means.
When his life is half gone, they will desert
    him,
  and in the end he will prove to be a fool.

12A glorious throne, exalted from the beginning,
  is the place of our sanctuary.
13O LORD, the hope of Israel,

all who forsake you will be put to shame.
Those who turn away from you will be
    written in the dust
  because they have forsaken the LORD,
    the spring of living water.

14Heal me, O LORD, and I will be healed;
  save me and I will be saved,
  for you are the one I praise.
15They keep saying to me,
  "Where is the word of the LORD?
  Let it now be fulfilled!"
16I have not run away from being your
    shepherd;
  you know I have not desired the day of
    despair.
  What passes my lips is open before you.
17Do not be a terror to me;
  you are my refuge in the day of disaster.
18Let my persecutors be put to shame,
  but keep me from shame;
let them be terrified,
  but keep me from terror.
Bring on them the day of disaster;
  destroy them with double destruction.

Discovering the Word 1. What geographical and human conditions in Jeremiah's society are described in relation to one another (vv. 5–8, 11, 15–18)? 2. Why will the person who relies on human strength be disappointed (vv. 5–6)? 3. How does God provide for the person who relies on him instead of on human strength (vv. 7–8)? 4. What is the state of the human heart before God (vv. 9–10)? 5. What did Jeremiah continue to hope for (vv. 14–18)?

Applying the Word 1. What "drought conditions" are you facing now? 2. In what ways do you find it easier to trust someone or something else besides God to see you through those circumstances? 3. How does God's promise in verses 7–8 give you confidence?

Responding in Prayer Bring the most difficult circumstances of your life to the Lord. Remembering the deceitfulness of the human heart, acknowledge any ways in which you are trusting something or someone besides God. Renew your trust in him and allow the "living water" (v. 13) to refresh you.

Jeremiah 17:19–27

19This is what the LORD said to me: "Go and stand at the gate of the people, through which the kings of Judah go in and out; stand also at all the other gates of Jerusalem. 20Say to them, 'Hear the word of the LORD, O kings of Judah and all people of Judah and everyone living in Jerusalem who come through these gates. 21This is what the LORD says: Be careful not to carry a load on the Sabbath day or bring it through the gates of Jerusalem.

22Do not bring a load out of your houses or do any work on the Sabbath, but keep the Sabbath day holy, as I commanded your forefathers. 23Yet they did not listen or pay attention; they were stiff-necked and would not listen or respond to discipline. 24But if you are careful to obey me, declares the LORD, and bring no load through the gates of this city on the Sabbath, but keep the Sabbath day holy by not doing any work on it,

²⁵then kings who sit on David's throne will come through the gates of this city with their officials. They and their officials will come riding in chariots and on horses, accompanied by the men of Judah and those living in Jerusalem, and this city will be inhabited forever. ²⁶People will come from the towns of Judah and the villages around Jerusalem, from the territory of Benjamin and the western foothills, from the hill country and the Negev, bringing burnt offerings and sacrifices, grain offerings, incense and thank offerings to the house of the LORD. ²⁷But if you do not obey me to keep the Sabbath day holy by not carrying any load as you come through the gates of Jerusalem on the Sabbath day, then I will kindle an unquenchable fire in the gates of Jerusalem that will consume her fortresses.' "

9 / *Jeremiah 18:1–17*
God's Shaping Hand

ONE OF MY sons just got braces. He is not happy about it. For the next three years his mouth is going to be full of metal and rubber bands that push and pull his teeth and jaw back into shape. Three years seems like a long time, but moving flesh and bone is difficult. Braces are inconvenient and painful, but they will improve my son's mouth and health for the rest of his life.

God is interested in shaping us, not just our teeth, but our whole being. It's a big task. Shaping souls is difficult, takes time, and requires divine power and skills. Unlike gums, teeth and bone, souls don't always yield to the shaping pressures of the divine hand. If they do, it takes a lifetime of God's pressures to conform to the end goal, the image of Christ. Jeremiah didn't know about braces, nor did he know the name of Jesus Christ, but he did know that God is in the business of shaping our lives.

 Warming Up to God   Recall one or two major events that have been a significant shaping influence in your life. How did they affect you for good or for ill?

 Read Jeremiah 18:1–17.

18 This is the word that came to Jeremiah from the LORD: ²"Go down to the potter's house, and there I will give you my message." ³So I went down to the potter's house, and I saw him working at the wheel. ⁴But the pot he was shaping from the clay was marred in his hands; so the potter formed it into another pot, shaping it as seemed best to him.

⁵Then the word of the LORD came to me: ⁶"O house of Israel, can I not do with you as this potter does?" declares the LORD. "Like clay in the hand of the potter, so are you in my hand, O house of Israel. ⁷If at any time I announce that a nation or kingdom is to be uprooted, torn down and destroyed, ⁸and if that nation I warned repents of its evil, then I will relent and not inflict on it the disaster I had planned. ⁹And if at another time I announce that a nation or kingdom is to be built up and planted, ¹⁰and if it does evil in my sight and does not obey me, then I will reconsider the good I had intended to do for it.

¹¹"Now therefore say to the people of Judah and those living in Jerusalem, 'This is what the LORD says: Look! I am preparing a disaster for you and devising a plan against you. So turn from your evil ways, each one of you, and reform your ways and your actions.' ¹²But they will reply, 'It's no use. We will continue with our own plans; each of us will follow the stubbornness of his evil heart.' "

¹³Therefore this is what the LORD says:

"Inquire among the nations:
  Who has ever heard anything like this?
A most horrible thing has been done
  by Virgin Israel.
¹⁴Does the snow of Lebanon
  ever vanish from its rocky slopes?
Do its cool waters from distant sources

ever cease to flow?[f]
15Yet my people have forgotten me;
  they burn incense to worthless idols,
which made them stumble in their ways
  and in the ancient paths.
They made them walk in bypaths
  and on roads not built up.
16Their land will be laid waste,
  an object of lasting scorn;

all who pass by will be appalled
  and will shake their heads.
17Like a wind from the east,
  I will scatter them before their enemies;
I will show them my back and not my face
  in the day of their disaster."

[f]14 The meaning of the Hebrew for this sentence is uncertain.

 Discovering the Word 1. What did Jeremiah see and hear at the potter's house (vv. 1–10)? 2. God makes it clear that his pronouncements and promises are conditional. How do you think God might respond to someone who objects that this makes him untrustworthy? 3. Jeremiah draws an analogy between human nations and clay in the potter's hand. How does the difference between humans and clay make this an analogy of hope? 4. In order to be reshaped by the potter, the clay has to be soft. How well is Judah going to do under God's hand (vv. 11–15)? 5. A primary cause of Judah's coming judgment was a determined forgetfulness (v. 15). How might forgetfulness be an expression of disobedience and unfaithfulness?

Applying the Word 1. Being reshaped by the divine potter isn't always a pleasant experience. Describe one or two times when you have been aware of God's shaping hand in your life. 2. God is the one who shapes us. What can we do to make sure that our hearts are responsive to him?

Responding in Prayer Picture yourself as clay. Ask God to make you soft and moldable. Pray that your trust in the Potter will grow stronger.

Jeremiah 18:18—21:14

18They said, "Come, let's make plans against Jeremiah; for the teaching of the law by the priest will not be lost, nor will counsel from the wise, nor the word from the prophets. So come, let's attack him with our tongues and pay no attention to anything he says."

19Listen to me, O Lord;
  hear what my accusers are saying!
20Should good be repaid with evil?
  Yet they have dug a pit for me.
Remember that I stood before you
  and spoke in their behalf
to turn your wrath away from them.
21So give their children over to famine;
  hand them over to the power of the sword.
Let their wives be made childless and widows;
  let their men be put to death,
  their young men slain by the sword in
      battle.
22Let a cry be heard from their houses
  when you suddenly bring invaders against
      them,
for they have dug a pit to capture me
  and have hidden snares for my feet.

23But you know, O Lord,
  all their plots to kill me.
Do not forgive their crimes
  or blot out their sins from your sight.
Let them be overthrown before you;
  deal with them in the time of your anger.

19 This is what the Lord says: "Go and buy a clay jar from a potter. Take along some of the elders of the people and of the priests 2and go out to the Valley of Ben Hinnom, near the entrance of the Potsherd Gate. There proclaim the words I tell you, 3and say, 'Hear the word of the Lord, O kings of Judah and people of Jerusalem. This is what the Lord Almighty, the God of Israel, says: Listen! I am going to bring a disaster on this place that will make the ears of everyone who hears of it tingle. 4For they have forsaken me and made this a place of foreign gods; they have burned sacrifices in it to gods that neither they nor their fathers nor the kings of Judah ever knew, and they have filled this place with the blood of the innocent. 5They have built the high places of Baal to burn their

sons in the fire as offerings to Baal—something I did not command or mention, nor did it enter my mind. ⁶So beware, the days are coming, declares the LORD, when people will no longer call this place Topheth or the Valley of Ben Hinnom, but the Valley of Slaughter.

⁷" 'In this place I will ruin⁸ the plans of Judah and Jerusalem. I will make them fall by the sword before their enemies, at the hands of those who seek their lives, and I will give their carcasses as food to the birds of the air and the beasts of the earth. ⁸I will devastate this city and make it an object of scorn; all who pass by will be appalled and will scoff because of all its wounds. ⁹I will make them eat the flesh of their sons and daughters, and they will eat one another's flesh during the stress of the siege imposed on them by the enemies who seek their lives.'

¹⁰"Then break the jar while those who go with you are watching, ¹¹and say to them, 'This is what the LORD Almighty says: I will smash this nation and this city just as this potter's jar is smashed and cannot be repaired. They will bury the dead in Topheth until there is no more room. ¹²This is what I will do to this place and to those who live here, declares the LORD. I will make this city like Topheth. ¹³The houses in Jerusalem and those of the kings of Judah will be defiled like this place, Topheth—all the houses where they burned incense on the roofs to all the starry hosts and poured out drink offerings to other gods.' "

¹⁴Jeremiah then returned from Topheth, where the LORD had sent him to prophesy, and stood in the court of the LORD's temple and said to all the people, ¹⁵"This is what the LORD Almighty, the God of Israel, says: 'Listen! I am going to bring on this city and the villages around it every disaster I pronounced against them, because they were stiff-necked and would not listen to my words.' "

20 When the priest Pashhur son of Immer, the chief officer in the temple of the LORD, heard Jeremiah prophesying these things, ²he had Jeremiah the prophet beaten and put in the stocks at the Upper Gate of Benjamin at the LORD's temple. ³The next day, when Pashhur released him from the stocks, Jeremiah said to him, "The LORD's name for you is not Pashhur, but Magor-Missabib.ʰ ⁴For this is what the LORD says: 'I will make you a terror to yourself and to all your friends; with your own eyes you will see them fall by the sword of their enemies. I will hand all Judah over to the king of Babylon,

who will carry them away to Babylon or put them to the sword. ⁵I will hand over to their enemies all the wealth of this city—all its products, all its valuables and all the treasures of the kings of Judah. They will take it away as plunder and carry it off to Babylon. ⁶And you, Pashhur, and all who live in your house will go into exile to Babylon. There you will die and be buried, you and all your friends to whom you have prophesied lies.' "

⁷O LORD, you deceivedⁱ me, and I was
    deceivedⁱ;
  you overpowered me and prevailed.
I am ridiculed all day long;
  everyone mocks me.
⁸Whenever I speak, I cry out
  proclaiming violence and destruction.
So the word of the LORD has brought me
  insult and reproach all day long.
⁹But if I say, "I will not mention him
  or speak any more in his name,"
his word is in my heart like a fire,
  a fire shut up in my bones.
I am weary of holding it in;
  indeed, I cannot.
¹⁰I hear many whispering,
  "Terror on every side!
  Report him! Let's report him!"
All my friends
  are waiting for me to slip, saying,
"Perhaps he will be deceived;
  then we will prevail over him
  and take our revenge on him."

¹¹But the LORD is with me like a mighty warrior;
  so my persecutors will stumble and not
    prevail.
They will fail and be thoroughly disgraced;
  their dishonor will never be forgotten.
¹²O LORD Almighty, you who examine the
    righteous
  and probe the heart and mind,
let me see your vengeance upon them,
  for to you I have committed my cause.

¹³Sing to the LORD!
  Give praise to the LORD!
He rescues the life of the needy
  from the hands of the wicked.

¹⁴Cursed be the day I was born!

ᵍ7 The Hebrew for *ruin* sounds like the Hebrew for *jar* (see verses 1 and 10). ʰ3 *Magor-Missabib* means *terror on every side.* ⁱ7 Or *persuaded*

May the day my mother bore me not be
   blessed!
¹⁵Cursed be the man who brought my father
   the news,
   who made him very glad, saying,
   "A child is born to you—a son!"
¹⁶May that man be like the towns
   the Lord overthrew without pity.
   May he hear wailing in the morning,
   a battle cry at noon.
¹⁷For he did not kill me in the womb,
   with my mother as my grave,
   her womb enlarged forever.
¹⁸Why did I ever come out of the womb
   to see trouble and sorrow
   and to end my days in shame?

21 The word came to Jeremiah from the Lord when King Zedekiah sent to him Pashhur son of Malkijah and the priest Zephaniah son of Maaseiah. They said: ²"Inquire now of the Lord for us because Nebuchadnezzar[j] king of Babylon is attacking us. Perhaps the Lord will perform wonders for us as in times past so that he will withdraw from us."

³But Jeremiah answered them, "Tell Zedekiah, ⁴'This is what the Lord, the God of Israel, says: I am about to turn against you the weapons of war that are in your hands, which you are using to fight the king of Babylon and the Babylonians[k] who are outside the wall besieging you. And I will gather them inside this city. ⁵I myself will fight against you with an outstretched hand and a mighty arm in anger and fury and great wrath. ⁶I will strike down those who live in this city—both men and animals—and they will die of a terrible plague. ⁷After that, declares the Lord, I will hand over Zedekiah king of Judah, his officials and the people in this city who survive the plague, sword and famine, to Nebuchadnezzar king of Babylon and to their enemies who seek their lives. He will put them to the sword; he will show them no mercy or pity or compassion.'

⁸"Furthermore, tell the people, 'This is what the Lord says: See, I am setting before you the way of life and the way of death. ⁹Whoever stays in this city will die by the sword, famine or plague. But whoever goes out and surrenders to the Babylonians who are besieging you will live; he will escape with his life. ¹⁰I have determined to do this city harm and not good, declares the Lord. It will be given into the hands of the king of Babylon, and he will destroy it with fire.'

¹¹"Moreover, say to the royal house of Judah, 'Hear the word of the Lord; ¹²O house of David, this is what the Lord says:

" 'Administer justice every morning;
   rescue from the hand of his oppressor
   the one who has been robbed,
or my wrath will break out and burn like fire
   because of the evil you have done—
   burn with no one to quench it.
¹³I am against you, ⌊Jerusalem,⌋
   you who live above this valley
   on the rocky plateau,
               declares the Lord—
you who say, "Who can come against us?
   Who can enter our refuge?"
¹⁴I will punish you as your deeds deserve,
               declares the Lord.
I will kindle a fire in your forests
   that will consume everything around you.' "

j2 Hebrew *Nebuchadrezzar*, of which *Nebuchadnezzar* is a variant; here and often in Jeremiah and Ezekiel   k4 Or *Chaldeans*; also in verse 9

10 / *Jeremiah 22*
To Know the Lord

THE BOOK *ANNA and the King of Siam*, from which the musical *The King and I* was made, tells the true story of Anna Leonowens, who in 1862 became governess to the royal Siamese family. For one of her first lessons she decided to teach the children geography. The only map in the palace showed Siam at the center of the world. The Siamese king was pictured wearing a splendid crown and holding symbols of plenty and authority. Next to Siam was poor Burma, full of demons, its king without clothes or crown. It was a matter of perspective. God often sees powerful figures quite differently from the way they see themselves.

Warming Up to God How often do you say that you "know the Lord"? What does that phrase mean for you?

Read Jeremiah 22.

22 This is what the LORD says: "Go down to the palace of the king of Judah and proclaim this message there: ²'Hear the word of the LORD, O king of Judah, you who sit on David's throne—you, your officials and your people who come through these gates. ³This is what the LORD says: Do what is just and right. Rescue from the hand of his oppressor the one who has been robbed. Do no wrong or violence to the alien, the fatherless or the widow, and do not shed innocent blood in this place. ⁴For if you are careful to carry out these commands, then kings who sit on David's throne will come through the gates of this palace, riding in chariots and on horses, accompanied by their officials and their people. ⁵But if you do not obey these commands, declares the LORD, I swear by myself that this palace will become a ruin.' "

⁶For this is what the LORD says about the palace of the king of Judah:

"Though you are like Gilead to me,
    like the summit of Lebanon,
I will surely make you like a desert,
    like towns not inhabited.
⁷I will send destroyers against you,
    each man with his weapons,
and they will cut up your fine cedar beams
    and throw them into the fire.

⁸"People from many nations will pass by this city and will ask one another, 'Why has the LORD done such a thing to this great city?' ⁹And the answer will be: 'Because they have forsaken the covenant of the LORD their God and have worshiped and served other gods.' "

¹⁰Do not weep for the dead ⌊king⌋ or mourn
        his loss;
    rather, weep bitterly for him who is exiled,
because he will never return
    nor see his native land again.

¹¹For this is what the LORD says about Shallum¹ son of Josiah, who succeeded his father as king of Judah but has gone from this place: "He will never return. ¹²He will die in the place where they have led him captive; he will not see this land again."

¹³"Woe to him who builds his palace by
        unrighteousness,
    his upper rooms by injustice,
making his countrymen work for nothing,
    not paying them for their labor.
¹⁴He says, 'I will build myself a great palace
    with spacious upper rooms.'
So he makes large windows in it,
    panels it with cedar
    and decorates it in red.

¹⁵"Does it make you a king
    to have more and more cedar?
Did not your father have food and drink?
    He did what was right and just,
    so all went well with him.
¹⁶He defended the cause of the poor and needy,
    and so all went well.
Is that not what it means to know me?"
    declares the LORD.
¹⁷"But your eyes and your heart
    are set only on dishonest gain,
on shedding innocent blood
    and on oppression and extortion."

¹⁸Therefore this is what the LORD says about Jehoiakim son of Josiah king of Judah:

"They will not mourn for him:
    'Alas, my brother! Alas, my sister!'
They will not mourn for him:
    'Alas, my master! Alas, his splendor!'
¹⁹He will have the burial of a donkey—
    dragged away and thrown
    outside the gates of Jerusalem."

²⁰"Go up to Lebanon and cry out,
    let your voice be heard in Bashan,
cry out from Abarim,
    for all your allies are crushed.
²¹I warned you when you felt secure,
    but you said, 'I will not listen!'
This has been your way from your youth;
    you have not obeyed me.
²²The wind will drive all your shepherds away,
    and your allies will go into exile.
Then you will be ashamed and disgraced

¹11 Also called *Jehoahaz*

because of all your wickedness.
²³You who live in 'Lebanon,ᵐ'
  who are nestled in cedar buildings,
how you will groan when pangs come upon
    you,
    pain like that of a woman in labor!

²⁴"As surely as I live," declares the LORD, "even
if you, Jehoiachinⁿ son of Jehoiakim king of Judah, were a signet ring on my right hand, I would
still pull you off. ²⁵I will hand you over to those
who seek your life, those you fear—to Nebuchadnezzar king of Babylon and to the Babylonians.ᵒ
²⁶I will hurl you and the mother who gave you
birth into another country, where neither of you
was born, and there you both will die. ²⁷You will

never come back to the land you long to return to."

²⁸Is this man Jehoiachin a despised, broken pot,
  an object no one wants?
Why will he and his children be hurled out,
  cast into a land they do not know?
²⁹O land, land, land,
  hear the word of the LORD!
³⁰This is what the LORD says:
"Record this man as if childless,
  a man who will not prosper in his lifetime,
for none of his offspring will prosper,
  none will sit on the throne of David
  or rule anymore in Judah."

ᵐ23 That is, the palace in Jerusalem (see 1 Kings 7:2)   ⁿ24 Hebrew
Coniah, a variant of *Jehoiachin;* also in verse 28   ᵒ25 Or *Chaldeans*

Discovering the Word 1. The kings named here were among the last to rule in Judah. What did they consider important (vv. 8–9, 14–15, 17, 20–21, 23)? 3. Verses 15–16 refer to Josiah, who led Judah into spiritual renewal a generation earlier. How is justice defined in these verses and in verse 3? 4. Why was the fate of Josaiah's son Jehoiakim to be so harsh (vv. 18–23)? 5. Why are the people told not to mourn for the king of Judah (vv. 10–12) and Jehoiakim (vv. 18–19)?

Applying the Word 1. How do you respond to the idea that doing justice is inseparable from knowing God (v. 16)? 2. How does your knowledge of God affect how fairly you treat others?

Responding in Prayer If this study reveals ways that you have been unfair or failed to stand up to injustice, confess that to the Lord. Pray for people who are being unjustly treated.

---

11 / *Jeremiah 23*
A Divine Coup

DURING WORLD WAR II the Japanese experimented with effective ways to run their prison camps. At one camp they removed the five percent of the prison population who had any experience in leadership or could articulate a defined set of religious beliefs and moral behavior. The results were amazing. There were less attempted escapes and more docile prisoners at that camp than at any other.

We need leaders and we need beliefs. But what happens when the leaders become corrupt or intentionally lead in an immoral way? Judah faced just such a crisis. The whole nation was headed for a cliff and the leaders weren't doing anything about it. In fact, they were leading the way to the edge. How will God respond? Jeremiah has some bad news for the leaders and some good news for the people.

Warming Up to God Recall someone who has been an influential leader in your life. What did they do, and how did it affect you?

Read Jeremiah 23.

---

23 "Woe to the shepherds who are destroying and scattering the sheep of
my pasture!" declares the LORD.
²Therefore this is what the LORD, the God of Is-

rael, says to the shepherds who tend my people:
"Because you have scattered my flock and driven
them away and have not bestowed care on them,
I will bestow punishment on you for the evil you

have done," declares the LORD. ³"I myself will gather the remnant of my flock out of all the countries where I have driven them and will bring them back to their pasture, where they will be fruitful and increase in number. ⁴I will place shepherds over them who will tend them, and they will no longer be afraid or terrified, nor will any be missing," declares the LORD.

⁵"The days are coming," declares the LORD,
  "when I will raise up to David^p a
    righteous Branch,
 a King who will reign wisely
    and do what is just and right in the land.
⁶In his days Judah will be saved
    and Israel will live in safety.
 This is the name by which he will be called:
    The LORD Our Righteousness.

⁷"So then, the days are coming," declares the LORD, "when people will no longer say, 'As surely as the LORD lives, who brought the Israelites up out of Egypt,' ⁸but they will say, 'As surely as the LORD lives, who brought the descendants of Israel up out of the land of the north and out of all the countries where he had banished them.' Then they will live in their own land."

⁹Concerning the prophets:

My heart is broken within me;
    all my bones tremble.
 I am like a drunken man,
    like a man overcome by wine,
 because of the LORD
    and his holy words.
¹⁰The land is full of adulterers;
    because of the curse^q the land lies
      parched^r
    and the pastures in the desert are withered.
 The ∟prophets⌐ follow an evil course
    and use their power unjustly.

¹¹"Both prophet and priest are godless;
    even in my temple I find their wickedness,"
                    declares the LORD.
¹²"Therefore their path will become slippery;
    they will be banished to darkness
    and there they will fall.
 I will bring disaster on them
    in the year they are punished,"
                    declares the LORD.

¹³"Among the prophets of Samaria
    I saw this repulsive thing:

They prophesied by Baal
    and led my people Israel astray.
¹⁴And among the prophets of Jerusalem
    I have seen something horrible:
    They commit adultery and live a lie.
 They strengthen the hands of evildoers,
    so that no one turns from his wickedness.
 They are all like Sodom to me;
    the people of Jerusalem are like Gomorrah."

¹⁵Therefore, this is what the LORD Almighty says concerning the prophets:

"I will make them eat bitter food
    and drink poisoned water,
 because from the prophets of Jerusalem
    ungodliness has spread throughout the
      land."

¹⁶This is what the LORD Almighty says:

"Do not listen to what the prophets are
      prophesying to you;
    they fill you with false hopes.
 They speak visions from their own minds,
    not from the mouth of the LORD.
¹⁷They keep saying to those who despise me,
    'The LORD says: You will have peace.'
 And to all who follow the stubbornness of
      their hearts
    they say, 'No harm will come to you.'
¹⁸But which of them has stood in the council of
      the LORD
    to see or to hear his word?
 Who has listened and heard his word?
¹⁹See, the storm of the LORD
    will burst out in wrath,
 a whirlwind swirling down
    on the heads of the wicked.
²⁰The anger of the LORD will not turn back
    until he fully accomplishes
    the purposes of his heart.
 In days to come
    you will understand it clearly.
²¹I did not send these prophets,
    yet they have run with their message;
 I did not speak to them,
    yet they have prophesied.
²²But if they had stood in my council,
    they would have proclaimed my words to
      my people

---

^p5 Or *up from David's line*   ^q10 Or *because of these things*
^r10 Or *land mourns*

and would have turned them from their evil
    ways
    and from their evil deeds.

23"Am I only a God nearby,"
                            declares the LORD,
    "and not a God far away?
24Can anyone hide in secret places
    so that I cannot see him?"
                            declares the LORD.
    "Do not I fill heaven and earth?"
                            declares the LORD.

25"I have heard what the prophets say who
prophesy lies in my name. They say, 'I had a
dream! I had a dream!' 26How long will this continue in the hearts of these lying prophets, who
prophesy the delusions of their own minds?
27They think the dreams they tell one another
will make my people forget my name, just as their
fathers forgot my name through Baal worship.
28Let the prophet who has a dream tell his dream,
but let the one who has my word speak it faithfully. For what has straw to do with grain?" declares the LORD. 29"Is not my word like fire," declares the LORD, "and like a hammer that breaks a
rock in pieces?

30"Therefore," declares the LORD, "I am against
the prophets who steal from one another words
supposedly from me. 31Yes," declares the LORD, "I
am against the prophets who wag their own
tongues and yet declare, 'The LORD declares.' 32In-
deed, I am against those who prophesy false

dreams," declares the LORD. "They tell them and
lead my people astray with their reckless lies, yet
I did not send or appoint them. They do not benefit these people in the least," declares the LORD.
33"When these people, or a prophet or a priest,
ask you, 'What is the oracle$ of the LORD?' say to
them, 'What oracle?ᵗ I will forsake you, declares
the LORD.' 34If a prophet or a priest or anyone else
claims, 'This is the oracle of the LORD,' I will punish that man and his household. 35This is what
each of you keeps on saying to his friend or relative: 'What is the LORD's answer?' or 'What has the
LORD spoken?' 36But you must not mention 'the
oracle of the LORD' again, because every man's
own word becomes his oracle and so you distort
the words of the living God, the LORD Almighty,
our God. 37This is what you keep saying to a
prophet: 'What is the LORD's answer to you?' or
'What has the LORD spoken?' 38Although you
claim, 'This is the oracle of the LORD,' this is what
the LORD says: You used the words, 'This is the
oracle of the LORD,' even though I told you that
you must not claim, 'This is the oracle of the
LORD.' 39Therefore, I will surely forget you and
cast you out of my presence along with the city I
gave to you and your fathers. 40I will bring upon
you everlasting disgrace—everlasting shame that
will not be forgotten."

$33 Or *burden* (see Septuagint and Vulgate)   ᵗ33 Hebrew; Septuagint
and Vulgate *'You are the burden.* (The Hebrew for *oracle* and *burden* is
the same.)

 Discovering the Word 1. How will the punishment fit the crime for Israel's leaders (vv. 1–4, 39–40)?
2. God promised a new ruler from the line of David. How will his reign be different from the current leader's
(vv. 5–8)? 3. Righteousness is central to a relationship with God. Why do you think the name "The LORD Our
Righteousness" (v. 6) might be significant? 4. What charges are brought against the religious leaders (vv. 9–32)?
5. What are the results of their leadership?

Applying the Word 1. If God were to bring charges against the spiritual leaders of today's church, what
do think they might be? 2. What effects might such leadership be having on the life of the church and
individual Christians? 3. God charges the religious leaders with failing to stand in his council (vv. 18, 22). We may
not be prophets or priests, but we can learn from their example. How do you receive the counsel of the Lord?

Responding in Prayer How have you experienced the benefits of Christ as God's Shepherd King? Offer
your praise to God.

12 / *Jeremiah 24*
Living with God's Judgment

AFTER THE EVENING service, a visiting preacher was invited to spend the night at the home of one of the wealthy members of the church. The host was proud of his new house and showed it off with obvious pride. He attributed his good fortune to the Lord, saying that God had blessed his business in the previous year with a fourfold increase in profits. The guest was not impressed. With a dismissive gesture he asked his host, "How do you know that your prosperity is not a trick of the devil to cause you to become proud, materialistic and greedy?"

Although the challenge of the preacher seems harsh, it's a good question. What appears to be good fortune at the present may not be so in the end. In Jeremiah's message to the exiles and those who stayed in the land after the first deportation in A.D. 596, he turns the concept of good fortune on its head and provides a different perspective.

 Warming Up to God   When have you changed your mind about what you initially thought was a great opportunity or positive development?

 Read Jeremiah 24.

24 After Jehoiachin[u] son of Jehoiakim king of Judah and the officials, the craftsmen and the artisans of Judah were carried into exile from Jerusalem to Babylon by Nebuchadnezzar king of Babylon, the LORD showed me two baskets of figs placed in front of the temple of the LORD. ²One basket had very good figs, like those that ripen early; the other basket had very poor figs, so bad they could not be eaten.

³Then the LORD asked me, "What do you see, Jeremiah?"

"Figs," I answered. "The good ones are very good, but the poor ones are so bad they cannot be eaten."

⁴Then the word of the LORD came to me: ⁵"This is what the LORD, the God of Israel, says: 'Like these good figs, I regard as good the exiles from Judah, whom I sent away from this place to the land of the Babylonians.[v] ⁶My eyes will watch over them for their good, and I will bring them back to this land. I will build them up and not tear them down; I will plant them and not uproot them. ⁷I will give them a heart to know me, that I am the LORD. They will be my people, and I will be their God, for they will return to me with all their heart.

⁸" 'But like the poor figs, which are so bad they cannot be eaten,' says the LORD, 'so will I deal with Zedekiah king of Judah, his officials and the survivors from Jerusalem, whether they remain in this land or live in Egypt. ⁹I will make them abhorrent and an offense to all the kingdoms of the earth, a reproach and a byword, an object of ridicule and cursing, wherever I banish them. ¹⁰I will send the sword, famine and plague against them until they are destroyed from the land I gave to them and their fathers.' "

---

u1 Hebrew *Jeconiah,* a variant of *Jehoiachin*   *v5* Or *Chaldeans*

 Discovering the Word   1. How does this vision of the figs display the continuing presence and power of God in the midst of a time of military defeat for Judah?   2. How does the vision of the figs change the way you might think about those who were taken in captivity to Babylon and those who got to stay in Jerusalem (vv. 5–10)?   4. God says that he is going to regard the exiles as "good" (v. 5). What do you think that means?   5. How might those who escaped captivity feel about themselves, the exiles and God (vv. 8–10)?

Applying the Word   1. Christians are to consider themselves blessed by God in the midst of difficult circumstances. What can we learn from the experience of the exiles that can help us experience God's blessing in difficult times?   2. What are some of the benefits that you have received from trying times?

Responding in Prayer   God's ultimate act of judgment is the resurrection. Praise him for the grace offered through Christ's sacrifice.

Jeremiah 25:1–14

25 The word came to Jeremiah concerning all the people of Judah in the fourth year of Jehoiakim son of Josiah king of Judah, which was the first year of Nebuchadnezzar king of Babylon. ²So Jeremiah the prophet said to all the people of Judah and to all those living in Jerusalem: ³For twenty-three years—from the thirteenth year of Josiah son of Amon king of Judah until this very day—the word of the LORD has come to me and I have spoken to you again and again, but you have not listened.

⁴And though the LORD has sent all his servants the prophets to you again and again, you have not listened or paid any attention. ⁵They said, "Turn now, each of you, from your evil ways and your evil practices, and you can stay in the land the LORD gave to you and your fathers for ever and ever. ⁶Do not follow other gods to serve and worship them; do not provoke me to anger with what your hands have made. Then I will not harm you."

⁷"But you did not listen to me," declares the LORD, "and you have provoked me with what your hands have made, and you have brought harm to yourselves."

⁸Therefore the LORD Almighty says this: "Because you have not listened to my words, ⁹I will summon all the peoples of the north and my servant Nebuchadnezzar king of Babylon," declares the LORD, "and I will bring them against this land and its inhabitants and against all the surrounding nations. I will completely destroy^w them and make them an object of horror and scorn, and an everlasting ruin. ¹⁰I will banish from them the sounds of joy and gladness, the voices of bride and bridegroom, the sound of millstones and the light of the lamp. ¹¹This whole country will become a desolate wasteland, and these nations will serve the king of Babylon seventy years.

¹²"But when the seventy years are fulfilled, I will punish the king of Babylon and his nation, the land of the Babylonians,^{x} for their guilt," declares the LORD, "and will make it desolate forever. ¹³I will bring upon that land all the things I have spoken against it, all that are written in this book and prophesied by Jeremiah against all the nations. ¹⁴They themselves will be enslaved by many nations and great kings; I will repay them according to their deeds and the work of their hands."

^{w}9 The Hebrew term refers to the irrevocable giving over of things or persons to the LORD, often by totally destroying them. ^{x}12 Or *Chaldeans*

13 / Jeremiah 25:15–38
International Judgment

READING ABOUT JESUS praying in the Garden of Gethsemane is painful. The night before Jesus was crucified "he fell with his face to the ground and prayed, 'My Father, if it is possible, may this cup be taken from me. Yet not as I will, but as you will' " (Mt 26:39). What was the cup Jesus was praying about? It no doubt had to do with the upcoming experience of the cross.

When we turn to this passage in Jeremiah, we can begin to get a glimpse of the pain Jesus must have felt. Jeremiah writes about the cup of God's wrath that was to be given to all the nations of the earth in order to bring judgment. The cup Jeremiah writes of was too much for the nations to drink. How then was Jesus Christ alone able to stand it? As you study this difficult passage, keep in mind the physical, spiritual and eternal issues at stake.

 Warming Up to God Violence is all around us. What wars or other forms of violence are on your mind as you begin? Take time to pray about the situations that concern you.

 Read Jeremiah 25:15–38.

¹⁵This is what the LORD, the God of Israel, said to me: "Take from my hand this cup filled with the wine of my wrath and make all the nations to whom I send you drink it. ¹⁶When they drink it, they will stagger and go mad because of the sword I will send among them."

¹⁷So I took the cup from the LORD's hand and made all the nations to whom he sent me drink it: ¹⁸Jerusalem and the towns of Judah, its kings and officials, to make them a ruin and an object of horror and scorn and cursing, as they are today; ¹⁹Pharaoh king of Egypt, his attendants, his officials and all his people, ²⁰and all the foreign people there; all the kings of Uz; all the kings of the Philistines (those of Ashkelon, Gaza, Ekron, and the people left at Ashdod); ²¹Edom, Moab and Ammon; ²²all the kings of Tyre and Sidon; the kings of the coastlands across the sea; ²³Dedan, Tema, Buz and all who are in distant places[y]; ²⁴all the kings of Arabia and all the kings of the foreign people who live in the desert; ²⁵all the kings of Zimri, Elam and Media; ²⁶and all the kings of the north, near and far, one after the other—all the kingdoms on the face of the earth. And after all of them, the king of Sheshach[z] will drink it too.

²⁷"Then tell them, 'This is what the LORD Almighty, the God of Israel, says: Drink, get drunk and vomit, and fall to rise no more because of the sword I will send among you.' ²⁸But if they refuse to take the cup from your hand and drink, tell them, 'This is what the LORD Almighty says: You must drink it! ²⁹See, I am beginning to bring disaster on the city that bears my Name, and will you indeed go unpunished? You will not go unpunished, for I am calling down a sword upon all who live on the earth, declares the LORD Almighty.'

³⁰"Now prophesy all these words against them and say to them:

" 'The LORD will roar from on high;
    he will thunder from his holy dwelling

and roar mightily against his land.
He will shout like those who tread the grapes,
    shout against all who live on the earth.
³¹The tumult will resound to the ends of the earth,
    for the LORD will bring charges against the nations;
he will bring judgment on all mankind
    and put the wicked to the sword,' "
                                        declares the LORD.

³²This is what the LORD Almighty says:

"Look! Disaster is spreading
    from nation to nation;
a mighty storm is rising
    from the ends of the earth."

³³At that time those slain by the LORD will be everywhere—from one end of the earth to the other. They will not be mourned or gathered up or buried, but will be like refuse lying on the ground.

³⁴Weep and wail, you shepherds;
    roll in the dust, you leaders of the flock.
For your time to be slaughtered has come;
    you will fall and be shattered like fine pottery.
³⁵The shepherds will have nowhere to flee,
    the leaders of the flock no place to escape.
³⁶Hear the cry of the shepherds,
    the wailing of the leaders of the flock,
    for the LORD is destroying their pasture.
³⁷The peaceful meadows will be laid waste
    because of the fierce anger of the LORD.
³⁸Like a lion he will leave his lair,
    and their land will become desolate
because of the sword[a] of the oppressor
    and because of the LORD's fierce anger.

y23 Or *who clip the hair by their foreheads*   *z26 Sheshach* is a cryptogram for Babylon.   *a38* Some Hebrew manuscripts and Septuagint (see also Jer. 46:16 and 50:16); most Hebrew manuscripts *anger*

Discovering the Word 1. The central image of these verses is a cup. What does the cup stand for? 2. There is an extensive list of nations in verses 18–26. What is God's point in mentioning them one by one? 3. The nations don't have a choice about this coming war. What is the reason for God's wide-ranging judgment (vv. 27–29)? 4. Verses 30–33 emphasize the sounds of war. What will be heard, and what will the sounds mean? 5. What justification can there be for God to cause such terrible experiences? 6. Jeremiah uses the images of shepherds and a lion to describe the leaders and God. How does that help the leaders understand their situation (vv. 34–38)?

Applying the Word 1. Consider wars in the twentieth century—World War I, World War II, Vietnam, the Gulf War or others that come to mind. How do you think leaders of nations involved viewed their participation in these wars? 2. In most wars, one or even both sides claim that God is on their side. How might you respond to such a claim in light of Jeremiah's prophecy?

Responding in Prayer Pray for victims of violence and war around the world.

Jeremiah 26

26 Early in the reign of Jehoiakim son of Josiah king of Judah, this word came from the LORD: 2"This is what the LORD says: Stand in the courtyard of the LORD's house and speak to all the people of the towns of Judah who come to worship in the house of the LORD. Tell them everything I command you; do not omit a word. 3Perhaps they will listen and each will turn from his evil way. Then I will relent and not bring on them the disaster I was planning because of the evil they have done. 4Say to them, 'This is what the LORD says: If you do not listen to me and follow my law, which I have set before you, 5and if you do not listen to the words of my servants the prophets, whom I have sent to you again and again (though you have not listened), 6then I will make this house like Shiloh and this city an object of cursing among all the nations of the earth.' "

7The priests, the prophets and all the people heard Jeremiah speak these words in the house of the LORD. 8But as soon as Jeremiah finished telling all the people everything the LORD had commanded him to say, the priests, the prophets and all the people seized him and said, "You must die! 9Why do you prophesy in the LORD's name that this house will be like Shiloh and this city will be desolate and deserted?" And all the people crowded around Jeremiah in the house of the LORD.

10When the officials of Judah heard about these things, they went up from the royal palace to the house of the LORD and took their places at the entrance of the New Gate of the LORD's house. 11Then the priests and the prophets said to the officials and all the people, "This man should be sentenced to death because he has prophesied against this city. You have heard it with your own ears!"

12Then Jeremiah said to all the officials and all the people: "The LORD sent me to prophesy against this house and this city all the things you have heard. 13Now reform your ways and your actions and obey the LORD your God. Then the LORD will relent and not bring the disaster he has pronounced against you. 14As for me, I am in your hands; do with me whatever you think is good and right. 15Be assured, however, that if you put me to death, you will bring the guilt of innocent blood on yourselves and on this city and on those who live in it, for in truth the LORD has sent me to you to speak all these words in your hearing."

16Then the officials and all the people said to the priests and the prophets, "This man should not be sentenced to death! He has spoken to us in the name of the LORD our God."

17Some of the elders of the land stepped forward and said to the entire assembly of people, 18"Micah of Moresheth prophesied in the days of Hezekiah king of Judah. He told all the people of Judah, 'This is what the LORD Almighty says:

" 'Zion will be plowed like a field,
    Jerusalem will become a heap of rubble,
      the temple hill a mound overgrown with
        thickets.'b

19"Did Hezekiah king of Judah or anyone else in Judah put him to death? Did not Hezekiah fear the LORD and seek his favor? And did not the LORD relent, so that he did not bring the disaster he pronounced against them? We are about to bring a terrible disaster on ourselves!"

20(Now Uriah son of Shemaiah from Kiriath Jearim was another man who prophesied in the name of the LORD; he prophesied the same things against this city and this land as Jeremiah did. 21When King Jehoiakim and all his officers and officials heard his words, the king sought to put

b18 Micah 3:12

him to death. But Uriah heard of it and fled in fear to Egypt. ²²King Jehoiakim, however, sent Elnathan son of Acbor to Egypt, along with some other men. ²³They brought Uriah out of Egypt and took him to King Jehoiakim, who had him struck down with a sword and his body thrown into the burial place of the common people.)

²⁴Furthermore, Ahikam son of Shaphan supported Jeremiah, and so he was not handed over to the people to be put to death.

14 / *Jeremiah 27*
How to Prosper Anyway

HIKING ALONG A narrow ledge on a path in the Alps, a tourist slipped and fell. Just before sliding off a cliff and down into the deep ravine below, he caught hold of a tree root. About five minutes later, across the ravine, he heard a voice calling out, "Let go of the tree and swing to the left." That didn't sound like a good idea, so he continued to cling to the tree although his hands were beginning to ache and his grip was slipping. The voice called out again: "From where I am standing I can see a ledge about twenty feet below you and just off at an angle. If you drop down, you can get back to the path and walk down." The hiker had to make a decision: did he trust the voice or not? From where he hung it looked like a straight drop of hundreds of feet down to certain death. But he couldn't hang on much longer. Finally, he asked, "Is anyone else up there?"

Judah was in a difficult situation and getting strange advice from Jeremiah. Like the voice from across the ravine his message went against common sense and everything they understood about being the special people of God. Would they believe him and let go?

 Warming Up to God How do you handle advice when you don't agree with it or it comes from someone you are suspicious of?

 Read Jeremiah 27.

27 Early in the reign of Zedekiah[c] son of Josiah king of Judah, this word came to Jeremiah from the LORD: ²This is what the LORD said to me: "Make a yoke out of straps and crossbars and put it on your neck. ³Then send word to the kings of Edom, Moab, Ammon, Tyre and Sidon through the envoys who have come to Jerusalem to Zedekiah king of Judah. ⁴Give them a message for their masters and say, 'This is what the LORD Almighty, the God of Israel, says: "Tell this to your masters: ⁵With my great power and outstretched arm I made the earth and its people and the animals that are on it, and I give it to anyone I please. ⁶Now I will hand all your countries over to my servant Nebuchadnezzar king of Babylon; I will make even the wild animals subject to him. ⁷All nations will serve him and his son and his grandson until the time for his land comes; then many nations and great kings will subjugate him.

⁸" 'If, however, any nation or kingdom will not serve Nebuchadnezzar king of Babylon or bow its neck under his yoke, I will punish that nation with the sword, famine and plague, declares the LORD, until I destroy it by his hand. ⁹So do not listen to your prophets, your diviners, your interpreters of dreams, your mediums or your sorcerers who tell you, 'You will not serve the king of Babylon.' ¹⁰They prophesy lies to you that will only serve to remove you far from your lands; I will banish you and you will perish. ¹¹But if any nation will bow its neck under the yoke of the king of Babylon and serve him, I will let that nation remain in its own land to till it and to live there, declares the LORD." ' "

¹²I gave the same message to Zedekiah king of Judah. I said, "Bow your neck under the yoke of the king of Babylon; serve him and his people, and you will live. ¹³Why will you and your people die by the sword, famine and plague with which the LORD has threatened any nation that will not serve the king of Babylon? ¹⁴Do not listen to the words of the prophets who say to you, 'You will not serve the king of Babylon,' for they are proph-

ᶜ1 A few Hebrew manuscripts and Syriac (see also Jer. 27:3, 12 and 28:1); most Hebrew manuscripts *Jehoiakim* (Most Septuagint manuscripts do not have this verse.)

esying lies to you. ¹⁵'I have not sent them,' declares the LORD. 'They are prophesying lies in my name. Therefore, I will banish you and you will perish, both you and the prophets who prophesy to you.'"

¹⁶Then I said to the priests and all these people, "This is what the LORD says: Do not listen to the prophets who say, 'Very soon now the articles from the LORD's house will be brought back from Babylon.' They are prophesying lies to you. ¹⁷Do not listen to them. Serve the king of Babylon, and you will live. Why should this city become a ruin? ¹⁸If they are prophets and have the word of the LORD, let them plead with the LORD Almighty that the furnishings remaining in the house of the LORD and in the palace of the king of Judah and in Jerusalem not be taken to Babylon. ¹⁹For this is

what the LORD Almighty says about the pillars, the Sea, the movable stands and the other furnishings that are left in this city, ²⁰which Nebuchadnezzar king of Babylon did not take away when he carried Jehoiachin*d* son of Jehoiakim king of Judah into exile from Jerusalem to Babylon, along with all the nobles of Judah and Jerusalem— ²¹yes, this is what the LORD Almighty, the God of Israel, says about the things that are left in the house of the LORD and in the palace of the king of Judah and in Jerusalem: ²²'They will be taken to Babylon and there they will remain until the day I come for them,' declares the LORD. 'Then I will bring them back and restore them to this place.'"

d20 Hebrew Jeconiah, a variant of Jehoiachin

Discovering the Word 1. Jeremiah continues to function as a prophet to the nations. What is his message and who is he speaking to in verses 1–11? 2. Jeremiah also continues his use of images and object lessons. What was the purpose of giving the leaders in the Jerusalem counsel an object lesson with the yoke and a message about the coming power of Babylon? 3. How do you think the counsel of kings and envoys would have responded when Jeremiah walked in with a yoke on his neck? 4. Zedekiah received the same message as the nations. Why would this be especially upsetting and confusing to the nation who considered themselves to be God's chosen people (vv. 12–15)? 5. What challenge does Jeremiah issue to the prophets (vv. 16–18)? 6. How does God communicate that he is in charge of the whole experience of Judah's defeat (vv. 21–22)?

Applying the Word 1. When you are going through difficult times, what comfort and wisdom does the knowledge of God provide for you? 2. Jeremiah called the counsel members to risk going against common sense to receive God's deliverance. What risks has following God meant for you? 3. How can Jeremiah's courage be an example for you in the challenges you face?

Responding in Prayer Ask God to give you courage as you face difficult and challenging places in your life.

15 / *Jeremiah 28*
Destroying False Hope

HOW DO GOD'S people handle hostility? John the Baptist told his listeners they should go the second mile. Jesus told the disciples to turn the other cheek. There is a tension here. We may be inclined to think that Christians should be doormats, giving way to the forces of hostile opposition. But that is not the point. Jesus confronted the religious leaders with their hypocrisy and called for the judgment of God on them. Matthew 23 records some of his hot rhetoric. Yet, while Jesus confronted, he didn't lead a jihad, a holy war, to destroy the opposition. He trusted God to bring judgment and justice in his way and his time.

Jeremiah's ministry was full of confrontation and hostility from the opposition. In this study it becomes physical and deadly. As we watch Jeremiah, we can learn how to trust God's guidance and power in threatening situations.

Warming Up to God Recall an experience of being publicly confronted or embarrassed by someone. How did you respond?

Read Jeremiah 28.

28

In the fifth month of that same year, the fourth year, early in the reign of Zedekiah king of Judah, the prophet Hananiah son of Azzur, who was from Gibeon, said to me in the house of the Lord in the presence of the priests and all the people: ²"This is what the Lord Almighty, the God of Israel, says: 'I will break the yoke of the king of Babylon. ³Within two years I will bring back to this place all the articles of the Lord's house that Nebuchadnezzar king of Babylon removed from here and took to Babylon. ⁴I will also bring back to this place Jehoiachin^c son of Jehoiakim king of Judah and all the other exiles from Judah who went to Babylon,' declares the Lord, 'for I will break the yoke of the king of Babylon.' "

⁵Then the prophet Jeremiah replied to the prophet Hananiah before the priests and all the people who were standing in the house of the Lord. ⁶He said, "Amen! May the Lord do so! May the Lord fulfill the words you have prophesied by bringing the articles of the Lord's house and all the exiles back to this place from Babylon. ⁷Nevertheless, listen to what I have to say in your hearing and in the hearing of all the people: ⁸From early times the prophets who preceded you and me have prophesied war, disaster and plague against many countries and great kingdoms. ⁹But the prophet who prophesies peace will be recognized as one truly sent by the Lord only if his prediction comes true."

¹⁰Then the prophet Hananiah took the yoke off the neck of the prophet Jeremiah and broke it, ¹¹and he said before all the people, "This is what the Lord says: 'In the same way will I break the yoke of Nebuchadnezzar king of Babylon off the neck of all the nations within two years.' " At this, the prophet Jeremiah went on his way.

¹²Shortly after the prophet Hananiah had broken the yoke off the neck of the prophet Jeremiah, the word of the Lord came to Jeremiah: ¹³"Go and tell Hananiah, 'This is what the Lord says: You have broken a wooden yoke, but in its place you will get a yoke of iron. ¹⁴This is what the Lord Almighty, the God of Israel, says: I will put an iron yoke on the necks of all these nations to make them serve Nebuchadnezzar king of Babylon, and they will serve him. I will even give him control over the wild animals.' "

¹⁵Then the prophet Jeremiah said to Hananiah the prophet, "Listen, Hananiah! The Lord has not sent you, yet you have persuaded this nation to trust in lies. ¹⁶Therefore, this is what the Lord says: 'I am about to remove you from the face of the earth. This very year you are going to die, because you have preached rebellion against the Lord.' "

¹⁷In the seventh month of that same year, Hananiah the prophet died.

^c4 Hebrew *Jeconiah*, a variant of *Jehoiachin*

Discovering the Word 1. How do you think Hananiah's message was received by the priests and people (vv. 1–4)? 2. How would you characterize Jeremiah's initial response to Hananiah (vv. 5–9)? 3. What test does Jeremiah give for discerning a true prophet? 4. Shortly after Hananiah broke the yoke off Jeremiah's neck, the Lord gives Jeremiah a stern rebuttal for Hananiah (vv. 12–14). Why might he have waited for a period of time instead of speaking when Hananiah broke the yoke? 5. What do you think those who heard the encounter between Jeremiah and Hananiah might have learned?

Applying the Word 1. What insight does this incident between Jeremiah and Hananiah provide in spotting false prophets or misleading messages given by false teachers? 2. The people who hear Jeremiah and Hananiah must choose who they believe is actually speaking the word of the Lord. How can you know that the words recorded in the Bible are really words from God and not merely human words of empty hopes and dreams?

 Responding in Prayer Thank God for the gifts of people and resources he has put in your life to strengthen your faith. If you have questions for God, let him know.

16 / *Jeremiah 29:1–23*
Living as Exiles

HAVING LIVED FOR several years in various countries, I admit there were times I honestly didn't want to be there. Life would have been much more familiar and comfortable in my home country where at least I understood how things were done. On those days when I really felt like a foreigner, it was good to remember that God had put me in these unfamiliar surroundings, and he would sustain me. He could transcend differences of culture and language, and he was carrying out his purposes in that place. Jeremiah needed to remind his people of these things as well.

Warming Up to God   When have you felt like a foreigner? (It may have been in your own hometown.) What difference did your faith in the Lord make at those times?

Read Jeremiah 29:1–23.

29 This is the text of the letter that the prophet Jeremiah sent from Jerusalem to the surviving elders among the exiles and to the priests, the prophets and all the other people Nebuchadnezzar had carried into exile from Jerusalem to Babylon. ²(This was after King Jehoiachin*f* and the queen mother, the court officials and the leaders of Judah and Jerusalem, the craftsmen and the artisans had gone into exile from Jerusalem.) ³He entrusted the letter to Elasah son of Shaphan and to Gemariah son of Hilkiah, whom Zedekiah king of Judah sent to King Nebuchadnezzar in Babylon. It said:

⁴This is what the LORD Almighty, the God of Israel, says to all those I carried into exile from Jerusalem to Babylon: ⁵"Build houses and settle down; plant gardens and eat what they produce. ⁶Marry and have sons and daughters; find wives for your sons and give your daughters in marriage, so that they too may have sons and daughters. Increase in number there; do not decrease. ⁷Also, seek the peace and prosperity of the city to which I have carried you into exile. Pray to the LORD for it, because if it prospers, you too will prosper." ⁸Yes, this is what the LORD Almighty, the God of Israel, says: "Do not let the prophets and diviners among you deceive you. Do not listen to the dreams you encourage them to have. ⁹They are prophesying lies to you in my name. I have not sent them," declares the LORD.

¹⁰This is what the LORD says: "When seventy years are completed for Babylon, I will come to you and fulfill my gracious promise to bring you back to this place. ¹¹For I know the plans I have for you," declares the LORD, "plans to prosper you and not to harm you, plans to give you hope and a future. ¹²Then you will call upon me and come and pray to me, and I will listen to you. ¹³You will seek me and find me when you seek me with all your heart. ¹⁴I will be found by you," declares the LORD, "and will bring you back from captivity.*g* I will gather you from all the nations and places where I have banished you," declares the LORD, "and will bring you back to the place from which I carried you into exile."

¹⁵You may say, "The LORD has raised up prophets for us in Babylon," ¹⁶but this is what the LORD says about the king who sits on David's throne and all the people who remain in this city, your countrymen who did not go with you into exile— ¹⁷yes, this is what the LORD Almighty says: "I will send the sword, famine and plague against them and I will make them like poor figs that are so bad they cannot be eaten. ¹⁸I will pursue them with the sword, famine and plague and will make them abhorrent to all the kingdoms of the earth and an object of cursing and horror, of scorn and reproach, among all the nations where I drive them. ¹⁹For they have not listened to my words," declares the LORD, "words that I sent to them again and again by my servants the prophets. And you exiles have not listened either," declares the LORD.

²⁰Therefore, hear the word of the LORD, all

*f*2 Hebrew *Jeconiah,* a variant of *Jehoiachin*   *g*14 Or *will restore your fortunes* you exiles whom I have sent away from Jerusalem to Babylon. ²¹This is what the LORD Almighty, the God of Israel, says about Ahab son of Kolaiah and Zedekiah son of Maaseiah, who are prophesying lies to you in my name: "I will hand them over to Nebuchadnezzar king of Babylon, and he will put them to death before your very eyes. ²²Because of them, all the exiles from Judah who are in Babylon will use this curse: 'The LORD treat you like Zedekiah and Ahab, whom the king of Babylon burned in the fire.' ²³For they have done outrageous things in Israel; they have committed adultery with their neighbors' wives and in my name have spoken lies, which I did not tell them to do. I know it and am a witness to it," declares the LORD.

Discovering the Word 1. What attitude did Jeremiah urge the Jews to have toward Babylon, where they were exiled (vv. 4–9)? 2. In verses 10–14 what gracious promise did the Lord make? 3. What would be the people's part in realizing God's promise (vv. 12–13)? 4. What was happening to contradict God's message to the exiles (vv. 8–9, 15, 20–23)? 5. What was the difference between the hope held out by the false prophets and the hope held out by the Lord?

Applying the Word 1. Consider any place, situation or circumstance where the Lord has placed you for now but where you don't want to be. How might verses 5–7 apply to your attitude and behavior? 2. What hope do you draw from God's promises in verses 11 and 14? 3. How can that situation drive you to seek the Lord more earnestly (v. 13)?

Responding in Prayer Taking verses 12–13 as your model, come to the Lord in very private prayer. Seek his will and his comfort for that situation which you chafe at. Rest in the assurance that he has only good plans for you.

Jeremiah 29:24—30:24

²⁴Tell Shemaiah the Nehelamite, ²⁵"This is what the LORD Almighty, the God of Israel, says: You sent letters in your own name to all the people in Jerusalem, to Zephaniah son of Maaseiah the priest, and to all the other priests. You said to Zephaniah, ²⁶'The LORD has appointed you priest in place of Jehoiada to be in charge of the house of the LORD; you should put any madman who acts like a prophet into the stocks and neck-irons. ²⁷So why have you not reprimanded Jeremiah from Anathoth, who poses as a prophet among you? ²⁸He has sent this message to us in Babylon: It will be a long time. Therefore build houses and settle down; plant gardens and eat what they produce.' "

²⁹Zephaniah the priest, however, read the letter to Jeremiah the prophet. ³⁰Then the word of the LORD came to Jeremiah: ³¹"Send this message to all the exiles: 'This is what the LORD says about Shemaiah the Nehelamite: Because Shemaiah has prophesied to you, even though I did not send him, and has led you to believe a lie, ³²this is what the LORD says: I will surely punish Shemaiah the Nehelamite and his descendants. He will have no one left among this people, nor will he see the good things I will do for my people, declares the LORD, because he has preached rebellion against me.' "

30 This is the word that came to Jeremiah from the LORD: ²"This is what the LORD, the God of Israel, says: 'Write in a book all the words I have spoken to you. ³The days are coming,' declares the LORD, 'when I will bring my people Israel and Judah back from captivity[h] and restore them to the land I gave their forefathers to possess,' says the LORD."

⁴These are the words the LORD spoke concerning Israel and Judah: ⁵"This is what the LORD says:

" 'Cries of fear are heard—
    terror, not peace.
⁶Ask and see:
    Can a man bear children?
Then why do I see every strong man
    with his hands on his stomach like a
        woman in labor,

ʰ3 Or *will restore the fortunes of my people Israel and Judah*

every face turned deathly pale?
⁷How awful that day will be!
  None will be like it.
It will be a time of trouble for Jacob,
  but he will be saved out of it.

⁸ 'In that day,' declares the LORD Almighty,
  'I will break the yoke off their necks
and will tear off their bonds;
  no longer will foreigners enslave them.
⁹Instead, they will serve the LORD their God
  and David their king,
  whom I will raise up for them.

¹⁰ 'So do not fear, O Jacob my servant;
  do not be dismayed, O Israel,'
                    declares the LORD.
'I will surely save you out of a distant place,
  your descendants from the land of their
    exile.
Jacob will again have peace and security,
  and no one will make him afraid.
¹¹I am with you and will save you,'
  declares the LORD.
'Though I completely destroy all the nations
  among which I scatter you,
  I will not completely destroy you.
I will discipline you but only with justice;
  I will not let you go entirely unpunished.'

¹²"This is what the LORD says:

" 'Your wound is incurable,
  your injury beyond healing.
¹³There is no one to plead your cause,
  no remedy for your sore,
  no healing for you.
¹⁴All your allies have forgotten you;
  they care nothing for you.
I have struck you as an enemy would
  and punished you as would the cruel,
because your guilt is so great
  and your sins so many.
¹⁵Why do you cry out over your wound,
  your pain that has no cure?
Because of your great guilt and many sins
  I have done these things to you.

¹⁶ 'But all who devour you will be devoured;
  all your enemies will go into exile.
Those who plunder you will be plundered;
  all who make spoil of you I will despoil.
¹⁷But I will restore you to health
  and heal your wounds,'
                    declares the LORD,
'because you are called an outcast,
  Zion for whom no one cares.'

¹⁸"This is what the LORD says:

" 'I will restore the fortunes of Jacob's tents
  and have compassion on his dwellings;
the city will be rebuilt on her ruins,
  and the palace will stand in its proper
    place.
¹⁹From them will come songs of thanksgiving
  and the sound of rejoicing.
I will add to their numbers,
  and they will not be decreased;
I will bring them honor,
  and they will not be disdained.
²⁰Their children will be as in days of old,
  and their community will be established
    before me;
I will punish all who oppress them.
²¹Their leader will be one of their own;
  their ruler will arise from among them.
I will bring him near and he will come close
    to me,
  for who is he who will devote himself
  to be close to me?'
                    declares the LORD.
²²" 'So you will be my people,
  and I will be your God.' "

²³See, the storm of the LORD
  will burst out in wrath,
a driving wind swirling down
  on the heads of the wicked.
²⁴The fierce anger of the LORD will not turn
    back
  until he fully accomplishes
  the purposes of his heart.
In days to come
  you will understand this.

17 / *Jeremiah 31*
Restoration

AN ACCIDENTAL DELETE on a computer feels like a disaster. Vital material suddenly vanishes as if it never existed. Fortunately, there are usually ways to restore the lost file. Other things like broken relationships and lost opportunities are not so easy to bring back. In exile Israel must have often thought their last chance and hope were gone, but the Lord still had his purposes for them.

 Warming Up to God Think of a time your closeness with the Lord was restored after something disrupted it. What brought about the restoration?

 Read Jeremiah 31.

31 "At that time," declares the LORD, "I will be the God of all the clans of Israel, and they will be my people."
²This is what the LORD says:

"The people who survive the sword
  will find favor in the desert;
  I will come to give rest to Israel."

³The LORD appeared to us in the past,[i] saying:

"I have loved you with an everlasting love;
  I have drawn you with loving-kindness.
⁴I will build you up again
  and you will be rebuilt, O Virgin Israel.
Again you will take up your tambourines
  and go out to dance with the joyful.
⁵Again you will plant vineyards
  on the hills of Samaria;
the farmers will plant them
  and enjoy their fruit.
⁶There will be a day when watchmen cry out
  on the hills of Ephraim,
'Come, let us go up to Zion,
  to the LORD our God.' "

⁷This is what the LORD says:

"Sing with joy for Jacob;
  shout for the foremost of the nations.
Make your praises heard, and say,
  'O LORD, save your people,
  the remnant of Israel.'
⁸See, I will bring them from the land of the
    north
  and gather them from the ends of the earth.
Among them will be the blind and the lame,
  expectant mothers and women in labor;
  a great throng will return.
⁹They will come with weeping;
  they will pray as I bring them back.

I will lead them beside streams of water
  on a level path where they will not
    stumble,
because I am Israel's father,
  and Ephraim is my firstborn son.

¹⁰"Hear the word of the LORD, O nations;
  proclaim it in distant coastlands:
'He who scattered Israel will gather them
  and will watch over his flock like a
    shepherd.'
¹¹For the LORD will ransom Jacob
  and redeem them from the hand of those
    stronger than they.
¹²They will come and shout for joy on the
    heights of Zion;
  they will rejoice in the bounty of the
    LORD—
the grain, the new wine and the oil,
  the young of the flocks and herds.
They will be like a well-watered garden,
  and they will sorrow no more.
¹³Then maidens will dance and be glad,
  young men and old as well.
I will turn their mourning into gladness;
  I will give them comfort and joy instead of
    sorrow.
¹⁴I will satisfy the priests with abundance,
  and my people will be filled with my
    bounty,"
                    declares the LORD.

¹⁵This is what the LORD says:

"A voice is heard in Ramah,
  mourning and great weeping,
Rachel weeping for her children
  and refusing to be comforted,

---
i 3 Or LORD *has appeared to us from afar*

because her children are no more."

16This is what the LORD says:

"Restrain your voice from weeping
    and your eyes from tears,
for your work will be rewarded,"
                                    declares the LORD.
  "They will return from the land of the
    enemy.
17So there is hope for your future,"
                                    declares the LORD.
  "Your children will return to their own
    land.

18"I have surely heard Ephraim's moaning:
  'You disciplined me like an unruly calf,
    and I have been disciplined.
  Restore me, and I will return,
    because you are the LORD my God.
19After I strayed,
    I repented;
  after I came to understand,
    I beat my breast.
  I was ashamed and humiliated
    because I bore the disgrace of my youth.'
20Is not Ephraim my dear son,
    the child in whom I delight?
  Though I often speak against him,
    I still remember him.
  Therefore my heart yearns for him;
    I have great compassion for him,"
                                    declares the LORD.

21"Set up road signs;
    put up guideposts.
  Take note of the highway,
    the road that you take.
  Return, O Virgin Israel,
    return to your towns.
22How long will you wander,
    O unfaithful daughter?
  The LORD will create a new thing on earth—
    a woman will surround[j] a man."

23This is what the LORD Almighty, the God of
Israel, says: "When I bring them back from captivity,[k] the people in the land of Judah and in its
towns will once again use these words: 'The LORD
bless you, O righteous dwelling, O sacred mountain.' 24People will live together in Judah and all
its towns—farmers and those who move about
with their flocks. 25I will refresh the weary and
satisfy the faint."

26At this I awoke and looked around. My sleep
had been pleasant to me.
27"The days are coming," declares the LORD,
"when I will plant the house of Israel and the
house of Judah with the offspring of men and of
animals. 28Just as I watched over them to uproot
and tear down, and to overthrow, destroy and
bring disaster, so I will watch over them to build
and to plant," declares the LORD. 29"In those days
people will no longer say,

  'The fathers have eaten sour grapes,
    and the children's teeth are set on edge.'

30Instead, everyone will die for his own sin; whoever eats sour grapes—his own teeth will be set
on edge.

31"The time is coming," declares the LORD,
  "when I will make a new covenant
with the house of Israel
  and with the house of Judah.
32It will not be like the covenant
  I made with their forefathers
when I took them by the hand
  to lead them out of Egypt,
because they broke my covenant,
  though I was a husband to[l] them,[m]"
                                    declares the LORD.
33"This is the covenant I will make with the
      house of Israel
  after that time," declares the LORD.
"I will put my law in their minds
  and write it on their hearts.
I will be their God,
  and they will be my people.
34No longer will a man teach his neighbor,
  or a man his brother, saying, 'Know the
    LORD,'
because they will all know me,
  from the least of them to the greatest,"
                                    declares the LORD.
"For I will forgive their wickedness
  and will remember their sins no more."

35This is what the LORD says,

he who appoints the sun
  to shine by day,
who decrees the moon and stars
  to shine by night,
who stirs up the sea

<hr>

j 22 Or will go about ˌseekingˌ; or will protect   k 23 Or I restore their
fortunes   l 32 Hebrew; Septuagint and Syriac l and I turned away from
m 32 Or was their master

so that its waves roar—
the LORD Almighty is his name:
[36]"Only if these decrees vanish from my
sight,"
declares the LORD,
"will the descendants of Israel ever cease
to be a nation before me."

[37]This is what the LORD says:

"Only if the heavens above can be measured
and the foundations of the earth below be
searched out
will I reject all the descendants of Israel

because of all they have done,"
declares the LORD.

[38]"The days are coming," declares the LORD, "when this city will be rebuilt for me from the Tower of Hananel to the Corner Gate. [39]The measuring line will stretch from there straight to the hill of Gareb and then turn to Goah. [40]The whole valley where dead bodies and ashes are thrown, and all the terraces out to the Kidron Valley on the east as far as the corner of the Horse Gate, will be holy to the LORD. The city will never again be uprooted or demolished."

Discovering the Word 1. How would you sum up God's message to Jeremiah in this passage? 2. What reasons does God give for restoring Israel (vv. 3, 9, 20)? 3. How does God depict the bounty and joy which he will restore to Israel (vv. 1–2, 4–5, 12–14, 22–25, 27–28)? 4. What change of heart will Israel experience concerning their sin (vv. 9, 18–19)? 5. How will the new covenant be different from the old (vv. 31–34)? 6. How long will God's blessings last (vv. 35–37)?

Applying the Word 1. In what ways do you need to be restored by God? 2. Think of someone you know who needs restoration. It may be someone's relationship with God, a friendship, a marriage, a church fellowship. If appropriate, how can you contribute to that restoration?

Responding in Prayer Thank God for his restoring love. Pray for areas in your life where you feel broken and need his restoration. Pray for damaged relationships which need to be restored by the touch of God.

---

18 / *Jeremiah 32:1–25*
The Promise of Renewed Land

SOCIOLOGISTS HAVE DISCOVERED a set of behaviors which they call "deferred gratification pattern." It describes the practice of putting off a purchase or action in hope that better dividends would come in the future. Most everyone who lives by deferred gratification expects to get a good return. But what if the benefits don't come in your lifetime? In this chapter Jeremiah makes a real-estate deal that on the surface looks foolish. It is the ultimate in deferred gratification. In the transaction he demonstrates the depth of his character and the quality of his obedience to God.

Warming Up to God How do you feel when you have to put off buying something that you really want immediately?

Read Jeremiah 32:1–25.

---

32 This is the word that came to Jeremiah from the LORD in the tenth year of Zedekiah king of Judah, which was the eighteenth year of Nebuchadnezzar. [2]The army of the king of Babylon was then besieging Jerusalem, and Jeremiah the prophet was confined in the courtyard of the guard in the royal palace of Judah.

[3]Now Zedekiah king of Judah had imprisoned him there, saying, "Why do you prophesy as you do? You say, 'This is what the LORD says: I am about to hand this city over to the king of Babylon, and he will capture it. [4]Zedekiah king of Judah will not escape out of the hands of the Babylonians[n] but will certainly be handed over

[n]4 Or *Chaldeans*; also in verses 5, 24, 25, 28, 29 and 43

to the king of Babylon, and will speak with him face to face and see him with his own eyes. ⁵He will take Zedekiah to Babylon, where he will remain until I deal with him, declares the Lᴏʀᴅ. If you fight against the Babylonians, you will not succeed.' "

⁶Jeremiah said, "The word of the Lᴏʀᴅ came to me: ⁷Hanamel son of Shallum your uncle is going to come to you and say, 'Buy my field at Anathoth, because as nearest relative it is your right and duty to buy it.'

⁸"Then, just as the Lᴏʀᴅ had said, my cousin Hanamel came to me in the courtyard of the guard and said, 'Buy my field at Anathoth in the territory of Benjamin. Since it is your right to redeem it and possess it, buy it for yourself.'

"I knew that this was the word of the Lᴏʀᴅ; ⁹so I bought the field at Anathoth from my cousin Hanamel and weighed out for him seventeen shekels⁰ of silver. ¹⁰I signed and sealed the deed, had it witnessed, and weighed out the silver on the scales. ¹¹I took the deed of purchase—the sealed copy containing the terms and conditions, as well as the unsealed copy— ¹²and I gave this deed to Baruch son of Neriah, the son of Mahseiah, in the presence of my cousin Hanamel and of the witnesses who had signed the deed and of all the Jews sitting in the courtyard of the guard.

¹³"In their presence I gave Baruch these instructions: ¹⁴This is what the Lᴏʀᴅ Almighty, the God of Israel, says: Take these documents, both the sealed and unsealed copies of the deed of purchase, and put them in a clay jar so they will last a long time. ¹⁵For this is what the Lᴏʀᴅ Almighty, the God of Israel, says: Houses, fields and vineyards will again be bought in this land.'

¹⁶"After I had given the deed of purchase to Baruch son of Neriah, I prayed to the Lᴏʀᴅ:

¹⁷"Ah, Sovereign Lᴏʀᴅ, you have made the heavens and the earth by your great power and outstretched arm. Nothing is too hard for you. ¹⁸You show love to thousands but bring the punishment for the fathers' sins into the laps of their children after them. O great and powerful God, whose name is the Lᴏʀᴅ Almighty, ¹⁹great are your purposes and mighty are your deeds. Your eyes are open to all the ways of men; you reward everyone according to his conduct and as his deeds deserve. ²⁰You performed miraculous signs and wonders in Egypt and have continued them to this day, both in Israel and among all mankind, and have gained the renown that is still yours. ²¹You brought your people Israel out of Egypt with signs and wonders, by a mighty hand and an outstretched arm and with great terror. ²²You gave them this land you had sworn to give their forefathers, a land flowing with milk and honey. ²³They came in and took possession of it, but they did not obey you or follow your law; they did not do what you commanded them to do. So you brought all this disaster upon them.

²⁴"See how the siege ramps are built up to take the city. Because of the sword, famine and plague, the city will be handed over to the Babylonians who are attacking it. What you said has happened, as you now see. ²⁵And though the city will be handed over to the Babylonians, you, O Sovereign Lᴏʀᴅ, say to me, 'Buy the field with silver and have the transaction witnessed.' "

⁰9 That is, about 7 ounces (about 200 grams)

 Discovering the Word 1. Jerusalem is in a state of siege. How might Jeremiah's willingness to purchase a field have been a means of comfort to the threatened citizens? 2. Why is Jeremiah imprisoned in the courtyard, and why is Zedekiah shut up in Jerusalem? 3. Jeremiah records in detail the process of the legal transaction for the purchase of the land (vv. 9–12). What impact would this have on those who watched? 4. Why would Jeremiah make a transaction from which he would never personally benefit (vv. 14–15)? 5. After the purchase Jeremiah offered a prayer (vv. 17–25). What themes are woven throughout the prayer? 6. What further comfort and confirmation of Jeremiah does God offer in verses 38–44?

Applying the Word 1. What can we learn about Christian service and character from Jeremiah's model? 2. Jeremiah's prayer shows a familiar knowledge of God's past actions. How can this study of Jeremiah be a resource for your prayers?

Responding in Prayer Prayer is a great source of comfort in times of trouble. Talk to God about the things that are on your mind today.

Jeremiah 32:26–44

26Then the word of the LORD came to Jeremiah: 27"I am the LORD, the God of all mankind. Is anything too hard for me? 28Therefore, this is what the LORD says: I am about to hand this city over to the Babylonians and to Nebuchadnezzar king of Babylon, who will capture it. 29The Babylonians who are attacking this city will come in and set it on fire; they will burn it down, along with the houses where the people provoked me to anger by burning incense on the roofs to Baal and by pouring out drink offerings to other gods.

30"The people of Israel and Judah have done nothing but evil in my sight from their youth; indeed, the people of Israel have done nothing but provoke me with what their hands have made, declares the LORD. 31From the day it was built until now, this city has so aroused my anger and wrath that I must remove it from my sight. 32The people of Israel and Judah have provoked me by all the evil they have done—they, their kings and officials, their priests and prophets, the men of Judah and the people of Jerusalem. 33They turned their backs to me and not their faces; though I taught them again and again, they would not listen or respond to discipline. 34They set up their abominable idols in the house that bears my Name and defiled it. 35They built high places for Baal in the Valley of Ben Hinnom to sacrifice their sons and daughtersᵖ to Molech, though I never commanded, nor did it enter my mind, that they should do such a detestable thing and so make Judah sin.

36"You are saying about this city, 'By the sword, famine and plague it will be handed over to the king of Babylon'; but this is what the LORD, the God of Israel, says: 37I will surely gather them from all the lands where I banish them in my furious anger and great wrath; I will bring them back to this place and let them live in safety. 38They will be my people, and I will be their God. 39I will give them singleness of heart and action, so that they will always fear me for their own good and the good of their children after them. 40I will make an everlasting covenant with them: I will never stop doing good to them, and I will inspire them to fear me, so that they will never turn away from me. 41I will rejoice in doing them good and will assuredly plant them in this land with all my heart and soul.

42"This is what the LORD says: As I have brought all this great calamity on this people, so I will give them all the prosperity I have promised them. 43Once more fields will be bought in this land of which you say, 'It is a desolate waste, without men or animals, for it has been handed over to the Babylonians.' 44Fields will be bought for silver, and deeds will be signed, sealed and witnessed in the territory of Benjamin, in the villages around Jerusalem, in the towns of Judah and in the towns of the hill country, of the western foothills and of the Negev, because I will restore their fortunes,ᑫ declares the LORD."

ᵖ35 Or *to make their sons and daughters pass through ⌐the fire⌐*
ᑫ44 Or *will bring them back from captivity*

19 / Jeremiah 33
The Sure and Certain Promise

WHEN JOHN THE Baptist was in prison, he sent messengers to Jesus asking if he was the Messiah or not. The question probably came from confusion and despair. After all, hadn't John proclaimed the Coming One who would take away the sins of the world? Surely the Messiah's coming would bring freedom and fulfillment for everyone. Why was John imprisoned?

God had warned Jeremiah from the moment of his call that his ministry would be difficult. Even so, like John the Baptist, there must have been days of frustration. He was ignored, rejected, despised and imprisoned. In the midst of that darkness, God comes to Jeremiah with a candle of light. Sometimes God doesn't rescue us. Sometimes he does. Either way, he extends his love and grace.

 Warming Up to God When things look dark and depressing, what do you do to gain encouragement and hope?

 Read Jeremiah 33.

33

While Jeremiah was still confined in the courtyard of the guard, the word of the LORD came to him a second time: ²"This is what the LORD says, he who made the earth, the LORD who formed it and established it—the LORD is his name: ³'Call to me and I will answer you and tell you great and unsearchable things you do not know.' ⁴For this is what the LORD, the God of Israel, says about the houses in this city and the royal palaces of Judah that have been torn down to be used against the siege ramps and the sword ⁵in the fight with the Babylonians[r]: 'They will be filled with the dead bodies of the men I will slay in my anger and wrath. I will hide my face from this city because of all its wickedness.

⁶" 'Nevertheless, I will bring health and healing to it; I will heal my people and will let them enjoy abundant peace and security. ⁷I will bring Judah and Israel back from captivity[s] and will rebuild them as they were before. ⁸I will cleanse them from all the sin they have committed against me and will forgive all their sins of rebellion against me. ⁹Then this city will bring me renown, joy, praise and honor before all nations on earth that hear of all the good things I do for it; and they will be in awe and will tremble at the abundant prosperity and peace I provide for it.'

¹⁰"This is what the LORD says: 'You say about this place, "It is a desolate waste, without men or animals." Yet in the towns of Judah and the streets of Jerusalem that are deserted, inhabited by neither men nor animals, there will be heard once more ¹¹the sounds of joy and gladness, the voices of bride and bridegroom, and the voices of those who bring thank offerings to the house of the LORD, saying,

"Give thanks to the LORD Almighty,
    for the LORD is good;
    his love endures forever."

For I will restore the fortunes of the land as they were before,' says the LORD.

¹²"This is what the LORD Almighty says: 'In this place, desolate and without men or animals—in all its towns there will again be pastures for shepherds to rest their flocks. ¹³In the towns of the hill country, of the western foothills and of the Negev, in the territory of Benjamin, in the villages around Jerusalem and in the towns of Judah, flocks will again pass under the hand of the one who counts them,' says the LORD.

¹⁴" 'The days are coming,' declares the LORD, 'when I will fulfill the gracious promise I made to the house of Israel and to the house of Judah.

¹⁵" 'In those days and at that time
    I will make a righteous Branch sprout from
        David's line;
    he will do what is just and right in the
        land.
¹⁶In those days Judah will be saved
    and Jerusalem will live in safety.
This is the name by which it[t] will be called:
    The LORD Our Righteousness.'

¹⁷For this is what the LORD says: 'David will never fail to have a man to sit on the throne of the house of Israel, ¹⁸nor will the priests, who are Levites, ever fail to have a man to stand before me continually to offer burnt offerings, to burn grain offerings and to present sacrifices.' "

¹⁹The word of the LORD came to Jeremiah: ²⁰"This is what the LORD says: 'If you can break my covenant with the day and my covenant with the night, so that day and night no longer come at their appointed time, ²¹then my covenant with David my servant—and my covenant with the Levites who are priests ministering before me—can be broken and David will no longer have a descendant to reign on his throne. ²²I will make the descendants of David my servant and the Levites who minister before me as countless as the stars of the sky and as measureless as the sand on the seashore.' "

---

[r]5 Or *Chaldeans*   [s]7 Or *will restore the fortunes of Judah and Israel*
[t]16 Or *he*

²³The word of the LORD came to Jeremiah: ²⁴"Have you not noticed that these people are saying, 'The LORD has rejected the two kingdomsᵘ he chose'? So they despise my people and no longer regard them as a nation. ²⁵This is what the LORD says: 'If I have not established my covenant with day and night and the fixed laws of heaven and earth, ²⁶then I will reject the descendants of Jacob and David my servant and will not choose one of his sons to rule over the descendants of Abraham, Isaac and Jacob. For I will restore their fortunesᵛ and have compassion on them.' "

ᵘ24 Or families   ᵛ26 Or will bring them back from captivity

Discovering the Word 1. Jeremiah is imprisoned in Jerusalem with the Babylonian army at the gates. What does God do to offer him comfort? 2. The Hebrew meaning of the Lord's name used here is "Promise Keeper." Why do you think God repeats his name four times in verses 2–4? 3. God invites Jeremiah to call out for assurance and then immediately offers his response (vv. 4–9). In what way would God's words be comforting? 4. What is God going to do to fulfill his promises to Judah and Israel (vv. 15–18)? 5. The destruction of Israel and Judah could lead to the accusation that God was a covenant breaker. How does God answer this (vv. 20–26)?

Applying the Word 1. Have there been times in your life when you felt confined, trapped or limited? 2. How could or did the knowledge of God help? 3. How would your experience of life and your relationship with God be different if he was untrustworthy?

Responding in Prayer Offer praise to the only God worthy of your trust.

Jeremiah 34—35

34 While Nebuchadnezzar king of Babylon and all his army and all the kingdoms and peoples in the empire he ruled were fighting against Jerusalem and all its surrounding towns, this word came to Jeremiah from the LORD: ²"This is what the LORD, the God of Israel, says: Go to Zedekiah king of Judah and tell him, 'This is what the LORD says: I am about to hand this city over to the king of Babylon, and he will burn it down. ³You will not escape from his grasp but will surely be captured and handed over to him. You will see the king of Babylon with your own eyes, and he will speak with you face to face. And you will go to Babylon.

⁴" 'Yet hear the promise of the LORD, O Zedekiah king of Judah. This is what the LORD says concerning you: You will not die by the sword; ⁵you will die peacefully. As people made a funeral fire in honor of your fathers, the former kings who preceded you, so they will make a fire in your honor and lament, "Alas, O master!" I myself make this promise, declares the LORD.' "

⁶Then Jeremiah the prophet told all this to Zedekiah king of Judah, in Jerusalem, ⁷while the army of the king of Babylon was fighting against Jerusalem and the other cities of Judah that were still holding out—Lachish and Azekah. These were the only fortified cities left in Judah.

⁸The word came to Jeremiah from the LORD after King Zedekiah had made a covenant with all the people in Jerusalem to proclaim freedom for the slaves. ⁹Everyone was to free his Hebrew slaves, both male and female; no one was to hold a fellow Jew in bondage. ¹⁰So all the officials and people who entered into this covenant agreed that they would free their male and female slaves and no longer hold them in bondage. They agreed, and set them free. ¹¹But afterward they changed their minds and took back the slaves they had freed and enslaved them again.

¹²Then the word of the LORD came to Jeremiah: ¹³"This is what the LORD, the God of Israel, says: I made a covenant with your forefathers when I brought them out of Egypt, out of the land of slavery. I said, ¹⁴'Every seventh year each of you must free any fellow Hebrew who has sold himself to you. After he has served you six years, you must let him go free.'ʷ Your fathers, however, did not listen to me or pay attention to me. ¹⁵Recently you repented and did what is right in my sight: Each of you proclaimed freedom to his

ʷ14 Deut. 15:12

countrymen. You even made a covenant before me in the house that bears my Name. ¹⁶But now you have turned around and profaned my name; each of you has taken back the male and female slaves you had set free to go where they wished. You have forced them to become your slaves again.

¹⁷"Therefore, this is what the LORD says: You have not obeyed me; you have not proclaimed freedom for your fellow countrymen. So I now proclaim 'freedom' for you, declares the LORD— 'freedom' to fall by the sword, plague and famine. I will make you abhorrent to all the kingdoms of the earth. ¹⁸The men who have violated my covenant and have not fulfilled the terms of the covenant they made before me, I will treat like the calf they cut in two and then walked between its pieces. ¹⁹The leaders of Judah and Jerusalem, the court officials, the priests and all the people of the land who walked between the pieces of the calf, ²⁰I will hand over to their enemies who seek their lives. Their dead bodies will become food for the birds of the air and the beasts of the earth.

²¹"I will hand Zedekiah king of Judah and his officials over to their enemies who seek their lives, to the army of the king of Babylon, which has withdrawn from you. ²²I am going to give the order, declares the LORD, and I will bring them back to this city. They will fight against it, take it and burn it down. And I will lay waste the towns of Judah so no one can live there."

35 This is the word that came to Jeremiah from the LORD during the reign of Jehoiakim son of Josiah king of Judah: ²"Go to the Recabite family and invite them to come to one of the side rooms of the house of the LORD and give them wine to drink."

³So I went to get Jaazaniah son of Jeremiah, the son of Habazziniah, and his brothers and all his sons—the whole family of the Recabites. ⁴I brought them into the house of the LORD, into the room of the sons of Hanan son of Igdaliah the man of God. It was next to the room of the officials, which was over that of Maaseiah son of Shallum the doorkeeper. ⁵Then I set bowls full of wine and some cups before the men of the Recabite family and said to them, "Drink some wine."

⁶But they replied, "We do not drink wine, because our forefather Jonadab son of Recab gave us this command: 'Neither you nor your descendants must ever drink wine. ⁷Also you must never build houses, sow seed or plant vineyards; you must never have any of these things, but must always live in tents. Then you will live a long time in the land where you are nomads.' ⁸We have obeyed everything our forefather Jonadab son of Recab commanded us. Neither we nor our wives nor our sons and daughters have ever drunk wine ⁹or built houses to live in or had vineyards, fields or crops. ¹⁰We have lived in tents and have fully obeyed everything our forefather Jonadab commanded us. ¹¹But when Nebuchadnezzar king of Babylon invaded this land, we said, 'Come, we must go to Jerusalem to escape the Babylonianˣ and Aramean armies.' So we have remained in Jerusalem."

¹²Then the word of the LORD came to Jeremiah, saying: ¹³"This is what the LORD Almighty, the God of Israel, says: Go and tell the men of Judah and the people of Jerusalem, 'Will you not learn a lesson and obey my words?' declares the LORD. ¹⁴Jonadab son of Recab ordered his sons not to drink wine and this command has been kept. To this day they do not drink wine, because they obey their forefather's command. But I have spoken to you again and again, yet you have not obeyed me. ¹⁵Again and again I sent all my servants the prophets to you. They said, "Each of you must turn from your wicked ways and reform your actions; do not follow other gods to serve them. Then you will live in the land I have given to you and your fathers." But you have not paid attention or listened to me. ¹⁶The descendants of Jonadab son of Recab have carried out the command their forefather gave them, but these people have not obeyed me.'

¹⁷"Therefore, this is what the LORD God Almighty, the God of Israel, says: 'Listen! I am going to bring on Judah and on everyone living in Jerusalem every disaster I pronounced against them. I spoke to them, but they did not listen; I called to them, but they did not answer.' "

¹⁸Then Jeremiah said to the family of the Recabites, "This is what the LORD Almighty, the God of Israel, says: 'You have obeyed the command of your forefather Jonadab and have followed all his instructions and have done everything he ordered.' ¹⁹Therefore, this is what the LORD Almighty, the God of Israel, says: 'Jonadab son of Recab will never fail to have a man to serve me.' "

ˣ11 Or Chaldean

20 / *Jeremiah 36*
The Burning Scroll

A WRITER'S GREATEST fear is that the sole copy of a book manuscript will be destroyed by fire. Once burned up, those thousands of lost words can never be reconstructed. An annoyed king once tossed God's words into the flames. Still the Word of God persists and lives through any fire.

 Warming Up to God Reflect on what God's Word has meant in your life. How is it precious to you?

 Read Jeremiah 36.

36 In the fourth year of Jehoiakim son of Josiah king of Judah, this word came to Jeremiah from the LORD: ²"Take a scroll and write on it all the words I have spoken to you concerning Israel, Judah and all the other nations from the time I began speaking to you in the reign of Josiah till now. ³Perhaps when the people of Judah hear about every disaster I plan to inflict on them, each of them will turn from his wicked way; then I will forgive their wickedness and their sin."

⁴So Jeremiah called Baruch son of Neriah, and while Jeremiah dictated all the words the LORD had spoken to him, Baruch wrote them on the scroll. ⁵Then Jeremiah told Baruch, "I am restricted; I cannot go to the LORD's temple. ⁶So you go to the house of the LORD on a day of fasting and read to the people from the scroll the words of the LORD that you wrote as I dictated. Read them to all the people of Judah who come in from their towns. ⁷Perhaps they will bring their petition before the LORD, and each will turn from his wicked ways, for the anger and wrath pronounced against this people by the LORD are great."

⁸Baruch son of Neriah did everything Jeremiah the prophet told him to do; at the LORD's temple he read the words of the LORD from the scroll. ⁹In the ninth month of the fifth year of Jehoiakim son of Josiah king of Judah, a time of fasting before the LORD was proclaimed for all the people in Jerusalem and those who had come from the towns of Judah. ¹⁰From the room of Gemariah son of Shaphan the secretary, which was in the upper courtyard at the entrance of the New Gate of the temple, Baruch read to all the people at the LORD's temple the words of Jeremiah from the scroll.

¹¹When Micaiah son of Gemariah, the son of Shaphan, heard all the words of the LORD from the scroll, ¹²he went down to the secretary's room in the royal palace, where all the officials were sitting: Elishama the secretary, Delaiah son of Shemaiah, Elnathan son of Acbor, Gemariah son of Shaphan, Zedekiah son of Hananiah, and all the other officials. ¹³After Micaiah told them everything he had heard Baruch read to the people from the scroll, ¹⁴all the officials sent Jehudi son of Nethaniah, the son of Shelemiah, the son of Cushi, to say to Baruch, "Bring the scroll from which you have read to the people and come." So Baruch son of Neriah went to them with the scroll in his hand. ¹⁵They said to him, "Sit down, please, and read it to us."

So Baruch read it to them. ¹⁶When they heard all these words, they looked at each other in fear and said to Baruch, "We must report all these words to the king." ¹⁷Then they asked Baruch, "Tell us, how did you come to write all this? Did Jeremiah dictate it?"

¹⁸"Yes," Baruch replied, "he dictated all these words to me, and I wrote them in ink on the scroll."

¹⁹Then the officials said to Baruch, "You and Jeremiah, go and hide. Don't let anyone know where you are."

²⁰After they put the scroll in the room of Elishama the secretary, they went to the king in the courtyard and reported everything to him. ²¹The king sent Jehudi to get the scroll, and Jehudi brought it from the room of Elishama the secretary and read it to the king and all the officials standing beside him. ²²It was the ninth month and the king was sitting in the winter apartment, with a fire burning in the firepot in front of him. ²³Whenever Jehudi had read three or four columns of the scroll, the king cut them off with a scribe's knife and threw them into the firepot, until the entire scroll was burned in the fire. ²⁴The king and all his attendants who heard all

these words showed no fear, nor did they tear their clothes. 25Even though Elnathan, Delaiah and Gemariah urged the king not to burn the scroll, he would not listen to them. 26Instead, the king commanded Jerahmeel, a son of the king, Seraiah son of Azriel and Shelemiah son of Abdeel to arrest Baruch the scribe and Jeremiah the prophet. But the LORD had hidden them.

27After the king burned the scroll containing the words that Baruch had written at Jeremiah's dictation, the word of the LORD came to Jeremiah: 28"Take another scroll and write on it all the words that were on the first scroll, which Jehoiakim king of Judah burned up. 29Also tell Jehoiakim king of Judah, 'This is what the LORD says: You burned that scroll and said, "Why did you write on it that the king of Babylon would cer-

tainly come and destroy this land and cut off both men and animals from it?" 30Therefore, this is what the LORD says about Jehoiakim king of Judah: He will have no one to sit on the throne of David; his body will be thrown out and exposed to the heat by day and the frost by night. 31I will punish him and his children and his attendants for their wickedness; I will bring on them and those living in Jerusalem and the people of Judah every disaster I pronounced against them, because they have not listened.' "

32So Jeremiah took another scroll and gave it to the scribe Baruch son of Neriah, and as Jeremiah dictated, Baruch wrote on it all the words of the scroll that Jehoiakim king of Judah had burned in the fire. And many similar words were added to them.

Discovering the Word 1. What was the purpose of the scroll's being written and read (vv. 1–10)? 2. What effect did the scroll have on King Jehoiakim's officials (vv. 11–19)? 3. When the king heard the scroll read aloud, how did he react (vv. 20–26)? 4. How would you describe the king's attitude toward God's words? 5. How did God overrule the king's contempt (vv. 27–32)?

Applying the Word 1. Which of God's words do people prefer to "cut out and burn" today? 2. Jeremiah was directed to rewrite the scroll, plus more. That took courage. How can you remind people that God's Word still stands despite the contempt of some?

Responding in Prayer Praise God that his Word is eternal and can never be destroyed by unbelief or contempt. Pray that you and believers all over the world will stand up for the truth of Scripture.

Jeremiah 37

37 Zedekiah son of Josiah was made king of Judah by Nebuchadnezzar king of Babylon; he reigned in place of Jehoiachinʸ son of Jehoiakim. 2Neither he nor his attendants nor the people of the land paid any attention to the words the LORD had spoken through Jeremiah the prophet.

3King Zedekiah, however, sent Jehucal son of Shelemiah with the priest Zephaniah son of Maaseiah to Jeremiah the prophet with this message: "Please pray to the LORD our God for us."

4Now Jeremiah was free to come and go among the people, for he had not yet been put in prison. 5Pharaoh's army had marched out of Egypt, and when the Babyloniansᶻ who were besieging Jerusalem heard the report about them, they withdrew from Jerusalem.

6Then the word of the LORD came to Jeremiah the prophet: 7"This is what the LORD, the God of

Israel, says: Tell the king of Judah, who sent you to inquire of me, 'Pharaoh's army, which has marched out to support you, will go back to its own land, to Egypt. 8Then the Babylonians will return and attack this city; they will capture it and burn it down.'

9"This is what the LORD says: Do not deceive yourselves, thinking, 'The Babylonians will surely leave us.' They will not! 10Even if you were to defeat the entire Babylonianᵃ army that is attacking you and only wounded men were left in their tents, they would come out and burn this city down."

11After the Babylonian army had withdrawn from Jerusalem because of Pharaoh's army, 12Jeremiah started to leave the city to go to the territory of Benjamin to get his share of the property

ʸ1 Hebrew *Coniah*, a variant of *Jehoiachin*   ᶻ5 Or *Chaldeans*; also in verses 8, 9, 13 and 14   ᵃ10 Or *Chaldean*; also in verse 11 among the people there. ¹³But when he reached the Benjamin Gate, the captain of the guard, whose name was Irijah son of Shelemiah, the son of Hananiah, arrested him and said, "You are deserting to the Babylonians!"

¹⁴"That's not true!" Jeremiah said. "I am not deserting to the Babylonians." But Irijah would not listen to him; instead, he arrested Jeremiah and brought him to the officials. ¹⁵They were angry with Jeremiah and had him beaten and imprisoned in the house of Jonathan the secretary, which they had made into a prison.

¹⁶Jeremiah was put into a vaulted cell in a dungeon, where he remained a long time. ¹⁷Then King Zedekiah sent for him and had him brought to the palace, where he asked him privately, "Is there any word from the LORD?"

"Yes," Jeremiah replied, "you will be handed over to the king of Babylon."

¹⁸Then Jeremiah said to King Zedekiah, "What crime have I committed against you or your officials or this people, that you have put me in prison? ¹⁹Where are your prophets who prophesied to you, 'The king of Babylon will not attack you or this land'? ²⁰But now, my lord the king, please listen. Let me bring my petition before you: Do not send me back to the house of Jonathan the secretary, or I will die there."

²¹King Zedekiah then gave orders for Jeremiah to be placed in the courtyard of the guard and given bread from the street of the bakers each day until all the bread in the city was gone. So Jeremiah remained in the courtyard of the guard.

21 / *Jeremiah 38*
Sunk in the Mud

WHAT A HARD time it has been for Jeremiah! God warned him it would be difficult. Certainly it was, more than he ever imagined. In this passage we see Jeremiah thrown in the mud of a deep well and left for dead. Although he gets out of the well, he is not released from confinement and is imprisoned in Jerusalem until the very end. However, Jeremiah's ministry of faithfulness to God and God's people helped prepare the way for you and me. We can know God in ways that are deeper, richer and more powerful because Jeremiah had the courage to be faithful and the wisdom to record his words.

Warming Up to God What sort of spiritual legacy would you like to leave for your friends and family?

Read Jeremiah 38.

38 Shephatiah son of Mattan, Gedaliah son of Pashhur, Jehucal*ᵇ* son of Shelemiah, and Pashhur son of Malkijah heard what Jeremiah was telling all the people when he said, ²"This is what the LORD says: 'Whoever stays in this city will die by the sword, famine or plague, but whoever goes over to the Babylonians*ᶜ* will live. He will escape with his life; he will live.' ³And this is what the LORD says: 'This city will certainly be handed over to the army of the king of Babylon, who will capture it.' "

⁴Then the officials said to the king, "This man should be put to death. He is discouraging the soldiers who are left in this city, as well as all the people, by the things he is saying to them. This man is not seeking the good of these people but their ruin."

⁵"He is in your hands," King Zedekiah answered. "The king can do nothing to oppose you."

⁶So they took Jeremiah and put him into the cistern of Malkijah, the king's son, which was in the courtyard of the guard. They lowered Jeremiah by ropes into the cistern; it had no water in it, only mud, and Jeremiah sank down into the mud.

⁷But Ebed-Melech, a Cushite,*ᵈ* an official*ᵉ* in

ᵇ1 Hebrew Jucal, a variant of Jehucal *ᶜ2 Or Chaldeans; also in verses 18, 19 and 23* *ᵈ7 Probably from the upper Nile region* *ᵉ7 Or a eunuch* the royal palace, heard that they had put Jeremiah into the cistern. While the king was sitting in the Benjamin Gate, [8]Ebed-Melech went out of the palace and said to him, [9]"My lord the king, these men have acted wickedly in all they have done to Jeremiah the prophet. They have thrown him into a cistern, where he will starve to death when there is no longer any bread in the city."

[10]Then the king commanded Ebed-Melech the Cushite, "Take thirty men from here with you and lift Jeremiah the prophet out of the cistern before he dies."

[11]So Ebed-Melech took the men with him and went to a room under the treasury in the palace. He took some old rags and worn-out clothes from there and let them down with ropes to Jeremiah in the cistern. [12]Ebed-Melech the Cushite said to Jeremiah, "Put these old rags and worn-out clothes under your arms to pad the ropes." Jeremiah did so, [13]and they pulled him up with the ropes and lifted him out of the cistern. And Jeremiah remained in the courtyard of the guard.

[14]Then King Zedekiah sent for Jeremiah the prophet and had him brought to the third entrance to the temple of the LORD. "I am going to ask you something," the king said to Jeremiah. "Do not hide anything from me."

[15]Jeremiah said to Zedekiah, "If I give you an answer, will you not kill me? Even if I did give you counsel, you would not listen to me."

[16]But King Zedekiah swore this oath secretly to Jeremiah: "As surely as the LORD lives, who has given us breath, I will neither kill you nor hand you over to those who are seeking your life."

[17]Then Jeremiah said to Zedekiah, "This is what the LORD God Almighty, the God of Israel, says: 'If you surrender to the officers of the king of Babylon, your life will be spared and this city will not be burned down; you and your family will live. [18]But if you will not surrender to the officers of the king of Babylon, this city will be handed over to the Babylonians and they will burn it down; you yourself will not escape from their hands.' "

[19]King Zedekiah said to Jeremiah, "I am afraid of the Jews who have gone over to the Babylonians, for the Babylonians may hand me over to them and they will mistreat me."

[20]"They will not hand you over," Jeremiah replied. "Obey the LORD by doing what I tell you. Then it will go well with you, and your life will be spared. [21]But if you refuse to surrender, this is what the LORD has revealed to me: [22]All the women left in the palace of the king of Judah will be brought out to the officials of the king of Babylon. Those women will say to you:

" 'They misled you and overcame you—
    those trusted friends of yours.
Your feet are sunk in the mud;
    your friends have deserted you.'

[23]"All your wives and children will be brought out to the Babylonians. You yourself will not escape from their hands but will be captured by the king of Babylon; and this city will[f] be burned down."

[24]Then Zedekiah said to Jeremiah, "Do not let anyone know about this conversation, or you may die. [25]If the officials hear that I talked with you, and they come to you and say, 'Tell us what you said to the king and what the king said to you; do not hide it from us or we will kill you,' [26]then tell them, 'I was pleading with the king not to send me back to Jonathan's house to die there.' "

[27]All the officials did come to Jeremiah and question him, and he told them everything the king had ordered him to say. So they said no more to him, for no one had heard his conversation with the king.

[28]And Jeremiah remained in the courtyard of the guard until the day Jerusalem was captured.

[f]23 Or and you will cause this city to

Discovering the Word 1. As Judah was besieged by Babylon, what were Jeremiah's enemies concerned about? 2. If you were in leadership and heard Jeremiah's message, what would have to happen before you would be willing to surrender to your enemies? 3. Jeremiah ends up in the well, sunk down deep into the mud. How had God prepared Jeremiah for just such a situation? 4. How did Jeremiah get out of the well (vv. 7–13)? 5. Zedekiah the king calls Jeremiah to ask for his advice (vv. 14–23). What personal and political reasons does Jeremiah give for Zedekiah to surrender? 6. How would you evaluate the success of Jeremiah's ministry?

Applying the Word 1. In what ways can Christians end up in wells today? 2. How can God help you to persevere even when you are stuck in the mud?

Responding in Prayer Ask God to mold you into his servant, someone who will leave a legacy of faith behind.

Jeremiah 39—43

39 This is how Jerusalem was taken: ¹In the ninth year of Zedekiah king of Judah, in the tenth month, Nebuchadnezzar king of Babylon marched against Jerusalem with his whole army and laid siege to it. ²And on the ninth day of the fourth month of Zedekiah's eleventh year, the city wall was broken through. ³Then all the officials of the king of Babylon came and took seats in the Middle Gate: Nergal-Sharezer of Samgar, Nebo-Sarsekimᵍ a chief officer, Nergal-Sharezer a high official and all the other officials of the king of Babylon. ⁴When Zedekiah king of Judah and all the soldiers saw them, they fled; they left the city at night by way of the king's garden, through the gate between the two walls, and headed toward the Arabah.ʰ

⁵But the Babylonianⁱ army pursued them and overtook Zedekiah in the plains of Jericho. They captured him and took him to Nebuchadnezzar king of Babylon at Riblah in the land of Hamath, where he pronounced sentence on him. ⁶There at Riblah the king of Babylon slaughtered the sons of Zedekiah before his eyes and also killed all the nobles of Judah. ⁷Then he put out Zedekiah's eyes and bound him with bronze shackles to take him to Babylon.

⁸The Babyloniansʲ set fire to the royal palace and the houses of the people and broke down the walls of Jerusalem. ⁹Nebuzaradan commander of the imperial guard carried into exile to Babylon the people who remained in the city, along with those who had gone over to him, and the rest of the people. ¹⁰But Nebuzaradan the commander of the guard left behind in the land of Judah some of the poor people, who owned nothing; and at that time he gave them vineyards and fields.

¹¹Now Nebuchadnezzar king of Babylon had given these orders about Jeremiah through Nebuzaradan commander of the imperial guard: ¹²"Take him and look after him; don't harm him but do for him whatever he asks." ¹³So Nebuzara-dan the commander of the guard, Nebushazban a chief officer, Nergal-Sharezer a high official and all the other officers of the king of Babylon ¹⁴sent and had Jeremiah taken out of the courtyard of the guard. They turned him over to Gedaliah son of Ahikam, the son of Shaphan, to take him back to his home. So he remained among his own people.

¹⁵While Jeremiah had been confined in the courtyard of the guard, the word of the LORD came to him: ¹⁶"Go and tell Ebed-Melech the Cushite, 'This is what the LORD Almighty, the God of Israel, says: I am about to fulfill my words against this city through disaster, not prosperity. At that time they will be fulfilled before your eyes. ¹⁷But I will rescue you on that day, declares the LORD; you will not be handed over to those you fear. ¹⁸I will save you; you will not fall by the sword but will escape with your life, because you trust in me, declares the LORD.'"

40 The word came to Jeremiah from the LORD after Nebuzaradan commander of the imperial guard had released him at Ramah. He had found Jeremiah bound in chains among all the captives from Jerusalem and Judah who were being carried into exile to Babylon. ²When the commander of the guard found Jeremiah, he said to him, "The LORD your God decreed this disaster for this place. ³And now the LORD has brought it about; he has done just as he said he would. All this happened because you people sinned against the LORD and did not obey him. ⁴But today I am freeing you from the chains on your wrists. Come with me to Babylon, if you like, and I will look after you; but if you do not want to, then don't come. Look, the whole country lies before you; go wherever you please." ⁵However, before Jeremiah turned to go,ᵏ Nebuzaradan added, "Go back to Gedaliah son of Ahikam, the son of Shaphan, whom the

---

g3 Or *Nergal-Sharezer, Samgar-Nebo, Sarsekim*   *h4* Or *the Jordan Valley*   *i5* Or *Chaldean*   *j8* Or *Chaldeans*   *k5* Or *Jeremiah answered* king of Babylon has appointed over the towns of Judah, and live with him among the people, or go anywhere else you please."

Then the commander gave him provisions and a present and let him go. ⁶So Jeremiah went to Gedaliah son of Ahikam at Mizpah and stayed with him among the people who were left behind in the land.

⁷When all the army officers and their men who were still in the open country heard that the king of Babylon had appointed Gedaliah son of Ahikam as governor over the land and had put him in charge of the men, women and children who were the poorest in the land and who had not been carried into exile to Babylon, ⁸they came to Gedaliah at Mizpah—Ishmael son of Nethaniah, Johanan and Jonathan the sons of Kareah, Seraiah son of Tanhumeth, the sons of Ephai the Netophathite, and Jaazaniah*l* the son of the Maacathite, and their men. ⁹Gedaliah son of Ahikam, the son of Shaphan, took an oath to reassure them and their men. "Do not be afraid to serve the Babylonians,*m*" he said. "Settle down in the land and serve the king of Babylon, and it will go well with you. ¹⁰I myself will stay at Mizpah to represent you before the Babylonians who come to us, but you are to harvest the wine, summer fruit and oil, and put them in your storage jars, and live in the towns you have taken over."

¹¹When all the Jews in Moab, Ammon, Edom and all the other countries heard that the king of Babylon had left a remnant in Judah and had appointed Gedaliah son of Ahikam, the son of Shaphan, as governor over them, ¹²they all came back to the land of Judah, to Gedaliah at Mizpah, from all the countries where they had been scattered. And they harvested an abundance of wine and summer fruit.

¹³Johanan son of Kareah and all the army officers still in the open country came to Gedaliah at Mizpah ¹⁴and said to him, "Don't you know that Baalis king of the Ammonites has sent Ishmael son of Nethaniah to take your life?" But Gedaliah son of Ahikam did not believe them.

¹⁵Then Johanan son of Kareah said privately to Gedaliah in Mizpah, "Let me go and kill Ishmael son of Nethaniah, and no one will know it. Why should he take your life and cause all the Jews who are gathered around you to be scattered and the remnant of Judah to perish?"

¹⁶But Gedaliah son of Ahikam said to Johanan

son of Kareah, "Don't do such a thing! What you are saying about Ishmael is not true."

41 In the seventh month Ishmael son of Nethaniah, the son of Elishama, who was of royal blood and had been one of the king's officers, came with ten men to Gedaliah son of Ahikam at Mizpah. While they were eating together there, ²Ishmael son of Nethaniah and the ten men who were with him got up and struck down Gedaliah son of Ahikam, the son of Shaphan, with the sword, killing the one whom the king of Babylon had appointed as governor over the land. ³Ishmael also killed all the Jews who were with Gedaliah at Mizpah, as well as the Babylonian*n* soldiers who were there.

⁴The day after Gedaliah's assassination, before anyone knew about it, ⁵eighty men who had shaved off their beards, torn their clothes and cut themselves came from Shechem, Shiloh and Samaria, bringing grain offerings and incense with them to the house of the Lord. ⁶Ishmael son of Nethaniah went out from Mizpah to meet them, weeping as he went. When he met them, he said, "Come to Gedaliah son of Ahikam." ⁷When they went into the city, Ishmael son of Nethaniah and the men who were with him slaughtered them and threw them into a cistern. ⁸But ten of them said to Ishmael, "Don't kill us! We have wheat and barley, oil and honey, hidden in a field." So he let them alone and did not kill them with the others. ⁹Now the cistern where he threw all the bodies of the men he had killed along with Gedaliah was the one King Asa had made as part of his defense against Baasha king of Israel. Ishmael son of Nethaniah filled it with the dead.

¹⁰Ishmael made captives of all the rest of the people who were in Mizpah—the king's daughters along with all the others who were left there, over whom Nebuzaradan commander of the imperial guard had appointed Gedaliah son of Ahikam. Ishmael son of Nethaniah took them captive and set out to cross over to the Ammonites.

¹¹When Johanan son of Kareah and all the army officers who were with him heard about all the crimes Ishmael son of Nethaniah had committed, ¹²they took all their men and went to fight Ishmael son of Nethaniah. They caught up with him near the great pool in Gibeon. ¹³When all the people Ishmael had with him saw Johanan son of Kareah and the army officers who were with him,

---

*l*8 Hebrew *Jezaniah,* a variant of *Jaazaniah*   *m*9 Or *Chaldeans*; also in verse 10   *n*3 Or *Chaldean* they were glad. ¹⁴All the people Ishmael had taken captive at Mizpah turned and went over to Johanan son of Kareah. ¹⁵But Ishmael son of Nethaniah and eight of his men escaped from Johanan and fled to the Ammonites.

¹⁶Then Johanan son of Kareah and all the army officers who were with him led away all the survivors from Mizpah whom he had recovered from Ishmael son of Nethaniah after he had assassinated Gedaliah son of Ahikam: the soldiers, women, children and court officials he had brought from Gibeon. ¹⁷And they went on, stopping at Geruth Kimham near Bethlehem on their way to Egypt ¹⁸to escape the Babylonians.ᵒ They were afraid of them because Ishmael son of Nethaniah had killed Gedaliah son of Ahikam, whom the king of Babylon had appointed as governor over the land.

42 Then all the army officers, including Johanan son of Kareah and Jezaniahᵖ son of Hoshaiah, and all the people from the least to the greatest approached ²Jeremiah the prophet and said to him, "Please hear our petition and pray to the Lord your God for this entire remnant. For as you now see, though we were once many, now only a few are left. ³Pray that the Lord your God will tell us where we should go and what we should do."

⁴"I have heard you," replied Jeremiah the prophet. "I will certainly pray to the Lord your God as you have requested; I will tell you everything the Lord says and will keep nothing back from you."

⁵Then they said to Jeremiah, "May the Lord be a true and faithful witness against us if we do not act in accordance with everything the Lord your God sends you to tell us. ⁶Whether it is favorable or unfavorable, we will obey the Lord our God, to whom we are sending you, so that it will go well with us, for we will obey the Lord our God."

⁷Ten days later the word of the Lord came to Jeremiah. ⁸So he called together Johanan son of Kareah and all the army officers who were with him and all the people from the least to the greatest. ⁹He said to them, "This is what the Lord, the God of Israel, to whom you sent me to present your petition, says: ¹⁰'If you stay in this land, I will build you up and not tear you down; I will plant you and not uproot you, for I am grieved over the disaster I have inflicted on you. ¹¹Do not be afraid of the king of Babylon, whom you now fear. Do not be afraid of him, declares the Lord,

for I am with you and will save you and deliver you from his hands. ¹²I will show you compassion so that he will have compassion on you and restore you to your land.'

¹³"However, if you say, 'We will not stay in this land,' and so disobey the Lord your God, ¹⁴and if you say, 'No, we will go and live in Egypt, where we will not see war or hear the trumpet or be hungry for bread,' ¹⁵then hear the word of the Lord, O remnant of Judah. This is what the Lord Almighty, the God of Israel, says: 'If you are determined to go to Egypt and you do go to settle there, ¹⁶then the sword you fear will overtake you there, and the famine you dread will follow you into Egypt, and there you will die. ¹⁷Indeed, all who are determined to go to Egypt to settle there will die by the sword, famine and plague; not one of them will survive or escape the disaster I will bring on them.' ¹⁸This is what the Lord Almighty, the God of Israel, says: 'As my anger and wrath have been poured out on those who lived in Jerusalem, so will my wrath be poured out on you when you go to Egypt. You will be an object of cursing and horror, of condemnation and reproach; you will never see this place again.'

¹⁹"O remnant of Judah, the Lord has told you, 'Do not go to Egypt.' Be sure of this: I warn you today ²⁰that you made a fatal mistake�q when you sent me to the Lord your God and said, 'Pray to the Lord our God for us; tell us everything he says and we will do it.' ²¹I have told you today, but you still have not obeyed the Lord your God in all he sent me to tell you. ²²So now, be sure of this: You will die by the sword, famine and plague in the place where you want to go to settle."

43 When Jeremiah finished telling the people all the words of the Lord their God—everything the Lord had sent him to tell them— ²Azariah son of Hoshaiah and Johanan son of Kareah and all the arrogant men said to Jeremiah, "You are lying! The Lord our God has not sent you to say, 'You must not go to Egypt to settle there.' ³But Baruch son of Neriah is inciting you against us to hand us over to the Babylonians,ᵒ so they may kill us or carry us into exile to Babylon."

⁴So Johanan son of Kareah and all the army officers and all the people disobeyed the Lord's command to stay in the land of Judah. ⁵Instead, Johanan son of Kareah and all the army officers

ᵒ18,3 Or Chaldeans   ᵖ1 Hebrew; Septuagint (see also 43:2) Azariah   �q20 Or you erred in your hearts led away all the remnant of Judah who had come back to live in the land of Judah from all the nations where they had been scattered. 6They also led away all the men, women and children and the king's daughters whom Nebuzaradan commander of the imperial guard had left with Gedaliah son of Ahikam, the son of Shaphan, and Jeremiah the prophet and Baruch son of Neriah. 7So they entered Egypt in disobedience to the LORD and went as far as Tahpanhes.

8In Tahpanhes the word of the LORD came to Jeremiah: 9"While the Jews are watching, take some large stones with you and bury them in clay in the brick pavement at the entrance to Pharaoh's palace in Tahpanhes. 10Then say to them, 'This is what the LORD Almighty, the God of Israel, says: I will send for my servant Nebuchadnezzar

king of Babylon, and I will set his throne over these stones I have buried here; he will spread his royal canopy above them. 11He will come and attack Egypt, bringing death to those destined for death, captivity to those destined for captivity, and the sword to those destined for the sword. 12Her will set fire to the temples of the gods of Egypt; he will burn their temples and take their gods captive. As a shepherd wraps his garment around him, so will he wrap Egypt around himself and depart from there unscathed. 13There in the temple of the suns in Egypt he will demolish the sacred pillars and will burn down the temples of the gods of Egypt.' "

r12 Or I   s13 Or in Heliopolis

22 / *Jeremiah 44*
Self-Destruction

THE HOUSE NEXT door to us is sinking. Not very fast, but it is definitely leaning—fortunately away from our house. It was built years ago where a ravine had been filled in. At the time the spot must have looked like a fine building site. Slowly but surely, the land has settled out from under that house.

We persist in our self-destructive habits because they offer some immediate payoff. But eventually they catch up with us when our shaky foundation starts to go.

Warming Up to God   What destructive habit have you had the greatest struggle with?

Read Jeremiah 44.

44 This word came to Jeremiah concerning all the Jews living in Lower Egypt—in Migdol, Tahpanhes and Memphis t—and in Upper Egypt u: 2"This is what the LORD Almighty, the God of Israel, says: You saw the great disaster I brought on Jerusalem and on all the towns of Judah. Today they lie deserted and in ruins 3because of the evil they have done. They provoked me to anger by burning incense and by worshiping other gods that neither they nor you nor your fathers ever knew. 4Again and again I sent my servants the prophets, who said, 'Do not do this detestable thing that I hate!' 5But they did not listen or pay attention; they did not turn from their wickedness or stop burning incense to other gods. 6Therefore, my

fierce anger was poured out; it raged against the towns of Judah and the streets of Jerusalem and made them the desolate ruins they are today.

7"Now this is what the LORD God Almighty, the God of Israel, says: Why bring such great disaster on yourselves by cutting off from Judah the men and women, the children and infants, and so leave yourselves without a remnant? 8Why provoke me to anger with what your hands have made, burning incense to other gods in Egypt, where you have come to live? You will destroy yourselves and make yourselves an object of cursing and reproach among all the nations on earth. 9Have you forgotten the wickedness committed by your fathers and by the kings and queens of

t1 Hebrew Noph   u1 Hebrew in Pathros

Judah and the wickedness committed by you and your wives in the land of Judah and the streets of Jerusalem? [10]To this day they have not humbled themselves or shown reverence, nor have they followed my law and the decrees I set before you and your fathers.

[11]"Therefore, this is what the LORD Almighty, the God of Israel, says: I am determined to bring disaster on you and to destroy all Judah. [12]I will take away the remnant of Judah who were determined to go to Egypt to settle there. They will all perish in Egypt; they will fall by the sword or die from famine. From the least to the greatest, they will die by sword or famine. They will become an object of cursing and horror, of condemnation and reproach. [13]I will punish those who live in Egypt with the sword, famine and plague, as I punished Jerusalem. [14]None of the remnant of Judah who have gone to live in Egypt will escape or survive to return to the land of Judah, to which they long to return and live; none will return except a few fugitives."

[15]Then all the men who knew that their wives were burning incense to other gods, along with all the women who were present—a large assembly—and all the people living in Lower and Upper Egypt,[v] said to Jeremiah, [16]"We will not listen to the message you have spoken to us in the name of the LORD! [17]We will certainly do everything we said we would: We will burn incense to the Queen of Heaven and will pour out drink offerings to her just as we and our fathers, our kings and our officials did in the towns of Judah and in the streets of Jerusalem. At that time we had plenty of food and were well off and suffered no harm. [18]But ever since we stopped burning incense to the Queen of Heaven and pouring out drink offerings to her, we have had nothing and have been perishing by sword and famine."

[19]The women added, "When we burned incense to the Queen of Heaven and poured out drink offerings to her, did not our husbands know that we were making cakes like her image and pouring out drink offerings to her?"

[20]Then Jeremiah said to all the people, both men and women, who were answering him,

[21]"Did not the LORD remember and think about the incense burned in the towns of Judah and the streets of Jerusalem by you and your fathers, your kings and your officials and the people of the land? [22]When the LORD could no longer endure your wicked actions and the detestable things you did, your land became an object of cursing and a desolate waste without inhabitants, as it is today. [23]Because you have burned incense and have sinned against the LORD and have not obeyed him or followed his law or his decrees or his stipulations, this disaster has come upon you, as you now see."

[24]Then Jeremiah said to all the people, including the women, "Hear the word of the LORD, all you people of Judah in Egypt. [25]This is what the LORD Almighty, the God of Israel, says: You and your wives have shown by your actions what you promised when you said, 'We will certainly carry out the vows we made to burn incense and pour out drink offerings to the Queen of Heaven.'

"Go ahead then, do what you promised! Keep your vows! [26]But hear the word of the LORD, all Jews living in Egypt: 'I swear by my great name,' says the LORD, 'that no one from Judah living anywhere in Egypt will ever again invoke my name or swear, "As surely as the Sovereign LORD lives." [27]For I am watching over them for harm, not for good; the Jews in Egypt will perish by sword and famine until they are all destroyed. [28]Those who escape the sword and return to the land of Judah from Egypt will be very few. Then the whole remnant of Judah who came to live in Egypt will know whose word will stand—mine or theirs.

[29]"'This will be the sign to you that I will punish you in this place,' declares the LORD, 'so that you will know that my threats of harm against you will surely stand.' [30]This is what the LORD says: 'I am going to hand Pharaoh Hophra king of Egypt over to his enemies who seek his life, just as I handed Zedekiah king of Judah over to Nebuchadnezzar king of Babylon, the enemy who was seeking his life.'"

[v]15 Hebrew in Egypt and Pathros

Discovering the Word 1. What example is Jeremiah told to remind the exiles in Egypt about (vv. 1–6)? 2. How are they in danger of bringing destruction on themselves (vv. 7–14)? 3. What reasons do the people give for persisting in their idolatry (vv. 15–19)? 4. Through Jeremiah, how does God warn them again

(vv. 20–25)? **5.** Because the Jews in Egypt failed to listen to the Lord's warning, what fate will they bring on themselves (vv. 26–30)?

Applying the Word 1. When has the Lord warned you about things in your life which harm you? **2.** How might the Lord be warning you now about some self-destructive practice or attitude?

Responding in Prayer Open your life to the light of the Lord's searching. Confess any excuses you make for harmful attitudes or habits. Thank the Lord for his warnings which come because he loves you.

Jeremiah 45—49

45 This is what Jeremiah the prophet told Baruch son of Neriah in the fourth year of Jehoiakim son of Josiah king of Judah, after Baruch had written on a scroll the words Jeremiah was then dictating: ²"This is what the LORD, the God of Israel, says to you, Baruch: ³You said, 'Woe to me! The LORD has added sorrow to my pain; I am worn out with groaning and find no rest.'"

⁴⌐The LORD said,⌐ "Say this to him: 'This is what the LORD says: I will overthrow what I have built and uproot what I have planted, throughout the land. ⁵Should you then seek great things for yourself? Seek them not. For I will bring disaster on all people, declares the LORD, but wherever you go I will let you escape with your life.'"

46 This is the word of the LORD that came to Jeremiah the prophet concerning the nations:

²Concerning Egypt:

This is the message against the army of Pharaoh Neco king of Egypt, which was defeated at Carchemish on the Euphrates River by Nebuchadnezzar king of Babylon in the fourth year of Jehoiakim son of Josiah king of Judah:

³"Prepare your shields, both large and small,
    and march out for battle!
⁴Harness the horses,
    mount the steeds!
Take your positions
    with helmets on!
Polish your spears,
    put on your armor!
⁵What do I see?
    They are terrified,
they are retreating,
    their warriors are defeated.
They flee in haste

without looking back,
    and there is terror on every side,"
                          declares the LORD.
⁶"The swift cannot flee
    nor the strong escape.
In the north by the River Euphrates
    they stumble and fall.

⁷"Who is this that rises like the Nile,
    like rivers of surging waters?
⁸Egypt rises like the Nile,
    like rivers of surging waters.
She says, 'I will rise and cover the earth;
    I will destroy cities and their people.'
⁹Charge, O horses!
    Drive furiously, O charioteers!
March on, O warriors—
    men of Cushʷ and Put who carry shields,
    men of Lydia who draw the bow.
¹⁰But that day belongs to the Lord, the LORD
        Almighty—
    a day of vengeance, for vengeance on his
        foes.
The sword will devour till it is satisfied,
    till it has quenched its thirst with blood.
For the Lord, the LORD Almighty, will offer
        sacrifice
    in the land of the north by the River
        Euphrates.

¹¹"Go up to Gilead and get balm,
    O Virgin Daughter of Egypt.
But you multiply remedies in vain;
    there is no healing for you.
¹²The nations will hear of your shame;
    your cries will fill the earth.
One warrior will stumble over another;
    both will fall down together."

¹³This is the message the LORD spoke to Jere-

ʷ9 That is, the upper Nile region

miah the prophet about the coming of Nebuchadnezzar king of Babylon to attack Egypt:

¹⁴"Announce this in Egypt, and proclaim it in Migdol;
　　proclaim it also in Memphisˣ and
　　　Tahpanhes:
'Take your positions and get ready,
　for the sword devours those around you.'
¹⁵Why will your warriors be laid low?
　They cannot stand, for the Lᴏʀᴅ will push
　　them down.
¹⁶They will stumble repeatedly;
　they will fall over each other.
They will say, 'Get up, let us go back
　to our own people and our native lands,
　away from the sword of the oppressor.'
¹⁷There they will exclaim,
'Pharaoh king of Egypt is only a loud noise;
　he has missed his opportunity.'

¹⁸"As surely as I live," declares the King,
　whose name is the Lᴏʀᴅ Almighty,
"one will come who is like Tabor among the
　　mountains,
　like Carmel by the sea.
¹⁹Pack your belongings for exile,
　you who live in Egypt,
for Memphis will be laid waste
　and lie in ruins without inhabitant.

²⁰"Egypt is a beautiful heifer,
　but a gadfly is coming
　against her from the north.
²¹The mercenaries in her ranks
　are like fattened calves.
They too will turn and flee together,
　they will not stand their ground,
for the day of disaster is coming upon them,
　the time for them to be punished.
²²Egypt will hiss like a fleeing serpent
　as the enemy advances in force;
they will come against her with axes,
　like men who cut down trees.
²³They will chop down her forest,"
　　　　　　　　　　　　declares the Lᴏʀᴅ,
　"dense though it be.
They are more numerous than locusts,
　they cannot be counted.
²⁴The Daughter of Egypt will be put to shame,
　handed over to the people of the north."

²⁵The Lᴏʀᴅ Almighty, the God of Israel, says: "I am about to bring punishment on Amon god of Thebes,ʸ on Pharaoh, on Egypt and her gods and her kings, and on those who rely on Pharaoh. ²⁶I will hand them over to those who seek their lives, to Nebuchadnezzar king of Babylon and his officers. Later, however, Egypt will be inhabited as in times past," declares the Lᴏʀᴅ.

²⁷"Do not fear, O Jacob my servant;
　do not be dismayed, O Israel.
I will surely save you out of a distant place,
　your descendants from the land of their
　　exile.
Jacob will again have peace and security,
　and no one will make him afraid.
²⁸Do not fear, O Jacob my servant,
　for I am with you," declares the Lᴏʀᴅ.
"Though I completely destroy all the nations
　among which I scatter you,
　I will not completely destroy you.
I will discipline you but only with justice;
　I will not let you go entirely unpunished."

47 This is the word of the Lᴏʀᴅ that came to Jeremiah the prophet concerning the Philistines before Pharaoh attacked Gaza:

²This is what the Lᴏʀᴅ says:

"See how the waters are rising in the north;
　they will become an overflowing torrent.
They will overflow the land and everything in
　　it,
　the towns and those who live in them.
The people will cry out;
　all who dwell in the land will wail
³at the sound of the hoofs of galloping steeds,
　at the noise of enemy chariots
　and the rumble of their wheels.
Fathers will not turn to help their children;
　their hands will hang limp.
⁴For the day has come
　to destroy all the Philistines
and to cut off all survivors
　who could help Tyre and Sidon.
The Lᴏʀᴅ is about to destroy the Philistines,
　the remnant from the coasts of Caphtor.ᶻ
⁵Gaza will shave her head in mourning;
　Ashkelon will be silenced.
O remnant on the plain,
　how long will you cut yourselves?

ˣ14 Hebrew *Noph*; also in verse 19　　ʸ25 Hebrew *No*　　ᶻ4 That is, Crete

⁶" 'Ah, sword of the LORD,' ⌊you cry,⌋
  'how long till you rest?
Return to your scabbard;
  cease and be still.'
⁷But how can it rest
  when the LORD has commanded it,
when he has ordered it
  to attack Ashkelon and the coast?"

48

Concerning Moab:

This is what the LORD Almighty, the God of Israel, says:

"Woe to Nebo, for it will be ruined.
  Kiriathaim will be disgraced and captured;
  the stronghold*a* will be disgraced and
    shattered.
²Moab will be praised no more;
  in Heshbon*b* men will plot her downfall:
  'Come, let us put an end to that nation.'
You too, O Madmen,*c* will be silenced;
  the sword will pursue you.
³Listen to the cries from Horonaim,
  cries of great havoc and destruction.
⁴Moab will be broken;
  her little ones will cry out.*d*
⁵They go up the way to Luhith,
  weeping bitterly as they go;
on the road down to Horonaim
  anguished cries over the destruction are
    heard.
⁶Flee! Run for your lives;
  become like a bush*e* in the desert.
⁷Since you trust in your deeds and riches,
  you too will be taken captive,
and Chemosh will go into exile,
  together with his priests and officials.
⁸The destroyer will come against every town,
  and not a town will escape.
The valley will be ruined
  and the plateau destroyed,
  because the LORD has spoken.
⁹Put salt on Moab,
  for she will be laid waste*f*;
her towns will become desolate,
  with no one to live in them.

¹⁰"A curse on him who is lax in doing the
    LORD's work!
  A curse on him who keeps his sword from
    bloodshed!

¹¹"Moab has been at rest from youth,
  like wine left on its dregs,
not poured from one jar to another—
  she has not gone into exile.
So she tastes as she did,
  and her aroma is unchanged.
¹²But days are coming,"
  declares the LORD,
"when I will send men who pour from jars,
  and they will pour her out;
they will empty her jars
  and smash her jugs.
¹³Then Moab will be ashamed of Chemosh,
  as the house of Israel was ashamed
  when they trusted in Bethel.

¹⁴"How can you say, 'We are warriors,
  men valiant in battle'?
¹⁵Moab will be destroyed and her towns
    invaded;
  her finest young men will go down in the
    slaughter,"
  declares the King, whose name is the LORD
    Almighty.
¹⁶"The fall of Moab is at hand;
  her calamity will come quickly.
¹⁷Mourn for her, all who live around her,
  all who know her fame;
say, 'How broken is the mighty scepter,
  how broken the glorious staff!'

¹⁸"Come down from your glory
  and sit on the parched ground,
  O inhabitants of the Daughter of Dibon,
for he who destroys Moab
  will come up against you
  and ruin your fortified cities.
¹⁹Stand by the road and watch,
  you who live in Aroer.
Ask the man fleeing and the woman escaping,
  ask them, 'What has happened?'
²⁰Moab is disgraced, for she is shattered.
  Wail and cry out!
Announce by the Arnon
  that Moab is destroyed.
²¹Judgment has come to the plateau—
  to Holon, Jahzah and Mephaath,
²² to Dibon, Nebo and Beth Diblathaim,
²³ to Kiriathaim, Beth Gamul and Beth Meon,
²⁴ to Kerioth and Bozrah—

a1 Or / *Misgab*   *b2* The Hebrew for *Heshbon* sounds like the
Hebrew for *plot*.   *c2* The name of the Moabite town Madmen sounds
like the Hebrew for *be silenced*.   *d4* Hebrew; Septuagint / *proclaim it
to Zoar*   *e6* Or *like Aroer*   *f9* Or *Give wings to Moab, / for she
will fly away*

to all the towns of Moab, far and near.
²⁵Moab's horn⁸ is cut off;
   her arm is broken,"
                   declares the Lord.

²⁶"Make her drunk,
   for she has defied the Lord.
Let Moab wallow in her vomit;
   let her be an object of ridicule.
²⁷Was not Israel the object of your ridicule?
   Was she caught among thieves,
that you shake your head in scorn
   whenever you speak of her?
²⁸Abandon your towns and dwell among the
      rocks,
   you who live in Moab.
Be like a dove that makes its nest
   at the mouth of a cave.

²⁹"We have heard of Moab's pride—
   her overweening pride and conceit,
her pride and arrogance
   and the haughtiness of her heart.
³⁰I know her insolence but it is futile,"
                   declares the Lord,
   "and her boasts accomplish nothing.
³¹Therefore I wail over Moab,
   for all Moab I cry out,
   I moan for the men of Kir Hareseth.
³²I weep for you, as Jazer weeps,
   O vines of Sibmah.
Your branches spread as far as the sea;
   they reached as far as the sea of Jazer.
The destroyer has fallen
   on your ripened fruit and grapes.
³³Joy and gladness are gone
   from the orchards and fields of Moab.
I have stopped the flow of wine from the
      presses;
   no one treads them with shouts of joy.
Although there are shouts,
   they are not shouts of joy.

³⁴"The sound of their cry rises
   from Heshbon to Elealeh and Jahaz,
from Zoar as far as Horonaim and Eglath
      Shelishiyah,
   for even the waters of Nimrim are dried up.
³⁵In Moab I will put an end
   to those who make offerings on the high
      places
   and burn incense to their gods,"
                   declares the Lord.

³⁶"So my heart laments for Moab like a flute;
   it laments like a flute for the men of Kir
      Hareseth.
   The wealth they acquired is gone.
³⁷Every head is shaved
   and every beard cut off;
every hand is slashed
   and every waist is covered with sackcloth.
³⁸On all the roofs in Moab
   and in the public squares
there is nothing but mourning,
   for I have broken Moab
   like a jar that no one wants,"
                   declares the Lord.
³⁹"How shattered she is! How they wail!
   How Moab turns her back in shame!
Moab has become an object of ridicule,
   an object of horror to all those around
      her."

⁴⁰This is what the Lord says:

"Look! An eagle is swooping down,
   spreading its wings over Moab.
⁴¹Kerioth ʰ will be captured
   and the strongholds taken.
In that day the hearts of Moab's warriors
   will be like the heart of a woman in labor.
⁴²Moab will be destroyed as a nation
   because she defied the Lord.
⁴³Terror and pit and snare await you,
   O people of Moab,"
                   declares the Lord.
⁴⁴"Whoever flees from the terror
   will fall into a pit,
whoever climbs out of the pit
   will be caught in a snare;
for I will bring upon Moab
   the year of her punishment,"
                   declares the Lord.

⁴⁵"In the shadow of Heshbon
   the fugitives stand helpless,
for a fire has gone out from Heshbon,
   a blaze from the midst of Sihon;
it burns the foreheads of Moab,
   the skulls of the noisy boasters.
⁴⁶Woe to you, O Moab!
   The people of Chemosh are destroyed;
your sons are taken into exile
   and your daughters into captivity.

ᵍ25 *Horn* here symbolizes strength.   ʰ41 Or *The cities*

47"Yet I will restore the fortunes of Moab
  in days to come,"
                                      declares the LORD.

Here ends the judgment on Moab.

49

Concerning the Ammonites:

This is what the LORD says:

"Has Israel no sons?
  Has she no heirs?
Why then has Molech[i] taken possession of
  Gad?
Why do his people live in its towns?
2But the days are coming,"
  declares the LORD,
"when I will sound the battle cry
  against Rabbah of the Ammonites;
it will become a mound of ruins,
  and its surrounding villages will be set on
    fire.
Then Israel will drive out
  those who drove her out,"
                                      says the LORD.
3"Wail, O Heshbon, for Ai is destroyed!
  Cry out, O inhabitants of Rabbah!
Put on sackcloth and mourn;
  rush here and there inside the walls,
for Molech will go into exile,
  together with his priests and officials.
4Why do you boast of your valleys,
  boast of your valleys so fruitful?
O unfaithful daughter,
  you trust in your riches and say,
  'Who will attack me?'
5I will bring terror on you
  from all those around you,"
                      declares the Lord, the LORD Almighty.
"Every one of you will be driven away,
  and no one will gather the fugitives.

6"Yet afterward, I will restore the fortunes of
  the Ammonites,"
                                      declares the LORD.

7Concerning Edom:

This is what the LORD Almighty says:

"Is there no longer wisdom in Teman?
  Has counsel perished from the prudent?
  Has their wisdom decayed?
8Turn and flee, hide in deep caves,
  you who live in Dedan,

for I will bring disaster on Esau
  at the time I punish him.
9If grape pickers came to you,
  would they not leave a few grapes?
If thieves came during the night,
  would they not steal only as much as they
    wanted?
10But I will strip Esau bare;
  I will uncover his hiding places,
  so that he cannot conceal himself.
His children, relatives and neighbors will
    perish,
  and he will be no more.
11Leave your orphans; I will protect their lives.
  Your widows too can trust in me."

12This is what the LORD says: "If those who do
not deserve to drink the cup must drink it, why
should you go unpunished? You will not go unpunished, but must drink it. 13I swear by myself,"
declares the LORD, "that Bozrah will become a ruin
and an object of horror, of reproach and of cursing; and all its towns will be in ruins forever."

14I have heard a message from the LORD:
  An envoy was sent to the nations to say,
"Assemble yourselves to attack it!
  Rise up for battle!"

15"Now I will make you small among the
    nations,
  despised among men.
16The terror you inspire
  and the pride of your heart have deceived
    you,
you who live in the clefts of the rocks,
  who occupy the heights of the hill.
Though you build your nest as high as the
    eagle's,
  from there I will bring you down,"
                                      declares the LORD.
17"Edom will become an object of horror;
  all who pass by will be appalled and will
    scoff
  because of all its wounds.
18As Sodom and Gomorrah were overthrown,
  along with their neighboring towns,"
                                      says the LORD,
"so no one will live there;
  no man will dwell in it.

19"Like a lion coming up from Jordan's thickets

i1 Or their king; Hebrew malcam; also in verse 3

to a rich pastureland,
I will chase Edom from its land in an instant.
　Who is the chosen one I will appoint for
　　　this?
Who is like me and who can challenge me?
　And what shepherd can stand against me?"
²⁰Therefore, hear what the Lord has planned
　　　against Edom,
　what he has purposed against those who
　　　live in Teman:
The young of the flock will be dragged away;
　he will completely destroy their pasture
　　　because of them.
²¹At the sound of their fall the earth will
　　　tremble;
　their cry will resound to the Red Sea.ʲ
²²Look! An eagle will soar and swoop down,
　spreading its wings over Bozrah.
In that day the hearts of Edom's warriors
　will be like the heart of a woman in labor.

²³Concerning Damascus:

"Hamath and Arpad are dismayed,
　for they have heard bad news.
They are disheartened,
　troubled likeᵏ the restless sea.
²⁴Damascus has become feeble,
　she has turned to flee
　and panic has gripped her;
anguish and pain have seized her,
　pain like that of a woman in labor.
²⁵Why has the city of renown not been
　　　abandoned,
　the town in which I delight?
²⁶Surely, her young men will fall in the streets;
　all her soldiers will be silenced in that day,"
　　　　　　　　　　declares the Lord Almighty.
²⁷"I will set fire to the walls of Damascus;
　it will consume the fortresses of
　　　Ben-Hadad."

²⁸Concerning Kedar and the kingdoms of Hazor, which Nebuchadnezzar king of Babylon attacked:

This is what the Lord says:

"Arise, and attack Kedar
　and destroy the people of the East.
²⁹Their tents and their flocks will be taken;
　their shelters will be carried off
　　　with all their goods and camels.
Men will shout to them,
　'Terror on every side!'

³⁰"Flee quickly away!
　Stay in deep caves, you who live in Hazor,"
　　　　　　　　　　declares the Lord.
"Nebuchadnezzar king of Babylon has plotted
　　　against you;
　he has devised a plan against you.

³¹"Arise and attack a nation at ease,
　which lives in confidence,"
　　　　　　　　　　declares the Lord,
"a nation that has neither gates nor bars;
　its people live alone.
³²Their camels will become plunder,
　and their large herds will be booty.
I will scatter to the winds those who are in
　　　distant placesˡ
　and will bring disaster on them from every
　　　side,"
　　　　　　　　　　declares the Lord.
³³"Hazor will become a haunt of jackals,
　a desolate place forever.
No one will live there;
　no man will dwell in it."

³⁴This is the word of the Lord that came to
Jeremiah the prophet concerning Elam, early in
the reign of Zedekiah king of Judah:

³⁵This is what the Lord Almighty says:

"See, I will break the bow of Elam,
　the mainstay of their might.
³⁶I will bring against Elam the four winds
　from the four quarters of the heavens;
I will scatter them to the four winds,
　and there will not be a nation
　where Elam's exiles do not go.
³⁷I will shatter Elam before their foes,
　before those who seek their lives;
I will bring disaster upon them,
　even my fierce anger,"
　　　　　　　　　　declares the Lord.
"I will pursue them with the sword
　until I have made an end of them.
³⁸I will set my throne in Elam
　and destroy her king and officials,"
　　　　　　　　　　declares the Lord.

³⁹"Yet I will restore the fortunes of Elam
　in days to come,"
　　　　　　　　　　declares the Lord.

ʲ21 Hebrew *Yam Suph*; that is, Sea of Reeds　　ᵏ23 Hebrew *on* or *by*
ˡ32 Or *who clip the hair by their foreheads*

23 / *Jeremiah 50:1–20*
Babylon Shouldn't Gloat

"IT WAS BAD enough that I fell down flat on the ice," said our friend who was just learning to ice skate, "but then this little kid skated around me in a circle and asked, 'Are you all right?' " At humiliating times like those, we need somebody to take our side and literally pick us up. When we've fallen on our faces and it feels like evil is gloating over good, God yearns jealously for us and does not forget us.

 Warming Up to God   Recall a time you felt defeated. How did the Lord show you he still cared?

 Read Jeremiah 50:1–20.

50 This is the word the LORD spoke through Jeremiah the prophet concerning Babylon and the land of the Babylonians[m]:

2"Announce and proclaim among the nations,
   lift up a banner and proclaim it;
   keep nothing back, but say,
'Babylon will be captured;
   Bel will be put to shame,
   Marduk filled with terror.
Her images will be put to shame
   and her idols filled with terror.'
3A nation from the north will attack her
   and lay waste her land.
No one will live in it;
   both men and animals will flee away.

4"In those days, at that time,"
   declares the LORD,
"the people of Israel and the people of Judah
      together
   will go in tears to seek the LORD their God.
5They will ask the way to Zion
   and turn their faces toward it.
They will come and bind themselves to the
   LORD
   in an everlasting covenant
   that will not be forgotten.

6"My people have been lost sheep;
   their shepherds have led them astray
   and caused them to roam on the
      mountains.
They wandered over mountain and hill
   and forgot their own resting place.
7Whoever found them devoured them;
   their enemies said, 'We are not guilty,
for they sinned against the LORD, their true
      pasture,

the LORD, the hope of their fathers.'

8"Flee out of Babylon;
   leave the land of the Babylonians,
   and be like the goats that lead the flock.
9For I will stir up and bring against Babylon
   an alliance of great nations from the land of
      the north.
They will take up their positions against her,
   and from the north she will be captured.
Their arrows will be like skilled warriors
   who do not return empty-handed.
10So Babylonia[n] will be plundered;
   all who plunder her will have their fill,"
                        declares the LORD.

11"Because you rejoice and are glad,
   you who pillage my inheritance,
because you frolic like a heifer threshing
      grain
   and neigh like stallions,
12your mother will be greatly ashamed;
   she who gave you birth will be disgraced.
She will be the least of the nations—
   a wilderness, a dry land, a desert.
13Because of the LORD's anger she will not be
      inhabited
   but will be completely desolate.
All who pass Babylon will be horrified and
      scoff
   because of all her wounds.

14"Take up your positions around Babylon,
   all you who draw the bow.
Shoot at her! Spare no arrows,
   for she has sinned against the LORD.
15Shout against her on every side!

---

[m]1 Or *Chaldeans*; also in verses 8, 25, 35 and 45   [n]10 Or *Chaldea*

She surrenders, her towers fall,
her walls are torn down.
Since this is the vengeance of the LORD,
take vengeance on her;
do to her as she has done to others.
¹⁶Cut off from Babylon the sower,
and the reaper with his sickle at harvest.
Because of the sword of the oppressor
let everyone return to his own people,
let everyone flee to his own land.

¹⁷"Israel is a scattered flock
that lions have chased away.
The first to devour him
was the king of Assyria;
the last to crush his bones
was Nebuchadnezzar king of Babylon."

¹⁸Therefore this is what the LORD Almighty, the
God of Israel, says:

"I will punish the king of Babylon and his
land
as I punished the king of Assyria.
¹⁹But I will bring Israel back to his own pasture
and he will graze on Carmel and Bashan;
his appetite will be satisfied
on the hills of Ephraim and Gilead.
²⁰In those days, at that time,"
declares the LORD,
"search will be made for Israel's guilt,
but there will be none,
and for the sins of Judah,
but none will be found,
for I will forgive the remnant I spare.

 Discovering the Word 1. What is going to happen to Babylon (vv. 1–3, 9–10, 14–16, 18)? 2. When God comes to their rescue, how will Israel respond (vv. 4–5)? 3. How had Babylon gotten the upper hand (vv. 6–7)? 4. Why is God so angry with Babylon (vv. 11–15)? 5. How will God vindicate Israel (v. 20)?

 Applying the Word 1. What are some ways that you feel wrong is triumphing over right? 2. In what areas are you tempted to gloat over others who have fallen?

Responding in Prayer Commit to the Lord any situations where you feel wrong is gloating over right. Confess any ways that you gloat over others. Thank the Lord that even in failure he remembers you.

Jeremiah 50:21—51:64

²¹"Attack the land of Merathaim
and those who live in Pekod.
Pursue, kill and completely destroyᵒ them,"
declares the LORD.
"Do everything I have commanded you.
²²The noise of battle is in the land,
the noise of great destruction!
²³How broken and shattered
is the hammer of the whole earth!
How desolate is Babylon
among the nations!
²⁴I set a trap for you, O Babylon,
and you were caught before you knew it;
you were found and captured
because you opposed the LORD.
²⁵The LORD has opened his arsenal
and brought out the weapons of his wrath,
for the Sovereign LORD Almighty has work to
do
in the land of the Babylonians.

²⁶Come against her from afar.
Break open her granaries;
pile her up like heaps of grain.
Completely destroy her
and leave her no remnant.
²⁷Kill all her young bulls;
let them go down to the slaughter!
Woe to them! For their day has come,
the time for them to be punished.
²⁸Listen to the fugitives and refugees from
Babylon
declaring in Zion
how the LORD our God has taken vengeance,
vengeance for his temple.

²⁹"Summon archers against Babylon,
all those who draw the bow.
Encamp all around her;
let no one escape.

ᵒ21 The Hebrew term refers to the irrevocable giving over of things or
persons to the LORD, often by totally destroying them; also in verse 26.

Repay her for her deeds;
  do to her as she has done.
For she has defied the LORD,
  the Holy One of Israel.
³⁰Therefore, her young men will fall in the
      streets;
  all her soldiers will be silenced in that day,"
                              declares the LORD.
³¹"See, I am against you, O arrogant one,"
  declares the Lord, the LORD Almighty,
"for your day has come,
  the time for you to be punished.
³²The arrogant one will stumble and fall
  and no one will help her up;
I will kindle a fire in her towns
  that will consume all who are around her."

³³This is what the LORD Almighty says:

"The people of Israel are oppressed,
  and the people of Judah as well.
All their captors hold them fast,
  refusing to let them go.
³⁴Yet their Redeemer is strong;
  the LORD Almighty is his name.
He will vigorously defend their cause
  so that he may bring rest to their land,
  but unrest to those who live in Babylon.

³⁵"A sword against the Babylonians!"
  declares the LORD—
"against those who live in Babylon
  and against her officials and wise men!
³⁶A sword against her false prophets!
  They will become fools.
A sword against her warriors!
  They will be filled with terror.
³⁷A sword against her horses and chariots
  and all the foreigners in her ranks!
  They will become women.
A sword against her treasures!
  They will be plundered.
³⁸A drought on ᴾ her waters!
  They will dry up.
For it is a land of idols,
  idols that will go mad with terror.

³⁹"So desert creatures and hyenas will live there,
  and there the owl will dwell.
It will never again be inhabited
  or lived in from generation to generation.
⁴⁰As God overthrew Sodom and Gomorrah
  along with their neighboring towns,"
                              declares the LORD,

"so no one will live there;
  no man will dwell in it.

⁴¹"Look! An army is coming from the north;
  a great nation and many kings
  are being stirred up from the ends of the
      earth.
⁴²They are armed with bows and spears;
  they are cruel and without mercy.
They sound like the roaring sea
  as they ride on their horses;
they come like men in battle formation
  to attack you, O Daughter of Babylon.
⁴³The king of Babylon has heard reports about
      them,
  and his hands hang limp.
Anguish has gripped him,
  pain like that of a woman in labor.
⁴⁴Like a lion coming up from Jordan's thickets
  to a rich pastureland,
I will chase Babylon from its land in an
      instant.
  Who is the chosen one I will appoint for
      this?
Who is like me and who can challenge me?
  And what shepherd can stand against me?"
⁴⁵Therefore, hear what the LORD has planned
      against Babylon,
  what he has purposed against the land of
      the Babylonians:
The young of the flock will be dragged away;
  he will completely destroy their pasture
      because of them.
⁴⁶At the sound of Babylon's capture the earth
      will tremble;
  its cry will resound among the nations.

51

This is what the LORD says:

  "See, I will stir up the spirit of a
      destroyer
against Babylon and the people of Leb
      Kamai. �q
²I will send foreigners to Babylon
  to winnow her and to devastate her land;
they will oppose her on every side
  in the day of her disaster.
³Let not the archer string his bow,
  nor let him put on his armor.

ᴾ38 Or A sword against   q1 Leb Kamai is a cryptogram for Chaldea,
that is, Babylonia.

Do not spare her young men;
    completely destroy[r] her army.
[4]They will fall down slain in Babylon,[s]
    fatally wounded in her streets.
[5]For Israel and Judah have not been forsaken
    by their God, the LORD Almighty,
though their land[t] is full of guilt
    before the Holy One of Israel.

[6]"Flee from Babylon!
    Run for your lives!
    Do not be destroyed because of her sins.
It is time for the LORD's vengeance;
    he will pay her what she deserves.
[7]Babylon was a gold cup in the LORD's hand;
    she made the whole earth drunk.
The nations drank her wine;
    therefore they have now gone mad.
[8]Babylon will suddenly fall and be broken.
    Wail over her!
Get balm for her pain;
    perhaps she can be healed.

[9]" 'We would have healed Babylon,
    but she cannot be healed;
let us leave her and each go to his own land,
    for her judgment reaches to the skies,
    it rises as high as the clouds.'

[10]" 'The LORD has vindicated us;
    come, let us tell in Zion
    what the LORD our God has done.'

[11]"Sharpen the arrows,
    take up the shields!
The LORD has stirred up the kings of the
        Medes,
    because his purpose is to destroy Babylon.
The LORD will take vengeance,
    vengeance for his temple.
[12]Lift up a banner against the walls of Babylon!
    Reinforce the guard,
station the watchmen,
    prepare an ambush!
The LORD will carry out his purpose,
    his decree against the people of Babylon.
[13]You who live by many waters
    and are rich in treasures,
your end has come,
    the time for you to be cut off.
[14]The LORD Almighty has sworn by himself:
    I will surely fill you with men, as with a
        swarm of locusts,
    and they will shout in triumph over you.

[15]"He made the earth by his power;
    he founded the world by his wisdom
    and stretched out the heavens by his
        understanding.
[16]When he thunders, the waters in the heavens
        roar;
    he makes clouds rise from the ends of the
        earth.
He sends lightning with the rain
    and brings out the wind from his
        storehouses.

[17]"Every man is senseless and without
        knowledge;
    every goldsmith is shamed by his idols.
His images are a fraud;
    they have no breath in them.
[18]They are worthless, the objects of mockery;
    when their judgment comes, they will
        perish.
[19]He who is the Portion of Jacob is not like
        these,
    for he is the Maker of all things,
including the tribe of his inheritance—
    the LORD Almighty is his name.

[20]"You are my war club,
    my weapon for battle—
with you I shatter nations,
    with you I destroy kingdoms,
[21]with you I shatter horse and rider,
    with you I shatter chariot and driver,
[22]with you I shatter man and woman,
    with you I shatter old man and youth,
    with you I shatter young man and maiden,
[23]with you I shatter shepherd and flock,
    with you I shatter farmer and oxen,
    with you I shatter governors and officials.

[24]"Before your eyes I will repay Babylon and all
who live in Babylonia[u] for all the wrong they
have done in Zion," declares the LORD.

[25]"I am against you, O destroying mountain,
    you who destroy the whole earth,"
                                    declares the LORD.
"I will stretch out my hand against you,
    roll you off the cliffs,
    and make you a burned-out mountain.
[26]No rock will be taken from you for a
        cornerstone,

---

[r]3 The Hebrew term refers to the irrevocable giving over of things or
persons to the LORD, often by totally destroying them.   [s]4 Or *Chaldea*
[t]5 Or *l and the land ⌊of the Babylonians⌋*   [u]24 Or *Chaldea*; also in
verse 35

nor any stone for a foundation,
   for you will be desolate forever,"
                              declares the LORD.

27"Lift up a banner in the land!
   Blow the trumpet among the nations!
Prepare the nations for battle against her;
   summon against her these kingdoms:
   Ararat, Minni and Ashkenaz.
Appoint a commander against her;
   send up horses like a swarm of locusts.
28Prepare the nations for battle against her—
   the kings of the Medes,
their governors and all their officials,
   and all the countries they rule.
29The land trembles and writhes,
   for the LORD's purposes against Babylon
      stand—
to lay waste the land of Babylon
   so that no one will live there.
30Babylon's warriors have stopped fighting;
   they remain in their strongholds.
Their strength is exhausted;
   they have become like women.
Her dwellings are set on fire;
   the bars of her gates are broken.
31One courier follows another
   and messenger follows messenger
to announce to the king of Babylon
   that his entire city is captured,
32the river crossings seized,
   the marshes set on fire,
   and the soldiers terrified."

33This is what the LORD Almighty, the God of
Israel, says:

"The Daughter of Babylon is like a threshing
      floor
   at the time it is trampled;
the time to harvest her will soon come."

34"Nebuchadnezzar king of Babylon has
      devoured us,
he has thrown us into confusion,
   he has made us an empty jar.
Like a serpent he has swallowed us
   and filled his stomach with our delicacies,
   and then has spewed us out.
35May the violence done to our fleshᵛ be upon
      Babylon,"
   say the inhabitants of Zion.
"May our blood be on those who live in
      Babylonia,"

says Jerusalem.

36Therefore, this is what the LORD says:

"See, I will defend your cause
   and avenge you;
I will dry up her sea
   and make her springs dry.
37Babylon will be a heap of ruins,
   a haunt of jackals,
an object of horror and scorn,
   a place where no one lives.
38Her people all roar like young lions,
   they growl like lion cubs.
39But while they are aroused,
   I will set out a feast for them
   and make them drunk,
so that they shout with laughter—
   then sleep forever and not awake,"
                              declares the LORD.
40"I will bring them down
   like lambs to the slaughter,
   like rams and goats.

41"How Sheshachʷ will be captured,
   the boast of the whole earth seized!
What a horror Babylon will be
   among the nations!
42The sea will rise over Babylon;
   its roaring waves will cover her.
43Her towns will be desolate,
   a dry and desert land,
a land where no one lives,
   through which no man travels.
44I will punish Bel in Babylon
   and make him spew out what he has
      swallowed.
The nations will no longer stream to him.
   And the wall of Babylon will fall.

45"Come out of her, my people!
   Run for your lives!
   Run from the fierce anger of the LORD.
46Do not lose heart or be afraid
   when rumors are heard in the land;
one rumor comes this year, another the next,
   rumors of violence in the land
   and of ruler against ruler.
47For the time will surely come
   when I will punish the idols of Babylon;
her whole land will be disgraced
   and her slain will all lie fallen within her.

ᵛ35 Or done to us and to our children   ʷ41 Sheshach is a cryptogram
for Babylon.

⁴⁸Then heaven and earth and all that is in them
    will shout for joy over Babylon,
for out of the north
    destroyers will attack her,"
                                    declares the LORD.

⁴⁹"Babylon must fall because of Israel's slain,
    just as the slain in all the earth
    have fallen because of Babylon.
⁵⁰You who have escaped the sword,
    leave and do not linger!
Remember the LORD in a distant land,
    and think on Jerusalem."

⁵¹"We are disgraced,
    for we have been insulted
    and shame covers our faces,
because foreigners have entered
    the holy places of the LORD's house."

⁵²"But days are coming," declares the LORD,
    "when I will punish her idols,
and throughout her land
    the wounded will groan.
⁵³Even if Babylon reaches the sky
    and fortifies her lofty stronghold,
I will send destroyers against her,"
                                    declares the LORD.

⁵⁴"The sound of a cry comes from Babylon,
    the sound of great destruction
    from the land of the Babylonians.ˣ
⁵⁵The LORD will destroy Babylon;
    he will silence her noisy din.
Waves ⌊of enemies⌋ will rage like great waters;
    the roar of their voices will resound.
⁵⁶A destroyer will come against Babylon;

her warriors will be captured,
    and their bows will be broken.
For the LORD is a God of retribution;
    he will repay in full.
⁵⁷I will make her officials and wise men drunk,
    her governors, officers and warriors as well;
they will sleep forever and not awake,"
    declares the King, whose name is the LORD
    Almighty.

⁵⁸This is what the LORD Almighty says:

"Babylon's thick wall will be leveled
    and her high gates set on fire;
the peoples exhaust themselves for nothing,
    the nations' labor is only fuel for the
    flames."

⁵⁹This is the message Jeremiah gave to the staff
officer Seraiah son of Neriah, the son of Mahseiah, when he went to Babylon with Zedekiah king
of Judah in the fourth year of his reign. ⁶⁰Jere-
miah had written on a scroll about all the disasters that would come upon Babylon—all that had
been recorded concerning Babylon. ⁶¹He said to
Seraiah, "When you get to Babylon, see that you
read all these words aloud. ⁶²Then say, 'O LORD,
you have said you will destroy this place, so that
neither man nor animal will live in it; it will be
desolate forever.' ⁶³When you finish reading this
scroll, tie a stone to it and throw it into the Euphrates. ⁶⁴Then say, 'So will Babylon sink to rise
no more because of the disaster I will bring upon
her. And her people will fall.' "

The words of Jeremiah end here.

ˣ54 Or Chaldeans

---

24 / *Jeremiah 52*
Jerusalem Plundered

THE MOVERS CAME while our friend was at work. She knew they were coming, of course, but still it was a shock
when she opened the front door and found all the rooms bare. She admits she broke down and cried. How much
worse if she had been robbed of everything against her will as Jerusalem was.

 Warming Up to God When do you feel that the Lord has taken away something you counted on? What
was that like?

 Read Jeremiah 52.

52

Zedekiah was twenty-one years old when he became king, and he reigned in Jerusalem eleven years. His mother's name was Hamutal daughter of Jeremiah; she was from Libnah. ²He did evil in the eyes of the LORD, just as Jehoiakim had done. ³It was because of the LORD's anger that all this happened to Jerusalem and Judah, and in the end he thrust them from his presence.

Now Zedekiah rebelled against the king of Babylon.

⁴So in the ninth year of Zedekiah's reign, on the tenth day of the tenth month, Nebuchadnezzar king of Babylon marched against Jerusalem with his whole army. They camped outside the city and built siege works all around it. ⁵The city was kept under siege until the eleventh year of King Zedekiah.

⁶By the ninth day of the fourth month the famine in the city had become so severe that there was no food for the people to eat. ⁷Then the city wall was broken through, and the whole army fled. They left the city at night through the gate between the two walls near the king's garden, though the Babylonians*ʸ* were surrounding the city. They fled toward the Arabah,*ᶻ* ⁸but the Babylonian*ᵃ* army pursued King Zedekiah and overtook him in the plains of Jericho. All his soldiers were separated from him and scattered, ⁹and he was captured.

He was taken to the king of Babylon at Riblah in the land of Hamath, where he pronounced sentence on him. ¹⁰There at Riblah the king of Babylon slaughtered the sons of Zedekiah before his eyes; he also killed all the officials of Judah. ¹¹Then he put out Zedekiah's eyes, bound him with bronze shackles and took him to Babylon, where he put him in prison till the day of his death.

¹²On the tenth day of the fifth month, in the nineteenth year of Nebuchadnezzar king of Babylon, Nebuzaradan commander of the imperial guard, who served the king of Babylon, came to Jerusalem. ¹³He set fire to the temple of the LORD, the royal palace and all the houses of Jerusalem. Every important building he burned down. ¹⁴The whole Babylonian army under the commander of the imperial guard broke down all the walls around Jerusalem. ¹⁵Nebuzaradan the commander of the guard carried into exile some of the poorest people and those who remained in the city, along with the rest of the craftsmen*ᵇ* and those who had gone over to the king of Babylon. ¹⁶But Nebuzaradan left behind the rest of the poorest people of the land to work the vineyards and fields.

¹⁷The Babylonians broke up the bronze pillars, the movable stands and the bronze Sea that were at the temple of the LORD and they carried all the bronze to Babylon. ¹⁸They also took away the pots, shovels, wick trimmers, sprinkling bowls, dishes and all the bronze articles used in the temple service. ¹⁹The commander of the imperial guard took away the basins, censers, sprinkling bowls, pots, lampstands, dishes and bowls used for drink offerings—all that were made of pure gold or silver.

²⁰The bronze from the two pillars, the Sea and the twelve bronze bulls under it, and the movable stands, which King Solomon had made for the temple of the LORD, was more than could be weighed. ²¹Each of the pillars was eighteen cubits high and twelve cubits in circumference*ᶜ*; each was four fingers thick, and hollow. ²²The bronze capital on top of the one pillar was five cubits*ᵈ* high and was decorated with a network and pomegranates of bronze all around. The other pillar, with its pomegranates, was similar. ²³There were ninety-six pomegranates on the sides; the total number of pomegranates above the surrounding network was a hundred.

²⁴The commander of the guard took as prisoners Seraiah the chief priest, Zephaniah the priest next in rank and the three doorkeepers. ²⁵Of those still in the city, he took the officer in charge of the fighting men, and seven royal advisers. He also took the secretary who was chief officer in charge of conscripting the people of the land and sixty of his men who were found in the city. ²⁶Nebuzaradan the commander took them all and brought them to the king of Babylon at Riblah. ²⁷There at Riblah, in the land of Hamath, the king had them executed.

So Judah went into captivity, away from her land. ²⁸This is the number of the people Nebuchadnezzar carried into exile:

in the seventh year, 3,023 Jews;
²⁹in Nebuchadnezzar's eighteenth year,
        832 people from Jerusalem;
³⁰in his twenty-third year,

---

*ʸ*7 Or *Chaldeans*; also in verse 17   *ᶻ*7 Or *the Jordan Valley*
*ᵃ*8 Or *Chaldean*; also in verse 14   *ᵇ*15 Or *populace*   *ᶜ*21 That is,
about 27 feet (about 8.1 meters) high and 18 feet (about 5.4 meters) in
circumference   *ᵈ*22 That is, about 7 1/2 feet (about 2.3 meters)

745 Jews taken into exile by Nebuzaradan the commander of the imperial guard. There were 4,600 people in all.

31In the thirty-seventh year of the exile of Jehoiachin king of Judah, in the year Evil-Merodach*e* became king of Babylon, he released Jehoiachin king of Judah and freed him from prison on the twenty-fifth day of the twelfth month. 32He spoke kindly to him and gave him a seat of honor higher than those of the other kings who were with him in Babylon. 33So Jehoiachin put aside his prison clothes and for the rest of his life ate regularly at the king's table. 34Day by day the king of Babylon gave Jehoiachin a regular allowance as long as he lived, till the day of his death.

e31 Also called Amel-Marduk

 Discovering the Word 1. Chapter 51 tells us that Jeremiah's words end there. How does the writer of chapter 52 describe what happened to the city of Jerusalem at the hands of the king of Babylon? 2. What explanation is given for the disaster (vv. 1–3)? 3. There was an excruciatingly long siege by the Babylonian army against Jerusalem. What were some results of it (vv. 4–11)? 4. How did the Babylonian commander treat the sacred items in the Lord's temple (vv. 12–23)? 5. What became of the priests and other Jewish officials (vv. 24–27)? 6. What surprising turn of events happened to Jehoiachin, the young previous king of Judah who had been deposed (vv. 31–34)?

Applying the Word 1. Why does a major loss sometimes shock people into returning to the Lord? 2. Why do you think it sometimes takes a major blow to bring people back? 3. How do you respond to big losses?

Responding in Prayer Pray about any wrenching losses you have had or which you fear happening. Ask the Lord what you should learn through losing. Trust him to restore what he wishes in his own time.

Lamentations

*L*amentations is a book that grips our emotions, not just our intellect. It is a personal account of the author's mourning over the fall of Jerusalem in 586 B.C. and the exile of the Jewish people to Babylon. But it is more than a book of grieving; it offers hope in the midst of suffering.

The title *Lamentations* is the translation of a Greek word that means "to cry aloud," aptly summarizing the content. This book has a different structure from other Bible books. It is composed of five melancholy poems (one per chapter) with a limping meter that was used for funeral dirges. In the Hebrew, the second line of two parallel lines is one beat short of the first one, thus producing a limp in the meter. In addition, four of the poems are written as acrostics. In chapters 1, 2 and 4 each verse starts with a word that begins with a letter of the Hebrew alphabet, progressing in order. In chapter 3 three verses go with each letter.

These poems focus on the events described in 2 Kings 25 when the Babylonian army invaded Jerusalem and razed the city, carrying away most of the population. They also provide a sequel to the book of Jeremiah that warns about the coming invasion and fall of the city. Because of the similarity in events described, some commentators believe that Jeremiah was the author. However, since it is anonymous, we cannot be sure.

But Lamentations is more than one man's reaction to the loss of his home. It gives us a biblical approach to suffering. The author teaches us that we can't deal with suffering by ignoring it, pretending it doesn't exist, trying to get out of it, or minimizing its pain. Instead, we have to go through it, remembering that God is with us in it.

Outline

1/ Lamentations 1—2 ——————————— *Mourning Over Sin*
2/ Lamentations 3 ——————————— *Hope in the Midst of Suffering*
3/ Lamentations 4—5 ——————————— *Suffering Is Not Forever*

1 / *Lamentations 1—2*
Mourning Over Sin

"SIN WOULD HAVE few takers if its consequences occurred immediately," said W. T. Purkiser. The history of the Jewish people certainly illustrates this saying. They sinned for years before experiencing the consequences of exile and destruction of their holy city, Jerusalem, as the author described in Lamentations.

 Warming Up to God How do you react when you suffer consequences of your sins? Talk to God about your reactions and ask him to show you what he wants to teach you.

 Read Lamentations 1—2.

---

1 ᵃHow deserted lies the city,
  once so full of people!
  How like a widow is she,
who once was great among the nations!
She who was queen among the provinces
  has now become a slave.

²Bitterly she weeps at night,
  tears are upon her cheeks.
Among all her lovers
  there is none to comfort her.
All her friends have betrayed her;
  they have become her enemies.

³After affliction and harsh labor,
  Judah has gone into exile.
She dwells among the nations;
  she finds no resting place.
All who pursue her have overtaken her
  in the midst of her distress.

⁴The roads to Zion mourn,
  for no one comes to her appointed feasts.
All her gateways are desolate,
  her priests groan,
her maidens grieve,
  and she is in bitter anguish.

⁵Her foes have become her masters;
  her enemies are at ease.
The LORD has brought her grief
  because of her many sins.
Her children have gone into exile,
  captive before the foe.

⁶All the splendor has departed
  from the Daughter of Zion.
Her princes are like deer
  that find no pasture;
in weakness they have fled
  before the pursuer.

⁷In the days of her affliction and wandering
  Jerusalem remembers all the treasures
  that were hers in days of old.
When her people fell into enemy hands,
  there was no one to help her.
Her enemies looked at her
  and laughed at her destruction.

⁸Jerusalem has sinned greatly
  and so has become unclean.
All who honored her despise her,
  for they have seen her nakedness;
she herself groans
  and turns away.

⁹Her filthiness clung to her skirts;
  she did not consider her future.
Her fall was astounding;
  there was none to comfort her.
"Look, O LORD, on my affliction,
  for the enemy has triumphed."

¹⁰The enemy laid hands
  on all her treasures;
she saw pagan nations
  enter her sanctuary—
those you had forbidden
  to enter your assembly.

¹¹All her people groan
  as they search for bread;
they barter their treasures for food
  to keep themselves alive.
"Look, O LORD, and consider,
  for I am despised."

¹²"Is it nothing to you, all you who pass by?
  Look around and see.
Is any suffering like my suffering
  that was inflicted on me,

ᵃThis chapter is an acrostic poem, the verses of which begin with the successive letters of the Hebrew alphabet.

that the Lord brought on me
    in the day of his fierce anger?

13"From on high he sent fire,
    sent it down into my bones.
He spread a net for my feet
    and turned me back.
He made me desolate,
    faint all the day long.

14"My sins have been bound into a yoke*b*;
    by his hands they were woven together.
They have come upon my neck
    and the Lord has sapped my strength.
He has handed me over
    to those I cannot withstand.

15"The Lord has rejected
    all the warriors in my midst;
he has summoned an army against me
    to*c* crush my young men.
In his winepress the Lord has trampled
    the Virgin Daughter of Judah.

16"This is why I weep
    and my eyes overflow with tears.
No one is near to comfort me,
    no one to restore my spirit.
My children are destitute
    because the enemy has prevailed."

17Zion stretches out her hands,
    but there is no one to comfort her.
The Lord has decreed for Jacob
    that his neighbors become his foes;
Jerusalem has become
    an unclean thing among them.

18"The Lord is righteous,
    yet I rebelled against his command.
Listen, all you peoples;
    look upon my suffering.
My young men and maidens
    have gone into exile.

19"I called to my allies
    but they betrayed me.
My priests and my elders
    perished in the city
while they searched for food
    to keep themselves alive.

20"See, O Lord, how distressed I am!
    I am in torment within,
and in my heart I am disturbed,
    for I have been most rebellious.

Outside, the sword bereaves;
    inside, there is only death.

21"People have heard my groaning,
    but there is no one to comfort me.
All my enemies have heard of my distress;
    they rejoice at what you have done.
May you bring the day you have announced
    so they may become like me.

22"Let all their wickedness come before you;
    deal with them
as you have dealt with me
    because of all my sins.
My groans are many
    and my heart is faint."

2 *d*How the Lord has covered the
    Daughter of Zion
    with the cloud of his anger*e*!
He has hurled down the splendor of Israel
    from heaven to earth;
he has not remembered his footstool
    in the day of his anger.

2Without pity the Lord has swallowed up
    all the dwellings of Jacob;
in his wrath he has torn down
    the strongholds of the Daughter of Judah.
He has brought her kingdom and its princes
    down to the ground in dishonor.

3In fierce anger he has cut off
    every horn*f* of Israel.
He has withdrawn his right hand
    at the approach of the enemy.
He has burned in Jacob like a flaming fire
    that consumes everything around it.

4Like an enemy he has strung his bow;
    his right hand is ready.
Like a foe he has slain
    all who were pleasing to the eye;
he has poured out his wrath like fire
    on the tent of the Daughter of Zion.

5The Lord is like an enemy;
    he has swallowed up Israel.
He has swallowed up all her palaces
    and destroyed her strongholds.

b14 Most Hebrew manuscripts; Septuagint *He kept watch over my sins*
c15 Or *has set a time for me / when he will*   *d*This chapter is an
acrostic poem, the verses of which begin with the successive letters of the
Hebrew alphabet.   *e1* Or *How the Lord in his anger / has treated the
Daughter of Zion with contempt*   *f3* Or / *all the strength;* or *every
king; horn* here symbolizes strength.

He has multiplied mourning and lamentation
  for the Daughter of Judah.

⁶He has laid waste his dwelling like a garden;
  he has destroyed his place of meeting.
The LORD has made Zion forget
  her appointed feasts and her Sabbaths;
in his fierce anger he has spurned
  both king and priest.

⁷The Lord has rejected his altar
  and abandoned his sanctuary.
He has handed over to the enemy
  the walls of her palaces;
they have raised a shout in the house of the
    LORD
  as on the day of an appointed feast.

⁸The LORD determined to tear down
  the wall around the Daughter of Zion.
He stretched out a measuring line
  and did not withhold his hand from
    destroying.
He made ramparts and walls lament;
  together they wasted away.

⁹Her gates have sunk into the ground;
  their bars he has broken and destroyed.
Her king and her princes are exiled among
    the nations,
  the law is no more,
and her prophets no longer find
  visions from the LORD.

¹⁰The elders of the Daughter of Zion
  sit on the ground in silence;
they have sprinkled dust on their heads
  and put on sackcloth.
The young women of Jerusalem
  have bowed their heads to the ground.

¹¹My eyes fail from weeping,
  I am in torment within,
my heart is poured out on the ground
  because my people are destroyed,
because children and infants faint
  in the streets of the city.

¹²They say to their mothers,
  "Where is bread and wine?"
as they faint like wounded men
  in the streets of the city,
as their lives ebb away
  in their mothers' arms.

¹³What can I say for you?

With what can I compare you,
  O Daughter of Jerusalem?
To what can I liken you,
  that I may comfort you,
  O Virgin Daughter of Zion?
Your wound is as deep as the sea.
  Who can heal you?

¹⁴The visions of your prophets
  were false and worthless;
they did not expose your sin
  to ward off your captivity.
The oracles they gave you
  were false and misleading.

¹⁵All who pass your way
  clap their hands at you;
they scoff and shake their heads
  at the Daughter of Jerusalem:
"Is this the city that was called
  the perfection of beauty,
  the joy of the whole earth?"

¹⁶All your enemies open their mouths
  wide against you;
they scoff and gnash their teeth
  and say, "We have swallowed her up.
This is the day we have waited for;
  we have lived to see it."

¹⁷The LORD has done what he planned;
  he has fulfilled his word,
  which he decreed long ago.
He has overthrown you without pity,
  he has let the enemy gloat over you,
  he has exalted the horn⁸ of your foes.

¹⁸The hearts of the people
  cry out to the Lord.
O wall of the Daughter of Zion,
  let your tears flow like a river
    day and night;
give yourself no relief,
  your eyes no rest.

¹⁹Arise, cry out in the night,
  as the watches of the night begin;
pour out your heart like water
  in the presence of the Lord.
Lift up your hands to him
  for the lives of your children,
who faint from hunger
  at the head of every street.

g17 Horn here symbolizes strength.

²⁰"Look, O Lᴏʀᴅ, and consider:
  Whom have you ever treated like this?
Should women eat their offspring,
  the children they have cared for?
Should priest and prophet be killed
  in the sanctuary of the Lord?

²¹"Young and old lie together
  in the dust of the streets;
my young men and maidens
  have fallen by the sword.

You have slain them in the day of your
    anger;
  you have slaughtered them without pity.

²²"As you summon to a feast day,
  so you summoned against me terrors on
    every side.
In the day of the Lᴏʀᴅ's anger
  no one escaped or survived;
those I cared for and reared,
  my enemy has destroyed."

 Discovering the Word 1. What words and images in chapter 1 describe Jerusalem's misery? 2. How did the author describe God's judgments on the nation (2:1–10)? 3. What various emotions is the author feeling as he writes this (2:11–22)? 4. How did the author view God in this situation (1:5, 18; 2:17)? 5. What do you learn about the cause and effect of sin from these chapters?

 Applying the Word 1. Recalling your own experiences with the aftermath of sin, in what ways can you identify with the description of Jerusalem's misery in chapter 1? 2. In what ways, if any, has Christ made your experience with sin different from what is described here? 3. When have you felt like the author in regard to the sins of those around you?

 Responding in Prayer Ask God to give you a desire to obey him in one area you are struggling with right now.

---

2 / *Lamentations 3*
Hope in the Midst of Suffering

HOPE IS SUCH an elusive quality. It's easy to be hopeful when life is going well. But it's harder to hang on to hope when trouble obscures our focus. In the midst of horrible suffering, however, the author of Lamentations learned how to experience hope when everything seemed hopeless.

Warming Up to God What experiences feel hopeless to you? Ask God to show you how you can have hope as you meet him in this chapter.

Read Lamentations 3.

---

3 ʰI am the man who has seen affliction
    by the rod of his wrath.
  ²He has driven me away and made me
    walk
  in darkness rather than light;
³indeed, he has turned his hand against me
  again and again, all day long.

⁴He has made my skin and my flesh grow old
  and has broken my bones.
⁵He has besieged me and surrounded me
  with bitterness and hardship.
⁶He has made me dwell in darkness

like those long dead.
⁷He has walled me in so I cannot escape;
  he has weighed me down with chains.
⁸Even when I call out or cry for help,
  he shuts out my prayer.
⁹He has barred my way with blocks of stone;
  he has made my paths crooked.

¹⁰Like a bear lying in wait,
  like a lion in hiding,

ʰ This chapter is an acrostic poem; the verses of each stanza begin with the successive letters of the Hebrew alphabet, and the verses within each stanza begin with the same letter.

11he dragged me from the path and mangled me
and left me without help.
12He drew his bow
and made me the target for his arrows.
13He pierced my heart
with arrows from his quiver.
14I became the laughingstock of all my people;
they mock me in song all day long.
15He has filled me with bitter herbs
and sated me with gall.

16He has broken my teeth with gravel;
he has trampled me in the dust.
17I have been deprived of peace;
I have forgotten what prosperity is.
18So I say, "My splendor is gone
and all that I had hoped from the LORD."

19I remember my affliction and my wandering,
the bitterness and the gall.
20I well remember them,
and my soul is downcast within me.
21Yet this I call to mind
and therefore I have hope:

22Because of the LORD's great love we are not
consumed,
for his compassions never fail.
23They are new every morning;
great is your faithfulness.
24I say to myself, "The LORD is my portion;
therefore I will wait for him."

25The LORD is good to those whose hope is in
him,
to the one who seeks him;
26it is good to wait quietly
for the salvation of the LORD.
27It is good for a man to bear the yoke
while he is young.

28Let him sit alone in silence,
for the LORD has laid it on him.
29Let him bury his face in the dust—
there may yet be hope.
30Let him offer his cheek to one who would
strike him,
and let him be filled with disgrace.

31For men are not cast off
by the Lord forever.
32Though he brings grief, he will show
compassion,
so great is his unfailing love.

33For he does not willingly bring affliction
or grief to the children of men.

34To crush underfoot
all prisoners in the land,
35to deny a man his rights
before the Most High,
36to deprive a man of justice—
would not the Lord see such things?

37Who can speak and have it happen
if the Lord has not decreed it?
38Is it not from the mouth of the Most High
that both calamities and good things come?
39Why should any living man complain
when punished for his sins?

40Let us examine our ways and test them,
and let us return to the LORD.
41Let us lift up our hearts and our hands
to God in heaven, and say:
42"We have sinned and rebelled
and you have not forgiven.

43"You have covered yourself with anger and
pursued us;
you have slain without pity.
44You have covered yourself with a cloud
so that no prayer can get through.
45You have made us scum and refuse
among the nations.

46"All our enemies have opened their mouths
wide against us.
47We have suffered terror and pitfalls,
ruin and destruction."
48Streams of tears flow from my eyes
because my people are destroyed.

49My eyes will flow unceasingly,
without relief,
50until the LORD looks down
from heaven and sees.
51What I see brings grief to my soul
because of all the women of my city.

52Those who were my enemies without cause
hunted me like a bird.
53They tried to end my life in a pit
and threw stones at me;
54the waters closed over my head,
and I thought I was about to be cut off.

55I called on your name, O LORD,
from the depths of the pit.
56You heard my plea: "Do not close your ears

to my cry for relief."
⁵⁷You came near when I called you,
and you said, "Do not fear."

⁵⁸O Lord, you took up my case;
you redeemed my life.
⁵⁹You have seen, O Lᴏʀᴅ, the wrong done to
me.
Uphold my cause!
⁶⁰You have seen the depth of their vengeance,
all their plots against me.

⁶¹O Lᴏʀᴅ, you have heard their insults,

all their plots against me—
⁶²what my enemies whisper and mutter
against me all day long.
⁶³Look at them! Sitting or standing,
they mock me in their songs.

⁶⁴Pay them back what they deserve, O Lᴏʀᴅ,
for what their hands have done.
⁶⁵Put a veil over their hearts,
and may your curse be on them!
⁶⁶Pursue them in anger and destroy them
from under the heavens of the Lᴏʀᴅ.

 Discovering the Word 1. Why did the author feel so hopeless (vv. 1–18)? 2. Why did his hopelessness turn to hope (vv. 19–24)? 3. What did he remember about God that changed his perspective on suffering (vv. 25–39)? 4. How did the author's prayer relate to his suffering (vv. 40–66)? 5. What do you learn in this chapter about the relationship between God's judgment and his love?

 Applying the Word 1. In what ways has God been faithful to you? 2. One way to deal with hopelessness is to be reminded of the character of God. How can you get to know God better?

Responding in Prayer Praise God for his specific attributes that can give you hope in the midst of suffering. Ask him to help you remember these the next time you hit hard times.

---

3 / *Lamentations 4—5*
Suffering Is Not Forever

WHEN SOMEONE WE know dies, when a spouse departs, when a dream is snatched away, we go through a grieving process. It isn't pleasant, but it's necessary for our emotional healing. Those are not the only times we need to mourn. Lamentations teaches us that grieving over our sins and confessing them to God is important for our spiritual health. As the author ended this book, he focused on steps beyond the grief.

 Warming Up to God How do you talk to God when you are suffering? Are you open with God? Are you afraid to voice certain questions? Do you tend to blame God? Evaluate yourself before you turn to the Scripture text.

 Read Lamentations 4—5.

---

4 ¹How the gold has lost its luster,
the fine gold become dull!
The sacred gems are scattered
at the head of every street.

²How the precious sons of Zion,
once worth their weight in gold,
are now considered as pots of clay,
the work of a potter's hands!

³Even jackals offer their breasts
to nurse their young,

but my people have become heartless
like ostriches in the desert.

⁴Because of thirst the infant's tongue
sticks to the roof of its mouth;
the children beg for bread,
but no one gives it to them.

⁵Those who once ate delicacies
are destitute in the streets.
Those nurtured in purple

ⁱThis chapter is an acrostic poem, the verses of which begin with the successive letters of the Hebrew alphabet.

now lie on ash heaps.

⁶The punishment of my people
  is greater than that of Sodom,
which was overthrown in a moment
  without a hand turned to help her.

⁷Their princes were brighter than snow
  and whiter than milk,
their bodies more ruddy than rubies,
  their appearance like sapphires.ʲ

⁸But now they are blacker than soot;
  they are not recognized in the streets.
Their skin has shriveled on their bones;
  it has become as dry as a stick.

⁹Those killed by the sword are better off
  than those who die of famine;
racked with hunger, they waste away
  for lack of food from the field.

¹⁰With their own hands compassionate women
  have cooked their own children,
who became their food
  when my people were destroyed.

¹¹The LORD has given full vent to his wrath;
  he has poured out his fierce anger.
He kindled a fire in Zion
  that consumed her foundations.

¹²The kings of the earth did not believe,
  nor did any of the world's people,
that enemies and foes could enter
  the gates of Jerusalem.

¹³But it happened because of the sins of her
    prophets
  and the iniquities of her priests,
who shed within her
  the blood of the righteous.

¹⁴Now they grope through the streets
  like men who are blind.
They are so defiled with blood
  that no one dares to touch their garments.

¹⁵"Go away! You are unclean!" men cry to
    them.
  "Away! Away! Don't touch us!"
When they flee and wander about,
  people among the nations say,
  "They can stay here no longer."

¹⁶The LORD himself has scattered them;
  he no longer watches over them.

The priests are shown no honor,
  the elders no favor.

¹⁷Moreover, our eyes failed,
  looking in vain for help;
from our towers we watched
  for a nation that could not save us.

¹⁸Men stalked us at every step,
  so we could not walk in our streets.
Our end was near, our days were numbered,
  for our end had come.

¹⁹Our pursuers were swifter
  than eagles in the sky;
they chased us over the mountains
  and lay in wait for us in the desert.

²⁰The LORD's anointed, our very life breath,
  was caught in their traps.
We thought that under his shadow
  we would live among the nations.

²¹Rejoice and be glad, O Daughter of Edom,
  you who live in the land of Uz.
But to you also the cup will be passed;
  you will be drunk and stripped naked.

²²O Daughter of Zion, your punishment will
    end;
  he will not prolong your exile.
But, O Daughter of Edom, he will punish
    your sin
  and expose your wickedness.

5 Remember, O LORD, what has happened
    to us;
  look, and see our disgrace.
²Our inheritance has been turned over to
    aliens,
  our homes to foreigners.
³We have become orphans and fatherless,
  our mothers like widows.
⁴We must buy the water we drink;
  our wood can be had only at a price.
⁵Those who pursue us are at our heels;
  we are weary and find no rest.
⁶We submitted to Egypt and Assyria
  to get enough bread.
⁷Our fathers sinned and are no more,
  and we bear their punishment.
⁸Slaves rule over us,

ʲ 17 Or lapis lazuli

and there is none to free us from their
     hands.
⁹We get our bread at the risk of our lives
     because of the sword in the desert.
¹⁰Our skin is hot as an oven,
     feverish from hunger.
¹¹Women have been ravished in Zion,
     and virgins in the towns of Judah.
¹²Princes have been hung up by their hands;
     elders are shown no respect.
¹³Young men toil at the millstones;
     boys stagger under loads of wood.
¹⁴The elders are gone from the city gate;
     the young men have stopped their
     music.
¹⁵Joy is gone from our hearts;
     our dancing has turned to mourning.

¹⁶The crown has fallen from our head.
     Woe to us, for we have sinned!
¹⁷Because of this our hearts are faint,
     because of these things our eyes grow dim
¹⁸for Mount Zion, which lies desolate,
     with jackals prowling over it.

¹⁹You, O LORD, reign forever;
     your throne endures from generation to
     generation.
²⁰Why do you always forget us?
     Why do you forsake us so long?
²¹Restore us to yourself, O LORD, that we may
     return;
     renew our days as of old
²²unless you have utterly rejected us
     and are angry with us beyond measure.

Discovering the Word 1. Contrast the people before and after Jerusalem's fall (4:1–12). 2. In what areas did the fall and captivity affect them (4:1–20)? 3. Why did God allow his people to be overtaken by their enemies (4:13–22)? 4. What did the author confess to God (5:1–18)? 5. How does the tone change at the end of this book (5:19–22)? Why?

Applying the Word 1. What part does prayer play in mourning the consequences of your sin? 2. How can talking to God be a help in the midst of suffering? 3. What do you need to confess to God today?

Responding in Prayer Confess whatever sins God brought to mind. Then focus on the miracle of grace that he offers, letting that be the source of your praise.

Ezekiel

"**T**hat you may know that I am the LORD" is a phrase that occurs sixty-six times in the book of Ezekiel. It captures the essence of the visions, parables and allegories that comprise this remarkable Old Testament book. It also locates our deepest need: to become increasingly aware of the glory of God as the ultimate reality.

Like Ezekiel, who wrote and ministered in exile in faraway Babylon after 597 B.C., we live an exilic existence in this world, longing for our ultimate homeland—heaven. Ezekiel and his compatriots were surrounded by the seductions of a sophisticated but pagan foreign culture. What they needed was not mere words about God but an empowering vision that would fortify their imagination and evoke their faith. This book is a revelation of God through images, signs and metaphors of God's glory, appealing to faith *through* the imagination. Ezekiel is hard for us to understand precisely because we are so alienated from a full biblical spirituality that includes a redeemed imagination.

But Ezekiel has another important reason for framing his message in allegories, metaphors and parables. His message is one of judgment and hope for Jerusalem—the church of his day. He prophesied not *to* Jerusalem but *of* Jerusalem to his fellow exiles who still lived for Jerusalem and home. News of Jerusalem was the supreme factor in the life of the exiles. Indeed, the book easily is divided between prophecies given before the final collapse of Jerusalem (chapters 1—24) and those given after (chapters 25—48).

But Ezekiel's message about Jerusalem would be hard to speak and harder still to hear. The people who remained in Jerusalem after the first deportation that took Ezekiel and his wife to Babylon in 597 B.C. were given to idolatrous and perverted imaginations. The people were like an unfaithful spouse. The leaders no longer led. The nation was like a valley of dry bones. To communicate the tragedy, as well as the hope of God's covenanted people, Ezekiel needed art to catch the people's attention and draw them into a divine perspective on the matter.

At times Ezekiel becomes an incarnated audio-visual aid when he lies on his side outside his house for part of each day for a year, makes models of Jerusalem with siege works and even forgoes mourning the death of his wife. In these things, too, Ezekiel's passion was that the people should "know that I am the LORD." For even in judging the church of that day, God will reveal himself as a faithful covenant partner. He will lead his own people when the leaders fail to shepherd the sheep. He will resurrect the dead bones of his own house. He will empower his people in exile to live godly lives by showing them the glory of his heavenly temple and his determination to renew the land and bring his whole creation to a worthy end.

Ezekiel is full of apocalyptic end-times visions and prophecies and therefore offers us an important perspective: a short-range pessimism and a long-range optimism. It is not surprising therefore that Ezekiel is a major source of images and metaphors for the "revelation of Jesus Christ" in the last book of the Bible (Rev 1:1). Besides this Ezekiel contains themes that are crucial to our ministry in the modern world: the desperate need for purification in both the outward ethical life and the inner imagination, the recovery of covenantal relationship with God, the restoration of pastoral leadership, the fundamental role of hope in the spiritual life, the wonderful destiny of the created order, and the primacy of the glory of God as the central motive for mission.

It is this passion for the glory of God and this appeal to our redeemed imagination that gives this book its universal and timeless quality. Like Ezekiel we are away from home, longing for our true homeland, distressed that the community that bears God's glory on earth does so in such a tawdry way, and wondering what will come of it all. The word we need, as it turns out, is not so much a word as a vision of the magnificence of God who is absolutely determined to glorify himself and to be known. So these visions, allegories and parables are, as Calvin Seerveld once said, like the sign given to Noah long before: rainbows for the fallen world.

Outline

1/ Ezekiel 1 —————————————— Envisioning the Glory of God

2/ Ezekiel 2:1—3:15 —————————— Experiencing the Call of God

3/ Ezekiel 4—5 ————————————— Warning the People of God

4/ Ezekiel 6—7 ————————————— Living in the End Times

5/ Ezekiel 8 ——————————————— The Darkened Inner Eye

6/ Ezekiel 11 —————————————— When Human Leaders Fail

7/ Ezekiel 16 —————————————— The Bride of God

8/ Ezekiel 18 —————————————— Assuming Personal Responsibility

9/ Ezekiel 24:15–27 ————————— Losing One's Beloved

10/ Ezekiel 27—28 ———————————— National Pride—National Downfall

11/ Ezekiel 33 ——————————————— The Watchman

12/ Ezekiel 34 —————————————— Past and Future Shepherds

13/ Ezekiel 37 —————————————— Can These Bones Live?

14/ Ezekiel 40—41 ————————————— The New Temple

15/ Ezekiel 43:1–12 ————————— The God Who Dwells with His People

16/ Ezekiel 47:1–12 ————————— The Vision of a Renewed Creation

Ezekiel's Temple

A. Wall (40:5,16-20)
B. East gate (40:6-14,16)
C. Portico (40:8)
D. Outer court (40:17)
E. Pavement (40:17)
F. Inner court (40:19)
G. North gate (40:20-22)
H. Inner court (40:23)
I. South gate (40:24-26)
J. South inner court (40:27)
K. Gateway (40:28-31)
L. Gateway (40:32-34)
M. Gateway (40:35-38)
N. Priests' rooms (40:44-45)

O. Court (40:47)
P. Temple portico (40:48-49)
Q. Outer sanctuary (41:1-2)
R. Most Holy Place (41:3-4)
S. Temple walls (41:5-7,9,11)
T. Base (41:8)
U. Open area (41:10)
V. West building (41:12)
W. Priests' rooms (42:1-10)
X. Altar (43:13-17)
AA. Rooms for preparing sacrifices (40:39-43)
BB. Ovens (46:19-20)
CC. Kitchens (46:21-24)

Ezekiel uses a long or "royal" cubit, 20.4 inches or 51.81 cm ("cubit and a handbreadth," Eze 40:5) as opposed to the standard Hebrew cubit of 17.6 inches or 44.7 cm.

Scripture describes a floor plan, but provides few height dimensions. This artwork shows an upward projection of the temple over the floor plan. This temple existed only in a vision of Ezekiel (Eze 40:2), and has never actually been built as were the temples of Solomon, Zerubbabel and Herod.

Floor plan of sanctuary

Side rooms

NORTH

NORTH

SOUTH

EAST

Height of this wall has been exaggerated slightly to avoid optical illusion

Kitchens were in all four corners

1 / *Ezekiel 1*
Envisioning the Glory of God

NO ONE CAN experience someone else's encounter with God. Therefore, Ezekiel's verbal record of his vision is, in one sense, unique to this prophet. But there are universal elements in Ezekiel's experience which can awaken our own faith if we are willing to not only think about the concept of God's glory, but also allow our imaginations to become a vehicle for faith-response to God's glory through this inspired word picture. We might then say, along with the theologian Karl Barth, "God is beautiful."

 Warming Up to God   What pictures, if any, have you had when you have thought about or experienced God's greatness?

 Read Ezekiel 1.

In the*a* thirtieth year, in the fourth month on the fifth day, while I was among the exiles by the Kebar River, the heavens were opened and I saw visions of God.

²On the fifth of the month—it was the fifth year of the exile of King Jehoiachin— ³the word of the LORD came to Ezekiel the priest, the son of Buzi,*b* by the Kebar River in the land of the Babylonians.*c* There the hand of the LORD was upon him.

⁴I looked, and I saw a windstorm coming out of the north—an immense cloud with flashing lightning and surrounded by brilliant light. The center of the fire looked like glowing metal, ⁵and in the fire was what looked like four living creatures. In appearance their form was that of a man, ⁶but each of them had four faces and four wings. ⁷Their legs were straight; their feet were like those of a calf and gleamed like burnished bronze. ⁸Under their wings on their four sides they had the hands of a man. All four of them had faces and wings, ⁹and their wings touched one another. Each one went straight ahead; they did not turn as they moved.

¹⁰Their faces looked like this: Each of the four had the face of a man, and on the right side each had the face of a lion, and on the left the face of an ox; each also had the face of an eagle. ¹¹Such were their faces. Their wings were spread out upward; each had two wings, one touching the wing of another creature on either side, and two wings covering its body. ¹²Each one went straight ahead. Wherever the spirit would go, they would go, without turning as they went. ¹³The appearance of the living creatures was like burning coals of fire or like torches. Fire moved back and forth among the creatures; it was bright, and lightning flashed out of it. ¹⁴The creatures sped back and forth like flashes of lightning.

¹⁵As I looked at the living creatures, I saw a wheel on the ground beside each creature with its four faces. ¹⁶This was the appearance and structure of the wheels: They sparkled like chrysolite, and all four looked alike. Each appeared to be made like a wheel intersecting a wheel. ¹⁷As they moved, they would go in any one of the four directions the creatures faced; the wheels did not turn about*d* as the creatures went. ¹⁸Their rims were high and awesome, and all four rims were full of eyes all around.

¹⁹When the living creatures moved, the wheels beside them moved; and when the living creatures rose from the ground, the wheels also rose. ²⁰Wherever the spirit would go, they would go, and the wheels would rise along with them, because the spirit of the living creatures was in the wheels. ²¹When the creatures moved, they also moved; when the creatures stood still, they also stood still; and when the creatures rose from the ground, the wheels rose along with them, because the spirit of the living creatures was in the wheels.

²²Spread out above the heads of the living creatures was what looked like an expanse, sparkling like ice, and awesome. ²³Under the expanse their wings were stretched out one toward the other, and each had two wings covering its body. ²⁴When the creatures moved, I heard the sound of their wings, like the roar of rushing waters, like the voice of the Almighty,*e* like the tumult of an army. When they stood still, they lowered their wings.

---

*a*1 Or ₒmyₒ   *b*3 Or *Ezekiel son of Buzi the priest*   *c*3 Or *Chaldeans*   *d*17 Or *aside*   *e*24 Hebrew *Shaddai*

²⁵Then there came a voice from above the expanse over their heads as they stood with lowered wings. ²⁶Above the expanse over their heads was what looked like a throne of sapphire,ᶠ and high above on the throne was a figure like that of a man. ²⁷I saw that from what appeared to be his waist up he looked like glowing metal, as if full of fire, and that from there down he looked like fire; and brilliant light surrounded him. ²⁸Like the appearance of a rainbow in the clouds on a rainy day, so was the radiance around him.

This was the appearance of the likeness of the glory of the LORD. When I saw it, I fell facedown, and I heard the voice of one speaking.

ᶠ26 Or *lapis lazuli*

 Discovering the Word 1. Ezekiel is by the Kebar River in faraway Babylonian exile. It is five years after he and his compatriots were forcibly removed from Jerusalem. You may find it helpful to close your eyes and allow each new dimension of the vision to unfold. Record your impressions of colors, changing light, sounds, movement and symbols. 2. In this vision of God what do we learn about the relationship between God and his creation (vv. 4–21)? 3. What do verses 4–21 suggest about the character of God? 4. As Ezekiel is directed from creation to Creator (vv. 22–28), what further images and sounds create a sense of the glory of God? 5. Why would no form but the human form be appropriate to represent God visually?

Applying the Word 1. That the God of Zion would appear to Ezekiel in far-off Babylon amidst the sordid heathenism must have been an immense encouragement to Ezekiel. What does this mean for your personal life and your church life? 2. What aspects of the vision point to new frontiers in your experience of God?

Responding in Prayer As you pray, allow God to redeem your imagination to envision the glory of God. (There are some thoughts on the use of the imagination in the introduction.)

---

2 / *Ezekiel 2:1—3:15*
Experiencing the Call of God

MENTION THE PHRASE "called of God" and most think of those special few, God's chosen prophets, preachers and missionaries. That was certainly the case under the old covenant (before Christ) even though the people of God as a *people* were called (Hos 11:1). But under the new covenant every Christian is called in three ways: to belong to God, to live a holy life and to serve God's purposes in the world (Eph 4:1). Ezekiel's call was special, setting him apart from the people as God's spokesperson. But we can learn much from it. In chapter one we see that Ezekiel's call is first to Someone. Then, in chapter two, he is called to something. The order is crucial.

 Warming Up to God What would it be like if God never called us and merely left us to make of our lives what we could?

 Read Ezekiel 2:1—3:15.

2He said to me, "Son of man, stand up on your feet and I will speak to you." ²As he spoke, the Spirit came into me and raised me to my feet, and I heard him speaking to me.

³He said: "Son of man, I am sending you to the Israelites, to a rebellious nation that has rebelled against me; they and their fathers have been in revolt against me to this very day. ⁴The people to whom I am sending you are obstinate and stubborn. Say to them, 'This is what the Sovereign LORD says.' ⁵And whether they listen or fail to listen—for they are a rebellious house—they will know that a prophet has been among them. ⁶And you, son of man, do not be afraid of them or their words. Do not be afraid, though briers and thorns are all around you and you live among scorpions. Do not be afraid of what they say or terrified by them, though they are a rebellious house. ⁷You must speak my words to them, whether they listen or fail to listen, for they are rebellious. ⁸But you, son of man, listen to what I say to you. Do

not rebel like that rebellious house; open your mouth and eat what I give you."

⁹Then I looked, and I saw a hand stretched out to me. In it was a scroll, ¹⁰which he unrolled before me. On both sides of it were written words of lament and mourning and woe.

3 And he said to me, "Son of man, eat what is before you, eat this scroll; then go and speak to the house of Israel." ²So I opened my mouth, and he gave me the scroll to eat.

³Then he said to me, "Son of man, eat this scroll I am giving you and fill your stomach with it." So I ate it, and it tasted as sweet as honey in my mouth.

⁴He then said to me: "Son of man, go now to the house of Israel and speak my words to them. ⁵You are not being sent to a people of obscure speech and difficult language, but to the house of Israel— ⁶not to many peoples of obscure speech and difficult language, whose words you cannot understand. Surely if I had sent you to them, they would have listened to you. ⁷But the house of Israel is not willing to listen to you because they are not willing to listen to me, for the whole house of Israel is hardened and obstinate. ⁸But I will make you as unyielding and hardened as they are. ⁹I will make your forehead like the hardest stone, harder than flint. Do not be afraid of them or terrified by them, though they are a rebellious house."

¹⁰And he said to me, "Son of man, listen carefully and take to heart all the words I speak to you. ¹¹Go now to your countrymen in exile and speak to them. Say to them, 'This is what the Sovereign LORD says,' whether they listen or fail to listen."

¹²Then the Spirit lifted me up, and I heard behind me a loud rumbling sound—May the glory of the LORD be praised in his dwelling place!— ¹³the sound of the wings of the living creatures brushing against each other and the sound of the wheels beside them, a loud rumbling sound. ¹⁴The Spirit then lifted me up and took me away, and I went in bitterness and in the anger of my spirit, with the strong hand of the LORD upon me. ¹⁵I came to the exiles who lived at Tel Abib near the Kebar River. And there, where they were living, I sat among them for seven days—overwhelmed.

Discovering the Word 1. What indications are there in the passage that Ezekiel heard God's call not only as an obligation but also as an empowering and motivating reality (2:2; 3:12–15)? 2. Why does God want Ezekiel to go on speaking God's word even though the people will not listen (2:5)? 3. What might keep Ezekiel from fulfilling God's call, and how does God deal with this (2:6–8)? 4. In the vision the scroll of God's word is given to Ezekiel. Why would "eating" the scroll (2:8; 3:2) be so important for God's spokesperson? 5. Ezekiel is overwhelmed (3:15). What do you think is happening to this servant of God while he sits among the exiles for seven days?

Applying the Word 1. Why do you think being a missionary to the church (God's people) will be harder than being a missionary to the strangers outside (3:5–9)? 2. Ezekiel found both sweetness and bitterness in being a called person. In what ways is your experience of Christian vocation (or calling) similar? 3. What have you learned that will help you be faithful in witnessing even to those who are obstinately opposed to the gospel or where there is no evident success?

Responding in Prayer Thank God that he now issues his call through Christ to each and every member of his family. Pray for grace to live out the whole of your life in response to God's call and with the provision of his Spirit.

Ezekiel 3:16–27

¹⁶At the end of seven days the word of the LORD came to me: ¹⁷"Son of man, I have made you a watchman for the house of Israel; so hear the word I speak and give them warning from me. ¹⁸When I say to a wicked man, 'You will surely die,' and you do not warn him or speak out to dissuade him from his evil ways in order to save his life, that wicked man will die for^g his sin, and I will hold you accountable for his blood. ¹⁹But if you do warn the wicked man and he does

818 Or in; also in verses 19 and 20

not turn from his wickedness or from his evil ways, he will die for his sin; but you will have saved yourself.

²⁰"Again, when a righteous man turns from his righteousness and does evil, and I put a stumbling block before him, he will die. Since you did not warn him, he will die for his sin. The righteous things he did will not be remembered, and I will hold you accountable for his blood. ²¹But if you do warn the righteous man not to sin and he does not sin, he will surely live because he took warning, and you will have saved yourself."

²²The hand of the LORD was upon me there, and he said to me, "Get up and go out to the plain, and there I will speak to you." ²³So I got up and went out to the plain. And the glory of the LORD was standing there, like the glory I had seen by the Kebar River, and I fell facedown.

²⁴Then the Spirit came into me and raised me to my feet. He spoke to me and said: "Go, shut yourself inside your house. ²⁵And you, son of man, they will tie with ropes; you will be bound so that you cannot go out among the people. ²⁶I will make your tongue stick to the roof of your mouth so that you will be silent and unable to rebuke them, though they are a rebellious house. ²⁷But when I speak to you, I will open your mouth and you shall say to them, 'This is what the Sovereign LORD says.' Whoever will listen let him listen, and whoever will refuse let him refuse; for they are a rebellious house.

3 / *Ezekiel 4—5*
Warning the People of God

HARDLY ANYONE THINKS of the wrath of God as a positive thing. Most think of it as a divine temper tantrum. But the wrath of God is God's giving people up to experience the results of their own choice (Ro 1:24, 26, 28). It is like a wood plane which if used with the grain produces a smooth surface, but if used against the grain tears up all the fibers even though it is the same tool and the same block of wood.

Ezekiel has a hard message for his people. In far-off Babylon, with hearts still focused on their beloved Jerusalem, the people must be warned about what is going to happen to the holy city. Under King Zedekiah Jerusalem had recovered some of its strength, and false prophets were predicting a time of favor (Jer 28:1–4). The truth was otherwise. If they repent, they will know God's grace; if they do not, they will know his wrath. Much later in history God's own Son bore the wrath they and we deserve outside the walls of that same city.

 Warming Up to God   Think of a time in your life when you had a hard but good warning. What made it a good thing even though it hurt at the time?

 Read Ezekiel 4—5.

4 "Now, son of man, take a clay tablet, put it in front of you and draw the city of Jerusalem on it. ²Then lay siege to it: Erect siege works against it, build a ramp up to it, set up camps against it and put battering rams around it. ³Then take an iron pan, place it as an iron wall between you and the city and turn your face toward it. It will be under siege, and you shall besiege it. This will be a sign to the house of Israel.

⁴"Then lie on your left side and put the sin of the house of Israel upon yourself.^h You are to bear their sin for the number of days you lie on your side. ⁵I have assigned you the same number of days as the years of their sin. So for 390 days you will bear the sin of the house of Israel.

⁶"After you have finished this, lie down again, this time on your right side, and bear the sin of the house of Judah. I have assigned you 40 days, a day for each year. ⁷Turn your face toward the siege of Jerusalem and with bared arm prophesy against her. ⁸I will tie you up with ropes so that you cannot turn from one side to the other until you have finished the days of your siege.

⁹"Take wheat and barley, beans and lentils, millet and spelt; put them in a storage jar and use them to make bread for yourself. You are to eat it

^h4 Or *your side*

during the 390 days you lie on your side. ¹⁰Weigh out twenty shekels¹ of food to eat each day and eat it at set times. ¹¹Also measure out a sixth of a hin¹ of water and drink it at set times. ¹²Eat the food as you would a barley cake; bake it in the sight of the people, using human excrement for fuel." ¹³The LORD said, "In this way the people of Israel will eat defiled food among the nations where I will drive them."

¹⁴Then I said, "Not so, Sovereign LORD! I have never defiled myself. From my youth until now I have never eaten anything found dead or torn by wild animals. No unclean meat has ever entered my mouth."

¹⁵"Very well," he said, "I will let you bake your bread over cow manure instead of human excrement."

¹⁶He then said to me: "Son of man, I will cut off the supply of food in Jerusalem. The people will eat rationed food in anxiety and drink rationed water in despair, ¹⁷for food and water will be scarce. They will be appalled at the sight of each other and will waste away because of ᵏ their sin.

5 "Now, son of man, take a sharp sword and use it as a barber's razor to shave your head and your beard. Then take a set of scales and divide up the hair. ²When the days of your siege come to an end, burn a third of the hair with fire inside the city. Take a third and strike it with the sword all around the city. And scatter a third to the wind. For I will pursue them with drawn sword. ³But take a few strands of hair and tuck them away in the folds of your garment. ⁴Again, take a few of these and throw them into the fire and burn them up. A fire will spread from there to the whole house of Israel.

⁵"This is what the Sovereign LORD says: This is Jerusalem, which I have set in the center of the nations, with countries all around her. ⁶Yet in her wickedness she has rebelled against my laws and decrees more than the nations and countries around her. She has rejected my laws and has not followed my decrees.

⁷"Therefore this is what the Sovereign LORD says: You have been more unruly than the nations around you and have not followed my decrees or kept my laws. You have not even¹ conformed to the standards of the nations around you.

⁸"Therefore this is what the Sovereign LORD says: I myself am against you, Jerusalem, and I will inflict punishment on you in the sight of the nations. ⁹Because of all your detestable idols, I will do to you what I have never done before and will never do again. ¹⁰Therefore in your midst fathers will eat their children, and children will eat their fathers. I will inflict punishment on you and will scatter all your survivors to the winds. ¹¹Therefore as surely as I live, declares the Sovereign LORD, because you have defiled my sanctuary with all your vile images and detestable practices, I myself will withdraw my favor; I will not look on you with pity or spare you. ¹²A third of your people will die of the plague or perish by famine inside you; a third will fall by the sword outside your walls; and a third I will scatter to the winds and pursue with drawn sword.

¹³"Then my anger will cease and my wrath against them will subside, and I will be avenged. And when I have spent my wrath upon them, they will know that I the LORD have spoken in my zeal.

¹⁴"I will make you a ruin and a reproach among the nations around you, in the sight of all who pass by. ¹⁵You will be a reproach and a taunt, a warning and an object of horror to the nations around you when I inflict punishment on you in anger and in wrath and with stinging rebuke. I the LORD have spoken. ¹⁶When I shoot at you with my deadly and destructive arrows of famine, I will shoot to destroy you. I will bring more and more famine upon you and cut off your supply of food. ¹⁷I will send famine and wild beasts against you, and they will leave you childless. Plague and bloodshed will sweep through you, and I will bring the sword against you. I the LORD have spoken."

---

¹10 That is, about 8 ounces (about 0.2 kilogram)   ¹11 That is, about 2/3 quart (about 0.6 liter)   ᵏ17 Or away in   ¹7 Most Hebrew manuscripts; some Hebrew manuscripts and Syriac You have

---

Discovering the Word   1. What audio-visual aids and personal dramatic acts is Ezekiel instructed to use to communicate what God intended to do with Jerusalem? **2.** The prophet is called to bear the sin of the people on his side (4:4–8). What could Ezekiel be communicating through this? **3.** What does 4:9–15 reveal about the relationship between Ezekiel and God? **4.** What reason does God give for his drastic action with Jerusalem (5:6–7, 11)? **5.** How does the punishment fit the crime (5:8–17)? **6.** What do you learn in this passage about God's zeal for righteousness (5:13)?

Applying the Word 1. What is the Lord's attitude toward believers who do not live by standards even as high as those who do not profess faith in God? 2. In what way might your life pale in comparison to a nonbeliever's life?

Responding in Prayer Ask the Lord to give you his perspective on what is happening in the world and in your life. Praise God that there is hope in his judgment.

4 / *Ezekiel 6—7*
Living in the End Times

THE FRENCH EXISTENTIALIST Albert Camus once said that he would wait for the judgment of God resolutely because he had known something far worse: the judgment of human beings. With men and women there are no extenuating circumstances. But with God there is hope, often signaled in the Bible by a "but" as in Ezekiel 6:8. Israel was called to be a kingdom of priests (Ex 19:6), declaring God's Word to the world that all may "know the LORD" (2Ki 19:19). In the end people expected the nations to be judged and Israel saved. But in this passage God's final judgment has begun and judgment begins at the house of God.

Warming Up to God What do you most fear and most long for when you hear that God is bringing history to a conclusion with a final judgment?

Read Ezekiel 6—7.

---

6 The word of the LORD came to me: 2"Son of man, set your face against the mountains of Israel; prophesy against them 3and say: 'O mountains of Israel, hear the word of the Sovereign LORD. This is what the Sovereign LORD says to the mountains and hills, to the ravines and valleys: I am about to bring a sword against you, and I will destroy your high places. 4Your altars will be demolished and your incense altars will be smashed; and I will slay your people in front of your idols. 5I will lay the dead bodies of the Israelites in front of their idols, and I will scatter your bones around your altars. 6Wherever you live, the towns will be laid waste and the high places demolished, so that your altars will be laid waste and devastated, your idols smashed and ruined, your incense altars broken down, and what you have made wiped out. 7Your people will fall slain among you, and you will know that I am the LORD.

8" 'But I will spare some, for some of you will escape the sword when you are scattered among the lands and nations. 9Then in the nations where they have been carried captive, those who escape will remember me—how I have been grieved by their adulterous hearts, which have turned away from me, and by their eyes, which have lusted after their idols. They will loathe themselves for the evil they have done and for all their detestable practices. 10And they will know that I am the LORD; I did not threaten in vain to bring this calamity on them.

11" 'This is what the Sovereign LORD says: Strike your hands together and stamp your feet and cry out "Alas!" because of all the wicked and detestable practices of the house of Israel, for they will fall by the sword, famine and plague. 12He that is far away will die of the plague, and he that is near will fall by the sword, and he that survives and is spared will die of famine. So will I spend my wrath upon them. 13And they will know that I am the LORD, when their people lie slain among their idols around their altars, on every high hill and on all the mountaintops, under every spreading tree and every leafy oak—places where they offered fragrant incense to all their idols. 14And I will stretch out my hand against them and make the land a desolate waste from the desert to Diblah[m]—wherever they live. Then they will know that I am the LORD.' "

7 The word of the LORD came to me: [2]"Son of man, this is what the Sovereign LORD says to the land of Israel: The end! The end has come upon the four corners of the land. [3]The end is now upon you and I will unleash my anger against you. I will judge you according to your conduct and repay you for all your detestable practices. [4]I will not look on you with pity or spare you; I will surely repay you for your conduct and the detestable practices among you. Then you will know that I am the LORD.

[5]"This is what the Sovereign LORD says: Disaster! An unheard-of[n] disaster is coming. [6]The end has come! The end has come! It has roused itself against you. It has come! [7]Doom has come upon you—you who dwell in the land. The time has come, the day is near; there is panic, not joy, upon the mountains. [8]I am about to pour out my wrath on you and spend my anger against you; I will judge you according to your conduct and repay you for all your detestable practices. [9]I will not look on you with pity or spare you; I will repay you in accordance with your conduct and the detestable practices among you. Then you will know that it is I the LORD who strikes the blow.

[10]"The day is here! It has come! Doom has burst forth, the rod has budded, arrogance has blossomed! [11]Violence has grown into[o] a rod to punish wickedness; none of the people will be left, none of that crowd—no wealth, nothing of value. [12]The time has come, the day has arrived. Let not the buyer rejoice nor the seller grieve, for wrath is upon the whole crowd. [13]The seller will not recover the land he has sold as long as both of them live, for the vision concerning the whole crowd will not be reversed. Because of their sins, not one of them will preserve his life. [14]Though they blow the trumpet and get everything ready, no one will go into battle, for my wrath is upon the whole crowd.

[15]"Outside is the sword, inside are plague and famine; those in the country will die by the sword, and those in the city will be devoured by famine and plague. [16]All who survive and escape will be in the mountains, moaning like doves of the valleys, each because of his sins. [17]Every hand will go limp, and every knee will become as weak as water. [18]They will put on sackcloth and be clothed with terror. Their faces will be covered with shame and their heads will be shaved. [19]They will throw their silver into the streets, and their gold will be an unclean thing. Their silver and gold will not be able to save them in the day of the LORD's wrath. They will not satisfy their hunger or fill their stomachs with it, for it has made them stumble into sin. [20]They were proud of their beautiful jewelry and used it to make their detestable idols and vile images. Therefore I will turn these into an unclean thing for them. [21]I will hand it all over as plunder to foreigners and as loot to the wicked of the earth, and they will defile it. [22]I will turn my face away from them, and they will desecrate my treasured place; robbers will enter it and desecrate it.

[23]"Prepare chains, because the land is full of bloodshed and the city is full of violence. [24]I will bring the most wicked of the nations to take possession of their houses; I will put an end to the pride of the mighty, and their sanctuaries will be desecrated. [25]When terror comes, they will seek peace, but there will be none. [26]Calamity upon calamity will come, and rumor upon rumor. They will try to get a vision from the prophet; the teaching of the law by the priest will be lost, as will the counsel of the elders. [27]The king will mourn, the prince will be clothed with despair, and the hands of the people of the land will tremble. I will deal with them according to their conduct, and by their own standards I will judge them. Then they will know that I am the LORD."

[m]14 Most Hebrew manuscripts; a few Hebrew manuscripts *Riblah*
[n]5 Most Hebrew manuscripts; some Hebrew manuscripts and Syriac *Disaster after*   [o]11 Or *The violent one has become*

Discovering the Word   1. Ezekiel now turns from God's condemnation of Jerusalem to Israel as a whole, especially the mountains of Israel (6:2) where the pagan shrines ("high places") and idol worship were located. What sins brings God's judgment on his own people?   2. Trace the various dimensions of God's wrath in chapters 6 and 7 where Ezekiel claims the season of final reckoning is upon them. What patterns do you see? (For example, why is God's judgment of their use of wealth fitting [7:9, 19–22]?)   3. What judgment in 7:25–27 will be particularly distressing (see also Ps 74:9)?   4. In what way could the silence of God in responding to prayers and initiating revelation be a further way in which they could know that God is God (7:4)?   5. What word of comfort and hope does Ezekiel's message contain for the exiles living dispersed in a foreign land far away from Jerusalem (6:8–10)?

 Applying the Word 1. What sins addressed by Ezekiel are found also in our contemporary society and church? 2. First Peter 4:17 tells us that God's people will be the first to be judged. What does this mean to you as you think about your life?

Responding in Prayer Ask God to reveal in what ways you have been taken in by the pollution of God's people and the world around you. Pray for a true spirit of repentance that finds hope in God's mercy.

5 / *Ezekiel 8*
The Darkened Inner Eye

IN THE OPENING vision Ezekiel was overwhelmed by the glory of God (1:28). But now as he is taken in a vision not only inside beloved Jerusalem but inside the hearts of God's people in Jerusalem, Ezekiel is overwhelmed by the sin of God's people. The root sin that concerns Ezekiel is not moral failures but the perversion of the human imagination so that people are wooed away from single-minded love of God. This passage reveals the truth that as people imagine in their hearts, so they will be.

 Warming Up to God Consider the ways in which imagination is being used in our contemporary culture. What aspects would be troubling to God?

 Read Ezekiel 8.

8 In the sixth year, in the sixth month on the fifth day, while I was sitting in my house and the elders of Judah were sitting before me, the hand of the Sovereign LORD came upon me there. 2I looked, and I saw a figure like that of a man.*p* From what appeared to be his waist down he was like fire, and from there up his appearance was as bright as glowing metal. 3He stretched out what looked like a hand and took me by the hair of my head. The Spirit lifted me up between earth and heaven and in visions of God he took me to Jerusalem, to the entrance to the north gate of the inner court, where the idol that provokes to jealousy stood. 4And there before me was the glory of the God of Israel, as in the vision I had seen in the plain.

5Then he said to me, "Son of man, look toward the north." So I looked, and in the entrance north of the gate of the altar I saw this idol of jealousy.

6And he said to me, "Son of man, do you see what they are doing—the utterly detestable things the house of Israel is doing here, things that will drive me far from my sanctuary? But you will see things that are even more detestable."

7Then he brought me to the entrance to the court. I looked, and I saw a hole in the wall. 8He said to me, "Son of man, now dig into the wall." So I dug into the wall and saw a doorway there.

9And he said to me, "Go in and see the wicked and detestable things they are doing here." 10So I went in and looked, and I saw portrayed all over the walls all kinds of crawling things and detestable animals and all the idols of the house of Israel. 11In front of them stood seventy elders of the house of Israel, and Jaazaniah son of Shaphan was standing among them. Each had a censer in his hand, and a fragrant cloud of incense was rising.

12He said to me, "Son of man, have you seen what the elders of the house of Israel are doing in the darkness, each at the shrine of his own idol? They say, 'The LORD does not see us; the LORD has forsaken the land.'" 13Again, he said, "You will see them doing things that are even more detestable."

14Then he brought me to the entrance to the north gate of the house of the LORD, and I saw women sitting there, mourning for Tammuz. 15He said to me, "Do you see this, son of man? You will see things that are even more detestable than this."

p2 Or saw a fiery figure

16He then brought me into the inner court of the house of the Lord, and there at the entrance to the temple, between the portico and the altar, were about twenty-five men. With their backs toward the temple of the Lord and their faces toward the east, they were bowing down to the sun in the east.

17He said to me, "Have you seen this, son of man? Is it a trivial matter for the house of Judah to do the detestable things they are doing here? Must they also fill the land with violence and continually provoke me to anger? Look at them putting the branch to their nose! 18Therefore I will deal with them in anger; I will not look on them with pity or spare them. Although they shout in my ears, I will not listen to them."

Discovering the Word 1. Fourteen months after the opening vision of the glory of God Ezekiel is caught up in another prophetic trance. While the glory of God is still there (v. 4), what in contrast does Ezekiel now see (vv. 5–6, 10–16)? 2. The "idol that provokes to jealousy" (vv. 3, 5–6) is probably the wooden image of Asherah, the Canaanite goddess that Manasseh had put in the temple (2Ki 21:7), which seems to have been returned to the prestigious northern gate next to the royal palace. "All kinds of crawling things and detestable animals" (v. 10) were likely serpent deities that had been part of Egyptian, Canaanite and Babylonian religions. "Mourning for Tammuz" (v. 14) refers to a Sumerian god of vegetation who died and became the god of the underworld and is worshiped here in a mourning ritual. Why do you think spiritual pollution, which so offended Ezekiel, is as serious as social sins and breaches in social justice? 3. Verse 12 tells us even the leaders are worshiping idols. What is the connection between what is happening on the inside of the minds of the leaders and what is taking place in the corporate life of the nation? 4. Why is the vision of the twenty-five men (v. 16), later called elders (9:6), the ultimate detestable picture?

Applying the Word 1. The leaders explain their private imaginative life by the words "the Lord does not see us" (v. 12). How does this same explanation help you understand the downfall of significant Christian leaders today? 2. What perversions of the imagination are threats to healthy spirituality for you? 3. One remarkable fact in this vision is the presence of the glory of God in the midst of spiritual perversion (v. 4). In what way is this both an encouragement and a warning to you as you struggle to have a pure thought life?

Responding in Prayer Pray that your vision of the glory of God will purify your imagination so that every thought will be taken captive.

Ezekiel 9—10

9 Then I heard him call out in a loud voice, "Bring the guards of the city here, each with a weapon in his hand." 2And I saw six men coming from the direction of the upper gate, which faces north, each with a deadly weapon in his hand. With them was a man clothed in linen who had a writing kit at his side. They came in and stood beside the bronze altar.

3Now the glory of the God of Israel went up from above the cherubim, where it had been, and moved to the threshold of the temple. Then the Lord called to the man clothed in linen who had the writing kit at his side 4and said to him, "Go throughout the city of Jerusalem and put a mark on the foreheads of those who grieve and lament over all the detestable things that are done in it."

5As I listened, he said to the others, "Follow him through the city and kill, without showing pity or compassion. 6Slaughter old men, young

men and maidens, women and children, but do not touch anyone who has the mark. Begin at my sanctuary." So they began with the elders who were in front of the temple.

7Then he said to them, "Defile the temple and fill the courts with the slain. Go!" So they went out and began killing throughout the city. 8While they were killing and I was left alone, I fell facedown, crying out, "Ah, Sovereign Lord! Are you going to destroy the entire remnant of Israel in this outpouring of your wrath on Jerusalem?"

9He answered me, "The sin of the house of Israel and Judah is exceedingly great; the land is full of bloodshed and the city is full of injustice. They say, 'The Lord has forsaken the land; the Lord does not see.' 10So I will not look on them with pity or spare them, but I will bring down on their own heads what they have done."

11Then the man in linen with the writing kit at

his side brought back word, saying, "I have done as you commanded."

10

I looked, and I saw the likeness of a throne of sapphire[q] above the expanse that was over the heads of the cherubim. ²The LORD said to the man clothed in linen, "Go in among the wheels beneath the cherubim. Fill your hands with burning coals from among the cherubim and scatter them over the city." And as I watched, he went in.

³Now the cherubim were standing on the south side of the temple when the man went in, and a cloud filled the inner court. ⁴Then the glory of the LORD rose from above the cherubim and moved to the threshold of the temple. The cloud filled the temple, and the court was full of the radiance of the glory of the LORD. ⁵The sound of the wings of the cherubim could be heard as far away as the outer court, like the voice of God Almighty[r] when he speaks.

⁶When the LORD commanded the man in linen, "Take fire from among the wheels, from among the cherubim," the man went in and stood beside a wheel. ⁷Then one of the cherubim reached out his hand to the fire that was among them. He took up some of it and put it into the hands of the man in linen, who took it and went out. ⁸(Under the wings of the cherubim could be seen what looked like the hands of a man.)

⁹I looked, and I saw beside the cherubim four wheels, one beside each of the cherubim; the wheels sparkled like chrysolite. ¹⁰As for their appearance, the four of them looked alike; each was like a wheel intersecting a wheel. ¹¹As they moved, they would go in any one of the four directions the cherubim faced; the wheels did not turn about[s] as the cherubim went. The cherubim went in whatever direction the head faced, without turning as they went. ¹²Their entire bodies, including their backs, their hands and their wings, were completely full of eyes, as were their four wheels. ¹³I heard the wheels being called "the whirling wheels." ¹⁴Each of the cherubim had four faces: One face was that of a cherub, the second the face of a man, the third the face of a lion, and the fourth the face of an eagle.

¹⁵Then the cherubim rose upward. These were the living creatures I had seen by the Kebar River. ¹⁶When the cherubim moved, the wheels beside them moved; and when the cherubim spread their wings to rise from the ground, the wheels did not leave their side. ¹⁷When the cherubim stood still, they also stood still; and when the cherubim rose, they rose with them, because the spirit of the living creatures was in them.

¹⁸Then the glory of the LORD departed from over the threshold of the temple and stopped above the cherubim. ¹⁹While I watched, the cherubim spread their wings and rose from the ground, and as they went, the wheels went with them. They stopped at the entrance to the east gate of the LORD's house, and the glory of the God of Israel was above them.

²⁰These were the living creatures I had seen beneath the God of Israel by the Kebar River, and I realized that they were cherubim. ²¹Each had four faces and four wings, and under their wings was what looked like the hands of a man. ²²Their faces had the same appearance as those I had seen by the Kebar River. Each one went straight ahead.

q1 Or *lapis lazuli*   *r5* Hebrew *El-Shaddai*   *s11* Or *aside*

6 / *Ezekiel 11*
When Human Leaders Fail

BECOMING DISILLUSIONED WITH leaders, whether in the realm of politics or the media, is always a painful experience. But the keenest loss of respect is most often associated with religious leaders who, instead of leading people to put their trust in God, gain trust for themselves and then lead their followers astray. In Ezekiel's case his pain at seeing the deceitful heart of Jerusalem's leadership is more than matched by the Lord's word of encouragement. Chapter 11 brings to a conclusion the vision given to Ezekiel that started in chapter 8. The fulfillment of his word of judgment came in 2 Kings 25:18–21 and of his word of hope with the restored kingdom (Ezra/Nehemiah) and the coming of Christ.

Warming Up to God Recall an experience of seeing a Christian leader prove to be proud, self-confident or deceitful. What did it do to your relationship with God?

Read Ezekiel 11.

11 Then the Spirit lifted me up and brought me to the gate of the house of the Lord that faces east. There at the entrance to the gate were twenty-five men, and I saw among them Jaazaniah son of Azzur and Pelatiah son of Benaiah, leaders of the people. ²The Lord said to me, "Son of man, these are the men who are plotting evil and giving wicked advice in this city. ³They say, 'Will it not soon be time to build houses?' This city is a cooking pot, and we are the meat.' ⁴Therefore prophesy against them; prophesy, son of man."

⁵Then the Spirit of the Lord came upon me, and he told me to say: "This is what the Lord says: That is what you are saying, O house of Israel, but I know what is going through your mind. ⁶You have killed many people in this city and filled its streets with the dead.

⁷"Therefore this is what the Sovereign Lord says: The bodies you have thrown there are the meat and this city is the pot, but I will drive you out of it. ⁸You fear the sword, and the sword is what I will bring against you, declares the Sovereign Lord. ⁹I will drive you out of the city and hand you over to foreigners and inflict punishment on you. ¹⁰You will fall by the sword, and I will execute judgment on you at the borders of Israel. Then you will know that I am the Lord. ¹¹This city will not be a pot for you, nor will you be the meat in it; I will execute judgment on you at the borders of Israel. ¹²And you will know that I am the Lord, for you have not followed my decrees or kept my laws but have conformed to the standards of the nations around you."

¹³Now as I was prophesying, Pelatiah son of Benaiah died. Then I fell facedown and cried out in a loud voice, "Ah, Sovereign Lord! Will you completely destroy the remnant of Israel?"

¹⁴The word of the Lord came to me: ¹⁵"Son of man, your brothers—your brothers who are your blood relatives ᵘ and the whole house of Israel— are those of whom the people of Jerusalem have said, 'They are ᵛ far away from the Lord; this land was given to us as our possession.'

¹⁶"Therefore say: 'This is what the Sovereign Lord says: Although I sent them far away among the nations and scattered them among the countries, yet for a little while I have been a sanctuary for them in the countries where they have gone.'

¹⁷"Therefore say: 'This is what the Sovereign Lord says: I will gather you from the nations and bring you back from the countries where you have been scattered, and I will give you back the land of Israel again.'

¹⁸"They will return to it and remove all its vile images and detestable idols. ¹⁹I will give them an undivided heart and put a new spirit in them; I will remove from them their heart of stone and give them a heart of flesh. ²⁰Then they will follow my decrees and be careful to keep my laws. They will be my people, and I will be their God. ²¹But as for those whose hearts are devoted to their vile images and detestable idols, I will bring down on their own heads what they have done, declares the Sovereign Lord."

²²Then the cherubim, with the wheels beside them, spread their wings, and the glory of the God of Israel was above them. ²³The glory of the Lord went up from within the city and stopped above the mountain east of it. ²⁴The Spirit lifted me up and brought me to the exiles in Babylonia ʷ in the vision given by the Spirit of God.

Then the vision I had seen went up from me, ²⁵and I told the exiles everything the Lord had shown me.

³ Or This is not the time to build houses.   ᵘ15 Or are in exile with you (see Septuagint and Syriac)   ᵛ15 Or those to whom the people of Jerusalem have said, 'Stay   ʷ24 Or Chaldea

---

Discovering the Word 1. Ezekiel is given a vision of twenty-five leaders by the gate to the temple who were a political pressure group led by the nobility that was left in Jerusalem. In what specific ways were they leading the people astray (vv. 1–13)? 2. The leaders claimed that the people were as safe in Jerusalem as meat kept from the fire in a pot (vv. 3, 11). Why is this reckless course so dangerous (see also Jer 21:8–10)? 3. The death of one of the leaders, Pelatiah (v. 13), provoked a deep crisis for Ezekiel. What insight do we gain about Ezekiel's spirituality (see also 9:8)? 4. What hopeful message does the Lord have for the people scattered in Babylon (vv. 14–25)?   5. The people felt God-forsaken (because they were away from the temple) and spiritually helpless. In what way does Ezekiel now see things differently?

Applying the Word   1. What help do you gain from this chapter on how to relate to leaders?   2. In what ways does the comforting message to the exiles bring hope for times when you feel God–forsaken and spiritually helpless?

Responding in Prayer   Thank God that he is your sanctuary (v. 17), that his presence will go with you everywhere, and that your covenantal relationship with God (v. 20) through Christ is secure.

Ezekiel 12—15

12 The word of the LORD came to me: [2]"Son of man, you are living among a rebellious people. They have eyes to see but do not see and ears to hear but do not hear, for they are a rebellious people.

[3]"Therefore, son of man, pack your belongings for exile and in the daytime, as they watch, set out and go from where you are to another place. Perhaps they will understand, though they are a rebellious house. [4]During the daytime, while they watch, bring out your belongings packed for exile. Then in the evening, while they are watching, go out like those who go into exile. [5]While they watch, dig through the wall and take your belongings out through it. [6]Put them on your shoulder as they are watching and carry them out at dusk. Cover your face so that you cannot see the land, for I have made you a sign to the house of Israel."

[7]So I did as I was commanded. During the day I brought out my things packed for exile. Then in the evening I dug through the wall with my hands. I took my belongings out at dusk, carrying them on my shoulders while they watched.

[8]In the morning the word of the LORD came to me: [9]"Son of man, did not that rebellious house of Israel ask you, 'What are you doing?'

[10]"Say to them, 'This is what the Sovereign LORD says: This oracle concerns the prince in Jerusalem and the whole house of Israel who are there.' [11]Say to them, 'I am a sign to you.'

"As I have done, so it will be done to them. They will go into exile as captives.

[12]"The prince among them will put his things on his shoulder at dusk and leave, and a hole will be dug in the wall for him to go through. He will cover his face so that he cannot see the land. [13]I will spread my net for him, and he will be caught in my snare; I will bring him to Babylonia, the land of the Chaldeans, but he will not see it, and there he will die. [14]I will scatter to the winds all those around him—his staff and all his troops—and I will pursue them with drawn sword.

[15]"They will know that I am the LORD, when I disperse them among the nations and scatter them through the countries. [16]But I will spare a few of them from the sword, famine and plague, so that in the nations where they go they may acknowledge all their detestable practices. Then they will know that I am the LORD."

[17]The word of the LORD came to me: [18]"Son of man, tremble as you eat your food, and shudder in fear as you drink your water. [19]Say to the people of the land: 'This is what the Sovereign LORD says about those living in Jerusalem and in the land of Israel: They will eat their food in anxiety and drink their water in despair, for their land will be stripped of everything in it because of the violence of all who live there. [20]The inhabited towns will be laid waste and the land will be desolate. Then you will know that I am the LORD.' "

[21]The word of the LORD came to me: [22]"Son of man, what is this proverb you have in the land of Israel: 'The days go by and every vision comes to nothing'? [23]Say to them, 'This is what the Sovereign LORD says: I am going to put an end to this proverb, and they will no longer quote it in Israel.' Say to them, 'The days are near when every vision will be fulfilled. [24]For there will be no more false visions or flattering divinations among the people of Israel. [25]But I the LORD will speak what I will, and it shall be fulfilled without delay. For in your days, you rebellious house, I will fulfill whatever I say, declares the Sovereign LORD.' "

[26]The word of the LORD came to me: [27]"Son of man, the house of Israel is saying, 'The vision he sees is for many years from now, and he prophesies about the distant future.'

28"Therefore say to them, 'This is what the Sovereign LORD says: None of my words will be delayed any longer; whatever I say will be fulfilled, declares the Sovereign LORD.' "

13

The word of the LORD came to me: 2"Son of man, prophesy against the prophets of Israel who are now prophesying. Say to those who prophesy out of their own imagination: 'Hear the word of the LORD! 3This is what the Sovereign LORD says: Woe to the foolishˣ prophets who follow their own spirit and have seen nothing! 4Your prophets, O Israel, are like jackals among ruins. 5You have not gone up to the breaks in the wall to repair it for the house of Israel so that it will stand firm in the battle on the day of the LORD. 6Their visions are false and their divinations a lie. They say, "The LORD declares," when the LORD has not sent them; yet they expect their words to be fulfilled. 7Have you not seen false visions and uttered lying divinations when you say, "The LORD declares," though I have not spoken?

8" 'Therefore this is what the Sovereign LORD says: Because of your false words and lying visions, I am against you, declares the Sovereign LORD. 9My hand will be against the prophets who see false visions and utter lying divinations. They will not belong to the council of my people or be listed in the records of the house of Israel, nor will they enter the land of Israel. Then you will know that I am the Sovereign LORD.

10" 'Because they lead my people astray, saying, "Peace," when there is no peace, and because, when a flimsy wall is built, they cover it with whitewash, 11therefore tell those who cover it with whitewash that it is going to fall. Rain will come in torrents, and I will send hailstones hurtling down, and violent winds will burst forth. 12When the wall collapses, will people not ask you, "Where is the whitewash you covered it with?"

13" 'Therefore this is what the Sovereign LORD says: In my wrath I will unleash a violent wind, and in my anger hailstones and torrents of rain will fall with destructive fury. 14I will tear down the wall you have covered with whitewash and will level it to the ground so that its foundation will be laid bare. When itʸ falls, you will be destroyed in it; and you will know that I am the LORD. 15So I will spend my wrath against the wall and against those who covered it with whitewash. I will say to you, "The wall is gone and so are

those who whitewashed it, 16those prophets of Israel who prophesied to Jerusalem and saw visions of peace for her when there was no peace, declares the Sovereign LORD." '

17"Now, son of man, set your face against the daughters of your people who prophesy out of their own imagination. Prophesy against them 18and say, 'This is what the Sovereign LORD says: Woe to the women who sew magic charms on all their wrists and make veils of various lengths for their heads in order to ensnare people. Will you ensnare the lives of my people but preserve your own? 19You have profaned me among my people for a few handfuls of barley and scraps of bread. By lying to my people, who listen to lies, you have killed those who should not have died and have spared those who should not live.

20" 'Therefore this is what the Sovereign LORD says: I am against your magic charms with which you ensnare people like birds and I will tear them from your arms; I will set free the people that you ensnare like birds. 21I will tear off your veils and save my people from your hands, and they will no longer fall prey to your power. Then you will know that I am the LORD. 22Because you disheartened the righteous with your lies, when I had brought them no grief, and because you encouraged the wicked not to turn from their evil ways and so save their lives, 23therefore you will no longer see false visions or practice divination. I will save my people from your hands. And then you will know that I am the LORD.' "

14

Some of the elders of Israel came to me and sat down in front of me. 2Then the word of the LORD came to me: 3"Son of man, these men have set up idols in their hearts and put wicked stumbling blocks before their faces. Should I let them inquire of me at all? 4Therefore speak to them and tell them, 'This is what the Sovereign LORD says: When any Israelite sets up idols in his heart and puts a wicked stumbling block before his face and then goes to a prophet, I the LORD will answer him myself in keeping with his great idolatry. 5I will do this to recapture the hearts of the people of Israel, who have all deserted me for their idols.'

6"Therefore say to the house of Israel, 'This is what the Sovereign LORD says: Repent! Turn from your idols and renounce all your detestable practices!

ˣ3 Or wicked   ʸ14 Or the city

7" 'When any Israelite or any alien living in Israel separates himself from me and sets up idols in his heart and puts a wicked stumbling block before his face and then goes to a prophet to inquire of me, I the LORD will answer him myself. 8I will set my face against that man and make him an example and a byword. I will cut him off from my people. Then you will know that I am the LORD.

9" 'And if the prophet is enticed to utter a prophecy, I the LORD have enticed that prophet, and I will stretch out my hand against him and destroy him from among my people Israel. 10They will bear their guilt—the prophet will be as guilty as the one who consults him. 11Then the people of Israel will no longer stray from me, nor will they defile themselves anymore with all their sins. They will be my people, and I will be their God, declares the Sovereign LORD.' "

12The word of the LORD came to me: 13"Son of man, if a country sins against me by being unfaithful and I stretch out my hand against it to cut off its food supply and send famine upon it and kill its men and their animals, 14even if these three men—Noah, Daniel[z] and Job—were in it, they could save only themselves by their righteousness, declares the Sovereign LORD.

15"Or if I send wild beasts through that country and they leave it childless and it becomes desolate so that no one can pass through it because of the beasts, 16as surely as I live, declares the Sovereign LORD, even if these three men were in it, they could not save their own sons or daughters. They alone would be saved, but the land would be desolate.

17"Or if I bring a sword against that country and say, 'Let the sword pass throughout the land,' and I kill its men and their animals, 18as surely as I live, declares the Sovereign LORD, even if these three men were in it, they could not save their own sons or daughters. They alone would be saved.

19"Or if I send a plague into that land and pour out my wrath upon it through bloodshed, killing its men and their animals, 20as surely as I live, declares the Sovereign LORD, even if Noah, Daniel and Job were in it, they could save neither son nor daughter. They would save only themselves by their righteousness.

21"For this is what the Sovereign LORD says: How much worse will it be when I send against Jerusalem my four dreadful judgments—sword and famine and wild beasts and plague—to kill its men and their animals! 22Yet there will be some survivors—sons and daughters who will be brought out of it. They will come to you, and when you see their conduct and their actions, you will be consoled regarding the disaster I have brought upon Jerusalem—every disaster I have brought upon it. 23You will be consoled when you see their conduct and their actions, for you will know that I have done nothing in it without cause, declares the Sovereign LORD."

15 The word of the LORD came to me: 2"Son of man, how is the wood of a vine better than that of a branch on any of the trees in the forest? 3Is wood ever taken from it to make anything useful? Do they make pegs from it to hang things on? 4And after it is thrown on the fire as fuel and the fire burns both ends and chars the middle, is it then useful for anything? 5If it was not useful for anything when it was whole, how much less can it be made into something useful when the fire has burned it and it is charred?

6"Therefore this is what the Sovereign LORD says: As I have given the wood of the vine among the trees of the forest as fuel for the fire, so will I treat the people living in Jerusalem. 7I will set my face against them. Although they have come out of the fire, the fire will yet consume them. And when I set my face against them, you will know that I am the LORD. 8I will make the land desolate because they have been unfaithful, declares the Sovereign LORD."

z14 Or Danel; the Hebrew spelling may suggest a person other than the prophet Daniel; also in verse 20.

7 / *Ezekiel 16*
The Bride of God

JESUS CHOSE PARABLES to express the deepest truths of God, and once even used a parable about the death warrant on himself (Mt 21:33–41) as an appeal to his executioners to have faith. In a similar way Ezekiel uses allegory to express the fundamental problem of Israel's relationship with God. He intends that his readers will eventually come to the conclusion that "he is talking about us!" Unlike a parable, which normally makes a single point, an allegory is intended to have symbolic meaning through every detail. By using a rags-to-riches story of a homeless waif who becomes a much-loved bride, Ezekiel makes an artistic and eloquent appeal to the source of true spirituality: gratitude. And he shows through this story how the heinous sin of ingratitude would be unforgivable but for the unconditional covenant love of the God of Israel, the God and Father of Jesus Christ.

 Warming Up to God   What feelings do you have when you hear of the sexual unfaithfulness of people you know and love?

 Read Ezekiel 16.

16 The word of the LORD came to me: ²"Son of man, confront Jerusalem with her detestable practices ³and say, 'This is what the Sovereign LORD says to Jerusalem: Your ancestry and birth were in the land of the Canaanites; your father was an Amorite and your mother a Hittite. ⁴On the day you were born your cord was not cut, nor were you washed with water to make you clean, nor were you rubbed with salt or wrapped in cloths. ⁵No one looked on you with pity or had compassion enough to do any of these things for you. Rather, you were thrown out into the open field, for on the day you were born you were despised.

⁶" 'Then I passed by and saw you kicking about in your blood, and as you lay there in your blood I said to you, "Live!"ᵃ ⁷I made you grow like a plant of the field. You grew up and developed and became the most beautiful of jewels.ᵇ Your breasts were formed and your hair grew, you who were naked and bare.

⁸" 'Later I passed by, and when I looked at you and saw that you were old enough for love, I spread the corner of my garment over you and covered your nakedness. I gave you my solemn oath and entered into a covenant with you, declares the Sovereign LORD, and you became mine.

⁹" 'I bathedᶜ you with water and washed the blood from you and put ointments on you. ¹⁰I clothed you with an embroidered dress and put leather sandals on you. I dressed you in fine linen and covered you with costly garments. ¹¹I adorned you with jewelry: I put bracelets on your arms and a necklace around your neck, ¹²and I put a ring on your nose, earrings on your ears and

a beautiful crown on your head. ¹³So you were adorned with gold and silver; your clothes were of fine linen and costly fabric and embroidered cloth. Your food was fine flour, honey and olive oil. You became very beautiful and rose to be a queen. ¹⁴And your fame spread among the nations on account of your beauty, because the splendor I had given you made your beauty perfect, declares the Sovereign LORD.

¹⁵" 'But you trusted in your beauty and used your fame to become a prostitute. You lavished your favors on anyone who passed by and your beauty became his.ᵈ ¹⁶You took some of your garments to make gaudy high places, where you carried on your prostitution. Such things should not happen, nor should they ever occur. ¹⁷You also took the fine jewelry I gave you, the jewelry made of my gold and silver, and you made for yourself male idols and engaged in prostitution with them. ¹⁸And you took your embroidered clothes to put on them, and you offered my oil and incense before them. ¹⁹Also the food I provided for you—the fine flour, olive oil and honey I gave you to eat—you offered as fragrant incense before them. That is what happened, declares the Sovereign LORD.

²⁰" 'And you took your sons and daughters whom you bore to me and sacrificed them as food to the idols. Was your prostitution not enough? ²¹You slaughtered my children and sacrificed

---

ᵃ6 A few Hebrew manuscripts, Septuagint and Syriac; most Hebrew manuscripts *"Live!" And as you lay there in your blood I said to you, "Live!"*   ᵇ7 Or *became mature*   ᶜ9 Or *I had bathed*   ᵈ15 Most Hebrew manuscripts; one Hebrew manuscript (see some Septuagint manuscripts) *by. Such a thing should not happen* them[e] to the idols. 22In all your detestable practices and your prostitution you did not remember the days of your youth, when you were naked and bare, kicking about in your blood.

23" 'Woe! Woe to you, declares the Sovereign LORD. In addition to all your other wickedness, 24you built a mound for yourself and made a lofty shrine in every public square. 25At the head of every street you built your lofty shrines and degraded your beauty, offering your body with increasing promiscuity to anyone who passed by. 26You engaged in prostitution with the Egyptians, your lustful neighbors, and provoked me to anger with your increasing promiscuity. 27So I stretched out my hand against you and reduced your territory; I gave you over to the greed of your enemies, the daughters of the Philistines, who were shocked by your lewd conduct. 28You engaged in prostitution with the Assyrians too, because you were insatiable; and even after that, you still were not satisfied. 29Then you increased your promiscuity to include Babylonia,[f] a land of merchants, but even with this you were not satisfied.

30" 'How weak-willed you are, declares the Sovereign LORD, when you do all these things, acting like a brazen prostitute! 31When you built your mounds at the head of every street and made your lofty shrines in every public square, you were unlike a prostitute, because you scorned payment.

32" 'You adulterous wife! You prefer strangers to your own husband! 33Every prostitute receives a fee, but you give gifts to all your lovers, bribing them to come to you from everywhere for your illicit favors. 34So in your prostitution you are the opposite of others; no one runs after you for your favors. You are the very opposite, for you give payment and none is given to you.

35" 'Therefore, you prostitute, hear the word of the LORD! 36This is what the Sovereign LORD says: Because you poured out your wealth[g] and exposed your nakedness in your promiscuity with your lovers, and because of all your detestable idols, and because you gave them your children's blood, 37therefore I am going to gather all your lovers, with whom you found pleasure, those you loved as well as those you hated. I will gather them against you from all around and will strip you in front of them, and they will see all your nakedness. 38I will sentence you to the punishment of women who commit adultery and who shed blood; I will bring upon you the blood vengeance of my wrath and jealous anger. 39Then I

will hand you over to your lovers, and they will tear down your mounds and destroy your lofty shrines. They will strip you of your clothes and take your fine jewelry and leave you naked and bare. 40They will bring a mob against you, who will stone you and hack you to pieces with their swords. 41They will burn down your houses and inflict punishment on you in the sight of many women. I will put a stop to your prostitution, and you will no longer pay your lovers. 42Then my wrath against you will subside and my jealous anger will turn away from you; I will be calm and no longer angry.

43" 'Because you did not remember the days of your youth but enraged me with all these things, I will surely bring down on your head what you have done, declares the Sovereign LORD. Did you not add lewdness to all your other detestable practices?

44" 'Everyone who quotes proverbs will quote this proverb about you: "Like mother, like daughter." 45You are a true daughter of your mother, who despised her husband and her children; and you are a true sister of your sisters, who despised their husbands and their children. Your mother was a Hittite and your father an Amorite. 46Your older sister was Samaria, who lived to the north of you with her daughters; and your younger sister, who lived to the south of you with her daughters, was Sodom. 47You not only walked in their ways and copied their detestable practices, but in all your ways you soon became more depraved than they. 48As surely as I live, declares the Sovereign LORD, your sister Sodom and her daughters never did what you and your daughters have done.

49" 'Now this was the sin of your sister Sodom: She and her daughters were arrogant, overfed and unconcerned; they did not help the poor and needy. 50They were haughty and did detestable things before me. Therefore I did away with them as you have seen. 51Samaria did not commit half the sins you did. You have done more detestable things than they, and have made your sisters seem righteous by all these things you have done. 52Bear your disgrace, for you have furnished some justification for your sisters. Because your sins were more vile than theirs, they appear more righteous than you. So then, be ashamed and bear

e21 Or and made them pass through ⌊the fire⌋   f29 Or Chaldea
g36 Or lust

your disgrace, for you have made your sisters appear righteous.

53" 'However, I will restore the fortunes of Sodom and her daughters and of Samaria and her daughters, and your fortunes along with them, 54so that you may bear your disgrace and be ashamed of all you have done in giving them comfort. 55And your sisters, Sodom with her daughters and Samaria with her daughters, will return to what they were before; and you and your daughters will return to what you were before. 56You would not even mention your sister Sodom in the day of your pride, 57before your wickedness was uncovered. Even so, you are now scorned by the daughters of Edom*h* and all her neighbors and the daughters of the Philistines— all those around you who despise you. 58You will bear the consequences of your lewdness and your detestable practices, declares the LORD.

59" 'This is what the Sovereign LORD says: I will deal with you as you deserve, because you have despised my oath by breaking the covenant. 60Yet I will remember the covenant I made with you in the days of your youth, and I will establish an everlasting covenant with you. 61Then you will remember your ways and be ashamed when you receive your sisters, both those who are older than you and those who are younger. I will give them to you as daughters, but not on the basis of my covenant with you. 62So I will establish my covenant with you, and you will know that I am the LORD. 63Then, when I make atonement for you for all you have done, you will remember and be ashamed and never again open your mouth because of your humiliation, declares the Sovereign LORD.' "

*h*57 Many Hebrew manuscripts and Syriac; most Hebrew manuscripts, Septuagint and Vulgate *Aram*

Discovering the Word 1. The allegory is best studied in three parts. First, look at verses 1–43. The term *Canaanite* (v. 3) was a byword for "moral degradation," thus the proverb in verse 44. While Israel was born of pure Aramean stock, the nation had assimilated the culture of its surrounding neighbors. What historical events of the nation's history are recounted in this allegory? **2.** In the second part, verses 44–58, Ezekiel links a new allegory of two sisters to the old one. If the mother is seen as Jerusalem and the daughters its suburbs, what further point is Ezekiel now making? **3.** In the last section, verses 59–63, the allegory takes a surprising turn, signaled by the word *yet* (v. 60). What does covenant faithfulness require of God and his reluctant bride? **5.** While Hosea had been the first prophet to explain the relationship between the Lord and his people as a marriage covenant, Ezekiel develops this metaphor (v. 8) in his allegory. In what way does the covenant metaphor reveal that the sin of Israel is even more inexcusable than merely law-breaking? **6.** It appears that this triumphant covenant love presupposed the fall of Jerusalem, which for Ezekiel was inevitable. What hope should this allegory inspire as the exiles wondered about their own future?

Applying the Word 1. What does the covenant allegory inspire in you as you consider the future of Christianity? **2.** In what way can this chapter help you deal with a person who is truly converted but has fallen back into sin? **3.** What light does this allegory shed on the need for continuous gratitude?

   Responding in Prayer Take a few minutes and walk through your life in the Lord's presence. Reflect on God's faithfulness and thank God for his covenant love.

Ezekiel 17

17 The word of the LORD came to me: 2"Son of man, set forth an allegory and tell the house of Israel a parable. 3Say to them, 'This is what the Sovereign LORD says: A great eagle with powerful wings, long feathers and full plumage of varied colors came to Lebanon. Taking hold of the top of a cedar, 4he broke off its topmost shoot and carried it away to a land of merchants, where he planted it in a city of traders.

5" 'He took some of the seed of your land and put it in fertile soil. He planted it like a willow by abundant water, 6and it sprouted and became a low, spreading vine. Its branches turned toward him, but its roots remained under it. So it became a vine and produced branches and put out leafy boughs.

7" 'But there was another great eagle with powerful wings and full plumage. The vine now sent out its roots toward him from the plot where it was planted and stretched out its branches to him for water. ⁸It had been planted in good soil by abundant water so that it would produce branches, bear fruit and become a splendid vine.'

⁹"Say to them, 'This is what the Sovereign LORD says: Will it thrive? Will it not be uprooted and stripped of its fruit so that it withers? All its new growth will wither. It will not take a strong arm or many people to pull it up by the roots. ¹⁰Even if it is transplanted, will it thrive? Will it not wither completely when the east wind strikes it— wither away in the plot where it grew?' "

¹¹Then the word of the LORD came to me: ¹²"Say to this rebellious house, 'Do you not know what these things mean?' Say to them: 'The king of Babylon went to Jerusalem and carried off her king and her nobles, bringing them back with him to Babylon. ¹³Then he took a member of the royal family and made a treaty with him, putting him under oath. He also carried away the leading men of the land, ¹⁴so that the kingdom would be brought low, unable to rise again, surviving only by keeping his treaty. ¹⁵But the king rebelled against him by sending his envoys to Egypt to get horses and a large army. Will he succeed? Will he who does such things escape? Will he break the treaty and yet escape?

¹⁶" 'As surely as I live, declares the Sovereign LORD, he shall die in Babylon, in the land of the king who put him on the throne, whose oath he despised and whose treaty he broke. ¹⁷Pharaoh with his mighty army and great horde will be of no help to him in war, when ramps are built and siege works erected to destroy many lives. ¹⁸He despised the oath by breaking the covenant. Because he had given his hand in pledge and yet did all these things, he shall not escape.

¹⁹" 'Therefore this is what the Sovereign LORD says: As surely as I live, I will bring down on his head my oath that he despised and my covenant that he broke. ²⁰I will spread my net for him, and he will be caught in my snare. I will bring him to Babylon and execute judgment upon him there because he was unfaithful to me. ²¹All his fleeing troops will fall by the sword, and the survivors will be scattered to the winds. Then you will know that I the LORD have spoken.

²²" 'This is what the Sovereign LORD says: I myself will take a shoot from the very top of a cedar and plant it; I will break off a tender sprig from its topmost shoots and plant it on a high and lofty mountain. ²³On the mountain heights of Israel I will plant it; it will produce branches and bear fruit and become a splendid cedar. Birds of every kind will nest in it; they will find shelter in the shade of its branches. ²⁴All the trees of the field will know that I the LORD bring down the tall tree and make the low tree grow tall. I dry up the green tree and make the dry tree flourish.

" 'I the LORD have spoken, and I will do it.' "

8 / *Ezekiel 18*
Assuming Personal Responsibility

"THE DEVIL MADE me do it" is one extreme statement of passing responsibility to someone else. Sometimes we try to excuse ourselves by the company we keep, as Adam did long ago (Ge 3:12). Up until now the prophet has been explaining how national sin will lead to national punishment. But what about God's dealings with individuals? Do good people suffer with the bad for sins they never condoned? In this chapter Ezekiel focuses on individual responsibility.

 Warming Up to God Recall an incident when you got blamed for something done by others. What was especially difficult to accept?

 Read Ezekiel 18.

18

The word of the LORD came to me: ²"What do you people mean by quoting this proverb about the land of Israel:

" 'The fathers eat sour grapes,
    and the children's teeth are set on edge'?

³"As surely as I live, declares the Sovereign LORD, you will no longer quote this proverb in Israel. ⁴For every living soul belongs to me, the father as well as the son—both alike belong to me. The soul who sins is the one who will die.

⁵"Suppose there is a righteous man
    who does what is just and right.
⁶He does not eat at the mountain shrines
    or look to the idols of the house of Israel.
He does not defile his neighbor's wife
    or lie with a woman during her period.
⁷He does not oppress anyone,
    but returns what he took in pledge for a
        loan.
He does not commit robbery
    but gives his food to the hungry
    and provides clothing for the naked.
⁸He does not lend at usury
    or take excessive interest.ⁱ
He withholds his hand from doing wrong
    and judges fairly between man and man.
⁹He follows my decrees
    and faithfully keeps my laws.
That man is righteous;
    he will surely live,
                declares the Sovereign LORD.

¹⁰"Suppose he has a violent son, who sheds blood or does any of these other thingsʲ ¹¹(though the father has done none of them):

"He eats at the mountain shrines.
He defiles his neighbor's wife.
¹²He oppresses the poor and needy.
He commits robbery.
He does not return what he took in pledge.
He looks to the idols.
He does detestable things.
¹³He lends at usury and takes excessive interest.

Will such a man live? He will not! Because he has done all these detestable things, he will surely be put to death and his blood will be on his own head.

¹⁴"But suppose this son has a son who sees all the sins his father commits, and though he sees them, he does not do such things:

¹⁵"He does not eat at the mountain shrines
    or look to the idols of the house of Israel.
He does not defile his neighbor's wife.
¹⁶He does not oppress anyone
    or require a pledge for a loan.
He does not commit robbery
    but gives his food to the hungry
    and provides clothing for the naked.
¹⁷He withholds his hand from sinᵏ
    and takes no usury or excessive interest.
He keeps my laws and follows my decrees.

He will not die for his father's sin; he will surely live. ¹⁸But his father will die for his own sin, because he practiced extortion, robbed his brother and did what was wrong among his people.

¹⁹"Yet you ask, 'Why does the son not share the guilt of his father?' Since the son has done what is just and right and has been careful to keep all my decrees, he will surely live. ²⁰The soul who sins is the one who will die. The son will not share the guilt of the father, nor will the father share the guilt of the son. The righteousness of the righteous man will be credited to him, and the wickedness of the wicked will be charged against him.

²¹"But if a wicked man turns away from all the sins he has committed and keeps all my decrees and does what is just and right, he will surely live; he will not die. ²²None of the offenses he has committed will be remembered against him. Because of the righteous things he has done, he will live. ²³Do I take any pleasure in the death of the wicked? declares the Sovereign LORD. Rather, am I not pleased when they turn from their ways and live?

²⁴"But if a righteous man turns from his righteousness and commits sin and does the same detestable things the wicked man does, will he live? None of the righteous things he has done will be remembered. Because of the unfaithfulness he is guilty of and because of the sins he has committed, he will die.

²⁵"Yet you say, 'The way of the Lord is not just.' Hear, O house of Israel: Is my way unjust? Is it not your ways that are unjust? ²⁶If a righteous man turns from his righteousness and commits sin, he will die for it; because of the sin he has

---

ⁱ8 Or *take interest*; similarly in verses 13 and 17   ʲ10 Or *things to a brother*   ᵏ17 Septuagint (see also verse 8); Hebrew *from the poor* committed he will die. ²⁷But if a wicked man turns away from the wickedness he has committed and does what is just and right, he will save his life. ²⁸Because he considers all the offenses he has committed and turns away from them, he will surely live; he will not die. ²⁹Yet the house of Israel says, 'The way of the Lord is not just.' Are my ways unjust, O house of Israel? Is it not your ways that are unjust?

³⁰"Therefore, O house of Israel, I will judge you, each one according to his ways, declares the Sovereign LORD. Repent! Turn away from all your offenses; then sin will not be your downfall. ³¹Rid yourselves of all the offenses you have committed, and get a new heart and a new spirit. Why will you die, O house of Israel? ³²For I take no pleasure in the death of anyone, declares the Sovereign LORD. Repent and live!

Discovering the Word 1. In this chapter Ezekiel compares the fates of unrighteous sons with righteous fathers (vv. 5–13), and righteous sons with unrighteous fathers (vv. 14–18). What are the outward marks of righteousness and unrighteousness? 2. How does Ezekiel answer the question "Why does the son not share in the guilt of his father" (vv. 19–20)? 3. In this chapter Ezekiel gives several fundamental principles about the way God relates to people (vv. 4, 20, 22, 24, 26, 30). Put these in your own words. 4. What hope is there for the righteous and the unrighteous? 5. What is revealed about the heart of God in his treatment of individuals (v. 23)? 6. What makes repentance a desirable alternative (vv. 30–32)?

Applying the Word 1. What answer do you now have for the common complaint "God is not fair"? 2. In what way does this chapter give you confidence to face God daily and finally on the day of judgment?

Responding in Prayer Pray that you may have God's perspective when you speak to others about the judgment of God, namely that God prefers people to turn and have life, not wanting anyone to perish (2Pe 3:9).

Ezekiel 19:1—24:14

19 "Take up a lament concerning the princes of Israel ²and say:

" 'What a lioness was your mother
    among the lions!
She lay down among the young lions
    and reared her cubs.
³She brought up one of her cubs,
    and he became a strong lion.
He learned to tear the prey
    and he devoured men.
⁴The nations heard about him,
    and he was trapped in their pit.
They led him with hooks
    to the land of Egypt.

⁵" 'When she saw her hope unfulfilled,
    her expectation gone,
she took another of her cubs
    and made him a strong lion.
⁶He prowled among the lions,
    for he was now a strong lion.
He learned to tear the prey
    and he devoured men.
⁷He broke down¹ their strongholds

and devastated their towns.
The land and all who were in it
    were terrified by his roaring.
⁸Then the nations came against him,
    those from regions round about.
They spread their net for him,
    and he was trapped in their pit.
⁹With hooks they pulled him into a cage
    and brought him to the king of Babylon.
They put him in prison,
    so his roar was heard no longer
    on the mountains of Israel.

¹⁰" 'Your mother was like a vine in your
        vineyard ᵐ
    planted by the water;
it was fruitful and full of branches
    because of abundant water.
¹¹Its branches were strong,
    fit for a ruler's scepter.
It towered high
    above the thick foliage,
conspicuous for its height

¹7 Targum (see Septuagint); Hebrew *He knew*   ᵐ10 Two Hebrew manuscripts; most Hebrew manuscripts *your blood*

and for its many branches.
12But it was uprooted in fury
and thrown to the ground.
The east wind made it shrivel,
it was stripped of its fruit;
its strong branches withered
and fire consumed them.
13Now it is planted in the desert,
in a dry and thirsty land.
14Fire spread from one of its main[n] branches
and consumed its fruit.
No strong branch is left on it
fit for a ruler's scepter.'

This is a lament and is to be used as a lament."

20

In the seventh year, in the fifth month on the tenth day, some of the elders of Israel came to inquire of the LORD, and they sat down in front of me.

2Then the word of the LORD came to me: 3"Son of man, speak to the elders of Israel and say to them, 'This is what the Sovereign LORD says: Have you come to inquire of me? As surely as I live, I will not let you inquire of me, declares the Sovereign LORD.'

4"Will you judge them? Will you judge them, son of man? Then confront them with the detestable practices of their fathers 5and say to them: 'This is what the Sovereign LORD says: On the day I chose Israel, I swore with uplifted hand to the descendants of the house of Jacob and revealed myself to them in Egypt. With uplifted hand I said to them, "I am the LORD your God." 6On that day I swore to them that I would bring them out of Egypt into a land I had searched out for them, a land flowing with milk and honey, the most beautiful of all lands. 7And I said to them, "Each of you, get rid of the vile images you have set your eyes on, and do not defile yourselves with the idols of Egypt. I am the LORD your God."

8" 'But they rebelled against me and would not listen to me; they did not get rid of the vile images they had set their eyes on, nor did they forsake the idols of Egypt. So I said I would pour out my wrath on them and spend my anger against them in Egypt. 9But for the sake of my name I did what would keep it from being profaned in the eyes of the nations they lived among and in whose sight I had revealed myself to the Israelites by bringing them out of Egypt. 10Therefore I led them out of Egypt and brought them into the desert. 11I gave them my decrees and made known to them my laws, for the man who obeys them will live by them. 12Also I gave them my Sabbaths as a sign between us, so they would know that I the LORD made them holy.

13" 'Yet the people of Israel rebelled against me in the desert. They did not follow my decrees but rejected my laws—although the man who obeys them will live by them—and they utterly desecrated my Sabbaths. So I said I would pour out my wrath on them and destroy them in the desert. 14But for the sake of my name I did what would keep it from being profaned in the eyes of the nations in whose sight I had brought them out. 15Also with uplifted hand I swore to them in the desert that I would not bring them into the land I had given them—a land flowing with milk and honey, most beautiful of all lands— 16because they rejected my laws and did not follow my decrees and desecrated my Sabbaths. For their hearts were devoted to their idols. 17Yet I looked on them with pity and did not destroy them or put an end to them in the desert. 18I said to their children in the desert, "Do not follow the statutes of your fathers or keep their laws or defile yourselves with their idols. 19I am the LORD your God; follow my decrees and be careful to keep my laws. 20Keep my Sabbaths holy, that they may be a sign between us. Then you will know that I am the LORD your God."

21" 'But the children rebelled against me: They did not follow my decrees, they were not careful to keep my laws—although the man who obeys them will live by them—and they desecrated my Sabbaths. So I said I would pour out my wrath on them and spend my anger against them in the desert. 22But I withheld my hand, and for the sake of my name I did what would keep it from being profaned in the eyes of the nations in whose sight I had brought them out. 23Also with uplifted hand I swore to them in the desert that I would disperse them among the nations and scatter them through the countries, 24because they had not obeyed my laws but had rejected my decrees and desecrated my Sabbaths, and their eyes ⌊lusted⌋ after their fathers' idols. 25I also gave them over to statutes that were not good and laws they could not live by; 26I let them become defiled through their gifts—the sacrifice of every firstborn[o]— that I might fill them with horror so they would know that I am the LORD.'

[n]14 Or from under its ⌊the fire⌋ [o]26 Or —making every firstborn pass through the fire

27"Therefore, son of man, speak to the people of Israel and say to them, 'This is what the Sovereign Lord says: In this also your fathers blasphemed me by forsaking me: 28When I brought them into the land I had sworn to give them and they saw any high hill or any leafy tree, there they offered their sacrifices, made offerings that provoked me to anger, presented their fragrant incense and poured out their drink offerings. 29Then I said to them: What is this high place you go to?' " (It is called Bamahᴾ to this day.)

30"Therefore say to the house of Israel: 'This is what the Sovereign Lord says: Will you defile yourselves the way your fathers did and lust after their vile images? 31When you offer your gifts—the sacrifice of your sons in�q the fire—you continue to defile yourselves with all your idols to this day. Am I to let you inquire of me, O house of Israel? As surely as I live, declares the Sovereign Lord, I will not let you inquire of me.

32" 'You say, "We want to be like the nations, like the peoples of the world, who serve wood and stone." But what you have in mind will never happen. 33As surely as I live, declares the Sovereign Lord, I will rule over you with a mighty hand and an outstretched arm and with outpoured wrath. 34I will bring you from the nations and gather you from the countries where you have been scattered—with a mighty hand and an outstretched arm and with outpoured wrath. 35I will bring you into the desert of the nations and there, face to face, I will execute judgment upon you. 36As I judged your fathers in the desert of the land of Egypt, so I will judge you, declares the Sovereign Lord. 37I will take note of you as you pass under my rod, and I will bring you into the bond of the covenant. 38I will purge you of those who revolt and rebel against me. Although I will bring them out of the land where they are living, yet they will not enter the land of Israel. Then you will know that I am the Lord.

39" 'As for you, O house of Israel, this is what the Sovereign Lord says: Go and serve your idols, every one of you! But afterward you will surely listen to me and no longer profane my holy name with your gifts and idols. 40For on my holy mountain, the high mountain of Israel, declares the Sovereign Lord, there in the land the entire house of Israel will serve me, and there I will accept them. There I will require your offerings and your choice gifts,ʳ along with all your holy sacrifices. 41I will accept you as fragrant incense when I bring you out from the nations and gather you from the countries where you have been scattered, and I will show myself holy among you in the sight of the nations. 42Then you will know that I am the Lord, when I bring you into the land of Israel, the land I had sworn with uplifted hand to give to your fathers. 43There you will remember your conduct and all the actions by which you have defiled yourselves, and you will loathe yourselves for all the evil you have done. 44You will know that I am the Lord, when I deal with you for my name's sake and not according to your evil ways and your corrupt practices, O house of Israel, declares the Sovereign Lord.' "

45The word of the Lord came to me: 46"Son of man, set your face toward the south; preach against the south and prophesy against the forest of the southland. 47Say to the southern forest: 'Hear the word of the Lord. This is what the Sovereign Lord says: I am about to set fire to you, and it will consume all your trees, both green and dry. The blazing flame will not be quenched, and every face from south to north will be scorched by it. 48Everyone will see that I the Lord have kindled it; it will not be quenched.' "

49Then I said, "Ah, Sovereign Lord! They are saying of me, 'Isn't he just telling parables?' "

21 The word of the Lord came to me: 2"Son of man, set your face against Jerusalem and preach against the sanctuary. Prophesy against the land of Israel 3and say to her: 'This is what the Lord says: I am against you. I will draw my sword from its scabbard and cut off from you both the righteous and the wicked. 4Because I am going to cut off the righteous and the wicked, my sword will be unsheathed against everyone from south to north. 5Then all people will know that I the Lord have drawn my sword from its scabbard; it will not return again.'

6"Therefore groan, son of man! Groan before them with broken heart and bitter grief. 7And when they ask you, 'Why are you groaning?' you shall say, 'Because of the news that is coming. Every heart will melt and every hand go limp; every spirit will become faint and every knee become as weak as water.' It is coming! It will surely take place, declares the Sovereign Lord."

8The word of the Lord came to me: 9"Son of

ᴾ29 Bamah means high place.　　�q31 Or —making your sons pass through　　ʳ40 Or and the gifts of your firstfruits man, prophesy and say, 'This is what the Lord says:

" 'A sword, a sword,
　　sharpened and polished—
10sharpened for the slaughter,
　　polished to flash like lightning!

" 'Shall we rejoice in the scepter of my son ⌐Judah⌐? The sword despises every such stick.

11" 'The sword is appointed to be polished,
　　to be grasped with the hand;
　it is sharpened and polished,
　　made ready for the hand of the slayer.
12Cry out and wail, son of man,
　　for it is against my people;
　　it is against all the princes of Israel.
They are thrown to the sword
　　along with my people.
Therefore beat your breast.

13" 'Testing will surely come. And what if the scepter ⌐of Judah⌐, which the sword despises, does not continue? declares the Sovereign Lord.'

14"So then, son of man, prophesy
　　and strike your hands together.
Let the sword strike twice,
　　even three times.
It is a sword for slaughter—
　　a sword for great slaughter,
　　closing in on them from every side.
15So that hearts may melt
　　and the fallen be many,
I have stationed the sword for slaughters
　　at all their gates.
Oh! It is made to flash like lightning,
　　it is grasped for slaughter.
16O sword, slash to the right,
　　then to the left,
　　wherever your blade is turned.
17I too will strike my hands together,
　　and my wrath will subside.
I the Lord have spoken."

18The word of the Lord came to me: 19"Son of man, mark out two roads for the sword of the king of Babylon to take, both starting from the same country. Make a signpost where the road branches off to the city. 20Mark out one road for the sword to come against Rabbah of the Ammonites and another against Judah and fortified Jerusalem. 21For the king of Babylon will stop at the fork in the road, at the junction of the two roads,

to seek an omen: He will cast lots with arrows, he will consult his idols, he will examine the liver. 22Into his right hand will come the lot for Jerusalem, where he is to set up battering rams, to give the command to slaughter, to sound the battle cry, to set battering rams against the gates, to build a ramp and to erect siege works. 23It will seem like a false omen to those who have sworn allegiance to him, but he will remind them of their guilt and take them captive.

24"Therefore this is what the Sovereign Lord says: 'Because you people have brought to mind your guilt by your open rebellion, revealing your sins in all that you do—because you have done this, you will be taken captive.

25" 'O profane and wicked prince of Israel, whose day has come, whose time of punishment has reached its climax, 26this is what the Sovereign Lord says: Take off the turban, remove the crown. It will not be as it was: The lowly will be exalted and the exalted will be brought low. 27A ruin! A ruin! I will make it a ruin! It will not be restored until he comes to whom it rightfully belongs; to him I will give it.'

28"And you, son of man, prophesy and say, 'This is what the Sovereign Lord says about the Ammonites and their insults:

" 'A sword, a sword,
　　drawn for the slaughter,
　polished to consume
　　and to flash like lightning!
29Despite false visions concerning you
　　and lying divinations about you,
　it will be laid on the necks
　　of the wicked who are to be slain,
whose day has come,
　　whose time of punishment has reached its
　　　climax.
30Return the sword to its scabbard.
　　In the place where you were created,
　in the land of your ancestry,
　　I will judge you.
31I will pour out my wrath upon you
　　and breathe out my fiery anger against you;
　I will hand you over to brutal men,
　　men skilled in destruction.
32You will be fuel for the fire,
　　your blood will be shed in your land,
　you will be remembered no more;
　　for I the Lord have spoken.' "

s15 Septuagint; the meaning of the Hebrew for this word is uncertain.

22

The word of the LORD came to me: [2]"Son of man, will you judge her? Will you judge this city of bloodshed? Then confront her with all her detestable practices [3]and say: 'This is what the Sovereign LORD says: O city that brings on herself doom by shedding blood in her midst and defiles herself by making idols, [4]you have become guilty because of the blood you have shed and have become defiled by the idols you have made. You have brought your days to a close, and the end of your years has come. Therefore I will make you an object of scorn to the nations and a laughingstock to all the countries. [5]Those who are near and those who are far away will mock you, O infamous city, full of turmoil.

[6]" 'See how each of the princes of Israel who are in you uses his power to shed blood. [7]In you they have treated father and mother with contempt; in you they have oppressed the alien and mistreated the fatherless and the widow. [8]You have despised my holy things and desecrated my Sabbaths. [9]In you are slanderous men bent on shedding blood; in you are those who eat at the mountain shrines and commit lewd acts. [10]In you are those who dishonor their fathers' bed; in you are those who violate women during their period, when they are ceremonially unclean. [11]In you one man commits a detestable offense with his neighbor's wife, another shamefully defiles his daughter-in-law, and another violates his sister, his own father's daughter. [12]In you men accept bribes to shed blood; you take usury and excessive interest[t] and make unjust gain from your neighbors by extortion. And you have forgotten me, declares the Sovereign LORD.

[13]" 'I will surely strike my hands together at the unjust gain you have made and at the blood you have shed in your midst. [14]Will your courage endure or your hands be strong in the day I deal with you? I the LORD have spoken, and I will do it. [15]I will disperse you among the nations and scatter you through the countries; and I will put an end to your uncleanness. [16]When you have been defiled[u] in the eyes of the nations, you will know that I am the LORD.' "

[17]Then the word of the LORD came to me: [18]"Son of man, the house of Israel has become dross to me; all of them are the copper, tin, iron and lead left inside a furnace. They are but the dross of silver. [19]Therefore this is what the Sovereign LORD says: 'Because you have all become dross, I will gather you into Jerusalem. [20]As men gather silver, copper, iron, lead and tin into a furnace to melt it with a fiery blast, so will I gather you in my anger and my wrath and put you inside the city and melt you. [21]I will gather you and I will blow on you with my fiery wrath, and you will be melted inside her. [22]As silver is melted in a furnace, so you will be melted inside her, and you will know that I the LORD have poured out my wrath upon you.' "

[23]Again the word of the LORD came to me: [24]"Son of man, say to the land, 'You are a land that has had no rain or showers[v] in the day of wrath.' [25]There is a conspiracy of her princes[w] within her like a roaring lion tearing its prey; they devour people, take treasures and precious things and make many widows within her. [26]Her priests do violence to my law and profane my holy things; they do not distinguish between the holy and the common; they teach that there is no difference between the unclean and the clean; and they shut their eyes to the keeping of my Sabbaths, so that I am profaned among them. [27]Her officials within her are like wolves tearing their prey; they shed blood and kill people to make unjust gain. [28]Her prophets whitewash these deeds for them by false visions and lying divinations. They say, 'This is what the Sovereign LORD says'—when the LORD has not spoken. [29]The people of the land practice extortion and commit robbery; they oppress the poor and needy and mistreat the alien, denying them justice.

[30]"I looked for a man among them who would build up the wall and stand before me in the gap on behalf of the land so I would not have to destroy it, but I found none. [31]So I will pour out my wrath on them and consume them with my fiery anger, bringing down on their own heads all they have done, declares the Sovereign LORD."

23

The word of the LORD came to me: [2]"Son of man, there were two women, daughters of the same mother. [3]They became prostitutes in Egypt, engaging in prostitution from their youth. In that land their breasts were fondled and their virgin bosoms caressed. [4]The older was named Oholah, and her sister was Oholibah. They were mine and gave birth to sons and daughters. Oholah is Samaria, and Oholibah is Jerusalem.

---

[t]12 Or *usury and interest*   [u]16 Or *When I have allotted you your inheritance*   [v]24 Septuagint; Hebrew *has not been cleansed or rained on*   [w]25 Septuagint; Hebrew *prophets*

5"Oholah engaged in prostitution while she was still mine; and she lusted after her lovers, the Assyrians—warriors 6clothed in blue, governors and commanders, all of them handsome young men, and mounted horsemen. 7She gave herself as a prostitute to all the elite of the Assyrians and defiled herself with all the idols of everyone she lusted after. 8She did not give up the prostitution she began in Egypt, when during her youth men slept with her, caressed her virgin bosom and poured out their lust upon her.

9"Therefore I handed her over to her lovers, the Assyrians, for whom she lusted. 10They stripped her naked, took away her sons and daughters and killed her with the sword. She became a byword among women, and punishment was inflicted on her.

11"Her sister Oholibah saw this, yet in her lust and prostitution she was more depraved than her sister. 12She too lusted after the Assyrians—governors and commanders, warriors in full dress, mounted horsemen, all handsome young men. 13I saw that she too defiled herself; both of them went the same way.

14"But she carried her prostitution still further. She saw men portrayed on a wall, figures of Chaldeansˣ portrayed in red, 15with belts around their waists and flowing turbans on their heads; all of them looked like Babylonian chariot officers, natives of Chaldea.ʸ 16As soon as she saw them, she lusted after them and sent messengers to them in Chaldea. 17Then the Babylonians came to her, to the bed of love, and in their lust they defiled her. After she had been defiled by them, she turned away from them in disgust. 18When she carried on her prostitution openly and exposed her nakedness, I turned away from her in disgust, just as I had turned away from her sister. 19Yet she became more and more promiscuous as she recalled the days of her youth, when she was a prostitute in Egypt. 20There she lusted after her lovers, whose genitals were like those of donkeys and whose emission was like that of horses. 21So you longed for the lewdness of your youth, when in Egypt your bosom was caressed and your young breasts fondled.ᶻ

22"Therefore, Oholibah, this is what the Sovereign Lord says: I will stir up your lovers against you, those you turned away from in disgust, and I will bring them against you from every side— 23the Babylonians and all the Chaldeans, the men of Pekod and Shoa and Koa, and all the Assyrians

with them, handsome young men, all of them governors and commanders, chariot officers and men of high rank, all mounted on horses. 24They will come against you with weapons,ᵃ chariots and wagons and with a throng of people; they will take up positions against you on every side with large and small shields and with helmets. I will turn you over to them for punishment, and they will punish you according to their standards. 25I will direct my jealous anger against you, and they will deal with you in fury. They will cut off your noses and your ears, and those of you who are left will fall by the sword. They will take away your sons and daughters, and those of you who are left will be consumed by fire. 26They will also strip you of your clothes and take your fine jewelry. 27So I will put a stop to the lewdness and prostitution you began in Egypt. You will not look on these things with longing or remember Egypt anymore.

28"For this is what the Sovereign Lord says: I am about to hand you over to those you hate, to those you turned away from in disgust. 29They will deal with you in hatred and take away everything you have worked for. They will leave you naked and bare, and the shame of your prostitution will be exposed. Your lewdness and promiscuity 30have brought this upon you, because you lusted after the nations and defiled yourself with their idols. 31You have gone the way of your sister; so I will put her cup into your hand.

32"This is what the Sovereign Lord says:

"You will drink your sister's cup,
    a cup large and deep;
it will bring scorn and derision,
    for it holds so much.
33You will be filled with drunkenness and
        sorrow,
    the cup of ruin and desolation,
    the cup of your sister Samaria.
34You will drink it and drain it dry;
    you will dash it to pieces
    and tear your breasts.

I have spoken, declares the Sovereign Lord.

35"Therefore this is what the Sovereign Lord says: Since you have forgotten me and thrust me behind your back, you must bear the consequences of your lewdness and prostitution."

ˣ14 Or Babylonians   ʸ15 Or Babylonia; also in verse 16
ᶻ21 Syriac (see also verse 3); Hebrew caressed because of your young breasts   ᵃ24 The meaning of the Hebrew for this word is uncertain.

36The Lord said to me: "Son of man, will you judge Oholah and Oholibah? Then confront them with their detestable practices, 37for they have committed adultery and blood is on their hands. They committed adultery with their idols; they even sacrificed their children, whom they bore to me,b as food for them. 38They have also done this to me: At that same time they defiled my sanctuary and desecrated my Sabbaths. 39On the very day they sacrificed their children to their idols, they entered my sanctuary and desecrated it. That is what they did in my house.

40"They even sent messengers for men who came from far away, and when they arrived you bathed yourself for them, painted your eyes and put on your jewelry. 41You sat on an elegant couch, with a table spread before it on which you had placed the incense and oil that belonged to me.

42"The noise of a carefree crowd was around her; Sabeansc were brought from the desert along with men from the rabble, and they put bracelets on the arms of the woman and her sister and beautiful crowns on their heads. 43Then I said about the one worn out by adultery, 'Now let them use her as a prostitute, for that is all she is.' 44And they slept with her. As men sleep with a prostitute, so they slept with those lewd women, Oholah and Oholibah. 45But righteous men will sentence them to the punishment of women who commit adultery and shed blood, because they are adulterous and blood is on their hands.

46"This is what the Sovereign Lord says: Bring a mob against them and give them over to terror and plunder. 47The mob will stone them and cut them down with their swords; they will kill their sons and daughters and burn down their houses.

48"So I will put an end to lewdness in the land, that all women may take warning and not imitate you. 49You will suffer the penalty for your lewdness and bear the consequences of your sins of idolatry. Then you will know that I am the Sovereign Lord."

24

In the ninth year, in the tenth month on the tenth day, the word of the Lord came to me: 2"Son of man, record this date, this very date, because the king of Babylon has laid siege to Jerusalem this very day. 3Tell this rebellious house a parable and say to them: 'This is what the Sovereign Lord says:

" 'Put on the cooking pot; put it on
    and pour water into it.
4Put into it the pieces of meat,
    all the choice pieces—the leg and the
        shoulder.
Fill it with the best of these bones;
5   take the pick of the flock.
Pile wood beneath it for the bones;
    bring it to a boil
    and cook the bones in it.

6" 'For this is what the Sovereign Lord says:

" 'Woe to the city of bloodshed,
    to the pot now encrusted,
    whose deposit will not go away!
Empty it piece by piece
    without casting lots for them.

7" 'For the blood she shed is in her midst:
    She poured it on the bare rock;
she did not pour it on the ground,
    where the dust would cover it.
8To stir up wrath and take revenge
    I put her blood on the bare rock,
    so that it would not be covered.

9" 'Therefore this is what the Sovereign Lord says:

" 'Woe to the city of bloodshed!
    I, too, will pile the wood high.
10So heap on the wood
    and kindle the fire.
Cook the meat well,
    mixing in the spices;
    and let the bones be charred.
11Then set the empty pot on the coals
    till it becomes hot and its copper glows
so its impurities may be melted
    and its deposit burned away.
12It has frustrated all efforts;
    its heavy deposit has not been removed,
    not even by fire.

13" 'Now your impurity is lewdness. Because I tried to cleanse you but you would not be cleansed from your impurity, you will not be clean again until my wrath against you has subsided.

14" 'I the Lord have spoken. The time has come

---

b37 Or even made the children they bore to me pass through ⌜the fire⌟
c42 Or drunkards

for me to act. I will not hold back; I will not have pity, nor will I relent. You will be judged according to your conduct and your actions, declares the Sovereign Lord.' "

9 / *Ezekiel 24:15–27*
Losing One's Beloved

"UNTIL DEATH DO us part" are some of the hardest words to utter in the marriage vows. The words stick in our throats not only because of the enduring length of the covenant implied, but also because they remind us that death will rob us of our beloved. In this chapter we see Ezekiel in a new light, not bringing God's searing (but hopeful) judgment on the people, but mourning the loss of his own wife. Ezekiel's marriage was to be a parable for the people. They too must lose their beloved temple in Jerusalem. The chapter opens with the date of the inauguration of the final siege of Jerusalem (January 15, 588 B.C.). It ends with the people being instructed how to mourn the loss of the epicenter of their faith. As always, the purpose is that "they will know that I am the Lord" (v. 27).

 Warming Up to God Reflect on the vow "until death us do part." What inner pain or loss does it bring to mind?

 Read Ezekiel 24:15–27.

¹⁵The word of the Lord came to me: ¹⁶"Son of man, with one blow I am about to take away from you the delight of your eyes. Yet do not lament or weep or shed any tears. ¹⁷Groan quietly; do not mourn for the dead. Keep your turban fastened and your sandals on your feet; do not cover the lower part of your face or eat the customary food ⌊of mourners⌋."

¹⁸So I spoke to the people in the morning, and in the evening my wife died. The next morning I did as I had been commanded.

¹⁹Then the people asked me, "Won't you tell us what these things have to do with us?"

²⁰So I said to them, "The word of the Lord came to me: ²¹Say to the house of Israel, 'This is what the Sovereign Lord says: I am about to desecrate my sanctuary—the stronghold in which you take pride, the delight of your eyes, the object of your affection. The sons and daughters you left behind will fall by the sword. ²²And you will do

as I have done. You will not cover the lower part of your face or eat the customary food ⌊of mourners⌋. ²³You will keep your turbans on your heads and your sandals on your feet. You will not mourn or weep but will waste away because of[d] your sins and groan among yourselves. ²⁴Ezekiel will be a sign to you; you will do just as he has done. When this happens, you will know that I am the Sovereign Lord.'

²⁵"And you, son of man, on the day I take away their stronghold, their joy and glory, the delight of their eyes, their heart's desire, and their sons and daughters as well— ²⁶on that day a fugitive will come to tell you the news. ²⁷At that time your mouth will be opened; you will speak with him and will no longer be silent. So you will be a sign to them, and they will know that I am the Lord."

[d]23 Or *away in*

Discovering the Word 1. What words does the Lord use to describe Ezekiel's affection for his wife (v. 16) and the people's affection for the temple sanctuary in Jerusalem (vv. 21, 25)? 2. What actions is Ezekiel told to forego in verses 16–17? 3. These were the normal practices of public mourning. What do Ezekiel's words to the people tell you about why God asked him to do this (vv. 20–27)? 4. This would have been very hard for Ezekiel. How did his painful experience become a ministry to the people? 5. The refusal to weep was for both Ezekiel and the Israelites a reflection of a tragedy so deep that any expression of grief would be too inadequate. What does God want to accomplish in all this?

Applying the Word 1. Paul advises the Corinthians that "because of the present crisis" and the short-ness of time "those who have wives should live as if they had none; those who mourn, as if they did not" (1Co 7:26, 29–30). In what way does Ezekiel give us a model of putting God first while still loving his family? 2. Why is it spiritually dangerous to live for others, even a family member? 3. How can you better strike a balance between family and spiritual responsibility?

Responding in Prayer Pray that in both life and death, in plenty and loss, you may glorify God and seek first his kingdom.

Ezekiel 25—26

25 The word of the LORD came to me: 2"Son of man, set your face against the Ammonites and prophesy against them. 3Say to them, 'Hear the word of the Sovereign LORD. This is what the Sovereign LORD says: Because you said "Aha!" over my sanctuary when it was desecrated and over the land of Israel when it was laid waste and over the people of Judah when they went into exile, 4therefore I am going to give you to the people of the East as a possession. They will set up their camps and pitch their tents among you; they will eat your fruit and drink your milk. 5I will turn Rabbah into a pasture for camels and Ammon into a resting place for sheep. Then you will know that I am the LORD. 6For this is what the Sovereign LORD says: Because you have clapped your hands and stamped your feet, rejoicing with all the malice of your heart against the land of Israel, 7therefore I will stretch out my hand against you and give you as plunder to the nations. I will cut you off from the nations and exterminate you from the countries. I will destroy you, and you will know that I am the LORD.' "

8"This is what the Sovereign LORD says: 'Because Moab and Seir said, "Look, the house of Judah has become like all the other nations," 9therefore I will expose the flank of Moab, beginning at its frontier towns—Beth Jeshimoth, Baal Meon and Kiriathaim—the glory of that land. 10I will give Moab along with the Ammonites to the people of the East as a possession, so that the Ammonites will not be remembered among the nations; 11and I will inflict punishment on Moab. Then they will know that I am the LORD.' "

12"This is what the Sovereign LORD says: 'Because Edom took revenge on the house of Judah and became very guilty by doing so, 13therefore this is what the Sovereign LORD says: I will stretch out my hand against Edom and kill its men and their animals. I will lay it waste, and from Teman to Dedan they will fall by the sword. 14I will take vengeance on Edom by the hand of my people Israel, and they will deal with Edom in accordance with my anger and my wrath; they will know my vengeance, declares the Sovereign LORD.' "

15"This is what the Sovereign LORD says: 'Because the Philistines acted in vengeance and took revenge with malice in their hearts, and with ancient hostility sought to destroy Judah, 16therefore this is what the Sovereign LORD says: I am about to stretch out my hand against the Philistines, and I will cut off the Kerethites and destroy those remaining along the coast. 17I will carry out great vengeance on them and punish them in my wrath. Then they will know that I am the LORD, when I take vengeance on them.' "

26 In the eleventh year, on the first day of the month, the word of the LORD came to me: 2"Son of man, because Tyre has said of Jerusalem, 'Aha! The gate to the nations is broken, and its doors have swung open to me; now that she lies in ruins I will prosper,' 3therefore this is what the Sovereign LORD says: I am against you, O Tyre, and I will bring many nations against you, like the sea casting up its waves. 4They will destroy the walls of Tyre and pull down her towers; I will scrape away her rubble and make her a bare rock. 5Out in the sea she will become a place to spread fishnets, for I have spoken, declares the Sovereign LORD. She will become plunder for the nations, 6and her settlements on the mainland will be ravaged by the sword. Then they will know that I am the LORD.

7"For this is what the Sovereign LORD says: From the north I am going to bring against Tyre Nebuchadnezzar*e* king of Babylon, king of kings,

e 7 Hebrew *Nebuchadrezzar*, of which *Nebuchadnezzar* is a variant; here and often in Ezekiel and Jeremiah with horses and chariots, with horsemen and a great army. [8]He will ravage your settlements on the mainland with the sword; he will set up siege works against you, build a ramp up to your walls and raise his shields against you. [9]He will direct the blows of his battering rams against your walls and demolish your towers with his weapons. [10]His horses will be so many that they will cover you with dust. Your walls will tremble at the noise of the war horses, wagons and chariots when he enters your gates as men enter a city whose walls have been broken through. [11]The hoofs of his horses will trample all your streets; he will kill your people with the sword, and your strong pillars will fall to the ground. [12]They will plunder your wealth and loot your merchandise; they will break down your walls and demolish your fine houses and throw your stones, timber and rubble into the sea. [13]I will put an end to your noisy songs, and the music of your harps will be heard no more. [14]I will make you a bare rock, and you will become a place to spread fishnets. You will never be rebuilt, for I the Lord have spoken, declares the Sovereign Lord.

[15]"This is what the Sovereign Lord says to Tyre: Will not the coastlands tremble at the sound of your fall, when the wounded groan and the slaughter takes place in you? [16]Then all the princes of the coast will step down from their thrones and lay aside their robes and take off their embroidered garments. Clothed with terror, they will sit on the ground, trembling every moment, appalled at you. [17]Then they will take up a lament concerning you and say to you:

" 'How you are destroyed, O city of renown,
　　peopled by men of the sea!
You were a power on the seas,
　　you and your citizens;
you put your terror
　　on all who lived there.
[18]Now the coastlands tremble
　　on the day of your fall;
the islands in the sea
　　are terrified at your collapse.'

[19]"This is what the Sovereign Lord says: When I make you a desolate city, like cities no longer inhabited, and when I bring the ocean depths over you and its vast waters cover you, [20]then I will bring you down with those who go down to the pit, to the people of long ago. I will make you dwell in the earth below, as in ancient ruins, with those who go down to the pit, and you will not return or take your place[f] in the land of the living. [21]I will bring you to a horrible end and you will be no more. You will be sought, but you will never again be found, declares the Sovereign Lord."

[f]20 Septuagint; Hebrew *return, and I will give glory*

10 / *Ezekiel 27—28*
National Pride—National Downfall

TYPICALLY CHRISTIANS ASSUME that God is interested only in individuals and the church. The newspaper and the Bible seem to be worlds apart. But the prophecies of Ezekiel show that in all things, even in national histories, God will reveal his holy nature. God's judgment of Jerusalem is part of his divine sovereignty over all nations and follows the same pattern. There exists not only personal sin, but national sin, not only personal grace, but national grace. The case we will study is Tyre, but Ezekiel's survey in chapters 25—32 includes all his other neighbors.

 Warming Up to God　Why do you think it is so hard to discern God's divine purpose in the affairs of nations when you read the newspaper?

 Read Ezekiel 27—28.

27

The word of the LORD came to me: [2]"Son of man, take up a lament concerning Tyre. [3]Say to Tyre, situated at the gateway to the sea, merchant of peoples on many coasts, 'This is what the Sovereign LORD says:

" 'You say, O Tyre,
  "I am perfect in beauty."
[4]Your domain was on the high seas;
  your builders brought your beauty to
    perfection.
[5]They made all your timbers
  of pine trees from Senir[g];
they took a cedar from Lebanon
  to make a mast for you.
[6]Of oaks from Bashan
  they made your oars;
of cypress wood[h] from the coasts of
    Cyprus[i]
  they made your deck, inlaid with ivory.
[7]Fine embroidered linen from Egypt was your
    sail
  and served as your banner;
your awnings were of blue and purple
  from the coasts of Elishah.
[8]Men of Sidon and Arvad were your oarsmen;
  your skilled men, O Tyre, were aboard as
    your seamen.
[9]Veteran craftsmen of Gebal[j] were on board
  as shipwrights to caulk your seams.
All the ships of the sea and their sailors
  came alongside to trade for your wares.

[10]" 'Men of Persia, Lydia and Put
  served as soldiers in your army.
They hung their shields and helmets on your
    walls,
  bringing you splendor.
[11]Men of Arvad and Helech
  manned your walls on every side;
men of Gammad
  were in your towers.
They hung their shields around your walls;
  they brought your beauty to perfection.

[12]" 'Tarshish did business with you because of
your great wealth of goods; they exchanged silver,
iron, tin and lead for your merchandise.

[13]" 'Greece, Tubal and Meshech traded with
you; they exchanged slaves and articles of bronze
for your wares.

[14]" 'Men of Beth Togarmah exchanged work

horses, war horses and mules for your merchandise.

[15]" 'The men of Rhodes[k] traded with you, and
many coastlands were your customers; they paid
you with ivory tusks and ebony.

[16]" 'Aram[l] did business with you because of
your many products; they exchanged turquoise,
purple fabric, embroidered work, fine linen, coral
and rubies for your merchandise.

[17]" 'Judah and Israel traded with you; they exchanged wheat from Minnith and confections,[m]
honey, oil and balm for your wares.

[18]" 'Damascus, because of your many products
and great wealth of goods, did business with you
in wine from Helbon and wool from Zahar.

[19]" 'Danites and Greeks from Uzal bought your
merchandise; they exchanged wrought iron, cassia and calamus for your wares.

[20]" 'Dedan traded in saddle blankets with you.

[21]" 'Arabia and all the princes of Kedar were
your customers; they did business with you in
lambs, rams and goats.

[22]" 'The merchants of Sheba and Raamah
traded with you; for your merchandise they exchanged the finest of all kinds of spices and precious stones, and gold.

[23]" 'Haran, Canneh and Eden and merchants of
Sheba, Asshur and Kilmad traded with you. [24]In
your marketplace they traded with you beautiful
garments, blue fabric, embroidered work and
multicolored rugs with cords twisted and tightly
knotted.

[25]" 'The ships of Tarshish serve
  as carriers for your wares.
You are filled with heavy cargo
  in the heart of the sea.
[26]Your oarsmen take you
  out to the high seas.
But the east wind will break you to pieces
  in the heart of the sea.
[27]Your wealth, merchandise and wares,
  your mariners, seamen and shipwrights,
your merchants and all your soldiers,
  and everyone else on board
will sink into the heart of the sea
  on the day of your shipwreck.
[28]The shorelands will quake

[g]5 That is, Hermon   [h]6 Targum; the Masoretic Text has a different
division of the consonants.   [i]6 Hebrew *Kittim*   [j]9 That is, Byblos
[k]15 Septuagint; Hebrew *Dedan*   [l]16 Most Hebrew manuscripts; some
Hebrew manuscripts and Syriac *Edom*   [m]17 The meaning of the
Hebrew for this word is uncertain.

when your seamen cry out.
²⁹All who handle the oars
　　will abandon their ships;
the mariners and all the seamen
　　will stand on the shore.
³⁰They will raise their voice
　　and cry bitterly over you;
they will sprinkle dust on their heads
　　and roll in ashes.
³¹They will shave their heads because of you
　　and will put on sackcloth.
They will weep over you with anguish of soul
　　and with bitter mourning.
³²As they wail and mourn over you,
　　they will take up a lament concerning you:
"Who was ever silenced like Tyre,
　　surrounded by the sea?"
³³When your merchandise went out on the
　　　　seas,
　　you satisfied many nations;
with your great wealth and your wares
　　you enriched the kings of the earth.
³⁴Now you are shattered by the sea
　　in the depths of the waters;
your wares and all your company
　　have gone down with you.
³⁵All who live in the coastlands
　　are appalled at you;
their kings shudder with horror
　　and their faces are distorted with fear.
³⁶The merchants among the nations hiss at you;
　　you have come to a horrible end
　　and will be no more.' "

28

The word of the LORD came to me:
²"Son of man, say to the ruler of
Tyre, 'This is what the Sovereign
LORD says:

" 'In the pride of your heart
　　you say, "I am a god;
I sit on the throne of a god
　　in the heart of the seas."
But you are a man and not a god,
　　though you think you are as wise as a god.
³Are you wiser than Daniel[n]?
　　Is no secret hidden from you?
⁴By your wisdom and understanding
　　you have gained wealth for yourself
and amassed gold and silver
　　in your treasuries.
⁵By your great skill in trading
　　you have increased your wealth,

and because of your wealth
　　your heart has grown proud.

⁶" 'Therefore this is what the Sovereign LORD
says:

" 'Because you think you are wise,
　　as wise as a god,
⁷I am going to bring foreigners against you,
　　the most ruthless of nations;
they will draw their swords against your
　　　　beauty and wisdom
　　and pierce your shining splendor.
⁸They will bring you down to the pit,
　　and you will die a violent death
　　in the heart of the seas.
⁹Will you then say, "I am a god,"
　　in the presence of those who kill you?
You will be but a man, not a god,
　　in the hands of those who slay you.
¹⁰You will die the death of the uncircumcised
　　at the hands of foreigners.

I have spoken, declares the Sovereign LORD.' "

¹¹The word of the LORD came to me: ¹²"Son of
man, take up a lament concerning the king of
Tyre and say to him: 'This is what the Sovereign
LORD says:

" 'You were the model of perfection,
　　full of wisdom and perfect in beauty.
¹³You were in Eden,
　　the garden of God;
every precious stone adorned you:
　　ruby, topaz and emerald,
　　chrysolite, onyx and jasper,
　　sapphire,[o] turquoise and beryl.[p]
Your settings and mountings[q] were made of
　　　　gold;
on the day you were created they were
　　　　prepared.
¹⁴You were anointed as a guardian cherub,
　　for so I ordained you.
You were on the holy mount of God;
　　you walked among the fiery stones.
¹⁵You were blameless in your ways
　　from the day you were created
　　till wickedness was found in you.
¹⁶Through your widespread trade
　　you were filled with violence,

---

n3 Or Danel; the Hebrew spelling may suggest a person other than the
prophet Daniel.　o13 Or lapis lazuli　p13 The precise
identification of some of these precious stones is uncertain.　q13 The
meaning of the Hebrew for this phrase is uncertain.

and you sinned.
So I drove you in disgrace from the mount of
    God,
    and I expelled you, O guardian cherub,
    from among the fiery stones.
¹⁷Your heart became proud
    on account of your beauty,
and you corrupted your wisdom
    because of your splendor.
So I threw you to the earth;
    I made a spectacle of you before kings.
¹⁸By your many sins and dishonest trade
    you have desecrated your sanctuaries.
So I made a fire come out from you,
    and it consumed you,
and I reduced you to ashes on the ground
    in the sight of all who were watching.
¹⁹All the nations who knew you
    are appalled at you;
you have come to a horrible end
    and will be no more.' "

²⁰The word of the LORD came to me: ²¹"Son
of man, set your face against Sidon; prophesy
against her ²²and say: 'This is what the Sovereign
LORD says:

" 'I am against you, O Sidon,
    and I will gain glory within you.
They will know that I am the LORD,
    when I inflict punishment on her
    and show myself holy within her.
²³I will send a plague upon her
    and make blood flow in her streets.
The slain will fall within her,
    with the sword against her on every side.
Then they will know that I am the LORD.

²⁴" 'No longer will the people of Israel have malicious neighbors who are painful briers and
sharp thorns. Then they will know that I am the
Sovereign LORD.

²⁵" 'This is what the Sovereign LORD says: When
I gather the people of Israel from the nations
where they have been scattered, I will show myself holy among them in the sight of the nations.
Then they will live in their own land, which I
gave to my servant Jacob. ²⁶They will live there in
safety and will build houses and plant vineyards;
they will live in safety when I inflict punishment
on all their neighbors who maligned them. Then
they will know that I am the LORD their God.' "

Discovering the Word 1. King Nebuchadnezzar's next move after laying siege to Jerusalem was to lay
siege to Tyre. The exiles in Babylon would be concerned to know whether this strong and affluent nation
would receive the same moral treatment as God's people. What do the people of Tyre think of themselves (27:3),
and what do others think of Tyre (27:4, 33)? 2. How do Tyre's trading partners respond to the demise of this
"invincible" nation (27:28–36)? 3. What is Tyre's consuming sin (28:1–10)? 4. God calls the prophet to take up
a lament over Tyre (28:12–19). What does this suggest about God's attitude toward this arrogant nation? 5. What
is God's method and purpose in executing judgment on Tyre (28:24–26)?

Applying the Word 1. The apostle Paul says that God has made the nations of the earth and determined
"the times set for them and the exact places where they should live. God did this so that men should seek
him and perhaps reach out for him" (Ac 17:26–27). Ezekiel's fellow exiles were invited to seek God through the
national and international events of his day. What national and international events of our day similarly invite us to
seek the Lord? 2. When is national pride a good thing, and when does it become idolatrous?

Responding in Prayer Pray, as Paul instructed, with requests, intercession and thanksgiving for kings
and those in authority, "that we may live peaceful and quiet lives in all godliness and holiness." Do so
knowing that this is both good and pleasing to God (1Ti 2:1–3).

Ezekiel 29—32

29 In the tenth year, in the tenth month on the twelfth day, the word of the LORD came to me: [2]"Son of man, set your face against Pharaoh king of Egypt and prophesy against him and against all Egypt. [3]Speak to him and say: 'This is what the Sovereign LORD says:

" 'I am against you, Pharaoh king of Egypt,
  you great monster lying among your
       streams.
You say, "The Nile is mine;
  I made it for myself."
[4]But I will put hooks in your jaws
  and make the fish of your streams stick to
       your scales.
I will pull you out from among your streams,
  with all the fish sticking to your scales.
[5]I will leave you in the desert,
  you and all the fish of your streams.
You will fall on the open field
  and not be gathered or picked up.
I will give you as food
  to the beasts of the earth and the birds of
       the air.

[6]Then all who live in Egypt will know that I am the LORD.

" 'You have been a staff of reed for the house of Israel. [7]When they grasped you with their hands, you splintered and you tore open their shoulders; when they leaned on you, you broke and their backs were wrenched.[r]

[8]" 'Therefore this is what the Sovereign LORD says: I will bring a sword against you and kill your men and their animals. [9]Egypt will become a desolate wasteland. Then they will know that I am the LORD.

" 'Because you said, "The Nile is mine; I made it," [10]therefore I am against you and against your streams, and I will make the land of Egypt a ruin and a desolate waste from Migdol to Aswan, as far as the border of Cush.[s] [11]No foot of man or animal will pass through it; no one will live there for forty years. [12]I will make the land of Egypt desolate among devastated lands, and her cities will lie desolate forty years among ruined cities. And I will disperse the Egyptians among the nations and scatter them through the countries.

[13]" 'Yet this is what the Sovereign LORD says: At the end of forty years I will gather the Egyptians from the nations where they were scattered. [14]I will bring them back from captivity and return them to Upper Egypt,[t] the land of their ancestry. There they will be a lowly kingdom. [15]It will be the lowliest of kingdoms and will never again exalt itself above the other nations. I will make it so weak that it will never again rule over the nations. [16]Egypt will no longer be a source of confidence for the people of Israel but will be a reminder of their sin in turning to her for help. Then they will know that I am the Sovereign LORD.' "

[17]In the twenty-seventh year, in the first month on the first day, the word of the LORD came to me: [18]"Son of man, Nebuchadnezzar king of Babylon drove his army in a hard campaign against Tyre; every head was rubbed bare and every shoulder made raw. Yet he and his army got no reward from the campaign he led against Tyre. [19]Therefore this is what the Sovereign LORD says: I am going to give Egypt to Nebuchadnezzar king of Babylon, and he will carry off its wealth. He will loot and plunder the land as pay for his army. [20]I have given him Egypt as a reward for his efforts because he and his army did it for me, declares the Sovereign LORD.

[21]"On that day I will make a horn[u] grow for the house of Israel, and I will open your mouth among them. Then they will know that I am the LORD."

30 The word of the LORD came to me: [2]"Son of man, prophesy and say: 'This is what the Sovereign LORD says:

" 'Wail and say,
  "Alas for that day!"
[3]For the day is near,
  the day of the LORD is near—
a day of clouds,
  a time of doom for the nations.
[4]A sword will come against Egypt,
  and anguish will come upon Cush.[v]

---

[r]7 Syriac (see also Septuagint and Vulgate); Hebrew *and you caused their backs to stand*   [s]10 That is, the upper Nile region   [t]14 Hebrew *to Pathros*   [u]21 *Horn* here symbolizes strength.   [v]4 That is, the upper Nile region; also in verses 5 and 9

When the slain fall in Egypt,
   her wealth will be carried away
   and her foundations torn down.

⁵Cush and Put, Lydia and all Arabia, Libyaʷ and the people of the covenant land will fall by the sword along with Egypt.

⁶" 'This is what the LORD says:

" 'The allies of Egypt will fall
   and her proud strength will fail.
From Migdol to Aswan
   they will fall by the sword within her,
         declares the Sovereign LORD.
⁷" 'They will be desolate
   among desolate lands,
and their cities will lie
   among ruined cities.
⁸Then they will know that I am the LORD,
   when I set fire to Egypt
   and all her helpers are crushed.

⁹" 'On that day messengers will go out from me in ships to frighten Cush out of her complacency. Anguish will take hold of them on the day of Egypt's doom, for it is sure to come.

¹⁰" 'This is what the Sovereign LORD says:

" 'I will put an end to the hordes of Egypt
   by the hand of Nebuchadnezzar king of
      Babylon.
¹¹He and his army—the most ruthless of
      nations—
   will be brought in to destroy the land.
They will draw their swords against Egypt
   and fill the land with the slain.
¹²I will dry up the streams of the Nile
   and sell the land to evil men;
by the hand of foreigners
   I will lay waste the land and everything in
      it.

I the LORD have spoken.

¹³" 'This is what the Sovereign LORD says:

" 'I will destroy the idols
   and put an end to the images in
      Memphis.ˣ
No longer will there be a prince in Egypt,
   and I will spread fear throughout the land.
¹⁴I will lay waste Upper Egypt,ʸ
   set fire to Zoan
   and inflict punishment on Thebes.ᶻ
¹⁵I will pour out my wrath on Pelusium,ᵃ

the stronghold of Egypt,
   and cut off the hordes of Thebes.
¹⁶I will set fire to Egypt;
   Pelusium will writhe in agony.
Thebes will be taken by storm;
   Memphis will be in constant distress.
¹⁷The young men of Heliopolisᵇ and Bubastisᶜ
   will fall by the sword,
   and the cities themselves will go into
      captivity.
¹⁸Dark will be the day at Tahpanhes
   when I break the yoke of Egypt;
   there her proud strength will come to an
      end.
She will be covered with clouds,
   and her villages will go into captivity.
¹⁹So I will inflict punishment on Egypt,
   and they will know that I am the LORD.' "

²⁰In the eleventh year, in the first month on the seventh day, the word of the LORD came to me: ²¹"Son of man, I have broken the arm of Pharaoh king of Egypt. It has not been bound up for healing or put in a splint so as to become strong enough to hold a sword. ²²Therefore this is what the Sovereign LORD says: I am against Pharaoh king of Egypt. I will break both his arms, the good arm as well as the broken one, and make the sword fall from his hand. ²³I will disperse the Egyptians among the nations and scatter them through the countries. ²⁴I will strengthen the arms of the king of Babylon and put my sword in his hand, but I will break the arms of Pharaoh, and he will groan before him like a mortally wounded man. ²⁵I will strengthen the arms of the king of Babylon, but the arms of Pharaoh will fall limp. Then they will know that I am the LORD, when I put my sword into the hand of the king of Babylon and he brandishes it against Egypt. ²⁶I will disperse the Egyptians among the nations and scatter them through the countries. Then they will know that I am the LORD."

31 In the eleventh year, in the third month on the first day, the word of the LORD came to me: ²"Son of man, say to Pharaoh king of Egypt and to his hordes:

" 'Who can be compared with you in majesty?
³Consider Assyria, once a cedar in Lebanon,

ʷ5 Hebrew *Cub*   ˣ13 Hebrew *Noph*; also in verse 16
ʸ14 Hebrew *waste Pathros*   ᶻ14 Hebrew *No*; also in verses 15 and 16   ᵃ15 Hebrew *Sin*; also in verse 16   ᵇ17 Hebrew *Awen* (or *On*)
ᶜ17 Hebrew *Pi Beseth*

with beautiful branches overshadowing the
forest;
it towered on high,
    its top above the thick foliage.
4The waters nourished it,
    deep springs made it grow tall;
their streams flowed
    all around its base
and sent their channels
    to all the trees of the field.
5So it towered higher
    than all the trees of the field;
its boughs increased
    and its branches grew long,
    spreading because of abundant waters.
6All the birds of the air
    nested in its boughs,
all the beasts of the field
    gave birth under its branches;
all the great nations
    lived in its shade.
7It was majestic in beauty,
    with its spreading boughs,
for its roots went down
    to abundant waters.
8The cedars in the garden of God
    could not rival it,
    nor could the pine trees
    equal its boughs,
nor could the plane trees
    compare with its branches—
no tree in the garden of God
    could match its beauty.
9I made it beautiful
    with abundant branches,
    the envy of all the trees of Eden
    in the garden of God.

10" 'Therefore this is what the Sovereign Lord
says: Because it towered on high, lifting its top
above the thick foliage, and because it was proud
of its height, 11I handed it over to the ruler of the
nations, for him to deal with according to its
wickedness. I cast it aside, 12and the most ruthless of foreign nations cut it down and left it. Its
boughs fell on the mountains and in all the valleys; its branches lay broken in all the ravines of
the land. All the nations of the earth came out
from under its shade and left it. 13All the birds of
the air settled on the fallen tree, and all the beasts
of the field were among its branches. 14Therefore
no other trees by the waters are ever to tower

proudly on high, lifting their tops above the thick
foliage. No other trees so well-watered are ever
to reach such a height; they are all destined for
death, for the earth below, among mortal men,
with those who go down to the pit.

15" 'This is what the Sovereign Lord says: On
the day it was brought down to the grave[d] I covered the deep springs with mourning for it; I held
back its streams, and its abundant waters were
restrained. Because of it I clothed Lebanon with
gloom, and all the trees of the field withered
away. 16I made the nations tremble at the sound
of its fall when I brought it down to the grave
with those who go down to the pit. Then all the
trees of Eden, the choicest and best of Lebanon,
all the trees that were well-watered, were consoled in the earth below. 17Those who lived in its
shade, its allies among the nations, had also gone
down to the grave with it, joining those killed by
the sword.

18" 'Which of the trees of Eden can be compared with you in splendor and majesty? Yet you,
too, will be brought down with the trees of Eden
to the earth below; you will lie among the uncircumcised, with those killed by the sword.

" 'This is Pharaoh and all his hordes, declares
the Sovereign Lord.' "

32

In the twelfth year, in the twelfth
month on the first day, the word of
the Lord came to me: 2"Son of man,
take up a lament concerning Pharaoh king of
Egypt and say to him:

" 'You are like a lion among the nations;
    you are like a monster in the seas
thrashing about in your streams,
    churning the water with your feet
    and muddying the streams.

3" 'This is what the Sovereign Lord says:

" 'With a great throng of people
    I will cast my net over you,
    and they will haul you up in my net.
4I will throw you on the land
    and hurl you on the open field.
I will let all the birds of the air settle on you
    and all the beasts of the earth gorge
       themselves on you.
5I will spread your flesh on the mountains
    and fill the valleys with your remains.

d15 Hebrew Sheol; also in verses 16 and 17

⁶I will drench the land with your flowing
    blood
  all the way to the mountains,
  and the ravines will be filled with your
    flesh.
⁷When I snuff you out, I will cover the
    heavens
  and darken their stars;
I will cover the sun with a cloud,
  and the moon will not give its light.
⁸All the shining lights in the heavens
  I will darken over you;
  I will bring darkness over your land,
          declares the Sovereign Lord.
⁹I will trouble the hearts of many peoples
  when I bring about your destruction among
    the nations,
  amongᵉ lands you have not known.
¹⁰I will cause many peoples to be appalled at
    you,
  and their kings will shudder with horror
    because of you
  when I brandish my sword before them.
On the day of your downfall
  each of them will tremble
  every moment for his life.

¹¹" 'For this is what the Sovereign Lord says:

  " 'The sword of the king of Babylon
    will come against you.
¹²I will cause your hordes to fall
  by the swords of mighty men—
  the most ruthless of all nations.
They will shatter the pride of Egypt,
  and all her hordes will be overthrown.
¹³I will destroy all her cattle
  from beside abundant waters
no longer to be stirred by the foot of man
  or muddied by the hoofs of cattle.
¹⁴Then I will let her waters settle
  and make her streams flow like oil,
          declares the Sovereign Lord.
¹⁵When I make Egypt desolate
  and strip the land of everything in it,
when I strike down all who live there,
  then they will know that I am the Lord.'

¹⁶"This is the lament they will chant for her.
The daughters of the nations will chant it; for
Egypt and all her hordes they will chant it, de-
clares the Sovereign Lord."

¹⁷In the twelfth year, on the fifteenth day of the
month, the word of the Lord came to me: ¹⁸"Son
of man, wail for the hordes of Egypt and consign
to the earth below both her and the daughters of
mighty nations, with those who go down to the
pit. ¹⁹Say to them, 'Are you more favored than
others? Go down and be laid among the uncircumcised.' ²⁰They will fall among those killed by
the sword. The sword is drawn; let her be dragged
off with all her hordes. ²¹From within the graveᶠ
the mighty leaders will say of Egypt and her allies, 'They have come down and they lie with the
uncircumcised, with those killed by the sword.'

²²"Assyria is there with her whole army; she is
surrounded by the graves of all her slain, all who
have fallen by the sword. ²³Their graves are in the
depths of the pit and her army lies around her
grave. All who had spread terror in the land of the
living are slain, fallen by the sword.

²⁴"Elam is there, with all her hordes around her
grave. All of them are slain, fallen by the sword.
All who had spread terror in the land of the living
went down uncircumcised to the earth below.
They bear their shame with those who go down
to the pit. ²⁵A bed is made for her among the
slain, with all her hordes around her grave. All of
them are uncircumcised, killed by the sword. Because their terror had spread in the land of the
living, they bear their shame with those who go
down to the pit; they are laid among the slain.

²⁶"Meshech and Tubal are there, with all their
hordes around their graves. All of them are uncircumcised, killed by the sword because they
spread their terror in the land of the living. ²⁷Do
they not lie with the other uncircumcised warriors who have fallen, who went down to the
grave with their weapons of war, whose swords
were placed under their heads? The punishment
for their sins rested on their bones, though the
terror of these warriors had stalked through the
land of the living.

²⁸"You too, O Pharaoh, will be broken and will
lie among the uncircumcised, with those killed by
the sword.

²⁹"Edom is there, her kings and all her princes;
despite their power, they are laid with those
killed by the sword. They lie with the uncircumcised, with those who go down to the pit.

³⁰"All the princes of the north and all the Sidonians are there; they went down with the slain in
disgrace despite the terror caused by their power.

ᵉ9 Hebrew; Septuagint *bring you into captivity among the nations, / to*
ᶠ21 Hebrew *Sheol*; also in verse 27

They lie uncircumcised with those killed by the sword and bear their shame with those who go down to the pit.

³¹"Pharaoh—he and all his army—will see them and he will be consoled for all his hordes that were killed by the sword, declares the Sovereign LORD. ³²Although I had him spread terror in the land of the living, Pharaoh and all his hordes will be laid among the uncircumcised, with those killed by the sword, declares the Sovereign LORD."

11 / *Ezekiel 33*
The Watchman

THE FIRST TWENTY-FOUR chapters of Ezekiel contain his prophecies *before* the fall of Jerusalem. They are concerned with what will happen to the spiritual epicenter of the Lord's people. Then Jerusalem falls and the temple is destroyed. In the interlude (chapters 25—32) Ezekiel surveys what God is doing with the surrounding nations. Now, in chapters 33—48, Ezekiel turns from the Jerusalem that was to the Jerusalem that will be. In this matter Ezekiel has, once again, a lonely role.

 Warming Up to God Think of a time when you stood alone for God's purposes or standards. What comforted you when you were not supported by others?

 Read Ezekiel 33.

33 The word of the LORD came to me: ²"Son of man, speak to your countrymen and say to them: 'When I bring the sword against a land, and the people of the land choose one of their men and make him their watchman, ³and he sees the sword coming against the land and blows the trumpet to warn the people, ⁴then if anyone hears the trumpet but does not take warning and the sword comes and takes his life, his blood will be on his own head. ⁵Since he heard the sound of the trumpet but did not take warning, his blood will be on his own head. If he had taken warning, he would have saved himself. ⁶But if the watchman sees the sword coming and does not blow the trumpet to warn the people and the sword comes and takes the life of one of them, that man will be taken away because of his sin, but I will hold the watchman accountable for his blood.'

⁷"Son of man, I have made you a watchman for the house of Israel; so hear the word I speak and give them warning from me. ⁸When I say to the wicked, 'O wicked man, you will surely die,' and you do not speak out to dissuade him from his ways, that wicked man will die for⁸ his sin, and I will hold you accountable for his blood. ⁹But if you do warn the wicked man to turn from his ways and he does not do so, he will die for his sin, but you will have saved yourself.

¹⁰"Son of man, say to the house of Israel, 'This is what you are saying: "Our offenses and sins weigh us down, and we are wasting away because of ʰ them. How then can we live?"' ¹¹Say to them, 'As surely as I live, declares the Sovereign LORD, I take no pleasure in the death of the wicked, but rather that they turn from their ways and live. Turn! Turn from your evil ways! Why will you die, O house of Israel?'

¹²"Therefore, son of man, say to your countrymen, 'The righteousness of the righteous man will not save him when he disobeys, and the wickedness of the wicked man will not cause him to fall when he turns from it. The righteous man, if he sins, will not be allowed to live because of his former righteousness.' ¹³If I tell the righteous man that he will surely live, but then he trusts in his righteousness and does evil, none of the righteous things he has done will be remembered; he will die for the evil he has done. ¹⁴And if I say to the wicked man, 'You will surely die,' but he then turns away from his sin and does what is just and right— ¹⁵if he gives back what he took in pledge for a loan, returns what he has stolen, follows the decrees that give life, and does no evil, he will

⁸8 Or *in; also in verse 9*   ʰ10 Or *away in*

surely live; he will not die. ¹⁶None of the sins he has committed will be remembered against him. He has done what is just and right; he will surely live.

¹⁷"Yet your countrymen say, 'The way of the Lord is not just.' But it is their way that is not just. ¹⁸If a righteous man turns from his righteousness and does evil, he will die for it. ¹⁹And if a wicked man turns away from his wickedness and does what is just and right, he will live by doing so. ²⁰Yet, O house of Israel, you say, 'The way of the Lord is not just.' But I will judge each of you according to his own ways."

²¹In the twelfth year of our exile, in the tenth month on the fifth day, a man who had escaped from Jerusalem came to me and said, "The city has fallen!" ²²Now the evening before the man arrived, the hand of the LORD was upon me, and he opened my mouth before the man came to me in the morning. So my mouth was opened and I was no longer silent.

²³Then the word of the LORD came to me: ²⁴"Son of man, the people living in those ruins in the land of Israel are saying, 'Abraham was only one man, yet he possessed the land. But we are many; surely the land has been given to us as our possession.' ²⁵Therefore say to them, 'This is what the Sovereign LORD says: Since you eat meat with the blood still in it and look to your idols and shed blood, should you then possess the land? ²⁶You rely on your sword, you do detestable

things, and each of you defiles his neighbor's wife. Should you then possess the land?'

²⁷"Say this to them: 'This is what the Sovereign LORD says: As surely as I live, those who are left in the ruins will fall by the sword, those out in the country I will give to the wild animals to be devoured, and those in strongholds and caves will die of a plague. ²⁸I will make the land a desolate waste, and her proud strength will come to an end, and the mountains of Israel will become desolate so that no one will cross them. ²⁹Then they will know that I am the LORD, when I have made the land a desolate waste because of all the detestable things they have done.'

³⁰"As for you, son of man, your countrymen are talking together about you by the walls and at the doors of the houses, saying to each other, 'Come and hear the message that has come from the LORD.' ³¹My people come to you, as they usually do, and sit before you to listen to your words, but they do not put them into practice. With their mouths they express devotion, but their hearts are greedy for unjust gain. ³²Indeed, to them you are nothing more than one who sings love songs with a beautiful voice and plays an instrument well, for they hear your words but do not put them into practice.

³³"When all this comes true—and it surely will—then they will know that a prophet has been among them."

Discovering the Word 1. In what ways is Ezekiel's role with God's people like that of a watchman on the walls of a city (vv. 1–20; 3:16–21)? 2. With what words will Ezekiel encourage the exiles who feel their sins are unforgivable and their punishment so final that there can be no deliverance (vv. 10–11)? 3. Why will Ezekiel's role as a watchman be especially important now that the news of Jerusalem's fall has arrived (v. 21)? 4. What apparently do the people assume they will be able to do (v. 24), and how must Ezekiel warn them (vv. 25–26)? 5. Why must Ezekiel keep speaking even though his words apparently have little effect (vv. 30–32; Mt 7:26–27)?

Applying the Word 1. In what way is the response of Ezekiel's contemporaries (vv. 30–32) similar to the response of church congregations to the weekly experience of listening to sermons? 2. On what issues of our day might God be calling you to stand apart from others? 3. What fears will you need to overcome to stand as a faithful watchman?

 Responding in Prayer Pray for Spirit-empowered boldness in standing for God and his righteousness on the issues of our day (Eph 6:19–20).

12 / *Ezekiel 34*
Past and Future Shepherds

SELF-INTEREST SHOULD NOT be the primary motivation of a spiritual leader. When an outstanding Christian leader is found to be sexually unfaithful, consumed with greed or on a power trip, not only are non-Christians tempted to become cynical; even the insiders wonder if there is any reality to the faith. Into such situations Ezekiel was called to speak God's word with searing honesty and triumphant hope. In choosing to address the leadership question by using the metaphor of shepherd, Ezekiel was using an image that was common in the Ancient Near East and is threaded through the Bible (Isa 44:28; Jer 10:21; Mic 5:4–5; Zec 11:4–17), one that can speak to us today.

 Warming Up to God Recall a pastor or Christian leader who has truly cared for you and helped you find strength in God. What were his or her characteristics?

 Read Ezekiel 34.

---

34 The word of the LORD came to me: ²"Son of man, prophesy against the shepherds of Israel; prophesy and say to them: 'This is what the Sovereign LORD says: Woe to the shepherds of Israel who only take care of themselves! Should not shepherds take care of the flock? ³You eat the curds, clothe yourselves with the wool and slaughter the choice animals, but you do not take care of the flock. ⁴You have not strengthened the weak or healed the sick or bound up the injured. You have not brought back the strays or searched for the lost. You have ruled them harshly and brutally. ⁵So they were scattered because there was no shepherd, and when they were scattered they became food for all the wild animals. ⁶My sheep wandered over all the mountains and on every high hill. They were scattered over the whole earth, and no one searched or looked for them.

⁷" 'Therefore, you shepherds, hear the word of the LORD: ⁸As surely as I live, declares the Sovereign LORD, because my flock lacks a shepherd and so has been plundered and has become food for all the wild animals, and because my shepherds did not search for my flock but cared for themselves rather than for my flock, ⁹therefore, O shepherds, hear the word of the LORD: ¹⁰This is what the Sovereign LORD says: I am against the shepherds and will hold them accountable for my flock. I will remove them from tending the flock so that the shepherds can no longer feed themselves. I will rescue my flock from their mouths, and it will no longer be food for them.

¹¹" 'For this is what the Sovereign LORD says: I myself will search for my sheep and look after

them. ¹²As a shepherd looks after his scattered flock when he is with them, so will I look after my sheep. I will rescue them from all the places where they were scattered on a day of clouds and darkness. ¹³I will bring them out from the nations and gather them from the countries, and I will bring them into their own land. I will pasture them on the mountains of Israel, in the ravines and in all the settlements in the land. ¹⁴I will tend them in a good pasture, and the mountain heights of Israel will be their grazing land. There they will lie down in good grazing land, and there they will feed in a rich pasture on the mountains of Israel. ¹⁵I myself will tend my sheep and have them lie down, declares the Sovereign LORD. ¹⁶I will search for the lost and bring back the strays. I will bind up the injured and strengthen the weak, but the sleek and the strong I will destroy. I will shepherd the flock with justice.

¹⁷" 'As for you, my flock, this is what the Sovereign LORD says: I will judge between one sheep and another, and between rams and goats. ¹⁸Is it not enough for you to feed on the good pasture? Must you also trample the rest of your pasture with your feet? Is it not enough for you to drink clear water? Must you also muddy the rest with your feet? ¹⁹Must my flock feed on what you have trampled and drink what you have muddied with your feet?

²⁰" 'Therefore this is what the Sovereign LORD says to them: See, I myself will judge between the fat sheep and the lean sheep. ²¹Because you shove with flank and shoulder, butting all the weak sheep with your horns until you have driven them away, ²²I will save my flock, and they will

no longer be plundered. I will judge between one sheep and another. ²³I will place over them one shepherd, my servant David, and he will tend them; he will tend them and be their shepherd. ²⁴I the LORD will be their God, and my servant David will be prince among them. I the LORD have spoken.

²⁵" 'I will make a covenant of peace with them and rid the land of wild beasts so that they may live in the desert and sleep in the forests in safety. ²⁶I will bless them and the places surrounding my hill.ⁱ I will send down showers in season; there will be showers of blessing. ²⁷The trees of the field will yield their fruit and the ground will yield its crops; the people will be secure in their land. They will know that I am the LORD, when I

break the bars of their yoke and rescue them from the hands of those who enslaved them. ²⁸They will no longer be plundered by the nations, nor will wild animals devour them. They will live in safety, and no one will make them afraid. ²⁹I will provide for them a land renowned for its crops, and they will no longer be victims of famine in the land or bear the scorn of the nations. ³⁰Then they will know that I, the LORD their God, am with them and that they, the house of Israel, are my people, declares the Sovereign LORD. ³¹You my sheep, the sheep of my pasture, are people, and I am your God, declares the Sovereign LORD.' "

ⁱ26 Or *I will make them and the places surrounding my hill a blessing*

 Discovering the Word 1. By reciting the failures of the kings and spiritual leaders before the exile, Ezekiel gives us several descriptions of what should and should not be done by good leaders. What are the characteristics of both? 2. Instead of proposing a leaderless community, Ezekiel offers an inspired vision of the Good Shepherd (vv. 10–16) in a remarkable foreshadowing of the parable of the lost sheep (Jn 10:1–21). What does God as Shepherd do that his human servant-leaders refuse to do? 3. Ezekiel switches the metaphor from shepherd as leader/feeder to shepherd as judge. The flock must be purified not only of bad leaders but also of bad members (vv. 17–22; Mt 25:31–46). Why are both leaders and members tested more by their care of the weak than of the strong and healthy? 4. Many of Ezekiel's visions are presented to us in a kind of dissolve-fade sequence. In verses 23–31 Ezekiel envisions the ultimate hope for the scattered exiles in Babylon. How does he describe it?

Applying the Word 1. Should Christians today long for such judgment by human shepherd–leaders? Why or why not? 2. In what ways does your own relationship with the weak and needy members of God's people express the justice desired by the Good Shepherd and true leader of the church? 3. Who needs your assistance?

Responding in Prayer Reflect on what "the LORD is [your] shepherd" (Ps 23:1) means to you, and turn this reflection into thanksgiving prayer.

Ezekiel 35—36

35

The word of the LORD came to me: ²"Son of man, set your face against Mount Seir; prophesy against it ³and say: 'This is what the Sovereign LORD says: I am against you, Mount Seir, and I will stretch out my hand against you and make you a desolate waste. ⁴I will turn your towns into ruins and you will be desolate. Then you will know that I am the LORD.

⁵" 'Because you harbored an ancient hostility and delivered the Israelites over to the sword at the time of their calamity, the time their punishment reached its climax, ⁶therefore as surely as I live, declares the Sovereign LORD, I will give you over to bloodshed and it will pursue you. Since

you did not hate bloodshed, bloodshed will pursue you. ⁷I will make Mount Seir a desolate waste and cut off from it all who come and go. ⁸I will fill your mountains with the slain; those killed by the sword will fall on your hills and in your valleys and in all your ravines. ⁹I will make you desolate forever; your towns will not be inhabited. Then you will know that I am the LORD.

¹⁰" 'Because you have said, "These two nations and countries will be ours and we will take possession of them," even though I the LORD was there, ¹¹therefore as surely as I live, declares the Sovereign LORD, I will treat you in accordance with the anger and jealousy you showed in your hatred of them and I will make myself known

among them when I judge you. ¹²Then you will know that I the LORD have heard all the contemptible things you have said against the mountains of Israel. You said, "They have been laid waste and have been given over to us to devour." ¹³You boasted against me and spoke against me without restraint, and I heard it. ¹⁴This is what the Sovereign LORD says: While the whole earth rejoices, I will make you desolate. ¹⁵Because you rejoiced when the inheritance of the house of Israel became desolate, that is how I will treat you. You will be desolate, O Mount Seir, you and all of Edom. Then they will know that I am the LORD.' "

36 "Son of man, prophesy to the mountains of Israel and say, 'O mountains of Israel, hear the word of the LORD. ²This is what the Sovereign LORD says: The enemy said of you, "Aha! The ancient heights have become our possession." ' ³Therefore prophesy and say, 'This is what the Sovereign LORD says: Because they ravaged and hounded you from every side so that you became the possession of the rest of the nations and the object of people's malicious talk and slander, ⁴therefore, O mountains of Israel, hear the word of the Sovereign LORD: This is what the Sovereign LORD says to the mountains and hills, to the ravines and valleys, to the desolate ruins and the deserted towns that have been plundered and ridiculed by the rest of the nations around you— ⁵this is what the Sovereign LORD says: In my burning zeal I have spoken against the rest of the nations, and against all Edom, for with glee and with malice in their hearts they made my land their own possession so that they might plunder its pastureland.' ⁶Therefore prophesy concerning the land of Israel and say to the mountains and hills, to the ravines and valleys: 'This is what the Sovereign LORD says: I speak in my jealous wrath because you have suffered the scorn of the nations. ⁷Therefore this is what the Sovereign LORD says: I swear with uplifted hand that the nations around you will also suffer scorn.

⁸" 'But you, O mountains of Israel, will produce branches and fruit for my people Israel, for they will soon come home. ⁹I am concerned for you and will look on you with favor; you will be plowed and sown, ¹⁰and I will multiply the number of people upon you, even the whole house of Israel. The towns will be inhabited and the ruins rebuilt. ¹¹I will increase the number of men and animals upon you, and they will be fruitful and become numerous. I will settle people on you as in the past and will make you prosper more than before. Then you will know that I am the LORD. ¹²I will cause people, my people Israel, to walk upon you. They will possess you, and you will be their inheritance; you will never again deprive them of their children.

¹³" 'This is what the Sovereign LORD says: Because people say to you, "You devour men and deprive your nation of its children," ¹⁴therefore you will no longer devour men or make your nation childless, declares the Sovereign LORD. ¹⁵No longer will I make you hear the taunts of the nations, and no longer will you suffer the scorn of the peoples or cause your nation to fall, declares the Sovereign LORD.' "

¹⁶Again the word of the LORD came to me: ¹⁷"Son of man, when the people of Israel were living in their own land, they defiled it by their conduct and their actions. Their conduct was like a woman's monthly uncleanness in my sight. ¹⁸So I poured out my wrath on them because they had shed blood in the land and because they had defiled it with their idols. ¹⁹I dispersed them among the nations, and they were scattered through the countries; I judged them according to their conduct and their actions. ²⁰And wherever they went among the nations they profaned my holy name, for it was said of them, 'These are the LORD's people, and yet they had to leave his land.' ²¹I had concern for my holy name, which the house of Israel profaned among the nations where they had gone.

²²"Therefore say to the house of Israel, 'This is what the Sovereign LORD says: It is not for your sake, O house of Israel, that I am going to do these things, but for the sake of my holy name, which you have profaned among the nations where you have gone. ²³I will show the holiness of my great name, which has been profaned among the nations, the name you have profaned among them. Then the nations will know that I am the LORD, declares the Sovereign LORD, when I show myself holy through you before their eyes.

²⁴" 'For I will take you out of the nations; I will gather you from all the countries and bring you back into your own land. ²⁵I will sprinkle clean water on you, and you will be clean; I will cleanse you from all your impurities and from all your idols. ²⁶I will give you a new heart and put a new spirit in you; I will remove from you your heart of

stone and give you a heart of flesh. 27And I will put my Spirit in you and move you to follow my decrees and be careful to keep my laws. 28You will live in the land I gave your forefathers; you will be my people, and I will be your God. 29I will save you from all your uncleanness. I will call for the grain and make it plentiful and will not bring famine upon you. 30I will increase the fruit of the trees and the crops of the field, so that you will no longer suffer disgrace among the nations because of famine. 31Then you will remember your evil ways and wicked deeds, and you will loathe yourselves for your sins and detestable practices. 32I want you to know that I am not doing this for your sake, declares the Sovereign LORD. Be ashamed and disgraced for your conduct, O house of Israel!

33" 'This is what the Sovereign LORD says: On the day I cleanse you from all your sins, I will resettle your towns, and the ruins will be rebuilt. 34The desolate land will be cultivated instead of lying desolate in the sight of all who pass through it. 35They will say, "This land that was laid waste has become like the garden of Eden; the cities that were lying in ruins, desolate and destroyed, are now fortified and inhabited." 36Then the nations around you that remain will know that I the LORD have rebuilt what was destroyed and have replanted what was desolate. I the LORD have spoken, and I will do it.'

37"This is what the Sovereign LORD says: Once again I will yield to the plea of the house of Israel and do this for them: I will make their people as numerous as sheep, 38as numerous as the flocks for offerings at Jerusalem during her appointed feasts. So will the ruined cities be filled with flocks of people. Then they will know that I am the LORD."

13 / *Ezekiel 37*
Can These Bones Live?

IMAGINATION IS THE vehicle through which faith finds expression, allowing us, as Cheryl Forbes says, "to complete the story." We have a profound need to see the conclusion of it all, especially what will come of God's own people. It is impossible for God to *tell* us the future. So he *shows* us. But an inspired vision of the end is different from invented endings. Ezekiel's word pictures envision what God will actually do, thereby feeding faith rather than fancy.

Warming Up to God What anxiety do you have about your future days and years? Pause to voice your fears to God.

Read Ezekiel 37.

37 The hand of the LORD was upon me, and he brought me out by the Spirit of the LORD and set me in the middle of a valley; it was full of bones. 2He led me back and forth among them, and I saw a great many bones on the floor of the valley, bones that were very dry. 3He asked me, "Son of man, can these bones live?"

I said, "O Sovereign LORD, you alone know."

4Then he said to me, "Prophesy to these bones and say to them, 'Dry bones, hear the word of the LORD! 5This is what the Sovereign LORD says to these bones: I will make breath*j* enter you, and you will come to life. 6I will attach tendons to you and make flesh come upon you and cover you with skin; I will put breath in you, and you will come to life. Then you will know that I am the LORD.' "

7So I prophesied as I was commanded. And as I was prophesying, there was a noise, a rattling sound, and the bones came together, bone to bone. 8I looked, and tendons and flesh appeared on them and skin covered them, but there was no breath in them.

9Then he said to me, "Prophesy to the breath; prophesy, son of man, and say to it, 'This is what

*j5 The Hebrew for this word can also mean *wind* or *spirit* (see verses 6-14).*

the Sovereign LORD says: Come from the four winds, O breath, and breathe into these slain, that they may live.' " ¹⁰So I prophesied as he commanded me, and breath entered them; they came to life and stood up on their feet—a vast army.

¹¹Then he said to me: "Son of man, these bones are the whole house of Israel. They say, 'Our bones are dried up and our hope is gone; we are cut off.' ¹²Therefore prophesy and say to them: 'This is what the Sovereign LORD says: O my people, I am going to open your graves and bring you up from them; I will bring you back to the land of Israel. ¹³Then you, my people, will know that I am the LORD, when I open your graves and bring you up from them. ¹⁴I will put my Spirit in you and you will live, and I will settle you in your own land. Then you will know that I the LORD have spoken, and I have done it, declares the LORD.' "

¹⁵The word of the LORD came to me: ¹⁶"Son of man, take a stick of wood and write on it, 'Belonging to Judah and the Israelites associated with him.' Then take another stick of wood, and write on it, 'Ephraim's stick, belonging to Joseph and all the house of Israel associated with him.' ¹⁷Join them together into one stick so that they will become one in your hand.

¹⁸"When your countrymen ask you, 'Won't you tell us what you mean by this?' ¹⁹say to them, 'This is what the Sovereign LORD says: I am going to take the stick of Joseph—which is in Ephraim's hand—and of the Israelite tribes associated with him, and join it to Judah's stick, making them a single stick of wood, and they will become one in my hand.' ²⁰Hold before their eyes the sticks you have written on ²¹and say to them, 'This is what the Sovereign LORD says: I will take the Israelites out of the nations where they have gone. I will gather them from all around and bring them back into their own land. ²²I will make them one nation in the land, on the mountains of Israel. There will be one king over all of them and they will never again be two nations or be divided into two kingdoms. ²³They will no longer defile themselves with their idols and vile images or with any of their offenses, for I will save them from all their sinful backsliding,ᵏ and I will cleanse them. They will be my people, and I will be their God.

²⁴" 'My servant David will be king over them, and they will all have one shepherd. They will follow my laws and be careful to keep my decrees. ²⁵They will live in the land I gave to my servant Jacob, the land where your fathers lived. They and their children and their children's children will live there forever, and David my servant will be their prince forever. ²⁶I will make a covenant of peace with them; it will be an everlasting covenant. I will establish them and increase their numbers, and I will put my sanctuary among them forever. ²⁷My dwelling place will be with them; I will be their God, and they will be my people. ²⁸Then the nations will know that I the LORD make Israel holy, when my sanctuary is among them forever.' "

ᵏ23 Many Hebrew manuscripts (see also Septuagint); most Hebrew manuscripts *all their dwelling places where they sinned*

Discovering the Word 1. What future does God present through both the vision (vv. 1–14) and the acted parable (vv. 15–23)? 2. To what condition of the people (vv. 11, 16–17) and of the prophet himself (v. 3) does this message minister? 3. Many people have interpreted verses 1–14 as an Old Testament doctrine of bodily resurrection or an allegory of individual spiritual regeneration in Christ. But in the context of Ezekiel's teachings after the fall of Jerusalem, why do you think "Can these bones live?" (v. 3) is an important question for the Lord to ask the prophet? 4. It appears that Ezekiel has the knowledge that God could resurrect his people, but not faith to believe God will do it. Why is it important for Ezekiel to be asked to speak to the dead bones (vv. 4, 7)? 5. The second part of Israel's resurrection in verses 15–28 is a development of the heart transplant image of 36:26–27. What further statements indicate that God has more in mind than the mere physical restoration of the nation of Israel (vv. 24–28)? 6. In 36:22 God says, "It is not for your sake, O house of Israel, that I am going to do these things, but for the sake of my holy name." Three times in the vision God says he will do this so that "you will know that I am the LORD" (37:6, 13, 14). Why is God's settled decision to renew his own people so crucial to the declaration of God's glory in the world?

Applying the Word 1. What hope does this vision give for Christians today who, viewing the state of the church, say, "Our bones are dried up and our hope is gone" (v. 11)? 2. For a host of skeletons to be turned into an effective army, God must work a miracle. Note the crucial role played by the prophet in the future of God's people. How could preaching and prayer on the part of the church today be part of our renewal process?

🤚 **Responding in Prayer** Pray for the unity of the church (vv. 15–23). Pray for the renewal of God's people (v. 24; 36:26–27). Pray that God's people will delight in being the sanctuary of God (v. 27). Pray that God's people will communicate the glory of God to the nations through mission (v. 28).

Ezekiel 38—39

38 The word of the LORD came to me: [2]"Son of man, set your face against Gog, of the land of Magog, the chief prince of[l] Meshech and Tubal; prophesy against him [3]and say: 'This is what the Sovereign LORD says: I am against you, O Gog, chief prince of[m] Meshech and Tubal. [4]I will turn you around, put hooks in your jaws and bring you out with your whole army—your horses, your horsemen fully armed, and a great horde with large and small shields, all of them brandishing their swords. [5]Persia, Cush[n] and Put will be with them, all with shields and helmets, [6]also Gomer with all its troops, and Beth Togarmah from the far north with all its troops—the many nations with you.

[7]" 'Get ready; be prepared, you and all the hordes gathered about you, and take command of them. [8]After many days you will be called to arms. In future years you will invade a land that has recovered from war, whose people were gathered from many nations to the mountains of Israel, which had long been desolate. They had been brought out from the nations, and now all of them live in safety. [9]You and all your troops and the many nations with you will go up, advancing like a storm; you will be like a cloud covering the land.

[10]" 'This is what the Sovereign LORD says: On that day thoughts will come into your mind and you will devise an evil scheme. [11]You will say, "I will invade a land of unwalled villages; I will attack a peaceful and unsuspecting people—all of them living without walls and without gates and bars. [12]I will plunder and loot and turn my hand against the resettled ruins and the people gathered from the nations, rich in livestock and goods, living at the center of the land." [13]Sheba and Dedan and the merchants of Tarshish and all her villages[o] will say to you, "Have you come to plunder? Have you gathered your hordes to loot, to carry off silver and gold, to take away livestock and goods and to seize much plunder?" '

[14]"Therefore, son of man, prophesy and say to Gog: 'This is what the Sovereign LORD says: In that day, when my people Israel are living in safety, will you not take notice of it? [15]You will come from your place in the far north, you and many nations with you, all of them riding on horses, a great horde, a mighty army. [16]You will advance against my people Israel like a cloud that covers the land. In days to come, O Gog, I will bring you against my land, so that the nations may know me when I show myself holy through you before their eyes.

[17]" 'This is what the Sovereign LORD says: Are you not the one I spoke of in former days by my servants the prophets of Israel? At that time they prophesied for years that I would bring you against them. [18]This is what will happen in that day: When Gog attacks the land of Israel, my hot anger will be aroused, declares the Sovereign LORD. [19]In my zeal and fiery wrath I declare that at that time there shall be a great earthquake in the land of Israel. [20]The fish of the sea, the birds of the air, the beasts of the field, every creature that moves along the ground, and all the people on the face of the earth will tremble at my presence. The mountains will be overturned, the cliffs will crumble and every wall will fall to the ground. [21]I will summon a sword against Gog on all my mountains, declares the Sovereign LORD. Every man's sword will be against his brother. [22]I will execute judgment upon him with plague and bloodshed; I will pour down torrents of rain, hailstones and burning sulfur on him and on his troops and on the many nations with him. [23]And so I will show my greatness and my holiness, and I will make myself known in the sight of many nations. Then they will know that I am the LORD.'

39 "Son of man, prophesy against Gog and say: 'This is what the Sovereign LORD says: I am against you, O Gog, chief prince of[m] Meshech and Tubal. [2]I will turn you around and drag you along. I will bring you from the far north and send you against the mountains of Israel. [3]Then I will strike your bow

---

[l]2 Or *the prince of Rosh,*   [m]3,1 Or *Gog, prince of Rosh,*   [n]5 That is, the upper Nile region   [o]13 Or *her strong lions*

from your left hand and make your arrows drop from your right hand. ⁴On the mountains of Israel you will fall, you and all your troops and the nations with you. I will give you as food to all kinds of carrion birds and to the wild animals. ⁵You will fall in the open field, for I have spoken, declares the Sovereign LORD. ⁶I will send fire on Magog and on those who live in safety in the coastlands, and they will know that I am the LORD.

⁷" 'I will make known my holy name among my people Israel. I will no longer let my holy name be profaned, and the nations will know that I the LORD am the Holy One in Israel. ⁸It is coming! It will surely take place, declares the Sovereign LORD. This is the day I have spoken of.

⁹" 'Then those who live in the towns of Israel will go out and use the weapons for fuel and burn them up—the small and large shields, the bows and arrows, the war clubs and spears. For seven years they will use them for fuel. ¹⁰They will not need to gather wood from the fields or cut it from the forests, because they will use the weapons for fuel. And they will plunder those who plundered them and loot those who looted them, declares the Sovereign LORD.

¹¹" 'On that day I will give Gog a burial place in Israel, in the valley of those who travel east toward*ᵖ* the Sea.*�q* It will block the way of travelers, because Gog and all his hordes will be buried there. So it will be called the Valley of Hamon Gog.*ʳ*

¹²" 'For seven months the house of Israel will be burying them in order to cleanse the land. ¹³All the people of the land will bury them, and the day I am glorified will be a memorable day for them, declares the Sovereign LORD.

¹⁴" 'Men will be regularly employed to cleanse the land. Some will go throughout the land and, in addition to them, others will bury those that remain on the ground. At the end of the seven months they will begin their search. ¹⁵As they go through the land and one of them sees a human bone, he will set up a marker beside it until the gravediggers have buried it in the Valley of Hamon Gog. ¹⁶(Also a town called Hamonah*ˢ* will be there.) And so they will cleanse the land.'

¹⁷"Son of man, this is what the Sovereign LORD says: Call out to every kind of bird and all the wild animals: 'Assemble and come together from all around to the sacrifice I am preparing for you, the great sacrifice on the mountains of Israel. There you will eat flesh and drink blood. ¹⁸You will eat the flesh of mighty men and drink the blood of the princes of the earth as if they were rams and lambs, goats and bulls—all of them fattened animals from Bashan. ¹⁹At the sacrifice I am preparing for you, you will eat fat till you are glutted and drink blood till you are drunk. ²⁰At my table you will eat your fill of horses and riders, mighty men and soldiers of every kind,' declares the Sovereign LORD.

²¹"I will display my glory among the nations, and all the nations will see the punishment I inflict and the hand I lay upon them. ²²From that day forward the house of Israel will know that I am the LORD their God. ²³And the nations will know that the people of Israel went into exile for their sin, because they were unfaithful to me. So I hid my face from them and handed them over to their enemies, and they all fell by the sword. ²⁴I dealt with them according to their uncleanness and their offenses, and I hid my face from them.

²⁵"Therefore this is what the Sovereign LORD says: I will now bring Jacob back from captivity*ᵗ* and will have compassion on all the people of Israel, and I will be zealous for my holy name. ²⁶They will forget their shame and all the unfaithfulness they showed toward me when they lived in safety in their land with no one to make them afraid. ²⁷When I have brought them back from the nations and have gathered them from the countries of their enemies, I will show myself holy through them in the sight of many nations. ²⁸Then they will know that I am the LORD their God, for though I sent them into exile among the nations, I will gather them to their own land, not leaving any behind. ²⁹I will no longer hide my face from them, for I will pour out my Spirit on the house of Israel, declares the Sovereign LORD."

ᵖ11 Or *of*　　*�q11* That is, the Dead Sea　　*ʳ11 Hamon Gog* means *hordes of Gog.*　　*ˢ16 Hamonah* means *horde.*　　*ᵗ25* Or *now restore the fortunes of Jacob*

14 / *Ezekiel 40—41*
The New Temple

EZEKIEL'S SPIRITUAL PILGRIMAGE was a parable of the experience of the Israelites in exile. He was removed from his ministry as priest in the temple and plunged into exile. There, stripped of his old securities, he was led by God to consider in parable, allegory and vision, the sin of Jerusalem, the holiness and otherness of God. Then Ezekiel suffered the loss of his beloved wife (24:15–24), a prophetic symbol of the speechless grief to be experienced by the exiles when their beloved Jerusalem would finally fall in 587 B.C. Now there was nothing left but God himself, the greatest treasure of all. So the last section of the book, chapters 40—48, is pure contemplation. The vision of the restored temple, the ideal Jerusalem and the renewed creation take us beyond "the things of God" to attend to God himself.

 Warming Up to God What comes to your mind when you think of heaven?

 Read Ezekiel 40—41.

40 In the twenty-fifth year of our exile, at the beginning of the year, on the tenth of the month, in the fourteenth year after the fall of the city—on that very day the hand of the LORD was upon me and he took me there. ²In visions of God he took me to the land of Israel and set me on a very high mountain, on whose south side were some buildings that looked like a city. ³He took me there, and I saw a man whose appearance was like bronze; he was standing in the gateway with a linen cord and a measuring rod in his hand. ⁴The man said to me, "Son of man, look with your eyes and hear with your ears and pay attention to everything I am going to show you, for that is why you have been brought here. Tell the house of Israel everything you see."

⁵I saw a wall completely surrounding the temple area. The length of the measuring rod in the man's hand was six long cubits, each of which was a cubitᵘ and a handbreadth.ᵛ He measured the wall; it was one measuring rod thick and one rod high.

⁶Then he went to the gate facing east. He climbed its steps and measured the threshold of the gate; it was one rod deep.ʷ ⁷The alcoves for the guards were one rod long and one rod wide, and the projecting walls between the alcoves were five cubits thick. And the threshold of the gate next to the portico facing the temple was one rod deep.

⁸Then he measured the portico of the gateway; ⁹itˣ was eight cubits deep and its jambs were two cubits thick. The portico of the gateway faced the temple.

¹⁰Inside the east gate were three alcoves on each side; the three had the same measurements, and the faces of the projecting walls on each side had the same measurements. ¹¹Then he measured the width of the entrance to the gateway; it was ten cubits and its length was thirteen cubits. ¹²In front of each alcove was a wall one cubit high, and the alcoves were six cubits square. ¹³Then he measured the gateway from the top of the rear wall of one alcove to the top of the opposite one; the distance was twenty-five cubits from one parapet opening to the opposite one. ¹⁴He measured along the faces of the projecting walls all around the inside of the gateway—sixty cubits. The measurement was up to the porticoʸ facing the courtyard.ᶻ ¹⁵The distance from the entrance of the gateway to the far end of its portico was fifty cubits. ¹⁶The alcoves and the projecting walls inside the gateway were surmounted by narrow parapet openings all around, as was the portico; the openings all around faced inward. The faces of the projecting walls were decorated with palm trees.

¹⁷Then he brought me into the outer court. There I saw some rooms and a pavement that had been constructed all around the court; there were thirty rooms along the pavement. ¹⁸It abutted the sides of the gateways and was as wide as they were long; this was the lower pavement. ¹⁹Then he measured the distance from the inside of the

ᵘ5 The common cubit was about 1 1/2 feet (about 0.5 meter).
ᵛ5 That is, about 3 inches (about 8 centimeters)   ʷ6 Septuagint;
Hebrew *deep, the first threshold, one rod deep*   ˣ8,9 Many Hebrew
manuscripts, Septuagint, Vulgate and Syriac; most Hebrew manuscripts
gateway facing the temple; it was one rod deep. ⁹*Then he measured the
portico of the gateway; it*   ʸ14 Septuagint; Hebrew *projecting wall*
ᶻ14 The meaning of the Hebrew for this verse is uncertain.

lower gateway to the outside of the inner court; it was a hundred cubits on the east side as well as on the north.

²⁰Then he measured the length and width of the gate facing north, leading into the outer court. ²¹Its alcoves—three on each side—its projecting walls and its portico had the same measurements as those of the first gateway. It was fifty cubits long and twenty-five cubits wide. ²²Its openings, its portico and its palm tree decorations had the same measurements as those of the gate facing east. Seven steps led up to it, with its portico opposite them. ²³There was a gate to the inner court facing the north gate, just as there was on the east. He measured from one gate to the opposite one; it was a hundred cubits.

²⁴Then he led me to the south side and I saw a gate facing south. He measured its jambs and its portico, and they had the same measurements as the others. ²⁵The gateway and its portico had narrow openings all around, like the openings of the others. It was fifty cubits long and twenty-five cubits wide. ²⁶Seven steps led up to it, with its portico opposite them; it had palm tree decorations on the faces of the projecting walls on each side. ²⁷The inner court also had a gate facing south, and he measured from this gate to the outer gate on the south side; it was a hundred cubits.

²⁸Then he brought me into the inner court through the south gate, and he measured the south gate; it had the same measurements as the others. ²⁹Its alcoves, its projecting walls and its portico had the same measurements as the others. The gateway and its portico had openings all around. It was fifty cubits long and twenty-five cubits wide. ³⁰(The porticoes of the gateways around the inner court were twenty-five cubits wide and five cubits deep.) ³¹Its portico faced the outer court; palm trees decorated its jambs, and eight steps led up to it.

³²Then he brought me to the inner court on the east side, and he measured the gateway; it had the same measurements as the others. ³³Its alcoves, its projecting walls and its portico had the same measurements as the others. The gateway and its portico had openings all around. It was fifty cubits long and twenty-five cubits wide. ³⁴Its portico faced the outer court; palm trees decorated the jambs on either side, and eight steps led up to it.

³⁵Then he brought me to the north gate and measured it. It had the same measurements as the others, ³⁶as did its alcoves, its projecting walls and its portico, and it had openings all around. It was fifty cubits long and twenty-five cubits wide. ³⁷Its portico[a] faced the outer court; palm trees decorated the jambs on either side, and eight steps led up to it.

³⁸A room with a doorway was by the portico in each of the inner gateways, where the burnt offerings were washed. ³⁹In the portico of the gateway were two tables on each side, on which the burnt offerings, sin offerings and guilt offerings were slaughtered. ⁴⁰By the outside wall of the portico of the gateway, near the steps at the entrance to the north gateway were two tables, and on the other side of the steps were two tables. ⁴¹So there were four tables on one side of the gateway and four on the other—eight tables in all—on which the sacrifices were slaughtered. ⁴²There were also four tables of dressed stone for the burnt offerings, each a cubit and a half long, a cubit and a half wide and a cubit high. On them were placed the utensils for slaughtering the burnt offerings and the other sacrifices. ⁴³And double-pronged hooks, each a handbreadth long, were attached to the wall all around. The tables were for the flesh of the offerings.

⁴⁴Outside the inner gate, within the inner court, were two rooms, one[b] at the side of the north gate and facing south, and another at the side of the south[c] gate and facing north. ⁴⁵He said to me, "The room facing south is for the priests who have charge of the temple, ⁴⁶and the room facing north is for the priests who have charge of the altar. These are the sons of Zadok, who are the only Levites who may draw near to the LORD to minister before him."

⁴⁷Then he measured the court: It was square— a hundred cubits long and a hundred cubits wide. And the altar was in front of the temple.

⁴⁸He brought me to the portico of the temple and measured the jambs of the portico; they were five cubits wide on either side. The width of the entrance was fourteen cubits and its projecting walls were[d] three cubits wide on either side. ⁴⁹The portico was twenty cubits wide, and twelve[e] cubits from front to back. It was reached

---

*a37 Septuagint (see also verses 31 and 34); Hebrew *jambs*
*b44 Septuagint; Hebrew *were rooms for singers, which were*
*c44 Septuagint; Hebrew *east*   *d48 Septuagint; Hebrew *entrance was*
*e49 Septuagint; Hebrew *eleven*

by a flight of stairs,[f] and there were pillars on each side of the jambs.

41

Then the man brought me to the outer sanctuary and measured the jambs; the width of the jambs was six cubits[g] on each side.[h] [2]The entrance was ten cubits wide, and the projecting walls on each side of it were five cubits wide. He also measured the outer sanctuary; it was forty cubits long and twenty cubits wide.

[3]Then he went into the inner sanctuary and measured the jambs of the entrance; each was two cubits wide. The entrance was six cubits wide, and the projecting walls on each side of it were seven cubits wide. [4]And he measured the length of the inner sanctuary; it was twenty cubits, and its width was twenty cubits across the end of the outer sanctuary. He said to me, "This is the Most Holy Place."

[5]Then he measured the wall of the temple; it was six cubits thick, and each side room around the temple was four cubits wide. [6]The side rooms were on three levels, one above another, thirty on each level. There were ledges all around the wall of the temple to serve as supports for the side rooms, so that the supports were not inserted into the wall of the temple. [7]The side rooms all around the temple were wider at each successive level. The structure surrounding the temple was built in ascending stages, so that the rooms widened as one went upward. A stairway went up from the lowest floor to the top floor through the middle floor.

[8]I saw that the temple had a raised base all around it, forming the foundation of the side rooms. It was the length of the rod, six long cubits. [9]The outer wall of the side rooms was five cubits thick. The open area between the side rooms of the temple [10]and the ⌐priests'⌐ rooms was twenty cubits wide all around the temple. [11]There were entrances to the side rooms from the open area, one on the north and another on the south; and the base adjoining the open area was five cubits wide all around.

[12]The building facing the temple courtyard on the west side was seventy cubits wide. The wall of the building was five cubits thick all around, and its length was ninety cubits.

[13]Then he measured the temple; it was a hundred cubits long, and the temple courtyard and the building with its walls were also a hundred cubits long. [14]The width of the temple courtyard on the east, including the front of the temple, was a hundred cubits.

[15]Then he measured the length of the building facing the courtyard at the rear of the temple, including its galleries on each side; it was a hundred cubits.

The outer sanctuary, the inner sanctuary and the portico facing the court, [16]as well as the thresholds and the narrow windows and galleries around the three of them—everything beyond and including the threshold was covered with wood. The floor, the wall up to the windows, and the windows were covered. [17]In the space above the outside of the entrance to the inner sanctuary and on the walls at regular intervals all around the inner and outer sanctuary [18]were carved cherubim and palm trees. Palm trees alternated with cherubim. Each cherub had two faces: [19]the face of a man toward the palm tree on one side and the face of a lion toward the palm tree on the other. They were carved all around the whole temple. [20]From the floor to the area above the entrance, cherubim and palm trees were carved on the wall of the outer sanctuary.

[21]The outer sanctuary had a rectangular doorframe, and the one at the front of the Most Holy Place was similar. [22]There was a wooden altar three cubits high and two cubits square[i]; its corners, its base[j] and its sides were of wood. The man said to me, "This is the table that is before the LORD." [23]Both the outer sanctuary and the Most Holy Place had double doors. [24]Each door had two leaves—two hinged leaves for each door. [25]And on the doors of the outer sanctuary were carved cherubim and palm trees like those carved on the walls, and there was a wooden overhang on the front of the portico. [26]On the sidewalls of the portico were narrow windows with palm trees carved on each side. The side rooms of the temple also had overhangs.

[f]49 Hebrew; Septuagint *Ten steps led up to it*   [g]1 The common cubit was about 1 1/2 feet (about 0.5 meter).   [h]1 One Hebrew manuscript and Septuagint; most Hebrew manuscripts *side, the width of the tent*   [i]22 Septuagint; Hebrew *long*   [j]22 Septuagint; Hebrew *length*

Discovering the Word 1. To better picture the temple take a look at the diagram in the introduction. The renewed temple of Ezekiel's vision was perfectly symmetrical and designed to exalt the holiness of God. Everything was a perfect fit in this ideal dwelling place for God. For whose benefit is Ezekiel shown this vision? 2. Take a look at the temple diagram. What is striking to you about the temple? 3. How would this physical space encourage worship? 4. The elaborate description of the temple has been interpreted by Christians in four ways: (1) as a prophetic blueprint of what Ezekiel intended to have rebuilt when the exiles would finally return to Jerusalem, (2) as symbolic of the spiritual reality of the Christian church, (3) as a literal future temple that will be built in the last times when Israel is consummated in the kingdom age with Jesus, and (4) as an accepted apocalyptic piece of literature which uses highly symbolic language to express realities that will be experienced when the story of God's people is brought to a worthy end with the coming of the Messiah. What would a vision like this have meant to the first readers? 5. Which interpretation does justice to the timelessness of Scripture, having a message for the Israelites in exile and Christians today longing for heaven?

Applying the Word 1. Revelation 21—22 draws heavily from the imagery of the new Jerusalem pictured in Ezekiel 40—48, but *without* the temple. Why would a future with a temple be essential for an Israelite "heaven," but a future without one be even more appropriate for followers of Jesus who want to dwell with him forever (Rev 21:22)? 2. What new meaning does this study bring to the Christian prayer "Come, Lord Jesus"?

Responding in Prayer In light of this passage, pray, "Your kingdom come, your will be done on earth as it is in heaven" (Mt 6:10).

Ezekiel 42

42 Then the man led me northward into the outer court and brought me to the rooms opposite the temple courtyard and opposite the outer wall on the north side. ²The building whose door faced north was a hundred cubits*ᵏ* long and fifty cubits wide. ³Both in the section twenty cubits from the inner court and in the section opposite the pavement of the outer court, gallery faced gallery at the three levels. ⁴In front of the rooms was an inner passageway ten cubits wide and a hundred cubits*ˡ* long. Their doors were on the north. ⁵Now the upper rooms were narrower, for the galleries took more space from them than from the rooms on the lower and middle floors of the building. ⁶The rooms on the third floor had no pillars, as the courts had; so they were smaller in floor space than those on the lower and middle floors. ⁷There was an outer wall parallel to the rooms and the outer court; it extended in front of the rooms for fifty cubits. ⁸While the row of rooms on the side next to the outer court was fifty cubits long, the row on the side nearest the sanctuary was a hundred cubits long. ⁹The lower rooms had an entrance on the east side as one enters them from the outer court.

¹⁰On the south side*ᵐ* along the length of the wall of the outer court, adjoining the temple courtyard and opposite the outer wall, were

rooms ¹¹with a passageway in front of them. These were like the rooms on the north; they had the same length and width, with similar exits and dimensions. Similar to the doorways on the north ¹²were the doorways of the rooms on the south. There was a doorway at the beginning of the passageway that was parallel to the corresponding wall extending eastward, by which one enters the rooms.

¹³Then he said to me, "The north and south rooms facing the temple courtyard are the priests' rooms, where the priests who approach the LORD will eat the most holy offerings. There they will put the most holy offerings—the grain offerings, the sin offerings and the guilt offerings—for the place is holy. ¹⁴Once the priests enter the holy precincts, they are not to go into the outer court until they leave behind the garments in which they minister, for these are holy. They are to put on other clothes before they go near the places that are for the people."

¹⁵When he had finished measuring what was inside the temple area, he led me out by the east gate and measured the area all around: ¹⁶He measured the east side with the measuring rod; it was five hundred cubits.*ⁿ* ¹⁷He measured the north

---

*ᵏ*2 The common cubit was about 1 1/2 feet (about 0.5 meter).
*ˡ*4 Septuagint and Syriac; Hebrew *and one cubit*   *ᵐ*10 Septuagint;
Hebrew *Eastward*   *ⁿ*16 See Septuagint of verse 17; Hebrew *rods*; also
in verses 18 and 19.

side; it was five hundred cubits° by the measuring rod. ¹⁸He measured the south side; it was five hundred cubits by the measuring rod. ¹⁹Then he turned to the west side and measured; it was five hundred cubits by the measuring rod. ²⁰So he measured the area on all four sides. It had a wall around it, five hundred cubits long and five hundred cubits wide, to separate the holy from the common.

°17 Septuagint; Hebrew *rods*

15 / *Ezekiel 43:1–12*
The God Who Dwells with His People

NINETEEN YEARS EARLIER (10:18–22; 11:22–24) Ezekiel had seen the glory of the Lord leaving the temple. Then the temple was destroyed. God gave Ezekiel an empowering vision of a renewed temple. But the building would be an empty shell without God's presence. Ezekiel's faith would also be empty without direct experience of God. So Ezekiel is given a second direct encounter with God like the one at the Kebar River in Babylon. As with all true encounters with God, this one means more than getting a personal blessing.

 Warming Up to God Does the thought of firsthand encounter with God frighten you or attract you? Why?

 Read Ezekiel 43:1–12.

43 Then the man brought me to the gate facing east, ²and I saw the glory of the God of Israel coming from the east. His voice was like the roar of rushing waters, and the land was radiant with his glory. ³The vision I saw was like the vision I had seen when he^p came to destroy the city and like the visions I had seen by the Kebar River, and I fell facedown. ⁴The glory of the LORD entered the temple through the gate facing east. ⁵Then the Spirit lifted me up and brought me into the inner court, and the glory of the LORD filled the temple.

⁶While the man was standing beside me, I heard someone speaking to me from inside the temple. ⁷He said: "Son of man, this is the place of my throne and the place for the soles of my feet. This is where I will live among the Israelites forever. The house of Israel will never again defile my holy name—neither they nor their kings—by their prostitution^q and the lifeless idols^r of their kings at their high places. ⁸When they placed their threshold next to my threshold and their doorposts beside my doorposts, with only a wall between me and them, they defiled my holy name by their detestable practices. So I destroyed them in my anger. ⁹Now let them put away from me their prostitution and the lifeless idols of their kings, and I will live among them forever.

¹⁰"Son of man, describe the temple to the people of Israel, that they may be ashamed of their sins. Let them consider the plan, ¹¹and if they are ashamed of all they have done, make known to them the design of the temple—its arrangement, its exits and entrances—its whole design and all its regulations^s and laws. Write these down before them so that they may be faithful to its design and follow all its regulations.

¹²"This is the law of the temple: All the surrounding area on top of the mountain will be most holy. Such is the law of the temple.

^p3 Some Hebrew manuscripts and Vulgate; most Hebrew manuscripts *I*   ^q7 Or *their spiritual adultery*; also in verse 9   ^r7 Or *the corpses*; also in verse 9   ^s11 Some Hebrew manuscripts and Septuagint; most Hebrew manuscripts *regulations and its whole design*

Discovering the Word 1. What sights, sounds, words and movement contribute to Ezekiel's sense of overpowering awe (vv. 1–5)? 2. What does God say to Ezekiel (vv. 6–9)? 3. What is God's declared reason for trusting this vision to Ezekiel (vv. 10–12)? 4. What needs among the Israelites in exile would be met by the Lord's summary statement "This is where I will live among the Israelites forever" (v. 7)? 5. The law of the temple

(v. 12) is the principle of holiness. From what we have studied in Ezekiel thus far, what will dwelling with God require of those who hunger for God's presence?

 Applying the Word   1. Malcolm Muggeridge said, "Only the heavenly-minded are of real earthly use. Those who made the most difference in this world are precisely those who longed most for the next." Do you agree or disagree? Why?   **2.** The holiness of the temple was secured by courts, walls, barriers and restrictions. Now that the barriers have been removed in Christ, on what conditions may we draw near to God in his glory (Heb 7:24–25; 10:14; 1Pe 2:5)?   **3.** What conditions for drawing near God remain (Heb 10:19–25)?

Responding in Prayer Pray that you will know the Lord better, drawing near with a sincere heart and being prepared to put aside all that disgraces God's holiness.

Ezekiel 43:13—46:24

¹³"These are the measurements of the altar in long cubits, that cubit being a cubit^t and a handbreadth^u: Its gutter is a cubit deep and a cubit wide, with a rim of one span^v around the edge. And this is the height of the altar: ¹⁴From the gutter on the ground up to the lower ledge it is two cubits high and a cubit wide, and from the smaller ledge up to the larger ledge it is four cubits high and a cubit wide. ¹⁵The altar hearth is four cubits high, and four horns project upward from the hearth. ¹⁶The altar hearth is square, twelve cubits long and twelve cubits wide. ¹⁷The upper ledge also is square, fourteen cubits long and fourteen cubits wide, with a rim of half a cubit and a gutter of a cubit all around. The steps of the altar face east."

¹⁸Then he said to me, "Son of man, this is what the Sovereign Lord says: These will be the regulations for sacrificing burnt offerings and sprinkling blood upon the altar when it is built: ¹⁹You are to give a young bull as a sin offering to the priests, who are Levites, of the family of Zadok, who come near to minister before me, declares the Sovereign Lord. ²⁰You are to take some of its blood and put it on the four horns of the altar and on the four corners of the upper ledge and all around the rim, and so purify the altar and make atonement for it. ²¹You are to take the bull for the sin offering and burn it in the designated part of the temple area outside the sanctuary.

²²"On the second day you are to offer a male goat without defect for a sin offering, and the altar is to be purified as it was purified with the bull. ²³When you have finished purifying it, you are to offer a young bull and a ram from the flock, both without defect. ²⁴You are to offer them before the Lord, and the priests are to sprinkle salt on them and sacrifice them as a burnt offering to the Lord.

²⁵"For seven days you are to provide a male goat daily for a sin offering; you are also to provide a young bull and a ram from the flock, both without defect. ²⁶For seven days they are to make atonement for the altar and cleanse it; thus they will dedicate it. ²⁷At the end of these days, from the eighth day on, the priests are to present your burnt offerings and fellowship offerings^w on the altar. Then I will accept you, declares the Sovereign Lord."

44 Then the man brought me back to the outer gate of the sanctuary, the one facing east, and it was shut. ²The Lord said to me, "This gate is to remain shut. It must not be opened; no one may enter through it. It is to remain shut because the Lord, the God of Israel, has entered through it. ³The prince himself is the only one who may sit inside the gateway to eat in the presence of the Lord. He is to enter by way of the portico of the gateway and go out the same way."

⁴Then the man brought me by way of the north gate to the front of the temple. I looked and saw the glory of the Lord filling the temple of the Lord, and I fell facedown.

⁵The Lord said to me, "Son of man, look carefully, listen closely and give attention to everything I tell you concerning all the regulations regarding the temple of the Lord. Give attention to the entrance of the temple and all the exits of the sanctuary. ⁶Say to the rebellious house of Israel, 'This is what the Sovereign Lord says: Enough of your detestable practices, O house of Israel! ⁷In

---

^{t}13 The common cubit was about 1 1/2 feet (about 0.5 meter).
^{u}13 That is, about 3 inches (about 8 centimeters) ^{v}13 That is, about 9 inches (about 22 centimeters) ^{w}27 Traditionally *peace offerings*

addition to all your other detestable practices, you brought foreigners uncircumcised in heart and flesh into my sanctuary, desecrating my temple while you offered me food, fat and blood, and you broke my covenant. ⁸Instead of carrying out your duty in regard to my holy things, you put others in charge of my sanctuary. ⁹This is what the Sovereign Lᴏʀᴅ says: No foreigner uncircumcised in heart and flesh is to enter my sanctuary, not even the foreigners who live among the Israelites.

¹⁰ 'The Levites who went far from me when Israel went astray and who wandered from me after their idols must bear the consequences of their sin. ¹¹They may serve in my sanctuary, having charge of the gates of the temple and serving in it; they may slaughter the burnt offerings and sacrifices for the people and stand before the people and serve them. ¹²But because they served them in the presence of their idols and made the house of Israel fall into sin, therefore I have sworn with uplifted hand that they must bear the consequences of their sin, declares the Sovereign Lᴏʀᴅ. ¹³They are not to come near to serve me as priests or come near any of my holy things or my most holy offerings; they must bear the shame of their detestable practices. ¹⁴Yet I will put them in charge of the duties of the temple and all the work that is to be done in it.

¹⁵ 'But the priests, who are Levites and descendants of Zadok and who faithfully carried out the duties of my sanctuary when the Israelites went astray from me, are to come near to minister before me; they are to stand before me to offer sacrifices of fat and blood, declares the Sovereign Lᴏʀᴅ. ¹⁶They alone are to enter my sanctuary; they alone are to come near my table to minister before me and perform my service.

¹⁷ 'When they enter the gates of the inner court, they are to wear linen clothes; they must not wear any woolen garment while ministering at the gates of the inner court or inside the temple. ¹⁸They are to wear linen turbans on their heads and linen undergarments around their waists. They must not wear anything that makes them perspire. ¹⁹When they go out into the outer court where the people are, they are to take off the clothes they have been ministering in and are to leave them in the sacred rooms, and put on other clothes, so that they do not consecrate the people by means of their garments.

²⁰ 'They must not shave their heads or let their hair grow long, but they are to keep the hair of their heads trimmed. ²¹No priest is to drink wine when he enters the inner court. ²²They must not marry widows or divorced women; they may marry only virgins of Israelite descent or widows of priests. ²³They are to teach my people the difference between the holy and the common and show them how to distinguish between the unclean and the clean.

²⁴ 'In any dispute, the priests are to serve as judges and decide it according to my ordinances. They are to keep my laws and my decrees for all my appointed feasts, and they are to keep my Sabbaths holy.

²⁵ 'A priest must not defile himself by going near a dead person; however, if the dead person was his father or mother, son or daughter, brother or unmarried sister, then he may defile himself. ²⁶After he is cleansed, he must wait seven days. ²⁷On the day he goes into the inner court of the sanctuary to minister in the sanctuary, he is to offer a sin offering for himself, declares the Sovereign Lᴏʀᴅ.

²⁸ 'I am to be the only inheritance the priests have. You are to give them no possession in Israel; I will be their possession. ²⁹They will eat the grain offerings, the sin offerings and the guilt offerings; and everything in Israel devotedˣ to the Lᴏʀᴅ will belong to them. ³⁰The best of all the firstfruits and of all your special gifts will belong to the priests. You are to give them the first portion of your ground meal so that a blessing may rest on your household. ³¹The priests must not eat anything, bird or animal, found dead or torn by wild animals.

45

" 'When you allot the land as an inheritance, you are to present to the Lᴏʀᴅ a portion of the land as a sacred district, 25,000 cubits long and 20,000ʸ cubits wide; the entire area will be holy. ²Of this, a section 500 cubits square is to be for the sanctuary, with 50 cubits around it for open land. ³In the sacred district, measure off a section 25,000 cubitsᶻ long and 10,000 cubitsᵃ wide. In it will be the sanctuary, the Most Holy Place. ⁴It will be the sacred portion of the land for the priests, who minister in the sanctuary and who draw near to minister before the Lᴏʀᴅ. It will be a place for their houses as well as a holy place for the sanctu-

ˣ29 The Hebrew term refers to the irrevocable giving over of things or persons to the Lᴏʀᴅ.   ʸ1 Septuagint (see also verses 3 and 5 and 48:9); Hebrew *10,000*   ᶻ3 That is, about 7 miles (about 12 kilometers)   ᵃ3 That is, about 3 miles (about 5 kilometers) ary. ⁵An area 25,000 cubits long and 10,000 cubits wide will belong to the Levites, who serve in the temple, as their possession for towns to live in.^b

⁶" 'You are to give the city as its property an area 5,000 cubits wide and 25,000 cubits long, adjoining the sacred portion; it will belong to the whole house of Israel.

⁷" 'The prince will have the land bordering each side of the area formed by the sacred district and the property of the city. It will extend westward from the west side and eastward from the east side, running lengthwise from the western to the eastern border parallel to one of the tribal portions. ⁸This land will be his possession in Israel. And my princes will no longer oppress my people but will allow the house of Israel to possess the land according to their tribes.

⁹" 'This is what the Sovereign LORD says: You have gone far enough, O princes of Israel! Give up your violence and oppression and do what is just and right. Stop dispossessing my people, declares the Sovereign LORD. ¹⁰You are to use accurate scales, an accurate ephah^c and an accurate bath.^d ¹¹The ephah and the bath are to be the same size, the bath containing a tenth of a homer^e and the ephah a tenth of a homer; the homer is to be the standard measure for both. ¹²The shekel^f is to consist of twenty gerahs. Twenty shekels plus twenty-five shekels plus fifteen shekels equal one mina.^g

¹³" 'This is the special gift you are to offer: a sixth of an ephah from each homer of wheat and a sixth of an ephah from each homer of barley. ¹⁴The prescribed portion of oil, measured by the bath, is a tenth of a bath from each cor (which consists of ten baths or one homer, for ten baths are equivalent to a homer). ¹⁵Also one sheep is to be taken from every flock of two hundred from the well-watered pastures of Israel. These will be used for the grain offerings, burnt offerings and fellowship offerings^h to make atonement for the people, declares the Sovereign LORD. ¹⁶All the people of the land will participate in this special gift for the use of the prince in Israel. ¹⁷It will be the duty of the prince to provide the burnt offerings, grain offerings and drink offerings at the festivals, the New Moons and the Sabbaths—at all the appointed feasts of the house of Israel. He will provide the sin offerings, grain offerings, burnt offerings and fellowship offerings to make atonement for the house of Israel.

¹⁸" 'This is what the Sovereign LORD says: In the first month on the first day you are to take a young bull without defect and purify the sanctuary. ¹⁹The priest is to take some of the blood of the sin offering and put it on the doorposts of the temple, on the four corners of the upper ledge of the altar and on the gateposts of the inner court. ²⁰You are to do the same on the seventh day of the month for anyone who sins unintentionally or through ignorance; so you are to make atonement for the temple.

²¹" 'In the first month on the fourteenth day you are to observe the Passover, a feast lasting seven days, during which you shall eat bread made without yeast. ²²On that day the prince is to provide a bull as a sin offering for himself and for all the people of the land. ²³Every day during the seven days of the Feast he is to provide seven bulls and seven rams without defect as a burnt offering to the LORD, and a male goat for a sin offering. ²⁴He is to provide as a grain offering an ephah for each bull and an ephah for each ram, along with a hinⁱ of oil for each ephah.

²⁵" 'During the seven days of the Feast, which begins in the seventh month on the fifteenth day, he is to make the same provision for sin offerings, burnt offerings, grain offerings and oil.

46 " 'This is what the Sovereign LORD says: The gate of the inner court facing east is to be shut on the six working days, but on the Sabbath day and on the day of the New Moon it is to be opened. ²The prince is to enter from the outside through the portico of the gateway and stand by the gatepost. The priests are to sacrifice his burnt offering and his fellowship offerings.^j He is to worship at the threshold of the gateway and then go out, but the gate will not be shut until evening. ³On the Sabbaths and New Moons the people of the land are to worship in the presence of the LORD at the entrance to that gateway. ⁴The burnt offering the prince brings to the LORD on the Sabbath day is to be six male lambs and a ram, all without defect. ⁵The grain offering given with the ram is to be an ephah,^k and the grain offering with the lambs is to be as much as he pleases, along with a hinⁱ of

---

^b5 Septuagint; Hebrew *temple; they will have as their possession 20 rooms*   ^c10 An ephah was a dry measure.   ^d10 A bath was a liquid measure.   ^e11 A homer was a dry measure.   ^f12 A shekel weighed about 2/5 ounce (about 11.5 grams).   ^g12 That is, 60 shekels; the common mina was 50 shekels.   ^h15 Traditionally *peace offerings*; also in verse 17   ⁱ24,5 That is, probably about 4 quarts (about 4 liters)   ^j2 Traditionally *peace offerings*; also in verse 12   ^k5 That is, probably about 3/5 bushel (about 22 liters)

oil for each ephah. ⁶On the day of the New Moon he is to offer a young bull, six lambs and a ram, all without defect. ⁷He is to provide as a grain offering one ephah with the bull, one ephah with the ram, and with the lambs as much as he wants to give, along with a hin of oil with each ephah. ⁸When the prince enters, he is to go in through the portico of the gateway, and he is to come out the same way.

⁹" 'When the people of the land come before the Lᴏʀᴅ at the appointed feasts, whoever enters by the north gate to worship is to go out the south gate; and whoever enters by the south gate is to go out the north gate. No one is to return through the gate by which he entered, but each is to go out the opposite gate. ¹⁰The prince is to be among them, going in when they go in and going out when they go out.

¹¹" 'At the festivals and the appointed feasts, the grain offering is to be an ephah with a bull, an ephah with a ram, and with the lambs as much as one pleases, along with a hin of oil for each ephah. ¹²When the prince provides a freewill offering to the Lᴏʀᴅ—whether a burnt offering or fellowship offerings—the gate facing east is to be opened for him. He shall offer his burnt offering or his fellowship offerings as he does on the Sabbath day. Then he shall go out, and after he has gone out, the gate will be shut.

¹³" 'Every day you are to provide a year-old lamb without defect for a burnt offering to the Lᴏʀᴅ; morning by morning you shall provide it. ¹⁴You are also to provide with it morning by morning a grain offering, consisting of a sixth of an ephah with a third of a hin of oil to moisten the flour. The presenting of this grain offering to the Lᴏʀᴅ is a lasting ordinance. ¹⁵So the lamb and the grain offering and the oil shall be provided morning by morning for a regular burnt offering.

¹⁶" 'This is what the Sovereign Lᴏʀᴅ says: If the prince makes a gift from his inheritance to one of his sons, it will also belong to his descendants; it is to be their property by inheritance. ¹⁷If, however, he makes a gift from his inheritance to one of his servants, the servant may keep it until the year of freedom; then it will revert to the prince. His inheritance belongs to his sons only; it is theirs. ¹⁸The prince must not take any of the inheritance of the people, driving them off their property. He is to give his sons their inheritance out of his own property, so that none of my people will be separated from his property.' "

¹⁹Then the man brought me through the entrance at the side of the gate to the sacred rooms facing north, which belonged to the priests, and showed me a place at the western end. ²⁰He said to me, "This is the place where the priests will cook the guilt offering and the sin offering and bake the grain offering, to avoid bringing them into the outer court and consecrating the people."

²¹He then brought me to the outer court and led me around to its four corners, and I saw in each corner another court. ²²In the four corners of the outer court were enclosed[l] courts, forty cubits long and thirty cubits wide; each of the courts in the four corners was the same size. ²³Around the inside of each of the four courts was a ledge of stone, with places for fire built all around under the ledge. ²⁴He said to me, "These are the kitchens where those who minister at the temple will cook the sacrifices of the people."

---

[l]22 The meaning of the Hebrew for this word is uncertain.

---

16 / *Ezekiel 47:1–12*
The Vision of a Renewed Creation

GEORGE BERNARD SHAW'S character Don Juan said, "Heaven is all right, of course. But for meeting old friends and acquaintances, you can't beat hell." He thus shows a complete misunderstanding of the attractiveness of heaven. In reality, heaven is no mere "pie in the sky by and by" but our true homeland: a total life in a total environment with the presence of God as the center and source of everything. Ezekiel's vision of the ultimate Temple, the new Jerusalem and the Israelites resettled in the redesigned land of Israel was the ultimate Old Testament hope. But drawing heavily on the imagery of Ezekiel, in Revelation 21—22 John depicts a completely renewed creation.

Warming Up to God What fears and hopes do you have when you consider the future of planet Earth?

 Read Ezekiel 47:1-12.

47 The man brought me back to the entrance of the temple, and I saw water coming out from under the threshold of the temple toward the east (for the temple faced east). The water was coming down from under the south side of the temple, south of the altar. ²He then brought me out through the north gate and led me around the outside to the outer gate facing east, and the water was flowing from the south side.

³As the man went eastward with a measuring line in his hand, he measured off a thousand cubits[m] and then led me through water that was ankle-deep. ⁴He measured off another thousand cubits and led me through water that was knee-deep. He measured off another thousand and led me through water that was up to the waist. ⁵He measured off another thousand, but now it was a river that I could not cross, because the water had risen and was deep enough to swim in—a river that no one could cross. ⁶He asked me, "Son of man, do you see this?"

Then he led me back to the bank of the river.

⁷When I arrived there, I saw a great number of trees on each side of the river. ⁸He said to me, "This water flows toward the eastern region and goes down into the Arabah,[n] where it enters the Sea.[o] When it empties into the Sea,[o] the water there becomes fresh. ⁹Swarms of living creatures will live wherever the river flows. There will be large numbers of fish, because this water flows there and makes the salt water fresh; so where the river flows everything will live. ¹⁰Fishermen will stand along the shore; from En Gedi to En Eglaim there will be places for spreading nets. The fish will be of many kinds—like the fish of the Great Sea.[p] ¹¹But the swamps and marshes will not become fresh; they will be left for salt. ¹²Fruit trees of all kinds will grow on both banks of the river. Their leaves will not wither, nor will their fruit fail. Every month they will bear, because the water from the sanctuary flows to them. Their fruit will serve for food and their leaves for healing."

[m]3 That is, about 1,500 feet (about 450 meters)   [n]8 Or *the Jordan Valley*   [o]8 That is, the Dead Sea   [p]10 That is, the Mediterranean; also in verses 15, 19 and 20

Discovering the Word 1. This passage is part of a larger section (43:13—48:35) which describes the arrangements for temple worship, the prince, Levites and priests, the division of the land with a kind of "green belt" separating the holy and the profane. What different elements of God's creation are a part of this picture of the temple? 2. What significant truths are communicated by this exquisitely beautiful vision? 3. Read Revelation 22:1–3. How does John draw on Ezekiel's vision now that Christ has been fully and finally revealed? 4. What evidence do we have that John is not giving us a literal description of the renewed land but a highly symbolic one: a figurative account of a literal future reality?

Applying the Word 1. What difference should this vision of a renewed creation (and not merely a renewed worship center) make to our stewardship of the created world? 2. How has this study changed your attitude toward heaven as your ultimate homeland? 3. How has your study of Ezekiel affected what it means to you "to know the Lord"?

Responding in Prayer Jesus says, "I am making everything new" (Rev 21:5), words which Ezekiel would have welcomed with all his heart. Thank God that he is determined to renew you, his people, and the entire creation.

Ezekiel 47:13—48:35

¹³This is what the Sovereign LORD says: "These are the boundaries by which you are to divide the land for an inheritance among the twelve tribes of Israel, with two portions for Joseph. ¹⁴You are to divide it equally among them. Because I swore with uplifted hand to give it to your forefathers, this land will become your inheritance.

¹⁵"This is to be the boundary of the land:

"On the north side it will run from the Great Sea by the Hethlon road past Lebo⁹ Hamath to Zedad, ¹⁶Berothahʳ and Sibraim (which lies on the border between Damascus and Hamath), as far as Hazer Hatticon, which is on the border of Hauran. ¹⁷The boundary will extend from the sea to Hazar Enan,ˢ along the northern border of Damascus, with the border of Hamath to the north. This will be the north boundary.

¹⁸"On the east side the boundary will run between Hauran and Damascus, along the Jordan between Gilead and the land of Israel, to the eastern sea and as far as Tamar.ᵗ This will be the east boundary.

¹⁹"On the south side it will run from Tamar as far as the waters of Meribah Kadesh, then along the Wadi ˻of Egypt˼ to the Great Sea. This will be the south boundary.

²⁰"On the west side, the Great Sea will be the boundary to a point opposite Leboᵘ Hamath. This will be the west boundary.

²¹"You are to distribute this land among yourselves according to the tribes of Israel. ²²You are to allot it as an inheritance for yourselves and for the aliens who have settled among you and who have children. You are to consider them as native-born Israelites; along with you they are to be allotted an inheritance among the tribes of Israel. ²³In whatever tribe the alien settles, there you are to give him his inheritance," declares the Sovereign LORD.

48 "These are the tribes, listed by name: At the northern frontier, Dan will have one portion; it will follow the Hethlon road to Leboᵛ Hamath; Hazar Enan and the northern border of Damascus next to Hamath will be part of its border from the east side to the west side.

²"Asher will have one portion; it will border the territory of Dan from east to west.

³"Naphtali will have one portion; it will border the territory of Asher from east to west.

⁴"Manasseh will have one portion; it will border the territory of Naphtali from east to west.

⁵"Ephraim will have one portion; it will border the territory of Manasseh from east to west.

⁶"Reuben will have one portion; it will border the territory of Ephraim from east to west.

⁷"Judah will have one portion; it will border the territory of Reuben from east to west.

⁸"Bordering the territory of Judah from east to west will be the portion you are to present as a special gift. It will be 25,000 cubitsʷ wide, and its length from east to west will equal one of the tribal portions; the sanctuary will be in the center of it.

⁹"The special portion you are to offer to the LORD will be 25,000 cubits long and 10,000 cubitsˣ wide. ¹⁰This will be the sacred portion for the priests. It will be 25,000 cubits long on the north side, 10,000 cubits wide on the west side, 10,000 cubits wide on the east side and 25,000 cubits long on the south side. In the center of it will be the sanctuary of the LORD. ¹¹This will be for the consecrated priests, the Zadokites, who were faithful in serving me and did not go astray as the Levites did when the Israelites went astray. ¹²It will be a special gift to them from the sacred portion of the land, a most holy portion, bordering the territory of the Levites.

¹³"Alongside the territory of the priests, the Levites will have an allotment 25,000 cubits long and 10,000 cubits wide. Its total length will be 25,000 cubits and its width 10,000 cubits. ¹⁴They must not sell or exchange any of it. This is the best of the land and must not pass into other hands, because it is holy to the LORD.

¹⁵"The remaining area, 5,000 cubits wide and 25,000 cubits long, will be for the common use of the city, for houses and for pastureland. The city will be in the center of it ¹⁶and will have these measurements: the north side 4,500 cubits, the south side 4,500 cubits, the east side 4,500 cubits,

---

ᵍ15 Or *past the entrance to*   ʳ15,16 See Septuagint and Ezekiel 48:1; Hebrew *road to go into Zedad,* ¹⁶*Hamath, Berothah*   ˢ17 Hebrew *Enan,* a variant of *Enan*   ᵗ18 Septuagint and Syriac; Hebrew *Israel. You will measure to the eastern sea*   ᵘ20 Or *opposite the entrance to*   ᵛ1 Or *to the entrance to*   ʷ8 That is, about 7 miles (about 12 kilometers)   ˣ9 That is, about 3 miles (about 5 kilometers) and the west side 4,500 cubits. ¹⁷The pastureland for the city will be 250 cubits on the north, 250 cubits on the south, 250 cubits on the east, and 250 cubits on the west. ¹⁸What remains of the area, bordering on the sacred portion and running the length of it, will be 10,000 cubits on the east side and 10,000 cubits on the west side. Its produce will supply food for the workers of the city. ¹⁹The workers from the city who farm it will come from all the tribes of Israel. ²⁰The entire portion will be a square, 25,000 cubits on each side. As a special gift you will set aside the sacred portion, along with the property of the city.

²¹"What remains on both sides of the area formed by the sacred portion and the city property will belong to the prince. It will extend eastward from the 25,000 cubits of the sacred portion to the eastern border, and westward from the 25,000 cubits to the western border. Both these areas running the length of the tribal portions will belong to the prince, and the sacred portion with the temple sanctuary will be in the center of them. ²²So the property of the Levites and the property of the city will lie in the center of the area that belongs to the prince. The area belonging to the prince will lie between the border of Judah and the border of Benjamin.

²³"As for the rest of the tribes: Benjamin will have one portion; it will extend from the east side to the west side.

²⁴"Simeon will have one portion; it will border the territory of Benjamin from east to west.

²⁵"Issachar will have one portion; it will border the territory of Simeon from east to west.

²⁶"Zebulun will have one portion; it will border the territory of Issachar from east to west.

²⁷"Gad will have one portion; it will border the territory of Zebulun from east to west.

²⁸"The southern boundary of Gad will run south from Tamar to the waters of Meribah Kadesh, then along the Wadi ⌊of Egypt⌋ to the Great Sea.ʸ

²⁹"This is the land you are to allot as an inheritance to the tribes of Israel, and these will be their portions," declares the Sovereign LORD.

³⁰"These will be the exits of the city: Beginning on the north side, which is 4,500 cubits long, ³¹the gates of the city will be named after the tribes of Israel. The three gates on the north side will be the gate of Reuben, the gate of Judah and the gate of Levi.

³²"On the east side, which is 4,500 cubits long, will be three gates: the gate of Joseph, the gate of Benjamin and the gate of Dan.

³³"On the south side, which measures 4,500 cubits, will be three gates: the gate of Simeon, the gate of Issachar and the gate of Zebulun.

³⁴"On the west side, which is 4,500 cubits long, will be three gates: the gate of Gad, the gate of Asher and the gate of Naphtali.

³⁵"The distance all around will be 18,000 cubits.

"And the name of the city from that time on will be:

THE LORD IS THERE."

ʸ28 That is, the Mediterranean

Daniel

I n the sweep of great world empires, the impact of military conquest on individual people is usually overlooked. For example, the fall of Jerusalem into the hands of Babylon six hundred years before Christ probably did not make much of a stir in the ancient world. It was an event so insignificant to the Babylonians that it wasn't even worth mentioning in their official chronicles.

This was the first of three defeats that those in Judah would suffer from the king of Babylon, Nebuchadnezzar. He simply established Babylonian authority over Judah and left. On the surface not much changed. But behind the scenes some Jewish families and especially some young Jewish men were deeply affected. A number of gifted young men from the families of the Jewish nobility were taken from their homes to a new land. They were thrust into a new lifestyle. Every effort was made to break down their former convictions. They had to make a difficult choice. Would they hold to their faith and to a life of obedience to the Lord God, or would they flow into the new culture? It was a time of crisis for these young men, including the man we will be studying together—Daniel.

It is precisely at this point that we identify with Daniel. Regardless of how sheltered our existence has been as children or how often we were taken to Sunday school, there comes a time when we are thrust into a pagan world. We are confronted in a modern university or on the job or in society with a lifestyle radically different from what is taught in the Bible. At each turn we have to make difficult decisions. Will we obey God regardless of the consequences, or will we become part of the surrounding culture?

Daniel gives us practical and personal help in our struggle. He was a man who rose to a position of great power and prestige in the world system but who never compromised essential biblical principles. He shows us how to live a life of spiritual integrity in the crush of a secular world. Anyone who has been tempted to cave in to such pressures will learn much from him.

The Historical Framework of the Book

Israel's great king Solomon died in 931 B.C. Solomon's son Rehoboam foolishly provoked the leaders of the northern part of the nation, and they split off from the south. The northern tribes (ten of them) were called Israel. They existed until 722 B.C. when they were destroyed by the Assyrians. The southern two tribes were called Judah. God spared Judah until 586 B.C. when the Babylonian armies crushed the nation.

Nebuchadnezzar, the Babylonian commander, had come to Judah and Jerusalem twice before to put down Jewish rebellion against the authority of the empire. In 605 B.C. the Jews had been treated fairly well. A few young men (including Daniel) from the leading families had been taken as hostages, but the nation was left relatively undisturbed. In 597 B.C. the treatment was harsher. More people were deported to Babylon, including the king, Jehoiachin, and the prophet Ezekiel. Finally, in 586 B.C. the Babylonian patience was exhausted. The temple of God was burned, the walls of Jerusalem were broken down, and the people were virtually all killed or deported to Babylon. A summary of these three "conquests" can be found in 2 Kings 24—25 and 2 Chronicles 36.

God judged Judah for seventy years (from 605 B.C. to 536 B.C.)—a period called the Babylonian captivity. In 536 B.C. Babylon was defeated by a new world power, Persia. Cyrus, the Persian ruler, allowed the Jews to return to Judah.

Daniel's ministry in Babylon extended through the entire seventy-year Babylonian captivity and on into the reign of the Persians. Daniel lived well into his eighties or nineties! His primary prophetic focus was on the Gentiles. Even during the period of Judah's humiliation God's voice was heard in the courtroom of the emperor.

The Theological Focus of the Book

If you read the book of Daniel and see only a den of lions and strange visions, you have missed the main character in the book—a sovereign God! Daniel wrote this book not to glorify himself but to exalt the Lord. In every circumstance, in every crisis, Daniel points us to a God who is sovereignly at work in human history.

To say that God is sovereign simply means that nothing happens that is not planned or permitted by God. That is true of kingdoms, and it is true in our lives. Daniel's God is not a weak, frustrated deity who sits in heaven, wringing his hands, hoping everything will turn out all right. He is a God who orders all events according to his own will.

The book of Daniel is apocalyptic literature designed to speak to us in those times when God seems to be absent. The crushed people of Judah in Daniel's day were saying, "Where is God?" Daniel answers their questions by showing them that, even in a national catastrophe, God is working out his purpose and plan.

Daniel is able to resist compromise because of his relationship to a sovereign God. His obedience was simply an expression of God's kingship in his life. Daniel's courage to proclaim God's message came from his allegiance to a sovereign God. He saw the Lord as the one who was King over the earthly kings of Babylon. Be prepared, then, in these quiet times to see God in a new way! It will be a stretching, convicting but life-changing adventure.

Daniel and the Future

The second part of the book of Daniel is less well known and markedly more difficult to understand than the first part of the book. But it is no less profitable! In Daniel 1—6 the focus is primarily on the life and character of Daniel as a *man* of God. In Daniel 7—12 the focus is on Daniel as the *messenger* of God. These chapters consist of a series of visions given to Daniel—visions of the future of the Gentile nations and of the nation of Israel.

The visions of Daniel are a source of controversy among students of the Bible. The first area of controversy centers around the *integrity* of the visions. Liberal and critical scholars maintain that what is recorded in these chapters is not prophecy at all. Instead the writer wrote after the events (sometime in the second century B.C.) but cast what he wrote in the literary form of predictions given by God to a wise man in Babylon four hundred years earlier. According to this view, these chapters record *history* (a record of events that have already transpired) and not *prophecy* (a prediction of events in the future).

For those who accept the Bible as God's revelation, this controversy is settled by the claims of the book itself and by the defense of those claims mounted by evangelical scholars. We also have Jesus' own confirmation of Daniel. In Matthew 24:15 he referred to Daniel as a real person and called him "the prophet." Jesus quoted from these later chapters of Daniel and took them as authoritative revelation from God (see Mt 24:30; Lk 21:27).

The second area of controversy centers on their *interpretation*. Even those who agree on the historical integrity of Daniel disagree on how these visions should be interpreted. Our objective in this guide is not to defend one particular prophetic system but rather to try to understand what Daniel says. Therefore, while we will refer to other biblical passages, the emphasis of each study will be on what we can learn from this book about God's program for human history. Not all the answers about the future will be found in one part of God's truth. If we understand this part, however, we will have a better understanding of the whole as we attempt to develop a biblical framework for future events. We will gain far more from Daniel if we try to learn what is revealed here rather than seeking to defend a preconceived idea of what we want Daniel to say.

While Daniel 7—12 is not an easy section of Scripture, it is just as much the Word of God as the rest. Therefore, it is profitable to us for instruction and correction. After spending many hours in these chapters, I can tell you that they expand not only our understanding of God's program for the future of the world, but also our capacity to trust a sovereign God for our own future. His cosmic, eternal plan includes us!

Outline

1/ Daniel 1 ———————————————— *Have You Got What It Takes?*

2/ Daniel 2:1–30 ———————————— *A Disturbing Dream*

3/ Daniel 2:31–49 ——————————— *The Future from a Divine Perspective*

4/ Daniel 3 ———————————————— *Bow or Burn!*

5/ Daniel 4 ———————————————— *The Sovereign God Rules*

6/ Daniel 5 ———————————————— *The Handwriting on the Wall*

7/ Daniel 6 ———————————————— *On the Menu at the Lions' Club*

8/ Daniel 7 ———————————————— *A Prophetic Panorama*

9/ Daniel 8 ———————————————— *World Powers in Conflict*

10/ Daniel 9 ——————————————— *Prayer and Prediction*

11/ Daniel 10:1—11:35 ————————— *Another Vision of the Future*

12/ Daniel 11:36—12:13 ———————— *A Dark Day and a Brilliant End*

1 / *Daniel 1*
Have You Got What It Takes?

HOW DID YOU feel when you first moved away from home and were launched out on your own? Daniel and his friends were torn from their land and taken to Babylon as young men. They were probably only twelve to fourteen years old. In Babylon they were placed in a three-year training program to prepare them to oversee Jewish affairs in the Babylonian Empire. A crisis of conscience erupted when the first meal was served.

 Warming Up to God In what way are you currently feeling pressured by culture? Talk openly with God about your struggles.

 Read Daniel 1.

1 In the third year of the reign of Jehoiakim king of Judah, Nebuchadnezzar king of Babylon came to Jerusalem and besieged it. ²And the Lord delivered Jehoiakim king of Judah into his hand, along with some of the articles from the temple of God. These he carried off to the temple of his god in Babylonia*ᵃ* and put in the treasure house of his god.

³Then the king ordered Ashpenaz, chief of his court officials, to bring in some of the Israelites from the royal family and the nobility— ⁴young men without any physical defect, handsome, showing aptitude for every kind of learning, well informed, quick to understand, and qualified to serve in the king's palace. He was to teach them the language and literature of the Babylonians.*ᵇ* ⁵The king assigned them a daily amount of food and wine from the king's table. They were to be trained for three years, and after that they were to enter the king's service.

⁶Among these were some from Judah: Daniel, Hananiah, Mishael and Azariah. ⁷The chief official gave them new names: to Daniel, the name Belteshazzar; to Hananiah, Shadrach; to Mishael, Meshach; and to Azariah, Abednego.

⁸But Daniel resolved not to defile himself with the royal food and wine, and he asked the chief official for permission not to defile himself this way. ⁹Now God had caused the official to show favor and sympathy to Daniel, ¹⁰but the official told Daniel, "I am afraid of my lord the king, who has assigned your*ᶜ* food and drink. Why should he see you looking worse than the other young men your age? The king would then have my head because of you."

¹¹Daniel then said to the guard whom the chief official had appointed over Daniel, Hananiah, Mishael and Azariah, ¹²"Please test your servants for ten days: Give us nothing but vegetables to eat and water to drink. ¹³Then compare our appearance with that of the young men who eat the royal food, and treat your servants in accordance with what you see." ¹⁴So he agreed to this and tested them for ten days.

¹⁵At the end of the ten days they looked healthier and better nourished than any of the young men who ate the royal food. ¹⁶So the guard took away their choice food and the wine they were to drink and gave them vegetables instead.

¹⁷To these four young men God gave knowledge and understanding of all kinds of literature and learning. And Daniel could understand visions and dreams of all kinds.

¹⁸At the end of the time set by the king to bring them in, the chief official presented them to Nebuchadnezzar. ¹⁹The king talked with them, and he found none equal to Daniel, Hananiah, Mishael and Azariah; so they entered the king's service. ²⁰In every matter of wisdom and understanding about which the king questioned them, he found them ten times better than all the magicians and enchanters in his whole kingdom.

²¹And Daniel remained there until the first year of King Cyrus.

ᵃ2 Hebrew *Shinar*   *ᵇ4* Or *Chaldeans*   *ᶜ10* The Hebrew for *your* and *you* in this verse is plural.

Discovering the Word 1. What specific tactics were used to give these young Jews a new Babylonian orientation (vv. 3–7)? 2. Why were the food regulations of the Old Testament Law so important to Daniel (vv. 8–10)? 3. Do you think he was making a big issue out of a minor problem? Explain. 4. What steps did Daniel take to provide a creative alternative to the king's plan (vv. 11–14)? **5.** What factors combined to produce the exceptional ability of Daniel and his friends?

 Applying the Word 1. What criteria can Christians use today to determine which activities we will engage in and which we won't? **2.** What can we learn from Daniel's attitude and actions when our biblical convictions are challenged?

Responding in Prayer Pray for refreshment and insight regarding the struggles you face.

2 / *Daniel 2:1–30*
A Disturbing Dream

IN *THE VOYAGE of the Dawn Treader* C. S. Lewis describes an island where dreams come true. "'This is the island I've been looking for this long time,' said one of the sailors. . . . 'Fools!' said a man from the island, stamping his foot with rage. 'That's the sort of talk that brought me here, and I'd better have been drowned or never born.' " Suddenly every man began rowing as they never had before, "for it had taken everyone just that half-minute to remember certain dreams they had had—dreams that make you afraid to sleep again." In Daniel 2 Nebuchadnezzar had such a dream, a dream that was both troubling and true.

 Warming Up to God Have you ever had a dream that was so real that it almost seemed true? How did you feel when you woke up?

 Read Daniel 2:1–30.

2 In the second year of his reign, Nebuchadnezzar had dreams; his mind was troubled and he could not sleep. ²So the king summoned the magicians, enchanters, sorcerers and astrologers*d* to tell him what he had dreamed. When they came in and stood before the king, ³he said to them, "I have had a dream that troubles me and I want to know what it means.*e*"

⁴Then the astrologers answered the king in Aramaic,*f* "O king, live forever! Tell your servants the dream, and we will interpret it."

⁵The king replied to the astrologers, "This is what I have firmly decided: If you do not tell me what my dream was and interpret it, I will have you cut into pieces and your houses turned into piles of rubble. ⁶But if you tell me the dream and explain it, you will receive from me gifts and rewards and great honor. So tell me the dream and interpret it for me."

⁷Once more they replied, "Let the king tell his servants the dream, and we will interpret it."

⁸Then the king answered, "I am certain that you are trying to gain time, because you realize that this is what I have firmly decided: ⁹If you do

not tell me the dream, there is just one penalty for you. You have conspired to tell me misleading and wicked things, hoping the situation will change. So then, tell me the dream, and I will know that you can interpret it for me."

¹⁰The astrologers answered the king, "There is not a man on earth who can do what the king asks! No king, however great and mighty, has ever asked such a thing of any magician or enchanter or astrologer. ¹¹What the king asks is too difficult. No one can reveal it to the king except the gods, and they do not live among men."

¹²This made the king so angry and furious that he ordered the execution of all the wise men of Babylon. ¹³So the decree was issued to put the wise men to death, and men were sent to look for Daniel and his friends to put them to death.

¹⁴When Arioch, the commander of the king's guard, had gone out to put to death the wise men of Babylon, Daniel spoke to him with wisdom and tact. ¹⁵He asked the king's officer, "Why did the king issue such a harsh decree?" Arioch then explained the matter to Daniel. ¹⁶At this, Daniel

d2 Or *Chaldeans*; also in verses 4, 5 and 10   *e3* Or *was*   *f4* The text from here through chapter 7 is in Aramaic.

went in to the king and asked for time, so that he might interpret the dream for him.

¹⁷Then Daniel returned to his house and explained the matter to his friends Hananiah, Mishael and Azariah. ¹⁸He urged them to plead for mercy from the God of heaven concerning this mystery, so that he and his friends might not be executed with the rest of the wise men of Babylon. ¹⁹During the night the mystery was revealed to Daniel in a vision. Then Daniel praised the God of heaven ²⁰and said:

"Praise be to the name of God for ever and
    ever;
wisdom and power are his.
²¹He changes times and seasons;
    he sets up kings and deposes them.
He gives wisdom to the wise
    and knowledge to the discerning.
²²He reveals deep and hidden things;
    he knows what lies in darkness,
    and light dwells with him.
²³I thank and praise you, O God of my fathers:
    You have given me wisdom and power,
you have made known to me what we asked
    of you,
    you have made known to us the dream of
    the king."

²⁴Then Daniel went to Arioch, whom the king had appointed to execute the wise men of Babylon, and said to him, "Do not execute the wise men of Babylon. Take me to the king, and I will interpret his dream for him."

²⁵Arioch took Daniel to the king at once and said, "I have found a man among the exiles from Judah who can tell the king what his dream means."

²⁶The king asked Daniel (also called Belteshazzar), "Are you able to tell me what I saw in my dream and interpret it?"

²⁷Daniel replied, "No wise man, enchanter, magician or diviner can explain to the king the mystery he has asked about, ²⁸but there is a God in heaven who reveals mysteries. He has shown King Nebuchadnezzar what will happen in days to come. Your dream and the visions that passed through your mind as you lay on your bed are these:

²⁹"As you were lying there, O king, your mind turned to things to come, and the revealer of mysteries showed you what is going to happen. ³⁰As for me, this mystery has been revealed to me, not because I have greater wisdom than other living men, but so that you, O king, may know the interpretation and that you may understand what went through your mind.

Discovering the Word 1. Why do you think Nebuchadnezzar demanded to know the content of his dream as well as its interpretation (vv. 1–13)? 2. What can we learn from Daniel's example about how we should react to a personal crisis (vv. 14–18)? 3. What do verses 19–23 tell you about how to respond to answered prayer? 4. Verses 20–23 have often been called "Daniel's psalm." What aspects of God's character are emphasized in these verses? 5. How did Daniel's knowledge of God's character reveal itself in his remarks to King Nebuchadnezzar (vv. 27–30)?

 Applying the Word 1. It is common to feel like we are at the mercy of the people and circumstances around us. How should a knowledge of God's wisdom, sovereignty and power affect our view of the people and circumstances in our lives? 2. Three aspects of Daniel's spiritual maturity stand out in this chapter: his *wisdom* in response to a crisis, his *prayer* in response to a problem and his *praise* in response to God's work in his life. How can Daniel's example help you grow in one of these areas?

Responding in Prayer Pray that your character will be remade in God's image.

3 / *Daniel 2:31–49*
The Future from a Divine Perspective

DANIEL 2 IS one of the most amazing prophetic passages in the Bible. It was written in 600 B.C., yet it predicted the future rise and fall of four great world empires! Some of Daniel 2 may seem like so much ancient history to us, but it was all future to Daniel. This passage gives us a long look at the sovereign authority of God, who not only has a plan for human history but is also carrying out that plan perfectly.

 Warming Up to God What experiences in your life have led you to put your trust in God?

 Read Daniel 2:31–49.

31"You looked, O king, and there before you stood a large statue—an enormous, dazzling statue, awesome in appearance. 32The head of the statue was made of pure gold, its chest and arms of silver, its belly and thighs of bronze, 33its legs of iron, its feet partly of iron and partly of baked clay. 34While you were watching, a rock was cut out, but not by human hands. It struck the statue on its feet of iron and clay and smashed them. 35Then the iron, the clay, the bronze, the silver and the gold were broken to pieces at the same time and became like chaff on a threshing floor in the summer. The wind swept them away without leaving a trace. But the rock that struck the statue became a huge mountain and filled the whole earth.

36"This was the dream, and now we will interpret it to the king. 37You, O king, are the king of kings. The God of heaven has given you dominion and power and might and glory; 38in your hands he has placed mankind and the beasts of the field and the birds of the air. Wherever they live, he has made you ruler over them all. You are that head of gold.

39"After you, another kingdom will rise, inferior to yours. Next, a third kingdom, one of bronze, will rule over the whole earth. 40Finally, there will be a fourth kingdom, strong as iron—for iron breaks and smashes everything—and as iron breaks things to pieces, so it will crush and break all the others. 41Just as you saw that the feet and toes were partly of baked clay and partly of iron, so this will be a divided kingdom; yet it will have some of the strength of iron in it, even as

you saw iron mixed with clay. 42As the toes were partly iron and partly clay, so this kingdom will be partly strong and partly brittle. 43And just as you saw the iron mixed with baked clay, so the people will be a mixture and will not remain united, any more than iron mixes with clay.

44"In the time of those kings, the God of heaven will set up a kingdom that will never be destroyed, nor will it be left to another people. It will crush all those kingdoms and bring them to an end, but it will itself endure forever. 45This is the meaning of the vision of the rock cut out of a mountain, but not by human hands—a rock that broke the iron, the bronze, the clay, the silver and the gold to pieces.

"The great God has shown the king what will take place in the future. The dream is true and the interpretation is trustworthy."

46Then King Nebuchadnezzar fell prostrate before Daniel and paid him honor and ordered that an offering and incense be presented to him. 47The king said to Daniel, "Surely your God is the God of gods and the Lord of kings and a revealer of mysteries, for you were able to reveal this mystery."

48Then the king placed Daniel in a high position and lavished many gifts on him. He made him ruler over the entire province of Babylon and placed him in charge of all its wise men. 49Moreover, at Daniel's request the king appointed Shadrach, Meshach and Abednego administrators over the province of Babylon, while Daniel himself remained at the royal court.

Discovering the Word 1. As you think about Daniel's description of the dream in verses 31–35 (not the interpretation of the dream in later verses), what was it about the dream that may have caused Nebuchadnezzar to be troubled (see v. 1)? 2. The interpretation of the dream begins in verse 36. Why do you think God referred to Nebuchadnezzar as the head of gold (vv. 36–38)? 3. While Daniel does not say who the future kingdoms are, we can identify them as Medo-Persia (silver), Greece (bronze) and Rome (iron). What does Daniel say about the relative nature and power of these kingdoms (vv. 36–43)? 4. What is the significance of the mixture of clay (ceramic) with iron (vv. 41–43)? 5. Verse 44 says that "in the time of those kings [the ones represented by the toes] the God of heaven will set up a kingdom." What characteristics of the kingdom of God are described in verses 44–45?

Applying the Word 1. What does this chapter teach you about God's activity in the course of human history? 2. How can the portrait of God in this chapter encourage us to trust God with our life and circumstances?

Responding in Prayer Take time to thank God for his control over the present and the future.

4 / *Daniel 3*
Bow or Burn!

THE STORY OF Shadrach, Meshach and Abednego in the fiery furnace ranks with Daniel in the lion's den and David and Goliath as one of the best-known and most exciting Bible stories. One of the problems with a story that's so familiar is that we tend to forget that it really happened. It is not a myth. It is history! It is also a very practical chapter for men and women who are trying to live for God in a secular society. We face the same pressure these three faced—the pressure to compromise what is right before God in order to be accepted by others.

Warming Up to God In what ways are you tempted to compromise your faith in order to be accepted by others?

Read Daniel 3.

3 King Nebuchadnezzar made an image of gold, ninety feet high and nine feet[g] wide, and set it up on the plain of Dura in the province of Babylon. ²He then summoned the satraps, prefects, governors, advisers, treasurers, judges, magistrates and all the other provincial officials to come to the dedication of the image he had set up. ³So the satraps, prefects, governors, advisers, treasurers, judges, magistrates and all the other provincial officials assembled for the dedication of the image that King Nebuchadnezzar had set up, and they stood before it.

⁴Then the herald loudly proclaimed, "This is what you are commanded to do, O peoples, nations and men of every language: ⁵As soon as you hear the sound of the horn, flute, zither, lyre, harp, pipes and all kinds of music, you must fall down and worship the image of gold that King Nebuchadnezzar has set up. ⁶Whoever does not

fall down and worship will immediately be thrown into a blazing furnace."

⁷Therefore, as soon as they heard the sound of the horn, flute, zither, lyre, harp and all kinds of music, all the peoples, nations and men of every language fell down and worshiped the image of gold that King Nebuchadnezzar had set up.

⁸At this time some astrologers[h] came forward and denounced the Jews. ⁹They said to King Nebuchadnezzar, "O king, live forever! ¹⁰You have issued a decree, O king, that everyone who hears the sound of the horn, flute, zither, lyre, harp, pipes and all kinds of music must fall down and worship the image of gold, ¹¹and that whoever does not fall down and worship will be thrown into a blazing furnace. ¹²But there are some Jews whom you have set over the affairs of the province of Babylon—Shadrach, Meshach and Abed-

g1 Aramaic sixty cubits high and six cubits wide *(about 27 meters high and 2.7 meters wide)*   *h8 Or* Chaldeans nego—who pay no attention to you, O king. They neither serve your gods nor worship the image of gold you have set up."

¹³Furious with rage, Nebuchadnezzar summoned Shadrach, Meshach and Abednego. So these men were brought before the king, ¹⁴and Nebuchadnezzar said to them, "Is it true, Shadrach, Meshach and Abednego, that you do not serve my gods or worship the image of gold I have set up? ¹⁵Now when you hear the sound of the horn, flute, zither, lyre, harp, pipes and all kinds of music, if you are ready to fall down and worship the image I made, very good. But if you do not worship it, you will be thrown immediately into a blazing furnace. Then what god will be able to rescue you from my hand?"

¹⁶Shadrach, Meshach and Abednego replied to the king, "O Nebuchadnezzar, we do not need to defend ourselves before you in this matter. ¹⁷If we are thrown into the blazing furnace, the God we serve is able to save us from it, and he will rescue us from your hand, O king. ¹⁸But even if he does not, we want you to know, O king, that we will not serve your gods or worship the image of gold you have set up."

¹⁹Then Nebuchadnezzar was furious with Shadrach, Meshach and Abednego, and his attitude toward them changed. He ordered the furnace heated seven times hotter than usual ²⁰and commanded some of the strongest soldiers in his army to tie up Shadrach, Meshach and Abednego and throw them into the blazing furnace. ²¹So these men, wearing their robes, trousers, turbans and other clothes, were bound and thrown into the blazing furnace. ²²The king's command was so urgent and the furnace so hot that the flames of the fire killed the soldiers who took up Shadrach, Meshach and Abednego, ²³and these three men, firmly tied, fell into the blazing furnace.

²⁴Then King Nebuchadnezzar leaped to his feet in amazement and asked his advisers, "Weren't there three men that we tied up and threw into the fire?"

They replied, "Certainly, O king."

²⁵He said, "Look! I see four men walking around in the fire, unbound and unharmed, and the fourth looks like a son of the gods."

²⁶Nebuchadnezzar then approached the opening of the blazing furnace and shouted, "Shadrach, Meshach and Abednego, servants of the Most High God, come out! Come here!"

So Shadrach, Meshach and Abednego came out of the fire, ²⁷and the satraps, prefects, governors and royal advisers crowded around them. They saw that the fire had not harmed their bodies, nor was a hair of their heads singed; their robes were not scorched, and there was no smell of fire on them.

²⁸Then Nebuchadnezzar said, "Praise be to the God of Shadrach, Meshach and Abednego, who has sent his angel and rescued his servants! They trusted in him and defied the king's command and were willing to give up their lives rather than serve or worship any god except their own God. ²⁹Therefore I decree that the people of any nation or language who say anything against the God of Shadrach, Meshach and Abednego be cut into pieces and their houses be turned into piles of rubble, for no other god can save in this way."

³⁰Then the king promoted Shadrach, Meshach and Abednego in the province of Babylon.

Discovering the Word 1. What do you think motivated Nebuchadnezzar to build this image of gold (vv. 1–7)? 2. Why do you think the astrologers reported the disobedience of Shadrach, Meshach and Abednego to Nebuchadnezzar (vv. 8–12)? 3. What temptations do you think Shadrach, Meshach and Abednego faced when they were brought before the king (vv. 13–15)? 4. What impresses you most about their response to these temptations (vv. 16–18)? 5. As you look at Nebuchadnezzar's response (vv. 13–15, 19–23), what evidence do you see that his basic conflict was with God rather than with these three men? 6. What specific actions did God take to bring assurance to the three men and to demonstrate his power to Nebuchadnezzar (vv. 24–30)?

Applying the Word 1. Some Christians claim that pain or sickness or trial are always the result of sin or lack of faith. How would you respond to that claim in light of this passage? 2. As you look back over this chapter, what lessons about the risks and rewards of obedience are most significant to you personally?

Responding in Prayer What commitments can you make to God today that will prepare you to face the pressures of a secular world? Speak to the Lord with honesty.

5 / *Daniel 4*
The Sovereign God Rules

WE ARE NOT accustomed to hearing our national leaders describe their sins in public. That's why Daniel 4 is such an unusual chapter! Nebuchadnezzar, the great, proud, powerful king of Babylon, writes a letter to the world describing in detail how God humiliated him for seven years and then graciously restored him.

Warming Up to God When have you been publicly humiliated?

Read Daniel 4.

4King Nebuchadnezzar,

To the peoples, nations and men of every language, who live in all the world:

May you prosper greatly!

²It is my pleasure to tell you about the miraculous signs and wonders that the Most High God has performed for me.

³How great are his signs,
    how mighty his wonders!
His kingdom is an eternal kingdom;
    his dominion endures from generation
        to generation.

⁴I, Nebuchadnezzar, was at home in my palace, contented and prosperous. ⁵I had a dream that made me afraid. As I was lying in my bed, the images and visions that passed through my mind terrified me. ⁶So I commanded that all the wise men of Babylon be brought before me to interpret the dream for me. ⁷When the magicians, enchanters, astrologersⁱ and diviners came, I told them the dream, but they could not interpret it for me. ⁸Finally, Daniel came into my presence and I told him the dream. (He is called Belteshazzar, after the name of my god, and the spirit of the holy gods is in him.)

⁹I said, "Belteshazzar, chief of the magicians, I know that the spirit of the holy gods is in you, and no mystery is too difficult for you. Here is my dream; interpret it for me. ¹⁰These are the visions I saw while lying in my bed: I looked, and there before me stood a tree in the middle of the land. Its height was enormous. ¹¹The tree grew large and strong and its top touched the sky; it was visible to the ends of the earth. ¹²Its leaves were beautiful, its fruit abundant, and on it was food for all. Under it the beasts of the field found shelter, and the birds of the air lived in its branches; from it every creature was fed.

¹³"In the visions I saw while lying in my bed, I looked, and there before me was a messenger,ʲ a holy one, coming down from heaven. ¹⁴He called in a loud voice: 'Cut down the tree and trim off its branches; strip off its leaves and scatter its fruit. Let the animals flee from under it and the birds from its branches. ¹⁵But let the stump and its roots, bound with iron and bronze, remain in the ground, in the grass of the field.

" 'Let him be drenched with the dew of heaven, and let him live with the animals among the plants of the earth. ¹⁶Let his mind be changed from that of a man and let him be given the mind of an animal, till seven timesᵏ pass by for him.

¹⁷" 'The decision is announced by messengers, the holy ones declare the verdict, so that the living may know that the Most High is sovereign over the kingdoms of men and gives them to anyone he wishes and sets over them the lowliest of men.'

¹⁸"This is the dream that I, King Nebuchadnezzar, had. Now, Belteshazzar, tell me what it means, for none of the wise men in my kingdom can interpret it for me. But you can, because the spirit of the holy gods is in you."

¹⁹Then Daniel (also called Belteshazzar) was greatly perplexed for a time, and his thoughts terrified him. So the king said,

ⁱ7 Or *Chaldeans*   ʲ13 Or *watchman*; also in verses 17 and 23
ᵏ16 Or *years*; also in verses 23, 25 and 32

"Belteshazzar, do not let the dream or its meaning alarm you."

Belteshazzar answered, "My lord, if only the dream applied to your enemies and its meaning to your adversaries! 20The tree you saw, which grew large and strong, with its top touching the sky, visible to the whole earth, 21with beautiful leaves and abundant fruit, providing food for all, giving shelter to the beasts of the field, and having nesting places in its branches for the birds of the air— 22you, O king, are that tree! You have become great and strong; your greatness has grown until it reaches the sky, and your dominion extends to distant parts of the earth.

23"You, O king, saw a messenger, a holy one, coming down from heaven and saying, 'Cut down the tree and destroy it, but leave the stump, bound with iron and bronze, in the grass of the field, while its roots remain in the ground. Let him be drenched with the dew of heaven; let him live like the wild animals, until seven times pass by for him.'

24"This is the interpretation, O king, and this is the decree the Most High has issued against my lord the king: 25You will be driven away from people and will live with the wild animals; you will eat grass like cattle and be drenched with the dew of heaven. Seven times will pass by for you until you acknowledge that the Most High is sovereign over the kingdoms of men and gives them to anyone he wishes. 26The command to leave the stump of the tree with its roots means that your kingdom will be restored to you when you acknowledge that Heaven rules. 27Therefore, O king, be pleased to accept my advice: Renounce your sins by doing what is right, and your wickedness by being kind to the oppressed. It may be that then your prosperity will continue."

28All this happened to King Nebuchadnezzar. 29Twelve months later, as the king was walking on the roof of the royal palace of Babylon, 30he said, "Is not this the great Bab-

ylon I have built as the royal residence, by my mighty power and for the glory of my majesty?"

31The words were still on his lips when a voice came from heaven, "This is what is decreed for you, King Nebuchadnezzar: Your royal authority has been taken from you. 32You will be driven away from people and will live with the wild animals; you will eat grass like cattle. Seven times will pass by for you until you acknowledge that the Most High is sovereign over the kingdoms of men and gives them to anyone he wishes."

33Immediately what had been said about Nebuchadnezzar was fulfilled. He was driven away from people and ate grass like cattle. His body was drenched with the dew of heaven until his hair grew like the feathers of an eagle and his nails like the claws of a bird.

34At the end of that time, I, Nebuchadnezzar, raised my eyes toward heaven, and my sanity was restored. Then I praised the Most High; I honored and glorified him who lives forever.

His dominion is an eternal dominion;
　his kingdom endures from generation to
　　generation.
35All the peoples of the earth
　are regarded as nothing.
He does as he pleases
　with the powers of heaven
　and the peoples of the earth.
No one can hold back his hand
　or say to him: "What have you done?"

36At the same time that my sanity was restored, my honor and splendor were returned to me for the glory of my kingdom. My advisers and nobles sought me out, and I was restored to my throne and became even greater than before. 37Now I, Nebuchadnezzar, praise and exalt and glorify the King of heaven, because everything he does is right and all his ways are just. And those who walk in pride he is able to humble.

All Proud will be humbled

📣 **Discovering the Word** 1. How does Nebuchadnezzar's proclamation in 4:1–3 differ from what he expressed in Daniel 3:28–29? 2. As you read Nebuchadnezzar's description of the dream (vv. 9–18), what aspects of the dream might have caused the king to be "terrified" (v. 5)? 3. Three times in this chapter God's purpose for giving the dream is repeated (vv. 17, 25, 32). Why do you think God was so intent on impressing Nebuchadnezzar with his sovereign authority instead of his grace or his love? 4. If Nebuchadnezzar had repented of his sins as Daniel advised, do you think God would have withheld his judgment, or was his decision irrevocable at this point (vv. 24–27)? Explain.   5. What specific steps did God take to humble Nebuchadnezzar (vv. 31–33)?

 Applying the Word 1. What does Nebuchadnezzar's experience teach us about the dangers of pride? 2. Sometimes we gain fresh insight into God's character and ways as we wrestle with a hard aspect of God's truth. What is the hardest thing about this chapter for you to accept? 3. What does that hard lesson teach you about how God works in our lives to bring us to Christlikeness?

Responding in Prayer It can be scary to have God at work in our lives. Talk to God about how you are feeling about his role in your life.

6 / *Daniel 5*
The Handwriting on the Wall

NEVER UNDERESTIMATE THE influence of one godly life! As chapter 5 opens, Daniel is an old man—more than eighty years old. The successors to Nebuchadnezzar's throne have ignored him. He has been shuffled off into some obscure office in the Babylonian bureaucracy. But when the king finds himself in trouble, he calls for God's man. Daniel shows us how to stand for God over the long haul.

 Warming Up to God Whose life has been an example to you? Thank God for that person's role in your life.

 Read Daniel 5.

5 King Belshazzar gave a great banquet for a thousand of his nobles and drank wine with them. ²While Belshazzar was drinking his wine, he gave orders to bring in the gold and silver goblets that Nebuchadnezzar his father[l] had taken from the temple in Jerusalem, so that the king and his nobles, his wives and his concubines might drink from them. ³So they brought in the gold goblets that had been taken from the temple of God in Jerusalem, and the king and his nobles, his wives and his concubines drank from them. ⁴As they drank the wine, they praised the gods of gold and silver, of bronze, iron, wood and stone.

⁵Suddenly the fingers of a human hand appeared and wrote on the plaster of the wall, near the lampstand in the royal palace. The king watched the hand as it wrote. ⁶His face turned pale and he was so frightened that his knees knocked together and his legs gave way.

⁷The king called out for the enchanters, astrologers[m] and diviners to be brought and said to these wise men of Babylon, "Whoever reads this writing and tells me what it means will be clothed in purple and have a gold chain placed around his

neck, and he will be made the third highest ruler in the kingdom."

⁸Then all the king's wise men came in, but they could not read the writing or tell the king what it meant. ⁹So King Belshazzar became even more terrified and his face grew more pale. His nobles were baffled.

¹⁰The queen,[n] hearing the voices of the king and his nobles, came into the banquet hall. "O king, live forever!" she said. "Don't be alarmed! Don't look so pale! ¹¹There is a man in your kingdom who has the spirit of the holy gods in him. In the time of your father he was found to have insight and intelligence and wisdom like that of the gods. King Nebuchadnezzar your father—your father the king, I say—appointed him chief of the magicians, enchanters, astrologers and diviners. ¹²This man Daniel, whom the king called Belteshazzar, was found to have a keen mind and knowledge and understanding, and also the ability to interpret dreams, explain riddles and solve difficult problems. Call for Daniel, and he will tell you what the writing means."

¹³So Daniel was brought before the king, and

---

[l]2 Or *ancestor*; or *predecessor*; also in verses 11, 13 and 18   [m]7 Or *Chaldeans*; also in verse 11   [n]10 Or *queen mother*

the king said to him, "Are you Daniel, one of the exiles my father the king brought from Judah? ¹⁴I have heard that the spirit of the gods is in you and that you have insight, intelligence and outstanding wisdom. ¹⁵The wise men and enchanters were brought before me to read this writing and tell me what it means, but they could not explain it. ¹⁶Now I have heard that you are able to give interpretations and to solve difficult problems. If you can read this writing and tell me what it means, you will be clothed in purple and have a gold chain placed around your neck, and you will be made the third highest ruler in the kingdom."

¹⁷Then Daniel answered the king, "You may keep your gifts for yourself and give your rewards to someone else. Nevertheless, I will read the writing for the king and tell him what it means.

¹⁸"O king, the Most High God gave your father Nebuchadnezzar sovereignty and greatness and glory and splendor. ¹⁹Because of the high position he gave him, all the peoples and nations and men of every language dreaded and feared him. Those the king wanted to put to death, he put to death; those he wanted to spare, he spared; those he wanted to promote, he promoted; and those he wanted to humble, he humbled. ²⁰But when his heart became arrogant and hardened with pride, he was deposed from his royal throne and stripped of his glory. ²¹He was driven away from people and given the mind of an animal; he lived with the wild donkeys and ate grass like cattle; and his body was drenched with the dew of heaven, until he acknowledged that the Most High God is sovereign over the kingdoms of men and sets over them anyone he wishes.

²²"But you his son,ᵒ O Belshazzar, have not humbled yourself, though you knew all this. ²³Instead, you have set yourself up against the Lord of heaven. You had the goblets from his temple brought to you, and you and your nobles, your wives and your concubines drank wine from them. You praised the gods of silver and gold, of bronze, iron, wood and stone, which cannot see or hear or understand. But you did not honor the God who holds in his hand your life and all your ways. ²⁴Therefore he sent the hand that wrote the inscription.

²⁵"This is the inscription that was written:

MENE, MENE, TEKEL, PARSINᵖ

²⁶"This is what these words mean:

Mene�q: God has numbered the days of your reign and brought it to an end.
²⁷*Tekel*ʳ: You have been weighed on the scales and found wanting.
²⁸*Peres*ˢ: Your kingdom is divided and given to the Medes and Persians."

²⁹Then at Belshazzar's command, Daniel was clothed in purple, a gold chain was placed around his neck, and he was proclaimed the third highest ruler in the kingdom.

³⁰That very night Belshazzar, king of the Babylonians,ᵗ was slain, ³¹and Darius the Mede took over the kingdom, at the age of sixty-two.

ᵒ22 Or *descendant*; or *successor*   ᵖ25 Aramaic UPARSIN (that is, AND PARSIN)   q26 *Mene* can mean *numbered* or *mina* (a unit of money).   ʳ27 *Tekel* can mean *weighed* or *shekel*.   ˢ28 *Peres* (the singular of *Parsin*) can mean *divided* or *Persia* or *a half mina* or *a half shekel*.   ᵗ30 Or *Chaldeans*

 Discovering the Word 1. The chapter begins with a party! As you read verses 1–4, what actions and attitudes on the part of Belshazzar and his guests do you think would have provoked the Lord's anger? 2. Three times Daniel has recorded the failure of the "wise men" of Babylon to interpret the message of God. What point is Daniel trying to make (vv. 7–9)? 3. Why do you think Daniel reminds Belshazzar of how God dealt with Nebuchadnezzar (vv. 18–21)? 4. What insights into the nature of Belshazzar's sins can you find in verses 22–23? 5. Based on what is recorded in verses 29–30, do you think Belshazzar accepted Daniel's interpretation as the authoritative message of the true God? Explain. 6. How has this chapter demonstrated that seventy years of life under Babylon's influence had not broken down Daniel's convictions?

 Applying the Word 1. In what areas might you be tempted to be proud or arrogant? 2. How can Daniel's words to Belshazzar help you become more humble and thankful to God (vv. 18–24)?

Responding in Prayer Ask God to make you an influencer.

7 / *Daniel 6*
On the Menu at the Lions' Club

DANIEL IN THE lions' den is a story that we never get tired of hearing. As a child, I was impressed by this story because Daniel was not thrown into the lion's den for being bad. He was thrown in for being godly! That is an important point to keep in mind as we study. We usually expect that when we do wrong we ought to be punished, and when we do right we ought to be praised. That is certainly the ideal, but it doesn't always work out that way. Sometimes those who do wrong are rewarded, and those who do right are persecuted. This chapter demonstrates that godliness can be costly.

 Warming Up to God How would you feel if the people you work with decided to watch everything about your public and private life?

 Read Daniel 6.

6 It pleased Darius to appoint 120 satraps to rule throughout the kingdom, ²with three administrators over them, one of whom was Daniel. The satraps were made accountable to them so that the king might not suffer loss. ³Now Daniel so distinguished himself among the administrators and the satraps by his exceptional qualities that the king planned to set him over the whole kingdom. ⁴At this, the administrators and the satraps tried to find grounds for charges against Daniel in his conduct of government affairs, but they were unable to do so. They could find no corruption in him, because he was trustworthy and neither corrupt nor negligent. ⁵Finally these men said, "We will never find any basis for charges against this man Daniel unless it has something to do with the law of his God."

⁶So the administrators and the satraps went as a group to the king and said: "O King Darius, live forever! ⁷The royal administrators, prefects, satraps, advisers and governors have all agreed that the king should issue an edict and enforce the decree that anyone who prays to any god or man during the next thirty days, except to you, O king, shall be thrown into the lions' den. ⁸Now, O king, issue the decree and put it in writing so that it cannot be altered—in accordance with the laws of the Medes and Persians, which cannot be repealed." ⁹So King Darius put the decree in writing.

¹⁰Now when Daniel learned that the decree had been published, he went home to his upstairs room where the windows opened toward Jerusalem. Three times a day he got down on his knees and prayed, giving thanks to his God, just as he had done before. ¹¹Then these men went as a group and found Daniel praying and asking God for help. ¹²So they went to the king and spoke to him about his royal decree: "Did you not publish a decree that during the next thirty days anyone who prays to any god or man except to you, O king, would be thrown into the lions' den?"

The king answered, "The decree stands—in accordance with the laws of the Medes and Persians, which cannot be repealed."

¹³Then they said to the king, "Daniel, who is one of the exiles from Judah, pays no attention to you, O king, or to the decree you put in writing. He still prays three times a day." ¹⁴When the king heard this, he was greatly distressed; he was determined to rescue Daniel and made every effort until sundown to save him.

¹⁵Then the men went as a group to the king and said to him, "Remember, O king, that according to the law of the Medes and Persians no decree or edict that the king issues can be changed."

¹⁶So the king gave the order, and they brought Daniel and threw him into the lions' den. The king said to Daniel, "May your God, whom you serve continually, rescue you!"

¹⁷A stone was brought and placed over the mouth of the den, and the king sealed it with his own signet ring and with the rings of his nobles, so that Daniel's situation might not be changed. ¹⁸Then the king returned to his palace and spent the night without eating and without any entertainment being brought to him. And he could not sleep.

¹⁹At the first light of dawn, the king got up and hurried to the lions' den. ²⁰When he came near

the den, he called to Daniel in an anguished voice, "Daniel, servant of the living God, has your God, whom you serve continually, been able to rescue you from the lions?"

²¹Daniel answered, "O king, live forever! ²²My God sent his angel, and he shut the mouths of the lions. They have not hurt me, because I was found innocent in his sight. Nor have I ever done any wrong before you, O king."

²³The king was overjoyed and gave orders to lift Daniel out of the den. And when Daniel was lifted from the den, no wound was found on him, because he had trusted in his God.

²⁴At the king's command, the men who had falsely accused Daniel were brought in and thrown into the lions' den, along with their wives and children. And before they reached the floor of the den, the lions overpowered them and crushed all their bones.

²⁵Then King Darius wrote to all the peoples,

nations and men of every language throughout the land:

"May you prosper greatly!

²⁶"I issue a decree that in every part of my kingdom people must fear and reverence the God of Daniel.

"For he is the living God
    and he endures forever;
his kingdom will not be destroyed,
    his dominion will never end.
²⁷He rescues and he saves;
    he performs signs and wonders
    in the heavens and on the earth.
He has rescued Daniel
    from the power of the lions."

²⁸So Daniel prospered during the reign of Darius and the reign of Cyrus ᵘ the Persian.

ᵘ28 Or Darius, that is, the reign of Cyrus

Discovering the Word 1. What do we learn about Daniel's character from the results of the investigation by his enemies (vv. 1–5)? 2. King Darius willingly signed the document prohibiting prayer to anyone but him (vv. 6–9). How does this action resemble the sins of his predecessors? 3. What specific evidences do you find in verse 10 of Daniel's consistent obedience to God? 4. How do verses 14–20 underscore the impact Daniel's life had on the king? 5. In what ways would the miracle Darius witnessed have reinforced Daniel's personal example (vv. 21–24)?

Applying the Word 1. How has Daniel encouraged you to be a more Christlike example to those around you? 2. Think back over the first six chapters. How can the fact that God "holds in his hand your life and all your ways" (5:23) help you to honor and obey him as Daniel did?

Responding in Prayer Make your prayer one of praise for the qualities of God you have been learning about like Daniel did (vv. 25–27).

---

8 / *Daniel 7*
A Prophetic Panorama

HAVE YOU EVER wondered if there was any order or plan to the course of human history? Nations and empires rise, expand, degenerate and fall. Leaders live, rule and die. But where is everything headed? Some in despair say that human history is going nowhere. Others try to sound optimistic and say that history is going wherever the human race takes it. Christians who know their God and his Word, however, realize that history does have a plan. That's the assurance God gave Daniel in what at first appeared to be a terrifying night vision!

Warming Up to God What questions do you have today about God's plan for you or for the world? Present your questions to the Lord, and ask him to use this text to give you greater understanding.

Read Daniel 7.

7 In the first year of Belshazzar king of Babylon, Daniel had a dream, and visions passed through his mind as he was lying on his bed. He wrote down the substance of his dream.

²Daniel said: "In my vision at night I looked, and there before me were the four winds of heaven churning up the great sea. ³Four great beasts, each different from the others, came up out of the sea.

⁴"The first was like a lion, and it had the wings of an eagle. I watched until its wings were torn off and it was lifted from the ground so that it stood on two feet like a man, and the heart of a man was given to it.

⁵"And there before me was a second beast, which looked like a bear. It was raised up on one of its sides, and it had three ribs in its mouth between its teeth. It was told, 'Get up and eat your fill of flesh!'

⁶"After that, I looked, and there before me was another beast, one that looked like a leopard. And on its back it had four wings like those of a bird. This beast had four heads, and it was given authority to rule.

⁷"After that, in my vision at night I looked, and there before me was a fourth beast—terrifying and frightening and very powerful. It had large iron teeth; it crushed and devoured its victims and trampled underfoot whatever was left. It was different from all the former beasts, and it had ten horns.

⁸"While I was thinking about the horns, there before me was another horn, a little one, which came up among them; and three of the first horns were uprooted before it. This horn had eyes like the eyes of a man and a mouth that spoke boastfully.

⁹"As I looked,

"thrones were set in place,
  and the Ancient of Days took his seat.
His clothing was as white as snow;
  the hair of his head was white like wool.
His throne was flaming with fire,
  and its wheels were all ablaze.
¹⁰A river of fire was flowing,
  coming out from before him.
Thousands upon thousands attended him;
  ten thousand times ten thousand stood
    before him.
The court was seated,

and the books were opened.

¹¹"Then I continued to watch because of the boastful words the horn was speaking. I kept looking until the beast was slain and its body destroyed and thrown into the blazing fire. ¹²(The other beasts had been stripped of their authority, but were allowed to live for a period of time.)

¹³"In my vision at night I looked, and there before me was one like a son of man, coming with the clouds of heaven. He approached the Ancient of Days and was led into his presence. ¹⁴He was given authority, glory and sovereign power; all peoples, nations and men of every language worshiped him. His dominion is an everlasting dominion that will not pass away, and his kingdom is one that will never be destroyed.

¹⁵"I, Daniel, was troubled in spirit, and the visions that passed through my mind disturbed me. ¹⁶I approached one of those standing there and asked him the true meaning of all this.

"So he told me and gave me the interpretation of these things: ¹⁷'The four great beasts are four kingdoms that will rise from the earth. ¹⁸But the saints of the Most High will receive the kingdom and will possess it forever—yes, for ever and ever.'

¹⁹"Then I wanted to know the true meaning of the fourth beast, which was different from all the others and most terrifying, with its iron teeth and bronze claws—the beast that crushed and devoured its victims and trampled underfoot whatever was left. ²⁰I also wanted to know about the ten horns on its head and about the other horn that came up, before which three of them fell— the horn that looked more imposing than the others and that had eyes and a mouth that spoke boastfully. ²¹As I watched, this horn was waging war against the saints and defeating them, ²²until the Ancient of Days came and pronounced judgment in favor of the saints of the Most High, and the time came when they possessed the kingdom.

²³"He gave me this explanation: 'The fourth beast is a fourth kingdom that will appear on earth. It will be different from all the other kingdoms and will devour the whole earth, trampling it down and crushing it. ²⁴The ten horns are ten kings who will come from this kingdom. After them another king will arise, different from the earlier ones; he will subdue three kings. ²⁵He will speak against the Most High and oppress his saints and try to change the set times and the

laws. The saints will be handed over to him for a time, times and half a time.ᵛ

²⁶" 'But the court will sit, and his power will be taken away and completely destroyed forever. ²⁷Then the sovereignty, power and greatness of the kingdoms under the whole heaven will be handed over to the saints, the people of the Most High. His kingdom will be an everlasting kingdom, and all rulers will worship and obey him.'

²⁸"This is the end of the matter. I, Daniel, was deeply troubled by my thoughts, and my face turned pale, but I kept the matter to myself."

ᵛ25 Or *for a year, two years and half a year*

 Discovering the Word 1. The sea is used in many prophetic passages to represent the nations of the world (see, for example, Is 17:12–13; 57:20 and Lk 21:25). If that is the picture here, how would you explain verses 2–3? 2. Daniel sees four beasts which, according to verse 17, represent four kingdoms. The lionlike appearance of the first beast may represent that kingdom's strength and majesty. What characteristics of the second, third and fourth kingdoms are suggested by verses 5–7? 3. What aspects of God's nature and power are suggested by Daniel's description of the Ancient of Days in verses 9–10? How can this vision of God give us hope and stability when the nations (or our lives) are in turmoil? 4. The final figure to appear in Daniel's vision is "one like a son of man" (vv. 13–14)—an apparent description of the Lord Jesus. Why do you think all the kings and kingdoms of the world are pictured as beasts but Christ looks like a son of man? 5. After the four kingdoms rise, "the saints of the Most High will receive the kingdom" (vv. 17–18). How is their conquest different from that of the four kingdoms? 6. Describe the political and military power of the "other horn" from the information found in this chapter (vv. 19–26).

Applying the Word 1. How does reading this passage affect your attitude toward the future? 2. Daniel is told that the saints of the Most High will share in the kingdom with the Son of man. What do you find most appealing about Daniel's description of God's kingdom (vv. 13–14, 27), and why?

Responding in Prayer Pray for those nations that are currently in turmoil. Ask God to bring hope to the people there.

9 / *Daniel 8*
World Powers in Conflict

GOD GAVE DANIEL the unique opportunity of looking at the future. But in chapter 8 that future gets very personal. The first seven chapters stressed the destinies of the Gentile world powers. In chapters 8—12, the emphasis is on the destiny of Israel.

 Warming Up to God Reflect on the current state of your country. What aspects of your nation's future concern you? Take time right now to pray for the future of your nation.

 Read Daniel 8.

8 In the third year of King Belshazzar's reign, I, Daniel, had a vision, after the one that had already appeared to me. ²In my vision I saw myself in the citadel of Susa in the province of Elam; in the vision I was beside the Ulai Canal. ³I looked up, and there before me was a ram with two horns, standing beside the canal, and the horns were long. One of the horns was longer than the other but grew up later. ⁴I watched the ram as he charged toward the west and the north and the south. No animal could stand against him, and none could rescue from his power. He did as he pleased and became great.

⁵As I was thinking about this, suddenly a goat with a prominent horn between his eyes came from the west, crossing the whole earth without touching the ground. ⁶He came toward the two-horned ram I had seen standing beside the canal and charged at him in great rage. ⁷I saw him attack the ram furiously, striking the ram and shat-

tering his two horns. The ram was powerless to stand against him; the goat knocked him to the ground and trampled on him, and none could rescue the ram from his power. ⁸The goat became very great, but at the height of his power his large horn was broken off, and in its place four prominent horns grew up toward the four winds of heaven.

⁹Out of one of them came another horn, which started small but grew in power to the south and to the east and toward the Beautiful Land. ¹⁰It grew until it reached the host of the heavens, and it threw some of the starry host down to the earth and trampled on them. ¹¹It set itself up to be as great as the Prince of the host; it took away the daily sacrifice from him, and the place of his sanctuary was brought low. ¹²Because of rebellion, the host ⌊of the saints⌋ʷ and the daily sacrifice were given over to it. It prospered in everything it did, and truth was thrown to the ground.

¹³Then I heard a holy one speaking, and another holy one said to him, "How long will it take for the vision to be fulfilled—the vision concerning the daily sacrifice, the rebellion that causes desolation, and the surrender of the sanctuary and of the host that will be trampled underfoot?"

¹⁴He said to me, "It will take 2,300 evenings and mornings; then the sanctuary will be reconsecrated."

¹⁵While I, Daniel, was watching the vision and trying to understand it, there before me stood one who looked like a man. ¹⁶And I heard a man's voice from the Ulai calling, "Gabriel, tell this man the meaning of the vision."

¹⁷As he came near the place where I was standing, I was terrified and fell prostrate. "Son of man," he said to me, "understand that the vision concerns the time of the end."

¹⁸While he was speaking to me, I was in a deep sleep, with my face to the ground. Then he touched me and raised me to my feet.

¹⁹He said: "I am going to tell you what will happen later in the time of wrath, because the vision concerns the appointed time of the end.ˣ ²⁰The two-horned ram that you saw represents the kings of Media and Persia. ²¹The shaggy goat is the king of Greece, and the large horn between his eyes is the first king. ²²The four horns that replaced the one that was broken off represent four kingdoms that will emerge from his nation but will not have the same power.

²³"In the latter part of their reign, when rebels have become completely wicked, a stern-faced king, a master of intrigue, will arise. ²⁴He will become very strong, but not by his own power. He will cause astounding devastation and will succeed in whatever he does. He will destroy the mighty men and the holy people. ²⁵He will cause deceit to prosper, and he will consider himself superior. When they feel secure, he will destroy many and take his stand against the Prince of princes. Yet he will be destroyed, but not by human power.

²⁶"The vision of the evenings and mornings that has been given you is true, but seal up the vision, for it concerns the distant future."

²⁷I, Daniel, was exhausted and lay ill for several days. Then I got up and went about the king's business. I was appalled by the vision; it was beyond understanding.

ʷ12 Or rebellion, the armies   ˣ19 Or because the end will be at the appointed time

---

Discovering the Word 1. Daniel is first given a rather strange vision involving a ram and a goat (vv. 1–14). No interpretation is given until after the scene has passed. Why do you think God chose to communicate future events to Daniel in this way? (Why not simply tell him the historical facts?) 2. In verse 20 Daniel is told that the ram represents the kings of the Medo-Persian Empire. From the events portrayed in verses 3–4, how would you expect this kingdom to come on the world scene? 3. The goat with one large horn is a symbol of the Greek Empire and their notable first king, Alexander the Great (v. 21). From the scene in verses 5–8, how would you describe the clash of these two empires? 4. From your experience and knowledge gained thus far in the "interpretation of visions," with Daniel as a guide, how would you interpret the symbolism of verses 9–12? 5. The "stern-faced king" (v. 23) whom Gabriel describes is probably Antiochus Epiphanes, who ruled Syria and Palestine from 175 to 164 B.C. He hated the Jews and their God. His most infamous act was desecrating the temple in Jerusalem in 168 B.C. For just over three years ("2,300 evenings and mornings," v. 14), no sacrifices to God were permitted. Finally, the Jews were able to drive Antiochus out of Israel and reclaim the temple. If you had been a Jew living under the tyranny of Antiochus, how would it have made you feel to read Daniel's prophetic prediction of the very events you were experiencing?

Applying the Word 1. In what ways can this chapter be an encouragement to you as you face emotional discouragement or spiritual attack (or even political tyranny)? 2. How does this chapter fit with Daniel's

main theme of God's sovereignty? **3.** What perspective does this chapter give us in understanding how a good God can permit evil?

 Responding in Prayer Ask God to make his ways known to you as you seek to understand who he is and how he works in the world.

10 / *Daniel 9*
Prayer and Prediction

ONE MORNING, SHORTLY after the Medes and the Persians had conquered Babylon, Daniel was reading the book of the prophet Jeremiah. Jeremiah had been a prophet in Jerusalem when Daniel was a boy. As he read the prophet's words, a couple of passages seemed to leap off the page (Jer 25:8–12; 29:10–11). God promised that Israel's captivity would last seventy years, and then God would bring them back to the land. Daniel began to add up the years since his deportation and realized that the captivity was almost over! As Daniel's mind was gripped by the written Word of God, the urge to pray was born. God's answer to Daniel's prayer was swift—and surprising! This passage not only teaches us about Daniel's response to God's Word; we also learn how we should respond to God's promises to us.

 Warming Up to God In times of deep personal crisis, men and women are often driven to pray. When have you experienced such a time in your life?

 Read Daniel 9.

9 In the first year of Darius son of Xerxes[y] (a Mede by descent), who was made ruler over the Babylonian[z] kingdom— ²in the first year of his reign, I, Daniel, understood from the Scriptures, according to the word of the LORD given to Jeremiah the prophet, that the desolation of Jerusalem would last seventy years. ³So I turned to the Lord God and pleaded with him in prayer and petition, in fasting, and in sackcloth and ashes.

⁴I prayed to the LORD my God and confessed:

"O Lord, the great and awesome God, who keeps his covenant of love with all who love him and obey his commands, ⁵we have sinned and done wrong. We have been wicked and have rebelled; we have turned away from your commands and laws. ⁶We have not listened to your servants the prophets, who spoke in your name to our kings, our princes and our fathers, and to all the people of the land.

⁷"Lord, you are righteous, but this day we are covered with shame—the men of Judah and people of Jerusalem and all Israel, both near and far, in all the countries where you

have scattered us because of our unfaithfulness to you. ⁸O LORD, we and our kings, our princes and our fathers are covered with shame because we have sinned against you. ⁹The Lord our God is merciful and forgiving, even though we have rebelled against him; ¹⁰we have not obeyed the LORD our God or kept the laws he gave us through his servants the prophets. ¹¹All Israel has transgressed your law and turned away, refusing to obey you.

"Therefore the curses and sworn judgments written in the Law of Moses, the servant of God, have been poured out on us, because we have sinned against you. ¹²You have fulfilled the words spoken against us and against our rulers by bringing upon us great disaster. Under the whole heaven nothing has ever been done like what has been done to Jerusalem. ¹³Just as it is written in the Law of Moses, all this disaster has come upon us, yet we have not sought the favor of the LORD our God by turning from our sins and giving attention to your truth. ¹⁴The

y1 Hebrew Ahasuerus   z1 Or Chaldean

Lord did not hesitate to bring the disaster upon us, for the Lord our God is righteous in everything he does; yet we have not obeyed him.

¹⁵"Now, O Lord our God, who brought your people out of Egypt with a mighty hand and who made for yourself a name that endures to this day, we have sinned, we have done wrong. ¹⁶O Lord, in keeping with all your righteous acts, turn away your anger and your wrath from Jerusalem, your city, your holy hill. Our sins and the iniquities of our fathers have made Jerusalem and your people an object of scorn to all those around us.

¹⁷"Now, our God, hear the prayers and petitions of your servant. For your sake, O Lord, look with favor on your desolate sanctuary. ¹⁸Give ear, O God, and hear; open your eyes and see the desolation of the city that bears your Name. We do not make requests of you because we are righteous, but because of your great mercy. ¹⁹O Lord, listen! O Lord, forgive! O Lord, hear and act! For your sake, O my God, do not delay, because your city and your people bear your Name."

²⁰While I was speaking and praying, confessing my sin and the sin of my people Israel and making my request to the Lord my God for his holy hill— ²¹while I was still in prayer, Gabriel, the man I had seen in the earlier vision, came to me in swift flight about the time of the evening sacrifice. ²²He instructed me and said to me, "Daniel, I have now come to give you insight and understanding. ²³As soon as you began to pray, an answer was given, which I have come to tell you, for you are highly esteemed. Therefore, consider the message and understand the vision:

²⁴"Seventy 'sevens'ᵃ are decreed for your people and your holy city to finishᵇ transgression, to put an end to sin, to atone for wickedness, to bring in everlasting righteousness, to seal up vision and prophecy and to anoint the most holy.ᶜ

²⁵"Know and understand this: From the issuing of the decreeᵈ to restore and rebuild Jerusalem until the Anointed One,ᵉ the ruler, comes, there will be seven 'sevens,' and sixty-two 'sevens.' It will be rebuilt with streets and a trench, but in times of trouble. ²⁶After the sixty-two 'sevens,' the Anointed One will be cut off and will have nothing.ᶠ The people of the ruler who will come will destroy the city and the sanctuary. The end will come like a flood: War will continue until the end, and desolations have been decreed. ²⁷He will confirm a covenant with many for one 'seven.'ᵍ In the middle of the 'seven'ᵍ he will put an end to sacrifice and offering. And on a wing ⌊of the temple⌋ he will set up an abomination that causes desolation, until the end that is decreed is poured out on him.ʰ"ⁱ

ᵃ24 Or 'weeks'; also in verses 25 and 26   ᵇ24 Or restrain   ᶜ24 Or Most Holy Place; or most holy One   ᵈ25 Or word   ᵉ25 Or an anointed one; also in verse 26   ᶠ26 Or off and will have no one; or off, but not for himself   ᵍ27 Or 'week'   ʰ27 Or it   ⁱ27 Or And one who causes desolation will come upon the pinnacle of the abominable ⌊temple⌋, until the end that is decreed is poured out on the desolated ⌊city⌋

Discovering the Word   1. In verses 4–19, which aspects of God's character did Daniel appeal to as the basis of his requests?   2. Daniel consistently uses the plural pronoun *we* throughout the prayer. Why do you think Daniel could confess for the whole nation?   3. In verse 24 Gabriel mentions six things that will happen for the people of Israel and the holy city of Jerusalem within seventy "sevens" (usually interpreted as 490 years; see Lev 25:8–24). What do you think these things mean individually and collectively?   4. Verse 26 states that "the people of the ruler who will come will destroy the city and the sanctuary." The Romans destroyed Jerusalem and its temple in A.D. 70. According to verse 27, how would you describe the course of events during the final "seven," or period of seven years?

Applying the Word   1. What aspects of God's character have you been learning about, and how?   2. What specific insights about your prayer life can you glean from Daniel's prayer?

Responding in Prayer   Consider your church and your nation. What corporate sins do you need to confess?

11 / *Daniel 10:1—11:35*
Another Vision of the Future

WARS, TERRORISM, ASSASSINATIONS—so often world events seem out of control. We are frustrated and frightened because of our inability to do anything to stop them. The last of four great visions given to Daniel presents God's perspective on world events.

 Warming Up to God What recent national or international crisis made you feel insecure or frightened? Explain.

 Read Daniel 10:1—11:35.

10 In the third year of Cyrus king of Persia, a revelation was given to Daniel (who was called Belteshazzar). Its message was true and it concerned a great war.*ʲ* The understanding of the message came to him in a vision.

²At that time I, Daniel, mourned for three weeks. ³I ate no choice food; no meat or wine touched my lips; and I used no lotions at all until the three weeks were over.

⁴On the twenty-fourth day of the first month, as I was standing on the bank of the great river, the Tigris, ⁵I looked up and there before me was a man dressed in linen, with a belt of the finest gold around his waist. ⁶His body was like chrysolite, his face like lightning, his eyes like flaming torches, his arms and legs like the gleam of burnished bronze, and his voice like the sound of a multitude.

⁷I, Daniel, was the only one who saw the vision; the men with me did not see it, but such terror overwhelmed them that they fled and hid themselves. ⁸So I was left alone, gazing at this great vision; I had no strength left, my face turned deathly pale and I was helpless. ⁹Then I heard him speaking, and as I listened to him, I fell into a deep sleep, my face to the ground.

¹⁰A hand touched me and set me trembling on my hands and knees. ¹¹He said, "Daniel, you who are highly esteemed, consider carefully the words I am about to speak to you, and stand up, for I have now been sent to you." And when he said this to me, I stood up trembling.

¹²Then he continued, "Do not be afraid, Daniel. Since the first day that you set your mind to gain understanding and to humble yourself before your God, your words were heard, and I have come in response to them. ¹³But the prince of the Persian kingdom resisted me twenty-one days.

Then Michael, one of the chief princes, came to help me, because I was detained there with the king of Persia. ¹⁴Now I have come to explain to you what will happen to your people in the future, for the vision concerns a time yet to come."

¹⁵While he was saying this to me, I bowed with my face toward the ground and was speechless. ¹⁶Then one who looked like a man*ᵏ* touched my lips, and I opened my mouth and began to speak. I said to the one standing before me, "I am overcome with anguish because of the vision, my lord, and I am helpless. ¹⁷How can I, your servant, talk with you, my lord? My strength is gone and I can hardly breathe."

¹⁸Again the one who looked like a man touched me and gave me strength. ¹⁹"Do not be afraid, O man highly esteemed," he said. "Peace! Be strong now; be strong."

When he spoke to me, I was strengthened and said, "Speak, my lord, since you have given me strength."

²⁰So he said, "Do you know why I have come to you? Soon I will return to fight against the prince of Persia, and when I go, the prince of Greece will come; ²¹but first I will tell you what is written in the Book of Truth. (No one supports me against them except Michael, your prince.

11 ¹And in the first year of Darius the Mede, I took my stand to support and protect him.)

²"Now then, I tell you the truth: Three more kings will appear in Persia, and then a fourth, who will be far richer than all the others. When he has gained power by his wealth, he will stir up everyone against the kingdom of Greece. ³Then a mighty king will appear, who will rule with great

ʲ1 Or *true and burdensome*   *ᵏ16* Most manuscripts of the Masoretic Text; one manuscript of the Masoretic Text, Dead Sea Scrolls and Septuagint *Then something that looked like a man's hand* power and do as he pleases. ⁴After he has appeared, his empire will be broken up and parceled out toward the four winds of heaven. It will not go to his descendants, nor will it have the power he exercised, because his empire will be uprooted and given to others.

⁵"The king of the South will become strong, but one of his commanders will become even stronger than he and will rule his own kingdom with great power. ⁶After some years, they will become allies. The daughter of the king of the South will go to the king of the North to make an alliance, but she will not retain her power, and he and his power[l] will not last. In those days she will be handed over, together with her royal escort and her father[m] and the one who supported her.

⁷"One from her family line will arise to take her place. He will attack the forces of the king of the North and enter his fortress; he will fight against them and be victorious. ⁸He will also seize their gods, their metal images and their valuable articles of silver and gold and carry them off to Egypt. For some years he will leave the king of the North alone. ⁹Then the king of the North will invade the realm of the king of the South but will retreat to his own country. ¹⁰His sons will prepare for war and assemble a great army, which will sweep on like an irresistible flood and carry the battle as far as his fortress.

¹¹"Then the king of the South will march out in a rage and fight against the king of the North, who will raise a large army, but it will be defeated. ¹²When the army is carried off, the king of the South will be filled with pride and will slaughter many thousands, yet he will not remain triumphant. ¹³For the king of the North will muster another army, larger than the first; and after several years, he will advance with a huge army fully equipped.

¹⁴"In those times many will rise against the king of the South. The violent men among your own people will rebel in fulfillment of the vision, but without success. ¹⁵Then the king of the North will come and build up siege ramps and will capture a fortified city. The forces of the South will be powerless to resist; even their best troops will not have the strength to stand. ¹⁶The invader will do as he pleases; no one will be able to stand against him. He will establish himself in the Beautiful Land and will have the power to destroy it. ¹⁷He will determine to come with the might of his entire kingdom and will make an alliance with the king of the South. And he will give him a daughter in marriage in order to overthrow the kingdom, but his plans[n] will not succeed or help him. ¹⁸Then he will turn his attention to the coastlands and will take many of them, but a commander will put an end to his insolence and will turn his insolence back upon him. ¹⁹After this, he will turn back toward the fortresses of his own country but will stumble and fall, to be seen no more.

²⁰"His successor will send out a tax collector to maintain the royal splendor. In a few years, however, he will be destroyed, yet not in anger or in battle.

²¹"He will be succeeded by a contemptible person who has not been given the honor of royalty. He will invade the kingdom when its people feel secure, and he will seize it through intrigue. ²²Then an overwhelming army will be swept away before him; both it and a prince of the covenant will be destroyed. ²³After coming to an agreement with him, he will act deceitfully, and with only a few people he will rise to power. ²⁴When the richest provinces feel secure, he will invade them and will achieve what neither his fathers nor his forefathers did. He will distribute plunder, loot and wealth among his followers. He will plot the overthrow of fortresses—but only for a time.

²⁵"With a large army he will stir up his strength and courage against the king of the South. The king of the South will wage war with a large and very powerful army, but he will not be able to stand because of the plots devised against him. ²⁶Those who eat from the king's provisions will try to destroy him; his army will be swept away, and many will fall in battle. ²⁷The two kings, with their hearts bent on evil, will sit at the same table and lie to each other, but to no avail, because an end will still come at the appointed time. ²⁸The king of the North will return to his own country with great wealth, but his heart will be set against the holy covenant. He will take action against it and then return to his own country.

²⁹"At the appointed time he will invade the South again, but this time the outcome will be different from what it was before. ³⁰Ships of the western coastlands[o] will oppose him, and he will lose heart. Then he will turn back and vent his fury against the holy covenant. He will return and

[l]6 Or *offspring*   [m]6 Or *child* (see Vulgate and Syriac)   [n]17 Or *but she*   [o]30 Hebrew *of Kittim*

show favor to those who forsake the holy covenant.

31"His armed forces will rise up to desecrate the temple fortress and will abolish the daily sacrifice. Then they will set up the abomination that causes desolation. 32With flattery he will corrupt those who have violated the covenant, but the people who know their God will firmly resist him.

33"Those who are wise will instruct many, though for a time they will fall by the sword or be burned or captured or plundered. 34When they fall, they will receive a little help, and many who are not sincere will join them. 35Some of the wise will stumble, so that they may be refined, purified and made spotless until the time of the end, for it will still come at the appointed time.

 Discovering the Word 1. Describe the man in Daniel's vision (10:4–6). 2. Why did the vision of verses 4–6 cause Daniel to react the way he did (10:7–11)? 3. What do the angel's words to Daniel tell us about God's response to those who seek him (10:12–14)? 4. In 11:5–35 the conflict between the Syrian division of the Greek Empire ruled by the Seleucid family ("the king of the North") and the Egyptian division of the Greek Empire ruled by the Ptolemies ("the king of the South") is outlined with amazing accuracy. The focus of the passage is on a man we have met in Daniel before—Antiochus Epiphanes. Verses 21–24 describe his conquest of the people of Israel who had regathered in Palestine after the exile. What do we learn from these verses about Antiochus's character and methods of operation? 5. Antiochus invaded Egypt the first time with relative success (11:25–28). The second time he met some new opposition and in his frustration vented his anger on "the holy covenant," the Jewish religion (11:29–31). What can we learn from 11:32–35 about why God may allow genuine believers to suffer under the hand of a godless tyrant?

 Applying the Word 1. How might Daniel's experience encourage us to be persistent in prayer? 2. If an evil power could hinder an angel in Daniel's day, what does this indicate about our own need for help against Satan's forces? 3. How can God's sovereign rule help us to stand firm when evil seems to triumph?

 Responding in Prayer Offer your praise to the Lord, who is sovereign over history.

12 / *Daniel 11:36—12:13*
A Dark Day and a Brilliant End

I HOPE AS a result of your quiet times in Daniel you have a new appreciation for the sovereign majesty of God—a God who can predict the future in detail, a God who raises up kings and kingdoms and who also brings them to ruin, a God who can protect Daniel in the lion's den, and a God who is just as concerned about us and our lives. The second part of Daniel's final prophetic vision in 11:36—12:13 projects Daniel far into the future to "the time of the end" of world history. The vision focuses on the nation of Israel, but gives us strong encouragement and hope during difficult times.

Warming Up to God In the course of your study in Daniel, what have you learned about the character of God that strengthened you spiritually?

Read Daniel 11:36—12:13.

36"The king will do as he pleases. He will exalt and magnify himself above every god and will say unheard-of things against the God of gods. He will be successful until the time of wrath is completed, for what has been determined must take place. 37He will show no regard for the gods of his fathers or for the one desired by women, nor will he regard any god, but will exalt himself above them all. 38Instead of them, he will honor a god of fortresses; a god unknown to his fathers he will honor with gold and silver, with precious stones and costly gifts. 39He will attack the mightiest fortresses with the help of a foreign god and will greatly honor those who acknowledge him. He will make them rulers over many people and will distribute the land at a price.ᵖ

⁴⁰"At the time of the end the king of the South will engage him in battle, and the king of the North will storm out against him with chariots and cavalry and a great fleet of ships. He will invade many countries and sweep through them like a flood. ⁴¹He will also invade the Beautiful Land. Many countries will fall, but Edom, Moab and the leaders of Ammon will be delivered from his hand. ⁴²He will extend his power over many countries; Egypt will not escape. ⁴³He will gain control of the treasures of gold and silver and all the riches of Egypt, with the Libyans and Nubians in submission. ⁴⁴But reports from the east and the north will alarm him, and he will set out in a great rage to destroy and annihilate many. ⁴⁵He will pitch his royal tents between the seas at�q the beautiful holy mountain. Yet he will come to his end, and no one will help him.

12 "At that time Michael, the great prince who protects your people, will arise. There will be a time of distress such as has not happened from the beginning of nations until then. But at that time your people—everyone whose name is found written in the book—will be delivered. ²Multitudes who sleep in the dust of the earth will awake: some to everlasting life, others to shame and everlasting contempt. ³Those who are wiseʳ will shine like the brightness of the heavens, and those who lead many to righteousness, like the stars for ever and ever. ⁴But you, Daniel, close up and seal the words of the scroll until the time of the end.

Many will go here and there to increase knowledge."

⁵Then I, Daniel, looked, and there before me stood two others, one on this bank of the river and one on the opposite bank. ⁶One of them said to the man clothed in linen, who was above the waters of the river, "How long will it be before these astonishing things are fulfilled?"

⁷The man clothed in linen, who was above the waters of the river, lifted his right hand and his left hand toward heaven, and I heard him swear by him who lives forever, saying, "It will be for a time, times and half a time.ˢ When the power of the holy people has been finally broken, all these things will be completed."

⁸I heard, but I did not understand. So I asked, "My lord, what will the outcome of all this be?"

⁹He replied, "Go your way, Daniel, because the words are closed up and sealed until the time of the end. ¹⁰Many will be purified, made spotless and refined, but the wicked will continue to be wicked. None of the wicked will understand, but those who are wise will understand.

¹¹"From the time that the daily sacrifice is abolished and the abomination that causes desolation is set up, there will be 1,290 days. ¹²Blessed is the one who waits for and reaches the end of the 1,335 days.

¹³"As for you, go your way till the end. You will rest, and then at the end of the days you will rise to receive your allotted inheritance."

ᵖ39 Or land for a reward   �q45 Or the sea and   ʳ3 Or who impart wisdom   ˢ7 Or a year, two years and half a year

---

Discovering the Word 1. Building from the prototype of the antichrist in Antiochus Epiphanes (11:21–32), the heavenly messenger now describes the final oppressor of Israel who will arise at "the time of the end" (11:35–40). This "king," following the example of Antiochus, will magnify himself as a god. How would you describe the "religious" character and actions of this king from 11:36–37? 2. From 11:40–43 trace the military career of this future king. 3. The king's defeat and the deliverance of the godly comes through the intervention of Michael, "the great prince" (12:1). How do you envision this intervention will take place? 4. Why do you think Daniel is given the instruction to seal the scroll "until the time of the end" (12:4, 9)? 5. In 12:9–13, do you think the messenger avoided Daniel's last question (12:8), or did he answer it? Explain.

Applying the Word 1. The antichrist's god will be "a god of fortresses"—the ancient god of war and militarism (11:38–39). How do we see the influence of this "god" at work today? 2. How can this victory and the messenger's description of the resurrection (12:1–3) encourage us during times of tribulation or persecution? 3. As you think back over the book of Daniel, what specific aspect of Daniel's character or example helped you most to live spiritually in a secular world? In what way?

 Responding in Prayer Ask God to continue to teach you what it means to live spiritually in a secular world.

Hosea

D o you think that the problems in our society are because people do not take responsibility for themselves or because the government is not taking responsibility for the people? Hosea's answer would be yes. He saw both as being at fault.

In the eighth century B.C. Hosea began his ministry in the northern kingdom of Israel (which he sometimes calls Ephraim, Jacob or Samaria). He probably preached at about the same time or a little after the prophet Amos during the prosperous reign of Jereboam II. Unfortunately, along with the strong growth of the economy, there were also increases in poverty, social injustice, religious prostitution, sexual immorality and sales of idols.

The century began without the threat of any superpowers in the Middle East. This allowed Jereboam II to consolidate politically and economically. Assyria (in the east) became the dominant military threat, while at the same time to a lesser degree Egypt experienced resurgence in the west. Israel, besides trying to play Egypt and Assyria against each other, utilized its military might to try to force Judah, the southern kingdom, to join them in a revolt against Assyria. This attempt failed and soon after (721 B.C.) Assyria destroyed Israel.

The book tells us little about Hosea's life; it is primarily about his message—a holistic critique of Israel. Using powerful metaphorical language, Hosea attacks theology, morals, economy and politics. God is passionately concerned for both the responsibility of the individual as well as the society to care for and to give justice to the poor. But the message he gives Hosea is not only one of drastic judgment, but also one of his astounding love, mercy and forgiveness. Carefully reading Hosea's message will help you flesh out these great truths.

Outline

1/ Hosea 1:1—2:1 ——————————— What's in a Name?

2/ Hosea 2:2—3:5 ——————————— Married to the Lord?

3/ Hosea 4 ——————————— How Not to Love God

4/ Hosea 5:1—6:11 ——————————— Destroying Evil

5/ Hosea 6:11—8:14 ——————————— What Do You See?

6/ Hosea 9—10 ——————————— What Are You Planting?

7/ Hosea 11:1–11 ——————————— Turning Away from God

8/ Hosea 11:12—13:16 ——————————— Chasing the Wind

9/ Hosea 14 ——————————— Who Is Wise?

1 / *Hosea 1:1—2:1*
What's in a Name?

WHY WERE YOU given the name that you have? Were you named after a relative or a famous person? The names of Hosea's children are chosen by the Lord because of their meaning. When you see their names, you may be grateful that it was your parents who chose your name!

 Warming Up to God Jesus' name, as well as Hosea's, means "the Lord saves" in Hebrew. How is the name of Jesus meaningful to you?

 Read Hosea 1:1—2:1.

---

1 The word of the Lord that came to Hosea son of Beeri during the reigns of Uzziah, Jotham, Ahaz and Hezekiah, kings of Judah, and during the reign of Jeroboam son of Jehoash*a* king of Israel:

²When the Lord began to speak through Hosea, the Lord said to him, "Go, take to yourself an adulterous wife and children of unfaithfulness, because the land is guilty of the vilest adultery in departing from the Lord." ³So he married Gomer daughter of Diblaim, and she conceived and bore him a son.

⁴Then the Lord said to Hosea, "Call him Jezreel, because I will soon punish the house of Jehu for the massacre at Jezreel, and I will put an end to the kingdom of Israel. ⁵In that day I will break Israel's bow in the Valley of Jezreel."

⁶Gomer conceived again and gave birth to a daughter. Then the Lord said to Hosea, "Call her Lo-Ruhamah,*b* for I will no longer show love to the house of Israel, that I should at all forgive them. ⁷Yet I will show love to the house of Judah; and I will save them—not by bow, sword or battle, or by horses and horsemen, but by the Lord their God."

⁸After she had weaned Lo-Ruhamah, Gomer had another son. ⁹Then the Lord said, "Call him Lo-Ammi,*c* for you are not my people, and I am not your God.

¹⁰"Yet the Israelites will be like the sand on the seashore, which cannot be measured or counted. In the place where it was said to them, 'You are not my people,' they will be called 'sons of the living God.' ¹¹The people of Judah and the people of Israel will be reunited, and they will appoint one leader and will come up out of the land, for great will be the day of Jezreel.

2 "Say of your brothers, 'My people,' and of your sisters, 'My loved one.'

---

*a*1 Hebrew *Joash,* a variant of *Jehoash*   *b*6 *Lo-Ruhamah* means *not loved.*   *c*9 *Lo-Ammi* means *not my people.*

 Discovering the Word 1. In 1:1—2:1 how do the names of Hosea's children play a key part in his message and ministry? 2. How do you react to God's calling Hosea to marry an adulterous wife (v. 2, in Hebrew, "a whore")? 3. Hosea names his firstborn Jezreel (vv. 4–5) after a valley where many bloody massacres had taken place. What would it have been like to have a name like Auschwitz, Hiroshima, Wounded Knee or Tiananmen Square? 4. The translation of the name Lo-Ruhamah (v. 6) is "not loved." How would this name speak to the people of Israel? 5. In the midst of the judgment of God, how would the reversal of the names in verses 1:10—2:1 give the people hope?

Applying the Word 1. Some find it offensive that God called Hosea to marry a whore, yet the point was to characterize God's people as being as unfaithful as a prostitute. How are you unfaithful to God? 2. In 1:10—2:1 God's reaction to the unfaithfulness is unexpected. What does it mean to you to be one of God's people? 3. The good news of 1:10—2:1 is realized today in Jesus Christ. Remember that those you meet today are loved by God and that he calls them his children. If you have an opportunity, offer this message of good news to someone else.

Responding in Prayer Each of us is prone to wander away from God at times. Thank God for his love and forgiveness in your life.

2 / *Hosea 2:2—3:5*
Married to the Lord?

DO YOU REMEMBER the adage "Sticks and stones will break my bones but names will never hurt me"? Children know better. They will tell you that words can hurt. Imagine how a wife of many years would react to hearing "You are not my wife, and I am not your husband." In Hosea 2:2 the Lord's words to Israel have much the same meaning.

 Warming Up to God In what ways has your unfaithfulness been a source of pain for God?

 Read Hosea 2:2—3:5.

2"Rebuke your mother, rebuke her,
  for she is not my wife,
  and I am not her husband.
Let her remove the adulterous look from her
    face
  and the unfaithfulness from between her
    breasts.
3Otherwise I will strip her naked
  and make her as bare as on the day she
    was born;
I will make her like a desert,
  turn her into a parched land,
  and slay her with thirst.
4I will not show my love to her children,
  because they are the children of adultery.
5Their mother has been unfaithful
  and has conceived them in disgrace.
She said, 'I will go after my lovers,
  who give me my food and my water,
  my wool and my linen, my oil and my
    drink.'
6Therefore I will block her path with
    thornbushes;
I will wall her in so that she cannot find
    her way.
7She will chase after her lovers but not catch
    them;
she will look for them but not find them.
Then she will say,
'I will go back to my husband as at first,
  for then I was better off than now.'
8She has not acknowledged that I was the one
  who gave her the grain, the new wine and
    oil,
who lavished on her the silver and gold—
  which they used for Baal.

9"Therefore I will take away my grain when it
    ripens,
and my new wine when it is ready.
I will take back my wool and my linen,
  intended to cover her nakedness.
10So now I will expose her lewdness
  before the eyes of her lovers;
  no one will take her out of my hands.
11I will stop all her celebrations:
  her yearly festivals, her New Moons,
  her Sabbath days—all her appointed feasts.
12I will ruin her vines and her fig trees,
  which she said were her pay from her
    lovers;
I will make them a thicket,
  and wild animals will devour them.
13I will punish her for the days
  she burned incense to the Baals;
she decked herself with rings and jewelry,
  and went after her lovers,
  but me she forgot,"

                declares the LORD.

14"Therefore I am now going to allure her;
  I will lead her into the desert
  and speak tenderly to her.
15There I will give her back her vineyards,
  and will make the Valley of Achorᵈ a door
    of hope.
There she will singᵉ as in the days of her
    youth,
  as in the day she came up out of Egypt.

16"In that day," declares the LORD,
  "you will call me 'my husband';
  you will no longer call me 'my master.'ᶠ
17I will remove the names of the Baals from her
    lips;
  no longer will their names be invoked.
18In that day I will make a covenant for them

ᵈ15 *Achor* means *trouble.*   ᵉ15 Or *respond*   ᶠ16 Hebrew *baal*

with the beasts of the field and the birds of
   the air
and the creatures that move along the
   ground.
 Bow and sword and battle
   I will abolish from the land,
   so that all may lie down in safety.
[19]I will betroth you to me forever;
   I will betroth you in[g] righteousness and
      justice,
   in[h] love and compassion.
[20]I will betroth you in faithfulness,
   and you will acknowledge the LORD.

[21]"In that day I will respond,"
   declares the LORD—
 "I will respond to the skies,
   and they will respond to the earth;
[22]and the earth will respond to the grain,
   the new wine and oil,
   and they will respond to Jezreel.[i]
[23]I will plant her for myself in the land;
   I will show my love to the one I called 'Not
      my loved one.'[j]

I will say to those called 'Not my people,[k]'
   'You are my people';
 and they will say, 'You are my God.' "

3 The LORD said to me, "Go, show your love to your wife again, though she is loved by another and is an adulteress. Love her as the LORD loves the Israelites, though they turn to other gods and love the sacred raisin cakes." [2]So I bought her for fifteen shekels[l] of silver and about a homer and a lethek[m] of barley. [3]Then I told her, "You are to live with[n] me many days; you must not be a prostitute or be intimate with any man, and I will live with[n] you."

[4]For the Israelites will live many days without king or prince, without sacrifice or sacred stones, without ephod or idol. [5]Afterward the Israelites will return and seek the LORD their God and David their king. They will come trembling to the LORD and to his blessings in the last days.

---

[g]19 Or *with*; also in verse 20   [h]19 Or *with*   [i]22 *Jezreel* means
God plants.   [j]23 Hebrew *Lo-Ruhamah*   [k]23 Hebrew *Lo-Ammi*
[l]2 That is, about 6 ounces (about 170 grams)   [m]2 That is, probably
about 10 bushels (about 330 liters)   [n]3 Or *wait for*

Discovering the Word **1.** How does Israel demonstrate that she is not God's wife (2:2–13)? **2.** Chapter 2 is organized by four "threats" (vv. 3, 6, 9, 14), each beginning with *otherwise* or *therefore*. What sets the fourth "threat" apart from the other three? **3.** After all the unfaithfulness (2:2–13), how can God do what is described in 2:14–23? **4.** Baal is a name for a false god and is translated "lord," "husband" or "master." In 2:16–17 Hosea tells the people to stop calling God "Baal" and to call him "my husband" instead. What significance do you see in that name change? **5.** What are the characteristics of a good "marriage" to God (2:18–23)? **6.** God has Hosea take back his unfaithful wife in chapter 3. How does Hosea's action mirror God's actions toward Israel?

Applying the Word **1.** Israel gave credit for her provisions of necessities and luxuries to other gods instead of to the Lord (2:2–13). Who do you give credit to? **2.** How is God calling you and your community to the desert (2:14–23)? **3.** We live in the "already" of being the bride of Christ, but we look forward to the "not yet" of perfect peace to come. Imagine what it will be like. How does that picture change your perspective on today?

Responding in Prayer Ask God to forgive you for your unfaithfulness and help you to know him as a God who makes you his bride.

---

3 / *Hosea 4*
How Not to Love God

HOW DO YOU know if you really love God? Look at how you treat God's people (1Jn 4:20). Hosea tells the people of Israel that they do not know God (4:1). This is revealed in the quality of their society and their worship.

Warming Up to God How do your actions confirm or deny your relationship with God?

Read Hosea 4.

4 Hear the word of the LORD, you
    Israelites,
  because the LORD has a charge to bring
against you who live in the land:
"There is no faithfulness, no love,
  no acknowledgment of God in the land.
²There is only cursing,ᵒ lying and murder,
  stealing and adultery;
they break all bounds,
  and bloodshed follows bloodshed.
³Because of this the land mourns,ᵖ
  and all who live in it waste away;
the beasts of the field and the birds of the air
  and the fish of the sea are dying.

⁴"But let no man bring a charge,
  let no man accuse another,
for your people are like those
  who bring charges against a priest.
⁵You stumble day and night,
  and the prophets stumble with you.
So I will destroy your mother—
⁶   my people are destroyed from lack of
        knowledge.

  "Because you have rejected knowledge,
    I also reject you as my priests;
because you have ignored the law of your
        God,
    I also will ignore your children.
⁷The more the priests increased,
  the more they sinned against me;
they exchanged�q theirʳ Glory for
  something disgraceful.
⁸They feed on the sins of my people
  and relish their wickedness.
⁹And it will be: Like people, like priests.
  I will punish both of them for their ways
  and repay them for their deeds.

¹⁰"They will eat but not have enough;
  they will engage in prostitution but not
        increase,
because they have deserted the LORD
  to give themselves ¹¹to prostitution,
to old wine and new,

which take away the understanding ¹²of my
        people.
They consult a wooden idol
  and are answered by a stick of wood.
A spirit of prostitution leads them astray;
  they are unfaithful to their God.
¹³They sacrifice on the mountaintops
  and burn offerings on the hills,
under oak, poplar and terebinth,
  where the shade is pleasant.
Therefore your daughters turn to prostitution
  and your daughters-in-law to adultery.

¹⁴"I will not punish your daughters
  when they turn to prostitution,
nor your daughters-in-law
  when they commit adultery,
because the men themselves consort with
        harlots
  and sacrifice with shrine prostitutes—
a people without understanding will come
        to ruin!

¹⁵"Though you commit adultery, O Israel,
  let not Judah become guilty.

  "Do not go to Gilgal;
    do not go up to Beth Aven.ˢ
  And do not swear, 'As surely as the LORD
        lives!'
¹⁶The Israelites are stubborn,
  like a stubborn heifer.
How then can the LORD pasture them
  like lambs in a meadow?
¹⁷Ephraim is joined to idols;
  leave him alone!
¹⁸Even when their drinks are gone,
  they continue their prostitution;
  their rulers dearly love shameful ways.
¹⁹A whirlwind will sweep them away,
  and their sacrifices will bring them shame.

ᵒ2 That is, to pronounce a curse upon   ᵖ3 Or *dries up*   q7 Syriac
and an ancient Hebrew scribal tradition; Masoretic Text *I will exchange*
ʳ7 Masoretic Text; an ancient Hebrew scribal tradition *my*   ˢ15 *Beth
Aven* means *house of wickedness* (a name for Bethel, which means *house
of God*).

Discovering the Word 1. What in verses 1–2 demonstrates that the knowledge of God is absent in Israel? 2. Why is the Lord angry with the priest (vv. 4–6)? 3. One way God provided for the priests was for them to receive a good portion of people's sacrifices. How had the priests corrupted their office (vv. 7–10)? 4. Verses 11–19 describe the people's worship habits. How had they deteriorated? 5. How are knowledge of God and worship interrelated?

 Applying the Word 1. The character of the people is described as stubborn in verse 16. In what way are you stubborn before God and his people? 2. The knowledge of God in this chapter is tied up with more than our relationship with the Lord. How can you and your community demonstrate your knowledge of God by your actions today? this year?

 Responding in Prayer Ask God to help you reflect on how you can love him more by loving others more.

---

4 / *Hosea 5:1—6:11*
Destroying Evil

"GOD IS LIKE rot." Wow! Can you imagine describing the Lord that way? Hosea did (5:12). He wanted to make a point about the God who will destroy evil in the community. The image of God as a moth (5:12) eating away at evil can be a source of comfort to us as we experience pain in this world.

Warming Up to God What evil would you like to see put under God's destructive power? Ask God to help you see what a mighty God he is.

Read Hosea 5:1—6:11.

---

5 "Hear this, you priests!
   Pay attention, you Israelites!
   Listen, O royal house!
   This judgment is against you:
You have been a snare at Mizpah,
   a net spread out on Tabor.
²The rebels are deep in slaughter.
   I will discipline all of them.
³I know all about Ephraim;
   Israel is not hidden from me.
Ephraim, you have now turned to
      prostitution;
   Israel is corrupt.

⁴"Their deeds do not permit them
   to return to their God.
A spirit of prostitution is in their heart;
   they do not acknowledge the LORD.
⁵Israel's arrogance testifies against them;
   the Israelites, even Ephraim, stumble in
      their sin;
   Judah also stumbles with them.
⁶When they go with their flocks and herds
   to seek the LORD,
they will not find him;

he has withdrawn himself from them.
⁷They are unfaithful to the LORD;
   they give birth to illegitimate children.
Now their New Moon festivals
   will devour them and their fields.

⁸"Sound the trumpet in Gibeah,
   the horn in Ramah.
Raise the battle cry in Beth Aven¹;
   lead on, O Benjamin.
⁹Ephraim will be laid waste
   on the day of reckoning.
Among the tribes of Israel
   I proclaim what is certain.
¹⁰Judah's leaders are like those
   who move boundary stones.
I will pour out my wrath on them
   like a flood of water.
¹¹Ephraim is oppressed,
   trampled in judgment,
   intent on pursuing idols.ᵘ
¹²I am like a moth to Ephraim,

¹8 *Beth Aven* means *house of wickedness* (a name for Bethel, which means *house of God*).   ᵘ11 The meaning of the Hebrew for this word is uncertain.

like rot to the people of Judah.
¹³"When Ephraim saw his sickness,
  and Judah his sores,
then Ephraim turned to Assyria,
  and sent to the great king for help.
But he is not able to cure you,
  not able to heal your sores.
¹⁴For I will be like a lion to Ephraim,
  like a great lion to Judah.
I will tear them to pieces and go away;
  I will carry them off, with no one to rescue
  them.
¹⁵Then I will go back to my place
  until they admit their guilt.
And they will seek my face;
  in their misery they will earnestly seek me."

6 "Come, let us return to the LORD.
  He has torn us to pieces
  but he will heal us;
he has injured us
  but he will bind up our wounds.
²After two days he will revive us;
  on the third day he will restore us,
  that we may live in his presence.
³Let us acknowledge the LORD;
  let us press on to acknowledge him.
As surely as the sun rises,
  he will appear;
he will come to us like the winter rains,
  like the spring rains that water the earth."

⁴"What can I do with you, Ephraim?
  What can I do with you, Judah?
Your love is like the morning mist,
  like the early dew that disappears.
⁵Therefore I cut you in pieces with my
    prophets,
  I killed you with the words of my mouth;
  my judgments flashed like lightning upon
    you.
⁶For I desire mercy, not sacrifice,
  and acknowledgment of God rather than
    burnt offerings.
⁷Like Adam,ᵛ they have broken the
    covenant—
  they were unfaithful to me there.
⁸Gilead is a city of wicked men,
  stained with footprints of blood.
⁹As marauders lie in ambush for a man,
  so do bands of priests;
they murder on the road to Shechem,
  committing shameful crimes.
¹⁰I have seen a horrible thing
  in the house of Israel.
There Ephraim is given to prostitution
  and Israel is defiled.

¹¹"Also for you, Judah,
  a harvest is appointed.

ᵛ7 Or As at Adam; or Like men

Discovering the Word 1. Ephraim/Israel has turned to prostitution (both literally and figuratively). How are the Israelites politically, socially and religiously unfaithful to the Lord in chapters 5—6? 2. What vivid language does Hosea use in these chapters to describe the Lord who is going to punish Israel? 3. Ephraim/Israel sees Assyria (5:13) as the answer to a military threat she faces. How is this unfaithfulness to the Lord? 4. What do you make of the people's call to worship in 6:1-3? 5. How does the Lord respond to their call to worship (6:4–6)?

Applying the Word 1. Thinking creatively, what word pictures would you use to characterize God? 2. How can your deeds hinder your discipleship? 3. While Hosea is not against the sacrificial system, it is clear that he is opposed to the empty religiosity of the people (6:6). How can we be sure that we are not merely going through the motions?

Responding in Prayer Ask God to show you the things that keep you from returning to him. Ask God to cleanse and restore you for his use and glory.

5 / Hosea 6:11—8:14
What Do You See?

HAVE YOU EVER looked at yourself in distorted carnival mirrors that make you look extremely tall and thin or incredibly short and fat? In the next few chapters of Hosea it seems that the Israelites had the opposite kinds of mirrors—they saw only the images of themselves that they wanted to see. Through Hosea the Lord tries to get the Israelites to see their reflection as it really is.

 Warming Up to God Ask God to open your eyes and your spirit to the truth about yourself.

 Read Hosea 6:11—8:14.

"Whenever I would restore the fortunes of my
    people,
7 ¹whenever I would heal Israel,
    the sins of Ephraim are exposed
    and the crimes of Samaria revealed.
They practice deceit,
    thieves break into houses,
    bandits rob in the streets;
²but they do not realize
    that I remember all their evil deeds.
Their sins engulf them;
    they are always before me.

³"They delight the king with their wickedness,
    the princes with their lies.
⁴They are all adulterers,
    burning like an oven
whose fire the baker need not stir
    from the kneading of the dough till it rises.
⁵On the day of the festival of our king
    the princes become inflamed with wine,
    and he joins hands with the mockers.
⁶Their hearts are like an oven;
    they approach him with intrigue.
Their passion smolders all night;
    in the morning it blazes like a flaming fire.
⁷All of them are hot as an oven;
    they devour their rulers.
All their kings fall,
    and none of them calls on me.

⁸"Ephraim mixes with the nations;
    Ephraim is a flat cake not turned over.
⁹Foreigners sap his strength,
    but he does not realize it.
His hair is sprinkled with gray,
    but he does not notice.
¹⁰Israel's arrogance testifies against him,
    but despite all this

he does not return to the LORD his God
    or search for him.

¹¹"Ephraim is like a dove,
    easily deceived and senseless—
now calling to Egypt,
    now turning to Assyria.
¹²When they go, I will throw my net over
        them;
    I will pull them down like birds of the air.
When I hear them flocking together,
    I will catch them.
¹³Woe to them,
    because they have strayed from me!
Destruction to them,
    because they have rebelled against me!
I long to redeem them
    but they speak lies against me.
¹⁴They do not cry out to me from their hearts
    but wail upon their beds.
They gather together^w for grain and new
        wine
    but turn away from me.
¹⁵I trained them and strengthened them,
    but they plot evil against me.
¹⁶They do not turn to the Most High;
    they are like a faulty bow.
Their leaders will fall by the sword
    because of their insolent words.
For this they will be ridiculed
    in the land of Egypt.

8 "Put the trumpet to your lips!
    An eagle is over the house of the LORD
    because the people have broken my
        covenant
    and rebelled against my law.

---
^w 14 Most Hebrew manuscripts; some Hebrew manuscripts and
Septuagint *They slash themselves*

2Israel cries out to me,
  'O our God, we acknowledge you!'
3But Israel has rejected what is good;
  an enemy will pursue him.
4They set up kings without my consent;
  they choose princes without my approval.
With their silver and gold
  they make idols for themselves
  to their own destruction.
5Throw out your calf-idol, O Samaria!
  My anger burns against them.
How long will they be incapable of purity?
6   They are from Israel!
This calf—a craftsman has made it;
  it is not God.
It will be broken in pieces,
  that calf of Samaria.

7"They sow the wind
  and reap the whirlwind.
The stalk has no head;
  it will produce no flour.
Were it to yield grain,
  foreigners would swallow it up.
8Israel is swallowed up;
  now she is among the nations

like a worthless thing.
9For they have gone up to Assyria
  like a wild donkey wandering alone.
Ephraim has sold herself to lovers.
10Although they have sold themselves among
     the nations,
  I will now gather them together.
They will begin to waste away
  under the oppression of the mighty king.
11"Though Ephraim built many altars for sin
     offerings,
  these have become altars for sinning.
12I wrote for them the many things of my law,
  but they regarded them as something alien.
13They offer sacrifices given to me
  and they eat the meat,
  but the LORD is not pleased with them.
Now he will remember their wickedness
  and punish their sins:
  They will return to Egypt.
14Israel has forgotten his Maker
  and built palaces;
  Judah has fortified many towns.
But I will send fire upon their cities
  that will consume their fortresses."

Discovering the Word 1. How does Hosea convey the wickedness of Israel (also called Samaria and Ephraim) in 7:1–7? 2. The Lord condemns the foreign policy of Israel. How do the images of 7:8–13 and 8:7–10 show their folly? 3. What did the Israelites need to do to change their future (7:14–15)? 4. The Israelites were convinced that they had turned to the Lord (8:2). What betrayed the reality of the situation (8:3–6)? 5. The Israelites asked for forgiveness through the sacrificial system that the Lord provided, so why was God angry (8:11–14)?

Applying the Word 1. Hosea uses vivid language to characterize the people of Israel in these chapters. What images would you use to describe your walk with God? 2. God condemns the Israelites for seeking help from idols or other nations. How are you like the Israelites? 3. The Israelites are incredibly self-deluded in these chapters. Where do you see this self-delusion in the church and in yourself?

Responding in Prayer Pray for forgiveness for the times that you delude yourself. Through the power of the Spirit pray that you will be able to face the truth and find freedom.

---

6 / *Hosea 9—10*
What Are You Planting?

DO YOU LIKE it when your refrigerator and cupboard are full? Isn't it great to have your debts paid and money in the bank? These are the times we thank and praise God. The Israelites were prosperous in the first part of Hosea's ministry, but here Hosea tells the Israelites not to rejoice. Their fertility (having babies, growing crops, increasing livestock) was coming to an end. It was not that they had not planted, but that they planted the wrong things. What we sow, we will reap.

Warming Up to God What are you planting in your life and in the lives of others? Consider whether you are letting God guide what you sow.

Read Hosea 9—10.

9 Do not rejoice, O Israel;
　　do not be jubilant like the other
　　　　nations.
For you have been unfaithful to your God;
　　you love the wages of a prostitute
　　at every threshing floor.
²Threshing floors and winepresses will not feed
　　　　the people;
　　the new wine will fail them.
³They will not remain in the LORD's land;
　　Ephraim will return to Egypt
　　and eat unclean[x] food in Assyria.
⁴They will not pour out wine offerings to the
　　　　LORD,
　　nor will their sacrifices please him.
Such sacrifices will be to them like the bread
　　　　of mourners;
　　all who eat them will be unclean.
This food will be for themselves;
　　it will not come into the temple of the
　　　　LORD.

⁵What will you do on the day of your
　　　　appointed feasts,
　　on the festival days of the LORD?
⁶Even if they escape from destruction,
　　Egypt will gather them,
　　and Memphis will bury them.
Their treasures of silver will be taken over by
　　　　briers,
　　and thorns will overrun their tents.
⁷The days of punishment are coming,
　　the days of reckoning are at hand.
　　Let Israel know this.
Because your sins are so many
　　and your hostility so great,
the prophet is considered a fool,
　　the inspired man a maniac.
⁸The prophet, along with my God,
　　is the watchman over Ephraim,[y]
yet snares await him on all his paths,
　　and hostility in the house of his God.
⁹They have sunk deep into corruption,
　　as in the days of Gibeah.
God will remember their wickedness
　　and punish them for their sins.

¹⁰"When I found Israel,

it was like finding grapes in the desert;
when I saw your fathers,
　　it was like seeing the early fruit on the fig
　　　　tree.
But when they came to Baal Peor,
　　they consecrated themselves to that
　　　　shameful idol
　　and became as vile as the thing they loved.
¹¹Ephraim's glory will fly away like a bird—
　　no birth, no pregnancy, no conception.
¹²Even if they rear children,
　　I will bereave them of every one.
Woe to them
　　when I turn away from them!
¹³I have seen Ephraim, like Tyre,
　　planted in a pleasant place.
But Ephraim will bring out
　　their children to the slayer."

¹⁴Give them, O LORD—
　　what will you give them?
Give them wombs that miscarry
　　and breasts that are dry.

¹⁵"Because of all their wickedness in Gilgal,
　　I hated them there.
Because of their sinful deeds,
　　I will drive them out of my house.
I will no longer love them;
　　all their leaders are rebellious.
¹⁶Ephraim is blighted,
　　their root is withered,
　　they yield no fruit.
Even if they bear children,
　　I will slay their cherished offspring."

¹⁷My God will reject them
　　because they have not obeyed him;
　　they will be wanderers among the nations.

10 Israel was a spreading vine;
　　he brought forth fruit for himself.
　　As his fruit increased,
he built more altars;
as his land prospered,
　　he adorned his sacred stones.
²Their heart is deceitful,

x3 That is, ceremonially unclean　　　y8 Or The prophet is the watchman over Ephraim, / the people of my God

and now they must bear their guilt.
The LORD will demolish their altars
and destroy their sacred stones.

³Then they will say, "We have no king
because we did not revere the LORD.
But even if we had a king,
what could he do for us?"
⁴They make many promises,
take false oaths
and make agreements;
therefore lawsuits spring up
like poisonous weeds in a plowed field.
⁵The people who live in Samaria fear
for the calf-idol of Beth Aven.ᶻ
Its people will mourn over it,
and so will its idolatrous priests,
those who had rejoiced over its splendor,
because it is taken from them into exile.
⁶It will be carried to Assyria
as tribute for the great king.
Ephraim will be disgraced;
Israel will be ashamed of its wooden
idols.ᵃ
⁷Samaria and its king will float away
like a twig on the surface of the waters.
⁸The high places of wickednessᵇ will be
destroyed—
it is the sin of Israel.
Thorns and thistles will grow up
and cover their altars.
Then they will say to the mountains, "Cover
us!"
and to the hills, "Fall on us!"

⁹"Since the days of Gibeah, you have sinned,
O Israel,
and there you have remained.ᶜ
Did not war overtake
the evildoers in Gibeah?

¹⁰When I please, I will punish them;
nations will be gathered against them
to put them in bonds for their double sin.
¹¹Ephraim is a trained heifer
that loves to thresh;
so I will put a yoke
on her fair neck.
I will drive Ephraim,
Judah must plow,
and Jacob must break up the ground.
¹²Sow for yourselves righteousness,
reap the fruit of unfailing love,
and break up your unplowed ground;
for it is time to seek the LORD,
until he comes
and showers righteousness on you.
¹³But you have planted wickedness,
you have reaped evil,
you have eaten the fruit of deception.
Because you have depended on your own
strength
and on your many warriors,
¹⁴the roar of battle will rise against your people,
so that all your fortresses will be
devastated—
as Shalman devastated Beth Arbel on the day
of battle,
when mothers were dashed to the ground
with their children.
¹⁵Thus will it happen to you, O Bethel,
because your wickedness is great.
When that day dawns,
the king of Israel will be completely
destroyed.

ᶻ5 Beth Aven means *house of wickedness* (a name for Bethel, which means *house of God*).   ᵈ6 Or *its counsel*   ᵇ8 Hebrew *aven*, a reference to Beth Aven (a derogatory name for Bethel)   ᶜ9 Or *there a stand was taken*

Discovering the Word 1. How do you see the theme of fertility in chapters 9—10? 2. Festival days were to celebrate the Lord's goodness to Israel. Why then would God take away the joy of the celebration? 3. Why was the prophet, God's lookout, considered a fool (9:7–8)? 4. Hosea describes the people using farming metaphors. What images stand out to you (9:10, 13, 16; 10:1, 4, 7, 11–13)? 5. How does the metaphor of planting describe the plight of Israel (10:11–15)?

Applying the Word 1. When do you find yourself focused more on what the Lord has blessed you with than on the Blesser himself? 2. How has the law of the farm—what you sow, you reap—shown itself in your life? 3. No one likes listening to prophets because they call into question those things which make us comfortable. How can we (as individuals and as the church) learn to keep our ears open to the prophets in our lives?

Responding in Prayer Ask God to help you to be a more faithful worker in the fields of your life, the church and the world.

---

7 / *Hosea 11:1–11*
Turning Away from God

YOU'VE PROBABLY HAD the experience of being nice to someone who did not appreciate it. It can result in a wedge in the relationship you were trying to nurture. But what about the reverse? Has there been a time when someone was nice to you, but you didn't realize it until much later? Your response to that kindness was probably much less than it should have been. Unfortunately for Israel, their response to God was horrible. God had nurtured them for years, but they gave their love to other gods.

 Warming Up to God When is it hard for you to experience God's love for you as his child? Ask God to make his love more than head knowledge for you.

 Read Hosea 11:1–11.

---

11 "When Israel was a child, I loved him,
and out of Egypt I called my son.
²But the more I*d* called Israel,
the further they went from me.*e*
They sacrificed to the Baals
and they burned incense to images.
³It was I who taught Ephraim to walk,
taking them by the arms;
but they did not realize
it was I who healed them.
⁴I led them with cords of human kindness,
with ties of love;
I lifted the yoke from their neck
and bent down to feed them.

⁵"Will they not return to Egypt
and will not Assyria rule over them
because they refuse to repent?
⁶Swords will flash in their cities,
will destroy the bars of their gates
and put an end to their plans.
⁷My people are determined to turn from me.
Even if they call to the Most High,
he will by no means exalt them.

⁸"How can I give you up, Ephraim?
How can I hand you over, Israel?
How can I treat you like Admah?
How can I make you like Zeboiim?
My heart is changed within me;
all my compassion is aroused.
⁹I will not carry out my fierce anger,
nor will I turn and devastate Ephraim.
For I am God, and not man—
the Holy One among you.
I will not come in wrath.*f*
¹⁰They will follow the LORD;
he will roar like a lion.
When he roars,
his children will come trembling from the
west.
¹¹They will come trembling
like birds from Egypt,
like doves from Assyria.
I will settle them in their homes,"
declares the LORD.

d2 Some Septuagint manuscripts; Hebrew they   e2 Septuagint;
Hebrew them   f9 Or come against any city

 Discovering the Word 1. What emotions do you sense as you read 11:1–11? 2. How did the Lord treat Israel (vv. 1, 3–4)? 3. Why does Israel respond to the Lord as she does (vv. 1–7)? 4. What do you make of God's anguish as he wrestles with treating Israel like the sister cities of Sodom and Gomorrah (vv. 8–9; Gen 14; Deut 29:23)? 5. Why will the Israelites finally respond to God's call (vv. 10–11)?

Applying the Word 1. How is your experience of God like the Israelites'? 2. What does it mean to you that the Lord is not human? 3. How are you affected by the descriptions of God's emotions?

 Responding in Prayer Pray that God will keep you from being determined to turn away. Ask him to help you realize the depth of his love and to give you the same love for him.

8 / *Hosea 11:12—13:16*
Chasing the Wind

IF YOU KNEW that two tornadoes were going to collide, would you stand in the middle of them? Israel did, because she thought she could play the two superpowers against each other. Hosea called this foolish practice "pursuing the wind." (The west wind was Egypt and the east wind was the more terrifying Assyria.) Instead of relying on the Lord, Israel thought she could control her future through foreign policy. History tells us that Israel was destroyed by Assyria.

 Warming Up to God Reflect before God on how you control your life and your future.

 Read Hosea 11:12—13:16.

¹²Ephraim has surrounded me with lies,
   the house of Israel with deceit.
And Judah is unruly against God,
   even against the faithful Holy One.

12 ¹Ephraim feeds on the wind;
   he pursues the east wind all day
   and multiplies lies and violence.
He makes a treaty with Assyria
   and sends olive oil to Egypt.
²The LORD has a charge to bring against Judah;
   he will punish Jacobᵍ according to his
      ways
   and repay him according to his deeds.
³In the womb he grasped his brother's heel;
   as a man he struggled with God.
⁴He struggled with the angel and overcame
      him;
   he wept and begged for his favor.
He found him at Bethel
   and talked with him there—
⁵the LORD God Almighty,
   the LORD is his name of renown!
⁶But you must return to your God;
   maintain love and justice,
   and wait for your God always.

⁷The merchant uses dishonest scales;
   he loves to defraud.
⁸Ephraim boasts,
   "I am very rich; I have become wealthy.

With all my wealth they will not find in me
   any iniquity or sin."

⁹"I am the LORD your God,
   ⌐who brought you⌐ out ofʰ Egypt;
I will make you live in tents again,
   as in the days of your appointed feasts.
¹⁰I spoke to the prophets,
   gave them many visions
   and told parables through them."

¹¹Is Gilead wicked?
   Its people are worthless!
Do they sacrifice bulls in Gilgal?
   Their altars will be like piles of stones
   on a plowed field.
¹²Jacob fled to the country of Aramⁱ;
   Israel served to get a wife,
   and to pay for her he tended sheep.
¹³The LORD used a prophet to bring Israel up
      from Egypt,
   by a prophet he cared for him.
¹⁴But Ephraim has bitterly provoked him to
      anger;
   his Lord will leave upon him the guilt of
      his bloodshed
   and will repay him for his contempt.

g2 Jacob means he grasps the heel (figuratively, *he deceives*).   *h9* Or
God / ever since you were in   *i12* That is, Northwest Mesopotamia

13

When Ephraim spoke, men
  trembled;
  he was exalted in Israel.
But he became guilty of Baal worship and
  died.
²Now they sin more and more;
  they make idols for themselves from their
    silver,
cleverly fashioned images,
  all of them the work of craftsmen.
It is said of these people,
  "They offer human sacrifice
  and kiss[j] the calf-idols."

³Therefore they will be like the morning mist,
  like the early dew that disappears,
  like chaff swirling from a threshing floor,
  like smoke escaping through a window.

⁴"But I am the LORD your God,
  ˍwho brought youˍ out of[k] Egypt.
You shall acknowledge no God but me,
  no Savior except me.
⁵I cared for you in the desert,
  in the land of burning heat.
⁶When I fed them, they were satisfied;
  when they were satisfied, they became
    proud;
  then they forgot me.
⁷So I will come upon them like a lion,
  like a leopard I will lurk by the path.
⁸Like a bear robbed of her cubs,
  I will attack them and rip them open.
Like a lion I will devour them;
  a wild animal will tear them apart.

⁹"You are destroyed, O Israel,
  because you are against me, against your
    helper.

¹⁰Where is your king, that he may save you?
  Where are your rulers in all your towns,
of whom you said,
  'Give me a king and princes'?
¹¹So in my anger I gave you a king,
  and in my wrath I took him away.
¹²The guilt of Ephraim is stored up,
  his sins are kept on record.
¹³Pains as of a woman in childbirth come to
    him,
  but he is a child without wisdom;
when the time arrives,
  he does not come to the opening of the
    womb.

¹⁴"I will ransom them from the power of the
    grave[l];
  I will redeem them from death.
Where, O death, are your plagues?
  Where, O grave,[l] is your destruction?

"I will have no compassion,
¹⁵ even though he thrives among his brothers.
An east wind from the LORD will come,
  blowing in from the desert;
his spring will fail
  and his well dry up.
His storehouse will be plundered
  of all its treasures.
¹⁶The people of Samaria must bear their guilt,
  because they have rebelled against their
    God.
They will fall by the sword;
  their little ones will be dashed to the
    ground,
  their pregnant women ripped open."

j2 Or "Men who sacrifice / kiss   k4 Or God / ever since you were in
l14 Hebrew Sheol

 Discovering the Word 1. How is Israel (also called Ephraim, Jacob and Samaria) revealed as lying, deceitful and manipulative in chapters 12 and 13? 2. How does God stand in contrast to Israel (12:5, 6, 9, 10, 13; 13:4–6)? 3. How does Hosea show the silliness of Israel's pride and idolatry (12:8; 13:2, 6, 13)? 4. Why does Hosea keep reminding Israel of what the Lord God did for them in the past? 5. What was the result of Israel's unfaithfulness to God and her manipulation of Assyria (13:15–16)?

Applying the Word 1. How do you lie to or manipulate God, others and yourself? 2. How can you let the Lord poke holes in your pride and idolatry? 3. How does the way God has saved you in the past change the way you look at the present and the future?

Responding in Prayer Pray that you will remember where to put your trust when the wind blows and when it is silent.

9 / *Hosea 14*
Who Is Wise?

SUPPOSE SOMEONE SAID to you, "Well, if you really knew me, I'm not sure that you would tell me that God loves me." What would you say? Have you ever wondered how God could love you? After reading Hosea, it is quite reasonable to wonder how God could love Israel. The Lord knew Israel to be thoroughly corrupt, and yet in chapter 14 God holds out incredible grace to this wicked nation.

 Warming Up to God Our sins are often too big for us to handle. When have you felt that your sins were too big even for God to handle?

 Read Hosea 14.

14 Return, O Israel, to the LORD your God.
　Your sins have been your downfall!
²Take words with you
　and return to the LORD.
Say to him:
　"Forgive all our sins
and receive us graciously,
　that we may offer the fruit of our lips.ᵐ
³Assyria cannot save us;
　we will not mount war-horses.
We will never again say 'Our gods'
　to what our own hands have made,
　for in you the fatherless find compassion."

⁴"I will heal their waywardness
　and love them freely,
　for my anger has turned away from them.
⁵I will be like the dew to Israel;
　he will blossom like a lily.
Like a cedar of Lebanon
　he will send down his roots;

⁶ his young shoots will grow.
His splendor will be like an olive tree,
　his fragrance like a cedar of Lebanon.
⁷Men will dwell again in his shade.
　He will flourish like the grain.
He will blossom like a vine,
　and his fame will be like the wine from Lebanon.
⁸O Ephraim, what more have Iⁿ to do with idols?
　I will answer him and care for him.
I am like a green pine tree;
　your fruitfulness comes from me."

⁹Who is wise? He will realize these things.
　Who is discerning? He will understand them.
The ways of the LORD are right;
　the righteous walk in them,
　but the rebellious stumble in them.

ᵐ2 Or *offer our lips as sacrifices of bulls*　　ⁿ8 Or *What more has Ephraim*

 Discovering the Word 1. How does this chapter act as a conclusion to Hosea? 2. What must Israel do to receive God's forgiveness (vv. 1–3)? 3. What promises are held out to a community who rebelled so greatly against the Lord (vv. 4–7)? 4. Israel sought help from other countries and from idols. How does the Lord stand in contrast to these "saviors" (vv. 8–9)?

Applying the Word 1. How do you need to heed and pray verses 1–3 or words like them? 2. In what way do you need to let God love you as he promises in verses 4–8? 3. Understanding and walking in the ways of the Lord are two critical partners for wisdom. How is that partnership of learning and doing manifested in your life? 4. Where should the partnership be strengthened?

Responding in Prayer Thank the Lord for forgiving and healing you. Pray that the Holy Spirit would help you to both know and walk in God's ways.

Joel

I n "The Great Stone Face" Nathaniel Hawthorne tells the story of a rock formation on the side of a mountain that resembled a human face. Legend had it that a truly great man resembling the great stone face would someday come to the nearby town. One boy made it his life's goal to study the face and search for its resemblance in others. Over the years he spent countless hours gazing with wonder at that awesome face. As the boy matured into manhood and as life's influences molded him, those around him were amazed to see what he had become—the great stone face!

The people of Judah were not being cautious about where they focused their attention. Joel's role was to warn them that their faces—and hearts—might be turning to stone.

We know little about the man Joel other than the fact that his message was geared toward Judah and that he was probably a resident of Jerusalem. The date of his writing is disputed among scholars. While some say Joel prophesied as late as 400 B.C., many believe he was a contemporary of Jonah and Amos.

Joel's prophecy came in the wake of a devastating locust plague. Joel saw this plague as a sign of God's judgment and warned that unless the people returned to the Lord they would face even greater judgment on the day of the Lord. But to those willing to "rend their hearts" he promised great blessings that would more than repay "the years the locusts have eaten" (2:25).

Outline

1/ Joel 1 ——————————————— *Responding to a Crisis*

2/ Joel 2:1–27 ——————————— *Return to the Lord!*

3/ Joel 2:28—3:21 ——————— *The Day of the Lord*

1 / *Joel 1*
Responding to a Crisis

A CRISIS CAN capture anyone's attention. But the response to a crisis can vary greatly from person to person. Some become bitter and hardened. Others quietly endure but learn nothing from the experience. A few, however, find their lives are purified, deepened and strengthened. In Joel 1 a major crisis has occurred—a swarm of locusts has invaded the land, with devastating results. In the aftermath of the devastation, Joel appears with a word from the Lord. His word still has the power to purify those who hear it.

 Warming Up to God What is the most traumatic event you have seen during your lifetime? Explain.

 Read Joel 1.

1 The word of the Lord that came to Joel son of Pethuel.

²Hear this, you elders;
  listen, all who live in the land.
Has anything like this ever happened in your
    days
  or in the days of your forefathers?
³Tell it to your children,
  and let your children tell it to their
    children,
  and their children to the next generation.
⁴What the locust swarm has left
  the great locusts have eaten;
what the great locusts have left
  the young locusts have eaten;
what the young locusts have left
  other locusts*ᵃ* have eaten.

⁵Wake up, you drunkards, and weep!
  Wail, all you drinkers of wine;
wail because of the new wine,
  for it has been snatched from your lips.
⁶A nation has invaded my land,
  powerful and without number;
it has the teeth of a lion,
  the fangs of a lioness.
⁷It has laid waste my vines
  and ruined my fig trees.
It has stripped off their bark
  and thrown it away,
  leaving their branches white.

⁸Mourn like a virgin*ᵇ* in sackcloth
  grieving for the husband*ᶜ* of her youth.
⁹Grain offerings and drink offerings
  are cut off from the house of the Lord.
The priests are in mourning,

those who minister before the Lord.
¹⁰The fields are ruined,
  the ground is dried up*ᵈ*;
the grain is destroyed,
  the new wine is dried up,
  the oil fails.
¹¹Despair, you farmers,
  wail, you vine growers;
grieve for the wheat and the barley,
  because the harvest of the field is
    destroyed.
¹²The vine is dried up
  and the fig tree is withered;
the pomegranate, the palm and the apple
    tree—
  all the trees of the field—are dried up.
Surely the joy of mankind
  is withered away.

¹³Put on sackcloth, O priests, and mourn;
  wail, you who minister before the altar.
Come, spend the night in sackcloth,
  you who minister before my God;
for the grain offerings and drink offerings
  are withheld from the house of your God.
¹⁴Declare a holy fast;
  call a sacred assembly.
Summon the elders
  and all who live in the land
to the house of the Lord your God,
  and cry out to the Lord.

¹⁵Alas for that day!
  For the day of the Lord is near;
  it will come like destruction from the
    Almighty.*ᵉ*

ᵃ4 The precise meaning of the four Hebrew words used here for locusts is uncertain.   ᵇ8 Or young woman   ᶜ8 Or betrothed   ᵈ10 Or ground mourns   ᵉ15 Hebrew Shaddai

¹⁶Has not the food been cut off
    before our very eyes—
joy and gladness
    from the house of our God?
¹⁷The seeds are shriveled
    beneath the clods.ᶠ
The storehouses are in ruins,
    the granaries have been broken down,
    for the grain has dried up.
¹⁸How the cattle moan!
    The herds mill about

because they have no pasture;
    even the flocks of sheep are suffering.
¹⁹To you, O LORD, I call,
    for fire has devoured the open pastures
    and flames have burned up all the trees of
        the field.
²⁰Even the wild animals pant for you;
    the streams of water have dried up
    and fire has devoured the open pastures.

ᶠ17 The meaning of the Hebrew for this word is uncertain.

 Discovering the Word   1. Describe the devastation left by the locust plague.   2. How will the plague affect the drunkards (v. 5), the priests (vv. 9, 13) and the farmers (v. 11)?   3. Why do you think these groups are singled out?   4. Joel compares the people of Judah to a virgin mourning for her husband (a fiancé[e] was referred to as *husband* or *wife*) (v. 8). What does this metaphor say about the depth of relationship between God and his people?   5. In verses 13–14 Joel calls the people to repent. How are they to demonstrate their repentance?

 Applying the Word   1. In what ways does God discipline his people today, either individually or corporately?   2. In what meaningful ways can you express your repentance today, both individually and corporately?

Responding in Prayer   Ask God to show you where your inner life is in crisis and how you need to repent.

---

2 / *Joel 2:1–27*
Return to the Lord!

IN ORDER TO get to the roses, we must first go through the thorns. The teaching of Joel in the first two chapters is hard. But roses—in the form of the promises of God—lie ahead. Because he loves us, the Father disciplines us when we wander from him. The warnings we see here are God's last resort to bring his people to true repentance— a *heart* relationship rather than one of empty ritual. As we read this chapter, we too must face questions of the heart.

 Warming Up to God   How do we sometimes serve God outwardly rather than from the heart?

 Read Joel 2:1–27.

---

2 Blow the trumpet in Zion;
    sound the alarm on my holy hill.
    Let all who live in the land tremble,
  for the day of the LORD is coming.
It is close at hand—
² a day of darkness and gloom,
    a day of clouds and blackness.
Like dawn spreading across the mountains
    a large and mighty army comes,
such as never was of old
    nor ever will be in ages to come.

³Before them fire devours,
    behind them a flame blazes.
Before them the land is like the garden of
        Eden,
    behind them, a desert waste—
    nothing escapes them.
⁴They have the appearance of horses;
    they gallop along like cavalry.
⁵With a noise like that of chariots
    they leap over the mountaintops,
    like a crackling fire consuming stubble,

like a mighty army drawn up for battle.

[6]At the sight of them, nations are in anguish;
  every face turns pale.
[7]They charge like warriors;
  they scale walls like soldiers.
They all march in line,
  not swerving from their course.
[8]They do not jostle each other;
  each marches straight ahead.
They plunge through defenses
  without breaking ranks.
[9]They rush upon the city;
  they run along the wall.
They climb into the houses;
  like thieves they enter through the
    windows.
[10]Before them the earth shakes,
  the sky trembles,
the sun and moon are darkened,
  and the stars no longer shine.
[11]The Lord thunders
  at the head of his army;
his forces are beyond number,
  and mighty are those who obey his
    command.
The day of the Lord is great;
  it is dreadful.
Who can endure it?

[12]"Even now," declares the Lord,
  "return to me with all your heart,
  with fasting and weeping and mourning."

[13]Rend your heart
  and not your garments.
Return to the Lord your God,
  for he is gracious and compassionate,
slow to anger and abounding in love,
  and he relents from sending calamity.
[14]Who knows? He may turn and have pity
  and leave behind a blessing—
grain offerings and drink offerings
  for the Lord your God.

[15]Blow the trumpet in Zion,
  declare a holy fast,
  call a sacred assembly.
[16]Gather the people,
  consecrate the assembly;
bring together the elders,
  gather the children,
  those nursing at the breast.

Let the bridegroom leave his room
  and the bride her chamber.
[17]Let the priests, who minister before the Lord,
  weep between the temple porch and the
    altar.
Let them say, "Spare your people, O Lord.
  Do not make your inheritance an object of
    scorn,
  a byword among the nations.
Why should they say among the peoples,
  'Where is their God?' "

[18]Then the Lord will be jealous for his land
  and take pity on his people.
[19]The Lord will reply[g] to them:

"I am sending you grain, new wine and oil,
  enough to satisfy you fully;
never again will I make you
  an object of scorn to the nations.

[20]"I will drive the northern army far from you,
  pushing it into a parched and barren land,
with its front columns going into the eastern
    sea[h]
and those in the rear into the western
    sea.[i]
And its stench will go up;
  its smell will rise."

Surely he has done great things.[j]
[21] Be not afraid, O land;
  be glad and rejoice.
Surely the Lord has done great things.
[22] Be not afraid, O wild animals,
  for the open pastures are becoming green.
The trees are bearing their fruit;
  the fig tree and the vine yield their riches.
[23]Be glad, O people of Zion,
  rejoice in the Lord your God,
for he has given you
  the autumn rains in righteousness.[k]
He sends you abundant showers,
  both autumn and spring rains, as before.
[24]The threshing floors will be filled with grain;
  the vats will overflow with new wine and
    oil.

[25]"I will repay you for the years the locusts
    have eaten—
  the great locust and the young locust,

[g]18,19 Or Lord was jealous . . . / and took pity . . . / [19]The Lord replied
[h]20 That is, the Dead Sea   [i]20 That is, the Mediterranean   [j]20 Or
rise. / Surely it has done great things."   [k]23 Or / the teacher for
righteousness:

the other locusts and the locust swarm[l]—
  my great army that I sent among you.
[26]You will have plenty to eat, until you are full,
  and you will praise the name of the LORD
      your God,
  who has worked wonders for you;
never again will my people be shamed.

[27]Then you will know that I am in Israel,
  that I am the LORD your God,
  and that there is no other;
never again will my people be shamed.

[l]25 The precise meaning of the four Hebrew words used here for locusts
is uncertain.

Discovering the Word 1. Joel compares the invasion to "the day of the LORD" (1:15; 2:1–2, 11). What can we learn about that day from these verses? 2. How can the day of the Lord be a warning against spiritual complacency? 3. "Even now," what hope does the Lord offer his people, and why (vv. 12–14)? 4. How do verses 12–17 help us understand repentance? 5. If his people repent, what promises does the Lord make (vv. 18–27)?

Applying the Word 1. In what ways would you like to renew your commitment to the Lord? 2. How have you experienced God's healing through the act of repentance?

Responding in Prayer Take time to "praise the name of the LORD your God" for the wonders he has worked for you (v. 26).

---

3 / Joel 2:28—3:21
The Day of the Lord

CHRISTIANS LONG FOR that great and final day when the Lord will return. But the day of the Lord will not be the same for everyone. For some it will be a day of indescribable joy and blessing. For others it will be a day of judgment and terror. In this final section of his book, Joel looks at both aspects of the day of the Lord.

Warming Up to God When you think of the Lord's return, what images come to mind?

Read Joel 2:28—3:21.

---

[28]"And afterward,
  I will pour out my Spirit on all people.
Your sons and daughters will prophesy,
  your old men will dream dreams,
  your young men will see visions.
[29]Even on my servants, both men and women,
  I will pour out my Spirit in those days.
[30]I will show wonders in the heavens
    and on the earth,
  blood and fire and billows of smoke.
[31]The sun will be turned to darkness
    and the moon to blood
  before the coming of the great and dreadful
      day of the LORD.
[32]And everyone who calls
  on the name of the LORD will be saved;
for on Mount Zion and in Jerusalem
  there will be deliverance,

as the LORD has said,
among the survivors
  whom the LORD calls.

3 "In those days and at that time,
  when I restore the fortunes of Judah
    and Jerusalem,
[2]I will gather all nations
  and bring them down to the Valley of
      Jehoshaphat.[m]
There I will enter into judgment against them
  concerning my inheritance, my people
    Israel,
for they scattered my people among the
    nations
  and divided up my land.
[3]They cast lots for my people

[m]2 Jehoshaphat means the LORD judges; also in verse 12.

and traded boys for prostitutes;
   they sold girls for wine
     that they might drink.

[4]"Now what have you against me, O Tyre and Sidon and all you regions of Philistia? Are you repaying me for something I have done? If you are paying me back, I will swiftly and speedily return on your own heads what you have done. [5]For you took my silver and my gold and carried off my finest treasures to your temples. [6]You sold the people of Judah and Jerusalem to the Greeks, that you might send them far from their homeland.

[7]"See, I am going to rouse them out of the places to which you sold them, and I will return on your own heads what you have done. [8]I will sell your sons and daughters to the people of Judah, and they will sell them to the Sabeans, a nation far away." The LORD has spoken.

[9]Proclaim this among the nations:
   Prepare for war!
Rouse the warriors!
   Let all the fighting men draw near and
     attack.
[10]Beat your plowshares into swords
   and your pruning hooks into spears.
Let the weakling say,
   "I am strong!"
[11]Come quickly, all you nations from every
     side,
   and assemble there.

   Bring down your warriors, O LORD!

[12]"Let the nations be roused;
   let them advance into the Valley of
     Jehoshaphat,
for there I will sit
   to judge all the nations on every side.
[13]Swing the sickle,

   for the harvest is ripe.
Come, trample the grapes,
   for the winepress is full
     and the vats overflow—
so great is their wickedness!"

[14]Multitudes, multitudes
   in the valley of decision!
For the day of the LORD is near
   in the valley of decision.
[15]The sun and moon will be darkened,
   and the stars no longer shine.
[16]The LORD will roar from Zion
   and thunder from Jerusalem;
   the earth and the sky will tremble.
But the LORD will be a refuge for his people,
   a stronghold for the people of Israel.
[17]"Then you will know that I, the LORD your
     God,
   dwell in Zion, my holy hill.
Jerusalem will be holy;
   never again will foreigners invade her.

[18]"In that day the mountains will drip new
     wine,
   and the hills will flow with milk;
   all the ravines of Judah will run with water.
A fountain will flow out of the LORD's house
   and will water the valley of acacias.[n]
[19]But Egypt will be desolate,
   Edom a desert waste,
   because of violence done to the people of
     Judah,
   in whose land they shed innocent blood.
[20]Judah will be inhabited forever
   and Jerusalem through all generations.
[21]Their bloodguilt, which I have not pardoned,
   I will pardon."

     The LORD dwells in Zion!

[n]18 Or Valley of Shittim

Discovering the Word **1.** According to 2:28–31, what signs will precede the "coming of the great and dreadful day of the LORD"? **2.** What have the nations done to provoke the Lord's judgment (3:1-8)? **3.** The Lord commands the nations to prepare for war (3:9). How does their battle relate to the Lord's judgment (3:9–16)? **4.** Joel describes the Lord as a lion, a thunderstorm, a refuge and a stronghold (3:16). What do these images reveal about the God we serve? **5.** What blessings does the Lord promise his people (3:16–21)?

Applying the Word **1.** Peter claimed Joel's prophecy was fulfilled on the day of Pentecost (Acts 2:17–21, 38–40). How then does Joel's promise of the Spirit and salvation apply to us (2:28–32)? **2.** What has Joel taught you about preparing for the day of the Lord? **3.** What steps do you need to take to be prepared?

 Responding in Prayer Ask God to make you always ready for his return.

Amos

Although Amos was a farmer from Judah, he prophesied to Israel, the northern kingdom, around 760 B.C. During this period the nation was secure and the upper classes prospered. Archaeological discoveries at Megiddo and Samaria have uncovered carved ivory inlays that were used in the furniture and decorative paneling in the homes of the wealthy. But instead of using their wealth to serve the needy, the upper classes were deaf to their cries. In fact, the wealthy maintained their lifestyle by oppressing the poor.

Although the Israelites continued to worship God, their worship was cold and self-serving. Jeroboam had built temples in Bethel and Dan so the people would worship in the north rather than traveling to Jerusalem. But God viewed this worship as idolatrous and declared, "I hate, I despise your religious feasts; I cannot stand your assemblies. Even though you bring me burnt offerings and grain offerings, I will not accept them" (Am 5:21–22).

God's judgment came against Israel in the form of famine, drought and plagues. But because the people failed to return to the Lord, Amos prophesied that all but a remnant would be destroyed. Still the Lord pleaded with Israel, "Seek good, not evil, that you may live!" (Am 5:14).

Amos has a powerful message today. We often seek the wrong things, forgetting the One who is the only source of true life. Amos challenges us to forsake anything and everything that hinders our relationship with God, proclaiming, "Seek the Lord and live!"

Outline

1/ Amos 1—2 ———————————— Judgment & Justice

2/ Amos 3 ———————————————— Sin & Wealth

3/ Amos 4 ———————————————— Prepare to Meet Your God!

4/ Amos 5—6 ————————————— Seek the Lord and Live!

5/ Amos 7—8 ————————————— Visions of Judgment

6/ Amos 9 ———————————————— Visions of Hope

1 / *Amos 1—2*
Judgment & Justice

PICTURE THIS, IF you will. It is about the middle of the eighth century B.C. People are flocking to the worship center at Bethel, people whom we might call "upper middle class." The design of the building is very appealing. The choirs are polished. Several brilliant orators are at hand. It feels good to come here—uplifting music, beautiful surroundings and comforting words. There is even opportunity for the people to placate their consciences by bringing offerings. But wait a minute! Who is that seedy-looking character? He speaks like a shepherd; he looks like a shepherd; he even smells like a shepherd—but he sure doesn't sound like a shepherd!

 Warming Up to God Recall something you never thought would happen to you. How did you feel when it *did* happen?

 Read Amos 1—2.

1 The words of Amos, one of the shepherds of Tekoa—what he saw concerning Israel two years before the earthquake, when Uzziah was king of Judah and Jeroboam son of Jehoash[a] was king of Israel.
²He said:

"The LORD roars from Zion
 and thunders from Jerusalem;
the pastures of the shepherds dry up,[b]
 and the top of Carmel withers."

³This is what the LORD says:

"For three sins of Damascus,
 even for four, I will not turn back ⌐my
  wrath⌐.
Because she threshed Gilead
 with sledges having iron teeth,
⁴I will send fire upon the house of Hazael
 that will consume the fortresses of
  Ben-Hadad.
⁵I will break down the gate of Damascus;
 I will destroy the king who is in[c] the
  Valley of Aven[d]
and the one who holds the scepter in Beth
  Eden.
 The people of Aram will go into exile to
  Kir,"
                                says the LORD.

⁶This is what the LORD says:

"For three sins of Gaza,
 even for four, I will not turn back ⌐my
  wrath⌐.
Because she took captive whole communities
 and sold them to Edom,
⁷I will send fire upon the walls of Gaza

that will consume her fortresses.
⁸I will destroy the king[e] of Ashdod
 and the one who holds the scepter in
  Ashkelon.
I will turn my hand against Ekron,
 till the last of the Philistines is dead,"
                        says the Sovereign LORD.

⁹This is what the LORD says:

"For three sins of Tyre,
 even for four, I will not turn back ⌐my
  wrath⌐.
Because she sold whole communities of
  captives to Edom,
 disregarding a treaty of brotherhood,
¹⁰I will send fire upon the walls of Tyre
 that will consume her fortresses."

¹¹This is what the LORD says:

"For three sins of Edom,
 even for four, I will not turn back ⌐my
  wrath⌐.
Because he pursued his brother with a sword,
 stifling all compassion,[f]
because his anger raged continually
 and his fury flamed unchecked,
¹²I will send fire upon Teman
 that will consume the fortresses of Bozrah."

¹³This is what the LORD says:

"For three sins of Ammon,
 even for four, I will not turn back ⌐my
  wrath⌐.

Because he ripped open the pregnant women
  of Gilead
  in order to extend his borders,
¹⁴I will set fire to the walls of Rabbah
  that will consume her fortresses
amid war cries on the day of battle,
  amid violent winds on a stormy day.
¹⁵Her king^g will go into exile,
  he and his officials together,"
                                   says the LORD.

2 This is what the LORD says:

"For three sins of Moab,
  even for four, I will not turn back ⌐my
    wrath⌐.
Because he burned, as if to lime,
  the bones of Edom's king,
²I will send fire upon Moab
  that will consume the fortresses of
    Kerioth.^h
Moab will go down in great tumult
  amid war cries and the blast of the trumpet.
³I will destroy her ruler
  and kill all her officials with him,"
                                   says the LORD.

⁴This is what the LORD says:

"For three sins of Judah,
  even for four, I will not turn back ⌐my
    wrath⌐.
Because they have rejected the law of the
    LORD
  and have not kept his decrees,
because they have been led astray by false
    gods,ⁱ
  the gods^j their ancestors followed,
⁵I will send fire upon Judah
  that will consume the fortresses of
    Jerusalem."

⁶This is what the LORD says:

"For three sins of Israel,

even for four, I will not turn back ⌐my
    wrath⌐.
They sell the righteous for silver,
  and the needy for a pair of sandals.
⁷They trample on the heads of the poor
  as upon the dust of the ground
  and deny justice to the oppressed.
Father and son use the same girl
  and so profane my holy name.
⁸They lie down beside every altar
  on garments taken in pledge.
In the house of their god
  they drink wine taken as fines.

⁹"I destroyed the Amorite before them,
  though he was tall as the cedars
  and strong as the oaks.
I destroyed his fruit above
  and his roots below.

¹⁰"I brought you up out of Egypt,
  and I led you forty years in the desert
  to give you the land of the Amorites.
¹¹I also raised up prophets from among your
    sons
  and Nazirites from among your young men.
Is this not true, people of Israel?"
                                   declares the LORD.

¹²"But you made the Nazirites drink wine
  and commanded the prophets not to
    prophesy.

¹³"Now then, I will crush you
  as a cart crushes when loaded with grain.
¹⁴The swift will not escape,
  the strong will not muster their strength,
  and the warrior will not save his life.
¹⁵The archer will not stand his ground,
  the fleet-footed soldier will not get away,
  and the horseman will not save his life.
¹⁶Even the bravest warriors
  will flee naked on that day,"
                                   declares the LORD.

^g15 Or / Molech; Hebrew malcam   ^h2 Or of her cities   ⁱ4 Or by lies   ^j4 Or lies

---

Discovering the Word 1. How does 1:2 set the tone for Amos's message? 2. Damascus, Gaza, Tyre, Edom, Ammon and Moab all represented enemies of Israel. How would the Israelites feel as they heard prophecies against these nations (1:3—2:3)? 3. The repeated phrase "For three sins . . . even for four" emphasizes God's patience before pronouncing judgment. What kinds of sin do the pagan nations have in common (1:3—2:3)? 4. How are Judah's sins different from those of the pagan nations (2:4–5)? 5. Amos cites a variety of sins of which Israel is guilty (2:6–8, 12). How would you categorize their sins? 6. How are Israel's sins all the more serious in light of their history (2:9–11)?

Applying the Word 1. As Christians, what can we do to bring relief and justice to the righteous, the needy, the poor and the oppressed? 2. How can Amos's warnings to Israel keep us from being presumptuous about our status as God's children?

 Responding in Prayer Ask God to grant you humility.

2 / *Amos 3*
Sin & Wealth

A WELL-KNOWN insurance company uses cartoons to advertise their product. One cartoon pictures a piano falling from an upper-story window toward an unsuspecting man below. As it speeds toward its destination, a friend politely asks, "By the way, what's the name of your insurance company?"

"Acme insurance, of course," the man replies. "Why do you ask?"

Disaster often comes unexpectedly. The people of Israel were wealthy, self-centered and complacent. Little did they realize that the full weight of God's judgment was about to fall on them.

 Warming Up to God How do you respond to the portrayal of God as judge?

 Read Amos 3.

3 Hear this word the LORD has spoken against you, O people of Israel—against the whole family I brought up out of Egypt:

²"You only have I chosen
  of all the families of the earth;
therefore I will punish you
  for all your sins."

³Do two walk together
  unless they have agreed to do so?
⁴Does a lion roar in the thicket
  when he has no prey?
Does he growl in his den
  when he has caught nothing?
⁵Does a bird fall into a trap on the ground
  where no snare has been set?
Does a trap spring up from the earth
  when there is nothing to catch?
⁶When a trumpet sounds in a city,
  do not the people tremble?
When disaster comes to a city,
  has not the LORD caused it?
⁷Surely the Sovereign LORD does nothing
  without revealing his plan
  to his servants the prophets.

⁸The lion has roared—

who will not fear?
The Sovereign LORD has spoken—
  who can but prophesy?

⁹Proclaim to the fortresses of Ashdod
  and to the fortresses of Egypt:
"Assemble yourselves on the mountains of
    Samaria;
  see the great unrest within her
  and the oppression among her people."

¹⁰"They do not know how to do right," declares
    the LORD,
  "who hoard plunder and loot in their
    fortresses."

¹¹Therefore this is what the Sovereign LORD says:

"An enemy will overrun the land;
  he will pull down your strongholds
  and plunder your fortresses."

¹²This is what the LORD says:

"As a shepherd saves from the lion's mouth
  only two leg bones or a piece of an ear,
  so will the Israelites be saved,
those who sit in Samaria
  on the edge of their beds

and in Damascus on their couches.^{k}"

^{13}"Hear this and testify against the house of
Jacob," declares the Lord, the LORD God Almighty.

^{14}"On the day I punish Israel for her sins,
    I will destroy the altars of Bethel;
the horns of the altar will be cut off
    and fall to the ground.

^{15}I will tear down the winter house
    along with the summer house;
the houses adorned with ivory will be
    destroyed
and the mansions will be demolished,"
                                        declares the LORD.

^{k}12 The meaning of the Hebrew for this line is uncertain.

Discovering the Word 1. The Israelites were confident that Yahweh was their God and they were his chosen people. But how had they misunderstood that call (vv. 1–2)? 2. In verses 3–6 Amos asks several rhetorical questions. How would you summarize what he is trying to say in these verses? 3. What do verses 9–10 say about Israel's morality and lifestyle in comparison with the pagan nations? 4. How would the Lord's judgment against Israel fit their crimes (vv. 10–11, 15)? 5. According to the law, people in danger could find refuge by grasping the horns of the altar (see 1Ki 1:50). How and why would this change (vv. 13–14)? 6. Try to view this chapter from the perspective of those who were oppressed by the wealthy. How would you feel as you heard Amos's prophecy?

Applying the Word 1. What does this chapter teach us about God's character? 2. This passage tells us that privilege brings responsibility. How is that true for you?

Responding in Prayer Ask the Lord to give you the strength of character needed to be responsible as a person of God.

---

3 / *Amos 4*
Prepare to Meet Your God!

IN 1741 JONATHAN Edwards preached his most famous sermon: "Sinners in the Hands of an Angry God." After using vivid imagery to make non-Christians feel the horror of their position, Edwards concluded: "Therefore, let every one that is out of Christ now awake and fly from the wrath to come!" God used that sermon to bring a powerful awakening to the town of Enfield, in New England. The prophet Amos preaches a similar sermon in this chapter. After warning Israel repeatedly to return to the Lord, he now declares: "Prepare to meet your God!"

 Warming Up to God Recall a time when you wandered from God. What brought you back?

 Read Amos 4.

---

4 Hear this word, you cows of Bashan on
    Mount Samaria,
you women who oppress the poor and
    crush the needy
and say to your husbands, "Bring us some
    drinks!"
^{2}The Sovereign LORD has sworn by his holiness:
    "The time will surely come
when you will be taken away with hooks,
    the last of you with fishhooks.
^{3}You will each go straight out
    through breaks in the wall,

and you will be cast out toward
    Harmon,^{l}"
                                        declares the LORD.
^{4}"Go to Bethel and sin;
    go to Gilgal and sin yet more.
Bring your sacrifices every morning,
    your tithes every three years.^{m}
^{5}Burn leavened bread as a thank offering
    and brag about your freewill offerings—
boast about them, you Israelites,

^{l}3 Masoretic Text; with a different word division of the Hebrew (see
Septuagint) *out, O mountain of oppression* ^{m}4 Or *tithes on the third
day*

for this is what you love to do,"
                    declares the Sovereign Lord.

6"I gave you empty stomachs[n] in every city
    and lack of bread in every town,
    yet you have not returned to me,"
                    declares the Lord.

7"I also withheld rain from you
    when the harvest was still three months
        away.
I sent rain on one town,
    but withheld it from another.
One field had rain;
    another had none and dried up.

8People staggered from town to town for water
    but did not get enough to drink,
    yet you have not returned to me,"
                    declares the Lord.

9"Many times I struck your gardens and
        vineyards,
I struck them with blight and mildew.
Locusts devoured your fig and olive trees,
    yet you have not returned to me,"
                    declares the Lord.

10"I sent plagues among you

as I did to Egypt.
I killed your young men with the sword,
    along with your captured horses.
I filled your nostrils with the stench of your
        camps,
    yet you have not returned to me,"
                    declares the Lord.

11"I overthrew some of you
    as I[o] overthrew Sodom and Gomorrah.
You were like a burning stick snatched from
        the fire,
    yet you have not returned to me,"
                    declares the Lord.

12"Therefore this is what I will do to you,
        Israel,
and because I will do this to you,
    prepare to meet your God, O Israel."

13He who forms the mountains,
    creates the wind,
    and reveals his thoughts to man,
he who turns dawn to darkness,
    and treads the high places of the earth—
    the Lord God Almighty is his name.

[n]6 Hebrew *you cleanness of teeth*   [o]11 Hebrew *God*

 Discovering the Word 1. The area of Bashan was noted for its fat, sleek cattle. How does the lifestyle of the women of Israel contrast with the judgment the Lord swears to bring upon them (vv. 2–3)? 2. Bethel and Gilgal were centers of worship for the northern kingdom (1Ki 12:26–33; Hos 4:15). What was sinful about Israel's worship at these places (vv. 4–5)? 3. What words would you use to describe each of the judgments the Lord brought on Israel (vv. 6–11)? 4. Amos proclaims to Israel, "Prepare to meet your God" (v. 12). In light of this chapter, what kind of "meeting" could Israel expect this to be? 5. The chapter closes with a brief hymn describing the God Israel would meet in judgment (v. 13). What do we learn about God from each aspect of Amos's description?

Applying the Word 1. How can we keep our worship from becoming empty ritual? 2. God's tenderness, even in the midst of judgment, is evident in the repeated words "yet you have not returned to me" (vv. 6, 8, 9, 10, 11). How have you experienced God's grace in the midst of discipline?

Responding in Prayer Take a few minutes to worship God, using this hymn as the basis for your prayers.

---

4 / Amos 5—6
Seek the Lord and Live!

SUCCESS, WEALTH, POWER, prestige—these are eagerly sought by many today. People are willing to sacrifice their marriages, their families and even their health to obtain these goals. But in the end most discover that the rewards were not worth the cost. How tragic! In chapters 5 and 6 Amos tells us how to avoid this tragedy in our lives—"Seek the Lord and live!"

 Warming Up to God Why do you think people are willing to sacrifice so much to obtain the things mentioned above? To what extent are you looking for these things?

 Read Amos 5—6.

5 Hear this word, O house of Israel, this lament I take up concerning you:

² "Fallen is Virgin Israel,
never to rise again,
deserted in her own land,
with no one to lift her up."

³This is what the Sovereign LORD says:

"The city that marches out a thousand strong
for Israel
will have only a hundred left;
the town that marches out a hundred strong
will have only ten left."

⁴This is what the LORD says to the house of Israel:

"Seek me and live;
⁵ do not seek Bethel,
do not go to Gilgal,
do not journey to Beersheba.
For Gilgal will surely go into exile,
and Bethel will be reduced to nothing.ᵖ"
⁶Seek the LORD and live,
or he will sweep through the house of
Joseph like a fire;
it will devour,
and Bethel will have no one to quench it.

⁷You who turn justice into bitterness
and cast righteousness to the ground
⁸(he who made the Pleiades and Orion,
who turns blackness into dawn
and darkens day into night,
who calls for the waters of the sea
and pours them out over the face of the
land—
the LORD is his name—
⁹he flashes destruction on the stronghold
and brings the fortified city to ruin),
¹⁰you hate the one who reproves in court
and despise him who tells the truth.

¹¹You trample on the poor
and force him to give you grain.

Therefore, though you have built stone
mansions,
you will not live in them;
though you have planted lush vineyards,
you will not drink their wine.
¹²For I know how many are your offenses
and how great your sins.

You oppress the righteous and take bribes
and you deprive the poor of justice in the
courts.
¹³Therefore the prudent man keeps quiet in
such times,
for the times are evil.

¹⁴Seek good, not evil,
that you may live.
Then the LORD God Almighty will be with
you,
just as you say he is.
¹⁵Hate evil, love good;
maintain justice in the courts.
Perhaps the LORD God Almighty will have
mercy
on the remnant of Joseph.

¹⁶Therefore this is what the Lord, the LORD God
Almighty, says:

"There will be wailing in all the streets
and cries of anguish in every public square.
The farmers will be summoned to weep
and the mourners to wail.
¹⁷There will be wailing in all the vineyards,
for I will pass through your midst,"
says the LORD.

¹⁸Woe to you who long
for the day of the LORD!
Why do you long for the day of the LORD?
That day will be darkness, not light.
¹⁹It will be as though a man fled from a lion
only to meet a bear,
as though he entered his house
and rested his hand on the wall

ᵖ5 Or grief; or wickedness; Hebrew aven, a reference to Beth Aven (a derogatory name for Bethel)

only to have a snake bite him.
20Will not the day of the Lord be darkness, not
　　light—
　pitch-dark, without a ray of brightness?

21"I hate, I despise your religious feasts;
　I cannot stand your assemblies.
22Even though you bring me burnt offerings
　　and grain offerings,
　I will not accept them.
Though you bring choice fellowship
　　offerings,q
　I will have no regard for them.
23Away with the noise of your songs!
　I will not listen to the music of your harps.
24But let justice roll on like a river,
　righteousness like a never-failing stream!

25"Did you bring me sacrifices and offerings
　forty years in the desert, O house of Israel?
26You have lifted up the shrine of your king,
　the pedestal of your idols,
　the star of your godr—
　which you made for yourselves.
27Therefore I will send you into exile beyond
　　Damascus,"
　says the Lord, whose name is God
　　Almighty.

6 Woe to you who are complacent in
　　Zion,
　and to you who feel secure on Mount
　　Samaria,
you notable men of the foremost nation,
　to whom the people of Israel come!
2Go to Calneh and look at it;
　go from there to great Hamath,
　and then go down to Gath in Philistia.
Are they better off than your two kingdoms?
　Is their land larger than yours?
3You put off the evil day
　and bring near a reign of terror.
4You lie on beds inlaid with ivory
　and lounge on your couches.
You dine on choice lambs
　and fattened calves.
5You strum away on your harps like David
　and improvise on musical instruments.

6You drink wine by the bowlful
　and use the finest lotions,
　but you do not grieve over the ruin of
　　Joseph.
7Therefore you will be among the first to go
　　into exile;
　your feasting and lounging will end.

8The Sovereign Lord has sworn by himself—
the Lord God Almighty declares:

"I abhor the pride of Jacob
　and detest his fortresses;
I will deliver up the city
　and everything in it."

9If ten men are left in one house, they too will
die. 10And if a relative who is to burn the bodies
comes to carry them out of the house and asks
anyone still hiding there, "Is anyone with you?"
and he says, "No," then he will say, "Hush! We
must not mention the name of the Lord."

11For the Lord has given the command,
　and he will smash the great house into
　　pieces
　and the small house into bits.

12Do horses run on the rocky crags?
　Does one plow there with oxen?
But you have turned justice into poison
　and the fruit of righteousness into
　　bitterness—
13you who rejoice in the conquest of Lo
　　Debars
　and say, "Did we not take Karnaimt by
　　our own strength?"

14For the Lord God Almighty declares,
　"I will stir up a nation against you,
　　O house of Israel,
　that will oppress you all the way
　　from Lebou Hamath to the valley of the
　　Arabah."

q22 Traditionally *peace offerings*　r26 Or *lifted up Sakkuth your king*
/ and Kaiwan your idols, / your star-gods; Septuagint *lifted up the shrine
of Molech / and the star of your god Rephan, / their idols*　s13 *Lo
Debar* means *nothing.*　t13 *Karnaim* means *horns; horn here
symbolizes strength.*　u14 Or *from the entrance to*

Discovering the Word　1. A *lament* (5:1) was a song or poem mourning someone's death. How does
Amos portray the death of Israel (5:2)?　**2.** What has Israel done to deserve the Lord's judgment (5:7, 10,
11, 12)?　**3.** The Lord pleads with Israel in verses 4, 6, 14 and 15. In this context, what would it mean for Israel to
seek the Lord?　**4.** How were the Israelites mistaken about the day of the Lord (5:18–20)?　**5.** How does Amos

portray the Israelites in 6:1–6?   **6.** How does the Lord promise to repay those who are complacent and proud (6:7–14)?

 Applying the Word   **1.** In their complacency and security, Israel failed to grieve over the ruin of their nation (5:6). What should grieve you today about your personal life?   **2.** What grieves you about your church and your nation?

 Responding in Prayer   Take time to pray about those things that cause you to grieve. Ask the Lord to help you seek his will in these areas.

5 / Amos 7—8
Visions of Judgment

IT IS EASY to side with Amos. After all, his prophecies are part of the Bible! But put yourself in Israel's place. How would you have responded if a farmer came to town and began announcing visions of judgment? In chapters 7—9 we will look at five of Amos's visions and one fairly typical response.

 Warming Up to God   Think of a time you have been confronted by a street preacher or visiting evangelist who warned of God's judgment. How do you respond to that approach?

 Read Amos 7—8.

7 This is what the Sovereign Lord showed me: He was preparing swarms of locusts after the king's share had been harvested and just as the second crop was coming up. ²When they had stripped the land clean, I cried out, "Sovereign Lord, forgive! How can Jacob survive? He is so small!"

³So the Lord relented.

"This will not happen," the Lord said.

⁴This is what the Sovereign Lord showed me: The Sovereign Lord was calling for judgment by fire; it dried up the great deep and devoured the land. ⁵Then I cried out, "Sovereign Lord, I beg you, stop! How can Jacob survive? He is so small!"

⁶So the Lord relented.

"This will not happen either," the Sovereign Lord said.

⁷This is what he showed me: The Lord was standing by a wall that had been built true to plumb, with a plumb line in his hand. ⁸And the Lord asked me, "What do you see, Amos?"

"A plumb line," I replied.

Then the Lord said, "Look, I am setting a plumb line among my people Israel; I will spare them no longer.

⁹"The high places of Isaac will be destroyed and the sanctuaries of Israel will be ruined; with my sword I will rise against the house of Jeroboam."

¹⁰Then Amaziah the priest of Bethel sent a message to Jeroboam king of Israel: "Amos is raising a conspiracy against you in the very heart of Israel. The land cannot bear all his words. ¹¹For this is what Amos is saying:

" 'Jeroboam will die by the sword,
      and Israel will surely go into exile,
      away from their native land.' "

¹²Then Amaziah said to Amos, "Get out, you seer! Go back to the land of Judah. Earn your bread there and do your prophesying there. ¹³Don't prophesy anymore at Bethel, because this is the king's sanctuary and the temple of the kingdom."

¹⁴Amos answered Amaziah, "I was neither a prophet nor a prophet's son, but I was a shepherd, and I also took care of sycamore-fig trees. ¹⁵But the Lord took me from tending the flock and said to me, 'Go, prophesy to my people Israel.' ¹⁶Now then, hear the word of the Lord. You say,

" 'Do not prophesy against Israel,

and stop preaching against the house of Isaac.'

¹⁷"Therefore this is what the Lord says:

" 'Your wife will become a prostitute in the
city,
and your sons and daughters will fall by
the sword.
Your land will be measured and divided up,
and you yourself will die in a pagan^v
country.
And Israel will certainly go into exile,
away from their native land.' "

8 This is what the Sovereign Lord showed
me: a basket of ripe fruit. ²"What do you
see, Amos?" he asked.

"A basket of ripe fruit," I answered.

Then the Lord said to me, "The time is ripe for
my people Israel; I will spare them no longer.

³"In that day," declares the Sovereign Lord,
"the songs in the temple will turn to wailing.^w
Many, many bodies—flung everywhere! Silence!"

⁴Hear this, you who trample the needy
and do away with the poor of the land,

⁵saying,

"When will the New Moon be over
that we may sell grain,
and the Sabbath be ended
that we may market wheat?"—
skimping the measure,
boosting the price
and cheating with dishonest scales,
⁶buying the poor with silver
and the needy for a pair of sandals,
selling even the sweepings with the wheat.

⁷The Lord has sworn by the Pride of Jacob: "I
will never forget anything they have done.

⁸"Will not the land tremble for this,

and all who live in it mourn?
The whole land will rise like the Nile;
it will be stirred up and then sink
like the river of Egypt.

⁹"In that day," declares the Sovereign Lord,

"I will make the sun go down at noon
and darken the earth in broad daylight.
¹⁰I will turn your religious feasts into mourning
and all your singing into weeping.
I will make all of you wear sackcloth
and shave your heads.
I will make that time like mourning for an
only son
and the end of it like a bitter day.

¹¹"The days are coming," declares the Sovereign
Lord,
"when I will send a famine through the
land—
not a famine of food or a thirst for water,
but a famine of hearing the words of the
Lord.
¹²Men will stagger from sea to sea
and wander from north to east,
searching for the word of the Lord,
but they will not find it.

¹³"In that day

"the lovely young women and strong young
men
will faint because of thirst.
¹⁴They who swear by the shame^x of Samaria,
or say, 'As surely as your god lives, O Dan,'
or, 'As surely as the god^y of Beersheba
lives'—
they will fall,
never to rise again."

^v17 Hebrew *an unclean*   ^w3 Or "*the temple singers will wail*
^x14 Or *by Ashima; or by the idol*   ^y14 Or *power*

Discovering the Word 1. What three visions of judgment does the Lord show Amos (7:1, 4, 7)? 2. Why does the Lord "relent" regarding the first two visions (7:1–6)? 3. In verses 10–17, Amos undergoes his own "plumb-line" test. What temptations might he have experienced? 4. How does Amos describe the lifestyle of those who are ripe for judgment (8:4–6)? 5. How does he describe the "harvest" they will experience (8:3–14)?

Applying the Word 1. Even though we can freely read the Bible, how does "famine" evidence itself among God's people? 2. How can the Lord's response to Amos's prayers (7:6) motivate us to pray for our nation? 3. How can Amos's response to Amaziah (7:10–17) be an example to us when we are tempted to compromise our beliefs?

Responding in Prayer Pray that God will use your study in Amos to mold you into the person he wants you to be.

6 / *Amos 9*
Visions of Hope

HOPE IS ONE of the three greatest gifts. It can lift our broken spirits, strengthen our feeble bodies and transform our darkest moments into lighthearted praise. Up to this point Amos has offered little hope to Israel. But in this final chapter, as the pace toward destruction quickens, he brings his prophecy to a surprising conclusion—one that is full of hope, promise and a renewed vision of God.

 Warming Up to God How does hope differ from wishful or "positive" thinking?

 Read Amos 9.

9 I saw the Lord standing by the altar, and he said:

"Strike the tops of the pillars
so that the thresholds shake.
Bring them down on the heads of all the
people;
those who are left I will kill with the
sword.
Not one will get away,
none will escape.
²Though they dig down to the depths of the
grave,^{z}
from there my hand will take them.
Though they climb up to the heavens,
from there I will bring them down.
³Though they hide themselves on the top of
Carmel,
there I will hunt them down and seize
them.
Though they hide from me at the bottom of
the sea,
there I will command the serpent to bite
them.
⁴Though they are driven into exile by their
enemies,
there I will command the sword to slay
them.
I will fix my eyes upon them
for evil and not for good."

⁵The Lord, the LORD Almighty,
he who touches the earth and it melts,

and all who live in it mourn—
the whole land rises like the Nile,
then sinks like the river of Egypt—
⁶he who builds his lofty palace^a in the
heavens
and sets its foundation^b on the earth,
who calls for the waters of the sea
and pours them out over the face of the
land—
the LORD is his name.

⁷"Are not you Israelites
the same to me as the Cushites^c?"
declares the LORD.
"Did I not bring Israel up from Egypt,
the Philistines from Caphtor^d
and the Arameans from Kir?

⁸"Surely the eyes of the Sovereign LORD
are on the sinful kingdom.
I will destroy it
from the face of the earth—
yet I will not totally destroy
the house of Jacob,"
declares the LORD.
⁹"For I will give the command,
and I will shake the house of Israel
among all the nations
as grain is shaken in a sieve,
and not a pebble will reach the ground.

^{z}2 Hebrew *to Sheol* ^{a}6 The meaning of the Hebrew for this phrase
is uncertain. ^{b}6 The meaning of the Hebrew for this word is
uncertain. ^{c}7 That is, people from the upper Nile region ^{d}7 That
is, Crete

¹⁰All the sinners among my people
    will die by the sword,
all those who say,
    'Disaster will not overtake or meet us.'

¹¹"In that day I will restore
    David's fallen tent.
I will repair its broken places,
    restore its ruins,
    and build it as it used to be,
¹²so that they may possess the remnant of
        Edom
    and all the nations that bear my name,ᵉ"
    declares the LORD, who will do these things.

¹³"The days are coming," declares the LORD,

"when the reaper will be overtaken by the
        plowman

and the planter by the one treading grapes.
New wine will drip from the mountains
    and flow from all the hills.
¹⁴I will bring back my exiledᶠ people Israel;
    they will rebuild the ruined cities and live
        in them.
They will plant vineyards and drink their
        wine;
    they will make gardens and eat their fruit.
¹⁵I will plant Israel in their own land,
    never again to be uprooted
    from the land I have given them,"

                                                    says the LORD your God.

ᵉ12 Hebrew; Septuagint *so that the remnant of men / and all the nations
that bear my name may seek ˻the Lord˼*   ᶠ14 Or *will restore the
fortunes of my*

Discovering the Word 1. How does Amos describe the fate of those who try to escape (vv. 1–4)? 2. How do you think the description of the Lord in verses 5–6 relates to the pronouncements of the previous verses? 3. The Israelites thought they were superior to other nations because God chose them and delivered them from Egypt. Why would they be shocked by verse 7 and the first part of verse 8? 4. What glimmer of hope does Amos offer the house of Jacob (vv. 8–10)? 5. Suddenly Israel's glimmer of hope begins to shine with intense brightness (vv. 11–15). How does Amos's final prophecy contrast with what he has said before?

Applying the Word 1. When in your life or in the life of your church has the Lord restored what was in ruins (v. 11)? 2. How can this portrait of God give us hope even when things seem hopeless?

Responding in Prayer Pray for hope in your life and in the lives of people you know who may feel hopeless.

Obadiah

I t's a little book, the shortest in the Old Testament. Tucked between its more famous neighbors, Amos and Jonah, it is so small you easily miss it. It makes its point briefly in vigorous language, and then it's over. What's more, it is directed to Edom, which most of us can't identify, let alone identify *with*. Yet as we read the prophecy of Obadiah, the words begin to sound strangely familiar. *Pride, exploitation, gloating, justice, deliverance, hope*—they're all here in these few succinct lines.

Who was Obadiah? The name means "servant of God," and there are several Obadiahs mentioned in the Bible from around the time of the book's events. All we know for sure is that this Obadiah received a vision (1:1). It was not a vision for the Jews, but for Edom.

Rivalry between Edom and Israel went way back. Abraham's son Isaac had twin sons, Jacob and Esau. Esau had the important right of firstborn, but in a moment of hunger he sold it to the opportunistic Jacob (Ge 25:27–34). Later Jacob tricked Esau out of their father's blessing (Ge 27). Jacob fled when he found out that Esau planned revenge. It was not till years later that they met again (Ge 33). Though the meeting was emotional, the breach was never entirely healed, and their descendants remained rivals—relatives with an unsettled score.

Esau was called "Edom" as early as Genesis 25:30, and the name is confirmed several times in Genesis 30. There is no doubt that Obadiah was talking about these relatives of Israel when he painted such a grim picture of their fate.

The Edomites had settled south of the Dead Sea, and there were frequent border clashes between Edom and Judah. When the Babylonian king Nebuchadnezzar conquered Jerusalem in 587 B.C. (2Ki 25:8–12), Edom saw their opportunity to move in on the spoils. They joined forces with the Babylonians, cut off the fleeing Judeans and grabbed what they could from the Jews (Ps 137:7). For that sin Obadiah said Edom would be brought down. The Edomites were assimilated into other peoples and never regained their identity as a nation.

In these twenty-one verses Obadiah has a lot to say about contemporary issues: greed, broken families, injustice, profit-taking. We are wise to pay attention to his warnings. If we are victims of those sins, we can take comfort that Obadiah ends on a note of hope—not for Edom, but for Israel. God will bring about justice. God sees the human disaster. God will restore what has been robbed. "And the kingdom will be the Lord's" (Ob 21).

Obadiah 1–21
Compassion for the Fallen

"SHOULD YOU BUY a house that's been repossessed, no matter how cheaply it's offered, or would that be profiting from someone else's misfortune?" To me, the questioner had an overly scrupulous conscience; but perhaps it's good that someone would bother to ask the question. Most of us take advantage of any opportunity that comes along, without caring where it came from.

 Warming Up to God When have you found the promise of God's righteous judgment a source of comfort?

 Read Obadiah 1–21.

---

¹The vision of Obadiah.

This is what the Sovereign LORD says about Edom—

We have heard a message from the LORD:
An envoy was sent to the nations to say,
"Rise, and let us go against her for battle"—

²"See, I will make you small among the
    nations;
  you will be utterly despised.
³The pride of your heart has deceived you,
  you who live in the clefts of the rocks*ᵃ*
  and make your home on the heights,
you who say to yourself,
  'Who can bring me down to the ground?'
⁴Though you soar like the eagle
  and make your nest among the stars,
  from there I will bring you down,"
                         declares the LORD.
⁵"If thieves came to you,
  if robbers in the night—
Oh, what a disaster awaits you—
  would they not steal only as much as they
    wanted?
If grape pickers came to you,
  would they not leave a few grapes?
⁶But how Esau will be ransacked,
  his hidden treasures pillaged!
⁷All your allies will force you to the border;
  your friends will deceive and overpower
    you;
those who eat your bread will set a trap for
    you,*ᵇ*
  but you will not detect it.

⁸"In that day," declares the LORD,
  "will I not destroy the wise men of Edom,

men of understanding in the mountains of
    Esau?
⁹Your warriors, O Teman, will be terrified,
  and everyone in Esau's mountains
  will be cut down in the slaughter.
¹⁰Because of the violence against your brother
    Jacob,
  you will be covered with shame;
  you will be destroyed forever.
¹¹On the day you stood aloof
  while strangers carried off his wealth
and foreigners entered his gates
  and cast lots for Jerusalem,
  you were like one of them.
¹²You should not look down on your brother
  in the day of his misfortune,
nor rejoice over the people of Judah
  in the day of their destruction,
nor boast so much
  in the day of their trouble.
¹³You should not march through the gates of
    my people
  in the day of their disaster,
nor look down on them in their calamity
  in the day of their disaster,
nor seize their wealth
  in the day of their disaster.
¹⁴You should not wait at the crossroads
  to cut down their fugitives,
nor hand over their survivors
  in the day of their trouble.

¹⁵"The day of the LORD is near
  for all nations.
As you have done, it will be done to you;
  your deeds will return upon your own
    head.

ᵃ3 Or of Sela   *ᵇ7 The meaning of the Hebrew for this clause is uncertain.*

¹⁶Just as you drank on my holy hill,
   so all the nations will drink continually;
they will drink and drink
   and be as if they had never been.
¹⁷But on Mount Zion will be deliverance;
   it will be holy,
and the house of Jacob
   will possess its inheritance.
¹⁸The house of Jacob will be a fire
   and the house of Joseph a flame;
the house of Esau will be stubble,
   and they will set it on fire and consume it.
There will be no survivors
   from the house of Esau."
             The Lord has spoken.

¹⁹People from the Negev will occupy

   the mountains of Esau,
and people from the foothills will possess
   the land of the Philistines.
They will occupy the fields of Ephraim and
   Samaria,
and Benjamin will possess Gilead.
²⁰This company of Israelite exiles who are in
   Canaan
will possess ⌊the land⌋ as far as Zarephath;
the exiles from Jerusalem who are in
   Sepharad
will possess the towns of the Negev.
²¹Deliverers will go up on^c Mount Zion
   to govern the mountains of Esau.
And the kingdom will be the Lord's.

^c21 Or *from*

 Discovering the Word 1. Edom (the descendants of Esau) had taken advantage of the fall of Jerusalem and even participated in its destruction. How did God respond to their actions? 2. What was Edom's attitude toward the future (vv. 3–4)? 3. Why would Edom be destroyed (vv. 10–14)? 4. How would justice be carried out in their downfall (vv. 15–18)? 5. What would be the fate of Edom's lands (vv. 19–21)?

Applying the Word 1. What warning do you see in Edom's example about how we should *not* respond to other people's misfortunes? 2. When have you been tempted to gloat over someone's downfall? 3. How can you show sympathy and compassion toward someone who has fallen?

Responding in Prayer Confess any feeling of superiority over those who have fallen. Ask the Lord to help you see others through his eyes of compassion.

Jonah

A wise professor once said, "What gets your attention, gets you." This is especially true in the book of Jonah. God takes drastic measures to get Jonah's attention. He does so not because he delights in calamity but because he desires our fellowship.

Jonah prophesied in the eighth century B.C., during or shortly before the reign of Jeroboam II (793–753 B.C.). God called him to preach to Nineveh, the capital of Assyria, which was the most powerful nation on earth. The more we know about Assyria, the more we understand why Jonah was reluctant to preach there. The Assyrians were a fierce, warring people who often treated their captives ruthlessly. Jonah had good reason to be afraid!

But fear was not the only thing that made Jonah reluctant. His attitude reflects the racial prejudice common in his day. The "chosen people" could not imagine that God could care about other nations—especially one as vile and idolatrous as Assyria. So the book of Jonah becomes a powerful illustration of the fact that God does not want "anyone to perish, but everyone to come to repentance" (2Pe 3:9).

The story of Jonah has been the subject of much controversy. Many people reject its historicity, preferring to view it as an allegory or parable. However, two things should be noted about this view. First, few people questioned the historicity of Jonah until the nineteenth century, when liberal scholars launched an attack on every book in the Bible. They objected to its historicity primarily because of the incident of Jonah's being swallowed by a fish. However, even from a natural standpoint this incident is quite possible. In his *Introduction to the Old Testament*, R. K. Harrison points out that there are other reliable records of people being swallowed by large fish and surviving. Second, Jesus himself viewed the story of Jonah as history (Mt 12:38–41; Lk 11:29–30, 32), comparing it to the greater miracle of his resurrection.

We can learn from Jonah, knowing there will be times when we run from God's will and need to return to him.

Outline

1/ Jonah 1 ———————————————— Jonah's Disobedience
2/ Jonah 2 ———————————————— Jonah's Prayer
3/ Jonah 3 ———————————————— Jonah's Obedience
4/ Jonah 4 ———————————————— Jonah's Anger

1 / *Jonah 1*
Jonah's Disobedience

"DON'T HIT YOUR sister!" Sometimes it takes all the willpower we have to obey. Yet how easy it is to do wrong in the first place. We get mad and we react. That's what it feels like with God sometimes too. He asks us to do things we don't want to do—things that are difficult, uncomfortable or even painful. So politely but firmly we refuse his command and try to put it out of our minds. Yet as Jonah discovered, our disobedience can be even more costly than our obedience.

 Warming Up to God   Have you ever wanted to turn away from something you knew God wanted you to do? Explain.

 Read Jonah 1.

1 The word of the Lord came to Jonah son of Amittai: ²"Go to the great city of Nineveh and preach against it, because its wickedness has come up before me."

³But Jonah ran away from the Lord and headed for Tarshish. He went down to Joppa, where he found a ship bound for that port. After paying the fare, he went aboard and sailed for Tarshish to flee from the Lord.

⁴Then the Lord sent a great wind on the sea, and such a violent storm arose that the ship threatened to break up. ⁵All the sailors were afraid and each cried out to his own god. And they threw the cargo into the sea to lighten the ship.

But Jonah had gone below deck, where he lay down and fell into a deep sleep. ⁶The captain went to him and said, "How can you sleep? Get up and call on your god! Maybe he will take notice of us, and we will not perish."

⁷Then the sailors said to each other, "Come, let us cast lots to find out who is responsible for this calamity." They cast lots and the lot fell on Jonah.

⁸So they asked him, "Tell us, who is responsible for making all this trouble for us? What do you do? Where do you come from? What is your country? From what people are you?"

⁹He answered, "I am a Hebrew and I worship the Lord, the God of heaven, who made the sea and the land."

¹⁰This terrified them and they asked, "What have you done?" (They knew he was running away from the Lord, because he had already told them so.)

¹¹The sea was getting rougher and rougher. So they asked him, "What should we do to you to make the sea calm down for us?"

¹²"Pick me up and throw me into the sea," he replied, "and it will become calm. I know that it is my fault that this great storm has come upon you."

¹³Instead, the men did their best to row back to land. But they could not, for the sea grew even wilder than before. ¹⁴Then they cried to the Lord, "O Lord, please do not let us die for taking this man's life. Do not hold us accountable for killing an innocent man, for you, O Lord, have done as you pleased." ¹⁵Then they took Jonah and threw him overboard, and the raging sea grew calm. ¹⁶At this the men greatly feared the Lord, and they offered a sacrifice to the Lord and made vows to him.

¹⁷But the Lord provided a great fish to swallow Jonah, and Jonah was inside the fish three days and three nights.

Discovering the Word   1. Nineveh was the capital of Assyria, a nation that was a fierce and powerful enemy of Israel's to the northeast. How does Jonah respond to the Lord's command to preach there (vv. 1–3)? 2. Tarshish, traditionally identified as Spain, was over two thousand miles in the opposite direction. While Jonah was journeying to Tarshish, what kinds of thoughts and feelings might he have experienced? 3. How do you think Jonah felt when the captain urged him to call on God for help (v. 6)? 4. Why do the sailors become even more terrified after they hear Jonah's story (vv. 7–10)? 5. Jonah acknowledges his guilt in verses 11–12. Do you think he is repentant at this point? Explain. 6. How does God use this calamity to demonstrate his grace and mercy (vv. 15–17)?

Applying the Word 1. How does this chapter illustrate the futility of running from God? 2. We run from God in ways that can be as obvious as Jonah's actions and in much more subtle daily ways. In what area of life are you currently running from God?

Responding in Prayer Pray that God will give you courage to be his representative to those he's calling you to minister to.

2 / *Jonah 2*
Jonah's Prayer

IN THE MOVIE *Pinnochio* a kindly woodcutter named Geppetto is swallowed by a whale named Monstro. Inside the dark, damp belly of the whale, Geppetto sits for what seems like an eternity. Then one day the whale violently coughs, and the woodcutter is expelled from his watery grave. Sound familiar? Every Sunday-school child would recognize this retelling of the story of Jonah. But unlike the Disney movie, Jonah's incredible adventure is not fantasy but fact.

 Warming Up to God What difficult situation has the Lord delivered you from? Offer your praises to God for his work in your life.

 Read Jonah 2.

From inside the fish Jonah prayed to the Lord his God. ²He said:

"In my distress I called to the Lord,
and he answered me.
From the depths of the grave*a* I called for help,
and you listened to my cry.
³You hurled me into the deep,
into the very heart of the seas,
and the currents swirled about me;
all your waves and breakers
swept over me.
⁴I said, 'I have been banished
from your sight;
yet I will look again
toward your holy temple.'
⁵The engulfing waters threatened me,*b*
the deep surrounded me;
seaweed was wrapped around my head.

⁶To the roots of the mountains I sank down;
the earth beneath barred me in forever.
But you brought my life up from the pit,
O Lord my God.

⁷"When my life was ebbing away,
I remembered you, Lord,
and my prayer rose to you,
to your holy temple.

⁸"Those who cling to worthless idols
forfeit the grace that could be theirs.
⁹But I, with a song of thanksgiving,
will sacrifice to you.
What I have vowed I will make good.
Salvation comes from the Lord."

¹⁰And the Lord commanded the fish, and it vomited Jonah onto dry land.

*a*2 Hebrew *Sheol*   *b*5 Or *waters were at my throat*

Discovering the Word 1. Describe the terrible sequence of events after Jonah was thrown overboard (vv. 3, 5–6). 2. What initial thoughts and feelings did Jonah have (vv. 3–6)? 3. How did these terrifying events affect Jonah's attitude toward God? 4. Why do you think God answered Jonah's prayer (vv. 2, 6, 9–10)? 5. Why can we be confident God will hear our prayers even if we are suffering the consequences of disobedience?

Applying the Word 1. When have you felt like you were in a deep, dark pit (v. 6), either physically, emotionally or spiritually? 2. Why do you think we sometimes have to sink so low before we remember God?

Responding in Prayer Take time now to thank God for his discipline and his grace. Quietly reaffirm your commitment to obey him.

3 / *Jonah 3*
Jonah's Obedience

GREAT REVIVALS HAVE occurred throughout history—among the Jews in the first century, the tribes of Ireland in the fifth century, the Protestants in the sixteenth century and the people of Wales in the twentieth century. Yet one of the greatest revivals of all time occurred hundreds of years before any of these—the amazing revival in Nineveh described in Jonah 3.

 Warming Up to God How have you seen God's compassion expressed when you are obedient?

 Read Jonah 3.

3 Then the word of the LORD came to Jonah a second time: ²"Go to the great city of Nineveh and proclaim to it the message I give you."

³Jonah obeyed the word of the LORD and went to Nineveh. Now Nineveh was a very important city—a visit required three days. ⁴On the first day, Jonah started into the city. He proclaimed: "Forty more days and Nineveh will be overturned." ⁵The Ninevites believed God. They declared a fast, and all of them, from the greatest to the least, put on sackcloth.

⁶When the news reached the king of Nineveh, he rose from his throne, took off his royal robes, covered himself with sackcloth and sat down in the dust. ⁷Then he issued a proclamation in Nineveh:

"By the decree of the king and his nobles:

Do not let any man or beast, herd or flock, taste anything; do not let them eat or drink. ⁸But let man and beast be covered with sackcloth. Let everyone call urgently on God. Let them give up their evil ways and their violence. ⁹Who knows? God may yet relent and with compassion turn from his fierce anger so that we will not perish."

¹⁰When God saw what they did and how they turned from their evil ways, he had compassion and did not bring upon them the destruction he had threatened.

 Discovering the Word 1. If you were Jonah, how would you feel when the word of the Lord came to you a second time (vv. 1–2)? 2. Assyria was one of the most powerful nations on earth, known especially for its military might and brutality. How would this make it difficult for Jonah to proclaim: "Forty more days and Nineveh will be overturned" (vv. 3–4)? 3. What evidence is there that the Ninevites were sincere in their repentance (vv. 5–9)? 4. How and why does the Lord respond to the Ninevites (v. 10)? 5. What view of God do the Ninevites express in this chapter? 6. If a genuine turning to God were to occur in this country, what results would you expect to see?

 Applying the Word 1. Describe one area in your life where you feel a need for repentance. 2. What actions can you take to demonstrate the sincerity of your repentance?

 Responding in Prayer Spend some time before the Lord expressing your repentance and experiencing God's grace.

4 / *Jonah 4*
Jonah's Anger

LIFE IS FULL of minor joys and irritations. Finding a parking place in rush hour can make us very happy. Finding a flat tire when we return can make us miserable. In chapter 4 we discover that Jonah also cared a great deal about life's little ups and downs. Although his petty passions seem amusing, they also invite us to reexamine what we really care about.

 Warming Up to God   What little things irritate you or bring you joy?

 Read Jonah 4.

But Jonah was greatly displeased and became angry. ²He prayed to the Lord, "O Lord, is this not what I said when I was still at home? That is why I was so quick to flee to Tarshish. I knew that you are a gracious and compassionate God, slow to anger and abounding in love, a God who relents from sending calamity. ³Now, O Lord, take away my life, for it is better for me to die than to live."

⁴But the Lord replied, "Have you any right to be angry?"

⁵Jonah went out and sat down at a place east of the city. There he made himself a shelter, sat in its shade and waited to see what would happen to the city. ⁶Then the Lord God provided a vine and made it grow up over Jonah to give shade for his head to ease his discomfort, and Jonah was very happy about the vine. ⁷But at dawn the next day God provided a worm, which chewed the vine so that it withered. ⁸When the sun rose, God provided a scorching east wind, and the sun blazed on Jonah's head so that he grew faint. He wanted to die, and said, "It would be better for me to die than to live."

⁹But God said to Jonah, "Do you have a right to be angry about the vine?"

"I do," he said. "I am angry enough to die."

¹⁰But the Lord said, "You have been concerned about this vine, though you did not tend it or make it grow. It sprang up overnight and died overnight. ¹¹But Nineveh has more than a hundred and twenty thousand people who cannot tell their right hand from their left, and many cattle as well. Should I not be concerned about that great city?"

 Discovering the Word   1. Why was Jonah greatly displeased and angry (vv. 1–3)?   2. Did these things give him any right to be angry (v. 4)? Explain.   3. Evidently the forty days had already passed (3:10). Why then do you think Jonah still waited to see what would happen to the city (v. 5)?   4. How does the Lord use the vine as an object lesson for Jonah (vv. 6–11)?   5. In what ways are we sometimes more concerned about petty things than about those under God's judgment?

Applying the Word   1. What can we do to begin seeing things more from God's perspective?   2. In your life, how have you seen God demonstrate the qualities Jonah mentions in 4:2?   3. How does God's treatment of you motivate you to reach out to those who don't know him?

Responding in Prayer   What have you learned from Jonah? Ask God to impress its message on your heart and life.

Micah

Have you ever learned from someone else's mistakes? We can save ourselves much pain by watching someone suffer the consequences of doing something that we easily could have done. The prophet Micah wonders why Judah does not learn from Israel.

After his death (922 B.C.) Solomon's kingdom was divided. To the north was Israel and to the south, Judah. Micah preaches before, during and after the time when Assyria comes from the east and destroys Israel (722 B.C.).

The society Micah portrays is not much different from what can be seen in the news today. People seize the property of others. The streets are filled with violence; widows and their children are thrown out of their homes. Yet Micah does not point to gangs as the source of the problem, but to the leaders. Prophet, priest and king alike commit wickedness toward those they are to protect. The prideful leaders sell prophecy for a price and cheat justice for a bribe.

Therefore Micah's message is largely one of judgment and doom. He knows that God will not ignore the plight of the innocent, nor will the Lord keep a blind eye toward the wicked. Micah boldly proclaims the impending destruction of God's people for their sins. In the first chapter Micah declares the impending destruction of Israel for her faithlessness. From the second chapter on he warns Judah of impending doom for the same faults as Israel. Yet Micah's message also contains clear messages of hope. At the end of chapters 2 and 7, along with chapters 4 and 5, we see that God will again have mercy on Judah. Micah holds out the promise of both a Messiah and a messianic age when all people will flock to the Lord's house.

Micah is not the first prophet to proclaim God's judgment against his people. He was preceded by Hosea and Amos. We can also be sure that the refugees from Israel, who quadrupled the population of Jerusalem, gave the Judeans eyewitness accounts of how God judged them. Unfortunately, the Judeans did not learn. Will we do any better?

Outline

1/ Micah 2 ———————————————— *Who Do You Listen To?*

2/ Micah 3 ———————————————— *How Not to Be a Leader*

3/ Micah 4 ———————————————— *Tomorrow and Today*

4/ Micah 5 ———————————————— *The Future of Our Enemies*

5/ Micah 6 ———————————————— *What God Requires*

6/ Micah 7 ———————————————— *How Long Will God Be Angry?*

Micah 1

1 The word of the LORD that came to Micah of Moresheth during the reigns of Jotham, Ahaz and Hezekiah, kings of Judah—the vision he saw concerning Samaria and Jerusalem.

²Hear, O peoples, all of you,
   listen, O earth and all who are in it,
that the Sovereign LORD may witness against
      you,
   the Lord from his holy temple.

³Look! The LORD is coming from his dwelling
      place;
   he comes down and treads the high places
      of the earth.
⁴The mountains melt beneath him
   and the valleys split apart,
like wax before the fire,
   like water rushing down a slope.
⁵All this is because of Jacob's transgression,
   because of the sins of the house of Israel.
What is Jacob's transgression?
   Is it not Samaria?
What is Judah's high place?
   Is it not Jerusalem?

⁶"Therefore I will make Samaria a heap of
      rubble,
   a place for planting vineyards.
I will pour her stones into the valley
   and lay bare her foundations.
⁷All her idols will be broken to pieces;
   all her temple gifts will be burned with fire;
   I will destroy all her images.
Since she gathered her gifts from the wages of
      prostitutes,
   as the wages of prostitutes they will again
      be used."

⁸Because of this I will weep and wail;
   I will go about barefoot and naked.
I will howl like a jackal
   and moan like an owl.
⁹For her wound is incurable;
   it has come to Judah.
It*a* has reached the very gate of my people,
   even to Jerusalem itself.
¹⁰Tell it not in Gath*b*;
   weep not at all.*c*
In Beth Ophrah*d*
   roll in the dust.
¹¹Pass on in nakedness and shame,
   you who live in Shaphir.*e*
Those who live in Zaanan*f*
   will not come out.
Beth Ezel is in mourning;
   its protection is taken from you.
¹²Those who live in Maroth*g* writhe in pain,
   waiting for relief,
because disaster has come from the LORD,
   even to the gate of Jerusalem.
¹³You who live in Lachish,*h*
   harness the team to the chariot.
You were the beginning of sin
   to the Daughter of Zion,
for the transgressions of Israel
   were found in you.
¹⁴Therefore you will give parting gifts
   to Moresheth Gath.
The town of Aczib*i* will prove deceptive
   to the kings of Israel.
¹⁵I will bring a conqueror against you
   who live in Mareshah.*j*
He who is the glory of Israel
   will come to Adullam.
¹⁶Shave your heads in mourning
   for the children in whom you delight;
make yourselves as bald as the vulture,
   for they will go from you into exile.

---

*a*9 Or He   *b*10 *Gath* sounds like the Hebrew for *tell*.
*c*10 Hebrew; Septuagint may suggest *not in Acco*. The Hebrew for *in Acco* sounds like the Hebrew for *weep*.   *d*10 *Beth Ophrah* means *house of dust*.   *e*11 *Shaphir* means *pleasant*.   *f*11 *Zaanan* sounds like the Hebrew for *come out*.   *g*12 *Maroth* sounds like the Hebrew for *bitter*.   *h*13 *Lachish* sounds like the Hebrew for *team*.   *i*14 *Aczib* means *deception*.   *j*15 *Mareshah* sounds like the Hebrew for *conqueror*.

1 / Micah 2
Who Do You Listen To?

JUST BECAUSE YOU have ears on your head does not mean that you listen. "Skilled incompetence" is a phrase that has been coined to characterize those who have become adept at protecting themselves from listening and learning. We practice it because we don't believe that the truth sets us free. Knowing that the truth can hurt, we have insulated ourselves from that pain. We are like those who tell Micah not to preach (v. 6).

Warming Up to God Ask God's Spirit to search you. Are you willing to hear the truth even if it is painful?

Read Micah 2.

2 Woe to those who plan iniquity,
to those who plot evil on their beds!
At morning's light they carry it out
because it is in their power to do it.
²They covet fields and seize them,
and houses, and take them.
They defraud a man of his home,
a fellowman of his inheritance.

³Therefore, the LORD says:

"I am planning disaster against this people,
from which you cannot save yourselves.
You will no longer walk proudly,
for it will be a time of calamity.
⁴In that day men will ridicule you;
they will taunt you with this mournful
song:
'We are utterly ruined;
my people's possession is divided up.
He takes it from me!
He assigns our fields to traitors.' "

⁵Therefore you will have no one in the
assembly of the LORD
to divide the land by lot.

⁶"Do not prophesy," their prophets say.
"Do not prophesy about these things;
disgrace will not overtake us."
⁷Should it be said, O house of Jacob:
"Is the Spirit of the LORD angry?
Does he do such things?"

"Do not my words do good

to him whose ways are upright?
⁸Lately my people have risen up
like an enemy.
You strip off the rich robe
from those who pass by without a care,
like men returning from battle.
⁹You drive the women of my people
from their pleasant homes.
You take away my blessing
from their children forever.
¹⁰Get up, go away!
For this is not your resting place,
because it is defiled,
it is ruined, beyond all remedy.
¹¹If a liar and deceiver comes and says,
'I will prophesy for you plenty of wine and
beer,'
he would be just the prophet for this
people!

¹²"I will surely gather all of you, O Jacob;
I will surely bring together the remnant of
Israel.
I will bring them together like sheep in a pen,
like a flock in its pasture;
the place will throng with people.
¹³One who breaks open the way will go up
before them;
they will break through the gate and go
out.
Their king will pass through before them,
the LORD at their head."

Discovering the Word 1. What sort of people is Micah preaching against (vv. 1–3, 8–9)? 2. In verses 1–2 we encounter people who apply the philosophy of modern success literature. It works for the prophet's audience, so why does Micah have a problem with it? 3. How does the punishment in verses 4–5 fit the crime of verses 1–3? 4. In verses 6–7 Micah's audience is offended at his message since they consider themselves quite safe. How does Micah respond to their false confidence? **5.** Why does Micah characterize the "perfect prophet" as he does (v. 11)?

 Applying the Word **1.** God cares about our thoughts and actions. How do you need him to transform you? **2.** How can you be better at hearing the truth even when it is painful? **3.** In what area do you and your church need to cry out for justice?

Responding in Prayer Ask God to make you rich and successful in doing good. Ask him to help you hear the truth.

---

2 / *Micah 3*
How Not to Be a Leader

PERHAPS YOU HAVE heard Lord Acton's saying "Power tends to corrupt. Absolute power corrupts absolutely." Yet strangely, God entrusts us with power. Even though his gifts of power can be used for evil (for example, David having Bathsheba's husband Uriah killed), God does not shield us from it. He gives us spiritual gifts, authority in the church and leadership positions in the world.

 Warming Up to God Consider the different parts of your life. What power has God given to you?

 Read Micah 3.

---

3 Then I said,

"Listen, you leaders of Jacob,
  you rulers of the house of Israel.
Should you not know justice,
² you who hate good and love evil;
who tear the skin from my people
  and the flesh from their bones;
³who eat my people's flesh,
  strip off their skin
  and break their bones in pieces;
who chop them up like meat for the pan,
  like flesh for the pot?"

⁴Then they will cry out to the LORD,
  but he will not answer them.
At that time he will hide his face from them
  because of the evil they have done.

⁵This is what the LORD says:

"As for the prophets
  who lead my people astray,
if one feeds them,
  they proclaim 'peace';
if he does not,
  they prepare to wage war against him.
⁶Therefore night will come over you, without
  visions,

and darkness, without divination.
The sun will set for the prophets,
  and the day will go dark for them.
⁷The seers will be ashamed
  and the diviners disgraced.
They will all cover their faces
  because there is no answer from God."

⁸But as for me, I am filled with power,
  with the Spirit of the LORD,
  and with justice and might,
to declare to Jacob his transgression,
  to Israel his sin.
⁹Hear this, you leaders of the house of
  Jacob,
  you rulers of the house of Israel,
who despise justice
  and distort all that is right;
¹⁰who build Zion with bloodshed,
  and Jerusalem with wickedness.
¹¹Her leaders judge for a bribe,
  her priests teach for a price,
  and her prophets tell fortunes for
  money.
Yet they lean upon the LORD and say,
  "Is not the LORD among us?
  No disaster will come upon us."
¹²Therefore because of you,

Zion will be plowed like a field,
Jerusalem will become a heap of rubble,
the temple hill a mound overgrown with
thickets.

 Discovering the Word 1. Describe the society and the leaders that Micah so vividly portrays in this chapter. 2. Why might God close his ears to our prayers (vv. 1–4)? 3. In verses 5–7 the prophets do not appear to be pretenders or con artists; rather they have gifts from God that they have turned to their own use. How then will the punishment of verse 6 be effective? 4. How does the Spirit of the Lord help Micah stand against his times (v. 8)? 5. The second half of verse 11 says that the leaders believe that the Lord will protect them. How can they think that?

Applying the Word 1. God sometimes calls us to stand against our culture as Micah did (especially v. 8). Where is he calling you to take a stand? 2. How can you guard yourself from using God's gifts for the wrong purpose? 3. All of us have the ability to be self-deluded like the leaders of Israel (v. 11). How can you guard yourself from thinking this way?

Responding in Prayer As you watch the news or read the newspaper, pray against the evil that you see.

3 / *Micah 4*
Tomorrow and Today

A BUMPER STICKER put it this way: "Life is hard, then you die." At the time of Micah's preaching life was tremendously difficult for the people of Israel. Yet in the midst of suffering Micah gives hope to the people that God will not let devastation be the last word.

 Warming Up to God Imagine what it will be like to finally be in God's presence. How does it change the way you look at today?

 Read Micah 4.

4 In the last days
the mountain of the LORD's temple will
be established
as chief among the mountains;
it will be raised above the hills,
and peoples will stream to it.
²Many nations will come and say,

"Come, let us go up to the mountain of the
LORD,
to the house of the God of Jacob.
He will teach us his ways,
so that we may walk in his paths."
The law will go out from Zion,
the word of the LORD from Jerusalem.
³He will judge between many peoples
and will settle disputes for strong nations
far and wide.
They will beat their swords into plowshares

and their spears into pruning hooks.
Nation will not take up sword against nation,
nor will they train for war anymore.
⁴Every man will sit under his own vine
and under his own fig tree,
and no one will make them afraid,
for the LORD Almighty has spoken.
⁵All the nations may walk
in the name of their gods;
we will walk in the name of the LORD
our God for ever and ever.

⁶"In that day," declares the LORD,

"I will gather the lame;
I will assemble the exiles
and those I have brought to grief.
⁷I will make the lame a remnant,
those driven away a strong nation.
The LORD will rule over them in Mount Zion
from that day and forever.

8As for you, O watchtower of the flock,
   O stronghold[k] of the Daughter of Zion,
the former dominion will be restored to you;
   kingship will come to the Daughter of
      Jerusalem."

9Why do you now cry aloud—
   have you no king?
Has your counselor perished,
   that pain seizes you like that of a woman in
      labor?
10Writhe in agony, O Daughter of Zion,
   like a woman in labor,
for now you must leave the city
   to camp in the open field.
You will go to Babylon;
   there you will be rescued.
There the LORD will redeem you
   out of the hand of your enemies.

11But now many nations
   are gathered against you.
They say, "Let her be defiled,
   let our eyes gloat over Zion!"
12But they do not know
   the thoughts of the LORD;
they do not understand his plan,
   he who gathers them like sheaves to the
      threshing floor.

13"Rise and thresh, O Daughter of Zion,
   for I will give you horns of iron;
I will give you hoofs of bronze
   and you will break to pieces many nations."
You will devote their ill-gotten gains to the
   LORD,
   their wealth to the Lord of all the earth.

   k8 Or hill

Discovering the Word 1. Notice the movement and tone of the major sections of the chapter (vv. 1–8, 9–11, 12–13). How would it have spoken to the people? 2. The mount on which the temple stands (Zion) is not even near the height of the highest mountains, so what will make it chief among the mountains (vv. 1–2)? 3. What will society be like in those days (vv. 3–8)? 4. The picture of the coming future is interrupted by the coming present. What does the society of Israel look like at this time (vv. 9–10)? 5. What sort of promise does God make to Israel (vv. 11–13)?

Applying the Word 1. How can you and your community better embody the picture in verses 1–5? 2. How can you participate in gathering in the lame, the exiled and the grieving into the body of Christ?

Responding in Prayer Ask God to give you hope that can sustain you in trials and that you can give to those who despair.

---

4 / *Micah 5*
The Future of Our Enemies

AS CHRISTIANS, WE often do not like to talk about the fact that we have enemies. We hesitate to label someone as an enemy. Yet enemies are real and sometimes quite evil. Dealing with them can occupy much of our time and our thoughts. Unfortunately, there are times when we do not even notice the greatest enemy of God's purpose. In the words of Pogo the cartoon character: "We have met the enemy and he is us."

Warming Up to God What concerns are weighing on your mind? Give God your fears and frustrations.

Read Micah 5.

---

5 Marshal your troops, O city of
      troops,[l]
   for a siege is laid against us.
They will strike Israel's ruler
   on the cheek with a rod.

2"But you, Bethlehem Ephrathah,
   though you are small among the clans[m] of
      Judah,

   l1 Or Strengthen your walls, O walled city   m2 Or rulers

out of you will come for me
   one who will be ruler over Israel,
whose origins[n] are from of old,
   from ancient times.[o] "

[3]Therefore Israel will be abandoned
   until the time when she who is in labor
      gives birth
and the rest of his brothers return
   to join the Israelites.

[4]He will stand and shepherd his flock
   in the strength of the LORD,
   in the majesty of the name of the LORD his
      God.
And they will live securely, for then his
      greatness
   will reach to the ends of the earth.
[5] And he will be their peace.

When the Assyrian invades our land
   and marches through our fortresses,
we will raise against him seven shepherds,
   even eight leaders of men.
[6]They will rule[p] the land of Assyria with the
      sword,
   the land of Nimrod with drawn sword.[q]
He will deliver us from the Assyrian
   when he invades our land
   and marches into our borders.

[7]The remnant of Jacob will be
   in the midst of many peoples
like dew from the LORD,
   like showers on the grass,

which do not wait for man
   or linger for mankind.
[8]The remnant of Jacob will be among the
      nations,
   in the midst of many peoples,
like a lion among the beasts of the forest,
   like a young lion among flocks of sheep,
which mauls and mangles as it goes,
   and no one can rescue.
[9]Your hand will be lifted up in triumph over
      your enemies,
   and all your foes will be destroyed.

[10]"In that day," declares the LORD,

"I will destroy your horses from among you
   and demolish your chariots.
[11]I will destroy the cities of your land
   and tear down all your strongholds.
[12]I will destroy your witchcraft
   and you will no longer cast spells.
[13]I will destroy your carved images
   and your sacred stones from among you;
you will no longer bow down
   to the work of your hands.
[14]I will uproot from among you your Asherah
      poles[r]
   and demolish your cities.
[15]I will take vengeance in anger and wrath
   upon the nations that have not obeyed me."

[n]2 Hebrew *goings out*   [o]2 Or *from days of eternity*   [p]6 Or *crush*
[q]6 Or *Nimrod in its gates*   [r]14 That is, symbols of the goddess
Asherah

 Discovering the Word **1.** Contrast the present-day ruler (v. 1) with the ruler who is to come (vv. 2–5).
2. How does the description of the future ruler give you comfort? **3.** How does Micah picture Israel's
future against Assyria (vv. 5–9)? **4.** While Israel feared her enemies that were outside her border, what enemies
within her borders did Micah expect destroyed (vv. 10–14)?

Applying the Word **1.** We no longer wait for the ruler to come from Bethlehem, so how can he give you
hope in the midst of your trials? **2.** Often we see others as our enemies, but what inside you is an enemy
to God's purposes (vv. 10–14)?

Responding in Prayer Ask God's Spirit to search you and to help you know what opposes his purpose.
Confess, and ask God to empower you to change and move on.

5 / *Micah 6*
What God Requires

IMAGINE THAT YOU are handed a summons to appear in court for breaching an agreement. Then to your surprise you read that the one who had initiated the suit is God. This is what happens to Judah in chapter 6. God calls them to court and argues his case by reminding them of his faithful acts and their faithlessness.

 Warming Up to God How has God recently shown you his faithfulness?

 Read Micah 6.

 Listen to what the Lord says:

"Stand up, plead your case before the
   mountains;
let the hills hear what you have to say.
²Hear, O mountains, the Lord's accusation;
   listen, you everlasting foundations of the
   earth.
For the Lord has a case against his people;
   he is lodging a charge against Israel.

³"My people, what have I done to you?
   How have I burdened you? Answer me.
⁴I brought you up out of Egypt
   and redeemed you from the land of slavery.
I sent Moses to lead you,
   also Aaron and Miriam.
⁵My people, remember
   what Balak king of Moab counseled
   and what Balaam son of Beor answered.
Remember ∟your journey⌐ from Shittim to
   Gilgal,
   that you may know the righteous acts of
   the Lord."

⁶With what shall I come before the Lord
   and bow down before the exalted God?
Shall I come before him with burnt offerings,
   with calves a year old?
⁷Will the Lord be pleased with thousands of
   rams,
   with ten thousand rivers of oil?
Shall I offer my firstborn for my
   transgression,
   the fruit of my body for the sin of my soul?
⁸He has showed you, O man, what is good.
   And what does the Lord require of you?

To act justly and to love mercy
   and to walk humbly with your God.

⁹Listen! The Lord is calling to the city—
   and to fear your name is wisdom—
"Heed the rod and the One who appointed
   it.ˢ
¹⁰Am I still to forget, O wicked house,
   your ill-gotten treasures
   and the short ephah,ᵗ which is accursed?
¹¹Shall I acquit a man with dishonest scales,
   with a bag of false weights?
¹²Her rich men are violent;
   her people are liars
   and their tongues speak deceitfully.
¹³Therefore, I have begun to destroy you,
   to ruin you because of your sins.
¹⁴You will eat but not be satisfied;
   your stomach will still be empty.ᵘ
You will store up but save nothing,
   because what you save I will give to the
   sword.
¹⁵You will plant but not harvest;
   you will press olives but not use the oil on
   yourselves,
   you will crush grapes but not drink the
   wine.
¹⁶You have observed the statutes of Omri
   and all the practices of Ahab's house,
   and you have followed their traditions.
Therefore I will give you over to ruin
   and your people to derision;
   you will bear the scorn of the nations.ᵛ"

ˢ9 The meaning of the Hebrew for this line is uncertain.   ᵗ10 An
ephah was a dry measure.   ᵘ14 The meaning of the Hebrew for this
word is uncertain.   ᵛ16 Septuagint; Hebrew *scorn due my people*

Discovering the Word 1. What kinds of complaints against Israel does the Lord list in this chapter? 2. What is the significance of the answer that God gives to his own question (vv. 3–5)? (These verses refer to Ex; Nu 22—24 and Jos 4.) 3. God requires the Israelites to sacrifice in worship. So why does he seem to be against it here (vv. 6–8)? 4. How do the actions of the people (vv. 9–12, 16) contrast with what God requires (v. 8)? 5. What sort of punishment awaits wicked towns or cities (vv. 13–15, 16)?

Applying the Word 1. How can remembering God's saving acts in the Bible and in your life (vv. 4–5) change your attitudes when you want to blame him (v. 3)? 2. Sometimes Christians reduce spirituality to simply doing certain things, like going to church or having consistent quiet times. How does this chapter expand your view? 3. Where is the voice of the Lord crying out (v. 9) against your town or city?

Responding in Prayer Ask God to show you how you can better embody verse 8. Ask the Holy Spirit to help you do so.

6 / *Micah 7*
How Long Will God Be Angry?

CDS ARE ABLE to store an amazing amount of information—from music to videos to entire encyclopedias. Imagine that someone had a complete CD of your life, so complete that they could even access your thoughts and actions with the touch of a button. What would someone find on your CD? What would you like to erase? The truth is that someone has all of that information about you—God.

Warming Up to God Reflect on what a CD of your life would be like—the type of music and the content. What brings you joy and what concerns you as you think of your life in this way?

Read Micah 7.

7 What misery is mine!
    I am like one who gathers summer fruit
      at the gleaning of the vineyard;
there is no cluster of grapes to eat,
    none of the early figs that I crave.
²The godly have been swept from the land;
    not one upright man remains.
All men lie in wait to shed blood;
    each hunts his brother with a net.
³Both hands are skilled in doing evil;
    the ruler demands gifts,
the judge accepts bribes,
    the powerful dictate what they desire—
they all conspire together.
⁴The best of them is like a brier,
    the most upright worse than a thorn hedge.
The day of your watchmen has come,
    the day God visits you.
    Now is the time of their confusion.
⁵Do not trust a neighbor;
    put no confidence in a friend.
Even with her who lies in your embrace
    be careful of your words.

⁶For a son dishonors his father,
    a daughter rises up against her mother,
a daughter-in-law against her
      mother-in-law—
a man's enemies are the members of his
    own household.

⁷But as for me, I watch in hope for the LORD,
    I wait for God my Savior;
    my God will hear me.

⁸Do not gloat over me, my enemy!
    Though I have fallen, I will rise.
Though I sit in darkness,
    the LORD will be my light.
⁹Because I have sinned against him,
    I will bear the LORD's wrath,
until he pleads my case
    and establishes my right.
He will bring me out into the light;
    I will see his righteousness.
¹⁰Then my enemy will see it
    and will be covered with shame,
she who said to me,

"Where is the LORD your God?"
My eyes will see her downfall;
    even now she will be trampled underfoot
    like mire in the streets.

¹¹The day for building your walls will come,
    the day for extending your boundaries.
¹²In that day people will come to you
    from Assyria and the cities of Egypt,
even from Egypt to the Euphrates
    and from sea to sea
    and from mountain to mountain.
¹³The earth will become desolate because of its
        inhabitants,
    as the result of their deeds.

¹⁴Shepherd your people with your staff,
    the flock of your inheritance,
which lives by itself in a forest,
    in fertile pasturelands.ʷ
Let them feed in Bashan and Gilead
    as in days long ago.

¹⁵"As in the days when you came out of Egypt,
    I will show them my wonders."

¹⁶Nations will see and be ashamed,

deprived of all their power.
They will lay their hands on their mouths
    and their ears will become deaf.
¹⁷They will lick dust like a snake,
    like creatures that crawl on the ground.
They will come trembling out of their dens;
    they will turn in fear to the LORD our God
    and will be afraid of you.
¹⁸Who is a God like you,
    who pardons sin and forgives the
        transgression
    of the remnant of his inheritance?
You do not stay angry forever
    but delight to show mercy.
¹⁹You will again have compassion on us;
    you will tread our sins underfoot
    and hurl all our iniquities into the depths
        of the sea.
²⁰You will be true to Jacob,
    and show mercy to Abraham,
as you pledged on oath to our fathers
    in days long ago.

ʷ14 Or *in the middle of Carmel*

Discovering the Word **1.** How do verses 1 and 7 frame 2–6? **2.** As Jerusalem speaks in verses 8–10, do you think she describes her situation correctly? **3.** Do you think Micah agrees with Jerusalem's self-assessment (vv. 8–10) as he speaks of the day to come (vv. 11–17)? **4.** The book ends with a powerful description of God. What character traits do you see?

Applying the Word **1.** In verses 1–6 Micah describes a society falling apart, yet in the midst of the chaos he is able to hope in God. How can you help others to the same? **2.** In Jerusalem's confession (v. 9) she is willing to bear the consequences of her guilt. How do you feel about your guilt? **3.** How can you make verses 18–20 a part of your life and the lives of others?

 Responding in Prayer Pray through this chapter, in particular verses 18–20. Confess your sins. Allow your heart to respond to God's grace.

Nahum

His name means *consolation*. His message carries little of it.

About the prophet Nahum we know little more than his hometown, Elkosh. His book is a poem of judgment directed to a city destined for judgment. At least a century earlier, Jonah had preached to Nineveh with reluctance. After all, the powerful Assyrian city was a particularly violent one, impaling its enemies and stacking their bodies at the gates. But Jonah's message broke through. Led by a shaken king, the city turned from their wickedness and was spared.

Then shortly before 612 B.C.—the fall of Nineveh—an angrier prophet brought a message of doom. Nahum sees that the city has fallen back into the cycle of wickedness which was their heritage. He prophesies that the Lord will use Babylon as his instrument of destruction. History confirms all of it: Nineveh was never heard from again.

The book is not a warning, but a hopeless prognosis. "The Lord is a jealous and avenging God," begins Nahum (1:2). Nearly every verse rings with the theme of inevitable judgment. "Nothing can heal your wound; your injury is fatal," concludes Nahum. Then he says that outsiders will *applaud* the downfall of the Ninevites (3:19).

What comfort can you gain from Nahum? The book speaks to the ultimate sovereignty of God. He judges those who, through the passage of time, ignore God's laws and persecute others. And despite the relentless prophecy of doom, we are assured, "the Lord is good, a refuge in times of trouble" (1:7). In a world which often seems to reward evil and suppress goodness, Nahum stands as a reminder of the absolute standards of God—and the inevitable fate of those who oppose him.

Outline

1/ Nahum 1 ———————————————— The God of Judgment
2/ Nahum 2 ———————————————— The Approach of Judgment
3/ Nahum 3 ———————————————— The Aftermath of Judgment

1 / *Nahum 1*
The God of Judgment

WHAT IS YOUR favorite of God's attributes? Love? Mercy? Grace? Comfort? Chances are you didn't name *judgment*. Yet that concept, however disquieting, is part of the divine equation. We cannot have a world of justice without judgment. Nahum reminds us that God is indeed just, and that when we break his laws, we break ourselves upon them. This chapter deals with the Lord's anger toward a city full of evil.

 Warming Up to God What world conflicts are you currently following in the news? How do you think God feels about some of these?

 Read Nahum 1.

1 An oracle concerning Nineveh. The book of the vision of Nahum the Elkoshite.

²The Lord is a jealous and avenging God;
  the Lord takes vengeance and is filled with
    wrath.
The Lord takes vengeance on his foes
  and maintains his wrath against his
    enemies.
³The Lord is slow to anger and great in power;
  the Lord will not leave the guilty
    unpunished.
His way is in the whirlwind and the storm,
  and clouds are the dust of his feet.
⁴He rebukes the sea and dries it up;
  he makes all the rivers run dry.
Bashan and Carmel wither
  and the blossoms of Lebanon fade.
⁵The mountains quake before him
  and the hills melt away.
The earth trembles at his presence,
  the world and all who live in it.
⁶Who can withstand his indignation?
  Who can endure his fierce anger?
His wrath is poured out like fire;
  the rocks are shattered before him.

⁷The Lord is good,
  a refuge in times of trouble.
He cares for those who trust in him,
⁸ but with an overwhelming flood
he will make an end of ⌞Nineveh⌟;
  he will pursue his foes into darkness.

⁹Whatever they plot against the Lord

he[a] will bring to an end;
  trouble will not come a second time.
¹⁰They will be entangled among thorns
  and drunk from their wine;
  they will be consumed like dry stubble.[b]
¹¹From you, ⌞O Nineveh,⌟ has one come forth
  who plots evil against the Lord
  and counsels wickedness.

¹²This is what the Lord says:

"Although they have allies and are numerous,
  they will be cut off and pass away.
Although I have afflicted you, ⌞O Judah,⌟
  I will afflict you no more.
¹³Now I will break their yoke from your neck
  and tear your shackles away."

¹⁴The Lord has given a command concerning
    you, ⌞Nineveh⌟:
"You will have no descendants to bear your
    name.
I will destroy the carved images and cast idols
  that are in the temple of your gods.
I will prepare your grave,
  for you are vile."

¹⁵Look, there on the mountains,
  the feet of one who brings good news,
  who proclaims peace!
Celebrate your festivals, O Judah,
  and fulfill your vows.
No more will the wicked invade you;
  they will be completely destroyed.

---

[a]9 Or *What do you foes plot against the Lord? / He*   [b]10 The meaning of the Hebrew for this verse is uncertain.

Discovering the Word 1. Why do you think Nahum uses poetry for such a subject as the anger of God? 2. Which description of God in verses 1–6 is most striking to you? Why? 3. How can you reconcile the statement in verse 7 with the rest of this chapter? 4. What charges against Nineveh are found in verses 9–14? 5. This book was written not directly to the Ninevites, but to Jewish readers. What might Nahum have intended the Jews to gain from hearing these words?

Applying the Word 1. What parallels can you find between Nineveh and today's world? 2. How should you respond today in the context of conditions that anger God? 3. Look again at verse 7. In what way do you need God's refuge from the world?

Responding in Prayer Pray that God will give you his perspective of the world and that you'll be angry toward the things which inspire his anger. Ask him to reassure you that "he cares for those who trust in him" (v. 7).

---

2 / *Nahum 2*
The Approach of Judgment

IMPENDING CATASTROPHE! THE news is full of it. Scientists warn us about global warming, coming earthquakes, acid rain and other dangers to the natural order. Politicians issue dire warnings about sinister movements and culture wars. Similarly, Nahum writes of a catastrophe soon to befall Nineveh. We see the culmination of the evils described in the first chapter as the Babylonian troops descend on the city.

Warming Up to God What crisis or challenge is on the outskirts of your life at present? How might God be working within this situation?

Read Nahum 2.

---

2 An attacker advances against you,
⌊Nineveh⌋.
Guard the fortress,
watch the road,
brace yourselves,
marshal all your strength!

²The LORD will restore the splendor of Jacob
like the splendor of Israel,
though destroyers have laid them waste
and have ruined their vines.

³The shields of his soldiers are red;
the warriors are clad in scarlet.
The metal on the chariots flashes
on the day they are made ready;
the spears of pine are brandished.ᶜ

⁴The chariots storm through the streets,
rushing back and forth through the squares.
They look like flaming torches;
they dart about like lightning.

⁵He summons his picked troops,
yet they stumble on their way.
They dash to the city wall;

the protective shield is put in place.

⁶The river gates are thrown open
and the palace collapses.

⁷It is decreedᵈ that ⌊the city⌋
be exiled and carried away.
Its slave girls moan like doves
and beat upon their breasts.

⁸Nineveh is like a pool,
and its water is draining away.
"Stop! Stop!" they cry,
but no one turns back.

⁹Plunder the silver!
Plunder the gold!
The supply is endless,
the wealth from all its treasures!

¹⁰She is pillaged, plundered, stripped!
Hearts melt, knees give way,
bodies tremble, every face grows pale.

¹¹Where now is the lions' den,
the place where they fed their young,
where the lion and lioness went,

ᶜ3 Hebrew; Septuagint and Syriac / *the horsemen rush to and fro*
ᵈ7 The meaning of the Hebrew for this word is uncertain.

and the cubs, with nothing to fear?
¹²The lion killed enough for his cubs
    and strangled the prey for his mate,
filling his lairs with the kill
    and his dens with the prey.

¹³"I am against you,"
    declares the LORD Almighty.

"I will burn up your chariots in smoke,
    and the sword will devour your young
       lions.
I will leave you no prey on the
      earth.
The voices of your messengers
    will no longer be heard."

Discovering the Word 1. How does chapter 1, which deals with God's power and anger, set the mood for the first verses of chapter 2? 2. Is Nahum actually warning Nineveh? Explain. 3. Given that moral evil is the cause of Nineveh's fall, what point does this chapter make about armies and power (vv. 3–6)? 4. Exactly how is Nineveh like a pool (v. 8)? 5. Nineveh had many lion sculptures. How is this metaphor turned against them in verses 11–13?

Applying the Word 1. Do you see God moving through political forces today? If so, how? 2. Nahum deals with the plundering of Ninevite wealth (vv. 9–10). How can you begin to better acknowledge God's control over your possessions?

Responding in Prayer In this chapter Nahum has described the thoroughness of God's judgment. Nineveh was never revived. Spend some time meditating on God's awesome power—terrifying yet reassuring. Praise and thank him that his power is always tied to justice.

3 / *Nahum 3*
The Aftermath of Judgment

AFTER TRAGEDY STRIKES, shock sets in. The victims become disoriented as they attempt to cope. Everyone else has an angle and an explanation for the tragedy. The question is pondered: could this have been avoided? Nahum closes with a woeful survey of the "city of blood" (3:1). We catch a glimpse of the sad aftermath of God's judgment.

Warming Up to God Recall the greatest crisis in your life over the last few years. How did you feel the day after it? How was your faith affected?

Read Nahum 3.

3 Woe to the city of blood,
    full of lies,
    full of plunder,
never without victims!
²The crack of whips,
    the clatter of wheels,
galloping horses
    and jolting chariots!
³Charging cavalry,
    flashing swords
    and glittering spears!
Many casualties,
    piles of dead,
bodies without number,
    people stumbling over the corpses—

⁴all because of the wanton lust of a harlot,
    alluring, the mistress of sorceries,
who enslaved nations by her prostitution
    and peoples by her witchcraft.

⁵"I am against you," declares the LORD
      Almighty.
"I will lift your skirts over your face.
I will show the nations your nakedness
    and the kingdoms your shame.
⁶I will pelt you with filth,
    I will treat you with contempt
    and make you a spectacle.
⁷All who see you will flee from you and say,
    'Nineveh is in ruins—who will mourn for
      her?'

Where can I find anyone to comfort you?"

⁸Are you better than Thebes,ᶜ
    situated on the Nile,
    with water around her?
The river was her defense,
    the waters her wall.
⁹Cushᶠ and Egypt were her boundless
        strength;
    Put and Libya were among her allies.
¹⁰Yet she was taken captive
    and went into exile.
Her infants were dashed to pieces
    at the head of every street.
Lots were cast for her nobles,
    and all her great men were put in chains.
¹¹You too will become drunk;
    you will go into hiding
    and seek refuge from the enemy.

¹²All your fortresses are like fig trees
    with their first ripe fruit;
when they are shaken,
    the figs fall into the mouth of the eater.
¹³Look at your troops—
    they are all women!
The gates of your land
    are wide open to your enemies;
fire has consumed their bars.

¹⁴Draw water for the siege,
    strengthen your defenses!

Work the clay,
    tread the mortar,
    repair the brickwork!
¹⁵There the fire will devour you;
    the sword will cut you down
    and, like grasshoppers, consume you.
Multiply like grasshoppers,
    multiply like locusts!
¹⁶You have increased the number of your
        merchants
    till they are more than the stars of the sky,
but like locusts they strip the land
    and then fly away.
¹⁷Your guards are like locusts,
    your officials like swarms of locusts
    that settle in the walls on a cold day—
but when the sun appears they fly away,
    and no one knows where.

¹⁸O king of Assyria, your shepherdsᵍ slumber;
    your nobles lie down to rest.
Your people are scattered on the mountains
    with no one to gather them.
¹⁹Nothing can heal your wound;
    your injury is fatal.
Everyone who hears the news about you
    claps his hands at your fall,
for who has not felt
    your endless cruelty?

ᶜ8 Hebrew *No Amon*   ᶠ9 That is, the upper Nile region   ᵍ18 Or
rulers

 Discovering the Word 1. How would you characterize the tone of this chapter? 2. What sins of Nineveh are recounted in this chapter? 3. Nineveh was famous for temple prostitution. How does Nahum appropriately use this reputation as a metaphor in verses 4–7? 4. What is the sin of the merchants (v. 16)? 5. Nahum often uses a mocking tone. How does verse 19 help explain this?

Applying the Word 1. What current areas of national or international life show the devastation of Nineveh? 2. How can you personally make God's sovereignty better known in your surroundings?

Responding in Prayer Nahum celebrates "the feet of one who brings good news, who proclaims peace!" (1:15). Thank God that in the midst of the most terrible events, God is fulfilling his own purposes. Ask him to empower you to bring good news and proclaim peace today.

Habakkuk

The period in which Habakkuk lived had a lot of international tension. Judah was caught between two treacherous world powers. Prior to the events of the book, the king of Egypt had murdered the king of Judah and set up a puppet government in Judah. The Babylonians were also a world power known for their treachery. They were enemies of the Egyptians. The Babylonians were soon to overthrow the Egyptians, but for Judah this was like going from the frying pan into the fire. Habakkuk wondered what God was going to do in this morass. He did not realize that God also saw Judah as a part of the problem in the world.

Habakkuk was a contemporary of Jeremiah's. Both prophets challenged the nation to give up their idolatry, pride and desire for wealth gained at the expense of the poor and by destroying the land. When Jeremiah delivered this message, he was persecuted for being unpatriotic (Jer 20:1–3).

Outline

1/ Habakkuk 1:1—2:1 —————————— Does God Care About Injustice?

2/ Habakkuk 2:2–20 —————————— The Log in Our Eyes

3/ Habakkuk 3 —————————— God's Creation

1 / *Habakkuk 1:1—2:1*
Does God Care About Injustice?

WHAT IF YOU cried out to God about the injustices in our world—the terrorism and trouble in various places—and God responded: "I am going to do something in your days that you would not believe. I'm raising up the nation you most distrust to sweep across the whole earth and seize dwelling places not their own." In this passage, Habakkuk gets that kind of message from God. Habakkuk had viewed Babylonia (modern-day Iraq) as the incarnation of evil. He was not prepared, therefore, when God announced he would use the Babylonians to judge his nation.

 Warming Up to God What injustices in your own life and in world news are on your mind as you begin this quiet time?

 Read Habakkuk 1:1—2:1.

1 The oracle that Habakkuk the prophet received.

²How long, O Lord, must I call for help,
but you do not listen?
Or cry out to you, "Violence!"
but you do not save?
³Why do you make me look at injustice?
Why do you tolerate wrong?
Destruction and violence are before me;
there is strife, and conflict abounds.
⁴Therefore the law is paralyzed,
and justice never prevails.
The wicked hem in the righteous,
so that justice is perverted.

⁵"Look at the nations and watch—
and be utterly amazed.
For I am going to do something in your days
that you would not believe,
even if you were told.
⁶I am raising up the Babylonians,ᵃ
that ruthless and impetuous people,
who sweep across the whole earth
to seize dwelling places not their own.
⁷They are a feared and dreaded people;
they are a law to themselves
and promote their own honor.
⁸Their horses are swifter than leopards,
fiercer than wolves at dusk.
Their cavalry gallops headlong;
their horsemen come from afar.
They fly like a vulture swooping to devour;
⁹ they all come bent on violence.
Their hordesᵇ advance like a desert wind
and gather prisoners like sand.

¹⁰They deride kings
and scoff at rulers.
They laugh at all fortified cities;
they build earthen ramps and capture them.
¹¹Then they sweep past like the wind and go on—
guilty men, whose own strength is their god."

¹²O Lord, are you not from everlasting?
My God, my Holy One, we will not die.
O Lord, you have appointed them to execute judgment;
O Rock, you have ordained them to punish.
¹³Your eyes are too pure to look on evil;
you cannot tolerate wrong.
Why then do you tolerate the treacherous?
Why are you silent while the wicked
swallow up those more righteous than themselves?
¹⁴You have made men like fish in the sea,
like sea creatures that have no ruler.
¹⁵The wicked foe pulls all of them up with hooks,
he catches them in his net,
he gathers them up in his dragnet;
and so he rejoices and is glad.
¹⁶Therefore he sacrifices to his net
and burns incense to his dragnet,
for by his net he lives in luxury
and enjoys the choicest food.
¹⁷Is he to keep on emptying his net,
destroying nations without mercy?

ᵃ6 Or *Chaldeans*   ᵇ9 The meaning of the Hebrew for this word is uncertain.

2 I will stand at my watch
and station myself on the ramparts;
I will look to see what he will say to
    me,

and what answer I am to give to this
    complaint.^{c}

^{c}1 Or and what to answer when I am rebuked

 Discovering the Word 1. What is Habakkuk's cry and complaint (vv. 2-4)? 2. What is amazing about the Lord's answer (vv. 5-11)? 3. How would you feel if you were in Habakkuk's shoes? 4. How does Habakkuk respond to God's answer (1:12—2:1)?

 Applying the Word 1. Do you ever feel like God doesn't care about the injustice in your life or in the world around you? Explain. 2. What can you learn from Habakkuk's relationship with God?

Responding in Prayer Follow Habakkuk's model and talk openly with God about the injustices you see.

---

2 / *Habakkuk 2:2-20*
The Log in Our Eyes

ONE OF THE great dangers for anyone who takes evil seriously is that in challenging evil we can begin to think that we are without sin. We can see evil in others much easier than in ourselves. This can result in a self-righteous attitude that denies the power of God in our lives and denies our constant need to seek God's forgiveness.

 Warming Up to God When have you found yourself so intent on "the enemy" that you have lost sight of your own sins?

 Read Habakkuk 2:2-20.

---

^{2}Then the LORD replied:

"Write down the revelation
    and make it plain on tablets
    so that a herald^d may run with it.
^{3}For the revelation awaits an appointed time;
    it speaks of the end
    and will not prove false.
Though it linger, wait for it;
    it^e will certainly come and will not delay.

^{4}"See, he is puffed up;
    his desires are not upright—
    but the righteous will live by his faith^f—
^{5}indeed, wine betrays him;
    he is arrogant and never at rest.
Because he is as greedy as the grave^g
    and like death is never satisfied,
he gathers to himself all the nations
    and takes captive all the peoples.

^{6}"Will not all of them taunt him with ridicule
and scorn, saying,

" 'Woe to him who piles up stolen goods
    and makes himself wealthy by extortion!
    How long must this go on?'
^{7}Will not your debtors^h suddenly arise?
    Will they not wake up and make you
        tremble?
    Then you will become their victim.
^{8}Because you have plundered many nations,
    the peoples who are left will plunder you.
For you have shed man's blood;
    you have destroyed lands and cities and
        everyone in them.

^{9}"Woe to him who builds his realm by unjust
        gain
    to set his nest on high,
    to escape the clutches of ruin!
^{10}You have plotted the ruin of many peoples,
    shaming your own house and forfeiting
        your life.
^{11}The stones of the wall will cry out,

^{d}2 Or so that whoever reads it ^{e}3 Or Though he linger, wait for him;
/ he ^{f}4 Or faithfulness ^{g}5 Hebrew Sheol ^{h}7 Or creditors

and the beams of the woodwork will echo
it.

12"Woe to him who builds a city with
bloodshed
and establishes a town by crime!
13Has not the LORD Almighty determined
that the people's labor is only fuel for the
fire,
that the nations exhaust themselves for
nothing?
14For the earth will be filled with the
knowledge of the glory of the LORD,
as the waters cover the sea.

15"Woe to him who gives drink to his
neighbors,
pouring it from the wineskin till they are
drunk,
so that he can gaze on their naked bodies.
16You will be filled with shame instead of glory.
Now it is your turn! Drink and be
exposed*!
The cup from the LORD's right hand is coming
around to you,

and disgrace will cover your glory.
17The violence you have done to Lebanon will
overwhelm you,
and your destruction of animals will terrify
you.
For you have shed man's blood;
you have destroyed lands and cities and
everyone in them.

18"Of what value is an idol, since a man has
carved it?
Or an image that teaches lies?
For he who makes it trusts in his own
creation;
he makes idols that cannot speak.
19Woe to him who says to wood, 'Come to life!'
Or to lifeless stone, 'Wake up!'
Can it give guidance?
It is covered with gold and silver;
there is no breath in it.
20But the LORD is in his holy temple;
let all the earth be silent before him."

*16 Masoretic Text; Dead Sea Scrolls, Aquila, Vulgate and Syriac (see also
Septuagint) *and stagger*

 Discovering the Word 1. In verse 2 God begins to explain his answer to Habakkuk. What is the challenge of verses 2–3? 2. Why must one have faith in order to meet the challenge? 3. What is the connection between faith and righteousness (v. 4)? 4. Chapter 2 lists five "woes" (vv. 6, 9, 12, 15, 19). For each, how is the consequence a direct result of the wrong committed? 5. How is the final woe connected to all the rest?

 Applying the Word 1. Why is it easier for us to see the idolatry of others than to see our own? 2. What are some of your idols?

Responding in Prayer Pray that God will help you to face your sins of idolatry and self-righteousness.

---

3 / *Habakkuk 3*
God's Creation

ONE SUMMER NIGHT at a girls' camp I enjoyed a solitary walk in the presence of God's creation. I walked past the beam of a barnyard pole light and out into a grassy meadow shrouded in twilight but still exhaling the warmth of afternoon sun. Myriad meadow insects sang their evening prayers. Tiny feet scurried through their own maze-world so deep in the grass that they barely fluttered the seeded canopy above. Children's voices laughed and sang, near enough to carry music to me, but too distant to bring their ever-present turmoil. A light breeze washed my face clean of sweat.

After hearing the shocking news that the Babylonians would destroy the nation of Judah, Habakkuk meditated on his beautiful land and its upcoming destruction. Then he wrote the prayer in Habakkuk 3.

 Warming Up to God When have you seen the wrath of God exercised in a way that surprised or confused you?

 Read Habakkuk 3.

3

A prayer of Habakkuk the prophet. On shigionoth.[j]

[2]LORD, I have heard of your fame;
I stand in awe of your deeds, O LORD.
Renew them in our day,
in our time make them known;
in wrath remember mercy.

[3]God came from Teman,
the Holy One from Mount Paran.   Selah[k]
His glory covered the heavens
and his praise filled the earth.
[4]His splendor was like the sunrise;
rays flashed from his hand,
where his power was hidden.
[5]Plague went before him;
pestilence followed his steps.
[6]He stood, and shook the earth;
he looked, and made the nations tremble.
The ancient mountains crumbled
and the age-old hills collapsed.
His ways are eternal.
[7]I saw the tents of Cushan in distress,
the dwellings of Midian in anguish.

[8]Were you angry with the rivers, O LORD?
Was your wrath against the streams?
Did you rage against the sea
when you rode with your horses
and your victorious chariots?
[9]You uncovered your bow,
you called for many arrows.   Selah
You split the earth with rivers;
[10] the mountains saw you and writhed.
Torrents of water swept by;
the deep roared
and lifted its waves on high.
[11]Sun and moon stood still in the heavens
at the glint of your flying arrows,

at the lightning of your flashing spear.
[12]In wrath you strode through the earth
and in anger you threshed the nations.
[13]You came out to deliver your people,
to save your anointed one.
You crushed the leader of the land of
wickedness,
you stripped him from head to foot.   Selah
[14]With his own spear you pierced his head
when his warriors stormed out to scatter
us,
gloating as though about to devour
the wretched who were in hiding.
[15]You trampled the sea with your horses,
churning the great waters.

[16]I heard and my heart pounded,
my lips quivered at the sound;
decay crept into my bones,
and my legs trembled.
Yet I will wait patiently for the day of
calamity
to come on the nation invading us.
[17]Though the fig tree does not bud
and there are no grapes on the vines,
though the olive crop fails
and the fields produce no food,
though there are no sheep in the pen
and no cattle in the stalls,
[18]yet I will rejoice in the LORD,
I will be joyful in God my Savior.

[19]The Sovereign LORD is my strength;
he makes my feet like the feet of a deer,
he enables me to go on the heights.

For the director of music. On my stringed
instruments.

[j]1 Probably a literary or musical term   [k]3 A word of uncertain
meaning; possibly a musical term; also in verses 9 and 13

Discovering the Word   1. Find as many references as you can to the natural environment.   2. What connections did Habakkuk see between God and nature?   3. Habakkuk prayed in verse 2, "In wrath remember mercy." What do you think he meant by that request?   4. Study the last line of verse 6 and the first two lines of verse 13. How might these words help you understand what appears to be senseless destruction?   5. What choices does Habakkuk make in light of his relationship with God (vv. 16–19)?

Applying the Word   1. If you could somehow know that your own nation would soon look like the description in Habakkuk 3, how do you think you would respond to God?   2. How does Habakkuk's prayer encourage you to continue worshiping God even when his actions confuse you?

Responding in Prayer   Pray for God's mercy on your land and people.

Zephaniah

O ld Testament prophets majored on the themes of God's coming judgment and future blessing. They often blended the near future with events that were so far distant they have yet to happen. Zephaniah was one of those prophets.

Zephaniah prophesied during King Josiah's reign over Judah, around 625–635 B.C. His messages focused on God's judgments on Judah, fulfilled when Babylon conquered the nation and carried most of the people into exile, and their restoration as a nation. Plus he spoke about the coming "day of the Lord," which is also a still-future time when God will judge the heathen nations and usher in the messianic kingdom of peace and blessing.

Even though it was written over 2600 years ago, Zephaniah's book is relevant to our times. He warned people of God's judgment on sins like materialism and injustice that are prevalent today. But he also offered hope of a better time to come, a message we also need to hear.

Outline

1/ Zephaniah 1 —————————————— *Complacent to the End*
2/ Zephaniah 2 —————————————— *Judgment to Come*
3/ Zephaniah 3 —————————————— *Better Days Are Coming*

1 / *Zephaniah 1*
Complacent to the End

SOMEONE ONCE SAID: "Complacency is a blight that saps energy, dulls attitudes, and causes a drain on the brain. The first symptom is satisfaction with things as they are. The second is rejection of things as they might be. 'Good enough' becomes today's watchword and tomorrow's standard." And as Zephaniah wrote, it gets in the way of spiritual progress.

 Warming Up to God　What image comes to mind when someone mentions complacency? Ask God to show you from this chapter how dangerous it can be.

 Read Zephaniah 1.

1 The word of the LORD that came to Zephaniah son of Cushi, the son of Gedaliah, the son of Amariah, the son of Hezekiah, during the reign of Josiah son of Amon king of Judah:

²"I will sweep away everything
　from the face of the earth,"
　　　　　　　　　declares the LORD.
³"I will sweep away both men and animals;
　I will sweep away the birds of the air
　and the fish of the sea.
The wicked will have only heaps of rubble[a]
　when I cut off man from the face of the
　　earth,"
　　　　　　　　　declares the LORD.

⁴"I will stretch out my hand against Judah
　and against all who live in Jerusalem.
I will cut off from this place every remnant of
　　Baal,
　the names of the pagan and the idolatrous
　　priests—
⁵those who bow down on the roofs
　to worship the starry host,
those who bow down and swear by the LORD
　and who also swear by Molech,[b]
⁶those who turn back from following the LORD
　and neither seek the LORD nor inquire of
　　him.
⁷Be silent before the Sovereign LORD,
　for the day of the LORD is near.
The LORD has prepared a sacrifice;
　he has consecrated those he has invited.
⁸On the day of the LORD's sacrifice
　I will punish the princes
　and the king's sons
and all those clad
　in foreign clothes.

⁹On that day I will punish
　all who avoid stepping on the threshold,[c]
who fill the temple of their gods
　with violence and deceit.
¹⁰"On that day," declares the LORD,
　"a cry will go up from the Fish Gate,
　wailing from the New Quarter,
　and a loud crash from the hills.
¹¹Wail, you who live in the market district[d];
　all your merchants will be wiped out,
　all who trade with[e] silver will be ruined.
¹²At that time I will search Jerusalem with
　　lamps
　and punish those who are complacent,
　who are like wine left on its dregs,
who think, 'The LORD will do nothing,
　either good or bad.'
¹³Their wealth will be plundered,
　their houses demolished.
They will build houses
　but not live in them;
they will plant vineyards
　but not drink the wine.

¹⁴"The great day of the LORD is near—
　near and coming quickly.
Listen! The cry on the day of the LORD will be
　　bitter,
　the shouting of the warrior there.
¹⁵That day will be a day of wrath,
　a day of distress and anguish,
　a day of trouble and ruin,
　a day of darkness and gloom,
　a day of clouds and blackness,
¹⁶a day of trumpet and battle cry
　against the fortified cities

---

*a*3 The meaning of the Hebrew for this line is uncertain.　　*b*5 Hebrew *Malcam,* that is, Milcom　　*c*9 See 1 Samuel 5:5.　　*d*11 Or *the Mortar*　　*e*11 Or *in*

and against the corner towers.
17I will bring distress on the people
and they will walk like blind men,
because they have sinned against the
Lord.
Their blood will be poured out like dust
and their entrails like filth.

18Neither their silver nor their gold
will be able to save them
on the day of the Lord's wrath.
In the fire of his jealousy
the whole world will be consumed,
for he will make a sudden end
of all who live in the earth."

 Discovering the Word 1. What did Zephaniah declare about God's coming judgment (vv. 1–3)? 2. For what sins would God judge his people (vv. 4–13)? 3. God's people responded to him with complacency. How did that attitude affect them (vv. 12–13)? 4. How did Zephaniah describe the coming day of the Lord (vv. 14–18)? 5. If you had been one of the people who received this message, how would you have reacted to it? Why?

 Applying the Word 1. In what areas do you tend to be complacent? 2. What would help you to overcome complacency in one area?

Responding in Prayer Ask God to help you trust him and to stretch you spiritually instead of being satisfied with your present comfort zone.

---

2 / *Zephaniah 2*
Judgment to Come

OUR NEEDS AND problems often keep us focused on ourselves. Sure we're going to heaven someday. But what about the people we know who do not have this assurance? Just as God fulfilled Zephaniah's warning to the nations around Judah, he will judge sinners as he declared in other portions of the Bible.

 Warming Up to God How often do you think about the judgment your unsaved friends and relatives will endure? Ask God to show you the seriousness of the judgment to come as you study this passage.

 Read Zephaniah 2.

---

2 Gather together, gather together,
O shameful nation,
2before the appointed time arrives
and that day sweeps on like chaff,
before the fierce anger of the Lord comes
upon you,
before the day of the Lord's wrath comes
upon you.
3Seek the Lord, all you humble of the land,
you who do what he commands.
Seek righteousness, seek humility;
perhaps you will be sheltered
on the day of the Lord's anger.

4Gaza will be abandoned
and Ashkelon left in ruins.
At midday Ashdod will be emptied
and Ekron uprooted.

5Woe to you who live by the sea,
O Kerethite people;
the word of the Lord is against you,
O Canaan, land of the Philistines.

"I will destroy you,
and none will be left."

6The land by the sea, where the Kerethites*f*
dwell,
will be a place for shepherds and sheep
pens.
7It will belong to the remnant of the house of
Judah;
there they will find pasture.
In the evening they will lie down
in the houses of Ashkelon.

*f*6 The meaning of the Hebrew for this word is uncertain.

The LORD their God will care for them;
he will restore their fortunes.[g]

[8]"I have heard the insults of Moab
and the taunts of the Ammonites,
who insulted my people
and made threats against their land.
[9]Therefore, as surely as I live,"
declares the LORD Almighty, the God of
Israel,
"surely Moab will become like Sodom,
the Ammonites like Gomorrah—
a place of weeds and salt pits,
a wasteland forever.
The remnant of my people will plunder them;
the survivors of my nation will inherit their
land."

[10]This is what they will get in return for their
pride,
for insulting and mocking the people of the
LORD Almighty.
[11]The LORD will be awesome to them
when he destroys all the gods of the land.
The nations on every shore will worship him,
every one in its own land.

[12]"You too, O Cushites,[h]
will be slain by my sword."

[13]He will stretch out his hand against the north
and destroy Assyria,
leaving Nineveh utterly desolate
and dry as the desert.
[14]Flocks and herds will lie down there,
creatures of every kind.
The desert owl and the screech owl
will roost on her columns.
Their calls will echo through the windows,
rubble will be in the doorways,
the beams of cedar will be exposed.
[15]This is the carefree city
that lived in safety.
She said to herself,
"I am, and there is none besides me."
What a ruin she has become,
a lair for wild beasts!
All who pass by her scoff
and shake their fists.

g 7 Or *will bring back their captives*   h 12 That is, people from the
upper Nile region

Discovering the Word   1. What did Zephaniah tell the people to do in order to avoid God's anger (vv. 1–3)?   2. What would God do to those who punished his people (vv. 4–15)?   3. What sins had the nations around Judah committed (vv. 4–15)?   4. What hope did Zephaniah offer God's people in the midst of this judgment (vv. 6–7)?   5. According to this chapter, what would the nations learn about God?

Applying the Word   1. In what ways is your nation in danger of God's judgment?   2. Reread verse 3. How can you seek the Lord today?

Responding in Prayer   Ask God for opportunities this week to tell others about him.

3 / *Zephaniah 3*
Better Days Are Coming

WHEN YOU THINK about the future, what comes to mind? Next year? Retirement? Heaven? Escape from the frustrations of today? No matter what you are going through now, you can look forward to some wonderful things, as God made clear through Zephaniah's prophecy.

Warming Up to God   If you were in charge of the future, what would you like to have happen?

Read Zephaniah 3.

3 Woe to the city of oppressors,
    rebellious and defiled!
    ²She obeys no one,
she accepts no correction.
She does not trust in the LORD,
    she does not draw near to her God.
³Her officials are roaring lions,
    her rulers are evening wolves,
    who leave nothing for the morning.
⁴Her prophets are arrogant;
    they are treacherous men.
Her priests profane the sanctuary
    and do violence to the law.
⁵The LORD within her is righteous;
    he does no wrong.
Morning by morning he dispenses his
       justice,
    and every new day he does not fail,
    yet the unrighteous know no shame.

⁶"I have cut off nations;
    their strongholds are demolished.
I have left their streets deserted,
    with no one passing through.
Their cities are destroyed;
    no one will be left—no one at all.
⁷I said to the city,
    'Surely you will fear me
    and accept correction!'
Then her dwelling would not be cut off,
    nor all my punishments come upon her.
But they were still eager
    to act corruptly in all they did.
⁸Therefore wait for me," declares the LORD,
    "for the day I will stand up to testify.ⁱ
I have decided to assemble the nations,
    to gather the kingdoms
and to pour out my wrath on them—
    all my fierce anger.
The whole world will be consumed
    by the fire of my jealous anger.

⁹"Then will I purify the lips of the peoples,
    that all of them may call on the name of
       the LORD
    and serve him shoulder to shoulder.
¹⁰From beyond the rivers of Cushʲ
    my worshipers, my scattered people,
    will bring me offerings.
¹¹On that day you will not be put to shame
for all the wrongs you have done to me,
because I will remove from this city
    those who rejoice in their pride.
Never again will you be haughty
    on my holy hill.
¹²But I will leave within you
    the meek and humble,
    who trust in the name of the LORD.
¹³The remnant of Israel will do no wrong;
    they will speak no lies,
    nor will deceit be found in their mouths.
They will eat and lie down
    and no one will make them afraid."

¹⁴Sing, O Daughter of Zion;
    shout aloud, O Israel!
Be glad and rejoice with all your heart,
    O Daughter of Jerusalem!
¹⁵The LORD has taken away your punishment,
    he has turned back your enemy.
The LORD, the King of Israel, is with you;
    never again will you fear any harm.
¹⁶On that day they will say to Jerusalem,
    "Do not fear, O Zion;
    do not let your hands hang limp.
¹⁷The LORD your God is with you,
    he is mighty to save.
He will take great delight in you,
    he will quiet you with his love,
    he will rejoice over you with singing."

¹⁸"The sorrows for the appointed feasts
    I will remove from you;
    they are a burden and a reproach to you.ᵏ
¹⁹At that time I will deal
    with all who oppressed you;
I will rescue the lame
    and gather those who have been scattered.
I will give them praise and honor
    in every land where they were put to
       shame.
²⁰At that time I will gather you;
    at that time I will bring you home.
I will give you honor and praise
    among all the peoples of the earth
when I restore your fortunesˡ
    before your very eyes,"
                  says the LORD.

ⁱ8 Septuagint and Syriac; Hebrew *will rise up to plunder*   ʲ10 That is,
the upper Nile region   ᵏ18 Or *"I will gather you who mourn for the
appointed feasts; / your reproach is a burden to you*   ˡ20 Or *I bring
back your captives*

Discovering the Word 1. After pronouncing judgments on the nations, Zephaniah came back to Judah. Why did God warn his people about judgment to come (vv. 1–7)? 2. How did the people respond to God's warning (v. 7)? 3. What did God promise his people in the future (vv. 8–20)? 4. What do you learn about God from this chapter?

 Applying the Word 1. Which promise are you looking forward to the most? Why? 2. Which description of God do you need to remember today as you wait for what he has promised in the future?

Responding in Prayer Look again at the sins mentioned in verse 2, and confess any sins God is warning you about. Thank him for what is to come in the future.

Haggai

If you're like most believers, you're pulled in a myriad of directions. Full schedules, necessary and worthwhile activities, family members, friends, other people, distractions and interruptions all clamor for attention. But where is God in the midst of our priorities? This is an ancient struggle that Haggai addressed over 2500 years ago.

To understand the messages of Haggai, we need to understand the historical context in which they were given. In 586 B.C. the Babylonians under Nebuchadnezzar defeated the southern kingdom of Judah and razed the city of Jerusalem, including the temple. They took many of the Jewish people captive as God's punishment for their sins, primarily idolatry. In 539 B.C. Cyrus, king of Persia, conquered Babylon, becoming the new ruler of the Jewish people. A year later, he issued a decree that permitted the exiles to return to their land.

The first group of exiles (about 50,000) returned in 536 B.C. under Zerubbabel's leadership to rebuild the temple. Apparently, Haggai was part of this group. After laying the foundation, the exiles quit when their enemies threatened them and hired lawyers to frustrate their work. So the temple rebuilding stopped for fifteen years. These events are recorded in Ezra 1—4.

Then God sent the prophets Haggai and Zechariah to call his people back to this work. Ezra 5 tells about this event while the books of Haggai and Zechariah give us the content of their preaching.

Rebuilding the temple was an important task for the Jewish people. The temple represented their relationship with God. It was the focal point of their worship and fellowship with the God who called them to be his chosen people. But other things had gotten in the way of finishing this task, much like other things—even good things—get in the way of our doing God's will today.

Haggai 1—2
Getting Priorities Straight

IT HAPPENED AGAIN. Even though Nathan had promised his wife their relationship would have greater priority in his schedule, he called to tell her he had to work late for the third night in a row. Then he spent a couple of hours Friday night paying the bills and bemoaning the fact that they didn't have enough money to fulfill their missions pledge. In spite of what we say, our actions are the clues to our priorities. Haggai had some things to say about lining up words and actions.

 Warming Up to God What would someone observing you for a week think your priorities are?

 Read Haggai 1—2.

1 In the second year of King Darius, on the first day of the sixth month, the word of the LORD came through the prophet Haggai to Zerubbabel son of Shealtiel, governor of Judah, and to Joshua[a] son of Jehozadak, the high priest:

²This is what the LORD Almighty says: "These people say, 'The time has not yet come for the LORD's house to be built.' "

³Then the word of the LORD came through the prophet Haggai: ⁴"Is it a time for you yourselves to be living in your paneled houses, while this house remains a ruin?"

⁵Now this is what the LORD Almighty says: "Give careful thought to your ways. ⁶You have planted much, but have harvested little. You eat, but never have enough. You drink, but never have your fill. You put on clothes, but are not warm. You earn wages, only to put them in a purse with holes in it."

⁷This is what the LORD Almighty says: "Give careful thought to your ways. ⁸Go up into the mountains and bring down timber and build the house, so that I may take pleasure in it and be honored," says the LORD. ⁹"You expected much, but see, it turned out to be little. What you brought home, I blew away. Why?" declares the LORD Almighty. "Because of my house, which remains a ruin, while each of you is busy with his own house. ¹⁰Therefore, because of you the heavens have withheld their dew and the earth its crops. ¹¹I called for a drought on the fields and the mountains, on the grain, the new wine, the oil and whatever the ground produces, on men and cattle, and on the labor of your hands."

¹²Then Zerubbabel son of Shealtiel, Joshua son

of Jehozadak, the high priest, and the whole remnant of the people obeyed the voice of the LORD their God and the message of the prophet Haggai, because the LORD their God had sent him. And the people feared the LORD.

¹³Then Haggai, the LORD's messenger, gave this message of the LORD to the people: "I am with you," declares the LORD. ¹⁴So the LORD stirred up the spirit of Zerubbabel son of Shealtiel, governor of Judah, and the spirit of Joshua son of Jehozadak, the high priest, and the spirit of the whole remnant of the people. They came and began to work on the house of the LORD Almighty, their God, ¹⁵on the twenty-fourth day of the sixth month in the second year of King Darius.

2 On the twenty-first day of the seventh month, the word of the LORD came through the prophet Haggai: ²"Speak to Zerubbabel son of Shealtiel, governor of Judah, to Joshua son of Jehozadak, the high priest, and to the remnant of the people. Ask them, ³'Who of you is left who saw this house in its former glory? How does it look to you now? Does it not seem to you like nothing? ⁴But now be strong, O Zerubbabel,' declares the LORD. 'Be strong, O Joshua son of Jehozadak, the high priest. Be strong, all you people of the land,' declares the LORD, 'and work. For I am with you,' declares the LORD Almighty. ⁵'This is what I covenanted with you when you came out of Egypt. And my Spirit remains among you. Do not fear.'

⁶"This is what the LORD Almighty says: 'In a little while I will once more shake the heavens and the earth, the sea and the dry land. ⁷I will shake all nations, and the desired of all nations will come, and I will fill this house with glory,'

---

*a 1 A variant of *Jeshua*; here and elsewhere in Haggai

says the LORD Almighty. 8'The silver is mine and the gold is mine,' declares the LORD Almighty. 9'The glory of this present house will be greater than the glory of the former house,' says the LORD Almighty. 'And in this place I will grant peace,' declares the LORD Almighty."

10On the twenty-fourth day of the ninth month, in the second year of Darius, the word of the LORD came to the prophet Haggai: 11"This is what the LORD Almighty says: 'Ask the priests what the law says: 12If a person carries consecrated meat in the fold of his garment, and that fold touches some bread or stew, some wine, oil or other food, does it become consecrated?' "

The priests answered, "No."

13Then Haggai said, "If a person defiled by contact with a dead body touches one of these things, does it become defiled?"

"Yes," the priests replied, "it becomes defiled."

14Then Haggai said, " 'So it is with this people and this nation in my sight,' declares the LORD. 'Whatever they do and whatever they offer there is defiled.

15" 'Now give careful thought to this from this day on[b]—consider how things were before one stone was laid on another in the LORD's temple. 16When anyone came to a heap of twenty mea-sures, there were only ten. When anyone went to a wine vat to draw fifty measures, there were only twenty. 17I struck all the work of your hands with blight, mildew and hail, yet you did not turn to me,' declares the LORD. 18'From this day on, from this twenty-fourth day of the ninth month, give careful thought to the day when the foundation of the LORD's temple was laid. Give careful thought: 19Is there yet any seed left in the barn? Until now, the vine and the fig tree, the pomegranate and the olive tree have not borne fruit.

" 'From this day on I will bless you.' "

20The word of the LORD came to Haggai a second time on the twenty-fourth day of the month: 21"Tell Zerubbabel governor of Judah that I will shake the heavens and the earth. 22I will overturn royal thrones and shatter the power of the foreign kingdoms. I will overthrow chariots and their drivers; horses and their riders will fall, each by the sword of his brother.

23" 'On that day,' declares the LORD Almighty, 'I will take you, my servant Zerubbabel son of Shealtiel,' declares the LORD, 'and I will make you like my signet ring, for I have chosen you,' declares the LORD Almighty."

b15 Or to the days past

 Discovering the Word 1. Getting priorities straight is not a 20th-century invention. According to chapter 1, what priority problems did the Jewish people have in Haggai's day? 2. What did God have to say about dealing with inappropriate priorities (1:3–8)? 3. What were the results of their wrong priorities (1:9–11)? 4. How did the people respond to Haggai's message (1:12–15)? Why? 5. In chapter 2 God gave Haggai three messages. What promises and warnings did he give his people?

 Applying the Word 1. What do you want your priorities to be? List them. 2. What changes do you need to make in your schedule for today to reflect those priorities?

Responding in Prayer Ask God to show you his priorities for you. Then pray that he will help you live them.

Zechariah

When God calls us to complete a task, we know we should be faithful and diligent until it is accomplished. But sometimes we grow tired or discouraged. Obstacles block our path; opponents mock us, and in time we are tempted to give up.

During such times, we need a fresh word from the Lord. He gently rebukes us, then offers us strong encouragement and genuine hope. Most of all, he gives us a renewed vision of how our task fits into his broader plans and purposes in the world.

If you have grown weary doing God's will, then the book of Zechariah can refresh and strengthen you. It was written to the 50,000 Jews who had returned to Jerusalem after the Babylonian captivity. God had called them to rebuild the temple, and initially they responded with great energy and zeal. But as they faced one problem after another, their zeal turned to apathy and the work on the temple ceased. Then God sent the prophet Zechariah (whose name means "The Lord remembers") to turn the people back to the Lord and to the task they needed to complete.

Zechariah is one of the most messianic books in the Bible. In order to encourage his people, the Lord looks beyond their immediate circumstances to the time when all God's enemies will be vanquished, all his purposes fulfilled and the whole earth will acknowledge his rightful rule as King.

Zechariah predicted the Messiah's triumphal entry into Jerusalem (9:9; Mt 21:5), his betrayal for thirty pieces of silver (11:12–13; Mt 26:14–16; 27:1–10), the desertion of his followers (13:7; Mt 26:31), the fact that the Messiah would be pierced (12:10; Jn 19:37) and his glorious return to the Mount of Olives (14:4; Ac 1:9–11). The book of Zechariah is quoted from or alluded to in the New Testament seventy-one times, and apart from Ezekiel had the greatest influence on the book of Revelation.

As you read Zechariah, may the Lord encourage you to complete whatever tasks he has given you and to see them from his eternal perspective.

Outline

1/ Zechariah 1 ——————————— *Return to the Lord*

2/ Zechariah 2—3 ——————————— *Joy and Cleansing*

3/ Zechariah 4—5 ——————————— *Overcoming Obstacles*

4/ Zechariah 6 ——————————— *The Priest and King*

5/ Zechariah 7 ——————————— *Justice and Mercy*

6/ Zechariah 8 ——————————— *The Lord's Return*

7/ Zechariah 9—10 ——————————— *The Coming of the King*

8/ Zechariah 11 ——————————— *The Two Shepherds*

9/ Zechariah 12—13 ——————————— *Preparing for the Lord*

10/ Zechariah 14 ——————————— *The Day of the Lord*

1 / *Zechariah 1*
Return to the Lord

DO YOU EVER wander from God? When you do things that displease him, does he seem far away? At such times we need to realize that the Lord longs for our return. Like a jealous lover, he wants our undivided loyalty and affection. In Zechariah 1:3 the Lord tells Israel and us, "Return to me . . . and I will return to you."

 Warming Up to God When you feel distant from the Lord, what makes you want to return to his love and care?

 Read Zechariah 1.

---

1 In the eighth month of the second year of Darius, the word of the LORD came to the prophet Zechariah son of Berekiah, the son of Iddo:

²"The LORD was very angry with your forefathers. ³Therefore tell the people: This is what the LORD Almighty says: 'Return to me,' declares the LORD Almighty, 'and I will return to you,' says the LORD Almighty. ⁴Do not be like your forefathers, to whom the earlier prophets proclaimed: This is what the LORD Almighty says: 'Turn from your evil ways and your evil practices.' But they would not listen or pay attention to me, declares the LORD. ⁵Where are your forefathers now? And the prophets, do they live forever? ⁶But did not my words and my decrees, which I commanded my servants the prophets, overtake your forefathers?

"Then they repented and said, 'The LORD Almighty has done to us what our ways and practices deserve, just as he determined to do.' "

⁷On the twenty-fourth day of the eleventh month, the month of Shebat, in the second year of Darius, the word of the LORD came to the prophet Zechariah son of Berekiah, the son of Iddo.

⁸During the night I had a vision—and there before me was a man riding a red horse! He was standing among the myrtle trees in a ravine. Behind him were red, brown and white horses.

⁹I asked, "What are these, my lord?"

The angel who was talking with me answered, "I will show you what they are."

¹⁰Then the man standing among the myrtle trees explained, "They are the ones the LORD has sent to go throughout the earth."

¹¹And they reported to the angel of the LORD, who was standing among the myrtle trees, "We have gone throughout the earth and found the whole world at rest and in peace."

¹²Then the angel of the LORD said, "LORD Almighty, how long will you withhold mercy from Jerusalem and from the towns of Judah, which you have been angry with these seventy years?" ¹³So the LORD spoke kind and comforting words to the angel who talked with me.

¹⁴Then the angel who was speaking to me said, "Proclaim this word: This is what the LORD Almighty says: 'I am very jealous for Jerusalem and Zion, ¹⁵but I am very angry with the nations that feel secure. I was only a little angry, but they added to the calamity.'

¹⁶"Therefore, this is what the LORD says: 'I will return to Jerusalem with mercy, and there my house will be rebuilt. And the measuring line will be stretched out over Jerusalem,' declares the LORD Almighty.

¹⁷"Proclaim further: This is what the LORD Almighty says: 'My towns will again overflow with prosperity, and the LORD will again comfort Zion and choose Jerusalem.' "

¹⁸Then I looked up—and there before me were four horns! ¹⁹I asked the angel who was speaking to me, "What are these?"

He answered me, "These are the horns that scattered Judah, Israel and Jerusalem."

²⁰Then the LORD showed me four craftsmen. ²¹I asked, "What are these coming to do?"

He answered, "These are the horns that scattered Judah so that no one could raise his head, but the craftsmen have come to terrify them and throw down these horns of the nations who lifted up their horns against the land of Judah to scatter its people."

Discovering the Word 1. In verses 1–6 Zechariah asks the people to recall Israel's captivity in Babylon. What lessons do the people need to learn from their forefathers? 2. If we want to return to the Lord, why must we turn from our evil ways (vv. 3–6)? 3. In Zechariah's first vision (vv. 7–17) he sees a horseman who is later identified as the angel of the Lord (v. 11). Why is the angel troubled by the state of the world in contrast to the conditions in Israel (vv. 12–13)? 4. What "comforting words" does the Lord give to the angel and to his people (vv. 13–17)? 5. The "four horns" in verses 18–21 are four rulers or nations "that scattered Judah, Israel and Jerusalem" (v. 19). How will the Lord use four other nations ("craftsmen") to bring justice to his people (vv. 20–21)?

Applying the Word 1. Think of the ways God has disciplined you in the past. How do these experiences make you want to be faithful to him in the present? 2. In what areas do you need to return to the Lord or turn from "evil ways"?

Responding in Prayer Confess any sins that have led you away from God. Ask him to help you return to him, and thank him for his forgiveness and love.

2 / *Zechariah 2—3*
Joy and Cleansing

DO YOU FEEL unclean and unworthy to stand before the Lord? Do your sins seem to be used as evidence against you, proving that you have no right to be called God's child? Zechariah 2—3 offers cleansing to those who feel defiled, hope to those who feel despair and joy to those who are overwhelmed with sorrow.

 Warming Up to God Do you ever feel unacceptable to God because of your sins? Express your feelings to the Lord and ask him to use this passage to see yourself as he sees you.

 Read Zechariah 2—3.

2 Then I looked up—and there before me was a man with a measuring line in his hand! ²I asked, "Where are you going?"

He answered me, "To measure Jerusalem, to find out how wide and how long it is."

³Then the angel who was speaking to me left, and another angel came to meet him ⁴and said to him: "Run, tell that young man, 'Jerusalem will be a city without walls because of the great number of men and livestock in it. ⁵And I myself will be a wall of fire around it,' declares the Lord, 'and I will be its glory within.'

⁶"Come! Come! Flee from the land of the north," declares the Lord, "for I have scattered you to the four winds of heaven," declares the Lord.

⁷"Come, O Zion! Escape, you who live in the Daughter of Babylon!" ⁸For this is what the Lord Almighty says: "After he has honored me and has sent me against the nations that have plundered you—for whoever touches you touches the apple of his eye— ⁹I will surely raise my hand against them so that their slaves will plunder them.*

Then you will know that the Lord Almighty has sent me.

¹⁰"Shout and be glad, O Daughter of Zion. For I am coming, and I will live among you," declares the Lord. ¹¹"Many nations will be joined with the Lord in that day and will become my people. I will live among you and you will know that the Lord Almighty has sent me to you. ¹²The Lord will inherit Judah as his portion in the holy land and will again choose Jerusalem. ¹³Be still before the Lord, all mankind, because he has roused himself from his holy dwelling."

3 Then he showed me Joshua* the high priest standing before the angel of the Lord, and Satan* standing at his right side to accuse him. ²The Lord said to Satan, "The Lord rebuke you, Satan! The Lord, who has chosen Jerusalem, rebuke you! Is not this man a burning stick snatched from the fire?"

³Now Joshua was dressed in filthy clothes as he stood before the angel. ⁴The angel said to those

*8,9 Or *says after . . . eye:* 9"I . . . *plunder them."*   *1 A variant of Jeshua; here and elsewhere in Zechariah   *1 *Satan* means *accuser.*

who were standing before him, "Take off his filthy clothes."

Then he said to Joshua, "See, I have taken away your sin, and I will put rich garments on you."

⁵Then I said, "Put a clean turban on his head." So they put a clean turban on his head and clothed him, while the angel of the LORD stood by.

⁶The angel of the LORD gave this charge to Joshua: ⁷"This is what the LORD Almighty says: 'If you will walk in my ways and keep my requirements, then you will govern my house and have charge of my courts, and I will give you a place among these standing here.

⁸" 'Listen, O high priest Joshua and your associates seated before you, who are men symbolic of things to come: I am going to bring my servant, the Branch. ⁹See, the stone I have set in front of Joshua! There are seven eyes*d* on that one stone, and I will engrave an inscription on it,' says the LORD Almighty, 'and I will remove the sin of this land in a single day.

¹⁰" 'In that day each of you will invite his neighbor to sit under his vine and fig tree,' declares the LORD Almighty."

d9 Or *facets*

Discovering the Word 1. At this point in history, Jerusalem lay in ruins because of the Babylonian conquest seventy years earlier. What hope do the angels offer Zechariah about the future of the city (2:1–5)? 2. "The land of the north" (2:6) is Babylon, the place of Israel's former captivity. Why does the Lord command those Israelites who remain there to "flee" and "escape" (2:6–9)? 3. In verses 10–13 the Lord himself promises to come and live among his people. How does this promise compare with the one in Revelation 21:1–4? 4. Joshua the high priest represents the nation of Israel (3:1–5). How does this courtroomlike scene illustrate what Christ has done for us on the cross? 5. Why must those who have been cleansed from their sins respond by walking in God's ways and keeping his requirements (3:6–10)?

Applying the Word 1. How does the promise of living with the Lord forever offer you hope, especially during those times when your life seems to be in ruins? 2. The name Satan means "accuser." When you feel accused and condemned because of your sins, what do you need to remember about what Christ has done for you?

Responding in Prayer Thank God for removing the filth of your sins and dressing you in the spotless clothes of Christ's righteousness. Praise him for his presence in your life and for the hope of living with him forever.

---

3 / *Zechariah 4—5*
Overcoming Obstacles

SOMETIMES WE FACE obstacles that seem insurmountable. We are confronted by challenges at work, at church or in our communities that are overwhelming. How should we respond in these situations? How can we have the strength to be victorious? This passage tells us: "'Not by might nor by power, but by my Spirit,' says the LORD Almighty" (4:6).

Warming Up to God What situation are you facing that seems overwhelming? Bring that situation to the Lord, asking him for the strength you need.

Read Zechariah 4—5.

4 Then the angel who talked with me returned and wakened me, as a man is wakened from his sleep. ²He asked me, "What do you see?"

I answered, "I see a solid gold lampstand with a bowl at the top and seven lights on it, with seven channels to the lights. ³Also there are two olive trees by it, one on the right of the bowl and the other on its left."

⁴I asked the angel who talked with me, "What are these, my lord?"

⁵He answered, "Do you not know what these are?"

"No, my lord," I replied.

⁶So he said to me, "This is the word of the Lᴏʀᴅ to Zerubbabel: 'Not by might nor by power, but by my Spirit,' says the Lᴏʀᴅ Almighty.

⁷"Whatᵉ are you, O mighty mountain? Before Zerubbabel you will become level ground. Then he will bring out the capstone to shouts of 'God bless it! God bless it!' "

⁸Then the word of the Lᴏʀᴅ came to me: ⁹"The hands of Zerubbabel have laid the foundation of this temple; his hands will also complete it. Then you will know that the Lᴏʀᴅ Almighty has sent me to you.

¹⁰"Who despises the day of small things? Men will rejoice when they see the plumb line in the hand of Zerubbabel.

"(These seven are the eyes of the Lᴏʀᴅ, which range throughout the earth.)"

¹¹Then I asked the angel, "What are these two olive trees on the right and the left of the lampstand?"

¹²Again I asked him, "What are these two olive branches beside the two gold pipes that pour out golden oil?"

¹³He replied, "Do you not know what these are?"

"No, my lord," I said.

¹⁴So he said, "These are the two who are anointed toᶠ serve the Lord of all the earth."

5 I looked again—and there before me was a flying scroll!

²He asked me, "What do you see?"

I answered, "I see a flying scroll, thirty feet long and fifteen feet wide.ᵍ"

³And he said to me, "This is the curse that is going out over the whole land; for according to what it says on one side, every thief will be banished, and according to what it says on the other, everyone who swears falsely will be banished. ⁴The Lᴏʀᴅ Almighty declares, 'I will send it out, and it will enter the house of the thief and the house of him who swears falsely by my name. It will remain in his house and destroy it, both its timbers and its stones.' "

⁵Then the angel who was speaking to me came forward and said to me, "Look up and see what this is that is appearing."

⁶I asked, "What is it?"

He replied, "It is a measuring basket.ʰ" And he added, "This is the iniquityⁱ of the people throughout the land."

⁷Then the cover of lead was raised, and there in the basket sat a woman! ⁸He said, "This is wickedness," and he pushed her back into the basket and pushed the lead cover down over its mouth.

⁹Then I looked up—and there before me were two women, with the wind in their wings! They had wings like those of a stork, and they lifted up the basket between heaven and earth.

¹⁰"Where are they taking the basket?" I asked the angel who was speaking to me.

¹¹He replied, "To the country of Babyloniaʲ to build a house for it. When it is ready, the basket will be set there in its place."

ᵉ7 Or Who   ᶠ14 Or two who bring oil and   ᵍ2 Hebrew twenty cubits long and ten cubits wide (about 9 meters long and 4.5 meters wide)   ʰ6 Hebrew an ephah; also in verses 7-11   ⁱ6 Or appearance   ʲ11 Hebrew Shinar

---

Discovering the Word 1. Oil is often used in Scripture as a symbol of God's Spirit. As Zerubbabel faces the overwhelming task of rebuilding the temple, what encouragement does the Lord give him (4:1–10)? 2. We may not have human might or power to face our mountains of opposition. How then can we be victorious (4:6–7)? 3. The two olive branches (4:11–14) represent the Lord's anointed servants: Zerubbabel the ruler and Joshua the priest. Why do you think God empowers frail humans to accomplish his mighty tasks? 4. How do the visions of the flying scroll and the woman in a basket challenge the Israelites to repent of their sins (5:1–11)? 5. How can sin become one of the greatest obstacles to accomplishing God's work?

Applying the Word 1. When confronted with overwhelming obstacles, why are we tempted to trust in human might or power? 2. Think of a mountain of difficulty you are currently facing. How can you rely on God's Spirit to level that mountain? 3. Is there any sin in your life that you need to confess and forsake before God anoints you with power?

Responding in Prayer Ask God to level the mountain of difficulty that rises up before you. Thank him for the abundant supply of his spiritual might and power in your life.

4 / Zechariah 6
The Priest and King

IN THE OLD Testament priests offered sacrifices and represented the people before God, and kings were divinely appointed leaders and shepherds over Israel. In Zechariah 6 the Lord combines the offices of priest and king. The symbolic crowning of Joshua, the high priest, foreshadows the coming of the ultimate Priest and King—the Messiah himself.

 Warming Up to God Like the people in Zechariah's day, we still look forward to the coming of the Messiah—although we anticipate his Second Coming. What do you long for most about the Lord's return? Express your longings to God.

Read Zechariah 6.

6 I looked up again—and there before me were four chariots coming out from between two mountains—mountains of bronze! ²The first chariot had red horses, the second black, ³the third white, and the fourth dappled—all of them powerful. ⁴I asked the angel who was speaking to me, "What are these, my lord?"

⁵The angel answered me, "These are the four spirits^k of heaven, going out from standing in the presence of the Lord of the whole world. ⁶The one with the black horses is going toward the north country, the one with the white horses toward the west,^{l} and the one with the dappled horses toward the south."

⁷When the powerful horses went out, they were straining to go throughout the earth. And he said, "Go throughout the earth!" So they went throughout the earth.

⁸Then he called to me, "Look, those going toward the north country have given my Spirit^m rest in the land of the north."

⁹The word of the LORD came to me: ¹⁰"Take ⌞silver and gold⌟ from the exiles Heldai, Tobijah and Jedaiah, who have arrived from Babylon. Go the same day to the house of Josiah son of Zephaniah. ¹¹Take the silver and gold and make a crown, and set it on the head of the high priest, Joshua son of Jehozadak. ¹²Tell him this is what the LORD Almighty says: 'Here is the man whose name is the Branch, and he will branch out from his place and build the temple of the LORD. ¹³It is he who will build the temple of the LORD, and he will be clothed with majesty and will sit and rule on his throne. And he will be a priest on his throne. And there will be harmony between the two.' ¹⁴The crown will be given to Heldai,^{n} Tobijah, Jedaiah and Hen^o son of Zephaniah as a memorial in the temple of the LORD. ¹⁵Those who are far away will come and help to build the temple of the LORD, and you will know that the LORD Almighty has sent me to you. This will happen if you diligently obey the LORD your God."

^{k}5 Or *winds* ^{l}6 Or *horses after them* ^{m}8 Or *spirit*
^{n}14 Syriac; Hebrew *Helem* ^{o}14 Or *and the gracious one, the*

 Discovering the Word 1. In Zechariah's eighth and final vision he sees four chariots drawn by various colored horses (vv. 1–8). How does this vision compare with the one in Zechariah 1:7–11 (see also Rev 6:1–8)? 2. The horses and chariots represent divine judgment. How do these chariots give the Lord's Spirit rest (v. 8), especially in the land of the north (Babylon)? 3. What does the Lord command Zechariah to do and to say to Joshua the high priest (vv. 9–13)? 4. Based on Zechariah 3:8 and other Old Testament passages such as Isaiah 11 and Jeremiah 23:5–6 and 33:14–16, we know that "the Branch" (v. 12) is ultimately the Messiah himself. Why is it significant that he will combine the offices of priest and king? 5. Why do you think the promises about the rebuilding of the temple are conditional on the people's obedience (vv. 14–15)?

 Applying the Word 1. Why do we need Jesus Christ, our High Priest, to represent us before God? 2. The Lord is also our ruler and king. In what areas do you need to "diligently obey" him this week?

Responding in Prayer Thank the Lord for his loving leadership in your life and for faithfully representing you before the Father. Ask him for the grace and strength to obey him diligently.

5 / *Zechariah 7*
Justice and Mercy

SOMETIMES OUR ACTIONS may appear to be pious, but our motives are misguided. How can we avoid this kind of hypocrisy? How can we get beyond an external legalism in order to serve the Lord from the heart? In Zechariah 7 the Lord tells his people the kind of obedience that really matters.

 Warming Up to God Do you ever feel as though you are merely going through the motions as you serve God? Ask the Lord to purify your motives as you study this passage.

 Read Zechariah 7.

7 In the fourth year of King Darius, the word of the LORD came to Zechariah on the fourth day of the ninth month, the month of Kislev. ²The people of Bethel had sent Sharezer and Regem-Melech, together with their men, to entreat the LORD ³by asking the priests of the house of the LORD Almighty and the prophets, "Should I mourn and fast in the fifth month, as I have done for so many years?"

⁴Then the word of the LORD Almighty came to me: ⁵"Ask all the people of the land and the priests, 'When you fasted and mourned in the fifth and seventh months for the past seventy years, was it really for me that you fasted? ⁶And when you were eating and drinking, were you not just feasting for yourselves? ⁷Are these not the words the LORD proclaimed through the earlier prophets when Jerusalem and its surrounding towns were at rest and prosperous, and the Negev and the western foothills were settled?' "

⁸And the word of the LORD came again to Zechariah: ⁹"This is what the LORD Almighty says: 'Administer true justice; show mercy and compassion to one another. ¹⁰Do not oppress the widow or the fatherless, the alien or the poor. In your hearts do not think evil of each other.'

¹¹"But they refused to pay attention; stubbornly they turned their backs and stopped up their ears. ¹²They made their hearts as hard as flint and would not listen to the law or to the words that the LORD Almighty had sent by his Spirit through the earlier prophets. So the LORD Almighty was very angry.

¹³" 'When I called, they did not listen; so when they called, I would not listen,' says the LORD Almighty. ¹⁴I scattered them with a whirlwind among all the nations, where they were strangers. The land was left so desolate behind them that no one could come or go. This is how they made the pleasant land desolate.' "

Discovering the Word 1. While they were in Babylon, the Israelites observed various fasts to commemorate the destruction of the temple. Now they ask if they need to continue (vv. 1–3). How does the Lord evaluate the seventy years of fasting by the people in exile (vv. 4–7)? 2. Why do you think the people are asking whether they should continue these fasts? 3. How can we know whether our actions are done for the Lord or merely for ourselves? 4. If our motives are pure, what kinds of actions will be evident in our lives (vv. 8–10)? 5. Why is it dangerous to harden our hearts against the Lord and against his Word (vv. 11–14)?

Applying the Word 1. In what areas are you merely practicing religious rituals rather than obeying the Lord from the heart? 2. How do you measure up to Zechariah's four tests of spiritual reality (vv. 8–10)? 3. In what practical ways can you begin to follow these commands?

Responding in Prayer Ask the Lord for insight into the areas of your life where your "obedience" is really self-serving or mere ritual. Pray for opportunities to administer true justice, and show mercy and compassion, while avoiding oppression and thinking evil of others.

6 / *Zechariah 8*
The Lord's Return

HARDSHIPS AND TRIALS often seem as though they will last forever. Our lives seem empty, and our days are dark and filled with pain. But Zechariah 8 offers us great hope. There will be a day when our mourning will be turned into laughter, and our sorrow into joy.

 Warming Up to God What do you imagine life will be like when the Lord returns? Thank God for this amazing promise and the great hope it offers.

 Read Zechariah 8.

8 Again the word of the LORD Almighty came to me. ²This is what the LORD Almighty says: "I am very jealous for Zion; I am burning with jealousy for her."

³This is what the LORD says: "I will return to Zion and dwell in Jerusalem. Then Jerusalem will be called the City of Truth, and the mountain of the LORD Almighty will be called the Holy Mountain."

⁴This is what the LORD Almighty says: "Once again men and women of ripe old age will sit in the streets of Jerusalem, each with cane in hand because of his age. ⁵The city streets will be filled with boys and girls playing there."

⁶This is what the LORD Almighty says: "It may seem marvelous to the remnant of this people at that time, but will it seem marvelous to me?" declares the LORD Almighty.

⁷This is what the LORD Almighty says: "I will save my people from the countries of the east and the west. ⁸I will bring them back to live in Jerusalem; they will be my people, and I will be faithful and righteous to them as their God."

⁹This is what the LORD Almighty says: "You who now hear these words spoken by the prophets who were there when the foundation was laid for the house of the LORD Almighty, let your hands be strong so that the temple may be built. ¹⁰Before that time there were no wages for man or beast. No one could go about his business safely because of his enemy, for I had turned every man against his neighbor. ¹¹But now I will not deal with the remnant of this people as I did in the past," declares the LORD Almighty.

¹²"The seed will grow well, the vine will yield its fruit, the ground will produce its crops, and the heavens will drop their dew. I will give all these things as an inheritance to the remnant of this people. ¹³As you have been an object of cursing among the nations, O Judah and Israel, so will I save you, and you will be a blessing. Do not be afraid, but let your hands be strong."

¹⁴This is what the LORD Almighty says: "Just as I had determined to bring disaster upon you and showed no pity when your fathers angered me," says the LORD Almighty, ¹⁵"so now I have determined to do good again to Jerusalem and Judah. Do not be afraid. ¹⁶These are the things you are to do: Speak the truth to each other, and render true and sound judgment in your courts; ¹⁷do not plot evil against your neighbor, and do not love to swear falsely. I hate all this," declares the LORD.

¹⁸Again the word of the LORD Almighty came to me. ¹⁹This is what the LORD Almighty says: "The fasts of the fourth, fifth, seventh and tenth months will become joyful and glad occasions and happy festivals for Judah. Therefore love truth and peace."

²⁰This is what the LORD Almighty says: "Many peoples and the inhabitants of many cities will yet come, ²¹and the inhabitants of one city will go to another and say, 'Let us go at once to entreat the LORD and seek the LORD Almighty. I myself am going.' ²²And many peoples and powerful nations will come to Jerusalem to seek the LORD Almighty and to entreat him."

²³This is what the LORD Almighty says: "In those days ten men from all languages and nations will take firm hold of one Jew by the hem of his robe and say, 'Let us go with you, because we have heard that God is with you.' "

Discovering the Word 1. If you were living in war-torn Jerusalem, which was a shadow of its former glory, why would you be encouraged by the Lord's promises in this chapter? 2. When the Lord returns to Jerusalem, what effects will he have on the city and its inhabitants (vv. 1–8)? 3. How will the future days be different from the former days for those who live in the city (vv. 9–13)? 4. How should God's graciousness to us affect us morally and spiritually (vv. 14–19)? 5. Do you think the promises of verses 20–23 were completely fulfilled in Zechariah's day, or do they look forward to a greater fulfillment in the future? Explain.

 Applying the Word 1. If we truly know the Lord, why must our actions reflect his character (vv. 16–17)? 2. What are some of the practical ways we can "love truth and peace" (v. 19)?

Responding in Prayer Thank God for the fact that he is already with us through the Holy Spirit. Praise him for the promise of his future return—when he will make all things new.

7 / *Zechariah 9—10*
The Coming of the King

DIFFICULT TIMES DO not last forever, nor do those who oppress us always have the upper hand. Israel had been defeated and humiliated by her enemies. However, in Zechariah 9—10 the Lord promises to conquer those who had conquered Israel and to restore peace to those troubled by war. But the high point of this passage looks beyond Israel's immediate future to the coming of the messianic King.

 Warming Up to God When you are in the midst of difficult times or have experienced defeat, how do the Lord's presence and promises give you hope?

 Read Zechariah 9—10.

An Oracle

9 The word of the LORD is against the land
     of Hadrach
     and will rest upon Damascus—
for the eyes of men and all the tribes
     of Israel
     are on the LORD—P
²and upon Hamath too, which borders on it,
     and upon Tyre and Sidon, though they are
     very skillful.
³Tyre has built herself a stronghold;
     she has heaped up silver like dust,
     and gold like the dirt of the streets.
⁴But the Lord will take away her possessions
     and destroy her power on the sea,
     and she will be consumed by fire.
⁵Ashkelon will see it and fear;
     Gaza will writhe in agony,
     and Ekron too, for her hope will
        wither.
  Gaza will lose her king
     and Ashkelon will be deserted.
⁶Foreigners will occupy Ashdod,

and I will cut off the pride of the
     Philistines.
⁷I will take the blood from their
        mouths,
     the forbidden food from between their
        teeth.
  Those who are left will belong to
        our God
     and become leaders in Judah,
     and Ekron will be like the Jebusites.
⁸But I will defend my house
     against marauding forces.
  Never again will an oppressor overrun my
        people,
     for now I am keeping watch.
⁹Rejoice greatly, O Daughter of Zion!
     Shout, Daughter of Jerusalem!
  See, your king�q comes to you,
     righteous and having salvation,
     gentle and riding on a donkey,
     on a colt, the foal of a donkey.

P 1 Or *Damascus. / For the eye of the* LORD *is on all mankind, / as well as on the tribes of Israel,*   q 9 Or *King*

10I will take away the chariots from
  Ephraim
and the war-horses from Jerusalem,
and the battle bow will be broken.
He will proclaim peace to the nations.
  His rule will extend from sea to sea
and from the River^r to the ends of the
  earth.^s
11As for you, because of the blood of my
  covenant with you,
I will free your prisoners from the waterless
  pit.
12Return to your fortress, O prisoners
  of hope;
even now I announce that I will restore
  twice as much to you.
13I will bend Judah as I bend my bow
and fill it with Ephraim.
I will rouse your sons, O Zion,
  against your sons, O Greece,
and make you like a warrior's sword.

14Then the LORD will appear over them;
  his arrow will flash like lightning.
The Sovereign LORD will sound the
  trumpet;
  he will march in the storms of the
  south,
15   and the LORD Almighty will shield
  them.
They will destroy
  and overcome with slingstones.
They will drink and roar as with wine;
  they will be full like a bowl
used for sprinkling^t the corners of the
  altar.
16The LORD their God will save them on that
  day
as the flock of his people.
They will sparkle in his land
  like jewels in a crown.
17How attractive and beautiful they will be!
Grain will make the young men thrive,
and new wine the young women.

10 Ask the LORD for rain in the
  springtime;
  it is the LORD who makes the
  storm clouds.
He gives showers of rain to men,
  and plants of the field to everyone.
2The idols speak deceit,
  diviners see visions that lie;

they tell dreams that are false,
  they give comfort in vain.
Therefore the people wander like sheep
  oppressed for lack of a shepherd.

3"My anger burns against the shepherds,
  and I will punish the leaders;
for the LORD Almighty will care
  for his flock, the house of Judah,
  and make them like a proud horse in
  battle.
4From Judah will come the cornerstone,
  from him the tent peg,
  from him the battle bow,
  from him every ruler.
5Together they^u will be like mighty men
  trampling the muddy streets in battle.
Because the LORD is with them,
  they will fight and overthrow the
  horsemen.

6"I will strengthen the house of Judah
  and save the house of Joseph.
I will restore them
  because I have compassion on them.
They will be as though
  I had not rejected them,
for I am the LORD their God
  and I will answer them.
7The Ephraimites will become like mighty
  men,
  and their hearts will be glad as with
  wine.
Their children will see it and be joyful;
  their hearts will rejoice in the LORD.
8I will signal for them
  and gather them in.
Surely I will redeem them;
  they will be as numerous as before.
9Though I scatter them among the peoples,
  yet in distant lands they will remember me.
They and their children will survive,
  and they will return.
10I will bring them back from Egypt
  and gather them from Assyria.
I will bring them to Gilead and Lebanon,
  and there will not be room enough for
  them.
11They will pass through the sea of trouble;
  the surging sea will be subdued

r10 That is, the Euphrates   s10 Or the end of the land
t15 Or bowl, / like   u4,5 Or ruler, all of them together. / 5They

and all the depths of the Nile will dry up.
  Assyria's pride will be brought down
    and Egypt's scepter will pass away.

¹²I will strengthen them in the Lᴏʀᴅ
    and in his name they will walk,"
                                declares the Lᴏʀᴅ.

 Discovering the Word 1. In 9:1–8 Zechariah describes the defeat of Israel's enemies, beginning in the north and ending in the south—a prediction fulfilled by Alexander the Great. How does it encourage you to know that the Lord punishes evil? 2. Why will the coming of the great King cause people to shout for joy (9:9–10)? 3. Before the Messiah can establish peace, he must assume the role of the Divine Warrior (9:11–17). How does Zechariah describe the Lord's battles? 4. Why will the Lord punish the shepherds of Israel and become their true Shepherd (10:1–4)? 5. Because the Lord is with his people and cares for them, what future blessings can they expect (10:5–12)?

 Applying the Word 1. The prophecy of Zechariah 9:9 was fulfilled during Jesus' triumphal entry into Jerusalem (see Mt 21:1–11). What is it about Christ's kingship that attracts you most? 2. How does it encourage you to know that the Messiah's reign will one day extend "to the ends of the earth" (9:10)? 3. How far does his reign extend in your life today? Explain.

 Responding in Prayer Ask the One who is Lord of all to extend his lordship to every area of your life. Thank him for his great promises and his infinite care.

8 / *Zechariah 11*
The Two Shepherds

LIKE SHEEP, GOD'S people need constant care. We need someone to feed us, to seek us when we are lost, and to heal our injuries. Zechariah 11 introduces us to two kinds of shepherds—the Good Shepherd, who represents the Messiah, and the worthless shepherd, who symbolizes all who prey on the flock from perverse motives and for selfish gain. Surprisingly, the prophet tells us that God's people treat both shepherds with equal contempt.

Warming Up to God In what ways do you need the kind of care a sheep receives from a good shepherd? Pray that God will open your eyes to the many ways he expresses his loving care to you.

Read Zechariah 11.

11 Open your doors, O Lebanon,
    so that fire may devour your
      cedars!
²Wail, O pine tree, for the cedar has fallen;
    the stately trees are ruined!
  Wail, oaks of Bashan;
    the dense forest has been cut down!
³Listen to the wail of the shepherds;
    their rich pastures are destroyed!
  Listen to the roar of the lions;
    the lush thicket of the Jordan is ruined!

⁴This is what the Lᴏʀᴅ my God says: "Pasture the flock marked for slaughter. ⁵Their buyers slaughter them and go unpunished. Those who sell them say, 'Praise the Lᴏʀᴅ, I am rich!' Their own shepherds do not spare them. ⁶For I will no longer have pity on the people of the land," de-

clares the Lᴏʀᴅ. "I will hand everyone over to his neighbor and his king. They will oppress the land, and I will not rescue them from their hands."

⁷So I pastured the flock marked for slaughter, particularly the oppressed of the flock. Then I took two staffs and called one Favor and the other Union, and I pastured the flock. ⁸In one month I got rid of the three shepherds.

The flock detested me, and I grew weary of them ⁹and said, "I will not be your shepherd. Let the dying die, and the perishing perish. Let those who are left eat one another's flesh."

¹⁰Then I took my staff called Favor and broke it, revoking the covenant I had made with all the nations. ¹¹It was revoked on that day, and so the

afflicted of the flock who were watching me knew it was the word of the LORD.

¹²I told them, "If you think it best, give me my pay; but if not, keep it." So they paid me thirty pieces of silver.

¹³And the LORD said to me, "Throw it to the potter"—the handsome price at which they priced me! So I took the thirty pieces of silver and threw them into the house of the LORD to the potter.

¹⁴Then I broke my second staff called Union, breaking the brotherhood between Judah and Israel.

¹⁵Then the LORD said to me, "Take again the equipment of a foolish shepherd. ¹⁶For I am going to raise up a shepherd over the land who will not care for the lost, or seek the young, or heal the injured, or feed the healthy, but will eat the meat of the choice sheep, tearing off their hoofs.

¹⁷"Woe to the worthless shepherd,
　who deserts the flock!
May the sword strike his arm and his right
　eye!
May his arm be completely withered,
　his right eye totally blinded!"

Discovering the Word 1. Verses 1–3 can refer either to arrogant nations and their rulers or to the region and people of Syro-Palestine. What is the fate of those described in these verses? 2. The Lord tells Zechariah to assume the role of the good shepherd over his flock—even though they are "marked for slaughter" (v. 4). How had the previous shepherds treated the flock (vv. 5–6)? 3. Even though the good shepherd shows God's favor to his sheep and seeks their unity, they detest him (v. 8). How does the shepherd respond to this abuse (vv. 9–11)? 4. After being rejected, the good shepherd asks for his wages but is paid only the price of a slave (v. 12; see also Ex 21:32 and Mt 27:9–10). How does the shepherd respond to this additional insult (vv. 13–14)? 5. In verse 15 Zechariah is told to assume the role of a foolish shepherd. When we reject God's care, what kind of treatment can we expect (vv. 16–17)?

Applying the Word 1. Which of the sheep's needs listed in verse 16 are areas of need in your life? 2. In what ways has the Good Shepherd met these needs in your life?

Responding in Prayer Ask the Lord to enable you to follow him and to submit to his tender care. Thank him for watching over you like a good and loving shepherd.

9 / Zechariah 12—13
Preparing for the Lord

THE LORD'S PEOPLE must be prepared for his return. Zechariah 12—13 describes how God delivers Jerusalem at the end of the age and then brings about national repentance. The passage climaxes with a vision of the pierced Messiah, who causes both mourning and spiritual transformation.

Warming Up to God In what ways is your life different because of your belief in the Lord's return? Ask him to use this passage to prepare your heart for his coming.

Read Zechariah 12—13.

An Oracle

12 This is the word of the LORD concerning Israel. The LORD, who stretches out the heavens, who lays the foundation of the earth, and who forms the spirit of man within him, declares: ²"I am going to make Jerusalem a cup that sends all the surrounding peoples reeling. Judah will be besieged as well as Jerusalem. ³On that day, when all the nations of the earth are gathered against her, I will make Jerusalem an immovable rock for all the nations. All who try to move it will injure themselves. ⁴On that day I will strike every horse with panic and its rider with madness," declares the LORD. "I will keep a watchful eye over the

house of Judah, but I will blind all the horses of the nations. ⁵Then the leaders of Judah will say in their hearts, 'The people of Jerusalem are strong, because the Lord Almighty is their God.'

⁶"On that day I will make the leaders of Judah like a firepot in a woodpile, like a flaming torch among sheaves. They will consume right and left all the surrounding peoples, but Jerusalem will remain intact in her place.

⁷"The Lord will save the dwellings of Judah first, so that the honor of the house of David and of Jerusalem's inhabitants may not be greater than that of Judah. ⁸On that day the Lord will shield those who live in Jerusalem, so that the feeblest among them will be like David, and the house of David will be like God, like the Angel of the Lord going before them. ⁹On that day I will set out to destroy all the nations that attack Jerusalem.

¹⁰"And I will pour out on the house of David and the inhabitants of Jerusalem a spirit^v of grace and supplication. They will look on^w me, the one they have pierced, and they will mourn for him as one mourns for an only child, and grieve bitterly for him as one grieves for a first-born son. ¹¹On that day the weeping in Jerusalem will be great, like the weeping of Hadad Rimmon in the plain of Megiddo. ¹²The land will mourn, each clan by itself, with their wives by themselves: the clan of the house of David and their wives, the clan of the house of Nathan and their wives, ¹³the clan of the house of Levi and their wives, the clan of Shimei and their wives, ¹⁴and all the rest of the clans and their wives.

13 "On that day a fountain will be opened to the house of David and the inhabitants of Jerusalem, to cleanse them from sin and impurity.

²"On that day, I will banish the names of the idols from the land, and they will be remembered no more," declares the Lord Almighty. "I will remove both the prophets and the spirit of impurity from the land. ³And if anyone still prophesies, his father and mother, to whom he was born, will say to him, 'You must die, because you have told lies in the Lord's name.' When he prophesies, his own parents will stab him.

⁴"On that day every prophet will be ashamed of his prophetic vision. He will not put on a prophet's garment of hair in order to deceive. ⁵He will say, 'I am not a prophet. I am a farmer; the land has been my livelihood since my youth.^{x}' ⁶If someone asks him, 'What are these wounds on your body^y?' he will answer, 'The wounds I was given at the house of my friends.'

⁷"Awake, O sword, against my shepherd,
　against the man who is close to me!"
　　declares the Lord Almighty.
"Strike the shepherd,
　and the sheep will be scattered,
　and I will turn my hand against the little
　　ones.
⁸In the whole land," declares the Lord,
　"two-thirds will be struck down and perish;
　yet one-third will be left in it.
⁹This third I will bring into the fire;
　I will refine them like silver
　and test them like gold.
They will call on my name
　and I will answer them;
I will say, 'They are my people,'
　and they will say, 'The Lord is our God.' "

^{v}10 Or *the Spirit*　^{w}10 Or *to*　^{x}5 Or *farmer; a man sold me in my youth*　^{y}6 Or *wounds between your hands*

Discovering the Word 1. How would you describe the siege against Jerusalem at the end of the age (12:1–9)? 2. In what ways do God's people discover that "the Lord Almighty is their God" (12:5) during this battle? 3. When Israel looks on (or "to") the one they have pierced, what effect does it have on the nation (12:10–14; see also Jn 19:37)? 4. For generations Israel was plagued by both sin and false prophets. How will the Lord deal with both of these problems (13:1–6)? 5. In 13:7 the scene shifts to a different point in time. How does Zechariah describe both the death of the Messiah and the events that follow (13:7–9; see also Mt 26:31)?

Applying the Word 1. How has looking to the One who was pierced brought both mourning and cleansing in your life? 2. The Lord speaks of a time when he will refine his people "like silver and test them like gold" (13:9). How do trials and testing purify us and make us fit for the Lord's return?

Responding in Prayer Thank the Lord for the great price he paid to cleanse us from sin and impurity. Ask him to purify your life of anything that displeases him so that your life will have the quality of pure silver and gold.

10 / *Zechariah 14*
The Day of the Lord

AT THE BEGINNING of history humanity rebelled against God and rejected his rule. But at the end of history the Lord will return to the earth and reestablish his place as King of kings and Lord of lords. Zechariah 14:1 describes that "day of the LORD" as the climax of both evil and of God's eternal salvation. At that time the Lord will "reign for ever and ever."

 Warming Up to God How does it encourage you to know that God is working to reestablish his rule over all the earth?

 Read Zechariah 14.

14 A day of the LORD is coming when your plunder will be divided among you.

²I will gather all the nations to Jerusalem to fight against it; the city will be captured, the houses ransacked, and the women raped. Half of the city will go into exile, but the rest of the people will not be taken from the city.

³Then the LORD will go out and fight against those nations, as he fights in the day of battle. ⁴On that day his feet will stand on the Mount of Olives, east of Jerusalem, and the Mount of Olives will be split in two from east to west, forming a great valley, with half of the mountain moving north and half moving south. ⁵You will flee by my mountain valley, for it will extend to Azel. You will flee as you fled from the earthquake² in the days of Uzziah king of Judah. Then the LORD my God will come, and all the holy ones with him.

⁶On that day there will be no light, no cold or frost. ⁷It will be a unique day, without daytime or nighttime—a day known to the LORD. When evening comes, there will be light.

⁸On that day living water will flow out from Jerusalem, half to the eastern sea² and half to the western sea,ᵇ in summer and in winter.

⁹The LORD will be king over the whole earth. On that day there will be one LORD, and his name the only name.

¹⁰The whole land, from Geba to Rimmon, south of Jerusalem, will become like the Arabah. But Jerusalem will be raised up and remain in its place, from the Benjamin Gate to the site of the First Gate, to the Corner Gate, and from the Tower of Hananel to the royal winepresses. ¹¹It will be inhabited; never again

will it be destroyed. Jerusalem will be secure.

¹²This is the plague with which the LORD will strike all the nations that fought against Jerusalem: Their flesh will rot while they are still standing on their feet, their eyes will rot in their sockets, and their tongues will rot in their mouths. ¹³On that day men will be stricken by the LORD with great panic. Each man will seize the hand of another, and they will attack each other. ¹⁴Judah too will fight at Jerusalem. The wealth of all the surrounding nations will be collected—great quantities of gold and silver and clothing. ¹⁵A similar plague will strike the horses and mules, the camels and donkeys, and all the animals in those camps.

¹⁶Then the survivors from all the nations that have attacked Jerusalem will go up year after year to worship the King, the LORD Almighty, and to celebrate the Feast of Tabernacles. ¹⁷If any of the peoples of the earth do not go up to Jerusalem to worship the King, the LORD Almighty, they will have no rain. ¹⁸If the Egyptian people do not go up and take part, they will have no rain. The LORDᶜ will bring on them the plague he inflicts on the nations that do not go up to celebrate the Feast of Tabernacles. ¹⁹This will be the punishment of Egypt and the punishment of all the nations that do not go up to celebrate the Feast of Tabernacles.

²⁰On that day HOLY TO THE LORD will be inscribed on the bells of the horses, and the cooking pots in the LORD's house will be like the sacred bowls in

---

ᶻ5 Or ⁵*My mountain valley will be blocked and will extend to Azel. It will be blocked as it was blocked because of the earthquake*   ᵃ8 That is, the Dead Sea   ᵇ8 That is, the Mediterranean   ᶜ18 Or *part, then the* LORD

front of the altar. ²¹Every pot in Jerusalem and Judah will be holy to the Lᴏʀᴅ Almighty, and all who come to sacrifice will take some of the pots and cook in them. And on that day there will no longer be a Canaaniteᵈ in the house of the Lᴏʀᴅ Almighty.

ᵈ21 Or *merchant*

 Discovering the Word 1. Verses 1–15 describe the final battle against Jerusalem (see also 12:1–9). Why do you think the Lord allows the city to be plundered before he intervenes (vv. 1–2)? 2. When the Lord returns to the Mount of Olives (v. 4; see also Ac 1:11–12), what dramatic events will occur (vv. 3–11)? 3. How will the Divine Warrior destroy the nations that came against Jerusalem (vv. 12–15)? 4. In what ways will Jerusalem become the geographic and religious center of the earth (vv. 9–21)? 5. Although the Lord will "be king over the whole earth" (v. 9), how does Zechariah's description of life on earth seem less than perfect and complete?

Applying the Word 1. Worship and celebration will be the central events of life on earth after the Lord's return (v. 16). To what extent do these activities characterize your life on earth now? 2. In what ways can you make worship and celebration more central to your daily activities?

Responding in Prayer Worship the Lord now in praise, thanksgiving and prayer. Celebrate the fact that the "king over the whole earth" has already become your King and Savior.

Malachi

*I*t's hard to wait—especially when that wait is open-ended. At first we are edgy and restless, glancing at a watch, adjusting hair and clothing, looking past the door. Then irritation builds. We are annoyed at the delay. We snap or complain to people nearby. Finally we stop waiting. We move on with our schedules but with less precision and enthusiasm. We give up. We believe that what we were waiting for will never happen.

The people of Malachi's era were in a period of waiting. Tragic and wonderful events had happened in the past. Their ancestors had heard the prophets warn of godlessness over and over—with no lasting reform. They had seen their kings subjected, then murdered, their beautiful three-hundred-year-old temple destroyed, their farms pillaged and burned, their friends hustled away as prisoners. They had spent seventy years living in Babylon under foreign rule.

But all that ended. Through the generosity of a Persian king (and God's own kindness), the Hebrew people returned to their homeland. With the help of Ezra and Nehemiah they rebuilt their homes, city walls and temple. They cleared their farmland and slowly resumed life as a worshiping people. Except for one thing. Where was God? They made the usual temple sacrifices, but saw no evidence of his presence. What did they expect? Freedom from poverty? Miracles? Shouting prophets? International respect? God himself? We cannot know. But as the wait grew long, the people grew lax. They married pagans. They took shortcuts in worship and sacrifices. They exploited the weak and poor among them. They prayed—and could not understand why God ignored their prayers.

Then God sent Malachi with a message. God would visit his people, Malachi explained. But they must prepare for his coming. And with these final words of the Old Testament, God showed his people how to wait. When he spoke again, it would be with the startling cry of the infant Jesus.

Outline

1/ Malachi 1:1—2:16 ———————— *How to Offend God*

2/ Malachi 2:17—3:18 ———————— *Me, God's Treasure?*

3/ Malachi 4 ———————— *Last Words*

1 / *Malachi 1:1—2:16*
How to Offend God

SOME OF US walk around under a cloud of guilt. We can't think of any particular sins, but we have a vague feeling that our every breath must offend God. Other people come from an opposite pole. We spend every day hardly aware of God, who establishes what is right and condemns all wrong. A small lie here, a lustful thought there, a brief grinding underfoot of a person at work. Yet on Sunday, we enter church all smiles. The book of Malachi is good for both kinds of people. It does not speak of vague guilt; it speaks of specific offenses against God. And it does not smile at these offenses. But beyond the guilt (or lack of guilt), Malachi speaks of God's power—and his love.

 Warming Up to God Meditate for a few moment on God's holiness—and his power. What does this reveal to you about yourself and your relationship to him?

 Read Malachi 1:1—2:16.

1 An oracle: The word of the LORD to Israel through Malachi.*a*

²"I have loved you," says the LORD.

"But you ask, 'How have you loved us?'

"Was not Esau Jacob's brother?" the LORD says. "Yet I have loved Jacob, ³but Esau I have hated, and I have turned his mountains into a wasteland and left his inheritance to the desert jackals."

⁴Edom may say, "Though we have been crushed, we will rebuild the ruins."

But this is what the LORD Almighty says: "They may build, but I will demolish. They will be called the Wicked Land, a people always under the wrath of the LORD. ⁵You will see it with your own eyes and say, 'Great is the LORD—even beyond the borders of Israel!'

⁶"A son honors his father, and a servant his master. If I am a father, where is the honor due me? If I am a master, where is the respect due me?" says the LORD Almighty. "It is you, O priests, who show contempt for my name.

"But you ask, 'How have we shown contempt for your name?'

⁷"You place defiled food on my altar.

"But you ask, 'How have we defiled you?'

"By saying that the LORD's table is contemptible. ⁸When you bring blind animals for sacrifice, is that not wrong? When you sacrifice crippled or diseased animals, is that not wrong? Try offering them to your governor! Would he be pleased with you? Would he accept you?" says the LORD Almighty.

⁹"Now implore God to be gracious to us. With such offerings from your hands, will he accept you?"—says the LORD Almighty.

¹⁰"Oh, that one of you would shut the temple doors, so that you would not light useless fires on my altar! I am not pleased with you," says the LORD Almighty, "and I will accept no offering from your hands. ¹¹My name will be great among the nations, from the rising to the setting of the sun. In every place incense and pure offerings will be brought to my name, because my name will be great among the nations," says the LORD Almighty.

¹²"But you profane it by saying of the Lord's table, 'It is defiled,' and of its food, 'It is contemptible.' ¹³And you say, 'What a burden!' and you sniff at it contemptuously," says the LORD Almighty.

"When you bring injured, crippled or diseased animals and offer them as sacrifices, should I accept them from your hands?" says the LORD. ¹⁴"Cursed is the cheat who has an acceptable male in his flock and vows to give it, but then sacrifices a blemished animal to the Lord. For I am a great king," says the LORD Almighty, "and my name is to be feared among the nations.

2 "And now this admonition is for you, O priests. ²If you do not listen, and if you do not set your heart to honor my name," says the LORD Almighty, "I will send a curse upon you, and I will curse your blessings. Yes, I have already cursed them, because you have not set your heart to honor me.

³"Because of you I will rebuke*b* your descendants*c*; I will spread on your faces the offal from your festival sacrifices, and you will be carried off with it. ⁴And you will know that I have sent you this admonition so that my covenant with Levi

---

a1 Malachi means my messenger.   *b3 Or cut off (see Septuagint)*
c3 Or will blight your grain

may continue," says the Lord Almighty. ⁵"My covenant was with him, a covenant of life and peace, and I gave them to him; this called for reverence and he revered me and stood in awe of my name. ⁶True instruction was in his mouth and nothing false was found on his lips. He walked with me in peace and uprightness, and turned many from sin.

⁷"For the lips of a priest ought to preserve knowledge, and from his mouth men should seek instruction—because he is the messenger of the Lord Almighty. ⁸But you have turned from the way and by your teaching have caused many to stumble; you have violated the covenant with Levi," says the Lord Almighty. ⁹"So I have caused you to be despised and humiliated before all the people, because you have not followed my ways but have shown partiality in matters of the law."

¹⁰Have we not all one Father^d? Did not one God create us? Why do we profane the covenant of our fathers by breaking faith with one another?

¹¹Judah has broken faith. A detestable thing has been committed in Israel and in Jerusalem: Judah has desecrated the sanctuary the Lord loves, by marrying the daughter of a foreign god. ¹²As for the man who does this, whoever he may be, may the Lord cut him off from the tents of Jacob^e— even though he brings offerings to the Lord Almighty.

¹³Another thing you do: You flood the Lord's altar with tears. You weep and wail because he no longer pays attention to your offerings or accepts them with pleasure from your hands. ¹⁴You ask, "Why?" It is because the Lord is acting as the witness between you and the wife of your youth, because you have broken faith with her, though she is your partner, the wife of your marriage covenant.

¹⁵Has not ⌊the Lord⌋ made them one? In flesh and spirit they are his. And why one? Because he was seeking godly offspring.^f So guard yourself in your spirit, and do not break faith with the wife of your youth.

¹⁶"I hate divorce," says the Lord God of Israel, "and I hate a man's covering himself^g with violence as well as with his garment," says the Lord Almighty.

So guard yourself in your spirit, and do not break faith.

^d10 Or *father*   ^e12 Or ¹²*May the Lord cut off from the tents of Jacob anyone who gives testimony in behalf of the man who does this* ^f15 Or ¹⁵*But the one ⌊who is our father⌋ did not do this, not as long as life remained in him. And what was he seeking? An offspring from God* ^g16 Or *his wife*

 Discovering the Word   1. Describe God as he reveals himself in this passage.   2. What warning might God's people heed because of his relationship with the descendants of Esau (1:1–5)?   3. The priests were descendants of Levi with special responsibility to guard the spiritual well-being of the people and lead them in worship. What accusations did God make against these Hebrew priests (1:6—2:9)?   4. What had the people of Judah done that offended God (2:10–16)?   5. What concepts does this passage contribute to biblical teachings on marriage, violence and divorce?

Applying the Word   1. The people of Judah went through the motions of worship, but God declared in 1:10 that it would have been better if they had "shut the temple doors." What flaws in your own worship might be an offense to God? (Consider your weekday behavior and your personal prayers, as well as your worship with other believers.)   2. What is one step you are willing to take toward more holy worship?

Responding in Prayer   Confess to God anything in your thoughts or actions that you know is an offense to him. Read the first sentence of Malachi 1:2 and wait quietly as you once again receive his love.

---

2 / *Malachi 2:17—3:18*
Me, God's Treasure?

"WHERE IS THE God of justice?" the people of Judah asked. Maybe God thinks that all the evil in our nation is fine with him, they thought. Surely if God cared he would pay them a visit. Maybe he would just shake hands and say everything was fine. Or maybe not. Malachi promised that longed-for visit from God, a "messenger," he said. But this messenger would not bring the warm, accepting comfort that they had hoped—except to some.

Warming Up to God If Christ were to visit you today, what would you expect him to say in your home? to your church? to your nation?

 Read Malachi 2:17—3:18.

---

¹⁷You have wearied the Lᴏʀᴅ with your words. "How have we wearied him?" you ask.

By saying, "All who do evil are good in the eyes of the Lᴏʀᴅ, and he is pleased with them" or "Where is the God of justice?"

3 "See, I will send my messenger, who will prepare the way before me. Then suddenly the Lord you are seeking will come to his temple; the messenger of the covenant, whom you desire, will come," says the Lᴏʀᴅ Almighty.

²But who can endure the day of his coming? Who can stand when he appears? For he will be like a refiner's fire or a launderer's soap. ³He will sit as a refiner and purifier of silver; he will purify the Levites and refine them like gold and silver. Then the Lᴏʀᴅ will have men who will bring offerings in righteousness, ⁴and the offerings of Judah and Jerusalem will be acceptable to the Lᴏʀᴅ, as in days gone by, as in former years.

⁵"So I will come near to you for judgment. I will be quick to testify against sorcerers, adulterers and perjurers, against those who defraud laborers of their wages, who oppress the widows and the fatherless, and deprive aliens of justice, but do not fear me," says the Lᴏʀᴅ Almighty.

⁶"I the Lᴏʀᴅ do not change. So you, O descendants of Jacob, are not destroyed. ⁷Ever since the time of your forefathers you have turned away from my decrees and have not kept them. Return to me, and I will return to you," says the Lᴏʀᴅ Almighty.

"But you ask, 'How are we to return?'

⁸"Will a man rob God? Yet you rob me.

"But you ask, 'How do we rob you?'

"In tithes and offerings. ⁹You are under a curse—the whole nation of you—because you are robbing me. ¹⁰Bring the whole tithe into the storehouse, that there may be food in my house. Test me in this," says the Lᴏʀᴅ Almighty, "and see if I will not throw open the floodgates of heaven and pour out so much blessing that you will not have room enough for it. ¹¹I will prevent pests from devouring your crops, and the vines in your fields will not cast their fruit," says the Lᴏʀᴅ Almighty. ¹²"Then all the nations will call you blessed, for yours will be a delightful land," says the Lᴏʀᴅ Almighty.

¹³"You have said harsh things against me," says the Lᴏʀᴅ.

"Yet you ask, 'What have we said against you?'

¹⁴"You have said, 'It is futile to serve God. What did we gain by carrying out his requirements and going about like mourners before the Lᴏʀᴅ Almighty? ¹⁵But now we call the arrogant blessed. Certainly the evildoers prosper, and even those who challenge God escape.' "

¹⁶Then those who feared the Lᴏʀᴅ talked with each other, and the Lᴏʀᴅ listened and heard. A scroll of remembrance was written in his presence concerning those who feared the Lᴏʀᴅ and honored his name.

¹⁷"They will be mine," says the Lᴏʀᴅ Almighty, "in the day when I make up my treasured possession.ʰ I will spare them, just as in compassion a man spares his son who serves him. ¹⁸And you will again see the distinction between the righteous and the wicked, between those who serve God and those who do not.

ʰ17 Or Almighty, "my treasured possession, in the day when I act

---

 Discovering the Word 1. Find all the questions in this passage. Give answers to each question based on information in the text. 2. In what ways will God's "messenger" be like soap or like fire (3:1–4)? 3. According to Malachi 3:5, how does God want his people to express their faith in their relationships with other people? 4. What reassurances do you find in Malachi 3:16–18? 5. Of what value might a scroll of remembrance be?

 Applying the Word 1. In Malachi 3:17 God speaks of his people as his "treasured possession." Take a look at the day ahead of you: your list of tasks, the potential joys and disappointments. How does knowing that God sees you as his treasured possession influence how you will walk through your day? 2. According to Malachi 3:16, people who feared God got together, talked with each other, and then wrote a scroll. Prepare a "scroll of remembrance" of your own. Record the names of people who have supported your faith. Add a simple statement of your faith and sign your name.

Responding in Prayer In Malachi 3:7 God says, "Return to me, and I will return to you." If it is appropriate, pray a prayer of return to God. If this is not one of your own needs, pray for a friend or family member who you hope will return to God. Ask for his mercy. Picture this person as one of God's treasured possessions and ask that God will bring it about.

3 / *Malachi 4*
Last Words

GOD'S LAST WORDS to readers of the Old Testament are a mixture of hope and warning. They speak of a coming "day of the LORD," a day God's people had long anticipated. But Malachi warns that not everyone will find this a comfortable day.

Warming Up to God Spend a few moments relaxing in God's presence. Invite him into the nooks and crannies of your being. Take inventory of those areas of your life that are warm to God and also those that bristle at his touch. Talk to him about both.

Read Malachi 4.

4 "Surely the day is coming; it will burn like a furnace. All the arrogant and every evildoer will be stubble, and that day that is coming will set them on fire," says the LORD Almighty. "Not a root or a branch will be left to them. ²But for you who revere my name, the sun of righteousness will rise with healing in its wings. And you will go out and leap like calves released from the stall. ³Then you will trample down the wicked; they will be ashes under the soles of your feet on the day when I do these things," says the LORD Almighty.

⁴"Remember the law of my servant Moses, the decrees and laws I gave him at Horeb for all Israel.

⁵"See, I will send you the prophet Elijah before that great and dreadful day of the LORD comes. ⁶He will turn the hearts of the fathers to their children, and the hearts of the children to their fathers; or else I will come and strike the land with a curse."

 Discovering the Word 1. According to Malachi, two kinds of people will be present at the day of the Lord. Who are these people, and how will that day impact each (vv. 1–3)? 2. Imagine yourself in the word pictures in verse 2. What would it be like to be there? 3. Verse 5 speaks of the day of the Lord as both great and dreadful. Why? 4. What part would Elijah (John the Baptist) play in the day of the Lord? 5. These verses may have been the final words of Old Testament writing before Christ's birth some four hundred years later. How do these words prepare us for Jesus?

 Applying the Word 1. What personal warnings can you take in the last six verses of the Old Testament? 2. What personal hope do you find?

Responding in Prayer Since you are in the last book of the Old Testament, take time to page backward, noticing familiar passages. Pause at several points and thank God for what he shows you about himself.

THE
NEW TESTAMENT

Matthew

What does it mean to be a disciple of Jesus Christ? How can we effectively disciple others? Christian bookstores are full of "how-to" manuals that seek to answer these questions. The early church had a discipling manual too—the book of Matthew. It was written to teach us how to be a disciple of Jesus Christ and how to disciple others. Before looking at current discipling manuals, why not go back to one of the originals?

Discipleship is the application of Christian truth to the present. "What does God want me to do about this relationship?" "How can I deal with anxiety?" We need to know what God expects of us on a daily basis. Discipleship is a very practical matter.

Practical questions are a concern of Matthew's as he writes his book. Matthew is a tax collector, so he knows how important it is to be practical. A tax collector has to know things like how much tax you owe, where you pay and who is authorized to collect it. And when a tax is paid, it must be recorded exactly. Otherwise government authorities tend to become hostile. Very practical stuff.

Matthew draws on all his background as he writes. Your most important need as a disciple is to know what the Lord is like. Matthew will help you. Through his work you will get to know Jesus better as he responds to needy people, handles conflict and faces opposition. You will also see what Jesus is like as a king. How does he handle authority? What type of laws does he give? How does he provide for his subjects?

For your daily living you will discover how to handle anger and envy. You will learn how to strengthen your faith, how to pray and how to grow in humility. You will gain insights into a biblical approach to evangelism. You will find out what attitudes the Lord thinks are important. And you will learn how to handle suffering and grief.

In short, a study of Matthew will help you become a better disciple and disciplemaker.

The contents of Matthew will be covered by dividing it into two equal sections, 1:1—16:20 and 16:21—28:20. The first half is entitled "Discovering the King." It focuses on the identity and authority of Jesus. The second half is entitled "The Rejection and Resurrection of the King." It focuses on Jesus as he encounters opposition and persecution culminating in the cross and resurrection.

From beginning to end Matthew is an exciting and challenging Gospel. Get ready for an adventure!

Outline

Part 1: Discovering the King

1/ Matthew 1—2 ——————————— *In Search of the King*

2/ Matthew 3 ——————————— *Preparing for the King*

3/ Matthew 4 ——————————— *The Beginning of the Kingdom*

4/ Matthew 5:1—6:18 ——————————— *The Law of the King (Part 1)*

5/ Matthew 6:19—7:29 ——————————— *The Law of the King (Part 2)*

6/ Matthew 8:1—9:34 ——————————— *The Powers of the King*

7/ Matthew 9:35—11:30 ——————————— *The Messengers of the King*

8/ Matthew 12 ——————————— *The Leaders and the King*

9/ Matthew 13 ——————————— *The Parables of the King*

10/ Matthew 14 ——————————— *The Revelation of the King (Part 1)*

11/ Matthew 15:1—16:20 ——————————— *The Revelation of the King (Part 2)*

Part 2: The Rejection and Resurrection of the King

12/ Matthew 16:21—17:27 ——————————— *The Work of the King*

13/ Matthew 18 ——————————— *The Greatest in the Kingdom*

14/ Matthew 19—20 ——————————— *Life in the Kingdom*

15/ Matthew 21:1–27 ——————————— *The King Occupies His Capital*

16/ Matthew 21:28—22:46 ——————————— *The King Silences the Opposition*

17/ Matthew 23 ——————————— *The King Condemns the Rebels*

18/ Matthew 24 ——————————— *The Return of the King*

19/ Matthew 25 ——————————— *Preparation for the King's Return*

20/ Matthew 26 ——————————— *The Betrayal of the King*

21/ Matthew 27 ——————————— *The Crucifixion of the King*

22/ Matthew 28 ——————————— *The Resurrection of the King*

1 / *Matthew 1—2*
In Search of the King

HAVE YOU EVER waited with anticipation for something only to find that when it came it was not what you wanted at all?

The long-awaited birth of the Messiah is recorded in Matthew 1—2. The nation of Israel waited for centuries for God's anointed King to be born. What a wonderful day that was to be. Jesus' birth, however, was not greeted with royal gladness by the nation and its leaders. Instead, there was intrigue and conflict. The political and religious establishment felt threatened by the coming of the Messiah. It was left to foreign leaders to welcome the newborn King.

 Warming Up to God Think of something you once strongly desired (a car, TV, stereo, a special relationship or whatever). When you got it, did it fulfill your expectations? Why or why not?

 Read Matthew 1—2.

1 A record of the genealogy of Jesus Christ the son of David, the son of Abraham:

²Abraham was the father of Isaac,
   Isaac the father of Jacob,
   Jacob the father of Judah and his brothers,
³Judah the father of Perez and Zerah, whose mother was Tamar,
   Perez the father of Hezron,
   Hezron the father of Ram,
⁴Ram the father of Amminadab,
   Amminadab the father of Nahshon,
   Nahshon the father of Salmon,
⁵Salmon the father of Boaz, whose mother was Rahab,
   Boaz the father of Obed, whose mother was Ruth,
   Obed the father of Jesse,
⁶and Jesse the father of King David.

David was the father of Solomon, whose mother had been Uriah's wife,
⁷Solomon the father of Rehoboam,
   Rehoboam the father of Abijah,
   Abijah the father of Asa,
⁸Asa the father of Jehoshaphat,
   Jehoshaphat the father of Jehoram,
   Jehoram the father of Uzziah,
⁹Uzziah the father of Jotham,
   Jotham the father of Ahaz,
   Ahaz the father of Hezekiah,
¹⁰Hezekiah the father of Manasseh,
   Manasseh the father of Amon,
   Amon the father of Josiah,
¹¹and Josiah the father of Jeconiah*ᵃ* and his

brothers at the time of the exile to Babylon.

¹²After the exile to Babylon:
   Jeconiah was the father of Shealtiel,
   Shealtiel the father of Zerubbabel,
¹³Zerubbabel the father of Abiud,
   Abiud the father of Eliakim,
   Eliakim the father of Azor,
¹⁴Azor the father of Zadok,
   Zadok the father of Akim,
   Akim the father of Eliud,
¹⁵Eliud the father of Eleazar,
   Eleazar the father of Matthan,
   Matthan the father of Jacob,
¹⁶and Jacob the father of Joseph, the husband of Mary, of whom was born Jesus, who is called Christ.

¹⁷Thus there were fourteen generations in all from Abraham to David, fourteen from David to the exile to Babylon, and fourteen from the exile to the Christ.*ᵇ*

¹⁸This is how the birth of Jesus Christ came about: His mother Mary was pledged to be married to Joseph, but before they came together, she was found to be with child through the Holy Spirit. ¹⁹Because Joseph her husband was a righteous man and did not want to expose her to public disgrace, he had in mind to divorce her quietly.

²⁰But after he had considered this, an angel of the Lord appeared to him in a dream and said, "Joseph son of David, do not be afraid to take

---

ᵃ11 That is, Jehoiachin; also in verse 12   ᵇ17 Or Messiah. "The Christ" (Greek) and "the Messiah" (Hebrew) both mean "the Anointed One."

Mary home as your wife, because what is conceived in her is from the Holy Spirit. ²¹She will give birth to a son, and you are to give him the name Jesus,ᶜ because he will save his people from their sins."

²²All this took place to fulfill what the Lord had said through the prophet: ²³"The virgin will be with child and will give birth to a son, and they will call him Immanuel"ᵈ—which means, "God with us."

²⁴When Joseph woke up, he did what the angel of the Lord had commanded him and took Mary home as his wife. ²⁵But he had no union with her until she gave birth to a son. And he gave him the name Jesus.

2 After Jesus was born in Bethlehem in Judea, during the time of King Herod, Magiᵉ from the east came to Jerusalem ²and asked, "Where is the one who has been born king of the Jews? We saw his star in the eastᶠ and have come to worship him."

³When King Herod heard this he was disturbed, and all Jerusalem with him. ⁴When he had called together all the people's chief priests and teachers of the law, he asked them where the Christᵍ was to be born. ⁵"In Bethlehem in Judea," they replied, "for this is what the prophet has written:

⁶" 'But you, Bethlehem, in the land of Judah,
    are by no means least among the rulers of
        Judah;
  for out of you will come a ruler
    who will be the shepherd of my people
        Israel.'ʰ "

⁷Then Herod called the Magi secretly and found out from them the exact time the star had appeared. ⁸He sent them to Bethlehem and said, "Go and make a careful search for the child. As soon as you find him, report to me, so that I too may go and worship him."

⁹After they had heard the king, they went on their way, and the star they had seen in the eastⁱ went ahead of them until it stopped over the place where the child was. ¹⁰When they saw the star, they were overjoyed. ¹¹On coming to the house, they saw the child with his mother Mary, and they bowed down and worshiped him. Then

they opened their treasures and presented him with gifts of gold and of incense and of myrrh. ¹²And having been warned in a dream not to go back to Herod, they returned to their country by another route.

¹³When they had gone, an angel of the Lord appeared to Joseph in a dream. "Get up," he said, "take the child and his mother and escape to Egypt. Stay there until I tell you, for Herod is going to search for the child to kill him."

¹⁴So he got up, took the child and his mother during the night and left for Egypt, ¹⁵where he stayed until the death of Herod. And so was fulfilled what the Lord had said through the prophet: "Out of Egypt I called my son."ʲ

¹⁶When Herod realized that he had been outwitted by the Magi, he was furious, and he gave orders to kill all the boys in Bethlehem and its vicinity who were two years old and under, in accordance with the time he had learned from the Magi. ¹⁷Then what was said through the prophet Jeremiah was fulfilled:

¹⁸"A voice is heard in Ramah,
    weeping and great mourning,
  Rachel weeping for her children
    and refusing to be comforted,
  because they are no more."ᵏ

¹⁹After Herod died, an angel of the Lord appeared in a dream to Joseph in Egypt ²⁰and said, "Get up, take the child and his mother and go to the land of Israel, for those who were trying to take the child's life are dead."

²¹So he got up, took the child and his mother and went to the land of Israel. ²²But when he heard that Archelaus was reigning in Judea in place of his father Herod, he was afraid to go there. Having been warned in a dream, he withdrew to the district of Galilee, ²³and he went and lived in a town called Nazareth. So was fulfilled what was said through the prophets: "He will be called a Nazarene."

ᶜ21 Jesus is the Greek form of Joshua, which means the Lᴏʀᴅ saves.
ᵈ23 Isaiah 7:14   ᵉ1 Traditionally Wise Men   ᶠ2 Or star when it
rose   ᵍ4 Or Messiah   ʰ6 Micah 5:2   ⁱ9 Or seen when it rose
ʲ15 Hosea 11:1   ᵏ18 Jer. 31:15

Discovering the Word 1. Considering Matthew's purpose to portray Jesus as a heavenly king, why would Matthew include a lineage at the very beginning of his book (1:1–17)? 2. Matthew highlights Jesus' birth in 1:18–25. What do these verses tell us about his origin and destiny? 3. In chapter 2, Matthew portrays Jesus' initial reception by the world. How does Jesus the heavenly king contrast with Herod the earthly king? 4. How are the Magi different from the religious leaders in this passage? 5. God is the unseen actor throughout chapter 2. In what ways can we see his "behind-the-scenes" actions (vv. 6, 15, 18 and 23)?

Applying the Word 1. How has knowing Jesus involved you in a search or journey? 2. The responses of the Magi and Herod are typical of the ways people respond to Jesus today. What factors might cause people to respond to Jesus in such radically different ways? 3. The Magi not only found Jesus, but they worshiped him and witnessed to the entire city of Jerusalem concerning his birth (2:2–3). In what ways has your search for the Lord resulted in worshiping him and telling others about him?

Responding in Prayer Spend time worshiping the King of kings. Then ask God to help you tell others about him.

2 / *Matthew 3*
Preparing for the King

IN ANCIENT TIMES the coming of a king required special preparation. A herald was sent ahead to prepare the road on which the king would be traveling. Holes were filled, rough places made smooth and crooked sections straightened. The same thing happened in recent times when Queen Elizabeth II visited the Bahamas. In preparation for her coming, the roads she would be traveling on were completely resurfaced. In Matthew 3, John the Baptist is sent to prepare the way for the coming of the Lord. But his arrival required a very different kind of preparation.

 Warming Up to God Spend some time in preparation for meeting the Lord by confessing your sins and listening for God's assurance of forgiveness.

 Read Matthew 3.

3 In those days John the Baptist came, preaching in the Desert of Judea ²and saying, "Repent, for the kingdom of heaven is near." ³This is he who was spoken of through the prophet Isaiah:

"A voice of one calling in the desert,
'Prepare the way for the Lord,
 make straight paths for him.' "¹

⁴John's clothes were made of camel's hair, and he had a leather belt around his waist. His food was locusts and wild honey. ⁵People went out to him from Jerusalem and all Judea and the whole region of the Jordan. ⁶Confessing their sins, they were baptized by him in the Jordan River.

⁷But when he saw many of the Pharisees and Sadducees coming to where he was baptizing, he said to them: "You brood of vipers! Who warned you to flee from the coming wrath? ⁸Produce fruit in keeping with repentance. ⁹And do not say to yourselves, 'We have Abraham as

our father.' I tell you that out of these stones God can raise up children for Abraham. ¹⁰The ax is already at the root of the trees, and every tree that does not produce good fruit will be cut down and thrown into the fire.

¹¹"I baptize you with^m water for repentance. But after me will come one who is more powerful than I, whose sandals I am not fit to carry. He will baptize you with the Holy Spirit and with fire. ¹²His winnowing fork is in his hand, and he will clear his threshing floor, gathering his wheat into the barn and burning up the chaff with unquenchable fire."

¹³Then Jesus came from Galilee to the Jordan to be baptized by John. ¹⁴But John tried to deter him, saying, "I need to be baptized by you, and do you come to me?"

¹⁵Jesus replied, "Let it be so now; it is proper

¹3 Isaiah 40:3   ^m11 Or *in*

for us to do this to fulfill all righteousness." Then John consented.

[16]As soon as Jesus was baptized, he went up out of the water. At that moment heaven was opened, and he saw the Spirit of God descending like a dove and lighting on him. [17]And a voice from heaven said, "This is my Son, whom I love; with him I am well pleased."

Discovering the Word 1. For Israel the desert was a place of both punishment and renewal (recall the wilderness wanderings). How does John's ministry convey both concepts (vv. 1–12)? 2. The religious leaders considered themselves children of Abraham (v. 9). According to verses 7–10, how were they abusing this privilege? 3. John calls us to produce "fruit in keeping with repentance" (v. 8). Give examples of the kind of fruit you think he has in mind. 4. Both John and Jesus have ministries of baptism (vv. 11–12). How are their baptisms similar and different? 5. What does Jesus' willingness to be baptized suggest about him (v. 15)?

Applying the Word 1. The coming of Christ either demands repentance or brings judgment. In what ways do you need to better prepare for his return? 2. Think of people around you who have rough places or valleys in their lives. How can you help them smooth out the rough places or fill in the valleys in preparation for Jesus' coming?

Responding in Prayer Ask God to help you show others how to prepare for Jesus.

---

3 / Matthew 4
The Beginning of the Kingdom

"IS IT TIME yet?" "How much longer?" Those are the questions children ask repeatedly as Christmas approaches. It's hard on them (and their parents) to wait. But when Christmas day comes, it's full of fun and surprises. After weeks of waiting, we all get to open our new gifts. The beginning of Jesus' ministry was like the coming of Christmas. After a long wait, the wrappings came off and the world got to see God's greatest gift.

Warming Up to God All of us have experienced something new—starting a new job, going to a new school, moving to a new community. What did it feel like?

Read Matthew 4.

---

4 Then Jesus was led by the Spirit into the desert to be tempted by the devil. [2]After fasting forty days and forty nights, he was hungry. [3]The tempter came to him and said, "If you are the Son of God, tell these stones to become bread."

[4]Jesus answered, "It is written: 'Man does not live on bread alone, but on every word that comes from the mouth of God.'[n]"

[5]Then the devil took him to the holy city and had him stand on the highest point of the temple. [6]"If you are the Son of God," he said, "throw yourself down. For it is written:

" 'He will command his angels concerning
        you,
    and they will lift you up in their hands,

so that you will not strike your foot against a
        stone.'[o]"

[7]Jesus answered him, "It is also written: 'Do not put the Lord your God to the test.'[p]"

[8]Again, the devil took him to a very high mountain and showed him all the kingdoms of the world and their splendor. [9]"All this I will give you," he said, "if you will bow down and worship me."

[10]Jesus said to him, "Away from me, Satan! For it is written: 'Worship the Lord your God, and serve him only.'[q]"

[11]Then the devil left him, and angels came and attended him.

[n]4 Deut. 8:3   [o]6 Psalm 91:11,12   [p]7 Deut. 6:16   [q]10 Deut. 6:13

¹²When Jesus heard that John had been put in prison, he returned to Galilee. ¹³Leaving Nazareth, he went and lived in Capernaum, which was by the lake in the area of Zebulun and Naphtali— ¹⁴to fulfill what was said through the prophet Isaiah:

¹⁵"Land of Zebulun and land of Naphtali,
    the way to the sea, along the Jordan,
    Galilee of the Gentiles—
¹⁶the people living in darkness
    have seen a great light;
on those living in the land of the shadow of
        death
    a light has dawned."ʳ

¹⁷From that time on Jesus began to preach, "Repent, for the kingdom of heaven is near."

¹⁸As Jesus was walking beside the Sea of Galilee, he saw two brothers, Simon called Peter and his brother Andrew. They were casting a net into the lake, for they were fishermen. ¹⁹"Come, follow me," Jesus said, "and I will make you fishers of men." ²⁰At once they left their nets and followed him.

²¹Going on from there, he saw two other brothers, James son of Zebedee and his brother John. They were in a boat with their father Zebedee, preparing their nets. Jesus called them, ²²and immediately they left the boat and their father and followed him.

²³Jesus went throughout Galilee, teaching in their synagogues, preaching the good news of the kingdom, and healing every disease and sickness among the people. ²⁴News about him spread all over Syria, and people brought to him all who were ill with various diseases, those suffering severe pain, the demon-possessed, those having seizures, and the paralyzed, and he healed them. ²⁵Large crowds from Galilee, the Decapolis,ˢ Jerusalem, Judea and the region across the Jordan followed him.

ʳ16 Isaiah 9:1,2   ˢ25 That is, the Ten Cities

 Discovering the Word 1. Look over the entire chapter to discover the locations mentioned. What do they tell us about Jesus' ministry? 2. The prerequisite for Jesus' ministry was his ability to resist temptation. What can we discover about Jesus from his encounter with Satan (vv. 1–11)? 3. Look specifically at each temptation (vv. 3–4, 5–7, 8–10). What was Satan trying to accomplish with each of them? 4. How does Jesus demonstrate his message "The kingdom of heaven is near" in verses 18–25? 5. One of Jesus' first functions as heavenly king is calling disciples. From verses 18–22 develop a brief definition of discipleship.

Applying the Word 1. What can we learn about temptation and how to resist it from Jesus' example? 2. Discipleship for the first disciples meant leaving job and family and following Jesus wherever he went. How has discipleship affected your life? 3. Imagine the excitement of the first disciples as they watched Jesus healing and teaching among the crowds. Put yourself in their place and describe how you would feel.

Responding in Prayer Recall the qualities of discipleship you saw. Pray that you will be made a faithful disciple.

---

4 / *Matthew 5:1—6:18*
The Law of the King (Part 1)

C. S. LEWIS was once criticized for not caring for the Sermon on the Mount. He replied, "As to 'caring for' the Sermon on the Mount, if 'caring for' here means 'liking' or enjoying, I suppose no one 'cares for' it. Who can like being knocked flat on his face by a sledge hammer? I can hardly imagine a more deadly spiritual condition than that of a man who can read that passage with tranquil pleasure" (*God in the Dock* [Grand Rapids, Mich.: Eerdmans, 1970], pp. 181–82).

Lewis was right. Studying the Sermon on the Mount can be a devastating experience. It exposes the depth of our sin and the shallowness of our commitment. But the pain it inflicts is meant to heal, not destroy, us. In fact, the Sermon on the Mount could be called the Christian's job description. It is the most complete summary we have of

Jesus' ethical expectations for his followers. Throughout church history it has been a helpful guide and a convincing challenge.

Warming Up to God When is it hard for you to follow God's law? Talk to God about your struggles with sin.

Read Matthew 5:1—6:18.

5 Now when he saw the crowds, he went up on a mountainside and sat down. His disciples came to him, ²and he began to teach them, saying:

³"Blessed are the poor in spirit,
for theirs is the kingdom of heaven.
⁴Blessed are those who mourn,
for they will be comforted.
⁵Blessed are the meek,
for they will inherit the earth.
⁶Blessed are those who hunger and thirst for righteousness,
for they will be filled.
⁷Blessed are the merciful,
for they will be shown mercy.
⁸Blessed are the pure in heart,
for they will see God.
⁹Blessed are the peacemakers,
for they will be called sons of God.
¹⁰Blessed are those who are persecuted because of righteousness,
for theirs is the kingdom of heaven.

¹¹"Blessed are you when people insult you, persecute you and falsely say all kinds of evil against you because of me. ¹²Rejoice and be glad, because great is your reward in heaven, for in the same way they persecuted the prophets who were before you.

¹³"You are the salt of the earth. But if the salt loses its saltiness, how can it be made salty again? It is no longer good for anything, except to be thrown out and trampled by men.

¹⁴"You are the light of the world. A city on a hill cannot be hidden. ¹⁵Neither do people light a lamp and put it under a bowl. Instead they put it on its stand, and it gives light to everyone in the house. ¹⁶In the same way, let your light shine before men, that they may see your good deeds and praise your Father in heaven.

¹⁷"Do not think that I have come to abolish the Law or the Prophets; I have not come to abolish them but to fulfill them. ¹⁸I tell you the truth, until heaven and earth disappear, not the smallest letter, not the least stroke of a pen, will by any means disappear from the Law until everything is accomplished. ¹⁹Anyone who breaks one of the least of these commandments and teaches others to do the same will be called least in the kingdom of heaven, but whoever practices and teaches these commands will be called great in the kingdom of heaven. ²⁰For I tell you that unless your righteousness surpasses that of the Pharisees and the teachers of the law, you will certainly not enter the kingdom of heaven.

²¹"You have heard that it was said to the people long ago, 'Do not murder,ᵗ and anyone who murders will be subject to judgment.' ²²But I tell you that anyone who is angry with his brotherᵘ will be subject to judgment. Again, anyone who says to his brother, 'Raca,ᵛ' is answerable to the Sanhedrin. But anyone who says, 'You fool!' will be in danger of the fire of hell.

²³"Therefore, if you are offering your gift at the altar and there remember that your brother has something against you, ²⁴leave your gift there in front of the altar. First go and be reconciled to your brother; then come and offer your gift.

²⁵"Settle matters quickly with your adversary who is taking you to court. Do it while you are still with him on the way, or he may hand you over to the judge, and the judge may hand you over to the officer, and you may be thrown into prison. ²⁶I tell you the truth, you will not get out until you have paid the last penny.ʷ

²⁷"You have heard that it was said, 'Do not commit adultery.'ˣ ²⁸But I tell you that anyone who looks at a woman lustfully has already committed adultery with her in his heart. ²⁹If your right eye causes you to sin, gouge it out and throw it away. It is better for you to lose one part of your body than for your whole body to be thrown into hell. ³⁰And if your right hand causes you to sin, cut it off and throw it away. It is better for you to lose one part of your body than for your whole body to go into hell.

ᵗ21 Exodus 20:13   ᵘ22 *Some manuscripts* brother *without cause*
ᵛ22 *An Aramaic term of contempt*   ʷ26 *Greek* kodrantes
ˣ27 Exodus 20:14

³¹"It has been said, 'Anyone who divorces his wife must give her a certificate of divorce.'*y* ³²But I tell you that anyone who divorces his wife, except for marital unfaithfulness, causes her to become an adulteress, and anyone who marries the divorced woman commits adultery.

³³"Again, you have heard that it was said to the people long ago, 'Do not break your oath, but keep the oaths you have made to the Lord.' ³⁴But I tell you, Do not swear at all: either by heaven, for it is God's throne; ³⁵or by the earth, for it is his footstool; or by Jerusalem, for it is the city of the Great King. ³⁶And do not swear by your head, for you cannot make even one hair white or black. ³⁷Simply let your 'Yes' be 'Yes,' and your 'No,' 'No'; anything beyond this comes from the evil one.

³⁸"You have heard that it was said, 'Eye for eye, and tooth for tooth.'*z* ³⁹But I tell you, Do not resist an evil person. If someone strikes you on the right cheek, turn to him the other also. ⁴⁰And if someone wants to sue you and take your tunic, let him have your cloak as well. ⁴¹If someone forces you to go one mile, go with him two miles. ⁴²Give to the one who asks you, and do not turn away from the one who wants to borrow from you.

⁴³"You have heard that it was said, 'Love your neighbor*a* and hate your enemy.' ⁴⁴But I tell you: Love your enemies*b* and pray for those who persecute you, ⁴⁵that you may be sons of your Father in heaven. He causes his sun to rise on the evil and the good, and sends rain on the righteous and the unrighteous. ⁴⁶If you love those who love you, what reward will you get? Are not even the tax collectors doing that? ⁴⁷And if you greet only your brothers, what are you doing more than others? Do not even pagans do that? ⁴⁸Be perfect, therefore, as your heavenly Father is perfect.

6 "Be careful not to do your 'acts of righteousness' before men, to be seen by them. If you do, you will have no reward from your Father in heaven.

²"So when you give to the needy, do not announce it with trumpets, as the hypocrites do in the synagogues and on the streets, to be honored by men. I tell you the truth, they have received their reward in full. ³But when you give to the needy, do not let your left hand know what your right hand is doing, ⁴so that your giving may be in secret. Then your Father, who sees what is done in secret, will reward you.

⁵"And when you pray, do not be like the hypocrites, for they love to pray standing in the synagogues and on the street corners to be seen by men. I tell you the truth, they have received their reward in full. ⁶But when you pray, go into your room, close the door and pray to your Father, who is unseen. Then your Father, who sees what is done in secret, will reward you. ⁷And when you pray, do not keep on babbling like pagans, for they think they will be heard because of their many words. ⁸Do not be like them, for your Father knows what you need before you ask him.

⁹"This, then, is how you should pray:

" 'Our Father in heaven,
hallowed be your name,
¹⁰your kingdom come,
    your will be done
      on earth as it is in heaven.
¹¹Give us today our daily bread.
¹²Forgive us our debts,
    as we also have forgiven our debtors.
¹³And lead us not into temptation,
    but deliver us from the evil one.'*c*

¹⁴For if you forgive men when they sin against you, your heavenly Father will also forgive you. ¹⁵But if you do not forgive men their sins, your Father will not forgive your sins.

¹⁶"When you fast, do not look somber as the hypocrites do, for they disfigure their faces to show men they are fasting. I tell you the truth, they have received their reward in full. ¹⁷But when you fast, put oil on your head and wash your face, ¹⁸so that it will not be obvious to men that you are fasting, but only to your Father, who is unseen; and your Father, who sees what is done in secret, will reward you.

---

*y*31 Deut. 24:1   *z*38 Exodus 21:24; Lev. 24:20; Deut. 19:21
*a*43 Lev. 19:18   *b*44 Some late manuscripts *enemies, bless those who curse you, do good to those who hate you*   *c*13 Or *from evil*; some late manuscripts *one, / for yours is the kingdom and the power and the glory forever. Amen.*

Discovering the Word 1. The Beatitudes describe the qualities Jesus desires in each of his disciples (5:3–12). Give a brief definition of each quality. 2. Jesus compares his followers to salt and light (5:13–16). What do these metaphors suggest about our role in society? 3. In the rest of chapter 5 Jesus discusses various misconceptions we might have about the Law (Old Testament Scriptures). Why do you think that Jesus stresses that he did not come to abolish the Law (5:17–20)? 4. How does Jesus' teaching on murder and adultery (5:21–30) differ from the traditional understanding? 5. How does Jesus want us to respond to evil people and enemies (5:38–47)? 6. What do we learn about proper and improper motives from Jesus' examples about giving, praying and fasting (6:1–18)?

 Applying the Word 1. Why are our motives just as important as our religious acts? 2. What does this reveal to you about your motives? 3. In what way do you need to experience Christ's blessing?

 Responding in Prayer Pray for Christ's blessing in the areas in which you feel needy.

---

5 / *Matthew 6:19—7:29*
The Law of the King (Part 2)

JIM ELLIOT, A missionary killed by the Auca Indians, once wrote: "He is no fool who gives what he cannot keep to gain what he cannot lose." His words echo this portion of the Sermon on the Mount. Jesus asks us to choose between two treasures, two masters, two roads and two destinies. But he clearly explains why following him is the only wise choice.

 Warming Up to God When are earthly treasures more tempting to you than heavenly ones?

Read Matthew 6:19—7:29.

¹⁹"Do not store up for yourselves treasures on earth, where moth and rust destroy, and where thieves break in and steal. ²⁰But store up for yourselves treasures in heaven, where moth and rust do not destroy, and where thieves do not break in and steal. ²¹For where your treasure is, there your heart will be also.

²²"The eye is the lamp of the body. If your eyes are good, your whole body will be full of light. ²³But if your eyes are bad, your whole body will be full of darkness. If then the light within you is darkness, how great is that darkness!

²⁴"No one can serve two masters. Either he will hate the one and love the other, or he will be devoted to the one and despise the other. You cannot serve both God and Money.

²⁵"Therefore I tell you, do not worry about your life, what you will eat or drink; or about your body, what you will wear. Is not life more important than food, and the body more important than clothes? ²⁶Look at the birds of the air; they do not sow or reap or store away in barns,

and yet your heavenly Father feeds them. Are you not much more valuable than they? ²⁷Who of you by worrying can add a single hour to his life[d]?

²⁸"And why do you worry about clothes? See how the lilies of the field grow. They do not labor or spin. ²⁹Yet I tell you that not even Solomon in all his splendor was dressed like one of these. ³⁰If that is how God clothes the grass of the field, which is here today and tomorrow is thrown into the fire, will he not much more clothe you, O you of little faith? ³¹So do not worry, saying, 'What shall we eat?' or 'What shall we drink?' or 'What shall we wear?' ³²For the pagans run after all these things, and your heavenly Father knows that you need them. ³³But seek first his kingdom and his righteousness, and all these things will be given to you as well. ³⁴Therefore do not worry about tomorrow, for tomorrow will worry about itself. Each day has enough trouble of its own.

d27 Or *single cubit to his height*

7 "Do not judge, or you too will be judged. ²For in the same way you judge others, you will be judged, and with the measure you use, it will be measured to you.

³"Why do you look at the speck of sawdust in your brother's eye and pay no attention to the plank in your own eye? ⁴How can you say to your brother, 'Let me take the speck out of your eye,' when all the time there is a plank in your own eye? ⁵You hypocrite, first take the plank out of your own eye, and then you will see clearly to remove the speck from your brother's eye.

⁶"Do not give dogs what is sacred; do not throw your pearls to pigs. If you do, they may trample them under their feet, and then turn and tear you to pieces.

⁷"Ask and it will be given to you; seek and you will find; knock and the door will be opened to you. ⁸For everyone who asks receives; he who seeks finds; and to him who knocks, the door will be opened.

⁹"Which of you, if his son asks for bread, will give him a stone? ¹⁰Or if he asks for a fish, will give him a snake? ¹¹If you, then, though you are evil, know how to give good gifts to your children, how much more will your Father in heaven give good gifts to those who ask him! ¹²So in everything, do to others what you would have them do to you, for this sums up the Law and the Prophets.

¹³"Enter through the narrow gate. For wide is the gate and broad is the road that leads to destruction, and many enter through it. ¹⁴But small is the gate and narrow the road that leads to life, and only a few find it.

¹⁵"Watch out for false prophets. They come to you in sheep's clothing, but inwardly they are ferocious wolves. ¹⁶By their fruit you will recognize them. Do people pick grapes from thornbushes, or figs from thistles? ¹⁷Likewise every good tree bears good fruit, but a bad tree bears bad fruit. ¹⁸A good tree cannot bear bad fruit, and a bad tree cannot bear good fruit. ¹⁹Every tree that does not bear good fruit is cut down and thrown into the fire. ²⁰Thus, by their fruit you will recognize them.

²¹"Not everyone who says to me, 'Lord, Lord,' will enter the kingdom of heaven, but only he who does the will of my Father who is in heaven. ²²Many will say to me on that day, 'Lord, Lord, did we not prophesy in your name, and in your name drive out demons and perform many miracles?' ²³Then I will tell them plainly, 'I never knew you. Away from me, you evildoers!'

²⁴"Therefore everyone who hears these words of mine and puts them into practice is like a wise man who built his house on the rock. ²⁵The rain came down, the streams rose, and the winds blew and beat against that house; yet it did not fall, because it had its foundation on the rock. ²⁶But everyone who hears these words of mine and does not put them into practice is like a foolish man who built his house on sand. ²⁷The rain came down, the streams rose, and the winds blew and beat against that house, and it fell with a great crash."

²⁸When Jesus had finished saying these things, the crowds were amazed at his teaching, ²⁹because he taught as one who had authority, and not as their teachers of the law.

Discovering the Word 1. In 6:19–24 Jesus talks about treasures, eyes and masters. What common themes tie these verses together? 2. Worry is a dominant theme in 6:25–34. How can we escape worrying about such things as food and clothes? 3. What is the difference between judging others and being properly discerning (7:1–6)? 4. How should our knowledge of the Father affect our prayers (7:7–11)? 5. In the final section of the Sermon (7:13–27) Jesus talks about narrow and wide gates, good and bad trees, and wise and foolish builders. How do these three metaphors work together to make a common point?

Applying the Word 1. What does seeking first God's kingdom and righteousness (6:33) mean practically for your life? 2. Putting Jesus' words in practice is the way to build a lasting foundation against the day of judgment (7:24–27). What will the practice of Jesus' Sermon require of you?

 Responding in Prayer Pray that you will be a person of wisdom and discernment and not of judgment.

6 / *Matthew 8:1—9:34*
The Powers of the King

SOMEONE ONCE COMMENTED about a U.S. president: "I don't know where he is going, but I sure like the way he leads."

Leaders must demonstrate authority. But wise leaders know they must not abuse their authority. They know people follow leaders who also demonstrate integrity and compassion. In chapters 8 and 9 Jesus demonstrates that he is a worthy king, one in whom we can safely put our trust.

 Warming Up to God How has Jesus' authority been a guide to you in recent days?

 Read Matthew 8:1—9:34.

8When he came down from the mountainside, large crowds followed him. ²A man with leprosy⁵ came and knelt before him and said, "Lord, if you are willing, you can make me clean."

³Jesus reached out his hand and touched the man. "I am willing," he said. "Be clean!" Immediately he was cured ᶠ of his leprosy. ⁴Then Jesus said to him, "See that you don't tell anyone. But go, show yourself to the priest and offer the gift Moses commanded, as a testimony to them."

⁵When Jesus had entered Capernaum, a centurion came to him, asking for help. ⁶"Lord," he said, "my servant lies at home paralyzed and in terrible suffering."

⁷Jesus said to him, "I will go and heal him."

⁸The centurion replied, "Lord, I do not deserve to have you come under my roof. But just say the word, and my servant will be healed. ⁹For I myself am a man under authority, with soldiers under me. I tell this one, 'Go,' and he goes; and that one, 'Come,' and he comes. I say to my servant, 'Do this,' and he does it."

¹⁰When Jesus heard this, he was astonished and said to those following him, "I tell you the truth, I have not found anyone in Israel with such great faith. ¹¹I say to you that many will come from the east and the west, and will take their places at the feast with Abraham, Isaac and Jacob in the kingdom of heaven. ¹²But the subjects of the kingdom will be thrown outside, into the darkness, where there will be weeping and gnashing of teeth."

¹³Then Jesus said to the centurion, "Go! It will be done just as you believed it would." And his servant was healed at that very hour.

¹⁴When Jesus came into Peter's house, he saw Peter's mother-in-law lying in bed with a fever. ¹⁵He touched her hand and the fever left her, and she got up and began to wait on him.

¹⁶When evening came, many who were demon-possessed were brought to him, and he drove out the spirits with a word and healed all the sick. ¹⁷This was to fulfill what was spoken through the prophet Isaiah:

"He took up our infirmities
    and carried our diseases."ᵍ

¹⁸When Jesus saw the crowd around him, he gave orders to cross to the other side of the lake. ¹⁹Then a teacher of the law came to him and said, "Teacher, I will follow you wherever you go."

²⁰Jesus replied, "Foxes have holes and birds of the air have nests, but the Son of Man has no place to lay his head."

²¹Another disciple said to him, "Lord, first let me go and bury my father."

²²But Jesus told him, "Follow me, and let the dead bury their own dead."

²³Then he got into the boat and his disciples followed him. ²⁴Without warning, a furious storm came up on the lake, so that the waves swept over the boat. But Jesus was sleeping. ²⁵The disciples went and woke him, saying, "Lord, save us! We're going to drown!"

²⁶He replied, "You of little faith, why are you so afraid?" Then he got up and rebuked the winds and the waves, and it was completely calm.

²⁷The men were amazed and asked, "What kind of man is this? Even the winds and the waves obey him!"

²⁸When he arrived at the other side in the re-

ᵉ2 The Greek word was used for various diseases affecting the skin—not necessarily leprosy.   ᶠ3 Greek *made clean*   ᵍ17 Isaiah 53:4

gion of the Gadarenes,[h] two demon-possessed men coming from the tombs met him. They were so violent that no one could pass that way. [29]"What do you want with us, Son of God?" they shouted. "Have you come here to torture us before the appointed time?"

[30]Some distance from them a large herd of pigs was feeding. [31]The demons begged Jesus, "If you drive us out, send us into the herd of pigs."

[32]He said to them, "Go!" So they came out and went into the pigs, and the whole herd rushed down the steep bank into the lake and died in the water. [33]Those tending the pigs ran off, went into the town and reported all this, including what had happened to the demon-possessed men. [34]Then the whole town went out to meet Jesus. And when they saw him, they pleaded with him to leave their region.

9 Jesus stepped into a boat, crossed over and came to his own town. [2]Some men brought to him a paralytic, lying on a mat. When Jesus saw their faith, he said to the paralytic, "Take heart, son; your sins are forgiven."

[3]At this, some of the teachers of the law said to themselves, "This fellow is blaspheming!"

[4]Knowing their thoughts, Jesus said, "Why do you entertain evil thoughts in your hearts? [5]Which is easier: to say, 'Your sins are forgiven,' or to say, 'Get up and walk'? [6]But so that you may know that the Son of Man has authority on earth to forgive sins. . . ." Then he said to the paralytic, "Get up, take your mat and go home." [7]And the man got up and went home. [8]When the crowd saw this, they were filled with awe; and they praised God, who had given such authority to men.

[9]As Jesus went on from there, he saw a man named Matthew sitting at the tax collector's booth. "Follow me," he told him, and Matthew got up and followed him.

[10]While Jesus was having dinner at Matthew's house, many tax collectors and "sinners" came and ate with him and his disciples. [11]When the Pharisees saw this, they asked his disciples, "Why does your teacher eat with tax collectors and 'sinners'?"

[12]On hearing this, Jesus said, "It is not the healthy who need a doctor, but the sick. [13]But go and learn what this means: 'I desire mercy, not sacrifice.'[i] For I have not come to call the righteous, but sinners."

[14]Then John's disciples came and asked him, "How is it that we and the Pharisees fast, but your disciples do not fast?"

[15]Jesus answered, "How can the guests of the bridegroom mourn while he is with them? The time will come when the bridegroom will be taken from them; then they will fast.

[16]"No one sews a patch of unshrunk cloth on an old garment, for the patch will pull away from the garment, making the tear worse. [17]Neither do men pour new wine into old wineskins. If they do, the skins will burst, the wine will run out and the wineskins will be ruined. No, they pour new wine into new wineskins, and both are preserved."

[18]While he was saying this, a ruler came and knelt before him and said, "My daughter has just died. But come and put your hand on her, and she will live." [19]Jesus got up and went with him, and so did his disciples.

[20]Just then a woman who had been subject to bleeding for twelve years came up behind him and touched the edge of his cloak. [21]She said to herself, "If I only touch his cloak, I will be healed."

[22]Jesus turned and saw her. "Take heart, daughter," he said, "your faith has healed you." And the woman was healed from that moment.

[23]When Jesus entered the ruler's house and saw the flute players and the noisy crowd, [24]he said, "Go away. The girl is not dead but asleep." But they laughed at him. [25]After the crowd had been put outside, he went in and took the girl by the hand, and she got up. [26]News of this spread through all that region.

[27]As Jesus went on from there, two blind men followed him, calling out, "Have mercy on us, Son of David!"

[28]When he had gone indoors, the blind men came to him, and he asked them, "Do you believe that I am able to do this?"

"Yes, Lord," they replied.

[29]Then he touched their eyes and said, "According to your faith will it be done to you"; [30]and their sight was restored. Jesus warned them sternly, "See that no one knows about this." [31]But they went out and spread the news about him all over that region.

---

[h]28 Some manuscripts *Gergesenes*; others *Gerasenes*   [i]13 Hosea 6:6

32While they were going out, a man who was demon-possessed and could not talk was brought to Jesus. 33And when the demon was driven out, the man who had been mute spoke. The crowd was amazed and said, "Nothing like this has ever been seen in Israel."

34But the Pharisees said, "It is by the prince of demons that he drives out demons."

 Discovering the Word 1. In chapters 8—9 Jesus' miracles occur in three groups, followed by a response, or reaction. Briefly describe how Jesus demonstrates his authority in 8:1–22. 2. In 8:18–22 Jesus begins to attract would-be followers. What do these verses teach us about the cost and urgency of following him? 3. What do we learn about the extent of Jesus' authority in 8:23—9:17? 4. What is the relationship between Jesus' claim to have authority to forgive sins and his healing of the paralytic (9:1–8)? 5. In 9:9–17 Jesus compares himself to a doctor and a bridegroom. Then he discusses garments and wineskins. What do these illustrations teach us about his ministry? 6. How do people respond to Jesus in 9:18–34?

 Applying the Word 1. Look back over chapters 8—9. How does Jesus want us to respond to his power and authority? 2. How can a knowledge of Jesus' power and authority strengthen your faith?

Responding in Prayer Spend time praising God for Jesus' leadership.

---

7 / *Matthew 9:35—11:30*
The Messengers of the King

DURING THE LATE 1800s a wealthy philanthropist decided to give away all his money. He announced he would give five hundred dollars to anyone with a legitimate need. The response was overwhelming! People lined up day after day to receive their gift.

The gospel is a priceless treasure. But as we offer it to people, their response is not always enthusiastic. In this passage Jesus warns us about those who oppose his message and his messengers. But he also encourages us as we reach out to blind and needy people.

 Warming Up to God Have you ever known someone who seemed to like you only for what you could give them? What did it feel like?

 Read Matthew 9:35—11:30.

35Jesus went through all the towns and villages, teaching in their synagogues, preaching the good news of the kingdom and healing every disease and sickness. 36When he saw the crowds, he had compassion on them, because they were harassed and helpless, like sheep without a shepherd. 37Then he said to his disciples, "The harvest is plentiful but the workers are few. 38Ask the Lord of the harvest, therefore, to send out workers into his harvest field."

10 He called his twelve disciples to him and gave them authority to drive out evilʲ spirits and to heal every disease and sickness.

2These are the names of the twelve apostles: first, Simon (who is called Peter) and his brother

Andrew; James son of Zebedee, and his brother John; 3Philip and Bartholomew; Thomas and Matthew the tax collector; James son of Alphaeus, and Thaddaeus; 4Simon the Zealot and Judas Iscariot, who betrayed him.

5These twelve Jesus sent out with the following instructions: "Do not go among the Gentiles or enter any town of the Samaritans. 6Go rather to the lost sheep of Israel. 7As you go, preach this message: 'The kingdom of heaven is near.' 8Heal the sick, raise the dead, cleanse those who have leprosy,ᵏ drive out demons. Freely you have received, freely give. 9Do not take along any gold or silver or copper in your belts; 10take no bag for

ʲ1 Greek unclean ᵏ8 The Greek word was used for various diseases affecting the skin—not necessarily leprosy.

the journey, or extra tunic, or sandals or a staff; for the worker is worth his keep.

11"Whatever town or village you enter, search for some worthy person there and stay at his house until you leave. 12As you enter the home, give it your greeting. 13If the home is deserving, let your peace rest on it; if it is not, let your peace return to you. 14If anyone will not welcome you or listen to your words, shake the dust off your feet when you leave that home or town. 15I tell you the truth, it will be more bearable for Sodom and Gomorrah on the day of judgment than for that town. 16I am sending you out like sheep among wolves. Therefore be as shrewd as snakes and as innocent as doves.

17"Be on your guard against men; they will hand you over to the local councils and flog you in their synagogues. 18On my account you will be brought before governors and kings as witnesses to them and to the Gentiles. 19But when they arrest you, do not worry about what to say or how to say it. At that time you will be given what to say, 20for it will not be you speaking, but the Spirit of your Father speaking through you.

21"Brother will betray brother to death, and a father his child; children will rebel against their parents and have them put to death. 22All men will hate you because of me, but he who stands firm to the end will be saved. 23When you are persecuted in one place, flee to another. I tell you the truth, you will not finish going through the cities of Israel before the Son of Man comes.

24"A student is not above his teacher, nor a servant above his master. 25It is enough for the student to be like his teacher, and the servant like his master. If the head of the house has been called Beelzebub,[l] how much more the members of his household!

26"So do not be afraid of them. There is nothing concealed that will not be disclosed, or hidden that will not be made known. 27What I tell you in the dark, speak in the daylight; what is whispered in your ear, proclaim from the roofs. 28Do not be afraid of those who kill the body but cannot kill the soul. Rather, be afraid of the One who can destroy both soul and body in hell. 29Are not two sparrows sold for a penny[m]? Yet not one of them will fall to the ground apart from the will of your Father. 30And even the very hairs of your head are all numbered. 31So don't be afraid; you are worth more than many sparrows.

32"Whoever acknowledges me before men, I will also acknowledge him before my Father in heaven. 33But whoever disowns me before men, I will disown him before my Father in heaven.

34"Do not suppose that I have come to bring peace to the earth. I did not come to bring peace, but a sword. 35For I have come to turn

" 'a man against his father,
      a daughter against her mother,
   a daughter-in-law against her mother-in-
      law—
36   a man's enemies will be the members of his
      own household.'[n]

37"Anyone who loves his father or mother more than me is not worthy of me; anyone who loves his son or daughter more than me is not worthy of me; 38and anyone who does not take his cross and follow me is not worthy of me. 39Whoever finds his life will lose it, and whoever loses his life for my sake will find it.

40"He who receives you receives me, and he who receives me receives the one who sent me. 41Anyone who receives a prophet because he is a prophet will receive a prophet's reward, and anyone who receives a righteous man because he is a righteous man will receive a righteous man's reward. 42And if anyone gives even a cup of cold water to one of these little ones because he is my disciple, I tell you the truth, he will certainly not lose his reward."

11 After Jesus had finished instructing his twelve disciples, he went on from there to teach and preach in the towns of Galilee.[o]

2When John heard in prison what Christ was doing, he sent his disciples 3to ask him, "Are you the one who was to come, or should we expect someone else?"

4Jesus replied, "Go back and report to John what you hear and see: 5The blind receive sight, the lame walk, those who have leprosy[p] are cured, the deaf hear, the dead are raised, and the good news is preached to the poor. 6Blessed is the man who does not fall away on account of me."

7As John's disciples were leaving, Jesus began to speak to the crowd about John: "What did you go out into the desert to see? A reed swayed by the wind? 8If not, what did you go out to see? A man dressed in fine clothes? No, those who wear

l25 Greek Beezeboul or Beelzeboul   m29 Greek an assarion
n36 Micah 7:6   o1 Greek in their towns   p5 The Greek word was used for various diseases affecting the skin—not necessarily leprosy.

fine clothes are in kings' palaces. ⁹Then what did you go out to see? A prophet? Yes, I tell you, and more than a prophet. ¹⁰This is the one about whom it is written:

" 'I will send my messenger ahead of you,
    who will prepare your way before you.'�q

¹¹I tell you the truth: Among those born of women there has not risen anyone greater than John the Baptist; yet he who is least in the kingdom of heaven is greater than he. ¹²From the days of John the Baptist until now, the kingdom of heaven has been forcefully advancing, and forceful men lay hold of it. ¹³For all the Prophets and the Law prophesied until John. ¹⁴And if you are willing to accept it, he is the Elijah who was to come. ¹⁵He who has ears, let him hear.

¹⁶"To what can I compare this generation? They are like children sitting in the marketplaces and calling out to others:

¹⁷" 'We played the flute for you,
    and you did not dance;
  we sang a dirge,
    and you did not mourn.'

¹⁸For John came neither eating nor drinking, and they say, 'He has a demon.' ¹⁹The Son of Man came eating and drinking, and they say, 'Here is a glutton and a drunkard, a friend of tax collectors and "sinners." ' But wisdom is proved right by her actions."

²⁰Then Jesus began to denounce the cities in which most of his miracles had been performed, because they did not repent. ²¹"Woe to you, Korazin! Woe to you, Bethsaida! If the miracles that were performed in you had been performed in Tyre and Sidon, they would have repented long ago in sackcloth and ashes. ²²But I tell you, it will be more bearable for Tyre and Sidon on the day of judgment than for you. ²³And you, Capernaum, will you be lifted up to the skies? No, you will go down to the depths.ʳ If the miracles that were performed in you had been performed in Sodom, it would have remained to this day. ²⁴But I tell you that it will be more bearable for Sodom on the day of judgment than for you."

²⁵At that time Jesus said, "I praise you, Father, Lord of heaven and earth, because you have hidden these things from the wise and learned, and revealed them to little children. ²⁶Yes, Father, for this was your good pleasure.

²⁷"All things have been committed to me by my Father. No one knows the Son except the Father, and no one knows the Father except the Son and those to whom the Son chooses to reveal him.

²⁸"Come to me, all you who are weary and burdened, and I will give you rest. ²⁹Take my yoke upon you and learn from me, for I am gentle and humble in heart, and you will find rest for your souls. ³⁰For my yoke is easy and my burden is light."

�q10 Mal. 3:1   ʳ23 Greek Hades

 Discovering the Word 1. How and why does Jesus demonstrate compassion for the crowds (9:35–38)? 2. As a result of his compassion, Jesus sends out the Twelve (10:1–15). Describe their mission. 3. Jesus warns the disciples that their compassionate ministry will not be warmly received (10:16–25). What will they experience? 4. In 10:26–33 Jesus prepares his present and future disciples for opposition. Why shouldn't we be afraid of those who oppose us? 5. What does Jesus promise to those who are receptive to our message (10:40–42)? 6. What does 11:7–19 tell us about John and those who heard his message?

 Applying the Word 1. In what ways have you found rest in your life by coming to Jesus? 2. What have you learned about Jesus and the nature of discipleship from this study?

Responding in Prayer Pray for the gift of rest in Jesus.

8 / *Matthew 12*
The Leaders and the King

POWER OVER PEOPLE is not easily shared. Wars have been fought, people assassinated and elections rigged in order to gain or maintain power.

The leaders of Israel were becoming concerned over the growing reputation and following of Jesus. Like ripples in a pool of water, the ministry of Jesus and his disciples continued to have a widening impact on the Jewish nation. If Jesus' followers became too numerous, the leaders would end up losing their positions of authority. In Matthew 12 they formulate a strategy to discredit him.

 Warming Up to God How would you feel if untrue rumors about you were being spread around?

 Read Matthew 12.

12 At that time Jesus went through the grainfields on the Sabbath. His disciples were hungry and began to pick some heads of grain and eat them. ²When the Pharisees saw this, they said to him, "Look! Your disciples are doing what is unlawful on the Sabbath."

³He answered, "Haven't you read what David did when he and his companions were hungry? ⁴He entered the house of God, and he and his companions ate the consecrated bread—which was not lawful for them to do, but only for the priests. ⁵Or haven't you read in the Law that on the Sabbath the priests in the temple desecrate the day and yet are innocent? ⁶I tell you that one⁵ greater than the temple is here. ⁷If you had known what these words mean, 'I desire mercy, not sacrifice,'ᵗ you would not have condemned the innocent. ⁸For the Son of Man is Lord of the Sabbath."

⁹Going on from that place, he went into their synagogue, ¹⁰and a man with a shriveled hand was there. Looking for a reason to accuse Jesus, they asked him, "Is it lawful to heal on the Sabbath?"

¹¹He said to them, "If any of you has a sheep and it falls into a pit on the Sabbath, will you not take hold of it and lift it out? ¹²How much more valuable is a man than a sheep! Therefore it is lawful to do good on the Sabbath."

¹³Then he said to the man, "Stretch out your hand." So he stretched it out and it was completely restored, just as sound as the other. ¹⁴But the Pharisees went out and plotted how they might kill Jesus.

¹⁵Aware of this, Jesus withdrew from that place. Many followed him, and he healed all their sick, ¹⁶warning them not to tell who he was. ¹⁷This was to fulfill what was spoken through the prophet Isaiah:

¹⁸"Here is my servant whom I have chosen,
  the one I love, in whom I delight;
 I will put my Spirit on him,
  and he will proclaim justice to the nations.
¹⁹He will not quarrel or cry out;
  no one will hear his voice in the streets.
²⁰A bruised reed he will not break,
  and a smoldering wick he will not snuff
   out,
 till he leads justice to victory.
²¹ In his name the nations will put their
   hope."ᵘ

²²Then they brought him a demon-possessed man who was blind and mute, and Jesus healed him, so that he could both talk and see. ²³All the people were astonished and said, "Could this be the Son of David?"

²⁴But when the Pharisees heard this, they said, "It is only by Beelzebub,ᵛ the prince of demons, that this fellow drives out demons."

²⁵Jesus knew their thoughts and said to them, "Every kingdom divided against itself will be ruined, and every city or household divided against itself will not stand. ²⁶If Satan drives out Satan, he is divided against himself. How then can his kingdom stand? ²⁷And if I drive out demons by Beelzebub, by whom do your people drive them out? So then, they will be your judges. ²⁸But if I drive

⁵6 Or *something*; also in verses 41 and 42   ᵗ7 Hosea 6:6
ᵘ21 Isaiah 42:1-4   ᵛ24 Greek *Beezeboul* or *Beelzeboul*; also in verse 27

out demons by the Spirit of God, then the kingdom of God has come upon you.

²⁹"Or again, how can anyone enter a strong man's house and carry off his possessions unless he first ties up the strong man? Then he can rob his house.

³⁰"He who is not with me is against me, and he who does not gather with me scatters. ³¹And so I tell you, every sin and blasphemy will be forgiven men, but the blasphemy against the Spirit will not be forgiven. ³²Anyone who speaks a word against the Son of Man will be forgiven, but anyone who speaks against the Holy Spirit will not be forgiven, either in this age or in the age to come.

³³"Make a tree good and its fruit will be good, or make a tree bad and its fruit will be bad, for a tree is recognized by its fruit. ³⁴You brood of vipers, how can you who are evil say anything good? For out of the overflow of the heart the mouth speaks. ³⁵The good man brings good things out of the good stored up in him, and the evil man brings evil things out of the evil stored up in him. ³⁶But I tell you that men will have to give account on the day of judgment for every careless word they have spoken. ³⁷For by your words you will be acquitted, and by your words you will be condemned."

³⁸Then some of the Pharisees and teachers of the law said to him, "Teacher, we want to see a miraculous sign from you."

³⁹He answered, "A wicked and adulterous generation asks for a miraculous sign! But none will be given it except the sign of the prophet Jonah. ⁴⁰For as Jonah was three days and three nights in the belly of a huge fish, so the Son of Man will be three days and three nights in the heart of the earth. ⁴¹The men of Nineveh will stand up at the judgment with this generation and condemn it; for they repented at the preaching of Jonah, and now oneʷ greater than Jonah is here. ⁴²The Queen of the South will rise at the judgment with this generation and condemn it; for she came from the ends of the earth to listen to Solomon's wisdom, and now one greater than Solomon is here.

⁴³"When an evilˣ spirit comes out of a man, it goes through arid places seeking rest and does not find it. ⁴⁴Then it says, 'I will return to the house I left.' When it arrives, it finds the house unoccupied, swept clean and put in order. ⁴⁵Then it goes and takes with it seven other spirits more wicked than itself, and they go in and live there. And the final condition of that man is worse than the first. That is how it will be with this wicked generation."

⁴⁶While Jesus was still talking to the crowd, his mother and brothers stood outside, wanting to speak to him. ⁴⁷Someone told him, "Your mother and brothers are standing outside, wanting to speak to you."ʸ

⁴⁸He replied to him, "Who is my mother, and who are my brothers?" ⁴⁹Pointing to his disciples, he said, "Here are my mother and my brothers. ⁵⁰For whoever does the will of my Father in heaven is my brother and sister and mother."

ʷ41 Or *something*; also in verse 42   ˣ43 Greek *unclean*
ʸ47 Some manuscripts do not have verse 47.

Discovering the Word 1. Consider the ways that religious leaders attacked Jesus in verses 1–14. What was their strategy? 2. As you compare the Pharisees' second accusation against Jesus (v. 10) with their own response (v. 14), what irony do you see? 3. Notice the startling contrast between the religious leaders' attitude toward Jesus and God's attitude (vv. 15–21). How do they differ? 4. In verses 43–45 Jesus tells the Pharisees and teachers of the law a story. What does it reveal about them? 5. Look back over chapter 12. What factors led to the hardness and unbelief of the Pharisees and teachers of the law?

Applying the Word 1. How can we avoid being like the Pharisees and teachers of the law? 2. What area of change in your life does this suggest you consider?

Responding in Prayer Ask God to teach you how to read and understand his Word so that you can use it to his glory.

9 / *Matthew 13*
The Parables of the King

CROWDS ARE FICKLE. One moment they follow with enthusiasm, the next they turn hostile and angry. In Matthew 13 Jesus speaks to a mixed and fickle crowd. Some are hungry to hear his message. Others are suspicious and hostile. In this setting Jesus begins to speak in parables. These stories test our spiritual sight and hearing. They also expose the condition of our hearts.

 Warming Up to God Prepare for this study by asking God to open your mind and heart to what is here for you.

 Read Matthew 13.

13 That same day Jesus went out of the house and sat by the lake. ²Such large crowds gathered around him that he got into a boat and sat in it, while all the people stood on the shore. ³Then he told them many things in parables, saying: "A farmer went out to sow his seed. ⁴As he was scattering the seed, some fell along the path, and the birds came and ate it up. ⁵Some fell on rocky places, where it did not have much soil. It sprang up quickly, because the soil was shallow. ⁶But when the sun came up, the plants were scorched, and they withered because they had no root. ⁷Other seed fell among thorns, which grew up and choked the plants. ⁸Still other seed fell on good soil, where it produced a crop—a hundred, sixty or thirty times what was sown. ⁹He who has ears, let him hear."

¹⁰The disciples came to him and asked, "Why do you speak to the people in parables?"

¹¹He replied, "The knowledge of the secrets of the kingdom of heaven has been given to you, but not to them. ¹²Whoever has will be given more, and he will have an abundance. Whoever does not have, even what he has will be taken from him. ¹³This is why I speak to them in parables:

"Though seeing, they do not see;
    though hearing, they do not hear or
        understand.

¹⁴In them is fulfilled the prophecy of Isaiah:

" 'You will be ever hearing but never
        understanding;
    you will be ever seeing but never
        perceiving.
¹⁵For this people's heart has become calloused;
    they hardly hear with their ears,
    and they have closed their eyes.

Otherwise they might see with their eyes,
    hear with their ears,
    understand with their hearts
    and turn, and I would heal them.'ᶻ

¹⁶But blessed are your eyes because they see, and your ears because they hear. ¹⁷For I tell you the truth, many prophets and righteous men longed to see what you see but did not see it, and to hear what you hear but did not hear it.

¹⁸"Listen then to what the parable of the sower means: ¹⁹When anyone hears the message about the kingdom and does not understand it, the evil one comes and snatches away what was sown in his heart. This is the seed sown along the path. ²⁰The one who received the seed that fell on rocky places is the man who hears the word and at once receives it with joy. ²¹But since he has no root, he lasts only a short time. When trouble or persecution comes because of the word, he quickly falls away. ²²The one who received the seed that fell among the thorns is the man who hears the word, but the worries of this life and the deceitfulness of wealth choke it, making it unfruitful. ²³But the one who received the seed that fell on good soil is the man who hears the word and understands it. He produces a crop, yielding a hundred, sixty or thirty times what was sown."

²⁴Jesus told them another parable: "The kingdom of heaven is like a man who sowed good seed in his field. ²⁵But while everyone was sleeping, his enemy came and sowed weeds among the wheat, and went away. ²⁶When the wheat sprouted and formed heads, then the weeds also appeared.

²⁷"The owner's servants came to him and said,

ᶻ15 Isaiah 6:9,10

'Sir, didn't you sow good seed in your field? Where then did the weeds come from?'

28" 'An enemy did this,' he replied.

"The servants asked him, 'Do you want us to go and pull them up?'

29" 'No,' he answered, 'because while you are pulling the weeds, you may root up the wheat with them. 30Let both grow together until the harvest. At that time I will tell the harvesters: First collect the weeds and tie them in bundles to be burned; then gather the wheat and bring it into my barn.' "

31He told them another parable: "The kingdom of heaven is like a mustard seed, which a man took and planted in his field. 32Though it is the smallest of all your seeds, yet when it grows, it is the largest of garden plants and becomes a tree, so that the birds of the air come and perch in its branches."

33He told them still another parable: "The kingdom of heaven is like yeast that a woman took and mixed into a large amount*a* of flour until it worked all through the dough."

34Jesus spoke all these things to the crowd in parables; he did not say anything to them without using a parable. 35So was fulfilled what was spoken through the prophet:

"I will open my mouth in parables,
    I will utter things hidden since the creation
        of the world."*b*

36Then he left the crowd and went into the house. His disciples came to him and said, "Explain to us the parable of the weeds in the field."

37He answered, "The one who sowed the good seed is the Son of Man. 38The field is the world, and the good seed stands for the sons of the kingdom. The weeds are the sons of the evil one, 39and the enemy who sows them is the devil. The harvest is the end of the age, and the harvesters are angels.

40"As the weeds are pulled up and burned in the fire, so it will be at the end of the age. 41The Son of Man will send out his angels, and they will weed out of his kingdom everything that causes sin and all who do evil. 42They will throw them into the fiery furnace, where there will be weep-

ing and gnashing of teeth. 43Then the righteous will shine like the sun in the kingdom of their Father. He who has ears, let him hear.

44"The kingdom of heaven is like treasure hidden in a field. When a man found it, he hid it again, and then in his joy went and sold all he had and bought that field.

45"Again, the kingdom of heaven is like a merchant looking for fine pearls. 46When he found one of great value, he went away and sold everything he had and bought it.

47"Once again, the kingdom of heaven is like a net that was let down into the lake and caught all kinds of fish. 48When it was full, the fishermen pulled it up on the shore. Then they sat down and collected the good fish in baskets, but threw the bad away. 49This is how it will be at the end of the age. The angels will come and separate the wicked from the righteous 50and throw them into the fiery furnace, where there will be weeping and gnashing of teeth.

51"Have you understood all these things?" Jesus asked.

"Yes," they replied.

52He said to them, "Therefore every teacher of the law who has been instructed about the kingdom of heaven is like the owner of a house who brings out of his storeroom new treasures as well as old."

53When Jesus had finished these parables, he moved on from there. 54Coming to his hometown, he began teaching the people in their synagogue, and they were amazed. "Where did this man get this wisdom and these miraculous powers?" they asked. 55"Isn't this the carpenter's son? Isn't his mother's name Mary, and aren't his brothers James, Joseph, Simon and Judas? 56Aren't all his sisters with us? Where then did this man get all these things?" 57And they took offense at him.

But Jesus said to them, "Only in his hometown and in his own house is a prophet without honor."

58And he did not do many miracles there because of their lack of faith.

a33 Greek three satas (probably about 1/2 bushel or 22 liters)
b35 Psalm 78:2

Discovering the Word 1. According to the parable of the sower, what responses does Jesus expect as he preaches his message of the kingdom (vv. 1–9, 18–23)? 2. In verse 10 the disciples ask Jesus why he speaks to the people in parables. Explain his reply (vv. 11–17). 3. Wheat and weeds look similar until the harvest. How does this parable explain God's delayed judgment of the wicked (vv. 24–30, 36–43)? 4. What do the parables of the mustard seed and yeast suggest about the way the kingdom grows (vv. 31–35)? 5. What do the parables of the hidden treasure and the pearl teach us about the value of the kingdom (vv. 44–46)?

Applying the Word 1. Jesus wants his disciples to understand the parables. How have they enlarged your understanding of the kingdom of heaven? 2. Jesus also wants us to respond to what we have heard and understood. Throughout this chapter, what types of responses does he desire?

Responding in Prayer Ask the Lord to help you respond to him in the ways you observed.

10 / *Matthew 14*
The Revelation of the King (Part 1)

CRISES ARE UNCOMFORTABLE. They force us to make painful decisions, even when we don't want to decide. In Matthew 14 Jesus places the disciples in tough situations where they must act on what they have learned about him. The focus shifts from parables about the kingdom to the identity of the king.

 Warming Up to God Teachers use tests during our school years. But tests are not limited to school; God also uses tests throughout our lives. How do you think you've been tested lately?

 Read Matthew 14.

14 At that time Herod the tetrarch heard the reports about Jesus, ²and he said to his attendants, "This is John the Baptist; he has risen from the dead! That is why miraculous powers are at work in him."

³Now Herod had arrested John and bound him and put him in prison because of Herodias, his brother Philip's wife, ⁴for John had been saying to him: "It is not lawful for you to have her." ⁵Herod wanted to kill John, but he was afraid of the people, because they considered him a prophet.

⁶On Herod's birthday the daughter of Herodias danced for them and pleased Herod so much ⁷that he promised with an oath to give her whatever she asked. ⁸Prompted by her mother, she said, "Give me here on a platter the head of John the Baptist." ⁹The king was distressed, but because of his oaths and his dinner guests, he ordered that her request be granted ¹⁰and had John beheaded in the prison. ¹¹His head was brought in on a platter and given to the girl, who carried it to her mother. ¹²John's disciples came and took his body and buried it. Then they went and told Jesus.

¹³When Jesus heard what had happened, he withdrew by boat privately to a solitary place. Hearing of this, the crowds followed him on foot from the towns. ¹⁴When Jesus landed and saw a large crowd, he had compassion on them and healed their sick.

¹⁵As evening approached, the disciples came to him and said, "This is a remote place, and it's already getting late. Send the crowds away, so they can go to the villages and buy themselves some food."

¹⁶Jesus replied, "They do not need to go away. You give them something to eat."

¹⁷"We have here only five loaves of bread and two fish," they answered.

¹⁸"Bring them here to me," he said. ¹⁹And he directed the people to sit down on the grass. Taking the five loaves and the two fish and looking up to heaven, he gave thanks and broke the loaves. Then he gave them to the disciples, and the disciples gave them to the people. ²⁰They all ate and were satisfied, and the disciples picked up twelve basketfuls of broken pieces that were left over. ²¹The number of those who ate was about five thousand men, besides women and children.

²²Immediately Jesus made the disciples get into the boat and go on ahead of him to the other side, while he dismissed the crowd. ²³After he had dismissed them, he went up on a mountainside by himself to pray. When evening came, he was there alone, ²⁴but the boat was already a considerable distance^c from land, buffeted by the waves because the wind was against it.

²⁵During the fourth watch of the night Jesus went out to them, walking on the lake. ²⁶When the disciples saw him walking on the lake, they were terrified. "It's a ghost," they said, and cried out in fear.

²⁷But Jesus immediately said to them: "Take courage! It is I. Don't be afraid."

²⁸"Lord, if it's you," Peter replied, "tell me to come to you on the water."

²⁹"Come," he said.

Then Peter got down out of the boat, walked on the water and came toward Jesus. ³⁰But when he saw the wind, he was afraid and, beginning to sink, cried out, "Lord, save me!"

³¹Immediately Jesus reached out his hand and caught him. "You of little faith," he said, "why did you doubt?"

³²And when they climbed into the boat, the wind died down. ³³Then those who were in the boat worshiped him, saying, "Truly you are the Son of God."

³⁴When they had crossed over, they landed at Gennesaret. ³⁵And when the men of that place recognized Jesus, they sent word to all the surrounding country. People brought all their sick to him ³⁶and begged him to let the sick just touch the edge of his cloak, and all who touched him were healed.

^c24 Greek *many stadia*

 Discovering the Word 1. In verses 1–2 Herod speculates about Jesus' identity. What led him to believe that Jesus is John the Baptist (vv. 3–12)? 2. How is the feeding of the five thousand (vv. 13–21) a test for the disciples? 3. Herod and Jesus, the two kings in this passage, both serve banquets. What does each king's banquet reveal about his character and authority? 4. Imagine you are in the boat with the anxious disciples (vv. 22–26). Describe what you would see, hear and feel. 5. How is Peter's trying experience on the water a vivid picture of faith and doubt (vv. 28–31)?

Applying the Word 1. When are you most tempted to take your eyes off the Lord and to sink in doubt? 2. In verse 33 the disciples worship Jesus and declare, "Truly you are the Son of God." What do you see in this incident that leads you to worship Jesus? 3. How can these things help you to trust Jesus the next time you are tempted to doubt?

Responding in Prayer Spend a few minutes worshiping Jesus, the Son of God.

---

11 / *Matthew 15:1—16:20*
The Revelation of the King (Part 2)

EUREKA! WHAT A relief and pleasure it is when something we have not quite understood becomes clear to us. In this section of Matthew the disciples come to a supernatural understanding of Jesus. What they thought they knew becomes a new and deeper knowledge. Peter, speaking for the disciples, declares who Jesus really is. Peter's words bring us to the climax of the first half of Matthew.

 Warming Up to God When you first recognized who Jesus is and what he offers to you, what were your thoughts and feelings?

 Read Matthew 15:1—16:20.

15

Then some Pharisees and teachers of the law came to Jesus from Jerusalem and asked, [2]"Why do your disciples break the tradition of the elders? They don't wash their hands before they eat!"

[3]Jesus replied, "And why do you break the command of God for the sake of your tradition? [4]For God said, 'Honor your father and mother'[d] and 'Anyone who curses his father or mother must be put to death.'[e] [5]But you say that if a man says to his father or mother, 'Whatever help you might otherwise have received from me is a gift devoted to God,' [6]he is not to 'honor his father'[f] with it. Thus you nullify the word of God for the sake of your tradition. [7]You hypocrites! Isaiah was right when he prophesied about you:

[8]" 'These people honor me with their lips,
    but their hearts are far from me.
[9]They worship me in vain;
    their teachings are but rules taught by
        men.'[g]

[10]Jesus called the crowd to him and said, "Listen and understand. [11]What goes into a man's mouth does not make him 'unclean,' but what comes out of his mouth, that is what makes him 'unclean.' "

[12]Then the disciples came to him and asked, "Do you know that the Pharisees were offended when they heard this?"

[13]He replied, "Every plant that my heavenly Father has not planted will be pulled up by the roots. [14]Leave them; they are blind guides.[h] If a blind man leads a blind man, both will fall into a pit."

[15]Peter said, "Explain the parable to us."

[16]"Are you still so dull?" Jesus asked them. [17]"Don't you see that whatever enters the mouth goes into the stomach and then out of the body? [18]But the things that come out of the mouth come from the heart, and these make a man 'unclean.' [19]For out of the heart come evil thoughts, murder, adultery, sexual immorality, theft, false testimony, slander. [20]These are what make a man 'unclean'; but eating with unwashed hands does not make him 'unclean.' "

[21]Leaving that place, Jesus withdrew to the region of Tyre and Sidon. [22]A Canaanite woman from that vicinity came to him, crying out, "Lord, Son of David, have mercy on me! My daughter is suffering terribly from demon-possession."

[23]Jesus did not answer a word. So his disciples came to him and urged him, "Send her away, for she keeps crying out after us."

[24]He answered, "I was sent only to the lost sheep of Israel."

[25]The woman came and knelt before him. "Lord, help me!" she said.

[26]He replied, "It is not right to take the children's bread and toss it to their dogs."

[27]"Yes, Lord," she said, "but even the dogs eat the crumbs that fall from their masters' table."

[28]Then Jesus answered, "Woman, you have great faith! Your request is granted." And her daughter was healed from that very hour.

[29]Jesus left there and went along the Sea of Galilee. Then he went up on a mountainside and sat down. [30]Great crowds came to him, bringing the lame, the blind, the crippled, the mute and many others, and laid them at his feet; and he healed them. [31]The people were amazed when they saw the mute speaking, the crippled made well, the lame walking and the blind seeing. And they praised the God of Israel.

[32]Jesus called his disciples to him and said, "I have compassion for these people; they have already been with me three days and have nothing to eat. I do not want to send them away hungry, or they may collapse on the way."

[33]His disciples answered, "Where could we get enough bread in this remote place to feed such a crowd?"

[34]"How many loaves do you have?" Jesus asked.

"Seven," they replied, "and a few small fish."

[35]He told the crowd to sit down on the ground. [36]Then he took the seven loaves and the fish, and when he had given thanks, he broke them and gave them to the disciples, and they in turn to the people. [37]They all ate and were satisfied. Afterward the disciples picked up seven basketfuls of broken pieces that were left over. [38]The number of those who ate was four thousand, besides women and children. [39]After Jesus had sent the crowd away, he got into the boat and went to the vicinity of Magadan.

16

The Pharisees and Sadducees came to Jesus and tested him by asking him to show them a sign from heaven.

[2]He replied,[i] "When evening comes, you say,

d4 Exodus 20:12; Deut. 5:16   e4 Exodus 21:17; Lev. 20:9
f6 Some manuscripts *father or his mother*   g9 Isaiah 29:13
h14 Some manuscripts *guides of the blind*   i2 Some early manuscripts do not have the rest of verse 2 and all of verse 3.

'It will be fair weather, for the sky is red,' ³and in the morning, 'Today it will be stormy, for the sky is red and overcast.' You know how to interpret the appearance of the sky, but you cannot interpret the signs of the times. ⁴A wicked and adulterous generation looks for a miraculous sign, but none will be given it except the sign of Jonah." Jesus then left them and went away.

⁵When they went across the lake, the disciples forgot to take bread. ⁶"Be careful," Jesus said to them. "Be on your guard against the yeast of the Pharisees and Sadducees."

⁷They discussed this among themselves and said, "It is because we didn't bring any bread."

⁸Aware of their discussion, Jesus asked, "You of little faith, why are you talking among yourselves about having no bread? ⁹Do you still not understand? Don't you remember the five loaves for the five thousand, and how many basketfuls you gathered? ¹⁰Or the seven loaves for the four thousand, and how many basketfuls you gathered? ¹¹How is it you don't understand that I was not talking to you about bread? But be on your guard against the yeast of the Pharisees and Sadducees." ¹²Then they understood that he was not telling them to guard against the yeast used in bread, but against the teaching of the Pharisees and Sadducees.

¹³When Jesus came to the region of Caesarea Philippi, he asked his disciples, "Who do people say the Son of Man is?"

¹⁴They replied, "Some say John the Baptist; others say Elijah; and still others, Jeremiah or one of the prophets."

¹⁵"But what about you?" he asked. "Who do you say I am?"

¹⁶Simon Peter answered, "You are the Christ,ʲ the Son of the living God."

¹⁷Jesus replied, "Blessed are you, Simon son of Jonah, for this was not revealed to you by man, but by my Father in heaven. ¹⁸And I tell you that you are Peter,ᵏ and on this rock I will build my church, and the gates of Hadesˡ will not overcome it.ᵐ ¹⁹I will give you the keys of the kingdom of heaven; whatever you bind on earth will beⁿ bound in heaven, and whatever you loose on earth will beⁿ loosed in heaven." ²⁰Then he warned his disciples not to tell anyone that he was the Christ.

ʲ16 Or *Messiah*; also in verse 20   ᵏ18 *Peter* means *rock*.   ˡ18 Or *hell*   ᵐ18 Or *not prove stronger than it*   ⁿ19 Or *have been*

 Discovering the Word 1. Top religious leaders from Jerusalem oppose Jesus by attacking the disciples (15:1–2). What is their complaint, and what does it suggest about Jesus? 2. How does Jesus respond to their accusation (15:3–20)? 3. How would you account for the unusual interaction between Jesus, the woman and the disciples (15:21–28)? 4. After Jesus heals the sick and feeds the four thousand, the religious leaders ask him for a sign from heaven (16:1). Why do you think Jesus resists them (16:2–4)? 5. In 16:5–12 the disciples misunderstand Jesus' allusion to yeast. How is their misunderstanding related to a lack of faith? 6. In 16:5–12 the disciples couldn't even grasp a simple figure of speech. How then does Peter have enough insight to confess that Jesus is the Christ, the Son of God (16:13–17)?

Applying the Word 1. Are there religious practices in your life that are in danger of becoming outward, empty forms? Explain. 2. How can you avoid this tendency? 3. Jesus' question to Peter is one that everyone will have to respond to at some point. Who do you say Jesus is, and why?

Responding in Prayer Offer praise to Jesus Christ for who he is.

---

12 / *Matthew 16:21—17:27*
The Work of the King

ONE OF THE rules of good management is "No surprises." While surprises can be fun, they can also be upsetting. Good corporate leadership seeks to eliminate surprises so that everything runs according to plan.

Now that the disciples have been with Jesus for a while, he must prepare them for the true nature of his kingdom. They are shocked at the cost of his mission and his requirements for discipleship.

 Warming Up to God Recall an unpleasant surprise you received. How did you handle it?

 Read Matthew 16:21—17:27.

21From that time on Jesus began to explain to his disciples that he must go to Jerusalem and suffer many things at the hands of the elders, chief priests and teachers of the law, and that he must be killed and on the third day be raised to life.

22Peter took him aside and began to rebuke him. "Never, Lord!" he said. "This shall never happen to you!"

23Jesus turned and said to Peter, "Get behind me, Satan! You are a stumbling block to me; you do not have in mind the things of God, but the things of men."

24Then Jesus said to his disciples, "If anyone would come after me, he must deny himself and take up his cross and follow me. 25For whoever wants to save his life° will lose it, but whoever loses his life for me will find it. 26What good will it be for a man if he gains the whole world, yet forfeits his soul? Or what can a man give in exchange for his soul? 27For the Son of Man is going to come in his Father's glory with his angels, and then he will reward each person according to what he has done. 28I tell you the truth, some who are standing here will not taste death before they see the Son of Man coming in his kingdom."

17 After six days Jesus took with him Peter, James and John the brother of James, and led them up a high mountain by themselves. 2There he was transfigured before them. His face shone like the sun, and his clothes became as white as the light. 3Just then there appeared before them Moses and Elijah, talking with Jesus.

4Peter said to Jesus, "Lord, it is good for us to be here. If you wish, I will put up three shelters—one for you, one for Moses and one for Elijah."

5While he was still speaking, a bright cloud enveloped them, and a voice from the cloud said, "This is my Son, whom I love; with him I am well pleased. Listen to him!"

6When the disciples heard this, they fell face-down to the ground, terrified. 7But Jesus came and touched them. "Get up," he said. "Don't be afraid." 8When they looked up, they saw no one except Jesus.

9As they were coming down the mountain, Jesus instructed them, "Don't tell anyone what you have seen, until the Son of Man has been raised from the dead."

10The disciples asked him, "Why then do the teachers of the law say that Elijah must come first?"

11Jesus replied, "To be sure, Elijah comes and will restore all things. 12But I tell you, Elijah has already come, and they did not recognize him, but have done to him everything they wished. In the same way the Son of Man is going to suffer at their hands." 13Then the disciples understood that he was talking to them about John the Baptist.

14When they came to the crowd, a man approached Jesus and knelt before him. 15"Lord, have mercy on my son," he said. "He has seizures and is suffering greatly. He often falls into the fire or into the water. 16I brought him to your disciples, but they could not heal him."

17"O unbelieving and perverse generation," Jesus replied, "how long shall I stay with you? How long shall I put up with you? Bring the boy here to me." 18Jesus rebuked the demon, and it came out of the boy, and he was healed from that moment.

19Then the disciples came to Jesus in private and asked, "Why couldn't we drive it out?"

20He replied, "Because you have so little faith. I tell you the truth, if you have faith as small as a mustard seed, you can say to this mountain, 'Move from here to there' and it will move. Nothing will be impossible for you.ᵖ"

22When they came together in Galilee, he said to them, "The Son of Man is going to be betrayed into the hands of men. 23They will kill him, and on the third day he will be raised to life." And the disciples were filled with grief.

24After Jesus and his disciples arrived in Caper-

°25 The Greek word means either *life* or *soul*; also in verse 26.
ᵖ20 Some manuscripts *you.* 21*But this kind does not go out except by prayer and fasting.*

naum, the collectors of the two-drachma tax came to Peter and asked, "Doesn't your teacher pay the temple tax*q*?"

²⁵"Yes, he does," he replied.

When Peter came into the house, Jesus was the first to speak. "What do you think, Simon?" he asked. "From whom do the kings of the earth collect duty and taxes—from their own sons or from others?"

²⁶"From others," Peter answered.

"Then the sons are exempt," Jesus said to him. ²⁷"But so that we may not offend them, go to the lake and throw out your line. Take the first fish you catch; open its mouth and you will find a four-drachma coin. Take it and give it to them for my tax and yours."

q24 Greek the two drachmas

 Discovering the Word   1. What were some of the surprises the disciples received?   2. Peter and Jesus seem to be at cross purposes in 16:22–23. Why do you think Jesus addresses Peter as Satan?   3. What does Jesus reveal about the cost and rewards of following him (16:24–28)?   4. What would the disciples learn about Jesus by his transformed appearance, his conversation with Moses and Elijah, and the voice from heaven (17:1–8)?   5. How might this help resolve their confusion about Jesus' impending death?   6. As a result of their powerlessness, what do the disciples learn about faith?

 Applying the Word   1. How has following Jesus produced times of confusion for you?   2. We don't always understand life from a heavenly perspective. How can this passage reorient your thinking?

Responding in Prayer   Ask God to help you understand his ways so that you can be a better disciple.

---

13 / *Matthew 18*
The Greatest in the Kingdom

WHO IS GREATEST in the kingdom of God? How can a subject of the kingdom earn true wealth? When should we forgive? These questions dominate the thoughts of the disciples as they approach Jerusalem. They are also important questions for us. How we answer them will directly affect the quality of our discipleship.

 Warming Up to God   When has someone sinned against you? How did it affect you?

 Read Matthew 18.

---

18 At that time the disciples came to Jesus and asked, "Who is the greatest in the kingdom of heaven?"

²He called a little child and had him stand among them. ³And he said: "I tell you the truth, unless you change and become like little children, you will never enter the kingdom of heaven. ⁴Therefore, whoever humbles himself like this child is the greatest in the kingdom of heaven.

⁵"And whoever welcomes a little child like this in my name welcomes me. ⁶But if anyone causes one of these little ones who believe in me to sin, it would be better for him to have a large mill-

stone hung around his neck and to be drowned in the depths of the sea.

⁷"Woe to the world because of the things that cause people to sin! Such things must come, but woe to the man through whom they come! ⁸If your hand or your foot causes you to sin, cut it off and throw it away. It is better for you to enter life maimed or crippled than to have two hands or two feet and be thrown into eternal fire. ⁹And if your eye causes you to sin, gouge it out and throw it away. It is better for you to enter life with one eye than to have two eyes and be thrown into the fire of hell.

¹⁰"See that you do not look down on one of these little ones. For I tell you that their angels in heaven always see the face of my Father in heaven.ʳ

¹²"What do you think? If a man owns a hundred sheep, and one of them wanders away, will he not leave the ninety-nine on the hills and go to look for the one that wandered off? ¹³And if he finds it, I tell you the truth, he is happier about that one sheep than about the ninety-nine that did not wander off. ¹⁴In the same way your Father in heaven is not willing that any of these little ones should be lost.

¹⁵"If your brother sins against you,ˢ go and show him his fault, just between the two of you. If he listens to you, you have won your brother over. ¹⁶But if he will not listen, take one or two others along, so that 'every matter may be established by the testimony of two or three witnesses.'ᵗ ¹⁷If he refuses to listen to them, tell it to the church; and if he refuses to listen even to the church, treat him as you would a pagan or a tax collector.

¹⁸"I tell you the truth, whatever you bind on earth will beᵘ bound in heaven, and whatever you loose on earth will beᵘ loosed in heaven.

¹⁹"Again, I tell you that if two of you on earth agree about anything you ask for, it will be done for you by my Father in heaven. ²⁰For where two or three come together in my name, there am I with them."

²¹Then Peter came to Jesus and asked, "Lord, how many times shall I forgive my brother when he sins against me? Up to seven times?"

²²Jesus answered, "I tell you, not seven times, but seventy-seven times.ᵛ

²³"Therefore, the kingdom of heaven is like a king who wanted to settle accounts with his ser-

vants. ²⁴As he began the settlement, a man who owed him ten thousand talentsʷ was brought to him. ²⁵Since he was not able to pay, the master ordered that he and his wife and his children and all that he had be sold to repay the debt.

²⁶"The servant fell on his knees before him. 'Be patient with me,' he begged, 'and I will pay back everything.' ²⁷The servant's master took pity on him, canceled the debt and let him go.

²⁸"But when that servant went out, he found one of his fellow servants who owed him a hundred denarii.ˣ He grabbed him and began to choke him. 'Pay back what you owe me!' he demanded.

²⁹"His fellow servant fell to his knees and begged him, 'Be patient with me, and I will pay you back.'

³⁰"But he refused. Instead, he went off and had the man thrown into prison until he could pay the debt. ³¹When the other servants saw what had happened, they were greatly distressed and went and told their master everything that had happened.

³²"Then the master called the servant in. 'You wicked servant,' he said, 'I canceled all that debt of yours because you begged me to. ³³Shouldn't you have had mercy on your fellow servant just as I had on you?' ³⁴In anger his master turned him over to the jailers to be tortured, until he should pay back all he owed.

³⁵"This is how my heavenly Father will treat each of you unless you forgive your brother from your heart."

ʳ10 Some manuscripts *heaven.* ¹¹*The Son of Man came to save what was lost.* ˢ15 Some manuscripts do not have *against you.* ᵗ16 Deut. 19:15 ᵘ18 Or *have been* ᵛ22 Or *seventy times seven* ʷ24 That is, millions of dollars ˣ28 That is, a few dollars

---

Discovering the Word 1. The disciples want to know who is the greatest in the kingdom of heaven (v. 1). How does Jesus' appeal to little children answer their question (vv. 2–5)? 2. Spiritually speaking, the "little ones" are those who humble themselves ("become like little children") and believe in Jesus. What is Jesus' attitude toward those who cause the little ones to sin (vv. 6–7)? 3. How do verses 10–14 further emphasize the value Jesus places on his "little ones"? 4. Greatness in the kingdom is also dependent on living a life of forgiveness and mercy. What guidelines does Jesus give for dealing with those who sin against us (vv. 15–20)? 5. Forgiving someone once does not always guarantee he or she will not offend us again. How can the parable of the unmerciful servant help us to keep on forgiving (vv. 21–35)?

Applying the Word 1. Children have little status in the eyes of adults. How can we assume the status of children in our circle of friends and coworkers? 2. How should the value Jesus places on his "little ones" affect the way we view ourselves and other believers? 3. How does this chapter challenge your ideas of value and greatness?

Responding in Prayer Ask God to help you forgive those who have hurt you.

14 / *Matthew 19—20*
Life in the Kingdom

WHAT IS REALLY important to you? What makes you feel important? Money? Success? Recognition? These are common answers. The values that Jesus teaches, however, have little to do with such things. In the previous study we learned that to be great in the kingdom, we must become "small." In this study we will see how the values of the kingdom conflict with the world's approach to wealth and leadership.

 Warming Up to God What does success mean to you? How does that compare to what our culture says about success?

 Read Matthew 19—20.

19 When Jesus had finished saying these things, he left Galilee and went into the region of Judea to the other side of the Jordan. ²Large crowds followed him, and he healed them there.

³Some Pharisees came to him to test him. They asked, "Is it lawful for a man to divorce his wife for any and every reason?"

⁴"Haven't you read," he replied, "that at the beginning the Creator 'made them male and female,'ʸ ⁵and said, 'For this reason a man will leave his father and mother and be united to his wife, and the two will become one flesh'ᶻ? ⁶So they are no longer two, but one. Therefore what God has joined together, let man not separate."

⁷"Why then," they asked, "did Moses command that a man give his wife a certificate of divorce and send her away?"

⁸Jesus replied, "Moses permitted you to divorce your wives because your hearts were hard. But it was not this way from the beginning. ⁹I tell you that anyone who divorces his wife, except for marital unfaithfulness, and marries another woman commits adultery."

¹⁰The disciples said to him, "If this is the situation between a husband and wife, it is better not to marry."

¹¹Jesus replied, "Not everyone can accept this word, but only those to whom it has been given. ¹²For some are eunuchs because they were born that way; others were made that way by men; and others have renounced marriageᵃ because of the kingdom of heaven. The one who can accept this should accept it."

¹³Then little children were brought to Jesus for him to place his hands on them and pray for them. But the disciples rebuked those who brought them.

¹⁴Jesus said, "Let the little children come to me, and do not hinder them, for the kingdom of heaven belongs to such as these." ¹⁵When he had placed his hands on them, he went on from there.

¹⁶Now a man came up to Jesus and asked, "Teacher, what good thing must I do to get eternal life?"

¹⁷"Why do you ask me about what is good?" Jesus replied. "There is only One who is good. If you want to enter life, obey the commandments."

¹⁸"Which ones?" the man inquired.

Jesus replied, " 'Do not murder, do not commit adultery, do not steal, do not give false testimony, ¹⁹honor your father and mother,'ᵇ and 'love your neighbor as yourself.'ᶜ "

²⁰"All these I have kept," the young man said. "What do I still lack?"

²¹Jesus answered, "If you want to be perfect, go, sell your possessions and give to the poor, and you will have treasure in heaven. Then come, follow me."

²²When the young man heard this, he went away sad, because he had great wealth.

²³Then Jesus said to his disciples, "I tell you the truth, it is hard for a rich man to enter the king-

ʸ4 Gen. 1:27   ᶻ5 Gen. 2:24   ᵃ12 *Or have made themselves eunuchs*   ᵇ19 Exodus 20:12-16; Deut. 5:16-20   ᶜ19 Lev. 19:18

dom of heaven. ²⁴Again I tell you, it is easier for a camel to go through the eye of a needle than for a rich man to enter the kingdom of God."

²⁵When the disciples heard this, they were greatly astonished and asked, "Who then can be saved?"

²⁶Jesus looked at them and said, "With man this is impossible, but with God all things are possible."

²⁷Peter answered him, "We have left everything to follow you! What then will there be for us?"

²⁸Jesus said to them, "I tell you the truth, at the renewal of all things, when the Son of Man sits on his glorious throne, you who have followed me will also sit on twelve thrones, judging the twelve tribes of Israel. ²⁹And everyone who has left houses or brothers or sisters or father or mother^d or children or fields for my sake will receive a hundred times as much and will inherit eternal life. ³⁰But many who are first will be last, and many who are last will be first.

20 "For the kingdom of heaven is like a landowner who went out early in the morning to hire men to work in his vineyard. ²He agreed to pay them a denarius for the day and sent them into his vineyard.

³"About the third hour he went out and saw others standing in the marketplace doing nothing. ⁴He told them, 'You also go and work in my vineyard, and I will pay you whatever is right.' ⁵So they went.

"He went out again about the sixth hour and the ninth hour and did the same thing. ⁶About the eleventh hour he went out and found still others standing around. He asked them, 'Why have you been standing here all day long doing nothing?'

⁷" 'Because no one has hired us,' they answered.

"He said to them, 'You also go and work in my vineyard.'

⁸"When evening came, the owner of the vineyard said to his foreman, 'Call the workers and pay them their wages, beginning with the last ones hired and going on to the first.'

⁹"The workers who were hired about the eleventh hour came and each received a denarius. ¹⁰So when those came who were hired first, they expected to receive more. But each one of them also received a denarius. ¹¹When they received it, they began to grumble against the landowner.

¹²'These men who were hired last worked only one hour,' they said, 'and you have made them equal to us who have borne the burden of the work and the heat of the day.'

¹³"But he answered one of them, 'Friend, I am not being unfair to you. Didn't you agree to work for a denarius? ¹⁴Take your pay and go. I want to give the man who was hired last the same as I gave you. ¹⁵Don't I have the right to do what I want with my own money? Or are you envious because I am generous?'

¹⁶"So the last will be first, and the first will be last."

¹⁷Now as Jesus was going up to Jerusalem, he took the twelve disciples aside and said to them, ¹⁸"We are going up to Jerusalem, and the Son of Man will be betrayed to the chief priests and the teachers of the law. They will condemn him to death ¹⁹and will turn him over to the Gentiles to be mocked and flogged and crucified. On the third day he will be raised to life!"

²⁰Then the mother of Zebedee's sons came to Jesus with her sons and, kneeling down, asked a favor of him.

²¹"What is it you want?" he asked.

She said, "Grant that one of these two sons of mine may sit at your right and the other at your left in your kingdom."

²²"You don't know what you are asking," Jesus said to them. "Can you drink the cup I am going to drink?"

"We can," they answered.

²³Jesus said to them, "You will indeed drink from my cup, but to sit at my right or left is not for me to grant. These places belong to those for whom they have been prepared by my Father."

²⁴When the ten heard about this, they were indignant with the two brothers. ²⁵Jesus called them together and said, "You know that the rulers of the Gentiles lord it over them, and their high officials exercise authority over them. ²⁶Not so with you. Instead, whoever wants to become great among you must be your servant, ²⁷and whoever wants to be first must be your slave— ²⁸just as the Son of Man did not come to be served, but to serve, and to give his life as a ransom for many."

²⁹As Jesus and his disciples were leaving Jericho, a large crowd followed him. ³⁰Two blind

^d29 Some manuscripts *mother or wife*

men were sitting by the roadside, and when they heard that Jesus was going by, they shouted, "Lord, Son of David, have mercy on us!"

³¹The crowd rebuked them and told them to be quiet, but they shouted all the louder, "Lord, Son of David, have mercy on us!"

³²Jesus stopped and called them. "What do you want me to do for you?" he asked.

³³"Lord," they answered, "we want our sight."

³⁴Jesus had compassion on them and touched their eyes. Immediately they received their sight and followed him.

 Discovering the Word 1. How do Jesus' teachings on divorce and remarriage contrast with the values and practices of our culture (19:1–12)? 2. In 19:16–22 a young man struggles between choosing wealth or eternal life. Why do you think Jesus required him to choose? 3. What wealth does Jesus offer those who follow him (vv. 27–30)? 4. What does the parable of the workers teach us about greatness and wealth in the kingdom of God (20:1–16)? 5. In what ways is Jesus a model of the values he teaches in 20:25–28? 6. How does Jesus' interaction with the two blind men illustrate the values he has just taught?

 Applying the Word 1. How have you experienced what Jesus describes in 19:29? 2. In what ways has Jesus' teaching on greatness and wealth (Mt 18—20) challenged you?

 Responding in Prayer Ask God to give you strength to stand against the world and to make his values your values.

15 / *Matthew 21:1–27*
The King Occupies His Capital

IT IS FASHIONABLE to believe in Jesus. Surveys reveal that millions profess to be Christians. Celebrities claim miraculous, overnight conversions. Politicians boast they are "born again." Religion has become big business.

In Matthew 21 Jesus' popularity reaches its zenith. In the midst of public acclamation he occupies Jerusalem, the capital of the Jewish nation. His clash with the religious leaders reveals the difference between genuine faith and empty profession.

 Warming Up to God Today we will see Jesus enter Jerusalem to the praise and acclamation of the crowd. Imagine you have an opportunity to see Jesus. How do you feel? Express your feelings to the Lord.

📖 **Read Matthew 21:1–27.**

21 As they approached Jerusalem and came to Bethphage on the Mount of Olives, Jesus sent two disciples, ²saying to them, "Go to the village ahead of you, and at once you will find a donkey tied there, with her colt by her. Untie them and bring them to me. ³If anyone says anything to you, tell him that the Lord needs them, and he will send them right away."

⁴This took place to fulfill what was spoken through the prophet:

⁵"Say to the Daughter of Zion,
  'See, your king comes to you,
   gentle and riding on a donkey,
     on a colt, the foal of a donkey.' "ᵉ

⁶The disciples went and did as Jesus had instructed them. ⁷They brought the donkey and the colt, placed their cloaks on them, and Jesus sat on them. ⁸A very large crowd spread their cloaks on the road, while others cut branches from the trees and spread them on the road. ⁹The crowds that went ahead of him and those that followed shouted,

"Hosannaᶠ to the Son of David!"

"Blessed is he who comes in the name of the Lord!"ᵍ

"Hosannaᶠ in the highest!"

ᵉ5 Zech. 9:9   ᶠ9 A Hebrew expression meaning "Save!" which became an exclamation of praise; also in verse 15   ᵍ9 Psalm 118:26

¹⁰When Jesus entered Jerusalem, the whole city was stirred and asked, "Who is this?"

¹¹The crowds answered, "This is Jesus, the prophet from Nazareth in Galilee."

¹²Jesus entered the temple area and drove out all who were buying and selling there. He overturned the tables of the money changers and the benches of those selling doves. ¹³"It is written," he said to them, " 'My house will be called a house of prayer,'ʰ but you are making it a 'den of robbers.'ⁱ "

¹⁴The blind and the lame came to him at the temple, and he healed them. ¹⁵But when the chief priests and the teachers of the law saw the wonderful things he did and the children shouting in the temple area, "Hosanna to the Son of David," they were indignant.

¹⁶"Do you hear what these children are saying?" they asked him.

"Yes," replied Jesus, "have you never read,

" 'From the lips of children and infants
    you have ordained praise'ʲ ?"

¹⁷And he left them and went out of the city to Bethany, where he spent the night.

¹⁸Early in the morning, as he was on his way back to the city, he was hungry. ¹⁹Seeing a fig tree by the road, he went up to it but found nothing on it except leaves. Then he said to it, "May you never bear fruit again!" Immediately the tree withered.

²⁰When the disciples saw this, they were amazed. "How did the fig tree wither so quickly?" they asked.

²¹Jesus replied, "I tell you the truth, if you have faith and do not doubt, not only can you do what was done to the fig tree, but also you can say to this mountain, 'Go, throw yourself into the sea,' and it will be done. ²²If you believe, you will receive whatever you ask for in prayer."

²³Jesus entered the temple courts, and, while he was teaching, the chief priests and the elders of the people came to him. "By what authority are you doing these things?" they asked. "And who gave you this authority?"

²⁴Jesus replied, "I will also ask you one question. If you answer me, I will tell you by what authority I am doing these things. ²⁵John's baptism—where did it come from? Was it from heaven, or from men?"

They discussed it among themselves and said, "If we say, 'From heaven,' he will ask, 'Then why didn't you believe him?' ²⁶But if we say, 'From men'—we are afraid of the people, for they all hold that John was a prophet."

²⁷So they answered Jesus, "We don't know."

Then he said, "Neither will I tell you by what authority I am doing these things.

ʰ13 Isaiah 56:7   ⁱ13 Jer. 7:11   ʲ16 Psalm 8:2

Discovering the Word 1. Excitement is building and emotions are intense. What words or phrases communicate something of the electrifying atmosphere? 2. What different perceptions does the crowd have of Jesus (vv. 9–11)? 3. Jesus clears the temple in verses 12–17. How does the condition of the temple contrast with what God intended? 4. A fig tree with leaves usually had fruit. How does Jesus' cursing of the fig tree relate to his clearing the temple (vv. 18–22)? 5. How does Jesus' encounter with the Pharisees (vv. 23–27) illustrate the danger of not responding to the light God gives us?

Applying the Word 1. In what ways do you see the modern church "buying and selling" like those in the temple? 2. Identify one area in which your actions need to be more consistent with your beliefs.

Responding in Prayer Praise God for who Jesus is and what you have seen about him in this passage.

16 / *Matthew 21:28—22:46*
The King Silences the Opposition

CONFRONTATION IS NEVER easy. Yet there are times when the situation demands it. The religious leaders refused to acknowledge that Jesus was God's Messiah sent to rule. Skillfully, Jesus seeks to expose their hardness of heart and bring them to repentance. They respond not in repentance but by plotting a trap for him.

 Warming Up to God From time to time we all have been involved in confrontations. How do you feel in these situations?

 Read Matthew 21:28—22:46.

---

²⁸"What do you think? There was a man who had two sons. He went to the first and said, 'Son, go and work today in the vineyard.'

²⁹" 'I will not,' he answered, but later he changed his mind and went.

³⁰"Then the father went to the other son and said the same thing. He answered, 'I will, sir,' but he did not go.

³¹"Which of the two did what his father wanted?"

"The first," they answered.

Jesus said to them, "I tell you the truth, the tax collectors and the prostitutes are entering the kingdom of God ahead of you. ³²For John came to you to show you the way of righteousness, and you did not believe him, but the tax collectors and the prostitutes did. And even after you saw this, you did not repent and believe him.

³³"Listen to another parable: There was a landowner who planted a vineyard. He put a wall around it, dug a winepress in it and built a watchtower. Then he rented the vineyard to some farmers and went away on a journey. ³⁴When the harvest time approached, he sent his servants to the tenants to collect his fruit.

³⁵"The tenants seized his servants; they beat one, killed another, and stoned a third. ³⁶Then he sent other servants to them, more than the first time, and the tenants treated them the same way. ³⁷Last of all, he sent his son to them. 'They will respect my son,' he said.

³⁸"But when the tenants saw the son, they said to each other, 'This is the heir. Come, let's kill him and take his inheritance.' ³⁹So they took him and threw him out of the vineyard and killed him.

⁴⁰"Therefore, when the owner of the vineyard comes, what will he do to those tenants?"

⁴¹"He will bring those wretches to a wretched end," they replied, "and he will rent the vineyard

to other tenants, who will give him his share of the crop at harvest time."

⁴²Jesus said to them, "Have you never read in the Scriptures:

" 'The stone the builders rejected
  has become the capstone*ᵏ*;
the Lord has done this,
  and it is marvelous in our eyes'*ˡ*?

⁴³"Therefore I tell you that the kingdom of God will be taken away from you and given to a people who will produce its fruit. ⁴⁴He who falls on this stone will be broken to pieces, but he on whom it falls will be crushed."*ᵐ*

⁴⁵When the chief priests and the Pharisees heard Jesus' parables, they knew he was talking about them. ⁴⁶They looked for a way to arrest him, but they were afraid of the crowd because the people held that he was a prophet.

22 Jesus spoke to them again in parables, saying: ²"The kingdom of heaven is like a king who prepared a wedding banquet for his son. ³He sent his servants to those who had been invited to the banquet to tell them to come, but they refused to come.

⁴"Then he sent some more servants and said, 'Tell those who have been invited that I have prepared my dinner: My oxen and fattened cattle have been butchered, and everything is ready. Come to the wedding banquet.'

⁵"But they paid no attention and went off—one to his field, another to his business. ⁶The rest seized his servants, mistreated them and killed them. ⁷The king was enraged. He sent his army and destroyed those murderers and burned their city.

ᵏ42 Or *cornerstone*   *ˡ42* Psalm 118:22,23   *ᵐ44* Some manuscripts do not have verse 44.

8"Then he said to his servants, 'The wedding banquet is ready, but those I invited did not deserve to come. 9Go to the street corners and invite to the banquet anyone you find.' 10So the servants went out into the streets and gathered all the people they could find, both good and bad, and the wedding hall was filled with guests.

11"But when the king came in to see the guests, he noticed a man there who was not wearing wedding clothes. 12'Friend,' he asked, 'how did you get in here without wedding clothes?' The man was speechless.

13"Then the king told the attendants, 'Tie him hand and foot, and throw him outside, into the darkness, where there will be weeping and gnashing of teeth.'

14"For many are invited, but few are chosen."

15Then the Pharisees went out and laid plans to trap him in his words. 16They sent their disciples to him along with the Herodians. "Teacher," they said, "we know you are a man of integrity and that you teach the way of God in accordance with the truth. You aren't swayed by men, because you pay no attention to who they are. 17Tell us then, what is your opinion? Is it right to pay taxes to Caesar or not?"

18But Jesus, knowing their evil intent, said, "You hypocrites, why are you trying to trap me? 19Show me the coin used for paying the tax." They brought him a denarius, 20and he asked them, "Whose portrait is this? And whose inscription?"

21"Caesar's," they replied.

Then he said to them, "Give to Caesar what is Caesar's, and to God what is God's."

22When they heard this, they were amazed. So they left him and went away.

23That same day the Sadducees, who say there is no resurrection, came to him with a question. 24"Teacher," they said, "Moses told us that if a man dies without having children, his brother must marry the widow and have children for him. 25Now there were seven brothers among us. The first one married and died, and since he had no children, he left his wife to his brother. 26The same thing happened to the second and third brother, right on down to the seventh. 27Finally, the woman died. 28Now then, at the resurrection, whose wife will she be of the seven, since all of them were married to her?"

29Jesus replied, "You are in error because you do not know the Scriptures or the power of God. 30At the resurrection people will neither marry nor be given in marriage; they will be like the angels in heaven. 31But about the resurrection of the dead—have you not read what God said to you, 32'I am the God of Abraham, the God of Isaac, and the God of Jacob'[n]? He is not the God of the dead but of the living."

33When the crowds heard this, they were astonished at his teaching.

34Hearing that Jesus had silenced the Sadducees, the Pharisees got together. 35One of them, an expert in the law, tested him with this question: 36"Teacher, which is the greatest commandment in the Law?"

37Jesus replied: "'Love the Lord your God with all your heart and with all your soul and with all your mind.'[o] 38This is the first and greatest commandment. 39And the second is like it: 'Love your neighbor as yourself.'[p] 40All the Law and the Prophets hang on these two commandments."

41While the Pharisees were gathered together, Jesus asked them, 42"What do you think about the Christ[q]? Whose son is he?"

"The son of David," they replied.

43He said to them, "How is it then that David, speaking by the Spirit, calls him 'Lord'? For he says,

44" 'The Lord said to my Lord:
   "Sit at my right hand
until I put your enemies
   under your feet." '[r]

45If then David calls him 'Lord,' how can he be his son?" 46No one could say a word in reply, and from that day on no one dared to ask him any more questions.

n32 Exodus 3:6   o37 Deut. 6:5   p39 Lev. 19:18   q42 Or Messiah   r44 Psalm 110:1

Discovering the Word 1. What does the parable of the two sons reveal about the chief priests and the elders (21:28–32)? 2. How does the parable of the tenants illustrate the character of the Father, the Son and the religious leaders (21:33–46)? 3. How is the kingdom of heaven like the banquet described in 22:1–14? 4. In 22:23–28 the Sadducees tell Jesus a story designed to refute the resurrection. How does the story illustrate their ignorance of Scripture and God's power (22:29–33)? 5. Love was the foundation of the Old Testament law (22:34–40). Why do you think we have so much trouble equating God's laws with love? 6. Jesus poses a dilemma to the Pharisees that silences them: "How can the Christ be both the son of David and his Lord?" (22:41–46). What does this paradox reveal about the Lord?

Applying the Word 1. What guidance does Jesus give for fulfilling our obligations to God and the government? 2. How can these accounts of Jesus in conflict strengthen our faith in him? 3. What do they teach you about handling conflict?

Responding in Prayer Ask for the help you need for whatever conflict you face today.

17 / *Matthew 23*
The King Condemns the Rebels

INFLUENCE IS A powerful force. Those who influence others are able to change minds and to direct actions. The religious leaders in Israel possessed the power of influence. After they decided to oppose Jesus, they tried to lead others to do the same. In Matthew 23 Jesus condemns them point-blank. They should have been the first to enter the kingdom of God because of their knowledge of Scripture and their standing in the Jewish community. Because they refused, Jesus calls them to judgment. This passage exposes the guilt of those who do not practice what they preach.

 Warming Up to God When have you been hurt by inconsistency in the life or teaching of an influential person you respected? Talk to God about any feelings of hurt you still have.

 Read Matthew 23.

23 Then Jesus said to the crowds and to his disciples: ²"The teachers of the law and the Pharisees sit in Moses' seat. ³So you must obey them and do everything they tell you. But do not do what they do, for they do not practice what they preach. ⁴They tie up heavy loads and put them on men's shoulders, but they themselves are not willing to lift a finger to move them.

⁵"Everything they do is done for men to see: They make their phylacteries⁵ wide and the tassels on their garments long; ⁶they love the place of honor at banquets and the most important seats in the synagogues; ⁷they love to be greeted in the marketplaces and to have men call them 'Rabbi.'

⁸"But you are not to be called 'Rabbi,' for you have only one Master and you are all brothers. ⁹And do not call anyone on earth 'father,' for you have one Father, and he is in heaven. ¹⁰Nor are

you to be called 'teacher,' for you have one Teacher, the Christ.ᵗ ¹¹The greatest among you will be your servant. ¹²For whoever exalts himself will be humbled, and whoever humbles himself will be exalted.

¹³"Woe to you, teachers of the law and Pharisees, you hypocrites! You shut the kingdom of heaven in men's faces. You yourselves do not enter, nor will you let those enter who are trying to.ᵘ

¹⁵"Woe to you, teachers of the law and Pharisees, you hypocrites! You travel over land and sea to win a single convert, and when he becomes one, you make him twice as much a son of hell as you are.

¹⁶"Woe to you, blind guides! You say, 'If any-

⁵5 That is, boxes containing Scripture verses, worn on forehead and arm ᵗ10 Or *Messiah* ᵘ13 Some manuscripts *to. ¹⁴Woe to you, teachers of the law and Pharisees, you hypocrites! You devour widows' houses and for a show make lengthy prayers. Therefore you will be punished more severely.*

one swears by the temple, it means nothing; but if anyone swears by the gold of the temple, he is bound by his oath.' ¹⁷You blind fools! Which is greater: the gold, or the temple that makes the gold sacred? ¹⁸You also say, 'If anyone swears by the altar, it means nothing; but if anyone swears by the gift on it, he is bound by his oath.' ¹⁹You blind men! Which is greater: the gift, or the altar that makes the gift sacred? ²⁰Therefore, he who swears by the altar swears by it and by everything on it. ²¹And he who swears by the temple swears by it and by the one who dwells in it. ²²And he who swears by heaven swears by God's throne and by the one who sits on it.

²³"Woe to you, teachers of the law and Pharisees, you hypocrites! You give a tenth of your spices—mint, dill and cummin. But you have neglected the more important matters of the law—justice, mercy and faithfulness. You should have practiced the latter, without neglecting the former. ²⁴You blind guides! You strain out a gnat but swallow a camel.

²⁵"Woe to you, teachers of the law and Pharisees, you hypocrites! You clean the outside of the cup and dish, but inside they are full of greed and self-indulgence. ²⁶Blind Pharisee! First clean the inside of the cup and dish, and then the outside also will be clean.

²⁷"Woe to you, teachers of the law and Pharisees, you hypocrites! You are like whitewashed tombs, which look beautiful on the outside but on the inside are full of dead men's bones and everything unclean. ²⁸In the same way, on the outside you appear to people as righteous but on the inside you are full of hypocrisy and wickedness.

²⁹"Woe to you, teachers of the law and Pharisees, you hypocrites! You build tombs for the prophets and decorate the graves of the righteous. ³⁰And you say, 'If we had lived in the days of our forefathers, we would not have taken part with them in shedding the blood of the prophets.' ³¹So you testify against yourselves that you are the descendants of those who murdered the prophets. ³²Fill up, then, the measure of the sin of your forefathers!

³³"You snakes! You brood of vipers! How will you escape being condemned to hell? ³⁴Therefore I am sending you prophets and wise men and teachers. Some of them you will kill and crucify; others you will flog in your synagogues and pursue from town to town. ³⁵And so upon you will come all the righteous blood that has been shed on earth, from the blood of righteous Abel to the blood of Zechariah son of Berekiah, whom you murdered between the temple and the altar. ³⁶I tell you the truth, all this will come upon this generation.

³⁷"O Jerusalem, Jerusalem, you who kill the prophets and stone those sent to you, how often I have longed to gather your children together, as a hen gathers her chicks under her wings, but you were not willing. ³⁸Look, your house is left to you desolate. ³⁹For I tell you, you will not see me again until you say, 'Blessed is he who comes in the name of the Lord.'ᵛ"

ᵛ39 Psalm 118:26

Discovering the Word 1. What attitude does Jesus teach the people to have toward the religious leaders, and why (vv. 1–4)? 2. Compare the motives of the religious leaders (vv. 5–7) with the motives and attitudes Jesus requires of his followers (vv. 8–12). 3. Jesus pronounces seven woes (judgments) against the teachers of the law and the Pharisees (vv. 13–32). Summarize each one. 4. The entire generation to whom Jesus is speaking is held accountable for the "righteous blood" shed in all previous generations (vv. 33–36). Why do you think they received such a terrible sentence? 5. What responses do you have as you observe Jesus as a judge? 6. In the midst of this overwhelming condemnation, how is the tender compassion of Jesus also evident (vv. 33–39)?

Applying the Word 1. Jesus condemns the religious leaders for confusing inward and outward righteousness (vv. 25–28). In what ways are we inclined to do that today? 2. Where does this point out a place that needs to change in your life?

 Responding in Prayer Ask God to make your Christian life consistent with your beliefs.

18 / *Matthew 24*
The Return of the King

WE ALL WANT to be safe and secure. Yet many things can threaten our security—losing our job, our income, our health, our loved ones. Our ability to handle these threats will depend on the source of our security. Matthew 24 focuses on the destruction of Jerusalem and the return of Christ. The true issue of Christ's return is not the "hows" or "whens" that fascinate us. Rather we must learn to live in the present in light of the future. We must learn the true source of our security.

Warming Up to God   What gives you a sense of security?

Read Matthew 24.

24 Jesus left the temple and was walking away when his disciples came up to him to call his attention to its buildings. ²"Do you see all these things?" he asked. "I tell you the truth, not one stone here will be left on another; every one will be thrown down."

³As Jesus was sitting on the Mount of Olives, the disciples came to him privately. "Tell us," they said, "when will this happen, and what will be the sign of your coming and of the end of the age?"

⁴Jesus answered: "Watch out that no one deceives you. ⁵For many will come in my name, claiming, 'I am the Christ,ʷ' and will deceive many. ⁶You will hear of wars and rumors of wars, but see to it that you are not alarmed. Such things must happen, but the end is still to come. ⁷Nation will rise against nation, and kingdom against kingdom. There will be famines and earthquakes in various places. ⁸All these are the beginning of birth pains.

⁹"Then you will be handed over to be persecuted and put to death, and you will be hated by all nations because of me. ¹⁰At that time many will turn away from the faith and will betray and hate each other, ¹¹and many false prophets will appear and deceive many people. ¹²Because of the increase of wickedness, the love of most will grow cold, ¹³but he who stands firm to the end will be saved. ¹⁴And this gospel of the kingdom will be preached in the whole world as a testimony to all nations, and then the end will come.

¹⁵"So when you see standing in the holy place 'the abomination that causes desolation,'ˣ spoken of through the prophet Daniel—let the reader understand— ¹⁶then let those who are in Judea flee to the mountains. ¹⁷Let no one on the roof of his house go down to take anything out of the house. ¹⁸Let no one in the field go back to get his cloak. ¹⁹How dreadful it will be in those days for pregnant women and nursing mothers! ²⁰Pray that your flight will not take place in winter or on the Sabbath. ²¹For then there will be great distress, unequaled from the beginning of the world until now—and never to be equaled again. ²²If those days had not been cut short, no one would survive, but for the sake of the elect those days will be shortened. ²³At that time if anyone says to you, 'Look, here is the Christ!' or, 'There he is!' do not believe it. ²⁴For false Christs and false prophets will appear and perform great signs and miracles to deceive even the elect—if that were possible. ²⁵See, I have told you ahead of time.

²⁶"So if anyone tells you, 'There he is, out in the desert,' do not go out; or, 'Here he is, in the inner rooms,' do not believe it. ²⁷For as lightning that comes from the east is visible even in the west, so will be the coming of the Son of Man. ²⁸Wherever there is a carcass, there the vultures will gather.

²⁹"Immediately after the distress of those days

" 'the sun will be darkened,
     and the moon will not give its light;
the stars will fall from the sky,
     and the heavenly bodies will be shaken.'ʸ

³⁰"At that time the sign of the Son of Man will appear in the sky, and all the nations of the earth will mourn. They will see the Son of Man coming on the clouds of the sky, with power and great glory. ³¹And he will send his angels with a loud

ʷ5 Or *Messiah*; also in verse 23   ˣ15 Daniel 9:27; 11:31; 12:11
ʸ29 Isaiah 13:10; 34:4

trumpet call, and they will gather his elect from the four winds, from one end of the heavens to the other.

32"Now learn this lesson from the fig tree: As soon as its twigs get tender and its leaves come out, you know that summer is near. 33Even so, when you see all these things, you know that it*z* is near, right at the door. 34I tell you the truth, this generation*a* will certainly not pass away until all these things have happened. 35Heaven and earth will pass away, but my words will never pass away.

36"No one knows about that day or hour, not even the angels in heaven, nor the Son,*b* but only the Father. 37As it was in the days of Noah, so it will be at the coming of the Son of Man. 38For in the days before the flood, people were eating and drinking, marrying and giving in marriage, up to the day Noah entered the ark; 39and they knew nothing about what would happen until the flood came and took them all away. That is how it will be at the coming of the Son of Man. 40Two men will be in the field; one will be taken and the other left. 41Two women will be grinding with a hand mill; one will be taken and the other left.

42"Therefore keep watch, because you do not

know on what day your Lord will come. 43But understand this: If the owner of the house had known at what time of night the thief was coming, he would have kept watch and would not have let his house be broken into. 44So you also must be ready, because the Son of Man will come at an hour when you do not expect him.

45"Who then is the faithful and wise servant, whom the master has put in charge of the servants in his household to give them their food at the proper time? 46It will be good for that servant whose master finds him doing so when he returns. 47I tell you the truth, he will put him in charge of all his possessions. 48But suppose that servant is wicked and says to himself, 'My master is staying away a long time,' 49and he then begins to beat his fellow servants and to eat and drink with drunkards. 50The master of that servant will come on a day when he does not expect him and at an hour he is not aware of. 51He will cut him to pieces and assign him a place with the hypocrites, where there will be weeping and gnashing of teeth.

z33 Or *he*   *a34* Or *race*   *b36* Some manuscripts do not have *nor the Son.*

Discovering the Word 1. Following Jesus' statement about the temple's destruction, the disciples ask two questions (v. 3). Look through chapter 24, briefly noting ways that Jesus answers these questions. 2. Throughout history people have set dates for Christ's return and have been mistaken. What events might deceive the disciples into thinking the end is at hand (vv. 4–8)? 3. Before the end comes, what dangers will believers face, and how are we to handle them (vv. 9–14)? 4. In 167 B.C. Antiochus Epiphanes attacked Jerusalem and set up a pagan altar in the temple—an event that anticipated "the abomination that causes desolation" spoken of by Jesus (v. 15). What occurs in the aftermath of this abomination (vv. 15–22)? 5. How will we be able to distinguish false Christs from the true (vv. 23–31)? 6. How do the parables of the thief and the wise and wicked servants (vv. 42–51) emphasize the importance of living in light of Christ's return?

Applying the Word 1. Few of us have ever faced deadly peril for our faith. What types of pressure do you face for your faith in Christ? 2. In what ways do you have need of greater watchfulness and perseverance?

Responding in Prayer Praise God for giving you an unfailing source of security.

19 / *Matthew 25*
Preparation for the King's Return

ACCOUNTABILITY can be uncomfortable and inconvenient. Our desires and preferences are subject to the demands of another. Most of us would prefer to do things our own way. A rule of thumb in management is that people don't do what you expect; they do what you inspect. Jesus is coming back to inspect our lives. He holds us accountable for how we conduct ourselves in his absence. In Matthew 25 he urges us to prepare for his coming.

 Warming Up to God Have you ever been in a situation where your work did not meet up to standards when it was reviewed or inspected? How did it affect you?

 Read Matthew 25.

25 "At that time the kingdom of heaven will be like ten virgins who took their lamps and went out to meet the bridegroom. ²Five of them were foolish and five were wise. ³The foolish ones took their lamps but did not take any oil with them. ⁴The wise, however, took oil in jars along with their lamps. ⁵The bridegroom was a long time in coming, and they all became drowsy and fell asleep.

⁶"At midnight the cry rang out: 'Here's the bridegroom! Come out to meet him!'

⁷"Then all the virgins woke up and trimmed their lamps. ⁸The foolish ones said to the wise, 'Give us some of your oil; our lamps are going out.'

⁹" 'No,' they replied, 'there may not be enough for both us and you. Instead, go to those who sell oil and buy some for yourselves.'

¹⁰"But while they were on their way to buy the oil, the bridegroom arrived. The virgins who were ready went in with him to the wedding banquet. And the door was shut.

¹¹"Later the others also came. 'Sir! Sir!' they said. 'Open the door for us!'

¹²"But he replied, 'I tell you the truth, I don't know you.'

¹³"Therefore keep watch, because you do not know the day or the hour.

¹⁴"Again, it will be like a man going on a journey, who called his servants and entrusted his property to them. ¹⁵To one he gave five talentsᶜ of money, to another two talents, and to another one talent, each according to his ability. Then he went on his journey. ¹⁶The man who had received the five talents went at once and put his money to work and gained five more. ¹⁷So also, the one with the two talents gained two more. ¹⁸But the man who had received the one talent went off,

dug a hole in the ground and hid his master's money.

¹⁹"After a long time the master of those servants returned and settled accounts with them. ²⁰The man who had received the five talents brought the other five. 'Master,' he said, 'you entrusted me with five talents. See, I have gained five more.'

²¹"His master replied, 'Well done, good and faithful servant! You have been faithful with a few things; I will put you in charge of many things. Come and share your master's happiness!'

²²"The man with the two talents also came. 'Master,' he said, 'you entrusted me with two talents; see, I have gained two more.'

²³"His master replied, 'Well done, good and faithful servant! You have been faithful with a few things; I will put you in charge of many things. Come and share your master's happiness!'

²⁴"Then the man who had received the one talent came. 'Master,' he said, 'I knew that you are a hard man, harvesting where you have not sown and gathering where you have not scattered seed. ²⁵So I was afraid and went out and hid your talent in the ground. See, here is what belongs to you.'

²⁶"His master replied, 'You wicked, lazy servant! So you knew that I harvest where I have not sown and gather where I have not scattered seed? ²⁷Well then, you should have put my money on deposit with the bankers, so that when I returned I would have received it back with interest.

²⁸" 'Take the talent from him and give it to the one who has the ten talents. ²⁹For everyone who has will be given more, and he will have an abundance. Whoever does not have, even what he has will be taken from him. ³⁰And throw that worth-

ᶜ15 A talent was worth more than a thousand dollars.

less servant outside, into the darkness, where there will be weeping and gnashing of teeth.'

³¹"When the Son of Man comes in his glory, and all the angels with him, he will sit on his throne in heavenly glory. ³²All the nations will be gathered before him, and he will separate the people one from another as a shepherd separates the sheep from the goats. ³³He will put the sheep on his right and the goats on his left.

³⁴"Then the King will say to those on his right, 'Come, you who are blessed by my Father; take your inheritance, the kingdom prepared for you since the creation of the world. ³⁵For I was hungry and you gave me something to eat, I was thirsty and you gave me something to drink, I was a stranger and you invited me in, ³⁶I needed clothes and you clothed me, I was sick and you looked after me, I was in prison and you came to visit me.'

³⁷"Then the righteous will answer him, 'Lord, when did we see you hungry and feed you, or thirsty and give you something to drink? ³⁸When did we see you a stranger and invite you in, or needing clothes and clothe you? ³⁹When did we see you sick or in prison and go to visit you?'

⁴⁰"The King will reply, 'I tell you the truth, whatever you did for one of the least of these brothers of mine, you did for me.'

⁴¹"Then he will say to those on his left, 'Depart from me, you who are cursed, into the eternal fire prepared for the devil and his angels. ⁴²For I was hungry and you gave me nothing to eat, I was thirsty and you gave me nothing to drink, ⁴³I was a stranger and you did not invite me in, I needed clothes and you did not clothe me, I was sick and in prison and you did not look after me.'

⁴⁴"They also will answer, 'Lord, when did we see you hungry or thirsty or a stranger or needing clothes or sick or in prison, and did not help you?'

⁴⁵"He will reply, 'I tell you the truth, whatever you did not do for one of the least of these, you did not do for me.'

⁴⁶"Then they will go away to eternal punishment, but the righteous to eternal life."

Discovering the Word 1. How does the parable of the ten virgins illustrate the need to prepare for the groom's delayed return (vv. 1–13)? 2. A talent was a vast sum of money. In the parable of the talents, what were the master's expectations of his servants (vv. 14–30)? 3. How does the master demonstrate his approval or disapproval? 4. In the parable of the sheep and the goats, identify the King, the sheep, the goats and the "brothers" of the King (vv. 31–46). 5. What criteria does the King use to separate the sheep from the goats? 6. According to Jesus' teaching in this chapter, what should we be doing until he returns?

Applying the Word 1. What resources and responsibilities has Jesus given you? 2. How can you handle them in a good and faithful manner? 3. How should the material in this chapter affect your current priorities?

Responding in Prayer Ask God to show you how to serve him.

---

20 / *Matthew 26*
The Betrayal of the King

ON THE DRIZZLY day of October 16, 1555, Hugh Latimer and Nicholas Ridley, two influential English reformers, were tied to the stake and bundles of sticks were piled at their feet. The crowd strained to hear what the two men were saying. Would they recant or would they persist in dying as heretics? As the executioner pushed a torch into the wood, Latimer said, "Be of good comfort, Master Ridley, and play the man; we shall this day light such a candle, by God's grace, in England, as I trust shall never be put out." Suffering and temptation reveal the quality of our discipleship. Nowhere is this more evident than in Matthew 26, as we move into the climax of the book.

Warming Up to God Have you ever been tempted to stop following Christ? Explain.

📖 **Read Matthew 26.**

26 When Jesus had finished saying all these things, he said to his disciples, ²"As you know, the Passover is two days away—and the Son of Man will be handed over to be crucified."

³Then the chief priests and the elders of the people assembled in the palace of the high priest, whose name was Caiaphas, ⁴and they plotted to arrest Jesus in some sly way and kill him. ⁵"But not during the Feast," they said, "or there may be a riot among the people."

⁶While Jesus was in Bethany in the home of a man known as Simon the Leper, ⁷a woman came to him with an alabaster jar of very expensive perfume, which she poured on his head as he was reclining at the table.

⁸When the disciples saw this, they were indignant. "Why this waste?" they asked. ⁹"This perfume could have been sold at a high price and the money given to the poor."

¹⁰Aware of this, Jesus said to them, "Why are you bothering this woman? She has done a beautiful thing to me. ¹¹The poor you will always have with you, but you will not always have me. ¹²When she poured this perfume on my body, she did it to prepare me for burial. ¹³I tell you the truth, wherever this gospel is preached throughout the world, what she has done will also be told, in memory of her."

¹⁴Then one of the Twelve—the one called Judas Iscariot—went to the chief priests ¹⁵and asked, "What are you willing to give me if I hand him over to you?" So they counted out for him thirty silver coins. ¹⁶From then on Judas watched for an opportunity to hand him over.

¹⁷On the first day of the Feast of Unleavened Bread, the disciples came to Jesus and asked, "Where do you want us to make preparations for you to eat the Passover?"

¹⁸He replied, "Go into the city to a certain man and tell him, 'The Teacher says: My appointed time is near. I am going to celebrate the Passover with my disciples at your house.' " ¹⁹So the disciples did as Jesus had directed them and prepared the Passover.

²⁰When evening came, Jesus was reclining at the table with the Twelve. ²¹And while they were eating, he said, "I tell you the truth, one of you will betray me."

²²They were very sad and began to say to him one after the other, "Surely not I, Lord?"

²³Jesus replied, "The one who has dipped his hand into the bowl with me will betray me. ²⁴The Son of Man will go just as it is written about him. But woe to that man who betrays the Son of Man! It would be better for him if he had not been born."

²⁵Then Judas, the one who would betray him, said, "Surely not I, Rabbi?"

Jesus answered, "Yes, it is you."ᵈ

²⁶While they were eating, Jesus took bread, gave thanks and broke it, and gave it to his disciples, saying, "Take and eat; this is my body."

²⁷Then he took the cup, gave thanks and offered it to them, saying, "Drink from it, all of you. ²⁸This is my blood of theᵉ covenant, which is poured out for many for the forgiveness of sins. ²⁹I tell you, I will not drink of this fruit of the vine from now on until that day when I drink it anew with you in my Father's kingdom."

³⁰When they had sung a hymn, they went out to the Mount of Olives.

³¹Then Jesus told them, "This very night you will all fall away on account of me, for it is written:

> " 'I will strike the shepherd,
>   and the sheep of the flock will be
>   scattered.'ᶠ

³²But after I have risen, I will go ahead of you into Galilee."

³³Peter replied, "Even if all fall away on account of you, I never will."

³⁴"I tell you the truth," Jesus answered, "this very night, before the rooster crows, you will disown me three times."

³⁵But Peter declared, "Even if I have to die with you, I will never disown you." And all the other disciples said the same.

³⁶Then Jesus went with his disciples to a place called Gethsemane, and he said to them, "Sit here while I go over there and pray." ³⁷He took Peter and the two sons of Zebedee along with him, and he began to be sorrowful and troubled. ³⁸Then he said to them, "My soul is overwhelmed with sor-

ᵈ25 Or "You yourself have said it"   ᵉ28 Some manuscripts the new
ᶠ31 Zech. 13:7

row to the point of death. Stay here and keep watch with me."

³⁹Going a little farther, he fell with his face to the ground and prayed, "My Father, if it is possible, may this cup be taken from me. Yet not as I will, but as you will."

⁴⁰Then he returned to his disciples and found them sleeping. "Could you men not keep watch with me for one hour?" he asked Peter. ⁴¹"Watch and pray so that you will not fall into temptation. The spirit is willing, but the body is weak."

⁴²He went away a second time and prayed, "My Father, if it is not possible for this cup to be taken away unless I drink it, may your will be done."

⁴³When he came back, he again found them sleeping, because their eyes were heavy. ⁴⁴So he left them and went away once more and prayed the third time, saying the same thing.

⁴⁵Then he returned to the disciples and said to them, "Are you still sleeping and resting? Look, the hour is near, and the Son of Man is betrayed into the hands of sinners. ⁴⁶Rise, let us go! Here comes my betrayer!"

⁴⁷While he was still speaking, Judas, one of the Twelve, arrived. With him was a large crowd armed with swords and clubs, sent from the chief priests and the elders of the people. ⁴⁸Now the betrayer had arranged a signal with them: "The one I kiss is the man; arrest him." ⁴⁹Going at once to Jesus, Judas said, "Greetings, Rabbi!" and kissed him.

⁵⁰Jesus replied, "Friend, do what you came for."ᵍ

Then the men stepped forward, seized Jesus and arrested him. ⁵¹With that, one of Jesus' companions reached for his sword, drew it out and struck the servant of the high priest, cutting off his ear.

⁵²"Put your sword back in its place," Jesus said to him, "for all who draw the sword will die by the sword. ⁵³Do you think I cannot call on my Father, and he will at once put at my disposal more than twelve legions of angels? ⁵⁴But how then would the Scriptures be fulfilled that say it must happen in this way?"

⁵⁵At that time Jesus said to the crowd, "Am I leading a rebellion, that you have come out with swords and clubs to capture me? Every day I sat in the temple courts teaching, and you did not arrest me. ⁵⁶But this has all taken place that the writings of the prophets might be fulfilled." Then all the disciples deserted him and fled.

⁵⁷Those who had arrested Jesus took him to Caiaphas, the high priest, where the teachers of the law and the elders had assembled. ⁵⁸But Peter followed him at a distance, right up to the courtyard of the high priest. He entered and sat down with the guards to see the outcome.

⁵⁹The chief priests and the whole Sanhedrin were looking for false evidence against Jesus so that they could put him to death. ⁶⁰But they did not find any, though many false witnesses came forward.

Finally two came forward ⁶¹and declared, "This fellow said, 'I am able to destroy the temple of God and rebuild it in three days.' "

⁶²Then the high priest stood up and said to Jesus, "Are you not going to answer? What is this testimony that these men are bringing against you?" ⁶³But Jesus remained silent.

The high priest said to him, "I charge you under oath by the living God: Tell us if you are the Christ,ʰ the Son of God."

⁶⁴"Yes, it is as you say," Jesus replied. "But I say to all of you: In the future you will see the Son of Man sitting at the right hand of the Mighty One and coming on the clouds of heaven."

⁶⁵Then the high priest tore his clothes and said, "He has spoken blasphemy! Why do we need any more witnesses? Look, now you have heard the blasphemy. ⁶⁶What do you think?"

"He is worthy of death," they answered.

⁶⁷Then they spit in his face and struck him with their fists. Others slapped him ⁶⁸and said, "Prophesy to us, Christ. Who hit you?"

⁶⁹Now Peter was sitting out in the courtyard, and a servant girl came to him. "You also were with Jesus of Galilee," she said.

⁷⁰But he denied it before them all. "I don't know what you're talking about," he said.

⁷¹Then he went out to the gateway, where another girl saw him and said to the people there, "This fellow was with Jesus of Nazareth."

⁷²He denied it again, with an oath: "I don't know the man!"

⁷³After a little while, those standing there went up to Peter and said, "Surely you are one of them, for your accent gives you away."

⁷⁴Then he began to call down curses on himself and he swore to them, "I don't know the man!"

Immediately a rooster crowed. ⁷⁵Then Peter remembered the word Jesus had spoken: "Before the rooster crows, you will disown me three times." And he went outside and wept bitterly.

ᵍ50 Or "Friend, why have you come?"   ʰ63 Or Messiah; also in verse 68

Discovering the Word 1. How do verses 1–16 set the stage for Jesus' betrayal and death? 2. In verses 17–30 Jesus celebrates the Passover with his disciples. How is this occasion both ominous and hopeful? 3. What insights can we gain about Jesus during his time in Gethsemane (vv. 36–45)? 4. Jesus' betrayal comes at the hand of one of his own disciples (vv. 47–50). As you look over the role of Judas in this chapter, why do you think the religious leaders used him? 5. Why do you think Jesus remained silent during the first part of his trial (vv. 57–63)? 6. In answer to the high priest's question (v. 63), Jesus declares that he is the Christ (alluding to Dan 7:13–14). Describe the immediate—and ultimate—impact of Jesus' words on those present (vv. 65–68).

Applying the Word 1. When have you been confronted with the weakness of your commitment to the Lord? 2. Both Jesus and the disciples faced temptation in this chapter. How can Jesus' example and the disciples' failures help us withstand temptation and testing?

Responding in Prayer Ask God to give you the courage to claim allegiance to Christ.

---

21 / *Matthew 27*
The Crucifixion of the King

MY GOD, MY God, why have you forsaken me?
Why are you so far from saving me, so far from the words of my groaning?
O my God, I cry out by day, but you do not answer, by night, and am not silent. (Ps 22:1–2)
Do you ever feel that God is absent when you need him most? You pray but receive no answer. You cry but no one seems to care. As Pilate and the religious leaders condemn, mock and crucify God's Son, God himself seems strangely absent. Those who trust in the midst of roaring silence will in the end discover that God was there all along.

 Warming Up to God When have you felt as though God were absent when you needed him? Talk to God about how you felt.

 Read Matthew 27.

---

27 Early in the morning, all the chief priests and the elders of the people came to the decision to put Jesus to death. ²They bound him, led him away and handed him over to Pilate, the governor.

³When Judas, who had betrayed him, saw that Jesus was condemned, he was seized with remorse and returned the thirty silver coins to the chief priests and the elders. ⁴"I have sinned," he said, "for I have betrayed innocent blood."

"What is that to us?" they replied. "That's your responsibility."

⁵So Judas threw the money into the temple and left. Then he went away and hanged himself.

⁶The chief priests picked up the coins and said, "It is against the law to put this into the treasury, since it is blood money." ⁷So they decided to use the money to buy the potter's field as a burial place for foreigners. ⁸That is why it has been called the Field of Blood to this day. ⁹Then what was spoken by Jeremiah the prophet was fulfilled: "They took the thirty silver coins, the price set on him by the people of Israel, ¹⁰and they used them to buy the potter's field, as the Lord commanded me."ⁱ

¹¹Meanwhile Jesus stood before the governor, and the governor asked him, "Are you the king of the Jews?"

"Yes, it is as you say," Jesus replied.

¹²When he was accused by the chief priests and the elders, he gave no answer. ¹³Then Pilate asked him, "Don't you hear the testimony they are bringing against you?" ¹⁴But Jesus made no reply,

ⁱ10 See Zech. 11:12,13; Jer. 19:1-13; 32:6-9.

not even to a single charge—to the great amazement of the governor.

¹⁵Now it was the governor's custom at the Feast to release a prisoner chosen by the crowd. ¹⁶At that time they had a notorious prisoner, called Barabbas. ¹⁷So when the crowd had gathered, Pilate asked them, "Which one do you want me to release to you: Barabbas, or Jesus who is called Christ?" ¹⁸For he knew it was out of envy that they had handed Jesus over to him.

¹⁹While Pilate was sitting on the judge's seat, his wife sent him this message: "Don't have anything to do with that innocent man, for I have suffered a great deal today in a dream because of him."

²⁰But the chief priests and the elders persuaded the crowd to ask for Barabbas and to have Jesus executed.

²¹"Which of the two do you want me to release to you?" asked the governor.

"Barabbas," they answered.

²²"What shall I do, then, with Jesus who is called Christ?" Pilate asked.

They all answered, "Crucify him!"

²³"Why? What crime has he committed?" asked Pilate.

But they shouted all the louder, "Crucify him!"

²⁴When Pilate saw that he was getting nowhere, but that instead an uproar was starting, he took water and washed his hands in front of the crowd. "I am innocent of this man's blood," he said. "It is your responsibility!"

²⁵All the people answered, "Let his blood be on us and on our children!"

²⁶Then he released Barabbas to them. But he had Jesus flogged, and handed him over to be crucified.

²⁷Then the governor's soldiers took Jesus into the Praetorium and gathered the whole company of soldiers around him. ²⁸They stripped him and put a scarlet robe on him, ²⁹and then twisted together a crown of thorns and set it on his head. They put a staff in his right hand and knelt in front of him and mocked him. "Hail, king of the Jews!" they said. ³⁰They spit on him, and took the staff and struck him on the head again and again. ³¹After they had mocked him, they took off the robe and put his own clothes on him. Then they led him away to crucify him.

³²As they were going out, they met a man from Cyrene, named Simon, and they forced him to carry the cross. ³³They came to a place called Gol-

gotha (which means The Place of the Skull). ³⁴There they offered Jesus wine to drink, mixed with gall; but after tasting it, he refused to drink it. ³⁵When they had crucified him, they divided up his clothes by casting lots.ʲ ³⁶And sitting down, they kept watch over him there. ³⁷Above his head they placed the written charge against him: THIS IS JESUS, THE KING OF THE JEWS. ³⁸Two robbers were crucified with him, one on his right and one on his left. ³⁹Those who passed by hurled insults at him, shaking their heads ⁴⁰and saying, "You who are going to destroy the temple and build it in three days, save yourself! Come down from the cross, if you are the Son of God!"

⁴¹In the same way the chief priests, the teachers of the law and the elders mocked him. ⁴²"He saved others," they said, "but he can't save himself! He's the King of Israel! Let him come down now from the cross, and we will believe in him. ⁴³He trusts in God. Let God rescue him now if he wants him, for he said, 'I am the Son of God.'" ⁴⁴In the same way the robbers who were crucified with him also heaped insults on him.

⁴⁵From the sixth hour until the ninth hour darkness came over all the land. ⁴⁶About the ninth hour Jesus cried out in a loud voice, *"Eloi, Eloi,ᵏ lama sabachthani?"*—which means, "My God, my God, why have you forsaken me?"ˡ

⁴⁷When some of those standing there heard this, they said, "He's calling Elijah."

⁴⁸Immediately one of them ran and got a sponge. He filled it with wine vinegar, put it on a stick, and offered it to Jesus to drink. ⁴⁹The rest said, "Now leave him alone. Let's see if Elijah comes to save him."

⁵⁰And when Jesus had cried out again in a loud voice, he gave up his spirit.

⁵¹At that moment the curtain of the temple was torn in two from top to bottom. The earth shook and the rocks split. ⁵²The tombs broke open and the bodies of many holy people who had died were raised to life. ⁵³They came out of the tombs, and after Jesus' resurrection they went into the holy city and appeared to many people.

⁵⁴When the centurion and those with him who were guarding Jesus saw the earthquake and all that had happened, they were terrified, and exclaimed, "Surely he was the Sonᵐ of God!"

⁵⁵Many women were there, watching from a

ʲ35 A few late manuscripts *lots that the word spoken by the prophet might be fulfilled: "They divided my garments among themselves and cast lots for my clothing"* (Psalm 22:18)   ᵏ46 Some manuscripts *Eli, Eli*   ˡ46 Psalm 22:1   ᵐ54 Or *a son*

distance. They had followed Jesus from Galilee to care for his needs. ⁵⁶Among them were Mary Magdalene, Mary the mother of James and Joses, and the mother of Zebedee's sons.

⁵⁷As evening approached, there came a rich man from Arimathea, named Joseph, who had himself become a disciple of Jesus. ⁵⁸Going to Pilate, he asked for Jesus' body, and Pilate ordered that it be given to him. ⁵⁹Joseph took the body, wrapped it in a clean linen cloth, ⁶⁰and placed it in his own new tomb that he had cut out of the rock. He rolled a big stone in front of the entrance to the tomb and went away. ⁶¹Mary Magdalene and the other Mary were sitting there opposite the tomb.

⁶²The next day, the one after Preparation Day, the chief priests and the Pharisees went to Pilate. ⁶³"Sir," they said, "we remember that while he was still alive that deceiver said, 'After three days I will rise again.' ⁶⁴So give the order for the tomb to be made secure until the third day. Otherwise, his disciples may come and steal the body and tell the people that he has been raised from the dead. This last deception will be worse than the first."

⁶⁵"Take a guard," Pilate answered. "Go, make the tomb as secure as you know how." ⁶⁶So they went and made the tomb secure by putting a seal on the stone and posting the guard.

Discovering the Word 1. After the religious leaders hand Jesus over to Pilate, Judas feels remorse (vv. 1–5). How is remorse different from repentance? 2. Jesus stands before Pilate in verses 11–26. How and why does Pilate seek to avoid sentencing Jesus? 3. The soldiers viciously mock Jesus in verses 27–31. What does their mockery reveal about their knowledge of Jesus? 4. As Jesus hangs on the cross, he is repeatedly mocked and insulted (vv. 32–44). How do these insults reveal the spiritual choices these people have made? 5. As death begins to engulf him, Jesus cries out to God (vv. 45–46). What does his cry, and the overshadowing darkness, reveal about his relationship to the Father during this torment? 6. Observe the role Jesus' followers play during the events of his crucifixion and burial (vv. 55–61). How do you think they felt?

Applying the Word 1. This chapter is filled with irony. Satan's "triumph" is actually his defeat. Christ's "defeat" is actually his triumph. How should this challenge our views about the way God works in our lives?

Responding in Prayer Pray for protection so that you won't succumb to social pressure.

---

22 / *Matthew 28*
The Resurrection of the King

VICTORY REQUIRES PROCLAMATION! Once a battle has been won, it's time to spread the word. Matthew 28 focuses on the messengers of Jesus' resurrection—the angel tells the women, the women tell the disciples, the disciples tell the nations, even the guards tell the religious leaders. As Matthew concludes his Gospel, we are invited to join with those who throughout history have been witnesses and messengers of Jesus, the victorious resurrected Lord.

Warming Up to God To prepare for this study, recall the joy of an Easter celebration you have experienced. What elements made that joyful for you?

Read Matthew 28.

---

28 After the Sabbath, at dawn on the first day of the week, Mary Magdalene and the other Mary went to look at the tomb.

²There was a violent earthquake, for an angel of the Lord came down from heaven and, going to the tomb, rolled back the stone and sat on it. ³His appearance was like lightning, and his clothes were white as snow. ⁴The guards were so afraid of him that they shook and became like dead men.

⁵The angel said to the women, "Do not be afraid, for I know that you are looking for Jesus, who was crucified. ⁶He is not here; he has risen, just as he said. Come and see the place where he lay. ⁷Then go quickly and tell his disciples: 'He has risen from the dead and is going ahead of you into Galilee. There you will see him.' Now I have told you."

⁸So the women hurried away from the tomb, afraid yet filled with joy, and ran to tell his disciples. ⁹Suddenly Jesus met them. "Greetings," he said. They came to him, clasped his feet and worshiped him. ¹⁰Then Jesus said to them, "Do not be afraid. Go and tell my brothers to go to Galilee; there they will see me."

¹¹While the women were on their way, some of the guards went into the city and reported to the chief priests everything that had happened. ¹²When the chief priests had met with the elders and devised a plan, they gave the soldiers a large sum of money, ¹³telling them, "You are to say, 'His disciples came during the night and stole him away while we were asleep.' ¹⁴If this report gets to the governor, we will satisfy him and keep you out of trouble." ¹⁵So the soldiers took the money and did as they were instructed. And this story has been widely circulated among the Jews to this very day.

¹⁶Then the eleven disciples went to Galilee, to the mountain where Jesus had told them to go. ¹⁷When they saw him, they worshiped him; but some doubted. ¹⁸Then Jesus came to them and said, "All authority in heaven and on earth has been given to me. ¹⁹Therefore go and make disciples of all nations, baptizing them in[n] the name of the Father and of the Son and of the Holy Spirit, ²⁰and teaching them to obey everything I have commanded you. And surely I am with you always, to the very end of the age."

[n] 19 Or into; see Acts 8:16; 19:5; Romans 6:3; 1 Cor. 1:13; 10:2 and Gal. 3:27.

Discovering the Word 1. The angel is the first messenger of the resurrection (vv. 2–7). What is the significance of his appearance and words? 2. Consider the mission of the women (vv. 1–9). How does it undergo a radical change? 3. The Roman guard and the Jewish leaders are confronted with a miracle. How do they respond, and why? 4. The disciples go to Galilee where they meet with Jesus. Describe the commission he gives to them and us (vv. 16–20). 5. How does Jesus equip them and future disciples to carry out his commission?

Applying the Word 1. What keeps people today from believing that Jesus is the resurrected Lord? 2. As you conclude this study of Matthew, how can you be more involved in making disciples and fulfilling the Great Commission?

 Responding in Prayer Pray that God will help you to be faithful to this task.

Mark

F ew Americans put much stock in royalty. We have been raised to treasure the spirit of democracy. But democracy, at least on any large scale, is a recent development in human history.

People in other eras were most accustomed to kings. For good or evil, kings and emperors left their mark on daily life. Thus when a new king came to power, whether through natural succession or through victory in battle, questions clamored in people's minds. What would the new king be like? Would he be kind and compassionate or selfish and ruthless? Would he use his power to serve his own ends, or would he seek the welfare of all his subjects?

The Jews of Jesus' day, long oppressed by foreign rulers, yearned for a new king—one whom God himself would anoint and use to establish his own rule of justice and peace, not only over Israel but over all the earth. Imagine the excitement as John the Baptist came announcing the coming of the Lord as king and as Jesus himself announced, "The time has come. The kingdom of God is near." Yet as Jesus continued his ministry, he met a growing wave of opposition. Not everyone was pleased with the kind of kingdom he seemed to be announcing or with who he proclaimed himself to be. The religious rulers especially opposed him, but the common people heard him gladly.

New Testament scholars, with few exceptions, agree that Mark's Gospel is the earliest written account of Jesus' life and ministry. Composed between A.D. 60 and 70, it likely served as the basis for the Gospels of Matthew and Luke. Mark himself, though not one of the Twelve, was probably an early convert (Acts 12:12) and a companion to both Peter (1 Pe 5:13) and Paul. Though Mark had an early falling out with Paul (Acts 15:36–41), the two were clearly reconciled later on (Co 4:10; 2Ti 4:11; Phm 24). Thus Mark is linked to two of the most prominent apostles.

More and more, scholars are coming to believe that Mark was not just a collector of stories about Jesus but that he gave form and shape to these stories to counteract some dangerous distortions of the gospel message. Apparently some Christians so focused on Jesus' deity and glorious resurrection that they began to ignore his humanity and suffering. As a result they expected to be spared suffering in this life and to quickly join Jesus in the glories of heaven. You can well imagine how their faith may have been shaken when Nero took to using some of them as torches!

Mark theologically and pastorally sets out to retell the story of Jesus, showing that the kingdom in its glory comes at the end of the path of suffering and service. While Matthew focuses on Jesus as the teacher from whom we should learn (Mt 11:29; 28:20) and John focuses on him as the Son of God in whom we should believe (Jn 20:31), Mark portrays Jesus principally as the servant-king whom we should follow (Mk 1:17). Thus, if we are to enjoy the glories of the kingdom, we too must follow the road of suffering and service.

May the Lord himself increase your understanding of who he is and the life to which he has called you.

Outline

1/ Mark 1:1–15 —————————————— *Gospel Beginnings*

2/ Mark 1:16–39 ————————————— *Four Portraits*

3/ Mark 1:40—2:17 ———————————— *The Clean and the Unclean*

4/ Mark 2:18—3:35 ———————————— *Conflict in Galilee*

5/ Mark 4:1–34 ——————————————— *Kingdom Parables*

6/ Mark 4:35—6:6 ————————————— *Desperate Straits*

7/ Mark 6:6–56 ——————————————— *Beyond Burnout*

8/ Mark 7 —————————————————— *Violating Tradition*

9/ Mark 8:1—9:1 —————————————— *Who Do You Say I Am?*

10/ Mark 9:2–32 ——————————————— *Suffering and Glory*

11/ Mark 9:33–50 ——————————————— *The First and the Last*

12/ Mark 10:1–31 ——————————————— *Divorce, Children and Eternal Life*

13/ Mark 10:32–52 —————————————— *Blindness and Sight*

14/ Mark 11:1–25 ——————————————— *Palm Sunday*

15/ Mark 11:27—12:27 ————————————— *Tempting Questions*

16/ Mark 12:28–44 —————————————— *An End to Questions*

17/ Mark 13 ————————————————— *Keep Watch*

18/ Mark 14:1–42 ——————————————— *The Betrayer Approaches*

19/ Mark 14:43–72 —————————————— *Betrayed!*

20/ Mark 15:1—16:8 ————————————— *Victory Snatched from Defeat*

1 / *Mark 1:1–15*
Gospel Beginnings

DO YOU HAVE any friends who begin mystery novels at the back? Like endings, beginnings tell us a lot. In them writers set the context for what is to come and often drop hints which later prove to be important. The beginning of Mark's Gospel is no exception. This passage introduces several important themes which will be developed in the following chapters.

 Warming Up to God What does it mean to you that Jesus is King? What images and feelings does that bring to mind? Meditate on Jesus as King for a while in preparation for reading Mark's Gospel.

 Read Mark 1:1–15.

1 The beginning of the gospel about Jesus Christ, the Son of God.*

²It is written in Isaiah the prophet:

"I will send my messenger ahead of you,
who will prepare your way"*b*—
³"a voice of one calling in the desert,
'Prepare the way for the Lord,
make straight paths for him.' "*c*

⁴And so John came, baptizing in the desert region and preaching a baptism of repentance for the forgiveness of sins. ⁵The whole Judean countryside and all the people of Jerusalem went out to him. Confessing their sins, they were baptized by him in the Jordan River. ⁶John wore clothing made of camel's hair, with a leather belt around his waist, and he ate locusts and wild honey. ⁷And this was his message: "After me will come one more powerful than I, the thongs of whose sandals I am not worthy to stoop down and untie. ⁸I baptize you with*d* water, but he will baptize you with the Holy Spirit."

⁹At that time Jesus came from Nazareth in Galilee and was baptized by John in the Jordan. ¹⁰As Jesus was coming up out of the water, he saw heaven being torn open and the Spirit descending on him like a dove. ¹¹And a voice came from heaven: "You are my Son, whom I love; with you I am well pleased."

¹²At once the Spirit sent him out into the desert, ¹³and he was in the desert forty days, being tempted by Satan. He was with the wild animals, and angels attended him.

¹⁴After John was put in prison, Jesus went into Galilee, proclaiming the good news of God. ¹⁵"The time has come," he said. "The kingdom of God is near. Repent and believe the good news!"

a1 Some manuscripts do not have *the Son of God.* *b2* Mal. 3:1 *c3* Isaiah 40:3 *d8* Or *in*

 Discovering the Word 1. Verses 2 and 3 combine quotations from Malachi and Isaiah. What do these two quotations have in common? 2. How does John's ministry prepare the way for Jesus? 3. How does John emphasize the greatness of the one who will come after him (vv. 7–8)? 4. Despite his greatness, Jesus came to John for baptism. What does this tell us about Jesus' relationship to us? 5. How do the events surrounding Jesus' baptism prepare him for his temptation in the desert? 6. How does Jesus summarize his mission at the beginning of his ministry?

 Applying the Word 1. What temptations are you currently struggling with? 2. What encouragement do you find here for facing your own temptations?

Responding in Prayer Ask God to help you find the encouragement and strength you need to face temptation.

2 / *Mark 1:16–39*
Four Portraits

WE ALL LIVE with authority—whether supervisors, professors, parents or police. And depending on how that authority is exercised, we feel either put upon, trapped and used, or we feel secure, free and useful.

In 1:1–15 Mark has told us that Jesus has come as king to fulfill the Old Testament longings for the Lord's rule over all the earth. But what kind of king is he? Mark, it seems, knows that a picture is worth a thousand words. So, rather than offering an abstract character analysis, he paints four verbal portraits of Jesus in action.

Warming Up to God In this passage we see Jesus going to a solitary place to pray after a busy day of ministry. But even here he is interrupted with more needs. When have you been in that kind of situation? Ask God to help you balance your need to be with him with the needs of others.

Read Mark 1:16–39.

---

¹⁶As Jesus walked beside the Sea of Galilee, he saw Simon and his brother Andrew casting a net into the lake, for they were fishermen. ¹⁷"Come, follow me," Jesus said, "and I will make you fishers of men." ¹⁸At once they left their nets and followed him.

¹⁹When he had gone a little farther, he saw James son of Zebedee and his brother John in a boat, preparing their nets. ²⁰Without delay he called them, and they left their father Zebedee in the boat with the hired men and followed him.

²¹They went to Capernaum, and when the Sabbath came, Jesus went into the synagogue and began to teach. ²²The people were amazed at his teaching, because he taught them as one who had authority, not as the teachers of the law. ²³Just then a man in their synagogue who was possessed by an evil*ᵉ* spirit cried out, ²⁴"What do you want with us, Jesus of Nazareth? Have you come to destroy us? I know who you are—the Holy One of God!"

²⁵"Be quiet!" said Jesus sternly. "Come out of him!" ²⁶The evil spirit shook the man violently and came out of him with a shriek.

²⁷The people were all so amazed that they asked each other, "What is this? A new teaching—and with authority! He even gives orders to evil spirits and they obey him." ²⁸News about him spread quickly over the whole region of Galilee.

²⁹As soon as they left the synagogue, they went with James and John to the home of Simon and Andrew. ³⁰Simon's mother-in-law was in bed with a fever, and they told Jesus about her. ³¹So he went to her, took her hand and helped her up. The fever left her and she began to wait on them.

³²That evening after sunset the people brought to Jesus all the sick and demon-possessed. ³³The whole town gathered at the door, ³⁴and Jesus healed many who had various diseases. He also drove out many demons, but he would not let the demons speak because they knew who he was.

³⁵Very early in the morning, while it was still dark, Jesus got up, left the house and went off to a solitary place, where he prayed. ³⁶Simon and his companions went to look for him, ³⁷and when they found him, they exclaimed: "Everyone is looking for you!"

³⁸Jesus replied, "Let us go somewhere else—to the nearby villages—so I can preach there also. That is why I have come." ³⁹So he traveled throughout Galilee, preaching in their synagogues and driving out demons.

ᵉ23 Greek unclean; also in verses 26 and 27

Discovering the Word 1. What different factors contributed to the ready response of Simon, Andrew, James and John to Jesus' invitation (vv. 16–20)? (Don't forget 1:1–15!) 2. What might be some of the reasons that Jesus silences the demon about who he is (vv. 21–28)? 3. What impression of Jesus do you get from the portrait of his visit to the home of Simon and Andrew (vv. 29–34)? 4. Thus far we have looked at three portraits of Jesus. What aspects of Jesus' character do we see in them? 5. How does Jesus exercise his authority differently from kings and dictators and other human authorities? 6. The quiet and solitude of verses 35–39 are quite a contrast from the previous events. What do these verses reveal about Jesus' priorities?

Applying the Word   1. How do you respond to Jesus' authority?   2. Jesus' priorities are clear in this passage. What steps do you need to take to bring your priorities more closely in line with his?

 Responding in Prayer   Ask God to help you reevaluate your priorities in light of Jesus' kingship.

3 / *Mark 1:40—2:17*
The Clean and the Unclean

"UNCLEAN! UNCLEAN!" THE man shouted, and everyone scattered to avoid contact with the leper—everyone except Jesus.

The religious wisdom of the day demanded that a holy man keep away from the common people, the "sinners." So Jesus was bound to encounter resistance as he openly welcomed them. This passage focuses on Christ's compassion toward those we normally avoid.

 Warming Up to God   What is it about yourself that you feel is "unclean"? Confess your sins to God and hear him declare you to be clean once again.

 Read Mark 1:40—2:17.

⁴⁰A man with leprosyᶠ came to him and begged him on his knees, "If you are willing, you can make me clean."

⁴¹Filled with compassion, Jesus reached out his hand and touched the man. "I am willing," he said. "Be clean!" ⁴²Immediately the leprosy left him and he was cured.

⁴³Jesus sent him away at once with a strong warning: ⁴⁴"See that you don't tell this to anyone. But go, show yourself to the priest and offer the sacrifices that Moses commanded for your cleansing, as a testimony to them." ⁴⁵Instead he went out and began to talk freely, spreading the news. As a result, Jesus could no longer enter a town openly but stayed outside in lonely places. Yet the people still came to him from everywhere.

2 A few days later, when Jesus again entered Capernaum, the people heard that he had come home. ²So many gathered that there was no room left, not even outside the door, and he preached the word to them. ³Some men came, bringing to him a paralytic, carried by four of them. ⁴Since they could not get him to Jesus because of the crowd, they made an opening in the roof above Jesus and, after digging through it, lowered the mat the paralyzed man was lying on. ⁵When Jesus saw their faith, he said to the paralytic, "Son, your sins are forgiven."

⁶Now some teachers of the law were sitting there, thinking to themselves, ⁷"Why does this fellow talk like that? He's blaspheming! Who can forgive sins but God alone?"

⁸Immediately Jesus knew in his spirit that this was what they were thinking in their hearts, and he said to them, "Why are you thinking these things? ⁹Which is easier: to say to the paralytic, 'Your sins are forgiven,' or to say, 'Get up, take your mat and walk'? ¹⁰But that you may know that the Son of Man has authority on earth to forgive sins . . . ." He said to the paralytic, ¹¹"I tell you, get up, take your mat and go home." ¹²He got up, took his mat and walked out in full view of them all. This amazed everyone and they praised God, saying, "We have never seen anything like this!"

¹³Once again Jesus went out beside the lake. A large crowd came to him, and he began to teach them. ¹⁴As he walked along, he saw Levi son of Alphaeus sitting at the tax collector's booth. "Follow me," Jesus told him, and Levi got up and followed him.

¹⁵While Jesus was having dinner at Levi's house, many tax collectors and "sinners" were eating with him and his disciples, for there were many who followed him. ¹⁶When the teachers of the law who were Pharisees saw him eating with

ᶠ40 The Greek word was used for various diseases affecting the skin—not necessarily leprosy.

the "sinners" and tax collectors, they asked his disciples: "Why does he eat with tax collectors and 'sinners'?"

¹⁷On hearing this, Jesus said to them, "It is not the healthy who need a doctor, but the sick. I have not come to call the righteous, but sinners."

 Discovering the Word 1. Leviticus 13:45–46 states that a leper "must wear torn clothes, let his hair be unkempt, cover the lower part of his face and cry out, 'Unclean! Unclean!' As long as he has the infection he remains unclean. He must live alone; he must live outside the camp." What risks did the leper take in coming to Jesus (1:40–45)? 2. What risks did Jesus take in responding to him as he did? 3. How does Jesus respond to the man's total need? 4. Imagine that you are the paralytic being lowered before Jesus (2:1–12). How do you feel, especially when Jesus announces, "Son, your sins are forgiven"? 5. Contrast the Pharisees' attitude toward tax collectors and "sinners" with that of Jesus.

 Applying the Word 1. Who do you consider to be some of the "unlovely" or "unreachable" for God's kingdom? 2. What steps can you take to bring your thoughts and actions toward them into line with those of Jesus?

 Responding in Prayer Ask Jesus to help you see people as he does and act toward them as he would.

4 / *Mark 2:18—3:35*
Conflict in Galilee

"A TRULY RELIGIOUS person wouldn't do such a thing!"
  "Religion is fine, but you're becoming a fanatic!"
  Such accusations are commonly leveled at Christians. They are difficult to bear under any circumstances. But when they come from family and friends, the pain is even greater. This passage looks at some of the pressures and privileges of following Jesus.

 Warming Up to God In what area of your life are you currently facing pressure or conflict? Ask God to provide you with the strength you need in that situation through his Word and the Holy Spirit.

Read Mark 2:18—3:35.

¹⁸Now John's disciples and the Pharisees were fasting. Some people came and asked Jesus, "How is it that John's disciples and the disciples of the Pharisees are fasting, but yours are not?"

¹⁹Jesus answered, "How can the guests of the bridegroom fast while he is with them? They cannot, so long as they have him with them. ²⁰But the time will come when the bridegroom will be taken from them, and on that day they will fast.

²¹"No one sews a patch of unshrunk cloth on an old garment. If he does, the new piece will pull away from the old, making the tear worse. ²²And no one pours new wine into old wineskins. If he does, the wine will burst the skins, and both the wine and the wineskins will be ruined. No, he pours new wine into new wineskins."

²³One Sabbath Jesus was going through the grainfields, and as his disciples walked along, they began to pick some heads of grain. ²⁴The Pharisees said to him, "Look, why are they doing what is unlawful on the Sabbath?"

²⁵He answered, "Have you never read what David did when he and his companions were hungry and in need? ²⁶In the days of Abiathar the high priest, he entered the house of God and ate the consecrated bread, which is lawful only for priests to eat. And he also gave some to his companions."

²⁷Then he said to them, "The Sabbath was made for man, not man for the Sabbath. ²⁸So the Son of Man is Lord even of the Sabbath."

3 Another time he went into the synagogue, and a man with a shriveled hand was there. ²Some of them were looking for a reason to accuse Jesus, so they watched him closely to see if he would heal him on the Sabbath. ³Jesus said to the man with the shriveled hand, "Stand up in front of everyone."

⁴Then Jesus asked them, "Which is lawful on the Sabbath: to do good or to do evil, to save life or to kill?" But they remained silent.

⁵He looked around at them in anger and, deeply distressed at their stubborn hearts, said to the man, "Stretch out your hand." He stretched it out, and his hand was completely restored. ⁶Then the Pharisees went out and began to plot with the Herodians how they might kill Jesus.

⁷Jesus withdrew with his disciples to the lake, and a large crowd from Galilee followed. ⁸When they heard all he was doing, many people came to him from Judea, Jerusalem, Idumea, and the regions across the Jordan and around Tyre and Sidon. ⁹Because of the crowd he told his disciples to have a small boat ready for him, to keep the people from crowding him. ¹⁰For he had healed many, so that those with diseases were pushing forward to touch him. ¹¹Whenever the evil⁸ spirits saw him, they fell down before him and cried out, "You are the Son of God." ¹²But he gave them strict orders not to tell who he was.

¹³Jesus went up on a mountainside and called to him those he wanted, and they came to him. ¹⁴He appointed twelve—designating them apostles^h—that they might be with him and that he might send them out to preach ¹⁵and to have authority to drive out demons. ¹⁶These are the twelve he appointed: Simon (to whom he gave the name Peter); ¹⁷James son of Zebedee and his brother John (to them he gave the name Boanerges, which means Sons of Thunder); ¹⁸Andrew, Philip, Bartholomew, Matthew, Thomas, James son of Alphaeus, Thaddaeus, Simon the Zealot ¹⁹and Judas Iscariot, who betrayed him.

²⁰Then Jesus entered a house, and again a crowd gathered, so that he and his disciples were not even able to eat. ²¹When his family heard about this, they went to take charge of him, for they said, "He is out of his mind."

²²And the teachers of the law who came down from Jerusalem said, "He is possessed by Beelzebub^i! By the prince of demons he is driving out demons."

²³So Jesus called them and spoke to them in parables: "How can Satan drive out Satan? ²⁴If a kingdom is divided against itself, that kingdom cannot stand. ²⁵If a house is divided against itself, that house cannot stand. ²⁶And if Satan opposes himself and is divided, he cannot stand; his end has come. ²⁷In fact, no one can enter a strong man's house and carry off his possessions unless he first ties up the strong man. Then he can rob his house. ²⁸I tell you the truth, all the sins and blasphemies of men will be forgiven them. ²⁹But whoever blasphemes against the Holy Spirit will never be forgiven; he is guilty of an eternal sin."

³⁰He said this because they were saying, "He has an evil spirit."

³¹Then Jesus' mother and brothers arrived. Standing outside, they sent someone in to call him. ³²A crowd was sitting around him, and they told him, "Your mother and brothers are outside looking for you."

³³"Who are my mother and my brothers?" he asked.

³⁴Then he looked at those seated in a circle around him and said, "Here are my mother and my brothers! ³⁵Whoever does God's will is my brother and sister and mother."

---

g11 Greek unclean; also in verse 30   *h14 Some manuscripts do not have designating them apostles.*   *i22 Greek Beezeboul or Beelzeboul*

Discovering the Word 1. On what grounds are Jesus and his disciples criticized in 2:18—3:6? 2. How are Jesus' and the Pharisees' attitudes toward the Sabbath different? 3. While the Pharisees and the Herodians are plotting to kill Jesus, how are the common people responding to him (3:7–12)? 4. What charge do the teachers of the law bring against Jesus in 3:20–30? 5. How does Jesus refute it?

Applying the Word 1. What types of opposition have you encountered as a Christian? 2. How have you dealt with experiences of opposition? 3. When you are opposed or rejected by those who are closest to you, what comfort can you receive from Jesus' words in verses 33–35?

Responding in Prayer Ask God to give you courage to follow him even when others stand against you.

5 / *Mark 4:1–34*
Kingdom Parables

SOME STORIES WEAR their points on their sleeves, as it were. Others, to borrow from P. G. Wodehouse's definition of a parable, keep something up their sleeves "which suddenly pops up and knocks you flat." Among Jesus' stories we find a variety—from those that are easy to understand to those that are so difficult they invite our thought and reflection again and again. The stories in this passage contain vital information about God's kingdom and its subjects—for those who have ears to hear!

 Warming Up to God What aspect in your life makes it difficult for you to hear the voice of Christ? Talk to Jesus about the barriers you face and ask him to show you how to remove them.

 Read Mark 4:1–34.

4 Again Jesus began to teach by the lake. The crowd that gathered around him was so large that he got into a boat and sat in it out on the lake, while all the people were along the shore at the water's edge. ²He taught them many things by parables, and in his teaching said: ³"Listen! A farmer went out to sow his seed. ⁴As he was scattering the seed, some fell along the path, and the birds came and ate it up. ⁵Some fell on rocky places, where it did not have much soil. It sprang up quickly, because the soil was shallow. ⁶But when the sun came up, the plants were scorched, and they withered because they had no root. ⁷Other seed fell among thorns, which grew up and choked the plants, so that they did not bear grain. ⁸Still other seed fell on good soil. It came up, grew and produced a crop, multiplying thirty, sixty, or even a hundred times."

⁹Then Jesus said, "He who has ears to hear, let him hear."

¹⁰When he was alone, the Twelve and the others around him asked him about the parables. ¹¹He told them, "The secret of the kingdom of God has been given to you. But to those on the outside everything is said in parables ¹²so that,

" 'they may be ever seeing but never
        perceiving,
    and ever hearing but never understanding;
    otherwise they might turn and be
        forgiven!'ʲ"

¹³Then Jesus said to them, "Don't you understand this parable? How then will you understand any parable? ¹⁴The farmer sows the word. ¹⁵Some people are like seed along the path, where the word is sown. As soon as they hear it, Satan comes and takes away the word that was sown in them. ¹⁶Others, like seed sown on rocky places, hear the word and at once receive it with joy. ¹⁷But since they have no root, they last only a short time. When trouble or persecution comes because of the word, they quickly fall away. ¹⁸Still others, like seed sown among thorns, hear the word; ¹⁹but the worries of this life, the deceitfulness of wealth and the desires for other things come in and choke the word, making it unfruitful. ²⁰Others, like seed sown on good soil, hear the word, accept it, and produce a crop—thirty, sixty or even a hundred times what was sown."

²¹He said to them, "Do you bring in a lamp to put it under a bowl or a bed? Instead, don't you put it on its stand? ²²For whatever is hidden is meant to be disclosed, and whatever is concealed is meant to be brought out into the open. ²³If anyone has ears to hear, let him hear."

²⁴"Consider carefully what you hear," he continued. "With the measure you use, it will be measured to you—and even more. ²⁵Whoever has will be given more; whoever does not have, even what he has will be taken from him."

²⁶He also said, "This is what the kingdom of God is like. A man scatters seed on the ground. ²⁷Night and day, whether he sleeps or gets up, the seed sprouts and grows, though he does not know how. ²⁸All by itself the soil produces grain—first the stalk, then the head, then the full kernel in the head. ²⁹As soon as the grain is ripe, he puts the sickle to it, because the harvest has come."

³⁰Again he said, "What shall we say the kingdom of God is like, or what parable shall we use to describe it? ³¹It is like a mustard seed, which is the smallest seed you plant in the ground. ³²Yet

j12 Isaiah 6:9,10

when planted, it grows and becomes the largest of all garden plants, with such big branches that the birds of the air can perch in its shade."

³³With many similar parables Jesus spoke the word to them, as much as they could understand. ³⁴He did not say anything to them without using a parable. But when he was alone with his own disciples, he explained everything.

 Discovering the Word 1. Watch especially for words and phrases that are repeated in verses 1–25. What idea or ideas seem to dominate these verses? 2. Jesus explains the parable of the sower, or the parable of the soils (vv. 3–8), in verses 14–20. Put this explanation in your own words, describing from your own experience examples of each kind of soil-seed combination. 3. On what grounds are people included or excluded from the secret of the kingdom? 4. How do verses 21–25 help explain verses 11–12? 5. What insights into kingdom growth do the parables of the growing seed and the mustard seed give us (vv. 26–34)?

Applying the Word 1. What kind of soil are you? 2. What can you do to become the kind of soil Jesus is looking for? 3. In this passage we see Jesus both spreading the message of the kingdom and teaching about how the kingdom grows. What lessons can we learn about evangelism both from his example and from his teaching?

Responding in Prayer Ask Jesus to work in you to make you receptive soil.

---

6 / *Mark 4:35—6:6*
Desperate Straits

"DON'T BE AFRAID; just believe." These words may ring rather hollow when we, and not someone else, face a fearful or life-threatening situation. Yet in the face of real danger we discover just how much faith we have. In this study we find a number of different people in desperate straits. Their experiences with Jesus can help us to trust him with the fearful areas of our own lives.

 Warming Up to God When do you feel afraid? Reflect on these words from Isaiah 12:2: "Surely God is my salvation; I will trust and not be afraid." Allow God to comfort you.

 Read Mark 4:35—6:6.

---

³⁵That day when evening came, he said to his disciples, "Let us go over to the other side." ³⁶Leaving the crowd behind, they took him along, just as he was, in the boat. There were also other boats with him. ³⁷A furious squall came up, and the waves broke over the boat, so that it was nearly swamped. ³⁸Jesus was in the stern, sleeping on a cushion. The disciples woke him and said to him, "Teacher, don't you care if we drown?"

³⁹He got up, rebuked the wind and said to the waves, "Quiet! Be still!" Then the wind died down and it was completely calm.

⁴⁰He said to his disciples, "Why are you so afraid? Do you still have no faith?"

⁴¹They were terrified and asked each other,

"Who is this? Even the wind and the waves obey him!"

5 They went across the lake to the region of the Gerasenes.ᵏ ²When Jesus got out of the boat, a man with an evilˡ spirit came from the tombs to meet him. ³This man lived in the tombs, and no one could bind him any more, not even with a chain. ⁴For he had often been chained hand and foot, but he tore the chains apart and broke the irons on his feet. No one was strong enough to subdue him. ⁵Night and day among the tombs and in the hills he would cry out and cut himself with stones.

⁶When he saw Jesus from a distance, he ran and fell on his knees in front of him. ⁷He shouted

---

ᵏ1 Some manuscripts *Gadarenes*; other manuscripts *Gergesenes*
ˡ2 Greek *unclean*; also in verses 8 and 13

at the top of his voice, "What do you want with me, Jesus, Son of the Most High God? Swear to God that you won't torture me!" 8For Jesus had said to him, "Come out of this man, you evil spirit!"

9Then Jesus asked him, "What is your name?"

"My name is Legion," he replied, "for we are many." 10And he begged Jesus again and again not to send them out of the area.

11A large herd of pigs was feeding on the nearby hillside. 12The demons begged Jesus, "Send us among the pigs; allow us to go into them." 13He gave them permission, and the evil spirits came out and went into the pigs. The herd, about two thousand in number, rushed down the steep bank into the lake and were drowned.

14Those tending the pigs ran off and reported this in the town and countryside, and the people went out to see what had happened. 15When they came to Jesus, they saw the man who had been possessed by the legion of demons, sitting there, dressed and in his right mind; and they were afraid. 16Those who had seen it told the people what had happened to the demon-possessed man—and told about the pigs as well. 17Then the people began to plead with Jesus to leave their region.

18As Jesus was getting into the boat, the man who had been demon-possessed begged to go with him. 19Jesus did not let him, but said, "Go home to your family and tell them how much the Lord has done for you, and how he has had mercy on you." 20So the man went away and began to tell in the Decapolis*m* how much Jesus had done for him. And all the people were amazed.

21When Jesus had again crossed over by boat to the other side of the lake, a large crowd gathered around him while he was by the lake. 22Then one of the synagogue rulers, named Jairus, came there. Seeing Jesus, he fell at his feet 23and pleaded earnestly with him, "My little daughter is dying. Please come and put your hands on her so that she will be healed and live." 24So Jesus went with him.

A large crowd followed and pressed around him. 25And a woman was there who had been subject to bleeding for twelve years. 26She had suffered a great deal under the care of many doctors and had spent all she had, yet instead of getting better she grew worse. 27When she heard about Jesus, she came up behind him in the crowd and touched his cloak, 28because she

thought, "If I just touch his clothes, I will be healed." 29Immediately her bleeding stopped and she felt in her body that she was freed from her suffering.

30At once Jesus realized that power had gone out from him. He turned around in the crowd and asked, "Who touched my clothes?"

31"You see the people crowding against you," his disciples answered, "and yet you can ask, 'Who touched me?' "

32But Jesus kept looking around to see who had done it. 33Then the woman, knowing what had happened to her, came and fell at his feet and, trembling with fear, told him the whole truth. 34He said to her, "Daughter, your faith has healed you. Go in peace and be freed from your suffering."

35While Jesus was still speaking, some men came from the house of Jairus, the synagogue ruler. "Your daughter is dead," they said. "Why bother the teacher any more?"

36Ignoring what they said, Jesus told the synagogue ruler, "Don't be afraid; just believe."

37He did not let anyone follow him except Peter, James and John the brother of James. 38When they came to the home of the synagogue ruler, Jesus saw a commotion, with people crying and wailing loudly. 39He went in and said to them, "Why all this commotion and wailing? The child is not dead but asleep." 40But they laughed at him.

After he put them all out, he took the child's father and mother and the disciples who were with him, and went in where the child was. 41He took her by the hand and said to her, *"Talitha koum!"* (which means, "Little girl, I say to you, get up!"). 42Immediately the girl stood up and walked around (she was twelve years old). At this they were completely astonished. 43He gave strict orders not to let anyone know about this, and told them to give her something to eat.

6 Jesus left there and went to his hometown, accompanied by his disciples. 2When the Sabbath came, he began to teach in the synagogue, and many who heard him were amazed.

"Where did this man get these things?" they asked. "What's this wisdom that has been given him, that he even does miracles! 3Isn't this the carpenter? Isn't this Mary's son and the brother of

m20 That is, the Ten Cities

James, Joseph,ⁿ Judas and Simon? Aren't his sisters here with us?" And they took offense at him.

⁴Jesus said to them, "Only in his hometown, among his relatives and in his own house is a prophet without honor." ⁵He could not do any

miracles there, except lay his hands on a few sick people and heal them. ⁶And he was amazed at their lack of faith.

ⁿ3 *Greek* Joses, *a variant of* Joseph

Discovering the Word 1. In the first incident the disciples are quite naturally afraid of the storm and disturbed that Jesus seems not to be concerned about their drowning. Once Jesus calms the storm, however, they are still terrified. How does their fear after the storm differ from their previous fears? 2. Who in the next incident is afraid and why (5:1–20)? 3. Many people find it hard to understand why Jesus allowed the demons to destroy the pigs. It could have been to prevent a violent exit from the man or to show him visibly that he was now free. Even if we can't pin down exactly why Jesus allowed this, what does the fate of the pigs show about what the demons were trying to do to the man? 4. In 5:21–43 two stories are woven together—that of Jairus's daughter and the woman with a hemorrhage. What sorts of fears are involved in these two incidents? 5. What are the relationships between fear and faith in each of these incidents?

Applying the Word 1. Fear can be a very powerful emotion. What kinds of fear keep you from doing some things you think you should? 2. What keeps you from turning your fears into faith? 3. How can Jesus' authority as shown here calm your fears and strengthen your faith?

Responding in Prayer Pray for your fears to become increased faith.

---

7 / *Mark 6:6–56*
Beyond Burnout

BURNOUT IS ALL too common an experience among Christians today. One of its most disastrous consequences is a hardened heart that keeps us from being refreshed by our Lord. In this study we see the disciples suffering from burnout and catch a vision of how Jesus can help us to counteract its effects.

Warming Up to God What is pressing on you and taking away your energy? Ask God to refresh your spirit and renew your commitment. Then consider how you could better handle your responsibilities.

Read Mark 6:6–56.

Then Jesus went around teaching from village to village. ⁷Calling the Twelve to him, he sent them out two by two and gave them authority over evilᵒ spirits.

⁸These were his instructions: "Take nothing for the journey except a staff—no bread, no bag, no money in your belts. ⁹Wear sandals but not an extra tunic. ¹⁰Whenever you enter a house, stay there until you leave that town. ¹¹And if any place will not welcome you or listen to you, shake the dust off your feet when you leave, as a testimony against them."

¹²They went out and preached that people should repent. ¹³They drove out many demons

and anointed many sick people with oil and healed them.

¹⁴King Herod heard about this, for Jesus' name had become well known. Some were saying,ᵖ "John the Baptist has been raised from the dead, and that is why miraculous powers are at work in him."

¹⁵Others said, "He is Elijah."

And still others claimed, "He is a prophet, like one of the prophets of long ago."

¹⁶But when Herod heard this, he said, "John, the man I beheaded, has been raised from the dead!"

¹⁷For Herod himself had given orders to have

ᵒ7 *Greek* unclean   ᵖ14 *Some early manuscripts* He was saying

John arrested, and he had him bound and put in prison. He did this because of Herodias, his brother Philip's wife, whom he had married. ¹⁸For John had been saying to Herod, "It is not lawful for you to have your brother's wife." ¹⁹So Herodias nursed a grudge against John and wanted to kill him. But she was not able to, ²⁰because Herod feared John and protected him, knowing him to be a righteous and holy man. When Herod heard John, he was greatly puzzled*q*; yet he liked to listen to him.

²¹Finally the opportune time came. On his birthday Herod gave a banquet for his high officials and military commanders and the leading men of Galilee. ²²When the daughter of Herodias came in and danced, she pleased Herod and his dinner guests.

The king said to the girl, "Ask me for anything you want, and I'll give it to you." ²³And he promised her with an oath, "Whatever you ask I will give you, up to half my kingdom."

²⁴She went out and said to her mother, "What shall I ask for?"

"The head of John the Baptist," she answered.

²⁵At once the girl hurried in to the king with the request: "I want you to give me right now the head of John the Baptist on a platter."

²⁶The king was greatly distressed, but because of his oaths and his dinner guests, he did not want to refuse her. ²⁷So he immediately sent an executioner with orders to bring John's head. The man went, beheaded John in the prison, ²⁸and brought back his head on a platter. He presented it to the girl, and she gave it to her mother. ²⁹On hearing of this, John's disciples came and took his body and laid it in a tomb.

³⁰The apostles gathered around Jesus and reported to him all they had done and taught. ³¹Then, because so many people were coming and going that they did not even have a chance to eat, he said to them, "Come with me by yourselves to a quiet place and get some rest."

³²So they went away by themselves in a boat to a solitary place. ³³But many who saw them leaving recognized them and ran on foot from all the towns and got there ahead of them. ³⁴When Jesus landed and saw a large crowd, he had compassion on them, because they were like sheep without a shepherd. So he began teaching them many things.

³⁵By this time it was late in the day, so his disciples came to him. "This is a remote place," they said, "and it's already very late. ³⁶Send the people away so they can go to the surrounding countryside and villages and buy themselves something to eat."

³⁷But he answered, "You give them something to eat."

They said to him, "That would take eight months of a man's wages*r*! Are we to go and spend that much on bread and give it to them to eat?"

³⁸"How many loaves do you have?" he asked. "Go and see."

When they found out, they said, "Five—and two fish."

³⁹Then Jesus directed them to have all the people sit down in groups on the green grass. ⁴⁰So they sat down in groups of hundreds and fifties. ⁴¹Taking the five loaves and the two fish and looking up to heaven, he gave thanks and broke the loaves. Then he gave them to his disciples to set before the people. He also divided the two fish among them all. ⁴²They all ate and were satisfied, ⁴³and the disciples picked up twelve basketfuls of broken pieces of bread and fish. ⁴⁴The number of the men who had eaten was five thousand.

⁴⁵Immediately Jesus made his disciples get into the boat and go on ahead of him to Bethsaida, while he dismissed the crowd. ⁴⁶After leaving them, he went up on a mountainside to pray.

⁴⁷When evening came, the boat was in the middle of the lake, and he was alone on land. ⁴⁸He saw the disciples straining at the oars, because the wind was against them. About the fourth watch of the night he went out to them, walking on the lake. He was about to pass by them, ⁴⁹but when they saw him walking on the lake, they thought he was a ghost. They cried out, ⁵⁰because they all saw him and were terrified.

Immediately he spoke to them and said, "Take courage! It is I. Don't be afraid." ⁵¹Then he climbed into the boat with them, and the wind died down. They were completely amazed, ⁵²for they had not understood about the loaves; their hearts were hardened.

⁵³When they had crossed over, they landed at Gennesaret and anchored there. ⁵⁴As soon as they got out of the boat, people recognized Jesus. ⁵⁵They ran throughout that whole region and carried the sick on mats to wherever they heard he was. ⁵⁶And wherever he went—into villages,

q20 Some early manuscripts he did many things   r37 Greek take two hundred denarii

towns or countryside—they placed the sick in the marketplaces. They begged him to let them touch

even the edge of his cloak, and all who touched him were healed.

 Discovering the Word 1. What do Jesus' instructions to the Twelve tell us about the kind of ministry they were to have (vv. 6–13)? 2. What kind of man was Herod (vv. 14–29)? 3. This flashback to the execution of John the Baptist interrupts the account of Jesus' sending out the Twelve to preach and heal. Why do you suppose Mark recounts it here? 4. What differences are there between Jesus' approach to the crowd and that of his disciples (vv. 30–44)? 5. Jesus and Herod, the two kings in this passage, both serve banquets. Compare the two.

 Applying the Word 1. When has tiredness blunted your desire to care for others? 2. Recognizing the contributing factors, what steps can you take to counteract burnout and a hardened heart?

Responding in Prayer Ask God to help you to give of yourself while maintaining balance in your life so that you don't burn out.

---

8 / Mark 7
Violating Tradition

ALL OF US are influenced by traditions of one sort or another—even those of us who *by tradition* don't put much stock in them! But at what point do traditions lose their value or even become counterproductive? When do religious practices become a substitute for really obeying God? In this study Jesus has some rather harsh words for the Pharisees and the traditions they choose to observe.

 Warming Up to God Consider your spiritual life. Are there any aspects of your devotional practices that you feel bound to? Consider before God whether you are putting unrealistic expectations on yourself.

 Read Mark 7.

---

7 The Pharisees and some of the teachers of the law who had come from Jerusalem gathered around Jesus and ²saw some of his disciples eating food with hands that were "unclean," that is, unwashed. ³(The Pharisees and all the Jews do not eat unless they give their hands a ceremonial washing, holding to the tradition of the elders. ⁴When they come from the marketplace they do not eat unless they wash. And they observe many other traditions, such as the washing of cups, pitchers and kettles.⁵)

⁵So the Pharisees and teachers of the law asked Jesus, "Why don't your disciples live according to the tradition of the elders instead of eating their food with 'unclean' hands?"

⁶He replied, "Isaiah was right when he prophesied about you hypocrites; as it is written:

" 'These people honor me with their lips,
    but their hearts are far from me.
⁷They worship me in vain;

their teachings are but rules taught by
    men.'ᵗ

⁸You have let go of the commands of God and are holding on to the traditions of men."

⁹And he said to them: "You have a fine way of setting aside the commands of God in order to observeᵘ your own traditions! ¹⁰For Moses said, 'Honor your father and your mother,'ᵛ and, 'Anyone who curses his father or mother must be put to death.'ʷ ¹¹But you say that if a man says to his father or mother: 'Whatever help you might otherwise have received from me is Corban' (that is, a gift devoted to God), ¹²then you no longer let him do anything for his father or mother. ¹³Thus you nullify the word of God by your tradition that you have handed down. And you do many things like that."

¹⁴Again Jesus called the crowd to him and said,

⁴4 Some early manuscripts *pitchers, kettles and dining couches*
ᵗ6,7 Isaiah 29:13   ᵘ9 Some manuscripts *set up*   ᵛ10 Exodus 20:12; Deut. 5:16   ʷ10 Exodus 21:17; Lev. 20:9

"Listen to me, everyone, and understand this. [15]Nothing outside a man can make him 'unclean' by going into him. Rather, it is what comes out of a man that makes him 'unclean.'[x]"

[17]After he had left the crowd and entered the house, his disciples asked him about this parable. [18]"Are you so dull?" he asked. "Don't you see that nothing that enters a man from the outside can make him 'unclean'? [19]For it doesn't go into his heart but into his stomach, and then out of his body." (In saying this, Jesus declared all foods "clean.")

[20]He went on: "What comes out of a man is what makes him 'unclean.' [21]For from within, out of men's hearts, come evil thoughts, sexual immorality, theft, murder, adultery, [22]greed, malice, deceit, lewdness, envy, slander, arrogance and folly. [23]All these evils come from inside and make a man 'unclean.' "

[24]Jesus left that place and went to the vicinity of Tyre.[y] He entered a house and did not want anyone to know it; yet he could not keep his presence secret. [25]In fact, as soon as she heard about him, a woman whose little daughter was possessed by an evil[z] spirit came and fell at his feet. [26]The woman was a Greek, born in Syrian Phoenicia. She begged Jesus to drive the demon out of her daughter.

[27]"First let the children eat all they want," he told her, "for it is not right to take the children's bread and toss it to their dogs."

[28]"Yes, Lord," she replied, "but even the dogs under the table eat the children's crumbs."

[29]Then he told her, "For such a reply, you may go; the demon has left your daughter."

[30]She went home and found her child lying on the bed, and the demon gone.

[31]Then Jesus left the vicinity of Tyre and went through Sidon, down to the Sea of Galilee and into the region of the Decapolis.[a] [32]There some people brought to him a man who was deaf and could hardly talk, and they begged him to place his hand on the man.

[33]After he took him aside, away from the crowd, Jesus put his fingers into the man's ears. Then he spit and touched the man's tongue. [34]He looked up to heaven and with a deep sigh said to him, *"Ephphatha!"* (which means, "Be opened!"). [35]At this, the man's ears were opened, his tongue was loosened and he began to speak plainly.

[36]Jesus commanded them not to tell anyone. But the more he did so, the more they kept talking about it. [37]People were overwhelmed with amazement. "He has done everything well," they said. "He even makes the deaf hear and the mute speak."

[x]15 Some early manuscripts *'unclean.'* [16]*If anyone has ears to hear, let him hear.* [y]24 Many early manuscripts *Tyre and Sidon* [z]25 Greek *unclean* [a]31 That is, the Ten Cities

---

Discovering the Word 1. What are the Pharisees concerned about (vv. 1–5)? 2. What specific complaints does Jesus raise against the Pharisees' approach to tradition (vv. 6–13)? 3. How does Jesus' view of becoming "unclean" differ from that of the Pharisees (vv. 14–23)? 4. Jesus responds to the Syrophoenician woman's request with a miniparable about children, bread and dogs (vv. 24–27). What is he actually saying? 5. What does the woman's response reveal about her? 6. The healing of the deaf man takes place in the Decapolis, where Jesus had exorcised the demons from the Gerasene man at the tombs (5:1–20). How do the events here demonstrate that man's success in telling about what Jesus had done for him (vv. 31–37)?

Applying the Word 1. What religious traditions influence your life? Is that influence good or bad? Explain. 2. What sorts of traditions do we observe today that get in the way of really honoring God? 3. In what ways do you sometimes emphasize appearance over internal reality?

Responding in Prayer Now, as then, those who are spiritually deaf—whether through hardness of heart or through substituting traditions for true obedience—can be healed by Jesus. Pray for yourself and others who need Jesus' healing touch.

9 / *Mark 8:1—9:1*
Who Do You Say I Am?

"WHO DO YOU say I am?" The whole Gospel of Mark so far has been supplying evidence for answering this question. It's a question Jesus asks each of us, and the answer we give ultimately determines our destiny. But our answer involves more than what we say with our lips. Our real answer is to be found in the way we live our lives.

 Warming Up to God What need in your life has God met recently? Spend time praising God and thanking him for meeting your needs.

 Read Mark 8:1—9:1.

8 During those days another large crowd gathered. Since they had nothing to eat, Jesus called his disciples to him and said, ²"I have compassion for these people; they have already been with me three days and have nothing to eat. ³If I send them home hungry, they will collapse on the way, because some of them have come a long distance."

⁴His disciples answered, "But where in this remote place can anyone get enough bread to feed them?"

⁵"How many loaves do you have?" Jesus asked.

"Seven," they replied.

⁶He told the crowd to sit down on the ground. When he had taken the seven loaves and given thanks, he broke them and gave them to his disciples to set before the people, and they did so. ⁷They had a few small fish as well; he gave thanks for them also and told the disciples to distribute them. ⁸The people ate and were satisfied. Afterward the disciples picked up seven basketfuls of broken pieces that were left over. ⁹About four thousand men were present. And having sent them away, ¹⁰he got into the boat with his disciples and went to the region of Dalmanutha.

¹¹The Pharisees came and began to question Jesus. To test him, they asked him for a sign from heaven. ¹²He sighed deeply and said, "Why does this generation ask for a miraculous sign? I tell you the truth, no sign will be given to it." ¹³Then he left them, got back into the boat and crossed to the other side.

¹⁴The disciples had forgotten to bring bread, except for one loaf they had with them in the boat. ¹⁵"Be careful," Jesus warned them. "Watch out for the yeast of the Pharisees and that of Herod."

¹⁶They discussed this with one another and said, "It is because we have no bread."

¹⁷Aware of their discussion, Jesus asked them: "Why are you talking about having no bread? Do you still not see or understand? Are your hearts hardened? ¹⁸Do you have eyes but fail to see, and ears but fail to hear? And don't you remember? ¹⁹When I broke the five loaves for the five thousand, how many basketfuls of pieces did you pick up?"

"Twelve," they replied.

²⁰"And when I broke the seven loaves for the four thousand, how many basketfuls of pieces did you pick up?"

They answered, "Seven."

²¹He said to them, "Do you still not understand?"

²²They came to Bethsaida, and some people brought a blind man and begged Jesus to touch him. ²³He took the blind man by the hand and led him outside the village. When he had spit on the man's eyes and put his hands on him, Jesus asked, "Do you see anything?"

²⁴He looked up and said, "I see people; they look like trees walking around."

²⁵Once more Jesus put his hands on the man's eyes. Then his eyes were opened, his sight was restored, and he saw everything clearly. ²⁶Jesus sent him home, saying, "Don't go into the village.ᵇ"

²⁷Jesus and his disciples went on to the villages around Caesarea Philippi. On the way he asked them, "Who do people say I am?"

²⁸They replied, "Some say John the Baptist; others say Elijah; and still others, one of the prophets."

²⁹"But what about you?" he asked. "Who do you say I am?"

ᵇ26 Some manuscripts *Don't go and tell anyone in the village*

Peter answered, "You are the Christ.ᶜ"

³⁰Jesus warned them not to tell anyone about him.

³¹He then began to teach them that the Son of Man must suffer many things and be rejected by the elders, chief priests and teachers of the law, and that he must be killed and after three days rise again. ³²He spoke plainly about this, and Peter took him aside and began to rebuke him.

³³But when Jesus turned and looked at his disciples, he rebuked Peter. "Get behind me, Satan!" he said. "You do not have in mind the things of God, but the things of men."

³⁴Then he called the crowd to him along with his disciples and said: "If anyone would come after me, he must deny himself and take up his cross and follow me. ³⁵For whoever wants to save his lifeᵈ will lose it, but whoever loses his life for me and for the gospel will save it. ³⁶What good is it for a man to gain the whole world, yet forfeit his soul? ³⁷Or what can a man give in exchange for his soul? ³⁸If anyone is ashamed of me and my words in this adulterous and sinful generation, the Son of Man will be ashamed of him when he comes in his Father's glory with the holy angels."

9 And he said to them, "I tell you the truth, some who are standing here will not taste death before they see the kingdom of God come with power."

ᶜ29 Or Messiah. "The Christ" (Greek) and "the Messiah" (Hebrew) both mean "the Anointed One."   ᵈ35 The Greek word means either life or soul; also in verse 36.

 Discovering the Word 1. Why do you suppose the disciples, having witnessed the feeding of the 5,000, have such a hard time believing Jesus can supply the needs of 4,000 here (8:1–13)? 2. What do the disciples fail to understand in verses 14–21 and why? 3. What unusual thing happens while Jesus is curing the blind man (vv. 22–26)? 4. How is Peter in verses 27–33 like the blind man in verses 22–26? 5. What does Jesus say it means to acknowledge him as the Christ and to follow him?

Applying the Word 1. When have you acted like the disciples in verses 1–13, not expecting God to work just after he has met a need in your life? 2. Is your life characterized more by seeking to lose your life or to save it? Explain. 3. In what way do you need to "lose your life"?

Responding in Prayer Ask Jesus to help you see more clearly those areas where you are not yet following him.

---

10 / *Mark 9:2–32*
Suffering and Glory

IN A FAMOUS short story, the main character is given the choice of opening one of two doors. Behind one is a beautiful maiden; behind the other, a ferocious tiger. It is easy to identify with the hero of the story, hoping for joy rather than suffering, pleasure rather than pain. But what if we cannot have one without the other? This passage examines the relationship between suffering and glory, human weakness and divine power.

 Warming Up to God In this passage God tells the disciples to "listen to" his Son. What does Christ want to say to you today?

 Read Mark 9:2–32.

---

²After six days Jesus took Peter, James and John with him and led them up a high mountain, where they were all alone. There he was transfigured before them. ³His clothes became dazzling white, whiter than anyone in the world could bleach them. ⁴And there appeared before them Elijah and Moses, who were talking with Jesus.

⁵Peter said to Jesus, "Rabbi, it is good for us to be here. Let us put up three shelters—one for you, one for Moses and one for Elijah." ⁶(He did not know what to say, they were so frightened.)

⁷Then a cloud appeared and enveloped them, and a voice came from the cloud: "This is my Son, whom I love. Listen to him!"

8Suddenly, when they looked around, they no longer saw anyone with them except Jesus.

9As they were coming down the mountain, Jesus gave them orders not to tell anyone what they had seen until the Son of Man had risen from the dead. 10They kept the matter to themselves, discussing what "rising from the dead" meant.

11And they asked him, "Why do the teachers of the law say that Elijah must come first?"

12Jesus replied, "To be sure, Elijah does come first, and restores all things. Why then is it written that the Son of Man must suffer much and be rejected? 13But I tell you, Elijah has come, and they have done to him everything they wished, just as it is written about him."

14When they came to the other disciples, they saw a large crowd around them and the teachers of the law arguing with them. 15As soon as all the people saw Jesus, they were overwhelmed with wonder and ran to greet him.

16"What are you arguing with them about?" he asked.

17A man in the crowd answered, "Teacher, I brought you my son, who is possessed by a spirit that has robbed him of speech. 18Whenever it seizes him, it throws him to the ground. He foams at the mouth, gnashes his teeth and becomes rigid. I asked your disciples to drive out the spirit, but they could not."

19"O unbelieving generation," Jesus replied, "how long shall I stay with you? How long shall I put up with you? Bring the boy to me."

20So they brought him. When the spirit saw Jesus, it immediately threw the boy into a convulsion. He fell to the ground and rolled around, foaming at the mouth.

21Jesus asked the boy's father, "How long has he been like this?"

"From childhood," he answered. 22"It has often thrown him into fire or water to kill him. But if you can do anything, take pity on us and help us."

23" 'If you can'?" said Jesus. "Everything is possible for him who believes."

24Immediately the boy's father exclaimed, "I do believe; help me overcome my unbelief!"

25When Jesus saw that a crowd was running to the scene, he rebuked the evil^c spirit. "You deaf and mute spirit," he said, "I command you, come out of him and never enter him again."

26The spirit shrieked, convulsed him violently and came out. The boy looked so much like a corpse that many said, "He's dead." 27But Jesus took him by the hand and lifted him to his feet, and he stood up.

28After Jesus had gone indoors, his disciples asked him privately, "Why couldn't we drive it out?"

29He replied, "This kind can come out only by prayer.^{f}"

30They left that place and passed through Galilee. Jesus did not want anyone to know where they were, 31because he was teaching his disciples. He said to them, "The Son of Man is going to be betrayed into the hands of men. They will kill him, and after three days he will rise." 32But they did not understand what he meant and were afraid to ask him about it.

^{c}25 Greek *unclean* ^{f}29 Some manuscripts *prayer and fasting*

Discovering the Word 1. What is the significance of the presence of Elijah and Moses with Jesus on the mount? 2. In verse 7 God's voice is heard for a second time in Mark's Gospel, the first being in 1:11. What purposes are accomplished by God's affirmation here? 3. Jesus descends the mountain and returns to his other disciples, only to find them in hot debate with the teachers of the law over their failure to exorcise a young boy robbed of speech (vv. 14–18). Why do you suppose Jesus is so harsh in verse 19? 4. At the end of this account, Jesus again tells his disciples about his death and resurrection (vv. 30–32). Why do you suppose the disciples failed to understand what he meant? 5. What details in the account of the boy's healing parallel those in Jesus' prediction of his coming suffering and victory?

Applying the Word 1. Which do you struggle with more—believing that Jesus *can* or that he *wants* to answer your prayers? Explain. 2. How can the dialogue between Jesus and the boy's father encourage you when your faith is weak? 3. How can this passage encourage you in the midst of pain and suffering? 4. The statement in verse 7, "Listen to him!" probably alludes to Deuteronomy 18:15–19. Explain how we can listen to Jesus today.

 Responding in Prayer Ask God to provide you with the encouragement you need in your life and to make you a channel of his grace to others.

11 / *Mark 9:33–50*
The First and the Last

ALL OF US, I imagine, struggle with the question of status and identity within a group. Where do I fit? How important am I to this group? Who is on our side? Who isn't? In this study we find out how Jesus turns conventional wisdom about status and group identity on its ear.

 Warming Up to God When have you put yourself before others? Be vulnerable before God as you consider your selfishness. Let him show you your sin.

 Read Mark 9:33–50.

---

³³They came to Capernaum. When he was in the house, he asked them, "What were you arguing about on the road?" ³⁴But they kept quiet because on the way they had argued about who was the greatest.

³⁵Sitting down, Jesus called the Twelve and said, "If anyone wants to be first, he must be the very last, and the servant of all."

³⁶He took a little child and had him stand among them. Taking him in his arms, he said to them, ³⁷"Whoever welcomes one of these little children in my name welcomes me; and whoever welcomes me does not welcome me but the one who sent me."

³⁸"Teacher," said John, "we saw a man driving out demons in your name and we told him to stop, because he was not one of us."

³⁹"Do not stop him," Jesus said. "No one who does a miracle in my name can in the next moment say anything bad about me, ⁴⁰for whoever is not against us is for us. ⁴¹I tell you the truth, anyone who gives you a cup of water in my name because you belong to Christ will certainly not lose his reward.

⁴²"And if anyone causes one of these little ones who believe in me to sin, it would be better for him to be thrown into the sea with a large millstone tied around his neck. ⁴³If your hand causes you to sin, cut it off. It is better for you to enter life maimed than with two hands to go into hell, where the fire never goes out.ᵍ ⁴⁵And if your foot causes you to sin, cut it off. It is better for you to enter life crippled than to have two feet and be thrown into hell.ʰ ⁴⁷And if your eye causes you to sin, pluck it out. It is better for you to enter the kingdom of God with one eye than to have two eyes and be thrown into hell, ⁴⁸where

" 'their worm does not die,
    and the fire is not quenched.'ⁱ

⁴⁹Everyone will be salted with fire.

⁵⁰"Salt is good, but if it loses its saltiness, how can you make it salty again? Have salt in yourselves, and be at peace with each other."

ᵍ43 Some manuscripts *out, ⁴⁴where / " 'their worm does not die, / and the fire is not quenched.'* ʰ45 Some manuscripts *hell, ⁴⁶where / " 'their worm does not die, / and the fire is not quenched.'* ⁱ48 Isaiah 66:24

 Discovering the Word 1. In verses 33–37, what is Jesus trying to get across to the disciples? 2. Why is a child so appropriate an illustration for Jesus' point (vv. 36–37)? 3. What perspective governs Jesus' response to John in verses 39–41? 4. Christian history has known some individuals to take Jesus' words in verses 43–47 quite literally. Why is cutting off a hand or foot or plucking out an eye not radical enough a way to deal with sin? 5. How are Jesus' attitudes about greatness and personal worth radically different from attitudes we often adopt from society?

Applying the Word 1. What individuals or groups are you tempted to silence because they are not one of us? 2. When should you oppose someone in Jesus' name (if ever)? 3. What attitudes and actions does this passage suggest should govern our relationships with rival individuals or groups who act in Jesus' name?

Responding in Prayer Look to God for his wisdom as you consider how to deal with groups and individuals you know who don't uphold the truth as you understand it.

12 / *Mark 10:1–31*
Divorce, Children and Eternal Life

FOR MANY OF us preachin' becomes meddlin' when it impinges on how we live. But Jesus and the New Testament, like the Old Testament before them, never allow religion to be divorced from family life and social relationships. This passage exposes some of the ways the gospel ought to transform these areas of our life.

 Warming Up to God Think about a child you know and how that child trusts his or her parents. Compare that picture to how you regard God. Talk to God about what you discover about yourself.

 Read Mark 10:1–31.

10 Jesus then left that place and went into the region of Judea and across the Jordan. Again crowds of people came to him, and as was his custom, he taught them.

²Some Pharisees came and tested him by asking, "Is it lawful for a man to divorce his wife?"

³"What did Moses command you?" he replied.

⁴They said, "Moses permitted a man to write a certificate of divorce and send her away."

⁵"It was because your hearts were hard that Moses wrote you this law," Jesus replied. ⁶"But at the beginning of creation God 'made them male and female.'ʲ ⁷For this reason a man will leave his father and mother and be united to his wife,ᵏ ⁸and the two will become one flesh.'ˡ So they are no longer two, but one. ⁹Therefore what God has joined together, let man not separate."

¹⁰When they were in the house again, the disciples asked Jesus about this. ¹¹He answered, "Anyone who divorces his wife and marries another woman commits adultery against her. ¹²And if she divorces her husband and marries another man, she commits adultery."

¹³People were bringing little children to Jesus to have him touch them, but the disciples rebuked them. ¹⁴When Jesus saw this, he was indignant. He said to them, "Let the little children come to me, and do not hinder them, for the kingdom of God belongs to such as these. ¹⁵I tell you the truth, anyone who will not receive the kingdom of God like a little child will never enter it." ¹⁶And he took the children in his arms, put his hands on them and blessed them.

¹⁷As Jesus started on his way, a man ran up to him and fell on his knees before him. "Good teacher," he asked, "what must I do to inherit eternal life?"

¹⁸"Why do you call me good?" Jesus answered. "No one is good—except God alone. ¹⁹You know the commandments: 'Do not murder, do not commit adultery, do not steal, do not give false testimony, do not defraud, honor your father and mother.'ᵐ"

²⁰"Teacher," he declared, "all these I have kept since I was a boy."

²¹Jesus looked at him and loved him. "One thing you lack," he said. "Go, sell everything you have and give to the poor, and you will have treasure in heaven. Then come, follow me."

²²At this the man's face fell. He went away sad, because he had great wealth.

²³Jesus looked around and said to his disciples, "How hard it is for the rich to enter the kingdom of God!"

²⁴The disciples were amazed at his words. But Jesus said again, "Children, how hard it isⁿ to enter the kingdom of God! ²⁵It is easier for a camel to go through the eye of a needle than for a rich man to enter the kingdom of God."

²⁶The disciples were even more amazed, and said to each other, "Who then can be saved?"

²⁷Jesus looked at them and said, "With man this is impossible, but not with God; all things are possible with God."

²⁸Peter said to him, "We have left everything to follow you!"

²⁹"I tell you the truth," Jesus replied, "no one who has left home or brothers or sisters or mother or father or children or fields for me and the gospel ³⁰will fail to receive a hundred times as much in this present age (homes, brothers, sis-

---

ʲ6 Gen. 1:27   ᵏ7 Some early manuscripts do not have *and be united to his wife.*   ˡ8 Gen. 2:24   ᵐ19 Exodus 20:12-16; Deut. 5:16-20   ⁿ24 Some manuscripts *is for those who trust in riches*

ters, mothers, children and fields—and with them, persecutions) and in the age to come, eternal life. ³¹But many who are first will be last, and the last first."

 Discovering the Word 1. What differences in approach to the question of divorce seem evident between Jesus and the Pharisees? 2. On the basis of verses 6–9, some Christian churches have refused to recognize divorce even when a couple has obtained a civil dissolution of their marriage. Do you think this is the intent of Jesus' statement? Why or why not? 3. In verses 13–16 we find that Jesus has used a child or children for the second time to illustrate a spiritual principle. What does it mean to receive the kingdom like a little child? 4. What kind of answer does the rich man expect from Jesus in response to his question (v. 17)? 5. How have the Pharisees (vv. 2–9) and the rich man (vv. 17–25) failed to receive the kingdom like a child (v. 15)?

Applying the Word 1. What obstacles were or are hardest for you to overcome in entering the kingdom? 2. What evidence has there been of God's help in your overcoming these obstacles? 3. In what areas of your life do you most need to express more childlike faith in God? 4. How have you experienced the truth of Jesus' words, "No one who has left home . . . will fail to receive a hundred times as much"?

Responding in Prayer Ask God to make you like a child.

---

13 / *Mark 10:32–52*
Blindness and Sight

THE BLIND SOMETIMES have uncanny "sight," and the deaf sometimes "hear" what others miss. Spiritual insight and alertness arise from the heart rather than from status or position. In this passage Mark seems to delight in the irony of a blind man who perceives what the sighted cannot see.

 Warming Up to God What does God want you to "see" or know? Sit quietly before him and listen for his voice.

 Read Mark 10:32–52.

---

³²They were on their way up to Jerusalem, with Jesus leading the way, and the disciples were astonished, while those who followed were afraid. Again he took the Twelve aside and told them what was going to happen to him. ³³"We are going up to Jerusalem," he said, "and the Son of Man will be betrayed to the chief priests and teachers of the law. They will condemn him to death and will hand him over to the Gentiles, ³⁴who will mock him and spit on him, flog him and kill him. Three days later he will rise."

³⁵Then James and John, the sons of Zebedee, came to him. "Teacher," they said, "we want you to do for us whatever we ask."

³⁶"What do you want me to do for you?" he asked.

³⁷They replied, "Let one of us sit at your right and the other at your left in your glory."

³⁸"You don't know what you are asking," Jesus said. "Can you drink the cup I drink or be baptized with the baptism I am baptized with?"

³⁹"We can," they answered.

Jesus said to them, "You will drink the cup I drink and be baptized with the baptism I am baptized with, ⁴⁰but to sit at my right or left is not for me to grant. These places belong to those for whom they have been prepared."

⁴¹When the ten heard about this, they became indignant with James and John. ⁴²Jesus called them together and said, "You know that those who are regarded as rulers of the Gentiles lord it over them, and their high officials exercise authority over them. ⁴³Not so with you. Instead, whoever wants to become great among you must be your servant, ⁴⁴and whoever wants to be first must be slave of all. ⁴⁵For even the Son of Man did not come to be served, but to serve, and to give his life as a ransom for many."

⁴⁶Then they came to Jericho. As Jesus and his disciples, together with a large crowd, were leaving the city, a blind man, Bartimaeus (that is, the Son of Timaeus), was sitting by the roadside begging. ⁴⁷When he heard that it was Jesus of Nazareth, he began to shout, "Jesus, Son of David, have mercy on me!"

⁴⁸Many rebuked him and told him to be quiet, but he shouted all the more, "Son of David, have mercy on me!"

⁴⁹Jesus stopped and said, "Call him."

So they called to the blind man, "Cheer up! On your feet! He's calling you." ⁵⁰Throwing his cloak aside, he jumped to his feet and came to Jesus.

⁵¹"What do you want me to do for you?" Jesus asked him.

The blind man said, "Rabbi, I want to see."

⁵²"Go," said Jesus, "your faith has healed you." Immediately he received his sight and followed Jesus along the road.

 Discovering the Word   1. Given what Jesus has just said in verses 33–34, what is ironic about James and John's request (vv. 35–37)?   2. What seems to motivate James and John's request?   3. When the other ten apostles hear about this status request, they become indignant. In response, what principle does Jesus bring out again (see 9:35, 10:31 and 10:42–45)?   4. From the brief account in verses 46–52, what kind of man does Bartimaeus seem to be?   5. Why do you suppose Jesus asked Bartimaeus what he wanted him to do for him?

Applying the Word   1. How can your life better conform to Jesus' view of greatness? (Consider what motivates your actions as well as what you do.)   2. Jesus is indeed on the road to glory, but that road will not bypass Jerusalem. Self-sacrifice and service mark the way. What are some present opportunities for you to follow him?   3. What may be some of the costs?

Responding in Prayer   Tell God how you want to sacrifice for him.

---

14 / *Mark 11:1–25*
Palm Sunday

THE TROUBLE WITH righteous anger is that it is so much easier to be angry than righteous. But it is possible to be both. This passage provides an example of how our emotions and attitudes can work toward God's purposes instead of against them.

 Warming Up to God   When have your emotions "gotten the better of you" lately? Evaluate that experience prayerfully.

 Read Mark 11:1–25.

As they approached Jerusalem and came to Bethphage and Bethany at the Mount of Olives, Jesus sent two of his disciples, ²saying to them, "Go to the village ahead of you, and just as you enter it, you will find a colt tied there, which no one has ever ridden. Untie it and bring it here. ³If anyone asks you, 'Why are you doing this?' tell him, 'The Lord needs it and will send it back here shortly.'"

⁴They went and found a colt outside in the street, tied at a doorway. As they untied it, ⁵some people standing there asked, "What are you doing, untying that colt?" ⁶They answered as Jesus

had told them to, and the people let them go. ⁷When they brought the colt to Jesus and threw their cloaks over it, he sat on it. ⁸Many people spread their cloaks on the road, while others spread branches they had cut in the fields. ⁹Those who went ahead and those who followed shouted,

"Hosanna!ᵒ"

"Blessed is he who comes in the name of the Lord!"ᵖ

ᵒ9 A Hebrew expression meaning "Save!" which became an exclamation of praise; also in verse 10   ᵖ9 Psalm 118:25,26

¹⁰"Blessed is the coming kingdom of our father
   David!"

"Hosanna in the highest!"

¹¹Jesus entered Jerusalem and went to the temple. He looked around at everything, but since it
was already late, he went out to Bethany with the
Twelve.

¹²The next day as they were leaving Bethany,
Jesus was hungry. ¹³Seeing in the distance a fig
tree in leaf, he went to find out if it had any fruit.
When he reached it, he found nothing but leaves,
because it was not the season for figs. ¹⁴Then he
said to the tree, "May no one ever eat fruit from
you again." And his disciples heard him say it.

¹⁵On reaching Jerusalem, Jesus entered the
temple area and began driving out those who
were buying and selling there. He overturned the
tables of the money changers and the benches of
those selling doves, ¹⁶and would not allow anyone to carry merchandise through the temple
courts. ¹⁷And as he taught them, he said, "Is it not
written:

" 'My house will be called
   a house of prayer for all nations'�q?

But you have made it 'a den of robbers.'ʳ"

¹⁸The chief priests and the teachers of the law
heard this and began looking for a way to kill
him, for they feared him, because the whole
crowd was amazed at his teaching.

¹⁹When evening came, theyˢ went out of the
city.

²⁰In the morning, as they went along, they saw
the fig tree withered from the roots. ²¹Peter remembered and said to Jesus, "Rabbi, look! The fig
tree you cursed has withered!"

²²"Haveᵗ faith in God," Jesus answered. ²³"I
tell you the truth, if anyone says to this mountain,
'Go, throw yourself into the sea,' and does not
doubt in his heart but believes that what he says
will happen, it will be done for him. ²⁴Therefore
I tell you, whatever you ask for in prayer, believe
that you have received it, and it will be yours.
²⁵And when you stand praying, if you hold anything against anyone, forgive him, so that your
Father in heaven may forgive you your sins.ᵘ"

---

q17 Isaiah 56:7   r17 Jer. 7:11   s19 Some early manuscripts he
t22 Some early manuscripts If you have   u25 Some manuscripts sins.
26But if you do not forgive, neither will your Father who is in heaven
forgive your sins.

 Discovering the Word 1. What progression of moods do you see in this passage? 2. In what ways is
the significance of Jesus' entry into Jerusalem reinforced? 3. Why is Jesus so angry with what is taking
place in the temple (vv. 15–17)? 4. Why do you suppose Mark has sandwiched this account of Jesus' clearing out
of the temple within that of the cursing of the fig tree? 5. What does Jesus teach us about prayer in verses 22–25?

 Applying the Word 1. When is anger righteous? 2. Are there activities or attitudes in your church or
fellowship which get in the way of God's purposes? 3. What can you do to help eliminate them?

Responding in Prayer Respond to this passage in prayer, praising the King of peace and asking that his
kingdom might be established.

---

15 / *Mark 11:27—12:27*
Tempting Questions

SOME PEOPLE ASK questions because they want to know the answers. Others take malicious delight in posing
unanswerable questions or in trying to trip up an opponent. Jesus often asked questions to get his hearers to think
deeply for themselves. Learning to look behind questions to motives and learning to pose effective questions can
help us all to be better evangelists and servants.

 Warming Up to God When is Jesus most real to you? Spend some time meditating on the privilege of
having Christ present with you.

 Read Mark 11:27—12:27.

²⁷They arrived again in Jerusalem, and while Jesus was walking in the temple courts, the chief priests, the teachers of the law and the elders came to him. ²⁸"By what authority are you doing these things?" they asked. "And who gave you authority to do this?"

²⁹Jesus replied, "I will ask you one question. Answer me, and I will tell you by what authority I am doing these things. ³⁰John's baptism—was it from heaven, or from men? Tell me!"

³¹They discussed it among themselves and said, "If we say, 'From heaven,' he will ask, 'Then why didn't you believe him?' ³²But if we say, 'From men' . . . ." (They feared the people, for everyone held that John really was a prophet.)

³³So they answered Jesus, "We don't know."

Jesus said, "Neither will I tell you by what authority I am doing these things."

12

He then began to speak to them in parables: "A man planted a vineyard. He put a wall around it, dug a pit for the winepress and built a watchtower. Then he rented the vineyard to some farmers and went away on a journey. ²At harvest time he sent a servant to the tenants to collect from them some of the fruit of the vineyard. ³But they seized him, beat him and sent him away empty-handed. ⁴Then he sent another servant to them; they struck this man on the head and treated him shamefully. ⁵He sent still another, and that one they killed. He sent many others; some of them they beat, others they killed.

⁶"He had one left to send, a son, whom he loved. He sent him last of all, saying, 'They will respect my son.'

⁷"But the tenants said to one another, 'This is the heir. Come, let's kill him, and the inheritance will be ours.' ⁸So they took him and killed him, and threw him out of the vineyard.

⁹"What then will the owner of the vineyard do? He will come and kill those tenants and give the vineyard to others. ¹⁰Haven't you read this scripture:

" 'The stone the builders rejected
    has become the capstoneᵛ;
¹¹the Lord has done this,
    and it is marvelous in our eyes'ʷ?"

¹²Then they looked for a way to arrest him because they knew he had spoken the parable against them. But they were afraid of the crowd; so they left him and went away.

¹³Later they sent some of the Pharisees and Herodians to Jesus to catch him in his words. ¹⁴They came to him and said, "Teacher, we know you are a man of integrity. You aren't swayed by men, because you pay no attention to who they are; but you teach the way of God in accordance with the truth. Is it right to pay taxes to Caesar or not? ¹⁵Should we pay or shouldn't we?"

But Jesus knew their hypocrisy. "Why are you trying to trap me?" he asked. "Bring me a denarius and let me look at it." ¹⁶They brought the coin, and he asked them, "Whose portrait is this? And whose inscription?"

"Caesar's," they replied.

¹⁷Then Jesus said to them, "Give to Caesar what is Caesar's and to God what is God's."

And they were amazed at him.

¹⁸Then the Sadducees, who say there is no resurrection, came to him with a question. ¹⁹"Teacher," they said, "Moses wrote for us that if a man's brother dies and leaves a wife but no children, the man must marry the widow and have children for his brother. ²⁰Now there were seven brothers. The first one married and died without leaving any children. ²¹The second one married the widow, but he also died, leaving no child. It was the same with the third. ²²In fact, none of the seven left any children. Last of all, the woman died too. ²³At the resurrectionˣ whose wife will she be, since the seven were married to her?"

²⁴Jesus replied, "Are you not in error because you do not know the Scriptures or the power of God? ²⁵When the dead rise, they will neither marry nor be given in marriage; they will be like the angels in heaven. ²⁶Now about the dead rising—have you not read in the book of Moses, in the account of the bush, how God said to him, 'I am the God of Abraham, the God of Isaac, and the God of Jacob'ʸ? ²⁷He is not the God of the dead, but of the living. You are badly mistaken!"

ᵛ10 Or cornerstone   ʷ11 Psalm 118:22,23   ˣ23 Some manuscripts resurrection, when men rise from the dead,   ʸ26 Exodus 3:6

Discovering the Word 1. In 11:27 the chief priests, the elders and the teachers of the law come asking a seemingly straightforward question about Jesus' authority. What does Jesus' reply and the subsequent discussion reveal about their motives? 2. The parable of the tenants is rich in meaning. If the tenants are Israel and its religious leaders, who are the owner, the servants and the son? 3. A common enemy can often draw together people who are not otherwise on good terms. In 12:13–17 we find Herodians (supporters of the puppet monarchy) and the Pharisees (ardent nationalists and opponents of Roman rule) joining forces. How does the question they pose to Jesus reflect their conflicting interests? 4. The Sadducees differed from their Jewish contemporaries because they rejected the idea of resurrection. What motives lie behind their question to Jesus (12:18–23)? 5. How do the Sadducees display ignorance of the Scriptures and the power of God?

Applying the Word 1. How are you experiencing the truth of the Scriptures and the power of God? 2. How can we get to know the Scriptures and the power of God better? 3. As we seek to share the good news of Christ and his kingdom, we will meet people with a wide variety of questions and motives. What can we learn about answering and asking questions from this passage?

Responding in Prayer Pray that you will be ready to answer questions about your beliefs.

16 / *Mark 12:28–44*
An End to Questions

PEOPLE ARE MOTIVATED by many things—ambition, money, power, recognition, the desire to please God. In this passage Jesus encounters or comments on a variety of people whose lives are governed by different goals. In so doing he exposes our own motivations to his searching glance.

 Warming Up to God What motivates your daily life and future plans? List each motivating factor. Reflect on your list before God.

 Read Mark 12:28–44.

---

²⁸One of the teachers of the law came and heard them debating. Noticing that Jesus had given them a good answer, he asked him, "Of all the commandments, which is the most important?"

²⁹"The most important one," answered Jesus, "is this: 'Hear, O Israel, the Lord our God, the Lord is one.ᶻ ³⁰Love the Lord your God with all your heart and with all your soul and with all your mind and with all your strength.'ᵃ ³¹The second is this: 'Love your neighbor as yourself.'ᵇ There is no commandment greater than these."

³²"Well said, teacher," the man replied. "You are right in saying that God is one and there is no other but him. ³³To love him with all your heart, with all your understanding and with all your strength, and to love your neighbor as yourself is more important than all burnt offerings and sacrifices."

³⁴When Jesus saw that he had answered wisely, he said to him, "You are not far from the kingdom of God." And from then on no one dared ask him any more questions.

³⁵While Jesus was teaching in the temple courts, he asked, "How is it that the teachers of the law say that the Christᶜ is the son of David? ³⁶David himself, speaking by the Holy Spirit, declared:

" 'The Lord said to my Lord:
"Sit at my right hand
until I put your enemies
under your feet." 'ᵈ

³⁷David himself calls him 'Lord.' How then can he be his son?"

The large crowd listened to him with delight.

³⁸As he taught, Jesus said, "Watch out for the teachers of the law. They like to walk around in flowing robes and be greeted in the marketplaces, ³⁹and have the most important seats in the syna-

ᶻ29 Or *the Lord our God is one Lord*   ᵃ30 Deut. 6:4,5   ᵇ31 Lev. 19:18   ᶜ35 Or *Messiah*   ᵈ36 Psalm 110:1

gogues and the places of honor at banquets. ⁴⁰They devour widows' houses and for a show make lengthy prayers. Such men will be punished most severely."

⁴¹Jesus sat down opposite the place where the offerings were put and watched the crowd putting their money into the temple treasury. Many rich people threw in large amounts. ⁴²But a poor widow came and put in two very small copper coins, ^e worth only a fraction of a penny. ^f

⁴³Calling his disciples to him, Jesus said, "I tell you the truth, this poor widow has put more into the treasury than all the others. ⁴⁴They all gave out of their wealth; but she, out of her poverty, put in everything—all she had to live on."

^e42 Greek *two lepta*   ^f42 Greek *kodrantes*

 Discovering the Word 1. Like the chief priests, elders, Pharisees and Sadducees of 11:27—12:27, another teacher of the law comes to Jesus with a pointed question (v. 28). What evidence is there that he is not out to trap Jesus? 2. Though Jesus is only asked for one commandment, in good rabbinic fashion he responds by adding a second to his reply. What relationship does this second commandment bear to the first? 3. To a Jew in Jesus' day a descendant was always inferior to an ancestor. A son might call his father or grandfather "lord," but never vice versa. How *can* Christ be both David's Lord and his descendant (vv. 35–37)? 4. In contrast to the teachers of the law and the rich, what motivates the widow's religious behavior?

Applying the Word 1. If you were to evaluate your daily activities on the basis of love for God and neighbor, how would you fare? Explain. 2. What steps can you take to make the love of God and love of neighbor a higher priority in your life? 3. What implications does the example of the widow have for our giving to the Lord's work?

Responding in Prayer Ask God to give you the attitude of the widow both in your love for him and toward others.

---

17 / *Mark 13*
Keep Watch

WAITING FOR CHRISTMAS can keep some children excited and on their best behavior for weeks. But what if Christmas never came? To many of us the Second Coming may seem like a Christmas that never comes. In this passage, Jesus answers some questions about the future, both near and far off, but above all he encourages an attitude we all need to develop.

 Warming Up to God When is it hard for you to wait for God? Ask him to give you insight and courage as you watch and wait.

 Read Mark 13.

---

13 As he was leaving the temple, one of his disciples said to him, "Look, Teacher! What massive stones! What magnificent buildings!"

²"Do you see all these great buildings?" replied Jesus. "Not one stone here will be left on another; every one will be thrown down."

³As Jesus was sitting on the Mount of Olives opposite the temple, Peter, James, John and Andrew asked him privately, ⁴"Tell us, when will these things happen? And what will be the sign that they are all about to be fulfilled?"

⁵Jesus said to them: "Watch out that no one deceives you. ⁶Many will come in my name, claiming, 'I am he,' and will deceive many. ⁷When you hear of wars and rumors of wars, do not be alarmed. Such things must happen, but the end is still to come. ⁸Nation will rise against nation, and kingdom against kingdom. There will be earthquakes in various places, and famines. These are the beginning of birth pains.

⁹"You must be on your guard. You will be handed over to the local councils and flogged in the synagogues. On account of me you will stand

before governors and kings as witnesses to them. [10]And the gospel must first be preached to all nations. [11]Whenever you are arrested and brought to trial, do not worry beforehand about what to say. Just say whatever is given you at the time, for it is not you speaking, but the Holy Spirit.

[12]"Brother will betray brother to death, and a father his child. Children will rebel against their parents and have them put to death. [13]All men will hate you because of me, but he who stands firm to the end will be saved.

[14]"When you see 'the abomination that causes desolation'[g] standing where it[h] does not belong—let the reader understand—then let those who are in Judea flee to the mountains. [15]Let no one on the roof of his house go down or enter the house to take anything out. [16]Let no one in the field go back to get his cloak. [17]How dreadful it will be in those days for pregnant women and nursing mothers! [18]Pray that this will not take place in winter, [19]because those will be days of distress unequaled from the beginning, when God created the world, until now—and never to be equaled again. [20]If the Lord had not cut short those days, no one would survive. But for the sake of the elect, whom he has chosen, he has shortened them. [21]At that time if anyone says to you, 'Look, here is the Christ[i]!' or, 'Look, there he is!' do not believe it. [22]For false Christs and false prophets will appear and perform signs and miracles to deceive the elect—if that were possible. [23]So be on your guard; I have told you everything ahead of time.

[24]"But in those days, following that distress,

" 'the sun will be darkened,
  and the moon will not give its light;
[25]the stars will fall from the sky,
  and the heavenly bodies will be shaken.'[j]

[26]"At that time men will see the Son of Man coming in clouds with great power and glory. [27]And he will send his angels and gather his elect from the four winds, from the ends of the earth to the ends of the heavens.

[28]"Now learn this lesson from the fig tree: As soon as its twigs get tender and its leaves come out, you know that summer is near. [29]Even so, when you see these things happening, you know that it is near, right at the door. [30]I tell you the truth, this generation[k] will certainly not pass away until all these things have happened. [31]Heaven and earth will pass away, but my words will never pass away.

[32]"No one knows about that day or hour, not even the angels in heaven, nor the Son, but only the Father. [33]Be on guard! Be alert[l]! You do not know when that time will come. [34]It's like a man going away: He leaves his house and puts his servants in charge, each with his assigned task, and tells the one at the door to keep watch.

[35]"Therefore keep watch because you do not know when the owner of the house will come back—whether in the evening, or at midnight, or when the rooster crows, or at dawn. [36]If he comes suddenly, do not let him find you sleeping. [37]What I say to you, I say to everyone: 'Watch!' "

g14 Daniel 9:27; 11:31; 12:11   h14 Or he; also in verse 29
i21 Or Messiah   j25 Isaiah 13:10; 34:4   k30 Or race
l33 Some manuscripts alert and pray

Discovering the Word   1. Jesus doesn't seem to answer the disciples' question directly, at least not at first. What is he concerned about (vv. 5-8)?   2. How would Jesus' warnings and encouragements (vv. 5-13) have helped the disciples in the early years of the church?   3. Christians have sometimes disagreed about how to interpret Jesus' words in verses 14-23. Some think Jesus is talking about the destruction of the temple in A.D. 70 and the events leading up to that. Others think these events are still future. What evidence is there to support each view?   4. How is the distress described in verses 24-27 different from that described in verses 5-23?   5. Many people throughout the ages have tried to make precise predictions about the return of Jesus. How does watching as Jesus urges differ from making such predictions?

Applying the Word   1. What relevance do the warnings and encouragements in verses 5-13 have for us today?   2. In what area of your life do you need to "be on guard"?   3. In what practical ways can we be alert for Jesus' return?

Responding in Prayer   Spend some time in praise and thanksgiving for the promises in this passage.

18 / *Mark 14:1–42*
The Betrayer Approaches

IF YOU'VE EVER caught yourself yawning at a critical moment or felt spiritually asleep when the Lord was calling you to a task, you'll have little difficulty in empathizing with the disciples in this account. We now enter into the last few days of Jesus' earthly ministry. The mood is somber as more and more people begin to fail and desert him.

Warming Up to God What task has God been calling you to? Spend some time prayerfully considering what God has for you.

Read Mark 14:1–42.

14 Now the Passover and the Feast of Unleavened Bread were only two days away, and the chief priests and the teachers of the law were looking for some sly way to arrest Jesus and kill him. ²"But not during the Feast," they said, "or the people may riot."

³While he was in Bethany, reclining at the table in the home of a man known as Simon the Leper, a woman came with an alabaster jar of very expensive perfume, made of pure nard. She broke the jar and poured the perfume on his head.

⁴Some of those present were saying indignantly to one another, "Why this waste of perfume? ⁵It could have been sold for more than a year's wages^m and the money given to the poor." And they rebuked her harshly.

⁶"Leave her alone," said Jesus. "Why are you bothering her? She has done a beautiful thing to me. ⁷The poor you will always have with you, and you can help them any time you want. But you will not always have me. ⁸She did what she could. She poured perfume on my body beforehand to prepare for my burial. ⁹I tell you the truth, wherever the gospel is preached throughout the world, what she has done will also be told, in memory of her."

¹⁰Then Judas Iscariot, one of the Twelve, went to the chief priests to betray Jesus to them. ¹¹They were delighted to hear this and promised to give him money. So he watched for an opportunity to hand him over.

¹²On the first day of the Feast of Unleavened Bread, when it was customary to sacrifice the Passover lamb, Jesus' disciples asked him, "Where do you want us to go and make preparations for you to eat the Passover?"

¹³So he sent two of his disciples, telling them, "Go into the city, and a man carrying a jar of water will meet you. Follow him. ¹⁴Say to the owner of the house he enters, 'The Teacher asks: Where is my guest room, where I may eat the Passover with my disciples?' ¹⁵He will show you a large upper room, furnished and ready. Make preparations for us there."

¹⁶The disciples left, went into the city and found things just as Jesus had told them. So they prepared the Passover.

¹⁷When evening came, Jesus arrived with the Twelve. ¹⁸While they were reclining at the table eating, he said, "I tell you the truth, one of you will betray me—one who is eating with me."

¹⁹They were saddened, and one by one they said to him, "Surely not I?"

²⁰"It is one of the Twelve," he replied, "one who dips bread into the bowl with me. ²¹The Son of Man will go just as it is written about him. But woe to that man who betrays the Son of Man! It would be better for him if he had not been born."

²²While they were eating, Jesus took bread, gave thanks and broke it, and gave it to his disciples, saying, "Take it; this is my body."

²³Then he took the cup, gave thanks and offered it to them, and they all drank from it.

²⁴"This is my blood of the^n covenant, which is poured out for many," he said to them. ²⁵"I tell you the truth, I will not drink again of the fruit of the vine until that day when I drink it anew in the kingdom of God."

²⁶When they had sung a hymn, they went out to the Mount of Olives.

²⁷"You will all fall away," Jesus told them, "for it is written:

" 'I will strike the shepherd,
    and the sheep will be scattered.'^o

^m5 Greek *than three hundred denarii*   ^n24 Some manuscripts *the new*
^o27 Zech. 13:7

²⁸But after I have risen, I will go ahead of you into Galilee."

²⁹Peter declared, "Even if all fall away, I will not."

³⁰"I tell you the truth," Jesus answered, "today—yes, tonight—before the rooster crows twice*ᵖ you yourself will disown me three times."

³¹But Peter insisted emphatically, "Even if I have to die with you, I will never disown you." And all the others said the same.

³²They went to a place called Gethsemane, and Jesus said to his disciples, "Sit here while I pray." ³³He took Peter, James and John along with him, and he began to be deeply distressed and troubled. ³⁴"My soul is overwhelmed with sorrow to the point of death," he said to them. "Stay here and keep watch."

³⁵Going a little farther, he fell to the ground and prayed that if possible the hour might pass from him. ³⁶"Abba,ᑫ Father," he said, "every-

thing is possible for you. Take this cup from me. Yet not what I will, but what you will."

³⁷Then he returned to his disciples and found them sleeping. "Simon," he said to Peter, "are you asleep? Could you not keep watch for one hour? ³⁸Watch and pray so that you will not fall into temptation. The spirit is willing, but the body is weak."

³⁹Once more he went away and prayed the same thing. ⁴⁰When he came back, he again found them sleeping, because their eyes were heavy. They did not know what to say to him.

⁴¹Returning the third time, he said to them, "Are you still sleeping and resting? Enough! The hour has come. Look, the Son of Man is betrayed into the hands of sinners. ⁴²Rise! Let us go! Here comes my betrayer!"

ᵖ30 Some early manuscripts do not have *twice*.   ᑫ36 Aramaic for *Father*

 Discovering the Word 1. What different motives are present in the conflict that arises at the home of Simon the Leper? 2. During the Passover feast Jesus tells the Twelve that one of them will betray him. What do you think they were feeling as they responded to his announcement (v. 19)? 3. Few words have spawned as much debate regarding their meaning as those Jesus spoke in verses 22–24. Regardless of how literally we take them, what are the bread and cup of the Lord's Supper to symbolize for us? 4. How might verses 32–36 help those who struggle with the question of whether Jesus is the only way to God?

Applying the Word 1. How can the exhortations in verses 34 and 38 make the difference in your own life between resisting or falling into temptation? 2. When have you felt like the disciples must have felt in verse 40? 3. What consolation and encouragement can you draw from the disciples' experience?

Responding in Prayer Thank God for his wonderful provision of forgiveness in Christ.

---

19 / *Mark 14:43–72*
Betrayed!

THE PERSECUTION OF enemies is one thing, the abandonment of friends another. In this study we find Jesus not only betrayed by one of his disciples but abandoned by all the others and ruefully denied by one of his closest friends. All this added to the cruel and unlawful treatment by the Sanhedrin. This account reveals how intense pressures can test the quality of our discipleship.

 Warming Up to God We all betray Christ in the things we say or do. How have you betrayed him recently? Spend time in sincere confession. Hear the words of forgiveness.

 Read Mark 14:43–72.

⁴³Just as he was speaking, Judas, one of the Twelve, appeared. With him was a crowd armed with swords and clubs, sent from the chief priests, the teachers of the law, and the elders. ⁴⁴Now the betrayer had arranged a signal with them: "The one I kiss is the man; arrest him and lead him away under guard." ⁴⁵Going at once to Jesus, Judas said, "Rabbi!" and kissed him. ⁴⁶The men seized Jesus and arrested him. ⁴⁷Then one of those standing near drew his sword and struck the servant of the high priest, cutting off his ear.

⁴⁸"Am I leading a rebellion," said Jesus, "that you have come out with swords and clubs to capture me? ⁴⁹Every day I was with you, teaching in the temple courts, and you did not arrest me. But the Scriptures must be fulfilled." ⁵⁰Then everyone deserted him and fled.

⁵¹A young man, wearing nothing but a linen garment, was following Jesus. When they seized him, ⁵²he fled naked, leaving his garment behind.

⁵³They took Jesus to the high priest, and all the chief priests, elders and teachers of the law came together. ⁵⁴Peter followed him at a distance, right into the courtyard of the high priest. There he sat with the guards and warmed himself at the fire.

⁵⁵The chief priests and the whole Sanhedrin were looking for evidence against Jesus so that they could put him to death, but they did not find any. ⁵⁶Many testified falsely against him, but their statements did not agree.

⁵⁷Then some stood up and gave this false testimony against him: ⁵⁸"We heard him say, 'I will destroy this man-made temple and in three days will build another, not made by man.'" ⁵⁹Yet even then their testimony did not agree.

⁶⁰Then the high priest stood up before them and asked Jesus, "Are you not going to answer? What is this testimony that these men are bringing against you?" ⁶¹But Jesus remained silent and gave no answer.

Again the high priest asked him, "Are you the Christ,ʳ the Son of the Blessed One?"

⁶²"I am," said Jesus. "And you will see the Son of Man sitting at the right hand of the Mighty One and coming on the clouds of heaven."

⁶³The high priest tore his clothes. "Why do we need any more witnesses?" he asked. ⁶⁴"You have heard the blasphemy. What do you think?"

They all condemned him as worthy of death. ⁶⁵Then some began to spit at him; they blindfolded him, struck him with their fists, and said, "Prophesy!" And the guards took him and beat him.

⁶⁶While Peter was below in the courtyard, one of the servant girls of the high priest came by. ⁶⁷When she saw Peter warming himself, she looked closely at him.

"You also were with that Nazarene, Jesus," she said.

⁶⁸But he denied it. "I don't know or understand what you're talking about," he said, and went out into the entryway.ˢ

⁶⁹When the servant girl saw him there, she said again to those standing around, "This fellow is one of them." ⁷⁰Again he denied it.

After a little while, those standing near said to Peter, "Surely you are one of them, for you are a Galilean."

⁷¹He began to call down curses on himself, and he swore to them, "I don't know this man you're talking about."

⁷²Immediately the rooster crowed the second time.ᵗ Then Peter remembered the word Jesus had spoken to him: "Before the rooster crows twiceᵘ you will disown me three times." And he broke down and wept.

ʳ61 Or Messiah   ˢ68 Some early manuscripts entryway and the rooster crowed   ᵗ72 Some early manuscripts do not have the second time.   ᵘ72 Some early manuscripts do not have twice.

Discovering the Word 1. How does Jesus respond to his betrayal? 2. What aspects of Jesus' trial before the Sanhedrin (vv. 53–65) does Mark emphasize? 3. Up until this point Jesus has regularly disguised his identity, but in verse 62 he openly confesses his identity as the Christ. Why do you think he does this now? 4. How is the charge against Jesus both justifiable and unjustifiable? 5. What mix of motives brings Peter into the high priest's courtyard yet keeps him from acknowledging his relationship to Jesus (vv. 66–72)?

Applying the Word 1. How are your motives mixed in following Jesus? 2. In what circumstances are you most tempted to be ashamed of Jesus or to deny him? 3. What warnings and encouragement can you draw from Peter's experience?

Responding in Prayer Ask God to keep you from betrayal.

20 / *Mark 15:1—16:8*
Victory Snatched from Defeat

TRUE GREATNESS, JESUS taught, is found in being a servant: "Whoever wants to be first must be slave of all. For even the Son of Man did not come to be served, but to serve, and to give his life as a ransom for many." Recorded here is the vivid testimony to Jesus' greatness and glory.

 Warming Up to God What about death is intimidating to you? Reflect on how Jesus would have felt going to the cross. Spend time responding in prayer.

 Read Mark 15:1—16:8.

15 Very early in the morning, the chief priests, with the elders, the teachers of the law and the whole Sanhedrin, reached a decision. They bound Jesus, led him away and handed him over to Pilate.

²"Are you the king of the Jews?" asked Pilate.

"Yes, it is as you say," Jesus replied.

³The chief priests accused him of many things. ⁴So again Pilate asked him, "Aren't you going to answer? See how many things they are accusing you of."

⁵But Jesus still made no reply, and Pilate was amazed.

⁶Now it was the custom at the Feast to release a prisoner whom the people requested. ⁷A man called Barabbas was in prison with the insurrectionists who had committed murder in the uprising. ⁸The crowd came up and asked Pilate to do for them what he usually did.

⁹"Do you want me to release to you the king of the Jews?" asked Pilate, ¹⁰knowing it was out of envy that the chief priests had handed Jesus over to him. ¹¹But the chief priests stirred up the crowd to have Pilate release Barabbas instead.

¹²"What shall I do, then, with the one you call the king of the Jews?" Pilate asked them.

¹³"Crucify him!" they shouted.

¹⁴"Why? What crime has he committed?" asked Pilate.

But they shouted all the louder, "Crucify him!"

¹⁵Wanting to satisfy the crowd, Pilate released Barabbas to them. He had Jesus flogged, and handed him over to be crucified.

¹⁶The soldiers led Jesus away into the palace (that is, the Praetorium) and called together the whole company of soldiers. ¹⁷They put a purple robe on him, then twisted together a crown of thorns and set it on him. ¹⁸And they began to call out to him, "Hail, king of the Jews!" ¹⁹Again and again they struck him on the head with a staff and spit on him. Falling on their knees, they paid homage to him. ²⁰And when they had mocked him, they took off the purple robe and put his own clothes on him. Then they led him out to crucify him.

²¹A certain man from Cyrene, Simon, the father of Alexander and Rufus, was passing by on his way in from the country, and they forced him to carry the cross. ²²They brought Jesus to the place called Golgotha (which means The Place of the Skull). ²³Then they offered him wine mixed with myrrh, but he did not take it. ²⁴And they crucified him. Dividing up his clothes, they cast lots to see what each would get.

²⁵It was the third hour when they crucified him. ²⁶The written notice of the charge against him read: THE KING OF THE JEWS. ²⁷They crucified two robbers with him, one on his right and one on his left.ᵛ ²⁹Those who passed by hurled insults at him, shaking their heads and saying, "So! You who are going to destroy the temple and build it in three days, ³⁰come down from the cross and save yourself!"

³¹In the same way the chief priests and the teachers of the law mocked him among themselves. "He saved others," they said, "but he can't save himself! ³²Let this Christ,ʷ this King of Israel, come down now from the cross, that we may see and believe." Those crucified with him also heaped insults on him.

³³At the sixth hour darkness came over the whole land until the ninth hour. ³⁴And at the ninth hour Jesus cried out in a loud voice, *"Eloi, Eloi, lama sabachthani?"*—which means, "My God, my God, why have you forsaken me?"ˣ

³⁵When some of those standing near heard this, they said, "Listen, he's calling Elijah."

³⁶One man ran, filled a sponge with wine vinegar, put it on a stick, and offered it to Jesus to drink. "Now leave him alone. Let's see if Elijah comes to take him down," he said.

³⁷With a loud cry, Jesus breathed his last.

ᵛ27 Some manuscripts *left, ²⁸and the scripture was fulfilled which says, "He was counted with the lawless ones"* (Isaiah 53:12)   ʷ32 Or *Messiah*   ˣ34 Psalm 22:1

³⁸The curtain of the temple was torn in two from top to bottom. ³⁹And when the centurion, who stood there in front of Jesus, heard his cry and^y saw how he died, he said, "Surely this man was the Son^z of God!"

⁴⁰Some women were watching from a distance. Among them were Mary Magdalene, Mary the mother of James the younger and of Joses, and Salome. ⁴¹In Galilee these women had followed him and cared for his needs. Many other women who had come up with him to Jerusalem were also there.

⁴²It was Preparation Day (that is, the day before the Sabbath). So as evening approached, ⁴³Joseph of Arimathea, a prominent member of the Council, who was himself waiting for the kingdom of God, went boldly to Pilate and asked for Jesus' body. ⁴⁴Pilate was surprised to hear that he was already dead. Summoning the centurion, he asked him if Jesus had already died. ⁴⁵When he learned from the centurion that it was so, he gave the body to Joseph. ⁴⁶So Joseph bought some linen cloth, took down the body, wrapped it in the linen, and placed it in a tomb cut out of rock. Then he rolled a stone against the entrance of the tomb. ⁴⁷Mary Magdalene and Mary the mother of Joses saw where he was laid.

16 When the Sabbath was over, Mary Magdalene, Mary the mother of James, and Salome bought spices so that they might go to anoint Jesus' body. ²Very early on the first day of the week, just after sunrise, they were on their way to the tomb ³and they asked each other, "Who will roll the stone away from the entrance of the tomb?"

⁴But when they looked up, they saw that the stone, which was very large, had been rolled away. ⁵As they entered the tomb, they saw a young man dressed in a white robe sitting on the right side, and they were alarmed.

⁶"Don't be alarmed," he said. "You are looking for Jesus the Nazarene, who was crucified. He has risen! He is not here. See the place where they laid him. ⁷But go, tell his disciples and Peter, 'He is going ahead of you into Galilee. There you will see him, just as he told you.'"

⁸Trembling and bewildered, the women went out and fled from the tomb. They said nothing to anyone, because they were afraid.

[The earliest manuscripts and some other ancient witnesses do not have Mark 16:9–20.]

⁹When Jesus rose early on the first day of the week, he appeared first to Mary Magdalene, out of whom he had driven seven demons. ¹⁰She went and told those who had been with him and who were mourning and weeping. ¹¹When they heard that Jesus was alive and that she had seen him, they did not believe it.

¹²Afterward Jesus appeared in a different form to two of them while they were walking in the country. ¹³These returned and reported it to the rest; but they did not believe them either.

¹⁴Later Jesus appeared to the Eleven as they were eating; he rebuked them for their lack of faith and their stubborn refusal to believe those who had seen him after he had risen.

¹⁵He said to them, "Go into all the world and preach the good news to all creation. ¹⁶Whoever believes and is baptized will be saved, but whoever does not believe will be condemned. ¹⁷And these signs will accompany those who believe: In my name they will drive out demons; they will speak in new tongues; ¹⁸they will pick up snakes with their hands; and when they drink deadly poison, it will not hurt them at all; they will place their hands on sick people, and they will get well."

¹⁹After the Lord Jesus had spoken to them, he was taken up into heaven and he sat at the right hand of God. ²⁰Then the disciples went out and preached everywhere, and the Lord worked with them and confirmed his word by the signs that accompanied it.

^y39 Some manuscripts do not have *heard his cry and*   ^z39 Or *a son*

 Discovering the Word 1. What kind of man is Pilate (vv. 1–15)? 2. What keeps him from doing what is right? 3. What ironies are present in the charges and jeers directed toward Jesus on the cross (vv. 25–32)? 4. Why do you think it was Joseph and the women who had followed Jesus, and not the eleven, who were present when Jesus died and his body needed a tomb (15:42—16:8)? 5. Why is it significant that Peter is mentioned by name in 16:7?

 Applying the Word 1. How can we keep from succumbing to the temptation Pilate faced? 2. How can this passage reinforce our commitment to sharing the good news of Christ with others?

Responding in Prayer Spend time in praise and thanksgiving for Christ's sacrifice and for his resurrection over death.

Luke

A t coffee break in a Paris conference, a third-year law student approached me with a good question. "You were talking about me when you spoke of church people who are respectfully bored with Jesus. You talk about him as if he's fascinating. How can I see Jesus this way?"

That opener with Jacques led to a fruitful discussion about the basic need to know the earthly life of Jesus Christ. Apart from Revelation 14:4, all references to "following Jesus" are of him as a man living in this world. The Son of God—*yes!* But just as emphatically we must say he is the Son of Humanity, authentically human!

How can we better know and follow Jesus Christ? Master the facts and implications of his earthly life and mission. That is how the first disciples gradually were dispelled of their wrong notions and came to see who Jesus of Nazareth really was—a divine Messiah, the Son of God, the universal Savior. They left behind historical records of his life. You have chosen to study the most comprehensive record of that life, *Luke's good news of new hope and new joy.*

The Uniqueness of Luke

Of the four Gospels, Luke's is the longest. It includes material not found elsewhere—for example, Jesus' childhood, his parables in chapters 10—19, his one-year ministry through Samaria and Berea during his final journey to Jerusalem. It includes unique characters—for instance, Zechariah and Elizabeth, Simeon and Anna, Simon the Pharisee and the prostitute, the Emmaus disciples (note the coupling) and Zaccheus.

Of the four Gospel writers, Luke was the only Gentile. As an initial outsider to God's chosen community, he was intrigued by Jesus' compassionate attention to foreigners (Syrians, Romans, Greeks, Africans) and social outcasts (tax collectors, lepers, prostitutes, beggars).

No other biblical author includes as many women—or as sympathetically as Luke does. No other writer talks about children and describes family life as he does. This is delightfully surprising for one who was apparently a bachelor.

Luke made a rich contribution to apostolic history, the period when the gospel was established in the Roman Empire. As a cosmopolitan traveler, he was admirably suited to become a coworker and "beloved doctor" of Paul, the apostle to the Gentiles. Acts and Paul's letters hint that this companionship had a tempering effect on the fiery apostle who became Christianity's foremost church planter, theologian and statesman.

The Writing of Luke

Luke's Gospel is accurate and well organized. Its formal introduction reflects the writer's Greek literary background (1:1–4). Here he claims to follow the principles for writing dependable history: (1) acquaintance with similar accounts, (2) interviews with primary sources—eyewitnesses and leading personages, (3) investigation of reported events, (4) orderliness in arranging materials, and (5) a stated aim.

Most scholars think that Luke (like Matthew) probably used Mark's older Gospel as the structural basis of his Gospel. When, however, he does use Mark's stories, he often touches them lightly with an extra personal detail. For example, compare the openings of the Jairus story in Mark 5:21–23 and Luke 8:40–42.

Luke addresses his Gospel (and Acts) to Theophilus. We know nothing else about this man. His name, "lover of God," was an aristocratic Roman one, and not uncommon among government officials. He could have been an actual person or a literary representative of this upper class of Gentile readers. According to Luke 1:4, he was either a seeker or a new Christian in need of historical substantiation of the good news.

Characteristics of Luke

Luke writes history like an artist. He employs prose and poetry, dialogue and description. In his choice of events and people he uses rhythm of emphasis, comparisons and contrasts. He uses this last teaching technique especially well with broad subjects—for example, Jesus' compassion for outcasts and his condemnation of the Pharisees, and Jesus' teachings on freedom of life with God and the cost of discipleship.

In transitions Luke is especially artistic. Note how the change of persons and locations in chapter 1 is smoothened by moving from one pregnancy to another. Likewise, his summaries of events also serve as links to the next train of events (for example, 2:39–40 or 5:15–16).

His book overflows with worship, prayer and praise, hope and joy. It begins with Old Testament believers in the temple, worshiping in messianic hope. It ends with New Testament believers also in the temple, rejoicing in resurrection hope. In between we see Jesus interacting personally with the widest range of human beings found in any book of the Bible (or any book in the world)—the old and the young, the very poor and the very rich, Jews and foreigners, national/international leaders and the rejects of society, the highly articulate and the nonarticulate.

Watch for bits of humor (for example, in Jesus' parables and in the Zaccheus story), the role of the Holy Spirit, medical terms, Jesus' habits of prayer, and the "divine necessity" Jesus felt (2:49; 4:43; 13:16, 33; 17:25; 24:26). Luke's portrait of Jesus is strong, warm, compassionate and cosmopolitan—like the writer himself.

My prayer for you as you study comes from Paul the apostle, Luke's friend:

May the God of hope fill you with all joy and peace as you trust in him, so that you may overflow with hope by the power of the Holy Spirit. (Ro 15:13)

Outline

Part 1: Mission in Galilee

1/ Luke 1 ———————————————— *People of Hope*

2/ Luke 2 ——————————————— Child of Hope

3/ Luke 3:1–20 ——————————— Public Preparation

4/ Luke 3:21—4:13 ————————— Personal Preparation

5/ Luke 4:14—5:16 ————————— Promising Yet Dangerous Blessings

6/ Luke 5:17—6:11 ————————— Radical Authority

7/ Luke 6:12–49 —————————— Radical Lifestyle

8/ Luke 7 ———————————————— Five People of Faith

9/ Luke 8:1–21 ——————————— Taking Care How You Listen

10/ Luke 8:22–56 —————————— Four Signs of Power and Identity

11/ Luke 9:1–50 —————————— Training for the Twelve

Part 2: Mission in Samaria, Berea and Judea

12/ Luke 9:51—10:24 ———————— Short-Term Costs for Long-Term Benefits

13/ Luke 10:25—11:13 ———————— Marks of Jesus' True Disciples

14/ Luke 11:14—12:12 ———————— Jesus the Controversialist

15/ Luke 12:13—13:21 ———————— Greed, Need & Judgment

16/ Luke 13:22—14:35 ———————— Are Only a Few People Going to Be Saved?

17/ Luke 15 ——————————————— The God Who Likes to Throw Parties

18/ Luke 16 ——————————————— Managing Your Money

19/ Luke 17:1—18:14 ————————— How to Grow Mustard-Seed Faith

20/ Luke 18:15—19:10 ————————— The Nobodies God Wants

21/ Luke 19:11–48 ——————————— False Hopes About the Kingdom of God

22/ Luke 20:1—21:4 —————————— Final Debates—Clear Rejection

23/ Luke 21:5–38 ———————————— Getting Ready for the End

24/ Luke 22:1–46 ———————————— Jesus' New Passover

25/ Luke 22:47—23:56 ————————— The Message of the Cross

26/ Luke 24 ——————————————— God Has the Last Word

1 / *Luke 1*
People of Hope

LUKE BEGINS HIS story of the extraordinary Christ by introducing some very ordinary people. They live in a small, second-rate country occupied by imperial Rome. It is around 4 B.C. For over 400 years their nation, Israel, has had no prophetic voice from God. Has God forgotten his chosen people? Has he left them to be the perennial pawns of aggressive neighbors? Is he going back on his many promises to send his Messiah to save them?

No. God is about to break into Israel's dark history with new light, and he chooses to do this through an elderly childless couple and a teenaged village girl.

 Warming Up to God   How do you feel when you are part of a hopeful minority among pessimistic people on a committee or in a group?

 Read Luke 1.

Many have undertaken to draw up an account of the things that have been fulfilled[a] among us, ²just as they were handed down to us by those who from the first were eyewitnesses and servants of the word. ³Therefore, since I myself have carefully investigated everything from the beginning, it seemed good also to me to write an orderly account for you, most excellent Theophilus, ⁴so that you may know the certainty of the things you have been taught.

⁵In the time of Herod king of Judea there was a priest named Zechariah, who belonged to the priestly division of Abijah; his wife Elizabeth was also a descendant of Aaron. ⁶Both of them were upright in the sight of God, observing all the Lord's commandments and regulations blamelessly. ⁷But they had no children, because Elizabeth was barren; and they were both well along in years.

⁸Once when Zechariah's division was on duty and he was serving as priest before God, ⁹he was chosen by lot, according to the custom of the priesthood, to go into the temple of the Lord and burn incense. ¹⁰And when the time for the burning of incense came, all the assembled worshipers were praying outside.

¹¹Then an angel of the Lord appeared to him, standing at the right side of the altar of incense. ¹²When Zechariah saw him, he was startled and was gripped with fear. ¹³But the angel said to him: "Do not be afraid, Zechariah; your prayer has been heard. Your wife Elizabeth will bear you a son, and you are to give him the name John. ¹⁴He will be a joy and delight to you, and many will rejoice because of his birth, ¹⁵for he will be great

in the sight of the Lord. He is never to take wine or other fermented drink, and he will be filled with the Holy Spirit even from birth.[b] ¹⁶Many of the people of Israel will he bring back to the Lord their God. ¹⁷And he will go on before the Lord, in the spirit and power of Elijah, to turn the hearts of the fathers to their children and the disobedient to the wisdom of the righteous—to make ready a people prepared for the Lord."

¹⁸Zechariah asked the angel, "How can I be sure of this? I am an old man and my wife is well along in years."

¹⁹The angel answered, "I am Gabriel. I stand in the presence of God, and I have been sent to speak to you and to tell you this good news. ²⁰And now you will be silent and not able to speak until the day this happens, because you did not believe my words, which will come true at their proper time."

²¹Meanwhile, the people were waiting for Zechariah and wondering why he stayed so long in the temple. ²²When he came out, he could not speak to them. They realized he had seen a vision in the temple, for he kept making signs to them but remained unable to speak.

²³When his time of service was completed, he returned home. ²⁴After this his wife Elizabeth became pregnant and for five months remained in seclusion. ²⁵"The Lord has done this for me," she said. "In these days he has shown his favor and taken away my disgrace among the people."

²⁶In the sixth month, God sent the angel Gabriel to Nazareth, a town in Galilee, ²⁷to a virgin pledged to be married to a man named Joseph, a descendant of David. The virgin's name was

a1 Or been surely believed   *b15 Or from his mother's womb*

Mary. 28The angel went to her and said, "Greetings, you who are highly favored! The Lord is with you."

29Mary was greatly troubled at his words and wondered what kind of greeting this might be. 30But the angel said to her, "Do not be afraid, Mary, you have found favor with God. 31You will be with child and give birth to a son, and you are to give him the name Jesus. 32He will be great and will be called the Son of the Most High. The Lord God will give him the throne of his father David, 33and he will reign over the house of Jacob forever; his kingdom will never end."

34"How will this be," Mary asked the angel, "since I am a virgin?"

35The angel answered, "The Holy Spirit will come upon you, and the power of the Most High will overshadow you. So the holy one to be born will be calledᶜ the Son of God. 36Even Elizabeth your relative is going to have a child in her old age, and she who was said to be barren is in her sixth month. 37For nothing is impossible with God."

38"I am the Lord's servant," Mary answered. "May it be to me as you have said." Then the angel left her.

39At that time Mary got ready and hurried to a town in the hill country of Judea, 40where she entered Zechariah's home and greeted Elizabeth. 41When Elizabeth heard Mary's greeting, the baby leaped in her womb, and Elizabeth was filled with the Holy Spirit. 42In a loud voice she exclaimed: "Blessed are you among women, and blessed is the child you will bear! 43But why am I so favored, that the mother of my Lord should come to me? 44As soon as the sound of your greeting reached my ears, the baby in my womb leaped for joy. 45Blessed is she who has believed that what the Lord has said to her will be accomplished!"

46And Mary said:

"My soul glorifies the Lord
47 and my spirit rejoices in God my Savior,
48for he has been mindful
    of the humble state of his servant.
From now on all generations will call me
    blessed,
49 for the Mighty One has done great things
    for me—
    holy is his name.
50His mercy extends to those who fear him,
    from generation to generation.

51He has performed mighty deeds with his arm;
    he has scattered those who are proud in
        their inmost thoughts.
52He has brought down rulers from their
        thrones
    but has lifted up the humble.
53He has filled the hungry with good things
    but has sent the rich away empty.
54He has helped his servant Israel,
    remembering to be merciful
55to Abraham and his descendants forever,
    even as he said to our fathers."

56Mary stayed with Elizabeth for about three months and then returned home.

57When it was time for Elizabeth to have her baby, she gave birth to a son. 58Her neighbors and relatives heard that the Lord had shown her great mercy, and they shared her joy.

59On the eighth day they came to circumcise the child, and they were going to name him after his father Zechariah, 60but his mother spoke up and said, "No! He is to be called John."

61They said to her, "There is no one among your relatives who has that name."

62Then they made signs to his father, to find out what he would like to name the child. 63He asked for a writing tablet, and to everyone's astonishment he wrote, "His name is John." 64Immediately his mouth was opened and his tongue was loosed, and he began to speak, praising God. 65The neighbors were all filled with awe, and throughout the hill country of Judea people were talking about all these things. 66Everyone who heard this wondered about it, asking, "What then is this child going to be?" For the Lord's hand was with him.

67His father Zechariah was filled with the Holy Spirit and prophesied:

68"Praise be to the Lord, the God of Israel,
    because he has come and has redeemed his
        people.
69He has raised up a hornᵈ of salvation for us
    in the house of his servant David
70(as he said through his holy prophets of long
        ago),
71salvation from our enemies
    and from the hand of all who hate us—
72to show mercy to our fathers
    and to remember his holy covenant,

ᶜ35 Or So the child to be born will be called holy,   ᵈ69 Horn here symbolizes strength.

73 the oath he swore to our father Abraham:
74to rescue us from the hand of our enemies,
and to enable us to serve him without fear
75 in holiness and righteousness before him all
our days.

76And you, my child, will be called a prophet of
the Most High;
for you will go on before the Lord to
prepare the way for him,
77to give his people the knowledge of salvation

through the forgiveness of their sins,
78because of the tender mercy of our God,
by which the rising sun will come to us
from heaven
79to shine on those living in darkness
and in the shadow of death,
to guide our feet into the path of peace."

80And the child grew and became strong in spirit; and he lived in the desert until he appeared publicly to Israel.

Discovering the Word 1. Gabriel announces some astounding facts to Zechariah about his son who is to be born (vv. 11–17). Do you find yourself sympathetic or critical of Zechariah's response of unbelief (vv. 18–22)? Explain. 2. Luke 1:26–56 has Gabriel's second birth announcement. How is it even more extraordinary than the first? 3. The visit to her cousin Elizabeth bolsters Mary's faith for the stupendous event to come. As expressed in her song of response, what kind of God does she believe in (vv. 46–55)? 4. Note the effects of John's birth on neighbors and relatives (vv. 57–66). What might be Luke's purpose in describing their response in such detail? 5. In Zechariah's inspired prophecy he sees (1) the great acts that God's Redeemer will do (vv. 68–75), and (2) his child's unique relation to this Redeemer (vv. 76–79). Suppose you were one of Zechariah's neighbors or relatives listening to him. Which part would have stirred you as a devout Jew? Explain.

Applying the Word 1. When is it difficult for you to hope in God? 2. Zechariah and Mary expressed their hope in God differently. What in their interaction with God gives you hope as you also seek to trust God totally?

Responding in Prayer Thank God for being the only source of true hope.

---

2 / *Luke 2*
Child of Hope

DID YOU HEAR the one about the woman shopper at Christmas who came upon a nativity scene in the store window? In disgust she exclaimed, "Now look what they're dragging into Christmas. Religion!"

Warming Up to God For you, what is most meaningful at Christmas?

Read Luke 2.

---

2 In those days Caesar Augustus issued a decree that a census should be taken of the entire Roman world. 2(This was the first census that took place while Quirinius was governor of Syria.) 3And everyone went to his own town to register.

4So Joseph also went up from the town of Nazareth in Galilee to Judea, to Bethlehem the town of David, because he belonged to the house and line of David. 5He went there to register with

Mary, who was pledged to be married to him and was expecting a child. 6While they were there, the time came for the baby to be born, 7and she gave birth to her firstborn, a son. She wrapped him in cloths and placed him in a manger, because there was no room for them in the inn.

8And there were shepherds living out in the fields nearby, keeping watch over their flocks at night. 9An angel of the Lord appeared to them, and the glory of the Lord shone around them, and

they were terrified. [10]But the angel said to them, "Do not be afraid. I bring you good news of great joy that will be for all the people. [11]Today in the town of David a Savior has been born to you; he is Christ[e] the Lord. [12]This will be a sign to you: You will find a baby wrapped in cloths and lying in a manger."

[13]Suddenly a great company of the heavenly host appeared with the angel, praising God and saying,

[14]"Glory to God in the highest,
　　and on earth peace to men on whom his
　　　　favor rests."

[15]When the angels had left them and gone into heaven, the shepherds said to one another, "Let's go to Bethlehem and see this thing that has happened, which the Lord has told us about."

[16]So they hurried off and found Mary and Joseph, and the baby, who was lying in the manger. [17]When they had seen him, they spread the word concerning what had been told them about this child, [18]and all who heard it were amazed at what the shepherds said to them. [19]But Mary treasured up all these things and pondered them in her heart. [20]The shepherds returned, glorifying and praising God for all the things they had heard and seen, which were just as they had been told.

[21]On the eighth day, when it was time to circumcise him, he was named Jesus, the name the angel had given him before he had been conceived.

[22]When the time of their purification according to the Law of Moses had been completed, Joseph and Mary took him to Jerusalem to present him to the Lord [23](as it is written in the Law of the Lord, "Every firstborn male is to be consecrated to the Lord"[f]), [24]and to offer a sacrifice in keeping with what is said in the Law of the Lord: "a pair of doves or two young pigeons."[g]

[25]Now there was a man in Jerusalem called Simeon, who was righteous and devout. He was waiting for the consolation of Israel, and the Holy Spirit was upon him. [26]It had been revealed to him by the Holy Spirit that he would not die before he had seen the Lord's Christ. [27]Moved by the Spirit, he went into the temple courts. When the parents brought in the child Jesus to do for him what the custom of the Law required, [28]Simeon took him in his arms and praised God, saying:

[29]"Sovereign Lord, as you have promised,
　　you now dismiss[h] your servant in peace.
[30]For my eyes have seen your salvation,
[31]　which you have prepared in the sight of all
　　　　people,
[32]a light for revelation to the Gentiles
　　and for glory to your people Israel."

[33]The child's father and mother marveled at what was said about him. [34]Then Simeon blessed them and said to Mary, his mother: "This child is destined to cause the falling and rising of many in Israel, and to be a sign that will be spoken against, [35]so that the thoughts of many hearts will be revealed. And a sword will pierce your own soul too."

[36]There was also a prophetess, Anna, the daughter of Phanuel, of the tribe of Asher. She was very old; she had lived with her husband seven years after her marriage, [37]and then was a widow until she was eighty-four.[i] She never left the temple but worshiped night and day, fasting and praying. [38]Coming up to them at that very moment, she gave thanks to God and spoke about the child to all who were looking forward to the redemption of Jerusalem.

[39]When Joseph and Mary had done everything required by the Law of the Lord, they returned to Galilee to their own town of Nazareth. [40]And the child grew and became strong; he was filled with wisdom, and the grace of God was upon him.

[41]Every year his parents went to Jerusalem for the Feast of the Passover. [42]When he was twelve years old, they went up to the Feast, according to the custom. [43]After the Feast was over, while his parents were returning home, the boy Jesus stayed behind in Jerusalem, but they were unaware of it. [44]Thinking he was in their company, they traveled on for a day. Then they began looking for him among their relatives and friends. [45]When they did not find him, they went back to Jerusalem to look for him. [46]After three days they found him in the temple courts, sitting among the teachers, listening to them and asking them questions. [47]Everyone who heard him was amazed at his understanding and his answers. [48]When his parents saw him, they were astonished. His mother said to him, "Son, why have you treated

---

[e]11 Or Messiah. "The Christ" (Greek) and "the Messiah" (Hebrew) both mean "the Anointed One"; also in verse 26.　[f]23 Exodus 13:2,12　[g]24 Lev. 12:8　[h]29 Or promised, / now dismiss　[i]37 Or widow for eighty-four years

us like this? Your father and I have been anxiously searching for you."

⁴⁹"Why were you searching for me?" he asked. "Didn't you know I had to be in my Father's house?" ⁵⁰But they did not understand what he was saying to them.

⁵¹Then he went down to Nazareth with them and was obedient to them. But his mother treasured all these things in her heart. ⁵²And Jesus grew in wisdom and stature, and in favor with God and men.

 Discovering the Word 1. As with other strategic events, Luke gives the historical setting of the birth of Jesus (vv. 1–4). What implications does this setting suggest about the world into which Jesus came? 2. Luke gives us few details of Jesus' birth in verses 6–7. But what impression does he leave with you? 3. We like shepherds on Christmas cards. But back then they were an outcast group. So what in the angels' message would be incredible to them (vv. 9–14)? 4. The second and third prophetic events (note that the naming of Jesus was a prophetic event) are closely tied together (2:22–28). In what ways are Simeon and Anna similar? 5. How are their prophetic messages about Jesus similar yet different?

 Applying the Word 1. Compare yourself with Jesus' development (vv. 40, 49, 51–52). In which area do you think you need more growth? 2. What can you begin to do to experience that growth?

Responding in Prayer Ask God to mold you into the person he wants you to be.

---

3 / *Luke 3:1–20*
Public Preparation

SEVERAL YEARS AGO, before Queen Elizabeth arrived in a British Commonwealth country, its people feverishly prepared a royal welcome. They gave special attention to the highway running from the airport to the capital. Each house along the way received from the government a fresh coat of paint—but only on the front of the house!

Superficial changes that people can notice—that's all some Christian leaders seem to ask for. Not so the preaching of John the Baptizer. He asked for radical moral changes, reversals of lifestyle.

 Warming Up to God In what way are you likely to be satisfied with superficial changes in your own life?

 Read Luke 3:1–20.

---

3 In the fifteenth year of the reign of Tiberius Caesar—when Pontius Pilate was governor of Judea, Herod tetrarch of Galilee, his brother Philip tetrarch of Iturea and Traconitis, and Lysanias tetrarch of Abilene— ²during the high priesthood of Annas and Caiaphas, the word of God came to John son of Zechariah in the desert. ³He went into all the country around the Jordan, preaching a baptism of repentance for the forgiveness of sins. ⁴As is written in the book of the words of Isaiah the prophet:

"A voice of one calling in the desert,
'Prepare the way for the Lord,
  make straight paths for him.

⁵Every valley shall be filled in,
  every mountain and hill made low.
The crooked roads shall become straight,
  the rough ways smooth.
⁶And all mankind will see God's salvation.' "ʲ

⁷John said to the crowds coming out to be baptized by him, "You brood of vipers! Who warned you to flee from the coming wrath? ⁸Produce fruit in keeping with repentance. And do not begin to say to yourselves, 'We have Abraham as our father.' For I tell you that out of these stones God can raise up children for Abraham. ⁹The ax is already at the root of the trees, and every tree that

j6 Isaiah 40:3-5

does not produce good fruit will be cut down and thrown into the fire."

10"What should we do then?" the crowd asked.

11John answered, "The man with two tunics should share with him who has none, and the one who has food should do the same."

12Tax collectors also came to be baptized. "Teacher," they asked, "what should we do?"

13"Don't collect any more than you are required to," he told them.

14Then some soldiers asked him, "And what should we do?"

He replied, "Don't extort money and don't accuse people falsely—be content with your pay."

15The people were waiting expectantly and were all wondering in their hearts if John might possibly be the Christ.[k] 16John answered them all, "I baptize you with[l] water. But one more powerful than I will come, the thongs of whose sandals I am not worthy to untie. He will baptize you with the Holy Spirit and with fire. 17His winnowing fork is in his hand to clear his threshing floor and to gather the wheat into his barn, but he will burn up the chaff with unquenchable fire." 18And with many other words John exhorted the people and preached the good news to them.

19But when John rebuked Herod the tetrarch because of Herodias, his brother's wife, and all the other evil things he had done, 20Herod added this to them all: He locked John up in prison.

[k]15 Or Messiah   [l]16 Or in

 Discovering the Word 1. Reflect on John's dominant preaching theme in verses 3–9. How would you paraphrase this theme with contemporary relevance? 2. John gladly answers three distinct groups asking about the practical fruits of repentance. What basic sin does John attack in each case (vv. 8–14)? 3. In verses 15–20 John introduces Jesus the Christ. He has been uncompromising about the need for repentance. Now he also refuses to let the crowds think he is the expected Christ. In warning them, what picture of the Christ does he paint? 4. Like repentance, judgment is not a popular topic today among many Christians. Yet how is this also part of "the good news" (v. 18)?

Applying the Word 1. What injustices in your society would John attack? 2. John's message and ministry show what repentance should be. How would you explain repentance to inquirers in terms that make sense to them?

Responding in Prayer Pray for a friend who needs this explanation.

---

4 / Luke 3:21—4:13
Personal Preparation

"THE BEST WAY to get rid of temptation is to give in to it," said Oscar Wilde. He was the brilliant, flamboyant Irish writer of the second half of the nineteenth century. He died young, gifted and dissipated by his unbridled passions.

Jesus also died young and gifted, but disciplined by his passion for God. His discipline began in childhood where we have already observed an early consciousness of his life mission. Now, at thirty, he submits himself to more tests to prepare him further for this goal.

 Warming Up to God What would you like to have achieved ten years from now?

 Read Luke 3:21—4:13.

21When all the people were being baptized, Jesus was baptized too. And as he was praying, heaven was opened 22and the Holy Spirit descended on him in bodily form like a dove. And a voice came from heaven: "You are my Son, whom I love; with you I am well pleased."

²³Now Jesus himself was about thirty years old when he began his ministry. He was the son, so it was thought, of Joseph,

the son of Heli, ²⁴the son of Matthat,
the son of Levi, the son of Melki,
the son of Jannai, the son of Joseph,
²⁵the son of Mattathias, the son of Amos,
the son of Nahum, the son of Esli,
the son of Naggai, ²⁶the son of Maath,
the son of Mattathias, the son of Semein,
the son of Josech, the son of Joda,
²⁷the son of Joanan, the son of Rhesa,
the son of Zerubbabel, the son of Shealtiel,
the son of Neri, ²⁸the son of Melki,
the son of Addi, the son of Cosam,
the son of Elmadam, the son of Er,
²⁹the son of Joshua, the son of Eliezer,
the son of Jorim, the son of Matthat,
the son of Levi, ³⁰the son of Simeon,
the son of Judah, the son of Joseph,
the son of Jonam, the son of Eliakim,
³¹the son of Melea, the son of Menna,
the son of Mattatha, the son of Nathan,
the son of David, ³²the son of Jesse,
the son of Obed, the son of Boaz,
the son of Salmon,ᵐ the son of Nahshon,
³³the son of Amminadab, the son of Ram,ⁿ
the son of Hezron, the son of Perez,
the son of Judah, ³⁴the son of Jacob,
the son of Isaac, the son of Abraham,
the son of Terah, the son of Nahor,
³⁵the son of Serug, the son of Reu,
the son of Peleg, the son of Eber,
the son of Shelah, ³⁶the son of Cainan,
the son of Arphaxad, the son of Shem,
the son of Noah, the son of Lamech,
³⁷the son of Methuselah, the son of Enoch,
the son of Jared, the son of Mahalalel,
the son of Kenan, ³⁸the son of Enosh,
the son of Seth, the son of Adam,
the son of God.

4 Jesus, full of the Holy Spirit, returned from the Jordan and was led by the Spirit in the desert, ²where for forty days he was tempted by the devil. He ate nothing during those days, and at the end of them he was hungry.

³The devil said to him, "If you are the Son of God, tell this stone to become bread."

⁴Jesus answered, "It is written: 'Man does not live on bread alone.'ᵒ"

⁵The devil led him up to a high place and showed him in an instant all the kingdoms of the world. ⁶And he said to him, "I will give you all their authority and splendor, for it has been given to me, and I can give it to anyone I want to. ⁷So if you worship me, it will all be yours."

⁸Jesus answered, "It is written: 'Worship the Lord your God and serve him only.'ᵖ"

⁹The devil led him to Jerusalem and had him stand on the highest point of the temple. "If you are the Son of God," he said, "throw yourself down from here. ¹⁰For it is written:

" 'He will command his angels concerning you
    to guard you carefully;
¹¹they will lift you up in their hands,
    so that you will not strike your foot against
    a stone.'�q"

¹²Jesus answered, "It says: 'Do not put the Lord your God to the test.'ʳ"

¹³When the devil had finished all this tempting, he left him until an opportune time.

ᵐ32 Some early manuscripts *Sala*   ⁿ33 Some manuscripts *Amminadab, the son of Admin, the son of Arni*; other manuscripts vary widely.   ᵒ4 Deut. 8:3   ᵖ8 Deut. 6:13   q11 Psalm 91:11,12   ʳ12 Deut. 6:16

Discovering the Word 1. Jesus did not have to be baptized for the forgiveness of his sins (v. 3). But by this public act he identified with our human race in need of repentance and forgiveness. What do Luke's details emphasize about Jesus' baptism? 2. Luke's genealogy of Jesus begins with his father, Joseph, and passing Abraham moves all the way back to "Adam, the son of God" (3:23–38). What does Luke want to bring out about Jesus? 3. Temptations are strong appeals to satisfy legitimate desires in wrong circumstances or by wrong means. What natural desire is the devil trying to get Jesus to satisfy in each appeal? 4. God created these desires. Why then would it become sin if Jesus were to satisfy each desire in his circumstances then?

Applying the Word 1. What do you learn from Jesus about dealing with temptations? 2. If we want to serve God wholeheartedly, we too must undergo tough training. In which area do you feel the greatest need for discipline? 3. What should be your first step in that direction?

 Responding in Prayer Pray that God would work in your life to prepare you for the ministry he has for you.

5 / *Luke 4:14—5:16*
Promising Yet Dangerous Beginnings

SOMETIMES PEOPLE SAY, "Everything has been going so well that I feel something awful coming." They know enough about life not to expect good things to continue forever. But we need not be fatalistic. We can be both realistic and positive about expectations in life. We have seen how well Jesus began. We shall also see how realistic he was about fickle human nature and how he drew out the best in people who wanted to follow him.

 Warming Up to God When you've felt rejection (on any level), what was your greatest fear?

 Read Luke 4:14—5:16.

---

¹⁴Jesus returned to Galilee in the power of the Spirit, and news about him spread through the whole countryside. ¹⁵He taught in their synagogues, and everyone praised him.

¹⁶He went to Nazareth, where he had been brought up, and on the Sabbath day he went into the synagogue, as was his custom. And he stood up to read. ¹⁷The scroll of the prophet Isaiah was handed to him. Unrolling it, he found the place where it is written:

¹⁸"The Spirit of the Lord is on me,
    because he has anointed me
    to preach good news to the poor.
He has sent me to proclaim freedom for the
    prisoners
    and recovery of sight for the blind,
to release the oppressed,
¹⁹   to proclaim the year of the Lord's favor." ˢ

²⁰Then he rolled up the scroll, gave it back to the attendant and sat down. The eyes of everyone in the synagogue were fastened on him, ²¹and he began by saying to them, "Today this scripture is fulfilled in your hearing."

²²All spoke well of him and were amazed at the gracious words that came from his lips. "Isn't this Joseph's son?" they asked.

²³Jesus said to them, "Surely you will quote this proverb to me: 'Physician, heal yourself! Do here in your hometown what we have heard that you did in Capernaum.' "

²⁴"I tell you the truth," he continued, "no prophet is accepted in his hometown. ²⁵I assure you that there were many widows in Israel in Elijah's time, when the sky was shut for three and a half years and there was a severe famine throughout the land. ²⁶Yet Elijah was not sent to any of them, but to a widow in Zarephath in the region of Sidon. ²⁷And there were many in Israel with leprosyᵗ in the time of Elisha the prophet, yet not one of them was cleansed—only Naaman the Syrian."

²⁸All the people in the synagogue were furious when they heard this. ²⁹They got up, drove him out of the town, and took him to the brow of the hill on which the town was built, in order to throw him down the cliff. ³⁰But he walked right through the crowd and went on his way.

³¹Then he went down to Capernaum, a town in Galilee, and on the Sabbath began to teach the people. ³²They were amazed at his teaching, because his message had authority.

³³In the synagogue there was a man possessed by a demon, an evilᵘ spirit. He cried out at the top of his voice, ³⁴"Ha! What do you want with us, Jesus of Nazareth? Have you come to destroy us? I know who you are—the Holy One of God!"

³⁵"Be quiet!" Jesus said sternly. "Come out of him!" Then the demon threw the man down before them all and came out without injuring him.

³⁶All the people were amazed and said to each other, "What is this teaching? With authority and power he gives orders to evil spirits and they come out!" ³⁷And the news about him spread throughout the surrounding area.

³⁸Jesus left the synagogue and went to the home of Simon. Now Simon's mother-in-law was suffering from a high fever, and they asked Jesus to help her. ³⁹So he bent over her and rebuked the fever, and it left her. She got up at once and began to wait on them.

⁴⁰When the sun was setting, the people brought to Jesus all who had various kinds of sickness, and laying his hands on each one, he

---

ˢ19 Isaiah 61:1,2   ᵗ27 The Greek word was used for various diseases affecting the skin—not necessarily leprosy.   ᵘ33 Greek *unclean*; also in verse 36

healed them. ⁴¹Moreover, demons came out of many people, shouting, "You are the Son of God!" But he rebuked them and would not allow them to speak, because they knew he was the Christ.ᵛ

⁴²At daybreak Jesus went out to a solitary place. The people were looking for him and when they came to where he was, they tried to keep him from leaving them. ⁴³But he said, "I must preach the good news of the kingdom of God to the other towns also, because that is why I was sent." ⁴⁴And he kept on preaching in the synagogues of Judea.ʷ

5 One day as Jesus was standing by the Lake of Gennesaret,ˣ with the people crowding around him and listening to the word of God, ²he saw at the water's edge two boats, left there by the fishermen, who were washing their nets. ³He got into one of the boats, the one belonging to Simon, and asked him to put out a little from shore. Then he sat down and taught the people from the boat.

⁴When he had finished speaking, he said to Simon, "Put out into deep water, and let downʸ the nets for a catch."

⁵Simon answered, "Master, we've worked hard all night and haven't caught anything. But because you say so, I will let down the nets."

⁶When they had done so, they caught such a large number of fish that their nets began to break. ⁷So they signaled their partners in the other boat to come and help them, and they came and filled both boats so full that they began to sink.

⁸When Simon Peter saw this, he fell at Jesus' knees and said, "Go away from me, Lord; I am a sinful man!" ⁹For he and all his companions were astonished at the catch of fish they had taken, ¹⁰and so were James and John, the sons of Zebedee, Simon's partners.

Then Jesus said to Simon, "Don't be afraid; from now on you will catch men." ¹¹So they pulled their boats up on shore, left everything and followed him.

¹²While Jesus was in one of the towns, a man came along who was covered with leprosy.ᶻ When he saw Jesus, he fell with his face to the ground and begged him, "Lord, if you are willing, you can make me clean."

¹³Jesus reached out his hand and touched the man. "I am willing," he said. "Be clean!" And immediately the leprosy left him.

¹⁴Then Jesus ordered him, "Don't tell anyone, but go, show yourself to the priest and offer the sacrifices that Moses commanded for your cleansing, as a testimony to them."

¹⁵Yet the news about him spread all the more, so that crowds of people came to hear him and to be healed of their sicknesses. ¹⁶But Jesus often withdrew to lonely places and prayed.

ᵛ41 Or *Messiah*   ʷ44 Or *the land of the Jews*; some manuscripts *Galilee*   ˣ1 That is, Sea of Galilee   ʸ4 The Greek verb is plural.   ᶻ12 The Greek word was used for various diseases affecting the skin—not necessarily leprosy.

Discovering the Word 1. What link do you see between Jesus' temptations and the beginning of his mission (4:14–15)? 2. Watch the people's changing attitudes to Jesus (vv. 14–15, 20–22, 28–29). What has caused the radical change? 3. What prejudices can make people today object to Jesus' good news or perhaps to Jesus himself? How would you respond to these objections? 4. Having been rejected by Nazareth, Jesus now makes Capernaum his base of operations. Here Luke describes what may be a typical work day for Jesus. Identify his activities during that period (4:31–44). 5. Read Luke 5:1–16. Note the progressive steps by which Jesus persuades Simon Peter to leave everything and follow him. When you met Jesus, what tensions arose as you recognized the need to leave everything to follow him?

Applying the Word 1. What can you learn from Jesus' example of dealing with rejection? 2. In its context Jesus' healing of the leper appears to be a personal encounter, typical of his opening ministry. As such then, what do you observe about Jesus as a people helper? 3. Think of your ministry to others. Which of Jesus' ministering qualities do you want to have added to or reinforced in your life?

 Responding in Prayer Praise God for such a practical Teacher and Lord!

6 / *Luke 5:17—6:11*
Radical Authority

GOD IS ALWAYS full of surprises. Those who know him delight in this. This, however, upsets people who feel secure only with neatly structured beliefs that are left untouched. One problem for them is that every now and then God chooses to do something new and fresh. Then packaged religions and secure traditions fall apart! This often happened when Jesus came on Israel's religious scene with surprising teaching and authority.

 Warming Up to God   Do you wish you had more or less authority in your life? Why?

 Read Luke 5:17—6:11.

---

¹⁷One day as he was teaching, Pharisees and teachers of the law, who had come from every village of Galilee and from Judea and Jerusalem, were sitting there. And the power of the Lord was present for him to heal the sick. ¹⁸Some men came carrying a paralytic on a mat and tried to take him into the house to lay him before Jesus. ¹⁹When they could not find a way to do this because of the crowd, they went up on the roof and lowered him on his mat through the tiles into the middle of the crowd, right in front of Jesus.

²⁰When Jesus saw their faith, he said, "Friend, your sins are forgiven."

²¹The Pharisees and the teachers of the law began thinking to themselves, "Who is this fellow who speaks blasphemy? Who can forgive sins but God alone?"

²²Jesus knew what they were thinking and asked, "Why are you thinking these things in your hearts? ²³Which is easier: to say, 'Your sins are forgiven,' or to say, 'Get up and walk'? ²⁴But that you may know that the Son of Man has authority on earth to forgive sins. . . ." He said to the paralyzed man, "I tell you, get up, take your mat and go home." ²⁵Immediately he stood up in front of them, took what he had been lying on and went home praising God. ²⁶Everyone was amazed and gave praise to God. They were filled with awe and said, "We have seen remarkable things today."

²⁷After this, Jesus went out and saw a tax collector by the name of Levi sitting at his tax booth. "Follow me," Jesus said to him, ²⁸and Levi got up, left everything and followed him.

²⁹Then Levi held a great banquet for Jesus at his house, and a large crowd of tax collectors and others were eating with them. ³⁰But the Pharisees and the teachers of the law who belonged to their sect complained to his disciples, "Why do you eat and drink with tax collectors and 'sinners'?"

³¹Jesus answered them, "It is not the healthy who need a doctor, but the sick. ³²I have not come to call the righteous, but sinners to repentance."

³³They said to him, "John's disciples often fast and pray, and so do the disciples of the Pharisees, but yours go on eating and drinking."

³⁴Jesus answered, "Can you make the guests of the bridegroom fast while he is with them? ³⁵But the time will come when the bridegroom will be taken from them; in those days they will fast."

³⁶He told them this parable: "No one tears a patch from a new garment and sews it on an old one. If he does, he will have torn the new garment, and the patch from the new will not match the old. ³⁷And no one pours new wine into old wineskins. If he does, the new wine will burst the skins, the wine will run out and the wineskins will be ruined. ³⁸No, new wine must be poured into new wineskins. ³⁹And no one after drinking old wine wants the new, for he says, 'The old is better.' "

6 One Sabbath Jesus was going through the grainfields, and his disciples began to pick some heads of grain, rub them in their hands and eat the kernels. ²Some of the Pharisees asked, "Why are you doing what is unlawful on the Sabbath?"

³Jesus answered them, "Have you never read what David did when he and his companions were hungry? ⁴He entered the house of God, and taking the consecrated bread, he ate what is lawful only for priests to eat. And he also gave some to his companions." ⁵Then Jesus said to them, "The Son of Man is Lord of the Sabbath."

⁶On another Sabbath he went into the syna-

gogue and was teaching, and a man was there whose right hand was shriveled. 7The Pharisees and the teachers of the law were looking for a reason to accuse Jesus, so they watched him closely to see if he would heal on the Sabbath. 8But Jesus knew what they were thinking and said to the man with the shriveled hand, "Get up and stand in front of everyone." So he got up and stood there.

9Then Jesus said to them, "I ask you, which is lawful on the Sabbath: to do good or to do evil, to save life or to destroy it?"

10He looked around at them all, and then said to the man, "Stretch out your hand." He did so, and his hand was completely restored. 11But they were furious and began to discuss with one another what they might do to Jesus.

Discovering the Word 1. Imagine yourself a part of the religious establishment mentioned in 5:17. How would you have viewed Jesus' growing popularity? 2. Compare the Pharisees' questions in 5:21, 30, 33; 6:2, 7—criticisms which climax in 6:11. What pattern(s) do you observe? 3. What skills in answering religious critics can you learn from Jesus?

Applying the Word 1. Jesus was relentless in his battle with the religious legalists of his day. He clearly saw that in distorting God's laws they also distorted God's image. What religious legalisms can keep you from enjoying the Lord and his true sabbath? 2. Over which area of your life do you see Jesus exercising authority? 3. Over which area of your life do you sense an absence of Jesus' authority?

Responding in Prayer Ask Jesus to rule over your *whole* life.

7 / *Luke 6:12–49*
Radical Lifestyle

MAHATMA MOHANDAS GANDHI was India's revered leader in the fight for national independence from British colonialism. As a child in India, a student in England and a lawyer in South Africa, he was exposed to Christianity—and racism. He admired the teachings of Jesus, especially the Sermon on the Mount. He admired the life of Jesus, and indeed was inspired to follow his example. But after years of observing Christians, he sadly concluded, "For me to believe in their Redeemer, their lives must show they are redeemed." He never became a Christian.

A Christian's lifestyle matters—not only correct words. The total teaching and example of Jesus demands a lifestyle that is noticeably different from the average person's.

Warming Up to God Describe someone you know who has a truly Christlike lifestyle.

Read Luke 6:12–49.

12One of those days Jesus went out to a mountainside to pray, and spent the night praying to God. 13When morning came, he called his disciples to him and chose twelve of them, whom he also designated apostles: 14Simon (whom he named Peter), his brother Andrew, James, John, Philip, Bartholomew, 15Matthew, Thomas, James son of Alphaeus, Simon who was called the Zealot, 16Judas son of James, and Judas Iscariot, who became a traitor.

17He went down with them and stood on a level place. A large crowd of his disciples was there and a great number of people from all over Judea, from Jerusalem, and from the coast of Tyre and Sidon, 18who had come to hear him and to be healed of their diseases. Those troubled by evil[a] spirits were cured, 19and the people all tried to touch him, because power was coming from him and healing them all.

20Looking at his disciples, he said:

a18 Greek unclean

"Blessed are you who are poor,
    for yours is the kingdom of God.
21Blessed are you who hunger now,
    for you will be satisfied.
Blessed are you who weep now,
    for you will laugh.
22Blessed are you when men hate you,
    when they exclude you and insult you
    and reject your name as evil,
        because of the Son of Man.

23"Rejoice in that day and leap for joy, because great is your reward in heaven. For that is how their fathers treated the prophets.

24"But woe to you who are rich,
    for you have already received your comfort.
25Woe to you who are well fed now,
    for you will go hungry.
Woe to you who laugh now,
    for you will mourn and weep.
26Woe to you when all men speak well of you,
    for that is how their fathers treated the
        false prophets.

27"But I tell you who hear me: Love your enemies, do good to those who hate you, 28bless those who curse you, pray for those who mistreat you. 29If someone strikes you on one cheek, turn to him the other also. If someone takes your cloak, do not stop him from taking your tunic. 30Give to everyone who asks you, and if anyone takes what belongs to you, do not demand it back. 31Do to others as you would have them do to you.

32"If you love those who love you, what credit is that to you? Even 'sinners' love those who love them. 33And if you do good to those who are good to you, what credit is that to you? Even 'sinners' do that. 34And if you lend to those from whom you expect repayment, what credit is that to you? Even 'sinners' lend to 'sinners,' expecting to be repaid in full. 35But love your enemies, do good to them, and lend to them without expecting to get anything back. Then your reward will be great, and you will be sons of the Most High, because he is kind to the ungrateful and wicked. 36Be merciful, just as your Father is merciful.

37"Do not judge, and you will not be judged. Do not condemn, and you will not be condemned. Forgive, and you will be forgiven. 38Give, and it will be given to you. A good measure, pressed down, shaken together and running over, will be poured into your lap. For with the measure you use, it will be measured to you."

39He also told them this parable: "Can a blind man lead a blind man? Will they not both fall into a pit? 40A student is not above his teacher, but everyone who is fully trained will be like his teacher.

41"Why do you look at the speck of sawdust in your brother's eye and pay no attention to the plank in your own eye? 42How can you say to your brother, 'Brother, let me take the speck out of your eye,' when you yourself fail to see the plank in your own eye? You hypocrite, first take the plank out of your eye, and then you will see clearly to remove the speck from your brother's eye.

43"No good tree bears bad fruit, nor does a bad tree bear good fruit. 44Each tree is recognized by its own fruit. People do not pick figs from thornbushes, or grapes from briers. 45The good man brings good things out of the good stored up in his heart, and the evil man brings evil things out of the evil stored up in his heart. For out of the overflow of his heart his mouth speaks.

46"Why do you call me, 'Lord, Lord,' and do not do what I say? 47I will show you what he is like who comes to me and hears my words and puts them into practice. 48He is like a man building a house, who dug down deep and laid the foundation on rock. When a flood came, the torrent struck that house but could not shake it, because it was well built. 49But the one who hears my words and does not put them into practice is like a man who built a house on the ground without a foundation. The moment the torrent struck that house, it collapsed and its destruction was complete."

Discovering the Word 1. In verses 17–19 Luke has carefully given us the setting for the "Sermon on the Plain." What kinds of people are in Jesus' audience? 2. Jesus begins with kingdom attitudes that shape one's lifestyle. What contrasts does he draw between his way of personal fulfillment and the world's way (vv. 20–26)? 3. Jesus knows that loving one's enemies is impossible without strong motivation. How does he argue that his disciples can have that motivation (vv. 31–36)? 4. In verse 37 Jesus is probably being facetious, for he knows it is impossible not to judge others. Rather we are to judge with good sense. What guidelines does he give to judge

in this way (vv. 37b–42)? 5. Jesus concludes by warning his listeners of the long-term results of their present choice of lifestyle (vv. 43–49). How do his logic and illustrations sharpen his argument?

 Applying the Word 1. In what ways have you found Jesus' road to happiness the right one? Or an unsatisfactory one? 2. Loving one's enemies is another aspect of a radical Christian lifestyle. In what ways does your enemy make it hard for you to love him/her? 3. What in this study gives you hope that you can maintain the kind of radical lifestyle Jesus expects of his followers?

Responding in Prayer Pray for the strength and wisdom you need to love your enemies.

---

8 / *Luke 7*
Five People of Faith

AN ARTIST FRIEND struggled over the exclusive claim of the Christian faith. Is Jesus really the only way to God? Growing up in a pluralistic society had conditioned her to resist such an intolerant position. Because she was still interested, some Christians pressured her to "accept Jesus as your Savior and Lord." She could not. But she privately pursued the Gospels. She began to note how differently people approached Jesus and how personally he treated each of them. Gradually she saw a distinction: There is indeed only one way to God—through Jesus Christ—but there are many ways to Jesus Christ. Today we meet five persons with diverse backgrounds and varying approaches to Jesus—all different in expressing faith in Jesus.

 Warming Up to God When is it hard for you to accept the idea that there is only one way to God?

 Read Luke 7.

---

7 When Jesus had finished saying all this in the hearing of the people, he entered Capernaum. ²There a centurion's servant, whom his master valued highly, was sick and about to die. ³The centurion heard of Jesus and sent some elders of the Jews to him, asking him to come and heal his servant. ⁴When they came to Jesus, they pleaded earnestly with him, "This man deserves to have you do this, ⁵because he loves our nation and has built our synagogue." ⁶So Jesus went with them.

He was not far from the house when the centurion sent friends to say to him: "Lord, don't trouble yourself, for I do not deserve to have you come under my roof. ⁷That is why I did not even consider myself worthy to come to you. But say the word, and my servant will be healed. ⁸For I myself am a man under authority, with soldiers under me. I tell this one, 'Go,' and he goes; and that one, 'Come,' and he comes. I say to my servant, 'Do this,' and he does it."

⁹When Jesus heard this, he was amazed at him, and turning to the crowd following him, he said, "I tell you, I have not found such great faith even in Israel." ¹⁰Then the men who had been sent returned to the house and found the servant well.

¹¹Soon afterward, Jesus went to a town called Nain, and his disciples and a large crowd went along with him. ¹²As he approached the town gate, a dead person was being carried out—the only son of his mother, and she was a widow. And a large crowd from the town was with her. ¹³When the Lord saw her, his heart went out to her and he said, "Don't cry."

¹⁴Then he went up and touched the coffin, and those carrying it stood still. He said, "Young man, I say to you, get up!" ¹⁵The dead man sat up and began to talk, and Jesus gave him back to his mother.

¹⁶They were all filled with awe and praised God. "A great prophet has appeared among us," they said. "God has come to help his people." ¹⁷This news about Jesus spread throughout Judea*ᵇ* and the surrounding country.

¹⁸John's disciples told him about all these things. Calling two of them, ¹⁹he sent them to the

ᵇ17 Or the land of the Jews

Lord to ask, "Are you the one who was to come, or should we expect someone else?"

20When the men came to Jesus, they said, "John the Baptist sent us to you to ask, 'Are you the one who was to come, or should we expect someone else?'"

21At that very time Jesus cured many who had diseases, sicknesses and evil spirits, and gave sight to many who were blind. 22So he replied to the messengers, "Go back and report to John what you have seen and heard: The blind receive sight, the lame walk, those who have leprosy[c] are cured, the deaf hear, the dead are raised, and the good news is preached to the poor. 23Blessed is the man who does not fall away on account of me."

24After John's messengers left, Jesus began to speak to the crowd about John: "What did you go out into the desert to see? A reed swayed by the wind? 25If not, what did you go out to see? A man dressed in fine clothes? No, those who wear expensive clothes and indulge in luxury are in palaces. 26But what did you go out to see? A prophet? Yes, I tell you, and more than a prophet. 27This is the one about whom it is written:

" 'I will send my messenger ahead of you,
    who will prepare your way before you.'[d]

28I tell you, among those born of women there is no one greater than John; yet the one who is least in the kingdom of God is greater than he."

29(All the people, even the tax collectors, when they heard Jesus' words, acknowledged that God's way was right, because they had been baptized by John. 30But the Pharisees and experts in the law rejected God's purpose for themselves, because they had not been baptized by John.)

31"To what, then, can I compare the people of this generation? What are they like? 32They are like children sitting in the marketplace and calling out to each other:

" 'We played the flute for you,
    and you did not dance;
we sang a dirge,
    and you did not cry.'

33For John the Baptist came neither eating bread nor drinking wine, and you say, 'He has a demon.' 34The Son of Man came eating and drinking, and

you say, 'Here is a glutton and a drunkard, a friend of tax collectors and "sinners." ' 35But wisdom is proved right by all her children."

36Now one of the Pharisees invited Jesus to have dinner with him, so he went to the Pharisee's house and reclined at the table. 37When a woman who had lived a sinful life in that town learned that Jesus was eating at the Pharisee's house, she brought an alabaster jar of perfume, 38and as she stood behind him at his feet weeping, she began to wet his feet with her tears. Then she wiped them with her hair, kissed them and poured perfume on them.

39When the Pharisee who had invited him saw this, he said to himself, "If this man were a prophet, he would know who is touching him and what kind of woman she is—that she is a sinner."

40Jesus answered him, "Simon, I have something to tell you."

"Tell me, teacher," he said.

41"Two men owed money to a certain moneylender. One owed him five hundred denarii,[e] and the other fifty. 42Neither of them had the money to pay him back, so he canceled the debts of both. Now which of them will love him more?"

43Simon replied, "I suppose the one who had the bigger debt canceled."

"You have judged correctly," Jesus said.

44Then he turned toward the woman and said to Simon, "Do you see this woman? I came into your house. You did not give me any water for my feet, but she wet my feet with her tears and wiped them with her hair. 45You did not give me a kiss, but this woman, from the time I entered, has not stopped kissing my feet. 46You did not put oil on my head, but she has poured perfume on my feet. 47Therefore, I tell you, her many sins have been forgiven—for she loved much. But he who has been forgiven little loves little."

48Then Jesus said to her, "Your sins are forgiven."

49The other guests began to say among themselves, "Who is this who even forgives sins?"

50Jesus said to the woman, "Your faith has saved you; go in peace."

---

[c]22 The Greek word was used for various diseases affecting the skin—not necessarily leprosy.   [d]27 Mal. 3:1   [e]41 A denarius was a coin worth about a day's wages.

Discovering the Word 1. Note the distinctive background of each of the five individuals who met Jesus. How are their backgrounds different? 2. What do they all have in common as they relate to Jesus? 3. Picture the two processions in verses 11–13 meeting just outside the town gate. There is no request for help, no sign of faith from the widow. But look at Jesus himself in verses 13–15. What does this focus suggest about another dimension of faith in God's power? 4. Despite the Pharisees' public rejection of Jesus, one of them invites him to dinner. A drama unfolds (vv. 36–50). The woman's faith in Jesus is obvious. But Simon shows signs of some kind of faith in Jesus (vv. 36a, 39, 40b). How does Jesus proceed to draw out his faith? 5. Jesus' interaction with the woman is vastly different from his interaction with Simon. What does this indicate about his understanding of each?

Applying the Word 1. It was physically easy for Jesus to touch the dead man. But in doing so, he ritualistically contaminated himself. In our society what comparable risks might we have to take to help needy people? 2. Of the five people you have looked at, with whom can you more readily identify? How does she/he challenge your faith in Jesus as Friend and Lord?

Responding in Prayer Pray for courage to take risks in reaching out to those around you who are open to learning about Christ.

9 / *Luke 8:1–21*
Taking Care How You Listen

WHEN THE BERLIN Wall fell in 1989, the West rejoiced. For Christians it symbolized evangelistic opportunities in East Europe. At first we heard much of "tremendous openness," "thousands accepting Christ," "demand for Bibles." This was probably true. Then we began hearing about growing materialism and power struggles among some Christian leaders. Journalists began to report that many who came to meetings were mainly eager for Western contacts to worldly opportunities. Wherever the gospel is preached, results vary, because people have different motives for listening and responding. Jesus knew this about his contemporary audience, and he dealt with it in a graphic way.

 Warming Up to God What were the two most significant factors that influenced your response to the Christian gospel?

 Read Luke 8:1–21.

8 After this, Jesus traveled about from one town and village to another, proclaiming the good news of the kingdom of God. The Twelve were with him, ²and also some women who had been cured of evil spirits and diseases: Mary (called Magdalene) from whom seven demons had come out; ³Joanna the wife of Cuza, the manager of Herod's household; Susanna; and many others. These women were helping to support them out of their own means.

⁴While a large crowd was gathering and people were coming to Jesus from town after town, he told this parable: ⁵"A farmer went out to sow his seed. As he was scattering the seed, some fell along the path; it was trampled on, and the birds of the air ate it up. ⁶Some fell on rock, and when it came up, the plants withered because they had no moisture. ⁷Other seed fell among thorns,

which grew up with it and choked the plants. ⁸Still other seed fell on good soil. It came up and yielded a crop, a hundred times more than was sown."

When he said this, he called out, "He who has ears to hear, let him hear."

⁹His disciples asked him what this parable meant. ¹⁰He said, "The knowledge of the secrets of the kingdom of God has been given to you, but to others I speak in parables, so that,

" 'though seeing, they may not see;
    though hearing, they may not
        understand.'ᶠ

¹¹"This is the meaning of the parable: The seed is the word of God. ¹²Those along the path are the ones who hear, and then the devil comes and

f10 Isaiah 6:9

takes away the word from their hearts, so that they may not believe and be saved. ¹³Those on the rock are the ones who receive the word with joy when they hear it, but they have no root. They believe for a while, but in the time of testing they fall away. ¹⁴The seed that fell among thorns stands for those who hear, but as they go on their way they are choked by life's worries, riches and pleasures, and they do not mature. ¹⁵But the seed on good soil stands for those with a noble and good heart, who hear the word, retain it, and by persevering produce a crop.

¹⁶"No one lights a lamp and hides it in a jar or puts it under a bed. Instead, he puts it on a stand, so that those who come in can see the light. ¹⁷For there is nothing hidden that will not be disclosed, and nothing concealed that will not be known or brought out into the open. ¹⁸Therefore consider carefully how you listen. Whoever has will be given more; whoever does not have, even what he thinks he has will be taken from him."

¹⁹Now Jesus' mother and brothers came to see him, but they were not able to get near him because of the crowd. ²⁰Someone told him, "Your mother and brothers are standing outside, wanting to see you."

²¹He replied, "My mother and brothers are those who hear God's word and put it into practice."

 Discovering the Word 1. Luke's description of the women followers in verses 2–3 is unique among the Gospels. What do these verses tell you about the changing nature of Jesus' ministry? 2. In Jesus' first parable the seeds sown are the same, but the soils are different. How are they different? 3. Jesus himself interprets this opening parable. What is his main point (vv. 11–15)? 4. As the crowds grow, Jesus increasingly teaches in parables. He gives his reason for this in verses 8b–10. How is the use of parables effective in testing a listener's sincerity? 5. Luke uses the family episode as a live illustration of listening to God (vv. 19–21). What does Jesus highlight by this illustration?

 Applying the Word 1. Think over 8:15, where Jesus spells out what good soil is. How do you aim to cultivate your good soil? 2. Reflecting on the parable of the lighted lamp (vv. 16–18), consider your habits of listening to God's truth. How can you be more open to God?

 Responding in Prayer Ask God to guide you to his truth and make you always open to what he has to say to you.

---

10 / *Luke 8:22–56*
Four Signs of Power and Identity

WHEN IS GOD present among people? Worshipers in a village in Portugal, in a village in Yugoslavia and more recently in an Illinois town all said he was present in a unique way. They claimed the Virgin Mary appeared to them, sometimes instructing or comforting and sometimes healing them. These locations drew thousands of people, either seeking the physical reality of God or simply curious. Visions, healing and deliverance services easily draw crowds all over the world. Whether people are believers or skeptics, they want to see, and perhaps experience, God's power—if it's there.

Warming Up to God To what extent do we today need unusual displays of God's power?

Read Luke 8:22–56.

---

²²One day Jesus said to his disciples, "Let's go over to the other side of the lake." So they got into a boat and set out. ²³As they sailed, he fell asleep. A squall came down on the lake, so that the boat was being swamped, and they were in great danger.

²⁴The disciples went and woke him, saying, "Master, Master, we're going to drown!"

He got up and rebuked the wind and the raging waters; the storm subsided, and all was calm. 25"Where is your faith?" he asked his disciples.

In fear and amazement they asked one another, "Who is this? He commands even the winds and the water, and they obey him."

26They sailed to the region of the Gerasenes,g which is across the lake from Galilee. 27When Jesus stepped ashore, he was met by a demon-possessed man from the town. For a long time this man had not worn clothes or lived in a house, but had lived in the tombs. 28When he saw Jesus, he cried out and fell at his feet, shouting at the top of his voice, "What do you want with me, Jesus, Son of the Most High God? I beg you, don't torture me!" 29For Jesus had commanded the evilh spirit to come out of the man. Many times it had seized him, and though he was chained hand and foot and kept under guard, he had broken his chains and had been driven by the demon into solitary places.

30Jesus asked him, "What is your name?"

"Legion," he replied, because many demons had gone into him. 31And they begged him repeatedly not to order them to go into the Abyss.

32A large herd of pigs was feeding there on the hillside. The demons begged Jesus to let them go into them, and he gave them permission. 33When the demons came out of the man, they went into the pigs, and the herd rushed down the steep bank into the lake and was drowned.

34When those tending the pigs saw what had happened, they ran off and reported this in the town and countryside, 35and the people went out to see what had happened. When they came to Jesus, they found the man from whom the demons had gone out, sitting at Jesus' feet, dressed and in his right mind; and they were afraid. 36Those who had seen it told the people how the demon-possessed man had been cured. 37Then all the people of the region of the Gerasenes asked Jesus to leave them, because they were overcome with fear. So he got into the boat and left.

38The man from whom the demons had gone out begged to go with him, but Jesus sent him away, saying, 39"Return home and tell how much God has done for you." So the man went away and told all over town how much Jesus had done for him.

40Now when Jesus returned, a crowd welcomed him, for they were all expecting him. 41Then a man named Jairus, a ruler of the synagogue, came and fell at Jesus' feet, pleading with him to come to his house 42because his only daughter, a girl of about twelve, was dying.

As Jesus was on his way, the crowds almost crushed him. 43And a woman was there who had been subject to bleeding for twelve years,i but no one could heal her. 44She came up behind him and touched the edge of his cloak, and immediately her bleeding stopped.

45"Who touched me?" Jesus asked.

When they all denied it, Peter said, "Master, the people are crowding and pressing against you."

46But Jesus said, "Someone touched me; I know that power has gone out from me."

47Then the woman, seeing that she could not go unnoticed, came trembling and fell at his feet. In the presence of all the people, she told why she had touched him and how she had been instantly healed. 48Then he said to her, "Daughter, your faith has healed you. Go in peace."

49While Jesus was still speaking, someone came from the house of Jairus, the synagogue ruler. "Your daughter is dead," he said. "Don't bother the teacher any more."

50Hearing this, Jesus said to Jairus, "Don't be afraid; just believe, and she will be healed."

51When he arrived at the house of Jairus, he did not let anyone go in with him except Peter, John and James, and the child's father and mother. 52Meanwhile, all the people were wailing and mourning for her. "Stop wailing," Jesus said. "She is not dead but asleep."

53They laughed at him, knowing that she was dead. 54But he took her by the hand and said, "My child, get up!" 55Her spirit returned, and at once she stood up. Then Jesus told them to give her something to eat. 56Her parents were astonished, but he ordered them not to tell anyone what had happened.

g26 Some manuscripts Gadarenes; other manuscripts Gergesenes; also in verse 37 h29 Greek unclean i43 Many manuscripts years, and she had spent all she had on doctors

Discovering the Word 1. Jesus' Galilean disciples were used to sudden, violent storms on their sea, but this one was ferocious. What emotions do they experience from the beginning to the end of this event (vv. 22–25)? 2. Luke 8:26–39 is the second power encounter—this time in foreign territory. What unusual elements do you observe in the interchange between the man and Jesus? 3. We should not get morbidly curious about the subject of demons. But from this text what can you know about them? 4. Jesus and his disciples are back in home territory, where two more astonishing events take place. How is the healing of the woman different from other Bible healings you know of (vv. 40–56)?

Applying the Word 1. Jesus insists on knowing who touched him. How has it helped to witness publicly to what God has done for you? 2. What signs of God's power in your world move you most to worship and obey Jesus Christ as Lord of the universe?

Responding in Prayer Be thankful that you may worship God, who is both all-powerful and all-loving.

11 / *Luke 9:1–50*
Training for the Twelve

"IT HAS BEEN my experience that superior people are attracted only by challenge. By setting our standards low and making our life soft we have, quite automatically and unconsciously, assured ourselves of mediocre people" (Ambassador MacWhite in *The Ugly American*, referring to his observations in the diplomatic corps). Looking at Jesus' diplomatic corps of twelve, we might wonder about his standards. The Gospels tell us little about their backgrounds, but they tell us much about how Jesus trained them. This is useful for us.

Warming Up to God In what area of your Christian life do you feel that you are growing?

Read Luke 9:1–50.

9 When Jesus had called the Twelve together, he gave them power and authority to drive out all demons and to cure diseases, ²and he sent them out to preach the kingdom of God and to heal the sick. ³He told them: "Take nothing for the journey—no staff, no bag, no bread, no money, no extra tunic. ⁴Whatever house you enter, stay there until you leave that town. ⁵If people do not welcome you, shake the dust off your feet when you leave their town, as a testimony against them." ⁶So they set out and went from village to village, preaching the gospel and healing people everywhere.

⁷Now Herod the tetrarch heard about all that was going on. And he was perplexed, because some were saying that John had been raised from the dead, ⁸others that Elijah had appeared, and still others that one of the prophets of long ago had come back to life. ⁹But Herod said, "I beheaded John. Who, then, is this I hear such things about?" And he tried to see him.

¹⁰When the apostles returned, they reported to Jesus what they had done. Then he took them with him and they withdrew by themselves to a town called Bethsaida, ¹¹but the crowds learned about it and followed him. He welcomed them and spoke to them about the kingdom of God, and healed those who needed healing.

¹²Late in the afternoon the Twelve came to him and said, "Send the crowd away so they can go to the surrounding villages and countryside and find food and lodging, because we are in a remote place here."

¹³He replied, "You give them something to eat."

They answered, "We have only five loaves of bread and two fish—unless we go and buy food for all this crowd." ¹⁴(About five thousand men were there.)

But he said to his disciples, "Have them sit down in groups of about fifty each." ¹⁵The disciples did so, and everybody sat down. ¹⁶Taking the

five loaves and the two fish and looking up to heaven, he gave thanks and broke them. Then he gave them to the disciples to set before the people. [17]They all ate and were satisfied, and the disciples picked up twelve basketfuls of broken pieces that were left over.

[18]Once when Jesus was praying in private and his disciples were with him, he asked them, "Who do the crowds say I am?"

[19]They replied, "Some say John the Baptist; others say Elijah; and still others, that one of the prophets of long ago has come back to life."

[20]"But what about you?" he asked. "Who do you say I am?"

Peter answered, "The Christ[j] of God."

[21]Jesus strictly warned them not to tell this to anyone. [22]And he said, "The Son of Man must suffer many things and be rejected by the elders, chief priests and teachers of the law, and he must be killed and on the third day be raised to life."

[23]Then he said to them all: "If anyone would come after me, he must deny himself and take up his cross daily and follow me. [24]For whoever wants to save his life will lose it, but whoever loses his life for me will save it. [25]What good is it for a man to gain the whole world, and yet lose or forfeit his very self? [26]If anyone is ashamed of me and my words, the Son of Man will be ashamed of him when he comes in his glory and in the glory of the Father and of the holy angels. [27]I tell you the truth, some who are standing here will not taste death before they see the kingdom of God."

[28]About eight days after Jesus said this, he took Peter, John and James with him and went up onto a mountain to pray. [29]As he was praying, the appearance of his face changed, and his clothes became as bright as a flash of lightning. [30]Two men, Moses and Elijah, [31]appeared in glorious splendor, talking with Jesus. They spoke about his departure, which he was about to bring to fulfillment at Jerusalem. [32]Peter and his companions were very sleepy, but when they became fully awake, they saw his glory and the two men standing with him. [33]As the men were leaving Jesus, Peter said to him, "Master, it is good for us to be here. Let us put up three shelters—one for you, one for Moses and one for Elijah." (He did not know what he was saying.)

[34]While he was speaking, a cloud appeared and enveloped them, and they were afraid as they entered the cloud. [35]A voice came from the cloud, saying, "This is my Son, whom I have chosen; listen to him." [36]When the voice had spoken, they found that Jesus was alone. The disciples kept this to themselves, and told no one at that time what they had seen.

[37]The next day, when they came down from the mountain, a large crowd met him. [38]A man in the crowd called out, "Teacher, I beg you to look at my son, for he is my only child. [39]A spirit seizes him and he suddenly screams; it throws him into convulsions so that he foams at the mouth. It scarcely ever leaves him and is destroying him. [40]I begged your disciples to drive it out, but they could not."

[41]"O unbelieving and perverse generation," Jesus replied, "how long shall I stay with you and put up with you? Bring your son here."

[42]Even while the boy was coming, the demon threw him to the ground in a convulsion. But Jesus rebuked the evil[k] spirit, healed the boy and gave him back to his father. [43]And they were all amazed at the greatness of God.

While everyone was marveling at all that Jesus did, he said to his disciples, [44]"Listen carefully to what I am about to tell you: The Son of Man is going to be betrayed into the hands of men." [45]But they did not understand what this meant. It was hidden from them, so that they did not grasp it, and they were afraid to ask him about it.

[46]An argument started among the disciples as to which of them would be the greatest. [47]Jesus, knowing their thoughts, took a little child and had him stand beside him. [48]Then he said to them, "Whoever welcomes this little child in my name welcomes me; and whoever welcomes me welcomes the one who sent me. For he who is least among you all—he is the greatest."

[49]"Master," said John, "we saw a man driving out demons in your name and we tried to stop him, because he is not one of us."

[50]"Do not stop him," Jesus said, "for whoever is not against you is for you."

[j]20 Or *Messiah*   [k]42 Greek *unclean*

Discovering the Word 1. For two years Jesus has been teaching, training and testing the Twelve. In what important ways has Jesus prepared them for this first short-term mission without him (vv. 1–9)? 2. The apostles have just returned from an intense and successful evangelistic mission. Their reluctance to help the crowd is understandable. But Jesus is insistent. What progressive steps do you see him take to involve them in feeding the people (vv. 10–17)? 3. Peter's "Great Confession" of Jesus' true identity is followed by two hard teachings—the first prediction of his ignominious death (vv. 21–22) and the costs of commitment to him as Lord (vv. 23–27). But what does Jesus say are the long-term benefits of these short-term costs? 4. Luke links Jesus' transfiguration to his final trip to Jerusalem, where death awaits (9:30–32, 51ff.). How then is the transfiguration important to Jesus himself and to the disciples? 5. On the plain with the mixed crowd we can sense Jesus' deep feelings. How can he be at once both compassionate and impatient?

 Applying the Word 1. When have you felt both God's compassion and impatience? 2. What is one blind spot, or area of spiritual immaturity, that you need to work on?

Responding in Prayer Talk to God about how you want to grow into spiritual maturity.

12 / *Luke 9:51—10:24*
Short-Term Costs for Long-Term Benefits

I THOUGHT ALL my problems would be solved when I became a Christian. But they have increased. Cost? Pain? Sacrifice? These elements don't fit into the American way of life of avoiding discomfort and inconvenience. Instant gratification is the order of the day. No goal could be further from Jesus' way of life for his disciples while here on earth.

 Warming Up to God What has been costly for you in following Jesus?

 Read Luke 9:51—10:24.

⁵¹As the time approached for him to be taken up to heaven, Jesus resolutely set out for Jerusalem. ⁵²And he sent messengers on ahead, who went into a Samaritan village to get things ready for him; ⁵³but the people there did not welcome him, because he was heading for Jerusalem. ⁵⁴When the disciples James and John saw this, they asked, "Lord, do you want us to call fire down from heaven to destroy them*l*?" ⁵⁵But Jesus turned and rebuked them, ⁵⁶and*m* they went to another village.

⁵⁷As they were walking along the road, a man said to him, "I will follow you wherever you go."

⁵⁸Jesus replied, "Foxes have holes and birds of the air have nests, but the Son of Man has no place to lay his head."

⁵⁹He said to another man, "Follow me."

But the man replied, "Lord, first let me go and bury my father."

⁶⁰Jesus said to him, "Let the dead bury their own dead, but you go and proclaim the kingdom of God."

⁶¹Still another said, "I will follow you, Lord; but first let me go back and say good-by to my family."

⁶²Jesus replied, "No one who puts his hand to the plow and looks back is fit for service in the kingdom of God."

10 After this the Lord appointed seventy-two*n* others and sent them two by two ahead of him to every town and place where he was about to go. ²He told them, "The harvest is plentiful, but the workers are few. Ask the Lord of the harvest, therefore, to send out workers into his harvest field. ³Go! I am sending you out like lambs among wolves. ⁴Do not take a purse or bag or sandals; and do not greet anyone on the road.

*l*54 Some manuscripts *them, even as Elijah did*   *m*55,56 Some manuscripts *them. And he said, "You do not know what kind of spirit you are of, for the Son of Man did not come to destroy men's lives, but to save them." ⁵⁶And*   *n*1 Some manuscripts *seventy*; also in verse 17

5"When you enter a house, first say, 'Peace to this house.' 6If a man of peace is there, your peace will rest on him; if not, it will return to you. 7Stay in that house, eating and drinking whatever they give you, for the worker deserves his wages. Do not move around from house to house.

8"When you enter a town and are welcomed, eat what is set before you. 9Heal the sick who are there and tell them, 'The kingdom of God is near you.' 10But when you enter a town and are not welcomed, go into its streets and say, 11'Even the dust of your town that sticks to our feet we wipe off against you. Yet be sure of this: The kingdom of God is near.' 12I tell you, it will be more bearable on that day for Sodom than for that town.

13"Woe to you, Korazin! Woe to you, Bethsaida! For if the miracles that were performed in you had been performed in Tyre and Sidon, they would have repented long ago, sitting in sackcloth and ashes. 14But it will be more bearable for Tyre and Sidon at the judgment than for you. 15And you, Capernaum, will you be lifted up to the skies? No, you will go down to the depths.o

16"He who listens to you listens to me; he who rejects you rejects me; but he who rejects me rejects him who sent me."

17The seventy-two returned with joy and said,

"Lord, even the demons submit to us in your name."

18He replied, "I saw Satan fall like lightning from heaven. 19I have given you authority to trample on snakes and scorpions and to overcome all the power of the enemy; nothing will harm you. 20However, do not rejoice that the spirits submit to you, but rejoice that your names are written in heaven."

21At that time Jesus, full of joy through the Holy Spirit, said, "I praise you, Father, Lord of heaven and earth, because you have hidden these things from the wise and learned, and revealed them to little children. Yes, Father, for this was your good pleasure.

22"All things have been committed to me by my Father. No one knows who the Son is except the Father, and no one knows who the Father is except the Son and those to whom the Son chooses to reveal him."

23Then he turned to his disciples and said privately, "Blessed are the eyes that see what you see. 24For I tell you that many prophets and kings wanted to see what you see but did not see it, and to hear what you hear but did not hear it."

o15 Greek *Hades*

 Discovering the Word 1. This is the beginning of Jesus' final, year-long journey to Jerusalem. What impressions of Jesus do the opening statements (9:51–53) leave with you? 2. In 9:56–62 Jesus interviews three would-be disciples. Each encounter reveals the person's inadequate understanding of what it means to follow Jesus. What issues are at stake for each of these people? 3. From Jesus' response to each what do you learn about some specific costs of discipleship in his kingdom? 4. How is the mission of the seventy-two in Luke 10:1–16 different from the mission of the Twelve in 9:1–6? 5. Verses 17–24 record a postmission report and evaluation. Of course celebration is in order! For Jesus the success of the seventy-two is a preview of the ultimate overthrow of Satan. But as one of them, how would you have felt on hearing Jesus' words in verse 20?

Applying the Word 1. Jesus' every instruction reveals a deep sense of urgency. How do we develop an urgency for mission and evangelism? 2. Jesus' demands in discipleship and mission are indeed serious (9:57–62; 10:2–12). But he accompanies them with positive appeals—explicit and implicit (9:60b, 62b; 10:2, 16, 18–24). Which of his appeals inspires you to pursue discipleship on his terms?

Responding in Prayer Ask for strength to bear the real cost of discipleship.

13 / *Luke 10:25—11:13*
Marks of Jesus' True Disciples

IT IS SOMETIMES hard to tell who is a real Christian. This is not necessarily because people indiscriminately claim to be Christian. One reason is that many people sincerely live by inherited Christian values and even show fruit of the Spirit. But they have no personal relationship with God. On the other hand, some claim such a relationship to God but do not live by his standards. Among the many who followed Jesus were those who also were not clear about true discipleship. So Jesus makes it absolutely clear what marks a true follower of his.

 Warming Up to God If you are not told, how can you tell if a person is a Christian?

 Read Luke 10:25—11:13.

---

²⁵On one occasion an expert in the law stood up to test Jesus. "Teacher," he asked, "what must I do to inherit eternal life?"

²⁶"What is written in the Law?" he replied. "How do you read it?"

²⁷He answered: " 'Love the Lord your God with all your heart and with all your soul and with all your strength and with all your mind'ᵖ; and, 'Love your neighbor as yourself.'�q "

²⁸"You have answered correctly," Jesus replied. "Do this and you will live."

²⁹But he wanted to justify himself, so he asked Jesus, "And who is my neighbor?"

³⁰In reply Jesus said: "A man was going down from Jerusalem to Jericho, when he fell into the hands of robbers. They stripped him of his clothes, beat him and went away, leaving him half dead. ³¹A priest happened to be going down the same road, and when he saw the man, he passed by on the other side. ³²So too, a Levite, when he came to the place and saw him, passed by on the other side. ³³But a Samaritan, as he traveled, came where the man was; and when he saw him, he took pity on him. ³⁴He went to him and bandaged his wounds, pouring on oil and wine. Then he put the man on his own donkey, took him to an inn and took care of him. ³⁵The next day he took out two silver coinsʳ and gave them to the innkeeper. 'Look after him,' he said, 'and when I return, I will reimburse you for any extra expense you may have.'

³⁶"Which of these three do you think was a neighbor to the man who fell into the hands of robbers?"

³⁷The expert in the law replied, "The one who had mercy on him."

Jesus told him, "Go and do likewise."

³⁸As Jesus and his disciples were on their way, he came to a village where a woman named Martha opened her home to him. ³⁹She had a sister called Mary, who sat at the Lord's feet listening to what he said. ⁴⁰But Martha was distracted by all the preparations that had to be made. She came to him and asked, "Lord, don't you care that my sister has left me to do the work by myself? Tell her to help me!"

⁴¹"Martha, Martha," the Lord answered, "you are worried and upset about many things, ⁴²but only one thing is needed.ˢ Mary has chosen what is better, and it will not be taken away from her."

One day Jesus was praying in a certain place. When he finished, one of his disciples said to him, "Lord, teach us to pray, just as John taught his disciples."

²He said to them, "When you pray, say:

" 'Father,ᵗ
hallowed be your name,
    your kingdom come.ᵘ
³Give us each day our daily bread.
⁴Forgive us our sins,
    for we also forgive everyone who sins
        against us.ᵛ
And lead us not into temptation.ʷ' "

⁵Then he said to them, "Suppose one of you has a friend, and he goes to him at midnight and says, 'Friend, lend me three loaves of bread, ⁶be-

---

*p*27 Deut. 6:5   *q*27 Lev. 19:18   *r*35 Greek *two denarii*
*s*42 Some manuscripts *but few things are needed—or only one*
*t*2 Some manuscripts *Our Father in heaven*   *u*2 Some manuscripts *come. May your will be done on earth as it is in heaven.*   *v*4 Greek *everyone who is indebted to us*   *w*4 Some manuscripts *temptation but deliver us from the evil one*

cause a friend of mine on a journey has come to me, and I have nothing to set before him.'

⁷"Then the one inside answers, 'Don't bother me. The door is already locked, and my children are with me in bed. I can't get up and give you anything.' ⁸I tell you, though he will not get up and give him the bread because he is his friend, yet because of the man's boldnessˣ he will get up and give him as much as he needs.

⁹"So I say to you: Ask and it will be given to you; seek and you will find; knock and the door will be opened to you. ¹⁰For everyone who asks receives; he who seeks finds; and to him who knocks, the door will be opened.

¹¹"Which of you fathers, if your son asks forʸ a fish, will give him a snake instead? ¹²Or if he asks for an egg, will give him a scorpion? ¹³If you then, though you are evil, know how to give good gifts to your children, how much more will your Father in heaven give the Holy Spirit to those who ask him!"

ˣ8 Or *persistence* ʸ11 Some manuscripts *for bread, will give him a stone; or if he asks for*

 Discovering the Word 1. The conversation begins with a man who "stood up," indicating he had been sitting with others listening to Jesus teach. What other facts about this man can you pick up in 10:25–29? 2. What does Jesus perceive about his understanding of the Law (10:25–28)? 3. To challenge the expert Jesus portrays the hero in his parable as a Samaritan. This despised outsider proves obedience to God's law of love by his actions (first mark). Note the specific ways that he "took pity" on the victim (10:33–35). What could be Jesus' reasons for including such details? 4. In verse 36 Jesus reverses the expert's original question in verse 29. If you were the expert, what effect would this have on you? 5. Martha displays both positive and negative qualities (10:38–42). What (second) mark does her sister Mary show? 6. Look at 11:1–13 for the third mark of Jesus' true disciples—praying. In verses 2–4 Jesus is not giving a prayer merely to be recited. Rather, he is giving prayer headings. What basic needs do these headings cover?

Applying the Word 1. What qualities do you observe in people who, like Mary, "choose what is better"? 2. By parable and commentary Jesus urges his disciples to pray with boldness. We can dare to be bold because of who God is—our Father and our King (vv. 2, 13). How should trust in such a God radicalize your praying?

Responding in Prayer Speak to God boldly and with trust.

---

14 / *Luke 11:14—12:12*
Jesus the Controversialist

WHEN I THINK of controversialists, Al comes to mind. He was one of the most effective missionaries I've known. Yet he stirred up controversy with almost everyone near him—his board, his colleagues, the local church leaders. They didn't know what to do with him, or what to do without him. But those he was evangelizing loved him!

Some people seem to be born controversialists. They're happiest when arguing with others, only half alive when the atmosphere is congenial. Jesus was a controversialist. But it was not for his ego that he engaged in fierce debates with the most highly trained Bible scholars of his day. He engaged in controversy because he loved the truth and hated lies.

 Warming Up to God How do you respond to controversies? Why?

 Read Luke 11:14—12:12.

---

¹⁴Jesus was driving out a demon that was mute. When the demon left, the man who had been mute spoke, and the crowd was amazed. ¹⁵But some of them said, "By Beelzebub,ᶻ the prince of

ᶻ15 Greek *Beezeboul* or *Beelzeboul*; also in verses 18 and 19

demons, he is driving out demons." ¹⁶Others tested him by asking for a sign from heaven.

¹⁷Jesus knew their thoughts and said to them: "Any kingdom divided against itself will be ruined, and a house divided against itself will fall. ¹⁸If Satan is divided against himself, how can his kingdom stand? I say this because you claim that I drive out demons by Beelzebub. ¹⁹Now if I drive out demons by Beelzebub, by whom do your followers drive them out? So then, they will be your judges. ²⁰But if I drive out demons by the finger of God, then the kingdom of God has come to you.

²¹"When a strong man, fully armed, guards his own house, his possessions are safe. ²²But when someone stronger attacks and overpowers him, he takes away the armor in which the man trusted and divides up the spoils.

²³"He who is not with me is against me, and he who does not gather with me, scatters.

²⁴"When an evil^a spirit comes out of a man, it goes through arid places seeking rest and does not find it. Then it says, 'I will return to the house I left.' ²⁵When it arrives, it finds the house swept clean and put in order. ²⁶Then it goes and takes seven other spirits more wicked than itself, and they go in and live there. And the final condition of that man is worse than the first."

²⁷As Jesus was saying these things, a woman in the crowd called out, "Blessed is the mother who gave you birth and nursed you."

²⁸He replied, "Blessed rather are those who hear the word of God and obey it."

²⁹As the crowds increased, Jesus said, "This is a wicked generation. It asks for a miraculous sign, but none will be given it except the sign of Jonah. ³⁰For as Jonah was a sign to the Ninevites, so also will the Son of Man be to this generation. ³¹The Queen of the South will rise at the judgment with the men of this generation and condemn them; for she came from the ends of the earth to listen to Solomon's wisdom, and now one^b greater than Solomon is here. ³²The men of Nineveh will stand up at the judgment with this generation and condemn it; for they repented at the preaching of Jonah, and now one greater than Jonah is here.

³³"No one lights a lamp and puts it in a place where it will be hidden, or under a bowl. Instead he puts it on its stand, so that those who come in may see the light. ³⁴Your eye is the lamp of your body. When your eyes are good, your whole body also is full of light. But when they are bad, your body also is full of darkness. ³⁵See to it, then, that the light within you is not darkness. ³⁶Therefore, if your whole body is full of light, and no part of it dark, it will be completely lighted, as when the light of a lamp shines on you."

³⁷When Jesus had finished speaking, a Pharisee invited him to eat with him; so he went in and reclined at the table. ³⁸But the Pharisee, noticing that Jesus did not first wash before the meal, was surprised.

³⁹Then the Lord said to him, "Now then, you Pharisees clean the outside of the cup and dish, but inside you are full of greed and wickedness. ⁴⁰You foolish people! Did not the one who made the outside make the inside also? ⁴¹But give what is inside ⌊the dish⌋^{c} to the poor, and everything will be clean for you.

⁴²"Woe to you Pharisees, because you give God a tenth of your mint, rue and all other kinds of garden herbs, but you neglect justice and the love of God. You should have practiced the latter without leaving the former undone.

⁴³"Woe to you Pharisees, because you love the most important seats in the synagogues and greetings in the marketplaces.

⁴⁴"Woe to you, because you are like unmarked graves, which men walk over without knowing it."

⁴⁵One of the experts in the law answered him, "Teacher, when you say these things, you insult us also."

⁴⁶Jesus replied, "And you experts in the law, woe to you, because you load people down with burdens they can hardly carry, and you yourselves will not lift one finger to help them.

⁴⁷"Woe to you, because you build tombs for the prophets, and it was your forefathers who killed them. ⁴⁸So you testify that you approve of what your forefathers did; they killed the prophets, and you build their tombs. ⁴⁹Because of this, God in his wisdom said, 'I will send them prophets and apostles, some of whom they will kill and others they will persecute.' ⁵⁰Therefore this generation will be held responsible for the blood of all the prophets that has been shed since the beginning of the world, ⁵¹from the blood of Abel to the blood of Zechariah, who was killed between the altar and the sanctuary. Yes, I tell you, this generation will be held responsible for it all.

⁵²"Woe to you experts in the law, because you

^{a}24 Greek unclean ^{b}31 Or something; also in verse 32 ^{c}41 Or what you have

have taken away the key to knowledge. You yourselves have not entered, and you have hindered those who were entering."

53When Jesus left there, the Pharisees and the teachers of the law began to oppose him fiercely and to besiege him with questions, 54waiting to catch him in something he might say.

12 Meanwhile, when a crowd of many thousands had gathered, so that they were trampling on one another, Jesus began to speak first to his disciples, saying: "Be on your guard against the yeast of the Pharisees, which is hypocrisy. 2There is nothing concealed that will not be disclosed, or hidden that will not be made known. 3What you have said in the dark will be heard in the daylight, and what you have whispered in the ear in the inner rooms will be proclaimed from the roofs.

4"I tell you, my friends, do not be afraid of those who kill the body and after that can do no more. 5But I will show you whom you should fear: Fear him who, after the killing of the body,

has power to throw you into hell. Yes, I tell you, fear him. 6Are not five sparrows sold for two pennies*d*? Yet not one of them is forgotten by God. 7Indeed, the very hairs of your head are all numbered. Don't be afraid; you are worth more than many sparrows.

8"I tell you, whoever acknowledges me before men, the Son of Man will also acknowledge him before the angels of God. 9But he who disowns me before men will be disowned before the angels of God. 10And everyone who speaks a word against the Son of Man will be forgiven, but anyone who blasphemes against the Holy Spirit will not be forgiven.

11"When you are brought before synagogues, rulers and authorities, do not worry about how you will defend yourselves or what you will say, 12for the Holy Spirit will teach you at that time what you should say."

d6 Greek two assaria

 Discovering the Word 1. In what two ways do Jesus' critics attack him (11:15–16)? 2. In 11:17–20 Jesus answers the first attack. How does he point out their illogical position? 3. Jesus answers his critics' second attack in 11:29–36. In what way is Jesus comparing himself to Jonah and Solomon? 4. In 11:37–38 the host is surprised that Jesus has not ritually washed his hands after contact with public "uncleanness." Jesus counters that criticism, then adds six more attacks on their religious practices! Of these accusations (11:42, 43, 44, 46, 47, 52), which reminds you of a contemporary practice? In what ways? 5. Jesus must now prepare his disciples for persecution by these same leaders (12:1–12). First, he deals with the fear of these men. How does he help them to distinguish between the wrong kind of fear and the proper kind (12:4–7)?

Applying the Word 1. Few of us would engage in public religious controversy as Jesus did. But we all have occasions when we need to stand against lies and speak the truth. What are your opportunities to do this? 2. In what ways is it difficult for you?

Responding in Prayer Ask the Lord Jesus to give you the help you need to take a stand.

---

15 / *Luke 12:13—13:21*
Greed, Need & Judgment

A CHRISTIAN YUPPIE? Is it possible to be Jesus' disciple on his terms and at the same time be a yuppie, for whom material values and the latest exotica are priorities? Some try to have it both ways and don't make it—either way. One such Christian yuppie described her experience. "For ten years I skillfully juggled both sets of values—Jesus' and Madison Avenue's. Then I collapsed." We are constantly tested in our value system, because we live between earth and heaven, time and eternity. Jesus gives us guidelines and solemn warnings on how to live productively in this creative tension.

 Warming Up to God Think about the past few days. In what ways have you been enticed by the material values of the world? Confess them before the Lord.

Read Luke 12:13—13:21.

¹³Someone in the crowd said to him, "Teacher, tell my brother to divide the inheritance with me."

¹⁴Jesus replied, "Man, who appointed me a judge or an arbiter between you?" ¹⁵Then he said to them, "Watch out! Be on your guard against all kinds of greed; a man's life does not consist in the abundance of his possessions."

¹⁶And he told them this parable: "The ground of a certain rich man produced a good crop. ¹⁷He thought to himself, 'What shall I do? I have no place to store my crops.'

¹⁸"Then he said, 'This is what I'll do. I will tear down my barns and build bigger ones, and there I will store all my grain and my goods. ¹⁹And I'll say to myself, "You have plenty of good things laid up for many years. Take life easy; eat, drink and be merry." '

²⁰"But God said to him, 'You fool! This very night your life will be demanded from you. Then who will get what you have prepared for yourself?'

²¹"This is how it will be with anyone who stores up things for himself but is not rich toward God."

²²Then Jesus said to his disciples: "Therefore I tell you, do not worry about your life, what you will eat; or about your body, what you will wear. ²³Life is more than food, and the body more than clothes. ²⁴Consider the ravens: They do not sow or reap, they have no storeroom or barn; yet God feeds them. And how much more valuable you are than birds! ²⁵Who of you by worrying can add a single hour to his life*? ²⁶Since you cannot do this very little thing, why do you worry about the rest?

²⁷"Consider how the lilies grow. They do not labor or spin. Yet I tell you, not even Solomon in all his splendor was dressed like one of these. ²⁸If that is how God clothes the grass of the field, which is here today, and tomorrow is thrown into the fire, how much more will he clothe you, O you of little faith! ²⁹And do not set your heart on what you will eat or drink; do not worry about it. ³⁰For the pagan world runs after all such things, and your Father knows that you need them. ³¹But seek his kingdom, and these things will be given to you as well.

³²"Do not be afraid, little flock, for your Father has been pleased to give you the kingdom. ³³Sell your possessions and give to the poor. Provide purses for yourselves that will not wear out, a treasure in heaven that will not be exhausted, where no thief comes near and no moth destroys. ³⁴For where your treasure is, there your heart will be also.

³⁵"Be dressed ready for service and keep your lamps burning, ³⁶like men waiting for their master to return from a wedding banquet, so that when he comes and knocks they can immediately open the door for him. ³⁷It will be good for those servants whose master finds them watching when he comes. I tell you the truth, he will dress himself to serve, will have them recline at the table and will come and wait on them. ³⁸It will be good for those servants whose master finds them ready, even if he comes in the second or third watch of the night. ³⁹But understand this: If the owner of the house had known at what hour the thief was coming, he would not have let his house be broken into. ⁴⁰You also must be ready, because the Son of Man will come at an hour when you do not expect him."

⁴¹Peter asked, "Lord, are you telling this parable to us, or to everyone?"

⁴²The Lord answered, "Who then is the faithful and wise manager, whom the master puts in charge of his servants to give them their food allowance at the proper time? ⁴³It will be good for that servant whom the master finds doing so when he returns. ⁴⁴I tell you the truth, he will put him in charge of all his possessions. ⁴⁵But suppose the servant says to himself, 'My master is taking a long time in coming,' and he then begins to beat the menservants and maidservants and to eat and drink and get drunk. ⁴⁶The master of that servant will come on a day when he does not expect him and at an hour he is not aware of. He will cut him to pieces and assign him a place with the unbelievers.

⁴⁷"That servant who knows his master's will and does not get ready or does not do what his master wants will be beaten with many blows. ⁴⁸But the one who does not know and does things deserving punishment will be beaten with few blows. From everyone who has been given much, much will be demanded; and from the one who

*25 Or *single cubit to his height*

has been entrusted with much, much more will be asked.

⁴⁹"I have come to bring fire on the earth, and how I wish it were already kindled! ⁵⁰But I have a baptism to undergo, and how distressed I am until it is completed! ⁵¹Do you think I came to bring peace on earth? No, I tell you, but division. ⁵²From now on there will be five in one family divided against each other, three against two and two against three. ⁵³They will be divided, father against son and son against father, mother against daughter and daughter against mother, mother-in-law against daughter-in-law and daughter-in-law against mother-in-law."

⁵⁴He said to the crowd: "When you see a cloud rising in the west, immediately you say, 'It's going to rain,' and it does. ⁵⁵And when the south wind blows, you say, 'It's going to be hot,' and it is. ⁵⁶Hypocrites! You know how to interpret the appearance of the earth and the sky. How is it that you don't know how to interpret this present time?

⁵⁷"Why don't you judge for yourselves what is right? ⁵⁸As you are going with your adversary to the magistrate, try hard to be reconciled to him on the way, or he may drag you off to the judge, and the judge turn you over to the officer, and the officer throw you into prison. ⁵⁹I tell you, you will not get out until you have paid the last penny.ᶠ"

13

Now there were some present at that time who told Jesus about the Galileans whose blood Pilate had mixed with their sacrifices. ²Jesus answered, "Do you think that these Galileans were worse sinners than all the other Galileans because they suffered this way? ³I tell you, no! But unless you repent, you too will all perish. ⁴Or those eighteen who died when the tower in Siloam fell on them—do you think they were more guilty than all the others living in Jerusalem? ⁵I tell you, no! But unless you repent, you too will all perish."

⁶Then he told this parable: "A man had a fig tree, planted in his vineyard, and he went to look for fruit on it, but did not find any. ⁷So he said to the man who took care of the vineyard, 'For three years now I've been coming to look for fruit on this fig tree and haven't found any. Cut it down! Why should it use up the soil?'

⁸"'Sir,' the man replied, 'leave it alone for one more year, and I'll dig around it and fertilize it. ⁹If it bears fruit next year, fine! If not, then cut it down.'"

¹⁰On a Sabbath Jesus was teaching in one of the synagogues, ¹¹and a woman was there who had been crippled by a spirit for eighteen years. She was bent over and could not straighten up at all. ¹²When Jesus saw her, he called her forward and said to her, "Woman, you are set free from your infirmity." ¹³Then he put his hands on her, and immediately she straightened up and praised God.

¹⁴Indignant because Jesus had healed on the Sabbath, the synagogue ruler said to the people, "There are six days for work. So come and be healed on those days, not on the Sabbath."

¹⁵The Lord answered him, "You hypocrites! Doesn't each of you on the Sabbath untie his ox or donkey from the stall and lead it out to give it water? ¹⁶Then should not this woman, a daughter of Abraham, whom Satan has kept bound for eighteen long years, be set free on the Sabbath day from what bound her?"

¹⁷When he said this, all his opponents were humiliated, but the people were delighted with all the wonderful things he was doing.

¹⁸Then Jesus asked, "What is the kingdom of God like? What shall I compare it to? ¹⁹It is like a mustard seed, which a man took and planted in his garden. It grew and became a tree, and the birds of the air perched in its branches."

²⁰Again he asked, "What shall I compare the kingdom of God to? ²¹It is like yeast that a woman took and mixed into a large amountᵍ of flour until it worked all through the dough."

ᶠ59 Greek lepton   ᵍ21 Greek three satas (probably about 1/2 bushel or 22 liters)

Discovering the Word 1. Nowhere does Jesus condemn possessions. But he has much to say about how to use them. From 12:15, 22–23 and 31, how could you summarize Jesus' teaching about life and material goods?   2. What view of God do worrying Christians apparently have?   3. The parable in 12:35–48 illustrates priorities Christians should have in view of Jesus' return after his departure—or in any crisis situation. (That Jesus was referring to his Second Coming would not be obvious to his listeners, as it is to us.) What are these priorities that apply to all servant disciples?   4. All three parables above speak or hint of God's judgment on the choices we make (12:20, 40, 46–48). The language and imagery of our present text also point to that judgment. In

the midst of these warnings, what hope does Jesus offer to the wise (12:57–59)? **5.** Provoked by Jesus' teaching on judgment (13:1–9), some people raise a question about a well-known atrocity. In reply, how does Jesus both correct their wrong assumption and still extend hope? **6.** This is the last time we see Jesus teaching in a synagogue (13:10–21). In what ways does this sabbath conflict with the synagogue ruler summarize the priorities and values of Jesus' total ministry?

 Applying the Word 1. The obviously rich are not the only ones in danger of being fools. How do poor and middle-class people also face the same dangers? **2.** Recall again your past week's activities and personal concerns. To what extent do they reflect the priorities and values of God's kingdom?

Responding in Prayer Ask God to mold your values and priorities into his own.

16 / *Luke 13:22—14:35*
Are Only a Few People Going to Be Saved?

STILL ANOTHER NEW group has come to our town, attracting scores of disaffected members of other churches. The leaders have convinced them that they alone have the right interpretation of "who is really saved." People in Jesus' day also wanted to be sure about salvation. They asked the question in different ways—"What must I do to inherit eternal life?" "How can a man be born again to enter the kingdom of God?" "Who then can be saved?" Even secular people ask, "Which life goal is right?" No matter the form, it is still an essential question for anyone to ask.

 Warming Up to God When are you likely to question your salvation?

 Read Luke 13:22—14:35.

22Then Jesus went through the towns and villages, teaching as he made his way to Jerusalem. 23Someone asked him, "Lord, are only a few people going to be saved?"

He said to them, 24"Make every effort to enter through the narrow door, because many, I tell you, will try to enter and will not be able to. 25Once the owner of the house gets up and closes the door, you will stand outside knocking and pleading, 'Sir, open the door for us.'

"But he will answer, 'I don't know you or where you come from.'

26"Then you will say, 'We ate and drank with you, and you taught in our streets.'

27"But he will reply, 'I don't know you or where you come from. Away from me, all you evildoers!'

28"There will be weeping there, and gnashing of teeth, when you see Abraham, Isaac and Jacob and all the prophets in the kingdom of God, but you yourselves thrown out. 29People will come from east and west and north and south, and will take their places at the feast in the kingdom of God. 30Indeed there are those who are last who will be first, and first who will be last."

31At that time some Pharisees came to Jesus and said to him, "Leave this place and go somewhere else. Herod wants to kill you."

32He replied, "Go tell that fox, 'I will drive out demons and heal people today and tomorrow, and on the third day I will reach my goal.' 33In any case, I must keep going today and tomorrow and the next day—for surely no prophet can die outside Jerusalem!

34"O Jerusalem, Jerusalem, you who kill the prophets and stone those sent to you, how often I have longed to gather your children together, as a hen gathers her chicks under her wings, but you were not willing! 35Look, your house is left to you desolate. I tell you, you will not see me again until you say, 'Blessed is he who comes in the name of the Lord.'ʰ"

14 One Sabbath, when Jesus went to eat in the house of a prominent Pharisee, he was being carefully watched. 2There in front of him was a man suffering from dropsy. 3Jesus asked the Pharisees and

ʰ35 Psalm 118:26

experts in the law, "Is it lawful to heal on the Sabbath or not?" ⁴But they remained silent. So taking hold of the man, he healed him and sent him away.

⁵Then he asked them, "If one of you has a son[i] or an ox that falls into a well on the Sabbath day, will you not immediately pull him out?" ⁶And they had nothing to say.

⁷When he noticed how the guests picked the places of honor at the table, he told them this parable: ⁸"When someone invites you to a wedding feast, do not take the place of honor, for a person more distinguished than you may have been invited. ⁹If so, the host who invited both of you will come and say to you, 'Give this man your seat.' Then, humiliated, you will have to take the least important place. ¹⁰But when you are invited, take the lowest place, so that when your host comes, he will say to you, 'Friend, move up to a better place.' Then you will be honored in the presence of all your fellow guests. ¹¹For everyone who exalts himself will be humbled, and he who humbles himself will be exalted."

¹²Then Jesus said to his host, "When you give a luncheon or dinner, do not invite your friends, your brothers or relatives, or your rich neighbors; if you do, they may invite you back and so you will be repaid. ¹³But when you give a banquet, invite the poor, the crippled, the lame, the blind, ¹⁴and you will be blessed. Although they cannot repay you, you will be repaid at the resurrection of the righteous."

¹⁵When one of those at the table with him heard this, he said to Jesus, "Blessed is the man who will eat at the feast in the kingdom of God."

¹⁶Jesus replied: "A certain man was preparing a great banquet and invited many guests. ¹⁷At the time of the banquet he sent his servant to tell those who had been invited, 'Come, for everything is now ready.'

¹⁸"But they all alike began to make excuses. The first said, 'I have just bought a field, and I must go and see it. Please excuse me.'

¹⁹"Another said, 'I have just bought five yoke of oxen, and I'm on my way to try them out. Please excuse me.'

²⁰"Still another said, 'I just got married, so I can't come.'

²¹"The servant came back and reported this to his master. Then the owner of the house became angry and ordered his servant, 'Go out quickly into the streets and alleys of the town and bring in the poor, the crippled, the blind and the lame.'

²²" 'Sir,' the servant said, 'what you ordered has been done, but there is still room.'

²³"Then the master told his servant, 'Go out to the roads and country lanes and make them come in, so that my house will be full. ²⁴I tell you, not one of those men who were invited will get a taste of my banquet.' "

²⁵Large crowds were traveling with Jesus, and turning to them he said: ²⁶"If anyone comes to me and does not hate his father and mother, his wife and children, his brothers and sisters—yes, even his own life—he cannot be my disciple. ²⁷And anyone who does not carry his cross and follow me cannot be my disciple.

²⁸"Suppose one of you wants to build a tower. Will he not first sit down and estimate the cost to see if he has enough money to complete it? ²⁹For if he lays the foundation and is not able to finish it, everyone who sees it will ridicule him, ³⁰saying, 'This fellow began to build and was not able to finish.'

³¹"Or suppose a king is about to go to war against another king. Will he not first sit down and consider whether he is able with ten thousand men to oppose the one coming against him with twenty thousand? ³²If he is not able, he will send a delegation while the other is still a long way off and will ask for terms of peace. ³³In the same way, any of you who does not give up everything he has cannot be my disciple.

³⁴"Salt is good, but if it loses its saltiness, how can it be made salty again? ³⁵It is fit neither for the soil nor for the manure pile; it is thrown out.

"He who has ears to hear, let him hear."

ⁱ5 Some manuscripts *donkey*

Discovering the Word 1. Jesus' journeying to Jerusalem gives the setting of our title question (13:22–23). What in Jesus' parable answer would startle his Jewish listeners or perhaps you? 2. The Pharisees' motive for warning Jesus is not clear. They are now allied with the Herodians, their political enemies, against Jesus. But he is fearless (13:31–33). Then he expresses other emotions (vv. 34–35). Why do you think Jesus is so deeply passionate about Jerusalem? 3. What explains the Pharisees' double silence to Jesus' questions (14:4,6)? 4. How does this third parable climax Jesus' answer to our study question of who ultimately will be saved

(14:15–24)? 5. Travelers nearing Jerusalem passed old wooden crosses along the way. Everyone knew their use—for criminal execution. So how would Jesus' fellow travelers understand his words in 14:27?

 Applying the Word 1. With two parables he teaches the guests about true honor (14:7–11) and his host about true hospitality (14:12–14). How should Jesus' lessons affect your social life? 2. Jesus lays down his conditions for discipleship by calling into question powerful loyalties—to family and to self. What would be a contemporary example of Christians "hating" their family? 3. Try counting the cost of not following Jesus on his terms. What to you is most sobering?

 Responding in Prayer Talk openly with God about how you are experiencing the cost of discipleship.

17 / *Luke 15*
The God Who Likes to Throw Parties

THE TITLE OF Rembrandt's famous painting "Return of the Prodigal Son" focuses on the father's younger son in Jesus' well-known parable. But by composition and lighting, the artist causes us to focus on the father—his face weathered by suffering, his hands lovingly embracing the ragged boy, his whole body bent to his returned son. Some people focus more on the sin and repentance of the young man than on God's compassion and purposes. Repentance is necessary. But Jesus' rejoicing Father completes, indeed dominates, the picture.

 Warming Up to God How have you recently experienced the joyful side of God's nature? Praise God for who he is.

Read Luke 15.

15 Now the tax collectors and "sinners" were all gathering around to hear him. ²But the Pharisees and the teachers of the law muttered, "This man welcomes sinners and eats with them."

³Then Jesus told them this parable: ⁴"Suppose one of you has a hundred sheep and loses one of them. Does he not leave the ninety-nine in the open country and go after the lost sheep until he finds it? ⁵And when he finds it, he joyfully puts it on his shoulders ⁶and goes home. Then he calls his friends and neighbors together and says, 'Rejoice with me; I have found my lost sheep.' ⁷I tell you that in the same way there will be more rejoicing in heaven over one sinner who repents than over ninety-nine righteous persons who do not need to repent.

⁸"Or suppose a woman has ten silver coins*ʲ* and loses one. Does she not light a lamp, sweep the house and search carefully until she finds it? ⁹And when she finds it, she calls her friends and neighbors together and says, 'Rejoice with me; I have found my lost coin.' ¹⁰In the same way, I tell you, there is rejoicing in the presence of the angels of God over one sinner who repents."

¹¹Jesus continued: "There was a man who had two sons. ¹²The younger one said to his father, 'Father, give me my share of the estate.' So he divided his property between them.

¹³"Not long after that, the younger son got together all he had, set off for a distant country and there squandered his wealth in wild living. ¹⁴After he had spent everything, there was a severe famine in that whole country, and he began to be in need. ¹⁵So he went and hired himself out to a citizen of that country, who sent him to his fields to feed pigs. ¹⁶He longed to fill his stomach with the pods that the pigs were eating, but no one gave him anything.

¹⁷"When he came to his senses, he said, 'How many of my father's hired men have food to spare, and here I am starving to death! ¹⁸I will set out and go back to my father and say to him: Father, I have sinned against heaven and against you. ¹⁹I am no longer worthy to be called your son; make me like one of your hired men.' ²⁰So he got up and went to his father.

"But while he was still a long way off, his father

ʲ8 Greek ten drachmas, each worth about a day's wages

saw him and was filled with compassion for him; he ran to his son, threw his arms around him and kissed him.

21"The son said to him, 'Father, I have sinned against heaven and against you. I am no longer worthy to be called your son.ᵏ'

22"But the father said to his servants, 'Quick! Bring the best robe and put it on him. Put a ring on his finger and sandals on his feet. 23Bring the fattened calf and kill it. Let's have a feast and celebrate. 24For this son of mine was dead and is alive again; he was lost and is found.' So they began to celebrate.

25"Meanwhile, the older son was in the field. When he came near the house, he heard music and dancing. 26So he called one of the servants and asked him what was going on. 27'Your brother has come,' he replied, 'and your father

has killed the fattened calf because he has him back safe and sound.'

28"The older brother became angry and refused to go in. So his father went out and pleaded with him. 29But he answered his father, 'Look! All these years I've been slaving for you and never disobeyed your orders. Yet you never gave me even a young goat so I could celebrate with my friends. 30But when this son of yours who has squandered your property with prostitutes comes home, you kill the fattened calf for him!'

31" 'My son,' the father said, 'you are always with me, and everything I have is yours. 32But we had to celebrate and be glad, because this brother of yours was dead and is alive again; he was lost and is found.' "

ᵏ21 Some early manuscripts son. Make me like one of your hired men.

Discovering the Word 1. What provoked Jesus' parables (vv. 1–2)? 2. In the first two parables the theme of an owner searching for something lost and rejoicing when it is found begins to answer Jesus' critics. The third parable repeats the basic theme. But how is it different from the first two? 3. What steps do you perceive in the young man's 180-degree turnabout? 4. The drama grows as Jesus describes the father in verses 20–24. In the light of verse 2, what does he want his critics to see about this man? 5. In the interaction with his older son, what other dimensions of the father's character and motives appear (vv. 28–32)? 6. The rejoicing nature of God is still foreign if not downright offensive to some religious people (see vv. 2, 6–7, 9–10, 22–24, 32 and 14:16–17). Why?

Applying the Word 1. How do these parables move you to believe in the possibilities of new or fresh changes in your relationship to family members and to God? 2. Which of your friends have like the older son an inadequate or wrong view of God?

Responding in Prayer Pray for an opportunity to share with your friends this appealing portrait of God.

---

18 / *Luke 16*
Managing Your Money

WE HAVE SUPPOSEDLY left the high-flying 1980s decade of greed. In 1985 Ivan Boesky was commencement speaker at a prestigious school of business administration in California. He said to the graduating class, "Greed is all right, by the way. I want you to know that I think greed is healthy. You can be greedy and still feel good about yourself." Sad, yes. And the response of those young men and women was just as sad. They laughed and applauded. A year and a half later Boesky was in prison for his runaway greed. The two parables in our present chapter show Jesus' judgment on the proper use of money.

Warming Up to God Why do you like money?

Read Luke 16.

16

Jesus told his disciples: "There was a rich man whose manager was accused of wasting his possessions. ²So he called him in and asked him, 'What is this I hear about you? Give an account of your management, because you cannot be manager any longer.'

³"The manager said to himself, 'What shall I do now? My master is taking away my job. I'm not strong enough to dig, and I'm ashamed to beg— ⁴I know what I'll do so that, when I lose my job here, people will welcome me into their houses.'

⁵"So he called in each one of his master's debtors. He asked the first, 'How much do you owe my master?'

⁶" 'Eight hundred gallons¹ of olive oil,' he replied.

"The manager told him, 'Take your bill, sit down quickly, and make it four hundred.'

⁷"Then he asked the second, 'And how much do you owe?'

" 'A thousand bushels^m of wheat,' he replied.

"He told him, 'Take your bill and make it eight hundred.'

⁸"The master commended the dishonest manager because he had acted shrewdly. For the people of this world are more shrewd in dealing with their own kind than are the people of the light. ⁹I tell you, use worldly wealth to gain friends for yourselves, so that when it is gone, you will be welcomed into eternal dwellings.

¹⁰"Whoever can be trusted with very little can also be trusted with much, and whoever is dishonest with very little will also be dishonest with much. ¹¹So if you have not been trustworthy in handling worldly wealth, who will trust you with true riches? ¹²And if you have not been trustworthy with someone else's property, who will give you property of your own?

¹³"No servant can serve two masters. Either he will hate the one and love the other, or he will be devoted to the one and despise the other. You cannot serve both God and Money."

¹⁴The Pharisees, who loved money, heard all this and were sneering at Jesus. ¹⁵He said to them, "You are the ones who justify yourselves in the eyes of men, but God knows your hearts. What is highly valued among men is detestable in God's sight.

¹⁶"The Law and the Prophets were proclaimed until John. Since that time, the good news of the kingdom of God is being preached, and everyone is forcing his way into it. ¹⁷It is easier for heaven and earth to disappear than for the least stroke of a pen to drop out of the Law.

¹⁸"Anyone who divorces his wife and marries another woman commits adultery, and the man who marries a divorced woman commits adultery.

¹⁹"There was a rich man who was dressed in purple and fine linen and lived in luxury every day. ²⁰At his gate was laid a beggar named Lazarus, covered with sores ²¹and longing to eat what fell from the rich man's table. Even the dogs came and licked his sores.

²²"The time came when the beggar died and the angels carried him to Abraham's side. The rich man also died and was buried. ²³In hell,^n where he was in torment, he looked up and saw Abraham far away, with Lazarus by his side. ²⁴So he called to him, 'Father Abraham, have pity on me and send Lazarus to dip the tip of his finger in water and cool my tongue, because I am in agony in this fire.'

²⁵"But Abraham replied, 'Son, remember that in your lifetime you received your good things, while Lazarus received bad things, but now he is comforted here and you are in agony. ²⁶And besides all this, between us and you a great chasm has been fixed, so that those who want to go from here to you cannot, nor can anyone cross over from there to us.'

²⁷"He answered, 'Then I beg you, father, send Lazarus to my father's house, ²⁸for I have five brothers. Let him warn them, so that they will not also come to this place of torment.'

²⁹"Abraham replied, 'They have Moses and the Prophets; let them listen to them.'

³⁰" 'No, father Abraham,' he said, 'but if someone from the dead goes to them, they will repent.'

³¹"He said to him, 'If they do not listen to Moses and the Prophets, they will not be convinced even if someone rises from the dead.' "

---

¹6 Greek *one hundred batous* (probably about 3 kiloliters)   ^m7 Greek *one hundred korous* (probably about 35 kiloliters)   ^n23 Greek *Hades*

Discovering the Word 1. Jesus' parable in verses 1–18 is quite straightforward. His application, how-ever, seems not to be clear (vv. 8b–9). At first reading, how does he seem to be applying the parable to his disciples? 2. Where in the context could you show that Jesus is not condoning greed and dishonesty? 3. According to Jesus in verses 10–15, what does our management of money have to do with our standing before God? 4. In the first part of the parable in verses 19–31 Jesus contrasts the earthly status of Lazarus and the rich man, and then their different eternal states. What does Jesus want the Pharisees to see about the relationship of money in this life and in the life after death? 5. In the second part of the parable we learn more about life after death (vv. 26–31). What facts and implications do you observe about this dimension of existence?

 Applying the Word 1. How should these parables affect your present use of money? 2. What practical actions would help you to use your money more effectively?

Responding in Prayer Our relatives and friends are not all skeptics. Pray that Jesus' teaching on life after death may spur you to more personal evangelism with those who are still open.

---

19 / *Luke 17:1—18:14*
How to Grow Mustard-Seed Faith

AS JESUS, HIS disciples and the crowds draw near Jerusalem, he knows disillusion will set in for them. No one understands his repeated predictions of death by the hands of the nation's leaders. They all expect political glory. Their faith is in a nationalistic, political Messiah come to overthrow the Roman rulers and reinstate their national independence. They had to learn what we also have to learn: Faith is not a complete package one receives at conversion. Our trust is not to be in a set program but in a dynamic Person. Faith is a growing response to God, and grows best in the adversities of life.

 Warming Up to God Since you first met Jesus, what disillusionments have you had about him and his way of life?

 Read Luke 17:1—18:14

---

17 Jesus said to his disciples: "Things that cause people to sin are bound to come, but woe to that person through whom they come. ²It would be better for him to be thrown into the sea with a millstone tied around his neck than for him to cause one of these little ones to sin. ³So watch yourselves.

"If your brother sins, rebuke him, and if he repents, forgive him. ⁴If he sins against you seven times in a day, and seven times comes back to you and says, 'I repent,' forgive him."

⁵The apostles said to the Lord, "Increase our faith!"

⁶He replied, "If you have faith as small as a mustard seed, you can say to this mulberry tree, 'Be uprooted and planted in the sea,' and it will obey you.

⁷"Suppose one of you had a servant plowing or looking after the sheep. Would he say to the servant when he comes in from the field, 'Come along now and sit down to eat'? ⁸Would he not rather say, 'Prepare my supper, get yourself ready and wait on me while I eat and drink; after that you may eat and drink'? ⁹Would he thank the servant because he did what he was told to do? ¹⁰So you also, when you have done everything you were told to do, should say, 'We are unworthy servants; we have only done our duty.'"

¹¹Now on his way to Jerusalem, Jesus traveled along the border between Samaria and Galilee. ¹²As he was going into a village, ten men who had leprosy° met him. They stood at a distance ¹³and called out in a loud voice, "Jesus, Master, have pity on us!"

¹⁴When he saw them, he said, "Go, show yourselves to the priests." And as they went, they were cleansed.

¹⁵One of them, when he saw he was healed, came back, praising God in a loud voice. ¹⁶He

---

°12 The Greek word was used for various diseases affecting the skin—not necessarily leprosy.

threw himself at Jesus' feet and thanked him—
and he was a Samaritan.

17Jesus asked, "Were not all ten cleansed?
Where are the other nine? 18Was no one found to
return and give praise to God except this foreigner?" 19Then he said to him, "Rise and go;
your faith has made you well."

20Once, having been asked by the Pharisees
when the kingdom of God would come, Jesus replied, "The kingdom of God does not come with
your careful observation, 21nor will people say,
'Here it is,' or 'There it is,' because the kingdom of
God is withinᵖ you."

22Then he said to his disciples, "The time is
coming when you will long to see one of the days
of the Son of Man, but you will not see it. 23Men
will tell you, 'There he is!' or 'Here he is!' Do not
go running off after them. 24For the Son of Man
in his day�q will be like the lightning, which
flashes and lights up the sky from one end to the
other. 25But first he must suffer many things and
be rejected by this generation.

26"Just as it was in the days of Noah, so also
will it be in the days of the Son of Man. 27People
were eating, drinking, marrying and being given
in marriage up to the day Noah entered the ark.
Then the flood came and destroyed them all.

28"It was the same in the days of Lot. People
were eating and drinking, buying and selling,
planting and building. 29But the day Lot left
Sodom, fire and sulfur rained down from heaven
and destroyed them all.

30"It will be just like this on the day the Son of
Man is revealed. 31On that day no one who is on
the roof of his house, with his goods inside,
should go down to get them. Likewise, no one in
the field should go back for anything. 32Remem-
ber Lot's wife! 33Whoever tries to keep his life
will lose it, and whoever loses his life will preserve it. 34I tell you, on that night two people will
be in one bed; one will be taken and the other
left. 35Two women will be grinding grain together; one will be taken and the other left.ʳ"

37"Where, Lord?" they asked.

He replied, "Where there is a dead body, there
the vultures will gather."

18 Then Jesus told his disciples a parable to show them that they should
always pray and not give up. 2He
said: "In a certain town there was a judge who
neither feared God nor cared about men. 3And
there was a widow in that town who kept coming
to him with the plea, 'Grant me justice against my
adversary.'

4"For some time he refused. But finally he said
to himself, 'Even though I don't fear God or care
about men, 5yet because this widow keeps bothering me, I will see that she gets justice, so that
she won't eventually wear me out with her coming!' "

6And the Lord said, "Listen to what the unjust
judge says. 7And will not God bring about justice
for his chosen ones, who cry out to him day and
night? Will he keep putting them off? 8I tell you,
he will see that they get justice, and quickly.
However, when the Son of Man comes, will he
find faith on the earth?"

9To some who were confident of their own
righteousness and looked down on everybody
else, Jesus told this parable: 10"Two men went up
to the temple to pray, one a Pharisee and the
other a tax collector. 11The Pharisee stood up and
prayed aboutˢ himself: 'God, I thank you that I
am not like other men—robbers, evildoers, adulterers—or even like this tax collector. 12I fast
twice a week and give a tenth of all I get.'

13"But the tax collector stood at a distance. He
would not even look up to heaven, but beat his
breast and said, 'God, have mercy on me, a sinner.'

14"I tell you that this man, rather than the
other, went home justified before God. For everyone who exalts himself will be humbled, and he
who humbles himself will be exalted."

ᵖ21 Or among　 q24 Some manuscripts do not have in his day.
ʳ35 Some manuscripts left. 36Two men will be in the field; one will be
taken and the other left.　s11 Or to

Discovering the Word 1. Consider the strong reaction of the disciples in 17:1–5. What has caused this
reaction? 2. In the story of the lepers Jesus seems surprised that only one of the ten returned in gratitude
for his healing. What relation can you see between faith and gratitude in his final words (17:17–19)? 3. For the
Pharisees, what emphasis about the kingdom of God does Jesus make (17:20–21)? Why? 4. To his disciples
Jesus stresses the need to be prepared for the coming of the Son of Man (himself). He uses two examples of
warning in the Old Testament. Why were those people unprepared for God's judgment (17:22–37)? 5. To encourage us to persist in praying Jesus draws a portrait of a certain judge as a contrast to God. In what ways is God

different from the judge (18:6–8)?   6. Persistence in praying is balanced by the caution in the second parable not to be presumptuous about God (18:9–14). Both men address "God." But how do their prayers reveal different concepts of God and their relation to him?

 Applying the Word   1. What might your prayers reveal about your concept of God and how you relate to him?   2. Faith often seems abstract and elusive. How has Jesus in this study made it more concrete and attainable for your daily living?

Responding in Prayer   Pray from your heart to the God who desires to hear you.

20 / *Luke 18:15—19:10*
The Nobodies God Wants

"ONLY THE LITTLE people pay taxes." This quote comes from the very rich hotel "queen," Leona Helmsley, who is now paying dearly for tax evasion. What a contrast of attitude with God's compassion for "the little people." Our study introduces us to three groups or individuals whom society considered insignificant—little children, a blind beggar and a tax collector. They represent the kind of people he wants in his messianic community.

 Warming Up to God   Reflect on the past week. Is it possible that you have treated someone as insignificant? If so, confess your sin to the Lord.

 Read Luke 18:15—19:10.

¹⁵People were also bringing babies to Jesus to have him touch them. When the disciples saw this, they rebuked them. ¹⁶But Jesus called the children to him and said, "Let the little children come to me, and do not hinder them, for the kingdom of God belongs to such as these. ¹⁷I tell you the truth, anyone who will not receive the kingdom of God like a little child will never enter it."

¹⁸A certain ruler asked him, "Good teacher, what must I do to inherit eternal life?"

¹⁹"Why do you call me good?" Jesus answered. "No one is good—except God alone. ²⁰You know the commandments: 'Do not commit adultery, do not murder, do not steal, do not give false testimony, honor your father and mother.'ᶜ"

²¹"All these I have kept since I was a boy," he said.

²²When Jesus heard this, he said to him, "You still lack one thing. Sell everything you have and give to the poor, and you will have treasure in heaven. Then come, follow me."

²³When he heard this, he became very sad, because he was a man of great wealth. ²⁴Jesus looked at him and said, "How hard it is for the rich to enter the kingdom of God! ²⁵Indeed, it is

easier for a camel to go through the eye of a needle than for a rich man to enter the kingdom of God."

²⁶Those who heard this asked, "Who then can be saved?"

²⁷Jesus replied, "What is impossible with men is possible with God."

²⁸Peter said to him, "We have left all we had to follow you!"

²⁹"I tell you the truth," Jesus said to them, "no one who has left home or wife or brothers or parents or children for the sake of the kingdom of God ³⁰will fail to receive many times as much in this age and, in the age to come, eternal life."

³¹Jesus took the Twelve aside and told them, "We are going up to Jerusalem, and everything that is written by the prophets about the Son of Man will be fulfilled. ³²He will be handed over to the Gentiles. They will mock him, insult him, spit on him, flog him and kill him. ³³On the third day he will rise again."

³⁴The disciples did not understand any of this. Its meaning was hidden from them, and they did not know what he was talking about.

³⁵As Jesus approached Jericho, a blind man was

ᶜ20 Exodus 20:12-16; Deut. 5:16-20

sitting by the roadside begging. 36When he heard the crowd going by, he asked what was happening. 37They told him, "Jesus of Nazareth is passing by."

38He called out, "Jesus, Son of David, have mercy on me!"

39Those who led the way rebuked him and told him to be quiet, but he shouted all the more, "Son of David, have mercy on me!"

40Jesus stopped and ordered the man to be brought to him. When he came near, Jesus asked him, 41"What do you want me to do for you?"

"Lord, I want to see," he replied.

42Jesus said to him, "Receive your sight; your faith has healed you." 43Immediately he received his sight and followed Jesus, praising God. When all the people saw it, they also praised God.

19 Jesus entered Jericho and was passing through. 2A man was there by the name of Zacchaeus; he was a chief tax collector and was wealthy. 3He wanted to see who Jesus was, but being a short man he could not, because of the crowd. 4So he ran ahead and climbed a sycamore-fig tree to see him, since Jesus was coming that way.

5When Jesus reached the spot, he looked up and said to him, "Zacchaeus, come down immediately. I must stay at your house today." 6So he came down at once and welcomed him gladly.

7All the people saw this and began to mutter, "He has gone to be the guest of a 'sinner.' "

8But Zacchaeus stood up and said to the Lord, "Look, Lord! Here and now I give half of my possessions to the poor, and if I have cheated anybody out of anything, I will pay back four times the amount."

9Jesus said to him, "Today salvation has come to this house, because this man, too, is a son of Abraham. 10For the Son of Man came to seek and to save what was lost."

Discovering the Word 1. The disciples represent their society's attitude to children—they're insignificant (18:15). How does Jesus give significance to them? 2. In contrast, 18:18–30 is about a "somebody" who disqualifies himself from the kingdom. He has everything society considers admirable and desirable. But what condition for eternal life does he lack (18:22)? 3. In Luke 18:31–34 Jesus' fourth prediction to the Twelve about his coming violent death again meets with lack of understanding. Their presuppositions about riches and their political agenda (19:11) deafens them to Jesus' intent. Then in 18:35–45 Luke introduces us to someone who represents another group of nobodies. What is unusual about the beggar's attitude and title that catches Jesus' attention? 4. Jericho was a rich agricultural town, a popular resort for royalty and priests. What kind of character would a chief tax collector in such a town likely develop? 5. What other side of Zaccheus surfaces in 19:3–6 and 8?

Applying the Word 1. How does Jesus' example with Zaccheus show you how you might share the gospel? 2. Which outsider or nobody from your circle of acquaintances could you introduce to Jesus?

Responding in Prayer Pray for those who are considered insignificant in your community.

---

21 / *Luke 19:11–48*
False Hopes About the Kingdom of God

MOST OF MY bosses have been hard drivers who regularly exasperated me. But in the long run we worked together productively. If we respect and like our bosses, we are often willing to work hard and even overtime. If we don't respect or like them, we usually are not willing. Then we probably become unproductive. Likewise our personal view of God affects our working relationship to him. In this case productivity has not just temporal but eternal consequences.

Warming Up to God How has work been for you this week? Talk to God about any frustrations you have experienced.

Read Luke 19:11–48.

¹¹While they were listening to this, he went on to tell them a parable, because he was near Jerusalem and the people thought that the kingdom of God was going to appear at once. ¹²He said: "A man of noble birth went to a distant country to have himself appointed king and then to return. ¹³So he called ten of his servants and gave them ten minas.ᵘ 'Put this money to work,' he said, 'until I come back.'

¹⁴"But his subjects hated him and sent a delegation after him to say, 'We don't want this man to be our king.'

¹⁵"He was made king, however, and returned home. Then he sent for the servants to whom he had given the money, in order to find out what they had gained with it.

¹⁶"The first one came and said, 'Sir, your mina has earned ten more.'

¹⁷" 'Well done, my good servant!' his master replied. 'Because you have been trustworthy in a very small matter, take charge of ten cities.'

¹⁸"The second came and said, 'Sir, your mina has earned five more.'

¹⁹"His master answered, 'You take charge of five cities.'

²⁰"Then another servant came and said, 'Sir, here is your mina; I have kept it laid away in a piece of cloth. ²¹I was afraid of you, because you are a hard man. You take out what you did not put in and reap what you did not sow.'

²²"His master replied, 'I will judge you by your own words, you wicked servant! You knew, did you, that I am a hard man, taking out what I did not put in, and reaping what I did not sow? ²³Why then didn't you put my money on deposit, so that when I came back, I could have collected it with interest?'

²⁴"Then he said to those standing by, 'Take his mina away from him and give it to the one who has ten minas.'

²⁵" 'Sir,' they said, 'he already has ten!'

²⁶"He replied, 'I tell you that to everyone who has, more will be given, but as for the one who has nothing, even what he has will be taken away. ²⁷But those enemies of mine who did not want me to be king over them—bring them here and kill them in front of me.' "

²⁸After Jesus had said this, he went on ahead, going up to Jerusalem. ²⁹As he approached Bethphage and Bethany at the hill called the Mount of Olives, he sent two of his disciples, saying to them, ³⁰"Go to the village ahead of you, and as you enter it, you will find a colt tied there, which no one has ever ridden. Untie it and bring it here. ³¹If anyone asks you, 'Why are you untying it?' tell him, 'The Lord needs it.' "

³²Those who were sent ahead went and found it just as he had told them. ³³As they were untying the colt, its owners asked them, "Why are you untying the colt?"

³⁴They replied, "The Lord needs it."

³⁵They brought it to Jesus, threw their cloaks on the colt and put Jesus on it. ³⁶As he went along, people spread their cloaks on the road.

³⁷When he came near the place where the road goes down the Mount of Olives, the whole crowd of disciples began joyfully to praise God in loud voices for all the miracles they had seen:

³⁸"Blessed is the king who comes in the name
of the Lord!"ᵛ

"Peace in heaven and glory in the highest!"

³⁹Some of the Pharisees in the crowd said to Jesus, "Teacher, rebuke your disciples!"

⁴⁰"I tell you," he replied, "if they keep quiet, the stones will cry out."

⁴¹As he approached Jerusalem and saw the city, he wept over it ⁴²and said, "If you, even you, had only known on this day what would bring you peace—but now it is hidden from your eyes. ⁴³The days will come upon you when your enemies will build an embankment against you and encircle you and hem you in on every side. ⁴⁴They will dash you to the ground, you and the children within your walls. They will not leave one stone on another, because you did not recognize the time of God's coming to you."

⁴⁵Then he entered the temple area and began driving out those who were selling. ⁴⁶"It is written," he said to them, " 'My house will be a house of prayer'ʷ; but you have made it 'a den of robbers.'ˣ "

⁴⁷Every day he was teaching at the temple. But

ᵘ13 A mina was about three months' wages.　ᵛ38 Psalm 118:26
ʷ46 Isaiah 56:7　ˣ46 Jer. 7:11

the chief priests, the teachers of the law and the leaders among the people were trying to kill him.

⁴⁸Yet they could not find any way to do it, because all the people hung on his words.

 Discovering the Word 1. Jesus' key words in verse 10 have inflamed the crowd's messianic expectations. Jesus' parable aims to counter any false hopes. In verses 12–15 what comparisons between the nobleman and himself does Jesus highlight? 2. Consider the hour of accountability when the master returns as king (vv. 15–26). The reward of the first two (representative) servants is simple. But the king's dialogue with the third servant is detailed. With this emphasis, what point is Jesus making (keep in mind v. 11)? 3. The adversaries of the nobleman-made-king are mentioned only at the beginning and the end (vv. 14, 27). Whom does Jesus intend them to represent? 4. How does he smash the false hopes of this group? 5. In verses 28–40 we see Jesus in various aspects of his messianic role. In a descriptive word or phrase, what concern of Jesus' do you see as he approaches Jerusalem? 6. What concern of Jesus' do you note as he reflects on Jerusalem (vv. 41–44)?

 Applying the Word 1. In this panoramic view of Jesus the Messiah, what do you find hard to understand about him? 2. What about Jesus here can you positively respond to? Why?

Responding in Prayer Worship Jesus the Messiah king with praise, awe and thanksgiving.

---

22 / *Luke 20:1—21:4*
Final Debates—Clear Rejection

I CAN REMEMBER when a humanist on campus branded the Christians a bunch of losers. He claimed he did not need religion for a crutch as they did. I was reduced to wordlessness by his hostile tone. Then I thought of three perfect answers—late that night in bed.

Most of us are not quick to think on our feet, and certainly not as quick and sharp as Jesus. We have seen him as a fearless controversialist in Galilee. Now we will see him in the capital, taking on four distinct authority groups as each mounts attacks on him.

 Warming Up to God When have you felt humiliated because you could not defend your faith?

 Read Luke 20:1—21:4.

---

20 One day as he was teaching the people in the temple courts and preaching the gospel, the chief priests and the teachers of the law, together with the elders, came up to him. ²"Tell us by what authority you are doing these things," they said. "Who gave you this authority?"

³He replied, "I will also ask you a question. Tell me, ⁴John's baptism—was it from heaven, or from men?"

⁵They discussed it among themselves and said, "If we say, 'From heaven,' he will ask, 'Why didn't you believe him?' ⁶But if we say, 'From men,' all the people will stone us, because they are persuaded that John was a prophet."

⁷So they answered, "We don't know where it was from."

⁸Jesus said, "Neither will I tell you by what authority I am doing these things."

⁹He went on to tell the people this parable: "A man planted a vineyard, rented it to some farmers and went away for a long time. ¹⁰At harvest time he sent a servant to the tenants so they would give him some of the fruit of the vineyard. But the tenants beat him and sent him away empty-handed. ¹¹He sent another servant, but that one also they beat and treated shamefully and sent away empty-handed. ¹²He sent still a third, and they wounded him and threw him out.

¹³"Then the owner of the vineyard said, 'What

shall I do? I will send my son, whom I love; perhaps they will respect him.'

¹⁴"But when the tenants saw him, they talked the matter over. 'This is the heir,' they said. 'Let's kill him, and the inheritance will be ours.' ¹⁵So they threw him out of the vineyard and killed him.

"What then will the owner of the vineyard do to them? ¹⁶He will come and kill those tenants and give the vineyard to others."

When the people heard this, they said, "May this never be!"

¹⁷Jesus looked directly at them and asked, "Then what is the meaning of that which is written:

" 'The stone the builders rejected
    has become the capstone'ʸ'ᶻ?

¹⁸Everyone who falls on that stone will be broken to pieces, but he on whom it falls will be crushed."

¹⁹The teachers of the law and the chief priests looked for a way to arrest him immediately, because they knew he had spoken this parable against them. But they were afraid of the people.

²⁰Keeping a close watch on him, they sent spies, who pretended to be honest. They hoped to catch Jesus in something he said so that they might hand him over to the power and authority of the governor. ²¹So the spies questioned him: "Teacher, we know that you speak and teach what is right, and that you do not show partiality but teach the way of God in accordance with the truth. ²²Is it right for us to pay taxes to Caesar or not?"

²³He saw through their duplicity and said to them, ²⁴"Show me a denarius. Whose portrait and inscription are on it?"

²⁵"Caesar's," they replied.

He said to them, "Then give to Caesar what is Caesar's, and to God what is God's."

²⁶They were unable to trap him in what he had said there in public. And astonished by his answer, they became silent.

²⁷Some of the Sadducees, who say there is no resurrection, came to Jesus with a question. ²⁸"Teacher," they said, "Moses wrote for us that if a man's brother dies and leaves a wife but no children, the man must marry the widow and have children for his brother. ²⁹Now there were seven brothers. The first one married a woman

and died childless. ³⁰The second ³¹and then the third married her, and in the same way the seven died, leaving no children. ³²Finally, the woman died too. ³³Now then, at the resurrection whose wife will she be, since the seven were married to her?"

³⁴Jesus replied, "The people of this age marry and are given in marriage. ³⁵But those who are considered worthy of taking part in that age and in the resurrection from the dead will neither marry nor be given in marriage, ³⁶and they can no longer die; for they are like the angels. They are God's children, since they are children of the resurrection. ³⁷But in the account of the bush, even Moses showed that the dead rise, for he calls the Lord 'the God of Abraham, and the God of Isaac, and the God of Jacob.'ᵃ ³⁸He is not the God of the dead, but of the living, for to him all are alive."

³⁹Some of the teachers of the law responded, "Well said, teacher!" ⁴⁰And no one dared to ask him any more questions.

⁴¹Then Jesus said to them, "How is it that they say the Christᵇ is the Son of David? ⁴²David himself declares in the Book of Psalms:

" 'The Lord said to my Lord:
    "Sit at my right hand
⁴³until I make your enemies
    a footstool for your feet." 'ᶜ

⁴⁴David calls him 'Lord.' How then can he be his son?"

⁴⁵While all the people were listening, Jesus said to his disciples, ⁴⁶"Beware of the teachers of the law. They like to walk around in flowing robes and love to be greeted in the marketplaces and have the most important seats in the synagogues and the places of honor at banquets. ⁴⁷They devour widows' houses and for a show make lengthy prayers. Such men will be punished most severely."

21

As he looked up, Jesus saw the rich putting their gifts into the temple treasury. ²He also saw a poor widow put in two very small copper coins.ᵈ ³"I tell you the truth," he said, "this poor widow has put in more than all the others. ⁴All these people gave their gifts out of their wealth; but she out of her poverty put in all she had to live on."

ʸ17 Or *cornerstone*   ᶻ17 Psalm 118:22   ᵃ37 Exodus 3:6
ᵇ41 Or *Messiah*   ᶜ43 Psalm 110:1   ᵈ2 Greek *two lepta*

Discovering the Word 1. By the end of the debate on Jesus' authority, what has each side achieved (20:1–8)? 2. By parable and commentary Jesus pronounces final judgment on the leaders (20:9–18). How do you respond to his stern characterization of God? 3. The Sadducees accepted only the first five Old Testament books, which they (wrongly) presumed said nothing about life after death. What, therefore, do they expect their hypothetical story to do to belief in the resurrection (20:27–47)? 4. Again Jesus points to wrong assumptions behind their question. What error does he identify in their view of life after death (vv. 34–36)? 5. How refreshing this widow must have been to Jesus after the controversies! What does this tell you about the kind of faith Jesus values (21:1–4)?

 Applying the Word 1. All four groups totally reject Jesus as God's Messiah king. After this, there are no more debates on the truth—only arrest and death. Besides valid debates, how can we maintain biblical truth against the enemies of Christianity? 2. What is a political/religious tension for you as a Christian? 3. In what way would you like to be more bold in defending your faith?

 Responding in Prayer Pray now for faith like the widow's.

23 / *Luke 21:5–38*
Getting Ready for the End

THE "EVIL EMPIRE" of the once-powerful USSR has disappeared, and its former allies are left dangling for military aid. We praise God for this. But some "scholars" of biblical prophecy have to rewrite their books about who the antichrist is and who the nations that will meet for battle in Magog are. Sensational interpretations of "the last days" can stir up some people, especially when the Middle East is in the news. Others react against what they perceive as scare tactics by avoiding any consideration of biblical prophecies. In today's chapter the Lord Jesus shows us how to keep a balance by being properly informed and obedient to his instructions.

Warming Up to God What feelings does talk about the last days create in you?

Read Luke 21:5–38.

⁵Some of his disciples were remarking about how the temple was adorned with beautiful stones and with gifts dedicated to God. But Jesus said, ⁶"As for what you see here, the time will come when not one stone will be left on another; every one of them will be thrown down."

⁷"Teacher," they asked, "when will these things happen? And what will be the sign that they are about to take place?"

⁸He replied: "Watch out that you are not deceived. For many will come in my name, claiming, 'I am he,' and, 'The time is near.' Do not follow them. ⁹When you hear of wars and revolutions, do not be frightened. These things must happen first, but the end will not come right away."

¹⁰Then he said to them: "Nation will rise against nation, and kingdom against kingdom. ¹¹There will be great earthquakes, famines and pestilences in various places, and fearful events and great signs from heaven.

¹²"But before all this, they will lay hands on you and persecute you. They will deliver you to synagogues and prisons, and you will be brought before kings and governors, and all on account of my name. ¹³This will result in your being witnesses to them. ¹⁴But make up your mind not to worry beforehand how you will defend yourselves. ¹⁵For I will give you words and wisdom that none of your adversaries will be able to resist or contradict. ¹⁶You will be betrayed even by parents, brothers, relatives and friends, and they will put some of you to death. ¹⁷All men will hate you because of me. ¹⁸But not a hair of your head will perish. ¹⁹By standing firm you will gain life.

²⁰"When you see Jerusalem being surrounded by armies, you will know that its desolation is near. ²¹Then let those who are in Judea flee to the

mountains, let those in the city get out, and let those in the country not enter the city. 22For this is the time of punishment in fulfillment of all that has been written. 23How dreadful it will be in those days for pregnant women and nursing mothers! There will be great distress in the land and wrath against this people. 24They will fall by the sword and will be taken as prisoners to all the nations. Jerusalem will be trampled on by the Gentiles until the times of the Gentiles are fulfilled.

25"There will be signs in the sun, moon and stars. On the earth, nations will be in anguish and perplexity at the roaring and tossing of the sea. 26Men will faint from terror, apprehensive of what is coming on the world, for the heavenly bodies will be shaken. 27At that time they will see the Son of Man coming in a cloud with power and great glory. 28When these things begin to take place, stand up and lift up your heads, because your redemption is drawing near."

29He told them this parable: "Look at the fig tree and all the trees. 30When they sprout leaves,

you can see for yourselves and know that summer is near. 31Even so, when you see these things happening, you know that the kingdom of God is near.

32"I tell you the truth, this generationᶜ will certainly not pass away until all these things have happened. 33Heaven and earth will pass away, but my words will never pass away.

34"Be careful, or your hearts will be weighed down with dissipation, drunkenness and the anxieties of life, and that day will close on you unexpectedly like a trap. 35For it will come upon all those who live on the face of the whole earth. 36Be always on the watch, and pray that you may be able to escape all that is about to happen, and that you may be able to stand before the Son of Man."

37Each day Jesus was teaching at the temple, and each evening he went out to spend the night on the hill called the Mount of Olives, 38and all the people came early in the morning to hear him at the temple.

ᶜ32 Or *race*

Discovering the Word   1. What are your general impressions of Jesus' discourse on the end of the age?   2. At least three important events are evident. The first is Jesus' delivering this discourse to his disciples in A.D. 30 in Jerusalem. What are the other two (vv. 20–24 and vv. 27–28)?   3. But Jesus also says some positive things will happen during this time (vv. 12–19). (These activities can also be applied between the second and third events.) What in Jesus' message gives you hope for an otherwise uncertain future?   4. In verses 8–9 Jesus has said that certain activities are not signs of the end. But what does he say will be signs of the end when he returns (vv. 25–28, and probably vv. 10–11)?   5. How is Jesus' parable of the fig tree (vv. 29–31) related to his preceding teachings (for example, 19:41–44; 20:16)?

Applying the Word   1. Earthly preoccupation can keep us insensitive to spiritual realities and unprepared "to stand before the Son of Man" (vv. 5, 34–36). What aspects of modern living tempt you this way?   2. Which one of Jesus' promises gives you strong incentive to be well prepared (vv. 14–15, 19, 24, 28, 31, 33)?

Responding in Prayer   Pray that you would be made ready.

---

24 / *Luke 22:1–46*
Jesus' New Passover

NOW WE ENTER deeply into the saddest days of history. With Judas' help the religious leaders, considered the most enlightened men in their nation, complete their plot to kill the Son of God. But these days are also the greatest days on earth for Jesus. He is about to complete his life mission, and he confirms to the eleven remaining that they will carry on that mission. So with them he privately establishes his new Passover to supersede the old Passover.

Warming Up to God   Recall your most moving celebration of the Lord's Supper. What made it so?

Read Luke 22:1–46.

22 Now the Feast of Unleavened Bread, called the Passover, was approaching, ²and the chief priests and the teachers of the law were looking for some way to get rid of Jesus, for they were afraid of the people. ³Then Satan entered Judas, called Iscariot, one of the Twelve. ⁴And Judas went to the chief priests and the officers of the temple guard and discussed with them how he might betray Jesus. ⁵They were delighted and agreed to give him money. ⁶He consented, and watched for an opportunity to hand Jesus over to them when no crowd was present.

⁷Then came the day of Unleavened Bread on which the Passover lamb had to be sacrificed. ⁸Jesus sent Peter and John, saying, "Go and make preparations for us to eat the Passover."

⁹"Where do you want us to prepare for it?" they asked.

¹⁰He replied, "As you enter the city, a man carrying a jar of water will meet you. Follow him to the house that he enters, ¹¹and say to the owner of the house, 'The Teacher asks: Where is the guest room, where I may eat the Passover with my disciples?' ¹²He will show you a large upper room, all furnished. Make preparations there."

¹³They left and found things just as Jesus had told them. So they prepared the Passover.

¹⁴When the hour came, Jesus and his apostles reclined at the table. ¹⁵And he said to them, "I have eagerly desired to eat this Passover with you before I suffer. ¹⁶For I tell you, I will not eat it again until it finds fulfillment in the kingdom of God."

¹⁷After taking the cup, he gave thanks and said, "Take this and divide it among you. ¹⁸For I tell you I will not drink again of the fruit of the vine until the kingdom of God comes."

¹⁹And he took bread, gave thanks and broke it, and gave it to them, saying, "This is my body given for you; do this in remembrance of me."

²⁰In the same way, after the supper he took the cup, saying, "This cup is the new covenant in my blood, which is poured out for you. ²¹But the hand of him who is going to betray me is with mine on the table. ²²The Son of Man will go as it has been decreed, but woe to that man who betrays him." ²³They began to question among themselves which of them it might be who would do this.

²⁴Also a dispute arose among them as to which of them was considered to be greatest. ²⁵Jesus said to them, "The kings of the Gentiles lord it over them; and those who exercise authority over them call themselves Benefactors. ²⁶But you are not to be like that. Instead, the greatest among you should be like the youngest, and the one who rules like the one who serves. ²⁷For who is greater, the one who is at the table or the one who serves? Is it not the one who is at the table? But I am among you as one who serves. ²⁸You are those who have stood by me in my trials. ²⁹And I confer on you a kingdom, just as my Father conferred one on me, ³⁰so that you may eat and drink at my table in my kingdom and sit on thrones, judging the twelve tribes of Israel.

³¹"Simon, Simon, Satan has asked to sift you ᶠ as wheat. ³²But I have prayed for you, Simon, that your faith may not fail. And when you have turned back, strengthen your brothers."

³³But he replied, "Lord, I am ready to go with you to prison and to death."

³⁴Jesus answered, "I tell you, Peter, before the rooster crows today, you will deny three times that you know me."

³⁵Then Jesus asked them, "When I sent you without purse, bag or sandals, did you lack anything?"

"Nothing," they answered.

³⁶He said to them, "But now if you have a purse, take it, and also a bag; and if you don't have a sword, sell your cloak and buy one. ³⁷It is written: 'And he was numbered with the transgressors' ᵍ; and I tell you that this must be fulfilled in me. Yes, what is written about me is reaching its fulfillment."

³⁸The disciples said, "See, Lord, here are two swords."

"That is enough," he replied.

³⁹Jesus went out as usual to the Mount of Olives, and his disciples followed him. ⁴⁰On reaching the place, he said to them, "Pray that you will not fall into temptation." ⁴¹He withdrew about a stone's throw beyond them, knelt down and prayed, ⁴²"Father, if you are willing, take this cup from me; yet not my will, but yours be done."

ᶠ31 The Greek is plural.   ᵍ37 Isaiah 53:12

⁴³An angel from heaven appeared to him and strengthened him. ⁴⁴And being in anguish, he prayed more earnestly, and his sweat was like drops of blood falling to the ground.ʰ

⁴⁵When he rose from prayer and went back to the disciples, he found them asleep, exhausted from sorrow. ⁴⁶"Why are you sleeping?" he asked them. "Get up and pray so that you will not fall into temptation."

ʰ44 Some early manuscripts do not have verses 43 and 44.

 Discovering the Word 1. What do verses 1–6 tell you about the authorities? 2. Look at verses 7–23, comparing Jesus' plans with the authorities' plans. As you examine his plans, what impresses you about Jesus himself? 3. Jesus chides the disciples for their preoccupation with power and prestige. What lesson does he teach about the kind of leaders he wants to carry on his work (vv. 26–27)? 4. Jesus further prepares them for coming tests. The first preparation is for Peter immediately ahead. The second is for all the apostles in the long run. Like him they would have to face official hostility (vv. 36–38). In either testing what should help them to persevere (vv. 28, 29–30, 31, 32, 35)? 5. What guidelines for praying do you see in each verse of 39–46, showing Jesus' example?

Applying the Word 1. Jesus' institution of his new Passover was interspersed with human weakness and failure. In redeeming his disciples, he used their shortcomings. What weaknesses and failures do you want to acknowledge as you contemplate afresh eating Jesus' new Passover? 2. What new, or renewed, truths about prayer do you discover in Jesus' example (22:39–46)?

Responding in Prayer Follow the guidelines for prayer in Jesus' example.

---

25 / Luke 22:47—23:56
The Message of the Cross

THE SYMBOL OF the cross is used in many ways—on and in Christian churches, by the Red Cross, on many European flags. It is used as jewelry even by non-Christians. But they would never think of wearing a burnished gold miniature of an electric chair around their necks. In the first century the wooden cross meant capital punishment for criminals. Jesus died as a criminal to be the substitute for us sinners. Some old hymns have well retained this essential truth of Jesus' cross. Not many contemporary songs about his death do that. Approach this study with prayer for a deeper understanding of the cross of Jesus.

 Warming Up to God What was your first understanding of the Christian cross?

 Read Luke 22:47—23:56.

---

⁴⁷While he was still speaking a crowd came up, and the man who was called Judas, one of the Twelve, was leading them. He approached Jesus to kiss him, ⁴⁸but Jesus asked him, "Judas, are you betraying the Son of Man with a kiss?"

⁴⁹When Jesus' followers saw what was going to happen, they said, "Lord, should we strike with our swords?" ⁵⁰And one of them struck the servant of the high priest, cutting off his right ear.

⁵¹But Jesus answered, "No more of this!" And he touched the man's ear and healed him.

⁵²Then Jesus said to the chief priests, the officers of the temple guard, and the elders, who had come for him, "Am I leading a rebellion, that you have come with swords and clubs? ⁵³Every day I was with you in the temple courts, and you did not lay a hand on me. But this is your hour—when darkness reigns."

⁵⁴Then seizing him, they led him away and took him into the house of the high priest. Peter followed at a distance. ⁵⁵But when they had kindled a fire in the middle of the courtyard and had

sat down together, Peter sat down with them. ⁵⁶A servant girl saw him seated there in the firelight. She looked closely at him and said, "This man was with him."

⁵⁷But he denied it. "Woman, I don't know him," he said.

⁵⁸A little later someone else saw him and said, "You also are one of them."

"Man, I am not!" Peter replied.

⁵⁹About an hour later another asserted, "Certainly this fellow was with him, for he is a Galilean."

⁶⁰Peter replied, "Man, I don't know what you're talking about!" Just as he was speaking, the rooster crowed. ⁶¹The Lord turned and looked straight at Peter. Then Peter remembered the word the Lord had spoken to him: "Before the rooster crows today, you will disown me three times." ⁶²And he went outside and wept bitterly.

⁶³The men who were guarding Jesus began mocking and beating him. ⁶⁴They blindfolded him and demanded, "Prophesy! Who hit you?" ⁶⁵And they said many other insulting things to him.

⁶⁶At daybreak the council of the elders of the people, both the chief priests and teachers of the law, met together, and Jesus was led before them. ⁶⁷"If you are the Christ,ⁱ" they said, "tell us."

Jesus answered, "If I tell you, you will not believe me, ⁶⁸and if I asked you, you would not answer. ⁶⁹But from now on, the Son of Man will be seated at the right hand of the mighty God."

⁷⁰They all asked, "Are you then the Son of God?"

He replied, "You are right in saying I am."

⁷¹Then they said, "Why do we need any more testimony? We have heard it from his own lips."

23

Then the whole assembly rose and led him off to Pilate. ²And they began to accuse him, saying, "We have found this man subverting our nation. He opposes payment of taxes to Caesar and claims to be Christ,^j a king."

³So Pilate asked Jesus, "Are you the king of the Jews?"

"Yes, it is as you say," Jesus replied.

⁴Then Pilate announced to the chief priests and the crowd, "I find no basis for a charge against this man."

⁵But they insisted, "He stirs up the people all over Judea^k by his teaching. He started in Galilee and has come all the way here."

⁶On hearing this, Pilate asked if the man was a Galilean. ⁷When he learned that Jesus was under Herod's jurisdiction, he sent him to Herod, who was also in Jerusalem at that time.

⁸When Herod saw Jesus, he was greatly pleased, because for a long time he had been wanting to see him. From what he had heard about him, he hoped to see him perform some miracle. ⁹He plied him with many questions, but Jesus gave him no answer. ¹⁰The chief priests and the teachers of the law were standing there, vehemently accusing him. ¹¹Then Herod and his soldiers ridiculed and mocked him. Dressing him in an elegant robe, they sent him back to Pilate. ¹²That day Herod and Pilate became friends—before this they had been enemies.

¹³Pilate called together the chief priests, the rulers and the people, ¹⁴and said to them, "You brought me this man as one who was inciting the people to rebellion. I have examined him in your presence and have found no basis for your charges against him. ¹⁵Neither has Herod, for he sent him back to us; as you can see, he has done nothing to deserve death. ¹⁶Therefore, I will punish him and then release him.^l"

¹⁸With one voice they cried out, "Away with this man! Release Barabbas to us!" ¹⁹(Barabbas had been thrown into prison for an insurrection in the city, and for murder.)

²⁰Wanting to release Jesus, Pilate appealed to them again. ²¹But they kept shouting, "Crucify him! Crucify him!"

²²For the third time he spoke to them: "Why? What crime has this man committed? I have found in him no grounds for the death penalty. Therefore I will have him punished and then release him."

²³But with loud shouts they insistently demanded that he be crucified, and their shouts prevailed. ²⁴So Pilate decided to grant their demand. ²⁵He released the man who had been thrown into prison for insurrection and murder, the one they asked for, and surrendered Jesus to their will.

²⁶As they led him away, they seized Simon from Cyrene, who was on his way in from the country, and put the cross on him and made him carry it behind Jesus. ²⁷A large number of people followed him, including women who mourned and wailed for him. ²⁸Jesus turned and said to

ⁱ67 Or Messiah   ^j2 Or Messiah; also in verses 35 and 39   ^k5 Or over the land of the Jews   ^l16 Some manuscripts him." ¹⁷Now he was obliged to release one man to them at the Feast.

them, "Daughters of Jerusalem, do not weep for me; weep for yourselves and for your children. ²⁹For the time will come when you will say, 'Blessed are the barren women, the wombs that never bore and the breasts that never nursed!' ³⁰Then

" 'they will say to the mountains, "Fall on
    us!"
  and to the hills, "Cover us!" ' ᵐ

³¹For if men do these things when the tree is green, what will happen when it is dry?"

³²Two other men, both criminals, were also led out with him to be executed. ³³When they came to the place called the Skull, there they crucified him, along with the criminals—one on his right, the other on his left. ³⁴Jesus said, "Father, forgive them, for they do not know what they are doing." ⁿ And they divided up his clothes by casting lots.

³⁵The people stood watching, and the rulers even sneered at him. They said, "He saved others; let him save himself if he is the Christ of God, the Chosen One."

³⁶The soldiers also came up and mocked him. They offered him wine vinegar ³⁷and said, "If you are the king of the Jews, save yourself."

³⁸There was a written notice above him, which read: THIS IS THE KING OF THE JEWS.

³⁹One of the criminals who hung there hurled insults at him: "Aren't you the Christ? Save yourself and us!"

⁴⁰But the other criminal rebuked him. "Don't you fear God," he said, "since you are under the same sentence? ⁴¹We are punished justly, for we are getting what our deeds deserve. But this man has done nothing wrong."

⁴²Then he said, "Jesus, remember me when you come into your kingdom.º"

⁴³Jesus answered him, "I tell you the truth, today you will be with me in paradise."

⁴⁴It was now about the sixth hour, and darkness came over the whole land until the ninth hour, ⁴⁵for the sun stopped shining. And the curtain of the temple was torn in two. ⁴⁶Jesus called out with a loud voice, "Father, into your hands I commit my spirit." When he had said this, he breathed his last.

⁴⁷The centurion, seeing what had happened, praised God and said, "Surely this was a righteous man." ⁴⁸When all the people who had gathered to witness this sight saw what took place, they beat their breasts and went away. ⁴⁹But all those who knew him, including the women who had followed him from Galilee, stood at a distance, watching these things.

⁵⁰Now there was a man named Joseph, a member of the Council, a good and upright man, ⁵¹who had not consented to their decision and action. He came from the Judean town of Arimathea and he was waiting for the kingdom of God. ⁵²Going to Pilate, he asked for Jesus' body. ⁵³Then he took it down, wrapped it in linen cloth and placed it in a tomb cut in the rock, one in which no one had yet been laid. ⁵⁴It was Preparation Day, and the Sabbath was about to begin.

⁵⁵The women who had come with Jesus from Galilee followed Joseph and saw the tomb and how his body was laid in it. ⁵⁶Then they went home and prepared spices and perfumes. But they rested on the Sabbath in obedience to the commandment.

ᵐ30 Hosea 10:8   ⁿ34 Some early manuscripts do not have this sentence.   º42 Some manuscripts come with your kingly power

---

 Discovering the Word 1. In a word or phrase, what describes the way Jesus relates to each individual or group during his arrest (22:47–62)? 2. Only a few hours after Peter swore loyalty to Jesus, he makes an about-face (vv. 57–60). In what kind of situation are you tempted to avoid identification with Jesus and his cause? 3. Three times Pilate says he finds no valid charge against Jesus, and seeks to release him (23:4, 13–16 and 22). Why then does he ultimately pronounce the death penalty on Jesus? 4. Luke gives few details of Jesus' physical death. Instead he focuses on people's attitudes. What attitude to the man on the center cross does each group or individual reveal (23:32–49)? 5. Throughout his six hours on the cross, Jesus is in touch with his Father. What do his brief words to the Father reflect about their relationship (23:34,46)?

 Applying the Word 1. What can you do to make the message of the cross relevant to your needy world? 2. How can the cross become more relevant to you as an individual?

Responding in Prayer Praise God for giving his Son over to this horrible death on the cross for your sake.

26 / *Luke 24*
God Has the Last Word

HOW MIGHT YOU destroy Christianity? Explain away Jesus' resurrection. For instance, you could say the overemotional women at the tomb were deluded. Or argue that they went to the wrong tomb. You might insist that the resurrection was spiritual, not physical, or that the disciples had hallucinations. From that first Easter till now the enemies of the church have tried to get rid of the historical facts (Mt 28:11–15). None has succeeded.

 Warming Up to God What does Christ's resurrection mean to you? What would the world lose if Jesus did not rise from death?

 Read Luke 24.

24 On the first day of the week, very early in the morning, the women took the spices they had prepared and went to the tomb. ²They found the stone rolled away from the tomb, ³but when they entered, they did not find the body of the Lord Jesus. ⁴While they were wondering about this, suddenly two men in clothes that gleamed like lightning stood beside them. ⁵In their fright the women bowed down with their faces to the ground, but the men said to them, "Why do you look for the living among the dead? ⁶He is not here; he has risen! Remember how he told you, while he was still with you in Galilee: ⁷'The Son of Man must be delivered into the hands of sinful men, be crucified and on the third day be raised again.' " ⁸Then they remembered his words.

⁹When they came back from the tomb, they told all these things to the Eleven and to all the others. ¹⁰It was Mary Magdalene, Joanna, Mary the mother of James, and the others with them who told this to the apostles. ¹¹But they did not believe the women, because their words seemed to them like nonsense. ¹²Peter, however, got up and ran to the tomb. Bending over, he saw the strips of linen lying by themselves, and he went away, wondering to himself what had happened.

¹³Now that same day two of them were going to a village called Emmaus, about seven miles[p] from Jerusalem. ¹⁴They were talking with each other about everything that had happened. ¹⁵As they talked and discussed these things with each other, Jesus himself came up and walked along with them; ¹⁶but they were kept from recognizing him.

¹⁷He asked them, "What are you discussing together as you walk along?"

They stood still, their faces downcast. ¹⁸One of them, named Cleopas, asked him, "Are you only a visitor to Jerusalem and do not know the things that have happened there in these days?"

¹⁹"What things?" he asked.

"About Jesus of Nazareth," they replied. "He was a prophet, powerful in word and deed before God and all the people. ²⁰The chief priests and our rulers handed him over to be sentenced to death, and they crucified him; ²¹but we had hoped that he was the one who was going to redeem Israel. And what is more, it is the third day since all this took place. ²²In addition, some of our women amazed us. They went to the tomb early this morning ²³but didn't find his body. They came and told us that they had seen a vision of angels, who said he was alive. ²⁴Then some of our companions went to the tomb and found it just as the women had said, but him they did not see."

²⁵He said to them, "How foolish you are, and how slow of heart to believe all that the prophets have spoken! ²⁶Did not the Christ[q] have to suffer these things and then enter his glory?" ²⁷And beginning with Moses and all the Prophets, he explained to them what was said in all the Scriptures concerning himself.

²⁸As they approached the village to which they were going, Jesus acted as if he were going farther. ²⁹But they urged him strongly, "Stay with us, for it is nearly evening; the day is almost over." So he went in to stay with them.

³⁰When he was at the table with them, he took bread, gave thanks, broke it and began to give it to them. ³¹Then their eyes were opened and they recognized him, and he disappeared from their sight. ³²They asked each other, "Were not our

p13 Greek sixty stadia (about 11 kilometers)   *q26 Or Messiah; also in verse 46*

hearts burning within us while he talked with us on the road and opened the Scriptures to us?"

³³They got up and returned at once to Jerusalem. There they found the Eleven and those with them, assembled together ³⁴and saying, "It is true! The Lord has risen and has appeared to Simon." ³⁵Then the two told what had happened on the way, and how Jesus was recognized by them when he broke the bread.

³⁶While they were still talking about this, Jesus himself stood among them and said to them, "Peace be with you."

³⁷They were startled and frightened, thinking they saw a ghost. ³⁸He said to them, "Why are you troubled, and why do doubts rise in your minds? ³⁹Look at my hands and my feet. It is I myself! Touch me and see; a ghost does not have flesh and bones, as you see I have."

⁴⁰When he had said this, he showed them his hands and feet. ⁴¹And while they still did not believe it because of joy and amazement, he asked them, "Do you have anything here to eat?" ⁴²They gave him a piece of broiled fish, ⁴³and he took it and ate it in their presence.

⁴⁴He said to them, "This is what I told you while I was still with you: Everything must be fulfilled that is written about me in the Law of Moses, the Prophets and the Psalms."

⁴⁵Then he opened their minds so they could understand the Scriptures. ⁴⁶He told them, "This is what is written: The Christ will suffer and rise from the dead on the third day, ⁴⁷and repentance and forgiveness of sins will be preached in his name to all nations, beginning at Jerusalem. ⁴⁸You are witnesses of these things. ⁴⁹I am going to send you what my Father has promised; but stay in the city until you have been clothed with power from on high."

⁵⁰When he had led them out to the vicinity of Bethany, he lifted up his hands and blessed them. ⁵¹While he was blessing them, he left them and was taken up into heaven. ⁵²Then they worshiped him and returned to Jerusalem with great joy. ⁵³And they stayed continually at the temple, praising God.

Discovering the Word 1. The women are a personal link between the cross and the empty tomb. Suppose you are one of them. How do you feel when the men respond with "Nonsense!" (vv. 1–12)? 2. What strikes you about the stranger's dialogue with the disciples (vv. 13–35)? 3. We can sympathize with the disciples' struggle between despair and hope. In his rebuke Jesus identifies the cause of their despair—reluctance to believe the Scriptures about a suffering Messiah (v. 25). How have the Scriptures ever moved you from despair to new hope? 4. Look at verses 36–53 as a seeker inquiring about Jesus' resurrection. Which facts and implications help you to believe his personal reality? 5. For three or so years Jesus has been preparing his disciples to carry on his world mission. He climaxes this mission training by stressing systematic, in-depth Bible understanding (vv. 25–27, 32, 44–47). In what ways can you testify to this importance?

Applying the Word 1. We have been carefully studying the life and mission of Jesus. What would you say are your three greatest incentives to be his "witness of these things"? 2. What a message we have! The Lord Jesus has come to bring new hope and new joy to the world! How can you (and your church or fellowship group) take Jesus' message of new hope and new joy to your community?

Responding in Prayer Pray that you will be a source of joy to many as you bring Jesus' message.

John

The most significant fact in history can be summed up in four words: *Jesus Christ is God!* The great declaration of the Bible is that God in human flesh was born in Bethlehem. It was God in the person of Jesus Christ who astonished the people of his day with his miracles and amazed them with his teaching. It was God who lived a perfect life and then allowed himself to be put to death on a Roman cross for humanity's sins. It was God who three days after he died broke the bonds of death and came out of the grave alive. The deity of Jesus—the fact that he was God in human flesh—is the bottom line of the Christian faith.

When the apostle John sat down to write his Gospel, he was not interested simply in adding one more biography of Jesus to the three already in existence. John wrote his book with a very specific purpose in mind. He tells us in 20:30–31:

> Jesus did many other miraculous signs in the presence of his disciples, which are not recorded in this book. But these are written that you may believe that Jesus is the Christ, the Son of God, and that by believing you may have life in his name.

John's book is not a biography; it's a theological argument. John wants to convince us that Jesus of Nazareth is God the Son. Then he wants to show us how that fact will change our lives in some rather amazing ways. It is by believing in Jesus Christ as the Son of God that we find life—real life, eternal life, a whole new kind of life!

Every event John records is designed to show us that Jesus is God. John pulls from the life of Jesus specific incidents that demonstrate his majesty and deity. Of particular interest to John are the sign miracles of Jesus. In the first twelve chapters of his book, John records seven miracles. These miracles were not performed simply to alleviate human suffering or to meet human need. The miracles were "signs." They pointed to the truth of Jesus' claim to be the Son of God.

John was the last Gospel writer. The best evidence points to a date around A.D. 90 for the composition of his Gospel. The other Gospels had been in circulation for some time. John wrote to add his unique perspective and to fill in some of the details not recorded by the other writers. He assumes his readers are familiar with the other Gospels. John does not mention, for example, the anguish of Jesus in the Garden of Gethsemane. The other writers had adequately described that incident. John does give us the details of Jesus' conversation with his disciples in the upper room. The other writers mention it only briefly.

John never mentions himself by name in the Gospel. He refers to himself simply as "the disciple whom Jesus loved." We have in this Gospel the memories of an intimate friend about the Lord Jesus. Jesus Christ had transformed John's life. I hope you are prepared to have that happen to you! You are about to begin a fascinating study focused on the greatest person who ever lived—Jesus Christ. If you will respond to what John writes in faith and obedience, you, like John, will experience a whole new kind of life.

Outline

Part 1: Jesus, the Living Word of God

1/ John 1 ——————————————— *The Master & Five Who Followed*

2/ John 2 ——————————————— *Wine & a Whip*

3/ John 3 ——————————————— *The New Birth*

4/ John 4 ——————————————— *Soul & Body—Saving & Healing*

5/ John 5 ——————————————— *Deity on Trial*

6/ John 6 ——————————————— *Jesus, the Bread of Life*

7/ John 7:1–52 —————————————— *Confusion over Christ*

8/ John 7:53—8:11 ————————————— *Caught in Adultery*

9/ John 8:12–59 ————————————— *Jesus, the Light of the World*

10/ John 9 ——————————————— *A Blind Man Sees the Light*

11/ John 10 ——————————————— *The Shepherd & His Sheep*

12/ John 11 ——————————————— *Resurrection & Life*

13/ John 12 ——————————————— *The King's Last Acts*

Part 2: Jesus, the Living Way to God

14/ John 13:1–17 —————————————— *The Son as a Slave*

15/ John 13:18–38 ————————————— *The Betrayer & the Boaster*

16/ John 14 ——————————————— *Comfort for a Troubled Heart*

17/ John 15:1–17 —————————————— *The Secret of Remaining*

18/ John 15:18—16:4 ————————————— *The Cost of Friendship with Jesus*

19/ John 16:5–33 —————————————— *Secrets of the Spirit*

20/ John 17 ——————————————— *The Master's Final Prayer*

21/ John 18:1–27 —————————————— *"Jesus, You're Under Arrest!"*

22/ John 18:28—19:16 ———————————— *Pilate on Trial*

23/ John 19:17–42 ————————————— *Obedient to Death*

24/ John 20 ——————————————— *The Son Is Up!*

25/ John 21 ——————————————— *A Walk with a Resurrected Man*

1 / *John 1*
The Master & Five Who Followed

IT WAS A great day in our history when a man first walked on the moon. But the Bible declares that a far greater event took place two thousand years ago. God walked on the earth in the person of Jesus Christ. John opens his Gospel with a beautiful hymn of exaltation to Christ. It is one of the most profound passages in all the Bible. It is written in simple, straightforward language, yet in studying the depths of its meaning, it is a passage where we never reach bottom. It is an ocean-sized truth, and we have to be content to paddle around in shallow water.

 Warming Up to God Consider the miracle of God becoming human. Give him your praise and worship for what he has done for you.

 Read John 1.

1 In the beginning was the Word, and the Word was with God, and the Word was God. ²He was with God in the beginning. ³Through him all things were made; without him nothing was made that has been made. ⁴In him was life, and that life was the light of men. ⁵The light shines in the darkness, but the darkness has not understood*ᵃ* it.

⁶There came a man who was sent from God; his name was John. ⁷He came as a witness to testify concerning that light, so that through him all men might believe. ⁸He himself was not the light; he came only as a witness to the light. ⁹The true light that gives light to every man was coming into the world.*ᵇ*

¹⁰He was in the world, and though the world was made through him, the world did not recognize him. ¹¹He came to that which was his own, but his own did not receive him. ¹²Yet to all who received him, to those who believed in his name, he gave the right to become children of God— ¹³children born not of natural descent,*ᶜ* nor of human decision or a husband's will, but born of God.

¹⁴The Word became flesh and made his dwelling among us. We have seen his glory, the glory of the One and Only,*ᵈ* who came from the Father, full of grace and truth. ¹⁵John testifies concerning him. He cries out, saying, "This was he of whom I said, 'He who comes after me has surpassed me because he was before me.' " ¹⁶From the fullness of his grace we have all received one blessing after another. ¹⁷For the law was given through Moses; grace and truth came through Jesus Christ. ¹⁸No one has ever seen God, but God the One and Only,*ᵈ,ᵉ* who is at the Father's side, has made him known.

¹⁹Now this was John's testimony when the Jews of Jerusalem sent priests and Levites to ask him who he was. ²⁰He did not fail to confess, but confessed freely, "I am not the Christ.*ᶠ*"

²¹They asked him, "Then who are you? Are you Elijah?"

He said, "I am not."

"Are you the Prophet?"

He answered, "No."

²²Finally they said, "Who are you? Give us an answer to take back to those who sent us. What do you say about yourself?"

²³John replied in the words of Isaiah the prophet, "I am the voice of one calling in the desert, 'Make straight the way for the Lord.' "*ᵍ*

²⁴Now some Pharisees who had been sent ²⁵questioned him, "Why then do you baptize if you are not the Christ, nor Elijah, nor the Prophet?"

²⁶"I baptize with*ʰ* water," John replied, "but among you stands one you do not know. ²⁷He is the one who comes after me, the thongs of whose sandals I am not worthy to untie."

²⁸This all happened at Bethany on the other side of the Jordan, where John was baptizing.

²⁹The next day John saw Jesus coming toward him and said, "Look, the Lamb of God, who takes away the sin of the world! ³⁰This is the one I meant when I said, 'A man who comes after me has surpassed me because he was before me.' ³¹I myself did not know him, but the reason I came

---

*ᵃ*5 Or *darkness, and the darkness has not overcome*   *ᵇ*9 Or *This was the true light that gives light to every man who comes into the world*   *ᶜ*13 Greek *of bloods*   *ᵈ*14,18 Or *the Only Begotten*   *ᵉ*18 Some manuscripts *but the only (or only begotten) Son*   *ᶠ*20 Or *Messiah.* "The Christ" (Greek) and "the Messiah" (Hebrew) both mean "the Anointed One"; also in verse 25.   *ᵍ*23 Isaiah 40:3   *ʰ*26 Or *in;* also in verses 31 and 33

baptizing with water was that he might be revealed to Israel."

³²Then John gave this testimony: "I saw the Spirit come down from heaven as a dove and remain on him. ³³I would not have known him, except that the one who sent me to baptize with water told me, 'The man on whom you see the Spirit come down and remain is he who will baptize with the Holy Spirit.' ³⁴I have seen and I testify that this is the Son of God."

³⁵The next day John was there again with two of his disciples. ³⁶When he saw Jesus passing by, he said, "Look, the Lamb of God!"

³⁷When the two disciples heard him say this, they followed Jesus. ³⁸Turning around, Jesus saw them following and asked, "What do you want?"

They said, "Rabbi" (which means Teacher), "where are you staying?"

³⁹"Come," he replied, "and you will see."

So they went and saw where he was staying, and spent that day with him. It was about the tenth hour.

⁴⁰Andrew, Simon Peter's brother, was one of the two who heard what John had said and who had followed Jesus. ⁴¹The first thing Andrew did was to find his brother Simon and tell him, "We have found the Messiah" (that is, the Christ). ⁴²And he brought him to Jesus.

Jesus looked at him and said, "You are Simon son of John. You will be called Cephas" (which, when translated, is Peterⁱ).

⁴³The next day Jesus decided to leave for Galilee. Finding Philip, he said to him, "Follow me."

⁴⁴Philip, like Andrew and Peter, was from the town of Bethsaida. ⁴⁵Philip found Nathanael and told him, "We have found the one Moses wrote about in the Law, and about whom the prophets also wrote—Jesus of Nazareth, the son of Joseph."

⁴⁶"Nazareth! Can anything good come from there?" Nathanael asked.

"Come and see," said Philip.

⁴⁷When Jesus saw Nathanael approaching, he said of him, "Here is a true Israelite, in whom there is nothing false."

⁴⁸"How do you know me?" Nathanael asked.

Jesus answered, "I saw you while you were still under the fig tree before Philip called you."

⁴⁹Then Nathanael declared, "Rabbi, you are the Son of God; you are the King of Israel."

⁵⁰Jesus said, "You believeʲ because I told you I saw you under the fig tree. You shall see greater things than that." ⁵¹He then added, "I tell youᵏ the truth, youᵏ shall see heaven open, and the angels of God ascending and descending on the Son of Man."

ⁱ42 Both *Cephas* (Aramaic) and *Peter* (Greek) mean *rock*.   ʲ50 Or *Do you believe . . . ?*   ᵏ51 The Greek is plural.

Discovering the Word 1. John records more than a dozen names or descriptions of Jesus in this chapter. What are some of these? 2. In verses 1–3 what facts does John declare to be true of the Word? 3. According to verses 14–18, what specific aspects of God's character are revealed to us through Jesus? 4. What steps did John take to guarantee that people would not look at him but at Christ? 5. In verses 35–51 we are introduced to five men: Andrew, Simon, Philip, Nathanael and one unnamed disciple (John). How did each man respond to the testimony he heard about Jesus?

Applying the Word 1. Which of the names of Jesus has the most significance to you personally? Explain why. 2. What do you hope will happen in your life as a result of studying the Gospel of John?

Responding in Prayer Ask God to bring the light and life of Jesus to you as you study his Word.

---

2 / John 2
Wine & a Whip

AFTER I HAD given a presentation on the claims of Christ, a skeptical student asked: "What proof do you have that Jesus really was who he claimed to be?" People have been asking that question for two thousand years! For John the convincing proof of Jesus' deity was found in his words and deeds. No one but God could say the things Jesus

said, and no one but God could do the things Jesus did. In this chapter are two signs that demonstrate that Jesus was the fullness of God clothed in humanity.

 Warming Up to God Thank God for revealing himself to you personally.

 Read John 2.

2 On the third day a wedding took place at Cana in Galilee. Jesus' mother was there, ²and Jesus and his disciples had also been invited to the wedding. ³When the wine was gone, Jesus' mother said to him, "They have no more wine."

⁴"Dear woman, why do you involve me?" Jesus replied. "My time has not yet come."

⁵His mother said to the servants, "Do whatever he tells you."

⁶Nearby stood six stone water jars, the kind used by the Jews for ceremonial washing, each holding from twenty to thirty gallons.[l]

⁷Jesus said to the servants, "Fill the jars with water"; so they filled them to the brim.

⁸Then he told them, "Now draw some out and take it to the master of the banquet."

They did so, ⁹and the master of the banquet tasted the water that had been turned into wine. He did not realize where it had come from, though the servants who had drawn the water knew. Then he called the bridegroom aside ¹⁰and said, "Everyone brings out the choice wine first and then the cheaper wine after the guests have had too much to drink; but you have saved the best till now."

¹¹This, the first of his miraculous signs, Jesus performed at Cana in Galilee. He thus revealed his glory, and his disciples put their faith in him.

¹²After this he went down to Capernaum with his mother and brothers and his disciples. There they stayed for a few days.

¹³When it was almost time for the Jewish Passover, Jesus went up to Jerusalem. ¹⁴In the temple courts he found men selling cattle, sheep and doves, and others sitting at tables exchanging money. ¹⁵So he made a whip out of cords, and drove all from the temple area, both sheep and cattle; he scattered the coins of the money changers and overturned their tables. ¹⁶To those who sold doves he said, "Get these out of here! How dare you turn my Father's house into a market!"

¹⁷His disciples remembered that it is written: "Zeal for your house will consume me."[m]

¹⁸Then the Jews demanded of him, "What miraculous sign can you show us to prove your authority to do all this?"

¹⁹Jesus answered them, "Destroy this temple, and I will raise it again in three days."

²⁰The Jews replied, "It has taken forty-six years to build this temple, and you are going to raise it in three days?" ²¹But the temple he had spoken of was his body. ²²After he was raised from the dead, his disciples recalled what he had said. Then they believed the Scripture and the words that Jesus had spoken.

²³Now while he was in Jerusalem at the Passover Feast, many people saw the miraculous signs he was doing and believed in his name.[n] ²⁴But Jesus would not entrust himself to them, for he knew all men. ²⁵He did not need man's testimony about man, for he knew what was in a man.

[l]6 Greek *two to three metretes* (probably about 75 to 115 liters)
[m]17 Psalm 69:9   [n]23 Or *and believed in him*

 Discovering the Word 1. When the groom's parents ran out of wine for their guests, Jesus' mother asked him to help (v. 3). What do you think Mary expected Jesus to do? (Remember, according to verse 11 Jesus had not yet performed any miracles.) 2. What did Jesus mean by his reply to Mary in verse 4? 3. According to verse 11, the purpose of Jesus' miracle was not to save the groom from embarrassment but to display Christ's glory. What aspects of Christ's glory does this miracle reveal to you? 4. How does John's picture of Jesus in verses 15–16 fit with today's popular concept of him? 5. Only the Messiah had the authority to cleanse the temple. The people recognized that and asked Jesus for a miraculous sign to confirm his identify (v. 18). To what "sign" did Jesus point them (vv. 19–22)? Why do you think that particular sign was so significant in Jesus' mind?

Applying the Word 1. In what practical ways can you demonstrate the same concern that Jesus does toward the holy character of God? 2. How do Jesus' presence and actions at this party serve as a model for you?

Responding in Prayer Ask God to help you to be his representative in everything you do.

3 / John 3
The New Birth

I TALKED TODAY to a junior in college who is only one month old. No, she isn't a child genius. Recently a friend explained to her the claims of Christ. As she responded in simple faith, she experienced the joys of spiritual birth.

The most beautiful explanation of the new birth is found here in John 3. It's a passage that children can understand, and one that the greatest saints of God have never fully grasped. It's a message not so much to be analyzed and dissected as it is to be received with joy.

 Warming Up to God Do you remember your spiritual birthday? Reflect on what that time meant for you.

 Read John 3.

3 Now there was a man of the Pharisees named Nicodemus, a member of the Jewish ruling council. ²He came to Jesus at night and said, "Rabbi, we know you are a teacher who has come from God. For no one could perform the miraculous signs you are doing if God were not with him."

³In reply Jesus declared, "I tell you the truth, no one can see the kingdom of God unless he is born again.ᵒ"

⁴"How can a man be born when he is old?" Nicodemus asked. "Surely he cannot enter a second time into his mother's womb to be born!"

⁵Jesus answered, "I tell you the truth, no one can enter the kingdom of God unless he is born of water and the Spirit. ⁶Flesh gives birth to flesh, but the Spiritᵖ gives birth to spirit. ⁷You should not be surprised at my saying, 'You�q must be born again.' ⁸The wind blows wherever it pleases. You hear its sound, but you cannot tell where it comes from or where it is going. So it is with everyone born of the Spirit."

⁹"How can this be?" Nicodemus asked.

¹⁰"You are Israel's teacher," said Jesus, "and do you not understand these things? ¹¹I tell you the truth, we speak of what we know, and we testify to what we have seen, but still you people do not accept our testimony. ¹²I have spoken to you of earthly things and you do not believe; how then will you believe if I speak of heavenly things? ¹³No one has ever gone into heaven except the one who came from heaven—the Son of Man.ʳ

¹⁴Just as Moses lifted up the snake in the desert, so the Son of Man must be lifted up, ¹⁵that everyone who believes in him may have eternal life.ˢ

¹⁶"For God so loved the world that he gave his one and only Son,ᵗ that whoever believes in him shall not perish but have eternal life. ¹⁷For God did not send his Son into the world to condemn the world, but to save the world through him. ¹⁸Whoever believes in him is not condemned, but whoever does not believe stands condemned already because he has not believed in the name of God's one and only Son.ᵘ ¹⁹This is the verdict: Light has come into the world, but men loved darkness instead of light because their deeds were evil. ²⁰Everyone who does evil hates the light, and will not come into the light for fear that his deeds will be exposed. ²¹But whoever lives by the truth comes into the light, so that it may be seen plainly that what he has done has been done through God."ᵛ

²²After this, Jesus and his disciples went out into the Judean countryside, where he spent some time with them, and baptized. ²³Now John also was baptizing at Aenon near Salim, because there was plenty of water, and people were constantly coming to be baptized. ²⁴(This was before John was put in prison.) ²⁵An argument developed between some of John's disciples and a certain Jewʷ over the matter of ceremonial washing.

ᵒ3 Or *born from above; also in verse 7*　　ᵖ6 Or *but spirit*　　�q7 The Greek is plural.　　ʳ13 Some manuscripts *Man, who is in heaven*　　ˢ15 Or *believes may have eternal life in him*　　ᵗ16 Or *his only begotten Son*　　ᵘ18 Or *God's only begotten Son*　　ᵛ21 Some interpreters end the quotation after verse 15.　　ʷ25 Some manuscripts *and certain Jews*

²⁶They came to John and said to him, "Rabbi, that man who was with you on the other side of the Jordan—the one you testified about—well, he is baptizing, and everyone is going to him."

²⁷To this John replied, "A man can receive only what is given him from heaven. ²⁸You yourselves can testify that I said, 'I am not the Christˣ but am sent ahead of him.' ²⁹The bride belongs to the bridegroom. The friend who attends the bridegroom waits and listens for him, and is full of joy when he hears the bridegroom's voice. That joy is mine, and it is now complete. ³⁰He must become greater; I must become less.

³¹"The one who comes from above is above all;

the one who is from the earth belongs to the earth, and speaks as one from the earth. The one who comes from heaven is above all. ³²He testifies to what he has seen and heard, but no one accepts his testimony. ³³The man who has accepted it has certified that God is truthful. ³⁴For the one whom God has sent speaks the words of God, for Godʸ gives the Spirit without limit. ³⁵The Father loves the Son and has placed everything in his hands. ³⁶Whoever believes in the Son has eternal life, but whoever rejects the Son will not see life, for God's wrath remains on him."ᶻ

ˣ28 Or *Messiah*   ʸ34 Greek *he*   ᶻ36 Some interpreters end the quotation after verse 30.

Discovering the Word 1. What is your impression of Nicodemus (vv. 1–21)? 2. Why do you suppose Nicodemus responds to Jesus' explanation of new birth with such amazement (v. 9)? 3. How does the story of Moses lifting up the snake in the desert (vv. 14–15; see Nu 21:4–9) illustrate our need and Christ's offer? 4. How and why does our response to God's Son determine our destiny (vv. 18–21)? 5. How would you summarize John's view of the character and ministry of Jesus (vv. 22–36)?

Applying the Word 1. John made it clear that Jesus was superior to him. What is one way you can demonstrate Christ's superiority in your life? 2. Who do you know that needs to know the truth about God? 3. How can you help that person see God?

Responding in Prayer Ask God to make you ready to testify of the role of Jesus in your life.

---

4 / John 4
Soul & Body—Saving & Healing

"I LOVE HUMANITY; it's people I can't stand!" Those well-known words from a member of the "Peanuts" gang still make us chuckle. But our smiles hide the fact that we sometimes feel exactly like that. John says very little about Jesus' contact with the multitudes. But long sections of the Gospel are devoted to conversations Jesus had with individuals. In John 4 we see Jesus reach out first to a woman, then to his disciples, and finally to a grieving father. Watching Jesus give himself to people with love and compassion will help us care for those God puts in our paths.

Warming Up to God When have you recently felt that you were being mobbed by the multitudes? Ask God to help you take care of yourself even as you try to help others.

Read John 4.

---

4 The Pharisees heard that Jesus was gaining and baptizing more disciples than John, ²although in fact it was not Jesus who baptized, but his disciples. ³When the Lord learned of this, he left Judea and went back once more to Galilee.

⁴Now he had to go through Samaria. ⁵So he came to a town in Samaria called Sychar, near the

plot of ground Jacob had given to his son Joseph. ⁶Jacob's well was there, and Jesus, tired as he was from the journey, sat down by the well. It was about the sixth hour.

⁷When a Samaritan woman came to draw water, Jesus said to her, "Will you give me a drink?" ⁸(His disciples had gone into the town to buy food.)

⁹The Samaritan woman said to him, "You are a Jew and I am a Samaritan woman. How can you ask me for a drink?" (For Jews do not associate with Samaritans.ᵃ)

¹⁰Jesus answered her, "If you knew the gift of God and who it is that asks you for a drink, you would have asked him and he would have given you living water."

¹¹"Sir," the woman said, "you have nothing to draw with and the well is deep. Where can you get this living water? ¹²Are you greater than our father Jacob, who gave us the well and drank from it himself, as did also his sons and his flocks and herds?"

¹³Jesus answered, "Everyone who drinks this water will be thirsty again, ¹⁴but whoever drinks the water I give him will never thirst. Indeed, the water I give him will become in him a spring of water welling up to eternal life."

¹⁵The woman said to him, "Sir, give me this water so that I won't get thirsty and have to keep coming here to draw water."

¹⁶He told her, "Go, call your husband and come back."

¹⁷"I have no husband," she replied.

Jesus said to her, "You are right when you say you have no husband. ¹⁸The fact is, you have had five husbands, and the man you now have is not your husband. What you have just said is quite true."

¹⁹"Sir," the woman said, "I can see that you are a prophet. ²⁰Our fathers worshiped on this mountain, but you Jews claim that the place where we must worship is in Jerusalem."

²¹Jesus declared, "Believe me, woman, a time is coming when you will worship the Father neither on this mountain nor in Jerusalem. ²²You Samaritans worship what you do not know; we worship what we do know, for salvation is from the Jews. ²³Yet a time is coming and has now come when the true worshipers will worship the Father in spirit and truth, for they are the kind of worshipers the Father seeks. ²⁴God is spirit, and his worshipers must worship in spirit and in truth."

²⁵The woman said, "I know that Messiah" (called Christ) "is coming. When he comes, he will explain everything to us."

²⁶Then Jesus declared, "I who speak to you am he."

²⁷Just then his disciples returned and were surprised to find him talking with a woman. But no one asked, "What do you want?" or "Why are you talking with her?"

²⁸Then, leaving her water jar, the woman went back to the town and said to the people, ²⁹"Come, see a man who told me everything I ever did. Could this be the Christᵇ?" ³⁰They came out of the town and made their way toward him.

³¹Meanwhile his disciples urged him, "Rabbi, eat something."

³²But he said to them, "I have food to eat that you know nothing about."

³³Then his disciples said to each other, "Could someone have brought him food?"

³⁴"My food," said Jesus, "is to do the will of him who sent me and to finish his work. ³⁵Do you not say, 'Four months more and then the harvest'? I tell you, open your eyes and look at the fields! They are ripe for harvest. ³⁶Even now the reaper draws his wages, even now he harvests the crop for eternal life, so that the sower and the reaper may be glad together. ³⁷Thus the saying 'One sows and another reaps' is true. ³⁸I sent you to reap what you have not worked for. Others have done the hard work, and you have reaped the benefits of their labor."

³⁹Many of the Samaritans from that town believed in him because of the woman's testimony, "He told me everything I ever did." ⁴⁰So when the Samaritans came to him, they urged him to stay with them, and he stayed two days. ⁴¹And because of his words many more became believers.

⁴²They said to the woman, "We no longer believe just because of what you said; now we have heard for ourselves, and we know that this man really is the Savior of the world."

⁴³After the two days he left for Galilee. ⁴⁴(Now Jesus himself had pointed out that a prophet has no honor in his own country.) ⁴⁵When he arrived in Galilee, the Galileans welcomed him. They had seen all that he had done in Jerusalem at the Passover Feast, for they also had been there.

⁴⁶Once more he visited Cana in Galilee, where he had turned the water into wine. And there was a certain royal official whose son lay sick at Capernaum. ⁴⁷When this man heard that Jesus had arrived in Galilee from Judea, he went to him and begged him to come and heal his son, who was close to death.

⁴⁸"Unless you people see miraculous signs and

ᵃ9 Or do not use dishes Samaritans have used　　ᵇ29 Or Messiah

wonders," Jesus told him, "you will never believe."

⁴⁹The royal official said, "Sir, come down before my child dies."

⁵⁰Jesus replied, "You may go. Your son will live."

The man took Jesus at his word and departed. ⁵¹While he was still on the way, his servants met him with the news that his boy was living. ⁵²When he inquired as to the time when his son got better, they said to him, "The fever left him yesterday at the seventh hour."

⁵³Then the father realized that this was the exact time at which Jesus had said to him, "Your son will live." So he and all his household believed.

⁵⁴This was the second miraculous sign that Jesus performed, having come from Judea to Galilee.

 Discovering the Word 1. What is surprising about Jesus' question to the Samaritan woman (vv. 8–9)? 2. Why does the woman suddenly change the subject and begin talking about the controversy over the proper place of worship (vv. 16–20)? 3. From verses 27–42, do you think the Samaritan woman genuinely believed? What do you see in the passage that supports your position? 4. After his encounter with the Samaritan woman, what specific lessons does Jesus apply to his disciples and to us (vv. 34–38)? 5. What does the "second miraculous sign" Jesus performs (vv. 43–54) reveal about him?

Applying the Word 1. What has Jesus taught you in this chapter about meeting the specific needs of those around you? 2. What present-day situations might arouse the same racial, religious and sexual prejudices as the Samaritan woman did? 3. How could you reach someone who has been rejected by the world, as Jesus did?

Responding in Prayer Ask God to help you be aware of the "Samaritans" around you. Ask him to help you reach out to them.

5 / John 5
Deity on Trial

IN MY HIGH-SCHOOL years, I was hooked on television lawyer programs. Those intrepid men and women always found the missing piece of evidence that would rescue the innocent and convict the guilty. I've learned since high-school days that sometimes judges and juries are wrong.

In John chapter five Jesus is on trial. A group of people are forced to make a decision about Jesus in their hearts. They hear all the evidence but make a disastrously wrong decision. Judgments are still made for and against Jesus. Whenever he is presented as Savior and Lord, people decide in their hearts to believe his claims or to turn and walk away.

 Warming Up to God How has God recently revealed the truth of his claims as Savior to you? Thank him for his powerful works in your life.

 Read John 5.

5 Some time later, Jesus went up to Jerusalem for a feast of the Jews. ²Now there is in Jerusalem near the Sheep Gate a pool, which in Aramaic is called Bethesda* and which is surrounded by five covered colonnades. ³Here a great number of disabled people used to lie—the blind, the lame, the paralyzed.* ⁵One who was there had been an invalid for thirty-eight years.

⁶When Jesus saw him lying there and learned that he had been in this condition for a long time, he asked him, "Do you want to get well?"

⁷"Sir," the invalid replied, "I have no one to help me into the pool when the water is stirred.

---

² Some manuscripts *Bethzatha*; other manuscripts *Bethsaida*
³ Some less important manuscripts *paralyzed—and they waited for the moving of the waters.* ⁴*From time to time an angel of the Lord would come down and stir up the waters. The first one into the pool after each such disturbance would be cured of whatever disease he had.*

While I am trying to get in, someone else goes down ahead of me."

[8]Then Jesus said to him, "Get up! Pick up your mat and walk." [9]At once the man was cured; he picked up his mat and walked.

The day on which this took place was a Sabbath, [10]and so the Jews said to the man who had been healed, "It is the Sabbath; the law forbids you to carry your mat."

[11]But he replied, "The man who made me well said to me, 'Pick up your mat and walk.' "

[12]So they asked him, "Who is this fellow who told you to pick it up and walk?"

[13]The man who was healed had no idea who it was, for Jesus had slipped away into the crowd that was there.

[14]Later Jesus found him at the temple and said to him, "See, you are well again. Stop sinning or something worse may happen to you." [15]The man went away and told the Jews that it was Jesus who had made him well.

[16]So, because Jesus was doing these things on the Sabbath, the Jews persecuted him. [17]Jesus said to them, "My Father is always at his work to this very day, and I, too, am working." [18]For this reason the Jews tried all the harder to kill him; not only was he breaking the Sabbath, but he was even calling God his own Father, making himself equal with God.

[19]Jesus gave them this answer: "I tell you the truth, the Son can do nothing by himself; he can do only what he sees his Father doing, because whatever the Father does the Son also does. [20]For the Father loves the Son and shows him all he does. Yes, to your amazement he will show him even greater things than these. [21]For just as the Father raises the dead and gives them life, even so the Son gives life to whom he is pleased to give it. [22]Moreover, the Father judges no one, but has entrusted all judgment to the Son, [23]that all may honor the Son just as they honor the Father. He who does not honor the Son does not honor the Father, who sent him.

[24]"I tell you the truth, whoever hears my word and believes him who sent me has eternal life and will not be condemned; he has crossed over from death to life. [25]I tell you the truth, a time is coming and has now come when the dead will hear the voice of the Son of God and those who hear

will live. [26]For as the Father has life in himself, so he has granted the Son to have life in himself. [27]And he has given him authority to judge because he is the Son of Man.

[28]"Do not be amazed at this, for a time is coming when all who are in their graves will hear his voice [29]and come out—those who have done good will rise to live, and those who have done evil will rise to be condemned. [30]By myself I can do nothing; I judge only as I hear, and my judgment is just, for I seek not to please myself but him who sent me.

[31]"If I testify about myself, my testimony is not valid. [32]There is another who testifies in my favor, and I know that his testimony about me is valid.

[33]"You have sent to John and he has testified to the truth. [34]Not that I accept human testimony; but I mention it that you may be saved. [35]John was a lamp that burned and gave light, and you chose for a time to enjoy his light.

[36]"I have testimony weightier than that of John. For the very work that the Father has given me to finish, and which I am doing, testifies that the Father has sent me. [37]And the Father who sent me has himself testified concerning me. You have never heard his voice nor seen his form, [38]nor does his word dwell in you, for you do not believe the one he sent. [39]You diligently study[e] the Scriptures because you think that by them you possess eternal life. These are the Scriptures that testify about me, [40]yet you refuse to come to me to have life.

[41]"I do not accept praise from men, [42]but I know you. I know that you do not have the love of God in your hearts. [43]I have come in my Father's name, and you do not accept me; but if someone else comes in his own name, you will accept him. [44]How can you believe if you accept praise from one another, yet make no effort to obtain the praise that comes from the only God[f]?

[45]"But do not think I will accuse you before the Father. Your accuser is Moses, on whom your hopes are set. [46]If you believed Moses, you would believe me, for he wrote about me. [47]But since you do not believe what he wrote, how are you going to believe what I say?"

[e]39 Or *Study diligently* (the imperative)   [f]44 Some early manuscripts *the Only One*

Discovering the Word 1. Based on the scene and conversation around the pool, how would you describe the feelings and attitudes of the invalid (vv. 1–15)? 2. The seventh commandment said: "Remember the Sabbath day by keeping it holy" (see Ex 20:8–11). In their zeal to apply this command, what were the Jews failing to see (vv. 9–15)? 3. What insights do verses 19–23 give us into (a) the Father's devotion to the Son and (b) the Son's dependence on the Father? 4. What "witnesses" does Jesus call forward to testify on his behalf (vv. 31–47)? 5. What counter-accusations does Jesus make against those who are attacking him? 6. According to this chapter, what really influences our verdict for or against Jesus?

 Applying the Word 1. When have you been more concerned about a religious activity than the reality behind it? Explain. 2. How can you avoid the kind of religion that is outwardly pious but inwardly bankrupt?

 Responding in Prayer Ask God to help you discover true religion.

---

6 / John 6
Jesus, the Bread of Life

DO YOU REALIZE that during your lifetime you will probably spend over thirty-five thousand hours eating? That's the equivalent of eight years of nonstop meals, twelve hours a day! The problem, of course, is that even after a big meal we get hungry again. At best, food only satisfies us for a few hours.

Yet in this chapter, Jesus offers us food that satisfies our hunger forever. You can't buy it in a grocery store. It is found only in Jesus himself.

 Warming Up to God How do you usually respond to an "impossible" situation—a problem in your life that doesn't seem to have a solution?

Read John 6.

---

6 Some time after this, Jesus crossed to the far shore of the Sea of Galilee (that is, the Sea of Tiberias), ²and a great crowd of people followed him because they saw the miraculous signs he had performed on the sick. ³Then Jesus went up on a mountainside and sat down with his disciples. ⁴The Jewish Passover Feast was near.

⁵When Jesus looked up and saw a great crowd coming toward him, he said to Philip, "Where shall we buy bread for these people to eat?" ⁶He asked this only to test him, for he already had in mind what he was going to do.

⁷Philip answered him, "Eight months' wages⁸ would not buy enough bread for each one to have a bite!"

⁸Another of his disciples, Andrew, Simon Peter's brother, spoke up, ⁹"Here is a boy with five small barley loaves and two small fish, but how far will they go among so many?"

¹⁰Jesus said, "Have the people sit down." There was plenty of grass in that place, and the men sat

down, about five thousand of them. ¹¹Jesus then took the loaves, gave thanks, and distributed to those who were seated as much as they wanted. He did the same with the fish.

¹²When they had all had enough to eat, he said to his disciples, "Gather the pieces that are left over. Let nothing be wasted." ¹³So they gathered them and filled twelve baskets with the pieces of the five barley loaves left over by those who had eaten.

¹⁴After the people saw the miraculous sign that Jesus did, they began to say, "Surely this is the Prophet who is to come into the world." ¹⁵Jesus, knowing that they intended to come and make him king by force, withdrew again to a mountain by himself.

¹⁶When evening came, his disciples went down to the lake, ¹⁷where they got into a boat and set off across the lake for Capernaum. By now it was dark, and Jesus had not yet joined them. ¹⁸A

8 7 Greek two hundred denarii

strong wind was blowing and the waters grew rough. ¹⁹When they had rowed three or three and a half miles,ʰ they saw Jesus approaching the boat, walking on the water; and they were terrified. ²⁰But he said to them, "It is I; don't be afraid." ²¹Then they were willing to take him into the boat, and immediately the boat reached the shore where they were heading.

²²The next day the crowd that had stayed on the opposite shore of the lake realized that only one boat had been there, and that Jesus had not entered it with his disciples, but that they had gone away alone. ²³Then some boats from Tiberias landed near the place where the people had eaten the bread after the Lord had given thanks. ²⁴Once the crowd realized that neither Jesus nor his disciples were there, they got into the boats and went to Capernaum in search of Jesus.

²⁵When they found him on the other side of the lake, they asked him, "Rabbi, when did you get here?"

²⁶Jesus answered, "I tell you the truth, you are looking for me, not because you saw miraculous signs but because you ate the loaves and had your fill. ²⁷Do not work for food that spoils, but for food that endures to eternal life, which the Son of Man will give you. On him God the Father has placed his seal of approval."

²⁸Then they asked him, "What must we do to do the works God requires?"

²⁹Jesus answered, "The work of God is this: to believe in the one he has sent."

³⁰So they asked him, "What miraculous sign then will you give that we may see it and believe you? What will you do? ³¹Our forefathers ate the manna in the desert; as it is written: 'He gave them bread from heaven to eat.'ⁱ"

³²Jesus said to them, "I tell you the truth, it is not Moses who has given you the bread from heaven, but it is my Father who gives you the true bread from heaven. ³³For the bread of God is he who comes down from heaven and gives life to the world."

³⁴"Sir," they said, "from now on give us this bread."

³⁵Then Jesus declared, "I am the bread of life. He who comes to me will never go hungry, and he who believes in me will never be thirsty. ³⁶But as I told you, you have seen me and still you do not believe. ³⁷All that the Father gives me will come to me, and whoever comes to me I will never drive away. ³⁸For I have come down from

heaven not to do my will but to do the will of him who sent me. ³⁹And this is the will of him who sent me, that I shall lose none of all that he has given me, but raise them up at the last day. ⁴⁰For my Father's will is that everyone who looks to the Son and believes in him shall have eternal life, and I will raise him up at the last day."

⁴¹At this the Jews began to grumble about him because he said, "I am the bread that came down from heaven." ⁴²They said, "Is this not Jesus, the son of Joseph, whose father and mother we know? How can he now say, 'I came down from heaven'?"

⁴³"Stop grumbling among yourselves," Jesus answered. ⁴⁴"No one can come to me unless the Father who sent me draws him, and I will raise him up at the last day. ⁴⁵It is written in the Prophets: 'They will all be taught by God.'ʲ Everyone who listens to the Father and learns from him comes to me. ⁴⁶No one has seen the Father except the one who is from God; only he has seen the Father. ⁴⁷I tell you the truth, he who believes has everlasting life. ⁴⁸I am the bread of life. ⁴⁹Your forefathers ate the manna in the desert, yet they died. ⁵⁰But here is the bread that comes down from heaven, which a man may eat and not die. ⁵¹I am the living bread that came down from heaven. If anyone eats of this bread, he will live forever. This bread is my flesh, which I will give for the life of the world."

⁵²Then the Jews began to argue sharply among themselves, "How can this man give us his flesh to eat?"

⁵³Jesus said to them, "I tell you the truth, unless you eat the flesh of the Son of Man and drink his blood, you have no life in you. ⁵⁴Whoever eats my flesh and drinks my blood has eternal life, and I will raise him up at the last day. ⁵⁵For my flesh is real food and my blood is real drink. ⁵⁶Whoever eats my flesh and drinks my blood remains in me, and I in him. ⁵⁷Just as the living Father sent me and I live because of the Father, so the one who feeds on me will live because of me. ⁵⁸This is the bread that came down from heaven. Your forefathers ate manna and died, but he who feeds on this bread will live forever." ⁵⁹He said this while teaching in the synagogue in Capernaum.

⁶⁰On hearing it, many of his disciples said, "This is a hard teaching. Who can accept it?"

ʰ19 Greek rowed twenty-five or thirty stadia (about 5 or 6 kilometers)
ⁱ31 Exodus 16:4; Neh. 9:15; Psalm 78:24,25   ʲ45 Isaiah 54:13

⁶¹Aware that his disciples were grumbling about this, Jesus said to them, "Does this offend you? ⁶²What if you see the Son of Man ascend to where he was before! ⁶³The Spirit gives life; the flesh counts for nothing. The words I have spoken to you are spirit*ᵏ* and they are life. ⁶⁴Yet there are some of you who do not believe." For Jesus had known from the beginning which of them did not believe and who would betray him. ⁶⁵He went on to say, "This is why I told you that no one can come to me unless the Father has enabled him."

⁶⁶From this time many of his disciples turned back and no longer followed him.

⁶⁷"You do not want to leave too, do you?" Jesus asked the Twelve.

⁶⁸Simon Peter answered him, "Lord, to whom shall we go? You have the words of eternal life. ⁶⁹We believe and know that you are the Holy One of God."

⁷⁰Then Jesus replied, "Have I not chosen you, the Twelve? Yet one of you is a devil!" ⁷¹(He meant Judas, the son of Simon Iscariot, who, though one of the Twelve, was later to betray him.)

ᵏ63 Or Spirit

 Discovering the Word 1. How would you characterize Philip's and Andrew's responses to the problem of feeding this enormous crowd (vv. 5–9)? 2. Imagine that you are one of the disciples, rowing the boat in dark, rough waters (vv. 16–21). How would your concept of Jesus have been altered by seeing him walk on water? 3. The next day the people were hungry again, so they came seeking Jesus (vv. 22–25). How does he try to redirect their thinking (vv. 26–33)? 4. Based on the remarks of some in the crowd (vv. 41–42), do you think they finally understood what Jesus was saying? Explain. 5. When Jesus said, "This bread is my flesh," the crowd could think only of cannibalism (v. 52). What do you think it means to eat Jesus' flesh and drink his blood (vv. 53–59)? Is this something we do once for all time, or is it an ongoing process? Explain. 6. In verses 60–71 Jesus turns away from the crowd and focuses on his disciples. How would you describe their responses to his "hard teaching"?

Applying the Word 1. Which response in question 6 best describes your present attitude toward Jesus? Explain. 2. Jesus has contrasted the two appetites found in every person—the appetite for food that perishes and the appetite for food that endures. In what ways has Jesus satisfied the spiritual hunger in your heart?

Responding in Prayer Praise God for satisfying all your needs.

---

7 / John 7:1–52
Confusion over Christ

NOT LONG AGO I had a series of conversations with a young man about Jesus Christ and why faith in him is so important. At first, the young man was interested. He was open to listen to God's Word and to consider Christ's claims. As time went on, however, he became more and more hostile to Christ. Finally, he told me that he didn't want to pursue his investigation any further. He had decided to reject Christ and his offer of salvation.

That is precisely the pattern that John traces in his Gospel. In the early chapters, men and women responded to Jesus with belief. Then some of those who were following him turned away. Now open warfare breaks out between Jesus and his enemies—and yet, some still seek the truth. This chapter will help you respond positively to the wide variety of attitudes toward Jesus today.

 Warming Up to God "If anyone is thirsty, let him come to me and drink." These are Jesus' words to us today. In what way do you need Jesus' spiritual refreshment? Be quiet before him and experience the "streams of living water."

Read John 7:1–52.

7 After this, Jesus went around in Galilee, purposely staying away from Judea because the Jews there were waiting to take his life. ²But when the Jewish Feast of Tabernacles was near, ³Jesus' brothers said to him, "You ought to leave here and go to Judea, so that your disciples may see the miracles you do. ⁴No one who wants to become a public figure acts in secret. Since you are doing these things, show yourself to the world." ⁵For even his own brothers did not believe in him.

⁶Therefore Jesus told them, "The right time for me has not yet come; for you any time is right. ⁷The world cannot hate you, but it hates me because I testify that what it does is evil. ⁸You go to the Feast. I am not yet[l] going up to this Feast, because for me the right time has not yet come." ⁹Having said this, he stayed in Galilee.

¹⁰However, after his brothers had left for the Feast, he went also, not publicly, but in secret. ¹¹Now at the Feast the Jews were watching for him and asking, "Where is that man?"

¹²Among the crowds there was widespread whispering about him. Some said, "He is a good man."

Others replied, "No, he deceives the people." ¹³But no one would say anything publicly about him for fear of the Jews.

¹⁴Not until halfway through the Feast did Jesus go up to the temple courts and begin to teach. ¹⁵The Jews were amazed and asked, "How did this man get such learning without having studied?"

¹⁶Jesus answered, "My teaching is not my own. It comes from him who sent me. ¹⁷If anyone chooses to do God's will, he will find out whether my teaching comes from God or whether I speak on my own. ¹⁸He who speaks on his own does so to gain honor for himself, but he who works for the honor of the one who sent him is a man of truth; there is nothing false about him. ¹⁹Has not Moses given you the law? Yet not one of you keeps the law. Why are you trying to kill me?"

²⁰"You are demon-possessed," the crowd answered. "Who is trying to kill you?"

²¹Jesus said to them, "I did one miracle, and you are all astonished. ²²Yet, because Moses gave you circumcision (though actually it did not come from Moses, but from the patriarchs), you circumcise a child on the Sabbath. ²³Now if a child can be circumcised on the Sabbath so that the law of Moses may not be broken, why are you angry with me for healing the whole man on the Sabbath? ²⁴Stop judging by mere appearances, and make a right judgment."

²⁵At that point some of the people of Jerusalem began to ask, "Isn't this the man they are trying to kill? ²⁶Here he is, speaking publicly, and they are not saying a word to him. Have the authorities really concluded that he is the Christ[m]? ²⁷But we know where this man is from; when the Christ comes, no one will know where he is from."

²⁸Then Jesus, still teaching in the temple courts, cried out, "Yes, you know me, and you know where I am from. I am not here on my own, but he who sent me is true. You do not know him, ²⁹but I know him because I am from him and he sent me."

³⁰At this they tried to seize him, but no one laid a hand on him, because his time had not yet come. ³¹Still, many in the crowd put their faith in him. They said, "When the Christ comes, will he do more miraculous signs than this man?"

³²The Pharisees heard the crowd whispering such things about him. Then the chief priests and the Pharisees sent temple guards to arrest him. ³³Jesus said, "I am with you for only a short time, and then I go to the one who sent me. ³⁴You will look for me, but you will not find me; and where I am, you cannot come."

³⁵The Jews said to one another, "Where does this man intend to go that we cannot find him? Will he go where our people live scattered among the Greeks, and teach the Greeks? ³⁶What did he mean when he said, 'You will look for me, but you will not find me,' and 'Where I am, you cannot come'?"

³⁷On the last and greatest day of the Feast, Jesus stood and said in a loud voice, "If anyone is thirsty, let him come to me and drink. ³⁸Whoever believes in me, as[n] the Scripture has said, streams of living water will flow from within him." ³⁹By this he meant the Spirit, whom those who believed in him were later to receive. Up to that time the Spirit had not been given, since Jesus had not yet been glorified.

⁴⁰On hearing his words, some of the people said, "Surely this man is the Prophet."

⁴¹Others said, "He is the Christ."

Still others asked, "How can the Christ come from Galilee? ⁴²Does not the Scripture say that

[8] Some early manuscripts do not have yet.   [m]26 Or Messiah; also in verses 27, 31, 41 and 42   [n]37,38 Or / If anyone is thirsty, let him come to me. / And let him drink, 38who believes in me. / As

the Christ will come from David's family° and from Bethlehem, the town where David lived?" ⁴³Thus the people were divided because of Jesus. ⁴⁴Some wanted to seize him, but no one laid a hand on him.

⁴⁵Finally the temple guards went back to the chief priests and Pharisees, who asked them, "Why didn't you bring him in?"

⁴⁶"No one ever spoke the way this man does," the guards declared.

⁴⁷"You mean he has deceived you also?" the Pharisees retorted. ⁴⁸"Has any of the rulers or of the Pharisees believed in him? ⁴⁹No! But this mob that knows nothing of the law—there is a curse on them."

⁵⁰Nicodemus, who had gone to Jesus earlier and who was one of their own number, asked, ⁵¹"Does our law condemn anyone without first hearing him to find out what he is doing?"

⁵²They replied, "Are you from Galilee, too? Look into it, and you will find that a prophet^P does not come out of Galilee."

[The earliest manuscripts and many other ancient witnesses do not have John 7:53—8:11.]

°42 Greek *seed*   P52 Two early manuscripts *the Prophet*

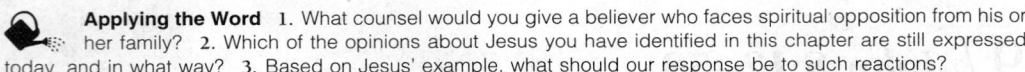

Discovering the Word 1. The first blast of hostility against Jesus comes from his own family (vv. 1–13). How would you characterize the statements made by Jesus' brothers (vv. 3–5)? 2. When Jesus makes his presence in Jerusalem known, people begin to challenge the origin (and, therefore, the authority) of his teaching. According to Jesus, how can we verify the truth of his teaching (vv. 16–18)? 3. What other opinions or questions do people have about Jesus in verses 20–36? 4. How does Jesus respond to each one? 5. On the last day of the Feast of Tabernacles, large vats of water were poured out on the pavement of the temple court as a reminder of God's provision of water in the wilderness. With that custom in mind, how would you explain the significance of Jesus' remarks in verses 37–39?

Applying the Word 1. What counsel would you give a believer who faces spiritual opposition from his or her family? 2. Which of the opinions about Jesus you have identified in this chapter are still expressed today, and in what way? 3. Based on Jesus' example, what should our response be to such reactions?

Responding in Prayer Pray for wisdom as you face various reactions to Jesus.

---

8 / John 7:53—8:11
Caught in Adultery

NOTHING IS MORE humiliating than being caught in an act of disobedience! Whether it's a child with his hand in the cookie jar or an adult driving over the speed limit, we all know the sinking feeling of being caught. In John 8, a woman is caught in the most awkward of situations—in the very act of adultery. The way Jesus responds to her may surprise you.

Warming Up to God Think of a time when you hurt someone and that person was willing to forgive you. How did it feel to be forgiven? Thank God for extending forgiveness to you.

Read John 7:53—8:11.

---

⁵³Then each went to his own home.

⁸But Jesus went to the Mount of Olives. ²At dawn he appeared again in the temple courts, where all the people gathered around him, and he sat down to teach them. ³The teachers of the law and the Pharisees brought in a woman caught in adultery. They made her stand before the group ⁴and said to Jesus, "Teacher, this woman was caught in the act of adultery. ⁵In the Law Moses commanded us to stone such women.

Now what do you say?" 6They were using this question as a trap, in order to have a basis for accusing him.

But Jesus bent down and started to write on the ground with his finger. 7When they kept on questioning him, he straightened up and said to them, "If any one of you is without sin, let him be the first to throw a stone at her." 8Again he stooped down and wrote on the ground.

9At this, those who heard began to go away one at a time, the older ones first, until only Jesus was left, with the woman still standing there. 10Jesus straightened up and asked her, "Woman, where are they? Has no one condemned you?"

11"No one, sir," she said.

"Then neither do I condemn you," Jesus declared. "Go now and leave your life of sin."

 Discovering the Word 1. What do we know about the character and motives of those who bring this woman to Jesus? 2. While it is obvious that the woman is guilty, what elements of injustice can you find in this situation? 3. The Pharisees and teachers were often very self-righteous. Why do you think they went away rather than stoning the woman (vv. 7–9)? 4. How would you describe Jesus' attitude toward the woman (vv. 10–11)?

Applying the Word 1. What can we learn from this passage about Christ's attitude toward us—even when we feel awful about ourselves? 2. What does it teach us about forgiving and accepting others? 3. Who do you need to offer your forgiveness to?

Responding in Prayer Ask God to show you what it means to forgive.

---

9 / *John 8:12–59*
Jesus, the Light of the World

JESUS NEVER SPOKE in public without creating controversy. In fact, he was constantly in trouble! Rather than retreating behind the safety of a pulpit, Jesus spoke in settings where people were bold enough to talk back. In this portion of John's story, Jesus makes a series of claims about himself. Each claim is met by a challenge from his enemies. Each challenge is then answered, and the answer leads to the next claim. Throughout this interchange, Jesus shows us how to speak the truth in the face of hostility. He also reveals some amazing things about himself.

 Warming Up to God Have you ever tried to talk about Christ with a family member or coworker who was hostile to your message? How did you feel at the time? Thank God for giving you a Savior who understands everything we experience.

 Read John 8:12–59.

12When Jesus spoke again to the people, he said, "I am the light of the world. Whoever follows me will never walk in darkness, but will have the light of life."

13The Pharisees challenged him, "Here you are, appearing as your own witness; your testimony is not valid."

14Jesus answered, "Even if I testify on my own behalf, my testimony is valid, for I know where I came from and where I am going. But you have no idea where I come from or where I am going.

15You judge by human standards; I pass judgment on no one. 16But if I do judge, my decisions are right, because I am not alone. I stand with the Father, who sent me. 17In your own Law it is written that the testimony of two men is valid. 18I am one who testifies for myself; my other witness is the Father, who sent me."

19Then they asked him, "Where is your father?"

"You do not know me or my Father," Jesus replied. "If you knew me, you would know my

Father also." 20He spoke these words while teaching in the temple area near the place where the offerings were put. Yet no one seized him, because his time had not yet come.

21Once more Jesus said to them, "I am going away, and you will look for me, and you will die in your sin. Where I go, you cannot come."

22This made the Jews ask, "Will he kill himself? Is that why he says, 'Where I go, you cannot come'?"

23But he continued, "You are from below; I am from above. You are of this world; I am not of this world. 24I told you that you would die in your sins; if you do not believe that I am ⌐the one I claim to be⌐,q you will indeed die in your sins."

25"Who are you?" they asked.

"Just what I have been claiming all along," Jesus replied. 26"I have much to say in judgment of you. But he who sent me is reliable, and what I have heard from him I tell the world."

27They did not understand that he was telling them about his Father. 28So Jesus said, "When you have lifted up the Son of Man, then you will know that I am ⌐the one I claim to be⌐ and that I do nothing on my own but speak just what the Father has taught me. 29The one who sent me is with me; he has not left me alone, for I always do what pleases him." 30Even as he spoke, many put their faith in him.

31To the Jews who had believed him, Jesus said, "If you hold to my teaching, you are really my disciples. 32Then you will know the truth, and the truth will set you free."

33They answered him, "We are Abraham's descendantsr and have never been slaves of anyone. How can you say that we shall be set free?"

34Jesus replied, "I tell you the truth, everyone who sins is a slave to sin. 35Now a slave has no permanent place in the family, but a son belongs to it forever. 36So if the Son sets you free, you will be free indeed. 37I know you are Abraham's descendants. Yet you are ready to kill me, because you have no room for my word. 38I am telling you what I have seen in the Father's presence, and you do what you have heard from your father.s "

39"Abraham is our father," they answered.

"If you were Abraham's children," said Jesus, "then you wouldt do the things Abraham did. 40As it is, you are determined to kill me, a man who has told you the truth that I heard from God. Abraham did not do such things. 41You are doing the things your own father does."

"We are not illegitimate children," they protested. "The only Father we have is God himself."

42Jesus said to them, "If God were your Father, you would love me, for I came from God and now am here. I have not come on my own; but he sent me. 43Why is my language not clear to you? Because you are unable to hear what I say. 44You belong to your father, the devil, and you want to carry out your father's desire. He was a murderer from the beginning, not holding to the truth, for there is no truth in him. When he lies, he speaks his native language, for he is a liar and the father of lies. 45Yet because I tell the truth, you do not believe me! 46Can any of you prove me guilty of sin? If I am telling the truth, why don't you believe me? 47He who belongs to God hears what God says. The reason you do not hear is that you do not belong to God."

48The Jews answered him, "Aren't we right in saying that you are a Samaritan and demon-possessed?"

49"I am not possessed by a demon," said Jesus, "but I honor my Father and you dishonor me. 50I am not seeking glory for myself; but there is one who seeks it, and he is the judge. 51I tell you the truth, if anyone keeps my word, he will never see death."

52At this the Jews exclaimed, "Now we know that you are demon-possessed! Abraham died and so did the prophets, yet you say that if anyone keeps your word, he will never taste death. 53Are you greater than our father Abraham? He died, and so did the prophets. Who do you think you are?"

54Jesus replied, "If I glorify myself, my glory means nothing. My Father, whom you claim as your God, is the one who glorifies me. 55Though you do not know him, I know him. If I said I did not, I would be a liar like you, but I do know him and keep his word. 56Your father Abraham rejoiced at the thought of seeing my day; he saw it and was glad."

57"You are not yet fifty years old," the Jews said to him, "and you have seen Abraham!"

58"I tell you the truth," Jesus answered, "before Abraham was born, I am!" 59At this, they picked up stones to stone him, but Jesus hid himself, slipping away from the temple grounds.

q24 Or I am he; also in verse 28   r33 Greek seed; also in verse 37
s38 Or presence. Therefore do what you have heard from the Father.
t39 Some early manuscripts "If you are Abraham's children," said Jesus, "then

Discovering the Word 1. The Pharisees challenge the validity of Jesus' claim (v. 13). How does Jesus answer their challenge (vv. 14–18)? 2. Jesus' reference to his Father leads to his second claim—that he came from God. How does this claim heighten the tension between Jesus and the Jews (vv. 19–30)? 3. Jesus makes another startling claim in verses 31–32: "If you hold to my teaching . . . then you will know the truth, and the truth will set you free." Why does holding to Jesus' teaching lead to true knowledge and freedom? 4. Jesus' opponents also claim to have both Abraham and God as their father. According to Jesus, how does their conduct contradict their claim (vv. 39–47)?

 Applying the Word 1. Why is our conduct the truest test of our beliefs? 2. In what ways does your lifestyle validate (or invalidate) your claim to be a follower of Christ?

Responding in Prayer Ask God to help you change the parts of your life that don't match your beliefs.

---

10 / *John 9*
A Blind Man Sees the Light

OUR SIGHT IS a wonderful gift from God. We marvel at the fiery colors of a sunset, the rich pastels of spring and the delicate beauty of a flower. How tragic it must be to never see the light of day. Yet there is a far greater tragedy than physical blindness. In this passage Jesus meets a man who has been blind from birth. The man illustrates that those who are blind often see clearly, while those with sight see nothing at all.

 Warming Up to God Before you begin this chapter about various kinds of blindness and sight, ask God to open your eyes so that you can see what he has for you.

 Read John 9.

---

9 As he went along, he saw a man blind from birth. ²His disciples asked him, "Rabbi, who sinned, this man or his parents, that he was born blind?"

³"Neither this man nor his parents sinned," said Jesus, "but this happened so that the work of God might be displayed in his life. ⁴As long as it is day, we must do the work of him who sent me. Night is coming, when no one can work. ⁵While I am in the world, I am the light of the world."

⁶Having said this, he spit on the ground, made some mud with the saliva, and put it on the man's eyes. ⁷"Go," he told him, "wash in the Pool of Siloam" (this word means Sent). So the man went and washed, and came home seeing.

⁸His neighbors and those who had formerly seen him begging asked, "Isn't this the same man who used to sit and beg?" ⁹Some claimed that he was.

Others said, "No, he only looks like him."

But he himself insisted, "I am the man."

¹⁰"How then were your eyes opened?" they demanded.

¹¹He replied, "The man they call Jesus made some mud and put it on my eyes. He told me to go to Siloam and wash. So I went and washed, and then I could see."

¹²"Where is this man?" they asked him.

"I don't know," he said.

¹³They brought to the Pharisees the man who had been blind. ¹⁴Now the day on which Jesus had made the mud and opened the man's eyes was a Sabbath. ¹⁵Therefore the Pharisees also asked him how he had received his sight. "He put mud on my eyes," the man replied, "and I washed, and now I see."

¹⁶Some of the Pharisees said, "This man is not from God, for he does not keep the Sabbath."

But others asked, "How can a sinner do such miraculous signs?" So they were divided.

¹⁷Finally they turned again to the blind man, "What have you to say about him? It was your eyes he opened."

The man replied, "He is a prophet."

¹⁸The Jews still did not believe that he had been blind and had received his sight until they

sent for the man's parents. ¹⁹"Is this your son?" they asked. "Is this the one you say was born blind? How is it that now he can see?"

²⁰"We know he is our son," the parents answered, "and we know he was born blind. ²¹But how he can see now, or who opened his eyes, we don't know. Ask him. He is of age; he will speak for himself." ²²His parents said this because they were afraid of the Jews, for already the Jews had decided that anyone who acknowledged that Jesus was the Christ ᵘ would be put out of the synagogue. ²³That was why his parents said, "He is of age; ask him."

²⁴A second time they summoned the man who had been blind. "Give glory to God, ᵛ " they said. "We know this man is a sinner."

²⁵He replied, "Whether he is a sinner or not, I don't know. One thing I do know. I was blind but now I see!"

²⁶Then they asked him, "What did he do to you? How did he open your eyes?"

²⁷He answered, "I have told you already and you did not listen. Why do you want to hear it again? Do you want to become his disciples, too?"

²⁸Then they hurled insults at him and said, "You are this fellow's disciple! We are disciples of Moses! ²⁹We know that God spoke to Moses, but as for this fellow, we don't even know where he comes from."

³⁰The man answered, "Now that is remarkable! You don't know where he comes from, yet he opened my eyes. ³¹We know that God does not listen to sinners. He listens to the godly man who does his will. ³²Nobody has ever heard of opening the eyes of a man born blind. ³³If this man were not from God, he could do nothing."

³⁴To this they replied, "You were steeped in sin at birth; how dare you lecture us!" And they threw him out.

³⁵Jesus heard that they had thrown him out, and when he found him, he said, "Do you believe in the Son of Man?"

³⁶"Who is he, sir?" the man asked. "Tell me so that I may believe in him."

³⁷Jesus said, "You have now seen him; in fact, he is the one speaking with you."

³⁸Then the man said, "Lord, I believe," and he worshiped him.

³⁹Jesus said, "For judgment I have come into this world, so that the blind will see and those who see will become blind."

⁴⁰Some Pharisees who were with him heard him say this and asked, "What? Are we blind too?"

⁴¹Jesus said, "If you were blind, you would not be guilty of sin; but now that you claim you can see, your guilt remains.

ᵘ22 Or *Messiah*   ᵛ24 A solemn charge to tell the truth (see Joshua 7:19)

 Discovering the Word   1. Based on the question the disciples ask Jesus (v. 2), how do they view the relation between sickness and sin?   2. What is Jesus' view of the same issue (vv. 3–5)?   3. Why do you think Jesus goes through the process of making mud and instructing the man to go wash, instead of simply healing him instantly?   4. On what grounds do the Pharisees object to this miracle (vv. 16, 22, 24, 29)?   5. How do the Pharisees react when the genuineness of the miracle becomes undeniable (vv. 28–34)?

 Applying the Word   1. When might Christians today exhibit the Pharisees' attitude to a marvelous work of God's grace or power?   2. What principles in this chapter could help you improve your spiritual eyesight?

Responding in Prayer   Ask God to strengthen your faith so that you might respond as the man did, "Lord, I believe."

11 / *John 10*
The Shepherd & His Sheep

JESUS WAS A master at using simple, everyday objects or events to illustrate profound spiritual truths. The farmer scattering seed, the vine sustaining the branches, and sparrows falling to the earth all took on a new dimension in Jesus' eyes. In John 10, Jesus uses the scene of a shepherd enclosing his sheep in a sheepfold to give us one of the most moving pictures of our salvation and security in Christ found anywhere in the Bible. If you've ever doubted the love of Christ, Jesus will give you a healthy dose of assurance in this chapter.

 Warming Up to God What usually prompts you to have doubts about your salvation or your walk with Christ—your own sin? feelings of unworthiness? personal failures? Be honest with Christ about your doubts.

 Read John 10.

10 "I tell you the truth, the man who does not enter the sheep pen by the gate, but climbs in by some other way, is a thief and a robber. ²The man who enters by the gate is the shepherd of his sheep. ³The watchman opens the gate for him, and the sheep listen to his voice. He calls his own sheep by name and leads them out. ⁴When he has brought out all his own, he goes on ahead of them, and his sheep follow him because they know his voice. ⁵But they will never follow a stranger; in fact, they will run away from him because they do not recognize a stranger's voice." ⁶Jesus used this figure of speech, but they did not understand what he was telling them.

⁷Therefore Jesus said again, "I tell you the truth, I am the gate for the sheep. ⁸All who ever came before me were thieves and robbers, but the sheep did not listen to them. ⁹I am the gate; whoever enters through me will be saved.ʷ He will come in and go out, and find pasture. ¹⁰The thief comes only to steal and kill and destroy; I have come that they may have life, and have it to the full.

¹¹"I am the good shepherd. The good shepherd lays down his life for the sheep. ¹²The hired hand is not the shepherd who owns the sheep. So when he sees the wolf coming, he abandons the sheep and runs away. Then the wolf attacks the flock and scatters it. ¹³The man runs away because he is a hired hand and cares nothing for the sheep.

¹⁴"I am the good shepherd; I know my sheep and my sheep know me— ¹⁵just as the Father knows me and I know the Father—and I lay down my life for the sheep. ¹⁶I have other sheep that are not of this sheep pen. I must bring them

also. They too will listen to my voice, and there shall be one flock and one shepherd. ¹⁷The reason my Father loves me is that I lay down my life— only to take it up again. ¹⁸No one takes it from me, but I lay it down of my own accord. I have authority to lay it down and authority to take it up again. This command I received from my Father."

¹⁹At these words the Jews were again divided. ²⁰Many of them said, "He is demon-possessed and raving mad. Why listen to him?"

²¹But others said, "These are not the sayings of a man possessed by a demon. Can a demon open the eyes of the blind?"

²²Then came the Feast of Dedicationˣ at Jerusalem. It was winter, ²³and Jesus was in the temple area walking in Solomon's Colonnade. ²⁴The Jews gathered around him, saying, "How long will you keep us in suspense? If you are the Christ,ʸ tell us plainly."

²⁵Jesus answered, "I did tell you, but you do not believe. The miracles I do in my Father's name speak for me, ²⁶but you do not believe because you are not my sheep. ²⁷My sheep listen to my voice; I know them, and they follow me. ²⁸I give them eternal life, and they shall never perish; no one can snatch them out of my hand. ²⁹My Father, who has given them to me, is greater than allᶻ; no one can snatch them out of my Father's hand. ³⁰I and the Father are one."

³¹Again the Jews picked up stones to stone him, ³²but Jesus said to them, "I have shown you many great miracles from the Father. For which of these do you stone me?"

ʷ9 Or *kept safe*   ˣ22 That is, Hanukkah   ʸ24 Or *Messiah*
ᶻ29 Many early manuscripts *What my Father has given me is greater than all*

33"We are not stoning you for any of these," replied the Jews, "but for blasphemy, because you, a mere man, claim to be God."

34Jesus answered them, "Is it not written in your Law, 'I have said you are gods'ᵃ? 35If he called them 'gods,' to whom the word of God came—and the Scripture cannot be broken— 36what about the one whom the Father set apart as his very own and sent into the world? Why then do you accuse me of blasphemy because I said, 'I am God's Son'? 37Do not believe me unless I do what my Father does. 38But if I do it, even though you do not believe me, believe the mira-

cles, that you may know and understand that the Father is in me, and I in the Father." 39Again they tried to seize him, but he escaped their grasp.

40Then Jesus went back across the Jordan to the place where John had been baptizing in the early days. Here he stayed 41and many people came to him. They said, "Though John never performed a miraculous sign, all that John said about this man was true." 42And in that place many believed in Jesus.

ᵃ34 Psalm 82:6

Discovering the Word 1. What spiritual truths is Jesus trying to convey in verses 1–5? 2. In verses 11–15 Jesus talks about the shepherd's care for his sheep. What can you learn from those verses about Jesus' care and relationship with you? 3. According to Jesus, how are the Jews in this passage different from his sheep (vv. 22–27)? 4. When Jesus claims that he and the Father are one, the Jews pick up stones to stone him (vv. 30–33). Do you think his defense is a denial of his deity (vv. 33–36)? Explain.

Applying the Word 1. How do you respond to promises and assurances Jesus gives his sheep in verses 28–29? 2. Which promise from Jesus in this chapter is most encouraging to you? 3. How can Jesus' promise help you when you have doubts?

Responding in Prayer Praise God for giving you such a Good Shepherd.

---

12 / *John 11*
Resurrection & Life

EVER SINCE GOD judged Adam and Eve, death has plagued humanity. It separates us from those we love and looms over our own lives like a menacing spirit. In this chapter Jesus reaches out to a family struggling with the pain of death. He shows us why we need never fear death again.

Warming Up to God When is it difficult for you to feel that God is with you? Talk to God about your feelings of abandonment.

Read John 11.

---

11 Now a man named Lazarus was sick. He was from Bethany, the village of Mary and her sister Martha. 2This Mary, whose brother Lazarus now lay sick, was the same one who poured perfume on the Lord and wiped his feet with her hair. 3So the sisters sent word to Jesus, "Lord, the one you love is sick."

4When he heard this, Jesus said, "This sickness will not end in death. No, it is for God's glory so

that God's Son may be glorified through it." 5Jesus loved Martha and her sister and Lazarus. 6Yet when he heard that Lazarus was sick, he stayed where he was two more days.

7Then he said to his disciples, "Let us go back to Judea."

8"But Rabbi," they said, "a short while ago the Jews tried to stone you, and yet you are going back there?"

9Jesus answered, "Are there not twelve hours of

daylight? A man who walks by day will not stumble, for he sees by this world's light. ¹⁰It is when he walks by night that he stumbles, for he has no light."

¹¹After he had said this, he went on to tell them, "Our friend Lazarus has fallen asleep; but I am going there to wake him up."

¹²His disciples replied, "Lord, if he sleeps, he will get better." ¹³Jesus had been speaking of his death, but his disciples thought he meant natural sleep.

¹⁴So then he told them plainly, "Lazarus is dead, ¹⁵and for your sake I am glad I was not there, so that you may believe. But let us go to him."

¹⁶Then Thomas (called Didymus) said to the rest of the disciples, "Let us also go, that we may die with him."

¹⁷On his arrival, Jesus found that Lazarus had already been in the tomb for four days. ¹⁸Bethany was less than two miles[b] from Jerusalem, ¹⁹and many Jews had come to Martha and Mary to comfort them in the loss of their brother. ²⁰When Martha heard that Jesus was coming, she went out to meet him, but Mary stayed at home.

²¹"Lord," Martha said to Jesus, "if you had been here, my brother would not have died. ²²But I know that even now God will give you whatever you ask."

²³Jesus said to her, "Your brother will rise again."

²⁴Martha answered, "I know he will rise again in the resurrection at the last day."

²⁵Jesus said to her, "I am the resurrection and the life. He who believes in me will live, even though he dies; ²⁶and whoever lives and believes in me will never die. Do you believe this?"

²⁷"Yes, Lord," she told him, "I believe that you are the Christ,[c] the Son of God, who was to come into the world."

²⁸And after she had said this, she went back and called her sister Mary aside. "The Teacher is here," she said, "and is asking for you." ²⁹When Mary heard this, she got up quickly and went to him. ³⁰Now Jesus had not yet entered the village, but was still at the place where Martha had met him. ³¹When the Jews who had been with Mary in the house, comforting her, noticed how quickly she got up and went out, they followed her, supposing she was going to the tomb to mourn there.

³²When Mary reached the place where Jesus was and saw him, she fell at his feet and said,

"Lord, if you had been here, my brother would not have died."

³³When Jesus saw her weeping, and the Jews who had come along with her also weeping, he was deeply moved in spirit and troubled. ³⁴"Where have you laid him?" he asked.

"Come and see, Lord," they replied.

³⁵Jesus wept.

³⁶Then the Jews said, "See how he loved him!" ³⁷But some of them said, "Could not he who opened the eyes of the blind man have kept this man from dying?"

³⁸Jesus, once more deeply moved, came to the tomb. It was a cave with a stone laid across the entrance. ³⁹"Take away the stone," he said.

"But, Lord," said Martha, the sister of the dead man, "by this time there is a bad odor, for he has been there four days."

⁴⁰Then Jesus said, "Did I not tell you that if you believed, you would see the glory of God?"

⁴¹So they took away the stone. Then Jesus looked up and said, "Father, I thank you that you have heard me. ⁴²I knew that you always hear me, but I said this for the benefit of the people standing here, that they may believe that you sent me."

⁴³When he had said this, Jesus called in a loud voice, "Lazarus, come out!" ⁴⁴The dead man came out, his hands and feet wrapped with strips of linen, and a cloth around his face.

Jesus said to them, "Take off the grave clothes and let him go."

⁴⁵Therefore many of the Jews who had come to visit Mary, and had seen what Jesus did, put their faith in him. ⁴⁶But some of them went to the Pharisees and told them what Jesus had done. ⁴⁷Then the chief priests and the Pharisees called a meeting of the Sanhedrin.

"What are we accomplishing?" they asked. "Here is this man performing many miraculous signs. ⁴⁸If we let him go on like this, everyone will believe in him, and then the Romans will come and take away both our place[d] and our nation."

⁴⁹Then one of them, named Caiaphas, who was high priest that year, spoke up, "You know nothing at all! ⁵⁰You do not realize that it is better for you that one man die for the people than that the whole nation perish."

⁵¹He did not say this on his own, but as high priest that year he prophesied that Jesus would die for the Jewish nation, ⁵²and not only for that

[b]18 Greek *fifteen stadia* (about 3 kilometers)   [c]27 Or *Messiah*
[d]48 Or *temple*

nation but also for the scattered children of God, to bring them together and make them one. ⁵³So from that day on they plotted to take his life.

⁵⁴Therefore Jesus no longer moved about publicly among the Jews. Instead he withdrew to a region near the desert, to a village called Ephraim, where he stayed with his disciples.

⁵⁵When it was almost time for the Jewish Passover, many went up from the country to Jerusalem for their ceremonial cleansing before the Passover. ⁵⁶They kept looking for Jesus, and as they stood in the temple area they asked one another, "What do you think? Isn't he coming to the Feast at all?" ⁵⁷But the chief priests and Pharisees had given orders that if anyone found out where Jesus was, he should report it so that they might arrest him.

 Discovering the Word 1. How can we resolve the apparent conflict between Jesus' love for Lazarus and his deliberate delay in helping him (vv. 4–6)? 2. What additional insight into God's purposes can we gain from Jesus' statement in verse 15? 3. What elements of doubt and faith do you see in Martha's statements to Jesus (vv. 17–27)? 4. How should Christ's statement in verses 25–26 radically alter our views of life and death? 5. Why do you think John emphasizes that Jesus was deeply moved by Mary's grief and the anguish of those with her (vv. 28–38)? 6. How would you explain the fact that the people who see the same miracle respond in two totally different ways (vv. 45–57)?

 Applying the Word 1. How can those verses help us when we feel abandoned by God in a time of great need? 2. In what ways will this chapter change the way you respond to personal difficulty or the apparent delay of God?

 Responding in Prayer Thank God for his personal presence with you.

---

13 / *John 12*
The King's Last Acts

IF YOU HAVE ever felt rejected or misunderstood, you know how Jesus felt as his public ministry came to an end. The hostility against him had risen to a fever pitch. His gentle compassion and abundant miracles were met with oppression and violence. Jesus knew what none of his friends knew—that he was about to die. In spite of the fleeting attempts of the crowd to make him King, Jesus chose the way of the cross.

Warming Up to God If you knew for sure that you had only one week to live, what would you do with that week?

Read John 12.

12 Six days before the Passover, Jesus arrived at Bethany, where Lazarus lived, whom Jesus had raised from the dead. ²Here a dinner was given in Jesus' honor. Martha served, while Lazarus was among those reclining at the table with him. ³Then Mary took about a pint*ᵉ* of pure nard, an expensive perfume; she poured it on Jesus' feet and wiped his feet with her hair. And the house was filled with the fragrance of the perfume.

⁴But one of his disciples, Judas Iscariot, who was later to betray him, objected, ⁵"Why wasn't this perfume sold and the money given to the poor? It was worth a year's wages.*ᶠ*" ⁶He did not say this because he cared about the poor but because he was a thief; as keeper of the money bag, he used to help himself to what was put into it.

⁷"Leave her alone," Jesus replied. "⌊It was intended⌋ that she should save this perfume for the day of my burial. ⁸You will always have the poor among you, but you will not always have me."

⁹Meanwhile a large crowd of Jews found out

ᵉ3 Greek a litra *(probably about 0.5 liter)*   *ᶠ5 Greek* three hundred denarii

that Jesus was there and came, not only because of him but also to see Lazarus, whom he had raised from the dead. ¹⁰So the chief priests made plans to kill Lazarus as well, ¹¹for on account of him many of the Jews were going over to Jesus and putting their faith in him.

¹²The next day the great crowd that had come for the Feast heard that Jesus was on his way to Jerusalem. ¹³They took palm branches and went out to meet him, shouting,

"Hosanna!ᵍ"

"Blessed is he who comes in the name of the
      Lord!"ʰ

"Blessed is the King of Israel!"

¹⁴Jesus found a young donkey and sat upon it, as it is written,

¹⁵"Do not be afraid, O Daughter of Zion;
      see, your king is coming,
      seated on a donkey's colt."ⁱ

¹⁶At first his disciples did not understand all this. Only after Jesus was glorified did they realize that these things had been written about him and that they had done these things to him.

¹⁷Now the crowd that was with him when he called Lazarus from the tomb and raised him from the dead continued to spread the word. ¹⁸Many people, because they had heard that he had given this miraculous sign, went out to meet him. ¹⁹So the Pharisees said to one another, "See, this is getting us nowhere. Look how the whole world has gone after him!"

²⁰Now there were some Greeks among those who went up to worship at the Feast. ²¹They came to Philip, who was from Bethsaida in Galilee, with a request. "Sir," they said, "we would like to see Jesus." ²²Philip went to tell Andrew; Andrew and Philip in turn told Jesus.

²³Jesus replied, "The hour has come for the Son of Man to be glorified. ²⁴I tell you the truth, unless a kernel of wheat falls to the ground and dies, it remains only a single seed. But if it dies, it produces many seeds. ²⁵The man who loves his life will lose it, while the man who hates his life in this world will keep it for eternal life. ²⁶Whoever serves me must follow me; and where I am, my servant also will be. My Father will honor the one who serves me.

²⁷"Now my heart is troubled, and what shall I say? 'Father, save me from this hour'? No, it was

for this very reason I came to this hour. ²⁸Father, glorify your name!"

Then a voice came from heaven, "I have glorified it, and will glorify it again." ²⁹The crowd that was there and heard it said it had thundered; others said an angel had spoken to him.

³⁰Jesus said, "This voice was for your benefit, not mine. ³¹Now is the time for judgment on this world; now the prince of this world will be driven out. ³²But I, when I am lifted up from the earth, will draw all men to myself." ³³He said this to show the kind of death he was going to die.

³⁴The crowd spoke up, "We have heard from the Law that the Christʲ will remain forever, so how can you say, 'The Son of Man must be lifted up'? Who is this 'Son of Man'?"

³⁵Then Jesus told them, "You are going to have the light just a little while longer. Walk while you have the light, before darkness overtakes you. The man who walks in the dark does not know where he is going. ³⁶Put your trust in the light while you have it, so that you may become sons of light." When he had finished speaking, Jesus left and hid himself from them.

³⁷Even after Jesus had done all these miraculous signs in their presence, they still would not believe in him. ³⁸This was to fulfill the word of Isaiah the prophet:

"Lord, who has believed our message
      and to whom has the arm of the Lord been
        revealed?"ᵏ

³⁹For this reason they could not believe, because, as Isaiah says elsewhere:

⁴⁰"He has blinded their eyes
      and deadened their hearts,
so they can neither see with their eyes,
      nor understand with their hearts,
      nor turn—and I would heal them."ˡ

⁴¹Isaiah said this because he saw Jesus' glory and spoke about him.

⁴²Yet at the same time many even among the leaders believed in him. But because of the Pharisees they would not confess their faith for fear they would be put out of the synagogue; ⁴³for they loved praise from men more than praise from God.

⁴⁴Then Jesus cried out, "When a man believes

ᵍ13 A Hebrew expression meaning "Save!" which became an exclamation of praise   ʰ13 Psalm 118:25, 26   ⁱ15 Zech. 9:9   ʲ34 Or *Messiah*   ᵏ38 Isaiah 53:1   ˡ40 Isaiah 6:10

in me, he does not believe in me only, but in the one who sent me. ⁴⁵When he looks at me, he sees the one who sent me. ⁴⁶I have come into the world as a light, so that no one who believes in me should stay in darkness.

⁴⁷"As for the person who hears my words but does not keep them, I do not judge him. For I did not come to judge the world, but to save it.

⁴⁸There is a judge for the one who rejects me and does not accept my words; that very word which I spoke will condemn him at the last day. ⁴⁹For I did not speak of my own accord, but the Father who sent me commanded me what to say and how to say it. ⁵⁰I know that his command leads to eternal life. So whatever I say is just what the Father has told me to say."

Discovering the Word 1. What motivates Mary to pour expensive perfume on Jesus' feet? 2. Judas objects to Mary's extravagance. What motives and wrong thinking lie behind his objection (vv. 4–8)? 3. What do the shouts of the crowd tell us about their expectations of Jesus (vv. 12–13)? 4. How do Christ's statements about his mission clash with the crowd's expectations (vv. 23–28)? 5. When we stubbornly refuse to believe, what happens to our spiritual senses, and why (vv. 37–41)? 6. Jesus' last public message to his people is recorded in verses 44–50. What indications do you find that he is still reaching out in love and grace to those who have rejected him?

Applying the Word 1. In what ways should we be extravagant in our devotion to Jesus? 2. How can you apply the example of Jesus to people who reject you or your testimony about Christ?

Responding in Prayer In your own life are you more interested in earthly acclaim and glory or are you willing to lose your life for Christ's sake? Examine your direction and life goals in the light of Jesus' commitment to do the will of the Father.

14 / *John 13:1–17*
The Son as a Slave

THERE WERE TWO things on Jesus' heart the night before his crucifixion—his Father and his disciples. In John 13—17, we have the privilege of listening to his conversations with them both. However, before Jesus can instruct his disciples about his death, he has to act out a lesson in servitude. Jesus also shows us the spirit he expects in those who follow him. Greatness in Christ's eyes does not come from having many servants but from being the servant of many.

Warming Up to God Have you ever been asked to do a demeaning, lowly job? What thoughts went through your mind at that time? Praise God for a Savior who was willing to take on the lowliest task of all.

Read John 13:1–17.

13 It was just before the Passover Feast. Jesus knew that the time had come for him to leave this world and go to the Father. Having loved his own who were in the world, he now showed them the full extent of his love.ᵐ

²The evening meal was being served, and the devil had already prompted Judas Iscariot, son of Simon, to betray Jesus. ³Jesus knew that the Father had put all things under his power, and that he had come from God and was returning to God; ⁴so he got up from the meal, took off his outer

clothing, and wrapped a towel around his waist. ⁵After that, he poured water into a basin and began to wash his disciples' feet, drying them with the towel that was wrapped around him.

⁶He came to Simon Peter, who said to him, "Lord, are you going to wash my feet?"

⁷Jesus replied, "You do not realize now what I am doing, but later you will understand."

⁸"No," said Peter, "you shall never wash my feet."

ᵐ1 Or *he loved them to the last*

Jesus answered, "Unless I wash you, you have no part with me."

⁹"Then, Lord," Simon Peter replied, "not just my feet but my hands and my head as well!"

¹⁰Jesus answered, "A person who has had a bath needs only to wash his feet; his whole body is clean. And you are clean, though not every one of you." ¹¹For he knew who was going to betray him, and that was why he said not every one was clean.

¹²When he had finished washing their feet, he put on his clothes and returned to his place. "Do you understand what I have done for you?" he asked them. ¹³"You call me 'Teacher' and 'Lord,' and rightly so, for that is what I am. ¹⁴Now that I, your Lord and Teacher, have washed your feet, you also should wash one another's feet. ¹⁵I have set you an example that you should do as I have done for you. ¹⁶I tell you the truth, no servant is greater than his master, nor is a messenger greater than the one who sent him. ¹⁷Now that you know these things, you will be blessed if you do them.

Discovering the Word 1. According to John, what did Jesus know about himself (vv. 1–3)? In light of that knowledge, what is remarkable about what Jesus did next (vv. 4–5)? 2. Footwashing was normally done by servants or slaves. Why do you think that Jesus washed his disciples' feet instead of simply talking to them about love? 3. Was Peter simply being humble when he refused to allow Jesus to serve him (vv. 6–8)? Explain. 4. What spiritual truth was Jesus trying to communicate to Peter (and to us) in verses 8–11? 5. Based on Jesus' words in verse 17, how would you describe the relationship between knowledge, action and joy in the Christian life?

Applying the Word 1. What has this chapter revealed to you about your attitude toward serving? 2. In what specific ways can you model the humility of Jesus toward those with whom you live or work?

Responding in Prayer Ask God to give you a humble spirit.

15 / John 13:18–38
The Betrayer & the Boaster

THERE ARE SOME people we just don't like to be around! They aren't necessarily our enemies. They simply have the uncanny ability to irritate us. If we had been one of Jesus' disciples, we would probably have found it difficult to be around Peter. He was blunt and, at times, arrogant. On the other hand, we might have regarded Judas with trust and respect. The only one who saw deeply enough to discern the true character of these men was Jesus.

Warming Up to God Has someone in your life ever hurt you deeply? How have you responded to that hurt? Tell God how you feel about what happened. Allow him to speak to your pain.

Read John 13:18–38.

¹⁸"I am not referring to all of you; I know those I have chosen. But this is to fulfill the scripture: 'He who shares my bread has lifted up his heel against me.'ⁿ

¹⁹"I am telling you now before it happens, so that when it does happen you will believe that I am He. ²⁰I tell you the truth, whoever accepts anyone I send accepts me; and whoever accepts me accepts the one who sent me."

²¹After he had said this, Jesus was troubled in spirit and testified, "I tell you the truth, one of you is going to betray me."

²²His disciples stared at one another, at a loss to know which of them he meant. ²³One of them, the disciple whom Jesus loved, was reclining next to him. ²⁴Simon Peter motioned to this disciple and said, "Ask him which one he means."

²⁵Leaning back against Jesus, he asked him, "Lord, who is it?"

ⁿ18 Psalm 41:9

²⁶Jesus answered, "It is the one to whom I will give this piece of bread when I have dipped it in the dish." Then, dipping the piece of bread, he gave it to Judas Iscariot, son of Simon. ²⁷As soon as Judas took the bread, Satan entered into him.

"What you are about to do, do quickly," Jesus told him, ²⁸but no one at the meal understood why Jesus said this to him. ²⁹Since Judas had charge of the money, some thought Jesus was telling him to buy what was needed for the Feast, or to give something to the poor. ³⁰As soon as Judas had taken the bread, he went out. And it was night.

³¹When he was gone, Jesus said, "Now is the Son of Man glorified and God is glorified in him. ³²If God is glorified in him,ᵒ God will glorify the Son in himself, and will glorify him at once.

³³"My children, I will be with you only a little longer. You will look for me, and just as I told the Jews, so I tell you now: Where I am going, you cannot come.

³⁴"A new command I give you: Love one another. As I have loved you, so you must love one another. ³⁵By this all men will know that you are my disciples, if you love one another."

³⁶Simon Peter asked him, "Lord, where are you going?"

Jesus replied, "Where I am going, you cannot follow now, but you will follow later."

³⁷Peter asked, "Lord, why can't I follow you now? I will lay down my life for you."

³⁸Then Jesus answered, "Will you really lay down your life for me? I tell you the truth, before the rooster crows, you will disown me three times!

ᵒ32 Many early manuscripts do not have *If God is glorified in him*.

 Discovering the Word 1. Jesus takes this opportunity to predict his betrayal. How would his prediction dispel any doubts the disciples might have and strengthen their faith (v. 19)? 2. Evidently, the disciples did not know who would betray Jesus (v. 22). What does this tell us about how Jesus had treated Judas? 3. Why does the kind of love Jesus describes convince all of humanity that we are Jesus' disciples (v. 35)? 4. Do you think Peter's declaration in verse 37 comes from pride or from sincerity? Explain. 5. Three people stand out in this passage—Jesus, Judas and Peter. What one character quality of each—good or evil—impresses you the most?

Applying the Word 1. How would you have treated Judas if you knew he would eventually betray you? 2. John later wrote: "This is how we know what love is: Jesus Christ laid down his life for us. And we ought to lay down our lives for our brothers" (1 Jn 3:16). In what practical ways can you exhibit this sacrificial love?

Responding in Prayer Pray for a strong faith that won't lead you into betrayal when times are tough.

---

16 / *John 14*
Comfort for a Troubled Heart

THE CALL CAME late at night. A broken sob was followed by these words: "Our son is dying. Will you please come to the hospital?" As I made the trip through darkened streets, I wondered what I could say to bring comfort to these heartbroken parents. Jesus faced that challenge too. In this chapter he comforts eleven disciples who feel like their world is coming unglued.

 Warming Up to God What is troubling you? Give it to God, and wait before him to receive his comfort.

 Read John 14.

14

"Do not let your hearts be troubled. Trust in God*P*; trust also in me. ²In my Father's house are many rooms; if it were not so, I would have told you. I am going there to prepare a place for you. ³And if I go and prepare a place for you, I will come back and take you to be with me that you also may be where I am. ⁴You know the way to the place where I am going."

⁵Thomas said to him, "Lord, we don't know where you are going, so how can we know the way?"

⁶Jesus answered, "I am the way and the truth and the life. No one comes to the Father except through me. ⁷If you really knew me, you would know*q* my Father as well. From now on, you do know him and have seen him."

⁸Philip said, "Lord, show us the Father and that will be enough for us."

⁹Jesus answered: "Don't you know me, Philip, even after I have been among you such a long time? Anyone who has seen me has seen the Father. How can you say, 'Show us the Father'? ¹⁰Don't you believe that I am in the Father, and that the Father is in me? The words I say to you are not just my own. Rather, it is the Father, living in me, who is doing his work. ¹¹Believe me when I say that I am in the Father and the Father is in me; or at least believe on the evidence of the miracles themselves. ¹²I tell you the truth, anyone who has faith in me will do what I have been doing. He will do even greater things than these, because I am going to the Father. ¹³And I will do whatever you ask in my name, so that the Son may bring glory to the Father. ¹⁴You may ask me for anything in my name, and I will do it.

¹⁵"If you love me, you will obey what I command. ¹⁶And I will ask the Father, and he will give you another Counselor to be with you forever— ¹⁷the Spirit of truth. The world cannot accept him, because it neither sees him nor knows him. But you know him, for he lives with you and will be*r* in you. ¹⁸I will not leave you as orphans; I will come to you. ¹⁹Before long, the world will not see me anymore, but you will see me. Because I live, you also will live. ²⁰On that day you will realize that I am in my Father, and you are in me, and I am in you. ²¹Whoever has my commands and obeys them, he is the one who loves me. He who loves me will be loved by my Father, and I too will love him and show myself to him."

²²Then Judas (not Judas Iscariot) said, "But, Lord, why do you intend to show yourself to us and not to the world?"

²³Jesus replied, "If anyone loves me, he will obey my teaching. My Father will love him, and we will come to him and make our home with him. ²⁴He who does not love me will not obey my teaching. These words you hear are not my own; they belong to the Father who sent me.

²⁵"All this I have spoken while still with you. ²⁶But the Counselor, the Holy Spirit, whom the Father will send in my name, will teach you all things and will remind you of everything I have said to you. ²⁷Peace I leave with you; my peace I give you. I do not give to you as the world gives. Do not let your hearts be troubled and do not be afraid.

²⁸"You heard me say, 'I am going away and I am coming back to you.' If you loved me, you would be glad that I am going to the Father, for the Father is greater than I. ²⁹I have told you now before it happens, so that when it does happen you will believe. ³⁰I will not speak with you much longer, for the prince of this world is coming. He has no hold on me, ³¹but the world must learn that I love the Father and that I do exactly what my Father has commanded me.

"Come now; let us leave.

P 1 Or You trust in God   q 7 Some early manuscripts If you really have known me, you will know   r 17 Some early manuscripts and is

---

Discovering the Word   1. How would the promises Jesus makes in verses 1–4 bring comfort to his disciples?   2. In light of verses 5–14, why is it crucial for our focus to be on Jesus himself?   3. According to Jesus, how will the Spirit bring comfort and help to his followers (vv. 15–27)?   4. What is the relationship between our love and obedience to Jesus and his love and presence in our lives (vv. 15–24)?   5. How does the peace Christ offers differ from that which the world offers (vv. 25–31)?

Applying the Word   1. Think of a friend who is going through a personal crisis. How could this chapter help you to minister to that person?   2. How can Jesus' words help you in a personal crisis or when you have a troubled heart?

Responding in Prayer Ask God to comfort someone you know who is troubled.

---

17 / *John 15:1–17*
The Secret of Remaining

THE FINAL WEEKEND before Christmas is not the time to visit a shopping mall. If you are fortunate enough to find a parking spot, the press of people inside makes shopping almost impossible. I overheard one mother giving these final instructions to her young son before plunging into the crowd: "Stay close to me and hold my hand all the time. We won't get separated if we hold on to each other."

As Jesus prepared his disciples to face life without his visible presence, he impressed on them the importance of staying close to him spiritually. He said, "Remain in me." If you've ever longed to understand the secret of spiritual growth, you will find it in Jesus' words to us in John 15.

 Warming Up to God Have you ever felt far from Christ since becoming a Christian? What circumstances made you feel that way? Be still before God and feel his presence with you now.

 Read John 15:1–17.

15 "I am the true vine, and my Father is the gardener. ²He cuts off every branch in me that bears no fruit, while every branch that does bear fruit he prunes⁵ so that it will be even more fruitful. ³You are already clean because of the word I have spoken to you. ⁴Remain in me, and I will remain in you. No branch can bear fruit by itself; it must remain in the vine. Neither can you bear fruit unless you remain in me.

⁵"I am the vine; you are the branches. If a man remains in me and I in him, he will bear much fruit; apart from me you can do nothing. ⁶If anyone does not remain in me, he is like a branch that is thrown away and withers; such branches are picked up, thrown into the fire and burned. ⁷If you remain in me and my words remain in you, ask whatever you wish, and it will be given you. ⁸This is to my Father's glory, that you bear much fruit, showing yourselves to be my disciples.

⁹"As the Father has loved me, so have I loved you. Now remain in my love. ¹⁰If you obey my commands, you will remain in my love, just as I have obeyed my Father's commands and remain in his love. ¹¹I have told you this so that my joy may be in you and that your joy may be complete. ¹²My command is this: Love each other as I have loved you. ¹³Greater love has no one than this, that he lay down his life for his friends. ¹⁴You are my friends if you do what I command. ¹⁵I no longer call you servants, because a servant does not know his master's business. Instead, I have called you friends, for everything that I learned from my Father I have made known to you. ¹⁶You did not choose me, but I chose you and appointed you to go and bear fruit—fruit that will last. Then the Father will give you whatever you ask in my name. ¹⁷This is my command: Love each other.

⁵2 The Greek for *prunes* also means *cleans*.

Discovering the Word 1. Jesus' instructions to his disciples in this passage revolve around three symbols—the vine, the gardener and the branches. What is Jesus trying to communicate by calling himself the *true vine*? 2. What does it mean to remain in Christ (v. 4)? 3. The Father prunes fruitful branches to make them more fruitful (v. 2). In what ways have you experienced the Father's "pruning"? 4. What spiritual benefits result from remaining in Christ (vv. 7–11)? 5. What are the requirements and benefits of friendship with Christ (vv. 14–17)?

Applying the Word 1. There are three categories of branches described in this passage—those bearing no fruit, those bearing some fruit, and those bearing much fruit. In which category would you place yourself and why? 2. If you are not bearing much fruit, what is Jesus' counsel to you in these verses?

Responding in Prayer Picture yourself as a tree laden with plump, healthy fruit. Ask God to help you become the person he wants you to be.

18 / *John 15:18—16:4*
The Cost of Friendship with Jesus

WHILE ON EARTH, Jesus did not surround himself with a group of students or even a group of followers. He placed himself in the company of friends. To admit that we need friends is a sign of maturity, not immaturity. Close relationships are Christlike! In this passage Jesus shows us what friendship with him is really like. There's both comfort and cost.

 Warming Up to God Are you ready to face the cost of following Christ? Talk openly with God about your fears—and excitement.

 Read John 15:18—16:4.

18"If the world hates you, keep in mind that it hated me first. 19If you belonged to the world, it would love you as its own. As it is, you do not belong to the world, but I have chosen you out of the world. That is why the world hates you. 20Remember the words I spoke to you: 'No servant is greater than his master.'[t] If they persecuted me, they will persecute you also. If they obeyed my teaching, they will obey yours also. 21They will treat you this way because of my name, for they do not know the One who sent me. 22If I had not come and spoken to them, they would not be guilty of sin. Now, however, they have no excuse for their sin. 23He who hates me hates my Father as well. 24If I had not done among them what no one else did, they would not be guilty of sin. But now they have seen these miracles, and yet they have hated both me and my Father. 25But this is

to fulfill what is written in their Law: 'They hated me without reason.'[u]

26"When the Counselor comes, whom I will send to you from the Father, the Spirit of truth who goes out from the Father, he will testify about me. 27And you also must testify, for you have been with me from the beginning.

16 "All this I have told you so that you will not go astray. 2They will put you out of the synagogue; in fact, a time is coming when anyone who kills you will think he is offering a service to God. 3They will do such things because they have not known the Father or me. 4I have told you this, so that when the time comes you will remember that I warned you. I did not tell you this at first because I was with you.

[t]20 John 13:16   [u]25 Psalms 35:19; 69:4

 Discovering the Word 1. If love is to characterize our relationship with other believers, hate will characterize our relationships with the world. What reasons does Jesus give for the world's hatred? 2. What does Jesus mean when he says that without his coming, his words and his miracles, the world "would not be guilty of sin" (15:22–25)? 3. In what specific ways will the Counselor and the disciples themselves continue the ministry begun by Jesus (15:26–27)? 4. What kind of treatment can the disciples expect from those who do not know Christ (16:1–4)?

Applying the Word 1. What kinds of persecution are more probable for us in our society? Explain. 2. If we as Christians are not persecuted in some way, what might that imply about our spiritual commitment? 3. How are you experiencing the world's hatred as a Christian?

Responding in Prayer Pray for those around the world who face persecution for their faith.

19 / *John 16:5–33*
Secrets of the Spirit

A LOVELY WOMAN in our church died not long ago. She knew for almost a year that, unless the Lord intervened, the cancer in her brain would kill her. That year gave her time of wonderful interaction with her husband and family. Her family had the opportunity to express their love for her, and the dying woman had the privilege of passing on her godly wisdom.

In John 16 Jesus knows that he will die in less than twenty-four hours. When his disciples are faced with that reality, Jesus responds to their concerns by talking about the coming Holy Spirit.

 Warming Up to God   Think about the people in your life who are important to you. What would you want to tell them if you knew that you had only a short time to live? Ask God to make you ready to hear what Jesus had to say in his last days.

 Read John 16:5–33.

⁵"Now I am going to him who sent me, yet none of you asks me, 'Where are you going?' ⁶Because I have said these things, you are filled with grief. ⁷But I tell you the truth: It is for your good that I am going away. Unless I go away, the Counselor will not come to you; but if I go, I will send him to you. ⁸When he comes, he will convict the world of guilt[v] in regard to sin and righteousness and judgment: ⁹in regard to sin, because men do not believe in me; ¹⁰in regard to righteousness, because I am going to the Father, where you can see me no longer; ¹¹and in regard to judgment, because the prince of this world now stands condemned.

¹²"I have much more to say to you, more than you can now bear. ¹³But when he, the Spirit of truth, comes, he will guide you into all truth. He will not speak on his own; he will speak only what he hears, and he will tell you what is yet to come. ¹⁴He will bring glory to me by taking from what is mine and making it known to you. ¹⁵All that belongs to the Father is mine. That is why I said the Spirit will take from what is mine and make it known to you.

¹⁶"In a little while you will see me no more, and then after a little while you will see me."

¹⁷Some of his disciples said to one another, "What does he mean by saying, 'In a little while you will see me no more, and then after a little while you will see me,' and 'Because I am going to the Father'?" ¹⁸They kept asking, "What does he mean by 'a little while'? We don't understand what he is saying."

¹⁹Jesus saw that they wanted to ask him about this, so he said to them, "Are you asking one another what I meant when I said, 'In a little while you will see me no more, and then after a little while you will see me'? ²⁰I tell you the truth, you will weep and mourn while the world rejoices. You will grieve, but your grief will turn to joy. ²¹A woman giving birth to a child has pain because her time has come; but when her baby is born she forgets the anguish because of her joy that a child is born into the world. ²²So with you: Now is your time of grief, but I will see you again and you will rejoice, and no one will take away your joy. ²³In that day you will no longer ask me anything. I tell you the truth, my Father will give you whatever you ask in my name. ²⁴Until now you have not asked for anything in my name. Ask and you will receive, and your joy will be complete.

²⁵"Though I have been speaking figuratively, a time is coming when I will no longer use this kind of language but will tell you plainly about my Father. ²⁶In that day you will ask in my name. I am not saying that I will ask the Father on your behalf. ²⁷No, the Father himself loves you because you have loved me and have believed that I came from God. ²⁸I came from the Father and entered the world; now I am leaving the world and going back to the Father."

²⁹Then Jesus' disciples said, "Now you are speaking clearly and without figures of speech. ³⁰Now we can see that you know all things and that you do not even need to have anyone ask you questions. This makes us believe that you came from God."

³¹"You believe at last!"[w] Jesus answered.

---

v8 Or will expose the guilt of the world   w31 Or "Do you now believe?"

32"But a time is coming, and has come, when you will be scattered, each to his own home. You will leave me all alone. Yet I am not alone, for my Father is with me.

33"I have told you these things, so that in me you may have peace. In this world you will have trouble. But take heart! I have overcome the world."

 Discovering the Word 1. Jesus said that it was for the disciples' good that he go away and that the Counselor come. Why was the Spirit's presence more profitable to the disciples than Jesus' presence? 2. What did Jesus say the Spirit's ministry would be toward the world (vv. 8–11)? 3. The Spirit's ministry is one of communication. What specific things did Jesus say the Spirit would communicate to the disciples (vv. 13–15)? 4. Jesus answers the questions the disciples ask in verses 17–18, not by giving them an explanation but by making them a promise (vv. 19–22). What was the promise? 5. Why would Jesus' promise bring them joy in the midst of their grief and confusion? 6. How would Jesus' assurance of the Father's love help the disciples in the days just ahead of them (vv. 25–33)?

 Applying the Word 1. How can this incident help us when our questions to the Lord seemingly go unanswered? 2. How do you respond to the promise in verses 23–24?

Responding in Prayer Give God the desires of your heart, knowing that he wants to make your joy complete.

---

20 / *John 17*
The Master's Final Prayer

THE APPROACH OF death has a way of bringing our priorities into focus. People who know death is imminent also know what is really important in life and who they really care about. In Jesus' final prayer with his disciples, he prays for himself, for them and for you! Every believer is on Jesus' mind as he faces the greatest trial of his life—the cross.

 Warming Up to God Spend some time reflecting on God's glory. To what extent is God's glory foremost in your mind on a daily basis? Explain.

 Read John 17.

---

17 After Jesus said this, he looked toward heaven and prayed:

"Father, the time has come. Glorify your Son, that your Son may glorify you. ²For you granted him authority over all people that he might give eternal life to all those you have given him. ³Now this is eternal life: that they may know you, the only true God, and Jesus Christ, whom you have sent. ⁴I have brought you glory on earth by completing the work you gave me to do. ⁵And now, Father, glorify me in your presence with the glory I had with you before the world began.

⁶"I have revealed youˣ to those whom you gave me out of the world. They were yours; you gave them to me and they have obeyed your word. ⁷Now they know that ev-

erything you have given me comes from you. ⁸For I gave them the words you gave me and they accepted them. They knew with certainty that I came from you, and they believed that you sent me. ⁹I pray for them. I am not praying for the world, but for those you have given me, for they are yours. ¹⁰All I have is yours, and all you have is mine. And glory has come to me through them. ¹¹I will remain in the world no longer, but they are still in the world, and I am coming to you. Holy Father, protect them by the power of your name—the name you gave me—so that they may be one as we are one. ¹²While I was with them, I protected them and kept them safe by that name you gave me. None

ˣ6 Greek *your name*; also in verse 26

has been lost except the one doomed to destruction so that Scripture would be fulfilled.

¹³"I am coming to you now, but I say these things while I am still in the world, so that they may have the full measure of my joy within them. ¹⁴I have given them your word and the world has hated them, for they are not of the world any more than I am of the world. ¹⁵My prayer is not that you take them out of the world but that you protect them from the evil one. ¹⁶They are not of the world, even as I am not of it. ¹⁷Sanctify^y them by the truth; your word is truth. ¹⁸As you sent me into the world, I have sent them into the world. ¹⁹For them I sanctify myself, that they too may be truly sanctified.

²⁰"My prayer is not for them alone. I pray also for those who will believe in me through their message, ²¹that all of them may be one, Father, just as you are in me and I am in you. May they also be in us so that the world may

believe that you have sent me. ²²I have given them the glory that you gave me, that they may be one as we are one: ²³I in them and you in me. May they be brought to complete unity to let the world know that you sent me and have loved them even as you have loved me.

²⁴"Father, I want those you have given me to be with me where I am, and to see my glory, the glory you have given me because you loved me before the creation of the world.

²⁵"Righteous Father, though the world does not know you, I know you, and they know that you have sent me. ²⁶I have made you known to them, and will continue to make you known in order that the love you have for me may be in them and that I myself may be in them."

^y17 Greek *hagiazo* (*set apart for sacred use* or *make holy*); also in verse 19

 Discovering the Word 1. Jesus makes only one request for himself—that the Father would glorify him so that he might glorify the Father. In what way would each one glorify the other (vv. 1–5)? Why do you think that was so important to Jesus? 2. According to verses 6–19, what specific ministries did Jesus have toward his disciples? 3. Twice Jesus asked the Father to protect his disciples from the evil one (vv. 11, 15). Why would that protection have been so important in Jesus' mind as he faced the cross? 4. Jesus prayed that those who believe in him would be one "so that the world may believe that you have sent me" (vv. 21, 23)? Why is our unity a powerful argument for the reality of Jesus?

Applying the Word 1. Jesus also asked the Father to sanctify his disciples through his word (v. 17). How can we allow God's Word to have that kind of effect on our lives? 2. Jesus obviously prayed this prayer out loud to bring comfort and assurance to his disciples. In what particular ways do Jesus' words encourage or assure you?

Responding in Prayer Ask God to bring unity to your church or fellowship.

---

21 / *John 18:1–27*
"Jesus, You're Under Arrest!"

MOST OF US would hate the thought of being arrested and brought to trial. If we were guilty of a crime, being arrested would be humiliating. But if we were innocent, it would be devastating. Yet in what should have been a demeaning experience for Jesus, we see again his majesty and glory. Jesus uses an experience of attack, betrayal and abandonment to demonstrate his confident trust in the Father. His calm assurance will help us face life's hurts and injustices with the same trust in the same Father.

 Warming Up to God Think about a time when you realized you had committed a deep sin. How did you feel when you took it before Christ? Thank him for his grace to you then and now.

Read John 18:1–27.

18

When he had finished praying, Jesus left with his disciples and crossed the Kidron Valley. On the other side there was an olive grove, and he and his disciples went into it.

²Now Judas, who betrayed him, knew the place, because Jesus had often met there with his disciples. ³So Judas came to the grove, guiding a detachment of soldiers and some officials from the chief priests and Pharisees. They were carrying torches, lanterns and weapons.

⁴Jesus, knowing all that was going to happen to him, went out and asked them, "Who is it you want?"

⁵"Jesus of Nazareth," they replied.

"I am he," Jesus said. (And Judas the traitor was standing there with them.) ⁶When Jesus said, "I am he," they drew back and fell to the ground.

⁷Again he asked them, "Who is it you want?"

And they said, "Jesus of Nazareth."

⁸"I told you that I am he," Jesus answered. "If you are looking for me, then let these men go." ⁹This happened so that the words he had spoken would be fulfilled: "I have not lost one of those you gave me."ᶻ

¹⁰Then Simon Peter, who had a sword, drew it and struck the high priest's servant, cutting off his right ear. (The servant's name was Malchus.) ¹¹Jesus commanded Peter, "Put your sword away! Shall I not drink the cup the Father has given me?"

¹²Then the detachment of soldiers with its commander and the Jewish officials arrested Jesus. They bound him ¹³and brought him first to Annas, who was the father-in-law of Caiaphas, the high priest that year. ¹⁴Caiaphas was the one who had advised the Jews that it would be good if one man died for the people.

¹⁵Simon Peter and another disciple were following Jesus. Because this disciple was known to the high priest, he went with Jesus into the high priest's courtyard, ¹⁶but Peter had to wait outside at the door. The other disciple, who was known to the high priest, came back, spoke to the girl on duty there and brought Peter in.

¹⁷"You are not one of his disciples, are you?" the girl at the door asked Peter.

He replied, "I am not."

¹⁸It was cold, and the servants and officials stood around a fire they had made to keep warm. Peter also was standing with them, warming himself.

¹⁹Meanwhile, the high priest questioned Jesus about his disciples and his teaching.

²⁰"I have spoken openly to the world," Jesus replied. "I always taught in synagogues or at the temple, where all the Jews come together. I said nothing in secret. ²¹Why question me? Ask those who heard me. Surely they know what I said."

²²When Jesus said this, one of the officials nearby struck him in the face. "Is this the way you answer the high priest?" he demanded.

²³"If I said something wrong," Jesus replied, "testify as to what is wrong. But if I spoke the truth, why did you strike me?" ²⁴Then Annas sent him, still bound, to Caiaphas the high priest.ᵃ

²⁵As Simon Peter stood warming himself, he was asked, "You are not one of his disciples, are you?"

He denied it, saying, "I am not."

²⁶One of the high priest's servants, a relative of the man whose ear Peter had cut off, challenged him, "Didn't I see you with him in the olive grove?" ²⁷Again Peter denied it, and at that moment a rooster began to crow.

ᶻ9 John 6:39   ᵃ24 Or (Now Annas had sent him, still bound, to Caiaphas the high priest.)

Discovering the Word 1. Why would Jesus go to a place where Judas knew he might be found (vv. 1–3)? 2. When the soldiers say they are seeking Jesus of Nazareth, Jesus replies, "I am he" (literally, "I am"; v. 5). How would you explain the reaction of the soldiers (v. 6)? 3. What insight do Peter's action and Jesus' rebuke (v. 11) give you about our attempts at times to "help God out" in our own strength and wisdom? 4. Think back to the deepest sin of your life. How does a look at your own sin change your attitude toward Peter's denial of Jesus? 5. What specific events in this passage display (a) Jesus' courage, (b) his power and (c) his obedience to the Father?

 Applying the Word 1. What can we learn from Peter's failure about being ready to stand against the world's challenges? 2. How will this study change the way you will face a time of testing in your own life?

Responding in Prayer Ask God to make you ready to face difficulties with grace.

22 / *John 18:28—19:16*
Pilate on Trial

"CHRIST KILLERS!" THE words made my stomach tighten. Someone had spray-painted the words and a series of swastikas on the Jewish synagogue in our city. Anti-Semitism had raised its ugly head again.

The New Testament does blame the Jewish leaders for condemning Jesus to die. But they weren't acting alone. The Roman governor, Pontius Pilate, also condemned Jesus to die. There is a sense, too, in which we killed Jesus. He died for *our* sins. The most amazing answer to the question of who killed Jesus is that no one did! Jesus said, "No one takes my life from me. I lay it down of my own choice."

 Warming Up to God What temptation to compromise your Christian faith or witness are you facing? Ask the One who has faced deep trials to give you strength.

 Read John 18:28—19:16.

²⁸Then the Jews led Jesus from Caiaphas to the palace of the Roman governor. By now it was early morning, and to avoid ceremonial uncleanness the Jews did not enter the palace; they wanted to be able to eat the Passover. ²⁹So Pilate came out to them and asked, "What charges are you bringing against this man?"

³⁰"If he were not a criminal," they replied, "we would not have handed him over to you."

³¹Pilate said, "Take him yourselves and judge him by your own law."

"But we have no right to execute anyone," the Jews objected. ³²This happened so that the words Jesus had spoken indicating the kind of death he was going to die would be fulfilled.

³³Pilate then went back inside the palace, summoned Jesus and asked him, "Are you the king of the Jews?"

³⁴"Is that your own idea," Jesus asked, "or did others talk to you about me?"

³⁵"Am I a Jew?" Pilate replied. "It was your people and your chief priests who handed you over to me. What is it you have done?"

³⁶Jesus said, "My kingdom is not of this world. If it were, my servants would fight to prevent my arrest by the Jews. But now my kingdom is from another place."

³⁷"You are a king, then!" said Pilate.

Jesus answered, "You are right in saying I am a king. In fact, for this reason I was born, and for this I came into the world, to testify to the truth. Everyone on the side of truth listens to me."

³⁸"What is truth?" Pilate asked. With this he went out again to the Jews and said, "I find no basis for a charge against him. ³⁹But it is your custom for me to release to you one prisoner at the time of the Passover. Do you want me to release 'the king of the Jews'?"

⁴⁰They shouted back, "No, not him! Give us Barabbas!" Now Barabbas had taken part in a rebellion.

19 Then Pilate took Jesus and had him flogged. ²The soldiers twisted together a crown of thorns and put it on his head. They clothed him in a purple robe ³and went up to him again and again, saying, "Hail, king of the Jews!" And they struck him in the face.

⁴Once more Pilate came out and said to the Jews, "Look, I am bringing him out to you to let you know that I find no basis for a charge against him." ⁵When Jesus came out wearing the crown of thorns and the purple robe, Pilate said to them, "Here is the man!"

⁶As soon as the chief priests and their officials saw him, they shouted, "Crucify! Crucify!"

But Pilate answered, "You take him and crucify him. As for me, I find no basis for a charge against him."

⁷The Jews insisted, "We have a law, and according to that law he must die, because he claimed to be the Son of God."

⁸When Pilate heard this, he was even more afraid, ⁹and he went back inside the palace.

"Where do you come from?" he asked Jesus, but Jesus gave him no answer. 10"Do you refuse to speak to me?" Pilate said. "Don't you realize I have power either to free you or to crucify you?"

11Jesus answered, "You would have no power over me if it were not given to you from above. Therefore the one who handed me over to you is guilty of a greater sin."

12From then on, Pilate tried to set Jesus free, but the Jews kept shouting, "If you let this man go, you are no friend of Caesar. Anyone who claims to be a king opposes Caesar."

13When Pilate heard this, he brought Jesus out and sat down on the judge's seat at a place known as the Stone Pavement (which in Aramaic is Gabbatha). 14It was the day of Preparation of Passover Week, about the sixth hour.

"Here is your king," Pilate said to the Jews. 15But they shouted, "Take him away! Take him away! Crucify him!"

"Shall I crucify your king?" Pilate asked.

"We have no king but Caesar," the chief priests answered.

16Finally Pilate handed him over to them to be crucified.

Discovering the Word   1. A Roman trial included four basic elements: the accusation (18:29–31), the interrogation (search for evidence) (18:32–35), the defense (18:36–37) and the verdict (18:38). What events or statements from the text are included in each?   2. Pilate obviously was trying to release Jesus. What specific attempts did he make (18:39; 19:4, 6, 10, 12, 15)?   3. The Jews' true charge against Jesus comes out in verse 7—"He claimed to be the Son of God." Why do you think Pilate reacted to that statement as he did (vv. 8–9)?   4. Why didn't Jesus say more to Pilate (vv. 9–11)? Shouldn't he have defended himself more vigorously?   5. What can you conclude about Pilate's character after reading this passage? What kind of man was he?

Applying the Word   1. How can you respond appropriately to Christ's grace to you?   2. What does this passage tell you about how you should respond when you are treated unjustly?

Responding in Prayer   Ask God to help you follow his example of grace when you are under pressure.

---

23 / John 19:17–42
Obedient to Death

THERE IS NOTHING pleasant or attractive about an execution. The only one I've ever seen was in a televised news report from Vietnam. A captured soldier was shot. It left a knot in my stomach for days.

In Jesus' day execution was designed to be public and painful. The account of the crucifixion is not easy to read. You may be tempted to think that Jesus' death was a cruel mistake. It wasn't. Jesus' life was not taken from him; he laid it down willingly. It was part of his plan—a plan that included you and me. His cross was in a very real sense our cross.

Warming Up to God   When you think about death, what feelings and thoughts come to mind?

Read John 19:17–42.

So the soldiers took charge of Jesus. 17Carrying his own cross, he went out to the place of the Skull (which in Aramaic is called Golgotha). 18Here they crucified him, and with him two others—one on each side and Jesus in the middle.

19Pilate had a notice prepared and fastened to the cross. It read: JESUS OF NAZARETH, THE KING OF THE JEWS. 20Many of the Jews read this sign, for the place where Jesus was crucified was near the city, and the sign was written in Aramaic, Latin and Greek. 21The chief priests of the Jews protested to Pilate, "Do not write 'The King of the Jews,' but that this man claimed to be king of the Jews."

²²Pilate answered, "What I have written, I have written."

²³When the soldiers crucified Jesus, they took his clothes, dividing them into four shares, one for each of them, with the undergarment remaining. This garment was seamless, woven in one piece from top to bottom.

²⁴"Let's not tear it," they said to one another. "Let's decide by lot who will get it."

This happened that the scripture might be fulfilled which said,

"They divided my garments among them
    and cast lots for my clothing."[b]

So this is what the soldiers did.

²⁵Near the cross of Jesus stood his mother, his mother's sister, Mary the wife of Clopas, and Mary Magdalene. ²⁶When Jesus saw his mother there, and the disciple whom he loved standing nearby, he said to his mother, "Dear woman, here is your son," ²⁷and to the disciple, "Here is your mother." From that time on, this disciple took her into his home.

²⁸Later, knowing that all was now completed, and so that the Scripture would be fulfilled, Jesus said, "I am thirsty." ²⁹A jar of wine vinegar was there, so they soaked a sponge in it, put the sponge on a stalk of the hyssop plant, and lifted it to Jesus' lips. ³⁰When he had received the drink, Jesus said, "It is finished." With that, he bowed his head and gave up his spirit.

³¹Now it was the day of Preparation, and the next day was to be a special Sabbath. Because the Jews did not want the bodies left on the crosses during the Sabbath, they asked Pilate to have the legs broken and the bodies taken down. ³²The soldiers therefore came and broke the legs of the first man who had been crucified with Jesus, and then those of the other. ³³But when they came to Jesus and found that he was already dead, they did not break his legs. ³⁴Instead, one of the soldiers pierced Jesus' side with a spear, bringing a sudden flow of blood and water. ³⁵The man who saw it has given testimony, and his testimony is true. He knows that he tells the truth, and he testifies so that you also may believe. ³⁶These things happened so that the scripture would be fulfilled: "Not one of his bones will be broken,"[c] ³⁷and, as another scripture says, "They will look on the one they have pierced."[d]

³⁸Later, Joseph of Arimathea asked Pilate for the body of Jesus. Now Joseph was a disciple of Jesus, but secretly because he feared the Jews. With Pilate's permission, he came and took the body away. ³⁹He was accompanied by Nicodemus, the man who earlier had visited Jesus at night. Nicodemus brought a mixture of myrrh and aloes, about seventy-five pounds.[e] ⁴⁰Taking Jesus' body, the two of them wrapped it, with the spices, in strips of linen. This was in accordance with Jewish burial customs. ⁴¹At the place where Jesus was crucified, there was a garden, and in the garden a new tomb, in which no one had ever been laid. ⁴²Because it was the Jewish day of Preparation and since the tomb was nearby, they laid Jesus there.

[b]24 Psalm 22:18   [c]36 Exodus 12:46; Num. 9:12; Psalm 34:20
[d]37 Zech. 12:10   [e]39 Greek *a hundred litrai* (about 34 kilograms)

Discovering the Word   1. Three groups were involved in Jesus' death—the soldiers, the Jewish leaders and Pilate. How would you characterize each one's attitude toward Jesus? In what ways do their attitudes toward Jesus parallel those of men and women today?   2. How is Jesus' tender care for Mary evident even while he is dying (vv. 26–27)?   3. What was the significance of Jesus' cry "It is finished" (v. 30; see Jn 17:4)?   4. What evidence does John give that Jesus really died?   5. Why was it so important for John to establish the certainty of Jesus' death?

Applying the Word   1. The disciples are not mentioned at the crucifixion; they were probably not there. When it comes to public identification with Jesus, under what circumstances are you tempted to respond in the same way?   2. What aspect of Jesus' death has made the deepest impression on you, and why?

  Responding in Prayer   Thank God for providing salvation to you through Christ's death.

24 / John 20
The Son Is Up!

THE STORY CIRCULATED for days in the hospital where my brother worked. An orderly was told to take a body to the morgue. Simply out of habit, the orderly felt the man's wrist for a pulse. When he realized his mistake, the orderly quickly dropped the arm, but not before his sensitive fingers told him something his mind struggled to believe. There was a pulse! The doctors were called, and the man revived.

That story may or may not be true. But I know of one account of a man coming back to life that is true. The man lived for years after the event. In fact, he is still alive.

 Warming Up to God   Imagine being with Joseph of Arimathea and Nicodemus preparing Jesus' body for burial. What thoughts and feelings would have gone through your mind?

 Read John 20.

20 Early on the first day of the week, while it was still dark, Mary Magdalene went to the tomb and saw that the stone had been removed from the entrance. ²So she came running to Simon Peter and the other disciple, the one Jesus loved, and said, "They have taken the Lord out of the tomb, and we don't know where they have put him!"

³So Peter and the other disciple started for the tomb. ⁴Both were running, but the other disciple outran Peter and reached the tomb first. ⁵He bent over and looked in at the strips of linen lying there but did not go in. ⁶Then Simon Peter, who was behind him, arrived and went into the tomb. He saw the strips of linen lying there, ⁷as well as the burial cloth that had been around Jesus' head. The cloth was folded up by itself, separate from the linen. ⁸Finally the other disciple, who had reached the tomb first, also went inside. He saw and believed. ⁹(They still did not understand from Scripture that Jesus had to rise from the dead.)

¹⁰Then the disciples went back to their homes, ¹¹but Mary stood outside the tomb crying. As she wept, she bent over to look into the tomb ¹²and saw two angels in white, seated where Jesus' body had been, one at the head and the other at the foot.

¹³They asked her, "Woman, why are you crying?"

"They have taken my Lord away," she said, "and I don't know where they have put him." ¹⁴At this, she turned around and saw Jesus standing there, but she did not realize that it was Jesus.

¹⁵"Woman," he said, "why are you crying? Who is it you are looking for?"

Thinking he was the gardener, she said, "Sir, if you have carried him away, tell me where you have put him, and I will get him."

¹⁶Jesus said to her, "Mary."

She turned toward him and cried out in Aramaic, "Rabboni!" (which means Teacher).

¹⁷Jesus said, "Do not hold on to me, for I have not yet returned to the Father. Go instead to my brothers and tell them, 'I am returning to my Father and your Father, to my God and your God.' "

¹⁸Mary Magdalene went to the disciples with the news: "I have seen the Lord!" And she told them that he had said these things to her.

¹⁹On the evening of that first day of the week, when the disciples were together, with the doors locked for fear of the Jews, Jesus came and stood among them and said, "Peace be with you!" ²⁰After he said this, he showed them his hands and side. The disciples were overjoyed when they saw the Lord.

²¹Again Jesus said, "Peace be with you! As the Father has sent me, I am sending you." ²²And with that he breathed on them and said, "Receive the Holy Spirit. ²³If you forgive anyone his sins, they are forgiven; if you do not forgive them, they are not forgiven."

²⁴Now Thomas (called Didymus), one of the Twelve, was not with the disciples when Jesus came. ²⁵So the other disciples told him, "We have seen the Lord!"

But he said to them, "Unless I see the nail marks in his hands and put my finger where the nails were, and put my hand into his side, I will not believe it."

²⁶A week later his disciples were in the house again, and Thomas was with them. Though the

doors were locked, Jesus came and stood among them and said, "Peace be with you!" ²⁷Then he said to Thomas, "Put your finger here; see my hands. Reach out your hand and put it into my side. Stop doubting and believe."

²⁸Thomas said to him, "My Lord and my God!"

²⁹Then Jesus told him, "Because you have seen me, you have believed; blessed are those who have not seen and yet have believed."

³⁰Jesus did many other miraculous signs in the presence of his disciples, which are not recorded in this book. ³¹But these are written that you may believe that Jesus is the Christ, the Son of God, and that by believing you may have life in his name.

ʃ31 Some manuscripts may continue to

 Discovering the Word 1. John records three witnesses to the empty tomb: Mary Magdalene, Peter and "the other disciple" (John himself). What important details do we learn from each one (vv. 1–9)? 2. John also records three appearances of the risen Christ: to Mary, to his disciples and to Thomas. Why do you think Mary doesn't immediately recognize Jesus (vv. 10–15)? 3. After she does recognize him, what impresses you most about their encounter (vv. 16–18)? 4. When Jesus appears to his disciples, what specific gifts and promises does he give them (vv. 19–23)? 5. Finally, Jesus appears to Thomas (vv. 24–29). How does Thomas's attitude—both before and after Jesus appears to him—add credibility to the resurrection?

Applying the Word 1. What do you learn from Jesus' encounter with Thomas about dealing with people who have doubts about Christianity? 2. Who could you help to understand and believe the claims of Christ? 3. John tells us why he has written his Gospel in verses 30–31. Of all the "miraculous signs" John has included, which have been most convincing to you? Why?

Responding in Prayer Praise God for what he has done in Christ.

---

25 / *John 21*
A Walk with a Resurrected Man

MOST OF US find it easier to forgive than to forget. We may be ready to forgive someone who has hurt us deeply, but we have a hard time trusting that person again. Peter failed Jesus miserably. He promised to give up his life if necessary to protect Jesus, but denied him a few hours later. Peter knew Jesus had forgiven him. But would Jesus still trust him? Could Jesus still use him to bring glory to God? Will Christ still use us after we've failed?

 Warming Up to God How do you feel when someone you have hurt refuses to forgive you?

 Read John 21.

---

21 Afterward Jesus appeared again to his disciples, by the Sea of Tiberias.ᵍ It happened this way: ²Simon Peter, Thomas (called Didymus), Nathanael from Cana in Galilee, the sons of Zebedee, and two other disciples were together. ³"I'm going out to fish," Simon Peter told them, and they said, "We'll go with you." So they went out and got into the boat, but that night they caught nothing.

⁴Early in the morning, Jesus stood on the shore, but the disciples did not realize that it was Jesus.

⁵He called out to them, "Friends, haven't you any fish?"

"No," they answered.

⁶He said, "Throw your net on the right side of the boat and you will find some." When they did, they were unable to haul the net in because of the large number of fish.

⁷Then the disciple whom Jesus loved said to

81 That is, Sea of Galilee

Peter, "It is the Lord!" As soon as Simon Peter heard him say, "It is the Lord," he wrapped his outer garment around him (for he had taken it off) and jumped into the water. 8The other disciples followed in the boat, towing the net full of fish, for they were not far from shore, about a hundred yards.ʰ 9When they landed, they saw a fire of burning coals there with fish on it, and some bread.

10Jesus said to them, "Bring some of the fish you have just caught."

11Simon Peter climbed aboard and dragged the net ashore. It was full of large fish, 153, but even with so many the net was not torn. 12Jesus said to them, "Come and have breakfast." None of the disciples dared ask him, "Who are you?" They knew it was the Lord. 13Jesus came, took the bread and gave it to them, and did the same with the fish. 14This was now the third time Jesus appeared to his disciples after he was raised from the dead.

15When they had finished eating, Jesus said to Simon Peter, "Simon son of John, do you truly love me more than these?"

"Yes, Lord," he said, "you know that I love you."

Jesus said, "Feed my lambs."

16Again Jesus said, "Simon son of John, do you truly love me?"

He answered, "Yes, Lord, you know that I love you."

Jesus said, "Take care of my sheep."

17The third time he said to him, "Simon son of John, do you love me?"

Peter was hurt because Jesus asked him the third time, "Do you love me?" He said, "Lord, you know all things; you know that I love you."

Jesus said, "Feed my sheep. 18I tell you the truth, when you were younger you dressed yourself and went where you wanted; but when you are old you will stretch out your hands, and someone else will dress you and lead you where you do not want to go." 19Jesus said this to indicate the kind of death by which Peter would glorify God. Then he said to him, "Follow me!"

20Peter turned and saw that the disciple whom Jesus loved was following them. (This was the one who had leaned back against Jesus at the supper and had said, "Lord, who is going to betray you?") 21When Peter saw him, he asked, "Lord, what about him?"

22Jesus answered, "If I want him to remain alive until I return, what is that to you? You must follow me." 23Because of this, the rumor spread among the brothers that this disciple would not die. But Jesus did not say that he would not die; he only said, "If I want him to remain alive until I return, what is that to you?"

24This is the disciple who testifies to these things and who wrote them down. We know that his testimony is true.

25Jesus did many other things as well. If every one of them were written down, I suppose that even the whole world would not have room for the books that would be written.

ʰ8 Greek *about two hundred cubits* (about 90 meters)

 Discovering the Word 1. What was Jesus trying to show the disciples by allowing them to catch such a large number of fish (vv. 4–6; see Lk 5:4–11)? 2. When Peter hears that "it is the Lord" (vv. 7–8), he jumps into the water and begins swimming ahead of the boat. What does this reveal about Peter and his relationship with Jesus? 3. What subtle differences do you notice in Jesus' three questions and Peter's responses (vv. 15–17)? 4. Why do you think Jesus chose this particular time to predict the kind of death Peter would die (vv. 18–19)? 5. What does Jesus' rebuke to Peter (v. 22) reveal about the danger of comparing ourselves with other Christians?

Applying the Word 1. What can we learn from this passage about the steps involved in restoring a Christian who has sinned? 2. How does it help to know that you can still serve and glorify God no matter what your past failures have been?

Responding in Prayer Respond to God with your heart and life for what you have learned about Jesus in your study of John.

Acts

The book of Acts should come with a warning label reading, "If you are open to God, this book will call you to new life."

Acts is an extraordinary work. In essence, it is the story of transformed lives—and the difference these lives made in the world.

Just before Acts begins, we see the disciples behind closed doors wallowing in the mire of their fear, self-doubt and personal shame. Apart from their master, they were a pathetic group indeed (Lk 24:11; Jn 20:19). However, by the second chapter of Acts, the same men who abandoned Jesus at Gethsemane have become irrepressible dynamos, preaching with utter conviction—and at great personal risk—"the mighty acts of God."

What changed them? And what impact did they make upon their generation and all subsequent ones? *This* is the story of Acts.

Acts is an important book for us today because it confirms that the power which transformed the disciples' lives is the same power that can transform our lives today! That power is, of course, God himself—coming to us through the Holy Spirit.

There are many benefits to studying Acts:

☐ *Acts serves as a distant mirror.* We will see the dynamics of the earliest church, the nature of their fellowship, the intensity of their prayer life and their out-and-out zeal to declare the saving gospel of Jesus Christ. Through this example, our own situation will be called into question. What does it mean to be the church today—and what are we to be doing?

☐ *Acts emphasizes the primary task of the church—evangelization.* Speaking the gospel is only part of the task. It is the formative process that we see in these earliest communities. In Acts we see the entire process of calling, healing, empowering and sending people forth to love and obey Jesus Christ. Acts will challenge us to a holistic-community spirituality that can renew our churches today.

☐ *Acts calls us to a vital experience with the Holy Spirit.* Jesus promised power to the disciples *after* the Holy Spirit came upon them. And the book of Acts reveals the Holy Spirit as the driving force behind all meaningful ministry in Jesus' name. Where do we look for spiritual power today? Education? Work? Religious heritage? Acts calls us to a Spirit-filled life.

☐ *Acts forges a new sense of identity.* The disciples gradually realized they were no longer Jews (at least from the confessional and ceremonial points of view). They slowly began to understand

that they were part of that new community of the Spirit which was prophesied in the Hebrew Scriptures. And they saw the need to call all people—Jews and Gentiles—to repentance and fellowship with this new community—the church. Baptism in the name of the Father, the Son and the Holy Spirit, and the Lord's Supper became the outward signs of the inward grace. The emphasis is on relationships.

The explosive power of this living document will touch you. As you work through these quiet times, may you experience the calling, healing, empowering and sending dynamic of the Holy Spirit.

Outline

Part 1: God's Power in Jerusalem and Judea

1/ Acts 1 —————————————— You Will Be My Witnesses

2/ Acts 2 —————————————— Receiving the Power

3/ Acts 3 —————————————— Healing Power

4/ Acts 4:1–31 ————————————— Called into Question

5/ Acts 4:32—5:16 ———————————— Oneness of Heart

6/ Acts 5:17—6:7 ————————————— Persecution and Expansion

7/ Acts 6:8—7:60 ————————————— Stephen, Full of Spirit and Wisdom

8/ Acts 8 —————————————— The Power of Suffering

9/ Acts 9:1–31 ————————————— Saul's Conversion

10/ Acts 9:32—10:48 ———————————— Salvation for Every Nation

11/ Acts 11 —————————————— The First Jewish-Gentile Church

12/ Acts 12 —————————————— Miraculous Escape

Part 2: God's Power at the Ends of the Earth

13/ Acts 13—14 ————————————— Paul's First Missionary Journey

14/ Acts 15 —————————————— Conflict in the Church

15/ Acts 16 —————————————— What Must I Do?

16/ Acts 17 —————————————— An Unknown God

17/ Acts 18 —————————————— Companions in Ministry

18/ Acts 19:1—20:12 ———————————— In the Name of Jesus

19/ Acts 20:13–38 ———————————— Paul's Farewell

20/ Acts 21:1—22:21 ———————————— Facing Opposition

21/ Acts 22:22—23:35 ——————————— God at Work

22/ Acts 24:1—25:12 ———————————— Falsely Accused

23/ Acts 25:13—26:32 ——————————— Testimony Before Agrippa

24/ Acts 27—28 ————————————— Paul in Rome!

[Handwritten note:] Feeling overwhelmed! God gave them the strength & power to accomplish this task. Trust God the help me thy anything that overwhelms me. The power to overcome is in the Holy Spirit.

1 / *Acts 1*
You Will Be My Witnesses

I REMEMBER TELLING a friend, "If I were dying, what I would most need would be confidence that all I had believed about Jesus was true. I would want you to read Scripture to me, pray with me, and talk to me about Jesus and heaven." This confidence is what I need most not only when I am dying, but also when I am living.

During the days between his resurrection and ascension, Jesus built the confidence of his disciples. He demonstrated and spoke truth about himself. And then he left them with a clearly defined task and the promise of the power to carry out that task. Thus, Luke was able to write with confidence to Theophilus about Jesus.

 Warming Up to God   Have you had days when you did not feel confident, but fearful? Let God encourage you this day with the power and strength contained in his Word.

 Read Acts 1.

In my former book, Theophilus, I wrote about all that Jesus began to do and to teach ²until the day he was taken up to heaven, after giving instructions through the Holy Spirit to the apostles he had chosen. ³After his suffering, he showed himself to these men and gave many convincing proofs that he was alive. He appeared to them over a period of forty days and spoke about the kingdom of God. ⁴On one occasion, while he was eating with them, he gave them this command: "Do not leave Jerusalem, but wait for the gift my Father promised, which you have heard me speak about. ⁵For John baptized with*ᵃ* water, but in a few days you will be baptized with the Holy Spirit."

⁶So when they met together, they asked him, "Lord, are you at this time going to restore the kingdom to Israel?"

⁷He said to them: "It is not for you to know the times or dates the Father has set by his own authority. ⁸But you will receive power when the Holy Spirit comes on you; and you will be my witnesses in Jerusalem, and in all Judea and Samaria, and to the ends of the earth."

⁹After he said this, he was taken up before their very eyes, and a cloud hid him from their sight.

¹⁰They were looking intently up into the sky as he was going, when suddenly two men dressed in white stood beside them. ¹¹"Men of Galilee," they said, "why do you stand here looking into the sky? This same Jesus, who has been taken from you into heaven, will come back in the same way you have seen him go into heaven."

¹²Then they returned to Jerusalem from the hill called the Mount of Olives, a Sabbath day's walk*ᵇ* from the city. ¹³When they arrived, they went upstairs to the room where they were staying. Those present were Peter, John, James and Andrew; Philip and Thomas, Bartholomew and Matthew; James son of Alphaeus and Simon the Zealot, and Judas son of James. ¹⁴They all joined together constantly in prayer, along with the women and Mary the mother of Jesus, and with his brothers.

¹⁵In those days Peter stood up among the believers*ᶜ* (a group numbering about a hundred and twenty) ¹⁶and said, "Brothers, the Scripture had to be fulfilled which the Holy Spirit spoke long ago through the mouth of David concerning Judas, who served as guide for those who arrested Jesus— ¹⁷he was one of our number and shared in this ministry."

¹⁸(With the reward he got for his wickedness, Judas bought a field; there he fell headlong, his body burst open and all his intestines spilled out. ¹⁹Everyone in Jerusalem heard about this, so they called that field in their language Akeldama, that is, Field of Blood.)

²⁰"For," said Peter, "it is written in the book of Psalms,

" 'May his place be deserted;
    let there be no one to dwell in it,'*ᵈ*

and,

" 'May another take his place of leadership.'*ᵉ*

²¹Therefore it is necessary to choose one of the men who have been with us the whole time the Lord Jesus went in and out among us, ²²beginning from John's baptism to the time when Jesus

ᵃ5 Or in   ᵇ12 That is, about 3/4 mile (about 1,100 meters)
ᶜ15 Greek brothers   ᵈ20 Psalm 69:25   ᵉ20 Psalm 109:8

was taken up from us. For one of these must become a witness with us of his resurrection."

23So they proposed two men: Joseph called Barsabbas (also known as Justus) and Matthias. 24Then they prayed, "Lord, you know everyone's heart. Show us which of these two you have chosen 25to take over this apostolic ministry, which Judas left to go where he belongs." 26Then they cast lots, and the lot fell to Matthias; so he was added to the eleven apostles.

 Discovering the Word 1. What did Luke, the author of Acts, report to Theophilus about Jesus' last days on earth (vv. 1–11)? 2. Put yourself in the shoes of the apostles. How would you feel if you were the first to be given the task described in verse 8? 3. How are we equipped for this task, according to the passage? 4. How did the disciples respond to all that they had seen and heard (vv. 12–26)? 5. Peter goes to Scripture immediately when he speaks. How do these words of David affect their confidence as well as give them direction (v. 20)?

Applying the Word 1. When has your faith in Jesus Christ been encouraged by the words of others? 2. How is your hope and confidence in Jesus affected by what you learn about him in the passage? 3. How are you affected when you pray with other believers—especially as you consider your part in God's mission for the church (v. 14)?

Responding in Prayer Thank God for giving you a task to carry out, and tell him about the fears and joys you feel as his servant.

2 / Acts 2
Receiving the Power

AT MY SCHOOL a group of upperclassmen wanted to communicate the message of Jesus to the incoming class of freshmen. They realized that there was only one source to accomplish this task—the power of the Holy Spirit. So they decided to pray for all the new students by name weeks before they arrived on campus. As a result, many who did not know Jesus when they arrived graduated as maturing Christians.

 Warming Up to God The Holy Spirit, although at times we do not sense him, is always there to help us. Let him quiet you now and open your heart to what he wants to tell you about himself.

 Read Acts 2.

2 When the day of Pentecost came, they were all together in one place. 2Suddenly a sound like the blowing of a violent wind came from heaven and filled the whole house where they were sitting. 3They saw what seemed to be tongues of fire that separated and came to rest on each of them. 4All of them were filled with the Holy Spirit and began to speak in other tongues*f* as the Spirit enabled them.

5Now there were staying in Jerusalem Godfearing Jews from every nation under heaven. 6When they heard this sound, a crowd came together in bewilderment, because each one heard them speaking in his own language. 7Utterly amazed, they asked: "Are not all these men who are speaking Galileans? 8Then how is it that each

of us hears them in his own native language? 9Parthians, Medes and Elamites; residents of Mesopotamia, Judea and Cappadocia, Pontus and Asia, 10Phrygia and Pamphylia, Egypt and the parts of Libya near Cyrene; visitors from Rome 11(both Jews and converts to Judaism); Cretans and Arabs—we hear them declaring the wonders of God in our own tongues!" 12Amazed and perplexed, they asked one another, "What does this mean?"

13Some, however, made fun of them and said, "They have had too much wine.*g*"

14Then Peter stood up with the Eleven, raised his voice and addressed the crowd: "Fellow Jews and all of you who live in Jerusalem, let me ex-

f4 Or languages; also in verse 11   *g13* Or sweet wine

plain this to you; listen carefully to what I say. ¹⁵These men are not drunk, as you suppose. It's only nine in the morning! ¹⁶No, this is what was spoken by the prophet Joel:

¹⁷" 'In the last days, God says,
    I will pour out my Spirit on all people.
  Your sons and daughters will prophesy,
    your young men will see visions,
    your old men will dream dreams.
¹⁸Even on my servants, both men and women,
    I will pour out my Spirit in those days,
    and they will prophesy.
¹⁹I will show wonders in the heaven above
    and signs on the earth below,
    blood and fire and billows of smoke.
²⁰The sun will be turned to darkness
    and the moon to blood
    before the coming of the great and glorious
        day of the Lord.
²¹And everyone who calls
    on the name of the Lord will be saved.'ʰ

²²"Men of Israel, listen to this: Jesus of Nazareth was a man accredited by God to you by miracles, wonders and signs, which God did among you through him, as you yourselves know. ²³This man was handed over to you by God's set purpose and foreknowledge; and you, with the help of wicked men,ⁱ put him to death by nailing him to the cross. ²⁴But God raised him from the dead, freeing him from the agony of death, because it was impossible for death to keep its hold on him. ²⁵David said about him:

" 'I saw the Lord always before me.
    Because he is at my right hand,
    I will not be shaken.
²⁶Therefore my heart is glad and my tongue
        rejoices;
    my body also will live in hope,
²⁷because you will not abandon me to the
        grave,
    nor will you let your Holy One see decay.
²⁸You have made known to me the paths of life;
    you will fill me with joy in your
        presence.'ʲ

²⁹"Brothers, I can tell you confidently that the patriarch David died and was buried, and his tomb is here to this day. ³⁰But he was a prophet and knew that God had promised him on oath

that he would place one of his descendants on his throne. ³¹Seeing what was ahead, he spoke of the resurrection of the Christ,ᵏ that he was not abandoned to the grave, nor did his body see decay. ³²God has raised this Jesus to life, and we are all witnesses of the fact. ³³Exalted to the right hand of God, he has received from the Father the promised Holy Spirit and has poured out what you now see and hear. ³⁴For David did not ascend to heaven, and yet he said,

" 'The Lord said to my Lord:
    "Sit at my right hand
³⁵until I make your enemies
    a footstool for your feet." 'ˡ

³⁶"Therefore let all Israel be assured of this: God has made this Jesus, whom you crucified, both Lord and Christ."

³⁷When the people heard this, they were cut to the heart and said to Peter and the other apostles, "Brothers, what shall we do?"

³⁸Peter replied, "Repent and be baptized, every one of you, in the name of Jesus Christ for the forgiveness of your sins. And you will receive the gift of the Holy Spirit. ³⁹The promise is for you and your children and for all who are far off—for all whom the Lord our God will call."

⁴⁰With many other words he warned them; and he pleaded with them, "Save yourselves from this corrupt generation." ⁴¹Those who accepted his message were baptized, and about three thousand were added to their number that day.

⁴²They devoted themselves to the apostles' teaching and to the fellowship, to the breaking of bread and to prayer. ⁴³Everyone was filled with awe, and many wonders and miraculous signs were done by the apostles. ⁴⁴All the believers were together and had everything in common. ⁴⁵Selling their possessions and goods, they gave to anyone as he had need. ⁴⁶Every day they continued to meet together in the temple courts. They broke bread in their homes and ate together with glad and sincere hearts, ⁴⁷praising God and enjoying the favor of all the people. And the Lord added to their number daily those who were being saved.

ʰ21 Joel 2:28-32   ⁱ23 Or of those not having the law (that is, Gentiles)   ʲ28 Psalm 16:8-11   ᵏ31 Or Messiah. "The Christ" (Greek) and "the Messiah" (Hebrew) both mean "the Anointed One"; also in verse 36.   ˡ35 Psalm 110:1

Discovering the Word 1. How do the Jews respond to the power of the Spirit which they witness (vv. 5–12)? 2. Here we see Peter as a dynamic leader and preacher. It is the power of the Holy Spirit that has changed this man who was once a coward who denied Jesus three times. Scripture, again, is the foundation of Peter's proclamation of truth. What message does the Old Testament book of Joel have for the bewildered crowd (vv. 17–21)? 3. What is there in Peter's sermon that would reassure Theophilus about his faith and help him "know the certainty of the things" that he'd been taught? 4. What does Peter have to offer to those who are responsive to his message (vv. 37–39)? 5. Describe the fellowship of the believers in this young church (vv. 42–47).

 Applying the Word 1. Imagine you were there on the day of Pentecost. What do you think it would have been like for you as one of the crowd looking on? 2. How has your life been affected by the gift of the Holy Spirit? 3. How does the life and purpose of your church or Christian fellowship group compare to that of this group?

Responding in Prayer Ask God to make the power of the Holy Spirit come alive in your life, and pray that God will use you through that power.

3 / Acts 3
Healing Power

I MET ANNE at the hospital where I was working one evening. She was in an isolation room. She had hepatitis from using contaminated needles to take drugs. In time our relationship grew, and Anne came to know Jesus. She recovered from hepatitis and went off drugs. She worked at healing her relationship with her parents. Later, she married and established a Christian home. Anne's story makes it clear that the power of the Holy Spirit is demonstrated not only through physical healing, but also in the "complete healing" that includes every aspect of our lives.

 Warming Up to God Recall a time when you felt broken and in need of healing. Thank God for the ways that he has transformed and healed you since then.

 Read Acts 3.

3 One day Peter and John were going up to the temple at the time of prayer—at three in the afternoon. ²Now a man crippled from birth was being carried to the temple gate called Beautiful, where he was put every day to beg from those going into the temple courts. ³When he saw Peter and John about to enter, he asked them for money. ⁴Peter looked straight at him, as did John. Then Peter said, "Look at us!" ⁵So the man gave them his attention, expecting to get something from them.

⁶Then Peter said, "Silver or gold I do not have, but what I have I give you. In the name of Jesus Christ of Nazareth, walk." ⁷Taking him by the right hand, he helped him up, and instantly the man's feet and ankles became strong. ⁸He jumped to his feet and began to walk. Then he went with them into the temple courts, walking and jumping, and praising God. ⁹When all the people saw him walking and praising God, ¹⁰they recognized him as the same man who used to sit begging at

the temple gate called Beautiful, and they were filled with wonder and amazement at what had happened to him.

¹¹While the beggar held on to Peter and John, all the people were astonished and came running to them in the place called Solomon's Colonnade. ¹²When Peter saw this, he said to them: "Men of Israel, why does this surprise you? Why do you stare at us as if by our own power or godliness we had made this man walk? ¹³The God of Abraham, Isaac and Jacob, the God of our fathers, has glorified his servant Jesus. You handed him over to be killed, and you disowned him before Pilate, though he had decided to let him go. ¹⁴You disowned the Holy and Righteous One and asked that a murderer be released to you. ¹⁵You killed the author of life, but God raised him from the dead. We are witnesses of this. ¹⁶By faith in the name of Jesus, this man whom you see and know was made strong. It is Jesus' name and the faith

that comes through him that has given this complete healing to him, as you can all see.

17"Now, brothers, I know that you acted in ignorance, as did your leaders. 18But this is how God fulfilled what he had foretold through all the prophets, saying that his Christ[m] would suffer. 19Repent, then, and turn to God, so that your sins may be wiped out, that times of refreshing may come from the Lord, 20and that he may send the Christ, who has been appointed for you—even Jesus. 21He must remain in heaven until the time comes for God to restore everything, as he promised long ago through his holy prophets. 22For Moses said, 'The Lord your God will raise up for

you a prophet like me from among your own people; you must listen to everything he tells you. 23Anyone who does not listen to him will be completely cut off from among his people.'[n]

24"Indeed, all the prophets from Samuel on, as many as have spoken, have foretold these days. 25And you are heirs of the prophets and of the covenant God made with your fathers. He said to Abraham, 'Through your offspring all peoples on earth will be blessed.'[o] 26When God raised up his servant, he sent him first to you to bless you by turning each of you from your wicked ways."

[m] 18 Or Messiah; also in verse 20   [n] 23 Deut. 18:15,18,19
[o] 25 Gen. 22:18; 26:4

 Discovering the Word 1. How does the response of the people to the miracle in verses 6–8 contrast with the beggar's response (vv. 8 and 11–12)? 2. When Peter noticed how the crowd reacted, he saw his opportunity and talked to them about Jesus. According to Peter's message, what had God done to Jesus (vv. 13–15)? What had the Jews done to him? 3. How is the authority of Jesus demonstrated in this miracle (v. 16)? 4. How did Peter explain that all that had happened to Jesus was a part of God's plan (vv. 17–26)?

Applying the Word 1. What healing do you need in your life? 2. How do you respond when you have opportunities like Peter's to talk about Jesus? 3. The "completely" healed man was a powerful testimony to the power of God and the truth of Peter's words. How have you seen the power of God demonstrated in your life and in the lives of others?

Responding in Prayer Thank God for working so powerfully to change your life, and ask him to give you the opportunity to talk about Jesus to one person this week.

---

4 / *Acts 4:1–31*
Called into Question

A DISABLED PERSON becomes abled! And a one-time burden to society, a beggar, becomes a contributing citizen! How do the religious leaders respond to these miraculous events? Instead of expressing gratitude, they become extremely upset. The two men responsible for the healing are arrested.

 Warming Up to God Today, in this new day that God has created, your Savior wants to come to you. With calmness, let the distractions around you—the voices and restless thoughts—slip away. As the spirit of God comes to dwell with you, allow yourself to enjoy his presence in quietness and gratitude.

Read Acts 4:1–31.

---

4 The priests and the captain of the temple guard and the Sadducees came up to Peter and John while they were speaking to the people. 2They were greatly disturbed because the apostles were teaching the people and proclaiming in Jesus the resurrection of the dead. 3They seized Peter and John, and because it was evening, they put them in jail until the next day.

4But many who heard the message believed, and the number of men grew to about five thousand.

5The next day the rulers, elders and teachers of the law met in Jerusalem. 6Annas the high priest was there, and so were Caiaphas, John, Alexander and the other men of the high priest's family. 7They had Peter and John brought before them

and began to question them: "By what power or what name did you do this?"

⁸Then Peter, filled with the Holy Spirit, said to them: "Rulers and elders of the people! ⁹If we are being called to account today for an act of kindness shown to a cripple and are asked how he was healed, ¹⁰then know this, you and all the people of Israel: It is by the name of Jesus Christ of Nazareth, whom you crucified but whom God raised from the dead, that this man stands before you healed. ¹¹He is

" 'the stone you builders rejected,
     which has become the capstone.ᵖ'q

¹²Salvation is found in no one else, for there is no other name under heaven given to men by which we must be saved."

¹³When they saw the courage of Peter and John and realized that they were unschooled, ordinary men, they were astonished and they took note that these men had been with Jesus. ¹⁴But since they could see the man who had been healed standing there with them, there was nothing they could say. ¹⁵So they ordered them to withdraw from the Sanhedrin and then conferred together. ¹⁶"What are we going to do with these men?" they asked. "Everybody living in Jerusalem knows they have done an outstanding miracle, and we cannot deny it. ¹⁷But to stop this thing from spreading any further among the people, we must warn these men to speak no longer to anyone in this name."

¹⁸Then they called them in again and commanded them not to speak or teach at all in the name of Jesus. ¹⁹But Peter and John replied, "Judge for yourselves whether it is right in God's sight to obey you rather than God. ²⁰For we can-

not help speaking about what we have seen and heard."

²¹After further threats they let them go. They could not decide how to punish them, because all the people were praising God for what had happened. ²²For the man who was miraculously healed was over forty years old.

²³On their release, Peter and John went back to their own people and reported all that the chief priests and elders had said to them. ²⁴When they heard this, they raised their voices together in prayer to God. "Sovereign Lord," they said, "you made the heaven and the earth and the sea, and everything in them. ²⁵You spoke by the Holy Spirit through the mouth of your servant, our father David:

" 'Why do the nations rage
     and the peoples plot in vain?
²⁶The kings of the earth take their stand
     and the rulers gather together
against the Lord
     and against his Anointed One.ʳ's

²⁷Indeed Herod and Pontius Pilate met together with the Gentiles and the peopleᵗ of Israel in this city to conspire against your holy servant Jesus, whom you anointed. ²⁸They did what your power and will had decided beforehand should happen. ²⁹Now, Lord, consider their threats and enable your servants to speak your word with great boldness. ³⁰Stretch out your hand to heal and perform miraculous signs and wonders through the name of your holy servant Jesus."

³¹After they prayed, the place where they were meeting was shaken. And they were all filled with the Holy Spirit and spoke the word of God boldly.

ᵖ 11 Or cornerstone   q 11 Psalm 118:22   r 26 That is, Christ or Messiah   s 26 Psalm 2:1,2   t 27 The Greek is plural.

Discovering the Word 1. What has upset the religious leaders (vv. 1–2)? 2. What action did they take (vv. 3–7)? 3. Just a few weeks have passed since Annas and Caiaphas had been involved in the condemnation of Jesus. In his response to their question "By what power or what name did you do this?" Peter is forcing them to encounter Jesus again. What does Peter say about him (vv. 10–12)? 4. In verses 13–22 what made it so difficult for the opposing religious leaders to bring this unacceptable behavior to a halt? 5. What was the reaction of the believers to John and Peter's account (vv. 24–30)? 6. What does their prayer tell you about their faith in the character, power and faithfulness of God (vv. 24–30)?

Applying the Word 1. When has your faith been challenged by others? 2. Imagine that you had been in a group of believers John and Peter returned to and told of what had happened. What would have been your reaction? 3. "After they prayed, the place where they were meeting was shaken. And they were all filled with the Holy Spirit and spoke the word of God boldly." In what ways do you need the power of the Holy Spirit to face the world today?

Responding in Prayer Ask God to fill you with the Spirit as you face constant challenge to the power for and the task of experiencing and communicating the gospel.

---

5 / Acts 4:32—5:16
Oneness of Heart

IT WAS WITH a heavy feeling of dread and pain that I read name after name engraved on the Vietnam Memorial in Washington, D.C. Then I saw that next to the memorial was a statue of three men—a black, a Hispanic and a white soldier. They were standing very close together. The tour guide, a former soldier who fought in Nam, explained the significance of the statue. He said that there were more minorities fighting for the U.S. than ever before. And the reason that they were standing so close together was that in Vietnam they learned, like never before, how very much they needed each other. In this study we will see that when the battle is spiritual, our need for each other is even more critical.

 Warming Up to God Who has God given you that meets a need in your life? Thank God for giving you such a valuable and loving gift.

 Read Acts 4:32—5:16.

---

³²All the believers were one in heart and mind. No one claimed that any of his possessions was his own, but they shared everything they had. ³³With great power the apostles continued to testify to the resurrection of the Lord Jesus, and much grace was upon them all. ³⁴There were no needy persons among them. For from time to time those who owned lands or houses sold them, brought the money from the sales ³⁵and put it at the apostles' feet, and it was distributed to anyone as he had need.

³⁶Joseph, a Levite from Cyprus, whom the apostles called Barnabas (which means Son of Encouragement), ³⁷sold a field he owned and brought the money and put it at the apostles' feet.

5 Now a man named Ananias, together with his wife Sapphira, also sold a piece of property. ²With his wife's full knowledge he kept back part of the money for himself, but brought the rest and put it at the apostles' feet.

³Then Peter said, "Ananias, how is it that Satan has so filled your heart that you have lied to the Holy Spirit and have kept for yourself some of the money you received for the land? ⁴Didn't it belong to you before it was sold? And after it was sold, wasn't the money at your disposal? What made you think of doing such a thing? You have not lied to men but to God."

⁵When Ananias heard this, he fell down and died. And great fear seized all who heard what had happened. ⁶Then the young men came for-

ward, wrapped up his body, and carried him out and buried him.

⁷About three hours later his wife came in, not knowing what had happened. ⁸Peter asked her, "Tell me, is this the price you and Ananias got for the land?"

"Yes," she said, "that is the price."

⁹Peter said to her, "How could you agree to test the Spirit of the Lord? Look! The feet of the men who buried your husband are at the door, and they will carry you out also."

¹⁰At that moment she fell down at his feet and died. Then the young men came in and, finding her dead, carried her out and buried her beside her husband. ¹¹Great fear seized the whole church and all who heard about these events.

¹²The apostles performed many miraculous signs and wonders among the people. And all the believers used to meet together in Solomon's Colonnade. ¹³No one else dared join them, even though they were highly regarded by the people. ¹⁴Nevertheless, more and more men and women believed in the Lord and were added to their number. ¹⁵As a result, people brought the sick into the streets and laid them on beds and mats so that at least Peter's shadow might fall on some of them as he passed by. ¹⁶Crowds gathered also from the towns around Jerusalem, bringing their sick and those tormented by evilᵘ spirits, and all of them were healed.

ᵘ 16 Greek *unclean*

Discovering the Word 1. How is oneness of heart and mind demonstrated in 4:32–37? 2. What have Ananias and Sapphira done that is not consistent with Christian community (5:1–2)? 3. Pretend you are watching the interaction between Peter and Ananias and Sapphira (5:3–9). How would you report this incident? 4. Verse 11 states that "great fear seized the whole church and all who heard about these events." How do you think the church was affected by this fear? 5. What are the tangible evidences of the power of the Holy Spirit in this community in 5:12–16?

Applying the Word 1. How does this story demonstrate the high value that God places on truth and unity within the body of Christ? 2. In what ways do we lie to each other today within our Christian communities? 3. How could you begin to help others in your church or fellowship understand what Christian community is about?

Responding in Prayer Ask God to uphold truth in his church and to help you speak the truth before others.

6 / Acts 5:17—6:7
Persecution and Expansion

IN 1956 TRAGIC news spread across the world. Five American men—sons, husbands and fathers—were massacred by a tribe of Auca Indians. Their purpose was to take the good news of Jesus Christ to the Aucas. The opposition to this endeavor cost them their lives.

That agonizing loss, which seemed at the time to be such a waste, has turned into great fruit for the kingdom of God. Over the years that same tribe of Indians has been transformed by the power of God. The message of Jesus was taken to them by the loved ones of those five young men. Another visible fruit of this great loss is the many who have gone into the world with the gospel, having been inspired by the lives and deaths of these missionaries. The church of Jesus Christ continues to expand today in spite of great persecution, even as it did in the day of the apostles.

 Warming Up to God Although we know that God is in complete control of the universe, we often forget that he also has specific plans for our individual lives. Thank him for being sovereign everywhere, including the secrecy of your own heart.

Read Acts 5:17—6:7.

17Then the high priest and all his associates, who were members of the party of the Sadducees, were filled with jealousy. 18They arrested the apostles and put them in the public jail. 19But during the night an angel of the Lord opened the doors of the jail and brought them out. 20"Go, stand in the temple courts," he said, "and tell the people the full message of this new life."

21At daybreak they entered the temple courts, as they had been told, and began to teach the people.

When the high priest and his associates arrived, they called together the Sanhedrin—the full assembly of the elders of Israel—and sent to the jail for the apostles. 22But on arriving at the jail, the officers did not find them there. So they went back and reported, 23"We found the jail securely locked, with the guards standing at the

doors; but when we opened them, we found no one inside." 24On hearing this report, the captain of the temple guard and the chief priests were puzzled, wondering what would come of this.

25Then someone came and said, "Look! The men you put in jail are standing in the temple courts teaching the people." 26At that, the captain went with his officers and brought the apostles. They did not use force, because they feared that the people would stone them.

27Having brought the apostles, they made them appear before the Sanhedrin to be questioned by the high priest. 28"We gave you strict orders not to teach in this name," he said. "Yet you have filled Jerusalem with your teaching and are determined to make us guilty of this man's blood."

29Peter and the other apostles replied: "We must obey God rather than men! 30The God of

our fathers raised Jesus from the dead—whom you had killed by hanging him on a tree. ³¹God exalted him to his own right hand as Prince and Savior that he might give repentance and forgiveness of sins to Israel. ³²We are witnesses of these things, and so is the Holy Spirit, whom God has given to those who obey him."

³³When they heard this, they were furious and wanted to put them to death. ³⁴But a Pharisee named Gamaliel, a teacher of the law, who was honored by all the people, stood up in the Sanhedrin and ordered that the men be put outside for a little while. ³⁵Then he addressed them: "Men of Israel, consider carefully what you intend to do to these men. ³⁶Some time ago Theudas appeared, claiming to be somebody, and about four hundred men rallied to him. He was killed, all his followers were dispersed, and it all came to nothing. ³⁷After him, Judas the Galilean appeared in the days of the census and led a band of people in revolt. He too was killed, and all his followers were scattered. ³⁸Therefore, in the present case I advise you: Leave these men alone! Let them go! For if their purpose or activity is of human origin, it will fail. ³⁹But if it is from God, you will not be able to stop these men; you will only find yourselves fighting against God."

⁴⁰His speech persuaded them. They called the apostles in and had them flogged. Then they ordered them not to speak in the name of Jesus, and let them go.

⁴¹The apostles left the Sanhedrin, rejoicing because they had been counted worthy of suffering disgrace for the Name. ⁴²Day after day, in the temple courts and from house to house, they never stopped teaching and proclaiming the good news that Jesus is the Christ.ᵛ

6 In those days when the number of disciples was increasing, the Grecian Jews among them complained against the Hebraic Jews because their widows were being overlooked in the daily distribution of food. ²So the Twelve gathered all the disciples together and said, "It would not be right for us to neglect the ministry of the word of God in order to wait on tables. ³Brothers, choose seven men from among you who are known to be full of the Spirit and wisdom. We will turn this responsibility over to them ⁴and will give our attention to prayer and the ministry of the word."

⁵This proposal pleased the whole group. They chose Stephen, a man full of faith and of the Holy Spirit; also Philip, Procorus, Nicanor, Timon, Parmenas, and Nicolas from Antioch, a convert to Judaism. ⁶They presented these men to the apostles, who prayed and laid their hands on them.

⁷So the word of God spread. The number of disciples in Jerusalem increased rapidly, and a large number of priests became obedient to the faith.

ᵛ42 Or Messiah

 Discovering the Word 1. List the expressions and causes of emotion throughout verses 5:17–42. 2. Describe the apostles' response, motivation and source of strength throughout this whole episode. 3. What was Gamaliel's message to the religious leaders (5:34–39)? 4. How was his influence in saving the apostles' lives an example of that truth which he spoke? 5. As the number of disciples increased, what practical needs began to present themselves (6:1–6)? 6. How did the Twelve respond to those needs (6:2–6)?

Applying the Word 1. When have you encountered internal and/or external opposition when you have attempted to proclaim the message of Jesus? 2. Is it more difficult for you to deal with internal or external opposition? Why? 3. As you observe the work of the Holy Spirit throughout this passage, what actions do you think you and/or your church should take to ensure his ministry among you?

Responding in Prayer Tell God about the difficulties and struggles you have been facing as a believer in him. Ask him to give you strength and to remind you that his ways are higher than your own.

7 / Acts 6:8—7:60
Stephen, Full of Spirit and Wisdom

I AM GLAD for those people in my life who make me long to know God better. God's character in them makes me hunger and thirst for him. That is what happens to me when I am exposed to Stephen. I read about him and I want to know God.

Stephen is described as "full of the Holy Spirit and wisdom, full of God's grace and power." He was a gift to the early church but could not be tolerated by her enemies.

 Warming Up to God Think of a person that makes you want to know God better. Reflect on the qualities you see in him or her.

 Read Acts 6:8—7:60.

---

⁸Now Stephen, a man full of God's grace and power, did great wonders and miraculous signs among the people. ⁹Opposition arose, however, from members of the Synagogue of the Freedmen (as it was called)—Jews of Cyrene and Alexandria as well as the provinces of Cilicia and Asia. These men began to argue with Stephen, ¹⁰but they could not stand up against his wisdom or the Spirit by whom he spoke.

¹¹Then they secretly persuaded some men to say, "We have heard Stephen speak words of blasphemy against Moses and against God."

¹²So they stirred up the people and the elders and the teachers of the law. They seized Stephen and brought him before the Sanhedrin. ¹³They produced false witnesses, who testified, "This fellow never stops speaking against this holy place and against the law. ¹⁴For we have heard him say that this Jesus of Nazareth will destroy this place and change the customs Moses handed down to us."

¹⁵All who were sitting in the Sanhedrin looked intently at Stephen, and they saw that his face was like the face of an angel.

7 Then the high priest asked him, "Are these charges true?"

²To this he replied: "Brothers and fathers, listen to me! The God of glory appeared to our father Abraham while he was still in Mesopotamia, before he lived in Haran. ³'Leave your country and your people,' God said, 'and go to the land I will show you.'ʷ

⁴"So he left the land of the Chaldeans and settled in Haran. After the death of his father, God sent him to this land where you are now living. ⁵He gave him no inheritance here, not even a foot of ground. But God promised him that he and his descendants after him would possess the land, even though at that time Abraham had no child. ⁶God spoke to him in this way: 'Your descendants will be strangers in a country not their own, and they will be enslaved and mistreated four hundred years. ⁷But I will punish the nation they serve as slaves,' God said, 'and afterward they will come out of that country and worship me in this place.'ˣ ⁸Then he gave Abraham the covenant of circumcision. And Abraham became the father of Isaac and circumcised him eight days after his birth. Later Isaac became the father of Jacob, and Jacob became the father of the twelve patriarchs.

⁹"Because the patriarchs were jealous of Joseph, they sold him as a slave into Egypt. But God was with him ¹⁰and rescued him from all his troubles. He gave Joseph wisdom and enabled him to gain the goodwill of Pharaoh king of Egypt; so he made him ruler over Egypt and all his palace.

¹¹"Then a famine struck all Egypt and Canaan, bringing great suffering, and our fathers could not find food. ¹²When Jacob heard that there was grain in Egypt, he sent our fathers on their first visit. ¹³On their second visit, Joseph told his brothers who he was, and Pharaoh learned about Joseph's family. ¹⁴After this, Joseph sent for his father Jacob and his whole family, seventy-five in all. ¹⁵Then Jacob went down to Egypt, where he and our fathers died. ¹⁶Their bodies were brought back to Shechem and placed in the tomb that Abraham had bought from the sons of Hamor at Shechem for a certain sum of money.

¹⁷"As the time drew near for God to fulfill his promise to Abraham, the number of our people in Egypt greatly increased. ¹⁸Then another king, who knew nothing about Joseph, became ruler of

ʷ3 Gen. 12:1   ˣ7 Gen. 15:13,14

Egypt. ¹⁹He dealt treacherously with our people and oppressed our forefathers by forcing them to throw out their newborn babies so that they would die.

²⁰"At that time Moses was born, and he was no ordinary child.ʸ For three months he was cared for in his father's house. ²¹When he was placed outside, Pharaoh's daughter took him and brought him up as her own son. ²²Moses was educated in all the wisdom of the Egyptians and was powerful in speech and action.

²³"When Moses was forty years old, he decided to visit his fellow Israelites. ²⁴He saw one of them being mistreated by an Egyptian, so he went to his defense and avenged him by killing the Egyptian. ²⁵Moses thought that his own people would realize that God was using him to rescue them, but they did not. ²⁶The next day Moses came upon two Israelites who were fighting. He tried to reconcile them by saying, 'Men, you are brothers; why do you want to hurt each other?'

²⁷"But the man who was mistreating the other pushed Moses aside and said, 'Who made you ruler and judge over us? ²⁸Do you want to kill me as you killed the Egyptian yesterday?'ᶻ ²⁹When Moses heard this, he fled to Midian, where he settled as a foreigner and had two sons.

³⁰"After forty years had passed, an angel appeared to Moses in the flames of a burning bush in the desert near Mount Sinai. ³¹When he saw this, he was amazed at the sight. As he went over to look more closely, he heard the Lord's voice: ³²'I am the God of your fathers, the God of Abraham, Isaac and Jacob.'ᵈ Moses trembled with fear and did not dare to look.

³³"Then the Lord said to him, 'Take off your sandals; the place where you are standing is holy ground. ³⁴I have indeed seen the oppression of my people in Egypt. I have heard their groaning and have come down to set them free. Now come, I will send you back to Egypt.'ᵇ

³⁵"This is the same Moses whom they had rejected with the words, 'Who made you ruler and judge?' He was sent to be their ruler and deliverer by God himself, through the angel who appeared to him in the bush. ³⁶He led them out of Egypt and did wonders and miraculous signs in Egypt, at the Red Seaᶜ and for forty years in the desert.

³⁷"This is that Moses who told the Israelites, 'God will send you a prophet like me from your own people.'ᵈ ³⁸He was in the assembly in the desert, with the angel who spoke to him on Mount Sinai, and with our fathers; and he received living words to pass on to us.

³⁹"But our fathers refused to obey him. Instead, they rejected him and in their hearts turned back to Egypt. ⁴⁰They told Aaron, 'Make us gods who will go before us. As for this fellow Moses who led us out of Egypt—we don't know what has happened to him!'ᵉ ⁴¹That was the time they made an idol in the form of a calf. They brought sacrifices to it and held a celebration in honor of what their hands had made. ⁴²But God turned away and gave them over to the worship of the heavenly bodies. This agrees with what is written in the book of the prophets:

" 'Did you bring me sacrifices and offerings
    forty years in the desert, O house of Israel?
⁴³You have lifted up the shrine of Molech
    and the star of your god Rephan,
    the idols you made to worship.
Therefore I will send you into exile'ᶠ beyond
    Babylon.

⁴⁴"Our forefathers had the tabernacle of the Testimony with them in the desert. It had been made as God directed Moses, according to the pattern he had seen. ⁴⁵Having received the tabernacle, our fathers under Joshua brought it with them when they took the land from the nations God drove out before them. It remained in the land until the time of David, ⁴⁶who enjoyed God's favor and asked that he might provide a dwelling place for the God of Jacob.ᵍ ⁴⁷But it was Solomon who built the house for him.

⁴⁸"However, the Most High does not live in houses made by men. As the prophet says:

⁴⁹" 'Heaven is my throne,
    and the earth is my footstool.
What kind of house will you build for me?
                                    says the Lord.
    Or where will my resting place be?
⁵⁰Has not my hand made all these things?'ʰ

⁵¹"You stiff-necked people, with uncircumcised hearts and ears! You are just like your fathers: You always resist the Holy Spirit! ⁵²Was there ever a prophet your fathers did not persecute? They even killed those who predicted the coming of the Righteous One. And now you have betrayed and murdered him— ⁵³you who have

ʸ20 Or *was fair in the sight of God*   ᶻ28 Exodus 2:14
ᵃ32 Exodus 3:6   ᵇ34 Exodus 3:5,7,8,10   ᶜ36 That is, Sea of Reeds
ᵈ37 Deut. 18:15   ᵉ40 Exodus 32:1   ᶠ43 Amos 5:25-27
ᵍ46 Some early manuscripts *the house of Jacob*   ʰ50 Isaiah 66:1,2

received the law that was put into effect through angels but have not obeyed it."

⁵⁴When they heard this, they were furious and gnashed their teeth at him. ⁵⁵But Stephen, full of the Holy Spirit, looked up to heaven and saw the glory of God, and Jesus standing at the right hand of God. ⁵⁶"Look," he said, "I see heaven open and the Son of Man standing at the right hand of God."

⁵⁷At this they covered their ears and, yelling at the top of their voices, they all rushed at him, ⁵⁸dragged him out of the city and began to stone him. Meanwhile, the witnesses laid their clothes at the feet of a young man named Saul.

⁵⁹While they were stoning him, Stephen prayed, "Lord Jesus, receive my spirit." ⁶⁰Then he fell on his knees and cried out, "Lord, do not hold this sin against them." When he had said this, he fell asleep.

 Discovering the Word 1. What do you learn about Stephen throughout this passage? 2. What do the accusations against Stephen tell us about why the Jewish religious leaders were so upset (6:13–14)? 3. Sometimes the speech in chapter 7 is called "Stephen's defense," although it is actually a defense of pure Christianity as God's appointed way to worship. What are the main points of this defense? 4. What did God tell Abraham would happen to his descendants, the Hebrews (7:1–7)? 5. What direct application does Stephen make concerning the religious leaders from 7:39–43 (see 7:51–53)?

Applying the Word 1. God told Abraham what would happen to the Hebrews years before it all happened, even before he had a son. How are you affected when you see all that unfolds in history? 2. Throughout this whole passage, we see in Stephen the evidence of being full of the Spirit and wisdom. What are the evidences today of being full of the Spirit and wisdom? 3. In what aspect of your life would you like to reflect more of the Spirit and wisdom?

Responding in Prayer Ask God to fill you with the Spirit and with wisdom.

8 / Acts 8
The Power of Suffering

STEPHEN IS DEAD. When he is buried, the people mourn deeply. The church has experienced the tragedy of her first martyr. In this study we meet Philip and Saul. Saul approves of Stephen's death. He is putting all his energy into destroying the rest of Jesus' followers. In contrast, Philip is one of the seven, full of the Spirit and wisdom. His energy goes into the proclamation of the truth about Jesus. People respond. And so both the persecution and the expansion of the church continue.

 Warming Up to God Has there been a time recently that you were confused about God's intentions behind the events that he placed in your life? Ask him to give you his understanding and peace.

 Read Acts 8.

8 And Saul was there, giving approval to his death.

On that day a great persecution broke out against the church at Jerusalem, and all except the apostles were scattered throughout Judea and Samaria. ²Godly men buried Stephen and mourned deeply for him. ³But Saul began to destroy the church. Going from house to house, he dragged off men and women and put them in prison.

⁴Those who had been scattered preached the word wherever they went. ⁵Philip went down to a city in Samaria and proclaimed the Christ[i] there. ⁶When the crowds heard Philip and saw the miraculous signs he did, they all paid close attention to what he said. ⁷With shrieks, evil[j] spirits came

i5 Or Messiah   j7 Greek unclean

out of many, and many paralytics and cripples were healed. [8]So there was great joy in that city.

[9]Now for some time a man named Simon had practiced sorcery in the city and amazed all the people of Samaria. He boasted that he was someone great, [10]and all the people, both high and low, gave him their attention and exclaimed, "This man is the divine power known as the Great Power." [11]They followed him because he had amazed them for a long time with his magic. [12]But when they believed Philip as he preached the good news of the kingdom of God and the name of Jesus Christ, they were baptized, both men and women. [13]Simon himself believed and was baptized. And he followed Philip everywhere, astonished by the great signs and miracles he saw.

[14]When the apostles in Jerusalem heard that Samaria had accepted the word of God, they sent Peter and John to them. [15]When they arrived, they prayed for them that they might receive the Holy Spirit, [16]because the Holy Spirit had not yet come upon any of them; they had simply been baptized into[k] the name of the Lord Jesus. [17]Then Peter and John placed their hands on them, and they received the Holy Spirit.

[18]When Simon saw that the Spirit was given at the laying on of the apostles' hands, he offered them money [19]and said, "Give me also this ability so that everyone on whom I lay my hands may receive the Holy Spirit."

[20]Peter answered: "May your money perish with you, because you thought you could buy the gift of God with money! [21]You have no part or share in this ministry, because your heart is not right before God. [22]Repent of this wickedness and pray to the Lord. Perhaps he will forgive you for having such a thought in your heart. [23]For I see that you are full of bitterness and captive to sin."

[24]Then Simon answered, "Pray to the Lord for me so that nothing you have said may happen to me."

[25]When they had testified and proclaimed the word of the Lord, Peter and John returned to Jerusalem, preaching the gospel in many Samaritan villages.

[26]Now an angel of the Lord said to Philip, "Go south to the road—the desert road—that goes down from Jerusalem to Gaza." [27]So he started out, and on his way he met an Ethiopian[l] eunuch, an important official in charge of all the treasury of Candace, queen of the Ethiopians. This man had gone to Jerusalem to worship, [28]and on his way home was sitting in his chariot reading the book of Isaiah the prophet. [29]The Spirit told Philip, "Go to that chariot and stay near it."

[30]Then Philip ran up to the chariot and heard the man reading Isaiah the prophet. "Do you understand what you are reading?" Philip asked.

[31]"How can I," he said, "unless someone explains it to me?" So he invited Philip to come up and sit with him.

[32]The eunuch was reading this passage of Scripture:

"He was led like a sheep to the slaughter,
    and as a lamb before the shearer is silent,
    so he did not open his mouth.
[33]In his humiliation he was deprived of justice.
    Who can speak of his descendants?
    For his life was taken from the earth."[m]

[34]The eunuch asked Philip, "Tell me, please, who is the prophet talking about, himself or someone else?" [35]Then Philip began with that very passage of Scripture and told him the good news about Jesus.

[36]As they traveled along the road, they came to some water and the eunuch said, "Look, here is water. Why shouldn't I be baptized?"[n] [38]And he gave orders to stop the chariot. Then both Philip and the eunuch went down into the water and Philip baptized him. [39]When they came up out of the water, the Spirit of the Lord suddenly took Philip away, and the eunuch did not see him again, but went on his way rejoicing. [40]Philip, however, appeared at Azotus and traveled about, preaching the gospel in all the towns until he reached Caesarea.

[k]16 Or in   [l]27 That is, from the upper Nile region   [m]33 Isaiah 53:7,8   [n]36 Some late manuscripts baptized?" [37]Philip said, "If you believe with all your heart, you may." The eunuch answered, "I believe that Jesus Christ is the Son of God."

Discovering the Word 1. In this passage the command to be witnesses in all of Judea and Samaria (Ac 1:8) is fulfilled. What are the causes and extent of the spread of the gospel at this time? 2. Look at the story of Simon the Sorcerer (vv. 9–25). How does he attempt to get spiritual power? What is his motivation for wanting this power (vv. 18–19)? 3. In contrast, what is God's way for his people to receive spiritual power (vv.

20–23)? **4.** What are the factors involved in the eunuch's coming to know the Lord (vv. 26–39)? **5.** How was Philip's ministry to the eunuch the beginning of the witness "to the ends of the earth" (Ac 1:8)?

 Applying the Word **1.** The story of Simon the Sorcerer demonstrates that becoming a Christian does not instantly resolve all problems and character flaws. What do you learn from Peter concerning nurturing young believers? **2.** What principles of evangelism have you observed throughout this passage? **3.** What have you learned from Acts 8 that might make you a more effective witness for Jesus?

Responding in Prayer Ask God for the guidance of his Holy Spirit, and ask him to help you follow the model of evangelism that Philip provides.

---

9 / Acts 9:1–31
Saul's Conversion

WHEN CHUCK COLSON became a Christian in prison, the whole nation reacted with skepticism—Christians and non-Christians alike. Of all the leading characters in the Watergate scandal, he was one of the most notorious. Could such a calculating man sincerely come to God?

 Warming Up to God Think back to what your life was like before you met Christ. Thank God for the transformation that he has made in your life—both your instant rebirth into his kingdom and the gradual remolding of your character since then.

 Read Acts 9:1–31.

---

9 Meanwhile, Saul was still breathing out murderous threats against the Lord's disciples. He went to the high priest ²and asked him for letters to the synagogues in Damascus, so that if he found any there who belonged to the Way, whether men or women, he might take them as prisoners to Jerusalem. ³As he neared Damascus on his journey, suddenly a light from heaven flashed around him. ⁴He fell to the ground and heard a voice say to him, "Saul, Saul, why do you persecute me?"

⁵"Who are you, Lord?" Saul asked.

"I am Jesus, whom you are persecuting," he replied. ⁶"Now get up and go into the city, and you will be told what you must do."

⁷The men traveling with Saul stood there speechless; they heard the sound but did not see anyone. ⁸Saul got up from the ground, but when he opened his eyes he could see nothing. So they led him by the hand into Damascus. ⁹For three days he was blind, and did not eat or drink anything.

¹⁰In Damascus there was a disciple named Ananias. The Lord called to him in a vision, "Ananias!"

"Yes, Lord," he answered.

¹¹The Lord told him, "Go to the house of Judas on Straight Street and ask for a man from Tarsus named Saul, for he is praying. ¹²In a vision he has seen a man named Ananias come and place his hands on him to restore his sight."

¹³"Lord," Ananias answered, "I have heard many reports about this man and all the harm he has done to your saints in Jerusalem. ¹⁴And he has come here with authority from the chief priests to arrest all who call on your name."

¹⁵But the Lord said to Ananias, "Go! This man is my chosen instrument to carry my name before the Gentiles and their kings and before the people of Israel. ¹⁶I will show him how much he must suffer for my name."

¹⁷Then Ananias went to the house and entered it. Placing his hands on Saul, he said, "Brother Saul, the Lord—Jesus, who appeared to you on the road as you were coming here—has sent me so that you may see again and be filled with the Holy Spirit." ¹⁸Immediately, something like scales fell from Saul's eyes, and he could see again. He got up and was baptized, ¹⁹and after taking some food, he regained his strength.

Saul spent several days with the disciples in Damascus. ²⁰At once he began to preach in the

synagogues that Jesus is the Son of God. ²¹All those who heard him were astonished and asked, "Isn't he the man who raised havoc in Jerusalem among those who call on this name? And hasn't he come here to take them as prisoners to the chief priests?" ²²Yet Saul grew more and more powerful and baffled the Jews living in Damascus by proving that Jesus is the Christ.ᵒ

²³After many days had gone by, the Jews conspired to kill him, ²⁴but Saul learned of their plan. Day and night they kept close watch on the city gates in order to kill him. ²⁵But his followers took him by night and lowered him in a basket through an opening in the wall.

²⁶When he came to Jerusalem, he tried to join the disciples, but they were all afraid of him, not believing that he really was a disciple. ²⁷But Bar-

nabas took him and brought him to the apostles. He told them how Saul on his journey had seen the Lord and that the Lord had spoken to him, and how in Damascus he had preached fearlessly in the name of Jesus. ²⁸So Saul stayed with them and moved about freely in Jerusalem, speaking boldly in the name of the Lord. ²⁹He talked and debated with the Grecian Jews, but they tried to kill him. ³⁰When the brothers learned of this, they took him down to Caesarea and sent him off to Tarsus.

³¹Then the church throughout Judea, Galilee and Samaria enjoyed a time of peace. It was strengthened; and encouraged by the Holy Spirit, it grew in numbers, living in the fear of the Lord.

ᵒ22 Or Messiah

 Discovering the Word 1. Review what you know about Saul (7:58—8:3). What further insights do you get about him from 9:1–2? 2. Describe Saul's encounter with Jesus Christ in verses 3–9. (What is the emotional, spiritual, physical and social climate?) 3. Ananias is the second person within three days to have a direct encounter with the Lord. Compare and contrast his encounter (vv. 10–16) with that of Saul. 4. What is the significance of Ananias addressing Saul as "Brother" (v. 17)? 5. What is the response of both believers and nonbelievers to Saul and his ministry (vv. 19–30)? 6. What role does Barnabas play in Saul's life and ministry?

Applying the Word 1. What do you learn about obedience to God through Saul and Ananias? 2. What does Saul's conversion teach us about those in our lives who are most likely not to believe? 3. Consider the people in your life who are most antagonistic to Christianity. How might God use you to bring them to Christ?

Responding in Prayer Pray for the salvation of someone you consider an unlikely convert. Ask God to increase your faith.

---

10 / *Acts 9:32—10:48*
Salvation for Every Nation

ONCE THE BERLIN Wall seemed impenetrable, and communism powerful and indestructible. For seventy years Christians wondered if Christmas would ever be openly celebrated in Russia. Then, dramatically, the wall fell. Communism collapsed. Nations that had been closed to the gospel for years began to welcome Christians, their help and their message with open arms. The historic breakthrough was like the one the early Christians experienced in this passage. A seemingly impenetrable spiritual wall was broken down. In both situations we see that from God's perspective there is always the potential for reaching every person in all the corners of the world with the wonderful news of Jesus Christ.

 Warming Up to God Think of an impossible feat that you have seen God accomplish. Thank him and allow him to show you again that he truly is almighty.

 Read Acts 9:32—10:48.

32As Peter traveled about the country, he went to visit the saints in Lydda. 33There he found a man named Aeneas, a paralytic who had been bedridden for eight years. 34"Aeneas," Peter said to him, "Jesus Christ heals you. Get up and take care of your mat." Immediately Aeneas got up. 35All those who lived in Lydda and Sharon saw him and turned to the Lord.

36In Joppa there was a disciple named Tabitha (which, when translated, is Dorcas*p*), who was always doing good and helping the poor. 37About that time she became sick and died, and her body was washed and placed in an upstairs room. 38Lydda was near Joppa; so when the disciples heard that Peter was in Lydda, they sent two men to him and urged him, "Please come at once!"

39Peter went with them, and when he arrived he was taken upstairs to the room. All the widows stood around him, crying and showing him the robes and other clothing that Dorcas had made while she was still with them.

40Peter sent them all out of the room; then he got down on his knees and prayed. Turning toward the dead woman, he said, "Tabitha, get up." She opened her eyes, and seeing Peter she sat up. 41He took her by the hand and helped her to her feet. Then he called the believers and the widows and presented her to them alive. 42This became known all over Joppa, and many people believed in the Lord. 43Peter stayed in Joppa for some time with a tanner named Simon.

10

At Caesarea there was a man named Cornelius, a centurion in what was known as the Italian Regiment. 2He and all his family were devout and God-fearing; he gave generously to those in need and prayed to God regularly. 3One day at about three in the afternoon he had a vision. He distinctly saw an angel of God, who came to him and said, "Cornelius!"

4Cornelius stared at him in fear. "What is it, Lord?" he asked.

The angel answered, "Your prayers and gifts to the poor have come up as a memorial offering before God. 5Now send men to Joppa to bring back a man named Simon who is called Peter. 6He is staying with Simon the tanner, whose house is by the sea."

7When the angel who spoke to him had gone, Cornelius called two of his servants and a devout soldier who was one of his attendants. 8He told

them everything that had happened and sent them to Joppa.

9About noon the following day as they were on their journey and approaching the city, Peter went up on the roof to pray. 10He became hungry and wanted something to eat, and while the meal was being prepared, he fell into a trance. 11He saw heaven opened and something like a large sheet being let down to earth by its four corners. 12It contained all kinds of four-footed animals, as well as reptiles of the earth and birds of the air. 13Then a voice told him, "Get up, Peter. Kill and eat."

14"Surely not, Lord!" Peter replied. "I have never eaten anything impure or unclean."

15The voice spoke to him a second time, "Do not call anything impure that God has made clean."

16This happened three times, and immediately the sheet was taken back to heaven.

17While Peter was wondering about the meaning of the vision, the men sent by Cornelius found out where Simon's house was and stopped at the gate. 18They called out, asking if Simon who was known as Peter was staying there.

19While Peter was still thinking about the vision, the Spirit said to him, "Simon, three*q* men are looking for you. 20So get up and go downstairs. Do not hesitate to go with them, for I have sent them."

21Peter went down and said to the men, "I'm the one you're looking for. Why have you come?"

22The men replied, "We have come from Cornelius the centurion. He is a righteous and God-fearing man, who is respected by all the Jewish people. A holy angel told him to have you come to his house so that he could hear what you have to say." 23Then Peter invited the men into the house to be his guests.

The next day Peter started out with them, and some of the brothers from Joppa went along. 24The following day he arrived in Caesarea. Cornelius was expecting them and had called together his relatives and close friends. 25As Peter entered the house, Cornelius met him and fell at his feet in reverence. 26But Peter made him get up. "Stand up," he said, "I am only a man myself."

27Talking with him, Peter went inside and found a large gathering of people. 28He said to

p36 Both *Tabitha* (Aramaic) and *Dorcas* (Greek) mean *gazelle.*
q19 One early manuscript *two;* other manuscripts do not have the number.

them: "You are well aware that it is against our law for a Jew to associate with a Gentile or visit him. But God has shown me that I should not call any man impure or unclean. ²⁹So when I was sent for, I came without raising any objection. May I ask why you sent for me?"

³⁰Cornelius answered: "Four days ago I was in my house praying at this hour, at three in the afternoon. Suddenly a man in shining clothes stood before me ³¹and said, 'Cornelius, God has heard your prayer and remembered your gifts to the poor. ³²Send to Joppa for Simon who is called Peter. He is a guest in the home of Simon the tanner, who lives by the sea.' ³³So I sent for you immediately, and it was good of you to come. Now we are all here in the presence of God to listen to everything the Lord has commanded you to tell us."

³⁴Then Peter began to speak: "I now realize how true it is that God does not show favoritism ³⁵but accepts men from every nation who fear him and do what is right. ³⁶You know the message God sent to the people of Israel, telling the good news of peace through Jesus Christ, who is Lord of all. ³⁷You know what has happened throughout Judea, beginning in Galilee after the baptism that John preached— ³⁸how God anointed Jesus of Nazareth with the Holy Spirit and power, and how he went around doing good and healing all who were under the power of the devil, because God was with him.

³⁹"We are witnesses of everything he did in the country of the Jews and in Jerusalem. They killed him by hanging him on a tree, ⁴⁰but God raised him from the dead on the third day and caused him to be seen. ⁴¹He was not seen by all the people, but by witnesses whom God had already chosen—by us who ate and drank with him after he rose from the dead. ⁴²He commanded us to preach to the people and to testify that he is the one whom God appointed as judge of the living and the dead. ⁴³All the prophets testify about him that everyone who believes in him receives forgiveness of sins through his name."

⁴⁴While Peter was still speaking these words, the Holy Spirit came on all who heard the message. ⁴⁵The circumcised believers who had come with Peter were astonished that the gift of the Holy Spirit had been poured out even on the Gentiles. ⁴⁶For they heard them speaking in tonguesʳ and praising God.

Then Peter said, ⁴⁷"Can anyone keep these people from being baptized with water? They have received the Holy Spirit just as we have." ⁴⁸So he ordered that they be baptized in the name of Jesus Christ. Then they asked Peter to stay with them for a few days.

ʳ46 Or other languages

Discovering the Word 1. How is God's power demonstrated in 9:32–43? 2. This is the first time Peter has been involved in raising someone from the dead. How might this prepare him for what happens in chapter 10? 3. How did God prepare Cornelius for Peter (10:1–8)? 4. In what ways did God prepare Peter for Cornelius (10:9–33)? 5. What evidence is there that Cornelius expected God to work (10:24–26)?

Applying the Word 1. What lessons do we learn from Cornelius's life? 2. In summary, how do you see God's purpose, as stated in Acts 1:8, "You will receive power when the Holy Spirit comes on you; and you will be my witnesses in Jerusalem, and in all Judea and Samaria, and to the ends of the earth," being fulfilled in this passage? 3. In what ways could you grow in relating to people of other cultures and races?

 Responding in Prayer Ask God to use your experiences in life and knowledge of him to bring others to Christ.

---

11 / *Acts 11*
The First Jewish-Gentile Church

LUKE SET UP the stories of Peter and Cornelius and Ananias with amazing symmetry. The Holy Spirit simultaneously prepared the hearts of Ananias and of Saul—as he simultaneously prepared those of Peter and Cornelius. Peter questioned and hesitated, as did Ananias. Peter doubted whether he could be friends with the Gentiles,

Ananias whether he could approach the enemy of the church. Both obey without hesitation when God makes his divine will known. These stories come together in today's study. Peter defends his ministry to Cornelius to the church at Jerusalem. He convinces them of God's work in the Gentiles. It is also here that Saul, the one-time enemy of the church, reappears as a minister to the church in Antioch, a church filled with both Jewish and Gentile Christians.

 Warming Up to God In the face of change, how do you handle the need for a new perspective? Resistance? Excitement? Uncertainty? Do you face a change now? Take time to put your response, whatever it is, in God's hands.

 Read Acts 11.

11 The apostles and the brothers throughout Judea heard that the Gentiles also had received the word of God. ²So when Peter went up to Jerusalem, the circumcised believers criticized him ³and said, "You went into the house of uncircumcised men and ate with them."

⁴Peter began and explained everything to them precisely as it had happened: ⁵"I was in the city of Joppa praying, and in a trance I saw a vision. I saw something like a large sheet being let down from heaven by its four corners, and it came down to where I was. ⁶I looked into it and saw four-footed animals of the earth, wild beasts, reptiles, and birds of the air. ⁷Then I heard a voice telling me, 'Get up, Peter. Kill and eat.'

⁸"I replied, 'Surely not, Lord! Nothing impure or unclean has ever entered my mouth.'

⁹"The voice spoke from heaven a second time, 'Do not call anything impure that God has made clean.' ¹⁰This happened three times, and then it was all pulled up to heaven again.

¹¹"Right then three men who had been sent to me from Caesarea stopped at the house where I was staying. ¹²The Spirit told me to have no hesitation about going with them. These six brothers also went with me, and we entered the man's house. ¹³He told us how he had seen an angel appear in his house and say, 'Send to Joppa for Simon who is called Peter. ¹⁴He will bring you a message through which you and all your household will be saved.'

¹⁵"As I began to speak, the Holy Spirit came on them as he had come on us at the beginning. ¹⁶Then I remembered what the Lord had said: 'John baptized withˢ water, but you will be baptized with the Holy Spirit.' ¹⁷So if God gave them the same gift as he gave us, who believed in the Lord Jesus Christ, who was I to think that I could oppose God?"

¹⁸When they heard this, they had no further objections and praised God, saying, "So then, God has granted even the Gentiles repentance unto life."

¹⁹Now those who had been scattered by the persecution in connection with Stephen traveled as far as Phoenicia, Cyprus and Antioch, telling the message only to Jews. ²⁰Some of them, however, men from Cyprus and Cyrene, went to Antioch and began to speak to Greeks also, telling them the good news about the Lord Jesus. ²¹The Lord's hand was with them, and a great number of people believed and turned to the Lord.

²²News of this reached the ears of the church at Jerusalem, and they sent Barnabas to Antioch. ²³When he arrived and saw the evidence of the grace of God, he was glad and encouraged them all to remain true to the Lord with all their hearts. ²⁴He was a good man, full of the Holy Spirit and faith, and a great number of people were brought to the Lord.

²⁵Then Barnabas went to Tarsus to look for Saul, ²⁶and when he found him, he brought him to Antioch. So for a whole year Barnabas and Saul met with the church and taught great numbers of people. The disciples were called Christians first at Antioch.

²⁷During this time some prophets came down from Jerusalem to Antioch. ²⁸One of them, named Agabus, stood up and through the Spirit predicted that a severe famine would spread over the entire Roman world. (This happened during the reign of Claudius.) ²⁹The disciples, each according to his ability, decided to provide help for the brothers living in Judea. ³⁰This they did, sending their gift to the elders by Barnabas and Saul.

ˢ16 Or in

Discovering the Word **1.** What kind of reception was awaiting Peter when he went back up to Jerusalem (vv. 1–3)? **2.** What seemed to be the final and most convincing proof to Peter of God's working in the Gentiles (vv. 15–17)? Why? **3.** In the meantime the gospel is spreading to Gentiles at a tremendous rate in Antioch. What kind of care is provided for new believers (vv. 22–30)? **4.** What was the reason for, and what were the results of, Barnabas's trip to Antioch (vv. 22–30)?

Applying the Word **1.** What can we learn from the way Peter responded to his critics? **2.** How does our care for new believers compare and contrast to the care given here? **3.** How do you see in this passage the true meaning of "Christian" being more fully discovered and lived out in a multicultural church?

Responding in Prayer Ask God to help you be more open and flexible to the changes that he desires to bring about in your life.

12 / *Acts 12*
Miraculous Escape

HUDSON TAYLOR, FAMOUS missionary to China, said, "Man is moved by God through prayer alone." We see the power of God demonstrated in this passage in response to the prayers of his people.

Warming Up to God Recall a time when God answered one of your prayers. Thank him for the joy and encouragement you received from his gracious blessing upon you.

Read Acts 12.

12 It was about this time that King Herod arrested some who belonged to the church, intending to persecute them. ²He had James, the brother of John, put to death with the sword. ³When he saw that this pleased the Jews, he proceeded to seize Peter also. This happened during the Feast of Unleavened Bread. ⁴After arresting him, he put him in prison, handing him over to be guarded by four squads of four soldiers each. Herod intended to bring him out for public trial after the Passover.

⁵So Peter was kept in prison, but the church was earnestly praying to God for him.

⁶The night before Herod was to bring him to trial, Peter was sleeping between two soldiers, bound with two chains, and sentries stood guard at the entrance. ⁷Suddenly an angel of the Lord appeared and a light shone in the cell. He struck Peter on the side and woke him up. "Quick, get up!" he said, and the chains fell off Peter's wrists.

⁸Then the angel said to him, "Put on your clothes and sandals." And Peter did so. "Wrap your cloak around you and follow me," the angel told him. ⁹Peter followed him out of the prison, but he had no idea that what the angel was doing was really happening; he thought he was seeing a vision. ¹⁰They passed the first and second guards and came to the iron gate leading to the city. It opened for them by itself, and they went through it. When they had walked the length of one street, suddenly the angel left him.

¹¹Then Peter came to himself and said, "Now I know without a doubt that the Lord sent his angel and rescued me from Herod's clutches and from everything the Jewish people were anticipating."

¹²When this had dawned on him, he went to the house of Mary the mother of John, also called Mark, where many people had gathered and were praying. ¹³Peter knocked at the outer entrance, and a servant girl named Rhoda came to answer the door. ¹⁴When she recognized Peter's voice, she was so overjoyed she ran back without opening it and exclaimed, "Peter is at the door!"

¹⁵"You're out of your mind," they told her. When she kept insisting that it was so, they said, "It must be his angel."

¹⁶But Peter kept on knocking, and when they opened the door and saw him, they were astonished. ¹⁷Peter motioned with his hand for them to be quiet and described how the Lord had brought him out of prison. "Tell James and the brothers

about this," he said, and then he left for another place.

18In the morning, there was no small commotion among the soldiers as to what had become of Peter. 19After Herod had a thorough search made for him and did not find him, he cross-examined the guards and ordered that they be executed.

Then Herod went from Judea to Caesarea and stayed there a while. 20He had been quarreling with the people of Tyre and Sidon; they now joined together and sought an audience with him. Having secured the support of Blastus, a trusted personal servant of the king, they asked for peace, because they depended on the king's country for their food supply.

21On the appointed day Herod, wearing his royal robes, sat on his throne and delivered a public address to the people. 22They shouted, "This is the voice of a god, not of a man." 23Immediately, because Herod did not give praise to God, an angel of the Lord struck him down, and he was eaten by worms and died.

24But the word of God continued to increase and spread.

25When Barnabas and Saul had finished their mission, they returned from*t* Jerusalem, taking with them John, also called Mark.

t25 Some manuscripts to

Discovering the Word 1. Describe the main characters in this passage. How do they respond to what is happening to and around them? 2. What seems to motivate Herod's actions (vv. 1–5)? 3. What does the church's response to James's death and Peter's being in prison (vv. 5 and 12) demonstrate about prayer? 4. Why was Herod struck down (vv. 21–23)? 5. Contrast Herod's end with what happened with the Word of God (vv. 19–24).

Applying the Word 1. How have you seen God respond to a group of people who were earnestly praying? 2. Why do you think the praying Christians reacted as they did to Peter's return? 3. The earnest prayer of the church significantly affected the outcome of the events of this chapter. How is your motivation to pray influenced by this truth?

Responding in Prayer Think of an "impossible" prayer request or need that you have. Place it before God and ask him to give you the faith to believe that he will answer your prayer and give you "the desires of your heart."

---

13 / *Acts 13—14*
Paul's First Missionary Journey

PETER HAS DISAPPEARED. We do not know where he is hiding. Luke is ushering Peter from the stage while Paul steps to the forefront. Peter, the apostle to the Jews, has played his part well and prepared the way for Paul, the apostle to the Gentiles. Paul and Barnabas have completed their mission of mercy in Jerusalem on behalf of the church in Antioch (11:29) and have returned to Antioch with John Mark. In this study we will look at Paul's first missionary journey—the beginning of his master plan of evangelism.

Warming Up to God Do you feel distant from God as you try to approach the Scriptures? Remember that God in his great mercy has come to us first and wants to meet us here. He longs to care for us, his little sheep, and capture us in his arms.

  Read Acts 13—14.

---

13 In the church at Antioch there were prophets and teachers: Barnabas, Simeon called Niger, Lucius of Cyrene, Manaen (who had been brought up with Herod the tetrarch) and Saul. 2While they were worshiping the Lord and fasting, the Holy Spirit said, "Set apart for me Barnabas and Saul for the work to which I have called them." 3So after they

had fasted and prayed, they placed their hands on them and sent them off.

[4]The two of them, sent on their way by the Holy Spirit, went down to Seleucia and sailed from there to Cyprus. [5]When they arrived at Salamis, they proclaimed the word of God in the Jewish synagogues. John was with them as their helper.

[6]They traveled through the whole island until they came to Paphos. There they met a Jewish sorcerer and false prophet named Bar-Jesus, [7]who was an attendant of the proconsul, Sergius Paulus. The proconsul, an intelligent man, sent for Barnabas and Saul because he wanted to hear the word of God. [8]But Elymas the sorcerer (for that is what his name means) opposed them and tried to turn the proconsul from the faith. [9]Then Saul, who was also called Paul, filled with the Holy Spirit, looked straight at Elymas and said, [10]"You are a child of the devil and an enemy of everything that is right! You are full of all kinds of deceit and trickery. Will you never stop perverting the right ways of the Lord? [11]Now the hand of the Lord is against you. You are going to be blind, and for a time you will be unable to see the light of the sun."

Immediately mist and darkness came over him, and he groped about, seeking someone to lead him by the hand. [12]When the proconsul saw what had happened, he believed, for he was amazed at the teaching about the Lord.

[13]From Paphos, Paul and his companions sailed to Perga in Pamphylia, where John left them to return to Jerusalem. [14]From Perga they went on to Pisidian Antioch. On the Sabbath they entered the synagogue and sat down. [15]After the reading from the Law and the Prophets, the synagogue rulers sent word to them, saying, "Brothers, if you have a message of encouragement for the people, please speak."

[16]Standing up, Paul motioned with his hand and said: "Men of Israel and you Gentiles who worship God, listen to me! [17]The God of the people of Israel chose our fathers; he made the people prosper during their stay in Egypt, with mighty power he led them out of that country, [18]he endured their conduct[u] for about forty years in the desert, [19]he overthrew seven nations in Canaan and gave their land to his people as their inheritance. [20]All this took about 450 years.

"After this, God gave them judges until the time of Samuel the prophet. [21]Then the people asked for a king, and he gave them Saul son of Kish, of the tribe of Benjamin, who ruled forty years. [22]After removing Saul, he made David their king. He testified concerning him: 'I have found David son of Jesse a man after my own heart; he will do everything I want him to do.'

[23]"From this man's descendants God has brought to Israel the Savior Jesus, as he promised. [24]Before the coming of Jesus, John preached repentance and baptism to all the people of Israel. [25]As John was completing his work, he said: 'Who do you think I am? I am not that one. No, but he is coming after me, whose sandals I am not worthy to untie.'

[26]"Brothers, children of Abraham, and you God-fearing Gentiles, it is to us that this message of salvation has been sent. [27]The people of Jerusalem and their rulers did not recognize Jesus, yet in condemning him they fulfilled the words of the prophets that are read every Sabbath. [28]Though they found no proper ground for a death sentence, they asked Pilate to have him executed. [29]When they had carried out all that was written about him, they took him down from the tree and laid him in a tomb. [30]But God raised him from the dead, [31]and for many days he was seen by those who had traveled with him from Galilee to Jerusalem. They are now his witnesses to our people.

[32]"We tell you the good news: What God promised our fathers [33]he has fulfilled for us, their children, by raising up Jesus. As it is written in the second Psalm:

" 'You are my Son;
    today I have become your Father.'[v][w]

[34]The fact that God raised him from the dead, never to decay, is stated in these words:

" 'I will give you the holy and sure blessings
    promised to David.'[x]

[35]So it is stated elsewhere:

" 'You will not let your Holy One see decay.'[y]

[36]"For when David had served God's purpose in his own generation, he fell asleep; he was buried with his fathers and his body decayed. [37]But the one whom God raised from the dead did not see decay.

[38]"Therefore, my brothers, I want you to know that through Jesus the forgiveness of sins is pro-

[u]18 Some manuscripts *and cared for them*   [v]33 Or *have begotten you*   [w]33 Psalm 2:7   [x]34 Isaiah 55:3   [y]35 Psalm 16:10

claimed to you. ³⁹Through him everyone who believes is justified from everything you could not be justified from by the law of Moses. ⁴⁰Take care that what the prophets have said does not happen to you:

⁴¹" 'Look, you scoffers,
        wonder and perish,
    for I am going to do something in your days
        that you would never believe,
        even if someone told you.'ᶻ"

⁴²As Paul and Barnabas were leaving the synagogue, the people invited them to speak further about these things on the next Sabbath. ⁴³When the congregation was dismissed, many of the Jews and devout converts to Judaism followed Paul and Barnabas, who talked with them and urged them to continue in the grace of God.

⁴⁴On the next Sabbath almost the whole city gathered to hear the word of the Lord. ⁴⁵When the Jews saw the crowds, they were filled with jealousy and talked abusively against what Paul was saying.

⁴⁶Then Paul and Barnabas answered them boldly: "We had to speak the word of God to you first. Since you reject it and do not consider yourselves worthy of eternal life, we now turn to the Gentiles. ⁴⁷For this is what the Lord has commanded us:

" 'I have made youᵃ a light for the Gentiles,
        that youᵃ may bring salvation to the ends
            of the earth.'ᵇ"

⁴⁸When the Gentiles heard this, they were glad and honored the word of the Lord; and all who were appointed for eternal life believed.

⁴⁹The word of the Lord spread through the whole region. ⁵⁰But the Jews incited the God-fearing women of high standing and the leading men of the city. They stirred up persecution against Paul and Barnabas, and expelled them from their region. ⁵¹So they shook the dust from their feet in protest against them and went to Iconium. ⁵²And the disciples were filled with joy and with the Holy Spirit.

14 At Iconium Paul and Barnabas went as usual into the Jewish synagogue. There they spoke so effectively that a great number of Jews and Gentiles believed. ²But the Jews who refused to believe stirred up the Gentiles and poisoned their minds against the brothers. ³So Paul and Barnabas spent consider-

able time there, speaking boldly for the Lord, who confirmed the message of his grace by enabling them to do miraculous signs and wonders. ⁴The people of the city were divided; some sided with the Jews, others with the apostles. ⁵There was a plot afoot among the Gentiles and Jews, together with their leaders, to mistreat them and stone them. ⁶But they found out about it and fled to the Lycaonian cities of Lystra and Derbe and to the surrounding country, ⁷where they continued to preach the good news.

⁸In Lystra there sat a man crippled in his feet, who was lame from birth and had never walked. ⁹He listened to Paul as he was speaking. Paul looked directly at him, saw that he had faith to be healed ¹⁰and called out, "Stand up on your feet!" At that, the man jumped up and began to walk.

¹¹When the crowd saw what Paul had done, they shouted in the Lycaonian language, "The gods have come down to us in human form!" ¹²Barnabas they called Zeus, and Paul they called Hermes because he was the chief speaker. ¹³The priest of Zeus, whose temple was just outside the city, brought bulls and wreaths to the city gates because he and the crowd wanted to offer sacrifices to them.

¹⁴But when the apostles Barnabas and Paul heard of this, they tore their clothes and rushed out into the crowd, shouting: ¹⁵"Men, why are you doing this? We too are only men, human like you. We are bringing you good news, telling you to turn from these worthless things to the living God, who made heaven and earth and sea and everything in them. ¹⁶In the past, he let all nations go their own way. ¹⁷Yet he has not left himself without testimony: He has shown kindness by giving you rain from heaven and crops in their seasons; he provides you with plenty of food and fills your hearts with joy." ¹⁸Even with these words, they had difficulty keeping the crowd from sacrificing to them.

¹⁹Then some Jews came from Antioch and Iconium and won the crowd over. They stoned Paul and dragged him outside the city, thinking he was dead. ²⁰But after the disciples had gathered around him, he got up and went back into the city. The next day he and Barnabas left for Derbe.

²¹They preached the good news in that city and won a large number of disciples. Then they returned to Lystra, Iconium and Antioch,

ᶻ41 Hab. 1:5   ᵃ47 The Greek is singular.   ᵇ47 Isaiah 49:6

²²strengthening the disciples and encouraging them to remain true to the faith. "We must go through many hardships to enter the kingdom of God," they said. ²³Paul and Barnabas appointed elders^c for them in each church and, with prayer and fasting, committed them to the Lord, in whom they had put their trust. ²⁴After going through Pisidia, they came into Pamphylia, ²⁵and when they had preached the word in Perga, they went down to Attalia.

²⁶From Attalia they sailed back to Antioch, where they had been committed to the grace of God for the work they had now completed. ²⁷On arriving there, they gathered the church together and reported all that God had done through them and how he had opened the door of faith to the Gentiles. ²⁸And they stayed there a long time with the disciples.

c23 Or Barnabas ordained elders; or Barnabas had elders elected

---

Discovering the Word   1. Antioch was the second greatest metropolis of the church and the mother of Gentile Christianity. What role did the church of Antioch play in Paul's first missionary journey (13:1–3; 14:26–28)?   2. Review Paul's message in the synagogue in Pisidian Antioch (13:16–41). What truths of the gospel are communicated?   3. How does Paul's message show sensitivity to his audience and the context?   4. List the different responses to the gospel (13:7–8, 13, 42–45, 48, 52; 14:1–5) that you see throughout this passage. 5. How did Paul respond to those who rejected the gospel (13:9–11, 46, 51)? to those who believed (14:9–10, 21–23)?

Applying the Word   1. People today are not apt to offer sacrifices to those who bring the good news of Jesus. However, in what ways are we faced with the temptation to be "God" in another's life or to take credit for what God has done?   2. How can we help one another when in the midst of such temptations?   3. Consider the qualities you see in Paul and Barnabas that made them effective in their ministry. Which of these qualities do you want God to develop in you to make you more effective in communicating the gospel?

Responding in Prayer   Is there a way God wants to change you? Talk to God about it.

---

14 / *Acts 15*
Conflict in the Church

IN MOST AREAS of life, I think I am pretty realistic. When it comes to conflict among believers, however, I tend to be an idealist. I believe that unity is something that God requires of us. Believers should be able to talk, pray and work through conflict—just the way it was worked through by the church at Jerusalem. However, I am becoming a little more realistic about this. I have been in several situations in which I felt like I did everything within my power to bring about reconciliation—but failed.

This seems to be the case with Paul and Barnabas. These two men who were used by God to keep a church from splitting could not resolve their own differences and ended up going separate ways. The late Kenneth Strachan of Latin American Mission said, "We all need to live and serve in the constant recognition of our own humanity."

Warming Up to God   Has there been a time recently when you were in conflict with someone? Tell God about it and let his peace and compassion wash over you as he teaches you.

Read Acts 15.

---

15 Some men came down from Judea to Antioch and were teaching the brothers: "Unless you are circumcised, according to the custom taught by Moses, you cannot be saved." ²This brought Paul and Barnabas into sharp dispute and debate with them. So Paul and Barnabas were appointed, along with some other believers, to go up to Jerusalem to see the apostles and elders about this question. ³The church sent them on their way, and as they traveled through Phoenicia and Samaria, they told how the Gentiles had been con-

verted. This news made all the brothers very glad. [4]When they came to Jerusalem, they were welcomed by the church and the apostles and elders, to whom they reported everything God had done through them.

[5]Then some of the believers who belonged to the party of the Pharisees stood up and said, "The Gentiles must be circumcised and required to obey the law of Moses."

[6]The apostles and elders met to consider this question. [7]After much discussion, Peter got up and addressed them: "Brothers, you know that some time ago God made a choice among you that the Gentiles might hear from my lips the message of the gospel and believe. [8]God, who knows the heart, showed that he accepted them by giving the Holy Spirit to them, just as he did to us. [9]He made no distinction between us and them, for he purified their hearts by faith. [10]Now then, why do you try to test God by putting on the necks of the disciples a yoke that neither we nor our fathers have been able to bear? [11]No! We believe it is through the grace of our Lord Jesus that we are saved, just as they are."

[12]The whole assembly became silent as they listened to Barnabas and Paul telling about the miraculous signs and wonders God had done among the Gentiles through them. [13]When they finished, James spoke up: "Brothers, listen to me. [14]Simon[d] has described to us how God at first showed his concern by taking from the Gentiles a people for himself. [15]The words of the prophets are in agreement with this, as it is written:

[16]" 'After this I will return
    and rebuild David's fallen tent.
Its ruins I will rebuild,
    and I will restore it,
[17]that the remnant of men may seek the Lord,
    and all the Gentiles who bear my name,
says the Lord, who does these things'[e]
[18]   that have been known for ages.[f]

[19]"It is my judgment, therefore, that we should not make it difficult for the Gentiles who are turning to God. [20]Instead we should write to them, telling them to abstain from food polluted by idols, from sexual immorality, from the meat of strangled animals and from blood. [21]For Moses has been preached in every city from the earliest times and is read in the synagogues on every Sabbath."

[22]Then the apostles and elders, with the whole church, decided to choose some of their own men and send them to Antioch with Paul and Barnabas. They chose Judas (called Barsabbas) and Silas, two men who were leaders among the brothers. [23]With them they sent the following letter:

The apostles and elders, your brothers,

To the Gentile believers in Antioch, Syria and Cilicia:

Greetings.

[24]We have heard that some went out from us without our authorization and disturbed you, troubling your minds by what they said. [25]So we all agreed to choose some men and send them to you with our dear friends Barnabas and Paul— [26]men who have risked their lives for the name of our Lord Jesus Christ. [27]Therefore we are sending Judas and Silas to confirm by word of mouth what we are writing. [28]It seemed good to the Holy Spirit and to us not to burden you with anything beyond the following requirements: [29]You are to abstain from food sacrificed to idols, from blood, from the meat of strangled animals and from sexual immorality. You will do well to avoid these things.

Farewell.

[30]The men were sent off and went down to Antioch, where they gathered the church together and delivered the letter. [31]The people read it and were glad for its encouraging message. [32]Judas and Silas, who themselves were prophets, said much to encourage and strengthen the brothers. [33]After spending some time there, they were sent off by the brothers with the blessing of peace to return to those who had sent them.[g] [35]But Paul and Barnabas remained in Antioch, where they and many others taught and preached the word of the Lord.

[36]Some time later Paul said to Barnabas, "Let us go back and visit the brothers in all the towns where we preached the word of the Lord and see how they are doing." [37]Barnabas wanted to take John, also called Mark, with them, [38]but Paul did not think it wise to take him, because he had deserted them in Pamphylia and had not contin-

---

[d]14 Greek *Simeon*, a variant of *Simon*; that is, Peter   [e]17 Amos 9:11,12   [f]17,18 Some manuscripts *things'— / [18]known to the Lord for ages is his work*   [g]33 Some manuscripts *them,* [34]*but Silas decided to remain there*

ued with them in the work. ³⁹They had such a sharp disagreement that they parted company. Barnabas took Mark and sailed for Cyprus, ⁴⁰but Paul chose Silas and left, commended by the brothers to the grace of the Lord. ⁴¹He went through Syria and Cilicia, strengthening the churches.

 Discovering the Word 1. Describe the conflict that arises between the Christians (vv. 1–35). 2. Describe the spirit of those involved and the steps that were taken to resolve this conflict. 3. What were the results? 4. In what ways do you see (or can you assume) unity between Paul and Barnabas (vv. 36–41)? 5. Paul and Barnabas came to the point of "agreeing to disagree" and going their separate ways. What were the benefits of this temporary solution?

Applying the Word 1. What principles do you observe that are vital to follow as we face conflict with others in our Christian community? 2. Which of these principles do you struggle with implementing the most? 3. Both Paul and Barnabas seemed to have strong cases for their points of view. Under what kinds of circumstances should we surrender deep convictions when they are challenged by another? 4. No matter how strongly we feel about an issue, we do not see the whole picture. How should that affect the way we respond to people with whom we are in conflict?

Responding in Prayer Ask God to give you discernment as you face conflict in both the church and in your personal life.

---

15 / *Acts 16*
What Must I Do?

THE MEMORY IS still vivid. The event was InterVarsity's Urbana Missionary Conference. The place, a dormitory room. The person, a young lady from the Bible study group that I led. I sensed the prompting of the Holy Spirit to stop by Susan's room. As I walked in to say "hi" she looked up from the booklet she was reading and said, "I would like to become a Christian. Will you help me?" This dormitory setting was not quite as dramatic as the Philippian jail. But it was just as exciting to hear Susan's words, as it was for Paul and Silas to hear the jailer's cry, "Sirs, what must I do to be saved?"

 Warming Up to God Think back to the time you uttered those words, either to a friend or to God himself. Praise God for creating a desire for him in you and thank him for giving his precious salvation to you.

 Read Acts 16.

---

16 He came to Derbe and then to Lystra, where a disciple named Timothy lived, whose mother was a Jewess and a believer, but whose father was a Greek. ²The brothers at Lystra and Iconium spoke well of him. ³Paul wanted to take him along on the journey, so he circumcised him because of the Jews who lived in that area, for they all knew that his father was a Greek. ⁴As they traveled from town to town, they delivered the decisions reached by the apostles and elders in Jerusalem for the people to obey. ⁵So the churches were strengthened in the faith and grew daily in numbers.

⁶Paul and his companions traveled throughout the region of Phrygia and Galatia, having been kept by the Holy Spirit from preaching the word in the province of Asia. ⁷When they came to the border of Mysia, they tried to enter Bithynia, but the Spirit of Jesus would not allow them to. ⁸So they passed by Mysia and went down to Troas. ⁹During the night Paul had a vision of a man of Macedonia standing and begging him, "Come over to Macedonia and help us." ¹⁰After Paul had seen the vision, we got ready at once to leave for Macedonia, concluding that God had called us to preach the gospel to them.

¹¹From Troas we put out to sea and sailed

straight for Samothrace, and the next day on to Neapolis. ¹²From there we traveled to Philippi, a Roman colony and the leading city of that district of Macedonia. And we stayed there several days.

¹³On the Sabbath we went outside the city gate to the river, where we expected to find a place of prayer. We sat down and began to speak to the women who had gathered there. ¹⁴One of those listening was a woman named Lydia, a dealer in purple cloth from the city of Thyatira, who was a worshiper of God. The Lord opened her heart to respond to Paul's message. ¹⁵When she and the members of her household were baptized, she invited us to her home. "If you consider me a believer in the Lord," she said, "come and stay at my house." And she persuaded us.

¹⁶Once when we were going to the place of prayer, we were met by a slave girl who had a spirit by which she predicted the future. She earned a great deal of money for her owners by fortune-telling. ¹⁷This girl followed Paul and the rest of us, shouting, "These men are servants of the Most High God, who are telling you the way to be saved." ¹⁸She kept this up for many days. Finally Paul became so troubled that he turned around and said to the spirit, "In the name of Jesus Christ I command you to come out of her!" At that moment the spirit left her.

¹⁹When the owners of the slave girl realized that their hope of making money was gone, they seized Paul and Silas and dragged them into the marketplace to face the authorities. ²⁰They brought them before the magistrates and said, "These men are Jews, and are throwing our city into an uproar ²¹by advocating customs unlawful for us Romans to accept or practice."

²²The crowd joined in the attack against Paul and Silas, and the magistrates ordered them to be stripped and beaten. ²³After they had been severely flogged, they were thrown into prison, and the jailer was commanded to guard them carefully. ²⁴Upon receiving such orders, he put them in the inner cell and fastened their feet in the stocks.

²⁵About midnight Paul and Silas were praying and singing hymns to God, and the other prisoners were listening to them. ²⁶Suddenly there was such a violent earthquake that the foundations of the prison were shaken. At once all the prison doors flew open, and everybody's chains came loose. ²⁷The jailer woke up, and when he saw the prison doors open, he drew his sword and was about to kill himself because he thought the prisoners had escaped. ²⁸But Paul shouted, "Don't harm yourself! We are all here!"

²⁹The jailer called for lights, rushed in and fell trembling before Paul and Silas. ³⁰He then brought them out and asked, "Sirs, what must I do to be saved?"

³¹They replied, "Believe in the Lord Jesus, and you will be saved—you and your household." ³²Then they spoke the word of the Lord to him and to all the others in his house. ³³At that hour of the night the jailer took them and washed their wounds; then immediately he and all his family were baptized. ³⁴The jailer brought them into his house and set a meal before them; he was filled with joy because he had come to believe in God—he and his whole family.

³⁵When it was daylight, the magistrates sent their officers to the jailer with the order: "Release those men." ³⁶The jailer told Paul, "The magistrates have ordered that you and Silas be released. Now you can leave. Go in peace."

³⁷But Paul said to the officers: "They beat us publicly without a trial, even though we are Roman citizens, and threw us into prison. And now do they want to get rid of us quietly? No! Let them come themselves and escort us out."

³⁸The officers reported this to the magistrates, and when they heard that Paul and Silas were Roman citizens, they were alarmed. ³⁹They came to appease them and escorted them from the prison, requesting them to leave the city. ⁴⁰After Paul and Silas came out of the prison, they went to Lydia's house, where they met with the brothers and encouraged them. Then they left.

Discovering the Word 1. In verses 6–10 how is Paul directed concerning where he should go? 2. What principles of guidance do you see in verses 6–10? 3. Paul responded immediately to God's message. How was his obedience confirmed on arriving in Macedonia (vv. 11–15)? 4. The slaveowners had Paul and Silas jailed. Their response to being in jail and being beaten was to pray and sing hymns. Describe the events that led up to the jailer's question "What must I do to be saved?" (vv. 23–30). 5. It is clear in the book of Acts that God is concerned about the world and the nations being reached with the gospel. But he is also concerned about reaching individuals. What individuals were affected by Paul's obedience to God's leading (vv. 14, 18, 30–31)? How?

Applying the Word 1. How does your response to opposition to and suffering for the gospel compare and contrast to that of Paul and Silas (v. 25)? 2. Paul and Silas speak the truth of the gospel as well as living it out. How do you give both a verbal and a living witness to Jesus? 3. Is there a person or task to which God is calling you? What steps do you need to take for immediate and unreserved obedience?

Responding in Prayer Ask God to give you courage as you step in faith to obey him, to tell those around you about the good news that has transformed your life.

16 / Acts 17
An Unknown God

ONLY A FEW short decades ago, Christians in the West could assume that most people they met belonged to a church or at least based their lives on Judeo-Christian values. Today, Christians in the West face what Christians in the East have had to cope with for centuries—a wide variety of religious beliefs and practices that often have little in common with Christianity. The world's major religions, Hinduism, Buddhism and Islam, are making inroads as are a variety of cults, New Age philosophies, occultic activities and even traditional paganism. How do we cope with a world that knows or cares so little about the truth of Jesus Christ? Paul left us a helpful model when he visited the world center of pagan philosophy and religion—Athens.

 Warming Up to God Do you often feel overwhelmed by the dismal spiritual conditions of this world? Remember and even savor the knowledge that Jesus is Lord over it all—the sin, deceit and pain around us are all subject to his will.

 Read Acts 17.

17 When they had passed through Amphipolis and Apollonia, they came to Thessalonica, where there was a Jewish synagogue. ²As his custom was, Paul went into the synagogue, and on three Sabbath days he reasoned with them from the Scriptures, ³explaining and proving that the Christ[h] had to suffer and rise from the dead. "This Jesus I am proclaiming to you is the Christ,[h]" he said. ⁴Some of the Jews were persuaded and joined Paul and Silas, as did a large number of God-fearing Greeks and not a few prominent women.

⁵But the Jews were jealous; so they rounded up some bad characters from the marketplace, formed a mob and started a riot in the city. They rushed to Jason's house in search of Paul and Silas in order to bring them out to the crowd.[i] ⁶But when they did not find them, they dragged Jason and some other brothers before the city officials, shouting: "These men who have caused trouble all over the world have now come here, ⁷and Jason has welcomed them into his house. They are all defying Caesar's decrees, saying that there is another king, one called Jesus." ⁸When they heard this, the crowd and the city officials were thrown into turmoil. ⁹Then they made Jason and the others post bond and let them go.

¹⁰As soon as it was night, the brothers sent Paul and Silas away to Berea. On arriving there, they went to the Jewish synagogue. ¹¹Now the Bereans were of more noble character than the Thessalonians, for they received the message with great eagerness and examined the Scriptures every day to see if what Paul said was true. ¹²Many of the Jews believed, as did also a number of prominent Greek women and many Greek men.

¹³When the Jews in Thessalonica learned that Paul was preaching the word of God at Berea, they went there too, agitating the crowds and stirring them up. ¹⁴The brothers immediately sent Paul to the coast, but Silas and Timothy stayed at Berea. ¹⁵The men who escorted Paul brought him to Athens and then left with instructions for Silas and Timothy to join him as soon as possible.

¹⁶While Paul was waiting for them in Athens, he was greatly distressed to see that the city was full of idols. ¹⁷So he reasoned in the synagogue with the Jews and the God-fearing Greeks, as well as in the marketplace day by day with those who

h3 Or Messiah   i5 Or the assembly of the people

happened to be there. ¹⁸A group of Epicurean and Stoic philosophers began to dispute with him. Some of them asked, "What is this babbler trying to say?" Others remarked, "He seems to be advocating foreign gods." They said this because Paul was preaching the good news about Jesus and the resurrection. ¹⁹Then they took him and brought him to a meeting of the Areopagus, where they said to him, "May we know what this new teaching is that you are presenting? ²⁰You are bringing some strange ideas to our ears, and we want to know what they mean." ²¹(All the Athenians and the foreigners who lived there spent their time doing nothing but talking about and listening to the latest ideas.)

²²Paul then stood up in the meeting of the Areopagus and said: "Men of Athens! I see that in every way you are very religious. ²³For as I walked around and looked carefully at your objects of worship, I even found an altar with this inscription: TO AN UNKNOWN GOD. Now what you worship as something unknown I am going to proclaim to you.

²⁴"The God who made the world and everything in it is the Lord of heaven and earth and does not live in temples built by hands. ²⁵And he is not served by human hands, as if he needed anything, because he himself gives all men life and breath and everything else. ²⁶From one man he made every nation of men, that they should inhabit the whole earth; and he determined the times set for them and the exact places where they should live. ²⁷God did this so that men would seek him and perhaps reach out for him and find him, though he is not far from each one of us. ²⁸'For in him we live and move and have our being.' As some of your own poets have said, 'We are his offspring.'

²⁹"Therefore since we are God's offspring, we should not think that the divine being is like gold or silver or stone—an image made by man's design and skill. ³⁰In the past God overlooked such ignorance, but now he commands all people everywhere to repent. ³¹For he has set a day when he will judge the world with justice by the man he has appointed. He has given proof of this to all men by raising him from the dead."

³²When they heard about the resurrection of the dead, some of them sneered, but others said, "We want to hear you again on this subject." ³³At that, Paul left the Council. ³⁴A few men became followers of Paul and believed. Among them was Dionysius, a member of the Areopagus, also a woman named Damaris, and a number of others.

 Discovering the Word 1. In this chapter Paul interacts with three cities and three different cultures. Compare and contrast Paul's ministry in Thessalonica and Berea. (What approach did he take? How was his message received by the people? What kind of results did he have?) 2. In Thessalonica and Berea, as in most places, Paul makes his contacts in the synagogues and speaks almost exclusively from Scripture. How does his ministry in Athens differ from this? 3. How do the people respond to his teaching in Athens? 4. Though Paul approaches people differently, some points in the content of his message are very consistent. Identify these (vv. 3, 18, 24–28, 30–31).

Applying the Word 1. In his lecture in Athens, Paul mentions "the objects of your worship." What are some of the objects of worship for people in our culture? 2. In Athens Paul begins to tell them about the living God with an inscription from one of their altars—"to an unknown god." What are the "points of truth" from which you can start to communicate the gospel to those in your world? 3. What are ways that you might be tempted to compromise the message of the gospel as you communicate it to certain people? 4. How do you need to better prepare yourself to effectively communicate the gospel of Jesus Christ to those to whom God has called you to minister?

Responding in Prayer Ask God to show you what you have in common with the non-Christians in your life.

17 / *Acts 18*
Companions in Ministry

JUST RECENTLY, I visited my childhood pastor and his wife. As I left them, my heart was full of gratitude. Gratitude not only for the Wrights, but also for the others past and present who have prepared me for outreach. I am thankful for those who have prayed for me, been my friends, walked along with me, listened to me, loved me and cared about my walk with God and my service to others, who have encouraged me and corrected me. I enjoy thinking about the people who have touched my life and who have been companions in ministry. I am not alone in this need for companionship. In this study we will look at some of the people in Paul's life who were his companions in ministry.

 Warming Up to God Close your eyes and think about one person who profoundly affects your life. Tell God how grateful you are to know such a wonderful friend and thank God for loving you through that person.

 Read Acts 18.

18 After this, Paul left Athens and went to Corinth. ²There he met a Jew named Aquila, a native of Pontus, who had recently come from Italy with his wife Priscilla, because Claudius had ordered all the Jews to leave Rome. Paul went to see them, ³and because he was a tentmaker as they were, he stayed and worked with them. ⁴Every Sabbath he reasoned in the synagogue, trying to persuade Jews and Greeks.

⁵When Silas and Timothy came from Macedonia, Paul devoted himself exclusively to preaching, testifying to the Jews that Jesus was the Christ.ʲ ⁶But when the Jews opposed Paul and became abusive, he shook out his clothes in protest and said to them, "Your blood be on your own heads! I am clear of my responsibility. From now on I will go to the Gentiles."

⁷Then Paul left the synagogue and went next door to the house of Titius Justus, a worshiper of God. ⁸Crispus, the synagogue ruler, and his entire household believed in the Lord; and many of the Corinthians who heard him believed and were baptized.

⁹One night the Lord spoke to Paul in a vision: "Do not be afraid; keep on speaking, do not be silent. ¹⁰For I am with you, and no one is going to attack and harm you, because I have many people in this city." ¹¹So Paul stayed for a year and a half, teaching them the word of God.

¹²While Gallio was proconsul of Achaia, the Jews made a united attack on Paul and brought him into court. ¹³"This man," they charged, "is persuading the people to worship God in ways contrary to the law."

¹⁴Just as Paul was about to speak, Gallio said to the Jews, "If you Jews were making a complaint about some misdemeanor or serious crime, it would be reasonable for me to listen to you. ¹⁵But since it involves questions about words and names and your own law—settle the matter yourselves. I will not be a judge of such things." ¹⁶So he had them ejected from the court. ¹⁷Then they all turned on Sosthenes the synagogue ruler and beat him in front of the court. But Gallio showed no concern whatever.

¹⁸Paul stayed on in Corinth for some time. Then he left the brothers and sailed for Syria, accompanied by Priscilla and Aquila. Before he sailed, he had his hair cut off at Cenchrea because of a vow he had taken. ¹⁹They arrived at Ephesus, where Paul left Priscilla and Aquila. He himself went into the synagogue and reasoned with the Jews. ²⁰When they asked him to spend more time with them, he declined. ²¹But as he left, he promised, "I will come back if it is God's will." Then he set sail from Ephesus. ²²When he landed at Caesarea, he went up and greeted the church and then went down to Antioch.

²³After spending some time in Antioch, Paul set out from there and traveled from place to place throughout the region of Galatia and Phrygia, strengthening all the disciples.

²⁴Meanwhile a Jew named Apollos, a native of Alexandria, came to Ephesus. He was a learned man, with a thorough knowledge of the Scriptures. ²⁵He had been instructed in the way of the Lord, and he spoke with great fervorᵏ and taught

ʲ5 Or *Messiah*; also in verse 28   ᵏ25 Or *with fervor in the Spirit*

about Jesus accurately, though he knew only the baptism of John. ²⁶He began to speak boldly in the synagogue. When Priscilla and Aquila heard him, they invited him to their home and explained to him the way of God more adequately.

²⁷When Apollos wanted to go to Achaia, the brothers encouraged him and wrote to the disciples there to welcome him. On arriving, he was a great help to those who by grace had believed. ²⁸For he vigorously refuted the Jews in public debate, proving from the Scriptures that Jesus was the Christ.

Discovering the Word 1. List the people in Paul's life that you see in this passage. 2. What did Silas and Timothy contribute to Paul's life and ministry (v. 5)? 3. In verses 18–23 what do you learn about Paul's relationships? 4. Describe Apollos (vv. 24–26). 5. How was Apollos's ministry affected by his relationship with Aquila and Priscilla (vv. 27–28)?

Applying the Word 1. When has someone encouraged you with good news of God's work elsewhere, entered into your ministry, shared themselves or their home with you, or supported you financially or in other ways? 2. What keeps you from allowing others to enter into your life and ministry in such ways? 3. As you review this passage, what ways do you recognize in which you need to develop, build and nurture relationships that will contribute to your spiritual growth and outreach?

Responding in Prayer Who are your companions in ministry? Thank God for their presence in your life as good gifts from him.

18 / *Acts 19:1—20:12*
In the Name of Jesus

WE LEFT PAUL in chapter 18 traveling throughout Galatia and Phrygia "strengthening all the disciples." In this chapter he returns to Ephesus, where he settles for two and a half years. Great work is done there during this time, and it radiates out to other cities in the province of Asia. Luke vividly portrays the effect of Paul's ministry in just a few scenes in this chapter.

Warming Up to God Often we feel that reading the Bible is our time to give to God. But he dearly wants to come to us as we study Scripture and pray. Lay aside your effort right now and commit yourself to accepting God's grace. Let God be your companion while you study the Word.

Read Acts 19:1—20:12.

19 While Apollos was at Corinth, Paul took the road through the interior and arrived at Ephesus. There he found some disciples ²and asked them, "Did you receive the Holy Spirit when¹ you believed?"

They answered, "No, we have not even heard that there is a Holy Spirit."

³So Paul asked, "Then what baptism did you receive?"

"John's baptism," they replied.

⁴Paul said, "John's baptism was a baptism of repentance. He told the people to believe in the one coming after him, that is, in Jesus." ⁵On hearing this, they were baptized into^m the name of the Lord Jesus. ⁶When Paul placed his hands on

them, the Holy Spirit came on them, and they spoke in tongues^n and prophesied. ⁷There were about twelve men in all.

⁸Paul entered the synagogue and spoke boldly there for three months, arguing persuasively about the kingdom of God. ⁹But some of them became obstinate; they refused to believe and publicly maligned the Way. So Paul left them. He took the disciples with him and had discussions daily in the lecture hall of Tyrannus. ¹⁰This went on for two years, so that all the Jews and Greeks who lived in the province of Asia heard the word of the Lord.

¹¹God did extraordinary miracles through Paul,

¹2 Or *after*   ^m5 Or *in*   ^n6 Or *other languages*

¹²so that even handkerchiefs and aprons that had touched him were taken to the sick, and their illnesses were cured and the evil spirits left them.

¹³Some Jews who went around driving out evil spirits tried to invoke the name of the Lord Jesus over those who were demon-possessed. They would say, "In the name of Jesus, whom Paul preaches, I command you to come out." ¹⁴Seven sons of Sceva, a Jewish chief priest, were doing this. ¹⁵⌊One day⌋ the evil spirit answered them, "Jesus I know, and I know about Paul, but who are you?" ¹⁶Then the man who had the evil spirit jumped on them and overpowered them all. He gave them such a beating that they ran out of the house naked and bleeding.

¹⁷When this became known to the Jews and Greeks living in Ephesus, they were all seized with fear, and the name of the Lord Jesus was held in high honor. ¹⁸Many of those who believed now came and openly confessed their evil deeds. ¹⁹A number who had practiced sorcery brought their scrolls together and burned them publicly. When they calculated the value of the scrolls, the total came to fifty thousand drachmas.ᵒ ²⁰In this way the word of the Lord spread widely and grew in power.

²¹After all this had happened, Paul decided to go to Jerusalem, passing through Macedonia and Achaia. "After I have been there," he said, "I must visit Rome also." ²²He sent two of his helpers, Timothy and Erastus, to Macedonia, while he stayed in the province of Asia a little longer.

²³About that time there arose a great disturbance about the Way. ²⁴A silversmith named Demetrius, who made silver shrines of Artemis, brought in no little business for the craftsmen. ²⁵He called them together, along with the workmen in related trades, and said: "Men, you know we receive a good income from this business. ²⁶And you see and hear how this fellow Paul has convinced and led astray large numbers of people here in Ephesus and in practically the whole province of Asia. He says that man-made gods are no gods at all. ²⁷There is danger not only that our trade will lose its good name, but also that the temple of the great goddess Artemis will be discredited, and the goddess herself, who is worshiped throughout the province of Asia and the world, will be robbed of her divine majesty."

²⁸When they heard this, they were furious and began shouting: "Great is Artemis of the Ephesians!" ²⁹Soon the whole city was in an uproar. The people seized Gaius and Aristarchus, Paul's traveling companions from Macedonia, and rushed as one man into the theater. ³⁰Paul wanted to appear before the crowd, but the disciples would not let him. ³¹Even some of the officials of the province, friends of Paul, sent him a message begging him not to venture into the theater.

³²The assembly was in confusion: Some were shouting one thing, some another. Most of the people did not even know why they were there. ³³The Jews pushed Alexander to the front, and some of the crowd shouted instructions to him. He motioned for silence in order to make a defense before the people. ³⁴But when they realized he was a Jew, they all shouted in unison for about two hours: "Great is Artemis of the Ephesians!"

³⁵The city clerk quieted the crowd and said: "Men of Ephesus, doesn't all the world know that the city of Ephesus is the guardian of the temple of the great Artemis and of her image, which fell from heaven? ³⁶Therefore, since these facts are undeniable, you ought to be quiet and not do anything rash. ³⁷You have brought these men here, though they have neither robbed temples nor blasphemed our goddess. ³⁸If, then, Demetrius and his fellow craftsmen have a grievance against anybody, the courts are open and there are proconsuls. They can press charges. ³⁹If there is anything further you want to bring up, it must be settled in a legal assembly. ⁴⁰As it is, we are in danger of being charged with rioting because of today's events. In that case we would not be able to account for this commotion, since there is no reason for it." ⁴¹After he had said this, he dismissed the assembly.

20 When the uproar had ended, Paul sent for the disciples and, after encouraging them, said good-by and set out for Macedonia. ²He traveled through that area, speaking many words of encouragement to the people, and finally arrived in Greece, ³where he stayed three months. Because the Jews made a plot against him just as he was about to sail for Syria, he decided to go back through Macedonia. ⁴He was accompanied by Sopater son of Pyrrhus from Berea, Aristarchus and Secundus from Thessalonica, Gaius from Derbe, Timothy also, and Tychicus and Trophimus from the province of Asia. ⁵These men went on ahead and waited for us at Troas. ⁶But we sailed from Philippi after the

---

ᵒ19 A drachma was a silver coin worth about a day's wages.

Feast of Unleavened Bread, and five days later joined the others at Troas, where we stayed seven days.

⁷On the first day of the week we came together to break bread. Paul spoke to the people and, because he intended to leave the next day, kept on talking until midnight. ⁸There were many lamps in the upstairs room where we were meeting. ⁹Seated in a window was a young man named Eutychus, who was sinking into a deep sleep as Paul talked on and on. When he was sound asleep, he fell to the ground from the third story and was picked up dead. ¹⁰Paul went down, threw himself on the young man and put his arms around him. "Don't be alarmed," he said. "He's alive!" ¹¹Then he went upstairs again and broke bread and ate. After talking until daylight, he left. ¹²The people took the young man home alive and were greatly comforted.

Discovering the Word 1. Scan chapter 19. Where do you see God's power revealed? 2. In 19:1–7 Paul encounters some disciples. What did he do to interact with them effectively? 3. Throughout this entire passage it is evident that Paul has a strategy for communicating the gospel. Specifically, what strategy does Paul have for his ministry in Ephesus (19:8–10)? 4. What is the cause of the riot in Ephesus (19:23–41)? How was it settled? 5. Paul continued to travel and encourage believers as he preached the gospel. What effect did the episode in 20:7–12 have on the crowd?

Applying the Word 1. What do you see in Paul's relationship with the disciples that might help you in relating to young Christians or your non-Christian friends? 2. What kind of plan for communicating the gospel would be helpful in your world? 3. How can you prepare yourself for both positive and negative responses as you are a part of communicating the gospel of Christ?

Responding in Prayer Thank God for the amazing fact that he uses us, sinful humanity, to spread the gospel and advance his kingdom. Thank him for using you.

19 / Acts 20:13–38
Paul's Farewell

"I WILL SEE you in heaven." I nodded, gave him a hug and a kiss and walked away from his bedside. When I left the room, I wept. Although it was twenty years ago that I said goodby to Pop Z, the memory is still deep in my heart. In this chapter we will enter into weeping as Paul says his final goodby to the elders at Ephesus. He knows that more hardship and prison await him in Jerusalem. And he will never see the faces of these elders again.

Warming Up to God Is the busyness of the world around you crowding you as you seek the face of God? Thank God that he has given you the grace that brought you to his Word right now, and ask him to still your restless heart as he comes to sit with you.

Read Acts 20:13–38.

¹³We went on ahead to the ship and sailed for Assos, where we were going to take Paul aboard. He had made this arrangement because he was going there on foot. ¹⁴When he met us at Assos, we took him aboard and went on to Mitylene. ¹⁵The next day we set sail from there and arrived off Kios. The day after that we crossed over to Samos, and on the following day arrived at Miletus. ¹⁶Paul had decided to sail past Ephesus to avoid spending time in the province of Asia, for he was in a hurry to reach Jerusalem, if possible, by the day of Pentecost.

¹⁷From Miletus, Paul sent to Ephesus for the elders of the church. ¹⁸When they arrived, he said to them: "You know how I lived the whole time I was with you, from the first day I came into the province of Asia. ¹⁹I served the Lord with great humility and with tears, although I was severely tested by the plots of the Jews. ²⁰You know that I have not hesitated to preach anything that would

be helpful to you but have taught you publicly and from house to house. ²¹I have declared to both Jews and Greeks that they must turn to God in repentance and have faith in our Lord Jesus.

²²"And now, compelled by the Spirit, I am going to Jerusalem, not knowing what will happen to me there. ²³I only know that in every city the Holy Spirit warns me that prison and hardships are facing me. ²⁴However, I consider my life worth nothing to me, if only I may finish the race and complete the task the Lord Jesus has given me—the task of testifying to the gospel of God's grace.

²⁵"Now I know that none of you among whom I have gone about preaching the kingdom will ever see me again. ²⁶Therefore, I declare to you today that I am innocent of the blood of all men. ²⁷For I have not hesitated to proclaim to you the whole will of God. ²⁸Keep watch over yourselves and all the flock of which the Holy Spirit has made you overseers.ᵖ Be shepherds of the church of God,�q which he bought with his own blood. ²⁹I know that after I leave, savage wolves will come in among you and will not spare the flock. ³⁰Even from your own number men will arise and distort the truth in order to draw away disciples after them. ³¹So be on your guard! Remember that for three years I never stopped warning each of you night and day with tears.

³²"Now I commit you to God and to the word of his grace, which can build you up and give you an inheritance among all those who are sanctified. ³³I have not coveted anyone's silver or gold or clothing. ³⁴You yourselves know that these hands of mine have supplied my own needs and the needs of my companions. ³⁵In everything I did, I showed you that by this kind of hard work we must help the weak, remembering the words the Lord Jesus himself said: 'It is more blessed to give than to receive.' "

³⁶When he had said this, he knelt down with all of them and prayed. ³⁷They all wept as they embraced him and kissed him. ³⁸What grieved them most was his statement that they would never see his face again. Then they accompanied him to the ship.

ᵖ28 Traditionally *bishops*   q28 Many manuscripts *of the Lord*

Discovering the Word   1. What does Paul say about his ministry to the Ephesians (vv. 18–21, 26–27, 31, 33–35)?   2. What are Paul's priorities (vv. 22–25)?   3. What instructions did Paul give to the leaders of the church at Ephesus (vv. 28–31)?   4. According to verse 32, why can Paul leave them with confidence?   5. In summary, according to this passage, why would Paul be able to say with integrity and humility to these leaders, "Follow my example. Do as I have done"?

Applying the Word   1. Who is in your spiritual care?   2. How are you preparing those that you nurture spiritually so that you can leave them with this same confidence?   3. Paul and the Ephesian elders were given the rare and special gift of being able to say goodby. What would you want to say to those in your spiritual care if you knew that you were going to die? Take time to express your hope and your love to that person in the near future.

Responding in Prayer   Ask God for the courage to say these most important words to those you love and for whom you care deeply.

---

20 / *Acts 21:1—22:21*
Facing Opposition

AS THEY WENT to their death, taking the gospel of Jesus Christ to the Auca Indians, five young men sang:
We go in faith, our own great weakness feeling,
And needing more each day Thy grace to know:
Yet from our hearts a song of triumph pealing;
We rest on Thee, and in Thy name we go.

We rest on Thee our Shield and our Defender!
Thine is the battle, thine shall be the praise
When passing through the gates of pearly splendor,
Victors—we rest with Thee, through endless days.

Like Paul, knowing that death was a very real possibility, they did not turn aside from what they knew God wanted them to do.

 Warming Up to God   There are times when we do not feel courageous about our faith, but question it. However, God is just as real when we doubt or fear as when our faith is strong. Let him come to you now in the midst of your fear and allow him to stretch your vision of how powerful he truly is.

 Read Acts 21:1—22:21.

21 After we had torn ourselves away from them, we put out to sea and sailed straight to Cos. The next day we went to Rhodes and from there to Patara. ²We found a ship crossing over to Phoenicia, went on board and set sail. ³After sighting Cyprus and passing to the south of it, we sailed on to Syria. We landed at Tyre, where our ship was to unload its cargo. ⁴Finding the disciples there, we stayed with them seven days. Through the Spirit they urged Paul not to go on to Jerusalem. ⁵But when our time was up, we left and continued on our way. All the disciples and their wives and children accompanied us out of the city, and there on the beach we knelt to pray. ⁶After saying good-by to each other, we went aboard the ship, and they returned home.

⁷We continued our voyage from Tyre and landed at Ptolemais, where we greeted the brothers and stayed with them for a day. ⁸Leaving the next day, we reached Caesarea and stayed at the house of Philip the evangelist, one of the Seven. ⁹He had four unmarried daughters who prophesied.

¹⁰After we had been there a number of days, a prophet named Agabus came down from Judea. ¹¹Coming over to us, he took Paul's belt, tied his own hands and feet with it and said, "The Holy Spirit says, 'In this way the Jews of Jerusalem will bind the owner of this belt and will hand him over to the Gentiles.'"

¹²When we heard this, we and the people there pleaded with Paul not to go up to Jerusalem. ¹³Then Paul answered, "Why are you weeping and breaking my heart? I am ready not only to be bound, but also to die in Jerusalem for the name of the Lord Jesus." ¹⁴When he would not be dissuaded, we gave up and said, "The Lord's will be done."

¹⁵After this, we got ready and went up to Jeru-salem. ¹⁶Some of the disciples from Caesarea accompanied us and brought us to the home of Mnason, where we were to stay. He was a man from Cyprus and one of the early disciples.

¹⁷When we arrived at Jerusalem, the brothers received us warmly. ¹⁸The next day Paul and the rest of us went to see James, and all the elders were present. ¹⁹Paul greeted them and reported in detail what God had done among the Gentiles through his ministry.

²⁰When they heard this, they praised God. Then they said to Paul: "You see, brother, how many thousands of Jews have believed, and all of them are zealous for the law. ²¹They have been informed that you teach all the Jews who live among the Gentiles to turn away from Moses, telling them not to circumcise their children or live according to our customs. ²²What shall we do? They will certainly hear that you have come, ²³so do what we tell you. There are four men with us who have made a vow. ²⁴Take these men, join in their purification rites and pay their expenses, so that they can have their heads shaved. Then everybody will know there is no truth in these reports about you, but that you yourself are living in obedience to the law. ²⁵As for the Gentile believers, we have written to them our decision that they should abstain from food sacrificed to idols, from blood, from the meat of strangled animals and from sexual immorality."

²⁶The next day Paul took the men and purified himself along with them. Then he went to the temple to give notice of the date when the days of purification would end and the offering would be made for each of them.

²⁷When the seven days were nearly over, some Jews from the province of Asia saw Paul at the temple. They stirred up the whole crowd and seized him, ²⁸shouting, "Men of Israel, help us! This is the man who teaches all men everywhere

against our people and our law and this place. And besides, he has brought Greeks into the temple area and defiled this holy place." 29(They had previously seen Trophimus the Ephesian in the city with Paul and assumed that Paul had brought him into the temple area.)

30The whole city was aroused, and the people came running from all directions. Seizing Paul, they dragged him from the temple, and immediately the gates were shut. 31While they were trying to kill him, news reached the commander of the Roman troops that the whole city of Jerusalem was in an uproar. 32He at once took some officers and soldiers and ran down to the crowd. When the rioters saw the commander and his soldiers, they stopped beating Paul.

33The commander came up and arrested him and ordered him to be bound with two chains. Then he asked who he was and what he had done. 34Some in the crowd shouted one thing and some another, and since the commander could not get at the truth because of the uproar, he ordered that Paul be taken into the barracks. 35When Paul reached the steps, the violence of the mob was so great he had to be carried by the soldiers. 36The crowd that followed kept shouting, "Away with him!"

37As the soldiers were about to take Paul into the barracks, he asked the commander, "May I say something to you?"

"Do you speak Greek?" he replied. 38"Aren't you the Egyptian who started a revolt and led four thousand terrorists out into the desert some time ago?"

39Paul answered, "I am a Jew, from Tarsus in Cilicia, a citizen of no ordinary city. Please let me speak to the people."

40Having received the commander's permission, Paul stood on the steps and motioned to the crowd. When they were all silent, he said to them in Aramaic[r]:

22

1"Brothers and fathers, listen now to my defense." 2When they heard him speak to them in Aramaic, they became very quiet.

Then Paul said: 3"I am a Jew, born in Tarsus of Cilicia, but brought up in this city. Under Gamaliel I was thoroughly trained in the law of our fathers and was just as zealous for God as any of you are today. 4I persecuted the followers of this Way to their death, arresting both men and women and throwing them into prison, 5as also the high priest and all the Council can testify. I even obtained letters from them to their brothers in Damascus, and went there to bring these people as prisoners to Jerusalem to be punished.

6"About noon as I came near Damascus, suddenly a bright light from heaven flashed around me. 7I fell to the ground and heard a voice say to me, 'Saul! Saul! Why do you persecute me?'

8" 'Who are you, Lord?' I asked.

" 'I am Jesus of Nazareth, whom you are persecuting,' he replied. 9My companions saw the light, but they did not understand the voice of him who was speaking to me.

10" 'What shall I do, Lord?' I asked.

" 'Get up,' the Lord said, 'and go into Damascus. There you will be told all that you have been assigned to do.' 11My companions led me by the hand into Damascus, because the brilliance of the light had blinded me.

12"A man named Ananias came to see me. He was a devout observer of the law and highly respected by all the Jews living there. 13He stood beside me and said, 'Brother Saul, receive your sight!' And at that very moment I was able to see him.

14"Then he said: 'The God of our fathers has chosen you to know his will and to see the Righteous One and to hear words from his mouth. 15You will be his witness to all men of what you have seen and heard. 16And now what are you waiting for? Get up, be baptized and wash your sins away, calling on his name.'

17"When I returned to Jerusalem and was praying at the temple, I fell into a trance 18and saw the Lord speaking. 'Quick!' he said to me. 'Leave Jerusalem immediately, because they will not accept your testimony about me.'

19" 'Lord,' I replied, 'these men know that I went from one synagogue to another to imprison and beat those who believe in you. 20And when the blood of your martyr[s] Stephen was shed, I stood there giving my approval and guarding the clothes of those who were killing him.'

21"Then the Lord said to me, 'Go; I will send you far away to the Gentiles.' "

r40 Or possibly *Hebrew*; also in 22:2   s20 Or *witness*

Discovering the Word 1. Describe the warnings to Paul concerning going to Jerusalem (21:4, 10–12). 2. How did Paul respond to these warnings (21:5, 13)? 3. Paul arrives in Jerusalem, is greeted by the elders and reports what God has done through his ministry. What are the elders concerned about for Paul (21:20–25)? 4. How does Paul demonstrate his desire to be at one with the Jewish Christians (21:26)? 5. Note how Paul was treated with mob hysteria, assumption and false evidence (21:27–36, 38). How does he respond to all of this (21:37—22:21)?

Applying the Word 1. Think of a person you know who is focused on obeying God. How are you affected by his/her obedience? 2. How do you usually respond when you find yourself in conflict with others as a result of your obedience to God? 3. What have you seen in this passage that will help you become more single-minded in your obedience to God's will?

Responding in Prayer Tell God of your desire to be obedient, but admit the difficulties you face because of your sin. Ask him again to cleanse you and help you run the race with fervor.

21 / *Acts 22:22—23:35*
God at Work

BEING UNDER GOD'S protection is not a guarantee of physical safety. Being under his protection does guarantee that our Father is with us and has a purpose for us and that nothing happens to us that does not come through his hands. We can live with confidence that our life on earth will not end until that purpose for us is complete. And that ultimately we will end up safe and protected in heaven. Paul was so sure of God's hand in his life that he continued to move out boldly with the message of Jesus Christ in spite of physical danger intensifying.

 Warming Up to God The protection of the Father's strong arms is always around us. Thank him for his mighty but unseen acts that keep you safe and secure as you walk through this life.

 Read Acts 22:22—23:35.

---

²²The crowd listened to Paul until he said this. Then they raised their voices and shouted, "Rid the earth of him! He's not fit to live!"

²³As they were shouting and throwing off their cloaks and flinging dust into the air, ²⁴the commander ordered Paul to be taken into the barracks. He directed that he be flogged and questioned in order to find out why the people were shouting at him like this. ²⁵As they stretched him out to flog him, Paul said to the centurion standing there, "Is it legal for you to flog a Roman citizen who hasn't even been found guilty?"

²⁶When the centurion heard this, he went to the commander and reported it. "What are you going to do?" he asked. "This man is a Roman citizen."

²⁷The commander went to Paul and asked, "Tell me, are you a Roman citizen?"

"Yes, I am," he answered.

²⁸Then the commander said, "I had to pay a big price for my citizenship."

"But I was born a citizen," Paul replied.

²⁹Those who were about to question him withdrew immediately. The commander himself was alarmed when he realized that he had put Paul, a Roman citizen, in chains.

³⁰The next day, since the commander wanted to find out exactly why Paul was being accused by the Jews, he released him and ordered the chief priests and all the Sanhedrin to assemble. Then he brought Paul and had him stand before them.

23 Paul looked straight at the Sanhedrin and said, "My brothers, I have fulfilled my duty to God in all good conscience to this day." ²At this the high priest Ananias ordered those standing near Paul to strike him on the mouth. ³Then Paul said to him, "God will strike you, you whitewashed wall! You sit there to judge me according to the law, yet you yourself violate the law by commanding that I be struck!"

⁴Those who were standing near Paul said, "You dare to insult God's high priest?"

⁵Paul replied, "Brothers, I did not realize that

he was the high priest; for it is written: 'Do not speak evil about the ruler of your people.'[*t*]"

[6]Then Paul, knowing that some of them were Sadducees and the others Pharisees, called out in the Sanhedrin, "My brothers, I am a Pharisee, the son of a Pharisee. I stand on trial because of my hope in the resurrection of the dead." [7]When he said this, a dispute broke out between the Pharisees and the Sadducees, and the assembly was divided. [8](The Sadducees say that there is no resurrection, and that there are neither angels nor spirits, but the Pharisees acknowledge them all.)

[9]There was a great uproar, and some of the teachers of the law who were Pharisees stood up and argued vigorously. "We find nothing wrong with this man," they said. "What if a spirit or an angel has spoken to him?" [10]The dispute became so violent that the commander was afraid Paul would be torn to pieces by them. He ordered the troops to go down and take him away from them by force and bring him into the barracks.

[11]The following night the Lord stood near Paul and said, "Take courage! As you have testified about me in Jerusalem, so you must also testify in Rome."

[12]The next morning the Jews formed a conspiracy and bound themselves with an oath not to eat or drink until they had killed Paul. [13]More than forty men were involved in this plot. [14]They went to the chief priests and elders and said, "We have taken a solemn oath not to eat anything until we have killed Paul. [15]Now then, you and the Sanhedrin petition the commander to bring him before you on the pretext of wanting more accurate information about his case. We are ready to kill him before he gets here."

[16]But when the son of Paul's sister heard of this plot, he went into the barracks and told Paul.

[17]Then Paul called one of the centurions and said, "Take this young man to the commander; he has something to tell him." [18]So he took him to the commander.

The centurion said, "Paul, the prisoner, sent for me and asked me to bring this young man to you because he has something to tell you."

[19]The commander took the young man by the hand, drew him aside and asked, "What is it you want to tell me?"

[20]He said: "The Jews have agreed to ask you to bring Paul before the Sanhedrin tomorrow on the pretext of wanting more accurate information about him. [21]Don't give in to them, because more than forty of them are waiting in ambush for him. They have taken an oath not to eat or drink until they have killed him. They are ready now, waiting for your consent to their request."

[22]The commander dismissed the young man and cautioned him, "Don't tell anyone that you have reported this to me."

[23]Then he called two of his centurions and ordered them, "Get ready a detachment of two hundred soldiers, seventy horsemen and two hundred spearmen[*u*] to go to Caesarea at nine tonight. [24]Provide mounts for Paul so that he may be taken safely to Governor Felix."

[25]He wrote a letter as follows:

[26]Claudius Lysias,

To His Excellency, Governor Felix:

Greetings.

[27]This man was seized by the Jews and they were about to kill him, but I came with my troops and rescued him, for I had learned that he is a Roman citizen. [28]I wanted to know why they were accusing him, so I brought him to their Sanhedrin. [29]I found that the accusation had to do with questions about their law, but there was no charge against him that deserved death or imprisonment. [30]When I was informed of a plot to be carried out against the man, I sent him to you at once. I also ordered his accusers to present to you their case against him.

[31]So the soldiers, carrying out their orders, took Paul with them during the night and brought him as far as Antipatris. [32]The next day they let the cavalry go on with him, while they returned to the barracks. [33]When the cavalry arrived in Caesarea, they delivered the letter to the governor and handed Paul over to him. [34]The governor read the letter and asked what province he was from. Learning that he was from Cilicia, [35]he said, "I will hear your case when your accusers get here." Then he ordered that Paul be kept under guard in Herod's palace.

[*t*]5 Exodus 22:28   [*u*]23 The meaning of the Greek for this word is uncertain.

Discovering the Word 1. Throughout this passage, we can see God's hand in the circumstances of Paul's life, protecting and directing him. In Acts 22:22–29 what is the source of the conflict? What is it that protects Paul? 2. In 23:1–10 what is the source of the conflict? How is Paul protected? 3. Why was Paul struck on the mouth for saying, "My brothers, I have fulfilled my duty to God in all good conscience to this day" (23:1)? 4. In Acts 23:12–25 the Jews are frustrated because they cannot get rid of Paul through the law, so they decide to ambush and kill him on their own. How is Paul protected? 5. We have observed God's protection of Paul. How do we see God's care for Paul in a more direct and supernatural way in 23:11?

Applying the Word 1. Think about God's hand in your life and ministry. How have you seen him work to protect and direct you toward his will? 2. In what ways do you need to grow in humbly acknowledging God's hand in your life? 3. How has your hope for God's will to be done in you been affected by looking at God's hand in Paul's life?

Responding in Prayer Ask God to show you his active hand in your life.

---

22 / *Acts 24:1—25:12*
Falsely Accused

OUR DEAR FRIEND George was falsely accused and on trial for heresy. My husband prayed fervently that God would shut the accusers' mouths, that he would bind their efforts, and that truth would prevail and bring freedom. He asked God to confound their actions so that their own words would bring out the truth and show up their false accusations. God chose to do what Andy asked for, and George was exonerated in a dramatic fashion. The words of the accusers brought condemnation on them. The defense did not even have to present their case. The pain, however, of being falsely accused is great. And the damage was not easily repaired. But George's consistent godly response throughout the whole ordeal reminded me of Jesus and Paul when they were falsely accused.

Warming Up to God Remember that today has been given to you by God, and he desires to be with you as you walk through it. Let him come to you now, knowing that he will show you more of himself through his Word.

 Read Acts 24:1—25:12.

---

24 Five days later the high priest Ananias went down to Caesarea with some of the elders and a lawyer named Tertullus, and they brought their charges against Paul before the governor. ²When Paul was called in, Tertullus presented his case before Felix: "We have enjoyed a long period of peace under you, and your foresight has brought about reforms in this nation. ³Everywhere and in every way, most excellent Felix, we acknowledge this with profound gratitude. ⁴But in order not to weary you further, I would request that you be kind enough to hear us briefly.

⁵"We have found this man to be a troublemaker, stirring up riots among the Jews all over the world. He is a ringleader of the Nazarene sect ⁶and even tried to desecrate the temple; so we seized him. ⁸By^v examining him yourself you

will be able to learn the truth about all these charges we are bringing against him."

⁹The Jews joined in the accusation, asserting that these things were true.

¹⁰When the governor motioned for him to speak, Paul replied: "I know that for a number of years you have been a judge over this nation; so I gladly make my defense. ¹¹You can easily verify that no more than twelve days ago I went up to Jerusalem to worship. ¹²My accusers did not find me arguing with anyone at the temple, or stirring up a crowd in the synagogues or anywhere else in the city. ¹³And they cannot prove to you the charges they are now making against me. ¹⁴However, I admit that I worship the God of our fathers

^{v}6-8 Some manuscripts *him and wanted to judge him according to our law.* ⁷*But the commander, Lysias, came and with the use of much force snatched him from our hands* ⁸*and ordered his accusers to come before you. By*

as a follower of the Way, which they call a sect. I believe everything that agrees with the Law and that is written in the Prophets, ¹⁵and I have the same hope in God as these men, that there will be a resurrection of both the righteous and the wicked. ¹⁶So I strive always to keep my conscience clear before God and man.

¹⁷"After an absence of several years, I came to Jerusalem to bring my people gifts for the poor and to present offerings. ¹⁸I was ceremonially clean when they found me in the temple courts doing this. There was no crowd with me, nor was I involved in any disturbance. ¹⁹But there are some Jews from the province of Asia, who ought to be here before you and bring charges if they have anything against me. ²⁰Or these who are here should state what crime they found in me when I stood before the Sanhedrin— ²¹unless it was this one thing I shouted as I stood in their presence: 'It is concerning the resurrection of the dead that I am on trial before you today.' "

²²Then Felix, who was well acquainted with the Way, adjourned the proceedings. "When Lysias the commander comes," he said, "I will decide your case." ²³He ordered the centurion to keep Paul under guard but to give him some freedom and permit his friends to take care of his needs.

²⁴Several days later Felix came with his wife Drusilla, who was a Jewess. He sent for Paul and listened to him as he spoke about faith in Christ Jesus. ²⁵As Paul discoursed on righteousness, self-control and the judgment to come, Felix was afraid and said, "That's enough for now! You may leave. When I find it convenient, I will send for you." ²⁶At the same time he was hoping that Paul would offer him a bribe, so he sent for him frequently and talked with him.

²⁷When two years had passed, Felix was succeeded by Porcius Festus, but because Felix wanted to grant a favor to the Jews, he left Paul in prison.

25 Three days after arriving in the province, Festus went up from Caesarea to Jerusalem, ²where the chief priests and Jewish leaders appeared before him and presented the charges against Paul. ³They urgently requested Festus, as a favor to them, to have Paul transferred to Jerusalem, for they were preparing an ambush to kill him along the way. ⁴Festus answered, "Paul is being held at Caesarea, and I myself am going there soon. ⁵Let some of your leaders come with me and press charges against the man there, if he has done anything wrong."

⁶After spending eight or ten days with them, he went down to Caesarea, and the next day he convened the court and ordered that Paul be brought before him. ⁷When Paul appeared, the Jews who had come down from Jerusalem stood around him, bringing many serious charges against him, which they could not prove.

⁸Then Paul made his defense: "I have done nothing wrong against the law of the Jews or against the temple or against Caesar."

⁹Festus, wishing to do the Jews a favor, said to Paul, "Are you willing to go up to Jerusalem and stand trial before me there on these charges?"

¹⁰Paul answered: "I am now standing before Caesar's court, where I ought to be tried. I have not done any wrong to the Jews, as you yourself know very well. ¹¹If, however, I am guilty of doing anything deserving death, I do not refuse to die. But if the charges brought against me by these Jews are not true, no one has the right to hand me over to them. I appeal to Caesar!"

¹²After Festus had conferred with his council, he declared: "You have appealed to Caesar. To Caesar you will go!"

Discovering the Word 1. What are the accusations brought against Paul by the Jews (24:1–27)? 2. How would you describe Paul's defense? (Consider the content and the attitude and tone.) 3. What do you think is the significance of the fact that Felix was well acquainted with the Way (v. 22)? 4. In Acts 25:1–12 two years have passed since his trial, and Festus has become the new governor. The Jews have not given up. They continue to plot to kill Paul and ask Festus to have him transferred to Jerusalem. Festus refuses and tells the Jewish leaders to come to Caesarea for the trial. What evidence is there in this passage that Festus knows that Paul is innocent? 5. Why does Festus suggest that Paul go back to Jerusalem to be on trial?

Applying the Word 1. When have you known someone to respond to the proclamation of the gospel as Felix did? What might this mean? 2. Describe a time you have been falsely accused because of your faith. 3. What can you learn about how to respond to accusers from the way Paul responded to his accusers?

Responding in Prayer Ask God to give you patience and a heart of love for the people who surround you—your coworkers, family—people you can show the example of Christ.

23 / *Acts 25:13—26:32*
Testimony Before Agrippa

THOUGH HIS INNOCENCE has been clearly stated many times, Paul remains a prisoner. He repeatedly has to face the unfair charges of the Jewish leaders. He has made his defense with integrity and power, and in return he gets only threats of death. In it all Paul's witness remains consistent. His greatest desire is that his accusers and those in judgment over him will become Christians.

 Warming Up to God How do you respond to the unfairness in the world around you—poverty, homelessness, the unfairness in your own life? It is difficult to assume an attitude like Paul's in the face of injustice. But God sees and knows what is right, and he understands the anger we feel. Express your thoughts and feelings to him. Let him calm the stirring in your heart with his gentle words.

📖 **Read Acts 25:13—26:32.**

¹³A few days later King Agrippa and Bernice arrived at Caesarea to pay their respects to Festus. ¹⁴Since they were spending many days there, Festus discussed Paul's case with the king. He said: "There is a man here whom Felix left as a prisoner. ¹⁵When I went to Jerusalem, the chief priests and elders of the Jews brought charges against him and asked that he be condemned.

¹⁶"I told them that it is not the Roman custom to hand over any man before he has faced his accusers and has had an opportunity to defend himself against their charges. ¹⁷When they came here with me, I did not delay the case, but convened the court the next day and ordered the man to be brought in. ¹⁸When his accusers got up to speak, they did not charge him with any of the crimes I had expected. ¹⁹Instead, they had some points of dispute with him about their own religion and about a dead man named Jesus who Paul claimed was alive. ²⁰I was at a loss how to investigate such matters; so I asked if he would be willing to go to Jerusalem and stand trial there on these charges. ²¹When Paul made his appeal to be held over for the Emperor's decision, I ordered him held until I could send him to Caesar."

²²Then Agrippa said to Festus, "I would like to hear this man myself."

He replied, "Tomorrow you will hear him."

²³The next day Agrippa and Bernice came with great pomp and entered the audience room with the high ranking officers and the leading men of the city. At the command of Festus, Paul was brought in. ²⁴Festus said: "King Agrippa, and all who are present with us, you see this man! The whole Jewish community has petitioned me about him in Jerusalem and here in Caesarea, shouting that he ought not to live any longer. ²⁵I found he had done nothing deserving of death, but because he made his appeal to the Emperor I decided to send him to Rome. ²⁶But I have nothing definite to write to His Majesty about him. Therefore I have brought him before all of you, and especially before you, King Agrippa, so that as a result of this investigation I may have something to write. ²⁷For I think it is unreasonable to send on a prisoner without specifying the charges against him."

26 Then Agrippa said to Paul, "You have permission to speak for yourself."

So Paul motioned with his hand and began his defense: ²"King Agrippa, I consider myself fortunate to stand before you today as I make my defense against all the accusations of the Jews, ³and especially so because you are well acquainted with all the Jewish customs and controversies. Therefore, I beg you to listen to me patiently.

⁴"The Jews all know the way I have lived ever since I was a child, from the beginning of my life in my own country, and also in Jerusalem. ⁵They have known me for a long time and can testify, if they are willing, that according to the strictest

sect of our religion, I lived as a Pharisee. ⁶And now it is because of my hope in what God has promised our fathers that I am on trial today. ⁷This is the promise our twelve tribes are hoping to see fulfilled as they earnestly serve God day and night. O king, it is because of this hope that the Jews are accusing me. ⁸Why should any of you consider it incredible that God raises the dead?

⁹"I too was convinced that I ought to do all that was possible to oppose the name of Jesus of Nazareth. ¹⁰And that is just what I did in Jerusalem. On the authority of the chief priests I put many of the saints in prison, and when they were put to death, I cast my vote against them. ¹¹Many a time I went from one synagogue to another to have them punished, and I tried to force them to blaspheme. In my obsession against them, I even went to foreign cities to persecute them.

¹²"On one of these journeys I was going to Damascus with the authority and commission of the chief priests. ¹³About noon, O king, as I was on the road, I saw a light from heaven, brighter than the sun, blazing around me and my companions. ¹⁴We all fell to the ground, and I heard a voice saying to me in Aramaic,ʷ 'Saul, Saul, why do you persecute me? It is hard for you to kick against the goads.'

¹⁵"Then I asked, 'Who are you, Lord?'

" 'I am Jesus, whom you are persecuting,' the Lord replied. ¹⁶'Now get up and stand on your feet. I have appeared to you to appoint you as a servant and as a witness of what you have seen of me and what I will show you. ¹⁷I will rescue you from your own people and from the Gentiles. I am sending you to them ¹⁸to open their eyes and turn them from darkness to light, and from the power of Satan to God, so that they may receive forgiveness of sins and a place among those who are sanctified by faith in me.'

¹⁹"So then, King Agrippa, I was not disobedient to the vision from heaven. ²⁰First to those in Damascus, then to those in Jerusalem and in all Judea, and to the Gentiles also, I preached that they should repent and turn to God and prove their repentance by their deeds. ²¹That is why the Jews seized me in the temple courts and tried to kill me. ²²But I have had God's help to this very day, and so I stand here and testify to small and great alike. I am saying nothing beyond what the prophets and Moses said would happen— ²³that the Christˣ would suffer and, as the first to rise from the dead, would proclaim light to his own people and to the Gentiles."

²⁴At this point Festus interrupted Paul's defense. "You are out of your mind, Paul!" he shouted. "Your great learning is driving you insane."

²⁵"I am not insane, most excellent Festus," Paul replied. "What I am saying is true and reasonable. ²⁶The king is familiar with these things, and I can speak freely to him. I am convinced that none of this has escaped his notice, because it was not done in a corner. ²⁷King Agrippa, do you believe the prophets? I know you do."

²⁸Then Agrippa said to Paul, "Do you think that in such a short time you can persuade me to be a Christian?"

²⁹Paul replied, "Short time or long—I pray God that not only you but all who are listening to me today may become what I am, except for these chains."

³⁰The king rose, and with him the governor and Bernice and those sitting with them. ³¹They left the room, and while talking with one another, they said, "This man is not doing anything that deserves death or imprisonment."

³²Agrippa said to Festus, "This man could have been set free if he had not appealed to Caesar."

ʷ14 Or Hebrew   ˣ23 Or Messiah

Discovering the Word 1. Describe the nature and content of Festus's report to Agrippa (25:13–22). 2. What are the main points about himself that Paul presents in his defense (26:1–23)? 3. Why does Paul say he is on trial (26:6–8)? 4. Contrast the commission of the Sanhedrin (26:9–11) to the commission of Christ (26:15–18). 5. Describe Paul's final interaction with King Agrippa (26:26–29).

Applying the Word 1. What motivates you to tell non-Christians about Jesus? 2. How does Paul's desire for King Agrippa compare or contrast with your desire for those around you who do not know Christ? 3. How might you move closer to where Paul was in this desire?

Responding in Prayer Ask God to give you the proper response to injustice and a heart that is soft toward those who do not know him.

24 / Acts 27—28
Paul in Rome!

ROME AT LAST! Paul was innocent. He could have been a free man. But he had appealed to Caesar—and to Caesar he was to go. As we look at these last two chapters of Acts and complete our study of the life of this marvelous servant of God, it might be worthwhile to ask the questions "Who was really free, and who were the real prisoners?"

 Warming Up to God Sit quietly for a few moments, without trying to force your thoughts to move in any direction. Let silence reign in your heart before you look to Scripture.

 Read Acts 27—28.

27 When it was decided that we would sail for Italy, Paul and some other prisoners were handed over to a centurion named Julius, who belonged to the Imperial Regiment. ²We boarded a ship from Adramyttium about to sail for ports along the coast of the province of Asia, and we put out to sea. Aristarchus, a Macedonian from Thessalonica, was with us.

³The next day we landed at Sidon; and Julius, in kindness to Paul, allowed him to go to his friends so they might provide for his needs. ⁴From there we put out to sea again and passed to the lee of Cyprus because the winds were against us. ⁵When we had sailed across the open sea off the coast of Cilicia and Pamphylia, we landed at Myra in Lycia. ⁶There the centurion found an Alexandrian ship sailing for Italy and put us on board. ⁷We made slow headway for many days and had difficulty arriving off Cnidus. When the wind did not allow us to hold our course, we sailed to the lee of Crete, opposite Salmone. ⁸We moved along the coast with difficulty and came to a place called Fair Havens, near the town of Lasea.

⁹Much time had been lost, and sailing had already become dangerous because by now it was after the Fast.ʸ So Paul warned them, ¹⁰"Men, I can see that our voyage is going to be disastrous and bring great loss to ship and cargo, and to our own lives also." ¹¹But the centurion, instead of listening to what Paul said, followed the advice of the pilot and of the owner of the ship. ¹²Since the harbor was unsuitable to winter in, the majority decided that we should sail on, hoping to reach Phoenix and winter there. This was a harbor in Crete, facing both southwest and northwest.

¹³When a gentle south wind began to blow,

they thought they had obtained what they wanted; so they weighed anchor and sailed along the shore of Crete. ¹⁴Before very long, a wind of hurricane force, called the "northeaster," swept down from the island. ¹⁵The ship was caught by the storm and could not head into the wind; so we gave way to it and were driven along. ¹⁶As we passed to the lee of a small island called Cauda, we were hardly able to make the lifeboat secure. ¹⁷When the men had hoisted it aboard, they passed ropes under the ship itself to hold it together. Fearing that they would run aground on the sandbars of Syrtis, they lowered the sea anchor and let the ship be driven along. ¹⁸We took such a violent battering from the storm that the next day they began to throw the cargo overboard. ¹⁹On the third day, they threw the ship's tackle overboard with their own hands. ²⁰When neither sun nor stars appeared for many days and the storm continued raging, we finally gave up all hope of being saved.

²¹After the men had gone a long time without food, Paul stood up before them and said: "Men, you should have taken my advice not to sail from Crete; then you would have spared yourselves this damage and loss. ²²But now I urge you to keep up your courage, because not one of you will be lost; only the ship will be destroyed. ²³Last night an angel of the God whose I am and whom I serve stood beside me ²⁴and said, 'Do not be afraid, Paul. You must stand trial before Caesar; and God has graciously given you the lives of all who sail with you.' ²⁵So keep up your courage, men, for I have faith in God that it will happen just as he told me. ²⁶Nevertheless, we must run aground on some island."

²⁷On the fourteenth night we were still being

ʸ9 That is, the Day of Atonement (Yom Kippur)

driven across the Adriatic[z] Sea, when about midnight the sailors sensed they were approaching land. 28They took soundings and found that the water was a hundred and twenty feet[a] deep. A short time later they took soundings again and found it was ninety feet[b] deep. 29Fearing that we would be dashed against the rocks, they dropped four anchors from the stern and prayed for daylight. 30In an attempt to escape from the ship, the sailors let the lifeboat down into the sea, pretending they were going to lower some anchors from the bow. 31Then Paul said to the centurion and the soldiers, "Unless these men stay with the ship, you cannot be saved." 32So the soldiers cut the ropes that held the lifeboat and let it fall away.

33Just before dawn Paul urged them all to eat. "For the last fourteen days," he said, "you have been in constant suspense and have gone without food—you haven't eaten anything. 34Now I urge you to take some food. You need it to survive. Not one of you will lose a single hair from his head." 35After he said this, he took some bread and gave thanks to God in front of them all. Then he broke it and began to eat. 36They were all encouraged and ate some food themselves. 37Altogether there were 276 of us on board. 38When they had eaten as much as they wanted, they lightened the ship by throwing the grain into the sea.

39When daylight came, they did not recognize the land, but they saw a bay with a sandy beach, where they decided to run the ship aground if they could. 40Cutting loose the anchors, they left them in the sea and at the same time untied the ropes that held the rudders. Then they hoisted the foresail to the wind and made for the beach. 41But the ship struck a sandbar and ran aground. The bow stuck fast and would not move, and the stern was broken to pieces by the pounding of the surf.

42The soldiers planned to kill the prisoners to prevent any of them from swimming away and escaping. 43But the centurion wanted to spare Paul's life and kept them from carrying out their plan. He ordered those who could swim to jump overboard first and get to land. 44The rest were to get there on planks or on pieces of the ship. In this way everyone reached land in safety.

28 Once safely on shore, we found out that the island was called Malta. 2The islanders showed us unusual kindness. They built a fire and welcomed us all because it was raining and cold. 3Paul gathered a pile of brushwood and, as he put it on the fire, a viper, driven out by the heat, fastened itself on his hand. 4When the islanders saw the snake hanging from his hand, they said to each other, "This man must be a murderer; for though he escaped from the sea, Justice has not allowed him to live." 5But Paul shook the snake off into the fire and suffered no ill effects. 6The people expected him to swell up or suddenly fall dead, but after waiting a long time and seeing nothing unusual happen to him, they changed their minds and said he was a god.

7There was an estate nearby that belonged to Publius, the chief official of the island. He welcomed us to his home and for three days entertained us hospitably. 8His father was sick in bed, suffering from fever and dysentery. Paul went in to see him and, after prayer, placed his hands on him and healed him. 9When this had happened, the rest of the sick on the island came and were cured. 10They honored us in many ways and when we were ready to sail, they furnished us with the supplies we needed.

11After three months we put out to sea in a ship that had wintered in the island. It was an Alexandrian ship with the figurehead of the twin gods Castor and Pollux. 12We put in at Syracuse and stayed there three days. 13From there we set sail and arrived at Rhegium. The next day the south wind came up, and on the following day we reached Puteoli. 14There we found some brothers who invited us to spend a week with them. And so we came to Rome. 15The brothers there had heard that we were coming, and they traveled as far as the Forum of Appius and the Three Taverns to meet us. At the sight of these men Paul thanked God and was encouraged. 16When we got to Rome, Paul was allowed to live by himself, with a soldier to guard him.

17Three days later he called together the leaders of the Jews. When they had assembled, Paul said to them: "My brothers, although I have done nothing against our people or against the customs of our ancestors, I was arrested in Jerusalem and handed over to the Romans. 18They examined me and wanted to release me, because I was not guilty of any crime deserving death. 19But when the Jews objected, I was compelled to appeal to Caesar—not that I had any charge to bring

z27 In ancient times the name referred to an area extending well south of Italy.　　a28 Greek twenty orguias (about 37 meters)　　b28 Greek fifteen orguias (about 27 meters)

against my own people. ²⁰For this reason I have asked to see you and talk with you. It is because of the hope of Israel that I am bound with this chain."

²¹They replied, "We have not received any letters from Judea concerning you, and none of the brothers who have come from there has reported or said anything bad about you. ²²But we want to hear what your views are, for we know that people everywhere are talking against this sect."

²³They arranged to meet Paul on a certain day, and came in even larger numbers to the place where he was staying. From morning till evening he explained and declared to them the kingdom of God and tried to convince them about Jesus from the Law of Moses and from the Prophets. ²⁴Some were convinced by what he said, but others would not believe. ²⁵They disagreed among themselves and began to leave after Paul had made this final statement: "The Holy Spirit spoke the truth to your forefathers when he said through Isaiah the prophet:

²⁶" 'Go to this people and say,
    "You will be ever hearing but never
        understanding;
    you will be ever seeing but never
        perceiving."
²⁷For this people's heart has become calloused;
    they hardly hear with their ears,
    and they have closed their eyes.
Otherwise they might see with their eyes,
    hear with their ears,
    understand with their hearts
and turn, and I would heal them.'ᶜ

²⁸"Therefore I want you to know that God's salvation has been sent to the Gentiles, and they will listen!"ᵈ

³⁰For two whole years Paul stayed there in his own rented house and welcomed all who came to see him. ³¹Boldly and without hindrance he preached the kingdom of God and taught about the Lord Jesus Christ.

ᶜ27 Isaiah 6:9,10   ᵈ28 Some manuscripts listen!" ²⁹After he said this, the Jews left, arguing vigorously among themselves.

 Discovering the Word 1. Though Paul had every reason by this time to become very self-centered, how do you see him continuing to minister to others throughout these two chapters (27:9–10, 21–25, 31–38, 42–43; 28:3, 8–9, 17–20, 23–31)? 2. What do you see of Paul's compassion as he ministers? 3. What do you think it says about Paul that Julius let him go see his friends (27:3)? 4. What do you see of Paul's confidence in God throughout this passage? 5. In conclusion, what from the book of Acts motivates and equips you to be a witness "to the ends of the earth" (1:8)?

Applying the Word 1. What are the situations or relationships in your life with non-Christians in which you are tempted to give up on your proclamation of the gospel? 2. What truths from this study of Acts encourage you to not give up? 3. The words "Boldly and without hindrance he preached the kingdom of God and taught about the Lord Jesus Christ" (28:31) summarize not only Paul's two years in Rome, but his whole Christian life. To what degree would you like this to be a summary of your life? Explain.

Responding in Prayer Thank God for the ways that he has taught you through the book of Acts. Ask him to continue to teach you as you try to live out the lessons you have learned.

Romans

Romans may be the most important letter you will ever read. It is Paul's masterpiece, the clearest and fullest explanation of the gospel in the Bible. John Calvin said that "if a man understands it, he has a sure road opened for him to the understanding of the whole Scripture." William Tyndale, the father of English Bible translators, believed that every Christian should learn it by heart. "The more it is studied," he wrote, "the easier it is; the more it is chewed, the pleasanter it is" (prologue to Romans in his 1534 English New Testament).

But watch out! Those who study Romans are rarely the same afterward. For example, in the summer of A.D. 386 Augustine sat weeping in the garden of his friend Alypius. He wanted to begin a new life but lacked the strength to break with the old. Taking up a scroll of Romans, he read, "Clothe yourselves with the Lord Jesus Christ, and do not think about how to gratify the desires of the sinful nature." "No further would I read," he tells us, "nor had I any need; instantly at the end of this sentence, a clear light flooded my heart and all the darkness of doubt vanished away."

In 1515 Martin Luther began to teach the book of Romans to his students. He wrote, "Night and day I pondered until . . . I grasped the truth that the righteousness of God is that righteousness whereby, through grace and sheer mercy, he justifies us by faith. Thereupon I felt myself to be reborn and to have gone through open doors into paradise. The whole scripture took on new meaning, and whereas before the 'righteousness of God' had filled me with hate, now it became to me inexpressibly sweet in greater love. This passage in Paul became to me a gateway to heaven." Two years later he nailed his ninety-five theses to the door of the castle church in Wittenberg, and the Protestant Reformation began!

The evening of May 24, 1738, John Wesley "went very unwillingly to a society in Aldersgate Street, where one was reading Luther's preface to the Epistle to the Romans. About a quarter before nine," he wrote in his journal, "while he was describing the change which God works in the heart through faith in Christ, I felt my heart strangely warmed. I felt I did trust in Christ, Christ alone, for my salvation; and an assurance was given me that he had taken *my* sins away, even *mine*; and saved me from the law of sin and death." This event in Wesley's life helped to launch the great Evangelical Revival of the eighteenth century.

We need to grasp the message of Romans in our day as well. Many are preaching a gospel that lacks clarity and substance. People are told to "invite Jesus into their heart" or simply to "follow Christ" without understanding the meaning of his death and resurrection.

We cannot correct this problem merely by memorizing gospel outlines or canned presentations. We need to immerse ourselves in Scripture through diligent study and thoughtful reflection. Only when the gospel grips us as it did Augustine, Luther and Wesley

will we realize why "it is the power of God for the salvation of everyone who believes" (Ro 1:16).

Romans is different from most of Paul's letters. He did not found the church in Rome; in fact, he had never been there. It has been suggested that the church in Rome was founded by some of those who were present on the day of Pentecost (Acts 2:10). However, Paul had met some of the Roman Christians, such as Priscilla and Aquila (Ro 16), during his missionary journeys to other cities.

Other letters were written to address specific problems within the churches. Romans seems relatively free of problems. Their only major "problem" was that they had never met the apostle. Therefore, Paul felt a need to fully explain to them in a letter what he would have said in person.

Paul probably wrote Romans between A.D. 57–58 while he was at Corinth in the home of his friend and convert Gaius. He planned to go first to Jerusalem to deliver a gift of money from the Gentile churches to the poor in Jerusalem. Then he hoped to visit Rome on his way to Spain. His hopes were later realized, but not as he had expected. When he finally arrived in Rome in early A.D. 60, he was a prisoner under house arrest (Acts 28:11–31).

May you be encouraged and challenged by the new life and the new lifestyle we have in Christ!

Outline

Part 1: A New Life

1/ Romans 1:1–17 ——————————— Good News from God
2/ Romans 1:18–32 ——————————— The Wrath of God
3/ Romans 2 ——————————————— The Judgment of God
4/ Romans 3:1–20 ——————————— The Verdict
5/ Romans 3:21–31 ——————————— The Righteousness from God
6/ Romans 4 ——————————————— The Example of Abraham
7/ Romans 5 ——————————————— Reasons to Rejoice
8/ Romans 6:1—7:6 ——————————— New Life, New Lifestyle
9/ Romans 7:7–25 ——————————— Our Struggle with Sin
10/ Romans 8:1–17 ——————————— The Spirit Brings Life
11/ Romans 8:18–39 ————————— Glorious Conquerors

Part 2: A New Lifestyle

12/ Romans 9:1–29 ——————————— The Potter and His Clay
13/ Romans 9:30—10:21 ————————— Misguided Zeal
14/ Romans 11 —————————————— The Future of Israel
15/ Romans 12 —————————————— Living Sacrifices
16/ Romans 13 —————————————— Submitting to Authorities
17/ Romans 14 —————————————— To Eat or Not to Eat
18/ Romans 15:1–13 ————————— Unity, Hope and Praise
19/ Romans 15:14—16:27 ——————— Brothers and Sisters in Christ

1 / *Romans 1:1–17*
Good News from God

"I'M ENGAGED!"

"I got a raise!"

"My wife's having a baby!"

What is our immediate response to good news? We tell others! We feel we will burst unless we share our joy with those around us.

Paul felt that way about the gospel, the good news about Jesus Christ. As we read these opening verses in his letter to the Romans, we find his excitement is contagious.

 Warming Up to God   Our days and weeks are often filled with bad news. Think of all the *good* news you can, and praise God for it.

 Read Romans 1:1–17.

Paul, a servant of Christ Jesus, called to be an apostle and set apart for the gospel of God— ²the gospel he promised beforehand through his prophets in the Holy Scriptures ³regarding his Son, who as to his human nature was a descendant of David, ⁴and who through the Spirit[a] of holiness was declared with power to be the Son of God[b] by his resurrection from the dead: Jesus Christ our Lord. ⁵Through him and for his name's sake, we received grace and apostleship to call people from among all the Gentiles to the obedience that comes from faith. ⁶And you also are among those who are called to belong to Jesus Christ.

⁷To all in Rome who are loved by God and called to be saints:

Grace and peace to you from God our Father and from the Lord Jesus Christ.

⁸First, I thank my God through Jesus Christ for all of you, because your faith is being reported all over the world. ⁹God, whom I serve with my whole heart in preaching the gospel of his Son, is my witness how constantly I remember you ¹⁰in my prayers at all times; and I pray that now at last by God's will the way may be opened for me to come to you.

¹¹I long to see you so that I may impart to you some spiritual gift to make you strong— ¹²that is, that you and I may be mutually encouraged by each other's faith. ¹³I do not want you to be unaware, brothers, that I planned many times to come to you (but have been prevented from doing so until now) in order that I might have a harvest among you, just as I have had among the other Gentiles.

¹⁴I am obligated both to Greeks and non-Greeks, both to the wise and the foolish. ¹⁵That is why I am so eager to preach the gospel also to you who are at Rome.

¹⁶I am not ashamed of the gospel, because it is the power of God for the salvation of everyone who believes: first for the Jew, then for the Gentile. ¹⁷For in the gospel a righteousness from God is revealed, a righteousness that is by faith from first to last,[c] just as it is written: "The righteous will live by faith."[d]

a4 Or who as to his spirit   b4 Or was appointed to be the Son of God with power   c17 Or is from faith to faith   d17 Hab. 2:4

Discovering the Word   1. Imagine that verses 1 and 5 are the only information you possess about Paul. Describe everything you would know about him.   2. In verses 1–5 Paul gives a summary of the gospel for which he had been set apart. What do we learn about the gospel from these verses?   3. What do verses 8–13 reveal about Paul's attitude toward the Romans?   4. Paul says we can be eager to preach the gospel or be ashamed of it (vv. 15–16). What might lead us to adopt one attitude or the other?

Applying the Word   1. Because he was an apostle ("one who is sent"), Paul felt obligated to preach the gospel to everyone (v. 14). Whom do you have the greatest opportunity for reaching with the gospel? 2. What steps can you take to reach them?

Responding in Prayer Pray that God will use Romans to give you Paul's attitude toward the gospel and toward those who need its message.

2 / *Romans 1:18–32*
The Wrath of God

"HOW ARE YOU?" someone asks. "I'm fine," we reply. But are we really, or do our words mask our true condition? In this passage Paul tells us that we are not fine—neither we nor our friends nor society. Something is dreadfully wrong.

 Warming Up to God Usually we have to admit we need help before we can be helped. Why do we often find it so difficult to admit a need? Give your needs to God's care.

 Read Romans 1:18–32.

[18]The wrath of God is being revealed from heaven against all the godlessness and wickedness of men who suppress the truth by their wickedness, [19]since what may be known about God is plain to them, because God has made it plain to them. [20]For since the creation of the world God's invisible qualities—his eternal power and divine nature—have been clearly seen, being understood from what has been made, so that men are without excuse.

[21]For although they knew God, they neither glorified him as God nor gave thanks to him, but their thinking became futile and their foolish hearts were darkened. [22]Although they claimed to be wise, they became fools [23]and exchanged the glory of the immortal God for images made to look like mortal man and birds and animals and reptiles.

[24]Therefore God gave them over in the sinful desires of their hearts to sexual impurity for the degrading of their bodies with one another. [25]They exchanged the truth of God for a lie, and worshiped and served created things rather than the Creator—who is forever praised. Amen.

[26]Because of this, God gave them over to shameful lusts. Even their women exchanged natural relations for unnatural ones. [27]In the same way the men also abandoned natural relations with women and were inflamed with lust for one another. Men committed indecent acts with other men, and received in themselves the due penalty for their perversion.

[28]Furthermore, since they did not think it worthwhile to retain the knowledge of God, he gave them over to a depraved mind, to do what ought not to be done. [29]They have become filled with every kind of wickedness, evil, greed and depravity. They are full of envy, murder, strife, deceit and malice. They are gossips, [30]slanderers, God-haters, insolent, arrogant and boastful; they invent ways of doing evil; they disobey their parents; [31]they are senseless, faithless, heartless, ruthless. [32]Although they know God's righteous decree that those who do such things deserve death, they not only continue to do these very things but also approve of those who practice them.

Discovering the Word 1. John Stott defines God's wrath (v. 18) as "his righteous reaction to evil, his implacable hostility to it, his refusal to condone it, and his judgment upon it" (John R. W. Stott, "God's Judgment," in *Believing and Obeying Jesus Christ*). According to this definition, how would God's wrath differ from the sinful anger or violent temper condemned by Scripture? 2. What does everyone know about God, according to verses 19–20? 3. Verses 21–32 describe the downward spiral of sin experienced by people who rebel against God. How would you summarize each level of their descent? 4. How might each level lead to the next? 5. People often raise the question of how God could condemn those who have never heard of him. How does this passage address this question?

Applying the Word 1. What evidence do you see of this moral and spiritual degeneration today?
2. How might this passage make you less ashamed of the gospel and more eager to preach it?

Responding in Prayer Pray that God would be revealed powerfully to those who are rejecting him.

3 / *Romans 2*
The Judgment of God

PROSTITUTES, DRUG ADDICTS, thieves—it's easy to see why these people need the gospel. But what about "respectable" people: doctors, business executives, the family next door? They seem so contented, so fulfilled, so . . . *nice*!

In Romans 1:18–32 Paul described the depravity of those who reject God. Now he imagines someone saying, "You're absolutely right, Paul. Such people are wicked and deserve everything that's coming to them! But of course *we* would never do such things and would be very critical of anyone who did." In this passage Paul shows why even "nice" people need the gospel.

Warming Up to God Have you ever wondered whether some non-Christians really need the gospel? Explain. Ask God to open your heart to understand what place he has in each of our lives.

Read Romans 2.

2 You, therefore, have no excuse, you who pass judgment on someone else, for at whatever point you judge the other, you are condemning yourself, because you who pass judgment do the same things. ²Now we know that God's judgment against those who do such things is based on truth. ³So when you, a mere man, pass judgment on them and yet do the same things, do you think you will escape God's judgment? ⁴Or do you show contempt for the riches of his kindness, tolerance and patience, not realizing that God's kindness leads you toward repentance?

⁵But because of your stubbornness and your unrepentant heart, you are storing up wrath against yourself for the day of God's wrath, when his righteous judgment will be revealed. ⁶God "will give to each person according to what he has done."ᵉ ⁷To those who by persistence in doing good seek glory, honor and immortality, he will give eternal life. ⁸But for those who are self-seeking and who reject the truth and follow evil, there will be wrath and anger. ⁹There will be trouble and distress for every human being who does evil: first for the Jew, then for the Gentile; ¹⁰but glory, honor and peace for everyone who does good: first for the Jew, then for the Gentile. ¹¹For God does not show favoritism.

¹²All who sin apart from the law will also perish apart from the law, and all who sin under the law will be judged by the law. ¹³For it is not those who hear the law who are righteous in God's sight, but it is those who obey the law who will be declared righteous. ¹⁴(Indeed, when Gentiles, who do not have the law, do by nature things required by the law, they are a law for themselves, even though they do not have the law, ¹⁵since they show that the requirements of the law are written on their hearts, their consciences also bearing witness, and their thoughts now accusing, now even defending them.) ¹⁶This will take place on the day when God will judge men's secrets through Jesus Christ, as my gospel declares.

¹⁷Now you, if you call yourself a Jew; if you rely on the law and brag about your relationship to God; ¹⁸if you know his will and approve of what is superior because you are instructed by the law; ¹⁹if you are convinced that you are a guide for the blind, a light for those who are in the dark, ²⁰an instructor of the foolish, a teacher of infants, because you have in the law the embodiment of knowledge and truth— ²¹you, then, who teach others, do you not teach yourself? You who preach against stealing, do you steal? ²²You who

ᵉ6 Psalm 62:12; Prov. 24:12

say that people should not commit adultery, do you commit adultery? You who abhor idols, do you rob temples? ²³You who brag about the law, do you dishonor God by breaking the law? ²⁴As it is written: "God's name is blasphemed among the Gentiles because of you."ⁱ

²⁵Circumcision has value if you observe the law, but if you break the law, you have become as though you had not been circumcised. ²⁶If those who are not circumcised keep the law's requirements, will they not be regarded as though they were circumcised? ²⁷The one who is not circum-

cised physically and yet obeys the law will condemn you who, even though you have theᵍ written code and circumcision, are a lawbreaker.

²⁸A man is not a Jew if he is only one outwardly, nor is circumcision merely outward and physical. ²⁹No, a man is a Jew if he is one inwardly; and circumcision is circumcision of the heart, by the Spirit, not by the written code. Such a man's praise is not from men, but from God.

ᶠ24 Isaiah 52:5; Ezek. 36:22   ᵍ27 Or who, by means of a

Discovering the Word 1. When people are judgmental, how do they reveal both an understanding and a misunderstanding of God's judgment (vv. 1–4)? 2. Verses 5–16 describe a future day of judgment known as "the day of God's wrath" (v. 5). What will God consider important and unimportant on that day? 3. How are God's standards of judgment both similar and different for the two groups described in verses 12–16? 4. In verses 17–29 Paul focuses his attention on a hypocritical Jew. How does such a person view himself and others (vv. 17–20)? 5. Jews placed great value on circumcision because it was the visible sign that they were God's people. How had some of them confused the sign with what it signified (vv. 25–29)?

Applying the Word 1. How has religious hypocrisy hurt the cause of Christ in our day? 2. Many non-Christians have high moral standards. How can we use their own standards to help them see their need of Christ? 3. How can this chapter help you to more effectively share the gospel with respectable, religious or moral non-Christians?

Responding in Prayer Ask God to make you bold in talking with a non-Christian.

---

4 / *Romans 3:1–20*
The Verdict

IF YOUR ETERNAL destiny were decided by the quality of your life and the level of your obedience to God, how would you fare? There is one sure way to find out. Take your case to the divine court. The Bible assures us that we will all have our day in court (Ro 2:5–6; 14:10–12). But we need not wait until then to find out the verdict. Paul tells us in advance in this passage.

Warming Up to God Describe some of the thoughts and feelings you might have if you were on trial for committing a serious crime—and you knew you were guilty. Now consider the fact that Christ has set you free despite your guilt. How do you feel?

Read Romans 3:1–20.

---

3 What advantage, then, is there in being a Jew, or what value is there in circumcision? ²Much in every way! First of all, they have been entrusted with the very words of God.

³What if some did not have faith? Will their lack of faith nullify God's faithfulness? ⁴Not at

all! Let God be true, and every man a liar. As it is written:

"So that you may be proved right when you
    speak
and prevail when you judge."ʰ

ʰ4 Psalm 51:4

5But if our unrighteousness brings out God's righteousness more clearly, what shall we say? That God is unjust in bringing his wrath on us? (I am using a human argument.) 6Certainly not! If that were so, how could God judge the world? 7Someone might argue, "If my falsehood enhances God's truthfulness and so increases his glory, why am I still condemned as a sinner?" 8Why not say—as we are being slanderously reported as saying and as some claim that we say— "Let us do evil that good may result"? Their condemnation is deserved.

9What shall we conclude then? Are we any better[i]? Not at all! We have already made the charge that Jews and Gentiles alike are all under sin. 10As it is written:

"There is no one righteous, not even one;
11 there is no one who understands,
     no one who seeks God.
12All have turned away,
     they have together become worthless;
there is no one who does good,

not even one."[j]
13"Their throats are open graves;
     their tongues practice deceit."[k]
"The poison of vipers is on their lips."[l]
14 "Their mouths are full of cursing and
          bitterness."[m]
15"Their feet are swift to shed blood;
16 ruin and misery mark their ways,
17and the way of peace they do not know."[n]
18 "There is no fear of God before their
          eyes."[o]

19Now we know that whatever the law says, it says to those who are under the law, so that every mouth may be silenced and the whole world held accountable to God. 20Therefore no one will be declared righteous in his sight by observing the law; rather, through the law we become conscious of sin.

i9 Or worse   j12 Psalms 14:1-3; 53:1-3; Eccles. 7:20   k13 Psalm 5:9   l13 Psalm 140:3   m14 Psalm 10:7   n17 Isaiah 59:7,8   o18 Psalm 36:1

Discovering the Word 1. Why might some Jews have accused God of unfaithfulness and injustice (vv. 3–8)? 2. How does Paul respond to these accusations? 3. In the role of prosecutor, Paul has charged that Jews and Gentiles alike are under sin (v. 9). How does Scripture support his charge (vv. 10–18)? 4. In verses 13–18 Paul describes how the various parts of our bodies are involved in sin. How does this figurative language graphically illustrate our condition as fallen people? 5. How would you reconcile the statements in verses 10–18 with the fact that some non-Christians *do* seem to seek after God and lead exemplary lives? 6. Imagine a courtroom scene with God as the judge and the world on trial. From what you have learned in Romans 1:18—3:20, summarize the charges against us, the supporting evidence and the verdict.

Applying the Word 1. Paul does not discuss the grace of God (3:21—5:21) until he has discussed the judgment of God (1:18—3:20). He does not proclaim the good news until we have understood the bad news. Why does he follow this order? 2. How should Paul's example affect our evangelism? (Be as specific as possible.)

Responding in Prayer The letter to the Romans could have ended with 3:20. God would be perfectly just to condemn us all and to leave us fearfully awaiting his wrath. Let this fact sink in for a moment, then take time to thank God for being not only just but also merciful and gracious.

---

5 / *Romans 3:21–31*
The Righteousness from God

LIKE PRISONERS ON death row, people are guilty, condemned and awaiting the execution of God's wrath. They sit silently in the miserable darkness of their cell, all hope extinguished.

Then abruptly, the door swings open and darkness becomes light, death becomes life, and bondage becomes freedom. "You are *pardoned*," a voice tells them. But how? Why? This passage answers these questions.

Warming Up to God Imagine that you are a judge, and someone you love is on trial. Would you be more tempted to compromise your justice or your love? Explain.

 Read Romans 3:21–31.

²¹But now a righteousness from God, apart from law, has been made known, to which the Law and the Prophets testify. ²²This righteousness from God comes through faith in Jesus Christ to all who believe. There is no difference, ²³for all have sinned and fall short of the glory of God, ²⁴and are justified freely by his grace through the redemption that came by Christ Jesus. ²⁵God presented him as a sacrifice of atonement,ᵖ through faith in his blood. He did this to demonstrate his justice, because in his forbearance he had left the sins committed beforehand unpunished— ²⁶he did it to demonstrate his justice at the present time, so as to be just and the one who justifies those who have faith in Jesus.

²⁷Where, then, is boasting? It is excluded. On what principle? On that of observing the law? No, but on that of faith. ²⁸For we maintain that a man is justified by faith apart from observing the law. ²⁹Is God the God of Jews only? Is he not the God of Gentiles too? Yes, of Gentiles too, ³⁰since there is only one God, who will justify the circumcised by faith and the uncircumcised through that same faith. ³¹Do we, then, nullify the law by this faith? Not at all! Rather, we uphold the law.

ᵖ25 Or *as the one who would turn aside his wrath, taking away sin*

 Discovering the Word 1. How is the righteousness from God (3:22–24) different from righteousness by law (2:5–13)? 2. The word *redemption* (v. 24) is borrowed from the slave market. It means to buy someone out of slavery. From what types of slavery has Christ delivered us? 3. The phrase *sacrifice of atonement* (v. 25) is borrowed from the Old Testament. Animal sacrifices turned away God's wrath from the sinner. Why does Christ's death turn away God's wrath from us? 4. How should we respond, emotionally and spiritually, to the fact that Jesus experienced God's wrath for us? 5. Some people find it difficult to understand how God can be perfectly just and gracious at the same time. How do the justice and grace of God meet at the cross (vv. 25–26)? 6. How does boasting about ourselves betray a fundamental misunderstanding of the gospel (vv. 27–31)?

 Applying the Word 1. At times do you still feel unacceptable to God? Explain. 2. In what ways might you feel or act differently if you more fully grasped what Jesus has done for you?

 Responding in Prayer Take time to praise and thank God for Jesus Christ.

6 / *Romans 4*
The Example of Abraham

"IT'S HOPELESS." NO words are more discouraging than these. Yet sometimes situations appear beyond hope, beyond help. Our natural response during such times is despair and depression.

Abraham knew what it meant to face insurmountable obstacles. He too was hopeless, yet somehow he found renewed reason to hope. For this reason he has become a timeless example and encouragement for us.

 Warming Up to God Recall a situation in which you felt hopeless. What restored you to hope?

 Read Romans 4.

4 What then shall we say that Abraham, our forefather, discovered in this matter? ²If, in fact, Abraham was justified by works, he had something to boast about—but not before God. ³What does the Scripture say? "Abraham believed God, and it was credited to him as righteousness."q

⁴Now when a man works, his wages are not credited to him as a gift, but as an obligation. ⁵However, to the man who does not work but trusts God who justifies the wicked, his faith is credited as righteousness. ⁶David says the same thing when he speaks of the blessedness of the man to whom God credits righteousness apart from works:

⁷"Blessed are they
   whose transgressions are forgiven,
   whose sins are covered.
⁸Blessed is the man
   whose sin the Lord will never count against
   him."r

⁹Is this blessedness only for the circumcised, or also for the uncircumcised? We have been saying that Abraham's faith was credited to him as righteousness. ¹⁰Under what circumstances was it credited? Was it after he was circumcised, or before? It was not after, but before! ¹¹And he received the sign of circumcision, a seal of the righteousness that he had by faith while he was still uncircumcised. So then, he is the father of all who believe but have not been circumcised, in order that righteousness might be credited to them. ¹²And he is also the father of the circumcised who not only are circumcised but who also walk in the footsteps of the faith that our father Abraham had before he was circumcised.

¹³It was not through law that Abraham and his offspring received the promise that he would be heir of the world, but through the righteousness that comes by faith. ¹⁴For if those who live by law are heirs, faith has no value and the promise is worthless, ¹⁵because law brings wrath. And where there is no law there is no transgression.

¹⁶Therefore, the promise comes by faith, so that it may be by grace and may be guaranteed to all Abraham's offspring—not only to those who are of the law but also to those who are of the faith of Abraham. He is the father of us all. ¹⁷As it is written: "I have made you a father of many nations."s He is our father in the sight of God, in whom he believed—the God who gives life to the dead and calls things that are not as though they were.

¹⁸Against all hope, Abraham in hope believed and so became the father of many nations, just as it had been said to him, "So shall your offspring be."t ¹⁹Without weakening in his faith, he faced the fact that his body was as good as dead—since he was about a hundred years old—and that Sarah's womb was also dead. ²⁰Yet he did not waver through unbelief regarding the promise of God, but was strengthened in his faith and gave glory to God, ²¹being fully persuaded that God had power to do what he had promised. ²²This is why "it was credited to him as righteousness." ²³The words "it was credited to him" were written not for him alone, ²⁴but also for us, to whom God will credit righteousness—for us who believe in him who raised Jesus our Lord from the dead. ²⁵He was delivered over to death for our sins and was raised to life for our justification.

q3 Gen. 15:6; also in verse 22   r8 Psalm 32:1,2   s17 Gen. 17:5
t18 Gen. 15:5

Discovering the Word 1. According to Paul, how were Old Testament saints, such as Abraham and David, justified (vv. 1–8)? 2. What are some of the differences between justification by faith and by works (vv. 4–8)? 3. It's easy to feel that God accepts us only when we are good. When we feel this way, how can the examples of Abraham and David give us hope? 4. Some people today claim that unless we are baptized, we have no hope of being saved. How might Abraham's experience refute this claim? 5. God promised that Abraham and his offspring would inherit the world (v. 13). Who are Abraham's offspring (vv. 13–17)? 6. How does Abraham illustrate our own hopeless predicament as non-Christians and the solution provided in Jesus Christ (vv. 18–25)?

Applying the Word 1. What situation are you currently facing that requires faith in the God of resurrection and creation? 2. How can you demonstrate faith and hope in that situation?

Responding in Prayer Know that God wants you to have hope. Pray with that assurance.

7 / *Romans 5*
Reasons to Rejoice

WE ALL LONG to be joyful, to experience the pure delight that life sometimes offers. But life's joys are elusive, momentary, gone as quickly as they come. How can we have an abiding, enduring joy—especially when suffering intrudes into our lives? In Romans 5 Paul gives us several firm and lasting reasons to rejoice.

 Warming Up to God What kinds of things make you joyful? If you are in a private place where you feel comfortable, sing a short song of praise to God.

 Read Romans 5.

5 Therefore, since we have been justified through faith, weᵘ have peace with God through our Lord Jesus Christ, ²through whom we have gained access by faith into this grace in which we now stand. And weᵘ rejoice in the hope of the glory of God. ³Not only so, but weᵘ also rejoice in our sufferings, because we know that suffering produces perseverance; ⁴perseverance, character; and character, hope. ⁵And hope does not disappoint us, because God has poured out his love into our hearts by the Holy Spirit, whom he has given us.

⁶You see, at just the right time, when we were still powerless, Christ died for the ungodly. ⁷Very rarely will anyone die for a righteous man, though for a good man someone might possibly dare to die. ⁸But God demonstrates his own love for us in this: While we were still sinners, Christ died for us.

⁹Since we have now been justified by his blood, how much more shall we be saved from God's wrath through him! ¹⁰For if, when we were God's enemies, we were reconciled to him through the death of his Son, how much more, having been reconciled, shall we be saved through his life! ¹¹Not only is this so, but we also rejoice in God through our Lord Jesus Christ, through whom we have now received reconciliation.

¹²Therefore, just as sin entered the world through one man, and death through sin, and in this way death came to all men, because all sinned— ¹³for before the law was given, sin was in the world. But sin is not taken into account when there is no law. ¹⁴Nevertheless, death

reigned from the time of Adam to the time of Moses, even over those who did not sin by breaking a command, as did Adam, who was a pattern of the one to come.

¹⁵But the gift is not like the trespass. For if the many died by the trespass of the one man, how much more did God's grace and the gift that came by the grace of the one man, Jesus Christ, overflow to the many! ¹⁶Again, the gift of God is not like the result of the one man's sin: The judgment followed one sin and brought condemnation, but the gift followed many trespasses and brought justification. ¹⁷For if, by the trespass of the one man, death reigned through that one man, how much more will those who receive God's abundant provision of grace and of the gift of righteousness reign in life through the one man, Jesus Christ.

¹⁸Consequently, just as the result of one trespass was condemnation for all men, so also the result of one act of righteousness was justification that brings life for all men. ¹⁹For just as through the disobedience of the one man the many were made sinners, so also through the obedience of the one man the many will be made righteous.

²⁰The law was added so that the trespass might increase. But where sin increased, grace increased all the more, ²¹so that, just as sin reigned in death, so also grace might reign through righteousness to bring eternal life through Jesus Christ our Lord.

ᵘ*1,2,3 Or let us*

Discovering the Word 1. How has faith in Jesus Christ changed our relationship with God (vv. 1–2)? 2. In verses 2–11 what reasons does Paul give for rejoicing? 3. How does suffering for Christ's sake produce the character changes mentioned in verses 3–4? 4. How do verses 5–8 emphasize the love God has for

us? 5. Read verses 12–21. How are Adam and Christ similar (vv. 12, 18–19)? 6. How is Christ's gift different from Adam's trespass (vv. 15–21)?

 Applying the Word 1. In what area of your life are you experiencing suffering? 2. How can a knowledge of the process of character change help us to rejoice in our sufferings?

 Responding in Prayer This passage gives us many reasons for rejoicing. Spend time thanking and praising God for all we have in Christ Jesus.

8 / *Romans 6:1—7:6*
New Life, New Lifestyle

SUBTLE ALLURE, PERSISTENT urges, passionate desires. Sin entices us in many ways. A thought enters our mind that we dare not acknowledge: "If I give in, I can always be forgiven." Sound familiar? Such thinking can become an excuse for immoral practices. But it betrays a fundamental misunderstanding of God's grace in our lives. In Romans 6:1—7:6 Paul explains why the idea of "sinning so that grace may increase" is unthinkable for Christians.

 Warming Up to God When you became a Christian, was the change in your life dramatic, gradual or imperceptible? Explain. Whether it has taken place slowly or quickly, praise God for the change he has worked in your life.

 Read Romans 6:1—7:6.

6 What shall we say, then? Shall we go on sinning so that grace may increase? ²By no means! We died to sin; how can we live in it any longer? ³Or don't you know that all of us who were baptized into Christ Jesus were baptized into his death? ⁴We were therefore buried with him through baptism into death in order that, just as Christ was raised from the dead through the glory of the Father, we too may live a new life.

⁵If we have been united with him like this in his death, we will certainly also be united with him in his resurrection. ⁶For we know that our old self was crucified with him so that the body of sin might be done away with,ᵛ that we should no longer be slaves to sin— ⁷because anyone who has died has been freed from sin.

⁸Now if we died with Christ, we believe that we will also live with him. ⁹For we know that since Christ was raised from the dead, he cannot die again; death no longer has mastery over him. ¹⁰The death he died, he died to sin once for all; but the life he lives, he lives to God.

¹¹In the same way, count yourselves dead to sin but alive to God in Christ Jesus. ¹²Therefore do not let sin reign in your mortal body so that you obey its evil desires. ¹³Do not offer the parts of

your body to sin, as instruments of wickedness, but rather offer yourselves to God, as those who have been brought from death to life; and offer the parts of your body to him as instruments of righteousness. ¹⁴For sin shall not be your master, because you are not under law, but under grace.

¹⁵What then? Shall we sin because we are not under law but under grace? By no means! ¹⁶Don't you know that when you offer yourselves to someone to obey him as slaves, you are slaves to the one whom you obey—whether you are slaves to sin, which leads to death, or to obedience, which leads to righteousness? ¹⁷But thanks be to God that, though you used to be slaves to sin, you wholeheartedly obeyed the form of teaching to which you were entrusted. ¹⁸You have been set free from sin and have become slaves to righteousness.

¹⁹I put this in human terms because you are weak in your natural selves. Just as you used to offer the parts of your body in slavery to impurity and to ever-increasing wickedness, so now offer them in slavery to righteousness leading to holiness. ²⁰When you were slaves to sin, you were free from the control of righteousness. ²¹What benefit did you reap at that time from the things

ᵛ6 Or *be rendered powerless*

you are now ashamed of? Those things result in death! ²²But now that you have been set free from sin and have become slaves to God, the benefit you reap leads to holiness, and the result is eternal life. ²³For the wages of sin is death, but the gift of God is eternal life in^w Christ Jesus our Lord.

7 Do you not know, brothers—for I am speaking to men who know the law—that the law has authority over a man only as long as he lives? ²For example, by law a married woman is bound to her husband as long as he is alive, but if her husband dies, she is released from the law of marriage. ³So then, if she marries another man while her husband is still alive, she is called an adulteress. But if her husband dies, she

is released from that law and is not an adulteress, even though she marries another man.

⁴So, my brothers, you also died to the law through the body of Christ, that you might belong to another, to him who was raised from the dead, in order that we might bear fruit to God. ⁵For when we were controlled by the sinful nature,^x the sinful passions aroused by the law were at work in our bodies, so that we bore fruit for death. ⁶But now, by dying to what once bound us, we have been released from the law so that we serve in the new way of the Spirit, and not in the old way of the written code.

^w23 Or through   ^x5 Or the flesh; also in verse 25

Discovering the Word   1. In what sense was our baptism both a funeral and a resurrection?   2. Our "old self" (6:6) refers to everything we were as non-Christians. When our old self was crucified with Christ, in what sense was sin rendered powerless (6:5–7)?   3. What does it mean to "count yourselves dead to sin but alive to God" (6:11)?   4. Paul compares both our old life and our new to slavery. Why is this analogy appropriate in each case (6:15–18)?   5. How is the principle "that the law has authority over a man only as long as he lives" illustrated by marriage (7:1–3)?   6. In 6:1—7:6 Paul uses baptism, slavery and marriage to illustrate the differences between our old life and our new life. What common themes are emphasized in these illustrations?

Applying the Word   1. What sins are you particularly struggling to free yourself of?   2. What assurance and encouragement is Paul giving you in your struggle against sin?

Responding in Prayer   Thank God that you are no longer a slave to sin. Pray that you will live as a slave to righteousness.

---

9 / *Romans 7:7–25*
Our Struggle with Sin

ARE YOU EVER baffled by your behavior? You know the right thing to do, but you fail to do it. You resolve to avoid certain things, and they become even more attractive and enticing. Why? What keeps us from translating our desires into actions? In Romans 7 Paul explores his own inner struggles to do good and avoid evil. As we look into his mind and heart, we see a reflection of ourselves and the power that opposes us.

Warming Up to God   Saying no to a piece of pie we don't need *seems* so simple, but is easier said than done. How have you recently struggled to do what you know you should do?

Read Romans 7:7–25.

---

⁷What shall we say, then? Is the law sin? Certainly not! Indeed I would not have known what sin was except through the law. For I would not have known what coveting really was if the law had not said, "Do not covet."^y ⁸But sin, seizing the opportunity afforded by the commandment,

produced in me every kind of covetous desire. For apart from law, sin is dead. ⁹Once I was alive apart from law; but when the commandment came, sin sprang to life and I died. ¹⁰I found that

^y7 Exodus 20:17; Deut. 5:21

the very commandment that was intended to bring life actually brought death. ¹¹For sin, seizing the opportunity afforded by the commandment, deceived me, and through the commandment put me to death. ¹²So then, the law is holy, and the commandment is holy, righteous and good.

¹³Did that which is good, then, become death to me? By no means! But in order that sin might be recognized as sin, it produced death in me through what was good, so that through the commandment sin might become utterly sinful.

¹⁴We know that the law is spiritual; but I am unspiritual, sold as a slave to sin. ¹⁵I do not understand what I do. For what I want to do I do not do, but what I hate I do. ¹⁶And if I do what I do not want to do, I agree that the law is good. ¹⁷As it is, it is no longer I myself who do it, but it is sin living in me. ¹⁸I know that nothing good lives in me, that is, in my sinful nature.ᶻ For I

have the desire to do what is good, but I cannot carry it out. ¹⁹For what I do is not the good I want to do; no, the evil I do not want to do—this I keep on doing. ²⁰Now if I do what I do not want to do, it is no longer I who do it, but it is sin living in me that does it.

²¹So I find this law at work: When I want to do good, evil is right there with me. ²²For in my inner being I delight in God's law; ²³but I see another law at work in the members of my body, waging war against the law of my mind and making me a prisoner of the law of sin at work within my members. ²⁴What a wretched man I am! Who will rescue me from this body of death? ²⁵Thanks be to God—through Jesus Christ our Lord!

So then, I myself in my mind am a slave to God's law, but in the sinful nature a slave to the law of sin.

ᶻ18 Or *my flesh*

Discovering the Word 1. How did the law create in Paul a vivid awareness of sin (vv. 7–12)? 2. Why would it be wrong to blame the law for Paul's spiritual death (vv. 13–14)? 3. According to verses 14–20, why does Paul feel so wretched? 4. In chapter 6 Paul stated that Christians are no longer slaves to sin. Yet here he claims he is a slave to sin (v. 14). How would you explain this difference? 5. How can a person's anguish and frustration with sin be beneficial (vv. 24–25)?

Applying the Word 1. To what extent can you identify with Paul's struggles in these verses? Explain. 2. Why is it important to realize that only Christ can rescue you from the power of your sin?

Responding in Prayer When Paul realized that Jesus could rescue him from his wretched condition, he cried out, "Thanks be to God!" If this is your response too, spend time thanking him.

---

10 / *Romans 8:1–17*
The Spirit Brings Life

IF WE WERE unable to obey God as non-Christians, then how can we as Christians? What has happened to turn our slavery into freedom, our sin into righteousness and our spiritual death into life?

The struggle described in Romans 7 does not end when we become Christians. But there is a new dimension to that struggle that totally changes its outcome. In chapter 8 Paul describes the life-giving effects of the Spirit.

Warming Up to God This chapter is one of celebration. What has the Holy Spirit recently done in you that gives you reason to rejoice?

Read Romans 8:1–17.

8 Therefore, there is now no condemnation for those who are in Christ Jesus,ᵃ ²because through Christ Jesus the law of the Spirit of life set me free from the law of sin and death. ³For what the law was powerless to do in that it was weakened by the sinful nature,ᵇ God did by sending his own Son in the likeness of sinful man to be a sin offering.ᶜ And so he condemned sin in sinful man,ᵈ ⁴in order that the righteous requirements of the law might be fully met in us, who do not live according to the sinful nature but according to the Spirit.

⁵Those who live according to the sinful nature have their minds set on what that nature desires; but those who live in accordance with the Spirit have their minds set on what the Spirit desires. ⁶The mind of sinful manᵉ is death, but the mind controlled by the Spirit is life and peace; ⁷the sinful mindᶠ is hostile to God. It does not submit to God's law, nor can it do so. ⁸Those controlled by the sinful nature cannot please God.

⁹You, however, are controlled not by the sinful nature but by the Spirit, if the Spirit of God lives in you. And if anyone does not have the Spirit of Christ, he does not belong to Christ. ¹⁰But if Christ is in you, your body is dead because of sin, yet your spirit is alive because of righteousness. ¹¹And if the Spirit of him who raised Jesus from the dead is living in you, he who raised Christ from the dead will also give life to your mortal bodies through his Spirit, who lives in you.

¹²Therefore, brothers, we have an obligation—but it is not to the sinful nature, to live according to it. ¹³For if you live according to the sinful nature, you will die; but if by the Spirit you put to death the misdeeds of the body, you will live, ¹⁴because those who are led by the Spirit of God are sons of God. ¹⁵For you did not receive a spirit that makes you a slave again to fear, but you received the Spirit of sonship.ᵍ And by him we cry, "Abba,ʰ Father." ¹⁶The Spirit himself testifies with our spirit that we are God's children. ¹⁷Now if we are children, then we are heirs—heirs of God and co-heirs with Christ, if indeed we share in his sufferings in order that we may also share in his glory.

ᵃ1 Some later manuscripts *Jesus, who do not live according to the sinful nature but according to the Spirit,*   ᵇ3 Or *the flesh; also in verses 4, 5, 8, 9, 12 and 13*   ᶜ3 Or *man, for sin*   ᵈ3 Or *in the flesh*   ᵉ6 Or *mind set on the flesh*   ᶠ7 Or *the mind set on the flesh*   ᵍ15 Or *adoption*   ʰ15 Aramaic for *Father*

Discovering the Word 1. Romans 7 described how the law of sin brought about our spiritual death. What has God done to free us from the law of sin and death (vv. 1–4)? 2. In verses 5–8 Paul divides all of humanity into two categories: those who live according to the sinful nature and those who live according to the Spirit. In your own words, what are some characteristics of each group? 3. There are many professing Christians whose lives seem very different from Paul's description of life in the Spirit. How do you think Paul would account for this fact? 4. In verse 12 Paul concludes that we have an obligation. Describe in your own words the negative and positive aspects of that obligation (vv. 12–14). 5. How do we experience the reality and privileges of being God's children (vv. 15–17)?

Applying the Word 1. What evidence do you see of your life being controlled by the Spirit? 2. Practically speaking, how can we put to death the misdeeds of the body by the Spirit?

Responding in Prayer Spend time thanking God for the gift of the Spirit and the difference he makes in our lives.

---

11 / *Romans 8:18–39*
Glorious Conquerors

"ROMAN CONQUERORS RETURNING from the wars enjoyed the honor of a triumph, a tumultuous parade. In the procession came trumpeters, musicians and strange animals from the conquered territories, together with carts laden with treasure and captured armaments. The conqueror rode in a triumphal chariot, the dazed prisoners walking in chains before him. Sometimes his children, robed in white, stood with him in the chariot or rode the trace horses. A slave stood behind the conqueror, holding a golden crown and whispering in his ear a warning: that all glory is fleeting." (At the end of the movie *Patton*, these words went through the mind of that famous general.)

In Romans 8 Paul describes Christians as glorious conquerors who by God's grace overcome all forces arrayed against us. But the glory we receive is eternal.

 Warming Up to God Why is it often difficult to feel like a glorious conqueror?

 Read Romans 8:18–39.

18I consider that our present sufferings are not worth comparing with the glory that will be revealed in us. 19The creation waits in eager expectation for the sons of God to be revealed. 20For the creation was subjected to frustration, not by its own choice, but by the will of the one who subjected it, in hope 21that*i* the creation itself will be liberated from its bondage to decay and brought into the glorious freedom of the children of God.

22We know that the whole creation has been groaning as in the pains of childbirth right up to the present time. 23Not only so, but we ourselves, who have the firstfruits of the Spirit, groan inwardly as we wait eagerly for our adoption as sons, the redemption of our bodies. 24For in this hope we were saved. But hope that is seen is no hope at all. Who hopes for what he already has? 25But if we hope for what we do not yet have, we wait for it patiently.

26In the same way, the Spirit helps us in our weakness. We do not know what we ought to pray for, but the Spirit himself intercedes for us with groans that words cannot express. 27And he who searches our hearts knows the mind of the Spirit, because the Spirit intercedes for the saints in accordance with God's will.

28And we know that in all things God works for the good of those who love him,*j* who*k* have been called according to his purpose. 29For those God foreknew he also predestined to be conformed to the likeness of his Son, that he might be the firstborn among many brothers. 30And

those he predestined, he also called; those he called, he also justified; those he justified, he also glorified.

31What, then, shall we say in response to this? If God is for us, who can be against us? 32He who did not spare his own Son, but gave him up for us all—how will he not also, along with him, graciously give us all things? 33Who will bring any charge against those whom God has chosen? It is God who justifies. 34Who is he that condemns? Christ Jesus, who died—more than that, who was raised to life—is at the right hand of God and is also interceding for us. 35Who shall separate us from the love of Christ? Shall trouble or hardship or persecution or famine or nakedness or danger or sword? 36As it is written:

"For your sake we face death all day long;
   we are considered as sheep to be
      slaughtered."*l*

37No, in all these things we are more than conquerors through him who loved us. 38For I am convinced that neither death nor life, neither angels nor demons,*m* neither the present nor the future, nor any powers, 39neither height nor depth, nor anything else in all creation, will be able to separate us from the love of God that is in Christ Jesus our Lord.

i20,21 Or subjected it in hope. 21For   j28 Some manuscripts And we know that all things work together for good to those who love God   k28 Or works together with those who love him to bring about what is good—with those who   l36 Psalm 44:22   m38 Or nor heavenly rulers

---

 Discovering the Word 1. What words and vivid images in these verses underscore the difficulties of the present time? 2. Explain why these difficulties don't compare with the glory that will be revealed in us (vv. 18–25). 3. How can the Spirit's help encourage us (vv. 26–27)? 4. In verse 28 Paul speaks of "the good" and "his purpose." What is God's good purpose for us (v. 29)? 5. How might trouble, hardship, persecution, famine, nakedness, danger or the threat of death cause us to question God's love for us (vv. 35–36)? 6. In spite of these things, why does Paul proclaim that we are "more than conquerors" (vv. 37–39)?

 Applying the Word 1. How can eager expectation of glory help us cope with our present problems and sufferings? 2. Look again at the powerful words of verses 38–39. How does this give you courage to persevere?

Responding in Prayer Ask God to make you ready for his future glory.

12 / *Romans 9:1–29*
The Potter and His Clay

"I DON'T BELIEVE in Christ." It grieves us to hear these words. But when they come from close friends or family members, the pain can be unbearable. Why doesn't God open their hearts to the gospel? Why did he save us and not them? Paul felt great pain and perplexity over Israel's unbelief. Their Messiah had come, and they had rejected him. In chapters 9—11 Paul wrestles with these questions.

 Warming Up to God Whose unbelief grieves you? Talk openly with God about your concerns.

 Read Romans 9:1–29.

9 I speak the truth in Christ—I am not lying, my conscience confirms it in the Holy Spirit— 2I have great sorrow and unceasing anguish in my heart. 3For I could wish that I myself were cursed and cut off from Christ for the sake of my brothers, those of my own race, 4the people of Israel. Theirs is the adoption as sons; theirs the divine glory, the covenants, the receiving of the law, the temple worship and the promises. 5Theirs are the patriarchs, and from them is traced the human ancestry of Christ, who is God over all, forever praised!*n* Amen.

6It is not as though God's word had failed. For not all who are descended from Israel are Israel. 7Nor because they are his descendants are they all Abraham's children. On the contrary, "It is through Isaac that your offspring will be reckoned."*o* 8In other words, it is not the natural children who are God's children, but it is the children of the promise who are regarded as Abraham's offspring. 9For this was how the promise was stated: "At the appointed time I will return, and Sarah will have a son."*p*

10Not only that, but Rebekah's children had one and the same father, our father Isaac. 11Yet, before the twins were born or had done anything good or bad—in order that God's purpose in election might stand: 12not by works but by him who calls—she was told, "The older will serve the younger."*q* 13Just as it is written: "Jacob I loved, but Esau I hated."*r*

14What then shall we say? Is God unjust? Not at all! 15For he says to Moses,

"I will have mercy on whom I have mercy,
 and I will have compassion on whom I
 have compassion."*s*

16It does not, therefore, depend on man's desire or effort, but on God's mercy. 17For the Scripture says to Pharaoh: "I raised you up for this very purpose, that I might display my power in you and that my name might be proclaimed in all the earth."*t* 18Therefore God has mercy on whom he wants to have mercy, and he hardens whom he wants to harden.

19One of you will say to me: "Then why does God still blame us? For who resists his will?" 20But who are you, O man, to talk back to God? "Shall what is formed say to him who formed it, 'Why did you make me like this?' "*u* 21Does not the potter have the right to make out of the same lump of clay some pottery for noble purposes and some for common use?

22What if God, choosing to show his wrath and make his power known, bore with great patience the objects of his wrath—prepared for destruction? 23What if he did this to make the riches of his glory known to the objects of his mercy, whom he prepared in advance for glory— 24even us, whom he also called, not only from the Jews but also from the Gentiles? 25As he says in Hosea:

"I will call them 'my people' who are not my
 people;

n5 Or Christ, who is over all. God be forever praised! Or Christ. God who is over all be forever praised! o7 Gen. 21:12
p9 Gen. 18:10,14 q12 Gen. 25:23 r13 Mal. 1:2,3
s15 Exodus 33:19 t17 Exodus 9:16 u20 Isaiah 29:16; 45:9

and I will call her 'my loved one' who is
  not my loved one," v

²⁶and,

"It will happen that in the very place where it
    was said to them,
  'You are not my people,'
they will be called 'sons of the living God.'" w

²⁷Isaiah cries out concerning Israel:

"Though the number of the Israelites be like
    the sand by the sea,

only the remnant will be saved.
²⁸For the Lord will carry out
    his sentence on earth with speed and
      finality." x

²⁹It is just as Isaiah said previously:

"Unless the Lord Almighty
    had left us descendants,
  we would have become like Sodom,
    we would have been like Gomorrah." y

v25 Hosea 2:23   w26 Hosea 1:10   x28 Isaiah 10:22,23
y29 Isaiah 1:9

Discovering the Word 1. Why does Paul have great sorrow for the people of Israel? 2. How do verses 6–13 demonstrate that God has not failed in his promises and purposes for Israel? 3. Many people feel it is unjust for God to choose some and not others (v. 14). In reply why does Paul speak of God's mercy rather than his justice or injustice (vv. 15–18)? 4. How does the illustration of the potter and his clay help us gain a proper perspective (vv. 20–23)? 5. How is God's mercy and justice revealed in his treatment of the Gentiles and Jews (vv. 24–29)?

Applying the Word 1. How do you respond to the idea of election (v. 11), God's choosing certain people to be the objects of his mercy? 2. When do you feel uncertain about your own salvation? 3. What would help you to feel more secure?

Responding in Prayer Thank God for the fact that although he would have been perfectly just to condemn us all, he mercifully chose to save some.

---

13 / *Romans 9:30—10:21*
Misguided Zeal

THE WORLD IS full of religious people: Jews, Christians, Muslims, Hindus, Buddhists and many others. Islam alone has over 800 million adherents. Many of these people are zealous, dedicated and sincere. But are zeal and sincerity enough? Are there many paths to God, or just one? In this passage Paul continues to wrestle with the problem of Israel's unbelief. He now focuses on Israel's and on our own responsibility to believe the gospel.

Warming Up to God Have you ever known a sincere and devout non-Christian? How did you respond to his or her zeal?

Read Romans 9:30—10:21

---

³⁰What then shall we say? That the Gentiles, who did not pursue righteousness, have obtained it, a righteousness that is by faith; ³¹but Israel, who pursued a law of righteousness, has not attained it. ³²Why not? Because they pursued it not by faith but as if it were by works. They stumbled over the "stumbling stone." ³³As it is written:

"See, I lay in Zion a stone that causes men to
    stumble

and a rock that makes them fall,
and the one who trusts in him will never be
    put to shame." z

10 Brothers, my heart's desire and prayer to God for the Israelites is that they may be saved. ²For I can testify about them that they are zealous for God, but their zeal is not based on knowledge. ³Since

z33 Isaiah 8:14; 28:16

they did not know the righteousness that comes from God and sought to establish their own, they did not submit to God's righteousness. ⁴Christ is the end of the law so that there may be righteousness for everyone who believes.

⁵Moses describes in this way the righteousness that is by the law: "The man who does these things will live by them."ᵃ ⁶But the righteousness that is by faith says: "Do not say in your heart, 'Who will ascend into heaven?'ᵇ" (that is, to bring Christ down) ⁷"or 'Who will descend into the deep?'ᶜ" (that is, to bring Christ up from the dead). ⁸But what does it say? "The word is near you; it is in your mouth and in your heart,"ᵈ that is, the word of faith we are proclaiming: ⁹That if you confess with your mouth, "Jesus is Lord," and believe in your heart that God raised him from the dead, you will be saved. ¹⁰For it is with your heart that you believe and are justified, and it is with your mouth that you confess and are saved. ¹¹As the Scripture says, "Anyone who trusts in him will never be put to shame."ᵉ ¹²For there is no difference between Jew and Gentile—the same Lord is Lord of all and richly blesses all who call on him, ¹³for, "Everyone who calls on the name of the Lord will be saved."ᶠ

¹⁴How, then, can they call on the one they have not believed in? And how can they believe in the one of whom they have not heard? And how can they hear without someone preaching to them?

¹⁵And how can they preach unless they are sent? As it is written, "How beautiful are the feet of those who bring good news!"ᵍ

¹⁶But not all the Israelites accepted the good news. For Isaiah says, "Lord, who has believed our message?"ʰ ¹⁷Consequently, faith comes from hearing the message, and the message is heard through the word of Christ. ¹⁸But I ask: Did they not hear? Of course they did:

"Their voice has gone out into all the earth,
 their words to the ends of the world."ⁱ

¹⁹Again I ask: Did Israel not understand? First, Moses says,

"I will make you envious by those who are
 not a nation;
 I will make you angry by a nation that has
 no understanding."ʲ

²⁰And Isaiah boldly says,

"I was found by those who did not seek me;
 I revealed myself to those who did not ask
 for me."ᵏ

²¹But concerning Israel he says,

"All day long I have held out my hands
 to a disobedient and obstinate people."ˡ

a5 Lev. 18:5   *b6* Deut. 30:12   *c7* Deut. 30:13   *d8* Deut. 30:14
e11 Isaiah 28:16   *j13* Joel 2:32   *g15* Isaiah 52:7
h16 Isaiah 53:1   *i18* Psalm 19:4   *j19* Deut. 32:21
k20 Isaiah 65:1   *l21* Isaiah 65:2

Discovering the Word 1. Why was Jesus Christ more of a stumbling stone to the Jews than to the Gentiles (9:30-33)? 2. Many people believe religious zeal and sincerity are all a person needs to be saved. How would Paul respond to this belief (10:1-4)? 3. How do verses 6-8 stress the simplicity of righteousness by faith? 4. First-century Christians publicly confessed that "Jesus is Lord" at their baptism. Why is public confession important in addition to the belief in one's heart (vv. 9-13)? 5. William Carey, the father of modern missions, once proposed to a group of ministers that they discuss the implications of the Great Commission. Dr. John C. Ryland retorted: "Young man, sit down. When God pleases to convert the heathen, he will do it without your aid or mine!" How does Dr. Ryland's understanding of God's sovereignty mesh with verses 14-15?

Applying the Word 1. Realizing the implications of verses such as Romans 10:14-15, William Carey responded to God's call and went to India. Where do you feel called to go with the gospel? 2. What steps can you take (or have you taken) to be obedient to that call?

Responding in Prayer Israel's unbelief did not stop Paul from praying for them (10:1). Spend time praying for those with whom you have the opportunity of sharing the gospel.

14 / *Romans 11*
The Future of Israel

FOR CENTURIES THE people of Israel awaited their Messiah. But when he came, very few believed in him. This situation has persisted to the point where Christianity is now considered a Gentile religion. What happened to God's promises and plans for Israel? Has God rejected his people? In this chapter Paul answers these questions.

 Warming Up to God We all have expectations of how God will work in our lives that come out of our desires rather than God's. In what way do you feel that God has failed to follow your plan? Express to God any feelings of disappointment or discouragement you might have.

Read Romans 11.

11 I ask then: Did God reject his people? By no means! I am an Israelite myself, a descendant of Abraham, from the tribe of Benjamin. ²God did not reject his people, whom he foreknew. Don't you know what the Scripture says in the passage about Elijah—how he appealed to God against Israel: ³"Lord, they have killed your prophets and torn down your altars; I am the only one left, and they are trying to kill me"*ᵐ*? ⁴And what was God's answer to him? "I have reserved for myself seven thousand who have not bowed the knee to Baal."*ⁿ* ⁵So too, at the present time there is a remnant chosen by grace. ⁶And if by grace, then it is no longer by works; if it were, grace would no longer be grace.*ᵒ*

⁷What then? What Israel sought so earnestly it did not obtain, but the elect did. The others were hardened, ⁸as it is written:

"God gave them a spirit of stupor,
    eyes so that they could not see
    and ears so that they could not hear,
to this very day."*ᵖ*

⁹And David says:

"May their table become a snare and a trap,
    a stumbling block and a retribution for
        them.
¹⁰May their eyes be darkened so they cannot
        see,
    and their backs be bent forever."*�q*

¹¹Again I ask: Did they stumble so as to fall beyond recovery? Not at all! Rather, because of their transgression, salvation has come to the Gentiles to make Israel envious. ¹²But if their transgression means riches for the world, and

their loss means riches for the Gentiles, how much greater riches will their fullness bring!

¹³I am talking to you Gentiles. Inasmuch as I am the apostle to the Gentiles, I make much of my ministry ¹⁴in the hope that I may somehow arouse my own people to envy and save some of them. ¹⁵For if their rejection is the reconciliation of the world, what will their acceptance be but life from the dead? ¹⁶If the part of the dough offered as firstfruits is holy, then the whole batch is holy; if the root is holy, so are the branches.

¹⁷If some of the branches have been broken off, and you, though a wild olive shoot, have been grafted in among the others and now share in the nourishing sap from the olive root, ¹⁸do not boast over those branches. If you do, consider this: You do not support the root, but the root supports you. ¹⁹You will say then, "Branches were broken off so that I could be grafted in." ²⁰Granted. But they were broken off because of unbelief, and you stand by faith. Do not be arrogant, but be afraid. ²¹For if God did not spare the natural branches, he will not spare you either.

²²Consider therefore the kindness and sternness of God: sternness to those who fell, but kindness to you, provided that you continue in his kindness. Otherwise, you also will be cut off. ²³And if they do not persist in unbelief, they will be grafted in, for God is able to graft them in again. ²⁴After all, if you were cut out of an olive tree that is wild by nature, and contrary to nature were grafted into a cultivated olive tree, how much more readily will these, the natural branches, be grafted into their own olive tree!

²⁵I do not want you to be ignorant of this mys-

m3 1 Kings 19:10,14   *n4* 1 Kings 19:18   *o6* Some manuscripts *by grace. But if by works, then it is no longer grace; if it were, work would no longer be work.*   *p8* Deut. 29:4; Isaiah 29:10   *q10* Psalm 69:22,23

tery, brothers, so that you may not be conceited: Israel has experienced a hardening in part until the full number of the Gentiles has come in. ²⁶And so all Israel will be saved, as it is written:

"The deliverer will come from Zion;
he will turn godlessness away from Jacob.
²⁷And this is' my covenant with them
when I take away their sins."ˢ

²⁸As far as the gospel is concerned, they are enemies on your account; but as far as election is concerned, they are loved on account of the patriarchs, ²⁹for God's gifts and his call are irrevocable. ³⁰Just as you who were at one time disobedient to God have now received mercy as a result of their disobedience, ³¹so they too have now become disobedient in order that they too may

now' receive mercy as a result of God's mercy to you. ³²For God has bound all men over to disobedience so that he may have mercy on them all.

³³Oh, the depth of the riches of the wisdom
andᵘ knowledge of God!
How unsearchable his judgments,
and his paths beyond tracing out!
³⁴"Who has known the mind of the Lord?
Or who has been his counselor?"ᵛ
³⁵"Who has ever given to God,
that God should repay him?"ʷ
³⁶For from him and through him and to him
are all things.
To him be the glory forever! Amen.

ʳ27 Or *will be*   ˢ27 Isaiah 59:20,21; 27:9; Jer. 31:33,34   ᵗ31 Some manuscripts do not have *now.*   ᵘ33 Or *riches and the wisdom and the*   ᵛ34 Isaiah 40:13   ʷ35 Job 41:11

 Discovering the Word 1. How does Paul know that God has not rejected his people (vv. 1–6)? 2. What were the spiritual consequences for those Israelites who rejected Jesus Christ (vv. 7–10)? 3. Why are these consequences inevitable for anyone who persistently rejects the gospel? 4. Why is Paul convinced that even greater blessings will come from Israel's acceptance of Christ (vv. 11–16)? 5. Why should Paul's illustration of the olive tree prevent Gentiles from feeling superior to unbelieving Israelites (vv. 17–24)? 6. In this chapter Paul has argued that Israel's unbelief is partial (vv. 1–10), purposeful (vv. 11–16) and temporary (vv. 25–32). How does this make him feel about God (vv. 33–36)?

 Applying the Word 1. Why is it foolish for Christians today to feel superior to non-Christians? 2. How can Paul's description of God in verses 33–36 also encourage us to trust and praise him?

Responding in Prayer Thank God that his plans are greater than anything we can conceive.

---

15 / *Romans 12*
Living Sacrifices

IN THE FIRST eleven chapters Paul has described God's gift of righteousness. In Christ we who were condemned are justified. We who were sinners are sanctified. And we who had no hope will be glorified. But what is our proper response to God's mercy, love and grace? Paul tells us in this and the following chapters.

 Warming Up to God Jesus once told a Pharisee that a person who is forgiven little loves little. But a person who is forgiven much loves much (Lk 7:47). Why do you think this is so?

 Read Romans 12.

---

12 Therefore, I urge you, brothers, in view of God's mercy, to offer your bodies as living sacrifices, holy and pleasing to God—this is your spiritualˣ act of worship. ²Do not conform any longer to the pattern of this world, but be transformed by the re-

newing of your mind. Then you will be able to test and approve what God's will is—his good, pleasing and perfect will.

³For by the grace given me I say to every one of

ˣ1 Or *reasonable*

you: Do not think of yourself more highly than you ought, but rather think of yourself with sober judgment, in accordance with the measure of faith God has given you. [4]Just as each of us has one body with many members, and these members do not all have the same function, [5]so in Christ we who are many form one body, and each member belongs to all the others. [6]We have different gifts, according to the grace given us. If a man's gift is prophesying, let him use it in proportion to his[y] faith. [7]If it is serving, let him serve; if it is teaching, let him teach; [8]if it is encouraging, let him encourage; if it is contributing to the needs of others, let him give generously; if it is leadership, let him govern diligently; if it is showing mercy, let him do it cheerfully.

[9]Love must be sincere. Hate what is evil; cling to what is good. [10]Be devoted to one another in brotherly love. Honor one another above yourselves. [11]Never be lacking in zeal, but keep your spiritual fervor, serving the Lord. [12]Be joyful in hope, patient in affliction, faithful in prayer. [13]Share with God's people who are in need. Practice hospitality.

[14]Bless those who persecute you; bless and do not curse. [15]Rejoice with those who rejoice; mourn with those who mourn. [16]Live in harmony with one another. Do not be proud, but be willing to associate with people of low position.[z] Do not be conceited.

[17]Do not repay anyone evil for evil. Be careful to do what is right in the eyes of everybody. [18]If it is possible, as far as it depends on you, live at peace with everyone. [19]Do not take revenge, my friends, but leave room for God's wrath, for it is written: "It is mine to avenge; I will repay,"[a] says the Lord. [20]On the contrary:

"If your enemy is hungry, feed him;
    if he is thirsty, give him something to
    drink.
In doing this, you will heap burning coals on
    his head."[b]

[21]Do not be overcome by evil, but overcome evil with good.

[y]6 Or *in agreement with the*   [z]16 Or *willing to do menial work*
[a]19 Deut. 32:35   [b]20 Prov. 25:21,22

 Discovering the Word   1. Why do you think Paul uses the imagery of "living sacrifices" to describe our proper response to God's mercy?   2. Sometimes we view God's will as something to be avoided rather than desired. How can the last part of verse 2 correct this distortion?   3. How can the realization that we are members of a body (vv. 3–8) prevent us from thinking too highly of ourselves (v. 3)?   4. How would the kind of love Paul describes in verses 9–16 transform our relationships with other Christians?   5. How would Paul's advice in verses 17–21 help us to overcome our enemies?

Applying the Word   1. What are some ways we can renew our minds (v. 2) and so be transformed?   2. As you think "with sober judgment" about yourself, what gift (or gifts) do you think God has given you (vv. 3–8)?   3. In what ways do you need to begin living more sacrificially before God, other Christians or the world?

Responding in Prayer   Ask God to use you in serving the body of Christ.

---

16 / *Romans 13*
Submitting to Authorities

THE SERGEANT GLARES at a delinquent recruit whose face is now only inches away.
    "That's an order!" he barks. "Do you understand?"
    "Yes, sir," replies the recruit.
    "I can't *hear* you!" shouts the sergeant.
    "YES, SIR!" screams the recruit, who has just had his first lesson in military authority.
    For many people the word *authority* conjures up images like the one just described. Those in authority are viewed as oppressors, and too often the impression is correct. Paul was no stranger to the abuses of authority. He had

experienced much persecution at the hands of civil and religious authorities all around the Mediterranean. In light of this, Paul's view of authority may be surprising.

 Warming Up to God What comes into your mind when you hear the word *authority*? Why?

 Read Romans 13.

13

Everyone must submit himself to the governing authorities, for there is no authority except that which God has established. The authorities that exist have been established by God. ²Consequently, he who rebels against the authority is rebelling against what God has instituted, and those who do so will bring judgment on themselves. ³For rulers hold no terror for those who do right, but for those who do wrong. Do you want to be free from fear of the one in authority? Then do what is right and he will commend you. ⁴For he is God's servant to do you good. But if you do wrong, be afraid, for he does not bear the sword for nothing. He is God's servant, an agent of wrath to bring punishment on the wrongdoer. ⁵Therefore, it is necessary to submit to the authorities, not only because of possible punishment but also because of conscience.

⁶This is also why you pay taxes, for the authorities are God's servants, who give their full time to governing. ⁷Give everyone what you owe him: If you owe taxes, pay taxes; if revenue, then revenue; if respect, then respect; if honor, then honor.

⁸Let no debt remain outstanding, except the continuing debt to love one another, for he who loves his fellowman has fulfilled the law. ⁹The commandments, "Do not commit adultery," "Do not murder," "Do not steal," "Do not covet,"ᶜ and whatever other commandment there may be, are summed up in this one rule: "Love your neighbor as yourself."ᵈ ¹⁰Love does no harm to its neighbor. Therefore love is the fulfillment of the law.

¹¹And do this, understanding the present time. The hour has come for you to wake up from your slumber, because our salvation is nearer now than when we first believed. ¹²The night is nearly over; the day is almost here. So let us put aside the deeds of darkness and put on the armor of light. ¹³Let us behave decently, as in the daytime, not in orgies and drunkenness, not in sexual immorality and debauchery, not in dissension and jealousy. ¹⁴Rather, clothe yourselves with the Lord Jesus Christ, and do not think about how to gratify the desires of the sinful nature.ᵉ

ᶜ9 Exodus 20:13-15,17; Deut. 5:17-19,21   ᵈ9 Lev. 19:18   ᵉ14 Or *the flesh*

 Discovering the Word 1. What is Paul's view of authority and those who exercise it (vv. 1–5)? 2. How would Paul's view of governing authorities apply to wicked and perverse rulers such as Nero or Hitler? 3. What are some reasons Paul gives for submitting to those in authority (vv. 1–5)? 4. In verse 8 Paul says, "Let no debt remain outstanding." Does this mean Christians should never incur any type of debts (mortgage, car and so on)? 5. In verses 11–14 Paul uses several vivid images to describe "the present time." How does each one give us a picture of how we should (or shouldn't) live?

Applying the Word 1. In verses 6–7 Paul suggests some practical ways we should submit to those in authority. What other examples can you think of? 2. Do you think it is ever appropriate to resist rather than to submit to the authorities? Explain. 3. Think back over this chapter. In what ways do you need to "clothe yourselves with the Lord Jesus Christ"?

Responding in Prayer Submission does not come to us naturally. Pray that you will learn to submit.

17 / *Romans 14*
To Eat or Not to Eat

IN THE LATE 1800s robed choirs were considered worldly by some Christians. More recently going to movies, watching television and drinking wine or beer have been viewed as sinful.

The Bible contains many clear commands. But it is also silent or ambiguous about many moral issues. These "gray" areas have always been a source of dispute and conflict among Christians, even though the specific areas of dispute change from time to time. What principles should guide us when our actions are criticized by others or when we feel critical toward them? Romans 14 helps us answer these questions.

 Warming Up to God What types of behavior do Christians disagree about today?

 Read Romans 14:1–23.

14 Accept him whose faith is weak, without passing judgment on disputable matters. ²One man's faith allows him to eat everything, but another man, whose faith is weak, eats only vegetables. ³The man who eats everything must not look down on him who does not, and the man who does not eat everything must not condemn the man who does, for God has accepted him. ⁴Who are you to judge someone else's servant? To his own master he stands or falls. And he will stand, for the Lord is able to make him stand.

⁵One man considers one day more sacred than another; another man considers every day alike. Each one should be fully convinced in his own mind. ⁶He who regards one day as special, does so to the Lord. He who eats meat, eats to the Lord, for he gives thanks to God; and he who abstains, does so to the Lord and gives thanks to God. ⁷For none of us lives to himself alone and none of us dies to himself alone. ⁸If we live, we live to the Lord; and if we die, we die to the Lord. So, whether we live or die, we belong to the Lord.

⁹For this very reason, Christ died and returned to life so that he might be the Lord of both the dead and the living. ¹⁰You, then, why do you judge your brother? Or why do you look down on your brother? For we will all stand before God's judgment seat. ¹¹It is written:

" 'As surely as I live,' says the Lord,
'every knee will bow before me;
   every tongue will confess to God.' "ᶠ

¹²So then, each of us will give an account of himself to God.

¹³Therefore let us stop passing judgment on one another. Instead, make up your mind not to put any stumbling block or obstacle in your brother's way. ¹⁴As one who is in the Lord Jesus, I am fully convinced that no foodᵍ is unclean in itself. But if anyone regards something as unclean, then for him it is unclean. ¹⁵If your brother is distressed because of what you eat, you are no longer acting in love. Do not by your eating destroy your brother for whom Christ died. ¹⁶Do not allow what you consider good to be spoken of as evil. ¹⁷For the kingdom of God is not a matter of eating and drinking, but of righteousness, peace and joy in the Holy Spirit, ¹⁸because anyone who serves Christ in this way is pleasing to God and approved by men.

¹⁹Let us therefore make every effort to do what leads to peace and to mutual edification. ²⁰Do not destroy the work of God for the sake of food. All food is clean, but it is wrong for a man to eat anything that causes someone else to stumble. ²¹It is better not to eat meat or drink wine or to do anything else that will cause your brother to fall.

²²So whatever you believe about these things keep between yourself and God. Blessed is the man who does not condemn himself by what he approves. ²³But the man who has doubts is condemned if he eats, because his eating is not from faith; and everything that does not come from faith is sin.

ᶠ11 Isaiah 45:23   ᵍ14 Or *that nothing*

Discovering the Word 1. What are some areas of dispute between the "weak" and the "strong" in verses 1–6? 2. What attitudes do the weak and the strong tend to have toward each other (vv. 1–4)? Why? 3. What types of Christians are you most likely to judge or look down on? Why? 4. Why is it wrong to pass judgment on other Christians (vv. 1–13)? 5. When we are *not* around those whose faith is weak, what principles should govern our Christian liberty (vv. 5–23)? 6. When we *are* around those whose faith is weak, what principles should guide our actions, and why (vv. 13–21)?

 Applying the Word 1. What practices offend you? 2. Which of your own practices might distress or destroy another brother or sister in Christ?

Responding in Prayer Ask God for wisdom to know how to respond in areas in which you are causing offense.

18 / *Romans 15:1–13*
Unity, Hope and Praise

YOU DESERVE THE best. Look out for number one. Pamper yourself. These are the watchwords of our age. But in this chapter Paul urges us to stop gazing at our own reflection. For the first time in Romans he holds up the example of Christ, the one who embodies all the qualities God desires in us.

 Warming Up to God When is self-concern appropriate, and when does it turn into selfishness?

 Read Romans 15:1–13.

15 We who are strong ought to bear with the failings of the weak and not to please ourselves. ²Each of us should please his neighbor for his good, to build him up. ³For even Christ did not please himself but, as it is written: "The insults of those who insult you have fallen on me."[h] ⁴For everything that was written in the past was written to teach us, so that through endurance and the encouragement of the Scriptures we might have hope.

⁵May the God who gives endurance and encouragement give you a spirit of unity among yourselves as you follow Christ Jesus, ⁶so that with one heart and mouth you may glorify the God and Father of our Lord Jesus Christ.

⁷Accept one another, then, just as Christ accepted you, in order to bring praise to God. ⁸For I tell you that Christ has become a servant of the Jews[i] on behalf of God's truth, to confirm the promises made to the patriarchs ⁹so that the Gentiles may glorify God for his mercy, as it is written:

"Therefore I will praise you among the
        Gentiles;
    I will sing hymns to your name."[j]

¹⁰Again, it says,

"Rejoice, O Gentiles, with his people."[k]

¹¹And again,

"Praise the Lord, all you Gentiles,
    and sing praises to him, all you peoples."[l]

¹²And again, Isaiah says,

"The Root of Jesse will spring up,
    one who will arise to rule over the nations;
the Gentiles will hope in him."[m]

¹³May the God of hope fill you with all joy and peace as you trust in him, so that you may overflow with hope by the power of the Holy Spirit.

h3 Psalm 69:9   *i8* Greek *circumcision*   *j9* 2 Samuel 22:50;
Psalm 18:49   *k10* Deut. 32:43   *l11* Psalm 117:1
m12 Isaiah 11:10

Discovering the Word 1. What personal attitudes might hinder or help us to bear with the failings of the weak (vv. 1–2)? Explain why. 2. If we follow Christ's example in this and other areas of our lives, why will we need endurance, encouragement and hope (vv. 4–5)? 3. In contrast to the discord and possible verbal abuse hinted at in Romans 14, what does God desire of us (vv. 5–6)? 4. In verses 9–12 Paul quotes from four different Old Testament passages. What words and phrases express the dominant mood of these verses? 5. Why is this mood appropriate for all who hope in Jesus?

 Applying the Word 1. Keeping in mind the context of verses 1–12, how can we become those whose lives overflow with joy, peace and hope (v. 13)? 2. Paul concludes this passage with a vivid prayer (v. 13). Consider these words, and try to picture this reality. How do you feel?

 Responding in Prayer Spend time praising God for the joy, peace and hope we have in Christ.

19 / *Romans 15:14—16:27*
Brothers and Sisters in Christ

IN CHRIST WE have a bond that is stronger than flesh and blood. We are now and will always be brothers and sisters in Christ, members of God's family. This passage introduces us to some of our first-century relatives. As you read about them, notice the care they had for each other.

Warming Up to God What images come to mind when you think of the first-century church?

Read Romans 15:14—16:27.

14I myself am convinced, my brothers, that you yourselves are full of goodness, complete in knowledge and competent to instruct one another. 15I have written you quite boldly on some points, as if to remind you of them again, because of the grace God gave me 16to be a minister of Christ Jesus to the Gentiles with the priestly duty of proclaiming the gospel of God, so that the Gentiles might become an offering acceptable to God, sanctified by the Holy Spirit.

17Therefore I glory in Christ Jesus in my service to God. 18I will not venture to speak of anything except what Christ has accomplished through me in leading the Gentiles to obey God by what I have said and done— 19by the power of signs and miracles, through the power of the Spirit. So from Jerusalem all the way around to Illyricum, I have fully proclaimed the gospel of Christ. 20It has always been my ambition to preach the gospel where Christ was not known, so that I would not be building on someone else's foundation. 21Rather, as it is written:

"Those who were not told about him will see,
    and those who have not heard will
        understand." [n]

22This is why I have often been hindered from coming to you.

23But now that there is no more place for me to work in these regions, and since I have been longing for many years to see you, 24I plan to do so when I go to Spain. I hope to visit you while passing through and to have you assist me on my journey there, after I have enjoyed your company for a while. 25Now, however, I am on my way to Jerusalem in the service of the saints there. 26For Macedonia and Achaia were pleased to make a contribution for the poor among the saints in Jerusalem. 27They were pleased to do it, and indeed they owe it to them. For if the Gentiles have shared in the Jews' spiritual blessings, they owe it to the Jews to share with them their material blessings. 28So after I have completed this task and have made sure that they have received this fruit, I will go to Spain and visit you on the way. 29I know that when I come to you, I will come in the full measure of the blessing of Christ.

[n]21 Isaiah 52:15

[30] I urge you, brothers, by our Lord Jesus Christ and by the love of the Spirit, to join me in my struggle by praying to God for me. [31] Pray that I may be rescued from the unbelievers in Judea and that my service in Jerusalem may be acceptable to the saints there, [32] so that by God's will I may come to you with joy and together with you be refreshed. [33] The God of peace be with you all. Amen.

16

I commend to you our sister Phoebe, a servant[o] of the church in Cenchrea. [2] I ask you to receive her in the Lord in a way worthy of the saints and to give her any help she may need from you, for she has been a great help to many people, including me.

[3] Greet Priscilla[p] and Aquila, my fellow workers in Christ Jesus. [4] They risked their lives for me. Not only I but all the churches of the Gentiles are grateful to them.

[5] Greet also the church that meets at their house.

Greet my dear friend Epenetus, who was the first convert to Christ in the province of Asia.

[6] Greet Mary, who worked very hard for you.

[7] Greet Andronicus and Junias, my relatives who have been in prison with me. They are outstanding among the apostles, and they were in Christ before I was.

[8] Greet Ampliatus, whom I love in the Lord.

[9] Greet Urbanus, our fellow worker in Christ, and my dear friend Stachys.

[10] Greet Apelles, tested and approved in Christ.

Greet those who belong to the household of Aristobulus.

[11] Greet Herodion, my relative.

Greet those in the household of Narcissus who are in the Lord.

[12] Greet Tryphena and Tryphosa, those women who work hard in the Lord.

Greet my dear friend Persis, another woman who has worked very hard in the Lord.

[13] Greet Rufus, chosen in the Lord, and his mother, who has been a mother to me, too.

[14] Greet Asyncritus, Phlegon, Hermes, Patrobas, Hermas and the brothers with them.

[15] Greet Philologus, Julia, Nereus and his sister, and Olympas and all the saints with them.

[16] Greet one another with a holy kiss.

All the churches of Christ send greetings.

[17] I urge you, brothers, to watch out for those who cause divisions and put obstacles in your way that are contrary to the teaching you have learned. Keep away from them. [18] For such people are not serving our Lord Christ, but their own appetites. By smooth talk and flattery they deceive the minds of naive people. [19] Everyone has heard about your obedience, so I am full of joy over you; but I want you to be wise about what is good, and innocent about what is evil.

[20] The God of peace will soon crush Satan under your feet.

The grace of our Lord Jesus be with you.

[21] Timothy, my fellow worker, sends his greetings to you, as do Lucius, Jason and Sosipater, my relatives.

[22] I, Tertius, who wrote down this letter, greet you in the Lord.

[23] Gaius, whose hospitality I and the whole church here enjoy, sends you his greetings.

Erastus, who is the city's director of public works, and our brother Quartus send you their greetings.[q]

[25] Now to him who is able to establish you by my gospel and the proclamation of Jesus Christ, according to the revelation of the mystery hidden for long ages past, [26] but now revealed and made known through the prophetic writings by the command of the eternal God, so that all nations might believe and obey him— [27] to the only wise God be glory forever through Jesus Christ! Amen.

---

o 1 Or *deaconess*   P 3 Greek *Prisca,* a variant of *Priscilla*
q 23 Some manuscripts *their greetings.* 24 *May the grace of our Lord Jesus Christ be with all of you. Amen.*

 Discovering the Word 1. What do we learn about Paul's apostolic ministry from 15:22? 2. What are Paul's immediate and future plans (15:23–33)? 3. What does 15:23–33 teach us about relationships among first-century Christians? 4. Use your imagination. From what we know about Paul and the Romans, how might the people in verses 1–16 have "risked their lives," "worked very hard" and "been a great help" to Paul and others? 5. How do the final words of this letter summarize the scope of our salvation (vv. 25–27)?

 Applying the Word 1. In what ways can we share material blessings with other Christians? 2. What can you do to strengthen relationships in your spiritual family?

Responding in Prayer Pray for your church and the needs of specific people you know.

1 Corinthians

I n 1938, just before World War II, Dietrich Bonhoeffer wrote *Life Together*, a moving little book on the principles of Christian community. Eighteen and a half centuries earlier the apostle Paul wrote what has come to be known as 1 Corinthians, a fascinating commentary on one Christian community that he founded. Why should we bother with either of these books?

Simply because we all have to live together with people, in Christian contexts and otherwise. Whether the situation involves a close friendship, a roommate, a spouse, a small group, a family, an office, a campus club, a neighborhood or a congregation, the challenges of life together will inevitably crop up. Church life is not immune to these problems, and Corinth was particularly susceptible. As a result, we can benefit from Paul's advice to that community.

Are there cliques and power struggles in the communities of which you are a part? Are you plagued by people who think they are spiritually or intellectually superior? How do you handle the immorality that seems so prevalent in the world, especially when it begins to invade the church? What is the proper way to exercise your rights, especially when a friend wrongs you or you feel that a matter of principle is at stake? How do we regulate marriage and singleness in the face of so many attacks on the health of both these life situations? How are we ever going to solve the battle of the sexes? What is the path to respecting one another's personality and gifts? Can eternity make a difference in how we live together today?

If any of these questions are relevant to your life and communities, then 1 Corinthians has something to say to you.

The relationship between Paul and the church at Corinth is a bittersweet chapter in church history. As the apostle traveled down the isthmus joining the two halves of Achaia (Greece) and first spotted the plain surrounding the city and the hill known as the Acrocorinth jutting up behind, he could hardly have imagined the depths and heights that would be reached by the church he left behind eighteen months later (see Acts 18 for the background of this part of Paul's second missionary journey). Nor could Paul have any idea of the depths and heights of emotion to which the members of that church would lead him, their spiritual father, over the next few years of visits and letters.

Both comedy and tragedy are found in the story of the Corinthian church. There was the

comedy of a dynamic, gifted Christian community composed of uneducated, uninfluential people. They were plucked out of one of the greatest centers of trade, political authority and pagan religion in the Roman empire. Morals were so bad in that city that its citizens had inspired a word for sexual license—to *Corinthianize!* The existence of a church in such a setting was a reason for comic rejoicing.

However, there was also the tragedy of the Corinthians forgetting their humble roots and placing themselves as kings over one another—even over Paul, their founder and friend. The resulting tensions and schisms would boil over with even greater heartache for Paul in 2 Corinthians.

In the first six chapters of 1 Corinthians Paul begins with the distressing matters he has learned about: factions, incest, court cases and freedom gone wild. In chapters 7—14 he treats a series of topics that the Corinthians have asked him about, from marriage to spiritual gifts, with each new topic signaled by the phrase *Now concerning.* Finally, he sums up the teaching of the book in chapter 15, which is devoted to a theology of the resurrection or "last things."

Understanding why chapter 15 and parts of chapters 1—4 fit into this book is the key to unlocking 1 Corinthians. As always, Paul is not only interested in correcting practice but also in grounding his instruction in theological principles. In fact, the Corinthians had two root problems: premature spirituality (they thought they had everything heaven could offer) and immature spirituality (they forgot that the heart of the gospel is love, servanthood and the cross). Perhaps our communities, too, need correction in both practice and theology.

Outline

1/ 1 Corinthians 1 ———————————— *Called in Christ*

2/ 1 Corinthians 2 ———————————— *Mind of Christ*

3/ 1 Corinthians 3 ———————————— *Founded on Christ*

4/ 1 Corinthians 4 ———————————— *Servants of Christ*

5/ 1 Corinthians 5—6 ————————— *Members of Christ*

6/ 1 Corinthians 7 ———————————— *Devoted to Christ*

7/ 1 Corinthians 8—9 ————————— *Living for Christ*

8/ 1 Corinthians 10:1—11:1 ———— *Eating with Christ*

9/ 1 Corinthians 11:2–34 ———————— *Headship of Christ*

10/ 1 Corinthians 12 ——————————— *Body of Christ*

11/ 1 Corinthians 13 ——————————— *Love of Christ*

12/ 1 Corinthians 14 ——————————— *Speaking for Christ*

13/ 1 Corinthians 15—16 ——————— *Hope in Christ*

1 / *1 Corinthians 1*
Called in Christ

HAVE YOU EVER found a Christian group that doesn't have any problems? If so, don't join it—you'll ruin everything! The church in Corinth was far from perfect. Paul had heard a long list of complaints about this eager but misguided flock. As he attempted some long-distance pastoring, where would he begin? Paul's starting point is very relevant for problem groups and individuals today.

 Warming Up to God When have you been hurt by division within a church or Christian group you were a part of?

 Read 1 Corinthians 1.

1 Paul, called to be an apostle of Christ Jesus by the will of God, and our brother Sosthenes,

²To the church of God in Corinth, to those sanctified in Christ Jesus and called to be holy, together with all those everywhere who call on the name of our Lord Jesus Christ—their Lord and ours:

³Grace and peace to you from God our Father and the Lord Jesus Christ.

⁴I always thank God for you because of his grace given you in Christ Jesus. ⁵For in him you have been enriched in every way—in all your speaking and in all your knowledge— ⁶because our testimony about Christ was confirmed in you. ⁷Therefore you do not lack any spiritual gift as you eagerly wait for our Lord Jesus Christ to be revealed. ⁸He will keep you strong to the end, so that you will be blameless on the day of our Lord Jesus Christ. ⁹God, who has called you into fellowship with his Son Jesus Christ our Lord, is faithful.

¹⁰I appeal to you, brothers, in the name of our Lord Jesus Christ, that all of you agree with one another so that there may be no divisions among you and that you may be perfectly united in mind and thought. ¹¹My brothers, some from Chloe's household have informed me that there are quarrels among you. ¹²What I mean is this: One of you says, "I follow Paul"; another, "I follow Apollos"; another, "I follow Cephas*a*"; still another, "I follow Christ."

¹³Is Christ divided? Was Paul crucified for you? Were you baptized into*b* the name of Paul? ¹⁴I am thankful that I did not baptize any of you except Crispus and Gaius, ¹⁵so no one can say

that you were baptized into my name. ¹⁶(Yes, I also baptized the household of Stephanas; beyond that, I don't remember if I baptized anyone else.) ¹⁷For Christ did not send me to baptize, but to preach the gospel—not with words of human wisdom, lest the cross of Christ be emptied of its power.

¹⁸For the message of the cross is foolishness to those who are perishing, but to us who are being saved it is the power of God. ¹⁹For it is written:

"I will destroy the wisdom of the wise;
    the intelligence of the intelligent I will
        frustrate."*c*

²⁰Where is the wise man? Where is the scholar? Where is the philosopher of this age? Has not God made foolish the wisdom of the world? ²¹For since in the wisdom of God the world through its wisdom did not know him, God was pleased through the foolishness of what was preached to save those who believe. ²²Jews demand miraculous signs and Greeks look for wisdom, ²³but we preach Christ crucified: a stumbling block to Jews and foolishness to Gentiles, ²⁴but to those whom God has called, both Jews and Greeks, Christ the power of God and the wisdom of God. ²⁵For the foolishness of God is wiser than man's wisdom, and the weakness of God is stronger than man's strength.

²⁶Brothers, think of what you were when you were called. Not many of you were wise by human standards; not many were influential; not many were of noble birth. ²⁷But God chose the foolish things of the world to shame the wise; God chose the weak things of the world to shame the strong. ²⁸He chose the lowly things of this world and the despised things—and the things

a12 That is, Peter   *b13* Or in; also in verse 15   *c19* Isaiah 29:14

that are not—to nullify the things that are, 29so that no one may boast before him. 30It is because of him that you are in Christ Jesus, who has become for us wisdom from God—that is, our righteousness, holiness and redemption. 31Therefore, as it is written: "Let him who boasts boast in the Lord."d

d31 Jer. 9:24

Discovering the Word 1. Before discussing the problems in Corinth, Paul affirms his readers (vv. 1–9). Why is he thankful for them? 2. Why do you think cliques had formed around Paul, Apollos and Cephas (v. 12)? 3. How did Paul conduct himself in Corinth to avoid, if possible, the problem of a personality cult (vv. 14–17)? 4. The Corinthians boasted in worldly wisdom and those who taught it. How does the message of the cross destroy all such boasting (vv. 18–25)? 5. The Corinthians also felt intellectually and spiritually superior to others. What had they forgotten about their past and the reason God chose them (vv. 26–29)? 6. What does it mean to "boast in the Lord" (vv. 30–31)?

Applying the Word 1. As you reflect on your own past, what reasons do you have for being humble rather than proud? 2. How can genuine humility promote unity in your church or fellowship?

Responding in Prayer Take time to thank the Lord for all he has done for you.

---

2 / 1 Corinthians 2
Mind of Christ

MANY PEOPLE THINK Christianity is for the mindless and dull. Someone has said, "I feel like unscrewing my head and putting it underneath the pew every time I go to church." Unfortunately, this chapter has been used to support an uneducated, unthinking approach to Christianity. But this misses the point. As Søren Kierkegaard, the Danish philosopher, once said: Christ doesn't destroy reason; he *dethrones* it.

Warming Up to God In what area of your life do you need wisdom?

Read 1 Corinthians 2.

---

2 When I came to you, brothers, I did not come with eloquence or superior wisdom as I proclaimed to you the testimony about God.e 2For I resolved to know nothing while I was with you except Jesus Christ and him crucified. 3I came to you in weakness and fear, and with much trembling. 4My message and my preaching were not with wise and persuasive words, but with a demonstration of the Spirit's power, 5so that your faith might not rest on men's wisdom, but on God's power.

6We do, however, speak a message of wisdom among the mature, but not the wisdom of this age or of the rulers of this age, who are coming to nothing. 7No, we speak of God's secret wisdom, a wisdom that has been hidden and that God destined for our glory before time began. 8None of the rulers of this age understood it, for if they had, they would not have crucified the Lord of glory. 9However, as it is written:

"No eye has seen,
  no ear has heard,
no mind has conceived
  what God has prepared for those who love
    him"f—

10but God has revealed it to us by his Spirit.

The Spirit searches all things, even the deep things of God. 11For who among men knows the thoughts of a man except the man's spirit within him? In the same way no one knows the thoughts of God except the Spirit of God. 12We have not

e1 Some manuscripts as I proclaimed to you God's mystery
f9 Isaiah 64:4

received the spirit of the world but the Spirit who is from God, that we may understand what God has freely given us. ¹³This is what we speak, not in words taught us by human wisdom but in words taught by the Spirit, expressing spiritual truths in spiritual words.ᵍ ¹⁴The man without the Spirit does not accept the things that come from the Spirit of God, for they are foolishness to him, and he cannot understand them, because they are spiritually discerned. ¹⁵The spiritual man makes judgments about all things, but he himself is not subject to any man's judgment:

¹⁶"For who has known the mind of the Lord
    that he may instruct him?"ʰ

But we have the mind of Christ.

ᵍ13 Or Spirit, interpreting spiritual truths to spiritual men
ʰ16 Isaiah 40:13

 Discovering the Word 1. Greek philosophers were often polished orators whose eloquence and wisdom dazzled their audiences. How does this contrast with Paul's preaching in Corinth (vv. 1–5)? 2. How is God's wisdom different from the wisdom of this age (vv. 6–10)? 3. Why are *secret* and *hidden* appropriate words to describe this wisdom? 4. When it comes to understanding God's wisdom, how does the person without the Spirit contrast with the spiritual person (vv. 14–16)? 5. Based on this passage, how would you define spiritual maturity?

 Applying the Word 1. Who has been an example of spiritual maturity to you? 2. What can you do to become more spiritually mature?

Responding in Prayer Ask that you would be given the true wisdom that comes from the Spirit.

---

3 / 1 Corinthians 3
Founded on Christ

THE DUKE OF Windsor, recalling his childhood discipline by George V, then King of England, said that his father used to daily remind him, "Never forget who you are." As the spiritual father of the Corinthians, Paul reminds them in this chapter, "Never forget *whose* you are."

The Corinthians were worldly and quarrelsome because they misunderstood both the message and the messengers of the cross. In chapters one and two, Paul focused on the message—the true wisdom from God. Now he looks at God's messengers. As he does so, Paul reminds the Corinthians and us of our true identity in Christ.

 Warming Up to God Think of a time when someone who really cared for you confronted you with a failure to live up to your values. What qualities of that encounter made it constructive? Praise God for giving you people who care about your spiritual life.

 Read 1 Corinthians 3.

---

3 Brothers, I could not address you as spiritual but as worldly—mere infants in Christ. ²I gave you milk, not solid food, for you were not yet ready for it. Indeed, you are still not ready. ³You are still worldly. For since there is jealousy and quarreling among you, are you not worldly? Are you not acting like mere men? ⁴For when one says, "I follow Paul," and another, "I follow Apollos," are you not mere men?

⁵What, after all, is Apollos? And what is Paul? Only servants, through whom you came to believe—as the Lord has assigned to each his task. ⁶I planted the seed, Apollos watered it, but God made it grow. ⁷So neither he who plants nor he who waters is anything, but only God, who makes things grow. ⁸The man who plants and the man who waters have one purpose, and each will be rewarded according to his own labor. ⁹For we are God's fellow workers; you are God's field, God's building.

¹⁰By the grace God has given me, I laid a foun-

dation as an expert builder, and someone else is building on it. But each one should be careful how he builds. ¹¹For no one can lay any foundation other than the one already laid, which is Jesus Christ. ¹²If any man builds on this foundation using gold, silver, costly stones, wood, hay or straw, ¹³his work will be shown for what it is, because the Day will bring it to light. It will be revealed with fire, and the fire will test the quality of each man's work. ¹⁴If what he has built survives, he will receive his reward. ¹⁵If it is burned up, he will suffer loss; he himself will be saved, but only as one escaping through the flames.

¹⁶Don't you know that you yourselves are God's temple and that God's Spirit lives in you? ¹⁷If anyone destroys God's temple, God will destroy him; for God's temple is sacred, and you are that temple.

¹⁸Do not deceive yourselves. If any one of you thinks he is wise by the standards of this age, he should become a "fool" so that he may become wise. ¹⁹For the wisdom of this world is foolishness in God's sight. As it is written: "He catches the wise in their craftiness"ⁱ; ²⁰and again, "The Lord knows that the thoughts of the wise are futile."ʲ ²¹So then, no more boasting about men! All things are yours, ²²whether Paul or Apollos or Cephasᵏ or the world or life or death or the present or the future—all are yours, ²³and you are of Christ, and Christ is of God.

ⁱ19 Job 5:13   ʲ20 Psalm 94:11   ᵏ22 That is, Peter

 Discovering the Word 1. Even though the Corinthians had the Spirit, why couldn't they be considered spiritual (vv. 1–4)? 2. What two illustrations does Paul use to describe himself and Apollos (vv. 6–9, 10–15)? 3. In what ways is God's church like a field being planted (vv. 6–9)? 4. In 3:10–15 Paul changes the metaphor from farming to building. Describe the various ways the church is like a building under construction. 5. In verse 3 Paul accused the Corinthians of being worldly. How can he say to the same people, "You are God's temple" and "God's Spirit lives in you" (v. 16)? 6. The Corinthians had initially claimed, "I belong to Paul" or "I belong to Apollos" (1:12 RSV). Paul claims something more important. In what sense do Paul, Apollos and everything else belong to the Corinthians—and to us (vv. 21–23)?

Applying the Word 1. How does this chapter affect your view of your own ministry in the church and that of professional ministers? 2. How does this way of evaluating our lives apply not only to so-called Christian work but also to other aspects of our vocation in Christ: relationships, occupations, avocations, community involvement and so on? 3. In what way are you challenged to "be careful" about how you build?

Responding in Prayer Everything we do must be founded on Christ. Before God, search your attitudes and actions, and pray that this would be true of you.

---

4 / 1 Corinthians 4
Servants of Christ

IN THE LAST study Paul called the Corinthians not to forget that they were God's holy temple. Now he calls them and all Christian communities to experience the power of radical servanthood for Christ's sake. St. Francis of Assisi exhibited this when he walked through Muslim battle lines during the Crusades in order to preach to the Sultan. Mother Teresa also is a "fool for Christ" when she bends down to care for a dying beggar in Calcutta. There is power in such actions, even though the wise ones of this age shake their heads in disbelief or wag their tongues in scorn.

 Warming Up to God How do you feel when you hear about people like St. Francis who give away all they have to the poor, or Mother Teresa who live sacrificially?

 Read 1 Corinthians 4.

4 So then, men ought to regard us as servants of Christ and as those entrusted with the secret things of God. ²Now it is required that those who have been given a trust must prove faithful. ³I care very little if I am judged by you or by any human court; indeed, I do not even judge myself. ⁴My conscience is clear, but that does not make me innocent. It is the Lord who judges me. ⁵Therefore judge nothing before the appointed time; wait till the Lord comes. He will bring to light what is hidden in darkness and will expose the motives of men's hearts. At that time each will receive his praise from God.

⁶Now, brothers, I have applied these things to myself and Apollos for your benefit, so that you may learn from us the meaning of the saying, "Do not go beyond what is written." Then you will not take pride in one man over against another. ⁷For who makes you different from anyone else? What do you have that you did not receive? And if you did receive it, why do you boast as though you did not?

⁸Already you have all you want! Already you have become rich! You have become kings—and that without us! How I wish that you really had become kings so that we might be kings with you! ⁹For it seems to me that God has put us apostles on display at the end of the procession, like men condemned to die in the arena. We have been made a spectacle to the whole universe, to angels as well as to men. ¹⁰We are fools for Christ, but you are so wise in Christ! We are weak, but you are strong! You are honored, we are dishonored! ¹¹To this very hour we go hungry and thirsty, we are in rags, we are brutally treated, we are homeless. ¹²We work hard with our own hands. When we are cursed, we bless; when we are persecuted, we endure it; ¹³when we are slandered, we answer kindly. Up to this moment we have become the scum of the earth, the refuse of the world.

¹⁴I am not writing this to shame you, but to warn you, as my dear children. ¹⁵Even though you have ten thousand guardians in Christ, you do not have many fathers, for in Christ Jesus I became your father through the gospel. ¹⁶Therefore I urge you to imitate me. ¹⁷For this reason I am sending to you Timothy, my son whom I love, who is faithful in the Lord. He will remind you of my way of life in Christ Jesus, which agrees with what I teach everywhere in every church.

¹⁸Some of you have become arrogant, as if I were not coming to you. ¹⁹But I will come to you very soon, if the Lord is willing, and then I will find out not only how these arrogant people are talking, but what power they have. ²⁰For the kingdom of God is not a matter of talk but of power. ²¹What do you prefer? Shall I come to you with a whip, or in love and with a gentle spirit?

Discovering the Word 1. In contrast to the hero worship in Corinth, how do Paul and his coworkers wish to be regarded (vv. 1–2)? 2. Paul fears the Corinthians are moving "beyond what was written"—probably a reference to the Old Testament Scriptures. How might going beyond the authority of Scripture result in taking "pride in one man over against another" (v. 6)? 3. Scripture teaches that the suffering of this present age precedes the glory of the age to come. In their own minds, how had the Corinthians taken a shortcut to glory (vv. 8, 10)? 4. How did their "glorious" description of themselves contrast with the experiences of Paul and the other apostles (vv. 9–13)? 5. We receive the first hint in this section that some in Corinth were not only boasting about other leaders but were also putting down Paul. How does the apostle choose to combat these opponents (vv. 18–21)?

 Applying the Word 1. How would imitating Paul's way of life (vv. 16–17) require changes in your thinking and actions? 2. In what ways does this passage challenge you to become a "fool for Christ"?

 Responding in Prayer Thank God for the leaders who have formed and impacted your Christian faith and walk.

5 / *1 Corinthians 5—6*
Members of Christ

THE NEW TESTAMENT church has inspired both exciting and disastrous experiments down through history. Hoping to create the perfect New Testament community, some have tried to design groups where all the gifts are expressed, worship is spontaneous and fellowship is deep. But they forget the common element of all New Testament churches—problems!

In chapters 1—4 Paul dealt with divisions in the church. Now he focuses on serious moral problems in Corinth. Incest and drunkenness during Communion are hardly what we hope to find in church. But we must remember that growing churches are not always filled with well-scrubbed Christians, but rather with a motley collection of sinners being saved.

 Warming Up to God How do you react when you hear about serious moral and spiritual problems of people in your church? What about your attitude do you think might be inappropriate or judgmental? Ask God to open your heart to this study.

Read 1 Corinthians 5—6.

5 It is actually reported that there is sexual immorality among you, and of a kind that does not occur even among pagans: A man has his father's wife. ²And you are proud! Shouldn't you rather have been filled with grief and have put out of your fellowship the man who did this? ³Even though I am not physically present, I am with you in spirit. And I have already passed judgment on the one who did this, just as if I were present. ⁴When you are assembled in the name of our Lord Jesus and I am with you in spirit, and the power of our Lord Jesus is present, ⁵hand this man over to Satan, so that the sinful nature[l] may be destroyed and his spirit saved on the day of the Lord.

⁶Your boasting is not good. Don't you know that a little yeast works through the whole batch of dough? ⁷Get rid of the old yeast that you may be a new batch without yeast—as you really are. For Christ, our Passover lamb, has been sacrificed. ⁸Therefore let us keep the Festival, not with the old yeast, the yeast of malice and wickedness, but with bread without yeast, the bread of sincerity and truth.

⁹I have written you in my letter not to associate with sexually immoral people— ¹⁰not at all meaning the people of this world who are immoral, or the greedy and swindlers, or idolaters. In that case you would have to leave this world. ¹¹But now I am writing you that you must not associate with anyone who calls himself a brother but is sexually immoral or greedy, an idolater or a slanderer, a drunkard or a swindler. With such a man do not even eat.

¹²What business is it of mine to judge those outside the church? Are you not to judge those inside? ¹³God will judge those outside. "Expel the wicked man from among you."[m]

6 If any of you has a dispute with another, dare he take it before the ungodly for judgment instead of before the saints? ²Do you not know that the saints will judge the world? And if you are to judge the world, are you not competent to judge trivial cases? ³Do you not know that we will judge angels? How much more the things of this life! ⁴Therefore, if you have disputes about such matters, appoint as judges even men of little account in the church![n] ⁵I say this to shame you. Is it possible that there is nobody among you wise enough to judge a dispute between believers? ⁶But instead, one brother goes to law against another—and this in front of unbelievers!

⁷The very fact that you have lawsuits among you means you have been completely defeated already. Why not rather be wronged? Why not rather be cheated? ⁸Instead, you yourselves cheat and do wrong, and you do this to your brothers.

⁹Do you not know that the wicked will not inherit the kingdom of God? Do not be deceived: Neither the sexually immoral nor idolaters nor adulterers nor male prostitutes nor homosexual offenders ¹⁰nor thieves nor the greedy nor drunkards nor slanderers nor swindlers will inherit the kingdom of God. ¹¹And that is what some of you

[l]5 *Or that his body; or that the flesh*   [m]13 Deut. 17:7; 19:19; 21:21; 22:21,24; 24:7   [n]4 *Or matters, do you appoint as judges men of little account in the church?*

were. But you were washed, you were sanctified, you were justified in the name of the Lord Jesus Christ and by the Spirit of our God.

12"Everything is permissible for me"—but not everything is beneficial. "Everything is permissible for me"—but I will not be mastered by anything. 13"Food for the stomach and the stomach for food"—but God will destroy them both. The body is not meant for sexual immorality, but for the Lord, and the Lord for the body. 14By his power God raised the Lord from the dead, and he will raise us also. 15Do you not know that your bodies are members of Christ himself? Shall I then take the members of Christ and unite them with a prostitute? Never! 16Do you not know that

he who unites himself with a prostitute is one with her in body? For it is said, "The two will become one flesh."*o 17But he who unites himself with the Lord is one with him in spirit.

18Flee from sexual immorality. All other sins a man commits are outside his body, but he who sins sexually sins against his own body. 19Do you not know that your body is a temple of the Holy Spirit, who is in you, whom you have received from God? You are not your own; 20you were bought at a price. Therefore honor God with your body.

*o16 Gen. 2:24

Discovering the Word 1. In Greece there was no shame in having sexual relationships before marriage or outside of marriage. What made the sexual problem in this church especially loathsome to Paul? 2. How is Paul's strategy of discipline designed to bring health to both the church and the individual (5:2–5)? 3. Paul compares the Christian life to the Passover and Feast of Unleavened Bread. According to Paul, what do the yeast, the bread without yeast and the Passover lamb symbolize (5:6–8)? 4. Some Christians practice a doctrine of "double separation." First, they separate themselves from the evil influences in the world. Second, they separate themselves from Christians who have not separated themselves from the world. What type of separation is taught in verses 9–13? 5. What commands and guidelines does Paul give for settling disputes between Christians (vv. 1–8)? Explain. 6. Paul calls the body "a temple of the Holy Spirit" (6:18–20). How does the biblical view of the body presented here contrast with the modern view?

Applying the Word 1. Why do you think so few churches today practice discipline of those who commit an immorality? 2. How can we distinguish between the kinds of people who should be put out of the church (5:2, 9–11; 6:9–10) and those who belong in the church even though they are "worldly" and immature (see 3:1)? 3. How can understanding your body as a temple of the Holy Spirit (v. 19) lead to a healthy balance of bodily control and bodily celebration?

Responding in Prayer Ask God to help you take whatever steps are necessary to maintain both personal and corporate purity.

---

6 / 1 Corinthians 7
Devoted to Christ

CORINTH, UNLIKE MOST modern cities today, did not have sex shops, *Playboy* magazines, porn videos and "adult entertainment" centers. But there was so much sexual immorality that the ancients had a word to describe engaging in raw sensual pleasure—to *Corinthianize*. In chapter six Paul dealt with those who justified a permissive lifestyle in the name of Christian freedom. In this chapter he battles on the opposite front. Some Corinthians claimed sex was sinful—or at least a second-class diversion—even in marriage. In response Paul answers questions about marriage, sexuality and singleness.

Warming Up to God How did you learn about sexuality? What attitudes did you learn that have been hurtful to you? Ask God to use this passage to help you better understand marriage and singleness.

Read 1 Corinthians 7.

7 Now for the matters you wrote about: It is good for a man not to marry.ᴾ ²But since there is so much immorality, each man should have his own wife, and each woman her own husband. ³The husband should fulfill his marital duty to his wife, and likewise the wife to her husband. ⁴The wife's body does not belong to her alone but also to her husband. In the same way, the husband's body does not belong to him alone but also to his wife. ⁵Do not deprive each other except by mutual consent and for a time, so that you may devote yourselves to prayer. Then come together again so that Satan will not tempt you because of your lack of self-control. ⁶I say this as a concession, not as a command. ⁷I wish that all men were as I am. But each man has his own gift from God; one has this gift, another has that.

⁸Now to the unmarried and the widows I say: It is good for them to stay unmarried, as I am. ⁹But if they cannot control themselves, they should marry, for it is better to marry than to burn with passion.

¹⁰To the married I give this command (not I, but the Lord): A wife must not separate from her husband. ¹¹But if she does, she must remain unmarried or else be reconciled to her husband. And a husband must not divorce his wife.

¹²To the rest I say this (I, not the Lord): If any brother has a wife who is not a believer and she is willing to live with him, he must not divorce her. ¹³And if a woman has a husband who is not a believer and he is willing to live with her, she must not divorce him. ¹⁴For the unbelieving husband has been sanctified through his wife, and the unbelieving wife has been sanctified through her believing husband. Otherwise your children would be unclean, but as it is, they are holy.

¹⁵But if the unbeliever leaves, let him do so. A believing man or woman is not bound in such circumstances; God has called us to live in peace. ¹⁶How do you know, wife, whether you will save your husband? Or, how do you know, husband, whether you will save your wife?

¹⁷Nevertheless, each one should retain the place in life that the Lord assigned to him and to which God has called him. This is the rule I lay down in all the churches. ¹⁸Was a man already circumcised when he was called? He should not become uncircumcised. Was a man uncircumcised when he was called? He should not be circumcised. ¹⁹Circumcision is nothing and uncir-

cumcision is nothing. Keeping God's commands is what counts. ²⁰Each one should remain in the situation which he was in when God called him. ²¹Were you a slave when you were called? Don't let it trouble you—although if you can gain your freedom, do so. ²²For he who was a slave when he was called by the Lord is the Lord's freedman; similarly, he who was a free man when he was called is Christ's slave. ²³You were bought at a price; do not become slaves of men. ²⁴Brothers, each man, as responsible to God, should remain in the situation God called him to.

²⁵Now about virgins: I have no command from the Lord, but I give a judgment as one who by the Lord's mercy is trustworthy. ²⁶Because of the present crisis, I think that it is good for you to remain as you are. ²⁷Are you married? Do not seek a divorce. Are you unmarried? Do not look for a wife. ²⁸But if you do marry, you have not sinned; and if a virgin marries, she has not sinned. But those who marry will face many troubles in this life, and I want to spare you this.

²⁹What I mean, brothers, is that the time is short. From now on those who have wives should live as if they had none; ³⁰those who mourn, as if they did not; those who are happy, as if they were not; those who buy something, as if it were not theirs to keep; ³¹those who use the things of the world, as if not engrossed in them. For this world in its present form is passing away.

³²I would like you to be free from concern. An unmarried man is concerned about the Lord's affairs—how he can please the Lord. ³³But a married man is concerned about the affairs of this world—how he can please his wife— ³⁴and his interests are divided. An unmarried woman or virgin is concerned about the Lord's affairs: Her aim is to be devoted to the Lord in both body and spirit. But a married woman is concerned about the affairs of this world—how she can please her husband. ³⁵I am saying this for your own good, not to restrict you, but that you may live in a right way in undivided devotion to the Lord.

³⁶If anyone thinks he is acting improperly toward the virgin he is engaged to, and if she is getting along in years and he feels he ought to marry, he should do as he wants. He is not sinning. They should get married. ³⁷But the man who has settled the matter in his own mind, who is under no compulsion but has control over his

ᴾ 1 Or "It is good for a man not to have sexual relations with a woman."

own will, and who has made up his mind not to marry the virgin—this man also does the right thing. ³⁸So then, he who marries the virgin does right, but he who does not marry her does even better.ᵠ

³⁹A woman is bound to her husband as long as he lives. But if her husband dies, she is free to marry anyone she wishes, but he must belong to the Lord. ⁴⁰In my judgment, she is happier if she

stays as she is—and I think that I too have the Spirit of God.

ᵠ36-38 Or ³⁶*If anyone thinks he is not treating his daughter properly, and if she is getting along in years, and he feels she ought to marry, he should do as he wants. He is not sinning. He should let her get married.* ³⁷*But the man who has settled the matter in his own mind, who is under no compulsion but has control over his own will, and who has made up his mind to keep the virgin unmarried—this man also does the right thing.* ³⁸*So then, he who gives his virgin in marriage does right, but he who does not give her in marriage does even better.*

 Discovering the Word 1. Although Paul agrees that celibacy is good (v. 1), why is it impractical for most people (vv. 2, 7)? 2. What practical advice does Paul give to the unmarried and the married for avoiding sexual immorality (vv. 2–9)? 3. According to Paul, what are some benefits of remaining in a marriage to a non-Christian (vv. 12–16)? 4. Under what circumstances would Paul seemingly allow for divorce, and why (vv. 15–16)? 5. Paul speaks of God calling us *to* a certain situation (vv. 17, 24) and of God calling us while we were *in* that situation (vv. 18–22). How are these two dimensions of calling different? 6. In verses 24–40 Paul addresses *those considering marriage*. Why does Paul call singleness a "better" way (v. 38) and a "happier" way (v. 40) when he has such a high view of marriage?

 Applying the Word 1. What principles from this passage could help us care for Christians who are considering separation or divorce? 2. Whether you are married or single, in what way do you struggle to be faithful to God's calling?

 Responding in Prayer Ask God to show you his calling for you.

---

7 / *1 Corinthians 8—9*
Living for Christ

A NOTE TACKED up on a refrigerator had these words: "It is better to be righteous than right!" Today individuals and groups are clamoring and clashing over rights: the right to free speech, the rights of the poor, the right to liberation, women's rights, aboriginal rights, the right not to be bothered by smokers (or nonsmokers), the rights of animals, the rights of blacks, the rights of whites.

So many of the struggles over rights, both legitimate and bogus, seem to revolve around attaining freedom to change the status quo. The apostle Paul, however, appears to be on opposite ground. For him rights and freedoms are unimportant compared to the privilege of living for Christ.

Warming Up to God In what area are you currently struggling with a person or group in opposition to you? Ask God to use this study to show you how to be righteous.

Read 1 Corinthians 8—9.

---

8 Now about food sacrificed to idols: We know that we all possess knowledge.ʳ Knowledge puffs up, but love builds up. ²The man who thinks he knows something does not yet know as he ought to know. ³But the man who loves God is known by God.

⁴So then, about eating food sacrificed to idols: We know that an idol is nothing at all in the

world and that there is no God but one. ⁵For even if there are so-called gods, whether in heaven or on earth (as indeed there are many "gods" and many "lords"), ⁶yet for us there is but one God, the Father, from whom all things came and for whom we live; and there is but one Lord, Jesus

ʳ1 Or *"We all possess knowledge,"* as you say

Christ, through whom all things came and through whom we live.

[7]But not everyone knows this. Some people are still so accustomed to idols that when they eat such food they think of it as having been sacrificed to an idol, and since their conscience is weak, it is defiled. [8]But food does not bring us near to God; we are no worse if we do not eat, and no better if we do.

[9]Be careful, however, that the exercise of your freedom does not become a stumbling block to the weak. [10]For if anyone with a weak conscience sees you who have this knowledge eating in an idol's temple, won't he be emboldened to eat what has been sacrificed to idols? [11]So this weak brother, for whom Christ died, is destroyed by your knowledge. [12]When you sin against your brothers in this way and wound their weak conscience, you sin against Christ. [13]Therefore, if what I eat causes my brother to fall into sin, I will never eat meat again, so that I will not cause him to fall.

9 Am I not free? Am I not an apostle? Have I not seen Jesus our Lord? Are you not the result of my work in the Lord? [2]Even though I may not be an apostle to others, surely I am to you! For you are the seal of my apostleship in the Lord.

[3]This is my defense to those who sit in judgment on me. [4]Don't we have the right to food and drink? [5]Don't we have the right to take a believing wife along with us, as do the other apostles and the Lord's brothers and Cephas[s]? [6]Or is it only I and Barnabas who must work for a living?

[7]Who serves as a soldier at his own expense? Who plants a vineyard and does not eat of its grapes? Who tends a flock and does not drink of the milk? [8]Do I say this merely from a human point of view? Doesn't the Law say the same thing? [9]For it is written in the Law of Moses: "Do not muzzle an ox while it is treading out the grain."[t] Is it about oxen that God is concerned? [10]Surely he says this for us, doesn't he? Yes, this was written for us, because when the plowman plows and the thresher threshes, they ought to do so in the hope of sharing in the harvest. [11]If we have sown spiritual seed among you, is it too much if we reap a material harvest from you? [12]If

others have this right of support from you, shouldn't we have it all the more?

But we did not use this right. On the contrary, we put up with anything rather than hinder the gospel of Christ. [13]Don't you know that those who work in the temple get their food from the temple, and those who serve at the altar share in what is offered on the altar? [14]In the same way, the Lord has commanded that those who preach the gospel should receive their living from the gospel.

[15]But I have not used any of these rights. And I am not writing this in the hope that you will do such things for me. I would rather die than have anyone deprive me of this boast. [16]Yet when I preach the gospel, I cannot boast, for I am compelled to preach. Woe to me if I do not preach the gospel! [17]If I preach voluntarily, I have a reward; if not voluntarily, I am simply discharging the trust committed to me. [18]What then is my reward? Just this: that in preaching the gospel I may offer it free of charge, and so not make use of my rights in preaching it.

[19]Though I am free and belong to no man, I make myself a slave to everyone, to win as many as possible. [20]To the Jews I became like a Jew, to win the Jews. To those under the law I became like one under the law (though I myself am not under the law), so as to win those under the law. [21]To those not having the law I became like one not having the law (though I am not free from God's law but am under Christ's law), so as to win those not having the law. [22]To the weak I became weak, to win the weak. I have become all things to all men so that by all possible means I might save some. [23]I do all this for the sake of the gospel, that I may share in its blessings.

[24]Do you not know that in a race all the runners run, but only one gets the prize? Run in such a way as to get the prize. [25]Everyone who competes in the games goes into strict training. They do it to get a crown that will not last; but we do it to get a crown that will last forever. [26]Therefore I do not run like a man running aimlessly; I do not fight like a man beating the air. [27]No, I beat my body and make it my slave so that after I have preached to others, I myself will not be disqualified for the prize.

[s]5 That is, Peter   [t]9 Deut. 25:4

Discovering the Word 1. Sacrificial animals offered in temples were dedicated to a pagan god, and most of them were sold in the public market. Understandably, many Christians in Corinth wondered whether they should eat such meat. According to Paul, what do mature Christians know about food sacrificed to idols (8:4–6, 8)? 2. What warning does Paul give about this kind of knowledge (8:1–3)? Explain. 3. What does Paul say is more important than exercising the freedom that comes from knowledge (8:9–13)? 4. Paul moves on from rights and freedoms based on *knowledge* to the topic of rights based on *position*. What apostolic rights has Paul given up (9:4–5, 11–12, 14, 18–19)? 5. How and why has Paul given up the freedom to live whatever lifestyle he prefers (9:19–23)? 6. In giving up the rights mentioned in chapters 8—9, how are we like athletes in training (9:24–27)?

 Applying the Word 1. In what situations today might our "knowledge" and freedom destroy a weaker brother? 2. What distinguishes actions that challenge the immature to grow from actions that wound them? 3. How might we adjust our lifestyles in order to reach people in various subcultures?

Responding in Prayer Ask God to help you train more rigorously so you will not be disqualified but will receive the victor's crown.

8 / *1 Corinthians 10:1—11:1*
Eating with Christ

SHOULD CHRISTIANS GO to R-rated movies—or any movies, for that matter? Should they drink alcoholic beverages such as beer or wine? Should they wear expensive clothes, makeup and jewelry? Debates over such "questionable" practices are as old as the church. How can we resolve them?

The Corinthians were divided over such issues. Some had overscrupulous consciences. They would not sit down to a meal if the meat had been purchased at a pagan meat market (and therefore offered to a "god"). Others were so "liberated" that they could eat the Lord's Supper and then commit sexual immorality. These liberated Christians regarded baptism and the Eucharist (Communion) as automatic protection against God's judgment. In 1 Corinthians 10 Paul finds a way of reaching both kinds of people: he calls them and us to do everything for the glory of God.

 Warming Up to God What "questionable" practices have you wrestled with personally?

 Read 1 Corinthians 10:1—11:1.

10 For I do not want you to be ignorant of the fact, brothers, that our forefathers were all under the cloud and that they all passed through the sea. ²They were all baptized into Moses in the cloud and in the sea. ³They all ate the same spiritual food ⁴and drank the same spiritual drink; for they drank from the spiritual rock that accompanied them, and that rock was Christ. ⁵Nevertheless, God was not pleased with most of them; their bodies were scattered over the desert.

⁶Now these things occurred as examplesᵘ to keep us from setting our hearts on evil things as they did. ⁷Do not be idolaters, as some of them were; as it is written: "The people sat down to eat and drink and got up to indulge in pagan revelry."ᵛ ⁸We should not commit sexual immoral-

ity, as some of them did—and in one day twenty-three thousand of them died. ⁹We should not test the Lord, as some of them did—and were killed by snakes. ¹⁰And do not grumble, as some of them did—and were killed by the destroying angel.

¹¹These things happened to them as examples and were written down as warnings for us, on whom the fulfillment of the ages has come. ¹²So, if you think you are standing firm, be careful that you don't fall! ¹³No temptation has seized you except what is common to man. And God is faithful; he will not let you be tempted beyond what you can bear. But when you are tempted, he will also provide a way out so that you can stand up under it.

ᵘ6 Or *types*; also in verse 11   ᵛ7 Exodus 32:6

¹⁴Therefore, my dear friends, flee from idolatry. ¹⁵I speak to sensible people; judge for yourselves what I say. ¹⁶Is not the cup of thanksgiving for which we give thanks a participation in the blood of Christ? And is not the bread that we break a participation in the body of Christ? ¹⁷Because there is one loaf, we, who are many, are one body, for we all partake of the one loaf.

¹⁸Consider the people of Israel: Do not those who eat the sacrifices participate in the altar? ¹⁹Do I mean then that a sacrifice offered to an idol is anything, or that an idol is anything? ²⁰No, but the sacrifices of pagans are offered to demons, not to God, and I do not want you to be participants with demons. ²¹You cannot drink the cup of the Lord and the cup of demons too; you cannot have a part in both the Lord's table and the table of demons. ²²Are we trying to arouse the Lord's jealousy? Are we stronger than he?

²³"Everything is permissible"—but not everything is beneficial. "Everything is permissible"—but not everything is constructive. ²⁴Nobody should seek his own good, but the good of others.

²⁵Eat anything sold in the meat market without raising questions of conscience, ²⁶for, "The earth is the Lord's, and everything in it."ʷ

²⁷If some unbeliever invites you to a meal and you want to go, eat whatever is put before you without raising questions of conscience. ²⁸But if anyone says to you, "This has been offered in sacrifice," then do not eat it, both for the sake of the man who told you and for conscience' sakeˣ— ²⁹the other man's conscience, I mean, not yours. For why should my freedom be judged by another's conscience? ³⁰If I take part in the meal with thankfulness, why am I denounced because of something I thank God for?

³¹So whether you eat or drink or whatever you do, do it all for the glory of God. ³²Do not cause anyone to stumble, whether Jews, Greeks or the church of God— ³³even as I try to please everybody in every way. For I am not seeking my own good but the good of many, so that they may be saved. ¹Follow my example, as I follow the example of Christ.

11

ʷ26 Psalm 24:1   ˣ28 Some manuscripts conscience' sake, for "the earth is the Lord's and everything in it"

 Discovering the Word 1. What experiences did all the Israelites have in common when they left Egypt and headed for the Promised Land (vv. 1–10)? 2. Why does Paul remind the Corinthians (and us) of these events (vv. 11–13)? 3. Why are some lifestyles incompatible with celebrating the Lord's Supper (vv. 14–22)? 4. According to verses 23–33, what principles should guide our behavior as Christians? 5. How does Paul apply these principles to the subject of eating meat offered to idols?

Applying the Word 1. Think of one or two areas where you are currently experiencing temptation. In which one of these are you least likely to believe that there is a way of escape? 2. In what way has God provided an escape for your temptation? 3. How can the principles discussed in this passage guide your behavior in areas that might be "permissible" but not beneficial?

Responding in Prayer Ask God to give you courage to flee temptation.

---

9 / 1 Corinthians 11:2–34
Headship of Christ

TWO TRENDS IN Western society contrive to make us independent people: the trend to blur the differences between the sexes (androgyny) and the human potential movement. In the movie *Tootsie* a male actor impersonating a woman said to a woman with whom he fell in love, "I was a better man with you when I was a woman than I am a woman with you now that I am a man." Such is the sexual confusion produced by the first trend. Fritz Perls verbalized the second trend this way: "I do my thing and you do your thing and if by chance we meet, it's beautiful."

Both trends work against our newness in Christ. Followers of Jesus are neither independent nor dependent but *inter*dependent. We discover interdependence in Christian worship in this passage.

Warming Up to God When you enter a worship service, do you tend to think mainly of your personal relationship to God or your relationship with your fellow worshipers? Explain.

 Read 1 Corinthians 11:2–34.

²I praise you for remembering me in everything and for holding to the teachings,ʸ just as I passed them on to you.

³Now I want you to realize that the head of every man is Christ, and the head of the woman is man, and the head of Christ is God. ⁴Every man who prays or prophesies with his head covered dishonors his head. ⁵And every woman who prays or prophesies with her head uncovered dishonors her head—it is just as though her head were shaved. ⁶If a woman does not cover her head, she should have her hair cut off; and if it is a disgrace for a woman to have her hair cut or shaved off, she should cover her head. ⁷A man ought not to cover his head,ᶻ since he is the image and glory of God; but the woman is the glory of man. ⁸For man did not come from woman, but woman from man; ⁹neither was man created for woman, but woman for man. ¹⁰For this reason, and because of the angels, the woman ought to have a sign of authority on her head.

¹¹In the Lord, however, woman is not independent of man, nor is man independent of woman. ¹²For as woman came from man, so also man is born of woman. But everything comes from God. ¹³Judge for yourselves: Is it proper for a woman to pray to God with her head uncovered? ¹⁴Does not the very nature of things teach you that if a man has long hair, it is a disgrace to him, ¹⁵but that if a woman has long hair, it is her glory? For long hair is given to her as a covering. ¹⁶If anyone wants to be contentious about this, we have no other practice—nor do the churches of God.

¹⁷In the following directives I have no praise for you, for your meetings do more harm than good. ¹⁸In the first place, I hear that when you come together as a church, there are divisions among you, and to some extent I believe it. ¹⁹No doubt there have to be differences among you to show which of you have God's approval. ²⁰When you come together, it is not the Lord's Supper you

eat, ²¹for as you eat, each of you goes ahead without waiting for anybody else. One remains hungry, another gets drunk. ²²Don't you have homes to eat and drink in? Or do you despise the church of God and humiliate those who have nothing? What shall I say to you? Shall I praise you for this? Certainly not!

²³For I received from the Lord what I also passed on to you: The Lord Jesus, on the night he was betrayed, took bread, ²⁴and when he had given thanks, he broke it and said, "This is my body, which is for you; do this in remembrance of me." ²⁵In the same way, after supper he took the cup, saying, "This cup is the new covenant in my blood; do this, whenever you drink it, in remembrance of me." ²⁶For whenever you eat this bread and drink this cup, you proclaim the Lord's death until he comes.

²⁷Therefore, whoever eats the bread or drinks the cup of the Lord in an unworthy manner will be guilty of sinning against the body and blood of the Lord. ²⁸A man ought to examine himself before he eats of the bread and drinks of the cup. ²⁹For anyone who eats and drinks without recognizing the body of the Lord eats and drinks judgment on himself. ³⁰That is why many among you are weak and sick, and a number of you have fallen asleep. ³¹But if we judged ourselves, we would not come under judgment. ³²When we are judged by the Lord, we are being disciplined so that we will not be condemned with the world.

³³So then, my brothers, when you come together to eat, wait for each other. ³⁴If anyone is hungry, he should eat at home, so that when you meet together it may not result in judgment.

And when I come I will give further directions.

ʸ2 Or *traditions*   ᶻ4-7 Or ⁴*Every man who prays or prophesies with long hair dishonors his head.* ⁵*And every woman who prays or prophesies with no covering ⌊of hair⌋ on her head dishonors her head—she is just like one of the "shorn women." ⁶If a woman has no covering, let her be for now with short hair, but since it is a disgrace for a woman to have her hair shorn or shaved, she should grow it again.* ⁷*A man ought not to have long hair.*

 Discovering the Word 1. What seems to be Paul's major concern for the church in this section? 2. The word *head* in verse 3 could mean either "chief" and "ruler" or "source" and "origin" (like the head of a stream). Which understanding of headship best fits Paul's concern here? Explain. 3. In the culture of Corinth a woman signaled that she was in right relationship with her husband either by wearing a veil which covered her hair

or by wearing her hair up (rather than letting it fall loose). What reasons does Paul give for continuing this practice (vv. 4–10, 13–16)? 4. Paul balances his previous statements by saying that "in the Lord" man is not independent of woman (vv. 11–12). Why is this balance important? 5. Why would eating and drinking "without recognizing the body of the Lord" be so dangerous (vv. 29–32)? 6. According to Paul, how can we eat and drink the Lord's Supper in a worthy manner (vv. 28–33)?

 Applying the Word 1. Although we may not have a cultural equivalent for head coverings, how should appropriate relationships between men and women be expressed in Christian community? 2. What has this chapter taught you about worship that is honoring or dishonoring to God? 3. How do you need to change your pattern of worship?

Responding in Prayer Thank God for making you part of a larger body.

10 / *1 Corinthians 12*
Body of Christ

THE CHURCH TODAY has enormous frozen assets. Only when we thaw these assets and release every member for ministry can the work of God be done in the world. After several decades of "gift" teaching, we have made surprisingly little progress. One reason is that gifts have been co-opted by the human potential movement. We view our gifts as part of our development and fulfillment rather than as one more glorious way to be interdependent in Christ. This passage focuses on the true nature and purpose of spiritual gifts.

 Warming Up to God What has God shown you about your gifts and how you should use them in the church?

 Read 1 Corinthians 12.

12 Now about spiritual gifts, brothers, I do not want you to be ignorant. ²You know that when you were pagans, somehow or other you were influenced and led astray to mute idols. ³Therefore I tell you that no one who is speaking by the Spirit of God says, "Jesus be cursed," and no one can say, "Jesus is Lord," except by the Holy Spirit.

⁴There are different kinds of gifts, but the same Spirit. ⁵There are different kinds of service, but the same Lord. ⁶There are different kinds of working, but the same God works all of them in all men.

⁷Now to each one the manifestation of the Spirit is given for the common good. ⁸To one there is given through the Spirit the message of wisdom, to another the message of knowledge by means of the same Spirit, ⁹to another faith by the same Spirit, to another gifts of healing by that one Spirit, ¹⁰to another miraculous powers, to another prophecy, to another distinguishing between spirits, to another speaking in different kinds of tongues,ᵃ and to still another the interpretation

of tongues.ᵃ ¹¹All these are the work of one and the same Spirit, and he gives them to each one, just as he determines.

¹²The body is a unit, though it is made up of many parts; and though all its parts are many, they form one body. So it is with Christ. ¹³For we were all baptized byᵇ one Spirit into one body—whether Jews or Greeks, slave or free—and we were all given the one Spirit to drink.

¹⁴Now the body is not made up of one part but of many. ¹⁵If the foot should say, "Because I am not a hand, I do not belong to the body," it would not for that reason cease to be part of the body. ¹⁶And if the ear should say, "Because I am not an eye, I do not belong to the body," it would not for that reason cease to be part of the body. ¹⁷If the whole body were an eye, where would the sense of hearing be? If the whole body were an ear, where would the sense of smell be? ¹⁸But in fact God has arranged the parts in the body, every one

ᵃ10 Or *languages*; also in verse 28   ᵇ13 Or *with*; or *in*

of them, just as he wanted them to be. ¹⁹If they were all one part, where would the body be? ²⁰As it is, there are many parts, but one body.

²¹The eye cannot say to the hand, "I don't need you!" And the head cannot say to the feet, "I don't need you!" ²²On the contrary, those parts of the body that seem to be weaker are indispensable, ²³and the parts that we think are less honorable we treat with special honor. And the parts that are unpresentable are treated with special modesty, ²⁴while our presentable parts need no special treatment. But God has combined the members of the body and has given greater honor to the parts that lacked it, ²⁵so that there should be no division in the body, but that its parts should have equal concern for each other. ²⁶If one

part suffers, every part suffers with it; if one part is honored, every part rejoices with it.

²⁷Now you are the body of Christ, and each one of you is a part of it. ²⁸And in the church God has appointed first of all apostles, second prophets, third teachers, then workers of miracles, also those having gifts of healing, those able to help others, those with gifts of administration, and those speaking in different kinds of tongues. ²⁹Are all apostles? Are all prophets? Are all teachers? Do all work miracles? ³⁰Do all have gifts of healing? Do all speak in tongues*ᶜ*? Do all interpret? ³¹But eagerly desire*ᵈ* the greater gifts.

And now I will show you the most excellent way.

ᶜ30 Or other languages   ᵈ31 Or But you are eagerly desiring

Discovering the Word 1. What particular problem in the Corinthian church may have led Paul to offer the "test" in verse 3? 2. What clue does Paul's test give us about the ultimate goal of spiritual gifts? 3. What do verses 4–6 reveal about the unity and diversity of spiritual gifts? 4. What might make some members of your church feel useless or envious of other parts of the body (vv. 12–26)? 5. According to Paul, how can we make every part of the body feel special (vv. 21–26)? 6. Paul does not give us a complete list of gifts in this chapter. What might the words *first, second, third* and *then* (v. 28) indicate?

Applying the Word 1. What can you do to help others in your group or church to discover their giftedness? 2. How would you like to develop and exercise your spiritual gifts?

Responding in Prayer Pray that both you and those you know would use your gifts to God's glory.

---

11 / *1 Corinthians 13*
Love of Christ

PERHAPS THE MOST abused phrase in the English language is "I love you." Instead of communicating unselfish caring, it often expresses enlightened self-interest, manipulative affection or sheer lust. In 1 Corinthians 13 Paul not only defines love for us but shows us why this is the most excellent way to relate to anyone—especially to members of the family of God.

Warming Up to God Think of a person who has truly loved you. What were the marks of that person's way of relating to you?

Read 1 Corinthians 13.

---

13 If I speak in the tongues*ᵉ* of men and of angels, but have not love, I am only a resounding gong or a clanging cymbal. ²If I have the gift of prophecy and can fathom all mysteries and all knowledge, and if I have a faith that can move mountains, but

have not love, I am nothing. ³If I give all I possess to the poor and surrender my body to the flames,*ᶠ* but have not love, I gain nothing.

⁴Love is patient, love is kind. It does not envy, it does not boast, it is not proud. ⁵It is not rude,

ᵉ1 Or languages   ᶠ3 Some early manuscripts body that I may boast

it is not self-seeking, it is not easily angered, it keeps no record of wrongs. 6Love does not delight in evil but rejoices with the truth. 7It always protects, always trusts, always hopes, always perseveres.

8Love never fails. But where there are prophecies, they will cease; where there are tongues, they will be stilled; where there is knowledge, it will pass away. 9For we know in part and we prophesy in part, 10but when perfection comes,

the imperfect disappears. 11When I was a child, I talked like a child, I thought like a child, I reasoned like a child. When I became a man, I put childish ways behind me. 12Now we see but a poor reflection as in a mirror; then we shall see face to face. Now I know in part; then I shall know fully, even as I am fully known.

13And now these three remain: faith, hope and love. But the greatest of these is love.

 Discovering the Word 1. What is so tragic about using our gifts without love (vv. 1–3)? 2. How would you define each of love's qualities (vv. 4–7)? 3. In verses 8–13 Paul summarizes the *supremacy of love*. Compared with love, why do the spiritual gifts have limited value? 4. Some understand the "perfection" in verse 10 as the completed New Testament, thus eliminating the need for tongues or prophecy today. Others understand it as the perfection we will experience when Christ returns. In light of Paul's other comparisons (vv. 11–12), which interpretation seems more likely? Explain. 5. Why is love greater than faith or hope (v. 13)?

Applying the Word 1. How can love lead to healthy interdependence in your relationships rather than unhealthy independence or dependence? 2. Which aspect of love do you most need to develop? 3. Besides telling us what love is, this passage gives us an incidental portrait of Jesus as the ultimate lover. Reread verses 4–7, replacing *love* with *Jesus*. What fresh picture of Jesus' care do you gain through this exercise?

Responding in Prayer Ask Jesus Christ to teach you what it means to love.

12 / *1 Corinthians 14*
Speaking for Christ

WORDS ARE CHEAP today. They can be digitized and processed. With one depressed button on a computer we can eliminate words forever, without even a trace remaining in memory. However, the Bible says words have great power, because they are an extension of our personality. God's Word always accomplishes his purposes, because it is spoken with his personal power. In this chapter Paul focuses on the exciting potential of God-inspired speech in the Christian community.

 Warming Up to God Recall a time when something that was shared from the congregation during a worship service (or in a small group) truly encouraged you. What characterized this word ministry?

 Read 1 Corinthians 14.

14 Follow the way of love and eagerly desire spiritual gifts, especially the gift of prophecy. 2For anyone who speaks in a tongue*g* does not speak to men but to God. Indeed, no one understands him; he utters mysteries with his spirit.*h* 3But everyone who prophesies speaks to men for their strengthening, encouragement and comfort. 4He who speaks in a tongue edifies himself, but he who prophesies edifies the church. 5I would like every one of you to

speak in tongues,*i* but I would rather have you prophesy. He who prophesies is greater than one who speaks in tongues,*i* unless he interprets, so that the church may be edified.

6Now, brothers, if I come to you and speak in tongues, what good will I be to you, unless I bring you some revelation or knowledge or prophecy or word of instruction? 7Even in the case of lifeless

*g*2 Or *another language*; also in verses 4, 13, 14, 19, 26 and 27
*h*2 Or *by the Spirit*   *i*5 Or *other languages*; also in verses 6, 18, 22, 23 and 39

things that make sounds, such as the flute or harp, how will anyone know what tune is being played unless there is a distinction in the notes? [8]Again, if the trumpet does not sound a clear call, who will get ready for battle? [9]So it is with you. Unless you speak intelligible words with your tongue, how will anyone know what you are saying? You will just be speaking into the air. [10]Undoubtedly there are all sorts of languages in the world, yet none of them is without meaning. [11]If then I do not grasp the meaning of what someone is saying, I am a foreigner to the speaker, and he is a foreigner to me. [12]So it is with you. Since you are eager to have spiritual gifts, try to excel in gifts that build up the church.

[13]For this reason anyone who speaks in a tongue should pray that he may interpret what he says. [14]For if I pray in a tongue, my spirit prays, but my mind is unfruitful. [15]So what shall I do? I will pray with my spirit, but I will also pray with my mind; I will sing with my spirit, but I will also sing with my mind. [16]If you are praising God with your spirit, how can one who finds himself among those who do not understand[j] say "Amen" to your thanksgiving, since he does not know what you are saying? [17]You may be giving thanks well enough, but the other man is not edified.

[18]I thank God that I speak in tongues more than all of you. [19]But in the church I would rather speak five intelligible words to instruct others than ten thousand words in a tongue.

[20]Brothers, stop thinking like children. In regard to evil be infants, but in your thinking be adults. [21]In the Law it is written:

"Through men of strange tongues
    and through the lips of foreigners
I will speak to this people,
    but even then they will not listen to me,"[k]
says the Lord.

[22]Tongues, then, are a sign, not for believers but for unbelievers; prophecy, however, is for believers, not for unbelievers. [23]So if the whole church comes together and everyone speaks in tongues, and some who do not understand[l] or some unbelievers come in, will they not say that you are out of your mind? [24]But if an unbeliever or someone who does not understand[m] comes in while everybody is prophesying, he will be convinced by all that he is a sinner and will be judged by all, [25]and the secrets of his heart will be laid bare. So he will fall down and worship God, exclaiming, "God is really among you!"

[26]What then shall we say, brothers? When you come together, everyone has a hymn, or a word of instruction, a revelation, a tongue or an interpretation. All of these must be done for the strengthening of the church. [27]If anyone speaks in a tongue, two—or at the most three—should speak, one at a time, and someone must interpret. [28]If there is no interpreter, the speaker should keep quiet in the church and speak to himself and God.

[29]Two or three prophets should speak, and the others should weigh carefully what is said. [30]And if a revelation comes to someone who is sitting down, the first speaker should stop. [31]For you can all prophesy in turn so that everyone may be instructed and encouraged. [32]The spirits of prophets are subject to the control of prophets. [33]For God is not a God of disorder but of peace.

As in all the congregations of the saints, [34]women should remain silent in the churches. They are not allowed to speak, but must be in submission, as the Law says. [35]If they want to inquire about something, they should ask their own husbands at home; for it is disgraceful for a woman to speak in the church.

[36]Did the word of God originate with you? Or are you the only people it has reached? [37]If anybody thinks he is a prophet or spiritually gifted, let him acknowledge that what I am writing to you is the Lord's command. [38]If he ignores this, he himself will be ignored.[n]

[39]Therefore, my brothers, be eager to prophesy, and do not forbid speaking in tongues. [40]But everything should be done in a fitting and orderly way.

[j]16 Or *among the inquirers*   [k]21 Isaiah 28:11,12   [l]23 Or *some inquirers*   [m]24 Or *or some inquirer*   [n]38 Some manuscripts *If he is ignorant of this, let him be ignorant*

Discovering the Word 1. Evidently, the Corinthians placed great value on the gift of tongues. Why does Paul prefer prophecy to uninterpreted tongues (vv. 1–5)? 2. What illustrations does Paul use to show why uninterpreted tongues do not build up the church (vv. 6–12)? 3. What remedy does Paul suggest (vv. 13–19)? 4. What does Paul say about the *purpose* of tongues and of prophecy (vv. 20–25)? 5. What guidelines does Paul

give for when someone should speak in tongues and when he should remain silent (vv. 27–28)? 6. How can Paul's statements in verses 33–35 be harmonized with his teaching about women praying and prophesying (11:5)?

 Applying the Word 1. In what ways might we be guilty of meaningless or mindless worship today? 2. How can Paul's counsel improve the quality of our worship?

 Responding in Prayer Ask that worship in your church might be meaningful and powerful for all who come.

13 / *1 Corinthians 15—16*
Hope in Christ

WHAT HAPPENS AFTER death? Do we live on as disembodied souls, as the Greeks taught? Do we go through countless cycles of reincarnation, as the Hindus believe? Do both body and soul cease to exist, as naturalism maintains?

Because of their Greek heritage, the Corinthians questioned the reality of the resurrection. In this passage Paul challenges their thinking by pointing out the absurd conclusions to which it leads. He reminds us that the resurrection is a crucial aspect of our hope in Christ.

 Warming Up to God Have you ever pondered what death will be like for you? How do you feel about it? Express your feelings to Christ. Allow him to prepare you for this study.

 Read 1 Corinthians 15—16.

15 Now, brothers, I want to remind you of the gospel I preached to you, which you received and on which you have taken your stand. ²By this gospel you are saved, if you hold firmly to the word I preached to you. Otherwise, you have believed in vain.

³For what I received I passed on to you as of first importance*: that Christ died for our sins according to the Scriptures, ⁴that he was buried, that he was raised on the third day according to the Scriptures, ⁵and that he appeared to Peter,ᴾ and then to the Twelve. ⁶After that, he appeared to more than five hundred of the brothers at the same time, most of whom are still living, though some have fallen asleep. ⁷Then he appeared to James, then to all the apostles, ⁸and last of all he appeared to me also, as to one abnormally born.

⁹For I am the least of the apostles and do not even deserve to be called an apostle, because I persecuted the church of God. ¹⁰But by the grace of God I am what I am, and his grace to me was not without effect. No, I worked harder than all of them—yet not I, but the grace of God that was with me. ¹¹Whether, then, it was I or they, this is what we preach, and this is what you believed.

¹²But if it is preached that Christ has been raised from the dead, how can some of you say that there is no resurrection of the dead? ¹³If there is no resurrection of the dead, then not even Christ has been raised. ¹⁴And if Christ has not been raised, our preaching is useless and so is your faith. ¹⁵More than that, we are then found to be false witnesses about God, for we have testified about God that he raised Christ from the dead. But he did not raise him if in fact the dead are not raised. ¹⁶For if the dead are not raised, then Christ has not been raised either. ¹⁷And if Christ has not been raised, your faith is futile; you are still in your sins. ¹⁸Then those also who have fallen asleep in Christ are lost. ¹⁹If only for this life we have hope in Christ, we are to be pitied more than all men.

²⁰But Christ has indeed been raised from the dead, the firstfruits of those who have fallen asleep. ²¹For since death came through a man, the resurrection of the dead comes also through a man. ²²For as in Adam all die, so in Christ all will be made alive. ²³But each in his own turn: Christ, the firstfruits; then, when he comes, those who belong to him. ²⁴Then the end will come, when

*3 Or *you at the first*   ᴾ5 Greek *Cephas*

he hands over the kingdom to God the Father after he has destroyed all dominion, authority and power. 25For he must reign until he has put all his enemies under his feet. 26The last enemy to be destroyed is death. 27For he "has put everything under his feet."*q* Now when it says that "everything" has been put under him, it is clear that this does not include God himself, who put everything under Christ. 28When he has done this, then the Son himself will be made subject to him who put everything under him, so that God may be all in all.

29Now if there is no resurrection, what will those do who are baptized for the dead? If the dead are not raised at all, why are people baptized for them? 30And as for us, why do we endanger ourselves every hour? 31I die every day—I mean that, brothers—just as surely as I glory over you in Christ Jesus our Lord. 32If I fought wild beasts in Ephesus for merely human reasons, what have I gained? If the dead are not raised,

"Let us eat and drink,
    for tomorrow we die."*r*

33Do not be misled: "Bad company corrupts good character." 34Come back to your senses as you ought, and stop sinning; for there are some who are ignorant of God—I say this to your shame.

35But someone may ask, "How are the dead raised? With what kind of body will they come?" 36How foolish! What you sow does not come to life unless it dies. 37When you sow, you do not plant the body that will be, but just a seed, perhaps of wheat or of something else. 38But God gives it a body as he has determined, and to each kind of seed he gives its own body. 39All flesh is not the same: Men have one kind of flesh, animals have another, birds another and fish another. 40There are also heavenly bodies and there are earthly bodies; but the splendor of the heavenly bodies is one kind, and the splendor of the earthly bodies is another. 41The sun has one kind of splendor, the moon another and the stars another; and star differs from star in splendor.

42So will it be with the resurrection of the dead. The body that is sown is perishable, it is raised imperishable; 43it is sown in dishonor, it is raised in glory; it is sown in weakness, it is raised in power; 44it is sown a natural body, it is raised a spiritual body.

If there is a natural body, there is also a spiritual body. 45So it is written: "The first man Adam became a living being"*s*; the last Adam, a life-giving spirit. 46The spiritual did not come first, but the natural, and after that the spiritual. 47The first man was of the dust of the earth, the second man from heaven. 48As was the earthly man, so are those who are of the earth; and as is the man from heaven, so also are those who are of heaven. 49And just as we have borne the likeness of the earthly man, so shall we*t* bear the likeness of the man from heaven.

50I declare to you, brothers, that flesh and blood cannot inherit the kingdom of God, nor does the perishable inherit the imperishable. 51Listen, I tell you a mystery: We will not all sleep, but we will all be changed— 52in a flash, in the twinkling of an eye, at the last trumpet. For the trumpet will sound, the dead will be raised imperishable, and we will be changed. 53For the perishable must clothe itself with the imperishable, and the mortal with immortality. 54When the perishable has been clothed with the imperishable, and the mortal with immortality, then the saying that is written will come true: "Death has been swallowed up in victory."*u*

55"Where, O death, is your victory?
    Where, O death, is your sting?"*v*

56The sting of death is sin, and the power of sin is the law. 57But thanks be to God! He gives us the victory through our Lord Jesus Christ.

58Therefore, my dear brothers, stand firm. Let nothing move you. Always give yourselves fully to the work of the Lord, because you know that your labor in the Lord is not in vain.

16

Now about the collection for God's people: Do what I told the Galatian churches to do. 2On the first day of every week, each one of you should set aside a sum of money in keeping with his income, saving it up, so that when I come no collections will have to be made. 3Then, when I arrive, I will give letters of introduction to the men you approve and send them with your gift to Jerusalem. 4If it seems advisable for me to go also, they will accompany me.

5After I go through Macedonia, I will come to you—for I will be going through Macedonia. 6Perhaps I will stay with you awhile, or even spend the winter, so that you can help me on my journey, wherever I go. 7I do not want to see you

q27 Psalm 8:6   *r32* Isaiah 22:13   *s45* Gen. 2:7   *t49* Some early manuscripts *so let us*   *u54* Isaiah 25:8   *v55* Hosea 13:14

now and make only a passing visit; I hope to spend some time with you, if the Lord permits. [8]But I will stay on at Ephesus until Pentecost, [9]because a great door for effective work has opened to me, and there are many who oppose me.

[10]If Timothy comes, see to it that he has nothing to fear while he is with you, for he is carrying on the work of the Lord, just as I am. [11]No one, then, should refuse to accept him. Send him on his way in peace so that he may return to me. I am expecting him along with the brothers.

[12]Now about our brother Apollos: I strongly urged him to go to you with the brothers. He was quite unwilling to go now, but he will go when he has the opportunity.

[13]Be on your guard; stand firm in the faith; be men of courage; be strong. [14]Do everything in love.

[15]You know that the household of Stephanas were the first converts in Achaia, and they have devoted themselves to the service of the saints. I urge you, brothers, [16]to submit to such as these and to everyone who joins in the work, and labors at it. [17]I was glad when Stephanas, Fortunatus and Achaicus arrived, because they have supplied what was lacking from you. [18]For they refreshed my spirit and yours also. Such men deserve recognition.

[19]The churches in the province of Asia send you greetings. Aquila and Priscilla[w] greet you warmly in the Lord, and so does the church that meets at their house. [20]All the brothers here send you greetings. Greet one another with a holy kiss.

[21]I, Paul, write this greeting in my own hand.

[22]If anyone does not love the Lord—a curse be on him. Come, O Lord[x]!

[23]The grace of the Lord Jesus be with you.

[24]My love to all of you in Christ Jesus. Amen.[y]

[w]19 Greek *Prisca*, a variant of *Priscilla*   [x]22 In Aramaic the expression *Come, O Lord* is *Marana tha.*   [y]24 Some manuscripts do not have *Amen.*

 Discovering the Word 1. Paul reminds the Corinthians of the gospel he preached to them. What are the essential elements of the gospel (15:1–11)? 2. If there is no resurrection, what are the consequences for Christ, for Paul and for us (15:12–19)? 3. How does belief or disbelief in the resurrection affect a person's lifestyle (15:29–34)? 4. What illustrations does Paul use to explain why the resurrection is not illogical but makes good sense (15:35–41)? 5. Although the resurrection body is somehow related to the natural body, how is it also radically different (15:42–49)? 6. How does chapter 16 give several illustrations of "the work of the Lord" Paul referred to in 15:58?

Applying the Word 1. To which specific area of service will you give yourself this week, knowing that your labor in the Lord is not in vain? 2. What is the most substantial change that studying 1 Corinthians has brought about in your life?

Responding in Prayer Praise God for what you have learned in 1 Corinthians.

2 Corinthians

Life is relational. We hope and hurt the most about relationships with people who matter to us. A special friend we are in danger of losing, an employer who misunderstands our actions, a spouse who seems distant and cold, a brother in Christ who has spoken behind our back, a family member long estranged are samples of the web of relationships that make up our lives. When a special relationship is hanging by a slender thread, we are often at a loss to know what to say or do. Should we tell the truth even if it hurts? Should we avoid confrontation? Should we share what is going on inside us even if it shows we are weak and struggling, far weaker than we would like others to know?

Second Corinthians is all about relationships—not perfect ones, but real ones. In this letter the apostle Paul reveals that he is struggling deeply in his relationship with the believers in Corinth. Though he founded this church, they have apparently rejected him. This letter is an attempt at reconciliation. What made Paul's relationship more complicated was the seeming contest between Paul and his converts. The Corinthians were enjoying charismatic ecstasy. They had their orators, theologians, super-saints and super-apostles. They were strong, wise and triumphant. Paul, in contrast, was weak, foolish and a seeming failure.

In similar circumstances most people try to use strength and wisdom to win their way back. They create just the right leadership image. But Paul chose to pour out his soul to them, trusting that in the process Christ would be revealed. In this letter Paul is both medium and message. This great Christian leader takes the enormous risk of telling how confused, upset and weak he is. In 1 Corinthians Paul lets us see inside a first-century church. But in 2 Corinthians Paul lets us see inside a first-century Christian, the apostle himself. Through his large heart we see into the heart of God and the heart of the Christian message.

Paul founded the church in Corinth about A.D. 50. It was a lively church composed of first-generation Christians but infected with many of the problems associated with a mission. Corinth was the Las Vegas of the Roman Empire. Some new believers polluted the church with their secular standards in business and sexuality. They argued that all things are permissible in Christ. Others got superspiritual and boasted about their visions, prophecies, words of knowledge and spiritual experiences. In the course of time they wrote Paul asking for advice. Paul write 1 Corinthians in about A.D. 55 to address these questions and various problems.

Then it seems the Corinthians turned against the founding apostle, a crucial fact to know in order to understand 2 Corinthians. This letter was born in hurt.

Paul paid a second "painful visit" (2Co 2:1) and wrote a sorrowful letter, now lost, from Ephesus (2:4). It is highly likely that Paul then came to Macedonia (2Co 7:5), modern Greece, where he was reunited with Titus from Corinth and from which he wrote 2 Corinthians, probably while in Philippi. Later in A.D. 56 Paul visited Corinth again to receive their gifts for the poor Christians in Jerusalem.

As 2 Corinthians was written, Paul had several problems with the Corinthians: he changed his travel plans and did not come when he said he would (2Co 1:12—2:4); they failed to discipline the person who caused a grievous offense (2:5–11); their contributions for his collection for the Jewish Christians had lapsed (2Co 8—9); he had accepted financial support from the Macedonians (Thessalonica and Philippi) but not from the Achaians, especially the Corinthians (11:7–11). Paul also conflicted with newly arrived ministers in Corinth who preached a different gospel, probably a return to a form of Judaism (2:14—7:4; 10:1—13:14). Some individual Corinthians criticized Paul because he was a powerful letter-writer but a weak speaker who was unimpressive in person.

This relational conflict becomes the medium for revealing the distinctive message of this book: Christ meets us at our point of desperate weakness, *not only before we are saved, but after*. Against the false triumphalism of his opponents, Paul proclaims a gospel in which God's power is demonstrated best in human weakness. We have the Christ-treasure in jars of clay or, as Phillips powerfully paraphrases, "in a common earthenware jar." In a day when authentic Christianity seems less attractive than superspirituality or the "gospel of health, wealth and prosperity," Paul's searing honesty offers exactly what the world so deeply hungers for: it tells us how to be really real. As we walk through Paul's relationship with the Corinthians step by step, we discover how God in Christ is prepared to meet our deepest relational needs just as we are and where we are.

Outline

1/ 2 Corinthians 1:1–11 ————————— Our Comforting God

2/ 2 Corinthians 1:12—2:11 ————————— Always Yes in Christ

3/ 2 Corinthians 2:12—3:6 ————————— A Letter from Christ

4/ 2 Corinthians 3:7–18 ————————— Becoming Like Christ

5/ 2 Corinthians 4:1—5:10 ————————— This Treasure, These Jars of Clay

6/ 2 Corinthians 5:11—6:13 ————————— Ambassadors for Christ

7/ 2 Corinthians 6:14—7:16 ————————— Good Grief

8/ 2 Corinthians 8:1—9:15 ————————— The Need to Give

9/ 2 Corinthians 10 ————————— Spiritual Warfare

10/ 2 Corinthians 11 ————————— Super–Apostles, Super–Leaders

11/ 2 Corinthians 12 ————————— My Burden Carries Me

12/ 2 Corinthians 13 ————————— Examine Yourselves

1 / 2 *Corinthians 1:1–11*
Our Comforting God

"LIFE IS DIFFICULT!" With these three words Scott Peck begins his bestselling book *The Road Less Traveled*. But in 2 Corinthians Paul says this and more. Just where life is difficult, where our relationships are strained, where our competence is questioned, where our health and security are threatened, God makes himself known in powerful comfort. We discover that one of the supreme greatnesses of Christianity is that it does not seek a supernatural escape from the difficulties of life. Instead it offers a supernatural use for them. Troubles become triumphs as God makes himself known in our weakness.

 Warming Up to God   What comfort do you need from God today? Sit and wait for him to visit you with his peace and reassurance.

 Read 2 Corinthians 1:1–11.

1 Paul, an apostle of Christ Jesus by the will of God, and Timothy our brother,

To the church of God in Corinth, together with all the saints throughout Achaia:

²Grace and peace to you from God our Father and the Lord Jesus Christ.

³Praise be to the God and Father of our Lord Jesus Christ, the Father of compassion and the God of all comfort, ⁴who comforts us in all our troubles, so that we can comfort those in any trouble with the comfort we ourselves have received from God. ⁵For just as the sufferings of Christ flow over into our lives, so also through Christ our comfort overflows. ⁶If we are distressed, it is for your comfort and salvation; if we are comforted, it is for your comfort, which produces in you patient endurance of the same suf-

ferings we suffer. ⁷And our hope for you is firm, because we know that just as you share in our sufferings, so also you share in our comfort.

⁸We do not want you to be uninformed, brothers, about the hardships we suffered in the province of Asia. We were under great pressure, far beyond our ability to endure, so that we despaired even of life. ⁹Indeed, in our hearts we felt the sentence of death. But this happened that we might not rely on ourselves but on God, who raises the dead. ¹⁰He has delivered us from such a deadly peril, and he will deliver us. On him we have set our hope that he will continue to deliver us, ¹¹as you help us by your prayers. Then many will give thanks on our*ᵃ* behalf for the gracious favor granted us in answer to the prayers of many.

ᵃ11 Many manuscripts your

 Discovering the Word   1. After his customary greeting and "signature," Paul breaks into praise. What evokes this spontaneous worship (vv. 3–7)?   2. What is the connection between the sufferings of Christ and the comfort of Christ (vv. 5–6)?   3. Paul's hardships in the province of Asia (modern-day Turkey) were evidently life-threatening. What did he discover about the meaning of such sufferings in the Christian life (vv. 8–11)? 4. How do you think Paul's openness in sharing the realities of his Christian experience affected his relationship with the Corinthians?

Applying the Word   1. In what ways have you experienced God's comfort in a difficult situation?   2. How does your experience of God's comfort enable you to comfort others who are suffering?   3. Based on what you have learned in these first eleven verses, how can hardships draw you closer to God instead of driving you away from him?

Responding in Prayer   Think of someone you know who needs to experience God's comfort. Ask God to comfort that person and to use you in offering comfort.

2 / 2 Corinthians 1:12—2:11
Always Yes in Christ

CONTRARY TO WHAT some misguided Christian parents think, affirming children does not make them proud and self-centered. Rather, it meets a fundamental need of the human personality. But often our attempts to affirm each other backfire.

Such was Paul's experience with the Corinthians. Paul had promised to visit them again, twice, in fact; first as he made his way to Macedonia and then on his way back. But he changed his plans, delaying his visit and deciding to visit only once. This led his opponents to claim that he was unreliable or fickle. In the process of defending his actions, Paul pointed the Corinthians to the ultimate ground of our affirmation: the eternal yes spoken to us by God in Christ.

 Warming Up to God Recall an experience of being affirmed by another, possibly a parent or a good friend. What made that word or action especially upbuilding for you?

 Read 2 Corinthians 1:12—2:11.

¹²Now this is our boast: Our conscience testifies that we have conducted ourselves in the world, and especially in our relations with you, in the holiness and sincerity that are from God. We have done so not according to worldly wisdom but according to God's grace. ¹³For we do not write you anything you cannot read or understand. And I hope that, ¹⁴as you have understood us in part, you will come to understand fully that you can boast of us just as we will boast of you in the day of the Lord Jesus.

¹⁵Because I was confident of this, I planned to visit you first so that you might benefit twice. ¹⁶I planned to visit you on my way to Macedonia and to come back to you from Macedonia, and then to have you send me on my way to Judea. ¹⁷When I planned this, did I do it lightly? Or do I make my plans in a worldly manner so that in the same breath I say, "Yes, yes" and "No, no"?

¹⁸But as surely as God is faithful, our message to you is not "Yes" and "No." ¹⁹For the Son of God, Jesus Christ, who was preached among you by me and Silas[b] and Timothy, was not "Yes" and "No," but in him it has always been "Yes." ²⁰For no matter how many promises God has made, they are "Yes" in Christ. And so through him the "Amen" is spoken by us to the glory of God. ²¹Now it is God who makes both us and you stand firm in Christ. He anointed us, ²²set his seal of ownership on us, and put his Spirit in our hearts as a deposit, guaranteeing what is to come. ²³I call God as my witness that it was in order

to spare you that I did not return to Corinth. ²⁴Not that we lord it over your faith, but we work with you for your joy, because it is by faith you stand firm. ¹So I made up my mind that I would not make another painful visit to you. ²For if I grieve you, who is left to make me glad but you whom I have grieved? ³I wrote as I did so that when I came I should not be distressed by those who ought to make me rejoice. I had confidence in all of you, that you would all share my joy. ⁴For I wrote you out of great distress and anguish of heart and with many tears, not to grieve you but to let you know the depth of my love for you.

⁵If anyone has caused grief, he has not so much grieved me as he has grieved all of you, to some extent—not to put it too severely. ⁶The punishment inflicted on him by the majority is sufficient for him. ⁷Now instead, you ought to forgive and comfort him, so that he will not be overwhelmed by excessive sorrow. ⁸I urge you, therefore, to reaffirm your love for him. ⁹The reason I wrote you was to see if you would stand the test and be obedient in everything. ¹⁰If you forgive anyone, I also forgive him. And what I have forgiven—if there was anything to forgive—I have forgiven in the sight of Christ for your sake, ¹¹in order that Satan might not outwit us. For we are not unaware of his schemes.

b 19 Greek *Silvanus*, a variant of *Silas*

Discovering the Word 1. Based on 1:12–22, what do you think Paul's opponents were saying about his motives and ministry style? 2. What reasons does Paul give for maintaining that his change of itinerary was not a change of mind about the Corinthians (1:12, 17)? 3. Why do you think Paul directs their attention away for his travel plans to the unqualified yes or "amen" of the gospel (1:18–20)? 4. What further reason does Paul give for his change of travel plans (1:23—2:4)? 5. In 2:5–11 Paul refers to the discipline of a member of the church, possibly because of a gross sexual sin (see 1Co 5:1). How does Paul's handling of this problem affirm his love not only for the Corinthians but also for the man who had sinned?

 Applying the Word 1. What experiences have you had with church discipline? 2. How would Paul's approach to discipline be one that would still allow the person confronted to hear God's affirmation in Christ? 3. What have you learned about the conditions of receiving the affirmation Christ wants us to give?

Responding in Prayer Praise God for his faithful promises and his yes in Christ.

---

3 / 2 Corinthians 2:12—3:6
A Letter from Christ

CHRISTIANITY IS ESSENTIALLY a lay movement. But one would not think so while visiting the average church. Often the impression we get is that ministry is for the theologically trained, the polished and proficient. With the professionalism of ministry in our society, many of us question our ability to minister. Like Paul, we ask, "Who is equal to such a task?" (2:16). In this chapter Paul tells us why all believers are competent for ministry in Christ.

 Warming Up to God How do you feel about being told that becoming a Christian means becoming a minister? Talk to God about any fears you may have about being a minister.

 Read 2 Corinthians 2:12—3:6.

12Now when I went to Troas to preach the gospel of Christ and found that the Lord had opened a door for me, 13I still had no peace of mind, because I did not find my brother Titus there. So I said good-by to them and went on to Macedonia.

14But thanks be to God, who always leads us in triumphal procession in Christ and through us spreads everywhere the fragrance of the knowledge of him. 15For we are to God the aroma of Christ among those who are being saved and those who are perishing. 16To the one we are the smell of death; to the other, the fragrance of life. And who is equal to such a task? 17Unlike so many, we do not peddle the word of God for profit. On the contrary, in Christ we speak before God with sincerity, like men sent from God.

3 Are we beginning to commend ourselves again? Or do we need, like some people, letters of recommendation to you or from you? 2You yourselves are our letter, written on our hearts, known and read by everybody. 3You show that you are a letter from Christ, the result of our ministry, written not with ink but with the Spirit of the living God, not on tablets of stone but on tablets of human hearts.

4Such confidence as this is ours through Christ before God. 5Not that we are competent in ourselves to claim anything for ourselves, but our competence comes from God. 6He has made us competent as ministers of a new covenant—not of the letter but of the Spirit; for the letter kills, but the Spirit gives life.

 Discovering the Word 1. Because Paul had no peace of mind in Troas, he couldn't take full advantage of the "door" the Lord had opened for him. How was he able to speak of his triumph in Christ (2:14) in the same breath as confessing his weakness? 2. What do you think Paul means in saying we are "the smell of death" to some and "the fragrance of life" to others (2:15–16)? 3. In contrast to those who boasted about their letters of

recommendation, Paul says the Corinthians are his letter (3:1–3). What sort of letter are they? 4. In 2:16 Paul asked, "Who is equal to such a task?" What answer does he give in 3:4–6? 5. According to Paul, how does our ministry under the New Covenant contrast with ministry under the Old (3:3–6)?

 Applying the Word 1. When has Christ enabled you to triumph in the midst of a personal struggle? 2. How does the thought that Christianity spreads like a fragrance challenge your church or Christian group? 3. How has this passage encouraged you to feel competent to minister as a disciple of Jesus?

 Responding in Prayer You are a letter from Christ. Pray that you would represent Christ to those around you.

4 / 2 Corinthians 3:7–18
Becoming Like Christ

IT SEEMS TO me that it ought to be that Christ is most revealed when we hide ourselves. But that is the Old Covenant with its fading glory, condemnation focus and death-dealing impact. The New Covenant ministry is paradoxically this: as I look at Christ and as I reveal myself, it is not I who am revealed but Christ. I am like a Kodachrome transparency. If I am looked *at,* one will see almost no image at all. But if I am held to the light and looked *through,* a beautiful image begins to appear. In this passage Paul celebrates the revelation that comes with the New Covenant.

 Warming Up to God Ask God to reveal that part of himself which is in you. Spend some time seeing yourself through his eyes. Praise him for the beauty he reveals.

 Read 2 Corinthians 3:7–18.

7Now if the ministry that brought death, which was engraved in letters on stone, came with glory, so that the Israelites could not look steadily at the face of Moses because of its glory, fading though it was, 8will not the ministry of the Spirit be even more glorious? 9If the ministry that condemns men is glorious, how much more glorious is the ministry that brings righteousness! 10For what was glorious has no glory now in comparison with the surpassing glory. 11And if what was fading away came with glory, how much greater is the glory of that which lasts!

12Therefore, since we have such a hope, we are very bold. 13We are not like Moses, who would put a veil over his face to keep the Israelites from gazing at it while the radiance was fading away. 14But their minds were made dull, for to this day the same veil remains when the old covenant is read. It has not been removed, because only in Christ is it taken away. 15Even to this day when Moses is read, a veil covers their hearts. 16But whenever anyone turns to the Lord, the veil is taken away. 17Now the Lord is the Spirit, and where the Spirit of the Lord is, there is freedom. 18And we, who with unveiled faces all reflect[c] the Lord's glory, are being transformed into his likeness with ever-increasing glory, which comes from the Lord, who is the Spirit.

c18 Or contemplate

 Discovering the Word 1. How does Paul demonstrate that ministry under the New Covenant is more glorious than under the Old (vv. 7–11)? 2. How are we contrasted with Moses (vv. 12–16)? 3. What does verse 18 reveal about the process and goal of our lives as Christians under the New Covenant? 4. Paul speaks of our boldness (v. 12) and freedom (v. 17). Why should each of these characterize our New Covenant ministry?

 Applying the Word 1. What evidence do you see in your life of the glorious transformation (metamorphosis) described in verse 18? 2. Is it easy or difficult for you to recognize God's glory as it is revealed in you? Explain. 3. In what area would you like to be made more like Christ?

Responding in Prayer Praise God for the transformation he has worked and is working in you.

5 / 2 Corinthians 4:1—5:10
This Treasure, These Jars of Clay

MARGERY WILLIAMS WROTE a delightful children's story about two nursery animals, a Velveteen Rabbit (after which the book is named) and a Skin Horse, who was very old and very wise. "What is real?" asked the Velveteen Rabbit. The Skin Horse said, "Real isn't how you are made, it is a thing that happens when you are loved for a long, long time. Generally, by the time you are real most of your hair has been loved off, and your eyes drop out and you get loose in the joints and very shabby. But these things don't matter at all, because once you are REAL you can't be ugly except to those who don't understand. Once you are real you can't become unreal again. It lasts for always" (Margery Williams, *The Velveteen Rabbit* [New York: Simon & Schuster, Inc., 1975]).

The gospel treasure is contained by people marked by weakness, frailty and a kind of living death. Paradoxically, as we shall see, this life situation serves to enhance the message we bring, not detract from it. Once real in Christ, you can't become ugly or unreal again.

 Warming Up to God Do you feel free to be real in your relationship with Christ? Talk to him about the parts of yourself you feel are shabby. Listen for his loving response.

 Read 2 Corinthians 4:1—5:10.

4 Therefore, since through God's mercy we have this ministry, we do not lose heart. ²Rather, we have renounced secret and shameful ways; we do not use deception, nor do we distort the word of God. On the contrary, by setting forth the truth plainly we commend ourselves to every man's conscience in the sight of God. ³And even if our gospel is veiled, it is veiled to those who are perishing. ⁴The god of this age has blinded the minds of unbelievers, so that they cannot see the light of the gospel of the glory of Christ, who is the image of God. ⁵For we do not preach ourselves, but Jesus Christ as Lord, and ourselves as your servants for Jesus' sake. ⁶For God, who said, "Let light shine out of darkness,"ᵈ made his light shine in our hearts to give us the light of the knowledge of the glory of God in the face of Christ.

⁷But we have this treasure in jars of clay to show that this all-surpassing power is from God and not from us. ⁸We are hard pressed on every side, but not crushed; perplexed, but not in despair; ⁹persecuted, but not abandoned; struck down, but not destroyed. ¹⁰We always carry around in our body the death of Jesus, so that the life of Jesus may also be revealed in our body. ¹¹For we who are alive are always being given over to death for Jesus' sake, so that his life may

be revealed in our mortal body. ¹²So then, death is at work in us, but life is at work in you.

¹³It is written: "I believed; therefore I have spoken."ᵉ With that same spirit of faith we also believe and therefore speak, ¹⁴because we know that the one who raised the Lord Jesus from the dead will also raise us with Jesus and present us with you in his presence. ¹⁵All this is for your benefit, so that the grace that is reaching more and more people may cause thanksgiving to overflow to the glory of God.

¹⁶Therefore we do not lose heart. Though outwardly we are wasting away, yet inwardly we are being renewed day by day. ¹⁷For our light and momentary troubles are achieving for us an eternal glory that far outweighs them all. ¹⁸So we fix our eyes not on what is seen, but on what is unseen. For what is seen is temporary, but what is unseen is eternal.

5 Now we know that if the earthly tent we live in is destroyed, we have a building from God, an eternal house in heaven, not built by human hands. ²Meanwhile we groan, longing to be clothed with our heavenly dwelling, ³because when we are clothed, we will not be found naked. ⁴For while we are in this tent, we groan and are burdened, because we do not wish

ᵈ6 Gen. 1:3   ᵉ13 Psalm 116:10

to be unclothed but to be clothed with our heavenly dwelling, so that what is mortal may be swallowed up by life. ⁵Now it is God who has made us for this very purpose and has given us the Spirit as a deposit, guaranteeing what is to come.

⁶Therefore we are always confident and know that as long as we are at home in the body we are away from the Lord. ⁷We live by faith, not by sight. ⁸We are confident, I say, and would prefer to be away from the body and at home with the Lord. ⁹So we make it our goal to please him, whether we are at home in the body or away from it. ¹⁰For we must all appear before the judgment seat of Christ, that each one may receive what is due him for the things done while in the body, whether good or bad.

Discovering the Word 1. How does Paul's ministry contrast with the practices of evangelists who discredit the gospel (4:2)? 2. What forces does Paul see at work behind those who reject and those who accept his gospel (4:4–6)? 3. In what ways does Paul contrast the glory of the gospel with the weakness of those who preach it (4:7–18)? 4. What images does Paul use to compare the shabbiness of life now with the glory of the life to come (5:1–5)? 5. How does Paul's wonderful destiny in Christ affect his view of life and death (5:6–10)? 6. Reviewing the entire passage, what do you now understand Paul to mean by saying, "we live by faith, not by sight" (5:7)?

Applying the Word 1. We often assume that our weakness will hinder the gospel and detract from it. On the contrary, how does our weakness reveal God's power? 2. How can Paul's perspective help you come to terms with your own weaknesses and mortality?

Responding in Prayer Praise God for what you have learned about yourself through this passage.

---

6 / 2 Corinthians 5:11—6:13
Ambassadors for Christ

DIETRICH BONHOEFFER DESCRIBES the emergence of the super-leader under Hitler:
It is essential for the image of the Leader that the group does not see the face of the one who goes before, but sees him only from behind as the figure stepping ahead. His humanity is veiled in his Leader's form. (Quoted in Ray Anderson, *Minding God's Business* [Grand Rapids, Mich.: Eerdmans, 1986], p. 5.)

Warming Up to God Think of a time when you defended yourself in the context of a strained relationship. To what did you appeal?

Read 2 Corinthians 5:11—6:13.

---

¹¹Since, then, we know what it is to fear the Lord, we try to persuade men. What we are is plain to God, and I hope it is also plain to your conscience. ¹²We are not trying to commend ourselves to you again, but are giving you an opportunity to take pride in us, so that you can answer those who take pride in what is seen rather than in what is in the heart. ¹³If we are out of our mind, it is for the sake of God; if we are in our right mind, it is for you. ¹⁴For Christ's love compels us, because we are convinced that one died for all, and therefore all died. ¹⁵And he died for all, that those who live should no longer live for themselves but for him who died for them and was raised again.

¹⁶So from now on we regard no one from a worldly point of view. Though we once regarded Christ in this way, we do so no longer. ¹⁷Therefore, if anyone is in Christ, he is a new creation; the old has gone, the new has come! ¹⁸All this is from God, who reconciled us to himself through Christ and gave us the ministry of reconciliation: ¹⁹that God was reconciling the world to himself in Christ, not counting men's sins against them. And he has committed to us the message of reconciliation. ²⁰We are therefore Christ's ambassa-

dors, as though God were making his appeal through us. We implore you on Christ's behalf: Be reconciled to God. ²¹God made him who had no sin to be sin*f* for us, so that in him we might become the righteousness of God.

6 As God's fellow workers we urge you not to receive God's grace in vain. ²For he says,

"In the time of my favor I heard you,
    and in the day of salvation I helped you."*g*

I tell you, now is the time of God's favor, now is the day of salvation.

³We put no stumbling block in anyone's path, so that our ministry will not be discredited. ⁴Rather, as servants of God we commend ourselves in every way: in great endurance; in troubles, hardships and distresses; ⁵in beatings, imprisonments and riots; in hard work, sleepless nights and hunger; ⁶in purity, understanding, patience and kindness; in the Holy Spirit and in sincere love; ⁷in truthful speech and in the power of God; with weapons of righteousness in the right hand and in the left; ⁸through glory and dishonor, bad report and good report; genuine, yet regarded as impostors; ⁹known, yet regarded as unknown; dying, and yet we live on; beaten, and yet not killed; ¹⁰sorrowful, yet always rejoicing; poor, yet making many rich; having nothing, and yet possessing everything.

¹¹We have spoken freely to you, Corinthians, and opened wide our hearts to you. ¹²We are not withholding our affection from you, but you are withholding yours from us. ¹³As a fair exchange—I speak as to my children—open wide your hearts also.

f21 Or be a sin offering   g2 Isaiah 49:8

 Discovering the Word 1. Paul defends his *ministry* and *message* of reconciliation in this passage. What accusations might Paul's opponents have made about his ministry (5:11–13)? 2. How does Paul explain his true motives and goals (5:11–14)? 3. In describing his message, Paul uses the words *reconciliation* and *reconciled* five times (5:18–20). What does it mean to be reconciled to God? 4. What would it mean for the Corinthians—or us today—to receive the grace of God in vain (6:1)? 5. To what further credentials does Paul point in order to commend himself to the Corinthians (6:3–10)?

Applying the Word 1. How might Paul's example help you be a more effective ambassador, especially to people who are "turned off" by Christianity? 2. Who, specifically, would you like to be an ambassador to? 3. How could you reach that person?

Responding in Prayer Ask God to make you an effective ambassador.

---

7 / 2 Corinthians 6:14—7:16
Good Grief

A GREAT THEOLOGIAN once said, "To be a sinner is our distress, but to know it, is our hope!" Paul would say "Amen." We have nothing to lose and everything to gain if we are in Christ and walking into the light. But the Corinthians were tempted to cover up a scandal and not to call it sin. In response, Paul patiently and effectively ministered to the Corinthians, urging them not to cover up the problem. The result was what Paul calls godly sorrow.

 Warming Up to God Recall an experience of deep sorrow, possibly a significant loss, hurt or disappointment. What were some of the good things, if any, that came after the sorrow had passed? Praise God for what you learned from that experience.

Read 2 Corinthians 6:14—7:16.

¹⁴Do not be yoked together with unbelievers. For what do righteousness and wickedness have in common? Or what fellowship can light have with darkness? ¹⁵What harmony is there between Christ and Belial*ʰ*? What does a believer have in common with an unbeliever? ¹⁶What agreement is there between the temple of God and idols? For we are the temple of the living God. As God has said: "I will live with them and walk among them, and I will be their God, and they will be my people."*ⁱ*

¹⁷"Therefore come out from them
　　and be separate,
　　　　　　　　　　　　　　says the Lord.
　Touch no unclean thing,
　　and I will receive you."*ʲ*
¹⁸"I will be a Father to you,
　　and you will be my sons and daughters,
　　　　　　　says the Lord Almighty."*ᵏ*

7 Since we have these promises, dear friends, let us purify ourselves from everything that contaminates body and spirit, perfecting holiness out of reverence for God.

²Make room for us in your hearts. We have wronged no one, we have corrupted no one, we have exploited no one. ³I do not say this to condemn you; I have said before that you have such a place in our hearts that we would live or die with you. ⁴I have great confidence in you; I take great pride in you. I am greatly encouraged; in all our troubles my joy knows no bounds.

⁵For when we came into Macedonia, this body of ours had no rest, but we were harassed at every turn—conflicts on the outside, fears within. ⁶But God, who comforts the downcast, comforted us by the coming of Titus, ⁷and not only by his com-

ing but also by the comfort you had given him. He told us about your longing for me, your deep sorrow, your ardent concern for me, so that my joy was greater than ever.

⁸Even if I caused you sorrow by my letter, I do not regret it. Though I did regret it—I see that my letter hurt you, but only for a little while— ⁹yet now I am happy, not because you were made sorry, but because your sorrow led you to repentance. For you became sorrowful as God intended and so were not harmed in any way by us. ¹⁰Godly sorrow brings repentance that leads to salvation and leaves no regret, but worldly sorrow brings death. ¹¹See what this godly sorrow has produced in you: what earnestness, what eagerness to clear yourselves, what indignation, what alarm, what longing, what concern, what readiness to see justice done. At every point you have proved yourselves to be innocent in this matter. ¹²So even though I wrote to you, it was not on account of the one who did the wrong or of the injured party, but rather that before God you could see for yourselves how devoted to us you are. ¹³By all this we are encouraged.

In addition to our own encouragement, we were especially delighted to see how happy Titus was, because his spirit has been refreshed by all of you. ¹⁴I had boasted to him about you, and you have not embarrassed me. But just as everything we said to you was true, so our boasting about you to Titus has proved to be true as well. ¹⁵And his affection for you is all the greater when he remembers that you were all obedient, receiving him with fear and trembling. ¹⁶I am glad I can have complete confidence in you.

ʰ15 Greek *Beliar,* a variant of *Belial*　　*ⁱ16* Lev. 26:12; Jer. 32:38; Ezek. 37:27　　*ʲ17* Isaiah 52:11; Ezek. 20:34,41　　*ᵏ18* 2 Samuel 7:14; 7:8

Discovering the Word　1. This passage is usually understood to apply to marriages between believers and unbelievers. However, what other types of close relationships or partnerships might Paul have in mind?　2. What reasons does Paul give for avoiding such unions (6:14–16)?　3. Although we may forfeit certain relationships, what positive promises does the Lord give us (6:16—7:1)?　4. What difference should our relationship with God make when we contemplate marriage or other close relationships (6:17; 7:1)?　5. In 7:2–6 Paul recalls how comforted he was when he met Titus in Macedonia and heard news of the Corinthians. What makes Paul so "confident," "proud" and "encouraged" (7:4) about the Corinthians?　6. Referring to their response to his "sorrowful letter" (7:8), Paul compares worldly sorrow with godly sorrow (7:9–10). What are the positive indications and constructive results of godly sorrow (7:10–11)?

Applying the Word　1. It is often counterproductive to try to persuade someone not to marry a person they deeply love, even if the intended partner is unsuitable. What clues does this passage give us for ministering to someone who is tempted to marry outside the faith?　2. If godly sorrow is so beneficial, why do you

think most Christians shrink from the relational work, discipline and tough love that are required to bring it about in others?   3. In what areas of your life are you most in need of godly sorrow?

 Responding in Prayer Ask Christ to teach you more about godly sorrow.

8 / *2 Corinthians 8:1—9:15*
The Need to Give

THE PRIVACY OF the purse makes it extremely difficult for Christians to talk about their money. The fig leaf has slipped from the genitals to the wallet. The problem is compounded by hard-sell media evangelists raising funds for their personal empires. But Paul devotes two whole chapters to the grace of giving, because both he and the Corinthians have a problem in this area.

 Warming Up to God Reflect on your own pattern of giving. When is it hard for you?

 Read 2 Corinthians 8:1—9:15.

8 And now, brothers, we want you to know about the grace that God has given the Macedonian churches. ²Out of the most severe trial, their overflowing joy and their extreme poverty welled up in rich generosity. ³For I testify that they gave as much as they were able, and even beyond their ability. Entirely on their own, ⁴they urgently pleaded with us for the privilege of sharing in this service to the saints. ⁵And they did not do as we expected, but they gave themselves first to the Lord and then to us in keeping with God's will. ⁶So we urged Titus, since he had earlier made a beginning, to bring also to completion this act of grace on your part. ⁷But just as you excel in everything—in faith, in speech, in knowledge, in complete earnestness and in your love for us*ⁱ*—see that you also excel in this grace of giving.

⁸I am not commanding you, but I want to test the sincerity of your love by comparing it with the earnestness of others. ⁹For you know the grace of our Lord Jesus Christ, that though he was rich, yet for your sakes he became poor, so that you through his poverty might become rich.

¹⁰And here is my advice about what is best for you in this matter: Last year you were the first not only to give but also to have the desire to do so. ¹¹Now finish the work, so that your eager willingness to do it may be matched by your completion of it, according to your means. ¹²For if the will-

ingness is there, the gift is acceptable according to what one has, not according to what he does not have.

¹³Our desire is not that others might be relieved while you are hard pressed, but that there might be equality. ¹⁴At the present time your plenty will supply what they need, so that in turn their plenty will supply what you need. Then there will be equality, ¹⁵as it is written: "He who gathered much did not have too much, and he who gathered little did not have too little."*ᵐ*

¹⁶I thank God, who put into the heart of Titus the same concern I have for you. ¹⁷For Titus not only welcomed our appeal, but he is coming to you with much enthusiasm and on his own initiative. ¹⁸And we are sending along with him the brother who is praised by all the churches for his service to the gospel. ¹⁹What is more, he was chosen by the churches to accompany us as we carry the offering, which we administer in order to honor the Lord himself and to show our eagerness to help. ²⁰We want to avoid any criticism of the way we administer this liberal gift. ²¹For we are taking pains to do what is right, not only in the eyes of the Lord but also in the eyes of men.

²²In addition, we are sending with them our brother who has often proved to us in many ways that he is zealous, and now even more so because of his great confidence in you. ²³As for Titus, he

7 Some manuscripts in our love for you   *ᵐ15 Exodus 16:18*

is my partner and fellow worker among you; as for our brothers, they are representatives of the churches and an honor to Christ. 24Therefore show these men the proof of your love and the reason for our pride in you, so that the churches can see it.

9 There is no need for me to write to you about this service to the saints. 2For I know your eagerness to help, and I have been boasting about it to the Macedonians, telling them that since last year you in Achaia were ready to give; and your enthusiasm has stirred most of them to action. 3But I am sending the brothers in order that our boasting about you in this matter should not prove hollow, but that you may be ready, as I said you would be. 4For if any Macedonians come with me and find you unprepared, we—not to say anything about you—would be ashamed of having been so confident. 5So I thought it necessary to urge the brothers to visit you in advance and finish the arrangements for the generous gift you had promised. Then it will be ready as a generous gift, not as one grudgingly given.

6Remember this: Whoever sows sparingly will also reap sparingly, and whoever sows generously will also reap generously. 7Each man should give what he has decided in his heart to give, not reluctantly or under compulsion, for God loves a cheerful giver. 8And God is able to make all grace abound to you, so that in all things at all times, having all that you need, you will abound in every good work. 9As it is written:

> "He has scattered abroad his gifts to the poor;
>   his righteousness endures forever."[n]

10Now he who supplies seed to the sower and bread for food will also supply and increase your store of seed and will enlarge the harvest of your righteousness. 11You will be made rich in every way so that you can be generous on every occasion, and through us your generosity will result in thanksgiving to God.

12This service that you perform is not only supplying the needs of God's people but is also overflowing in many expressions of thanks to God. 13Because of the service by which you have proved yourselves, men will praise God for the obedience that accompanies your confession of the gospel of Christ, and for your generosity in sharing with them and with everyone else. 14And in their prayers for you their hearts will go out to you, because of the surpassing grace God has given you. 15Thanks be to God for his indescribable gift!

[n]9 Psalm 112:9

Discovering the Word 1. In what ways are the Macedonians excellent examples of generosity (8:1–5)? 2. In both chapters Paul refrains from using the word *money*. Instead he speaks of *sharing* (8:4; 9:13), *service* (8:4, 18; 9:1, 12–13), *offering* (8:19), *grace* (8:6–7) and *gift* (8:12, 20; 9:5). What insights do these words give us into the nature of giving? 3. Paul never raised money for himself, for his own missionary organization or even for Corinth Community Church. What is the primary goal that governs his appeal for gifts (8:10–15)? 4. What care does Paul take to avoid any suspicion of dishonesty or self-interest as he handles this large gift (8:16–24)? 5. Some people teach that giving money to the Lord's work results in your getting more money yourself. What does Paul say about the personal benefits of giving (9:6–11)?

Applying the Word 1. What positive and negative feelings do you have about people raising money for a Christian cause? 2. Paul encourages *cheerful* giving (9:7). The word is the root of our English *hilarious*. It is the exact opposite of calculated giving under compulsion. According to these two chapters, how could you become a more cheerful giver? 3. What difference will this study make in the stewardship of your resources?

 Responding in Prayer Pray for the needs of believers around the world, especially those who suffer persecution.

9 / *2 Corinthians 10*
Spiritual Warfare

SOMETIMES WHEN THINGS seem to be getting better we hear news that the situation is worse than we thought. While Paul was writing this letter, or after completing and sending chapters 1—9, he got fresh news that some outside leaders, some so-called super-apostles, had usurped his rightful place. Now Paul engages in spiritual warfare with principalities, powers and persons who oppose not only Paul but Christ himself. Unlike many of us, Paul wants to make peace, not keep the peace by covering over the problem.

 Warming Up to God In what area do you feel that you are currently battling evil? What help do you need from God?

 Read 2 Corinthians 10.

10 By the meekness and gentleness of Christ, I appeal to you—I, Paul, who am "timid" when face to face with you, but "bold" when away! ²I beg you that when I come I may not have to be as bold as I expect to be toward some people who think that we live by the standards of this world. ³For though we live in the world, we do not wage war as the world does. ⁴The weapons we fight with are not the weapons of the world. On the contrary, they have divine power to demolish strongholds. ⁵We demolish arguments and every pretension that sets itself up against the knowledge of God, and we take captive every thought to make it obedient to Christ. ⁶And we will be ready to punish every act of disobedience, once your obedience is complete.

⁷You are looking only on the surface of things.ᵒ If anyone is confident that he belongs to Christ, he should consider again that we belong to Christ just as much as he. ⁸For even if I boast somewhat freely about the authority the Lord gave us for building you up rather than pulling you down, I will not be ashamed of it. ⁹I do not want to seem to be trying to frighten you with my letters. ¹⁰For some say, "His letters are weighty and forceful, but in person he is unimpressive and his speaking amounts to nothing." ¹¹Such people should realize that what we are in our let-

ters when we are absent, we will be in our actions when we are present.

¹²We do not dare to classify or compare ourselves with some who commend themselves. When they measure themselves by themselves and compare themselves with themselves, they are not wise. ¹³We, however, will not boast beyond proper limits, but will confine our boasting to the field God has assigned to us, a field that reaches even to you. ¹⁴We are not going too far in our boasting, as would be the case if we had not come to you, for we did get as far as you with the gospel of Christ. ¹⁵Neither do we go beyond our limits by boasting of work done by others.ᵖ Our hope is that, as your faith continues to grow, our area of activity among you will greatly expand, ¹⁶so that we can preach the gospel in the regions beyond you. For we do not want to boast about work already done in another man's territory. ¹⁷But, "Let him who boasts boast in the Lord."�q ¹⁸For it is not the one who commends himself who is approved, but the one whom the Lord commends.

ᵒ7 Or *Look at the obvious facts*   ᵖ13-15 Or ¹³*We, however, will not boast about things that cannot be measured, but we will boast according to the standard of measurement that the God of measure has assigned us—a measurement that relates even to you.* ¹⁴ . . . . ¹⁵*Neither do we boast about things that cannot be measured in regard to the work done by others.*   �q17 Jer. 9:24

Discovering the Word 1. What apparent disadvantages did Paul suffer in comparison to his opponents in Corinth? (See especially verses 1 and 9.) 2. Paul says he is not waging war "as the world does" (v. 3). What types of worldly weapons and strategies do you think he has in mind? 3. What is Paul's strategy in this spiritual warfare (vv. 4–6)? 4. Trace, in verses 7 and 10, the arguments of Paul's opponents. 5. What is wrong with the boasting of Paul's opponents (vv. 7–18)?

Applying the Word 1. In what situations are we tempted to use worldly weapons and strategies today? 2. What similar arguments and pretensions oppose the knowledge of God today? 3. Which of your own thoughts need to be "taken captive" (v. 5) to obedience to Christ?

Responding in Prayer Ask God to guard your words, that your boasting might be only in the Lord.

---

10 / *2 Corinthians 11*
Super-Apostles, Super-Leaders

IN HIS BOOK *Servant Leadership* Robert K. Greenleaf wrote, "We live in the age of the anti-leader, and our vast educational structure devotes little care to nurturing leaders or to understanding followership" (Robert K. Greenleaf, *Servant Leadership* [New York: Paulist Press, 1977], p. 4).

Warming Up to God Whose leadership are you under? Reflect before Christ on the positive or negative impact of that leadership in your life.

Read 2 Corinthians 11.

---

11 I hope you will put up with a little of my foolishness; but you are already doing that. ²I am jealous for you with a godly jealousy. I promised you to one husband, to Christ, so that I might present you as a pure virgin to him. ³But I am afraid that just as Eve was deceived by the serpent's cunning, your minds may somehow be led astray from your sincere and pure devotion to Christ. ⁴For if someone comes to you and preaches a Jesus other than the Jesus we preached, or if you receive a different spirit from the one you received, or a different gospel from the one you accepted, you put up with it easily enough. ⁵But I do not think I am in the least inferior to those "super-apostles." ⁶I may not be a trained speaker, but I do have knowledge. We have made this perfectly clear to you in every way.

⁷Was it a sin for me to lower myself in order to elevate you by preaching the gospel of God to you free of charge? ⁸I robbed other churches by receiving support from them so as to serve you. ⁹And when I was with you and needed something, I was not a burden to anyone, for the brothers who came from Macedonia supplied what I needed. I have kept myself from being a burden to you in any way, and will continue to do so. ¹⁰As surely as the truth of Christ is in me, nobody in the regions of Achaia will stop this boasting of mine. ¹¹Why? Because I do not love

you? God knows I do! ¹²And I will keep on doing what I am doing in order to cut the ground from under those who want an opportunity to be considered equal with us in the things they boast about.

¹³For such men are false apostles, deceitful workmen, masquerading as apostles of Christ. ¹⁴And no wonder, for Satan himself masquerades as an angel of light. ¹⁵It is not surprising, then, if his servants masquerade as servants of righteousness. Their end will be what their actions deserve.

¹⁶I repeat: Let no one take me for a fool. But if you do, then receive me just as you would a fool, so that I may do a little boasting. ¹⁷In this self-confident boasting I am not talking as the Lord would, but as a fool. ¹⁸Since many are boasting in the way the world does, I too will boast. ¹⁹You gladly put up with fools since you are so wise! ²⁰In fact, you even put up with anyone who enslaves you or exploits you or takes advantage of you or pushes himself forward or slaps you in the face. ²¹To my shame I admit that we were too weak for that!

What anyone else dares to boast about—I am speaking as a fool—I also dare to boast about. ²²Are they Hebrews? So am I. Are they Israelites? So am I. Are they Abraham's descendants? So am I. ²³Are they servants of Christ? (I am out of my mind to talk like this.) I am more. I have worked much harder, been in prison more frequently,

been flogged more severely, and been exposed to death again and again. ²⁴Five times I received from the Jews the forty lashes minus one. ²⁵Three times I was beaten with rods, once I was stoned, three times I was shipwrecked, I spent a night and a day in the open sea, ²⁶I have been constantly on the move. I have been in danger from rivers, in danger from bandits, in danger from my own countrymen, in danger from Gentiles; in danger in the city, in danger in the country, in danger at sea; and in danger from false brothers. ²⁷I have labored and toiled and have often gone without sleep; I have known hunger and thirst and have often gone without food; I have been cold and naked. ²⁸Besides everything else, I face daily the pressure of my concern for all the churches. ²⁹Who is weak, and I do not feel weak? Who is led into sin, and I do not inwardly burn?

³⁰If I must boast, I will boast of the things that show my weakness. ³¹The God and Father of the Lord Jesus, who is to be praised forever, knows that I am not lying. ³²In Damascus the governor under King Aretas had the city of the Damascenes guarded in order to arrest me. ³³But I was lowered in a basket from a window in the wall and slipped through his hands.

 Discovering the Word 1. What are Paul's motives for challenging the so-called super-apostles who are winning over the Corinthians (vv. 1–6)? 2. Why do you think betrothal rather than marriage is such a good image of the goal of Christian ministry (vv. 2–3)? 3. Why do you think Paul's decision to "preach the gospel free of charge" was so important in defending his ministry (vv. 7–12)? 4. Looking at the whole chapter, what marks of the super-apostles justified Paul's description of them as *false, deceitful* and *masquerading*? 5. In contrast, what does Paul boast about as the mark of his own leadership (vv. 16–33)?

Applying the Word 1. What kind of Christian leadership today might fall under the apostle's judgment? 2. What have you learned from this study about the marks of true Christian leadership? 3. What have you learned about being a healthy follower?

Responding in Prayer Pray for your pastor and other Christian leaders.

11 / *2 Corinthians 12*
My Burden Carries Me

UNINTENTIONALLY, A GERMAN philosopher captured the genius of Paul's spirituality with these arresting words: "My burden carries me." Normally we think about the difficulty of carrying our burdens. But in reality our burdens carry us to Christ by convincing us that we are not self-sufficient. They are spiritual assets, not liabilities. "When I am weak, then I am strong" is Paul's final distinction between super-spirituality and the real thing.

 Warming Up to God What burdens are you carrying today? Turn them over to Christ one by one. Feel the weight lifted from you.

 Read 2 Corinthians 12.

12 I must go on boasting. Although there is nothing to be gained, I will go on to visions and revelations from the Lord. ²I know a man in Christ who fourteen years ago was caught up to the third heaven. Whether it was in the body or out of the body I do not know—God knows. ³And I know that this man—whether in the body or apart from the body I do not know, but God knows—⁴was caught up to paradise. He heard inexpressible things, things that man is not permitted to tell. ⁵I will boast about a man like that, but I will not boast about myself, except about my weaknesses. ⁶Even if I should choose to boast, I would not be a fool, because I would be speaking the truth. But I refrain, so no one will think more of me than is warranted by what I do or say.

⁷To keep me from becoming conceited because

of these surpassingly great revelations, there was given me a thorn in my flesh, a messenger of Satan, to torment me. [8]Three times I pleaded with the Lord to take it away from me. [9]But he said to me, "My grace is sufficient for you, for my power is made perfect in weakness." Therefore I will boast all the more gladly about my weaknesses, so that Christ's power may rest on me. [10]That is why, for Christ's sake, I delight in weaknesses, in insults, in hardships, in persecutions, in difficulties. For when I am weak, then I am strong.

[11]I have made a fool of myself, but you drove me to it. I ought to have been commended by you, for I am not in the least inferior to the "super-apostles," even though I am nothing. [12]The things that mark an apostle—signs, wonders and miracles—were done among you with great perseverance. [13]How were you inferior to the other churches, except that I was never a burden to you? Forgive me this wrong!

[14]Now I am ready to visit you for the third time, and I will not be a burden to you, because what I want is not your possessions but you. After all, children should not have to save up for their parents, but parents for their children. [15]So I will very gladly spend for you everything I have and expend myself as well. If I love you more, will you love me less? [16]Be that as it may, I have not been a burden to you. Yet, crafty fellow that I am, I caught you by trickery! [17]Did I exploit you through any of the men I sent you? [18]I urged Titus to go to you and I sent our brother with him. Titus did not exploit you, did he? Did we not act in the same spirit and follow the same course?

[19]Have you been thinking all along that we have been defending ourselves to you? We have been speaking in the sight of God as those in Christ; and everything we do, dear friends, is for your strengthening. [20]For I am afraid that when I come I may not find you as I want you to be, and you may not find me as you want me to be. I fear that there may be quarreling, jealousy, outbursts of anger, factions, slander, gossip, arrogance and disorder. [21]I am afraid that when I come again my God will humble me before you, and I will be grieved over many who have sinned earlier and have not repented of the impurity, sexual sin and debauchery in which they have indulged.

Discovering the Word 1. Paul describes his experience of being caught up to paradise by referring to "a man in Christ" (vv. 1–6). Why do you think he refrains from boasting about such an exalted experience? 2. Opinions concerning Paul's "thorn in my flesh" (v. 7) range from eye disease (Acts 9:9; Gal 4:15) to defective speech to his ever-present opponents. While no conclusive answer can be given about the details, what do we know about this bitter reality Paul faced? 3. How does Paul view Satan's part and God's part in his "thorn"? 4. In contrast to Paul's ecstatic experiences, the simple answer to his prayer (v. 9) is considered to be the summit from which we gain the most complete view of Paul's apostleship. What effect did this answer have on Paul himself? 5. To what credentials does Paul point while pleading for his rightful place in the Corinthians' hearts (vv. 11–21)?

Applying the Word 1. Reflecting on the whole chapter, what kind of weaknesses or problems can we legitimately expect God to transform into a means of grace? 2. What kinds of problems or weaknesses should we not expect God to transform? 3. How does this help you to understand an ongoing problem in your life?

 Responding in Prayer Pray that you will be made strong even in your weak places, that you might serve Christ.

---

12 / 2 Corinthians 13
Examine Yourselves

IMAGINE LIFE WITHOUT a final examination. At first it strikes us as a wonderful vacation, like school without tests and report cards. But without accountability life quickly loses its meaning. The whole Bible looks toward the final Day with vibrant hope. Those genuinely in Christ have nothing to fear and everything to anticipate. But what of those who are not sure, or who like the Corinthians might have false confidence about the outcome of the final exam? Paul deals with this matter in his final passionate plea.

Warming Up to God When is God's power real to you?

 Read 2 Corinthians 13.

13 This will be my third visit to you. "Every matter must be established by the testimony of two or three witnesses."[r] [2]I already gave you a warning when I was with you the second time. I now repeat it while absent: On my return I will not spare those who sinned earlier or any of the others, [3]since you are demanding proof that Christ is speaking through me. He is not weak in dealing with you, but is powerful among you. [4]For to be sure, he was crucified in weakness, yet he lives by God's power. Likewise, we are weak in him, yet by God's power we will live with him to serve you.

[5]Examine yourselves to see whether you are in the faith; test yourselves. Do you not realize that Christ Jesus is in you—unless, of course, you fail the test? [6]And I trust that you will discover that we have not failed the test. [7]Now we pray to God that you will not do anything wrong. Not that people will see that we have stood the test but that you will do what is right even though we

may seem to have failed. [8]For we cannot do anything against the truth, but only for the truth. [9]We are glad whenever we are weak but you are strong; and our prayer is for your perfection. [10]This is why I write these things when I am absent, that when I come I may not have to be harsh in my use of authority—the authority the Lord gave me for building you up, not for tearing you down.

[11]Finally, brothers, good-by. Aim for perfection, listen to my appeal, be of one mind, live in peace. And the God of love and peace will be with you.

[12]Greet one another with a holy kiss. [13]All the saints send their greetings.

[14]May the grace of the Lord Jesus Christ, and the love of God, and the fellowship of the Holy Spirit be with you all.

[r] Deut. 19:15

 Discovering the Word 1. What can the Corinthians expect from Paul's third visit (vv. 1–3, 10)? 2. Verse 4 sums up the whole book. Why does the cross represent the heart of what Paul has been saying to the Corinthians? 3. Paul asks them to examine themselves not so much in their doctrine as in their experience (vv. 5–6). How could the Corinthians know experientially that they truly belonged to Christ? 4. In what ways does Paul show that he cares more for *their* passing the test than for *his* seeming to pass the test in the eyes of others (vv. 7–9)? 5. In what specific ways does Paul pray they will be built up (vv. 11–14)?

 Applying the Word 1. In what ways do you shrink from your daily cross and find your power elsewhere? 2. If you are unsure of your position in Christ, what can you do about it in light of this chapter?

Responding in Prayer Pray for courage to take up your cross and follow Christ.

Galatians

W e all want to be accepted—by our family, by our friends and most of all by God. But so often people accept us only *if* we are attractive, smart, wealthy or powerful. So we work hard to project the right image and to conceal our faults. We often transfer this attitude to our relationship with God. We feel we must earn his acceptance. If we could only work harder, live better, pray longer, witness to more people—then we might get on God's good side.

In Galatians Paul challenges this kind of thinking. He exposes the futility of trying to earn God's acceptance when we are already accepted in Christ. His message frees us from living out of a sense of guilt. We find fresh assurance of God's love and renewed power to serve him.

Galatians was written by Paul sometime between A.D. 48–49. It was probably addressed to the churches in Antioch, Iconium, Lystra and Derbe, which were located in the Roman province of Galatia. Paul and Barnabas visited these cities during their first missionary journey. Their reception was unforgettable. Acts 13—14 tells us that they were driven out of Antioch, that they fled from Iconium and that Paul was stoned in Lystra! Yet in spite of the opposition against Paul and Barnabas, people believed the gospel and churches were formed.

The real threat arose shortly thereafter. Certain people infiltrated the new churches with a different message. "Paul omitted an important part of the gospel," they claimed. "You must also be circumcised and keep the law of Moses if you want to be saved" (see Acts 15:1). Their arguments were impressive and the religious zeal was undeniable. The Galatians were almost persuaded when Paul received word of what was happening. Quickly he dictated this letter and sent it to be read in each of the churches. Centuries later it still radiates the heat of Paul's anger. These preachers were impostors. Their gospel was perverted. The Galatians were in grave danger!

Outline

1/ Galatians 1:1–10 ——————————— Good News and Bad

2/ Galatians 1:11—2:10 ——————————— Why Believe the Gospel?

3/ Galatians 2:11–21 ——————————— Accepting Others

4/ Galatians 3:1–14 ——————————— Why God Accepts Us

5/ Galatians 3:15–29 ——————————— *Exposing Our Needs*

6/ Galatians 4:1–20 ———————————— *The Joys of Growing Up*

7/ Galatians 4:21—5:1 ————————— *Do-It-Yourself Religion*

8/ Galatians 5:2–15 ————————————— *Heavenly Help*

9/ Galatians 5:13–26 ——————————— *Living by the Spirit*

10/ Galatians 6:1–10 ——————————— *The Law of Love*

11/ Galatians 6:11–18 —————————— *Getting Motivated*

1 / *Galatians 1:1–10*
Good News and Bad

THE CHURCH HAS always been plagued by false teachers, heretics and followers of various cults. Usually such people have an aggressive program for winning new converts. How are we to respond to those who preach or accept a twisted gospel? Paul gives us an example in this passage.

 Warming Up to God Read and reflect on Galatians 1:3–5. Allow these verses to speak to you. Let them soak into your mind and heart. Praise God for what he has done in Christ.

 Read Galatians 1:1–10.

1 Paul, an apostle—sent not from men nor by man, but by Jesus Christ and God the Father, who raised him from the dead— ²and all the brothers with me,

To the churches in Galatia:

³Grace and peace to you from God our Father and the Lord Jesus Christ, ⁴who gave himself for our sins to rescue us from the present evil age, according to the will of our God and Father, ⁵to whom be glory for ever and ever. Amen.

⁶I am astonished that you are so quickly deserting the one who called you by the grace of Christ and are turning to a different gospel— ⁷which is really no gospel at all. Evidently some people are throwing you into confusion and are trying to pervert the gospel of Christ. ⁸But even if we or an angel from heaven should preach a gospel other than the one we preached to you, let him be eternally condemned! ⁹As we have already said, so now I say again: If anybody is preaching to you a gospel other than what you accepted, let him be eternally condemned!

¹⁰Am I now trying to win the approval of men, or of God? Or am I trying to please men? If I were still trying to please men, I would not be a servant of Christ.

 Discovering the Word 1. In three brief verses (3–5) Paul tells us an enormous amount about the gospel. What do we learn? 2. In verses 6–7 Paul summarizes the problem that caused him to write this letter. What was happening in the Galatian churches? 3. Verse 6 implies that if we desert the gospel, we also desert God. Why would this be true? 4. Why do you think Paul is so harsh in his judgment of those who preach a different gospel (vv. 8–9)? 5. How might the way we present the gospel be different if we were seeking the approval of people instead of God (v. 10)?

Applying the Word 1. What are some ways the gospel is being perverted today? 2. According to this passage, how can we ensure that the gospel we believe and preach is the true gospel? 3. What can you do to increase your understanding of the gospel?

Responding in Prayer Confess before God the ways in which you are seeking the approval of others before him. Ask God to help you turn your priorities around.

2 / *Galatians 1:11—2:10*
Why Believe the Gospel?

HAVE YOU EVER been talking with someone about the gospel when suddenly he or she says, "But that's just *your* opinion!"? This raises an important question. If the gospel is merely our opinion, then why should they listen to us? There are many other religions in the world, each one claiming to be a path to God. Who are we to assert that the

gospel is the only true message of salvation? This objection isn't new. Paul's opponents questioned the authenticity of the gospel he preached.

Warming Up to God We all struggle to believe at times. When is belief difficult for you? Don't be afraid to talk to God about it. Express your struggles and doubts to him.

Read Galatians 1:11—2:10.

[11]I want you to know, brothers, that the gospel I preached is not something that man made up. [12]I did not receive it from any man, nor was I taught it; rather, I received it by revelation from Jesus Christ.

[13]For you have heard of my previous way of life in Judaism, how intensely I persecuted the church of God and tried to destroy it. [14]I was advancing in Judaism beyond many Jews of my own age and was extremely zealous for the traditions of my fathers. [15]But when God, who set me apart from birth[a] and called me by his grace, was pleased [16]to reveal his Son in me so that I might preach him among the Gentiles, I did not consult any man, [17]nor did I go up to Jerusalem to see those who were apostles before I was, but I went immediately into Arabia and later returned to Damascus.

[18]Then after three years, I went up to Jerusalem to get acquainted with Peter[b] and stayed with him fifteen days. [19]I saw none of the other apostles—only James, the Lord's brother. [20]I assure you before God that what I am writing you is no lie. [21]Later I went to Syria and Cilicia. [22]I was personally unknown to the churches of Judea that are in Christ. [23]They only heard the report: "The man who formerly persecuted us is now preaching the faith he once tried to destroy." [24]And they praised God because of me.

2 Fourteen years later I went up again to Jerusalem, this time with Barnabas. I took Titus along also. [2]I went in response to a revelation and set before them the gospel that I preach among the Gentiles. But I did this privately to those who seemed to be leaders, for fear that I was running or had run my race in vain. [3]Yet not even Titus, who was with me, was compelled to be circumcised, even though he was a Greek. [4]This matter arose⌋ because some false brothers had infiltrated our ranks to spy on the freedom we have in Christ Jesus and to make us slaves. [5]We did not give in to them for a moment, so that the truth of the gospel might remain with you.

[6]As for those who seemed to be important— whatever they were makes no difference to me; God does not judge by external appearance— those men added nothing to my message. [7]On the contrary, they saw that I had been entrusted with the task of preaching the gospel to the Gentiles,[c] just as Peter had been to the Jews.[d] [8]For God, who was at work in the ministry of Peter as an apostle to the Jews, was also at work in my ministry as an apostle to the Gentiles. [9]James, Peter[e] and John, those reputed to be pillars, gave me and Barnabas the right hand of fellowship when they recognized the grace given to me. They agreed that we should go to the Gentiles, and they to the Jews. [10]All they asked was that we should continue to remember the poor, the very thing I was eager to do.

[a]15 Or *from my mother's womb*   [b]18 Greek *Cephas*   [c]7 Greek *uncircumcised*   [d]7 Greek *circumcised*; also in verses 8 and 9   [e]9 Greek *Cephas*; also in verses 11 and 14

Discovering the Word 1. In 1:11–12 Paul claims he received the gospel from Jesus Christ, not people. How does his brief autobiography in 1:13–24 confirm this claim? 2. Paul obviously did not need human authorization to preach the gospel. Why then did he present his gospel to the leaders in Jerusalem (2:1–2)? 3. Why was it significant that Titus (a Gentile) was not compelled to be circumcised (the sign of becoming a Jew) (2:3–5)? 4. Paul refused to give in to false brothers on the matter of circumcision "so that the truth of the gospel might remain with you" (2:5). How do you show your concern to preserve the gospel? 5. How did the leaders in Jerusalem respond to Paul's message and ministry (2:6–10)?

Applying the Word 1. The apostles were not simply zealous to preserve the gospel. They also felt called to proclaim the gospel (2:7–10). To whom do you feel called to bring the gospel? 2. What step can you take this week to bring the good news to someone? 3. How can Paul's testimony in this passage increase our confidence in the truth of the gospel?

Responding in Prayer Ask God to help you be a bearer of the good news.

3 / Galatians 2:11–21
Accepting Others

HAVE YOU EVER felt like avoiding certain types of Christians? Perhaps you don't like their theology. You may disapprove of their lifestyle. Or you may prefer to avoid people of their race, nationality or economic background. This passage helps us see why such attitudes conflict with the basic message of the gospel.

 Warming Up to God We have been justified by faith and are no longer under the law. In this way we have been accepted by God. How does God's acceptance help you feel good about who you are?

 Read Galatians 2:11–21.

¹¹When Peter came to Antioch, I opposed him to his face, because he was clearly in the wrong. ¹²Before certain men came from James, he used to eat with the Gentiles. But when they arrived, he began to draw back and separate himself from the Gentiles because he was afraid of those who belonged to the circumcision group. ¹³The other Jews joined him in his hypocrisy, so that by their hypocrisy even Barnabas was led astray.

¹⁴When I saw that they were not acting in line with the truth of the gospel, I said to Peter in front of them all, "You are a Jew, yet you live like a Gentile and not like a Jew. How is it, then, that you force Gentiles to follow Jewish customs?

¹⁵"We who are Jews by birth and not 'Gentile sinners' ¹⁶know that a man is not justified by observing the law, but by faith in Jesus Christ. So we, too, have put our faith in Christ Jesus that we may be justified by faith in Christ and not by observing the law, because by observing the law no one will be justified.

¹⁷"If, while we seek to be justified in Christ, it becomes evident that we ourselves are sinners, does that mean that Christ promotes sin? Absolutely not! ¹⁸If I rebuild what I destroyed, I prove that I am a lawbreaker. ¹⁹For through the law I died to the law so that I might live for God. ²⁰I have been crucified with Christ and I no longer live, but Christ lives in me. The life I live in the body, I live by faith in the Son of God, who loved me and gave himself for me. ²¹I do not set aside the grace of God, for if righteousness could be gained through the law, Christ died for nothing!"ⱼ

ⱼ21 Some interpreters end the quotation after verse 14.

 Discovering the Word 1. How were Peter and the other Jews not "acting in line with the truth of the gospel" (vv. 11–14)? 2. How might their actions have forced "Gentiles to follow Jewish customs" (v. 14)? 3. Why is it wrong to make such customs a basis for fellowship (vv. 15–16)? 4. How does Paul refute the accusation that Christ promotes sin (vv. 17–19)? 5. How has Christ enabled us to die to the law and to live for God (v. 20)?

Applying the Word 1. What nonessential customs do Christians sometimes force on each other? (For example, certain ways of praying, certain dress at worship, certain lifestyle habits and so on.) 2. Which of these are you most likely to be concerned about? 3. How can God's acceptance of you help you to be more accepting of others?

Responding in Prayer Pray for discernment about your own attitudes toward others, asking God to make you more accepting.

4 / *Galatians 3:1–14*
Why God Accepts Us

WE ALL WANT to be accepted. We do everything we can to win people's approval and avoid their rejection. But if we work so hard to please people, then what about God? How can we possibly meet his standards? The Galatians felt these inner struggles. They wanted to be fully accepted by God. But they seemed to forget that God had already accepted them. They also forgot *why*.

 Warming Up to God When have you felt unacceptable to God recently? Describe your feelings to God. Listen for his reassurance.

 Read Galatians 3:1–14.

3 You foolish Galatians! Who has bewitched you? Before your very eyes Jesus Christ was clearly portrayed as crucified. [2]I would like to learn just one thing from you: Did you receive the Spirit by observing the law, or by believing what you heard? [3]Are you so foolish? After beginning with the Spirit, are you now trying to attain your goal by human effort? [4]Have you suffered so much for nothing—if it really was for nothing? [5]Does God give you his Spirit and work miracles among you because you observe the law, or because you believe what you heard?

[6]Consider Abraham: "He believed God, and it was credited to him as righteousness."[g] [7]Understand, then, that those who believe are children of Abraham. [8]The Scripture foresaw that God would justify the Gentiles by faith, and announced the gospel in advance to Abraham: "All nations will be blessed through you."[h] [9]So those who have faith are blessed along with Abraham, the man of faith.

[10]All who rely on observing the law are under a curse, for it is written: "Cursed is everyone who does not continue to do everything written in the Book of the Law."[i] [11]Clearly no one is justified before God by the law, because, "The righteous will live by faith."[j] [12]The law is not based on faith; on the contrary, "The man who does these things will live by them."[k] [13]Christ redeemed us from the curse of the law by becoming a curse for us, for it is written: "Cursed is everyone who is hung on a tree."[l] [14]He redeemed us in order that the blessing given to Abraham might come to the Gentiles through Christ Jesus, so that by faith we might receive the promise of the Spirit.

g6 Gen. 15:6   h8 Gen. 12:3; 18:18; 22:18   i10 Deut. 27:26
j11 Hab. 2:4   k12 Lev. 18:5   l13 Deut. 21:23

 Discovering the Word 1. From verses 1–5 try to reconstruct in chronological order the Galatians' spiritual biography. 2. In what ways did the Galatians' behavior seem "bewitched" and "foolish" according to verses 1–5? 3. When we follow the example of Abraham's faith, what are the results (vv. 6–9)? 4. How does Abraham's experience contrast with that of the person who seeks to earn God's acceptance (vv. 10–12)? 5. How does the gift of the Spirit affirm that God accepts us completely in Christ?

Applying the Word 1. In what ways do we sometimes try to earn God's favor by what we do? 2. How can a vivid image of Christ's crucifixion (v. 1) guard us from this warped way of thinking? 3. How have you been blessed by the Spirit's presence in your life?

Responding in Prayer Spend some time thanking God for what Christ has done for us as described in these verses.

5 / *Galatians 3:15–29*
Exposing Our Needs

"HONEY," JILL CALLED out, "you'd better call the repairman. Our TV is on the blink again."

"Who needs a repairman!" Ron replied confidently. "I can fix this myself."

Four hours later. "There, that should do it." As he plugs it in, there's a loud buzzing noise, smoke rises from the TV, the lights begin to flicker, then darkness blacks out the room.

"Uh . . . maybe you're right, dear," Ron said sheepishly. "I suppose calling a repairman couldn't hurt."

People must admit they need help before they can receive it. Yet often this is very difficult. In Galatians 3:15–29 Paul tells us how God exposes our need for Christ.

 Warming Up to God What needs are pressing on you right now? Give them to God one by one.

 Read Galatians 3:15–29.

15Brothers, let me take an example from everyday life. Just as no one can set aside or add to a human covenant that has been duly established, so it is in this case. 16The promises were spoken to Abraham and to his seed. The Scripture does not say "and to seeds," meaning many people, but "and to your seed,"ᵐ meaning one person, who is Christ. 17What I mean is this: The law, introduced 430 years later, does not set aside the covenant previously established by God and thus do away with the promise. 18For if the inheritance depends on the law, then it no longer depends on a promise; but God in his grace gave it to Abraham through a promise.

19What, then, was the purpose of the law? It was added because of transgressions until the Seed to whom the promise referred had come. The law was put into effect through angels by a mediator. 20A mediator, however, does not represent just one party; but God is one.

21Is the law, therefore, opposed to the promises of God? Absolutely not! For if a law had been given that could impart life, then righteousness would certainly have come by the law. 22But the Scripture declares that the whole world is a prisoner of sin, so that what was promised, being given through faith in Jesus Christ, might be given to those who believe.

23Before this faith came, we were held prisoners by the law, locked up until faith should be revealed. 24So the law was put in charge to lead us to Christⁿ that we might be justified by faith. 25Now that faith has come, we are no longer under the supervision of the law.

26You are all sons of God through faith in Christ Jesus, 27for all of you who were baptized into Christ have clothed yourselves with Christ. 28There is neither Jew nor Greek, slave nor free, male nor female, for you are all one in Christ Jesus. 29If you belong to Christ, then you are Abraham's seed, and heirs according to the promise.

ᵐ16 Gen. 12:7; 13:15; 24:7   ⁿ24 Or *charge until Christ came*

 Discovering the Word 1. Why is the law unable to set aside or add to the promises spoken to Abraham (vv. 15–18)? 2. If the law did not set aside or add to the promises given to Abraham, then why was it given (vv. 19–25)? 3. How does a clear grasp of God's law help us to realize our need for Christ (vv. 22–25)? 4. In verse 28 Paul lists several ways in which people have been categorized. How have these categories sometimes functioned as barriers? 5. In light of the context, how have these barriers been broken down in Christ?

Applying the Word 1. When is it difficult for you to admit to God that you have a need or problem? 2. When is it difficult for you to ask others for help? 3. What would help you allow both God and others to help you?

Responding in Prayer Ask God to help you put aside your pride and expose your needs to him and to your Christian friends and church family.

6 / Galatians 4:1–20
The Joys of Growing Up

HAVE YOU EVER longed to be a child again—to be free from work, mortgage payments, bills and taxes? Remember the carefree days, when from morning till night your job was to play? The Galatians did. They longed to return to the spiritual childhood of the law. But aren't we forgetting something? Just think of all the things we *couldn't* do as children. In Galatians 4:1–20 Paul reminds us of the joys of growing up.

 Warming Up to God What is frustrating you today? Take time to journal or talk to God about how you are feeling and why. Work at it until your mind is clear and you are ready to study.

 Read Galatians 4:1–20.

4 What I am saying is that as long as the heir is a child, he is no different from a slave, although he owns the whole estate. ²He is subject to guardians and trustees until the time set by his father. ³So also, when we were children, we were in slavery under the basic principles of the world. ⁴But when the time had fully come, God sent his Son, born of a woman, born under law, ⁵to redeem those under law, that we might receive the full rights of sons. ⁶Because you are sons, God sent the Spirit of his Son into our hearts, the Spirit who calls out, *"Abba,ᵒ* Father." ⁷So you are no longer a slave, but a son; and since you are a son, God has made you also an heir.

⁸Formerly, when you did not know God, you were slaves to those who by nature are not gods. ⁹But now that you know God—or rather are known by God—how is it that you are turning back to those weak and miserable principles? Do you wish to be enslaved by them all over again? ¹⁰You are observing special days and months and seasons and years! ¹¹I fear for you, that somehow I have wasted my efforts on you.

¹²I plead with you, brothers, become like me, for I became like you. You have done me no wrong. ¹³As you know, it was because of an illness that I first preached the gospel to you. ¹⁴Even though my illness was a trial to you, you did not treat me with contempt or scorn. Instead, you welcomed me as if I were an angel of God, as if I were Christ Jesus himself. ¹⁵What has happened to all your joy? I can testify that, if you could have done so, you would have torn out your eyes and given them to me. ¹⁶Have I now become your enemy by telling you the truth?

¹⁷Those people are zealous to win you over, but for no good. What they want is to alienate you ⌐from us⌐, so that you may be zealous for them. ¹⁸It is fine to be zealous, provided the purpose is good, and to be so always and not just when I am with you. ¹⁹My dear children, for whom I am again in the pains of childbirth until Christ is formed in you, ²⁰how I wish I could be with you now and change my tone, because I am perplexed about you!

ᵒ6 Aramaic for *Father*

 Discovering the Word 1. How was life under the law like spiritual childhood (vv. 3–7)? 2. Verse 4 states, "When the time had fully come, God sent his Son." How did things change because of his coming (vv. 4–7)? 3. In view of Paul's discussion in verses 1–7, how does the Galatians' behavior seem incredible (vv. 8–11)? 4. How and why had the Galatians' attitude toward Paul changed (vv. 12–20)? 5. What do these verses reveal about Paul's feelings toward the Galatians? 6. How do verses 12–20 illustrate the care and concern we should have for other members of God's family?

 Applying the Word 1. In what ways do you sometimes act like a spiritual slave? 2. How can you begin acting more like God's beloved son or daughter?

Responding in Prayer Spend a few minutes of intimate prayer with the Father, thanking him for the privileges of being a member of his family.

7 / *Galatians 4:21—5:1*
Do-It-Yourself Religion

TRUSTING GOD CAN seem risky. What if he lets us down? Still worse, what if our faith is simply foolishness? When such thoughts enter our minds, it's easy to panic. We are tempted to take back what we have entrusted to God. We feel safer taking matters into our own hands. Abraham felt these struggles while waiting for God's promise of a son. He rushed God's plan and had a son through his slave Hagar. Later, even though he and Sarah were very old, the promised son was born. This story has become a timeless illustration of do-it-yourself religion versus trust in the promises of God.

 Warming Up to God What promises has God kept with you? Spend time in reflection, thanksgiving and worship.

 Read Galatians 4:21—5:1.

21Tell me, you who want to be under the law, are you not aware of what the law says? 22For it is written that Abraham had two sons, one by the slave woman and the other by the free woman. 23His son by the slave woman was born in the ordinary way; but his son by the free woman was born as the result of a promise.

24These things may be taken figuratively, for the women represent two covenants. One covenant is from Mount Sinai and bears children who are to be slaves: This is Hagar. 25Now Hagar stands for Mount Sinai in Arabia and corresponds to the present city of Jerusalem, because she is in slavery with her children. 26But the Jerusalem that is above is free, and she is our mother. 27For it is written:

"Be glad, O barren woman,
  who bears no children;
break forth and cry aloud,

you who have no labor pains;
because more are the children of the desolate
    woman
  than of her who has a husband."*p*

28Now you, brothers, like Isaac, are children of promise. 29At that time the son born in the ordinary way persecuted the son born by the power of the Spirit. It is the same now. 30But what does the Scripture say? "Get rid of the slave woman and her son, for the slave woman's son will never share in the inheritance with the free woman's son."*q* 31Therefore, brothers, we are not children of the slave woman, but of the free woman.

5 It is for freedom that Christ has set us free. Stand firm, then, and do not let yourselves be burdened again by a yoke of slavery.

P27 Isaiah 54:1   430 Gen. 21:10

 Discovering the Word 1. What does Paul mean when he says that the son of the slave woman was born the "ordinary way" but the son of the free woman was "the result of a promise" (v. 23; see also v. 29)? 2. In verse 24 Paul says that the story of Hagar and Sarah may be understood "figuratively." What do Hagar, the covenant from Sinai and "the present city of Jerusalem" have in common (vv. 24–25)? 3. How is Sarah (who, although unnamed, is the other woman in the story) similar to the new covenant and to the Jerusalem that is above (vv. 26–27)? 4. How does Paul describe the ultimate fate of the slave woman's and the free woman's spiritual descendants (v. 30)? 5. In 5:1 Paul states that Christ set us free so that we could experience freedom! Given the thrust of Galatians 1—4, what does Paul mean when he says we are free?

Applying the Word 1. The spiritual principle described in this passage has broad application. Throughout Scripture God promises to accomplish that which we cannot do on our own. Think of Abraham, Moses, Joshua, Gideon, the apostles and others. In what areas are you trusting in the promises of God and the power of the Spirit to accomplish the extraordinary? 2. What are some present-day threats to our spiritual freedom? 3. What are some practical ways we can "stand firm" against them?

Responding in Prayer Ask God to help you stand against any threat to spiritual freedom in society and in your life.

8 / *Galatians 5:2–15*
Heavenly Help

"HELP!" THE MAN cried as he dangled helplessly from the edge of a cliff. "Can anyone up there help me?"
"Yes," answered a heavenly voice, "I'll help you. But first you must let go."
"Let go!" gasped the man. "But then I'd fall!"
"I'll catch you," replied the voice.
There was a long pause, then the man cried out, "Can anyone *else* up there help me?"
If we want Christ to save us, we must let go of the idea that we can save ourselves—even a little.

 Warming Up to God In what area of your life are you ignoring the help that God is offering? Humble yourself before the Lord as you give him this area of concern.

 Read Galatians 5:2–15.

²Mark my words! I, Paul, tell you that if you let yourselves be circumcised, Christ will be of no value to you at all. ³Again I declare to every man who lets himself be circumcised that he is obligated to obey the whole law. ⁴You who are trying to be justified by law have been alienated from Christ; you have fallen away from grace. ⁵But by faith we eagerly await through the Spirit the righteousness for which we hope. ⁶For in Christ Jesus neither circumcision nor uncircumcision has any value. The only thing that counts is faith expressing itself through love.

⁷You were running a good race. Who cut in on you and kept you from obeying the truth? ⁸That kind of persuasion does not come from the one who calls you. ⁹"A little yeast works through the whole batch of dough." ¹⁰I am confident in the Lord that you will take no other view. The one who is throwing you into confusion will pay the penalty, whoever he may be. ¹¹Brothers, if I am still preaching circumcision, why am I still being persecuted? In that case the offense of the cross has been abolished. ¹²As for those agitators, I wish they would go the whole way and emasculate themselves!

¹³You, my brothers, were called to be free. But do not use your freedom to indulge the sinful nature*ʳ*; rather, serve one another in love. ¹⁴The entire law is summed up in a single command: "Love your neighbor as yourself."*ˢ* ¹⁵If you keep on biting and devouring each other, watch out or you will be destroyed by each other.

ʳ13 Or *the flesh*; also in verses 16, 17, 19 and 24   *ˢ14* Lev. 19:18

 Discovering the Word 1. What were the Judaizers (those preaching against Paul) urging the Galatians to do and why (vv. 2–4)? 2. In verses 2–4 Paul gave stern warnings to those who desired to be circumcised. Now he says, "neither circumcision nor uncircumcision has any value" (v. 6). How can both of these views be true? 3. Paul compares the Galatians to runners in a race and to a batch of dough (vv. 7–9). How do these comparisons illustrate the nature and perils of the Christian life? 4. In verses 10–12 Paul makes some severe statements about those who are troubling the Galatians (especially v. 12!). Even by today's standards they are harsh. Why was he so upset? 5. What is the difference between the two concepts of freedom described in verses 13–14?

Applying the Word 1. Are you running the good race? In what area do you need to ask God to help you stay on track? 2. When have you "cut in on" someone and kept them from "obeying the truth" (v. 7)? 3. How can you encourage someone you know to stay in the race?

Responding in Prayer Ask God to help you be both a good runner and a good companion in the race.

9 / *Galatians 5:16–26*
Living by the Spirit

IF CHRIST HAS set us free, then why not live as we please? Why not grab all the money, sex and power we can get? Afterward, we can simply ask for forgiveness! Paul challenges this kind of thinking with the true meaning of Christian freedom.

 Warming Up to God Spend some time in quiet before the Lord, opening yourself to what he wants to say to you in prayer and through the Scripture.

 Read Galatians 5:16–26.

16So I say, live by the Spirit, and you will not gratify the desires of the sinful nature. 17For the sinful nature desires what is contrary to the Spirit, and the Spirit what is contrary to the sinful nature. They are in conflict with each other, so that you do not do what you want. 18But if you are led by the Spirit, you are not under law.

19The acts of the sinful nature are obvious: sexual immorality, impurity and debauchery; 20idolatry and witchcraft; hatred, discord, jealousy, fits of rage, selfish ambition, dissensions, factions 21and envy; drunkenness, orgies, and the like. I warn you, as I did before, that those who live like this will not inherit the kingdom of God.

22But the fruit of the Spirit is love, joy, peace, patience, kindness, goodness, faithfulness, 23gentleness and self-control. Against such things there is no law. 24Those who belong to Christ Jesus have crucified the sinful nature with its passions and desires. 25Since we live by the Spirit, let us keep in step with the Spirit. 26Let us not become conceited, provoking and envying each other.

 Discovering the Word 1. What does it mean to "live by the Spirit" (v. 16)? 2. How is being led by the Spirit different from living under law (v. 18)? 3. Why is it so easy to recognize the acts of the sinful nature (vv. 19–21)? 4. How can Paul's warning in verse 21 be reconciled with his emphasis on justification by faith? 5. Why is *fruit* a good description of the Spirit's work in us (vv. 22–23)?

Applying the Word 1. Paul assumes that even though all Christians live by the Spirit, we do not always keep in step with the Spirit (vv. 25–26). In what ways do you struggle to keep in step with the Spirit? 2. In what ways do you see the Spirit's fruit ripening in your life? 3. What fruit would you like to cultivate more?

Responding in Prayer Spend time thanking God for the Spirit's work in your life. Pray for the Spirit's help in those areas where you feel out of step.

---

10 / *Galatians 6:1–10*
The Law of Love

THE FRUIT OF the Spirit is most clearly demonstrated in our relationships with others. They are a visible and practical measure of our spirituality. In this passage Paul describes how we should relate to the family of believers and to all people.

 Warming Up to God This is a passage about relationships. Who are you having difficulty loving right now? Talk to God about it.

 Read Galatians 6:1–10.

6 Brothers, if someone is caught in a sin, you who are spiritual should restore him gently. But watch yourself, or you also may be tempted. ²Carry each other's burdens, and in this way you will fulfill the law of Christ. ³If anyone thinks he is something when he is nothing, he deceives himself. ⁴Each one should test his own actions. Then he can take pride in himself, without comparing himself to somebody else, ⁵for each one should carry his own load.

⁶Anyone who receives instruction in the word must share all good things with his instructor.

⁷Do not be deceived: God cannot be mocked. A man reaps what he sows. ⁸The one who sows to please his sinful nature, from that nature' will reap destruction; the one who sows to please the Spirit, from the Spirit will reap eternal life. ⁹Let us not become weary in doing good, for at the proper time we will reap a harvest if we do not give up. ¹⁰Therefore, as we have opportunity, let us do good to all people, especially to those who belong to the family of believers.

⁸ Or his flesh, from the flesh

 Discovering the Word 1. What guidelines does Paul offer for dealing with a person who is "caught in a sin," and why is each important (v. 1)? 2. How does the law of Christ (v. 2) differ from the kind of law-keeping urged by Paul's opponents? 3. The sins or burdens of others can lead us to feel superior. How can proper methods of self-examination correct this attitude (vv. 3–5)? 4. What other application of the principle of sowing and reaping does Paul make in verses 9 and 10?

Applying the Word 1. What burdens are people you know carrying? 2. What are some ways you can help a friend carry these? 3. What are one or two new ways you could begin sowing to please the Spirit (a) personally, (b) in relationships with other Christians and (c) in relationships with non-Christians?

Responding in Prayer Ask God to help you "do good to all people," especially to those in the family of God.

---

11 / *Galatians 6:11–18*
Getting Motivated

PEER PRESSURE CAN exert a powerful influence on us. The style of our clothes, the kind of music we listen to, our vocabulary, even the soft drinks we buy are affected by what others do and say. We are often tempted to change our behavior so others will accept us. But such approval can have a high price tag. In this final passage Paul helps us to consider whose approval we desire most.

 Warming Up to God In what areas are you feeling cultural pressure? Consider work, family, Christian and non-Christian friendships, how you dress, what you do or don't buy and so on. Bring each of these pressures to God.

Read Galatians 6:11–18.

---

¹¹See what large letters I use as I write to you with my own hand!

¹²Those who want to make a good impression outwardly are trying to compel you to be circumcised. The only reason they do this is to avoid being persecuted for the cross of Christ. ¹³Not even those who are circumcised obey the law, yet they want you to be circumcised that they may boast about your flesh. ¹⁴May I never boast except

in the cross of our Lord Jesus Christ, through which" the world has been crucified to me, and I to the world. ¹⁵Neither circumcision nor uncircumcision means anything; what counts is a new creation. ¹⁶Peace and mercy to all who follow this rule, even to the Israel of God.

" 14 Or whom

¹⁷Finally, let no one cause me trouble, for I bear on my body the marks of Jesus.

¹⁸The grace of our Lord Jesus Christ be with your spirit, brothers. Amen.

 Discovering the Word   1. What do verses 12–13 reveal about the motives of Paul's opponents?   2. How will boasting in the cross affect our desire for the world's approval (v. 14)?   3. Why does the new creation have value in contrast to the worthlessness of circumcision or uncircumcision (v. 15)?   4. In Paul's closing blessing and benediction he mentions peace, mercy and the grace of our Lord Jesus Christ (vv. 16, 18). Why is each of these appropriate for those who follow the "rule" of verses 14–15?

Applying the Word   1. In what situations are you tempted to hide your Christianity in order to "make a good impression outwardly"?   2. Paul bore on his body the marks of Jesus (the evidence of faithful service). What are the "marks of Jesus" in your life?   3. How has this passage helped to purify your motives and goals in life?

Responding in Prayer   Ask God to make the "marks of Jesus" more evident in your life.

Ephesians

L et's face it. Most of us are problem centered. How will I get all my work done on time? What can I do to be a better witness? Why do I get angry so easily?

Solving all these problems is good. But so often we lack a broader perspective. We put Band-Aids over gaping wounds instead of looking for long-term solutions. We lack vision, so we fail to ask why we are involved in certain activities at all.

I have enjoyed going back again and again to Paul's letter to the Ephesians because it communicates the Christian vision more powerfully and succinctly than any of his other letters. Most of Paul's other letters are directed to the particular problems of a given church. For example, he wrote to the Galatians about the threat of legalism. He addressed a variety of problems at the church at Corinth. But his letter to the Ephesians is blissfully free from turmoil.

Some believe the letter has this quality because it was not written solely for the church at Ephesus. Rather, it was probably a circular letter sent to the Christian communities of Asia and other provinces, especially where Paul was not personally known. While most of his letters are full of personal greetings, no individuals are mentioned here or greeted by name. In fact some early manuscripts even lack the words "in Ephesus" (1:1). They are addressed generally "to the saints who are also faithful in Christ Jesus." But at an early date the letter became associated with the Ephesian church, so most later manuscripts have "to the saints in Ephesus, the faithful in Christ Jesus."

Ultimately, however, this letter is written to us, whoever the original readers were. It enables us to see the full sweep of God's program from before creation to the ultimate union of everyone and everything in Jesus Christ. It puts our problems and our entire lives in the context of eternity.

May Ephesians expand your vision of what God is doing in history and give you wholeness in this broken world.

Outline

1/ Ephesians 1:1–14 ———————— *The Purpose of God*

2/ Ephesians 1:15–23 ———————— *"I Keep Asking"*

3/ Ephesians 2:1–10 —————————— *Amazing Grace*

4/ Ephesians 2:11–22 —————————— *We Are One*

5/ Ephesians 3 —————————— *Prisoner and Preacher*

6/ Ephesians 4:1–16 —————————— *Unity and Uniqueness*

7/ Ephesians 4:17–32 —————————— *Something Old, Something New*

8/ Ephesians 5:1–20 —————————— *Live in Love, Live in Light*

9/ Ephesians 5:21–33 —————————— *Wives and Husbands*

10/ Ephesians 6:1–9 —————————— *Children, Parents, Slaves, Masters*

11/ Ephesians 6:10–24 —————————— *Prayer Wars*

1 / *Ephesians 1:1–14*
The Purpose of God

WE HAVE A love-hate relationship with God's will. We dearly want to discover it and obey it, to be secure in knowing we are following the path he desires. On the other hand, we definitely don't want to find out what he wants, because deep down we suspect it may not be to our liking. In this study, we'll see what Paul says about God's will.

 Warming Up to God Reflect on the ways that God has revealed his will to you over the course of your life. What patterns do you see? Thank God for his guidance.

 Read Ephesians 1:1–14.

1 Paul, an apostle of Christ Jesus by the will of God,

To the saints in Ephesus,[a] the faithful[b] in Christ Jesus:

²Grace and peace to you from God our Father and the Lord Jesus Christ.

³Praise be to the God and Father of our Lord Jesus Christ, who has blessed us in the heavenly realms with every spiritual blessing in Christ. ⁴For he chose us in him before the creation of the world to be holy and blameless in his sight. In love ⁵he[c] predestined us to be adopted as his sons through Jesus Christ, in accordance with his pleasure and will— ⁶to the praise of his glorious grace, which he has freely given us in the One he loves. ⁷In him we have redemption through his blood, the forgiveness of sins, in accordance with the riches of God's grace ⁸that he lavished on us with all wisdom and understanding. ⁹And he[d] made known to us the mystery of his will according to his good pleasure, which he purposed in Christ, ¹⁰to be put into effect when the times will have reached their fulfillment—to bring all things in heaven and on earth together under one head, even Christ.

¹¹In him we were also chosen,[e] having been predestined according to the plan of him who works out everything in conformity with the purpose of his will, ¹²in order that we, who were the first to hope in Christ, might be for the praise of his glory. ¹³And you also were included in Christ when you heard the word of truth, the gospel of your salvation. Having believed, you were marked in him with a seal, the promised Holy Spirit, ¹⁴who is a deposit guaranteeing our inheritance until the redemption of those who are God's possession—to the praise of his glory.

ᵃ1 Some early manuscripts do not have in Ephesus.   ᵇ1 Or believers who are   ᶜ4,5 Or sight in love. ⁵He   ᵈ8,9 Or us. With all wisdom and understanding, ⁹he   ᵉ11 Or were made heirs

 Discovering the Word 1. According to verses 3–6, what blessings are ours from the Father? 2. What other blessings, according to verses 7–12, do we have in Jesus Christ? 3. From the information given in 1:1–14 alone, try to formulate a clear statement of what it means to be chosen by God. 4. What additional blessings do we receive through the Holy Spirit (vv. 13–14)? 5. What does it mean to live "to the praise of his glory" (vv. 6, 12, 14)?

Applying the Word 1. How do you respond emotionally to knowing you are chosen by God? 2. How has this passage increased your sense of participation in God's total purpose for the universe? 3. How could your life be more in keeping with the phrase "to the praise of his glory"?

Responding in Prayer Spend time in praise to the God and Father of our Lord Jesus Christ who has blessed us with every spiritual blessing.

2 / *Ephesians 1:15–23*
"I Keep Asking"

SOMETIMES PRAYER CAN be like pushing a full wheelbarrow—with no wheel. At other times it's like rushing down the rapids of a mountain river. What makes the difference? In this passage, we'll see why Paul's prayers overflow with praise and thanksgiving.

 Warming Up to God Talk to God about the times prayer was hard for you. Describe your disappointment or pain. Take time to allow him to listen to you fully.

 Read Ephesians 1:15–23.

¹⁵For this reason, ever since I heard about your faith in the Lord Jesus and your love for all the saints, ¹⁶I have not stopped giving thanks for you, remembering you in my prayers. ¹⁷I keep asking that the God of our Lord Jesus Christ, the glorious Father, may give you the Spirit/ of wisdom and revelation, so that you may know him better. ¹⁸I pray also that the eyes of your heart may be enlightened in order that you may know the hope to which he has called you, the riches of his glorious inheritance in the saints, ¹⁹and his incomparably great power for us who believe. That power is like the working of his mighty strength, ²⁰which he exerted in Christ when he raised him from the dead and seated him at his right hand in the heavenly realms, ²¹far above all rule and authority, power and dominion, and every title that can be given, not only in the present age but also in the one to come. ²²And God placed all things under his feet and appointed him to be head over everything for the church, ²³which is his body, the fullness of him who fills everything in every way.

/17 Or *a spirit*

 Discovering the Word 1. How do Paul's prayers for his readers throughout this passage cover the past, the present and the future? 2. How does Paul emphasize the tremendous power available "for us who believe" (v. 19)? 3. How do verses 20–23 expand on Paul's discussion of Christ's headship begun in verses 9–10? 4. How is the church, the body of believers, central to God's plans for the universe (vv. 22–23)?

Applying the Word 1. When you pray for fellow Christians, how do you usually pray for them? 2. In what ways would you like your prayers to be more like Paul's? 3. How could you make the church a more central part of your life?

Responding in Prayer Pray for Christ's church and individuals in your church, following Paul's example.

3 / *Ephesians 2:1–10*
Amazing Grace

ONE OF THE best-known verses in the book of Ephesians is 2:8, "By grace you have been saved, through faith." Grace has often been defined by the acrostic God's Riches At Christ's Expense. With this passage, we'll consider some of the riches we have been given in Christ.

 Warming Up to God Focus on God's graciousness to you in the past days, weeks and months. Allow yourself to experience the depth of his goodness. Respond to him in prayer and praise.

 Read Ephesians 2:1–10.

2 As for you, you were dead in your transgressions and sins, ²in which you used to live when you followed the ways of this world and of the ruler of the kingdom of the air, the spirit who is now at work in those who are disobedient. ³All of us also lived among them at one time, gratifying the cravings of our sinful nature⁸ and following its desires and thoughts. Like the rest, we were by nature objects of wrath. ⁴But because of his great love for us, God, who is rich in mercy, ⁵made us alive with Christ even when we were dead in transgressions—it is by grace you have been saved. ⁶And God raised us up with Christ and seated us with him in the heavenly realms in Christ Jesus, ⁷in order that in the coming ages he might show the incomparable riches of his grace, expressed in his kindness to us in Christ Jesus. ⁸For it is by grace you have been saved, through faith—and this not from yourselves, it is the gift of God— ⁹not by works, so that no one can boast. ¹⁰For we are God's workmanship, created in Christ Jesus to do good works, which God prepared in advance for us to do.

⁸3 Or *our flesh*

 Discovering the Word 1. In verse 1 Paul says, "You were dead in your transgressions and sins." How does sin kill? 2. In verses 2–3 Paul mentions three negative influences on our lives, which the church later put into the formula of "the world, the flesh and the devil." According to Paul, how did each of these affect our lives as non-Christians? 3. What does Paul mean when he says we have been "made alive," "raised" and "seated" with Christ (vv. 5–6)? 4. When Paul says that our salvation is not from ourselves (vv. 8–9), is he saying that we play no role in our salvation? Explain. 5. What do you learn about God's grace from verses 4–10?

 Applying the Word 1. What good works has God prepared you to do? 2. What has hindered you from doing these?

Responding in Prayer Thank God specifically for some of the many ways he has been gracious to you. Ask him to remove the barriers to the good works he has created for you to do.

---

4 / *Ephesians 2:11–22*
We Are One

MANY OF US have sung, "We are one in the Spirit; we are one in the Lord." But we also continue to find ourselves at odds with Christians who believe or live differently than we do. Such problems were just as common in Paul's day as in ours.

 Warming Up to God Consider what groups of Christians you disagree with or have trouble getting along with. Reflect on what causes these tensions. Ask God to open your mind and heart so that you can develop understanding.

Read Ephesians 2:11–22.

---

¹¹Therefore, remember that formerly you who are Gentiles by birth and called "uncircumcised" by those who call themselves "the circumcision" (that done in the body by the hands of men)— ¹²remember that at that time you were separate from Christ, excluded from citizenship in Israel and foreigners to the covenants of the promise, without hope and without God in the world. ¹³But now in Christ Jesus you who once were far away have been brought near through the blood of Christ.

¹⁴For he himself is our peace, who has made the two one and has destroyed the barrier, the dividing wall of hostility, ¹⁵by abolishing in his flesh the law with its commandments and regulations. His purpose was to create in himself one new man out of the two, thus making peace, ¹⁶and in this one body to reconcile both of them

to God through the cross, by which he put to death their hostility. ¹⁷He came and preached peace to you who were far away and peace to those who were near. ¹⁸For through him we both have access to the Father by one Spirit.

¹⁹Consequently, you are no longer foreigners and aliens, but fellow citizens with God's people and members of God's household, ²⁰built on the foundation of the apostles and prophets, with Christ Jesus himself as the chief cornerstone. ²¹In him the whole building is joined together and rises to become a holy temple in the Lord. ²²And in him you too are being built together to become a dwelling in which God lives by his Spirit.

Discovering the Word   1. Paul uses vivid imagery in this passage. What are some of these images?   2. What divided Gentiles from Jews (vv. 11–13)?   3. How are the two reconciliations Christ achieves related (vv. 14–18)?   4. How do the images Paul uses in verses 19–22 emphasize the unity Christians have with one another?

Applying the Word   1. What kinds of name-calling (perhaps even using biblical terms) do Christians in your church engage in?   2. What rules and requirements would you be inclined to enforce (like the law in verse 15) that might hinder people from coming into the kingdom?   3. What practical first step toward unity with another Christian can you take in the next week?

Responding in Prayer   Pray for unity in the church, that people would not be turned away from Christ by Christians who don't get along with each other.

---

5 / *Ephesians 3*
Prisoner and Preacher

WHAT DO YOU think of when you hear the word *church*? A building on the corner? A stuffy group of religious hypocrites? A vibrant fellowship? Paul's special ministry enables him to enlarge our conception of the church. In this passage he clarifies and exalts its place in God's plan.

 Warming Up to God   When have you had a particularly powerful experience in the church? It might have been worship, teaching or fellowship. Reflect on what made it special and thank God for it.

Read Ephesians 3.

---

3 For this reason I, Paul, the prisoner of Christ Jesus for the sake of you Gentiles—

²Surely you have heard about the administration of God's grace that was given to me for you, ³that is, the mystery made known to me by revelation, as I have already written briefly. ⁴In reading this, then, you will be able to understand my insight into the mystery of Christ, ⁵which was not made known to men in other generations as it has now been revealed by the Spirit to God's holy apostles and prophets. ⁶This mystery is that through the gospel the Gentiles are heirs together with Israel, members together of one body, and sharers together in the promise in Christ Jesus.

⁷I became a servant of this gospel by the gift of God's grace given me through the working of his power. ⁸Although I am less than the least of all God's people, this grace was given me: to preach to the Gentiles the unsearchable riches of Christ, ⁹and to make plain to everyone the administration of this mystery, which for ages past was kept hidden in God, who created all things. ¹⁰His intent was that now, through the church, the manifold wisdom of God should be made known to the rulers and authorities in the heavenly realms, ¹¹according to his eternal purpose which he accomplished in Christ Jesus our Lord. ¹²In him and through faith in him we may approach God with freedom and confidence. ¹³I ask you, therefore, not to be discouraged because of my sufferings for you, which are your glory.

¹⁴For this reason I kneel before the Father, ¹⁵from whom his whole family[h] in heaven and on earth derives its name. ¹⁶I pray that out of his glorious riches he may strengthen you with power through his Spirit in your inner being, ¹⁷so that Christ may dwell in your hearts through faith. And I pray that you, being rooted and established in love, ¹⁸may have power, together with all the saints, to grasp how wide and long and high and deep is the love of Christ, ¹⁹and to know this love that surpasses knowledge—that you may be filled to the measure of all the fullness of God.

²⁰Now to him who is able to do immeasurably more than all we ask or imagine, according to his power that is at work within us, ²¹to him be glory in the church and in Christ Jesus throughout all generations, for ever and ever! Amen.

[h] 15 Or whom all fatherhood

Discovering the Word   1. What gifts of God's grace does Paul say he has received (vv. 2–3, 8)?   2. Explain the meaning of the mystery revealed to Paul (vv. 2–6).   3. How is the mystery connected with the ministry given to him (vv. 7–13)?   4. Three times in verses 14–21 Paul mentions "love" and "power." What do we learn about power and love in these verses?   5. How does the benediction in verses 20–21 tie together the main themes that have run through the first three chapters of Ephesians?

Applying the Word   1. What is your attitude toward the church?   2. What about your attitude matches Paul's?   3. What about your attitude would you like to change?

Responding in Prayer   Choose at least one item from Paul's prayer and make it a prayer of your own, for yourself and your church.

---

6 / *Ephesians 4:1–16*
Unity and Uniqueness

WHILE EPHESIANS 1—3 provides a doctrinal foundation, Ephesians 4—6 shows in practical detail how to give glory to God in the church. Paul now considers the quality of life that is demanded of believers individually and in the fellowship of Christ's church.

 Warming Up to God   Ephesians 4:2 reads, "Be completely humble and gentle; be patient, bearing with one another in love." Reflect on these words. Measure your recent behavior against them. Talk to God about what you discover.

 Read Ephesians 4:1–16.

---

4 As a prisoner for the Lord, then, I urge you to live a life worthy of the calling you have received. ²Be completely humble and gentle; be patient, bearing with one another in love. ³Make every effort to keep the unity of the Spirit through the bond of peace. ⁴There is one body and one Spirit—just as you were called to one hope when you were called— ⁵one Lord, one faith, one baptism; ⁶one God and Father of all, who is over all and through all and in all.

⁷But to each one of us grace has been given as Christ apportioned it. ⁸This is why it[i] says:

"When he ascended on high,

he led captives in his train
   and gave gifts to men."[j]

⁹(What does "he ascended" mean except that he also descended to the lower, earthly regions[k]? ¹⁰He who descended is the very one who ascended higher than all the heavens, in order to fill the whole universe.) ¹¹It was he who gave some to be apostles, some to be prophets, some to be evangelists, and some to be pastors and teachers, ¹²to prepare God's people for works of service, so that the body of Christ may be built up ¹³until we all reach unity in the faith and in the knowledge

[i] 8 Or God   [j] 8 Psalm 68:18   [k] 9 Or the depths of the earth

of the Son of God and become mature, attaining to the whole measure of the fullness of Christ.

¹⁴Then we will no longer be infants, tossed back and forth by the waves, and blown here and there by every wind of teaching and by the cunning and craftiness of men in their deceitful scheming. ¹⁵Instead, speaking the truth in love, we will in all things grow up into him who is the Head, that is, Christ. ¹⁶From him the whole body, joined and held together by every supporting ligament, grows and builds itself up in love, as each part does its work.

 Discovering the Word 1. What are the characteristics of a life that is worthy of our calling (vv. 1–3)? 2. Paul says we have one body, one Spirit, one hope, one Lord, one faith, one baptism, and one God and Father of all. How do these seven "ones" contribute to actually living out true unity? 3. In verses 8–10 Christ is compared to a conquering hero whose victory parade fills "the whole universe," from the highest heaven to the lowest earth. He then generously distributes gifts (the spoils of victory) to his loyal followers. What is the nature and purpose of these gifts (vv. 11–13)? 4. How does spiritual infancy differ from spiritual maturity (vv. 14–16)?

 Applying the Word 1. What spiritual gifts do you think you might have? 2. How do they fulfill the purposes described in verses 11–13? 3. In verse 16 Paul says that the body "grows and builds itself up in love, as each part does its work." What steps must you take to more fully work toward this goal?

Responding in Prayer Pray that your spiritual gifts will be used to help others grow in Christ and to build the church.

7 / *Ephesians 4:17–32*
Something Old, Something New

ALREADY AND NOT YET. That's how we experience Christ. Already we have come out of spiritual darkness and into his light. Already we have received his grace and come to know him. But not yet do we live completely the way God wants. We have not yet arrived. Still, Jesus is right beside us on this journey.

 Warming Up to God When have you felt that you were lost in the darkness? What brought you into the light? Spend time praising God for his redemption.

 Read Ephesians 4:17–32.

¹⁷So I tell you this, and insist on it in the Lord, that you must no longer live as the Gentiles do, in the futility of their thinking. ¹⁸They are darkened in their understanding and separated from the life of God because of the ignorance that is in them due to the hardening of their hearts. ¹⁹Having lost all sensitivity, they have given themselves over to sensuality so as to indulge in every kind of impurity, with a continual lust for more.

²⁰You, however, did not come to know Christ that way. ²¹Surely you heard of him and were taught in him in accordance with the truth that is in Jesus. ²²You were taught, with regard to your former way of life, to put off your old self, which is being corrupted by its deceitful desires; ²³to be made new in the attitude of your minds; ²⁴and to put on the new self, created to be like God in true righteousness and holiness.

²⁵Therefore each of you must put off falsehood and speak truthfully to his neighbor, for we are all members of one body. ²⁶"In your anger do not sin"ʲ: Do not let the sun go down while you are still angry, ²⁷and do not give the devil a foothold. ²⁸He who has been stealing must steal no longer, but must work, doing something useful with his own hands, that he may have something to share with those in need.

²⁹Do not let any unwholesome talk come out of your mouths, but only what is helpful for building others up according to their needs, that it may benefit those who listen. ³⁰And do not grieve the

ʲ26 Psalm 4:4

Holy Spirit of God, with whom you were sealed for the day of redemption. ³¹Get rid of all bitterness, rage and anger, brawling and slander, along with every form of malice. ³²Be kind and compassionate to one another, forgiving each other, just as in Christ God forgave you.

Discovering the Word 1. How does Paul contrast the life of the Gentile (unbeliever) with that of a true believer throughout these verses? 2. What are the effects of hard-heartedness (vv. 17–19)? 3. What does it mean to put off the old self (v. 22)? 4. In verses 25–32 what does Paul tell us to put off, what does he say to put on and what reason does he give (or imply) for doing these things?

Applying the Word 1. Which of the commands in verses 25–32 do you have the most difficulty following? Explain. 2. What practical steps could you take this week to improve your relationships with others in this area of difficulty? 3. Which of the commands in verses 25–32 have you seen God strengthen you to obey?

Responding in Prayer Spend time praising God for his work in your life, and pray that he will give you grace in the areas needing improvement.

---

8 / *Ephesians 5:1–20*
Live in Love, Live in Light

NOT DOING WHAT is wrong is one thing. But sometimes it can be even more difficult to do what is right. In Ephesians 5 Paul continues to outline what it means "to live a life worthy of the calling you have received" (4:1). He does this by considering ways we shouldn't act and ways we should.

 Warming Up to God Spend some time singing and making music in your heart to the Lord with "psalms, hymns and spiritual songs" (5:19).

 Read Ephesians 5:1–20.

---

5 Be imitators of God, therefore, as dearly loved children ²and live a life of love, just as Christ loved us and gave himself up for us as a fragrant offering and sacrifice to God.

³But among you there must not be even a hint of sexual immorality, or of any kind of impurity, or of greed, because these are improper for God's holy people. ⁴Nor should there be obscenity, foolish talk or coarse joking, which are out of place, but rather thanksgiving. ⁵For of this you can be sure: No immoral, impure or greedy person— such a man is an idolater—has any inheritance in the kingdom of Christ and of God.ᵐ ⁶Let no one deceive you with empty words, for because of such things God's wrath comes on those who are disobedient. ⁷Therefore do not be partners with them.

⁸For you were once darkness, but now you are light in the Lord. Live as children of light ⁹(for the fruit of the light consists in all goodness, righteousness and truth) ¹⁰and find out what pleases the Lord. ¹¹Have nothing to do with the fruitless deeds of darkness, but rather expose them. ¹²For it is shameful even to mention what the disobedient do in secret. ¹³But everything exposed by the light becomes visible, ¹⁴for it is light that makes everything visible. This is why it is said:

"Wake up, O sleeper,
    rise from the dead,
  and Christ will shine on you."

¹⁵Be very careful, then, how you live—not as unwise but as wise, ¹⁶making the most of every opportunity, because the days are evil. ¹⁷Therefore do not be foolish, but understand what the Lord's will is. ¹⁸Do not get drunk on wine, which leads to debauchery. Instead, be filled with the Spirit. ¹⁹Speak to one another with psalms,

ᵐ5 Or *kingdom of the Christ and God*

hymns and spiritual songs. Sing and make music in your heart to the Lord, [20]always giving thanks to God the Father for everything, in the name of our Lord Jesus Christ.

 Discovering the Word 1. How is Christ the perfect example of what Paul asks of us (v. 2)? 2. How is thanksgiving an appropriate replacement for the behavior Paul condemnns in verses 2–4? 3. Why will immoral, impure or greedy people be unable to inherit the kingdom (vv. 5–7)? 4. In verses 8–14 Paul contrasts light and darkness to say more about holy living. According to these verses, what does it mean to "live as children of light"? 5. Verses 19–20 describe several beneficial results of being filled with the Spirit. In your own words, explain the characteristics of those who are filled with the Spirit.

Applying the Word 1. Look again at verses 1–2. What have you observed about God that you have begun or could begin to imitate? 2. Looking again at verses 3–4, how could you use thanksgiving to replace improper behavior in your life? 3. According to the characteristics in verses 15–17, how could you live more wisely?

Responding in Prayer Talk to God as a child to a father. Tell him how you would like to imitate him.

9 / *Ephesians 5:21–33*
Wives and Husbands

A LOT OF emotion and misunderstanding surrounds the word *submit*. So try to come to this text as if you had never seen it before. Try to set aside your own biases and see what Paul really has to say on the subject of submission.

 Warming Up to God How has God shown you that he is faithful and trustworthy? Express your thanksgiving for his care.

 Read Ephesians 5:21–33.

[21]Submit to one another out of reverence for Christ.

[22]Wives, submit to your husbands as to the Lord. [23]For the husband is the head of the wife as Christ is the head of the church, his body, of which he is the Savior. [24]Now as the church submits to Christ, so also wives should submit to their husbands in everything.

[25]Husbands, love your wives, just as Christ loved the church and gave himself up for her [26]to make her holy, cleansing[n] her by the washing with water through the word, [27]and to present her to himself as a radiant church, without stain or wrinkle or any other blemish, but holy and blameless. [28]In this same way, husbands ought to love their wives as their own bodies. He who loves his wife loves himself. [29]After all, no one ever hated his own body, but he feeds and cares for it, just as Christ does the church— [30]for we are members of his body. [31]"For this reason a man will leave his father and mother and be united to his wife, and the two will become one flesh."[o] [32]This is a profound mystery—but I am talking about Christ and the church. [33]However, each one of you also must love his wife as he loves himself, and the wife must respect her husband.

[n]26 Or *having cleansed*   [o]31 Gen. 2:24

 Discovering the Word 1. How does verse 21 set the tone for this passage? 2. Why is the church's submission to the Lord a helpful illustration of a wife's submission to her husband (vv. 22–24)? 3. How are husbands to show love for their wives (vv. 25–30)? 4. Why do you think Paul calls on wives to respect their

husbands while he calls on husbands to love their wives (v. 33)? 5. How do verses 31–33 summarize his teaching on the unity that is to exist between wives and husbands?

 Applying the Word 1. How do you react to the idea of being told to submit to someone? 2. If you are married, how would you like to grow in your ability to love and submit to your spouse? 3. Whether you are married or single, how would you like to grow in your submission to Christ?

Responding in Prayer Tell Christ how you would like to more fully submit your life to him.

10 / *Ephesians 6:1–9*
Children, Parents, Slaves, Masters

HOW MUCH OUR parents mean to us—yet how difficult they can be! How much we love our children—yet how exasperating they are at times! In nine packed verses Paul delves not only into these important relationships but into those of the work world as well.

 Warming Up to God Reflect on the finest qualities of your parents (or of parenting in general). Consider which of these qualities you have experienced in your relationship with God and thank him.

 Read Ephesians 6:1–9.

6 Children, obey your parents in the Lord, for this is right. ²"Honor your father and mother"—which is the first commandment with a promise— ³"that it may go well with you and that you may enjoy long life on the earth."ᴾ

⁴Fathers, do not exasperate your children; instead, bring them up in the training and instruction of the Lord.

⁵Slaves, obey your earthly masters with respect and fear, and with sincerity of heart, just as you would obey Christ. ⁶Obey them not only to win their favor when their eye is on you, but like slaves of Christ, doing the will of God from your heart. ⁷Serve wholeheartedly, as if you were serving the Lord, not men, ⁸because you know that the Lord will reward everyone for whatever good he does, whether he is slave or free.

⁹And masters, treat your slaves in the same way. Do not threaten them, since you know that he who is both their Master and yours is in heaven, and there is no favoritism with him.

P3 Deut. 5:16

 Discovering the Word 1. What reasons are given for obeying and honoring parents (vv. 1–3)? 2. Why does Paul contrast making children exasperated with bringing "them up in the training and instruction of the Lord" (v. 4)? 3. What is implied about the way slaves normally worked for their masters (vv. 5–8)? 4. Paul says masters should treat slaves the way slaves should treat masters because both have the same Master in heaven. Why should this make a difference in how slaves are treated? 5. How do verses 1–9 contribute to the theme of the church glorifying God through visible unity?

Applying the Word 1. What are some practical ways you can obey or honor your parents? 2. If you are a parent, what can you do this week to follow verse 4 more closely? (If you are not a parent, how have you seen verse 4 in action?) 3. How could the principles Paul considers in verses 5–9 be lived out in situations you have been in or are in?

Responding in Prayer Pray that in all you do you would serve "wholeheartedly, as if you were serving the Lord."

11 / *Ephesians 6:10–24*
Prayer Wars

IN A WAR of bullets, careful aim and heavy armor win battles. In a war of words, eloquent speech and sharp pens overcome the opposition. But if the fight is outside the realm of sight, sound and touch, how are victories won?

 Warming Up to God How have you recently seen God protecting you as you face spiritual battles?

 Read Ephesians 6:10–24.

---

¹⁰Finally, be strong in the Lord and in his mighty power. ¹¹Put on the full armor of God so that you can take your stand against the devil's schemes. ¹²For our struggle is not against flesh and blood, but against the rulers, against the authorities, against the powers of this dark world and against the spiritual forces of evil in the heavenly realms. ¹³Therefore put on the full armor of God, so that when the day of evil comes, you may be able to stand your ground, and after you have done everything, to stand. ¹⁴Stand firm then, with the belt of truth buckled around your waist, with the breastplate of righteousness in place, ¹⁵and with your feet fitted with the readiness that comes from the gospel of peace. ¹⁶In addition to all this, take up the shield of faith, with which you can extinguish all the flaming arrows of the evil one. ¹⁷Take the helmet of salvation and the sword of the Spirit, which is the word of God. ¹⁸And pray in the Spirit on all occasions with all kinds of prayers and requests. With this in mind, be alert and always keep on praying for all the saints.

¹⁹Pray also for me, that whenever I open my mouth, words may be given me so that I will fearlessly make known the mystery of the gospel, ²⁰for which I am an ambassador in chains. Pray that I may declare it fearlessly, as I should.

²¹Tychicus, the dear brother and faithful servant in the Lord, will tell you everything, so that you also may know how I am and what I am doing. ²²I am sending him to you for this very purpose, that you may know how we are, and that he may encourage you.

²³Peace to the brothers, and love with faith from God the Father and the Lord Jesus Christ. ²⁴Grace to all who love our Lord Jesus Christ with an undying love.

 Discovering the Word 1. Four times in verses 10–14 Paul urges his readers to stand firm in the battle against the devil's stratagems. How are we as Christians susceptible to instability? 2. How does the "armor of God" (vv. 13–17) prepare us for spiritual battle? 3. In verses 18–20 Paul urges all kinds of prayers. How has he been a model prayer warrior throughout this letter?

Applying the Word 1. How do you sense a battle around you with more than physical forces and foes? 2. Which piece of armor do you need most to fight your spiritual battles? Explain. 3. What main obstacle do you face in fighting the battle of prayer more effectively?

Responding in Prayer Take time now to pray about your fight in spiritual warfare.

Philippians

"**R**ejoice in the Lord always," the author of Philippians exhorts us, "I will say it again: Rejoice!" Coming from most people, such words might sound trite and simplistic, but this is the apostle Paul speaking, a man who was not writing from a padded-leather office chair surrounded by books on how to be happy. On the contrary, he was a prisoner awaiting news that could result in his death. It isn't hard to get behind the words of Philippians and see the tension and uncertainty there. Yet through all this we see the example of a man whose life is filled with joy.

As we study Philippians, we discover Paul's secret: that a life lived for the glory of God will overflow with joy. What a message for our hurting world!

Philippi was an important city because it straddled the great east-west highway known as the Egnatian Way. The population of this city was cosmopolitan, being made up of Tracians, Greeks, Romans and a few Jews. In the center of the city was a large forum surrounded by temples, a library, fountains, monuments and public baths.

In 42 B.C. Antony and Octavian defeated Brutus and Cassius near Philippi. In honor of his victory, Antony made Philippi a Roman colony. This provided the Philippians with special rights and privileges as Roman citizens, and they responded with a great deal of pride and loyalty. Women enjoyed a high status in Philippi—taking an active part in both public and business life. Because of this, women also had important responsibilities in the Philippian church.

Paul founded this church sometime around the year A.D. 50, during his second missionary journey (Acts 16:12-40). From the letter to the Philippians we learn that this church was taking its share of suffering (1:29), it was in some danger of division (1:27; 2:2; 4:2), it may have been leaning toward a doctrine of perfectionism (3:12-13), and it was threatened by the teaching of Judaizers—a group which insisted that all Christians adhere to Jewish laws and customs. But despite these problems, Paul's love for this church was obvious. He sincerely rejoiced at the progress they were making.

We know that Paul was writing to the Philippians from prison (1:12-14). Unfortunately, it is not clear which prison he was writing from. If he was writing during his imprisonment in Rome, then the letter can be dated sometime between A.D. 61-63. However, many scholars have pointed out that the conditions which Paul describes seem much harsher than what we

know of the Roman imprisonment (Acts 28:16, 30-31). It could be that there was an earlier imprisonment not recorded in Acts. A good case has been made for Ephesus. If this is true, Philippians would have been written about A.D. 54.

Paul had several reasons for writing this letter. He wanted to explain why he was sending a man named Epaphroditus back to Philippi. He also wanted to thank the Philippians for the gift of money they had sent and to reassure his friends of his condition. Also, the news Paul had received concerning the Philippians made him long to encourage and advise a church he loved.

I hope that these quiet times will help you learn and apply Paul's secret to joyful living.

Outline

1/ Philippians 1:1-11 ——————————— A Church Is Born

2/ Philippians 1:12-30 ——————————— A Joyful Imprisonment

3/ Philippians 2:1-18 ——————————— The Path of Humility

4/ Philippians 2:19-30 ——————————— Servants of Christ

5/ Philippians 3 ——————————— Rejoice in the Lord

6/ Philippians 4:1-9 ——————————— Stand Firm in the Lord

7/ Philippians 4:10-23 ——————————— Paul's Thank-You Note

1 / *Philippians 1:1–11*
A Church Is Born

HAVE ANY OF your good friends ever told you what they appreciate about you? Have you ever listened while others prayed for you? If so, you know what a warm feeling it is to be assured that others care. In Philippians 1:1–11 Paul prays and thanks God for his friends in Philippi. As you read the passage, try to imagine yourself sitting with the Philippian Christians as this letter is read for the first time. You might be meeting in the home of Lydia, a Christian businesswoman. Perhaps you would be seated next to the jailer who heard about Christ while guarding Paul and Silas.

 Warming Up to God When has someone encouraged you by praying for you?

 Read Philippians 1:1–11.

1 Paul and Timothy, servants of Christ Jesus,

To all the saints in Christ Jesus at Philippi, together with the overseers*a* and deacons:

²Grace and peace to you from God our Father and the Lord Jesus Christ.

³I thank my God every time I remember you. ⁴In all my prayers for all of you, I always pray with joy ⁵because of your partnership in the gospel from the first day until now, ⁶being confident of this, that he who began a good work in you will carry it on to completion until the day of Christ Jesus.

⁷It is right for me to feel this way about all of you, since I have you in my heart; for whether I am in chains or defending and confirming the gospel, all of you share in God's grace with me. ⁸God can testify how I long for all of you with the affection of Christ Jesus.

⁹And this is my prayer: that your love may abound more and more in knowledge and depth of insight, ¹⁰so that you may be able to discern what is best and may be pure and blameless until the day of Christ, ¹¹filled with the fruit of righteousness that comes through Jesus Christ—to the glory and praise of God.

a 1 Traditionally bishops

 Discovering the Word 1. What are Paul's feelings toward the Philippians (vv. 3–8)? 2. Why does he feel this way about them? 3. What do verses 3–8 reveal about healthy Christian relationships? 4. What are Paul's prayer requests for the Philippians (vv. 9–11)? 5. Why would each of these qualities be essential to spiritual maturity?

 Applying the Word 1. How can your present relationships be strengthened to become more like what is described in verses 3–8? 2. What does Paul's prayer teach about how we should pray for others?

Responding in Prayer Using Paul's prayer as a model, spend a few minutes thanking God and praying for someone you love in Christ.

2 / *Philippians 1:12–30*
A Joyful Imprisonment

IN THIS PASSAGE we discover that Paul is writing to the Philippians from prison. This puts a whole new perspective on the joyful mood of the letter. While Paul is writing, he is experiencing what most of us would describe as awful

circumstances. Yet even at a time like this, Paul's first concern is that Christ is praised. This passage can teach us how to honor Christ in a difficult situation.

 Warming Up to God What people or things in life bring you the greatest joy?

 Read Philippians 1:12–30.

[12]Now I want you to know, brothers, that what has happened to me has really served to advance the gospel. [13]As a result, it has become clear throughout the whole palace guard[b] and to everyone else that I am in chains for Christ. [14]Because of my chains, most of the brothers in the Lord have been encouraged to speak the word of God more courageously and fearlessly.

[15]It is true that some preach Christ out of envy and rivalry, but others out of goodwill. [16]The latter do so in love, knowing that I am put here for the defense of the gospel. [17]The former preach Christ out of selfish ambition, not sincerely, supposing that they can stir up trouble for me while I am in chains.[c] [18]But what does it matter? The important thing is that in every way, whether from false motives or true, Christ is preached. And because of this I rejoice.

Yes, and I will continue to rejoice, [19]for I know that through your prayers and the help given by the Spirit of Jesus Christ, what has happened to me will turn out for my deliverance.[d] [20]I eagerly expect and hope that I will in no way be ashamed, but will have sufficient courage so that now as always Christ will be exalted in my body, whether by life or by death. [21]For to me, to live is Christ

and to die is gain. [22]If I am to go on living in the body, this will mean fruitful labor for me. Yet what shall I choose? I do not know! [23]I am torn between the two: I desire to depart and be with Christ, which is better by far; [24]but it is more necessary for you that I remain in the body. [25]Convinced of this, I know that I will remain, and I will continue with all of you for your progress and joy in the faith, [26]so that through my being with you again your joy in Christ Jesus will overflow on account of me.

[27]Whatever happens, conduct yourselves in a manner worthy of the gospel of Christ. Then, whether I come and see you or only hear about you in my absence, I will know that you stand firm in one spirit, contending as one man for the faith of the gospel [28]without being frightened in any way by those who oppose you. This is a sign to them that they will be destroyed, but that you will be saved—and that by God. [29]For it has been granted to you on behalf of Christ not only to believe on him, but also to suffer for him, [30]since you are going through the same struggle you saw I had, and now hear that I still have.

[b]13 Or *whole palace*   [c]16,17 Some late manuscripts have verses 16 and 17 in reverse order.   [d]19 Or *salvation*

 Discovering the Word 1. What does Paul say has happened as a result of his imprisonment (vv. 12–14)? 2. Compare the motives of the two groups described in verses 15–18. 3. What are Paul's considerations in choosing between life and death (vv. 20–26)? 4. What does it mean to conduct ourselves in a manner worthy of the gospel (vv. 27–30)?

Applying the Word 1. To what extent have you adopted Paul's attitude toward life and death? 2. What are the most difficult circumstances you are presently facing? 3. How can Christ be exalted in that situation?

Responding in Prayer Pray that you would learn to experience the joy that can emerge amidst sorrow.

3 / *Philippians 2:1–18*
The Path of Humility

IS IT POSSIBLE to have a good self-image and still be humble? Can a person want to be the best without being conceited? In Philippians 2:1–18 Paul directs us to Jesus Christ, a person equal with God yet whose incarnation and life are the supreme example of humility. This passage urges us to imitate Christ's attitude.

 Warming Up to God What is the difference between humility and a poor self-image?

 Read Philippians 2:1–18.

2 If you have any encouragement from being united with Christ, if any comfort from his love, if any fellowship with the Spirit, if any tenderness and compassion, ²then make my joy complete by being like-minded, having the same love, being one in spirit and purpose. ³Do nothing out of selfish ambition or vain conceit, but in humility consider others better than yourselves. ⁴Each of you should look not only to your own interests, but also to the interests of others.

⁵Your attitude should be the same as that of Christ Jesus:

⁶Who, being in very nature*ᵉ* God,
did not consider equality with God
something to be grasped,
⁷but made himself nothing,
taking the very nature*ᶠ* of a servant,
being made in human likeness.
⁸And being found in appearance as a man,
he humbled himself
and became obedient to death—
even death on a cross!
⁹Therefore God exalted him to the highest place
and gave him the name that is above every name,
¹⁰that at the name of Jesus every knee should bow,
in heaven and on earth and under the earth,
¹¹and every tongue confess that Jesus Christ is Lord,
to the glory of God the Father.

¹²Therefore, my dear friends, as you have always obeyed—not only in my presence, but now much more in my absence—continue to work out your salvation with fear and trembling, ¹³for it is God who works in you to will and to act according to his good purpose.

¹⁴Do everything without complaining or arguing, ¹⁵so that you may become blameless and pure, children of God without fault in a crooked and depraved generation, in which you shine like stars in the universe ¹⁶as you hold out*ᵍ* the word of life—in order that I may boast on the day of Christ that I did not run or labor for nothing. ¹⁷But even if I am being poured out like a drink offering on the sacrifice and service coming from your faith, I am glad and rejoice with all of you. ¹⁸So you too should be glad and rejoice with me.

ᵉ6 Or in the form of   ᶠ7 Or the form   ᵍ16 Or hold on to

 Discovering the Word 1. How can our experience of Christ and his Spirit (v. 1) help us to achieve the unity Paul desires in verse 2? 2. How do verses 3–4 help us to understand the nature of humility? 3. How did each of Christ's actions illustrate humility and a concern for the interests of others (vv. 6–8)? 4. In your own words, describe God's response to Jesus' humility (vv. 9–11). 5. In verses 12–13 Paul says you are to "work out your salvation" because God "works in you." How are these ideas related?

 Applying the Word 1. Who might you be tempted to impress during the next few days? 2. What act of humble service could you do for this person instead?

Responding in Prayer Pray for the opportunity to serve others as Christ has served you.

4 / *Philippians 2:19–30*
Servants of Christ

WHEN THE PHILIPPIANS heard that Paul was in prison, they sent one of their members—a man named Epaphroditus—to Paul with a gift of money. It was his job to help Paul in any way necessary. Epaphroditus returned home carrying the letter to the Philippians.

In this section of the letter, Paul outlines his future plans and explains why he is sending Epaphroditus back. The passage gives several beautiful examples of Christian service as displayed in the lives of Timothy, Epaphroditus, Paul and the Philippians.

 Warming Up to God What do you enjoy most and least about serving others?

 Read Philippians 2:19–30.

¹⁹I hope in the Lord Jesus to send Timothy to you soon, that I also may be cheered when I receive news about you. ²⁰I have no one else like him, who takes a genuine interest in your welfare. ²¹For everyone looks out for his own interests, not those of Jesus Christ. ²²But you know that Timothy has proved himself, because as a son with his father he has served with me in the work of the gospel. ²³I hope, therefore, to send him as soon as I see how things go with me. ²⁴And I am confident in the Lord that I myself will come soon.

²⁵But I think it is necessary to send back to you Epaphroditus, my brother, fellow worker and fellow soldier, who is also your messenger, whom you sent to take care of my needs. ²⁶For he longs for all of you and is distressed because you heard he was ill. ²⁷Indeed he was ill, and almost died. But God had mercy on him, and not on him only but also on me, to spare me sorrow upon sorrow. ²⁸Therefore I am all the more eager to send him, so that when you see him again you may be glad and I may have less anxiety. ²⁹Welcome him in the Lord with great joy, and honor men like him, ³⁰because he almost died for the work of Christ, risking his life to make up for the help you could not give me.

 Discovering the Word 1. Imagine that Timothy is being sent to visit your church or fellowship group. What might he do to help you? 2. Why is Paul sending Epaphroditus back to Philippi (vv. 25–28)? 3. How is Christ's attitude evident in the relationships among Paul, Epaphroditus and the Philippians (vv. 25–30)? 4. Why is it important to honor people like Epaphroditus, especially in light of Christ's exaltation (2:9–11)?

Applying the Word 1. Examine your plans and goals during the coming week. How can you bring your own interests into closer harmony with those of Jesus Christ? 2. What are some practical ways you can serve those around you during the coming week?

Responding in Prayer Pray that Christ will continue to give you the heart of a servant.

---

5 / *Philippians 3*
Rejoice in the Lord

HAVE YOU EVER become excited about an idea only to be deflated by the realities of making it work? Sometimes trying to live a Christian life is like that. We start off very excited about knowing the Lord, but it isn't long before the pressure of keeping "all the right rules" drains us of our joy. Unfortunately, we can then swing too far in the other direction and decide, "I'm not going to be concerned about Christian conduct. If Jesus has saved me, then it

doesn't matter how I live." This attitude will destroy our joy as quickly as the first. So what is the solution? Paul tells us in this passage.

 Warming Up to God What are some of your most important goals in life?

 Read Philippians 3.

3 Finally, my brothers, rejoice in the Lord! It is no trouble for me to write the same things to you again, and it is a safeguard for you.

²Watch out for those dogs, those men who do evil, those mutilators of the flesh. ³For it is we who are the circumcision, we who worship by the Spirit of God, who glory in Christ Jesus, and who put no confidence in the flesh— ⁴though I myself have reasons for such confidence.

If anyone else thinks he has reasons to put confidence in the flesh, I have more: ⁵circumcised on the eighth day, of the people of Israel, of the tribe of Benjamin, a Hebrew of Hebrews; in regard to the law, a Pharisee; ⁶as for zeal, persecuting the church; as for legalistic righteousness, faultless.

⁷But whatever was to my profit I now consider loss for the sake of Christ. ⁸What is more, I consider everything a loss compared to the surpassing greatness of knowing Christ Jesus my Lord, for whose sake I have lost all things. I consider them rubbish, that I may gain Christ ⁹and be found in him, not having a righteousness of my own that comes from the law, but that which is through faith in Christ—the righteousness that comes from God and is by faith. ¹⁰I want to know Christ and the power of his resurrection and the fellowship of sharing in his sufferings, becoming like him in his death, ¹¹and so, some-

how, to attain to the resurrection from the dead.

¹²Not that I have already obtained all this, or have already been made perfect, but I press on to take hold of that for which Christ Jesus took hold of me. ¹³Brothers, I do not consider myself yet to have taken hold of it. But one thing I do: Forgetting what is behind and straining toward what is ahead, ¹⁴I press on toward the goal to win the prize for which God has called me heavenward in Christ Jesus.

¹⁵All of us who are mature should take such a view of things. And if on some point you think differently, that too God will make clear to you. ¹⁶Only let us live up to what we have already attained.

¹⁷Join with others in following my example, brothers, and take note of those who live according to the pattern we gave you. ¹⁸For, as I have often told you before and now say again even with tears, many live as enemies of the cross of Christ. ¹⁹Their destiny is destruction, their god is their stomach, and their glory is in their shame. Their mind is on earthly things. ²⁰But our citizenship is in heaven. And we eagerly await a Savior from there, the Lord Jesus Christ, ²¹who, by the power that enables him to bring everything under his control, will transform our lowly bodies so that they will be like his glorious body.

 Discovering the Word 1. How does rejoicing in the Lord (v. 1) differ from other reasons for joy? 2. Why were the people Paul warns against in verses 2–3 so dangerous? 3. Contrast Paul the Pharisee (vv. 4–6) with Paul the Christian (vv. 7–11). How have his reasons for confidence changed? 4. In verses 12–14 Paul compares himself to an athlete who is running a race. Why is this such an appropriate description of the Christian life? 5. In verses 17–21 Paul contrasts Christians with "enemies of the cross." What are the concerns and destiny of each group?

Applying the Word 1. Have you ever placed your confidence in something, thinking it would bring you closer to God, that you now consider to be rubbish? Explain. 2. In verse 6 Paul speaks of "legalistic righteousness." What legalisms are today's Christians pressured to keep? 3. How do these legalisms get in the way of knowing Christ and rejoicing in the Lord?

Responding in Prayer Reflect on Paul's words "We eagerly await . . . the Lord Jesus Christ." Worship Christ with your anticipation of his return.

6 / *Philippians 4:1–9*
Stand Firm in the Lord

TAKE A MOMENT to think of the people you care about most. What is your greatest desire for these people? As Paul thinks of the Philippians, his greatest desire is that they will stand firm in what they have been taught. But he is also aware of some problems which may cause their faith to weaken. He writes to warn them that in order to stand firm they must put an end to disagreements, rejoice always and fill their thoughts with good things.

 Warming Up to God Do you find your stand in the Lord to be firmer or weaker than it was a year ago? What has made the difference?

 Read Philippians 4:1–9.

4 Therefore, my brothers, you whom I love and long for, my joy and crown, that is how you should stand firm in the Lord, dear friends!

²I plead with Euodia and I plead with Syntyche to agree with each other in the Lord. ³Yes, and I ask you, loyal yokefellow,*ʰ* help these women who have contended at my side in the cause of the gospel, along with Clement and the rest of my fellow workers, whose names are in the book of life.

⁴Rejoice in the Lord always. I will say it again: Rejoice! ⁵Let your gentleness be evident to all. The Lord is near. ⁶Do not be anxious about any-

thing, but in everything, by prayer and petition, with thanksgiving, present your requests to God. ⁷And the peace of God, which transcends all understanding, will guard your hearts and your minds in Christ Jesus.

⁸Finally, brothers, whatever is true, whatever is noble, whatever is right, whatever is pure, whatever is lovely, whatever is admirable—if anything is excellent or praiseworthy—think about such things. ⁹Whatever you have learned or received or heard from me, or seen in me—put it into practice. And the God of peace will be with you.

ʰ3 Or loyal Syzygus

 Discovering the Word 1. Paul opens this chapter with the statement "that is how you should stand firm in the Lord." Look back at 3:12–21. How are we to stand firm in the Lord? 2. In verse 2 Paul pleads with Euodia and Syntyche "to agree with each other in the Lord." Why do you think he is so concerned about their relationship? 3. How can each of the promises and commands listed in verses 4–7 help you to be joyful, peaceful and free from anxiety? 4. How can improper thoughts rob us of the peace God desires for us? 5. How can true, noble, right, pure, lovely, admirable, excellent or praiseworthy thoughts help to cleanse our minds and restore our tranquility (v. 8)?

 Applying the Word 1. What should be your response to disagreements within your church or fellowship group? 2. In verse 9 Paul tells us that the God of peace will be with us as we practice what we have learned. What have you learned in this passage that you need to put into practice?

Responding in Prayer Ask God to show you the thoughts and attitudes which are robbing you of joy and weakening your faith.

7 / *Philippians 4:10–23*
Paul's Thank-You Note

WE'VE ALL WRITTEN thank-you notes for gifts received for a birthday or for Christmas. Such notes usually include rather conventional phrases about the thankfulness of the recipient and the thoughtfulness of the giver. In Philippians 4 Paul thanks the Philippians for a gift of money they sent. However, it is a most unusual thank-you note. First

he breaks the conventional rules by waiting until the very end of the letter to say thank you. Then he writes as though he didn't really need the gift!

 Warming Up to God Have you thanked God for his many gifts to you lately? Take time to do so before you begin.

 Read Philippians 4:10–23.

---

¹⁰I rejoice greatly in the Lord that at last you have renewed your concern for me. Indeed, you have been concerned, but you had no opportunity to show it. ¹¹I am not saying this because I am in need, for I have learned to be content whatever the circumstances. ¹²I know what it is to be in need, and I know what it is to have plenty. I have learned the secret of being content in any and every situation, whether well fed or hungry, whether living in plenty or in want. ¹³I can do everything through him who gives me strength.

¹⁴Yet it was good of you to share in my troubles. ¹⁵Moreover, as you Philippians know, in the early days of your acquaintance with the gospel, when I set out from Macedonia, not one church shared with me in the matter of giving and receiving, except you only; ¹⁶for even when I was in Thessalonica, you sent me aid again and again when I was in need. ¹⁷Not that I am looking for a gift, but I am looking for what may be credited to your account. ¹⁸I have received full payment and even more; I am amply supplied, now that I have received from Epaphroditus the gifts you sent. They are a fragrant offering, an acceptable sacrifice, pleasing to God. ¹⁹And my God will meet all your needs according to his glorious riches in Christ Jesus.

²⁰To our God and Father be glory for ever and ever. Amen.

²¹Greet all the saints in Christ Jesus. The brothers who are with me send greetings. ²²All the saints send you greetings, especially those who belong to Caesar's household.

²³The grace of the Lord Jesus Christ be with your spirit. Amen.ⁱ

ⁱ23 Some manuscripts do not have *Amen*.

 Discovering the Word 1. Paul thanks the Philippians not for the money but for the concern they have shown (v. 10). Why would this have been more important to Paul? 2. Many people believe they can only be content once they have reached a certain level of economic prosperity. How does their view differ from Paul's secret of contentment (vv. 11–13)? 3. How had the Philippians helped Paul both in the past and the present (vv. 14–18)? 4. What benefits does Paul expect the Philippians to receive from their giving (vv. 17–19)?

Applying the Word 1. Many people complain that missionaries are always asking for money. How does this passage provide a model for both missionaries and those who support them? 2. How will this passage affect your giving?

Responding in Prayer Pray for Christian workers you know, that they would have the emotional and financial support they need.

Colossians

"**M**ore! More!" urged our son John when I laid down the spoon after feeding him. "Again! Again!" pleaded our daughter Sara as I turned the last page in the book I was reading to her.

Their cries for more pudding or stories are echoed in our culture's search for more—more power, more money, more knowledge, more gadgets, more furniture, more clothes—more everything!

Books on self-improvement and success flood the market. Gurus gain eager followers by offering enlightenment, power and secret wisdom. Millions read horoscopes every day.

We cry for "more" not only in our society but also in the church. If only we had more wisdom, more maturity, more power, more faith. To fill these needs we attend seminars, go to concerts, hear celebrity speakers and read their latest books.

Colossians was written to Christians with similar longings. They didn't know who and what they already had. False teachers urged them to add rules, ascetic practices and new philosophies to their Christian faith. Then they would have fullness of life. Paul writes to satisfy their desire for more by showing that they already had fullness in Christ.

Paul never traveled to Colossae, a city in the Lycus River valley about a hundred miles east of Ephesus and twelve miles from Laodicea. But somehow he met Epaphras, the man who had taken the gospel to Colossae, and Philemon, the host for the local house church. While in prison in Rome, Paul learned from Epaphras about the Colossian church and the pressures threatening their peace and stability.

These "faithful brothers" had not turned away from faith in Christ. Paul's warm, friendly letter affirms their positive qualities and the changes in their lives. But he warns them against being deceived by "fine-sounding arguments" (2:4) or being captured by "hollow and deceptive philosophy, which depends on human tradition and on the basic principles of this world rather than on Christ" (2:8).

The temptation to add ascetic practices, regulations or "superior knowledge" threatened their dependence on Christ alone for the fullness of life they wanted. The early Gnostics boasted about a spiritual "fullness" not previously experienced. They promised to complete and perfect the simple and elementary faith introduced by Paul and Epaphras. They

emphasized a deeper knowledge of God, reserved for a special few, and an experience of greater power.

Colossians is Paul's strongest declaration of the uniqueness and sufficiency of Christ, his full authority over all powers, and the fullness of life he gives. Paul spells out the implications of this fullness of life again and again in the letter.

Like the Colossians, we are bombarded by longings for something more. But Paul thunders in Colossians, You already have fullness in Christ. Enjoy it! "For in Christ all the fullness of the Deity lives in bodily form, and you have been given fullness in Christ" (2:9–10). The purpose of these quiet times is to help you discover the scope, reality and implications of the fullness of life you have in Christ. Paul's letter to Philemon gives principles for mending broken relationships that apply to us as well.

Outline

1/ Colossians 1:1–14 ——————————— *Thanks and Prayer*

2/ Colossians 1:15–23 —————————— *Jesus Is Supreme*

3/ Colossians 1:24—2:5 ————————— *Struggles for Maturity*

4/ Colossians 2:6–23 ——————————— *No Additions Needed*

5/ Colossians 3:1–11 ——————————— *New Life, New Lifestyle (Part 1)*

6/ Colossians 3:12–17 —————————— *New Life, New Lifestyle (Part 2)*

7/ Colossians 3:18—4:1 ————————— *At Home and On the Job*

8/ Colossians 4:2–18 ——————————— *Making the Most of Opportunities*

1 / *Colossians 1:1–14*
Thanks and Prayer

"GOD BLESS JENNIFER today" may be a typical prayer for a friend as she comes to mind. But what am I specifically asking for? How will I know if my prayer is answered? What difference would it make in Jennifer's life? Paul begins his letter by telling the Colossians why he is thankful for them and what he asks God to do in them. Paul's example gives us a model for encouraging and praying for one another.

 Warming Up to God How does it make you feel when a friend tells you the specific things he or she notices and appreciates about you?

 Read Colossians 1:1–14.

1 Paul, an apostle of Christ Jesus by the will of God, and Timothy our brother,

²To the holy and faithful[a] brothers in Christ at Colosse:

Grace and peace to you from God our Father.[b]

³We always thank God, the Father of our Lord Jesus Christ, when we pray for you, ⁴because we have heard of your faith in Christ Jesus and of the love you have for all the saints— ⁵the faith and love that spring from the hope that is stored up for you in heaven and that you have already heard about in the word of truth, the gospel ⁶that has come to you. All over the world this gospel is bearing fruit and growing, just as it has been doing among you since the day you heard it and understood God's grace in all its truth. ⁷You learned it from Epaphras, our dear fellow servant, who is a faithful minister of Christ on our[c] be-

half, ⁸and who also told us of your love in the Spirit.

⁹For this reason, since the day we heard about you, we have not stopped praying for you and asking God to fill you with the knowledge of his will through all spiritual wisdom and understanding. ¹⁰And we pray this in order that you may live a life worthy of the Lord and may please him in every way: bearing fruit in every good work, growing in the knowledge of God, ¹¹being strengthened with all power according to his glorious might so that you may have great endurance and patience, and joyfully ¹²giving thanks to the Father, who has qualified you[d] to share in the inheritance of the saints in the kingdom of light. ¹³For he has rescued us from the dominion of darkness and brought us into the kingdom of the Son he loves, ¹⁴in whom we have redemption,[e] the forgiveness of sins.

ª2 Or *believing*   b2 Some manuscripts *Father and the Lord Jesus Christ*   c7 Some manuscripts *your*   d12 Some manuscripts *us*   e14 A few late manuscripts *redemption through his blood*

 Discovering the Word 1. What characteristics of the Colossians cause Paul to always be thankful for them (vv. 3–6)? 2. What impresses you about how the gospel was spreading (vv. 5–8)? 3. After affirming their strengths, Paul tells the Colossians what he prays for them. What are Paul's requests for how they think and act? 4. How might spiritual wisdom and understanding help us to understand God's will (v. 9)? 5. According to Paul, true knowledge leads to a "life worthy of the Lord" (v. 10). What qualities does such a life include (vv. 10–12)? How are these qualities related to each other?

Applying the Word 1. In what specific ways do you see the qualities in verses 10–12 developing in your life? 2. Reread verses 12–14, putting your name in each sentence. How would meditating on these verses help you to appreciate what God has done for you?

Responding in Prayer Take time to pray for your church or fellowship group, using verses 9–14 as your model.

2 / *Colossians 1:15–23*
Jesus Is Supreme

WE FREQUENTLY HEAR: "All roads lead to God. Everyone is trying to get to the same place. That belief is fine for you, but I don't buy it for myself. Only bigots and fanatics label belief *true* or *false*."

The Colossians heard, "Worship Jesus, but not exclusively. Jesus is just one spirit among many to be worshiped." In this passage we'll study Paul's adamant declaration of Christ's supremacy over every being and idea which invites our attention.

 Warming Up to God What problems have you encountered in helping someone understand why Jesus is the only way to God?

 Read Colossians 1:15–23.

---

¹⁵He is the image of the invisible God, the firstborn over all creation. ¹⁶For by him all things were created: things in heaven and on earth, visible and invisible, whether thrones or powers or rulers or authorities; all things were created by him and for him. ¹⁷He is before all things, and in him all things hold together. ¹⁸And he is the head of the body, the church; he is the beginning and the firstborn from among the dead, so that in everything he might have the supremacy. ¹⁹For God was pleased to have all his fullness dwell in him, ²⁰and through him to reconcile to himself all things, whether things on earth or things in heaven, by making peace through his blood, shed on the cross.

²¹Once you were alienated from God and were enemies in your minds because of ʲ your evil behavior. ²²But now he has reconciled you by Christ's physical body through death to present you holy in his sight, without blemish and free from accusation— ²³ if you continue in your faith, established and firm, not moved from the hope held out in the gospel. This is the gospel that you heard and that has been proclaimed to every creature under heaven, and of which I, Paul, have become a servant.

ʲ21 Or minds, as shown by

Discovering the Word 1. Make as many statements as you can about why Jesus is supreme (vv. 15–18). Begin each with "Christ is . . ." 2. What does it mean that Christ is the "head of the body, the church" (v. 18)? 3. What actions was God pleased to take to reconcile us to himself (vv. 19–22)? 4. How does understanding God's actions help you explain why Jesus is the only way to God?

Applying the Word 1. How do the words *reconciled, holy in his sight, without blemish* and *free from accusation* (vv. 22–23) motivate you to continue firm in your faith in Christ? 2. How might those words appeal to unspoken needs of the friends you want to introduce to Jesus? 3. How did some recent choice you made about your time or money reflect Christ's supreme place in your life?

 Responding in Prayer Spend some time worshiping Jesus Christ for who he is and what he has done for you and your friends who don't yet know him.

---

3 / *Colossians 1:24—2:5*
Struggles for Maturity

FOR A WHOLE year a young man lived in isolation on a remote Arctic mountain. He risked his life on the flight in and on trails over thin ice (which gave way when he struggled under a heavy backpack). He shared his cold tent with mice and mosquitoes. He experimented with a diet of boiled, fried or charred mice. Why would anyone willingly

subject himself to such hardships? Farley Mowat had a goal. He wanted to learn the relationship between wolves and the diminishing caribou herds. In this study Paul describes his compelling goal, his struggles and his resources to reach it.

 Warming Up to God Recall a time when a goal was compelling enough to cause you to suffer for it. What helped you to keep going?

 Read Colossians 1:24—2:5.

²⁴Now I rejoice in what was suffered for you, and I fill up in my flesh what is still lacking in regard to Christ's afflictions, for the sake of his body, which is the church. ²⁵I have become its servant by the commission God gave me to present to you the word of God in its fullness— ²⁶the mystery that has been kept hidden for ages and generations, but is now disclosed to the saints. ²⁷To them God has chosen to make known among the Gentiles the glorious riches of this mystery, which is Christ in you, the hope of glory.

²⁸We proclaim him, admonishing and teaching everyone with all wisdom, so that we may present everyone perfect in Christ. ²⁹To this end I labor, struggling with all his energy, which so powerfully works in me.

2 I want you to know how much I am struggling for you and for those at Laodicea, and for all who have not met me personally. ²My purpose is that they may be encouraged in heart and united in love, so that they may have the full riches of complete understanding, in order that they may know the mystery of God, namely, Christ, ³in whom are hidden all the treasures of wisdom and knowledge. ⁴I tell you this so that no one may deceive you by fine-sounding arguments. ⁵For though I am absent from you in body, I am present with you in spirit and delight to see how orderly you are and how firm your faith in Christ is.

 Discovering the Word 1. How does Paul define God's commission to him (1:24–29)? 2. In the New Testament the term *mystery* refers not to something mysterious but to something previously hidden which God now wishes to make clear. What is the mystery that represents the "word of God in its fullness" (1:26–27; 2:2–3)? 3. According to Paul, what are the marks of Christian maturity (2:2–5)? 5. The Gnostics taught that their secret knowledge was the key to salvation. How would Paul's description of Christ (2:3–4) protect the Colossians from the "fine-sounding arguments" of the Gnostics?

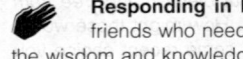 **Applying the Word** 1. What "fine-sounding arguments" today lure us away from Christ and hinder our spiritual maturity? 2. What can you do to refocus your attention on Christ and on his goals for you?

Responding in Prayer Thank God for the people who labored to help you mature in Christ. Pray for friends who need to be encouraged in heart and united in love. Ask God to increase your awareness of the wisdom and knowledge in Jesus Christ.

4 / *Colossians 2:6–23*
No Additions Needed

KIM YENG AND his family celebrated the day they became American citizens. Now they were no longer refugees but free citizens with full privileges and endless opportunities. But soon the neighbors began to question Kim. "Why are you making your kids superpatriots? They don't have to wear flags on their shirts every day." "Why did you spend all that money installing a tall flagpole in your yard?" "Don't you know that making your family eat hamburgers instead of eggrolls doesn't make you a better citizen?" In this study Paul questions the Colossians about the foolish human additions they are trying to add to all they have in Christ.

Warming Up to God How would you finish the following sentence? "I would feel fulfilled if . . ."

Read Colossians 2:6–23.

⁶So then, just as you received Christ Jesus as Lord, continue to live in him, ⁷rooted and built up in him, strengthened in the faith as you were taught, and overflowing with thankfulness.

⁸See to it that no one takes you captive through hollow and deceptive philosophy, which depends on human tradition and the basic principles of this world rather than on Christ.

⁹For in Christ all the fullness of the Deity lives in bodily form, ¹⁰and you have been given fullness in Christ, who is the head over every power and authority. ¹¹In him you were also circumcised, in the putting off of the sinful nature,ᵍ not with a circumcision done by the hands of men but with the circumcision done by Christ, ¹²having been buried with him in baptism and raised with him through your faith in the power of God, who raised him from the dead.

¹³When you were dead in your sins and in the uncircumcision of your sinful nature,ʰ God made youⁱ alive with Christ. He forgave us all our sins, ¹⁴having canceled the written code, with its regulations, that was against us and that stood opposed to us; he took it away, nailing it to the cross. ¹⁵And having disarmed the powers and authorities, he made a public spectacle of them, triumphing over them by the cross.ʲ

¹⁶Therefore do not let anyone judge you by what you eat or drink, or with regard to a religious festival, a New Moon celebration or a Sabbath day. ¹⁷These are a shadow of the things that were to come; the reality, however, is found in Christ. ¹⁸Do not let anyone who delights in false humility and the worship of angels disqualify you for the prize. Such a person goes into great detail about what he has seen, and his unspiritual mind puffs him up with idle notions. ¹⁹He has lost connection with the Head, from whom the whole body, supported and held together by its ligaments and sinews, grows as God causes it to grow.

²⁰Since you died with Christ to the basic principles of this world, why, as though you still belonged to it, do you submit to its rules: ²¹"Do not handle! Do not taste! Do not touch!"? ²²These are all destined to perish with use, because they are based on human commands and teachings. ²³Such regulations indeed have an appearance of wisdom, with their self-imposed worship, their false humility and their harsh treatment of the body, but they lack any value in restraining sensual indulgence.

g11 Or the flesh   *h13 Or your flesh*   *i13 Some manuscripts us*
j15 Or them in him

Discovering the Word 1. How do each of the images *rooted, built up, strengthened* and *overflowing* (v. 7) help us understand how we should continue to live in Christ? 2. In verse 8 we get the first real glimpse of the heresy being taught to the Colossians. What do we learn about it? 3. How would Paul's two statements about fullness in Christ (vv. 9–10) protect the Colossians from those deceptive ideas? 4. In verses 11–15 Paul describes some of what "fullness in Christ" includes. Which of our basic needs did Jesus' death, burial and resurrection meet? 5. What "shadows" were the Colossians adding to the "reality" they had found in Christ (vv. 16–17, 20–23)?

Applying the Word 1. Silently reread verses 9–15, inserting your name every time Paul says *you* or *us.* How do these facts affect your view of yourself? 2. What "shadows" are we tempted to add today?

Responding in Prayer Consider the fact that we are made complete in Christ. Allow your prayer and praise to arise out of that fact.

5 / *Colossians 3:1–11*
New Life, New Lifestyle (Part 1)

HAVE YOU SEEN pictures of marathon runners? Concentration and determination seem to ooze from every pore. These people set their hearts and minds on one thing—finish this race. They focus on the next step, the next checkpoint, until the race is complete. They shed pounds, unnecessary clothing or anything else that might slow them down. Attach their official number and they are ready to run.

As Christians, we are to live like marathon runners. We are to take off anything that slows us down and set our hearts and minds on the finish line.

 Warming Up to God As a child, how did setting your heart on a certain toy or gift affect how you acted and what you thought about?

 Read Colossians 3:1–11.

3 Since, then, you have been raised with Christ, set your hearts on things above, where Christ is seated at the right hand of God. ²Set your minds on things above, not on earthly things. ³For you died, and your life is now hidden with Christ in God. ⁴When Christ, who is your^k life, appears, then you also will appear with him in glory.

⁵Put to death, therefore, whatever belongs to your earthly nature: sexual immorality, impurity, lust, evil desires and greed, which is idolatry. ⁶Because of these, the wrath of God is coming.^{l} ⁷You used to walk in these ways, in the life you once lived. ⁸But now you must rid yourselves of all such things as these: anger, rage, malice, slander, and filthy language from your lips. ⁹Do not lie to each other, since you have taken off your old self with its practices ¹⁰and have put on the new self, which is being renewed in knowledge in the image of its Creator. ¹¹Here there is no Greek or Jew, circumcised or uncircumcised, barbarian, Scythian, slave or free, but Christ is all, and is in all.

^{k}4 Some manuscripts *our* ^{l}6 Some early manuscripts *coming on*
those who are disobedient

Discovering the Word 1. What do you think Paul means by *things above* and *earthly things* (vv. 1–2)? 2. How can we set our hearts and minds on things above rather than on earthly things? 3. What do the things we are to "put to death" have in common (v. 5)? 4. Our old ways of reacting are compared to a garment we took off at conversion (vv. 8–10). Why is each type of behavior inconsistent with our new life in Christ? 5. Although we may still struggle with these sins, what resources for change do we now have (vv. 9–11)?

Applying the Word 1. How can we keep God's perspective on immorality and greed when our culture accepts them as the norm? 2. What has been the effect on you and others when you have fallen back into these old motives or actions (vv. 5, 8–9)? 3. In verse 11 Paul lists the distressing divisions between people in the Colossian culture. How would becoming aware of Christ in other Christians help us to eliminate our cultural divisions?

Responding in Prayer Paul has shown the necessary blending of our emotions, mind and will in order to live like people who have been raised with Christ. Pray for help in the area where you feel weak. Spend time thanking God for the changes he has already made in you.

6 / *Colossians 3:12–17*
New Life, New Lifestyle (Part 2)

MARATHON RUNNERS NOT only shed anything that might slow them down, they also dress carefully. They choose the best running shoes and the most comfortable shorts and shirt possible. After telling us what to get rid of, Paul now speaks about the new clothes we are to wear because of our new life in Christ.

 Warming Up to God When you were a child, what was one behavior your parents insisted on just because you were a member of their family?

 Read Colossians 3:12–17.

¹²Therefore, as God's chosen people, holy and dearly loved, clothe yourselves with compassion, kindness, humility, gentleness and patience. ¹³Bear with each other and forgive whatever grievances you may have against one another. Forgive as the Lord forgave you. ¹⁴And over all these virtues put on love, which binds them all together in perfect unity.

¹⁵Let the peace of Christ rule in your hearts, since as members of one body you were called to peace. And be thankful. ¹⁶Let the word of Christ dwell in you richly as you teach and admonish one another with all wisdom, and as you sing psalms, hymns and spiritual songs with gratitude in your hearts to God. ¹⁷And whatever you do, whether in word or deed, do it all in the name of the Lord Jesus, giving thanks to God the Father through him.

 Discovering the Word 1. Why does Paul begin by reminding us of who we are in God's sight (v. 12)? 2. Why is the description "God's chosen people, holy and dearly loved" (v. 12) not dependent on our feelings or efforts (1:12–14; 2:9–10)? 3. Paul recognizes that grievances occur even in the church. How are his instructions for handling grievances different from the way our culture handles them (vv. 13–14)? 4. Paul also recognizes that Christians conflict with each other. How could conflicts be better managed with peace ruling (literally, "functioning like an umpire") in our hearts (v. 15)? 5. What does it mean to let the word of Christ "dwell" in us richly (v. 16; see also Eph 5:18–20)?

 Applying the Word 1. What "new clothes" (v. 12) would you like to put on? 2. How would doing everything "in the name of the Lord Jesus" transform what you have to say and do today (v. 17)?

Responding in Prayer Let your prayer grow out of the need to put on specific "new clothes." If there is someone you need to forgive, confess that and ask for power and determination to forgive.

7 / *Colossians 3:18—4:1*
At Home and On the Job

FACTORY WORKERS IN the Philippines had been meeting for months for a lunch-hour Bible study. One day the supervisor came to the leader and asked, "Could you start some more Bible studies in the factory? The men in the study have become the best workers on my shift."

That wouldn't have surprised the apostle Paul. In this section he instructs us about the distinctive attitudes and behavior that should mark Christians at home and on the job.

 Warming Up to God When is it easiest for you to have a "Christian" attitude toward your work?

 Read Colossians 3:18—4:1.

18Wives, submit to your husbands, as is fitting in the Lord.

19Husbands, love your wives and do not be harsh with them.

20Children, obey your parents in everything, for this pleases the Lord.

21Fathers, do not embitter your children, or they will become discouraged.

22Slaves, obey your earthly masters in everything; and do it, not only when their eye is on you and to win their favor, but with sincerity of heart and reverence for the Lord. 23Whatever you do, work at it with all your heart, as working for the Lord, not for men, 24since you know that you will receive an inheritance from the Lord as a reward. It is the Lord Christ you are serving. 25Anyone who does wrong will be repaid for his wrong, and there is no favoritism.

4 Masters, provide your slaves with what is right and fair, because you know that you also have a Master in heaven.

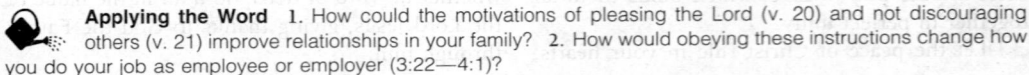

Discovering the Word   1. How do Paul's commands to wives/husbands, children/fathers and slaves/masters address our tendency to do the opposite?   2. The wife is to submit to the husband "as is fitting in the Lord" (v. 18). From what you learned in 3:5–17, what would that kind of submission include? What would it not include?   3. The husband is to love his wife and not be harsh with her (v. 19). How would 3:12–17 help him understand what that love should be like in actions and attitudes?   4. What attitudes and actions of parents embitter or discourage their children?   5. When and how are slaves to obey their masters (vv. 22–25)? With what motives?   6. What would it demand of a master to "provide your slaves with what is right and fair" (4:1)?

Applying the Word   1. How could the motivations of pleasing the Lord (v. 20) and not discouraging others (v. 21) improve relationships in your family?   2. How would obeying these instructions change how you do your job as employee or employer (3:22—4:1)?

Responding in Prayer   Ask God to show you any attitudes or actions toward your family or at work that you need to change. Ask for grace to begin making one small change today.

---

8 / *Colossians 4:2–18*
Making the Most of Opportunities

NO ONE EVER becomes a Christian by just watching how a Christian lives. An observer might think the Christian is earning his way to heaven by trying to be good. How could anyone ever guess how to become a Christian? Debating if what we say or how we live is more important in witnessing is like asking which leg is more important for walking. In this study Paul shows that witnessing is an interplay between prayer, living and speaking. His closing greetings illustrate many ways Christians help and encourage each other.

Warming Up to God   What one piece of advice about witnessing would you give to a younger Christian?

Read Colossians 4:2–18.

2Devote yourselves to prayer, being watchful and thankful. 3And pray for us, too, that God may open a door for our message, so that we may proclaim the mystery of Christ, for which I am in chains. 4Pray that I may proclaim it clearly, as I should. 5Be wise in the way you act toward outsiders; make the most of every opportunity. 6Let your conversation be always full of grace, sea- soned with salt, so that you may know how to answer everyone.

7Tychicus will tell you all the news about me. He is a dear brother, a faithful minister and fellow servant in the Lord. 8I am sending him to you for the express purpose that you may know about our*m* circumstances and that he may encourage

*m*8 Some manuscripts *that he may know about your*

your hearts. ⁹He is coming with Onesimus, our faithful and dear brother, who is one of you. They will tell you everything that is happening here.

¹⁰My fellow prisoner Aristarchus sends you his greetings, as does Mark, the cousin of Barnabas. (You have received instructions about him; if he comes to you, welcome him.) ¹¹Jesus, who is called Justus, also sends greetings. These are the only Jews among my fellow workers for the kingdom of God, and they have proved a comfort to me. ¹²Epaphras, who is one of you and a servant of Christ Jesus, sends greetings. He is always wrestling in prayer for you, that you may stand firm in all the will of God, mature and fully as-

sured. ¹³I vouch for him that he is working hard for you and for those at Laodicea and Hierapolis. ¹⁴Our dear friend Luke, the doctor, and Demas send greetings. ¹⁵Give my greetings to the brothers at Laodicea, and to Nympha and the church in her house.

¹⁶After this letter has been read to you, see that it is also read in the church of the Laodiceans and that you in turn read the letter from Laodicea.

¹⁷Tell Archippus: "See to it that you complete the work you have received in the Lord."

¹⁸I, Paul, write this greeting in my own hand. Remember my chains. Grace be with you.

 Discovering the Word 1. In verses 2–6 Paul teaches us how to speak to God about people and how to speak to people about God. Why would he tell us to *devote* ourselves to prayer (v. 2)? 2. Paul might have asked the church to pray for his release from prison. What requests does he make instead (vv. 3–4)? Why? 3. What advice does Paul give us about the way we live and converse with non-Christians (vv. 5–6)? 4. Paul concludes this letter with numerous personal messages and greetings. What qualities in people does Paul affirm, and why (vv. 7–18)?

Applying the Word 1. In what ways might you "be wise in the way you act toward outsiders" and "make the most of every opportunity" (v. 5)? 2. How could you encourage or comfort a fellow Christian this week by following the example of someone named here?

Responding in Prayer Use verses 3–4 to pray for yourself, your church leaders and missionaries. Ask God to make you aware of every opportunity to influence nonbelievers to consider Jesus.

1 Thessalonians

C onventional wisdom tells us that nothing is certain except death and taxes, but for most of us that is not enough. Wouldn't you like to be just as sure about where you stand with God? That's what the Thessalonians were looking for, and Paul's letters to them can help you find that assurance as well.

In the year A.D. 50, Paul entered Thessalonica while on his second missionary journey. He preached there for three weeks and was able to establish a church. However, a group of jealous Jews interpreted Paul's message to mean that he was proclaiming another ruler in opposition to the Roman emperor, and he was forced to leave town (Acts 17:1–10).

Because of Paul's concern for this young church, he sent his coworker, Timothy, to learn how the Thessalonians were doing. Timothy reported that the Christians' faith remained strong but that they continued to be persecuted by those who had banished Paul. Timothy also brought back questions which Paul had not had time to answer during his short stay.

First Thessalonians was Paul's first attempt at offering encouragement and answering questions—in fact it was probably the first of Paul's epistles. It was written from Corinth only a few months after Paul had left Thessalonica.

In 1 Thessalonians Paul offers encouragement in four major areas: (1) How can I be sure that I will be with Jesus after death? (2) How can I be sure that Jesus is coming again? (3) How can I be sure that Jesus hasn't forgotten me when I am suffering persecution? (4) How can I be sure that my life is pleasing to God?

Through your study of these letters, it is my hope that you will become sure of your faith and of your salvation and that, as a result, you will be able to "encourage each other with these words" (1Th 4:18).

Outline

1/ 1 Thessalonians 1 ——————— *Faith That Shows*

2/ 1 Thessalonians 2:1–16 ——————— *Gentle Evangelism*

3/ 1 Thessalonians 2:17—3:13 ——————— *Unmistakable Love*

4/ 1 Thessalonians 4:1–12 ——————— *A Life That Pleases God*

5/ 1 Thessalonians 4:13—5:11 ——————— *The Hope of Christ's Coming*

6/ 1 Thessalonians 5:12–28 ——————— *Life Among Friends*

1 / *1 Thessalonians 1*
Faith That Shows

A LIGHTHOUSE HAS become a common analogy for a church. Just as a lighthouse stands in a dark and dangerous spot flashing its message of warning and pointing to safe harbor, a church should also be a prominent and unmistakable sign to the community in which it exists. How can you help your church or fellowship group become such a shining light? This passage describes how the church in Thessalonica was able to do it.

 Warming Up to God What is the reputation of your church or fellowship group throughout the community?

 Read 1 Thessalonians 1.

---

1 Paul, Silas*a* and Timothy,

To the church of the Thessalonians in God the Father and the Lord Jesus Christ:

Grace and peace to you.*b*

²We always thank God for all of you, mentioning you in our prayers. ³We continually remember before our God and Father your work produced by faith, your labor prompted by love, and your endurance inspired by hope in our Lord Jesus Christ.

⁴For we know, brothers loved by God, that he has chosen you, ⁵because our gospel came to you not simply with words, but also with power, with the Holy Spirit and with deep conviction. You know how we lived among you for your sake.

⁶You became imitators of us and of the Lord; in spite of severe suffering, you welcomed the message with the joy given by the Holy Spirit. ⁷And so you became a model to all the believers in Macedonia and Achaia. ⁸The Lord's message rang out from you not only in Macedonia and Achaia—your faith in God has become known everywhere. Therefore we do not need to say anything about it, ⁹for they themselves report what kind of reception you gave us. They tell how you turned to God from idols to serve the living and true God, ¹⁰and to wait for his Son from heaven, whom he raised from the dead—Jesus, who rescues us from the coming wrath.

a1 Greek Silvanus, a variant of Silas   b1 Some early manuscripts you from God our Father and the Lord Jesus Christ

---

 Discovering the Word 1. Paul writes that he remembers the Thessalonians' "work produced by faith," "labor prompted by love" and "endurance inspired by hope" (v. 3). How do you think he could tell that faith, love and hope were behind their actions? 2. What role has the Holy Spirit played in the Thessalonians' faith (vv. 5–6)? 3. What role did Paul, Silas and Timothy have in the Thessalonians' conversion (v. 6)? 4. When is it wise and when is it unwise to imitate another Christian (vv. 6–7)? 5. What were the results of the Thessalonians' strong faith (vv. 8–10)?

 Applying the Word 1. What do you think your reputation is with non-Christians? 2. How can your faith (and the faith of your church or fellowship group) become more of a witness to others?

Responding in Prayer Ask to be made a genuine witness, and pray for the witness of your church.

2 / 1 Thessalonians 2:1–16
Gentle Evangelism

WHAT THOUGHTS COME to your mind when you hear the word *evangelism*? Pushy people trying to get you to see things their way? Guilt for not saying enough about your Savior? People swarming down the aisles at a gigantic rally? Or friends sharing the excitement of the good news with each other? For Paul, evangelism was always delightful and exciting. In this passage he tells us why talking about Christ is such a positive experience for him.

 Warming Up to God How do you feel about telling others about your faith? Talk with God about any fears or guilt you experience.

 Read 1 Thessalonians 2:1–16.

2 You know, brothers, that our visit to you was not a failure. ²We had previously suffered and been insulted in Philippi, as you know, but with the help of our God we dared to tell you his gospel in spite of strong opposition. ³For the appeal we make does not spring from error or impure motives, nor are we trying to trick you. ⁴On the contrary, we speak as men approved by God to be entrusted with the gospel. We are not trying to please men but God, who tests our hearts. ⁵You know we never used flattery, nor did we put on a mask to cover up greed—God is our witness. ⁶We were not looking for praise from men, not from you or anyone else.

As apostles of Christ we could have been a burden to you, ⁷but we were gentle among you, like a mother caring for her little children. ⁸We loved you so much that we were delighted to share with you not only the gospel of God but our lives as well, because you had become so dear to us. ⁹Surely you remember, brothers, our toil and hardship; we worked night and day in order not to be a burden to anyone while we preached the gospel of God to you.

¹⁰You are witnesses, and so is God, of how holy, righteous and blameless we were among you who believed. ¹¹For you know that we dealt with each of you as a father deals with his own children, ¹²encouraging, comforting and urging you to live lives worthy of God, who calls you into his kingdom and glory.

¹³And we also thank God continually because, when you received the word of God, which you heard from us, you accepted it not as the word of men, but as it actually is, the word of God, which is at work in you who believe. ¹⁴For you, brothers, became imitators of God's churches in Judea, which are in Christ Jesus: You suffered from your own countrymen the same things those churches suffered from the Jews, ¹⁵who killed the Lord Jesus and the prophets and also drove us out. They displease God and are hostile to all men ¹⁶in their effort to keep us from speaking to the Gentiles so that they may be saved. In this way they always heap up their sins to the limit. The wrath of God has come upon them at last.ᶜ

ᶜ16 Or *them fully*

 Discovering the Word 1. What excuses might Paul have had not to preach to the Thessalonians (vv. 1–2)? 2. What attitudes enable Paul to continue preaching despite opposition (vv. 3–6)? 3. What does this teach you about proper and improper reasons for witnessing to others? 4. Paul claims to have been "holy, righteous and blameless" (v. 10) among the Thessalonians. If this is important, how can imperfect people dare to do evangelism? 5. How is a father dealing with his children a good example of an evangelist (vv. 11–12)?

Applying the Word 1. In what specific ways can gentleness and caring become more a part of your evangelistic efforts? 2. In what ways have you found evangelism to be difficult? 3. What ideas and encouragement from this passage can help you to overcome these difficulties?

Responding in Prayer Ask God to give you encouragement to be a gentle evangelist.

3 / *1 Thessalonians 2:17—3:13*
Unmistakable Love

STUDIES SHOW THAT more people leave their churches today for lack of love than for any other reason (Win Arn, Carroll Nyquist and Charles Arn, *Who Cares About Love?* [Pasadena, Calif.: Church Growth Press, 1986], p. 7). It is indeed sad that even those who are committed to the Lord of love are unable to offer that love to others. How can your church become a place where love will "increase and overflow for each other and for everyone else" (1Th 3:12)? This passage provides some practical examples.

 Warming Up to God On a scale of 1 to 10, how loved do you feel by the members of your church or fellowship group?

 Read 1 Thessalonians 2:17—3:13.

¹⁷But, brothers, when we were torn away from you for a short time (in person, not in thought), out of our intense longing we made every effort to see you. ¹⁸For we wanted to come to you—certainly I, Paul, did, again and again—but Satan stopped us. ¹⁹For what is our hope, our joy, or the crown in which we will glory in the presence of our Lord Jesus when he comes? Is it not you? ²⁰Indeed, you are our glory and joy.

3 So when we could stand it no longer, we thought it best to be left by ourselves in Athens. ²We sent Timothy, who is our brother and God's fellow worker*d* in spreading the gospel of Christ, to strengthen and encourage you in your faith, ³so that no one would be unsettled by these trials. You know quite well that we were destined for them. ⁴In fact, when we were with you, we kept telling you that we would be persecuted. And it turned out that way, as you well know. ⁵For this reason, when I could stand it no longer, I sent to find out about your faith. I was afraid that in some way the tempter might have tempted you and our efforts might have been useless.

⁶But Timothy has just now come to us from you and has brought good news about your faith and love. He has told us that you always have pleasant memories of us and that you long to see us, just as we also long to see you. ⁷Therefore, brothers, in all our distress and persecution we were encouraged about you because of your faith. ⁸For now we really live, since you are standing firm in the Lord. ⁹How can we thank God enough for you in return for all the joy we have in the presence of our God because of you? ¹⁰Night and day we pray most earnestly that we may see you again and supply what is lacking in your faith.

¹¹Now may our God and Father himself and our Lord Jesus clear the way for us to come to you. ¹²May the Lord make your love increase and overflow for each other and for everyone else, just as ours does for you. ¹³May he strengthen your hearts so that you will be blameless and holy in the presence of our God and Father when our Lord Jesus comes with all his holy ones.

*d*2 Some manuscripts *brother and fellow worker*; other manuscripts *brother and God's servant*

 Discovering the Word 1. What evidence do you find in this passage that Paul really did love the Thessalonians (2:17, 20; 3:2, 5, 10)? 2. What phrases does Paul use to express his love (2:17–18; 3:5)? 3. What fears caused Paul to send Timothy to Thessalonica (3:2–5)? 4. What are Paul's desires for the Thessalonians (3:10–13)? 5. How do these desires reflect Paul's love and caring?

Applying the Word 1. How do you most often express your love for others? 2. What ideas from this passage can help you become even better at expressing love? 3. How can you (as an individual or group) help love increase within your church or fellowship group?

 Responding in Prayer Ask God to help you show love to someone in your church this week.

4 / 1 Thessalonians 4:1–12
A Life That Pleases God

ALL OF US want to please the people we love the most. That is why a wife will surprise her husband with his favorite meal, a husband will plan a special evening at a concert he knows will excite his wife, or a child will pick a bouquet of dandelions to present to Mom and Dad. What can Christians do to please God, whom they love so dearly?

 Warming Up to God If a Christian brother or sister asked you for advice on how to make their life more pleasing to God, what is the first thing you would say?

 Read 1 Thessalonians 4:1–12.

Finally, brothers, we instructed you how to live in order to please God, as in fact you are living. Now we ask you and urge you in the Lord Jesus to do this more and more. ²For you know what instructions we gave you by the authority of the Lord Jesus.

³It is God's will that you should be sanctified: that you should avoid sexual immorality; ⁴that each of you should learn to control his own body*e* in a way that is holy and honorable, ⁵not in passionate lust like the heathen, who do not know God; ⁶and that in this matter no one should wrong his brother or take advantage of him. The Lord will punish men for all such sins, as we have already told you and warned you. ⁷For God did not call us to be impure, but to live a holy life.

⁸Therefore, he who rejects this instruction does not reject man but God, who gives you his Holy Spirit.

⁹Now about brotherly love we do not need to write to you, for you yourselves have been taught by God to love each other. ¹⁰And in fact, you do love all the brothers throughout Macedonia. Yet we urge you, brothers, to do so more and more.

¹¹Make it your ambition to lead a quiet life, to mind your own business and to work with your hands, just as we told you, ¹²so that your daily life may win the respect of outsiders and so that you will not be dependent on anybody.

e4 Or learn to live with his own wife; or learn to acquire a wife

 Discovering the Word 1. Why would Paul give these instructions on holy living to people whom he says are already living a life which pleases God (vv. 1,10)? 2. What clues does this passage give as to how Paul would define sexual immorality (vv. 3–6)? 3. How does sexual immorality "wrong" or "take advantage of" a brother (v. 6)? 4. Scholars agree that verses 11 and 12 were directed toward members of the church who had quit working and were relying on the kindness of their fellow Christians to provide them with necessities. Why would Paul have been concerned about the effect this attitude was having on outsiders?

Applying the Word 1. What work habits detract from your Christian witness? 2. How can this passage help you to resist sexual temptation? 3. Paul has given commands in this passage concerning sexual immorality, love for fellow Christians and work. What can you do this week to become more obedient in one of these areas?

Responding in Prayer Give your life to the Lord, praying that it will be made pleasing to him.

5 / 1 Thessalonians 4:13—5:11
The Hope of Christ's Coming

A CRISIS OCCURRED in the Thessalonian church when one of their members died. Since they had expected to all be alive when Christ returned, they were now confused. Did this mean their friend would miss out on Christ's coming? Had this person died because God was angry with them? How much longer would it be before Christ finally did return? Maybe you have fears about what will happen when you die or when Christ returns. In this passage, Paul seeks to calm our fears and encourage us to look forward to the day we meet our Maker.

 Warming Up to God What fears do you have about death?

 Read 1 Thessalonians 4:13—5:11.

---

¹³Brothers, we do not want you to be ignorant about those who fall asleep, or to grieve like the rest of men, who have no hope. ¹⁴We believe that Jesus died and rose again and so we believe that God will bring with Jesus those who have fallen asleep in him. ¹⁵According to the Lord's own word, we tell you that we who are still alive, who are left till the coming of the Lord, will certainly not precede those who have fallen asleep. ¹⁶For the Lord himself will come down from heaven, with a loud command, with the voice of the archangel and with the trumpet call of God, and the dead in Christ will rise first. ¹⁷After that, we who are still alive and are left will be caught up together with them in the clouds to meet the Lord in the air. And so we will be with the Lord forever. ¹⁸Therefore encourage each other with these words.

5 Now, brothers, about times and dates we do not need to write to you, ²for you know very well that the day of the Lord will come like a thief in the night. ³While peo-

ple are saying, "Peace and safety," destruction will come on them suddenly, as labor pains on a pregnant woman, and they will not escape.

⁴But you, brothers, are not in darkness so that this day should surprise you like a thief. ⁵You are all sons of the light and sons of the day. We do not belong to the night or to the darkness. ⁶So then, let us not be like others, who are asleep, but let us be alert and self-controlled. ⁷For those who sleep, sleep at night, and those who get drunk, get drunk at night. ⁸But since we belong to the day, let us be self-controlled, putting on faith and love as a breastplate, and the hope of salvation as a helmet. ⁹For God did not appoint us to suffer wrath but to receive salvation through our Lord Jesus Christ. ¹⁰He died for us so that, whether we are awake or asleep, we may live together with him. ¹¹Therefore encourage one another and build each other up, just as in fact you are doing.

 Discovering the Word 1. In what ways is grief different for a Christian than it is for a non-Christian (4:13)? 2. What sequence of events does Paul say will occur when Christ returns (4:16–17)? 3. Why are the examples of a thief (5:2) and labor pains (5:3) good analogies of what will happen on the day of the Lord? 4. What dangers are associated with living in darkness (5:5–7)? 5. What instructions does Paul give for living in the light (5:8)?

Applying the Word 1. How do Paul's words help you to face your own fears about death? 2. Paul tells us that our defensive weapons against darkness are faith, love and hope (v. 8). What are some practical ways in which these virtues can defend you?

Responding in Prayer Pray that you will be made ready for the day of the Lord.

6 / *1 Thessalonians 5:12–28*
Life Among Friends

ANY GROUP OF people needs rules for getting along, and the church is no exception. Paul so wants the Thessalonians to "live in peace with each other" (1Th 5:13) that he closes his first letter to them with several instructions on how they can do this. These are instructions which have never gone out of date and can still be used to end the quarrels, hurt feelings and resentments in your church or fellowship group.

 Warming Up to God If you had the power to make one rule for helping people get along, what would it be?

 Read 1 Thessalonians 5:12–28.

---

¹²Now we ask you, brothers, to respect those who work hard among you, who are over you in the Lord and who admonish you. ¹³Hold them in the highest regard in love because of their work. Live in peace with each other. ¹⁴And we urge you, brothers, warn those who are idle, encourage the timid, help the weak, be patient with everyone. ¹⁵Make sure that nobody pays back wrong for wrong, but always try to be kind to each other and to everyone else.

¹⁶Be joyful always; ¹⁷pray continually; ¹⁸give thanks in all circumstances, for this is God's will for you in Christ Jesus.

¹⁹Do not put out the Spirit's fire; ²⁰do not treat prophecies with contempt. ²¹Test everything. Hold on to the good. ²²Avoid every kind of evil.

²³May God himself, the God of peace, sanctify you through and through. May your whole spirit, soul and body be kept blameless at the coming of our Lord Jesus Christ. ²⁴The one who calls you is faithful and he will do it.

²⁵Brothers, pray for us. ²⁶Greet all the brothers with a holy kiss. ²⁷I charge you before the Lord to have this letter read to all the brothers.

²⁸The grace of our Lord Jesus Christ be with you.

 Discovering the Word 1. What does it mean for someone to be "over you in the Lord" (v. 12)? 2. How can you warn a person about something they are doing wrong (v. 14) or prevent them from taking revenge (v. 15) and still live in peace with them? 3. What does it mean to be joyful "always," pray "continually" and give thanks "in all circumstances" (vv. 16–18)? 4. How can you test things like prophecy or teaching to find out if they are good or evil (vv. 19–22)? 5. Look through the passage again and pick out the actions and attitudes (stated or implied) which are displeasing to God. What are they?

 Applying the Word 1. When have you found God faithful in keeping you from sin (v. 24)? 2. In what way do you currently need God's faithfulness to keep you from sin?

Responding in Prayer Follow the discipline of giving thanks in all circumstances by finding as many things in your life as you can to be thankful for.

2 Thessalonians

S econd Thessalonians was written a short time after 1 Thessalonians to clear up misconceptions about the Second Coming that the first letter had failed to answer. Although the letter was written to Gentiles, it assumes some knowledge of the Old Testament. According to Donald Guthrie, this was typical of early Christian teaching (*New Testament Introduction,* rev. ed. [Downers Grove, Ill.: InterVarsity Press, 1990], p. 596).

Paul most likely wrote the letter from Corinth. In addition to clarifying their understanding about Christ's return, Paul addressed some ongoing problems in the church in dealing with idleness. This book offered its readers comfort and insight about faith and end times, as well as a call to take responsibility. May it both challenge and encourage you as well.

Outline

1/ 2 Thessalonians 1 —————————— *Evidence of Faith*

2/ 2 Thessalonians 2 —————————— *Lawlessness on the Loose*

3/ 2 Thessalonians 3 —————————— *Lazy Christians*

1 / *2 Thessalonians 1*
Evidence of Faith

CAN I KNOW for sure that I will go to heaven?

This is a question that plagued the Thessalonians to such an extent that even after the comfort of his first letter, Paul has to write again and give further encouragement. It was difficult for these young Christians to believe that the suffering of their present life would really be followed by the eternal joy of heaven. Perhaps you also wonder if heaven really exists and if you can be sure of going there. If so, you will find Paul writing this passage directly to you.

 Warming Up to God Have you ever met a person and gone away thinking, "They must be a Christian." What gave you that impression?

 Read 2 Thessalonians 1.

1 Paul, Silas*a* and Timothy,

To the church of the Thessalonians in God our Father and the Lord Jesus Christ:

²Grace and peace to you from God the Father and the Lord Jesus Christ.

³We ought always to thank God for you, brothers, and rightly so, because your faith is growing more and more, and the love every one of you has for each other is increasing. ⁴Therefore, among God's churches we boast about your perseverance and faith in all the persecutions and trials you are enduring.

⁵All this is evidence that God's judgment is right, and as a result you will be counted worthy of the kingdom of God, for which you are suffering. ⁶God is just: He will pay back trouble to those who trouble you ⁷and give relief to you who are troubled, and to us as well. This will happen when the Lord Jesus is revealed from heaven in blazing fire with his powerful angels. ⁸He will punish those who do not know God and do not obey the gospel of our Lord Jesus. ⁹They will be punished with everlasting destruction and shut out from the presence of the Lord and from the majesty of his power ¹⁰on the day he comes to be glorified in his holy people and to be marveled at among all those who have believed. This includes you, because you believed our testimony to you.

¹¹With this in mind, we constantly pray for you, that our God may count you worthy of his calling, and that by his power he may fulfill every good purpose of yours and every act prompted by your faith. ¹²We pray this so that the name of our Lord Jesus may be glorified in you, and you in him, according to the grace of our God and the Lord Jesus Christ.*b*

*a*1 Greek *Silvanus,* a variant of *Silas*   *b*12 Or *God and Lord, Jesus Christ*

 Discovering the Word 1. What good things does Paul notice about the lives of the Thessalonians (vv. 3–4)? 2. Why do you think that in times of persecution, some people's faith and love grow while others' fail (v. 4)? 3. Paul proclaims that "God is just." How does he describe God's justice (vv. 5–10)? 4. According to this passage, what makes a person "worthy of the kingdom" (v. 5) or "worthy of [God's] calling" (v. 11)? 5. In light of his teaching about God's judgment, why does Paul pray as he does in verses 11–12?

Applying the Word 1. How can God's justice encourage you when things are "just not fair"? 2. If someone were to pray for you as Paul did in verses 11–12, what is one specific way in which you would want God to change your life?

Responding in Prayer Pray that God's justice would be done in your life and throughout the world.

2 / 2 Thessalonians 2
Lawlessness on the Loose

HOW WILL THE world end? Will there be nuclear war? An evil empire? The destruction of civilization? Paul advises us that Satan has yet to attack us with the worst he has, and when he does, it will be a fearful time to be alive. However, Paul also promises that God will always be in control.

 Warming Up to God What potential threats to the safety of the world do you see right now (for example, attitudes, weapon building, warfare and so on)? What personal fears or concerns do you have about that?

 Read 2 Thessalonians 2.

2 Concerning the coming of our Lord Jesus Christ and our being gathered to him, we ask you, brothers, ²not to become easily unsettled or alarmed by some prophecy, report or letter supposed to have come from us, saying that the day of the Lord has already come. ³Don't let anyone deceive you in any way, for ˻that day will not come˼ until the rebellion occurs and the man of lawlessnessᶜ is revealed, the man doomed to destruction. ⁴He will oppose and will exalt himself over everything that is called God or is worshiped, so that he sets himself up in God's temple, proclaiming himself to be God.

⁵Don't you remember that when I was with you I used to tell you these things? ⁶And now you know what is holding him back, so that he may be revealed at the proper time. ⁷For the secret power of lawlessness is already at work; but the one who now holds it back will continue to do so till he is taken out of the way. ⁸And then the lawless one will be revealed, whom the Lord Jesus will overthrow with the breath of his mouth and destroy by the splendor of his coming. ⁹The coming of the lawless one will be in accordance with the work of Satan displayed in all kinds of coun-

terfeit miracles, signs and wonders, ¹⁰and in every sort of evil that deceives those who are perishing. They perish because they refused to love the truth and so be saved. ¹¹For this reason God sends them a powerful delusion so that they will believe the lie ¹²and so that all will be condemned who have not believed the truth but have delighted in wickedness.

¹³But we ought always to thank God for you, brothers loved by the Lord, because from the beginning God chose youᵈ to be saved through the sanctifying work of the Spirit and through belief in the truth. ¹⁴He called you to this through our gospel, that you might share in the glory of our Lord Jesus Christ. ¹⁵So then, brothers, stand firm and hold to the teachingsᵉ we passed on to you, whether by word of mouth or by letter.

¹⁶May our Lord Jesus Christ himself and God our Father, who loved us and by his grace gave us eternal encouragement and good hope, ¹⁷encourage your hearts and strengthen you in every good deed and word.

ᶜ3 Some manuscripts sin   ᵈ13 Some manuscripts because God chose you as his firstfruits   ᵉ15 Or traditions

---

 Discovering the Word 1. In 1 Thessalonians 4:13–18 Paul responded to the fears of the Thessalonians that if they died before Christ returned, they would miss the joy Christ had for them. Apparently, after Paul sent the first letter, someone tried to convince the Thessalonians that the day of the Lord had already come. What is Paul's proof that the day of the Lord has not come (vv. 3, 9)?   2. What can you learn about the "man of lawlessness" from this passage (vv. 3–4, 7–10)?   3. In what ways have you noticed the "secret power of lawlessness" (v. 7) to be already at work?   4. What contrasts do you find between those whom God condemns (vv. 10–12) and those whom he chooses for salvation (vv. 13–17)?

 Applying the Word 1. Even for Christians, the lawless one will bring fear and testing. What can you do to prepare yourself to withstand him?   2. How can this passage encourage you about facing the future?

Responding in Prayer Talk openly with God about any fears or concerns you have regarding the future.

3 / 2 Thessalonians 3
Lazy Christians

MEMBERS OF THE Thessalonian church were refusing to take responsibility. Some had quit working because they thought Jesus would be back any moment and didn't see any reason to exert themselves. Others relaxed because there were plenty of wealthier members in the church who were always willing to share. Regardless of the reason, Paul was abhorred by such laziness, and set the rule "If a man will not work, he shall not eat." How can our laziness affect the work of Christ? What can we do about the laziness of others? Paul addresses those questions in this study.

 Warming Up to God When is it hard for you to feel motivated to do the work of your church?

 Read 2 Thessalonians 3.

3 Finally, brothers, pray for us that the message of the Lord may spread rapidly and be honored, just as it was with you. ²And pray that we may be delivered from wicked and evil men, for not everyone has faith. ³But the Lord is faithful, and he will strengthen and protect you from the evil one. ⁴We have confidence in the Lord that you are doing and will continue to do the things we command. ⁵May the Lord direct your hearts into God's love and Christ's perseverance.

⁶In the name of the Lord Jesus Christ, we command you, brothers, to keep away from every brother who is idle and does not live according to the teaching*ᶠ* you received from us. ⁷For you yourselves know how you ought to follow our example. We were not idle when we were with you, ⁸nor did we eat anyone's food without paying for it. On the contrary, we worked night and day, laboring and toiling so that we would not be a burden to any of you. ⁹We did this, not because we do not have the right to such help, but in order to make ourselves a model for you to follow. ¹⁰For even when we were with you, we gave

you this rule: "If a man will not work, he shall not eat."

¹¹We hear that some among you are idle. They are not busy; they are busybodies. ¹²Such people we command and urge in the Lord Jesus Christ to settle down and earn the bread they eat. ¹³And as for you, brothers, never tire of doing what is right.

¹⁴If anyone does not obey our instruction in this letter, take special note of him. Do not associate with him, in order that he may feel ashamed. ¹⁵Yet do not regard him as an enemy, but warn him as a brother.

¹⁶Now may the Lord of peace himself give you peace at all times and in every way. The Lord be with all of you.

¹⁷I, Paul, write this greeting in my own hand, which is the distinguishing mark in all my letters. This is how I write.

¹⁸The grace of our Lord Jesus Christ be with you all.

ᶠ6 Or tradition

 Discovering the Word 1. In what ways did Paul expect that his ministry could be enhanced because of the Thessalonians' prayer (vv. 1–2)? 2. How is Paul's confidence in the Lord expressed in this request for prayer (vv. 3–5)? 3. How would you describe the problem the Thessalonian church was experiencing (v. 11)? 4. How did Paul make himself an example of the proper attitude toward work (vv. 7–9)? 5. What actions are to be taken against those who refuse to work (vv. 12–15)?

Applying the Word 1. What encouragement and ideas do these verses give you concerning your own prayer life? 2. In what ways do lazy Christians still continue to take advantage of the work of others? 3. What principles for discipline that could be applied in the church today do you find in this passage?

Responding in Prayer Pray that like Paul you will be a good example to others in your attitude toward work.

1 Timothy

E phesus, a key seaport for Asia Minor, was a swinging commercial center. Without an army, it maintained its place in the world through deal-making. It was the crowded home of about 350,000 people.

Dominating the economy of Ephesus was the temple of Artemis, "goddess of the Ephesians." It was regarded as one of the seven wonders of the ancient world. A huge structure of solid marble, it was the largest temple in the world outside Egypt, and the biggest *bank* east of Rome! You can read in Acts 19 about the riot Paul's preaching triggered among the guilds that depended on temple business. Artemis herself was a 37-breasted fertility goddess who stood for bringing prosperity out of constant change.

And change there was.

Various cultures mixed in Ephesus. Its heritage was Greek, but Romans pushed in when it became part of the Empire. A sizeable Jewish community took root, as well as smaller communities of many ethnic groups. Different religions, philosophies and ethics coexisted while everybody sought some piece of the economic action.

Sports were a major entertainment. The Greeks had two gymnasia built for athletic contests, while the Romans built a stadium for gladiator combat. By the mid-second century, the Roman approach of spectacular violence won the day over the Greek ideal of simple competition.

Sex was also big business. Art depicting various sex acts adorned the garden walls of large villas. Bestiality and homosexuality were celebrated. The Romans built baths—a kind of ancient country club where the upper-class members of both sexes went nude. Prostitution, divorce, multiple marriages, abandoned children and neglect of the elderly were common. Religious opinion ranged from advocating deviant sex to shunning sex totally.

A confusing mix of religions existed in the shadow of the dominant Artemis. The large Jewish community coexisted with it. Smaller ethnic groups had their own religions but didn't seek prominence. The Romans argued the case to rename Artemis as Diana, while thinking Greeks argued over mystical experiences and whether the names of gods were just diverse labels for the "One Prime Mover."

Although Artemis ruled in the public square, magic influenced the personal lives of most people and invaded all of the formal religions. A striking example is the account in Acts

19:13–17, which involved even the family of the Jewish high priest. In magic, the Ephesian spirit of deal-making was applied to spirituality. Ephesian magic became famous throughout the Roman world.

Paul, for his part, saw Ephesus as a great place to preach the gospel. He began with preaching to his fellow Jews on his second missionary journey. On his third journey, he invested two solid years evangelizing and developing Christian leaders. Christian faith became so popular that the magic trade and temple business fell sharply.

Paul's farewell message (Acts 20), however, shows that he was bracing for a spiritual counterattack on the Christian community. He predicted even some of his converts would set themselves up as Christian "gurus" and carve out followings around their own blend of Scripture, the gospel and mystical teachings. The issue Paul saw as crucial was spiritual authority: When should we accept spiritual teachings? When should we reject them? How do we know if Christian teachers are trustworthy? This, in fact, was just the situation when Paul wrote his first letter to Timothy.

Paul had turned over the leadership of the church in Ephesus, the most strategic in Asia Minor, to Timothy, a bright, sensitive associate. Timothy was about forty years old at that time, which was considered young for such leadership. False teaching was coming from people within the church. Since some of these were leaders (see Acts 20:30), Paul could not write to the church at Ephesus directly, but instead went through Timothy whom he had confidence in (Gordon Fee, "Issues in Evangelical Hermeneutics," *Crux* 26, no. 4 [December 1990]). Timothy's mission was to deal with false teaching, and it seems he was a capable teacher.

From references in 1 and 2 Corinthians, Acts, and the letters to Timothy, we know Timothy was a committed, but very human, person with some insecurities. Hebrews 13:23 shows that he spent some time in prison for his faith. We don't know what finally happened to Timothy, but we do know that John became the leader of the church not too long after these letters were written.

In these letters we can see Paul coaching the younger leader. In the process he raises issues which bear on us all—leaders or not.

Outline

1/ 1 Timothy 1 —————————— *What Difference Does It Make?*

2/ 1 Timothy 2 —————————— *Barriers to Renewal*

3/ 1 Timothy 3 —————————— *Who Can Lead?*

4/ 1 Timothy 4 —————————— *True and False Ministry*

5/ 1 Timothy 5:1—6:2 —————— *Implementing Spiritual Teaching*

6/ 1 Timothy 6:3–20 ————————— *Find Your Riches in Christ*

1 / *1 Timothy 1*
What Difference Does It Make?

"CHRIST CONSCIOUSNESS—MYSTICAL Teaching in the Bible," advertises a poster. "The mystical core of Christ's teaching has been obscured by centuries of dogma," it announces, inviting Christians to come to lectures by a young lady who follows a Hindu sect. And at the other extreme, some Christian leaders, dismayed by a low level of commitment, seek to create high-intensity groups with special teachings on top of the gospel and extra rules that regulate the social lives of their members. These modern examples are the kinds of thing that were rampant in the church at Ephesus; Paul sent Timothy to Ephesus to deal with them.

 Warming Up to God How do you distinguish between true and false spirituality?

 Read 1 Timothy 1.

1 Paul, an apostle of Christ Jesus by the command of God our Savior and of Christ Jesus our hope,

²To Timothy my true son in the faith:

Grace, mercy and peace from God the Father and Christ Jesus our Lord.

³As I urged you when I went into Macedonia, stay there in Ephesus so that you may command certain men not to teach false doctrines any longer ⁴nor to devote themselves to myths and endless genealogies. These promote controversies rather than God's work—which is by faith. ⁵The goal of this command is love, which comes from a pure heart and a good conscience and a sincere faith. ⁶Some have wandered away from these and turned to meaningless talk. ⁷They want to be teachers of the law, but they do not know what they are talking about or what they so confidently affirm.

⁸We know that the law is good if one uses it properly. ⁹We also know that law*ᵃ* is made not for the righteous but for lawbreakers and rebels, the ungodly and sinful, the unholy and irreligious; for those who kill their fathers or mothers, for murderers, ¹⁰for adulterers and perverts, for slave traders and liars and perjurers—and for whatever else is contrary to the sound doctrine ¹¹that conforms to the glorious gospel of the blessed God, which he entrusted to me.

¹²I thank Christ Jesus our Lord, who has given me strength, that he considered me faithful, appointing me to his service. ¹³Even though I was once a blasphemer and a persecutor and a violent man, I was shown mercy because I acted in ignorance and unbelief. ¹⁴The grace of our Lord was poured out on me abundantly, along with the faith and love that are in Christ Jesus.

¹⁵Here is a trustworthy saying that deserves full acceptance: Christ Jesus came into the world to save sinners—of whom I am the worst. ¹⁶But for that very reason I was shown mercy so that in me, the worst of sinners, Christ Jesus might display his unlimited patience as an example for those who would believe on him and receive eternal life. ¹⁷Now to the King eternal, immortal, invisible, the only God, be honor and glory for ever and ever. Amen.

¹⁸Timothy, my son, I give you this instruction in keeping with the prophecies once made about you, so that by following them you may fight the good fight, ¹⁹holding on to faith and a good conscience. Some have rejected these and so have shipwrecked their faith. ²⁰Among them are Hymenaeus and Alexander, whom I have handed over to Satan to be taught not to blaspheme.

ᵃ9 Or that the law

Discovering the Word 1. How does Paul describe Timothy's job (vv. 3–5)? 2. Finding hidden meanings in the Old Testament was big business in first-century religion. False teachers here tried to mix these "secret teachings" with the gospel. What results were the false teachers getting for their efforts (vv. 4–6)? 3. From what Paul says about the proper use of the law, how does it seem that the false teachers use it (vv. 8–11)? 4. In what ways was Paul himself like the false teachers before his conversion (vv. 12–17)? 5. Note the places where

the word *conscience* comes up (vv. 5, 19). When we speculate and theorize instead of dealing with our own issues of sin, what happens to conscience?

 Applying the Word 1. How can the kind of faith Paul shows in verse 15 help you face your own issues of conscience? 2. As in Paul's day, Christians can wander into groups that make unusual claims and demands. They may have impressive features, but engage in certain practices and pressures which make members feel uneasy. A lot of energy goes into keeping faith and conscience apart in these groups. Are you involved with some "spiritual" activities which bother your own conscience? (Be as honest as possible.)

Responding in Prayer Close in prayer by putting your own name in place of the general word *sinners* in verse 15. Now read verses 16–17 as your own prayer of thanks to God.

2 / *1 Timothy 2*
Barriers to Renewal

DO YOU EVER have difficulty approaching God in prayer? The Christians in Ephesus did. The barriers to prayer described here are anger, an over-emphasis on appearance, and an inappropriate role for women. Having sized up the situation and reminded Timothy of his mission, Paul outlines first steps to dealing with the needs of the church.

 Warming Up to God When do you find prayer difficult?

 Read 1 Timothy 2.

2 I urge, then, first of all, that requests, prayers, intercession and thanksgiving be made for everyone— ²for kings and all those in authority, that we may live peaceful and quiet lives in all godliness and holiness. ³This is good, and pleases God our Savior, ⁴who wants all men to be saved and to come to a knowledge of the truth. ⁵For there is one God and one mediator between God and men, the man Christ Jesus, ⁶who gave himself as a ransom for all men—the testimony given in its proper time. ⁷And for this purpose I was appointed a herald and an apostle—I am telling the truth, I am not lying—and a teacher of the true faith to the Gentiles.

⁸I want men everywhere to lift up holy hands in prayer, without anger or disputing.

⁹I also want women to dress modestly, with decency and propriety, not with braided hair or gold or pearls or expensive clothes, ¹⁰but with good deeds, appropriate for women who profess to worship God.

¹¹A woman should learn in quietness and full submission. ¹²I do not permit a woman to teach or to have authority over a man; she must be silent. ¹³For Adam was formed first, then Eve. ¹⁴And Adam was not the one deceived; it was the woman who was deceived and became a sinner. ¹⁵But women* will be saved* through childbearing—if they continue in faith, love and holiness with propriety.

*15 Greek *she*   *15 Or *restored*

Discovering the Word 1. Find all the times Paul says "all" and "everyone" (vv. 1–6). What does the use of these terms communicate about God? 2. Why do you think Paul emphasizes the word *one* in verse 5? 3. This entire chapter deals with worship. The church in Ephesus was probably a network of house churches. Their worship may have been patterned after the Jewish synagogues which separated men and women. What problem hindered the worship by men (v. 8)? 4. What problem hindered the worship by women (v. 9)? 5. In verses 11–12, Paul forbids women to teach men. But in 1 Corinthians 11:5, he tells them how to dress when they preach (or prophesy). How do you reconcile these texts?

Applying the Word 1. According to this passage, what could hinder worship and sharing the gospel? 2. Consider which of those are problems for you. How can you better deal with them?

Responding in Prayer Pray for your church's worship and for your personal worship.

---

3 / 1 Timothy 3
Who Can Lead?

SOME CHURCHES AND fellowships have a few people who are willing to lead. Those people may end up feeling burdened and alone. Other churches have people who are willing to lead, but not ready. If there are not enough leaders, however, the work of the church will not get done. The church of Ephesus was in the latter category. Those who were willing to lead were immature. And Timothy could not hope to carry out his mission against false teachers unless the leadership was healthy.

Warming Up to God What have your experiences of Christian leadership been like?

Read 1 Timothy 3.

---

3 Here is a trustworthy saying: If anyone sets his heart on being an overseer,[d] he desires a noble task. ²Now the overseer must be above reproach, the husband of but one wife, temperate, self-controlled, respectable, hospitable, able to teach, ³not given to drunkenness, not violent but gentle, not quarrelsome, not a lover of money. ⁴He must manage his own family well and see that his children obey him with proper respect. ⁵(If anyone does not know how to manage his own family, how can he take care of God's church?) ⁶He must not be a recent convert, or he may become conceited and fall under the same judgment as the devil. ⁷He must also have a good reputation with outsiders, so that he will not fall into disgrace and into the devil's trap.

⁸Deacons, likewise, are to be men worthy of respect, sincere, not indulging in much wine, and not pursuing dishonest gain. ⁹They must keep hold of the deep truths of the faith with a clear conscience. ¹⁰They must first be tested; and then if there is nothing against them, let them serve as deacons.

¹¹In the same way, their wives[e] are to be women worthy of respect, not malicious talkers but temperate and trustworthy in everything.

¹²A deacon must be the husband of but one wife and must manage his children and his household well. ¹³Those who have served well gain an excellent standing and great assurance in their faith in Christ Jesus.

¹⁴Although I hope to come to you soon, I am writing you these instructions so that, ¹⁵if I am delayed, you will know how people ought to conduct themselves in God's household, which is the church of the living God, the pillar and foundation of the truth. ¹⁶Beyond all question, the mystery of godliness is great:

> He[f] appeared in a body,[g]
>   was vindicated by the Spirit,
> was seen by angels,
>   was preached among the nations,
> was believed on in the world,
>   was taken up in glory.

---

d1 Traditionally bishop; also in verse 2   e11 Or way, deaconesses
f16 Some manuscripts God   g16 Or in the flesh

Discovering the Word 1. Consider two categories of qualification—*character* and *ability*. How do the qualities mentioned in these verses divide into these two categories? 2. What do you think is Paul's reason for insisting that a leader's relationships must work in the spheres of both church and family (vv. 5–6)? 3. How have you seen the principle in verse 7 obeyed or disobeyed? 4. "Deacon" simply means "servant." In the

passage it seems that deacons deal with the more practical affairs of church life, rather than with teaching. Given that, why do you think the point about doctrine in verse 9 is made with so much emphasis? 5. What do verses 14–16 tell us about Paul's purpose in writing this letter?

 Applying the Word 1. Verse 16 was probably a hymn sung in the church at Ephesus. The word translated as "deep truths" in verse 9 is rendered "mystery" here. We can say that the result Paul wanted from good Christian leadership was that these truths would be revealed. Therefore, when people look at our fellowship, what should they see? 2. How can you serve your church through leadership, or encourage others who lead?

 Responding in Prayer Pray for your pastor and church leaders.

4 / 1 Timothy 4
True and False Ministry

WITH THIS CHAPTER Paul's strategy for Timothy starts to emerge clearly. Timothy's mission was to deal with the false teachers. Paul sees, however, that fighting false teachers with ideology alone is fruitless. The real mission is that the church be healthy so that Jesus Christ is communicated through it. So he spoke of prayer and leadership first. With that foundation in place, Timothy will be able to turn his attention directly to the problems at hand.

 Warming Up to God Is there an older Christian in your family or church who has given you good advice? What was it?

 Read 1 Timothy 4.

4 The Spirit clearly says that in later times some will abandon the faith and follow deceiving spirits and things taught by demons. ²Such teachings come through hypocritical liars, whose consciences have been seared as with a hot iron. ³They forbid people to marry and order them to abstain from certain foods, which God created to be received with thanksgiving by those who believe and who know the truth. ⁴For everything God created is good, and nothing is to be rejected if it is received with thanksgiving, ⁵because it is consecrated by the word of God and prayer.

⁶If you point these things out to the brothers, you will be a good minister of Christ Jesus, brought up in the truths of the faith and of the good teaching that you have followed. ⁷Have nothing to do with godless myths and old wives' tales; rather, train yourself to be godly. ⁸For physical training is of some value, but godliness has value for all things, holding

promise for both the present life and the life to come.

⁹This is a trustworthy saying that deserves full acceptance ¹⁰(and for this we labor and strive), that we have put our hope in the living God, who is the Savior of all men, and especially of those who believe.

¹¹Command and teach these things. ¹²Don't let anyone look down on you because you are young, but set an example for the believers in speech, in life, in love, in faith and in purity. ¹³Until I come, devote yourself to the public reading of Scripture, to preaching and to teaching. ¹⁴Do not neglect your gift, which was given you through a prophetic message when the body of elders laid their hands on you.

¹⁵Be diligent in these matters; give yourself wholly to them, so that everyone may see your progress. ¹⁶Watch your life and doctrine closely. Persevere in them, because if you do, you will save both yourself and your hearers.

Discovering the Word 1. What is the nature of the teachings described in verses 2–3? 2. Why is this teaching—which could seem to be "superspiritual"—really a doctrine of demons (vv. 3–4)? 3. When you think of "false teaching," do you think of teachers who are morally too loose or too strict? Explain. 4. What was Timothy's personal life to be like (vv. 7–16)? 5. How was it to differ from that of the false teachers?

Applying the Word 1. Why do you think you are motivated at some times and *not* motivated at other times for training in godliness (v. 7)? 2. Timothy's primary ministry was teaching. What in this passage encourages you to develop and use your ministry gifts?

Responding in Prayer Pray for those who might be under the hold of false teachers, that the truth would be revealed to them.

---

5 / 1 Timothy 5:1—6:2
Implementing Spiritual Teaching

AT ONE TIME or another all of us have probably been in a situation in which we felt that someone in our church or fellowship was sinning. Whether or not we act on the situation and how we communicate to that person have a big effect on the outcome. Often when we rebuke others about their lifestyles, we come off as being judgmental and self-righteous. When Paul tells Timothy about specific persons and groups he needed to confront about certain issues, he is careful to show how to do so in love. Paul's teaching here gives us valuable guidance on being both direct and loving with other Christians.

 Warming Up to God When have you found—or seen—rebuke to have a positive impact?

 Read 1 Timothy 5:1—6:2.

---

5 Do not rebuke an older man harshly, but exhort him as if he were your father. Treat younger men as brothers, ²older women as mothers, and younger women as sisters, with absolute purity.

³Give proper recognition to those widows who are really in need. ⁴But if a widow has children or grandchildren, these should learn first of all to put their religion into practice by caring for their own family and so repaying their parents and grandparents, for this is pleasing to God. ⁵The widow who is really in need and left all alone puts her hope in God and continues night and day to pray and to ask God for help. ⁶But the widow who lives for pleasure is dead even while she lives. ⁷Give the people these instructions, too, so that no one may be open to blame. ⁸If anyone does not provide for his relatives, and especially for his immediate family, he has denied the faith and is worse than an unbeliever.

⁹No widow may be put on the list of widows unless she is over sixty, has been faithful to her husband,ʰ ¹⁰and is well known for her good deeds, such as bringing up children, showing hospitality, washing the feet of the saints, helping those in trouble and devoting herself to all kinds of good deeds.

¹¹As for younger widows, do not put them on such a list. For when their sensual desires overcome their dedication to Christ, they want to marry. ¹²Thus they bring judgment on themselves, because they have broken their first pledge. ¹³Besides, they get into the habit of being idle and going about from house to house. And not only do they become idlers, but also gossips and busybodies, saying things they ought not to. ¹⁴So I counsel younger widows to marry, to have children, to manage their homes and to give the enemy no opportunity for slander. ¹⁵Some have in fact already turned away to follow Satan.

¹⁶If any woman who is a believer has widows in her family, she should help them and not let the church be burdened with them, so that the church can help those widows who are really in need.

ʰ9 Or *has had but one husband*

¹⁷The elders who direct the affairs of the church well are worthy of double honor, especially those whose work is preaching and teaching. ¹⁸For the Scripture says, "Do not muzzle the ox while it is treading out the grain,"ⁱ and "The worker deserves his wages."ʲ ¹⁹Do not entertain an accusation against an elder unless it is brought by two or three witnesses. ²⁰Those who sin are to be rebuked publicly, so that the others may take warning.

²¹I charge you, in the sight of God and Christ Jesus and the elect angels, to keep these instructions without partiality, and to do nothing out of favoritism.

²²Do not be hasty in the laying on of hands, and do not share in the sins of others. Keep yourself pure.

²³Stop drinking only water, and use a little wine because of your stomach and your frequent illnesses.

²⁴The sins of some men are obvious, reaching the place of judgment ahead of them; the sins of others trail behind them. ²⁵In the same way, good deeds are obvious, and even those that are not cannot be hidden.

6 All who are under the yoke of slavery should consider their masters worthy of full respect, so that God's name and our teaching may not be slandered. ²Those who have believing masters are not to show less respect for them because they are brothers. Instead, they are to serve them even better, because those who benefit from their service are believers, and dear to them. These are the things you are to teach and urge on them.

ⁱ18 Deut. 25:4   ʲ18 Luke 10:7

 Discovering the Word 1. Paul touches on the different age and gender groups Timothy must lead. How is Timothy to regard the people he ministers to? 2. How is a godly widow to be distinguished from an ungodly one (vv. 3–8)? 3. What criteria did a widow need to meet to receive a place on the list of those who received financial aid from the church (vv. 9–10)? 4. Why do you think Paul gives these specific instructions about rebuking an elder in verses 19–20? 5. How have you found verses 24–25 to be true? 6. From 6:1–2 what do you think has been happening when slaves become believers?

Applying the Word 1. How can you rebuke someone in ways that are clear but also affirm the other person as a member of God's family? 2. In affluent Ephesus, like twentieth-century America, many elderly people were evidently abandoned. What obligations do you have to your own parents? 3. What ideas does this passage give you for new areas of ministry?

Responding in Prayer Pray for those in your church who are needy and who may be without family.

---

6 / 1 Timothy 6:3–20
Find Your Riches in Christ

SOME WELL-KNOWN Christian teachers and authors tell us that being a Christian means success and prosperity. If we are faithful, God will bless us with wealth. Other Christians advocate a simple lifestyle without interest in material possessions. What does Scripture say about how we are to regard money? In this chapter Paul concludes his agenda of how to lead the powerful and the powerless by addressing the wealthy members of the church.

 Warming Up to God What do you believe is the place of money in the life of a Christian?

 Read 1 Timothy 6:3–20.

---

³If anyone teaches false doctrines and does not agree to the sound instruction of our Lord Jesus Christ and to godly teaching, ⁴he is conceited and understands nothing. He has an unhealthy interest in controversies and quarrels about words that result in envy, strife, malicious talk, evil suspi-

cions ⁵and constant friction between men of corrupt mind, who have been robbed of the truth and who think that godliness is a means to financial gain.

⁶But godliness with contentment is great gain. ⁷For we brought nothing into the world, and we can take nothing out of it. ⁸But if we have food and clothing, we will be content with that. ⁹People who want to get rich fall into temptation and a trap and into many foolish and harmful desires that plunge men into ruin and destruction. ¹⁰For the love of money is a root of all kinds of evil. Some people, eager for money, have wandered from the faith and pierced themselves with many griefs.

¹¹But you, man of God, flee from all this, and pursue righteousness, godliness, faith, love, endurance and gentleness. ¹²Fight the good fight of the faith. Take hold of the eternal life to which you were called when you made your good confession in the presence of many witnesses. ¹³In the sight of God, who gives life to everything, and of Christ Jesus, who while testifying before Pontius Pilate made the good confession, I charge you ¹⁴to keep this command without spot or blame until the appearing of our Lord Jesus Christ, ¹⁵which God will bring about in his own time— God, the blessed and only Ruler, the King of kings and Lord of lords, ¹⁶who alone is immortal and who lives in unapproachable light, whom no one has seen or can see. To him be honor and might forever. Amen.

¹⁷Command those who are rich in this present world not to be arrogant nor to put their hope in wealth, which is so uncertain, but to put their hope in God, who richly provides us with everything for our enjoyment. ¹⁸Command them to do good, to be rich in good deeds, and to be generous and willing to share. ¹⁹In this way they will lay up treasure for themselves as a firm foundation for the coming age, so that they may take hold of the life that is truly life.

²⁰Timothy, guard what has been entrusted to your care. Turn away from godless chatter and the opposing ideas of what is falsely called knowledge, ²¹which some have professed and in so doing have wandered from the faith.

Grace be with you.

Discovering the Word 1. What do you think Paul means by an "unhealthy interest" (v. 4)? 2. According to verses 6–8, how are we to find contentment? 3. In your own words, how would you explain Paul's teaching on riches in verses 9–10? 4. What was Paul commanding Timothy to do in this context (vv. 11–14)? 5. How is Christ pictured in verses 13–16? 6. Why do you think Paul told Timothy to turn away from "godless chatter" (v. 20)?

Applying the Word 1. In what ways does your Christian life feel like a fight? 2. Describe how you have seen Christians use riches to do good work. 3. What has God entrusted to your care, and how do you guard it?

Responding in Prayer Pray that you would be a good steward of what you have been given.

How many of us will pause today to thank the Lord because we have something to wear and something to eat? And how would our lives change if we did?

2 Timothy

Second Timothy is Paul's last letter. He is in prison in Rome again—under Nero. He is an older man and does not expect to get out, but to die in prison (contrast with Php 1:23–25).

Opposition to Paul both inside and outside the church has intensified. Many former associates have deserted him. His loneliness and desire to see Timothy come through clearly. Further, Nero's persecution is under way, and many Christians are facing the choice of suffering or leaving the faith. Much of what he has built is at risk. When Paul's personal resources are at their lowest, he faces the greatest test. In this context he reflects on his own life and gives his final counsel.

This letter has fantastic value for us. It gives us insight into facing persecution and supporting others who are persecuted. It also shows both how to give away leadership and how to assume it at the right time. Finally, it provides encouragement to us in facing our own death.

Outline

1/ 2 Timothy 1 —————————————— *Rejected but Not Ashamed*

2/ 2 Timothy 2 —————————————— *Pass It On*

3/ 2 Timothy 3 —————————————— *How to Recognize God's Voice*

4/ 2 Timothy 4 —————————————— *It's Your Turn Now*

1 / 2 Timothy 1
Rejected but Not Ashamed

SHAME MEANS BEING revealed to others as weak and inadequate. Rejection is always cause for shame unless we are quite sure of both our ideas and our approach. We are prone to believe what others say about us, especially if they are more successful or in authority. We often need support from our own friends to maintain our dignity even in the face of unjust charges.

It is remarkable but true that when Paul was imprisoned, the church in Rome did not come to Paul's defense. Only one believer came looking for him. The rest probably held back from fear or considered the imprisonment something shameful. But although he has been rejected, Paul tells us he is *not* ashamed.

 Warming Up to God When have non-Christian friends or pressures from the world caused you to feel ashamed of the gospel?

 Read 2 Timothy 1.

1 Paul, an apostle of Christ Jesus by the will of God, according to the promise of life that is in Christ Jesus,

²To Timothy, my dear son:

Grace, mercy and peace from God the Father and Christ Jesus our Lord.

³I thank God, whom I serve, as my forefathers did, with a clear conscience, as night and day I constantly remember you in my prayers. ⁴Recalling your tears, I long to see you, so that I may be filled with joy. ⁵I have been reminded of your sincere faith, which first lived in your grandmother Lois and in your mother Eunice and, I am persuaded, now lives in you also. ⁶For this reason I remind you to fan into flame the gift of God, which is in you through the laying on of my hands. ⁷For God did not give us a spirit of timidity, but a spirit of power, of love and of self-discipline.

⁸So do not be ashamed to testify about our Lord, or ashamed of me his prisoner. But join with me in suffering for the gospel, by the power of God, ⁹who has saved us and called us to a holy life—not because of anything we have done but because of his own purpose and grace. This grace was given us in Christ Jesus before the beginning of time, ¹⁰but it has now been revealed through the appearing of our Savior, Christ Jesus, who has destroyed death and has brought life and immortality to light through the gospel. ¹¹And of this gospel I was appointed a herald and an apostle and a teacher. ¹²That is why I am suffering as I am. Yet I am not ashamed, because I know whom I have believed, and am convinced that he is able to guard what I have entrusted to him for that day.

¹³What you heard from me, keep as the pattern of sound teaching, with faith and love in Christ Jesus. ¹⁴Guard the good deposit that was entrusted to you—guard it with the help of the Holy Spirit who lives in us.

¹⁵You know that everyone in the province of Asia has deserted me, including Phygelus and Hermogenes.

¹⁶May the Lord show mercy to the household of Onesiphorus, because he often refreshed me and was not ashamed of my chains. ¹⁷On the contrary, when he was in Rome, he searched hard for me until he found me. ¹⁸May the Lord grant that he will find mercy from the Lord on that day! You know very well in how many ways he helped me in Ephesus.

Discovering the Word 1. What information are we given about the relationship between Paul and Timothy (vv. 2–6)? 2. What is Paul's situation (vv. 1, 8, 11–12, 15–16)? 3. Find the references to shame (vv. 12, 16). Why would *shame* be a response to Paul's imprisonment? 4. How did Paul reject shame in this situation (vv. 3, 8–12)?

Applying the Word 1. Imprisonment can take many forms beyond the literal example here, such as chronic disease, financial collapse, abuse, or anything that severely restricts your freedom and separates you from people. How can we apply Paul's example of resisting the shame that arises from such situations?

2. Consider Timothy's situation: his mentor has been disgraced; many of his associates have deserted the ministry; many of his church's members are drifting from the faith or cowed by the threat of persecution. How have you struggled or are you struggling with similar situations? **3.** How do you believe God is calling you to testify about him in your own situation?

 Responding in Prayer With your call to witness in mind, pray through what the text affirms about God in verses 8–12. As you pray, think especially about how you might be ashamed of sharing your faith, and ask for God's help.

2 / 2 Timothy 2
Pass It On

BARBARA BOYD ONCE said, "Paul had no dead-end disciples." The essence of Paul's ministry was to be certain that the gospel was handed on to other people in such a way that they came to regard this task as their own. This approach, which was very radical in its time, puts the "power" of the movement into the hands of thousands. Paul, having been deserted by many, wants to make sure the gospel won't die when he does—or when Timothy does.

 Warming Up to God Think of a time when an older Christian has entrusted some aspect of ministry to you. How did this create growth and maturity in your life?

 Read 2 Timothy 2.

2 You then, my son, be strong in the grace that is in Christ Jesus. ²And the things you have heard me say in the presence of many witnesses entrust to reliable men who will also be qualified to teach others. ³Endure hardship with us like a good soldier of Christ Jesus. ⁴No one serving as a soldier gets involved in civilian affairs—he wants to please his commanding officer. ⁵Similarly, if anyone competes as an athlete, he does not receive the victor's crown unless he competes according to the rules. ⁶The hardworking farmer should be the first to receive a share of the crops. ⁷Reflect on what I am saying, for the Lord will give you insight into all this.

⁸Remember Jesus Christ, raised from the dead, descended from David. This is my gospel, ⁹for which I am suffering even to the point of being chained like a criminal. But God's word is not chained. ¹⁰Therefore I endure everything for the sake of the elect, that they too may obtain the salvation that is in Christ Jesus, with eternal glory.

¹¹Here is a trustworthy saying:

If we died with him,
   we will also live with him;
¹²if we endure,
   we will also reign with him.

If we disown him,
   he will also disown us;
¹³if we are faithless,
   he will remain faithful,
   for he cannot disown himself.

¹⁴Keep reminding them of these things. Warn them before God against quarreling about words; it is of no value, and only ruins those who listen. ¹⁵Do your best to present yourself to God as one approved, a workman who does not need to be ashamed and who correctly handles the word of truth. ¹⁶Avoid godless chatter, because those who indulge in it will become more and more ungodly. ¹⁷Their teaching will spread like gangrene. Among them are Hymenaeus and Philetus, ¹⁸who have wandered away from the truth. They say that the resurrection has already taken place, and they destroy the faith of some. ¹⁹Nevertheless, God's solid foundation stands firm, sealed with this inscription: "The Lord knows those who are his,"ᵃ and, "Everyone who confesses the name of the Lord must turn away from wickedness."

²⁰In a large house there are articles not only of gold and silver, but also of wood and clay; some are for noble purposes and some for ignoble. ²¹If a man cleanses himself from the latter, he will be

ᵃ19 Num. 16:5 (see Septuagint)

an instrument for noble purposes, made holy, useful to the Master and prepared to do any good work.

²²Flee the evil desires of youth, and pursue righteousness, faith, love and peace, along with those who call on the Lord out of a pure heart. ²³Don't have anything to do with foolish and stupid arguments, because you know they produce quarrels. ²⁴And the Lord's servant must not quarrel; instead, he must be kind to everyone, able to teach, not resentful. ²⁵Those who oppose him he must gently instruct, in the hope that God will grant them repentance leading them to a knowledge of the truth, ²⁶and that they will come to their senses and escape from the trap of the devil, who has taken them captive to do his will.

 Discovering the Word 1. Paul begins with the call to Timothy to "be strong in grace." Why does he give that instruction rather than "be strong in your gifts," "be strong in knowledge" or "be strong in willpower"? 2. What does each of the three images in verses 3–7 illustrate about the ministry of entrusting the gospel to others who can pass it on? 3. Why does Paul cite these specific aspects of Christ that Timothy should remember (v. 8)? 4. How does this explain Paul's own confidence even while he is imprisoned (v. 9)? 5. Why does Paul say he endures (vv. 10–13)? 6. What do verses 18–19 say is both the potential and the limitation of false teaching?

 Applying the Word 1. Which of the images in verses 3–7 seems most applicable to your life right now? Why? 2. How should the trustworthy saying in verses 11–13 motivate us?

Responding in Prayer Where is your own character being tested as you try to entrust the gospel to others? Pray that God will encourage you and strengthen you in those areas.

---

3 / 2 Timothy 3
How to Recognize God's Voice

MOST OF US go through stages in our lives where we are vulnerable to false teachers. Campus cults make their biggest outreaches during the opening days of school and during finals week—when students are under the greatest stress. Life crises are doors of change—for good or evil. In addition, guilt, greed and other lusts often distort judgment and give false teachers their opportunity.

Philetus and Hymanaeus represent a tradition of potent religious falsehood Timothy fought against his whole career. We can expect the same kind of struggle. In spite of the power and appeal of such groups, however, Paul had great confidence in both Scripture and those who live by it. In this chapter he encourages Timothy to have confidence in God's teaching as well.

 Warming Up to God What factors do you think would make a person particularly susceptible to heresy?

 Read 2 Timothy 3.

---

3 But mark this: There will be terrible times in the last days. ²People will be lovers of themselves, lovers of money, boastful, proud, abusive, disobedient to their parents, ungrateful, unholy, ³without love, unforgiving, slanderous, without self-control, brutal, not lovers of the good, ⁴treacherous, rash, conceited, lovers of pleasure rather than lovers of God— ⁵having a form of godliness but denying its power. Have nothing to do with them.

⁶They are the kind who worm their way into homes and gain control over weak-willed women, who are loaded down with sins and are swayed by all kinds of evil desires, ⁷always learning but never able to acknowledge the truth. ⁸Just as Jannes and Jambres opposed Moses, so also these men oppose the truth—men of depraved minds, who, as far as the faith is concerned, are rejected. ⁹But they will not get very far because, as in the case of those men, their folly will be clear to everyone.

¹⁰You, however, know all about my teaching,

my way of life, my purpose, faith, patience, love, endurance, ¹¹persecutions, sufferings—what kinds of things happened to me in Antioch, Iconium and Lystra, the persecutions I endured. Yet the Lord rescued me from all of them. ¹²In fact, everyone who wants to live a godly life in Christ Jesus will be persecuted, ¹³while evil men and impostors will go from bad to worse, deceiving and being deceived. ¹⁴But as for you, continue in what you have learned and have become con-vinced of, because you know those from whom you learned it, ¹⁵and how from infancy you have known the holy Scriptures, which are able to make you wise for salvation through faith in Christ Jesus. ¹⁶All Scripture is God-breathed and is useful for teaching, rebuking, correcting and training in righteousness, ¹⁷so that the man of God may be thoroughly equipped for every good work.

 Discovering the Word 1. What evidence do we have here that these people are religious? 2. Notice the way those controlled by these religious leaders are described (v. 6). Why are we vulnerable to spiritual manipulation when we are "weak-willed," "loaded down with sins" and "swayed by evil desires"? 3. Why could Timothy trust Paul's spiritual influence (vv. 10–13)? 4. Paul does not expect blind faith from Timothy. What does he expect, and what two reasons does he give for it (vv. 14–15)? 5. Where does Scripture come from, and what is its power (vv. 15–17)?

Applying the Word 1. What would enhance your own trustworthiness among those you influence (children, students, coworkers or employees, and friends)? 2. In Hebrew (conceptually) to hear is to obey and do God's will. During this study, how have you sensed that God wants you to change in order to hear his voice more clearly?

Responding in Prayer Pray that you would hear God's voice and be kept safe from false teaching.

4 / 2 Timothy 4
It's Your Turn Now

THE STORY IS told of the umpire who called a strike on Babe Ruth. The Babe turned around and angrily shouted, "Hey, meathead! Me and 40,000 people here know that pitch was a ball!" The umpire replied, "Yeah, and mine is the only opinion that matters."

The gospel is not often popular. As he gears up for ministry, Timothy needs to know that only God's opinion matters. In this passage, the last written words of Paul we have, Paul instructs Timothy to think of eternity.

 Warming Up to God How do you respond (inwardly and outwardly) when you see friends turning away from the faith?

 Read 2 Timothy 4.

4 In the presence of God and of Christ Jesus, who will judge the living and the dead, and in view of his appearing and his kingdom, I give you this charge: ²Preach the Word; be prepared in season and out of season; correct, rebuke and encourage—with great patience and careful instruction. ³For the time will come when men will not put up with sound doctrine. Instead, to suit their own desires, they will gather around them a great number of teachers to say what their itching ears want to hear. ⁴They will turn their ears away from the truth and turn aside to myths. ⁵But you, keep your head in all situations, endure hardship, do the work of an evangelist, discharge all the duties of your ministry.

⁶For I am already being poured out like a drink offering, and the time has come for my departure. ⁷I have fought the good fight, I have finished the race, I have kept the faith. ⁸Now there is in store

for me the crown of righteousness, which the Lord, the righteous Judge, will award to me on that day—and not only to me, but also to all who have longed for his appearing.

⁹Do your best to come to me quickly, ¹⁰for Demas, because he loved this world, has deserted me and has gone to Thessalonica. Crescens has gone to Galatia, and Titus to Dalmatia. ¹¹Only Luke is with me. Get Mark and bring him with you, because he is helpful to me in my ministry. ¹²I sent Tychicus to Ephesus. ¹³When you come, bring the cloak that I left with Carpus at Troas, and my scrolls, especially the parchments.

¹⁴Alexander the metalworker did me a great deal of harm. The Lord will repay him for what he has done. ¹⁵You too should be on your guard against him, because he strongly opposed our message.

¹⁶At my first defense, no one came to my sup-

port, but everyone deserted me. May it not be held against them. ¹⁷But the Lord stood at my side and gave me strength, so that through me the message might be fully proclaimed and all the Gentiles might hear it. And I was delivered from the lion's mouth. ¹⁸The Lord will rescue me from every evil attack and will bring me safely to his heavenly kingdom. To him be glory for ever and ever. Amen.

¹⁹Greet Priscilla*ᵇ* and Aquila and the household of Onesiphorus. ²⁰Erastus stayed in Corinth, and I left Trophimus sick in Miletus. ²¹Do your best to get here before winter. Eubulus greets you, and so do Pudens, Linus, Claudia and all the brothers.

²²The Lord be with your spirit. Grace be with you.

ᵇ19 Greek *Prisca*, a variant of *Priscilla*

 Discovering the Word 1. What charge was Timothy to keep (vv. 3–5)? 2. Paul is seeing a big part of what he labored so hard to build under God's power dissolve. How can he still feel such satisfaction about his life (vv. 6–8)? 3. What do verses 9–13 reveal about Paul's situation? 4. Rome had a big Christian community, but they shunned Paul when he came to trial (vv. 16–17, see also 1:8, 12, 16–18). Paul could have chosen to burn with resentment. What clues in the passage show why he was not bitter? 5. The names in verses 19–20 denote men, women, Romans, Greeks, nobles and commoners. What comfort would that fact give both Paul and Timothy?

 Applying the Word 1. What life tasks do you need to finish in order to share Paul's satisfaction? 2. Who is taking a public stand for the gospel in your community, and how can you support him or her?

Responding in Prayer Pray for the spread of the gospel locally and around the world.

Titus

Titus was no stranger to conflict. He was a long-term companion of Paul who was a valuable aid in two of Paul's greatest crises.

Titus first appears in the New Testament in Galatians 2:1, where Paul says he took Titus along on his trip to Jerusalem with Barnabas. Titus was a Gentile, and the issue at hand was whether Gentiles should have to comply with Jewish ceremonial rites (circumcision, diet restrictions and so on) in order to be full members of the Christian community. With the young Paul at one side and Barnabas at the other, he was essentially "tried" (and acquitted) by the leaders in Jerusalem.

Titus appears again in the middle of Paul's struggle with the church at Corinth. In that deeply divided church, he represented Paul. He had the unwelcome job of delivering what we call the "severe letter," which Paul refers to in 2 Corinthians 2:1–4 and 7:5–13, and then staying there for about a year. Then he delivered the letter we now call 2 Corinthians in which Paul takes on his critics and calls the church to honor an unfulfilled financial pledge.

Titus was in Crete at the time Paul wrote him. Crete was a seaport, a sleazy port of call for cargo ships traversing the Mediterranean. It had been socially backward for 1400 years since the Minoan civilization was destroyed by a devastating earthquake. We do not know exactly when Titus went with Paul to Crete, but one possible scenario places it after Paul's release from his first imprisonment in Rome.

Paul had preached in Crete and was giving Titus the job of following through with developing a healthy church. This letter was sent while he was in the midst of his task and reviews his assignment. It shows Titus as a forceful personality and skilled administrator. It seems he was made of tougher stuff than Timothy, but his assignments were shorter. By the time Paul had written 2 Timothy, the job in Crete was done, and Titus had been sent on to Dalmatia (part of modern Yugoslavia).

This letter gives us two very valuable things: (1) a showcase of Paul's strategy for leadership in the midst of chaos (Timothy was given a long-term assignment in an established church; Titus was sent to follow up an evangelistic movement and give the Christian body some coherence) (2) a model of hope in the face of a very messy situation (Paul's confidence in the power of the gospel shines throughout the letter).

Titus 1—3
Great Expectations

GREAT EXPECTATIONS IS the well-known title of a novel by Charles Dickens. It is the story of a young man's early experiences out in the "real world" as he seeks to gain the fortune he has inherited. Similarly, the book of Titus tells of Paul's expectations for Titus during his first ministry experience on his own. Paul's promise to Titus is that he will become an heir of eternity.

Warming Up to God Think of a person in your life who expects great things from you. How do you feel about that person's expectations? Are they realistic?

Read Titus 1—3.

1 Paul, a servant of God and an apostle of Jesus Christ for the faith of God's elect and the knowledge of the truth that leads to godliness— ²a faith and knowledge resting on the hope of eternal life, which God, who does not lie, promised before the beginning of time, ³and at his appointed season he brought his word to light through the preaching entrusted to me by the command of God our Savior,

⁴To Titus, my true son in our common faith:

Grace and peace from God the Father and Christ Jesus our Savior.

⁵The reason I left you in Crete was that you might straighten out what was left unfinished and appoint*ᵃ* elders in every town, as I directed you. ⁶An elder must be blameless, the husband of but one wife, a man whose children believe and are not open to the charge of being wild and disobedient. ⁷Since an overseer*ᵇ* is entrusted with God's work, he must be blameless—not overbearing, not quick-tempered, not given to drunkenness, not violent, not pursuing dishonest gain. ⁸Rather he must be hospitable, one who loves what is good, who is self-controlled, upright, holy and disciplined. ⁹He must hold firmly to the trustworthy message as it has been taught, so that he can encourage others by sound doctrine and refute those who oppose it.

¹⁰For there are many rebellious people, mere talkers and deceivers, especially those of the circumcision group. ¹¹They must be silenced, because they are ruining whole households by teaching things they ought not to teach—and that for the sake of dishonest gain. ¹²Even one of their own prophets has said, "Cretans are always liars, evil brutes, lazy gluttons." ¹³This testimony is true. Therefore, rebuke them sharply, so that

they will be sound in the faith ¹⁴and will pay no attention to Jewish myths or to the commands of those who reject the truth. ¹⁵To the pure, all things are pure, but to those who are corrupted and do not believe, nothing is pure. In fact, both their minds and consciences are corrupted. ¹⁶They claim to know God, but by their actions they deny him. They are detestable, disobedient and unfit for doing anything good.

2 You must teach what is in accord with sound doctrine. ²Teach the older men to be temperate, worthy of respect, self-controlled, and sound in faith, in love and in endurance.

³Likewise, teach the older women to be reverent in the way they live, not to be slanderers or addicted to much wine, but to teach what is good. ⁴Then they can train the younger women to love their husbands and children, ⁵to be self-controlled and pure, to be busy at home, to be kind, and to be subject to their husbands, so that no one will malign the word of God.

⁶Similarly, encourage the young men to be self-controlled. ⁷In everything set them an example by doing what is good. In your teaching show integrity, seriousness ⁸and soundness of speech that cannot be condemned, so that those who oppose you may be ashamed because they have nothing bad to say about us.

⁹Teach slaves to be subject to their masters in everything, to try to please them, not to talk back to them, ¹⁰and not to steal from them, but to show that they can be fully trusted, so that in every way they will make the teaching about God our Savior attractive.

¹¹For the grace of God that brings salvation has appeared to all men. ¹²It teaches us to say "No" to

ᵃ5 Or ordain   ᵇ7 Traditionally bishop

ungodliness and worldly passions, and to live self-controlled, upright and godly lives in this present age, ¹³while we wait for the blessed hope—the glorious appearing of our great God and Savior, Jesus Christ, ¹⁴who gave himself for us to redeem us from all wickedness and to purify for himself a people that are his very own, eager to do what is good.

¹⁵These, then, are the things you should teach. Encourage and rebuke with all authority. Do not let anyone despise you.

3 Remind the people to be subject to rulers and authorities, to be obedient, to be ready to do whatever is good, ²to slander no one, to be peaceable and considerate, and to show true humility toward all men.

³At one time we too were foolish, disobedient, deceived and enslaved by all kinds of passions and pleasures. We lived in malice and envy, being hated and hating one another. ⁴But when the kindness and love of God our Savior appeared, ⁵he saved us, not because of righteous things we had done, but because of his mercy. He saved us through the washing of rebirth and renewal by the Holy Spirit, ⁶whom he poured out on us generously through Jesus Christ our Savior, ⁷so that, having been justified by his grace, we might be-

come heirs having the hope of eternal life. ⁸This is a trustworthy saying. And I want you to stress these things, so that those who have trusted in God may be careful to devote themselves to doing what is good. These things are excellent and profitable for everyone.

⁹But avoid foolish controversies and genealogies and arguments and quarrels about the law, because these are unprofitable and useless. ¹⁰Warn a divisive person once, and then warn him a second time. After that, have nothing to do with him. ¹¹You may be sure that such a man is warped and sinful; he is self-condemned.

¹²As soon as I send Artemas or Tychicus to you, do your best to come to me at Nicopolis, because I have decided to winter there. ¹³Do everything you can to help Zenas the lawyer and Apollos on their way and see that they have everything they need. ¹⁴Our people must learn to devote themselves to doing what is good, in order that they may provide for daily necessities and not live unproductive lives.

¹⁵Everyone with me sends you greetings. Greet those who love us in the faith.

Grace be with you all.

Discovering the Word 1. Note all you can from the book about the social situation (family, public and private morality). 2. What do you learn about the economic situation (work, wealth and poverty)? 3. What is revealed about the religious situation (spirituality, doctrine, church life)? 4. Paul expected enormous things of Titus. And he wanted Titus to meet him in Nicopolis (3:12) in about eight months. When it comes to what others expect of us, our first response is often to question whether they are fair. How fair do you think Paul's expectations of Titus were? 5. Paul's expectations were built not only on his knowledge of Titus, but on solid theological grounds as well. What were they (see 1:1–3; 2:11–14; 3:3–7)? 6. Do you think Paul's expectations helped Titus to accomplish his mission? Why or why not?

Applying the Word 1. Do your own Christian leaders expect too much or too little of you? 2. What effect does that have on your own walk with Jesus Christ? 3. At work, home, school or church, whether you are a follower or a leader, you have a responsibility to communicate your expectations. Name one step you could take to do this more effectively.

  Responding in Prayer What expectations are you wrestling with? Ask God for insight to know which come from him and which do not.

Philemon

T he little book of Philemon is the only surviving letter of Paul to an individual friend and convert about a private matter. In it we learn that Onesimus, one of Philemon's slaves, had stolen from his master and run away to Rome. In that great city he met Paul and became a Christian. Under Roman law, Philemon had the right to brand a returned slave and even kill him.

Paul applies what he wrote in Colossians: "Here there is no Greek or Jew . . . slave or free, but Christ is all, and is in all" (Col 3:11). Philemon and Onesimus are given the chance to participate in a revolutionary new process for reconciliation.

Philemon 1–25
Mending Fractured Relationships

DAVE AND ANDY enjoyed a prosperous business partnership for several years. Their families became closest friends, sharing vacations made possible by their growing computer business. Then one day Andy disappeared, along with the company bank account. Dave lost his friend, his business and his home. Three years later Andy returned, having squandered the money but having found Christ. Could Dave forgive him? Could they ever be friends again?

In Paul's letter to Philemon, you'll find principles for bringing reconciliation between two Christians who know the pain of wronging another and being wronged.

 Warming Up to God Recall a time when you wanted to restore a broken relationship. What were some of your fears in approaching the situation?

 Read Philemon 1–25.

¹Paul, a prisoner of Christ Jesus, and Timothy our brother,

To Philemon our dear friend and fellow worker, ²to Apphia our sister, to Archippus our fellow soldier and to the church that meets in your home:

³Grace to you and peace from God our Father and the Lord Jesus Christ.

⁴I always thank my God as I remember you in my prayers, ⁵because I hear about your faith in the Lord Jesus and your love for all the saints. ⁶I pray that you may be active in sharing your faith, so that you will have a full understanding of every good thing we have in Christ. ⁷Your love has given me great joy and encouragement, because you, brother, have refreshed the hearts of the saints.

⁸Therefore, although in Christ I could be bold and order you to do what you ought to do, ⁹yet I appeal to you on the basis of love. I then, as Paul—an old man and now also a prisoner of Christ Jesus— ¹⁰I appeal to you for my son Onesimus,ᵃ who became my son while I was in chains. ¹¹Formerly he was useless to you, but now he has become useful both to you and to me. ¹²I am sending him—who is my very heart— back to you. ¹³I would have liked to keep him with me so that he could take your place in help-

ing me while I am in chains for the gospel. ¹⁴But I did not want to do anything without your consent, so that any favor you do will be spontaneous and not forced. ¹⁵Perhaps the reason he was separated from you for a little while was that you might have him back for good— ¹⁶no longer as a slave, but better than a slave, as a dear brother. He is very dear to me but even dearer to you, both as a man and as a brother in the Lord.

¹⁷So if you consider me a partner, welcome him as you would welcome me. ¹⁸If he has done you any wrong or owes you anything, charge it to me. ¹⁹I, Paul, am writing this with my own hand. I will pay it back—not to mention that you owe me your very self. ²⁰I do wish, brother, that I may have some benefit from you in the Lord; refresh my heart in Christ. ²¹Confident of your obedience, I write to you, knowing that you will do even more than I ask.

²²And one thing more: Prepare a guest room for me, because I hope to be restored to you in answer to your prayers.

²³Epaphras, my fellow prisoner in Christ Jesus, sends you greetings. ²⁴And so do Mark, Aristarchus, Demas and Luke, my fellow workers.

²⁵The grace of the Lord Jesus Christ be with your spirit.

ᵃ10 Onesimus means useful.

Discovering the Word 1. Based on what you have read, how would you reconstruct the events that led up to this letter? 2. Having described Philemon's loving character, Paul appeals to him on the basis of love (v. 9). Why is love so essential for mending a fractured relationship? 3. In what ways has Onesimus changed since running away from Philemon (vv. 10–16)? 4. What will it require of Onesimus to return to Philemon? 5. What will it require of Philemon to do what Paul asks?

Applying the Word 1. What principles in this letter could you use for mending a fractured relationship? 2. Paul intervened to restore these two brothers in Christ. When might we need the help of a friend or counselor?

Responding in Prayer Pray for God's grace for you to follow these principles in a situation where you may be an Onesimus or Philemon or Paul.

Hebrews

A former Olympic distance runner and veteran missionary wrote the following letter of encouragement to a friend who was caught in the throes of a horrendous personal crisis:

In this race . . . I suddenly hit a branch of a tree (and) . . . the blow almost knocked me out. . . . It knocked me out of my race, stopped me cold. . . . Somehow I staggered back on the track and stumbled along. . . . I remember one clear conclusion. I must keep going, even if I come in long behind. I must not quit. So I kept going. I won the race. . . . Whatever the difficulty, the blow, we must keep on. God will lead to the result that will glorify him. (Gordon MacDonald, *Rebuilding Your Broken World* [Nashville: Oliver-Nelson, 1988], p. 224.)

The sentence "Whatever . . . the blow, we must keep on" captures the theme of the letter to the Hebrews, which I have entitled "Race to Glory." The author of Hebrews states it very clearly: "Let us run with perseverance the race marked out for us" (12:1).

Throughout, the author emphasizes this chief concern for the readers—that they finish their faith-race with Jesus Christ gloriously and triumphantly. "Pay more careful attention," the author warns, "so that we do not drift away" (2:1). "Let us be careful that none of you be found to have fallen short of it [God's promised rest]" (4:1). "Let us leave the elementary teachings about Christ and go on to maturity," the writer appeals (6:1). "We want each of you to show this same diligence to the very end, in order to make your hope sure" (6:11).

After convincingly showing how Jesus Christ meets all of our needs, the writer cries out, "Let us draw near to God with a sincere heart in full assurance of faith. . . . Let us hold unswervingly to the hope we profess, for he who promised is faithful" (10:22–23). "Do not throw away your confidence. . . . You need to persevere so that when you have done the will of God, you will receive what he has promised" (10:35–36).

The author devotes an entire chapter (11) to drawing the readers to the stories of great heroes who finished the race to glory, people like Moses, Abraham, Noah, Jacob and Joseph. These witnesses are summoned to inspire us onward in our own faith-race.

A friend of mine loves to joke that when he gets to heaven he is going to find out who wrote Hebrews. The letter bears no byline, so scholars have had a field day speculating about its possible authors. Included in this list are Paul, Silas, Titus, Mark, Clement, Luke, Aquila, Priscilla and Barnabas. If you took a poll among these scholars, Luke, Barnabas and Apollos would be strongly

favored. At any rate, whoever the author was, he or she knew the Hebrews very well.

The readers were knowledgeable Jews who had converted to faith in Jesus Christ. The entire scaffolding of the letter is Jewish history, theology and practice. These Jews were old enough in the faith to be teachers and to recall older leaders (5:12; 13:7). They had served one another and had suffered (6:10; 10:32–34). Their city can only be guessed at—possibly Jerusalem, Alexandria, Corinth, Ephesus or Rome.

What is completely clear about the audience is their spiritual peril. They were in danger of reverting to Judaism. The letter is chock full of warnings about it. They were being taunted by Jews as apostates from God and renegades from Moses. They were accused of abandoning their law and forfeiting the Old Testament promises.

So the writer goes to great lengths to prove that Jesus Christ is far superior to everything they had left behind for his sake. In that context, he warns them against neglect, unbelief, disobedience, immaturity and rejection. He stands in the grandstand, as it were, wildly cheering them on to stay on the track, not to quit, and to reach the finish line in the power of Jesus Christ.

Today's readers most likely will not have come to faith in Christ out of such a deeply embedded cultural and religious tradition. But every Christian at some time or other is tempted to quit and to ask, "What's the use?" As problems and roadblocks mount, as faith seems unproductive, as doors slam, we find it easy to think about quitting our personal faith-race.

We also need current reminders about the supremacy of Jesus Christ. There is no stronger enticement to stay in the race than to "fix our eyes on Jesus" (12:2). As the Pioneer of our salvation, he brings us to glory (2:10).

We run our faith-race in vital communion with God through prayer, by giving God's Word command of our lives, by faithfully worshiping him and loving fellow Christians, and by knowing and serving Jesus Christ better each day as our daily companion, guide and master.

Outline

1/ Hebrews 1 ———————————— Starting the Race

2/ Hebrews 2 ———————————— Warning Signs

3/ Hebrews 3 ———————————— Winning the Race

4/ Hebrews 4:1–13 ——————— Receiving God's Blessings

5/ Hebrews 4:14—5:10 ————— Overcoming Weakness

6/ Hebrews 5:11—6:20 ————— The Race to Maturity

7/ Hebrews 7 ———————————— Eternal Companion

8/ Hebrews 8 ———————————— God's "New Deal"

9/ Hebrews 9 ———————————— The Runner's Power

10/ Hebrews 10 —————————— Staying in the Race

11/ Hebrews 11 —————————— Models of Faith

12/ Hebrews 12 —————————— The Runner's Discipline

13/ Hebrews 13 —————————— Running by the Rules

1 / Hebrews 1
Starting the Race

WHEN THE ANCIENT church father John Chrysostom, bishop of Constantinople, was summoned by Emperor Arcadius and threatened with banishment, he responded, "You cannot banish me, for the whole world is my Father's kingdom."

"Then I will take away your life," said the emperor.

"You cannot," answered Chrysostom, "for my life is hid with Christ in God."

"I will take away your treasure," roared the emperor.

"You can't," replied Chrysostom, "for my treasure is in heaven, where my heart is."

"Then I will drive you away from all your friends," the emperor said.

"You cannot, for I have one friend from whom you can never separate me. I defy you," said Chrysostom, "because you can do me no harm."

Such conviction grows out of a firm grasp of who Jesus Christ really is. Hebrews 1 will get you started on the race with a look at the majesty, power and glory of Jesus Christ.

 Warming Up to God Focus on what you have experienced of the majesty, power and glory of Jesus Christ. Praise Jesus for who he is.

 Read Hebrews 1.

---

1 In the past God spoke to our forefathers through the prophets at many times and in various ways, ²but in these last days he has spoken to us by his Son, whom he appointed heir of all things, and through whom he made the universe. ³The Son is the radiance of God's glory and the exact representation of his being, sustaining all things by his powerful word. After he had provided purification for sins, he sat down at the right hand of the Majesty in heaven. ⁴So he became as much superior to the angels as the name he has inherited is superior to theirs.

⁵For to which of the angels did God ever say,

"You are my Son;
today I have become your Father*a"b*?

Or again,

"I will be his Father,
and he will be my Son"*c*?

⁶And again, when God brings his firstborn into the world, he says,

"Let all God's angels worship him."*d*

⁷In speaking of the angels he says,

"He makes his angels winds,
his servants flames of fire."*e*

⁸But about the Son he says,

"Your throne, O God, will last for ever and ever,

and righteousness will be the scepter of your kingdom.

⁹You have loved righteousness and hated wickedness;
therefore God, your God, has set you above your companions
by anointing you with the oil of joy."*f*

¹⁰He also says,

"In the beginning, O Lord, you laid the foundations of the earth,
and the heavens are the work of your hands.

¹¹They will perish, but you remain;
they will all wear out like a garment.

¹²You will roll them up like a robe;
like a garment they will be changed.
But you remain the same,
and your years will never end."*g*

¹³To which of the angels did God ever say,

"Sit at my right hand
until I make your enemies
a footstool for your feet"*h*?

¹⁴Are not all angels ministering spirits sent to serve those who will inherit salvation?

*a5 Or have begotten you   b5 Psalm 2:7   c5 2 Samuel 7:14;
1 Chron. 17:13   d6 Deut. 32:43 (see Dead Sea Scrolls and Septuagint)
e7 Psalm 104:4   f9 Psalm 45:6,7   g12 Psalm 102:25-27
h13 Psalm 110:1*

Discovering the Word 1. How do verses 1–3 reveal the essential truth of Christ's supremacy and sufficiency? 2. Based on what we learn in verses 2–3, how would you answer the question "Who is Jesus Christ?" 3. To drive his point home, the author uses seven Old Testament citations. What characteristics or attributes of Jesus does the writer find in the Old Testament to prove his claim that Jesus is superior to angels (vv. 4–14)? 4. Who is the source of all these astounding statements (vv. 5–8, 10, 13)? 5. What do you learn about angels from these verses? 6. Based on what you have observed in verses 5–14, how would you expand your answer to the question "Who is Christ?"

 Applying the Word 1. What needs in your life do these qualities of Jesus address? 2. What kind of life should you have because all this is true of Jesus?

Responding in Prayer Pray that your life will reflect your knowledge of Jesus.

2 / *Hebrews 2*
Warning Signs

"WARNING!" A BLACK-and-white lettered sign that I encounter on the Fox River in St. Charles, Illinois, warns me of a dam ahead. In that placid stream it would be easy to drive over the dam. Cigarette packs, cans of weed killer, fences around nuclear power plants—they all carry impressive warnings designed to steer us from life-threatening perils. In Hebrews 2, the writer erects the first of six prominent warning signs in the letter. The first, in effect, alerts us to the danger of drifting off the course of our faith-race. It tells us to concentrate on staying in the race.

 Warming Up to God What might cause you to "drive away" from Christ, or to let "such a great salvation" slip away like a loose ring that falls off your finger?

 Read Hebrews 2.

2 We must pay more careful attention, therefore, to what we have heard, so that we do not drift away. ²For if the message spoken by angels was binding, and every violation and disobedience received its just punishment, ³how shall we escape if we ignore such a great salvation? This salvation, which was first announced by the Lord, was confirmed to us by those who heard him. ⁴God also testified to it by signs, wonders and various miracles, and gifts of the Holy Spirit distributed according to his will.

⁵It is not to angels that he has subjected the world to come, about which we are speaking. ⁶But there is a place where someone has testified:

"What is man that you are mindful of him,
the son of man that you care for him?
⁷You made him a little[i] lower than the
angels;
you crowned him with glory and honor
⁸ and put everything under his feet."[j]

In putting everything under him, God left noth-

ing that is not subject to him. Yet at present we do not see everything subject to him. ⁹But we see Jesus, who was made a little lower than the angels, now crowned with glory and honor because he suffered death, so that by the grace of God he might taste death for everyone.

¹⁰In bringing many sons to glory, it was fitting that God, for whom and through whom everything exists, should make the author of their salvation perfect through suffering. ¹¹Both the one who makes men holy and those who are made holy are of the same family. So Jesus is not ashamed to call them brothers. ¹²He says,

"I will declare your name to my brothers;
in the presence of the congregation I will
sing your praises."[k]

¹³And again,

"I will put my trust in him."[l]

And again he says,

i7 Or him for a little while; also in verse 9   *j8 Psalm 8:4-6*
k12 Psalm 22:22   *l13 Isaiah 8:17*

"Here am I, and the children God has given me."[m]

[14]Since the children have flesh and blood, he too shared in their humanity so that by his death he might destroy him who holds the power of death—that is, the devil—[15]and free those who all their lives were held in slavery by their fear of death. [16]For surely it is not angels he helps, but Abraham's descendants. [17]For this reason he had to be made like his brothers in every way, in order that he might become a merciful and faithful high priest in service to God, and that he might make atonement for[n] the sins of the people. [18]Because he himself suffered when he was tempted, he is able to help those who are being tempted.

[m]13 Isaiah 8:18   [n]17 Or and that he might turn aside God's wrath, taking away

---

 Discovering the Word 1. In verse 1 we read, "pay more careful attention . . . to," and in verse 3 we are told not to "ignore." What is it that we are to focus our lives on? 2. What logic does the writer use in verses 2–3 to further focus our attention on the peril of drifting away? 3. How does the writer strengthen the warning that God's salvation in Christ is well worth our most intense obedience (vv. 3–4)? 4. To prove that Jesus is too great and too valuable to neglect, the writer tells us more about him (vv. 5–9). What major facts does he cite here? 5. Why did Jesus have "to be made like his brothers [you and me] in every way" (vv. 16–18)?

Applying the Word 1. How does Jesus help you when you are tempted? 2. What helps you to maintain a warm, life-changing relationship with Jesus? 3. "Be sure your seatbelts are securely fastened," the aircraft's captain warns you because of approaching turbulence. How can you help other believers to be "securely fastened" into Jesus?

Responding in Prayer Ask God to keep you securely fastened to Jesus.

---

3 / *Hebrews 3*
Winning the Race

COACHES TELL US that what distinguishes average from superior athletes is the will to win. Endowed with equal physical strengths, one reaches the heights of stardom while the other slips into obscurity. In this chapter, the writer describes two equally endowed Christian runners in the faith-race. One succeeded and the other failed. What made the difference? The will to win. One held firmly to Christ, but the other fell by the wayside because of a hard heart.

 Warming Up to God What makes the difference between vibrant, growing Christians you know and those who appear to be dull and uninterested in the implications of their profession of faith?

 Read Hebrews 3.

3 Therefore, holy brothers, who share in the heavenly calling, fix your thoughts on Jesus, the apostle and high priest whom we confess. [2]He was faithful to the one who appointed him, just as Moses was faithful in all God's house. [3]Jesus has been found worthy of greater honor than Moses, just as the builder of a house has greater honor than the house itself. [4]For every house is built by someone, but God is the builder of everything. [5]Moses was faithful as a servant in all God's house, testifying to what would be said in the future. [6]But Christ is faithful as a son over God's house. And we are his house, if we hold on to our courage and the hope of which we boast.

[7]So, as the Holy Spirit says:

"Today, if you hear his voice,
[8] do not harden your hearts
  as you did in the rebellion,
    during the time of testing in the desert,
[9]where your fathers tested and tried me

and for forty years saw what I did.
¹⁰That is why I was angry with that generation,
   and I said, 'Their hearts are always going
      astray,
   and they have not known my ways.'
¹¹So I declared on oath in my anger,
   'They shall never enter my rest.' "ᵒ

¹²See to it, brothers, that none of you has a sinful, unbelieving heart that turns away from the living God. ¹³But encourage one another daily, as long as it is called Today, so that none of you may be hardened by sin's deceitfulness. ¹⁴We have come to share in Christ if we hold firmly till the end the confidence we had at first. ¹⁵As has just been said:

"Today, if you hear his voice,
   do not harden your hearts
   as you did in the rebellion."ᵖ

¹⁶Who were they who heard and rebelled? Were they not all those Moses led out of Egypt? ¹⁷And with whom was he angry for forty years? Was it not with those who sinned, whose bodies fell in the desert? ¹⁸And to whom did God swear that they would never enter his rest if not to those who disobeyed�q? ¹⁹So we see that they were not able to enter, because of their unbelief.

ᵒ11 Psalm 95:7-11   ᵖ15 Psalm 95:7,8   q18 Or *disbelieved*

Discovering the Word   1. What does the writer emphasize about Jesus in verses 1–6 that would encourage us to "fix [our] thoughts" on him (v. 1) and "hold on" to our courage and hope (v. 6)?   2. In verses 7–11 the writer hoists his second warning—unbelief and disobedience. These verses describe the nation of Israel after they crossed the Red Sea. They refused to obey God's command to take the Promised Land because they were afraid of the military might they would face. So they were forced to wander forty years till that whole generation died off. How does the psalmist describe God's perspective on the Israelites?   3. In what ways might Christians "test and try" God (v. 9)? Why?   4. How did God judge the Israelites whom Moses led out of Egypt (vv. 15–19)? 5. Why did he judge them in this way?

Applying the Word   1. Review the facts about the hardhearted (vv. 8, 10, 12–13, 15–18). Which aspects of this lifestyle come closest to your experience?   2. What are you doing to avoid the peril of "falling in the desert" (v. 17)?

Responding in Prayer   Pray for your own salvation.

---

4 / *Hebrews 4:1–13*
Receiving God's Blessings

AMERICAN BUSINESS TYCOON Roger Babson once observed, "Opportunities are greater today than ever before in history. Young people have greater chances for health, happiness, and prosperity than had the children of any previous generation." The same is true for Christians in God's faith-race.

It was true for God's people, Israel, yet they missed the opportunity for living in God's land of blessing and perished in a wilderness of unbelief and disobedience. This chapter tells Christians in the race that there is something to fear, but also something to strive for—experiencing God's promised rest now.

Warming Up to God   Do you need more times of rest in your life? In what areas?

Read Hebrews 4:1–13.

4 Therefore, since the promise of entering his rest still stands, let us be careful that none of you be found to have fallen short of it. ²For we also have had the gospel preached to us, just as they did; but the message they heard was of no value to them, because those who heard did not combine it with faith.ʳ ³Now we who have believed enter that rest, just as God has said,

"So I declared on oath in my anger,
'They shall never enter my rest.' "ˢ

And yet his work has been finished since the creation of the world. ⁴For somewhere he has spoken about the seventh day in these words: "And on the seventh day God rested from all his work."ᵗ ⁵And again in the passage above he says, "They shall never enter my rest."

⁶It still remains that some will enter that rest, and those who formerly had the gospel preached to them did not go in, because of their disobedience. ⁷Therefore God again set a certain day, calling it Today, when a long time later he spoke through David, as was said before:

"Today, if you hear his voice,
do not harden your hearts."ᵘ

⁸For if Joshua had given them rest, God would not have spoken later about another day. ⁹There remains, then, a Sabbath-rest for the people of God; ¹⁰for anyone who enters God's rest also rests from his own work, just as God did from his. ¹¹Let us, therefore, make every effort to enter that rest, so that no one will fall by following their example of disobedience.

¹²For the word of God is living and active. Sharper than any double-edged sword, it penetrates even to dividing soul and spirit, joints and marrow; it judges the thoughts and attitudes of the heart. ¹³Nothing in all creation is hidden from God's sight. Everything is uncovered and laid bare before the eyes of him to whom we must give account.

ʳ2 Many manuscripts *because they did not share in the faith of those who obeyed*   ˢ3 Psalm 95:11; also in verse 5   ᵗ4 Gen. 2:2   ᵘ7 Psalm 95:7,8

Discovering the Word 1. What do you think the promise of entering God's rest means in verse 1? 2. The tragic fate of the Israelites who perished in the desert serves as the basis of God's warning to those who have heard the gospel. Why did some who had the gospel preached to them miss their opportunity to receive God's rest (v. 2)? 3. From what you have observed in Hebrews thus far, how would you describe the faith which is required to receive God's rest? 4. We are told to do our best to reach God's rest (3:11, 18; 4:1, 3, 5–6, 9–11). How do you picture such rest? 5. Verses 6–8 refer to the Israelites. How did they refuse to receive God's rest? 6. The "word of God" that judges our thoughts and attitudes (vv. 12–13) is the specific promise of God's rest. How can God's Word show you the condition of your heart?

Applying the Word 1. God rested from all of his work (v. 4), and he offers us a "Sabbath-rest" on the seventh day of the week. What does it mean to you to rest from your work? 2. What role does Scripture have in your life right now? 3. How would you like to deepen or change that relationship?

Responding in Prayer Praise God for the gifts in this passage—of Scripture and of rest.

---

5 / *Hebrews 4:14—5:10*
Overcoming Weakness

THE PULITZER PRIZE-winning book *City of Joy* tells about the intense suffering of a Polish priest in a Calcutta slum. His superiors offered him a comfortable lodging, but he chose to live just like the slum-dwellers. By his suffering he learned what it was like to be a slum-dweller. He could not have learned that any other way. Likewise, the Hebrews needed to be reminded of their God-appointed, suffering high priest, Jesus Christ, so they would hold firmly to him.

Warming Up to God What experiences have you had that have helped you to better understand another person?

Read Hebrews 4:14—5:10.

¹⁴Therefore, since we have a great high priest who has gone through the heavens,ᵛ Jesus the Son of God, let us hold firmly to the faith we profess. ¹⁵For we do not have a high priest who is unable to sympathize with our weaknesses, but we have one who has been tempted in every way, just as we are—yet was without sin. ¹⁶Let us then approach the throne of grace with confidence, so that we may receive mercy and find grace to help us in our time of need.

5 Every high priest is selected from among men and is appointed to represent them in matters related to God, to offer gifts and sacrifices for sins. ²He is able to deal gently with those who are ignorant and are going astray, since he himself is subject to weakness. ³This is why he has to offer sacrifices for his own sins, as well as for the sins of the people.

⁴No one takes this honor upon himself; he must be called by God, just as Aaron was. ⁵So Christ also did not take upon himself the glory of becoming a high priest. But God said to him,

"You are my Son;
today I have become your Father."ʷ ˣ

⁶And he says in another place,

"You are a priest forever,
in the order of Melchizedek."ʸ

⁷During the days of Jesus' life on earth, he offered up prayers and petitions with loud cries and tears to the one who could save him from death, and he was heard because of his reverent submission. ⁸Although he was a son, he learned obedience from what he suffered ⁹and, once made perfect, he became the source of eternal salvation for all who obey him ¹⁰and was designated by God to be high priest in the order of Melchizedek.

ᵛ14 Or gone into heaven   ʷ5 Or have begotten you   ˣ5 Psalm 2:7
ʸ6 Psalm 110:4

 Discovering the Word 1. What commands are given in 4:14 and 16? 2. What is there about the character of Jesus that encourages us to obey these commands? 3. Jesus, as our merciful and faithful high priest, made atonement for our sins. The writer reminds the Hebrews of their earthly high priest in Judaism. What was the high priest like (5:1–4)? 4. How would you compare Jesus' high appointment with the life he lived (5:7–8)? 5. What was the result of Christ's suffering (5:8–10)?

 Applying the Word 1. When you are tempted, what difference does it make to know that Jesus was likewise tempted and therefore sympathizes with your weakness? 2. How does Christ's suffering help you to take a positive attitude toward suffering?

Responding in Prayer Pray that your life would reflect your high appointment as the adopted son or daughter of God.

6 / *Hebrews 5:11—6:20*
The Race to Maturity

PETER SNELL, FORMER Olympic gold medalist, said that the only way to win a race is to get in front and go flat out. Prior to that, he said, it takes a whole lot of hard training and self-discipline. The Hebrews were in desperate danger of quitting the race, so the writer urged them to go forward. This is a chapter with four strong appeals: "Let us go on to maturity" (v. 1). "Show diligence" (v. 11). "Do not become lazy" (v. 12). "Take hold of the hope " (v. 18).

 Warming Up to God When are you most tempted to drop out of the faith-race? Why?

 Read Hebrews 5:11—6:20.

11We have much to say about this, but it is hard to explain because you are slow to learn. 12In fact, though by this time you ought to be teachers, you need someone to teach you the elementary truths of God's word all over again. You need milk, not solid food! 13Anyone who lives on milk, being still an infant, is not acquainted with the teaching about righteousness. 14But solid food is for the mature, who by constant use have trained themselves to distinguish good from evil.

6 Therefore let us leave the elementary teachings about Christ and go on to maturity, not laying again the foundation of repentance from acts that lead to death,z and of faith in God, 2instruction about baptisms, the laying on of hands, the resurrection of the dead, and eternal judgment. 3And God permitting, we will do so.

4It is impossible for those who have once been enlightened, who have tasted the heavenly gift, who have shared in the Holy Spirit, 5who have tasted the goodness of the word of God and the powers of the coming age, 6if they fall away, to be brought back to repentance, becausea to their loss they are crucifying the Son of God all over again and subjecting him to public disgrace.

7Land that drinks in the rain often falling on it and that produces a crop useful to those for whom it is farmed receives the blessing of God. 8But land that produces thorns and thistles is worthless and is in danger of being cursed. In the end it will be burned.

9Even though we speak like this, dear friends,

we are confident of better things in your case— things that accompany salvation. 10God is not unjust; he will not forget your work and the love you have shown him as you have helped his people and continue to help them. 11We want each of you to show this same diligence to the very end, in order to make your hope sure. 12We do not want you to become lazy, but to imitate those who through faith and patience inherit what has been promised.

13When God made his promise to Abraham, since there was no one greater for him to swear by, he swore by himself, 14saying, "I will surely bless you and give you many descendants."b 15And so after waiting patiently, Abraham received what was promised.

16Men swear by someone greater than themselves, and the oath confirms what is said and puts an end to all argument. 17Because God wanted to make the unchanging nature of his purpose very clear to the heirs of what was promised, he confirmed it with an oath. 18God did this so that, by two unchangeable things in which it is impossible for God to lie, we who have fled to take hold of the hope offered to us may be greatly encouraged. 19We have this hope as an anchor for the soul, firm and secure. It enters the inner sanctuary behind the curtain, 20where Jesus, who went before us, has entered on our behalf. He has become a high priest forever, in the order of Melchizedek.

z1 Or from useless rituals   a6 Or repentance while
b14 Gen. 22:17

Discovering the Word 1. How would you describe the failures of the Hebrews (5:11–14)? 2. In view of their resources and opportunities for growth, how do you account for their problems? 3. According to 6:6, why is it absolutely essential to develop Christian maturity? 4. What hope does the writer see for better things to come (vv. 9–10)? Why? 5. What essential part of God's nature encourages the Hebrews to be positive and hopeful about their future (vv. 13–18)?

Applying the Word 1. Two kinds of land production vividly portray the reason to go on to maturity (6:7–8). How does each characterize your life? 2. As you reflect on your track record, of both diligence and laziness (6:11–12), how can you improve? 3. In verses 19–20 the writer returns to the Hebrews' familiar religion of priests and their temple with its holy place curtained off. In other words, it was a picture of a more profound spiritual reality in Christ. How does Jesus fulfill your deepest aspirations and help you to go on to maturity in your faith-race?

Responding in Prayer Ask God to firmly anchor your soul with hope in Christ.

7 / *Hebrews 7*
Eternal Companion

IN THE OLD Testament, religion and priests go hand in hand. Moses had carefully laid out all the rules for the Levites, the priestly clan of Israel. But the Hebrew Christians had departed from their old religion that was centered on priestly functions. Yet some of them hankered to return to their old ways. "Don't turn back," the writer appeals. "You have something far better in Christ." In chapters 7—10 the author tells of Christ's superior priestly origin, his better covenant and his sufficient-for-all-time sacrifice of himself. Regardless of whether we have had to move away from old traditions to find Christ, we all need confidence builders like chapter 7 so that as we run our faith-race, we will stick with Jesus no matter what.

 Warming Up to God "He always makes me feel so strong," a church member said of his pastor after a sermon. What relationships strengthen your knowledge of Christ and build you up?

 Read Hebrews 7.

7 This Melchizedek was king of Salem and priest of God Most High. He met Abraham returning from the defeat of the kings and blessed him, ²and Abraham gave him a tenth of everything. First, his name means "king of righteousness"; then also, "king of Salem" means "king of peace." ³Without father or mother, without genealogy, without beginning of days or end of life, like the Son of God he remains a priest forever.

⁴Just think how great he was: Even the patriarch Abraham gave him a tenth of the plunder! ⁵Now the law requires the descendants of Levi who become priests to collect a tenth from the people—that is, their brothers—even though their brothers are descended from Abraham. ⁶This man, however, did not trace his descent from Levi, yet he collected a tenth from Abraham and blessed him who had the promises. ⁷And without doubt the lesser person is blessed by the greater. ⁸In the one case, the tenth is collected by men who die; but in the other case, by him who is declared to be living. ⁹One might even say that Levi, who collects the tenth, paid the tenth through Abraham, ¹⁰because when Melchizedek met Abraham, Levi was still in the body of his ancestor.

¹¹If perfection could have been attained through the Levitical priesthood (for on the basis of it the law was given to the people), why was there still need for another priest to come—one in the order of Melchizedek, not in the order of Aaron? ¹²For when there is a change of the priesthood, there must also be a change of the law. ¹³He of whom these things are said belonged to a different tribe, and no one from that tribe has ever served at the altar. ¹⁴For it is clear that our Lord descended from Judah, and in regard to that tribe Moses said nothing about priests. ¹⁵And what we have said is even more clear if another priest like Melchizedek appears, ¹⁶one who has become a priest not on the basis of a regulation as to his ancestry but on the basis of the power of an indestructible life. ¹⁷For it is declared:

"You are a priest forever,
in the order of Melchizedek." *c*

¹⁸The former regulation is set aside because it was weak and useless ¹⁹(for the law made nothing perfect), and a better hope is introduced, by which we draw near to God.

²⁰And it was not without an oath! Others became priests without any oath, ²¹but he became a priest with an oath when God said to him:

"The Lord has sworn
and will not change his mind:
'You are a priest forever.' " *c*

²²Because of this oath, Jesus has become the guarantee of a better covenant.

²³Now there have been many of those priests, since death prevented them from continuing in office; ²⁴but because Jesus lives forever, he has a permanent priesthood. ²⁵Therefore he is able to save completely*d* those who come to God through him, because he always lives to intercede for them.

²⁶Such a high priest meets our need—one who is holy, blameless, pure, set apart from sinners,

c 17,21 Psalm 110:4   *d 25* Or *forever*

exalted above the heavens. ²⁷Unlike the other high priests, he does not need to offer sacrifices day after day, first for his own sins, and then for the sins of the people. He sacrificed for their sins once for all when he offered himself. ²⁸For the law appoints as high priests men who are weak; but the oath, which came after the law, appointed the Son, who has been made perfect forever.

Discovering the Word 1. Jesus is our high priest, not of the ancient Jewish line of Aaron but of the line of the pre-Aaronic Melchizedek. "Just think how great he [Melchizedek] was," commands the writer (v. 4). What was there about Melchizedek that made him so great (vv. 1–3)? 2. Great as his name and position were, there was one incident that proved Melchizedek's superiority to the Hebrews: Their patriarch Abraham tithed (gave one tenth of his income) to him (v. 4). According to verses 5–10, why does this prove that Jesus' high priesthood is superior to that of Levi (Aaron's son)? 3. Jesus inaugurated a new era and set aside the old because he was not of the priestly tribe (vv. 11–14). On what does his priestly authority rest (vv. 15–17)? 4. In what sense were the ancient rules of the Jews "weak and useless" (vv. 18–19)? 5. God's oath set aside Jesus as a distinctive high priest (vv. 20–21). How does Jesus guarantee our faith-agreement (covenant) with him (vv. 22–25)? 6. What about Christ's character and sacrifice sets him far above other earthly priests (vv. 26–28)?

Applying the Word 1. Twice the writer tells us to come to God through Christ's high priesthood (vv. 19, 25). Why do you need to do this? 2. How can you practice it in your faith-race?

Responding in Prayer Praise God for giving you a high priest over all in Jesus Christ.

8 / Hebrews 8
God's "New Deal"

BACK IN 1932, President Franklin Roosevelt sought to rescue the country from the pit of the Great Depression by launching the New Deal. The concept caught the imagination of the people. The time was ripe for a radically new economic and social program. In this chapter, the writer of Hebrews announces God's "new deal"—a covenant, or agreement, between God and humanity. It offers far superior promises to those of the "old deal" (Old Testament laws and regulations).

Warming Up to God What does knowing you are God's child mean to you?

Read Hebrews 8.

8 The point of what we are saying is this: We do have such a high priest, who sat down at the right hand of the throne of the Majesty in heaven, ²and who serves in the sanctuary, the true tabernacle set up by the Lord, not by man.

³Every high priest is appointed to offer both gifts and sacrifices, and so it was necessary for this one also to have something to offer. ⁴If he were on earth, he would not be a priest, for there are already men who offer the gifts prescribed by the law. ⁵They serve at a sanctuary that is a copy and shadow of what is in heaven. This is why Moses was warned when he was about to build the tabernacle: "See to it that you make everything according to the pattern shown you on the mountain."ᵉ ⁶But the ministry Jesus has received is as superior to theirs as the covenant of which he is mediator is superior to the old one, and it is founded on better promises.

⁷For if there had been nothing wrong with that first covenant, no place would have been sought for another. ⁸But God found fault with the peopleᶠ and said:

"The time is coming, declares the Lord,
    when I will make a new covenant

ᵉ5 Exodus 25:40   ᶠ8 Some manuscripts may be translated *fault and said to the people.*

with the house of Israel
and with the house of Judah.
⁹It will not be like the covenant
I made with their forefathers
when I took them by the hand
to lead them out of Egypt,
because they did not remain faithful to my
covenant,
and I turned away from them,
declares the Lord.
¹⁰This is the covenant I will make with the
house of Israel
after that time, declares the Lord.
I will put my laws in their minds
and write them on their hearts.

I will be their God,
and they will be my people.
¹¹No longer will a man teach his neighbor,
or a man his brother, saying, 'Know the
Lord,'
because they will all know me,
from the least of them to the greatest.
¹²For I will forgive their wickedness
and will remember their sins no more."ᵍ

¹³By calling this covenant "new," he has made
the first one obsolete; and what is obsolete and
aging will soon disappear.

ᵍ12 Jer. 31:31-34

Discovering the Word 1. "We do have such a high priest" (v. 1) refers to the description of Jesus in 7:23–28. What additional facts do you learn about him (vv. 1–2)? 2. What is Christ's heavenly ministry (vv. 3–6)? 3. Verse 6 looks back to prove Christ's superior ministry and ahead to prove that we have a superior covenant with God. The key is "better promises." What was the problem with the first covenant (vv. 7–12)? 4. What guarantees God's "new deal" (v. 12)? (See also vv. 1–3; 9:14.)

Applying the Word 1. Do you function better under external restraint (the law) or inner constraint (God's Spirit) (v. 10)? Why? 2. What happens to you when you say to God, "Thank you for forgiving and forgetting my sin"? 3. A magazine ad for dishwashers offers more power, more pizzazz and more performance. How could your understanding and application of God's "new deal" offer all of that to you in your walk with him?

Responding in Prayer Ask God to forgive your sins, naming those you can think of specifically.

---

9 / *Hebrews 9*
The Runner's Power

IN VIEW OF the colossal problems besetting us—drugs, divorce, depression, to name a few—it seems like a gross oversimplification to say that the blood of Jesus Christ is the solution. But, in a different context, the Hebrews faced similar problems of neglect, unbelief and immaturity. They were in danger of dropping out of the race and turning back to their old ways. Seemingly, they lacked the power and purpose to advance and press on in their faith-race. What was the solution given to them? The blood of Jesus. Only a full and perfect knowledge of what Jesus is and does for us can bring us to a full and perfect Christian life.

Warming Up to God When do you feel like dropping out of the race?

Read Hebrews 9.

---

9 Now the first covenant had regulations for worship and also an earthly sanctuary. ²A tabernacle was set up. In its first room were the lampstand, the table and the consecrated bread; this was called the Holy Place. ³Behind the second curtain was a room called the Most Holy Place, ⁴which had the golden altar of incense and the gold-covered ark of the covenant. This ark contained the gold jar of manna, Aaron's staff that had budded, and the stone tablets of the cov-

enant. ⁵Above the ark were the cherubim of the Glory, overshadowing the atonement cover.ʰ But we cannot discuss these things in detail now.

⁶When everything had been arranged like this, the priests entered regularly into the outer room to carry on their ministry. ⁷But only the high priest entered the inner room, and that only once a year, and never without blood, which he offered for himself and for the sins the people had committed in ignorance. ⁸The Holy Spirit was showing by this that the way into the Most Holy Place had not yet been disclosed as long as the first tabernacle was still standing. ⁹This is an illustration for the present time, indicating that the gifts and sacrifices being offered were not able to clear the conscience of the worshiper. ¹⁰They are only a matter of food and drink and various ceremonial washings—external regulations applying until the time of the new order.

¹¹When Christ came as high priest of the good things that are already here,ⁱ he went through the greater and more perfect tabernacle that is not man-made, that is to say, not a part of this creation. ¹²He did not enter by means of the blood of goats and calves; but he entered the Most Holy Place once for all by his own blood, having obtained eternal redemption. ¹³The blood of goats and bulls and the ashes of a heifer sprinkled on those who are ceremonially unclean sanctify them so that they are outwardly clean. ¹⁴How much more, then, will the blood of Christ, who through the eternal Spirit offered himself unblemished to God, cleanse our consciences from acts that lead to death,ʲ so that we may serve the living God!

¹⁵For this reason Christ is the mediator of a new covenant, that those who are called may receive the promised eternal inheritance—now that he has died as a ransom to set them free from the sins committed under the first covenant.

¹⁶In the case of a will,ᵏ it is necessary to prove the death of the one who made it, ¹⁷because a will is in force only when somebody has died; it never takes effect while the one who made it is living. ¹⁸This is why even the first covenant was not put into effect without blood. ¹⁹When Moses had proclaimed every commandment of the law to all the people, he took the blood of calves, together with water, scarlet wool and branches of hyssop, and sprinkled the scroll and all the people. ²⁰He said, "This is the blood of the covenant, which God has commanded you to keep."ˡ ²¹In the same way, he sprinkled with the blood both the tabernacle and everything used in its ceremonies. ²²In fact, the law requires that nearly everything be cleansed with blood, and without the shedding of blood there is no forgiveness.

²³It was necessary, then, for the copies of the heavenly things to be purified with these sacrifices, but the heavenly things themselves with better sacrifices than these. ²⁴For Christ did not enter a man-made sanctuary that was only a copy of the true one; he entered heaven itself, now to appear for us in God's presence. ²⁵Nor did he enter heaven to offer himself again and again, the way the high priest enters the Most Holy Place every year with blood that is not his own. ²⁶Then Christ would have had to suffer many times since the creation of the world. But now he has appeared once for all at the end of the ages to do away with sin by the sacrifice of himself. ²⁷Just as man is destined to die once, and after that to face judgment, ²⁸so Christ was sacrificed once to take away the sins of many people; and he will appear a second time, not to bear sin, but to bring salvation to those who are waiting for him.

ʰ5 Traditionally *the mercy seat*   ⁱ11 Some early manuscripts *are to come*   ʲ14 Or *from useless rituals*   ᵏ16 Same Greek word as *covenant*; also in verse 17   ˡ20 Exodus 24:8

Discovering the Word 1. Contrast what Jesus did (vv. 11–14) with the old system (vv. 1–10). 2. Why was the shedding of sacrificial blood required even under the old covenant (vv. 16–22)? 3. The writer explains why the offering of Jesus' blood is not only necessary, but also a superior sacrifice. Why is it important to direct our attention to "heavenly things" (v. 23)? 4. What difference would it make to those steeped in Old Testament religion to know that Jesus once-for-all offered his own blood, rather than offering animal blood (vv. 25–26)?

Applying the Word 1. How can you deepen your understanding of and appreciation for Christ's self-sacrifice? 2. Death and judgment are certain. In view of that, how would you encourage someone to face eternity with hope and peace, based on what you have learned in this chapter? 3. Also certain is Jesus' Second Coming (v. 28). In light of his blood offering, how should you spend your time waiting for him?

Responding in Prayer Pray that you will use your time to serve Jesus even as you wait for him.

10 / *Hebrews 10*
Staying in the Race

FACED WITH SEEMINGLY eternal years of schoolwork and a multitude of rules to obey, children get discouraged. When that happens, parents say, "Look at your great opportunities. Take advantage of what you have now. Don't throw it away."

The writer of Hebrews, in chapter 10, reaches the heights of Mt. Everest with a picture of Jesus that offers his readers encouragement. From those lofty heights he tells them to warm up to God, hold their faith in him, and stir up one another in Christian faith and practice.

 Warming Up to God Recall an opportunity you missed because it sounded too good. What did you miss by not believing the evidence?

 Read Hebrews 10.

10 The law is only a shadow of the good things that are coming—not the realities themselves. For this reason it can never, by the same sacrifices repeated endlessly year after year, make perfect those who draw near to worship. ²If it could, would they not have stopped being offered? For the worshipers would have been cleansed once for all, and would no longer have felt guilty for their sins. ³But those sacrifices are an annual reminder of sins, ⁴because it is impossible for the blood of bulls and goats to take away sins.

⁵Therefore, when Christ came into the world, he said:

"Sacrifice and offering you did not desire,
  but a body you prepared for me;
⁶with burnt offerings and sin offerings
  you were not pleased.
⁷Then I said, 'Here I am—it is written about
  me in the scroll—
I have come to do your will, O God.' "ᵐ

⁸First he said, "Sacrifices and offerings, burnt offerings and sin offerings you did not desire, nor were you pleased with them" (although the law required them to be made). ⁹Then he said, "Here I am, I have come to do your will." He sets aside the first to establish the second. ¹⁰And by that will, we have been made holy through the sacrifice of the body of Jesus Christ once for all.

¹¹Day after day every priest stands and performs his religious duties; again and again he offers the same sacrifices, which can never take away sins. ¹²But when this priest had offered for all time one sacrifice for sins, he sat down at the right hand of God. ¹³Since that time he waits for his enemies to be made his footstool, ¹⁴because by one sacrifice he has made perfect forever those who are being made holy.

¹⁵The Holy Spirit also testifies to us about this. First he says:

¹⁶"This is the covenant I will make with them
  after that time, says the Lord.
I will put my laws in their hearts,
  and I will write them on their minds."ⁿ

¹⁷Then he adds:

"Their sins and lawless acts
  I will remember no more."ᵒ

¹⁸And where these have been forgiven, there is no longer any sacrifice for sin.

¹⁹Therefore, brothers, since we have confidence to enter the Most Holy Place by the blood of Jesus, ²⁰by a new and living way opened for us through the curtain, that is, his body, ²¹and since we have a great priest over the house of God, ²²let us draw near to God with a sincere heart in full assurance of faith, having our hearts sprinkled to cleanse us from a guilty conscience and having our bodies washed with pure water. ²³Let us hold

ᵐ7 Psalm 40:6-8 (see Septuagint)   ⁿ16 Jer. 31:33   ᵒ17 Jer. 31:34

unswervingly to the hope we profess, for he who promised is faithful. ²⁴And let us consider how we may spur one another on toward love and good deeds. ²⁵Let us not give up meeting together, as some are in the habit of doing, but let us encourage one another—and all the more as you see the Day approaching.

²⁶If we deliberately keep on sinning after we have received the knowledge of the truth, no sacrifice for sins is left, ²⁷but only a fearful expectation of judgment and of raging fire that will consume the enemies of God. ²⁸Anyone who rejected the law of Moses died without mercy on the testimony of two or three witnesses. ²⁹How much more severely do you think a man deserves to be punished who has trampled the Son of God under foot, who has treated as an unholy thing the blood of the covenant that sanctified him, and who has insulted the Spirit of grace? ³⁰For we know him who said, "It is mine to avenge; I will repay,"ᴾ and again, "The Lord will judge his people."�q ³¹It is a dreadful thing to fall into the hands of the living God.

³²Remember those earlier days after you had received the light, when you stood your ground in a great contest in the face of suffering. ³³Sometimes you were publicly exposed to insult and persecution; at other times you stood side by side with those who were so treated. ³⁴You sympathized with those in prison and joyfully accepted the confiscation of your property, because you knew that you yourselves had better and lasting possessions.

³⁵So do not throw away your confidence; it will be richly rewarded. ³⁶You need to persevere so that when you have done the will of God, you will receive what he has promised. ³⁷For in just a very little while,

"He who is coming will come and will not
       delay.
³⁸   But my righteous oneʳ will live by faith.
   And if he shrinks back,
       I will not be pleased with him."ˢ

³⁹But we are not of those who shrink back and are destroyed, but of those who believe and are saved.

ᴾ30 Deut. 32:35   q30 Deut. 32:36; Psalm 135:14   ʳ38 One early manuscript *But the righteous*   ˢ38 Hab. 2:3,4

 Discovering the Word 1. The writer continues to discuss Jesus and the Old Testament offerings. How do verses 1–4 prove that the Old Testament system was a shadow, not the real thing? 2. Contrast Jesus' sacrifice (the reality) with the shadow (vv. 5–10). Why is his sacrifice better? 3. As you meditate on verses 11–18 and the awesome love and power of Jesus to take away your sins, what are the responses in your heart and mind? 4. In light of what God has done for us in Christ (vv. 19–21), what three commands does the writer feel compelled to issue (vv. 22–24)? 5. If we fail to draw near to God, hold fast our faith and stir up one another, what is likely to happen (vv. 25–26, 38–39)?

 Applying the Word 1. How can you help hold someone you know "unswervingly" to faith? 2. What purposes could be achieved in your life by both this strong encouragement and this stern warning?

Responding in Prayer Pray for your church, that you would support and encourage one another.

---

11 / *Hebrews 11*
Models of Faith

PROBABLY NO SUBJECT is so glibly misunderstood as faith. Nearly everyone professes to have some of it. Many people would like to have more. The writer to the Hebrews takes faith out of religious theory and clothes it with flesh and blood. The author does this with what we today call *role models*. These models inspire us to go on believing in Jesus.

 Warming Up to God Complete the sentence: "Faith is . . ."

Read Hebrews 11.

11 Now faith is being sure of what we hope for and certain of what we do not see. ²This is what the ancients were commended for.

³By faith we understand that the universe was formed at God's command, so that what is seen was not made out of what was visible.

⁴By faith Abel offered God a better sacrifice than Cain did. By faith he was commended as a righteous man, when God spoke well of his offerings. And by faith he still speaks, even though he is dead.

⁵By faith Enoch was taken from this life, so that he did not experience death; he could not be found, because God had taken him away. For before he was taken, he was commended as one who pleased God. ⁶And without faith it is impossible to please God, because anyone who comes to him must believe that he exists and that he rewards those who earnestly seek him.

⁷By faith Noah, when warned about things not yet seen, in holy fear built an ark to save his family. By his faith he condemned the world and became heir of the righteousness that comes by faith.

⁸By faith Abraham, when called to go to a place he would later receive as his inheritance, obeyed and went, even though he did not know where he was going. ⁹By faith he made his home in the promised land like a stranger in a foreign country; he lived in tents, as did Isaac and Jacob, who were heirs with him of the same promise. ¹⁰For he was looking forward to the city with foundations, whose architect and builder is God.

¹¹By faith Abraham, even though he was past age—and Sarah herself was barren—was enabled to become a father because he ᵗ considered him faithful who had made the promise. ¹²And so from this one man, and he as good as dead, came descendants as numerous as the stars in the sky and as countless as the sand on the seashore.

¹³All these people were still living by faith when they died. They did not receive the things promised; they only saw them and welcomed them from a distance. And they admitted that they were aliens and strangers on earth. ¹⁴People who say such things show that they are looking for a country of their own. ¹⁵If they had been thinking of the country they left, they would

have had opportunity to return. ¹⁶Instead, they were longing for a better country—a heavenly one. Therefore God is not ashamed to be called their God, for he has prepared a city for them.

¹⁷By faith Abraham, when God tested him, offered Isaac as a sacrifice. He who had received the promises was about to sacrifice his one and only son, ¹⁸even though God had said to him, "It is through Isaac that your offspring ᵘ will be reckoned." ᵛ ¹⁹Abraham reasoned that God could raise the dead, and figuratively speaking, he did receive Isaac back from death.

²⁰By faith Isaac blessed Jacob and Esau in regard to their future.

²¹By faith Jacob, when he was dying, blessed each of Joseph's sons, and worshiped as he leaned on the top of his staff.

²²By faith Joseph, when his end was near, spoke about the exodus of the Israelites from Egypt and gave instructions about his bones.

²³By faith Moses' parents hid him for three months after he was born, because they saw he was no ordinary child, and they were not afraid of the king's edict.

²⁴By faith Moses, when he had grown up, refused to be known as the son of Pharaoh's daughter. ²⁵He chose to be mistreated along with the people of God rather than to enjoy the pleasures of sin for a short time. ²⁶He regarded disgrace for the sake of Christ as of greater value than the treasures of Egypt, because he was looking ahead to his reward. ²⁷By faith he left Egypt, not fearing the king's anger; he persevered because he saw him who is invisible. ²⁸By faith he kept the Passover and the sprinkling of blood, so that the destroyer of the firstborn would not touch the firstborn of Israel.

²⁹By faith the people passed through the Red Sea ʷ as on dry land; but when the Egyptians tried to do so, they were drowned.

³⁰By faith the walls of Jericho fell, after the people had marched around them for seven days.

³¹By faith the prostitute Rahab, because she welcomed the spies, was not killed with those who were disobedient. ˣ

³²And what more shall I say? I do not have time

ᵗ11 Or *By faith even Sarah, who was past age, was enabled to bear children because she*   ᵘ18 Greek *seed*   ᵛ18 Gen. 21:12
ʷ29 That is, Sea of Reeds   ˣ31 Or *unbelieving*

to tell about Gideon, Barak, Samson, Jephthah, David, Samuel and the prophets, 33who through faith conquered kingdoms, administered justice, and gained what was promised; who shut the mouths of lions, 34quenched the fury of the flames, and escaped the edge of the sword; whose weakness was turned to strength; and who became powerful in battle and routed foreign armies. 35Women received back their dead, raised to life again. Others were tortured and refused to be released, so that they might gain a better resurrection. 36Some faced jeers and flogging, while still others were chained and put in prison.

37They were stoned*y*; they were sawed in two; they were put to death by the sword. They went about in sheepskins and goatskins, destitute, persecuted and mistreated— 38the world was not worthy of them. They wandered in deserts and mountains, and in caves and holes in the ground.

39These were all commended for their faith, yet none of them received what had been promised. 40God had planned something better for us so that only together with us would they be made perfect.

y37 Some early manuscripts stoned; they were put to the test;

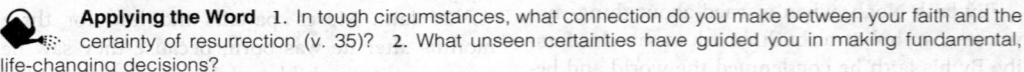

Discovering the Word 1. Look for both assured confidence and calm expectation (v. 1) in the role models of faith in this chapter. How did Abel, Enoch and Noah express their faith (vv. 4–7)? 2. Considering the foolishness of his choices by human standards, what do you think Abraham's emotions were like (vv. 8–10)? 3. How does the promise of a heavenly country help us to keep our faith, even when we don't see our hopes fulfilled immediately (vv. 13–16)? 4. Why do you think Abraham's faith triumphed when he was asked to give up Isaac (vv. 17–19)? 5. How would you compare the faith of the named heroes and heroines who achieved greatness (vv. 20–35) with those unnamed persons who suffered grievously (vv. 35–38)? 6. Some Christians believe that faith always leads to material and physical blessing. What does this passage tell you about the role of both blessing and suffering for the faithful?

Applying the Word 1. In tough circumstances, what connection do you make between your faith and the certainty of resurrection (v. 35)? 2. What unseen certainties have guided you in making fundamental, life-changing decisions?

Responding in Prayer Pray for the faith you need in your life right now to do God's will.

12 / *Hebrews 12*
The Runner's Discipline

WE OFTEN WONDER why thousands of marathoners seem to enjoy punishing themselves in grueling races. Certainly, for most, it's not the hope of winning. What is it then? Explaining it to his readers, writer Art Carey said, "The real joy of the Boston Marathon is just finishing, just winning the contest with yourself—doing what you have set out to do." That's the attitude the Hebrews were supposed to have: Stay in the faith-race to the end.

Warming Up to God Who has been a model of perseverance and endurance for you? Thank God for that person.

Read Hebrews 12.

12 Therefore, since we are surrounded by such a great cloud of witnesses, let us throw off everything that hinders and the sin that so easily entangles, and let us run with perseverance the race marked out for us. 2Let us fix our eyes on Jesus, the author and

perfecter of our faith, who for the joy set before him endured the cross, scorning its shame, and sat down at the right hand of the throne of God. 3Consider him who endured such opposition from sinful men, so that you will not grow weary and lose heart.

[4]In your struggle against sin, you have not yet resisted to the point of shedding your blood. [5]And you have forgotten that word of encouragement that addresses you as sons:

"My son, do not make light of the Lord's
    discipline,
  and do not lose heart when he rebukes
    you,
[6]because the Lord disciplines those he loves,
  and he punishes everyone he accepts as a
    son."[z]

[7]Endure hardship as discipline; God is treating you as sons. For what son is not disciplined by his father? [8]If you are not disciplined (and everyone undergoes discipline), then you are illegitimate children and not true sons. [9]Moreover, we have all had human fathers who disciplined us and we respected them for it. How much more should we submit to the Father of our spirits and live! [10]Our fathers disciplined us for a little while as they thought best; but God disciplines us for our good, that we may share in his holiness. [11]No discipline seems pleasant at the time, but painful. Later on, however, it produces a harvest of righteousness and peace for those who have been trained by it.

[12]Therefore, strengthen your feeble arms and weak knees. [13]"Make level paths for your feet,"[a] so that the lame may not be disabled, but rather healed.

[14]Make every effort to live in peace with all men and to be holy; without holiness no one will see the Lord. [15]See to it that no one misses the grace of God and that no bitter root grows up to cause trouble and defile many. [16]See that no one is sexually immoral, or is godless like Esau, who for a single meal sold his inheritance rights as the oldest son. [17]Afterward, as you know, when he wanted to inherit this blessing, he was rejected.

He could bring about no change of mind, though he sought the blessing with tears.

[18]You have not come to a mountain that can be touched and that is burning with fire; to darkness, gloom and storm; [19]to a trumpet blast or to such a voice speaking words that those who heard it begged that no further word be spoken to them, [20]because they could not bear what was commanded: "If even an animal touches the mountain, it must be stoned."[b] [21]The sight was so terrifying that Moses said, "I am trembling with fear."[c]

[22]But you have come to Mount Zion, to the heavenly Jerusalem, the city of the living God. You have come to thousands upon thousands of angels in joyful assembly, [23]to the church of the firstborn, whose names are written in heaven. You have come to God, the judge of all men, to the spirits of righteous men made perfect, [24]to Jesus the mediator of a new covenant, and to the sprinkled blood that speaks a better word than the blood of Abel.

[25]See to it that you do not refuse him who speaks. If they did not escape when they refused him who warned them on earth, how much less will we, if we turn away from him who warns us from heaven? [26]At that time his voice shook the earth, but now he has promised, "Once more I will shake not only the earth but also the heavens."[d] [27]The words "once more" indicate the removing of what can be shaken—that is, created things—so that what cannot be shaken may remain.

[28]Therefore, since we are receiving a kingdom that cannot be shaken, let us be thankful, and so worship God acceptably with reverence and awe, [29]for our "God is a consuming fire."[e]

[z]6 Prov. 3:11,12 [a]13 Prov. 4:26 [b]20 Exodus 19:12,13
[c]21 Deut. 9:19 [d]26 Haggai 2:6 [e]29 Deut. 4:24

 Discovering the Word 1. Of what value is it to keep your eyes on Jesus (vv. 2–3)? 2. What discipline of the Hebrews do you think the writer alludes to (vv. 3–4, 7; 11:35–38)? 3. How do the values of God's discipline cited here help us to respond positively to discipline (vv. 10–12)? 4. Identify the writer's specific instructions in verses 14–17. On what principles are they based? 5. How could you identify a "bitter root" or a "godless Esau" in your life (vv. 15–16)? 6. We've all been tempted to drop out of the race. Why would the warning of verses 25–29 cause us to reconsider?

 Applying the Word 1. What hindrances and entanglements get in the way of your Christian faith-race (v. 1)? Why? 2. What encouragement do you find in verses 18–24 to run the faith-race with perseverance?

Responding in Prayer Let your prayer be one of worship for the God who is a "consuming fire."

13 / *Hebrews 13*
Running by the Rules

BEN JOHNSON OF Canada was stripped of the Olympic gold medals he won at Seoul in 1988 because he broke the rules about drug use. Similarly, the Christian's faith-race is much more than a sprint to the finish line. It's a race which brings glory to God by the way the runners behave. In the concluding chapter, the writer to the Hebrews sketches a variety of duties to God and humanity. Together they reveal an exalted level of personal morality and duty.

 Warming Up to God   Consider your attitude to God's law. At what times do you find it a burden? When does it help you?

 Read Hebrews 13.

---

13 Keep on loving each other as brothers. ²Do not forget to entertain strangers, for by so doing some people have entertained angels without knowing it. ³Remember those in prison as if you were their fellow prisoners, and those who are mistreated as if you yourselves were suffering.

⁴Marriage should be honored by all, and the marriage bed kept pure, for God will judge the adulterer and all the sexually immoral. ⁵Keep your lives free from the love of money and be content with what you have, because God has said,

"Never will I leave you;
never will I forsake you."*ƒ*

⁶So we say with confidence,

"The Lord is my helper; I will not be afraid.
What can man do to me?"*g*

⁷Remember your leaders, who spoke the word of God to you. Consider the outcome of their way of life and imitate their faith. ⁸Jesus Christ is the same yesterday and today and forever.

⁹Do not be carried away by all kinds of strange teachings. It is good for our hearts to be strengthened by grace, not by ceremonial foods, which are of no value to those who eat them. ¹⁰We have an altar from which those who minister at the tabernacle have no right to eat.

¹¹The high priest carries the blood of animals into the Most Holy Place as a sin offering, but the bodies are burned outside the camp. ¹²And so Jesus also suffered outside the city gate to make the people holy through his own blood. ¹³Let us, then, go to him outside the camp, bearing the disgrace he bore. ¹⁴For here we do not have an enduring city, but we are looking for the city that is to come.

¹⁵Through Jesus, therefore, let us continually offer to God a sacrifice of praise—the fruit of lips that confess his name. ¹⁶And do not forget to do good and to share with others, for with such sacrifices God is pleased.

¹⁷Obey your leaders and submit to their authority. They keep watch over you as men who must give an account. Obey them so that their work will be a joy, not a burden, for that would be of no advantage to you.

¹⁸Pray for us. We are sure that we have a clear conscience and desire to live honorably in every way. ¹⁹I particularly urge you to pray so that I may be restored to you soon.

²⁰May the God of peace, who through the blood of the eternal covenant brought back from the dead our Lord Jesus, that great Shepherd of the sheep, ²¹equip you with everything good for doing his will, and may he work in us what is pleasing to him, through Jesus Christ, to whom be glory for ever and ever. Amen.

²²Brothers, I urge you to bear with my word of exhortation, for I have written you only a short letter.

²³I want you to know that our brother Timothy has been released. If he arrives soon, I will come with him to see you.

²⁴Greet all your leaders and all God's people. Those from Italy send you their greetings.

²⁵Grace be with you all.

ƒ5 Deut. 31:6   g6 Psalm 118:6,7

Discovering the Word 1. Verses 1–3 tie in with verse 16. In what sense should loving others, doing good, sharing, entertaining strangers, and helping the prisoners and the mistreated be considered "sacrifices" to God? 2. Sexual purity is one of God's absolutes (v. 4). How do you account for sexual impurity among professing Christians—some of them well-known public figures? 3. What facts about God help to keep you from loving money (vv. 5–6)? 4. Obligation to spiritual leaders are laid out in verses 7, 17–18. What is here that we should follow? 5. In what sense is our praise a sacrifice to God (v. 15)?

 Applying the Word 1. Which of these exhortations do you need to apply to yourself? 2. On the basis of your study of Hebrews, what do you think God would like to "work" in you that would please him?

Responding in Prayer Verses 20–21 are a benediction, a summary prayer. Make that your prayer for yourself.

James

What does James have to say to me? James is practical.

Take problems. James knows nobody's perfect. So he doesn't tell us how to live trouble-free. He tells us how to live when troubles hit. Do I complain? Or do I use difficulties as an opportunity for growth?

Take words. We all talk. And sometimes we say things we wish we hadn't. James helps us use words more carefully, more positively. Do my words hurt others? Do they advance God's kingdom? Are they truthful? Are they loving?

Take money. It flows around us (despite our complaints about tight budgets and taxes). Do I withhold my money when others are in need? Do I put more value on worldly things than on the things of God?

Take time. If we have enough money, we know we never have enough time. We do all we can to get the most out of each hour of each day, filling our calendars with activity. But am I missing God's will and perspective in the midst of schedule making?

James is practical—maybe too practical! So expect these quiet times to be challenging—not because they will be hard to understand but because they will be all too easy to understand.

Who is this fellow James? There are several people in the New Testament called James, including two apostles. Though they have never been completely certain, most church scholars have believed that a third man, James the brother of Jesus (Mt 13:55; Mk 6:3), wrote this letter. While he probably joined the others in Jesus' family in rejecting Jesus during his earthly ministry, James certainly started following Jesus after his resurrection. In fact, James soon became the head of the church in Jerusalem.

He probably led the first church council in Jerusalem (Acts 15), which decided that Gentiles did not have to become Jews before they could be saved. This is an important factor in assessing James's view of faith and works (which is to be noted in light of 2:14–16).

Yet James was aware of the very Jewish makeup of the church in Jerusalem and required Paul to squelch the rumor that he, Paul, was telling Jews to abandon the law of Moses. James himself apparently followed Jewish law closely, enough so that he was known as "James the Just." He died a martyr in A.D. 62.

James addresses his letter to "the twelve tribes scattered among the nations." "Twelve tribes" could refer to Jewish Christians who through exile, enslavement and trade were spread

throughout the entire Mediterranean basin. More likely it refers simply to Christians, since the New Testament compares the church to Israel (Gal 6:16 RSV; 1Pe 2:9–10). In any case, the letter is not addressed to one specific congregation, as Paul's letters were. It is therefore called a general, or catholic, epistle.

These quiet times will help you face squarely James's call for a consistent Christian life, for a practical faith—a faith that works.

Outline

1/ James 1:1–18 —————————————— *Dependable or Double-minded?*

2/ James 1:19–27 ——————————————— *Words, Words, Words*

3/ James 2:1–13 ——————————————— *Who's the Judge?*

4/ James 2:14–26 —————————————— *Just Works*

5/ James 3:1–12 ——————————————— *Preventing Forest Fires*

6/ James 3:13—4:10 ————————————— *Keeping the Peace*

7/ James 4:11–17 —————————————— *Getting Perspective*

8/ James 5:1–11 ——————————————— *What Awaits*

9/ James 5:12–20 —————————————— *Making Others Whole*

1 / *James 1:1–18*
Dependable or Double-minded?

NO PAIN, NO gain. Or so the saying goes. Athletes remind themselves of this to get their best possible performance. Sometimes they have to go through grueling training. Without it there is no improvement. James suggests it is the same for Christians.

 Warming Up to God Enduring pain is not pleasant! What fears do you have as you think about what it means to face trials? Be honest with yourself. Describe your fears to God. Allow him to comfort you.

 Read James 1:1–18.

1 James, a servant of God and of the Lord Jesus Christ,

To the twelve tribes scattered among the nations:

Greetings.

²Consider it pure joy, my brothers, whenever you face trials of many kinds, ³because you know that the testing of your faith develops perseverance. ⁴Perseverance must finish its work so that you may be mature and complete, not lacking anything. ⁵If any of you lacks wisdom, he should ask God, who gives generously to all without finding fault, and it will be given to him. ⁶But when he asks, he must believe and not doubt, because he who doubts is like a wave of the sea, blown and tossed by the wind. ⁷That man should not think he will receive anything from the Lord; ⁸he is a double-minded man, unstable in all he does.

⁹The brother in humble circumstances ought to take pride in his high position. ¹⁰But the one who is rich should take pride in his low position, because he will pass away like a wild flower. ¹¹For the sun rises with scorching heat and withers the plant; its blossom falls and its beauty is destroyed. In the same way, the rich man will fade away even while he goes about his business.

¹²Blessed is the man who perseveres under trial, because when he has stood the test, he will receive the crown of life that God has promised to those who love him.

¹³When tempted, no one should say, "God is tempting me." For God cannot be tempted by evil, nor does he tempt anyone; ¹⁴but each one is tempted when, by his own evil desire, he is dragged away and enticed. ¹⁵Then, after desire has conceived, it gives birth to sin; and sin, when it is full-grown, gives birth to death.

¹⁶Don't be deceived, my dear brothers. ¹⁷Every good and perfect gift is from above, coming down from the Father of the heavenly lights, who does not change like shifting shadows. ¹⁸He chose to give us birth through the word of truth, that we might be a kind of firstfruits of all he created.

 Discovering the Word 1. How are perseverance and maturity developed in us by enduring trials (vv. 3–4)? 2. Under pressure, how does the faithful Christian (described in vv. 5–6) contrast with the person described in verses 6–8? 3. In the context of trials and perseverance, why does James contrast rich and poor Christians (vv. 9–11)? 4. How are temptations different from trials (vv. 2–16)? 5. How is God the ultimate example of goodness and dependability (vv. 16–18)?

Applying the Word 1. What difficult experiences have increased your perseverance and maturity? 2. In what ways do you tend to rely on your possessions? 3. Think of trials or temptations you are currently facing. How can this passage encourage you to depend on God?

Responding in Prayer Take time now to talk to God about your needs. Ask him to help you be like him in his goodness and dependability.

2 / James 1:19–27
Words, Words, Words

WE ALL DO it. It's as common as flies around a horse. While someone else is talking, we're thinking about what we're going to say next instead of about what is being said to us. We know others are worth more care and attention. But the habit is hard to break.

God wants us to slow down and listen too. But even when we've really listened to him, we're still not done. This study gives us practical help on listening and more.

 Warming Up to God There's so much to listen to all around us. What different voices and messages are on your mind? Tell God about them and ask him to help you clear your mind and focus on his Word.

 Read James 1:19–27.

19My dear brothers, take note of this: Everyone should be quick to listen, slow to speak and slow to become angry, 20for man's anger does not bring about the righteous life that God desires. 21Therefore, get rid of all moral filth and the evil that is so prevalent and humbly accept the word planted in you, which can save you.

22Do not merely listen to the word, and so deceive yourselves. Do what it says. 23Anyone who listens to the word but does not do what it says is like a man who looks at his face in a mirror 24and, after looking at himself, goes away and immediately forgets what he looks like. 25But the man who looks intently into the perfect law that gives freedom, and continues to do this, not forgetting what he has heard, but doing it—he will be blessed in what he does.

26If anyone considers himself religious and yet does not keep a tight rein on his tongue, he deceives himself and his religion is worthless. 27Religion that God our Father accepts as pure and faultless is this: to look after orphans and widows in their distress and to keep oneself from being polluted by the world.

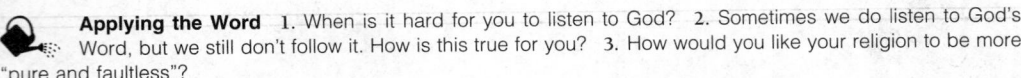 **Discovering the Word** 1. How can being quick to listen and slow to speak help us to be slow to become angry (v. 19)? 2. James tells us that God's Word was planted in us. What weeds can choke that Word and keep it from growing (v. 21)? Explain. 3. In your own words explain how the person who merely listens to God's Word is different from the one who puts it into practice (vv. 22–25). 4. According to verses 26 and 27, how do people who think they are religious differ from those who are truly religious? 5. Based on what you've read in this chapter, do you think James would be satisfied with good works apart from our listening to and receiving God's Word? Explain.

 Applying the Word 1. When is it hard for you to listen to God? 2. Sometimes we do listen to God's Word, but we still don't follow it. How is this true for you? 3. How would you like your religion to be more "pure and faultless"?

Responding in Prayer Ask God to help you become a better listener and doer of his Word.

3 / James 2:1–13
Who's the Judge?

LABELS AREN'T JUST found on soup cans. We put them on people all the time. Funny or dull. Smart or thick-headed. Friendly or cold. There are all kinds of ways we can categorize people. And our categories can have a profound influence on the way we treat people. As you might suspect, James has a few words to say about favoritism.

Warming Up to God Reflect on judgmental words and thoughts you have had this week. Confess them to God. Allow yourself to experience his mercy.

Read James 2:1–13.

2 My brothers, as believers in our glorious Lord Jesus Christ, don't show favoritism. ²Suppose a man comes into your meeting wearing a gold ring and fine clothes, and a poor man in shabby clothes also comes in. ³If you show special attention to the man wearing fine clothes and say, "Here's a good seat for you," but say to the poor man, "You stand there" or "Sit on the floor by my feet," ⁴have you not discriminated among yourselves and become judges with evil thoughts?

⁵Listen, my dear brothers: Has not God chosen those who are poor in the eyes of the world to be rich in faith and to inherit the kingdom he promised those who love him? ⁶But you have insulted the poor. Is it not the rich who are exploiting you? Are they not the ones who are dragging you into court? ⁷Are they not the ones who are slan-dering the noble name of him to whom you be-long?

⁸If you really keep the royal law found in Scrip-ture, "Love your neighbor as yourself,"ᵃ you are doing right. ⁹But if you show favoritism, you sin and are convicted by the law as lawbreakers. ¹⁰For whoever keeps the whole law and yet stum-bles at just one point is guilty of breaking all of it. ¹¹For he who said, "Do not commit adultery,"ᵇ also said, "Do not murder."ᶜ If you do not com-mit adultery but do commit murder, you have become a lawbreaker.

¹²Speak and act as those who are going to be judged by the law that gives freedom, ¹³because judgment without mercy will be shown to anyone who has not been merciful. Mercy triumphs over judgment!

ᵃ8 Lev. 19:18   ᵇ11 Exodus 20:14; Deut. 5:18   ᶜ11 Exodus 20:13; Deut. 5:17

Discovering the Word 1. How would you react if someone came into your church who wore sloppy clothes, was dirty or had body odor (vv. 2–4)? 2. Why is it wrong to give preferential treatment to those who have money (vv. 5–7)? 3. Verse 5 says God has chosen the poor to be rich in faith. Is God guilty of showing favoritism in this way? Explain. 4. How can "the royal law" (v. 8) guide our treatment of both poor and rich? 5. In what sense is violating one law as serious as breaking every law (vv. 9–11)?

Applying the Word 1. Toward what people or groups do you show favoritism? 2. How can you change your attitude and actions?

Responding in Prayer Ask God to work in your heart and mind to help you see beneath the surface as you relate to people.

4 / James 2:14–26
Just Works

"IT IS EASIER said than done" is a cliché that certainly applies to our Christian life. It is much easier to talk about God than to obey him. James said that even the demons believe there is one God. But that certainly does not make them Christians! That's why someone can have all his or her doctrine perfectly straight and still have missed out on God's will. James helps us stay on target.

Warming Up to God What has God been asking you to do that you have been ignoring? Talk to him about it.

Read James 2:14–26.

¹⁴What good is it, my brothers, if a man claims to have faith but has no deeds? Can such faith save him? ¹⁵Suppose a brother or sister is without clothes and daily food. ¹⁶If one of you says to him, "Go, I wish you well; keep warm and well fed," but does nothing about his physical needs, what good is it? ¹⁷In the same way, faith by itself, if it is not accompanied by action, is dead.

¹⁸But someone will say, "You have faith; I have deeds."

Show me your faith without deeds, and I will show you my faith by what I do. ¹⁹You believe that there is one God. Good! Even the demons believe that—and shudder.

²⁰You foolish man, do you want evidence that faith without deeds is useless*d*? ²¹Was not our ancestor Abraham considered righteous for what he did when he offered his son Isaac on the altar? ²²You see that his faith and his actions were working together, and his faith was made complete by what he did. ²³And the scripture was fulfilled that says, "Abraham believed God, and it was credited to him as righteousness,"*e* and he was called God's friend. ²⁴You see that a person is justified by what he does and not by faith alone.

²⁵In the same way, was not even Rahab the prostitute considered righteous for what she did when she gave lodging to the spies and sent them off in a different direction? ²⁶As the body without the spirit is dead, so faith without deeds is dead.

d20 Some early manuscripts dead   *e23 Gen. 15:6*

Discovering the Word 1. According to James, what good is faith without deeds (vv. 14–17)? Explain why he says this. 2. How does James answer the objection "You have faith; I have deeds" (vv. 18–19)? 3. James gives two Old Testament examples of faith in action. The first is the familiar story of God testing Abraham by asking him to sacrifice his son Isaac. Abraham obeyed but was stopped by an angel at the last minute. How was Abraham's faith made complete by what he did (vv. 21–24)? 4. The second Old Testament example is Rahab, the prostitute who hid two Israelite spies sent to Jericho before Israel's attack. How did Rahab's belief affect her (v. 25)? 5. How does James's closing analogy (v. 26) summarize his teaching on faith and actions?

Applying the Word 1. How do your actions demonstrate the reality of your faith? 2. In what ways can you bring your actions more in line with your beliefs?

Responding in Prayer Ask God to help you follow through with the works that will reveal your true faith.

---

5 / *James 3:1–12*
Preventing Forest Fires

ONE OF THE most distressing crises is a fire out of control. The pain of seeing the destruction can be almost unbearable. Personal belongings going up in smoke. The beauty of nature destroyed. Even loss of life itself. In this passage James compares the destructive power of the tongue to that of a forest fire.

 Warming Up to God How have you been hurt by someone's destructive words recently? Give your pain to God. Let him comfort you.

 Read James 3:1–12.

3 Not many of you should presume to be teachers, my brothers, because you know that we who teach will be judged more strictly. ²We all stumble in many ways. If anyone is never at fault in what he says, he is a perfect man, able to keep his whole body in check.

³When we put bits into the mouths of horses to make them obey us, we can turn the whole animal. ⁴Or take ships as an example. Although they are so large and are driven by strong winds, they are steered by a very small rudder wherever the pilot wants to go. ⁵Likewise the tongue is a small part of the body, but it makes great boasts. Consider what a great forest is set on fire by a small

spark. ⁶The tongue also is a fire, a world of evil among the parts of the body. It corrupts the whole person, sets the whole course of his life on fire, and is itself set on fire by hell.

⁷All kinds of animals, birds, reptiles and creatures of the sea are being tamed and have been tamed by man, ⁸but no man can tame the tongue. It is a restless evil, full of deadly poison.

⁹With the tongue we praise our Lord and Father, and with it we curse men, who have been made in God's likeness. ¹⁰Out of the same mouth come praise and cursing. My brothers, this should not be. ¹¹Can both fresh water and salt*f* water flow from the same spring? ¹²My brothers, can a fig tree bear olives, or a grapevine bear figs? Neither can a salt spring produce fresh water.

f11 Greek bitter (see also verse 14)

 Discovering the Word   1. James compares the tongue (the words we speak) to a bit and a rudder (vv. 3–4). Why do you think the tongue has such control over our lives?   2. James also compares the tongue to a fire and to a world of evil (vv. 5–6). What is the point of these two comparisons?   3. Verses 7–8 emphasize what a challenge it is to control the tongue. What makes this so difficult?   4. In what ways can the tongue poison people and relationships?   5. In verses 9–12 James uses a series of analogies from nature (springs, trees, vines). How do they highlight the inconsistencies of the tongue?

Applying the Word   1. What damage has your tongue done recently?   2. What in this text gives you added strength and motivation to be more careful with your words?   3. What can you do to give God more praise? Be specific.   4. How can you give more affirmation to those you come in contact with each day?

Responding in Prayer   Ask God to help you to be self-controlled about the ways that you speak to others.

---

6 / *James 3:13—4:10*
Keeping the Peace

WHY DO PEOPLE who love each other the most often fight the most too? Husbands and wives, parents and children, brothers and sisters—it's all too common. James offers a valuable remedy for this sickness.

 Warming Up to God   How have you gotten caught up in fighting recently? If that conflict continues to be a concern to you, talk to God about it. Ask God to clear your mind of anger and distrust so that you can focus on his healing Word.

Read James 3:13—4:10.

---

¹³Who is wise and understanding among you? Let him show it by his good life, by deeds done in the humility that comes from wisdom. ¹⁴But if you harbor bitter envy and selfish ambition in your hearts, do not boast about it or deny the truth. ¹⁵Such "wisdom" does not come down from heaven but is earthly, unspiritual, of the devil. ¹⁶For where you have envy and selfish ambition, there you find disorder and every evil practice.

¹⁷But the wisdom that comes from heaven is first of all pure; then peace-loving, considerate, submissive, full of mercy and good fruit, impartial and sincere. ¹⁸Peacemakers who sow in peace raise a harvest of righteousness.

4 What causes fights and quarrels among you? Don't they come from your desires that battle within you? ²You want something but don't get it. You kill and covet, but you cannot have what you want. You quarrel and fight. You do not have, because you do not ask God. ³When you ask, you do not receive, because you ask with wrong motives, that you may spend what you get on your pleasures.

⁴You adulterous people, don't you know that friendship with the world is hatred toward God?

Anyone who chooses to be a friend of the world becomes an enemy of God. ⁵Or do you think Scripture says without reason that the spirit he caused to live in us envies intensely?ᵍ ⁶But he gives us more grace. That is why Scripture says:

"God opposes the proud
    but gives grace to the humble."ʰ

⁷Submit yourselves, then, to God. Resist the devil, and he will flee from you. ⁸Come near to God and he will come near to you. Wash your hands, you sinners, and purify your hearts, you double-minded. ⁹Grieve, mourn and wail. Change your laughter to mourning and your joy to gloom. ¹⁰Humble yourselves before the Lord, and he will lift you up.

ᵍ5 Or that God jealously longs for the spirit that he made to live in us; or that the Spirit he caused to live in us longs jealously   ʰ6 Prov. 3:34

 Discovering the Word 1. In 3:13–18 James discusses earthly and heavenly wisdom. What are the characteristics of each? 2. What does James say is the source of quarrels (4:1–2)? 3. What does James say is necessary to come to God in prayer (vv. 3–10)? 4. What does it mean to be humble, to submit to God (vv. 6–7)? 5. In verses 7–10 James gives several suggestions for humbling ourselves before God. How does each contribute to a humble spirit?

Applying the Word 1. As you look at 4:3, what might be examples of right and wrong motives in your prayer? 2. In what area are you an enemy of God (see v. 4 and consider your attitude toward material possessions, friends, study or work, and leisure time)? How can you restore your relationship to him? 3. In what situations could humility help you become a source of peace? Explain.

Responding in Prayer Take a few minutes to quietly humble yourself before God. Ask him to help you become a peacemaker.

---

7 / *James 4:11–17*
Getting Perspective

"I AM THE master of my fate. I am the captain of my soul." How subtly we convince ourselves that we control our lives. Sometimes only a crisis or even death itself convinces us otherwise. If we are truly wise and humble, we will listen carefully when James says, "You are a mist that appears for a little while and then vanishes."

 Warming Up to God How have you been trying to control your life? Confess it to God and experience the freedom of giving him control.

 Read James 4:11–17.

---

¹¹Brothers, do not slander one another. Anyone who speaks against his brother or judges him speaks against the law and judges it. When you judge the law, you are not keeping it, but sitting in judgment on it. ¹²There is only one Lawgiver and Judge, the one who is able to save and destroy. But you—who are you to judge your neighbor?

¹³Now listen, you who say, "Today or tomorrow we will go to this or that city, spend a year there, carry on business and make money." ¹⁴Why, you do not even know what will happen tomorrow. What is your life? You are a mist that appears for a little while and then vanishes. ¹⁵Instead, you ought to say, "If it is the Lord's will, we will live and do this or that." ¹⁶As it is, you boast and brag. All such boasting is evil. ¹⁷Anyone, then, who knows the good he ought to do and doesn't do it, sins.

Discovering the Word 1. Why does James say we shouldn't slander or speak against a Christian brother or sister (vv. 11–12)? 2. If we judge the law, what does this say about our attitude toward the lawgiver (v. 11)? 3. How can a proper attitude toward God (v. 12) enable us to have a proper attitude toward others? 4. How would you describe the two attitudes toward the future found in verses 13–17? 5. If our life is like a mist, what should be our attitude toward tomorrow?

Applying the Word 1. If you knew you were going to die tomorrow, how would your attitude toward life today be different? 2. What future plans do you often dwell on? 3. In what area of your life do you need to turn your plans over to God's will?

Responding in Prayer Ask God to help you love those around you rather than judge them. Humbly commit your future plans to the Lord.

8 / *James 5:1–11*
What Awaits

YOU HAVE PROBABLY heard of the young man who cried out, "Lord, I want patience and I want it now!" James encourages us in this passage to wait on God and to be patient, and warns us against wanting it all now.

 Warming Up to God God wants to know your concerns and frustrations. Tell God what has been making you impatient lately.

 Read James 5:1–11.

5 Now listen, you rich people, weep and wail because of the misery that is coming upon you. ²Your wealth has rotted, and moths have eaten your clothes. ³Your gold and silver are corroded. Their corrosion will testify against you and eat your flesh like fire. You have hoarded wealth in the last days. ⁴Look! The wages you failed to pay the workmen who mowed your fields are crying out against you. The cries of the harvesters have reached the ears of the Lord Almighty. ⁵You have lived on earth in luxury and self-indulgence. You have fattened yourselves in the day of slaughter.ⁱ ⁶You have condemned and murdered innocent men, who were not opposing you.

⁷Be patient, then, brothers, until the Lord's coming. See how the farmer waits for the land to yield its valuable crop and how patient he is for the autumn and spring rains. ⁸You too, be patient and stand firm, because the Lord's coming is near. ⁹Don't grumble against each other, brothers, or you will be judged. The Judge is standing at the door!

¹⁰Brothers, as an example of patience in the face of suffering, take the prophets who spoke in the name of the Lord. ¹¹As you know, we consider blessed those who have persevered. You have heard of Job's perseverance and have seen what the Lord finally brought about. The Lord is full of compassion and mercy.

ⁱ5 Or *yourselves as in a day of feasting*

 Discovering the Word 1. James declares that misery awaits rich people. What crimes have they committed (vv. 1–6)? 2. Is James condemning all rich people? Explain. 3. James goes on to give three examples of patient people: a farmer, the prophets and Job. How is each an example of patience? 4. What different reactions would you expect the rich and those who suffer to have to the prospect of the Lord's return (vv. 7–9)? 5. How is piling up riches the opposite of patience that waits in faith for God to provide?

Applying the Word 1. When are you tempted to hoard rather than to give and wait on God? 2. In what areas of your life are you impatient? 3. What do you learn about patience from the examples James mentions?

Responding in Prayer Pray that God would make you a person who can wait for God to answer prayer.

9 / *James 5:12–20*
Making Others Whole

BROKEN HOMES, shattered relationships, damaged emotions—we live in a fragmented and hurting world. As we see all the wounded people around us, we long to help, to offer a healing touch. James gives us very practical suggestions for helping people become whole.

Warming Up to God God wants you to be whole. In what area are you struggling with emotional pain? Tell God how you want him to help you.

Read James 5:12–20.

¹²Above all, my brothers, do not swear—not by heaven or by earth or by anything else. Let your "Yes" be yes, and your "No," no, or you will be condemned.

¹³Is any one of you in trouble? He should pray. Is anyone happy? Let him sing songs of praise. ¹⁴Is any one of you sick? He should call the elders of the church to pray over him and anoint him with oil in the name of the Lord. ¹⁵And the prayer offered in faith will make the sick person well; the Lord will raise him up. If he has sinned, he will be forgiven. ¹⁶Therefore confess your sins to each other and pray for each other so that you may be healed. The prayer of a righteous man is powerful and effective.

¹⁷Elijah was a man just like us. He prayed earnestly that it would not rain, and it did not rain on the land for three and a half years. ¹⁸Again he prayed, and the heavens gave rain, and the earth produced its crops.

¹⁹My brothers, if one of you should wander from the truth and someone should bring him back, ²⁰remember this: Whoever turns a sinner from the error of his way will save him from death and cover over a multitude of sins.

Discovering the Word 1. What different types of prayer are mentioned in verses 13–18? 2. In verses 14–16 James discusses physical and spiritual healing. What are the steps in this process? 3. How is physical healing connected with the forgiveness of sins? 4. How does the Old Testament prophet Elijah illustrate the effectiveness of prayer (vv. 17–18)? 5. According to verses 19–20, how, if at all, are we our brother's keeper?

Applying the Word 1. Do you pray more when you are in trouble or when things are going well? Explain. 2. How could you make one of the types of prayer James describes more a part of your life? 3. How can you help others become whole physically, emotionally or spiritually?

Responding in Prayer Ask God for grace as you minister to others.

1 Peter

I t was a shaky time for Christians in the Roman Empire. In A.D. 68 Emperor Nero saw himself surrounded by political enemies and took the easy way out: suicide. In the next year three emperors, in rapid succession, took his place, but couldn't hold the job. So in A.D. 69 troops proclaimed the military leader Vespasian as emperor—and saw that he stayed there.

Vespasian hated Jews, and he counted Christians among them. Prior to becoming emperor, his goal had been to trample Judea and erase it from existence. As emperor, he sent his oldest son, Titus, to finish the job. Titus put Jerusalem under siege for three months. Then he tightened the noose. Troops leveled buildings to the ground. The temple became a crumble of stones. Jerusalem fell. Jews (and Christians) became Roman captives.

Aftershocks vibrated throughout the Roman Empire, blending with the general persecution against "atheists" (people who refused to worship Roman gods) that Nero had begun. Christians everywhere suffered. They were driven from their homes, deported to the outer borders of the empire, forbidden to worship openly and, worse yet, splintered by their own internal doctrinal disputes.

It is possible that the apostle Paul was martyred under Nero. And Peter was martyred as well—crucified upside-down, tradition says, because he felt unworthy to die in the same position as his Lord. It was a dark season for Christians.

How were they to endure?

Peter, through God's inspiration, sensed this coming darkness. If conservative scholars are correct, Peter's first letter can be dated about A.D. 64, written probably from the city of Rome —which Peter called Babylon in 5:13.

This is not a bleak letter. Indeed, it is full of hope and practical counsel on how to endure. It tells us to balance holy living with correct doctrine, to nurture spiritual growth, to work within existing authority structures, and to take care of each other.

This letter, sent with prophetic love to first-century Christians, still lives today. It provides a compass for our own dark road.

Outline

1/ 1 Peter 1:1–12 ——————— *Strangers in the World*

2/ 1 Peter 1:13–25 ——————— *Called to Be Different*

3/ 1 Peter 2:1–12 ——————— *Do I Want to Grow Up?*

4/ 1 Peter 2:13—3:7 ——————— *In His Steps*

5/ 1 Peter 3:8–22 ——————— *If I'm Living Right, Then Why Do I Hurt So Much?*

6/ 1 Peter 4 ——————— *The Christian Path of Nails*

7/ 1 Peter 5 ——————— *TLC for Trying Times*

1 / 1 Peter 1:1–12
Strangers in the World

A SMALL YOUNG man stood in the front of my classroom and spoke anxiously of home. He pointed to South Korean newspaper clippings that hinted of takeover by the North. He worried that the end was near: Ten years? Five? Two? If he is correct, Christians in South Korea have a right to feel nervous. Will they still have a church five years from now? Will they still have Bibles? Will they have to shutter their windows and lower their voices when they pray with their children?

How can a believer prepare for that kind of suffering? And what is it, anyway, that makes Christians strangers to the rest of the world?

 Warming Up to God If you knew you were about to enter a difficult set of circumstances that would test your faith, how would you prepare yourself?

 Read 1 Peter 1:1–12.

---

1 Peter, an apostle of Jesus Christ,

To God's elect, strangers in the world, scattered throughout Pontus, Galatia, Cappadocia, Asia and Bithynia, ²who have been chosen according to the foreknowledge of God the Father, through the sanctifying work of the Spirit, for obedience to Jesus Christ and sprinkling by his blood:

Grace and peace be yours in abundance.

³Praise be to the God and Father of our Lord Jesus Christ! In his great mercy he has given us new birth into a living hope through the resurrection of Jesus Christ from the dead, ⁴and into an inheritance that can never perish, spoil or fade—kept in heaven for you, ⁵who through faith are shielded by God's power until the coming of the salvation that is ready to be revealed in the last time. ⁶In this you greatly rejoice, though now for a little while you may have had to suffer grief in all kinds of trials. ⁷These have come so that your faith—of greater worth than gold, which perishes even though refined by fire—may be proved genuine and may result in praise, glory and honor when Jesus Christ is revealed. ⁸Though you have not seen him, you love him; and even though you do not see him now, you believe in him and are filled with an inexpressible and glorious joy, ⁹for you are receiving the goal of your faith, the salvation of your souls.

¹⁰Concerning this salvation, the prophets, who spoke of the grace that was to come to you, searched intently and with the greatest care, ¹¹trying to find out the time and circumstances to which the Spirit of Christ in them was pointing when he predicted the sufferings of Christ and the glories that would follow. ¹²It was revealed to them that they were not serving themselves but you, when they spoke of the things that have now been told you by those who have preached the gospel to you by the Holy Spirit sent from heaven. Even angels long to look into these things.

Discovering the Word 1. Study Peter's description of the people who were about to receive his letter (vv. 1–2). How does his description of them help explain why they were "strangers in the world"? 2. Peter says in verse 6, "Now for a little while you may have had to suffer grief in all kinds of trials." If you were to hear that kind of message, what information in this paragraph might help you through the suffering (vv. 3–9)? 3. What did Peter believe to be true of genuine faith (vv. 7–9)? 4. By what different routes did news of salvation come to the readers of Peter's letter (vv. 10–12)?

Applying the Word 1. How does the future, as Peter describes it here, offer you hope in your own setting? 2. When have you seen Jesus (through a person or event) in a way that increased your faith? 3. Peter refers to new birth, or salvation, throughout this passage as a central difference between Christians and the world. What tensions have you experienced because of this difference?

 Responding in Prayer Praise God for his gift of salvation that can help us cope with tensions with the world.

2 / 1 Peter 1:13–25
Called to Be Different

I GREW UP in a church of fervent Christians. We knelt to pray, carried Bibles to school, wore "modest" clothes—even to gym class—and talked a lot about Jesus. Needless to say, kids from our church never made the "most popular" lists at the local public high school. Instead, we feared the taunt "Holy Roller."

It's possible that our attempts to be separate and holy did more to close people out of our beliefs than to invite them in. Yet God does call his people to be different; different from what they would be if they did not believe in Jesus and different from the unbelievers around them.

Warming Up to God Think of a Christian you admire. In what ways does that person resemble Christ? Praise God for what you learn about him through others.

Read 1 Peter 1:13–25.

---

¹³Therefore, prepare your minds for action; be self-controlled; set your hope fully on the grace to be given you when Jesus Christ is revealed. ¹⁴As obedient children, do not conform to the evil desires you had when you lived in ignorance. ¹⁵But just as he who called you is holy, so be holy in all you do; ¹⁶for it is written: "Be holy, because I am holy."[a]

¹⁷Since you call on a Father who judges each man's work impartially, live your lives as strangers here in reverent fear. ¹⁸For you know that it was not with perishable things such as silver or gold that you were redeemed from the empty way of life handed down to you from your forefathers, ¹⁹but with the precious blood of Christ, a lamb without blemish or defect. ²⁰He was chosen before the creation of the world, but was revealed in these last times for your sake. ²¹Through him you

believe in God, who raised him from the dead and glorified him, and so your faith and hope are in God.

²²Now that you have purified yourselves by obeying the truth so that you have sincere love for your brothers, love one another deeply, from the heart.[b] ²³For you have been born again, not of perishable seed, but of imperishable, through the living and enduring word of God. ²⁴For,

"All men are like grass,
    and all their glory is like the flowers of the field;
the grass withers and the flowers fall,
²⁵   but the word of the Lord stands forever."[c]

And this is the word that was preached to you.

[a]16 Lev. 11:44,45; 19:2; 20:7   [b]22 Some early manuscripts *from a pure heart*   [c]25 Isaiah 40:6-8

Discovering the Word 1. Peter lists several ways that followers of Jesus ought to respond to his gift of salvation. Define each of these responses more fully (vv. 13–16). 2. Select one of these responses. If you were to put that response on the "front burner" of your priorities, what changes would you have to make in your life? 3. What events from the past would help the recipients of Peter's letter to appreciate God's concern for them (vv. 18–21)? 4. How could the conditions that Peter describes in verses 21–25 promote sincere love among Christians? 5. Peter links the Word of God with salvation and new birth. (Compare verses 10, 12, 23 and 25.) What do you think Peter meant when he said that this Word is "enduring" and "stands forever"?

Applying the Word 1. How might an honest attempt to "be holy" improve your relationships with people close to you? 2. In what situations might it make you, as verse 17 says, more like a stranger? 3. Jot a quick list of all you have to do today (or tomorrow). How could you begin to tackle this list with the goal "Be holy in all you do"?

Responding in Prayer Pray specifically from your list that you would be holy and would improve relationships with those around you.

3 / *1 Peter 2:1–12*
Do I Want to Grow Up?

"WOULD YOU SEND me to school?" [Peter] inquired craftily.

"Yes . . ."

"I don't want to go to school and learn solemn things," he told her passionately. "I don't want to be a man. O Wendy's mother, if I was to wake up and feel there was a beard!"

"Peter," said Wendy the comforter, "I should love you in a beard." Mrs. Darling stretched out her arms to him. "Keep back, lady, no one is going to catch me and make me a man." (James M. Barrie, *Peter Pan* [New York: Charles Scribner's Sons, 1911], p. 228.)

 Warming Up to God In what ways are you tempted to follow Peter Pan's approach to life?

 Read 1 Peter 2:1–12.

2 Therefore, rid yourselves of all malice and all deceit, hypocrisy, envy, and slander of every kind. ²Like newborn babies, crave pure spiritual milk, so that by it you may grow up in your salvation, ³now that you have tasted that the Lord is good.

⁴As you come to him, the living Stone—rejected by men but chosen by God and precious to him— ⁵you also, like living stones, are being built into a spiritual house to be a holy priesthood, offering spiritual sacrifices acceptable to God through Jesus Christ. ⁶For in Scripture it says:

"See, I lay a stone in Zion,
a chosen and precious cornerstone,
and the one who trusts in him
will never be put to shame." *d*

⁷Now to you who believe, this stone is precious. But to those who do not believe,

"The stone the builders rejected
has become the capstone, *e* " *f*

⁸and,

"A stone that causes men to stumble
and a rock that makes them fall." *g*

They stumble because they disobey the message—which is also what they were destined for.

⁹But you are a chosen people, a royal priesthood, a holy nation, a people belonging to God, that you may declare the praises of him who called you out of darkness into his wonderful light. ¹⁰Once you were not a people, but now you are the people of God; once you had not received mercy, but now you have received mercy.

¹¹Dear friends, I urge you, as aliens and strangers in the world, to abstain from sinful desires, which war against your soul. ¹²Live such good lives among the pagans that, though they accuse you of doing wrong, they may see your good deeds and glorify God on the day he visits us.

*d6 Isaiah 28:16 e7 Or cornerstone f7 Psalm 118:22
g8 Isaiah 8:14*

Discovering the Word 1. Peter speaks here of two aspects of Christian growth: individual and corporate. How might the five inner sins of verse 1 damage outer relationships with other believers? 2. What does the metaphor in verses 2–3 contribute to your understanding of how to nurture spiritual growth? 3. How does belief or unbelief influence the way a person understands Jesus, the "living Stone" (vv. 4–8)? 4. What reasons do the people here have to praise God (vv. 9–10)? 5. Verse 11 repeats a now familiar theme in 1 Peter—that Christians are aliens and strangers in the world. How might living up to the description of verse 9 cause a Christian to be alienated from the world?

Applying the Word 1. The *New Bible Commentary* interprets verse 12, "the day [God] visits us," as "the day God will visit the earth and search out man's hearts in judgment." If this were to occur in your lifetime, what evidence would you want God to find of your own spiritual growth? 2. How could today's passage help you overcome a tendency to become a spiritual Peter Pan?

Responding in Prayer Ask God to rid you of "all malice and all deceit, hypocrisy, envy, and slander of every kind."

4 / 1 Peter 2:13—3:7
In His Steps

IN THE LATE 1800s a young social worker tramped the streets of Topeka, Kansas. Disguised as an unemployed printer, he begged for food, work, hope. The social-worker-turned-tramp was a believer in Jesus and knew the giving, caring moral code that Jesus lived and taught. So he assumed that fellow Christians, even though they could not see through his disguise, would be among the first to help. He was wrong. He found that a tramp's life was tough—and that Christians didn't make it any easier.

Charles Sheldon went home to write a book about his experience—a novel that introduced a dying tramp to the Reverend Henry Maxwell and his congregation. In it, a body of believers begins to see the submissive suffering of Jesus and what it means to walk *In His Steps.*

 Warming Up to God If you were to rate your natural inclination for being submissive on a scale of one to ten, where would you place yourself and why? (One is a mud-covered doormat; ten is a banner-waving firebrand.)

 Read 1 Peter 2:13—3:7.

¹³Submit yourselves for the Lord's sake to every authority instituted among men: whether to the king, as the supreme authority, ¹⁴or to governors, who are sent by him to punish those who do wrong and to commend those who do right. ¹⁵For it is God's will that by doing good you should silence the ignorant talk of foolish men. ¹⁶Live as free men, but do not use your freedom as a cover-up for evil; live as servants of God. ¹⁷Show proper respect to everyone: Love the brotherhood of believers, fear God, honor the king.

¹⁸Slaves, submit yourselves to your masters with all respect, not only to those who are good and considerate, but also to those who are harsh. ¹⁹For it is commendable if a man bears up under the pain of unjust suffering because he is conscious of God. ²⁰But how is it to your credit if you receive a beating for doing wrong and endure it? But if you suffer for doing good and you endure it, this is commendable before God. ²¹To this you were called, because Christ suffered for you, leaving you an example, that you should follow in his steps.

²²"He committed no sin,
and no deceit was found in his mouth."ʰ

²³When they hurled their insults at him, he did not retaliate; when he suffered, he made no threats. Instead, he entrusted himself to him who judges justly. ²⁴He himself bore our sins in his body on the tree, so that we might die to sins and live for righteousness; by his wounds you have been healed. ²⁵For you were like sheep going astray, but now you have returned to the Shepherd and Overseer of your souls.

3 Wives, in the same way be submissive to your husbands so that, if any of them do not believe the word, they may be won over without words by the behavior of their wives, ²when they see the purity and reverence of your lives. ³Your beauty should not come from outward adornment, such as braided hair and the wearing of gold jewelry and fine clothes. ⁴Instead, it should be that of your inner self, the unfading beauty of a gentle and quiet spirit, which is of great worth in God's sight. ⁵For this is the way the holy women of the past who put their hope in God used to make themselves beautiful. They were submissive to their own husbands, ⁶like Sarah, who obeyed Abraham and called him her master. You are her daughters if you do what is right and do not give way to fear.

⁷Husbands, in the same way be considerate as you live with your wives, and treat them with respect as the weaker partner and as heirs with you of the gracious gift of life, so that nothing will hinder your prayers.

ʰ22 Isaiah 53:9

Discovering the Word 1. According to Peter, why should Christians treat their governing leaders with respect (2:13–15)? 2. How could the teachings of 2:16–17 keep you from becoming a "muddy doormat" to your government? 3. How might being a Christian bring some meaning to the suffering that comes from being a slave (2:18–21)? 4. 2:23 says that in his suffering, Jesus "entrusted himself to him who judges justly." How might a similar trust in God help you to submit to the necessary suffering that has come into your own life?

Applying the Word 1. Finding a balance between responsible action for healthy change and submission to authority is a constant tension for the Christian who wants to obey this passage. How can you draw together both ends of this tension? (In what situations would you take action? At what point would you submit?) 2. How do you balance the tension of submission versus responsible action in your job? in your marriage? in other relationships?

Responding in Prayer Pray for courage to walk "in his steps" even in the face of suffering.

5 / *1 Peter 3:8–22*
If I'm Living Right, Then Why Do I Hurt So Much?

WE OFTEN ASSUME a direct connection between "right living" and "easy living." It's an added pat on the back when life runs smoothly. But it is an unspoken accusation when trauma strikes. Peter contemplated this connection—even added a link or two to the chain. (Sure there are ways to live that will decrease our chances for unjust conflict.) But Peter made no promises of easy living. Sometimes suffering comes—whether or not we earn it. It came to Jesus.

Warming Up to God When in your life has suffering been hard to understand?

Read 1 Peter 3:8–22.

⁸Finally, all of you, live in harmony with one another; be sympathetic, love as brothers, be compassionate and humble. ⁹Do not repay evil with evil or insult with insult, but with blessing, because to this you were called so that you may inherit a blessing. ¹⁰For,

"Whoever would love life
and see good days
must keep his tongue from evil
and his lips from deceitful speech.
¹¹He must turn from evil and do good;
he must seek peace and pursue it.
¹²For the eyes of the Lord are on the righteous
and his ears are attentive to their prayer,
but the face of the Lord is against those who
do evil."ⁱ

¹³Who is going to harm you if you are eager to do good? ¹⁴But even if you should suffer for what is right, you are blessed. "Do not fear what they

fearʲ; do not be frightened."ᵏ ¹⁵But in your hearts set apart Christ as Lord. Always be prepared to give an answer to everyone who asks you to give the reason for the hope that you have. But do this with gentleness and respect, ¹⁶keeping a clear conscience, so that those who speak maliciously against your good behavior in Christ may be ashamed of their slander. ¹⁷It is better, if it is God's will, to suffer for doing good than for doing evil. ¹⁸For Christ died for sins once for all, the righteous for the unrighteous, to bring you to God. He was put to death in the body but made alive by the Spirit, ¹⁹through whomˡ also he went and preached to the spirits in prison ²⁰who disobeyed long ago when God waited patiently in the days of Noah while the ark was being built. In it only a few people, eight in all, were saved through water, ²¹and this water symbolizes bap-

ⁱ12 Psalm 34:12-16   ʲ14 Or *not fear their threats*   ᵏ14 Isaiah 8:12
ˡ18,19 Or *alive in the spirit,* ¹⁹*through which*

tism that now saves you also—not the removal of dirt from the body but the pledge*m* of a good conscience toward God. It saves you by the resurrection of Jesus Christ, ²²who has gone into

heaven and is at God's right hand—with angels, authorities and powers in submission to him.

m21 Or response

 Discovering the Word 1. Find as many phrases as you can in verses 8–12 that describe what a Christian ought to be and do. 2. What do you find difficult about the way of life described in verses 8–12? 3. In spite of godly living, Peter knew that Christians may encounter hardship. What counsel does Peter offer for coping with suffering (vv. 13–17)? 4. Why might unbelievers be willing to listen to reasons for hope from a person who is living the way Peter describes (vv. 15–17)? 5. Verse 18 is a "capsule" description of Christ's work and purpose. What all can you know from this verse about why Jesus came and what he accomplished?

 Applying the Word 1. How could setting apart Christ as Lord, as verse 15 commands, help you endure suffering? 2. Our world is often unjust. Bring to mind some of your past or current sufferings. In the context of these sufferings, how can the picture of Christ portrayed by this passage bring you hope?

Responding in Prayer Thank God for the hope we have been given in Christ.

6 / *1 Peter 4*
The Christian Path of Nails

SHUSAKO ENDO, THE Japanese novelist, tells the story of two missionary priests in *Silence*. The priests came from Portugal to Japan in the mid–1600s. At that time the Christian faith in Japan was one hundred years old. It had some 300,000 followers, a cluster of colleges, seminaries, hospitals and local clergy. But persecution had struck the church. A fragmented government united under a single cause: to become truly Japanese. And that meant erasing foreign religion, especially Christianity. Christians suffered horrible deaths. Endo's book asks why. Why the suffering? Why did God appear to sit through it in silence? And these questions are just as relevant for us today as we continue to suffer because of our beliefs.

 Warming Up to God When you learn of Christians suffering because of their faith, what questions come to your mind? Voice your questions to God.

 Read 1 Peter 4.

4Therefore, since Christ suffered in his body, arm yourselves also with the same attitude, because he who has suffered in his body is done with sin. ²As a result, he does not live the rest of his earthly life for evil human desires, but rather for the will of God. ³For you have spent enough time in the past doing what pagans choose to do—living in debauchery, lust, drunkenness, orgies, carousing and detestable idolatry. ⁴They think it strange that you do not plunge with them into the same flood of dissipation, and they heap abuse on you. ⁵But they will have to give account to him who is ready to judge the living and the dead. ⁶For this is the reason the gospel was preached even to those who are now

dead, so that they might be judged according to men in regard to the body, but live according to God in regard to the spirit.

⁷The end of all things is near. Therefore be clear minded and self-controlled so that you can pray. ⁸Above all, love each other deeply, because love covers over a multitude of sins. ⁹Offer hospitality to one another without grumbling. ¹⁰Each one should use whatever gift he has received to serve others, faithfully administering God's grace in its various forms. ¹¹If anyone speaks, he should do it as one speaking the very words of God. If anyone serves, he should do it with the strength God provides, so that in all things God may be

praised through Jesus Christ. To him be the glory and the power for ever and ever. Amen.

¹²Dear friends, do not be surprised at the painful trial you are suffering, as though something strange were happening to you. ¹³But rejoice that you participate in the sufferings of Christ, so that you may be overjoyed when his glory is revealed. ¹⁴If you are insulted because of the name of Christ, you are blessed, for the Spirit of glory and of God rests on you. ¹⁵If you suffer, it should not be as a murderer or thief or any other kind of criminal, or even as a meddler. ¹⁶However, if you suffer as a Christian, do not be ashamed, but praise God that you bear that name. ¹⁷For it is

time for judgment to begin with the family of God; and if it begins with us, what will the outcome be for those who do not obey the gospel of God? ¹⁸And,

"If it is hard for the righteous to be saved,
    what will become of the ungodly and the
        sinner?"ⁿ

¹⁹So then, those who suffer according to God's will should commit themselves to their faithful Creator and continue to do good.

ⁿ18 Prov. 11:31

 Discovering the Word 1. According to this passage, how is a Christian different from a pagan (vv. 1–6)? (Note attitudes as well as actions.) 2. Our doubts may sometimes taunt us, "Of what use is your Christian faith? God does not protect you. When your time comes, you die like the rest." How might the information in verses 4–6 help us deal with those doubts? 3. What specific instructions does Peter give suffering Christians who are aware that the end of all things is coming (vv. 7–11)? 4. Of what spitirual and practical value are these instructions? 5. Verse 11 speaks of two forms of leadership in the early church: those who speak (teach) and those who serve. How would the purpose of church leadership as it is described here prevent a misuse of power between Christians? 6. According to verses 12–19, what are some right and wrong ways for a Christian to suffer?

 Applying the Word 1. Think back to the questions you posed in question one. How do Peter's teachings help you deal with these questions? 2. How might verse 19 become both a comfort and a challenge to you when you suffer because of your faith?

 Responding in Prayer Pray for Christians in many parts of the world who face suffering for their beliefs.

---

7 / 1 Peter 5
TLC for Trying Times

RELATIONSHIPS BRING COLOR to life. Sure, the mountaintop hermit has a spectacular view outside the window. But the colors inside the cabin are browns and grays. It is people who bring sparkle and fire to existence.

When Peter concluded his first letter, a work frequently pointing to suffering, he did not tell his readers to escape to the isolation of a spiritual or literal mountaintop. Instead, he pointed to their relationships and said, "Here's how to take care of each other."

Warming Up to God What has been one of your most valuable relationships, and what made it valuable?

Read 1 Peter 5.

---

5 To the elders among you, I appeal as a fellow elder, a witness of Christ's sufferings and one who also will share in the glory to be revealed: ²Be shepherds of God's flock that is under your care, serving as overseers—not

because you must, but because you are willing, as God wants you to be; not greedy for money, but eager to serve; ³not lording it over those entrusted to you, but being examples to the flock. ⁴And when the Chief Shepherd appears, you will re-

ceive the crown of glory that will never fade away.

5Young men, in the same way be submissive to those who are older. All of you, clothe yourselves with humility toward one another, because,

"God opposes the proud
but gives grace to the humble."⁰

6Humble yourselves, therefore, under God's mighty hand, that he may lift you up in due time. 7Cast all your anxiety on him because he cares for you.

8Be self-controlled and alert. Your enemy the devil prowls around like a roaring lion looking for someone to devour. 9Resist him, standing firm in the faith, because you know that your brothers throughout the world are undergoing the same kind of sufferings.

10And the God of all grace, who called you to his eternal glory in Christ, after you have suffered a little while, will himself restore you and make you strong, firm and steadfast. 11To him be the power for ever and ever. Amen.

12With the help of Silas,ᵖ whom I regard as a faithful brother, I have written to you briefly, encouraging you and testifying that this is the true grace of God. Stand fast in it.

13She who is in Babylon, chosen together with you, sends you her greetings, and so does my son Mark. 14Greet one another with a kiss of love.

Peace to all of you who are in Christ.

⁰5 Prov. 3:34   ᵖ12 Greek Silvanus, a variant of Silas

 Discovering the Word 1. Peter speaks, in verse 1, to his fellow elders. In what ways did Peter see himself as like the elders he was writing to (vv. 1–4)? 2. When have you appreciated a person who acted toward you as a spiritual elder? 3. With what different beings or groups do these verses describe a Christian's relationships (vv. 5–11)? 4. What reasons did Peter give for following each of the commands in verses 5–9? 5. Peter points out three sets of relationships for all Christians—relationships with other believers, relationship with Satan, relationship with God. How would you summarize Peter's ideal for each of these?

Applying the Word 1. God's Word speaks to us in a variety of ways. What joy, comfort or warning do Peter's instructions in verses 5–11 point to in your own experience? 2. How could Peter's teachings about relationships in this chapter help you to "stand fast" in your own faith?

Responding in Prayer Ask God to comfort you, and wait before him to experience his care.

2 Peter

P
eter's second letter refers appreciatively to Paul's letters in 3:15–16, but bears no hint that Paul is dead. On the other hand, Peter seems to anticipate his own death. Soon (see 1:13–14). Scholars therefore date this letter in the same decade of the sixties as 1 Peter—but closer to the end.

This letter does not tell us how to escape suffering, but instead to expect it. It shows us that throughout suffering we can enjoy our fellowship with other believers and look forward to a new heaven and a new earth, a "home of righteousness," with an end to pain.

Outline

1/ 2 Peter 1:1–11 ——————————— *The Long Way Home*

2/ 2 Peter 1:12–21 —————————— *If I Should Die . . .*

3/ 2 Peter 2 ————————————— *Follow Which Leader?*

4/ 2 Peter 3 ————————————— *The Fire Next Time*

1 / 2 Peter 1:1–11
The Long Way Home

HOW DOES A person get to heaven? Is it by proper knowledge of Christian doctrines? Or by godly living? Is it by faith in Christ's gift of salvation? Or by working according to Christ's goals and principles? Is it by God's call to us to be his own? Or by our own endurance with God until the day we die? Weighty issues. And with them, Peter opens his second letter.

 Warming Up to God Reflect on your life. What qualities of godliness is God developing within you?

 Read 2 Peter 1:1–11.

Simon Peter, a servant and apostle of Jesus Christ,

To those who through the righteousness of our God and Savior Jesus Christ have received a faith as precious as ours:

²Grace and peace be yours in abundance through the knowledge of God and of Jesus our Lord.

³His divine power has given us everything we need for life and godliness through our knowledge of him who called us by his own glory and goodness. ⁴Through these he has given us his very great and precious promises, so that through them you may participate in the divine nature and escape the corruption in the world caused by evil desires.

⁵For this very reason, make every effort to add to your faith goodness; and to goodness, knowledge; ⁶and to knowledge, self-control; and to self-control, perseverance; and to perseverance, godliness; ⁷and to godliness, brotherly kindness; and to brotherly kindness, love. ⁸For if you possess these qualities in increasing measure, they will keep you from being ineffective and unproductive in your knowledge of our Lord Jesus Christ. ⁹But if anyone does not have them, he is nearsighted and blind, and has forgotten that he has been cleansed from his past sins.

¹⁰Therefore, my brothers, be all the more eager to make your calling and election sure. For if you do these things, you will never fall, ¹¹and you will receive a rich welcome into the eternal kingdom of our Lord and Savior Jesus Christ.

 Discovering the Word 1. In verses 1–2 we are told that we will receive the gifts of faith, grace and peace through Christ's righteousness and knowledge of God. How does your own spiritual well-being depend in part on Christ's righteousness and in part on your knowledge of God? 2. Verse 3 speaks of both knowledge and holy living as a part of the Christian life. Think of the balance between knowledge of Jesus and holy living that you have seen in Christians. What happens if one area or the other is weak? 3. Peter writes in verse 4 that because of God's promises, Christians "may participate in the divine nature and escape the corruption in the world." What does he then expect believers to do to nurture their own holy living (vv. 5–7)? 4. How are knowledge of Jesus and godly living related to each other (vv. 8–9)? 5. What do you think it means for a person to be called and elected by God (vv. 10–11)?

Applying the Word 1. Select one of the Christian qualities mentioned in verses 5–7 that you would like to become more prominent in your own life. If you were to practice this quality more faithfully, how would it help you escape the pollution of evil influences around you? 2. Verse 3 says that the divine power of Jesus has given us everything we need for godliness here and also for eternal life. If you were to draw more fully on this power that Jesus makes available to you, what changes would you hope to see in yourself?

Responding in Prayer Pray for the changes you think God is calling for within you.

2 / 2 Peter 1:12–21
If I Should Die . . .

IN 1976 JOE Bayly lay on a gurney outside an operating room at the Mayo Clinic's Methodist Hospital. He was scheduled for a minor operation. He'd probably be shuffling through the hospital hallway in a couple of days. But what if he just didn't wake up?

Joe's musings on that possibility left readers with a small thought-provoking book titled, appropriately, *Heaven*. In it he speaks of his faith in Jesus Christ and his hope here—and hereafter. It has influenced children and adults, believers and nonbelievers to follow Christ. Ten years later, Joe again lay on a gurney outside the operating room. The operation was a little more serious this time—his heart. But still, at Mayo, it was routine. But in 1986, when Joe woke up, it was hereafter.

 Warming Up to God As you think back over why you believe what you believe, who or what were the major influences in your life? Praise God for the privilege of knowing him.

 Read 2 Peter 1:12–21.

¹²So I will always remind you of these things, even though you know them and are firmly established in the truth you now have. ¹³I think it is right to refresh your memory as long as I live in the tent of this body, ¹⁴because I know that I will soon put it aside, as our Lord Jesus Christ has made clear to me. ¹⁵And I will make every effort to see that after my departure you will always be able to remember these things.

¹⁶We did not follow cleverly invented stories when we told you about the power and coming of our Lord Jesus Christ, but we were eyewitnesses of his majesty. ¹⁷For he received honor and glory from God the Father when the voice came to him from the Majestic Glory, saying, "This is my Son, whom I love; with him I am well pleased."ᵃ ¹⁸We ourselves heard this voice that came from heaven when we were with him on the sacred mountain.

¹⁹And we have the word of the prophets made more certain, and you will do well to pay attention to it, as to a light shining in a dark place, until the day dawns and the morning star rises in your hearts. ²⁰Above all, you must understand that no prophecy of Scripture came about by the prophet's own interpretation. ²¹For prophecy never had its origin in the will of man, but men spoke from God as they were carried along by the Holy Spirit.

ᵃ17 Matt. 17:5; Mark 9:7; Luke 9:35

 Discovering the Word 1. What phrases here create a picture of Peter's view of death (vv. 13–15)? 2. Based on these phrases, how would you describe Peter's attitude about death? 3. What difference would it make to those who knew Peter that his teachings about Jesus came from an "eyewitness of his majesty" (v. 16)? 4. What do verses 19–21 show about the origin and purpose of Scripture?

Applying the Word 1. What do you hope will be your own feelings when you approach death? 2. What could you be doing during your lifetime to build toward a "good death"? 3. Peter did not want his readers to be so dependent on him that their faith would fall apart after his death. Who would you like to influence with your faith in your lifetime, and how can you best go about it?

Responding in Prayer Thank God for the gift of Scripture and the ways in which it increases our faith.

3 / 2 Peter 2
Follow Which Leader?

"I HUGGED HER, and it was like hugging a statue. I looked into her eyes, and I felt that 'the lights were on, but no one was home.' She had been my best friend in a Christian college! What happened?"

For months my friend puzzled over this strange reunion with her college housemate. Later the puzzle pieces fell into place. A cult. "Someone got to her," she said later. "That person had to be very persuasive, and very tricky. My friend knew the Bible, and she wasn't dumb. I wish I knew what happened."

Warming Up to God   Jesus Christ is always faithful to his promises. Reflect on that fact and allow praise to well up within you in response.

Read 2 Peter 2.

---

2 But there were also false prophets among the people, just as there will be false teachers among you. They will secretly introduce destructive heresies, even denying the sovereign Lord who bought them—bringing swift destruction on themselves. ²Many will follow their shameful ways and will bring the way of truth into disrepute. ³In their greed these teachers will exploit you with stories they have made up. Their condemnation has long been hanging over them, and their destruction has not been sleeping.

⁴For if God did not spare angels when they sinned, but sent them to hell,ᵇ putting them into gloomy dungeonsᶜ to be held for judgment; ⁵if he did not spare the ancient world when he brought the flood on its ungodly people, but protected Noah, a preacher of righteousness, and seven others; ⁶if he condemned the cities of Sodom and Gomorrah by burning them to ashes, and made them an example of what is going to happen to the ungodly; ⁷and if he rescued Lot, a righteous man, who was distressed by the filthy lives of lawless men ⁸(for that righteous man, living among them day after day, was tormented in his righteous soul by the lawless deeds he saw and heard)— ⁹if this is so, then the Lord knows how to rescue godly men from trials and to hold the unrighteous for the day of judgment, while continuing their punishment.ᵈ ¹⁰This is especially true of those who follow the corrupt desire of the sinful natureᵉ and despise authority.

Bold and arrogant, these men are not afraid to slander celestial beings; ¹¹yet even angels, although they are stronger and more powerful, do not bring slanderous accusations against such beings in the presence of the Lord. ¹²But these men blaspheme in matters they do not understand. They are like brute beasts, creatures of instinct, born only to be caught and destroyed, and like beasts they too will perish.

¹³They will be paid back with harm for the harm they have done. Their idea of pleasure is to carouse in broad daylight. They are blots and blemishes, reveling in their pleasures while they feast with you.ᶠ ¹⁴With eyes full of adultery, they never stop sinning; they seduce the unstable; they are experts in greed—an accursed brood! ¹⁵They have left the straight way and wandered off to follow the way of Balaam son of Beor, who loved the wages of wickedness. ¹⁶But he was rebuked for his wrongdoing by a donkey—a beast without speech—who spoke with a man's voice and restrained the prophet's madness.

¹⁷These men are springs without water and mists driven by a storm. Blackest darkness is reserved for them. ¹⁸For they mouth empty, boastful words and, by appealing to the lustful desires of sinful human nature, they entice people who are just escaping from those who live in error. ¹⁹They promise them freedom, while they themselves are slaves of depravity—for a man is a slave to whatever has mastered him. ²⁰If they have escaped the corruption of the world by knowing our Lord and Savior Jesus Christ and are again entangled in it and overcome, they are worse off at the end than they were at the beginning. ²¹It would have been better for them not to have

ᵇ4 Greek *Tartarus*   ᶜ4 Some manuscripts *into chains of darkness*
ᵈ9 Or *unrighteous for punishment until the day of judgment*   ᵉ10 Or
the flesh   ᶠ13 Some manuscripts *in their love feasts*

known the way of righteousness, than to have known it and then to turn their backs on the sacred command that was passed on to them. 22Of them the proverbs are true: "A dog returns to its vomit,"g and, "A sow that is washed goes back to her wallowing in the mud."

g22 Prov. 26:11

Discovering the Word 1. Why are false teachers dangerous (2:1-3, also 1:20-21)? 2. Study verses 4-9. What did Peter want his readers to learn from these Old Testament events? 3. What characteristics should alert us that we are encountering a false teacher (vv. 10-19)? 4. Why might some people be attracted to teachers with these characteristics? 5. Why might it be better if a false teacher had never known the truth (vv. 20-22)?

Applying the Word 1. How can you protect yourself from the influence of false teachers? 2. What cautions can you institute to keep from becoming a false teacher yourself?

Responding in Prayer Pray for those who are victims of false teachers.

---

4 / 2 *Peter 3*
The Fire Next Time

AS A TEEN and young adult, when someone mentioned the end of the world, I shuddered and hoped, "Not yet." I wanted to graduate, fall in love, get married, raise children, work at a career—not necessarily in that order. At the very least I wanted to see how the weekend's date turned out. My sunsets looked like sunrise. And God's promised end of the world seemed a cruel interruption.

But at this writing, my twenty-two-year-old daughter and her unborn child lie cold in a country cemetery, a teenage son struggles with severe depression in a nearby psychiatric ward, my husband's colleague of over twenty years just revealed a secret life that includes distributing drugs to teens. My sunrises long for sunset. And the end of the world promises welcome relief.

Warming Up to God When are you likely to wish the world would end? Explain.

Read 2 Peter 3.

---

3 Dear friends, this is now my second letter to you. I have written both of them as reminders to stimulate you to wholesome thinking. 2I want you to recall the words spoken in the past by the holy prophets and the command given by our Lord and Savior through your apostles.

3First of all, you must understand that in the last days scoffers will come, scoffing and following their own evil desires. 4They will say, "Where is this 'coming' he promised? Ever since our fathers died, everything goes on as it has since the beginning of creation." 5But they deliberately forget that long ago by God's word the heavens existed and the earth was formed out of water and by water. 6By these waters also the world of that time was deluged and destroyed. 7By the same word the present heavens and earth are reserved for fire, being kept for the day of judgment and destruction of ungodly men.

8But do not forget this one thing, dear friends: With the Lord a day is like a thousand years, and a thousand years are like a day. 9The Lord is not slow in keeping his promise, as some understand slowness. He is patient with you, not wanting anyone to perish, but everyone to come to repentance.

10But the day of the Lord will come like a thief. The heavens will disappear with a roar; the elements will be destroyed by fire, and the earth and everything in it will be laid bare.h

h10 Some manuscripts be burned up

¹¹Since everything will be destroyed in this way, what kind of people ought you to be? You ought to live holy and godly lives ¹²as you look forward to the day of God and speed its coming.ⁱ That day will bring about the destruction of the heavens by fire, and the elements will melt in the heat. ¹³But in keeping with his promise we are looking forward to a new heaven and a new earth, the home of righteousness.

¹⁴So then, dear friends, since you are looking forward to this, make every effort to be found spotless, blameless and at peace with him. ¹⁵Bear in mind that our Lord's patience means salvation, just as our dear brother Paul also wrote you with the wisdom that God gave him. ¹⁶He writes the same way in all his letters, speaking in them of these matters. His letters contain some things that are hard to understand, which ignorant and unstable people distort, as they do the other Scriptures, to their own destruction.

¹⁷Therefore, dear friends, since you already know this, be on your guard so that you may not be carried away by the error of lawless men and fall from your secure position. ¹⁸But grow in the grace and knowledge of our Lord and Savior Jesus Christ. To him be glory both now and forever! Amen.

ⁱ12 Or *as you wait eagerly for the day of God to come*

Discovering the Word 1. What reasons did Peter give his readers to pay attention to this writing? (Look especially at verses 1–3 and 15–18.) 2. What mistakes will the last-day scoffers make (vv. 4–7)? 3. What reasons does Peter offer for a delay in Christ's return (vv. 8–9, 15)? 4. Compare and contrast the use of fire and water in this passage. What is the significance of each? 5. Notice the question of verse 11, "What kind of people ought you to be?" What answers can you find through the remainder of the chapter?

Applying the Word 1. If the day of the Lord were to come in your lifetime, what would you like to accomplish first? 2. In what condition would you like God to find your work? 3. How would you like God to find your relationships?

Responding in Prayer Pray that you will be always ready for Christ's return.

1 John

Today many people claim to be Christians. In fact, a 1986 Gallup Survey revealed that ninety-four percent of adult Americans believe in God, and that seventy-six percent believe that Jesus is either God or the Son of God. Furthermore, when the question "Would you describe yourself as a 'born again' Christian or not?" was asked, thirty-three percent said yes.

The problem, of course, is that actions speak louder than words. The same survey revealed that many of the mainline Protestant denominations have experienced sharp losses in membership since the mid sixties. For example, only forty percent told Gallup that they had attended church in the last week, and only ten percent claimed to read the Bible on a daily basis.

This credibility problem is intensified when we move from the pew to the pulpit. A shocking number of Christian leaders have been found guilty of sexual sin or financial misconduct. Sadly, their moral failures have been brought to our national attention by the secular news media, anxious to expose such blatant hypocrisy. If such leaders are representative of the church in general, it seems that we are indeed experiencing a period of unprecedented moral decline.

How are we to respond to this kind of situation? How can we tell the difference between genuine Christians and those who merely profess to know Christ?

John's letters were written for that very purpose. John writes to expose the false claims of those whose conduct contradicts their claims. He also provides strong assurance to those whose lifestyle is consistent with their Christian faith.

First John was written between A.D. 85 and 95 by the apostle John, the author of the Gospel of John and Revelation. Evidently the letter was circulated among a number of churches in Asia who were threatened by false teachers.

These false teachers embraced an early form of heresy known as Gnosticism. They taught that matter was entirely evil and spirit was entirely good. This teaching resulted in two fundamental errors:

A "new" theology. This centered in a denial of the incarnation. Since God could not be contaminated by a human body, these false teachers did not believe God became man in Jesus Christ. Some taught that he merely seemed to have a body, a view known as Docetism. Others claimed that the divine Christ descended on Jesus at his baptism but departed before the

crucifixion, a view known as Cerinthianism. This latter view seems to be in the background of much of 1 John.

A *"new" morality*. These false teachers also claimed "to have reached such an advanced stage in spiritual experience that they were 'beyond good and evil.' They maintained that they had no sin, not in the sense that they had attained moral perfection but in the sense that what might be sin for people at a less mature stage of inner development was no longer sin for the completely 'spiritual' man. For him ethical distinctions had ceased to be relevant" (F. F. Bruce, *The Epistles of John* [Grand Rapids, Mich.: Eerdmans, 1978], p. 26).

What intensified this problem was that these false teachers had once been an active part of the fellowship which John's readers were continuing to enjoy (see 2:19). But because their "new" teaching was so contrary to the apostolic truths of the gospel, they had to part company with the faithful. As you can well imagine, those who remained in the true fellowship were unsettled and shaken by the defection of these new teachers and needed to be reassured. But in the process, the others also needed to be exposed for what they truly were—unbelieving heretics.

In order to accomplish both purposes, John provides a series of tests for distinguishing between genuine Christians and those who falsely claim to know Christ. In response to the "new" theology, he provides us with a doctrinal test: What does the person believe about Christ? In response to the "new" morality, he provides us with a moral test: How does the person respond to the commandments of Christ? Finally, he provides us with a social test: Does the person love other Christians?

In fact, John's entire first letter is structured around these three tests, each of which appears in three separate groups, or cycles, in the letter. After the prologue (1:1–4), there is the first cycle (1:5—2:27), followed by the second (2:28—4:6) and third (4:7—5:12). Then in the conclusion (5:13–21) John again emphasizes his theme of Christian assurance.

In view of this purpose and structure, it is important to realize that the contrasts in John's letter are not between two types of Christians but between genuine Christians and those who merely claim to be Christians. For in the words of John Stott: "John's argument is double-edged. If he seeks to bring believers to the knowledge that they have eternal life, he is equally at pains to show that unbelievers have not. His purpose is to destroy the false assurance of the counterfeit as well as to confirm the right assurance of the genuine" (John Stott, *The Epistles of John* [Grand Rapids, Mich.: Eerdmans, 1964], p. 52).

Outline

1/ 1 John 1 —————————— *Fellowship & Forgiveness*

2/ 1 John 2:1–11 —————————— *Talking & Walking the Truth*

3/ 1 John 2:12–17 —————————— *Encouragement & Warning*

4/ 1 John 2:18–27 —————————— *How Important Is Theology?*

5/ 1 John 2:28—3:10 —————————— *Like Father, Like Son*

6/ 1 John 3:11–24 —————————— *Blessed Assurance*

7/ 1 John 4:1–12 —————————— *Discernment & Devotion*

8/ 1 John 4:13–21 —————————— *Fear's Remedy*

9/ 1 John 5:1–12 —————————— *Faith Is the Victory*

10/ 1 John 5:13–21 —————————— *What We Know as Christians*

1 / *1 John 1*
Fellowship & Forgiveness

CHRISTIANS EVERYWHERE SEEM to be interested in fellowship. They gather in fellowship halls, attend fellowship dinners and participate in well-organized activities with fellow believers. But what really constitutes biblical fellowship? A covered-dish supper? Coffee and doughnuts? Social events and activities? Perhaps more than any other passage of Scripture, these opening verses of 1 John establish the basis of true fellowship that is to be enjoyed and experienced by all Christians. More importantly, they enable us to understand how we can know we have fellowship with God.

 Warming Up to God What thoughts and feelings come to your mind when you think of Christian fellowship?

 Read 1 John 1.

That which was from the beginning, which we have heard, which we have seen with our eyes, which we have looked at and our hands have touched—this we proclaim concerning the Word of life. ²The life appeared; we have seen it and testify to it, and we proclaim to you the eternal life, which was with the Father and has appeared to us. ³We proclaim to you what we have seen and heard, so that you also may have fellowship with us. And our fellowship is with the Father and with his Son, Jesus Christ. ⁴We write this to make our*ᵃ* joy complete.

⁵This is the message we have heard from him and declare to you: God is light; in him there is no darkness at all. ⁶If we claim to have fellowship with him yet walk in the darkness, we lie and do not live by the truth. ⁷But if we walk in the light, as he is in the light, we have fellowship with one another, and the blood of Jesus, his Son, purifies us from all*ᵇ* sin.

⁸If we claim to be without sin, we deceive ourselves and the truth is not in us. ⁹If we confess our sins, he is faithful and just and will forgive us our sins and purify us from all unrighteousness. ¹⁰If we claim we have not sinned, we make him out to be a liar and his word has no place in our lives.

ᵃ4 Some manuscripts your   *ᵇ7 Or* every

 Discovering the Word 1. John begins this chapter by announcing an apostolic message. What is the content of that message (vv. 1–2)? 2. What are John's reasons for announcing his message (vv. 3–4)? 3. John provides a test by which we can know if we have fellowship with God (vv. 5–10). 4. The first part of John's test concerns the way we live or "walk" (vv. 6–7). What is the relationship between our conduct and our claim to have fellowship with God? 5. The second part of John's test concerns our attitude toward sin (vv. 8–10). What does our denial or confession of sin reveal about the reality of our relationship with God? 6. Based on your study of this passage, what does it mean to have fellowship with God—and each other?

 Applying the Word 1. Does John's test strengthen or weaken your assurance of fellowship with God? Explain. 2. How can we enjoy a greater fellowship with those who know the Father and the Son?

Responding in Prayer Pray that the level of fellowship in your church would be deepened and enriched.

Translated word confess means to speak the same thing or agree with." When we confess, we agree with God about our sin, our need to be cleansed & our need to forgive others.

2 / 1 John 2:1–11
Talking & Walking the Truth

FROM THE VERY beginning of Jesus' ministry, he emphasized that it is not what we profess but what we *possess* that counts for eternity. In his first major message he declared, "By their fruit you will recognize them." He then went on to teach, "Not everyone who says to me, 'Lord, Lord,' will enter the kingdom of heaven, but only he who does the will of my Father who is in heaven" (Mt 7:20–21). In the same way, John emphasizes that our claim to know Jesus must be backed by our conduct. This is necessary if we are to be certain about the reality of our faith.

 Warming Up to God When have you been impacted by someone saying one thing and doing another?

 Read 1 John 2:1–11.

2 My dear children, I write this to you so that you will not sin. But if anybody does sin, we have one who speaks to the Father in our defense—Jesus Christ, the Righteous One. ²He is the atoning sacrifice for our sins, and not only for ours but also for^c the sins of the whole world.

³We know that we have come to know him if we obey his commands. ⁴The man who says, "I know him," but does not do what he commands is a liar, and the truth is not in him. ⁵But if anyone obeys his word, God's love^d is truly made complete in him. This is how we know we are in him: ⁶Whoever claims to live in him must walk as Jesus did.

⁷Dear friends, I am not writing you a new command but an old one, which you have had since the beginning. This old command is the message you have heard. ⁸Yet I am writing you a new command; its truth is seen in him and you, because the darkness is passing and the true light is already shining.

⁹Anyone who claims to be in the light but hates his brother is still in the darkness. ¹⁰Whoever loves his brother lives in the light, and there is nothing in him^e to make him stumble. ¹¹But whoever hates his brother is in the darkness and walks around in the darkness; he does not know where he is going, because the darkness has blinded him.

^{c}2 Or *He is the one who turns aside God's wrath, taking away our sins, and not only ours but also* ^{d}5 Or *word, love for God* ^{e}10 Or *it*

Discovering the Word 1. According to John, how can we tell whether we truly know Christ or merely claim to know him (vv. 3–6)? 2. Practically speaking, what does it mean to "walk as Jesus did" (v. 6)? 3. In verses 7–11, John focuses on one of the commands. How can this command be both old and new (vv. 7–8)? 4. Why would love for our brother rather than love for God serve as a test of being in the light (vv. 9–11)? 5. In view of the overall context of this passage, what does it mean to *live* in the light (v. 10)? to live in Christ (v. 6)?

 Applying the Word 1. Although John does not want us to sin, he knows that we sometimes do (vv. 1–2). How does the realization that Jesus speaks "in our defense" provide comfort and assurance when you sin? 2. How does this passage encourage you to obey Christ and love other members of his body?

Responding in Prayer Ask that your life would reflect the integrity of Christ.

write notecards of integrity

3 / *1 John 2:12–17*
Encouragement & Warning

PILGRIM'S PROGRESS IS the classic tale of Christian's escape from the City of Destruction to the Heavenly City. It is true to experience because all of us can identify with his encounters along the way. In the Valley of Humiliation he enters into combat with Apollyon, his fiercest foe. At the Hill of Difficulty he meets Adam-the-First and his three daughters: Lust-of-the-Flesh, Lust-of-the-Eyes and Pride-of-Life. In the town of Folly he narrowly escapes its greatest attraction, Vanity Fair. These encounters are John Bunyan's well-known descriptions of the threefold arena of all Christian conflict—the world, the flesh and the devil. They are the same three foes that appear here in 1 John.

 Warming Up to God How far did you progress as a Christian before you became aware of these three foes? Explain.

 Read 1 John 2:12–17.

¹²I write to you, dear children,
  because your sins have been forgiven on
    account of his name.
¹³I write to you, fathers,
  because you have known him who is from
    the beginning.
 I write to you, young men,
  because you have overcome the evil one.
 I write to you, dear children,
  because you have known the Father.
¹⁴I write to you, fathers,
  because you have known him who is from
    the beginning.

 I write to you, young men,
  because you are strong,
  and the word of God lives in you,
  and you have overcome the evil one.

¹⁵Do not love the world or anything in the world. If anyone loves the world, the love of the Father is not in him. ¹⁶For everything in the world—the cravings of sinful man, the lust of his eyes and the boasting of what he has and does—comes not from the Father but from the world. ¹⁷The world and its desires pass away, but the man who does the will of God lives forever.

 Discovering the Word 1. Who is represented by the three groups being addressed (vv. 12–14)? 2. What is the source of our victory over the evil one (vv. 13–14)? 3. Why can there be no middle ground between our love for God and love for the world (vv. 15–17)? 4. What are the reasons we are to resist such temptations (vv. 15–17)? 5. How does the realization that the world is passing away (v. 17) lessen its appeal in your life?

 Applying the Word 1. How does this passage help us gain a better understanding of our spiritual battle? 2. On a daily basis, how can that truth help us overcome the tactics and schemes of the evil one?

Responding in Prayer Praise God for giving you the strength you need to overcome the evil one.

4 / *1 John 2:18–27*
How Important Is Theology?

THERE IS AN increasingly popular mindset within the church today that seeks to divorce Christian teaching from Christian living. "We don't want more theology," we are told, "just more about Jesus." But how can we learn more about Jesus apart from a proper understanding of who he is and what he has accomplished? The fact is, there is nothing more basic to Christianity than the person and work of Christ. Apart from understanding Christ, there can

be no real Christian living. That is why John goes to great lengths to protect his "dear children" from false views about Christ and to instruct them in the truth.

 Warming Up to God What have you been learning about the person and work of Christ recently?

 Read 1 John 2:18–27.

¹⁸Dear children, this is the last hour; and as you have heard that the antichrist is coming, even now many antichrists have come. This is how we know it is the last hour. ¹⁹They went out from us, but they did not really belong to us. For if they had belonged to us, they would have remained with us; but their going showed that none of them belonged to us.

²⁰But you have an anointing from the Holy One, and all of you know the truth.ᶠ ²¹I do not write to you because you do not know the truth, but because you do know it and because no lie comes from the truth. ²²Who is the liar? It is the man who denies that Jesus is the Christ. Such a man is the antichrist—he denies the Father and the Son. ²³No one who denies the Son has the

Father; whoever acknowledges the Son has the Father also.

²⁴See that what you have heard from the beginning remains in you. If it does, you also will remain in the Son and in the Father. ²⁵And this is what he promised us—even eternal life.

²⁶I am writing these things to you about those who are trying to lead you astray. ²⁷As for you, the anointing you received from him remains in you, and you do not need anyone to teach you. But as his anointing teaches you about all things and as that anointing is real, not counterfeit— just as it has taught you, remain in him.

f20 Some manuscripts and you know all things

 Discovering the Word 1. What characteristics of false teachers and their teaching is John exposing in these verses? 2. All the New Testament authors viewed the first coming of Christ as the event which marked the beginning of the end—"the last hour." What are some of the signs of the last hour (vv. 18–19)? 3. To deny that "Jesus is the Christ" (v. 22) is to deny that the man Jesus is the eternal, divine Christ—the God-Man. Why is John so harsh toward those who believe and teach such a view (vv. 22–23)? 4. Why is remaining in the truth so important in the Christian life (vv. 24–25)? 5. How does his instruction (v. 27) help us understand what it means to remain in Christ?

 Applying the Word 1. What does this passage teach us about the Holy Spirit's ministry of *preserving* us from error? 2. What does it teach about our responsibility of *persevering* in the truth?

Responding in Prayer Ask God to fill your heart and mind with truth about himself.

---

5 / *1 John 2:28—3:10*
Like Father, Like Son

A NUMBER OF years ago *Newsweek* featured an article on the increasing amount of people within our society who are claiming to be "born again." The article included the following report:

> According to a recent Gallup survey based on personal interviews with 1,553 Americans of voting age, half of all Protestants—and a third of all Americans—say they have been "born again." That figure comes to nearly 50 million adult Americans who claim to have experienced a turning point in their lives by making a personal commitment to Jesus Christ as their Savior. ("Born Again," *Newsweek*, October 25, 1976, p. 68.)

How would we go about discovering if the results of that survey were true? Where would we turn in God's Word to validate such a claim? Without question, 1 John 2:28—3:10 provides one of the clearest tests in Scripture for determining whether one who claims to be a Christian has truly been born of God.

Warming Up to God What do you think your local community would be like if one third of everyone who lived there was born again?

Read 1 John 2:28—3:10.

²⁸And now, dear children, continue in him, so that when he appears we may be confident and unashamed before him at his coming.

²⁹If you know that he is righteous, you know that everyone who does what is right has been born of him.

3 How great is the love the Father has lavished on us, that we should be called children of God! And that is what we are! The reason the world does not know us is that it did not know him. ²Dear friends, now we are children of God, and what we will be has not yet been made known. But we know that when he appears,ᵍ we shall be like him, for we shall see him as he is. ³Everyone who has this hope in him purifies himself, just as he is pure.

⁴Everyone who sins breaks the law; in fact, sin is lawlessness. ⁵But you know that he appeared so that he might take away our sins. And in him is no sin. ⁶No one who lives in him keeps on sinning. No one who continues to sin has either seen him or known him.

⁷Dear children, do not let anyone lead you astray. He who does what is right is righteous, just as he is righteous. ⁸He who does what is sinful is of the devil, because the devil has been sinning from the beginning. The reason the Son of God appeared was to destroy the devil's work. ⁹No one who is born of God will continue to sin, because God's seed remains in him; he cannot go on sinning, because he has been born of God. ¹⁰This is how we know who the children of God are and who the children of the devil are: Anyone who does not do what is right is not a child of God; nor is anyone who does not love his brother.

g2 Or when it is made known

Discovering the Word 1. Based on John's emphasis at the beginning and the end of the passage (2:28–29; 3:9–10), what test is he using to validate a person's claim of being born again? 2. Throughout this passage John teaches that God's children resemble their Father. In what ways does he reinforce this principle (2:29—3:10)? 3. How does John's definition of sin (v. 4) compare with some of the viewpoints people have today? 4. Although Christians can and do sin, how does knowing Christ change our relationship to sin (v. 6)? 5. Why does the new birth make it impossible for God's children to have a life characterized by sin (v. 9)?

Applying the Word 1. As one who has been born of God, what are some ways you see the family traits of obedience and love developing in your life? 2. In what area would you like to be more obedient?

Responding in Prayer Pray that your family resemblance to God and to Christ would be increased.

6 / *1 John 3:11–24*
Blessed Assurance

IN HIS CLASSIC book *Holiness* J. C. Ryle expresses concern for believers who doubt: "I heartily wish that assurance was more sought after than it is. Too many among those who believe begin doubting and go on doubting, live doubting and die doubting, and go to heaven in a kind of mist" (J. C. Ryle, *Holiness* [Grand Rapids, Mich.: Baker, 1979], p. 158). He goes on to say:

Doubts and fears have power to spoil much of the happiness of a true believer in Christ. Uncertainty and suspense are bad enough in any condition—in the matter of our health, our property, our families, our affections, our earthly callings—but never so bad as in the affairs of our souls. (Ryle, *Holiness*, p. 159.)

Without question, doubt and fear have robbed many of the joys of Christian assurance. That is why this passage is so important for Christian living. It overflows with the confidence and assurance that ought to characterize every member of God's family.

 Warming Up to God Have you ever questioned whether you were a member of God's family? Explain.

 Read 1 John 3:11–24.

¹¹This is the message you heard from the beginning: We should love one another. ¹²Do not be like Cain, who belonged to the evil one and murdered his brother. And why did he murder him? Because his own actions were evil and his brother's were righteous. ¹³Do not be surprised, my brothers, if the world hates you. ¹⁴We know that we have passed from death to life, because we love our brothers. Anyone who does not love remains in death. ¹⁵Anyone who hates his brother is a murderer, and you know that no murderer has eternal life in him.

¹⁶This is how we know what love is: Jesus Christ laid down his life for us. And we ought to lay down our lives for our brothers. ¹⁷If anyone has material possessions and sees his brother in need but has no pity on him, how can the love of God be in him? ¹⁸Dear children, let us not love with words or tongue but with actions and in truth. ¹⁹This then is how we know that we belong to the truth, and how we set our hearts at rest in his presence ²⁰whenever our hearts condemn us. For God is greater than our hearts, and he knows everything.

²¹Dear friends, if our hearts do not condemn us, we have confidence before God ²²and receive from him anything we ask, because we obey his commands and do what pleases him. ²³And this is his command: to believe in the name of his Son, Jesus Christ, and to love one another as he commanded us. ²⁴Those who obey his commands live in him, and he in them. And this is how we know that he lives in us: We know it by the Spirit he gave us.

 Discovering the Word 1. John begins this passage by talking about love and hate. How do Cain and Abel illustrate the two basic categories of humanity (vv. 11–15)? 2. Why is Christ's death on the cross the supreme example of love (v. 16)? 3. How can John's assurances in verses 19–20 help us deal with times of doubt? 4. Why would our obedience to God's commands affect our confidence in prayer (vv. 21–22)? 5. Why do you think John reduces the commandments to a single command to be obeyed (v. 23)?

Applying the Word 1. In verse 17 John mentions one specific way we can follow Christ's example. How have you and those in your church sought to love those with material needs? 2. In what other practical ways might we "lay down our lives" for each other? 3. Based on this passage, how would you counsel someone who lacked assurance that he or she was a Christian?

Responding in Prayer Pray about the needs on your heart with confidence before God.

7 / *1 John 4:1–12*
Discernment & Devotion

EVERY CHRISTIAN VIRTUE bears within itself the seeds of its own destruction. A zeal for the truth, for example, if not tempered by love and compassion can cause us to become arrogant, harsh and cold. Likewise, love for others if unchecked by the truth can cause us to be wishy-washy and even tolerant toward sin. If one of these virtues is not governed by the other, it can become a liability and not a strength. Like everything else, obtaining a proper balance is of utmost importance. In this passage, both doctrinal discernment and devotion to other Christians are held before us in perfect balance. They are not either/or, but both/and. One without the other is not enough.

Warming Up to God Which of these two aspects of the Christian life do you tend to emphasize above the other? Why?

Read 1 John 4:1–12.

4 Dear friends, do not believe every spirit, but test the spirits to see whether they are from God, because many false prophets have gone out into the world. ²This is how you can recognize the Spirit of God: Every spirit that acknowledges that Jesus Christ has come in the flesh is from God, ³but every spirit that does not acknowledge Jesus is not from God. This is the spirit of the antichrist, which you have heard is coming and even now is already in the world.

⁴You, dear children, are from God and have overcome them, because the one who is in you is greater than the one who is in the world. ⁵They are from the world and therefore speak from the viewpoint of the world, and the world listens to them. ⁶We are from God, and whoever knows God listens to us; but whoever is not from God does not listen to us. This is how we recognize the Spirit[h] of truth and the spirit of falsehood.

⁷Dear friends, let us love one another, for love comes from God. Everyone who loves has been born of God and knows God. ⁸Whoever does not love does not know God, because God is love. ⁹This is how God showed his love among us: He sent his one and only Son[i] into the world that we might live through him. ¹⁰This is love: not that we loved God, but that he loved us and sent his Son as an atoning sacrifice for[j] our sins. ¹¹Dear friends, since God so loved us, we also ought to love one another. ¹²No one has ever seen God; but if we love one another, God lives in us and his love is made complete in us.

[h]6 Or spirit   [i]9 Or his only begotten Son   [j]10 Or as the one who would turn aside his wrath, taking away

Discovering the Word 1. Why is there such a great need for Christians to be discerning (v. 1)? 2. What test does John give us for determining whether a person's teaching is from "the Spirit of God" or the "spirit of the antichrist" (vv. 2–3)? 3. As Christians, how can we overcome the doctrinal errors that continually confront us (vv. 4–6)? 4. Why must we be diligent in our devotion to one another (vv. 7–8)? 5. How does our love for each other make the invisible God visible in our midst (v. 12)?

Applying the Word 1. How does God's love for you motivate you to love others (v. 11)? 2. In what practical way can you show love this week to a brother or sister in Christ?

Responding in Prayer Ask that you would be filled with love.

8 / 1 John 4:13–21
Fear's Remedy

IN THE SEQUEL to *Pilgrim's Progress*, Mr. Great-Heart and Father Honest engage in a conversation about an old friend, Mr. Fearing. At one point in the dialogue he is portrayed in the following way: "He was a man that had the root of the matter in him, but he was one of the most troublesome Pilgrims that I ever met with in all my days."

That is Bunyan's way of describing many who are on the road to heaven: thoroughly sincere (the root of the matter is in them) yet so overloaded with doubts and fears that their pilgrimage is indeed "troublesome." How is Mr. Fearing to fare in this life? How does he, and how do we, overcome this kind of problem? The answer, in part, lies within this passage in 1 John.

Warming Up to God In what ways do you feel burdened by fear? Pause to voice your fears to God and listen for his assurance.

Read 1 John 4:13–21.

¹³We know that we live in him and he in us, because he has given us of his Spirit. ¹⁴And we have seen and testify that the Father has sent his Son to be the Savior of the world. ¹⁵If anyone acknowledges that Jesus is the Son of God, God lives in him and he in God. ¹⁶And so we know and rely on the love God has for us.

God is love. Whoever lives in love lives in God, and God in him. ¹⁷In this way, love is made complete among us so that we will have confidence on the day of judgment, because in this world we are like him. ¹⁸There is no fear in love. But perfect love drives out fear, because fear has to do with punishment. The one who fears is not made perfect in love.

¹⁹We love because he first loved us. ²⁰If anyone says, "I love God," yet hates his brother, he is a liar. For anyone who does not love his brother, whom he has seen, cannot love God, whom he has not seen. ²¹And he has given us this command: Whoever loves God must also love his brother.

 Discovering the Word 1. What three tests does John give for determining whether "we live in him and he in us" (vv. 13–16)? 2. How is our experience of God's love related to our ability to love others (vv. 16, 19)? 3. What insights does verse 18 give us into why we sometimes fear God and others? 4. Why is it impossible to love God and yet hate one of the members of his family (vv. 19–21)?

 Applying the Word 1. How can the principle "perfect love drives out fear" (v. 18) help you overcome your fears? 2. In what ways can this passage strengthen our confidence before God?

 Responding in Prayer Ask God to fill you with love for someone whom you find difficult to love.

9 / *1 John 5:1–12*
Faith Is the Victory

CHRISTIANS WITH A variety of theological views have wholeheartedly sung the words to the well-known hymn:
   Faith is the victory! Faith is the victory!
   O glorious victory, That overcomes the world.
But in light of the daily battles in the Christian life, not all agree on what this victory is, when it is accomplished, or how we go about achieving it. In this passage John clears up some of our confusion. He focuses our attention on not only the victory we have in Christ, but also on Christ himself. For, first and foremost, an overcoming faith is one that is centered in a correct understanding of who Christ is.

 Warming Up to God What spiritual battles are the focus of your attention?

 Read 1 John 5:1–12.

5Everyone who believes that Jesus is the Christ is born of God, and everyone who loves the father loves his child as well. ²This is how we know that we love the children of God: by loving God and carrying out his commands. ³This is love for God: to obey his commands. And his commands are not burdensome, ⁴for everyone born of God overcomes the world. This is the victory that has overcome the world, even our faith. ⁵Who is it that overcomes the world? Only he who believes that Jesus is the Son of God.

⁶This is the one who came by water and blood—Jesus Christ. He did not come by water only, but by water and blood. And it is the Spirit who testifies, because the Spirit is the truth. ⁷For there are three that testify: ⁸the*ᵏ* Spirit, the water

ᵏ 7,8 Late manuscripts of the Vulgate testify in heaven: the Father, the Word and the Holy Spirit, and these three are one. 8And there are three that testify on earth: the (not found in any Greek manuscript before the sixteenth century)

and the blood; and the three are in agreement. ⁹We accept man's testimony, but God's testimony is greater because it is the testimony of God, which he has given about his Son. ¹⁰Anyone who believes in the Son of God has this testimony in his heart. Anyone who does not believe God has made him out to be a liar, because he has not believed the testimony God has given about his Son. ¹¹And this is the testimony: God has given us eternal life, and this life is in his Son. ¹²He who has the Son has life; he who does not have the Son of God does not have life.

Discovering the Word 1. What are some inevitable results of the new birth (vv. 1–2)? 2. Why is obedience to God's commandments not burdensome for Christians (v. 3)? 3. How then can we explain the struggle we sometimes have to obey? 4. Reflect for a moment on the two major characteristics of the world described earlier (see 2:15–17; 4:1–6). What then does it mean for us to "overcome the world" (vv. 4–5)? 5. The heretics of John's day taught that the divine Christ descended on Jesus at his baptism but left before his death (v. 6). What is wrong with this view? 6. The Old Testament law required two or three witnesses to prove a claim. Who are John's three witnesses, and what do they testify (vv. 7–8)?

Applying the Word 1. What evidence of the victory over the world do you see in your life? 2. How does your own experience confirm the truth that eternal life is found in Jesus (vv. 10–12)?

Responding in Prayer Take time to thank God for his son, and for the victory and eternal life we have in him.

---

10 / *1 John 5:13–21*
What We Know as Christians

ALMOST IMMEDIATELY AFTER his well-known conversion experience at Aldersgate Street, John Wesley struggled for months over the uncertainty of his own salvation. Receiving little help from his friends or his church, his thoughts began to turn inward. Focusing on his sinful failures, he became increasingly despondent and dejected. He sought relief by opening passages within the Bible at random, but when that also proved unfruitful he continued his downward spiral. Finally he sank to such depths of despair that he made the following shocking notation in his journal: "My friends affirm that I am mad because I said I was not a Christian a year ago. I affirm I am not a Christian now" (Arnold A. Dallimore, *George Whitefield*, Vol. I [Carlisle, Penn.: Banner of Truth, 1975], p. 196).

What was Wesley's problem? Unfortunately, it is the same problem that afflicts many sincere Christians today—a lack of knowledge. There are certain truths that all of us as Christians must know if we are to avoid an experience like his. Those truths are found in this passage.

Warming Up to God How well can you relate to Wesley's experience? Explain.

Read 1 John 5:13–21.

---

¹³I write these things to you who believe in the name of the Son of God so that you may know that you have eternal life. ¹⁴This is the confidence we have in approaching God: that if we ask anything according to his will, he hears us. ¹⁵And if we know that he hears us—whatever we ask—we know that we have what we asked of him.

¹⁶If anyone sees his brother commit a sin that does not lead to death, he should pray and God will give him life. I refer to those whose sin does not lead to death. There is a sin that leads to death. I am not saying that he should pray about that. ¹⁷All wrongdoing is sin, and there is sin that does not lead to death.

¹⁸We know that anyone born of God does not continue to sin; the one who was born of God keeps him safe, and the evil one cannot harm him. ¹⁹We know that we are children of God, and that the whole world is under the control of the

evil one. ²⁰We know also that the Son of God has come and has given us understanding, so that we may know him who is true. And we are in him who is true—even in his Son Jesus Christ. He is the true God and eternal life.

²¹Dear children, keep yourselves from idols.

 Discovering the Word 1. What assurance does John give us in these verses? 2. Verse 13 is a summary statement of purpose for the entire epistle. What then are those "things" which assure us we have eternal life? 3. How can we get to the point where we want what God wants (vv. 14–15)? 4. In light of the whole context of this epistle, what might be the distinction between the sin that does not lead to death and the one that does (vv. 16–17)? 5. How does the coming of God's Son enable us to know the true God in contrast to the false conceptions of God that continually surround us (vv. 20–21)?

 Applying the Word 1. What certainties in this passage are the most encouraging to you? 2. In what way do you need greater assurance from God?

Responding in Prayer Pray that God will make your desires his own will.

2 John

*L*ike 1 John, 2 John was written by the apostle John between A.D. 85 and 95. It was written to provide guidance about hospitality. During the first century, traveling evangelists relied on the hospitality of church members. Because inns were few and unsafe, believers would take such people into their homes and then give them provisions for their journey. Since Gnostic teachers also relied on hospitality, John warned his readers against taking such people into their homes lest they participate in spreading heresy.

2 John 1–13
Truth & Love

THERE ARE TWO equally extreme misconceptions many people have concerning what it means to be a Christian or to live the Christian life. One view says, "It doesn't matter what you believe as long as you are sincere and loving." The other one says, "It doesn't matter how you live as long as you believe the truth." The reason why both views are just as wrong is because the Word of God binds both truth and love inseparably together. They are friends, not enemies. Nowhere will you see this perspective more clearly than in John's second epistle. His major purpose is to demonstrate how love and truth are designed to support and complement one another as only good friends can.

 Warming Up to God Have you ever been in a situation where you felt you were torn between doing the right thing and the loving thing? Explain.

 Read 2 John 1–13.

---

¹The elder,

To the chosen lady and her children, whom I love in the truth—and not I only, but also all who know the truth— ²because of the truth, which lives in us and will be with us forever:

³Grace, mercy and peace from God the Father and from Jesus Christ, the Father's Son, will be with us in truth and love.

⁴It has given me great joy to find some of your children walking in the truth, just as the Father commanded us. ⁵And now, dear lady, I am not writing you a new command but one we have had from the beginning. I ask that we love one another. ⁶And this is love: that we walk in obedience to his commands. As you have heard from the beginning, his command is that you walk in love.

⁷Many deceivers, who do not acknowledge Jesus Christ as coming in the flesh, have gone out into the world. Any such person is the deceiver and the antichrist. ⁸Watch out that you do not lose what you have worked for, but that you may be rewarded fully. ⁹Anyone who runs ahead and does not continue in the teaching of Christ does not have God; whoever continues in the teaching has both the Father and the Son. ¹⁰If anyone comes to you and does not bring this teaching, do not take him into your house or welcome him. ¹¹Anyone who welcomes him shares in his wicked work.

¹²I have much to write to you, but I do not want to use paper and ink. Instead, I hope to visit you and talk with you face to face, so that our joy may be complete.

¹³The children of your chosen sister send their greetings.

 Discovering the Word 1. In the brief introductory address and greeting (vv. 1–3), notice how many times *truth* and *love* are mentioned together. What does it mean to love someone "in the truth" (v. 1)? 2. We tend to love only those Christians who agree with us or who we feel are compatible with us. But what does it mean to love them "because of the truth" (v. 2)? 3. In verses 4–6 the unity of truth and love is applied to our relationships within the church. What distinction is made between the *commandment* and the *commandments*? 4. In verses 7–11 the unity of truth and love is applied to our relationships outside the church. By denying that Christ had come in the flesh (v. 7), what fundamental truths were the false teachers rejecting? 5. Obtaining a future reward for faithful service was a strong motivation for John (v. 8). In what sense does the prospect of receiving a reward from Jesus Christ motivate you to walk in truth and love?

 Applying the Word 1. Would you identify yourself as someone whose truth needs to be balanced by love or whose love needs to be balanced by truth? Explain. 2. What can you do to gain a better balance?

Responding in Prayer Pray that your life would reveal an understanding of both truth and love.

3 John

*L*ike 2 John, 3 John was written to provide us with guidance about hospitality, but in a much more positive way. Whereas 2 John tells us what we are *not* to do, 3 John emphasizes what we *are* to do. For those genuine teachers who are totally dependent upon the body of Christ for all of their needs, we are to open not only our hearts but also our homes. This instruction is primarily found in John's commendation of Gaius, who has done this very thing, and in his denunciation of Diotrephes, who has refused. These two men become living examples of good and evil, truth and error.

It is my hope that these studies will encourage and assure you that you "walk in the truth."

3 John 1–14
Opening Our Hearts & Homes

IMAGINE LIVING IN a world where there were no bed-and-breakfasts, no hotels and headwaiters. If traveling evangelists and teachers were to come to your town, you would have the privilege of inviting them into your home for the night and giving them provisions for their journey. Such was the world of John and his readers. Their hospitality was one of the clearest testimonies of their love for the brethren and obedience to God.

The same is true today. For in the words of Helga Henry, wife of noted theologian Carl F. H. Henry, "Christian hospitality is not a matter of choice; it is not a matter of money; it is not a matter of age, social standing, sex, or personality. Christian hospitality is a matter of obedience to God" (V. A. Hall, *Be My Guest* [Chicago: Moody Press, 1979], p. 9). For that reason the instruction concerning hospitality in this letter takes on added significance.

 Warming Up to God When is showing hospitality difficult?

 Read 3 John 1–14.

---

¹The elder,

To my dear friend Gaius, whom I love in the truth.

²Dear friend, I pray that you may enjoy good health and that all may go well with you, even as your soul is getting along well. ³It gave me great joy to have some brothers come and tell about your faithfulness to the truth and how you continue to walk in the truth. ⁴I have no greater joy than to hear that my children are walking in the truth.

⁵Dear friend, you are faithful in what you are doing for the brothers, even though they are strangers to you. ⁶They have told the church about your love. You will do well to send them on their way in a manner worthy of God. ⁷It was for the sake of the Name that they went out, receiving no help from the pagans. ⁸We ought therefore to show hospitality to such men so that we may work together for the truth.

⁹I wrote to the church, but Diotrephes, who loves to be first, will have nothing to do with us. ¹⁰So if I come, I will call attention to what he is doing, gossiping maliciously about us. Not satisfied with that, he refuses to welcome the brothers. He also stops those who want to do so and puts them out of the church.

¹¹Dear friend, do not imitate what is evil but what is good. Anyone who does what is good is from God. Anyone who does what is evil has not seen God. ¹²Demetrius is well spoken of by everyone—and even by the truth itself. We also speak well of him, and you know that our testimony is true.

¹³I have much to write you, but I do not want to do so with pen and ink. ¹⁴I hope to see you soon, and we will talk face to face.

Peace to you. The friends here send their greetings. Greet the friends there by name.

Discovering the Word 1. Why is Gaius an especially good example for us to follow? 2. How are both love and faithfulness demonstrated in Christian hospitality (vv. 5–6)? 3. Why do you think Christian workers are to look to Christians for support and not to non-Christians (vv. 7–8)? 4. In addition to hospitality, how else can we "work together" with such people? 5. How are the actions of Diotrephes consistent with his true heart's desire (vv. 9–11)?

Applying the Word 1. In contrast to Diotrephes, Demetrius was "well spoken of by everyone" (v. 12). If those who know you best were asked about your love and hospitality, what might they say? 2. In light of this passage, what practical steps could you take to develop more of a ministry of hospitality?

 Responding in Prayer Pray for an open heart that will lead you to an open home.

Jude

Jude wrote in the same era as Peter. In fact, much of the information in Jude is found also in 2 Peter 2.

Jude was the brother of James and the half-brother of Jesus. Both Matthew 13:55 and Mark 6:3 speak of James and Jude (along with Joseph and Simon) as brothers of Jesus. Though, according to John 7:5, Christ's brothers were not believers in him during his lifetime, these two at least became converts after his death.

James became a leader in the early church. We see him in action in 1 Corinthians 15:7; Acts 12:17 and 15:13; Galatians 1:19 and 2:9, 12; and Acts 21:18. We hear from Jude only in this book, except perhaps in 1 Corinthians 9:5. It is interesting to note that while Jude claims James as brother, both he and James refer to themselves as servants of Jesus.

The book of Jude was written to oppose false teachers who were sexually immoral and were teaching arrogantly. This letter would have been used as a sermon in the writer's absence (Craig S. Keener, *The IVP Bible Background Commentary: New Testament* [Downers Grove, Ill.: InterVarsity Press, 1993], pp. 752–53).

Jude 1–25
The Twisted Fate of Twisted Faith

IN NOVEMBER OF 1978, in a jungle clearing in Guyana, more than nine hundred people committed suicide by drinking cyanide-treated punch. Those too young to act on their own were given the punch by their parents. The Jonestown massacre sends a shudder through all Christians—and well it should—because Jim Jones, who prescribed this "White Night" of death, at one time claimed to be among us. It's enough to cause Christians to take a hard, critical look at the life and faith of their leaders—and themselves. The book of Jude shows us how.

Warming Up to God How do you think that people get tricked into perverted versions of the Christian faith?

Read Jude 1–25.

---

¹Jude, a servant of Jesus Christ and a brother of James,

To those who have been called, who are loved by God the Father and kept by*ᵃ* Jesus Christ:

²Mercy, peace and love be yours in abundance.

³Dear friends, although I was very eager to write to you about the salvation we share, I felt I had to write and urge you to contend for the faith that was once for all entrusted to the saints. ⁴For certain men whose condemnation was written about*ᵇ* long ago have secretly slipped in among you. They are godless men, who change the grace of our God into a license for immorality and deny Jesus Christ our only Sovereign and Lord.

⁵Though you already know all this, I want to remind you that the Lord*ᶜ* delivered his people out of Egypt, but later destroyed those who did not believe. ⁶And the angels who did not keep their positions of authority but abandoned their own home—these he has kept in darkness, bound with everlasting chains for judgment on the great Day. ⁷In a similar way, Sodom and Gomorrah and the surrounding towns gave themselves up to sexual immorality and perversion. They serve as an example of those who suffer the punishment of eternal fire.

⁸In the very same way, these dreamers pollute their own bodies, reject authority and slander celestial beings. ⁹But even the archangel Michael, when he was disputing with the devil about the body of Moses, did not dare to bring a slanderous accusation against him, but said, "The Lord rebuke you!" ¹⁰Yet these men speak abusively against whatever they do not understand; and what things they do understand by instinct, like

unreasoning animals—these are the very things that destroy them.

¹¹Woe to them! They have taken the way of Cain; they have rushed for profit into Balaam's error; they have been destroyed in Korah's rebellion.

¹²These men are blemishes at your love feasts, eating with you without the slightest qualm—shepherds who feed only themselves. They are clouds without rain, blown along by the wind; autumn trees, without fruit and uprooted—twice dead. ¹³They are wild waves of the sea, foaming up their shame; wandering stars, for whom blackest darkness has been reserved forever.

¹⁴Enoch, the seventh from Adam, prophesied about these men: "See, the Lord is coming with thousands upon thousands of his holy ones ¹⁵to judge everyone, and to convict all the ungodly of all the ungodly acts they have done in the ungodly way, and of all the harsh words ungodly sinners have spoken against him." ¹⁶These men are grumblers and faultfinders; they follow their own evil desires; they boast about themselves and flatter others for their own advantage.

¹⁷But, dear friends, remember what the apostles of our Lord Jesus Christ foretold. ¹⁸They said to you, "In the last times there will be scoffers who will follow their own ungodly desires." ¹⁹These are the men who divide you, who follow mere natural instincts and do not have the Spirit.

²⁰But you, dear friends, build yourselves up in your most holy faith and pray in the Holy Spirit. ²¹Keep yourselves in God's love as you wait for the mercy of our Lord Jesus Christ to bring you to eternal life.

ᵃ1 Or *for;* or *in*   *ᵇ4* Or *men who were marked out for condemnation*
ᶜ5 Some early manuscripts *Jesus*

²²Be merciful to those who doubt; ²³snatch others from the fire and save them; to others show mercy, mixed with fear—hating even the clothing stained by corrupted flesh.

²⁴To him who is able to keep you from falling and to present you before his glorious presence without fault and with great joy— ²⁵to the only God our Savior be glory, majesty, power and authority, through Jesus Christ our Lord, before all ages, now and forevermore! Amen.

Discovering the Word 1. What can you know of the circumstances of the people receiving this letter and of Jude's purpose in writing to them (vv. 3–4)? 2. Find as many words and phrases as you can in this letter that describe those "certain men" who have "secretly slipped in among you." 3. What harm could people like these do within a body of believers? 4. Jude used a series of six metaphors in verses 12–13. How does each illustrate the danger of teachers who have perverted the gospel? 5. In the face of this problem, Jude gives his readers two sets of instructions: "Remember" (v. 17) and "Build yourselves up" (v. 20). Notice the specific instructions under each of these. How would remembering, in the way Jude describes, help believers keep the essential ingredients of the Christian faith? 6. How would building ourselves up in the ways Jude outlines (vv. 17–23) help us keep on living in a way that is true to our faith?

Applying the Word 1. What errors in faith and life do you see as subtle dangers to today's Christians? 2. How can you protect yourself, and other believers whose lives you touch, from falling into these errors?

Responding in Prayer Pray that you and your church would be protected from false religion.

Revelation

The human spirit is like a little child on a long journey asking, "Are we almost there?" Yet today many of us have stopped thinking about the future. Fear of the bomb and an unthinkable holocaust drives us to squeeze what we can from the present. We become obsessed with momentary gratification. This erodes our capacity to plan and build for the future—if there is one—and paralyzes us from living faithfully in the present.

Unlike people today, New Testament Christians eagerly awaited and longed for the future. They believed the complete reign of Christ on earth was a more certain reality than the seeming victory of evil. Jesus gave John the strangely beautiful vision recorded in the book of Revelation to give us hope. Of the three Christian virtues—faith, hope and love—the one most needing attention today is hope. Revelation touches us at the point of our despair, our world-weariness, our future shock, our fear of persecution, our collaboration with a sick (though friendly) society. It is quite possibly the most relevant book of the Bible for this moment in history.

But how are we to understand this highly symbolic book? Since Revelation was meant to be read at one sitting (1:3), we do well to put aside the charts, sermons and films we have seen that claim to unravel its mysteries. It is better just to read it. A child might understand Revelation better than adults who approach it with preconceived systems. If a child were to hear this as a story and were to conclude, "I'm so glad the Lamb won over the awful beast," he or she would have truly heard it and taken to heart what is written in it (1:3).

Two Common Misconceptions

Many people misunderstand the book because of two commonly held misconceptions. First, Revelation is not difficult to understand. Though it is highly symbolic, it is not a lock whose key has been lost. The major reason we have difficulty decoding the symbolism of this book is that, unlike the first readers, we are largely illiterate when it comes to the Bible.

The Old Testament provides the most important clues for decoding Revelation. Of the 404 verses in Revelation, 278 allude to the Old Testament (though not one direct citation is actually quoted). The book is a biblical implosion. Old Testament ideas, symbols, names and themes have been powerfully pulled together through the inspiration of the Spirit to form a collage, a kaleidoscopic effect in the message John brings.

For example, a phrase like "God will wipe away every tear from their eyes" (7:17) is a cre-

ative adaptation of Isaiah 25:8. Proper names like "Balaam," "Jerusalem" and "Sodom" and concepts like "the tree of life" are adapted from John's Bible. Numbers like "forty-two months" are used symbolically, as numbers like "seven" are in the Old Testament (Dan 9:27). This book above all others in the New Testament must be interpreted by Scripture.

Second, we misunderstand Revelation when we treat it as a book of predictions. It is not so much a prediction of future events as it is an exposé of spiritual realities that affect us now and will bring the events of history to a worthy end. John shows us how the world looks to someone in the Spirit.

John wrote Revelation between A.D. 90 and 95 from his place of exile on Patmos Island. Tradition tells us that prior to his exile John left Israel to live in Ephesus, capital of the Roman province of Asia. The seven churches to whom this book is addressed were visited by a courier traveling on the circular road through modern Turkey. His letter described John's vision of Christ as Lord of the churches (1:12–3:22), as the Lamb on the throne (5:1–14), as the liberating Word of God (19:11–16) and as the Leader in the new creation (21—22). This book is truly *the Revelation of Jesus Christ* (1:1).

John says, "Blessed is the one who reads the words of this prophecy, and blessed are those who hear it" (1:3). Look forward to this blessing as you study Revelation.

Outline

1/ Revelation 1:1–8 —————————— The Illustrated Letter

2/ Revelation 1:9–20 ————————— Surprised by Magnificence

3/ Revelation 2 —————————————— Pardon My Speaking the Truth

4/ Revelation 3 —————————————— My Dear Compromised People

5/ Revelation 4—5 ————————————— Worship the Omnipotent Lamb

6/ Revelation 6 —————————————— The Beautiful Wrath of God

7/ Revelation 7 —————————————— Living Faithfully Through the Holocaust

8/ Revelation 8—9 ————————————— The Message of the Angels

9/ Revelation 10—11 ———————————— God's Messenger

10/ Revelation 12 ————————————— Conflict with the Accuser

11/ Revelation 13 ————————————— The Beast

12/ Revelation 14—15 ——————————— Tale of Two Choices

13/ Revelation 16 ————————————— Who's to Blame?

14/ Revelation 17—18 ——————————— Beneath the Surface

15/ Revelation 19 ————————————— Are You Going to the Wedding?

16/ Revelation 20 ————————————— The Last Battle

17/ Revelation 21—22 ——————————— God Dwelling with His People

1 / *Revelation 1:1–8*
The Illustrated Letter

PERSECUTION, IMPRISONMENT, MARTYRDOM. These seem far removed from the lives of many Christians today. Yet we do suffer. Who can witness the breakup of families, the death of unborn children, the threat of war and the plight of the poor without crying out, "Come, Lord Jesus"? In this passage he does come in a vision to give us hope in a suffering world.

Warming Up to God Following Jesus brings many benefits. It also causes new pressures and problems. In what ways have you found being a Christian difficult?

Read Revelation 1:1–8.

1 The revelation of Jesus Christ, which God gave him to show his servants what must soon take place. He made it known by sending his angel to his servant John, ²who testifies to everything he saw—that is, the word of God and the testimony of Jesus Christ. ³Blessed is the one who reads the words of this prophecy, and blessed are those who hear it and take to heart what is written in it, because the time is near.

⁴John,

To the seven churches in the province of Asia:

Grace and peace to you from him who is, and who was, and who is to come, and from the seven spirits*ᵃ* before his throne, ⁵and from Jesus Christ, who is the faithful witness, the firstborn from the dead, and the ruler of the kings of the earth.

To him who loves us and has freed us from our sins by his blood, ⁶and has made us to be a kingdom and priests to serve his God and Father—to him be glory and power for ever and ever! Amen.

⁷Look, he is coming with the clouds,
   and every eye will see him,
even those who pierced him;
   and all the peoples of the earth will mourn
     because of him.

           So shall it be! Amen.

⁸"I am the Alpha and the Omega," says the Lord God, "who is, and who was, and who is to come, the Almighty."

ᵃ4 Or the sevenfold Spirit

Discovering the Word 1. The word *reveal* means "to bring to light what was formerly hidden, veiled and secret." Who and what will be unveiled by the revelation given to John (vv. 1–3)? 2. How would John's description of God be a comfort to his readers (vv. 4–5)? 3. Why would it help discouraged believers to know they are "a kingdom and priests to serve his God and Father" (v. 6)? 4. John presents a vision of Jesus as both coming (v. 7) and already and always here (v. 8). What would it be like to have only one of these two perspectives?

Applying the Word 1. In what ways has a knowledge of Christ's coming encouraged you in the midst of suffering? 2. John states that we will be blessed if we hear his message and take it to heart (v. 3). In what ways do you think he expects us to take this message to heart?

Responding in Prayer Ask God to fill your heart with hope.

2 / Revelation 1:9–20
Surprised by Magnificence

THE EXPERIENCE OF meeting a famous person is sometimes disconcerting. He or she may be less impressive than we had imagined. But when John sees Jesus face to face, he is overwhelmed with his magnificence. John's experience challenges us to ask whether we have ever met the same Person. Or do we follow a pale, distorted copy of the real Lord?

Warming Up to God From all that you have read or experienced before opening Revelation, what images or pictures do you have of Jesus?

Read Revelation 1:9–20.

⁹I, John, your brother and companion in the suffering and kingdom and patient endurance that are ours in Jesus, was on the island of Patmos because of the word of God and the testimony of Jesus. ¹⁰On the Lord's Day I was in the Spirit, and I heard behind me a loud voice like a trumpet, ¹¹which said: "Write on a scroll what you see and send it to the seven churches: to Ephesus, Smyrna, Pergamum, Thyatira, Sardis, Philadelphia and Laodicea."

¹²I turned around to see the voice that was speaking to me. And when I turned I saw seven golden lampstands, ¹³and among the lampstands was someone "like a son of man,"[b] dressed in a robe reaching down to his feet and with a golden sash around his chest. ¹⁴His head and hair were white like wool, as white as snow, and his eyes were like blazing fire. ¹⁵His feet were like bronze glowing in a furnace, and his voice was like the sound of rushing waters. ¹⁶In his right hand he held seven stars, and out of his mouth came a sharp double-edged sword. His face was like the sun shining in all its brilliance.

¹⁷When I saw him, I fell at his feet as though dead. Then he placed his right hand on me and said: "Do not be afraid. I am the First and the Last. ¹⁸I am the Living One; I was dead, and behold I am alive for ever and ever! And I hold the keys of death and Hades.

¹⁹"Write, therefore, what you have seen, what is now and what will take place later. ²⁰The mystery of the seven stars that you saw in my right hand and of the seven golden lampstands is this: The seven stars are the angels[c] of the seven churches, and the seven lampstands are the seven churches.

[b]13 Daniel 7:13   [c]20 Or *messengers*

Discovering the Word 1. John pictures the seven churches as seven golden lampstands (to hold oil lamps). What does John's picture tell us about the function of the churches? 2. How would Jesus' relationship to these churches (v. 13) encourage them to fulfill their function during hard times? 3. John's vision of Jesus is rich with biblical symbolism. Instead of trying to picture all these characteristics at once, allow them to impress you one at a time, like a slide presentation. Which images impress you most with the magnificence of Jesus, and why (vv. 13–16)? 4. Why do you think a godly person like John would be so powerfully overcome by the presence of the One he loved (v. 17)? 5. How would Jesus' words encourage John not to be fearful in his presence (vv. 17–18)?

Applying the Word 1. Revelation was written to churches persecuted under a totalitarian regime. Our society seems more friendly. Yet how is it hostile to us both morally and spiritually? 2. How has this passage enlarged your vision of who Jesus is? 3. How can this vision of Jesus encourage us to resist the seductions of our society?

Responding in Prayer Praise Jesus for who he is and for what you have learned about him here.

3 / *Revelation 2*
Pardon My Speaking the Truth

WHAT CAN WE do to help a fellow Christian who is ready to cave in under pressure? Usually we wouldn't say that things are going to get worse before they get better! But that's what Christ does in the seven letters to churches in Asia (Rev 2—3). He confronts believers who have compromised morally and spiritually. But he also encourages them. This kind of tough love is essential for spiritual health.

 Warming Up to God In what area of your life do you feel pressured (spiritually or otherwise)?

 Read Revelation 2.

2 "To the angel*d* of the church in Ephesus write:

These are the words of him who holds the seven stars in his right hand and walks among the seven golden lampstands: ²I know your deeds, your hard work and your perseverance. I know that you cannot tolerate wicked men, that you have tested those who claim to be apostles but are not, and have found them false. ³You have persevered and have endured hardships for my name, and have not grown weary.

⁴Yet I hold this against you: You have forsaken your first love. ⁵Remember the height from which you have fallen! Repent and do the things you did at first. If you do not repent, I will come to you and remove your lampstand from its place. ⁶But you have this in your favor: You hate the practices of the Nicolaitans, which I also hate.

⁷He who has an ear, let him hear what the Spirit says to the churches. To him who overcomes, I will give the right to eat from the tree of life, which is in the paradise of God.

⁸"To the angel of the church in Smyrna write:

These are the words of him who is the First and the Last, who died and came to life again. ⁹I know your afflictions and your poverty—yet you are rich! I know the slander of those who say they are Jews and are not, but are a synagogue of Satan. ¹⁰Do not be afraid of what you are about to suffer. I tell you, the devil will put some of you in prison to test you, and you will suffer persecution for ten days. Be faithful, even to the point of death, and I will give you the crown of life.

¹¹He who has an ear, let him hear what the Spirit says to the churches. He who overcomes will not be hurt at all by the second death.

¹²"To the angel of the church in Pergamum write:

These are the words of him who has the sharp, double-edged sword. ¹³I know where you live—where Satan has his throne. Yet you remain true to my name. You did not renounce your faith in me, even in the days of Antipas, my faithful witness, who was put to death in your city—where Satan lives.

¹⁴Nevertheless, I have a few things against you: You have people there who hold to the teaching of Balaam, who taught Balak to entice the Israelites to sin by eating food sacrificed to idols and by committing sexual immorality. ¹⁵Likewise you also have those who hold to the teaching of the Nicolaitans. ¹⁶Repent therefore! Otherwise, I will soon come to you and will fight against them with the sword of my mouth.

¹⁷He who has an ear, let him hear what the Spirit says to the churches. To him who overcomes, I will give some of the hidden manna. I will also give him a white stone with a new name written on it, known only to him who receives it.

¹⁸"To the angel of the church in Thyatira write:

These are the words of the Son of God, whose eyes are like blazing fire and whose feet are like burnished bronze. ¹⁹I know your deeds, your love and faith, your service and

d1 Or messenger; also in verses 8, 12 and 18

perseverance, and that you are now doing more than you did at first.

²⁰Nevertheless, I have this against you: You tolerate that woman Jezebel, who calls herself a prophetess. By her teaching she misleads my servants into sexual immorality and the eating of food sacrificed to idols. ²¹I have given her time to repent of her immorality, but she is unwilling. ²²So I will cast her on a bed of suffering, and I will make those who commit adultery with her suffer intensely, unless they repent of her ways. ²³I will strike her children dead. Then all the churches will know that I am he who searches hearts and minds, and I will repay each of you according to your deeds. ²⁴Now I say to the rest of you in Thyatira, to you who do not hold to her teaching and have

not learned Satan's so-called deep secrets (I will not impose any other burden on you): ²⁵Only hold on to what you have until I come.

²⁶To him who overcomes and does my will to the end, I will give authority over the nations—

²⁷'He will rule them with an iron scepter;
    he will dash them to pieces like
        pottery'ᶜ—

just as I have received authority from my Father. ²⁸I will also give him the morning star. ²⁹He who has an ear, let him hear what the Spirit says to the churches.

ᶜ27 Psalm 2:9

Discovering the Word 1. Why would forsaking "your first love" (v. 4) be so tragic for the church at Ephesus? 2. Why do you think Christ's judgment would be so severe if they did not repent (v. 5)? 3. Smyrna was noted for emperor worship. Refusal to worship the emperor brought martyrdom to some Christians. What does Jesus know about the believers in Smyrna (vv. 8–11)? 4. The letter to Smyrna is the only one of the seven that mentions no problem and gives no warning. What role does affirmation play in helping Christians who are under spiritual pressure? 5. Pergamum was also a center of emperor worship. This may be why it is called the place "where Satan has his throne." In addition, temple prostitution was prevalent. How had the church responded to the lure of these temptations (vv. 12–17)? 6. Jezebel (v. 20) is an Old Testament character who symbolizes spiritual adultery (1 Kings 16:31). How was the so-called prophetess in Thyatira like her namesake (vv. 18–29)?

Applying the Word 1. Jesus charges the godly and loving church at Thyatira with being too tolerant of evil in their midst. In what areas are Christians today too tolerant? 2. Each of the letters (except the one to Smyrna) contains an affirmation, a problem, a warning and a promise. How might Jesus' example guide us as we care for a brother or sister ready to cave in under pressure?

Responding in Prayer Pray for someone you know who is under pressure to compromise.

---

4 / *Revelation 3*
My Dear Compromised People

EXPERTS TELL US we are exposed to fourteen hundred advertisements a day. It takes an enormous act of will not to be conformed to our environment, to be in but not of the world. The remaining three churches in the crownlike array of towns in Asia would be visited by a postal courier completing his circuit in the exact order of John's letters. Each letter helps us resist this powerful threat of being conformed to the world.

Warming Up to God In what ways do Christian groups and churches you know resemble the surrounding culture?

Read Revelation 3.

3 "To the angel[f] of the church in Sardis write:

These are the words of him who holds the seven spirits[g] of God and the seven stars. I know your deeds; you have a reputation of being alive, but you are dead. 2Wake up! Strengthen what remains and is about to die, for I have not found your deeds complete in the sight of my God. 3Remember, therefore, what you have received and heard; obey it, and repent. But if you do not wake up, I will come like a thief, and you will not know at what time I will come to you.

4Yet you have a few people in Sardis who have not soiled their clothes. They will walk with me, dressed in white, for they are worthy. 5He who overcomes will, like them, be dressed in white. I will never blot out his name from the book of life, but will acknowledge his name before my Father and his angels. 6He who has an ear, let him hear what the Spirit says to the churches.

7"To the angel of the church in Philadelphia write:

These are the words of him who is holy and true, who holds the key of David. What he opens no one can shut, and what he shuts no one can open. 8I know your deeds. See, I have placed before you an open door that no one can shut. I know that you have little strength, yet you have kept my word and have not denied my name. 9I will make those who are of the synagogue of Satan, who claim to be Jews though they are not, but are liars—I will make them come and fall down at your feet and acknowledge that I have loved you. 10Since you have kept my command to endure patiently, I will also keep you from the hour of trial that is going to come upon the whole world to test those who live on the earth.

11I am coming soon. Hold on to what you have, so that no one will take your crown. 12Him who overcomes I will make a pillar in the temple of my God. Never again will he leave it. I will write on him the name of my God and the name of the city of my God, the new Jerusalem, which is coming down out of heaven from my God; and I will also write on him my new name. 13He who has an ear, let him hear what the Spirit says to the churches.

14"To the angel of the church in Laodicea write:

These are the words of the Amen, the faithful and true witness, the ruler of God's creation. 15I know your deeds, that you are neither cold nor hot. I wish you were either one or the other! 16So, because you are lukewarm—neither hot nor cold—I am about to spit you out of my mouth. 17You say, 'I am rich; I have acquired wealth and do not need a thing.' But you do not realize that you are wretched, pitiful, poor, blind and naked. 18I counsel you to buy from me gold refined in the fire, so you can become rich; and white clothes to wear, so you can cover your shameful nakedness; and salve to put on your eyes, so you can see.

19Those whom I love I rebuke and discipline. So be earnest, and repent. 20Here I am! I stand at the door and knock. If anyone hears my voice and opens the door, I will come in and eat with him, and he with me.

21To him who overcomes, I will give the right to sit with me on my throne, just as I overcame and sat down with my Father on his throne. 22He who has an ear, let him hear what the Spirit says to the churches."

f1 Or *messenger*; also in verses 7 and 14   g1 Or *the sevenfold Spirit*

Discovering the Word 1. In the first century, Sardis exhibited a stark contrast between its past splendor as a Persian capital and its current decay. What indications does the Lord give that the church's reputation does not match its reality (vv. 1–6)? Why is this such a serious problem? 2. Of the seven churches, only the church in Philadelphia received nothing but praise and promises. Why would a weak church be encouraged by Jesus' promise of an open door of opportunity (v. 8)? 3. As the Philadelphian church faced opposition, how would Jesus' other promises encourage them (vv. 9–13)? 4. Laodicea's northern neighbor, Hierapolis, had famous hot springs. Its southern neighbor, Colossae, had refreshing cool water. A six-mile aqueduct brought water to Laodicea, but by the time it arrived it was lukewarm. How does this help us understand Christ's statements in verses 14–16? 5. Laodicea was so self-sufficient that when they suffered an earthquake in A.D. 60 they rejected help from Rome. How did this attitude affect them spiritually?

Applying the Word 1. Many churches today feel weak, insignificant and discouraged. What can we learn from Christ's words to the Philadelphians? 2. As you review all seven letters (Rev 2—3), what has the Spirit taught you about being an overcomer?

 Responding in Prayer Pray that the church would be a powerful force in the world.

5 / *Revelation 4—5*
Worship the Omnipotent Lamb

IN A PLAY by George Bernard Shaw, Don Juan says, "Heaven is all right, of course, but for meeting old friends and acquaintances you can't beat hell." There is a powerful truth in this facetious remark. While most people *say* they want to go to heaven, they might prefer hell if heaven is like the picture given in these two chapters. People concerned only about themselves would find the ceaseless praise of God and the Lamb intolerable. Worship on earth, a foretaste of heaven, is just as unpalatable. But worship is the deepest need of the seven churches just described. And it is our deepest need too, as this study will show.

 Warming Up to God What was the most significant worship experience you have ever had, and what made it so special?

 Read Revelation 4—5.

4 After this I looked, and there before me was a door standing open in heaven. And the voice I had first heard speaking to me like a trumpet said, "Come up here, and I will show you what must take place after this." ²At once I was in the Spirit, and there before me was a throne in heaven with someone sitting on it. ³And the one who sat there had the appearance of jasper and carnelian. A rainbow, resembling an emerald, encircled the throne. ⁴Surrounding the throne were twenty-four other thrones, and seated on them were twenty-four elders. They were dressed in white and had crowns of gold on their heads. ⁵From the throne came flashes of lightning, rumblings and peals of thunder. Before the throne, seven lamps were blazing. These are the seven spirits*h* of God. ⁶Also before the throne there was what looked like a sea of glass, clear as crystal.

In the center, around the throne, were four living creatures, and they were covered with eyes, in front and in back. ⁷The first living creature was like a lion, the second was like an ox, the third had a face like a man, the fourth was like a flying eagle. ⁸Each of the four living creatures had six wings and was covered with eyes all around, even under his wings. Day and night they never stop saying:

"Holy, holy, holy
is the Lord God Almighty,
who was, and is, and is to come."

⁹Whenever the living creatures give glory, honor and thanks to him who sits on the throne and who lives for ever and ever, ¹⁰the twenty-four elders fall down before him who sits on the throne, and worship him who lives for ever and ever. They lay their crowns before the throne and say:

¹¹"You are worthy, our Lord and God,
to receive glory and honor and power,
for you created all things,
and by your will they were created
and have their being."

5 Then I saw in the right hand of him who sat on the throne a scroll with writing on both sides and sealed with seven seals. ²And I saw a mighty angel proclaiming in a loud voice, "Who is worthy to break the seals and open the scroll?" ³But no one in heaven or on earth or under the earth could open the scroll or even look inside it. ⁴I wept and wept because no one was found who was worthy to open the scroll or look inside. ⁵Then one of the elders said to me,

h5 Or the sevenfold Spirit

"Do not weep! See, the Lion of the tribe of Judah, the Root of David, has triumphed. He is able to open the scroll and its seven seals."

6Then I saw a Lamb, looking as if it had been slain, standing in the center of the throne, encircled by the four living creatures and the elders. He had seven horns and seven eyes, which are the seven spirits[i] of God sent out into all the earth. 7He came and took the scroll from the right hand of him who sat on the throne. 8And when he had taken it, the four living creatures and the twenty-four elders fell down before the Lamb. Each one had a harp and they were holding golden bowls full of incense, which are the prayers of the saints. 9And they sang a new song:

"You are worthy to take the scroll
     and to open its seals,
because you were slain,
     and with your blood you purchased men
          for God
     from every tribe and language and people
          and nation.
10You have made them to be a kingdom and
     priests to serve our God,

and they will reign on the earth."

11Then I looked and heard the voice of many angels, numbering thousands upon thousands, and ten thousand times ten thousand. They encircled the throne and the living creatures and the elders. 12In a loud voice they sang:

"Worthy is the Lamb, who was slain,
to receive power and wealth and wisdom and
     strength
and honor and glory and praise!"

13Then I heard every creature in heaven and on earth and under the earth and on the sea, and all that is in them, singing:

"To him who sits on the throne and to the
     Lamb
be praise and honor and glory and power,
          for ever and ever!"

14The four living creatures said, "Amen," and the elders fell down and worshiped.

[i]6 Or the sevenfold Spirit

Discovering the Word   1. Instead of trying to decode every part of the throne room of God, try to imagine what can be seen and heard. What are some of your initial impressions of God's glory as envisioned here (Rev 4)?   2. How do the four creatures and the twenty-four elders respond to God's glory (vv. 8, 10–11)?   3. How does their reaction help us define and practice worship?   4. While John leaves us in suspense about the contents of the scroll and its seals, there is no doubt about the central figure in the unfolding drama. Why do you think he superimposes the image of the Lamb on the image of the Lion (5:5–6)?   5. The heavenly choir gets larger and larger as the scene unfolds (5:8, 11, 13). What do we see in this vision of heavenly worship that is timelessly relevant?

Applying the Word   1. Worship is not an action but a reaction, a response evoked by a vision of God's glory. If we have difficulty worshiping God, what might we need to do?   2. If earthly worship is to be modeled after heavenly, what is most lacking in your experience of worship?

Responding in Prayer   Take time now to worship the Lamb and the One who sits on the throne.

---

6 / *Revelation 6*
The Beautiful Wrath of God

JUDGMENT IS NOT something we normally long for. But if we are suffering unjustly in an evil social system, God's judgment—far from being a dreaded prospect—is our only hope. Like a wood plane that is used against the grain rather than with it, so wrath is how people opposing the rule of God will experience his grace.

In Revelation 6—19 there is a complicated and rather confusing pattern of disaster and suffering. If we seek to unravel these pictures as a timetable for the future, we will be disappointed and perplexed. But if we want to learn

how to live in the present and find hope for the future, there is much here to encourage us. These chapters inspire trust in a God who is faithful and just.

 Warming Up to God As you approach the subject of God's wrath, what thoughts and feelings do you have? Explain.

 Read Revelation 6.

6 I watched as the Lamb opened the first of the seven seals. Then I heard one of the four living creatures say in a voice like thunder, "Come!" ²I looked, and there before me was a white horse! Its rider held a bow, and he was given a crown, and he rode out as a conqueror bent on conquest.

³When the Lamb opened the second seal, I heard the second living creature say, "Come!" ⁴Then another horse came out, a fiery red one. Its rider was given power to take peace from the earth and to make men slay each other. To him was given a large sword.

⁵When the Lamb opened the third seal, I heard the third living creature say, "Come!" I looked, and there before me was a black horse! Its rider was holding a pair of scales in his hand. ⁶Then I heard what sounded like a voice among the four living creatures, saying, "A quart^j of wheat for a day's wages,^{k} and three quarts of barley for a day's wages,^{k} and do not damage the oil and the wine!"

⁷When the Lamb opened the fourth seal, I heard the voice of the fourth living creature say, "Come!" ⁸I looked, and there before me was a pale horse! Its rider was named Death, and Hades was following close behind him. They were given power over a fourth of the earth to kill by sword, famine and plague, and by the wild beasts of the earth.

⁹When he opened the fifth seal, I saw under the altar the souls of those who had been slain because of the word of God and the testimony they had maintained. ¹⁰They called out in a loud voice, "How long, Sovereign Lord, holy and true, until you judge the inhabitants of the earth and avenge our blood?" ¹¹Then each of them was given a white robe, and they were told to wait a little longer, until the number of their fellow servants and brothers who were to be killed as they had been was completed.

¹²I watched as he opened the sixth seal. There was a great earthquake. The sun turned black like sackcloth made of goat hair, the whole moon turned blood red, ¹³and the stars in the sky fell to earth, as late figs drop from a fig tree when shaken by a strong wind. ¹⁴The sky receded like a scroll, rolling up, and every mountain and island was removed from its place.

¹⁵Then the kings of the earth, the princes, the generals, the rich, the mighty, and every slave and every free man hid in caves and among the rocks of the mountains. ¹⁶They called to the mountains and the rocks, "Fall on us and hide us from the face of him who sits on the throne and from the wrath of the Lamb! ¹⁷For the great day of their wrath has come, and who can stand?"

j6 Greek a choinix (probably about a liter) *k6 Greek a denarius*

 Discovering the Word 1. The scene shifts back to earth as the Lamb opens the book of destiny. Summarize the events during the first four seals (vv. 1–8). 2. Are the events during the seals normal bad times (compare vv. 1–8 with vv. 12–14)? Explain. 3. How does the experience of the saints (vv. 9–11) contrast with that of the unbelievers (vv. 15–17) as they anticipate the impending wrath of God? 4. What evidence, if any, do you see of this contrast among people today?

Applying the Word 1. If we realize that the wrath of God will one day be fully expressed, what difference should it make in our attitude toward sin? 2. In our attitude toward unjust suffering? 3. In our attitude toward non-Christians?

Responding in Prayer Pray for non-Christians you know, that they would come to know the love of the Lord.

7 / *Revelation 7*
Living Faithfully Through the Holocaust

SOME PREACHERS SPEAK of the Christian life as one great success story. They say that if we attend church, live right, tithe and exercise faith, we will prosper financially and be free of illness and distress.

But the relative peace some of us enjoy at this moment is exceptional in the world and in history. From the ascension of Christ to his return, the normal lot of believers is tribulation.

Most of the Christians John pictures for us are martyrs. They are dead to the threats of this life but gloriously alive to God. Their experience reminds us that the call to discipleship is a call to radical obedience.

 Warming Up to God What feelings do you have when you hear of Christians today who lose their jobs, are thrown into prison or are martyred for Christ?

 Read Revelation 7.

---

7 After this I saw four angels standing at the four corners of the earth, holding back the four winds of the earth to prevent any wind from blowing on the land or on the sea or on any tree. ²Then I saw another angel coming up from the east, having the seal of the living God. He called out in a loud voice to the four angels who had been given power to harm the land and the sea: ³"Do not harm the land or the sea or the trees until we put a seal on the foreheads of the servants of our God." ⁴Then I heard the number of those who were sealed: 144,000 from all the tribes of Israel.

⁵From the tribe of Judah 12,000 were sealed,
   from the tribe of Reuben 12,000,
   from the tribe of Gad 12,000,
⁶from the tribe of Asher 12,000,
   from the tribe of Naphtali 12,000,
   from the tribe of Manasseh 12,000,
⁷from the tribe of Simeon 12,000,
   from the tribe of Levi 12,000,
   from the tribe of Issachar 12,000,
⁸from the tribe of Zebulun 12,000,
   from the tribe of Joseph 12,000,
   from the tribe of Benjamin 12,000.

⁹After this I looked and there before me was a great multitude that no one could count, from every nation, tribe, people and language, standing before the throne and in front of the Lamb. They were wearing white robes and were holding palm branches in their hands. ¹⁰And they cried out in a loud voice:

"Salvation belongs to our God,
   who sits on the throne,

and to the Lamb."

¹¹All the angels were standing around the throne and around the elders and the four living creatures. They fell down on their faces before the throne and worshiped God, ¹²saying:

"Amen!
Praise and glory
and wisdom and thanks and honor
and power and strength
be to our God for ever and ever.
Amen!"

¹³Then one of the elders asked me, "These in white robes—who are they, and where did they come from?"

¹⁴I answered, "Sir, you know."

And he said, "These are they who have come out of the great tribulation; they have washed their robes and made them white in the blood of the Lamb. ¹⁵Therefore,

"they are before the throne of God
   and serve him day and night in his temple;
and he who sits on the throne will spread his
      tent over them.
¹⁶Never again will they hunger;
   never again will they thirst.
The sun will not beat upon them,
   nor any scorching heat.
¹⁷For the Lamb at the center of the throne will
      be their shepherd;
   he will lead them to springs of living water.
And God will wipe away every tear from their
      eyes."

Discovering the Word 1. In verses 1–8 an angel seals 144,000 people. What do you think "the seal of the living God" means (7:2; 9:4)? 2. In verse 9 the scene shifts from earth to heaven. How did the great multitude in verse 9 come to stand before the Lamb? 3. Why does the multitude cry out with praise, worship and thanksgiving (vv. 10–12)? 4. How do the blessings these martyred Christians enjoy compare with the tribulations they suffered (vv. 13–17)? 5. How does their experience help us understand the ultimate benefit of being a faithful Christian?

Applying the Word 1. In the first century, persecution of Christians came from three basic sources: emperor worshipers, heretics and those whose commercial interests were threatened by the radical lifestyle of Christians. Why might faithful Christians suffer today? 2. This vision comes at the point of maximum dramatic intensity: between the sixth and seventh seals. How can the vision encourage us to be faithful no matter what happens in the world?

Responding in Prayer Pray for those who suffer for their faith.

---

8 / *Revelation 8—9*
The Message of the Angels

ANGELS ARE QUITE popular these days. We see them depicted on T-shirts, mugs and cards. You can get little pins picturing charming angels. And there's a growing category of books available to show you how to get in touch with your "inner angels" and other such things. None of this has much to do with the angels we meet in Scripture. In the next few passages you will meet some of God's angels—and you will be confronted with their terrible power.

Warming Up to God What positive feelings or experiences have you had about angels?

Read Revelation 8—9.

---

8 When he opened the seventh seal, there was silence in heaven for about half an hour.

²And I saw the seven angels who stand before God, and to them were given seven trumpets.

³Another angel, who had a golden censer, came and stood at the altar. He was given much incense to offer, with the prayers of all the saints, on the golden altar before the throne. ⁴The smoke of the incense, together with the prayers of the saints, went up before God from the angel's hand. ⁵Then the angel took the censer, filled it with fire from the altar, and hurled it on the earth; and there came peals of thunder, rumblings, flashes of lightning and an earthquake.

⁶Then the seven angels who had the seven trumpets prepared to sound them.

⁷The first angel sounded his trumpet, and there came hail and fire mixed with blood, and it was hurled down upon the earth. A third of the earth was burned up, a third of the trees were burned up, and all the green grass was burned up.

⁸The second angel sounded his trumpet, and something like a huge mountain, all ablaze, was thrown into the sea. A third of the sea turned into blood, ⁹a third of the living creatures in the sea died, and a third of the ships were destroyed.

¹⁰The third angel sounded his trumpet, and a great star, blazing like a torch, fell from the sky on a third of the rivers and on the springs of water— ¹¹the name of the star is Wormwood.¹ A third of the waters turned bitter, and many people died from the waters that had become bitter.

¹²The fourth angel sounded his trumpet, and a third of the sun was struck, a third of the moon, and a third of the stars, so that a third of them turned dark. A third of the day was without light, and also a third of the night.

¹³As I watched, I heard an eagle that was flying in midair call out in a loud voice: "Woe! Woe!

¹ 11 That is, Bitterness

Woe to the inhabitants of the earth, because of the trumpet blasts about to be sounded by the other three angels!"

9 The fifth angel sounded his trumpet, and I saw a star that had fallen from the sky to the earth. The star was given the key to the shaft of the Abyss. ²When he opened the Abyss, smoke rose from it like the smoke from a gigantic furnace. The sun and sky were darkened by the smoke from the Abyss. ³And out of the smoke locusts came down upon the earth and were given power like that of scorpions of the earth. ⁴They were told not to harm the grass of the earth or any plant or tree, but only those people who did not have the seal of God on their foreheads. ⁵They were not given power to kill them, but only to torture them for five months. And the agony they suffered was like that of the sting of a scorpion when it strikes a man. ⁶During those days men will seek death, but will not find it; they will long to die, but death will elude them.

⁷The locusts looked like horses prepared for battle. On their heads they wore something like crowns of gold, and their faces resembled human faces. ⁸Their hair was like women's hair, and their teeth were like lions' teeth. ⁹They had breastplates like breastplates of iron, and the sound of their wings was like the thundering of many horses and chariots rushing into battle. ¹⁰They had tails and stings like scorpions, and in their tails they had power to torment people for five months. ¹¹They had as king over them the angel of the Abyss, whose name in Hebrew is Abaddon, and in Greek, Apollyon.ᵐ

¹²The first woe is past; two other woes are yet to come.

¹³The sixth angel sounded his trumpet, and I heard a voice coming from the hornsⁿ of the golden altar that is before God. ¹⁴It said to the sixth angel who had the trumpet, "Release the four angels who are bound at the great river Euphrates." ¹⁵And the four angels who had been kept ready for this very hour and day and month and year were released to kill a third of mankind. ¹⁶The number of the mounted troops was two hundred million. I heard their number.

¹⁷The horses and riders I saw in my vision looked like this: Their breastplates were fiery red, dark blue, and yellow as sulfur. The heads of the horses resembled the heads of lions, and out of their mouths came fire, smoke and sulfur. ¹⁸A third of mankind was killed by the three plagues of fire, smoke and sulfur that came out of their mouths. ¹⁹The power of the horses was in their mouths and in their tails; for their tails were like snakes, having heads with which they inflict injury.

²⁰The rest of mankind that were not killed by these plagues still did not repent of the work of their hands; they did not stop worshiping demons, and idols of gold, silver, bronze, stone and wood—idols that cannot see or hear or walk. ²¹Nor did they repent of their murders, their magic arts, their sexual immorality or their thefts.

---

m 11 Abaddon and Apollyon mean Destroyer.   *n 13 That is, projections*

Discovering the Word   1. List the events that happen when each of the angels blows his trumpet.   2. What similarities do you note between all of these events?   3. The seventh seal (8:1–5) contains the seven trumpet judgments (8:6—11:15). What apparently is God's purpose in allowing these judgments to fall on the whole creation (9:20–21)?   4. Does such a response by God seem justified? Explain.   5. It is sometimes maintained that Christians are removed from the world before God's wrath falls. What alternate view is possibly suggested by 9:4 (see also 7:3)?

Applying the Word   1. Those mentioned in 9:20–21 did not repent. How do our sins today compare to theirs?   2. Where do you see yourself in this list of sins?   3. In what way do you feel that you need to be ready for the judgment that takes place here?

 Responding in Prayer   Repent of your sins before God.

9 / Revelation 10—11
God's Messenger

IN THE OLD Testament, God often used specific persons to deliver a message to another person, or sometimes to entire groups. Sometimes these messages were positive and easy to hear. However, they were often condemnations of the way things were, and those who delivered the messages, the prophets, were often ridiculed or threatened. In chapter 10, John is given a message which is not easy to deliver.

In chapter 11, two of God's prophets have a life experience which roughly parallels Jesus' time on earth. Their example can give us hope that the God who calls us to be a light in the darkness is also the one who will vindicate us.

Warming Up to God When has God used someone else to give you a message? How did you react to the message and the messenger?

Read Revelation 10—11.

10 Then I saw another mighty angel coming down from heaven. He was robed in a cloud, with a rainbow above his head; his face was like the sun, and his legs were like fiery pillars. ²He was holding a little scroll, which lay open in his hand. He planted his right foot on the sea and his left foot on the land, ³and he gave a loud shout like the roar of a lion. When he shouted, the voices of the seven thunders spoke. ⁴And when the seven thunders spoke, I was about to write; but I heard a voice from heaven say, "Seal up what the seven thunders have said and do not write it down."

⁵Then the angel I had seen standing on the sea and on the land raised his right hand to heaven. ⁶And he swore by him who lives for ever and ever, who created the heavens and all that is in them, the earth and all that is in it, and the sea and all that is in it, and said, "There will be no more delay! ⁷But in the days when the seventh angel is about to sound his trumpet, the mystery of God will be accomplished, just as he announced to his servants the prophets."

⁸Then the voice that I had heard from heaven spoke to me once more: "Go, take the scroll that lies open in the hand of the angel who is standing on the sea and on the land."

⁹So I went to the angel and asked him to give me the little scroll. He said to me, "Take it and eat it. It will turn your stomach sour, but in your mouth it will be as sweet as honey." ¹⁰I took the little scroll from the angel's hand and ate it. It tasted as sweet as honey in my mouth, but when I had eaten it, my stomach turned sour. ¹¹Then I was told, "You must proph-

esy again about many peoples, nations, languages and kings."

11 I was given a reed like a measuring rod and was told, "Go and measure the temple of God and the altar, and count the worshipers there. ²But exclude the outer court; do not measure it, because it has been given to the Gentiles. They will trample on the holy city for 42 months. ³And I will give power to my two witnesses, and they will prophesy for 1,260 days, clothed in sackcloth." ⁴These are the two olive trees and the two lampstands that stand before the Lord of the earth. ⁵If anyone tries to harm them, fire comes from their mouths and devours their enemies. This is how anyone who wants to harm them must die. ⁶These men have power to shut up the sky so that it will not rain during the time they are prophesying; and they have power to turn the waters into blood and to strike the earth with every kind of plague as often as they want.

⁷Now when they have finished their testimony, the beast that comes up from the Abyss will attack them, and overpower and kill them. ⁸Their bodies will lie in the street of the great city, which is figuratively called Sodom and Egypt, where also their Lord was crucified. ⁹For three and a half days men from every people, tribe, language and nation will gaze on their bodies and refuse them burial. ¹⁰The inhabitants of the earth will gloat over them and will celebrate by sending each other gifts, because these two prophets had tormented those who live on the earth.

¹¹But after the three and a half days a breath of life from God entered them, and they stood on

their feet, and terror struck those who saw them. ¹²Then they heard a loud voice from heaven saying to them, "Come up here." And they went up to heaven in a cloud, while their enemies looked on.

¹³At that very hour there was a severe earthquake and a tenth of the city collapsed. Seven thousand people were killed in the earthquake, and the survivors were terrified and gave glory to the God of heaven.

¹⁴The second woe has passed; the third woe is coming soon.

¹⁵The seventh angel sounded his trumpet, and there were loud voices in heaven, which said:

"The kingdom of the world has become the
    kingdom of our Lord and of his Christ,
    and he will reign for ever and ever."

¹⁶And the twenty-four elders, who were seated on their thrones before God, fell on their faces and worshiped God, ¹⁷saying:

"We give thanks to you, Lord God Almighty,
    the One who is and who was,
because you have taken your great power
    and have begun to reign.
¹⁸The nations were angry;
    and your wrath has come.
The time has come for judging the dead,
    and for rewarding your servants the
        prophets
and your saints and those who reverence your
      name,
    both small and great—
and for destroying those who destroy the
      earth."

¹⁹Then God's temple in heaven was opened, and within his temple was seen the ark of his covenant. And there came flashes of lightning, rumblings, peals of thunder, an earthquake and a great hailstorm.

Discovering the Word   1. What are the actions of the "mighty angel" introduced in 10:1?   2. What is the significance of the mystery of God which will be revealed without further delay (10:6–7)?   3. What happens to the two witnesses empowered by God (11:3–14)?   4. Why do you think the witnesses caused such turmoil? 5. What happens when the seventh trumpet is blown (11:15–19)?

Applying the Word   1. The "little scroll" that John eats (10:8–11) probably refers to the gospel. When has the gospel tasted like honey or turned your stomach sour?   2. 11:10 says that the two witnesses had "tormented those who live on the earth." When have you felt that God was calling you to deliver a message of bad news?   3. What feelings about God and his actions do you have after reading the description of worship in 11:15–19?

Responding in Prayer   Pray that you will be willing to be God's messenger to those around you.

---

10 / *Revelation 12*
Conflict with the Accuser

DRAGONS SYMBOLIZE ALL that is terrifying, evil and loathsome. In Revelation 12 Satan appears as an enormous red dragon, full of rage. Knowing that his time is short, he unleashes his fury as never before. During such dark moments of history, it seems as though God is absent and Satan is victorious. Yet in this passage John describes a heavenly vision that puts all earthly tribulation in proper perspective.

Warming Up to God   In what ways are you experiencing the reality of spiritual warfare?

Read Revelation 12.

12

A great and wondrous sign appeared in heaven: a woman clothed with the sun, with the moon under her feet and a crown of twelve stars on her head. ²She was pregnant and cried out in pain as she was about to give birth. ³Then another sign appeared in heaven: an enormous red dragon with seven heads and ten horns and seven crowns on his heads. ⁴His tail swept a third of the stars out of the sky and flung them to the earth. The dragon stood in front of the woman who was about to give birth, so that he might devour her child the moment it was born. ⁵She gave birth to a son, a male child, who will rule all the nations with an iron scepter. And her child was snatched up to God and to his throne. ⁶The woman fled into the desert to a place prepared for her by God, where she might be taken care of for 1,260 days.

⁷And there was war in heaven. Michael and his angels fought against the dragon, and the dragon and his angels fought back. ⁸But he was not strong enough, and they lost their place in heaven. ⁹The great dragon was hurled down—that ancient serpent called the devil, or Satan, who leads the whole world astray. He was hurled to the earth, and his angels with him.

¹⁰Then I heard a loud voice in heaven say:

"Now have come the salvation and the power
    and the kingdom of our God,
    and the authority of his Christ.
For the accuser of our brothers,
who accuses them before our God day and
    night,
    has been hurled down.
¹¹They overcame him
    by the blood of the Lamb
    and by the word of their testimony;
they did not love their lives so much
    as to shrink from death.
¹²Therefore rejoice, you heavens
    and you who dwell in them!
But woe to the earth and the sea,
    because the devil has gone down to you!
He is filled with fury,
    because he knows that his time is short."

¹³When the dragon saw that he had been hurled to the earth, he pursued the woman who had given birth to the male child. ¹⁴The woman was given the two wings of a great eagle, so that she might fly to the place prepared for her in the desert, where she would be taken care of for a time, times and half a time, out of the serpent's reach. ¹⁵Then from his mouth the serpent spewed water like a river, to overtake the woman and sweep her away with the torrent. ¹⁶But the earth helped the woman by opening its mouth and swallowing the river that the dragon had spewed out of his mouth. ¹⁷Then the dragon was enraged at the woman and went off to make war against the rest of her offspring—those who obey God's commandments and hold to the testimony of Jesus.

Discovering the Word 1. Three of the characters in this chapter are the woman (perhaps the Lord's people or the Holy Spirit), the red dragon (Satan) and the male child (the Lord Jesus). What conflict does John observe among them (vv. 1–6)? 2. In verses 7–9 John describes a war in heaven. What does the war reveal about the dragon? 3. What does the dragon's defeat mean in heaven (vv. 10, 12) and on earth (vv. 12–17)? 4. What does it mean to overcome Satan's accusations by the blood of the Lamb and the word of our testimony (v. 11)?

Applying the Word 1. How can we help a fellow Christian who is no longer under God's condemnation but who still feels condemned and defeated? 2. In what other ways do we experience Satan's attacks? 3. How can the victory of Christ help us face these battles and struggles of the Christian life?

Responding in Prayer Pray for those who are struggling against Satan.

11 / *Revelation 13*
The Beast

IN *BRAVE NEW World* Aldous Huxley described a future too close for comfort: "As political and economic freedom diminishes, sexual freedom tends compensatingly to increase. And the dictator will do well to encourage that freedom." Faithful Christianity inevitably involves conflict, tension and suffering for followers of Jesus. We cannot be fully at home in our own culture. Even where we do not face open hostility, we are pressured—indeed seduced—by a seemingly friendly society. Revelation 13 demonstrates that the church must always deal with radical evil. In these visions John unmasks the powers of darkness at work in everyday life and at the end of history.

 Warming Up to God Why do you think it is so difficult for believers to make substantial changes in society? (For example, in the areas of justice, protection of the unborn or making peace.)

 Read Revelation 13.

13 ¹And the dragon° stood on the shore of the sea.

And I saw a beast coming out of the sea. He had ten horns and seven heads, with ten crowns on his horns, and on each head a blasphemous name. ²The beast I saw resembled a leopard, but had feet like those of a bear and a mouth like that of a lion. The dragon gave the beast his power and his throne and great authority. ³One of the heads of the beast seemed to have had a fatal wound, but the fatal wound had been healed. The whole world was astonished and followed the beast. ⁴Men worshiped the dragon because he had given authority to the beast, and they also worshiped the beast and asked, "Who is like the beast? Who can make war against him?"

⁵The beast was given a mouth to utter proud words and blasphemies and to exercise his authority for forty-two months. ⁶He opened his mouth to blaspheme God, and to slander his name and his dwelling place and those who live in heaven. ⁷He was given power to make war against the saints and to conquer them. And he was given authority over every tribe, people, language and nation. ⁸All inhabitants of the earth will worship the beast—all whose names have not been written in the book of life belonging to the Lamb that was slain from the creation of the world.ᴾ

⁹He who has an ear, let him hear.

¹⁰If anyone is to go into captivity,
  into captivity he will go.

If anyone is to be killed�q with the sword,
  with the sword he will be killed.

This calls for patient endurance and faithfulness on the part of the saints.

¹¹Then I saw another beast, coming out of the earth. He had two horns like a lamb, but he spoke like a dragon. ¹²He exercised all the authority of the first beast on his behalf, and made the earth and its inhabitants worship the first beast, whose fatal wound had been healed. ¹³And he performed great and miraculous signs, even causing fire to come down from heaven to earth in full view of men. ¹⁴Because of the signs he was given power to do on behalf of the first beast, he deceived the inhabitants of the earth. He ordered them to set up an image in honor of the beast who was wounded by the sword and yet lived. ¹⁵He was given power to give breath to the image of the first beast, so that it could speak and cause all who refused to worship the image to be killed. ¹⁶He also forced everyone, small and great, rich and poor, free and slave, to receive a mark on his right hand or on his forehead, ¹⁷so that no one could buy or sell unless he had the mark, which is the name of the beast or the number of his name.

¹⁸This calls for wisdom. If anyone has insight, let him calculate the number of the beast, for it is man's number. His number is 666.

ᵒ1 Some late manuscripts *And I*   ᴾ8 Or *written from the creation of the world in the book of life belonging to the Lamb that was slain*   q10 Some manuscripts *anyone kills*

Discovering the Word 1. In what ways is the beast a satanic imitation of Christ? 2. What is the mission of the beast (vv. 5–8)? 3. Why do you think John tells us about this formidable enemy of the soul? 4. What new powers are given to the second beast (vv. 11–18)? 5. How does this beast ensure that people worship the first beast?

Applying the Word 1. John seems to be describing a conflict with Satan and his puppets that is going on now but will one day be fully realized (see 1Jn 2:18). How might we expect to see this satanic influence at work today? 2. How can we prepare ourselves to face this conflict?

Responding in Prayer Pray that you will be equipped to face Satan.

12 / *Revelation 14—15*
Tale of Two Choices

AS YOU STRUGGLE to live according to God's laws, do you ever wonder if there will really be any reward? Will there be any difference between those who love God and those who live their lives in rebellion against God's love? In these chapters, John makes it clear that the choices we make now will have an impact on God's judgement on us in the future. These chapters are a tale of two choices.

Warming Up to God When have you really tried to do what is right, only to see those who didn't play by the rules seem to come out better than you? How did you feel about the outcome?

Read Revelation 14—15.

14 Then I looked, and there before me was the Lamb, standing on Mount Zion, and with him 144,000 who had his name and his Father's name written on their foreheads. ²And I heard a sound from heaven like the roar of rushing waters and like a loud peal of thunder. The sound I heard was like that of harpists playing their harps. ³And they sang a new song before the throne and before the four living creatures and the elders. No one could learn the song except the 144,000 who had been redeemed from the earth. ⁴These are those who did not defile themselves with women, for they kept themselves pure. They follow the Lamb wherever he goes. They were purchased from among men and offered as firstfruits to God and the Lamb. ⁵No lie was found in their mouths; they are blameless.

⁶Then I saw another angel flying in midair, and he had the eternal gospel to proclaim to those who live on the earth—to every nation, tribe, language and people. ⁷He said in a loud voice, "Fear God and give him glory, because the hour of his judgment has come. Worship him who made the heavens, the earth, the sea and the springs of water."

⁸A second angel followed and said, "Fallen! Fallen is Babylon the Great, which made all the nations drink the maddening wine of her adulteries."

⁹A third angel followed them and said in a loud voice: "If anyone worships the beast and his image and receives his mark on the forehead or on the hand, ¹⁰he, too, will drink of the wine of God's fury, which has been poured full strength into the cup of his wrath. He will be tormented with burning sulfur in the presence of the holy angels and of the Lamb. ¹¹And the smoke of their torment rises for ever and ever. There is no rest day or night for those who worship the beast and his image, or for anyone who receives the mark of his name." ¹²This calls for patient endurance on the part of the saints who obey God's commandments and remain faithful to Jesus.

¹³Then I heard a voice from heaven say, "Write: Blessed are the dead who die in the Lord from now on."

"Yes," says the Spirit, "they will rest from their labor, for their deeds will follow them."

[14]I looked, and there before me was a white cloud, and seated on the cloud was one "like a son of man"[r] with a crown of gold on his head and a sharp sickle in his hand. [15]Then another angel came out of the temple and called in a loud voice to him who was sitting on the cloud, "Take your sickle and reap, because the time to reap has come, for the harvest of the earth is ripe." [16]So he who was seated on the cloud swung his sickle over the earth, and the earth was harvested.

[17]Another angel came out of the temple in heaven, and he too had a sharp sickle. [18]Still another angel, who had charge of the fire, came from the altar and called in a loud voice to him who had the sharp sickle, "Take your sharp sickle and gather the clusters of grapes from the earth's vine, because its grapes are ripe." [19]The angel swung his sickle on the earth, gathered its grapes and threw them into the great winepress of God's wrath. [20]They were trampled in the winepress outside the city, and blood flowed out of the press, rising as high as the horses' bridles for a distance of 1,600 stadia.[s]

15

I saw in heaven another great and marvelous sign: seven angels with the seven last plagues—last, because with them God's wrath is completed. [2]And I saw what looked like a sea of glass mixed with fire and, standing beside the sea, those who had been victorious over the beast and his image and over the number of his name. They held harps given them by God [3]and sang the song of Moses the servant of God and the song of the Lamb:

"Great and marvelous are your deeds,
  Lord God Almighty.
Just and true are your ways,
  King of the ages.
[4]Who will not fear you, O Lord,
  and bring glory to your name?
For you alone are holy.
All nations will come
  and worship before you,
for your righteous acts have been revealed."

[5]After this I looked and in heaven the temple, that is, the tabernacle of the Testimony, was opened. [6]Out of the temple came the seven angels with the seven plagues. They were dressed in clean, shining linen and wore golden sashes around their chests. [7]Then one of the four living creatures gave to the seven angels seven golden bowls filled with the wrath of God, who lives for ever and ever. [8]And the temple was filled with smoke from the glory of God and from his power, and no one could enter the temple until the seven plagues of the seven angels were completed.

[r]14 Daniel 7:13   [s]20 That is, about 180 miles (about 300 kilometers)

Discovering the Word 1. What differences do you notice between the 144,000 who are with the Lamb (14:1–5) and Babylon (14:8), the beast and those who worship it (14:6–11)? 2. What harvest is reaped in 14:14–20? 3. What connections do you find between the angels who give warnings in 14:6–11 and the beings who reap the harvest? 4. Who sings the hymn to God in 15:1–4? 5. What are the righteous acts that have been revealed (15:4)?

Applying the Word 1. In 14:12 John states that this passage "calls for patient endurance on the part of the saints." How does this passage encourage you to endure in your faith? 2. The hymn beginning in 15:3 is called the song of Moses, which was sung by Moses after crossing the Red Sea. When have you been delivered by God from danger, spiritual or physical?

 Responding in Prayer Thank God for the assurance you have of your salvation.

13 / *Revelation 16*
Who's to Blame?

WHEN SOMETHING GOES wrong, who do we blame? Often, God's name is among the first to come up. When we are inclined to blame God, we must ask ourselves what it is we expect out of life. Do we feel that we have an innate right to health, wealth and happiness? In understanding God's working in the world it's important that we learn to see beyond our private world to God's vast creation.

Warming Up to God Be honest with yourself about your feelings toward God. When are you inclined to place blame on God for events in your life?

Read Revelation 16.

16 Then I heard a loud voice from the temple saying to the seven angels, "Go, pour out the seven bowls of God's wrath on the earth."

²The first angel went and poured out his bowl on the land, and ugly and painful sores broke out on the people who had the mark of the beast and worshiped his image.

³The second angel poured out his bowl on the sea, and it turned into blood like that of a dead man, and every living thing in the sea died.

⁴The third angel poured out his bowl on the rivers and springs of water, and they became blood. ⁵Then I heard the angel in charge of the waters say:

"You are just in these judgments,
    you who are and who were, the Holy One,
    because you have so judged;
⁶for they have shed the blood of your saints
        and prophets,
    and you have given them blood to drink as
        they deserve."

⁷And I heard the altar respond:

"Yes, Lord God Almighty,
    true and just are your judgments."

⁸The fourth angel poured out his bowl on the sun, and the sun was given power to scorch people with fire. ⁹They were seared by the intense heat and they cursed the name of God, who had control over these plagues, but they refused to repent and glorify him.

¹⁰The fifth angel poured out his bowl on the throne of the beast, and his kingdom was plunged into darkness. Men gnawed their tongues in agony ¹¹and cursed the God of heaven because of their pains and their sores, but they refused to repent of what they had done.

¹²The sixth angel poured out his bowl on the great river Euphrates, and its water was dried up to prepare the way for the kings from the East. ¹³Then I saw three evilᶜ spirits that looked like frogs; they came out of the mouth of the dragon, out of the mouth of the beast and out of the mouth of the false prophet. ¹⁴They are spirits of demons performing miraculous signs, and they go out to the kings of the whole world, to gather them for the battle on the great day of God Almighty.

¹⁵"Behold, I come like a thief! Blessed is he who stays awake and keeps his clothes with him, so that he may not go naked and be shamefully exposed."

¹⁶Then they gathered the kings together to the place that in Hebrew is called Armageddon.

¹⁷The seventh angel poured out his bowl into the air, and out of the temple came a loud voice from the throne, saying, "It is done!" ¹⁸Then there came flashes of lightning, rumblings, peals of thunder and a severe earthquake. No earthquake like it has ever occurred since man has been on earth, so tremendous was the quake. ¹⁹The great city split into three parts, and the cities of the nations collapsed. God remembered Babylon the Great and gave her the cup filled with the wine of the fury of his wrath. ²⁰Every island fled away and the mountains could not be found. ²¹From the sky huge hailstones of about a hundred pounds each fell upon men. And they cursed God on account of the plague of hail, because the plague was so terrible.

ᶜ13 Greek *unclean*

Discovering the Word 1. Note the similarity between these plagues and those brought on Egypt (blood, frogs, gnats, flies, livestock, boils, hail, locusts, darkness, firstborn). What might be meant by this comparison? 2. How could the same events lead to worship on the part of some (vv. 5–7) and cursing on the part of others (vv. 9, 21)? 3. How can we see this happening in our culture? 4. What is the result of the plagues (vv. 19–21)?

 Applying the Word 1. When has God's judgment been a source of praise for you? 2. When has God's judgment caused you to curse or blame God?

Responding in Prayer Talk honestly with God about any feelings of blame and responsibility that have been revealed to you during this study.

---

14 / *Revelation 17—18*
Beneath the Surface

IN EVERY AGE there is at least one symbol for everything that goes against God. For several of the Old Testament writers it was Babylon, the beautiful city that held captive God's chosen people. Babylon represented everything that was evil and unsightly about humanity. John uses this powerful symbol to interpret his own age and the powers that opposed God in his generation. In these two chapters we see not only John's vision of how those powers opposed God, but the ultimate outcome of that opposition.

 Warming Up to God When have you noticed someone or something that looked appealing, but upon closer scrutiny was unappealing or revolting?

 Read Revelation 17—18.

---

17 One of the seven angels who had the seven bowls came and said to me, "Come, I will show you the punishment of the great prostitute, who sits on many waters. ²With her the kings of the earth committed adultery and the inhabitants of the earth were intoxicated with the wine of her adulteries."

³Then the angel carried me away in the Spirit into a desert. There I saw a woman sitting on a scarlet beast that was covered with blasphemous names and had seven heads and ten horns. ⁴The woman was dressed in purple and scarlet, and was glittering with gold, precious stones and pearls. She held a golden cup in her hand, filled with abominable things and the filth of her adulteries. ⁵This title was written on her forehead:

MYSTERY

BABYLON THE GREAT

THE MOTHER OF PROSTITUTES

AND OF THE ABOMINATIONS OF THE EARTH.

⁶I saw that the woman was drunk with the blood of the saints, the blood of those who bore testimony to Jesus.

When I saw her, I was greatly astonished. ⁷Then the angel said to me: "Why are you astonished? I will explain to you the mystery of the woman and of the beast she rides, which has the seven heads and ten horns. ⁸The beast, which you saw, once was, now is not, and will come up out of the Abyss and go to his destruction. The inhabitants of the earth whose names have not been written in the book of life from the creation of the world will be astonished when they see the beast, because he once was, now is not, and yet will come.

⁹"This calls for a mind with wisdom. The seven heads are seven hills on which the woman sits. ¹⁰They are also seven kings. Five have fallen, one is, the other has not yet come; but when he does come, he must remain for a little while. ¹¹The beast who once was, and now is not, is an eighth king. He belongs to the seven and is going to his destruction.

¹²"The ten horns you saw are ten kings who have not yet received a kingdom, but who for one hour will receive authority as kings along with the beast. ¹³They have one purpose and will give their power and authority to the beast. ¹⁴They

will make war against the Lamb, but the Lamb will overcome them because he is Lord of lords and King of kings—and with him will be his called, chosen and faithful followers."

¹⁵Then the angel said to me, "The waters you saw, where the prostitute sits, are peoples, multitudes, nations and languages. ¹⁶The beast and the ten horns you saw will hate the prostitute. They will bring her to ruin and leave her naked; they will eat her flesh and burn her with fire. ¹⁷For God has put it into their hearts to accomplish his purpose by agreeing to give the beast their power to rule, until God's words are fulfilled. ¹⁸The woman you saw is the great city that rules over the kings of the earth."

18

After this I saw another angel coming down from heaven. He had great authority, and the earth was illuminated by his splendor. ²With a mighty voice he shouted:

"Fallen! Fallen is Babylon the Great!
　She has become a home for demons
and a haunt for every evilᵘ spirit,
　a haunt for every unclean and detestable
　　bird.
³For all the nations have drunk
　the maddening wine of her adulteries.
The kings of the earth committed adultery
　with her,
　and the merchants of the earth grew rich
　　from her excessive luxuries."

⁴Then I heard another voice from heaven say:

"Come out of her, my people,
　so that you will not share in her sins,
　so that you will not receive any of her
　　plagues;
⁵for her sins are piled up to heaven,
　and God has remembered her crimes.
⁶Give back to her as she has given;
　pay her back double for what she has done.
　Mix her a double portion from her own
　　cup.
⁷Give her as much torture and grief
　as the glory and luxury she gave herself.
In her heart she boasts,
　'I sit as queen; I am not a widow,
　and I will never mourn.'
⁸Therefore in one day her plagues will
　　overtake her:
　death, mourning and famine.

She will be consumed by fire,
　for mighty is the Lord God who judges her.

⁹"When the kings of the earth who committed adultery with her and shared her luxury see the smoke of her burning, they will weep and mourn over her. ¹⁰Terrified at her torment, they will stand far off and cry:

" 'Woe! Woe, O great city,
　O Babylon, city of power!
In one hour your doom has come!'

¹¹"The merchants of the earth will weep and mourn over her because no one buys their cargoes any more— ¹²cargoes of gold, silver, precious stones and pearls; fine linen, purple, silk and scarlet cloth; every sort of citron wood, and articles of every kind made of ivory, costly wood, bronze, iron and marble; ¹³cargoes of cinnamon and spice, of incense, myrrh and frankincense, of wine and olive oil, of fine flour and wheat; cattle and sheep; horses and carriages; and bodies and souls of men.

¹⁴"They will say, 'The fruit you longed for is gone from you. All your riches and splendor have vanished, never to be recovered.' ¹⁵The merchants who sold these things and gained their wealth from her will stand far off, terrified at her torment. They will weep and mourn ¹⁶and cry out:

" 'Woe! Woe, O great city,
　dressed in fine linen, purple and scarlet,
　and glittering with gold, precious stones
　　and pearls!
¹⁷In one hour such great wealth has been
　　brought to ruin!'

"Every sea captain, and all who travel by ship, the sailors, and all who earn their living from the sea, will stand far off. ¹⁸When they see the smoke of her burning, they will exclaim, 'Was there ever a city like this great city?' ¹⁹They will throw dust on their heads, and with weeping and mourning cry out:

" 'Woe! Woe, O great city,
　where all who had ships on the sea
　became rich through her wealth!
In one hour she has been brought to ruin!
²⁰Rejoice over her, O heaven!
　Rejoice, saints and apostles and prophets!

ᵘ2 Greek unclean

God has judged her for the way she treated you.' "

²¹Then a mighty angel picked up a boulder the size of a large millstone and threw it into the sea, and said:

"With such violence
  the great city of Babylon will be thrown
    down,
      never to be found again.
²²The music of harpists and musicians,
  flute players and trumpeters,
    will never be heard in you again.

No workman of any trade

will ever be found in you.
The sound of a millstone
  will never be heard in you.
²³The light of a lamp
  will never shine in you again.
The voice of bridegroom and bride
  will never be heard in you again.
Your merchants were the world's great men.
  By your magic spell all the nations were led astray.
²⁴In her was found the blood of prophets and of the saints,

 Discovering the Word 1. Who or what do you think John had in mind when he described the prostitute (17:3–6)? 2. What are the crimes of the prostitute, identified as Babylon (17:3–6; 18:1–3)? As it changes from prostitute see herself at the fall of Babylon? 3. What is the reaction of the kings (18:9–10), merchants (18:11–17a) and does the captains (18:17b– sea

 Applying the Word 1. Who or what is a contemporary parallel to the prostitute? 2. In what ways modern "prostitute" a temptation to you? 3. How can you avoid this temptation?

Responding in Prayer Ask God for protection from the temptations of those who are prideful and oppose God.

---

15 / Revelation 19
Are You Going to the Wedding?

JOHN USES A metaphor that has lost much of its meaning in our generation—marriage. In this day of interchangeable marriage roles, five-year renewable relationships and serial monogamy, it is difficult to grasp the splendor of marriage as God intends it. John chooses a wedding to describe the consummation of the deepest longing of the human soul: Christ's coming to receive us. Our present engagement (betrothal) to Christ will be followed by the wedding service and a joyous feast. Then and only then can we experience complete unity with Christ. This vision seems a welcome relief after the long passage on tribulation and judgment (chapters 6—18). In fact, the marriage is the logical result of all that has gone before, as we shall see.

Warming Up to God In your opinion, what are some of the best things about marriage?

Read Revelation 19.

---

19 After this I heard what sounded like the roar of a great multitude in heaven shouting:

"Hallelujah!
Salvation and glory and power belong to our God,

² for true and just are his judgments.
He has condemned the great prostitute
  who corrupted the earth by her adulteries.
He has avenged on her the blood of his
  servants."

³And again they shouted:

□ Revelation 19:4

"Hallelujah! ... goes up for ever and
The smoke fro...
ever. ...elders and the four living
...nd worshiped God, who was
⁴The tw... e. And they cried:
creatures...
seated ...!"

...ame from the throne, saying:

"A...
...,
...ervants,
...ike a great multi-
...ar of rushing waters and like loud
...der, shouting:

...Lord God Almighty reigns.
...o...ice and be glad
...us re...him glory!
...an...dding of the Lamb has come,
F...the...bride has made herself ready.
...nen, bright and clean,
...as given her to wear."

...ne linen stands for the righteous acts of the
saints.)

⁹Then the angel said to me, "Write: 'Blessed are
those who are invited to the wedding supper of
the Lamb!' " And he added, "These are the true
words of God."

¹⁰At this I fell at his feet to worship him. But he
said to me, "Do not do it! I am a fellow servant
with you and with your brothers who hold to the
testimony of Jesus. Worship God! For the testimony of Jesus is the spirit of prophecy."

¹¹I saw heaven standing open and there before

me was a white horse, whose rider is called Faithful and True. With justice he judges and makes
war. ¹²His eyes are like blazing fire, and on his
head are many crowns. He has a name written on
him that no one knows but he himself. ¹³He is
dressed in a robe dipped in blood, and his name
is the Word of God. ¹⁴The armies of heaven were
following him, riding on white horses and
dressed in fine linen, white and clean. ¹⁵Out of
his mouth comes a sharp sword with which to
...an iron scepter. ...He will rule them with
fury of the wrath of God Almighty. ¹⁶On his robe
and on his th...has this name written:

KING OF KINGS AND L...E LORDS.

¹⁷And I saw an angel standing in the sun, who
cried in a loud voice t...all the birds flying in
midair, "Come, gather together for the great supper of God, ¹⁸so that you may eat the flesh of
kings, generals, and mighty men, of horses and
their riders, and the flesh of all people, free and
slave, small and great."

¹⁹Then I saw the beast and the kings of the
earth and their armies gathered together to make
war against the rider on the horse and his army.
²⁰But the beast was captured, and with him the
false prophet who had performed the miraculous
signs on his behalf. With these signs he had deluded those who had received the mark of the
beast and worshiped his image. The two of them
were thrown alive into the fiery lake of burning
sulfur. ²¹The rest of them were killed with the
sword that came out of the mouth of the rider on
the horse and all the birds gorged themselves on
their flesh.

v 15 Psalm 2:9

Discovering the Word 1. Why is the great multitude shouting praise in heaven? 2. John does not
describe the details of the marriage, he simply proclaims it. Why is marriage such a good image for the
believer's hope (vv. 7–9)? 3. Like a champion ready for battle, Jesus appears on horseback. What do we learn
about him (vv. 11–16)? 4. Why must this battle take place before the marriage can begin and the kingdom of God
can fully come (vv. 17–21)?

Applying the Word 1. In what ways would you like to see Christ triumph in your life or in the world around
you? 2. How can we confidently know we are invited to the "wedding supper of the Lamb"?

Responding in Prayer Allow praise for this future celebration to flow forth out of your prayer.

16 / *Revelation 20*
The Last Battle

FINALITY IS SOMETHING we crave and which God graciously provides. A relationship needs to be broken, an assignment needs to be completed, an extended friendship needs to become a committed marriage—all require closure. The previous study explored our inexpressible hope to be reunited with our Lord. This chapter enlarges our appreciation of God's master plan: his settled decision to be with us forever and to establish his glorious rule over everything.

 Warming Up to God What do you look forward to most about Christ's return?

 Read Revelation 20.

20 And I saw an angel coming down out of heaven, having the key to the Abyss and holding in his hand a great chain. ²He seized the dragon, that ancient serpent, who is the devil, or Satan, and bound him for a thousand years. ³He threw him into the Abyss, and locked and sealed it over him, to keep him from deceiving the nations anymore until the thousand years were ended. After that, he must be set free for a short time.

⁴I saw thrones on which were seated those who had been given authority to judge. And I saw the souls of those who had been beheaded because of their testimony for Jesus and because of the word of God. They had not worshiped the beast or his image and had not received his mark on their foreheads or their hands. They came to life and reigned with Christ a thousand years. ⁵(The rest of the dead did not come to life until the thousand years were ended.) This is the first resurrection. ⁶Blessed and holy are those who have part in the first resurrection. The second death has no power over them, but they will be priests of God and of Christ and will reign with him for a thousand years.

⁷When the thousand years are over, Satan will be released from his prison ⁸and will go out to deceive the nations in the four corners of the earth—Gog and Magog—to gather them for battle. In number they are like the sand on the seashore. ⁹They marched across the breadth of the earth and surrounded the camp of God's people, the city he loves. But fire came down from heaven and devoured them. ¹⁰And the devil, who deceived them, was thrown into the lake of burning sulfur, where the beast and the false prophet had been thrown. They will be tormented day and night for ever and ever.

¹¹Then I saw a great white throne and him who was seated on it. Earth and sky fled from his presence, and there was no place for them. ¹²And I saw the dead, great and small, standing before the throne, and books were opened. Another book was opened, which is the book of life. The dead were judged according to what they had done as recorded in the books. ¹³The sea gave up the dead that were in it, and death and Hades gave up the dead that were in them, and each person was judged according to what he had done. ¹⁴Then death and Hades were thrown into the lake of fire. The lake of fire is the second death. ¹⁵If anyone's name was not found written in the book of life, he was thrown into the lake of fire.

 Discovering the Word 1. This chapter, out of the whole book, has sparked the greatest controversy. Why is Satan, previously thrown to earth (12:9), now bound (20:1–3)? 2. The thousand-year reign of Christ (vv. 4–6) has been interpreted as referring to: (a) a period of righteousness and peace on earth *before* Christ's return; (b) Christ's reign in heaven *between* his First and Second Coming; (c) Christ's reign on earth *after* his return. Which view (if any) do you think best fits this passage and the book of Revelation? 3. What is the nature and outcome of Satan's last fling (vv. 7–10)? 4. Who will be judged at the great-white-throne judgment (vv. 11–15)? 5. What does it say about God's character that he should keep a record of each person's deeds?

Applying the Word 1. How can verses 4–6 help us to see life and death in proper perspective? 2. How should the ultimate judgment of evil and the reward of faithfulness affect the way we live now?

Responding in Prayer Pray that you will be made faithful in every way.

17 / *Revelation 21—22*
God Dwelling with His People

W. H. AUDEN said, "Nobody is ever sent to hell; he or she insists on going there." Could the same be said of heaven? Far from being "pie in the sky by and by" or a hedonistic longing for pleasure, John's vision of God dwelling with his people is the consummation of faith. Creation is renewed. Evil is finally excluded. The face of God is seen. But John's vision is, at the same time, unsettling to the normal view held by Christians about "last things." It goes beyond not only our imagination but even our faith.

 Warming Up to God What do you think about when you hear the word *heaven*?

 Read Revelation 21—22.

21 Then I saw a new heaven and a new earth, for the first heaven and the first earth had passed away, and there was no longer any sea. ²I saw the Holy City, the new Jerusalem, coming down out of heaven from God, prepared as a bride beautifully dressed for her husband. ³And I heard a loud voice from the throne saying, "Now the dwelling of God is with men, and he will live with them. They will be his people, and God himself will be with them and be their God. ⁴He will wipe every tear from their eyes. There will be no more death or mourning or crying or pain, for the old order of things has passed away."

⁵He who was seated on the throne said, "I am making everything new!" Then he said, "Write this down, for these words are trustworthy and true."

⁶He said to me: "It is done. I am the Alpha and the Omega, the Beginning and the End. To him who is thirsty I will give to drink without cost from the spring of the water of life. ⁷He who overcomes will inherit all this, and I will be his God and he will be my son. ⁸But the cowardly, the unbelieving, the vile, the murderers, the sexually immoral, those who practice magic arts, the idolaters and all liars—their place will be in the fiery lake of burning sulfur. This is the second death."

⁹One of the seven angels who had the seven bowls full of the seven last plagues came and said to me, "Come, I will show you the bride, the wife of the Lamb." ¹⁰And he carried me away in the Spirit to a mountain great and high, and showed me the Holy City, Jerusalem, coming down out of heaven from God. ¹¹It shone with the glory of God, and its brilliance was like that of a very precious jewel, like a jasper, clear as crystal. ¹²It had a great, high wall with twelve gates, and with twelve angels at the gates. On the gates were written the names of the twelve tribes of Israel. ¹³There were three gates on the east, three on the north, three on the south and three on the west. ¹⁴The wall of the city had twelve foundations, and on them were the names of the twelve apostles of the Lamb.

¹⁵The angel who talked with me had a measuring rod of gold to measure the city, its gates and its walls. ¹⁶The city was laid out like a square, as long as it was wide. He measured the city with the rod and found it to be 12,000 stadia*ʷ* in length, and as wide and high as it is long. ¹⁷He measured its wall and it was 144 cubits*ˣ* thick,*ʸ* by man's measurement, which the angel was using. ¹⁸The wall was made of jasper, and the city of pure gold, as pure as glass. ¹⁹The foundations of the city walls were decorated with every kind of precious stone. The first foundation was jasper, the second sapphire, the third chalcedony, the fourth emerald, ²⁰the fifth sardonyx, the sixth carnelian, the

---

ʷ16 That is, about 1,400 miles (about 2,200 kilometers) *ˣ17* That is, about 200 feet (about 65 meters) *ʸ17* Or **high**

seventh chrysolite, the eighth beryl, the ninth topaz, the tenth chrysoprase, the eleventh jacinth, and the twelfth amethyst.ᶻ ²¹The twelve gates were twelve pearls, each gate made of a single pearl. The great street of the city was of pure gold, like transparent glass.

²²I did not see a temple in the city, because the Lord God Almighty and the Lamb are its temple. ²³The city does not need the sun or the moon to shine on it, for the glory of God gives it light, and the Lamb is its lamp. ²⁴The nations will walk by its light, and the kings of the earth will bring their splendor into it. ²⁵On no day will its gates ever be shut, for there will be no night there. ²⁶The glory and honor of the nations will be brought into it. ²⁷Nothing impure will ever enter it, nor will anyone who does what is shameful or deceitful, but only those whose names are written in the Lamb's book of life.

22

Then the angel showed me the river of the water of life, as clear as crystal, flowing from the throne of God and of the Lamb ²down the middle of the great street of the city. On each side of the river stood the tree of life, bearing twelve crops of fruit, yielding its fruit every month. And the leaves of the tree are for the healing of the nations. ³No longer will there be any curse. The throne of God and of the Lamb will be in the city, and his servants will serve him. ⁴They will see his face, and his name will be on their foreheads. ⁵There will be no more night. They will not need the light of a lamp or the light of the sun, for the Lord God will give them light. And they will reign for ever and ever.

⁶The angel said to me, "These words are trustworthy and true. The Lord, the God of the spirits of the prophets, sent his angel to show his servants the things that must soon take place."

⁷"Behold, I am coming soon! Blessed is he who keeps the words of the prophecy in this book."

⁸I, John, am the one who heard and saw these things. And when I had heard and seen them, I fell down to worship at the feet of the angel who had been showing them to me. ⁹But he said to me,

"Do not do it! I am a fellow servant with you and with your brothers the prophets and of all who keep the words of this book. Worship God!"

¹⁰Then he told me, "Do not seal up the words of the prophecy of this book, because the time is near. ¹¹Let him who does wrong continue to do wrong; let him who is vile continue to be vile; let him who does right continue to do right; and let him who is holy continue to be holy."

¹²"Behold, I am coming soon! My reward is with me, and I will give to everyone according to what he has done. ¹³I am the Alpha and the Omega, the First and the Last, the Beginning and the End.

¹⁴"Blessed are those who wash their robes, that they may have the right to the tree of life and may go through the gates into the city. ¹⁵Outside are the dogs, those who practice magic arts, the sexually immoral, the murderers, the idolaters and everyone who loves and practices falsehood.

¹⁶"I, Jesus, have sent my angel to give youᵃ this testimony for the churches. I am the Root and the Offspring of David, and the bright Morning Star."

¹⁷The Spirit and the bride say, "Come!" And let him who hears say, "Come!" Whoever is thirsty, let him come; and whoever wishes, let him take the free gift of the water of life.

¹⁸I warn everyone who hears the words of the prophecy of this book: If anyone adds anything to them, God will add to him the plagues described in this book. ¹⁹And if anyone takes words away from this book of prophecy, God will take away from him his share in the tree of life and in the holy city, which are described in this book.

²⁰He who testifies to these things says, "Yes, I am coming soon."

Amen. Come, Lord Jesus.

²¹The grace of the Lord Jesus be with God's people. Amen.

ᶻ20 The precise identification of some of these precious stones is uncertain. ᵃ16 The Greek is plural.

Discovering the Word 1. What aspects of the "old order" must be eliminated before God can fully dwell with his people (21:1–5)? 2. What in the passage suggests that the new Jerusalem is nothing other than the church in its final, consummated life (21:10)? 3. Why do you think John gives such a detailed description of the splendor of the city (21:11–21)? 4. Why do you think a city (rather than a glorious garden like Eden) is used

to describe our final home? **5.** Taken together, chapters 21 and 22 describe a place of exquisite beauty. Yet what statements indicate that the real significance of the city lies in something else (22:1–21)? **6.** What are the requirements for entering the city (21:6–7, 27; 22:12, 14)?

Applying the Word **1.** Why must the requirements for entering the city be met during the times of testing we experience in this life? **2.** As you review what you have learned in Revelation, what new insight do you have into the early Christian prayer "Come, Lord Jesus!"?

Responding in Prayer Pray for Jesus' coming.

ACKNOWLEDGMENTS

The following articles were revised and adapted from InterVarsity Press publications:

"Why Have a Quiet Time?" by John White, from pp. 136-43 of *The Race* © 1984 by InterVarsity Christian Fellowship of the United States of America.

"How to Have a Quiet Time" by Stephen D. Eyre, from pp. 3-12 and 28-31 of *Quiet Time Dynamics* © 1989 by InterVarsity Press.

"How to Study the Bible" by James F. Nyquist and Jack Kuhatschek, from pages 25-35 of *Leading Bible Discussions,* 2d ed. © 1985 by InterVarsity Christian Fellowship of the United States of America.

"Prayer and Journaling" by Bill Hybels, from pages 39-44 and 59-60 of *Too Busy Not to Pray* © 1988 by InterVarsity Christian Fellowship of the United States of America.

The quiet times in the following books of the Bible were adapted from InterVarsity Press LifeGuide® Bible Studies:

Genesis by Charles and Anne Hummel © 1985 by InterVarsity Christian Fellowship of the United States of America.

Exodus © 1989 by James Reapsome.

Deuteronomy by Stephen Eyre. LifeGuide® Bible Study to be published in 1998.

Joshua © 1988 by Donald Baker.

Judges © 1995 by Donald Baker.

Nehemiah by Don Fields © 1994 by InterVarsity Christian Fellowship of the United States of America.

Esther © 1995 by Patty Pell.

Job © 1995 by R. Paul Stevens.

Psalms © 1987 by Eugene H. Peterson. Introduction and quiet times 1-3, 6-7, 16, 39, 47, 52, 60, 76 and 83.

Psalms II © 1995 by Juanita Ryan. Quiet times 34, 41-45, 50-51, 54, 59, 74, 78.

Proverbs © 1990 by William Mouser.

Ecclesiastes © 1992 by Bill and Teresa Syrios

Isaiah © 1991 by Howard Peskett.

Jeremiah © 1996 by Stephen Eyre. Introduction and quiet times 1, 4, 7, 9, 11-15, 18-19 and 21.

Daniel by Douglas Connelly © 1986 by InterVarsity Christian Fellowship of the United States of America.

Jonah, Joel & Amos © 1988 by Doug and Doris Haugen.

Matthew © 1987 by Stephen and Jacalyn Eyre.

Mark by James Hoover © 1985 by InterVarsity Christian Fellowship of the United States of America.

Luke © 1992 by Ada Lum.

John © 1990 by Douglas Connelly.

Acts © 1992 by Phyllis J. Le Peau.

Romans by Jack Kuhatschek © 1986 by InterVarsity Christian Fellowship of the United States of America.

1 Corinthians © 1988 by Paul Stevens and Dan Williams.

2 Corinthians © 1990 by Paul Stevens.

Galatians by Jack Kuhatschek © 1986 by InterVarsity Christian Fellowship of the United States of America.

Ephesians by Andrew T. and Phyllis J. Le Peau © 1985 by InterVarsity Christian Fellowship of the United States of America.

Philippians by Donald Baker © 1985 by InterVarsity Christian Fellowship of the United States of America.

Colossians & Philemon © 1989 by Martha Reapsome.

1 & 2 Thessalonians © 1991 by Donald E. Baker.

1 & 2 Timothy and Titus © 1991 by Pete Sommer.

Hebrews © 1991 by James Reapsome.

James by Andrew T. and Phyllis J. Le Peau, rev. ed. © 1987.

1 & 2 Peter and Jude © 1992 by Carolyn Nystrom.

John's Letters © 1990 by Ron Blankley.

Revelation © 1987 by R. Paul Stevens. (Quiet times 9, 12 and 14 of Revelation are by Scott Hotaling.)

Quiet times in the Psalms are taken from the following sources (all titles are published by InterVarsity Press):

Quiet times 13, 15, 17, 36, 49, 53, 55-57, 64-65, 67, 70-71, 75 and 82 are by Dietrich Gruen.

Quiet times 21-32 taken from *Waiting on the Lord* by Stephen D. and Jacalyn Eyre © 1994.

Quiet times 20 and 35 are by Linda Gehrs.

Quiet times 38 and 72 are by Cindy Bunch.

Quiet time 4 taken from *Healing for Broken People* © 1990 by Dan Harrison.

Quiet time 5 taken from *Prayer* © 1994 by David Healey.

Quiet times 8, 9 and 12 taken from *Recovery from Abuse* © 1990 by Dale and Juanita Ryan.

Quiet time 10 taken from *Pursuing Holiness* © 1992 by Carolyn Nystrom.

Quiet time 11 taken from *Created Male* © 1993 by Brian M. Wallace and Cindy Bunch.

Quiet time 14 taken from *Resources for Caring People* © 1991 by Phyllis J. Le Peau and NCF.

Quiet time 19 taken from *Suffering* © 1992 by Jack Kuhatschek.

Quiet time 33 taken from *Caring for Emotional Needs* © 1991 by Phyllis J. Le Peau and NCF.

Quiet time 37 taken from *Entering God's Presence* © 1992 by Stephen D. Eyre.

Quiet times 40 and 66 taken from *Recovery from Family Dysfunctions* © 1990 by Dale and Juanita Ryan.

Quiet time 46 taken from *Multi-Ethnicity* © 1990 by Isaac Canales.

Quiet time 48 taken from *Women Facing Temptation* © 1993 by Cindy Bunch.

Quiet time 58 taken from *Recovery from Distorted Images of Self* by Juanita and Dale Ryan © 1993.

Quiet time 61 taken from *Loving the World* © 1992 by Carolyn Nystrom.

Quiet time 62 taken from *The Fruit of the Spirit* by Hazel Offner, revised ed. © 1987.

Quiet time 63 taken from *Recovery from Bitterness* © 1990 by Dale and Juanita Ryan.

Quiet time 68 taken from *Deciding Wisely* © 1992 by Bill Syrios.

Quiet times 69 and 79 taken from *Recovery: A Lifelong Journey* © 1993 by Juanita and Dale Ryan.

Quiet time 73 taken from *People and Technology* © 1990 by Mary Fisher.

Quiet time 77 taken from *Self-Esteem* © 1990 by Jack Kuhatschek.

Quiet time 80 taken from *Recovery from Distorted Images of God* © 1990 by Dale and Juanita Ryan.

Quiet time 81 taken from *Recovery from Depression* © 1993 by Juanita and Dale Ryan.

Other quiet times are from the following sources (all titles are published by InterVarsity Press unless otherwise noted):

Leviticus: Introduction and quiet times 1-3, 5-6 and 8 by Dale and Sandy Larsen. Quiet time 4 taken from *Pursuing Holiness* by Carolyn Nystrom © 1992. Quiet time 7 taken from *Environmental Stewardship* © 1990 by Ruth Goring Stewart.

Numbers: Introduction and quiet times 1-3 and 6-10 by Rob Suggs. Quiet time 4 taken from *Women of the Old Testament* by Gladys Hunt © 1990. Quiet time 5 taken from *Staying Faithful* by Andrea Sterk Louthan and Howard Louthan.

Ruth: Taken from *Women of the Old Testament* © 1990 by Gladys Hunt.

1 Samuel: Introduction and quiet times 6-7, 9-11 and 13 taken from *David* © 1990 by Jack Kuhatshek. Quiet times 2 and 5 taken from *Old Testament Characters* © 1988 by Peter Scazzero. Quiet time 2 taken from *Fruit of the Spirit*, revised edition © 1987 by Hazel Offner.

2 Samuel: Quiet times 1-2 and 4-5 taken from *David* © 1990 by Jack Kuhatshek. Quiet times 3 and 7-8 taken from *Created Male* © 1993 by Brian Wallace and Cindy Bunch. Quiet time 6 taken from *Sexual Wholeness* © 1993 by Cindy Bunch and Scott Hotaling. Introduction by Cindy Bunch.

1 Kings: Introduction and quiet times 1-3 and 8 taken from *Old Testament Kings*, revised edition © 1993 by Carolyn Nystrom. Quiet time 5 taken from *Old Testament Characters* © 1988 by Peter Scazzero. Quiet time 6 taken from *Caring for Emotional Needs* © 1991 by Phyllis J. Le Peau and NCF. Quiet time 7 taken from *Women Facing Temptation* © 1993 by Cindy Bunch. Quiet time 4 taken from *Following God Together* © 1993 by Cindy Bunch and Scott Hotaling.

2 Kings: Introduction and quiet times 7-8 and 11-13 taken from *Old Testament Kings*, revised edition © 1993 by Carolyn Nystrom. Quiet times 1 and 4-6 taken from *Characters and Kings*, Part 2 by Carolyn Nystrom (Grand Rapids, Mich.: Zondervan, 1985) and used by permission of the author. Quiet times 9-10 taken from *Staying Faithful* © 1992 by Andrea Sterk Louthan and Howard Louthan. Quiet time 2 taken from *Women of the Old Testament* © 1990 by Gladys Hunt. Quiet time 3 taken from *Caing for Physical Needs* © 1991 by Phyllis J. Le Peau and NCF.

1 Chronicles: Introduction and quiet times 1-4 and 6 by Dale and Sandy Larsen. Quiet times 5 and 7 taken from *David* © 1990 by Jack Kuhatschek.

2 Chronicles: Quiet times 3 and 5 taken from *Old Testament Kings* by Carolyn Nystrom rev. ed. © 1993. Quiet time 2 taken from *Characters and Kings*, Part 1 by Carolyn Nystrom (Grand Rapids, Mich.: Zondervan, 1985) and used by permission of the author. Quiet time 6 taken from *Characters and Kings*, Part 2 by Carolyn Nystrom (Grand Rapids, Mich.: Zondervan, 1985) and used by permission of the author. Quiet time 7 taken from *Following God Together* © 1993 by Cindy Bunch and Scott Hotaling. Introduction and quiet times 3 and 5 by Dale and Sandy Larsen.

Ezra: Introduction and quiet times by Tom Parker.

Song of Songs: Adapted from *Sexual Wholeness* by Cindy Bunch and Scott Hotaling © 1993 and *Created for Relationships* by Cindy Bunch and Scott Hotaling.

Jeremiah: Quiet times 2-3, 5-6, 8, 10, 16-17, 20 and 22-24 by Dale and Sandy Larsen.

Lamentations: Introduction and quiet times by Lin Johnson.

Ezekiel: Introduction and quiet times by Paul Stevens.

Hosea: Introduction and quiet times by Tom Parker.

Obadiah: Introduction and quiet times by Dale and Sandy Larsen.

Micah: Introduction and quiet times by Tom Parker.

Nahum: Introduction and quiet times by Rob Suggs.

Habakkuk: Introduction and quiet times 1-2 taken from *Loving Justice* © 1990 by Bob and Carol Hunter. Quiet time 3 taken from *Loving the World* © 1992 by Carolyn Nystrom.

Zephaniah: Introduction and quiet times by Lin Johnson.

Haggai: Introduction and quiet time by Lin Johnson.

Zechariah: Introduction and quiet times by Jack Kuhatschek.

Malachi: Introduction and quiet times by Carolyn Nystrom.

INDEX OF QUIET TIME SUBJECTS

Abandonment
Hos 2:2—3:5 1058
Mt 27 1190

Acceptance
Gal 2:11-21 1430

Accountability
Mt 25 1186
1Ti 5:1—6:2 1487

Adultery
Jn 7:53—8:11 1289

Adversity
Ex 5:1—7:7 72

Advice
2Sa 18:19—19:10 363
Est 3 561
Jer 27 926

Affirmation
2Co 1:12—2:11 1412

Ambition
Ecc 4:4—5:7 788

Angels
Ps 91 695
Heb 1 1504
Rev 8—9 1578

Anger
Job 9—10 580
Ps 4 615
Ps 18:1-24 626
Ps 94 697
Ps 109 712
Jnh 4 1096
Na 1 1108
Mk 11:1-25 1214

Assurance
Lk 13:22—14:35 1255
2Co 1:1-11 1411

Authority
Ro 13 1381

Baptism
Mt 3 1153

Belief
Mt 15:1—16:20 1170

Betrayal
Mk 14:43-72 1221
Jn 13:18-38 1300

Bitterness
1Sa 18 324

Blame
Rev 16 1586

Blessings of God
Job 42 607

Blessings of Jesus
Mt 5:1—6:18 1155

Burnout
1Ki 19:1-18 399
Mk 6:6-56 1204

Calling
Ex 3—4 70
Lev 8 124
Jer 1 890

Celebration
Lev 23 142
1Ch 15:1—16:6 463
Ne 8 545
Est 9—10 569
Isa 25 837

Character
Ge 50 64
Da 2:1-30 1036
Jn 2 1278
2Pe 1:1-11 1543

Choices
Jdg 3:12-31 271

Christ
Zec 6 1132
Mal 4 1146

Christlikeness
Ro 12 1380
2Co 3:7-18 1414

Christmas
Lk 2 1230

Christ's Return
Zec 12—13 1138
Zec 14 1140
1Th 4:13—5:11 1475

2Pe 3 1546

The Church
1Co 5—6 1394
1Co 11:2-34 1400
Eph 3 1444

Citizenship
1Sa 9:1—10:9 312

City
Ps 122 726

Comfort
Ps 19 629
Ps 86 690
Ps 121 726
Ps 145 740
Zec 9—10 1135
Jn 14 1301
1Pe 5 1540

Commitment
Ge 34—36 43
1Ki 11 387
Jer 13 907

Communication
Ge 9:18—11:32 14

Compassion
Isa 54—55 871
Mk 1:40—2:17 1198
Lk 18:15—19:10 1262
Jn 4 1281

Complacency
Zep 1 1118

Complaining to God
Jer 12 906

Compromise
Ezr 10 531
Rev 3 1572

Confession
Ps 32 641

Conflict
Ge 30:25—31:55 38
Jdg 14—15 286
1Ki 12 390
1Ch 19 468
Mt 21:28—22:46 1180
Ac 15 1339

Col 3:12-17 1467
Jas 3:13—4:10 1528

Contentment
Nu 11 164
Ps 77 683

Control
Jas 4:11-17 1529

Courage
Dt 31:1-13 230
1Ch 11 459
Ac 1 1317

Covenant
Ex 20:1-21 91
Ex 23:20—24:18 95
Eze 16 989

Creation
Ge 1:1—2:3 4
Ps 104 706
Eze 47:1-12 1028

Crisis
Nu 21:1-9 177
1Sa 30 338
Da 10:1—11:35 1052
Na 2 1109

Criticism
Nu 12 166
Ac 11 1333

Death
Ps 39 651
Ps 90 694
Ecc 9:1-12 794
Mk 15:1—16:8 1223
Jn 11 1295
Ac 20:13-38 1348
1Co 15—16 1406
2Pe 1:12-21 1544

Debate
Lk 11:14—12:12 1250

Deceit
Jos 9 247

Decision-Making
Ne 11 551
Ps 119:1-24 720
Pr 21 769
1Co 3 1391

Rev 14—15 1584

Defending Your Faith
Lk 20:1—21:4 1265

Deliverance
Ex 12:29—13:16 81

Despair
Ps 88 691

Desperation
Ps 142 737

Difficulties
1Sa 17 322

Disagreements
Php 4:1-9 1458

Disappointment
1Ch 28 477
Nu 20:1-13 175

Discernment
Mk 10:32-52 1213

Discipleship
Jer 18:1-17 914
Mt 4 1154
Mt 9:35—11:30 1162
Mt 16:21—17:27 1172
Lk 9:1-50 1245
Lk 10:25—11:13 1249

Discipleship (Cost of)
Lk 9:51—10:24 1247

Discipline
2Sa 12 354
Am 4 1081
Lk 3:21—4:13 1233

Discipline from God
Ps 38 650
Heb 12 1518

Disillusionment
Eze 11 984

Disobedience
Ex 32 105

Distress
2Ki 16 428
Ps 57 667

Divorce						
Mk 10:1-31	1212	2Ki 6:24—7:20	416	**Friends**		
		Mic 6	1104	Pr 27	776	
Doubt		Lk 17:1—18:14	1260			
Job 2:11—4:17	574	Heb 11	1516	**Friendship**		
Ps 25	634	Rev 7	1577	1Sa 20	327	
Ps 73	680			Job 6	577	
Mt 14	1169	**Faith and Works**				
Jn 20	1312	Jas 2:14-26	1526	**Fulfillment**		
Ro 9:1-29	1376			Ecc 1:12—2:16	785	
2Co 13	1424	**Faithfulness of God**				
1Jn 3:11-24	1554	Est 8	567	**Future**		
1Jn 5:13-21	1558			Hos 11:12—13:16	1068	
		False Gods		Mic 4	1101	
Drifting Away		1Ki 18	397	Zep 3	1120	
Heb 2	1505			2Th 2	1479	
		False Religion				
Encouragement		Mt 21:1-27	1178	**Giving**		
Pr 10	755			Ex 35—36	110	
SS 5—6	805	**False Teachers**		1Ch 29	479	
Mk 14:1-42	1220	Gal 1:1-10	1428	Pr 19	766	
		1Ti 4	1486			
End Times		2Ti 3	1493	**God**		
Isa 2	814	2Pe 2	1545	2Ch 6—7	486	
Eze 6—7	980	Jude	1565	2Ch 14—15	493	
Joel 2:28—3:21	1075			Ac 6:8—7:60	1326	
Lk 21:5-38	1267	**Family**				
		Ge 25:12—27:40	31	**God the Father**		
Enemies		Ge 37—38	47	Gal 4:1-20	1433	
Lk 6:12-49	1238					
		Family Dysfunctions		**Godly Living**		
Environmentalism		Jdg 11:1—12:7	282	Da 11:36—12:13	1054	
Lev 25	144					
Isa 24	835	**Family History**		**God's Character**		
		Ne 7	543	Dt 6	206	
Evangelism				Job 38	603	
Lk 7	1240	**Fear**				
Ac 19:1—20:12	1346	Ps 23	633	**God's Glory**		
Ro 1:1-17	1363	Isa 40	852	Eze 1	975	
2Co 5:11—6:13	1416	Mk 4:35—6:6	1202			
Col 4:2-18	1468	1Jn 4:13-21	1556	**God's Goodness**		
1Th 2:1-16	1472			Ps 107	710	
		Fellowship				
Evil		1Th 2:17—3:13	1473	**God's Holiness**		
Ps 2	613	1Th 5:12-28	1476	Ex 19	90	
Jer 50:1-20	955	1Jn 1	1550	Ex 28:1—29:37	100	
Da 8	1048			2Sa 6	346	
Hos 5:1—6:11	1061	**Fools**		Isa 6	818	
		Pr 17—18	764			
Excellence				**God's Love**		
Ex 39:32—40:38	115	**Forgiveness**		Ps 45	657	
		Ge 41—42	51	Ps 67	675	
Expectations		Ex 34	108	Ps 118	718	
Tit 1—3	1497	Zec 2—3	1129	Isa 43:1—44:5	857	
		Mt 18	1174	Isa 62	880	
Faith		Jn 21	1313	Hos 14	1070	
Ge 12—13	16					
Ge 14—15	18	**Freedom**		**God's Power**		
Jos 2	239	Ezr 1—2	519	Ex 7:8—10:29	75	
Jdg 6:33—7:25	276	Col 2:6-23	1464	Ezr 5—6	524	
				Na 3	1110	

Ac 9:32—10:48	1331	**Isa 61**	878	
		Ac 3	1320	
God's Provision		Jas 5:12-20	1531	
Ex 15:22—17:16	86			
Zec 11	1137	**Heaven**		
		Rev 21—22	1592	
God's Supremacy				
Ecc 3:1—4:3	787	**Help from God**		
		2Ki 19	434	
God's Will		Ps 3	614	
Ex 25—27	97	Gal 3:15-29	1432	
Jos 1	238			
1Sa 15	319	**Helplessness**		
1Sa 24	331	Ps 10	621	
1Ch 18:1—19:3	467			
Eph 1:1-14	1441	**Holiness**		
		Dt 7	207	
God's Wrath		Eze 43:1-12	1024	
Eze 4—5	978	Eph 5:1-20	1447	
Habakkuk 3	1115	Col 3:1-11	1466	
Ro 1:18-32	1364	1Th 1	1471	
		1Pe 1:13-25	1535	
Gospel				
Gal 1:11—2:10	1428	**Holy Spirit**		
		Ac 2	1318	
Gossip		Ac 4:1-31	1321	
Mt 12	1165	Gal 5:16-26	1436	
Jas 3:1-12	1527			
		Honesty		
Grace		Ps 15	624	
Jdg 16	288	Jer 5	896	
2Ch 34	513			
Hos 1:1—2:1	1057	**Hope**		
Eph 2:1-10	1442	Ge 45:16—47:31	58	
		Job 35	600	
Grief		Ps 33	642	
Ps 102	703	Ps 42—43	654	
2Co 6:14—7:16	1417	Ps 146	741	
		Isa 11—12	825	
Guidance		Isa 49	865	
Ge 24:1—25:11	29	Isa 65:17—66:24	884	
Nu 9	162	Am 9	1087	
Ezr 8	527	Zec 8	1134	
Ps 29	638	Lk 1	1228	
Ps 143	738	Ro 4	1368	
Jer 29:1-23	929	1Pe 1:1-12	1534	
		Rev 1:1-8	1569	
Guilt				
Lev 16	134	**Hospitality**		
Ps 130	730	2Ki 4:8-37	412	
1Ti 1	1483	3Jn	1563	
Hardheartedness		**Humility**		
Heb 3	1506	Est 5	564	
		Da 4	1041	
Hate		Php 2:1-18	1455	
Ps 137	734			
		Hypocrisy		
Healing		Mt 23	1182	
2Ki 5	414			

Identity
Nu 1 152
2Ki 18:17—37 433

Idolatry
2Ki 17 430
Ps 115 716
Jer 10:1-16 903
Hab 2:2-20 1114

Inconsistency
Isa 5 816

Influence
Da 5 1043

Injustice
Ecc 8:2-17 793
Hab 1:1—2:1 1113

Inner Peace
Ps 37:1-17 648

Integrity
Jdg 9 279
1Sa 25 332
2Sa 9 350
1Jn 2:1-11 1551

Internal Conflict
Ne 5 540

Intimidation
Ne 6 542
Isa 36—37 848

Israel (Future of)
Ro 11 1379

Jesus Christ
Isa 8:11—9:7 822
Isa 42 856
Isa 52:13—53:12 870
Mt 1—2 1151
Mk 8:1—9:1 1208
Jn 1 1277
Col 1:15-23 1463
Heb 7 1511
Rev 1:9-20 1570

Joy
Ru 3—4 300
Ps 66 673
Ps 126 728
Lk 15 1257
Ro 5 1370
Php 3:1-21 1456

Judging
1Sa 16 320

Judgment of God
Ge 6—7 10
Ge 18—19 22
Jer 24 922
Eze 27—28 1003
Am 7—8 1085
Zep 2 1119
Ro 2 1365
Ro 3:1-20 1366
Rev 6 1575
Rev 20 1591

Judgmentalism
Jas 2:1-13 1525

Justice
Est 7 566
Jer 22 917
Am 1—2 1078
Zec 7 1133
Ac 25:13—26:32 1356
2Th 1 1478

Justice (God's)
Eze 18 992

Kingdom
Da 7 1046

Knowing God
Ex 33 107

Law (God's)
Ex 20:22—23:19 92
Lev 19 137
Dt 4:1-14 201
Dt 23:15-25 222
2Ki 22:1—23:35 439
Heb 13 1520

Leadership
Ex 18 88
Nu 17 173
Nu 27:12-23 185
Jos 23 263
2Ki 23:36—25:30 442
Jer 23 919
Eze 34 1013
Mic 3 1100
Mt 8:1—9:34 1160
2Co 11 1422
1Ti 3 1485

Legacy
Jer 38:1-26 942

Lies
Ezr 4 522

Lifestyle
Jn 8:12-59 1290
1Co 8—9 1397

Listening
Lk 8:1-21 1242

Listening to God
1Sa 3 307
1Ki 22:1-40 404
Ps 34 644
Mic 2 1099
Jas 1:19-27 1525

Longing for God
Ps 63 671
Ps 84 688

Lordship
Lk 5:17—6:11 1237

Loss
Jer 52 960
Eze 24:15-27 1001

Love
Ps 36 646
SS 3 802
Hos 4 1059
1Co 13 1403

Loving Others
1Jn 4:1-12 1555
2Jn 1561

Loyalty
Ru 1—2 298

Manipulation
1Ki 21 402

Marriage
Ge 2:4-25 5
SS 4 803
SS 7—8 806
1Co 7 1395
Eph 5:21-33 1448

Materialism
Ecc 5:8—6:12 790
Lk 12:13—13:21 1252

Maturity
Col 1:24—2:5 1463
Heb 5:11—6:20 1509

Meaning in Life
Ecc 1:1-11 784
Ecc 12:9-14 798

Mentoring
2Ti 2 1492

Mercy
Ge 27:41—30:24 35

Ministry
Ac 13—14 1336
Ac 18 1345
2Co 2:12—3:6 1413

Money
Dt 15:1-11 216
Pr 30 779
Lk 16:1-31 1258
1Ti 6:3-20 1488

New Covenant
Heb 8 1512

Obedience
Lev 26 146
Dt 30 229
Jos 24 264
Jdg 2:6-23 269
Jnh 3 1095
Mk 7:1-37 1206
Jn 19:17-42 1310
Ro 8:1-17 1373
1Jn 2:28—3:10 1553

Obstacles
Zec 4—5 1130

Offending Other Christians
Ro 14 1383
1Co 10:1—11:1 1399

Opposition
Ne 4 539
Ac 21:1—22:21 1349

Other Religions
Ac 17 1343
Ro 9:30—10:21 1377

Parables
Mt 13 1167

Parenting
Eph 6:1-9 1449

Persecution
Ex 1 68
Ps 5 616
Ps 31 640
Da 6 1045
Jn 15:18—16:4 1304
Ac 5:17—6:7 1324

(Mentoring col. continued)
Ac 24:1—25:12 1354

Perseverance
Ge 48—49 61
Ro 8:18-39 1374
Gal 5:2-15 1435
2Ti 4 1494
Heb 10 1515

Planning
Ne 2 536

Praise
Ps 150 744

Prayer
1Ki 3 377
Ps 1 613
Ps 55 665
Ps 116 717
Ps 119:25-40 721
Pr 15—16 761
Isa 38:1—39:8 851
Jnh 2 1094
Jn 17 1306
Ac 12 1335
Eph 1:15-23 1442
Php 1:1-11 1453

Pressure
Da 1 1035
Mk 2:18—3:35 1199
Gal 6:11-18 1437
Rev 2 1571

Priorities
Ezr 3 521
Hag 1—2 1124
Mk 1:16-39 1197
Mk 12:28-44 1217

Privilege
Ezr 7 526

Procrastination
Pr 24:23-34 773

Promises
Jdg 21 295

Promises of God
Ge 8:1—9:17 12
Ge 16—17 20
Jos 20—21 259
2Sa 7 348
1Ch 17 466
Jer 33 936
Da 9 1050
Jn 10 1294
Jn 16:5-33 1305

Prophecy
Da 2:31-49   1038
Rev 10—11   1580

Protection
Ps 18:25-50   628
Ac 22:22—23:35 1352

Providence of God
2Ki 20:1—21:18 436

Purity
Eze 8   982

Questioning
Mk 11:27—12:27 1215

Rebellion
Job 13—14   583
Jnh 1   1093

Reconciliation
Ge 32—33   41
Ge 43:1—45:15   55
Phm   1500

Rejection
Ps 22   631
Jn 12   1297
Lk 4:14—5:16   1235
Gal 3:1-14   1431

Relationships
Gal 6:1-10   1436

Religion
Isa 1   812

Renewal
Eze 37   1016

Repentance
Jdg 6:1-32   275
Ne 9   547
Job 40   605
Jer 3:6—4:4   893
Joel 1   1072
Joel 2:1-27   1073
Zec 1   1128
Lk 3:1-20   1232

Respect
Est 1   559

Responding to God
Hos 11:1-11   1067

Rest
Ps 95   698
Heb 4:1-13   1507

Restoration
Jer 31   932

Resurrection
Mt 28   1192
Lk 24:1-53   1273

Returning to God
Mal 2:17—3:18   1144

Revenge
2Ki 9—10   420
Ps 35   645

Reverence
Dt 5   204

Revival
Is 63:7—64:12   881

Rewards from God
Ps 37:18-40   649

Righteousness
Eze 33   1011
Ro 3:21-31   1367

Risk-taking
Ex 2   69
Nu 13:1—14:9   167
Est 4   563
Ecc 11:1—12:8   797

Sacrifice
Ge 22—23   27
Lev 1   119

Salvation
Ex 11:1—12:28   79
Dt 4:15-40   202
Ps 103   705
Isa 45   861
Jn 3   1280
Ac 9:1-31   1330

Satisfaction
Jn 6   1285

Scripture
Jer 36   940

Security
1Ch 21:1—22:1   470
Ps 30   639
Ps 46   658
Mt 24   1184

Self-Control
1Sa 26   334

Spiritual Growth
Jos 14—18   253

Self-Destructive Habits
Jer 44   947

Self-Doubt
Ps 13   623

Self-Image
Ps 8   619
Ps 100   702
Ps 139   735

Service
1Ki 17   396
Ne 12   552
Php 2:19-30   1456

Serving Christ
1Co 4   1392

Sexual Immorality
1Th 4:1-12   1474

Sexual Violence
2Sa 13   355

Sexuality
SS 1—2   801

Shame
2Ti 1   1491

Sin
Ge 3   7
Ge 4—5   8
Jos 7—8   244
Ezr 9   529
Est 6   565
Ps 51   663
La 1—2   964
Hos 6:11—8:14   1063
Mic 5   1102
Mic 7   1105
Ro 6:1—7:6   1371
Ro 7:7-25   1372

Society
Jdg 17—18   290

Spiritual Decay
Ne 13   554

Spiritual Direction
2Ch 23—24   502

Spiritual Gifts
Ex 37:1—39:31   112
1Co 12   1402

Mk 4:1-34   1201
Jn 15:1-17   1303
Eph 4:17-32   1446

Spiritual Maturity
1Pe 2:1-12   1536

Spiritual Warfare
Jos 5:13—6:27   243
Ps 110   714
Jn 7:1-52   1287
2Co 10   1421
Eph 6:10-24   1450
1Jn 2:12-17   1552
1Jn 5:1-12   1557
Rev 12   1581
Rev 13   1583
Rev 17—18   1587

Status
Mk 9:33-50   1211

Stewardship
2Co 8:1—9:15   1419

Stress
2Sa 15   359

Success
Hos 9—10   1064
Am 5—6   1082

Suffering
Job 20—21   589
Ps 6   617
La 3   967
La 4—5   969
Mk 9:2-32   1209
Lk 22:47—23:56 1270
Jn 18:28—19:16 1309
Ac 8   1328
2Co 12   1423
Php 1:12-30   1453
Heb 4:14—5:10   1508
Jas 1:1-18   1524
1Pe 3:8-22   1538
1Pe 4   1539

Superiority
Ob   1090

Supernatural Power
Lk 8:22-56   1243

Talk
Pr 6:1-19   750

Teamwork
Ne 3   537

Temptation
2Sa 11   352
Da 3   1039
Mk 1:1-15   1196

Tension with the World
1Pe 2:13—3:7   1537

Testing
Job 1:1—2:10   573
Mt 26   1187
Lk 22:1-46   1268
Jn 18:1-27   1307

Thankfulness
Ps 47   659
Ps 50   661
Ps 65   672
Php 4:10-23   1458
Col 1:1-14   1462

Tithing
Ne 10   549

Transition
Dt 3:21-29   200
2Ki 13   425

Unity
Nu 32   189
Jos 22   261
Ps 133   732
Ac 4:32—5:16   1323
Ro 15:1-13   1384
Ro 15:14—16:27 1385
1Co 1   1389
Eph 2:11-22   1443
Eph 4:1-16   1445

Values
Ps 16   625
Mt 19—20   1176

Vocation
Eze 2:1—3:15   976

Waiting
1Sa 1   304
Job 23   592
Ps 27   636
Ps 40   652
Ps 44   656
Jer 32:1-25   934
Mk 13:1-37   1218
Heb 9   1513
Jas 5:1-11   1530

War
Jer 25:15-38   923

Weakness
2Co 4:1—5:10   1415

Wealth
Am 3   1080

Weariness
2Ch 20:1-30   498

Wisdom
2Ch 1   482

Pr 7   752
Pr 9   754
Pr 13—14   759
Ecc 7:1—8:1   791
Ecc 9:13—10:20   795
Jn 9   1292
1Co 2   1390

Witness
Ac 16   1341
Ac 27—28   1358

Work
Ps 127   729
Ecc 2:17-26   786
Lk 19:11-48   1263
Jn 13:1-17   1299
Col 3:18—4:1   1467
2Th 3   1480

Worry
Mt 6:19—7:29   1158

Worship
Ex 15:1-21   84
Ex 29:38—31:18   103
Lev 10   127
Dt 12:1-14   212
Jos 3:1—5:12   240
Ps 24   633
Ps 96   699
Ps 99   701
Ps 148   743
Isa 58   875

Jer 7:1-20   899
Eze 40—41   1020
Mal 1:1—2:16   1143
1Co 14   1404
1Ti 2   1484
Rev 4—5   1574
Rev 19   1589